WORLD

CIVILIZATIONS

WORLD

THE GLOBAL EXPERIENCE

CIVILIZATIONS

PETER N. STEARNS
CARNEGIE MELLON UNIVERSITY

MICHAEL ADAS
RUTGERS UNIVERSITY

STUART B. SCHWARTZ
UNIVERSITY OF MINNESOTA

HarperCollinsPublishers

Executive Editor: Bruce Borland
Development Editor: Rebecca Strehlow
Project Coordination, Text and Cover Design:
    Proof Positive/Farrowlyne Associates, Inc.
Cover Photo: Jack Demuth
Photo Researcher: Roberta Knauf
Production Manager: Michael Weinstein
Compositor: The Clarinda Company
Printer and Binder: Courier Corporation
Cover Printer: The Lehigh Press, Inc.

World Civilizations: The Global Experience

Library of Congress Cataloging-in-Publication Data

Stearns, Peter N.
    World civilizations:the global experience/Peter N. Stearns, Michael Adas, Stuart B. Schwartz.— 1st ed.
            p.   cm.
    Also published as a single volume ed.
    Includes bibliographical references and index.
    Contents: v. 1. Beginnings to 1750—v. 2. 1450 to present.
    ISBN 0-06-046431-3 (student ed.)—ISBN 0-06-500469-8 (inst. ed.)
    1. Civilization—History. 2. Civilization—History—Sources.
I. Adas, Michael. II. Schwartz, Stuart B. III. Title.
CB69.S84 1992
909—dc20   91-33476
                                         CIP

    92 93 94 9 8 7 6 5 4 3 2

Brief Contents

Detailed Contents

3

4

5

6

7

8

9

10

11

THE END OF THE CLASSICAL ERA: WORLD HISTORY IN TRANSITION, A.D. 200–700 · 235

PART 3 · THE POSTCLASSICAL ERA · 257

12

THE FIRST GLOBAL CIVILIZATION: THE RISE AND SPREAD OF ISLAM · 265

13

ABBASID DECLINE AND THE SPREAD OF ISLAMIC CIVILIZATION TO SOUTH AND SOUTHEAST ASIA · 289

14

15

16

17

18

19

20

21

PART 4   THE WORLD SHRINKS, 1450–1750   489

22

23

24

25

26

Depart des Heroines de Paris pour Versailles le 5 Octobre 1789.

31

32

33

PART 6   THE 20TH CENTURY IN WORLD

34

40

41

42

Maps

Preface

World history provides an exciting introduction both to the world and to the historian's craft, and this text builds on these two themes. The survey course in world history has been gaining ground steadily as a staple of the history and social science curriculum. The reasons are immediately evident. First, the composition of the American population perpetually changes, adding to our need for international understanding. The European heritage, though still vital, now logically shares attention with our sources in Africa, various parts of Asia, and Latin America.

Second, American involvement in world affairs continues to grow. Long a Pacific, Caribbean, and Atlantic power, the United States nevertheless has tended to define its primary interests in terms of Europe. In the second half of the 20th century, after participation in three wars in Asia, plus massive economic and cultural interaction around the globe, the United States and its citizens have embraced a global perspective. This perspective involves emphasis on international currents and on a full range of civilizations.

GOALS

To meet the needs of a global perspective—to explain the emergence of the present world and its major civilizations—teachers of world history have created an increasingly sophisticated and comprehensive structure. Several decades of scholarship in world history and in area studies by historians and other social scientists and humanists have yielded a wealth of information and interpretive generalizations. This text reflects a synthesis of teaching and historical scholarship, a synthesis that grasps world history not as a list of facts recorded for routine memorization but as a set of processes open to analysis that builds an understanding of how world study has been shaped.

We have taught and written widely on topics central to world history. This text reflects our experience and our conviction of the role of world history in improving students' ability to handle issues of interpretation. By showing students how to assess change and continuity, the text helps them learn how to relate past to present.

As in many world history texts, we include excerpts from original documents in order to enhance student contact with diverse voices of the past. As with several other writers, we also share a firm commitment to include social history that involves women, the nonelite, and experiences and events outside the spheres of politics and high culture.

This text is no clone, however. It offers a number of distinctive qualities that pioneer in the presentation of world history.

❧ APPROACH

The two most important and distinguishing features of this text involve its genuine global orientation and its analytical style. This is a real *world* history text. It deals seriously with the Western tradition, but does not allocate extra space to it that might blur the distinction between a Western civilization text and a world history text. Correspondingly, civilizations or societies sometimes slighted in world texts—such as the nomadic societies of Asia, Latin American societies, and nations and states of the Pacific Rim—receive additional attention here. This global orientation makes *World Civilizations: The Global Experience* the first of a logical new generation, one that will decide coverage in terms of international criteria, giving the West its respectful due but not pride of place.

This text also seeks to upgrade the analytical level of the presentation of world history. Many world history texts function as factual compendia, leaving analytical challenge to the classroom. Our goal throughout has been to relate fact to interpretation while still allowing ample room for classroom exploration. Analytical emphasis is evident in the attention to periodization, which presents strands of interpretation amid the parade of facts. Comparative issues are strongly emphasized, as a means both of raising the level of reading above that of memorization and of bridging the gap between discrete civilization segments.

By happy accident, this text was written during one of those moments in world history (1989–1991) when all sorts of established patterns seem to change. Thus, the text incorporates the recent upheavals in Russia, Eastern Europe, and the Middle East, not as completed events, to be sure, but in integral relationship with other coverage. The text is thus up-to-date not only in its presentation of facts but also in relating recent events to larger analytical patterns.

❧ THEMES AND STRUCTURE

This text pays a great deal of attention to periodization. Some texts range through one civilization and then the next without much attention to coherent time periods. This book, in contrast, identifies themes for each major period of world history that help locate some common experiences or at least common forces in individual societies. Part introductions set clear definitions for each period, identifying new kinds of global contacts and parallel developments. Basic characteristics of each period are referred to in chapters dealing with specific civilizations and also in a number of crosscutting chapters that return to larger world trends.

The book is divided into six major parts, each defined by fundamental new characteristics in world history. After sketching the hunting-and-gathering phase of the human experience, Part 1 focuses on several major developmental stages. The rise of agriculture and then the development of civilization—with initial examples in different parts of Asia, Africa, Central America, and southeastern Europe—constitute the sequence that set world history in motion, from the origin of the human species until about 3000 years ago.

Part 2 deals with the elaboration of major civilizations in several parts of the world. Civilizations in this classical phase developed a new capacity to integrate large regions and diverse groups of people through overarching cultural and political systems. They also established many durable values that continue to mark the character of major societies to the present day. Part 3 of the book, covering the period from A.D. 500 to A.D. 1400, gains coherence through the spread of major religions to many different societies, by further expansion of the civilization form, and above all by the establishment of new commercial and cultural linkages that brought most civilizations into great contact with each other.

The final three parts of the book deal with world history in the past 550 years. During these years, previous international systems were fundamentally redefined, and well-established traditional civilizations encountered new forces of change. Part 4 of the book deals with the three centuries after 1450, when new technology and modes of military and political organization allowed the establishment of a variety of important empires and when western Europe gained primary control of international trade, redefining its own society in the process. Western global power increased in the 170 years after 1750 (Part 5), mainly through the ramifications of the Industrial Revolution. Other civilizations had to take a position toward Western power and toward industrialization—a common set of pressures that evoked diverse responses.

A new period of world history opened up in the middle decades of the 20th century with the retreat of Western imperialism, the rise of new political systems such as communism, the surge of the United States and the Soviet Union, and a variety of economic innovations including the achievements of Japan and the Pacific Rim. Part 6 deals with this most recent period of world history and some of its portents for the future.

❧ PEDAGOGICAL AIDS

Teachers (and students) of world history come from a wide range of backgrounds, personal and academic. To support the thematic and analytical features of the text and to make all facets of world history as accessible as possible, the authors have integrated a number of pedagogical features into the book.

In addition to narrative part openers that set forth key themes in each unit, parts begin with an extensive but manageable timeline that establishes the period under consideration. The timeline includes events in all the societies involved.

Chapters open with an outline for a quick overview of major topics and with a detailed timeline specific to the groups to be discussed. Chapter introductions highlight key themes and analytical issues to consider in reading.

Within each chapter, one or more documents appear in a discrete section. The documents are preceded by a brief, scene-setting narration and followed by probing questions. Each chapter also contains an analytical essay on a topic of broad application; the essay is followed by questions intended both to probe student appreciation of the topic and to suggest questions or interpretive issues for further thought.

The text is accompanied by photographs, line drawings, and a series of maps specially developed to enhance the global orientation. Maps in the part introductions and in the chapters highlight major developments during each period and familiarize students with many non-Western arenas.

Each chapter ends with a conclusion that goes beyond a mere summary of events. Conclusions reiterate the key themes and issues raised in the chapter and again suggest areas for reflection and anticipation. Obvious examples can be found in the unit on the 20th century, in which conclusions highlight developments leading to events of which students have had first-hand experience. Each chapter also includes several paragraphs of annotated suggested readings, so that readers can pursue additional topics on their own.

At the back of the book (in addition to the index) is a comprehensive glossary, another feature that sets this book apart. It includes conceptual terms, frequently used foreign terms, and names of important geographical regions and key characters on the world stage. Much of world history will be new to most students, and this glossary will greatly assist them in developing a global vocabulary.

ACKNOWLEDGMENTS

Grateful acknowledgment is made to the following colleagues and reviewers, who made many useful suggestions during the development of this book:

Claire Adas
Rutgers University

Jay Pascal Anglin
The University of Southern Mississippi

Norman R. Bennett
Boston University

Deborah D. Buffton
University of Wisconsin—LaCrosse

Victoria Chandler
Georgia College

Allen Cronenberg
Auburn University

Kevin Deuschle
Rutgers University

William T. Eagan
University of Southern Colorado

James Forse
Bowling Green State University

Peter Golden
Rutgers University

Dana Greene
Saint Mary's College—Maryland

William Kent Hackmann
University of Idaho

Eric G. Haines
Bellevue Community College

Howard R. Holter
California State University—Dominquez Hills

Jon E. Mandaville
Portland State University

Robert M. Maxon
West Virginia University

John A. Mears
Southern Methodist University

Vera Blinn Reber
Shippensburg University

Timothy A. Ross
Arkansas State University

John P. Ryan
Kansas City, Kansas Community College

Martin F. Seedorf
Eastern Washington University

S. Henry Tsai
University of Arkansas

Ralph V. Turner
Florida State University

Richard S. Williams
Washington State University

Donald R. Wright
SUNY College—Cortland

Herbert F. Zeigler
University of Hawaii—Manoa

PETER N. STEARNS
MICHAEL ADAS
STUART B. SCHWARTZ

Supplements

The following supplements are available for use in conjunction with this book:

✥ FOR THE STUDENT

Student Study Guide and Practice Quizzes, in two volumes. Volume I (Chapters 1 through 23) and Volume II (Chapters 22 through 42), prepared by John Paul Bischoff, Oklahoma State University. Includes chapter outlines, timeline and map exercises, two multiple-choice practice tests, and sample essay questions.

Mapping World Civilizations: Student Activities. A free student map workbook by Gerald Danzer, University of Illinois, Chicago. Features numerous map skill exercises written to enhance students' basic geographical literacy. The exercises provide ample opportunities for interpreting maps and analyzing cartographic materials as historical documents. The instructor is entitled to one free copy of *Mapping World Civilizations: Student Activities* for each copy of the text purchased from HarperCollins.

SuperShell II Computerized Tutorial. An interactive program for computer-assisted learning, prepared by John Paul Bischoff, Oklahoma State University. Features multiple-choice, true-false, and completion quizzes; comprehensive chapter outlines; "flash cards" for key terms and concepts; and diagnostic feedback capabilities. Available for IBM computers.

Timelink: World History Computerized Atlas, by William Hamblin, Brigham Young University. A highly graphic, Hypercard-based computerized atlas and historical geography tutorial for the Macintosh.

Documents in World History, in two volumes. Volume I, *The Great Traditions—From Ancient Times to 1500*; Volume II, *The Modern Centuries—From 1500 to the Present,* edited by Peter N. Stearns, Carnegie Mellon University. A collection of primary source documents that illustrates the human characteristics of key civilizations during major stages of world history.

✥ FOR THE INSTRUCTOR

Instructor's Resource Manual, by John Paul Bischoff, Oklahoma State University. Includes chapter outlines, discussion, term paper and essay topics. Also bound in the *Instructor's Resource Manual* is the *Experiencing World Music* audio cassette (see below). The *Instructor's Resource Manual* includes a commentary on each piece in the audiocassette.

Experiencing World Music. A 60-minute audiocassette. Contains over 20 selections of important music from a wide range of times and cultures. Selections range between one and four minutes in length. Commentaries about the pieces and suggestions for using them in lectures, prepared by Evan Tonsing, Oklahoma State University, and Jane Adas, Rutgers University, are included in the *Instructor's Resource Manual*. Western pieces include short selections from the medieval period to the present. Non-Western pieces include short selections from China, India, Japan, Iran, Africa, Turkey, and others.

Test Bank, by John Paul Bischoff, Oklahoma State University. A total of 2300 questions, including 50 multiple-choice questions and five essay questions per text chapter. Each test item is referenced by topic, type, and text page number. Available in print and computerized format.

TestMaster Computerized Testing System. A test-generation software package available for IBM and Macintosh computers. Allows users to add, delete, edit, and print test items. Available free to adopters.

World History Through Maps and Views, by Gerald Danzer, University of Illinois, Chicago, winner of the AHA's James Harvey Robinson Award for his work in the development of map transparencies. This set of 100 four-color transparencies from selected sources is bound in a three-ring binder and available free to adopters. Also contains an introduction on teaching history with maps and detailed commentary on each transparency. The collection includes cartographic and pictorial maps, views and photos, urban plans, building diagrams, classic maps, and works of art.

Map Transparencies. A set of 48 two- and four-color transparencies of basic maps designed to be used in teaching world civilization courses.

The HarperCollins World Civilization Media Program. A wide variety of media enhancements for use in teaching world civilization courses. Offered to qualified adopters of HarperCollins's western civilization texts.

Grades. A grade-keeping and classroom management software program that maintains data for up to 200 students.

Prologue

The study of history is the study of the past. Knowledge of the past gives us perspective on our societies today. It shows different ways people have identified problems and tried to resolve them, as well as important common impulses in the human experience. History can inform through its variety, remind us of some human constants, and provide a common vocabulary and examples that aid in mutual communication. One of the ways in which peoples from different cultures understand one another is through shared historical information.

The study of history is also the study of change. Historians seek to describe major changes in the human experience over time and to examine the ways in which those changes connect the past to the present. They try to distinguish between superficial and fundamental change, as well as between sudden and gradual change, and to explain why change occurs and what impact it has. Finally, they are attentive to the ongoing nature of change, pinpointing continuities from the past along with innovations. History, in other words, is a study of human society in motion.

World history is not simply a collection of the histories of various societies, but a subject in its own right. World history is the study of historical events in a global context. It does not attempt to sum up everything that has happened in the past. It focuses on two principal subjects: the evolution of leading civilizations and the framework for international contacts among different societies. In the first category, world history identifies major stages in the development of important societies. In the second category, world history emphasizes major stages in the interaction between different peoples and societies around the globe.

THE EMERGENCE OF WORLD HISTORY

Serious attempts to deal with world history are relatively recent. Many historians have attempted to locate the evolution of their own societies in the context of developments in a larger "known world": Herodotus, though particularly interested in the origins of Greek culture, wrote also of developments around the Mediterranean; Ibn-Khaldūn wrote of what he knew about developments in Africa and Europe as well as in the Muslim world; and unsystematically, European historians in the 18th-century Enlightenment liked to compare the evolution of various societies along with their own. But it was not until the 20th century, with an increase in international contacts and a vastly expanded knowledge of the historical patterns of major societies, that a complete world history became possible. In the West, world history depended on a growing realization that the world could not be understood simply as a mirror reflecting the West's greater glory or as a stage for Western-dominated power politics. This hard-won realization continues to meet some resistance. Nevertheless, at various points since 1900, historians in several societies have attempted to develop an international approach to the subject that includes but goes beyond merely establishing a context for the study of the emergence of their own civilization.

There are many other approaches to the study of history. The most familiar uses a purely national framework, such as the study of American history or French history, which at best is enlivened by some awareness of how one national tradition compares with the traditions of other societies. World history does not replace national histories entirely. The history of the United States, France, or China can be enhanced when there is a larger context to fit it in, for this facilitates more precise comparisons and underlines the ways in which national patterns were shaped by more general forces.

The need to study world history, however, goes beyond the provision of a good starting point for examining one's own society. The surge of interest in world history has been fueled by three other, interrelated factors. The first factor has been an explosion of knowledge about the histories of societies outside the Western tradition, in some cases also older than that tradition. The known past is much larger than ever before. The perspectives and the interpretive insights history provides have greatly expanded. Analysis of a host of issues—the effects of a classical tradition on later cultural development, the relationship between religion and commerce, or the impact of the Industrial Revolution on women—simply cannot be confined to Western examples.

The second factor involves the realization of the increasingly international context in which we live. Much of what happens in the United States can still be explained by national or even local contexts, but our economy and culture, as well as our military and diplomatic framework, are vitally shaped by developments around the world. For example, wars and revolutions in the Middle East and economic and population trends in Latin America have direct impact on the way we live. Living in an international context creates the need to understand this context and to apply to it the knowledge and perspectives of history. We need to know how other traditions besides our own have evolved, what beliefs and attitudes they produce, and what kinds of economic and political behaviors they generate.

One world historian has put the case this way: History in the United States first concentrated on the national experience alone, as part of an attempt at self-understanding and as a means of building agreed-upon national values. In the 20th century Americans realized that they were caught up in a network of which Europe was a vital part. One response was the creation of programs in the study of the history of Western civilization that made us better able to deal with European issues in the post–World War II era. Now we need, and are developing, the same types of programs on a wider international level—and world history plays a key role here.

The third factor follows from the growing analytical challenge world history poses. Historians increasingly understand that key aspects of past and present alike have been shaped by global forces—exchanges of technologies, ideas, religions, foods, and diseases. Defining and assessing the emergence of global forces and tracing their interaction with individual societies stand at the forefront of the world history agenda as a research area. Our understanding of these forces, though still incomplete, is steadily improving.

In addition to explaining the need for world history, it is necessary to offer a few words at the outset about its manageability. No world history includes everything, or even most things, about the past. It focuses on the activities of human civilizations, rather than human history as a whole. No world history would be manageable if this distinction were not kept in mind.

WHAT CIVILIZATION MEANS

In dealing with *civilizations*—societies that generate and use an economic surplus beyond basic survival needs—world history focuses on only a tiny portion of the more than 2.5 million years since the genus *Homo* first appeared in the savanna of eastern Africa. The era of civilized life makes up about 9000 of the 40,000 years that our own human species, *Homo sapiens sapiens,* has inhabited the earth. Civilized life has made possible human population densities unimaginable in precivilized time periods; it has given human groups the capacity to reshape their environments in fundamental ways and to dominate most other living creatures. The history of civilizations embraces most of the people who have ever lived; their literature, formal scientific discoveries, art, music, architecture, and inventions; their most sophisticated social, political, and economic systems; their brutality and destruction caused by conflicts; their exploitation of other species; and their degradation of the environment—a result of advances in technology and economic organization.

To be truly global in scope, our inquiry into the history of civilizations must not be constricted by the narrow, Western-centric standards for determining what is civilized. Many peoples have seen themselves as "civilized," regarding outsiders with different physical features and cultures as uncouth "barbarians" or even subhumans. For example, in awarding a society civilized status, most European and American writers have insisted that monumental buildings, cities, writing, and a high level of technology be present. These criteria banished from the realm of the civilized many societies that were highly advanced in other areas but deficient in the ones Western writers deemed critical. Clearly, another approach to the meaning of civilization has to be taken if one is to write a truly global history of the human experience.

Different civilizations have stressed and therefore excelled in different facets of human creativity. The Chinese have consistently demonstrated the capacity to build large and effective political systems. But Chinese thinkers have formulated only one major religion, Daoism, and this has had only a limited appeal both within and beyond East Asia. By contrast, the peoples of India have produced some of humankind's most sophisticated and sublime religions, but they have rarely known periods of political unity and strong government. The civilizations of the Maya made remarkable discoveries in astronomy and mathematics, but their technology remained roughly equivalent to that of stone-age peoples as late as the arrival of the Spaniards in the 16th century. These examples suggest that, rather than stressing particular attainments such as the capacity to build pyramids or wheeled vehicles, a genuinely global definition of what it means to be civilized should focus on underlying patterns of social development that are common to complex societies throughout history. The attributes that determine whether a particular society is civilized or not should be freed from the *ethnocentrism*—or the tendency to judge other peoples' cultural forms solely on the basis of how they compare to one's own—and sense of moral superiority that have dominated definitions of civilization.

For our purposes, civilization is a form of human social organization that arises from the capacity of certain peoples to produce food supplies beyond their basic needs, and to develop a variety of specialized occupations, a heightened social differentiation on a class and gender basis, intensified economic exchanges between social groups, and regional and long-distance trading networks. Surplus agricultural production spurs the growth of large towns and then cities inhabited by merchants, artisans, ritual specialists, and political leaders. Both specialization and town life contribute to an increase in creativity and innovation that have been characteristic of all civilizations.

THE COMPARATIVE APPROACH TO THE HISTORY OF CIVILIZATIONS

In concentrating on civilizations, world history offers an initial focus that greatly reduces the time period world his-

tory covers, and also draws attention to civilizations that covered particularly extensive geographical areas. Even in emphasizing major civilizations, however, world history must offer other ways to select and highlight significant developments. One vital step involves a comparative approach to the major societies. Much of world history can be organized through careful comparisons of the leading characteristics of the principal civilizations, such as formal governments, family structures, and art. Remembering what civilizations have in common helps us to manage the complexity of world history and to highlight key distinctions among major societies. Comparison gives us a means of connecting historical developments within different civilizations and allows us to identify key patterns that ought to be remembered and explained.

Comparison can also help capture the process of historical change. A single civilization can be compared across time, before and after change. Furthermore, a situation new to one society can be compared with similar situations that exist elsewhere. Consider the introduction of a new slave system, as happened in the Americas in the 16th and 17th centuries. By comparing the American slave system with slave systems developed elsewhere, one can get a better fix on what American slavery involved and what changes it brought to the emerging society.

INTERNATIONAL CONTACTS AND TIME PERIODS

World history is not, however, simply a progression of separate civilizations that can be compared in various ways. An understanding of the kinds of contacts different civilizations developed—and their responses to the forces that crossed their boundaries—is as important as the story of the great societies themselves. For example, when the rate of international trade picked up, it presented questions for each major society to answer: How would the society participate in the trading system? What domestic impact did international trade have? How did one society's reactions to the new levels of trade compare with those of other major societies?

World history is organized into major time periods primarily on the basis of changes in the nature and level of international exchange. Because of parallel developments, contacts, and crosscutting global forces, many civilizations display some common chronological features that suggest an international framework encompassing the individual societies. Establishing a sense of each time period of world history in terms of the characteristics of international interactions gives coherence to the larger story of world history. Some time periods see a particular trend toward the formation of empires; others involve the spread of major religions; others stress the impact of new technologies or production systems. Not all societies, in a given time period, neatly responded to the larger world forces—isolation from the wider world remained possible until just a few centuries ago—but enough did to enable us to define the basic chronology of world history.

This book emphasizes six major time periods in world history. The first, covered in Part 1, involved the emergence of civilization. Early civilizations arose after people had formed a wide variety of local societies over most of the inhabitable globe. The early civilizations were regional, but they pulled more localized groups together into some shared institutions and beliefs; some of them developed limited contacts with other civilizations.

· The second period of world history saw the formation of much larger civilization units—the great classical societies of China, India, and the Mediterranean. Emphasis in the classical period rests on the integration of and the level of contact among these larger civilization areas. This was the period when elites in many parts of the world created systems of thought and artistic styles that continue to have force today: Confucian ideas about polite behavior and the social good, Greek ideas about nature, and Buddhist ideas about spirituality.

The third, postclassical period in world history emerged as the classical civilizations underwent new challenge and decline. After about A.D. 500, civilization spread to new areas and new kinds of contact developed, involving the spread of novel religious systems, the increase of commercial exchange, and even the acceleration of international disease transmission.

The fourth period of world history, beginning around A.D. 1450, saw the Americas and other previously isolated areas brought into the international framework as trade and exchange reached yet another level of intensity. Humble American crops such as corn and potatoes encouraged massive population growth in many societies—a trend that continues into our own time.

Between about 1750 and 1920, the fifth period of world history was shaped particularly through the advent of industrial society in western Europe. Industrial technology brought new rates of international interaction and a new, and complex, balance of forces among the major civilization areas. Habits of work changed in response to new ideas of discipline and productivity; leisure changed as well. This was the time when key sports won an international audience.

Finally, world history periodization took a sixth turn during the 20th century, again because of complicated changes in the nature of international contacts and the impact these contacts have on particular societies. The new global patterns of this century gain added meaning against the perspective of previous world trends.

The basic framework for managing and understanding world history resembles a weaving loom, in which two sets of threads interweave. One set consists of the major civilizations, identified through their principal characteristics and traced over time; the second set involves parallel processes and contacts that delineate the principal time periods of world history. The interaction between civilizations and international forces form the warp and weave of world history, from civilization's origin to the present day.

ANALYSIS IN WORLD HISTORY

In addition to comparison and periodization, which link the historical experience of individual civilizations, some world historians have been fascinated by a third, even more sweeping formula: regularities in historical development that can be identified and applied on a global basis. Do all civilizations rise, mature, and then fall in a process like that of human growth? Is there a historical law that proves that societies that begin to neglect the welfare of their lowest classes are doomed to decay? A variety of historical laws have been proposed, and even if some of them prove simplistic, the more insightful ones can raise valid questions about the larger processes of world history.

World history involves comparison, assessment of global interaction, and consideration of more general formulas about how human societies operate. There are facts to be learned, but the greater analytical challenge is to use the facts to compare civilizations, to identify key periods of world history and the patterns of change from one period to the next, and to test general propositions about historical causation and development. Using this approach, world history becomes something to think about, not simply something to regurgitate. With this approach the task of learning world history gains focus and purpose.

WORLD

CIVILIZATIONS

Paleolithic Age

1 million Further development of species into *Homo erectus*, an upright, tool-using human

30,000 Passage of people to Americas

8500–3500 Neolithic Age; development of farming in Middle East

2.5 million Emergence of more humanlike species, initially in eastern Africa

600,000 Wide spread of species across Asia, Europe, Africa; development of fire use

12,000 Domestication of dogs

40,000 Completion to date of basic human evolution; *Homo sapiens sapiens* displaces other human species

8500–6500 Domestication of sheep, pigs, goats, cattle

1 THE AGRARIAN REVOLUTION AND THE BIRTH OF CIVILIZATION

2 THE RISE OF CIVILIZATION IN THE MIDDLE EAST AND AFRICA

3 ASIA'S FIRST CIVILIZATIONS: INDIA AND CHINA

This 3d millennium B.C. stone frieze from the temple of the birth goddess Ninhursag depicts Sumerian priests probably processing milk into butter.

3100–1087 Initial kingdoms, then flowering of Egyptian civilization

7000 Full-fledged town in Jericho

5000 Domestication of maize (corn)

4000–3000 Age of innovation in Middle East: writing, bronze metalworking, wheel, plow

2500–1500 Indus civilization in South Asia

5600 Beans domesticated in Western Hemisphere

5000–2000 Yangshao culture in North China

3500–1800 Sumerian civilization, with some disruptions through conquest

PART

1

The Origins of Civilizations

This first section focuses on how human societies started and particularly on how initial civilization emerged. The key markers are the advent of the first production system—agriculture—and the achievements and diversities of the first complex societies that resulted. The section ends around 1000 B.C., when several civilizations were poised to develop more elaborate cultural and political forms and to embrace wider areas beyond their river-valley cores.

Because world history concentrates on the evolution of civilizations, there is no need here to inquire into the gradual evolution of the species itself or the stages of early stone tool use. Though human beings first appeared over two million years ago, major stages in the physical development of the species ended only about 40,000 years ago. Long before this, it was clear that humans were capable of using tools and improving the tools they used.

It was this capacity that produced a particularly crucial break in the context of human history, by allowing groups of people to move away from the hunting-and-gathering economy that had shaped human society from its inception. Hunting for meat and gathering nuts and seeds allowed people to form organized units, but only rather small ones. The system permitted people to locate in many areas, but it could not sustain large numbers of people.

This is why the capacity to effect a major transformation in basic economic organization, by substituting agriculture for hunting and gathering as the primary source of food, constituted such a decisive change in the human record. This transformation, based on the improved tools of the New Stone (Neolithic) Age, began after 9000 B.C. With this change, the possibility of more elaborate forms of social and political organization—civilization itself—gradually emerged. The Neolithic revolution ushered in agriculture and thus stands as a landmark of the human experience, as the prehistoric development moved toward the world history of more organized societies.

1850 Shang kingdom   **1600** Beginnings of Indo-European invasions   **1000–500** Olmec civilization in Mesoamerica   **400** Potatoes domes-
in China   **1122** Western Zhou kings,   **800** Beginning of writing of Bible (Israel)   ticated (Andes)
                                           1600 Spread of civiliza-   China; writing develops   **700** Composition of first of the sacred Vedas (India)
1800 Babylonian   tion to Crete (Minoan)   **1000** Kush independent kingdom in Africa (Upper Nile)
Empire in Middle East   **550** Persian Empire
                                                                                 1250 Moses and Jewish   **770** Later Zhou kings   (Middle East)
                                                                                 exodus from Egypt
        1700–1300 Rise of village
        culture in Mesoamerica   **1000** Spread of Phoenician settlements, Western
                                                                                                   Mediterranean; Indo-European invasions of Greece

Patterns of Human Migration

THE NEOLITHIC REVOLUTION

It is also vital to realize how adaptable we are as a species. Humankind had spread to all major continents and many island groups at least 15,000 years before agriculture was invented. The species proved able to adapt to a wide variety of climates and environments even before elaborate technologies further aided survival. Hunting and gathering encouraged dispersal of the population. When agriculture made larger cultural and political systems possible, the differences and divisions among segments of the far-flung population posed major barriers that could not completely be overcome. Much of human history involves gradual efforts to introduce wider connections—first in small regions, then in larger empires, religious areas, and trading networks—among peoples painfully and incompletely won from local attachments. Certainly the first phases of human history, once agriculture started gaining ground, are understandable only if the existing disunity of the species is established as a baseline. The first civilizations which appeared about 3500 B.C., though they were foreshadowed by the earlier development of stationary settlements and the first towns, began regional processes of linking local groups more closely around shared beliefs, regional trade, and vital river systems that provided irrigation for agriculture.

Much of human history, in other words, from about 9000 B.C. onward involves tensions between new capacities to organize larger groups of people and larger areas—based initially on the superior productive power of agriculture—and the fact that, from even earlier history, people had strongly rooted attachments to scattered local groupings.

In fact, many people resisted agriculture itself. The new economic system allowed more people to exist, but it also brought many disadvantages. These included changes in relationships between men and women and a need to work harder. Agriculture thus constituted progress only in some ways; it could be seen as deterioration in others. It also, by requiring settling down and more coordination among larger groups of people, could rouse resentments based on attachments to a wandering life and small, scattered units of human organization.

Two other complexities that attended the emergence of agriculture and civilization are covered primarily in Chapters 1 and 2. First, while change sped up it hardly rocketed. New political forms emerged very slowly. There is an agonizing gap of many centuries between the first signs of civilization in the Middle East and its full initial development. Technology did not develop at an even pace. Agriculture gave rise to the use of new materials, particularly metals, and new manufacturing techniques, but the transformation of the production process took many centuries. For example, several thousand years passed between the discovery of grain growing and the invention of bread.

The second complexity involves place. The development of agriculture and then civilization did not proceed evenly across the globe. The dispersion of the species inhibited the rapid spread of new ideas, as did deliberate resistance to novelty. In some areas agriculture and then civilization emerged separately, well after their initial advent in western Asia (what we today call the Middle East). It is essential to combine some sense of common patterns of these developments with a recognition of their diverse starting points. Several separate "inventions" of agriculture oc-

curred; other areas learned of agriculture from contact with one of the pioneering centers. Vast differences in timing help explain later historical patterns in the Asian and North African regions where innovation had first occurred, and in Europe and the Americas.

CIVILIZATION'S FIRST PHASE: THE RIVER VALLEYS

Four major centers of early civilization developed by 2500 B.C.: Mesopotamia, Egypt, northwestern India, and northern China. All four were regional concentrations, though each exhibited some capacity to fan out slightly into adjacent territories. They had limited contact with one another. These civilizations created basic devices to facilitate more effective government and trade, a system of writing, some bureaucratic forms and legal procedures, increasingly elaborate commercial practices, and characteristic styles in art and architecture. They can be seen as pioneers in generating basic elements common to later, more organized, and more expansive civilizations. These key ingredients of civilized life would never have to be fully reinvented by later civilizations. In some cases—most clearly Mesopotamia and China—the early civilizations also projected ideas about humanity and nature that would continue to shape civilization in these and other areas, long after these rather constricted river-valley societies had given way to great empires.

The pioneering phase of civilization in Asia and parts of Europe and Africa lasted for many centuries, up to 2500 years. A number of the early civilizations were deliberately conservative, which helps account for their durability and their lack of striking internal change. Yet, in part because of some widespread invasions, the early civilizations either ended or paused to regroup around 1000 B.C. This date signaled a definable break between the initial phase of civilization's history and a more mature phase.

ISSUES FOR INTERPRETATION: PROBLEMS IN ANALYZING EARLY WORLD HISTORY

The early phases of world history—from late prehistory through the invention of agriculture to the emergence of civilization in several distinct and separate varieties—involve one obvious but creative tension. The focus of early societies deliberately oscillates between technology and culture—between tools and ideas—as they built a growing mastery over nature while also producing a wide variety of values and styles of art and science. Both facets of development involve important encounters between evolving forms of human society and their physical environments. Both

Early Civilizations

technology and culture must be used to analyze how and why change occurred and to establish the characteristics of any civilization.

The early phases of world history introduce not only key initial concepts, such as civilization, and vital early forms of what became separate civilized traditions, but also introduce analytical issues of interpretation that can be tested in the first millennia of agriculture and metal-working.

Comparison is an essential feature of analysis. The early civilizations all had to devise institutions and techniques. Although they had some characteristics in common, they also differed in political structure and cultural styles. Comparison centers on the exploration of these similarities and differences.

Periodization comes into play as well. It is not too hard to establish the beginning of the first periods of world history: one needs only to look for the advent of agriculture, then for the initial manifestation of civilization. What makes the task complex is the variation in the timing of the starting point for each civilization. Mesopotamia came first, followed by the rise of civilizations in Egypt and India, followed to some extent by gradual expansion from the initial Mesopotamian centers. Chinese civilization developed later and more separately; civilizations emerged even more distinctly in other areas, notably parts of the Americas.

Heritage constitutes another important interpretive issue for these first periods in world history. For example, how much did later civilizations borrow from earlier examples, beyond basic techniques, and how much did they invent separately? Was a basic difference in outlook between the Middle East and eastern Asia set as early as 1000 B.C.?

Early civilizations obviously introduced some techniques that have lasted to our own day—though by 1000 B.C. they had not yet spread to most areas of the world. These techniques included writing and the use of money. Whether the early civilizations also set the tone for later, larger societies is open to greater debate. A recent argument that Egypt, as an African society, really provided basic institutions and ideas for Greek and later European culture is an instance of this important effort to explore how much of the later shape of major civilizations was prepared in the long river-valley phase.

Defining the close of the first period of world history is considerably tougher than identifying its origins and main features. Even in Asia and North Africa, quite apart from the Americas, the four main river-valley civilizations met different fates. Those in Mesopotamia and India almost completely disappeared, while that of Egypt persisted after 1000 B.C. The Chinese civilization that still exists today is in some ways directly linked to its early river-valley phase.

PART 1 THE ORIGINS OF CIVILIZATIONS   5

Blending separate civilizations into common time periods is not a tidy process. Nevertheless, the crucial characteristics of the first period in world history can be identified. Aided by some mutual contact, people in several regions of Asia, North Africa, and southeastern Europe learned to master some common problems in setting up agricultural civilizations and spreading the resulting institutions and beliefs over significant regional areas.

One final analytical approach can be fruitfully applied to the first period of world history. Many people, including some who are dubious about outright historical laws, find in the past informative analogies that help them interpret later human experience. Two major potential analogies leap out from the formative civilization period. First, the ways the first civilizations arose set patterns that can be applied to the study of the genesis of civilization in other areas. This analogy applies particularly vividly to the Americas, where early civilizations, arising independently and somewhat later, are often compared to Egypt or Mesopotamia (see Chapter 9). It can also apply to early civilizations in Italy, Africa, or the Polynesian islands.

The second analogy is even more grandiose. With the development of agriculture the first period of civilized development produced one of the two basic shifts in human production methods ever developed. (Industrialization was the second.) The nature, causes, and limitations of the agrarian revolution of the late-Neolithic period set patterns and raised questions that have helped us understand the much more recent Industrial Revolution. Because recent human history involves almost unprecedented alterations in basic living habits, we can only benefit from understanding prior experiences that are at all comparable.

We do not assess early human history simply as an exercise in the study of remote origins. We do so because it aids our exploration of human dynamics—including processes active in the modern world.

	LATE PALEOLITHIC	TRANSITION PHASE	NEOLITHIC AGE	
Eastern Hemisphere	18,000–10,000 Central Russian mammoth bone settlements		8500–5000 Development of farming in the Middle East 7000 Full-fledged town at Jericho	
		10,500–8000 Natufian settlements		
		12,000 Domestication of dogs	8500 Domestication of sheep	6250–5400 Catal Huyuk at its peak
			7500–6500 Domestication of pigs, goats, cattle	
Western Hemisphere				5600 Beans domesticated

18,000 B.C.	12,000 B.C.	10,000 B.C.	8,000 B.C.	6,000 B.C.

The Agrarian Revolution and the Birth of Civilization

INTRODUCTION. This history of human civilizations focuses on only a tiny portion—roughly 9000 years—of the more than 2.5 million years since the genus *Homo* first appeared in the savannas of eastern Africa. Within this 9000-year time span, we will concentrate on societies that we consider civilized by virtue of their reliance on sedentary agriculture for sustenance and their ability to produce crop surpluses that support specialized elites as well as nonfarming, trading, and manufacturing groups. In most civilizations, farming surpluses and specialization have also given rise to the concentration of human populations in towns and cities and complex social divisions and social stratification based on a mix of birth, sex, and occupation. The era of civilized life so defined makes up less than a quarter of the 40,000 years that our own human species, *Homo sapiens*, has inhabited the earth. But within the civilized societies that developed in this limited time span, most of human history has been lived.

Our emphasis in defining civilizations on the basis of the economic circumstances that give rise to them and the social patterns that characterize them makes necessary our exploration of the origins of early civilizations. We need to understand why humans opted for this form of organization and path of development, and how they were able to make the transition from small-scale, nonspecialized, subsistence societies to city-states with their increasingly complex division of labor. Before studying the varying patterns of civilized life that are the focus of world history, we will examine some of the alternative modes of human organization that had evolved by the end of the transition period

METAL AGE

5000–2000 Yangshao culture in North China   c. 1766 Emergence of Shang kingdom in China

c. 3100 Rise of Egyptian civilization

3500–2350 Civilization of Sumer

2500–1500 Indus civilization in South Asia

4000–3000 Age of Innovation in the Middle East: Introduction of writing, metalworking, the wheel, and the plow

5000 Domestication of maize (corn)   2000 Kotosh culture in Peru   1000–500 Olmec civilization in Mesoamerica

3500 Llama domesticated   400 Potatoes domesticated

1700–1300 Rise of village culture in Mesoamerica

between the Paleolithic or Old Stone Age and the Neolithic or New Stone Age. In this period, from roughly 12,000 to 8000 B.C., changes in human organization and food production that made possible the surpluses and specialization that were essential to the first stirrings of civilized life in the 8th millennium B.C. occurred. The economic and social patterns that developed after 8000 B.C. were in turn critical to the surge of invention between 4000 and 3000 B.C. that laid the basis for the first civilizations.

The rise of farming in the Neolithic era (between roughly 8000 and 5000 B.C.) is generally regarded as the source of the first truly revolutionary transformations in human history. But the thousands of years over which this process occurred suggest that it was not revolutionary in the usual sense of a rapid or abrupt change. Rather, the development of agriculture profoundly altered the relationship between human societies and their environments and between humans and other, often competing, animal species. The shift to agriculture also altered the way humans lived their daily lives.

Sedentary farming was made possible by technological breakthroughs that made the survival of the human species more secure, and gave humans a much greater capacity to remake their environments to suit their needs. The most visible signs of this capacity were the spread of regularly cultivated fields and especially the development of towns, such as Jericho between 8500 and 7500 B.C. and Çatal Huyuk around 5500 B.C. Human control over other animal species was evidenced by the growing herds of domesticated goats, sheep, and cattle that became important sources of food and materials for clothing and shelter. Trade between these centers of settlement and production greatly increased contacts between different human groups, enhancing the innovation and increase of resources that were key features of the Neolithic era. Transformations of this sort occurred in all the areas of the world where civilizations emerged in the last two or three millennia B.C. Indeed, these transformations proved to be an essential prelude to the emergence of a variety of civilizations.

ANALYSIS
THE IDEA OF CIVILIZATION IN WORLD HISTORICAL PERSPECTIVE

The perception that there are fundamental differences between civilized and "barbaric" or "savage" peoples is very ancient and widespread. For thousands of years the Chinese, the civilized inhabitants of the "Middle Kingdom," set themselves off from neighboring peoples, including the pastoralist or nomadic cattle- and sheep-herding peoples of the vast plains or steppes to the north and west of China proper, whom they regarded as barbarians. For the Chinese being civilized was cultural, not biological or racial. If barbarians learned the Chinese language and adopted Chinese ways, from the clothes they wore to the food they ate, the outsiders were admitted into the exalted circle of the civilized.

A very similar pattern of demarcation and cultural absorption was found among the Amerindian peoples of present-day Mexico. Those who settled in the valleys of the moutainous interior, where they built great civilizations, lived in fear of invasions by peoples they regarded as barbarous and referred to as the *chichimecs,* meaning "sons of the dog." The latter were nomadic hunters and gatherers who periodically moved down from the desert regions of North Mexico into the fertile central valleys in search of game and settlements to pillage. The Aztecs were simply the last, and perhaps the most fierce, of a long line of chichimec peoples who entered the valleys and either destroyed or conquered the urban-based empires that had developed there. But after the raiders conquered and settled down in the mountain valleys, they adopted many of the religious beliefs and institutional patterns and much of the material culture of the vanquished peoples.

The word *civilization* is derived from the Latin word *civilis* meaning "of the citizens." The term was coined by the Romans to distinguish between themselves as citizens of a cosmopolitan, urban-focused civilization and the "inferior" peoples who lived in the forests and deserts on the fringes of their Mediterranean empire. Centuries earlier the Greeks, who had contributed much to the rise of Roman civilization, made a similar distinction between themselves and outsiders. Because the languages that non-Greek peoples to the north of the Greek heartlands spoke sounded like senseless blabber to the Greeks, they lumped all the outsiders together as *barbarians,* which meant literally "those who cannot speak Greek." As in the case of the Chinese and Aztecs, the boundaries between civilized and barbarian for the Greeks and Romans were cultural, not biological. Regardless of the color of one's skin or the shape of one's nose, it was possible for free individuals to become members of a Greek *polis*—city-state—or Roman citizens by adopting Greek or Roman customs and swearing allegiance to the *polis* or the emperor.

Until the 17th and 18th centuries, the primacy of cultural attributes (language, dress, manners, etc.) as the means by which civilized peoples set themselves off from barbaric ones had been rarely challenged. But in those centuries two major changes occurred among thinkers in western Europe. First, efforts were made to define systematically not only the differences between civilized and barbarian, but to identify a series of stages in human development that ranged from the lowest savagery to the highest civilization. Depending on the writer in question, candidates for civilization ranged from Greece and Rome to (not surprisingly) Europe of the 17th and 18th centuries. Most of the other peoples of the globe, whose "discovery" since the 15th century had prompted the efforts to classify them in the first place, were ranked in increasingly complex hierarchies. Peoples like the Chinese and Arabs, who had created great cities and monumental architecture, writing, advanced technology, and large empires, usually won a place along with the Europeans near the top of these ladders of human achievement. Nomadic, cattle- and sheep-herding peoples, such as the Mongols, were usually classified as barbarians. Civilized and barbarian peoples were in turn pitted against various sorts of *savages*. These ranged from the hunters and gatherers who inhabited much of North America and Australia before the arrival of the Europeans to the slash-and-burn or migratory cultivators in the hill and forest zones on most of the continents.

The second major shift that European writers brought about in our ideas rgarding civilization began at the end of the 18th century, but did not really take hold until a century later. In keeping with a growing emphasis in European thinking and social interaction on racial or biological differences, modes of human social organization and cultural expression were increasingly linked to what were alleged to be the innate capacities of each human *race*. Though no one could agree on what a race was or how many races there were, most European writers argued that some races were more inventive, more moral, more courageous, more artistic—thus more capable of building civilizations—than others. "White" or Caucasian Europeans were, of course, considered by white European authors to be the most capable of all. The hierarchy from savage to civilized took on a color dimension from white at the top, where the civilized peoples clustered, to yellow, red, brown, and black in descending order.

Some authors sought to reserve all the attainments of civilization for whites, or as some preferred to call them, "Aryans." Confronted with clear evidence of civilization in places such as China and the Middle East, these writers categorized Arabs as Caucasian and argued that Aryan migrants had carried the essence of civilization to places like India and China. As the evolutionary theories of thinkers such as Charles Darwin came into vogue, race and level of cultural development were seen in the perspective of thousands of years of human change and adaptation rather than as being fixed in time. Nevertheless, this new perspective had little effect on the rankings of different human groups. Civilized whites were simply seen as having evolved much further than backward and barbaric peoples.

The perceived correspondence between race and level of development and the hardening of the boundaries between civilized and "inferior" peoples affected much more than intellectual discourse about the nature and history of human society. These beliefs were used to justify European imperialist expansion, which was seen as a "civilizing mission" aimed at uplifting barbaric and savage peoples across the globe. In the last half of the 19th century virtually all non-Western peoples came to be dominated by the Europeans, who were confident that they, as representatives of the highest civilization ever created, were best equipped to govern lesser breeds of humans.

In the 20th century much of the intellectual baggage that had made credible racially embedded hierarchies of civilized and savage peoples has been jettisoned. Racist thinking has been discredited by 20th-century developments, including the revolt of the colonized peoples and the persistent failure of racial supremacists to provide convincing proof for innate differences in mental and physical aptitudes among various human groups. These trends as well as research that has resulted in a much more sophisticated understanding of the evolutionary process have led to the abandonment of rigid and self-serving 19th-century ideas about civilization. Yet even though non-European peoples such as the Indians and Chinese are increasingly given credit for their civilized attainments, much ethnocentrism remains in the ways social theorists determine who is civilized and who is not. Perhaps the best way to avoid the tendency to define the term with reference to one's own society is to view civilization as one of a number of human approaches to social organization, rather than attempting to identify specific kinds of cultural achievement (writing, cities, monumental architecture, etc.). All peoples, from small bands of hunters and gatherers to farmers and factory workers, live in *societies*. All societies produce *cultures*—combinations of the ideas, objects, and patterns of behavior that result from human social interaction. But all societies and cultures do not generate the surplus production that permits the levels of specialization, scale, and complexity that distinguish civilizations from other modes of social organization. All peoples are intrinsically capable of building civilizations, but many have lacked the resource base, historical circumstances, or, quite simply, the motivation for doing so.

Questions: Identify a society you consider to be civilized. What criteria did you use to determine that it was civilized? Can you apply those criteria to other societies? Can you think of societies that might not fit your criteria and yet be civilizations?

❧ HUMAN LIFE IN THE ERA OF HUNTERS AND GATHERERS

By the end of the Paleolithic or Old Stone Age in 12,000 B.C., humans had evolved in physical appearance and mental capacity to roughly the same level as today. Our species, *Homo sapiens,* had been competing with increasing success for game and campsites with other human-like creatures for nearly 30,000 years. *Homo sapiens'* enlarged brain, critical to the survival of all of the branches of the genus *Homo,* was virtually the same size as that of modern humans. The erect posture of Stone Age humans produced a tendency toward spinal strain and backaches that was more than compensated for by the fact that an upright posture freed their hands, as it had those of

earlier human species. The combination of a larger brain and free hands with opposable thumbs made it possible for different human species to craft and manipulate tools and weapons of increasing sophistication. These implements helped to offset the humans' marked inferiority in body strength and speed to rival predators, such as wolves and wild cats, as well as to many of the creatures that humans themselves preyed on. A more highly developed brain also allowed humans to transform cries and grunts into the patterned sounds that make up language. Language greatly enhanced the possibilities for cooperation and a sense of cohesion within the small bands that were the predominant form of human social organization in this era. By the last phase of the Paleolithic epoch these advantages had made *Homo sapiens* a species capable of mastering the earth.

The *Homo sapiens'* upright posture, which freed their hands, meant that over long periods of time homonoids could develop weapons and tools.

PALEOLITHIC CULTURE

No matter how much *Homo sapiens sapiens* may have developed in physical appearance and brain capacity by around 12,000 B.C., its culture, with some exceptions, was not radically different from the cultures of the rival human species such as the Neanderthals, who had died out thousands of years earlier. Fire, which was perhaps the most central element in the material culture of Paleolithic peoples, had been mastered nearly a half million years earlier. Originally snatched from conflagrations caused by lightning or lava flows, fire was domesticated as humans developed techniques to preserve glowing embers and to start fires by rubbing sticks and other materials together. The control of fire led to numerous improvements in the lives of Stone Age peoples. It rendered edible a much wider range of foods, particularly animal flesh, which was virtually the only source of protein in a culture without cows, goats, or chickens and thus lacking in milk, cheese, and eggs. Cooked meat, which was easier to digest, may also have been more effectively preserved and stored, thus giving Stone Age peoples an additional buffer against the constant threat of starvation. In addition, fire was used in treating animal hides for clothing and hardening wooden weapons and tools. Its light and warmth became the focal point of human campsites.

By Late Paleolithic or Old Stone Age times, human groups survived by combining hunting and fishing with the gathering of fruits, berries, grains, and root crops that grew in the wild. They had created a considerable number of tools to assist them in these critical endeavors. Tools of wood and bone have perished; thus surviving stone tools are our main evidence of the technology of this epoch. These tools had advanced considerably by the late Old Stone Age. Early human tools, discovered by archeologists at sites that date back well over 2 million years, were made by breaking off the edges of stone cores to create crude points or rough cutting surfaces. By the Late Paleolithic period, humans had grown much more adept at working stone. They preferred to chip and sharpen flakes broken off the core stone. These chips could be fashioned into knife blades, arrow points, or choppers, which had a wide range of uses from hunting and warfare to skinning animal carcasses and harvesting wild plants.

Earlier human groups had produced evidence of artistic expression, small figurines and decorated implements; the Late Paleolithic was a period of particularly intense creativity. Fine miniature sculpture, beads and other forms of jewelry, and carved bones were produced by Paleolithic peoples, but their most impressive artistic contributions were the cave paintings that have been discovered at sites

Early human groups developed a variety of stone tools. The tools shown here include weapon points (second row from the top), scrapers for peeling off animal hides or working wood (third row from the top), and a hammerstone (lower left).

in southern France and Spain. Remarkably realistic and colorful depictions of a variety of animals from woolly mammoths to horses were found deep in the caverns at these sites.

Because the peoples who created these paintings did not write, we cannot be certain of the reasons for this surge in artistic creativity. These paintings may have been done for the sake of artistic expression itself. But the location of the paintings deep in the cave complexes and the rather consistent choice of game animals as subject matter suggest that they served a ritual purpose. Perhaps capturing the images of animals in art was seen as a way of assisting hunting parties in the wild. It is also possible that those who painted the animal figures hoped to acquire some of the strength and speed of the animals depicted, to improve their chances in the hunt and to ward off the animals that preyed on the human hunters themselves. Some paintings may have been done to celebrate and commemorate particularly successful hunting expeditions or other key events.

Other paintings and in many cases small sculptures, including those found at a number of Middle Eastern sites, appear to have religious significance. They may have been intended, for example, to depict prominent deities or to promote fertility. There is also speculation that paintings at a number of sites may represent early counting systems or primitive calendars. Whatever their purpose, the paintings of the Old Stone Age era suggest quite a sophisticated level of thinking. They also indicate that humans were becoming increasingly interested in expressing themselves artistically and leaving lasting images of their activities and concerns.

THE SPREAD OF HUMAN CULTURE

The possession of fire and tools with which to make clothing and shelters made it possible for different human species to extend the range of their habitation far beyond the East African savanna (grassy plain) zone where they

had originated. During the last Ice Age, which began about 2.5 million years ago and ended around 8000 B.C., humans first moved northward from Africa into Europe and eastward across the present-day Middle East into central Asia, India, and East Asia. Neanderthals and related peoples were found across this zone as late as 35,000 B.C., and some archeologists claim that by then they may also have begun to migrate across a land bridge into the New World. By 10,000 B.C., groups of the *Homo sapiens sapiens* species had colonized all of the continents except Antarctica. Glaciation, which had caused a significant drop in sea levels, resulted in land bridges to the New World and Australia. By the late Paleolithic period, around 12,000 B.C., human colonies were found in North and South America and in the south and west of Australia. Thus, long before the rise of civilizations, human societies had proven themselves capable of surviving in widely varying climates and terrains.

HUMAN SOCIETY AND DAILY LIFE AT THE END OF THE OLD STONE AGE

Most human societies in the Old Stone Age consisted of small groups that migrated regularly in pursuit of game animals and wild plants. But recent archeological research has shown that in a number of places natural conditions

The Spread of Human Populations, About 10,000 B.C.

and human ingenuity permitted some groups to establish settlements where they lived for much of the year, and in some cases for generation after generation. These settled communities harvested wild grains that grew in abundance in many areas. After surviving for centuries in this way, some of these communities made the transition to true farming by domesticating plants and animals near their permanent village sites. Many Paleolithic peoples who established enduring settlements did not advance to domesticated agricultural production, and in fact often reverted to a migratory hunting-and-gathering existence.

The rejection of full-fledged agriculture and the reversion to migratory life-styles caution us against seeing farming as an inevitable stage in human development. There was no simple progression from hunting-and-gathering peoples to settled foraging societies and then to genuine farming communities. Rather, human groups experimented with different strategies for survival. Climatic changes, the availability of water for crop irrigation, dietary preferences, and patterns of procreation affected the strategy a particular group adopted. Only those groups involved in crop and animal domestication, however, have proved capable of producing civilizations.

THE WANDERERS

However successful a particular group proved to be at hunting and gathering, few could support a band larger than 20 to 30 men, women, and children. Dependence on migrating herds of game dictated that these bands were nomadic, though many moved back and forth between the same forest and grazing areas year after year. The migration patterns meant that small numbers of humans needed an extensive land area to support themselves, and consequently human population densities were very low.

Though we imagine Stone Age peoples living in caves, recent research suggests that most preferred to live on open ground. The migratory peoples who lived on hilltops or in forest clearings built temporary shelters of skins and leaves or grass thatching. Their flimsy campsites were readily abandoned when herd movements or threats from competing bands prompted migration. Though it is likely that bands developed a sense of territoriality, boundaries were vague and much interhuman strife focused on rival claims to sources of game and wild foods.

Within each band, labor was divided on a gender basis. Males hunted and fished in riverine or coastal areas. Because they became skilled in the use of weapons in the hunt, it is also likely that males protected the band from animal predators and raids by other human groups. Though women's roles were less adventuresome and aggressive, they were arguably more critical to the survival of the band. The foods women gathered provided the basic subsistence of the band and permitted its survival in times when hunting parties were unsuccessful. Women also became adept in the application of medicinal plants, which were the only means that Paleolithic peoples had to ward off disease. Because life expectancy was short—20 years or less on the average—and mortality rates for women in labor and infants were very high, women had to give birth many times in order for the band to increase its numbers even slightly. The early appearance (c. 25,000 B.C.) of figurines carved by *Homo sapiens sapiens* that depict voluptuous and pregnant women suggest the existence of cults devoted to earth and mother goddesses. The centrality of feminine symbolism in early art and religion may also be indicative of the considerable influence that women wielded within the band.

SETTLING DOWN: DEAD ENDS AND TRANSITIONS

Though most humans lived in small hunting-and-gathering bands until well into the era of the agrarian revolution between 8000 and 5000 B.C., some prefarming peoples worked out a very different strategy of survival. They managed to devise more intensive hunting-and-gathering patterns that permitted them to establish semipermanent and even permanent settlements and support larger and more complex forms of social organization. Among the most spectacular of the Paleolithic settlements are those of central Russia. Apparently there was an abundance of large but slow woolly mammoths in the region some 20,000 years ago. The hunting techniques of the local peoples produced a supply of meat that, when supplemented by wild plant foods gathered in the area, made it possible for them to live in the same place throughout much of the year. Their dependence on the mammoths is suggested by the bones found in refuse pits at the settlement sites and by the bones of the larger mammoths that were used extensively for the walls and roofing of dwellings. The storage pits for food and the other materials found at the sites of the central Russian settlements suggest that the mammoth-bone dwellers participated in trading networks that involved groups in the Black Sea region nearly 500 miles away. Burial patterns and differing degrees of bodily decoration also indicate that there were clear status differences among the groups that inhabited the settlements. Mammoth-bone communities lasted from about 18,000 to 10,000 B.C., when they suddenly disappeared for reasons that are still unknown.

Even more sophisticated than the central Russian settlements were those of the Natufian complex, which extended over much of present-day Israel, Jordan, and Lebanon.

Among the most common artifacts of early human cultures are figurines or rock carvings of female fertility figures. This carving of a wonderfully robust and very pregnant woman, called the "Venus of Laussel," was found at an early campsite in St.-Germain-en-Laye in France.

Climate changes that occurred between 12,000 and 11,000 B.C. enabled wild barley and wheat plants to spread over much of this area. When supplemented with nuts and the meat of gazelles and other game, these wild grains proved sufficient to support numerous and quite densely populated settlements on a permanent basis. Between about 10,500 and 8000 B.C., the Natufian culture flourished in this area. The population at Natufian settlement sites reached as high as six to seven times that of other early Neolithic communities. The Natufians developed quite sophisticated techniques of storing grain, and they devised pestles and grinding slabs to prepare it to eat. They built circular and oval dwellings of stone that were occupied year-round for centuries.

The evidence we have from housing layout, burial sites, jewelry, and other materials indicates that, like the mammoth-bone dwellers of central Russia, Natufian society was stratified. Clothing appears to have been used to distinguish a person's rank, and grand burial ceremonies marked the passing of community chieftains. There is also evidence that Natufian society was *matrilocal*—young men went to live with their wives' families—and *matrilineal*—family descent and inheritance were traced through the female line. The fact that women gathered food crops in the wild may explain the importance of women and the power and influence they enjoyed in Natufian settlements.

The Natufian strategy for survival did not involve the development of new tools or techniques for production. It rested primarily on the intensification of gathering wild grains and the improvement of storage techniques. The Natufians' concentration on a couple of grain staples, gazelle meat, and nuts rendered the culture vulnerable through overspecialization. After 9000 B.C. the climate of the region where the Natufian settlements were located grew more and more arid. The grains and game on which they had grown dependent were reduced or vanished from many locations. One thousand years later, all the Natufian sites had been abandoned. Some villagers reverted to migratory hunting and gathering in an effort to broaden the range of animals they could hunt and the foods they could harvest from the wild. Other villagers—usually those located near large and reliable sources of water—domesticated the grains they had once gathered in the woodlands.

A PRECARIOUS EXISTENCE

Until the late Old Stone Age era around 12,000 B.C., advances in human technology and social organization were remarkably slow when compared to the advances that have occurred since about 8000 B.C. Millions of years of evolution of the genus *Homo* had produced small numbers of humans mostly scattered in tiny bands across six continents. On the average the lives of members of these bands were—to paraphrase a cynical, 17th-century English philosopher, Thomas Hobbes—violent and short. They crouched around their campfires in constant fear of animal predators and human enemies. They were at the mercy of the elements and helpless in the face of injury or disease. They had a few crude tools and weapons; their nomadic existence reflected their dependence on the feeding cycles of migrating animals.

The smaller numbers of human groups that lived in permanent settlements had better shelters, a more secure supply of food, and larger communities on which to draw in their relentless struggle for survival. But their life-styles

This sketch of a mammoth-bone hut suggests the ingenuity in the design and construction of these single-room structures.

were precarious in that their specialized hunting-and-gathering practices meant that shifts in grazing patterns or the climate could undermine their carefully developed cultures. Late Paleolithic humans had considerably improved on earlier and by then extinct versions of the species. But there was little to suggest that within a few thousand years they would radically transform the environments in which they lived and dominate all other forms of life.

AGRICULTURE AND THE ORIGINS OF CIVILIZATION: THE NEOLITHIC REVOLUTION

There was nothing natural or inevitable about the development of agriculture. Because cultivation of plants requires more labor than hunting and gathering, we can assume that Stone Age humans gave up their former ways of life reluctantly and slowly. In fact, peoples such as the Bushmen of Southwest Africa still follow them today. But between about 8000 and 3500 B.C., increasing numbers of humans shifted to dependence on cultivated crops and domesticated animals for their subsistence. By about 7000 B.C., their tools and skills had advanced sufficiently for cultivating peoples to support towns with over one thousand people, such as Jericho in the valley of the Jordan River and Çatal Huyuk in present-day Turkey. By 3500 B.C., agricultural peoples in the Middle East could support sufficient numbers of noncultivating specialists to give rise to the first civilizations. As this pattern spread to or devel-

oped independently in other centers across the globe, the character of most human lives and the history of the species as a whole were fundamentally transformed.

CAUSES OF THE AGRARIAN TRANSFORMATION

Because there are no written records of the transition period between 8000 and 5000 B.C. when many animals were first domesticated and plants were cultivated on a regular basis, we cannot be certain why and how some peoples adopted these new ways of producing food and other necessities of life. Climatic changes associated with the retreat of the glaciers at the end of the last Ice Age (about 12,000 B.C.), may have played an important role. These climatic shifts prompted the migration of many big game animals to new pasturelands in northern areas. They also left a dwindling supply of game for human hunters in areas such as the Middle East, where agriculture first arose and many animals were first domesticated. Climatic shifts also led to changes in the distribution and growing patterns of wild grains and other crops on which hunters and gatherers depended. In addition, it is likely that the shift to sedentary farming was prompted in part by an increase in human populations in certain areas. It is possible that the population growth was caused by changes in the climate and plant and animal life, forcing hunting bands to move into the territories where these shifts had been minimal. It is also possible that population growth occurred within these unaffected regions, because the hunting-and-gathering pattern reached higher levels of productivity. Peoples like the Natufians found their human communities could grow significantly by intensively harvesting grains that grew in the wild. As the population grew, more and more attention was given to the grain harvest, which eventually led to the conscious and systematic cultivation of plants and thus the agrarian revolution.

THE DOMESTICATION OF PLANTS AND ANIMALS

The peoples who first cultivated cereal grains had long observed them growing in the wild and gleaned their seeds as they gathered other plants for their leaves and roots. In Late Paleolithic times both wild barley and wheat grew over large areas in present-day Turkey, Iraq, Syria, Jordan, Lebanon, and Israel. Hunting-and-gathering bands in these areas may have consciously experimented with planting and nurturing seeds taken from the wilds or they may have accidentally discovered the principles of domestication by observing the growth of seeds dropped near their campsites. However it began, the practice of agriculture caught on only gradually. Archeological evidence suggests that the first agriculturists retained their hunting-and-gathering activities as a hedge against the ever-present threat of starvation. But as Stone Age peoples became more adept at cultivating a growing range of crops, including protein-rich legumes such as peas and beans, various fruits, and olives, the effort they expended on activities outside agriculture diminished.

It is probable that the earliest farmers broadcast wild seeds, a practice that cut down on labor but sharply reduced the potential yield. Over the centuries, more and more care was taken to select the best grain for seed and to mix different strains in ways that improved both crop yields and resistance to plant diseases. As the time required to tend growing plants and the dependence on agricultural production for subsistence increased, some roving bands chose to settle down while others practiced a mix of hunting and *shifting cultivation* that allowed them to continue to move about.

Though several animals may have been domesticated before the discovery of agriculture, the two processes combined to make up the critical transformation in human culture called the *Neolithic* (New Stone Age) *revolution*. Different animal species were tamed in different ways that reflected both their own natures and the ways in which they interacted with humans. Dogs, for example, were originally wolves that hunted humans or scavenged at their campsites. As early as 12,000 B.C., Stone Age peoples found that wolf pups could be tamed and trained to track and corner game. The strains of dogs that gradually developed proved adept at controlling herd animals like sheep. Relatively docile and defenseless herds of sheep could be controlled once their leaders had been captured and tamed. Sheep, goats, and pigs (which also were scavengers at human campsites) were first domesticated in the Middle East between 8500 and 7000 B.C. Horned cattle, which were faster and better able to defend themselves than wild sheep, were not tamed until about 6500 B.C. The central place of bull and cattle symbolism in the sacrificial and fertility cults of many early peoples has led some archeologists to argue that their domestication was originally motivated by religious sentiments rather than a desire for new sources of food and clothing.

Domesticated animals such as cattle and sheep provided New Stone Age humans with additional sources of protein-rich meat and in some cases milk. Animal hides and wool greatly expanded the materials from which clothes, containers, shelters, and crude boats could be crafted. Animal horns and bones could be carved or used for needles and other utensils. Because plows and wheels did not come into use until the Bronze Age (c. 4000–3500 B.C.), most Neo-

lithic peoples made little use of animal power for farming, transportation, or travel. There is evidence, however, that peoples in northern areas used tamed reindeer to pull sledges, and those farther South used camels for transporting goods. More importantly, the Neolithic peoples used domesticated herd animals as a steady source of manure to enrich the soil and thus improve the yield of the crops that were gradually becoming the basis of their livelihood.

THE SPREAD OF THE NEOLITHIC REVOLUTION

The greater labor involved in cultivation and the fact that it did not at first greatly enhance the peoples' security or living standards caused many bands to stay with long-tested subsistence strategies. Through most of the Neolithic period, sedentary agricultural communities coexisted with more numerous bands of hunters and gatherers, migratory cultivators, and hunters and fishers. Even after sedentary agriculture became the basis for the livelihood of the majority of humans, hunters and gatherers and shifting cultivators held out in many areas of the globe. For example, due to the absence of the horse and most herd animals in the Americas, nomadic hunting cultures became the main alternatives there.

The domestication of animals gave rise to *pastoralism* which has proven the strongest competitor to sedentary agriculture throughout most of the world. Pastoralism has thrived in semiarid areas such as central Asia, the Sudanic belt south of the Sahara desert in Africa, and the savanna zone of East and South Africa. These areas were incapable of supporting dense or large populations. The nomadic, herding way of life has tended to produce independent and hardy peoples, well-versed in the military skills needed not only for their survival but also to challenge more heavily populated agrarian societies. Horse-riding nomads who herd sheep or cattle have destroyed powerful kingdoms and laid the foundations for vast empires. The camel nomads of Arabia played critical roles in the rise of Islamic civilization. The cattle-herding peoples of central, East, and South Africa produced some of the most formidable preindustrial military organizations. Only with the rather recent period of the Industrial Revolution has the power of nomadic peoples been irreparably broken and the continuation of their cultures threatened by the steady encroachment of sedentary peoples.

In the era of the Neolithic revolution (roughly 8000–5000 B.C.), agriculture was far from the dominant mode of support for human societies. But those who adopted it survived and increased, and passed their techniques of production to other peoples. The cultivation of wheat and barley spread throughout the Middle East and eastward to India. These crops also spread northward to Europe, where oats and rye were added later. From Egypt, the cultivation of grain crops and fibers, such as flax and cotton that were used for clothing, spread to peoples along the Nile in the interior of Africa, along the North African coast, and across the vast savanna zone south of the Sahara desert.

Agriculture in the African rain forest zone farther south evolved independently in the 2d millennium B.C., and was based on root crops such as cassava and tree crops such as bananas and palm nuts. In northern China during the Neolithic period, a millet-based agricultural system developed along the Huanghe or Yellow River basin. From this core region, it spread in the last millennia B.C. east toward the North China Sea and southward toward the Yangtze basin. A later, but independent, agricultural revolution based on rice began in mainland Southeast Asia sometime before 5000 B.C. and slowly spread into South China and India and to the islands of Southeast Asia. In the Americas *maize*- (or corn), manioc-, and sweet potato-based agrarian systems arose in Mesoamerica (Mexico and Central America today) and present-day Peru. Long before the arrival of

Columbus in the Americas in A.D. 1492, these and other crops had spread through large portions of the continents of the Western Hemisphere, from the temperate woodlands of the North Atlantic coast to the rain forests of the Amazon region. Thus, varying patterns of agricultural production were disseminated on all the inhabited continents except Australia, to virtually all the regions of the globe where there were sufficient rainfall and suitable temperatures.

THE NEOLITHIC TRANSITION

With the development of agriculture, humans began to radically transform the environments in which they lived. A growing portion of humans became sedentary cultivators who cleared the lands around their settlements and controlled the plants that grew and the animals that grazed on them. The greater presence of humans was also apparent in the steadily growing size and numbers of settlements. These were found both in areas that they had long inhabited and in new regions that farming allowed them to settle. This great increase in the number of sedentary farmers is primarily responsible for the leap in human population

The Spread of Agriculture

during the Neolithic transition. For tens of thousands of years before agriculture was developed, the total number of humans had fluctuated between an estimated five and eight million persons. By 4000 B.C., after four or five millennia of farming, their number had risen to 60 or 70 million. Hunting-and-gathering bands managed to subsist in the zones between cultivated areas and continued to war and trade with sedentary peoples. But villages and cultivated fields became the dominant features of human habitation over much of the globe.

THE TRANSFORMATION OF MATERIAL LIFE

The growth of sedentary farming communities in the Neolithic era greatly accelerated the pace of technological and social change. The relatively sudden surge in invention and social complexity in the Neolithic era marks one of the great turning points in human history. Increased reliance on sedentary cultivation led to the development of a wide variety of agricultural implements, from digging sticks used to break up the soil and axes to clear forested areas to the introduction of the plow. Techniques of seed selection, planting, fertilization, and weeding improved steadily. By the end of the Neolithic period, human societies in a number of areas had devised ways of storing rainwater and re-channeling river water to irrigate plants. The reservoirs and canals, dikes and sluices that permitted water storage

and control represented another major advance in the ability of humans to remake their environment. These changes protected the thin and fragile soils of the tropical or semi-tropical areas from the sun and torrential rains.

More and better tools and permanent settlements gave rise to larger, more elaborate, and commodious housing and the construction of community ritual centers. Building materials varied greatly by region, but sun-dried bricks, *wattle* (interwoven branches, usually plastered with mud), and stone structures were associated with early agricultural communities. Seasonal harvests made improved techniques of food storage essential. At first, baskets and leather containers were employed, but by the early Neolithic period pottery, which protected stored foods better from moisture and dust, was known to a number of cultures in the Middle East.

Houses in early agricultural settlements usually included special storage areas, and most were centered on clay or stone hearths that were ventilated by a hole in the roof. The presence of stored food in early villages made the houses tempting targets for nomadic bands or rival settlements. For that reason they were increasingly fortified. More dependable and varied food supplies, walls, and sturdy houses greatly enhanced the security and comfort of human groups. These conditions spurred higher rates of procreation and lowered mortality rates, at least in times when crop yields were high.

Early Neolithic settlements, such as this artist's reconstruction of one in Denmark, often included stockades, which were built to protect the precious supply of grain and stock animals. The farmer's houses are outside the stockade on the right.

By the end of the Neolithic period in the 6th millennium B.C., many of the major food plants that humans cultivate today had been domesticated. In addition to food crops, plants, such as flax and cotton whose fibers could be woven into clothing, tents, and rugs, had begun to be cultivated in the Middle East and other areas. New tools and ready supplies of hides also led to new forms of water transport. Axes made possible the carving of paddles and dug-out canoes capable of crossing large bodies of water. Skin-covered boats and reed-and-log rafts were also surprisingly effective forms of water transport. Even after the introduction of the wheel in Afroasia in the 4th millennium B.C., water transport remained much more efficient than land, particularly when bulk goods were involved. Not until railways revolutionized land transport in the 19th century A.D. was this situation reversed.

SOCIAL CHANGE

The surplus production that agriculture made possible was the key to the social transformations that made up another dimension of the Neolithic revolution. Surpluses meant that cultivators could exchange part of their harvest for the specialized services and productions of noncultivators, such as toolmakers and weavers. Human communities became differentiated on an occupational basis. Political and religious leaders arose who eventually formed elite classes that intermarried and became involved in ruling and ceremonies on a full-time basis. But in the Neolithic period the specialized production of stone tools, weapons, and perhaps pottery was a more important consequence of the development of agriculture than the formation of elites. Originally, each household crafted the tools and weapons it required, just as it wove its own baskets and produced its own clothing. Over time, however, families or individuals who proved particularly skilled in these tasks began to manufacture implements beyond their own needs and exchange them for grain, milk, or meat.

Villages in certain regions specialized in the production of materials in demand in other areas. For example, flint, which was extremely hard, was the preferred material for the blades of axes. Axes were needed for forest clearing, which was essential to the extension of cultivation throughout much of Europe. The demand was so great that villagers who lived near flint deposits could support themselves either by mining the flint or by crafting the flint heads that were then traded, often with peoples who lived far from the sources of production. Exchanges such as these set precedents for regional specialization and interregional trade. But the emergence of full-time merchants appears to have been associated with the rise of cities in a later period.

It is difficult to know precisely what impact the shift to agriculture had on the social structure of the communities that made the transition. It is likely that social distinctions were heightened due to occupational differences, but that well-defined social stratification, such as that which produces class identity, was nonexistent. Leadership remained largely communal, though village alliances may have existed in some areas. Judging by research on peoples who still live at roughly Stone Age levels, such as in New Guinea, property in Neolithic times was held in common by the community, or at least all households in the community were given access to village lands and water.

By virtue of their key roles as plant gatherers in pre-farming cultures, it can be surmised that women played a critical part in the domestication of plants. Nonetheless, there is evidence that their position declined in many agricultural communities. They worked, and have continued to work the fields in most cultures. But men took over tasks involving heavy labor, for example, land clearing, hoeing, and plowing. Men monopolized the new tools and weapons devised in the Neolithic era and later times, and they controlled the vital irrigation systems that developed in most of the early centers of agriculture. As far as we can tell, men also took the lead in taming, breeding, and raising the large animals associated with both farming and pastoral communities. Thus, though Neolithic art suggests that earth and fertility cults, which focused on feminine deities, retained their appeal, the social and economic position of women may have begun to decline with the shift to sedentary agriculture.

THE FIRST TOWNS: SEEDBEDS OF CIVILIZATION

By about 7000 B.C., techniques of agricultural production in the Middle East had reached a level at which it was possible to support thousands of people, many of whom were not engaged in agriculture, in densely populated settlements. Two of the earliest of these settlements were at Jericho in what is today the Israeli-occupied West Bank, and at Çatal Huyuk in present-day southern Turkey. With populations of about 2000 and from 4000 to 6000 people respectively, Jericho and Çatal Huyuk would be seen today as little more than large villages or small towns. But in the perspective of human cultural development they represented the first stirrings of urban life. In these and other Middle Eastern Neolithic settlements, occupational specialization and the formation of religious and political-military elite groups advanced significantly. Trade became essential for the community's survival and was carried on, perhaps by specialized merchants, with peoples at considerable distances. Crafts such as pottery, metalworking, and jewelry making were highly developed. At Çatal Huyuk in particular, both sculpture and wall painting were carried to a high level of sophistication.

In these earliest town centers, the key ingredients of civilization came together. Agricultural surpluses were sufficient to support specialized nonfarming producers and nonfarming political and religious leaders. The interaction of these groups resulted in a burst of creativity and innovation in a wide variety of fields. But these earliest centers were quite isolated. They were merely tiny islands of sedentary cultivators and small numbers of townspeople, surrounded by vast plains and woodlands. The earliest town centers appear to have traded rather extensively but to have maintained only intermittent and limited contacts with neighboring hunting-and-gathering peoples. Though small in size and not highly specialized in comparison with the cities of Sumer and other early civilizations, the first towns, settled during this period, nonetheless played critical roles in continuing the Neolithic transformation. The ruling elites and craft specialists of these towns contributed in several major ways to the introduction in the 4th millennium B.C. of critical inventions—inventions such as the wheel, the plow, writing, and the use of bronze—that secured the future of civilized life as the central pattern of human history.

JERICHO

Proximity to the Jordan River and the deep and clear waters of an oasis spring account for repeated human settlement at the place where the town of Jericho was built. By 7000 B.C., over ten acres at the site were occupied by round houses of mud and brick resting on stone foundations. Most early houses had only a single room with mud plaster floors and a domed ceiling, but some houses had as many as three rooms. Entry to these windowless dwellings was provided by a single wood-framed doorway and steps down to the floor of the main room underground. Although there is no evidence that the town was fortified in the early stages of its growth, its expanding wealth made the building of walls for protection from external enemies increasingly imperative. The town was enclosed by a ditch cut into the rocky soil and a wall reaching almost 12 feet in height. The extensive excavation required for this construction is quite impressive because the peoples who undertook it possessed neither picks nor shovels. The stones for the wall were dragged from a riverbed nearly a mile away. These feats of transport and construction suggest not only a sizable labor force but one that was well organized and disciplined.

This village street at Jericho included rectangular houses made of bricks with large, elaborately decorated wooden doorways.

When Jericho was rebuilt in later centuries, the wall reached a height of nearly 15 feet, and the fortifications included a stone tower at least 25 feet high. The area covered by the town increased. Round houses gave way to rectangular ones, entered through larger and more elaborately decorated wooden doorways. Houses were built of improved bricks, were provided with plaster hearths and stone mills for grinding grain, and were furnished with storage baskets and straw mats. In addition, small buildings that were used as religious shrines were found in the later stages of the city's history.

Though the economy of Jericho was based primarily upon the farming of wheat and barley, there is considerable evidence of reliance on both hunting and trade. Domesticated goats provided meat and milk, while gazelles and various marsh birds were hunted for their flesh, hides, and feathers. The town was close to large supplies of salt, sulfur, and pitch. These materials, which were in great demand in this era, were traded for *obsidian*—dark, glasslike volcanic rock—semiprecious stones from Anatolia, turquoise from the Sinai, and cowrie shells from the Red Sea.

The ruins excavated at Jericho indicate that the city was governed by a distinct and quite powerful ruling group, which was probably allied to the keepers of the shrine centers. There probably were specialized artisans and a small merchant class. In addition to the fertility figurines and animal carvings found at many other sites, the inhabitants of Jericho sculpted life-sized, highly naturalistic human figures and heads. These sculptures, which may have been used in ancestor cults, give us vivid impresions of the physical features of the people who enjoyed the wealth and security of Jericho.

ÇATAL HUYUK

The first community at this site in southern Turkey was founded around 7000 B.C., somewhat later than the earliest settlements at Jericho. But the town that grew up at Çatal Huyuk was a good deal more extensive than that at Jericho and contained a larger and more diversified population. Çatal Huyuk was in fact the most advanced human center of the Neolithic period. At the peak of its power and prosperity the city occupied 32 acres and contained as many as 6000 people. Its rectangular buildings, which were centers of family life and community interaction, were remarkably uniform—built of mud-dried bricks. They had windows high in their walls and were entered from holes in their flat roofs. These entryways also served as chimneys for the fireplaces that the houses contained. The houses were joined together to provide fortification for the town. Movement within the settlement was mainly across the roofs and terraces of the houses. Since each dwelling had a substantial storeroom, when the ladder to the roof entrance was pulled up, each became a separate fortress within the larger complex.

This artist's reconstruction depicts the layout of living units in the town of Çatal Huyuk. A family dwelling included an open hearth and an oven in the wall, clearly demarcated and slightly raised sleeping areas, and benches along the walls.

DOCUMENT
EVIDENCE OF LIFE IN THE EARLIEST TOWNS

Because writing had not yet been invented at the time that towns such as Jericho and Çatal Huyuk were settled, the remains of buildings and artifacts dug up at these sites provide our best sources about the lives of the people who lived there. The artifacts and the town plan shown are from the town of Hacilar that was built in present-day Turkey about 1000 years after the town of Çatal Huyuk.

Questions: What do these illustrations tell you about the life of the town's inhabitants? How had town life changed in the millennium since Çatal Huyuk? In what ways had it remained the same? Does change or persistence seem to be dominant?

This artist's reconstruction shows the town plan of one of the sites at Hacilar.

This picture shows a pottery deer found at Hacilar.

These drawings show the baked-clay statuettes of a mother goddess and fertility figurines found at Hacilar sites.

The standardization of housing and construction at Çatal Huyuk suggests an even more imposing ruling group than that found at Jericho. The many religious shrines found at the site also indicate the existence of a powerful priesthood. The shrines were built in the same way as ordinary houses, but they contained sanctuaries surrounded by four or five rooms related to the ceremonies of the shrine's cult. The walls of these religious centers were filled with paintings of bulls and carrion eaters, especially vultures, suggesting fertility cults and rites associated with death. The statuary that has survived indicates that the chief deity of the Çatal Huyuk peoples was a goddess, who is variously depicted as a young woman giving birth or nursing a small child, and as an old woman accompanied by a vulture.

The obvious importance of the cult shrines and the elaborate burial practices of the peoples of Çatal Huyuk reveal the growing role of religion in the lives of Neolithic peoples. The carefully carved sculptures associated with the sanctuaries and the fine jewelry, mirrors, and weapons found buried with the dead attest to the high level of material culture and artistic proficiency achieved by these town dwellers. Excavations of the settlement also reveal an economic base that was much broader and richer than that of Jericho. Hunting remained a factor, but the breeding of goats, sheep, and cattle vastly surpassed that associated with Jericho. A wide range of foods were consumed by Çatal Huyuk's inhabitants, including several grains, peas, berries, berry wine, and vegetable oils made from nuts. Trade was extensive both with the peoples in the surrounding hills and with places as distant as present-day Syria and the Mediterranean region. Çatal Huyuk was also a major center of artisan production. Its flint and obsidian weapons, jewelry, and obsidian mirrors were some of the finest produced in the Neolithic era. The remains of the town's culture leave little doubt that its inhabitants had achieved a civilized level of existence.

CONCLUSION

THE WATERSHED OF THE 4TH MILLENNIUM B.C.

Though Jericho, Çatal Huyuk, and similar settlements can best be seen as towns rather than cities, they displayed many of the characteristics that have come to be associated with urban life. Perhaps they were too small and too dependent on crops grown by their own inhabitants to be labeled cities. But they clearly set the patterns for layout, fortification, and standardization that would be found in the first cities in neighboring regions such as Sumer in Mesopotamia and Egypt, and in distant urban complexes such as those of Harappa in Northwest India and of Kush and Axum in Africa. The level of specialization and political organization these early townspeople had attained proved critical to the invention and dissemination of new tools and production techniques during the 4th millennium B.C. The years from 4000 to 3000 B.C. saw a second wave of major transformations in human culture in the Middle East and nearby regions. These shifts marked the transition from the last of the Stone Ages to the Bronze Age and succeeding epochs of metalworking.

During this transition era, the use of the plow significantly increased crop yields; wheeled vehicles made it possible to carry a greater volume of food and other raw materials over greater distances. Both developments meant that larger noncultivating populations could be supported and concentrated in particular locales. Though copper ore had been used for spear and axe heads for millennia, accident and experiment revealed that when copper was mixed with other ores such as tin, it formed bronze, a harder and more durable material. The bronze tools that resulted further enhanced agricultural production. Trade-oriented, specialized, and wealthy urban peoples were also more likely than relatively isolated nomadic hunters and gatherers to acquire and manufacture bronze weapons, which were much lighter and more lethal than those made of stone. Finally, the development of writing, first in Mesopotamia and later in India, China, and other centers of agrarian production, greatly improved communications in ways that made it possible to expand trading networks and enlarge bureaucracies. Both were essential to the maintenance of large urban complexes.

The development in the Middle East of wheeled vehicles, metalworking, ox-drawn plows, and writing in the 4th millennium B.C. also marks one of the great points of divergence in the history of human civilizations. Except for writing, which was used by some Amerindian peoples on a limited basis, none of these pivotal inventions was known in the Western Hemisphere until the Spaniards invaded it at the end of the 15th century A.D. The great civilizations that Amerindian peoples have produced without these technological breakthroughs suggest that their absence in Mesoamerica and Peru had nothing to do with lack of human ingenuity. The distinctive environment in which Amerindian civilizations developed was critical. The absence of large draft animals everywhere but the Andes Mountains, for example, made wheeled vehicles an unlikely innovation. The difficult terrain in the Andes rendered the use of llamas as pack animals much more advantageous than employing them as haulers of sledges or carts.

In addition, the long isolation of Amerindian peoples from the centers of civilization in Africa, Asia, and Europe prevented the diffusion of the new technology that was developed in a variety of centers at different times. This diffusion and ongoing exchange of objects and ideas between the civilized peoples of the Eastern Hemisphere had played a key role in the founding of new civilizations and the continued growth and development of those already established. Lacking these contacts, the peoples of the Americas built civilizations that were wonderfully sophisticated in many areas, but far behind those of the "Old World" in critical areas such as technological innovation and the harnessing of animal and machine power. Because

their civilizations also developed in very different plant, animal, and disease environments from those in the Eastern Hemisphere, the peoples (and plant and animal life) of areas, such as the Americas, Australia, and the South Pacific, proved even more vulnerable to the diseases introduced from Africa and Eurasia after A.D. 1492. These differences would eventually have catastrophic consequences for these peoples, who had long been isolated from the critical exchanges between the peoples of the Eastern Hemisphere.

FURTHER READINGS

A very considerable literature has developed in recent years on early humans and the critical Neolithic transformations. Sonia Cole's *The Neolithic Revolution* (1970) remains a concise and authoritative survey of this process in the Middle East and parts of Europe. For a broader overview that takes into account more recent research and includes early farming cultures in the Americas, see Robert J. Wenke's *Patterns in Prehistory* (1984). For a sense of the debates that have raged on various aspects of this process, see the sometimes quite technical essays in Stuart Streuver, ed., *Prehistoric Agriculture* (1971), which also covers the Americas extensively.

Even more lively, though often quite technical, are Donald O. Henry's *From Foraging to Agriculture* (1989); and Douglas Price and James A. Brown, eds., *Prehistoric Hunter-Gatherers: The Emergence of Cultural Complexity* (1986). M. C. and H. B. Quennell's *Everyday Life in the New Stone, Bronze and Early Iron Ages* (1955) is difficult to top for an imaginative reconstruction of life in the Neolithic epoch, though some of it is now dated. The most reliable treatment of technology in this era can still be found in volume one of C. Singer, et al., *A History of Technology* (1954). The best introduction to the earliest towns are in James Mellaart's *Earliest Civilizations of the Near East* (1965) and *The Neolithic of the Near East* (1975).

7000–4000 Spread of agriculture through most of Middle East   3000 Introduction of bronze tools
                                4000 Sumerians settle in Tigris-Euphrates valley
                5000 Farming along Nile River   3500 Early Sumerian alphabet

Middle East

2400–2200 Akkadian
empire conquers Sumer

**Egypt and
Upper Nile**

3100–2700 Initial kingdoms   2600 First great pyramid

2700–2200 Old Kingdom period

**Other
Mediterranean**

2 The Rise of Civilization in the Middle East and Africa

INTRODUCTION. The first full civilization emerged by 3500 B.C. in the Tigris-Euphrates valley in the Middle East. Relatively soon thereafter civilization developed along the Nile in Egypt, and later spread to other parts of the Middle East and one region in Africa. The advent of civilization provided a framework for most of the developments in world history. Additionally, the specific early civilizations that arose in the Middle East and Africa had several distinctive features, in political structure and cultural tone, for example. These features secured the evolution of these societies until the partial eclipse of the river-valley civilizations after about 1000 B.C. The early civilizations in the Middle East and North Africa served as generators of a number of separate and durable civilization traditions, which can still be found in civilizations around the Mediterranean, in parts of Europe, and even across the Atlantic.

The central subject of this chapter is the nature of early civilization and its manifestations in two key cases. Both of these early civilizations formed around major rivers—the Tigris and Euphrates in Mesopotamia and the Nile in northeastern Africa. Explaining how civilizations emerged in the Middle East and then Africa requires a reminder of the conditions that contributed to change after 4000 B.C. and a more precise definition of civilization. Once that is done, we can turn to the characteristics of *Mesopotamian civilization*, from its origins around 3500 B.C. until it experienced an important period of disunity around 1000 B.C. Next comes Egypt,

---

2000 B.C.	1000 B.C.	A.D. 1
	1100 Spread of use of iron	
2000 Gilgamesh epic written **1400–1200** Hittite empire; use of iron	**665–617** Assyrian empire	
1800 Babylonian empire; Hammurabi, 1796–1750		
1600 Settlement of Jews in southeast Mediterranean	**539** Persian empire	
2052–1786 Middle Kingdom period; civilization to Upper Nile	**1575–1087** New Kingdom period	**A.D. 100** Decline of Kush and its capital Meroe
	1000 Kush independent kingdom	
1700 Hyksos invasion	**730** Kushite rule of Egypt	**A.D. 300** Rise of Axum [Ethiopia]
2000 Phoenician state	**1000–970** Kingdom of Israel under King David	
1250 Moses and Jewish exodus from Egypt	**800** Beginning of writing of Bible	
	1000 Indo-European invasion of Greece	
	1000 Spread of Phoenician settlements in western Mediterranean	
1600 Minoan civilization [Crete]	**721** Assyrian invasion conquers northern Israel	

the world's second civilization in time, which again can be traced until about 1000 B.C. The two early civilizations had very different cultures and political structures reflecting their very separate origins. By 1000 B.C. both of these two early civilizations produced offshoots in eastern Africa, southern Europe, and additional centers in the Middle East. These smaller centers of civilization made important contributions of their own, for example, the monotheistic religion created among the Jewish people in Palestine.

THE MIDDLE EAST BY 4000 B.C.: THE CAUSES OF CIVILIZATION

As you have seen, one reason that civilization first appeared in the Middle East was because agriculture had taken hold in this region. Over many centuries agriculture became more common and productive in the Middle East; it began to create the conditions for further innovations—including civilization. But the first civilization also required an additional set of *stimuli*, the new inventions and organizations that had taken shape around 4000 B.C.

Much time elapsed between the development of agriculture and the rise of civilization in the Middle East and many other places. The successful agricultural communities that formed were based primarily on very localized production, which normally sustained a population despite recurrent disasters caused by bad weather or harvest problems. Localized agriculture did not consistently yield the kind of surplus that would allow specializations among the population, and therefore it could not generate civilization.

Even the formation of small regional centers, such as Jericho or Çatal Huyuk, did not assure a rapid pace of change. Their economic range remained localized, with little trade or specialization. Most families who inhabited them produced for their own needs and nothing more. It was important that more and more regions in the Middle East were pulled into the orbit of agriculture as the Neolithic revolution gained ground. By 4000 B.C. large nomadic groups still flourished only at the southern end of the region in the deserts of the Arabian peninsula. Even the knowledge of agriculture spread slowly, so the gradual conversion of virtually the whole Middle East and some surrounding areas was no small achievement. But the shape of agricultural communities themselves in 4000 B.C. differed little from that of pioneering agricultural centers 4000 years before.

Based on the expansion of agriculture in the Middle East, a detached observer who lived a little before 4000 B.C. might have predicted the gradual spread or independent development of agriculture in many parts of the world. Portions of India, northern Africa, central Asia, and southern Europe were already drawn in (though other nearby regions, such as Italy, remained immune for another millennium and a half). A separate Neolithic revolution was beginning to take shape in Central America. All this was vital, but it did not assure the civilizational revolution within key agricultural regions themselves.

DYNAMIC IMPLICATIONS OF AGRICULTURE

Several factors flowed together to create the unexpected development of civilization. While the establishment of agriculture did not guarantee further change, it did ultimately contribute to change by encouraging new forms of social organization. Settled agriculture, as opposed to slash-and-burn varieties, usually implied some forms of property so that land could be identified as belonging to a family, a village, or a landlord. Only with property was there incentive to introduce improvements, such as wells or irrigation measures, that could be monopolized by those who created them or left to their heirs. But property meant the need for new kinds of laws and enforcement mechanisms, which in turn implied more extensive government. Here agriculture could create some possibilities for trade and could spur innovation—new kinds of regulations and some government figures who could enforce them.

Farming encouraged the formation of larger and more stable communities than had existed before Neolithic times. Most hunting peoples moved in small groups containing no more than 60 individuals who could not settle in a single spot lest the game run out. With settled agriculture the constraints changed. Communities developed around the cleared and improved fields. In many early agricultural areas including the Middle East, a key incentive to stability was the need for irrigation systems. Irrigated agriculture depended on arrangements that would allow farmers to cooperate in building and maintaining irrigation ditches and sluices. The needs of irrigation, plus protection from marauders, help explain why most early agricultural peoples settled in village communities, rather than isolated farms. Villages that grouped several hundred people constituted the characteristic pattern of residence in almost all agricultural societies from Neolithic days to our own times. Some big rivers encouraged elaborate irrigation projects that could channel water in virtually assured quantities to vast stretches of land. To create larger irrigation projects along major rivers such as Tigris-Euphrates or the Nile, large gangs of laborers had to be assembled. Further, regulations had to assure that users along the river and in the villages near the river's source would have equal access to the water supply. This implied an increase in the scale of political and economic organization. A key link between the advantages of irrigation and the gradual emergence of civilization was that irrigated land produced surpluses with greater certainty and required new kinds of organization.

It is no accident that the earliest civilizations arose along large rivers and amid irrigation projects. Civilization in Mesopotamia and then Egypt involved not only the central fact of economic surplus but also the ability to integrate tens, even hundreds of square miles along rivers. Regional coordination, based first on irrigation needs, could easily lead to other contacts: shared cultures, including artistic styles and religious beliefs; economic contacts, including trade; and common political institutions.

FURTHER INNOVATIONS: NEW TOOLS AND SPECIALIZATIONS IN THE 4TH MILLENNIUM WATERSHED

The first civilization also required the technological developments whose impact coalesced around 4000 B.C. These developments addressed problems faced by agricultural peoples who were encouraged by opportunities available in individual villages to share ideas and encourage inventive colleagues. Most of the inventions thus occurred in regions where agriculture was best developed, which for a long time meant the Middle East. At the same time, the new inventions enhanced the productivity of Middle Eastern agriculture, creating the consistent surpluses that would ultimately shape civilization itself. The result was a recurrent series of technological changes. The first potter's wheel was invented by about 6000 B.C. It encouraged faster and higher-quality ceramic pottery production, which facilitated food storage and improved the reliability of food supplies. Pottery production promoted the emergence of a group of specialized manufacturing workers who made pots to exchange for food produced by others.

Better tools allowed improvements in other products made out of wood or stone. Obsidian, a hard stone, began to be used for tools in the late Neolithic centuries. The wheel was another Middle-Eastern innovation. Wheeled vehicles long remained slow but they were vital to many monumental construction projects where large blocks of stone were moved to the construction sites of temples. Shipbuilding also gradually improved. Developments of this sort, enhancing production and possibilities for trade, set the framework for the outright emergence of civilization with the rise of Sumerian society along the Tigris-Euphrates.

A key technological change, which occurred slightly after the emergence of the first civilization, was the introduction of metal for use in tools and weapons. By about 3000 B.C., copper began to be mixed with tin to make bronze;

this development occurred around the Black Sea and in the Middle East. Use of metal allowed manufacture of a greater variety of tools than could be made of stone or bone, and the tools were lighter and more quickly made. The Middle East was the first region to move from the Neolithic (stone tool) Age to the Bronze Age. Other parts of the eastern Mediterranean soon made the transition. Metal hoes, plows, and other implements proved extremely useful to agricultural societies and also to herding peoples in central Asia. Again new technology promoted further specialization as groups of artisans concentrated on metal production, exchanging their wares for food. Widespread use of bronze also encouraged greater trade, because tin, in particular, was hard to find; by 2000 B.C. trade had become a motivation for extensive development of sea routes.

EARLY CIVILIZATION IN MESOPOTAMIA

Even the technological innovations that shaped the context for the rise of civilization took many centuries to win full impact. Soon after 4000 B.C. however, conditions were ripe for a final set of changes that constituted the arrival of civilization. These changes were based on the use of economic surplus and the growing needs of a coordinated regional network of villages.

THE SUMERIANS

The scene for the first civilization was the northeastern section of what we today call the Middle East, along the great rivers that led to the Persian Gulf. The agents were a newly-arrived people called the Sumerians.

The first civilization developed in a part of the Middle East slightly south of the hilly country in which the first agricultural villages had emerged several thousand years earlier. Between the northern hills and the deserts of the Arabian peninsula, running from the eastern Mediterranean coast to the fall plain of the Tigris and Euphrates rivers, lies a large swath of arable land called the Fertile Crescent. The rivers rise in the spring, depositing immensely fertile soil. Rainfall was scant in the region, so as population pressure increased, farming communities began to find ways to tame and use the rivers through irrigation ditches. Construction of the ditches required improved tools that were not available much before 4000 B.C., and from that point onward developments in the region were swift. Irrigation plus the fertility of the Tigris-Euphrates region generated substantial food surpluses promoting population growth and village expansion, as well as increasing trade and specialization. The region was vulnerable in one respect: It was so flat that it was open to frequent invasion.

By 3500 B.C. farmers in Mesopotamia, as the Tigris-Euphrates region is also called, were benefiting not only from rich agriculture, but also from flourishing pottery and obsidian tool production. The wheel had been introduced, and community coordination was steadily improving to support the irrigation network.

The final boost toward establishing civilization was provided by the Sumerians, a people who had migrated into the area from the north around 4000 B.C. They settled in an area of about 700 square miles where they mixed with other local races in a pattern of cultural mingling that has remained characteristic of the region. Sumerian culture early developed important religious values with centers of pilgrimage and worship. Well before 3000 B.C. many of these centers were provided with elaborately decorated temples, built with mud brick. Sumerians were impressed with the power of grim gods who ultimately controlled human destiny.

SUMERIAN CULTURE AND POLITICS. Into this rich economy and culture writing—the most important invention between the advent of agriculture and the age of the steam engine—was introduced around 3500 B.C. The Sumerian invention of writing was probably rather sudden, based on new needs for commercial, property, and political records including a celebration of the deeds of proud local kings. Writing was preceded by the invention of clay cylinder seals, on which little pictures of objects could be recorded. The earliest Sumerian writing simply evolved from these pictures baked on clay tablets, which were turned into symbols and gradually transformed into phonetic elements. The early Sumerian *alphabet*—set of symbols representing sounds—may have had as many as 2000 symbols derived from the early pictures. Before long writers began to use more abstract symbols to represent sounds which allowed Sumerians and their successors to reduce the alphabet to about 300 symbols. Sumerian writers used a wedge-shaped stick to impress the symbols on clay tablets. The resulting writing is called *cuneiform*, meaning "wedge shaped," and it was used for several thousand years in the Middle East for many different languages. Cuneiform writing was difficult to learn, so specialized scribes monopolized most of it, but the Sumerians in fact believed that every object in nature should have a separate name to assure its place in the universe; knowing the name gave a person some power over the object. Writing, in other words, quickly took on essentially religious purposes, allowing people to impose an abstract order over nature and the social world.

Sumerian civilization lasted intact until about 2000 B.C. Its political organization was based on tightly organized city-states, where the agricultural hinterland was ruled by an urban-based king who claimed great authority. In some cases local councils advised the king. One of the functions of Sumerian states was to define boundaries, unlike the less formal territories of precivilized villages in the region. The government helped regulate religion and enforce its duties. It also provided a system of courts for justice. Kings were originally war leaders whose leadership of a trained army in defense and war remained vital in Sumerian politics where fighting loomed large. Kings, the noble class, and the priesthood controlled considerable land. Slaves, conquered in wars with nearby tribes, were used to work this land.

Sumerian political and social organization set up traditions that would long endure in this region. City-state government established a tradition of regional rule, that would often be overlaid by larger empires but would frequently return as the principal organizational form. The reliance on slaves was maintained in the economy of many successor civilizations. Use of slaves along with the lack of natural barriers to invasion help explain recurrent warfare, for war was often needed to supply labor. At the same time, slavery in the Middle Eastern tradition was a variable condition, and many slaves were able to earn their own keep and even buy their freedom.

The Sumerians, aided by regional political stability and the use of writing, added to their region's economic prosperity. Agriculture gained as farmers learned how to cultivate date trees, onions, and garlic. Oxen were used to pull plows, donkeys to carry goods. Wheeled carts helped transport goods as well. The Sumerians introduced the use of fertilizer and adopted silver as a means of exchange for buying and selling. Major cities expanded—one city reached a population of over 70,000—with substantial housing units in rows of flat-roofed, mud-brick shops and apartments. More commonly, cities contained as many as 10,000 people. The Sumerians improved the potter's wheel, which expanded the production of pottery. Because of the skill level and commercial importance involved, men began to take the trade away from women. The Sumerians also invented glass. Trade expanded to the lower Persian Gulf and to the western portion of the Middle East along the Mediterranean. By 2000 B.C. the Sumerians had trading contacts with India.

The Sumerians also steadily elaborated their culture, again using writing to advance earlier forms. By about 2000 B.C. they managed to write down the world's oldest story, the Gilgamesh epic, which went back at least to the 7th millennium B.C. in oral form. Gilgamesh, a real person who had ruled a city-state, became the first hero in world literature. The epic describes a great flood that obliterated humankind except for a favored family who sur-

Mesopotamia and the Middle East

vived by building an ark and producing descendants who formed a new race of people. The overall tone of the epic and of Sumerian culture (perhaps reflecting the frequently disastrous floods of the region) was somber. Gilgamesh does great deeds but constantly bumps up against the iron laws of the gods, ensuring human failure as the gods triumph in the end.

> The heroes, the wise men, like the new moon have their waxing and waning. Men will say, "Who has ever ruled with might and with power like Gilgamesh?" As in the dark month, the month of shadows; so without him there is no light. O Gilgamesh, this was the meaning of your dream. You were given the kingship, such was your destiny; everlasting life was not your destiny . . . . Gilgamesh, why do you search? The life you seek you will never find. When the gods created the world, they made death a part of human fate.

Along with early literature, Sumerian art developed steadily. Statues and painted frescoes adorned the temples of the gods, and statues of the gods decorated individual homes. Sumerian science aided a complex agricultural society, as people sought to learn more about the movement of the sun and stars—thus founding the science of astronomy—and to improve their mathematical knowledge. The Sumerians employed a system of numbers based on units of 12, 60, and 360, which we still use in calculations involving circles and hours. They also introduced specific systems, such as charts of major constellations, that have been used for 5000 years in the Middle East and through later imitation in India and Europe. In other words, Sumerians and their successors in Mesopotamia created patterns of observation and abstract thought about nature on which a number of later societies, including our own, still rely.

Religion played a vital role in Sumerian culture and politics. Gods were associated with various forces of nature. At the same time gods were seen as having a human form and many of humanity's more disagreeable characteristics. Thus the gods often quarreled and used their power in selfish and childish ways—which made for interesting stories but also created a fear that the gods might make life difficult and hard to control. The gloomy cast of Sumerian

One of the early uses of writing involved marking property boundaries. This picture shows cuneiform writing on a Mesopotamian map from about 1300 B.C. The map focuses on defining the king's estate.

religious ideas also included an afterlife of suffering—an original version of the concept of hell. Because gods were believed to regulate natural forces such as flooding in a region where nature was often harsh and unpredictable, they were more feared than loved. Priests played a central role because of their responsibility for placating the gods through proper prayers, sacrifices, and magic. Priests became full-time specialists, running the temples and also performing the astronomical calculations necessary to run the irrigation systems. Each city had a patron god, and erected impressive shrines to please and honor this god and other deities. Massive towers, called *ziggurats*, formed the monumental architecture for this civilization. Prayers and offerings to prevent floods as well as to protect good health were a vital part of Sumerian life. Sumerian ideas about the divine force behind and within natural objects—in rivers, trees, and mountains—were common among agricultural peoples. A religion of this sort is known as *animism*. More specifically, Sumerian religious notions, notably their

ideas about the creation of the earth by the gods from a chaos of water and about divine punishment of humans through floods, continue to have force in Jewish, Christian, and Muslim cultures, all of which were born much later in the Middle East.

Sumerian activities in trade and war spread beyond the regional limits of the civilization in the Middle East. The adoption of portions of the Gilgamesh tale in later literature such as the Jewish Bible developed well to the west of Sumer. Even after Sumer itself collapsed, the Sumerian language was still used in religious schools and temples, showing the power of this early culture and its decidedly religious emphasis.

WHAT CIVILIZATION MEANT

The emergence of the world's first civilization in Sumer brought to fruition the key features of this form of organization. Sumerian society certainly met the basic criterion of civilization in that it built on fairly regular economic surpluses. Sumerian farmers produced enough that they could be taxed in order to support a small but crucial number of priests and government officials. They produced enough to allow some trade and specialization, thus encouraging groups of artisans and merchants who did not farm. The Sumerian economy also stretched out along the great irrigation systems of the Tigris-Euphrates. One of the tasks of regional government was to elaborate and maintain these systems: regional coordination was thus a vital feature.

The advent of civilization in Sumer also involved additional innovations building on the key features of surplus and coordination: the creation of cities beyond the scope of individual centers, such as Jericho, where at least several thousand people lived and considerable specialization developed; and the invention of writing. While these innovations were not found in all civilizations, they were vital in Sumer and other early centers such as Egypt and the Indus River.

THE IMPORTANCE OF CITIES.

In Middle-Eastern agricultural civilization (all civilizations were fundamentally agricultural until about 200 years ago), most people did not live in cities. The cities that existed were crucial, however, because they amassed wealth and power; allowed relatively easy exchange of ideas, encouraging intellectual and artistic changes; and promoted further specialization in manufacture and trade. Early Middle-Eastern cities radiated considerable influence and power into surrounding countrysides. Cities also relied on broader attributes of civilization, the most notable being relatively extensive trade and political organization. Cities could not be founded until the Middle East produced a significant agricultural surplus above what farmer families needed to live on and had groups—merchants—to organize trade that brought food to the city and carried urban-made goods to the countryside and other cities. Cities could not be founded until there was a sufficiently solid political organization—a government, with some recognized legitimacy, and some full-time officials—that could run essential urban services, such as a court system for disputes, and help regulate the relationship between cities and the countryside.

Saying that early Middle-Eastern civilizations were based on cities, then, even when most people remained in the countryside as agricultural producers, is partly saying that civilizations had generated more elaborate trade and political structures than initial agricultural societies had managed. This helps explain, also, why civilizations generally covered a fairly wide area, breaking out of the localism that described the economics and political activities of the initial agricultural communities.

THE IMPORTANCE OF WRITING.

The second key ingredient that emerged in the Middle East after 4000 B.C. was the invention of writing. Some historians and anthropologists urge against focusing too much on the development of writing, because concentrating only on this aspect, albeit important, can leave out some civilizations, such as the civilization of the Incas in the Andes region of South America, that produced significant political forms without this intellectual tool. We now appreciate the sophistication societies can attain without writing, and rate the division of early human activities between hunting and gathering and agriculture as more fundamental than the invention of writing.

Writing was a genuinely important development even so. Societies with writing can organize more elaborate records including the lists essential for effective taxation. Writing is a precondition for most formal bureaucracies which depend on standardized communication and the ability to maintain some documentation. Societies with writing can also organize a more elaborate intellectual life because of their ability to record data and build on past, written wisdom. For example, it is no accident that with writing many early civilizations began to generate more formal scientific knowledge. Societies before the development of writing typically depended on poetic sagas to convey their value systems, with the poetry designed to aid in memorization. With writing, the importance of sagas such as Gilgamesh might at first have continued but usually the diversity of cultural expressions soon increased with other kinds of literature supplementing the long, rhymed epics. Some experts argue that the very fact of becoming literate changes the way people think—encouraging a greater sense that the world can be understood by organized human inquiry as opposed to a belief in whimsical magical spirits. Writing, in other words, can produce more abstract religious thinking and also secular thinking that seeks to describe nature and human affairs in nonreligious terms.

Writing, like the existence of cities, certainly helps explain how civilizations could develop more extensive trading and political systems than those of most earlier agricultural societies. As a basis for even small bureaucracies—and as a basis of record-keeping for merchant dealings beyond purely personal contacts—writing played a considerable role in extending the geographical range of key civilizations and in developing new forms of economic and political organization. It is vital to recognize, however, that the advent of writing in the early history of civilizations also created new divisions within the population, for only a small minority of people—mainly priests, scribes, and a few merchants—had time to master writing skills.

CIVILIZATION: DRAWBACKS AND LIMITS. Because civilizations are by definition well organized compared to the societies that preceded them, it is not surprising that almost all history is about what has happened to civilized societies. We know most about such societies, and we are likely to be particularly impressed by their great art or powerful rulers. It is also true that civilizations tended to be far more populous than noncivilized societies. Because civilizations depend on some trade, they allow greater specialization that increases productivity and sustenance of larger populations. Their political structure allows whole regions or even a number of regions to be unified. But the history of civilization does not embrace everybody. In the days of the river-valley civilizations, even long after Sumer, most inhabited parts of the world were not in the civilization orbit.

There is inevitable confusion between defining a society as a civilization and assuming that civilization produces a monopoly on higher values and controlled behavior. In the first place, civilization brings losses as well as gains. As the Middle East moved toward civilization, distinctions based on social class and wealth increased. This was clearly the case in Sumer, where social structure ranged from slaves, who were treated as property, to powerful kings and priests. Civilizations typically have firmer class or caste divisions and greater separations between ruler and ruled than "simpler" societies. Civilizations also often create greater inequality between men and women than noncivilized societies do. Many early civilizations, including those of the Middle East, went to considerable pains to organize the inferiority of women on a more structured basis than ever before, treating women as the property of fathers or husbands. Finally, as Sigmund Freud noted, civilizations impose a host of restraints on people in order to keep them organized in a complex social unit. Such restraints can create a great deal of personal tension and even mental illness. "Civilization," then, should not be taken as a synonym for "a 'good' or 'progressive' society."

Furthermore, people in noncivilized societies may be exceptionally well regulated and possessed of interesting, important culture. They are not "merely" barbarians or uncouth wild men. Some societies that were most eager to repress anger and aggression in human dealings, such as several Eskimo groups, were not part of a civilization until recently. In contrast, many civilized societies produce a great deal of aggressive behavior and build warlike qualities into their list of virtues. While some noncivilized societies treat old people cruelly, others display respect and veneration. A civilized society does not invariably enhance the human capacity for restrained, polite behavior or an interest in the higher values of life. Civilizations do not even clearly promote greater human happiness.

The development of civilization continued the process of enhancing human capacity for technological and political organization, and the production of increasingly elaborate and diverse artistic and intellectual forms. In this quite restricted sense, the term has meaning and legitimately commands the attention of most historians. Because of the power and splendor civilizations could provide, they did tend to spread as other societies came under their influence or deliberately tried to imitate their achievements. Early civilizations, however, spread slowly because many peoples had no contact with them and because their disadvantages, such as greater social inequality, might be repellent. Thus the initial advent of civilization, while an important historical milestone, came in clearly circumscribed regions like the Tigris-Euphrates valley. The history of early civilization focuses attention on the generation of the first forms of civilized activity—writing and city administration—and on the construction of linkages in medium-sized geographical units.

THE COURSE OF MESOPOTAMIAN CIVILIZATION: A SERIES OF CONQUESTS

The general characteristics of civilization, from economic surplus to writing, cities, and social inequality, are vital, but must be combined with the specific qualities of particular civilizations such as those of Mesopotamia, where writing was of a certain style; social organization was distinctive, for example, in the power of priests; and overall culture had some special qualities.

A key ingredient of Mesopotamian civilization was frequent instability as one ruling people gave way to another invading force. The Sumerians, themselves invaders of the fertile river valleys, did not set up a sufficiently strong and united political force to withstand pressures from outside, particularly when other peoples of the Middle East began to copy key achievements, such as the formation of cities.

LATER MESOPOTAMIAN EMPIRES

Shortly after 2400 B.C. a king from a non-Sumerian city, Akkad, conquered the Sumerian city-states and inaugurated an Akkadian Empire. This empire soon sent troops as far as Egypt and Ethiopia. The initial Akkadian ruler, *Sargon I,* the first clearly identified individual in world history, set up a unified empire integrating the city-states into a whole, and added to Sumerian art a new style marked by the theme of royal victory. Professional military organization expanded since Sargon maintained a force of 5400 troops. Extensive tax revenues were needed to support his operations. The Akkadians were the first people to use writing for more than commercial and temple records, kingdoms were springing up in various parts of the Middle East, while new invading groups, including Indo-European tribes that came from the Balkans in southeastern Europe, added to the region's confusion. A civilization derived from Sumerian culture spread more widely in the Middle East, though political unity was rarely achieved in the expanded setting.

Another new empire arose around 1800 B.C., for the first time unifying the whole of Mesopotamia. This Babylonian Empire was headed by *Hammurabi,* one of the great rulers of early civilized history. Hammurabi set up an extensive network of officials and judges, while maintaining a separate priesthood. He also codified the laws of the region, to deal with a number of criminal, property, and family issues. Large cities testified to the wealth and power

This bronze stag, a common theme in Mesopotamian art, comes from royal tombs near the Hittite capital in present-day Turkey.

This bronze head of Sargon, founder of the Akkadian dynasty, dates from about 2350 B.C. The elaborate metalwork displays the artistic talents acquired by leading craftsmen.

producing a number of literary works. The Akkadian empire, however, lasted only about 200 years, and then it was overthrown by another invading force. Sumerian regional states reappeared, in what turned out to be the final phase of this particular civilization. It was then that the *Epic of Gilgamesh* was written. By this time, around 2000 B.C., of this new empire. At the same time, Sumerian cultural traditions were maintained and elaborated. The famous *Hammurabic code* thus was built on earlier codifications by Sumerian kings.

A Babylonian poem testified to the continued sobriety of the dominant culture: "I look about me and see only evil. My troubles grow and I cannot find justice. I have prayed to the gods and sacrificed, but who can understand the gods in heaven? Who knows what they plan for us? Who has ever been able to understand a god's conduct?"

Finally, Babylonian scientists extended the Sumerian work in astronomy and mathematics. Scholars were able to predict lunar eclipses and trace the paths of some of the planets. Babylonians also worked out mathematical tables and an algebraic geometry of great practical utility. The modern 60-minute hour and 360-degree circle are heritages of the Babylonian system of measurement. The study of astronomy is another Babylonian legacy.

Indeed, of all the successors of the Sumerians, the Babylonians constructed the most elaborate culture, though their rule was not long-lived. The Babylonians expanded commerce and a common cultural zone, both based on growing use of cuneiform writing and a shared language. During the empire itself, new government strength showed both in the extensive legal system and in the opulent public buildings and royal palaces. The hanging gardens of one king dazzled visitors from the entire region.

The Babylonian empire fell by about 1600 B.C. An invading Hittite people, pressing in from central Asia, adapted the Sumerian cuneiform script to their own Indo-

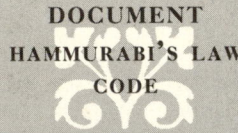

DOCUMENT
HAMMURABI'S LAW CODE

Hammurabi, as king of Babylon, united Mesopotamia under his rule from about 1800 to 1750 B.C. His law code, the earliest such compilation still in existence, was discovered on a stone slab in Iran in A.D. 1901. Not a systematic presentation, it was a collection of exemplary cases designed to set general standards of

The Stele of Hammurabi shows the king in front of the sun god, Shamash. Hammurabi's code of law is carved below.

justice. The code provides vital insights into the nature of social relations and family structure in this ancient civilization. Examples of the Hammurabic code follow:

When Marduk commanded me to give justice to the people of the land and to let [them] have [good] governance, I set forth truth and justice throughout the land [and] prospered the people.

At that time:

If a man has accused a man and has charged him with manslaughter and then has not proved [it against] him, his accuser shall be put to death.

If a man has charged a man with sorcery and then has not proved [it against] him, he who is charged with the sorcery shall go to the holy river; he shall leap into the holy river and, if the holy river overwhelms him, his accuser shall take and keep his house; if the holy river proves that man clear [of the offense] and he comes back safe, he who has charged him with sorcery shall be put to death; he who leapt into the holy river shall take and keep the house of his accuser.

If a man has come forward in a case to bear witness to a felony and then has not proved the statement that he has made, if that case [is] a capital one, that man shall be put to death.

If he has come forward to bear witness to [a claim for] corn or money, he shall remain liable for the penalty for that suit.

If a judge has tried a suit, given a decision, caused a sealed tablet to be executed, [and] thereafter varies his judgment, they shall convict that judge of varying [his] judgment and he shall pay twelve-fold the claim in that suit; then they shall remove him from his place on the bench of judges in the assembly, and he shall not [again] sit in judgment with the judges.

If a free person helps a slave to escape, the free person will be put to death.

If a man has committed robbery and is caught, that man shall be put to death.

If the robber is not caught, the man who has been robbed shall formally declare whatever he has lost before a god, and the city and the mayor in whose territory or district the robbery has been committed shall replace whatever he has lost for him.

If [it is] the life [of the owner that is lost], the city or the mayor shall pay one *maneh* of silver to his kinsfolk.

If a person owes money and Adad [the river god] has flooded the person's field, the person will not give any grain [tax] or pay any interest in that year.

If a person is too lazy to make the dike of his field strong and there is a break in the dike and water destroys his own farmland, that person will make good the grain [tax] that is destroyed.

If a merchant increases interest beyond that set by the king and collects it, that merchant will lose what was lent.

If a trader borrows money from a merchant and then denies the fact, that merchant in the presence of god and witnesses will prove the trader borrowed the money and the trader will pay the merchant three times the amount borrowed.

If the husband of a married lady has accused her but she is not caught lying with another man, she shall take an oath by the life of a god and return to her house.

If a man takes himself off and there is not the [necessary] maintenance in his house, his wife [so long as] her [husband is delayed], shall keep [herself chaste; she shall not] enter [another man's house].

If that woman has not kept herself chaste but enters another man's house, they shall convict that woman and cast her into the water.

If a son strikes his father, they shall cut off his forehand.

If a man has put out the eye of a free man, they shall put out his eye.

If he breaks the bone of a [free] man, they shall break his bone.

If he puts out the eye of a villein or breaks the bone of a villein, he shall pay 1 maneh of silver.

If he puts out the eye of a [free] man's slave or breaks the bone of a [free] man's slave, he shall pay half his price.

If a man knocks out the tooth of a [free] man equal [in rank] to him[self], they shall knock out his tooth.

If he knocks out the tooth of a villein, he shall pay ⅓ maneh of silver.

If a man strikes the cheek of a [free] man who is superior [in rank] to him[self], he shall be beaten with 60 stripes with a whip of ox-hide in the assembly.

If the man strikes the cheek of a free man equal to him[self in rank], he shall pay 1 maneh of silver.

If a villain strikes the cheek of a villein, he shall pay 10 *shekels* of silver.

If the slave of a [free] man strikes the cheek of a free man, they shall cut off his ear.

Questions: What can you tell from the Hammurabic code about the social and family structure of Mesopotamia? What is the relationship between law and trade? Why did agricultural civilizations such as Babylon insist on harsh punishments for crimes?

European language and set up an empire of their own. The Hittites soon yielded, and a series of smaller kingdoms disputed the region for several centuries, between about 1200 and 900 B.C. This period allowed a number of regional cultures, such as the Hebrew and the Phoenician, to develop greater autonomy, thus adding to the diversity and the achievements of the Middle East. Then, after about 900 B.C., another series of empires began in the Middle East, including the Assyrian Empire and later the Persian Empire based on invasions of new groups from central Asia. These new invaders had mastered the produc-

tion of iron weapons and also used horses and chariots in fighting, sketching a new framework for the development of empires and a new chapter in the history of the Middle East and of civilization more generally.

ANCIENT EGYPT

A second civilization grew up in northeastern Africa, along the Nile River. Egyptian civilization, formed by 3000 B.C., benefited from trade and technological influence from Mesopotamia, but it produced a quite different society and culture. Because its values and its tightly knit political organization encouraged monumental building, we know more about Egypt than about Mesopotamia, even though the latter was in most respects more important and richer in subsequent heritage.

BASIC PATTERNS OF EGYPTIAN SOCIETY

Unlike Mesopotamia and the Middle East, where an original river-valley basis to civilization ultimately gave way to the spread of civilization throughout an entire region, Egyptian civilization from its origins to its decline was focused on the Nile River and the deserts around it. The Nile focus also gave a more optimistic cast to Egyptian culture, for it could be seen as a source of never-failing bounty to be thankfully received, rather than a menacing cause of floods. Egyptian civilization may at the outset have received some inspiration from Sumer, but a distinctive pattern soon developed in both religion and politics.

Farming had been developed along the Nile by about 5000 B.C., but some time before 3200 B.C. economic development accelerated, in part because of growing trade with other regions including Mesopotamia. This economic acceleration provided the basis for the formation of regional kingdoms. Unlike Sumer, Egypt moved fairly directly from precivilization to large government units, without passing through a city-state phase, though the first *pharaoh*, Narmer, had to conquer a number of petty local

kings around 3100 B.C. Indeed Egypt always had fewer problems with political unity than Mesopotamia did, in part because of the unifying influence of the course of the Nile River. By the same token, however, Egyptian politics tended to be more authoritarian as well as centralized, for city-states in the Mesopotamian style, though often ruled by kings, also provided the opportunity for councils and other participatory institutions.

By 3100 B.C. Narmer, king of southern Egypt, conquered the northern regional kingdom and created a unified state 600 miles long. This state was to last 3000 years. Despite some important disruptions, this was an amazing record of stability even though the greatest vitality of the civilization was exhausted by about 1000 B.C. During the 2000-year span in which Egypt displayed its greatest vigor, the society went through three major periods of monarchy (the Old, the Intermediate, and the New Kingdoms), each divided from its successor by a century or two of confusion.

In all its phases, Egyptian civilization was characterized by the strength of the pharaoh. The pharaoh was held to be descended from gods, with the power to assure prosperity and control the rituals that assured the flow of the Nile and the fertility derived from irrigation. Soon, the pharaoh was regarded as a god. Much Egyptian art was devoted to demonstrating the power and sanctity of the king. From the king's authority also flowed an extensive bureaucracy, recruited from the landed nobles but specially trained in writing and law. Governors were appointed for key regions

Egypt, Kush, and Axum, Successive Dynasties

and were responsible for supervising irrigation and arranging for the great public works that became a hallmark of Egyptian culture. Most Egyptians were peasant farmers, closely regulated and heavily taxed. Labor requisition by the states allowed construction of the great pyramids and other huge public buildings. These monuments were triumphs of human coordination, for the Egyptians were not particularly advanced technologically. They even lacked pulleys or other devices to hoist the huge slabs of stone that formed the pyramids.

Given the importance of royal rule and the belief that pharaohs were gods, it is not surprising that each of the main periods of Egyptian history was marked by some striking kings. Early in each dynastic period leading pharaohs conquered new territories, sometimes pressing up the Nile River into present-day Sudan, once even moving up the Mediterranean coast of the Middle East. One pharaoh, Akhenaton, late in Egyptian history, tried to use his power to install a new, one-god religion, replacing the Egyptian pantheon. Many pharaohs commemorated their greatness by building huge pyramids to house themselves and their retinues after death, commanding work crews of up to 100,000 men to haul and lift the stone. The first great pyramid was built around 2600 B.C.; the largest pyramid followed about a century later, taking 20 years to complete and containing 2 million blocks of stone, each weighing 5½ tons.

Some scholars have seen even larger links between Egypt's stable, centralized politics and its fascination with an orderly death, including massive funeral monuments and preservation through mummification. Death rituals suggested a concern with extending organization to the afterlife, based on a belief that, through politics, death as well as life could be carefully controlled. A similar connection between strong political structures and careful funeral arrangements developed in Chinese civilization, though with quite different specific religious beliefs.

IDEAS AND ART

Despite some initial inspiration, Egyptian culture separated itself from Mesopotamia in a number of ways beyond politics and monument building. The Egyptians did not take to the Sumerian cuneiform alphabet and developed a hieroglyphic alphabet instead. *Hieroglyphics*, though more pictorial than Sumerian cuneiform, were based on simplified pictures of objects abstracted to represent concepts or sounds. As in Mesopotamia the writing system was complex, and its use was, for the most part, monopolized by the powerful priestly caste. Egyptians ultimately developed a new material to write on, *papyrus*, which was cheaper to manufacture and use than clay tablets or animal skins and

allowed the proliferation of elaborate record keeping. On the other hand, Egypt did not generate an epic literary tradition.

Egyptian science focused on mathematics and astronomy, but its achievements were far less advanced than those of Mesopotamia. The Egyptians were, however, the first people to establish the length of the solar year, which they divided into 12 months each with three weeks of ten days. The week was the only division of time not based on any natural cycles. The achievement of this calendar suggests Egyptian concern about predicting the flooding of the Nile and their abilities in astronomical observation. The Egyptians also made important advances in medicine, including knowledge of the workings of a variety of medicinal drugs and some contraceptive devices. Elements of Egyptian medical knowledge were gained by the Greeks, and so passed into later Middle Eastern and European civilizations.

The pillar of Egyptian culture was not science, however, but religion, which was firmly established as the basis of a whole world view. The religion promoted the worship of many gods. It mixed magical ceremonies and beliefs with worship, in a fashion common to early religions almost everywhere. A more distinctive focus involved the concern with death and preparation for life in another world, where in contrast to the Mesopotamians the Egyptians held that a happy, changeless well-being could be achieved. The care shown in preparing tombs and mummifying bodies, along with elaborate funeral rituals particularly for the rulers and bureaucrats, was designed to assure a satisfactory afterlife, though Egyptians also believed that favorable judgment by a key god, Osiris, was essential as well. Other Egyptian deities included a creation goddess, similar to other Middle Eastern religious figures later adapted into Christian worship of the Virgin Mary; and a host of gods represented by partial animal figures. Egyptian art focused heavily on the gods, though earthly, human scenes were portrayed as well in a characteristic, stylized form that lasted without great change for many centuries.

Stability was a hallmark of Egyptian culture. Given the duration of Egyptian civilization, there were surprisingly few basic changes in styles and beliefs. Egyptian emphasis on stability was reflected in their view of a changeless afterlife, suggesting a conscious attempt to argue that persistence was a virtue. Change did, however, occur in some key areas. Egypt was long fairly isolated, which helped preserve continuity. The invasions of Egypt by Palestine toward the end of the Old Kingdom period (about 2200 B.C.) were distinct exceptions to Egypt's usual self-containment. They were followed by attacks from the Middle East by tribes of Asian origin, which brought a period

This detail from tomb art shows a husband and wife doing harvesting work. Appropriately for
patriarchial values, the husband takes the lead in work, the wife following to assist.

of division and chaos, including rival royal dynasties. But
the unified monarchy was reestablished during the Middle
Kingdom period, during which Egyptian settlements spread
southward into what is now the Sudan, setting origins for
the later African kingdom of Kush.

Then followed another period of social unrest and invasion, ending in the final great kingdom period, the New
Kingdom, around 1570 B.C. During this period trade and
other contacts with the Middle East and the eastern Mediterranean, including the island of Crete, gained ground.
These contacts spread certain Egyptian influences, notably
in monumental architecture, to other areas. It was during
the New Kingdom that Egyptians first installed formal slavery, subjecting people such as the Jews. It was also in this
period that the pharaoh Akhenaton tried to impose a new
monotheistic religion, reflecting some foreign influence, but
his effort was renounced by his successor Tutankhamen,
who restored the old capital city and built a lavish tomb to
celebrate the return to the traditional gods. After about
1150 B.C., new waves of invasion and internal conspiracies
and disorganization, including strikes and social protest,
brought fairly steady decline. It was around this period
that one people, the Hebrews, followed their leader Moses
out of Egypt and into the deserts of Palestine.

EGYPT AND MESOPOTAMIA COMPARED

The development of two great early civilizations in the Middle East and North Africa encourages a first effort at comparative analysis. Because of different geography, different degrees of exposure to outside invasion and influence, and different prior beliefs, Egypt and Mesopotamia were in contrast to one another in many ways. Egypt emphasized strong central authority, while Mesopotamian politics shifted more frequently over a substructure of regional city-states. Mesopotamian art focused on less monumental structures, while embracing a pronounced literary element that Egyptian art lacked.

These cultural differences can be explained partly by geography: Mesopotamians lacked access to the great stones that Egyptians could import for their monuments. The differences also owed something to different politics, for Egyptian ability to organize masses of laborers followed from its centralized government structures and strong bureaucracy. The differences owed something, finally, to different beliefs, for the Mesopotamians lacked the Egyptian concern for preparations for the afterlife, which so motivated the great tombs and pyramids that have made Egypt and some of the pharaohs live on in human memory.

Both societies traded extensively, but there was a difference in economic tone. Mesopotamia was more productive of technological improvements, because their environment was more difficult to manage than the Nile valley. Trade contacts were more extensive, and the Mesopotamians gave attention to a merchant class and commercial law.

Social differences were less obvious because it is difficult to obtain information on daily life for early civilizations. It is probable, though, that the status of women was greater in Egypt than in Mesopotamia (where women's position seems to have deteriorated after Sumer). Egyptians paid great respect to women at least in the upper classes, in part because marriage alliances were vital to the preservation and stability of the monarchy. Also, Egyptian religion included more pronounced deference to goddesses as sources of creativity.

Comparisons in politics, culture, economics, and society suggest civilizations that varied substantially because of largely separate origins and environments. The distinction in overall tone was striking, with Egypt being more stable and cheerful than Mesopotamia not only in beliefs about gods and the afterlife but in the colorful and lively pictures the Egyptians emphasized in their decorative art. Also striking was the distinction in internal history, with Egyptian civilization far less marked by disruption than its Mesopotamian counterpart.

Comparison must also note important similarities, some of them characteristic of early civilizations. Both Egypt and Mesopotamia emphasized social stratification, with a

This tomb painting from about 1300 B.C. highlights black-skinned people from the rising kingdom of Kush, who interacted increasingly with Egyptian society and would at one point control Egypt directly.

noble, landowning class on top and masses of peasants and slaves at the bottom. A powerful priestly group also figured in the elite. While specific achievements in science differed, there was a common emphasis on astronomy and related mathematics, which produced durable findings about units of time and measurement. Both Mesopotamia and Egypt changed only slowly by the standards of more modern societies. Details of change have not been preserved, but it is true that having developed successful political and economic systems there was a strong tendency toward conservation. Change, when it came, was usually brought by outside forces—natural disasters or invasions. Both civilizations demonstrated extraordinary durability in the basics. Egyptian civilization and a fundamental Mesopotamian culture lasted far longer than the civilizations that came later, in part because of relative isolation within each respective region and because of the deliberate effort to maintain what had been achieved, rather than experiment widely.

Both civilizations, finally, left an important heritage in their region and adjacent territories. A number of smaller civilization centers were launched under the impetus of Mesopotamia and Egypt, and some would produce important innovations of their own by about 1000 B.C.

ANALYSIS
WOMEN IN PATRIARCHAL SOCIETIES

Most agricultural civilizations downgraded the status and potential of women, at least according to modern Western standards and to the implicit standards of hunting-and-gathering societies. Agricultural civilizations were characteristically *patriarchal*; that is, they were run by men and based on the assumption that men directed political, economic, and cultural life. Furthermore, as agricultural civilizations developed over time and became more prosperous and more elaborately organized, the status of women deteriorated from its initial level. Individual families were normally set up on a patriarchal basis, with the husband and father determining fundamental conditions and making the key decisions, and with humble obedience owed to this male authority. Patriarchal family structure rested on men's control of most or all property, starting with land itself; marriage was based on property relationships and it was assumed that marriage, and therefore subordination to men, was the normal condition for the vast majority of women. A revealing symptom of patriarchal families was the fact that, after marrying, a woman usually moved to the orbit (and often the residence) of her husband's family.

This piece of Egyptian art shows the sun god extending blessings to King Akhenaton and his family.

Characteristic patriarchal conditions developed in Mesopotamian civilization. Marriages were arranged for women by their parents, with a formal contract being drawn up. The husband served as authority over his wife and children just as he did over his slaves. Early Sumerians may have given women greater latitude than came to be the case later on. Their religion attributed considerable power to female sexuality and their early law gave women important rights, so that they could not be treated as outright property. Still, even in Sumerian law the adultery of a wife was punishable by death, while a husband's adultery was treated far more lightly—a double standard characteristic of patriarchalism. Mesopotamian societies after Sumerian times began to emphasize the importance of a woman's virginity on marriage and imposed the veil on respectable women when in public to emphasize their modesty. These changes showed a progressive cramping of women's social position and daily freedoms. At all points, a good portion of Mesopotamian law (such as the Hammurabic code) was given over to prescriptions for women, assuring certain basic protections but clearly emphasizing limits and inferiority.

Patriarchal conditions also could vary from one agricultural civilization to another. Egyptian civilization gave women, at least in the upper classes, more credit and witnessed a number of powerful queens. The beautiful Nefertiti, wife of Akhenaton, seemed to have been influential in the religious disputes in this reign. Some agricultural societies gave women a certain importance by tracing descendants from mothers rather than fathers. This was true, for example, of Jewish law. But even these matrilineal societies held women to be inferior to men; for example, Jewish law insisted that men and women worship separately. So while variety is truly important, it usually operated within a framework of basic patriarchalism. It was around 2000 B.C. that an Egyptian writer, Ptah Hotep, put patriarchal beliefs as clearly as anyone in the early civilizations: "If you are a man of note, found for yourself a household, and love your wife at home, as it beseems. Fill her belly, clothe her back. . . . But hold her back from getting the mastery. Remember that her eye is her stormwind, and her vulva and mouth are her strength."

Why was patriarchalism so pervasive? As agriculture improved using better techniques, women's labor, though still absolutely vital, became less important than it had been in hunting-and-gathering or early agricultural societies. This was particularly true in the upper classes and in cities where men frequently took over the most productive work, craft production, or political leadership, for example. The inferior position of women in the upper classes was usually more marked than in peasant villages where women's labor remained essential. More generally, agricultural societies were based on concepts of property, beginning with the ways land was organized. Early law codes were based on property relationships. It seemed essential in these circumstances for a man to be sure who his heirs were—that is, to try to make sure that he monopolized the sexual activities of his wife or wives. This situation helps account for the strong legal emphasis placed on women's sexual fidelity and the tendency to treat women themselves as part of a man's property. Within this framework, in turn, it became possible to think of women as inferior and partly ornamental, so that when groups achieved a certain prosperity they often tried to demonstrate this by further reducing the status of women. This was a very clear pattern in Chinese civilization and may have operated also in India and, later, in western Europe. Patriarchalism, in sum, responded to economic and property conditions in agricultural civilizations and might deepen over time.

Patriarchalism raises important questions about women themselves. Many women internalized the culture of patriarchalism, holding that it was their job to obey and to serve men and accepting arguments that their aptitudes were inferior to those of men. But patriarchalism did not preclude some important options for women. In many societies a minority of women could gain some relief through religious functions, which could provide a chance to operate independent of family structures. Patriarchal laws defined some rights for women even within marriage, protecting them in theory from the worst abuses. Sumerian law, for example, gave women as well as men the right to divorce on certain conditions when their spouse had not lived up to obligations. Women could also wield informal power in patriarchal societies by the emotional hold they gained over husbands or sons; this was behind the scenes

and indirect, but a forceful woman might use these means to figure prominently in a society's history. Women also could form networks, if only within a large household. Older women, who commanded the obedience of many daughters-in-law as well as unmarried daughters, could powerfully shape the activities of the family.

The fact remains that patriarchalism was a commanding theme in most agricultural civilizations, from the early centuries onward. Enforcing patriarchalism, through law and culture, provided one means by which these societies regulated their members and tried to achieve order. While women were not reduced to literal servitude by most patriarchal systems, they might have come close. Their options were severely constrained. Girls were raised to assume patriarchal conditions, and boys were raised with full consciousness of their distinctiveness. In many agricultural civilizations patriarchalism dictated that boys, because of their importance in carrying on the family name and the chief economic activities, were more likely to survive. When population excess threatened a family or a community, patriarchal assumptions dictated that female infants should be killed as a means of population control.

Questions: How do you think most women, raised in patriarchal society, would react to their conditions? What might cause differences in women's conditions in patriarchal societies? Why were upper-class women often more inferior to men in power than peasant women were?

KUSH AND THE EASTERN MEDITERRANEAN

Toward the end of the early civilization period, a number of partially separate civilization centers sprang up on the fringes of the civilized world in Africa and the Middle East, extending also into parts of southern Europe. These centers built heavily on the achievements of the great early centers. They resulted from the expansion efforts of these centers, as in the Egyptian push southward during the New Kingdom period and from new organizational problems within the chief centers themselves; in the Middle East, separate societies emerged during the chaotic centuries following the collapse of the Hittite empire.

KUSH AND AXUM: CIVILIZATION SPREADS IN AFRICA

The kingdom of Kush sprang up along the upper (southern) reaches of the Nile. Kush was the first African state other than Egypt of which there is record. This was a state on the frontiers of Egyptian activity, where Egyptian garrisons had been stationed from time to time. By 1000 B.C. it emerged as an independent political unit, though strongly influenced by Egyptian forms. By 730 B.C., as Egypt declined, Kush was strong enough to conquer its northern neighbor and rule it for several centuries, though this conquest was soon ended by Assyrian invasion from the Middle East. After this point the Kushites began to push their frontiers farther south, gaining a more diverse African population and weakening the Egyptian influence. It was at this point that the new capital was established at Meroe. Kushites became skilled in iron use and had access to substantial African ore and fuel. The use of iron tools extended the area that could be brought into agriculture. Kush formed a key center of metal technology in the ancient world, as a basis of both military and economic strength.

Kushites developed a form of writing derived from Egyptian hieroglyphics (and which has not yet been fully deciphered). They established a number of significant cities. Their political organization, also derived from Egypt, emphasized a strong monarchy with elaborate ceremonies based on the belief that the king was a god. Kushite economic influence extended widely in sub-Saharan Africa.

Extensive trade was conducted with people to the west, and this trade may have brought knowledge of iron making to much of the rest of Africa. The greatest period of the kingdom at Meroe, where activities centered from the early 6th century onward, lasted from about 250 B.C. to A.D. 50. By this time the kingdom served as a channel for African goods—animal skins, ebony and ivory, gold and slaves—into the commerce of the Middle East and the Mediterranean. Many monuments were built during these centuries, including huge royal pyramids and an elaborate palace in Meroe. Much fine pottery and jewelry were produced. Meroe began to decline from about A.D. 100 onward and was defeated by a kingdom to the south, Axum, around A.D. 300. Prosperity and extensive political and economic activity did not end in this region, but extended into the formation of a kingdom in present-day Ethiopia.

The outreach of Kush is not entirely clear beyond its trading network set up with neighboring regions. Whether African peoples outside the Upper Nile region learned much from Kush about political forms is unknown. Certainly there was little imitation of its writing, and the region of Kush and Ethiopia would long remain somewhat isolated from the wider stream of African history. Nevertheless, the formation of a separate society stretching below

The Eastern Mediterranean, about 1100 B.C.

the eastern Sahara was an important step in setting the bases for technological and economic change throughout much of upper Africa. Though its achievements flow less fully into later African development, Kush holds for Africa what Sumer achieved for the Middle East—it set a wider process of civilization in motion.

THE MEDITERRANEAN REGION

Smaller centers in the Middle East began to spring up after about 1500 B.C. Though dependent on the larger Mesopotamian culture for many features, these centers added important new ingredients and in some cases also extended the hold of civilization westward to the Asian coast of the Mediterranean. The smaller cultures also added to the diversity of the Middle East, creating a varied array of identities that would continue to mark the region even under the impetus of later empires, such as Rome, or the sweeping religion of Islam. Several of these smaller cultures proved immensely durable and would influence other parts of the world as well.

THE JEWS.   The most important of the smaller Middle Eastern groups were the Jews, who gave the world one of its most influential religions. The Jews were a Semitic people (a population group that also includes the Arabs). They were influenced by Babylonian civilization but also marked by a period of enslavement in Egypt. They settled in the southeast corner of the Mediterranean around 1600 B.C., probably migrating from Mesopotamia. Some moved into Egypt where they were treated as a subject people. In the 13th century B.C., Moses led these Jews to Palestine, in search of a homeland promised by the Jewish God, Yahweh. This was later held to be the central development in Jewish history. The Jews began at this point to emerge as a people with a self-conscious culture and some political identity. At most points, however, the Jewish state was small and relatively weak, retaining independence only while other parts of the Middle East were disorganized. A few Jewish kings were able to unify their people, but at many points the Jews were divided into separate regional states. Most of Palestine came under foreign (initially Assyrian) domination from 722 B.C. onward, but the Jews were able to maintain their cultural identity and key religious traditions.

MONOTHEISM.   The distinctive achievement of the Jews was the development of a strong monotheistic religion. Early Jewish leaders probably emphasized a particularly strong, creator god as the most powerful of many divinities—a hierarchy not uncommon in animism— but

this encouraged a focus on the father God for prayer and loyalty. By the time of Moses, Jews were urged increasingly to abandon worship of all other gods and to receive from Yahweh the *Torah* (a holy Law), the keeping of which would assure divine protection and guidance. From this point onward Jews regarded themselves as a chosen people under God's special guidance. As Jewish politics deteriorated due to increasing foreign pressure, prophets sprang up to call Jews back to faithful observance of God's laws. By the 9th century B.C. some religious ideas and the history of the Jews began to be written down in what would become the Jewish Bible (the Old Testament of the Christian Bible).

Besides the emphasis on a single God, Jewish religion had two important features. First was the idea of an overall divine plan. God guided Jewish history, and when disasters came they constituted punishment for failures to live up to divine laws. Second was the concept of a divinely organized morality. The Jewish God demanded not empty sacrifices or selfish prayers, but righteous behavior. God, though severe, was ultimately merciful and would help the Jews to regain morality. This system was not only monotheistic but also intensely ethical; God was actively concerned with the doings of people and so enjoined good behavior. By the 2d century B.C., these concepts were clearly spelled out in the Torah and the other writings that were formed into the Old Testament of the Bible. By their emphasis on a written religion the Jews were able to retain their identity under foreign rule and even under outright dispersion from their Mediterranean homeland.

The impact of Jewish religion beyond the Jewish people was complex. The Jews saw God's guidance in all of human history, and not simply their own. Ultimately all peoples would be led to God. But God's special pact was with the Jews, and there was little premium placed on missionary activity or converting others to the faith. This limitation helps explain the intensity and durability of the Jewish faith; it also kept the Jewish people a minority within the Middle East though at various points substantial conversions to Judaism did spread the religion somewhat more widely. Jewish monotheism, though a landmark in world religious history, is noteworthy for sustaining a distinctive Jewish culture to our own day, not for immediately altering a wider religious map.

Yet the elaboration of monotheism had a wide significance. In Jewish hands the concept of God became less humanlike, more abstract—a basic change not only in religion but in overall outlook. Yahweh had a power and a planning quality far different from the attributes of the traditional gods of the Middle East or Egypt. The gods, particularly in Mesopotamia, were whimsical and capricious; Yahweh was orderly and just, and individuals could know

This Jewish wall painting, from a synagogue at Dura Europas (about A.D. 239) reflects the artistic style of the Roman Empire. The scene, though, is central to Jewish tradition in that it shows Abraham and the convenant of God, rejecting the apparatus of pagan idolatry symbolized by the material items of worship to the right.

what to expect if they adhered to God's rules. The link to ethical conduct and moral behavior was also central. Religion for the Jews was a system of life, not merely a set of rituals and ceremonies. The full impact of this religious transformation on Middle Eastern and Mediterranean civilization would come only later, when Jewish ideas were taken up by the proselytizing faiths of Christianity and Islam. But the basic concept formed one of the legacies of the twilight period from the first great civilizations to the new cultures that would soon arise in their place.

THE MINOANS.   The Jews were not alone among the distinct societies popping up in the eastern Mediterranean. Around 1600 B.C. a civilized society developed on the island of Crete. This Minoan society traded widely with both Mesopotamia and Egypt, and probably acquired many of its civilized characteristics from this exchange. Minoan society, for example, copied Egyptian architectural forms and mathematics, though it developed important new artistic styles in the colossal palace built in the capital city, Knossos. The alphabet, too, was adapted from Egypt. Political structures similar to those of Egypt or the Mesopotamian empires emphasized elaborate bureaucratic controls, complete with massive record keeping, under a powerful monarch. Minoan navies at various points conquered parts of the mainland of Greece, eventually leading to the

establishment of the first civilization there. Centered particularly in the kingdom of Mycenae, this early Greek civilization developed considerable capacity for monumental building, and also conducted important wars with city-states in the Middle East, including the famous conflict with Troy.

Civilizations in Crete and in Greece were overturned by a wave of Indo-European invasions, culminating around 1000 B.C., that temporarily reduced the capacities of these societies to maintain elaborate art or writing, or extensive political or economic organizations. While the civilization that would arise later, to form classical Greece, had somewhat separate origins, it would build extensively on the memories of this first civilized society and on its roots in Egyptian and Mesopotamian achievements.

THE PHOENICIANS.   Another distinct society grew up in the Middle East itself, in what is now the nation of Lebanon. Around 2000 B.C. a people called the Phoenicians settled on the Mediterranean coast. Like the Minoans, they quickly turned to seafaring because their agricultural hinterland was not extensive. The Phoenicians used their elaborate trading contacts to gain knowledge from the major civilization centers, and then in several key cases improved upon what they learned. Around 1300 B.C. they devised a much simplified alphabet based on the Mesopotamian cuneiform. The Phoenician alphabet had only 22 letters, and so was learned relatively easily. It served as ancestor to the Greek and Latin lettering systems. The Phoenicians also upgraded the Egyptian numbering system.

The Phoenicians were, however, a merchant people, not vested in extensive cultural achievements. They advanced manufacturing techniques in several areas, particularly the production of dyes for cloth. Above all, for commercial purposes, they dispersed and set up colonies at a number of points along the Mediterranean. They benefited from the growing weakness of Egypt and the earlier collapse of Minoan society and its Greek successor, for there were few competitors for influence in the Mediterranean by 1000 B.C. Phoenician sailors moved steadily westward, setting up a major trading city on the coast of North Africa at Carthage, and lesser centers in Italy, Spain, and southern France. The Phoenicians even traded along the Atlantic coast of Europe, reaching Britain where they sought a supply of tin. Ultimately Phoenicia collapsed in the wake of the Assyrian invasions of the Middle East, though several of the colonial cities long survived.

THE END OF THE EARLY CIVILIZATION PERIOD

The proliferation of spin-off civilizations brought important innovations within the framework set by the achievements of the great progenitors in Mesopotamia and Egypt. The simplified alphabet, the major cultural shift described by the first great monotheistic system, and a number of quite practical improvements—the introduction by another Mediterranean coastal peoples, the Lydians, of coined money—considerably advanced the level of civilization itself. The spread of civilization into Kush and into some European portions of the Mediterranean, fed by deliberate expansion and growing trade, also set the basis for the development of major civilization centers beyond the original core. By 1000 B.C. the civilization zone initially established by separate developments in Mesopotamia and Egypt had fanned out widely, sketching the basis for later societies in the Middle East, Africa, and parts of Europe.

No sharp line divides the long early phase of the development of civilization in the Middle East and North Africa from the next, classical period; there was no total overturning by invasion, as would characterize the first civilization in India. Developments such as the spread of the Kushite kingdom, the survival of the Egyptian kingdom, or the elaboration of the Jewish religion continued well into the final centuries B.C. Successive empires in the Middle East would revive or preserve many features of the Mesopotamian pattern.

Around 1000 B.C., and for several centuries thereafter, there was a somewhat pervasive pause in the development of civilizations in this general region. The pause did not disrupt the Phoenician or Kushite expansion on the fringes, nor did it shatter all civilized forms. But Mesopotamia did undergo an unusual several-century span in which regional city-states and considerable internal warfare brought political chaos. Egyptian politics were also deteriorating. Early civilizations in Greece were overwhelmed (almost as completely as their counterpart in India) by waves of invasions by Indo-Europeans from eastern Europe. These invasions for a time reduced politics to essentially tribal levels and virtually destroyed cultural activities that depended on writing or elaborate workmanship.

The waves of Indo-European invasion form the clearest breaking point. These invaders were hunters and herders initially from central Asia, who pressed into western Asia and Europe in successive waves. The Hittites were an Indo-European people capable of assimilating Mesopotamian values to the extent of setting up a major empire. They also pushed back the Egyptian sphere of influence, launching the decline of the New Kingdom and also freeing up the southeastern Mediterranean corner for the rise of smaller states such as the Jewish kingdom. But by 1200 B.C. the Hittites were swept away by another invading force of Indo-Europeans (the same group that interrupted civilization in Greece).

The Indo-Europeans, beginning with the Hittites, introduced iron use which gave rise to more powerful weaponry and the possibility of geographically more extensive empires based on military power. The first group to exploit this new weaponry were the Assyrians, who began a pattern of conquest from their base along the Tigris River. By 665 B.C. they had conquered the whole of the civilized Middle East down to the Persian Gulf as well as Egypt. This was a cruel people, eager to terrorize their enemies. The Assyrians used iron, a strong and widely available metal, to arm more men more cheaply than societies relying on bronze were able to do. Their empire was unprecedentedly large and also unusually systematic as they collected tribute, assimilated diverse cultural achievements, and even moved whole peoples (as they did the Jews) in order to maintain control. The Assyrian state was not long lived. By 612 B.C. it fell to a combination of pressures from invading frontier tribes and internal revolt. A number of smaller successor kingdoms followed, until another great eastern empire, the Persian, arose in 539 B.C.

The key points are these: The characteristic boundaries of the early civilizations that had lasted so long amid a relatively slow pace of change were beginning to yield. Invading peoples brought new ideas. The Indo-Europeans, for example, ignored the Mesopotamian or Egyptian beliefs about the divine attributes of kings. Rather, kings were selected by councils formed by nobles and the army. Also, where Indo-European culture took deep root, as in Greece, political patterns would begin to diverge from those set in the earlier civilizations of the region. Geographical boundaries were shifting too. Egypt faded as a major independent actor, while the Middle East was open to new empires with greater unifying potential than ever before; and new centers of vitality were beginning to be sketched in Africa and along the European coast of the Mediterranean.

The stage was beginning to be shaped for the emergence of a new set of civilizations, such as in Persia and Greece, that would build on earlier precedents in many ways but advance new cultural and political forms. Based on the new military technology brought by iron and on steady improvements in shipping, these new civilizations would reach out to wider regions than the early civilizations had usually managed. More extensive civilization zones and new cultural and political principles, though both prepared by developments in the early civilization period, would define the era of classical civilizations in the Middle East and Mediterranean that began to emerge by about 800 B.C. with the recovery of civilization in Greece and, soon, the rise of the great Persian empire.

CONCLUSION

THE ISSUE OF HERITAGE

The centuries in which early civilizations took hold and spread in Mesopotamia and Egypt, and then in surrounding regions, provide a fascinating insight into the ways civilization took shape, the reasons it developed, and the mixtures of advantages and disadvantages it involved. The period of early civilization, stretching over more than 2000 years, also allows a clear understanding of the mixtures of diversity and contact that would long shape history in the Middle East, northern Africa, and southern Europe. Separate centers arose, particularly along the Tigris-Euphrates and the Nile, that had relatively little interaction and differed in numerous ways.

Civilization, though it grouped unprecedented numbers of people in common cultures and common political structures, was also a separating phenomenon because of its diverse points of origin. Because of the way in which two distinct civilizations began in the Middle East and North Africa, supplemented by successive invasions and the for-

mation of smaller regional cultures, the area would be permanently marked as a complex, vibrant, but often disputed and disputatious part of the world.

As a new set of civilizations began to emerge to replace the societies born of the river-valley achievements, it is important to ask more specifically what traces of the river-valley civilizations would survive. Diversity in the region is one important trace, as is the persistence of specific developments such as the Jewish religion. So too, at another level, were the monumental achievements of the early civilizations, notably of course the great Egyptian structures.

Beyond specifics, however, there were two levels of heritage from the river-valley civilizations, one vital and precisely measurable, the other vital but harder to assess.

TECHNIQUES

The basic apparatus of civilization never had to be reinvented in the Middle-Eastern or Mediterranean regions, or in those areas that received civilization from these regions. This apparatus includes the idea of writing, calendars, basic mathematical and scientific discoveries, and improved technologies, such as irrigation, iron use, more productive grain seeds, the potter's wheel, and the wheel. Money and the idea of written, collected law did not have to be rediscovered in this part of the world, nor did the use of certain medicinal drugs. A large number of the attributes or consequences of civilization were so obviously advantageous that they would be taken over by any successor society and carefully preserved amid vast political or cultural change. Other parts of the world had to invent some of these civilization features separately, but in this considerable region the river-valley civilizations produced a framework that never had to be redone.

CULTURES

Whether the early civilizations also produced a set of basic political and cultural impulses that would survive into later societies is harder to determine. Certainly there are some important traces. The flood story of Mesopotamia passed into the Jewish Bible and so into the cultural arsenal of both Christian and Muslim civilizations in the world today—some of them far distant, geographically, from the story's place of origin. We use words that come directly from the ancient Middle East or Egypt—such as the Sumerian-derived word *alcohol*— that suggest important transmissions. It is increasingly believed that modern music owes much to discoveries in early Mesopotamian civilization in the form of specific instruments (harps, drums, flutes) as well as in the development of the seven- and eight-token scales now used in the West and passed from

Mesopotamia through Greece. Towers and columns now common in Muslim and in European and American architecture were based on the ziggurats and perhaps Egyptian columns. These continuities in style or vocabulary were not of course unchanged as they were transmitted, but they show the ongoing influence of the early civilizations on societies that succeeded Mesopotamia and Egypt.

The heritage of the early civilizations in politics, though incomplete, is fairly obvious. Ideas of divine kingship, worked out in Mesopotamia and Egypt, were remembered and revived in the later Roman empire, and may also have influenced later African monarchies. The importance of regional city-states recurrently marked Middle-Eastern history, with some bearing on the political fragmentation of the region even in recent times.

Some historians have gone further still, in suggesting an ongoing link between certain modern civilizations and their river-valley progenitors. It has been argued, for example, that cultures that accepted Mesopotamian influence, including classical Greece and later Christian cultures, emphasized a division between humanity and nature quite different from the civilization traditions launched by early societies in India, China, and probably sub-Saharan Africa. Instead of seeing humanity as part of a larger natural harmony, the Mesopotamian tradition held humans separate from nature, capable of observing and exploiting it from a different vantage point, seeing nature as antagonistic rather than seeking a peace within it. From this basic division in early cultures would come different scientific approaches, religions, and religious goals. The Middle East and Europe have long been centers of religions that encourage action and anxiety, as opposed to religious traditions of greater tranquility that arose in India; some of these characteristics may go back to the Sumerian world view. Distinctive attitudes toward women might even result, as the Mesopotamian tradition tended to argue that women were closer to nature than men and so more inherently inferior. Whether this basic cultural divide holds up in general may be debated; it may presume too much on what is known about later scientific or religious outlooks, not on what is known about the early civilizations themselves. Much would depend, of course, on how any Mesopotamian core tradition was transmitted into subsequent cultures such as the Greek, the Christian, and the Muslim.

Nevertheless, the idea of some basic guidelines passing down from the early civilizations is a fascinating one. Not fully provable and certainly not definite fact, the idea legitimately suggests the power and complexity of the values, not just the specific technical and social inventions, that early civilizations developed. There is one point that might give support to the idea of distinctive, durable frameworks of values: The civilizations that inherited from Egypt and Mesopotamia were not all the civilizations in the world. Other, quite separate early civilization centers, notably those in India, China, and later the Americas, would send out different signals, duplicating through separate invention some of the practical features of Egypt and Mesopotamia but inevitably producing quite different versions of culture and politics. More people in the world today look back to these other early civilizations for points of origin, than lay claim directly to the heritage of the Middle East and North Africa.

FURTHER READINGS

Two excellent studies can guide additional work on early civilization in Mesopotamia: C. L. Redman's *The Rise of Civilization: From Early Farmers to Urban Society in the Ancient Near East* (1988); and N. J. Nissen's *The Early History of the Ancient Near East, 9000–2000 B.C.* (1988). See also S. N. Kramer's *History Begins at Sumer* (1981). Two fine studies of Egypt are A. Gardiner's *Egypt of the Pharaohs* (1966), a very readable treatment, and A. Nibbi's *Ancient Egypt and Some Eastern Neighbors* (1981). Patterns of life with some useful comparison are the subject of J. Hawkes's *Life in Mesopotamia, the Indus Valley, and Egypt* (1973). Two recent books deal with important special topics: M. Silver's *Economic Structures of the Ancient Near East* (1987); and T. Jacobsen's *The Treasures of Darkness: A History of Mesopotamian Religion* (1976).

Two studies of Israel are J. Bright's *A History of Israel* (1981); and the first two volumes of W. D. Davies and L. Finkelstein, eds., *The Cambridge History of Judaism* (1984, 1987). For a study of Phoenicia, see N. K. Sandars's *The Sea Peoples* (1985). Early civilization in the Upper Nile is the subject of Roland Oliver, ed., *The Dawn of African History* (1968).

THE INDUS VALLEY AND THE GENESIS OF
SOUTH ASIAN CIVILIZATION

THE ARYAN INVASIONS AND EARLY ARYAN
SOCIETY IN INDIA
  ∞∞∞ **DOCUMENT:** Aryan Poetry in Praise of a War-horse

A BEND IN THE RIVER AND THE BEGINNINGS
OF CHINA

THE DECLINE OF THE SHANG AND THE ERA
OF ZHOU DOMINANCE
  ∞∞∞ **ANALYSIS:** The Legacy of Asia's First Civilizations
  ∞∞∞ **CONCLUSION:** Beginnings and Transitions
  ∞∞∞ **FURTHER READINGS**

India

4000–2500 Spread of farming and villages in western India

China   400,000–350,000 Peking man   8000–4000 Transition to sedentary agriculture; silkweaving
                                                    4000 Yangshao

| 400,000 B.C. | 8,000 B.C. | 4,000 B.C. | 3,000 B.C. |

Asia's First Civilizations: India and China

3

INTRODUCTION. Like Sumer, Egypt, and other early civilizations in the Middle East, civilizations first developed in East and South Asia in the vicinity of great river systems. When irrigated by the massive spring floods of the Yellow River, the rich soil of the North China plain proved a superb basis for what has been the largest and most enduring civilization in human history. Civilization first developed in the Indus River valley in present-day Pakistan in the middle of the 3d millennium B.C., more than a thousand years earlier than it did in China. In fact, the civilization of the Indus valley, usually called Harappan after its chief city, rivals Sumer and Egypt as humanity's oldest. But like Sumer and its successor civilizations in the Middle East, Harappan civilization was unable to survive natural catastrophes and nomadic invasions. In contrast to the civilization of the Shang rulers in China around 1500 B.C., Harappa vanished from history. Until the mid-19th century it was "lost" or forgotten, even by the peoples who lived in the vicinity of its sand-covered ruins. Important elements of Harappan society were transmitted to later civilizations in the Indian subcontinent. But unlike the Shang kingdom, Harappa did not survive to be the core and geographical center from which a unified and continuous civilization developed like that found in China. The difference in the fate of these two great civilizations provides one of the key questions in dealing with the history of civilized societies: What factors permitted some civilizations to endure for millennia while others rose and fell within a few centuries?

The early sections of this chapter are devoted to the rise and decline of Harappan civilization in India and to the history of the nomadic peoples who supplanted the Harappans. Between about 1500 and 1000 B.C., as the great cities of the Indus region crumbled into ruins, nomadic Aryan invaders from central Asia moved into the fertile

---

c. 2500 Emergence of Harappan civilization	**1600–1500** Beginning of Aryan nomadic invasions	**600–500** Age of the Buddha and Hindu-Buddhist rivalry
	1600–1200 Collapse of the Harappan civilization	**700** The composition of the first of the sacred Vedas
2200 Longshan	**1122** Former or western Zhou kings	**550–480** Age of Confucius
	1766 Shang kingdom; writing develops	**770** Later or eastern Zhou kings

Indus plains and pushed into the Ganges River valleys to the east. It took these unruly, warlike peoples many centuries to build a civilization that rivaled that of the Harappans. The Aryans concentrated on assaulting Harappan settlements and different Aryan tribal groups. As peoples who depended primarily on great herds of cattle to provide their subsistence, they had little use for the great irrigation works and advanced agricultural technology of the Indus valley peoples. Though they conserved some Harappan beliefs and symbols, the Aryan invaders did little to restore or replace the great cities and engineering systems of the peoples they had supplanted.

Eventually, however, many of the Aryan groups began to settle down, and increasingly they relied on farming to support their communities. By about 700 B.C., their priests had begun to orally record the sacred hymns and ritual incantations that had long been central to Aryan culture. In the following centuries, strong warrior leaders built tribunal units into larger kingdoms. The emergence of priestly and warrior elites signaled the beginning of a new pattern of civilization in South Asia. By the 6th century B.C., the renewal of civilized life in India was marked by the emergence of great world religions, such as Hinduism and Buddhism, and a renewal of trade, urban life, and splendid artistic and architectural achievements.

The early development of civilization in China combined the successive phases of advancement of Mesopotamian history with the continuity of Egyptian civilization. Civilization in China coalesced around 1500 B.C. Chinese civilization emerged gradually out of Neolithic farming and potterymaking cultures that had long been present in the Yellow River region of East Asia. The establishment of the Shang kingdom at this point in time gave political expression to a combination of civilizing trends. The appearance of a distinctive and increasingly specialized elite supported by the peasant majority of the Chinese people, the growth of towns and the first cities, the spread of trade, and the formulation of a written language all indicated that a major civilization was emerging in China.

Though the political dominance of the Shang came to an end in 1122 under the new royal house of the Zhou, civilized development in China was enriched and extended as the Chinese people migrated east and south from their original Yellow River heartland. By the end of the Zhou era, which would last officially until 256 B.C., many of the central elements in Chinese civilization, one of humankind's oldest, were firmly established. Some of those elements have persisted to the present day.

THE INDUS VALLEY AND THE GENESIS OF SOUTH ASIAN CIVILIZATION

Great torrents of water from the world's highest mountain range, the Himalayas, carved out the vast Indus River system that was to nurture the first civilization in the Indian subcontinent. As the rapidly running mountain streams reached the plains of the Indus valley, they branched out into seven great rivers, of which five remain today. These rivers in turn converge midway down the valley to form the Indus River, which runs for hundreds of miles to the southwest and empties into the Arabian Sea. The streams that flow from high in the Himalayas are fed by monsoon rains. Rain clouds are carried from the seas surrounding the Indian subcontinent by *monsoons*—seasonal winds—across the lowlands to the mountains where, cooled and trapped, they release their life-giving waters. These "summer" or wet monsoons, which blow toward central Asia from the sea, are also a critical source of moisture for the plains and valleys they cross before they reach the mountain barriers. The streams from the mountains also carry prodigious amounts of rich soil to these plains, con-

India in the Age of Harappa and the Early Aryan Invasions

This wheeled model clay cart—which was found during the excavation at Mohenjo-daro, one of the two great Indus cities—tells us a good deal about the main mode of land transport employed in South Asia's first civilization. Similar models have been found in almost all Indus valley settlements, and in some respects they resemble the ox-drawn, nearly solid-wheeled carts in use in India today.

stantly enlarging them and giving them the potential for extensive cultivation and dense human habitation. The Indus is only one of many river systems in the Indian subcontinent formed by melting snow and monsoon rains, but it was the first to nurture a civilization.

The lower Indus plains were a very different place in the 3d millennium B.C. than they are today. Most of the region is now arid and desolate, crisscrossed by dried-up riverbeds and virtually devoid of forests. In Harappan times, it was green and heavily forested. Game animals and pasturage for domesticated animals were plentiful. Long before the first settlements associated with the Harappan complex appeared, the plains were dotted with the settlements of sedentary agriculturists. By at least 3000 B.C., these pre-Harappan peoples cultivated wheat and barley, and had developed sophisticated agricultural implements and cropping techniques.

The pre-Harappan peoples knew how to make bronze weapons, tools, and mirrors, and they had mastered the art of potterymaking. Recurring motifs, such as bulls and long-horned cattle on elaborately decorated bowls and storage urns, suggest links to early agricultural communities in the Middle East, while fish designs indicate a preoccupation with what was probably a major source of food. The long-horned bull was a central image in the Harappan culture and remains important in Indian *iconography*, the art

of pictorial representation. Pre-Harappan peoples in the Indus valley also carved large numbers of small figurines of women. These statuettes differ from those found in many other early cultures in the detailed attention given to hairstyles and jewelry. Early village sites also contained tiny carts with clay wheels that may be the earliest children's toys yet discovered.

THE DISCOVERY AND MYSTERY OF HARAPPA

In the late 1850s, the British were directing the building of railway lines through the Indus valley. In need of bricks for the railway bed, the engineers allowed the construction workers to plunder those bricks found in the dirt mounds of long-abandoned cities in the valley. A British general named Cunningham, who would later be the head of the Indian Archeological Survey, visited one of these sites in 1856. While there, he was given a number of artifacts including several soapstone seals imprinted with various carvings, including the figure of a bull and what were apparently letters in a script. Cunningham was convinced that the artifacts were of ancient origin and was intrigued by the strange script, which bore little resemblance to that of any of the languages then in use in various parts of India. As head of the archeological survey, Cunningham took steps to ensure the full-scale excavation of what came to be recognized as one of the earliest and most mysterious of all human civilizations.

Today the script still has not been deciphered and much of the original mystery remains. But decades of extensive excavation at the original site and hundreds of other sites throughout the Indus valley have uncovered a huge complex of cities and villages that made up the first civilization in South Asia. The evidence found so far indicates that Harappan civilization developed quite rapidly in the middle centuries of the 3d millennium B.C. There are sharp divergences from the village cultures that preceded it in levels of material culture, scale, and organization. Equally notable is the lack of strong resemblances to other early civilizations to the west of Mesopotamia, which indicates that Harappa was not a colony. Skeletal remains, however, show that the dominant human type of the peoples who built the civilization was a tall, long faced, dark-haired strain much like those from the Mediterranean region.

The civilization was anchored on two cities: Harappa in the north on one of the five great rivers that forms the Indus, and Mohenjo-daro, 400 miles to the south on the banks of the Indus proper. These cities formed the town capitals of a complex of smaller urban centers and villages that covered an area four times the size of Sumer and twice the size of Egypt during the Old Kingdom. That the many sites associated with the Harappan complex were part of one civilization has been established due to excavations of layer after layer of cities and towns rebuilt in the same way, with the same proportions, at the same locations.

THE GREAT CITIES

Though hundreds of miles apart, Harappa and Mohenjo-daro were remarkably similar in layout and construction. Both were built on a square grid pattern that was divided by main thoroughfares into 12 smaller and precisely measured grids. Each of the cities was surrounded by walls, which extended one mile from east to west and one-half mile from north to south. The buildings of the cities and the surrounding walls were made of standardized kiln-dried bricks. Controlled building on such a massive scale would have required an autocratic government with the capacity to organize and supervise the daily tasks of large numbers of laborers. This control appears to have extended to the Harappans' domestic lives as well.

The existence of a strong ruling class is also indicated by the presence of large and well-fortified citadels in each of the capital cities. These citadels served as sanctuaries for the cities' populations in times of attack and as community centers in times of peace. The citadel at Mohenjo-daro in-

This artist's reconstruction of Mohenjo-daro conveys a sense of the impressive size and well-planned layout of the city. Note the fortified walls and gates, and the fortress-like construction of the blocks of buildings within the city.

cluded a very large building that may have been a palace. Both citadels contained what are believed to have been audience and assembly halls or places of worship, and bathing tanks for public use. The elaborately decorated bath at Mohenjo-daro was surrounded by a cloister, which opened onto many small rooms that may have housed priests of the city's cults. Large granaries were located near each of the citadels, which suggest that the state stored grain for ceremonial purposes, times of shortage, and possibly the regulatation of grain production and sale.

Though the main avenues of the cities were straight and about 30 feet wide, the lanes and paths in the cities' quarters were narrow and twisting. Brick houses of one to three stories were jumbled together in these areas, which must have been densely populated at the height of Harappan civilization. The layout of the houses was strikingly uniform in that each consisted of a courtyard surrounded by rooms for sleeping, cooking, and, in the larger homes, receiving visitors. Entrance to the houses was gained through a long passageway from the street, which in combination with few

windows reflects a concern for security. The lack of ornamentation on the houses and the dun-colored brick walls
must have given the cities a very drab appearance. Each of
the homes had a bathing area and drains that emptied into
a covered, citywide sewage system, which was the best in
the ancient world. The Harappans apparently bathed standing up by pouring pitchers of water over their bodies.
Some scholars believe that bathing was related to religious
rituals rather than hygiene.

HARAPPAN CULTURE AND SOCIETY

The great cities and many towns of the Harappan complex were supported by a rather advanced agricultural system based on the cultivation of wheat, rye, peas, and
possibly rice. Cotton was widely cultivated and numerous
domesticated animals were reared. It is likely that irrigation systems were built to catch and control waters from
the monsoon and the rivers, and that fish caught in the
rivers provided an additional dietary staple.

The cities of Harappa were major trading centers. The
mysterious seals from the Indus civilization have been
found in urban ruins as far away as Sumer in Mesopotamia. Jade from present-day China and precious jewels
from what is now Burma have been unearthed at various
Indus sites. Despite these overseas contacts, Harappan peoples appear to have been intensely conservative and highly
resistant to innovations introduced from the outside. They
cast tools and weapons in bronze, but most of their tools
were inferior to those of Mesopotamian peoples with whom
they had contacts, and their weapons were even more primitive. They lacked swords, tipped their spears with bronze
points so thin that they would crumble on contact, and
used stone for their arrowheads. These shortcomings may
have proven fatal to the survival of the Harappan civilization.

Harappan society was dominated by a powerful priestly
class that ruled from the citadel of each of the capitals.
Though there may have been specialized warriors, the
priests appear to have been the main coordinators of fortress construction and preparation for defense. The location
of granaries and artisan dwellings near the citadels indicates
that the priests may have also overseen handicraft production and supervised both regional and long-distance trade.

The priests derived their impressive control over city
and town dwellers from their role as the intermediaries between the Harappan populace and a number of gods and
goddesses, whose provision of fertility was of paramount
concern. Several of the gods are depicted on the undeci-
phered seals that are dominated by a naked male figure
with a horned head and a fierce facial expression. On some

of the seals he is pictured in a crossed-legged posture of
meditation similar to that which was later known as the lotus position. Numerous figurines of females, also naked except for a great deal of jewelry, have been found. These
"mother goddesses" appear to have been objects of worship
for the common people, while the horned god was apparently favored by the priests and upper classes.

The obsession with fertility was also reflected in the
veneration of sacred animals, especially bulls, and by the
large quantity of phallic-shaped objects that have been
found at Harappan sites. Along with a handful of superbly
carved figurines of male notables, dancing girls, and animals, these cult objects represent the pinnacle of artistic expression for the rather unimaginative and practical-minded
peoples of Harappa.

The control exhibited by the uniformity and rigid ordering of Harappan culture would not have been possible
without an extensive administrative class serving the
priests. It is probable that members of this class and possibly wealthy mercantile families lived in the large two- and
three-story houses. Characteristically, size—not decoration—set their dwellings off from the artisans, laborers,
and slaves that made up the rest of the urban population.
Outside of the two great cities, the subjects of the priest-
rulers were agriculturists, whose surplus production was essential to urban life and the maintenance of very vulnerable
defenses against natural calamities and human aggressors.

THE SLOW DEMISE OF HARAPPAN CIVILIZATION

It was once widely accepted that Harappan civilization
was the victim of assaults by nomadic invaders eager to
claim the rich Indus valley as pasturelands for their herds
of cattle. A dramatic vision of a wave of "barbarian" invaders smashing town dwellers' skulls made for good storytelling but bad history. Archeological investigations carried
out in recent decades demonstrate rather conclusively that
Harappa declined gradually in the middle centuries of the
2d millennium B.C. The precise causes of that decline remain a matter of dispute. The later layers of building at
Harappa and Mohenjo-daro as well as at other sites show a
clear deterioration in the quality of construction and building materials. There also are a few smashed skulls, but
these have been dated somewhat earlier than the period
when the civilization disappears from history.

It is likely that a combination of factors led to Harappa's demise. There is evidence of severe flooding at Mohenjo-daro and other sites. Short-term natural disasters may
have compounded the adverse effects of long-term climatic
changes. Shifts in the monsoon pattern and changes in tem-

perature may have begun the process of desertification that eventually transformed the region into the arid steppe that it has remained for most of recorded history. Rapid changes in types of pottery suggest a series of sudden waves of migrants into the region. It is possible that the Harappans were too weak militarily to prevent these incoming peoples from settling in or taking over their towns and cities.

The marked decline in the quality of building and town planning indicates that the priestly elite was losing control. Some of the migrants probably were bands of Aryan herders who entered the Indus region over an extended period of time, rather than in militant waves. But the Aryan pastoralists may have consciously destroyed or neglected the dikes and canals on which the agrarian life of the Harappan peoples depended. Extensive cattle raising would then have replaced intensive crop cultivation, further undermining the economic basis of the civilization. That there was a good deal of violent conflict in this transition cannot be ruled out. Groups of skeletons in postures of flight have been found on the stairways at some sites. There is evidence of burned-out settlements and the flight of refugees through the passes into the Himalayas to the north. Thus, a combination of factors brought an end to India's first civilization. These factors also gave rise to an extended transition period, dominated increasingly by the nomadic Aryan invaders.

THE ARYAN INVASIONS AND EARLY ARYAN SOCIETY IN INDIA

All through the centuries when Harappan civilization was crumbling from the blows dealt by natural calamities and human aggression, new peoples were moving into the Indus valley. Of these migrants, those of Aryan descent gradually gained the upper hand in the Indus basin, to the west on the Ganges plains, and in the northeast in the foothills of the Himalayas. Despite the claims of 19th-century racist writers, such as Arthur Gobineau, and 20th-century demagogues, such as Hitler, the Aryans were not a race or distinct biological group. The term *Aryan* is properly a linguistic one.

The Aryans were originally herders who spoke one variant of a group of related Indo-European languages and lived in the area between the Caspian and Black seas. For reasons probably related to climatic shifts and conflicts over grazing lands, these nomadic, Indo-Aryan peoples began to migrate in large numbers from their homelands in the 3d and 2d millennia B.C. The first migrations were westward into Asia Minor and eventually Europe. The second waves were eastward toward Iran and the Indus valley.

The Indo-Europeans' mobility and military prowess made it possible for them to prevail over peoples who occupied the areas into which they moved. The remarkable extent of the zone affected by their expansion is illustrated by the great variety and prominence of modern languages that belong to the Indo-European family. From the Celtic, Germanic, and Romance languages of western Europe and the Slavonic tongues to the east, to the speech of the ancient Persians and modern Iranians and the Sanskrit-derived languages of North India, the ancient Indo-European invaders have left a lasting legacy. Despite millennia of separation and differing paths of cultural development on the part of Indo-European groups, the similarities between their widely dispersed languages remains striking. The word for father, for example, is *pater* in Latin, *vater* in German, *pitar* in Sanskrit, and *athir* in Celtic.

A WARRIOR CULTURE

To the Aryan branch of the Indo-European nomads, the Indus and the valleys beyond were a veritable paradise of lush, well-watered, and underpopulated grasslands and forests. After spreading across the Indus plains (and probably driving the Harappan peoples farther south) the Aryans moved in waves of small bands to the southeast, into the rich plains and valleys formed by the Ganges River system that surpassed the great Indus complex in size. Like the Indus plains in earlier times, the Ganges region provided the combination of monsoon rains and great river systems that made the heartland for different variations of civilized life possible. The Aryans took many centuries to approach the level of civilization achieved by the Harappan peoples. But the potential for agriculture was so obvious that herding bands began to settle down and cultivate lands cleared from the forests in the first generations after their arrival.

The Aryans in India did not develop writing until long after they entered the subcontinent. But we can learn a good deal about their way of life from the hymns they composed for religious-based animal sacrifices, entertainment, and historical chronicles. Transmitted orally for centuries by priests and bards, the hymns were written down in sacred books called the *Vedas* in the 6th century B.C.

The Vedic hymns describe the Aryan invaders as a restless and warlike people organized at first in tribes and later in small kingdoms. The tribes and kingdoms fought constantly among themselves, often over cattle and pasturelands, and warred with the indigenous peoples. The chief deity of the Aryans was Indra, the god of battle and lightning. He was described as a colossal, hard-drinking warrior with a huge pot belly. Indra was revered as the smasher of dams and the destroyer of cities. The Aryans were superb horsemen, who also employed chariots in their wars. Their bows and arrows and metal-tipped spears were a good deal more effective than the weapons of the indigenous peoples. Altogether the Vedas describe the Aryans as a rowdy crew fond of beer, who engaged in and bragged about their gambling, fighting, horseracing, and womanizing.

ARYAN SOCIETY

When they entered the Indian subcontinent, the Aryan bands were divided into three main social groups: warriors, priests, and commoners. Conflict with the indigenous peoples added a fourth group, slaves or serfs. Though social differentiation between the first three groups was pronounced, the dividing line between the Aryans, who were freeborn, and the enslaved population was particularly rigid. Apparently, there was also a physical dimension to the sharp division between the free and enslaved. The Aryans pictured themselves as light-skinned conquerors in a sea of dark-skinned "Dasas," their name for the indigenous peoples. Attempts to prohibit *miscegenation*, sexual relations and procreation, between Aryans and Dasas, gave rise to the caste system that came to form the basis for Indian social organization throughout subsequent history. Marriages between the two groups were forbidden; penalties were proscribed according to the rank of males and females who had sexual liaisons.

As the Aryans settled down, social divisions became more complex, with groups such as cultivators, merchants, and artisans joining the ruling groups of warriors, priests, and herders. Social distinctions were further complicated by the miscegenation that did in fact occur on a large scale. Over the centuries, four broad *varnas*—social classes—developed: *brahmans*—or priests—warriors, merchants, and peasants. Beneath them were the outcaste and untouchable descendants of the Dasas and other non-Aryan migrants.

The culture of the Aryan invaders placed great emphasis on physical strength, martial skills, and heroic exploits. Descent and inheritance were *patrilineal*, through the male line. Elder males monopolized authority within the household, though it was possible for their mothers and wives to influence decisions behind the scenes. At marriage, brides left their own households and families and went to live with those of their husbands. Monogamous marriages were the norm, but *polygamy*, one husband with several wives, and *polyandry*, one wife with several husbands, are recounted in the Aryan epics.

Sizeable *dowries*, or marriage payments, in the form of cattle, food, or precious objects were commonly given to the husband's family. The fact that some prospective husbands paid a "bride-price" to his wife-to-be's family suggests that female children had not yet become the economic burden that they have been considered through much of Indian history. Nonetheless, sons were preferred to daughters because of the males' important family ritual roles and

---

DOCUMENT
ARYAN POETRY IN PRAISE OF A WAR-HORSE

The following early Vedic hymn exults in the power of a great Aryan war-horse.

Rushing to glory, to the capture of herds,
Swooping down as a hungry falcon,
Eager to be first, he darts amid the ranks of the chariots
Happy as a bridegroom making a garland,
Spurning the dust and champing at the bit.

And the victorious steed and faithful,
His body obedient to his driver in battle,
Speeding on through the melee,
Stirs up the dust to fall on his brows.

And at his deep neigh, like the thunder of heaven,
The foemen tremble in fear,
For he fights against thousands, and none can resist him,
So terrible is his charge.

Questions: How did the Aryans regard war and fight their battles? What does the passage tell us about Aryan ideals of manliness and heroism, and their attitude toward death, loyalty, and the herd animals that were central to their culture?

their key roles as warriors and priests. These positions were never held by women, nor were women allowed to be the chieftains of tribal bands or rulers of the kingdoms that developed in the early centuries of Aryan invasions.

ARYAN RELIGION AND ARTISTIC EXPRESSION

As the central position of the god Indra suggests in the figure below, the early Aryans were polytheists who worshipped a wide range of deities that physically resembled humans and displayed human emotions and needs. Like those of the ancient Greeks, each of the gods and goddesses of the Aryans had the power to assist their supplicants in a particular aspect of their lives. Thus, there were gods for creation, fire and death, and goddesses of dawn or light, the forest, and fertility. Like the human society that propitiated these deities, the Aryan pantheon was dominated by male gods, particularly those relating to war, fire, and rain. Religious worship was centered on animal sacrifices and ritual offerings of food that were designed to win specific favors from individual deities. The major function of the Vedic priests was to perform these critical sacrifices, a role that later allowed them to amass great power.

This graceful bronze statuette depicts the war god Indra in what is perhaps a deceptively relaxed pose. Supplicants worshiped a variety of gods and goddesses, often with very specific requests, such as for success in business (the goddess Lakshmi), the means to overcome obstacles in their lives (Ganesha), and the good fortune to conceive children (Shiva, as well as a number of feminine deities).

In contrast to their Hindu and Buddhist descendants, there was apparently little inclination toward introspection among the early Aryans. The oldest of the Vedas consist mainly of songs, some of them quite beautiful, in praise of the various deities and incredibly detailed formulas for sacrifices. There is little speculation on issues that would later preoccupy Indian priests and philosophers such as the purpose of creation, the fate of the dead, and the nature of the soul. There was no concept of reincarnation or the transmigration of the soul. Much like the ancient Greeks, evildoers went to the "House of Clay" after death, while the virtuous were rewarded in the "World of the Fathers." In an early hymn to Vishvakarman, the creator god, however, there is a vision of a primal essence and oneness that prefigures later Indian thinking:

What was the germ primeval which the waters received
where all the gods were seen together?
The waters, they received that germ primeval
wherein the gods were gathered all together.
It rested set upon the unborn's navel,
that One wherein abide all things existing.

Excepting military hardware, early Aryan material culture represented a marked decline from the level reached during the Harappan period. Wood and thatch villages replaced stone and brick cities and towns. There is little evidence of interest in sculpture or painting and thus it is unlikely that great works of art were produced. The Aryans were, however, extremely fond of music. They played flutes, harps, lutes, and a variety of cymbals and drums, and they delighted in singing and dancing. If the Vedic hymns are to be believed, they were also much addicted to gambling, particularly dice. One of the few secular poems in the early Vedic corpus, "The Gambler's Lament," vividly captures the pleasures and pitfalls of the gamblers' den. One passage reminds the tempted youth that:

The dice are armed with hooks and piercing,
they are deceptive, hot and burning.
Like children they give and take again,
they strike back at their conquerors.
They are sweetened with honey through the magic they
work on the gambler.

Gambling has remained a recurring theme in Indian religious and philosophical discourses throughout South Asian history.

HARAPPA'S FALL AND ARYAN DOMINANCE

During the early centuries of the Aryan invasions, which began around 1500 B.C., civilization disappeared from India. Itinerant pastoralism dominated Indian economic life as sedentary agriculture retreated with the fleeing Harappan peoples. A well-defined elite gave way to rowdy chieftains, chosen for their popularity among their warrior followers. A rather complex division of labor and responsibility gave way to tribal egalitarianism and occupational interchangeability. State control and standardization were replaced by fractious warrior bands and something resembling political chaos.

With the spread of cultivation among the invading tribes and the growth of trade some centuries after the fall of Harappa, the basis for civilization again emerged. The small kingdoms that arose in the foothills of the Himalayas and the upper Gangetic plains combined the ingredients that would give rise to India's great classical civilizations. These civilizations produced a succession of wealthy and far-flung empires; gave rise to two major religions, Hinduism and Buddhism, as well as a variety of lesser-known faiths; and produced splendid art, architecture, philosophy, and literature. But the new patterns of civilized life that developed in the last centuries B.C. diverged widely from those established by the Harappans. Though some of the Harappans' symbols and beliefs were adopted by the Aryans and other invaders, the Harappan civilization became little more than a memory.

A BEND IN THE RIVER AND THE BEGINNINGS OF CHINA

The region that gave birth to Chinese civilization was less promising than the once-fertile Indus plains. The Yellow River, from its source on the Tibetan plateau, turns and bends its way through the desolate Ordos Desert region to the Yellow Sea thousands of miles to the east.

Like the semi-arid steppelands to the north and west, the great bend in the river receives a limited and uncertain amount of rainfall. The wet monsoons that inundate much of south and coastal China are so spent by the time they reach the Ordos region that the northern part of the area is desert. Thus, the Ordos bend does not seem to be a place in which to settle, much less one in which to lay the foundations for one of humankind's greatest civilizations.

HUMAN SETTLEMENTS

Humanlike creatures as well as humans have lived on the north China plain for hundreds of thousands of years. Peking man, one of the most famous of the *hominids*—

China in the Shang and Zhou Eras

two-legged primates—had campsites along the Fen River nearly 400,000 years ago, and several Paleolithic sites have been uncovered along the Yellow River where it arcs through the Ordos Desert. From Neolithic times (c. 8000–1800 B.C.) cultivating peoples gravitated to the lands that make up the base of the Ordos bulge, where conditions were surprisingly suitable for sedentary agriculture and human settlement.

The region abounded in rich *loess*, a fine-grained, yellowish-brown soil that was deposited by powerful winds from central Asia in prehistoric times. In places, this extremely fertile soil built up over thousands of millennia to depths of over 300 feet. The Yellow River derived its name from the peculiar color of the soil that permeates the river as it is carried eastward toward the sea. Rich soil and the abundant supplies of water in areas near the Yellow River and its tributaries made the southern portions of the Ordos bulge, and the areas eastward along the North China plain suitable for intensive cultivation of grain crops and dense settlement. In addition, the region was shielded by mountains to the west and south, but open to trade with and migratory movements from the grasslands to the north.

By 4000 B.C. human communities supported by sedentary agriculture were spread across the loess zone. These communities coalesced into two widely spread cultural complexes that laid the basis for the Shang dynasty and Chinese civilization. Both the Yangshao culture (c. 2500–2000

B.C.) and the Longshan culture (c. 2000–1500 B.C.) that followed it were based on very different mixes of agriculture and hunting. In the Yangshao period, hunting and fishing predominated, while foods supplied by shifting cultivation were supplementary. By the Longshan period, the cultivation of grain, millet in particular, was the central preoccupation, while sedentary cropping techniques made it possible for them to support large, permanent villages surrounded by walls of stamped earth. Hunting and fishing continued, but domesticated pigs, cattle, and sheep became important sources of food and materials for shelter and tools. The finely crafted and painted pottery, and the production of silk which were prominent features of each culture, suggest the beginnings of specialized labor.

THE ROLE OF IRRIGATION

Increasingly elaborate irrigation systems were vital to the expansion of the agrarian base of society. Some of China's most ancient and venerated cultural heroes were linked to the building and restoration of the system of dikes and canals that grew up along the Yellow River. The shallow bed of the river after it empties onto the plains of north China, and the large quantities of silt it carries, render the river particularly treacherous in the springtime when the melting snows of the Tibetan plateau and Kunlun mountains turn the river into a raging torrent. From ancient times, controlling the river by building and maintaining great earthen dikes has been a major preoccupation of peasants and rulers.

These concerns may have given rise to China's first rulers and prompted a high level of community and intervillage cooperation. It is significant that one of the most abused of China's early and semi-mythical leaders was a man named Kun, who proved incapable of controlling a succession of great floods. His son, Yu, who devised an effective system of flood control, has been revered for millennia as one of the great monarchs of China's mythical golden age. When later thinkers such as Confucius searched China's past for leaders whose skill and virtue might be emulated in their own times, men such as Yu came readily to mind.

We know little about the social organization and daily life of the Yangshao and Longshan cultures, but two practices are worthy of note. China's first agriculturists buried their dead. Their rather extensive cemeteries and burial mounds may reflect a veneration for the deceased that was to become a central feature of Chinese social life and religious practice. The peoples of both cultures also employed animal bones for divination. When seared by heated pokers, the collar bones of cattle and other animals cracked in a variety of ways. The meaning of the patterns produced were then interpreted, probably by specialized seers or priests. This key mode of religious expression was, in the next phase of Chinese development, to be linked to the development of writing. And writing was to provide for the Chinese, perhaps more than any other people, the core ingredient of civilized life.

THE WARRIOR KINGS OF THE SHANG ERA

Semi-legendary Chinese accounts tell us that Yu, the father of north China's great network of dikes and canals, also founded China's first kingdom, Xia. Because no archeological sites connected to Xia have been found, it is possible that it was purely the fabrication of later writers. But in the centuries before 1500 B.C., numerous small kingdoms had begun to emerge south of the Ordos bulge and east along the north China plain. Most of these were ruled by nomadic tribal groups that continued to filter into the area from the north and west.

This region of different ethnic and linguistic groups formed a distinctive Chinese culture. Key features of this culture included its cooking vessels and cuisine, its reliance on cracked animal bones for divination, its domestication of the silkworm and use of silk fabrics for clothing, and its practice of ancestor worship. The form of ancestor worship followed also suggests that Chinese culture was already patrilineal. By 1500 B.C. one of the tribes in the Ordos region, the Shang, conquered most of the rest and founded a kingdom that would lay the foundations of Chinese civilization.

Until recent decades we knew little more about the Shang than their Xia predecessors. But extensive excavation of Shang sites at Anyang, Zhengzhou, and elsewhere in recent decades have given us insights into many aspects of Shang culture and society. In some respects they were very like those of the Aryans who were in the process of conquering northern India in this same era. Like the Aryans, the Shang were warlike nomads. They fought on horseback and from chariots with highly lethal bronze weapons. Non-Shang subject peoples provided the foot soldiers that made up the bulk of their armies. Like those of Aryan India and Homeric Greece, Shang battles were wild melees that hinged on hand-to-hand combat between a few champions on each side. But unlike the Indo-Aryans and ancient Greeks, the Shang warriors were ruled by strong kings who drew on their vassals' energies and military prowess to build a remarkably extensive empire.

The Shang monarch was seen as the intermediary between the Supreme Being, *Shangdi*, and ordinary mortals. His kingdom was viewed as the center of the world, and

On this inscribed oracle bone from ancient China, note both the characters written on the bone—which were the precursors of the Chinese writing system—and the holes where the hot pokers were inserted to crack the bone, thus forming the patterns on which events could be foretold.

he claimed universal dominion over all humankind. Shang rulers directed the affairs of state and bore ritual responsibilities for the fertility of their kingdom and the well-being of their subjects. In the springtime, they participated in special ceremonies that included a symbolic mating with female fertility spirits. In times of drought and famine,

Shang rulers or perhaps designated surrogates were obliged to perform ritual dances in the nude. The dancer, presumably the surrogate, was later burned alive to placate the spirits whose anger had caused the natural calamities.

SHANG SOCIETY

Though Shang monarchs were served by a sizeable regular bureaucracy in the capital city and the surrounding areas, most of the peasant and artisan population of the kingdom was governed by vassal retainers. These were recruited from the former ruling families and the aristocratic classes of the many small states. The vassals depended on the produce and labor from the commoners in these areas to support their families and military retainers. In return for these grants of control over the bonded peasants, warrior aristocrats collected tribute that went to support the monarch and his court. They supplied soldiers for the king's armies in times of war, and kept the peace and administered justice among the peasants and townspeople.

Shang rulers and their families, servants, and noble retainers lived within walled towns in large compounds that housed *extended families*. The extended families consisted of several generations of the family patriarch. As in Aryan India, family life at least among the upper classes was dominated by the elder males in the household. At marriage women went to live with their husband's family who were virtual strangers. Unswerving obedience was expected of both women and younger males. Within their own household and family spheres, patriarchs and husbands exercised absolute authority. Their wishes and commands were carried down the family hierarchy from elder to younger brother and mother-in-law to young bride.

Judging from later social arrangements in China, the extended-family pattern was widespread only among elite groups who had the resources to support the large households and many servants it required. Ordinary peasants, who made up the great majority of the population, lived in modified *nuclear families*—households consisting of husband and wife, their children, and perhaps a grandmother or orphaned cousin. It is likely that peasant families were as male-dominated and *patrilocal*—the wife went to live with her husband's family—as those of the elite.

Peasants were in effect the servants of the nobles. By Shang times they grew a wide range of crops, but the staple foods were millet, wheat, beans, and rice. They worked the land in the village in cooperative work teams using a variety of wooden hoes, spades, and crude plows. They lived in sunken houses of stamped earth, and made offerings to local gods of the soil and kitchen hearth.

This carving from the Shang era depicts a two-pronged digging stick that probably was used to turn over the soil for cultivation. This wooden hoe is possibly the single most important tool of the Shang era.

Though the peasants had only very limited opportunities for social and economic advancement, they were better off than most of the slaves who made up the lowest strata of society in the Shang era. The large numbers of slaves in the Shang era indicate that the Shang warrior elite relied on a variety of systems to control and extract resources from the artisan, cultivating, and herding population that came under their rule. Though it is likely that many of the artisans were slaves, some were free and quite prosperous. It is probable that this latter group was engaged in the manufacture of products that required a high degree of skill, such as silk textiles (one of the earliest of many inventions the Chinese have bequeathed to humanity) and the casting of bronze. Though their dwellings were located outside the walls of Shang towns, some were surprisingly large and commodious.

Life for the majority of the commoners was generally a good deal less rewarding than that of the skilled artisans. Much of what the commoners produced with long hours of backbreaking labor went to support an increasingly rapacious warrior elite. Given the vast tracts of unoccupied, arable land that existed both within the Shang domains and beyond to the south and east, it is not surprising that the elite resorted to measures such as enslavement and the bonding of peasants to the land they worked. These devices were employed to discourage flight to the nearby forests or long-distance migration to the frontier wilderness.

This elaborately decorated, bronze incense vessel from the Shang era, with its whimsical horse and catlike figure, testifies to the high level of artistic expression that had been achieved very early in Chinese history.

SHANG CULTURE AND THE DEVELOPMENT OF WRITING

Given their frequent involvement in warfare and concern for controlling peasant groups, it is not surprising that the Shang elites were preoccupied with rituals, oracles, and sacrifices. In addition to the fertility functions of the ruler the entire elite was also involved in propitiating spirits to provide good crops and numerous offspring. Shang artistic expression reached its peak in the ornately carved and expertly cast bronze vessels that were used to make these offerings. Shang bronzes have been compared favorably to the great bronze sculptures that were produced in Italy during the Renaissance some 2500 years later.

Some offerings, such as fine grain, incense, wine, and animals, to the spirit world were sometimes a good deal less innocuous than others. Shang records tell of water festivals at which ritual contests were waged between rival boats, each seeking to sink the other. Those aboard the losing craft drowned when it capsized and were offered up to the deities responsible for fertility and good harvests. War captives and servants were also buried with deceased Shang rulers and major officials. Like the pharaohs of ancient Egypt, the kings of Shang went to the other world accompanied by their wives, servants, and loyal retainers as well as their favorite horses and hunting dogs, war chariots, and weapons. The ancestral veneration grew into a cult of the royal clan that involved sacrifices of war captives, mass burials, and the construction of tombs for each of the emperors.

Concerns for abundant harvests and victory in war led the Shang elite to put great stock in the predictions provided by the *shamans,* priests who performed oracular rituals. Warriors about to go into battle, officials embarking on long journeys, or families negotiating marriage alliances routinely consulted the shamans to ensure that their enterprises would turn out well. This reliance on the shamans strongly influenced beliefs and behavior in the Shang era. The actual procedures followed by the shamans also gave rise to perhaps the single most important element in Chinese culture—writing.

As in pre-Shang times, oracles made their prognostications on the basis of "readings" taken from animal bones or tortoise shells. Each of the bones or shells was drilled with a hole and touched by a red-hot iron poker. The bones or shells then cracked and the patterns of cracks were then interpreted by the shaman. Gradually the practice evolved of inscribing the bones and shells with painted designs that became part of the patterns the shamans "read." Over time, these designs became standardized and came to form the basis for an *ideographic*— relating to graphic symbols—written Chinese language.

The development of writing became the key to Chinese identity and the growth of civilization in China. The many and diverse peoples of the loess region and the north China plain spoke a bewildering variety of languages that were often mutually unintelligible from one group to the next. They were surrounded by nomadic herders on the north and shifting cultivators to the south, whose contacts with and movements into the loess zone further complicated the linguistic muddle. But the written language that developed made communications possible between the educated elites of many of these peoples.

Like the hieroglyphics of the ancient Egyptians, early Chinese characters were pictographic. Thus, they readily conveyed the ideas they were intended to express. The original character for the sun, for example, was a circle with a dot in the center, while the character for a tree was a single tree and a forest was a set of three tree characters. Combinations of characters made it possible for the Chinese literati to convey increasingly complex ideas. The character for emperor, for example, combined elements of the ideographs for king, heaven, earth, and harmony.

Over time the number of characters has increased substantially. By the end of the Shang period, there were an estimated 3000 characters. A well-educated scholar in the modern era would need to master some 8000 characters. The way they are written has also changed significantly. The character for the sun, for example, has been modernized.

Originally the characters were carved into bones or bronze vessels rather than written. Bones and shells gradually gave way to bamboo slips, silk scrolls, and wooden plates, and they in turn were supplanted in the 1st century A.D. by paper (another critical Chinese invention). An assortment of fine brushes and inks were developed to "paint" the characters, which in later periods became a major mode of artistic expression.

Use of the increasingly standardized and more sophisticated characters provided the bond that gave growing numbers of the peoples of the loess zone a common identity. This sense of identity was felt most keenly by the elite groups that monopolized the use of the characters, but eventually the sense of identity filtered down to the cultivating and artisan classes. After centuries of use, the characters gave the Chinese a powerful sense of continuity in time and space. With the persistence and growth of this identity, the Chinese people entered history for the first time. Increasingly distinct from the many nomadic herders and shifting cultivators with whom they continued to war, trade, and intermarry, the Chinese used their written language to build the educational and bureaucratic systems that would become the hallmarks of humankind's most extensive and enduring civilization.

THE DECLINE OF THE SHANG AND THE ERA OF ZHOU DOMINANCE

By the 11th century B.C., the decentralized Shang political system had long been in decline. In the west of the polyglot kingdom a newly arrived nomadic people, the Zhou, had set up a vassal state that originally recognized Shang overlordship. The Zhou are believed to have been Turkic-speaking peoples from central Asia. They may have been driven from their original homelands by Indo-Aryan invaders.

As time passed and the Shang hold over its many vassal states weakened, Zhou emissaries began to infiltrate neighboring states. They strove to convince the vassal leaders of these states to abandon their allegiance to the Shang and back the Zhou bid for paramountcy. By the last decades of the 12th century, a substantial majority of the vassals had shifted to support of the Zhou. In 1122 B.C., Wu, the king of the Zhou, openly challenged the authority of the last Shang ruler. When the Shang ruler's armies were defeated by those loyal to Wu, the last Shang king committed suicide. With the fall of the Shang, Wu proclaimed the kings of Zhou its successor as sovereigns of China.

THE NEW KINGDOM

In the early centuries of their overlordship, the Zhou rulers exercised more power than their Shang predecessors. Under Wu and his brother, the Duke of Zhou, the empire was greatly expanded, especially to the east and south. Because the original Zhou capital at Xian was too far to the west to effectively control these areas, a second capital was built at Loyang hundreds of miles to the east. Wu and other early Zhou rulers governed their vast domains through a hierarchy of vassals who were controlled to a much greater extent than had been the case under the Shang.

Many of the most powerful vassals were relatives, fellow clansmen, or longstanding allies of the Zhou household. Thus, ties of kinship cemented their loyalty and obedience to the Zhou overlords. They in turn held in check vassals further down the hierarchy, who were often their own subordinates or relations. In addition, the lords of Zhou formally annexed the vassal states. The Zhou overlords claimed ownership of all of the land in their domains, which was then parcelled out to their vassals for their support. Peoples whose loyalty to the Zhou dynasty was suspect were uprooted and forced to migrate to areas within the empire controlled by Zhou strongmen.

ZHOU FEUDALISM

In the Early Zhou period, formal oaths of allegiance and regularized fief-granting procedures transformed the Shang vassal system into a more genuine *feudal* order. Here, as in the later systems, feudalism stressed mutual obligation and benefits within the ruling clan. *Fiefs,* in Europe and Japan varying considerably in size and consisting of peasant villages, were given to selected aristocratic and warrior retainers. In return, the favored vassals pledged their loyalty to the dynasty in a special ceremony in the ruler's palace. During the ceremony the new fiefholder was given a clump of earth, symbolizing the land and villages granted to him by the monarch. At the same time, a charter of his duties to his ruler and his rights as fiefholder was presented to the assembled court.

Zhou monarchs had virtually no control over how fiefdoms, beyond those in the central core regions, were run and no way to ensure that they were getting their fair share of revenues or troops. If a vassal stopped sending tribute to the capital or refused requests to muster troops for war or laborers for Zhou building projects, he was in effect declaring war and risking annihilation. As long as the Zhou overlords were strong, it was safer and profitable enough to pass on the revenue to the court and to rally to the Zhou overlord's call to battle. When the dynasty weakened, the flow of revenue from the vassals' domains dried up and their troops were increasingly used for wars between the feudal lords or in alliances against the Zhou rulers.

CHANGES IN THE SOCIAL ORDER

Two developments worked against the continuance of the feudal system. The first was the elaboration of an ideology that the Zhou rulers used to legitimize their rule. When King Wu overthrew the Shang dynasty, he claimed that the Shang had lost the Mandate of Heaven and thus no longer deserved the allegiance of their vassals. The concept of the Mandate of Heaven provided a powerful rationale for the Zhou monarchs to strive to centralize authority. Wu charged that his successful bid for the throne was proof that the Zhou had the moral probity and leadership potential to inherit the heavenly mandate the Shang had betrayed.

This appeal to a supernatural source of legitimation was a common feature of preindustrial monarchies throughout the world, and it became a pillar of the political system in China. It also meant that the Zhou had established the principle that supreme political authority was granted by Heaven, not a ruler's vassals or common people. This claim would greatly enhance the capacity of the Zhou and subsequent royal houses to rule as absolutist and authoritarian monarchs. But it also contained a potentially critical check on their powers that was to be explored by Chinese social thinkers in the Late Zhou era. If a ruler governed by virtue of the Mandate of Heaven, it was possible, as the Shang precedent clearly demonstrated, for a monarch and royal house to fail in their duties and lose the mandate. Subsequently it was legitimate for their subjects to overthrow them and replace them with a new imperial house.

The second development working against the persistence of feudalism in China involved the emergence of an alternative to the military retainers who governed most of the empire. From the Early Zhou era, the small corps of professional bureaucrats that had once served the Shang rulers began to grow in size and expertise. These administrators, who were the best educated men in the empire, came to be known in the Late Zhou period (c. 770–400 B.C.) as *shi*, or men of service. Their literacy and willingness to serve as scribes, clerks, advisors, and overseers won them a livelihood as administrators both at the court and in the palaces of the fiefholders and their subordinate vassals. Some of these aspiring administrators were supported by grants of villages, but others, particularly those at the royal court, were paid regular salaries out of the imperial treasury. Many performed a wide range of services that at times could be embarrassingly menial; some even had to cultivate small plots of land to supplement their meager salaries. Increasingly, however, they came to specialize in keeping records, running particular departments, such as public works or war, or organizing palace rituals and ceremonies.

There is some evidence that even before the end of the Early Zhou era in the middle of the 8th century B.C., the most favored of these administrators had begun to amass considerable influence as advisors to the ruler and powerful nobles. As representatives of the great lords, they sometimes exercised direct authority over lesser vassals. Though the rise of a large and skilled corps of professional bureaucrats did not occur until the Late Zhou era, these early administrators were the forerunners of a scholarly governing class that would become the chief guardian of civilization in China.

NEW PATTERNS OF LIFE

In the Early Zhou era, the conquerors lived separately from the subjugated "black-haired people." This division appears to confirm the supposition that the Zhou were originally Turkic tribespeople with lighter hair and eye coloring than the peoples they found in the loess soil region and along the north China plain. In the twin capitals of Xian and Loyang, the Zhou and their servants lived in one side of the walled city, while peoples of other ethnic groups inhabited the rest.

Early in the Zhou period, some of the non-Zhou populace in Xian revolted against their foreign overlords. The revolt was brutally repressed and large numbers of the deeply implicated artisans were forced to migrate to Loyang where they lived for generations in poverty. With the passage of time, Loyang became the main seat of the royal house. The palace of Loyang was considered the center of the earth, and each spring critical sacrifices to Heaven and the fertility spirits were performed by the Zhou monarchs.

Zhou vassals, living away from the capitals, resided in walled garrison towns. Each town was laid out on a rectangular grid with two main roads that crossed at a central square. Servants, artisans, and slaves resided in or near the garrisons. Beyond them stretched the villages and tilled fields of the enserfed farmers who made up the great majority of the empire's population. Their staple crops remained millet and wheat, but rice was widely cultivated in the eastern and southern portions of the Zhou domains. Peasants worked their lands on a pattern similar to the later so-called well-field system because it resembled the Chinese character for a well. Each of eight peasant households cultivated one of eight plots that were arranged around a central plot. This middle plot was farmed by all of the families to provide the produce that would be given to the lord as tribute.

The introduction of iron farm implements and the extension of the irrigation system contributed to higher levels of productivity. But much of the increase went to fill the coffers of the lords and Shang court, rather than to the peasants themselves. The peasants were burdened by their lords' regular demands for labor on road, building, and irrigation projects. They were also obliged to feed and find shelter for the lords' retainers when they journeyed from the garrison towns. In times of war, the peasants marched on foot alongside the chariots and cavalry of the lords' army. As time passed, the lords' demands grew more and more oppressive. A rare insight into the peasants' plight is provided by a poem from the *Book of Odes* that was written in the Late Zhou era:

Big rat, big rat,
Do not eat my millet!
Three years I have served you,
But you will not care for me.
I am going to leave you
And go to that happy land;
Happy land, happy land;
Where I will find my place.

Big rat, big rat,
Do not eat my sprouts!
Three years I have served you
But you give me no comfort.
I am going to leave you
And go to those happy fields;
Happy fields, happy fields;
Who there shall long moan?

Peasants at some distance from their lords' garrison towns appear to have been the best off. In fact, communications were so poor in many parts of the empire that local lords were content to leave peasant communities alone if they regularly supplied tribute and gifts on special occasions. The peasants in these outlying villages were in effect free cultivators. Perhaps it was these peasant communities that later Chinese writers remembered in idyllic terms—peaceful, well-fed, living in harmony among themselves and with their kindly and protective overlords. It is likely, however, that the peasant lament previously quoted more accurately captures the reality of peasant life in the Zhou period.

MIGRATIONS AND THE EXPANSION OF THE CHINESE CORE

Throughout the centuries of Zhou rule, both the area controlled by its vassals and the lands occupied by peoples who identified themselves as Chinese grew steadily. New agricultural tools and techniques of production stimulated population growth that in turn led to the extension of cultivation into new areas along the north China plain and then southward along the coast. Periodic nomadic raids and, at times, lasting conquests pushed Chinese peasant migrants to the south and east. Other peasants fled the oppression of feudal lords or sought large tracts of fertile frontier land.

Whatever the reasons for migrating, in the Zhou era the Chinese moved in the tens of thousands down the Yellow River, into the Shandong peninsula, and then south across the flatlands to first the Huai and later the great Yangtze River basins. As they advanced, non-Chinese peoples, who were hunters and gatherers and shifting cultivators, fell back into the hills to the west of the great plains and then to the mountainous region south of the Yangtze. By the end of the Zhou era, the two great river systems, the Yellow and the Yangtze, that have been the heart of Chinese civilization for thousands of years had been straddled. The basin of the Yellow River was securely theirs, despite the continuing nomadic threat. The Yangtze had barely been reached, but the enormous agricultural potential of the rice-growing, monsoon-watered south had begun to be tapped.

CULTURAL CHANGE IN THE EARLY ZHOU PERIOD

The Zhou influx into the loess heartland of early China strengthened the dominance of males within the family and in society. Perhaps the key roles males played in ancestor veneration contributed to their increased authority. The cults of royal and familial ancestors became the central foci of religious observance. Human sacrifice ended and philosophical speculation remained minimal as increasingly elaborate rites and ceremonies developed around the worship of deceased members of the family, clan, and dynasty. Family patriarchs and monarchs monopolized the role of celebrant in these ceremonies designed to win the blessings of the ancestors or Heaven, which was conceptualized rather abstractly and called Tian.

As in Aryan India, more and more stress was placed on the importance of performing these and other ceremonies flawlessly. An obsession with correctly performed rites led to the elite's more generalized concern with refined manners and proper decorum. The rough nomads had rapidly settled down to enjoy the amenities of the rich and powerful among the civilized.

THE END OF THE EARLY OR WESTERN ZHOU

By the 8th century B.C., Zhou power was in decline. Its control over its vassals had diminished dramatically and the size and strength of several of the vassals' domains had grown to the point that they were openly challenging the overlordship of the dynasty. In 771 B.C., an allied group of northern nobles attacked Xian. The Zhou ruler was killed in a battle, and in the months that followed most of the western portions of the kingdom were lost to leaders of the vassal alliance or nomadic invaders eager to take advantage of internal divisions among the Chinese. Retainers loyal to the Zhou managed to rescue a young prince and escort him safely to Loyang. The shift to the eastern capital marks the end of the Early or Western Zhou era.

A less powerful Zhou kingdom would survive for over five centuries more. The territories it effectively controlled shrank to little more than the capital and its immediate environs. Zhou vassals warred continuously, using the defense of the royal house to legitimize their attacks and conquests. Over time, successful lords annexed the holdings of defeated neighbors and several rival kingdoms emerged in place of the fiefdoms that had existed in the Early Zhou. The growing chaos and widespread suffering eventually produced a reaction on the part of the shi bureaucrats, a reaction that would produce some of China's greatest thinkers and radically alter the course of Chinese civilization.

ANALYSIS
THE LEGACY OF ASIA'S FIRST CIVILIZATIONS

In their size, complexity, and longevity, the first civilizations to develop in South Asia and China match and in some respects surpass the earliest civilizations that arose in Mesopotamia and Egypt. But the long-term impact of the Harappan civilization of the Indus basin and the Shang-Zhou civilization in north China was strikingly different. The loess zone and north China plain where the Shang and Zhou empires took hold became the center of a continuous civilization that was to last into the 20th century A.D., and, many historians would argue, to the present day. Though regions farther south, such as the Yangtze basin, would in some time periods enjoy political, economic, and cultural predominance within China, the capital and center of Chinese civilization repeatedly returned to the Yellow River area and the north China plain. The Indus valley proved capable of nurturing a civilization that endured for over a thousand years. But when Harappa collapsed, the plains of the Indus were bypassed in favor of the far more lush and extensive lands in the basin of the Ganges River network to the east. Though the Indus would later serve, for much shorter time spans, as the seat of empires, the core areas of successive Indian civilization were far to the east and south.

The contrast between the fate of the original geographical centers of Indian and Chinese civilizations is paralleled by the legacy of the civilizations themselves. Harappa was destroyed and it disappeared from history for thousands of years. Though the peoples who built the Indus complex left their mark on subsequent Indian culture, they did not pass on the fundamental patterns of civilized life that had evolved. Their mother goddess and the dancing god of fertility endured, and some of their symbols, such as the swastika and *lingam* (usually stone, phallic images), were prominent in later artistic and religious traditions. Harappan tanks or public bathing ponds remain a central feature of Indian cities, particularly in the south. Their techniques of growing rice and cotton were preserved by cultivating peoples fleeing nomadic invaders, and were later taken up by the newly arrived Indo-Aryan tribes.

Virtually everything else was lost. In contrast to the civilizations of Mesopotamia, which fell but were replaced by new civilizations that preserved and built on the achievements of their predecessors, much of what the Harappan peoples had accomplished had to be redone by later civilized peoples. The cities of the Indus civilization were destroyed and comparable urban centers did not reappear in

South Asia for hundreds or, by some scholars' reckoning, thousands of years. Their remarkably advanced standards for the measurement of distance and weight ceased to be used. Their system of writing was forgotten, and when rediscovered, it was celebrated as an intriguing but very dead language from the past. Harappan skills in community planning, sewage control, and engineering were meaningless to the nomadic peoples who took control of their homelands. The Harappan penchant for standardization, discipline, and state control was profoundly challenged by the brawling, independent-minded warriors who supplanted them as masters of the Indian subcontinent.

In contrast to the civilization of the Indus valley, the original civilization of China has survived nomadic incursions and natural catastrophes and profoundly influenced the course of all Chinese history. Shang irrigation and dike systems and millet and wheat cultivation provided the basis upon which subsequent dynasties innovated and expanded. Shang and Zhou walled towns and villages surrounded with stamped earth have persisted as the predominant patterns of settlement throughout Chinese history. The founders of the Shang and Zhou dynasty have been revered by scholar and peasant alike as philosopher-kings who ought to be emulated by leaders at all levels. The Shang and Zhou worship of Heaven and their ancestral veneration have remained central to Chinese religious belief and practice for thousands of years. The concept of the Mandate of Heaven has been pivotal in Chinese political thinking and organization.

Above all, the system of writing that developed in connection with Shang oracles developed into the key means of communication between the elites of the many peoples who lived in the core regions of Chinese civilization. The scholar-bureaucrats who both developed this written language and profited the most from it soon emerged as the dominant force in Chinese culture and society. Chinese characters provided the basis for the educational system and bureaucracy that were to hold Chinese civilization together through thousands of years of invasions and political crises. In contrast to India, many of the key ingredients of China's early civilizations have remained central throughout Chinese history. This persistence has made for a continuity of identity that is unique to the Chinese people.

It has also meant that China, like the early civilizations of Mesopotamia, was one of the great sources of civilizing influences in human history as a whole. Though the area affected by ideas and institutions developed in China was less extensive than that to which the peoples of Mesopotamia bequeathed writing, law, and their other great achievements, contacts with the Chinese led to the spread of civilization to Japan, Korea, and Vietnam. Writing and political organization were two areas in which the earliest formulations of Chinese civilization vitally affected other peoples. In later periods Chinese thought and other modes of cultural expression such as art, architecture, and etiquette also strongly influenced the growth of civilized life.

China's technological innovation was to have an impact on civilized development on a global scale comparable to that of early Mesopotamia. Beginning with the increasingly sophisticated irrigation systems, the Chinese have devised a remarkable share of humankind's basic machines and engineering principles. In the Shang-Zhou era they also pioneered key manufacturing processes such as *sericulture*—the manufacture of silk cloth through the domestication of silkworms.

The reasons for the differing legacies of India and China are numerous and complex. But critical to the disappearance of the first and the resilience of the second were different patterns of interaction between the sedentary peoples who built the early civilizations and the nomadic herders who challenged them. In the Indian case, the nomadic threat was remote, perhaps nonexistent for centuries. The Harappan peoples were deficient in military technology and organization. When combined with natural calamities, the waves of warlike nomads migrating into the Indus region proved too much for the Harappan peoples to resist or absorb. The gap between the nomads' herding culture and the urban, agriculture-based Harappan civilization was too great to be bridged. Conflict between them may well have proven fatal to a civilization long in decline.

The loess regions of northern China were open to invasions or migrations on the part of the nomadic herding peoples who lived to the north and west. Peoples from these areas were moving almost continuously into the core zones of Chinese civilization. The constant threat the nomads posed forced the peoples of the north China plain to develop the defenses and military technology essential to defending against nomadic raids or bids for lasting conquest. Contrasting cultures and ways of life enhanced the sense of identity of the cultivating peoples. The obvious nomadic presence prodded these same peoples to unite under strong rulers against the outsiders who did not share Chinese culture. Constant interaction with the nomads led the Shang peoples to develop a culture that was malleable and receptive to outside influences, social structures, and political systems. Nomadic energies reinvigorated and enriched the kingdom of the Shang and Zhou, in contrast to India where they proved catastrophic for the relatively isolated and unprepared peoples of Harappa.

Questions: Compare the early civilizations of India and China to that of Sumer in Mesopotamia and that which developed in Egypt. Which are more similar in terms of longevity? Why does Sumer have a greater impact on subsequent civilizations than the Indus valley complex, which is also destroyed? Are the factors that explain the persistence of Chinese civilization comparable to those responsible for the longevity of Egypt? Are there major differences between the two in terms of their interaction with nomadic peoples? Which of these four civilizations do you think has left the greatest legacy to civilized peoples throughout the world? What is the main legacy of each?

CONCLUSION

BEGINNINGS AND TRANSITIONS

The spread of the Aryan pastoralists into the hills and plains of northern and eastern India between 1500 and 500 B.C. and the establishment and decline of the Zhou kingdom in the latter half of the same time span marked key transition phases in the development of civilization in India and China. But in each case a very different sort of transition occurred. Like Mesopotamia, the well-watered Indus valley had given rise to one of humankind's earliest civilizations. In contrast to the succession of more limited civilized centers that arose in Mesopotamia, Harappa extended over the largest territory of any of the first civilizations, and it existed without interruption for over a millennium. Its longevity invites comparison with Egypt. But Egypt proved more able than either Harappa or individual Mesopotamian civilizations to absorb massive invasions of nomadic peoples.

Faced with major climatic shifts, the Harappans proved unable to also withstand the steady and prolonged pressure of the Aryan incursions. Thus, the dominance of these invaders in the Harappan core regions and much of the rest of northern India by 1000 B.C. meant the end of India's first civilization.

The Zhou conquest and later the slow disintegration of the Zhou dynasty represented a continuation rather than a break in the development of civilization in China. Though civilization arose later in China than in the other three original centers in the Eastern Hemisphere, like the others it emerged independently and resulted in a distinctive pattern of development. In its capacity to endure, China resembled Egypt more than Mesopotamia or Harappa.

Perhaps as a result, the Chinese proved the most adept at absorbing and assimilating outside invaders while preserving their own sense of identity and their basic beliefs and institutions. The Chinese both originated and perpetuated these key ingredients for thousands of years. The conquering Zhou did not destroy Chinese society and culture; they were assimilated by them so thoroughly that they became Chinese. Thus, though the Zhou period brought major changes in the nature and direction of civilized development in China, fundamental themes and patterns persisted from the Shang era, and the Zhou rulers strove to conserve and build upon the achievements of their predecessors.

FURTHER READINGS

The best introduction to the Indus valley civilization remains that found in A. L. Basham's *The Wonder That Was India* (1954). Perhaps the best book-length studies that place Harappa in the context of Indian prehistory more generally are Stuart Piggot's *Prehistoric India* (1950) and Briget and Stuart Allchin's *The Birth of Indian Civilization* (1968). For a sense of more recent findings on the Indus complex, see the sometimes quite technical essays in G. L. Possehl, ed., *Harappan Civilization: A Contemporary Perspective* (1982). Romila Thapar's *History of India* (1966) has a superb chapter on Aryan culture and society. Also interesting are C. Chakraborty's account of *Common Life in the Rigeveda and Atharvaveda* (1977) and the lively and contentious analysis of *Ancient India* (1969) by D. D. Kosambi.

For ancient China, Wolfram Eberhard's *History of China* (1977 ed.) and the early portions of Michael Loewe's *Imperial China* (1965) are good places to start. More detailed (and technical) accounts of the formation of China through the Early Zhou include Kwang-chih Chang's *The Archeology of Ancient China* (1977) and *Shang Civilization* (1980); H. G. Creel's *The Origins of Statecraft in Ancient China* (1970); and Ping-ti Ho's *The Cradle of the East* (1975). K. C. Wu's *The Chinese Heritage* (1982) provides the fullest political history of the Shang and Early Zhou. While somewhat dated by recent archeological research, H. G. Creel's *The Birth of China* (1967 ed.) remains the liveliest and broadest account of these epochs.

5000 B.C.	2000 B.C.	1000 B.C.	750 B.C.

China

1122–770 Initial Zhou kingdom

770–403 Later Zhou kingdom; beginning of China's classical period

Mediterranean and Middle East

800 Rise of Greek city-states

600 Zoroastrian religion in Iran

India

1200–700 Vedas composed

The Americas

900 Maya begins

850–250 Chavin culture (Andes)

Other Societies

2000 Germans settle in Denmark

5000 Early Japanese settlement

800 B.C.–A.D.1000 Bantu migration, sub-Saharan Africa

1500–500 Polynesian migrations

750–600 Meroe (Kush) rules Egypt

1000 Germans expand southward

600 Legendary ruler in Japan

4 NOMADIC CHALLENGES AND CIVILIZED RESPONSES

This statue is an example of the bronze figures crafted during the eastern Han dynasty in the 2d century. The figure was excavated at Wu-Wei in Kansu, China, in 1969.

202 B.C.–A.D. 9 Initial Han dynasty; key technical developments of horse collar and water mill

88 Beginning of Han decline

551-c. 233 Period of the great Chinese philosophers: Confucius, Laozi, Menicus, the Legalists, etc.

221 Shih Huangdi proclaimed first emperor of China

23–220 Later Han dynasty; invention of paper and the compass

500–449 Wars with Persia; Persia defeated

300–100 Hellenistic period

27 Augustus founds Roman Empire

330 Alexander the Great

133 ff. Decline of Roman republic

106 Height of Roman territory

500–450 Beginnings of Roman republic

30 Crucifixion of Christ

264–140 Roman expansion in North Africa (Punic wars) and eastern Mediterranean

550 Formation of Persian Empire

470–430 Height of Athenian culture; Socrates and Greek philosophical style

180 Beginning of the decline of Rome

431 ff. Peloponnesian wars; decline of Greece

327–325 Alexander's invasion

200 B.C.–A.D. 200 Greater Buddhist influence

c. 542–483 Buddha

322–185 Mauryan Empire

300 B.C.–A.D.900 Height of Maya

100 Germans begin contact with Rome; Slavs migrate into eastern Europe

PART 2

The Classical Period in World History

INTRODUCTION. Between 1000 and 500 B.C. a classical period took shape in several centers of Asia, North Africa, and southern Europe. These centers lasted until roughly the fifth century A.D. The classical civilizations built on the achievements of earlier river-valley civilizations. Centered in China, India, and the Mediterranean, each major classical civilization overlapped one or more of the earlier centers geographically. Because of the ability to build on earlier achievement, the pace of change accelerated in Asia, North and northeastern Africa, and southern Europe.

The innovations of the classical civilizations were dramatic: empires developed as a political form and great thinkers and religious leaders drew traditional cultural elements together in striking new statements that served as the basis for whole new cultures.

However, many regions and human societies were not connected to the classical centers, or gained connections only as the period drew to a close. In these regions, too, important developments occurred during the classical period, yielding new civilizations, as in the Americas, or more advanced

220 Last Han emperor deposed

300 Spread of Buddhism

589–618 Sui dynasty

618 Tang dynasty

312–337 Constantine; formation of Eastern Empire; adoption of Christianity

401 ff. Germanic invasions

527–565 Justinian Eastern emperor

476 Last Roman emperor in West

319–540 Gupta Empire

606–647 Harsha's Empire

451 First Hun invasions

200–1300 Anasazi in North American Southwest

800–1300 Mississippian culture

200–700 Mochica culture (Andes)

200–500 Nasca culture (Andes)

900–1200 Toltecs

300–900 Intermediate Horizon period (Andes)

300–1000 Second wave of Polynesian migrations to Hawaii

900 Polynesians to New Zealand

300–700 Rise of Axum; conversion to Christianity

401 ff. Large-scale Germanic invasions in Roman Empire

700 ff. Spread of Islam; trans-Sahara trade in Africa

1000 Height of kingdom of Ghana, Africa

300–400 Yamato claim imperial control of Japan

580 ff. Spread of Buddhism in Japan

300 Decline of Meroe

400 Chinese script imported

agricultural economies. Crudely put, the world after 1000 B.C. divided into two main parts, one where the roots of civilization were well established and the other where complex societies were first forming. Coverage of the classical period must embrace both major sectors.

 ### THE NATURE OF CLASSICAL CIVILIZATIONS

It is important to gain some sense of the dynamics of the classical period before turning to developments in the individual civilization areas of the world. Essentially, classical civilizations differed from their river-valley ancestors in complexity, though they built on river-valley foundations in many ways and initially took shape in the same parts of the world. They also differed in geographic extent: the classical civilizations extended over a much larger territory than the river-valley societies had done, which meant a major expansion not simply of civilization, but of the ability of leading civilizations to integrate diverse regions and peoples.

The nature of the classical period can be amplified in two ways: first, by sketching the currents that set the new period in motion and those that drew it to a close; and second, by defining the greater sophistication of the classical civilizations more precisely. Any period in history must be definable in terms of starting and stopping processes, and must have some internal coherence in terms of definable main features.

 ### ORIGINS OF THE CLASSICAL PERIOD

No single event ushered in the classical period of history, which is one reason that pinning down a starting date is difficult. Too few connections existed among the civilization centers to make a clean single beginning very likely. Nor was there a dramatic set of technological breakthroughs of the sort that had prepared the rise of the first river-valley civilizations. The classical era did witness important technological changes, particularly in Asia, but they were not fundamental and their results emerged gradually. The classical period began soon after 1000 B.C., because all the main centers of established civilization were ripe for new developments due to a faltering of traditional forms and the influx of new nomadic elements. Indo-European invasions toppled empires in Mesopotamia and Egypt around 1200 B.C., as they had done earlier along the Indus River. One sign of the resultant change was the partial relocation of civilization centers: The heart of Indian civilization shifted from the Indus to the Ganges River valley, as the Aryans cleared the dense forests of the northern Indian plains and spread cultivation. The expansion of China to the south had already begun under the Early Zhou, but it continued with the spread of Chinese culture and political forms into the Yangtze River valley and the mountain regions to the south and west. In the Middle East a Persian state arose in Mesopotamia, recalling the earlier series of empires from Babylon onward.

This map portrays the Romans' view of the world about A.D. 150.

Geographical change was more dramatic in the eastern Mediterranean. An important new center began to develop in Greece, from 800 B.C. onward, as the Indo-European peoples of the peninsula settled down. Greece used but greatly altered the scope of earlier civilization achievements from Crete, Mesopotamia, and Egypt, thus proving to be a major source of innovation throughout the Mediterranean region.

The expansion of the civilization centers also brought new peoples into contact with civilization on the fringes of the great empires. During the classical period nomadic groups in Europe and agricultural peoples outside China in eastern Asia began to learn what civilization involved. Civilization had already moved into parts of sub-Saharan Africa through contacts with Egypt; some of the results now fanned out into other parts of Africa south of the desert.

THE END OF THE CLASSICAL PERIOD

The end of the classical period, between the 3d and 6th centuries A.D., was clearer than its beginning, though hardly a unified event. Internal decay in the classical em-

pires combined with a new surge of invasions from central Asia to topple great states from China in the east to Rome in the west. Civilization was not destroyed, but from Asia to Africa it was strongly threatened, forcing reassessments and redefinitions. This reworking of civilization patterns was the trigger for yet another new period in world history after about A.D. 500. The classical period was thus bounded in its beginnings by new sources of vigor and innovation, produced by adaptations in the original river-valley centers after 1000 B.C., and in its end by huge dislocations caused by decay and invasion following a creative period stretching over a thousand years.

THE NATURE OF THE CLASSICAL PERIOD: REGIONAL INTEGRATION

More important than sketching the boundaries of the classical era, however, is understanding its defining characteristics. The possibility of identifying a few widely shared features is the mark of an analytically useful period in history, and the classical era offers three or four headline items.

In the three major civilization areas—China, India, and the Middle East plus the Mediterranean—that could build on earlier river-valley achievements, the increasing ability to integrate large regions was the main shared achievement. This achievement might be compared to the halting steps visible in our own day to absorb separate civilizations into larger unities that share trading links and political and cultural values such as democracy and modern architecture. In the classical era, separate small areas were pulled into larger, unified orbits. China and India constructed integrated societies that in many respects have survived to the present day, while the integration efforts in the Mediterranean region proved somewhat more ephemeral. In all three cases, however, integration marked new abilities in the cultural, economic, and political spheres.

In the economic sphere, for example, classical civilizations created larger trading zones. The Mediterranean became a single economic region, first under Greek control and then under the imperial Romans. In this common market, local areas could maintain profitable specializations by trading with other Mediterranean areas. China helped link two major growing regions, one of wheat and millet and one of rice, through rising internal trade. Indian trade, both from the Ganges region and through the efforts of sea-going merchants, fanned out through the subcontinent and across the Indian Ocean into Sri Lanka and much of Southeast Asia. The economic interdependence of large regions was basic to the integration of large civilization zones.

Expansion of trading units also had wider implications. Trade with sub-Saharan Africa extended from the Mediterranean zone. In the Americas a separate regional-trading zone developed. Trade of some significance also occurred among major civilizations in Asia, North Africa, and Europe, though it did not rival the internal dynamics.

Cultural integration was also important in defining new civilization areas. Important cultural innovations emerged in the 6th and 5th centuries B.C. in all three classical centers and Persia. This cultural integration indicated a common need for a new definition of basic cultural values. Socratic philosophy and the great philosophical tradition in Greece, Confucianism and Daoism in China, and Buddhism in India all emerged at roughly the same time, serving as major cultural orientations for the ongoing development of civilization in and beyond the various regions involved. Basic classical styles in art and architecture also were shaped in this period, and again would continue to define standard patterns. Hindu-derived art in India and classical Greco-Roman buildings in the West still shape artistic expression in the later 20th century.

Cultural innovation, in setting new ideas and styles in motion, was matched by dissemination through each civilization. Indian religious values spread through the subcontinent and moved steadily southward from centers along the northern rivers. Chinese philosophies and religions also spread among elites throughout the Middle Kingdom, building on the unified elite language, Mandarin. Greek language, art, and philosophy spread through the Mediter-

Centers of Classical Civilization, 1st Century A.D.

ranean basin and the Middle East. By no means was everyone in each major civilization brought into the same belief systems, for elite-commoner divisions remained crucial. Some civilizations were more fiercely assimilationist than others, for tolerance of internal diversity varied. Nevertheless, the emergence of wide cultural zones defined by distinctive styles and systems of thought was a crucial development.

Finally, there was substantial political integration. Each of the three centers of classical civilization managed to form huge regional empires for periods of several centuries. The ability to construct such large political units both reflected and promoted the other kinds of integration with each civilization.

Economic, cultural, and political integration meant that the great classical civilizations developed new abilities in internal communications, with enough shared language and shared technical systems to send messages, for example, across a wide expanse. Road systems fanned out in classical China and in the great Indian and Roman empires. Bureaucracies and laws provided new unity as well, and military forces moved easily within each of the civilization units. The precise nature of integration varied with the civilization.

CONTACTS AND HERITAGE

The integration theme has two other ramifications, each of which involved all the classical centers: mutual contacts and ongoing heritage.

The growth of civilization's geographical scope allowed some important contacts among the major civilizations. In addition to trade from China to the Mediterranean, there were even more important cases of cultural borrowing or diffusion at several points in the classical period. India was particularly affected by cultural exchange from the Mediterranean region. More important was India's key role in facilitating international trade and cultural influence, westward and eastward alike, as the economies of the classical civilizations reached their high points in the first centuries A.D. Cross-civilizational contacts were limited still, and they did not shape the period as a whole. For example, while elite Romans bought silk cloth made in China, they did not know it came from China—China was too distant, and regional traders controlled segments of the relevant trading route. Nevertheless, a rudimentary intercivilizational framework was established that has steadily increased in scale and intensity in each successive world history period to the present day.

The establishment of massive empires and cultural networks gave the classical era an awe-inspiring majesty to peoples who came later in time. This accounts for use of the word *classical* to describe this period. Though civilization had been invented before, it was in this period that great monuments of thought, politics, and art were developed that would provide the foundations for most of humankind's later civilizations. The civilizations of the classical era set in motion fundamental patterns of development whose effects can still be felt today in art, philosophy, political institutions, and economic habits.

Each of the main classical civilizations differed greatly from the others in culture, politics, and economic and social forms. The chapters that follow will encourage a comparison among the great civilizations. The similarities among the classical civilizations are very general, but they are all the more important in determining a common framework of analysis.

OUTSIDE THE GREAT EMPIRES

By no means was all the world absorbed in the doings of the classical civilizations, however. Each of the classical centers radiated some wider influence. China began to affect a larger East Asian zone, including Vietnam, Japan, and Korea; Indian influence spread through much of Southeast and central Asia. The Mediterranean societies interacted with the budding civilization of the Upper Nile in Africa, and of course spread directly to North Africa and parts of Europe.

The classical period also saw the rise of civilizations in Asia and the Americas that were independent of the first river-valley cores. The independent emergence or spread of civilization or pre-civilization revealed that the world was still not moving at the same pace, for most of these developments were remote from the activities of the older civilization centers. The great expansion in the portion of the globe controlled by civilized societies, however, must rank with the specific achievements of the classical societies in defining the period as a whole, as the map of civilization changed in many ways.

The closing of the classical period returns attention to the core civilizations. The "fall" of Rome or the collapse of the great classical dynasty in China had no impact whatsoever on the Americas. The sheer achievement of the leading classical civilizations virtually assured, however, that any collapse would reverberate well beyond their official borders. The end or interruption of the great empires, while significant *within* each civilization, had consequences that affected a still larger territory in Asia, Africa, and Europe. This in turn would lead to the next major civilization map, and the next world history period after about A.D. 500.

Eurasia and Africa				
7500–7000 Domestication of sheep and goats; first pastoralists		**1900–1000** Hittite (Indo-European) expansion throughout the Middle East		
		2000–1500 Domestication of horse and camel		**1122** Zhou nomads establish dominance in China
7000–6500 Domestication of cattle		**1800–1575** Hyksos invade Egypt		
			c. 1600–600 Indo-European nomadic expansion	
	c. 3000 First use of donkeys as pack animals			

The Americas   c. 5000 Llama is domesticated by Andes mountain dwellers

Nomadic Challenges and Civilized Responses

INTRODUCTION. By the end of the 2d millennium B.C., civilizations based on the Neolithic innovations of livestock domestication and sedentary agriculture had evolved in several core regions across all the continents of the globe except Australia and Antarctica. The Middle East had proven the earliest and most fertile source of civilizations, having produced Sumer and the Akkadian and Babylonian empires. In South Asia the great Harappan complex spread throughout the Indus valley and beyond in the middle centuries of the 3d millennium B.C. In the Nile delta 500 years earlier, and in the bend in the Yellow River about a millennium later, two of the most durable civilizations, the Egyptian and the Chinese, had begun to flourish. Between about 2000 and 1500 B.C., Mesopotamian- and Egyptian-influenced civilizations also spread to the island of Crete in the Mediterranean and into what was to become Greece in southeastern Europe. At the very end of the 2d millennium, a separate Kush civilization developed in Africa up the Nile from Egypt and for several generations dominated its older, northern neighbor. In the Americas, seed civilizations emerged on the western Mexican coast, at Monte Alban and far to the south at Chavin in the Andean highlands and along the coast of present-day Peru.

The achievements of the peoples who established the centers of civilized development were truly impressive. But the total area occupied by civilized sedentary agriculturists and town dwellers remained only a small portion of the regions of the earth. Seen in this larger context, the different centers of civilization were rather constricted pools, usually separated by thousands of miles and surrounded by peoples

400–300 Hun invasions of China

450–500 Hun invasions in India

650–750 Bedouin Arabs spearhead Islamic expansion across North Africa and the Middle East and into central Asia

200–580 Era of nomadic dominance in China

1050–1250 Age of nomadic dominance in Northwest Africa and the western Sudan

170 B.C.–A.D. 100 Waves of nomadic invasions into India

c. 370–480 First wave of nomadic incursions into western Europe

1050–1420 Prolonged phase of expansion by Turkic and Mongol nomads

c. 750–850 Nomad invasions from North Mexico central valley

1375–1440 Rise of the Aztecs

970–985 Toltec expansion throughout the central valley

c. 850 Teotihucan destroyed by invading nomads

Earliest Civilizations and the Migrations of Nomadic Peoples

whom the civilized regarded as distinct and hostile. Perhaps as high as 90 percent of the human population of the earth, which is estimated to have reached between two and three hundred million in this era, were sedentary agriculturists concentrated in the civilized cores.

However, most of the inhabited earth was occupied by migratory peoples who either practiced shifting rather than sedentary cultivation, were nomadic herders, or followed a hunting-and-gathering existence much like that of the Stone Age peoples before the Neolithic revolution. Shifting cultivators predominated in the rain-forest zones of Central and South America, West Africa, east and central India, and much of south China and the Southeast Asian mainland and islands. Nomads who herded domesticated animals ranged over the great swaths of grassy plains that stretched across central Eurasia and fringed desert areas, such as the central Arabian peninsula and the Sudanic zone in Africa. In the Americas, hunters and gatherers occupied similar areas as well as the arid wastes between the plains of North America and the fertile valleys of central Mexico.

Though none of the peoples following these migratory modes of existence produced its own civilization, many of them significantly influenced the course of development of the civilizations that arose in different areas. In some instances the impact of non-sedentary peoples was largely destructive, such as the nomadic Indo-Aryans' contribution to the decline of the Harappan complex in the Indus valley and the role of the hunting-and-gathering chichimecs in the collapse of early civilizations in Mesoamerica.

Other incursions of migratory peoples into the zones occupied by sedentary agriculturists and townspeople were disruptive only initially. Eventually they led either to the establishment of new civilizations or to even stronger dynastic control over existing civilizations that had come under assault. Such was the case in Mesopotamia after the Hittite (Indo-European) invasions at the end of the 2d millennium B.C., in China with the rise of the Zhou kingdom in roughly the same period, and in the Americas with the establishment of great Toltecan and Aztecan cities and empires. Finally, in key phases of global historical development, nomadic peoples served as links rather than barriers to civilization. Thus, they furthered the development of trading networks, carried new religious ideas far from the lands where they were first conceived, and transmitted key inventions between the different pools of human civilization.

In regions such as South India and China and Southeast Asia, where there were no great civilized centers until the last centuries B.C. and where sedentary agriculture was confined to small pockets in the lowland valleys, contacts with the shifting cultivators of the hills were more limited and less dramatic. But peoples practicing the two patterns did exchange goods and periodically raided each others' domains in search of slaves and booty. They also clashed over the control of the river valleys, where irrigated wet-rice cultivators could be practiced on a large enough scale to support the cities and kingdoms that became the foci of early civilization in these areas. The outcome of these struggles often determined which people would go on to play major roles in the history of the regions in which they lived, and which would sink into obscurity and extended struggles to defend their territories from lowland dominance.

Migratory peoples have had such a great impact on human history that it is essential to have a clear sense of their life-styles and the nature of their interaction with farming and urban populations. Migratory peoples can be divided into several main types depending on the means by which they supported themselves and responded to different environments. After discussing these basic types of migratory peoples and contrasting their lifestyles and patterns of social organization with those of the sedentary agriculturists, the remainder of this chapter will be devoted to one variant of the migratory pattern—pastoral nomadism. Pastoral nomadism has had a great and continuing impact on the development of individual civilizations and on the contacts between the civilized cores. After exploring the ways in which pastoralism shaped all aspects of nomadic life and culture and considering different forms of nomadic social and political organization, key patterns of interaction between nomads and sedentary peoples will be identified. Insights into the nature of nomadic life-styles and persistent modes of response to civilized peoples will prove essential to a full understanding of the history of virtually all civilizations, from the early ones we have already studied through those that flourished in the centuries just before the Industrial Revolution.

None of the variants of the migratory pattern posed as formidable a challenge to agrarian, town-based peoples as the pastoral nomads. These nomads raided and conquered the kingdoms and empires of the civilized peoples and on occasion forged huge empires of their own that spanned several of the great civilizations. Though they remained powerful rivals of the civilized peoples until the advent of the Industrial Revolution just 200 years ago, the nomads were tied to patterns of economic sustenance and social and political organization that fundamentally constricted their

ability to dominate agrarian and urban zones on a long-term basis. Contacts between the two invariably led to the nomads' assimilation by sedentary cultures or their retreat to the grasslands or desert margins whence they had come.

ANALYSIS
VARIETIES OF HUMAN ADAPTATION AND THE POTENTIAL FOR CIVILIZATION

Perhaps the best way both to understand individual modes of human adaptation to environmental conditions and to compare these different responses is to relate them to the two extreme types of adaptation ecologists call the *niche* and the *holding*. In the first instance, the human group works its way into the environment in which it lives rather than transforming that environment. Like the plants and other kinds of animals with whom they share a particular ecosystem, these peoples simply occupy one of many niches available in the overall ecosystem. Their activities have only a minimal impact on the other niches or the life forms that occupy them. In the most extreme manifestations of the niche pattern, exhibited by rain-forest peoples of Central and South America, Southeast Asia, and Africa, small human groups hunt game and gather fruits and vegetables in the jungle without altering the forest environment.

These peoples move continuously through large areas of the forest, ingeniously tapping the many sources of plant and animal food available. They seldom contact other bands, and when they do it is often to contest, frequently violently, the use of portions of the forest they consider part of the large territory from which they draw their livelihood. This pattern of subsistence is virtually identical to the pattern practiced by hunting-and-gathering peoples in the pre-farming Stone Age. In addition to the forest farmers, the niche pattern has been adopted in the past by Amerindian and African peoples in prairie and semidesert regions.

Before the Industrial Revolution sedentary agriculturists, whose cultivation was dependent on elaborate irrigation systems, represented the most developed form of the holding approach to ecological adaptation. Peoples who practice variants of this approach transform the natural environments in which they live. In the case of sedentary cultivators, they clear forests, haul away stones, and plow grasses and weeds to prepare large tracts of land for the cultivation of plants. In addition to land for cultivation, fields and forests are cleared to support the domesticated animals. Thus, both the original vegetation and animal life in regions brought under cultivation are supplanted by domesticated plants and livestock. The domesticated plants are arranged in patterns designated by human decision rather than natural processes. They are protected from wild animals, and rival plant life is removed by weeding.

Because a very large investment in labor hours is needed to prepare fields for farming and to grow and harvest the various crops, sedentary cultivators settle in permanent dwellings near the fields they work. In time, some of these settlements have grown into towns and cities, which have proven to be key elements in most civilizations. Thus, both farming and settlement in the holding mode have made for major transformations of the natural landscape in the regions in which they have been practiced. These transformations represent the most extreme form of the holding response that occurred before the Industrial Revolution.

Between the niche pattern and the holding pattern, a number of intermediary forms of human adaptation have developed. Two of the most important of these adaptations are closer to the niche than the holding pattern. The first of these alternatives is represented by the shifting or slash-and-burn farmers who are concentrated in the rain-forest zones of both the Eastern and Western Hemispheres. Shifting cultivators burn off the jungle undergrowth but leave the large trees and the cover they provide to protect the fragile tropical soils. Using the ashes created by their fires as a natural fertilizer, shifting farmers then cultivate the area cleared on the forest floor on a limited basis. The foods grown in this manner form the staples of their diet, which are supplemented by meat, wild berries, and other forest plants.

After working a particular clearing for a year or two, shifting cultivators move on to another patch in the forest where they again begin the burning-cultivating sequence. Like the hunters and gatherers, shifting cultivators require large amounts of land because it takes anywhere from 20 to 30 years for burnt-off forest to be restored to the point where it can be reused. Generally, they move from patch to patch in a huge circle in the forest zone, eventually returning after 20 or so years to the patch they had originally worked. Though more substantial than those of the hunters and gatherers, their shelters tend to be flimsy because they are regularly abandoned.

The pastoral nomads provide the second major alternative between hunting-and-gathering and sedentary agriculture. Though nomadic groups differ according to the kinds of animals they herd and whether they ride horses or camels or work their herds on foot, their pattern of adaptation to their natural environment is similar. Like the shifting cultivators, nomads do not seek to transform their natural environments in major ways. In the steppe and savanna grasslands where they live in the winter and spring months, they introduce large herds of domesticated livestock. Their herds in effect harvest the plant cover in these areas. The nomads also set up temporary camps of tents or wagons near their herds. When the hot and dry summer season arrives, the nomads break camp and move with their herds to riverine or hilly areas where there is sufficient plant life to sustain their livestock.

The energy expended by the nomads in transforming their environment is minimal. Like the shifting cultivators and the hunters and gatherers, nomadic peoples need large tracts of land to maintain their subsistence life-style. But some nomadic groups, particularly those of the Eurasian steppes, have proven able to support far larger bands than either the shifting-farming or the hunting-and-gathering responses have allowed. Horse- and camel-riding nomads have also achieved a degree of mobility and a potential for large-scale organization that has proven impossible for shifting cultivators or hunters and gatherers. These advantages have given the nomads the capacity to challenge the peoples of the sedentary farming zones to a degree undreamed of by groups practicing any other migratory approach to ecological adaptation. In fundamental ways, human history until the Industrial Revolution can be seen as an extended contest between the nomadic peoples, who were the most expansive and warlike of all who followed migratory or nichelike adaptations, and the sedentary agriculturists, whose civilizations rested on their capacity to establish advanced holdings in fertile and well-watered areas.

Questions: Given the patterns of adaptation discussed, why would it be easier to build a civilization on the basis of the sedentary-farming holding pattern than on any of the migratory-niche responses described? What would a people gain in opting for the holding pattern and developing a civilization? What might they lose in giving up a nomadic or shifting-cultivating way of life?

THE RISE AND SPREAD OF PASTORAL NOMADISM

The domestication of animals also made possible an alternative basis for the support and organization of human societies—nomadic pastoralism. We do not know when genuinely nomadic societies first came into existence because the peoples who developed them had no written records and their wood-, hide-, and bone-based material culture deteriorated rapidly in the harsh steppe and semi-desert environments in which they lived. But it is likely that the nomadic alternatives to sedentary agriculture emerged sometime after the first civilizations, and that nomadic herders were quite widely distributed by 1500 B.C. It is also probable that pastoral nomadism originated among peoples who had been driven with their herds from the fertile river valleys of the civilized cores or among hunting-and-gathering bands that captured domesticated livestock in raids on agricultural villages.

The nomadic peoples led their herds into the grassy but sparsely inhabited plains of central Eurasia. In this vast area and in similar zones in Sudanic and East Africa, Arabia, and highland South America, refugees and raiders found ample pasturage for their herds and discovered that they could subsist on the products the animals supplied. The regions into which nomadism spread received enough rainfall (considerably more then than today) to support the grasses and other plant life on which herd animals feed, but not nearly enough for sedentary farming. Thus, nomadic peoples occupied lands that could not be claimed by rapidly growing farming populations. As they spread through the steppes and savannas, the pastoralists displaced the original hunting-and-gathering peoples or prompted them to adopt the herding life-style, which was better suited to the plains environment. The pastoralists in turn continued to hunt the abundant game animals for both the meat and the furs they provided.

THE HORSE NOMADS

The first nomadic peoples about whom we know a good deal are the Indo-European tribes of the middle centuries of the 2d millennium B.C. For over a millennium thereafter they threatened the early civilizations of the Middle East and the Indus plains. Some Indo-European peoples, such as the Hittites and Hyksos, also established their own empires and centers of civilization, while others, such as the early Greeks, settled in the lands to which they migrated. As late as the last centuries B.C., these settled groups still struggled to fight off the incursions of later Indo-European migrants such as the Scythians, who invaded Europe and Asia Minor, and the Kushanas, who established an empire spanning Northwest India and central Asia. Some Indo-European peoples migrated eastward, where they contested with other nomadic peoples for grazing lands, and invaded northwest India, where they proved an increasing menace to Harappan civilization.

Interestingly, the earliest Indo-European invaders did not ride the horses that they raised in great numbers and prized as symbols of wealth and status. Instead they fought from war chariots drawn by one or two horses. With the development of increasingly effective bridles and stirrups, however, Indo-European warriors increasingly rode horses to migrate or do battle.

Another nomadic group that played a major role in the age of classical civilizations were the Hsiung-nu (later known in Europe as the Huns). The devastation wrought by Hsiung-nu incursions into China, beginning in the 4th century B.C., presaged the calamities that would befall India and Europe centuries later when the Huns toppled the Gupta Empire and smashed into the crumbling Roman Empire. The eastern branches of the Hsiung-nu tribes also competed for pasturelands with peoples such as the Tungus, while the Huns to the west fought constantly with sheep- and goat-herding nomadic peoples speaking a variety of Turkic languages. From the era of the Indo-European migrations, droughts and intertribal warfare periodically drove large bands of central Asian nomads into the sedentary agricultural zones that fringed their far-flung steppe homelands. Their migrations played a major role in the rise and fall of empires in the civilized cores from the time of these first incursions to the era of the Turkic and Mongol explosions of the 11th through the 14th centuries A.D.

THE REINDEER HERDERS OF THE NORTH

It is possible that reindeer-herding nomads like the Lapps were migrating with their flocks across the tundra of northern Europe even before the nomadic pattern spread to the steppe regions of central Asia. In the bogs of Scandinavia archeologists have found the remains of sledges dating as early as the Late Paleolithic era. The earliest of these sledges were probably pulled by teams of dogs or men on rudimentary skis. But by the early Neolithic period, tamed reindeer were used, suggesting that pastoral nomadism had been established in the region. Despite their early appearance, the reindeer-herding nomads lived far from the centers of civilization, an isolation that rendered their influence on the course of human history marginal at best.

THE CAMEL NOMADS

The spread of pastoral nomadism in the central Asian steppes had hinged largely upon the domestication of the horse. Farther west in the Arabian peninsula and the Sudanic zone that stretches across north-central Africa, another animal played the pivotal role in the diffusion of the nomadic pattern. As early as 1700 B.C. the camel was mentioned in Egyptian sources as a pack animal, but it was not yet ridden by humans. It is likely that pastoralism based on the camel had been established in western Asia even before they were first ridden in the last centuries B.C.

Awkward-looking and peevish creatures, camels have proven remarkably adapted to the barren and parched regions that fringe the Sahara and Arabian deserts. They can

Desert nomads trek with their heavily burdened camels through the arid terrain of sand and scrub near Tripoli in present-day Libya. The loss of one's camel or failure to keep one's bearings could prove fatal in such an unforgiving environment.

carry loads of up to 400 pounds and travel 60 miles a day. Once they have filled the reservoirs in their paunches with water, camels are able to sustain this pace for over 20 days without water in temperatures averaging 120 degrees Fahrenheit. If they are occasionally fed a little green fodder on the journey, the camels will plod on indefinitely. Without the fodder, they will continue on for another five days before lying down to die. Though horses were introduced into both Arabia and the Sudan and cattle-herding nomads came to predominate on the savannas south of the Sahara, the camel has remained central to most of the nomadic cultures that have developed in these regions. These "ships of the desert" have been essential to the great trading systems that developed in these areas and the formidable capacity of their nomadic masters for making war.

THE CATTLE HERDERS

Beginning in the upper reaches of the Nile River in the southern portions of the present-day nation of Sudan, and expanding over the centuries from north to south across the rift valleys and plains of East and southern Africa, yet an-

The steppes provided a vast expanse of grazing ground for central Asian pastoralists herding cattle. Nomadic peoples, however, had to move about to find sufficient water and vegetation, the supply of which varied according to seasonal conditions in different areas.

other major variant of pastoral nomadism developed. In this vast and varied expanse, warrior-dominated societies based on cattle herding coalesced and expanded. Because the climate and especially the disease environment posed major barriers to horse breeding, the cattle nomads migrated, hunted, and fought their wars on foot. But cattle provided their sustenance and the basis of their material culture. Cattle were the prime gauge of wealth and status, the focus of religious rituals, and the key item given to the bride's family in arranging a marriage alliance.

Like those of the reindeer herders of the northern tundras, the regions occupied by the cattle nomads were initially distant from major civilized centers. As a consequence, we know little of the early history of these peoples. However, in contrast to the Lapps and other sub-arctic pastoralists, the cattle herders of Africa were eventually to play major roles in the history of different areas of the continent.

NOMADIC PEOPLES OF THE AMERICAS

Because most of the large mammals of the Americas had died out by the end of the last Ice Age, pastoral nomadism played almost no part in the history of these continents until horses, cattle, and other domesticated animals were introduced by the Europeans after A.D. 1492. Only in the highlands of the Andes, where llamas and alpacas survived in large numbers, was it possible for truly nomadic cultures to develop. But even in this limited area, pastoralists played a minor and subordinate role. The prairie and semidesert regions of the Americas that might have supported pastoralists were occupied instead by hunting-and-gathering peoples. The incursions of some of these peoples, such as the dreaded chichimecs, into the sedentary farming zones of Mesoamerica appear to be similar to the assaults on the civilized core regions of Eurasia by the steppe and camel nomads.

The absence of large mammals, however, prevented the nomadic peoples of the prairies and arid plains from fully tapping the potential of their environments and deprived them of the superior mobility necessary for raiding and conquering in the civilized heartlands. If the Aztecs can be taken as typical, however ferocious the chichimecs were in battle, they were impoverished wanderers until they established themselves in the sedentary zones. The Aztecs' arrival in the central valley of Mexico was little noticed by the civilized peoples who lived in great cities along its lakes. During the decades when they struggled to establish themselves in the region, the hapless and weak Aztecs were beaten in battle, enslaved in large numbers, and finally driven to a marshy island refuge in Lake Texcoco. The

contrast between the reception accorded in civilized Mesoamerica to incoming migratory peoples and the shock waves sent repeatedly through the civilized centers of Eurasia by invading horse- and camel-herding nomads is indeed striking evidence of the power that could be generated by pastoral adaptation.

NOMADIC SOCIETY AND CULTURE

More than any other feature, migratory patterns define and structure the lives of pastoral nomads. These movements reflect both the nomads' dependence on domesticated animals and the extent to which humans and animals have adapted to their environments. Nomads and herds migrate to survive. The steppe and prairie areas in which they live experience extreme fluctuations in temperature and weather conditions. Temperatures in the steppe regions of central Asia, for example, can range from 45 degrees Fahrenheit below zero in the winter to over 120 degrees in midsummer. In the steppe and the desert fringes of the Sahara and Arabia, there are also extreme variations in temperature on a daily basis. In the heat of the mid-afternoon sun, temperatures can soar well above 100 degrees and then plummet after nightfall to below freezing. In both regions, powerful winds, easily able to throw a rider from the saddle, stir up dust and sand storms and batter the sparse plant life that is able to survive in the thin and desiccated soils.

In this harsh environment, nomadic peoples must regularly migrate to feed and water the herds on which their own survival depends. Year after year they usually follow the same routes between the different areas in which they pasture their herds. In late winter or early spring, they drive their herds onto the plains where the seasonal rains provide a cover of rich vegetation to nourish their calving or lambing animals. When the dry winds and incessant heat of summer begin to wither the grasses and shrubs of the steppe or the desert fringe, the nomads drive their herds into hilly regions, the lower slopes of distant mountains, or to riverine areas where pasturage can still be found. After wintering in these regions, they return to the plains to celebrate rituals of renewal and fertility amid their feeding and growing herds.

The distances nomadic groups migrate on a regular basis vary greatly, from tens to hundreds of miles, depending on the size and needs of their herds and the environment in which they live. In addition to temperature and rainfall, their movements may be determined by a variety of factors. In East Africa and the western Sudan, for example, cattle-raising peoples must drive their herds from areas where the tsetse fly thrives in certain seasons or risk the decimation of their livestock by disease. The camel-herding nomads of the Arabian peninsula must ensure that their animals feed on the salt-laden grasses at the desert fringe on a regular basis, for without the salt the camels will sicken and die.

Prolonged drought in regions where nomadic peoples normally pasture their animals can lead to temporary, and at times permanent, alterations in their routes and destinations. But shifts in migratory routines are adopted reluctantly, both because of the risks involved in moving into unknown regions and the potential for conflict with other nomadic groups. Though the nomad's sense of property is focused on livestock, pastoral groups stake out particular areas and watering places as their own. The use of another tribe's migration route, wells, or pasture lands has invariably provoked violent conflict and the expulsion or elimination of one of the competing groups. Thus, the nomads' struggle to survive in the harsh environment of the steppe and desert fringe is complemented by an ongoing contest to preserve their own pasturelands from rivals or to wrest control of additional or alternative areas in times of population increase or natural calamity.

LIVESTOCK AND SURVIVAL

Though most nomadic peoples have traded with or raided the settlements of sedentary agriculturists, their survival has depended primarily on the well-being of their livestock. Whether cattle, camels, or sheep, the nomads' herds supply the meat, milk, and dairy products that are their staple foods. They use the hides or fleece of their livestock to make their clothing, tent and wagon covers, weapons, eating utensils, jewelry, and works of art. Animal sacrifices are at the center of the nomads' religious rituals, and the size and quality of a nomad's herd is the prime indicator of one's wealth and status.

Peoples who raise camels and horses also depend on their animals to transport their worldly goods from one pastureland to another and to carry to market those items they wish to trade with sedentary peoples. The goods the nomads trade are in turn primarily products they derive from their herds—meat, milk products, skins, wool, and bone sculptures. The mobility they gain from the animals they raise plays a key role in their survival. It allows them to flee from powerful enemies or to reap the advantages of speed and surprise in attacks on rival encampments or town and village dwellers. For the horse- or camel-herding nomads, the loss of the animals they ride is in effect a sentence of death. For this reason, in the steppes and desert fringe, horse and camel stealers are severely punished, very often by death.

"COURAGE CULTURES" AND NOMADIC PATRIARCHY

The harsh environment in which nomadic peoples struggle to survive not only takes a very real physical toll; it shapes virtually all aspects of their social organization and cultural expression. The lives of nomadic peoples have tended to be punctuated by intermittent violence. It is likely that the life expectancy of nomads, male and female, has been considerably shorter than that of sedentary peoples at comparable points in time. The hard-skinned, sun and wind cracked faces of nomadic peoples testify to the constancy of their struggles for mere survival. Their history of intertribal feuds, warfare, and forced migrations reflects the ways in which these struggles set human group against human group. Their harsh environment and the chronic violence in their lives prompted nomadic peoples to develop what anthropologists have aptly labelled *courage cultures*. Cultures of this type are dominated by physically strong and warlike males bound to each other by strong ties of personal loyalty. Members of this type of society place a premium on personal honor and value physical courage and heroic deeds above all other human attributes and accomplishments.

Although there are regional variations, most nomadic peoples live in kin-related bands that range in numbers from 10 or 20 to over 100. In times of crisis and exceptionally strong leadership, these bands have been brought together in great encampments numbering in the tens of thousands. But most nomads have lived most of their lives among their clanspeople who were often linked to those in neighboring bands by tribal membership. This meant that each traced their origins back to a common, often mythical, ancestor. The fact or fiction of common origins did not prevent clans from clashing over pasturelands, campsites, or livestock. In fact, interclan quarrels accounted for much of the social violence experienced in a nomad's lifetime. Oral traditions suggest that these quarrels could erupt from the flimsiest of pretexts—a snub in the marketplace or a dispute over the ownership of a fine horse or camel.

Whether arising out of insults or competition for herds or pastureland, the violent confrontations that erupted from interclan rivalries set in motion cycles of raids, killings, and reprisals that could span generations and even centuries. The deep-felt hostility these vendettas entrenched was a major barrier to interclan and tribal cooperation and alliances that would have allowed them to project more consistently and effectively their power beyond the steppes and desert margins. They also had a devastating effect on nomadic society. As the following verse describing conditions in Mongol and nomadic Arab society illustrates, clans became fixated on revenge at great cost to both sides:

> The starry sky used
> to turn away—
> For there was such discord
> Amongst all the people.
> Nobody lay in bed there.
> Mother earth trembled—
> For there was such discord
> Amongst all the people.
> Nobody wrapped up in a blanket,
> Everything was pierced through with swords.
> Each man encroached on another,
> Nobody lived by his own free will.
> Who will get out in this general scramble,
> Who will survive this deadly battle?

The following verse describes the consequences of their quarrels:

> Clan Amir's broken and gone. Nothing is left of her
>   good.
> In the meadows of A'raf now—only ruined dwelling
>   places.
> Ragged shadows of tents and penfold-walls and shelters
> Bough torn from bough, all spoiled by wind and
>   weather.
> All gone, the ancients gone, all her wise counsel gone.
> None of us left but folk whose war-mares are only fillies
> [thus timid people whose horses are not fit for war].

CULTURES MADE FOR WAR

Because stock raising did not require the labor that was involved in sedentary cultivation, males in nomadic society could devote long hours to honing the martial skills needed to fight these vendettas or for warfare with the armies of agrarian states. In horse and camel societies, young boys could ride almost as soon as they could walk. Man and animal came to function as one. Horse nomads, such as the Mongols, learned to depend on their legs alone to grip and direct their war steeds, thus freeing their arms and hands to make deadly use of their powerful bows and arrows. In the assault, they could swing beneath the belly of their horse and let loose arrow after arrow while denying their enemies a clear target. Horse and camel nomads could literally live on their mounts for days, giving them a mobility denied to all other peoples until the advent of the railway.

This mobility has also proven critical in the nomadic peoples' ability to ward off the assaults of revenge-minded armies of sedentary peoples. In one of the earliest recorded instances of this capacity to defend themselves through retreat, the Scythians drew the Persian emperor Darius and a large army into a prolonged and futile chase through the steppes of western Asia in the 6th century B.C. As recently as the late 19th century, this pattern was followed by the cattle- and camel-herding nomads of the Sudan. They drew a British-led, Egyptian army of over 5000 soldiers into the desert wastes of the Upper Nile region. When the invaders were exhausted and dying of thirst and disease, the nomadic warriors ambushed and exterminated them.

In the daytime, the flaps of this nomad's tent, pitched near an abandoned town in the central Arabian desert, are opened to catch desert breezes. At night, the flaps are closed to hold in warmth as the desert temperature falls sharply.

This drawing depicts a Mongol hunter in pursuit of wild game. Note how the hunter's ability to ride and guide his horse with his legs alone leaves his arms free to shoot his bow and arrow.

The very considerable skills that both mounted nomads and those who fought on foot displayed in battle gave them a reputation for ferocity among sedentary peoples. Many of the tales of their "barbarities" were hearsay or pure fiction, but some of them were quite accurate. The Scythians and Hsiung-nu, for example, had drinking cups fashioned from the skulls of defeated rivals. The leaders of the Huns lined these skull-goblets with gold. Some nomadic peoples regularly drank blood drained from their animals, which was quite rich in protein. Both the Scythians and Hsiung-nu practiced head-hunting, and on the death of their rival's chief they slit the throats of the deceased leader's wives and servants and buried them with him. The exploits of Turkic warriors (whom the Chinese called the T'u-chueh) were commemorated by stones piled on their tombs, one stone for every enemy they had killed in battle during their lifetime.

HOSPITALITY AND FAMILY TIES

This harsh side of nomadic life was offset among many peoples by traditions of hospitality and generosity. Once accepted as a guest within a nomadic encampment, an individual was safe from bodily harm—a tradition that a nomadic band broke only at its own peril. Nomads went out of their way to fête and feast their guests. Some have been immortalized for slaughtering their best camels or cattle to feed kinsmen or allies. Physical courage; endurance; a strong sense of honor; and loyalty to one's kin, clan, or chosen leader have also been exemplified by nomadic peoples.

Male monopolization of animal husbandry, band security, and warfare ensured that men would dominate gender relationships. Males controlled the herds that were the most valued property for pastoralists, traded with outside peoples for goods, and strictly controlled their households. Inheritance was through the male line. Though marriage patterns varied somewhat, young girls usually went to live in the households of older husbands. Polygamy was common and a woman's position in her new household depended on her ability to produce healthy children, preferably sons.

Though the bards of many nomadic peoples told of young men's infatuation with legendary beauties and ill-fated romances, marriages were primarily alliances between families and clans. In some societies, the bride was virtually reduced to a piece of property with the males from her own family and prospective in-laws haggling over the number of camels or mares to be included in her dowry or paid as a bride-price to her kinsmen. Once married, young women had little choice but to make the best of a life in transit dominated by domestic tasks such as breaking and reestablishing camp, cooking, sewing, and rearing children. Women of all ages had to endure the natural hardships and insecurities of nomadic life with little of the honor or excitement that could be enjoyed by their warrior fathers, husbands, and sons.

In some nomadic societies, women were given positions of prestige and power. The Sarmatians, for example, expected their women to serve as priests, fight in wars, and even rule. Among the Mongols, it was the custom for the young widows of deceased tribal leaders to rule as regents until their infant or adolescent sons came of age. Instances of strong-willed and domineering women, such as the Mongol dowager Nomolun who was slain attempting to avenge the death of six of her seven sons at the hands of a raiding band, do appear in nomadic tales and legends. But such instances of female dominance are remarkable for their rarity, rather than suggestive of a recurring pattern or a social norm.

SOCIAL STRATIFICATION

Despite the persistence of the notion that nomadic societies have been much more egalitarian and nurturing of self-reliant individualism than have been sedentary, agrarian societies, pastoral groups have generally displayed both social stratification and dependence. Some households and kin groups control much larger herds and pasturelands than others; some families possess neither. The kin groups who control substantial resources become the patrons and protectors of weaker and less fortunate families within the band or tribal group. In exchange for access to the resources of their patrons, the less well-to-do become the loyal clients of clan and tribal notables and warrior-leaders. These clients assist in raising the patrons' livestock, rally to their side in times of feuding, raiding, or war, and defer to their decisions in matters of tribal politics or family difficulties. In many nomadic societies, some of the notables' dependents have been little more than slaves, albeit domestic ones with personal ties to their masters.

Beyond gender and patron-client distinctions, there is little social differentiation in nomadic societies, owing largely to the lack or low level of occupational specialization. Though smiths who could forge tools and weapons were revered specialists in some nomadic societies, in most societies only the shamans were distinguished by occupation from the rest of the population. In addition to their cere-

monial roles, shamans also served as healers, soothsayers, and in some cultures, keepers of the tribal traditions.

ANIMAL TOTEMS AND TROUSERS

Like all else in their lives, the material culture of nomadic peoples is dominated by the animals they herd and hunt. These animals also dictate artistic themes and styles. Much of the artwork of nomadic peoples, such as bone sculptures, wood carvings, and woven rugs, depicts stylized animals. Sometimes the animals are domesticated, such as bulls, hawks, and horses; more often they are wild creatures, such as lions, serpents, and deer. Often the animal depicted is a clan or tribal totem, which is seen as a mythic ancestor of the group and venerated as progenitor and protector. Frequently the animal is shown fighting with one of its own kind, preying on another species, or struggling to free itself from a predator.

Nomadic artwork is largely utilitarian, with carvings incorporated in the poles and entrance ways of tents or in the sides of wagons. Animal motifs appear on belt buckles, jewelry, weapons, or rugs that are used to pad and insulate the interiors of wagons or tents. It is rare to find art for art's sake because the highly mobile existence of pastoral peoples renders paintings or sculptures excessively burdensome.

Like their art, the other aspects of nomadic culture are linked to their pastoral life cycle. Their housing, whether tent or wagon, is easily dismantled and reassembled. Their clothing is adapted to both their animals and the environment. Pants or trousers were an invention of the horse nomads of the central Asian steppes. The horse nomads also used skins or wool to fashion leather or felt shirts and pointed caps with ear flaps to protect them from the icy blasts of the winter steppe. Not surprisingly, nomadic peoples from central Asia also invented the stirrup, bits and reins, and the saddle.

Nomadic weapons have varied by region and type of domestic animals. But before gunpowder was introduced, bows and arrows and battle axes predominated among the horsemen of the Eurasian steppes; spears and hide shields among the cattle herders of Africa; and spears and swords among the camel herders of Arabia. The nomads' mobility and martial inclinations meant that all but the most isolated nomads were a constant threat to agrarian peoples. The wealth and vulnerability of the latter proved tempting targets for the fierce warriors from the steppe and desert fringe. It is small wonder that nomadic peoples often pioneered in weapons development and military tactics, ultimately forcing changes in the military patterns of sedentary peoples as well.

NOMADS AND CIVILIZATION

The image of nomadic peoples in the millennia of recorded history has been created mainly by hostile town-dwelling writers. Not surprisingly, that image has rarely been a flattering one. In Biblical times, prophets such as Jeremiah depicted the nomads as "cruel" and without mercy, and declared that they were agents by which Yahweh, the God of the Hebrews, chastised his people for their wickedness. The peoples of the crumbling Roman Empire believed that the Huns were the offspring of evil spirits and witches, and that their most infamous leader, Attila, was "the scourge of God." The Chinese regarded the many nomadic peoples who pressed in on their walled northern borders as uncouth and backward barbarians, whose brutality and delight in destruction posed a constant threat to the very life of their civilization. The coming of the chichimecs in Mesoamerica or the Mongols in the regions that fringed the steppes of central Asia was equated with great natural catastrophes, such as earthquakes in Mesoamerica and the spread of the plague in central Asia.

In fact, contacts between nomadic and farming or town-dwelling peoples were often more regular and peaceful and mutually beneficial than these stereotypes would suggest. Many accounts of pastoral peoples depict them living in self-sufficient isolation. In this view, pastoralists have had little need of contacts with sedentary peoples in normal times. Thus, nomadic incursions into settled agrarian regions are routinely accounted for by either natural calamities, which push hard-pressed pastoralists into civilized domains, or political weaknesses in the latter, which tempt nomadic warriors to loot and pillage.

DOCUMENT
NOMADIC VERSE AND NOMADIC VALUES

Much of what we know about nomadic attitudes and social interaction in the centuries before some of them adopted writing systems (based on languages such as Arabic and Chinese) has been gleaned from ancient myths, legends, and poetry. These works, which are among the finest artistic creations of nomadic peoples, were originally sung or declaimed at clan and tribal gatherings and passed down orally from one generation to the next. The three excerpts that follow are verses composed by camel-herding peoples of the Arabian peninsula. They provide some of our surest insights into pre-Islamic culture among the nomads of that region and reflect values characteristic of pastoral cultures in most areas of the globe.

1. Yet envy not even him of whom they say:
   Ripeness and wisdom came with length of days.
   Love life—live long—live safely—
   All the same
   Long living leaves its furrow on thy face.
2. Time has taught me something; all other things have lied;
   The wasting of the days lets things unguessed stand clear.
   And I know this at last: how powerful men use power.

   All powerful men get praise, whatever shame they earn.
   This too I know: poverty wears great hearts down,
   And the wearing's like the lick of a rawhide whip.
   A poor man looks at glories he can never climb
   And sits among the rest silent, silent, silent.
3. Endure. For a man free-born only endurance is honor.
   Time is fell; there's neither help nor heal of his hurt.
   Even if it availed a man to obey his fear,
   Or a man could parry trouble by any low consent,
   Still to endure the full brunt, cut and thrust
   Of Fate with a manly front, to endure's the only honor.

Questions: What sorts of attitudes toward life does the first verse reflect? Do these verses picture humans in charge of their own fate or at the mercy of some predetermined destiny? What does the second verse tell us about nomadic social structure among the early Arabs? Does it suggest that birth or merit decides one's place in the social order? How much social mobility do you think there is in this society? What sorts of values does the third verse express? How would you compare them to those dominant in your own culture?

Recent research suggests that this view both distorts the nature of nomadic-sedentary interaction and greatly over-simplifies the motives that have periodically led nomads to move into areas dominated by agrarian-based states. In fact, most nomadic groups have been dependent upon farming or town-dwelling populations for foods and manu-factured goods that they cannot produce themselves. Though nomads have sought at times to take these by force, more often they have gained them through peaceful exchanges or services provided.

AN ONGOING EXCHANGE

Though their contacts have often involved violent clashes, it is critical to counterbalance these admittedly dra-matic historical moments with a sense of the ongoing and long-term patterns of peaceful exchange and cohabitation of pastoral and sedentary farming or urban-based peoples.

All but the most isolated of nomadic peoples maintained regular contacts with farming villages and urban centers. Most nomadic peoples traded regularly with peasants and

town dwellers for grains and vegetables that could not be grown on the steppes or desert fringe. They also bartered their animals and animal products for cotton or silk cloth-ing, iron tools and weapons, and at times food for their animals. Sedentary peoples were normally less in need than the nomads were of what the two exchanged in trade, but the meat and dairy products bartered by pastoralists could provide important supplements to the largely vegetarian diet of many cultivating peoples. For sedentary peoples in areas such as China, India, and western Asia, the nomadic steppes were also a prime source of the horses their cavalry rode into war.

NOMADS, TRADE, AND CONTACTS
BETWEEN CIVILIZATIONS

In addition to their involvement in regular trade on a local basis, nomads have played and continue to play criti-cal roles in the development of long-distance trade. No-madic peoples pioneered all the great overland routes that linked the civilized cores of Eurasia in both ancient times

Main African-Eurasian Trade Routes in the Classical Age

and the Middle Ages. The most famous of these were the fabled silk routes that ran from western China across the mountains and steppes of central Asia to the civilized centers of Mesopotamia in the last millennium B.C., and in the 1st millennium A.D. to Rome, the Islamic heartlands, and western Europe.

Chinese rulers at one end of these trading networks and Roman emperors and later Islamic sultans at the other end frequently had to send their armies to do battle with hostile nomads whose raids threatened to cut off the flow of trade. But perhaps more often pastoral peoples played critical roles in establishing and expanding trading links. For periodic payments by merchants and imperial bureaucrats, they provided protection from bandits and raiding parties for caravans passing through their grazing lands. For further payments, nomadic peoples would supply animals to transport both the merchants' goods and the food and drink for the sustenance of those in the caravan parties. At times, pastoralists themselves took charge of both transport and trading, but it was more common for the trading operations to be controlled by specialized merchants. These merchants were based either in the urban centers of the civilized cores or in the trading towns that grew up along the Silk Road in central Asia, the oases of Arabia, or the savanna zones that bordered the vast Sahara desert in Africa on the north and south.

Until they were supplanted by the railroads and steamships of the Industrial Revolution, the overland trading routes of Eurasia and the Americas were, along with comparable networks established for sailing vessels, the most important channels for contacts between civilizations. Religions, such as Buddhism and Islam, spread peacefully along the trading routes throughout central Asia, Persia, and Africa. Artistic motifs and styles, such as those developed in the cosmopolitan Hellenistic world created by Alexander the Great's conquests, were diffused by trading contacts in North Africa, northern India, and western China.

Inventions that were vital to the continued growth and expansion of the civilized cores were carried in war and peace by traders or nomadic peoples from one center to another. For example, central Asian steppe nomads who had been converted to Islam clashed with the armies of the Chinese Empire in the 8th century A.D. The victorious Muslims found craftsmen among their prisoners who knew the secrets of making paper, which had been invented many centuries earlier by the Chinese. The combination of nomadic mobility and established trading links resulted in the rapid diffusion of papermaking techniques to Mesopotamia and Egypt in the 8th and 9th centuries and across North Africa to Europe in the centuries that followed.

NOMADS AS MERCENARIES AND EMPIRE BUILDERS

Despite ongoing contacts and nomadic contributions to civilized development, the predominant responses of settled peoples to pastoralists have been fear and hostility. Both the military prowess and the periodic ecological crises that have forced large numbers of them to raid sedentary areas go a long way in explaining these reactions. Very often, sedentary peoples have sought to ward off nomadic assaults by ensuring through tribute payments, which the Chinese aptly called "goodwill gifts," that their pastoral neighbors were well supplied with the goods they might covet in "civilized" towns and villages. Rulers of sedentary states have also paid generous sums for the services of nomadic peoples as mercenary soldiers. Those recruited in this manner both rode into battle with the ruler's own armies and served as frontier defenders against other pastoralists or the forces of rival empires. In the period before the rise of the first Islamic empires, for example, the rulers of both Byzantium and Persia guarded their common borderlands with colonies of both sedentary and nomadic Arabs.

This practice could prove costly to the patron state. With the conversion of these frontier peoples to Islam in the 7th century A.D., both Byzantium and Persia were particularly vulnerable to attack by the very peoples who had once defended them. In China, border guardians, such as the Zhou, have repeatedly built rival states of their own that have overthrown the dynasties they had originally been used to protect. Even when nomadic mercenaries have remained loyal to the sedentary rulers who recruited them, they have proven difficult to tax or prevent from looting the peasants who live near their encampments. These dangers may explain why strong dynasties have been reluctant to recruit nomadic allies, preferring instead to build long walls, such as that built in China, or chains of fortified garrisons, such as those built by the Romans, to keep pastoral peoples beyond the boundaries of their empires.

Whether they have begun as mercenaries within sedentary zones or raiders from without, again and again nomadic groups have overthrown dynasties established in the agrarian cores. At times, nomadic victories have meant interruptions in civilized development, such as with the Hyksos' invasion of Egypt in the 2d millennium B.C. In other instances, nomadic invasions have hastened the end of once-flourishing civilizations, as was the case with the Aryan incursions into India in the 1st millennium B.C. and the assaults of peoples such as the Hittites and Kassites into the empires of Mesopotamia throughout the ancient period.

Just as often, however, nomadic invaders have captured rather than destroyed the targeted empire and civilization

For millennia, camel caravans like this one have made their way through the desert terrain of Arabia. Caravans have provided key links for trade and cultural exchange between the civilizations of Africa and Eurasia.

After seizing the throne of the defeated dynasty, nomads have governed largely through the institutions and personnel of the conquered peoples. When this pattern has been followed, the nomadic warriors who settled down in the sedentary zone have often gradually adopted elements of the culture of the farmers and town dwellers of the new empires they establish. Chinese history provides some of the best examples of this pattern, but as the experience of invaders like the Mongol conquerors of China in the 13th century A.D. demonstrates, often the nomads struggled with considerable success to remain culturally distinct from the subject peoples.

Despite the attractions of the luxuries and sophistication of the civilized to the new rulers, nomadic peoples have been suspicious or downright antagonistic toward the "soft" living of town dwellers. The great Muslim historian, Ibn Khaldun (A.D. 1332–1406), incorporated this ambivalence in his three-generation cycle for dynasties founded by nomadic warriors. In the first generation, the ruler is vigor-

ous and the kingdom strong. But each succeeding ruler, raised amid the temptations and luxury of palace and harem, is weaker and less occupied with the affairs of state that are the central concern of strong kings and emperors. By the third (or fourth) generation, the successor of the hearty nomadic warrior-conquerors is a dissolute wastrel, incapable of defending his throne from internal enemies and foreign invasions. The dynasty collapses and another vigorous warrior dynasty is established by new invaders from the steppes or desert fringe.

Though the histories of dynasties founded by nomadic chieftains have varied greatly in duration and vigor, the general patterns that Ibn Khaldun discerned have proven remarkably accurate. At times, warrior-conquerors fled the soft living of the palace centers for the rugged life of their steppe or desert encampments. Some may have remained in the new capital, but longed for the simpler life of their homelands, a sentiment that is wonderfully captured in the following verse by the wife of an early Islamic ruler:

This 18th-century painting shows Kazak nomads bringing tribute horses to the emperor of China. Painted by an Italian artist Guiseppe Castiglione, this work exhibits a striking cross-civilizational mixture of European and Chinese artistic styles.

A tent flapping in the desert air is dearer than this tower-
  ing house;
Wind rustling over the sandy waste hath a sweeter
  sound than all the king's trumpets;
A crust in the nook of a wandering tent more relish
  than all these delicate cates [sweetmeats];
And a noble clansman's more to my lust than the
  paunchy longbeards about me here.

It is said that the great Mongol conqueror, Chinggis Khan, saw only potential pasturelands in the intensely cultivated millet fields of northern China. Most pastoral conquerors, such as the Aryans in India, tended to destroy or neglect the irrigation systems of the areas that came under their rule. Frequently, the dynasties established by nomadic conquerors were overthrown within a century or two by internal rebellions or the successful challenges of new invaders from the steppes or desert. Those who had not assimilated the culture of the conquered peoples or become mercenary troops in the armies of the new dynasty returned to the steppes from which their forebears had come.

CONCLUSION

NOMADS AND THE PATTERN OF GLOBAL HISTORY

Their military prowess and greater dependence on the products of sedentary peoples have given nomadic pastoralists a far greater role in world history than other more isolated peoples following variants of the niche pattern of ecological adaptation. But the harsh environments in which nomads lived and the limitations in scale and occupational restrictiveness imposed by their mode of adaptation have made it impossible for nomads to build civilizations of their own or to dominate, on a long-term basis, those developed by sedentary peoples. Though steppe peoples, such as the Hittites, Mongols, and Turks, could forge great empires by winning political control over one or more of the civilized cores, their dynasties were usually short-lived and their rule dependent on the personnel, skills, and institutions of the conquered sedentary peoples. The more stable and productive economic base of sedentary peoples has allowed them to carry much larger populations on much more limited land areas than nomads. It has also led to an occupational diversity; a capacity to build enduring, large-scale state systems; and a level of accomplishment in invention, science, and the arts that was far beyond anything nomadic peoples could dream of matching.

As a result, nomadic peoples have periodically affected the course of civilized history and for brief periods have dominated it. For example, Indo-European nomadic invaders, such as the Aryans and Hittites, played major roles in the rise and fall of civilizations in western India, Egypt, and the Fertile Crescent. In China, nomadic peoples vitally affected the rise of both the Shang and Zhou kingdoms that laid the basis for civilization in eastern Asia. In later chapters we will see that new waves of nomadic assaults in Eurasia, Africa, and the Americas had much to do with the rise of great classical dynasties, such as the Guptas in India and the Han in China, and even whole civilizations, such as the Roman Empire in the Mediterranean. This impact continues throughout the five continents where civilizations developed, building to the great Mongol and Turkic explosions from the steppes of central Asia from the 11th to 14th centuries A.D. But most of human history has been lived and made by sedentary agrarian peoples and the city dwellers they support. With the coming of the Industrial Revolution and the greatly enhanced firepower and mobility that transformation gave to the already far more numerous peoples of the civilized zones from the late 18th century onward, the nomads' already subordinate position has been further reduced and their way of life increasingly threatened.

FURTHER READINGS

The best general work on nomadic societies, which covers a wide range of different types over much of Eurasia and Africa, is A. M. Khazanov's *Nomads and the Outside World* (1984). The volume edited by Wolfgang Weissleder on *The Nomadic Alternative* (1978) contains a number of excellent case studies on different types of Afroasian nomads. For insights into the ecological underpinnings of both nomadic and sedentary societies and the interaction between the two, see Owen Lattimore's *Studies in Frontier History* (1962). Rene Grousset's *Empire of the Steppes: A History of Central Asia* (1970), covers some of the most important nomadic societies in terms of their impact on sedentary peoples from prehistoric times through the centuries of Mongol dominance. On the development of nomadism among the Middle Eastern Arabs, see Richard Bulliet's *The Camel and the Wheel* (1975). Jacques Maquet's *Civilizations of Black Africa* (1972) includes introductory sections on the cattle-herding nomads of Africa. For a highly readable application of the holding and niche variants of ecological adaptation, one cannot go wrong with Lucien M. Hanks's *Rice and Man: Agricultural Ecology in Southeast Asia* (1972).

Unification and the Consolidation of Civilization in China

INTRODUCTION. China formed one of the first areas where interaction between nomadic pressure and the power of a river-valley civilization produced the characteristics of a larger, more complex classical society. The breakdown of the Zhou dynasty's ability to control its vassals in the 8th century B.C. led to an extended period of political conflict and social turmoil throughout China. In both the Yellow and Yangtze river basins numerous states rose and fell, each seeking to replace the Zhou as the paramount power in East Asia. Internal conflicts left China vulnerable to outside invaders, and between the 8th and 3d centuries B.C. nomadic peoples frequently raided the farming areas of the north China plain. Many of the nomads stayed. They settled down and eventually assimilated the distinct culture that had been developing in the region since the age of the Shang warrior kings. Some of these invaders captured existing states; others established new dynasties that further intensified the already complex political maneuvers and wars for supremacy.

Though the human suffering caused by the prolonged struggles between the warring states was enormous, these conflicts also provided the impetus for intellectual and political changes that, in the long run, greatly strengthened Chinese civilization. In the 6th and 5th centuries B.C., thinkers, such as Confucius and his disciples, sought to find ways to end the conflict and turmoil. They advocated changes that would both stabilize China's fluid social structure and promote the establishment of a strong and unified political system. Other philosophers, such as Laozi, the founder of Daoism, proposed contemplative ways of life that would put an end to the vicious rivalries and chaos.

The yearning for unity and an end to civil strife appeared to be answered by the emergence, in the 3d century B.C., of the warrior strongman Shi Huangdi. By 221 B.C., Shi Huangdi's state of Qin had vanquished all its rivals, and he founded a new imperial dynasty that promised to bring an end to the centuries of division and strife. But Shi Huangdi proved a tyrant. Driven by his own ambition

---

202 B.C.–A.D. 9 Former Han dynasty; development of the horse collar, stern-post rudder, and water mill

202–195 Reign of Liu Bang (Gaozu emperor)   **9–23** Interregnum of Wang Mang   **2nd century A.D.** Development of porcelain

141–87 Reign of Han Wudi   **23–220** Later Han dynasty; invention of paper and the compass and the advice of ruthless ministers, he embarked on a series of grandiose building projects. These exhausted the common people and angered the regional elites whose cooperation was vital to Qin rule. Shi Huangdi's death in 210 B.C. was the signal for resistance throughout the empire to the rule of his less despotic and less capable son and his inner circle of advisors. A rapidly spreading revolt, led by two peasants, toppled the Qin dynasty in 207 B.C. and gave rise to its much longer-lived successor, the Han.

The Han era, which was to last with a brief interruption for over 400 years, saw the consolidation of Chinese civilization. Unity was established in the old core regions and Chinese political control was greatly extended in all directions. Perhaps more critically, the Han rulers founded what was to be the largest, most effective, and most enduring bureaucracy in the preindustrial world. They oversaw the development of the first civil service examinations and the professionalization of Chinese administration. The shi, or scholar-bureaucrats, were the greatest beneficiaries of these initiatives, and from the Han era onward they set the tone for Chinese social and cultural development. The shi were responsible for great achievements in literature and the arts. They provided the support and at times the creative ingenuity that were critical to the great advances in technology—advances that vaulted China far ahead of all other civilizations in war, shipbuilding, civil administration, and many areas of mining and manufacturing. Above all, a sense of Chinese distinctiveness and identity was set, which was reflected in later centuries by Chinese references to themselves as the "sons of Han." This identity was to prove critical to the survival of Chinese civilization in the centuries of war, foreign invasion, and internal division that returned when the Han dynasty collapsed in the early 3d century A.D.

The chaos of the Zhou period, in other words, eventually led to important developments in Chinese culture and political institutions that provided considerable unity to a wide region. These same developments formed a heritage that would long identify Chinese civilization. The result constituted one of the clearest achievements of any of the great classical civilizations; a standard against which these other civilizations can be compared.

PHILOSOPHICAL REMEDIES FOR THE PROLONGED CRISIS OF THE LATER ZHOU

The protracted warfare that raged throughout China after the Zhou rulers were reduced to powerless figureheads proved a major setback for both the emerging shi elite and the ordinary people. Military skills and physical prowess were valued over the literary and ceremonial aptitudes of the shi. Local lords, whose kingdoms were constantly threatened by their neighbors, tended to concentrate all power in their own hands and put little stock in the council of men who stayed behind in the palace while they risked their lives on the field of battle. The military leaders who wore trousers—which were widely adopted following the example of the horse-riding northern nomads—were contemptuous of the scholars who wore robes and gowns. In most kingdoms the power of the old aristocratic families was strengthened, often at the expense of the shi who were reduced to little more than clerks and fawning courtiers of the local strongmen. Rituals were neglected, and court etiquette, which had been so prized in the Early Zhou era, was replaced by the rough manners of nomadic invaders. Many shi found themselves without political positions and were forced to eke out a living as village school teachers and local scribes.

With rulers concentrating on the very survival of their kingdoms, resources were consumed by expenditures on warfare. Public works, including dikes, canals, and regional granaries, were neglected and some fell into ruin. Marauding armies confiscated or destroyed crops on which the peasantry depended for its livelihood. Hard-pressed rulers taxed the farmers heavily and conscripted them to transport military supplies and, increasingly, to fight in the incessant wars of the Late Zhou period. Armies spread disease and destruction throughout China. The severity of the suffering caused by natural calamities was increased many times by the breakdown of public works and social support systems.

Perhaps because most of the kingdoms depended on outside areas for their supply of at least some vital materials, such as iron, horses, or salt, trade continued to increase despite political fragmentation and social disruption. The introduction of copper money and the growing acceptance of private property did much to advance the fortunes of the Chinese merchant class. By the end of the Zhou era, traders were growing wealthy as the suppliers of courts, armies, and town populations and as major investors in land ownership, which became widespread as the control of feudal vassals over villages and croplands broke down. The rulers of some kingdoms turned the lucrative task of taxing the peasantry over to prominent merchant families. Wealth and political connections brought these big traders considerable power. A legendary merchant named Zu Kung, for example, was said in the course of a single business trip to have saved one kingdom from destruction, strengthened two others, and caused the decline and fall of two more.

As trade and artisan production increased, towns, particularly walled administrative centers, grew in size. By the last centuries of the Zhou period, China could boast of several urban centers with hundreds of thousands of people. For many centuries to come no other civilization could support cities of this size.

CONFUCIUS AND THE RESTORATION OF THE SHI

Threatened by the greatly enhanced power of the warrior overlords of rival kingdoms and the rising wealth and influence of the mercantile class, the aspiring shi scholar-bureaucrats found a champion in Kung Fuzi, or Confucius as he has been known in the West. Confucius was born in the middle of the 6th century B.C. into a poor shi family. Like many others, Confucius's father had lost his place at the local court and the family had fallen on hard times. As a consequence, young Confucius had to take jobs, such as accounting, that were considered demeaning for a young man of his education and abilities. He was apparently an outspoken and opinionated individual, who had a talent for putting people off by the brutally frank expression of his views. He had hoped for a high post in the state of Lu, near the Shandung Peninsula in the present day, but having been passed over, he took to the road in search of the ideal ruler. He never found his ideal and thus spent most of his life traveling from one kingdom to another. But during his travels he met many leaders and local shi, supported himself by teaching, and earned a growing reputation for his learning and wisdom. Soon Confucius had attracted a considerable following. Some traveled with him as loyal disciples; others promoted his ideas at the courts of local rulers and compiled his sayings in what would come to be known as the *Analects*—meaning "the collected sayings"; thus, "Confucius says."

Though frustrated in his search for an ideal king to serve and unable to test his ideas as an actual administrator and advisor, Confucius developed ethical principles and a view of the proper ordering of society that would shape Chinese civilization for the next 2000 years. He was not a religious teacher like the Jewish prophets or the Buddha, but rather a social philosopher. Ancestral veneration played a role, but his thinking was focused on the earthly realm and the proper ways to arrange social relationships and achieve good government. He was obsessed with the need for order and harmony. He believed that these could come about only if Chinese rulers relied on the advice of wise and educated men, who in Confucius's view could only be recruited from among the shi.

This stone rubbing was taken from a portrait of Confucius painted by a Chinese prince in the mid-18th century. Here Confucius is idealized as a wise, fatherly member of the scholar-gentry class, replete with official headgear and robes of office.

Confucius was convinced that a small minority of superior men were destined by their talents and sense of duty to govern and set an example for the common people. In a rather revolutionary bit of thinking, he argued that these men (women were quite explicitly excluded) were superior not by virtue of aristocratic birth but by virtue of their education and training. Superior men in this view were made, not born, which meant that even a lowly peasant could aspire to this exalted status. However, most of the superior men were drawn from the elite classes, especially the old aristocracy and established shi households.

There was a strong ethical dimension to all of Confucian thought. Confucius believed that superior men should be given the power to rule, not to enrich or glorify themselves but to serve society as a whole; that the interests and welfare of the common people must be paramount in the decisions of good emperors and their advisors; and that in return for their concern and protection, the common people should respect, support, and acknowledge the superior status of their overlords. Social harmony depended on each person accepting his or her allotted place and performing the tasks that his or her social station required. Obedience and deference were owed to one's superiors and elders, to males from females, and to teachers from students. A good man for Confucius was one who

Treats his betters as betters,
Wears an air of respect,
Who in serving father and mother
Knows how to put in his whole strength,
Who in the service of his prince will
    lay down his life
Who in intercourse with friends is
    true to his word.

Society according to Confucius was held together by personal ties of loyalty and obedience. Five links were stressed: three family links (father and son, elder brother and younger brother, husband and wife), one political link (ruler and subject), and one social link (friend and friend). If these links were faithfully honored, Confucius believed that only a minimum of intervention by the state in the lives of its subjects would be necessary.

THE CONFUCIAN GENTLEMAN

According to Confucius, the superior or educated man was a person of courage who made decisions on his own and then defended them no matter how strong the opposition. Shi in positions of power were to pay proper deference to rulers, but not be afraid to criticize them for errors in judgment or neglecting the welfare of their subjects. A superior man, which became synonymous with membership in the shi class, was moderate in demeanor and controlled his emotions. He presented a calm and composed "face" to rivals, subordinates, and friends. He was well mannered and observant of proper rituals and forms of address and behavior that varied depending on the social status of the person with whom he was interacting. Above all, the shi gentleman was a generalist rather than a specialist. He strove to be equally accomplished at running a government department, directing the repair of irrigation works, composing poetry, or painting the plum blossoms in his garden. Power and status were accorded him as a

moral exemplar, not for specific tasks he performed. Confucius reckoned that with such men in charge of China, war and social strife would be forever brought under control.

THE HEIRS OF CONFUCIUS

During his lifetime and after his death in the early 5th century B.C., Confucius had many disciples who both spread his teachings and debated over their interpretation. The most important division arose between the followers of Mencius (Meng Ko) and those of Xunzi, who lived in the 3d and 2d centuries B.C. Mencius began with the assumption that humans were inclined to be good and thus ought to be ruled in such a way that their goodness could develop to the fullest extent. His thinking, which had a strong egalitarian strain, stressed the consent of the common people as the basis for political power. It provided the philosophical underpinnings for the longstanding Chinese notion that the people had the right to rise up and overthrow incompetent or oppressive rulers.

Xunzi rejected the basic assumption on which Mencius's system rested. Xunzi argued that humans were inclined to be lazy and evil. He concluded that a strong, authoritarian government was necessary to curb their selfish desires and capacity to harm each other. Xunzi believed that humans could be improved through strong laws and education, but he had little sympathy with the notion that the people were the ultimate source of political power. The ideas of both thinkers and those of Confucius continued to influence intellectual discourse in China for millennia. But in the short term, the views of Xunzi, bolstered by the arguments of later political philosophers who were known as the Legalists, would prove the most influential.

DAOIST ALTERNATIVES

A very different sort of cure for China's ills in the Late Zhou era was offered by the recluse and philosopher Laozi (often called Lao Tsu in popular Daoist texts). Laozi's life history has been obscured by fantastic legends including those relating that his mother was pregnant with him for decades and that when he was finally born he was an old man with a white beard. Whatever his actual background, his ideas were very different from those of Confucius and his disciples. Laozi had little use for government or absolute ethical prescriptions in any form. As a solution for the sufferings brought on by human greed and ambition, Laozi recommended a retreat from society and civilization into nature. Through the contemplation of nature, he believed, the individual could become attuned with the Dao, or the cosmic force and source of all creation. Laozi stressed nonaction over political power and self-examination over the mastery of others. He taught:

It is wisdom to know others.
It is enlightenment to know one's self.

The conqueror of men is powerful.
The master of himself is stronger.

It is wealth to be content.
It is willful to force one's way on others.

Though much of Laozi's message concerned withdrawal from the world, he could not resist giving a good deal of advice to those who remained in society, particularly the rulers of China's many kingdoms. He chastised them for enjoying war and the excessive pursuit of pleasure in their palaces while the mass of the population went hungry. He wrote:

When the court is arrayed in splendor,
The fields are full of weeds,
And the granaries are bare.

Laozi exhorted rulers and men of affairs to cultivate the virtues of patience, selflessness, and concern for the welfare of all creatures. He argued that these virtues were consistent with the nature of the Dao. Like Confucius he believed that wise rulers and honest administrators made for happy and peaceful kingdoms. But Laozi differed from Confucius in his views on how a good ruler was made and what qualities he possessed. And where Confucius viewed a strong state and sound society as the primary goals, Laozi saw them as temporary concerns that were of little relevance to the wise man in search of the hidden meanings of creation and human life.

RIVAL SCHOOLS AND POLITICAL POWER

Like Confucius, Laozi had many disciples both in his own lifetime and in later centuries. His poetic sayings were interpreted by these followers in widely varying ways. Some held to his original stress on withdrawal from the world, communion with nature, and meditation. Others mixed his ideas with magic, eroticism, and a search for a concoction that would bring bodily immortality to those who drank it. The meditative followers had the greatest appeal to the shi elite and courtiers of later ages, who drew on Daoist ideas to enhance their sensitivity to art and the natural world and to satisfy their interest in questions regarding the supernatural. In contrast, the masses were attracted by the magical solutions to everyday problems emphasized by conjurers and con men with rather dubious claims to being Laozi's disciples.

Though both Confucianism and Daoism would eventually be blended in the composite ideology associated with civilized life in China, they had first to survive an often violent challenge from another school of philosophers. The Legalists, the thinkers of this alternative school, were the first to win the patronage of a powerful ruler. That man was Shi Huangdi, who at the end of the 3d century B.C. became the first true emperor of China.

DOCUMENT
TEACHINGS OF THE RIVAL CHINESE SCHOOLS

The brief passages quoted below are taken from the writings of Confucius, Mencius, Xunzi, and Laozi. Identify the author of each passage and explain why you believe it was written by the person you chose.

1. I take no action and the people are reformed.
I enjoy peace and people become honest.
I do nothing and people become rich.
I have no desires and people return to the good and simple life.
2. The gentleman cherishes virtue; the inferior man cherishes possessions.

The gentleman thinks of sanctions; the inferior man thinks of personal favors.
3. The nature of man is evil; his goodness is acquired.
His nature being what it is, man is born, first, with a desire for gain.
If this desire is followed, strife will result and courtesy will disappear.
4. Keep your mouth closed.
Guard your senses.
Temper your sharpness.
Simplify your problems.
Mask your brightness.
Be at one with the dust of the earth.

This is primal union.

5. Personal cultivation begins with poetry, is made firm with rules of decorum, and is perfected by music.

6. When it is left to follow its natural feelings, human nature will do good. That's why I say it is good. If it becomes evil, it is not the fault of man's original capability.

Questions: Which of these ideas are most compatible? Which of them could best be termed religious; which are most secular? Which philosophers propose ideas that are best suited to people who wish to build a strong and unified political order?

THE TRIUMPH OF THE QIN AND ESTABLISHMENT OF IMPERIAL UNITY

By the end of the 5th century B.C., the long wars had considerably reduced the number of the states striving to supplant the house of Zhou. The failure of larger states, such as Ju and Wu, based in the Yangtze river valley to conquer the kingdoms of the north China plain in the preceding centuries left only seven main rivals and the rump kingdom that was still ruled by the descendants of Zhou. In the 4th and 3d centuries B.C., one of these kingdoms, the westernmost state of Qin, grew steadily more powerful at the expense of its rivals. Like the original Zhou dynasty, the ruling dynasty of Qin was of nomadic origins. The warriors of Qin had in earlier centuries served as the defenders of the western boundaries of the Zhou empire. They had gradually expanded their power eastward as the

The Later Zhou and Qin Empires

- Later Zhou, ca. 550 B.C.
- Boundaries of principal states, ca. 550 B.C.
- Boundary of Qin Empire, ca. 221 B.C.

0   500 Miles
0   500 Kilometers

effective control of their overlords declined. As a backward land ruled by "barbarians," Qin was the object of ridicule by the rulers and administrators of states to the east, who considered themselves more civilized. Ambassadors and travelers from eastern states, such as Wei and Lu, complained of the crude living quarters in the Qin capital, the gross manners found even at the court, and the utter disregard for ceremony in the affairs of state. They failed to note the innovations in the kingdom of Qin that would, in time, give it greater political and military power than all of its rivals combined.

THE TRANSFORMATION OF A "BARBARIAN" LAND

It is true that the Qin state lagged behind most of its rivals in the fine arts and refined etiquette. But from as early as the 5th century B.C. they had initiated a number of critical social and political changes that greatly increased their capacity to wage war against their snobbish rivals to the east and south. The rulers of Qin had long supported experimentation with bronze and ironworking that had transformed tool- and weapons-making in the Zhou era. In order to encourage the peasantry to adopt new tools and more productive cultivation techniques, the Qin freed them from bondage to local lords and allowed them to claim and hold their own land. Over time these measures substantially increased the resource base on which Qin political ambitions depended. Because freeing the peasants undermined the support of the vassal warriors who originally carried out local administration, the Qin sought to build a regular bureaucracy supported by and totally loyal to the dynasty. These efforts attracted considerable numbers of shi administrators, who were presumably willing to put up with bad manners if well-paying positions were to be had.

Qin power and military prowess were also increased by the many wars the state fought, first to survive and later to conquer the rest of China. The Qin conscripted for military service the peasants it had freed and given land, thus rendering its armies a good deal larger than those of rival states. The superior bureaucracy of the Qin meant that its forces were better supplied and organized. The nomadic background of the Qin elite ensured an ample supply of able military leaders. It also made the Qin more receptive to military innovations than many of their adversaries. They were, for example, one of the first states to use massed cavalry, which gave their armies a high degree of mobility, and to adopt the crossbow, which came into widespread use in the Late Zhou era. Good leadership and free peasants, who may have felt they had more to fight for than the vassals and serfs of other kingdoms, made the Qin armies famous for their ferocity and speed.

THE LEGALIST SANCTION

From at least the 4th century B.C., Qin efforts to break the power of their vassals and local lords were justified by the writings of a number of statesmen who came to be known collectively as the Legalists. The semilegendary Shang Yang, who served a Qin ruler of the mid 4th century B.C., was the founder of the Legalist school of political philosophy. In the *Book of Lord Shang,* he contended that the power of China's rulers should be absolute. Their major objective as sovereigns should be to enhance the strength and wealth of the state. Shang Yang argued that the people existed to serve the state, and he had little to say about the ruler's duty to promote their welfare. He believed that the main responsibility of the state with regard to the people was to enforce strict laws with harsh punishments for offenders. Though the ruler was absolute, even he should not be above the law. To drive this point home, Shang Yang once had the crown prince punished for breaking the law—the cheek of the prince's tutor was tattooed in retribution for the offense.

As Shang Yang discovered at the end of his life, he too was subject to the strict laws. When he fled the court after the death of the ruler who was his patron and protector, the aged statesman sought refuge at a roadside inn. But a law had been enacted which stated that a traveler could not stay at an inn without a permit, which Shang Yang did not have. The innkeeper, who faced death if he did not obey the law, turned out the old man. Shang Yang later led an unsuccessful rebellion that resulted in his being tied to chariots and ripped apart in punishment.

Two of Shang Yang's intellectual heirs, Li Si and Han Feizi, were high officials at the court of a later Qin monarch, Shi Huangdi, who would conquer all of China at the end of the 3d century B.C. They enlisted the Confucian philosopher Xunzi's supposition that humans were naturally evil to bolster the authoritarian claims of their master.

They differed from Shang Yang in their contention that the ruler was above the law, but followed his prescriptions for harsh punishments and strong state control over its subjects. Perhaps in response to the favorable reception accorded the ideas of Confucius and his disciples in other kingdoms, Li Si and Han Feizi declared that philosophers were unnecessary, even dangerous to the ruler. They advocated strict control of ideas within his realm, and Li Si provided the inspiration for Shi Huangdi's book burning campaign after he became the emperor of China.

EMPEROR OF CHINA

Shi Huangdi, the "tiger" of Qin, was extremely receptive to the Legalist approach to government. A man of unbounded ambition, energy, and physical courage, he was also a megalomaniac who did not tolerate the slightest challenge to his absolute rule. Because of complaints from his officials, he once had hundreds of shi buried alive. His solution to "leaks" of news from the palace was similarly draconian. When his disapproval of the overuse of carriages by his courtiers became known throughout the capital and no one would admit to repeating comments he had made in confidence, Shi Huangdi executed all who were present when the criticism was made. After becoming emperor, his megalomania knew no bounds. When it was reported that a chain of hills was blocking the critical wet monsoons, he had the trees on them cut down and their surface dyed red, the color associated with criminals in China.

By 221 B.C., Shi Huangdi had completed the work of his predecessors. He had defeated the last of rival states of the Qin and unified China under the upstart dynasty. To strengthen his hold over the vast domains that he now ruled, Shi Huangdi ordered all regional fortresses destroyed and the weapons of local warrior groups collected and melted down. Former states disappeared and 36 provinces were created in their place. Vassal overlords and regional commanders were replaced by Qin bureaucrats. Surviving princes and aristocrats, as well as very wealthy merchants, were ordered to live in the capital at Xianyang, where Shi Huangdi's huge palace loomed over hundreds of others. The emperor's scribes developed a standard script and coinage, and weights and measures were unified throughout the empire.

Shi Huangdi's greatest passion was for building. His architects joined and expanded the walls that had been built by the northern kingdoms to keep out nomadic invaders, thus creating China's Great Wall. The Great Wall and other public works projects, such as canals and roadways, were constructed by millions of forcibly recruited peasant

This portion of the Great Wall runs through the mountainous terrain of northwest China. When kept in good repair and supplied with sufficient numbers of soldiers, the high walls and broad battlements that are clearly shown in this photo presented a formidable obstacle for nomads who sought to invade China.

laborers, of which 700,000 were said to have been used to build the emperor's palace alone. Even his death did not put an end to Shi Huangdi's building projects. In preparation for his own burial, the emperor ordered the construction of a large tomb at Mount Li, which was not uncovered until 1971. As a final gesture of grandeur, he had over 7000 life-sized, terra cotta statues of soldiers made, which would be buried with him. Each had individual features and all were arranged in proper battle formation.

STRIVING FOR STATE CONTROL

Within the empire, Shi Huangdi and his Legalist advisors sought to control all aspects of daily life. Laws were proclaimed for every possible occasion and activity. One law forbad two grown males to live under the same roof, thus ensuring an increase in tax revenues based on household units. Another law decreed that after a man's death, his lands were to be divided among his sons but not his daughters. This measure was intended to ensure that individuals were not able to build up wealth and a local power base. It also strengthened the position of males by denying females a portion of inherited property, which was the main source of wealth.

Qin control efforts even extended to ideas. At Li Si's instigation Shi Huangdi ordered the burning of all books except an official history, Legalist texts, and works on technology, medicine, and astrology. At this point in time, books were written by hand on bamboo strips that were then bound together. Their high cost and the relatively

Hundreds of these clay warriors were found in the tomb of the first Chinese emperor, Shi Huangdi. Remarkably, each of the warriors has individualized facial features. Together with the clay horses also found in the tomb, these massed forces provide striking evidence of the power wielded by the founder of China's first and short-lived imperial dynasty.

small numbers of literate elite meant that books were scarce and easily confiscated. Provision was made for one copy of each of the works that was destroyed to be preserved in the imperial library, but the library was burned when the dynasty was overthrown in 207 B.C. Many precious works were lost, but some books had been hidden in secret caches and were later recovered.

THE COLLAPSE OF A TYRANNICAL REGIME

Shi Huangdi's building frenzy and the harsh rule of his Legalist administrators aroused resistance throughout the Qin's newly won empire. The shi were particularly angered by his book burning and the repression of ideas that rivaled those of the Legalists. The peasantry was alienated by the Qin's endless demands for taxes and labor. In fact, Shi Huangdi's seemingly limitless appetite for building projects proved the immediate cause of the revolt that led to the abrupt collapse of the dynasty in 207 B.C., just three years after the emperor's death. The two peasants who began the revolt were conscripted for labor service on the Great Wall. On the journey from their village to the construction site, they realized that they could not arrive on time. Because the typical penalty for arriving late for a labor assignment was death, the two men concluded that they had little to lose by rousing others to revolt. Their calls for resistance found a ready audience among the weary

peasantry and angry shi elite. The revolt spread rapidly and within months the Qin dynasty was toppled. Shi Huangdi's son was murdered by a band of conspirators and the emperor's huge palace was burned to the ground.

THE QIN ACHIEVEMENT

Although Qin rule over all of China lasted only a matter of decades, its short reign marked a watershed in Chinese history. Shi Huangdi not only unified China, but strove to govern it with a centralized bureaucracy staffed by salaried officials. This meant that he was not dependent on unsteady and potentially hostile vassals—a dependency that had been the undoing of earlier dynasties. It also involved strengthening the shi who increasingly provided the social and political bonds that would hold China together through times of dynastic crisis and foreign invasion.

Though oppressive for the peasantry, the public works projects of the Qin provided the grid of roads and canals that made it possible for succeeding dynasties to hold the far-flung territories together. The construction of the Great Wall reinforced the longstanding division between the nomads of central and north Asia and the farmers to the south. Improved communications and a unified currency advanced the efforts of China's merchants to establish interregional markets and the interdependence of the often very different geographical areas of the Chinese empire. Though the threat of a return to the warring states' anarchy loomed briefly after the sudden collapse of the Qin, the foundations that Shi Huangdi had laid for a centralized empire permitted another remarkable leader to establish a far milder and more lasting dynasty in China, the house of Han.

ANALYSIS
SUNZI AND THE SHIFT FROM RITUAL COMBAT TO "REAL" WAR

For better or worse, the development of classical civilizations in the Middle East, Greece, China, and India greatly advanced the business of making war. Agricultural surpluses made it possible to support specialized fighters and military commanders. Population growth made for larger armies that required armor and weapons and a certain amount of training. Horses, and in some areas camels and elephants, were raised to carry men into battle or pull war chariots. Advances in metalworking meant steadily improving weaponry, and the art of fortification became a major concern for early engineers and architects. Warfare came to involve more soldiers who fought for longer periods and suffered greater numbers of casualties. Frontier defenses and military campaigns became one of the prime concerns and main expenses for those who ruled civilized states.

Despite advances in weaponry and training at least for warrior elites, warfare in most early civilizations was a combination of ritual and chaotic brawl. Wars were not fought during harvest times, winter months, or months when the monsoon rains arrived. A ruler was expected to announce his intention to attack a neighboring kingdom well in advance. Before battle, the high priests of each ruler offered sacrifices to the gods and their readings of various sorts of omens, not strategic considerations, determined the time and place of combat. Battles consisted primarily of formal duels between trained and well-armed warriors in the midst of rather confused collisions of masses of poorly trained and armed foot soldiers, who were usually slaves or forcibly recruited peasants. Though often fierce, the warriors' duels were in theory regulated by codes of honor and fair play. It was unseemly, for example, for one champion to strike another from behind or when his opponent had fallen. Defeated champions, if they lived, were treated with great respect. Individual initiative and deeds of heroism were at a premium.

Duels between warrior champions were the setpiece of a battle. As the great epics of early civilizations, such as the Indian *Mahabharata* and the Greek *Iliad*, demonstrate

graphically, great warriors cut bloody swaths through the ranks of poorly prepared infantry and lesser fighters to get to each other and set up the hand-to-hand combats that normally determined the outcome of battle. The death of a commander, who was often the ruler of the kingdom at war or a renowned champion, meant the collapse of his forces and their chaotic flight from the field. Normally the victorious army did not destroy or capture what remained of the opposing soldiers. The game had been played and won. The winners either retired with their booty to prepare for the next round or began negotiations to determine the terms on which the defeated party would submit to their overlordship.

The Shang and Early Zhou periods of Chinese history were filled with wars and most of them were fought according to this ritualized pattern. But by the Late Zhou period, some commanders and thinkers had become highly critical of the indecisiveness and waste of the endless conflicts between the warring states. In the 4th century B.C., Sunzi, an advisor to one of the warring monarchs, responded to these concerns with a treatise on *The Art of War*, which stands as one of the great classics of military theory. In opposition to the ritualized approach to war, Sunzi proposed a very different vision of military conflict. He argued that war was merely an extension of statecraft. Wars ought not to be games or macho contests for bragging rights; they ought to be fought only for ends that increased the territory, wealth, and power of the state. With these aims in mind, Sunzi insisted that speed was of the essence in warfare, and that long wars burdened the subjects of the warring rulers and bred rebellions. He also urged that target kingdoms be captured as swiftly as possible and with as little damage as possible. Sunzi argued that war was a science and as such it should be the object of extensive study. Rather than brawny warriors, commanders ought to be men well versed in organization, strategy, and tactics. He proposed, and Chinese rulers subsequently set up, special schools to train officers in the art of war.

Sunzi's ideas transformed warfare in China. Rulers made every effort to bring down rivals short of war. Bluffs, spies, threats, and saboteurs were employed before armies were actually sent to war. Both before and after war was actually declared, substantial state resources and large bureaucracies were devoted to building and training armies and supplying them in the field. Here the greater power of the shi officials in the Late Zhou era played a critical role. As the backup for victorious armies, Shi thinkers stressed the importance of a ruler's ability to mobilize the resources and population of his kingdom as fully as possible. Sneak attacks were considered fair, and feints and ruses were regularly employed by field commanders. Weather conditions and advantageous terrain rather than the auguries of soothsayers determined the time and place of battle. Successful generals were trained, and their soldiers were far better drilled than in earlier times.

Psychological devices were strongly recommended. For example, techniques were used to make the enemy commanders angry and cause them to make foolish moves that might demoralize their armies. Discipline rather than individual heroics was required. This point was driven home by a ruler who had one of his commanders beheaded because the general's troops attacked ahead of schedule, despite the fact that this action was the key to victory. In combat, regular formations replaced mass brawls; soldiers fought as units under the direction of a chain of commanders. Good fighters were still valued, but now as unit leaders rather than accomplished duelists. Quarter for a wounded enemy was less likely to be given. The main object of battle became the destruction of the enemy's forces as quickly as possible. The aim of warfare became the conquest of a rival kingdom or the defense of one's own.

Shi Huangdi's military and political successes demonstrated how effective the reorganization of warfare along the lines suggested by Sunzi might be. Halfway across the globe, the Greeks were independently developing comparable patterns of warfare. In roughly the same era as Sunzi and Shi Huangdi, the discipline and training of the smaller Greek armies culminated in Alexander the Great's unprecedented conquests. But these successes by no means put an end to ritual warfare between civilized peoples. Though Chinese armies tended to be organized and led according to the prescriptions of Sunzi and other theorists, the chivalric codes and battles centered on the duels of champions showed a remarkable staying power. This was particularly true of societies that were dominated by warrior elites, such as those that later developed in India, Japan, and Europe. But conditions in the warring states and the genius of Sunzi had led to a radically new vision of what wars were about and how they would be fought. The effects of this vision are still felt by civilized societies.

Questions: Do the ideas of Sunzi strike you as a force for the advance or retreat of civilized life? Why? What features of Chinese political systems and society may have contributed to the rise of this alternative way of warfare? If two societies—one employing Sunzi's brand of warfare, the other following ritual patterns—clashed, what advantages and disadvantages would each have?

THE FOUNDING OF THE HAN DYNASTY AND THE BEGINNINGS OF CHINA'S CLASSICAL AGE

The sudden collapse of the Qin Empire threatened again to plunge China into incessant warfare and social strife. The pent-up anger produced by one and one-half decade of harsh state demands and repression flared into regional riots and rebellions throughout the former Qin territories. Vassal chiefs fought former Qin bureaucrats for local control, and some dreamed of founding a renewed empire. The unlikely winner of these many-sided contests for power was a man of peasant birth named Liu Bang. Liu Bang's early life scarcely suggests that he would become the founder of one of China's longest-lived and most illustrious dynasties. In his youth Liu Bang was lazy, uneducated, and without work. He was best known for his fondness of wine and women, tastes that remained pronounced throughout his life. In the years before the end of the Qin dynasty, Liu Bang, either because he had changed his shiftless ways or through clever maneuvers, had managed to establish himself as a village headman. In the confusion that followed the fall of the Qin, he built up a considerable following of soldiers, ex-bureaucrats, and disgruntled peasants.

Liu Bang was apparently not much of a military commander; in fact, legend has it that he lost all the battles he fought for control of China except the last one. But he did have a gift for picking able subordinates and then giving them a real chance to exercise their talents. His skill at mediating between quarrelsome subordinates allowed him to hold his motley alliance of followers together, while the forces of his enemies dissolved in violent factional fights. In 202 B.C., after years of campaigning and negotiation, Liu Bang proclaimed himself the new emperor of China, thus founding the Han dynasty that would rule China, with a brief interruption, for the next 400 years.

THE RESTORATION OF IMPERIAL CONTROL

For a time it looked like the new emperor, whose official name was Gaozu, would restore the system of vassalage that had formed the basis for royal administration in the Zhou era. He raised many of his followers to the ranks of the nobility, and rewarded them and existing lords, who had supported his efforts to win the throne, with grants of large estates. It soon became clear, however, that even his once-loyal followers were not above using the domains they had been granted to build up independent bases of power that could eventually threaten the dynasty itself. In addition to this threat, Liu Bang's determination to establish a more centralized imperial administration was promoted by the shi officials who attached themselves to his cause during his struggle for power and after he became emperor. Perhaps because Liu Bang was illiterate, he came to rely heavily on his shi advisors, even though he personally despised them. His efforts at bureaucratic centralization focused on enhancing their training and responsibilities. His successors would continue this trend as they moved aggressively to undercut the position of the regional vassals.

Liu Bang's initiatives toward bureaucratic centralization were taken up by a number of strong and able rulers who succeeded him on the Han throne, most notably Han Wudi (140–87 B.C.). First, the larger fiefs granted to the highest nobles were broken up by a royal decree that required the domains of the vassals to be divided between all their sons at the time of their death rather than pass intact to their eldest son. At the same time, regular government appointees, especially regional governors and district magistrates, expanded their authority at the expense of local lords. In the time of Han Wudi, vassals were forbidden to bequeath their domains to heirs they adopted. When a noble died without legitimate offspring his estates were confiscated by the central government. Under a variety of pretexts, Han Wudi's administrators also seized the fiefs of many other vassals, who were relegated to the status of commoners. These measures were resisted violently by the regional lords, but in each case the military strength of the dynasty proved too great for the rebels. Attempted rebellion provided a superb reason to remove a vassal and add his lands to the imperial domains.

HAN EXPANSION

The Han rulers also used the impressive military might at their disposal to enlarge the empire and neutralize external threats. The most formidable of the external enemies were the Hsiung-nu nomads who lived north of the Great Wall. From the time of the first Han emperor, these skilled horsemen of Mongol descent had raided and looted territories south of the wall. Liu Bang sought to buy them off with presents and by marrying one of his daughters to the paramount Hsiung-nu chieftain. By the time of Han Wudi it was clear that major expeditions would be necessary to put an end to the Hsiung-nu incursions. Han Wudi's forces defeated the nomads and annexed their pasturelands to the north and west of the Great Wall to the Han domains. But these great victories in the 120s B.C. provided only temporary relief. Under weaker Han rulers and when divisions arose within the empire, the Hsiung-

China in the Han Era

nu and other nomadic raiders repeatedly managed to breach the defenses of the Great Wall and raid deep into Han territory.

Han armies also expanded the empire to the east and south. In the east, the northern parts of Korea were conquered in 108 B.C. and were ruled by the Chinese for over 400 years. Conquests in the south extended Chinese civilization into the mountainous interior and down the coast of the South China Sea to Vietnam. The many different ethnic groups who lived in these areas either submitted to Han rule and assimilated to Chinese civilization or, like the various branches of the T'ai-speaking peoples, migrated farther south into present-day Burma, Thailand, and Laos. Small groups of these peoples continued to resist absorption by the Chinese. The southernmost of the resisting peoples were subjects of the kingdom the Chinese called Nam Viet. After many attempts, Han armies finally managed to conquer this state and establish control over the Vietnamese people in 111 B.C. The Chinese would maintain control of the area for over a thousand years and would play a major role in the spread of civilization to the Vietnamese people.

THE REVENGE OF THE SHI

The majority of the shi, who were followers of Confucius and his disciples, had deeply resented the favoritism shown by Shi Huangdi for the Legalists. His thought control and book-burning campaigns, which had taken a heavy toll on the Confucian texts, enraged most of the shi and left them eager for a chance to strike back. The fall of the Qin provided just such an opportunity. At the urging of the advocates of the Confucian school, Liu Bang and his successors banned the works of the Legalists, and members of the school were hounded from the court and in some cases killed in local risings. The harsh law codes of the Qin were replaced by the milder edicts of the Han. Legalist ideas were eventually blended into the mix of philosophies and religious beliefs that came to make up China's official ideology.

Confucianism in its varying forms soon became the dominant thought system in Chinese civilization. Its full ascendancy was delayed in the early Han era by the suspicions of rulers, such as Liu Bang who strongly favored Daoism, and the rivalry of non-Confucian thinkers. But by the end of the 2d century B.C., the shi scholar-officials and the Confucian ideas they championed had won the preeminent place among the ruling classes of China that they would enjoy for much of the next 2000 years.

While downgrading the Legalists, Han rulers after Liu Bang increasingly promoted the Confucian cause. A systematic effort was launched to locate Confucian texts that had been hidden away during the book-burning campaign. Lost texts were reconstructed from memory, and official versions of the Confucian classics were inscribed in stone by a team of scholars and artisans. A thorough knowledge of Confucian teachings became essential to employment and promotion in the Han administrative hierarchy. This prerequisite for success in Han politics was institutionalized by the founding of an imperial university at the capital at Xian in 124 B.C.

By the end of the Han era there were over 30,000 students at this state-supported center, which was designed primarily to turn out trained bureaucrats. Many of its graduates went on to become the heads of government departments and the close advisors of emperors. Even while still at school, the offspring of shi families who flocked to Xian were known as an activist lot, prone to demonstrations and petitions to the emperor and government officials. In the decades after the imperial university was founded, similar institutions were set up in the provinces to recruit and educate local talent. Shi teachers flourished both in positions at the formal schools and as tutors for the sons of shi and aristocratic households bent on acquiring the education that was increasingly vital to careers in government.

EDUCATION, EXAMINATIONS, AND SHI DOMINANCE

Though students studying at the imperial university were expected to master law and a choice of specialized fields, including history, astronomy, and music, all concentrated on the memorization and interpretation of the Con-

fucian classics. These were given even greater emphasis when formal exams for government positions were established at the beginning of the last century B.C. The Chinese examination system marked the establishment of the first professional civil service in human history. Though exams were at first confined to the upper levels of government, local and regional exams were later established to identify and test local talent. Theoretically, any Chinese could take the exams. But no one could hope to pass them without a proper education, and education required considerable sums of money. This meant that members of established shi families, the old aristocracy, and local landlord households had a decisive advantage.

Each elite family supported the brightest of its sons. They were tutored at home as children, then enrolled in local schools, where they mastered the Chinese characters and the Confucian texts. On occasion a particularly bright child from a peasant household was adopted by a shi or landlord family and given the support he needed to do well on the exams and advance in the bureaucracy.

Though in general individuals from the lower classes lacked a proper education and the means to get it, a number of exceptional examples are recounted by Chinese historians of enterprising farmers or merchants who rose to high administrative posts. In one instance at the end of the

This brick bas-relief carving depicts a Confucian scholar lecturing degree holders and three young students. The dress, formal postures, and seating arrangements were characteristic of the scholar-gentry class by Han times.

2d century B.C., a dismissed police official, who had resorted to pig breeding to support himself, had in his later years so impressed the emperor with his responses to the examiners' questions that he was eventually elevated to the post of imperial chancellor.

Merchants, who had the resources to get a good education, were prohibited from taking the exams. By virtue of their wealth and moneymaking talents, some prominent merchants were given official positions in times when the Han rulers were hard-pressed for money. But posts, such as those involving the administration of the salt and iron mining monopolies, were usually low level and often reverted to shi degree holders or noble appointees once the crisis had passed.

In addition to the fact that education and success on the exams were monopolized by elite families, opportunities for government jobs were limited by the fact that only a small percentage of jobs were allotted by competitive examination. Though the Han rulers sought to put an end to hereditary rank, in fact many political positions automatically passed from father to son. Many offices were appointive, and an individual's chance of winning an office depended on personal links to the emperor or high official who distributed the political spoils. In later dynasties the percentage of offices earned by success in the examinations increased steadily at the expense of those appointed or won by connections. But in the Han era offices that were won by passing exams remained relatively limited. Despite this fact, the Han system nurtured a revolutionary idea—that administrative office and the exercise of political power ought to depend on personal merit and effort rather than birth alone.

FAMILY AND SOCIETY IN CLASSICAL CHINA

The growing influence of the shi in government circles was also felt in Chinese social life as a whole. In effect, three main social strata came to be recognized by those who wrote the official documents and histories: the literate shi, the ordinary but free subjects, and the underclass referred to as the "mean people." Within each of these large groupings there were important occupational and status divisions. The shi ranged, for example, from the powerful families that served the imperial household to local tutors and petty clerks stationed in frontier provinces. The common people included groups that we would identify as separate classes. The majority were peasants, but even they differed greatly in wealth and social status. Some controlled large amounts of land, lived in extended family compounds, and aspired to provide their sons with the educa-

tion that would elevate the family to shi status. These large landowners were the target of Han decrees requiring that a father divide his property equally between his sons. These measures prevented local notables from amassing too much land and wealth, and thus becoming a potential political threat to the dynasty.

THE EMERGENCE OF THE SCHOLAR-GENTRY

Increasingly, local landlord families were linked by marriage or the success of their sons to the shi. This combination gave rise to what was a new class configuration, the scholar-gentry, which superseded the shi. As their dual label suggests, the scholar-gentry upheld their position through both their landholdings in the rural areas and the

This painted pottery model reflects a gentry house from the Han era (about the first century A.D.). The walls, strong gates, and numerous stories were prominent features of extended-family dwellings.

political posts they won in the bureaucracy, which was housed mainly in the towns. Families tended to maintain branches in both areas. Wealth from landholding provided the means to educate the brightest males, who increased the family's fortunes by winning lucrative administrative positions. Well-placed family members in the town looked after the interests of their rural elders and cousins when it came to things, such as tax quotas, military protection, or civil litigation. If bandits or nomads raided the area where the rural branch of the family resided, they could take refuge with their relatives in town. When towns became the object of warring armies, the city dwellers fled to the countryside. This double base and mutual support made for remarkable durability. Some families played major roles for centuries in Chinese politics and society. Some lasted for thousands of years—far longer than any imperial dynasty.

In both town and country, scholar-gentry families lived in large walled compounds, which often had separate buildings for each unit of the extended family. Surviving clay figurines of gentry homes show that they were multistoried structures with stucco or wooden walls and tiled roofs. Most compounds included an inner garden where children could play and their elders could chat and enjoy nature. In times of peace, scholar-gentry families lived the

This rubbing was taken from a stone carving showing a horse carriage from the Later Han dynastic period. The racing horses and decorated carriage suggest the confidence and opulence of the elite classes, who alone could afford such a vehicle.

good life. Family granaries ensured a ready supply of good food, and numerous household servants took care of tedious chores, such as cleaning, cooking, and washing clothes. Male and female members of the family dressed in silks, which commoners, including merchants, were not permitted to wear (at least in public). A family's standing in the official and social hierarchy was further advertised by the color of the emblems and ribbons males were permitted to wear.

When a member of a scholar-gentry household who held an administrative position left the compound for work or a night on the town, he rode in a horse-drawn carriage that, like his clothing, was of a size and design that indicated his government rank. Both male and female members of the family enjoyed the deference of the common people. Merchants plied them with their finest goods, servants scurried to do their bidding, and peasants bowed politely as they passed in their carriages. A commoner who forgot his place could expect to be chided by his peers or roughed up by the toughs that most gentry families employed to look after their physical safety.

CLASS AND GENDER ROLES

There is considerable evidence that women, particularly those from powerful scholar-gentry households, enjoyed more freedom and status in the Han era than they were to have in later periods of Chinese history. Because marriages, especially among the elite, were arranged with family alliances rather than romantic concerns in mind, young men had as little say in the choice of their future spouses as women. Though the woman's father paid a dowry to the family of his son-in-law and his daughter went to her husband's house to live, the young bride could usually rely on her powerful relatives to ensure that she was well-treated in her new home. She was often allowed to take along her servants and even a sister as live-in companions. Widowed women were permitted to remarry, and all women participated in family ceremonies. Perhaps most important, women of upper-class families were often tutored in writing, the arts, and music. There were a number of important female poets in the Han era and at least one prominent court historian was a woman.

Despite these promising trends, women at all social levels remained subordinated to men. Family households were run by the older males, and though women could inherit, male children normally received the greater share of family property. The following verse from the *Book of Poetry*, which indicates the appropriate responses to the birth into an aristocratic family of a son and daughter, clearly illustrates the preference for and consequent privileges of males:

> *Sons shall be born to him—*
> *They will be put to sleep on couches;*
> *They will be clothed in robes;*
> *They will have scepters to play with;*
> *Their cry will be loud.*
> *(Hereafter) they will be resplendent with red knee-*
> *   covers,*
> *The (future) king, the princes of the land.*

> *Daughters shall be born to him—*
> *They will be put to sleep on the ground;*
> *They will be clothed in wrappers;*
> *They will have tiles to play with.*
> *It will be theirs neither to do wrong nor to do good.*
> *Only about the liquor and the food will they have to*
> *   think,*
> *And to cause no sorrow to their parents.*

Political positions were reserved for males, though women could sometimes exert powerful influence from behind the throne. But this backstage plotting and scheming at the court merely served to confirm the view of the Confucian scholars that women were unfit for politics. Again, their shortcomings are bluntly set forth in the *Book of Poetry*:

> *A woman with a long tongue*
> *Is a stepping-stone to disorder.*
> *Disorder does not come down from Heaven—*
> *It is produced by women.*
> *Those from whom come no lessons, no instruction,*
> *Are women and eunuchs.*

At the level of the scholar-gentry, young married women were subjected to the demands and criticisms of notoriously domineering mothers-in-law. This was less of a problem among the lower classes where residence in extended households was not common. But women from peasant families were expected to cook, clean house, and labor long hours in the fields. Some found social outlets and even a degree of financial independence as market women in nearby towns, but all were legally subordinated to their fathers and husbands. At all class levels, women were expected to marry and, whatever their individual talents, their most vital social function remained bearing children, preferably male children.

PEASANT LIFE

Ordinary cultivators held varying amounts of land, but few produced more than they needed to subsist and pay taxes. Moderately prosperous farmers sold their surplus to traders or their agents, or in a local market town. Most

A glimpse of early Chinese peasant life is provided by this brick painting from the era of the Wei-Jin dynasties that struggled to control China after the fall of the Han.

peasants who had a decent-sized plot of land lived well. But many peasants had little or no land of their own and were forced to labor for well-to-do landlords in order to earn a meager living. Peasants with plots that were too small to support their families complained to Han officials that they "did not have enough husks and beans to eat and [that] their coarse clothing was not in good condition." Those who worked the land of others as tenants or landless laborers were even more miserable. According to an official description, they "wore the coverings of oxen and horses and ate the food of dogs and pigs."

Key Chinese inventions, such as the shoulder collar (which permitted horses to pull greater loads) and the wheelbarrow, eased the physical burdens placed on farmers at all levels. These devices, expanding irrigation networks, improved iron tools, and new cropping patterns made for larger agricultural yields that were mostly consumed by upper-class groups and the town populations. The governing classes required all peasants to devote a designated number of days each year to labor on public works. In addition, peasants were liable to conscription for the imperial armies.

The existence of available, arable land in many areas, particularly the south, relieved population pressure and provided frontier outlets where hard-pressed laborers could clear land and start life anew. Some peasants took to banditry in the rugged hill country or the forested zones that still existed in large parts of the Yellow and Yangtze river basins. Others scraped by as beggars in provincial towns or lived with vagabonds who traveled the roads of the empire in search of temporary employment or vulnerable merchants and country houses to rob. Many more peasants joined *secret societies*, which provided financial support in times of shortage and physical protection in case of disputes

with other cultivators or local notables. The most famous of the secret societies was called the Red Eyebrows because painted eyebrows served as its badge of membership. Usually the activities of the secret societies were localized, but in times of great social stress, groups, such as the Red Eyebrows, could play major roles in widespread popular insurrections.

THE HAN CAPITAL

The urban growth that had been one of the most notable social developments in the Late Zhou era continued unabated in the Han period. The new capital city at Xian took on the basic features of Chinese imperial cities from that time forward. Laid out on a somewhat distorted grid, Xian had a number of great roadways that gave access to and defined the main quarters of the city. Much of the city was protected by long earth and brick walls broken at regular intervals by towers and gates. Estimates of Xian's population range from about 100,000, which probably refer to those people living within the walls, to 250,000, which probably include those people living outside the walls and in neighboring villages.

The emperor resided in an inner or forbidden city, which only his family, servants, and closest advisors were permitted to enter. The inner city was an impressive complex of palaces, towers, and decorated gateways. Each palace included audience halls and banquet rooms, large gardens and fish ponds, and luxurious living quarters for the emperor, his wife and many concubines, and their numerous children. To the west of Xian beyond the city walls a large pleasure garden was laid out for the imperial family, which included, among other things, one of the earliest known zoos.

The forbidden city was surrounded by administrative buildings and the palaces of the most powerful aristocratic and scholar-gentry households. Under later dynasties, this zone would become a distinct imperial city within the capital. Some of the imperial palaces and government buildings were made of stone or brick, but many were made of clay covered with brightly colored plaster. Most were roofed with the glazed tiles with upturned edges that would become characteristic of Chinese architecture in the following millennia. The structures in the inner city were a good deal more imposing than the buildings in the rest of the capital, which were made of wood or stamped earth. Palace buildings, ordinary houses, and the city as a whole were oriented to the south, which, as the direction where the sun reached the highest point in the sky, was considered most auspicious.

TOWNS AND TRADERS

The Han capital at Xian was only one of many imposing cities found in China in this era. It is likely that China was the most urbanized civilization in the world at this time, a fact that tells us much about the productivity of its agricultural sector. There were large numbers of towns with over ten thousand people and several towns, such as Xian, with populations in the tens of thousands. Most towns were walled, and many were administrative centers dominated by the multi-story residences and offices of imperial officials and scholar-gentry notables. But other towns grew up around mining and manufacturing centers, and many were centers of trade, which continued to grow in the Han era. This growth was greatly advanced by Han military expansion to the west and south. It resulted in the establishment of new overland trade routes into central Asia and south China. Overseas links were also established with northern Vietnam, the rest of Southeast Asia, and westward to the rich trading towns of coastal India.

Large mercantile firms controlled these long-distance trading networks. They grew wealthy from the transport and sale of bulk items, such as grain and horses, as well as from supplying the elite classes with exotic luxury items, such as incense, fragrant woods, and rhinoceros horn, which when ground into an edible powder was believed to enhance male potency. Merchant families also made great fortunes by lending money and investing in mining, ship construction, sheep raising, and less legitimate enterprises such as gambling halls, brothels, and grave robbing.

Though the merchant classes became wealthier and more numerous, they found it increasingly difficult to translate profits into political power or social status. Fearing their rivalry, the scholar-gentry induced successive Han rulers to issue laws that restricted merchant activities and privileges. Under most Han rulers, for example, merchants were not permitted to hold administrative posts, though they often exerted considerable local influence. They were not allowed to own carriages, carry weapons, or wear silk clothing. Scholar-gentry writers consistently classed merchants below the peasants in terms of their social usefulness, arguing that peasants produced food and essential services, while traders produced nothing but rather lived off the labor of others. The merchants, however, enjoyed a living standard that was higher than that of most of the peasants and artisans. In addition, they could very often translate wealth into considerable political clout, at least at the local level.

A GENIUS FOR INVENTION AND ARTISAN PRODUCTION

Long before the Han, the Chinese had displayed a special aptitude for invention and technological innovation. They had built massive irrigation systems, canal networks, and fortifications and devised cropping techniques that remained for millennia some of the most productive known to humanity. In the centuries of Han rule, however, their talent for invention reached new heights, and with it rose the excellence of their artisan production. There is little doubt that China was the most technologically innovative and advanced of all the classical civilizations.

At the level of the elite, the introduction of the brush pen and paper at the end of the 2d century B.C. greatly facilitated the administrative work of the scholar-gentry and advanced their literary and artistic production. The Han Chinese also developed watermills to grind grain and power artisan workshops, and rudders and compasses to steer and guide ships (though in the Han era compasses were employed primarily for divination and not used by sailors until the 9th century A.D.). They devised ingenious mining techniques to allow them to fully exploit the iron and copper resources that had become critical to warfare and domestic artisan production. From this point until the 15th and 16th centuries, Chinese shipbuilding techniques were among the most advanced in the world. In the centuries of Han rule, silk making was carried to new levels of refinement, and techniques for making lacquerware and porcelain were pioneered, which allowed China to remain a leader in ceramics until well into the modern era.

All these advances, of course, promoted the growth of the artisan, manufacturing classes. Artisans tended to be clustered in special sectors of Chinese towns but, in some regions, villages devoted almost exclusively to crafts such as silkweaving or pottery manufacture existed. Skilled artisans were in high demand and probably had a higher living standard than most peasants, though the scholar-gentry accorded them a lower official social status. Again, the ideal and reality did not necessarily correspond, for some members of the artisan classes amassed wealth and were allowed to carry weapons, ride horses, and wear silk clothing. In addition, evidence of scholar-gentry scientific experimentation suggests considerable interaction between members of the scholar-gentry elite and the artisan classes. The development of paper, the compass, and elaborate astronomical equipment would not have been possible without artisan skills and cooperation.

THE ARTS AND SCIENCES IN THE HAN ERA

Chinese art during the classical period was largely decorative, stressing careful detail and expert craftsmanship. Artistic styles often reflected the precision and geometric qualities of the many symbols of Chinese writing, and indeed calligraphy itself became a highly prized art form. Chinese painting was much less developed than it was to become under later Chinese dynasties. But the bronzes and ceramic figurines, bowls, and vases produced in this era set a very high standard for later Chinese artists. Important work was also done in jade and ivory carving and woven silk screens. Han artwork provides some of our most vivid insights into the fashions and life-styles of the Chinese in the classical era, from the aristocracy to the peasants. Most of the monumental building was concentrated on the ongoing construction of the Great Wall and on the palaces and tombs of the imperial city. But the extensive irrigation works that crisscrossed the countryside and the long walls, multi-tiered towers, and elaborate gates that became prominent features of China's many towns were engineering and architectural feats.

In the sciences, the Chinese were more drawn to experimentation with practical applications than grand theorizing. By 444 B.C. court astronomers had developed an accurate calendar based on a year of 365.5 days. Later astronomers calculated the movements of the planets Saturn and Jupiter, and observed sunspots—more than 1500 years before comparable observations were made in Europe. The main purpose of Chinese astronomy was to make celestial phenomena predictable, as part of a wider interest in ensuring harmony between heaven and earth. In astronomy and other areas, Chinese scientists steadily improved their instruments, even inventing a kind of seismograph to register the strength of earthquakes. The Chinese were also active in medical research. They made great strides in the diagnosis of diseases and in the prescription of herbal remedies and drugs to cure them. Recent evidence suggests that physicians in the Han era had begun to explore the principles of acupuncture, which remains the most distinctive and one of the most beneficial Chinese contributions to the advance of medicine.

Chinese mathematics also stressed the practical. Daoism encouraged some interest in studying the orderly processes of nature, but most research focused on how things work. For example, Chinese scholars studied the mathematics of music in ways that promoted advances in acoustics. They also sought to work out standards for the measurement of distance, volume, and weight. This kind of scientific and mathematical learning won substantial backing from the government and was generally approved by the shi scholar-officials. These achievements in the arts and sciences added to the richness and diversity of the classical heritage of Chinese civilization. Educated Chinese could concentrate their careers on political, artistic, or scientific-technological pursuits, or they could shift from one field to the next at various points in their lives.

IMPERIAL CRISIS AND HAN RESTORATION

For over two centuries the Han maintained its hold over a unified Chinese empire. But by the end of the last century B.C., a number of problems centering on the court itself threatened to bring an end to Han rule. After Han Wudi, the quality of the emperors declined markedly. Many of his successors neglected the duties of government and, like the monarchs of the late Shang and Zhou, indulged heavily in the pleasures of food, drink, and concubines. As the hold of the emperors over state affairs weakened, the powerful families of their wives sought to take charge of imperial administration. In A.D. 6, the fact that the only male heir of the Han dynasty was a small child gave one of these families, the Wang, the opportunity to seize the throne in its own right.

With the initial support of the scholar-gentry and the general populace, an ambitious nephew of the Empress Dowager Wang, named Wang Mang, proclaimed himself emperor in A.D. 9. But Wang Mang's numerous and well-intended reforms rapidly alienated the very groups that had originally greeted his accession with great joy. Attempts to exert imperial control over land ownership angered the scholar-gentry. Government monopolies, which sent the price of food and other essentials soaring, led to widespread peasant unrest. In A.D. 23, the hapless Wang Mang was overthrown, and the Han dynasty was restored.

THE LATER HAN AND IMPERIAL COLLAPSE

The Later Han dynasty ruled a unified China for nearly 200 years. For a time the peace and prosperity of the Former Han era returned. Internal rebels were suppressed and the nomads were again beaten into submission. The last centuries of the dynasty witnessed little of the innovation and creativity of the early centuries of Han rule. Inventions were improved and scholars commented on the works of earlier thinkers; the population of the empire continued to grow; and trading networks expanded. But major breakthroughs in government, the arts, and invention would have to wait for centuries and the next great dynasty, the Tang.

Politically, the Later Han was a period of steady decline. Han rulers were plagued by incessant struggles among factions at the court, which had been transferred from Xian eastward to the city of Loyang. Challenges from the families of the emperors' wives continued, but they were complicated by the growing power of the *eunuchs*— males who had been castrated in order to make them reliable guardians of the emperor's concubines. Some eunuchs were orphans, but many were sons of families who viewed their recruitment into the eunuch corps at the palace as a sure way to financial security and political advancement.

Over the years, the number of eunuchs increased, and after the Han dynasty was restored they gained substantially in power as palace administrators and inner advisors of the later emperors. In the last decades of Han rule, these beleaguered monarchs sought to use them to check the power of their wives' families. The three-way struggles that developed among the scholar-gentry, the families of the rulers' wives, and the eunuchs eventually ripped the court apart. Divisions at the center of the empire weakened the emperor's ability to check nomadic incursions and remedy the worsening conditions of the mass of the people. An enfeebled imperial administration meant growing power for landlords and the increasing autonomy of regional officials. Local notables pressed the peasantry that worked their lands for more taxes and higher rents. Secret societies spread like wildfire and peasant risings broke out throughout the empire. Military commanders and regional lords seized power in their own right and fought against each other for the right to claim the Han throne.

The dynasty was not officially overthrown until A.D. 220, but decades earlier its power had been usurped. The end of the Han meant the return of the warring states. It began nearly 400 years of division, strife, and turmoil that would end only with the rise of the Sui dynasty at the end of the 6th century A.D.

AN ERA OF ACCOMPLISHMENT AND AFFLUENCE

The four centuries of Han rule from roughly 200 B.C. to A.D. 200 represented the first wave in a cyclic succession of dynasties that would rule China until the 20th century. Through more than two millennia, a fairly predictable pattern was followed. Local rebellions would culminate in the overthrow of an existing dynasty, which had either become overly oppressive, such as the Qin, or too weak to rule effectively. For a century or so, the rulers of the new dynasty would be effective and consequently China would be relatively peaceful and prosperous. After a period of decline, one or two capable emperors would restore the dynasty's fortunes for a time. But then, roughly two centuries after the dynasty had been founded, prolonged decline would set in. Foreign invasions, natural calamities, corruption, and civil strife would sap whatever strength the dynasty had and turn the populace against it. Rebellions, usually led by disaffected members of the army and shi elite but sometimes led by peasants would erupt. The dynasty would be overthrown and a new one proclaimed to succeed it. The cycle would begin anew.

Prolonged periods of political division and civil strife followed the fall of some dynasties, most notably the Han. Yet there was considerable social and institutional continuity from one dynasty to the next. Though Chinese civilization expanded and changed significantly in areas as fundamental as the social composition of the ruling elite, marriage arrangements, and religion, key elements came together in the Han period that persisted into the 20th century. Among these were the assumption that political unity was natural and desirable; the principle of rule by an emperor served by a professional bureaucracy; and the dominance in political, social, and cultural life of the educated shi elite. Most Chinese also had a deep veneration for tradition and their ancestors, and laid great stress on the importance of maintaining social harmony, self-restraint, and decorum in dealings within the family and in the wider society. These core elements ensured not just that Chinese civilization would survive, but that the Han would be just the first of a succession of dynastic eras marked by major achievements in virtually all spheres of human endeavor.

Classical China did not produce an entirely unified culture or complete social harmony. Major philosophical and religious schools disagreed widely about the nature of "man" and the goals of life. Many ordinary people knew little of the ideas of the great Chinese philosophers such as

Confucius and Laozi. They continued to believe in a variety of gods and spirits, which were often associated with the home and kitchen, and developed rituals and offerings to placate these supernatural beings. The elite-mass gap in Chinese culture was considerable, in part because Chinese writing was so difficult to master that only a small elite had time and money enough to learn to read and write.

Despite these divisions and differences, the short-lived Qin dynasty and four centuries of Han rule had established the basic components of a civilization that would last for thousands of years. As the achievements of the classical age demonstrate, it was to be one of the most creative and influential civilizations of all human history. The strength of its agrarian base has allowed China to carry about one-fourth of the total human population from the last centuries B.C. to the present day. The productivity of its peasants has allowed the Chinese to support some of the world's largest cities and one of history's largest and most creative elites. Over the centuries, Chinese textiles, porcelain, and inventions have been traded over much of the globe and have spurred technological revolutions in regions as distant as Japan and Europe.

In the Han era, the Chinese established the first universities, the first civil service exams, and humanity's most enduring bureaucracy. In the same period, they consolidated a distinguished tradition in political philosophy, and began artistic experimentation that would yield rich rewards under later dynasties. The civilization of China that came together in the classical age of the Qin and Han was destined to dominate the history of much of Asia and contribute significantly to the advance of civilized life throughout the globe.

places Chinese thought in a comparative context can be found in Benjamin Schwartz's *The World of Thought in Ancient China* (1983). Michael Loewe's *Everyday Life in Early Imperial China* (1968) is excellent for Han society, as is the more detailed and scholarly work on *Han Social Structure* (1972) by T'ung-Tsu Ch'u, which includes extensive quotations from Chinese texts and valuable insights into the position of women, merchants, artisans, and eunuchs. A detailed survey of the archeological work done on Han sites and what they tell us about Han society is provided by Wang Shongshu's *Han Civilization* (1982). Michele Pirazzoli-t'Serstevens's lavishly illustrated study of *The Han Civilization of China* (1982) contains the most comprehensive, up-to-date, and readable overview of Han civilization available. Edmund Capon and William MacQuitty's *Princes of Jade* (1973) is less informative and reliable, but it also contains superb plates and illustrations. The most authoritative and detailed account of science and technology in the Han and later dynastic periods can be found in Joseph Needham's multivolume study on *Science and Civilization in China* (1954–). Burton Watson's *Courtier and Commoner in Ancient China* (1974), which is a translation of portions of Ban Ku's *History of the Former Han*, can be perused for examples and anecdotes that allow the student to gain a vivid sense of the day-to-day workings of Han society.

FURTHER READINGS

Good introductions to life in China in the classical age can be found in Wolfram Eberhard's *A History of China* (1977), Dun J. Li's *The Ageless Chinese* (1965), and E. Reischauer and J. K. Fairbank's *East Asia: The Great Tradition* (1960). *China's Civilization* (1976) by Arthur Cotterell and David Morgan contains useful illustrations and incorporates more recent interpretations of developments in early China. Two works deal extensively with the life and reign of Shi Huangdi: Arthur Cotterell's *The First Emperor of China* (1981) and Li Yu-Ning's *The First Emperor of China* (1975).

A relatively brief and clear introduction to Chinese thought is provided by Frederic Mote's *Intellectual Foundations of China* (1971). A much more detailed study that

1600 Indo-European invasions

1400 Kingdom
of Mycenae;
Trojan War

1000–800 Greek
"Dark Ages" after
Dorian invasions

800–700 Rise of
Greek city-states
and economy;
Homeric epics,
Iliad and *Odyssey*

600–500 Spread of commercial agriculture; rise of social protest

546–527 Pisistratus tyrant in Athens

550 Cyrus the Great forms Persian Empire

Classical Greece and the Hellenistic World

6

INTRODUCTION. Beginning about B.C. 800 on the peninsula and islands of Greece and surrounding territory in the eastern Mediterranean, a second center of classical civilization began to emerge. As in China, classical Greek civilization built on earlier regional civilizations, which had constructed elaborate monuments, developed a form of writing, and produced strong monarchies. Influenced by cultures in the Middle East and Egypt, civilization on the island of Crete and around Mycenae on the Greek mainland had flourished for several centuries around 2000 B.C. These regional civilizations were able to assimilate initial Indo-European invaders who spoke the language that came to be known as Greek.

Internal warfare, however, plus a second wave of Indo-European invasions by a Greek-speaking people called the Dorians, virtually ended the first phase of civilization in this part of the Mediterranean by about 1100 B.C. Rich capital cities, including Mycenae itself, were abandoned. For a time agriculture itself deteriorated as some Greeks turned to nomadic life and purely local governments predominated. Greek-speaking people spread around the Aegean Sea, setting the basis for a culture that could include important parts of modern Turkey, Greece, and the Balkans, but a new civilization emerged only after 800 B.C.

GREECE AS A CLASSICAL CIVILIZATION

At this point, a full-fledged classical society began to take shape, exhibiting many basic features in common with the classical phase of civilization in China and India. Like the other classical societies, Greek civilization would extend over a wide region, embracing ultimately a far larger area than any of the earlier cultures of the eastern Mediterranean. Greek influence would spread well beyond the peninsula itself, to much of the Middle East, part of North Africa, Sicily, and southern Italy. Greece began to sketch a Mediterranean civilization zone that combined earlier cen-

---

470–430 Athens at its height—Pericles, Phidias, Sophocles, Socrates, etc. **338–323** Macedonian Empire; Alexander the Great

525–456 Aeschylus launches tradition of dramatic tragedy **431–404** Peloponnesian Wars **359–336** Philip II of Macedon **300–100** Hellenistic period

500–449 Greek defeat of Persia; spread of Athenian Empire **384–322** Aristotle **399** Socrates condemned **250–126** Flourishing of Hellenistic astronomy and mathematics

| 500 B.C. | 400 B.C. | 300 B.C. |

ters, notably in the Middle East, with more western shores new to civilization in any form. Classical Greece easily passed the test of geographical expansion, as classical China had done. The Greeks produced less tidy political unities than the Chinese emperors, but their cultural and commercial outreach and periodic military forays affected a large portion of western Asia and southern Europe.

Classical Greece developed the second major feature of all the classical civilizations by demonstrating new political and cultural capacities compared to the earlier regional cultures of Egypt, Mesopotamia, and Greece. A greater diversity of philosophies and political forms developed; science and mathematics advanced, building on previous achievements; the ability to organize large empires arose, though somewhat haltingly. More elaborate forms of trade, philosophy, and government define this classical society, just as they define the classical period in India and China. Finally, there was an ongoing heritage of values and institutions between classical civilization in the Mediterranean and successor cultures, making the long classical period in this part of the world a truly formative one like that in eastern and southern Asia.

While Greek civilization had enduring impact, it was less clearly focused, geographically or institutionally, than that of China. Nothing like the Chinese cycles of dynasties described classical Greek history, for Greek political experience was more varied with more unexpected innovations.

There were also important rivals to Greek civilization and a distinct break within Greek history itself that add further complexity.

 PERSIA

After the fall of the great Babylonian and Hittite empires in the Middle East by 1200 B.C. and the ensuing regional states including some Greek colonies in the Middle East, a series of new invasions took shape. First came the Assyrians and then an influx of Iranians. From a network of small kingdoms in this region, a great conqueror emerged by 550 B.C. Cyrus the Great established a massive Persian Empire that ran across the northern Middle East and into northwestern India. The new empire formed the clearest successor to the great Mesopotamian states of the past, and Cyrus carefully tolerated traditional cultures. The Iranians advanced iron technology in the Middle East. A religious leader, Zoroaster, revised an animist religious tradition by seeing life as a battle between two divine forces, of good and evil. Zoroastrianism stressed the importance of personal moral choice in picking one side or the other, with a Last Judgment ultimately deciding the eternal fate of each person; the righteous would live on in a heaven, the "House of Song"; the evil would be condemned to eternal pain. Zoroastrianism converted Persia's later emperors and added to the cultural richness of this civilization.

Greece and Greek Colonies of the World

[Map: Greece and Greek Colonies of the World showing the Mediterranean Sea, Black Sea, Atlantic Ocean, and Red Sea regions. Labeled locations include Tanais, Olbia, Panticapaeum, Chersonesus, Dioscurias, Istros, Sinope, Trapezus, Byzantium, Heraclea, Chalcedon, Abdera, Abydos, Assos, Sestos, Potidaea, Phocaea, Ephesus, Aspendus, Chalcis, Eretria, Miletus, Megara, Athens, Corinth, Rhodes, Thera, Cyprus, Tyre, Crete, Naucratis, Cyrene, Barca, Carthage, Syracuse, Naxos, Selinus, Himera, Rhegium, Zancle (Messina), Croton, Sybaris, Ambracia, Tarentum, Poseidonia, Neapolis, Epidamnus, Apollonia, Corsica, Alalia, Sardinia, Emporiae, Massilia (Marseille), Nicaea, Agathe, Saguntum, Hemeroscopium, Mainaca, IBERIA, AFRICA, ASIA MINOR. Rivers shown: Rhône R., Danube R., Nile R. Legend: Areas of Greek settlement, Parent cities, Major colonies. Scale: 500 Miles / 500 Kilometers]

Using ceremonial styles similar to those of earlier Mesopotamia, the great Persian Empire celebrated its powerful emperors. This wall-relief shows Darius and Xerxes surrounded by courtiers.

Later emperors expanded Persian holdings. They were unable to defeat Greece and enter Europe, but they long dominated the Middle East, providing an extensive period of peace and prosperity. Ultimately, the Persian Empire was toppled by Alexander the Great, a Greek-educated conqueror. Persian language and culture survived in the northeastern portion of the Middle East, periodically affecting developments in the region as a whole.

The rise of classical civilization in Greece must thus be seen in competition with a parallel and powerful classical civilization in Persia. Greek achievements would ultimately prove more influential—Zoroastrianism, for example, faded in importance—but they were not unrivaled.

HELLENISM

Greek politics and culture flourished between about 800–400 B.C. and then began to decline. A military empire then emerged, formed initially by Alexander the Great. The empire itself was short-lived, but it helped spread elements of Greek culture through the Middle East and Europe. The resultant Hellenistic period—the word *Hellenism* means "derived from the Greek"—thus saw a reconfiguration of the geography of the Mediterranean world and the Middle East. Greek styles and values spread through the whole region, reaching out to parts of Italy in the west, North Africa, and the entire Middle East.

The Hellenistic period involved more than the dissemination of Greek culture. New political styles resembled Middle-Eastern monarchies more than the earlier Greek city-states. Philosophers and scientists introduced new themes to Greek culture, though without revising it entirely. Innovation, then, must be added to dissemination in describing this distinct Hellenistic pattern, which would flourish for about two centuries.

The Hellenistic period blended, finally, with the rise of a new center of Mediterranean civilization based in Rome.

Once more, regional geography was altered and important additions were made to both the Greek and Hellenistic legacies.

The main point is clear: Mediterranean civilization, as launched by the Greeks, moved around, with the eastern region as its center. The civilization never generated a single set of institutions comparable to the Chinese dynasties and their bureaucracy. Because it also passed through several major phases of development, the civilization is not easy to define. This means that its longer-run heritage was more diffuse than in China or India, where the geographic center, though not immobile, remained more consistent.

A VITAL LEGACY

The final complexity in dealing with classical Greece (and then Rome) involves its relationship to us—to contemporary residents of North America. For most Americans, Greece constitutes the first phase of "our own" classical past. The framers of the Constitution of the United States were intensely conscious of Greek precedents. Designers of public buildings in the United States have dutifully copied Greek and Roman models. Plato and Aristotle continue to be thought of as founders of our philosophical tradition, skillful teachers still imitate the Socratic method in seeking dialogues with students, and reliance on scientific methods of inquiry owes much to Greek formulations. The United States and Western Europe unquestionably owe a great debt to the achievements of the classical Mediterranean. We need to understand Greek civilization in order to understand our own society; yet this fact may tempt us to seek in Greek history a particularly rich detail or meaning. The Western educational tradition has long invited elaborate explorations of the Greco-Roman past as part of the standard intellectual equipment for the educated person.

The world history approach requires the classical Mediterranean to be seen in a larger framework—one in which its development is compared with other great classical traditions. Although less familiar to the West, the classical patterns of China and India are no less important and no less valid. From a comparative standpoint, the civilization of the classical Mediterranean was inferior to that of China and India in key respects. The challenge is to comprehend the leading features of Greek and Roman civilization and recognize our debt to them while recognizing the vital importance of equally fascinating formative periods in other parts of the world. The sense of reverence to Greece and the Hellenistic world, which remains an identifiable feature of Western culture today, must not preclude comparisons with the other creative classical civilizations—civilizations to which even more people in southern and eastern Asia feel reverence as they define their own identities in the late 20th century.

THE RISE OF THE CITY-STATES: THE POLITICAL CORE OF GREEK CIVILIZATION

The rapid development of civilization in Greece had two obvious roots. First was the continued existence of small cities, as well as the memories of the earlier achievements of Crete and Mycenae, even during the Indo-European invasions. This heritage was combined with an Indo-European culture that included a vivid polytheistic religion. Oral poems chanted to local aristocracies preserved knowledge of a pantheon of gods and goddesses and of values from which more elaborate philosophies and ethical systems could be devised.

The second spur to Greek civilization was a general revival of trade in the eastern Mediterranean, abetted by the introduction of coined money. Trade allowed many Greek city-states (including Greek-dominated cities in Greece and Mediterranean Asia, particularly in what is now Turkey) to increase their wealth and their range of contacts. By 800 B.C. several Greek centers had trading connections around the Black Sea and also in Egypt and southern Italy. Economic revival, in turn, spurred population growth and social change in the Greek centers, which encouraged new political structures that challenged dominance by the owners of landed estates.

THE EMERGENCE OF GREEK FORMS

As it developed, Greek civilization placed particular emphasis on political and cultural values comparable with those in other classical civilizations. Greek political evolution occurred at an often dizzying pace from the civiliza-

tion's early days until a period of decline set in after a major internal war at the end of the 5th century B.C. Cultural development, in contrast, continued into the following Hellenistic centuries, while the civilization's geographical range widened on the heels of Alexander the Great's conquests. In the Greek and Hellenistic periods, political and cultural patterns depended on a complex social and economic structure that both explained and drove the Greek thirst for expansion.

During the 8th century B.C., the Greeks adapted the Phoenician alphabet for writing their own language, therefore creating the literal basis for a new civilization. This alphabet was easier to learn than any writing system previ-

Vase art, with realistic figures from Greek legends surrounded by geometric designs, played a prominent role in Greece. In this myth a female athlete wrestles with a male. The male is portrayed with black skin, reflecting the real-life fact that men spent more time in the sun.

ously devised. The advancement of literacy further stimulated trade by aiding in the exchange of commercial information, and also enhanced cultural life. It was at this point that two great poems, the *Iliad* and the *Odyssey,* which focused on the legendary Mycenean War with Troy, were written down, possibly by the poet Homer to whom they were attributed or by a larger group of writers gradually formalizing oral tradition. The Homeric achievement drew together many separate stories and set forth definitions of the gods and human nature that shaped later Greek thinking profoundly. Soon after the Homeric epics were written, other writers in several cities, including the famous woman poet Sappho, began writing poems that ranged from military songs to lyric statements. A distinctive Greek art also began to emerge. Architects defined the shape of the Greek temple as an oblong building framed by pillars. Early Greek sculptors used Egyptian models, but then moved toward more realistic portrayals including full profile figures. Geometric designs on pottery similarly yielded to more realistic scenes of human activities, reflecting yet again the growing appreciation of human beauty and the centrality of human life.

THE *POLIS* (CITY-STATE) EMERGES AS A POLITICAL UNIT

Greek politics also took shape in the three centuries after 800 B.C. Greek government in this early period and thereafter revolved around the city-state unit—that is, a regional government centered in a major city but embracing the agricultural hinterland as well. These units could be quite tiny or, like Sparta (one of the key city-states), they could embrace a substantial area. Athens, the most famous city-state, was about the size of the state of Rhode Island; by the 5th century B.C. Athens had a population of roughly 250,000, of whom 100,000 lived in the city proper. The city-state government came naturally to Greece, partly because of the traditions set in earlier Middle Eastern civilizations where regional states often predominated and partly because a mountainous terrain made larger connections difficult. Many city-states were formed in a valley or bay with a single city organizing the surrounding agricultural enclave. Greek settlements in other areas, however, such as the northern Middle East or southern Italy, also adopted the city-state form even when natural conditions did not require it. By 600 B.C., nearly 300 independent poleis had developed in Greece. While the city-state format promoted frequent wars, as no single unit predominated, it did encourage a political life of unusual intensity. So much was this the case that the Greek word for city-state government—*polis*—serves as the origin of our word politics.

Early Greek poleis were mainly ruled by landowning aristocrats, mostly descendants of the Indo-European warrior class who were still responsible for most military activities. Free farmers were also citizens, supporting the government and often participating in periodic assemblies though not ruling directly. Councils of various sorts played a vital role in the early Greek city-states, even when there was a single king or other ruler. Warrior-aristocrats frequently met with the ruler to advise on matters of state, and they expected their advice to be taken seriously. Independent farmers also had a chance to meet occasionally to discuss political issues; one historian has described this form of government as a real peasant democracy.

This mixed system was increasingly challenged from about 700 B.C. onward. With the commercial expansion that began in the 8th century, aristocratic rule was often disputed. Some city-states escaped major contests, for they remained largely agricultural; Sparta, for example, maintained a strong militaristic rule under aristocratic leadership. But in active trading centers, merchants and a growing urban manufacturing group chafed under aristocratic rule. Furthermore, in many areas agriculture itself changed. Landlords began to specialize in growing olives and grapes and in manufacturing cooking oil and wines. These were commercial products, requiring substantial capital to develop; the landlords began importing cheap grain from colonies in Asia, Egypt, and Sicily in order to provide basic foodstuffs. These imports progressively squeezed out local independent farmers, creating a growing gulf between the rich and poor. The ideals of widespread citizenship were contradicted by these developments.

The result, by the 6th century B.C., was a growing crescendo of social protest, pitting urban groups and dispossessed farmers against the aristocratic elite. One common outcome was a series of tyrants who won popular support against the aristocratic interest. These tyrants often developed public works and other activities that benefited the lower classes and the cities, while maintaining pressures against aristocratic opposition. But the idea of one-man rule contradicted traditions of political legitimacy, which held that the community should govern itself, and of course it antagonized the aristocracy without destroying this class completely. Hence in many cases reformers arose to try to restore earlier ideals of citizenship while dealing with the new social tensions. Many reformers emphasized developing new laws to regulate economic relationships without resorting to tyrants. Solon, a reformer in Athens early in the 6th century, set up laws that would ease the burden of debts on the farmers by prohibiting slavery for such debts. The idea developed that laws could be written and revised, rather than being passed down unaltered from tradition; here was one source of new political interest and participation.

Other forces pressed for political change. Military activity increasingly involved larger numbers of citizens who formed tightly organized and well-coordinated lines of infantry; naval forces, in the port cities, such as Athens, also depended on extensive recruitment. This development increased the need for strong bonds among citizens within the polis, regardless of its previous constitutional form. By 500 B.C., most poleis strongly believed in the importance of loyalty to the community, which itself would be regulated by law rather than custom or purely personal relationships. Participation in public life became a widespread ideal, and it corresponded to the busy functions that grouped city dwellers together in the marketplace.

The dominant religion also supported this ideal of political unity and involvement. Each city-state had its own patron god or goddess, and regular rituals called forth prayer and ceremony on behalf of the city's well-being. These ceremonies included plays, choruses, sporting events, and religious exercises, all calling attention to the power and cohesion of the polis. When, in 399 B.C., the philosopher Socrates was condemned by a jury in Athens for corrupting his students by encouraging skepticism and doubt, he was given a choice between exile and death: he chose death because, as he said, the city had been the source of his character and he owed it obedience; better to die than to be apart.

This spirit of political devotion and participation was the most common ingredient of city-state life. It showed itself in the willingness of citizens to serve in the military at their own expense and to sponsor plays, poetry contests, temples, and other public buildings. The specific constitutional structures of the Greek city-states, as they hit their stride after the period of most pronounced social unrest, varied greatly. Some city-states remained monarchies; Sparta in fact had two kings who helped check each other. Other city-states reverted to aristocratic councils, while in a few city-states tyrants still ruled. Generally, however, by the 5th century, there was some evolution toward more democratic structures, and here Athens proudly took the lead.

THE RISE OF DEMOCRACY IN ATHENS

Athens had undergone a fairly standard, if highly dramatic, political evolution prior to its democratic flowering in the 5th century B.C. It started when smaller villages were unified into a single city-state as an aristocratic domain. Powerful nobles held the best land and dominated political and religious life through their council. There was no written law. During the 7th century, tensions between aristocrats and commoners mounted as family farmers increasingly went into debt when harvests failed, often losing their land and in some cases being enslaved when they could not repay. Solon's reforms, which limited indebtedness while also encouraging greater commerce, resolved this crisis, and Solon also expanded the citizenship rights of most adult males. Citizens could elect a council that monitored the aristocratic government. But these reforms did not prevent the rise of an outright tyranny as an aristocratic leader, Pisastratus, gained popular support against the traditional noble councils, ruling from 546–527 B.C. Pisastratus sponsored major new buildings and public works, which created new jobs, while dominating the major councils. Soon after his death an invasion from Sparta sought to restore the aristocracy, but while the tyranny was toppled, the Athenian people refused to revert to traditional forms. A new reform leader, Clisthenes, reestablished a council, elected by all citizens, that prepared agendas for an assembly composed of the citizens themselves. Athens was ready to become not only the most powerful but also the most fully developed of the Greek democracies of the 5th century.

Full-blown Athenian democracy, after a few additional reforms around 462 B.C., continued to depend on the popular assembly as sovereign authority. All decisions of state emanated from this body or had to be approved by it, and there were no restrictions on who could debate or propose in assembly meetings. This was direct democracy—the word itself comes from the Greek word for people, *demos*—not rule through elected representatives. Since the assembly met frequently, only a minority of citizens actually had time to attend regularly, and a few leading speakers usually predominated.

Citizen voice, however, had other outlets. The army was composed of citizens, whose active service and coordinated maneuvers expressed the spirit of the democratic polis. Citizens also served as jurors in court trials, and every judicial decision could be appealed to a citizen board. Most officials were selected by lot on grounds that any citizen could and should serve as administrator. A few key officials—the generals and imperial treasurers—were elected, usually from the nobility, but like all officials they were carefully assessed by the assembly and might be removed or punished for faulty service. Terms of office were brief, further to encourage popular control. Only a few positions in the area of military leadership were reserved for appointment.

This was a democracy of a different sort from the version common in the contemporary world. It depended on the small size of the city-state and the intensive participation of its citizens. Furthermore, many adults were excluded from political rights. Women, though they might be citizens in terms of treatment by the law, had no rights of political participation. Half of all adult males were not citizens in any sense, being slaves or foreigners. Even at its most democratic, the Athenian government was shaped by considerable behind-the-scenes control by the aristocracy. The Athenian leader Pericles, who guided Athens during its decades of greatest glory after the mid-5th century, was an aristocrat who managed to direct affairs year after year through wise manipulation of political groups and his own prestige, whether or not he held formal office. Many Athenians, and even more Greeks in city-states where democracy did not go as far, continued to believe that real political virtue lay in aristocratic rule (*aristocracy* being derived from the Greek word *aristos* or "rule of the best"). Sparta continued to represent the aristocratic alternative.

Yet if democracy was qualified, and far from general throughout Greece, its principles were articulated clearly. Athenian democracy rested far more directly on the public devotion and talent of those who were citizens than modern democracies do. Pericles offered a classic definition of the democratic ideal:

> The administration is in the hands of the many and not of the few. But while the law secures equal justice to all alike in their private disputes, the claim of excellence is also recognized; and when a citizen is in any way distinguished he is preferred to the public service, not as a matter of privilege but as the reward of merit. Neither is poverty a bar, but a man may benefit his country whatever be the obscurity of his condition.

In truth, for many Athenians politics could provide both excitement and responsibility. Huge juries handled crucial trials, including political cases such as that of Socrates. Officials judged to have served badly could be ostracized for ten years, a measure introduced to prevent tyranny. Names of politicians judged to be potential tyrants were inscribed on *ostraka*, or pottery fragments, and if one name was listed often enough the person was forced to leave.

By the end of the 5th century, when Athens plunged into a devastating war with Sparta, the polis demonstrated some of the weaknesses as well as the strengths of democracy. Ordinary citizens worked hard in the war, but the lower-class citizens, eager to get government jobs and spoils, often pressed for reckless expeditions that weakened the state in its military efforts and contributed substantially to ultimate defeat. In a famous instance, popular leaders won approval for a major attack on Sicily, designed to expand Athens's empire and bring booty for the naval forces involved, even though this diverted dangerously from the Spartan threat. Cautious leaders were overturned in favor of crowd-pleasers who promised lucrative colonial ventures or an expansion of government payments to poorer citizens.

A COMPARISON OF GREEK AND CHINESE POLITICAL STYLES

The Greek political approach, overall, involved intense emphasis on political virtue and responsibility. Participation in politics was part of the ideal life, particularly in the aristocracy. There was in this approach, with its concern for a sound political system and well-defined relationships among various social elements, more than a hint of the values Confucianism emphasized in China. But in the decentralized atmosphere of Greek politics, a far larger array of political structures was tossed up than was true in China with its greater stress on a single centralized system. Compared to Chinese political principles also, the Greeks placed more value on various councils, and on participation rather than on hierarchy and obedience (including the very idea of citizenship); there was more emphasis on formal preparation of law (a theme the Romans would later extend) and far less stress on a bureaucracy and bureaucratic codes. Democracy was not a fully typical form, as even in Athens it proved short-lived. The idea of intense citizen involvement and responsibility—with the corollary that citizenship was restricted—was more characteristic of Greek political life, compatible with mixed aristocratic council systems as well as with democracy.

GREEK DIPLOMACY AND THE TENSIONS OF UNITED EFFORT

During the four centuries when Greek political forms evolved, many city-states sent out additional colonies, which expanded exposure to Greek political values. Colonies helped relieve population pressure at home. They also provided vital grain supplies to the mainland while serving as markets for processed products, including wine, cooking oil, and manufactured goods. By the 5th century, Greek colonies dotted the Mediterranean coast of present-day Turkey, the entire coastline of the Black Sea, and key points in North Africa, Italy, and even southern France and Spain. By providing new wealth, colonies greatly supported political and cultural vigor in Greece itself. They reduced, though did not eliminate, quarrels among city-states back home. They also helped Greeks realize their common values beyond the intense, divisive loyalties of the poleis.

At their best from 750–420 B.C., Greek politics included some important common efforts, in addition to the focus on separate government units. The Greek city-states were capable of sufficient coordination to deal with a variety of general problems. They joined in regular celebrations such as the athletic competitions of the Olympic games, which grouped wrestlers and runners in often bitter (and occasionally rigged) competitions. They supported some common religious organizations, such as the oracle priests at Delphi whose predictions and advice were widely sought. More important was the collaboration that allowed Greece to defeat its most pressing outside enemy, the great

This statue of a discus thrower by the sculptor Myron shows Greek love for athletics and the realistic but heroic style adopted for human figures by the classical Greek artists.

empire of Persia. Soon after Cyrus the Great created the Persian Empire, he turned against wealthy Greek colonies along the Asian side of the Mediterranean, conquering them by about 540 B.C. Persian power became an obvious threat to the Greek mainland, impelling cooperation between Athens and Sparta, the most powerful city-states. In 499 B.C. the conquered Greek cities rebelled against the Persians, and were aided by the Athenian navy. The rebellion failed, and the Persian kings (Darius I, then Xerxes) moved against Greece in punishment. In 480 B.C. a Persian army of 100,000 troops moved down the Greek peninsula, initially winning great success and capturing Athens. But the Athenians built a new fleet, which defeated the Persian navy and cut off supplies, and then a Spartan-led force bested the Persian army. While Persia continued to dominate the Middle East, Greek independence was preserved. The greatest age of Greek politics and culture followed, including the perfection of Athenian political institutions and the Age of Pericles.

The wars against Persia provided some of the most dramatic moments in classical Greek history. In the battle at Thermopylae, 300 Spartans and a few thousand Greek soldiers blocked a huge Persian army until they were betrayed by local Greeks and caught from behind. After a crucial Athenian naval victory at Marathon, a runner labored over 26 miles to bring news to the city, collapsing after the word was passed. The final Greek triumph, celebrated later by the historian Herodotus, who praised Greek justice over the excessive ambition of the Persians, helped the Greeks define their separate identity as a society different from the Asian empire.

In the years following the Persian defeat Athens began to form an empire of its own. The Athenians quickly rebuilt their city, leading to a huge impetus for Greek art and architecture. Athenian naval power helped organize an alliance of lesser Greek cities, which Athens quickly dominated. Officially designed to guard against the Persian threat, this Delian league was headed by an Athenian admiral, its treasury controlled by Athens. Increasingly, many cities became completely dependent on Athenian rule without having a voice in policy. The empire provided great resources for Athens, but it also complicated Athenian politics because the city grew to include increasing numbers of noncitizens while the spoils of political office, given imperial wealth, became increasingly attractive and highly contested. Many Athenians wondered if authoritarian control of colonies based on military force and heavy tribute payment was compatible with free political life at home. Domestic political infighting to compete for crowd favor became increasingly nasty as dependence on the empire increased.

Even as new problems loomed, Greek political development during the three centuries prior to the mid-5th century had produced a number of key results. An initial aristocratic tone, though often modified, had demonstrated continued validity even in democratic centers such as Athens. Greek aristocrats could agree on the need for wise political service and devotion to political life. Some of their ideals had extended to a wider group of citizens and underwrote the intense political loyalties of the city-states. At the same time, other political trends had modified aristocratic rule, particularly through the advance of democracy.

Greek political and economic control had spread widely along the eastern and northern coasts of the Mediterranean, and around the Black Sea. And temporary union among the Greeks had pushed back the Persian advance, where defeat would have opened quite a different chapter in Mediterranean history.

Yet the Greek political structure was also fragile. With so many different government units, division could easily override common purpose. Diversity also produced animosity, with democrats and aristocrats glaring at each other both within and among poleis. A new and bitter conflict between the leading states set the stage for declining political vigor within Greece itself.

ATHENS VS. SPARTA

The growing imperial power of Athens attracted competition from Sparta, which had its own alliance system of land-based city-states. Competition for power in the Greek peninsula in the later 5th century B.C.—each side fearing that the other might gain a dominant position—was heightened by ideological conflicts that some historians have compared in their intensity though not their precise nature to "cold war" battles between the capitalist United States and the communist Soviet Union in the decades after World War II. Sparta stood for the old Greece before extensive commerce and massive political change. Aristocratic rule had been transformed into a highly military regime in which boys were trained for battle and girls for the bearing of brave sons; Spartan militarism was designed to keep a large force of near-slaves, who did the agricultural work, under control. Use of money was discouraged by minting coins of unwieldy size. Discipline and control were the themes of Spartan society.

Athens contrasted with Sparta by encouraging extensive trade and a vibrant, creative culture, while its democracy contrasted with the narrow aristocratic dominance of Sparta. Both sides were quite aware of their differences and disliked the principles of the rival society intensely. Both also drew allies from like-minded poleis. Sparta had unex-pected advantages because its traditional principles were widely admired, even by some conservative Athenians. The heavy-handedness of Athens's empire also drew hostility from many smaller cities.

For a few decades, around 450 B.C., an uneasy peace prevailed between the Greek rivals. Pericles, though aggressively proud of Athens's values, judged that Athenian welfare rested on a cautious foreign policy and in peace with the Spartans. But in 435 B.C. a revolt in a colonial city-state, Corcyra, disrupted the precarious balance. Corcyra had been neutral between Athens and Sparta, but it had a large navy that now risked coming under the control of a Spartan ally. Athens insisted that Corcyra was under its protection, for it feared a rival navy; but this persuaded Sparta that Athens was insatiably power hungry. War broke out in 431 B.C., as Spartan forces marched into Athenian territory.

In the resultant Peloponnesian War, the Athenian strategy was to let Sparta invade its outlying lands, while relying on its fleet to maintain supplies and to raid the Spartan coast. But during the second year of the war a massive plague broke out in Athens, ultimately killing one-third of the population, including Pericles. Grievances rose in Athens, and there was no longer a leader to provide consistent guidance. A victory over Spartan troops brought a chance for peace, but a warlike faction in Athens insisted on continuing the war, seeking to conquer new territory while wasting precious Athenian resources. The attempt to invade Sicily failed, costing Athens over 200 ships, 4,500 men, and the support of many allies. Finally, in 404 B.C. a Spartan general cut off the Athenian food supply, and the city had to surrender. Athens was deprived of its remaining fleet, and the city walls were torn down. A political age came to an end not only in Athens, but in all of Greece.

HELLENISTIC POLITICS

The collapse of Athens opened the way for Spartan domination of the Greek mainland. During the war, Sparta had accepted Persian help, particularly on the seas, and in return it handed over control of the Greek states in Asia. In Greece, the Spartans installed tight controls supported by a local military garrison, while requiring almost as much tribute as Athens had once collected from its dependencies in the Delian league. These policies plus Sparta's unyielding hostility to any democratic forms soon caused resentments, which among other things gave Athens a chance to regain some independence.

Periodic wars against the Persians and among key Greek states dominated the first half of the 4th century. An alliance between Athens and the city-state of Thebes successfully attacked the Spartans, briefly setting up a Theban Empire in northern Greece. Athens formed a new league of its own, but soon began to abuse its allies through tribute demands and interference. Having defeated Thebes, Athens's federation collapsed amid revolt. By 355 B.C. Greece had returned to a setting of independent, disorganized city-states, many of them exhausted by decades of war and civil strife.

The Peloponnesian War destroyed the basis for informal Greek unity, while weakening both the major combatants. It took only a few decades to realize that Greek politics had lost its luster. The larger Greek empire began to break up as colonies were pulled away, while a dangerous vacuum of power opened in the mainland itself.

A NEW EMPIRE REPLACES CLASSICAL GREECE

Into this vacuum came a new force from the kingdom of Macedon on the borders of Greece. Macedonian conquests in turn opened a period of three centuries in which Greek culture spread widely in Egypt and far into western Asia. Greek city-states persisted in this new Hellenistic world, but they were no longer the dominant forms. Greek culture also mixed with new elements from the Middle East and India, though on the whole Hellenistic culture built more clearly on Greek themes than Hellenistic politics did. In geography, politics, and to an extent culture, a new era opened in the 4th century, just as Greek institutions lost their vitality. The roots of the new order lay in the rise of a Macedonian dynasty that conquered first Greece and then the Persian Empire within two generations.

Macedon, a kingdom to the north of Greece, was semi-barbaric by Greek standards and loosely organized under a king. Its residents spoke Greek, and Macedonian kings had long been interested in Greek culture. When King Philip II (359–336 B.C.) seized power, he strengthened the monarchy within Macedon and then turned his attention to the chaos of Greece. Skilled both as a general and diplomat, Philip soon developed a strong army that had more flexible tactics than the standard citizen force of the poleis. By seizing some northern Greek territory, he gained the resources to pay mercenary troops and peasant soldiers. Then he turned to the divided city-states of central Greece.

Despite warnings by insightful leaders, states such as Athens were no longer willing to make major sacrifices for self-defense. Philip also found allies in Greek statesmen who wanted a new unity, even if imposed from the outside. Finally, in 338 B.C., Philip won a decisive battle, aided by a cavalry charge led by his 18-year-old son Alexander. Macedon now ruled the bulk of Greece, and while the city-states retained their governments with rights of internal administration, Macedonian garrisons assured tax tributes and loyalty to the new kingdom.

ALEXANDER THE GREAT

Philip's death left the next stage of Macedonian expansion to Alexander, who gained power at the age of 20. Alexander, eager to continue his father's thrust for conquest, logically turned to the target of the Persian Empire, still vast but now weakly ruled. In 334 B.C., Alexander moved into Asia with about 35,000 troops. Daring triumphs brought him control of the Persian side of the Mediterranean coast. Then, in 333 B.C., Alexander defeated the main Persian army led by its emperor in Syria.

Persian efforts to sue for peace were ignored: Alexander wanted the whole empire and more, if possible. He moved into Egypt, now a weakened regional state, where he was greeted as pharaoh and son of a god. By 331 B.C., he en-

This bust of Alexander the Great is in the heroic style of Greek sculpture. The youthful emperor was one of the greatest conquerors of the world.

tered Babylon and then seized the vast Persian treasury, as the Greeks and Macedonians gained revenge for the many Persian threats to their homeland. Alexander pressed into India, but he finally had to stop because his men refused to go farther.

Alexander planned a dazzling future for his new empire, hoping to merge Greek and Asian institutions and values and add further conquests. He founded many cities bearing his name, the most famous one in Egypt. He spread Macedonian and Greek officials through his vast new Middle Eastern holdings. Alexander also encouraged intermarriage with Persian and other local women, a practice in which he himself set an example. Eager to promote a Hellenistic culture, evidenced by his founding centers of scholarship in Greek learning, Alexander also recognized the need to accommodate various traditions in a multinational empire. Whether he could have succeeded in consolidating his unprecedented holdings, given his vision and organizational skills, cannot be known for he died of a fever in Babylon at the age of 33.

LATER HELLENISTIC STATES

Alexander's unexpected death quickly brought disunity to the new empire, though not an end to the Hellenistic enterprise. Quarrels among his successors allowed key generals to seize the major provinces as kings. Three major regional dynasties resulted—one in Egypt (the Ptolemies) that ended with the suicide of the famous queen, Cleopatra, in 31 B.C.; one in Mesopotamia (the Seleucids); and one in Macedonia, Greece, and the northern Middle East (the Antigonids).

The three major successor states enjoyed about 75 years of vigor and prosperity. Trade in Greek goods continued to flourish, and all the new kings encouraged commerce. Many Greeks moved toward the government jobs and merchant positions available in the Middle East. Wealth centered, however, on the city dwellers and the Hellenized upper classes (whether of Greek origin or not), while native peasants suffered from high taxes and the lack of adequate land. Internal divisions caused a decline in production and combined with warfare among the kingdoms to weaken the successor states and open them to outside attack. By the 2d century B.C.—just as Rome was beginning to expand—all the Hellenistic kingdoms except the one in Egypt had vanished.

The two centuries of Hellenism marked the end of the characteristically Greek political style. City-states continued officially to exist, and they would maintain some functions even later under Roman control. But they no longer served as intense focal points because of the control exercised by foreign monarchs. Hellenistic politics centered on military empires. While few dramatic or enduring political principles emerged from this approach, Alexander and his successors provided vital service in preserving large segments of Greek culture after city-state quarrels had exhausted earlier government systems. They also creatively extended this culture well beyond Greece and its earlier colonies to a larger Mediterranean and Middle Eastern zone, as well as to India. Hellenistic kingdoms also developed trade and artistic contacts with the African kingdom of Kush, bringing new impulses to this civilization.

Hellenism did not bring cultural unity or political cohesion to the Middle East and eastern Mediterranean. There was new interchange, however, and some common interests in Greek science and philosophy that would outlast the Hellenistic period, continuing into the Roman era and beyond. Hellenist leaders also generated innovations, particularly in science. The spread of a Greek-derived culture, then, set a new framework for intellectual life in a large and diverse portion of the civilized world. This heritage would have pleased the Hellenistic conquerors, who saw cultural expansion as part of their mission.

GREEK CREATIVITY IN CULTURE

The genius of Greek civilization lay more obviously in various facets of culture than in politics. It was Greek culture that determined the most lasting contributions of this civilization to the Mediterranean world, and that served as the key linkage in the larger Hellenistic orbit sketched by Alexander.

The Greeks did not create a major religion, and in this they differed from India and to a lesser extent from China. Greek ideas would ultimately influence great religions, particularly Christianity and to some degree Islam, but this came later. The characteristic Greek religion was a rather primitive affair, derived from animist belief in the spirits of nature elevated into a complex set of gods and goddesses who were seen as interfering in human life. The Greeks thus had a creator or father god, Zeus, who presided over an unruly assemblage of divinities whose functions ranged from regulating the daily passage of the sun (Apollo) or the oceans (Poseidon) to inspiring war or human love and beauty. Specific gods patronized other human activities such as metalworking, the hunt, literature, and history. Regular ceremonies to the gods had real political importance, and many individuals sought the gods' aid in foretelling the future or in assuring a good harvest or good health. Stories of the gods' activities provided rich entertainment and could drive home lessons about appropriate moral behavior, including courage and humility.

This was a religion, then, passed down from earlier Indo-European experience, that served many human needs and cemented community loyalties. It was not, however, intensely spiritual. Interestingly the basic Indo-European pantheon was the same as that brought to India, which in both cases assumed human form. The Greek use of religion, however, differed considerably from the more otherworldly Indian outcome. Greek religion tended toward a human-centered, worldly approach. Stories of the gods allowed illustration of human qualities, rather like soap operas on a vaster scale; the gods could be jealous, sneaky, lustful, and powerful. Greek religion, like the Indian religion, helped engender an important literary tradition. In the Greek religion the gods primarily provided good stories or served as foils to inquire deeply into human passions and vulnerabilities. Greek gods were used mainly in terms of what they could do for humankind and what they could reveal about human nature, rather than as sources pushing people toward consideration of higher planes of spirituality or some ultimately divine experience.

Greek religion also had a number of limitations. Its lack of spiritual passion failed to satisfy many ordinary workers and peasants, particularly when times were hard due to political chaos or economic distress. Popular "mystery" religions, which had more exciting rituals and promised greater spiritual insight in contrast to worldly cares, often swept through Greece with secret ceremonies, a strong sense of fellowship, and a greater implication of contact with unfathomable divine powers. The importance of mystery religions to an extent paralleled the role of Daoism in providing a contrast to more politically-directed religion or philosophy, though none of the mystery religions won the currency or durability of Daoism in China.

PHILOSOPHY

The limitations of Greek religion also left many literate and educated people dissatisfied. The religion provided stories about how the world came to be as it is, but scant basis for systematic inquiry into nature or human society. And while the dominant religion promoted political loyalty, it did not provide an elaborate basis for ethical thought. Hence, from at least the 6th century onward, many Greek thinkers attempted to generate philosophical systems separate from a primarily religious base. The attempt to understand humankind, society, and nature by rational observation and deduction became one of the hallmarks of Greek and Hellenistic culture. The approach was not entirely dissimilar from that of Confucianism in China, but it had different specifics and a different and wider-ranging scope.

Many thinkers sought to generate ethical systems on the basis of rational definitions of right and wrong and some sense of the purpose of life on earth. Socrates (born in 465 B.C. and the tutor of Plato, who in turn would teach Aristotle) urged people to consider the bases of right action in terms of rational reflection on goals and consequences; in contrast to earlier Middle-Eastern traditions, he thus formulated secular criteria, rather than devising rewards and punishments from an otherworldly system. Aristotle, perhaps the most important of the Greek philosophers, maintained this ethical system through stressing the importance of moderation in human behavior against the instability of political life in Athens and the excesses of the gods.

During the Hellenistic period other ethical systems were devised. Thus a group called the Stoics emphasized an inner moral independence to be cultivated by strict discipline of the body and personal bravery. These ethical systems were major contributions in their own right, attracting many disciples and generating much literary debate; they also would, later, be blended with Christian religious thought.

Greek philosophy further devoted much attention to defining appropriate political structures. Various constitutional systems were discussed, often in light of ongoing political disputes between Athens and Sparta. The Athenian philosopher Plato, in the 5th century, devised an ideal government structure in which philosophers would rule. Most Greek political theory stressed the importance of balance with due outlet for aristocratic principles and some popular contribution. Again, religious justifications for political behavior were played down in favor of arguments in terms of utility and practicality or more general definitions of justice. It was in this vein, also, that philosophers, such as Aristotle, discussed social topics such as slavery or the conditions of women (providing vigorous defenses for the inevitability and usefulness of slavery and for family structures that would assume women's inferiority).

The idea of a philosophy separate from official religion, though not necessarily hostile to it, also encouraged considerable emphasis on the powers of human thought. In Athens, Socrates encouraged his pupils to question received wisdom on the ground that the chief human duty was "the improvement of the soul." Socrates himself ran afoul of the Athenian government in the aftermath of the tensions of the Peloponnesian War, for he seemed to be undermining political loyalty itself with his constant questions. But the Socratic principle of thinking things through by means of skeptical questioning, rather than assuming on the basis of authority or faith, became a recurrent strand in classical Greek thinking and education and was part of its heritage to later societies. Socrates' great pupil, Plato, accentuated the positive somewhat more strongly in suggesting that human reason could approach an understanding of the perfect forms—the absolutely True, Good, and Beautiful—that he believed underlay nature. Thus a philosophical tradition arose in Greece that tended to play down the importance of human spirituality in favor of a celebration of the human power to think. The result bore some similarities to Chinese Confucianism, though with greater emphasis on skeptical questioning and abstract speculations about the basic nature of humanity and the universe.

Greek interest in rationality carried over into inquiry into the underlying order of physical nature. The Greeks were not great empirical scientists. Relatively few new scientific findings emanated from Athens, though philosophers such as Aristotle did collect large amounts of biological data. The Greek interest lay in speculations about nature's order, and many non-Westerners believe that this tradition continues to inform what they see as an excessive Western passion for seeking sweeping rationality in the universe. Greek belief in rational theorizing produced widespread philosophical commitment to a scientific method that would combine empirical data with general concepts. In practice, the Greek concern translated into a host of theories about the motions of the planets and the organization of elemental principles of earth, fire, air, and water, and into a considerable interest in mathematics as a means of rendering nature's patterns comprehensible. Greek and later Hellenistic work in geometry was particularly impressive, featuring among other achievements the basic theorems of Pythagoras and Euclid's compendium of geometry.

Scientists in the Hellenistic period added some important empirical contributions, especially in studies of anatomy; medical treatises by Galen were not improved upon in the Western world for many centuries. Less fortunately, the Hellenistic astronomer Ptolemy formalized an elaborate theory of the sun's motion around a stationary earth; this new Hellenistic theory contradicted much earlier Middle Eastern astronomy, which had recognized the earth's rotation. The idea of an earth-centered universe seemed to explain many observed phenomena, including eclipses, and this fact along with the sheer reputation of Greek science assured that Ptolemy's theory was long taken as fixed wisdom in Western thought. (Ptolemy's views followed those of Aristotle. Aristotle had combined what he thought were observed data plus rationalistic deductions about nature's properties—the earth's core is heavier than its shell and so must be the center of the system—to prove that the sun and the planets revolved around the earth.)

Other Hellenistic scientists added more constructively to the observations about planetary motion. Archimedes (c. 287–212 B.C.) wrote about mathematics and the measurement of water power. He devised pulley systems to pump out flooded ships and fields and invented novel kinds of fortifications. Other Hellenistic scientists, using dissection on the corpses of criminals, made important discoveries about digestion and the vascular system.

THE ARTS

Despite the importance of the rationalist tradition, science and mathematics loomed far less large than art and literature in conveying key cultural values in Greek and Hellenistic culture. The official religion inspired themes for artistic expressions and justifications for temples, statues, and plays devoted to the glories of the gods. But the human-centered qualities of the Greeks also showed through, as artists emphasized the beauty of realistic portrayals of the human form and poets and playwrights used the gods as foils for inquiries into the human condition.

All the arts received some attention in classical Mediterranean civilization. Performances of music and dance were vital parts of religious festivals, but their precise styles have not been preserved. Far more durable was the Greek interest in drama, for plays took a central role in this culture. Greek dramatists worked both on comedy and on tragedy, indeed making a formal division between the two approaches that is still part of the Western tradition. On the whole, in contrast to Indian writers, the Greeks placed greatest emphasis on tragedy. Their belief in human reason and balance also involved a sense that these virtues were precarious, so that a person could easily overstep and be ensnared in situations of powerful emotion and uncontrollable consequences. The Athenian dramatist Sophocles, for example, so insightfully portrayed the psychological flaws of his hero Oedipus that modern psychology long used the term *Oedipus complex* to refer to potentially tragic attachments between a man and his mother. Another Athenian playwright, Aristophanes, used similar beliefs in the limitations of human experience to produce a sense of comedy, poking fun at the failures of human nature.

In addition to defining the concept of drama, enriching the language, providing powerful themes, and maintaining a society that appreciated compelling plays, the Greeks established rules for future societies about how a drama should be written. These rules included an insistence on a coherent plot as opposed to a jumble of unrelated events. These specific precedents, along with the knowledge that the Greeks had perfected drama, helped shape dramatic writing in societies that looked back on the Greek example.

Greek literature contained a strong epic tradition as well, starting with the beautifully crafted tales of the *Iliad* and the *Odyssey*. By the 5th century B.C., interest in human

Varied column designs marked the progression of Greek architecture from the square Doric simplicity (as shown in the first two pictures of the Parthenon), through Ionic, to the more ornate Corinthian. These columns marked temples and other public buildings.

Greek dramas were staged in this theater of Dionysus. This magnificent outdoor facility was nestled in a hillside, with the stage at the base of seating risers sculpted in stone. The location of the theater reflected its wide public functions.

affairs led to a new kind of formal historical writing with Herodotus trying to sort out fact from myth in dealing with various Mediterranean cultures and Thucydides composing a vivid account of the Peloponnesian War.

In the visual arts, the emphasis of classical Mediterranean civilization lay in sculpture and architecture, though Greek artists also advanced in ceramic work. In Athens's brilliant 5th century B.C.—the age of Pericles, Socrates, Sophocles, Aristophanes, and many other intensely creative figures—sculptors such as Phidias developed unprecedented skill in simultaneously realistic yet beautiful portrayals of the human form, from lovely goddesses to muscled warriors and athletes.

Greek architecture, from the 8th century B.C. onward, emphasized monumental construction, square or rectangular in shape, with columned porticoes. The Greeks devised three distinct styles for their massive buildings, each more ornate than the last: the Doric, the Ionic, and the Corinthian. The Greeks, in short, invented what Westerners and others in the world today still regard as "classical" architecture, though the Greeks themselves were influenced by Egyptian and Cretan models in their preferences. Greece provided abundant stone for ambitious temples, markets, and other public buildings. Many of these same structures were filled with products of the sculptors' workshops. They were also brightly painted, though over the centuries the paint would fade so that later imitators came to think of the classical as involving unadorned stone.

Classical Mediterranean art and architecture were intimately linked with the society that produced them. There is temptation, because of the formal role of classical styles in later societies, to attribute a stiffness to Greek art that was not present in the original. Greek structures were built to be used. Temples and marketplaces were part of daily urban life. Classical art was also flexible, according to need. Classical dramas were not merely examples of high art performed in front of a cultural elite. Indeed, Athens lives in the memory of many intellectuals because of the creativity of the writers and philosophers and of the large audiences that trooped to performances of plays by authors, such as Sophocles. Literally thousands of people periodically gathered in the big hillside theaters of Athens and other cities for the new plays and the music and poetry competitions that simultaneously honored the gods.

THE PRINCIPLES OF GREEK CULTURE

Overall, the Greek and Hellenistic cultural achievement rested on four major principles. First, the interest in formal political theory, with a strong emphasis on debating the merits of different constitutional structures and assuming that government forms could be planned, obviously reflected the distinctive political atmosphere of Greece. If Greek politics faced frequent crises, its incorporation in political thought and history gave it a longer life and wider subsequent influence.

Second, art and sculpture served on the whole to glorify human achievement, starting with a celebration of the beauties of the ideal human form, used also to represent the gods.

Third, drama and philosophy stressed the importance of human striving, though comedy might poke fun and tragedy might emphasize the inevitable limits. This characteristic joined with the emphases of the visual arts in stressing secular over otherworldly themes. And while ethical philosophers might enjoin moderation, there was a fascination with human energy and striving rather different from the more consistent restraint urged in secular Chinese thought.

Fourth, the philosophical and scientific tradition emphasized the validity of logical constructs in understanding the natural world.

The characteristics of Greek philosophy were not totally distinctive, of course, and they built on some earlier features of Middle Eastern culture. Nor was the resultant cultural package uniformly successful. Greek and Hellenistic science was open to more error than the more practical sci-

entific traditions established in classical China and India. The Greek approach also tended to emphasize a significant cultural gap between the educated elite and common masses. The debates of the philosophers formed part of an aristocratic tradition closed to the ordinary folk. The absence of a strong religious link helped to separate popular beliefs and folklore from the reasoning of the creative intellectuals.

Some gap between literate and nonliterate culture was built into all the classical civilizations. But formal Greek culture was particularly uninterested in adopting popular values, which meant that there were fewer shared assumptions among various levels of Greek and Hellenistic society in terms of styles of thought, than was true in China or India. Popular and widely accessible dramatic performances and the public art of the Greek cities modified this gap. With the decline of the city-states, however, and the rise of more general Hellenistic forms in which community art played a lesser role, the cultural gaps stood out in sharper relief.

DOCUMENT
THE POWER OF GREEK DRAMA

This section consists of two passages, one by the great tragedian, Aeschylus (525–456 B.C.), and one by Athens's leading writer of comedies, Aristophanes (c. 450–385 B.C.). Aeschylus's passage, from the play *Libation Bearers*, sees Orestes confront his mother Clytemnestra after having killed her lover and suspecting that she had earlier killed his father. Clytemnestra has learned what Orestes did and knows what is to come; she asks a slave:

Clytemnestra: Swift! Bring me an axe that can slay. I will know now if I am to win or lose. I stand here on the height of misery.
[Orestes *enters with his companion* Pylades.]
Orestes: It is you I seek. The other has had his fill. You love him—you shall lie in the same grave.
Clytemnestra: Stop—oh, my son. Look—my breast. Your heavy head dropped on it and you slept, oh, many a time, and your baby mouth where never a tooth was, sucked the milk and so you grew—
Orestes: Oh, Pylades, what shall I do? My mother—Awe holds me. May I spare?
Pylades: Where then Apollo's words and the dread compact? Make all men enemies but not the gods.

Orestes: Good counsel. I obey. You—follow me. I lead you where he lies to kill you there.
Clytemnestra: It seems, my son, that you will kill your mother.
Orestes: Not I. You kill yourself.
Clytemnestra: I am alive—I stand beside my grave. I hear the song of death. [*They go out and the* Chorus *sings that her fate is just.*] Lift up your head, oh, house. I see the light.
[*The palace doors roll back.* Orestes *stands over the two dead bodies.*]
Orestes: I am blameless of the one. He died the death adulterers must die. But she who planned this thing of horror against her husband by whom she had borne beneath her girdle the burden of children—what think you of her? Snake or viper was she? Her very touch would rot a man.
Chorus: Woe—woe—Oh, fearful, deeds!
Orestes: Did she do it or did she not? The proofs you know—the deed and the death. I am victor but vile, polluted.
Chorus: One trouble is here—another comes.
Orestes: Hear me and learn, for I know how it will end. I am borne along a runaway horse. My thoughts are out of bounds. Fear at my heart is

leaping up. Before my reason goes—oh, you my friends, I say I killed my mother—yet not without reason—she was vile and she killed my father and God hated her—Look—Look—Women—there—there—Black—all black, and long hair twisting like snakes. Oh, let me go.

Chorus: What fancies trouble you, O son, faithful to your father? Do not fear.

Orestes: No fancies. My mother has sent them. They throng upon me and from their eyes blood drips, blood of hate. You see them not? I—I see them. They drive me. I cannot stay.

[He rushes out.]

Chorus: Oh, where will this frenzy of evil end.

Aristophanes' play *Plutus* mocks what he sees as the reigning values of Athens. The passage begins with a slave asking his respectable looking master why they are following a blind man:

Chremylus: I'll tell you why, straight out. Of all my slaves I know that you are the best, most constant—thief. Well—I have been a good, religious man, but always poor—no luck.

Slave: And so you have.

Chremylus: So then I want to ask—not for myself, I've pretty well shot all my arrows now—but for my son, my only son. I prayed that he might change his ways and turn into a scoundrel, wicked, rotten through and through, and so live happily ever after. The god replied, the first man I fell in with to follow.

Slave: Yes—Quite good. Of course, a blind man can see it's better nowadays to be a rotten scoundrel.

[*The man in front proves to be Wealth himself, not aware of his power because he is blind. The two others proceed to enlighten him.*]

Chremylus: Why everything there is, is just Wealth's slave. The girls, now, if a poor man comes along, will they look at him? But just let a rich one, and he can get a deal more than he wants.

Slave: Oh, not the sweet, good, modest girls. They never would ask a man for money.

Chremylus: No? What then?

Slave: Presents—the kind that cost a lot—that's all.

Chremylus: Well, all the voting's done for Wealth of course. You man our battleships. You own our army. When you're an ally, that side's sure to win. Nobody ever has enough of you. While all things else a man can have too much of—of love.

Slave: Of loaves.

Chremylus: Of literature.

Slave: Of candy.

Chremylus: Of fame.

Slave: Of figs.

Chremylus: Of manliness.

Slave: Of mutton.

Questions: What were the purposes of comedy and tragedy in classical Athens? How does Aeschylus's passage move toward a starkly tragic view? How is a truly tragic situation for a person defined? What values might an Athenian audience have had in order to enjoy a satire such as that by Aristophanes? Are the Greek ideas of comedy and tragedy suggested in the passage different from American definitions today?

HELLENISTIC CULTURE DURING AND AFTER ALEXANDER

Greek intellectual and artistic life was not a constant. Literature changed considerably between the epic style of Homer and the more controlled dramatic forms of the great Athenian playwrights of the 5th century B.C. History-writing, similarly, moved away from epic storytelling toward more analytical inquiries into the characteristics of different cultures or (with Thucydides) the causes of major developments such as the Peloponnesian War. In architecture, change was more limited, but there was a tendency to move toward more elaborate decorative motifs over time.

Inevitably, the decline of the Greek city-states and the emergence of the larger Hellenistic zone, from the 4th to the 3d centuries B.C., produced still more innovation in the Greek cultural tradition. Literature, for example, declined. Alexandria in Egypt became a dominant center of literary studies, based on a vast Greek library. Older stories and plays were preserved and analyzed, often with great intelligence. Historical information was elaborated, and historical biography came into its own. There were also many disputes, some learned and some very petty, about the principles of literary excellence. But there was little new drama produced.

Greek art and sculpture continued to dominate Hellenistic output, and the commercial wealth of the early Hellenistic kingdoms encouraged a vast amount of new building and decoration. While no new styles emerged, there was some movement toward more sentimental, emotional statuary.

Hellenistic intellectuals, in addition to their concerns with ethical systems, concentrated heavily on developing new knowledge in science and mathematics. Alexander and the Hellenistic dynasty in Egypt encouraged this work, and the expansion of cultural exchange in the Mediterranean in the Middle East also encouraged new research. Hellenistic thinkers thus preserved Greek scientific achievements and added significant new elements. Their work provided most of the scientific learning available to the Western world for almost 2000 years, and it also set a durable basis for scientific research in the Middle East and North Africa. Astronomical charts and maps improved greatly, despite the confusion about the Earth as the center of the universe. Geography also improved, and one scientist was able to calculate the circumference of the Earth within 200 miles. In biology and medicine, however, there was little advancement, beyond summing up Greek research in textbook fashion. Interest in astrology and magic in fact increased. And in general, partly because of political decline, Hellenistic science won few new achievements after the end of the third century.

Thus, along with an understanding of the main Greek-Hellenistic cultural emphases as they added up over time, a grasp of changing strengths is also essential. Hellenistic thinkers performed signal service simply in preserving Greek learning, particularly in blending it with Middle Eastern cultures and in spreading it to North Africa. In some facets, they also added important contributions of their own. Their vigor and the comprehensive art and philosophy they took over from the classical Greeks, greatly impressed the Romans as they moved into wider contacts with the Mediterranean world, just as the Hellenistic era was fading away.

ANALYSIS
DEFINING SOCIAL HISTORY

What constitutes a society, either in the past or in the present? Until fairly recently, many historians wrote as if the principal elements of the past that were worth recapturing involved formal politics—the changes in the structure of the state, the rise and fall of major political leaders and their military battles—and the generation of major new ideas. Other elements of a society's structure might be recognized. How the masses of people lived was relevant insofar as it affected taxation levels (and thus what political leaders could do), political protest, and military service. New inventions or big changes in the economic or social system, such as an increase of slavery, could figure in. But the detailed work of the historian focused on charting and explaining what the leading statesmen and intellectuals were doing.

This type of historical focus has much to recommend it. Often, the key legacies of a major time period or civilization seem to lie in its dominant political forms, artistic styles, and religious notions. In classical Greece, as we have seen, political and intellectual achievements not only commanded great attention at the time, at least in the upper classes, but also contributed most obviously to later societies after the Greek and Hellenistic ages had ended.

Yet modern historical research does not begin or end with the doings of the greatest statesmen and thinkers. A new field called *social history*, gaining momentum in the United States and elsewhere over the past 25 years, increasingly defines a wider agenda. Social historians do not deny the significance of political structures, wars, or philosophical systems, but they argue that history also consists of the doings of ordinary people and other facets of life such as family activities, death, disease, work, and leisure. For social historians, the past is much larger than was once the case. It includes many groups of actors besides the elite—women, peasants and craftsmen, and children and youth. It tries to integrate great ideas with the beliefs large numbers of people had about how the universe worked or what the good life was, and it tries to combine attention to political forms with an understanding of the social structures and problems that helped generate these forms.

Social historians do not always have an easy time fleshing out their topics. Ordinary people, for example, did not conveniently describe their beliefs for posterity the way thinkers like Aristotle or Confucius did. Particularly for early and classical civilizations, when records have been lost and most people were illiterate, it is not easy to characterize work and family values beneath the elite.

Furthermore, social history, even when based on a great deal of evidence, does not always mesh easily with the more conventional discussions of wars or the rise and fall of kings. Social historians focus on defining and explaining change, just as all historians do. But change in social history involves the advent of new processes—new work systems or new ways of treating children—not a series of major events. The social history style, in other words, and its substance differ from what many people think history is supposed to be. There are critics who continue to argue that the social history surge is a great mistake, and that what we need to know about the past is the major achievements, as conventionally defined, because these convey the only things that matter and can alone inspire our youth to greatness.

Until recently, many world histories defined their domains in terms of formal governments and intellectual history alone. One world historian leaves ordinary people out simply because, in his view, only the groups that produce major milestones are worth attending to; the supporting cast is irrelevant. Another world historian once argued that the lives of ordinary people changed little, at least during the long reign of agriculturally based civilizations, and so there is little to know about them in comparison with the obvious ups and downs of governments or artistic styles. Yet social history, for all its complexity, continues to gain ground, determining much of the subject matter of world history, for three major reasons.

First, the history of "unconventional" groups or topics helps us understand these same topics in societies today. It is just as important to have a historical perspective on women's roles, to see how they changed and varied in the past, as it is to understand the evolution of judicial systems. We comprehend current work patterns better in our own society and elsewhere if we see what they emerged from. At certain times work, women's roles, or family forms may change only gradually, even amid lively political developments. But the reverse may also be true, and there is no question that social-historical change can be charted and assessed.

Second, patterns and changes in the social history realm intimately affect the ways governments and intellectuals function, and the reverse is true as well. In classical civilizations, such as China and Greece, a substantial gulf often separated wealthy, literate aristocrats or bureaucrats and ordinary peasants or slaves. Yet governments had to be organized in such a way as to keep ordinary people contented or repressed (or contend with protest). Confucianism tried to deal with this issue; Greek city-state governments experimented almost constantly with systems that would preserve a class structure yet provide sufficient harmony for political life. Intellectuals might spin out new ideas from their own creative genius, but their ideas interacted in the long run with popular beliefs. One key way to grasp a civilization or the causes of change is to talk about how formal institutions and intellectual styles related to the masses of people and the basic structures of life.

Finally, ordinary people and the structures they were involved with could leave legacies, just as intellectual and political leaders did. Later periods or societies would thus build on earlier patterns of work, ways to treat children, or definitions of slavery.

Social history provides a means of testing the relationship between the people and their daily institutions, and the more heralded ideas and institutions of officialdom. We will see that the view of the world of a Greek slave or wife would differ substantially from that of Pericles or Aristotle. This is not just an isolated finding; it reflects a certain lack of coherence among different groups in overall Greek culture that limited the staying power of the civilization.

Among the social sciences during the past 20 years, social history has proved to be one of the most fruitful sources of new knowledge and analysis. This result is a redefinition of the past and of the kinds of questions to raise about how societies function.

Questions: What are some of the key problems of social history? What would a social historian emphasize in discussing the major features of classical Chinese civilization? Besides knowing about Greek and Hellenistic political development and intellectual styles, what else would the social historian try to pinpoint in summing up this classical civilization?

ECONOMY AND SOCIETY IN CLASSICAL GREECE

The economic and social structure of classical Greece, including the colonies it sent out around the Mediterranean, had many features in common with other agricultural civilizations. It particularly resembled other civilizations in which an invading, warlike group settled down to agriculture. Thus, while 8th-century Greece depended clearly on farming, it had an aristocracy based on ownership of large estates and special claims to military service. At the same time many farmers were independent, owning their plots of land and claiming some political and social status just as tribal soldiers had once done. But — again in a common pattern — the Greek economy evolved, particularly as trade rose and cities grew. Social structure became accordingly more complex, and inequalities widened in many ways.

There were also, however, distinctive features in the Greek pattern. Because mainland Greece was so rocky and mountainous, discouraging easy grain growing, many city-states came to depend unusually heavily on seagoing trade (and colonies). Frequent wars and colonization produced abundant opportunities to seize slaves, and classical Mediterranean society maintained greater dependence on slavery than was true of Indian or Chinese civilizations in the same period. Correspondingly, while Greece developed many craft products, somewhat less attention was paid to the improvement of manufacturing technology than either China or India displayed. This reflected Greek concern for science as a philosophical system rather than a collection of useful empirical data. It also reflected widespread slavery, which reduced the need to think about better ways to produce because many of the hardest tasks were done by cheap, coerced labor.

The pronounced aristocratic tone persisted in society as well as politics, based on the importance of the landed elite. Despite important differences among political forms, aristocratic assemblies and officials formed the most coherent single city-state theme in Greek politics. Aristocrats had the time to devote to political life as the Greeks defined it, and they argued that they brought special virtues, of education and disinterest, to the political process. Aristocratic cultural patronage also helped give shape to Mediterranean art, literature, and the education of aristocratic youth (boys above all).

The aristocratic tenor of Greek society showed in the ambiguous position of merchants. Greece progressively became involved with growing trade. Yet aristocratic suspicion of merchant values persisted, particularly among conservatives who blasted change in the name of traditional austerity. Sparta, which had unusually fertile land, tried to downplay trade altogether. The deliberately cumbersome coinage discouraged commerce, while aristocratic estate-owners concentrated on directing a semi-slave population of farm workers. Even in bustling Athens, most merchants were foreigners (mainly from the Middle East). Overall, merchants held higher status in the classical Mediterranean than in Confucian China, but their standing was less firm than in India (see Chapter 7).

RURAL LIFE AND AGRICULTURE

The bulk of the population of the Greek and Hellenistic world was rural. The agricultural base of Mediterranean society must be kept in mind even though the leading political and cultural activities occurred in cities. Rural peoples preserved distinctive rituals and beliefs. Many Greek farmers, for example, annually gathered for a spring passion play to celebrate the recovery of the goddess of fertility from the lower world, an event that was seen as a vital preparation for planting and that also carried hints of the possibility of life after death—a prospect important to many people who endured a life of hard labor and poverty. A substantial population of free farmers played a vital role in the early politics of the Greek city-states.

At the same time there was a constant tendency for large landlords to force these farmers to become tenants or laborers or to join the swelling crowds of the urban lower class. Tensions between tyrants and aristocrats, as well as between democratic reformers and aristocratic conservatives, often revolved around farmers' attempts to preserve their independence and shake off the heavy debts they had incurred. Waves of popular protest were not uncommon. Class tension was encouraged by special features of Greek agriculture. Farming was complicated by the fact that soil conditions were not ideal for grain growing, and yet grain was the staple of life. As Greek society advanced, there was a natural tendency to specialize in cash crops, which would allow importation of grain from areas more appropriate to its production—parts of the northern Middle East, Sicily, and North Africa. In mainland Greece, production of olives and grapes for cooking oil and wine making spread widely. The products were well suited to soil conditions, but they required capital to install—a five-year wait was necessary before either vines or olive trees would begin to yield significant fruit. To convert to olives and grapes, farmers went into debt and often failed; aristocratic estate owners with more abundant resources converted more successfully, buying up the land of failed farmers in the process.

Mediterranean agriculture thus became unusually market-oriented. Compared to other agricultural civilizations, relatively few farmers produced simply for their own needs, except in the early period before civilization fully developed. Imports of basic foods were more extensive here than in India or China. This was one obvious spur to empire: to try to assure access to adequate grain supplies. Greek expansion pushed out mainly toward sources of grain in Sicily and around the Black Sea.

Large estate agriculture gained further momentum in the Hellenistic kingdoms. Vast estates spread in Egypt and the Middle East, requiring specialized banks and financial agents. Elements of this capitalistic agriculture affected Mediterranean history later under both the Roman Empire and Arab rule. The system also helped generate the surpluses needed for spreading Hellenistic culture and its urban monuments.

For peasants themselves, the importance of commercial farming created an unusual tendency for farming families to cluster in small towns rather than the villages typical of other parts of Europe, Asia, and Africa. Towns of a few thousand people provided trading facilities for grain and other goods, while the peasants who lived there could still travel to the surrounding fields for work. These rural agglomerations would remain typical around the Mediterranean even after the classical period had ended and the region underwent new political and cultural divisions.

The importance of trade in basic goods dictated extensive concern with commercial arrangements, despite the ambiguous status of merchants themselves. Private merchants operated most of the ships that carried foodstuffs and other goods. But Greek governments supervised the grain trade, providing not only transportation facilities but also storage depots to try to minimize the chance of famines. Other kinds of trade were vital also. Luxury products from the shops of urban artists and craftworkers played a vital role in the life-style of the upper classes, and some commodities, such as tools and pots, were sold more widely. There also was some trade beyond the borders of the Mediterranean civilization for goods from India and China.

SLAVERY AND PRODUCTION

Slavery was another key ingredient of the classical Mediterranean economy. Philosophers, such as Aristotle, produced elaborate justifications for the necessity of slavery to a proper society, for without slaves how would aristocrats learn what must be learned to maintain culture or have the time to cultivate political virtue? Slaves were acquired as a result of wars, unusually frequent in the Mediterranean world compared to China and India. Athenians used slaves for household service and also as workers in their vast silver mines, which hastened the progress of Athens's empire and commercial operations, although working conditions were appallingly bad. Sparta used *helots*, or unfree labor, extensively for agricultural work. The Spartan system relied less on prisoners taken from war, for it was imposed by Indo-European conquerors over previous residents in the area. Of the approximately 270,000 people in 5th-century Athens 80,000 to 100,000 were slaves, while helots in Sparta outnumbered their masters by a ratio of nearly ten to one. In cities such as Athens some slaves enjoyed considerable independence and could earn money on their own. *Manumission*, or freeing, of valued slaves was also common. Yet slave systems also required extensive military controls.

Slavery also helps explain why Greece was not especially interested in technological innovations applicable to agriculture or manufacturing. The Greeks made important advances in shipbuilding and navigation, which were vital for their trading economy. But technology designed to improve production of food or manufactured goods did not figure largely in this civilization. Abundant slave labor probably discouraged concern for more efficient production methods. So did a sense that the true goals of humankind were artistic and political. One Hellenistic scholar, for example, refused to write a handbook on engineering because "the work of an engineer and everything that ministers to

the needs of life is ignoble and vulgar." As a result of this outlook, Mediterranean society lagged behind both India and China in production technology. Population growth, also, was less substantial. A host of features of Greek life, including aspects of politics, thus hinged on the slave system and its requirements.

GREEK PATRIARCHY

Greek society emphasized the importance of a tight family structure, with husband and father firmly in control. Women had vital economic functions, particularly in farming and artisan families. A woman with a powerful personality could command a major place within a household, and a free woman's responsibility for family possessions was protected by law. Socrates spent so much time teaching in the marketplace because of his wife Xantippe's sharp tongue when he was at home. But in law and culture, women were held inferior. Even the activities of free women were directed toward their husbands' interests. The raping of a free woman, though a crime, was a lesser offense than seducing her, since seduction meant winning her affections away from her husband. Families burdened with too many children sometimes put female infants to death. Pericles stated common beliefs about women when he noted, "For a woman not to show more weakness than is natural to her sex is a great glory, and not to be talked about for good or for evil among men." On the other hand, the oppression of women was probably less severe in this civilization than in China, for many Greek women were active in business and controlled a substantial minority of all urban property holdings.

Though Greek culture represented women abundantly as goddesses, often with revered powers, and celebrated the female form as well as male form in art, the real cultural status of women was low. Aristotle even argued that women provided only an abode for a child developing before birth, as male seed alone continued the full germ of the child. Marriages were arranged by a woman's father; husbands could divorce wives at will, whereas women had to go to court. Adultery was tolerated for men, but was grounds for divorce in the case of women. Even within the upper-class household, where women had vital functions including supervision of domestic slaves, men entertained in separate rooms.

HOMOSEXUALITY

Relations between men and women in Greek society, at least in the aristocracy, help explain the Greek attitude toward homosexuality. Upper-class boys and girls were often brought up separately, which increased the likelihood of homosexual relationships. While some Athenians ridiculed homosexual love, most saw love affairs between two young people of the same sex as a normal stage of life. Homosexuality was not defined as an exclusive preference, and many people in later life emphasized heterosexuality. Older men sometimes took younger men as partners, a practice which the philosopher Plato and others praised as a means of training the young in practical wisdom. Spartans stressed same-sex love as a means of inspiring heroic deeds in battle. Some contemporary psychologists have speculated that the Greeks' frank acceptance of homosexual impulses limited neurosis among adults, without conflict with substantial devotion to marriage.

SOCIAL DIVISIONS

As with many aspects of Greek culture, homosexuality was almost certainly more pronounced in the aristocracy than in other social groups. Male and female peasants and urban workers worked together and generally mingled more freely, which may have promoted greater emphasis on heterosexuality, and these groups simply lacked the time for some of the more elaborate sexual arrangements.

Other cultural divisions complicated Greek society. Peasants shared beliefs in the gods and goddesses about which the playwrights wrote, but their religious celebrations were largely separate from those of the upper classes. At times Greek peasants showed their interest in some of the more emotional religious practices imported from the Middle East, which provided more color than the official ceremonies of the Greek pantheon and spiced the demanding routines of work.

Different beliefs reflected and furthered the real social tensions of Greek and Hellenistic societies, particularly as these societies became more commercial and large estates challenged the peasant desire for independent property ownership. Popular rebellions did not succeed in dislodging the landowning aristocracy, but they contributed to a number of political shifts in classical Greece and to the ultimate decline in the political stability of the city-states and later the Hellenistic kingdoms.

Interestingly, conditions for women improved somewhat in the Hellenistic period, in an atypical trend. Artists and playwrights began to display more interest in women and their conditions. Women in Hellenistic cities appeared more freely in public, and some aristocratic women gained new functions, for example, in forming cultural clubs. A number of queens exercised great power, often ruling harshly. Cratesiclea, the mother of a Hellenistic king in Sparta, willingly served as a hostage to help form an alliance with a more powerful state; she reputedly said, "send me away, wherever you think this body of mine will be most useful to Sparta." More widely, Hellenistic women began to take an active role in commerce, though they still needed male guardianship over property.

A COMPLEX LEGACY

Classical Greece and its Hellenistic successors lasted for about 600 years. While major political and social changes took place during this span, some durable characteristics also developed. Durability resulted from the power of key cultural forms, the settled routines of the peasants, and the absence of major technological shifts.

Yet the legacy of classical Greece and Hellenism was complicated by the shifts in location and by the recurrent changes in political forms. Hellenism left an important mark, particularly in science and philosophy, that provided a new audience for some of the institutions and values first pioneered in Greece, but also brought important new emphases. Later, the Roman Empire would reshape the boundaries of the Mediterranean world yet again, while adding additional new themes. The legacy of the classical Mediterranean was comparable to that of China or India, but the sequence of its achievements must be traced with care.

The Greek and Hellenistic patterns formed an important variant on general features of classical civilizations after 800 B.C. Integration of a large region into a common system was not based primarily on large empires, despite Athens's expansion and Alexander's massive conquests. Rather, the Greek and Hellenistic zones depended largely on the spread of particular cultural forms in language, art, monuments, science, and philosophy, and on the trading network essential for exchange of grain for processed goods.

The Greek legacy was primarily cultural as well. When Romans or subsequent civilizations looked back to Greece, they looked to styles and ideas, sometimes embellished by some historical sense of how Greek politics operated. Thus definitions of political life, including constitutional forms such as democracy and ideas such as citizenship, were amply preserved and recurrently revived. Specific institutions, such as the Athenian assembly or the Spartan dual monarchy, died with classical Greece—again in contrast to China where institutional continuities combined with cultural heritage between the classical centuries and later ages. Yet Greek culture also had a vivid power in its compelling mode of comprehending and representing nature.

Classical Greece also developed an interesting tension between its compelling culture and the lives and beliefs of ordinary people in its orbit—women, slaves, merchants, and farmers. Aspects of the culture, like aspects of politics, were rather open. A useful, public art was designed to be experienced by all sorts of urban groups as part of their daily lives. Dramatic productions drew substantial audiences from various classes and included women as well as men. At the same time the most intense cultural life was reserved for aristocratic men, and key philosophical principles were not widely disseminated. Popular religion and some popular rituals remained distinct in many ways, which was another reason that the Greek achievement survived incompletely. Here, interesting contrasts developed with the final center of classical civilization in India, where the cohesion of the civilization also rested heavily on the culture—but a much more religious culture. Despite a rigid social hierarchy, India was in some ways more successful than Greece in developing a sufficiently flexible and diverse culture in which a variety of groups could participate.

FURTHER READINGS

Two good surveys on classical Greece are K. Dover's *The Greeks* (1981) and F. J. Frost's *Greek Society* (1980), both with recent bibliographies. An older study on Greek culture is extremely solid: H. D. F. Kitto's *The Greeks* (1957). On Hellenism, M. M. Austin's *The Hellenistic World from Alexander to the Roman Conquest* (1981) is an excellent introduction.

Works on key special topics are M. Crawford and D. Whitehead's *Archaic and Classical Greece* (1983); A. R. Burn's *Persia and the Greeks* (1962); and M. M. Austin and P. Vidal-Naquet's *Economic and Social History of Ancient Greece* (1978). On Greek intellectual life, see W. Burkert's *Greek Religions* (1985) and G. E. R. Lloyd's *The Revolutions of Wisdom: Studies in the Claims and Practices of Ancient Greek Science* (1987). Particular features of Greek society are treated in Moses Finley's *Slavery in the Ancient World* (1972), an exciting study, and Sarah Pomeroy's *Goddesses, Whores, Wives, and Slaves: Women in Classical Antiquity* (1975).

An excellent way to approach Greek history is through documents from the period itself. See Herodotus's *The Histories* (trans. de Selincourt) (1972) and M. Crawford, ed., *Sources for Ancient History* (1983).

1600–1000 Period of Aryan invasions   700–c. 550 Era of unrivalled Brahman dominance   322–185 Reign of the Mauryan Empire

1200–700 Sacred Vedas composed   322–298 Chandragupta Maurya rules

c. 542–483 Life of the Buddha

327–325 Alexander the Great's invasion

c. 1500 Fall of Harappan civilization

7

Religious Rivalries and India's Golden Age

INTRODUCTION. The development of a new civilization in India after the long period of disruption following Harappa's fall around 1500 B.C. completed—along with those in China and the Mediterranean—the basic roster of classical civilizations that arose after 1000 B.C. The new foundations for this civilization were laid between 1500 and 500 B.C. by the nomadic Aryan invaders who were moving into India during the centuries when Harappa collapsed. By the end of this period, fairly large states, ruled by kings who claimed divine descent, controlled much of the fertile farmland that made up the Ganges River plains. Cities had developed, originally around the palaces of these monarchs and later at the sites of important religious shrines and regional market centers. A rich and increasingly influential merchant class joined the Aryan priests and warriors at the top of the Indian social hierarchy.

Ritual divisions and restrictions on intermarriage between these three groups grew more rigid as the increasingly complex caste hierarchy became a pervasive force in Indian life. Above all, the Vedic priests, or brahmans, emerged as the dominant force in Indian society and culture. Their literacy and the magical aura that surrounded the vital ceremonies they performed rendered them the makers and chief advisors of kings, the dispensers of the blessings (or curses) of the gods, and the most revered and privileged of India's elite social groups.

Even as the brahmans' power peaked, however, forces were building in Indian society that threatened to alter fundamentally the course of civilized development in South Asia. Weary of the empty rituals associated with sacrifices to the gods and the power seeking and materialism of the priestly class, numerous holy men and religious seers had arisen by the 6th century B.C. From these holy men a number of major religious thinkers emerged who sought to discover and propagate more meaningful forms of religious belief and worship.

170–165 Yueh-chih invasions   **1–105** Kushana empire in the northwest   **319–540** Gupta Empire

268–237 Ashoka is emperor of India

405 Fa-hsien's (Fa-xian's) pilgrimage

200 B.C.–A.D. 200 Period of greatest Buddhist influence

451 First Hun invasions

c. 150 Indo-Greek invasions

c. 300 Kautilya's *Arthashastra* is written

606–647 Harsha's empire

| 300 B.C. | 100 B.C. | A.D. 100 | A.D. 300 |

The most successful of these thinkers, the Buddha, founded one of the great world religions, a religion that for centuries provided a powerful challenge to the brahmans and many of the ancient Vedic beliefs and practices. The rivalry that developed between the followers of the Buddha and the brahmans helped define and reshape India's cultural core. The brahmans defended and reinvigorated the ancient Vedic rites and beliefs, and, drawing heavily on these beliefs, they promoted the growth of the religion we know as Hinduism. By the first centuries A.D., it was clear that a revived Hinduism had survived the Buddhist challenge. Though Buddhism would remain an important force in many parts of India for another millennium, it would eventually all but die out in the land of its birth.

The Buddha's teachings also contributed to the establishment of India's first genuine empire. Beginning in the late 4th century B.C., the rulers of a local dynasty in eastern India, the Maurya, began to build what would become the largest empire in premodern India. The most successful of the Mauryan monarchs, Ashoka (268–232 B.C.), converted to Buddhism and then sought to govern according to Buddhist precepts and to spread the religion to neighboring parts of Asia. The Mauryan Empire proved to be short-lived, however. When it collapsed it was then followed by another round of nomadic invasions through the Himalaya passes in the northwest, and the subcontinent was again fragmented politically. Many of the dynasties that followed the Mauryas dedicated themselves to the promotion of either Buddhism or the brahman counteroffensive. But in the early 4th century A.D., there arose in north India a powerful new dynasty, the Gupta, that was firmly committed to the reassertion of the brahmans' dominance.

The Gupta rulers' patronage of Hinduism reaffirmed the position of the brahmans as high priests and political advisors and led to an age of splendid Hindu achievement in architecture, painting, and sculpture as well as philosophy, literature, and the sciences. The Gupta Empire was considerably smaller than that established by the Mauryas, and the dynasty did not rule a good deal longer. But the ideas and institutions that were solidified during the Gupta era gave Indian civilization the strength and resilience to withstand the shock of a yet another round of foreign invasions, beginning with the ravages of the Huns in the first half of the 6th century A.D.

This overview of the critical millennium of Indian history between c. 500 B.C. and A.D. 500 suggests a number of underlying patterns. One of the most critical of these patterns is the predominance in Indian history of political disunity and the short life of even the most powerful Indian empires and dynasties. In contrast to China, where unity was the norm and disunity viewed as unnatural and harmful, India has been divided into rival kingdoms throughout most of its history. This has meant that regional cultural diversity and local identities have been more pronounced in India than in China. In fact, the very name India and the idea of the continent as a single political unit did not exist until foreign rulers, the British, conceived them in the 19th century A.D.

Also in contrast to China, where scholar-bureaucrats and strong states were the mainstays of civilization, the brahmans and social institutions, such as the caste system, have been the key to the remarkable persistence of civilization in India. Rather than vanquish the brahmans and destroy the caste system, foreign invaders have frequently been converted by them and have established themselves as warrior-kings near the top of the caste hierarchy. Thus, despite periodic foreign invasions and persistent political divisions, common religious ideas and distinctive forms of social organization have provided the basis for an underlying unity for most of the diverse ethnic groups of South Asia, from Vedic times to the present. Religion and social organization held together Indian civilization durably but more loosely than political culture united China. Here, processes of regional integration in India common to all the classical civilizations were at work through most of the subcontinent, though in distinctive fashion.

THE AGE OF BRAHMAN DOMINANCE

The forces that made for the renewal of civilization in South Asia after the fall of Harappa were initially centered, not on the great plains of the Ganges and Indus river systems, but in the foothills of the Himalaya mountains. Tribes of Aryan warrior-herders settled in the lush valleys of the cool hills. The hills provided abundant pasturage for their herds of horses and cattle, and the wooded valleys were easier to clear for farming than the jungle-covered plains along the Ganges and its tributaries. In the hill regions, single Aryan tribes or confederations of tribal groups developed small states—in many ways similar to those in Homeric Greece—that were based on a combination of sedentary agriculture and livestock breeding. The territory of most of these states extended no farther than the hills surrounding a single large valley or several adjoining valley systems. Most of the states were republics ruled collectively by a council made up of the free warrior elite. Individual leaders were usually called kings, even though their offices and powers more closely resembled those of tribal chieftains. They were elected or removed from office by a vote of the warriors' councils.

The hill republics provided an environment well-suited to the preservation of traditional Aryan values and life-styles. Wars between the numerous hill states were frequent, as were feuds and cattle raids. Thus, the warrior elites were kept busy at pastimes that brought them both wealth and honor. The republics nurtured the spirit of independence that had been strong among the invading Aryan tribes and hostility toward those who sought to concentrate political authority in the hands of a single ruler.

The warrior elites were also careful to keep the power of the brahmans in check, and the hill cultures fostered a healthy skepticism with regard to the priests and the gods they worshipped. One early hymn reported, for example, that "One and another say, There is no Indra [the god of thunder and war]. Who hath beheld him? Whom then shall we honor?" In another hymn the brahmans, chanting their prayers, are compared to croaking frogs gathered about a pond in the rainy season. Given these trends, it is not surprising that the hill regions were major centers of religious ferment from the 6th century B.C. onward. Perhaps the greatest religious reformer of all time, the Buddha, was from one of these republics, as were the founders of a number of other, less well-known Indian religions, such as Jainism.

THE KINGDOMS OF THE GANGES PLAINS

As Aryan settlement spread in the last millennium B.C. from the Indus region and Himalaya foothills to vast plains of the Ganges River system, republics and religious skeptics gave way to kings and powerful brahman priests. It is possible that the large amounts of labor and higher degree of organization required to clear the heavy jungle growth and build irrigation networks in the low-lying plains were key factors in the development of more centralized and authoritarian states in the Ganges region. The communications links provided by the Ganges and its tributaries, and the greater ease with which armies could move across the plains (once they were cleared of forest cover), may also help to explain why larger states, ruled by kings rather than warrior councils, developed across much of north-central and eastern India. Though these regions eventually became the heartlands of great empires, in the middle centuries of the last millennium B.C. they were divided into a patchwork of rival kingdoms.

Kings in the lowlands were often drawn from the warrior elite, but they ruled in their own right rather than due to their selection by warrior councils. Excepting their influential brahman advisors, there were no formal checks on the power and authority of the kings. Many kings claimed descent from divine ancestors, and their thrones were normally inherited by their sons. All considered themselves the supreme war leaders, chief judges, and protectors of the peoples in their domains. As these roles suggest, the powers and privileges these kings enjoyed were justified by the duties they performed. The great epic the *Ramayana* and other sources from this period stress the duties and obligations of righteous monarchs. They were expected to protect the realm from outside invaders and internal social conflicts. They were instructed to revere the brahmans and follow their advice, to patronize public works, and to rule in ways that promoted the welfare of their people. Ideally, Vedic kings were supposed to be hardworking, honest, and accessible to their most lowly subjects. There are even passages in the ancient texts that justify the violent overthrow of evil rulers.

It is highly unlikely that monarchs who lived up to all these high ideals would have long survived the court intrigues and the assaults of rival rulers that were commonplace in the Vedic era. In fact, the sources from this period suggest a darker side to kingship that may have been closer to the realities of the age. Kings lived in constant fear for their thrones and lives. They were threatened by both internal rivals, including their own sons, and neighboring monarchs who periodically tested their strength in battle. A ruler's survival depended on the extensive use of spies and informers, a strong and loyal palace guard, and his courage and skills as a military commander.

Interstate rivalries were formalized in the horse sacrifice, which involved the release of a strong horse that was followed by the king and his armies wherever it roamed. If the horse crossed into neighboring realms, the king in pursuit claimed them as his own. If the rulers of the lands claimed could not defeat the forces of the king performing the sacrifice, their kingdoms were annexed in a ceremony in which the horse was sacrificed to the gods. These practices help to explain more fully why most dynasties and kingdoms in this era were short-lived and why the power of the Aryan warrior elite was rivaled only by that of the brahmans who consecrated kings and then served as their main advisors.

SOURCES OF BRAHMAN POWER

Though most of the rulers of the kingdoms on the Ganges plains were members of the warrior elite, brahmans residing at the court centers often exercised more real power. Their positions as the educators of the princes who would someday rule and as the chief advisors to the rulers themselves naturally made them influential figures in the ruling circles. Like the scholar-gentry in China, their literacy in a society where few could read or write made the brahmans obvious candidates for administrative positions, from heads of bureaucratic departments to judges and tax collectors. In addition, only the brahmans knew how to perform the sacred rituals that were essential to the coronation of a new king. They alone knew the rites that conferred divine status on a monarch, and without divine status a ruler's legitimacy was in doubt. Once the ruler was installed, brahman astrologers foretold his future and regulated his daily schedule, instructing him when to make war or mate with his wives.

As the brahmans' pivotal role in court ceremonies and prophecy indicates, their positions of power and prestige were linked above all to their capacity to mediate between the gods and humans. The key function of the priests of the early Aryan invaders was to offer sacrifices to the gods and spirits who intervened continuously in human affairs. By the 7th and 6th centuries B.C., the sacrifices themselves had in a very real sense become more powerful than the gods to which they were offered. By this time it was widely believed that if the sacrifice was done correctly, the god to whom it was directed had no choice but to grant the wish of the petitioner for whom the brahmans had performed the ceremony. Thus, a king could ensure victory, a peasant village sufficient rainfall, or a barren woman fertility if the proper ceremony was conducted flawlessly. Only the brahmans were capable of performing the ceremony and allowed to read the sacred Vedic texts where the prayers and instructions for various types of sacrifices were set forth. Only they had memorized the steps of the sacrificial rituals and mastered the techniques of preparing the sacrificial offerings correctly. Their monopoly over the sacred rites ensured that brahmans would be honored and feared, even by the strongest of warrior-kings.

Only a small percentage of the brahmans in a given kingdom served as advisors at the court or as state administrators. Many were the personal priests or physicians of wealthy high-caste families; most were village priests, schoolteachers, and wandering ascetics. Some were alchemists and sorcerers, and even downright charlatans, living off the gullibility of the masses who believed in their ability to tell fortunes and turn magic spells to good and evil purposes. But all brahmans from the palaces of kings to the most remote villages were privileged beings, exempt from taxes and protected from bodily injury by the harsh punishments meted out to those who dared to assault them.

As the following passage from one of the ancient Vedas makes clear, not even kings were considered exempt from the horrible fate that befell those who did injury to a brahman.

> Whenever a king, fancying himself mighty,
> seeks to devour a Brahman, [his] kingdom is broken up. . . .
> [Ruin] overflows that kingdom as water swamps a leaky boat;
> calamity smites that country in which a priest is wronged.
> Even trees . . . repel, and refuse their shade to, the man who claims a right to the property of a Brahman.

AN ERA OF WIDESPREAD SOCIAL CHANGE

The rise of kings and increasing brahman dominance were only two of the many social changes that occurred as full civilization took shape for the second time in Indian history. Around the court centers of the lowland kings, towns grew up as servant, artisan, and merchant groups sought to cater to the needs of the rulers, their courtiers, and often large numbers of brahman advisors and administrators. Along the Ganges and other rivers, towns developed that were mainly trading centers or devoted to the specialized manufacture of key products such as pottery, tools, and cotton textiles. With the increase in commerce and specialized production, merchants and artisans became established as distinctive social groups. The great wealth amassed by the larger trading houses allowed the merchants to win a prominent place in the Indian social hierarchy, which became both more complex and more rigid in this era.

Another social stratum that assumed major importance in this period was the peasantry. As farming supplanted herding as the basis for the economies of the lowland kingdoms, peasants came to make up a large percentage of India's population. Mud-walled farming villages spread across the plains of northern India, though throughout the classical era they continued to be dwarfed in most places by massive primeval rain forests. Irrigation networks and new agricultural tools steadily increased productivity and hence the capacity of the peasants to support ever larger numbers of nonfarming specialists. Most peasants grew staples such as rice, millet, and wheat, but some villages specialized in cotton, plants for dyes such as indigo, and luxury crops such as sugar cane. Though presumably eager to market

This artist's recreation (based on classical Indian stone sculptures) depicts an Indian city from the 2d or 1st century B.C. Like many of the larger Indian towns, the one depicted has walls and a moat, and most of its buildings are constructed of intricately carved wood.

their surplus or specialized crops, the peasants only grudgingly paid the tribute demanded by the tax collectors of the lowland monarchs. If a ruler was weak and his court in disarray, it is likely that the peasants paid nothing at all.

THE CASTE SYSTEM

The tripartite class division in India between warriors, priests, and commoners that made up the tribal social order of the early Aryan invaders had altered radically over the centuries. New social groups, such as merchants and peasants, were added to these broad social categories (varna) and each was subdivided into occupational subgroups, or *castes*. Broad categories and occupational subgroups were arranged in a hierarchical pyramid based on the degree to which the tasks they performed were considered polluting. Those who dealt with human waste or slaughtered animals, for example, were regarded as extremely defiling, while scholars and wandering holy men who eschewed physical labor and refused to eat animal flesh were revered for their purity.

At the top of the pyramid were the brahman, warrior, and merchant castes whose members made up only a small minority of the total population. The bulk of the population belonged to peasant and artisan castes, which made up most of the central and lower layers of the caste pyramid. Beneath the peasants and artisans were the untouchables, who performed the most despised tasks in Indian society, including removing human waste from towns and villages, street sweeping, and the tanning of leather hides. The Indians' reverence for cows, which may have been present in Harappan society, and their aversion to dead animals rendered the latter occupation particularly polluting. Even the untouchables were divided into caste subgroups, with sweepers looking down upon manure handlers, and they in turn despising leatherworkers.

Over the centuries, the boundaries between caste groups hardened. In addition to occupation, a caste's position in the Indian social hierarchy was distinguished by its diet and the caste groups with which its members could dine or exchange different kinds of food. A caste's status also determined the social groups with which it was allowed to intermarry and whether or not it was permitted to read the Vedas. Only members of castes belonging to the three highest varnas (brahmans, warriors, and merchants) were allowed to read the texts. Rama, perhaps the greatest of Indian cultural heroes, was celebrated in the *Ramayana* for cutting off the head of a peasant holy man who presumed to recite hymns from the Vedas while hanging upside down from a tree.

A person was born into a caste group and could not change his or her caste status. Over considerable periods of time, a caste group could collectively rise or fall in status, but individuals were tied to the fortunes of their caste as a whole. An individual's refusal to accept the duties and status associated with the caste into which he or she was born could lead to beatings and other forms of physical abuse. If the rebellious individual continued to violate caste laws, he or she would be ostracized or quite literally outcast. This penalty normally meant certain death because no one, including members of their own family, was allowed to pay them for labor or offer them food, drink, or other services.

In addition to physical punishment and local sanctions, the caste system was upheld by Indian rulers and the belief that it was supernaturally ordained. One of the chief duties of a righteous monarch was to preserve the caste hierarchy and see to it that persons at each level carried out the tasks and behaved in the manner appropriate to those at that rank. Ideally, the caste system was to provide for a harmonious exchange of products and services at all levels of Indian society. Peasants, for example, provided food for the brahmans, who saw to their religious and ritual needs, and for the warriors, who defended them from bandits and foreign invaders. In reality, high-caste groups, particularly brahmans and warriors, enjoyed a disproportionate share of wealth and power. But except in times of severe natural calamity or social crisis, even the lowliest of untouchables was guaranteed a livelihood, however meager.

In classical Indian texts the creation of the caste system is depicted as the work of the gods. Different sorts of humans were created to perform different sorts of tasks and were allotted varying degrees of status and honor. The caste position and career determined by a person's birth was called one's *dharma*. The concept of transmigration of the soul helped to explain why some were given the enviable dharma of a brahman, while others were consigned to the lowly status of an untouchable tanner. In the Vedic era, the notion was widely accepted that a person's soul existed through many human lives and was transferred from one body to another after death. In each of its lives, the soul accumulated varying amounts of merit and demerit, depending on the actions of the person in whose body it dwelled. The sum of these merits and demerits at any given point in time made up one's *karma*. An individual's karma in turn determined the sort of person that soul would be attached to in its next reincarnation. Thus, a person who was born as a brahman possessed a soul that had built up a large surplus of merit; a person born as a sweeper was paying the penalty for the sins of his or her past lives.

One of the greatest sins was to violate one's dharma, to refuse the duties and status attached to the caste into which one was born. The only way to ensure a better situation in the next rebirth was to accept one's situation in the present and fully perform the tasks one was allotted. Thus, the concepts of the transmigration of the soul and reincarnation provided both an explanation for the inequities of the caste system and a religious rationale for an individual's acceptance of his or her place in the caste hierarchy.

ANALYSIS
INEQUALITY AS THE SOCIAL NORM

The Indian caste system is perhaps the most extreme expression of a mode of social organization that violates the most basic principles on which modern Western societies are based. Like the Egyptian division between a noble and a commoner and the Greek division between a freeperson and a slave, the caste system rests on the assumption that humans are inherently unequal and that their lot in life is determined by the family and social strata into which they are born. The caste system, like the social systems of all other classical civilizations, presumed that social divisions were relatively fixed and stable and that individuals ought to be content with the station they had been allotted at birth. Furthermore, all classical social systems (with the partial exception of the Greeks, at least in Athens) played down the importance of the individual and stressed the primacy of collective obligations and loyalties that were centered in the family, extended kin groups, or broader occupational or social groupings. One's family or caste affiliation, not one's individual ambition, determined a person's career goals and activities.

All of these assumptions, of course, directly contradict some of our most cherished beliefs. They run counter to the most basic organizing principles of modern Western culture that are rooted in a commitment to equality of opportunity. This principle is enshrined in our constitutions and legal systems, taught in our schools and churches, and proclaimed in our media from literature to television. The belief in human equality, or at least equality of opportunity, has also been one of the most important ideas that modern Western civilization has exported to the peoples of Africa, Asia, and Latin America.

The notion of equality rests on two assumptions. The first is that a person's place in society should be determined not by the class or family into which he or she is born but by personal abilities and hard work. The second is that the opportunity to rise—or fall—in social status should be open to everyone and protected by law. Some of our most cherished myths reflect these assumptions: that anyone can aspire to be president of the United States, for example, or that an ordinary person has the right to challenge the actions of the politically and economically powerful.

Of course, equality is a social ideal rather than something any human society has achieved. No one pretends that all humans are equal in intelligence or talent, and in fact there are important barriers to equality of opportunity. But the belief persists that all humans should have an equal chance to better themselves by making use of the brains and skills they have. In the real world, race, class, and gender differences have often favored some individuals over others, and laws and government agencies have often not corrected these inequities. But the citizens of modern Western societies, and increasingly the rest of the world, champion the principles of equality of opportunity and the potential for social mobility as the just and natural bases for social organization and interaction.

What is just and natural for modern societies, however, would have been incomprehensible to the peoples of the classical age. In fact, most human societies through most of human history have been organized on assumptions that are much closer to those underlying the Indian caste system than those we assume to be the norm. Ancient Egyptians or Greeks, or for that matter medieval Europeans or early modern Chinese, believed that career possibilities, political power, and social privileges should be set by law according to the position of one's family in the social hierarchy. The Indian caste structure was the most rigid and complex of the systems by which occupations, resources, and status were allotted. But all classical civilizations had similar social mechanisms to determine the obligations and prerogatives of members of each social stratum from the aristocracy to the slaves.

In some ways classical Chinese and Greek societies provided exceptions to these general patterns. In China, individuals from lowly social origins could rise to positions of great status and power, and well-placed families could fall on hard times and lose their gentry status. But "rags to riches" success stories were the exception rather than the rule, and mobility between different social strata was lim-

ited even in the best of times. In fact, Chinese thinkers made much of the distinctions between the scholar-gentry elite and the common people. Though some of the Greeks, particularly the Athenians, developed the idea of equality for all citizens in a particular city-state, the great majority of the populations of their societies were not citizens, and many were slaves. By virtue of their birth the latter were assigned lives of servitude and physical drudgery. Democratic participation and the chance to make full use of their talents were confined only to the freemen of the city-states.

In virtually all societies these fixed social hierarchies were upheld by creation myths and religious beliefs that proclaimed their divine origins and the dangers of supernatural retribution if they were challenged or altered. Elite thinkers stressed the importance of the established social order to human peace and well-being; rulers were duty bound to defend it with all the force at their disposal. Few challenged the naturalness of the hierarchy itself; fewer still proposed alternatives to it. Each individual was expected to accept his or her place and concentrate on the duties and obligations that his or her place required, rather than worry about their rights or personal desires. Male and female were required to subordinate their individual yearnings and talents to the needs of their families, clans, communities, or social superiors. In return for a person's acceptance of his or her allotted place in the hierarchy, he or she received material sustenance and a social slot. These, of course, were denied to those people who fought the system. They were outcast or exiled, physically punished, imprisoned or killed.

Thus, the social organization of most societies has contradicted the ideals that we take for granted. Most of humankind has accepted inequality as natural; birth as the prime determinant of social standing and ambition; and fixed social hierarchies with low degrees of mobility.

Questions: What sorts of arguments did the thinkers of the classical civilizations of Greece, China, and India use to explain and justify the great differences in social status and material wealth that existed? Why did the vast majority of persons who lived in these societies, including oppressed groups such as slaves and untouchables, accept these divisions? In what ways were the fixed hierarchies and the idea of little or no social mobility modified in ancient Greece and China? Comparing this mode of social organization to the ideal in your own society, what do you see as the advantages and drawbacks of each? Are real social inequalities as different from classical systems as beliefs about social justice are?

THE FAMILY AND THE CHANGING
STATUS OF WOMEN

Some of our best insights into family life and gender relationships in this era are provided by the two great Indian epics, the *Mahabharata* and the *Ramayana*. Though these tales of war and princely honor, love and social duty were not written down until the last centuries B.C., they were related in oral form long before. They suggest that by the middle centuries of the last millennium B.C., the extended family was increasingly regarded as the ideal. Those who could support the large household that extended family arrangements required, which normally meant only the highest caste groups, gathered all the male members of a given family and their wives and children under the same roof. At times up to four generations, from great-grandfathers and mothers to great-grandsons and daughters, lived together in the same dwelling or family compound.

Though these arrangements restricted individual privacy and often led to family quarrels, they also provided a high degree of security and human companionship. Lower-caste groups from the peasants and artisans rarely possessed the wealth required to support extended households. As a consequence, the great majority of Indian families were nuclear, or made up of parents and their children with perhaps a widowed grandparent sharing their dwelling.

Somewhat contradictory visions of the positions and roles of women emerge from the epics, which suggest that attitudes toward women may have been in flux. On the one hand, women are seen as weak, passionate, frivolous, and fond of gossip and slander. Female demons in the *Ramayana* take on the roles of jealous temptresses and vengeful jilted lovers. Within the family, women remain clearly subordinated to men. Though youths are charged to obey and honor their mothers, parental veneration is focused on the father to whom complete obedience and loyalty are expected. Wives are instructed to be attentive to their husbands' needs and be ready to obey their every command. Rama's wife Sita is chosen for her physical beauty and absolute devotion to her husband. When he is forced into exile in the forest, she follows without question or complaint. When she is carried off to Sri Lanka by the demon Ravanna, Rama races to defend her honor and his own. Having rescued her after a mighty battle with Ravanna and his evil minions, Rama then refuses to take her back because he suspects that she may have been raped while in captivity. Only when she proves her virtue by walking unscathed through a fire will he accept her again as his wife. Throughout both epics, the fate of women is controlled by men, be they gods, demons, or mortal humans.

In places in the epics, on the other hand (and in other sources from this period), there are indications that in some ways women had greater freedom and opportunities for self-expression than was the case by the last centuries B.C. Women in the epics are often depicted as strong-willed and cunning. Sita and Draupadi, two of the wives of the five Pandava brothers who are the heroes of the *Mahabharata*, display remarkable courage and strength of character at various points in their respective ordeals. Contemporary sources mention women who were renowned scholars of the sacred Vedic texts, which they later would not even be permitted to read. Women in this era also made their mark as teachers, poets, musicians, and artists, though the last two activities were not highly esteemed. Like their brothers, girls from high-caste families were allowed to undergo the special ceremonies that celebrated their twice-born or exalted status—an honor boys continued to enjoy but which gradually died out for young women. Women were even famed for their skills in the martial arts, as the amazon (female warrior) palace guards of a number of monarchs demonstrated.

THE END OF AN ERA

Roughly 1000 years after the first Aryan tribes entered India a new civilization had come into being that was very different from the Harappan complex it had replaced. Sedentary agriculture was well-established and productive enough to support a variety of specialized elites, true cities, extensive trade, and nonagrarian artisan manufacturers. In the caste system, the Indians had developed perhaps the most complex system of social stratification and labor division known to human history. They had also made notable accomplishments in philosophy and religious speculation, invention, and artistic creativity, though most of the art works were done in wood and thus have perished over time. But these considerable achievements pale in comparison with what was about to occur in the final centuries B.C. The unchallenged and increasingly self-serving dominance of the brahmans, the endless succession of petty wars between the kings they advised, and the religious bankruptcy displayed by the excesses of the sacrificial cults all prompted major challenges. These challenges and the brahman responses to them would both remake and enrich Indian civilization in the millennium before and after the birth of Christ.

Even before these late-classical developments, some of the persisting features of Indian civilization were in place. The rigid social structure of the caste system guided behavior and provided stability and a sense of order for social relationships, amid the political divisions and frequent wars of the multitude of regional kingdoms. Duty to one's caste, much more than state loyalties, guided classical Indian civilization, in contrast to the greater stress on political allegiances in China and Greece. Religious beliefs and practices provided powerful buttresses for the social system. These were exercised both through the power of the brahmans and through the ethical prescriptions and regulations found in the sacred Vedic texts. These texts were orally compiled and systematically transmitted by the brahman priests between 1200 and 900 B.C. In the last centuries B.C., the Vedas were written in the Sanskrit language, which thereafter became the standard and scholarly language of India, akin to Greek and Latin in the West. From the chants and ritual formulas of the early Vedas, the texts were increasingly devoted to religious and philosophical speculation and moral prescriptions for the faithful. This highly religious culture provided the context for further changes, as Indian civilization moved to even greater complexity.

RELIGIOUS FERMENT AND THE RISE OF BUDDHISM

The 6th and 5th centuries B.C. were a time of great social turmoil and philosophical speculation throughout Eurasia. In China, Confucius and Laozi proposed very different views of the proper organization of human society and purposes of life. In Persia, Zoroaster founded a new religion, while the prophets Ezekiel and Isaiah strove to improve the Hebrews' understanding of the intentions of their single, almighty God. In Greece, the writings of Thales and Pythagorous laid the basis for unprecedented advances in philosophy, the sciences, and mathematics. India too was caught up in this transcontinental trend of social experimentation and intellectual probing.

Indian reformers questioned the brahmans' dominance and the efficacy of the sacrifices on which it ultimately rested. They sought to find alternatives to the caste system as the basis for India's social order. They posed questions about the nature of the universe and ends of life that the Vedic thinkers had debated for centuries, and often came up with very different answers. Some experimented with new techniques of meditation and self-mortification; others sought to establish new religions that would free the masses from what were viewed as the oppressive teachings of the brahmans. One holy man and thinker, the Buddha, did all of these things and in the process made the most influential religious and philosophical breakthroughs of an age of remarkable intellectual ferment. Though Zoroaster trans-

formed Persian thinking and Confucius proclaimed an ethical system that was adopted in China and neighboring lands, the Buddha founded a religion that became a key ingredient in the life of civilized peoples throughout most of Asia.

THE MAKING OF A HOLY MAN

Accounts of the Buddha's life are so cluttered with myths and miracles that it is difficult to know what kind of man he actually was and what sort of message he originally preached. We are fairly certain, however, that he lived from the middle of the 6th century to the second decade of the 5th century B.C. He was born into one of the warrior clans of the hill states south of the Himalayas, where as we have seen the rule of kings and the hold of the brahmans was weak. Buddhist traditions relate that he was the son of the local ruler who was haunted by a prophecy made by a holy man at the time of the Buddha's birth. The holy man predicted that the child would someday become a wandering ascetic like himself, thus refusing his father's throne.

To prevent this, the king confined his son to the palace grounds and provided him with every imaginable human pleasure and comfort. But as he approached manhood, the prince grew curious about the world beyond the palace gardens and walls. With the aid of a trusted servant, the Buddha ventured forth into the nearby countryside where he encountered for the first time illness, old age, death, and an ascetic. Unsettled by these encounters with human suffering, the prince became moody and withdrawn. Finally, as the holy man had predicted, he renounced all claims to succeed his father as king and set off with a group of wandering ascetics to meditate and ponder the many questions his discoveries beyond the palace walls had posed.

FROM HOLY MAN TO TEACHER

In the wilderness, the Buddha experimented with the many ways Indian holy men had devised to reach a higher understanding of the nature of humanity and the supernatural world. He did yogic exercises, fasted almost to death, chanted sacred prayers for days on end, and conversed with every seer he encountered. Discouraged by his failure to find the answer to the questions that had driven him to take up the life of a wandering ascetic and exhausted by the self-punishment he had inflicted, the Buddha collapsed, legend has it, under a huge bo tree. Saved from death by the care of a young girl who took pity on him, the Buddha turned to meditation in his search for understanding. Ultimately, by disciplining his mind and body, he achieved en-

This beautifully detailed sandstone statue of the enlightened Buddha meditating in a standing position was carved in the 5th century A.D. Note the nimbus or halo—which was commonly employed in later Buddhist iconography—as well as the calm and composure radiated by the Buddha's facial expression.

lightenment, which rested on his discovery of what Buddhists came to call the Four Noble Truths.

The central issue for the Buddha was the problem of suffering, which he believed all living things experienced because all living things and the objects to which they are attached are impermanent. The moment we are born we begin to die, he reasoned. Persons one loves or befriends may turn indifferent or hostile or simply move away; love and friendship are inevitably ended by death. The goals to which humans devote their lives, such as fame and wealth, are empty and once attained can easily be lost. These attachments to the illusory and impermanent things of the world are the source of suffering; one can escape suffering only by ceasing to desire the things of the world and realizing that even one's sense of self is part of the illusion. This realization or enlightenment can be achieved by following the eight-step process of right action, thinking, and meditation. Once enlightenment has been attained, the individual is released from suffering because he or she is free from desire and attachment. He or she has attained *nirvana*—not heaven in the Christian sense, but simply a state of tranquility.

Having attained enlightenment, the Buddha, due to his great compassion for all living creatures, sought to spread his message to all humanity (and, Buddhist legends relate, to the creatures of the forest as well). He became the most successful of the numerous holy men who traveled through the hill and lowland kingdoms in this era, challenging the teachings of the brahmans and offering alternative modes of worship and paths to salvation. The Buddha soon gained a considerable following that ranged from exalted monarchs to humble sweepers, and included both men and women. As he predicted, his followers turned his teachings into an organized religion. In the process, what had begun as a starkly pessimistic and antiworldly vision of existence, without gods or a god or the promise of heaven, became one of the great salvationist faiths of all human history.

THE MAKING OF A RELIGION

After his death (again as he feared), the Buddha was worshiped as a divinity. His most faithful disciples became monks who devoted their lives to spreading his message and achieving nirvana. They held conferences where they sought to compile authoritative collections of his teachings and traditions concerning his life. Not surprisingly, disagreements over points of doctrine and meaning arose at these sessions. These disputes led to the formation of rival schools of monks who vied with each other, the brahmans, and other sects to build a popular following.

Over time the rival schools created elaborate philosophical systems. But in seeking to attract a broader following, the monks stressed more accessible aspects of what had become a new religion. They offered miraculous tales of the Buddha's life, which included traditions that his mother had been a virgin and that he had been visited by revered scholars from afar soon after his birth. In the popular mind nirvana became equated with heaven. Graphic visions of heavenly pleasures and the tortures of hell became central features of popular Buddhism. The Buddha was worshiped as a savior who returned periodically to help the faithful find the way to heaven. Though within the monastic communities Buddhist monks continued to stress meditation and the achievement of nirvana, lay people were encouraged to perform good deeds that would earn enough merit for their soul to go to one of the Buddhist heavens after their death.

THE BUDDHIST CHALLENGE

Though other philosopher-holy men criticized the religious beliefs and caste system that the brahmans had done so much to establish, none was as successful as the Buddha and the many monastic orders committed to his teachings at winning converts among the Indian people. The monks and monastic organizations provided a very viable alternative to the brahman priesthood as centers of scholarship, education, and religious ritual, and often directly opposed the beliefs that the brahmans championed. Though the Buddha retained the ideas of karma and reincarnation, he rejected the Vedas as divinely inspired teachings that ought to be accepted as the ultimate authority on all issues. He ridiculed the powers the brahmans claimed for their sacrifices and the gods for whom they were intended. He favored introspection and self-mastery over ritual. In so doing, he struck at the very heart of the brahmans' social and religious dominance.

The Buddha rejected the life-style of both the brahmans who had become addicted to worldly power and brahman ascetics who practiced extreme forms of bodily mortification. He sought to do away with the caste system, an aim that gave his teachings great potential appeal among the untouchables and other groups. The Buddha also accepted women as his followers and taught that they were capable of attaining nirvana. These opportunities were institutionalized in Buddhist monastic organizations, which normally included provisions for communities of nuns. The evidence we have suggests that the monastic life became a fulfilling career outlet for women in many parts of India. This outlet proved doubly meaningful in an era when educational and other occupational opportunities for women were declining and upper-caste women in particular were increasingly confined to the home.

BRAHMAN REACTION

In virtually all spheres of life from religious worship to social organization, Buddhism offered potentially revolutionary challenges to the long-established brahmanical order. As the numbers of the converts to the new faith multiplied, the brahmans grew more and more sensitive to the challenge posed by Buddhism. But the brahmans drew comfort from the fact that they still controlled the kings of the lowland states where most of the population and Indian civilization was concentrated. The kings in turn were committed to upholding their positions and the caste hierarchy that was the key to the world they dominated. When in the 4th and 3d centuries B.C. these kings were displaced by the powerful Mauryan Empire, and when the most talented ruler of that empire converted to Buddhism, the brahmans could no longer ignore their peril. The rise of the Mauryan Empire then was very much a factor in a largely peaceful, but nonetheless increasingly intense, struggle between the brahmans and the Buddhist monastic orders.

GREEK INVASIONS AND THE MAURYA EMPIRE

The intellectual and social ferment that swept northern India in the 6th century B.C. was intensified by political upheavals touched off by the invasion of northwestern India by Alexander the Great in 327 B.C. Though Alexander's designs to add India to his domains were frustrated, his victories in India threw the patchwork of Indian regional kingdoms into turmoil. Capitalizing on the crisis, the leaders of one of the kingdoms, the Mauryas, forged a mighty empire of their own. Under the ruler Ashoka, Buddhism peaked in its influence on Indian civilization. But even as Ashoka sent monks to spread the teachings overseas, a brahman counter-offensive was building. Though the rapid fall of the Maurya Empire after Ashoka's death was a factor in the success of the brahmanical response, major changes in the religious system they sought to defend were more decisive in the neutralization of the Buddhist challenge.

THE GREEK INTERLUDE

Alexander the Great had a number of reasons for invading India. To begin with, he believed that except for India, Arabia, North Africa, and some remote and barbaric parts of Europe, he had run out of places to conquer. He knew of the Indians because some of them had fought with the Persians against his armies; he knew little or nothing of the Chinese. In Alexander's view, invading India would complete his subjugation of the world and allow him to surpass all other conquerors, including the semimythical Hercules and the Greek god Dionysus. A new campaign would keep his soldiers in fighting trim and his generals from quarreling among themselves. It is also likely that Alexander found the prospect of further adventures in India a good deal more exciting than the humdrum tasks involved in administering the huge empire his armies had won in less than a decade.

Whatever his motives, in 327 B.C. Alexander's armies crossed the Hindu Kush into India, thus beginning what would be his last major campaign of conquest. It was a rousing success. His greatly outnumbered armies won a series of battles against the peoples living in the upper Indus valley, the most notable of which was against an Indian ruler named Porus. As had been the case in his Persian campaigns, Alexander's well-trained troops proved more than a match for the war chariots, archers, and massed cavalry of his Indian adversaries. Once the surprise wore off, his veteran soldiers also proved able to cope with the numbers of war elephants that had spooked their horses.

Victory stirred Alexander's passion for further conquests. But his soldiers, weary of endless battles and fearful of the stiffening resistance of numerous Indian princes in an exotic and very distant land, refused to go farther to the east. After considerable debate, Alexander agreed to lead his forces out of India. Those in his armies who survived an epic march through the desert wastes to the north and west of the Indus River returned to Persia in 324 B.C. Alexander's death a year later left his Indian conquests to be fought over by the commanders who divided up his empire.

THE IMPACT OF THE GREEK INVASIONS

Though a number of Greek rulers controlled territory in India's northwest for some decades after Alexander's invasion, the impact of his campaign was largely indirect. It stimulated some trade and considerable cultural exchange between India and the Mediterranean region. Of particular importance was the flow of Greek astronomical and mathematical ideas to India and the impact of Indian thinking on religious movements in the Mediterranean. The Greek Stoics and the mystery religions that swept the eastern Mediterranean in the centuries around the birth of Christ owe much to Indian philosophical influences. In the arts, the combination of Indian and Greek styles led to an Indo-Greek school of sculpture that was both distinctive and influential in shaping approaches to the depiction of the Buddha. Indian motifs were blended with Greek physical features and artistic techniques (see the figure below).

This Buddhist sculpture shows the Gandhara school of the early centuries A.D. The work of the Gandharan artists represented a fusion of Greek and Indian artistic styles and religious motifs. Particularly noteworthy are the handling of the Greek-style clothing and the Greek hairdos.

THE RISE OF THE MAURYAS

Appropriately, the most lasting effects of Alexander's invasion were military and political. The defeat of Porus and other rulers in the northwest and the establishment of Greek control over hostile peoples there created a political vacuum that was soon filled by the ablest of the regional lords, Chandragupta Maurya (322–298 B.C.). After some initial setbacks, Chandragupta embarked on a sustained campaign to build a great empire bit by bit. After conquering much of the northwest and driving the Greek successors of Alexander out of India, his armies began the conquest of the kingdoms of the Ganges plain that would later form the heartland of the Maurya Empire.

In addition to his skills as a military commander, Chandragupta owed his success to a clever advisor named Kautilya. Kautilya was one of a number of thinkers who contributed to a manual on statecraft, the *Arthashastra,* that developed the darker side of the approaches to kingship that had emerged in the preceding centuries. The writers of the *Arthashastra* argued that in the pursuit of political power any measure was justified. Powerful kingdoms, they felt, must constantly expand, while weak rulers should accept the most humiliating terms in order to attach themselves to strong monarchs.

In great detail, Kautilya and his fellow political strategists described the techniques a ruler must use to attain and hold power. Spies disguised as beggars, barbers, and even holy men should be stationed everywhere in a king's own domains and those of his enemies. Crime or internal dissent must be harshly punished. The authors of the *Arthashastra* sanctioned removing rival rulers by bribery and assassination (for which specially trained prizefighters were recommended) and by employing traitors to undermine the resistance in neighboring kingdoms. Like Sun-zi (Sun Tzu) in China, they scorned the notion of chivalrous warfare where great champions fought each other in single combat. Enemies wounded and fallen should be killed, they advised, lest they rise up again. Kautilya and his coauthors approved of the use of poison-tipped arrows and chariots with sword blades attached to their wheel hubs. With such advice, it is little wonder that Chandragupta rapidly conquered adversaries who were apparently operating by a much less ruthless set of rules.

THE NEW IMPERIAL STYLE

As Chandragupta's empire grew, the folksy atmosphere of earlier localized court centers gave way to a new imperial style. He reigned from an elaborately carved and decorated palace set in large and well-tended gardens. Adopting the Persian example, Chandragupta proclaimed himself an absolute emperor and on state occasions sat on a high throne above hundreds of his splendidly attired courtiers. He was guarded by a special corps of amazons, and elaborate precautions were taken to safeguard his life. The food he ate was first tasted by servants to ensure that *he* did not die of poisoning. Parrots were bred for the trees of the palace gardens to make sure that poisonous snakes did not find their way into the ruler's chambers. There were hollow pillars in which to hide palace spies; secret passages to enable the king to move about the palace undetected; and an obligatory bath and frisking for all who entered. Chandragupta built a standing army that Greek writers estimated (overly generously) was 500,000 strong and sought with some success to replace regional lords with his own administrators.

Chandragupta's son and successor, Bindusara, extended the Maurya Empire to the east along the Ganges plains and far to the south of the subcontinent. Little is known about Bindusara, but he was apparently a highly cultured man. He once requested wine, figs, and a philosopher as presents from one of the Greek rulers in western Asia. He received the wine and figs, but not the philosopher because, as the ruler informed him, the Greeks did not trade in philosophers. Bindusara's son, Ashoka, completed the conquests begun by his father and grandfather, and in his long reign from 268–232 B.C. northern India enjoyed a time of unprecedented political unity, prosperity, and cultural splendor.

India at the Time of Ashoka

ASHOKA'S CONVERSION AND HIS REFORMS

In the early years of his rule, Ashoka showed little of the wisdom and tolerance that were to set off his reign as one of the great periods in Indian history. He won his throne only after a bloody struggle in which he eliminated several brothers. He was apparently bad tempered and impetuous, as evidenced by his order that a woman from his harem be put to death for telling him that he was ugly. He also delighted in conquest—at least until he witnessed the horrible sufferings that were caused by his conquest of Orissa in eastern India. That experience and regret for his earlier dissolute life led to his conversion to Buddhism.

From the time of his conversion onward Ashoka became a ruler who strove to serve his people and promote their welfare. He ceased to enlarge his domains by conquest; used his revenues to build roads, hospitals, and rest houses; and sought to reduce the slaughter of animals in his kingdom by encouraging vegetarianism. His attempts to curb the slaughter of cows were particularly important, since those attempts, in conjunction with a reverence for cattle, contributed to the sacred status that this animal attained in Indian civilization. Because Ashoka's edicts were also aimed at restricting animal sacrifices, they aroused the anxiety of the brahmans who saw them as a threat to the rituals that were vital to their dominance in Indian society.

The influence of Buddhism on Ashoka's personal life spilled over into his state policy. Drawing on the Buddhist notion of a righteous world ruler spreading peace and good government, Ashoka sought to build an imperial bureaucracy that would enforce his laws and sanctions against war and animal slaughter. Though his efforts to establish meaningful control by a centralized administration met with some success, they also aroused considerable opposition. The brahmans, resentful of their displacement as political advisors and administrators by Ashoka's bureaucrats, sought to stir up local resistance to imperial edicts. Warrior families that had once ruled the small states also sought to retain their control over local politics. They waited for signs of dynastic weakness in the hope of reviving their lost kingdoms. There is also a sense that snooping and sermonizing by Ashoka's deputies soon became tiresome for the populace as a whole, which was not accustomed to strong state intervention in their lives.

SOCIAL CHANGE AND REACTIONS TO ASHOKA'S RULE

There were, however, a number of social groups that gained greatly from Ashoka's attempts to recast Indian society in a Buddhist mold. The period of Maurya rule coin-

cided with a great expansion from the Roman Empire in the west to China in the east. Indian merchants and artisans participated eagerly in this process. India established itself as one of the great preindustrial manufacturing centers of the classical world, specializing in cotton cloth and clothing. In fact, Indian cloth makers were so skilled that for many centuries Roman writers would lament the flow of gold to the east to pay for Indian textiles, for which the Romans had little else to exchange. Seeing in Buddhism an advantageous alternative to the caste system, the growing and increasingly prosperous merchant and artisan social strata supported Ashoka's efforts. They generously patronized the different orders of Buddhist monks that increased greatly in wealth and membership. Women also had good reasons to support the Buddhist alternative. Their position within the family was strengthened under Buddhist law, and the monastic life gave them opportunities for achievement and self-expression as nuns, scholars, and artists.

BUDDHIST ART IN THE MAURYAN AGE

One of the chief signs of the Buddhist surge under Ashoka and his successors was the spread of great monastery complexes throughout the subcontinent. Most of the monasteries were made of wood and thus were lost in fires or destroyed by later invaders. But the Buddhist architectural legacy was preserved in the great stone shrines, or *stupas*, that were built to house pieces of bone or hair and personal possessions, which were said to be relics of the Buddha. Most of the freestanding stupas were covered mounds of dirt surrounded by intricately carved stone gateways and fences. But the Indian genius for decoration and design reached a higher level of expression in the centuries after the fall of the Maurya dynasty. In the 2d century B.C., Buddhists and the devotees of other holy men carved temples out of solid granite in the hills of western India. Here Indian painting also reached its apex in wonderful wall paintings depicting events in the life of the Buddha and, in the process, giving us a magnificent glimpse into the housing, dress, life-styles, and natural environment of classical India.

ASHOKA AND THE SPREAD OF BUDDHISM

Another major effect of Ashoka's dedication to Buddhism resulted from his efforts to spread the faith beyond the Indian subcontinent. He sent missions, including one led by one of his sons, to Sri Lanka to the south and to the Himalayan kingdoms and the steppes of central Asia to the north. The establishment of Buddhism in each region was critical, because converted rulers and monks in these

This photo shows the great Buddhist stupa at Sanchi in central India. Stupas were built to house
relics of the Buddha, and they became major sites of pilgrimage for the Buddhist faithful.

areas were instrumental in spreading the religion to much of the rest of Asia. From Sri Lanka Buddhism was carried to Burma, Java, and many other parts of Southeast Asia. From Nepal and central Asia it was disseminated into Tibet, China, and the rest of East Asia.

ASHOKA'S DEATH AND THE DECLINE OF THE MAURYAS

Ashoka's bold experiments in religious and social change and the empire that he and his forebears had established did not long survive his death. Weaker rulers followed him to the throne. The empire was first divided between rival claimants within the Maurya household, and then pulled apart by internal strife and local lords who sought to reestablish the many kingdoms that had been absorbed into the Maurya imperium. By 185 B.C., the Maurya Empire had disappeared. Political fragmentation returned to the subcontinent; new warrior invaders compounded rapidly growing divisions. Though some of these conquerors built substantial empires and were devoted to the continued spread of Buddhism, none of them could match Ashoka in power and resolution. Within the fragmented political order that emerged after the decline of the Mauryas, the brahmans initiated a religious revival that gradually, and usually without overt persecution, pushed Buddhism to the fringes of Indian social and intellectual life.

BRAHMANICAL RECOVERY AND THE SPLENDORS OF THE GUPTA AGE

In the centuries after the end of the Mauryan Empire new waves of invaders entered the Indian subcontinent. Indo-Greek rulers, whose kingdoms were based in central Asia, attempted to establish provinces in the northwest. Their kingdoms were attacked by Scythian nomads who then raided and plundered and later settled in North India. The Scythians were overrun by a new wave of nomads, the Yueh-chih, from the eastern steppes. The Yueh-chih conquests gave rise to the Kushana dynasty that was based in the northwest and was the most powerful in India between the end of the 1st and the early 3d centuries A.D.

Under the Kushanas, Buddhism experienced its last great era of imperial patronage. But the Kushanas' domains did not extend to the Ganges plains or central and South India, so in those areas kingdoms arose where the brahmans were able to reestablish their old political and religious dominance. Across the subcontinent in the centuries between the fall of the Mauryas and the rise of the Guptas in the late 3d century A.D., Buddhism and Hinduism, as the brahmanical beliefs and modes of worship would come to be known, vied largely without violence for the patronage of Indian rulers and the support of the Indian masses. By the time of the founding of the Gupta Empire in the 4th century A.D., it was clear that the brahmans would be able to meet the Buddhist challenge.

KEYS TO THE BRAHMAN COUNTEROFFENSIVE

Even in the centuries before the rise of the Guptas, when the influence of Buddhism in Indian society was at its height, a number of patterns had developed that rendered it quite vulnerable to a brahman counteroffensive. The monastic orders became more and more concentrated in huge monasteries. Increasingly isolated from village and urban life, the monks grew obsessed with fine points of philosophy that often had little or no relevance to ordinary believers. Because Buddhism in India had not developed a sequence of family and life-cycle rituals or folk festivals, the monks had little occasion to interact with the mass of the people. They focused their services more and more on wealthy patrons, whose donations supported the monasteries. This support made the daily rounds to collect alms unnecessary for the monks in many areas, and led to luxurious life-styles and lax discipline at some of the more prominent Buddhist centers.

While the Buddhist monks became more remote from the Indian populace, the brahmans strove to effect changes in belief and worship that would make Hinduism more ap-

pealing to ordinary people. They played down the need for grand and expensive sacrifices and stressed the importance of personal worship and small, everyday offerings of food and prayers to the gods. Increasing stress was placed on intense devotion to gods such as Shiva and Vishnu and their female consorts Kali and Lakshmi. Special gods were allotted to particular occupational groups, such as Ganesh, the elephant-headed, pot-bellied deity who was especially revered by merchants.

Temples, both large and small, sprang up to house the multitude of statues that provided the focus for popular worship of the gods. Devotional cults were open to persons at all caste levels, including in some cases the untouchables. Women were also allowed to participate, at times, as cult poets and singers. In addition, the brahmans multiplied or enriched special festivals and rites-of-passage ceremonies, such as child naming celebrations, weddings, and funerals, which enlarged the role they played in the everyday life of the Indian people. Over a period of centuries, revived Hinduism simply absorbed the salvationist Buddhism that alone had a mass appeal. The brahmans treated the Buddha as another god of the Hindu pantheon and allowed their followers to worship him as one of the worldly forms of the preserver god Vishnu.

At the elite level, brahman holy men and scholars placed increasing emphasis on the sophisticated and sublime philosophical ideas associated with the later books of the Vedas, which were called the *Upanishads*. Not heavens or hells, but the release of the soul from the endless cycle of rebirths was stressed in these teachings. Moderated asceticism and meditation were the means by which this release was achieved. In contrast to the Buddha who preached that the soul itself was an illusion, the orthodox Hindu schools taught that the soul was real and its ultimate purpose was to fuse with the godhead from which it had come. The world was *maya*, or illusion, only because it was wrongly perceived by most humans. Those who had achieved realization and release understood that the world was in fact an extension of a single reality that encompassed everything.

Building on earlier religious practices and the themes of the Vedas, the brahmans managed to provide spiritual solace for people at virtually all social levels. Their religion offered concrete ceremonies to mark life's passages, festivals to enliven the lives of princes, artisans, and peasants alike, and sublime philosophical speculation that stressed the oneness of all creation. Hinduism spread to only limited areas beyond India—most notably to island Southeast Asia. But its importance within the subcontinent and its subtlety in accommodating a variety of cultures and beliefs gave it the stature of Buddhism and the other great world religions of the Middle East.

Perhaps the most frequently depicted Indian religious image is the god Shiva, here portrayed in a South Indian bronze. The position of the god's hands or the objects held in them each represent a different aspect of his power, which is simultaneously creative and destructive.

SOCIAL AND POLITICAL CHANGE AND BUDDHIST DECLINE

In addition to monastic weaknesses and brahman reforms, Buddhism in India was weakened by underlying economic changes that altered the social circumstances that had favored the new religion. Most critical was the decline of the Rome-China trading axis with the fall of the Han empire in the 3d century A.D. and the weakening position of Rome in the same era. This not only undermined the position of merchant groups that had been major patrons of Buddhism, it made large-scale traders more and more dependent on local kings and warrior households, which remained the chief allies of the brahmans.

The damage done to Buddhism by the losses of the mercantile classes was compounded by the collapse of the Mauryan and later the Kushana empires, which had been the monastic orders' supreme source of patronage. Their eventual replacement by the Guptas, who were enthusiastic supporters of the brahmans and Hinduism, all but sealed the fate of Buddhism in India. Its demise would be gradual and only occasionally hastened by violent persecution. But centuries of rule by the Guptas in north India and Hindu kingdoms in the south left only pockets of Buddhist strength that would decay over time.

The Gupta Empire

THE GUPTA EMPIRE

In the last decades of the 3d century A.D., a family of wealthy landholders in the eastern Ganges plains first infiltrated the court of the local ruler and then seized his throne. Through a succession of clever alliances and timely military victories, the Gupta family built an empire that by the end of the 4th century A.D. extended across most of northern India. The Guptas' domains were not nearly as extensive as those of the Mauryas, and they had far less control over the regional lords and villages that fell under their sway than had briefly been the case with the Mauryas, particularly under Ashoka. The Gupta rulers never attempted to build a genuine bureaucracy or to regulate effectively affairs at the local level. Their empire was in fact a massive tributary edifice, in which former kings were left to rule in the name of the Guptas and regional warrior elites were virtually autonomous governors of all but the empire's heartlands in the Ganges basin. Even the villages in the Ganges area were parceled out among the generals and retainers of the Gupta emperors.

The Guptas were content to be acknowledged as supreme overlords and draw as much tribute as possible from the many vassals who were forced to accede to their rule. Weak control from the center meant that local lords periodically revolted or squabbled among themselves. Though internal warfare continued, it was at a low level compared

to the centuries after the fall of the Mauryas. Until the 5th century, foreign invaders were kept beyond the Himalayas and internal conflicts were short and localized. Gupta dominance brought over two and one-half centuries of relative peace and unprecedented prosperity to much of north India.

A HINDU RENAISSANCE

From the outset the Guptas had been staunch defenders of Hinduism and patrons of the brahmans. With the family's rise to power the brahmans' roles as sanctifiers of and advisors to kings were fully restored. Buddhist monks were increasingly confined to their monasteries, which, lacking the patronage of the imperial court, had to depend on wealthy local merchants or landowners. The brahmans' roles as *gurus*, or teachers, for the princes of the imperial court and the sons of local notables also became entrenched. Brahmans regained the aura of mystery and supernatural power that they had enjoyed in the Vedic age. In *The Signet Ring of Rakshasa*, one of the great dramas that was produced in the Gupta epoch, king Chandragupta prostrates himself at the feet of his teacher and advisor Chanyaka. The ruler lavishes presents on brahmans linked to the court and relies on their stratagems to thwart the schemes of his adversaries. With their power base and sources of patronage restored, brahman priests, poets, scholars, and patrons of the arts became the driving force behind an era of splendid achievement in literature, music, art, architecture, and the natural sciences.

The most dramatic expressions of the Hindu resurgence were the great temples that rose above the rapidly growing urban centers both within the Gupta domains and in the independent kingdoms in the far south. In many cases the temples themselves provided the impetus for urban growth. Merchants, artisans, servants, and laborers migrated to the towns where the temples were located to serve the growing numbers of pilgrims who journeyed to the sacred sites to worship and win favors from the Hindu deities. The intricately carved stone gateways and sanctuary towers of these edifices proclaimed the majesty of the Hindu gods and goddesses to both townspeople and peasants in nearby villages. The temple towers literally teemed with sculptures of deities and friezes of their legendary exploits; with animals which were often the vehicles or manifestations of major gods or goddesses; and with humans in all manner of activities, including explicit depictions of sexual intercourse on temples in eastern India and elsewhere.

The jumble of sculpture and the structure of the temples as a whole were very much reflections of the Hindu world view. Compared to medieval European cathedrals

These temple towers are in the pilgrimage town of Madurai in south India. Like medieval cathedrals and Islamic mosques, these great structures attest to the intense faith and outpouring of devotion that were associated with the Hindu resurgence of the early centuries A.D.

and Muslim mosques that soar to the heavens, Hindu temples were heavy and earthbound. These qualities were in part explained by limitations in construction techniques, but they resulted equally from the Hindu view that the divine is everywhere, not simply in the heavens. The towers, cluttered with statuary, mirrored the Hindu view of space as a realm alive with life. The worldly and even profane preoccupations of gods and goddesses (as well as ordinary mortals) depicted in temple sculptures suggest the Hindu conviction that divinity encompasses all life. It also reflects the symbolic parallels drawn in Indian religions between the union of male and female and the individual's search for oneness with the divine.

As these examples suggest, Hindu art stressed symbolism rather than accurate representation, which was so highly valued by the ancient Greeks. The sculpture and the god or goddess it depicted stood for something else— including creation (Brahma), destruction (Shiva), fertility (Lakshmi), and death (Kali as Durga). In fact, the temple complexes as a whole were massive *mandalas,* or cosmic diagrams, measured precisely and laid out according to established conventions.

LITERATURE AND THE SCIENCES

Though written languages had developed in India in the centuries before the rise of the Gupta dynasty, the Gupta reign initiated one of the great ages of Indian literary achievement. In the Gupta period and the following centuries many of the great classics of both Sanskrit, the sacred and classical Indian language, and Tamil, one of the major languages of the South, were written. The poet Kalidasa, who is acknowledged as the greatest of Sanskrit authors, lived in a period when Gupta power was at its height. In the "Cloud Messenger" and numerous other poems, he provided vivid pictures of life in the Gupta age. In the following passage, for example, the clouds bringing the monsoon rains pass over a town where the poet exclaims:

Your body will grow fat with the smoke of incense
   from open windows where women dress their hair.
You will be greeted by palace peacocks, dancing to welcome you, their friend.
If your heart is weary from travel you may pass the
   night above mansions fragrant with flowers
Whose pavements are marked with red dye from the
   feet of lovely women.

In addition to poetry and drama, Hindu scholars in the classical era wrote treatises on the nature of time, space, and causality in which there are arguments that have much in common with the findings of modern science on these issues. In fact, the era of the Hindu revival was a time of great Indian achievement both in mathematics and the sciences. In addition to advances in geometry and algebra that

DOCUMENT
A GUARDIAN'S
FAREWELL SPEECH
TO A YOUNG WOMAN
ABOUT TO BE
MARRIED

One of the great plays written during the Hindu revival of the early centuries A.D. was *Shakuntala* by Kalidasa. The play is a Cinderella-style tale about a beautiful young woman, Shakuntala, who is loved by a king and the travails she must endure before they are happily united. In the following exchange as Shakuntala sets out to join her husband at his palace, she is instructed by her guardians (the hermits Kashyapa and Gautami) on the proper behavior for a young wife, in a manner that recalls the famous speech by Polonius to his son Laertes in Shakespeare's *Hamlet*.

Kashyapa: Now you Shakuntala . . . Respect your superiors,
Be friendly toward the ladies of the palace.
Never be angry with your husband, no matter what happens.
Be polite with the maids;

In everything be humble.
These qualities make a woman; those without them are black sheep in their families.
What is your opinion, Gautami?

Gautami: A bride needs nothing more. Remember his advice, Shakuntala.

Shakuntala: How will I ever manage in the palace? I feel so lost. I belong here, Father.

Kashyapa: Don't worry, my child; you are privileged.
You will be his great wife;
He is noble and great.
You will give him a son, as the East gives us light.
The pain of separation will then pass.

Questions: What does this conversation tell you about gender relationships and marriage in classical India? What does it say about attitudes toward women? How do these relationships and attitudes compare to those found in China and Greece in this era? How do they compare to those in our own society?

---

were made quite independently of the work in these fields by the Greeks, Indian thinkers calculated the circumference of the globe and the value of π (pi) with remarkable accuracy. They also used the concept of zero and devised decimals and, most critically, the "Arabic" number system that we use today. Research at the great university center of Nalanda was devoted to mathematics, theoretical science, and applied sciences such as astronomy. In the Gupta age and afterward, the Indians also made major breakthroughs in medicine. They developed hospitals, surgical techniques, and sophisticated treatments for a variety of illnesses.

SOCIETY IN THE GUPTA AGE

As the brahmans recovered their earlier social dominance, the caste hierarchy they had long promoted was established as the backbone of the Indian social system. Caste divisions grew even more complex and came to vary significantly between different areas in the subcontinent. Styles of dress increasingly distinguished members of each varna grouping, and restrictions on untouchables and other low-

caste groups grew harsher and more pervasive. In some areas, for example, untouchables traveling on roadways between towns had to clap sticks together or continually shout that they were on the road in order to warn high-caste groups that they were in danger of being polluted. If a brahman or merchant was seen approaching, the untouchable was required to leave the road and pass by through the fields at a considerable distance. The untouchables were not allowed to use any wells but their own or to worship in the temples frequented by other caste groups. Even their living quarters were segregated from the rest of the towns and rural villages.

Like the untouchables, women at all caste levels suffered a further reduction of their status and restriction of career outlets. They were no longer allowed to read the sacred Vedas, though small numbers remained prominent in the devotional cults. Hindu law declared that women were legally minors, subject to the supervision and protection of their fathers, husbands, and, if widowed, their sons. Except for their personal clothing and jewelry, women were not allowed to inherit property. The fact that family fortunes could only pass from father to son and that large dowries were required to arrange marriages with suitable spouses meant that girls were seen as an economic liability, and often as a crushing burden. As popular sayings and poems from this period attest, sons were prized and pampered, while daughters were overlooked and neglected. In some regions where dowry amounts were highly inflated, female infanticide was practiced to save families from financial ruin.

Women were tied to the home, their lives decided by males. Marriages were primarily a means of establishing alliances between families. They were arranged with the groom having little say and the bride none. Child marriages were not uncommon among the upper castes. Young girls left the familiar surroundings of their own homes to live with their husband's families. In the new household they were at the mercy of their mothers-in-law, who could

These stylized sculptures show young women from the Hindu temple at Khajurāho in eastern India. These figures represent a standardized form of feminine beauty in South Asian culture — large breasts, small waist, and ornate jewelry.

be caring and reassuring but, if the literature from this and later periods is any gauge, were very often bossy and critical. A young girl's place in the new household depended almost wholly on her ability to bear *sons* who would be devoted to her and care for her in old age. A woman whose husband died before she bore him a son was doomed to a lonely life in the remote corners of the family compound. Even widows who bore sons were not to be envied. They were not allowed to remarry or go out alone, lest they defile the memory of their deceased husbands.

Other than marriage, few avenues were open to women. A single woman was regarded as an economic liability and a blot on her family's honor. As the Buddhist monasteries shrank in numbers and size, the possibility of becoming a nun diminished sharply. Only by becoming a courtesan or a woman accomplished in all of the arts, including sexual intercourse, could a woman establish some degree of independence. Courtesans, who are sometimes celebrated in the literature of this period, could become wealthy, well educated, and find outlets for their talents. But though they were far above the despised common prostitutes in status, they could not hope to have social respectability or raise families of their own. Unlike married women, whose husbands were duty bound to provide them with the requirements of life, courtesans were dependent on the tastes and whims of males who dominated all aspects of interaction between the sexes in the Gupta age.

THE PLEASURES OF ELITE LIFE

Though women were restricted in career options and largely confined to their households, life for those of the upper castes was not without its rewards, at least once they had established their place in their husband's family by having sons. Well-to-do families lived in large compounds set in gardens filled with flowering plants and colorful birds. They were waited on by servants and entertained at periodic festivals and in their own compounds by swings, games such as chess and parchesi (both of which the Indians invented), and wandering musicians. Males and females dressed in silks and fine cottons and at mealtimes enjoyed one of the world's great cuisines. When they ventured away from the family compound, the very wealthy were carried in litters born by servants and given the place of honor to which their caste rank entitled them.

Males from the upper castes were particularly privileged. They were expected to experience the four stages of the ideal Hindu life that were firmly established in this era for men only. In their youth they were to work hard as students, but many diversions and pleasures were available to the fashionable sons of well-to-do families. Many of these pastimes are described in the famous (or infamous)

Kamasutra by Vatsayana who lived in the Gupta era. Though often dismissed as little more than a glorified sex manual, Vatsayana's work in fact contains detailed instructions on virtually all aspects of the life of the young man-about-town. There are recommendations for grooming and hygiene; discussions of good etiquette in various situations; advice on the best way to select a wife; and, of course, instructions in making love to either a witty and knowledgeable courtesan or one's future wife. There was, of course, a double standard: young men were expected to come to marriage knowledgeable in the ways of love; girls who were not virgins were disgraced and unmarriageable. The manual indicates that the pleasures of youth were varied—from poetry readings and dancing contests to hunting and gambling.

The student was expected in the second stage of life to become a householder and ideally a faithful husband. Preserving or adding to the family fortune was a major task in this phase of life, and bearing sons to perform one's funeral rites and continue the family line was essential. At some point in middle age, the householder was supposed to bid farewell to his family and go off to the forest to join the hermits in meditation. In his final years, the upper caste male was expected to enter the fourth stage of life by becoming a wandering holy man, completely dependent on the charity of others. Few individuals actually advanced beyond the householder stage. But the fact that the sequence had become the social ideal indicates that Indian religion and society could readily accommodate scholarship and worldly pursuits, bodily denial, and meditation as valid paths to self-fulfillment.

LIFE-STYLES OF THE ORDINARY PEOPLE

For most Indians who labored as peasants, artisans, or sweepers at the lower levels of the caste system, the delights of upper-caste youths or the ability to set off as a wandering holy man were unattainable. Most Indians experienced lives of hard work, if not sheer drudgery. Most knew no deference but rather spent their lives bowing to and serving their caste superiors. At the lower-caste levels, women were somewhat freer in their ability to move about the town and countryside and buy and sell in the local marketplace. But they had no servants to perform their many household chores and were required to do backbreaking farming tasks, such as weeding fields or transplanting rice. There were, of course, small pleasures. Even low-caste groups could attend temple festivals, watch dances and dramatics performed in the open air, and risk their meager wages in dice games or betting on roosters specially bred to fight with each other. In an age when India was one of the most fertile and productive regions on the earth,

it is probable that all but the untouchables lived as well as ordinary people did anywhere in the world.

The Indian economy continued to grow in the Gupta age, despite the decline of long-distance trade with China and Rome. Leadership in international commerce increasingly shifted to the trading cities on the east and west coasts and the southern seaports of the subcontinent. Strong trading links were maintained with kingdoms in Sri Lanka and throughout Southeast Asia, which were strongly influenced by Indian cultural exports. In fact, India became the pivot of the great Indian Ocean trading network that stretched from the Red Sea and Persian Gulf in the west to the South China Sea in the east—a position it would maintain until the age of European overseas expansion after the 16th century A.D.

Regional trade and manufacturing also increased over much of India. Indians developed new uses for chemistry in manufacturing processes, such as the bleaching and dyeing of cloth. Their cotton cloth manufacturing techniques and tools were the best in the world. Most production occurred in artisan shops, as was the case in other agrarian-based civilizations. The strength of India's handicraft manufacturing sector combined with the unusual power and prestige of merchants to give its urban economy a decided boost. It is no small wonder that India was known by the time of the Guptas as a land of great wealth as well as the home of many religions. A Chinese Buddhist, Fa-hsien, on a pilgrimage to India, exclaimed:

> The people are many and happy. They do not have to register their households with the police. There is no death penalty. Religious sects have houses of charity where rooms, couches, beds, food, and drink are supplied to travelers.

GUPTA DECLINE AND A RETURN TO POLITICAL FRAGMENTATION

For nearly 250 years the Guptas managed to hold together the collection of vassal kingdoms that they passed off as an empire. Signs of future danger appeared in the northwest with the first of the Hun probes across the Himalayas in the early decades of the 5th century A.D. Preoccupied by the growing threat on their northern frontier, the later Gupta rulers failed to crush resistance from their vassals and challenges from states to the south of the Gupta domains. By the middle of the century, Gupta efforts to hold back repeated assaults by greater and greater numbers of Hun invaders were faltering. With the death of Skanda Gupta, the last of the truly able Gupta monarchs, a flood of nomadic invaders broke into the empire. Their pillaging and widely dispersed assaults finished off what remained of

Gupta military might, and the empire dissolved into a patchwork of local kingdoms and warring states. In the seventh century, Harsha, an exceptionally able ruler of one of these kingdoms, sought to reestablish imperial rule in the north. But his successes in this formidable endeavor ended with his death in 647.

From the mid-7th century until the establishment of the Delhi Sultanate in the early 13th century, northern India was divided and vulnerable to outside invasions. The first invasions were by nomadic peoples who raided and conquered, then settled down and became assimilated to Indian ways. From the 8th century onward, however, the invaders tended to be Muslims seeking not just booty and kingdoms to conquer but converts to a foreign religion. The faith they sought to spread, Islam, clashed in fundamental ways with the Hindu beliefs and social arrangements that had dominated life in the subcontinent since the age of the Guptas.

CONCLUSION

THE LEGACY OF THE CLASSICAL AGE IN INDIA

The civilization the Aryan invaders began to build in the centuries after settling in India in the middle of the 2d millennium B.C. proved a good deal more adaptable and long lasting than the Harappan complex it replaced. Though its growth was marked by a couple of notable attempts to build a centralized political system to shield and nurture it, unlike China its genius and strength did not rest in political organization or military innovation. By the last centuries B.C., the central bulwarks of civilization in India were the caste system and the Hindu religion that provided its ideological underpinnings. What has come to be viewed as a system of social oppression, served then as an intricate and ingenious mode of dividing labor and allotting social roles. The Hindu social order that rested on the caste hierarchy not only proved able to withstand the very formidable challenge of Buddhism, it rather easily absorbed wave after wave of foreign invaders.

Though the contributions of the Buddhists and other non-Hindu religions were not inconsiderable, the brahman-dominated, caste ordered civilization of India produced some of humanity's most sublime art and philosophy; important breakthroughs in mathematics, the sciences, and technology; prosperous urban centers; and a population that in numbers has been second only to that of China through much of human history. Neither the rigidity of the caste system nor the pronounced religious emphasis of Indian

culture prevented the range of diversity common in the achievements of the other classical civilizations. In India's case these achievements included an often sensual art and literature, a sizeable corpus of tough-minded political theory, and a sophisticated trading system—all of which defy persisting characterizations of India as otherworldly and antimaterial. Truly, India was one of the great civilized centers of the classical age.

FURTHER READINGS

Perhaps the most readable introductions to life and society in India's classical age can be found in either A. L. Basham's *The Wonder That Was India* (1954) or Jeannine Auboyer's *Daily Life in Ancient India* (1961). The works of Romilla Thapar, especially her *Ashoka and the Decline of the Mauryas* (1961), are the best on the political history of the era. But even her more general *A History of India* (1966) is very detailed and quite technical, certainly a challenge for the beginner. Fine narrative histories of all aspects of Indian civilization in this period can be found in the appropriate chapters of *The History and Culture of the Indian People* (1964), ed. R. C. Majumdar, A. K. Majumdar, and D. K. Ghose. One of the best works on the position of women and social life more generally is Pandharinath Prabhu's *Hindu Social Organization* (1940). A wide range of other aspects of ancient Indian culture are covered in the fine essays in A. L. Basham's *A Cultural History of India* (1975).

Superb introductions to various branches of Indian religious and philosophical thinking with well-selected portions of the appropriate texts can be found in S. Radhakrishnan and Charles Moore, eds., *A Source Book in Indian Philosophy* (1957). Of the many books on Buddhism, Trevor Ling's *The Buddha* (1973) has the dual advantage of incorporating recent scholarship and being very readable. S. Radhakrishnan's *Hindu View of Life* (1927) provides a useful insider's view of Hindu religious beliefs and social organization. Heinrich Zimmer's *Philosophies of India* (1956), though somewhat dated, remains a good place to begin an exploration of the riches and diversity of Indian mythology and religious thinking. Benjamin Rowland's *The Art and Architecture of India* (1953) is the most objective and comprehensive work available in English on Indian art. For a taste of Indian literature in the classical age, there are English translations of the *Ramayana* and the *Mahabharata* and P. Lal's fine translations of *Great Sanskrit Plays* (1957).

400 Rome completes control of central Italy   **146–133** Decline of Roman republic   **70–19** Vergil

167 Rome begins conquests in eastern Mediterranean   **44** Assassination of Caesar

106–43 Cicero

500–450 Beginnings of Roman   **264–146** Rome's   **133–121** Gracchus brothers' reform attempts   **46** Julius Caesar dictator
republic; Twelve Tables of Law   Punic Wars   **107 ff.** Increasing power of generals

500 B.C.   300 B.C.   100 B.C.

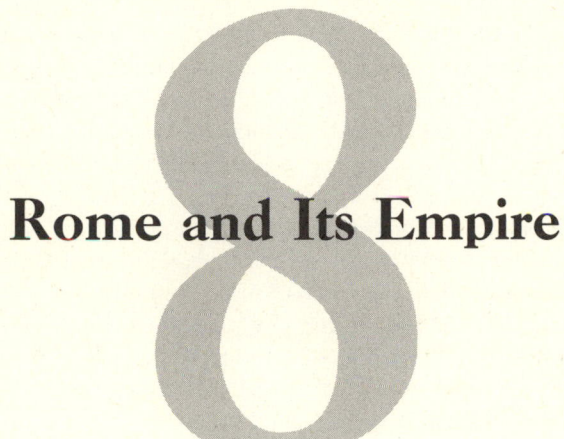

Rome and Its Empire

INTRODUCTION.   As classical civilizations took shape in India and China by the 5th century B.C., they maintained considerable coherence for the next 800–1000 years. This does not mean they were changeless: China experienced new dynasties and sharp debates among proponents of different ideologies. Change was even more pronounced in classical India, with recurrent invasions and the shifting fortunes of Buddhism and Hinduism. Nevertheless, there was continuity in many of the key issues and structures through the entire classical period, and while political boundaries shifted, the geographical cores of each of these Asian civilizations remained fairly constant.

This stability was not present in the Mediterranean. Greece, the cradle of classical Mediterranean civilization, had declined by the 4th century B.C. and its Hellenistic successor began to fade about two centuries later. This chapter deals with the final center of the classical Mediterranean, based around Rome. Rome preserved and extended many features of Greek and Hellenistic politics, culture, and economic organization; here too, as in southern and eastern Asia, there are some coherent classical themes. Rome also had a distinct tone and history, however, requiring separate treatment of the final 700 years of classical experience in the Mediterranean.

The earliest phases of Roman history occurred at a time when Greece and then Alexander and his successors held center stage to the east. It was during the 5th century B.C. that a new city-state near the middle of the Italian peninsula began to define a separate existence. Soon, Rome took on the trappings of a regional civilization, complete with its own language and an alphabet derived from the Greek alphabet. Rome was not the first civilization center in Italy. Greek settlements had long occupied much of southern Italy, and an Etruscan culture, still poorly understood in key respects, had developed to the north of Rome. Roman influence in Italy gradually expanded, however, making Italy a focus of activity in the western Mediterranean.

---

c. **4** B.C. Birth of Jesus   **35** Paul converts to Christianity

27 B.C. Augustus Caesar;
rise of Roman Empire   c. **30** Crucifixion of Jesus

180 Death of Emperor Marcus Aurelius; beginning of decline of empire

476 Fall of Rome

101–106 Under Trajan, Rome's greatest territory

313 Constantine legalizes Christianity

During the first centuries of Rome's advance, Greece and then the Hellenistic kingdoms held the leading position in the Mediterranean region. As these kingdoms declined, however, Rome prepared to advance, soon taking over the dominant role in Mediterranean civilization. By the 2d century B.C., Rome ruled Greece and the eastern Mediterranean directly, though it never penetrated fully into the Middle East's heartland where Hellenism had flourished. Yet Rome established a civilization zone around the Mediterranean that overlapped with much of the earlier Greek and Hellenistic orbit, while extending it to the west and further into North Africa. The Romans' massive empire flourished for four centuries and then limped through another 250 years in decline—an achievement in political organization and durability that the Greeks had never attained. Consequently the fall of the Roman Empire around A.D. 476 had a far more dramatic quality than the more gradual evolution of Greece and the Hellenistic world.

 ## ROME IN THE CLASSICAL MEDITERRANEAN TRADITION

Roman society was not, however, a fully independent creation. Despite its distinctive origins and location, Rome paralleled Greece in many ways—in social and economic structure, in city-state government, and in the pantheon of gods and goddesses. Rome also deliberately imitated many features of Greek culture—in literary forms and styles of art and architecture most notably, but also to a degree in philosophy.

At the same time, Rome was not identical with classical Greece, particularly in cultural emphases but to an extent in politics and economic life. Many historians treat Roman and Greek civilizations as separate entities, though granting important relationships between the two. While the Romans carefully preserved most Greek achievements, they lacked Greek interest or aptitude in philosophy or science; their genius lay more in engineering and administration. Rome's long republican phase expressed political impulses similar to those of the Greek city-states, but when it established a formal empire it developed more novel structures, including the great legal codes. It is true, also, that Greek and Roman influences did not entirely coincide geographically, even though Rome took over most of the areas that the Greeks had ruled. Greek values remained stronger in the eastern Mediterranean, whereas western Europe encountered a fuller Greek-Roman mixture with Roman contributions predominating in language and law.

Nevertheless, at the world history level a partial merger is justified. Greek and Roman societies shared many political impulses. Because of their common Indo-European background, imitation, and parallel developments, Greece

and Rome coincided more than they differed. Correspondingly the heritage they produced was conjoint; later European civilizations, particularly, would use both Greek and Roman elements indiscriminately, as part of a common classical past. Finally, the differences that did exist between Greece and Rome were not necessarily greater than those that emerged at distinct stages of classical development in Asia; classical India, after all, produced Buddhist periods and periods more devoted to the evolution of Hindu values, while China had Legalist episodes as well as the somewhat more characteristic Confucianism. Internal diversity and change over time were not peculiar to the classical Mediterranean, even though the separate auspices of Greece and Rome did give this common complexity a distinctive twist. The amalgam that ultimately emerged from the Mediterranean blended a number of varied elements of diverse origin—as was the case with the classical mixtures in Asia.

This chapter, dealing with Rome's rise and evolution, essentially treats the second main phase (third, when Hellenism is separated from classical Greece) of a classical Mediterranean civilization, comparable as a whole to the development of China and India during the same span of time. Thus, just as the classical period in China runs from the early Zhou dynasty around 1000–800 B.C. to the fall of the Han some 1100 years later, so a classical Mediterranean civilization was launched in Greece around 800 B.C., spread through Hellenism, and then solidified through the expansion of Rome in institutions that came crashing down only in the 5th century A.D.—again, about 1300 years after Greece had developed its alphabet, launched its city-state politics, and begun to write down its epic legends.

 ## ROME AND GREECE

Four points can be emphasized in defining the Roman-Greek relationship as part of a larger world history in the classical era. First, Rome served a vital role in preserving many features of Greek society. Romans used and copied Greek science, monumental architectural styles, and drama. They built on Greek political and ethical theory and used Greek ideas to shape and explain their own constitutional structure. They revived many Greek commercial patterns and copied Greek justifications of slavery. Rome had its own additions and modifications to make in many of these areas, but its eagerness to preserve and use Greek achievements was impressive.

Second, Rome spread civilization to new parts of Europe and North Africa. Greek influence had touched mainly coastal portions of the western Mediterranean. Rome moved inland, bringing all of North Africa, Spain, France, Romania and important parts of present-day Britain, the Low Countries, and Germany into contact with Greco-Roman values and institutions—including writing in the Latin language. Rome did not create a permanent unity for Mediterranean civilization, nor was it able to control the bulk of the Middle East. However, its achievement in bringing a larger part of Europe and North Africa into the orbit of civilization did have lasting impact.

Third, along with preserving and adapting classical Mediterranean civilization and spreading it geographically, Rome sponsored major innovations in politics. Rome used Greek political ideas and paralleled many features of the Greek polis. But it also established an imperial administration that had its own principles particularly in law, providing an important new ingredient for the political legacy of Mediterranean civilization. This is why the Roman Empire was so much more durable than the colonial leagues of Athens or the Hellenistic kingdoms, leaving a more vivid impression.

Finally, the Roman Empire served as a breeding ground for one of the great religious changes in world history—the advent and initial dissemination of Christianity. Christianity did not spring directly from the mainstream principles of Greco-Roman civilization, but it did use many of these principles selectively and, in its spread and church structure, depended heavily on what Rome had achieved.

Overall, by preserving vital aspects of Greek and Hellenistic politics and culture, but also in its own major innovations, Rome created a new version of Mediterranean civilization—a final major statement of classical institutions in this part of the world. Greco-Roman civilization, in turn, would provide the classical background to several successor civilizations—in western Europe, where later medieval and Renaissance leaders harked back to what they understood from Greece and Rome; in eastern Europe, where Greek influence merged with Roman imperial government and Christianity; and to a degree in the next phase of civilization in the Middle East, under the spur of Islam.

THE DEVELOPMENT OF ROME'S REPUBLIC

Agriculture developed late in Italy, which helps explain why this part of Europe entered the mainstream of world history later than Greece. The Neolithic revolution occurred only around 2500 B.C., and metalworking was introduced 1000 years later.

The people of Rome were Indo-European and migrated to Italy about 2000 B.C. They gradually assimilated agriculture and, by around 800 B.C., gained some contact with Greek settlements farther south on the peninsula. Rome

was ruled for a time by a group called the Etruscans, who provided powerful kings and organized tightly knit armies skilled in the use of horses and war chariots. The Etruscans imposed a strong government, but around 510 B.C. the local Roman aristocracy rebelled and devised a constitution carefully crafted to avoid tyrannical control. The Romans stressed a republic because they had found monarchy contrary to the public good (respublica). By this time the Romans had also adapted the Greek alphabet to form their own Latin alphabet, which remains in use throughout western Europe and the Americas today.

This statue of a Roman patrician—the class that filled the Senate—comes from the time of the empire. The family patriarch, clad in his toga, holds busts of his two sons.

The constitution of the early Roman republic favored the dominant aristocracy. Aristocrats staffed the powerful Senate, which advised on policy, and also served as magistrates. But lower-class citizens gained some voice. As in Greece, citizenship gave some people definite legal and political rights. At about 450 B.C. a law code was written to protect the property holdings of ordinary people and facilitate commerce. Soon, the ordinary citizens, or *plebeians*, won the right to elect their own representatives, the *tribunes*, to voice their interests. It was the Senate, however, that continued to serve as the center of Roman political life throughout the existence of the republic. The two chief executives, or consuls, were elected by an annual assembly in which the wealthy predominated. The rule of two consuls was designed to guard against arbitrary rule, and the consuls served normally for only a year, which meant that independent executive authority was hard to establish. This basic political structure, which balanced various interests to a degree but resembled many Greek city-states in leaning heavily on aristocratic voice, lasted for several centuries as Rome moved from a small local state to the center of a growing empire. The republic's balance of elements and the strong political loyalty it commanded from various classes was not only successful at the time; it would also inspire respect from later political reformers in Europe and the Americas seeking models for their own states and alternatives to monarchy.

Like its city-state politics, the early Roman economy resembled that of Greece about three centuries before. Aristocrats controlled large estates, but there were many grain growing farmers, who were also independent citizens capable of military service. By introducing the idea of written law early on (which placed some check on arbitrary aristocratic actions) and by allowing popular assemblies and elected officials to give some voice alongside the aristocratic Senate, the Roman republic constructed more explicit balances than most of the early Greek city-states had done. Social strife was long minimized as a result, even as many similar political ingredients appeared. More than the Greeks, the Romans emphasized clientage relationships by which landlords would aid and protect lesser citizens in return for loyalty and work source.

Rome's diplomatic and military directions departed even more markedly from the patterns of the early Greek poleis, because there were fewer social tensions to distract the government and because no checkerboard of successful city-state rivals emerged to restrain the dynamic newcomer.

THE EXPANSION OF ROME

Rome's career differed most notably from that of its Greek counterparts by more promptly and wholeheartedly embracing expansion. Rome developed a solid army based on the service of citizen-farmers; while not as rigidly organized as Sparta, Rome stressed discipline and self-sacrifice within the framework of a largely agricultural economy. Rome was not, however, as sheltered from outside attack by natural boundaries as many of the Greek poleis had been. It faced challenges from other areas in Italy, including a league of city-states to the north. Rome dealt with these challenges, from 496 B.C. onward, through a combination of alliances and military attacks; by about 400 B.C. it had gained control over the whole of central Italy. A second wave of expansion, toward the southern end of the peninsula, began around 360 B.C., gradually winning over rival tribes on grounds of superior military organization and tight control over allied states.

Roman infantry units—the famous *legions*— were disciplined and flexible fighting forces, trained never to give up; they endowed Rome with a deserved reputation for being able to bounce back from specific defeats through a persistent will to win. The Roman military was supported by the rich agricultural economy of central Italy, which provided an abundant population base; and each wave of expansion simply strengthened the military and economic resources available. Once established, Roman rule proved flexible, though it provoked some resentments and rebellions. Some areas were granted Roman citizenship, while others retained local self-governments; in a few cases colonies of Roman soldiers were planted to assure order.

By the early part of the 3d century B.C., Roman expansion brought them in conflict with the Greek cities of the south, which soon accepted Roman governance. This made Rome a rival of the former Phoenician colony, Carthage, for control of the western Mediterranean. Carthage, located in North Africa in the modern nation of Tunisia, had a substantial navy and was quick to see the threat from Roman control over Sicily. A series of Punic wars (*Punic* is the Roman word for Phoenician) began in 264 B.C. Thus Rome developed its own navy for the first time; both Carthage and Rome generated new allies and colonies in Spain, as competition steadily escalated. During the Second Punic War the great Carthaginian general, Hannibal, brought a large army to Italy, including 50 war elephants. But gradually the Romans wore Carthage down. In the third Punic War (146 B.C.) the Romans finally decided to kill or enslave every inhabitant. Rome now had a substantial overseas empire, including much of Spain and substantial parts of North Africa, held either outright or through allied states.

Rome's growing power also drew the new empire toward the eastern Mediterranean, partly from a search for new conquests and partly because rival states in the region appealed for help. The collapse of the Hellenistic king-

The Expansion of the Roman Republic, 146 B.C.

doms left a vacuum of power in this region that Rome was increasingly called to fill. From 167 B.C. onward the Romans began to conquer Macedonia and Greece, and soon set up a protectorate over the Asian coast of the Mediterranean and also Egypt.

The republic was often brutal in its treatment of areas conquered outside Italy. Opponents of Roman rule in Greece were punished severely; much booty and many prisoners were taken. The conquest of Spain during the 2d century B.C. produced repeated atrocities; in North Africa, Carthage was destroyed, its land plowed up, and salt scattered in its fields as a symbol of its abandonment.

Imperial expansion inevitably changed Roman society and politics, to the great dismay of traditionalists. New trade and wealth enriched the upper classes, creating new gaps between rich and poor and making it increasingly difficult to manage Rome's balanced constitution. Aristocrats bought out many farmers who could not compete with cheap grains imported from Sicily and later North Africa. Older clientage relationships deteriorated, sharpening class conflicts. The devastation caused by Hannibal's invasions also produced widespread indebtedness, allowing estate owners to buy out ordinary farmer-citizens. Central Italy, like Greece before it, turned into a grape and olive region, highly commercial and organized mainly in large estates. Ruined farmers either worked as rural laborers or moved to the city, swelling an impoverished urban lower class easily open to appeals from ambitious politicians. Adding to social complexity was the rise of an important business class that also helped the state to help collect taxes. Slavery also increased as a result of military conquests. Many slaves worked in households or craft production, even tutoring Roman children, but bands of slaves were used in mining

and on some of the great agricultural estates. By A.D. 14 (after the republic's collapse) three million slaves—40 percent of the total population—worked in Italy.

THE CRISIS OF THE REPUBLIC

What was happening around Rome closely resembled earlier patterns in Greece where accelerating social and economic tensions produced increasing political unrest. But the Roman crisis was in many ways greater, because the expanding empire created so many new opportunities for the upper classes to gain new lands and augment their supply of slaves. While some former farmers sank into debt-slavery, others flooded into the city of Rome, beginning a process that would push the city's population to one million, much of it consisting of poor, irregularly-employed laborers.

Roman politics had long depended not only on some balance between farmers and landowners, but also on aristocratic protection of the farmers as their clients. Thus free farmers had direct participation in the Roman state through the popular assemblies. They could also count on aristocratic landlords to help them protect their interests in courts of law or even tide them over economically in bad times. Now this community of interest was split, as the landlords tried to buy out the farmers to add to their estates and as many farmers, though still citizens, massed in the city of Rome. The result, first economically and then politically, was a durable class conflict between popular leaders and aristocrats, during the final decades of the republic. In this setting many ambitious leaders in both camps, including successful army generals, maneuvered for personal advantage.

In 133 B.C. a new tribune, Tiberius Gracchus, tried to limit the size of large estates, with the government redistributing some land to the poor. The Senate rejected the plan, and Tiberius was soon assassinated by conservatives. During the following decades, Gaius Gracchus, Tiberius's brother, tried to introduce land reforms, with a special attempt to appeal to the rising business class of wealthy men eager for greater power and continued expansion of the empire but below the aristocracy in status. Gracchus also proposed extending Roman citizenship to more of the Italian people, but the Roman masses opposed this dilution of their authority. The Senate decreed that Gracchus, undefended, was to be put to death; a servant helped him fall on his sword.

Soon after this, in 107 B.C., a successful army general, Marius, who had put down a rebellion in one of Rome's client kingdoms in North Africa, became consul. Marius began using paid volunteers from the lower classes for his army, creating a permanent military group, with great political potential through their ability to coerce the Senate. Then another general, Sulla, siding with the Senate, which he packed with his supporters, drove out Marius and his followers. The republic, though most of its institutions were still intact, had become little more than a battleground for opposing ambitions. Clearly, a republican constitution designed for an agrarian city-state was proving unsuitable for governing a vast empire with a highly commercial economy.

In 77 B.C., another general, Pompey, surged to the fore. Like his predecessors, he enhanced his power by winning new conquests—first in Spain, then in the Middle East. His success, plus renewed civil war at home, prompted the Senate to give him special powers. A middle-class political leader, Cicero, eloquently pleaded for a return to republican balance, arguing against the generals and popular demagogues, but he was not heeded. Pompey joined with other generals, including Julius Caesar, to form a new government that could override the Senate. Caesar, who won considerable support from the Roman lower classes, then pursued his own goals through winning new territory across the Alps in Gaul (present-day France). He then defied Pompey and the Senate by bringing his troops back to Italy and taking over the government in 49 B.C. Effectively, Caesar's victory in the ensuing civil war ended the republic.

Caesar introduced few formal changes in government institutions. The Senate, which was packed with Caesar's men, still existed and debated, but its acts were a sham because of Caesar's control of the army. Caesar brought more Italians and other provincials into politics, at the expense of old Roman families. Made dictator for ten years and then

This sculpture of the emperor Augustus in military regalia renders him with god-like solemnity.

for life, Caesar named many new officials and judges and introduced important reforms, such as a more scientific calendar that formed the basis for the one we use today. Suspected of wanting to set up a monarchy, Caesar was assassinated by traditionalist senators in 44 B.C.

This led to 13 more years of civil war, with Caesar's cause defended by his grand nephew and adopted son Octavian, who fought the armies of the Senate. Octavian soon took the name Caesar, which would come to mean emperor. In a series of wars, particularly in Egypt and the Middle East, Octavian finally won out. His last opponents, Mark Anthony and his wife Cleopatra, queen of Egypt, committed suicide, ending the civil strife and making Octavian absolute master of Rome and the entire Mediterranean world. Octavian then proceeded to create a new set of institutions that would be suited to Rome's altered position, including its vast empire, while not unduly offending the republican traditions still cherished by many citizens. His response was the creation of an outright empire, with himself as first emperor under the name of Augustus Caesar.

This empire was a success, as Rome unlike earlier Greek poleis made a successful transition to a new form of government that decisively broke with city-state bounds.

DOCUMENT
ROME AND A VALUES CRISIS

Rome's increasing contact with the eastern Mediterranean, particularly with Greece, brought important debates about culture. Many conservatives deplored Greek learning, arguing that it would corrupt Roman virtue. Cicero, a leading politician in the Senate and a major Latin writer, here defends Greek literature, using Hellenistic justifications of beauty and utility. Cicero played a major role in the popularization of Greek culture during the 1st century B.C.

Do you think that I could find inspiration for my daily speeches on so manifold a variety of topics, did I not cultivate my mind with study, or that my mind could endure so great a strain, did not study too provide it with relaxation? I am a votary of literature, and make the confession unashamed; shame belongs rather to the bookish recluse, who knows not how to apply his reading to the good of his fellows, or to manifest its fruits to the eyes of all. But what shame should be mine, gentlemen, who have made it a rule of my life for all these years never to allow the sweets of a cloistered ease or the seductions of pleasure or the enticements of repose to prevent me from aiding any man in the hour of his need? How then can I justly be blamed or censured, if it shall be found that I have devoted to literature a portion of my leisure hours no longer than others without blame devote to the pursuit of material gain, to the celebration of festivals or games, to pleasure and the repose of mind and body, to protracted banqueting, or perhaps to the gaming-board or to ballplaying? I have the better right to indulge herein, because my devotion to letters strengthens my oratorical powers, and these, such as they are, have never failed my friends in their hour of peril. Yet insignificant though these powers may seem to be, I fully realize from what source I draw all that is highest in them. Had I not persuaded myself from my youth up, thanks to the moral lessons derived from a wide reading, that nothing is to be greatly sought after in this life save glory and honour, and that in their quest all bodily pains and all dangers of death or ex-

ile should be lightly accounted, I should never have borne for the safety of you all the brunt of many a bitter encounter, or bared my breast to the daily onsets of abandoned persons. All literature, all philosophy, all history, abounds with incentives to noble action, incentives which would be buried in black darkness were the light of the written word not flashed upon them. How many pictures of high endeavor the great authors of Greece and Rome have drawn for our use, and bequeathed to us, not only for our contemplation, but for our emulation! These I have held ever before my vision throughout my public career, and have guided the workings of my brain and my soul by meditating upon patterns of excellence.

But let us for the moment waive these solid advantages; let us assume that entertainment is the sole end of reading; even so, I think you would hold that no mental employment is so broadening to the sympathies or so enlightening to the understanding. Other pursuits belong not to all times, all ages, all conditions; but this gives stimulus to our youth and diversion to our old age; this adds a charm to success, and offers a haven of consolation to failure. In the home it delights, in the world it hampers not. Through the night watches, on all our journeying, and in our hours of country ease, it is an unfailing companion.

If anyone thinks that the glory won by the writing of Greek verse is naturally less than that accorded to the poet who writes in Latin, he is entirely in the wrong. Greek literature is read in nearly every nation under heaven, while the vogue of Latin is confined to its own boundaries, and they are, we must grant, narrow. Seeing, therefore, that the activities of our race know no barrier save the limits of the round earth, we ought to be ambitious that whithersoever our arms have penetrated there also our fame and glory should extend; for the reason that literature exalts the nation whose high deeds it sings, and at the same time there can be no doubt that those who stake their lives to fight in honour's cause find therein a lofty incentive to peril and endeavor. We read that Alexander the Great carried in his train numbers of epic poets and historians. And yet, standing before the tomb of Achilles at Sigeum, he exclaimed, "Fortunate youth, to have found in Homer an herald of thy valor!" Well might he so exclaim, for had the *Iliad* never existed, the same mound which covered Achilles' bones would also have overwhelmed his memory.*

*Cicero, *Pro Archia Poeta*. Translated by N. H. Watts. Loeb Classical Library. Cicero, *Pro Archia* (Harvard University Press, 1965), 12–14, 16, 23–24.

Questions: What kind of objections to Greek learning is Cicero arguing against? Which of his arguments had most lasting appeal in reshaping Roman culture? Can you think of similar debates about foreign culture in other times and places in history?

ROMAN CULTURE

As Rome struggled with its political crisis, a major cultural transformation was taking place that merged earlier Roman values and the Latin language with the impressive heritage of Greek and Hellenistic learning. Roman leaders were increasingly schooled in philosophy and a rich literary culture, blended with the earlier republican ideas of active citizenship.

Roman intellectual life was never as vibrant as that of the glory days of 5th-century Athens, in part because Roman writers and artists were so eager to adopt Greek forms. But Rome had its own strengths, while preserving and modifying many Greek cultural achievements.

THE RANGE OF ROMAN ART

Greek artistic styles and literary influence increasingly shaped Roman upper-class life, from the 2d century into the days of the empire. Many aristocratic families were educated by Greek slaves, who as tutors had considerable independence and in a few cases produced important literary or historical work of their own. Imitation of Greece was aided by the similarity between Roman and Greek religions where essentially the same pantheon of gods and goddesses merely had different names. Roman religion was more political than Greek, bent toward divine protection of the state and colder in tone, but the similarities encouraged shared stories and literary symbolism. Rome's literary creativity was less impressive than that of the Greeks, partly because Greek authors were so widely read. The Roman poet Vergil picked up the Greek epic tradition, seeking to link Roman history and mythology with the great stories of the *Iliad* and the *Odyssey*. Roman poets and biographers were also active, shaping the Latin language and providing stylistic models. Roman sculptors worked mainly in the Greek tradition, producing busts of great men and statues and scenes of heroic grandeur. Rome also developed activ-

ity in painting, producing lively (sometimes pornographic) decorations for the houses of the wealthy.

Roman architecture benefited as the city's wealth grew. Again, Greek styles provided primary inspiration, with the

These columns surround the Arch of Titus near the Colosseum in Rome. The use of decorative styles that originated in classical Greece was a central feature of Roman public design.

This public lavatory was part of a new building in the prosperous Italian port city of Ostia Antica. Other buildings, some of which were made of bricks, were used for commercial and storage purposes, as well as for apartments.

Romans preferring the more ornate designs for columns and arches. But Rome added its own genius to Greek architecture mainly through engineering advances that allowed structures of greater size to be built. Huge stadiums, public baths, temples, massive aqueducts to carry water to cities, great stretches of paved road, and huge port facilities began to appear in the later republic. Roman ability to construct elaborate arches, which allowed buildings to carry great structural weight, was unsurpassed anywhere in the world. Under Augustus, statues, fountains, and temples to the gods spread through Rome, making the city the showcase as well as the capital of the new empire.

Greek influence and the practical issues of politics in an increasingly complex society prompted creativity in a number of other areas. Roman leaders valued skill in oratory and advanced discussions of the arts of rhetoric. Ethical philosophy received considerable attention. Hellenistic schools, including Stoicism, won many converts because

Roman leaders were eager to develop arguments for moral behavior that had strong logical support. Writers, such as Cicero, discussed the joys and sorrows of human life, urging moderation and a dedication to the public good.

Roman intellectuals did not, in the main, embrace the full range of Greek interests. They did little in science or formal philosophy, though the Greek and Hellenistic works were translated and read. Textbooks that compiled key concepts and discoveries aided this transmission process, as Rome extended classical Mediterranean culture by additional contributions in key areas and by the sheer process of bringing this culture to North Africa and southwestern Europe.

Again, architecture provides a useful guide. Roman monuments, in the styles adapted from the Greeks, were built from England in the north to the desert fringes of North Africa, from Spain to present day Hungary and Romania, and down the Middle Eastern coast of the Mediterranean. Temples, stadiums, villas for transplanted Romans or the local upper class, and the ubiquitous baths brought Roman styles and building knowledge through the expanded Mediterranean world. Awesome ruins of these structures, which still dot the former empire, give testimony to Rome's power as a cultural disseminator.

MAJOR THEMES IN ROMAN LITERATURE

Prosperity and greater stability during the reign of Augustus and his successors brought growing attention to other cultural activities. While some of Rome's best poets flourished during the late republic as Greek themes were transmuted into Latin language and style, the early empire saw a flowering of history and biography. Many writers praised the new imperial house, but poets, such as Horace, combined this loyalty with considerable humor and creative skill in adapting Greek poetic meters to the Latin language. Horace, initially a republican, shifted to support of Augustus; his odes were lyrical poems, many of them praising the emperor and his family.

Another poet, Ovid, stressed the growing sensuality of the aristocracy in his writing on the arts of love. Exiled by the emperor, who wanted to defend family values, he also wrote about the Roman religion and translated Greek nature stories. Historians, such as Livy, wrote elaborate accounts of Rome, linking the empire to the republican past.

Vergil's great epic poem the *Aeneid* was itself dedicated to the glories of Augustus and his empire:

> *Now fix your sight, and stand intent, to see your Roman*
> *race, and Julian progeny.*
> *There mighty Caesar waits his vital hour, Impatient for*
> *the world, and grasps his promised power.*
> *But next behold the youth of form divine—Caesar him-*
> *self, exalted in his line—Augustus, promised oft, and*
> *long foretold,*
> *Sent to the realm that Saturn ruled of old; born to re-*
> *store a better age of gold.*
> *Africa and India shall his power obey;*
> *He shall extend his propagated sway Beyond the solar*
> *year, without the starry way . . .*
> *But Rome! 'tis thine alone, with awful sway, To*
> *rule mankind, and make the world obey,*
> *Disposing peace and war, thy own majestic way. . . .*

After the cultural surge of the late republic and early empire and spurred by the assimilation of Greek forms, Roman cultural activity declined somewhat. Intellectual life continued, but it stressed preservation, imitation, textbook summaries, and education of the upper classes. Dissemination and additional building continued, but well before the politics of the empire began to deteriorate, mainstream literary and artistic vitality began to decline. Only the new religious spur of Christianity brought new uses for Latin and Greek literary skill, elements of philosophy, and ultimately art.

 ## THE INSTITUTIONS OF EMPIRE

If Roman culture had a certain limited quality, Roman political creativity continued at a high level. The evolution of the Roman republic was interesting in its parallels with Greek city-states and its increasingly dramatic death throes. Marked innovation awaited the critical decades of the republic when behind the scenes new principles of imperial administration were worked out and the legal system elaborated. These developments were then capped by the work of Augustus and his successors, in replacing the republic itself.

Rome's rule of its growing empire rested less on detailed control or an elaborate bureaucracy than on tolerance and cohesion through law. Military force was used as needed, and in troubled periods Rome briefly seized administration of a distant province.

In general, considerable autonomy was given to local governments, including the old Greek city-states, as the harsh colonial policies of the republic were revised. Some whole kingdoms, as in parts of North Africa, were preserved though required to obey Roman foreign policy and obtain permission for any new succession to the throne. This policy of tolerance greatly facilitated Roman control, for an elaborate bureaucratic apparatus did not have to be developed; only much later, in different circumstances, did lack of centralization prove to be a partial liability. At the same time, however, Rome maintained small military garrisons in most areas and large outposts in newly-conquered or threatened regions. Army generals doubled as provincial governors in such cases, which created the possibility of building considerable regional power even to the point of challenging the consuls and Senate back in Rome. Again, in contrast to Chinese principles of imperial rule, Roman efforts were marked by the absence of coordinated bureaucratic hierarchies or formal training.

Rome's greatest addition to its principles of politics and empire was careful attention to the development of codes of law. While local laws continued to apply in many areas of the empire, Roman law provided an overarching system accessible to citizens at any part of the empire and capable of facilitating commercial exchange. Roman jurists carefully constructed statements of general legal principles—what they regarded as "natural law" and case precedents—that applied consistent standards to specific civil or criminal issues, building one of the most extensive legal systems anywhere. In the early republic they collected the statutes passed by the Roman assembly and the interpretations of judicial officials. As the republic expanded and encountered other legal systems, judicial officials had to formulate more general principles of equity. By the end of the republic the idea of natural law, applicable to all societies and related to Stoic ethical theory, emerged as a result. Here was a substantial addition to the political traditions established by the Greek city-states and the early Roman republic.

Roman law focused heavily on protection of private property and on family stability. It also carried forward some central concepts. Law, in the Roman view, should evolve to meet changing conditions without, however, fluctuating wildly. Rules and objective judgments, rather than personal whim, should govern social relationships; thus Roman law steadily took over judgment functions earlier reserved for fathers of families or landlords. Roman law also promoted the importance of common-sense fairness. In one case cited in the law texts, a slave was being shaved by a barber in a public square. Two men were playing ball nearby and one accidentally hit the barber with the ball, causing him to cut the slave's throat. Who was responsible: barber, catcher, or pitcher? According to Roman law, the slave himself: for anyone so foolish as to be shaved in a public place was asking for trouble and bore the responsibility himself.

The extension of Roman law was supplemented by a willingness to extend citizenship to important groups outside Rome and its environs. This was a marked contrast to earlier Greek policy, bent more on defending the primacy of the polis. Italians had gained this right during the republic, and a minority of people in France, Spain, North Africa, and the eastern Mediterranean acquired citizenship in the early decades of the empire. Paul, a key figure in early Christianity and born a Jew, was a Roman citizen and proud of it. Several North Africans served as emperors and led in intellectual and religious life (including the early Christian church). More generally, citizenship gave selected individuals full access to Roman law and its courts, and obviously encouraged loyalty.

The combination of systematic law, military organization, and tolerance for local autonomy (including a welter of diverse religions) allowed Rome long to maintain its empire amid considerable internal peace, an achievement far greater than conquering the empire in the first place.

AUGUSTUS AND HIS SUCCESSORS

In building an imperial government after his final victory in 31 B.C., Octavian was able to utilize the tolerant principles of treatment for conquered provinces, and the developing system of law. He also appealed carefully to remaining republican loyalties. He talked sincerely about the validity of republican virtues and the importance of discipline and family virtues. He also retained many of the agencies of the republic, including the Senate, while eviscerating most of them by installing his own supporters in full control. Symbolizing the transition, in 27 B.C. the Senate voted the title *Augustus* on Octavian, a word often applied to gods and appropriate to an office that now dominated the state. The emperor now controlled the apparatus of government, making major appointments and military decisions and establishing new laws and policies.

Augustus set about consolidating his new regime by instituting moral reforms, banning mystery religions, and insisting on adherence to traditional Roman ceremonies. He revised the law to strengthen family stability, while encouraging people to have children by ruling, for example, that women with at least three children might gain new rights. Augustus launched an ambitious new building program in Rome, which brought new jobs to the Roman masses and new entertainments as well. Augustus also tried to regularize control over the provinces. He relied heavily on his army of 250,000 men, giving them abundant rewards for long service and loyalty. He maintained the earlier policy of considerable local autonomy to accompany military strength, while encouraging the development of Romanized colonies in many provinces, particularly in North Africa and western Europe.

The empire Augustus created maintained its basic organizational structure and its heady success for approximately two centuries. Incompetent emperors were no rarity in this period, in part because no clear lines of succession were established. Effectively, the army controlled basic power, which worked well when a strong emperor held the army's loyalty, but badly when an emperor lost command of the troops. Succession battles among rival generals were common. By A.D. 96 emperors began to reduce succession problems by adopting their own successors. This practice yielded a series of five good emperors who brought Rome to its greatest power.

The emperor Trajan adopted a more aggressive foreign policy in A.D. 101–106. The boundaries of the empire were pressed to the greatest extent ever, with fortifications in northern England and along the Rhine and Danube rivers signaling the inclusion of much of western Europe in the new geography of Mediterranean civilization. The empire also reached deeper into the Middle East, with new provinces in Armenia, Assyria, and Mesopotamia. But the expenses of maintaining the vast boundaries placed growing burdens on the imperial economy. A turn from expansion to defense, though probably inevitable, reduced some of the easy conquests characteristic of earlier years.

The Roman Empire from Augustus to A.D. 150

By A.D. 180 the empire poised on a pinnacle of power that would quickly turn to descent. Foreign policy turned defensive, a matter of building walls and trying to finance border garrisons to keep invaders out. The later Roman Empire, though still capable of impressive achievements, was enmeshed in a pattern of gradual decline, which in turn was part of the general collapse of the classical world.

THE EMPIRE AND CLASSICAL MEDITERRANEAN TRADITION

The creation of the Roman Empire added a final ingredient to the political characteristics of Mediterranean civilization more generally. The Greco-Roman world had already tossed up a diversity of political forms and institutions designed to balance various principles, such as aristocracy and democracy; it had focused attention on the obligations of citizenship and on the process of formally creating laws and constitutions. Articulate political theories, spelled out by Greek philosophers as well as practical Roman politicians, such as Cicero, defended various constitu-

tional alternatives and promoted the idea of responsible, active citizenship. Here was a distinctive political brew, different, for example, from Confucian traditions in China in the amount of attention given to state structure and citizen activities, particularly legislative activities, instead of bureaucratic service and obedience in hierarchy.

At its height the empire continued to rest on the principles established in the later republic and with Augustus. Local autonomy remained strong. In only a few cases, such as the forced dissolution of the independent Jewish state in 63 B.C. after a major local rebellion, did the Romans take over distant areas completely. Military garrisons, with provincial governors wielding necessary controls, were supplemented by considerable decentralization, the unifying features of Roman law, and the extension of citizenship to the well-placed minority. The idea of fair and reasoned law, to which officers of the state should themselves be subject, was a key political achievement of the Roman Empire, comparable in importance, though quite different in nature, to the Chinese elaboration of a bureaucratic structure.

Beyond the idea of law, the Roman imperial state did not innovate, particularly in the functions ascribed to government. Regulation of commerce was essential, as the Roman state tried to assure vital stocks of grain from Sicily and North Africa. The administration of food supplies and prices for huge cities, such as Rome, required a substantial official staff. Public works in the form of roads and harbors facilitated military transport as well as commerce, while government-sponsored amenities, such as public baths and stadiums, attracted public loyalty. The building of aqueducts to carry water to cities was another major state activity. All these public works and regulations required substantial tax revenues.

Government-supported religious ceremonies continued, but there was little attempt to impose this religion on all subjects and various other religions were usually tolerated. Only Jews and later Christians found the state's claim to primary loyalty unacceptable, and only they drew Roman reprisals; the Roman government tolerated Jewish monotheism but reacted fiercely to Jewish revolt. Even the later Roman emperors, who as a means of shoring up authority enhanced the idea that the emperor himself was a god, were normally tolerant of other religions, inconsistently attacking Christianity because of the Christians' refusal to place the state first in their devotion.

The significance of political achievements to classical Mediterranean civilization, in both its Greek and Roman versions, is abundantly clear. The main political principles, particularly in law and model forms of government structure, also formed a heritage to later societies, though not exactly a tidy one.

Localism and fervent political interests, including a sense of intense loyalty to the state; a diversity of political systems together with the preference for aristocratic rule; and the importance of law and the existence, in the Roman Empire, of an unusually elaborate and uniform set of legal principles—these were the chief political legacies of the classical Mediterranean world. Added to them was the sheer accomplishment of the Roman Empire itself, which united a region never before or since brought together and which still stands as one of the great political monuments of world history. This was not a political heritage of the sort that most modern Americans would fully admire, even aside from its diversity. Above all, while there was attention to careful legal procedures, there was no clear definition of individuals' rights; indeed, the emphasis on duties to the state could lead, as in Sparta, to an authoritarian framework in which the state administered even the raising of children. Nor, until the peaceful centuries of the early Roman Empire, was it an entirely successful political structure, as wars and instability were fully as prominent in this

civilization as in classical India. But there can be no question of the richness of this political culture or of its central importance to the Greeks and Romans.

THE CLASSICAL MEDITERRANEAN IN COMPARATIVE PERSPECTIVE

The three great classical civilizations lend themselves to a variety of comparisons. The general tone of each differed, ranging from India's otherworldly strain to China's emphasis on government centralization—though it is important to note the varieties of activities and interests and the changes that occurred within each of the three societies.

Basic comparisons embrace the substantial similarities that resulted from the tendency in each classical society to move toward empire or from the features imposed by primary reliance on an agricultural economy. Greco-Roman interest in secular culture bears some resemblance to Confucian emphasis in China, though in each case religious currents, including popular animism, remained as well. But Greco-Roman political values and institutions differed from Confucian stress on deference and bureaucratic training. India differed greatly from Greece and Rome in its use of the Indo-European pantheon of gods. Greek definitions of science contrasted with those of India and China. There are a number of focal points for comparison.

Each of the classical civilizations emphasized a fairly rigid social hierarchy, with substantial distance between elites and the majority of people who did the manual and menial work. This vital similarity among the civilizations reflected common tensions between complex leadership demands and life-styles and the limited economic resources of the agricultural economy. Groups at the top of the social hierarchy judged that they had to subordinate lower groups rather carefully to assure their own economic margins. Each classical society generated ideologies that explained and justified the great social divisions. Philosophers and religious leaders devoted considerable attention to this subject, either explicitly or by implication.

Within this common framework, however, there were obvious differences. Groups at the top of the social pyramid reflected varied value systems: hence in India the priests, in China the bureaucrats, and in Greece the cultivated aristocrats ruled the roost, though in all cases this elite evolved from an earlier pattern that gave stress to a warrior leadership. The status of merchants varied despite the vital role commerce played in all three civilizations.

Mobility opportunities varied also. India's caste system allowed movement within castes, if wealth was acquired, but little overall mobility; this was the most rigid classical social structure, because it tied people to their basic social and occupational position by birth. China's bureaucratic system allowed a very small number of talented people from below to rise substantially on the basis of education, though it must be emphasized that most bureaucrats continued to come from the landed aristocracy. Mediterranean society, with its aristocratic emphasis, limited the chance to rise to the top, but the importance of acquired wealth (particularly in Rome) did give some nonaristocrats important economic and political opportunities—Cicero, for example, came from a family of merchant background. Various classes also shared some political power in city-state assemblies; the idea of basic political rights among citizens (see "Analysis" in Chapter 7) was unusual in classical civilizations. Although most people were excluded even in the Greek democracies, this degree of mixing would have been impossible in a caste system.

Each classical civilization distinctively defined the position of the lowest orders. India's untouchables performed duties culturally evaluated as demeaning, though often vital. Classical Mediterranean society relied heavily on the legal and physical compulsions of slavery to provide both menial service and the most demanding kinds of labor, particularly as Greece and then Rome entered their expansion phases. Greece and Rome gave unusual voice to farmers when they maintained their own property, but tended to scorn manual labor per se—a view that helped justify slavery and was perpetuated by slavery in turn. The position of the peasantry tended to get worse over time in the Mediterranean when the economy became more complex. In this respect, India's caste system, which involved less direct control over labor, was more stable.

Finally, each of the classical civilizations developed a different kind of cultural "glue" to help hold its social hierarchy together. Greece and Rome left much of the task of managing the social hierarchy to local authorities; community bonds, as in the city-states, were meant to pull different groups into a sense of common purpose. They also relied on military force and clear legal statements that defined rights according to station. Force and legal inequalities played important roles in China and India as well, but there were additional bonds. India's Hinduism obviously helped justify and sustain hierarchy by promising rewards through reincarnation for submission to one's place in any given existence. Within this framework a network of caste laws and customs encouraged people to internalize their understanding of the jobs and social contacts permitted to

them. China, in addition to government enforcement, urged general cultural values of obedience and self-restraint, creating some agreement—despite varied religions and philosophies—on the legitimacy of social ranks through the definition of how gentlemen and commoners should behave.

In no case did the social cement work perfectly; social unrest surfaced in all the classical civilizations, as in major slave rebellions in Rome or recurrent peasant uprisings in China. At the same time, the rigidity of all classical social structures gave many common people some leeway. Elites viewed the masses as so different that they did not try to revamp all their beliefs or community institutions.

Differences in approach to social inequality nevertheless had important results. China and particularly India generated value systems that might convince people in the lower classes and the upper ranks that there was some legitimacy in the social hierarchy. Greece and Rome attempted a more difficult task in emphasizing the importance of aristocracy while offering some other elements a share in the political system. This combination could work well, though some groups, including slaves, were always excluded. It tended to deteriorate, however, when poorer citizens lost property. Yet no sweeping new social theory emerged to offer a different kind of solace to the masses—at least until Christianity began to spread. It is no accident, then, that Indian and Chinese social structures survived better than Mediterranean structures did, lasting well beyond the classical period into the 20th century.

Questions: Why did the classical civilizations seem to need radical social inequalities? What was the relationship between wealth and social position in each of the classical civilizations? If India used religion to compensate for social inequalities, what did China and the Mediterranean use?

THE EVOLUTION OF ROME'S ECONOMIC AND SOCIAL STRUCTURE

Several basic features of Roman economic and social development closely paralleled earlier patterns in Greece. A local agricultural economy that yielded two social groups—aristocracy and free farmers—became increasingly complex as a result of urban and commercial growth.

As earlier in the Greek city-states, a class of merchants expanded during the final centuries of the republic. Many merchants were foreigners, for Romans did not take well to seafaring and built clumsy boats that hugged the shores.

Traders from Greece and the Middle East played a vital role. But a native business group expanded as well, and its prestige was somewhat higher than its counterpart in classical Greece had been even though aristocratic suspicion of merchants persisted in Rome. Merchants gained political voice in the Roman Senate in the later days of the republic, though they never matched aristocratic prestige.

Rome and other imperial cities also developed large artisanal and shopkeeping groups, and of course a substantial, sometimes troubling, propertyless lower class.

Rome's family structure resembled that of classical Greece and all the major classical civilizations that showed tendencies toward strong central government. The family structure was firmly patriarchal. Roman law stipulated that "the husband is the judge of his wife. If she commits a fault, he punishes her; if she has drunk wine, he condemns her; if she has been guilty of adultery, he kills her." Later, however, the power of husbands was modified by the need for approval by a family court composed of members of both families. If divorced because of adultery, a Roman woman lost one-third of her property and had to wear a special garment that set her apart like a prostitute. The oppression of women was less severe in Rome than in either Greece or China, however. As wives and mothers, a number of aristocratic Roman women wielded considerable political power, if only through their husbands. Women freely appeared in public and attended major entertainments; some were educated, though rarely as well as men in the same class.

As Roman agriculture became increasingly commercialized from the 2d century B.C. onward, additional changes rocked Mediterranean society. The free-farming class de-

This Roman painting features a young woman in an unusual role, as a student of the early Greek poetess Sappho.

clined, while slavery spread steadily. As in Greece, many Roman slaves performed household tasks. Some were quite independent, particularly if they came from a civilized province such as Greece. Slaves were also used, however, for arduous manual labor, and large supplies of these slaves were brought in from Britain and Germany, the Slavic lands of the northern Balkans, and from Africa. Slave labor manned the mines, amid brutal conditions. It also increasingly staffed the large estates, along with some paid laborers and tenant farmers. Far more than in Greece earlier on, the Roman economy became dependent on slave labor; grain supplies and other marketed agricultural products relied on this labor extensively. This was a pattern that foreshadowed the use of slaves on commercial estates in the Americas from the 16th century onward, where slave labor provided the production on which the economy depended, but it was unusual in the classical world.

The spread of Roman slavery contributed further to the decline of free farmers. It also contributed to the unusual militarism of Rome in the late republic and early empire. Slave revolts, though not common, required a military presence. Displaced Italian farmers increasingly sought a longer term career in the military, where they could earn pay and have some prospect of acquiring property as veterans. Most obviously, military expansion was a vital source of additional slaves, for the Roman slave population did not reproduce itself. Here was an obvious contrast to China and India, where an expansionist foreign policy was not a central issue in labor supply.

Finally, Roman slavery, like Greek slavery, helps explain the relatively stagnant production technology in manufacturing and agriculture. The Romans displayed real engineering genius in their buildings, roads, and city design, but they paid little attention to techniques of food supply or manufacturing. Estate agriculture and government organization of ports and markets, not production methods, seized center stage with abundant slave labor a vital ingredient.

In Harappa, the first river-valley civilization in India, ingenious city design had combined with stagnant technology in other fields. Although Roman methods were far superior to those of Harappa simply because of subsequent advances, particularly in ironworking, its combination was somewhat similar: innovative urban plans and systems, but little attention to other technologies. A few engine designs were sketched but merely as exercises; there was no interest in building or using them. Some manufacturing operations used waterwheels for power, and there is evidence that these spread in the 2d century A.D. Still, the number of new inventions was few. One result was an ongoing lag behind the economies of India and China in sophisticated manufacturing. The Roman upper classes eagerly purchased silks and other processed goods that came from Asia, reaching the Mediterranean overland through the Middle East. In return the Romans offered exotic African animals, skins, and gold—not products they made.

The empire was not joined in a single economic and social structure. The social arrangements characteristic of Italy were not uniform through the Roman empire. Rome established vigorous cities in Spain, France, and England, populating them with the families of soldiers, who married local women, and with colonists. Only gradually and incompletely, however, did estate agriculture spread to Europe north of the Mediterranean. Many local farmers continued to practice subsistence agriculture, even hunting. The gap between new, Romanized cities and the rural population, usually ignorant of Latin as well as illiterate, was often considerable. In North African provinces, Romans pressed a policy of economic exploitation more ruthlessly. Peasants in Egypt and in other parts of North Africa were forced to produce grain for sale in the Italian markets, and large estates quickly predominated. There was little effort to set up Romanized cities or to encourage mutually beneficial trade. Even in more prestigious North African provinces, agricultural exploitation was so intense that resulting soil exhaustion and desert conditions have not been reversed in our own day. A third distinctive region was the portion of the empire in Greece and western Asia, where more active commerce and larger merchant groups maintained pre-Roman traditions and wielded greater wealth than existed in much of the Western Empire.

Because of the divisions of classical Mediterranean society, by region as well as class and gender, no easy generalizations about overall social achievement can be made. An 18th-century English historian called the high point of the Roman Empire before A.D. 180, the period in human history "during which the condition of the human race was most happy or prosperous." This is doubtful, given the technological accomplishments of China and India. And certainly many slaves, women, and ordinary male farmers might have disagreed even in the Mediterranean world itself. Quite apart from the huge social divisions and stark gaps between the slaves and the free people, Mediterranean society was, like most classical civilizations, massively split between upper-class and urban populations on the one hand, and the rural majority on the other. Few farmers actively participated in the political structures or cultural opportunities that were the most obvious mark of this civilization. Many farmers continued to work largely as their ancestors had done, with quite similar tools and very similar poverty, untouched by the doings of the great or the bustle of the cities except when wars swept over their lands.

We are tempted to remember particularly the urban achievements, for they carried the greatest influence to later ages that recalled the glories of Greece and Rome. The distinctive features of classical Mediterranean social and family structure had less enduring impact, though ideas about slavery or women were revived in subsequent periods. But the structures of ordinary life had their impact in helping to shape Roman politics and in contributing to new cultural changes and a declining vigor after about A.D. 180, in many facets of imperial life.

THE ORIGINS OF CHRISTIANITY

In the initial decades of the Roman Empire, at the eastern end of the Mediterranean, a new religion, Christianity, emerged. Much of the impetus for this new religion rested in issues in the Jewish religion, including a long-standing belief in the coming of a Messiah and rigidities that had developed in the Jewish priesthood. Whether or not Christianity was created by God, as Christians believe, the early stages of the religion focused on cleansing the Jewish religion of stiff rituals and haughty leaders. It had little at first to do with Roman culture. Christianity arose in a remote province and appealed particularly to the poorer classes. It is not easy, as a result, to fit Christianity neatly into the patterns of Roman history: It was deliberately separate, and only gradually had wider impact.

Christianity originated with Jesus of Nazareth, a Jewish prophet and teacher who probably came to believe he was the Son of God and certainly was regarded as such by his disciples. Jesus preached in Israel during the time of Augustus, urging a purification of the Jewish religion that would free Israel and establish the kingdom of God on earth. He urged a moral code based on love, charity, and humility, and he asked the faithful to follow his lessons, abandoning worldly concern. Many disciples believed that a Final Judgment day was near at hand, on which God would reward the righteous with immortality and condemn sinners to everlasting hell.

Jesus won many followers among the poor. He also roused suspicion among the upper classes and the leaders of the Jewish religion. These helped persuade the Roman governor, already concerned about unrest among the Jews, that Jesus was a dangerous agitator. Jesus was put to death as a result, crucified like a common criminal, about A.D. 30. His followers believed that he was resurrected on the third day after his death, a proof that he was the Son of

God. This belief helped the religion spread farther among Jewish communities in the Middle East, both within the Roman Empire and beyond. As they realized that the Messiah was not immediately returning to earth to set up the Kingdom of God, the disciples of Jesus began to fan out, particularly around the eastern Mediterranean, to spread the new Christian message.

Initially, Christian converts were Jewish by birth and followed the basic Jewish law. Their belief that Christ was divine as well as human, however, roused hostility among other Jews. When one early convert, Stephen, was stoned to death, many disciples left Israel and traveled throughout western Asia.

CHRISTIANITY GAINS CONVERTS AND RELIGIOUS STRUCTURE

Gradually over the next 250 years, Christianity won a growing number of converts. By the 4th century A.D., about 10 percent of the residents of the Roman Empire were Christian, and the new religion had also made converts elsewhere in the Middle East and Ethiopia. As it spread, Christianity connected increasingly with larger themes in Roman history.

With its particularly great appeal to some of the poor, Christianity was well positioned to reflect social grievances in an empire increasingly marked by inequality. Slaves, dispossessed farmers and impoverished city dwellers found hope in a religion that promised rewards after death. Christianity also answered cultural and spiritual needs—especially but not exclusively among the poor—left untended by mainstream Roman religion and culture. Roman values had stressed political goals and ethics suitable for life in this world. They did not join peoples of the empire in more spiritual loyalties, and they did not offer many emotionally satisfying rituals. As the empire consolidated, reducing direct political participation, a number of mystery religions spread from the Middle East and Egypt, religions that offered emotionally charged rituals. Worship of gods such as Mithra or Isis, derived from earlier Mesopotamian or Egyptian beliefs, attracted some Roman soldiers and others with rites of sacrifice and a strong sense of religious community. Christianity, though far more than a mystery religion, had some of these qualities and won converts on this basis as well. Christianity, in sum, gained ground in part because of features of Roman political and cultural life.

The spread of Christianity also benefited from some of the positive qualities of Rome's great empire. Political stability and communications over a wide area aided missionary efforts, while the Roman example helped inspire the government forms of the growing Christian church. Early Christian communities regulated themselves, but with expansion more formal government was introduced, with *bishops* playing a role not unlike Rome's provincial governors. Bishops headed churches in regional centers and supervised the activities of other churches in the area. Bishops in politically powerful cities, including Rome, gained particular authority. Roman principles also helped move what initially had been a religion among Jews to a genuinely cosmopolitan stance. Under the leadership of Paul, converted to Christianity about A.D. 35, Christian missionaries began to move away from insistence that adherents of the new religion must follow Jewish law. Rather, in the spirit of Rome and of Hellenism, the new faith was seen as universal, open to all whether or not they followed Jewish practices in diet, male circumcision, and so on.

Paul's conversion to Christianity proved vital. Paul was Jewish, but he had been born in a Greek city and was familiar with Greco-Roman culture. He helped explain basic Christian beliefs in terms other adherents of this culture could grasp, and he preached in Greece and Italy as well as the Middle East. Paul essentially created Christian theology, as a set of intellectual principles that followed from, but generalized, the message of Jesus. Paul also modified certain initial Christian impulses. Jesus himself had drawn a large number of women followers, but Paul emphasized women's subordination to men and the dangers of sexuality. It was Paul's stress on Christianity as a universal religion, requiring abandonment of other religious beliefs, and his related use of Greek—the dominant language of the day throughout the eastern Mediterranean—that particularly transformed the new faith.

RELATIONS WITH THE ROMAN EMPIRE

Gradually, Christian theological leaders made further contact with Greco-Roman intellectual life. They began to develop a body of Christian writings beyond the Bible messages written by the disciples of Jesus. By the 4th century A.D., Christian writings became the only creative cultural expressions in the Roman Empire, as theologians sought not only to explain issues in the new religion but

This sarcophagus, or tomb, from the 4th century shows Christ and the apostles in typical Roman dress.

This wall painting, in the style characteristic of the Roman Empire, shows Mary and Jesus. It was situated in a catacomb in Rome, where early Christians worshiped in tunneled caves to protect themselves from persecution.

also to relate it to Greek philosophy and Roman ethics. Ironically, as the Roman Empire was in most respects declining, Christianity produced an outpouring of complex thought and often elegant use of language. In this effort, Christianity redirected Roman culture (never known for abundant religious subtlety) but also preserved many earlier literary and philosophical achievements.

Adherents of the new religion clashed with Roman authorities, to be sure. Christians, who put their duties to God first, would not honor the emperor as a divinity and might seem to reject the authority of the state in other spheres. Several early emperors, including the mad Nero, persecuted Christians, killing some and driving their worship underground. Persecution was not constant, however, which helps explain why the religion continued to spread. It resumed only in the 4th century, when several emperors sought to use religious conformity and new claims to divinity as a way of cementing loyalties to a declining state. Ro-

man beliefs, including periodic tolerance, helped shape a Christian view that the state had a legitimately separate if subordinate sphere; Western Christians would often cite Christ as saying "Render unto Caesar that which is Caesar's, and unto God that which is God's."

The full story of early Christianity goes beyond the history of Rome, and we will turn to it again in Chapter 11. Christianity had more to do with opening a new era in the history of the Mediterranean region than with shaping the later Roman Empire. Yet important connections did exist that explain features of Christianity and of later Roman history. Though not a Roman product and though benefiting in part from the empire's decline, Christianity in some of its qualities can be counted as part of the Greco-Roman legacy.

CONCLUSION

THE MEDITERRANEAN HERITAGE

Well before Christianity became a major factor in Mediterranean life, the Roman Empire began to show important signs of decay. Its political-social framework became increasingly vulnerable. Defending the borders of the empire and maintaining government establishments was a costly business, yet many regions and groups found it difficult to meet their tax requirements. Further expansion of the empire became impossible after A.D. 180, because the government could not afford troops needed to keep order in more distant provinces and because pressures from border groups, particularly the Germanic tribes in central Europe, began to increase. Yet without expansion, needed labor supplies and rewards for army units became more difficult to come by.

Other economic disruptions followed from regional changes. The Italian economy, for example, began to suffer by the 3d century A.D., as African grain and French-grown wine cut into production, reducing prosperity and tax revenues at the empire's core. Disruptions of this sort contributed to political weakness, which forced new, more subsistence-oriented economic arrangements. More estates turned into local economic and political units rather than commercial operations, as connections that had cemented the empire at its height began to come undone.

Economic problems were not alone. Assuring high quality emperors, never easy, became more difficult after the final series of able leaders at the end of the 2d century A.D.

The declining authority of the imperial government began to reduce the willingness of upper-class individuals to sacrifice individual interest for service to the public good. Exactly what mixture produced Rome's gradual unraveling is not easy to determine. Rome was not eternal. Yet even as its fortune waned, it had established a legacy that would survive the empire itself. Roman institutions and values, Greek ideas and artistic forms that Rome had used and preserved, indeed the Greco-Roman ingredients in the ascending Christian religion—all would help shape successor societies around the Mediterranean.

Each of the classical civilizations created institutions and values that survived the classical period itself, helping to shape distinctive societies identifiable today. Each inspired great awe and veneration, causing later generations to look back on the classical period with genuine reverence.

Classical Mediterranean civilization fit that pattern neatly. Successor societies, including those in North America that can trace definite lineage back to Greece and Rome, have often defined the Mediterranean in such glowing terms that the existence of other (and in some ways, more successful) classical societies might be almost ignored. Certainly, the classical Mediterranean generated traditions in science and philosophy, in political theory and definitions of citizenship that, continuing or later revived after the fall of Rome, we value as part of our civilization today. Other values, such as those concerning the roles of women, also had lingering influence though in ways we now regard as less beneficent. Important features of classical Mediterranean society did not survive, however. On the whole, cultural emphases and artistic styles traveled best, though even here important features, such as the dominant Greco-Roman religion, were largely jettisoned. Political traditions were significant also, but they were more selectively used, certainly combined with a number of other, subsequent innovations.

In contrast to India and to an extent China, where caste or social ranking systems long endured, the characteristic social structure of the classical Mediterranean did not have much ongoing impact—though it had more impact in the eastern Mediterranean region than the west. It was already blurring, in fact, as Rome declined.

One of the key means of approaching the later history of China, India, or the Mediterranean region involves asking what happened to the basic features of the classical period—what persisted, what lasted if in modified form, and what was uprooted through change.

A recognition of the force of change is particularly important in the case of Greece and Rome. Classical Mediterranean society, along with its important positive qualities,

had one final impact on world history: its rather messy collapse. Unlike China, classical civilization in the Mediterranean region was not simply disrupted only to revive. Unlike India, there was no central religion derived from the civilization itself to serve as the link between the classical period and what followed. Furthermore, the fall of Rome was not a uniform decline; in essence, Rome "fell" more in some parts of the Mediterranean than it did in others. The result, among other things, was that no single civilization ultimately arose to claim the mantle of Greece and Rome. At the same time, there was no across-the-board maintenance of the classical Mediterranean institutions and values in any of the civilizations that later claimed a relationship to the Greek and Roman past. Greece and Rome would live on, in more than idle memory, but their heritage was unquestionably more complex and more selective than proved to be the case for India or China.

We turn to the process of Mediterranean decline under Rome in Chapter 11, and there we will determine more fully the initial process through which some Greco-Roman achievements survived while others perished. Two other phenomena need attention first, as part of an awareness that much of the world remained outside the orbit of the most extensive classical civilizations. In the Americas, something like a classical civilization period took shape though slightly later than the Chinese, Indian, and Mediterranean versions. In several other key regions, an initial, sometimes halting penetration of early civilization held center stage.

FURTHER READINGS

A solid recent survey with bibliography is K. Christ's *The Romans: An Introduction to Their History and Civilization* (1984). See also M. Crawford's *The Roman Republic* (1982) and B. W. Cunliffe's *Rome and Her Empire* (1978). On Rome's early history, see H. H. Scullard's *A History of the Roman World 753–146 B.C.* (1961).

An excellent analysis of basic features of Roman cultural and social life is P. Garnsey and R. Saller's *The Roman Empire: Economy, Society and Culture* (1987). See also R. MacMullen's *Roman Social Relations 50 B.C to A.D. 284* (1981). A bold quantitative study is R. Duncan-Jones's *The Economy of the Roman Empire* (1982). On slavery, the best recent works are K. Hopkins's *Conquerors and Slaves, Slaves and Masters in the Roman Empire* (1987) and K. R. Bradley and W. Philips, Jr.'s *Slavery from Roman Times to the Early Transatlantic Trade* (1985). On women, see J. F. Gardner's *Women in Roman Law and Society* (1986).

For war and diplomacy, see Y. Garlan's *War in the Ancient World* (1975) and E. N. Luttwak's *The Grand Strategy of the Roman Empire* (1976).

Collections of source materials include M. Crawford, ed., *Sources for Ancient History* (1983) and C. Fornara's *Translated Documents of Greece and Rome* (1977).

The rise and spread of Christianity are treated in two outstanding studies: R. MacMullen's *Christianizing the Roman Empire* (1984) and Peter Brown's *The World of Late Antiquity, A.D. 150–750* (1971). (Brown has also written a number of more specialized studies on early Christianity in the West.)

General Americas and North America	20,000–8000 Earliest migrations from Asia 9500 Earliest evidence of human occupation 9000–7000 "Clovis" and "Folsom" style weapons and tools in North America	7000 Evidence of agriculture; Guitarrero cave in Peru 5000 Plant domestication becoming widespread 4000 Maize domesticated in Mexico 3000 Early pottery of Puerto Hormiga, Colombia	2000 B.C.–A.D. 500 Early southwestern cultures 2000 Pottery in use in Mesoamerica
Mesoamerica		4000–2000 Archaic cultures	1500–800 Olmec civilization flourishes 900 Maya civilization beginnings; classic period in Mesoamerica	300 B.C.–A.D. 900 Height of Maya civilization
Andean Region		c. 3000–1500 B.C. Initial period; evidence of cotton cultivation, metallurgy, ceramics 1800–1200 Ceremonial centers in the highlands	200 B.C.–A.D. 500 Nasca culture 850–250 Early Horizon; Chavin flourishes

20,000 B.C.	9000 B.C.	5000 B.C.	1000 B.C.

The Peoples and Civilizations of the Americas

INTRODUCTION. This chapter, covering the diverse cultures and early civilizations in the Americas, pulls well away from the classical world of Asia, North Africa, and southern Europe. What took place in the Americas seems to have had no connection whatsoever to that classical world. The advent of civilization in the Americas did display some parallels with developments in Asia and North Africa in terms of the earlier river-valley stages and the contemporary elaboration of classical forms. This was, however, a vital period in the history of the Americas, setting certain institutional, cultural, and social patterns that outlasted the formative period itself.

American separateness was vital also, making the achievements of civilization all the more impressive, but constraining them as well. Separateness meant that American chronology had only accidental connections with the classical civilizations, based on the regional interchanges and the similar problems of internal deterioration and outside attack. Civilization in the New World moved to its own rhythm. While crucial developments in American civilization occurred during the classical period of world history, exploration of American developments in this chapter will also range before and after the 1000 B.C.–A.D. 500 span.

When Europeans set foot in the Americas in 1492, the criteria they used to describe and evaluate the peoples they encountered were drawn directly from their own heritage and understanding of their past. Using the known and familiar to explain the unknown and strange was perhaps

---

800–1300 Mississippian culture in Cahokia flourishes

100–600 Mound Builders of Adena

c. 100–700 Hopewell culture

200–1300 Anasazi culture in Southwest

900–1500 Post-classic era

1–650 Teotihuacan flourishes in central Mexico

900–1500 Maya cities under Mexican influence flourish in Yucatan

400–800 Monte Alban flourishes in Oaxaca

900–1200 Toltec empire in central Mexico

1350 Rise of the Aztecs

600–1000 Huari state

200–700 Mochica culture

1200–1400 Chimu state

300–900 Intermediate Horizon

300–900 Tihuanaco

inevitable, but it has continued to recent times in evaluations of the Americas and their peoples. The separate chronology of civilization in the Americas and the physical resources available there were essential differences. America, for example, had no horses or cattle, but American Indians had domesticated a number of plants whose caloric output was greater than any of the grains raised in Europe or Asia. The different resources available had a definite impact on the development of American societies.

In dealing with the Americas and their indigenous populations, we must be aware of the tendency to judge accomplishments and deficiencies by the standards of the Old World. Western societies have always used technology and writing as the measure of civilization. We tend to divide the past into periods based on technology or tools (the Stone Age, the Bronze Age, the Iron Age), to mark progress by the acquisition of certain important implements (the wheel, plow, etc.), and to assign the term *civilization* to peoples who build permanent buildings, create cities, and develop writing systems. This is understandable given our own development, but it imposes our standards on other peoples and on the past. Certainly complex societies can develop monumental buildings, specialized crafts, and writing systems, but why we value that set of features above the complicated cosmographies and kinship systems of peoples with simpler material cultures tells us more about ourselves than about civilization. When we thus encounter a people, such as the Incas of Peru, with no writing system, limited metallurgy for tools, and no use of the wheel or the plow but with a complex, organized empire almost 3000 miles in extent, great accomplishments in weaving and architecture, and a highly developed political system, our categories for civilization seem inadequate.

The history of the Western Hemisphere is part of the greater story of human development, and the cultures and civilizations of the Americas bear marked similarities to those of the Old World. But there were also important differences in the pace of development and the level of technology that ultimately placed the inhabitants of the Americas at a disadvantage. By the time Europeans arrived in the early 16th century, they encountered great empires, such as the Aztecs, with a technology not much different from that of earlier American civilizations that had preceded them by 1000 years, and in some ways similar to the civilizations of the ancient Near East.

ORIGINS OF AMERICAN SOCIETIES

Most archeologists agree that the Americas were originally populated by peoples from Asia, who moved during the period of the last Ice Age when the level of the oceans

fell. Possibly due to increasing population pressure, *Homo sapiens sapiens* in Europe and Asia had been able to move onto the northern steppes and tundra by about 20,000 B.C. and by that time were hunting large game, wearing clothes, and living in small groups. These people moved across the land bridge that formed in the present Bering Strait between Siberia and Alaska. During the last period of the Pleistocene, or Ice Age (Wisconsin glaciation), the capture of great quantities of water in the ice lowered the level of the oceans and made it possible to cross from Siberia to Alaska on dry land.

Perhaps one-third of the earth's surface was under ice during the greatest extent of the expanding glacial sheets. The land bridge itself was not covered with ice but was probably a grassy tundra. The mammoths, mastodons, ancestors of the bison, and other large game probably followed this route, and the hunters followed after. A subsequent rise in the world's temperature about 10,000 years ago caused the ice to melt and eventually raised the level of the oceans so that the land bridge disappeared and the land migrations from Asia stopped. The last migrations by the ancestors of the Inuit (Eskimos) and Aleuts were probably made in boats or across the polar ice.

THE ANCIENT HUNTERS

These migrations took place over a long period between about 20,000 B.C. and 8,000 B.C. The earliest definite archeological evidence of people in the Americas dates from about 9500 B.C., but many scholars believe that occupation is much older than that. Some evidence from South America points to human presence by at least 20,000 B.C., but that leaves unexplained the lack of such evidence farther north along the track of the supposed migration. How long it took for the area of the American continents to be occupied is open to question; it may have taken thousands of years, but one scholar has estimated that from a group of only 25 original migrants that doubled every generation, a population of 10 million would result in 500 years. A population of 10 million, or about 1 person per square mile, seems reasonable for these peoples given what we know about more modern hunting societies, but other scholars have estimated the whole world's population before agriculture at only 10 million.

The earliest migrants may have had a technology that did not include projectiles (spears) since the only evidence of their tools are small stones used for scraping or cutting. Crude spearheads, associated with the remains of animals that became extinct about 12,000 years ago, document the presence of hunting bands in the Americas. By about 11,000 years ago stone tools and simple spear points (with

Early spearheads indicating the presence of human populations in the Americas by 10,000 B.C. were discovered at Folsom (2d from right) and Clovis (center), New Mexico. Folsom points found in 1927 in conjunction with extinct bison species changed scientific thinking about the timing of human occupation in the New World.

short side channels or flutes allowing them to be bound onto shafts) associated with these early hunters were widely dispersed over North America. Originally discovered at Clovis, New Mexico, these projectile points demonstrate widely shared techniques of production.

Other tool traditions followed, some of them relatively localized. In New Mexico between 11,000 and 9,000 years ago, Folsom points were beautifully crafted with a flute that ran the length of the blade. These are usually found in conjunction with the bones of the ancestor of the bison. By about 6000 B.C. a longer, well-crafted point was in use for hunting not only the ancient long-horned bison, but also antelope and the modern bison.

As the climate became dryer and warmer, the ice began to melt. The great mammal herds diminished and some of the species disappeared. The ancient Americans seem to

have been particularly successful hunters, and it has been argued that the disappearance of animals such as the mammoths, the ancient horse, the camel, and the giant anteater was, at least in part, due to the hunters' skills. After all, the climate changed in Eurasia as well, but nowhere else in the world did the number of mammals that became extinct equal that of the Americas, especially North America.

Little is known about the society of these early Ice Age hunters. Most likely, they lived in small groups or bands of 20 to 25 people, following the game in a seasonal pattern. Sites where the bones of the hunters' kills are found indicate that these people probably hunted the mammals in large groups. Kinship provided the basis of social organization, and there was little specialization or hierarchy in society. Age and gender were the main determinants of a person's roles and what he or she contributed to the group.

AMERICAN DIVERSITY

Over the long period of the migrations, different peoples of different physical types and languages came out of Asia. Some of the first migrants came into the Western Hemisphere prior to the predominance of the Mongoloid peoples in Asia. Consequently there were Caucasoid and Australoid genetic features in the ancestors of the first Americans, or what are sometimes called the Paleo-Indians. The fact that all Indians of South America are of blood type O while in Asia type B predominates indicates the diversity of physical types involved in the migration and perhaps the early date of the migration prior to the creation of the present genetic situation of Asian populations. The Eskimos (Inuit), who genetically are most like contemporary Asians, were probably the last group to migrate.

While there was considerable physical variation among the American Indian populations, the genetic and physical similarity among them is very strong. This indicates a large degree of common ancestry and a relative isolation from other human populations. The variations among Indians can be attributed to adaptations and localized natural selection.

American Indian languages also display considerable diversity. There were over 2000 languages spoken in the Americas when Europeans arrived in the 16th century. While scholars differ in interpreting linguistic data, there is general agreement that there were a number of language groups or parent language stocks. People of related languages may have shared cultural elements at one time, but peoples of widely differing cultures sometimes spoke similar languages. For example, the nomadic Utes and the city-dwelling Aztecs spoke related tongues.

Language, however, can be used to trace the movement of peoples. The Navajo and Apaches of the American Southwest speak Athapascan languages related to the speech of the inhabitants of northwestern Canada and Alaska, and quite unlike that of their Pueblo neighbors. It is assumed that they were later migrants who split off from their linguistic relatives to the north.

OUTSIDE CONTACTS?

The problem of later contacts with the Americas across the Pacific or the Atlantic continues to fascinate archeologists and cause heated debate. Definite mysteries and gaps in the history of pre-Columbian cultures remain unresolved. Artistic motifs and styles similar to those of Shang China and Southeast Asia seem to indicate contact. Early pottery found at Valdivia on the coast of Ecuador seems remarkably like Japanese Jomon-period ceramics. Plants, such as cotton and bottle gourds, seem of definite Old World origin and their presence in the Americas suggests diffusion by human agents. While many scholars admit the possibility of sporadic transoceanic contacts with Chinese, Phoenicians, Polynesians, and others, the evidence is still mostly circumstantial. No identifiable Old World object has ever been positively identified in a pre-Columbian archeological site, and if Phoenicians or Chinese introduced pottery or writing to the Americas, why they failed to introduce the wheel or bronze at the same time remains an unanswered question.

The biological and archeological records indicate that the peopling of the Americas had taken place long before the beginnings of agriculture in the Old World and that, with the disappearance of the Bering land bridge, this population had lived in comparative isolation from the rest of humankind. While some archeologists have argued that the invention of agriculture and pottery may have taken place only once and then been diffused all over the world, most scholars believe that the peoples of the Americas developed agriculture, domestication of animals (except perhaps the dog), weaving, ceramics, complex societies, urbanism, numerical systems, and religious ideas—in short, their cultures—independently of the Old World. Still, occasional contacts were possible and the introduction of ideas and material things from elsewhere into American Indian cultures certainly may have taken place.

The processes of cultural development and the growth of Indian civilizations were long and complex, and they gave American Indian societies and cultures great resilience and an ability to survive even the shock of conquest. This independent development and relative isolation also had some negative results when American Indian populations came into contact with the peoples of Europe, Africa, and Asia. The development of a technology that did not include the wheel, the plow, or iron tools and weapons put American Indians at a disadvantage. Dogs, turkeys, and the guinea pig were domesticated, but with the exception of the llama in the Andes, the lack of large mammals, cattle, and horses was also a disadvantage in terms of diet, transportation, and power. With the exception of a limited area in the high Andes, pastoralism, so important in the Old World, was not a way of life in the Americas. Most importantly, the relative isolation of American populations from the disease environment of the larger Old World populations left the inhabitants of the Americas with no immunities to a number of diseases that became endemic in Asia, Europe, and Africa. This would prove disastrous after permanent contact was established.

THE ARCHAIC CULTURES

By about 9000 B.C. small bands of hunters were widely dispersed over the American continents. Changes in climate with the ending of the last Ice Age may lie behind changes in diet and ways of life. The disappearance of large game animals, whatever the cause, was probably met with the less-specialized hunting of smaller game, fishing, and an increased dependence on gathering wild fruits and other plant foods. The culture of these early populations is usually called the Archaic period. It represented an adaptation to the changing environment and possibilities of subsistence. People made baskets and used stone grinding tools to prepare the roots and plants they collected for food. They used a wide range of animals and plants. As the seacoasts stabilized between 5000 and 4000 B.C., populations concentrated around lagoons and river mouths to exploit fish and shellfish. Enormous debris mounds or shell middens found in Chile and Tierra del Fuego indicate long human dependence on these maritime resources. In Brazil, the middens indicate intensive use of these resources and permanent occupation sites.

AGRICULTURE IN THE AMERICAS. The move toward agriculture was a natural extension of a process in which a wide range of animal and plant resources was used with less dependence on the hunting of big game. Agriculture may thus have been brought about first by women, since in many simple hunting societies women are responsible for gathering plant foods. There is early evidence from Guitarrero caves in highland Peru of cultivation as early as 7000 B.C., and by 5000 B.C. plant domestication had taken place in a number of regions in the Americas.

The introduction of agriculture, the American version of the Neolithic revolution, was not so complete and drastic a change as we once thought, and many peoples continued to practice hunting and gathering along with some cultivation. In many places agriculturalists and hunter-gatherers eventually lived in close contact with each other as a result of different adaptations to environments and opportunities and of social choices. The movement from hunting to agriculture did not always happen. In a particularly rich environment on the seacoast or where game was plentiful, peoples might avoid agriculture and the regimentation of life it could represent.

Eventually, however, agriculture was practiced all over the Americas from the woodlands of eastern North America to the tropical forests of the Amazon basin. American Indians eventually cultivated over 100 different crops from peppers, squash, and tomatoes to amaranth and quinoa.

Some crops, particularly maize, potatoes, and manioc, became essential sources of food to dense populations. As in Asia earlier, agriculture imposed restrictions on human behavior and the patterns of human action; as American societies depended increasingly on agriculture, a series of processes were sometimes set in motion that resulted in complex social, economic, and political systems.

MAIZE, MANIOC, AND POTATOES. By about 4000 B.C. the domestication of maize had taken place in central Mexico and along with it came the cultivation of peppers, squash, and beans. These expanded and more dependable food resources resulted in population growth (although some scholars argue that the growth of populations may have stimulated the search for new food sources and the domestication of plants). The cultivation of maize spread far and wide. By 2000 B.C. it was grown in Peru, along with the potato and other crops native to that region. Maize spread northward to the present southern United States, and by about A.D. 1000 it was grown by groups such as the Iroquois in Canada.

In the tropical forests of the Orinoco and Amazon basins, people had developed an agriculture based on varieties of manioc or cassava, a root that could be made into a flour. The introduction of maize in areas that had depended only on manioc probably resulted in population growth and, with it, the rise of more complex societies. While varieties of potatoes were the staple in highland South America, and manioc was the principal crop of peoples of the lowlands of South America and the islands of the Caribbean, maize cultivation spread in all directions and was often practiced in those areas in conjunction with other staples. In Mesoamerica, the area from north central Mexico to Nicaragua, maize dominated the diet of agricultural peoples.

It seems clear that, in most cases, agriculture is a major feature in determining the ability of societies to achieve the surplus production and complexity needed for those elements usually associated with civilization. With the adoption of agriculture and a sedentary way of life, the process of civilization was set in motion in the Americas.

CULTURAL HEARTHS AND SOCIAL SYSTEMS

Traditionally, archeologists have seen two major cultural hearths in the Americas: Mesoamerica and the Peruvian orbit, including the coastal areas of Ecuador and Peru and the Andean highlands. In these two areas, processes of development, based on intensive agriculture and including most of the features usually associated with Old World civ-

Cultural Hearths—
Regions in the
Americas

ilizations, could be seen. In both areas a number of cycles of cultural advance and, sometimes, of empire-building took place long before the rise of the Incas and Aztecs, who were in power when the Europeans arrived. Artistic styles flourished and declined, and states rose and fell over thousands of years.

Some scholars have suggested that the area between these cultural hearths, including present-day Panama and Colombia, also contained a number of advanced societies with considerable cultural achievements (especially in metallurgy and goldworking) that differed only in that they did not build large stone buildings. Thus the whole region from central Mexico southward to Chile formed a continuous nucleus of American civilizations. On the peripheries of this nucleus, due to influence and imitation, other Indian peoples adopted features characteristic of the civilizations.

TYPES OF AMERICAN INDIAN SOCIETIES

The idea of a relatively contiguous area of cultural development makes more sense than the previous concept of independent centers. That earlier concept produced an image of the Americas in which isolated civilizations and cultural traditions developed along parallel lines with little contact or interchange. Emphasis on artistic variation and regional diversity contributed to this view, but scholars are increasingly beginning to examine the broad similarities among ancient American cultures. While many differences and variations existed, there were also uniformities of organization, subsistence, technology, and belief that made them more alike than any one of them was to civilizations of the Old World.

To some extent we can make distinctions among ancient American societies on the basis of their economic and political organization. Sedentary agriculture, and with it population density, was a key. Hunters and gatherers, living much as the early migrants to the Americas, continued to occupy large portions of the continents, dividing in small bands and moving seasonally to take advantage of the resources. These peoples sometimes were organized in larger tribes and might recognize a chief, but generally their societies were organized around family groups or clans and there was little hierarchy or specialization of skills. With some exceptions, the material culture of these people tended to be relatively simple.

Peoples who had made a partial transition to agriculture lived in larger and more complex societies. Here the village of 100 or 200 rather than the band of 25 was more common. Men often continued to hunt or make war, but women tilled the fields. Agricultural techniques tended to be simple and often necessitated periodic migration when soils played out. The villages of these tribes of semisedentary farmers and hunters have been found on the Brazilian coast and in the woodlands of eastern North America.

It was among peoples who had made a full transition to sedentary agriculture that the complex societies emerged most clearly, for it was here that surplus production was most firmly established. These populations could reach the millions. Men shifted into agriculture, forming a peasant base for a hierarchical society that might have included classes of nobles, merchants, and priests. Strong states and even empires could result, and the extraction of tribute from subject peoples and redistribution by central authority formed the basis of rule.

CHIEFDOMS AND STATES

Sedentary peoples and hunters often lived near each other and shared mutual hostility and disregard, but, in fact, the categories of sedentary, semisedentary, and hunter-gatherers were never clear-cut and many aspects of life were shared by them all. To some extent the large imperial states with highly developed religious and political systems and monumental architecture (which we call civilizations such as Teotihuacan in Mexico or Chimor in Peru) were variants of a widely diffused pattern, the chiefdom.

From the Amazon to the Mississippi valley, populations—sometimes in the tens of thousands—were governed by hereditary chieftains who ruled from central towns over a large territory, including smaller towns or villages that paid tribute to the ruler. The predominant town often had a ceremonial function, with large temples and a priest class. Beautiful pottery and other goods indicate specialization.

The existence of social hierarchy with a class of nobles and commoners was also a characteristic of many of the chiefdoms. It is sometimes argued that in the state-building societies ceremonial centers became true cities, and clan or family relations were replaced by social classes. The scale of the society was greater, but the differences are not always so obvious. Both the Aztecs and the Incas with their complex social hierarchies maintained aspects of earlier clan organization. In fact, in terms of social organization, warfare, and ceremonialism there seems to be little that differentiates the Maya city-states from some of the chiefdoms in South America or southeastern North America. Cahokia near St. Louis, an important town of the Mississippian culture (c. A.D. 1050–1200) with its great earthen mounds covering an area of five square miles, probably supported a population of over 30,000, as large as the great cities of the Maya civilization.

A distinction between sedentary agriculturists and nomadic hunters may be more useful than the distinctions between "civilized" and "uncivilized." Building and carving in stone, and thus the ability of archaeologists to reconstruct a culture, seem to have become a major feature in determining the difference between a state or chiefdom—and by extension between "civilizations"—and societies that do not seem to merit the title. At the same time, we should recognize that the settled peoples and the hunters recognized the difference between their ways of life, and when they were in contact, they often shared a mutual jealousy and a hostility toward each other. The Incas looked down on the peoples of the Amazonian rain forest and referred to them as *chunchos,* or barbarians, but they could never conquer these peoples. They traded with them from time to time, and sometimes used them as mercenaries.

The Aztecs called the nomads who lived to the north chichimecs, which came to mean "uncivilized," but the Aztecs themselves may have originated as one of these groups, which were constantly pushing in on the wealthier and better-fed settled areas. To some extent the pattern of tension between the nomad and the "civilized" Old World was reproduced in the Americas.

MESOAMERICA

Geographically, the region of Mesoamerica is a complex patchwork of zones that is also divided vertically into cooler highlands, tropical lowlands and coasts, and an intermediate temperate zone. These variations created a number of environments with different possibilities for human exploitation. They also created a basis for trade, as peoples sought to acquire goods not available locally. Much trade flowed from the tropical lowlands to the cooler central plateau.

The long slow process of change by which the hunters and gatherers of Mexico began to settle into small villages and domesticate certain plants is poorly known. Human beings were probably in Mesoamerica by 20,000 B.C. with men hunting the large game animals and, most likely, women involved in the gathering activities. Beginning around 5000 B.C. gathering and an increasing use of plant foods eventually led to the domestication of certain plants.

Mesoamerican Settlements

■ Primary cultural hearth

▥ Secondary cultural hearth

0   1000 Miles
0   1000 Kilometers

Beans, peppers, avocados, squash, and eventually maize served as the basis of agriculture in the region. Later innovations such as the introduction or development of pottery took place around 2000 B.C., but there was little to differentiate one small village from the next.

As the Shang dynasty ruled in China, permanent sedentary villages based to some extent on agriculture were first beginning to appear in Mesoamerica. These were small and modest settlements. The lack of elaborate burials indicates that these were societies without much hierarchy or social differentiation, and the uniform and simple nature of pottery and other material goods indicates a lack of craft specialization. But the number of these Archaic period villages proliferated, and population densities rose.

THE OLMEC MYSTERY

Quite suddenly a new phenomenon appeared. On the southeastern coast of Mesoamerica (Veracruz and Tabasco), without much evidence of gradual development in the archeological record, a cultural tradition emerged that included irrigated agriculture, monumental sculpture, urbanism, an elaborate religion, and the beginnings of calendrical and writing systems. The origin of the Olmecs remains unknown, but their impressive sites at La Venta and Tres Zapotes attest to a high degree of social organization and artistic skill. The major Olmec sites at San Lorenzo (1200–900 B.C.) and La Venta (900–500 B.C.) are in the wet tropical forests of the Gulf coast of eastern Mexico, but Olmec objects and art style spread to the drier highlands of central Mexico and toward the Pacific coast to the south.

The Olmecs have been called the "mother civilization" of Mesoamerica. Maize cultivation, especially along the rivers, provided the basis for a state ruled by a hereditary elite and in which the ceremonialism of a complex religion dominated much of life. At about the time that Tutankhamen ruled in Egypt, the Olmec civilization flourished in Mesoamerica.

The Olmecs remain a mystery. Some of their monumental sculptures seem to bear Negroid features; others appear to be representations of humans with feline attributes. They were great carvers of jade and traded or conquered to obtain it. They developed a *vigesimal* numerical system—based on 20—and a calendar that combined a 365-day year with a 260-day ritual cycle. This became the basis of all Mesoamerican calendar systems. What language they spoke and what became of their civilization remain unknown, but some scholars believe that they were the ancestors of the great Maya civilization that followed.

Olmec objects and, probably, Olmec influence and religious ideas spread into many areas of the highlands and lowlands, creating the first generalized culture in the region. By 900 B.C. Olmec style and symbols were widely diffused in Mesoamerica.

During this preclassic period (c. 2000–300 B.C.), other civilizations were developing elsewhere in middle America. At Monte Alban in the valley of Oaxaca, the Zapotec people created a large hilltop center based on terraced and irrigated agriculture in the surrounding valley. A writing system and calendar are also apparent here, perhaps borrowed from the Olmecs, as is considerable evidence of warfare and conquest. By about A.D. 500 Monte Alban had become a chief ceremonial center covering over 15

The origins of the Olmecs remain shrouded in mystery, but some of the enormous stone sculptures seem to have definite African features that indicate trans-Atlantic contact.

square miles and including some 30,000 people. Farther to the south, some early Maya centers began to appear. In the central valley of Mexico, Olmec artistic influence could be seen in expanding communities.

Much of what we know about these cultures must be interpreted from their architecture and art and the symbols these contain. Art, and especially public art, was both decorative and functional. It defined the place of the individual in society and in the universe. It had political and religious functions; in the Americas, as in many civilizations, these aspects were usually united. Interpreting artistic styles and symbols presents a variety of problems in the absence of written sources. The diffusion of Olmec symbols is a good example of the problem. Did the use of these symbols among other peoples in distant places indicate trade networks, missionary activity, colonies, conquest, or aesthetic appreciation? We do not know, but clearly Olmec influence was widely felt throughout the region.

THE CLASSIC ERA

After the Olmec initiative, the period from about A.D. 150 to 900 was a great age of cultural achievement in Mesoamerica. Archeologists refer to it as the classic period, and during it great civilizations flourished in a number of places. The two main centers of civilization were the high central valley of Mexico and the more humid tropical lands of southern Mexico, Yucatan, and Guatemala.

THE VALLEY OF MEXICO: TEOTIHUACAN. In central Mexico the city of Teotihuacan, near modern Mexico City, emerged as an enormous urban center with important religious functions. It was supported by intensive agriculture in the surrounding region and probably by crops planted around the great lake in the central valley of Mexico. Teotihuacan's enormous temple pyramids rival those of ancient Egypt and suggest a considerable state apparatus with the power to mobilize large numbers of workers. Population estimates for this city, which covered nine square miles, are as high as 200,000. This would make it greater than the cities of ancient Egypt or Mesopotamia and probably second only to ancient Rome of the cities of classical antiquity.

There were residential districts for certain trades and ethnic groups, and there is considerable evidence of wide social distinctions between the priests, nobles, and the common folk. The many gods of Mesoamerica, still worshiped when the Europeans arrived in the 16th century, were already honored at Teotihuacan. The god of rain, the feathered serpent, the goddess of corn, and the goddess of

waters are all apparent in the murals and decorations that adorned the palaces and temples. In fact, almost all Teotihuacan art seems to be religious in nature.

The influence of Teotihuacan extended as far to the south as Guatemala, and tribute was probably exacted from many regions. Teotihuacan objects, such as pottery and finely worked obsidian—and Teotihuacan artistic style—are found in many other areas. Teotihuacan influence was strong at Monte Alban in Oaxaca. Warriors dressed in the style of Teotihuacan can be found far to the south in the Maya region.

Teotihuacan represented either a political empire or a dominant cultural and ideological style that spread over much of central Mexico. The lack of battle scenes on the walls of Teotihuacan have led some scholars to believe that the dominance of Teotihuacan led to a long period of peace maintained by the authority and power of the great city. Internally, the fact that the later buildings tend to be secular palaces rather than temple pyramids perhaps indicates a shift in power and orientation from religious to civil authority.

THE CLASSIC MAYA. Between about A.D. 300 and 900, at roughly the same time that Teotihuacan dominated the central plateau, the Maya peoples were developing Mesoamerican civilization to its highest point in southern Mexico and Central America. While the Tang dynasty ruled China, Charlemagne created his domain in Europe, and Islam spread its influence from Spain to India, after the classical period had ended in the Old World, a great civilization flourished in the American tropics. The American classic period, launched as the Old World classical civilizations were coming to an end, lasted well into the next period of world history. Because of the richness of the archeological records and because Maya peoples still retained many aspects of the classic period when the Spanish arrived and observed them, it is possible to reconstruct the world of the classic Maya in some detail. We can use the Maya as an example of the classic period in Mesoamerican development, for while their civilization was distinctive it was based on some principles common to the area.

The Maya culture extended over a broad region that now includes parts of five different countries (Mexico, Guatemala, Belize, Honduras, and El Salvador). It included a number of related languages, and it had considerable regional variation as can be seen in its art styles. The whole region shared a common culture that included monumental architecture, a written language, a calendrical and mathematical system, a highly developed religion, and concepts of statecraft and social organization. With an essen-

At classic Maya cities like Tikal (Guatemala), stone columns with extensive inscriptions were erected to mark important historical events and to commemorate certain dates in the calendar system.

tially Neolithic technology in an area of dense forests plagued by insects and often poor soils, as many as 50 city-states flourished.

How did the large classic Maya urban-religious centers, such as Tikal, Copan, Quirigua, and Palenque, with populations between 30,000 and 80,000, support themselves? Slash-and-burn agriculture as practiced today in the region was not enough. The classic Maya used a number of agricultural systems. Evidence of irrigation, swamp drainage, and a system of artificially constructed "ridged fields" at river mouths (where intensive agriculture was practiced) has now appeared and seems to explain the Maya ability to support large urban centers and a total population of perhaps five million. While some authorities still believe that the Maya centers were essentially ceremonial and were occupied primarily by rulers, artisans, and an elite, it seems clear that populations concentrated in and around these cen-

ters to create a densely occupied landscape. The Maya cities vary in size and layout but almost all include large pyramids surmounted by temples, complexes of masonry buildings that served administrative or religious purposes, elite residences, a ritual ball court, and often a series of altars and memorial pillars. These memorial monuments, or *stelae*, were erected to commemorate triumphs and events in the lives of the Maya rulers or to mark ceremonial occasions. The stelae were usually dated and inscribed with hieroglyphic script. A complex calendar and a sophisticated writing system were two of the greatest Maya achievements.

RELIGION, WRITING, AND SOCIETY. The calendar system and sophisticated astronomical observations were made possible by a vigesimal system of mathematics. The Maya knew the concept of zero and used it in conjunction

The ritual ball game was played throughout Mesoamerica on courts at the Maya center of Copán. It was apparently both a sport and a religious ceremony. Players wore special pads. Stakes were high, and losers were sometimes sacrificed.

with the concept of place value or position. With elegant simplicity and only signs for one, five, and zero, they could make complex calculations. As among all the Mesoamerican peoples, the Maya calendar was based on a concept of recurring cycles of different length. They had a sacred cycle of 260 days divided into months of 20 days, within which there was a cycle of 13 numbers. This ritual calendar meshed with a solar calendar of 365 days, or 18 months of 20 days with a remainder of 5 "dead" or inauspicious days at the end of the year. The two calendars operated simultaneously so any day would have two names, but the particular combination of those two days would reoccur only once every 52 years. Thus among the Maya and most Mesoamericans, cycles of 52 years were sacred.

The classic Maya, however, differed from their neighbors in that they also kept a "long count" or a system of dating from a fixed date in the past. This date, 3114 B.C. by our calendar, probably marked the beginning of a great cycle of 5200 years since the world was created. Like other Mesoamericans (and the ancient Peruvians) the Maya believed in great cycles of creation and destruction of the universe. The long count enabled the Maya to date events with precision. The earliest recorded Maya date that survives is A.D. 292 and the last is A.D. 928.

A second great Maya accomplishment was the creation of a writing system. The Maya "wrote" on stone monuments, murals, and ceramics, and in books of folded bark paper and deerskin, only four of which survive. Scribes were honored and held an important place in society. Al-

though we still cannot read many inscriptions, recent advances now permit the reading of many texts. The Maya written language was, like Chinese and Sumerian, a logographic system that combined phonetic and semantic elements. With this system and about 287 symbols they were able to record and transmit complex concepts and ideas. The few remaining books are religious and astronomical texts, and many inscriptions on ceramics deal with the cult of the dead and with the complex Maya cosmology.

The Maya view of the universe was a flat earth, whose cardinal points and center were each dominated by a god who supported the sky. Above the sky extended 13 levels of heavens and below nine underworlds, each dominated by a god. Through these levels the sun and the moon, also conceived as deities, passed each day. A basic concept of Mesoamerican dualism—male and female, good and bad, day and night—emphasized the unity of all things, similar to that found in some Asian religions. Thus each god often had a parallel female consort or feminine form and often an underworld equivalent as well. In addition, there were patron deities of various occupations and classes. Thus the number of deities in the inscriptions seems overwhelming, but these should be understood as manifestations of a more limited set of supernatural forces, much like the *avatars*, or incarnations, of the Hindu gods.

While the few surviving books are religious in character, the majority of inscriptions on monuments are historical records of the ruling families of the Maya cities. The major Maya centers were the cores of city-states that con-

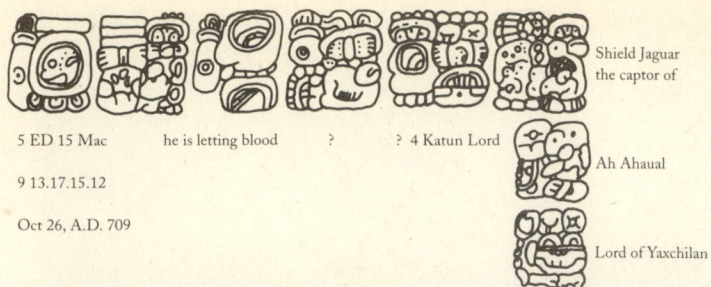

5 ED 15 Mac

9 13.17.15.12

Oct 26, A.D. 709

he is letting blood

?

? 4 Katun Lord

Shield Jaguar
the captor of

Ah Ahaual

Lord of Yaxchilan

This relief from the Mayan palace complex at Yaxchilan shows a kneeling woman pulling a rope barbed with thorns through her tongue to draw blood. Her husband, a king named Shield-Jaguar, holds a torch above her head. The king's hair is adorned with the shrunken head of a sacrificial victim.

she is letting blood

name or titles

Lady Xoc

Lady Batab

trolled outlying territories. There was constant warfare, and rulers, such as Pacal of Palenque (who died in A.D. 683), expanded their territories by conquest. Pacal's victories were recorded on his funerary monuments and in his lavish tomb discovered inside a pyramid at Palenque.

The rulers exercised considerable civil and probably religious power, and their rule was aided by an elite that exercised administrative functions. A class of scribes or perhaps priests tended to the cult of the state and specialized in the complex calendrical observations and calculations. The ruler and the scribes organized and participated in rituals of self-mutilation and human sacrifice that among the Maya, as in much of Mesoamerica, formed an important aspect of religion. Also, as a form of both worship and sport, the Maya like other Mesoamerican peoples wagered on and played a ritual ball game on specially constructed courts in which players moved a ball with their hips or elbows. Losers might forfeit their possessions or their lives.

Builders, potters, scribes, sculptors, and painters worked in the cities for the glory of the gods and the rulers. Most people, however, were peasant farmers whose labor supported the elaborate ritual and political lives of the elite. Captives were enslaved. Patrilineal families probably formed the basis of social life as they did among the Maya of later days. The elite, however, traced their families through both their fathers and mothers. Elite women are often represented in dynastic monuments in positions of importance. State marriages were important and elite women retained considerable rights. Among the common folk, women took over the preparation of food and domestic duties, including the production of fine cloth using the backstrap loom. The division of tasks by gender was probably supported by religious belief and custom if present-day Maya practices are a guide.

DOCUMENT
DECIPHERING THE
MAYA GLYPHS

Of all the peoples of ancient America, the Maya developed the most complex system of writing to record their history, religion, philosophy, and politics. Maya hieroglyphs have baffled and fascinated researchers since the 1820s, when the first steps toward deciphering the rich glyphs and symbols of Maya monuments, ceramics, and the few surviving Maya books were made. This process continues, and although we are not yet able to read all the surviving texts, those that have been deciphered have altered our view of Maya society and its underlying beliefs.

One of the problems of decipherment was a false start. In the 16th century, a Spanish bishop of Yucatan, Diego de Landa, burned many books in an attempt to stamp out Maya religion. Landa's attempt to describe the Maya writing based on his questioning of Indian informants was badly flawed. Landa thought the glyphs were letters, not syllables, and so his description confused scholars for many years. Despite his deficiencies, however, for many years Landa provided the only guide available. Unlike the decipherment of Egyptian hieroglyphs, no text with Maya and some other known language side by side exists, and so the problem of reading the Maya glyphs remains difficult.

The first modern advances were made in reading Maya numbers and identifying glyphs for the months in the calendar cycle. By the 1940s, scholars could read the dates rather well, and because so many inscriptions and the four remaining books seemed to be numerical and related to the calendar, most specialists believed that the Maya writing was primarily about the calendar system and that the Maya were obsessed with time. Many things complicated the reading of the other glyphs, such as the fact that scholars were not sure which of the various Maya languages that survive was the language of the inscriptions. In 1952, a young Russian researcher argued that the Maya glyphs combined signs that stood for whole words with others that represented sounds. In this, the Maya script was like ancient Egyptian and cuneiform writings. Although the theory was not fully accepted at first, it has proven to be accurate.

A major breakthrough took place in 1960, when art historian Tatiana Proskouriakoff noted that on certain sets of monuments the earliest and last dates were never more than 62 years apart, and that the first date was always accompanied by one certain glyph and the next always by another. She recognized that the images on the monuments were not gods or mythical figures, but kings, and that the first glyph indicated birth and the second accession. Sixty-two years was consistent with a human life span. With this approach, scholars have figured out the names of the rulers and their families and something about the dynastic history of a number of Maya cities.

Scholars now understand that, despite regional variations, the texts were written in a language widely understood throughout the Maya region. The glyphs combine syllables, symbols, emblems, and ideas in what is basically a complex phonetic system. Now that we are able to read numbers, dates, place or city emblems, and a few nouns and verbs, a new window has been opened on the ancient Maya.

Art historians Linda Schele and Mary Ellen Miller, in their excellent volume *The Blood of Kings: Ritual and Dynasty in Maya Art* (1986), provide a reading and interpretation of a famous Maya sculpture (see the figure on page 196). Here Lord Shield Jaguar, a ruler of Yaxchilan who was between 40 and 60 years old at the time, holds a torch to illumine a ceremony of blood-letting self-sacrifice. His wife, Lady Xoc, draws a rope with thorns through her tongue, after which he too will sacrifice his blood to sustain the gods. This ceremony took place on October 28, 709. The short accompanying text in glyphs dates the ceremony, identifies the people portrayed, and describes their actions.

Questions: What do the elaborate ritual life and sumptuous clothing suggest about the nature of Maya society? Do the complex calendar and writing system indicate widespread literacy or the power of an elite class that controlled this esoteric knowledge? Does the role of writing in Mesoamerican civilization seem like that in ancient Egypt, Sumer, and China?

CLASSIC COLLAPSE

Between about A.D. 700 and 900, the Mesoamerican world was shaken by the cataclysmic decline of the great cultural centers. The reasons for this collapse are not fully understood, but the phenomenon was general. In the central plateau, Teotihuacan was destroyed around A.D. 650 by outside invaders, probably nomadic hunters from the north perhaps with the collaboration of some of the groups under the dominance of Teotihuacan. The city may have already been in decline due to increasing problems with agriculture. Whereas the fall of Teotihuacan seems to have been sudden, Monte Alban, the Zapotec center, went into a phase of slow decline and eventual abandonment.

The most mysterious aspect of the collapse was the abandonment of the Maya cities. During the 8th century A.D. Maya rulers stopped erecting commemorative stelae and large buildings; population sizes dwindled. By A.D. 900 most of the major Maya centers were deserted. Scholars do not agree whether this process was the result of ecological problems and climatic change, agricultural exhaustion, internal revolt, or foreign pressure. The collapse took place at different times in different places and seems to be the result of a number of processes, of which increasing warfare was either a cause or symptom. The warfare may be related to the decline of Teotihuacan and the attempt of Maya city-states to position themselves to control old trade routes.

Chief among the explanations for the Maya collapse has been agricultural exhaustion. The Maya ability to create a civilization in the dense rain forest of the Peten in Guatemala and in the Chiapas lowlands had been based on a highly productive agricultural system. By the 8th century, the limits of that system, given the size and density of population, may have been reached. Tikal had an estimated density of over 300 people per square mile. Maintaining the great population centers was an increasing burden. Epidemic disease has also been suggested as a cause of the collapse, perhaps indicating some unrecorded contact with the Old World. Others believe that the peasantry simply refused to bear the burdens of serving and feeding the political and religious elite and that internal rebellion led to the end of ruling dynasties and their cities.

The reasons for the collapse of the classic civilization remain unclear, but the period was clearly ending, and while a few centers continued to be occupied by squatters and some traditions persisted, the cultural achievements of the classic period were not attained again. Long-count dating ended, the stelae cult ceased, and ceramic quality and architectural accomplishments declined. But as the great Maya centers of the southern lowlands and highlands were abandoned or declined, Maya cities in the Yucatan and in the Guatemala highlands expanded and carried on some of the traditions, along with considerable cultural influences from central Mexico. Mexicanized ruling families established themselves at Chichen Itzá and other towns in Yucatan, and Mexicanized Maya groups from the Gulf coast penetrated into the southern Maya areas. The northern Maya area was able to accommodate these influences and create a new synthesis of Maya and central Mexican culture. In the great southern Maya cities, such as Tikal, Palenque, and Quirigua, no such adjustment was made and the rain forest soon overran the temples and palaces.

After A.D. 1000 one of the new groups that occupied the central plateau after the fall of Teotihuacan, the Nahuatl-speaking Toltecs, established political control over a large territory and eventually extended their influence into Maya territory. Their genius seems to have been military, and much of their culture derived from classic traditions. From their capital at Tula in central Mexico, Toltec influence and trade may have spread as far as the American Southwest, where the cliff-dwelling Anasazi people, the ancestors of the Pueblo Indians, produced beautiful ceramics and cultivated maize in the desert valleys. In Yucatan, ruling families claimed descent from Toltec invaders. Even when the Toltec empire fell around A.D. 1200, the cultural traditions of Mesoamerica did not die, for imperial states and civilization do not necessarily go together. Eventually, however, a new power, the Aztecs, rose in the central plateau of Mexico. The Aztecs initiated yet another cycle of expansion based on the deep-rooted ways of life and thought of Mesoamerica.

❧ THE PEOPLES TO THE NORTH

Archeologists have been able to distinguish various stages of Archaic culture, from Alaska to northern Mexico, among the ancestors of the North American Indians. We cannot deal in detail with the many cultural traditions which evolved from those Archaic period cultures, but there are two broad regions in North America that merit special attention because of the complex, sedentary agricultural societies that developed there: the eastern woodlands of what is now the southern United States and the arid Southwest.

THE MOUND BUILDERS

In the valleys of the Mississippi and Ohio rivers, people began to practice agriculture by 2000 B.C., and by 700 B.C. a society that combined hunting and agriculture had begun to emerge. The Adena culture, which developed in southern Ohio and neighboring areas, was characterized by large earthen constructions and mounds. Some of the mounds were defensive while others served as places for burials. These burials contain pottery, pipes (indicating the use of tobacco), jewelry, and copper objects that indicate long-distance trade from as far away as Michigan. The Adena tradition may have been spread by migrants or by trade contacts to places, such as New York State and Maryland, where it lasted as late as A.D. 700. In Ohio and southern Illinois, however, Adena was then already being replaced by a more complex culture.

The Hopewell culture (c. A.D. 200–500) introduced new levels of scale and complexity. Elaborate mounds, some of great size and often organized into groups, were characteristic of this mound-builder culture. Some of the mounds, such as Serpent Mound in Ohio, were built as effigies of animals. Burials contained jewelry, personal items, weapons, and religious symbols of copper, quartz, galena, and mica. Conch shells and shark teeth indicate long-distance trade to the Gulf coast, and other materials were brought from as far away as the Rocky Mountains. Hopewell artisans worked in stone and clay and produced beautiful luxury items of pottery, pipes, and effigies, many seemingly designed specifically for the cult of the dead. By about A.D. 400 the main centers of Hopewell culture had ceased the large-scale construction of mounds, and the trade network had begun to break down.

After a hiatus of about 400 years, the Hopewell culture was succeeded by a new complex that spread widely throughout the Mississippi valley. Between A.D. 800 and 1300 very large towns and ceremonial centers, such as Moundville (Alabama) and Cahokia (Illinois), flourished throughout the southeastern region. Mound building here was not only for burials or effigies, but also for fortification and large pyramid platforms. Cahokia had one temple mound over 30 meters high, containing over 600,000 cubic meters of earth. These Mississippian centers were surrounded by large populations and other smaller towns. For example, at least 50 communities seem to have been under Cahokia's influence. Except for the absence of stone architecture, Cahokia seemed to parallel the urban development of Mesoamerica.

The rich variety of artifacts of excellent workmanship indicates social divisions within this society, but in fact we know little about its social organization. The best clues come from the 18th-century observations of the Natchez Indians who carried on the Mississippian tradition. They were organized as a powerful chiefdom under a ruler known as the Great Sun, who ruled a society composed of four distinct social classes, the lowest of which were called the *stinkards*. The Natchez were the last remnants of a culture that had mostly disappeared by A.D. 1400.

One explanation for the rise of Mississippian culture was the introduction of new strains of maize from Mesoamerica and the adoption of the maize-beans-squash complex developed there. Mississippians depended more fully on agriculture than their Hopewell and Adena predecessors. Mississippian populations were larger than those of previous cultures, and the search for new agricultural lands seems to have been a motive for political expansion. The large towns and urban centers, temple complexes, pyramid mounds, religious symbols, and crops appear to reflect a strong Mesoamerican influence, but no identifiable Mesoamerican artifacts have been found in Mississippian sites.

THE DESERT PEOPLES

Across the American Southwest a different cultural tradition developed with considerable local variation. By around 300 B.C. settled communities developed in this region, living first in pit houses partially beneath the ground and later living in stone structures. Irrigation was used to grow maize, beans, and other crops, and by A.D. 600 ball courts and temple mounds suggest the influence of Mesoamerican cultures. Distinctive pottery developed in each cultural region, and there seems to have been trade between these areas and with Mexico. In southern New Mexico by about A.D. 1000 multiroom stone dwellings were being used.

Perhaps the most famous of the southwestern regional traditions is that of the Anasazi (Navajo for "the ancient ones"), who lived in the Four Corners region of New Mexico, Arizona, Colorado, and Utah. Settled in the region from about 200 B.C. they began to live in large, multistory adobe and stone dwellings by A.D. 700. Apparently, pressure from hostile neighbors caused them to construct these groups of buildings in protected canyons or in cliffs where access is difficult. The existing cliff-dwelling ruins at Mesa Verde and Canyon de Chelly are excellent examples of Anasazi settlements. A characteristic feature of these villages and towns is the circular pit or *kiva* used for religious meetings by the men of the community. This structure may still be found today among the Pueblo Indians of the region.

Kivas are also found in another type of Anasazi settlement. The ruins of about 125 towns in Chaco Canyon, New Mexico, and surrounding areas are remarkable for their planning and the care of their construction in stone or adobe. Many of these towns were connected by an extensive system of what seem to be roads or ritual lines that linked the city to celestial or natural phenomena. The Anasazi produced excellent pottery without the potter's wheel and they had trading contacts with Mesoamerica, where the turquoise of their region was traded for items such as parrots, valued for their feathers.

A long period of drought in the late 13th century seems to explain the decline of the Anasazi and other southwestern traditions. This, followed by pressure from nomads, such as the Navajo and Apache, eventually led to the abandonment of the towns, but many scholars believe that the traditions of the Anasazi continued on in the culture of the modern Hopi and other Pueblo Indians of the American Southwest.

Among the ancient peoples of southwestern United States the contacts with Mesoamerican civilization are clearer than in the eastern woodlands. Both regions, however, demonstrate the diffusion of many aspects of civilization and the development of settled, agricultural societies throughout the Americas.

ANALYSIS
DIFFERENT TIME FOR DIFFERENT PEOPLES

While presenting the indigenous civilizations of the Americas that were often so concerned with time, it is appropriate to examine the importance of time and its measurement in world history. The calendar and the keeping of time are

so much a part of everyday life that we often think of these measures only as aspects of nature and of the natural order. We divide the day into 24 hours of 60 minutes, and the year into 12 months of 365 or so days, without much reflection on the meaning or origins of these divisions. Our lives are guided by the clock and marked by its division into working hours, doctor's appointments, class periods, and TV time slots, all of which reflect a widely accepted system not only of measurement, but also of an ideology of time and its value.

The marking and division of time is a complex matter with its cultural, political, and even biological aspects (as anyone who has flown across the international dateline or suffered from jet lag can testify). The concept and meaning of time has varied greatly from culture to culture and has changed historically within cultures. The leaders of both the French Revolution of 1789 and the Russian Revolution of 1917 created new calendar systems to represent what they hoped were to be the beginnings of new historical ages. Calendar systems and time measurement reflect ideas about politics and history as well as perceptions of the natural world.

Observation of the cyclical motion of the heavens was the key for constructing a yearly calendar by which agriculture could be regulated and religious cycles could be set. Early peoples observed the recurring patterns of the stars and planets. Clearly observed stages of the moon provided the guide for the ancient Babylonians, but because the annual cycle of the moon differed from the solar cycle, the lunar calendar did not provide an accurate guide to the seasons. It was in constant need of adjustment or *intercalation*, which added extra days or months if the seasons were to occur in the same place in the cycle in each calendar year. Despite its difficulties, the lunar calendar was adopted by the Hebrews. It is still in use by Jews and is also the basis of the Muslim calendar.

The ancient Egyptians were the first to use a solar year, and as early as 4000 B.C. they had devised a calendar of 12 months of 30 days each, to which they added 5 days of celebration at the start of each year. (The Mayas and other peoples of Mesoamerica had a similar solution, but added their 5 "inauspicious" days at the end of the year.) The Egyptian solar calendar, while not exact and also in need of periodic adjustments, served as the basis for the Julian calendar of the Roman Empire established by Julius Caesar in 45 B.C. This calendar was modified and improved in the Gregorian calendar, instituted by Pope Gregory XIII in the late 16th century and adopted slowly thereafter throughout Europe.

Other peoples and civilizations also worked out calendar systems based on observation of the heavens, and these in turn were related to concepts about time and history.

Among the ancient peoples of Mesoamerica, India, and Sumer, time was cyclical. Thus the events of history fit into recurring patterns that might reveal a divine purpose or plan but did not lead in any particular direction. Both the ancient Hindus and the Maya calculated great cycles of thousands of years as part of a divine plan.

The ancient Chinese were concerned with the measurement of time, and water clocks were in use during the Shang period around 1500 B.C. By the 11th century, an elaborate clock regulated by the flow of water had been designed for the emperor by Su Sung, a court official. But Chinese interest in mechanical clocks did not continue, and time did not figure prominently in Chinese philosophical thought or in the lives of most people. A new emperor often introduced a new calendar, for control of the calendar was viewed as an attribute of power. The Chinese conception of history was marked by belief in a divine mandate that was given to each dynasty and then withdrawn when it failed in its duties and obligations. Thus time and history recurred as each dynasty sought to fulfill this mandate of heaven.

For the ancient Hebrews and Christians history was not cyclical but linear; it moved toward an end, the revelation of God's will. The present was influenced by the past and the future. It has been suggested that a concept of the future and of progress depends on a linear view of time and history.

Prior to the 19th century, the vast majority of the world's people, including the peasants of the most technologically advanced societies, measured time by the cycle of work and daily tasks—when the cows had to be milked, how much time until dinner, how many hours of daylight remained. These "natural" rhythms kept work and life close together, and there was little concern for time as a separate "thing" that could be precisely measured and accounted, or "lost" or "gained." The day might be divided by the hours of daily prayer or by the duration of a task, but exact time was of little importance.

Although the Chinese had experimented with clocks, and other cultures had used sundials, candles, and water clocks to measure the passage of time, the synchronization and precision of these instruments was difficult. Clocks were curiosities and vehicles for artistic expression, more likely to be found in royal collections than in private homes. In A.D. 807, for example, Europeans marveled at a mechanical water clock sent as a gift by the Muslim leader Haroun al-Rashid to Charlemagne; but despite such wonders, the inaccurate instruments of antiquity were of limited use.

It was in Europe that the transformation of time measurement took place. Perhaps it was because of the deficiencies of sundials and water clocks in the cloudy and frosty climates of northern Europe that the mechanical clock was perfected there. It could have been simply because of Europe's growing interest in machines.

Between the 14th and 17th centuries, the measurement of time experienced a profound if gradual transformation. Church and town clocks appeared in the major urban centers, and clocks began to appear in private homes, especially after the introduction of the pendulum clocks about 1660. By the end of the 17th century, pocket watches based on balance springs made accurate timekeeping a "private" matter, and the aristocrats, master craftsmen, and merchants of Europe began to live their lives by the clock. When Catholic missionaries arrived in China in the 17th century, the Chinese were amazed by the complexity and accuracy of the clocks they brought. Some authors see Europe's fascination with time and perfection of the clock as a symbol of changes in attitudes about labor and nature. Moreover, accurate clocks were precise machines and symbolized the development of technology that accompanied the scientific revolution of the 17th Century and then the Industrial Revolution of the 18th century.

The "revolution in time," as historian David Landes has called it, was related to changes in work discipline needed in the new industries, where the synchronization of tasks in a factory called for precision and a sense of time different from that of rural labor. Such coordination had already begun to appear in activities such as shipbuilding or on sugar plantations. Time became something that workers sold and employers bought, and the concept of productivity measured by the amount of work done in a specific amount of time became a basic part of the industrial work ethic. The shift was difficult, however. Older working patterns were slow to change and industrialists complained that workers still honored "Saint Monday" by not showing up for work on that day, or that they preferred to work not by the hour but by the task. Early industrial workers were not eager to become captives of the machine and the clock.

Those earlier preindustrial attitudes toward work—the rhythm of intense labor at some times of year and less work at others, labor measured by the job and not by the amount of time it took to do it—persisted in most of the world outside Europe in the 19th century. European travelers to Asia, Africa, the Pacific, and the Americas commented on the natives' lack of punctuality, the natural or religious rhythms of their life, their inability to measure time, and often their seeming disregard for it. The "Myth of the Lazy Native" was being born. The clock became a measure of what Europeans and North Americans valued and what set them apart. When an English missionary in southern Africa wrote in his diary, "Today we have unpacked our clock and we seem a little more civilized," he summarized a great deal of modern world history.

Questions: To what extent did the measurement of time become important in the early civilizations of Egypt, the Near East, and China? Do concepts of time influence a people's view of history? What are the implications of the technological changes in keeping time? ☸

THE ANDEAN WORLD

The rise of civilization in South America paralleled many of the processes in Mesoamerica, but it was also conditioned by the specific geographical features of that continent. The Andean world presented to men and women a peculiar geography of complex microregions with extreme changes in altitude and temperature. The narrow and arid strip on the western coast, cut by a few rivers that flow to the Pacific, gives way quickly to the high Andes where some peaks rise to over 15,000 feet. Between the two major chains of the Andes lie high valleys and steppes, or *puna,* that form the highlands, or *altiplano.* On these cool uplands (usually above 10,000 feet) the land is relatively level and there is adequate water. Here potatoes and maize could be grown and the puna provided good grazing for llamas and alpacas, the "sheep of the Andes." Andean populations concentrated here or down on the arid coast in the river valleys that made irrigation possible. On the eastern slopes of the Andes a number of large rivers run down into the tropical rain forest concentrated at the basins of the Amazon and La Plata rivers. This is the humid *montaña,* where tropical fruits and coca leaf can be obtained.

This rugged topography imposed limitations and created opportunities for civilization to develop. The arid coastal valleys demanded irrigation, and this spurred population growth and social complexity. Irrigation projects were enormous, involving miles of canals and ditches and requiring constant maintenance and construction. Did the need for irrigation create the state, or did irrigation result from the formation of centralized authority? Scholars disagree, but it is clear that once formed, a major function of the coastal states was to irrigate. In the highlands, irrigation and terracing increased the food supply in regions where the amount of arable land was limited. Populations concentrated in the fertile valleys but were separated from each other by steep mountains. Trade and communication were difficult. It took large and well-organized projects to build roads, bridges, and agricultural terraces. The reasons for state building were good. The warfare, military images, and trophy heads seen in much ancient Peruvian art represent a world of limited resources and competition.

Recall that, in the Andean world, sharp vertical changes created microclimates within relatively short distances. Peo-

ples and even individual communities or families strove to control a number of ecological zones where different kinds of crops could be raised. A community might reside in the altiplano growing potatoes and *quinoa,* an Andean grain,

Andean Societies

but could also have fields in lower valleys to grow maize, pastures miles away at a higher elevation for their llamas, and even an outer colony in the montaña to provide cotton, coca, and other tropical products. In fact, access to a variety of these ecological zones by colonization, occupation, conquest, or trade seems to have been a constant feature in Andean life that determined pre-Columbian patterns of settlement and influenced the historical development of the Andean world.

EARLY DEVELOPMENTS AND THE RISE OF CHAVÍN

Much of early Andean history fits a pattern of alternation between periods of decentralization, in which various local or regional centers developed distinctive cultures, and periods when one of these centers seems to have spread its control over very large areas, establishing a cultural *horizon* under centralized authority. Between 3000 and 2000 B.C. permanent agricultural villages were established in both the Andean highlands and on the arid Pacific coast. Maize was introduced from Mesoamerica and was grown along with indigenous crops such as the potato. By about 2700 B.C., pottery was produced, first on the north coast in present-day Ecuador and then in the highlands of central Peru. This early pottery, called Valdivia ware, indicates advanced techniques of production. It is remarkably similar to Japanese Jomon-period ceramics, and this has led some scholars to hypothesize a transpacific contact by Japanese fishermen. Whatever the origins of pottery in the region, the presence of sedentary agriculture, ceramics, weaving, and permanent villages marked a level of productivity that

The Andean region contains a number of environments, from the arid coasts to the highland grasslands shown here. Their resources made access to different environmental niches a goal of Andean peoples.

was soon followed by evidence of political organization. Early sites, such as El Paraiso on the Peruvian coast, contain monumental buildings of great size, but we know little of the societies that built them.

Between 1800 and 1200 B.C. ceremonial centers with large stone buildings were constructed both in the highlands and on the coast. Pottery was now widely distributed; the domestication of the llama had taken place; and agriculture had become more complex, with evidence of simple irrigation at some places. The most important of these centers was Chavín de Huantar (850–250 B.C.) in the Peruvian highlands. Chavín contained a number of large temple platforms and adobe and stone constructions. Its craftsmen worked in ceramics, textiles, and gold. Chavín culture was characterized by artistic motifs that were widely diffused through much of the Andean region and seem to represent a cult or a system of religious beliefs. Jaguars, snakes, birds of prey, and humans with feline characteristics were used as decorations, often along with scenes of war and violence.

The artistic style was so widely diffused that archeologists refer to this epoch as a horizon, a period when there seems to have been a broad central authority that integrated a widely dispersed region. In truth, we do not know if the religion of Chavín was spread by conquest, trade, or missionary activity, nor do we know its origins. It does have some remarkable stylistic similarities with Olmec art in Mesoamerica; some archeologists have pointed out certain tropical features in both and have suggested the Amazonian lowlands as a possible point of origin for both traditions.

The evidence of warfare in early Peruvian agricultural societies may indicate a general process. With the development of intensive agriculture and a limited amount of arable land, the organization of irrigation and the creation of political authority and eventually states that could mobilize to protect or expand available land, was a vital necessity.

REGIONAL CULTURES AND A NEW HORIZON

By 300 B.C. Chavín was in decline, and whatever unity the widely spread Chavín style indicated was lost. The Andean world was now characterized by regional centers, each with its own cultural and artistic traditions. This was a period without political unity, but it produced some of the Andean world's finest art. Irrigated agriculture producing a wide variety of crops, the domestication of llamas and related animals, dense populations, and hierarchical societies could be found in a number of places. Some societies, such as Nazca on the south coast and Moche to the north, produced remarkable pottery and weaving.

Nazca weaving reached a high point for the Americas. Discovery in the 1920s of a group of richly dressed mummies at Paracas near Nazca revealed the artistic accomplishments of these ancient weavers. Over 100 colors were used and many techniques of weaving and cloth types were produced; designs were often abstract. The plain near Nazca is also the scene of great figures of various animals, which cover many hundreds of feet and can only be seen from the air. There are also great straight lines or paths that cut across the plain and seem to be oriented toward distant mountains or celestial points. Why these lines and designs were drawn is unknown.

The Mochica state (A.D., 200–700), in the Moche valley and on the coast to the north of Chavín, mobilized workers to construct great clay-brick temples, residences, and platforms. Artisans produced gold and silver jewelry and copper tools. The potters' art reached a high point; scenes on Mochica ceramics depict rulers receiving tribute and executing prisoners. Nobles, priests, farmers, soldiers, and slaves are also portrayed in remarkably lifelike ways; many vessels are quite clearly portraits of individual members of the elite. The Mochica also produced a great number of extremely explicit pottery vessels showing a variety of sexual activities. These scenes are almost always in a domestic setting and indicate descriptions of everyday life rather than ritual unions.

Moche expanded its control by conquest. Mochica art contains many representations of war, prisoners, and taking heads as trophies. There is also archeological evidence of hilltop forts and military posts. Politically, Moche and the other regional states seem to have been military states or chiefdoms, supported by extensive irrigated agriculture and often at war.

Some idea of life in Moche society has been spectacularly revealed with the discovery in 1988 of the tomb of a warrior-priest. Buried with retainers, servants, and his dog, this nobleman was covered with gold, silver, and copper ornaments, fine cloth, and jewelry. The scenes depicted on these objects and in the pottery buried with him include scenes of captive prisoners, ritual sacrifice, and warfare.

This pattern of regional development continued until about A.D. 300 when two large centers, Tihuanaco on the shores of Lake Titicaca and Huari, farther to the north in southern Peru, began to emerge as large states. How much centralized political control they exerted is unclear, but as in the earlier case of Chavín, the religious symbols and artistic style associated with these centers became widely diffused in the Andean world, creating perhaps a second or Intermediate Horizon (c. A.D. 300–900) roughly contemporary with the classic Maya and Teotihuacan in Mesoamerica.

At the plain of Nazca on the southern Peruvian coast, mysterious geometric designs and the shapes of animals, like this spider, were traced on the ground. The purpose of these shapes, which can only be seen from the air, remains unknown.

Tihuanaco was an urban ceremonial center with a population of perhaps 40,000, supported by extensive irrigated agriculture. Recent archeological work has revealed an extensive system of raised fields, irrigated by canals, that could produce high yields. Tihuanaco's inhabitants probably spoke Aymara, the language of the southern Andes that is spoken today in Bolivia. The art style of Tihuanaco and representations of its gods, especially the Staff God, spread all over the southern Andean zone.

In typical Andean fashion, Tihuanaco extended its political control through colonies as far away as Chile and the eastern Andean slopes in order to assure access to fish, coca, and tropical plants—the products of different ecological zones. Huari may have begun as a colony of Tihua-

naco, but it eventually exercised wide influence over much of the North Andean zone. While the period of its control was relatively short, the urban area of Huari eventually covered over six square miles and its influence was spread by the construction of a system of roads.

The Intermediate Horizon, represented by Tihuanaco and Huari, came to an end in the 9th century A.D., about the same time as the end of the classic period in Mesoamerica. Whether these two processes were connected remains unknown. With the decline of these expansive cultures in Peru another period of regional development followed as different peoples, especially those along the coast, sought to establish control over their neighbors. The Chimu state on the north coast, based on its magnificent capital city of Chau, eventually controlled over 600 miles of the coastal zone.

The Chimu state, founded about A.D. 800, was still expanding when it fell to the Incas in 1465. In this period other small states had formed. From Lake Titicaca westward to the Pacific coast, the Lupacqa created a kingdom. On the eastern margins of the lake and into the rich valleys on the eastern slope of the Andes other small chiefdoms formed. Meanwhile, in the highlands various ethnic groups were struggling for control of their neighbors. One of these, a group of Quechua-speaking clans, or *ayllus*, took control of the highlands around Cuzco and began to expand, especially after A.D. 1400. These were the Incas, who were in the midst of creating a new horizon of centralized control and considerable cultural influence over the various ethnic and linguistic groups of the Andean world from Ecuador to Chile, when the Europeans arrived in 1532.

ANDEAN LIFEWAYS

Although it is difficult to reconstruct much of the social and political organization of early Andean societies on the basis of archeological evidence, by using later observations from Inca times along with archeological materials we can identify some characteristic features. We have already spoken of *verticality*, or the control of a number of economic niches at different altitudes, as a principle of Andean life. This control and related self-sufficiency was sometimes the objective of states, but it was also the goal of families and communities. Kin groups were another constant of the Andean world.

Andean peoples were divided into ethnic groups and spoke a number of languages, although Aymara came to predominate in the Bolivian highlands and the Incas later spread Quechua from the central Andes to the coast and north to Ecuador. Despite ethnic and linguistic differences, communities were generally composed of households, which together recognized some form of kinship. These kinship units, or ayllus, traced descent from some common, sometimes mythical ancestor and they referred to other members of the ayllu as brother and sister. People usually married within their ayllu. The ayllu assigned each household land and access to herds and water to each household. But rights and access were not equal for every household or family within an ayllu. Ayllus were often divided into halves, which might have different functions or roles. This was a form of organization the peoples of the highland civilizations shared with many tribes of the Amazonian forests.

There were also community leaders and ayllu chiefs, or *curacas*, with privileges of dress and access to resources. Groups of ayllus sharing a similar dialect, customs and distinctive dress were bound together into ethnic groups, and sometimes a number of these were forged into a state. The ties of kinship were used to mobilize the community for cooperative labor and war. The ayllu was a basic organization, and kinship provided an understanding of the cooperation and conflict from the village to the empire. Some authors have suggested that, even in the large states, conflicts were more often between ayllus or groups of ayllus than between secondary social classes.

The principle of reciprocity that lay beneath the cooperative organization of the ayllu infused much Andean social life. Reciprocal obligations existed at many levels—within the family between men and women, between households within the ayllu, and between the curacas who were expected to represent the interests of the ayllu. Eventually, in theory at least, reciprocity also existed between communities and a large state such as Huari, which in return for labor and tribute was expected to provide access to goods or to mobilize large projects, such as irrigation or terracing, that would benefit the community. Reciprocity also infused religious belief. Andean peoples lived in a world where sacred spirits and powers, or *huacas*, were apparent in caves, mountains, rocks, rivers, and other natural phenomena. Worship of the huacas and of the mummies of ancestors (which were also considered holy and part of Andean religious life), at least from the Nazca period, was a matter of reciprocal exchange as well.

CONCLUSION

AMERICAN CIVILIZATIONS

There are striking parallels in the cultural development and the chronology of the two major areas of civilization in the Americas. This may be due to convergence—that is,

people in different places often work out similar solutions to the same problems—but there also seems to have been considerable contact between these regions over a long period of time. Much of this contact was probably indirect, funneled through the intermediate areas of Colombia and Panama. Peoples such as the Tairona and Muisca of Colombia created large-scale chiefdoms based on intensive cultivation. Their societies were hierarchical and their artisan crafts, especially metallurgy, were highly developed: South American gold metallurgy turns up in offerings at Maya shrines in Yucatan. Through such intermediate societies, contact between Mesoamerica and the Andean world may have been made. There are other examples of cultural diffusion and contact. The ritual ball game that was played for sport and worship throughout Mesoamerica and the Maya area on special courts has been found as far away as the American Southwest and even among the peoples of the Caribbean islands.

American Indian peoples and civilizations shared much, but there were differences as well. The Peruvian cultures developed metallurgy to a greater degree than elsewhere in the Americas and eventually produced bronze tools. The puna supported herds of llamas and permitted a form of pastoralism unknown in Mesoamerica. Unlike the Maya, the ancient peoples of the Andes never invented a writing system. Still, in many ways the civilizations of the Americas had more in common with each other than with those of the Old World, and that fact probably indicated their shared origins and their contacts over thousands of years.

In this brief survey it should be clear that we have not done justice to the variety and complexity of American Indian cultures and civilizations. It should also be clear that there is much that we do not know about the history of the Western Hemisphere. The long history of civilization in the New World, the strength of Indian languages, traditions, and beliefs, and the crops of the Americas domesticated by the ancestors of the Indians all had an impact on the subsequent history of these continents. The long relative isolation of the Americas from the populations, and therefore from the diseases, of the Old World and the inability of the Americas to share in the technological advances of the Old World proved disastrous after first contact. Ultimately, however, the resilience of Indian cultures would shape the societies of the Americas in many ways.

FURTHER READINGS

An excellent and up to date survey of the early history of the Americas is Stuart Fiedel's *Prehistory of the Americas* (1987). Also extremely useful for its information and for its excellent maps is Michael Coe, et al., *Atlas of Ancient America* (1986).

On the early history of Peru, Edward P. Lanning's *Peru before the Incas* (1967) remains, despite its age, a classic account, sensitive to the geography and ecology of the Andean region. Nigel Davies's *The Ancient Kingdoms of Mexico* (1983) offers a broad overview which combines archeology, art history, and history.

One of the best books on the Maya is Norman Hammond's *Ancient Maya Civilization* (1982). Well-illustrated and well-written, this book covers the major aspects of classic Maya culture and is especially good on the calendar system. An excellent short survey is Michael D. Coe's *The Maya,* 4th ed. (1987).

Two good introductions to the ancient cultures of North America are Robert Silverberg's *Mound Builders of Ancient America* (1968) and George G. Gumerman, ed., *The Anasazi in a Changing Environment* (1988). George S. Stuart's *America's Ancient Cities* (1988) uses a good text and excellent photos to emphasize the continuity between the peoples of North and middle America.

A fine example of a scholarly monograph and one that demonstrates that exciting discoveries about the ancient Americas do not all center on great cities and "lost" civilizations is Anna C. Roosevelt's *Parmana: Prehistoric Maize and Manioc Subsistence along the Amazon and Orinoco* (1980). This scientific study shows how archeologists are probing questions such as the origins and diffusion of agriculture.

Africa				
	3200 Unification of Upper and Lower Egypt		**800 B.C.–A.D.1000** Migration of Bantu-speakers throughout sub-Saharan Africa	
	7000–3000 Desiccation of the Sahara		**600 B.C.–A.D.1000** Iron diffused throughout Africa	
		c. 1500–300 Horses introduced to Africa by way of Egypt		
	3000–1000 Spread of agriculture south of the Sahara	**750–666** Kings of Meroe rule Egypt		

Northern Europe				
Germans	**2000 B.C. ff.** Germanic peoples settle in Scandinavia (present-day Denmark)		**100** Germans in southern Germany, on Roman borders	
		1000 B.C. ff. Germans spread through Germany, displacing Celts		
Slavs		**7th–3rd centuries** Scythian state in southern Russia		

Japan				
	c. 5000 Early migrations and settlement of Japan			
	3000–2000 Jomon culture	**600** Legendary Emperor Jimmu establishes state in Japan		

Polynesia				
		1500–500 Beginnings of Polynesian migrations; Lapita pottery found in Fiji, Tonga, Samoa		

The Spread of Peoples and Civilizations

10

INTRODUCTION. We have concentrated thus far on the centers of civilization and their internal developments in the classical societies of the Old World and the emerging civilizations in the Americas. In this chapter we will explore the connections between the established centers and the rest of the world's peoples. The major civilizations have historically been expansive, and their innovations and cultures have influenced their immediate neighbors and sometimes peoples who lived at great distances from them. While scholars still debate the issue of diffusion versus independent development, many believe that important early breakthroughs, such as agriculture, the domestication of animals, pottery, and metallurgy, did not need to be continually reinvented across the globe, but were rather diffused by contacts and migration. Agriculture, for example, may have been "invented" more than once, but most people learned about it by contact with those who already practiced it.

Throughout history, the process and means of cultural expansion have varied greatly. At times, as in the case of Rome, conquest has been the means of imposing ideas, language, and institutions. Roman culture and law was carried to the far ends of the empire in the wake of the conquering Roman legions. In other places, long-distance traders have carried ideas as well as goods. The ship, the caravan, and the sword have thus been instruments of cultural diffusion.

1076 Ghana conquered by Almoravids

1000 Ghana at height of its power

100–200 Camels introduced from Asia **300** Meroë declines **985** Conversion to Islam of king of Gao

700–800 Islam sweeps across North Africa

100 Rise of kingdom of Axum **300–700** Conversion to Christianity of Nubian kingdoms in Axum **800–1100** Growth of the trans-Sahara trade for gold

---

c. 55–112 Tacitus writes about Germans **401 ff.** Larger Germanic invasions of Roman Empire

100 ff. Improvements in German political organization, rise of local kings; movement of some Germans into Roman Empire

4th c. Germans pressed by Huns

---

100 ff. Increasing movement of Slavs into eastern Europe **679** Bulgars (Turkic people) migrate to Balkans, become largely Slavicized, set up first Slavic kingdom in Balkans

---

300–400 Yamato clan establishes imperial control

580s Buddhism adopted

400 Chinese script introduced

300–1000 Polynesian migrations; settlement of Hawaii and Easter Island **900** New Zealand settled **1100–1300** Recurring voyages from Hawaii to Tahiti

A.D. I   A.D. 500   A.D. IOOO

The later history of Rome after the empire was invaded demonstrates another possibility. It is not always conquerors who spread their culture; sometimes it is the conquered. In late Rome, as in pre-Colombian Mesoamerica and China, the "barbarian" conquerors of a civilization absorbed its culture and adopted its ways. The result was a new fusion of cultural elements. In other places, trade or missionary activity has been the means by which civilization has spread. In this chapter, for example, our discussion of early Japanese society will demonstrate the peaceful diffusion of Chinese culture and its transformation in Japan, a process in which Buddhism played a major role.

In this chapter we cannot deal with all the peoples of the globe who were influenced by the spread of civilization or who contributed to that process. Instead we shall examine four areas of the world, sub-Saharan Africa, northern Europe, Japan, and the Pacific islands, which at the time their cultures took shape were not among the civilization centers. Nevertheless, the peoples of these areas were influenced by developments or innovations in those centers, or, in the case of Polynesia, by earlier cultural developments on the Asian mainland. In each case, we will also see how ideas, techniques, and material objects were adapted to new environments and different social circumstances so that the spread of civilization and the contact of cultures was usually a creative process, not simply a matter of copying. Finally, important developments occurred during the classical period, though in Polynesia and the Americas there was no connection with the major Old World centers.

It may at first seem strange to discuss peoples as different as the Polynesians, the Germanic tribes, the Slavs, the Japanese, and the early sub-Saharan Africans together. But we should remember that the processes of migration, diffusion, and cultural development are the basis for our discussion. Moreover, unlike earlier chapters where the chronological limits have been relatively precise, our discussion will have to range more broadly over time because the pace and rhythm of the diffusion process varied greatly in these widely separated parts of the world. Here, too, the story of how these peoples began to develop their distinctive cultures, often in contact with centers of civilization, should be our focus, rather than a limited time frame. Finally, this chapter also serves the purpose of introducing some peoples whose role in world history would later become particularly important.

THE SPREAD OF CIVILIZATION IN AFRICA

Africa is a continent of great size, almost 12 million square miles or about three times the size of the United States. Most of it lies in the tropics and, although we often think of Africa in terms of its rain forests, less than ten percent of the continent is covered by tropical forests, and those are mostly in West Africa. Much of the African surface is covered by *savannas*, or open grasslands, and by arid plains and deserts. In geological terms, the continent is really formed by a series of high plateaus broken in the east by the Great Rift valley and the mountains that surround it. Large rivers—the Congo, the Nile, the Zambezi, and the Niger—begin in the interior of the continent and flow to the sea over great falls and cataracts that mark the passage from the plateau to the coast. These falls have historically made movement from the coast to the interior difficult, but the great river systems have also provided the interior of Africa with routes of communication.

We have already noted the origins of humankind in East Africa where some of the earliest fossil remains of protohominids have been found. Even before the appearance about 300,000 years ago of *Homo sapiens*, the ancestors of modern human beings, other hominid species, such as *Homo erectus*, had moved outward from Africa to Asia and Europe. Africa, therefore, holds a special place in the development of the human species. It was the scene of human origins. Moreover, in cultural terms, Africa participated in the early development of civilization. In Chapter 2 we discussed the remarkable civilization of Egypt in the Nile valley, and its extension to the Upper Nile Kingdoms of Kush and Ethiopia. In this chapter, we will examine the spread of elements of civilization to other areas of Africa.

Although an obstacle, the Sahara could be traversed, especially after the introduction of the camel, and an active trade developed between black Africa and the Mediterranean world.

Despite the false image of Africa as the "dark" and isolated continent, it was, in fact, often in contact with other areas of the world. It received from them technology, crops, ideas, and material goods that in turn stimulated social and cultural innovations. Moreover, the contacts were not always in the same direction, and there is now considerable evidence that not only early humans but also certain languages, crops, political, and cultural influences spread outward from Africa.

It is useful to begin this discussion by noting the climatic change that altered the appearance of the African continent and seems to have set a whole series of historical processes in motion. That change centers on the area of the Sahara, which during the Late Stone Age appears to have been far better watered than it is today, receiving between 10 and 50 times as much rain as at present. Archeological evidence indicates that a number of peoples, such as the ancestors of the modern-day Berbers and Tuaregs of North Africa, who speak languages related to ancient Egyptian, and the ancestors of the Negro peoples of sub-Saharan Africa, some of whom also spoke these Afro-Asiatic languages and others who did not, inhabited the area of the Sahara during this period. Around 9000 years ago this situation

began to change as temperatures rose and rainfall became erratic. By about 3000 B.C., much of the area was desert. The droughts that have recently affected Africa indicate that the *desiccation*, or drying up, of the Sahara is continuing and the desert is growing.

As the Sahara became less habitable, the populations moved north toward the Mediterranean coast and south into the area of the dry *sahel*, or fringe, and, especially, onto the grassy savannas suitable for agriculture and grazing. Savannas stretch across Africa from the mouth of the Senegal River on the west coast to Lake Chad and the Upper Nile valley. This broad region, the Sudan, became a center of cultural development. The movement of peoples into the Sudan and toward the Nile valley and the Mediterranean set the stage for major developments in the subsequent history of Africa.

AGRICULTURE, IRON, AND THE BANTU PEOPLES

Agriculture may have developed independently in Africa, but many scholars believe that the spread of agriculture and iron throughout Africa linked that continent to the

Africa: Variations in Climate

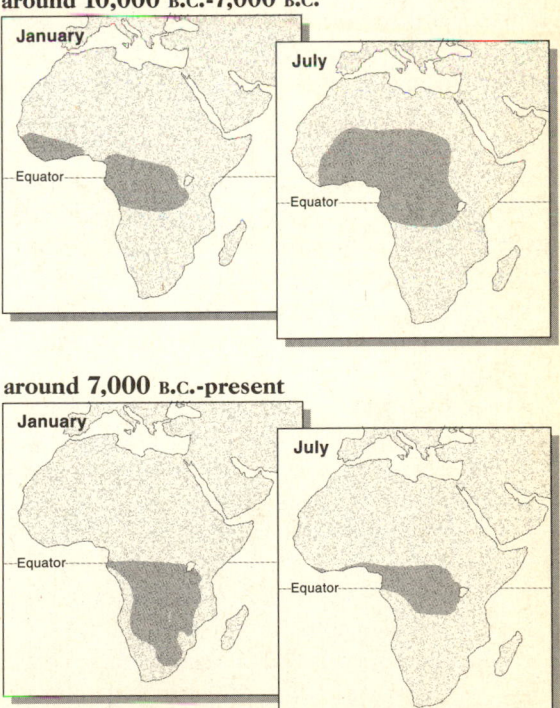

Areas of Heavy Rainfall around 10,000 B.C.-7,000 B.C.

around 7,000 B.C.-present

major centers of civilization in the Near East and Mediterranean world. The drying up of the Sahara had pushed many peoples to the south into sub-Saharan Africa. These were the ancestors of the Negro peoples. They settled at first in scattered hunting-and-gathering bands, although in some places near lakes and rivers people who fished, with a more secure food supply, lived in larger population concentrations. Agriculture seems to have reached these people from the Near East, since the first domesticated crops were millets and sorghums whose origins are not African but West Asian. The route of agricultural distribution may have gone through Egypt or Ethiopia, which long had contacts across the Red Sea with the Arabian peninsula. There is evidence of agriculture prior to 3000 B.C.

Once the idea of planting diffused, Africans began to develop their own crops, such as certain varieties of rice, and they demonstrated a continued receptiveness to new imports. The proposed areas of the domestication of African crops lie in a band that extends from Ethiopia across the southern Sudan to West Africa. Subsequently, other crops, such as bananas, were introduced from Southeast Asia, and in the 16th century A.D. American crops, such as maize and manioc, spread widely throughout Africa.

Livestock also came from outside Africa. Cattle were introduced from Asia, as probably were domestic sheep and goats. Horses were apparently introduced to Africa from West Asia by the Hyksos invaders of Egypt (1780–1560 B.C.) and then spread across the Sudan to West Africa. Rock paintings in the Sahara indicate that horses and chariots were used to traverse the desert and that by 300–200 B.C. there were trade routes across the Sahara. Horses were adopted by peoples of the West African savanna, and later their powerful cavalry forces allowed a number of them to carve out large empires. Finally, the camel was introduced from Asia around the first century A.D. This was an important innovation, because the camel's ability to thrive in harsh desert conditions and to carry large loads cheaply made it an effective and efficient means of transportation. The camel transformed the desert from a barrier into a still difficult, but more accessible, route of trade and communication.

Livestock provided a living to peoples in the arid portions of the savanna belt and the Sahara, and permitted a nomadic or seasonally moving, or *transhumant*, way of life to flourish in certain inhospitable regions. In some areas, it appears that livestock and agriculture arrived about the same time. The spread of cattle was seriously limited in some places by the tsetse fly, which carries a disease (sleeping sickness) dangerous to humans and especially cattle. The tsetse flourished in wet lowlands below 3500 feet, and it severely limited pastoralism and also the use of animals for farming and transport as a way of life in large areas of West and central Africa.

Iron also came from West Asia, although its routes of diffusion were somewhat different than those of agriculture. Most of Africa presents a curious case in which societies moved directly from a technology of stone to iron without passing through the intermediate stage of copper or bronze metallurgy, although some early copper-working sites have been found in West Africa. Iron had been worked in the Near East and Anatolia for at least a thousand years before it began to penetrate into sub-Saharan Africa. The Phoenicians carried the knowledge of iron smelting to their colonies, such as Carthage in North Africa, and from there to their trading ports along the coast of Morocco. By sea down the coast or by land across the Sahara, this knowledge penetrated into the forests and savannas of West Africa during the thousand years before Christ, or at roughly the same time that iron making was reaching western Europe. Evidence of iron making has been found in Nigeria, Ghana, and Mali, and iron implements seem to have slowly replaced stone ones at a number of sites.

This technological shift could cause profound changes in the complexity of African societies. Iron represented power. In West Africa the blacksmith who made tools and weapons had an important place in society, often with special religious powers and functions. Iron hoes, which made the land more productive, and iron weapons, which made the warrior more powerful, had symbolic meaning in a number of West African societies. Those who knew the secrets of iron making gained ritual and sometimes political power.

Iron entered Africa by other routes as well. Iron making seems to have traveled from the Red Sea into Ethiopia and East Africa and down the Nile from Egypt into the Sudan where, as we have seen, large African states, such as Meroe, were in close contact with dynastic Egypt. Meroe's contact with peoples to the south led to the further diffusion of iron technology. By the first century A.D., iron was known in sub-Saharan Africa, and within about a thousand years it had reached the southern end of the continent. Iron tools and weapons increased efficiency in agriculture and war. In the later stages of this story, the adoption of agriculture and the use of iron tools and weapons were roughly simultaneous processes.

Unlike in the Americas, where metallurgy was a very late and limited development, Africans had iron from a relatively early date, developing ingenious furnaces to produce the high heat (1100°F) needed for production and to

Remarkable bronze figures were cast at Ife (Nigeria) by Yoruba craftsmen.

control the amount of air that reached the carbon and iron ore necessary for making iron. Except for those regions directly influenced by the great Bronze Age civilization of Pharonic Egypt, much of Africa skipped right into the Iron Age, taking the basic technology and adapting it to local conditions and resources. The working of bronze was also known to Africans and by A.D. 1000 remarkably lifelike bronze sculptures of great technical virtuosity were cast at the city-state of Ife in Nigeria by the Yoruba people.

THE BANTU DISPERSAL

The diffusion of agriculture and later of iron was accompanied by a great movement of people who may have carried these innovations. These people probably originated in eastern Nigeria in West Africa. Their migration may have been set in motion by an increase in population caused by a movement into their homelands of peoples fleeing the desiccation of the Sahara. They spoke a language, proto-Bantu (*bantu* means "the people"), which is the parent tongue of a large number of related Bantu languages still spoken throughout sub-Saharan Africa. In fact, about 90 percent of the languages south of a line from the Bight of Benin on the west coast to Somalia on the east coast are part of the Bantu family.

Why and how these people spread out into central and southern Africa remains a mystery, but archeologists believe that at some stages their iron weapons allowed them to conquer their hunting-and-gathering opponents, who still used stone implements. Still, the process is uncertain, and peaceful migration — or simply rapid demographic growth — may have also caused the Bantu expansion.

The migrations moved first to the central Sudan and then into the forests of West and central Africa. The rivers, and especially the Congo basin, provided the means of movement; the migration was a long, gradual, and intermittent process. Moving outward from central Africa, Bantu peoples arrived at the east coast, where they contacted cattle-raising peoples of a different linguistic tradition. By the 12th century, the Bantu speakers, the ancestors of the Shona and Nguni peoples, pushed south of the Zambezi River into modern Zimbabwe and eventually into South Africa.

From the study of the related Bantu languages, it is possible to learn something about the original culture of the proto-Bantu speakers. The early Bantu depended on agriculture and fishing. They raised goats and perhaps cattle. They were village dwellers who organized their societies around kinship ties. Leadership of the villages was probably in the hands of a council of elders. The spirits of the natural world played a large role in the lives of these people. They looked to their ancestors to help deal with those spirits, and depended on village religious specialists to deal with calamity and to combat witchcraft, which they greatly feared.

In about a thousand years the Bantu-speaking peoples expanded over much of the continent, spreading their languages and cultures among the existing populations, absorbing those original peoples and being absorbed by them. By the 13th century A.D., cattle-raising, iron-using Bantu peoples had reached the southern end of the continent. By that time, Black Africa's major features were in place. A few pure hunting peoples remained, such as the Pygmies of central Africa, but their way of life was not that of most Africans. Agricultural and herding societies with knowledge of iron metallurgy could be found throughout sub-Saharan Africa. While pockets of peoples still speaking non-Bantu languages existed, such as the Khoi-Khoi and Bushmen of southern Africa, and in East Africa the influence of Ethiopian culture was still strong, Bantu languages predominated all over southern and central Africa and marked the trail of one of the world's great migrations.

AFRICA, CIVILIZATION, AND THE WIDER WORLD

We have viewed the development of Egyptian civilization in conjunction with the parallel developments of the Fertile Crescent, yet we should also recognize that many aspects of Egyptian life, such as ideas about religion and kingship, strongly resembled those of other African societies. There is much debate on whether the Egyptian idea of the king as a divine being with special powers over natural phenomena (an idea also found in some West African kingdoms), is due to the common origins of both or whether these concepts were diffused from Egypt to other areas of Africa. There are other striking parallels, such as brother-sister marriage among rulers or in the rituals of taking authority, that seem to tie cultures of sub-Saharan Africa to Egypt. Whatever the African origins of Egyptian civilization (a matter of considerable controversy), there is no doubt of extensive contact between Egypt and peoples living southward along the Nile valley in the Sudan and northern Ethiopia.

AXUM: A CHRISTIAN KINGDOM. We discussed the Egyptian contacts with Kush in Chapter 2, and the fact that the Kushites and their capitals became thoroughly influenced by Egyptian culture. For a short period, from 751 B.C. until the invasion of Egypt by the Assyrians in

666 B.C., the kings of Meroe also ruled as pharaohs of Egypt. Meroe possessed the ores and fuels needed to produce iron on a large scale. That technology, and its extensive trade with Egypt and the Mediterranean, allowed Meroe to flourish. But Meroe was not alone. Other town-based societies also existed in the region of the Sudan and Ethiopia.

The kingdom of Axum in the Ethiopian highlands, which eventually surpassed Meroe in importance around the 1st century A.D., introduces another cultural stream into the history of Africa. Axum seems to have received strong influences and perhaps settlers from the Arabian peninsula. Its population probably consisted of a mixture of these immigrants and peoples of Eritrea and the Ethiopian highlands. Axum became a great city with large palaces and monuments. It developed a writing system based on a South Arabian script. Geez, the language of the people of Axum, is a Semitic language, but Axum's rulers also spoke Greek and perhaps used it as a language of trade.

Axum was a powerful state. It controlled a number of ports, such as Adulis along the Red Sea coast, and it participated in the commerce of the Indian Ocean where its ivory, salt, and slaves were in great demand. It also traded with Alexandrian Egypt, and eventually with Rome, Byzantium, and India. Those contacts led to a fusion of cultural elements. By about A.D. 200, Axum was involved in military and political affairs across the Red Sea on the Arabian peninsula. By the middle of the 3d century A.D., Axum had defeated Meroe and emerged as the dominant power in the horn of Africa. The history of the kingdom of Axum underlines the cross-fertilization of cultures across the Red Sea.

Around A.D. 350, Ezana, the king of Axum, converted to Christianity, and that religion spread among Axum's peoples over the following centuries. Monasteries and churches were established, the Bible was translated, and a religious literature was developed that linked the Queen of Sheba, wife of King Solomon of the Old Testament, to Axum and demonstrated the area's supposed progression from Judaism to Christianity. All this established a certain religious legitimacy to the *negus*, or ruler of Axum. The form of Christianity that spread among the Axumites during the 5th and 6th centuries A.D. increased the kingdom's ties to the Greeks of the Eastern Mediterranean, although eventually Ethiopian Christianity became somewhat isolated.

All this indicates considerable influence and contact between this African kingdom and the outside world well before the arrival of Islam. The civilization of Axum became the basis for much of the distinctive culture of Christian Ethiopia in the centuries that followed. Here, as along the long-distance external influences were paralleled by an extended period of internal development among peoples of West Africa, such as the Yoruba, Mande, and Fulbe.

GOLDEN GHANA. The peoples of the savanna took advantage of their location to serve as intermediaries between the southern gold-producing forest zone in the region of the Niger and Senegal river valleys and the markets of North Africa. Trading salt for gold to the peoples of the forest, and then sending the gold northward along established caravan routes that crossed the Sahara, a number of states took form before the 8th century A.D. Strung in a line across the southern edge of the desert, the states of Takur, Ghana, Gao, and Kanem were located to serve as intermediaries in the trans-Sahara trade.

The trans-Sahara trade was the basis for the growth of the first great sub-Saharan state, the empire of Ghana, which lay squarely astride the route of exchange. This was a trading state created by the West African Soninke people, perhaps with some participation by the nomadic North African Tuaregs. Early Arab chroniclers wrote that in Ghana, 20 kings had ruled prior to the time of Muhammad, which was a way of saying that the kingdom was an ancient one. By the time Arab visitors began to write about Ghana and other Sudanic states in the 9th century A.D., these states were already well-established kingdoms, the product of their advantageous geographic position and apparently a joint heritage of internal development and external influences and trade. The external influences increased considerably with the arrival of Islam. In A.D. 985, the king of Gao converted to Islam and set in motion a series of conversions among the elites of the West African states. Conversion of the masses proceeded at a slower rate.

The ancient kingdom of Ghana (not to be confused with the modern nation of Ghana) lay mostly within the boundaries of the present-day Republic of Mali. It became a major trading state, receiving salt, cloth, and manufactured goods from North Africa and the Mediterranean in return for gold. The power of Ghana depended on its location and control over subject states and provinces, especially Bambuk and other gold-producing regions in the forest zones to the south. By the 9th century A.D., Ghana was known as a major source of gold within the Mediterranean world. In A.D. 1067, al-Bakri, a scholar from Muslim Spain, wrote a description of Ghana that provides us a view of its life and power. At that time the capital of Ghana, Kumbi Saleh, appears to have been divided into two adjoining cities about six miles apart. One was occupied by the king and his court, surrounded by the dwellings of the people. This city also contained buildings for worship and shrines to the local deities. The adjoining city

Axum, a large state in the Ethiopian highlands, received cultural influences from Arabia and traded widely in the Indian Ocean. Its capital contained large buildings and monuments like this 70-foot high solid granite obelisk.

Mediterranean coast of Africa where Phoenician, Greek, and Roman settlements were established, or up the Nile valley the ideas, techniques, and material goods from the Mediterranean and western Asia mixed with African peoples and practices.

Finally, we can mention the area of the grassy savanna extending across the Sudan into West Africa. The defeated leaders of Meroe apparently moved westward into the Sudan and reestablished themselves at Darfur and Kordofan in the 4th century A.D. Their influence may have extended even farther to the west. There are a number of accounts and myths associated with royal families and ancient kingdoms in West Africa that point to Egypt, Arabia, and even Persia as the original home of the founders. But in West Africa there is also evidence of long-term contact with the Mediterranean world directly across the Sahara. These

West African States

was inhabited by long-distance Muslim traders, religious leaders, and scholars. Its mosques and houses were built in the style of the mud-walled architecture of North Africa. Together, the population of these cities may have reached 20,000.

The gold and salt trades were taxed by the king of Ghana, and these taxes provided the revenues of the kingdom. The wealth allowed for growth of the kingdom and thus its power. The historian al-Bakri reported that Ghana could field an army of 200,000 men. Even if we allow for exaggeration, it should be noted that the Normans invaded England at about this time with fewer than 5000 men, so al-Bakri's statement indicates the existence of a powerful and well-organized kingdom. The accounts of Ghana suggest the existence of a large kingdom dominated by the royal family and a group of elite retainers, whose strength rested on control of the trade and on the tribute collected from neighboring peoples.

The image of Ghana in contemporaneous Arab sources was one of fabled wealth. The account of al-Bakri stated that the king had a monopoly on all gold nuggets found, but that the people could gather as much gold dust as they

wanted for trade. His description of a royal audience noted guards with gold and silver ornaments and weapons, the royal princes in attendance splendidly attired with gold plaited in their hair, and the doors of the chamber guarded by "dogs of excellent breed, who never leave the king's seat; they wear collars of gold and silver, ornamented with the same metals." The king was known as *Kaya-Maghan*, or "the king of Gold."

While there was a certain amount of fantasy mixed in these accounts, Ghana was obviously a powerful kingdom. Its influence eventually spread into the Sahara, and major trading towns like Awdagust were brought under its control. The Berber and Tuareg tribes of the Sahara had converted to Islam in the 7th century, and by the 11th century a new movement whose followers were called the Almoravids had begun to sweep across the western desert, Morocco, and Spain. One branch of this movement under Abu Bakr ibn Umar (d. 1087) launched a series of campaigns in the western Sudan. The Almoravids controlled the gold trade across the Sahara and began to move toward its sources. Ghana was conquered in 1076, and a new fusion of Sudanic and Saharan peoples took place.

While Ghana continued to exist, its power was considerably weakened and other states emerged to challenge its leadership. Islamization weakened the kingdom and perhaps caused a deepening division between its elites and the common folk. Former provinces broke away, and a period of political instability and fragmentation followed in which new states emerged among the Soninke, Fulbe, and Malinke peoples. The power of Ghana ended, but its tradition of trade and military power and the fusion of African and Islamic traditions continued among the successor states. Eventually, a new kingdom, Mali, emerged from this struggle. In many ways Mali was the heir to the power in the region, and it ruled a territory that extended from the bend of the Niger River to the Atlantic coast, which included much of the ancient kingdom of Ghana.

ANALYSIS
LANGUAGE AS A HISTORICAL SOURCE

Historians constantly search for new ways to understand the past and penetrate the haze that separates us from it. For much of the early history of the world we must depend on the archeological record. Cultures leave their traces not only in pottery, weapons, temples and mummies, but also in language, written or not. Language is a guide to the thought patterns of a people and to their society and their institutions. Language, moreover, is a guide to its speakers' historical relationships to others. The development of *historical linguistics* has greatly furthered our understanding of the past and has provided a set of theories and techniques that, along with archeology, have become indispensable aids to the study of both preliterate and literate societies.

The early study of languages was motivated by a recognition of the intimate relation between thought and language and the relationship between the structure of thought and language and the overall culture of a people. Early students of language, such as the French thinker Condillac who wrote in the mid-18th century, believed that "each language expresses the character of the people that speak it." However, linguistic insights were sometimes influenced by cultural bias. Later linguists, like the learned Wilhelm von Humboldt in his essay *On Language* (1836), wrote that some languages were "more perfect" and better suited to the "mental cultivation of mankind." Not surprisingly, von Humboldt believed that the Sanscritic languages (what we would call Indo-European) best fit that definition. By the

20th century, however, the early work of people like von Humboldt had laid the foundation for the modern study of historical linguistics.

We have already discussed (in Chapter 4) the great migration of the Indo-European peoples from central Asia into India and western Europe. In this chapter we examine two other great migrations in human history, the movement of the Bantu peoples throughout southern Africa and the spread of the Polynesians across the Pacific. To a large extent, much of what can be said in all three cases—and in the study of the early settlement of the Americas—is based on a study of the vocabulary, structure, and diffusion of languages.

The study of language as a historical record is based on some fundamental ideas. Languages change over time, as any reading of Chaucer or Shakespeare immediately reveals. As they change, they may diverge from related languages. Languages with strong similarities in structure and vocabulary that cannot be explained by borrowing or contacts are considered to be part of the same family, and it is assumed that sometime in the past an original language was the parent of all the languages in that family. As groups of people separated, their language changed and diverged. Further separation resulted in further divergence so that over time a large number of related languages could result from the original language. The proto-Indo-European language was the parent of both Persian and Latin, but Latin later split into French, Italian, Rumanian, Portuguese, Spanish and other related languages. By looking at structural and vocabulary similarities, it is possible to establish linguistic subgroups and their relationship to each other as well as to the parent language.

It can be assumed that the more diversity between languages, the longer the time that has elapsed since their separation from each other. For a while some linguists thought that if they could establish the rate at which linguistic changes took place, they could calculate the time that had elapsed since one language and its speakers had separated from another. On the basis of 100 or 200 basic words, they attempted to calculate the percentage of change or loss from one language to another. This technique, called *glottochronology*, is no longer popular since it is clear that languages do not change at a constant rate of speed but probably in spurts, and such change depends on many factors. Still, with written languages rates of change can be studied, and when used in conjunction with archeology, language can provide another and corroborating kind of historical evidence.

It is simple enough to see that the similarity of words in languages (barring random coincidence or words borrowed directly from a foreign language) can indicate a common origin. *Mother* in English, *mater* in Latin, and *mata* in Hindi all point to their common Indo-European origins. The word for eye in Tahiti was *mata*, in Hawaii, *maka*, and among the New Zealand Maori, *mata;* similarities that point to their common heritage as Polynesian languages. Despite the similar sounds involved in these two sets, the meanings indicate that we are dealing with two different language families.

In other cases, similarities and differences are less apparent and are not based only on a common vocabulary but on structure and pronunciation. While historical linguistics has developed various techniques and methods for establishing these relationships, explaining the divergence or the reason for the separation of the peoples that speak the languages is another story. Without the help of archeology, oral traditions, or written records, historical linguistics cannot describe the course of change.

The study of languages can tell us much about the values, social structure, and material life of peoples in the past. A language with 12 adjectives to describe the color of the sea between the speaker and the horizon, or another language that has 20 ways of describing the color of a llama's coat, indicates the importance of those things to the people involved. A language that has no word for private property or nobility probably lacked those concepts. The grammar and pronunciation of a language can be relatively independent of the physical world of its speakers, but the vocabulary cannot. It reflects what people knew and thought about. It can be assumed that if all the languages that split off from a parent tongue have the same word for iron, dog, cattle, or canoe, then the original speakers must have possessed these things. This kind of reasoning lies behind much of what we can say about the early Polynesians, the Bantu, or the Indo-Europeans. For example, by studying the distribution of words in various Polynesian languages, linguists have argued that, even though we do not know the original home of the Polynesians, the original speakers of the parent language were inhabitants of some mountainous tropical island or islands in the western Pacific islands, and they grew taro, yams, bananas, and sugar cane before their expansion and dispersal.

Of course, such analysis is a complicated and risky enterprise. A word may have existed at one point for a thing that no longer exists and thus the word disappeared or was transformed to mean something else, leaving no trace of its past use. Putting the linguistic evidence together with the historical record is a challenging task. When that record is available, such as in the case of Aztec or Roman expansion, we can see that language change and diffusion is sometimes the result of intentional policies rather than undirected change.

Historical linguistics also concerns itself with variations and subdivisions within languages, or *dialects,* and with their geographical distribution. What is the difference between a dialect and a language? Linguists argue on this point, but some unknown skeptic once said, "a language is a dialect with an army behind it." That comment should focus our attention on the social and historical reasons for the predominance of some languages. It also underlines the necessary relationship between linguistics and other methods of knowing the past, as tools that should be used together whenever possible.

Questions: In what way are language and literacy expressions of social or political power? What are some ways in which changes in our own language indicate broad historical changes? Is there a problem in using language as historical evidence because spoken language often differs from formal written forms and usage?

THE SLAVS AND GERMANS ON THE NORTHERN RIM

Beyond the boundaries of the Hellenistic kingdoms in the Middle East and southern Europe, and to the north of the expanding Roman Empire, lived a mixture of peoples mostly of Indo-European origin. Celtic peoples, for example, formed Europe's first culture that stretched from Spain northward. They were organized in small regional kingdoms with fierce warrior-leaders, and mixed agricultural and hunting economies. They had no cities and no writing, and their most impressive buildings were crude stone forts and arrays of stone set up to honor the gods of nature. The Romans considered the Celtic peoples barbarians, but as Rome expanded its empire into Gaul, Spain, and Britain, various Celtic peoples came under Roman influence. A population of Romanized Celts developed in villages and towns across western Europe.

THE GERMANS IN NORTHWESTERN EUROPE

Much of the northwestern portion of the European continent was populated by Germanic peoples whose culture and institutions in many ways resembled that of the Celts (whom they had in some regions displaced). Certainly, to Roman observers, the Germanic tribes north of the empire's boundaries were undistinguished barbarians, pure and simple. As the Roman historian Tacitus wrote: "Who, indeed, would leave Asia, Africa, or Italy to seek Ger-

The great religious monument of Stonehenge was a centerpiece of pre-Celtic worship in England.

many, with its desert scenery, its harsh climate, its sullen manners and aspect?" He might have added, "and its warlike people," for by Tacitus's time the Romans had already developed a wary respect for the German warriors.

Tacitus had other comments on the Germans, although at times he emphasized their virtues as a way of criticizing what he considered to be Rome's moral degeneracy. The strength and bravery of the German warriors impressed him. He pointed out that warriors were pledged to support their chiefs, and that these in turn led by example and sought to outdo their men in battle. The size of a chief's retinue was a measure of his power and distinction, and men strove to gain a place in such a following.

The role of women was particularly notable. Agriculture and all household duties were carried out by women, the elderly, and slaves. Women were thought to have an element of holiness and the gift of prophecy. Their advice was sought and respected. Men and women married rather late, and usually a bride-price was paid to the woman. This included oxen, a horse, and arms, which symbolized the union of the couple and their shared responsibilities. Women were supposed to pass these gifts on to their children. Strong matrilineal ties existed, and the relation between a man and his sisters' sons was particularly strong. The married state was respected, adultery was rare, and infanticide was not practiced. In a criticism of the Rome of his day, Tacitus said: "Good morality is more effective in Germany than good laws are elsewhere."

But Tacitus also commented on the rude material life of the Germans, their lack of cities, their simple dwellings, their lack of writing, and their constant fighting. Judgments of this sort accurately reflected the fact that the peoples of northwestern Europe had not formulated a civilization. They overlooked, however, several important achievements and also changes among some groups, such as the Germanic tribes, that accelerated during the final centuries of the classical era. Like the Celts, the Germanic peoples typically mixed agriculture and hunting, and they also herded cattle in a nomadic pattern. They had no cities. However, among many Germans agriculture steadily improved in the 1st centuries A.D. There were also marked improvements in iron use and the manufacture of cloth and other items. Some of these improvements resulted from knowledge of Roman skills, which spread gradually and incompletely northward beyond the empire's boundaries.

Political cohesion among some German groups improved by the 3d and 4th centuries A.D. As with many traditionally nomadic peoples, the Germans had long been organized in decentralized tribes of a few thousand members each, and even the tribes were loosely organized, with individual family groups settling most disputes. A tribe might have a king or an assembly of warrior chiefs; in either case, vigorous discussion of any policy issue among all fighting men was essential. Group loyalty and a certain amount of political equality were important parts of this tradition and would affect European institutions in the centuries after the classical era. After about A.D. 200, some German tribes coalesced into larger units as they learned to copy Roman military structure to an extent and were forced by Roman pressure to improve their organizational ability. The power of individual kings increased, as they ruled large confederations of tribes. Thus, even apart from the Germans who filtered into the Roman Empire or joined its armies, integrating portions of Roman civilization directly, there were important changes in the Germanic lands during the classical era, with improvements in agriculture, trade, manufacture, and politics.

Germanic culture, however, seems to have changed little outside Rome's boundaries. The German religion, like that of the Bantu, was animistic, with sacrifices and worship to the spirits of nature. Horses were the most common sacrifice, leading to a prejudice against eating horsemeat, which is still lively in German influenced parts of the world today.

The Germans would make their first clear mark in world history as growing bands began to move southward into the Roman Empire, ultimately probing into Italy, Spain, and North Africa. Their movement, the *Völkerwanderungen,* resulted from population growth in their own lands, the nomadic tradition, Rome's attractiveness and growing weakness, and, finally, invasions by Asian groups on the eastern flanks of the Germanic region. German pressure within the Roman Empire played a major role in toppling the empire, as we will see in the following chapter.

Growing coherence among some Germanic groups, however, had an influence beyond the pressures on Rome. It helped prepare larger areas of Europe for the gradual development of civilization in the centuries after Rome's fall. This new civilization would reflect many Roman legacies and a strong Christian influence, but it would also build on some Germanic elements. Even as Rome fell, in fact, a new Germanic center was taking shape in Scandinavia that would have wide influence in the following centuries. Far from Roman influence, Scandinavian populations were growing, and political confederations were being formed by the 5th century. This would soon lead to invasions and trade throughout much of the Mediterranean world.

THE SLAVS IN EASTERN EUROPE

While developments among various Germanic peoples held the stage in northwestern Europe, a somewhat similar pattern of precivilizational advance emerged in various parts of eastern Europe, with some influence from the Hellenistic kingdoms and then the eastern portions of the Ro-

man Empire. As early as 3000 B.C. agriculture had been established in the southern part of what is now Russia, spreading from the Middle East. Bronze tools were also introduced, and then a wave of Indo-European invasions, around 1000 B.C., brought iron. Several new invasions from central Asia followed, with a loosely organized Scythian state controlling the region from the 7th to the 3d centuries B.C. The Scythians were nomadic warriors, but agriculture continued to flourish in the plain north of the Black Sea. Scythian rule was followed by an invasion by a people known as the Sarmatians, some of whose descendants live in the central Caucasus region of the Soviet Union today. Under both Scythians and Sarmatians, Greek and Persian trade and cultural influence, including artistic styles, spread into this region.

By the final centuries of the classical era, Slavic peoples were increasingly migrating into Russia and other parts of eastern Europe. Some Slavs had been in this region before, and there is a dispute on the origin of these people. What is known is that the Slavic people were an Indo-European group; that they became increasingly noticeable in Russia and the Balkans by the time of the early Roman Empire; and that they would ultimately dominate much of eastern Europe from the Balkans northward. While Slavic political organization was perhaps a bit less well developed than Germanic, by the 5th century A.D. some regional kingdoms had been formed, notably in Bulgaria. Agriculture and manufacturing, including skilled iron work, gained ground steadily, and (in advance of the Germanic northwest) some trading cities had been formed.

Again, as with the Germans to the west, it would be premature to refer to a civilization of eastern Europe beyond the Mediterranean zone at the time of Rome's fall. And the Slavic peoples were severely disrupted, along with Rome itself, by invasions from central Asia, as the Huns and others cut across their lands. Nevertheless, an increasingly prosperous agricultural economy and rudiments of political organization beyond the tribal level described parts of the Slavic world toward the end of the Classical era, and presaged more important developments to come.

THE SPREAD OF CHINESE CIVILIZATION TO JAPAN

Although its full impact on global history has not been felt until the last century or so, the transmission of key elements in Chinese culture to the offshore islands that came to make up Japan clearly provides one of the most important examples of the spread of civilization from a central core area to neighboring or overseas peoples. In the 1st centuries A.D., the peoples of Japan imported a wide range

The most venerated of the Shinto shrines is that dedicated to the sun goddess, Amaterasu, at Ise in central Honshu. The thatched roof, unpainted cypress wood, simplicity of design, and the beautiful forest setting in which the shrine is located are characteristics of Shinto architecture.

of ideas, techniques of production, institutional models, and material objects from the Chinese mainland. After adapting these imports to make them compatible with the quite sophisticated culture they had previously developed, the Japanese used what they had borrowed from China to build a civilization of their own. New patterns of rice growing and handicraft production enhanced the economic base of the Yamato clan chieftains who, beginning in the 3d century A.D., extended their control over the most populous regions of the main Japanese island of Honshu.

The Chinese writing system was laboriously adapted to the spoken language of the Japanese and provided key vehicles for intellectual creativity and building a more centralized political system. Often transmitted from China through Korea, Buddhist religious beliefs and art forms enriched Japanese culture at both the elite and popular levels. At the Japanese court and in the peasant villages, these new influences were blended with well-established indigenous traditions of nature worship, which came to be known collectively as Shintoism. Thus, the Japanese developed a unique civilization from a blend of their own culture and a selective importation and conscious refashioning of Chinese influences.

The capacity of the Japanese to adopt Chinese culture distinguishes them from many of the other peoples who were also strongly affected by the expansion of Chinese civilization from its core regions along the Yellow River. For the most part, this expansion was overland and more or less connected to the regions that formed the original Chinese core. It moved southward to the series of river valleys and coastal plains that stretched from the Yangtze basin to northern Vietnam; eastward to the tributary kingdoms of the Korean peninsula; and west and north to the nomadic peoples, who exchanged goods and borrowed cultural elements from the Chinese but fought to resist their overlordship. Very often Chinese civilization, as in the areas south of the Yangtze River and in Vietnam, was spread by war and conquest and imposed as a unified whole on conquered peoples rather than being selectively adopted by them.

Few of these more typical patterns of Chinese expansion were found in the interaction between China and Japan. The extension of Chinese influences to the Japanese islands was necessarily by sea rather than overland. Instead of conquering armies, merchants and traveling monks—and eventually Japanese students who studied in China—were the most important agents by which elements of Chinese culture were transmitted. Especially in the early centuries of borrowing, from the 1st to the 5th centuries A.D., interchange between China and Japan was largely indirect. It was mediated by the peoples and kingdoms of Korea, who had grafted key aspects of Chinese civilization to their own cultures somewhat earlier than the Japanese.

In contrast to the Vietnamese and the peoples of South China, the Japanese initiated and controlled the process of cultural borrowing from China. Despite a willingness to acknowledge the cultural superiority of the Chinese Middle Kingdom, the Japanese retained their political independence throughout the centuries of intense borrowing. Consequently, the Japanese could be more selective in their adoption of Chinese ideas and institutions than most of the other peoples who came under the influences emanating from China.

NATURAL SETTING AND THE PEOPLING OF THE ISLANDS

The four main islands that make up the homeland of the Japanese people rise abruptly and dramatically from the Pacific Ocean along the northeast coast of Asia. Formed by volcanic eruptions that still occur periodically, the islands are dominated by mountains and rugged hills. Only a small portion of their surface area is level and extensive enough for the cultivation of wet rice, which from prehistoric times has been the staple of the Japanese diet. Thus, from the period of the earliest settlements, the Japanese have mainly occupied the coastal plains, especially in the south-central portions of the largest island of Honshu, which remain the most heavily populated areas of the islands today.

Though poor in natural resources, the islands are difficult to match in their combination of temperate climate and subtle natural beauty. Their forest-covered and mist-shrouded hills and glittering inland seas have instilled in the Japanese people a refined aesthetic sensibility and sensitivity to the natural world that have been reflected in their religion, art, and architecture from prehistoric ages to the

The Rise of Japanese Civilization

present. At the same time, the islands' limited resource base nurtured a disciplined, hardworking population that was regulated by strict legal codes and ruled through much of the islands' history by warrior elites. These characteristics of the Japanese people have been commented on by foreign visitors from the Chinese in the early centuries A.D. to Europeans and Americans in the modern era.

Archeological evidence suggests that as early as 5000 B.C. the ancestors of the Japanese people had begun to migrate to the islands. Drawn from numerous and diverse East Asian ethnic groups (and perhaps Southeast Asia and Polynesia), the migrants came in small bands and, periodically, larger waves over many centuries. One of these waves of migrants produced the Jomon culture in the 3d millennium B.C. The Jomon were a hunting-and-gathering people, who lived in pits dug in the ground. They produced a distinctive pottery, whose cordlike decoration gave the people their name.

Most of the new settlers crossed to the islands from the Korean peninsula and Manchuria. Because they were relatively isolated from political upheavals and social transformations occurring on the mainland, by the 1st centuries A.D. the diverse migrant streams had blended into a relatively homogenous population with a distinctive Japanese language, culture, and physical appearance. By then they had driven the Ainu, who had settled the islands before them, into northern Honshu and Hokkaido. Over the past

The critical role played by Buddhism in the transmission of key elements of Chinese civilization to Japan is strikingly illustrated by early Buddhist monasteries and temples such as this one at Nara. Comparison with the Shinto shrine at Ise underscores the contrast between the sparse indigenous art and architectural styles and the more ornate Buddhist structures that were modeled on Chinese prototypes.

two millennia, the Japanese have gradually displaced or absorbed the remaining Ainu, building in the process a strong sense of cultural and ethnic identity.

INDIGENOUS CULTURE AND SOCIETY

Long before distinctively Chinese cultural influences began to shape Japanese historical development, the indigenous peoples of the islands had taken significant steps toward the creation of a civilization of their own. In the last centuries B.C., migrants from the mainland introduced wet-rice agriculture and iron working into Japan. In this period, which is known as the Yayoi epoch, the Japanese also produced wheel-turned pottery and very sophisticated bronzeware, including elaborately decorated bells that were sometimes four and five feet high.

Until the early 5th century A.D., most of the Japanese population was divided into hundreds of clans, whose members worshiped a clan deity and claimed common descent from a real or fictitious ancestor. Each of these clans was dominated by a small warrior aristocracy. The clan elites drew their support from the peasantry, which made up over 90 percent of the population of the islands. It was also served by slaves, who like their counterparts in China were only a small minority of the Japanese people. Early visitors from the mainland noted the rigid social distinctions, including different sorts of tattoos and other body markings, that separated the warrior elite from the mass of the people. They also remarked on the strong position women enjoyed in early Japanese culture, in marked contrast to their clear subordination in China. Early Japanese households appear to have been *matriarchal*, that is, dominated by childbearing women. Women also played key roles as shamans—who were central to Japanese religious ceremonies and worship—as leaders of some of the clans, and later as empresses.

The importance of women in early Japanese culture is also indicated by their legends regarding the creation of the world. In these tales the sun goddess, Amaterasu, played a central role, and her worship became the central element in the Shinto religion developed by the island peoples. Shinto devotees worshipped numerous gods and spirits associated with the natural world. Some of these deities were identified with objects, such as huge trees or mountains like the famous Mount Fuji. Others were linked to animals, such as foxes and snakes, that were believed to possess special powers. Gods and spirits were believed to be capable of doing good or evil to humans. To ensure that they brought blessings rather than misfortune, the Japanese made offerings of food and prayers to the gods and nature spirits at special shrines. These structures were built of unfinished wood and notable for their simple lines and lack of ornamentation. They gave rise to a unique Shinto style of Japanese architecture that persists to the present day and has had a considerable impact on architecture in the modern world.

In the 4th and 5th centuries A.D., when one of the clans, the Yamato, gained increasing dominance over the others, an imperial cult developed around the sun goddess and Shinto worship. A central shrine was established on the island of Ise, and the priest-chief heads of the Yamato clan claimed descent from the sun goddess herself. Building upon this powerful source of legitimacy, the Yamato brought most of the lowland plains of the southern islands under their control through alliances and conquest. By the late 4th century A.D., their sway also extended to southern Korea. Though marginal in the amount of territory involved, this overseas extension of the Yamato domains

This hollow jar with a head is representative of the clay earthenware produced by the Japanese during the mid-Yayoi period.

brought intensified contacts with Chinese civilization, then about to enter into one of its most illustrious phases. The combination of these contacts and the Yamatos' successful campaigns to unify the Japanese people led to profound transformations in Japanese society and culture in the following centuries.

THE CHINESE MODEL AND THE REMAKING OF JAPAN

Though trade and the continued influx of migrants from the mainland had brought the Japanese peoples into contact with Chinese civilization from the last centuries B.C., the introduction of the Chinese script in the 4th century A.D. marks a major turning point in Japanese cultural development. Writing with the Chinese characters, which were adapted only with great difficulty to the Japanese language, made it possible for the Yamato to begin to build a real bureaucracy and thus more firmly establish their control over vassal clan heads and the peasantry. The use of the Chinese written language also meant that the Japanese could learn from Chinese texts on all manner of subjects, from science and philosophy to art and religion. These works, as well as Chinese scribes to make additional copies and interpret them, were imported from the 5th century onward. Later, Japanese students and scholars who were fluent in Chinese were sent to China to acquire new learning firsthand.

From the middle of the 6th century, the Buddhist religion became a pivotal factor in the transmission of Chinese influence to Japan. In the period of disunity and chaos that followed the fall of the Han dynasty in the early 3d century A.D., Buddhism was widely adopted by the distressed populace of China and the rulers of the warring kingdoms that succeeded the Han. The pervasive influence of the religion in China in this era and the powerful position of Buddhist monks at the courts of Chinese rulers gave great impetus to its spread to Korea and Japan. In the middle of the 6th century, a Korean ruler sent Buddhist images and scriptures as presents to the Japanese emperor and urged him to adopt the religion and convert his subjects to it. After considerable debate and even open strife among the families serving the imperial household over the advantages and dangers of introducing Buddhism into Japan, it was officially adopted as the religion of the Yamato domains in the late 580s.

From that time onward, Japanese rulers sought to propagate the new religion among their subjects. Warrior aristocrats and peasants converted to the new beliefs, but without giving up their long-standing reverence for Shinto spirits and deities. Thus, Shintoism and Buddhism developed side by side as twin pillars of state and society in Japan. The Japanese elite supported the efforts of Buddhist monks to spread their faith, and the monks in turn served as advisors to the emperor and regional lords. In their teachings of Buddhism the monks stressed scriptural passages and Buddhist ethical prescriptions that supported rule by a strong monarch and a unified and centralized state. In addition, Buddhist monks provided the emperor with a calendar based on that devised by the Chinese. The monks also greatly increased the number of Chinese texts available to Japanese scholars, and introduced the Chinese chronicles that served as the models for the first written histories of Japan.

Though converts from aristocratic Japanese families studied the complex beliefs of Buddhist philosophy and practiced its highly developed meditation techniques, to the illiterate mass of the Japanese people Buddhism was little more than a magical cult. Buddhist monks provided colorful rituals that enriched the peasants' monotonous lives and charms to ward off sickness or evil spirits, but the common people knew little of Buddhist teachings beyond highly mythologized versions of the Buddha's life. Nonetheless, the growing importance of the new faith was brought home to peasants as well as educated aristocrats by the construction of Buddhist monasteries and shrines throughout the islands. Buddhist sculptures and paintings of scenes of the Buddha's life or the heavens and hells of the supernatural world became major preoccupations of Japanese artists. Here again, Chinese influence was evident, particularly in architecture. In fact, because many of the great Buddhist centers in China have been destroyed by periodic persecutions and warfare, the great Buddhist temples and monasteries at former Japanese court centers, such as Nara, provide some of the best examples of early Chinese architecture in existence today.

POLITICAL AND SOCIAL CHANGE

Beginning in the early 7th century, the Yamato rulers proclaimed themselves absolute monarchs in imitation of the emperors of China. They styled themselves the "emperors of the rising sun" in official letters to (one imagines) the somewhat dismayed Chinese "emperors of the setting sun." Inspired by Chinese examples, they established councils and government departments and sought to introduce genuine bureaucratic control at the local level. At Nara and later Heian, the Japanese emperors laid out courts and capital cities patterned after the ancient imperial centers of China. The Yamato rulers strove to build a peasant conscript army and impose legal codes and a landholding system similar to those found in China.

In the centuries after the introduction of Buddhism, Chinese influences were felt in virtually all spheres of Japanese society. Alongside the traditional warrior elite, a class of monks and scholars developed that for several centuries exercised considerable power at the imperial court. Trade with China and Korea and improved communications within Japan enriched existing merchant groups and led to their emergence as a distinct class. New tools and techniques imported from the mainland increased the output of Japanese cultivators and made possible a great expansion of the islands' previously marginal mining industry. All social classes benefited greatly from the introduction of China's advanced medicines and methods of treating diseases and bodily injuries resulting from accidents or warfare.

The introduction into Japan of the ideal of the patriarchal and patrilineal family, which had long been dominant in China, presented a major challenge to traditional Japanese approaches to gender roles and relationships. For some centuries, the position of women within the family remained strong, and the ideal of wives and lovers who were accomplished in literature and the arts was preserved by the courtly elites at the imperial capitals of Nara and Heian. But the adoption of Chinese law codes eroded first the control that Japanese women were able to exercise with regard to their own children, and eventually their overall status relative to males. These changes were reflected in the spread of polygamy among the Japanese aristocracy. From the early 9th century, the changes were even more emphatically underscored by the elite's refusal to allow women from the imperial family to rule in their own right, as they had periodically in the early centuries of Japanese history. Increasingly Japanese women, like those in China and India, were subordinated to their fathers and husbands and

valued mainly for their domestic skills and ability to produce many healthy sons. As in China and India, entry into religious orders or successful careers as courtesans provided virtually the only alternatives to careers as subordinated wives and mothers.

CHINESE INFLUENCE AND JAPANESE RESISTANCE

Contacts with China and innovations based on the Chinese model were pushed, from the 4th century A.D. onward, by those at the top of Japanese society. Japanese rulers and their chief advisors were motivated mainly by the desire to increase the power of the state to control the warrior nobles and to extract resources from the peasantry. Buddhist ethics and Confucian legal codes enhanced the rulers' legitimacy; Chinese rituals gave a new dignity and luster to court routines; and the growth of a Chinese-style bureaucracy provided the means for the creation of the first genuine state in Japanese history. Because the Japanese remained politically independent from China, their rulers could convincingly argue that the adoption of Chinese ways was voluntary and carefully controlled. Only imports that would strengthen the Japanese state or contribute to the well-being of the Japanese populace need be accepted. Chinese ideas and institutions could be reworked to suit conditions in Japan and fit the needs of the Japanese people. Selective borrowing from their ancient and advanced Chinese neighbors, the innovators argued, allowed the Japanese to become fully civilized without destroying their own culture and identity.

Because Japanese rulers lacked the resource base of the Chinese emperors and worked with a society that differed greatly in scale and organization, many of their efforts to imitate Chinese patterns ended in failure. The bloated bureaucracies that resulted from the imitation of China were top-heavy and a growing burden for the peasants who had to support them. Efforts to establish local control and reorganize landholding along Chinese lines floundered due to the opposition of regional lords and their retainers. The warrior elite also frustrated the attempt to make soldiers of the peasantry. Conscripts in Japan in this era were little more than forced laborers. Many of the imported Chinese legal injunctions bore little relation to social conditions in Japan and were simply not enforced. The impressive capital cities laid out by the emperors' architects remained half-built and underpopulated, even at the height of the early dynasties' power.

More than differences in scale and social compatibility limited the extent to which Japan could be remade in the image of China. From the outset, the introduction of writing, Buddhism, and other imports from China had given

Legends and myths have long fascinated anthropologists, literary scholars, and folklorists because they offer an opportunity to see how various peoples have explained the universe and themselves within it. The noted French anthropologist Claude Levy-Strauss believed that all myths were constructed around certain basic structures of human thought, and that those structures could be revealed by the comparative study of myths. He also argued that for some cultures, such as those of South American Indians, myths with their essentially recurring structures were the primary means of explaining life, while in other cultures, such as those of western Europe and China, a sense of change, of history, came to predominate in these explanations. Recent scholarship has begun to question the separation of myth and history and has begun to look at the possible historical context and content of myths.

In this chapter, we have examined a number of peoples whose origins are shrouded in mystery and about whom many questions remain unanswered. The following excerpts provide these peoples' explanations of their own origins or those of their world.

DOCUMENT
MYTHS OF ORIGIN

brought forth twins, who lived in the same incestuous manner, far from their parents. This new generation took up trapping. So pairs of twins, moving each generation a little farther westward, populated the country.*

A GERMANIC MYTH: THE BIRTH OF THE GODS

This tale from the rich Norse mythology deals with the birth of the gods. Drawn from the songs and sagas of the Germanic peoples, these stories were part of an oral literature until about the 12th century, when they were committed to writing.

In the beginning of the ages there lived a cow, whose breath was sweet and whose milk was bitter. The cow was called Audhumla and she lived by herself in a frosty, misty plain, where there was nothing to be seen but heaps of snow and ice. A giant named Ymir came out of the dark north and lay down on the ice near Audhumla. "You must let me drink of your milk," said the giant to the cow; and though her milk was bitter, he liked it well. The cow saw a few grains of salt sprinkled over the ice; so she licked the salt and breathed with her sweet breath. Then long golden locks rose out of the ice, and the southern day shone on them, making them bright and glittering. The giant frowned but the cow continued to lick the salt, and after three licks an entire man arose—a hero strong and beautiful.

When the giant looked full in the face of that beautiful man, he hated him with all his heart and he took a terrible oath that he would never cease fighting until either he or Bur, the hero, should lie dead on the ground. He kept this vow.

Afterwards when the sons of the hero began to grow up, the giant and his sons fought against them too, and were very near conquering them many times. There was one of the sons of these heroes, called Odin, who after many combats, did at last slay the great old giant Ymir, and pierced his body with a keen spear. The blood poured forth in a torrent and drowned all the hideous brood, except for one who fled.

After this, Odin gathered around him his sons, brothers, and cousins and spoke to them thus:

"Heroes, we have won a great victory; our enemies

A BANTU MYTH OF MIGRATION

A series of origin epics and tales among the Luba peoples, who lived in central Africa to the east of the Kongo kingdom, were collected in the 20th century. The concept of splitting off from an existing village and settling in new territory is part of many African origin myths.

In the country of the east, on the right bank of the Lualaba River, there once was a man and a woman. Their names mean respectively "he who builds many houses," and "she who makes much pottery." They lived in ignorance of each other. Guided by the sound of chopping, the man discovered the woman, who was preparing firewood. They lived for a long time under the same roof, sleeping in separate beds. The copulation of a pair of jackals gave them the idea of sleeping together. They brought forth twins of opposite sex, who became inseparable companions. One day the twins found a locality that was exceptionally rich in fish. They finally obtained permission from their parents to leave the village and devote themselves entirely to fishing. In their turn, they are dead, or have fled. We cannot stay any longer here where there is nothing evil for us to fight against." The heroes looked around them at the words of Odin. They spoke out with one voice, "It is well spoken, Odin; we will follow you."

"Southward," answered Odin, "heat lies, and northward night. From the dim east the sun begins his journey westward home."

"Westward home!" they shouted all.

Odin rode in the midst of them and they all paid to him reverence and homage as to a king and father. On his right hand rode Thor, Odin's strong, warlike, eldest son. On his left hand rode Baldur, the most beautiful of his children. After him came Tyr, the Brave; the silent Vidar; and many more mighty lords and heroes; and then came a shell chariot, in which sat Frigga, the wife of Odin, with all her daughters, friends, and maids.†

THE BIRTH OF JAPAN

According to Japanese legend, the Lord of Heaven sent two young gods, Izanagi and his consort Izanami, to subdue chaos and create beauty after the earth had been created. Descending on a carriage of clouds, Izanagi took the divine spear given to him by the Lord of Heaven and, stirring the fog, created a beautiful island in the midst of the sea. But the island was too small for goodness to grow. Izanagi and Izanami became man and wife and built a shrine.

When Izanagi and his wife came out of the shrine, they stood transfixed. Before them stretched the long, curving shore of a vast island, and on the far horizon were the shapes of others. In great joy the two set out to view their new domains. From island to island they went, marveling at each new land; and when they had traveled them all, they found that there were eight, and to them they gave these names in the order of their birth; first the island of Shikoku, followed by Kyushu; Oki and Sado which [each] were born as twins; Tsushima; and finally Iki. Together they were called the country of the eight great islands, and as time passed they became known as Japan.

More and more islands appeared, and every day Izanagi traveled the land and sea watching over them. Sometimes Izanami went with him, but serving in the shrine took much of her time and she found the long journeys exhausting. . . .

"My dear husband, there is nothing I wish to do

more than to live here with you in peace and contentment. But now that so many islands have been born I pray that we too may bear children for our help and delight."

Her prayers were answered and in the years that followed many children were born to them. The first was the Sea Spirit, the next a Mountain Spirit, and then in succession, the spirits of fields, trees, rivers, and all natural things. Under their care and guidance the islands grew more and more verdant and beautiful. Soon the seasons were born, and the breaths of the winds and rains brought their changing cycles to the mountains and fields. Everywhere the forests grew thick and dense, and in the groves flocks of birds gathered and sang. Crops and harvests multiplied and flowers and bushes bloomed in profusion.

Izanagi and his wife lived in utmost contentment among their family, and when a daughter was born to them, who was the goddess of the Sun, their joy was unbounded. She was the most beautiful and radiant being . . . everywhere she went she filled the darkest air with light and brilliance. Her they named Amaterasu. . . .‡

A POLYNESIAN CREATION STORY

In this tale from Tahiti, Tangaroa, the ancestor of all the gods and the creator of Havaiki, the birthplace of the land, the gods, the chiefs, and humanity, creates the world. This version of the story was collected in Tahiti in 1822.

For a long time Tangaroa lived within his shell. It was round like an egg and in the lasting darkness it revolved in the void. There was no sun, there was no moon, there was no land nor mountain, all was moving in the void. There was no man, no fowl, no dog, no living thing; there was no water, salt or fresh.

At the end of a great time Tangaroa flicked his shell, and it cracked and fell apart. Then Tangaroa stepped forth and stood upon that shell and called:

"Who is above there? Who is below there?"

No voice replied. He called again:

"Who is in front there? Who is behind there?"

Still no voice answered. Only Tangaroa's voice was heard, there was no other.

Then Tangaroa said, "O rock crawl here!"

But no rock was to crawl to him.

He therefore said, "O sand crawl here!"

There was no sand to crawl to him. And Tangaroa

became angry because he was not obeyed. He therefore overturned his shell and raised it up to form a dome for the sky, and he named it Rumia, that is, Overturned.

After a time great Tangaroa, wearied from confinement, stepped out from another shell that covered him; and he took this shell for rock and sand.

But his anger was not finished, and so he took his backbone for a mountain range and his ribs for the ridges that ascend. He took his innards for the broad floating clouds and his flesh for the fatness of the earth, and his arms and legs for the strength of the earth. . . . Of his feathers he made trees and shrubs and plants to clothe the land.

And the blood of Tangaroa became hot, and it floated away to make the redness of the sky, and also rainbows. All that is red is made from Tangaroa's blood.

Tangaroa called forth gods. It was only later that he called forth man [people], when Tu was with him.

As Tangaroa had shells, so everything has a shell. The sky is a shell, which is endless space, where the gods placed the sun, the moon, the constellations, and the other stars.

The land is a shell to the stones and the water, and to the plants that spring from it. The shell of a man is woman, since it is from her that he comes forth. And a woman's shell is woman, since it is from her that she comes forth.

No one can name the shells of all the things that are in this world.[§]

Questions: Do myths seem to encode history or are they an alternative way to explain the past? What are the roles of men and women in the myths recorded here and what do they indicate about these early societies? Do the origin myths of the civilizations, such as China, Greece, and Rome, differ greatly from those recorded here?

*Luc de Heusch, *The Drunken King or the Origin of the State* (Bloomington: Indiana University Press, 1982), 11-12.

†Adapted from A. and E. Keary, *The Heroes of Asgard: Tales from Scandinavian Mythology* (New York: Macmillan Co., 1909), 1-4.

‡Helen and William McAlpine, *Japanese Tales and Legends* (London: Oxford University Press, 1958), 13-14.

§Anthony Alpers, *Legends of the South Seas* (New York: Thomas Crowell, 1970), 51-54.

concerns about preserving Japan's own culture, produced continuing opposition to foreign influences.

At times, as in the 580s and the mid-7th century, controversy over the extent of foreign influences became a central element in violent factional struggles between the aristocratic families closest to the throne. But until the 8th century each struggle resulted in the victory of the forces favoring continuing imports from abroad and the further transformation of Japan along Chinese lines. In Chapter 19, we will explore the rise and full flowering of the ultrarefined pattern of courtly life that these victories made possible between the 7th and 9th centuries. We will also consider the forces that eroded both the power of the court and factions that resisted influences from China with increasing success. As the landholding, aristocratic families around the throne reasserted their power from the 8th century onward, there was a conscious effort to restore what were believed to be indigenous customs and institutions at the expense of Chinese imports and to refashion Buddhism into a distinctively Japanese religion.

and Japan was paralleled in other areas of Asia by the outward spread of ideas, products, skills, and peoples from China or India. Sometimes this diffusion was accomplished through trade and borrowings, and sometimes it was the result of military action, but the spread of Indian civilization into Southeast Asia or of Chinese civilization into Vietnam and Korea underlined the process.

The peoples of the far Pacific who had departed the Asian mainland prior to the rise of classical China and India were unaffected by the spread of Chinese and Indian civilization. They had brought with them the cultural features of Late Neolithic Asia, and in relative isolation had developed these features on the islands of the vast Pacific.

Certainly one of the great epics of human achievement for which we have only fragmentary evidence is the peopling of the islands of the Pacific Ocean. The distance across the Pacific from Southeast Asia to Central America is some 20,000 miles, and the waters of that ocean are dotted with thousands of islands. These islands vary in size from tiny atolls formed by coral reefs, to large "high" islands with volcanic peaks and lush valleys, to the great continent of Australia. Most of these islands lie in the tropics, although some, such as New Zealand, do not. They are inhabited by a variety of peoples of quite different physical appearance, language, and culture, but whose origins for the most part seem to be in Asia.

We cannot deal with all the peoples of the Pacific, but the remarkable story of the Polynesians can serve as a case study of the spread of culture by long-distance maritime migration. Here we are not dealing with the spread from a great center of civilization, but with the migration of peoples and their adaptation to new challenges in relative isolation.

Roughly between 1500 B.C. and A.D. 1000 almost all the major islands west of New Guinea were visited, and many were settled, by the ancestors of the peoples we call Polynesians. They left no written records, so we must depend on the evidence of archeology and linguistics, their own oral traditions, and the observations of Europeans who first contacted them in order to reconstruct the history of their societies.

Linguistic evidence is a starting point. The Polynesians speak about 30 related languages from a family of languages called Austronesian, which is also found in the Philippines, Indonesia, and Southeast Asia. The Austronesians were clearly peoples from Asia, but they were not the first migrants in the Pacific. By the time of their expansion about 4000 years ago, New Guinea and Australia had al-

ready long been settled (probably since 38,000 B.C.) by dark-skinned peoples who spoke languages unrelated to Austronesian.

THE GREAT MIGRATION

Groups of these Austronesians, speaking a language ancestral to the Polynesian languages, began to expand eastward from Melanesia to Fiji, Tonga, and Samoa. By the time of this expansion, these people practiced agriculture of yams, taro (a tuber), and other crops, raised dogs, pigs, and chickens, and had already developed a variety of complex fishing techniques. Archeologists can identify their scattered settlements by a distinctive type of pottery called Lapita, with stamped decorations, and by the polished stone adzes, fishhooks, and other implements.

From Tonga and Samoa, these peoples began to spread eastward to Polynesia proper. Polynesia includes the islands contained in a rough imaginary triangle whose points lie at Hawaii to the north, New Zealand to the south, and Easter Island far to the east. Another group of these peoples seems to have moved westward, eventually settling on the island of Madagascar off the African coast.

On the widely dispersed islands of the Pacific, each culture and language began to adapt and evolve differently, and thus to diverge from the ancestral Polynesian forms. There remained some constants in the shared heritage of the ancestral Polynesian culture that also provided similari-

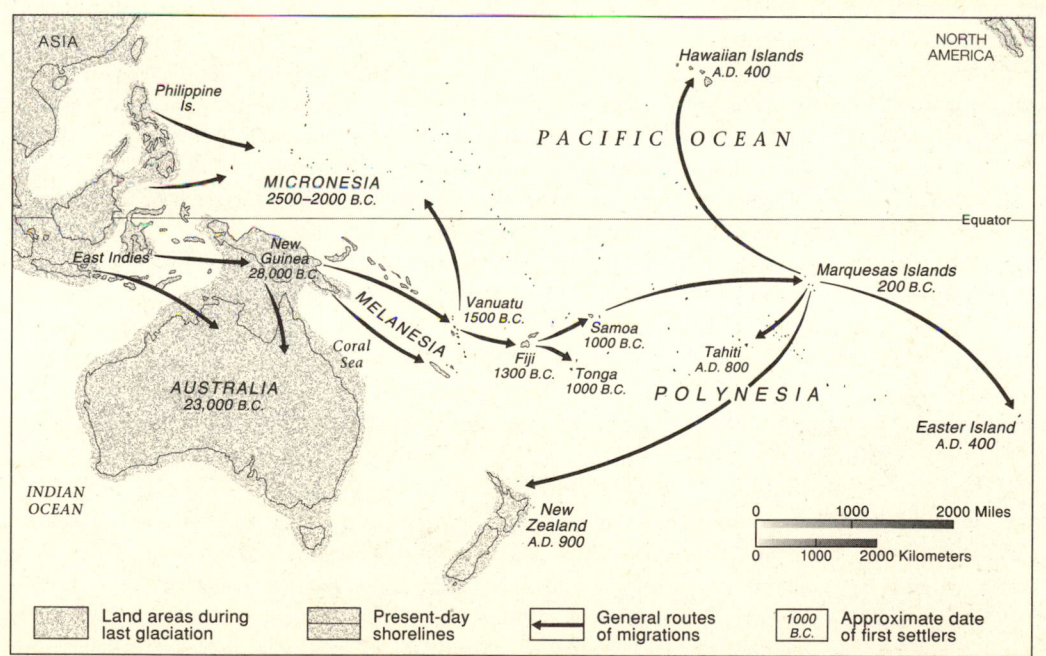

The Spread of Polynesian Peoples

ties. For example, the English explorer Captain James Cook in the 18th century was surprised to find that the words he had learned from the Tahitians were understandable to the Hawaiians, although almost 2500 miles separated those two island groups; also, a Tahitian named Tupia served Captain Cook effectively as a translator when he contacted the Maoris of New Zealand.

Basic principles of economy and social organization could also be found throughout Polynesia, especially on the larger islands. From relatively small groups of original colonists, island populations grew in size and density. By the late-18th century the island populations totaled perhaps 700,000. While the making of pottery was abandoned or forgotten, in many places agriculture became increasingly complex and intensive. Stratified societies with powerful chiefdoms based on lineage characterized many Polynesian islands and in some places, such as Hawaii, they became extremely hierarchical. Chiefs were able to mobilize their followers to build ceremonial or public architecture, or for wars and interisland raiding. Ritual and religion oriented many aspects of life and served as the basis of chiefly power.

THE VOYAGERS OF THE PACIFIC

How did these ancient Polynesians discover and occupy the islands of the vast Pacific? The Polynesians knew how to make a variety of seaworthy vessels. Small outrigger canoes were used for fishing and moving along island coasts, but for long-distance voyaging, they used great double canoes, or *pahi*. These vessels usually carried a platform between the two hulls on which shelter could be given to the passengers—people, animals, and plants. With large triangular sails, these vessels, some of which were between 60 and 100 feet long, were capable of long voyages at sea and could travel over 200 kilometers a day in good weather. They were capable of sailing to the windward, against the winds and tides of the Pacific, which tend to move from east to west. They were impressive craft, as the first European visitors to Hawaii and Tahiti noted enthusiastically.

Navigation was naturally a problem. Some scholars have held that the voyages were accidental—boats blown off course, which led to the occupation of new islands—but Polynesian traditions and the continuing ability of some Pacific islanders to navigate long distances by observing the stars, wave patterns, and other techniques of observation support the idea that voyages of colonization were planned. Moreover, sometimes they were two-way. For example, Hawaiian traditions commemorate the arrival of Tahitian chiefs who made voyages to and from Hawaii for about 200 years (A.D. 1100–1300). In 1976, to establish the

possibility of such voyaging, the *Hōkūlé a*, a reconstructed double canoe based on traditional proportions and using only traditional navigational techniques, was sailed from Hawaii to Tahiti in about 35 days. In the main, however, much of the voyaging seems to have been sporadic as groups pushed by war, population pressure, famine, or a spirit of exploration followed a chief or a navigator into the unknown. In the 18th century when the Europeans arrived, in much of Polynesia such long-range voyaging was rarely practiced. By that time, however, the Polynesians had explored and colonized almost every habitable island in the vast Pacific.

ANCIENT HAWAII

We can use the widely separated large islands, New Zealand and Hawaii, as examples of Polynesian societies that developed in relative isolation in response to particular environmental conditions. Hawaii includes eight major islands in a chain about 300 miles long. The volcanic nature of the islands and the tropical climate created an environment of great beauty and majesty that impressed the early inhabitants. The islands were probably settled in at least two migratory waves beginning around A.D. 300. There, early Polynesian culture was adapted and elaborated in relative isolation over a long period of time. The islands had good soil, and the population grew large, reaching, at contact in the 1700s, about 200,000 people. Towns and cities were absent, and houses, here as elsewhere in Polynesia, were scattered along the coast and in valleys leading to the higher interior. Islands were divided politically into wedge-shaped territories, broadest at the coast and narrowing toward the less-desired interior. A number of chiefly families competed for control of the islands. It was not until after European contact that in 1810 King Kamehameha I united all the islands under his control.

Of all the Polynesian societies Hawaii became the most hierarchical. The high chiefs, or *ali'i* claimed descent from the gods and rested their claims on their ability to recite in great detail their genealogical lineages. In some cases, marriage to their sisters ensured the purity of the chiefly family. Their power, authority, and sacredness, or *mana*, emanated from their lineages and enabled them to extract labor or tribute from their subjects or even take their land. Feathered capes and helmets as well as tattoos distinguished the chiefs. The ali'i were revered and feared. They were above and beyond the constraints of society. "The chief is a shark that swims on land," was a Hawaiian proverb. A class of lesser nobility and subchiefs of their relatives supported the rule of the ali'i

Society rested on the commoners who tilled the fields of taro and sweet potatoes, raised the pigs and chickens, and exploited the resources of the sea. Hawaiian society was intensely agricultural and the community's control of land was a central aspect of social and political relations. Within the hierarchy, commoners were viewed almost as a separate people or at least as a people lacking in lineage. Their lives were constrained and limited by a complex set of *kapu* (*tapu* in Tahiti), or taboo, which forbade certain activities and regulated social discourse. It was kapu for women to eat certain foods, to enter the house of a chief, to eat together with men, to view certain ceremonies limited to the chiefs, or even to cast a shadow on a chief. And there were many other limits imposed according to rank. Violations could lead to death. The number of kapu surrounding a chief was a measure of his status and his sanctity, as much a sign of his position in his society as materials goods might be in our society.

Many aspects of life were ritualized. The numerous gods were honored at ceremonial centers whose precincts were sacred. Ritual feasting and *hula*, or dancing, accompanied many ceremonies. Human and other sacrifices were offered to Ku, God of War, and to the other deities. Lono, the God of Fertility and Agricultural rebirth, held special importance to the Hawaiians. The great Makahiki festival of thanksgiving, which lasted for four months and at which the chiefs received their tribute from the commoners, was celebrated in honor of the annual return of Lono. During this time war was kapu, hulas were danced, and sexual activity was engaged in frequently in hopes of stimulating fertility. In fact, lovemaking was an art and a preoccupation of the Hawaiians, with important religious, kinship, and political meanings.

Of the various Polynesian societies, Hawaii perhaps can be seen as the most successful in terms of its political and social complexity, its economic foundations, its art and material culture, and its religion. With a neolithic technology, the Hawaiians created a complex culture on their islands. Lacking a written language, their legends and oral histories, which could trace the genealogies of chiefly families back to the original canoes of the first migrants, were remarkable achievements that formed and preserved their culture.

THE NEW ZEALAND LANDFALL AND THE DEVELOPMENT OF MAORI CULTURE

Perhaps as early as the 8th century A.D., the crews of canoes or rafts from the Society Islands and other parts of eastern Polynesia had sailed thousands of miles to the southwest and by chance discovered the two large islands that today make up New Zealand. Over the centuries additional bands of seafarers reached the islands, where they embarked on a struggle to survive in an environment that was colder and harsher than their home islands in Polynesia. Their success is evidenced by the large numbers of Maoris—the people descended from the Polynesian seafarers—who lived in the islands when the Europeans first came to stay in the late-18th century. If the high estimates of 200,000 people at this point in time are correct, the islands contained the highest concentration of Polynesian peoples anywhere in the world.

EARLY SETTLEMENT AND MODES OF SURVIVAL. The "land of the long white clouds," as the Polynesians referred to the mist-covered islands that made up New Zealand, had few edible plants beyond berries and fern roots. There were no native land mammals except bats and various kinds of *moa*, or large wingless birds. However, overhunting led to the extinction of the moa, and both early settlers and later migrants had to find new sources of subsistence. Fishing and the introduction by later migrants of many of the staple crops of Polynesia, including the sweet potato, taro, and yams, filled the dietary gap left by the disappearance of the moa. Perhaps to compensate for the shortage of protein in their diet, settlers ate dogs and rats, which had also been brought to the islands by migrants from Polynesia, and human flesh, usually carved from enemies killed in war.

The relatively moderate climate and rich soils of the north island rendered it more suitable for settlement than the cold and desolate south island that stretched beneath the fortieth parallel toward the South Pole. Consequently, Maori tribes numbering in the thousands warred over control of the forests and croplands on the north island. Long before the arrival of the Europeans, tribal territories with clearly defined boundaries had been established throughout most of the north island.

MAORI CULTURE AND SOCIETY. Maori tribes were given the names of the semimythical canoes that were believed to have carried their ancestors to the islands. Each tribe was divided into subgroups called *hapu*, the primary unit of identity and community. Within hapu villages the Maori lived in extended families, which included up to five generations, in large, elaborately carved wooden houses. All the land the Maoris farmed for their subsistence was owned by the hapu village and allotted by a communal council to each of the extended families for their support.

Each hapu was led by a male chief who was not a specialized political leader, but rather a particularly skillful warrior. Chieftainships were hereditary although weak leaders were soon displaced by more able warriors. Despite the magical aura associated with the hapu and tribal chieftains, their actual power was limited by village and tribal councils made up of the free males of a given group. Virtually all hapu communities also included slaves, who were usually prisoners of war or their descendants.

Though they had a strong voice within the family, women were clearly subordinated to men. Male dominance was evidenced by the monopoly they enjoyed with regard to positions of leadership and to highly prestigious activities such as making war and wood carving.

Maori society had not reached the level of development where full-time specialists could be supported, but many kinds of religious and craft experts were recognized. Several kinds of priests varied according to social status and functions. The most esteemed were the chiefs who were also trained as priests. The chief-priest presided over communal ceremonies and knew the special prayers designed to protect the tribe or hapu from human or supernatural enemies. The Maori world was alive with spirits, gods, and goddesses who intervened constantly in human affairs. At the other end of the social scale were shamans who specialized in healing and served as the mediums, by which gods and spirits made their desires known to humans.

A SOCIETY ORIENTED TO WAR. In addition to priests there was a wide variety of experts in Maori society, ranging from those who built canoes and made the ornate wood carvings that decorated Maori homes to those who tattooed the men's faces, thighs, and buttocks and women's lips and chins. The most important experts, however, were those with skills relating to making war. Maori society was obsessed with war. During the appropriate season, tribes and hapus fought regularly with their neighbors or distant confederations. Young males proved their worth as warriors, and leaders could not long maintain their positions without demonstrating their martial prowess. Much of the time and energy of Maori males was devoted to planning campaigns against neighboring tribes or building the intricate hilltop fortresses found throughout the north island. Though the loss of life in Maori wars was low by European standards, their combats were fierce. Hand-to-hand fighting with spears and exquisitely carved war clubs was the preferred mode of combat. Successful ambushes and surprise attacks were highly admired. The priest-leader of a hapu or tribe would cut out the heart of the first enemy killed in battle and offer it to the gods of his people. Enemy casualties were sometimes eaten; enemy prisoners, including women and children, were enslaved.

ON THE THRESHOLD OF CIVILIZATION. Polynesian seafarers had accomplished much in the harsh but beautiful environment of their New Zealand landfall. Mainly on the basis of imported crops, they had developed a fairly steady and productive agricultural system. Though they did not work metals, their material culture was quite impressive. In woodworking and decoration in particular they excelled the Polynesian societies from which their ancestors had come. They had also developed a wonderfully rich oral tradition, which placed a premium on oratorical skills and produced a complex and fascinating collection of myths and legends. Though divided and politically decentralized, the Maori had developed closely knit and well-organized communities within the hapu and tribe.

Their isolation and limited resource base prevented the Maoris from achieving the full occupational specialization that we have seen was critical to the advance to true civilization elsewhere. Isolation limited technological advance and Maori resistance to disease. These limits rendered them vulnerable to peoples such as the Europeans, who possessed more sophisticated tools and weapons and transmitted diseases that decimated the tribes of New Zealand severely. Though their skills in war and their adaptability allowed the Maori to survive in the long run, they could do little to prevent the disintegration of their culture and the destruction of much of the world they had known before the coming of the Europeans.

CONCLUSION

THE EMERGING CULTURES

The societies, forming on the fringes of the major core of world civilizations during the classical period and slightly beyond, shared two important features. First, as they adopted or imported agriculture, they were able to form more structured political units and develop a more complex social hierarchy. The second similarity was that each of the emerging societies exhibited important characteristics from its own past. These characteristics would carry forward into the subsequent history of these regions, even as other influences were encountered.

The four emerging areas also displayed one vital difference in addition to particular distinctions in art, language, and the like. Three of the areas—northern Europe, Japan, and sub-Saharan Africa—were in contact with more established civilization centers, at least to some extent. Polynesia stood apart by its early separation from Asia. This resulted in an impressive set of independent achievements as Polynesian society advanced and spread, but also in important constraints, most obviously in technology. Availability of outside influence, in other words, can explain important differences among societies.

Further development of contacts with more established centers for the Japanese, Slavs and Germans, and the Sudanic kingdoms of Africa depended on changes in the classical civilizations themselves. The explosion of the great classical empires after the 2d century A.D., then the new influences that helped reestablish vigorous societies in the same areas, had a vital spillover effect in northern Europe and Asia, and in sub-Saharan Africa. This fact returns us to the classical centers, as they declined but also birthed dynamic new forces, capable of transforming wide stretches of the Old World.

FURTHER READINGS

The general process of cultural migration and the problems of interpreting archeological and linguistic evidence are the subjects of Irving Rouse's *Migrations in Prehistory* (1986), which includes excellent chapters on the Japanese and the Polynesians.

Geography, society, and history of Africa are all treated in an informative way in Paul Bohannan and Philip Curtin's *Africa and the Africans*, 3d ed. (1988). A very useful introduction to and synthesis of Africa's ancient past is provided by David Phillipson's *African Archaeology* (1985). The *Horizon History of Africa* (1971) contains excellent articles by specialists and integrates these with origi-

nal texts, well-chosen illustrations, and good maps. Philip Curtin et al., *African History* (1978), contains excellent chapters on various regions. Nehemia Levitzion's *Ancient Ghana and Mali* (1973) provides a succinct survey based on the original sources.

Justine Davis Randers-Pehrson's *Barbarians and Romans: The Birth Struggle of Europe, A.D. 400–700* (1983) gives a broad overview of the Germans and Slavs during this period. Tacitus's classic on the Germans is easily available in the translation by H. Mattingly, *The Agricola and the Germania* (1970).

The fullest, though now somewhat dated, account of early Japanese cultural development available in English is included in G. B. Sansom's *A History of Japan to 1334* (1958). Useful introductions to the early period can also be found in Mikiso Hane's *Japan: A Historical Survey* (1972), E. O. Reischauer's *Japan: The Story of a Nation* (1974), and (especially for political developments) John W. Hall's *Japan from Prehistory to Modern Times* (1970). The best introductions to society and culture in the early period are provided by G. B. Sansom's *Japan: A Short Cultural History* (1943) and H. Paul Varley's *Japanese Culture: A Short History* (1973).

Peter Bellwood's *The Polynesians: Prehistory of an Island People* (rev. ed., 1978) is an excellent short introduction to the Polynesians. Jesse D. Jennings, ed., *The Prehistory of Polynesia* (1979), contains survey articles on various areas of Polynesia. Patrick Vinton Kirch's *Feathered Gods and Fishhooks* (1985) surveys the archeology of Hawaii. Classic accounts of Maori society and customs include Te Rangi Hiroa's (Peter Buck), *The Coming of the Maori* (1949) and the works of Elsdon Best, especially *Some Aspects of Maori Myth and Religion* (1923).

China	88 Beginning of Han decline	184 Daoist Yellow Turban rebellion	300–700 Spread of Buddhism
		220 Last Han emperor deposed; "Time of Troubles" begins; nomadic invasions in north	
India			
Rome and Christianity		284–305 Diocletian emperor	330–379 Basil organizes Eastern monasticism
		180 ff. Beginning of Rome's decline; population decline	
	231 Initial Germanic invasion effort		312–337 Constantine; division of empire administration; toleration of Christianity
Middle East			
	A.D. 100	A.D. 200	A.D. 300

The End of the Classical Era: World History in Transition, A.D. 200–700

II

INTRODUCTION. Between A.D. 200 and 600, all three of the great classical civilizations collapsed at least in part. The western portion of the Roman Empire declined and fell, suffering major eclipse. The fate of Han China, Gupta India, and indeed the eastern part of the Roman Empire was less dire, but here too there was substantial change. The coincidence of these developments in time raises one of the principal issues in world history: What causes civilizations to lose vigor? It also focuses attention on the close of one major period in time—characterized by the development and flowering of the classical societies—and the opening of a new, postclassical era in world history. For while decline and fall rivet attention from the 3d through the 6th centuries, important new developments, including the spread of great religions, also set up many of the positive characteristics of the next stage in world history, differentiating this stage from the classical era itself. This transitional aspect, as well as classical decline, requires analysis, as we examine developments that began to emerge around A.D. 200 and reached fruition between the 5th and the 8th centuries from Asia through North Africa and Europe.

This chapter returns to a primary focus on the centers of classical civilization in Eurasia and North Africa. The collapse or deterioration in all three classical civilization centers provides a vital set of comparable themes, concerning the process of decline, its causes, and its results. The end of the classical era is predicated on changes in Asia and the Mediterranean, not the whole world. Nevertheless, the fading of the great classical empires did have consequences beyond their borders. The reshuffling of civilization boundaries that resulted

---

589–618 Sui dynasty   **618** Tang dynasty

606–647 Loose empire under Harsha

400–500 Decline of Buddhism; evolution of popular Hinduism

c. 540 collapse of Gupta dynasty

657 ff. Rajput (regional princes) predominate; periodic clashes with Islamic armies in northwest

450 Hun invasions begin

401 ff. Increased Germanic invasions

527–565 Justinian, Eastern emperor

354–430 Augustine

480–547 Benedict and Western monasticism

410 Rome sacked by Germanic tribe

476 Last Roman emperor in West deposed

610 Beginning of Islam

would soon unleash new kinds of expansive forces that would touch sub-Saharan Africa, northern Europe, and various additional parts of Asia. Africans in the Sudan, Germans, Slavs, and Japanese were all affected. The changing map of civilization would still leave certain parts of the world entirely separate, but the number of isolated areas dropped. Before turning to this dynamic trend in the next unit, we must first chart the crumbling of the classical structures and the signs of subsequent trends over roughly five centuries.

It is worth remembering also that the classical period in American Indian civilizations, notably the Maya, ended not long after the collapse of the great empires in Asia and the Mediterranean, though the processes had no direct connection. We know much more about the nature and causes of decline in Rome or China because of available records, but some of the factors may have been similar. The process of civilization decline is invariably challenging and difficult to grasp, and it always has wide-ranging consequences, including unforeseen turns that led to the end of the classical era both in the Old World and the New.

All three classical civilizations in Asia, North Africa, and Europe suffered from outside invasions during the centuries of decline, the common results of growing incursions by nomadic herding groups from central Asia. This renewed wave of nomadic expansion was neither as sweeping, nor as damaging as the Indo-European outpourings on the civilization of the Indus valley many centuries before; but the new attack severely tested the civilized regimes. Western Rome, including the capital city itself, fell to Germanic invaders from northern Europe, though there was one fierce incursion by Asiatic Huns. The Germanic peoples pressed in partly because they were harassed by these same Huns and moved south for greater safety. Another Hun group from central Asia overthrew the Gupta dynasty in India, while similar nomadic tribes had earlier contributed to the disorder of China after the Han dynasty.

The central Asian nomads may have been spurred by population increase in their native lands, which prompted them to seek new territory. They were certainly encouraged by a growing realization of the weakness of the classical regimes. Han China as well as the later Roman Empire suffered from serious internal problems long before the invaders applied additional blows, and the Guptas had not permanently resolved India's tendency to political fragmentation. Thus, although outside invasion by warlike nomads forms the clearest common thread in the pattern of classical decline, the whole phenomenon invites consideration of some shared processes of internal decay that humbled once-proud empires before small but fierce bands of barbarian invaders.

In addition, then, to conveying what happened in the final centuries of the great classical empires, some assessment of causation—of the factors that explain roughly simultaneous decline—is essential. While invasions are part of the explanation, they would have been brushed aside with relative ease a few centuries before. Other changes had occurred, which accounted for the invaders' devastating success.

The process of decline, however, was far from identical across civilization boundaries. Everywhere the crisis was severe; even in China, which ultimately recovered most completely, the collapse of the Han dynasty led to an unusual period of disarray. But the image of destruction many Westerners learn on the basis of Rome's demise is really atypical. Most civilizations retained more of their earlier achievements than the Roman Europe managed to do. Differential patterns of revival and continuity raise additional prospects for a comparative analysis that sums up many of the emphases of the larger classical era that now drew to a close. What survived from classical China was different from the continuities in India, and both contrasted sharply with the much more complex Mediterranean patterns after the collapse of the Roman Empire. These differences must be explained, and they must also be used to anticipate subsequent developments.

The collapse or temporary eclipse of the classical civilizations forms a significant break in world history, and this too must be explored. The fall of the Han dynasty and the Guptas in India rather clearly ended formative periods in each civilization's history. This did not preclude further change. Indeed the period of decline ushered in new forces, such as a novel Chinese interest in Buddhism. Each civilization had to alter somewhat, simply in reaction to invasion and extensive chaos. What the period of decline did in India and China and to an extent in the eastern Mediterranean was to define the essentials of the classical achievement that could endure or revive, to establish the crucial heritage, even as other features of the classical period were winnowed away. India, to use the clearest example, found it relatively easy to build on the religious tradition already sketched in the classical era and to amplify the distinctive social structure; here was a heritage that would survive, though with modifications and adjustments, into India's postclassical period and beyond. But other features of the classical achievement did not continue. Buddhism faded in the religious tradition, while recurrent ability to form internal empires lapsed. India began a long experience in which political fragmentation alternated with larger structures established through invasion from the outside. The next time Indians formed more than large regional kingdoms was in A.D. 1947; here was a major change from the classical precedents set by the Mauryans and then the Guptas. In China as well as India, the centuries of decline brought important changes but also a process of selection in which crucial characteristics maintained the civilizations' definitions into a new age.

DECLINE AND PERIODIZATION

Decline and fall had still wider ramifications, beyond the classical civilizations, in ushering in a new period in world history. Separating one major time period from another must not be undertaken lightly, for it is too easy to look at change in one or two key regions and misleadingly assume that a larger framework had developed for all the civilizations. Generally, three overlapping shifts must occur for a new period to be identified in world history, and not just in some individual societies. First, the world map must change significantly, which means that at least some civilization areas are divided in new ways and new patterns of dynamism are established. Second, new kinds of contacts must be established among civilization areas. And third, perhaps in part because of new contacts, some new parallelisms must arise in the patterns displayed by the major civilization areas. Obviously, additional facets may develop as part of world history periodization, including some important new technologies. Nevertheless, the notion of three guidelines provides at least a minimum checklist.

The fall of the great empires and its consequences easily meets the three tests. Cultural and political boundaries shifted with the renewed openness of India to invasion and with the irrevocable division of the Mediterranean world. Boundary changes encouraged a number of civilizations to seek new outlets for expansion and influence, thus radiating contacts from the old classical core to new parts of Europe, Africa, and East and Southeast Asia. India's role as the most expansive civilization in terms of trade and cultural influence also declined, in favor of the newcomer Muslim civilization based in the Middle East.

New contacts among civilizations developed after the 5th century A.D., through patterns of warfare that brought Middle Easterners briefly to the borders of China, where among other things they learned about the manufacture of paper and spread this knowledge westward. New contacts developed also from new trade patterns and from the unprecedented outreach of great world religions—Buddhism, Christianity, and Islam—which spread across civilization boundaries without, however, erasing them.

Finally, new parallelisms developed among civilizations from Europe and North Africa through Japan, in addition to numerous developments within individual societies. Most civilizations witnessed important changes in belief

systems in the aftermath of classical decline. More systematic religious movements spread increasingly, challenging, replacing or merging with more traditional animism.

THE GREAT RELIGIONS

All of this means that the end of the classical period was not simply a story of decay and collapse. As the great empires fell or receded, after A.D. 200, the major world religions—the same religions practiced today—arose or spread. From Spain to China, growing political instability clearly prompted many people to seek solace in joys of the spirit, and while this religious surge was not entirely new, the resulting changes in the religious map of Europe, Africa, and Asia, plus the nature and intensity of religious interests, were significant new forces. Christianity became an extensive religion through the Mediterranean region as the Roman Empire's political strength weakened, though it used the empire's political structure to form its own institutional framework and channels of communication. Buddhism's surge into East Asia accompanied the growing problems of Han China in decline. Thus two major world faiths, different in many ways but similar in their emphasis on the life of the spirit and the importance of divine power, as well as in their desire to unseat popular animism with beliefs in a single divine force and more abstract religious concepts, began to reshape major portions of Europe and Asia precisely as the political edifice of the classical period declined or disappeared. Even in India, Hinduism continued an evolution that produced new levels of spirituality among large sectors of the population. Finally, shortly after A.D. 600, an entirely new religion, Islam, started a career that would make it the most dynamic force in world history during the next several centuries; its early expansion owed much to the political disunity and uncertainty in the eastern Mediterranean after Rome's demise.

In sum, the religious map of the world, while by no means completed in the aftermath of classical decline, began to take on new contours, many of which are recognizable today in Christian, Islamic, or Buddhist influence. The chronological coincidence of this set of religious changes suggests the importance of classical decline in setting in motion new opportunities for missionaries and new needs for ordinary people to reassess what and why they believed. Never before had single religions spread so widely, crossing so many previous cultural and political boundaries. Not since before the classical era had masses and elites been so joined in common religious institutions and interests.

The decline and fall of the great empires thus marks more than some parallel processes of political change. A larger set of changes was involved, ranging from redefinitions of geographical boundaries to some basic alterations in both formal and popular culture. Differences among civilizations remained great, and in some ways the collapse of the great empires and the rise of new religious divisions made international contacts more complex than before. Yet the centuries of decline did bring something of a common moment in the history of most major civilizations, which not only brought certain patterns to an end but launched a new dynamic.

UPHEAVALS IN EASTERN AND SOUTHERN ASIA

After a brief faltering following the reign of Wu ti, the Han dynasty seemed to recover, and by about A.D. 100 the central government was about as effective and the economy about as prosperous as before. The Chinese launched a new expansion campaign, pushing westward with attacks in central Asia across the Gobi desert, that may have helped spark the westward and then southerly movement of the groups known in Europe as the Huns. After about A.D. 88, however, the quality of the individual emperors began to decline. Most reigns were short and full of plotting; empresses and officials joined in the fray (see Chapter 5). On several occasions numerous bureaucrats and popular protesters were massacred.

DECLINE AND FALL IN HAN CHINA

At a basic level conditions among the peasantry began to deteriorate. Large landowners, always powerful under the Han, grew more so, avoiding taxes and forming private armies. Taxes on peasants increased, and many farmers, forced into serfdom, provided labor service and turned over much of their own produce as fees to the landlords. Social protest increased, often laced with Daoist beliefs.

Peasant unrest culminated in a great revolutionary effort led by the Daoists in A.D. 184. Leaders, called the Yellow Turbans, promised a golden age to be brought about by divine magic. Han generals suppressed this rebellion but set themselves up as regional rulers, a clear sign of the collapse of the central state. The last Han emperor was deposed in A.D. 220. China divided into three kingdoms for several decades, but finally even these began to collapse. China was ruled for several centuries by the landowning class, who managed huge numbers of serfs and directed private armies, operating beyond the control of formal government. Southern and northern China also pulled apart, with the south maintaining higher levels of economic growth and continuing to absorb tribal peoples into Chinese culture.

No firm dynasties could be established in this 350 year period, though there were short-lived regimes in the south. Northern China was pressed by invasions from central Asia. Nomadic peoples had been incorporated into Chinese armies, much as later Roman rulers tried to use Germanic troops; but as the government deteriorated, the nomads broke loose and began to invade the Middle Kingdom. Several nomad-dominated states were formed, though all lasted only briefly. Internal warfare became endemic in what was an unusually long breakdown in Chinese stability.

Into this chaos came a new fascination with Buddhism, which responded to political uncertainty and economic distress by offering spiritual solace and which also, like Christianity in Europe, provided a form of cultural cohesion at a time when political links had broken down. Imported from India—the only case until modern times when China borrowed a major idea from abroad—and disseminated by silk merchants and missionaries, Buddhism spread among both the Chinese and the nomadic warriors, helping gradually to mold a common culture in which Chinese ingredients predominated. Buddhist influence also brought to China a new spur for art and sculpture, altering established styles and themes.

Buddhism earned periodic attack by Daoist regional rulers, but the faith reached throughout China by the 5th century A.D. Buddhist monasteries for women as well as men gained ground. Many Chinese monks made pilgrimages to India, and Buddhist literature and philosophy spread widely. Chinese Buddhists blended practices from many Indian Buddhist sects, using meditation, recitation of prayers, and devotional exercises. The Chinese imposed some of their own values on Buddhism as well, as in insisting on the importance of forming families so that the ancestral line could be preserved; typically, as a result, only second sons became Buddhist monks, with first sons maintaining the family responsibilities. Buddhists were also pressed into political loyalty, paying taxes to the government and submitting to government regulations on the formation of monasteries.

Growing Buddhist influence also had an impact on Daoism, forcing greater formalization of Daoist doctrine and more efforts to reach the common people. Many Chinese found great similarities between the two faiths, though Buddhism continued to have the advantage of offering a clearer doctrine of personal salvation—the chance of holy life after death—and a firmer set of personal ethics. Daoist leaders developed a variety of practices, including meditation and dietary restrictions, that might bring immortality. Popular Daoism, mixing Daoist beliefs with an animistic pantheon of many gods, tended to hold that good or evil done in this life would be compensated by heavens or hells

The spread of Buddhism produced major new themes in Chinese art, many of which focused on stylized figures of Buddha himself. Buddha became an object of worship in this process, with great statues conveying his majesty.

hereafter. Popular Daoism also, of course, could have political implications in protesting social injustice. And Daoism often provided priests and shamans who practiced faith healing in cases of disease. These ramifications of Daoism proved quite durable among the Chinese peasantry, lasting in some parts of eastern Asia even today.

Confucianism, obviously, lost ground during this confused period in Chinese history, eclipsed by the more otherworldly interests. But the legacy of Chinese institutions and secular beliefs did not disappear, and as nomadic invaders were partly converted to Chinese ways, the opportunity for political revival reemerged toward the end of the 6th century. A series of strong rulers in the north drove out nomadic bands, and then merged, under a general of Chinese-Turkish background, into a new Sui dynasty. Under this brief dynasty the whole of northern China was united and South China was reconquered. New canals were built and the Great Wall repaired. Attempts to expand into Korea and central Asia brought financial collapse, however, along with new rebellions, and only in 618 was the more durable T'ang dynasty established. The time of troubles had ended.

The decline and fall of the Han had thus brought important disruption to China and had opened the civilization to new religious influences. But old values survived as well. Even the competing landlords retained some training in Confucianism, and with that training the idea of a united empire. New religious interests, though important, did not capture full attention. In this sense China, with greater cultural homogeneity established in the classical era, differed markedly from the Mediterranean, where Christianity and Islam came close to displacing older philosophical concerns while challenging earlier political loyalties. Many nomadic invaders found that they could do little better than to imitate Chinese styles, and this process ultimately encouraged the revival of older political habits. Chaos and innovation must not be forgotten, but eventually the main Chinese story was the ability to recapture continuity.

THE END OF THE GUPTAS: DECLINE IN INDIA

The decline of classical civilization in India was in one sense less drastic than the collapse of Han China in that India had not depended so heavily on political structures to hold its civilization together. The fall of the Guptas, in other words, did not initially entail an opening to dramatic new cultural or social influences. Yet the Gupta collapse

Chinese Buddhism, unlike most Chinese beliefs, spread among all regions and social groups. While it divided into many sects that disagreed over details of theology and rituals by commenting on earlier Buddhist scriptures (the Sutras), many ordinary Chinese believers cared little for such niceties, concerned rather with direct spiritual benefits. Often they arranged to have Buddhist sermons copied, as a means of obtaining merit, while adding a note of their own. The following passages come from such notes, written mainly in the 6th century.

Recorded on the 15th day of the fourth month of 531.

The Buddhist lay disciple Yuan Jung—having lived in this degenerate era for many years, fearful for his life, and yearning for home—now makes a donation of a thousand silver coins to the Three Jewels [the Buddha, the Law, and the Monastic Order]. This donation is made in the name of the Celestial King Vaisravana. In addition, he makes a donation of a thousand to ransom himself and his wife and children [from their earthly existence], a thousand more to ransom his servants, and a thousand more to ransom his domestic animals. This money is to be used for copying sutras. It is accompanied by the prayer that the Celestial King many attain Buddhahood; that the disciple's family, servants, and animals may be blessed with long life, many attain enlightenment, and may all be permitted to return to the capital.

Dated the 29th day of the fourth month of 550.

Happiness is not fortuitous: pray for it and it will respond. Results are not born of thin air: pay heed to causes and results will follow. This explains how the Buddhist disciple and nun Tao-jung—because her conduct in her previous life was not correct—came to be born in her present form, a woman, vile and unclean.

Now if she does not honor the awesome decree of Buddha, how can future consequences be favorable for her? Therefore, having cut down her expenditures on food and clothing, she reverently has had the *Nirvana Sutra* copied once. She prays that those who read it carefully will be exalted in mind to the highest realms and that those who communicate its meaning will cause others to be so enlightened.

She also prays that in her present existence she will have no further sickness or suffering, that her parents in seven other incarnations (who have already died or will die in the future) and her present family and close relatives may experience joy in the four realms [earth, water, fire, and air], and that whatever they seek may indeed come to pass. Finally, she prays that all those endowed with knowledge may be included within this prayer.

Recorded on the 28th day of the fifth month of 583.

The Army Superintendent, Sung Shao, having suffered the heavy sorrow of losing both his father and mother, made a vow on their behalf to read one section each of [many] sutras. He prays that the spirits of his parents will someday reach the Pure Land [paradise] and will thus be forever freed from the three unhappy states of existence and the eight calamities and that they may eternally listen to the Buddha's teachings.

He also prays that the members of his family, both great and small, may find happiness at will, that blessings may daily rain down upon them while hardships disperse like clouds. He prays that the imperial highways may be open and free of bandits, that the state may be preserved from pestilence, that wind and rain may obey their proper seasons, and that all suffering creatures may quickly find release. May all these prayers be granted!

The preceding incantation has been translated and circulated.

If this incantation is recited 7, 14, or 21 times daily (after having cleansed the mouth in the morning with a willow twig, having scattered flowers and incense before the image of Buddha, having knelt and joined the palms of the hands), the four grave sins, the five wicked acts, and all other transgressions will be wiped away. The present body will not be afflicted by untimely calamities; one will at last be born into the realm of immeasurably long life; and reincarnation in the female form will be escaped forever.

Now, the Sanskrit text has been re-examined and the Indian Vinaya monk Buddhasangha and other monks have been consulted; thus we know that the awesome power of this incantation is beyond comprehension. If it is recited 100 times in the evening and again at noon, it will destroy the four grave sins and five wicked acts. It will pluck out the very roots of sin and will ensure rebirth in the Western Regions. If, with sincerity of spirit, one is able to complete 200,000 recitations, perfect intelligence will be born and there will be no relapses. If 300,000 recitations are completed, one will see Amita Buddha face to face and will certainly be reborn into the Pure Land of tranquility and bliss.

Copied by the disciple of pure faith Sun Szu-chung on the 8th day of the fourth month of 720.

Questions: Why did Buddhism spread widely in China by the 6th century? How did popular Buddhism compare with original Buddhist teachings (see Chapter 7)? How did Chinese Buddhists define holy life?

left more durable traces in later Indian history, for internally generated political unity became more difficult than ever before.

While the high point of Gupta rule came under Chandragupta II early in the 5th century, his immediate successors managed to sustain considerable prosperity. India around A.D. 450 was probably the most stable and peaceful area in the world. However, in A.D. 440 a series of invasions began, from the nomadic Huns, that would gradually reduce the empire's strength. The Gupta pattern of somewhat decentralized rule, where vassal princes were treated as partial allies rather than subject to direct central administration, may have made response to invasion more difficult. The Huns controlled much of northwestern India— the classic invasion route of the subcontinent— by A.D. 500. By this juncture the quality of Gupta kings was also diminishing, which added to the problem (see Chapter 7). It was a regional prince, not the Guptas themselves, who broke the hold of the Huns in the northwest around A.D. 530, and the Guptas were too weak to restore their claims. The dynasty collapsed entirely around A.D. 550.

A few echoes of Gupta splendor developed during the 7th century. Harsha, a descendant of the Guptas through his grandmother, constructed a loose empire across northern India between 616 and 657. But he died without heirs, and his empire broke up again. From this point onward, until a better-organized series of outside invasions began, northern India was politically divided. Regional dynasties were occasionally powerful, but none controlled a large region and few managed to last very long. The regional princes, collectively called the *Rajput*, emphasized military prowess; but while there were many local wars, few political events had great significance.

In this localized framework, Indian culture continued to evolve. Buddhism declined steadily in India proper. The Guptas had preferred Hinduism, and the Hun invaders disliked the pronouncedly otherworldly tone of the Buddhists as well. Military-minded princes had little sympathy for Buddhist principles of calm and contemplation. Hindu beliefs, in contrast, gained ground, converting the Hun

leaders among other groups. Within Hinduism, worship of a mother goddess, Devi, spread widely, which encouraged a new popular emotionalism in religious ritual. In essence, India partially redefined its core culture by emphasizing the Hindu strain more clearly, while relying primarily on cultural cohesion to maintain the civilization at a time when political life became more difficult. The reassertion of Hinduism also helped the caste system, now spreading to southern India. The number and complexity of castes increased as invaders were assimilated into the system, but basic principles persisted from the classical period.

India's economic activity also continued at a relatively high level, though in periods of outright invasion there were new hardships. Here too, Indian civilization did not collapse to the extent of Han China, or the western Mediterranean. The decades after the fall of the Guptas indeed saw new outreach in trade and even some conquest by southern Tamil kingdoms who looked to establish firmer strongholds along the Indian Ocean in Southeast Asia.

While Indian civilization substantially maintained its position, though with new political disunity, another threat was to come after A.D. 600 from the new Middle Eastern

Hindu statues gave vivid forms to holy figures, many of them female. This scene portrays a goddess subduing a mythological cosmic monster.

This expressive Hindu religious representation of the goddess Indra is from a cave painting dating from about A.D. 500.

religion of Islam. (See Chapters 12 and 13.) At first, India's contacts with this new force were somewhat tangential. Arab armies, fighting under the banners of their god Allah, reached India's porous northwestern frontier during the 7th century, and while there was initially little outright conquest as opposed to raids for booty, Islam did win some converts in the north, particularly among lower-caste Indians drawn to the Islamic message of spiritual equality.

The challenge of Islam continued the evolutionary process within mainstream Hinduism. Hindu leaders strengthened their emphasis on religious and popular devotion, playing down some traditional intellectual interests. Popularization involved language change—as would occur in

Christianity in western Europe several centuries later. Hindu texts began to be written in vernacular languages such as Hindi, while the old classical language, Sanskrit, declined in usage. These reactions helped prevent more than a minority of Indians from abandoning Hinduism, but they also tended to narrow Indian culture more strictly toward the religious focus. Earlier Indian achievements in science and mathematics were not matched by new work.

By the 8th century Islamic competition also began to hit hard at India's international economic position. Arab traders soon wrested control of the Indian Ocean from Tamil merchants, and India, though still prosperous and productive, saw its commercial dynamism reduced. No political

Asia, About A.D. 600

response to these new challenges emerged, and with persistent regionalism the subcontinent was open by the 11th century to conquest by Muslim rulers from the outside. Clearly, the glory days of the Guptas were long past, and while classical traditions survived through Hinduism, the caste system, and active patterns of internal trade, the focus of the civilization, and its larger impact on Asia, were seriously reduced.

Here, then, is an important pattern of decline, though one rather different from that of China. India's political retreat from empire was longer lasting than China's political setbacks; only in the 20th century did India regain an ability to form large states on the basis of internal rule rather than regimes imposed from the outside. Obviously, earlier weaknesses in the classical past help explain this Indian-Chinese contrast. Classical India had generated neither a set of political values nor a durable institution like the Chinese bureaucracy that could allow a large political unit to bounce back from a period of invasion and chaos. Though India's regional states were often well run, combining the power of a prince with some sort of wider council, they were not strong enough to prevent recurrent threat of invasion, mainly by Muslim forces coming in from the northwest. On the other hand, India's culture and caste system showed great resiliency, for they did not depend on any single pattern of political support. India in this sense experienced fewer sharp cultural shifts and showed more ability to modify gradually, than did China under the Buddhist influence. Indian identity and key traditions could thus be preserved amid political disunity or even under foreign rule.

 DECLINE AND FALL: ROME

The decline of the Roman Empire fit, chronologically, between the collapse of the Han and that of the Gupta dynasty. It was more disruptive than either of these Asian developments. For this reason, and because memories and assessments of the fall of this great empire became part of the Western tradition, the process of deterioration deserves careful attention. Every so often, Americans or West Europeans concerned about changes in their own society wonder if there might be lessons in Rome's decline that apply to the uncertain future of Western civilization today. In contrast, a strong tradition in China (though not the only historical approach among the Chinese) argues that decline is part of a cyclical process that will also see a civilization regain its vigor; the focus on an overwhelming disaster is, in terms of the Chinese experience, less logical. For many educated Westerners (similar to some Indians who view the Gupta dynasty as India's finest era and its collapse therefore as an unredeemed misfortune) the fall of Rome has a powerful impact on the imagination, and commands a particular effort of explanation.

CAUSATION: WHY DID ROME DECLINE?

Signs of decay began to emerge in the Roman Empire from the late 2d century onward, at various levels. The statistical symptoms were declining population size, as birth rates no longer kept pace with mortality rates, and growing difficulties in recruiting effective armies. Political symptoms showed in the greater brutality and arbitrariness of many later Roman emperors—victims, according to one commentator at the time, of "lustful and cruel habits." Tax collection became increasingly difficult as residents of the empire fell on hard times. The governor of Egypt complained that "the once numerous inhabitants of the aforesaid villages have now been reduced to a few, because some have fled in poverty and others have died . . . and for this reason we are in danger owing to impoverishment of having to abandon the tax-collectorship." Above all there were the human symptoms. Inscriptions on Roman tombstones increasingly ended with the motto "I was not, I was, I am not, I have no more desires," suggesting a pervasive despondency at the futility of this life and despair at the absence of any life after death. As the structures of the empire deteriorated, meaning in life became harder to find—and this mood made efforts at structural revival all the more difficult.

The signs of change in the quality of political and economic life in the empire began to emerge after about A.D. 180, at which point the empire's geographical expansion had already slightly receded from its high point. The end of expansion was itself a problem, though the results would only gradually become apparent. Unlike Han China or Gupta India, the Roman Empire had depended extensively on expansion, not simply to provide prestige but to recruit the necessary slave labor force. With the empire's boundaries now pushed to the limits it could support, and with resistance emerging to further expansion on the part of tribes in northern Europe and the Parthian Empire in the Middle East, Rome almost inevitably had to restructure its labor policies on the great commercial estates and in the mines. This restructuring gradually occurred, but it involved a reduction of economic vitality and market production.

More pressing, initially, were the internal issues of politics and population. Growing political confusion, including disputes over how emperors should be appointed and controlled, produced a series of weak rulers and many battles over succession to the throne. Intervention of the army in the selection of emperors, as the army became an increasingly separate but vital institution, complicated political life and contributed to the worsening of rule from the top. The deterioration of the state, in other words, was not simply an accident in terms of personalities.

Still more important in launching the process of decline was a series of plagues that swept over the empire toward the end of the 2d century A.D. These plagues decimated the population and severely disrupted economic life. Some authorities have argued that Rome's urban population also suffered lead poisoning from the pipes leading from the aqueducts, which further weakened people and reduced population size. Lower population obviously added to problems of finding labor. Recruiting of troops became more difficult, as the empire was increasingly reduced to hiring Germanic soldiers to guard its frontiers. The need to pay troops added to the demands on the state's budget, just as declining production cut into tax revenues and the absence of new conquests cut into other rewards for soldiers.

Here, perhaps, is the key to the process of decline: a set of general problems, triggered by a cycle of plagues that could not be prevented, resulting in a rather mechanistic spiral that steadily worsened. But there is another side to Rome's downfall, though whether as cause or result of the initial difficulties is hard to say. Rome's upper classes became steadily more pleasure-seeking and individualistic, turning away from the political devotion and economic vigor that had characterized the republic and early empire. Cultural life decayed. Aside from some truly creative Christian writers—the fathers of Western theology—there was very little sparkle to the art or literature of the later empire. Many Roman scholars contented themselves with

writing textbooks that rather mechanically summarized earlier achievements in science, mathematics, and literary style. Writing textbooks is not, of course, proof of absolute intellectual incompetence—at least not in all cases—but the point was that new knowledge or artistic styles were not being generated, and even the levels of previous accomplishment began to slip. The later Romans wrote textbooks about rhetoric instead of displaying rhetorical talent in actual political life; they wrote simple compendiums about animals or geometry that barely captured the essentials of what earlier intellectuals had known, and often added superstitious beliefs that previous generations would have scorned. This cultural decline, finally, was not clearly due to disease or economic collapse, for it began in some ways before these larger problems hit. Something was happening to the Roman elite, perhaps because of the deadening hand of authoritarian political rule, perhaps because of a new commitment to luxuries and sensual indulgence. Revealingly, the upper classes were no longer willing to reproduce themselves, for bearing and raising children seemed incompatible with a pleasure-seeking life. Military service became less attractive to these groups, again forcing recruitment of paid soldiers from groups such as the Germanic tribes along the northern borders of the empire.

Rome's fall, in other words, can be blamed on large, impersonal forces that would have been hard for any society to control, or on moral and political decay that reflected growing corruption among the society's leaders. Probably elements of both were involved. Thus the plagues would have weakened even a vigorous society but would not necessarily have produced an irremediable downward spiral had not the morale of the ruling classes been sapped by unproductive values. Cultural stagnation and even the fall of a particular ruling group might have been survivable had the larger problems of population decline and waning prosperity prevented the ability to rebound. It is certainly noteworthy that Rome's economic disruption ran much deeper than the problems of Han China or Gupta India, causing not just temporary hardships but a real regression in the levels of production and forms of economic organization, at least in the empire's western half.

THE PROCESS OF DECLINE

Regardless of precise causes, the course of Roman decay is quite clear. As the quality of imperial rule declined, and as life became more dangerous and economic survival more precarious, many farmers clustered around the protection of large landlords, surrendering full control over their plots of land in the hope of military and judicial protection. The decentralization of political and economic authority, which was greatest in the Western, or European, portions of the empire, foreshadowed the manorial system of Europe in the Middle Ages. The estate system gave great political power to the landlords and could provide some local stability. But it weakened the hold of the emperor, and also tended to drive the economy away from the elaborate trade patterns of Mediterranean civilization in its heyday. Many estates sought to produce almost everything needed on the spot. Trade and production declined further, causing tax revenues to drop and cities to shrink in size. The empire was locked in a vicious circle, in which responses to initial deterioration merely lessened the chances of recovery.

Some later emperors tried vigorously to reverse the flow. Diocletian, who ruled from A.D. 284 to 305, tightened up the administration of the empire and tried to improve tax collection. Regulation of the dwindling economy increased. Diocletian also attempted to concentrate political loyalties on his own person, enhancing the pressure to worship the emperor as god. This was what prompted him to persecute Christians with particular viciousness, for they would not give Caesar preference over their God. The emperor Constantine, who ruled from 312 to 337, tried other experiments. He set up a second capital city, Constantinople, to regulate the eastern half of the empire more efficiently. He tried to use the religious force of Christianity to unify the empire spiritually, extending toleration and adopting it as his own faith. These measures were not

without result. The Eastern Empire, ruled from Constantinople (formerly the Greek colony of Byzantium, now the Turkish city of Istanbul), remained an effective political and economic unit. Christianity spread under official sponsorship, though there were some new problems attached to success.

But none of these measures revived the empire as a whole. Division merely made the weakness of the western half worse. Attempts to regulate the economy reduced economic initiative and lowered production; ultimately tax revenues declined once again. The army deteriorated further. And when the Germanic invasions began in earnest in the 400s, there was scant basis to resist. Many peasants, burdened by the social and economic pressures of the decaying empire, actually welcomed the barbarians. A priest noted that "in all districts taken over by the Germans, there is one desire among all the Romans, that they should never again find it necessary to pass under Roman jurisdiction." German kingdoms were set up in many parts of the empire by 425, and the last Roman emperor in the West was displaced in 476. The Germanic invaders numbered at most five percent of the population of the empire, but so great was the earlier decline that this small, uncoordinated force put an end to one of the world's great political structures.

The fall of Rome echoes some of the same questions that apply to China and India. Do civilizations inevitably fall, or at least undergo cycles of decline? When the col-

Patterns of Germanic Invasions

Germanic warriors become a new aristocracy. This mosaic from Italy shows a landowner from the Vandal tribe.

lapse involves outside invading forces, does one look primarily at internal decay? Germanic or central Asian invaders were less civilized than the Roman, Indian, or Chinese areas they attacked. Their reliance on hunting and herding gave them some skills, including excellent horsemanship in the case of the Huns, that allowed them easily to overrun more populous peasant settlements where people were unaccustomed to battle. Germans had also learned new organizational methods, from their contacts on the Roman borders, that made them a more formidable force. But there is no question that in their glory days, the professional armies of Rome or Han China could have contained the invaders; it was internal weakness that allowed the invaders to have such disruptive effects. Rome, indeed, seemed headed for downfall even before the Germanic intruders applied the final blows. At the same time, ironically, the luxurious living of the upper classes and the impressive reputation of the classical empires helped lure the invaders in.

RESULTS OF THE "FALL" OF ROME

The collapse of Rome echoed mightily through the later history of Europe and the Middle East. Rome's fall split the unity of the Mediterranean lands that had been so arduously won through Hellenistic culture and then the Roman Empire itself. This was one sign that the end of the Roman Empire was a more serious affair than the displacement of the last classical dynasties in India and China. Greece and Rome had not produced the shared political culture and bureaucratic traditions of China that could allow revival after a period of chaos. Nor had Mediterranean civilization, for all its vitality, generated a common religion that reached deeply enough, or satisfied enough needs, to maintain unity amid political fragmentation as in India. Such religions would reach the Mediterranean world as Rome fell, but they came too late to save the empire and produced a deep rift in this world, between Christian and Muslim, that has not been healed to this day.

Rome's collapse, though profound, was uneven. In effect, the fall of Rome divided the Mediterranean world into three zones—the starting point of three distinct civilizations that would develop in later centuries.

In the northeastern part of the empire, centered now on Constantinople, the empire in a sense did not fall. Civilization was more deeply entrenched here than in some of the western European portions of the empire, and there were fewer pressures from invaders. Emperors continued to rule Greece and other parts of Southeast Europe, plus the northern Middle East. This Eastern Empire—later to be known as the Byzantine Empire—was a product of the Hellenistic era and late imperial Rome, not a balanced result of the whole span of classical Mediterranean civilization. Thus, though its language became Greek, the Eastern Empire maintained the authoritarian tone of the late Roman rulers. Yet the empire itself was vibrant, artistically creative, and active in trade. Briefly, especially under the emperor Justinian (who ruled from 527 to 565), the Eastern emperors tried to regain the whole heritage of Rome. But Justinian was unable to maintain a hold in Italy, after some conquests at great cost, and a reconquered province of North Africa soon split away. He did issue one of the most famous compilations of Roman law, in the code that bore his name. But his was the last European-based effort to restore Mediterranean unity.

Still, Rome's fall did not disrupt the northern Middle East or southeastern Europe as much as might have been expected. The Sassanid (Persian) Empire, which had replaced the Parthian Empire in A.D. 227, maintained considerable strength in the northeastern portion of the Middle East. As the Roman Empire weakened, the Sassanids joined the attack, at times pushing into parts of southeastern Europe. Ultimately, however, the Byzantine Empire managed to create a stable frontier, dividing the northern Middle East into Byzantine and Sassanid zones. The division, in turn, would last until the Persians were overwhelmed by Arab Islamic armies in the 7th century. In Byzantium, which proved able to withstand even the Arab onslaught though with further loss of Middle Eastern territory, many of the important traditions of the later Roman Empire persisted, not only in the imperial political structure of the empire but through maintenance of many aspects of classical Greek culture, now conjoined with Christianity.

The second zone that devolved from Rome's fall was more seriously disrupted, though more in political terms than in terms of a marked economic or cultural decline. This zone consisted of North Africa and the southeastern shores of the Mediterranean. Here a number of regional kingdoms briefly succeeded the empire. And while Christianity spread in the area—indeed, one of the greatest Christian theologians, Augustine, was a bishop in North Africa—it was not so uniformly triumphant as in the Byzantine Empire or western Europe. Further, variant beliefs and doctrines soon split North African Christianity from the larger branches, producing most notably the Coptic church in Egypt, which still survives as a Christian minor-

The Mediterranean, Middle East, Europe, and North Africa, about A.D. 500

ity in that country, and in Ethiopia. And soon much of North Africa would be filled with the still newer doctrines of Islam and a new Arab Empire.

Finally, there was the western part of the empire—Italy, Spain, and points north. Here is where Rome's fall not only shattered unities but reduced the level of civilization itself. Crude, regional Germanic kingdoms grew in parts of Italy, in France, and elsewhere. The only clearly vital force in this region emanated not from Roman traditions but from the spread of Christianity. Even Christianity could not sustain a sophisticated literature or art or even theology, however. In the mire of Rome's collapse, this part of the world forgot for several centuries what it had previously known.

In this western domain what we call the fall of Rome was scarcely noted at the time, for decay had been progressing for so many decades that the failure to name a new emperor meant little. There was some comprehension of loss, some realization that the present could not rival the past. Thus Christian scholars were soon apologizing for their inability to write well or to understand some of the sophisticated doctrines of the earlier theologians such as Augustine. This sense of inferiority to classical achievements would long mark the culture of this western zone—even as times got better.

ANALYSIS
THE PROBLEM OF DECLINE AND FALL

Explaining the decline of civilizations has fascinated observers since civilizations began to decline. As Rome's vitality ebbed, many writers tried to figure out what was going on. Christian theologians, such as Augustine, wrote massive tomes to prove that Christianity was not to blame, for some non-Christian philosophers had argued that the religion's otherworldly emphasis and primary loyalty to the church had sapped Rome's strength. Both Christian and pagan writers worried that the cause of Rome's collapse was immorality, a loss of the virtues of self-denial and devotion to the common good that had made Rome great in the first place.

Many of these arguments have been taken up by world historians in more recent times. In the 18th century Edward Gibbon, a British philosopher-historian who was hostile to religion, returned to the attack on Christianity, holding that it contradicted key Roman qualities of military valor and civic devotion and so brought the empire's fall.

A number of 20th-century historians have preferred to examine Rome's moral decline, the growing self-indulgence and pleasure-seeking of the aristocracy and the urban masses, that led them to accept forms of government in which they no longer participated, caused them to turn away from a willingness to serve in the army, and removed them from concern about the common good. This argument is interesting because it corresponds to some undeniable changes in the culture of the later Roman Empire. It also has won attention because of anxieties contemporary Westerners have about their own society—too materialistic, too drawn to sexual indulgence, too dominated by the tastes of the masses. Analogy—that is, real or imagined similarities between situations such that a historical phenomenon is seen to correspond to a current one and vice versa—plays a big role in the moral decline concern.

Both the religious and moral decline arguments point to factors that in principle might have been addressed before the Roman Empire fell. A society deteriorating morally might pull itself together, accept a sterner set of virtues, and recover its earlier vigor. Those who point to analogies between Roman decay and Western self-indulgence may of course hope that Westerners might regain earlier self-control and reverse their presumed decline.

Another approach to the problem of decline, however, argues that it is almost inevitable. Civilizations, like individual humans, go through a period of vigor, reach the mature height of their powers, but then inevitably begin to lose their grip and deteriorate. At the civilization level this means that governments become stultified, with officials bent on protecting their position rather than seeking new ways to do things; that aristocracies, once bent on military glory and willing to endure hardships in its quest, become soft and leave the fighting to others; that territories expand farther than a society can really control, leaving supply routes and armaments overextended and vulnerable to attack. An American diplomatic historian has recently argued that this last process of overextension that reduces internal economic vitality through its sheer costliness occurred not only with Rome, but with 19th-century Britain and, now, the United States and the Soviet Union.

World history certainly lends itself to a search for patterns in the life cycles of civilizations. But it also generates some warnings. Civilizational decline does not occur in the same ways in all cases. It does seem true that many civilizations go through periods of confusion, when leadership worsens and new troubles ensue. The result, however, is not necessarily the death of a civilization, but rather a period of regrouping after which the civilization may re-emerge with a new combination of tradition and innovation. Rome's fall, after all, was unusual at the end of the classical era, and really occurred only in the western portion of the empire. Eastern Rome remained highly civilized and successful. China and India, though not unchanged by the decline of the great classical empires, did not suffer a full loss of achievement and certainly did not perish as civilizations. So the question of decline needs to be phrased carefully, with awareness of the diverse examples world history yields.

Possibly some special features of Western Rome made it an exceptional case. The advent of new epidemic diseases, producing population loss and economic decline, may have underlain the peculiar experience of the Western Roman Empire. Certainly relatively sparse populations left the Roman Empire far more vulnerable than China, India, or even the eastern Mediterranean to the disruptive effects of relatively small numbers of outside invaders. Dense populations, undiminished by new epidemics, help explain the resiliency of Chinese and Indian cultures, which could be disrupted but not destroyed by outside attack.

Many people seek laws in history. Perhaps there are some laws, or at least high probabilities, that argue for civilizations experiencing some normal growing phases which will produce serious weaknesses in the course of time. But world history also complicates many of the attempts that have been made to find laws, because so much depends on the characteristics of each particular society. Predictable patterns, such as inevitable rises and falls, are hard to find. Western historians, long mesmerized by the undeniable collapse of Rome and perhaps uncomfortable with some of the changes they see in their own society, may sometimes have generalized too widely from a single case.

Questions: How great a role did moral decline play in the collapse of the classical empires? What historical "laws" accurately describe what happened not only in Rome but in Gupta India and Han China? Why can it be argued that the eastern part of the Roman Empire did not decline?

DEVELOPMENT AND SPREAD OF WORLD RELIGIONS

The decline of the classical empires contributed several ingredients to the spread of what turned out to be the great world religions. Previously, most religion had been regional. Buddhism, spreading through India at various points in the classical period, could embrace a whole subcontinent. As Hinduism evolved from the Brahman religion, it did the same and also spread to a few other areas of Indian commerical influence in Southeast Asia. Christi-

anity showed an ability to win a growing minority in the Roman Empire and at a few points beyond its borders, in the Middle East and North Africa.

The waning of the great empires so confused and reshuffled geographical boundaries, from the Mediterranean to the Pacific, that the regional confines of religion were modified more dramatically. The same political decline encouraged people to turn to more spiritual institutions and rewards. The result was one of the world's key periods in which beliefs shifted and cultural allegiances took on new territorial patterns. Even religions still essentially regional, such as Daoism in China and Hinduism in India, worked to win new levels of active popular adherence. Just as the 5th century B.C. had clustered the origins of major philosophical systems for the educated elites in China and the Mediterranean, so the period A.D. 200–700 grouped fundamental changes in religious alignments.

CHRISTIANITY AND BUDDHISM COMPARED

As during the period of chaos in China, Rome's decline brought vital new religious influences to societies around the Mediterranean. Christianity moved westward from its original center in the Middle East, just as in Asia, Buddhism was spreading east from India. Though initially less significant then Buddhism in terms of numbers of converts, Christianity would ultimately prove to be one of the two largest world faiths. It would play a direct role in the formation of two postclassical civilizations, those of eastern and western Europe.

Christianity resembled Buddhism in important ways. It could stress the unimportance of things of this world, urging the centrality of people's spiritual destiny and the focus on divinity. Not surprisingly, Christianity, like Buddhism, produced an important monastic movement, in which especially holy individuals grouped to live a spiritual life and serve their religion through their sanctity. Christianity resembled the version of Buddhism that spread to China (and later Korea and Japan) by stressing the possibility of an afterlife and the role that holy leaders could play in helping to attain it.

The Chinese version of Buddhism, called Mahayana or the Greater Vehicle, placed considerable emphasis on Buddha as god or savior. Statues of the Buddha as god violated earlier Buddhist hostility to religious images, but they served to emphasize the religion as a channel of salvation. Well-organized temples, with priests and rituals, also helped bring religious solace to ordinary people in East Asia. The idea developed also that Buddhist holy men, or *bodhisattvas*, built up spiritual merits such that their prayers, even after death, could aid people and allow them to achieve some reflected holiness. Christianity in many respects moved in similar directions. It too came to emphasize salvation, with well-organized rituals designed to promote its achievement. Religious images, though contrary to Jewish beliefs against idol-worship, helped focus popular belief in most versions of Christianity. Holy men, sometimes granted the title *saint* after their death, were revered not only as models but also because their spiritual attainments could lend merit to the strivings of more ordinary folk. The broad similarities between Christianity and the evolving Buddhism of East Asia remind us of the common processes apparently at work as new religions spread amid the ruins of great empires.

Yet Christianity had a flavor of its own. More than any of the forms of Buddhism, it came to place great emphasis on church organization and structure, copying the example of the Roman Empire. It also placed greater value on missionary activity and widespread conversions, believing that error must be actively combated in God's name. More perhaps than any other major religion, certainly more than contemplative and tolerant Buddhism, Christianity stressed its possession of exclusive truth and its intolerance of competing beliefs. Such fierce confidence was not the least of the reasons for the new religion's success. The common dynamic and chronology shared by Christianity and spreading Buddhism suggest a similar process at work, as ordinary people sought a well-organized spiritual outlet different from traditional animism, more focused on otherworldly salvation. Christianity must also be understood, however, in the particular context of earlier Mediterranean religious traditions and the declining Roman Empire. Its emphasis on doctrines and exclusive loyalty differentiated it from the more tranquil religions of eastern and southern Asia, India as well as China, where a larger variety of beliefs and practices could be combined with Buddhism or Hinduism.

Christianity began, as was discussed in Chapter 8, as part of a Jewish reform movement. During the two centuries before the birth of Christ many insurgent Jews had preached the coming of a Messiah, or savior, who would bring a Last Judgment on humankind. Many reformed Jews also stressed the possibility of a life after death for the virtuous, which was a new element in Judaism. Jesus of Nazareth, believed by Christians to be the son of God sent to earth to live a sinless life so that the sacrifice of his body on the cross would redeem human sin, crystallized this radical reform movement. Combining extraordinary gentleness of spirit and great charisma, Jesus preached widely in Israel and gathered a group of loyal disciples around him. Initially, there seems to have been no intent to found a new religion. After Jesus's crucifixion, the disciples expected his imminent return and with it the end of the world. Only gradually when the Second Coming did not transpire, did the disciples begin to fan out and, through preaching, pick up growing numbers of supporters in various parts of the Roman Empire.

The message of Jesus and his disciples seemed clear: There was a single God, who loved humankind despite earthly sin. A virtuous life should be dedicated to the worship of God and fellowship among other believers; worldly concerns were secondary, and a life of poverty might be most conducive to holiness. God sent Jesus, called "Christ" from the Greek word Christos for "God's anointed," to preach his holy word and through his sacrifice to prepare for the possibility of wider attainment of an afterlife of heavenly communion with God. Belief, good works, and discipline of fleshly concerns would lead toward heaven; rituals, such as commemorating Christ's Last Supper with wine and bread, would promote the same goal.

This message spread at an opportune time. The official religion of the Greeks and Romans had long seemed rather sterile, particularly to many of the poor. The Christian emphasis on the beauty of poverty and the spiritual equality of all people, plus the fervor of the early Christians and the satisfying rituals they provided, gained growing attention. The wide reach of the Roman Empire made it relatively easy for Christian missionaries to travel extensively in Europe and the Middle East and spread the new word. Then, when conditions began to deteriorate in the empire, the solace of this otherworldly religion won even wider response.

The adjustments affected by early Christian leaders maximized their conversions. Under the guidance of Paul, Christians began to see themselves as part of a new religion rather than a Jewish reform movement, and they welcomed non-Jewish converts. Paul also encouraged more formal organization in the new church, with local groups selecting elders to govern them; soon, a single leader, or bishop, was appointed for each major city. This structure paralleled the provincial government of the empire. Finally, Christian doctrine became increasingly organized, as the writings of several disciples and others were collected into what became the New Testament of the Christian Bible.

CHRISTIANITY GAINS GROUND

During the first three centuries after Christ, the new religion competed among a number of Eastern mystery religions. It also faced, as we have seen, periodic persecution from the normally tolerant imperial government. Even so, by the time Constantine converted to the religion and accepted it as a legitimate faith, Christianity had won perhaps 10 percent of the empire's population. One convert was Constantine's mother, who visited the Holy Land and founded many churches there. Constantine's tolerant favor brought some new troubles to Christianity, particularly some interference by the state in matters of doctrine. But it became much easier to spread Christianity with official favor. Christian writers began to claim that both church and empire were works of God. At the same time continued deterioration of the empire added to the motives to join this amazingly successful new church. In the eastern Mediterranean, where imperial rule remained strong, state control of the church became a way of life. But in the west, where conditions were far more chaotic, bishops had a freer hand. A centralized church organization under the leadership of the bishop of Rome, called "Pope" from the word *papa*, or father, gave the Western church unusual strength and independence.

By the time Rome collapsed, Christianity thus had demonstrated immense spiritual power and possessed a solid organization, though one that differed from east to west. The new church faced a number of controversies over doctrine but managed to promote certain standard beliefs as against several heresies. A key tenet involved a complex doctrine of the Trinity, which held that the one God had three persons, the Father, the Son (Christ), and the Holy Ghost. In A.D. 325 a church council met in Nicaea, under imperial sponsorship, to debate a doctrine known as Arianism, which argued that Christ was divine but not of the same nature as God the Father. Ruling against Arianism, the resultant Nicene Creed insisted on the shared Godhead of all three parts of the Trinity. An important if complex decision in itself, the council also showed how important unified doctrine was to Christianity, in contrast to the greater toleration of diversity in Hinduism and Buddhism. Experience in fighting heresies promoted Christian interest in defending a single belief and strengthened its intolerance for any competing doctrine or faith.

Early Christianity also produced an important formal theology, through formative writers such as Augustine. This theology incorporated many elements of classical philosophy with Christian belief, and helped the church gain respectability among intellectuals. Theologians like Augustine grappled with such problems as freedom of the will: If God is all-powerful, can mere human beings have free will? And if not, how can human beings be justly punished for sin? By working out these issues in elaborate doctrine, the early theologians, or church fathers, provided an important role for formal, rational thought in a religion that continued to emphasize the primary importance of faith.

This painting by Hieronymous Bosch is of St. Jerome, who fled to the desert to avoid temptation. Christian monasticism institutionalized this renunciation of the world but also disciplined it toward socially useful works.

Like all successful religions, Christianity combined a number of appeals. It offered blind devotion to an all-powerful God. One church father, denying the validity of human thought, simply stated, "I believe because it is absurd." But Christianity also developed its own complex and fascinating intellectual system for those so inclined. Mystical holy men and women flourished under Christian banners, particularly in the Middle East. In the west soon after the empire's collapse, this impulse was partially disciplined through the institution of monasticism, which gained ground in Italy under Benedict of Nursia early in the 6th century. Benedict started a monastery to demonstrate the true holy life to Italian peasants in a region still

Conversion of kings, such as Clovis, king of the Franks, helped inspire wider conversions, while giving churchmen some symbolic power over the state.

(to Benedict's horror) practicing the worship of the sun-god Apollo. The Benedictine Rule, which soon spread to many other monasteries and convents, urged a disciplined life with prayer and spiritual excitement alternating with hard work in agriculture and in study. Monastic movements also developed in the eastern empires, in Greece and Turkey, and also in Egypt. Eastern monasticism was organized by St. Basil in the 4th century.

Thus Christianity attempted to encourage but also discipline intense piety, and to avoid a complete gulf between the lives of saintly men and women and the spiritual concerns of ordinary people. Christianity's success and organizational strength obviously appealed to political leaders. But the new religion never became the creature of the upper classes alone, as its popular message of ritual and salvation continued to draw the poor. Rather like Hinduism in India, Christianity provided some religious unity among different social groups. There was even a special interest for women. Christianity did not create equality among men and women, but it did preach the equal importance of women's and men's souls; and it encouraged men and women to worship together, unlike many other faiths.

Christianity promoted a new culture among those won to its banners. The rituals, the otherworldly emphasis, the interest in spiritual equality—these were far different from the central themes of classical Mediterranean civilization. Christianity modified classical beliefs in the central importance of the state and political loyalties. Though Christians accepted the state, they did not put it first. Christianity also worked against other classical institutions, such as slavery, in the name of brotherhood (though later Christians would accept slavery in other contexts). Christianity may have fostered a greater respectability for disciplined work than had been current in the aristocratic ethic of Mediterranean civilization, particularly through the values promoted by Western monasticism.

Certainly, Christianity sought some changes in classical culture, including greater emphasis on sexual restraint, beyond its central religious message. But Christianity preserved important classical values in addition to the interest in solid organization and some of the themes of classical philosophy. Church buildings in western Europe retained Roman architectural styles, though often with greater simplicity if only because of the poverty of the later empire and subsequent Germanic states. Latin remained the language of the church in the West, Greek the language of most Christians in the eastern Mediterranean. Monasticism played an immensely valuable role in preserving classical as well as Christian learning through the patient librarianship of the monks.

THE EMERGING RELIGIOUS MAP

When the Roman Empire fell, Christian history was still in its infancy. The Western church would soon spread its missionary zeal to northern Europe, and the Eastern church would reach into the Slavic lands of the Balkans and Russia. But Christianity was already established as a significant world religion—one of the few ever generated. A world religion is defined by unusual durability and drawing power and by a complexity that can win adherence from many different kinds of people. Major world religions, such as Christianity and Buddhism, show some ability to cut across different cultures, to win converts in a wide geographic area and amid considerable diversity.

One final world religion remained to enter the lists. Islam, launched in A.D. 610, would initially surpass Christianity in geographical extent and has remained Christianity's most tenacious rival. With Islam added, the roster of world religions was essentially complete. Changes would follow, but no totally new religion of major significance arose—unless one counts some of the secular faiths, such as communism, that have appeared in the past century. The centuries after the rise of Christianity, the spread of Buddhism, and the inception of Islam would see the conversion of most of the civilized world to one or another of the great faiths, producing a religious map that, in Europe and Asia and even parts of Africa, would not alter greatly until our own time. Table 11.1 shows the distribution of religions in the world today.

The spread of major religions—Hinduism in India, Buddhism in East and Southeast Asia, a more popular Daoism in China, Christianity in Europe and parts of the Mediterranean world, and ultimately Islam—was a vital result of the changes in the classical civilizations brought on by attack and decay. Despite the important diversity among these great religions, which included fierce mutual hatreds, particularly between Christian and Muslim, the overall development suggests that important basic currents could run through the civilized world, crossing political and cultural borders. Common difficulties, including invading forces that pressed out from central Asia and contagious epidemics that knew no boundaries, help explain

TABLE 11.1

Religions and Their Distribution in the World Today

Religion	Distribution*
Christianity	995 million
Roman Catholic	(580 million)
Protestant	(340 million)
Eastern Orthodox	(75 million)
Islam	600 million
Hinduism	480 million
Buddhism	255 million
Shintoism	57 million
Daoism	31 million
Judaism	14 million

*Figures for several religions have been reduced over the past 50 years by the impact of communism in Eastern Europe and parts of Asia.

parallel changes in separate civilizations. Contacts among the societies through trade and travel also provided common bonds. Chinese travelers learned of Buddhism through trading expeditions to India. Trade and diffusion of artistic styles linked the Mediterranean world to the Middle East and India.

There was a world framework, in other words, that affected the separate currents of the major civilizations. The new religions brought to each of the major civilizations and other parts of the world a greater interest in speculation about spiritual matters and a greater tendency to focus on a single basic divinity instead of a multitude of gods. Animist beliefs and practices continued to flourish as part of popular Hinduism and popular Daoism, and they were not entirely displaced among ordinary people who converted to Christianity, Buddhism, or Islam. But the new religious surge reduced the hold of literal animism in much of Asia and Europe, and this too was an important development across boundaries.

The development or spread of the major world religions—which so clearly related to the process of decline in the great empires, while depending on the communication channels these same empires had created—constituted a major change at a world-historical level. Obviously, some regions were still exempt: the great religions had yet to touch the Americas or parts of Africa and central Asia, and they spread only gradually northward in Europe. Obviously also, each religion had its own flavor; the idea of common process must not be exaggerated. And even where the new religions spread, they often merged with important animist elements. Thus Islam long would leave rural beliefs intact, concentrating on urban religious practice; Christianity often compromised with animist beliefs in magic and in ritual properties of natural objects, such as mistletoe or the bones of saints.

Nevertheless, the spread of the great religions did subject many people in many different societies to a tendency to shift beliefs away from age-old adherence to the idea of a host of divine spirits in nature, to a great concentration on a powerful, single divine force and, often, the spirituality attendant on new hopes for an afterlife. This change reflected the religious needs of people living amid new political uncertainties. The great religions could provide solace, and they also helped create new bonds of cohesion in societies where strictly political ties were loosening. Not only Hindu civilization, but also Christianity and Islam provided shared beliefs that could transcend divided, bickering political units.

The great religions could facilitate international trade, for they did not depend on local customs but on an ever-present God as organizer of all nature or at least a coherent divine order; successful trade could, in turn, help spread the new religions. Despite different ideas, the new religions also tended to promote more abstract scholarship than animistic religions had done, as part of defining a less tangible but more orderly divine presence. The characteristics of world religions in gradually challenging animism were very general, but they did suggest some parallel basic processes occurring in various parts of Asia, Europe, and Africa in the aftermath of the great classical empires.

CONCLUSION

IN THE WAKE OF DECLINE AND FALL

By A.D. 600 the major civilizations looked much different from the classical world at its height, and many of the differences would never be erased. The results of classical decline showed, obviously, in the new belief patterns, in the opportunities created for an amazing set of shifts in religious allegiance. They showed also in important revisions of the civilization map and in some related shifts in characteristic political styles.

The first geographical change resulted from the differential effects of classical decline: Some areas, as we have seen, altered far more than others. China proved unique in its ability to recapture so many classical ingredients. China and India shared, in contrast to the Mediterranean, an ability to maintain substantial cultural cohesion, based on widespread beliefs as well as, in China's case, restored politics. Traditional continuities would as a result play a more obvious role in eastern and southern Asia than in western Asia and Europe, though this fact resulted in part from the greater cultural homogenization achieved even earlier. Today, Indian and Chinese civilizations remain located in essentially the same places where they had taken root by late classical times, and at least until quite recent developments they still abundantly reflected the classical heritage: India in the caste system and an otherworldly cultural tone, China in Confucian beliefs and a fascination with a strong, bureaucratic state.

The case was quite different in the Mediterranean zone. The Roman Empire split asunder without repair, in part because it had not been able to spread shared beliefs very widely. China and India developed an ability to change without deep disruption, whereas the diverse heirs of Rome would oscillate, often, between innovative dynamism and sheer confusion. Classical Mediterranean civilization left a very real heritage, but, in part because geographical unity was lost, this heritage was used by successor civilizations far more selectively, with considerably more new (and diverse) ingredients than was true in eastern or southern Asia.

The geographical changes resulting from classical decline also promoted outreach to new areas. Powerful civilization centers, once they recovered from internal confusion and invasion, tended to reach out for new areas of influence, and given the larger changes in the geography of civilizations this often prompted them to look to areas not previously involved in the civilizational orbit. Thus China, once it rebounded from the centuries of chaos, extended new levels of influence to Vietnam, Korea, and even Japan. Also, regional states in southern India, already molded in a seagoing tradition and unable to expand northward because of the confusion in the upper part of the subcontinent, briefly increased their activities in Southeast Asia.

The division of the Mediterranean world prompted still more general diffusion effects. The Byzantine Empire, regarding itself as Rome's heir but blocked from recovering Rome's territory (particularly because of the powerful Arab presence in most of the eastern Mediterranean and north Africa), pushed its influence northward into the vast Slavic lands. The Arab Empire, less interested or less able than Rome to press into Europe beyond Spain and southern Italy, turned not only to some attacks on India and incursions into central Asia, but also to a wider array of contacts with Africa below the Sahara than Rome had ever developed. Finally, the clearest organizational heir to Rome in the West, the Catholic church, unable because of Byzantine and Arab power to control most previous imperial territory religiously, itself turned northward, sending missions that brought civilization to the fierce peoples of northwestern Europe.

Thus civilization fanned out. The strongest centers, those with the most sophisticated cultures and most elaborate political forms—including new or revived empires—remained located where the classical civilizations had taken full root before: China, India, the Middle East, North Africa, and southeastern Europe. But a new zone began to be created quite soon after the end of the classical period, as a result of new contacts and explicit missionary efforts; it embraced Japan, newly involved sections of Southeast Asia, northern Europe (both east and west) and parts of sub-Saharan Africa. This extension of civilization resulted directly from the tensions produced by the remaking of the classical map and from new forces such as the great missionary religions.

The centuries of transition at the end of the classical age must thus be seen not simply in terms of decline and confusion, though this element was definitely present, but in terms of a considerable reshuffling of peoples, boundaries, and beliefs that would soon give rise to a new period in world history. Elements of the classical era were irretrievably lost, particularly Mediterranean unity and, in western Europe and in India, the ability to form durable empires. In a few cases—again, most notably in western Europe—the levels of economic and cultural activity deteriorated for some centuries. Elsewhere, however, key features of civilization proved extremely resilient, even as new beliefs or boundaries were added to the mix; the ability to extend civilization's range to new regions was one sign of this ongoing vitality. Redefinition and realignment formed the key challenge for most of the civilized world in the new period beginning to take shape by the 6th century.

FURTHER READINGS

The fall of the Roman Empire has generated rich and interesting debate. For recent interpretations and discussion of earlier views, see A. H. M. Jones's *The Decline of the Ancient World* (1966); J. Vogt's *The Decline of Rome* (1965); F. W. Walbank's *The Awful Revolution—The Decline of the Roman Empire in the West* (1960).

On India and China in decline, worthwhile sources include R. Thaper's *History of India*, vol. I, (1966); R. C. Majumdar, ed., *The Classical Age* (1966); Raymond Dawson's *Imperial China* (1972); J. A. Harrison's *The Chinese Empire* (1972). See also Twitchett and Fairbanks, eds., *The Cambridge History of China*, vol. 3, part I, (1979).

On the role of disease in imperial decline, W. McNeill's *Plagues and Peoples* (1977) is provocative and useful.

For the rise and spread of new religions, a good introduction is Geoffrey Parinder, ed., *World Religions* (1971); see also Lewis M. Hopke's *Religions of the World* (1983) and Jamail Ragi al Farugi, ed., *Historical Atlas of the Religions of the World* (1974). On Hinduism, see N. C. Chandhuri's *Hinduism, A Religion to Live By* (1979); see also C. Eliot's *Hinduism and Buddhism* (1954). Two good studies of Buddhism are C. Humphreys's *Buddhism* (1962) and A. F. Wright's *Buddhism in Chinese History* (1959). Christianity's spread is the subject of S. Renko's *Pagan Rome and the Early Christians* (1986) and M. Hengel's *Acts and the History of Earliest Christianity* (1986). Important special topics are covered in J. Bowker's *Problems of Suffering in Religions of the World* (1975), a fascinating comparative effort; A. Sharma, ed., *Women in World Religions* (1987); and on Christianity, B. Witherington's *Women in the Earliest Churches* (1988).

527–565 Justinian,
Eastern Roman
(Byzantine) emperor

618–907 Tang dynasty

610–613 Origins of Islam

711 First Islamic attack in India

960–1127 Song dynasty (China)

864 Cyril and Methodius missionaries in eastern Europe

1055 Seljuk
Turks con-
trol Abbasid
caliphate

878 Last Japanese embassy to Chinn

570–632 Muhammad

661–750 Ummayad Caliphate

800–814 Charlemagne Empire in western Europe

634–750 Arab invasions in Middle
East; spread of Islam in North Africa

777 Independent Islamic kingdoms begin in North Africa

980–1015 Conversion of Vladimir I of Russia

968 Tula established by Toltecs (Mesoamerica)

589–618 Sui dynasty (China)

718 Byzantines defeat Arab attack on Constantinople

750 Abbasid caliphate

1000 Ghana Empire at its height (Africa)

1054 Schism between
Eastern and Western
Christianity

c. 855 Russian kingdom around Kiev

668 Korea becomes independent from China

Ptolemy, an astronomer, mathematician, and geographer, constructed this map and many others during the 2d century. He compiled his maps in a guide of eight books that also explained map construction.

1150–1350 Spread of Gothic style; scholasticism in western Europe

1066 Norman conquest of England; rise of feudal monarchy in western Europe

1231–1392 Mongols rule Korea

1150 Disintegration of Toltec Empire

1258 Capture of Baghdad by Mongols; end of Abbasid caliphate

1236 Capture of Russia by Mongols

1200 Rise of empire of Mali

c. 1100 Invention of explosive powder (China)

1260 Death of Sundiata

1206 Delhi sultanate in India

1096–1099 First Christian Crusade to Palestine

1185–1333 Kamakura Shogunate (Japan)

1265 First English parliament

1392–1910 Yi dynasty (Korea)

1320–1340 Bubonic plague breaks out in Gobi desert and spreads to other parts of Asia

1453 Turks capture Constantinople; end of Byzantine Empire

1405–1433 Chinese trading expeditions

1400 End of Polynesian expeditions

1279–1368 Mongol Empire in China

1439 Portugal acquires Azores

1325 Rise of Aztec Empire

1290s Islam begins to spread to Southeast Asia

1350 Rise of Incas (Andes)

1471–1493 Peak of Inca Empire

1338–1453 Hundred Years' War in Europe

1320s Europeans first use cannon in war

PART

3

The Postclassical Era

The next ten chapters concentrate primarily on the time period that runs from the 5th to the 15th century A.D., or from about 450 to about 1450. Most of the individual chapters deal with specific civilizations, for there were many changes occurring in old civilization centers (in the aftermath of the decline of the great classical empires) and in newer ones. Before turning to individual cases, however, it is vital to get a sense of some overall patterns in this thousand-year period, for a number of developments cut across single civilization boundaries. The postclassical period witnessed the emergence of an international framework, so that instead of the parallelisms and tentative contacts among individual civilizations that described the classical period, a genuine world-historical dynamic was taking shape.

Ironically, there is no widely accepted label for the millennium in world history after the fall of the classical empires. Historians have disagreed about the main dynamics of the period. One source of confusion involves the disparity between what was going on in Western civilization and what was going on in the world as a whole. In Western history this period is called the Middle Ages, and it denotes a time of recovery from the collapse of Rome's Western Empire based among other things on the spread of Christianity and the power of the Catholic church. In the early part of the Middle Ages, the West was at a low ebb, with weak political structures and scant commercial activity; this means that the Middle Ages as a whole can be seen as a somewhat complicated interlude between the higher ground of classical Rome and a new period of expansion called the Renaissance. This characterization is not entirely accurate for Western history, and it certainly is misleading for world history as a whole.

Many civilizations experienced not a halting recovery, but a brilliant period of development during the postclassical centuries; thus the idea of a "middle ages" between high points simply does not fit.

A more general reason for confusion about the nature of the postclassical era involves the tension between the undeniable spread of civilization to new areas, which tended to divide the world into separate units, and the linkage that also developed among many civilizations. Instead of a single, if diverse, Mediterranean civilization, for example, the Mediterranean world split into three segments: the Middle East and North Africa, eastern Europe and what is now Turkey, and western Europe. Yet all three of these now distinct areas were linked through economic, cultural, and sometimes military contacts, and not only with each other but with other parts of Asia and Africa. The tension between the proliferation of separate civilization areas and the network of world contacts is a vital characteristic of the postclassical period, and we will come back to it. Rather than advancing a jazzy label for the period 450–1450, the term *postclassical* will be used, for the key point is not the name but a sense in advance of what the period entailed.

THE NATURE OF THE POSTCLASSICAL PERIOD

As with the classical period, there are two ways to define the postclassical age: first, in terms of what events opened and closed it, and second in terms of coherent trends that lay between the overture and finale.

The stage for the postclassical era was set by the same developments that ended its predecessor: the collapse of the Roman Empire and thus the end of Mediterranean unity, and the decline of classical empires in Asia. The 5th century saw most of these developments draw together, though India's full transition with the fall of the Guptas occurred slightly later and China's period of chaos occurred a bit earlier. Capped by invasions of nomadic peoples, the classical decline produced huge changes in the world's civilizational map.

The end of the postclassical era was heralded by another set of invasions from central Asia, even more powerful than the surge of the Huns that had helped close the classical period. During the 13th and 14th centuries Mongol invaders poured through much of Asia and eastern Europe, ending or altering a host of specific governments and also encouraging new kinds of exchanges across civilization bor-

The Postclassical World Takes Shape, about A.D. 900

The Postclassical World in Transition, About A.D. 1400

ders, thanks to the vast if brief unity the Mongols produced in much of the civilized world. By 1400 much of Asia was beginning to recover from the Mongol onslaught, but a series of new empires and expansions was taking shape, including the beginning of the West's explorations into the wider world. These developments spanned about two centuries from the early 13th to the mid-15th century; as before, the end of a world history period was not an overnight affair. The postclassical period closes, then, with Mongol invasions and subsequent realignments. The realignments included the collapse of two key political units in the Middle East—the Arab caliphate and the Byzantine Empire—as well as the advent of a new empire under the Ottoman Turks, new stirrings in Russia, and the first phases of the West's explosion into the mainstream of world history. By about 1450 the emergence of new empires and the beginnings of Europe's global expansion provide clear evidence of a shift to another phase of world development.

The postclassical period thus opened with the collapse of big empires and ended with the collapse of others more recently formed. Identifying the beginning and end of the period, however, is far less important for the postclassical era than grasping the great trends that lie in between, and

gives character and considerable consistency to the period itself. Within this span, four overarching developments define the postclassical centuries, as they summarize key international factors amid the trends of individual societies. The expanding influence of the Arabs and Islam, within their Middle Eastern base and well beyond, is one basic feature. The sheer spread of civilization to additional regions of the world is another. A widespread trend toward a shift in basic belief systems, from animism to one of several great world religions, is a third. Finally, the development of a world network, consisting of increasingly regular and influential relations among many of the individual civilizations, constitutes the fourth general theme. This short list of items might be explained in slightly greater detail, and then their complex mutual relationships assessed.

THE RISE OF ISLAM

Soon after the period began, a "leading civilization" emerged in terms of its expansionist capacity and ability to influence other civilizations. Islamic civilization, initially spread by the Arabs, spearheaded the creation of a new empire in the Middle East and North Africa as well as important political initiatives in India, southern Europe, and central Asia. Its missionary outreach brought conversions to Islam over other parts of Africa and Asia. Arab commerce spread through the Indian Ocean to the western Pacific, down the east coast of Africa, and across the Sahara Desert. In the classical period, the three major civilization areas had been roughly balanced in dynamism, though India's outreach was particularly impressive. The postclassical era reshuffled the balance of power and created a definite world leader. Correspondingly, the decline of the Islamic imperial system was one of the key features leading to the end of this period and the emergence of a new era in world history.

THE EXPANSION OF CIVILIZATION

In the postclassical era civilization began to spread geographically, covering many parts of the world not previously embraced by this system of social organization. These were the centuries, for example, when the structures of civilization, including great regional trading kingdoms, spread across sub-Saharan Africa, in contrast to the previous concentration in a few centers such as the Upper Nile River basin. Civilization also spread widely in northern Europe, both east and west, and became more fully established in Japan. The zones of civilization expanded in the Americas, while Polynesian culture in the Pacific fanned out to include important new areas. The "civilization map" of the world was much larger in 1450 than it had been a thousand years before. At least eight diverse areas command attention during the postclassical era: the Middle East and North Africa; India; China and East Asia; eastern Europe; western Europe; sub-Saharan Africa; Southeast Asia (where various influences from other civilizations intermingled); and the Americas.

THE WORLD RELIGIONS

The postclassical era was also defined by the spread of major religions across much of Asia, Europe, and Africa. This process had begun in the later phases of the classical era, but it defined the new period far more clearly. While Hinduism took fuller shape as the majority religion in India and a few pockets in Southeast Asia, Buddhism spread to China and other parts of central and East Asia, including Japan, and also to much of Southeast Asia. Islam ran across the Middle East and North Africa and became an important minority religion in India, western China, and parts of sub-Saharan Africa. It also began to make inroads in Southeast Asia toward the end of the period. Finally, Christianity spread northward in Europe, both east and

west. The major world religions differed widely in many respects, but they did bring a new focus on issues of spirituality and an afterlife, and a new concentration on an overarching divine force. Relatedly, they shared an ability to extend beyond local cultures and win the adherence of diverse peoples to a core of beliefs and rituals. The world religions competed, with increasing success although amid many compromises, with the previous traditions of popular belief, particularly with animism and, in many areas, polytheism.

The postclassical era, in other words, saw widespread and quite fundamental shifts in religious belief and practices that encompassed elites and ordinary people alike. In many cases this huge change brought new institutions to the fore, such as the leading Christian churches, Buddhist monasteries, or the religious and legal experts of Islam. People began to move away from a belief in a multiplicity of nature spirits or gods, activating various forces of nature, and toward a greater concentration on an overriding divinity or single supernatural force. This involved an increase in abstraction in that the universe now came to be envisaged as part of a large divine plan. Various devices were used to modify this abstraction, thus making it more accessible to the ordinary populace. Some religions stressed intermediaries between humanity and divinity, including the powers of holy people and some continued beliefs in magical forces.

Nevertheless, an understanding of the postclassical era as one of the key turning points in the world history of culture allows us to focus on one of the central processes of this age. Pressed by political change and confusion after the fall of the classical empires, many people looked for new religious structure. Other people were converted to one of the new religions by the persuasion of missionaries—the greatest world religions (Islam, Christianity, and Buddhism) were active missionary faiths—and by the powerful example of political and commercial splendor in the seats of the new religious authority. Thus, Russia moved toward Christianity in part because of its leaders' awe of the civilized power of the Byzantine Empire and in part because of missionary preachments, while Islam won converts through a combination of missionary zeal and the political and commercial strength of the Arab Empire. A growth in international trade also encouraged religious change, for local gods made less sense to people who exchanged goods with diverse and distant areas. This combination of forces operated in a common direction in otherwise very different civilizations. The result was no agreement on belief—several of the new religions competed fiercely, with mutual detestation—but a vital underlying pattern nonetheless.

In the early phases of the classical period—notably, during the 5th and 4th centuries B.C.—an important pattern of cultural change had emerged in Greece, India, and China. Each civilization set some basic intellectual frameworks through the activities of such thinkers as the Buddha, Socrates, Confucius, and their various followers. Each great civilization reached a stage of needing some integrating beliefs.

The postclassical spread of world religions was a transformation of beliefs of a somewhat different sort. Though less tidy in that only one of the religions—Islam—was new at this point, it was even more important because of the large numbers of people affected through conversion. The world religions with their expansive understanding of the divine order—and in the case of Christianity and Islam, their strong emphasis on monotheism—made greater inroads into traditional popular beliefs, particularly animism, than the great thinkers of the classical world had done. Furthermore, the world religions not only cut across some civilization lines—as the earlier intellectual systems had not done—but also responded to common causes in the need various people felt in Asia, Europe, and North Africa for a new spiritual framework given the collapse of political units at the end of the classical age. The spread of religions, in other words, was neither coincidence nor accident; it flowed from some common events and was then enhanced by the extension of international contacts through trade and missionary activity.

THE WORLD NETWORK

The fourth major characteristic of the postclassical period, emerging with great force by around A.D. 1000, was ultimately the most important of all. An increasing level of interchange developed among the major civilizations of Asia, Europe, and parts of Africa. International trade grew, particularly thanks to the surge of Arab commerce but also as a result of continued activity by Indian merchants, Chinese exchanges with other parts of eastern and Southeast Asia, the development of new north-south trading connections in both eastern and western Europe, and the rise of African merchant routes along the eastern coast and overland through the Sahara. With growing trade and periodic military encounters, as civilizations new and old redefined their boundaries, other kinds of exchanges occurred across civilizations. Technology spread. Thus knowledge of paper, developed earlier in China, was gained by Muslim troops fighting on China's western border in the 9th century. Paper production in the Middle East resulted, and as western Europeans gained new links with this region through trade and religious wars, they learned of the new

product as well. The first European paper manufacture was set up in Italy in the 13th century. Technological dissemination of this sort was hardly speedy, but it did occur at a more rapid pace than with previous innovations. Cultural exchange was another vital source of contact. Religious ideas spread from India to China and thence to Japan, Korea, and Indochina; they spread from the Middle East to Africa and many parts of Asia. This was part of the great missionary wave. But other kinds of ideas spread as well. Arabs gained knowledge of Indian mathematics, including the number system; later in the period, West Europeans began to learn Arab mathematics, including the same number system, and they formed a more elaborate philosophy by using and reacting to Arab thought.

Defining the world network is not easy; there are no clear statistical measurements, no trenchant comments by farsighted contemporary observers. The exchange of technologies, such as papermaking, is a useful preliminary indication. Another measurement directly compares the world network as of about 1300 with the more limited contacts of the classical era. Affluent Romans under the empire had bought small amounts of silk cloth made in China and transported over the silk road, but the Romans did not know from where the silk came, and they had scant influence over its delivery. International trade was limited and it passed through a variety of groups, as it moved from region to region. In contrast, wealthy Westerners in 1300 bought silks and other goods from Asia in larger quantities and with a fair idea of from where they came. They also could identify key agents of international trade, notably Arab merchants. Further, Western leaders were beginning to wish they could control the source of the trade, which they would soon be able to do thanks to improved mapmaking pioneered by the Arabs, navigational techniques devised by the Chinese and transmitted via the Arabs, and shipbuilding and artillery innovations developed in the West. The world network was tightening. World trade continued to involve luxury products for the most part, but the volume was higher, the geographic range was more extensive, and the impact on the economies of many civilizations was greater.

Civilizations still defined key differences in institutions and values; new contacts did not destroy separate cultures and political institutions. Most people were still far removed from any direct contact with international trade. Increasingly, however, many civilizations operated in a genuinely international framework in which the world network of commercial, technological, and cultural exchanges was sufficiently influential to affect their operations. The development of the world network, contrasting markedly with the much more occasional and haphazard contacts among civilizations during the classical era, distinguished the postclassical era and all subsequent ages, including our own, from the earlier periods in which regional isolation predominated.

One qualification: The world network was a phenomenon of the Old World, extending an active framework of exchange among the various societies of Asia, northern, central, and eastern Africa, and Europe. It was not yet literally international, as the Americas, Polynesia, Australia, and several other regions were entirely excluded.

The postclassical era was not a time of fundamental technological innovation, though important advances occurred particularly in China and at the end of the period in the West. Existing technical knowledge spread more widely. The postclassical era witnessed a great variety of political forms, but no dominant political definition. Yet the period was clearly defined by dramatic new religious cultures, a new civilization map, and an active if still rudimentary world network.

FRAGMENTATION VS. INTERACTION

The postclassical period embraced important tensions between the fragmenting effect of separate civilizations and the new contacts and cultural parallelisms. This tension followed from the overriding characteristics of the period as different civilizations fanned out amid new links and contacts among societies in Asia, Europe, and Africa. It was revealing that empires, as political forms, became less common in this period than in the classical age, for many postclassical civilizations were not open to this kind of political integration or relied on religious ties instead.

The tension between fragmentation and interaction was modified by the fact that much of the spread of civilization extended from established bases. New civilizations, in other words, were in contact with old centers, and this provided some real coherence even as the number of major civilizations expanded. Lines of contact extended between the eastern Mediterranean and northeastern Europe, including Russia; between China and Korea, Vietnam and Japan; between the Arab Middle East and North Africa, and important parts of sub-Saharan Africa; and between various parts of the Mediterranean world and the rising civilization of western Europe.

The postclassical world, in fact, divided among three major categories of civilizations, defined according to newness and contacts with the emerging world network. The best established civilizations sat essentially in the same centers that had witnessed the key developments in the classical period. Arab society took over much of the Middle East

and North Africa; China dominated East Asia; India, though slightly in eclipse, continued to sponsor extensive trade and cultural development; and the Byzantine Empire took over the heritage of classical Greece and the eastern part of the Roman Empire. All the civilization centers differed to some extent from their classical predecessors; even China, with the greatest continuity, added new elements. The other centers were even more clearly marked by the impact of new religions and by new geographical boundaries. But they all built on previous strengths in art, commerce, and politics. They were, as a result, wealthier, more populous, and more sophisticated in style and manners than most other civilizations, particularly in the early centuries of the postclassical era. They embraced the greatest cities of the age—Constantinople, Baghdad, Zhangan, and Hangzhou.

Hovering around these centers were areas in which civilization was newer and many activities were less strongly organized. Japan, much of Southeast Asia, northern Europe, and parts of sub-Saharan Africa were defining their characteristics as civilizations, while also imitating key features of one of the more established centers. These areas participated to some degree in the world network, though their level of participation changed over time (as with the West's growing involvement from the 12th century onward). Societies in this second zone usually participated in world exchange at some disadvantage, receiving more influence than they sent out.

There was a third zone of civilizations where important developments occurred with no link whatsoever to the world network; isolation prevailed. Neither technological exchange nor the kinds of shared cultural impulse involved in the replacement of animism by a new religion occurred. Civilizations in the Americas and Polynesian societies best illustrate this third zone where no contacts modified an independent existence despite frequent exchanges within each area. Some parts of sub-Saharan Africa also saw the creation of vigorous cultures that were largely isolated. For the important civilizations evolving outside the world network, the main features of the postclassical era have little salience. Important developments occurred but within separate frameworks and with only a few, accidental parallels to patterns elsewhere. As for even larger parts of the world earlier, the dynamics of change were regional and no more.

The chapters dealing with the postclassical millennium are arranged as follows in relation to the major themes. Three initial chapters explore the emergence of the Arabs as major historical actors, the rise of Islam, and the spread of Islam to key regions such as India, Southeast Asia, and

Africa. The parts of the world particularly influenced by Islam illustrate all the overriding themes of the period: the rise of a worldwide civilization, expansion of civilization, change in beliefs, and the impact of international exchange in the four civilization areas covered in these chapters. Civilization expansion, religious change, and complex links to the world network focus the treatment of eastern and western Europe in Chapters 15 and 16. The separate ex- pansion of civilizations in the Americas is covered in Chapter 17. Chapter 18 turns to China, linked to larger patterns and the world network but in distinctive ways. The expansion of East Asian civilization—another part of the expansion-of-civilization theme—and the rise of the Mongol Empire lead to a final chapter on the changing world balance at the end of the postclassical period in the 15th century.

c. 570–632 Lifetime of the prophet Muhammad

597–626 Wars between the Byzantine and Sasanian (Persian) Empires

610 Muhammad's first revelations

613 Muhammad begins to preach the new faith

628 Muslim-Meccan truce

622 Muhammad's flight (*hijra*) from Mecca to Medina

624–627 Wars between the followers of
Muhammad and the Quraysh of Mecca
630 Muhammad enters Mecca in triumph

632–634 Caliph Abu Bakr
632 Death of Muhammad

633–634 Ridda
Wars in Arabia

634–644 Caliph Umar

634–643 Early Muslim Conquests in the
Byzantine Empire

637 Arab invasion
and destruction of
Sasanian Empire

A.D. 600   A.D. 620

The First Global Civilization: The Rise and Spread of Islam

12

INTRODUCTION. Although there were important contacts between the civilized centers of the classical world, no single civilization had bound together large portions of the ancient world in either the Western or the Eastern Hemisphere. But in the 7th century A.D., the followers of a new religion, *Islam,* which literally means "submission, the self-surrender of the believer to the will of the one, true God, Allah," charged out of the Arabian peninsula and began a sequence of conquest and conversion that would forge the first truly global civilization. Until then Arabia had been a nomadic backwater on the periphery of the civilizations of the eastern Mediterranean. Within decades, the *Muslims* (as the followers of the new faith and its prophet, Muhammad, were called) had conquered an empire extending from Spain in the west to central Asia in the east, an empire that combined the classical civilizations of Greece, Egypt, and Persia. In succeeding centuries, Islamic civilization would be spread by merchants, holy men, and warriors across the steppes of Asia (including most of what is today southern Russia) to western China, into the Indian subcontinent and across maritime Southeast Asia, and down the eastern coast of Africa and into the vast savanna zone to the west. Muslim conquerors would also capture Asia Minor and advance into the European heartland of Islam's great rival, Christendom.

During most of the millennium after the 7th century A.D., this great civilization, which cut a huge swath across the middle of the continents of Africa and Asia, provided key links and channels for exchange among the civilized centers of the classical era in the Eastern Hemisphere. Muslim merchants, often in cooperation with Jewish, Armenian, Indian, and other regional commercial groups, became key middlemen in the trade between civilizations from the western Mediterranean to the South China Sea. Muslim traders and conquerors became the prime agents

---

656–661 Caliph Ali; first civil war

680–692 Second civil war

744–750 Third civil war; Abbasid revolt

644–656 Caliph Uthman

661–680 Mu'awiya

680 Karbala; death of Ali's son Husayn

750 Abbasid caliphate

661–750 Ummayad caliphate

The Expansion of Islam from the 7th to the 13th Centuries

for the transfer of food crops, technology, and ideas among the many centers of civilization in the Eastern Hemisphere. Muslim scholars studied, preserved, and improved on the learning of the ancient civilizations of the Old World, including most critically those of Greece, Persia, and Egypt. For several centuries, Muslim works in philosophy, literature, mathematics, and the sciences elevated Arabic (the language of the *Quran*, the holy book containing God's revelations to Muhammad) to the status of *the* international language of the educated and informed. Thus, building on the achievements of earlier civilizations, Muslim peoples forged a splendid new civilization that excelled in most areas of human endeavor, from poetry and architecture to the sciences and urban development. Islam not only joined existing centers of civilization, it provided the foundations on which a truly global civilization would eventually be built.

Although unified by a common allegiance to the religious rituals and teachings proclaimed by Muhammad and to some extent by the Arabic language, the Islamic world was divided by political rivalries, vast cultural and linguistic diversity, and religious sectarianism. The agrarian cores of earlier civilizations provided the base of support for Muslim empires and kingdoms that fought to expand their territorial control at each other's expense and warred for the right to claim that their rulers were the true leaders of the Islamic world. It was unrealistic to expect that such a large area as that encompassed by Islamic civilization could be united under a single ruler, particularly given the primitive state of sea and overland communications. In any case, from the 7th to the 14th centuries, political rivalries prompted technological and organizational innovations that strengthened the Islamic world as a whole. Diversity and the continuing influx of new ideas, objects, and peoples from areas newly brought into the Islamic fold enriched Muslim civilization and enhanced its accomplishments in the arts, invention, and the sciences.

Only with the rise of Europe, beginning in the 14th century, from a besieged and peripheral outlier on the western fringes of the Islamic empires to a mighty aggressor on a global scale, did the divisions within the Islamic world begin to undermine seriously the continued strength and prosperity of Muslim civilization. By playing rival Islamic rulers and sects against each other, the emerging Christian powers could further their designs for territorial expansion. In the 15th and 16th centuries, Muslim divisions and rivalries allowed the Europeans to gain footholds, however precarious, in Africa and the East Indies.

This chapter begins with an exploration of the Arabian origins of Muhammad and the Islamic faith. It traces the emergence of the Muslim religion and community of Muhammad's faithful followers in the middle decades of the 7th century A.D. It then presents the early conquests of the Arabs, united by the new religion, and examines the achievements of early Islamic civilization. The chapter concludes with an account of a major shift in leadership that occurred within the Islamic community in the mid-8th century and the early history of the Abbasid Empire, which was a product of that shift. Chapter 13 focuses on the later centuries of Abbasid rule and the spread of Islam into South and Southeast Asia from the 10th through the 14th centuries. These chapters note the reasons for Islamic expansion and the ways in which that expansion made it the first truly global civilization.

DESERT AND TOWN: THE ARABIAN WORLD AND THE BIRTH OF ISLAM

The Arabian peninsula was a very unlikely birthplace for the first global civilization. Much of the area is covered by some of the most inhospitable desert regions in the world. An early traveler wrote of the region:

> All about us is an iron wilderness; a bare and black shining beach of heated volcanic stones . . . a vast bed and banks of rusty and basaltic bluish rocks . . . stubborn as heavy matter, as iron and sounding like bell metal; lying out eternally under the sand-driving desert wind. . . .

In the scrub zones on the edges of the *empty quarters*, or uninhabitable desert zones, a wide variety of *bedouin*, or nomadic cultures, had developed over the centuries on the basis of camel and goat herding. In the oases that dotted the dry landscape, towns and agriculture flourished on a limited scale. Only in the far south, on the Yemen and Hadramaut coasts, had extensive sedentary agriculture, sizeable cities, and regional kingdoms developed in ancient times. Over much of the rest of the peninsula, the camel nomads, organized in tribes and clans, were dominant. Yet in the rocky regions adjacent to the Red Sea, several trading towns had developed that would play pivotal roles in the emergence of Islam.

Though the urban roots of Islam have often been stressed by writers on Muslim civilization, the bedouin world in which the religion arose shaped the career of its prophet, his teachings, and the spread of the new beliefs in major ways. In fact, key towns, such as Mecca and Me-

With their supply of portable water, shade, and date palms, oases like this one in central Arabia have long been key centers of settlement and trade in the desert.

dina, were largely extensions of the tribal culture of the camel nomads. Their populations were linked by kinship to bedouin peoples. Mecca, for example, had been founded by bedouins and at the time of Muhammad was ruled by former bedouin clans. The safety of the trade routes on which the towns depended for their livelihood was in the hands of nomadic tribes who lived along the vulnerable caravan routes to the north and south. In addition, the town dwellers' social organization, which focused on clan and family, as well as their culture, including language and religion, were much like those of the nomads.

CLAN IDENTITY, CLAN RIVALRIES, AND THE CYCLE OF VENGEANCE

The harsh desert and scrub environment of Arabia gave rise to forms of social organization and a life-style that were similar to those of other nomadic peoples. Bedouin herders lived in kin-related clan groups that dwelt in highly mobile tent encampments. Clans were in turn clus-

Arabia and Surrounding Areas Before and During the Time of Muhammad

from another clan drawing water from one of their wells, they were likely to kill them. Wars very often broke out as a result of one clan encroaching on the pasture areas of another clan. In a culture where one's honor depended on respect for one's clan, the flimsiest of pretexts could lead to interclan violence. For instance, an insult to a warrior in a market town, the theft of a prize stallion, or one clan's drubbing in a horse race by another clan could end in pitched battles between clan groups. All the males of a given clan joined in these melees, which were normally won by the side that could field several champions who were famed for their strength and skill with spears or bows and arrows.

These battles were fought according to a code of chivalry that was quite common in early cultures. Though battles were usually small in terms of the numbers involved, they were hard fought and often bloody affairs. Almost invariably the battles either initiated or perpetuated clan feuds, which could continue for hundreds of years. The deaths of the warriors of one clan required that revenge be taken on the clan that had killed them. Their deaths led in turn to reprisals. Though one function of this pattern of reprisals was to maintain a rough balance between clan and tribal groups, it could get out of hand and lead to the virtual annihilation of one of the parties to the conflict. In addition, this constant infighting drained resources and energies that might have been put to constructive ends. It also weakened the bedouins' vis-à-vis neighboring peoples and empires and allowed them to be manipulated and set against each other.

DATES AND LONG-DISTANCE TRADE

Though bedouin herders occupied most of the habitable portions of Arabia, agriculturists and town dwellers carved out small enclaves in the western and southern parts of the peninsula in the classical era. Foreign invasions and the inroads of bedouin peoples had all but destroyed these civilizations centuries before the birth of Muhammad. But a number of cities had developed farther north as entrepots in the transcontinental trading system that stretched from the Mediterranean to Southeast Asia. The most important of these cities was Mecca, which was located in the mountainous region along the Red Sea on the western coast of Arabia. The town had been founded by the Umayyad clan of the Quraysh bedouin tribe, and members of the clan dominated its politics and commercial economy. The wealth and status of both Mecca and its merchant elite were also enhanced by the fact that the city was the site of the Ka'ba, one of the most revered religious shrines in pre-Islamic Arabia. The shrine not only attracted pilgrims *and* custom-

tered in larger tribal groupings, but these were rarely, if ever, congregated together and then only in times of war or severe crisis. The struggle for subsistence in the unforgiving Arabian environment resulted in a strong dependence on and loyalty to one's family and clan. Survival literally depended on cooperation with and support from kin. To be cut off from them or expelled from the clan encampment was in most cases fatal.

The use of watering places and grazing lands, which were essential to maintaining the herds on which bedouin life depended, was regulated by clan councils. But there could be wide disparities of wealth and status within clan groups and between clans of the same tribe. Though normally elected by councils of elder advisors, the *shaykhs*, or leaders of the tribes and clans, were almost always men with large herds, several wives, many children, and numerous retainers. The shaykhs' dictates were enforced by bands of free warriors, whose families made up a majority of a given clan group. Beneath the warriors were slave families, often the remnants of rival clans defeated and decimated by war, who served the shaykhs or the clan as a whole.

Clan cohesion and loyalty was reinforced by fierce interclan rivalries and struggles to control vital pasturelands and watering places. If the warriors from one clan found those ers for Mecca's bazaars, but at certain times of the year it was the focus of an obligatory truce in the interclan feuds. Freed from fears of assault by rival groups, traders and bedouin herdsmen flocked to the town to trade, exchange gossip, and partake in the delights (however limited in such a provincial environment) of city life.

This 15th-century Persian miniature shows Muslim pilgrims visiting the Ka'ba in Mecca, the most sacred of all Muslim shrines.

Northeast of Mecca was a second town, Yathrib or Medina, which—like most of the other towns in the peninsula—was established in an oasis. Wells and springs made sedentary agriculture possible. In addition to wheat and other staples, Medina's inhabitants grew date palms, whose fruit and seeds (which were fed to camels) they traded to the bedouins. Medina was also engaged, though on a much smaller scale than Mecca, in the long-distance caravan trade that passed through Arabia. In contrast to Umayyad-dominated Mecca, control in Medina was contested by two bedouin and three Jewish clans. Their quarrels left the city a poor second to Mecca as a center of trade, and these divisions proved critical to the very survival of the prophet Muhammad and the Islamic faith.

MARRIAGE AND FAMILY IN PRE-ISLAMIC ARABIA

Though the evidence is thin, there are a number of indications that women in pre-Islamic Arabian bedouin culture enjoyed greater freedom and higher status than those who lived in neighboring civilized centers, such as the Byzantine and Sasanian empires that then dominated the Middle East. Women played key economic roles in clan life, from milking camels and weaving cloth to raising children. Because male members of the clan were often on the move, many tribes traced descent through the mother rather than the father. In some tribes, *both* males and females were allowed multiple marriage partners, and the male was required to pay a bride-price, rather than the father of the female paying a dowry, in order to seal a marriage contract. In contrast to women (especially elite women) in neighboring Syria and Persia, women in pre-Islamic Arabia were not secluded and went about without veils. Their advice was highly regarded in clan and tribal councils, and they often authored the poems that were the focus of bedouin cultural life in the pre-Islamic era.

However, women were not by any means the equals of men. They could not gain glory as warriors, the most prized occupation of the bedouins; and often they were little more than drudge laborers. Their treatment and status depended on the custom of individual clans and tribes rather than on legal codes, and thus varied widely from one clan or family to the next. Customary practices regarding property control, inheritance, and divorce heavily favored males. Though remarkably skilled women, such as Muhammad's first wife Khadija, prospered in the urban environment of trading centers like Mecca, the rise of a mercantile elite and social stratification in these areas appears to have set back the position of women on the whole. The more stable family life of the towns led to the practice of tracing descent through the male line, and while males continued to practice polygamy, females were expected to be monogamous.

POETS AND NEGLECTED GODS

Because of the relative isolation of Arabia in the pre-Islamic age and the harshness and poverty of the natural environment (no one knew of or had any use for the vast reservoirs of oil hidden beneath its sands), Arab material culture was not highly developed. Except in the far south, there was little art or architecture of worth, and even Mecca made little impression on the cosmopolitan merchants who passed through the city in caravans from the fabled cities of the ancient civilizations farther north. The main focus of bedouin cultural creativity in the pre-Islamic era was poetry, which was composed and transmitted orally as there was as yet no written language. Clan and tribal bards narrated poems that told of their kinsmen's heroics in war and the clan's great deeds. Some poets were said to possess magical powers or to be possessed by demons. More than any other source, their poems provide a vision of life and society in pre-Islamic Arabia. They tell of lovers spurned and passion consummated, war and vendettas, loyalty, and generosity.

Bedouin religion was for most clans a blend of animism and *polytheism*, or the worship of many gods and goddesses. Some tribes, such as the Quraysh, recognized a supreme God named Allah. But they seldom prayed or sacrificed to Allah, concentrating instead on less abstract spirits who seemed more relevant to their daily lives. Both spirits and gods (for example, the moon god Hubal) tended to be associated with night, a cool period when dew covered the earth which had been parched by the blaze of the desert sun. Likewise, worship of nature spirits focused on sacred caves, pure springs, and groves of trees—places where the bedouins could take shelter from the heat and wind. Religion appears to have had little to do with ethics. Rather standards of morality and proper behavior were rooted in tribal customs and unwritten codes of honor.

How seriously the bedouins took their gods is also a matter of some doubt. Their lukewarm adherence is illustrated by the famous tale of a bedouin warrior who had set out to avenge his father's death at the hands of a rival clan. He stopped at an oracle along the way to seek advice by means of drawing arrows that indicated various courses of action he might take. Three times he drew arrows that advised him to abandon his quest for revenge. Infuriated by this counsel, he hurled the arrows at the idol of the oracle and exclaimed, "Accursed one! Had it been thy father who was murdered, thou would not have forbidden my avenging him."

 ## THE LIFE OF MUHAMMAD AND THE GENESIS OF ISLAM

By the 6th century A.D., the camel nomads were dominant throughout much of Arabia. The civilized centers to the south were in ruins, and trading centers, such as Mecca and Medina, depended on alliances with neighboring bedouin tribes to keep the caravan routes open. The constricted world of clan and kin, nomadic camp, blood feud, and local gods persisted despite the lure of the extensive empires and cosmopolitan urban centers that stretched in a great arc to the north and east of the Arabian peninsula. But pressures for change were mounting. Both the Byzantine and Sasanian empires struggled to assert greater control over the nomadic tribes of the peninsula, and Arab peoples migrated into Mesopotamia and other areas to the north, where they came increasingly under foreign influences. From these regions, the influence of monotheistic religions, especially Judaism and Christianity, entered Arabia, and Arab holy men urged the bedouin tribes to renounce idol worship and rely on a single, almighty God.

Equally critical, in trading towns such as Mecca and Medina, the personal bonds and mutual support systems that had made for survival within the clan gradually eroded. Their weakening gave rise to a sense of unease and disorientation and to growing indignation over glaring disparities in wealth and the neglect of the poor and weak. The prophet Muhammad and the new religion, which he sought to propagate in the early decades of the 7th century, responded both to the influences flowing into Arabia and to the social dislocations that were disrupting Arab life.

THE MAKING OF A PROPHET

The hardships of Muhammad's early life underscore the importance of clan ties in the Arabian world. He was born around A.D. 570 into a prominent clan of the Quraysh tribe, the Banu Hashim, in a bedouin encampment where he would spend the first six years of his life. Because his father died before he was born, Muhammad was raised by his father's kinsmen. The loss of his father was compounded by the death of Muhammad's mother shortly after he went to live with her some years later. The loss of his parents may have instilled in the young boy a desire to be revered and loved by his kinsmen; it certainly left him with a strong sense of compassion for the orphaned and downtrodden. Despite these early losses, Muhammad had the good fortune to be born into a respected clan and powerful tribe. His paternal uncle, Abu Talib, was particularly fond of the boy and served as his protector and supporter through much of his early life. Muhammad's grandfather, who like other leading members of the clan was engaged in commerce, educated the young man in the ways of the merchant. With Abu Talib, Muhammad made his first caravan journey to Syria, where on this and later trips he encountered adherents of the Christian and Jewish faiths whose beliefs and practices were to have such a great impact on his own teachings. In his adolescence, Muhammad took up residence in Mecca and prospered as a trader. In his early 20s, he went to work for Khadijah, the widow of a wealthy trader, who had successfully expanded her deceased husband's enterprises. Some years later, Muhammad married Khadijah, thus firmly establishing his place among the merchant elite of the city.

His life as a trader in Mecca and on the caravan routes not only exposed Muhammad to the world beyond Arabia; it made him acutely aware of the clan rivalries that had divided the peoples of the region for millennia. He was also increasingly concerned about new forces undermining solidarity within the clans. The growth of the towns and trade had enriched some clan families and left others behind, often in poverty. It had also introduced a new source of tension between clan and tribal groupings, because some clans, such as the Umayyads, grew rich on the profits from commerce, where others maintained their herding life-style. As a trader and traveler, Muhammad would have been aware of the new religious currents that were sweeping the region in the early 7th century, particularly the spread of monotheistic ideas and the growing dissatisfaction with the old gods. In Muhammad's time a number of prophets had arisen proclaiming a new faith for the Arabs. Some of these prophets would continue to compete with him for adherents after he received the divine revelations that would provide the basis for Islam.

Though socially prominent, economically well-off, and widely admired for his trading skills and trustworthiness, the middle-aged Muhammad grew increasingly distracted and dissatisfied with a life focused on material gain. He took to spending increasing amounts of time in meditation in the hills and wilderness that surrounded Mecca. In 610 or earlier, he received the first of many revelations, which his followers believe God transmitted to him through the angel Gabriel. These revelations were later written in Arabic and collected in the Quran. The teachings and injunctions of the Quran were to form the basis for the new religion that Muhammad began to preach to his clanspeople and the population of Mecca.

PERSECUTION, FLIGHT, AND VICTORY

At first Muhammad's following was small, consisting mainly of his wife, several clanspeople, and some servants and slaves. As his message was clarified with successive revelations, the circle of the faithful grew to the point where he began to be seen by the Umayyad notables who

dominated Meccan life as a threat to their own wealth and power. Above all, the new faith threatened to supplant the gods of the Ka'ba whose shrines had done so much to establish the city as a center of commerce and bedouin interchange. Though he was protected for a time by his own clan, Muhammad was increasingly threatened by the Umayyads. A plot was formulated to murder the prophet—a plot that involved participants from several clans and thus, it was hoped, would discourage reprisals on the part of the Banu Hashim. It was clear that Muhammad must flee Mecca, but where was he to find refuge?

Muhammad's reputation as a skillful and fair negotiator prepared the way for his successful flight from Umayyad persecution. The quarrels between the clans in the nearby city of Medina had increasingly precipitated violent clashes, and the oasis community was on the verge of civil war. Leaders of the bedouin clans in Medina sent a delegation to invite Muhammad, who was related to them on his mother's side, to arbitrate their disputes and put an end to the strife that had so long plagued the town. Clever ruses and the courage of his clansman Ali—who at one point took Muhammad's place and thus risked becoming the target of assassins—secured in 622 the safe passage of Muhammad and a small band of followers from Mecca to Medina. In Medina he was given a hero's welcome, which he soon earned by deftly settling the quarrels between the bedouin clans. His wisdom and skill as a political leader won him new followers, who joined those who had accompanied him from Mecca as the core believers of the new faith.

In the eyes of the Umayyad notables, Muhammad's successes made him a greater threat than ever. Not only was he preaching a faith that rivaled their own, but his leadership was strengthening Mecca's neighbor and competitor, Medina. Muslim raids on Meccan caravans provided yet another source of danger. Determined to put an end to these threats, the Quraysh launched a series of attacks in the mid-620s on Muhammad and his followers in Medina. These attacks led to several pitched battles, which were fought in the old chivalric style. In these clashes, Muhammad proved an able leader and courageous fighter. He was also an innovative strategist, who at one point "broke the rules" by having a ditch dug to protect the flanks of his badly outnumbered followers.

The ultimate victory of Muhammad and his followers was signaled by a treaty in 628 that included a provision granting them permission to visit the shrine at Ka'ba in Mecca during the season of truce. By then Muhammad's successful community had won numerous bedouin allies, and over 10,000 converts accompanied him on his triumphal return to his hometown in 629. After proving the power of Allah, the single God he proclaimed, by smash-

In this miniature, Muhammad is shown joining his disciples in laying the brick foundation for a large house for the Prophet that also served as the main mosque in Yathrib, or Medina.

ing the idols of the shrine, Muhammad converted the Umayyads and most of the other inhabitants of Mecca to the new faith.

ARABS AND ISLAM

Although Islam was soon to become one of the great world religions, the beliefs and practices enjoined by the prophet Muhammad were initially adopted only by the Arab town dwellers and bedouins among whom he had grown up—just as very early Christianity had focused on Jewish converts. The new religion had much to offer the divided peoples of Arabia. It gave them a form of pristine monotheism that belonged to no single tribe and transcended clan and class divisions. It provided a religion that was distinctly Arab in origin and yet the equal of the monotheistic faiths held by the Christians and Jews, who lived near and in the midst of the bedouin tribes. If anything, the monotheism preached by Muhammad was even more uncompromising than that of the Christians because it allowed for no intermediaries between the individual and God. God was one; there were no saints, and angels were nothing more than messengers; nor were there priests in the Christian or Jewish sense.

Adherence to Islam offered the possibility of an end to the vendettas and feuds that had so long divided the peoples of Arabia and undermined their attempts to throw off the domination of neighboring empires. The *umma*, or community of the faithful, transcended old tribal boundaries and made possible a degree of political unity undreamed of before Muhammad's time. The new religion provided a single and supernaturally sanctioned source of authority and discipline. With unity, the skills and energies that the bedouins had once channeled toward warring with each other were turned outward in a burst of conquest that is perhaps unmatched in human history in its speed and extent. From vassals, march warriors, or contemptible "savages" of the desert waste, the Arab bedouins were transformed into the conquerors and rulers of much of the Middle Eastern world.

The new religion also provided an ethical system that did much to heal the deep social rifts within Arabian society that had appeared in the time of the prophet. Islam stressed the dignity of all believers and their equality in the eyes of Allah. It promulgated an ethical code that stressed the responsibility of the well-to-do and strong for the poor and weak, the aged and infirm. Payment of the *zakat*, a tax for charity, was obligatory in the new faith. In both his revelations and personal behavior, Muhammad enjoined his followers to be kind and generous to their dependents, including slaves. He forbade the rich to exploit the poor through exorbitant rents or usurious rates of interest charged for loans. The prophet's teachings and the revelations of the Quran were soon incorporated into an extensive body of law that regulated all aspects of the lives of the Muslim faithful. Held accountable before Islamic law on earth, they lived in a manner that would prepare them for the Last Judgement that in Islam, as in Christianity, would determine their fate in eternity. A stern but compassionate God and a strict but socially minded body of law set impressive standards for the social interaction between adherents of the new faith.

UNIVERSALISTIC ELEMENTS IN ISLAM

Although almost exclusively a religion of the Arabs in its early years, from the outset Islam contained beliefs and practices that would give it a strong appeal to peoples at virtually all stages of social development and in widely varying cultural settings. Some of these beliefs—Islam's uncompromising monotheism, highly developed legal codes, egalitarianism, and strong sense of community—were the same as the attributes that had won it support among the peoples of Arabia. Its potential as a world religion was enhanced by the fact that most of the attributes of Islam were to some degree anticipated by the other Semitic religions with which Muhammad had contact. Muhammad accepted the validity of earlier divine revelations, which had given rise to the Jewish and Christian faiths. He taught that the revelations that he had received were a refinement and reformulation of earlier ones, and that they were the last and culminating divine instructions for human behavior and worship.

In addition to beliefs and practices that have given Islam a universal appeal, its "five pillars," which must be accepted and followed by all believers, provided the basis for an underlying religious unity. (1) The confession of faith was simple and powerful: "There is no God but God, and Muhammad is his Prophet." The injunctions (2) to pray, facing the holy city of Mecca, five times a day and (3) to fast during the month of Ramadan enhanced community solidarity and allowed the faithful to demonstrate their fervor. (4) The zakat or tithe for charity also strengthened community cohesion and won converts from those seeking an ethical code that stressed social responsibility and the "brotherhood" of all believers. (5) The *hajj*, or pilgrimage to the holy city of Mecca, to worship Allah at the Ka'ba (which was converted from an idolaters' shrine into the sacred center of the Islamic world) drew together the faithful from Morocco to China. No injunction did more to give Islam a truly cosmopolitan and universalistic character.

THE ARAB EMPIRE OF THE UMAYYADS

Muhammad's victory over the Umayyads, his capture of Mecca, and the resulting allegiance of many of the bedouin tribes of Arabia created a wholly new center of power in the Middle Eastern cradle of civilizations. A backward, non-

Whether in a nearby mosque or in their homes and shops, Muslims are required to pray five times a day, facing the holy city of Mecca.

agrarian area outside the core zones of Egypt, Mesopotamia, and Persia suddenly emerged as the source of religious and political forces that would eventually affect the history of much of the known world. But when the prophet Muhammad died quite suddenly in 632, it appeared that his religion might altogether disappear. Many of the bedouin tribes that had converted to Islam renounced the new faith in the months after Muhammad's death, and his remaining followers quarreled over who should succeed him. Though these quarrels were never fully resolved, the community managed to find new leaders who directed a series of campaigns to force those who had abandoned Islam to return to the fold.

Having united most of Arabia under the Islamic banner by 633, Muslim military commanders began to mount serious expeditions beyond the peninsula, where only probing attacks had occurred during the lifetime of the prophet and in the period of tribal warfare after his death. The courage, military prowess, and religious zeal of the warriors of Islam and the weaknesses of the empires that bordered on Arabia resulted in stunning conquests in Mesopotamia, North Africa, and Persia that dominated the next two decades of Islamic history. The empire built from these conquests was Arab rather than Islamic. Most of it was ruled by a small Arab-warrior elite, led by the Umayyads and other prominent clans, which had little desire to convert the subject populations, either Arab or otherwise, to the new religion.

Unaccustomed wealth and political power, which was reflected in the growth of new cities around Arab garrisons and the expansion of older urban centers, were the Arabs' rewards for these startling victories. The Umayyads, to the dismay of many of the faithful, developed into autocratic rulers who were more concerned with perpetuating their dynastic power than advancing the interests of the Islamic faithful as a whole. Their growing arrogance and adoption of a life-style stressing luxury and material gain exacerbated divisions within the Islamic community that had begun to emerge soon after Muhammad's death.

CONSOLIDATION AND DIVISION IN THE ISLAMIC COMMUNITY

The leadership crisis brought on by Muhammad's death in 632 was compounded by the fact that he had not appointed a successor or even established a procedure by which a new leader might be chosen. Opinion within the Muslim community was deeply divided as to who should succeed him. In addition, many bedouin tribes broke from the Islamic fold after hearing of the prophet's passing. Several of these tribes produced prophets of their own and some of the larger ones launched attacks on Mecca.

In this moment of extreme danger, there was an urgent need to find a new leader who could rally the faithful and put down the bedouin challenges to the community and the new faith. On the afternoon Muhammad died, one of the loyal clans called a meeting to select a new leader who would be designated as the *caliph*, the political and religious successor to Muhammad. Several choices were possible, and a deadlock between the clans appeared likely—a deadlock that would almost certainly have been fatal to a community threatened by enemies on all sides. One of the main candidates, Ali, the cousin and son-in-law of Muhammad, was passed over because he was considered too young to assume a position of such great responsibility. This decision was later to prove a major source of division in the Islamic community. But in 632, it appeared that a difficult reconciliation had been won by the choice of one of Muhammad's earliest followers and closest friends, Abu Bakr (caliph from 632 to 634). In addition to his personal courage, warmth, and wisdom, Abu Bakr was well versed in the genealogical histories of the bedouin tribes, which meant that he was well placed to determine which tribes could be turned against each other and which ones could be enticed into alliances. Initially at least, his mandate was very limited. He received no financial support from the Muslim community. Thus, he had to continue his previous occupation as a merchant on a part-time basis, and he only loosely controlled the better military commanders of the faithful.

These commanders turned out to be very able indeed. After turning back attacks on Mecca, the Islamic faithful routed one after another of the bedouin tribes. The defeat of rival prophets and some of the larger clans in what were known as the Ridda Wars soon brought about the return of one tribe after another to the Islamic fold. Emboldened by the proven skills of his generals and the swelling ranks of the Muslim faithful, Abu Bakr did nothing to stop raids to the north of Arabia into the sedentary zones in present-day Iraq and Syria and eastward into Egypt. There is evidence that Muhammad envisioned expansion into these areas, but his death left whatever plans he had unfulfilled.

The unified bedouin forces had originally intended merely to raid for booty and then retreat back into the desert. But their initial probes revealed the deep-seated rot and vulnerability of the Byzantine and Persian empires, which dominated or ruled directly the territories into which the Muslim warriors rode. The invaders were also prodded onward by the growing support of the Arab bedouin peoples who had migrated to the Fertile Crescent decades and even centuries earlier. These peoples had long served as the vassals and frontier guardians of the Byzantine and Persian empires. Now they joined their Arab brethren in a combined assault on the two empires.

MOTIVES FOR CONQUEST

The Arab warriors were driven by a number of forces. The unity the Islamic faith provided gave them a new sense of common cause and strength. United they could stand up to the non-Arab rulers who had so long played them against each other and despised them as unwashed and backward barbarians from the desert wastelands. It is also probable that the early leaders of the community saw the wars of conquest as a good way to release the pent-up energies of the martial bedouin tribes they now sought to lead. Above all, the bedouin warriors were drawn to the campaigns of expansion by the promise of a share in the booty to be won in the rich farmlands raided and the tribute that could be exacted from the towns and cities that came under Arab rule. As an early Arab writer remarked, the bedouins forsook their life as desert nomads not out of a promise of religious rewards, but due to a "yearning after bread and dates."

The chance to glorify their new religion may have been a motive for the Arab conquests, but they were not driven by a desire to win converts to it. In fact, other than fellow bedouin tribes of Arab descent, the invaders had good reason to avoid mass conversions. Not only would Arab warriors have to share the booty of their military expeditions with ever larger numbers if converts were made, but Muslims were exempted from some of the more lucrative taxes levied on Christian and other non-Muslim groups. Thus, the vision of Islamic *jihads*, or holy wars, launched to forcibly spread the faith, which has been associated with Islam, distorts the forces behind the early Arab expansion.

WEAKNESSES OF THE ADVERSARY EMPIRES

Of the two great empires that had once contested for dominance in the Fertile Crescent transit zone, the Sasanian Empire of Persia proved the more vulnerable. Power in the extensive Sasanian domains was formally concentrated in the hands of an autocratic emperor. By the time of the Arab explosion, the emperor was manipulated by a landed, aristocratic class that harshly exploited the cultivators who made up most of the population of the empire. Zoroastrianism, the official religion of the emperor, lacked popular roots. By contrast, the religion of a visionary reformer named Mazdak, which had won considerable support among the peasantry, had been brutally suppressed by the Sasanian rulers in the period before the rise of Islam.

At first the Sasanian commanders had little more than contempt for the Arab invaders and set out against them with poorly prepared forces. By the time the seriousness of the Islamic threat was made all too clear by decisive Arab victories in the Fertile Crescent region and the defection of the Arab tribes on the frontier, Muslim warriors had bro-

ken into the Sasanian heartland. Further Muslim victories brought about the rapid collapse of the vast empire. The Sasanian rulers and their forces retreated eastward in the face of the Muslim advance. The capital was taken, armies were destroyed, and generals were slain. When, in 651, the last of the Sasanian rulers was assassinated, Muslim victory and the destruction of the empire were ensured.

Despite an equally impressive string of Muslim victories in the provinces of their empire, the Byzantines proved a more resilient adversary (see Chapter 15). Their ability to resist the Muslim onslaught, however, was impeded both by the defection of their own frontier Arabs and the support the Muslim invaders received from the Christians of Syria and Egypt. Members of the Christian sects dominant in these areas, such as the Copts and Nestorians, had long resented the rule of the Orthodox Byzantines, who taxed them heavily and, periodically, openly persecuted them as heretics. When it became clear that the Muslims would not only tolerate the Christians but tax them less heavily than the Byzantines did, these Christian groups rallied to the Arabs.

Weakened from within and exhausted by the long wars fought with Persia in the decades before the Arab explosion, the Byzantines reeled from the Arab assaults. Syria, western Iraq, and Palestine were quickly taken by the Arab invaders, and by 640 a series of probes had been made into Egypt, one of the richest provinces of the empire. In the early 640s, the ancient center of learning and commerce, Alexandria, was taken; most of Egypt was occupied; and Arab armies extended their conquests into Libya to the west. Perhaps even more astounding from the point of view of the Byzantines, by the mid-640s the desert bedouins were putting together war fleets that increasingly challenged the long-standing Byzantine mastery of the Mediterranean. The rise of Muslim naval supremacy in the eastern end of the sea sealed the loss of Byzantium's rich provinces in Syria and Egypt and opened the way to further Muslim conquests in North Africa, the Mediterranean islands, and even southern Italy. For a time the Byzantines managed to rally their forces and stave off further inroads into their Balkan and Asia Minor heartlands. But the early triumphs of the Arab invaders had greatly reduced the strength and magnificence of the empire. Though it would survive for centuries, it would henceforth be a kingdom under siege.

THE LINGERING PROBLEM OF
SUCCESSION AND SECTARIAN STRIFE

The stunning successes of Muslim armies and the sudden rise of an Arab empire covered over for a time continuing divisions within the community. The old division between the tribes of Mecca and Medina was compounded by differences between the tribes of north and south Arabia as well as those who came to identify Syria as their homeland and those who settled in Iraq. Though these divisions were often generations old and the result of personal animosities, resentments had also begun to build over how the booty from the conquests ought to be divided among the tribal blocks that made up the Islamic community. In 656, just over two decades after the death of the prophet, the growing tensions broke into open violence. The spark that began the conflict was the murder of the third caliph, Uthman, by mutinous warriors returning from Egypt. Uthman's death was the signal for the supporters of Ali to proclaim him as caliph. In part Uthman's unpopularity among many of the tribes, particularly those from Medina and the prophet's earliest followers, arose from the fact that he was the first caliph to be chosen from Muhammad's early enemies, the Umayyad clan. Already angered by the murder of their kinsman, the Umayyads rejected Ali's claims and swore revenge when he failed to punish Uthman's assassins. Warfare erupted between the two factions.

Ali was a famed warrior and experienced commander, and his deeply committed supporters soon gained the upper hand. After his victory at the Battle of the Camel in late 656, most of the Arab garrisons shifted to his side in opposition to the Umayyads, whose supporters were concentrated in the province of Syria and the holy city of Mecca. Just as Ali was on the verge of routing the Umayyad forces at the battle of Siffin in 657, he was won over by a plea for mediation of the dispute. His decision to accept arbitration was fatal to his cause. Some of his most fervent adherents repudiated his leadership and had to be violently suppressed. While representatives of both parties sought unsuccessfully to work out a compromise, the Umayyads regrouped their forces and added Egypt to the provinces backing their claims. In 660, Mu'awiya, the new leader of the Umayyads, was proclaimed caliph in Jerusalem, thereby directly challenging Ali's position. A year later, Ali was assassinated, and his son, Hasan, was pressured by the Umayyads into renouncing his claims to the caliphate.

THE SUNNI-SHI'A DIVISION

In the generation after the prophet's death, the question of succession, which has proved to be a persistent problem in Islamic political systems, generated deep divisions within the Muslim community. The *Sunnis*, who backed the Umayyads, and the *Shi'as*, or dissenters who supported Ali, remain to this day the most fundamental divisions in the Islamic world. Hostility between these two branches of the Islamic faithful was further heightened in the years after Ali's death by the continuing struggle between the Umayyads and Ali's second son, Husayn. After being abandoned by the clans in southern Iraq, who had promised to rise in a revolt supporting his claims against the Umayyads, Husayn and a small party were overwhelmed and killed at Karbala in 680. From that point the Shi'as mounted determined and sustained resistance to the Umayyad caliphate.

Over the centuries factional disputes about who had the right to succeed Muhammad, with the Shi'ites recognizing none of the early caliphs except Ali, have been compounded by differences in belief, ritual, and law that have steadily widened the gap between Sunnis and Shi'as. These divisions have been further complicated by the formation of splinter sects within the Shi'a community in particular, beginning with those who defected from Ali when he agreed to arbitration of his and the Umayyads' claims.

THE UMAYYAD IMPERIUM

After a pause to settle internal disputes over succession, the remarkable sequence of Arab conquest was renewed in the last half of the 7th century. Muslim armies broke into central Asia, thus inaugurating a rivalry with Buddhism in the region that continues to the present day. By the early 8th century, the southern prong of this advance had reached into northwest India. Far to the west, Arab armies swept across North Africa and crossed the Straits of Gibraltar to conquer Spain and threaten France. Though the Muslim advance into western Europe was in effect checked by the hard-fought victory of Charles Martel and the Franks at Poitiers in 732, the Arabs did not fully retreat beyond the Pyrenees into Spain until decades later. Muslim warriors and sailors dominated much of the Mediterranean, a position that would be solidified by the conquest of key islands, such as Crete, Sicily, and Sardinia, in the early decades of the 9th century. By the early 700s, the Umayyads ruled an empire that extended from Spain in the west to the steppes of central Asia in the east. Not since the Romans had there been an empire to match it; never had an empire of its size been built so rapidly.

Though Mecca remained the holy city of Islam, under the Umayyads the political center of community shifted to Damascus in Syria, where the Umayyads chose to reside after the murder of Uthman. From Damascus a succession of Umayyad caliphs strove to build a bureaucracy that would bind together the vast domains they claimed to rule. The empire was very much an Arab conquest state. Except in the Arabian peninsula and parts of the Fertile Crescent, a small Arab and Muslim aristocracy ruled over peoples who were neither Arab nor Muslim. Only Muslim Arabs were first-class citizens of this great empire. They made up the core of the army and imperial administration, and only they received a share of the booty derived from the ongoing conquests. They could be taxed only for charity. The Umayyads sought to keep the Muslim warrior elite concentrated in garrison towns and separated from the local population. It was hoped that isolation would keep them from assimilating to the subjugated cultures, because intermarriage meant conversion and the loss of taxable subjects.

CONVERTS AND "PEOPLES OF THE BOOK"

Umayyad attempts to block extensive interaction between the Muslim warrior elite and the mass of their non-Muslim subjects had little chance of succeeding. The citified bedouin tribesmen were soon interacting intensively and intermarrying in considerable numbers with the local populations of the areas conquered. Equally critical, increasing numbers of these peoples were voluntarily converting to Islam, despite the fact that conversion did little to advance them socially or politically in the Umayyad period. *Mawali,* or Muslim converts, in this era still had to pay property taxes and in some cases the *jizya,* or head tax, levied on nonbelievers. They received no share of the booty and found it difficult, if not impossible, to acquire important positions in the army or bureaucracy. They were not even considered full members of the umma but were accepted only as clients of the powerful Arab clans. As a result, the number of conversions in the Umayyad era was low, and mawali were frequently found in the ranks of the dissident sects generated by the struggles over succession.

By far the greater portion of the population of the empire were *dhimmis,* or people of the book. As the title suggests, it was originally applied to Christians and Jews who shared the Bible with the Muslims. As Islamic conquests spread to peoples, such as the Zoroastrians of Persia and the Hindus of India, the designation "dhimmi" was necessarily stretched to accommodate the majority groups within these areas of the empire. The Muslim overlords generally displayed tolerance toward the religions of dhimmi peoples. Though they had to pay the jizya and both commercial and property taxes, their communities and legal systems were left intact and they were allowed to worship as they pleased. This approach made it a good deal easier for these peoples to accept Arab rule, particularly since many had been oppressed by their pre-Muslim rulers.

FAMILY AND GENDER ROLES IN THE UMAYYAD AGE

Broader social changes within the Arab and widening Islamic community were accompanied by significant shifts in the position of women, both within the family and in society at large. In the first centuries of Arab expansion, the greatly strengthened position of women under Islam prevailed over the seclusion and domination by males that were characteristic features of women's lives through much of the rest of the Middle East. Muhammad's teachings and the dictates of the Quran stressed the moral and ethical dimensions of marriage. The kindness and concern the prophet displayed for his own wives and daughters did much to strengthen the bonds between husband and wife and the nuclear family in the Islamic community. Muhammad encouraged marriage as a replacement for the casual and often commercial sexual liaisons that had been widespread in pre-Islamic Arabia. He vehemently denounced adultery on the part of both husbands and wives, though the punishment he recommended (100 lashes) was a good deal less draconian than the death by stoning later prescribed by some versions of Islamic law. He forbade female infanticide, which had apparently been widely practiced in Arabia in pre-Islamic times.

Though men were allowed to take up to four wives, the Quran forbade multiple marriages if the husband was not able to support more than one wife or treat all of his wives equally. Women could not take more than one husband, but Muhammad gave his own daughters a say as to whom they might marry and greatly strengthened the legal rights of women regarding inheritance and divorce. He insisted that the bride-price paid by the husband's family be given to his future wife, rather than to her father as before. By his own example, Muhammad greatly strengthened the position of women within the family. Not only were his wives and daughters prominent figures in the early Islamic community, but he treated them with great respect and even on occasion was known to take a hand in the household chores.

The prophet's teachings proclaimed the equality of men and women before God and in Islamic worship. Women, such as Kadijah, the prophet's first wife, were some of Muhammad's earliest and bravest followers. They accompanied his forces to battle (as did the wives of their adversaries) with the Meccans, and a woman was the first martyr for the new faith. Many of the traditions of the prophet, which have played such a critical role in Islamic law and ritual, were recorded by women, and his wives and daughters played an important role in the compilation of the Quran. Though women were not allowed to be prayer leaders, they played an active role in the politics of the early community. Muhammad's wife Aisha actively promoted the claims of the Umayyad party against Ali, while Zainab, his daughter by Fatima, went into battle with the ill-fated Husayn. Through much of the Umayyad period, little is heard of veiled Arab women, and they appear to have pursued a wide range of occupations, including scholarship, law, and commerce. Perhaps one of Zainab's nieces best epitomizes the independent-mindedness of Muslim women in the early Islamic era. When chided for going about without a veil, she replied that God in His wisdom had chosen to give her a beautiful face and that she intended to make sure that it was seen in public so that all might appreciate God's grace.

ANALYSIS
CIVILIZATION AND GENDER

Within a century of Muhammad's death, the relatively strong position women had enjoyed as a result of the teachings and example of the prophet had begun to erode. We do not fully understand all the forces that account for this decline. But almost certainly critical were the beliefs and practices of the urbanized, sedentary peoples in the areas the Arabs conquered and where many of them settled from the mid-7th century onward. The example of these ancient and long-civilized peoples increasingly influenced the Arab bearers of Islam. They developed a taste for city life and sought to partake of the superior material and artistic culture of the peoples they ruled. In terms of gender roles, most of these influences weakened the position of women.

We have seen this apparent connection between increasing political centralization and urbanization and the declining position of women in many of the ancient and classical civilizations. In China, India, Greece, and the Middle East, women appear (on the basis of the limited sources available) to have enjoyed broader occupational options and a stronger voice both within the family and in society in the periods before centralized kingdoms and highly stratified social systems emerged. In each case, the rise of what we have termed civilizations strengthened paternal control within the family, inheritance through the male line, and male domination of positions of power and the most lucrative occupational roles. Women in these societies became more and more subjected to men—their fathers and brothers, husbands and sons—and more and more confined to the roles of homemakers and bearers of children. Women's legal rights were reduced, at times almost to the vanishing point, and various ways were devised to shut them off from the world.

As we have seen, women played active and highly valued roles in the bedouin tribes of pre-Islamic Arabia. They experienced considerable freedom (in terms of sexual and marriage partners), occupational choices (within the limited range available in a rather isolated pastoral society), and opportunities to influence clan decisions. The impact of the bedouin pattern of gender roles and relationships is clear in the teachings and personal behavior of Muhammad. Islam did much to legalize the rather strong, but by no means equal, status of women vis-à-vis men and gave greater uniformity to their position from one tribe, town, or region to the next. For a century or two after the prophet's death, women in the Islamic world enjoyed unprecedented opportunities for education, religious expression, and social fulfillment.

Then the influences of the cultures into which the Arabs had expanded began to take hold. The practices of veiling and female seclusion that were long followed among the non-Arab dwellers of Syria and Persia were increasingly adopted by Muslim, Arab women. Increasingly confined to the home, women's occupational options decreased, and men served as their go-betweens in legal and commercial matters.

The erosion of the position of women was especially pronounced among those who lived in the cities that became the focus of Islamic civilization. Upper-class women in particular felt growing restrictions on their movement and activities. In the great residences that sprang up in the wealthy administrative centers and trading towns of the Middle East, the women's quarters were separate from the rest of the household and set off by high walls and gardens. In the palaces of Islamic rulers and provincial governors, this separation was marked by the development of the *harem*, or forbidden area. In the harem the notables' wives and concubines lived in seclusion, guarded by the watchful eyes and sharp swords of corps of eunuchs, who were males castrated specifically to qualify them for the task. When women of the upper classes went forth into the city, they were veiled from head to toe and were often carried in covered sedan chairs by servants who guarded them from the glances of the townsmen and travelers. In their homes, upper-class women were spared the drudgery of domestic chores by large numbers of female slaves, who, if we are to judge from stories, such as those related in the *Arabian Nights*, were fair game for their male masters.

Though veiling and seclusion and other practices that limited the physical and occupational mobility of women also spread to the lower urban classes and rural areas, they were never as stringently observed as in urban, upper-class households. Women from poorer families had to work to survive. Thus they had to go out—veiled but often unchaperoned—to the market or to work as domestic servants. Lower-class women also worked hard at home, not just at housekeeping but at weaving, rug making, and other crafts that provided key supplements to the family income. In rural areas and in towns distant from the main urban centers, veiling and confinement were also less strictly observed. Peasant women worked the family or local landlord's fields, planted their own kitchen gardens, and tended the livestock.

Because of Islamic religion and law, in all locales and at all class levels the position of women in the Middle East never deteriorated to the extent that it did in India, China, and many other civilized centers. And because of the need to read the Quran, women continued to be educated, family resources permitting, even if they rarely were able to use their learning for scholarship or artistic expression. Islamic law preserved for women property, inheritance, divorce, and remarriage rights that were frequently denied in other civilized societies. Thus, the strong position women had enjoyed in bedouin cultures and that had been in many respects built into Islam was never entirely undone by the customs and practices of the civilized centers in the rest of the Middle East.

The fact that the position of women has also been relatively strong in other cultural areas where authority is decentralized and social organization not highly stratified, such as in West Africa, suggests that at least in certain stages of its development civilization works against the interests of women. The control women in decentralized societies have over their own property; the necessity, given limited labor power, for them to become involved in key economic activities; and their important roles in political councils (which are closely tied to each family in the clan or village) suggest areas that might be explored in trying to understand why there has been a greater balance in gender roles and power in precivilized societies. The very immediate connection between women and agriculture or stock-raising chores, which are central to survival in these societies, may also account for the greater respect accorded them as well as their often prominent roles in fertility rituals and religious cults. Whatever the explanation, until the present era, higher degrees of centralization and social stratification—both characteristic features of civilized societies—have almost always favored males in the allotment of power and career opportunities.

Questions: Compare the position of women in classical Indian, Chinese, Roman, and Greek societies with regard to their ability to hold property, pursue careers outside the home, marriage and divorce rights, and level of education. Why are women relatively better off in societies such as Islam and Rome? Are differences in the position of women at various class levels in these societies similar? In what ways were women better off in decentralized pastoral or forest-farming societies? What advantages have they enjoyed in urbanized and centralized civilizations?

UMAYYAD DECLINE AND FALL

The ever-increasing size of the royal harem was just one manifestation of the Umayyad caliphs' growing addiction to luxury and soft living. Their legitimacy had been disputed by various Muslim factions from the outset of their seizure of the caliphate. But the Umayyads further alienated the Muslim faithful as they became more aloof in the early decades of the 8th century and retreated from the dirty business of war into their pleasure gardens and marble palaces. Their abandonment of the frugal, simple life-style followed by Muhammad and the earliest caliphs—including Abu Bakr, who made a trip to the market the day after he was selected to succeed the prophet—enraged the dissenting sects and sparked revolts throughout the empire. The uprising that would prove fatal to the short-lived dynasty began among the frontier warriors who had fought and settled in distant Iran.

By the middle decades of the 8th century, more than 50,000 warriors had settled near the oasis town of Merv in the eastern Iranian borderlands of the empire. Many of them had married local women, and over time they had come to identify with the region and to resent the dictates of governors sent from distant Damascus. The warrior settlers were also angered by the fact that they were rarely given the share of the booty, which was now officially tallied in the account books of the royal treasury, that they had earned by fighting the wars of expansion and defending the frontiers. They were contemptuous of the Umayyads and the Damascus elite, whom they viewed as corrupt and decadent. In the early 740s an attempt by Umayyad palace officials to introduce new troops into the Merv area touched off a revolt that soon spread over much of the eastern portions of the empire.

Marching under the black banners of the Abbasid party, which traced its descent from Muhammad's uncle, al-Abbas, the frontier warriors were openly challenging Umayyad armies by 747. Deftly forging alliances with Shi'ite rebels and other dissident groups that challenged the Umayyads throughout the empire, their leader, Abu al-Abbas, the great-great-grandson of the prophet's uncle, led his forces from victory to victory. Persia and then Iraq fell to the rebels. In 750, they met an army led by the Umayyad caliph himself in a massive battle on the river

Zab near the Tigris. The Abbasid victory resulted in the conquest of Syria and the capture of the Umayyad capital. Desiring to eliminate the Umayyad family altogether to prevent recurring challenges to his rule, Abu al-Abbas invited numerous members of the clan to what was styled as a reconciliation banquet in the same year. As the Umayyads were enjoying the feast, guards covered them with carpets and they were slaughtered by Abbas's troops. An effort was then made to hunt down and kill all the remaining members of the family throughout the empire. Most were slain, but the grandson of a former caliph fled to distant Spain, where he founded the Caliphate of Cordoba that was to live on for centuries after the rest of the empire had disappeared.

FROM ARAB TO ISLAMIC EMPIRE: THE EARLY ABBASID ERA

The sudden shift from Umayyad to Abbasid leadership within the Islamic Empire reflected a series of even more fundamental transformations within evolving Islamic civilization. The revolts against the Umayyads had arisen in part from a lingering hostility toward the Umayyad clan. But they were even more a product of growing regional identities and divisions within the Islamic world. As Islamic civilization spread even farther under the Abbasids, these regional interests and loyalties made it increasingly difficult to hold together the vast areas the Arabs had conquered. They also gave rise to new cleavages in the Islamic community that have sapped its strength from within, from Abbasid times to the present day. The revolts against the Umayyads were also an expression of the growing displeasure, if not disgust, of the Muslim faithful with the absolutist pretensions and extravagant life-styles of the Umayyad elite. There was a very strong puritanical thrust to the resistance of the Abbasids and their Shi'ite allies. Ironically, as we shall see, the victory of the Abbasids led to bureaucratic expansion, absolutism, and luxury on a scale beyond the wildest dreams of the Umayyads.

Finally, the coalition of forces that overthrew the Umayyads was strengthened by the support of the mawali who were weary of being second-class citizens in the Muslim world. They saw the Abbasids as champions of a policy of active conversion and their admission as full members of the Islamic community. Of all the major transformations that were marked by the Abbasids' rise to power, the last was the most significant for the development of Islamic civilization. From the religion of a small, Arab warrior elite, Islam became a cosmopolitan and genuinely universal faith with tens of millions of adherents from Spain to the Philippine islands.

ABBASID ABSOLUTISM

The rough treatment the Umayyad clan had received at the hands of the victorious Abbasids ought to have forewarned their Shi'ite and mawali allies of what was to come. But the Shi'a and other dissenting groups continued the support that allowed the Abbasids to level all other centers of political rivalry until it was too late. Gradually, the Abbasids rejected many of their old allies, becoming in the process more and more righteous in their defense of Sunni Islam and less and less tolerant of what they termed the heretical views of the various sects of Shi'ism. With the Umayyads all but eliminated and their allies brutally suppressed, the way was clear for the Abbasids to build a centralized, absolutist imperial order.

The fact that they chose to build their new capital, Baghdad, in Iraq near the ancient Persian capital of Ctesiphon was a clear sign of things to come. Soon the Abbasid caliphs were perched atop jewel-encrusted thrones, reminiscent of those of the ancient Persian emperors, gazing down on the great gatherings of courtiers and petitioners who bowed before them in their gilt and marbled audience halls. The caliphs' palaces and harems expanded to keep pace with their claims to absolute power over the Islamic faithful as well as the non-Muslim subjects of their vast empire.

The ever expanding corps of bureaucrats, servants, and slaves, who strove to translate Abbasid political claims into reality, lived and worked within the circular walls of the new capital at Baghdad. The bureaucratization of the Islamic Empire was reflected above all in the growing power of the *wazir*, or chief administrator and head of the caliph's inner councils, and the sinister figure of the royal executioner, who stood close to the throne in the public audiences of the Abbasid rulers. The wazirs, who were initially recruited mainly from the Persian provinces of the empire, oversaw the building of an administrative infrastructure that allowed the Abbasids to project their demands for tribute to the most distant provinces of the empire. Sheer size, poor communications, and collusion between Abbasid officials and local notables meant that the farther the town or village was from the capital, the less effectively royal commands were carried out. But for well over a century, the Abbasid regime was fairly effective at collecting revenue from its subject peoples and preserving law and order over much of the empire.

The presence of the executioner perhaps most strikingly symbolized the absolutist pretensions of the Abbasid rulers. With a wave of his hand, a caliph could condemn the highest of Muslim nobles to death. Thus, even in matters of life and death, the Abbasids claimed a status above the

This 15th-century Persian miniature shows the Tigris River flooding portions of the Abbasid capital at Baghdad.

rest of the Muslim faithful and even Islamic law that would have been rejected as heretical by the early community of believers. Though they stopped short of declaring themselves divine, the Abbasid rulers styled themselves the "shadow of God on earth," clearly beings superior to ordinary mortals—Muslim or otherwise. The openness and accessibility of the earlier caliphs, including the Umayyads, was increasingly unimaginable. The old days, when members of the Muslim community could request an audience with the caliph merely by ringing a bell announcing their presence in the palace, were clearly gone. Now, just to get into the vast and crowded throne room, one had to bribe and petition numerous officials, and more often than not the best result would be to win a few minutes with the wazir or one of his assistants. If an official or notable were lucky enough to buy and beg an audience with the caliph, he had to observe an elaborate sequence of bowing and prostration in approaching the throne. Positions at court and throughout the bureaucracy were won and lost depending on one's standing with powerful officials in the Abbasid hierarchy, and these great men could in turn be elevated or dismissed on the whim of the caliph.

THE "GOOD LIFE" AND ITS ENEMIES IN THE ABBASID AGE

The luxurious life-style of the Abbasid rulers and their courtiers both reflected the new wealth of the political and commercial elites of the Islamic Empire and intensified sectarian and social divisions within the Islamic community. As the compilation of folk tales, *The Thousand and One Nights*, from many parts of the empire testifies, life for much of the elite in Baghdad and other major urban centers was luxurious and oriented to the delights of the flesh. Caliphs and wealthy merchants lived in palatial residences of stone and marble, complete with gurgling fountains and elaborate gardens, which served as retreats from the glare and heat of the southern Mediterranean climate. In the Abbasid palaces luxurious living and ostentation soared to fantastic heights. In the Hall of the Tree, for example, there was a huge artificial tree, made entirely of gold and silver and filled with gold mechanical birds that chirped to keep the caliph in good cheer.

Sexual enjoyment, which within the confines of marriage had been condoned rather than restricted by the Quran, often degenerated into eroticism for its own sake. The harem, replete with fierce eunuchs, insatiable sultans, and veiled damsels, provided outside observers with a stereotypic image of the Abbasid world that had little to do with the life of the average citizen of the empire—and often even with that of the caliph and high officials. Yet as the following passage from *The Thousand and One Nights* describing the interior of the mansion of a Baghdad notable illustrates, the material delights of the Abbasid era were enjoyed far beyond the confines of the palace:

They reached a spacious ground-floor hall, built with admirable skill and beautified with all manner of colors and carvings, with upper balconies and groined arches and galleries and cupboards and recesses whose curtains hung before them. In the midst stood a great basin full of water surrounding a fine fountain, and at the upper end on the raised dais was a couch of juniper wood set with gems and pearls, with a canopy like mosquito curtain of red satin-silk looped up with pearls as big as filberts and bigger.

Since the tales were just that, tall stories, there is some exaggeration of the wealth, as well as the romantic exploits and human excesses, of the world depicted. But for the free-living members of the elite classes, the luxuries, frivolities, and vices of the Abbasid age were very real indeed.

This sort of living was, of course, highly offensive to the pious, particularly those of the dissenting sects, such as the Shi'as. Members of these sects also built up an abiding hatred for what they perceived as the arrogance and heresy of the Abbasid rulers and high officials. Thus, throughout their reign, the Abbasid rulers were threatened by periodic revolts on the part of sectarian groups. The leaders of these risings promised to cleanse the Islamic community of the excesses of the court and notables. In the centuries of Abbasid decline, when real power passed to a succession of regional dynasties, there emerged a number of violence-prone sects, such as the Assassins whose members were devoted to striking down Abbasid officials whenever the opportunity arose. Even for less-radical Muslims, the excesses of the Abbasid court and elite classes made a mockery of their claims to be the religious successors of Muhammad and the upholders of Islamic law. The resulting erosion of their legitimacy had much to do with the extended decline of the caliphates' authority, particularly from the middle of the 9th century onward.

ISLAMIC CONVERSION AND MAWALI ACCEPTANCE

Popular enmity for the political elite was offset to some extent by the fact that the Abbasid era saw the full integration of new converts, both Arab and non-Arab, into the Islamic community. In the last decades of the Umayyad period there was a growing acceptance of the mawali as equals and some effort to win new converts to the faith, particularly among Arab peoples outside the Arabian peninsula. In the Abbasid era, mass conversions to Islam were encouraged for all peoples of the empire from the Berbers of North Africa in the west to the Persians and Turkic peoples of Central Asia in the east. Converts were admitted on an equal footing with the first generations of believers, and over time the distinction between mawali and the earlier converts all but disappeared.

Most converts were won over peacefully, due to the great appeal of Islamic beliefs and to the considerable advantages they enjoyed over non-Muslim peoples in the empire. Not only were converts exempt from paying the head tax, but greater opportunities were open to them to get advanced schooling and launch careers as administrators, traders, or judges. No group demonstrated the new opportunities open to converts as dramatically as the Persians, who soon came to dominate the upper levels of imperial administration. In fact, as the Abbasid rulers became more dissolute and consequently less interested in affairs of state, a number of powerful Persian families close to the throne became the real locus of power within the imperial system.

COMMERCIAL BOOM AND URBAN GROWTH

The rise of the mawali was paralleled in the Abbasid era by the growth in wealth and social status of the commercial and landlord classes of the empire. The Abbasid age was a time of great urban expansion that was linked to a revival of the Afro-Eurasian trading network, which had declined with the fall of the Han dynasty in China in the early 3d century A.D. and the slow collapse of the Roman Empire in the 4th and 5th centuries. The Abbasid domains in the west and the great Tang and Song empires in the east became the pivots of the revived commercial system. From the western Mediterranean to the South China Sea, Arab *dhows*, or sailing vessels with triangular, or *lateen*, sails that later strongly influenced European ship design, carried the goods of one civilized core to be exchanged with those of another.

Muslim merchants, often in joint ventures with Christians and Jews (which, because each merchant had a different Sabbath, meant that the firm could carry on business all week), grew rich by supplying the cities of the empire with provisions and by taking charge of the long-distance trade that specialized in luxury products for the elite classes. The great profits made from the trade were reinvested in new commercial enterprises or the purchase of land and in the construction of the great mansions that dominated the central quarters of the political and commercial hubs of the empire. Some wealth also went to charity, as required by the Quran. A good deal of the wealth was spent on building and running mosques and religious schools, baths and rest houses for weary travelers, and hospitals, which in the numbers of patients served and the quality of their medical care surpassed those of any other civilization to that time.

DOCUMENT
THE MOSQUE AS A
SYMBOL OF ISLAMIC
CIVILIZATION

From one end of the Islamic world to the other, Muslim towns and cities could (and can today) be readily identified by the domes and minarets of the mosques where the faithful were (and are) called to prayer five times daily. The following illustrations trace the development of the mosque and the refinement of mosque architecture—the crowning glory of Islamic material culture—during the early centuries of Muslim expansion. As you look at these photos and follow the development of the mosque, consider what the functions of the mosque and the evolving style of mosque architecture can tell us about Muslim beliefs and values and the impact of earlier religions such as Judaism and Christianity on Islam.

between. The outer perimeter of the earliest mosques were made of reed mats, but soon more permanent stone walls surrounded the courtyard and prayer areas.

After Mecca was taken and the Ka'ba became the central shrine of the new faith, each mosque was oriented to the *qibla*, or Mecca wall, that always faced in the direction of the holy city.

In the last years of the prophet, the place where his chair was located was raised so that the faithful could see and hear him during prayer sessions. During the time of the first caliphs, the raised area became the place from which sermons were delivered. From the middle of the 8th century, this space evolved into a genuine pulpit. Somewhat earlier, the practice of build-

Given the low level of material culture in pre-Islamic Arabia, it is not surprising that the earliest prayer houses were simple in design and construction. In fact, these first mosques were laid out along the lines suggested by Muhammad's own house. They were square enclosures with a shaded porch on one side, a columned shelter on the other, and an open courtyard in

ing a special and often elaborately decorated niche in in the qibla had developed.

Over time the construction of the mosque became more elaborate. Very often the remains of Greek or Roman temples or abandoned Christian churches formed the core of major mosques, or the ruins of these structures were mined for stone for mosque construction. In

the larger cities, the courtyards of the great mosques were surrounded by columns and arches, and eventually they were enclosed by great domes such as that at the Dome of the Rock in Jerusalem.

The first minarets or towers from which the faithful were called to prayer were added in the early 8th century and soon became a key feature of the mosque complex. As mosques grew larger and more architecturally refined, elaborate decoration in brightly colored ceramic tiles, semiprecious stones, and gold and silver filigree adorned their sides and domes. Because human and animal images were forbidden, geometric designs, passages from the Quran in swirling Arabic, and flower and plant motifs were favored. Nowhere were these decorations more splendid than in the great mosques of Persia. Thus, in the early centuries of Islam, these great houses of worship became the focal points of Islamic cities, key places of community worship and socialization, and, with the schools that were often attached, vital intellectual and educational centers of the Islamic world.

Questions: What do the design and decoration of Muslim mosques tell us about the Islamic view of God and the relationship between God and humans? Discuss the Christian and Jewish influences you detect in mosque design and the pattern of the religious worship conducted there. What do you think is the significance of the lavish application of color and the frequent use of floral and plant motifs and Arabic verses from the Quran in the decoration of mosques through much of the Muslim world?

TOWN AND COUNTRY

In addition to the expanding bureaucracy and servant classes and the boom in commerce, the growth of Abbasid cities was fed by a great increase in artisan handicraft production. Both government-run and privately owned artisan workshops expanded or were established for the production of a wide range of products, from necessities, such as furniture and carpets, to luxury items such as glassware, jewelry, and tapestries. Though the artisans were frequently poorly paid and some worked in great workshops, they were not slaves or drudge laborers. They owned their own tools and were often highly valued for their craft skills. The most skilled of the artisans formed guildlike organizations that negotiated wages and working conditions with the merchant oligarchy and provided support for their members in times of financial difficulty or personal crisis.

In towns and the countryside, much of the unskilled labor was left to slaves, who were frequently attached in considerable numbers to prominent families as domestic servants. Large numbers of slaves were also in the service of the caliphs and their highest advisors. It was possible for the more clever and ambitious of these to rise to positions of considerable power, and many were able eventually to be granted or to buy their freedom. Less fortunate were the slaves forced into lives of hard labor under the overseer's whip on rural estates and government projects, such as those devoted to draining marshlands, or into a lifetime of labor in the nightmare conditions of the great salt mines in southern Iraq. Most of these drudge laborers, who were called the Zanj slaves, were non-Muslims captured on slaving raids in East Africa. With little hope of mobility, much less manumission, they had little reason to convert to Islam, and from the middle of the 9th century they became a major source of social unrest.

In the countryside a wealthy and deeply entrenched landed elite, referred to as the *ayan*, emerged in the early decades of Abbasid rule. Many of the landlords had been long established. Others were newcomers—Arab soldiers who invested their share of the booty in land, or merchants and administrators who funneled their profits and kickbacks into the acquisition of sizeable estates. In many regions, the vast majority of the peasantry did not own the land they worked. They occupied it as tenants, sharecroppers, or migratory laborers who were required to give the greater portion of the crops they harvested to the estate owners. In densely populated areas, the bargaining power of the agricultural tenants and laborers was greatly reduced by the ready supply of extra hands to replace those who would not agree to a division of the harvest that the landlord found sufficiently to his advantage. The control the ayan exercised over the cultivating classes gave them more and more independence from the Abbasid regime. In times of crisis, the ayan readily shifted their allegiance to regional challengers of the imperial administration or foreign invaders eager to carve out independent kingdoms within the Abbasid domains.

THE FIRST FLOWERING OF ISLAMIC LEARNING

When the Arabs first came out of the desert, they were for the most part illiterate and ignorant of the wider world. Their provincialism and cultural backwardness was no better revealed than at the moment when the victorious Muslim armies came within sight of the city of Alexandria in Egypt. Chroniclers of the great conquests record how the veteran Arab warriors halted and sat on their horses, mouths literally open in wonderment, before the great walls of the city that stretched across the horizon from the Pharos lighthouse in the north to perhaps the greatest library in the ancient world in the south.

As this confrontation suggests, the Arab conquerors burst quite suddenly into some of the most ancient and highly developed centers of civilization known to human history. Within the confines of the Islamic domains were located the centers of the Hellenistic, Persian, Indian, Egyptian, and Mesopotamian civilizations as well as the widely dispersed Christian and Jewish traditions of thought and learning. The rather sparse cultural tradition of the Arabs, which one author has fittingly captured with reference to their "mental virginity," made them highly receptive to influences percolating from the subject peoples and remarkably tolerant of the great diversity of their styles and approaches to thought and artistic creativity.

In the first phase of Abbasid rule, the Islamic contribution to human artistic expression focused on the great mosques and palaces. In addition to advances in religious, legal, and philosophical discourse, the Islamic contribution to learning was focused on the sciences and mathematics. In the early Abbasid period, the main tasks were recovering and preserving the learning of the ancient civilizations of the Mediterranean and Middle East. Beyond the works of Plato, for example, much of Greek learning had been lost to the peoples of western Europe. Thanks to Muslim and Jewish scholars in the Abbasid domains, the priceless writings of the Greeks on key subjects such as medicine, algebra, geometry, astronomy, anatomy, and ethics were saved, recopied in Arabic, and dispersed throughout the empire. From Spain in the west, Greek writings found their way into Christendom. Among the authors rescued in this manner, one need only mention Aristotle, Galen, Hippocrates, Ptolemy, and Euclid to demonstrate the importance of the preservation effort.

In addition, scholars working in Arabic played a role as transmitters of ideas that paralleled the rise of Arab traders and merchants as the carriers of goods and inventions. Indian numbers, for example—which, along with Greek mathematics, would prove critical to the development of scientific thinking in western Europe—were learned by Muslim invaders of India, carried to the Middle Eastern centers of Islamic civilization, and eventually transmitted across the Mediterranean to Italy and from there to northern Europe. But the best was yet to come. It is no exaggeration that from the 9th to about the 13th century,

Arabic was the most important and the first language of science and learning that extended across civilizations. In this era, Islamic scientific discoveries and imagination significantly affected the thinking and creativity of virtually all Old World civilizations from western Europe to China.

CONCLUSION

THE MEASURE OF THE ISLAMIC ACHIEVEMENT

By the 9th century, growing social stratification, sectarian divisions, and regional separatism had noticeably eroded the hold of the Abbasid caliphs on their vast empire. Non-Arab peoples such as the Turks, who had converted to Islam and migrated into the Muslim heartlands of Mesopotamia and North Africa, increasingly dominated political life. These newcomers carved out kingdoms within the Abbasid realm that soon outstripped the nominally sovereign caliphate in real military and political power. As we shall see in Chapter 13, Turkic peoples and on occasion new Arab contenders for influence became the chief defenders of Islamic civilization against growing challenges from western Europe and central Asia.

Though political power steadily passed to other groups within the Muslim community, the Arab accomplishment had been stunning. Not only had the largely nomadic peoples from the Arabian backwater managed to build one of the greatest empires of the preindustrial world, they had laid the basis for the first truly global civilization—if one excludes the Americas, which they cannot be expected to have influenced since they were as yet unknown. Building on earlier religious traditions, especially Christianity and Judaism, Arab culture had nurtured Islam—one of the great universal religions of humankind. The mosques, the prayer rituals and pilgrimages of the faithful, and the influence of Islamic law proclaimed the pervasive effects of this new creed on societies from Spain to eastern Indonesia and from central Asia to the savannas of West Africa.

Religion and politics had been conjoined from the time of the prophet Muhammad in the early 7th century. But under the Umayyad caliphs (661–750) and the early Abbasids who followed them, religious legitimacy was used to build a powerful, absolutist political order to govern the vast domains won by Islamic armies. Again, the Muslims drew on the bureaucratic institutions, royal precedents, and even the personnel of preexisting civilizations, particularly those of Persia and the Byzantine Empire.

In the arts and sciences the Muslims also initially relied heavily on the achievements of the classical civilizations of Greece and Mesopotamia. But the work of preserving and combining the discoveries of earlier peoples soon led to reformulation and innovation. As in religion and politics, in learning, invention, and artistic creativity Muslim peoples were soon making important original contributions, which were carried by their armies and religious teachers to other civilizations in Europe, Africa, and Asia.

Never before had a civilization spanned so many different cultures and combined such a patchwork of linguistic groups, religions, and ethnic types. Never before had a single civilization mediated so successfully between the other centers of civilized life. Never had a civilized lifestyle so deeply affected so many of the nomadic cultures that still surrounded the pools of sedentary agriculture and urban life. Ironically, the contacts Islamic mediation made possible between the civilized cores of the Eastern Hemisphere would contribute much to the transformations in technology and organization that would increasingly tilt the balance of power against the Muslim peoples. But those reversals were still far in the future. In the short run Islamic conversion and contact appeared to have ushered in an age of unprecedented nomadic intervention in and dominance over global history.

FURTHER READINGS

There are many accounts of Muhammad's life and the rise of Islam. A sense of these pivotal historical events from different perspectives can be gained from W. Montgomery Watt's *Muhammad: Prophet and Statesman* (1961), Tor Andrae's *Mohammed: The Man and His Faith* (1960),

Maxime Rodinson's *Mohammad* (1971), and the more recent revisionist (and somewhat less accessible for the general reader) writings of Elizabeth Crone and Michael Cook. Despite its unfortunate title, H. A. R. Gibb's *Mohammedism* (1962) remains a useful introduction to Islam as a religion. On early Islamic expansion and civilization through the first centuries of the Abbasid caliphate, see G. E. von Grunebaum's *Classical Islam* (1970), M. A. Shaban's *Islamic History: An Interpretation* (1971), and *The Abbasid Revolution* (1970). On virtually all of these topics, it is difficult to surpass Marshall G. S. Hodgson's brilliant analysis of *The Venture of Islam* (1974, vol. 1), but some grounding in the history and beliefs of the Muslims is highly recommended before attempting this sweeping and provocative work. More accessible to the nonspecialist reader but still authoritative and highly interpretive is Ira M. Lapidus's *A History of Islamic Societies* (1988).

On early Islamic society generally, see M. M. Ahsan's *Social Life Under the Abbasids* (1979). On women in Islam specifically, there is a superb essay by Guity Nashat, "Women in the Middle East, 8,000 B.C.–A.D. 1800," in the collection titled *Restoring Women to History*, published in 1988 by the Organization of American Historians. See also the relevant portions of the essays in Lois Beck and Nikki Keddi, eds., *Women in the Muslim World* (1978). For insights into Islamic culture and civilization from a literary perspective, a good place to begin is Eric Schroeder's delightful *Muhammad's People: A Tale by Anthology* (1955) and N. J. Dawood's translation of *Tales from the Thousand and One Nights* (1954). Of the many works on Muslim architecture, John D. Hoag's *Western Islamic Architecture* (1963) gives a good overview, but K. A. Creswell's *Early Muslim Architecture*, 2 vols. (1932–1940) provides greater detail and far better illustrations.

604–646 Harsha's empire in India

711–713 First Muslim raids into India

750 Establishment of the Abbasid caliphate (Baghdad)

775–785 Reign of al-Mahdi

788 Independent dynasty established in Morocco

813–833 Reign of al-Ma'mun; first mercenary forces recruited

865–925 Life of al-Razi, physician and scientist

809 First war of succession between Abbasid princes

786–809 Reign of al-Rashid

800 Independent dynasty established in Tunisia

661–750 Umayyad caliphate (Damascus)

777 Independent dynasty established in Algeria

A.D. 700   A.D. 800

Abbasid Decline and the Spread of Islamic Civilization to South and Southeast Asia

INTRODUCTION. By the middle decades of the 9th century A.D., the Abbasid dynasty had clearly begun to lose control over the vast Muslim Empire that had been won from the Umayyads a century earlier. From North Africa in the west to the Iranian heartlands in the east, rebellious governors and new dynasties arose to challenge the Abbasid caliphs' claims to be the rightful overlords of all Islamic peoples. As had been the case with the Umayyads before them, the Abbasids' ability to hold together the highly diversified empire they claimed in the 750s was greatly hampered by the difficulties of moving armies and compelling local administrators to obey orders across the great distances that separated the capital at Baghdad from the far-flung provinces they sought to rule. Travel by land and sea was slow and often dangerous; most of the peoples of the empire maintained regional identities rather than an attachment to the caliphal regime at Baghdad; and the military technology of the rebel forces was often on a par with, and at times superior to, that of Abbasid armies.

In addition to the splintering of the empire into often hostile states, the Abbasids had to contend with periodic revolts within the regions where they managed to maintain their rule. Here Shi'a dissenters, belonging to an ever proliferating variety of sects, were particularly troublesome. Major slave revolts and more localized peasant risings also sapped the strength of the empire. The Abbasids' capacity to meet these challenges was steadily diminished by the decline in the quality of Abbasid leadership. In addition, there was a sharp decrease in resources available to even the more able of the later caliphs, owing to losses in territory and control over the revenues collected by regional officials. When Mongol invasions finally put an end to the caliphate in the middle of the 13th century, it was only a shadow of the great empire that had once ruled much of the Islamic world.

973–1050 Life of al-Biruni, scientist

998 Beginning of Ghanzi raids into western India

c. 1020 Death of Firdawsi, author of the *Shah-Nama*

945 Persian Buyids capture Baghdad; caliphs made into puppet rulers

1055 Seljuk Turks overthrow Buyids, control caliphate

1096–1099 First Christian Crusade in Palestine

1206 Establishment of the Delhi sultanate in India

1111 Death of al-Ghazali, philosopher and scientist

1123 Death of Omar Khayyam, scientist and poet

1290s Beginning of the spread of Islam in Southeast Asia

1291 Fall of Acre; last Crusader stronghold in Middle East

1258 Fall of Baghdad to Mongols; end of Abbasid caliphate

A.D. 900   A.D. 1000   A.D. 1200

The Spread of Islam from the 10th to the 16th Centuries

Paradoxically, even as the political power of the Abbasids declined and the Muslim world broke into a patchwork of rival kingdoms and empires, Islamic civilization reached new heights of creativity and entered a new age of expansion in both the east and west. In architecture and the fine arts, in literature and philosophy, and in mathematics and the sciences, the centuries during which the Abbasid Empire was slowly dismembered were a era of remarkable achievement. At the same time, political fragmentation did little to slow the process of the growth of the Islamic world through political conquest and more enduring peaceful conversion. From the 10th to the 14th century, Muslim warriors, traders, and holy men carried the faith of Muhammad into the savanna and desert of West Africa, down the coast of East Africa, to the Turks and numerous other nomadic peoples of central Asia, and into South and Southeast Asia. For over five centuries, the spread of Islam played a central role in the rise, extension, or transformation of civilization in much of the Afro-Asian world.

In the early sections of this chapter, we will consider the forces that led to the prolonged disintegration of the Abbasid caliphate and the resulting political fragmentation of the Islamic world. The next sections of this chapter will present the great artistic and scientific accomplishments that Muslim peoples managed in the midst, and often in defiance, of political and social turmoil. Central to these achievements were contacts between the many ancient centers of civilization that had been or were being brought into the Muslim orbit. New converts, such as the Turkic peoples of central Asia, brought a revival of military and political strength that restored the authority of the caliphal regime for a time and enabled the Muslims to fend off the assaults of the crusading Europeans. Muslim trading contacts and conversions in areas such as Africa, India, Malaya, and the Indonesian archipelago drew new peoples, food crops, tools, and knowledge into the Islamic heartland areas. At the same time, the influx of conversion-minded Muslim peoples with their own very substantial cultural

The Abbasid Empire at Its Peak, c. A.D. 900

baggage brought fundamental transformations to virtually all of these regions. In the latter sections of this chapter, we will focus on the patterns and impact of Islamic expansion into South and Southeast Asia. In the next chapter, we will examine the ways in which the coming of Islam affected the development of civilization in various parts of Africa.

THE ISLAMIC HEARTLANDS IN THE MID- AND LATE ABBASID ERA

As early as the reign of the third Abbasid caliph, al-Mahdi (775–785), the courtly excesses and political divisions that would eventually contribute significantly to the decline of the empire were quite apparent. Al-Mahdi's efforts to reconcile the moderates among the Shi'a opposition to Abbasid rule ended in failure, and Shi'a revolts and assassination attempts against Abbasid officials would plague the dynasty to the end of its days. Al-Mahdi abandoned the frugal ways of his predecessor and, in the brief span of his reign, established the taste for luxury and monumental building and the habit of surrounding himself with a multitude of dependent wives, concubines, and courtiers that would prove an ever greater financial drain in the reigns of succeeding caliphs.

Perhaps most critically, al-Mahdi failed to find a solution to the vexing problem of succession. He not only wavered between which of his older sons ought to succeed him, he allowed his wives and concubines, the mothers of different candidates, to become involved in the palace in-

trigues that henceforth became a standard feature of the transfer of power from one caliph to the next. Though a full-scale civil war was avoided after al-Mahdi's death, within a year his eldest son and successor was poisoned. That perfidious act cleared the way for one of the most famous and enduring of the Abbasid caliphs, al-Rashid (786–809), to ascend the throne.

IMPERIAL EXTRAVAGANCE AND SUCCESSION DISPUTES

Emissaries sent in the early years of the 9th century to Baghdad from Charlemagne, then the most powerful monarch in Christian Europe, provide ample evidence that al-Rashid continued and enhanced his father's precedents for sumptuous and costly living among the courtly elite. Al-Rashid dazzled the Christians with the splendor of Baghdad's mosques, palaces, and treasure troves, and he also sent them back to Charlemagne with presents, including an intricate water clock and an elephant, that were quite literally worth a king's ransom. The luxury and intrigue of al-Rashid's court have also been immortalized by the tales of *The Thousand and One Nights*, which are set in the Baghdad of his day. The plots and maneuvers of courtesans, eunuchs, and royal ministers related in the tales suggest yet another source of dynastic weakness. Partly because he was only 23 at the time of his accession to the throne, al-Rashid became heavily dependent, particularly in the early years of his reign, on a family of Persian advisors. Though al-Rashid eventually put a halt to their usurpation

The richness and vitality of urban life in the Islamic world in the Abbasid age and succeeding eras are wonderfully captured in this 16th-century Persian illustration from the *Khamsah (Five Poems)* of Nizami.

the sons, significantly the victor in the next round of succession struggles, recruited a "bodyguard" of some 4000 slaves, mostly Turkic-speaking nomads from central Asia. On becoming caliph, he increased this mercenary force to over 70,000. Not surprisingly, this impressive force soon became a power center in its own right, much like the Praetorian Guard had in the later centuries of the Roman Empire. In 846, slave mercenaries murdered the reigning caliph and placed one of the caliph's sons on the throne. In the next decade, four more caliphs were assassinated or poisoned by the mercenary forces. From this time onward, the leaders of the slave mercenary armies were often the real power behind the Abbasid throne and consistently a major player in the factional contests for control of the capital and empire.

The mercenary troops also became a disruptive force in the life of Baghdad and other cities of the empire. Between stints of military service, which the mercenaries became more and more adept at keeping to a minimum or avoiding altogether, they became a rowdy and volatile element in the capital and garrison towns into which they crowded. They bullied the local populace and quarreled, often violently, among themselves. When their salaries and provisions were meager or late in coming (a situation that became increasingly frequent as the central government's share of the revenues fell to a small fraction of the taxes actually collected), they sacked and pillaged or became a leading element in the food riots that broke out periodically in the urban centers.

As defenders of the caliphate the slave soldiers were at first essential replacements for the Arab warriors who gradually drifted back to their homelands in Arabia or settled down on rural lands purchased with their share of the booty. But within decades the mercenaries had become a major source of instability within the empire and a constant threat to the very dynasty they had been recruited to protect.

IMPERIAL BREAKDOWN AND AGRARIAN DISORDER

In the last decades of the 9th century, the dynasty brought the slave armies under control for a time, but at a great cost. Incessant civil violence drained the treasury and alienated the subjects of the Abbasids. A further strain was placed on the empire's dwindling revenues by some caliphs' attempts to escape the perils and turmoil of Baghdad by establishing new capitals in the vicinity of the original capital. The construction of palaces, mosques, and public works for each of these new imperial centers added to the

of his powers and had these ambitious ministers executed or imprisoned, the growth of the power of royal advisors at the expense of the caliphs became a clear trend in succeeding reigns. In fact, from the mid-9th century onward, most of the caliphs were pawns in the power struggles between different factions at the court.

Al-Rashid's death was the signal for the first of a number of full-scale civil wars over succession. In itself the precedent set by the struggle for the throne was deeply damaging to the dynasty, but it had an additional consequence that would all but put an end to the real power of the caliphs. The first civil war convinced the sons of al-Ma'mun (813–33), the winner, that they needed to build personal armies in anticipation of the fight for the throne that would break out on the death of their father. One of already exorbitant costs of maintaining the court and imperial administration. The burden of footing the bill, of course, fell heavily on the already hard-pressed peasantry of the central provinces of the empire, where some semblance of imperial control still remained.

The need to support growing numbers of mercenary troops also increased the revenue demands on the peasantry. Lacking the bureaucratic means to pay a regular salary to the commanders of the mercenary forces and stipends for their troops, the Abbasid regime farmed out the revenues from various parts of the empire to these military chiefs and their retainers. Some of the commanders were concerned for the welfare of the village populations under their control and sought to make improvements in irrigation and cropping patterns that would enhance the revenues they received over the long term. Unfortunately, the majority of the mercenary leaders tried to exact as much as possible from the hapless peasants.

Spiraling taxation and outright pillaging led to the destruction or abandonment of many villages in the richest provinces of the empire. The great irrigation works that had for centuries been essential to agricultural production in the fertile Tigris-Euphrates basin fell into disrepair and in some areas collapsed entirely. Some peasants perished through flood, famine, or violent assault; others fled to wilderness areas beyond the reach of the Abbasid tax farmers

DOCUMENT

IMPERIAL ORDERS AND POLITICAL REALITIES IN THE LATE ABBASID ERA

The following instructions were sent in the 920s by Ali Ibn Isa, one of the most distinguished wazirs of the Abbasid Empire, to the governors and chief officials of the realm. They concern tax collection and the remittance of the caliph's rightful share of the revenues to Baghdad. They also contain requests for reports on the condition of the populace these officials administered.

It is now the commencement of the fiscal year and the beginning of a new season; a period during which Land Tax should yield considerable sums. I know of no special questions which I need to ask, not of any special matter of which I should remind you. I will only instruct you to remit a substantial portion of the proceeds of the this tax without delay, and to send in advice of the remittance together with your acknowledgement of this dispatch as soon as you have received it and noted its contents. You are then to write me a report on the state of your province, including a statement of account which will be readily intelligible here, and showing both how you have discharged your official duties and what additional measures you have taken to render the resources of your province large and productive. . . . Make up your mind to the fact that I shall tolerate no laxity nor intromission [interference] with what is due to the Prince of the True Believers; nor shall I leave a single dirham [an Abbasid coin] of his money unaccounted for; nor shall I put up with any negligence of the interests of Government, whether the offending party be a stranger to me or a member of my own family. You should be less concerned to earn my favor by personal considerations than to deal justly and equitably with the subjects under your charge, and to ease them of every improper burden, light or grave. On these heads I shall hold you no less responsible than I hold you answerable for the honest administration of the Sovereign's revenues and the due protection of his property. Advise me at regular intervals without fail of your various proceedings, so that I may know what you are doing. All if God so please.

Questions: What do these instructions tell us about the amount of control that the central government had over its provincial functionaries and the ways in which that control was exercised? Do the measures that Ali Ibn Isa states he will use to ensure that the caliph gets his fair share of the revenue and that the people are fairly treated strike you as likely to be very effective? What do his instructions tell you about the ideals of Islamic politics as opposed to the realities of the way the government was actually run?

or to neighboring kingdoms. Some formed bandit gangs that grew in size and audacity or joined the crowds of vagabonds that trudged the highways and camped in the towns of the imperial heartland. At times, bandits and vagabonds were involved in the food riots in the towns or the local peasant rebellions that broke out periodically in the later Abbasid period. In many cases dissident religious groups, such as the various Shi'a sects, instigated these uprisings, thereby making them movements that not only challenged the legitimacy of the Abbasid regime but were dedicated to its utter destruction.

THE DECLINING POSITION OF WOMEN IN THE FAMILY AND SOCIETY

The harem and the veil became the twin emblems of women's increasing subjugation to men and confinement to the home in the Abbasid era. Though the seclusion of women had been practiced by some Middle Eastern peoples since ancient times, the harem was a creation of the Abbasid court. Both the wives and concubines of the Abbasid caliphs were restricted to the forbidden quarters of the imperial palace. Many of the concubines were slaves, who could win their freedom and amass considerable power by bearing healthy sons for the rulers. The growing wealth of the Abbasid elite generated a large demand for female and male slaves, who were found in the tens of thousands in Baghdad and other large cities. Most of these urban slaves continued to perform domestic services in the homes of the wealthy. One of the 10th-century caliphs is reputed to have had 11,000 eunuchs among his slave corps, another is said to have kept 4,000 slave concubines. Most of the slaves had been captured or purchased in the non-Muslim regions surrounding the empire, including the Balkans, central Asia, and Sudanic Africa. They were purchased, with the highest prices going for the most physically appealing, in the slave markets found in all of the larger towns of the empire. Female and male slaves were prized both for their beauty and intelligence. Some of the best educated men and women in the Abbasid Empire were slaves, and caliphs and high officials frequently spent a good deal more time with their clever and talented slave concubines than with their less well-educated wives. Slave concubines and servants often also had a good deal more personal liberty than freeborn wives. Slave women could go to the market and were not required to wear the veils and robes that free women wore in public.

Over the centuries the practice of veiling spread from women of the urban elite to all classes in town and country. As the stories in *The Thousand and One Nights* make clear, seclusion and veiling were seen as essential ways of curbing the insatiable lust that many writers argued pos-

sessed all women from puberty. Because men were considered incapable of resisting the lures and temptations of women, men needed to be segregated from all but those women in their families.

Though women from poor households farmed, wove clothing and rugs, or raised silkworms to help support their families, rich women were allowed virtually no career outlets beyond the home. Often married at puberty (which was legally set at the age of nine) women were raised to devote their lives to running a household and serving their husbands. Their main purpose in life was to make a good marriage and have lots of children, preferably sons. For ordinary women bearing children secured a place in the household and provided insurance for their old age. For the women of the caliphal palace and the great houses of the elite, children provided an entree into political life. Wives and concubines cajoled their husbands and plotted with eunuchs and royal advisors to advance the interests of their sons and win for them the ruler's backing for succession to the throne. Despite these brief incursions into power politics, by the end of the Abbasid era the considerable freedom and influence both within the family and in the wider world that women had enjoyed had been severely constricted.

NOMADIC INCURSIONS AND THE ECLIPSE OF CALIPHAL POWER

Preoccupied by struggles in the capital and central provinces, the caliphs and their advisors were powerless to prevent further losses of territory in the outer reaches of the empire in addition to areas as close to the capital as Egypt and Syria. More alarmingly, by the mid-10th century, kingdoms that had formed in areas once part of the empire had begun to aspire to supplant the Abbasids as paramount lords of the Islamic world. In 945, the armies of one of these regional splinter dynasties, the Buyids of Persia, invaded the heartlands of the Abbasid Empire and captured Baghdad. From this point onward, the caliphs were little more than puppets controlled by families such as the Buyids, whose heads took the title of sultan and became the real rulers of what was left of the Abbasid Empire.

The Buyids controlled the caliph and court, but they could not prevent the further disintegration of the empire. In just over a century the Buyids' control over the caliphate was broken, and they were supplanted in 1055 by another group of nomadic invaders from central Asia via Persia, the Seljuk Turks. For the next two centuries, Turkic military leaders ruled the remaining portions of the Abbasid Empire in the name of caliphs, who were usually of Arab or Persian extraction. The Seljuks were staunch Sunnis, and they moved quickly to purge the Shi'a officials who had risen to power under the Buyids and to rid the caliph's domains of the Shi'ite influences the Buyids had sought to promote. For a time, the Seljuk military machine was also able to restore political initiative to the much reduced caliphate. Seljuk victories ended the threat of conquest by a rival Shi'a dynasty centered in Egypt and humbled the Byzantines, who had hoped to take advantage of Muslim divisions to regain some of their long-lost lands. The Byzantines' crushing defeat was particularly important because it opened the way to the settlement of Asia Minor, or Anatolia, by nomadic peoples of Turkic origins. The region later formed the nucleus for the powerful Ottoman Empire, and it comprises today the greater part of Turkey, the national home of the Turkic peoples.

THE CRUSADING INTERLUDE

Soon after seizing power, the Seljuks were confronted by another and very different challenge to Islamic civilization. It came from Christian Crusaders, knights from western Europe (see Chapter 16) who were determined to capture the portions of the Islamic world that made up the Holy Land of biblical times. Muslim divisions and the element of surprise made the first of the Crusaders' assaults between 1096–1099 by far the most successful. Much of the Holy Land was captured and divided into Christian kingdoms. In June of 1099, the main objective of the Crusade, Jerusalem, was taken while its Muslim and Jewish inhabitants were massacred by the rampaging Christian knights.

For nearly two centuries the Europeans, who eventually mounted eight Crusades that varied widely in strength and success, were able to maintain their precarious beachhead in the eastern Mediterranean. But they posed little threat to the more powerful Muslim princes, whose disregard for the Christians was demonstrated by the fact that they continued to quarrel among themselves despite the intruders' aggressions. When united under a strong leader, as they were under Saladin in the last decades of the 12th century, the Muslims rapidly reconquered most of the crusader outposts. Saladin's death in 1193 and the subsequent breakup of his kingdom gave the remaining Christian citadels some respite, but the last of the crusader kingdoms was lost with the fall of Acre in 1291.

Undoubtedly, the impact of the Crusades was much greater on the Christians who launched them than on the Muslim peoples who had to fend them off. Because there had long been so much contact between western Europe and the Islamic world through trade and the Muslim kingdoms in Spain and southern Italy, it is difficult to be sure which influences to attribute specifically to the Crusades. But the Crusaders' firsthand experiences in the eastern Mediterranean certainly intensified European borrowing from the Muslim world that had been going on for centuries. Muslim weapons, such as the famous damascene swords (named after the city of Damascus), were highly prized and sometimes copied by the Europeans who were always eager to improve on their methods of making war. Muslim techniques of building fortifications were adopted by many Christian rulers, as can be seen in the castles built in Normandy and coastal England by William the Conqueror and his successors in the 11th and 12th centuries. Richard the Lionhearted's legendary preference for Muslim over Christian physicians was but one manifestation of the Europeans' avid and centuries-old interest in the superior scientific learning of Muslim peoples.

From Muslims and Jews in Spain, Sicily, Egypt, and the Middle East, the Europeans recovered much of the Greek learning that had been lost to northern Europe during the waves of nomadic invasions after the fall of Rome. They also mastered Arabic numerals and the decimal system, and benefited from the great advances Arab and Persian thinkers had made in mathematics and many of the sciences. The European demand for Middle Eastern rugs and textiles is amply demonstrated by the Oriental rugs and tapestries that adorned the homes of the upper classes in Renaissance and early modern paintings as well as by names for cloth such as fustian, taffeta, muslin, and damask, which are derived from Persian terms or the names of Muslim cities where the cloth was produced and sold.

Muslim influences, from Persian and Arabic words and games such as chess (passed on from India) to chivalric ideals, troubadour ballads, and foods such as dates, coffee, and yogurt, permeated both the elite and popular cultures of much of western Europe in this period. Some of these imports—namely the songs of the troubadours—can be traced quite directly to the contacts the Crusaders made in the Holy Land. But most were part of a process of exchange that extended over centuries. In fact, the Italian merchant communities that remained after the political and military power of the Crusaders had been extinguished in the Middle East probably contributed a good deal more to this exchange than all the forays of Christian knighthood.

Of perhaps even greater significance, the "exchange" was largely a one-way process. Though they imported items such as fine glassware, weapons, and horses from Christian Italy and Byzantium and beeswax, slaves, and timber from Russia and the Balkans, Muslim peoples displayed little interest in the learning and products of the West in this era. The Crusades reflected this imbalance. They had only a marginal effect on political and military developments in the Middle East, and, if anything, their cultural impact on Islamic civilization was even less. There were, for example, few counterparts in the Islamic world to the songs and great heroic epics the Crusaders' feats in Spain and the Holy Land inspired in the West.

AN AGE OF LEARNING AND ARTISTIC REFINEMENT

The avid interest in Muslim ideas and material culture displayed by European knights and merchants who journeyed to the centers of Islamic civilization in this era cautions us against placing too great an emphasis on the political divisions and struggles that were such a prominent feature of the later Abbasid era. It also invites comparison with neighboring civilizations, such as India and western Europe, that were a good deal more fragmented and racked by endless warfare in late-Abbasid times. In the midst of the political turmoil and social tensions of the Abbasid age, Muslim thinkers and craftsmen living in kingdoms from Spain to Persia created, refined, and made discoveries in a remarkable range of fields. Their collective accomplishments mark one of the great ages of human ingenuity and creativity. Their thought and techniques influenced their counterparts in virtually all the civilized centers of the Old World from the Sudanic peoples of Africa to the Iberians and Franks of western Europe, and from the Hindus of India to the distant and relatively isolated Chinese.

URBAN GROWTH AND CONTINUING PROSPERITY

Though town life became somewhat more dangerous, the rapid growth and increasing prosperity that had been dominant trends in the first centuries of Muslim expansion continued until quite late in the Abbasid era. Expanding bureaucracies and caliphal building projects meant that employment opportunities for the well-educated and for skilled craftsmen remained surprisingly abundant. Despite the declining revenue base of the caliphate and deteriorating conditions in the countryside, there was a great expansion of the professional classes, particularly doctors, scholars, and legal and religious experts. Muslim, Jewish, and in some areas Christian entrepreneurs amassed great fortunes supplying the cities of the empire with staples such as grain and barley, essentials such as cotton and woolen textiles for clothing, and luxury items such as precious gems, citrus fruits, and sugar cane. Long-distance trade with coastal India and island Southeast Asia as well as the overland caravan trade with China flourished through much of the Abbasid era, despite periodic interruptions due to warfare between rival kingdoms. Trade across the Mediterranean to western Europe, both from North Africa and the Middle East, also increased. Merchants of Italian towns, such as Venice and Genoa, expanded their opera-

tions in the eastern Mediterranean, ironically as a by-product of the Crusades. Nonetheless, the continuing prosperity of many urban centers of the Islamic world gave a false impression of the economic state of Muslim lands as a whole. In the later centuries of Abbasid rule, the agrarian base on which the townspeople and rulers were ultimately dependent was rapidly eroding through much of the Middle East.

Among the chief beneficiaries of the sustained urban prosperity were the artists and artisans, who continued the great achievements in architecture and the crafts that had begun in the Umayyad era. Mosques and palaces grew larger and more ornate in most parts of the empire, and even in outlying areas, such as Cordoba in Spain, Muslim engineers and craftsmen created some of the great architectural treasures of all time. The tapestries and rugs of Muslim peoples, such as the Persians, were in great demand

A forest of graceful arches fills the interior of the mosque at Cordoba in Spain. Such an architectural feat testifies to the depth and expansive power of Islamic civilization.

The artist of this bronze incense burner from 12th-century Iran molded the burner into a caricature of a lion and intricately decorated the creature's body. The holes in the body allow smoke from the incense to escape.

from Europe to China. To this day, Muslim rugs have rarely been matched for their exquisite designs, vivid colors, and the skill with which they are woven. Muslim craftsmen also produced superb ceramics. Particularly stunning were the blue-glazed tiles, which were used to decorate the mosques and palaces of Persia, and the wonderfully designed pitchers and bowls, which were fashioned for everyday use in the Abbasid era but have become museum pieces in our day. Though the great age of miniature painting still lay ahead, Persian and Arab artists were famed for their lifelike depictions of plants and animals.

THE FULL FLOWERING OF PERSIAN LITERATURE

As Persian wives, concubines, advisors, bureaucrats, and—after the mid-10th century—Persian caliphs came to play central roles in imperial politics, Persian gradually replaced Arabic as the primary written language at the Abbasid court. Arabic remained the language of religion, law, and the natural sciences, but Persian was favored by Arabs, Turks, and those of Persian descent as the language of literary expression, administration, and scholarship. In Baghdad and major cities throughout the Abbasid Empire and in neighboring kingdoms, Persian was the chief language of "high culture," the language of polite exchanges between courtiers as well as of history, poetic musings, and mystical revelations.

Written in a modified Arabic script and drawing selectively on Arabic vocabulary, the Persian of the Abbasid age was a supple language as beautiful to look at when drafted by a skilled calligrapher as it was to read aloud. Though catch phrases ("A jug of wine, a loaf of bread—and Thou") from *Rubiyat* of Omar Khayya´m are certainly the pieces of Persian literature best known in the West, other writers from this period surpassed Khayyam in profundity of thought and elegance of style. Perhaps the greatest single work was the lengthy epic poem, *Shah-Nama* (Book of Kings), written by Firdawsi in the late 10th and early 11th centuries. The work relates the history of Persia from Creation to the Islamic conquests, and it abounds in dramatic details of battles, intrigues, and illicit love affairs. Firdawsi's Persian has been extolled for its grand, yet musical, virtuosity, and portions of the *Shah-Nama* and other Persian works were actually read aloud to musical accompaniment. Brilliantly illustrated manuscripts of Firdawsi's epic history are among the most exquisite works of Islamic art.

In addition to historical epics, Persian writers in the Abbasid era wrote on all manner of subjects, from doomed love affairs and the elements of statecraft to incidents from everyday life and mystical striving for communion with the divine. One of the great poets of the age, Sa'di, fuses an everyday and a religious message in the following relation of a single moment in his own life:

> *Often I am minded, from the days of my childhood,*
> *How once I went out with my father on a festival;*
> *In fun I grew preoccupied with all the folk about,*
> *Losing touch with my father in the popular confusion;*
> *In terror and bewilderment I raised up a cry,*
> *Then suddenly my father boxed my ears:*
> *"You bold-eyed child, how many times, now,*
> *Have I told you not to lose hold of my skirt?"*
> *A tiny child cannot walk out alone,*
> *For it is difficult to take a way not seen;*
> *You too, poor friend, are but a child upon endeavour's way:*
> *Go, seize the skirts of those who know the way!*

This blend of the mystical and commonplace was widely adopted in the literature of this period. It is epitomized in *Rubiyat*, whose author is much more concerned with finding meaning in life and a path to union with the divine than with extolling the delights of picnics in the garden with beautiful women.

ACHIEVEMENTS IN THE SCIENCES

From the preservers and compilers of the learning of the ancient civilizations they had conquered in the early centuries of expansion, Muslim peoples—and the Jewish scholars who lived peacefully in Muslim lands—increasingly became creators and inventors in their own right. For several centuries, which spanned much of the period of Abbasid rule, Islamic civilization outstripped all others in scientific discoveries, devising new techniques of investigation, and in the innovation and dissemination of technology. Their many accomplishments in these areas include major corrections to the algebraic and geometric theories of the ancient Greeks and great advances in the use of the concepts of the sine, cosine, and tangent that are basic to trigonometry.

Among numerous discoveries in chemistry, two that were fundamental to all subsequent investigation were the creation of the objective experiment and al-Razi's scheme

This illustrated page from the Persian epic-history, the *Shah-Nama*, or *Book of Kings*, portrays Bahram Gur winning the Persian throne by single-handedly overcoming two raging tigers.

of classifying all material substances into three categories: animal, vegetable, and mineral. The sophistication of Muslim scientific techniques is indicated by the fact that in the 11th century al-Biruni was able to calculate the exact specific weight of 18 major minerals. This sophistication was also manifested in the astronomical instruments and observations made through the cooperation of Muslim scholars and skilled craftsmen. Muslim technicians greatly improved devices, such as the astrolabe and armillary sphere, for measuring and mapping the position of celestial bodies. Muslim astronomers devised the names, which we still use today, of many of the constellations and individual stars. Their astronomical tables and maps of the stars were in great demand among scholars of other civilizations, including those of Europe and China.

Muslim scientific instruments, such as this intricately designed armillary sphere for mapping the stars and planets, were among the most advanced in the world as late as the 13th and 14th centuries. Muslim prototypes inspired European artisans, cartographers, and scientists to develop instruments and maps, which were essential to European overseas expansion from the 14th century onward.

As these breakthroughs suggest, much of the Muslims' work in scientific investigation had very practical applications. This practical bent was even more pronounced in a number of other fields. In medicine, for example, Muslim cities, such as Cairo, boasted some of the best hospitals in the world; doctors and pharmacists had to follow a regular course of study and pass a formal exam before they were allowed to practice; and Muslim scientists did important work on optics and bladder ailments. Muslim traders and craftsmen introduced into the Islamic world and Europe many basic machines and techniques—namely, paper making, silk weaving, and ceramic firing—that had been devised earlier in China. Muslim scholars made some of the world's best maps, which were envied and copied by geographers from Portugal to Poland. Muslim travelers, such as Ibn Khaldun and al-Biruni, wrote ethnographic and historical accounts of the lands they visited, which remain to the present day some of our fullest and most accurate sources on these regions. The Arab dhow was one of the finest sailing vessels of its day, and its hull and sail design later greatly influenced the shipbuilders of Italy and Iberia who would pioneer European overseas exploration from the 13th century onward. As these achievements testify, despite continuing political instability, Islamic civilization remained vibrant, receptive, and highly creative through much of the era of Abbasid decline and the political fragmentation of the Muslim heartlands.

RELIGIOUS TRENDS AND THE NEW IMPETUS FOR EXPANSION

The contradictory trends in Islamic civilization—social strife and political divisions versus expanding trading links and intellectual creativity—were strongly reflected in divergent trends in religious development in the later centuries of the caliphate. On the one hand, *Sufist* mysticism injected Islam with a new vibrancy and expansiveness; on the other hand, orthodox religious scholars, such as the *ulama*, grew increasingly suspicious of and hostile to non-Islamic ideas and scientific thinking. The Crusades had given great impetus to the latter trend, particularly with regard to Muslim borrowing from ancient Greek learning that the ulama associated with the aggressive civilizations of Christian Europe. Many orthodox scholars came to suspect that the propensity for empirical testing and seemingly endless questioning of the Greek tradition posed potential challenges to the absolute authority of the Quran, which they insisted was the final, perfect, and complete revelation of an all-knowing divinity. Brilliant thinkers like al-Ghazali, who was perhaps the greatest of Islamic theologians and whose ideas indirectly influenced major European philosophers such as Thomas Aquinas, struggled to fuse the Greek and Quranic traditions, achieving mixed success in terms of acceptance by orthodox scholars.

Much of the religious vitality in Islam in the later Abbasid period was centered in the Sufist movement. Like the Buddhist and Hindu holy men earlier in India, Sufis (whose title was derived from the woolen robes they wore) were wandering mystics who sought a personal union with God. In its various guises—including both Sunni and Shi'a manifestations—Sufism was a reaction against the impersonal and abstract divinity that many ulama scholars argued was the true God of the Quran. Like the Indian mystics, the Sufis and their followers sought to see beyond what they believed to be the illusory existence of everyday life and to delight in the presence of God in the world. True to the uncompromising monotheism of Islam, most Sufis insisted on a clear distinction between God and humans—a distinction Hindu and Buddhist mystics tended to deny or blur. But in some Sufist teachings God permeated the universe in ways that appeared to compromise his transcendent status.

Some Sufis gained reputations as great healers and workers of miracles; others led militant bands that sought to spread Islam to infidel peoples. To find God some Sufis used asceticism or bodily denial; others used meditation, songs, drugs, or (in the case of the famous *dervishes*) ecstatic dancing. Most Sufis built up a sizeable popular following, and the movement as a whole was a central factor in the continuing expansion of the Muslim religion and Islamic civilization in the later centuries of the Abbasid caliphate.

NEW WAVES OF NOMADIC INVASIONS AND THE END OF THE CALIPHATE

As we have seen, in the 10th and 11th centuries the Abbasid domains were divided by ever-growing numbers of rival successor states. Independent kingdoms or empires threatened the Islamic heartlands from Egypt and North Africa, northern Syria, and Persia. Asia Minor was divided between different bands of Seljuk Turks; much of Arabia was occupied for decades by Shi'a rebels; and the Tigris-Euphrates core of the empire was controlled by Turkic sultans who manipulated the caliphs they chose to put on the throne.

In the early decades of the 13th century, a new threat arose at the eastern extremities of the original Abbasid domains. Another central Asian nomadic people, the Mongols, united by their great war commander, Chinggis Khan, first raided in the 1220s and then smashed the Turko-Persian kingdoms that had developed in the regions to the east of Baghdad. Chinggis Khan died before the heartlands of the Muslim world were invaded, but his grandson, Hulegu, renewed the Mongol assault on the rich centers of Islamic civilization in the 1250s. In 1258, the Abbasid capital at Baghdad was taken by the Mongols and much of it was sacked. The thirty-seventh and last Abbasid caliph was put to death by the Mongols, who continued westward until they were finally defeated by the Mamluks, or Turkic slaves, who then ruled Egypt. Baghdad never recovered from the Mongol depredations and in 1401 a second capture of the city and another round of pillaging by the even fiercer forces of Tamerlane. Baghdad shrank from the status of one of the great cities of the world—from the cultural, if not the political center of Islamic civilization—to a provincial backwater, supplanted by Cairo to the west and soon thereafter Istanbul to the north.

THE COMING OF ISLAM TO SOUTH ASIA

The pattern of political fragmentation that had left the much-reduced Abbasid caliphate vulnerable to nomadic invasions was also found in the regions of South Asia to which Islam spread during the centuries of Abbasid decline. As in the Islamic heartland, internal political rivalries left openings for nomadic warrior bands to raid the towns and villages on the outer frontiers of the subcontinent. When the indigenous Indian lords failed to patch up their differences in order to effectively repel these incursions, more powerful foreign rulers and ever larger armies descended upon the subcontinent, first to raid and pillage but soon with the intention of conquering and settling. As they had been since ancient times, the fertile and heavily populated river valleys and irrigated plains of west and central India were tempting targets for nomadic chiefs in search of booty or displaced lords in search of a strong base on which to anchor their kingdoms.

All through the millennia when a succession of civilizations from Harappa to the Brahmanic Empire of the Guptas developed in the subcontinent, foreigners had entered India in waves of nomadic invaders or as small bands of displaced peoples seeking refuge. Invariably, those who chose to remain were assimilated into the civilizations they encountered in the lowland areas. They converted to the Hindu or Buddhist religion, found a place in the caste hierarchy, and adopted the dress, foods, and life-styles of the farming and city-dwelling peoples of the subcontinent. This capacity to absorb peoples moving into the area owed much to both the strength and flexibility of India's civilizations and the fact that they usually enjoyed a higher level of material culture than peoples entering the subcontinent.

As a result, the persistent failure of Indian rulers to unite in the face of aggression on the part of outsiders meant periodic disruptions and localized destruction, but not fundamental challenges to the existing order. All of this changed with the arrival of the Muslims in the last years of the 7th century A.D.

With the coming of the Muslims, the peoples of India encountered for the first time a large-scale influx of bearers of a civilization as sophisticated, if not as ancient, as their own. They were also confronted by a religious system that was in many ways the very opposite of their own. Hinduism (the predominant Indian religion at that time) was open, tolerant, and inclusive of widely varying forms of religious devotion—from idol worship to meditation—in search of union with the supernatural source of all creation. Islam was doctrinaire, proselytizing, and committed to the exclusive worship of a single, transcendent God.

In contrast to the egalitarianism of Islam, which proclaimed all believers equal in the sight of God, Hindu beliefs did much to validate the caste hierarchy, which rested on the acceptance of inborn differences between individuals and groups and the widely varying levels of material wealth, status, and religious purity these differences produced. Thus, where the faith of the invading Muslims was religiously more rigid than that of the absorptive and adaptive Hindus, the caste-based social system of the great majority of the indigenous peoples was much more compartmentalized and closed than those of the Muslim invaders, with their emphasis on mobility and the community of believers.

Because growing numbers of Muslim warriors, traders, holy men, and ordinary farmers and herders were able to enter and settle in the subcontinent, extensive interaction between invaders and the indigenous peoples was inevitable. In the early centuries of the Muslim influx, conflict, often involving violent clashes between the two, predominated. But there was also a good deal of trade and even religious interchange between them. As time passed, peaceful (if wary) interaction became the norm. Muslim rulers employed large numbers of Hindus to govern the largely non-Muslim populations they ruled; mosques and temples dominated different quarters within Indian cities; and Hindu and Muslim holy men strove to find areas of agreement between their two faiths. Tensions remained, and periodically they erupted into communal rioting or sustained warfare between Hindu and Muslim lords. From the 11th century, however, Islam became a major force in Indian history. Islam added further layers of richness and complexity to Indian civilization and some of its most enduring channels to the peoples and cultures of neighboring lands.

NORTH INDIA ON THE EVE OF THE MUSLIM INVASIONS

In the years after the collapse of the Gupta Empire at the end of the 5th century, the heads of numerous regional dynasties aspired to restore imperial unity in North India. But until Harsha in the early 7th century, all imperial ambitions were frustrated by timely alliances of rival lords that checked the rise of a single and unifying power center. Harsha was the second son of one of these rival kings, who through a series of wars had carved out a modest domain in the Panjab region to the southeast of the Indus River system. Upon his father's death in 604, Harsha's elder brother ascended the throne. He was soon killed—some accounts say treacherously murdered by the agents of a rival confederation of kings centered in Bengal. Although still a youth, Harsha agreed to accept the imperiled throne and was soon at war with the kingdoms of Bengal. The young king proved skillful at forging alliances with other rulers who were the enemies of those in the Bengali confederation; he also was a talented military commander. Soon after ascending the throne, he won a series of battles that both revenged the murder of his brother and led to a great increase in the territories under his control. Within a matter of years he had pieced together the largest empire India had seen since the fall of the Gupta dynasty over a century earlier.

HARSHA'S EMPIRE

At the height of his power Harsha ruled much of the central and eastern Gangetic plain, but his "empire" was a good deal smaller than that of the Guptas. He beat the Bengali lords in battle but was unable to control their lands on a sustained basis, and his attempts to expand into southern India were unsuccessful. Harsha also never conquered most of the Indus valley to the northwest of his original kingdom or the region to the south, called Rajputana, which was divided into a patchwork of tiny kingdoms, dominated by a proud and fierce warrior elite. Thus, though he was one of the most powerful rulers India was to know from the time of the Guptas until the establishment of the Delhi sultanate in the 13th century, Harsha's conquests fell far short of uniting even the northern regions of the Indian subcontinent.

The wars that dominated the early years of Harsha's reign gave way to a long period of peace and prosperity for his empire. Content with his early conquests and too greatly feared by rival rulers to be attacked, Harsha turned his considerable energies to promoting the welfare of his subjects. Like Ashoka, he built roads and numerous rest

302 PART 3 THE POSTCLASSICAL ERA

houses for weary travelers, established hospitals, and endowed temples and Buddhist monasteries. In many cases, Harsha personally supervised the building of these public works projects, and he frequently toured the provinces of his empire to inquire about the condition and needs of his subjects. A Chinese pilgrim named Xuan Zang, who visited the Buddhist shrines of India during Harsha's reign, wrote that as the king toured the provinces he would hold audiences for the common people in a special pavilion that was set up alongside the main roads. Judging from Xuan Zang's account, the prosperity of the Gupta age had been largely restored during Harsha's reign. This was particularly the case in large towns such as the capital, Kanauj, which had formidable walls, palatial homes, and beautiful gardens with man-made tanks or pools. Some of the artistic creativity of the Gupta age was also revived during Harsha's long reign. The ruler was an author of some talent who wrote at least three Sanskrit plays, and he befriended and generously patronized philosophers, poets, artists, and historians.

Though he was probably a Hindu devotee of the god Shiva in his early years, Harsha was tolerant of all faiths and increasingly attracted to Buddhism. His generous patronage of Buddhist monasteries and the Buddhist monkhood attracted pilgrims like Xuan Zang. If Xuan Zang's account can be trusted, Harsha came close to converting to Buddhism in the last years of his life. He sponsored great religious assemblies, which were dominated by Buddhist monks and religious rituals, and prohibited eating meat and putting an end to human life. His lavish patronage of the Buddhists led on one occasion to a Brahmininspired assassination attempt, which appears only to have strengthened his preference for Buddhist ceremonies and beliefs. Despite his favoritism, however, Buddhism was clearly in decline. Monasteries were large and wealthy, but monastic discipline was lax and most monks had little contact with the populace at large. Much like a Hindu god, the Buddha was the object of cult veneration, and a variety of corrupt practices had crept into popular worship. Buddhist centers would prove vulnerable targets for Muslim raiders, and in some areas a substantial portion of the dwindling numbers of Buddhist lay believers would soon convert to Islam.

POLITICAL DIVISIONS AND THE FIRST MUSLIM INVASIONS

Harsha died without a successor in 646, and his kingdom was quickly pulled apart by ambitious ministers seeking to found a new dynasty of their own. Though Hindu culture flourished in both north and south India in the centuries after Harsha's death—as evidenced by the great

temples that were constructed and the works of sculpture, literature, and music that were produced—no paramount kingdom emerged. Political divisions in the north and west-central regions of the subcontinent proved the most significant because they left openings for a succession of invasions by different Muslim peoples.

The first and the least lasting Muslim intrusion, which came in 711, resulted indirectly from the peaceful trading contacts that had initially brought Muslims into contact with Indian civilization. Since ancient times, Arab seafarers and traders had been major carriers in the vast trading network that stretched from Italy in the Mediterranean to the South China Sea. After converting to Islam, these traders continued to frequent the ports of India, particularly those on the western coast. An attack by pirates sailing from Debul (in Sind in western India) on ships owned by some of these Arab traders prompted Hajjaj, the viceroy of the eastern provinces of the Umayyad Empire, to launch a punitive expedition against the king of Sind. An able Arab general, Muhammad ibn Qasim, who was only 17 years old when the campaign began, led over 10,000 horse- and camel-mounted warriors into Sind to avenge the assault on Arab shipping.

After victories in several fiercely fought battles and successful sieges of the great stone fortresses that stood guard over various parts of the arid and thinly peopled Sind interior, Muhammad ibn Qasim declared the region, as well as the Indus valley to the northeast, provinces of the Umayyad Empire. Soon after the territories had been annexed to the Umayyad Empire, a new caliph, who was a bitter enemy of Hajjaj, came to power in Damascus. He purged Hajjaj and recalled and executed his son-in-law, Muhammad ibn Qasim. Though the personnel of the ruling Arab elite shifted as a result, the basic policies established by Muhammad ibn Qasim were followed by his Umayyad and Abbasid successors for several centuries.

In these early centuries, the coming of Islam brought little change for most of the inhabitants of the Indian subcontinent. In fact, in many areas local leaders and the mass of the populace had surrendered towns and districts willingly to the conquerors, who offered the promise of lighter taxation and greater religious tolerance. The Arab overlords decided to treat both Hindus and Buddhists as protected "people of the book," despite the fact that their faiths had no connection to the Bible, the book in question. This meant that though they were obliged to pay special taxes, non-Muslims enjoyed the freedom to worship as they pleased and to maintain their temples and monasteries.

As in other areas conquered by the Arabs, most of the indigenous officials and functionaries retained their positions, which did much to reconcile them to Muslim rule. The status and privileges of the Brahmin castes were also respected. Virtually all the Arabs, who made up only a tiny minority of the population, lived in the cities or special garrison towns. Because little effort was expended in converting the peoples of the conquered areas, they remained overwhelmingly Hindu or Buddhist and, initially at least, displayed scant interest in the beliefs or culture of their new overlords.

INDIAN INFLUENCES ON ISLAMIC CIVILIZATION

Though the impact of Islam on the Indian subcontinent in this period was limited, the Arab foothold in Sind provided contacts by which Indian learning could be transmitted to the Muslim heartlands in the Middle East. As a result, Islamic civilization was enriched by the skills and discoveries of yet another great civilization. Of particular importance was Indian scientific learning, which rivaled that of the Greeks as the most advanced of the ancient world. Hindu mathematicians and astronomers traveled to Baghdad after the Abbasids came to power in the mid-8th century. Their works on algebra and geometry were translated into Arabic, and their instruments for celestial observation were copied and improved upon by Arab astronomers. Most critically, Arab thinkers in all fields began to use the numerals that Hindu scholars had devised centuries earlier. Because these numbers were passed on to the Europeans through contacts with the Arabs in the early Middle Ages, we call them Arabic numerals today, but they originated in India. Because of the linkages between civilized centers established by the spread of Islam, this system of numerical notation has proved central to two scientific revolutions: the first in the Middle East, which was discussed previously, and a second, more sustained and fundamental transformation first in Europe and subsequently in much of the rest of the world from the 16th century onward.

In addition to science and mathematics, Indian treatises on subjects ranging from medicine to music were translated and studied by Arab scholars. Indian physicians were brought to Baghdad to run the well-endowed hospitals that the Christian Crusaders found a source of wonderment and a cause for envy. On a number of occasions, Indian doctors were able to cure Arab rulers and high officials whom Greek physicians had pronounced beyond help. Indian works on statecraft, alchemy, and palmistry were also translated into Arabic, and it is believed that some of the tales in the *Arabian Nights* were based on ancient Indian stories. Indian musical instruments and melodies made their way into the repertoires of Arab performers, and the Indian game of chess became a favorite of both princes and ordinary townspeople. Arabs who emigrated to Sind and

other Muslim-ruled areas often adopted Indian dress and hairstyles, ate Indian foods, and rode on elephants as the Hindu *rajas* (kings) did. In this era additional Arab colonies were established in coastal areas, such as Malabar to the south and Bengal in the east. These trading enclaves would later provide the staging areas from which Islam was transmitted to island and mainland Southeast Asia.

MUSLIM INVASIONS: THE SECOND WAVE

After the initial conquests by Muhammad ibn Qasim's armies, little territory was added to the Muslim foothold on the subcontinent. In fact, disputes between the Arabs occupying Sind and quarrels with first the Umayyad and later the Abbasid caliphs gradually weakened the Muslim hold on the area and led to the reconquest of parts of the lower Indus valley by Hindu rulers. The slow Muslim retreat was dramatically reversed by a new series of military invasions, this time launched by a Turkish slave dynasty that in 962 had seized power in Afghanistan to the north of the Indus valley. The third ruler of this dynasty, Mahmud of Ghazni, led a series of expeditions that initiated nearly two centuries of Muslim raiding and conquest in northern India. Drawn by the legendary wealth of the subcontinent and a zeal to spread the Muslim faith, Mahmud repeatedly raided northwest India in the first decades of the 11th century. He defeated one confederation of Hindu princes after another and drove deeper and deeper into the subcontinent in the quest of ever richer temples to sack and loot.

Mahmud's raids and those of his successors became a lasting source of enmity between Hindus and Muslims in South Asia. After capturing and looting a rich Hindu temple in 1008, he became obsessed with the promise of treasure and the chance to strike a blow at the infidel Hindu faith, which the great temple complexes provided. His most spectacular raid was directed in 1024 at the massive Somanth temple in Gujarat. The temple was served by more than 1,000 Hindu priests and hundreds of temple dancers and singers, supported by 10,000 villages, and defended by nearly 50,000 warriors. Its capture marked the high point of Mahmud's career as general and religious zealot. After stripping the captured shrine of its legendary jewels and golden decorations, Mahmud ordered his followers to smash its idols and destroy the intricate complex of shrines and passageways that housed them. The main idol of the temple was cut into many pieces, and the parts were placed in the floors and stairways at the entrances to Muslim mosques, where the faithful would regularly trod on them when going to prayer. The persecution of both Hindus and Buddhists by invaders, such as Mahmud, gave the Muslims a reputation among the Indian peoples for in-

Built in 1626 at Agra, this exquisite tomb of white marble encrusted with semiprecious stones provides a superb example of the blending of Islamic and Hindu architectural forms and artistic motifs.

tolerance and aggression that would greatly hinder the efforts of later and more tolerant Muslim potentates to reconcile Hindu subjects to their rule.

FROM BOOTY TO EMPIRE

The raids mounted by Mahmud of Ghazni and his successors, which were devoted primarily to pillaging, gave way in the last decades of the 12th century to sustained campaigns aimed at seizing political control in North India. The key figure in this transition was a tenacious military commander of Persian extraction, Muhammad of Ghur. The breakup of the Ghazni Empire as a result of the ceaseless quarrels of Mahmud's successors made it possible for the small mountain kingdom of Ghur, near Herat in western Afghanistan, to emerge as a formidable regional power center. Vendettas to avenge the death of relatives in the protracted struggle with the Ghaznis and the support of his elder brother prepared Muhammad for ambitious military expeditions into India, which began in 1178. After barely surviving several severe defeats at the hands of Hindu rulers, Muhammad put together a string of military victories that brought the Indus valley, Sind, and much of north-central India under his control.

Muhammad's conquests were extended in the following years by several of his most gifted subordinate commanders, who, as was quite common in Muslim kingdoms, were slaves who had risen to positions of power on the basis of their military skills. These commanders established Muslim rule in the Gangetic plain as far as Bengal and throughout Rajputana to the south and west. After Muhammad of Ghur was assassinated in 1206, Qutb-ud-din Aibak, one of his slave lieutenants, formed a separate kingdom in the Indian portions of the Ghuri Empire.

Significantly the capital of the new kingdom was at Delhi along the Jumna River on the Gangetic plain. Delhi's location in the very center of northern India graphically proclaimed that a Muslim dynasty rooted in the subcontinent itself, not an extension of a central Asian empire, had been founded. For the next 300 years a succession of dynasties would rule much of north and central India. Alternatively of Persian, Afghan, Turkic, and mixed descent, the rulers of these imperial houses, who proclaimed themselves the sultans of Delhi, fought each other, Mongol and Turkic invaders, and the indigenous Hindu princes for control of the Indus and Gangetic heartlands of Indian civilization.

All the dynasties that laid claim to the sultanate based their power on large military machines, which were anchored on massive contingents of cavalry and, increasingly, on corps of war elephants patterned after those that indigenous rulers had used for centuries. The support of their armies and sumptuous court establishments became the main objectives of the extensive bureaucracies that each of the rulers at Delhi sought to maintain. Though some rulers patronized public works projects, the arts, and charitable relief, most rulers concentrated on maximizing the revenues they could collect from the peasants and townspeople in their domains. Throughout the Delhi sultanate era, however, factional struggles among the ruling Muslims and their dependence on Hindu lords and village notables in administration at the local level greatly limited the actual control exercised by any of the dynasties that emerged. Through the collusion and cheating of lower-level officials, who had no sense of loyalty to the Muslim overlords, much of what the peasants produced was retained by the villagers or appropriated by local and regional elite groups.

CONVERSION

Though the Muslims literally fought their way into India, their interaction with the indigenous peoples soon came to be dominated by accommodation and peaceful exchanges. Over the centuries when much of the north was ruled by dynasties centered at Delhi, sizeable Muslim communities developed in different areas of the subcontinent, particularly in Bengal to the east and in the northwestern provinces in the Indus valley that were the points of entry for most of the Muslim peoples who migrated into India. Few of these converts were won by forcible conversion. The main carriers of the new faith were traders, who played a growing role in both coastal and inland trade, and Sufi mystics, whom in both style and message shared much with Indian holy people and wandering ascetics. Belief in their magical and healing powers did much to enhance the stature and increase the following of the Sufis, whose mosques and schools often became centers of regional political power. Sufis organized their devotees in militias to fend off bandits or the depredations of rival princes, oversaw the clearing of forests for farming and settlement, and welcomed low and outcaste Hindu groups into the Muslim brotherhood. After their deaths, the tombs of Sufi holy men became objects of veneration for Hindus and Buddhists as well as for Muslims. They were sites of pilgrimage, where travelers from many regions congregated and from which Islamic teachings were further spread throughout the subcontinent.

Most of the indigenous converts, who came to form a majority of the Muslims living in India, were drawn from specific regions and social groups. Surprisingly small numbers of converts were found in the Indo-Gangetic centers of Muslim political power, a fact that suggests the very limited importance of forced conversions. Most Indians who converted to Islam were from Buddhist or low-caste groups. In areas such as western India and Bengal, where Buddhism had survived as a popular religion until the era of the Muslim invasions, esoteric rituals and corrupt practices had debased Buddhist teachings and undermined the morale of the monastic orders. This decline was accelerated by Muslim raids on Buddhist temples and monasteries, which provided vulnerable and lucrative targets for the early invaders. Without monastic supervision, local congregations sank further into orgies and experiments with magic, and in some areas into practices, such as human sacrifice, that also disregarded the Buddha's social concerns and religious message. Disorganized and misdirected, Buddhism proved no match for the confident and vigorous new religion the Muslim invaders carried into the subcontinent, particularly when those who sought to spread the new faith possessed the charisma and organizing skills of the Sufi holy men.

Though Buddhist converts probably made up the larger portion of the Indians who converted to Islam, untouchables and low-caste Hindus, as well as animistic tribal peoples, were also attracted to the more egalitarian social arrangements promoted by the new faith. As was the case with the Buddhists, group conversions were essential since those who remained in the Hindu caste system would have little to do with those who converted. Some conversions were also prompted by the desire of Hindus or Buddhists to escape the hated head tax the Muslim rulers levied on unbelievers and by intermarriage between the indigenous peoples and Muslim migrants, whose communities usually included far fewer women than men. The migrants themselves also increased the size of the Muslim population in the subcontinent. This was particularly true in periods of crisis in central Asia, as in the 13th and 14th centuries when Turkic, Persian, and Afghan peoples retreated to the comparative sanctuary of India in the face of the Mongol and Timurid conquests.

ACCOMMODATION

Although Islam won large numbers of converts in certain areas and communities, it initially made little impression on the Hindu community as a whole. Despite military reverses and the imposition of Muslim political rule over large areas of the subcontinent, high-caste Hindus in particular persisted in regarding the invaders as the bearers of an upstart religion and as polluting outcastes. Al-Biruni, one of the chief chroniclers of the Muslim conquests, complained openly about the prevailing Indian disdain for the newcomers:

> The Hindus believe that there is no country but theirs, no nation like theirs, no kings like theirs, no religion like theirs, no science like theirs. They are haughty, foolishly vain, self-conceited and stolid.

Many Hindus were quite willing to take positions as administrators in the bureaucracies of Muslim overlords or as soldiers in their armies and to trade with Muslim merchants, but they remained socially aloof from their conquerors. Separate living quarters in both cities and rural villages were established everywhere Muslim communities developed; genuine friendships between members of high-caste groups and Muslims were rare and sexual liaisons between them were severely restricted.

During the early centuries of the Muslim influx, the Hindus were convinced that, like so many of the peoples who had entered the subcontinent in the preceding millennia, the Muslims would soon be absorbed by the superior religions and more sophisticated cultures of India. Many signs pointed to that outcome. Hindus staffed the bureaucracies and made up a good portion of the armies of Muslim rulers. In addition, Muslim princes adopted regal styles and practices that were Hindu-inspired and contrary to the Quran. Some Hindus proclaimed themselves to be of divine descent, while others minted coins decorated with Hindu images such as Nandi, the bull associated with a major Hindu god, Shiva.

More broadly, Muslim communities became socially divided along caste lines. Recently arrived Muslims were generally on top of the hierarchies that developed, and

even they were divided depending on whether they were Arab, Turk, or Persian. High-caste Hindu converts came next, followed by "clean" artisan and merchant groups. Lower caste and untouchable converts remained at the bottom of the social hierarchy, which may well explain why conversions by these groups were not as numerous as one would expect, given the original egalitarian thrust of Islam. Muslims also adopted Indian foods and styles of dress and took to chewing *pan,* or betel leaves. Their intrusion had unfortunate consequences for women in both Muslim and Hindu communities. The invaders increasingly adopted the lower age of women at the time of their marriage and the prohibitions against widow remarriage found especially at the high-caste levels of Indian society. Some upper "caste" Muslim groups even performed the ritual of *sati,* the immolation of widows with the bodies of their deceased husbands.

ISLAMIC CHALLENGE AND HINDU REVIVAL

Despite a significant degree of acculturation to Hindu life-styles and social organization, Muslim migrants to the subcontinent held to their own, quite distinctive religious beliefs and rituals. The Hindus found Islam impossible to absorb and soon realized that they were confronted by an actively proselytizing religion that had great appeal to substantial segments of the Indian population. Partly in response to this challenge, the Hindus placed ever greater emphasis on the devotional cults of gods and goddesses that faith. They were also strongly repudiated by the guardians of orthodoxy in each religious community. Sensing the long-term threat to Hinduism posed by Muslim political had earlier proved so effective in neutralizing the challenge of Buddhism and other indigenous religious rivals. Membership in these devotional, or *bhaktic,* cult groups was open to all, including women and untouchables. In fact, some of the most celebrated writers of religious poetry and songs of worship were women, such as Mira Bai. Saints from low-caste origins were revered by warriors and Brahmins as well as by farmers, merchants, and outcastes. Because many songs and poems were composed in regional languages, such as Bengali, Marathi, and Tamil, they were more accessible to the common people and became prominent expressions of popular culture in many areas.

Bhaktic holy people and gurus stressed the importance of a strong emotional bond between devotee and the god or goddess who was their object of veneration. Chants, dances, and in some settings drugs were used to reach the state of spiritual intoxication that was the key to individual salvation. Once one had achieved the state of ecstasy that came through intense emotional attachment to a god or

This Indian miniature painting of milk maidens serving the Hindu god, Krishna, reflects the highly personalized, devotional worship that was characteristic of the *bhaktic* movement.

goddess, all past sins were removed and caste distinctions rendered meaningless. The divine objects of these devotional cults varied not only by region and social group but also by the holy person followed. The most widely worshipped divine objects, however, were the gods Shiva and Vishnu—particularly in the guise of Krishna the goatherd—and the goddess Kali in any one of several manifestations. By increasing popular involvement in Hindu worship and enriching and extending modes of prayer and ritual, the bhaktic movement may have done much to stem the flow of converts to Islam, particularly at the level of low-caste groups. Once again, the Hindu tradition demonstrated its remarkable adaptability and tolerance for widely varying modes of divine worship.

ATTEMPTS TO BRIDGE THE DIFFERENCES BETWEEN HINDUISM AND ISLAM

The similarities in style and religious message between the Sufis, who sought to spread Islam to the Indian masses, and the gurus, who championed bhaktic devotion to the Hindu gods and goddesses, led to a number of attempts to find common ground between the two communities. One of these attempts can be traced in the teachings, recorded in the form of religious poems, of the 15th century mystic Kabir. A man of humble origins who was raised by Muslim weavers in Banaras, one of the most sacred Hindu cities, Kabir played down the importance of ritual differences between Hinduism and Islam. He declared:

O servant, where doest thou seek Me?
Lo! I am beside thee.
I am neither in temple nor in mosque:
Neither am I in rites and ceremonies, nor in Yoga and renunciation.

Though he saw both religions as valid paths to God, Kabir taught that the ultimate truths transcended Hinduism and Islam. Sheer devotion, not prayers or sacrifices, he argued, would lead the devotee to divine bliss:

If you have not drunk of the nectar of that One Love, what does it matter that you purge yourself of all sins?

The Kazi [judge] is searching the words of the Koran [Quran], and instructing others but if his heart is not steeped in that love, what does it avail, though he be a teacher of men? The Yogi dyes his garments with red: but if he knows nothing of the color of love, what does it avail though his garments be tinted?

Kabir says: "Whether I be in the temple or the balcony, in the camp or in the flower garden, I tell you truly that every moment my Lord is taking His delight in me."

The attempts of mystics like Kabir to minimize the differences between Hindu and Islamic beliefs and worship influenced only small numbers of the followers of either faith. They were also strongly repudiated by the guardians of orthodoxy in each religious community. Sensing the long-term threat to Hinduism posed by Muslim political dominance and conversion efforts, the Brahmins denounced the Muslims as infidel destroyers of Hindu temples and polluted meat eaters. Later Hindu mystics, such as the 15th-century holy man Chaitanya, composed songs that focused on love for Hindu deities and set out to convince Indian Muslims to renounce Islam in favor of Hinduism.

For their part, Muslim ulama, or religious experts, grew increasingly aware of the dangers that Hinduism posed for Islam. Attempts to fuse the two faiths, such as that by Kabir, were rejected on the grounds that though Hindus might argue that specific rituals and beliefs were not essential, they were fundamental for Islam. If one played down the teachings of the *Quran*, prayer, and the pilgrimage, one was no longer a true Muslim. Thus, the ulama and even some Sufi mystics stressed the teachings of Islam that separated it from Hinduism. They worked to promote unity within the Indian Muslim community and to strengthen its contacts with Muslims in neighboring lands and the Middle Eastern centers of the faith.

STAND-OFF: THE MUSLIM PRESENCE IN INDIA AT THE END OF THE SULTANATE PERIOD

After centuries of invasion and migration, a sizeable Muslim community had been established in the Indian subcontinent. Converts had been won, political control had been established throughout much of the area, and strong links had been forged with Muslims in other lands such as Persia and Afghanistan. But non-Muslims, particularly Hindus, remained the overwhelming majority of the population of the vast and diverse lands south of the Himalayas. Unlike the Zoroastrians in Persia or the animistic peoples of the Maghrib and the Sudan, most of the Indians showed little inclination to convert to the religion of the Muslim conquerors. On the contrary, despite their subjugation, they remained convinced that they possessed a superior religion and civilization and that the Muslims would eventually be absorbed into the expansive Hindu fold. The Muslim adoption of Hindu social forms and Indian customs certainly pointed in this direction. The teachings of Hindu and Muslim holy persons threatened to blur the religious boundaries between the two faiths, a process that favored the ascendancy of the more amorphous faith of the Hindu majority. Thus, though Muslim conquests and migration had carried Islam into the heart of one of the most ancient and populous centers of civilization, after centuries of political dominance and missionary activity, India remained one of the least converted and integrated of all the areas to which the message of Muhammad had spread.

 ## THE SPREAD OF ISLAM TO SOUTHEAST ASIA

The spread of Islam to various parts of coastal India set the stage for its further expansion to island Southeast Asia. As we have seen, Arab traders and sailors regularly visited the ports of Southeast Asia long before they converted to Islam. Initially the region was little more than a middle ground, where the Chinese segment of the great Euroasian trading complex met the Indian Ocean trading zone to the west. At ports on the coast of the Malayan peninsula, east Sumatra, and somewhat later north Java, goods from China were transferred from East Asian vessels to Arab or Indian ships, and products from as far west as Rome were loaded into the emptied Chinese ships to be carried to East Asia. By the 7th and 8th centuries A.D., sailors and ships from areas within Southeast Asia—particularly Sumatra and Malaya—had become active in the seaborne trade of the region. Southeast Asian products, especially luxury items, such as aromatic woods from the rainforests of Borneo and Sumatra, and spices, such as cloves, nutmeg, and mace from the far end of the Indonesian archipelago, had also become important exports to both China in the east

and India and the Mediterranean area in the west. These trading links were to prove even more critical to the expansion of Islam in Southeast Asia than they had earlier been to the spread of Buddhism and Hinduism.

As the coastal trade and shipping of India came to be controlled (from the 8th century onward) increasingly by Muslims from such regions as Gujarat and various parts of south India, elements of Islamic culture began to filter into island Southeast Asia. But only in the 13th century after the collapse of the far-flung trading empire of Shrivijaya, which was centered on the Straits of Malacca between Malaya and the north tip of Sumatra, was the way open for the widespread proselytization of Islam. With its great war fleets, Shrivijaya controlled trade in much of the area and was at times so powerful that it could launch attacks on rival empires in south India. Indian traders, Muslim or otherwise, were welcome to trade in the chain of ports controlled by Shrivijaya. Since the rulers and officials of Shrivijaya were devout Buddhists, however, there was little incentive for the traders and sailors of Southeast Asian ports to convert to Islam, the religion of growing numbers of the merchants and sailors from India. With the fall of Shrivijaya, the way was open for the establishment of Muslim trading centers and efforts to preach the faith to the coastal peoples. Muslim conquests in areas such as Gujarat and Bengal, which separated Southeast Asia from Buddhist centers in India from the 11th century onward, also played a role in opening the way for Muslim conversion.

THE PATTERN OF CONVERSION

As was the case in most of the areas to which Islam spread, peaceful and voluntary conversion was far more important than conquest and force in spreading the faith in Southeast Asia. Almost everywhere in the islands of the region, trading contacts paved the way for conversion. Muslim merchants and sailors introduced local peoples to the ideas and rituals of the new faith and impressed on them how much of the known world had already been converted. Muslim ships also carried Sufis to various parts of Southeast Asia, where they were destined to play as vital a role in conversion as they had in India. The first areas to be won to Islam in the last decades of the 13th century were several small port centers on the northern coast of Sumatra. From these ports, the religion spread in the following centuries across the Strait of Malacca to Malaya.

On the mainland the key to widespread conversion was the powerful trading city of Malacca, whose smaller trading empire had replaced the fallen Shrivijaya. From the capital at Malacca, Islam spread down the east coast of Sumatra, up the east and west coasts of Malaya, to the island of Borneo, and to the trading center of Demak on the north coast of Java. From Demak, the most powerful of the trading states on north Java, the Muslim faith was disseminated to other Javanese ports and, after a long struggle with a Hindu-Buddhist kingdom in the interior, to the rest of the island. From Demak, Islam was also carried to the Celebes, the spice islands in the eastern archipelago, and from there to Mindanao in the southern Philippines.

This progress of Islamic conversion shows that port cities in coastal areas were particularly receptive to the new faith. Here the trading links were critical. Once one of the key cities in a trading cluster converted, it was in the best interest of others to follow suit in order to enhance personal ties and provide a common basis in Muslim law to regulate business deals. Conversion to Islam also linked these centers, culturally as well as economically, to the merchants and ports of India, the Middle East, and the Mediterranean. Islam made slow progress in areas such as central Java, where Hindu-Buddhist dynasties contested its spread. But the fact that the earlier conversion to these Indian religions had been confined mainly to the ruling elites in Java and other island areas left openings for mass conversions to Islam that the Sufis eventually exploited. The island of Bali, where Hinduism had taken deep root at the popular level, remained largely impervious to the spread of Islam. The same was true of most of mainland Southeast Asia, where centuries before the coming of Islam, Theravada Buddhism had spread from India and Ceylon and won the fervent adherence of both the ruling elites and the peasant masses.

SUFI MYSTICS AND THE NATURE OF SOUTHEAST ASIAN ISLAM

The fact that Islam came to Southeast Asia primarily from India and that it was spread in many areas by Sufis had much to do with the mystical quality of the religion and its tolerance for coexistence with earlier animist, Hindu, and Buddhist beliefs and rituals. Just as they had in the Middle East and India, the Sufis who spread Islam in Southeast Asia varied widely in personality and approach. Most were believed by those who followed them to have magical powers, and virtually all Sufis established mosque and school centers from which they traveled in neighboring regions to preach the faith.

In winning converts, the Sufis were willing to allow the inhabitants of island Southeast Asia to retain pre-Islamic beliefs and practices that orthodox scholars would clearly have found contrary to Islamic doctrine. Pre-Islamic customary law remained important in regulating social interaction, while Islamic law was confined to specific sorts of agreements and exchanges. Women retained a much stronger position, both within the family and in society, than

they had in the Middle East and India. Local and regional markets, for example, continued to be dominated by the trading of small-scale female buyers and sellers. In such areas as western Sumatra, lineage and inheritance continued to be traced through the female line after the coming of Islam, despite its tendency to promote male dominance and descent through the male line. Perhaps most tellingly, pre-Muslim religious beliefs and rituals were incorporated into Muslim ceremonies. Indigenous cultural staples, such as the brilliant Javanese shadow plays that were based on the Indian epics of the Brahmanic age, were refined, and they became even more central to popular and elite belief and practice than they had been in the pre-Muslim era.

ANALYSIS
CONVERSION AND ACCOMMODATION IN THE SPREAD OF WORLD RELIGIONS

Although not all great civilizations have produced world religions, the two have tended to be closely associated throughout human history. World religions are those that have the capacity to spread across many cultures and societies, forge links between civilized centers, and diffuse civilized life-styles to nomadic pastoral or shifting-cultivating peoples. Religions with these characteristics had appeared before the rise of Islam. As we have seen, India alone produced two of these faiths in ancient times: Hinduism, which spread to parts of Southeast and central Asia, and Buddhism, which spread even more widely in the Asian world. At the other end of the Eastern Hemisphere, Christianity spread throughout the Mediterranean region before claiming northern and western Europe as its core area. Judaism spread not because it won converts in non-Jewish cultures but because the Jewish people were driven from their homeland by Roman persecution and scattered throughout the Middle East, North Africa, and Europe.

Because religious conversion affects all aspects of life, from the way one looks at the universe to everyday decisions about whom one may marry or how one ought to treat others, a world religion must be broad and flexible enough to permit the retention of much of the existing culture of peoples who are potential converts. At the same time, it must possess core beliefs and practices that are well enough defined to allow its followers to maintain a clear sense of common identity, despite their great differences in culture and society. These beliefs and practices must also be sufficiently profound and sophisticated to convince potential converts that their own cultures can be enriched and their lives improved by adopting the new religion.

Until the 16th century, when Christianity claimed the two continents of the Western Hemisphere, no world religion could match Islam in the extent to which it spread across the globe and in the diversity of peoples and cultures that identified themselves as Muslims. Given its uncompromising monotheism, very definite doctrines, and elaborately prescribed rituals and principles of social organization, Islam's success at winning converts from very different cultural backgrounds is at first glance quite surprising. This is particularly true if it is compared with the much more amorphous beliefs and more variable ceremonial patterns of earlier world religions such as Buddhism and Hinduism. Closer examination, however, reveals that the apparent rigidity of Islamic beliefs and social practices as written in the Quran and interpreted in the abstract by the ulama proved much more flexible and adaptable in the actual situations in which the religion was introduced into new, non-Islamic cultures. Like all world religions, Islam had the capacity to adjust to widely varying cultural norms and modes of expression at the same time it converted the peoples who exhibited these differences to a common set of religious beliefs, ritual forms, and social practices.

The fact that, in most areas to which it spread, Islam won converts overwhelmingly through the peaceful contacts between long-distance traders and the preaching and organizational skills of Sufis exemplifies this capacity for accommodation in the conversion process. Those adopting the new religion did not do so because they were pressured or forced to convert but because they saw Islam as a way to enhance their understanding of the supernatural, enrich their ceremonial expression, improve the quality of their social interaction, and establish ongoing links to a transcultural community beyond their local world.

Because Islam was adopted rather than imposed, those who converted had a good deal to say about how much of their own cultures they would change and which aspects of Islam they would emphasize or accept. Certain beliefs and practices were obligatory for all true believers—the worship of a single God, adherence to the prophet Muhammad and the divine revelations he received as recorded in the Quran, observance of the five pillars of the faith, etc.—but even these were liable to reinterpretation and reworking. In virtually all cultures to which it spread, for example, Islamic monotheism supplanted but did not eradicate the animistic veneration of nature spirits or personal and place deities. Allah was acknowledged as the most powerful and all-purpose of the supernatural agents, but people continued to make offerings to spirits that could heal or bring fertility, protect one's home, or punish one's enemies. In such areas as Africa and western China, where the veneration of ancestral spirits was a key aspect of religious life, the spirits were retained not as powers in themselves but as emissaries to Allah. In cultures like those found in India and Southeast Asia, Islamic doctrines were recast in a heavily mystical, even magical, mode.

The capacity of Islam for accommodation was exhibited in the social as well as the religious sphere. In Islamic Southeast Asia and, as we shall see in the next chapter, sub-Saharan Africa, the position of women remained a good deal stronger in critical areas, such as occupational outlets and family law, than it had become in the Middle East and India. In both regions, the male-centric features of Islam that had grown more pronounced through centuries of accommodation in ancient Middle Eastern and Persian cultures were played down in adapting to societies where women had traditionally enjoyed considerable influence, both within the extended family and in occupations such as farming, marketing, and craft production. Even an institution like the caste system of India, which in principle is so opposed to the strong egalitarian strain in Islam, survived in indigenous South Asian communities that converted to Islam and developed among Muslim groups who migrated into the subcontinent.

Beyond basic forms of social organization and interaction, Islam accommodated diverse aspects of the societies into which it spread. The African solar calendar, for example, which was essential for the coordination of the planting cycle, was retained alongside the Muslim lunar calendar. In India, Hindu-Buddhist symbols of kingship were appropriated by Muslim rulers and acknowledged by both their Hindu and Muslim subjects. In island Southeast Asia, exquisitely forged knives, called *krises*, which were believed to have magical powers, were among the most treasured possessions of local rulers both before and after they converted to Islam.

There was always the danger that accommodation could go too far, that in winning converts Islamic precepts and rituals would be so watered down and remolded that they no longer resembled and, in fact, actually contradicted the teachings of the Quran. Sects, for example, that came to worship Muhammad or his nephew Ali as godlike had clearly moved beyond the Muslim pale. This danger was a key source of the periodic movements for purification and revival that have been a notable feature of virtually all Islamic societies, particularly those on the frontier fringes of the Islamic world. But even these movements, which were built around the insistence that the Muslim faith had been corrupted by alien ideas and practices and that there had to be a return to Islamic fundamentals, were invariably cast in the modes of cultural expression of the peoples who rallied to them. What was considered fundamental varied by culture, and perhaps more important, the ways in which basic beliefs were interpreted and rituals enacted differed significantly from one Islamic culture to the next.

Questions: Can you think of ways in which world religions, such as Christianity, Hinduism, and Buddhism, changed to accommodate the cultures and societies to which they spread? Do these religions strike you as more or less flexible than Islam? Why? Do you think it is possible for a set of religious beliefs and practices to become a world religion without changing as it moves from one culture to the next? If not, why? If so, can you think of a religion that has?

world contained all requirements for civilized life, caused Muslim peoples to grow less receptive to outside influences and innovations. These tendencies became increasingly pronounced at precisely the time when their Christian rivals were entering a period of unprecedented curiosity, experimentation, and exploration of the world beyond their own civilized regions. The combination of these trends would put the Islamic world at a growing disadvantage vis-à-vis the West and would eventually engender a profound crisis in Islamic civilization that continues in the present day.

CONCLUSION

THE LEGACY OF THE ABBASID AGE

Though problems of political control and succession continued to plague the kingdoms and empires that divided the Muslim world, in the centuries of Abbasid rule the central position of Islamic civilization in global history was solidified. Its role as the go-between for the other, more ancient civilizations of the Eastern Hemisphere grew as Arab trading networks expanded and reached into new areas. More than ever it became the civilizer of nomadic peoples, from the Turks and Mongols of central Asia to the Berbers of North Africa and the camel herders of the Sudan. Equally critically, Islam's original contributions to the growth and refinement of civilized life greatly increased. From its great cities and universities and the accomplishments they generated in the fine arts, sciences, and literature to its vibrant religious and philosophical life, Islam pioneered patterns of organization and thinking that would affect the development of human societies in major ways for centuries to come.

In the midst of all this achievement, however, there were tendencies that would put the Muslim peoples at a growing disadvantage, particularly in relation to their longstanding European rivals. Muslim divisions would leave openings for political expansion that the Europeans would eagerly exploit, beginning with the island Southeast Asian extremities of the Islamic world and then working their way across Muslim North India. The Muslims' inclination to leave commerce and entrepreneurship increasingly in the hands of non-Muslim groups, such as Jews and Christians, would hamper effective responses to their growing economic dependence on and increasing backwardness relative to the West and other civilizations, particularly China. Above all, the growing orthodoxy and intolerance of the ulama, as well as the Muslim conceit that the vast Islamic

FURTHER READINGS

M. A. Shaban's *Islamic History: An Interpretation*, 2 vols. (1971) contains the most readable and thematic survey of early Islam, concentrating on the Abbasid period. Though Philip Hitti's monumental *History of the Arabs* (1967) and J. J. Saunders's *A History of Medieval Islam* (1965) are now somewhat dated, they contain much valuable information and some fine insights into Arab history. Also useful are the works of G. E. von Gruenenbaum, especially *Classical Islam* (1970), which covers the Abbasid era. On changes in Islamic religion and the makeup of the Muslim community, Marshall Hodgson's *Venture of Islam* (1974, vol. 2) is indispensable, but again it should not be tackled by the beginner. The *Cambridge History of Islam*, 2 vols. (1970) and Ira Lapidus's *A History of Islamic Societies* (1988) provide excellent reference works for the political events of the Abbasid era and Muslim achievements in various fields. D. M. Dunlop's *Arab Civilization to A.D. 1500* (1971) also contains detailed essays on the latter aspects of Islamic culture as well as an article on the accomplishments of Muslim women in this era.

On social history, B. F. Musallam's *Sex and Society in Islam* (1983) has material on the Abbasid period, and Ira Lapidus's study of *Muslim Cities in the Later Middle Ages* (1967) remains the standard work on urban life in the premodern era. Two essential works on the spread of Islam to India are S. M. Ikram's *Muslim Civilization in India* (1964) and Aziz Ahmad's *Studies in Islamic Culture in the Indian Environment* (1964). For the role of the Sufis in Islamic conversion, Richard Eaton's *Sufis of Bijapur* (1978) is particularly revealing. The best introduction to the pattern of Islamic conversion in Southeast Asia is H. J. de Graaf's essay in *Cambridge History of Islam* (1976, vol. 2). Clifford Geertz's *Islam Observed* (1968) provides a sweeping and provocative interpretation of the process of conversion in general, and of the varying forms Islam takes in the Javanese and Moroccan milieux in particular.

100–200 Camels introduced for trade in the Sahara　　**600–700** Islam spreads across North Africa

1000 Ghana at height of its power

300 Origins of the kingdom of Ghana

1100 Almoravid movement in the Sahara

A.D. 100　　　　　　600　　　　　　1000

African Civilizations and the Spread of Islam

INTRODUCTION. The spread of Islam, from its heartland in the Middle East and North Africa to India and Southeast Asia, revealed the power of the religion and its commercial and sometimes military attributes. Civilizations were altered without being fully drawn into a single Islamic statement. A similar pattern developed in sub-Saharan Africa, as Islam provided new influences and contacts without amalgamating African culture as a whole to the Middle Eastern core. New religious, economic, and political patterns developed in relation to the Islamic surge, but great diversity remained.

Africa below the Sahara was never totally isolated from the centers of civilization in Egypt, west Asia, or the Mediterranean, but for long periods the contacts were difficult and intermittent. During the ascendancy of Rome, sub-Saharan Africa like northern Europe was on the periphery of the major centers of civilization. After the fall of Rome, the civilizations of Byzantium and the Islamic world provided a link between the civilizations of the Middle East and the Mediterranean as well as the areas, such as northern Europe and Africa, on their frontiers. In Africa, between roughly A.D. 800 and 1500, the frequency and intensity of contact with the outside world increased as part of the growing international network. A number of social, religious, and technological changes took place that influenced many of the different peoples throughout the vast and varied continent. Chief among these changes was the arrival of the followers of the Prophet Muhammad.

The spread of Islam across much of the northern third of Africa produced profound effects on both those who converted and those who resisted the new faith. Islamization also served to link Muslim Africa even more closely to the outside world through trade, religion, and politics. Trade and long-distance commerce, in fact, was carried out in many parts of the continent and linked regions beyond the orbit of Muslim penetration. Until about 1450, however, Islam provided the major external contact between sub-Saharan Africa and the world.

State building took place in many areas of the continent under a variety of conditions. West Africa, for example, experienced both the cultural influence of Islam and its own internal dynamic of state building and civilizational developments that produced, in some places, great artistic accomplishments. The formation of some powerful states, such as Mali and Songhay, depended more on military power and dynastic alliances than on ethnic or cultural unity. In this aspect and in the process of state formation itself, Africa paralleled the roughly contemporaneous developments of western Europe. The development of city-states, with strong merchant communities in West Africa and on the Indian Ocean coast of East Africa, bore certain similarities to the urban developments of Italy and Germany in this period. However, disparities between the technologies and ideologies of Europeans and Africans by the end of this period also created marked differences in the way in which their societies developed. The arrival of western Europeans—the Portuguese—in the 15th century set in motion a series of exchanges that would draw Africans increasingly into the world economy and create a new set of relationships that would characterize African development for centuries to come.

Several emphases thus highlight the history of Africa in the postclassical centuries. Northern Africa and the East African coast became increasingly incorporated into the Arab Muslim world, but even other parts of the continent reflected the power of Islamic thought and institutions. New centers of civilization and political power arose in several parts of sub-Saharan Africa, illustrating the geographical diffusion of civilization. African civilizations, however, built somewhat less clearly on prior precedent than was the case in other postclassical societies. Some earlier themes, such as the Bantu migration and the formation of large states in the western Sudan, persisted. Overall, sub-Saharan Africa remained a varied and distinctive setting, parts of it drawn into new contacts with the growing world network, but much of it retaining a certain isolation.

AFRICAN SOCIETIES: DIVERSITY AND SIMILARITIES

The continent of Africa is so vast and the nature of its societies so diverse that it is almost impossible to generalize about them. Differences in geography, language, religion, politics, and other aspects of life contributed to the diversity and to Africa's lack of political unity over long periods of time. Unlike many parts of Asia, Europe, and North Africa, neither universal states nor universal religions characterized the history of sub-Saharan Africa. Yet universal religions, first Christianity and later Islam, did find adherents in Africa and sometimes contributed to the formation of large states and empires.

ISSUES IN UNDERSTANDING AFRICA

Perhaps because of the trends of European history, much of the history of Africa, like the history of the rest of the world, has been written in terms of organized political entities, states and empires. These political entities have been the units for understanding the past, and their rise and fall have provided the flow of history. Historians of Africa have realized, however, that while some African societies had rulers who exercised control through a hierarchy of officials in what can be called states, other African societies were "stateless," organizing around kinship or other forms of obligation and lacking the concentration of political power and authority we normally associate with the state. The African past reveals that the movement from stateless to state societies was not necessarily an evolutionary development. Stateless peoples who lived in villages organized around either lineages or *age sets*—that is, groups of people of the same age who are considered to have similar responsibilities to society—did not need rulers or bureaucracies and existed side by side with states; sometimes the stateless societies were larger and more extensive than the neighboring states. Stateless societies had forms of government, but the authority and power normally exercised by a ruler and his court in a kingdom could be held instead by a council of families or by the community, with no need to tax the population to support the ruler, the bureaucrats, the army, or the nobles as was usually the case in state-building societies. Stateless societies had little concentration of authority, and that authority only affected a small part of the peoples' lives. In these societies, government was rarely a full-time occupation.

Other alternatives to formal government were also possible. Among peoples of the West African forest, secret societies of men and women exercised considerable control over customs and beliefs and were able to limit the authority of rulers. Especially among peoples who had sharp rivalries between lineages or family groupings, secret societies developed that cut across the lineage divisions. The secret societies incorporated their members after an initiation that might have been based on knowledge, skills, physical tests, an initiation fee, or all of these. Members took on an allegiance to the society that transcended their lineage ties. The secret societies settled village disputes; enforcement or punishment was carried out by masked junior members acting on behalf of the secret society so that no feuding between families resulted. The secret societies acted to maintain stability within the community, and they served as an alternative to the authority of state institutions.

Throughout Africa many stateless societies thrived, perhaps aided by the fact that internal social pressures or disputes could often be resolved by the splitting off of dissidents and the establishment of a new village in the relatively sparsely populated continent. Fragmentation and a "frontier" open to new settlement were constant features in much of African history. Still, stateless societies found it difficult to meet external pressures, mobilize for warfare, organize large building projects, or create stable conditions for continuous long-distance trade with other peoples. All these needs or goals contributed in various ways to the formation of states in sub-Saharan Africa. Finally, stateless societies left fewer records or traditions of the exploits of great heroes; thus, we know less about them. The existence of stateless societies and their transformation into states are a constant of African history even beyond 1500.

COMMON ELEMENTS IN AFRICAN SOCIETIES

Amid the diversity of African cultures, it is also useful to note certain similarities in language, thought, and religion that provide some underlying unities. As we saw in Chapter 10, the spread of the Bantu-speaking peoples provided a linguistic base across much of Africa, so that even though specific languages differed, structure and vocabulary allowed for some mutual understanding between neighboring Bantu-speakers.

The same might be said of the animistic religion that characterized much of Africa. The belief in the power of natural forces personified as spirits or gods and the role of ritual and worship—often in the form of dancing, drumming, divination, and sacrifice—in influencing their actions was central to the religion of many African peoples, although local practice varied widely. African religions had well-developed concepts of good and evil. Africans, like Europeans, believed that some evil, disasters, and illnesses were produced by witchcraft. Specialists were needed to combat the power of evil and eliminate the witches. This led in many societies to the existence of a class of diviners or priests who guided religious practice and helped protect the community. Above all, African religion provided a *cosmology*—a view of how the universe worked—and a guide to ethics and behavior.

Many African peoples shared an underlying belief in a creator deity whose power and action were expressed through spirits or lesser gods and through the founding ancestors of the group. The ancestors were often viewed as the first settlers and thus the "owners" of the land or the local resources, and through them the fertility of the land, the game, the people, and the herds could be ensured. Among some groups working the land took on religious significance, so the land itself had a meaning beyond its economic usefulness.

Religion, economics, and history were thus closely intertwined. Then too, the family, lineage, or clan around which many African societies were organized had an important role in dealing with the gods. Deceased ancestors were often a direct link between their living relatives and the spirit world. Veneration of the ancestors and gods were part of the same system of belief. Such a system was strongly linked to specific places and people. It showed remarkable resiliency even in the face of contact with the more generalized principles of religions such as Islam and Christianity.

The economies of Africa are harder to describe in common terms than some basic aspects of politics and culture. North Africa was fully involved in the Mediterranean and Arab economic world, and stands clearly apart. Sub-Saharan Africa varied greatly from one region to the next. In many areas, settled agriculture and skilled ironwork had been established before the postclassical period or advanced rapidly during the period itself. Specialization encouraged active local and regional trade, the basis for many lively markets and the many large cities that grew both in the structured states and in the decentralized areas. The bustle and gaiety of market life were important ingredients of African society, and women as well as men participated actively. Trade was handled by professional merchants, in many cases in hereditary kinship groupings. Participation in international trade increased in many regions in this period, mainly toward the Islamic world and often through the intermediary of Arab traders.

While African states benefited from their ability to tax the trade, they stood at some disadvantage in trading unprocessed goods, such as gold, ivory, salt, or slaves, for more elaborate products made elsewhere. International trade stimulated political and cultural change and furthered the growth of African merchant groups, but it did not induce rapid technical or manufacturing shifts within Africa, except for some important innovations in the excavation of mines.

Finally, we should note that one of the least known aspects of African societies prior to the 20th century is the size and dynamic of their populations. This is true not only of Africa, but of much of the world. Archeological evidence, travelers' reports, and educated guesses are used to estimate the population of early African societies, but, in truth, our knowledge of how Africa fits into the general trends of the world population is very slight. By 1500, Africa may have had 30 to 60 million inhabitants.

THE ARRIVAL OF ISLAM IN NORTH AFRICA

Africa north of the Sahara had long been part of the world of classical antiquity, where Phoenicians, Greeks, Romans, and Vandals traded, settled, built, battled, and destroyed. The Greek city of Cyrene (c. 600 B.C.) in modern Libya or the great Phoenician outpost at Carthage (founded c. 814 B.C.) in Tunisia attest to the part North Africa played in the classical world. After the age of the Pharaohs, Egypt (conquered by Alexander in 331 B.C.) had become an important part of the Greek world and then later a key province in the Roman Empire, valued especially for its grain. Toward the end of the Roman Empire, Christianity had taken a firm hold in Mediterranean Africa but in the warring between the Vandals and the Byzantines in North Africa in the 5th and 6th centuries A.D., considerable disruption had taken place. During that period, the Berber peoples of the Sahara had raided the coastal cities. As we have seen with Egypt, North Africa was also linked across the Sahara to the rest of Africa in many ways. With the rise of Islam, those ties became even closer.

Between A.D. 640 and 700 the followers of Muhammad swept across North Africa from Suez to the Pillars of Hercules on Morocco's Atlantic shore. By A.D. 670 Muslims ruled Tunisia, or *Ifriqiya,* what the Romans had called Africa. (The Arabs originally used this word as the name for eastern North Africa and *Maghrib* for lands to the West.) By 711, Arab and Berber armies had crossed into Spain. Only their defeat in France by Charles Martel at Poitiers in 732 brought the Muslim advance in the West to a halt. The message of Islam found fertile ground among the populations of North Africa. Conversion took place rapidly within a certain political unity provided by the Abbasid dynasty. This unity eventually broke down and North Africa divided into a number of separate states and competing groups.

In opposition to the states dominated by the Arabic rulers, the peoples of the desert, the Berbers, formed states of their own at places such as Fez in Morocco and at Sijilimasa, the old city of the trans-Saharan caravan trade. By the 11th century, under pressure from new Muslim invaders from the East, a great puritanical reformist movement, whose followers were called the Almoravids, grew among the desert Berbers of the western Sahara. Launched on the course of a jihad, a holy war waged to purify, spread, or protect the faith, the Almoravids moved southward against the African kingdoms of the savanna and westward into Spain. In 1130 another reformist group, the Almohades, followed the same pattern. These North African and Spanish developments were an essential background to the penetration of Islam into sub-Saharan Africa.

Islam offered a number of attractions within Africa. Its fundamental teaching that all Muslims are equal within the community of believers made the acceptance of conquerors and new rulers easier. The Islamic tradition of uniting the powers of the state and religion in the person of the ruler or caliph appealed to some African kings as a way of reinforcing their authority. The concept that all members of the ummah, or community of believers, were equal put the newly converted Berbers and later Africans on an equal footing with the Arabs, at least in law. Despite these egalitarian and somewhat utopian ideas within Islam, practice differed considerably at local levels. Social stratification remained important in Islamicized societies and ethnic distinctions also divided the believers. Despite certain teachings on the relative equality between men and women, the law recognized that the monetary penalty for killing a man was twice that for killing a woman. The disparity between law and practice, between equality before God and inequality within the world, sometimes led to reform movements of a utopian type. Groups like the Almohades are characteristic within Islamic history, often developing in peripheral areas and dedicated to a purification of society by returning to the original teachings of the Prophet.

THE CHRISTIAN KINGDOMS: NUBIA AND ETHIOPIA

Islam, of course, was not the first universalistic religion to take root in Africa, and the wave of Arab conquests across northern Africa had left behind it islands of Christianity at various places. Christianity had made converts in Egypt and Ethiopia even before the conversion of the Roman Empire in the 4th century A.D. Aside from the Christian kingdom of Axum, Christian communities thrived in Egypt and Nubia. The Christians of Egypt, the Copts, developed a rich tradition in contact with Byzantium, translating the gospels and other religious literature from Greek to Coptic, their own tongue, which was based on the language of ancient Egypt. On doctrinal and political issues they eventually split from the Byzantine connection. When Egypt was conquered by Arab armies and then converted to Islam, the Copts were able to maintain their faith, recognized by Muslim rulers as followers of a revealed religion and thus entitled to a certain tolerance. The Coptic influence had already spread up the Nile into Nubia, the

The 13th-century churches of Lalaibela, some cut from a single rock, represent the power of early Christianity in Ethiopia.

ancient land of Kush. Muslim attempts to penetrate Nubia were met with such stiff resistance in the 9th century that the Christian descendants of ancient Kush were left in relative peace as independent Christian kingdoms until the 13th century.

The Ethiopian kingdom that grew from Axum was perhaps the most important of the African Christian outposts. Cut off from Christian Byzantium by the Muslim conquest of Egypt and the Red Sea coast, surrounded by pagan neighbors, and probably influenced by pagan and Jewish immigrants from Yemen, the Christian kingdom turned inward. Its people occupied the Ethiopian highlands, living in fortified towns and supporting themselves with agriculture on terraced hillsides. Eventually through a process of warfare, conversion, and compromise with non-Christian neighbors, a new dynasty appeared, which under King Lalaibela (d. 1221) sponsored a remarkable building project in which eleven great churches were sculpted from the rock in the town that bore his name.

In the 13th and 14th centuries an Ethiopian Christian state emerged under a dynasty that traced its origins back to the marriage of Solomon and Sheba. Using the Geez language of Axum as a religious language and Amharic as the common speech, this state maintained its brand of Christianity, in relative isolation while facing constant pressure from its increasingly Muslim neighbors.

The struggle between the Christian state in the Ethiopian highlands and the Muslim peoples in Somalia and on the Red Sea coast shaped much of the consequent history of the region and continues to do so today. When one of these Muslim states, with help from the Ottoman Turks, threatened the very existence of the Ethiopian kingdom, a Portuguese expedition arrived in 1542 at Massawa on the Red Sea and turned the tide in favor of its Christian allies. Portuguese attempts thereafter to bring Ethiopian Christianity into the Roman Catholic church failed, and Ethiopia remained isolated, Christian, and fiercely independent.

KINGDOMS OF THE GRASSLANDS

Islam spread through North Africa by conquest, much as it had done on the Indian subcontinent and in the Middle East. The situation differed in Africa south of the Sahara. The old caravan routes now carried Muslim merchants, teachers, and mystics who settled among the African peoples and the states south of the Sahara. Sometimes by war, but more often by peaceful conversion, Africans were brought into the new faith.

As the Islamic wave spread across North Africa, it sent ripples across the Sahara, not in the form of invading armies, but at first in the merchants and travelers who trod the dusty and ancient caravan routes toward the savanna. Africa had three important "coasts" of contact: the Atlantic, the Indian Ocean, and the savanna on the southern edge of the Sahara. On the edge of the desert, where a number of resource zones came together, African states such as Ghana had already formed by the 8th century by exchanging gold from the forests of West Africa for salt or dates from the Sahara or for goods from Mediterranean North Africa. Camels, which had been introduced from Asia to the Sahara between the 1st and 5th centuries A.D., had greatly improved the possibilities of trade, but these animals that thrived in arid and semiarid environments could not penetrate into the humid forest zones because of disease. Thus the *Sahel*, the extensive grassland belt at the southern edge of the Sahara, became a point of exchange between the forests to the south and North Africa—an active "coast" where ideas, trade, and people from the Sahara and beyond arrived in increasing numbers. Along that coast a number of African states developed between trading cities, taking advantage of their position as intermediaries in the trade. But location on the relatively open plains of the dry Sahel also meant that these states were subject to attack and periodic droughts.

In Chapter 10 we discussed the rise of the kingdom of Ghana among the Soninke peoples of the western Sudan. Founded probably in the 3d century A.D., Ghana rose to power by taxing the salt and gold exchanged within its borders. By the 10th century its rulers had converted to Islam and Ghana was at the height of its power. At a time when William the Conqueror could muster perhaps 10,000 troops for his invasion of England, Muslim accounts reported that the king of Ghana could field an army many times that size. Eventually, however, Almoravid armies in-

The Savanna Kingdoms, about 1400

vaded Ghana from North Africa in 1076, and although the kingdom survived, its power was in decline so that by the beginning of the 13th century new states had risen in the savanna to take its place of leadership.

SUDANIC STATES

There were a number of Sudanic kingdoms, and even during the height of Ghana's power neighboring and competing states persisted, such as Takrur on the Senegal River to the west and Gao (Kawkaw) on the Niger River to the east. Before dealing with the most important kingdoms that followed Ghana, it will be useful to review some of the elements these states had in common.

The Sudanic states were often led by the patriarch or council of elders of a particular family or group of lineages that established control over its neighbors. Usually these states had a territorial core area in which the people were of the same linguistic or ethnic background, but their power extended over subordinate communities. These were conquest states that drew on the taxes, tribute, and military support of the subordinate areas, lineages, and villages. The effective control of subordinate societies and the legal or informal control of their sovereignty are the usual definition of empires. Ghana, Mali, and Songhay and some of their neighbors were imperial states.

The rulers of these states were considered to be sacred individuals and were surrounded with rituals that separated them from their subjects. With the conversion of the rulers of Ghana and Takrur after the 10th century, Islam was used to reinforce indigenous ideas of kingship so that Islam became something of a royal cult. Much of the population never converted, and the Islamicized ruling families also drew on their traditional powers to fortify their rule.

A number of savanna states rose among the various peoples in the Sudan. We can trace the development and the culture of two of the most important, Mali and Songhay, as an example of the fusion of Islamic and indigenous African cultures, within the context of trade and military expansion, that these states represented.

THE EMPIRE OF MALI

The empire of Mali, centered between the Senegal and Niger rivers, was the creation of the Malinke peoples, who in the 13th century broke away from the control of Ghana, which was by then in steady decline. In Mali the old forms of kingship were reinforced by Islam. As in many of the Sudanic states, rulers supported Islam by building mosques, attending public prayers, and supporting preachers. In return, sermons to the faithful emphasized obedience and support of the king. Mali became a model of these Islamicized Sudanic kingdoms. The economic basis of society in the Mali Empire was successful agriculture. This was combined with an active tradition of trade in many products, although like Ghana, Mali also depended on its access to gold-producing areas to the south. Malinke merchants, or *juula*, formed small partnerships and groups to carry out trade throughout the area. They spread beyond the borders of the empire and throughout much of West Africa.

SUNDIATA: MALI'S "LION PRINCE"

The beginning of Malinke expansion is attributed to Sundiata (sometimes written *Sunjata*), a brilliant leader whose exploits serve as the foundation of a great oral tradition. The *griots,* professional oral historians who also served as keepers of traditions and advisors to kings, began their epic histories of Mali with Sundiata, the "Lion Prince."

> Listen then sons of Mali, children of the black people, listen to my word, for I am going to tell you of Sundiata, the father of the Bright Country, of the savanna land, the ancestor of those who draw the bow, the master of a hundred vanquished kings. . . . He was great among kings, he was peerless among men; he was beloved of God because he was the last of the great conquerors.

After a difficult childhood, Sundiata, representing the Keita clan, emerged from a period of interfamily and regional fighting to create a unified state. Oral histories ascribed to him the creation of the basic rules and relationships of Malinke society and the outline of the government of the empire of Mali. He became the *mansa,* or emperor. Provincial leaders and subkings ruled with the approval of the mansa, who also served as supreme judge and leader. Sundiata, it was said, "divided up the world," which meant that he was considered the originator of social arrangements. There were 16 clans of freemen entitled to bear arms and carry the bow and quiver of arrows as the symbol of their status, five clans devoted to religious du-

ties, and four clans of specialists and tradesmen such as the blacksmiths and the griots. Division and grouping by clans had apparently existed and represented traditional patterns among the peoples of the savanna in ancient Ghana as well, but Sundiata as the hero of origins was credited with the creation of this social arrangement. While he created the political institutions of rule that allowed for considerable regional and ethnic differences in the federated provinces, he also stationed garrisons to maintain loyalty and security. Travel was secure and crime was severely punished as Ibn Battuta, the Arab traveler, reported: "Of all peoples," he said "the Blacks are those who most hate injustice, and their emperor pardons none who is guilty of it." The security of travelers and their goods was an essential element in a state where commerce played so important a role.

THE SUCCESSORS OF SUNDIATA

Sundiata died about 1260, but his successors expanded the borders of Mali till it controlled most of the Niger valley almost to the Atlantic coast. A sumptuous court was established that hosted a large number of traders. Mali grew wealthy from the trade. Perhaps the most famous of Sundiata's successors was Mansa Kankan Musa (c. 1312–1337). As a Muslim he decided to make the hajj, or pilgrimage to Mecca, in 1324 and his trip brought the glory and wealth of Mali to the attention of the Muslim world

This illustration of a 14th-century map of Abraham Cresques shows Mansa Musa of Mali, "the richest and most noble king," receiving a trade caravan with a gold nugget in his hand.

and eventually to the Europeans as well. Accompanied by hundreds of richly-dressed servants and retainers and distributing gold along the way, Mansa Musa's pilgrimage created a sensation in Egypt and across the Sudan. It was said that so much gold was spent or distributed while he was in Egypt that it caused a devaluation of the currency. In 1375, a Jewish mapmaker in Spain illustrated one of his maps with the image of the Emperor of Mali who held a golden scepter in his hand, evidence that the fame of Mali was spreading.

Mali's contact with the outer world brought changes and innovations. Mansa Musa brought back from Muslim Spain the poet and architect Ishak as-Sahili, whom he had met in Mecca. He directed the building of a number of important mosques and expanded the use of sun-dried bricks as a major building material. A distinctive form of Sudanic architecture developed, making use of local materials, especially beaten clay. This can still be seen in the great mosque of Jenne.

CITY FOLK AND VILLAGERS

The cities of the western Sudan began to resemble those of North Africa, but with a distinctive local architectural style. The towns were commercial and often included craft

The spread of Islam and the importance of trade in Africa is represented by the great mosque at Jenne on the Niger River in the modern Republic of Mali.

specialists and a resident foreign merchant community. The military expansion of states, such as Ghana, Mali, and later Songhay, contributed to their commercial success because the power of the state protected traders. Also, the booty and captives acquired in conquest became part of the trade itself, exchanged for luxury goods and horses from North Africa.

A cosmopolitan court life developed as merchants and scholars were attracted by the power and protection of Mali. Mandinka juula traders ranged across the Sudan and exploited their position as middlemen. "Port" cities flourished, such as Jenne and Timbuktu, which lay just off the flood plain on the great bend in the Niger River. Timbuktu was reported to have a population of 50,000, and by the 14th century its great Sankore mosque contained a library and an associated university where scholars, jurists, and Muslim theologians studied. The book was the symbol of civilization in the Islamic world, and it was said that the book trade in Timbuktu was the most lucrative business of all.

For the vast majority of people in the empire of Mali or any of the other Sudanic states, life was not centered on the royal court, the great Mosque, or long-distance trade, but rather on the agricultural cycle and the village. Making a living from the land was the preoccupation of most people, and about 80 percent of the villagers lived by farming. This was a difficult life. The soils of the savanna were sandy and shallow. Plows were rarely used. The villagers were people of the hoe who looked to the skies in the spring for the first rains to start their planting. Rice in the river valleys, millet, sorghums, some wheat, fruits, and vegetables provided the basis of daily life in the village and supplied the caravan trade. Even a large farm would rarely exceed ten acres and most were much smaller. Clearing land was often done communally, accompanied by feasts and competition, but the farms belonged to families and were worked by them. A man with two wives and a number of unmarried sons could work more land than a man with one wife and a smaller family. *Polygyny*, or the practice of having multiple wives, therefore, was common in the region and it remains so today.

Given the difficulties of the soil, the periodic droughts, insect pests, storage problems, and the limitations of technology, the farmers of the Sudanic states—by the methods of careful cultivation, crop rotation, and, in places like Timbuktu, the use of irrigation—were able to provide for their people the basic foods that supported them and the imperial states on which they were based. The hoe and the bow became symbols of the common people of the savanna states.

Oral traditions are of various kinds. Some are simply the shared stories of a family or people, but in a number of West African societies the mastery of oral traditions is a skill practiced by griots. Although today's griots are professional musicians and bards, historically they held important places at the courts of West African kingdoms. The epic of Sundiata, the great ruler of Mali, has been passed down orally for centuries. In the following excerpts from a version collected among the Mandingo (Malinke) people in Guinea by the African scholar D. T. Niane, the role of the griot and the advantages of oral tradition are outlined.

We are now coming to the great moments in the life of Sundiata. The exile will end and another sun will rise. It is the sun of Sundiata. Griots know the history of kings and kingdoms and that is why they are the best counsellors of kings. Every king wants to have a singer to perpetuate his memory, for it is the griot who rescues the memories of kings from oblivion, as men have short memories. Kings have prescribed destinies just like men, and seers who probe the future know it. They have knowledge of the future, whereas we griots are depositories of the knowledge of the past. But whoever knows the history of a country can read its future.

Other peoples use writing to record the past, but this invention has killed the faculty of memory among them. They do not feel the past any more, for writing lacks the warmth of the human voice. With them everybody thinks he knows, whereas learning should be a secret. The prophets did not write and their words have been all the more vivid as a result. What paltry learning is that which is concealed in dumb books!

The following excerpt describes the preparation for a major battle fought by Sundiata against the forces of Soumaoro, king of the Sossos, who had taken control of Mali and who is referred to in the epic as an evil sorcerer. Note the interweaving of proverbs, the presence of aspects of Muslim and animist religion, the celebration of Sundiata's prowess, the recurring references to iron, and the high value placed on the cavalry, the key to military power in the savanna. Note how the story of Alexander the Great inspires this "African Alexander."

DOCUMENT
THE GREAT ORAL TRADITION AND THE EPIC OF SUNDIATA

Every man to his own land! If it is foretold that your destiny should be fulfilled in such and such a land, men can do nothing against it. Mansa Tounkara could not keep Sundiata back because the destiny of Songolon's son was bound up with that of Mali. Neither the jealousy of a cruel stepmother, nor her wickedness could alter for a moment the course of great destiny.

The snake, man's enemy, is not long-lived, yet the serpent that lives hidden will surely die old. Djata (Sundiata) was strong enough now to face his enemies. At the age of eighteen he had the stateliness of the lion and the strength of the buffalo. His voice carried authority, his eyes were live coals, his arm was iron, he was the husband of power.

Moussa Tounkara, king of Mema, gave Sundiata half of his army. The most valiant came forward of their own free will to follow Sundiata in the great adventure. The cavalry of Mema, which he had fashioned himself, formed his iron squadron. Sundiata, dressed in the Muslim fashion of Mema, left the town at the head of his small but redoubtable army. The whole population sent their best wishes with him. He was surrounded by five messengers from Mali, and Manding Bory [Sundiata's brother] rode proudly at his side. The horsemen of Mema formed behind Djata a bristling iron squadron. The troop took the direction of Wagadou, for Djata did not have enough troops to confront Soumaoro directly, and so the king of Mema advised him to go to Wagadou and take half the men of the king, Soumaba Cissé. A swift messenger had been sent there and so the king of Wagadou came out in person to meet Sundiata and his troops. He gave Sundiata half of his cavalry and blessed the weapons. Then Manding Bory said to his brother, "Djata, do you think yourself able to face Soumaoro now?"

"No matter how small a forest may be, you can always find there sufficient fibers to tie up a man. Numbers mean nothing; it is worth that counts. With my cavalry I shall clear myself a path to Mali."

Djata gave out his orders. They would head south, skirting Soumaoro's kingdom. The first objective to be reached was Tabon, the iron-gated town in the midst of the mountains, for Sundiata had promised Fran Kamara that he would pass Tabon before returning to Mali. He hoped to find that his childhood companion had become king. It was a forced march and during the halts the divines, Singbin Mara Cissé and Mandjan Bérété, related to Sundiata the history of Alexander the Great and several other heroes, but of all of them Sundiata preferred Alexander, the king of gold and silver, who crossed the world from west to east. He wanted to outdo his prototype both in the extent of his territory and in the wealth of his treasury.

Questions: Can "oral" traditions be used like other sources? Even if they are not entirely "true," do they have historical value? Judging from this epic, how did people of the Sudan define the qualities of a king? What aspects of the epic reveal contacts between this part of Africa and the wider world?

THE SONGHAY KINGDOM

As the power of Mali began to wane, a successor state from within the old empire was already beginning to emerge. The people of Songhay dominated the middle reaches of the Niger valley. Traditionally, the society of Songhay was made up of "masters of the soil," that is, farmers, herdsmen, and "masters of the waters," or fisherfolk. Songhay had begun to form in the 7th century as an independent kingdom perhaps under a Berber dynasty. By 1010 a capital was established at Gao on the Niger River, and the rulers had become Muslims, although the majority of the population remained pagan. Dominated by Mali for a while, by the 1370s Songhay had established its independence again and began to thrive, as new sources of gold from the West African forests began to pass through its territory. Gao became a large city with a resident foreign merchant community and a number of mosques. Under a dynamic leader, Sunni Ali (1464–1492), the empire of Songhay was forged.

Sunni Ali was a great tactical commander and a ruthless leader. His cavalry expanded the borders to the north and south and seized the traditional trading cities of Timbuktu and Jenne. The whole middle Niger valley fell under his control, and he developed a system of provincial administration to mobilize recruits for the army and rule the far-flung conquests. Although apparently a Muslim, he met any challenge to his authority even when it came from the Muslim scholars of Timbuktu, whom he persecuted. Sunni Ali was followed by a line of Muslim rulers who took the military title of *askia*. These rulers, especially Askia Muhammad, the "Great," extended the boundaries of the empire so that by the mid-16th century Songhay dominated the central Sudan.

Life in the Songhay Empire followed many of the patterns established in the previous savanna states. The fusion of Islamic and pagan populations and traditions continued. Muslim clerics and jurists were sometimes upset by the pagan beliefs and practices that continued among the population, and even more by the local interpretation of Islamic law. The facts that men and women mixed freely in the markets and streets, that women went unveiled, and that at Jenne young girls went naked shocked Muslim clerics, who wanted to impose a strict interpretation of the law of Islam.

Songhay remained the dominant power in the region until the end of the 16th century. In 1591, a Muslim army from Morocco, equipped with muskets, crossed the Sahara and defeated the vastly larger forces of Songhay. This sign of weakness stimulated internal revolts against the ruling family, and eventually the parts of the old empire broke away.

The demise of the Songhay imperial structure did not mean the end of the political and cultural tradition of the western Sudan. Other states that combined Muslim and pagan traditions rose among the Hausa peoples of northern Nigeria, based on cities such as Kano. The Hausa states developed to the east of Mali and Songhay and to the west of Kanem-Bornu, a major state of the central Sudan. The earliest Muslim ruler of Kano took control in the late-14th century and turned the city into a center of Muslim learning. In Kano, Katsina, and other Hausa cities of the region an urbanized royal court in a fortified capital ruled over the essentially animistic villages, where the majority of the population lived. With powerful cavalry forces these states were able to extend their rule and protect their active trade in salt, grains, and cloth. Internecine warfare, however, kept any one of them from dominating the others. While these later Islamicized African states tended to be small in size and local in their goals, they reproduced many of the social, political, and religious forms of the great empires of the grasslands.

Beyond the Sudan, Muslim penetration came in various forms. Merchants became established in most of the major trading cities; religious communities developed in each of these, often associated with particular families. Networks of trade and contact were established widely over the region as juula merchants and groups of pastoralists established their outposts in the area of Guinea. Muslim traders, herdsmen, warriors, and religious leaders became important minorities within these segmented African societies, composed of elite families, occupational groups, free men, and slaves. Intermarriage often took place, but Muslim influence varied widely from region to region. Nevertheless, families of juula traders and lineages that became known as specialists in Muslim law spread widely through the region, so that by the 18th century there were Muslim minorities scattered widely throughout West Africa, even in those areas where no Islamicized state had emerged.

POLITICAL AND SOCIAL LIFE IN THE SUDANIC STATES

We can generalize from these brief descriptions of Mali and Songhay about the nature of the Sudanic states. The village communities, clans, and various ethnic groups continued to organize many aspects of life in the savanna. The development of unified states provided an overarching structure that allowed the various groups and communities to coexist. The large states usually represented the political aims and power of a particular group and often of a dominant family. Many states pointed to the immigrant origins of the ruling families, and in reality the movement and fusion of populations was a constant feature in the Sudan. Islam provided a universalistic faith that served the interests of many groups. Common religion and law provided solidarity and trust to the merchants who resided in the cities and whose caravans brought goods to and from the savanna. The ruling families used Islamic titles, such as *emir* or caliph, to reinforce their authority, and they surrounded themselves with literate Muslim advisors and scribes who aided in the administration of government. The Muslim concept of a ruler who united civil and religious authority reinforced traditional ideas of kingship. It is also important to note that in Africa, as elsewhere in the world, the formation of states heightened social differences and made these societies more hierarchical.

In all the Sudanic states, Islam was fused with the existing traditions and beliefs. Rulership and authority was still based on the ability to intercede with local spirits, and while Sundiata or Sunni Ali might be nominally Muslim, they did not ignore the traditional basis of their rule. Because of this, Islam in these early stages in the Sudan tended to accommodate pagan practice and belief. Large proportions of the populations of Mali and Songhay never converted to Islam, and those who did convert often maintained many of the old beliefs as well.

We can see this fusion of traditions clearly in the position of women. A number of the Sudanic societies were matrilineal and some recognized the role of women within the lines of kinship, contrary to the normal patrilineal customs inscribed in the *Sharia*, or Islamic law. As we have just noted in the case of Songhay, North African visitors to the Sudan were shocked by the easy familiarity between men and women and the freedom enjoyed by women.

Finally, we must also take note that slavery and the slave trade between black Africa and the rest of the Islamic world had a major impact on women and children in these societies. Various forms of slavery and dependent labor had existed in Africa prior to the arrival of Islam. While we know little about slavery in central Africa in this period, slavery had been a relatively marginal aspect in the Sudanic states. Africans had been enslaved by others before, and Nubian (African) slaves had been known in the classical world, but with the Muslim conquests of North Africa and commercial penetration to the south, slavery became a more widely diffused phenomenon, and a slave trade in Africans developed on a new scale.

In theory, slavery was viewed by Muslims as a stage in the process of conversion—a way of preparing pagans to become Muslims—but in reality conversion did not guarantee freedom. Slaves in the Islamic world were used in a variety of occupations, such as domestic servants and laborers, but they were also used as soldiers and administrators who, having no local ties and affiliations, were considered to be dependent and thus trustworthy by their masters. Slaves were also used as eunuchs and concubines; thus the emphasis on women and children. The trade caravans from the Sahel across the Sahara often transported slaves as well as gold, and as we shall see, other slave-trade routes developed from the African interior to the east African coast. The tendency for the children of slave mothers to eventually be freed and integrated into Muslim society, while positive in one sense, also meant a constant demand for more slaves. Estimates of the volume of this trade vary widely. One scholar places the total in the trans-Saharan trade at 4.8 million, with another 2.4 million sent to the Muslim ports on the Indian Ocean coast. Actual figures may have been considerably lower, but the trade extended over 700 years and affected a large area. In a way, it was one more fashion in which the Islamic civilization touched and modified sub-Saharan Africa.

THE SWAHILI COAST OF EAST AFRICA

While the kingdoms of West Africa came under the influence of Islam from across the Sahara, another center of Islamic civilization was developing on the seaboard and offshore islands of Africa's Indian Ocean coast. Along that coast, extending southward from the horn of Africa to modern-day Mozambique, a string of Islamicized trading cities developed that reflected their cosmopolitan contacts with trading partners from Arabia, Persia, India, and China. Islam provided the residents of these towns a universal set of ethics and beliefs that made their maritime contacts easier; but in East Africa, as in the savanna kingdoms of West Africa, Islamization was slow to penetrate among the general population, and when it did, the result was often a compromise between indigenous ways and the new faith.

THE COASTAL TRADING PORTS

A 1st century Greek account of the Indian Ocean, *The Periplus of the Erythraean Sea*, mentioned some ports in East Africa but was somewhat vague as to the nature of the local inhabitants; that is, whether they were Africans or immigrants from the Arabian peninsula. From that century to the 10th century, the wave of Bantu migration had clearly reached the East African interior. Bantu-speaking pastoralists in the north and agriculturalists in the south mixed with older populations in the region. Other peoples were also moving to the African coast. Contact across the Indian Ocean dated back to at least the 2d century B.C. From Indonesia or Malaya, seaborne immigrants settled on the large island of Madagascar and from there introduced foods, such as bananas and coconuts, to the African coast. These were widely adopted and spread rapidly along the coast and into central Africa. Small coastal villages of fishermen and farmers, making rough pottery and working iron, dotted this coast. By the 8th and 9th centuries visitors and refugees from Oman and the Persian Gulf had established themselves at some of these villages, attracted by the possibilities of trade with the land of *Zanj,* the Arabic term for the East African coast. The villages were transformed from relatively homogeneous and egalitarian societies with shared language, ancestors, and traditions into more cosmopolitan and diverse communities.

By the 13th century, a string of urbanized trading ports sharing the common Bantu-based and Arabic-influenced Swahili language and other cultural traits—although governed by separate Muslim ruling families—had developed along the coast. Towns such as Mogadishu, Mombasa, Malindi, Kilwa, Pate, and Zanzibar eventually contained mosques, tombs, and palaces of cut stone and coral. Ivory, gold, iron, slaves, and exotic animals were exported from these ports in exchange for silks from Persia and porcelain from China for the ruling Muslim families. The Arab traveler Ibn Batuta was impressed with the beauty and refinement of these towns. He described Kilwa as "one of the most beautiful and well-constructed towns in the world" and was also impressed by the pomp and luxury of its ruler. Kilwa, in fact, was particularly wealthy because it controlled the southern port of Sofala, which had access to

The Swahili Coast; African Monsoon Routes and Major Trade Routes

the gold produced in the interior (near "Great Zimbabwe"), and because of its location as the farthest point south at which ships from India could hope to sail and return in a single monsoon season.

From the 13th to the 15th centuries, Kilwa flourished in the context of international trade, but it was not alone. At their height, perhaps as many as 30 of these port towns dotted the coast. These were tied to each other by an active coastal commerce and, in a few places, to the interior by a caravan trade, although it was usually Africans who brought the goods to the coast. Kilwa and Mogadishu minted their own coins by the 14th century, and cowrie shells were also used as a means of exchange. Textiles from India and porcelain from China were brought by Arab traders. Some Chinese ports sent goods directly to Africa in the 13th century, and as late as 1417 and 1431 state-sponsored expeditions sailing directly from China stopped at the East African coast to load ivory, gold, and rare woods. Such contact was discontinued after 1431 by the Chinese, and goods from China came to the coast thereafter in the ships of Arab or Indian traders.

THE MIXTURE OF CULTURES ON THE SWAHILI COAST

The Islamic overlay in these towns benefited this long-distance commerce. The 13th century was a period of considerable Islamic expansion, and as that faith spread eastward to India and Indonesia, it provided a religious bond of trust and law that facilitated trade throughout ports of the Indian Ocean. The ruling families in the East African trading ports built mosques and palaces; the mosque at Mogadishu was begun in 1238. Many of these ruling families claimed to be descendants of immigrants from Shiraz in Persia, a claim intended to legitimize their position and orthodoxy. In fact, some evidence indicates that the original Muslim families had emigrated to the Somali coast and from there to other towns farther south.

The institutions and forms of the Muslim world operated in these cities. Merchants, scholars, and travelers from elsewhere in Islam visited the towns. Ibn Batuta noted in his description of Mogadishu his reception by the local *quadi*, or judge, and sultan, the formality of worship in the mosque, and the similarity between local customs and those of Yemen. Yet while Islam tended to be the faith of the rulers and the merchants, the majority of the population on the East African coast, and perhaps even in the towns themselves, retained their previous beliefs and culture.

African culture remained strong throughout the area. Swahili language was essentially a Bantu language into which a large number of Arabic words were incorporated,

though many of them were not incorporated until the 16th century. The language was written in an Arabic script sometime prior to the 13th century; the ruling families could also converse in Arabic. Islam itself penetrated very little into the interior among the hunters, pastoralists, and farmers. Even the areas of the coast near the trading towns remained relatively unaffected. In the towns, the stone and coral buildings of the Muslim elite were surrounded by mud and thatch houses of the non-Muslim common people, so that Islamization was to some extent class-based. Still, a culture developed that fused Islamic and traditional elements. Family lineage, for example, was traced both through the maternal line, which controlled property (the traditional African practice), and through the paternal line, as was the Muslim custom. Swahili culture was a dynamic hybrid, and the Swahili people spread their language and culture along the coast of East Africa.

By the time the Portuguese arrived on this coast around 1500, the Swahili culture was widely diffused. Kilwa was no longer the predominant city, and the focus of trade had shifted to Malindi and Mombassa on the Kenya coast; but the commerce across the Indian Ocean continued. Vasco da Gama's ships arrived at Kilwa in 1498 and acquired a Hindu pilot to guide them to India, certainly nothing unusual except for the European involvement. Eventually, the Portuguese raided Kilwa and Mombassa in an attempt to shift the focus of trade into their own hands. Their outpost on Mozambique island and control of Sofala put much of the gold trade in their hands. The Portuguese discovered, however, that since most of the gold was produced by alluvial washings rather than in fixed mines it was difficult to control production, and some gold continued to pass through the network of Muslim traders. Although the Portuguese built a major outpost at Fort Jesus in Mombassa in 1592, they were never able to control the trade on the northern Swahili coast. The East African patterns, as established by 1500, persisted even more straightforwardly than those of the Sudanic kingdoms.

ANALYSIS
TWO TRANSITIONS IN THE HISTORY OF WORLD POPULATION

In this chapter and in those dealing with the ancient Americas, it is clear that establishing the size and structure of the historical populations is very difficult. Estimates based on fragmentary sources, the amount of available resources, and analysis of agricultural or hunting techniques have been used to make rough guesses about population size.

The results are often inadequate or controversial, but historians believe that the question is important.

Demography, the study of population, has increasingly become a valued tool of historical inquiry. Clearly, unless we have knowledge of the size, density, age structure, health, and reproductive capacity of a population, it is difficult to understand many aspects of its society, politics, and economy. In the contemporary world, most nations conduct periodic censuses in order to know the present situation of their populations and to plan for the future. Before the mid-18th century, when census taking became a regular procedure, population estimates and counts were sporadic and usually highly inaccurate. Estimating populations in the past, especially in nonliterate societies, is therefore a highly speculative exercise in which archeological evidence and estimates of productive capacity of agricultural practices and technology are used. The earliest date for a population estimate with a margin of error less than 20 percent is probably 1750.

The history of human population can be divided into two basic periods: a long era—almost all of human history—of very slow growth, and a very short period—about 200 years from 1750 to the present—of very rapid growth. For most of this history, the human population was very small and grew very slowly. Before the development of agriculture, the hunting-and-gathering economies of the world's populations supported between five and ten million people, if modern studies of such populations can be used as a guide. After about 8000 B.C. when domestication of plants and animals took place, population began to increase more rapidly but still at a modest level. Agriculture provided a more secure and larger food supply, but population concentration in villages and towns may have made people more susceptible to disease. Other historians believe that the settled agricultural life also led to intensified warfare (because of the struggle for land and water) and increasing social stratification within societies. Still, the Neolithic revolution and the development of agriculture stimulated population growth. It was the first major transition in the history of world population. One estimate, based on Roman and Chinese population counts and some informed guesses for the rest of the world, is an annual growth rate of about 0.36 per million. By A.D. 1 the world population may have been about 300 million people. It increased between A.D. 1 and 1750 to about 500 million people. We should bear in mind that during this period of general increase, there were always areas that suffered decline, sometimes of a violent nature due to warfare, epidemics, or natural catastrophes. The disastrous decline of American Indian populations, after contact with Europeans, due to disease, conquest, and social disruption is a case in point. The effects of the slave trade on Africa, while still debated, is another.

A second and extremely important transition took place between the mid-17th and the mid-18th centuries. Initially based on new food resources, this transition is often associated with the Industrial Revolution, when new sources of energy were harnessed to production. The growth rate greatly increased during this period in those countries most affected. Between 1750 and 1800, the population grew at a rate of over four percent a year to over a billion people. By the mid-20th century, the world growth rate had tripled, and by 1990 world population had risen to over 5 billion.

This Demographic Transition took place first in Europe and is still more characteristic of the developed world. Most premodern agrarian economies were characterized by a relative balance between the annual number of births and deaths; both were high. Life expectancy was usually less than 35 years, and the high mortality was compensated by high fertility—that is, women had many children. Improvements in medicine, hygiene, diet, and the general standard of living contributed to a decrease in mortality in the 18th century. This allowed populations to begin to grow at a faster rate. By the 19th century in most of western Europe, the decline in mortality was followed by a decline in fertility due to contraception. In some countries such as France, these two transitions took place at about the same time, so the growth of population was limited. In much of Europe, however, the decline in fertility lagged behind the decrease in mortality, so there was a period of rapid population growth. Until the 1920s, the population growth in western Europe and the United States was higher than in the rest of the world, especially the "less-developed countries." In recent times, that situation has been reversed.

Some demographers believe that the Demographic Transition is part of the process of shifting from a basically agrarian society to an industrial, urbanized one and that the improvements in medicine, technology, and higher standards of living will necessarily result in a change to a modern demographic regime. They believe that a decreasing need for children as part of the family economic unit, laws against child labor, and state intervention in family planning will eventually lower the birth rate and decrease the pressure of population on economic growth. This assumption remains to be proven, and responses may vary greatly from one region of the world to another due to economic conditions and cultural attitudes about proper family size.

Finally, we should also note that responses to the Demographic Transition can vary greatly according to historical conditions. In the 18th and 19th centuries, Europe resolved the problem of population growth by an enormous wave of emigration to the Americas, Australia, and various colonies around the globe. Present-day political circumstances make this solution less possible.

Still, it is clear that the Demographic Transition has begun to take place in the developing world of Latin America, Africa, and Asia. Mortality has dropped very rapidly since 1950 because of modern medical technology, and life expectancy has doubled. To cite a single example, in Sri Lanka the mortality rate was almost cut in half between 1945 and 1952 simply by eliminating malarial mosquitoes. Fertility has declined in many places in Asia and Latin America, but in Africa, where children have an important economic and social role in the extended family, it remains high. It is difficult to project how the Demographic Transition will take place in these areas of the world. However, all countries are faced with the problem of balancing their population's growth against the ability of the society to feed and provide an adequate standard of living to their people.

At present, the world's population is growing because of a moderate rate of growth in the industrialized nations and a high rate in the developing countries. In the 1970s, demographer Ansley Coale pointed out that the rate of growth, about two percent a year, is 100 times greater than it had been for most of human history. At this rate the world's population would be multiplied by 1000 every 350 years. The results of such growth would be disastrous. Coale concluded, therefore, that the present period of growth was a transitory one in the history of the world's population. Some concerned with the "population explosion" believe the fundamental answer is to limit population growth in the developing nations by state intervention, through incentives to have smaller families and education about birth control. Others believe that a redistribution of resources from rich nations to poor nations would alleviate the human misery created by population pressure and eventually lead to political and social conditions that would contribute to a gradual lowering of the birth rates. Clearly, the demographic questions must always be set in political, economic, and social contexts.

Questions: Why do nations differ about the need to control population growth? Why has the rate of population growth varied in different areas of the world? Is "population" essentially a biological, social, or political problem?

 PEOPLES OF THE FOREST AND PLAINS

As important as the Islamic impact was on the societies of the savanna and the East African coast, other African peoples in the continent's interior and in the forests of West Africa were following their own trajectories of development. By A.D. 1000, most of these societies were based on a varied agriculture sometimes combined with herding, and most societies used iron tools and weapons. Many were still organized in small village communities in which lineage, age sets, or other forms of social organization predominated. In various places, however, states had formed. Some of these began to resolve the problems of integrating large territories under a single government and ruling subject peoples. While Egypt, Kush, and Ethiopia had developed writing, and other areas borrowed the Arabic script, many sub-Saharan African societies were preliterate and transmitted their knowledge, skills, and traditions by oral methods and direct instruction. The presence or absence of writing has often been used as a measure of civilization by western observers, but as in pre-Colombian Peru, various African societies produced considerable accomplishments in the arts, building, and statecraft—sometimes in the context of highly urbanized settings—without a system of writing.

ARTISTS AND KINGS: YORUBA AND BENIN

In the forests of central Nigeria objects in terra-cotta of a realistic and highly stylized form have been discovered near the village of Nok. These objects, most of which date from about 500 B.C. to A.D. 200, display considerable artistic skill. The inhabitants of ancient Nok and its region practiced agriculture and used iron tools. They remain something of a mystery, but it appears that their artistic traditions spread widely through the forest areas and influenced other peoples. Nevertheless, there is a long hiatus in the historical and archeological record between the Nok sculptures and the renewed flourishing of artistic traditions in the region after about A.D. 1000.

Among the Yoruba-speaking peoples of Nigeria at the city of Ile-Ife, remarkable terra-cotta and bronze portrait heads of past rulers were produced in the period after A.D. 1200. The lifelike representations of these portraits and the skill of their execution place them among the greatest achievements of African art. The craftsmen of Ile-Ife also worked in wood and ivory. Much of the art seems to be associated with kings and the authority of kingship. Ile-Ife, like other Yoruba states, seems to have been an agricultural society supported by a peasantry and dominated by a ruling family and an aristocracy. Ile-Ife was considered by many peoples in the region to be the original cultural center, and a number of them traced their own beginnings to it.

Yoruba origins are, in fact, obscure. The Yoruba themselves believed that Olodumare, the Divine Spirit, created the world and then was moved to create humankind. He placed humans at Ile-Ife, and from there people migrated and eventually occupied the world. Thus Ile-Ife was seen as the holiest city of the Yoruba, their place of birth. Another legend maintained by the royal historians was that Oduduwa, a son of the king of Mecca, migrated from the east and settled in Yoruba. Modern historians have suggested that the real origins were perhaps Meroe and Nubia, or at least in the savanna south of the Sahara. In any case, the Yoruba spoke a non-Bantu language of the West African Kwa family and recognized a certain affinity between themselves and neighboring peoples, such as the Hausa, who spoke Afro-Asian languages.

The Yoruba were organized in a number of small city-states, each controlling perhaps a radius of 50 miles. The Yoruba were, in fact, highly urbanized, although many of the town inhabitants farmed in the surrounding countryside. These city-states developed under the strong authority of regional kings, who were considered divine. The person of the king was surrounded with a royal court of great size that included secondary wives, musicians, magicians, and bodyguards of soldier-slaves. His rule was not absolute, however, and it was limited by other forces in society. We can use the example of the Yoruba state of Oyo, which had emerged by the 14th century. Its king, the *alafin*, controlled subject peoples through "princes" in the provinces, drawn from local lineages, who were allowed to exercise traditional rule as long as they continued to pay tribute to Oyo. In the capital a council of state, made up of nobles from the seven city districts, advised the ruler and limited his power, and the *Ogboni*, or secret society of religious and political leaders, reviewed decisions of the king and the council. The union of civil and supernatural powers in the person of the ruler was the basis of power. The highly urbanized nature of Yoruba society and the flourishing of artisan traditions within these towns bears some similarity to the city-states of medieval Italy or Germany.

Patterns similar to the Yoruba city-states could be found among Edo peoples to the east of Yoruba. A large city-state called Benin was formed sometime in the 14th century under Ewuare, "The Great" (1440–1473). Benin's control was extended from the Niger River to the coast near modern Lagos. Benin City was described by early European visitors in the 16th century as a city of great population and broad avenues. The *Oba*, or ruler, lived in a large royal compound surrounded by a great entourage, and his authority was buttressed by ritual and ceremony.

In the 13th and 14th centuries Ife artists worked in terra-cotta, as well as bronze, and produced personalized portraits.

That authority was also the theme of the magnificent artistic output in ivory and cast bronze that became characteristic of Benin. Tradition had it that Iguegha, an artisan in bronze casting, was sent from Ile-Ife to introduce the techniques of making bronze sculptures. Benin then developed its own distinctive style, less naturalistic than that of Ile-Ife, but no less impressive. Celebration of the powers and majesty of the royal lineage as well as objects for the rituals surrounding kingship were the subjects of much of this art. When the first Europeans, the Portuguese, visited Benin in the 1480s, they were impressed by the power of the ruler and the extent of his territory. Similarly, the artists of Benin were impressed with the Portuguese, and Benin bronzes and ivories began to include representations of Portuguese soldiers and other themes that reflected the contact with outsiders.

CENTRAL AFRICAN KINGDOMS

South of the rain forest that stretched across Africa almost to Lake Victoria lay a broad expanse of savanna and plain, cut by a number of large rivers such as the Kwango and the Zambezi. From their original home in Nigeria, the Bantu peoples had spread into the southern reaches of the rain forest along the Congo River, then southward onto the southern savannas, and eventually to the east coast. By the 5th century A.D. Bantu farmers and fishermen had reached beyond the Zambezi, and by the 13th century they were approaching the southern end of the continent. Mostly beyond the influence of Islam, a number of these central African peoples had begun their own process of state formation by around A.D. 1000, replacing the pattern of kinship-based societies with forms of political authority based on kingship.

Whether the idea of kingship developed in one place and was diffused elsewhere or had multiple origins is unknown, but the older system based on seniority within the kinship group was replaced with rule based on the control of territory and the parallel development of rituals that reinforced the power of the ruler. A number of important kingdoms developed. In Katanga, the Luba peoples modified the older system of village headmen to a form of divine kinship in which the ruler and his relatives were thought to have a special power that ensured fertility of people and crops; thus only the royal lineage was fit to rule. A sort of bureaucracy grew to administer the state, but it was hereditary so that brothers or male children succeeded to the position. In a way, it was a half-step toward more modern concepts of bureaucracy, but it provided a way of integrating large numbers of people in a large political unit.

THE KINGDOMS OF KONGO AND MWENE MUTAPA

Beginning about the 13th century, another kingdom was forming on the lower Congo River. By the late 15th century this kingdom of the Kongo was flourishing. On a firm agricultural base, its people also developed the skills of weaving, pottery, blacksmithing, and carving. Individual artisans, skilled in the working of wood, copper, and iron, were highly esteemed. There was a sharp division of labor between men and women. Men took responsibility for clearing the forest and scrub, producing palm oil and palm

wine, building houses, hunting, and long-distance trade. Women took charge of cultivation in all its aspects, the care of domestic animals, and household duties. On the seacoast, women made salt from sea water and they also collected the seashells that served as currency in the Kongo kingdom. The population was distributed in small family-based villages and in towns. The area around the capital, Mbanza Kongo, had a population of 60,000–100,000 by the early 16th century.

The kingship of the Kongo was hereditary but local chieftainships were not, and this gave the central authority considerable power to control subordinates. In a way, the Kongo kingdom was a confederation of smaller states brought under the control of the manikongo, or king, and by the 15th century it was divided into eight major provinces. The word mani means blacksmith, and it demonstrated the importance that iron and the art of working it had in its association with political and ritual power.

Farther to the east another large Bantu confederation developed among the farming and cattle-herding Shona-speaking peoples in the region between the Zambezi and Limpopo rivers. Beginning in the 9th century A.D., migrants from the west began to build royal courts in stone, to which later immigrants added more polished constructions. There were a number of these zimbabwe, or stone house, sites (about 200 have been found) that housed local rulers and subchiefs, but the largest site, called Great Zimbabwe, was truly impressive. It was the center of the kingdom and had a religious importance as well, associated with the "bird of God," an eagle that served as a link between the world and the spirits. The symbol of the "bird of God" is found at the ruins of Great Zimbabwe and throughout the area of its control. Great Zimbabwe (not to be confused with the modern nation of Zimbabwe) included a number of structures, some with strong stone walls 15-feet thick and 30-feet high, a large conical tower, and extensive cut-stone architecture made without the use of mortar to join the bricks together. Observers in the 19th century suspected that Phoenicians or Arabs had built these structures, but archeologists have since established that a Bantu kingdom had begun construction in stone by the 11th century A.D. and had done its most sophisticated building in the 14th and 15th centuries.

By the 15th century, a centralized state had begun to form centered on Great Zimbabwe. It controlled a large portion of the interior of southeast Africa all the way to the Indian Ocean. Under a king who took the title of Mwene Mutapa (which the Portuguese later pronounced as Monomotapa), this kingdom experienced a short period of considerable expansion in the late 15th and 16th centuries. Its dominance over the sources of gold in the interior eventually gave it great advantages in commerce, which it devel-

Great Zimbabwe was one of a number of stone settlement complexes in southeastern Africa. Added to at different times, it served as the royal court of the Monomotapa empire.

oped with the Arab port of Sofala on the coast. Evidence of this trade is found in the glass beads and porcelain unearthed by archeologists at Great Zimbabwe. By the 16th century, internal divisions and rebellion had split the kingdom apart, but control of the gold fields still provided a source of power and trade. Representatives of the Mwene Mutapa called at the East Coast ports to buy Indian textiles, and their regal bearing and fine iron weapons impressed the first Europeans who saw them. As late as the 19th century, a much-reduced kingdom of Muenemutapa survived in the interior and provided some leadership against European encroachment.

CONCLUSION

INTERNAL DEVELOPMENT AND EXTERNAL CONTACTS

This chapter has concentrated on the Sudanic states and the Swahili coast, where the impact of Islam was the most profound and where, because of the existence of written sources, it is somewhat easier to reconstruct the region's history. Sub-Saharan Africa had never been totally isolated from the Mediterranean world or other outside contacts, but the spread of Islam obviously brought large areas of Africa to the global community more intensely, even though Africa remained something of an Islamic frontier. Still, the fusion of Islamic and indigenous African cultures created a synthesis that restructured the life of many Africans.

While the arrival of Islam in Africa in the period from 800 to 1500 was obviously a major event, it would be wrong to see Africa's history in this period exclusively in terms of the Islamic impact. Great Zimbabwe and the Kongo kingdom, to cite only two examples, represented the development of Bantu concepts of kingship and state building relatively independent of trends taking place elsewhere on the continent. Similar processes and accomplishments could also be noted in Benin and among the Yoruba of West Africa. Meanwhile in Ethiopia, East Africa, and the eastern Sudan the impact of the pre-Islamic Mediterranean world had been long felt.

By the late 15th century when the first Europeans, the Portuguese, began to arrive on the west and east coasts of Africa, they encountered in many places well-developed and powerful kingdoms that were able to deal with the Portuguese as equals from a position of strength. This was even more the case in those parts of Africa that had come under the influence of Islam, and through it had established various links with other areas of Muslim civilization. In this period, Africa had increasingly become part of the general cultural trends of the wider world, even though many of these contacts had been brought by outsiders rather than Africans. Moreover, the intensification of the export trade in ivory, slaves, and especially gold from Africa drew Africans, even those far from the centers of trade, into a widening network of relations. With the arrival of Europeans in sub-Saharan Africa in the late 15th century, the pace and intensity of the cultural and commercial contacts became even greater, and many African societies were presented with new and profound challenges.

FURTHER READINGS

A number of the books recommended on Africa in Chapter 10 are also useful for further reading in relation to this chapter. The period covered in this chapter is summarized in Roland Oliver and Anthony Atmore's *The African Middle Ages, 1400–1800* (1981). Basil Davidson has produced many excellent popular books that provide a sympathetic view of African development. A good example, prepared to accompany a television series, is *The Story of Africa* (1984). A readable book that gives an overview of African history and emphasizes broad common themes and everyday life is Robert W. July's *Precolonial Africa* (1975).

A very good survey of the early history of Africa with interesting comments on the Nok culture is Susan Keech McIntosh and Roderick J. McIntosh's "From Stone to Metal: New Perspectives on the Later Prehistory of West Africa," *Journal of World History* vol. 2, no. 1 (1988), 89–133. Basil Davidson has also written, with F. K. Buah, *A History of West Africa* (1966), which presents a good introduction for that region. More detailed, however, is J. F. Ade Ajayi and Michael Crowder's *History of West Africa*, 2 vols. (1971), which contains excellent review chapters by specialists. For the East African coast an excellent survey and introduction is provided by Derek Nurse and Thomas Spear in *The Swahili. Reconstructing the History and Language of an African Society* (1985).

Two good books on the Kongo kingdom are Anne Hilton's *The Kingdom of the Kongo* (1985), which shows how African systems of thought accommodated the arrival of Europeans and their culture, and Georges Balandier's *Daily Life in the Kingdom of the Kongo* (1969), which makes good use of travelers' reports and other documents to give a rounded picture of Kongo society. David Birmingham and Phyllis Martin's *History of Central Africa*, 2 vols. (1983) provides an excellent regional history.

Two multivolume general histories of Africa which provide synthetic articles by leading scholars on many of the topics discussed in this chapter are *The Cambridge History of Africa*, 8 vols. (1975–1986) and the *UNESCO General History of Africa*, 7 vols. to date (1981–).

Some important source materials on African history for this period are D. T. Niane's *Sundiata, an Epic of Old Mali* (1986); G. R. Crone, ed., *The Voyages of Cadamosto* 2d ser., vol. 80 (1937), which deals with Mali, Cape Verde, Senegal, and Benin; and H. A. R. Gibb's *The Travels of Ibn Batuta*, 2 vols. (1962), which in vol. 2 includes his visit to the Swahili coast.

THE BYZANTINE EMPIRE

 THE BYZANTINE EMPIRE IN MATURITY, 8TH
TO 11TH CENTURIES

    ∞∞∞ **ANALYSIS:** The Classical Heritage from Greece and
            Rome

 THE SPREAD OF CIVILIZATION IN EASTERN
EUROPE

    ∞∞∞ **DOCUMENT:** Russia Turns to Christianity

    ∞∞∞ **CONCLUSION:** The End of an Era in Eastern Europe

    ∞∞∞ **FURTHER READINGS**

1st century A.D.–650 Slavic migrations into eastern Europe

527–565 Justinian

330s Constantinople made capital of Eastern Roman Empire

718 Defeat of Arab attack on Constantinople

855 According to legend, Rurik king of Kievan Russia
864 Beginning of missionary work of brothers Cyril and Methodius in Slavic lands
896 Magyars settle in Hungary   **c. 960** Emergence of
870 First kingdom in what is now Czechoslovakia   Polish state

A.D. 1   600   800

15

Civilization in Eastern Europe: Byzantium and Russia

INTRODUCTION. The world of Islam extended from its core civilization in the Middle East and North Africa into parts of India and Southeast Asia as well as into many of the societies formed in sub-Saharan Africa. The Islamic network affected the various parts of Europe also, but less completely. In Europe, as in India, a different religion predominated. Moreover, most of Europe was not subjected to political or military control from the Islamic world.

Two major, though related, civilizations took shape in Europe, colored by Islamic dynamism but operating according to different principles. Comparable to African civilization in some ways—for example, in building political institutions—the European civilizations carved out new and distinctive features as well.

In addition to the great civilizations of Asia and North Africa, one other society, which in fact straddled western Asia and southeastern Europe, maintained particularly high levels of political, economic, and cultural life during much of the period 500–1450. The Byzantine Empire controlled an important, though somewhat fluctuating, swath of territory in the Balkans and the northern Middle East (in such present-day countries as Turkey). The empire was based on a civilization that predated Islam. Leaders of the empire regarded themselves as Roman emperors, and indeed their government was in many ways a direct continuation of the eastern portion of the late-Roman Empire. This was not really Rome moved eastward, however, though the governmental structure built on traditions of late-Roman emperors such as Diocletian and Constantine. The term *Byzantine*, though not used at the time, accurately suggests the distinction from Rome itself: This was a political heir to Rome, but with geography and focus of its own.

The real significance of the Byzantine Empire goes well beyond its ability to keep Rome's memory alive. The empire lasted for almost a thousand years, between Rome's collapse in the West and the final overthrow of the regime by Turkish invaders. The empire's capital, Constantinople,

---

1019–1054 Yaroslav king of Russia

1054 Schism between Eastern and Western Christianity

980–1015 Conversion of Vladimir I of Russia to Christianity

1018 Defeat of first Bulgarian Empire, taken over by Byzantines

1203–1204 Capture of Constantinople during the Fourth Crusade

1100–1453 Byzantine decline; growing Turkish attack

1236 Capture of Russia by Mongols (Tartars)

1480 Expulsion of Tartars from Russia

1453 Capture of Constantinople by Ottoman Turks; end of Byzantine Empire

1000   1200   1400

was one of the truly great cities of the world, certainly the most opulent and important city in Europe in this period. From Constantinople radiated one of the two major branches of Christianity, the Orthodox Christian churches that became dominant throughout most of eastern Europe.

Like the other great civilizations of the period, the Byzantine Empire spread its cultural and political influence to parts of the world that had not previously been controlled by any major civilization. Just as Muslim influence helped shape civilization in parts of Africa south of the Sahara, and Indian and Chinese dynamism helped define cultural zones in Southeast Asia, the Byzantines began to create a new civilization area in the Balkans and particularly in western Russia. Here was a major case, indeed, of the remaking of the civilizational map that formed such an important characteristic of the early centuries of the postclassical millennium.

The patterns of Byzantine cultural expansion, however, differed from those of the other great Asian centers in one important particular: The Byzantine Empire itself did not survive the postclassical period, and it did not leave direct successor states. There is, as a result, less of an explicit continuum between the Byzantine experience and later history—that is, the history of eastern Europe after 1453 when Constantinople fell to the surging Muslim Empire of the Ottoman Turks—than proved to be the case in eastern or southern Asia or even the Arab-dominated portions of the Middle East. During the postclassical period, the Byzantine Empire experienced more radical gyrations, more alternations between dynamism and eclipse, than the Asian civilizations on the whole, and ultimately it could not directly sustain itself.

A vital legacy remained, however. Even in the Balkans, which were long to be controlled by the Ottoman Turks, Orthodox Christianity remained the dominant faith. Byzantine cultural traditions continue to influence the Balkan area in the 20th century. The Byzantine achievement also influenced the Turkish Empire that, in the 15th century, seized its territory in southeastern Europe and the northern Middle East (present-day Turkey). In other words, although the Byzantine Empire perished, it did leave a vital heritage—this heritage, along with the sheer duration of the empire, defines the importance of Byzantine society in world history.

The empire's most important ultimate stepchild was Russia, whose rise as a civilized area relied heavily on influences from the Byzantines to the south. Russia took many initial cultural and political characteristics from the Byzantine Empire and would ultimately claim to inherit the mantle of the empire itself. However, the postclassical millennium formed a preliminary, somewhat tentative gestation period for civilization in Russia, and historians must be cautious in drawing too many parallels between the patterns displayed at this point and subsequent developments when Russia more fully hit its stride. A Byzantine or Byzantine-influenced heritage would remain, but it was highly selective, a less complete mold than had developed in many parts of Asia. East European civilization in the centuries after Rome's fall thus includes the turbulent existence of an important Byzantine center, plus the spread of culture northward—in a process that would include one of the important instances of conversion to a major monotheistic faith from a previously animistic belief system, as well as the partially separate political and cultural stirrings in Russia and other northern kingdoms.

The history of civilization in eastern Europe in this period involves one other interpretive issue in addition to the complexity of the relationship between Byzantine flourish and decline and the patterns to the north. This issue consists quite simply of how to frame the story of the spread of Christianity in Europe, between eastern and western portions of the continent. There were many commonalities between developments in eastern Europe and those of the Christian West. In both cases civilization spread northward, due to the missionary appeal of the religion itself. In both cases animism gave way to monotheism—though important compromises were made, particularly at the popular level. In both cases more northerly political units, such as Russia, Germany, and France, struggled for political definition without as yet being able to rival the political sophistication of the more advanced civilization areas in Asia and North Africa—or in Byzantium itself. In both cases new trading activities brought northern regions into contact with the major centers of world commerce including Constantinople, with important long-range as well as short-term results. In both cases newly civilized areas looked back to the Greco-Roman past, as well as to Christianity, for cultural inspiration, using as a result some of the same political myths and, with due modifications, artistic styles.

Yet, with all these shared ingredients, the civilizations that expanded in the East and developed in the West operated largely on separate tracks. They produced different versions of Christianity, which culturally as well as organizationally were rather separate, even hostile. The civilizations had little mutual contact, particularly in the formative centuries before western Europe became strong enough to trade significantly with Constantinople. Commercial patterns in both cases ran south-north, rather than east-west. Political evolution was also somewhat distinct. The fact was that, during most of the postclassical millennium, major portions of eastern Europe were significantly more advanced than the West in political sophistication, cultural range, and economic vitality. Even the relationship with the classical-Mediterranean past differed, as eastern Europe maintained important features of the late-Roman Empire directly whereas Western leaders ultimately turned to a much more selective borrowing and imitation. Thus eastern Europe worked directly from the classical architectural tradition, whereas western Europe, after a modest classicism, developed a much different dominant style.

By 1400 essentially two civilizations existed in Europe, with very few contacts and only a handful of basic similarities. This relationship would later change, with new contacts developing on the basis of contiguous geography, the common adherence to Christianity, and new commercial exchanges. In this formative period, however, the distinct paths must be emphasized along with the undeniably greater importance, in terms of larger world history before 1450, of the East European civilization. The boundary line between East and West was somewhat fuzzy, embracing important regions, such as Hungary, where overlapping and competing influences between western and eastern Europe helped define a special identity—where indeed a special identity exists to this day. In the major centers of the two European civilizations, however—in Byzantium and Russia, or France and the Low Countries—different paths were defined after the fall of Rome, marked by different cycles of dynamism and decline. When the two civilizations did meet, in this period as later, they met as distant cousins, related but not close kin.

THE BYZANTINE EMPIRE

The Byzantine Empire unfolded initially as part of the greater Roman Empire and then, as this framework shattered with Roman decline, took on a life of its own particularly from the reign of the emperor Justinian onward. During its formative period, which lasted through the first encounters with the new Arab and Muslim threat, the Byzantine Empire blended Greco-Roman political and intellectual traditions with new impulses. It also centered on a territory both different from and smaller than the eastern Mediterranean as Rome had defined it—this was the result of new pressures, particularly from the surge of Islam throughout North Africa and the bulk of the Middle East. The territorial definition of the Byzantine Empire emerged only gradually; again Justinian's reign formed an important step prior to Arab pressure. This definition was crucial in pushing Byzantine influences northward, toward sketching the larger East European civilization.

ORIGINS OF THE EMPIRE

The Byzantine Empire in some senses began in the 4th century A.D., when the Romans set up their Eastern capital in Constantinople. This city quickly became the most vig-

orous center of the otherwise fading imperial structure. The emperor Constantine constructed a host of elegant buildings, including Christian churches, in his new city, which was built on the foundations of a previously modest town called Byzantium. Soon, separate Eastern emperors ruled from the new metropolis, even before the Western portion of the empire fell to the Germanic invaders. They warded off invading Huns and other intruders, while enjoying a solid tax base in the peasant agriculture of the eastern Mediterranean. Constantinople was responsible for the Balkan peninsula, the northern Middle East, the Mediterranean coast, and North Africa. Although for several centuries Latin served as the court language of the Eastern Empire, Greek was the common tongue and, after the emperor Justinian in the 6th century, it became the official language as well. Indeed, in the eyes of the Easterners, Latin became an inferior, barbaric means of communication. Knowledge of Greek enabled the scholars of the Eastern Empire to read freely in the ancient Athenian philosophical and literary classics and in the Hellenistic writings and scientific treatises.

The new empire benefited from the high levels of civilization long present in the eastern Mediterranean. Commerce continued at a considerable pace, though the merchant classes declined and state control of trade increased. New blood was drawn into administration and trade, as Hellenized Egyptians and Syrians, long excluded from Roman administration, moved to Constantinople and entered the expanding bureaucracy of the Byzantine rulers. The empire faced many foreign enemies, though the pressure was less severe than that provided by the Germanic tribes in the West. It responded, however, by recruiting armies in the Middle East itself, not by relying on barbarian troops. And the empire increasingly turned from the emphasis on army power, so characteristic of Rome in its later phases, to add a growing, highly trained civilian bureaucracy. Tension between strong generals and bureaucratic leaders remained, but the empire did not rely primarily on force for its internal rule. Complex administration around a remote emperor, who was surrounded by elaborate ceremonies, increasingly defined the empire's political style.

EASTERN ORTHODOX CHRISTIANITY

As an Eastern Empire took shape politically, Christianity also began to split between East and West. In the West the pope, based in Rome, officially headed the framework of church organization. He claimed control over bishops, sent missionaries to the north, and tried to regulate doctrine. No comparable single leader developed in the Eastern church. For several centuries the Eastern church acknowledged the pope's authority as first among equals, but in practice papal directives had no hold over the Byzantine church. Rather, it was the emperors themselves who regulated church organization, creating a pattern of state control over church structure far different from the tradition that developed in the West, where the church insisted, though not always successfully, on its independence. Byzantine emperors used their claim to be God's representative on earth to cement their own power. Correspondingly, they kept a close eye on church affairs while trying to force non-Christians to convert. From the time of Justinian the number of non-Christians allowed in Constantinople was carefully limited.

Furthermore, the Eastern church experienced a number of different influences from those prevalent in Western Christianity. Monasticism developed earlier in the East than in the West. Many individual holy men and groups of monks sought to follow Christ in a more complete way, through special lives of fasting, celibacy, and prayer, staying apart from worldly concerns. Several leaders undertook to regulate this holy life, and a rule for monasteries developed by Basil, the patriarch of Constantinople in the mid-4th century, became particularly important in the East. Basil's rule helped formalize the separation between monasteries and ordinary people, pledging monks to lives of poverty, charity, and prayer. Unlike Western monastic orders, Eastern monks devoted little attention to scholarship. Their social role was great, however, for Eastern people venerated holy men and gave them considerable authority in the larger affairs of the church. Monasteries, along with traveling missionaries, provided food and medical care while seeking to drive away demons; they were far closer to popular Christianity than the official religion of the imperial court.

Eastern Christianity was also marked by a host of religious controversies different from those in the West. Particularly troubling was the 8th-century dispute over religious imagery, or icons, with one group seeking to purify Christianity from the physical representations of statues and pictures of Christ and the saints. Religious disputes made Eastern emperors and church officials all the more reluctant to allow interference from Western popes, for religious affairs were politically sensitive given the need to maintain unity in the realm.

Orthodox Christianity, in sum, shared a host of features with its Western cousin, including intolerance for other beliefs. Different political organizations, however, launched a largely separate pattern of religious development, in terms of specific church structures, monasticism, religious art, and theology. These differences in turn caused ongoing mutual suspicion and hostility. A late 12th-century church

patriarch in Constantinople even argued that Muslim rule would be preferable to that of the pope: "For if I am subject to the Muslim, at least he will not force me to share his faith. But if I have to be under the Frankish rule and united with the Roman Church, I may have to separate myself from God."

JUSTINIAN'S ACHIEVEMENTS

The early history of the Byzantine Empire was marked by a recurrent threat of invasion. Eastern emperors, relying on their local military base plus able generalship by upper-class Greeks, beat off attacks by the Sassanid Empire in Persia and by Germanic invaders.

Then, in 533, with the empire's borders reasonably well assured, a new emperor, Justinian, attempted to reconquer western territory in a last, futile effort to restore an empire like that of Rome. Justinian's reign would, ironically, confirm Byzantium's basis in the Greco-Roman heritage, through massive architectural and legal achievements in the classical mode, while also furthering the empire's relocation toward the Balkans and the western part of present-day Turkey, away from the Mediterranean coast.

Justinian himself, who faced and brutally suppressed serious social unrest, has been variously judged by contemporaries and later historians alike. He was a somber personality, autocratic, and prone to grandiose ideas. A contemporary historian named Procopius, no friend of the emperor, described him as "at once villainous and amenable; as people say colloquially, a moron. He was never truthful with anyone, but always guileful in what he said and did, yet easily hoodwinked by any who wanted to deceive him." The emperor was also heavily influenced by his wife Theodora, a courtesan connected with Constantinople's horse-racing world, who was eager for power. It was Theodora who stiffened Justinian's backbone in response to popular unrest and who prodded expansion plans.

Justinian's positive contributions to the Byzantine Empire lay in rebuilding Constantinople, ravaged by earlier riots against high taxes, and systematizing the Roman legal code. Extending later-Roman architecture, with its addition of domes to earlier classical styles, Justinian's builders constructed many new structures—the most inspiring of which was the huge new church, the Hagia Sophia, long one of the wonders of the Christian world. This was an achievement in engineering as well as architecture, for no one had previously been able to support a dome of comparable size. Justinian's codification of Roman law reached a goal earlier emperors had sought but not achieved. Unified law not only reduced confusion, but also served to unite and organize the new empire itself, paralleling the state's bureaucracy. Justinian's code, called the Body of Civil Law, stands as one of the clearest and most comprehensive systems created by any culture. The code summed up and reconciled a host of Roman edicts and decisions, making Roman law a coherent basis for political and economic life throughout the empire. Recurrently updated by later emperors, the code would also ultimately help spread Roman legal principles in various parts of Europe.

Justinian's military exploits had more ambiguous results. The emperor wanted to recapture the old Roman Empire itself. Aided by a brilliant general, Belisarius, new gains were made in North Africa and Italy. The Byzantines hoped to restore North Africa to its role as grain producer for the Mediterranean world, while Italy would be the symbol of past imperial glories. Unable to hold Rome against the Germans, Justinian's forces made their temporary capital, Ravenna, a key artistic center, embellished by some of the most beautiful Christian mosaics known any-

Mosaics in Ravenna, Italy, from the early period of the Byzantine Empire, illustrate some of the highest achievements of Byzantine religious art and provide a dazzling, ornate environment for worship. This mosaic features a rather militant Christ the Redeemer.

where in the world. But the major Italian holdings were short-lived, unable to withstand Germanic pressure, while North African territory was soon besieged as well.

Furthermore, Justinian's westward ambitions had weakened the empire in its own sphere. Persian forces attacked in the northern Middle East, while new Slavic groups, moving into the Balkans, pressed on another front. Justinian finally managed to create a new line of defense and even pushed Persian forces back again, but some Middle Eastern territory was irretrievably lost. Furthermore, all these wars, offensive and defensive alike, created new tax pressures on the government and forced Justinian to exertions that almost literally wore him to his death in 565.

THE EMPIRE'S DEFENSES

Justinian's successors, after some renewed hesitations and setbacks, began to concentrate more fully on defending the Eastern Empire itself. Persian successes in the northern Middle East were reversed in the 7th century, and the population was forcibly reconverted to Christianity. The resultant empire, centered in the southern Balkans and the western and central portions of present-day Turkey, was a far cry from Rome's greatness, far even from the wealth of the Eastern Empire itself when it had a firmer hold on the rich lands of the northern Middle East. It was sufficient, however, to amplify a rich Hellenistic culture and blend it more fully with Christianity, while advancing Roman achievements in engineering and military tactics as well as law.

The Byzantine Empire was also sufficiently strong to withstand the great new threat of the 7th century, though not without great loss: the surge of the Arab Muslims. The Arabs by the mid-7th century had built a fleet that challenged Byzantine naval supremacy in the eastern Mediterranean, while repeatedly attacking Constantinople. They quickly swallowed the empire's remaining provinces along the eastern seaboard of the Mediterranean, and soon cut into the northern Middle Eastern heartland as well. Considerable Arab cultural and commercial influence also affected patterns of life in Constantinople.

The Byzantine Empire, however reduced, held out nevertheless. A major siege of the capital in A.D. 717–718 was beaten back, partly due to a new weapon called Greek fire (a petroleum, quicklime, and sulfur mixture) that devastated Arab ships. The Arab threat was never entirely removed. Furthermore, wars with the Muslims had added new economic burdens to the empire, as invasions and taxation, weakening the position of small farmers, resulted in greater aristocratic estates and new power for aristocratic generals. The free rural population that had served the empire—providing military recruits and paying the bulk of πῦρρκῶν· Ηραΐοδὲ καὶτοὀσκλαςτῶπϝπολόωῖπυρί ·

τὸλεϝϝωμϙϳ   πυρπολ   ΤΟΝ ΤῶΝ Ε·Η ΔΗΠΙθΧΛΟΝ ·

"Greek fire" helped protect the Byzantine Empire from being overwhelmed by Arab forces.

the taxes—during its early centuries was forced into greater dependence. Greater emphasis was given to careful organization of the army and navy. For all the problems, however, the imperial core displayed real strength, governing a territory about half the size of the previous eastern portion of the Roman Empire and withstanding a series of enemies. More than a long-standing barrier to the Arabs, the empire would soon make its greatest contributions to subsequent world history by reaching northward in trade and culture, creating a new zone of civilization precisely because so much of the Mediterranean had fallen to Arab hands.

THE BYZANTINE EMPIRE IN MATURITY, 8TH TO 11TH CENTURIES

The history of the empire, after the greatest Arab onslaughts had been faced and their results assimilated, offered a dizzying series of weak and strong emperors, periods of vigor alternating with seeming decay. Arab pressure continued. Conquest of the island of Crete in the 9th century allowed Muslim harassment of Byzantine shipping in the Mediterranean for several centuries. Slavic kingdoms, especially that of Bulgaria, periodically pressed Byzantine territory in the Balkans, though at times military success and marriage alliances brought Byzantine control over the feisty Bulgarian kingdom. Thus while a Bulgarian

king in the 10th century took the title of tsar, a Slavic version of the word *Caesar*, steady Byzantine pressure through war eroded the regional kingdom. In the 11th century the Byzantine emperor Basil II, known appropriately enough as Bulgaroktonos, or slayer of the Bulgarians, used the empire's wealth to bribe many Bulgarian nobles and generals. He defeated the Bulgarian army in 1014, blinding as many as 15,000 captive soldiers—the sight of whom brought on the Bulgarian king's death. Thus did Bulgaria become part of the empire, its aristocracy settling in Constantinople and merging with the leading Greek families.

THE EMPIRE'S FLUCTUATING FORTUNES

Obviously, the Byzantine Empire was a state frequently beleaguered, where military arrangements continued to command great attention. On balance, however, the empire flourished until the 11th century. It entered a particularly stable period during the 9th and 10th centuries, when a new ruling dynasty managed to avoid the quarrels over succession to the imperial throne that had bedeviled many heirs before and after Justinian. The result was growing prosperity and solid political rule. The luxury of the court and its buildings steadily increased. Elaborate ceremonies and rich imperial processions created a magnificence designed to dazzle the empire's subjects. Briefly, at the end of the 10th century, the Byzantine emperor may have been

The Byzantine Empire, 565–1400

the most powerful single monarch on earth, with a capital city whose rich buildings and abundant popular entertainments awed visitors from western Europe and elsewhere, while giving Eastern rulers a growing confidence in the validity of their own institutions and values.

Rather than charting the details of specific rulers and some of the bloody battles the empire won or lost, it is important to emphasize the three crucial features of Byzantine society before its long but definitive decline: first, what the main social and political characteristics were—what defined the Byzantine; second, how the empire moved steadily apart from Western Christendom; and third, how Byzantine influence spread steadily northward.

BYZANTINE SOCIETY AND POLITICS

The Byzantine political system bore unusual resemblance to the earlier patterns in China. The emperor was held to be ordained by God, head of church as well as state. He appointed church bishops and passed religious and secular laws. The elaborate court rituals symbolized the ideals of a divinely inspired, all-powerful ruler, though they also often immobilized rulers and inhibited innovative policy. At key points women held the imperial throne, while maintaining the ceremonial power of the office.

Supplementing the centralized imperial authority was one of history's most elaborate bureaucracies. Trained in Greek classics, philosophy, and science in a secular school system that paralleled but contrasted with church education for the priesthood, Byzantine bureaucrats could be recruited from all social classes. As in China, aristocrats predominated, but there was some openness to talent among this elite of highly educated scholars. Bureaucrats were spe-

cialized into various offices, with officials close to the emperor being mainly eunuchs. Provincial governors were appointed from the center and charged with keeping tabs on military authorities. An elaborate system of spies helped preserve loyalty, while also creating intense distrust even among friends. It is small wonder that the word *Byzantine* came to refer to complex and convoluted institutional arrangements. At the same time, the system was sufficiently successful to constitute one of the cements that preserved the longest-lived single government structure the Mediterranean world has ever known.

Much of the empire's success depended on careful military organization. Byzantine rulers adapted the later Roman system by recruiting troops locally and rewarding them with grants of land in return for their military service. The land could not be sold, but sons inherited its administration in return for continued military responsibility. Many outsiders, particularly Slavs and Armenian Christians, were recruited for the army in this fashion. Increasingly, hereditary military leaders assumed considerable regional power, displacing more traditional and better-educated aristocrats. One emperor, Michael II, was a product of this system and was notorious for his hatred of Greek education and his overall personal ignorance. On the other hand, the military system had obvious advantages in protecting a state recurrently under attack from Muslims of various sorts—Persians, Arabs, and later Turks—as well as nomadic intruders from central Asia. Until the 15th century, the Byzantine Empire effectively blocked the path to Europe for most of these groups.

Socially and economically the empire depended on Constantinople's control over the countryside, with the bureaucracy regulating trade and controlling food prices. The large peasant class was vital in supplying goods and also in providing the bulk of tax revenues; food prices were kept artificially low—in order to content the numerous urban lower classes—in a system supported largely by taxes on the hard-pressed peasantry. Other cities were modest in size—Athens, for example, dwindled—with the focus on the capital city and its food needs. The empire developed a far-flung trading network with Asia to the east and Russia and Scandinavia to the north. Silk production expanded in the empire—with silk worms and techniques initially imported from China—and various luxury products, including cloth, carpets, and spices were sent northward. This gave the empire a favorable trading position with less sophisticated lands. Only China produced luxury goods of comparable quality. The empire also traded actively with India, the Arabs, and East Asia, while receiving simple products from western Europe and Africa. At the same time the large merchant class never gained significant political power, in part because of the elaborate network of governmental controls. In this, Byzantium again resembled China somewhat and differed notably from the looser social and political networks of the West, where rising merchants gained greater voice.

Byzantine cultural life centered on the secular traditions of Hellenism, so important in the education of bureaucrats, and on the evolving traditions of Eastern, or Orthodox, Christianity. While a host of literary and artistic creations resulted from this climate, there was little fundamental innovation outside of art and architecture. The Byzantine strength lay in preserving and commenting on past forms more than in developing new ones. A distinct Byzantine style had developed fairly early in art and architecture. The adaptation of Roman domed buildings, the elaboration of powerful and richly colored religious mosaics, and a tradition of *icon painting*—paintings of saints and other religious figures, often richly ornamented—expressed this artistic impulse and its marriage with Christianity. The blue and gold backgrounds set with richly dressed religious figures were meant to display on earth the unchanging brilliance of heaven. The important controversy over religious art arose in the 8th century, when a new emperor attacked the use of religious images in worship (probably responding to Muslim claims that Christians were idol-worshipers). This attack, called *iconoclasm* because of the breaking of images, roused huge protest from Byzantine monks, which briefly threatened a split between church and state. After a long and complex battle, icon use was gradually restored, while the tradition of state control over church affairs was also reasserted. Cultural issues in Byzantium reflected strong feelings, in part the fruit of the great diversity of peoples and cultural habits under the empire's

In this mosaic of Christ, dating from about A.D. 1100, note the difference from the images of Christ common in Western Christianity, which place more emphasis on suffering and less on divine majesty.

sway, even if major new intellectual principles did not result. A certain amount of diversity could be accepted, because of common allegiance to Christianity and the military and administrative effectiveness of the empire at its best.

THE SCHISM BETWEEN EAST AND WEST

Byzantine culture and politics, as well as its economic orientation toward Asia and northeastern Europe, helped explain the growing break between its Eastern version of Christianity and the Western version headed by the pope in Rome. There were many milestones in this rift. Different rituals opened as the West translated the Greek Bible into Latin in the 4th century. Later, Byzantine emperors deeply resented papal attempts to interfere in the iconoclastic dispute, for the popes, understandably enough, hoped to loosen state control over the Eastern church in order to make it conform more fully to their own idea of church-state relations. There was also scornful hostility to efforts

The Byzantine Empire developed a distinctively stylized religious art, adapted from earlier Roman painting styles and conveying the solemnity of the holy figures of the faith. This 11th century miniature features the holy women at the Sepulchre.

by a Frankish ruler, Charlemagne, to proclaim himself a Roman emperor in the 9th century—Byzantine officials knew full well that they were the true heirs of Rome and that Western rulers were crude and unsophisticated. They did, however, extend some recognition to the "Emperor of the Franks."

Contact between the two branches of Christianity trailed off, though neither East nor West cared to make a definitive break. Then in 1054 an ambitious church patriarch in Constantinople raised a host of old issues, including a quarrel over what kind of bread to use for the celebration of Christ's last supper in church mass. He also attacked the Roman Catholic practice, developed some centuries earlier, of insisting on celibacy for its priests; Eastern Orthodox priests could marry. Delegations of the two churches discussed these disputes, but this led only to new bitterness. The Roman pope finally *excommunicated* the patriarch and his followers—that is, banished them from Christian fellowship and the sacraments; the patriarch, no slouch, responded by excommunicating all Roman Catholics. Thus the split between the Roman Catholic church and Eastern Orthodoxy—the Byzantine or Greek, as well as the Russian Orthodox, Serbian Orthodox, and others—became formal and has endured to this day.

The East-West split fell short of complete divorce. A common Christianity with many shared or revived classical traditions and frequent commercial and cultural contacts continued to enliven the relationship between the two European civilizations. But the split did represent more than a passing quarrel or even the numerous differences that had developed in religious practices. It also reflected significant distinctions in political systems, most obviously in the principles of church-state relations but also between an imperial administration and the more divided Western state system. And it reflected the different patterns of development the two civilizations followed during the postclassical millennium. Byzantium, for all its ups and downs, was well aware of its advantages over the West during the early centuries following Rome's collapse. The East-West split occurred right at the end of Byzantium's period of greatest glory. By this point, however, the West was beginning to develop new strengths of its own, and its dynamism would over the next few centuries eclipse that of most of eastern Europe.

THE EMPIRE'S DECLINE

Shortly after the schism between East and West, the Byzantine Empire entered a long period of decline. Turkish invaders who had converted to Islam in central Asia began to press on its eastern borders, having already gained increasing influence in the Muslim caliphate. In the later 11th century, Turkish troops, the Seljuks, seized almost all the Asiatic provinces of the empire, thus cutting off the most prosperous sources of tax revenue as well as the territories that had supplied most of the empire's food. The empire staggered along for another four centuries, but its doom, at least as a significant power, was virtually sealed.

Eastern emperors appealed to Western leaders for help against the Turks, but their requests were largely ignored. The appeal helped motivate Western Crusades to the Holy Land, but this did not help the Byzantines. At the same time, Italian cities, blessed with powerful navies, gained in Constantinople increasing advantages, such as special trading privileges, a sign of the shift in power balance between East and West. One Western Crusade, in 1204, ostensibly set up to conquer the Holy Land from the Muslims, actually turned against Byzantium. Led by greedy Venetian merchants, the Crusade attacked and conquered Constantinople, briefly unseating the emperor altogether and weakening the whole imperial structure. But the West was not yet powerful enough to hold this ground, and a small Byzantine Empire was restored, able through careful diplomacy to survive for another two centuries. Not only Western and Turkish pressure but also the creation of new, independent Slavic kingdoms in the Balkans, such as Serbia, showed the empire's diminished power. Turkish settlements pressed ever closer to Constantinople in the northern Middle East—in the area that is now Turkey—and finally, in 1453, a Turkish sultan brought a powerful army, equipped by artillery purchased from the West, against the city, which fell after two months. By 1461 the Turks had conquered remaining pockets of Byzantine control, including most of the Balkans, bringing Islamic power farther into eastern Europe than ever before. The great Eastern Empire was no more.

The fall of Byzantium was one of the great events in world history, and we will deal with its impact in several later chapters. It was a great event because the Byzantine Empire had been so durable and important, anchoring a vital corner of the Mediterranean even amid the rapid surge of Islam. The empire's trading contacts and its ability to preserve and disseminate classical and Christian learning made it a vital unit during the whole postclassical period. Its influence easily survived its demise. The Turks as well as the major Slavic regions carried on the key Byzantine traditions. Ottoman Turkish administration, once installed in Constantinople, reproduced many Byzantine administrative procedures and some of their military techniques. Turkish architects began to build bigger domed mosques, as they learned how the Byzantines had built their churches. The Ottoman Empire, pushed through much of the Middle East, was an Islamic state, and no single set of traditions defined its operation. Particularly as

it functioned in what is now Turkey and southeastern Europe, however, it carried on many of the features that had marked its Byzantine predecessor and made it so successful.

ANALYSIS

THE CLASSICAL HERITAGE FROM GREECE AND ROME

Understanding the Byzantine Empire—its characteristics and importance alike—must raise questions about common assumptions many Americans have about their own relationship to the classical Mediterranean. These assumptions, at their crudest, risk seeing Greece and Rome as sort of a dress rehearsal for the greater glories of the modern West.

One of the characteristics of many civilizations in the postclassical period was their use of their society's history to help reinforce the identity of their own culture. China built heavily on a selective sense of Chinese history in the classical period and before, to provide an active tradition that would guide present generations. Confucianism, the basis for formal education in the bureaucracy, urged respect for the past and an effort to live up to its model. Historical sense in India was somewhat more diffuse, but memory of the great empires, especially the Guptas, along with earlier cultural achievements enshrined in the epic stories, remained active.

The classical civilizations in the Mediterranean—Greece and Rome—lent themselves to similar enshrinement, but with some obvious complexities. No single society inherited their mantle, in contrast to the situation in postclassical India and China. Further, all three civilizations that could lay claim as successors of Greece and Rome—western Europe, Byzantine and eastern Europe, and the Muslim civilization in the Middle East and North Africa (an active user of Hellenistic science)—differed from Greece and Rome in their basic religion. This automatically forced them to be wary and selective in what they chose to appropriate from the past. Finally the Greco-Roman traditions were very diverse, which meant that one society's "classical past" could differ notably from another's.

Western civilization, as it began to develop in the postclassical period, made strong claims of inheritance from Greece and Rome. These claims would solidify still further later on, and they remain an active ingredient of Western education today. Most history textbooks in the United States, for example, confidently assume a straight line between key features of Greece and Rome and desirable American institutions today: an obvious example is the idea that Athenian democracy led to modern American democracy. Classical heritage is used to highlight and dignify values educators feel young people should learn—a standard justification for history's usefulness, and not of course unique to Western society.

The Western use of classical heritage has three important limitations, however, whatever its moral or political utility. First, the classical past is treated selectively. Emphasis is placed on Athenian democracy and Greek rationalism, far more than on the central importance of slavery (though at one time, Greek arguments in favor of slavery were also used by Western apologists). Second, some modern institutions are given a classical cachet that may in fact have little to do with Greek or Roman precedent. Modern democracy, for example, did not in fact flow from classical models, which were rarely referred to in the postclassical West. Rather, the models were invoked much later, as inspiration, once democratic forms began to emerge for other reasons. Finally, the Greco-Roman past is "classical" for East European civilizations as well as for the West.

The Byzantine Empire was the most direct heir to Greece and Rome, almost a continuation state in fact. Societies that learned from Byzantium, like Russia, had less solid classical claims, but they could argue that the Greco-Roman mantle had been passed through assimilation. Further, what these societies meant by classical heritage was different from the Western version. Both East and West could look to Greek art for stylistic models, and to Roman law, but what they sought from classical philosophy and political tradition differed. Byzantium and its heirs stressed imperial majesty and orderly, authoritarian politics, which they could readily find in Greek city-states as in the Roman Empire, more than the West came to do. While both East and West copied classical architecture, only the West revived interest in the principles of Greek drama.

Moralistic or inspirational usage of the past is a common impulse, as leaders try to reinforce values they find important. By the same token, this usage can be tricky in terms of historical accuracy. All societies tend to downplay less savory aspects of their heritage, while giving disproportionate weight to other features judged useful. This tricky quality in heritage is particularly obvious for the heirs of Greece and Rome. Disagreements over what Greece and Rome really stood for followed from the diversities that sprang up around the Mediterranean in the postclassical centuries. This complexity, in turn, drives home the desirability of testing any claims of heritage against the realities of the historical record. History can easily be manipulated to create idealized, educationally inspiring pasts, yet even if this purpose is accepted it is vital to understand what distortions can result.

Questions: Why did Europeans (East or West) have more trouble identifying a classical past than Chinese leaders did? How might European educators in the East and West disagree over what lessons to emphasize from Greece and Rome? What did Byzantine leaders think the essential features of their heritage from Greece and Rome consisted of?

THE SPREAD OF CIVILIZATION IN EASTERN EUROPE

Long before Byzantine decline after the 11th century, the empire had been the source of a new northward surge of Christianity. Orthodox missionaries sent from Constantinople busily converted most people in the Balkans—in what is now Bulgaria, Yugoslavia, and parts of Romania and Hungary—to their version of Christianity, and some other trappings of Byzantine culture came in their wake. In 864 the Byzantine government sent the missionaries

East European Kingdoms in the 12th Century

Cyril and Methodius to the territory that is now Czechoslovakia. Here the effort failed in that Roman Catholic missionaries were more successful. But Cyril and Methodius continued their efforts in the Balkans and in southern Russia, where their ability to speak the Slavic language greatly aided their efforts. They devised a written script for this language, derived from Greek letters; to this day, the Slavic alphabet is known as Cyrillic. Thus the possibility of literature and some literacy developed in eastern Europe along with Christianity, well beyond the political borders of Byzantium. Byzantine missionaries were quite willing to have local languages used in church services, another contrast with Western Catholicism.

ORTHODOX MISSIONARIES AND OTHER INFLUENCES

Eastern missionaries did not monopolize the borderlands of eastern Europe. Roman Catholicism and the Latin alphabet prevailed not only in Czechoslovakia but also in most of Hungary (taken over in the 9th century by a Turkic people, the Magyars) and in Poland. Much of this region would long be an area of competition between Eastern and Western political and intellectual models. During the centuries after the conversion to Christianity, this stretch of eastern Europe north of the Balkans was organized in a series of regional monarchies, loosely governed amid a powerful, landowning aristocracy. Kingdoms of Poland, Bohemia (Czechoslovakia), and Lithuania easily surpassed most Western kingdoms in territory. This was also a moderately active area for trade and industry. Ironworking, for example, was more developed than in the West until the 12th century. Eastern Europe during these centuries also received an important influx of Jews, migrating away from the Middle East. Poland gained the largest single concentration of Jews. Eastern Europe's Jews, largely barred from agriculture and often resented by the Christian majority, gained strength in local commerce while maintaining their own religious and cultural traditions. A strong emphasis on extensive education and literacy, though primarily for males, distinguished Jewish culture not only in eastern Europe but also compared to most societies in the world at this time.

This was an early phase of the development of eastern Europe beyond the Byzantine heartland, for by Asian (or Byzantine) standards the region remained backward, lightly populated, and not yet able to produce a significant written or artistic culture beyond rudimentary church buildings and monkish chronicles of events. Many features of Byzantium, including its elaborate bureaucracy, were irrelevant to what was, like most of western Europe at the same time, a developing region.

THE EARLY RUSSIAN PHASE

Russia shared many features with the rest of northeastern Europe before the 15th century, including rather hesitant advances in economy and politics. A full-fledged Russian civilization had yet to emerge. Yet, as with much of eastern Europe, the centuries of Byzantine influence were an important formative period that would influence later developments considerably. During the postclassical centuries Russia was not a particularly significant society. It was in an initial stage as a civilization and primarily serves as one of the important cases in which civilization fanned out from more established centers—in this instance, Byzantium. Russia can be compared in this sense to other areas that were taking clear shape as civilizations but whose world-historical importance would come later—for example, Japan and in many ways western Europe itself.

Slavic peoples had moved into the sweeping plains of Russia and eastern Europe from an Asian homeland, during the time of the Roman Empire. They mixed with and

This 14th-century illustrated German-Jewish prayer book is a remnant from the spread of Jews and Jewish culture during the postclassical period.

incorporated some earlier inhabitants and some additional invaders, such as the Bulgarians who adopted Slavic language and customs. The Slavs already knew the use of iron, and they extended agriculture in the rich soils of what is now western Russia, where no durable civilization had previously taken root. Slavic political organization long rested in family tribes and villages; the Slavs maintained an animist religion with gods for the sun, thunder, wind, and fire. The early Russians also had a rich tradition of folk music and oral legends, and they developed some very loose regional kingdoms.

During the 6th and 7th centuries, traders from Scandinavia began to work through the Slavic lands, moving along the great rivers of western Russia, which run south to north—particularly the Dnieper. Through this route the Norse traders were able to reach the Byzantine Empire, and a regular, flourishing trade developed between Scandinavia and Constantinople. Luxury products from Byzantium and the Arab world traveled north, in return for furs and other relatively crude products. The Scandinavian traders, militarily superior to the Slavs, gradually set up some governments along their trade route, particularly in the city of Kiev. A monarchy emerged, and according to legend a man named Rurik, a native of Denmark, became the first king of Russia around A.D. 855. The Kievan kingdom, though still loosely organized through alliances with regional, landed aristocrats, flourished until the 12th century. It was from the Scandinavians also that the word *Russia* was coined, possibly from a Greek word for red, which applied to the hair color of many of the Norse traders. In turn, the Scandinavian minority gradually mingled with the Slavic population, particularly among the aristocracy.

Contacts between Kievan Russia and Byzantium extended steadily. Kiev, centrally located, became a prosperous trading center, and from there many Russians visited Constantinople. These exchanges led to growing knowledge of Christianity. King Vladimir I, a Rurik descendant who ruled from 980 to 1015, finally took the step of converting to Christianity not only in his own name but in that of all his people. He was eager to avoid the papal influence that came with Roman Catholicism, which he knew about through the experiences of the Polish kingdom; Orthodox Christianity gave a valid alternative that still provided a sophisticated replacement for prevailing animism. Islam was rejected, according to one account, because Vladimir could not accept a religion that forbade alcoholic drink. Russian awe at the splendor of religious services in Constantinople also played a role. Having made his decision, Vladimir proceeded to organize mass baptisms for his subjects, forcing conversions by military pressure. Early church leaders were imported from Byzantium, and they helped train a literate Russian priesthood. As in Byzantium, the king characteristically controlled major appointments, and a separate Russian church institution soon developed.

As Russia became Christian, it was the largest single state in Europe, though highly decentralized. Rurik's descendants managed for some time to avoid damaging battles over succession to the throne. Following Byzantine example they issued a formal law code, which among other things reduced the severity of traditional punishments and replaced community vendettas with state-run courts, at least in principle. The last of the great Kievan princes, Yaroslav, issued the legal codification, while also building numerous churches and arranging the translation of religious literature from Greek to Slavic.

This painting shows the Russian king, Vladimir, accepting Christianity.

DOCUMENT
RUSSIA TURNS TO
CHRISTIANITY

This document (from a monk's chronicle), describing Vladimir's conversion policy, indicates what was officially believed about the power of Russian kings, Russian social structure, and the relationship between Christianity and earlier animism. These official claims are important, but they may not reflect the whole reality of this important transition in Russian history.

For at this time the Russes were ignorant pagans. The devil rejoiced thereat, for he did not know that his ruin was approaching. He was so eager to destroy the Christian people, yet he was expelled by the true cross even from these very lands. . . . Vladimir was visited by Bulgars of the Mohammedan faith. . . . [He] listened to them for he was fond of women and indulgence, regarding which he heard with pleasure. But . . . abstinence from pork and wine were disagreeable to him. "Drinking," said he, "is the joy of the Russes. We cannot exist without that pleasure." [Russian envoys sent to Constantinople were astonished by the beauty of the churches and the chanting], and in their wonder praised the Greek ceremonial. . . .

[Later, Vladimir was suffering from blindness; a Byzantine bishop baptized him] and as the bishop laid his hand upon him, he straightway recovered his sight. Upon experiencing this miraculous cure, Vladimir glorified God, saying, "I have now perceived the one true God." When his followers beheld this miracle, many of them were also baptized. . . . Thereafter Vladimir sent heralds throughout the whole city to proclaim that if any inhabitant, rich or poor, did not betake himself to the river [for mass baptism] he would risk the Prince's displeasure. When the people heard these words, they wept for joy and exclaimed in their enthusiasm, "If this were not good, the Prince and his nobles would not have accepted it." . . . There was joy in heaven and upon earth to behold so many souls saved. But the devil groaned, lamenting, "Woe is me. How am I driven out hence . . . my reign in these regions is at an end." . . .

He [Vladimir] ordered that wooden churches should be built and established where [pagan] idols have previously stood. He founded the Church of Saint Basil on the hill where the idol of Perun and the other images had been set, and where the prince and the people had offered their sacrifices. He began to found churches, to assign priests throughout the cities and towns, and to bring people in for baptism from all towns and villages. He began to take the children of the best families and send them for instruction from books.

Questions: In what ways might the account be oversimple in describing royal powers and popular response? What explanations does this religious chronicler offer for the conversion of Russians to Christianity? Which of the explanations are most likely, and which are the results of some kind of bias? What kind of church-state relationship did this conversion procedure predict?

RUSSIAN INSTITUTIONS AND CULTURE

Russia borrowed much from Byzantium, but it was in no position to replicate major institutions such as the bureaucracy or an elaborate educational system. Russian kings were attracted to Byzantine ceremonials and luxury and to the concept (if not yet the reality) that a central ruler should have wide powers.

Many characteristics of Orthodox Christianity gradually penetrated Russian culture. Fervent devotion to the power of God and to many Eastern saints helped organize worship. Churches were relatively ornate, filled with icons and the sweet smell of incense. A monastic movement developed that stressed prayer and charity. Traditional practices, such as polygamy, gradually yielded to the Christian family ethic that insisted on only one wife. The emphasis on almsgiving as a manifestation of religious feeling long described the sense of obligation wealthy Russians felt toward the poor, and would actually delay the formation of more institutionalized welfare arrangements.

The Russian literature that developed, using the Cyrillic alphabet, mainly summed up a mixture of religious and royal events and was filled with praises to the saints and invocations of the power of God. Disasters were seen as just expressions of the wrath of God against human wickedness, while success in war followed from the aid of God and the saints in the name jointly of Russia and the Orthodox faith. This tone also was common in Western Christian writing during these centuries, but in Russia it monopolized formal culture more fully: a distinct, additional philosophical or scientific current did not emerge in the postclassical period.

Russian art focused on the religious also, with icon painting and illuminated religious manuscripts becoming something of a Kievan specialty. Orthodox churches, built in the form of a cross surmounted by a dome, similarly aped Byzantine styles, though frequently the building materials were wood rather than stone. Religious art and music were rivaled by continued popular entertainments in the oral tradition, which combined music, street performances, and some theater. The Russian church tried to suppress these forms, regarded as pagan, but with incomplete success.

Overall, this formative period in Russian society saw the development of a powerful religious sentiment, with particular cultural emphasis on art and music. This cultural development, although parallel to some features in emerging Western culture because of the common process of creating a new literary tradition from an animist background and because of shared Christian beliefs, operated quite separately from specific patterns in the West. Russian-Western contacts, at this point and for several centuries to come, were virtually nonexistent, though Yaroslav, interestingly, married his daughter to a French king, indicating awareness of possible beneficial interchange.

The same separate development marked Russian social and economic patterns. Russian peasants at this juncture were fairly free farmers, though an aristocratic landlord class existed. Russian aristocrats, called *boyars*, had less political power than their counterparts in western Europe, though the Kievan kings had to negotiate with them.

KIEVAN DECLINE

The Kievan kingdom began to fade in the 12th century. Rival princes set up regional governments, while the royal family frequently squabbled over succession to the throne. Invaders from Asia whittled at Russian territory. The rapid eclipse of Byzantium reduced Russian trade and wealth, for the kingdom had always depended heavily on the greater prosperity and sophisticated manufacturing of its southern neighbor. A new kingdom was briefly established around a city near what is now Moscow, but by

1200 Russia was weak and disunited. The final blow in this first chapter of Russian history came in 1236, when a large force of Mongols from central Asia moved through Russia and into other parts of eastern Europe. The initial Mongol intent was to add the whole of Europe to their growing empire. The Mongols, or Tartars as they are called in the Russian tradition, easily captured the major Russian cities, but they did not penetrate much farther west because of political difficulties in their Asian homeland. For over two centuries, however, Russia would remain under Tartar control.

This control, in turn, further separated the dynamic of Russian history from that of western Europe. Russian literature languished under Tartar supervision. Trade lapsed in western Russia, and indeed the vigorous north-south commerce of the Kievan period never returned. At the same time, loose Tartar supervision did not destroy Russian Christianity or a native Russian aristocratic class. So long as tribute was paid, Tartar overlords left day-to-day Rus-

St. Sophia in Kiev, though built after the postclassical period, utilized artistic themes developed earlier in Byzantium.

sian affairs alone. Thus when Tartar control was finally forced out, in the second half of the 15th century, a Russian cultural and political tradition could reemerge, serving as a partial basis for the further, fuller development of Russian society.

Russian leaders, moreover, retained during the period of eclipse an active memory of the glories of Byzantium. When Constantinople fell to the Turks in 1453, just as Russia was beginning to assert its independence from the Tartars, it was logical to claim and quite probable to believe, that the mantle of east European leadership had fallen on Russia. A monk, currying favor, wrote the Russian king in 1511 that while heresy had destroyed the first Roman Empire, and the Turks had cut down the second, Byzantium, a "third, new Rome," under the king's "mighty rule" "sends out the Orthodox Christian faith to the ends of the earth and shines more brightly than the sun." "Two Romes have fallen, but the third stands, and there will be no fourth." This sense of an Eastern Christian mission, inspiring a Russian resurgence, was not the least of the products of this complicated formative period in the emergence of a separate European civilization in the Slavic lands.

CONCLUSION

THE END OF AN ERA IN EASTERN EUROPE

With Byzantium and Russia both under siege, East European civilization unquestionably fell on hard times at the end of the postclassical era. Brighter days were ahead, though the struggle to define anew a full civilization after 1453 would not prove easy. In the meantime the connection of key border territories, such as Poland, to the west European cultural zone would deepen, another complication for the subsequent history of the region, while the Balkans lay under Turkish rule.

These difficulties confirmed the largely separate trajectories of West and East in Europe, for western Europe remained free from outside control and, despite some new problems, maintained a clearer vigor in politics, economy, and culture. When eastern Europe did reemerge, it would be at some disadvantage to the West, in terms of power and economic-cultural sophistication—a quite different balance from that which had prevailed during the glory days of Byzantium and the cruder vigor of Kievan Russia.

At the same time, the disruption caused by Tartar invasion and Byzantine collapse warns against projecting too much continuity between these early east European centuries and what would come later. Byzantine patterns were never recaptured. Key features of Kievan social structure would not characterize the later development of imperial Russia. Yet continuity was not entirely lost. Not only Christianity but the particular east European assumptions about political rulers and church-state relations as well as the pride in a lively artistic culture would serve as organizing threads when Russia and other Slavic societies turned to rebuilding.

The Byzantine Empire was one of the great centers of civilization during the postclassical period, though smaller than the other three centers in the Middle East (plus North Africa), India, and China. Alone of the great centers, it did not simply decline but disappeared, and this suggests some of the limitations of its final centuries of existence. Yet the empire was not simply a random feature of the postclassical period that must be inserted to keep the historical record straight. Its role in shaping one of the major versions of Christianity and its active effort in spreading religion, commerce, and the trappings of civilization northward helped prepare for later developments in the east European region. These developments, headed by the rise of Russia, began to take shape when the shock of Byzantium's fall and the Mongol invasions finally wore off.

FURTHER READINGS

J. M. Hussey's *The Byzantine World* (1982) provides a useful overview. Byzantine Christianity is studied in G. Every's *The Byzantine Patriarchate, 451–1204* (1978) and S. Runciman's The *Byzantine Theocracy* (1977); see also D. M. Nicol's *Church and Society in the Last Centuries of Byzantium* (1979). On culture, see E. Kitzinger's *Byzantine Art in the Making* (1977). Byzantine relations with the West form the main topic in H. J. Magoulias's *Byzantine Christianity: Emperor, Church and the West* (1982).

On Byzantine influence in eastern Europe, D. Obolensky's *The Byzantine Commonwealth: Eastern Europe, 500–1453* (1971) is an excellent analysis. See also S. Runciman's *A History of the First Bulgarian Empire* (1930).

On Russian history the best survey is Nicholas Riasanovsky's *A History of Russia* (4th ed., 1984), with a good bibliography. Three books deal with early Russian culture: N. P. Kondakov's *The Russian Icon* (1927), J. H. Billington's *The Icon and the Axe: An Interpretive History of Russian Culture* (1966), and Arthur Voyce's *The Art and Architecture of Medieval Russia* (1967).

Two source collections are also very helpful on early Russian history: T. Riha, ed., *Readings in Russian Civilization*, vol. 1, *Russia before Peter the Great, 900–1700* (1969); and especially S. A. Zenkovsky, ed. and trans., *Medieval Russia's Epics, Chronicles and Tales* (1963).

500–900 Recovery period after Rome's fall; missionary work in northern Europe

732 Franks defeat Muslims in France

800–814 Charlemagne's empire

900–1000 Spread of new plows; use of horses in agriculture, transport

962 Germanic kings revive "Roman" Empire

1066 Norman conquest of England; strong feudal monarchy

1018 Beginning of Christian reconquest of Spain

1073–1085 Gregory VII, reform Pope

1070–1141 Peter Abelard

1096–1270 Crusades

A.D. 500   A.D. 800   A.D. 1000

A New Civilization Emerges in Western Europe

16

INTRODUCTION. The postclassical period in western Europe began with the decline and fall of the Roman Empire and extended until the 15th century. Known as the Middle Ages in European history, the period featured gradual recovery from the shock of Rome's collapse and growing interaction with other societies, particularly around the Mediterranean.

Developments in Western civilization during the Middle Ages reflected many of the larger themes of postclassical world history. The spread of civilization underlay medieval history. Although western Europe had been touched by the Roman Empire at its height, contacts had been somewhat superficial outside the Mediterranean zone. And much of the north—most of Germany, northern Britain, and Scandinavia—had been entirely outside the Roman orbit. During the Middle Ages civilization extended, gradually, to the whole of western Europe.

Western Europe also witnessed the spread of new religious beliefs. The missionary activity of Christianity was the chief bearer of civilization to northwestern Europe in the early centuries of the Middle Ages. Most West Europeans converted from animistic faiths to Christian monotheism as part of this process, though in fact many produced an amalgam in which important traces of animism, including beliefs in magic and supernatural spirits, coexisted with often fervent Christianity.

Finally, medieval western Europe participated in the emerging international community, the network of expanding contacts among major societies in Asia, Europe, and parts of Africa. From such contacts medieval Europeans learned new technologies. New implements introduced from Asia by invading tribes helped spur medieval agriculture from the 10th century onward. Trade in the Mediterranean, bringing contacts with the Arabs, yielded other technological gains, such as the first European paper fac-

---

1150–1300 Gothic style spreads

1180 University of Paris

1200–1274 Thomas Aquinas and flowering of scholasticism

1215 Magna Carta

1226–1270 Louis IX of France

1303 Seizure of papacy by French king

1265 First English parliament

1338–1453 Hundred Years' War

1348 Black Death (bubonic plague)

1469 Formation of single Spanish monarch

A.D. 1150   A.D. 1300   A.D. 1450

tory set up in southern Italy in the 13th century. Medieval culture was at least as powerfully shaped by connections with the wider world. From the Byzantines and the Arabs, Western scholars by the 11th and 12th centuries learned new and challenging lessons in mathematics, science, and philosophy that spurred them to change and elaborate their own world view. The medieval West unquestionably took more from the emerging world network than it contributed, but it was also challenged by its international position to seek new world roles.

THE FLAVOR OF THE MIDDLE AGES

Medieval western Europe was not, however, simply an illustration of larger themes. It had its own characteristics, both positive and negative. The West was, during this entire period, a backward society by the standards of the great civilizations of the Middle East and Asia. Muslims, for example, scorned the West Europeans as barbarians, incapable of knowing science. "Their bodies are large, their manners harsh, their understanding dull and their tongues heavy . . . those of them who are farthest to the north are the most subject to stupidity, grossness and brutishness," said a 10th-century Arab geographer. Culturally and economically medieval Europeans were regarded as "underdeveloped" by those in other societies—including Christian Byzantium—who were aware of them. It is small wonder that before 1100 Europeans were not infrequently seized as slaves; or that even as their medieval society gained in strength, its international reputation rested mainly on the prowess of its warriors, not on more sophisticated achievements. Western Europe's inferior position explains why contacts with the wider world proved so important.

Medieval backwardness certainly accounts for a long-standing anxiety about, as well as hostility toward, the more powerful Muslim world. Fears of Arab invasion did not die with the end of the actual Arab threat, and Arab control of Spain and portions of southern Italy constituted a longstanding challenge to Europe's Christian leaders. Only toward the end of the Middle Ages could Europeans even begin to presume they were capable of grappling with Arab learning, and superior Arab wealth and commerce caused medieval traders no small concern. Yet inferiority was galling in that Europeans believed Islam to be a false religion (despite many features shared with Christianity) and sought ways to push back or circumvent Muslim power. The Crusades were one result of this belligerent outlook; explorations that sought trade routes free from Muslim power at the end of the Middle Ages were another.

Medieval Europe's backwardness means, finally, that it can most fruitfully be compared with other societies in which civilization was a fairly new achievement in these centuries, rather than with the more established centers. Western political structures had interesting points in common with those of Japan and sub-Saharan Africa. The European Middle Ages certainly serve as a reminder that the West has not always been among the front-runners of civilizations; the period also serves as evidence that societies can make important transitions in world position from one period to the next, through decline as well as advance. Societies regarded as underdeveloped today can point to the European Middle Ages as proof that unusual dynamism can develop amid apparent backwardness, allowing a civilization not only to catch up but in some ways to surge ahead of the traditional standard setters.

SIGNS OF VITALITY

The Middle Ages also served western Europe as something of a crucible for institutions and values that helped propel Western civilization forward. The postclassical West advanced mightily, by almost all relevant measurements, after some centuries of serious instability following the fall of the Roman Empire. Population grew, the economy blossomed, political units became more effective and covered larger territories, and a complex artistic and intellectual life took shape. Technological innovations included the use of new water-driven mills and improvements in iron casting for the manufacture of great church bells. In strictly Western terms, then, the Middle Ages, from at least the 10th to the 14th centuries, is a story of progress. Leaders in several fields were able to select aspects of the Greco-Roman heritage for their use. The postclassical centuries also formed a seedbed for certain new values and institutions that would outlast the medieval period itself. In politics and social structure, particularly, the Middle Ages contributed more to the ongoing heritage of Western civilization than the classical era had done. And even in intellectual life, where medieval thinkers grappled with the legacy of classical philosophy and science, the distinctive contributions of the Middle Ages would leave a durable mark. It was from the Middle Ages, thus, that the Western world gained the institution of the university (including rituals and degrees still associated with university life), the architectural forms (towers and vaulting arches of the Gothic style) we still associate with intellectual and religious life, and some new concepts of limited government.

The West's postclassical period, beyond ultimate service as a preliminary version of a Western way of life, also had its own flavor and its own particular tensions. It was, by later Western standards, an unusually religious age. Post-classical Europe, never united by a single government, was joined above all by its new Christian culture and a single Church headed by the pope in Rome. Politics as well as art and intellectual activity were powerfully shaped by the role of religion and the institutional church. Yet the Middle Ages also produced characteristic government forms and economic institutions, some of which coexisted uneasily with the strong current of spirituality. This was not a simple age, but it was a distinctive one, which some Westerners in later periods of commercial secularism and power politics have looked back on with real nostalgia.

 STAGES OF POSTCLASSICAL DEVELOPMENT: FROM RECOVERY ONWARD

From about A.D. 550 until about 900, western Europe seemed to be groping for civilization. Rome's decline had left Italy fragmented—its cities and commerce shrinking and its intellectual life in tatters. Rome continued to serve as the center of the growing Catholic church, in turn the most powerful institution and the central Christian agency in the West. And Italy's trade and urban life continued to surpass the levels of the remainder of western Europe, as the area retained stronger links with the Roman past than did newer centers such as France. But Italy could hardly claim anything but a shadow of the Roman Empire's grandeur, and its political weakness would indeed last until the later 19th century. Spain, another key region of the Roman Empire in the West, lay in the hands of the Muslims through much of the Middle Ages. A vibrant intellectual and economic life focused there, and it would have an important influence on Western developments by dint of its superiority, but it was for the time being out of the Western mainstream. The center of the postclassical West lay in France, the Low Countries, and southern and western Germany, with England increasingly drawn in. These were areas in which civilization was relatively recent, then only to be shaken by the Roman Empire's collapse. The relocation of the West's focal geography, as well as Rome's decline, explain why society had to struggle to keep afloat during the early postclassical centuries.

Frequent invasions reflected and prolonged the West's weakness, making it difficult to develop durable government or economic forms. Raids by the seagoing Vikings from Scandinavia periodically disrupted life from Ireland to Sicily. The Scandinavians attacked a number of coastal areas, while other invaders from eastern areas also disrupted politics, trade, and production. With weak rulers and little more than subsistence agriculture, it was small

wonder that intellectual activity almost ground to a halt. The few who could read and write were concentrated in the hierarchy and the monasteries of the Catholic church, where they provided signal service simply by keeping learning alive. But they could do little more than copy older manuscripts, including those of the great Christian thinkers of the later Roman Empire. They could not, by their own admission, understand much of the philosophy involved, and they often apologized for their inability even to write good Latin.

This was the setting in which a number of characteristic institutions began to provide greater structure to postclassical Western society; some of them carried implications that would long affect civilization in this area.

MANORIALISM AND FEUDALISM

Between Rome's fall and the 10th century, effective political organization was largely local, though Germanic kings ruled some territories such as a portion of what is France today. *Manorialism* was the system that described economic and political relations between landlords and their peasant laborers. Most people were *serfs* living on self-sufficient agricultural estates called manors. Serfs were agricultural workers who received some protection, including the administration of justice, from the landlords; in return they were obligated to turn over part of their goods and to remain on the land. The manorial system had originated in the later Roman Empire; it was strengthened by the decline of trade and the lack of larger political structures. Serfs needed the military forces the landlords could muster, given the instability of society. Without much market economy to stimulate production and specialization, these same landlords used the serfs' produce and labor to support their own modest establishments.

Manorialism thus involved a hierarchy of reciprocal obligations between the masses and the ruling class. Life for most serfs was difficult. Agricultural equipment was limited, which kept production low. Available plows, copied from Mediterranean models, were too light to work the heavy soils of France and Germany effectively. Only from the 9th century onward was a better plow, called the moldboard, introduced that allowed deeper turning of the soil. Most Western peasants early in the postclassical period also left half their land uncultivated each year to restore nutrients. This again limited productivity, though by the 9th century, a new three-field system, reserving only one-third of the land for fallow, improved the situation.

The obligations of the manorial system bore as heavily on most serfs as did technological limits. Serfs had to give their lord part of their crops in return for grazing their animals on his land or milling their grain. They also provided many days of labor repairing the lord's castle or working the lands under his control. Serfs were not slaves—they could not be bought or sold, and they retained essential ownership of their houses and lands so long as they kept up with their obligations; they could also pass their property rights on through inheritance. Peasants also grouped in their own villages, which provided them a rich community life of festivals and a political structure through which they could resolve most internal disputes. Nevertheless, life remained hard, particularly during the early postclassical centuries. Some serfs escaped landlord control, creating a host of vagabond wanderers who added to the disorder of the early Middle Ages.

On top of manorialism, as a result of the lack of strong political structures in postclassical western Europe, a second system, called *feudalism,* developed. Feudalism described relationships among military elites, mostly landlords, who could afford the horses and iron weaponry necessary to fight. Greater lords provided protection and aid to lesser lords, called vassals; vassals in turn owed their lords military service, some goods or payments, and advice. This system formed the beginnings of the European version of feudalism. In the long run, the feudal network of ties was a building block toward greater political stability. In the short run, after Rome's fall feudalism fed local disorder. Many landlords had armed bands of five or ten local vassals, easily converted into raiding parties. Many local wars occurred, as well as the attacks by Vikings and other groups.

THE CHURCH

During the recovery centuries after A.D. 500, the Catholic church provided the only extensive example of solid organization. Roman popes built a partial hierarchy by trying to control some of their local bishops. The popes did not always appoint the bishops, for monarchs and local lords often claimed this right, but they did send directives and received information. The popes also regulated doctrine, beating back several heresies that threatened a unified Christian faith. Moreover, they sponsored extensive missionary activity. Papal missionaries converted the English to Christianity. They brought the religion to northern and eastern Germany, beyond the borders of the previous Roman Empire, and ultimately, by the 10th century, to Scandinavia. They were active, of course, in the border regions of eastern Europe, sometimes competing directly with Orthodox missionaries. In theory, and to an extent in fact, the Church copied the government of the Roman Empire in order to administer Christendom. The pope in Rome was

the top authority. Regional churches were headed by bishops, who were supposed to owe allegiance to the Church's central authority; bishops, in turn, appointed and to some degree supervised local priests.

The solid structure of the church, which gave it a vital organizational edge over what secular government there was in the West, and the spread of Christianity constituted significant developments in the history of the West. Christian values increasingly became the essential cement of the newly located civilization that covered virtually the whole of western Europe.

The interest of early Germanic kings in Christianity was a testimony to the political as well as spiritual power of the Church. A warrior chieftain, Clovis, converted to Christianity around A.D. 496 in order to gain greater prestige over local rivals who were still pagan. This authority, in turn, gave him a vague dominion over the Franks, located in much of what is France today. Conversion of this sort also strengthened beliefs by Western religious leaders, particularly the popes, that they had a legitimate authority separate from and superior to the political sphere.

The Church also developed an important chain of monasteries during the Dark Ages. Western monasteries helped discipline the intense spirituality, felt by some individual Christians, expressed by a desire to escape the limits of ordinary material life. By locating those particularly dedicated to piety in groups and subjecting them to common rules, the Church could use the monastic movement to promote Christian unity in the West. The most important set of rules for monasteries was developed by Benedict of Nursia (in Italy) in the 6th century. Monasteries also served ordinary people as examples of a holy life, adding to the spiritual focus that formed part of the fabric of medieval society. They served more prosaic functions as well. Many monasteries helped improve the cultivation of the land at a time when agricultural techniques were at a low ebb. Benedict urged the holy importance of productive work. Study and prayer formed part of monastic discipline, and Western monks, in copying and pondering ancient manuscripts by Roman authors as well as Christian theologians, helped set the basis for later intellectual inquiry in this emerging civilization. Thus monasteries also provided some education, promoting literacy.

CHARLEMAGNE AND HIS SUCCESSORS

One significant development occurred during the early postclassical centuries in the more strictly political sphere. The royal house of the Franks grew in strength during the 8th century. A new family, the Carolingians, took over this monarchy, which was based in northern France, Belgium, and western Germany. One founder of the Carolingian line—Charles Martel, or Charles the Hammer—was responsible for defeating the Muslims in the battle of Tours in 732, though his victory had more to do with Arab exhaustion and an over-extended invasion force than Carolingian strength. This defeat helped confine the Muslims to Spain and, along with the Byzantine defeat of the Arabs in the same period, preserved Europe for Christianity.

A later Carolingian ruler in this same royal line, Charles the Great, or Charlemagne, established a substantial empire in France and Germany around the year 800. Briefly, it looked as if a new Roman Empire might revive in the West, and indeed the imperial title continued to be used by Charlemagne's successors in Germany. Charlemagne helped to restore some church-based education in western Europe, and the level of intellectual activity began

a slow recovery in part due to these efforts. When Charlemagne died in 814, however, his empire did not long survive him. Rather, it was split into three portions—the outlines of modern France, Germany, and a middle strip consisting of the Low Countries, Switzerland, and northern Italy. Several of Charlemagne's successors, with nicknames like "the Bald" or "the Fat," were not models of political dynamism even in their regional kingdoms.

From this point onward, the essential political history of western Europe consisted of the gradual emergence of regional monarchies; a durable empire proved impossible, given competing loyalties and the absence of a strong bureaucracy. Western Europe proved to be a civilization with strong cultural unity, initially centered in Catholic Christianity, but with pronounced political division. No single language united this civilization, any more than did a single government. Latin was used by intellectuals and by the church officials, but during the Middle Ages separate spo-

The pope's coronation of the emperor Charlemagne was a vital precedent for the idea that Church approval was essential for a legitimate state in western Europe, though in fact Charlemagne's power greatly exceeded the pope's.

Charlemagne's Empire and Successor States

Charlemagne's Empire at his accession, 768

Territories added before his death in 814

Tributary Slavic states

Both maps are shown at same scale

ken languages evolved, usually merging Germanic and Latin elements. These separate languages, such as French and English, in turn helped form the basis of some halting national identity when political and national boundaries roughly coincided—which is what began to happen in key cases after the 9th century.

The royal houses of several lands gained new visibility soon after Charlemagne's empire split. At first, the rulers who reigned over Germany and northern Italy were in the strongest position. It was they who claimed the title "emperor," beginning around the 10th century. Later they called themselves "holy Roman emperors," merging Christian and classical claims. By this time, however, their rule had become increasingly hollow, precisely because they relied too much on their imperial claims and did not build a solid monarchy from regional foundations. Local feudal lords often went their own way in Germany, while city-states showed independence in northern Italy. The future lay elsewhere, with the rise of monarchies in individual states—states that ultimately would become nations.

Throughout the early postclassical centuries, with Charlemagne's rule as only a brief and ambiguous exception, the key political institutions throughout western Europe continued to be the structures of manorialism and feudalism, supplemented by the religious bureaucracy of the Church. Ordinary people were effectively governed by their landlords, who taxed them in goods and in labor and provided some judicial courts; more formal governments counted for little as far as serfs were concerned.

Landlords extended government somewhat through feudalism; this system linked landlord-warriors over a considerable region. By pledging mutual, personal loyalty, vassals could obtain protection and property, and greater lords got military allies. Charlemagne, unable to develop an independent bureaucracy, confirmed the central importance of feudalism by rewarding his officials with land, which they quickly converted to family property in return for pledges of loyalty and service. His failure to surmount feudalism, like his failure to pass down an empire intact, confirmed the political weaknesses of early postclassical Europe. Yet feudalism could also be built upon. By forming feudal alliances carefully and by turning promises of loyalty and service to good use, regional rulers could form armies of unusual strength (by prevailing Western standards) and damp down internal warfare and raiding. It was by using feudalism, rather than vainly hoping to revive imperial glory, that western Europe began politically to emerge from its early-medieval trough.

The overriding theme of the early postclassical centuries in the West was the spread of Christianity through most of the region. This was backed by the extension of the institutional church, the only durable organization in Western society that passed a purely regional level. The monastic movement, another key institution throughout western Europe, promoted religion, learning, and certain values, such as productive labor, that provided wider cultural models. Both in monastic and parish churches, the Christian clergy emerged as a distinctive force in the society.

TOWARD THE HIGH MIDDLE AGES: NEW WESTERN VIGOR

A series of developments began, by the 9th and 10th centuries, to introduce new sources of strength into Western society that ultimately had clear political and cultural repercussions. New agricultural techniques were learned, mostly as a result of contacts with eastern Europe and with Asian raiders into central Europe. The new moldboard plow and the three-field system were crucial gains; so was a new horse collar that allowed horses to be yoked without choking. Use of horse collars and stirrups also confirmed the military dominance of the feudal lords who monopolized fighting on horseback. But better plows aided ordinary people by allowing deeper working of heavy soil and the opening of new land. Monasteries also promoted better agricultural methods (in contrast to the less-worldly orientation of monks in eastern Europe).

Shortly after this time, in the 10th century, Viking raids began to taper off, partly because regional feudal governments became stronger (sometimes when Vikings themselves took over, as in the French province of Normandy) and partly because the Vikings, now Christianized, began to settle down. Greater regional political stability and improved agriculture went hand in hand to encourage population growth, an important fact of Western history from the 10th through the 13th centuries.

Population growth, in turn, encouraged further economic innovation. More people created new markets. There was a wedge here for growing trade, which in turn encouraged towns to expand. During the early postclassical centuries, towns had barely held on in most of western Europe outside of Italy, serving mainly as church centers. Now, however, by A.D. 1000, they began to serve as regional centers of trade, developing a merchant class and some craft production. Growing towns required more food. Landlords and serfs alike began to look to lands that had not previously been converted to agriculture. Whole regions, such as northeastern Germany, became colonized by eager farmers, and new centers sprang up throughout settled regions such as France. To woo labor to the new farms, landlords typically had to loosen the bonds of serfdom, requiring less outright labor service, sometimes simply charging a money rent. Harsh serfdom still existed, but most serfs gained greater independence and some free peasants emerged. The pace of economic life, in other words, created a less rigid social structure, and more commercial, market-oriented economic motives began to coexist with earlier feudal and Christian ideals.

The growth of towns reflected the new vigor of West Europe's agriculture. In parts of Italy and the Low Countries, where trade and urban manufacturing were especially

This scene, from a manuscript of the 15th century, shows peasant labor and tools in France, near a stylized great palace.

brisk, urban populations soared to almost 20 percent of the total by the 13th century. Overall, they constituted about 5 percent of the West's population—a significant figure though below levels of the advanced Asian civilizations. A few European cities approached a population level of 100,000 people (in contrast to China, which had 52 still larger cities), but the multiplicity of modest regional centers was an important development. Town growth in turn added to the vitality of the postclassical West. Western thinkers tended to assume three basic social classes, or estates: the nobles, the clergy, and ordinary people. With towns, many merchants, though still "commoners," gained considerable wealth and power. Towns were appalling: Streets were filled with open sewage, poured from the windows of houses built so the upper floors hung over the first level; death rates were high, so that city populations depended on steady immigration from the countryside; beggars and criminals flocked. Cities were also exciting: Literacy spread in the commercial atmosphere, spurring the popular languages; professional entertainers introduced new songs as well as dazzling tricks like fire eating or bear baiting; urban interests spurred new forms of religious life including city-based monastic orders dedicated to teaching or hospital work. These new orders relished interaction with society to promote religious goals, in contrast to the more isolated traditional monasteries.

Europe's economic and urban surge helped feed formal cultural life, which had already gained somewhat under Charlemagne's encouragement. By the 9th and 10th centuries schools began to form around important cathedrals, training children particularly when destined for church careers. By the 11th century there was enough demand for trained personnel to allow the first universities to emerge. Italy offered universities to train in medicine and law; the legal faculties profited from a growing revival in knowledge of Roman law, while medicine benefited from new learning imported from the Arabs and from revived Greek and Hellenistic science. By the 12th century a more characteristic university was forming in Paris, specializing in training churchmen, with theology as the culminating subject but with faculties in other subjects as well. The Parisian example in turn inspired universities in England (Oxford and Cambridge), Germany, and elsewhere. Solid educational institutions, though destined for only a small minority of Europe's population, undergirded increasingly diverse and sophisticated efforts in philosophy and theology. At the same time, medieval art and architecture reached a new high point spurred by the same prosperity, conjoined in large part with the intense religious fervor that guided the growing intellectual vitality. The new-found vigor of western Europe, which owed something at the outset to partial political stabilization, fed further political developments, particularly in the form of the expanding monarchies of France and Britain.

FEUDAL MONARCHIES

Kings of France began to win growing authority from the 10th century onward. At first they mainly exploited their position as regional feudal lords in the area around Paris. They controlled a number of serf-stocked manors directly, and they held most other local landlords as vassals. More attentive administration of this regional base produced better revenues and armies. The kings also formed feudal links with great lords in other parts of France, often through marriage alliances, gradually bringing more territory under their effective control. They experimented with the beginnings of bureaucratic administration by separating

their personal accounts from government accounts, thus developing a small amount of specialization among the officials who served them. The growth of a strong feudal monarchy in France took several centuries, but it provided a clear evolutionary thread throughout the later postclassical centuries.

Feudal monarchy in England was introduced more abruptly. The Duke of Normandy, of Viking descent, who had already built a strong feudal domain in his French province, invaded England in 1066. The Duke, now known as William the Conqueror, extended his tight feudal system to his new kingdom. He tied the great lords of England to his royal court by bonds of loyalty, giving them estates in return for their military service. But he also utilized throughout the kingdom some royal officials, called sheriffs, to help supervise the administration of justice. He and his successors created, in essence, a merger of feudal principles with a slightly more centralized approach, including more standardized, national law codes issued by the royal court.

England's political gains spurred the French monarchy to further consolidation. English kings long held territories in France, including Normandy, as feudal lords. French kings wanted to press them back. This effort required greater attention to tax revenues and organization of armies, though these were still drawn mainly from the ranks of the king's feudal vassals. Success in wars gave the French kings new territory that they administered directly, including wealthy urban areas in northern France. Mistreatment of a French vassal by King John of England (who was also lord over many French lands including Normandy) allowed the Capetian king to deprive him of his French fiefs under feudal law, as a disobedient vassal. Local lords supported this effort, and Normandy was gained for France. At this point the Capetian king began to send out his own officials to aid in regional administration, while allowing the provinces to keep their own laws and courts.

By the 13th century France's feudal monarchy was essentially complete. Louis IX (1226–1270) inherited a stable kingdom. He improved the quality and particularly the ethical standards of royal bureaucrats sent to check on activities in distant provinces. The king gained a reputation as provider of justice. Louis was also extremely pious, ultimately sainted; many French people believed that such kings had virtually miraculous powers, including the ability to heal illness by the laying on of hands. Louis also sponsored vicious attacks on religious heretics in southern France and organized two futile Crusades against the Arab Muslims; he died of a fever during the second effort, but his memory continued to support the prestige of the French monarchy.

By the early 14th century the process of cautious centralization had gone far enough in France that a king could claim rights to make the Church pay taxes (an issue that caused great conflict). The king could coin money and employ some professional soldiers apart from the feudal armies that still did most of the fighting.

Strong monarchies did not, to be sure, develop evenly throughout Europe. The West remained politically divided and diverse. Germany and Italy, though nominally controlled by the Holy Roman emperor, were actually split into dukedoms and city-states. The pope directly ruled the territory of central Italy. The Low Countries, a vigorous trade and manufacturing region, remained divided into regional units. Spain formed somewhat larger, though still regional, monarchies as Christian lords began to push back the Muslims from 1018 onward; but a national royal house was formed only in the 15th century, with the marriage of Ferdinand and Isabella.

Clearly uneven, and by Asian standards still woefully limited, Europeans did develop more capacity for central administration during the later Middle Ages, though they built on, rather than displaced, the powers of feudal lords. Local wars gave way to larger conflicts, as between the proud rulers of France and England. In the 14th century a long battle began—the Hundred Years War, between the national monarchies of France and England—over territories the English King controlled in France and relatedly over feudal rights versus the emerging claims of national states.

THE WEST'S EXPANSIONIST IMPULSE: PHASE I

It was during the period of political development and economic advance that the West began to show its muscle beyond its initial postclassical borders. Population growth explains part of the expansionist impulse. So do memory of Rome's lost greatness and the righteous zeal provided through Christianity. Some Western leaders were aware of the superior wealth and sophistication of Arab and Byzantine civilizations and wanted either to stake a Western claim or to find other areas for conquest while promoting the glory of the Christian God. Whatever the mix of motives, an expansionist thrust early entered the West's policy toward the wider world.

The most concrete expansion took place in east-central Europe from the 11th century onward. Germanic knights and agricultural settlers poured into sparsely settled areas in what is now eastern Germany and Poland, changing the population balance considerably. Another important surge occurred in Spain. Small Christian states remained in northern Spain by the 10th century, and they gradually be-

gan to attack the Muslim government that held most of the peninsula. The "reconquest" stepped up in pace by the 11th century, as Christian forces, swelled by feudal warriors from various areas, pushed into central Spain, conquering the great Muslim center of Toledo. Full expulsion of the Muslims occurred only at the end of the Middle Ages in 1492, but the trend of the Christian offensive was clear even earlier. At Europe's other extreme, Viking voyagers had, along with their raids to the south, pushed out into the northern Atlantic, establishing settlements in Iceland. By the 11th century further voyages had pushed to Greenland and the Hudson Bay area in what is now Canada, where short-lived outposts were created. By the 13th century, Spanish and Italian seafarers entered the Atlantic from the Mediterranean, though without much initial result except several lost expeditions.

The most dramatic expansionist move involved the great Crusades against the Muslim control of the Holy Land. Pope Urban II called for the First Crusade in 1095, appealing to the undeniable piety of the West's rulers and common people. Crusaders were promised full forgiveness of sins if they died in battle, assuring them entry to heaven. The attraction of winning spoils from the rich Arab lands added to the inducement, as did the thirst for excitement among the West's feudal warriors. Three great armies, with tens of thousands of Crusaders from various parts of the West, assembled in Constantinople in 1097— much to the distress of the Byzantine government. The Western Crusaders moved toward Jerusalem, winning it from the Turkish armies that held the area by that time. For almost a century Western knights ruled the "kingdom of Jerusalem," losing it to a great Muslim general, Saladin, during the 12th century. A number of later Crusades attempted to win back the Holy Land, though many subsequent efforts turned toward other goals—or toward pure farce. The Third Crusade at the end of the 12th century led to the death of the German emperor and the imprisonment of the English king, though it did produce a brief truce with Saladin that allowed Christian pilgrims to visit Jerusalem. The Fourth Crusade was manipulated by merchants in Venice, who turned it into an attack on their commercial rivals in Constantinople.

The Crusades did not demonstrate a new Western superiority in the wider world, despite some limited successes. But as an expression of a combination of religious zeal and growing commercial and military vigor on the part of the knights and merchants who organized the largest efforts, the Crusades unquestionably showed the distinctive spirit of the Western Middle Ages at their height. They also helped open the West to new cultural and economic influences from the Middle East, a major spur to further change and to the West's interaction with the larger world.

This imaginary duel between the noble Christian champion, King Richard of England, and the Muslim leader Saladin, shows good guys and bad guys without hesitation.

RELIGIOUS EVOLUTION

As medieval society developed, the Catholic church went through several periods of decline and renewal. At times, church officials and the leading monastic groups became preoccupied with their holdings in land and their political interests. The Church was a wealthy institution; it was tempting for many priests and monks to behave like ordinary feudal lords in pursuit of greater worldly power. A reform movement arose in the 11th century to combat this growing secularism. Purified monastic orders, centered in Cluny in France, inspired fresh vigor to this branch of the Church. Later, in the 13th century, another monastic reform movement created orders such as the Franciscans, devoted to poverty and service in Europe's bustling cities.

Reform-minded popes, such as Gregory VII (1073–1085), sought to purify the Church generally and free it from interference by feudal lords. One technique was insistence on the particularly holy character of the priesthood. Reformers stipulated that all priests remain unmarried, to separate the priesthood from the ordinary world of the flesh. Gregory also endeavored to free the Church from any vestige of state control. He quarreled vigorously with the Holy Roman Emperor Henry IV over the practice of state appointment, or *investiture*, of bishops in Germany. Ultimately, by excommunicating the emperor from the Church, Gregory won his point. The emperor appealed on his knees in the snow of a northern Italian winter, and the investiture controversy ended apparently in the Church's favor. Gregory and several later popes made clear their beliefs that the Church was not only to be free from state interference but was superior to the state in its function as direct channel of God's word. These claims were not entirely accurate, as governments influenced religious affairs still, but they were not hollow. It was this sort of affirmation, indeed, that enabled the Church to inspire kings and warriors to fight in the Crusades, and also to war against several heresies that broke out during the same centuries. Independent of the state, a network of church courts developed to rule on matters of religious, or *canon*, law and to bring heretics to trial and, occasionally, to execution. Here, in long-run terms, was the origin of recurrent Western beliefs in church-state separation.

THE HIGH MIDDLE AGES

Even in the centuries of its greatest strength, the Church was by no means the dominant institution during the High Middle Ages. As feudal monarchs extended their power, particularly in France and England, they became increasingly involved in the administration of justice and, through taxation, in the economic affairs of their subjects. They also solidified their military power. While the German ruler, or holy Roman emperor, frequently had to do battle against regional lords, French and English kings usually managed to avoid this kind of internal conflict. At the same time, military strength made it possible for the royal families to assert their power against the claims of the Church. Early in the 14th century, the French king actually imprisoned the pope in a dispute over taxation policy.

The postclassical version of Western civilization reached its high mark in the 12th and 13th centuries. Fed by the growing dynamism of western Europe's population, agriculture, and cities, the High Middle Ages were characterized above all by a series of creative tensions. Feudal political structures, which derived from local and personal allegiances, were balanced by nascent central monarchies. The unquestionable authority of the Church and the cultural dominance of Christianity jostled with the intellectual vitality and diversity that formed part of university life. A social order and economy, based primarily on agriculture and the semi-free labor of serfs, now had to come to terms with important cities, merchants, and some new opportunities even for ordinary farmers.

Overall, the Western postclassical experience divided into three chronological sectors: the early centuries, in which Christianity's spread combined with pronounced limitations in politics and the economy; the period of expansion, culminating in the most glorious medieval centuries from 1100 to 1300, in which the most characteristic institutions and values fully flowered; and then a somewhat unusual transitional interlude, in which the West declined in many respects while experimenting with new forms in other areas.

ANALYSIS
THE SOURCES OF VITALITY IN THE POSTCLASSICAL WEST

Why did western Europe begin to demonstrate new vigor around A.D. 1000—forming new schools and a more elaborate culture; expanding trade and towns, while loosening the most restrictive aspects of manorial social organization; launching new, sometimes aggressive contacts with other areas, as in the Crusades? The question is really the reverse of the more familiar analysis of societal decline. It is at least as important to know what causes civilizations to rise as to probe the reasons for their fall. At various points in history (including the 20th century) certain societies begin to be more dynamic than they had been before, sometimes more dynamic also than many other societies in the same period. Determining causes in one case may help in evaluating other cases. Furthermore, an understanding of causes may help explain directions of new vigor—what kinds of new cultural forms are generated, for example, or why some dynamic societies are more expansionistic than others. The causes that produced new energy in the medieval West are particularly interesting in that they galvanized not only a backward society, but one that in some respects—in levels of trade and learning, for instance—had retrogressed from previous achievements.

The legacy of Greece and Rome had something to do with the medieval surge. Key Europeans knew the empire had existed; a sense of lost greatness might have inspired them. More concretely, revival of specific political achieve-

ments like Roman law helped stabilize medieval politics by the 11th century, starting with the organization of the Church itself. Continued use of Latin for intellectual life facilitated encounters with classical learning. One approach to an explanation, then, might suggest a certain inevitability: Classical achievements were so inspiring that, after a few centuries of chaos, the West almost automatically resurrected key elements of the Greco-Roman experience. By the 12th century medieval writers suggested this pattern, arguing that though they could not rival the sheer intellectual power of the classical philosophers, they actually could forge beyond them by "standing on their shoulders." This model would suggest a Western experience similar to that of China after its centuries of chaos subsequent to the fall of the Han dynasty, for here new vigor was based directly on the ability to revive past strengths (see Chapter 18).

Another model for the West stresses the impact of cultural change, notably the results of conversions to Christianity. To be sure, Christianity incorporated elements of classical learning and the institutional patterns of the Roman Empire, but it was in many ways a new force. It took some time for Christianity to be assimilated, but ultimately it began to reshape habits in important ways. Thus Christian pleas for peace, while they did not end war in Europe, did have a taming effect, allowing more stable political structures to develop by around A.D. 1000. The example of the Church as a bureaucratic institution similarly helped inspire secular rulers to improve their administration, while the interest in reading and interpreting the Bible and the writings of the church fathers spurred medieval intellectual and educational life. Some scholars have even argued for a special, unanticipated technological result of assimilation of Christianity. By arguing that humankind is superior to the animal world—made in God's image—the new religion encouraged medieval people toward a less reverent, more utilitarian view of nature as something to be exploited. It prepared medieval Europeans' receptivity to new technologies that would subdue nature. More specifically, Christian interest in bells, for use in church celebrations, stimulated medieval interest in metalworking, with results that were applied to other fields by the 15th century. Development of clocks, a major technological advance, followed from an interest in timing the start of religious services. Certainly Christianity encouraged some of the expansionist tone of a more dynamic western Europe, as part of a desire to convert unbelievers and beat back the infidel.

A third line of explanation stresses more purely technological factors. Moldboard plows began to spread in northwestern Europe by the 9th century, though they had been introduced earlier by Celtic or Germanic farmers. The moldboards worked much better in the moist, clinging soil of northern Europe than the lighter models the Romans had used. The moldboard in turn encouraged better iron-work and also improved village organization, for the new plows were costly and required cooperation. At the same time food production improved, spurring population growth, the rise of cities, and the important push into sparsely populated lands in eastern Germany.

A second innovation, again taking shape by the 9th and 10th centuries, was the new collar that allowed harnessing and shoeing of horses instead of oxen for field work—horses being notably faster in their work. Use of horses also encouraged land transport and roads. Finally, European farmers began to convert to the three-field system (in which a third of the land was left fallow, to replenish fertility, each year) instead of the Roman two-field system—again a clear basis for rising food production. What was happening—in advance of new political and cultural forms, bigger cities, and growing trade—was a quiet agricultural revolution, accomplished by nameless farmers. Perhaps Christian beliefs about nature inspired them to an extent. Certainly contact with other people helped—thus in Charlemagne's time, Europeans learned about horseshoes and stirrups from invaders from central Asia. But it was the technological thrust that directly set other, more dramatic signs of dynamism in motion, such as the growth of cities and the creation of universities.

Western Europe was not of course the only dynamic new society to emerge in the later centuries of the postclassical era. Russia, parts of Africa, Japan, and other areas showed vigor as well, and in some of the same ways, such as with more stable politics and commercial expansion. Whatever the specific combination of factors operating in western Europe, it is important to remember the larger typology: A number of societies were able to blend their own cultural traditions and the advantages of new contacts with more established centers of civilization to produce various kinds of growth and innovation. The motivation of trying to catch up with the richer centers, along with sufficient contacts to allow some hope of figuring out how to advance, played no small role in this general process.

Questions: Which of the causation models—heritage, religious change, or technology—seems more appealing, and why? Which of the causes began to have an impact first? Do the models contradict each other, or can they be combined? Which models might also be applied to explain the rise of medieval Russia or the kingdoms of sub-Saharan Africa?

CHARACTERISTICS OF WESTERN CIVILIZATION IN THE POSTCLASSICAL ERA

This section traces more general characteristics of the reviving civilization of the West between 500 and 1400, starting with formal intellectual and religious thought. Most key features became particularly refined and clarified during the West's dynamic centuries between 1000 and 1300. Shifts in the postclassical characteristics expressed the transition and partial decline that defined the century and a half after 1300. The characteristics of the postclassical West never resurfaced in the same combination, for key elements were distinctive to the age. But subsequent changes did not erase strong traces of this stage of Western history, from architecture to rationalism to ideas about the state.

CHANGE VS. REVIVAL

What kind of civilization did the postclassical centuries produce in the West, in what was a formative stage of civilization itself in much of the region? What was the balance between new elements and revivals of the Greco-Roman heritage?

In the late Roman and early postclassical centuries, for example, leading Christian thinkers worked out a decidedly nonclassical view of human sexuality. For Romans, sexual activity was a normal human expression, even an obligation in terms of procreation. For Western Christian leaders, humanity should emphasize its status as God's special creation on earth by remaining as separate as possible from base, animal instincts. Sexuality, on these grounds, became suspect. Family advice through the Middle Ages, by the same token, stressed the need to restrict sex to a minimum, while the holiest callings were celibate. Sexual activity continued, of course, outside the clergy and sometimes within it, but a religious disdain for sexuality became an important aspect of Western culture that lasted well beyond the Middle Ages. Change, here, overwhelmed the classical Mediterranean heritage.

All civilizations are defined in large part by a common culture. Some, however—like China, or periodically the Middle East—also combine considerable political unity. This was not the case in the medieval West, as we have seen, nor was it ever to be the case before the 1990s. Cultural characteristics thus form a key to what defined the Middle Ages and Western civilization itself, across the welter of political units that dotted western Europe. A common culture does not, of course, mean uniformity. Urban centers had different cultural expressions from rural areas, as was always the case in agricultural societies. As cities grew in western Europe they spawned new kinds of drama, more professional entertainers for ordinary folk, and the clearest masterpieces of Gothic architecture. The common culture of the Middle Ages also did not mean absolute unity around the Christian religion. Religion was the focal point of medieval cultural life, as was true of eastern Europe and Islam during the same centuries. But Western Christianity sponsored a number of creative cultural tensions and coexisted with an increasingly diverse intellectual and artistic endeavor, so that a substantial array of interests described the philosophy and literature of the High Middle Ages.

THEOLOGY

During the centuries before about 1000, a small number of churchmen continued the efforts of preserving and interpreting past wisdom, particularly the writings of church fathers like Augustine, but also some non-Christian Latin authors. During Charlemagne's time, a favorite practice was to gather quotations from ancient writers around key subjects. Efforts of this sort showed little creativity, but they gradually produced a fuller understanding of past thought and improvements in Latin writing style and in organizing philosophical materials. Interest in classical principles of rhetoric and, particularly, logic reflected the concern for coherent organization; Aristotle, known to the Middle Ages as the philosopher, was valued because of his clear exposition of rational thought.

From 1000 onward, a series of outstanding clerics advanced the logical exposition of philosophy and theology to new levels. They stressed the importance of absolute faith in God's word, but they believed that human reason could move toward an understanding of some aspects of religion and the natural order as well. Thus, according to several theologians, it was possible to prove the existence of God, to use logic to help explain the Trinity, and to develop certain moral principles. A concomitant interest in collecting Roman law and in codifying canon law also promoted the use of careful logical exposition. Fascination with logic led some intellectuals to a certain zeal in pointing out inconsistencies in past wisdom, even in the writings of the church fathers. In the 12th century, Peter Abelard in Paris wrote a treatise called "Yes or No" in which he showed a number of logical contradictions in established interpretations of doctrine. Though Abelard protested his faith, saying that "I would not be an Aristotle if this were to part me from Christ," he clearly took an impish delight in suggesting skepticism.

This logical-rationalist current in Western philosophy was hardly unopposed. Quite apart from the fact that most ordinary Christians knew nothing of these debates, seeing their religion as a matter of received belief and appointed sacraments that would remove sin and promote salvation, many church leaders emphasized the role of faith alone. A powerful monk, St. Bernard of Clairvaux, successfully challenged Abelard. Bernard, an intellectual of a different sort, stressed the importance of mystical union with God, attainable even on this earth in brief blissful glimpses, rather than rationalist endeavor. Bernard believed that reason was dangerous and prideful, and that God's truth must be received through faith alone.

The debates over how, and whether, to combine the classical Mediterranean philosophical and scientific tradition with revealed religious faith had much in common with debates among Arab intellectuals during the 10th and 11th centuries. Both Christianity and Islam relied heavily on faith in a revealed word, through the Bible or Koran respectively, yet some intellectuals in both cultures strained to include other approaches. Arab philosophers who had already advanced rationalist arguments helped shape the most characteristic Western approach. At the same time, because Christian thinkers interpreted the Bible in terms of allegories as well as literal truths, their theological speculations could range even more widely.

The thirst to assimilate rational philosophy and Christian faith was the dominant intellectual theme in the postclassical West. It represented the need to come to terms with both the Christian and the classical heritage. This assimilation of rational philosophy and Christian faith also posed formidable and fascinating problems of reconciliation. By the 12th century the zeal for this kind of knowledge produced several distinctive results. It explained the intellectual vitality of most of the emerging universities, where students flocked to hear the latest debates among leading theologians. Higher education certainly benefited students through resultant job opportunities; trained lawyers, for example, could hope for advancement in the growing bureaucracies of church or state. In contrast to China, however, the new universities were not directly tied into a single bureaucratic system, and the excitement they engendered during the Middle Ages did not follow from opportunism alone. A large number of students, from the whole of western Europe, sought out the mixture of spiritual and rational understanding that leading thinkers were trying to work out. Many early universities had students pay teachers directly if they were interested in attending a given set of lectures, and the eagerness for learning could make this system work.

The postclassical intellectual drive also motivated a growing interest in knowledge newly imported from the classical past and from the Arab world, and this knowledge in turn fed the highest achievements of medieval learning. By the 12th century Western scholars were consuming vast amounts of material translated from Greek in centers in the Byzantine Empire, Italy, and Muslim Spain. They gained familiarity with the bulk of ancient Greek and Hellenistic philosophy and science. They also read translations of Arab or Jewish learning, particularly those works where Middle Eastern thinkers had wrestled with the problems of mixing human reasoning with truths gained by faith. Translators in Spain and Constantinople could barely keep up with the growing Western demand to discover everything there was to know.

With much fuller knowledge of Aristotelian and Hellenistic science, plus the work of Arab rationalists, such as Ibn-Rushd (known in the West as Averroës), Western philosopher-theologians in the 13th century proceeded to the final great synthesis of medieval learning. The leading figure was Thomas Aquinas, an Italian-born monk who taught at the University of Paris. Aquinas maintained the basic belief that faith came first, but he greatly expanded the scope given to reason. Through reason alone, humans could know much of the natural order, of moral law, and of the nature of God. Thomas had complete confidence that all essential knowledge could be coherently organized, and he produced a host of *Summas,* or highest works, that disposed through careful logic of all possible objections to truth as revealed by reason and faith. Here was a masterful demonstration of medieval confidence in the fundamental orderliness of learning and God's creation. Essentially, this work restated in Christian terms Greek efforts to seek a rationality in nature that would correspond to the rational capacities of the human mind. To be sure, a few philosophers carried the interest in logic to absurd degrees; after the 13th century, scholasticism—as the dominant medieval philosophical approach was called because of its base in the schools—sometimes degenerated into silly debates such as the conundrum of how many angels could dance on the head of a pin. But at its height, and particularly with Aquinas, scholasticism demonstrated an unusual confidence in the logical orderliness of knowledge and in human ability to know clearly most of what needed to be known.

Medieval philosophy did not encourage a great deal of new scientific work. The emphasis on mastering past learning and organizing it logically could lead to overemphasis on previous discoveries, rather than empirical research. Thus university-trained doctors stressed memorization of Galen, the Hellenistic authority, rather than systematic practical experience. Toward the end of the 13th century, a current of practical science developed. In Oxford, members of the clergy, such as Roger Bacon, did experimental work with optics, pursuing research earlier done by Muslim scholars. An important by-product of this interest was the invention of eyeglasses, an indispensable aid to many Western (and other) scholars ever since. During the 14th and 15th centuries, experimentalists also advanced knowledge in chemistry and astronomy. This early work set the stage for the flourishing of Western science later on.

POPULAR RELIGION

Far less is known about popular beliefs than about formal intellectual life in the Middle Ages. Christian devotion undoubtedly ran deep and may well have increased with time among many ordinary people. The rise of cities saw the formation of laymen's groups to develop spirituality and express their love of God. The content of popular belief evolved as well. Enthusiasm for the veneration of Mary, the mother of Jesus, expanded by the 12th century, showing a desire to stress the merciful side of Christianity, as against the sternness of God the Father, and new hopes for assistance in gaining salvation. Worship of various saints showed a similar desire for intermediaries between people and God. At the same time, ordinary people continued to believe in various magical rituals, and they celebrated essentially pagan festivals, which might have involved much dancing and merriment. They blended their version of Christianity with considerable earthiness and spontaneity, some of which was conveyed by late-medieval writers such as the English writer Geoffrey Chaucer.

ART AND LITERATURE

Christian art in many ways reflected both the popular outlook and the more formal religion of theologians and church leaders. Religious art was another cultural area where the medieval West came to excel, as it was in other societies, such as the Islamic Middle East or Hindu India, where religious enthusiasm ran strong. As with philosophy, medieval art and architecture were intended to serve the glory of God. Western painters used religious subjects almost exclusively. Painting mainly on wooden panels, artists in most parts of western Europe depicted Christ's birth and suffering and the lives of the saints, using stiff, stylized figures. By the 14th and 15th centuries, artists improved their ability to render natural scenes realistically and portrayed a host of images of medieval life as backdrops to their religious subjects. Designs and scenes in stained glass for churches constituted another important artistic expression.

Medieval architecture initially followed Roman models, particularly in church building, using a rectangular, or Romanesque, style sometimes surmounted by domes. During the 11th century, however, a new style took hold that was far more original, though it benefited from knowledge of Muslim design plus advances in structural engineering in the West itself. Gothic architects, taking advantage of growing engineering expertise, built soaring church spires and massive, arched windows. While their work focused on the creation of churches and great cathedrals, some civic buildings and palaces also picked up the Gothic motif. The Gothic was one of the three main architectural styles (the others being the earlier classical and the later modern) ever developed in Western culture. It is not far-fetched to see the Gothic style as representative of Western postclassical

culture more generally. Its spiritual orientation showed in the towers cast up to the heavens. It built also on growing technical skills and deep popular devotion, shown in the monies collected to build the huge monuments as well as in the patient labor required for often many decades of construction. The originality of the Gothic reflected the growing Western ability to find suitable new means of expression, just as the heritage of Gothic in the later Western world showed the ongoing power of medieval models.

Medieval literature and music reflected strong religious interests. Most Latin writing dealt with points of philosophy, law, or political theory. There was little concern for stylistic niceties for their own sake. However, alongside writing in Latin came the development of a growing literature in the spoken languages, or *vernaculars*, of western

Gothic architecture constituted one of the creative expressions of postclassical western Europe and was used particularly in churches great and small. This major cathedral in Amiens, France, was built over many centuries and dwarfs the surrounding buildings.

Europe. The pattern was not unlike that of India a few centuries earlier after the fall of the Gupta empire, when Sanskrit served as a scholarly language but increasing power was given to popular languages such as Hindi. A number of oral sagas were written down, dealing with the deeds of great knights and mythic figures in the past. From this tradition came the first known writing in early English, *Beowulf,* and in French, the *Song of Roland.* Late in the Middle Ages, a number of writers created adventure stories, comic tales, and poetry in the vernacular tongues, such as Chaucer's *Canterbury Tales.* Much of their work, and also a number of plays written for performance in the growing cities, reflected the tension between Christian values and a desire to portray the richness and coarseness of life on this earth. Chaucer's narrative thus shows a fascination with bawdy behavior, a willingness to poke fun at the hypocrisy of many Christians, and an ability to capture some of the tragedies of human existence. In France, a long poem called the *Romance of the Rose* used vivid sexual imagery, while the poet Villon wrote, in largely secular terms, of the terror and poignancy of death. Finally, again in vernacular language, a series of courtly poets, or *troubadours,* based particularly in southern France in the 14th century, wrote hymns to the love that could flourish between men and women. While their verses stressed platonic devotion rather than sexual love and paid homage to courtly ceremonies and polite behavior, their concern with love was the first sign of a new valuation of this emotional experience in the Western tradition.

Medieval intellectual and artistic life, in sum, created a host of important themes. Religion served as the centerpiece, but it did not prevent a growing range of interests from science to romantic poetry. Medieval culture was a rich intellectual achievement in its own right. It also set in motion a series of developments—in rationalist philosophy, science, artistic representations of nature, and vernacular literature—that would serve as building blocks for later Western thought and art.

 ## ECONOMY AND SOCIETY IN THE POSTCLASSICAL CENTURIES

While culture provided the clearest cement for Western society during the medieval centuries, framed of course by the institutional sweep of the Catholic church, a number of common features also described economic activity and social structure. Here too, the postclassical West demonstrated impressive powers of innovation, for the hold of classical patterns was slight. As trade revived by the 10th century, the West became something of a common commercial zone. Most regions produced primarily for local consumption, as was true in agricultural societies generally. But

Italian merchants actively sought cloth manufactured in the Low Countries, and merchants in many areas traded for wool grown in England or timber supplies and furs brought from Scandinavia and the Baltic lands. Great ports and trading fairs, particularly in the Low Countries and northern France, served as centers for Western exchange, as well as markets for a few exotic products such as spices brought in from other civilizations.

Furthermore, despite great diversity in local detail, something of a common spirit and some common institutions developed in medieval social and economic life, and these in turn expressed important features of the larger civilization of the postclassical West. Western thinkers of this time liked to picture their society in rather simple terms, not unlike the metaphors of classical India. Borrowing from classical Greek and Roman concepts, John of Salisbury, an English churchman, likened society to the human body: Peasants were the feet, without which society could not function. Knightly warriors were the hands, to defend. Priests provided heart and soul, and the king was the head. Each part was essential, but each fit into a clear hierarchy in which lower segments were properly ruled by those above. Except for priests, most people were born into their status, with privileges or limits legally defined.

In fact, postclassical Western society was more complicated, and it evolved toward ever-greater complexity. The West did not develop a caste system, despite the emphasis on inherited positions, for there was always some mobility and creation of new groups. The landlord-serf relationship, which was both political and economic, remained crucial, but it tended to change considerably as peasants gained greater freedom of maneuver. Even under powerful landlords, rural villages regulated agriculture and controlled some land for common use, giving a strong community flavor to peasant life. Some peasants began producing for sale to urban markets, thus generating tensions with village traditions as well as with landlord control.

As in most agricultural societies, economic demands conditioned family life, as families formed the chief units of agricultural production. Choosing a spouse who was a good worker and winning an appropriate dowry or inheritance were vital ingredients of family life—and marriages, typically arranged by parents, placed economic criteria above all else. Children were expected to work at an early age, while adult men and women roughly divided labor between field and household.

AGRICULTURAL CHANGE

The improvements in agriculture after A.D. 800 brought important new ingredients to rural life. Some peasants were able to shake off the most severe constraints of manorialism, becoming almost free farmers with only a few obligations to their landlords, though rigid manorialism remained in place in many areas. Noble landlords still served mainly military functions, for ownership of a horse and armor were prerequisites for fighting until the end of the medieval period. But while most nobles shunned the taint of commerce—like aristocrats in many societies, they found too much money-grubbing demeaning—they did use trade to improve their standard of living and adopt more polished habits. The courtly literature of the late Middle Ages reflected this new style of life.

As many lords sought improved conditions, they were often tempted to press their serfs to pay higher rents and taxes—even as serfs themselves were gaining a new sense of freedom and control over their own land. This tension produced, from the late Middle Ages until the 19th century, a recurrent series of peasant-landlord battles in Western society. Peasants sought what they viewed as their natural and traditional right to the land, free and clear of any exactions. They talked of Christian equality, turning phrases such as "When Adam delved and Eve span, Who was then a gentleman?" A more complex economy clearly brought new social strains, not totally unlike the recurrent wave of popular unrest in China or the rural risings in the Middle East, where religion helped prompt egalitarian sentiments as well.

Yet on the whole the conditions of Western peasants improved during the most dynamic part of the Middle Ages. Landlord controls were less tight than they had become in other societies such as the Middle East. Western agriculture was not yet particularly advanced technologically, compared for example with East Asia, but it had improved notably over early medieval levels and also surpassed the productivity of the classical Mediterranean world.

CITIES AND COMMERCE

Gains in agriculture of course promoted larger changes in medieval economic life. Urban growth allowed more specialized manufacturing and commercial activities, which in turn promoted still greater trade. Banking was introduced to the West, spearheaded by Italian businessmen, to facilitate long-distance exchange of money and goods. The use of money spread steadily, to the dismay of many Christian moralists and many ordinary people who preferred the more direct, personal ways of traditional society. The largest trading and banking operations, not only in Italy but in southern Germany, the Low Countries, France, and Britain, were clearly capitalistic. Big merchants invested funds in trading ships and the goods they carried, hoping to make large profits on this capital. Profit making was not judged kindly by Christian thinkers like Thomas Aquinas,

who urged that all prices should be "just," reflecting only the labor put into the good; but it clearly, sometimes avidly, occurred.

Rising trade took a number of forms. There were exchanges between western Europe and other parts of the known world. Wealthy Europeans developed a taste for some of the spices and luxury goods of Asia; the Crusades played a role in bringing these products to wider attention. A Mediterranean trade redeveloped, mainly in the hands of Italian merchants, in which European cloth and some other products were exchanged for the more polished goods of the East. Commerce within Europe involved exchanges of timber and grain from the north for cloth and metal products manufactured in Italy and the Low Countries. England, at first an exporter of raw wool, developed some manufactured goods for exchange by the later Middle Ages. Commercial alliances developed. Cities in northern Germany and southern Scandinavia grouped together in the Hanseatic League to encourage trade. With growing banking facilities, it became possible to organize commercial transactions throughout much of western Europe. Bankers, including a number of Jewish businessmen, were valued for their service in lending money to monarchs and the papacy.

The growth of trade and banking in the Middle Ages served as the genesis of capitalism in Western civilization. The greater Italian and German bankers, the long-distance merchants of the Hanseatic cities, were clearly capitalistic in their willingness to invest considerable sums of money in trading ventures with the expectation of substantial profit. Given the continued dangers of trade by land and sea, the risks in these investments were substantial, but profits of up to 100 percent or more were also possible. In many cities, such as London, groups of powerful merchants banded together to invest in international trade, each buying shares in the venture and profiting or losing accordingly.

This was not, by world standards, a totally unprecedented merchant spirit. European traders were still less venturesome and less wealthy than some of their Muslim counterparts. Nor was Western society yet as tolerant of merchants as Muslim or Indian societies. Yet Western commercial endeavors were clearly gaining in dynamism. Because Western governments were weak, with few economic functions, merchants had a freer hand than in many other civilizations. Many of the growing cities, in particular, were ruled by commercial leagues. Monarchs liked to encourage the cities as a counterbalance to the power of the landed aristocracy, and, in the later Middle Ages and beyond, traders and kings were typically allied. However, aside from taxing merchants and using them as sources of loans, royal governments did not interfere extensively with trading activities. Merchants even developed their own codes of commercial law, administered by city courts. Thus the rising merchant class, though not unusual in strength or venturesomeness, was staking out an unusually powerful and independent role in European society.

Capitalism was not yet typical of the Western economy, even aside from the moral qualms fostered by the Christian tradition. Most peasants and landlords had not become enmeshed in a market system. In the cities, the dominant economic ethic stressed group protection, not untrammeled profit seeking. The characteristic institution was not the international trading firm, but the merchant or artisan guild. Guilds grouped people in the same business or trade in a single city, sometimes with loose links to similar guilds in other cities. These organizations were new in western Europe, though they resembled guilds in various parts of Asia but with greater independence from the state. They stressed security and mutual control. Merchant guilds thus sought to assure all members a share in any endeavor. If a ship pulled in loaded with wool, the clothiers' guild of the city insisted that all members participate in the purchasing, so that no one member would monopolize the profits.

Artisan guilds were composed of the people in the cities who actually made cloth, bread, jewelry, or furniture. These guilds tried to limit membership so that all members would be assured of work. They regulated apprenticeships, to guarantee good training but also to make sure that no member would employ too many apprentices and so gain undue wealth. They discouraged new methods because security and a rough equality, not maximum individual profit, were the goals; here was their alternative to the capitalistic approach. Guilds also tried to guarantee good workmanship, so that consumers would not have to worry about shoddy quality on the part of some unscrupulous profit seeker. Guilds played an important political and social role in the cities, assuring their members of recognized status and, often, a voice in city government. Their statutes were in turn upheld by municipal law and were often backed by the royal government as well.

Despite the traditionalism and security-mindedness of the guilds, manufacturing as well as commercial methods did improve in medieval Europe. Western Europe was not yet as advanced as Asia in iron making or textile manufacture, but it was beginning to catch up. In a few areas, such as clock making—which involved both sophisticated technology and an interesting concern for precise time—European artisans in fact had forged a world lead. Furthermore, some manufacturing spilled beyond the bounds of guild control. Particularly in the Low Countries and parts of Italy, groups of manufacturing workers were employed by capitalists to produce for a wide market. Their

This illustration shows the simple tools and painstaking labor of skilled artisans, whose shops fronted the narrow city streets.

techniques were simple, and they worked in their own homes, often alternating manufacturing labor with agriculture. Their work was regulated not by the motives of the guilds but by the inducements of merchant capitalists, who provided them with raw materials and then paid them for their production.

The simple fact was that, by the later Middle Ages, western Europe's economy and society embraced a number of contradictory groups and principles. Commercial and capitalist elements joined against the slower pace of economic life in the countryside and even against the dominant group protectionism of most urban guilds. Most people remained peasants, but a minority had escaped to the cities where they found more excitement, though also increased danger and higher rates of disease. Medieval tradition held that a serf who managed to live in the city for a year and a day became a free person. A few prosperous capitalists flourished, but most people operated according to quite different economic values, directed toward group welfare rather than individual profit. This was not either a static society or an early model of a modern commercial society. It had its own flavor, and its own tensions—the fruit of several centuries of economic and social change.

WOMEN AND FAMILY LIFE

The increasing complexity of medieval social and economic life may have had one final effect which is familiar from patterns in other agricultural societies: setting new limits on the conditions of women. Women's work remained of course vital in most families. Christian emphasis on the equality of all souls, and the practical importance of monastic groups organized for women, giving some an alternative to marriage, continued to offer distinctive features for women's lives in Western society. The veneration of Mary and other female religious figures gave women real cultural prestige, counterbalancing the Biblical emphasis on Eve as the source of human sin. In some respects women in the West had higher status than their sisters under Islam: They were less segregated in religious services (though they could not lead them) and less confined to the household. Still, women's effective voice in the family may have declined in the Middle Ages. Urban women often played important roles in local commerce and even operated some craft guilds, but they found themselves increasingly hemmed in by male-dominated organizations. By the late Middle Ages a literature arose that stressed women's roles as the assistants and comforters to men, listing supplemental household tasks and docile virtues as women's distinctive sphere. Patriarchal structures seemed to be taking deeper root.

DOCUMENT
CHANGING ROLES FOR WOMEN

A late-14th century Parisian manual entitled *The Good Wife* revealed the kind of thinking about gender that became more pronounced as medieval society developed in the West. It invites comparison with patriarchal views you have studied in other agricultural civilizations. Is any room left for initiatives by women?

Wherefore I counsel you to make such cheer to your husband at all his comings and stayings, and to persevere therein; and also be peaceable with him, and remember the rustic proverb, which saith that there be three things which drive the goodman from home, to wit, a leaking roof, a smoky chimney, and a scolding woman. And therefore, fair sister, I beseech you that you keep yourself in the love and good favour of your husband, you be unto him gentle, and amiable, and debonair. Do unto him what the good simple women of our country say hath been done to their sons, when these have set their love elsewhere and their mothers cannot wean them therefrom.

Wherefore, dear sister, I beseech you thus to bewitch and bewitch again your husband that shall be, and beware of roofless house and of smoky fire, and scold him not, but be unto him gentle and amiable and peaceable. Have a care that in winter he have a good fire and smokeless and let him rest well and be well covered between your breasts, and thus bewitch him. . . .

And thus shall you preserve and keep your husband from all discomforts and give him all the comforts whereof you can bethink you, and serve him and have him served in your house, and you shall look to him for outside things, for if he be good he will take even more pains and labour therein than you wish, and by doing what I have said, you will cause him ever to miss you and have his heart with you and your loving service and he will shun all other houses, all other women, all other services and households.

Questions: Is this a distinctively "Christian" view of women? How does it compare with Muslim or Chinese views of women in the postclassical period? Why might postclassical values have become more rigorous in the late medieval centuries in the West?

THE POLITICAL VALUES OF THE MIDDLE AGES

The key values and tensions of medieval society and culture were expressed in characteristic styles and institutions: the Gothic cathedral, the scholastic *Summas*, the manors, and the guilds. Medieval politics produced a similar summary expression in the feudal monarchy as it flowered during the High Middle Ages. There was, to be sure, greater basic diversity in medieval politics than in social or cultural forms, and feudal monarchy by no means took hold universally across Western society. However, some of the principles this institution captured were more widely held, wherever feudalism evolved to permit somewhat more centralized governing structures, in duchies or other regional states as well as the more eye-catching kingdoms like England and France.

In addition to its unusual, sometimes overwhelming chaos, the early postclassical West developed a number of implicit political principles that were carried over, though also modified, when more sophisticated government structures began to emerge with the rise of monarchies. Principle number one, clearly articulated in Church writings, held that laws of God were superior to those of humans. The Church, as an instrument of God, was separate from the state and in some ways above it, even though in the rough and tumble of actual medieval politics secular rulers often seized the upper hand. Principle number two involved the ineradicable local and regional divisions. Effective imperial governments could not be formed, as the collapse of Charlemagne's empire demonstrated; the West would be politically divided. Even regional governments had to recognize the strength of the local interests and power clusters. Principle number three, closely related to the impediments to centralization, involved the values embodied in feudalism. Feudal bonds—the relationships between lords and vassals—stressed mutuality. Each party in the relationship should contribute, each should gain. Vassals received protection and, usually, land (the fief or *feudum*, from which feudalism took its name) from their lord; lords won some payments, military service, and loyalty from their vassals. While feudalism permitted hierarchy among lords, it did not permit, at least in theory, unilateral assertions of power. It also encouraged mutual consultation. Vassals were supposed to advise their lords on judicial matters or issues of policy; lords were supposed to consult their vassals, rather than acting arbitrarily.

Unadulterated feudalism might of course function very badly. For all the high-sounding principles, there was a great deal of outright bullying and power display among the local lords during the postclassical period, quite apart from ill treatment of the masses of ordinary serfs who were underneath the feudal system. Effective government required some modifications of feudalism. Yet feudalism could be blended with other political systems, without losing many of its distinctive features.

MONARCHY AND ITS LIMITS

The new ingredient in medieval politics, as medieval society developed greater vigor from the 10th century onward, was of course the growth of royal power (or in some regions such as much of present-day Belgium, ducal power). Here the key steps are in many ways familiar, for they duplicated, unwittingly, the centralization principles developed earlier and more extensively in China and elsewhere. Medieval kings followed particular patterns of alliances and gradual aggrandizement because of their initially weak positions, and there were important specific events involved such as the Norman Conquest of England. Centralization is centralization, however, and though often reinvented it has some standard features.

Thus, as they began to expand their resources and aspirations, medieval kings developed small armies of their own, paid for by lands under their direct control, and they ventured a small central bureaucracy. Often they chose urban business or professional people to serve in this bureaucracy, partly because such people had expertise in financial matters and partly because, unlike the aristocracy, they would owe allegiance to the crown alone. French and English monarchs began to introduce bureaucratic specialties, so that some of their ministers would handle justice, others finance, and still others military matters. They found ways to send centrally appointed emissaries to the provinces to supervise tax collection and the administration of justice. It was in this vein that English kings, from the Norman Conquest onward, appointed local sheriffs to oversee the administration of justice. None of these activities gave the monarchs extensive contacts with ordinary subjects; for most people, effective governments were still local. Once the principle of central control was established, however, a steady growth of state-sponsored rule followed. By the end of the Middle Ages, monarchs were gaining the right to tax their subjects directly, and they were beginning to recruit professional armies, instead of relying solely on an aristocratic cavalry whose loyalties depended on feudal bonds or alliances. Several medieval kings, such as Louis IX in France, also gained solid reputations as law givers, which allowed a gradual centralization of legal codes and court systems. Rediscovery of Roman law in countries like France encouraged this centralization effort.

Feudal monarchy was always a delicately balanced institution, of which the central government formed only one of the key ingredients. The power of the Church served to check royal ambitions. As we have seen, the Church could often win in a clash with the state by excommunicating rulers and thus threatening to turn the loyalties of the population against them. Although the Church entered a period of decline at the end of the Middle Ages, the principle was rather clearly established that there were areas of belief and morality not open to manipulation by the state. And during most of the Middle Ages, the sheer authority of church organization and religious doctrine made this limitation on royal power a telling reality.

The second limitation on the royal families came from the traditions of feudalism and from the landed aristocracy as a powerful class. Aristocrats tended to resist too much monarchical control in the West, and they had the strength to make their objections heard. These aristocrats, even when vassals of the king, had their own economic base and their own military force—sometimes, in the case of great nobles, they had an army greater than that of the king. The growth of the monarchy cut into aristocratic power, but this led to new statements of the limits of kings. In 1215 the unpopular English king John faced opposition to his taxation measures from an alliance of nobles, townspeople, and church officials. Defeated in his war with France and then forced down by the leading English lords, John was forced to sign the Great Charter, or Magna Carta, which confirmed basically feudal rights against monarchical claims. John promised to observe restraint in his dealings with the nobles and the Church, agreeing for example not to institute new taxes without the lords' permission or to appoint bishops without the Church's permission. A few modern-sounding references to general rights of the English people against the state that were included in Magna Carta largely served to show where the feudal idea of mutual limits and obligations between rulers and ruled could later expand.

This same feudal balance led, late in the 13th century, to the creation of parliaments as bodies representing not individual voters but privileged groups such as the nobles and the Church. The first full English parliament convened in 1265, with the House of Lords representing the nobles and the church hierarchy, and the Commons made up of elected representatives from wealthy citizens of the towns. The parliament institutionalized the feudal principle that monarchs should consult with their vassals. In particular, parliaments gained the right to rule on any proposed changes in taxation; through this power, they could also advise the crown on other policy issues. While the parliamentary tradition became strongest in England, similar institutions arose in France, Spain, and several of the regional governments in Germany. Here too, parliaments represented the key estates: Church, nobles, and urban leaders. They were not widely elected.

Feudal government was not modern government. People had rights according to the estate into which they were born; there was no general concept of citizenship and no democracy. Thus parliaments represented only a minority, and even this minority only in terms of the three or four estates voting as units (nobles, clergy, urban merchants, and sometimes wealthy peasants), not some generalized collection of voters. Still, by creating a concept of limited government and some hint of representative institutions, Western feudal monarchy produced the beginnings of a distinctive political tradition. This tradition differed from the political results of Japanese feudalism, which emphasized group loyalty more than checks on central power.

During the postclassical period, a key result of the establishment of feudal monarchy was a comparatively weak central core; although several monarchies gained ground steadily, they wielded very few general powers. This would change, as kings attained far more extensive powers in military affairs, cultural patronage, and the like. However, some solid remnants of medieval traditions, embodied in institutions like parliaments and ideas like the separation between God's authority and state power, would define a basic thread in the Western political process even in the later 20th century.

THE WANING OF THE MIDDLE AGES

After about 1300 some of the characteristics of medieval life at its height began to give way. One problem, both symptom and cause of larger issues, was the major war that engulfed France and England during the 14th and 15th centuries. The Hundred Years' War, which sputtered into the mid-15th century, lasted even longer than its name and initially went very badly for France, a sign of new weakness in the French monarchy. Not very bloody, the war nevertheless consumed precious resources, brought confusion to key medieval centers in France, and ultimately demonstrated the futility of some of the military and organizational methods attached to feudalism. As the war dragged on, kings reduced their reliance on the prancing forces of the nobility in favor of paid armies of their own. New military methods challenged the key monopoly of the feudal lords, as ordinary paid archers learned how to unseat armored knights with powerful bows and arrows and with crossbows. The war ended with a French victory, sparked in part by the heroic leadership of the inspired peasant woman Joan of Arc, but both its devastation and the anti-feudal innovations it encouraged suggested a time of change.

Concurrently, from about 1300 onward, key sources of Western vitality threatened to disappear. Medieval agriculture could no longer keep pace with population growth; the

Western Europe toward the End of the Middle Ages, about 1360

readily available new lands had been used up, and there were no major new technological gains to compensate. The result included severe famines and an actual decline in population levels until the end of the century. A devastating series of plagues that persisted for several centuries, beginning with the Black Death in 1348, further challenged Europe's population and social structure. The West's economy did not go into a tailspin; in some respects, as in manufacturing technology, progress may even have sped up. Again, the contours were novel. The 150 to 200 years after 1300 form in Western history something of a transition period in which the features of the Middle Ages began to blur, while new problems and developments began to take center stage. Western civilization was not in a spiral of decline as a result, but the postclassical version of this civilization was.

THE SIGNS OF STRAIN

The decline of medieval society after about 1300 had two facets. In the first place, several of the sources of vigor that had sustained a varied culture and political life during the High Middle Ages stagnated or even changed course. The downward population trends showed the limits of Western resources at this point. Plagues cut the labor force. Ironically, as the West developed new international contacts it became more vulnerable to epidemic disease. New social disputes arose, heightening some of the tensions noted earlier between peasants and landlords, artisans and their employees. Not until the 16th century would the West begin to work out a new social structure.

The second aspect of decline involved the increasing challenges to several typical medieval institutions or compromises. Here decline was not absolute, but rather a sign

This artist's depiction of Florence, Italy, in the wake of the Black Death combines suffering with religious solace.

of change, as Western society began to shed part of its earlier skin only to emerge, with renewed dynamism, in somewhat different garb by the middle of the 15th century. The fading of medievalisms showed in many key areas, three of which we will present here.

During the 14th century, the ruling class of medieval society, the landowning aristocracy, began to show signs of confusion of function. It had long staked its claim to power on its control of much of the land and also on its military prowess, but its skill in warfare was now open to question. The growth of professional armies and new weaponry—such as the crossbow and, by the 15th century, the cannon and gunpowder—made traditional fighting methods, including fortified castles, increasingly irrelevant. The aristocracy did not, as a result, simply disappear. Rather, the nobility chose to emphasize a rich ceremonial style of life, featuring tournaments in which military expertise could be turned into competitive games. The spread of courtly love poems signaled another new interest in a more refined culture. The idea of *chivalry*—carefully con-

trolled, polite behavior, including behavior toward women—gained ground. This was a potentially fruitful development in indicating increased cultivation among the upper class. We have seen similar transformations in dealing with earlier changes in the Chinese and Muslim aristocracy. Yet at the time of transition in the West, some of the elaborate ceremonies of chivalry seemed rather hollow, even a bit silly—a sign that medieval values were losing hold, without being replaced by a new set of purposes.

Another key area involved decisive shifts in the balance between church and state that had characterized medieval life. For several decades in the aftermath of the taxation disputes in the early 14th century, French kings wielded great influence on the papacy, which they relocated from Rome to Avignon, a town surrounded by French territory; then rival claimants to the papacy confused the issue further. Ultimately a single pope was returned to Rome, but the Church was clearly weakened. Moreover, the Church began to lose some of its grip over Western religious life. Church leaders were so preoccupied with their political in-

In the Hundred Years' War, English archers fought France's feudal cavalry—the beginning of the end of feudal warfare in Europe. This 14th-century battle of Crécy was a resounding defeat for France's noble army, though it outnumbered the English army.

volvement that they tended to neglect the spiritual side. Religion was not declining; indeed, signs of intense popular piety continued to blossom, with the formation of new religious groups in the towns. But devotion became partially separated from the institution of the Church. One result, again beginning from the 14th century, was a series of popular heresies, with leaders in places like England and Bohemia preaching against the hierarchical apparatus of the Church in favor of direct popular experience of

God. Another result was an important new series of mystics, many of them women, who claimed direct, highly emotional contacts with God.

A third area in which medievalism faded was in the breaking down of the intellectual and even artistic synthesis. After the work of Aquinas, the sterile philosophical pursuits of the later scholastics seemed petty. Church officials became less tolerant of intellectual daring, and they even declared some of Aquinas's writings heretical. The earlier blend of rationalism and religion no longer seemed feasible. Ultimately, this would turn some thinkers away from religion, but this daring development took time to coalesce. In art, growing interest in realistic portrayals of nature, though fruitful, suggested the beginnings of a shift away from medieval artistic standards. Some medieval artistic styles became trite—a symptom of waning creativity. The various constraints on postclassical culture forms prompted many Western intellectuals to look for different emphases. In Italy most clearly, new kinds of literature and art took shape that differed from the styles and subjects of the postclassical centuries.

WORLD POSITION: SURPRISING STRENGTH

The adjustment of medieval culture and politics, and even the more basic problems of food supply and disease, did not seriously affect the West's position in the world during the 14th and 15th centuries. Medieval decline was not as sweeping or fundamental as the reduction of Arab power and the narrowing of Muslim culture, for example, during approximately the same centuries. Furthermore, the West was spared the Mongol invasions that so disrupted much of Asia and eastern Europe. It benefited from the new Mongol empires by gaining greater access to the knowledge and technology of Asian civilizations. However, the decline of medieval forms did cause confusion in the West at various social levels. This confusion helped prepare a series of fundamental changes in Western society, which began to take shape in the 15th and 16th centuries. It also prompted Westerners to seek new access to other parts of the world, in hopes of redressing the West's continued inferiorities. These initiatives, leading among other things to new Western explorations and trading patterns, also began to emerge in the 15th century. The decline of the Middle Ages helped prepare a new chapter in the West's relationship to the larger streams of world history.

CONCLUSION

THE POSTCLASSICAL WEST AND ITS HERITAGE

The term *Middle Ages* long suggested a rather unpleasant, backward period in Western history between the glories of classical Greece and Rome and the return of

vigorous civilization in the 15th century. In this view, the Middle Ages might be regarded as an unfortunate interlude in which Westerners were dominated by poverty and superstition, pulled away from mainstream Western values. Western leaders might be given credit for keeping a few classical ideals alive, copying documents and venerating the glories of the past. Western leaders, however, should be given credit for little else.

The harsh view of the Middle Ages is not entirely wrong, though it neglects the extent to which much activity centered in parts of Europe that had never before been integrated into a major civilization and therefore were building appropriate institutions and culture for the first time. Postclassical Europe was backward in some respects, even at its height. It did not participate in world contacts as an equal to the great Asian societies. The Middle Ages was not simply an awkward interlude in Western history, however. It had a formative force of its own.

THE DISTINCTIVE FLAVOR

In culture, medieval thinkers did recapture and repackage key elements of the classical heritage, particularly in their view of humanity's rational powers and their definition of reason in terms of logic. By linking classical rationalism with a strong belief in a divine plan they may indeed have advanced the idea of a fundamentally orderly universe and so set the stage for further advances in rationalistic scientific thought. Stylistically, medieval artists did not mainly work in classical modes, and their contributions added important ingredients to the larger cultural heritage. William Shakespeare, for example, writing in the later 16th century, borrowed freely from Greek literary themes, but he owed still more to the earthy popular drama that began in the Middle Ages.

In politics, the Middle Ages largely bypassed the classical heritage, despite a few longings for empire and the important usage of principles of Roman law. The most characteristic institutions were built on the Church and feudalism, and their heritage to later Western political developments was almost certainly greater than that of Greece or Rome. Medieval politics were not of course the final Western form, but in ideas of higher law and in the institutional restraints on central government they did prefigure values and institutions that have had enduring impact in the West. Similarly, medieval economics, with the new interest in merchant life and technical innovation that developed by the 10th century, set a much more direct stage for subsequent Western developments than classical economic patterns had done; here too, medieval developments were quite different from their Greek and Roman analogues, as was evident from the greater prestige of merchants and the absence of extensive slavery.

The Middle Ages, in sum, created its own culture, relying only in part on earlier classical models. Preservation of classical patterns was important, and Western leaders would later select a larger number of Greek and Roman ingredients to challenge certain medieval impulses. Medieval precedents would remain strong as well, even for periods in which Western pacesetters professed to scorn the Middle Ages. One world historian has suggested that a key historical source of Western vitality in more modern centuries has been the ability to select among a quite diverse set of pasts, rather than building, Chinese-fashion, upon more unified traditions. Certainly, the Middle Ages contributed greatly to the range of options available for later Western development, even as specifically medieval syntheses began to unravel by the 14th century.

WESTERN CIVILIZATION IN THE POSTCLASSICAL PERIOD: A COMPARATIVE BALANCE SHEET

The Middle Ages formed a distinctive period in Western history while contributing durable values for the civilization later on. Parliamentary institutions are one example of heritage, even though their medieval form differed considerably from their more modern guise.

Postclassical Europe can also be compared with other societies in a number of developmental respects. Growing complexity over time brought tensions between the merchant spirit and older agricultural values, which other civilizations had faced before; it also brought some familiar changes in the conditions of women. Conversion to Christianity had features that resembled conversion to Islam elsewhere, though Christian religious institutions differed considerably from Muslim institutions. Christian and Muslim thinkers shared problems in coming to terms with other intellectual traditions, though ultimately the balance struck turned out to differ. On another front, as feudal monarchies developed more specialized bureaucracies they unwittingly duplicated elements pioneered much earlier by Chinese rulers, and they copied contemporary bureaucracies they learned about in the Byzantine Empire and Muslim Spain.

The most important comparisons involve juxtaposing western Europe with other areas where civilization was partially novel in this period and where change was correspondingly rapid. Divided political rule in Europe resembled conditions in African regions and, even more

obviously, in Japan, the only other feudal society in this period. Rapidly growing trade and an orientation toward richer, more established centers was another common feature, shared also with Russia's north-south links. The West's contact levels were higher than those of most of sub-Saharan Africa, however, and its expansionist interests—witness the crusades—were much greater than Japan's. Again, the postclassical West constituted a type of civilization with many similarities to other emerging regions but with its own distinctive combinations, including the aggressive interest in the wider world.

FURTHER READINGS

For the Middle Ages generally, Joseph Strayer's *Western Europe in the Middle Ages* (1982) is a fine survey, with an extensive bibliography. Key topics are covered in R. S. Lopez's *The Commercial Revolution of the Middle Ages, 950–1350* (1976) and C. H. Lawrence's *Medieval Monasticism: Forms of Religious Life in Western Europe in the Middle Ages* (1984). National histories are important for the period, particularly on political life: see J. W. Baldwin's *The Government of Philip Augustus: Foundations of French Royal Power in the Middle Ages* (1986); G. Barraclough's *The Origins of Modern Germany* (1984); and M. Chibnall's *Anglo-Norman England, 1066–1166* (1986).

Social history has dominated much recent research on the period. See P. Ariès and G. Duby, eds., *A History of Private Life*, vol. 2 (1984) and Barbara Hanawalt's *The Ties That Bound: Peasant Families in Medieval England* (1986) for important orientation in this area. David Herlihy's *Medieval Households* (1985) is a vital contribution, as is J. Chapelot and R. Fossier's *The Village and House in the Middle Ages* (1985). J. Kirshner and S. F. Wemple, eds., *Women of the Medieval World* (1985) is a good collection. On tensions in popular religion, see C. Bynum's *Jesus as Mother: Studies in the Spirituality of the High Middle Ages* (1982) and L. Little's *Religious Poverty and the Profit Economy in Medieval Europe* (1978). A highly readable account of medieval life is E. Leroy Ladurie's *Montaillou: The Promised Land of Error* (1979).

Several excellent studies take up the theme of technological change: J. Gimpel's *The Medieval Machine: The Industrial Revolution of the Middle Ages* (1977); Lynn White, Jr.'s *Medieval Technology and Social Change* (1962); and David Landes's *Revolution in Time: Clocks and the Making of the Modern World* (1985).

On intellectual and artistic life, E. Gilson's *History of Christian Philosophy in the Middle Ages* (1954) is a brilliant sketch, while his *Reason and Revelation* (1956) focuses on key intellectual issues of the age. S. C. Ferruolo's *The Origins of the University* (1985) and N. Pevsner's *An Outline of European Architecture* (1963) deal with other important features; see also H. Berman's *Law and Revolution: The Formation of the Western Legal Tradition* (1983). An intriguing classic, focused primarily on culture, is J. Huizinga's *Waning of the Middle Ages* (1973).

Mesoamerica

1200–1500 Mississippian culture flourishes

1000 Toltec conquest of Chichen Itzá and influence in Yucatan

1150 Fall of Tula, disintegration of Toltec Empire

968 Tula established by Toltecs

Andean World

900–1465 Chimor Empire based on Chan Chan on north coast

900 End of Intermediate Horizon and decline of Tihuanaco and Huari

17

The Americas on the Eve of Invasion

INTRODUCTION. During the postclassic period, societies in the Americas remained entirely separate from those of the Old World. Some displayed features similar to the great centers of Asia and the Mediterranean in that they were able to build on earlier precedents from the classic period. Thus Mesoamerican civilizations formed large cities, based on elaborate political and economic organization, that would later dazzle European intruders much as Constantinople or the great cities of China did. But these similarities were accidental, and they were outweighed by the vast differences that resulted from American isolation.

As in the classical centuries, American societies continued to display extraordinary diversity. Other continuities marked the pre-Columbian experience up to the year of Columbus's arrival and indeed beyond. Great American civilizations were marked by elaborate cultural systems and a highly developed agriculture, yielding a distinctive array of foods. The postclassic period saw significant changes in the Americas also, particularly in the increasingly extensive organization of agriculture and in the ability to form larger political units.

By 1500 the Americas were densely populated in many places by Indian peoples long indigenous to the New World. The term *Indian* is, of course, a misnomer created by Columbus when he thought he had reached the Indies, but the label is also somewhat misleading because it implies a certain recognition of commonality among the peoples of the Americas that did not exist until after the arrival of Europeans. *Indian* as a term to describe all the peoples of the Americas only could have a meaning when there were non-Indians to apply it. Still, the term has been used for so long—and is still in use by many Native Americans today—that we will continue to use it.

As should already be clear, there were many Indian peoples with a vast array of cultural achievements. This variety of cultural patterns and ways of life of pre-Columbian

1325 Aztecs established in central Mexico; Tenochtitlan founded

1434–1472 Rule of Nezhualcoyotl at Texcoco

1486–1502 Ahuitzotl

1502–1520 Moctezuma II

1434 Creation of triple alliance   **1440–1469** Moctezuma I

1471–1493 Inca Topac Yupanqui increases areas under control

1438–1471 Great expansion under Inca Pachakuti

1350 Incas established in Cuzco area

1438 Incas dominate Cuzco and southern highlands

1493–1527 Huayna Capac expands into Ecuador; his death results in civil war civilizations prohibits a detailed discussion of each, but we can concentrate our attention on a few areas where major civilizations developed, based on earlier achievements. By concentrating on these regions we can demonstrate the continuity of civilization in the Americas. We shall examine in some detail Mesoamerica, especially central Mexico, and the Andean heartland. In both these areas great imperial states were in place when European expansion brought them into direct and continual contact with the Old World. That contact produced a vast literature on Indian societies by European observers, so that we have the advantage of a record of observation and interpretation by Europeans that can be added to the archeological record. Of course, this external evidence must be used carefully and the biases of the authors taken into account. We shall also discuss in less detail a few areas influenced by the centers of civilization—and some whose development seems to have been independent of them—in order to provide an overview of the Americas on the eve of invasion.

POSTCLASSIC MESOAMERICA, A.D. 1000–1500

As noted in Chapter 9, the collapse of Teotihuacan in central Mexico and the abandonment of the classical Maya cities in the 8th century A.D. signaled a significant political and cultural change in Mesoamerica. The civilizations that followed built on the achievements of their classic predecessors but rarely surpassed them, except in the area of political and military organization.

In central Mexico, nomadic peoples from beyond the northern frontier of the sedentary agricultural area took advantage of the political vacuum to move into the richer lands. Among these peoples were the Toltecs who established a capital at Tula in about 968. They adopted many cultural features from the sedentary peoples, to which they added a strongly militaristic ethic. This included the cult of sacrifice and war that is often portrayed in Toltec art. Later Mesoamerican peoples, such as the Aztecs, had some historical memory of the Toltecs and thought of them as culture heroes, the givers of civilization. Thus, being able to trace one's lineage back to the Toltecs later became a highly prized pedigree. The archeological record, however, indicates that Toltec accomplishments were often fused or confused with those of Teotihuacan in the memory of the Toltec's successors.

THE TOLTEC HERITAGE

Among the legends that survived about the Toltecs were those of Topiltzin, a Toltec leader and apparently a priest dedicated to the god Quetzalcoatl (the Feathered Serpent)

who later became confused with the god himself in the legends. Apparently, Topiltzin, a religious reformer, was involved in a struggle for priestly or political power with another faction. When he lost, Topiltzin and his followers went into exile, promising to return in the future to claim his throne on the same date according to the cyclical calendar system. Supposedly, Topiltzin and his followers sailed for Yucatan; there is considerable evidence of Toltec influence in that region. The legend of Topiltzin-Quetzalcoatl was well known to the Aztecs and may have influenced their response when the Europeans later arrived.

The Toltecs created an empire that extended over much of central Mexico, and their influence spread far beyond the region. Although the Maya had abandoned many cities and no longer kept long-count dates, large cities, especially in Yucatan, were still occupied. Around A.D. 1000, Chichen Itzá was conquered by Toltec warriors, and it and a number of other cities were then ruled for a long time by central Mexican dynasties or by Maya rulers under Toltec influence. The architecture at Chichen Itzá—with its pyramid of the god Quetzalcoatl (Feathered Serpent) and artistic motifs of warriors, feathered serpents, and the symbols of death—reflects the Toltec influence. Some Maya states in Guatemala, such as the Quiché kingdom, also had Toltecized ruling families.

Toltec influence spread northward as well. Obsidian mines were exploited in northern Mexico, and the Toltecs may have traded for turquoise in the American Southwest. There is evidence of contact between Mesoamerica and the cliff-dwellers of Colorado and New Mexico, who are the ancestors of the modern Pueblo Indians of the Southwest. It has been suggested that the great Anasazi adobe town at Chaco canyon in New Mexico was abandoned when the Toltec Empire fell and the trade for local turquoise ended.

How far eastward that influence spread is a matter of dispute. Was there contact between Mesoamerica and the elaborate culture and concentrated towns of the Hopewell peoples of the Ohio and Mississippi valleys discussed in Chapter 9? Scholars disagree. Eventually, in the lower Mississippi valley from about 700, elements of Hopewell culture seem to have been enriched by external contact perhaps with Mexico. This Mississippian culture, which flourished between 1200 and 1500, was based on maize and bean agriculture. Towns, usually located along rivers, had stepped temples made of earth and sometimes large burial mounds. Some of the burials include well-produced pottery and other goods and seem to be accompanied by ritual executions or sacrifices of servants or wives. This indicates social stratification in the society. Cahokia, near East St. Louis, Illinois, covered five square miles and may have had over 30,000 people in and around its center. Its largest earthen pyramid, called Monk's Mound, covers 15 acres and is comparable in size to the largest classic period pyramids in Mexico. Many of these cultural features seem to suggest contact with Mesoamerica, although no definitely Mexican object has been found in a Mississippian site. Still, certain artistic traits and subjects, including the feathered serpent, strongly suggest contact.

THE AZTEC RISE TO POWER

The Toltec Empire lasted until about 1150, at which time it was apparently destroyed by nomadic invaders from the north who also seem to have sacked Tula around that date. In the period after the fall of Tula, the center of population and political power in central Mexico shifted to the valley of Mexico and especially to the shores of the large chain of lakes in that basin. The three largest lakes were connected by marshes; together they provided a rich aquatic environment. While the eastern lakes tended to be brackish from the minerals that emptied in them from surrounding rivers, the southern and western portions contained fresh water. The shores of the lakes were dotted with settlements and towns. A dense population lived around the lakes to take advantage of their life-giving water for agriculture, the fish and aquatic plants and animals, and the advantages of transportation. Of the approximately 3000 square miles in the basin of the valley, about 400 square miles were underwater.

The lakes became the cultural heartland and population center of Mexico in the postclassic period. In the unstable world of post-Toltec Mesoamerica, various peoples and cities jockeyed for supremacy of the lakes and the advantages they offered. The winners of this struggle, the Aztecs, eventually built a great empire, but when they emerged on the historical scene they were the most unlikely candidates for power.

From their obscure origins, the Aztec (or as they called themselves, the Mexica) rise to power and formation of an imperial state was as spectacular as it was rapid. According to some of their legends, the Mexica had once inhabited the central valley and had known agriculture and the "civilized" life but had lived in exile to the north in a place called Aztlan (from whence we get the name *Aztec*). This may be an exaggeration by people who wished to lay claim to a distinguished heritage. Other sources indicate that the Aztecs were simply one of the nomadic tribes that used the political anarchy, following the fall of the Toltecs, to penetrate into the area of sedentary agricultural peoples. Like the ancient Egyptians, the Aztecs rewrote history to suit their purposes. Their ruler Itzcoatl (1427–1440) ordered all the old books destroyed and had history rewritten in a manner more favorable to the Aztec "official" version. Later observers, both Spaniards and Indians, wrote with

Central Mexico and Lake Texcoco

their own biases. Thus, it is difficult to piece the story together and to eliminate intentional bias, political manipulation, and later rewriting, but with the help of archeology and *ethnohistory*, or the use of anthropological techniques by historians, it is possible to outline the major features of Aztec life and history.

What seems clear is that the Aztecs were a group of about 10,000 people who migrated to the shores of Lake Texcoco in the central valley of Mexico around the year 1325. After the fall of the Toltec Empire, the central valley was inhabited by a mixture of peoples—Chichimec migrants from the northwest and various groups of sedentary agriculturalists. These peoples were divided into small political units that claimed greater or lesser authority on the basis of their military power and their connections to Toltec culture or Toltec descendants. Many of these peoples spoke Nahuatl, the language the Toltecs had spoken. The Aztecs too spoke this language, a fact that made their rise to power and their eventual claims to legitimacy more acceptable.

The Toltec political and cultural influence spread from its capital at Tula in northern Mexico (shown here) to places as far south as Chichén Itzá in Yucatán.

In this period the area around the lake was dominated by a number of tribes organized into city-states. The city of Azcapotzalco was the real power but was challenged by an alliance centered in the city of Texcoco. Another city, Culhuacan, which had been part of the Toltec Empire, used its heritage as legitimate heir to the Toltecs as a means of creating alliances by marrying its princes and princesses to more powerful but less distinguished states. This was a world of political manuever and state marriages, competing powers and shifting alliances.

An intrusive and militant group, such as the Aztecs, were distrusted and disliked by the dominant powers of the area, but their fighting skills could be put to use, and this made them attractive as mercenaries or allies. For about a century the Aztecs wandered around the shores of the lake, being allowed to settle for a while and then driven out by more powerful neighbors. An alliance with Culhuacan failed when instead of arranging a royal marriage of a princess sent from that city, the Aztecs executed her as an offering to their gods.

In a period of militarism and warfare, the Aztecs had a reputation as tough warriors and fanatical followers of their gods, to whom they offered continual human sacrifices. This reputation made them both valued and feared. Their own legends foretold that their wanderings would end when they saw an eagle perched on a cactus with a serpent in its beak. Supposedly, this sign was seen on a marshy island in Lake Texcoco and there, on that island and one nearby, the Aztecs settled. The city of Tenochtitlan was founded about 1325 and on the neighboring island the city of Tlatelolco was established shortly thereafter. The two cities eventually grew together, although they maintained separate administrations.

From this secure base the Aztecs began to take a more active role in regional politics. Azcapotzalco and Texcoco were locked in a struggle, and the Aztecs now began to serve Azcapotzalco as mercenaries. This alliance brought prosperity to the Aztecs, especially to their ruler and the warrior nobility, which was now acquiring lands and tribute from conquered towns. By 1428, however, the Aztecs had rebelled against Azcapotzalco and had joined with Texcoco in destroying it. From that victory the Aztecs emerged as an independent power. In 1434, Tenochtitlan, Texcoco, and a smaller city, Tlacopan, joined together in a triple alliance that exercised control over much of the central plateau. Nezhualcoyotl, the philosopher king in Texcoco (1434–1472), used his personal prestige and political wisdom to keep some balance in the alliance, but in reality, Tenochtitlan and the Aztecs dominated their allies and controlled the major share of the tribute and lands taken.

THE AZTEC SOCIAL CONTRACT

According to the Aztec accounts of this history, a social and political transformation had also taken place. Acampichtli, the first ruler, had created a nobility, or *pipiltin*, from the leading families by marriage with some Culhuacan nobles who could trace their roots to the Toltecs. When the war with Azcapotzalco broke out, the commoners were reluctant to fight; but the nobility urged them on and promised victory. According to the Aztec official version, the pipiltin promised to obey the commoners forever if they lost, and the commoners made a similar promise if the nobles could bring victory. The conquest of Azcapotzalco assured the position of the nobility. Moreover, the ruler of Tenochtitlan emerged from this process no longer as a spokesman for a general council, but as a supreme ruler with wide powers. Succeeding rulers expanded that power and the boundaries of Aztec control. Moctezuma I (1440–1469) conquered areas around the central plateau. Under his brother Ahuitzotl (1486–1502), the empire reached its greatest extent—from coast to coast and with some subject areas far to the south, although the Tarascan kingdom to the northwest remained independent. Moctezuma II (1502–1520) consolidated the conquest of central Mexico, and although a few independent states remained within central Mexico, Aztec domination extended from the Tarascan frontier southward to the Maya area. Subject peoples were forced to pay tribute, surrender lands, and sometimes do military service for the growing Aztec Empire.

Whatever the official explanation of events, it seems clear that Aztec society had been transformed in the process of expansion and conquest. From a loose association of clans, the Mexica had become a stratified society under the authority of a supreme ruler of great power. A central figure in these changes was Tlacaelel, a man who served as a sort of prime minister and advisor under three rulers from 1427 to his death around 1480. Under his direction, the histories were rewritten and the Mexica were given a self-image as a people chosen to serve the gods. Human sacrifice, long a part of Mesoamerican religion, was greatly expanded under his direction into a cult of enormous proportions in which the military class played a central role as suppliers of war captives to be used as sacrificial victims. Supposedly, at the dedication of the great temple during the reign of Ahuitzotl, over 10,000 victims were put to death. It was also a policy of Tlacaelel to leave a few territories unconquered so that periodic "flower wars" could be staged in which both sides could obtain captives for sacrifice. Whatever the religious motivations of this cult, Tlacaelel and the Aztec rulers manipulated it as an effective means of political terror. By the time of Moctezuma II, the Aztec state was dominated by a king who represented civil power and served as a representative of the gods on earth. The cult of human sacrifice and conquest was united with the political power of the ruler and the nobility.

RELIGION AND THE IDEOLOGY OF CONQUEST

Aztec religion incorporated many features that had long been part of the Mesoamerican system of beliefs. Religion was a vast, uniting, and sometimes oppressive force in which little distinction was made between the world of the gods and the natural world. The traditional deities of Mesoamerica—the gods of rain, fire, water, corn, the sky, and the sun, many of whom were worshiped as far back as the time of Teotihuacan—were known and venerated among the Aztecs. There were at least 128 major deities, but the number of gods, in fact, seemed innumerable for often each deity had a female consort or feminine form. This was because a basic duality was recognized in all things. Moreover, gods might have different forms or manifestations somewhat like the avatars of the Hindu deities. Often each god had at least five aspects, each associated with one of the cardinal directions and the center. Certain gods were thought to be the patrons of specific cities, ethnic groups, or occupations. It was an extensive pantheon supported by a round of yearly festivals and a highly complex ceremonialism that involved various forms of feasting and dancing along with penance and sacrifice.

This bewildering array of gods can be organized into three major themes or cults. The first were the gods of fertility and the agricultural cycle, such as Tlaloc, or the god of rain (called Chac by the Maya), and the gods and goddesses of water, maize, and fertility. Xipe Totec, for example, represented agricultural rebirth. His cult was horrible. Victims sacrificed to him were flayed, and a priest then donned the skin to represent the new growth of the maize. A second theme centered on the creator deities, the great gods and goddesses who had brought the universe into being. The story of their actions played a central role in Aztec cosmography. Tonatiuh, the warrior god of the sun, and Tezcatlipoca, the god of the night sky, were among the most powerful and respected gods among the peoples of central Mexico. Much of Aztec abstract and philosophical thought was devoted to the theme of creation. Finally, the cult of warfare and sacrifice built on the preexisting Mesoamerican traditions that had been expanding since Toltec times but which, under the militaristic Aztec state, became the cult of the state. Huitzilopochtli, the Aztec tribal patron, became the central figure of this cult, but it included Tezcatlipoca, Tonatiuh, and other gods as well.

The Aztecs revered the great traditional deities—such as Tlaloc and Quetzalcoatl, the ancient god of civilization—so holy to the Toltecs, but their own tribal deity Huitzilopochtli became paramount. The Aztecs identified him with the old sun god, and they saw him as a warrior in the daytime sky fighting to give life and warmth to the world against the forces of the night. In order to carry out that struggle, the sun needed strength—and just as the gods had sacrificed themselves for humankind, the nourishment the gods needed most was that which was most precious, human life in the form of hearts and blood. The great temple of Tenochtitlan was dedicated to both Huitzilopochtli and Tlaloc. The tribal deity of the Aztecs and the ancient agricultural god of the sedentary peoples of Mesoamerica were thus united.

In fact, while human sacrifice had long been a part of Mesoamerican religion, it had expanded considerably in the postclassic period of militarism. Warrior cults and the militaristic images of jaguars and eagles devouring human hearts were characteristic of Toltec art. The Aztecs simply took an existing tendency and carried it to an unprecedented scale. Both the types and frequency of sacrifice increased, and a whole symbolism and ritual, which included ritual cannibalism, developed as part of the cult. How much of Aztec sacrifice was the result of religious conviction and how much was imposed as a tactic of terror and political control by the rulers and the priest class is a question still open to debate (see "Analysis" in this chapter).

Beneath the surface of this polytheism, there was, however, also a sense of spiritual unity. Nezhualcoyotl, the king of Texcoco, composed hymns to the "lord of the close vicinity," an invisible creative force that supported all the gods. Yet, his conception of a kind of monotheism, much like that of Pharaoh Akhnaten in Egypt, was too abstract and never gained great popularity.

While the bloody aspects of Aztec religion have gained much attention, we must also realize that the Aztecs concerned themselves with many of the great religious and spiritual questions that have preoccupied other civilizations: Is there life after death? What is the meaning of life? What does it mean to live a good life? Do the gods really exist?

Nezhualcoyotl, whose poetry survived in oral form and was written down in the 16th century, wondered about life after death:

> Do flowers go to the land of the dead?
> In the Beyond, are we dead or do we still live?
> Where is the source of light, since that which gives
> life hides itself?

He also wondered about the existence of the gods:

> Are you real, are you fixed?
> Only You dominate all things
> The Giver of Life.
> Is this true?
> Perhaps, as they say, it is not true.

Aztec religious art and poetry is filled with images of flowers, birds, and song—all of which the Aztecs greatly admired—as well as human hearts and blood—the "precious water" needed to sustain the gods. It is this mixture of images that makes the symbolism of Aztec religion so difficult for modern observers to understand.

Aztec religion depended on a complex mythology that explained the birth and history of the gods and their relation to peoples and on a religious symbolism that infused all aspects of life. As we have seen, the Mesoamerican calendar system was religious in nature, and many ceremonies coincided with particular points in the calendar cycle. Moreover, the Aztecs also believed in a cyclical view of history and believed that the world had been destroyed four times before and would be destroyed again. Thus there was a certain fatalism in Aztec thought and a premonition that, eventually, the sacrifices would be insufficient and the gods would again bring catastrophe. Characteristically, at the end of each 52-year cycle, all the fires in the kingdom were extinguished, and while the people waited apprehensively, the priests attempted to kindle a new fire in the chest cavity of a sacrificial victim. If the gods approved and the sparks caught, the world would continue; the new fire was then taken by runners with torches to relight all the fires in the realm.

THE FOUNDATION OF HEAVEN: TENOCHTITLAN, THE GREAT CITY

The city-state with its ruler-spokesman was a key central Mexican concept and it applied to Tenochtitlan, the Aztec capital. The Mexica thought of themselves as inheritors of Toltec traditions and of their city as the new Tula. From its modest beginnings, Tenochtitlan became a great metropolis, with a central zone of palaces and whitewashed temples surrounded by adobe brick residential districts, smaller palaces, and markets. The temple precinct was dominated by the great pyramid and twin temple of Huizilopochtli and Tlaloc. (This has recently been excavated by archeologists.) The round temple of Quetzalcoatl, the school for the priesthood, and some seventy other buildings stood in or near the precinct. The craftsmanship and architecture was outstanding. Hernán Cortés, the Spanish conqueror who viewed the city, personally reported, "The stone masonry and the woodwork are equally good, they could not be bettered anywhere." There were gardens and a zoo kept for the ruler. The nobility had houses two stories high, sometimes with gardens on the roofs.

Tlatelolco, at first a separate island city, was eventually incorporated as part of Tenochtitlan. It too had impressive temples and palaces, and its large market remained the most important place of trade and exchange. Building projects by various Mexican rulers increased the size and beauty of the city. By 1519, the city covered about five square miles. It had a population of 150,000, larger than contemporary European cities such as Seville or Paris.

The great Aztec capital of Tenochtitlán was dominated by the pyramid and twin temples of Huitzilopochtli shown here in a modern miniature reconstruction.

Its island location gave Tenochtitlan a peculiar character. Set in the midst of a lake, the city was connected to the shores by four broad causeways. Since the city was built on an island and reclaimed land, it was crisscrossed by canals that allowed the constant canoe traffic on the lake access to the city. Away from the center of the city, households practiced floating garden, or *chinampa*, cultivation within the city. Each of the more than 60 city wards was controlled by a *calpulli*, or kin group, and each maintained its neighborhood temples and civic buildings. The city was supplied primarily by canoe transportation, although there were aqueducts that brought in fresh water. A dike had been constructed to keep the brackish waters of the eastern portion of the lake away from the agriculture in and around the city. There were smaller island communities and along the shores of the lake were other densely populated towns and cities. The structural achievement was impressive. A Spanish foot-soldier who saw it in 1519 wrote:

> Gazing on such wonderful sights, we did not know what to say, or whether what appeared before us was real, for on one side, on the land, there were great cities, and in the lake ever many more, and the lake was crowded with canoes, and in the causeway were many bridges at intervals, and in front of us stood the great city of Mexico. . . .

Such vivid descriptions by Western observers tell only a portion of the story. Tenochtitlan had an internal organization that reproduced the Aztec religious and social universe. Its four causeways were associated with the four cardinal directions and the gods of each. Within the city, neighborhoods were organized in pairs of 20 communal corporate groups and in a number of temple upkeep groupings, each with its neighborhood temple and school to maintain. The round of festivals, the calendar system, and the cosmology of Aztec religion was represented physically by the city's organization and the place and hierarchy of the corporate groups within it. Such groupings were based on occupations, residence, or ethnicity. This last grouping was important because Tenochtitlan and the Aztecs themselves had included large non-Aztec ethnic populations even in their origins. In fact, much of Aztec myth and official history was designed to create a unified people out of an agglomeration of groups.

Tenochtitlan was the heart of an empire and drew tribute and support from its allies and dependents, but in theory it was still just a city-state ruled by a headman, just like the other 50 or more city-states that dotted the central plateau. Even so, the Aztecs called it the "foundation of heaven," the basis of their might. It was a great world city, but unlike Rome or Athens, it was later so completely obliterated that even in the lifetime of its conquerors, one

Human sacrifice existed among many Mesoamerican peoples, but the Aztecs apparently expanded its practice for political reasons and religious belief.

of them could lament that "all is overthrown and lost, nothing left standing." Present-day Mexico City rises on the site of the former Aztec capital.

FEEDING THE PEOPLE: THE ECONOMY OF THE EMPIRE

Feeding the great population of Tenochtitlan and the Aztec confederation in general depended on traditional forms of agriculture and on innovations developed by the Aztecs. Lands of conquered peoples were often appropriated, and food was sometimes demanded as tribute. In fact, the quantities of maize, beans, and other foods brought into Tenochtitlan annually were staggering. In and around the lake, however, the Aztecs adopted an ingenious system of irrigated agriculture by constructing chinampas for agriculture. These were beds of aquatic weeds, mud, and earth that had been placed in frames made of cane and rooted to the lake floor. They formed artificial floating islands about five meters long and 30 to 100 meters wide. This narrow, striplike construction allowed the water to reach all the plants, and willow trees were also planted at intervals to give shade and help fix the roots. Much of the land of Tenochtitlan itself was chinampa in origin, and in the southern end of the lake over 20,000 acres of chinampas were constructed.

The yield from chinampa agriculture was high and four corn crops a year were possible. Apparently, this system of irrigated agriculture had been used in preclassic days, but a rise in the level of the lakes had made it impossible to continue. After 1200, however, lowering of the lake levels once again stimulated chinampa construction, which the Aztecs carried out on a grand scale. They also constructed dikes to close off the fresh waters in the southern and western parts of the lake from the brackish waters elsewhere. Today, the floating gardens of Xochimilco represent the remnants of the lake agriculture.

Production by the Aztec peasantry and tribute provided the basic foods. In each Aztec community the local clan apportioned the lands, some of which were also set aside for support of the temples and the state. In addition, individual nobles might also have private estates that were worked by servants or slaves from conquered peoples. Each community had periodic markets—according to various cycles in the calendar system such as every five and 13 days—in which a wide variety of goods were exchanged. Cacao beans and gold dust were sometimes used as currency, but much trade was done as barter. The great market at Tlatelolco operated daily and was controlled by the special merchant class, or *pochteca*, which specialized in long-distance trade in luxury items such as plumes of tropical birds and cacao. The markets were highly regulated and under the

MAIZE

WILLOW TREE

DAHLIA

DUCKWEED

STAKE

FRESH MUD
WATERWEED

SEDIMENT

Chinampas were an imaginative agricultural adaptation that permitted the Aztecs to produce high crop yields to supply the dense populations of the valley of Mexico.

control of inspectors and special judges. Despite the existence and importance of markets, this was not a market economy as we usually understand it.

The state controlled the use and distribution of many commodities and served to redistribute the vast levies of tribute received from subordinate peoples. Tribute levels were assigned according to whether the subject peoples had accepted Aztec rule or had fought against it. Those who surrendered paid less. Tribute payments, such as food, slaves, and sacrificial victims, served political and economic ends and a wide variety of commodities. Over 120,000 mantles of cotton cloth alone were collected as tribute each year and sent to Tenochtitlan. The Aztec state redistributed these goods. After the original conquests, it rewarded its nobility richly, but the commoners received far less. Still, the redistribution of many goods by the state interfered with the normal functioning of the market and created a peculiar state-controlled mixed economy.

AZTEC SOCIETY IN TRANSITION

During their wanderings, the Aztecs had been divided into seven *calpulli*, or clans, a form of organization that they would later expand and adapt to their imperial position. By the 16th century there were about 20 major calpulli and 40 associated ones in Tenochtitlan alone. The

calpulli were no longer only kinship groups but also residential groupings that might include neighbors, allies, and dependents. Much of Aztec local life remained based on the calpulli, which performed important functions such as distributing land to heads of households, organizing labor gangs and military units in times of war, and maintaining a temple and school. Calpulli were governed by councils of family heads, but not all families were equal, nor were all calpulli of equal status.

The calpulli had obviously been the ancient and basic building block of Aztec society. In the origins of Aztec society every person—noble and commoner—had belonged to a calpulli, but Aztec power increased and the rule of the empire expanded. The calpulli had been transformed, and other forms of social stratification had emerged. Legends of their origins emphasized that at one time the Aztecs had all been peasants and had worked for others. As Aztec power expanded, a class of nobility emerged, based on certain privileged families in the most distinguished calpulli. Originating from the lineages that headed calpulli—especially those that had married into non-Mexica families or could claim Toltec background—and by marriages, military achievements, or service to the state, this group of nobility accumulated high office, private lands, and other advantages. The most prominent families in the calpulli, those who had dominated leadership roles and formed a kind of local nobility, were eventually overshadowed by the military and administrative nobility of the Aztec state.

While some commoners might receive promotion to noble status, most nobles were born into the class—although birth merely qualified an individual for high position, which ultimately depended on performance and ability. Nobles controlled the priesthood and the military leadership. The military, in fact, was organized into various ranks based on experience and success in taking captives. Military virtues were linked to the cult of sacrifice and infused the whole society; they became the justification for the nobility's predominance and the ideology of the nobility's identity. The "flowery death," or death while taking prisoners for the sacrificial knife, was the fitting end to a noble life and assured eternity in the highest heaven, a reward also promised to women who died in childbirth. The military was highly ritualized: There were orders of warriors—the jaguar, eagle, and other groups each had a distinctive uniform and ritual and fought together as units. Distinctive banners, cloaks, and other insignia marked off the military ranks.

The social gulf that separated the nobility from the commoners was widening as the empire grew and the pipiltin accumulated the lands and tribute that the expansion implied. Egalitarian principles that may have once existed in Aztec life disappeared—a situation similar to what happened among the warring German tribes of early medieval Europe. Social distinctions were made apparent by the use and restrictions on clothing, hairstyles, uniforms, and other outward symbols of rank. The imperial family became the most distinguished of the pipiltin families. Moctezuma II was particularly anxious to favor the nobility, and under his rule aristocratic domination of society was intensified and commoners were increasingly limited in their opportunities for advancement and recognition.

As the nobility broke free from their old calpulli and acquired private lands, a new class of workers was created to serve as laborers on these lands. These *mayeques*, or serfs, were sometimes from dependent clans or more often from conquered peoples. Unlike the commoners attached to the land-controlling calpulli, the mayeques did not control land and worked at the will of others. Their status was low, but it was still above that of the slaves who might have been war captives, persons punished for crimes, or those who had sold themselves into bondage to escape hunger. The mayeques often did domestic work, and while they could buy their freedom, they could also be offered as sacrifices by their owner. Together, the mayeques and the slaves formed a growing sector of the population whose situation was directly tied to the fortunes of the nobility and the strength of the Aztec Empire and who had little to gain from its success. Finally, there were other social

In the militarized society of the Aztec Empire, warriors were organized into regiments and groups distinguished by their distinctive uniforms. They gained rank and respect by capturing enemies for sacrifice.

groups. The scribes, artisans, and healers all constituted part of a kind of intermediate group, especially important in the larger cities. The long-distance merchants formed a sort of calpulli with their own patron gods, privileges, and internal divisions. They sometimes served as spies or agents for the Aztec military, but despite this role and their wealth, they were subject to restrictions that hindered their entry into or rivalry with the nobility.

It is possible to see an emerging conflict between the nobility and the commoners and to interpret this as a class struggle, but some specialists emphasize that to interpret Aztec society on that basis is to impose Western concepts on a different reality. Corporate bodies, such as the calpulli, temple maintenance associations, and occupational groups, cut across class and remained important in Aztec life. Competition between corporate groups was often more apparent and more violent than between social classes.

DOCUMENT

AZTEC WOMEN AND MEN

In the mid-16th century, Bernardino de Sahagún, a Spanish missionary, prepared an extraordinary encyclopedia of Aztec culture. His purpose was to gather this information to learn the customs and beliefs of the Indians and their language in order to better convert them. While Sahagún hated the Indian religion, he came to admire many aspects of their culture. His work, *The General History of the Things of New Spain*, is one of the first ethnographies and a remarkable compendium of Aztec culture. Sahagún used numerous Indian informants to tell him about the days before the European arrival and so, even though this work dates from the postconquest era, it contains much useful information about earlier Aztec life.

In the following excerpts, the proper behavior for different roles of both women and men in Aztec society are described by the Aztecs themselves.

FATHER

One's father is the source of lineage. He is the sincere one. One's father is diligent, solicitous, compassionate, sympathetic; a careful administrator of his household. He rears, he teaches others, he advises, he admonishes one. He is exemplary; he leads a model life. He stores up for himself; he stores up for others. He cares for his assets; he saves for others. He is thrifty; he saves for the future, teaches thrift. He regulates, distributes with care, establishes order.

The bad father is incompassionate, negligent, unreliable. He is unfeeling . . . a shirker, a loafer, a sullen worker.

MOTHER

One's mother has children; she suckles them. Sincere, vigilant, agile, she is an energetic worker—diligent, watchful, solicitous, full of anxiety. She teaches people; she is attentive to them. She caresses, she serves others; she is apprehensive for their welfare; she is careful, thrifty—constantly at work.

The bad mother is evil, dull, stupid, sleepy, lazy. She is a squanderer, a petty thief, a deceiver, a fraud. Unreliable, she is one who loses things through neglect or anger, who heeds no one. She is disrespectful, inconsiderate, disregarding, careless.

She shows the way to disobedience; she expounds nonconformity.

THE RULER

The ruler is a shelter—fierce, revered, famous, esteemed; well-reputed, renowned.

The good ruler is a protector; one who carries his subjects in his arms, who unites them, who brings them together. He rules, he takes responsibilities, assumes burdens. He carries his subjects in his cape; he bears them in his arms. He governs; he is obeyed. To him as a shelter, as refuge, there is recourse. . . .

The bad ruler is a wild beast, a demon of the air, an ocelot, a wolf—infamous, avoided, detested as a respecter of nothing. He terrifies with his gaze; he makes the earth rumble; he implants, he spreads fear. He is wished dead.

THE NOBLE

The noble has a mother, a father. He resembles his parents. The good noble is obedient, cooperative, a follower of his parents' ways, a discreet worker; attentive, willing. He follows the ways of his parents; he resembles his father; he becomes his father's successor, he assumes his lot.

One of noble lineage is a follower of the exemplary life, a taker of the good example of others; a seeker, a follower of the exemplary life. He speaks eloquently, he is soft-spoken, virtuous, deserving of gratitude. He is noble of heart, gentle of word, discreet, well-reared, well-taught. He is moderate, energetic, inquiring, inquisitive. He scratches the earth with a thorn. He is one who fasts, who starves his entrails, who parches his lips. He provides nourishment to others. He sustains one, he serves food, he provides comfort. He is a concealer [of himself], a belittler of himself. He magnifies and praises others. He is a mourner for the dead, a doer of penances, a gracious speaker; devout, godly, desirable, wanted, memorable.

The bad noble is ungrateful and forgetful; a debaser, a disparager of things, contemptuous of others, arrogant, bragging. He creates disorder, glories over his lineage, extols his own virtues.

THE MATURE COMMON WOMAN

The good mature woman is candid. She is resolute, firm of heart, constant—not to be dismayed; brave like a man; vigorous, resolute, persevering—not one to falter. She is long-suffering; she accepts reprimands calmly—endures things like a man. She becomes firm—takes courage. She is intent. She gives of herself. She goes in humility. She exerts herself.

The bad woman is thin, tottering, weak—an inconstant companion, unfriendly. She annoys others, chagrins them, shames, oppresses one. She becomes impatient, she loses hope, becomes embarrassed—chagrined. Evil is her life, she lives in shame.

THE WEAVER OF DESIGNS

She concerns herself with using thread, works with thread. The good weaver of designs is skilled—a maker of varicolored capes, an outliner of designs, a blender of colors, a joiner of pieces, a matcher of pieces, a person of good memory. She does things dexterously. She weaves designs. She selects. She weaves tightly. She forms borders. She forms the neck. . . .

The bad weaver of designs is untrained—silly, foolish, unobservant, unskilled of hand, ignorant, stupid. She tangles the thread, she harms her work—she spoils it.

THE PHYSICIAN

The physician is a knower of herbs, of roots, of trees, of stones; she is experienced in these. She is one who conducts examinations; she is a woman of experience, of trust, of professional skill: a counselor.

The good physician is a restorer, a provider of health, a relaxer—one who makes people feel well, who envelops one in ashes. She cures people; she provides them health, she lances them, she bleeds them . . . pierces them with an obsidian lancet.

Questions: In what ways do the expectations for men and women differ in Aztec society? To what extent do the roles for men and women in Aztec society differ from our own? Did the Aztecs value the same characteristics as our own and other historical societies?

FEATURES OF AZTEC SOCIETY: OVERCOMING TECHNOLOGICAL CONSTRAINTS

Membership in society was defined by participation in various wider groups, such as the calpulli or a specific social class, and by gender roles and definitions. Aztec women assumed a variety of roles. Peasant women helped in the fields, but their primary domain was the household, where child-rearing and cooking took up much time. Above all, skill at weaving was highly regarded. Responsibility for training young girls fell on the mature and elderly women of the calpulli. Marriages were often arranged between lineages and virginity at marriage was highly regarded for young women. Polygamy existed among the nobility, but the peasants were monogamous. Aztec women could inherit property and pass it to their heirs. The rights of Aztec women seem to have been fully recognized, but in political and social life their role, while complementary to that of men, remained subordinate.

The technology of the Americas limited social development in a variety of ways. Here we can note a significant difference between the life of women in Mesoamerica and in the Mediterranean world. In the maize-based economies of Mesoamerica, women spent six hours a day grinding the corn by hand on stone boards, or *metates*, to prepare the household's food. Although similar hand techniques were used in ancient Egypt, they were eventually replaced by animal- or water-powered mills that turned wheat into flour. The miller or baker of Rome or medieval Europe could do the work of hundreds of women. Maize was among the simplest and most productive cereals to grow, but among the most time-consuming to prepare. Without the wheel or suitable animals for power, the Indian civilizations were unable to free women from the 30 to 40 hours a week that went into the preparation of the basic food.

Finally, we must consider the size of the population of the Aztec state. Estimates have varied widely from as little as 1.5 million to over 25 million, but there is now considerable evidence that population density was high, resulting in a total population that was far greater than previously suspected. Historical demographers now estimate that the population of central Mexico under Aztec control reached over 20 million, excluding the Maya areas. This underlines the extraordinary ability of the Aztec state to intimidate and control such vast numbers of people.

A TRIBUTE EMPIRE

Each of the city-states was ruled by a speaker chosen from the nobility. The Great Speaker, the ruler of Tenochtitlan, became first among supposed equals. He was in effect the emperor, with great private wealth and public power, and was increasingly attributed with the symbols and status of a living god. His court was magnificent and surrounded with elaborate rituals. Those who approached him could not look him in the eyes and were required to throw dirt upon their heads as a sign of humility. In theory, he was elected, but his election was really a choice between siblings of the same royal family. The prime minister held a position of tremendous power and was usually a close relative of the ruler. There was a governing council and, in theory, the rulers of the other cities of the triple alliance also had a say in government; but in reality most power was in the hands of the Aztec ruler and his chief advisor.

Over the course of a century of Aztec expansion a social and political transformation had taken place. The position and nature of the old calpulli clans had changed radically, and a newly powerful nobility with a deified and virtually absolute ruler had emerged. Under the sponsorship of the prime minister, Tlacaelel, the ancient cult of military virtues had been elevated to a supreme position as the religion of the state, and the double purpose of securing increasing tribute for the state and more victims for Huitzilopochtli combined to drive further Aztec conquests.

The empire was never integrated, and local rulers often stayed in place to act as surrogates and tribute collectors for the Aztec overlords. In many ways the Aztec Empire was simply an expansion of long-existing Mesoamerican concepts and institutions of government, and was not unlike the subject city-states over which it gained control. These city-states, in turn, were often left relatively unchanged, provided they recognized Aztec supremacy and met their obligations of labor and tribute. Tribute payments served both an economic and a political function, concentrating power and wealth in the Aztec capital. Archeologists at the recent excavations of the Great Temple beneath the center of Mexico City have been impressed by the large number of offerings and objects that came from the farthest ends of the empire and beyond. At the frontiers, neighboring states, such as Michoacan, preserved their freedom; while within the empire, independent kingdoms, such as Tlaxcala, maintained a fierce opposition to the Aztecs. There were many revolts against Aztec rule or a particular tribute burden, which the Aztecs often put down ruthlessly.

In general, the Aztec system was a success because it aimed at exerting political domination and not necessarily direct administrative or territorial control. In the long run, however, the increasing social stresses created by the rise of the pipiltin and the system of terror and tribute imposed over subject peoples were internal weaknesses that ultimately contributed to the Aztec Empire's collapse.

The Aztecs, then, represented a continuation of the long process of civilization in Mesoamerica. The civilizations of the classic era did not simply disappear in central Mexico or among the Maya in Yucatan and Central America, but they were reinterpreted and adapted to new political and social realities. When Europeans arrived in Mexico, they assumed that what they found was the culmination of Indian civilization, when, in fact, it was the militarized afterglow of earlier achievements.

ANALYSIS
THE "TROUBLING" CIVILIZATIONS OF THE AMERICAS

From the first encounter with the peoples of the Americas, European concepts and judgments about civilization, barbarism, morality, power, politics, and justice were constantly called into question. The American Indian societies had a number of religious ideas and practices that shocked Christian observers, and there were aspects of their social and familial arrangements that also clashed with European sensibilities. Those sensibilities were often influenced by religious and political considerations. Many of those who most condemned human sacrifice, polygamy, or the despotism of Indian rulers were also those who sought to justify European conquest and control. In contrast, not long after the Spanish conquests in the 16th century, defenders of Indian rights came forward to argue that despite certain "unfortunate" habits, Indian civilization was no less to be admired than that of the ancient (and pagan) Romans and Greeks. Not only conquest and power were involved in the ways Europeans viewed and used Indian cultures. Occasionally, European thinkers, such as the French writer Michel de Montaigne in his essay "On Cannibals" (1580), might ironically contrast Indian cultures with European society in order to point out the deficiencies of Europe. By the 18th and 19th centuries, aristocratic whites in Mexico, Brazil, and Peru extolled the glories of the Indian past as a way of criticizing the colonial present. For them, Indian civilization became a justification and metaphor for American liberty.

For Western civilization, evaluating and judging non-Western or past societies has always been a complex business which has mixed elements of morality, politics, religion, and self-perception along with the record of what is observed or considered to be "reality." That complexity is probably just as true for Chinese, Persian, or any culture trying to understand the "other." Still, Western society seems to have been particularly troubled by the American civilizations with their peculiar combination of neolithic technology and imperial organization. At times this has led to abhorrence and rejection—as in the case of Aztec sacrifice—but at other times, it has led to a kind of utopian romanticism in which the accomplishments of the Indian past are used as a critique of the present and a political program for the future.

The existence of "Inca socialism" is a case in point. While some early Spanish authors portrayed Inca rule as despotic, others saw it as a kind of utopia. Shortly after the conquest of Peru, Garcilaso de la Vega, the son of a Spaniard and Indian noblewoman, wrote a glowing history of his mother's people in which he presented an image of the Inca Empire as a carefully organized system in which every community collectively contributed to the whole and the state regulated the distribution of resources on a basis of need and reciprocity. In the 20th century, Peruvian socialists, faced with the problems of underdevelopment and social inequality in their country, used this view of Inca society as a possible model for their own future. Their interpretation and that of historians who later wrote of Inca "socialism" tended to ignore the high degree of hierarchy in the Inca Empire and the fact that the state extracted labor and goods from the subject communities to support the nobles who held extensive power. The utopian view of the Incas was no less political than the despotic view. Perhaps the lesson here is that what we see in the past often depends on what we think about the present or what we want for the future.

But if Inca socialism or despotism was a matter that has fascinated students of the past, Aztec religion has caught the imagination of historians and of the general public. It causes us to ask how a civilization as advanced and accomplished as this could engage in a practice so cruel and, to us, so morally reprehensible. Perhaps nothing challenges our appreciation of the American civilizations more than the extensive evidence of ritual torture and human sacrifice,

which among the Aztecs reached staggering proportions—on some occasions thousands of people were slain, usually by having their hearts ripped out.

First, we must put these practices in some perspective. Cruelty and violence can be found in many cultures and to a world that has witnessed genocide, mass killings, and atomic warfare, the Aztec practices do not stand in such marked contrast to what our own age has witnessed. Certain customs in many past civilizations and in present cultures seem to us strange, cruel, and immoral. We find Aztec human sacrifice particularly abhorrent, but we should be aware that such practices were found among the ancient Canaanites and the Celtic peoples and that the story of Abraham and Isaac in the Old Testament, while its message is against such sacrifice, reflects what was a known practice. Human sacrifice was practiced in pre-Christian Scandinavia and in ancient India. Although by the time of Confucius, human sacrifice of wives and retainers at the burial of a ruler was no longer practiced in China, the custom had been known and the issue of *suttee*, the Hindu ritual suicide of the widow on the funeral pyre of her husband, raged in India in the 20th century. The Aztecs were certainly not alone in the taking of human life as a religious rite. Whatever our moral judgments about such customs, it remains the historian's responsibility to understand them in the context of their own culture and time.

How have historians tried to explain or understand the extent of Aztec human sacrifice? Some defenders of Aztec culture have seen it as a limited phenomenon, greatly exaggerated by the Spanish for political purposes. Many scholars have seen it as essentially a religious act central to their belief that humans must sacrifice that which was most precious to them, life, in order to receive in return the sun, rain, and other blessings of the gods that make life possible. Others have viewed Aztec practice as the intentional manipulation and expansion of a widespread phenomenon that had long existed among many American peoples. In other words, the Aztec rulers, priests, and nobility used the cult of war and large-scale human sacrifice for political purposes, to terrorize their neighbors, and to keep the lower classes subordinate. Another possible explanation is demographic. If central Mexico was as densely populated as we believe, then the sacrifices may have served as a kind of population control.

Other interpretations have been even more startling. Anthropologist Marvin Harris has suggested that Aztec sacrifice, accompanied by ritual cannibalism was, in fact, a response to the lack of available protein. He argued that in the Old World human sacrifice was replaced by animal sacrifice, but in Mesoamerica which lacked cattle and sheep, that transformation never took place. The Aztec Empire was, as Harris called it, a "cannibal kingdom." Other scholars have strongly objected to Harris's interpretation of the evidence. But it is clear that the shadow of human sacrifice shades all assessments of Aztec civilization.

These debates ultimately raise important questions about the role of moral judgments in historical analysis and the way in which our vision of the past is influenced by our own political, moral, ethical, and social programs. In thinking about the past and about societies other than our own, we cannot, and perhaps should not abandon those programs, but we must always try to understand other times and other peoples in their own terms.

Questions: What special features of Aztec civilization have to be explained? Are they really distinctive? What explanations are most persuasive, in terms of historical sensitivity and contemporary standards? Are there features of 20th-century society that are similar to those of Aztec civilization, and that will require explanation for later generations?   ☯

TWANTINSUYU: WORLD OF THE INCAS

Almost at the same time that the Aztecs extended their control over much of Mesoamerica, a great imperial state was rising in the Andean highlands, and it eventually held sway over an empire some 3000 miles in extent. The Inca Empire incorporated many aspects of previous Andean cultures but fused them together in new ways—and with a genius for state organization and bureaucratic control over peoples of different cultures and languages, it achieved a level of integration and domination previously unknown in the Americas.

Throughout the Andean cultural hearth, during the period following the breakup or disintegration of the large "horizon" states of Tihuanaco and Huari (c. A.D. 550–1000), a number of smaller regional states continued to exercise some power. Rather than the breakdown of power that took place in postclassic Mesoamerica, in the Andean zone a number of relatively large states continued to be important. Some states in the Andean highlands on the broad open areas near Lake Titicaca, and those states along rivers on the north coast, such as in the Moche valley, remained centers of agricultural activity and population density. This time in the ultimate development of the Andean imperial state was a period of considerable warring between rival local chiefdoms and small states and in some ways was an Andean parallel to the post-Toltec militaristic era in Mesoamerica. Of these states the coastal kingdom of Chimor, centered on its capital of Chan Chan, emerged as the most powerful. Between 900 and its conquest by the Incas in 1465, it gained control of most of the north coast of Peru.

The great mud-walled city of Chan Chan in northern Peru, capital of the Chimu state, covered an area of six square kilometers. The Chimu Empire dominated the region prior to the rise of the Incas.

THE INCA RISE TO POWER

While Chimor spread its control over 600 miles of the coast, in the southern Andean highlands where there were few large urban areas, ethnic groups and polities struggled over the legacy of Tihuanaco. Among these groups were a number of related Quechua-speaking clans or ayllus living near Cuzco, an area that had been under the influence of Huari but had not been particularly important. Their own legends stated that ten related clans emerged from caves in the region and were taken to Cuzco by a mythical leader. Wherever their origins, by about A.D. 1350 they resided in and around Cuzco and by 1438 they had defeated their hostile neighbors in the area. At this point under their ruler, or *Inca,* Pachacuti (1438-1471), they launched a series of military alliances and campaigns that brought them control of the whole area from Cuzco to the shores of Lake Titicaca.

Over the next 60 years Inca armies were constantly on the march, extending control over a vast territory. Pachacuti's son and successor, Topac Yupanqui (1471-1493) conquered the northern coastal kingdom of Chimor by seizing its irrigation system, and he extended Inca control into the southern area of what is now Ecuador. At the other end of the empire, Inca armies reached the Maule River in Chile against stiff resistance from the Araucanian Indians. The next ruler, Huayna Capac (1493-1527) consolidated these conquests and suppressed a number of rebellions on the frontiers. By the time of his death, the Inca Empire—or as they called it, Twantinsuyu—stretched from what is now Colombia to Chile and eastward across Lake Titicaca and Bolivia to northern Argentina. Between nine and 13 million people of different ethnic backgrounds and languages came under Inca rule, a remarkable feat given the extent of the empire and the technology available for transportation and communication.

CONQUEST AND RELIGION

What impelled the Inca conquest and expansion? The usual desire for economic gain and political power that we have seen in other empires provides one suitable explanation, but there may be others more in keeping with Inca culture and ideology. The cult of the ancestors was extremely important in Inca belief. Deceased rulers were mummified and then treated as intermediaries with the gods, paraded in public during festivals, offered food and gifts, and consulted on important matters by special oracles. From the Chimor kingdom the Incas adopted the practice of royal "split inheritance" in which all the political power and titles of the ruler went to his successor, but all his palaces, wealth, land, and possessions remained in the hands of his male descendants who used them to support the cult of the dead Inca's mummy for eternity. Each new Inca, then, in order to ensure his own cult and place for eternity, needed to secure land and wealth, and these normally came as part of new conquests. In effect, the greater the number of past Inca rulers, the greater the number of royal courts to support and the greater the demand for labor, lands, and tribute. This system created a self-perpetuating need for expansion, tied directly to ancestor worship and the cult of the royal mummies, as well as tensions between the various royal lineages. In a way, the cult of the dead weighed increasingly heavily on the living.

Inca political and social life was infused with religious meaning. Like the Aztecs, the Incas held the sun to be the highest deity and considered the Inca to be the sun's representative on earth. The magnificent Temple of the Sun in Cuzco was the center of the state religion, and in its confines the mummies of the past Incas resided. The cult of the sun was spread throughout the empire, but the Inca did not prohibit the worship of local gods.

Inca Expansion

PACIFIC OCEAN

ANDES MOUNTAINS

Quito
Amazon R.
Marañon R.
Ucayali R.
Cajamarca
Huánuco
Urubamba R.
Pachacamac
Machu Picchu
Cuzco
Apurímac R.
Lake Titicaca
Santiago
Maule R.

Inca Empire

- To 1438
- To 1471
- To 1493
- To 1527

0 — 600 Miles
0 — 600 Kilometers

Other deities were also worshiped as part of the state religion. Viracocha, a creator god, was a favorite of Inca Pachacuti and remained important. Popular belief was based on a profound animism that endowed many natural phenomena with spiritual power. Mountains, stones, rivers, caves, or tombs and temples were considered to be huacas, or holy shrines. At these places, prayers were offered and sacrifices of animals, goods, and humans were made. In the Cuzco area imaginary lines running from the Temple of the Sun organized the huacas into groups for which certain ayllus took responsibility. The temples were served by many priests and women dedicated to the preparation of cloth and food for sacrifice. The temple priests were mainly responsible for the great festivals and celebrations and for divinations upon which state actions often depended.

The role of women in Inca agriculture is emphasized in this 16th-century drawing of the symbolic irrigation of the fields. Complex Inca irrigation systems permitted the farming of steep hillsides and marginal lands.

THE TECHNIQUES OF INCA IMPERIAL RULE

The Inca were able to keep control over their vast empire by using of a number of techniques and practices that assured either cooperation or subordination. The empire was ruled by the Inca who was considered virtually a god. He ruled from his court at Cuzco, which was also the site of the major temple; the high priest was usually a close relative. Twantinsuyu was divided into four great provinces, each under a governor, and then divided again. The Incas developed a state bureaucracy in which almost all the nobility played a role—while some chroniclers spoke of a state organization based on decimal units of 10,000; 1,000; 100; and smaller numbers of households to mobilize taxes and labor, recent research reveals that many local practices and variations were allowed to continue under Inca rule. Local rulers, or curacas, were allowed to maintain their position and were given privileges by the Inca in return for their loyalty. The curacas were exempt from tribute obligations and usually received labor or produce from those under their control. For insurance, the sons of conquered chieftains were taken to Cuzco for their education.

The Incas intentionally spread the Quechua language as a means of integrating the empire. The Incas also made extensive use of *mitmaq*, or colonists. Sometimes Quechua-speakers from Cuzco might be settled in a newly won area to provide an example and a garrison. On other occasions, a restive conquered population was moved to a new home. Throughout the empire, a complex system of roads was constructed with bridges and causeways when needed. Along these roads, way stations, or *tambos*, were placed about a day's walk apart to serve as inns, storehouses, and supply centers for Inca armies on the move. Tambos also served as relay points for the system of runners who carried messages throughout the empire. The Inca probably maintained over 10,000 tambos.

The Inca Empire functioned to extract land and labor from subject populations. Conquered peoples were enlisted in the Inca armies under Inca officers and were rewarded with goods from new conquests. Subject peoples received access to goods not previously available to them, and the Inca state undertook large projects of building and irrigation that formerly would have been impossible. In return the Incas demanded loyalty and tribute. The state claimed all resources and redistributed them. The Incas divided conquered areas into lands for the people, lands for the state, and lands for the sun—that is, for religion and the support of priests. There were also private estates held by some nobles.

With few exceptions the Incas, unlike the Aztecs, did not demand tribute in kind, but rather exacted labor on the lands assigned to the state and the religion. Communities were expected to take turns working on state and church lands and sometimes on building projects or in mining. These labor turns, or *mita*, were an essential aspect of Inca control. In addition, the Inca required women to weave high-quality cloth for the court and for religious purposes. The Incas provided the wool, but each household was required to produce cloth. Woven cloth, a great Andean art form, had political and religious significance. Some women were taken as concubines for the Inca and others were selected as servants at the temples, the so-called "Virgins of the Sun." In all this, the Inca had an overall imperial system, but remained sensitive to local variations so that its application accommodated regional and ethnic differences.

In theory, each community aimed at self-sufficiency and depended on the state for goods difficult to acquire. The ayllus of each community controlled the land, and the vast majority of the male population were peasants and herdsmen. Women aided in the fields, wove cloth, and cared for the household. Roles and obligations were gender specific and theoretically equal and interdependent. Andean peoples recognized parallel descent, so that property rights within the ayllus and among the nobility passed in both the male and female lines. Women passed rights and property to daughters, men to sons. Whether in pre-Inca times women may have served as leaders of ayllus is open to question, but under the Incas this seems to have been uncommon. Inca emphasis on military virtues reinforced the inequality of men and women even though an ideology of complementarity of the sexes was very strong.

The concept of close cooperation of men and women was also reflected in the Inca view of the cosmos. Gods and goddesses were worshiped by men and women but women felt a particular affinity for the moon and the goddesses of the earth and corn, the fertility deities. The Inca queen, the Inca's senior wife (who was usually also a sister of the Inca), was viewed as a link to the moon, queen and sister of the sun; she represented imperial authority to all women. But, despite an ideology of gender equality, Inca practice created a hierarchy of gender relationships that meshed with the dominance of the Inca state over subject peoples. This fact is supported and the power of the empire over local ethnic groups is demonstrated in that the Incas were able to select the most beautiful young women to serve the temples or be given to the Inca.

The integration of imperial policy with regional and ethnic diversity was a political achievement. Ethnic headmen were left in place, but over them were Inca administrators drawn from the Inca nobility in Cuzco. Reciprocity and verticality continued to characterize Andean groups as they came under Inca rule with reciprocity between the state and the local community simply an added level. The Inca state could provide roads, irrigation projects, and hard to get goods. Maize, for example, was usually grown on irrigated land and was particularly important as a ritual crop. State sponsored irrigation added to its cultivation. The Inca state manipulated the idea of reciprocity to extract labor power, and it dealt harshly with resistance and revolt. In addition to the ayllu peasantry there was also a class of people, the *yanas*, who were removed from their ayllus and served permanently as servants, artisans, or workers for the Inca or the Inca nobility.

The Inca nobility was greatly privileged and those related to the Inca himself held the highest positions. The nobility were all drawn from the ten royal ayllus. In addition, the residents of Cuzco were given noble status to enable them to serve in high bureaucratic posts. The nobles were distinguished by dress and custom. Only they were entitled to wear the large ear spools that enlarged the ears and caused the Spaniards to later call them *orejones*, or "big ears." Noticeably absent in most of the Inca Empire was a distinct merchant class. Unlike Mesoamerica where long-distance trade was so important, Inca emphasis on self-sufficiency and state regulation of production and surplus limited trade. Only in the northern areas of the empire, in the chiefdoms of Ecuador, the last region brought under Inca control, did a specialized class of traders exist.

The Inca imperial system which controlled an area almost 3000 miles in extent was a stunning achievement of statecraft, but like all empires it lasted only as long as it could control its subject populations and its own mechanisms of government. A system of royal multiple marriages as a way of forging alliances created rival claimants for power and the possibility of civil war. That is exactly what happened in the 1520s, just before the arrival of the Europeans. When the Spanish first arrived in Peru, they saw an empire weakened and wasted by civil strife.

INCA CULTURAL ACHIEVEMENTS

The Incas drew on the artistic traditions of their Andean predecessors and the skills of subject peoples. Beautiful pottery and cloth was produced in specialized workshops. Inca metallurgy was among the most advanced of the Americas, and Inca artisans worked gold and silver with great technical skill. The Incas also used copper and some bronze for weapons and tools. Like the Mesoamerican peoples, the Incas made no practical use of the wheel, but unlike them, they had no system of writing. The Incas, however, did make use of a system of knotted strings, or *quipu*, with which numerical and perhaps other information could be recorded. It functioned something like an abacus, and with it the Incas took censuses and kept financial records. The Incas had a passion for numerical order, and the population was divided into decimal units from which

population, military enlistment, and work details could be calculated. The existence of so many traits associated with civilization in the Old World and yet the absence of a system of writing among the Incas should make us realize the variation of human development and the dangers of becoming too attached to certain characteristics or cultural features in defining civilizations.

Inca genius was best displayed in their statecraft and in their architecture and public buildings. Inca stonecutting was remarkably accurate and the best buildings were constructed of large fitted stones without the use of masonry. Some of these buildings were immense. These constructions, the large agricultural terraces and irrigation projects, and the extensive system of roads were among the Incas' greatest achievements, displaying their technical ability and workmanship as well as their ability to mobilize large amounts of manpower.

COMPARING THE INCAS AND AZTECS

Both the Inca and the Aztec empires were based on a long development of civilization that preceded them; and while in some areas of artistic and intellectual achievement earlier peoples had surpassed their accomplishments, both represented the success of imperial and military organization. Both empires were based on intensive agriculture organized by a state that accumulated surplus production and then controlled the circulation of goods and their redistribution to groups or social classes. In both states older semikinship-based institutions, the ayllu and the calpulli, were being transformed by the emergence of a social hierarchy in which the nobility was increasingly predominant. In both areas this nobility was also the personnel of the state, so that the state organization was almost an image of society.

While the Incas attempted to create an overarching political state and made conscious attempts to integrate their empire as a unit (the Aztecs did less in this regard), both empires recognized local ethnic groups and political leaders and were willing to allow considerable variation from one group or region to another—that is, provided that Inca or Aztec sovereignty was recognized and tribute paid. Both the Aztecs and the Incas, like the Spaniards who followed them, found that their military power was less effective against nomadic peoples who lived on their frontiers. Essentially, the empires were created by the conquest of sedentary agricultural peoples and the extraction of tribute and labor from them.

We cannot overlook the considerable differences between Mesoamerica and the Andean region in terms of climate and geography nor ignore the differences between the Inca and Aztec civilizations. Trade and markets, for example, were far more developed in the Aztec Empire and earlier in Mesoamerica in general than in the Andean world. There were considerable differences in metallurgy, in writing systems, and in social definition and hierarchy. But within the context of world civilizations, it is probably best to view these two empires and the cultural areas they represent as variations of similar patterns and processes of which sedentary agriculture is the most important. Basic similarities underlying variation can also be seen in systems of belief and cosmology and in social structure. Whether similar origins, direct or indirect contact between the areas, or parallel development in Mesoamerica and the Andean area explains the similarity remains to be explored. But the American Indian civilizations shared much with each other, and that factor plus their relative isolation from external cultural and biological influences gave them their peculiar character and ultimately their vulnerability. At the same time, their ability to survive the shock of conquest and to contribute to the formation of societies after conquest demonstrates much of their strength and resiliency. Long after the Aztec and Inca empires had ceased to exist, the peoples of the Andes and Mexico continue to draw on these cultural traditions.

THE OTHER INDIANS

The civilizations of Mesoamerica and the Andes and the imperial states in place at the moment of contact with the wider world were high points of an Indian cultural achievement cut short by subsequent contact and conquest. The Americas, however, continued to be occupied by a wide variety of peoples who lived in different ways, ranging from the highly complex sedentary agricultural empires to simple kin-based bands of hunters and gatherers. Before ending, we can review that variety of lifeways.

Rather than a division between "primitive" and "civilized" Indians, it is more useful to consider series of gradations according to material culture and social complexity that also recognize similarities. Groups like the Incas had many things in common with the tribal peoples of the Amazon basin, such as the division into clans or into *halves*—that is, a division of villages or communities into two major groupings with mutually agreed upon roles and obligations. Moreover, as we have seen, the diversity of ancient America forces a reconsideration of ideas of human development based on Old World examples. If social complexity is supposedly dependent on an agricultural base for society, in the Americas some groups of fishermen and hunters and gatherers, such as the Indians of the northwest coast of the United States and British Columbia, developed hierarchical societies. For those who see control of water

for agriculture as the starting point for political authority and the state, there are examples such as the Pimas of Colorado and some of the chiefdoms of South America, who practiced irrigated agriculture but did not develop states.

HOW MANY INDIANS?

One of the major questions that has fascinated students of the Americas for centuries is the question of population size. For many years after the European conquests many people discounted the early descriptions of large and dense Indian populations as the exaggeration of the conquerors and missionaries who wished to make their own exploits seem more impressive. In the early 20th century, the most repeated estimate of Indian population around 1492 was 8.4 million (4 million in Mexico, 2 million in Peru, and 2.4 million in the rest of the hemisphere). Since that time, new archeological discoveries, a better understanding of the impact of disease on indigenous populations, new historical and demographic studies, and improved estimates of agricultural techniques and productivity have led to major revisions. Estimates still vary widely, and some have gone as high as 112 million at the time of contact. Despite disagreements, most scholars agree that Mesoamerica and the Andes supported the largest populations. Table 17.1 summarizes one of the most careful estimates, which places the total figure at over 57 million, although an American Indian demographer has adjusted this figure upward to 72 million.

TABLE 17.1

A Population Estimate for the Western Hemisphere, 1492

Area	Population in thousands
North America	4,400
Mexico	21,400
Central America	5,650
Caribbean	5,850
Andes	11,500
Lowland South America	8,500
Total	57,300

Sources: William M. Deneven, *The Native Population of the Americas in 1492* (1976), 289–292; John D. Durand, "Historical Estimates of World Population," *Population and Development Review*, 3 (1957), 253–296; Russell Thornton, *American Indian Holocaust and Survival* (1987).

TABLE 17.2

World Population c. 1500

Area	Population in thousands
China	100,000–150,000
Indian subcontinent	75,000–150,000
Southwestern Asia	20,000–30,000
Japan	15,000–20,000
Rest of Asia (except Russia)	15,000–30,000
Europe (except Russia)	60,000–70,000
Russia (USSR)	10,000–18,000
Northern Africa	6,000–12,000
Remainder of Africa	30,000–60,000
Oceania	1,000–2,000
Americas	57,000–72,000
Total	389,000–614,000

Sources: William M. Deneven, *The Native Population of the Americas in 1492* (1976), 289–292; John D. Durand, "Historical Estimates of World Population," *Population and Development Review*, 3 (1957), 253–296; Russell Thornton, *American Indian Holocaust and Survival* (1987).

These figures should be set in a global context. Around 1500 the population of the rest of the world was probably about 500 million, of which China and India each had 75–100 million people and Europe had 60–70 million, a figure roughly equivalent to the Americas. The peoples of the Americas clearly made up a major segment of humanity.

DIFFERING CULTURAL PATTERNS

While it is impossible to summarize the variety of cultural patterns and lifeways that existed in the Americas on the eve of contact, we can mention the major patterns outside the main civilizational areas. In Chapter 9 we noted that the area of northern South America and part of Central America was an intermediate area, which shared many features with the Andes and some with Mesoamerica and perhaps served at times as a point of cultural and material exchange between the two regions. In the mountain valleys of central Colombia large chiefdoms of the Muisca and Tairona peoples, based on sedentary agriculture, mobilized large numbers of peasant agriculturalists for building projects and extracted surpluses from them. Warfare seems to have been endemic in these societies and there was a strong religious cult associated with political authority. In fact, with the exception of monumental architecture, the in-

termediate-zone chieftainships resemble the sedentary agriculture states in many ways.

Similar kinds of chieftainships based on sedentary agriculture were found elsewhere in the Americas. There is strong evidence of large and populous chieftainships along the Amazon, where the rich aquatic environment supported complex and perhaps hierarchical societies. The island Arawaks that Columbus first encountered in the Caribbean on the island of Hispaniola were agriculturalists organized in a hierarchical society and divided into a number of chiefdoms. These Indian chiefdom-level societies bear a strong resemblance to the societies of Polynesia. On the bigger Caribbean islands, such as Hispaniola and Puerto Rico, chieftainships ruled over dense populations that lived primarily from the production of manioc.

Agriculture was widely diffused throughout the Americas by 1500. Some peoples, like those of the eastern North American woodlands and the coast of Brazil, combined agriculture with hunting and fishing. Techniques such as slash-and-burn farming led to the periodic movement of villages when production declined. Social organization in these societies often remained without strong class divisions, craft specializations, or the demographic density of people who practiced permanent, intensive agriculture. Unlike Europe, Asia, and Africa, nomadic herdsmen were lacking in the Americas. However, throughout the Americas from Tierra del Fuego to the Canadian forests remained peoples who lived in small, mobile, kin-based groups of hunters and gatherers. Their material culture was simple and their societies were more egalitarian.

Nowhere is the problem of American Indian diversity more apparent than in North America. In that vast continent perhaps as many as 200 languages were spoken by 1500, and a variety of cultures reflected Indian adaption to different ecological situations. By that time, the concentrated towns of the Mississipian Mound Builder cultures had mostly been abandoned and only a few groups in southeastern North America still maintained the social hierarchy and religious ideas of those earlier cultures. In the Southwest, the descendants of the Anasazi and other cliff dwellers had taken up residence in the adobe pueblos along the Rio Grande, where they practiced various forms of terracing and irrigation to support their agriculture. Their rich religious life, their artistic ceramic and weaving traditions, and their agricultural base reflected their own historical traditions.

Elsewhere in North America most groups were hunters and gatherers or combined those activities with some agriculture. Sometimes an environment was so rich that complex social organization and artistic specialization could develop without an agricultural base. This was the case among the Indians of the northwest coast, who depended on the rich resources of the sea. In other cases, technology was a limiting factor. The tough grasses of the prairies could not be easily farmed without the use of metal plows, nor could the buffalo be effectively hunted prior to the European introduction of the horse. Thus, the Great Plains were only sparsely occupied.

Finally, we should note that while there was great variation among the Indian cultures, some aspects stood in marked contrast to contemporary societies in Europe and Asia. With the exception of the state systems of Mesoamerica and the Andes, most Indian societies were strongly kin-based. Communal action and ownership of resources, such as land or hunting grounds, was emphasized, and material wealth was often disregarded or placed in a ritual or religious context. It was not that these societies were necessarily egalitarian, but rather that ranking was usually not based on wealth. Women, although often subordinate, in some societies held important political and social roles and usually played a central role in crop production. Indians tended to view themselves as part of the ecological system and not in control of it. These attitudes stood in marked contrast to those of the contemporary Eurasian civilizations.

CONCLUSION

AMERICAN INDIAN DIVERSITY IN WORLD CONTEXT

By the end of the 15th century, two great imperial systems had risen to dominate the two major centers of civilization in Mesoamerica and the Andes. Both of these empires were built on the achievements of their predecessors, and both reflected a militaristic phase in their area's development. These empires proved to be fragile—weakened by their own internal strains and the conflicts that any imperial system creates, but also limited by their technological inferiority when challenged by Eurasian civilization.

The Aztec and Inca empires were one end of a continuum of cultures that went from the most simple to the most complex. The Americas contained a broad range of societies, from great civilizations with millions of people to small bands of hunters. In many of these societies religion played a dominant role in defining the relationship between people and their environment and between the individual and society. How these societies would have developed and

what course the American civilizations might have taken in continued isolation remains an interesting and unanswerable question. The first European observers were simultaneously shocked by the "primitive" tribesmen and astounded by the wealth and accomplishments of civilizations like that of the Aztecs. Europeans generally saw the Indians as curiously anachronistic. In comparison with Europe and Asia, the Americas did seem strange—more like ancient Babylon or Egypt than contemporary China or Europe—except that without the wheel, large domesticated animals, the plow, and to a large extent metal tools and written languages, even that comparison is misleading. The relative isolation of the Americas had remained important in physical and cultural terms, but that isolation came to an end in 1492—often with disastrous results.

FURTHER READINGS

Alvin M. Josephy, Jr.'s *The Indian Heritage of America* (1968) is a broad, comprehensive history that deals with North and South America and provides much detail without being tedious. It is a logical starting point for further study. Frederich Katz's *The Ancient Civilizations of the Americas* (1972) is now somewhat out of date, but it still provides the best overall survey that compares Mesoamerica and Peru. It traces the rise of civilization in both areas.

The literature on the Aztecs is growing rapidly. Sahagún's *Florentine Codex: The General History of the Things of New Spain*, Charles Dibble and Arthur J. O. Anderson, eds. and trans., 11 vols. (1950–1968) is a fundamental source. A good overview is Jacques Soustelle's *Daily Life of the Aztecs* (1961), but more recent is Frances Berdan's *The Aztecs of Central Mexico: An Imperial Society* (1982). Miguel Leon-Portilla's *Aztec Thought and Culture* (1963) deals with religion and philosophy in a sympathetic way. Burr Cartwright Brundage has traced the history of the Aztec rise in a number of books such as *A Rain of Darts* (1972); his *The Jade Steps* (1985) provides a good analysis of religion. Nigel Davies's *The Aztec Empire* (1987) is a political and social analysis. Susan D. Gillespie's *The Aztec Kings* (1989) views Aztec history in terms of myth.

On Peru, a good overview through solid scholarly articles is provided in Richard W. Keatinge, ed., *Peruvian Prehistory* (1988). The article on Inca archeology by Craig Morris is especially useful. Alfred Metraux's *The History of the Incas* (1970) is an older, but still useful and very readable book. John Murra's *The Economic Organization of* the Inca State (1980) is a classic that has influenced much thinking about the Incas. J. Hyslop's *The Inka Road System* (1984) examines the building and function of the road network. The series of essays in John V. Murra, Nathan Wachtel, and Jacques Revel, eds., *Anthropological History of Andean Polities* (1986) shows how new approaches in ethnohistory are deepening our understanding of Inca society. Interesting social history is now being done. Irene Silverblatt's *Moon, Sun, and Witches: Gender Ideologies and Class in Inca and Colonial Peru* (1987) is a controversial

book on the position of women before, during, and after the Inca rise to power.

From a comparative perspective is Geoffrey W. Conrad and Arthur A. Demerest's *Religion and Empire: The Dynamics of Aztec and Inca Expansionism* (1984). These two archeologists compare the political systems of the two empires and the motivations for expansion. The authors find more similarities than differences. Excellent studies on specific themes on Mexico and Peru are found in George A. Collier, ed. et. al., *The Inca and Aztec States, 1400–1800* (1982).

220–589 Era of the Six Dynasties; political division in China; time of great Buddhist influence

618–907 Tang dynasty

690–705 Empress Wu; Buddhist influence in China peaks

220 End of the Han dynasty

589–618 Sui dynasty; building of the Grand Canal

618–626 Gaozu emperor   **668** Korean conquest; vassal state of Silla

627–649 Tang Taizong emperor   **712–756** Xuanzong emperor

840s Period of Buddhist persecution

Reunification and Renaissance in Chinese Civilization: The Eras of the Tang and Song Dynasties

INTRODUCTION. The postclassical period saw a vital consolidation of basic themes in Chinese civilization, where the ability to innovate on the basis of tradition was unparalleled. Less fundamental innovation occurred in China than in civilization areas such as the Americas or the two parts of Europe. Yet Chinese civilization contributed important new developments, some of which, notably in technology, soon affected the wider world network. Attention to postclassical China obviously returns to the core civilization areas of Asia and to the network of relationships that developed among societies in Asia and around the Mediterranean. Chinese achievements— for example, the size of cities—are best compared with the Middle East or India. China also formed its own wider orbit in eastern Asia. Relatively isolated compared to the Islamic world and India, China nevertheless contributed vitally to a number of other areas as it flourished under two vigorous dynasties.

In the era of political division and civil strife after the breakdown of the Han dynasty in the last decades of the 2d century A.D., most of the advances of the Qin-Han era (221 B.C. to A.D. 220) appeared to have been lost. Writers in the "period of the Six Dynasties" (A.D. 220–589) feared that the very basis for maintaining civilization in China had been swept away by a new wave of nomadic invasions and the seemingly endless wars fought by the patchwork of regional kingdoms that vied with each other to claim the imperial throne of the fallen Han. The bureaucratic apparatus of the empire collapsed, though many of the successor states aspired to the Qin-Han ideal of state centralization. In most kingdoms the position of the scholar-gentry declined sharply, as landed families with aristocratic pretensions dominated regional rulers. The reemergence of bickering and self-serving aristocratic elites could not help but remind the scholars who recorded China's history of the chaos and suffering of the Warring

960–1279 Song dynasty; Neo-Confucian revival

907 End of the Tang dynasty

1127–1279 Southern Song dynasty

1067–1085 Shenzong emperor; reforms of Wang Anshi

c. 1050 Invention of block printing

c. 1100 Invention of gunpowder

1119 First reference to the use of the compass for sea navigation

1115 Jurchen (Qin) kingdom in North China

1279–1368 Mongol (Yuan) dynasty rules all China

A.D. 950

A.D. 1100

A.D. 1250

States period before the rise of the Qin. In the centuries after the fall of the Han, non-Chinese nomads ruled much of China, and a foreign religion, Buddhism, eclipsed Confucian teachings as the prime force in Chinese political and cultural life. The Great Wall was divided between kingdoms and usually poorly defended as nomadic peoples raided and conquered across the north China plain. Trade and city life declined; technology stagnated; and, with mainly Buddhist exceptions, thought degenerated into the quest for magical cures and the elixir of immortality.

Given the magnitude of these reverses and the fact that Chinese civilization was battered and dislocated for nearly four centuries, its revival at the very end of the 6th century A.D. appears at first glance abrupt and incomprehensible. But the reestablishment of a centralized empire under the short-lived Sui dynasty and the restoration and growth of Chinese civilization during the 300-year Tang reign (A.D. 618–907) that followed demonstrated convincingly the great strength of the patterns of civilized life that had coalesced in the Qin-Han era. The rapid revival of empire and civilization under the Tang was also made possible by the preservation, in the kingdoms that carved up the Han Empire, of the Confucian institutions and ideas that had been so central to the development of civilization in China. Not only did the rulers of these kingdoms aspire to reunify China—an ideal that was a key ingredient of civilization as it had come to be understood in China—but the destruction and human suffering of the Six Dynasties era led to an intense longing at all social levels for a return to imperial order.

The victories of the two Sui emperors laid the basis for political unity that would be fully exploited by the early Tang rulers. Under the Tang, the Chinese imperial regime was again able to extend its control over the nomadic peoples who lived on the fringes of the empire as well as over the quarrelsome nobles who competed for political power. The first sections of this chapter will trace the rise of Sui-Tang rule and focus on the process of bureaucratic reconstruction that these dynasties undertook to solidify their power. The next sections will cover the major changes in Chinese economic and social life that occurred in the Tang era, with emphasis on the monumental shifts in the center of population, production, and trade from the north China plain to the Yangtze valley and coastal areas to the south. With political unification and the rapid expansion of the agricultural and commercial sectors came a renaissance in the arts, scholarship, and invention. These developments, with an emphasis on the often creative tensions between Chinese Buddhism and a revived Confucianism, will be discussed in the final sections on the Tang.

In a very real sense, particularly in thought and the arts, the revival begun in the Tang was continued and in some ways brought to full fruition under the Song dynasty (960–1279), which came to power after Tang authority collapsed in the first decades of the 10th century. The Song Empire never attained the size of the Tang, and Song political control at home was not as effectively exercised. But the Song era saw the full restoration of the scholar-gentry and the Confucian order. It was also perhaps the most glorious age of Chinese artistic and literary production, as well as a period of technological innovation that has few parallels in all human history. These latter accomplishments will be the focus of the section on the Song, which will end with a discussion of the underlying political failings of the dynasty. These shortcomings left China open to new nomadic incursions and, finally, to the conquest in 1279 of what was left of the Song Empire by the Mongols. As we shall see in Chapter 20, however, the high level of civilization China had attained in the Tang and Song eras limited the level of disruption caused by the new conquests. It also rendered the Mongols, the most powerful nomadic invaders the Chinese had ever seen, quite willing to adopt key elements in Chinese culture and lifestyles.

REBUILDING THE IMPERIAL EDIFICE IN THE SUI-TANG ERA

The initial steps of the rise of the Sui dynasty in the early 580s looked at first to be just another factional struggle of the sort that had occurred repeatedly in the splinter states fighting for control of China in the centuries after the fall of the Han. Wendi, a member of a prominent north Chinese noble family that had long been active in these contests, struck a marriage alliance between his daughter and the ruler of the northern Zhou empire, who had only recently defeated several rival rulers and united much of the north China plain. After considerable intrigue, Wendi seized the throne of his son-in-law and proclaimed himself emperor. Though Wendi claimed to be an ethnic Chinese and his son-in-law was from nomadic origins, the nomadic peoples who had long dominated the thrones of north China rallied to the usurper. In part, their support reflected the degree to which the nomadic warrior elite, who made up only a small minority of the population of the north China kingdoms, had been assimilated into the culture of the Chinese majority. In addition, Wendi went out of his way to win over the nomadic military commanders by reconfirming their titles and showing little inclination to favor the Confucian scholar-gentry class

China during the Periods of the Six Dynasties, the Sui Dynasty, and the Tang Dynasty

at their expense. With the support of many of these nomadic commanders, Wendi completed the extension of the empire across north China and in 589 attacked and conquered the weak and divided Chen kingdom, which had long ruled much of the south. With his victory over the Chen, Wendi reunited the traditional core areas of Chinese civilization for the first time in three and a half centuries.

Wendi won widespread popular support by lowering taxes and establishing *ever-ready granaries* throughout his domains. These bins for storing grain were established in all the large cities and in each village of the empire to ensure that there would be a reserve food supply in case floods or drought destroyed the peasants' crops and threatened the people with famine. Large landholders and poor peasants alike were taxed a portion of their crop to ensure that the granaries were filled for times of crisis. Beyond warding off famine, the surplus grain was dumped on the market in times of food shortages to hold down the price of the peoples' staple food. The experience of previous Chinese dynasties had revealed that food shortages and sharp price increases were major sources of social unrest, including riots and rebellions that could end in widespread movements to overthrow the government.

SUI EXCESSES AND COLLAPSE

The foundations Wendi laid for political unification and economic prosperity were at first strengthened even further by his son Yangdi, who murdered his father to reach the throne. Yangdi extended his father's conquests and drove back nomadic intruders who threatened the northern frontiers of the empire. He promulgated a new and milder legal code and devoted considerable resources to upgrading Confucian education and restoring the examination system for regulating entry into the bureaucracy. These latter measures were part of a broader policy of promoting the scholar-gentry in the imperial administration, often to the detriment of the great aristocratic families and nomadic military commanders.

Yangdi was overly fond of luxury and delighted in construction projects that reached megalomaniacal proportions. He forcibly conscripted hundreds of thousands of peasants to build numerous palaces, a new capital city at Loyang, and above all a series of great canals to link the various parts of his empire. His demands on the people seemed limitless. In his new capital at Loyang, for example, Yangdi had a vast, heavily forested game park laid out. Because there were not enough trees on the site chosen, tens of thousands of laborers were forced to dig up huge trees in the nearby hills and cart them miles to be replanted in the artificial mounds that tens of thousands of other laborers had built.

Even before work on his many construction projects had been completed, Yangdi led his exhausted and angry subjects into a series of unsuccessful wars to bring Korea again under Chinese rule. His failures in the Korean campaigns between 611 and 614 and the near-fatal reverse he suffered in central Asia at the hands of Turkic nomads in 615 set in motion widespread revolts throughout the empire. Provincial governors declared themselves independent rulers;

bandit gangs roved and raided at will; and nomadic peoples again established control over large sections of the north China plain. Faced with a crumbling empire, an increasingly deranged emperor retreated to his pleasure palaces in the city of Yangzhou on the Yangtze River to the south. When he was assassinated by his own ministers in 618, it looked very much as if China would return to the state of political division and social turmoil it had endured in the preceding centuries.

THE EMERGENCE OF THE TANG AND THE RESTORATION OF THE EMPIRE

The dissolution of the imperial order was averted by the military skills and political savvy of one of Yangdi's most illustrious officials, Li Yuan, the Duke of Tang. Of noble and mixed Chinese-nomadic origins, Li Yuan was for many years a loyal supporter of the Sui ruler. In fact, on one occasion, Li Yuan had rescued the impetuous Yangdi, whose forces had been trapped by a far larger force of Turkish cavalry in a small fort that was part of the Great Wall defenses. But as Yangdi grew more and more irrational and unrest spread from one end of the empire to another, Li Yuan was convinced by his sons and allies that only rebellion could save his family and the empire. From the many-sided struggle for the throne that followed Yangdi's death and continued until 623, Li Yuan emerged the victor. In 618, after major military successes in north China, he took the imperial name, Gaozu, and founded the Tang dynasty that would rule China for nearly three centuries.

Together with his second son Tang Taizong, in whose favor he abdicated in 626, Gaozu laid the basis for the golden age of the Tang. Tang armies conquered deep into central Asia as far as present-day Afghanistan, thereby forcing many of the nomadic peoples who had dominated China in the Six Dynasties era to submit to Tang overlordship. Of all the nomadic peoples on the empire's borders, the Turkic tribes posed the greatest threat. Therefore, the early Tang rulers sought to play one Turkic people off another, a stratagem that very often succeeded. They also completed the repairs begun by the Sui and earlier dynasties on the Great Wall and created frontier armies, partly recruited from the nomadic peoples, that gradually became the most potent military forces in the empire. Leaders of Turkic tribes were compelled to submit as vassals to the Tang rulers, who took the title of "heavenly khan." The daughters of the Turkic khans were often married into the imperial family. The sons were sent to the capital both as hostages to guarantee the good behavior of the tribe in

question and as students who were to be educated in Chinese ways in the hope of their eventual assimilation into Chinese culture.

The empire was also extended to parts of Tibet in the west, the Red River valley homeland of the Vietnamese in the south, and Manchuria in the north. In the Tang period, the Yangtze River basin and much of the south were fully integrated with North China for the first time since the Han. In 668, under the emperor Kaozong, Korea, whose peoples' resistance had done so much to bring down the Sui dynasty, was overrun by Chinese armies, and a vassal kingdom called Silla was established that long remained loyal to the Tang. In a matter of decades the Tang had built an empire that was far larger than even that of the early Han, an empire whose boundaries in many directions extended beyond the borders of China today.

REBUILDING THE BUREAUCRACY

Crucial for the restoration of Chinese unity were efforts undertaken by the early Tang monarchs to rebuild and expand the imperial bureaucracy. A revived scholar-gentry elite and reworked Confucian ideology played central roles in this process. From the time of the second Sui emperor, Yangdi, the fortunes of the scholar-gentry had begun to improve markedly. This trend continued under the early Tang emperors, who desperately needed loyal and well-educated officials to govern the vast empire they had put together in a matter of decades. The Tang rulers also used the scholar-gentry bureaucrats to offset the power of the aristocracy.

As the control of the aristocratic families over court life and administration declined, their role in Chinese history was much reduced. From the Tang era onward, political power in China was shared by a succession of imperial families and the bureaucrats of the civil service system. Members of the hereditary aristocracy continued to occupy administrative positions, but the scholar-gentry class came to staff most of the posts in the secretariats and executive department that oversaw a huge bureaucracy. This bureaucracy reached from the imperial palace down to the *subprefecture*, or district level, which was roughly equivalent to an American county. One secretariat drafted imperial decrees; a second monitored the reports of regional and provincial officials and the petitions of local notables. The executive department, which was divided into six ministries—including war, justice, and public works—ran the empire on a day-to-day basis. In addition, there was a powerful Bureau of Censors, whose chief task was to keep track of officials at all levels and report their misdeeds or failures to perform their duties. Finally, there was a very large staff to run the imperial household, both the palaces in the capital at Changan and the subsidiary residences of the princes of the imperial line and other dignitaries.

THE GROWING IMPORTANCE OF THE EXAMINATION SYSTEM

Like Yangdi, the Tang emperors patronized academies to train state officials and educate them in the Confucian classics. In the Tang era and under the Song dynasty that followed, the numbers of the educated scholar-gentry rose far above those in the Han era, though this elite and its dependents remained only a tiny fraction of the total Chinese population. In the Tang and Song periods, the examination system was also greatly enlarged, and the pattern of advancement in the civil service was much more regularized. Several different kinds of examinations were administered by the Ministry of Rites to students from the government schools or those recommended by distinguished scholars. Specialized exams in law, calligraphy, or mathematics could earn the successful candidate only a lower-level position in the Tang bureaucracy.

The highest offices could be gained only by those who were able to pass exams on the classics or the even more difficult exams on Chinese literature. Those who passed the latter earned the title of *jinshi*. Their names were announced throughout the empire; their families' positions were secured by the prospect of high office that was opened up by their success; and they became overnight dignitaries,

whom even their former student friends addressed formally and treated with deference. A further round of written and oral examinations determined the jinshi holder's ranking in the pool of civil servants who were eligible for the highest positions in the imperial administration, and thus the office he actually received. Success in exams at all levels won the candidate special social status, which included the right to wear certain types of clothing, freedom from corporal punishment, and the power to demand services and outward signs of respect, such as bowing, from the common people.

Even though a much higher proportion of Tang bureaucrats won their positions through success in civil service examinations than had been the case in the Han era, birth and family connections continued to be important in securing high office. Established bureaucrats not only saw that their sons and cousins got into the imperial academies, they could pull strings to see that even failed candidates from their families received government posts. Ethnic and regional ties also played a role in the staffing of bureaucratic departments. This meant that though bright commoners could rise to upper level positions in the bureaucracy, the central administration was dominated by a rather small number of established families. Sons followed fathers in positions of power and influence, and prominent households bought a disproportionate share of the places available in the imperial academies. Many positions were reserved for members of the old aristocracy and the low-ranking sons and grandsons of lesser wives and concubines belonging to the imperial family. Merit and ambition counted for something, but birth and family influence often counted for a good deal more.

DOCUMENT
TIES THAT BIND; PATHS TO POWER

The following letter was included in a short story by the Tang author Niu Su. It was sent by a local functionary named Wu Bao to a high official to whom Wu hoped to attach himself and thus win advancement in the imperial bureaucracy. What can this letter tell us about the ways in which the Chinese bureaucracy worked in the Tang and Song eras?

To my great good fortune, we share the same native place, and your renown for wise counsel is well known to me. Although, through gross neglect, I have omitted to prostrate myself before you, my heart has always been filled with admiration and re-

spect. You are the nephew of the Prime Minister, and have made use of your outstanding talents in his service. In consequence of this, your high ability has been rewarded with a commission. General Li is highly-qualified both as a civil and a military official, and he has been put in full command of the expedition [to put down "barbarian" rebellions in the southern parts of the empire]. In his hands he unites mighty forces, and he cannot fail to bring these petty brigands to order. By the alliance of the General's heroic valor and your own talent and ability, your armies' task of subjugation will be the work of a day. I, in my youth, devoted myself to study.

Reaching manhood, I paid close attention to the [Confucian] classics. But in talent I do not compare with other men, and so far I have held office only as an officer of the guard. I languish in this out-of-the-way corner beyond the Chien [mountains], close to the haunts of the barbarians. My native place is thousands of miles away, and many passes and rivers lie between. What is more, my term of office here is completed, and I cannot tell when I shall receive my next appointment. So lacking in talent, I fear I am but poorly fitted to be selected for an official post; far less can I entertain the hope of some meager salary. I can only retire, when old age comes, to some rustic retreat, and "turn aside to die in a ditch." I have heard by devious ways of your readiness to help those in distress. If you will not overlook a man from your native place, be quick to bestow your spe-cial favour on me, so that I may render you service "as a humble groom." Grant me some small salary, and a share however slight in your deeds of merit. If by your boundless favour I could take part in this triumphal progress, even as a member of the rear-most company, the day would live engraved on my memory.

Questions: What techniques does Wu employ to win the high official's favor? How does Wu expect the official to help him? What does he promise in return? Does birth or merit appear to be more important in his appeals? What does this suggest about the place of the examinations in the political system? What dangers to the imperial system are contained in the sorts of ties that Wu argues bind him to the high official?

THE MANY SCHOOLS CONTEND: STATE AND RELIGION IN THE TANG AND SONG ERAS

The Confucian revival threatened not only the old aristocratic families, whose power diminished as that of the scholar-gentry bureaucrats grew, but also the Buddhists, who had become a major force in Chinese life in the Six Dynasties era. Many of the rulers in the pre-Tang era, particularly the ones from nomadic origins, had been devout Buddhists and strong patrons of the Buddhist establishment. As we have seen, in the centuries after the fall of the Han, Buddhist sects had proliferated in China. The most popular were those founded by Chinese monks, in part because they soon took on distinctively Chinese qualities. Among the masses, the salvationist "pure land" strain of Mahayana Buddhism won widespread conversions as a refuge from an age of war and turmoil. Members of the elite classes, on the other hand, were more attracted to the Chan variant of Buddhism, or Zen as it is known in Japan and the West. With its stress on meditation and the appreciation of natural and artistic beauty and its Daoist hostility to written texts and scholasticism, Zen had great appeal for the educated classes of China. The riddlelike quality of Zen sayings was apparently particularly intriguing to Chinese intellectuals. The following sequence of questions and answers provides a fairly typical example:

The Master asked the monk: "What are you doing?"
The monk answered: "Sweeping the floor."
The Master said: "In front of the Buddha figure or behind it?"
The monk answered: "Both at the same time."
The Master said: "Give your sandals to Ts'ao-shan."

The combination of royal patronage and widespread conversion at both the elite and mass levels had made Buddhism a strong social, economic, and political force by the time of the Tang unification. The early Tang rulers continued to patronize Buddhism while they sought to promote education in the Confucian classics. Emperors like Taizong endowed monasteries, sent emissaries to India to collect texts and relics, and commissioned Buddhist paintings and statuary. On one occasion, Taizong displayed remarkable veneration for Buddhism by personally traveling to welcome home the famed pilgrim-monk Xuanzang, who was returning with Buddhist scriptures collected during 17 years of travel in India. No Tang ruler, however, matched the empress Wu (690–705) in supporting the Buddhist establishment. Not only did she contribute large sums to build or improve monasteries and reward Buddhist cooperation with impressive grants of land, at one point she sought to elevate Buddhism to the status of a state religion. The empress Wu also commissioned numerous Buddhist paintings and sculptures.

At sites such as Lungmen near the Yangtze River and Yunkang far to the north, massive statues of the Buddha were carved out of rocky cliffsides beginning in the 6th century A.D.

The sculptures are particularly noteworthy due to their colossal size. She had statues of the Buddha, which were as much as two and three stories high, carved from stone or cast in bronze. Some of these statues were housed in great caves near her capital at Loyang; for others she had equally huge pagodas built. With this sort of support, it is not surprising that Buddhism flourished in the early centuries of Tang rule. By the middle of the 9th century, there were nearly 50,000 monasteries and hundreds of thousands of Buddhist monks and nuns in China.

THE ANTI-BUDDHIST BACKLASH

Buddhist successes inevitably aroused the envy and enmity of both Confucian and Daoist rivals. Some of these attacked the religion as alien, even though the faith followed by most of the Chinese was very different from that originally preached by the Buddha or that practiced in India. Daoist monks sought to counter Buddhism's appeals to the masses by stressing their own magical and predictive powers, a tendency that led to a continuation of a long-standing Chinese fascination with alchemy and potions for fertility and longevity. Most damaging to the fortunes of Buddhism, however, was the growing campaign of Confucian scholar-administrators to convince the Tang rulers that the large Buddhist monastic establishment posed a fundamental economic challenge to the imperial order. Because monastic lands and resources were not taxed, the Tang regime lost huge amounts of revenue due to imperial grants to Buddhist monasteries or the wills of ordinary Chinese, which turned family properties over to Buddhist monasteries as an act of religious devotion. The state was also denied labor power, because it could neither tax nor conscript peasants who worked monastic estates.

By the mid-8th century, it was clear that the rapidly growing Buddhist monastic orders were a major drain on China's resources and a clear economic competitor of the Tang dynasty. Measures to limit the flow of land and resources to the monastic orders gave way in the 840s to open persecution of Buddhism under the emperor Wuzong (841–847). Thousands of monasteries and Buddhist shrines were destroyed, and hundreds of thousands of monks and nuns were forced to abandon their monastic existence and return to ordinary civilian lives. They and the slaves and peasants who worked their lands were again subject to taxation, and monastery lands were parceled out to taxpaying landlords and peasant smallholders.

Though Chinese Buddhism survived this and other bouts of repression, it did so in a much reduced state. Never again would the Buddhist monastic orders possess the political influence and control the wealth they enjoyed in the first centuries of Tang rule. The great age of Buddhist painting and cave sculptures gave way to art dominated by Daoist-Confucian subjects and styles in the late Tang and the Song dynastic era that followed. The Zen and "pure land" sects of Buddhism continued to attract adherents—those of the latter numbering in the millions. But Confucianism emerged as the central ideology of Chinese civilization for most of the period from the 9th to the early 20th century. Buddhism left its mark on the arts, the Chinese language, and Chinese thinking about things such as heaven, charity, and law, but it ceased to be a dominant influence. Buddhism's fate in China contrasts sharply with its ongoing and pivotal impact on the civilizations of mainland Southeast Asia, Tibet, and parts of central Asia.

Because many of the great Buddhist temples and monasteries in China were destroyed in various waves of persecution, some of the best surviving examples of East Asian Buddhist architecture, such as this monastery at Kyoto, are found in Japan.

 TANG DECLINE AND THE RISE OF THE SONG

The motives behind the mid-9th century Tang assault on the Buddhist monastic order were symptomatic of a general weakening of imperial control that had begun almost a century earlier. Following the decades of controversial but strong rule between 690 and 705 by the empress Wu, who actually sought to establish a new dynasty, a second attempt to control the throne was made by a highborn woman who had married into the imperial family. Backed by her powerful relatives and an extensive clique of prominent courtiers, Empress Wei poisoned her husband, the son of Empress Wu, and placed her own small child on the throne. But Empress Wei's attempt to seize power was thwarted by another prince who led a palace revolt that ended with the destruction of Wei and her supporters. The early decades of the long reign of this prince, who became the emperor Xuanzong (713–756), marked the peak of Tang power and the high point of Chinese civilization under the Tang dynasty.

Initially Xuanzong took a strong interest in political and economic reforms, which were pushed by the very capable officials he was able to appoint to high positions. Increasingly, his interest in running the vast Tang Empire waned, and he devoted himself more and more to patronizing the arts and to the enjoyment of the considerable pleasures available within the confines of the imperial city.

These diversions included music, which he played and also had performed by the numerous musicians he summoned and the thousands of concubines who vied in the imperial apartments for the attention of the monarch. After the death of his second wife, the aged and lonely emperor became infatuated with Yang Guifei, a beautiful young woman from the harem of one of the imperial princes.

Their relationship proved to be one of the most famous and ill-starred romances in all of Chinese history. While Xuanzong promenaded in the imperial gardens and gave flute lessons to Yang, who was raised to the status of royal concubine, she packed the upper levels of the government with her avaricious relatives and assumed an ever greater role in court politics. The arrogance and greed of Yang Guifei and her family angered rival cliques at court who took every opportunity to turn Yang's excesses into a cause for popular unrest. Xuanzong's long neglect of state affairs resulted in economic distress that fed this unrest and in chronic military weaknesses that rendered the government unable to deal with the disorders effectively. The deepening crisis came to a head in 755, when one of the emperor's main military leaders, a general of nomadic origins named An Lushan, led a widely supported revolt with the aim of founding a new dynasty to supplant the Tang.

Though the revolt was eventually crushed and the Tang dynasty preserved, victory was won at a very high cost. Early in the rebellion, Xuanzong's retreating and demoral-

This painting of Yang Guifei gives a vivid impression of the opulence and refinement of Chinese court life in the late-Tang era.

ized troops mutinied, first killing several members of the Yang family and then forcing the emperor to do away with Yang Guifei herself. Xuanzong lived on for a time, but his grief and disillusionment rendered him utterly incapable of continuing as emperor. None of the Tang monarchs who followed him could compare with the able leaders the dynasty had rather consistently produced in the first century and a half of its rule.

Equally critical, in order to defeat the rebels the Tang had both sought alliances with nomadic peoples living on the northern borders of the empire and delegated resources and political power to regional commanders. As had happened so often in the past, in the late-8th and 9th centuries the nomads used political divisions within China to gain entry into and eventually assert their control over large areas of the north China plain. At the same time, many provincial governors became in effect independent rulers. They collected their own taxes, passing little or none on to the imperial treasury; raised their own armies; and bequeathed their titles to their sons without asking for permission from the Tang court. Worsening economic conditions led to a succession of revolts in the 9th century. Some of these were popular risings led by peasants. The largest and most dangerous revolt for the dynasty was the

Huang-chao, which was named after its Robin Hood-style leader, a former salt merchant. Though it raged from the mid-870s into the 880s and at one point engulfed much of south China, the Huang-chao rebellion failed to win scholar-gentry support. As had been the case in many earlier popular risings, this failure, in combination with internal divisions and poor organization, eventually led to the defeat of the movement. But Tang efforts to put down the massive rising meant additional concessions to provincial lords and nomadic military commanders, and thus a further weakening of the dynasty.

THE FOUNDING OF THE SONG DYNASTY

By the end of the 9th century, little remained of the once-glorious Tang Empire. By 907, when the last emperor of the Tang dynasty was forced to resign, China appeared to be entering yet another era of nomadic dominance, political division, and social strife. For several decades, control over various regions was contested by upstart dynasties—some established by nomadic invaders, others founded by former provincial officers of the Tang. In 960, however, yet another military commander emerged to reunite China under a single dynasty. Zhao Kuangyin had established a far-flung reputation as one of the most honest and able of the generals of the last of the "Five Dynasties" that had struggled to control north China after the fall of the Tang. Though a fearless warrior, Zhao was a man of scholarly leanings, who collected books rather than booty while out campaigning. In the midst of the continuing struggles for control in the north, Zhao's subordinates and regular troops insisted that he proclaim himself emperor. In the next few years, Zhao, renamed Emperor Taizu, routed all his rivals except one, thus founding the Song dynasty that was to rule much of China for the next three centuries.

The one rival Taizu could not overcome was the northern Liao dynasty that had been founded in 907 by the nomadic Khitan peoples from Manchuria. This failure set a precedent for weakness in dealing with the nomadic peoples of the north that would plague the Song dynasty from its earliest years to its eventual destruction by the Mongols in the late 13th century. Beginning in 1004, the Song rulers were forced by military defeats at the hands of the Khitans to sign a series of humiliating treaties with their smaller but more militarily adept northern neighbors. These treaties committed the Song to paying what was in effect a very heavy tribute to the Liao dynasty to deter it from raiding and possibly conquering the Song domains. The Khitans, who had been highly Sinified during a century of rule in north China, were apparently content with this arrangement. They clearly regarded the ethnic Chinese empire of the Song as culturally superior, an area from which they could learn much in statecraft, the arts, and economic organization. They may also have reasoned that their own numbers were too small to govern all of China, even if they were able to conquer it, and that they would dangerously overextend themselves if they tried.

SONG POLITICS: SETTLING FOR PARTIAL RESTORATION

A comparison of the boundaries of the early Song Empire with that of the Tang domains reveals that the Song never matched its predecessor in political or military strength. In part these relative weaknesses of the Song resulted from imperial policies that were designed to ward off the conditions that had destroyed the Tang Empire. From the outset, the military was clearly subordinated to the civilian administrators of the scholar-gentry class. Only civil officials were allowed to be governors, thereby removing the temptation of regional military commanders to seize power in their own right. In addition, all military commanders were rotated to prevent them from building up a power base in the areas where they were stationed.

At the same time, the early Song rulers strongly promoted the interests of the Confucian scholar-gentry, who touted themselves as the key bulwark against the revival of warlordism. Officials' salaries were significantly increased and numerous perks—including additional servants and payments of luxury goods such as silk and wine—made government posts more lucrative than ever before. The civil service exams were fully routinized. They were given every three years at three levels—district, provincial, and imperial. Song examiners passed a far higher percentage of those taking the exams, and these successful candidates were much more likely to receive an official post than their counterparts in the Tang era. As a result, the bureaucracy soon became bloated with well-paid officials who often had little to do.

Thus, the ascendancy of the scholar-gentry class over its aristocratic and Buddhist rivals was fully secured in the Song era. In the coming centuries, emperors and rebels,

China in the Song and Southern Song Dynastic Periods

nomadic conquerors and wealthy merchants would rely on the scholar-gentry to run the great bureaucratic apparatus that served as the backbone of Chinese society. Even rulers who distrusted them and eunuchs and nobles who continued to vie with them for power could not imagine the government functioning without them. The *mandarins*, as they would be called by Western visitors, had established themselves as the indispensable guardians of Chinese civilization.

THE REVIVAL OF CONFUCIAN THOUGHT

The great influence of the scholar-gentry in the Song era was mirrored in the revival of Confucian ideas and values that dominated intellectual life. Many scholars sought to recover long-neglected texts and decipher ancient inscriptions. New academies, devoted to the study of the classical texts, were founded, and impressive libraries were established. In some cases these institutions of learning were located, like the imperial academies, in major urban centers. Some of the most renowned of the new schools were situated in remote mountain and forest regions, where students could pursue their studies free of the many distractions of urban life and in a setting where they could gain inner tranquility and wisdom by observing nature.

The adherents of new schools of philosophy propounded rival interpretations of the teachings of Confucius and other ancient thinkers and sought to prove the superiority of indigenous thought systems, such as Confucianism and Daoism, to imported ones, especially Buddhism. The most prominent thinkers of the era, such as Zhu Xi, stressed the importance of applying philosophical principles to everyday life and action. These neo-Confucianists believed that the cultivation of personal morality was the highest goal to which humans could aspire. They argued that virtue could be attained through the acquisition of knowledge gained by book learning and personal observation as well as through contact with men of wisdom and high morality. In these ways, the basically good nature of humans could be cultivated, and superior men, fit to govern and teach others, could be developed.

Neo-Confucian thinking, which would have a great impact on Chinese intellectual life during the eras of all the dynasties that followed the Song, affected many aspects of Chinese life. Its hostility to foreign philosophical systems, such as Buddhism, rendered Chinese rulers and bureaucrats less receptive to outside ideas and influences at a time when it was increasingly critical for them to be aware of developments in other civilizations. The neo-Confucian stress on tradition and past precedents was one of a number of forces that eventually did much to stifle innovation and critical thinking among the Chinese elite (though these effects were not strongly felt in the Song era, when there were persuasive alternatives to neo-Confucian philosophical positions). The neo-Confucian stress on rank, obligation, deference, and proper decorum and the performance of traditional rituals reinforced class, age, and gender distinctions, particularly as these were expressed in occupational roles. Great importance was given to upholding the authority of the patriarchal head of the Chinese household, which paralleled that of the male emperor of the Chinese people as a whole. If men and women kept to their place and performed the tasks allotted by their age and social rank, the neo-Confucians argued, there would be social harmony and prosperity. If problems arose, the best solutions could be found in examples drawn from the past; historical experience was thought to be the best guide for navigating the uncertain terrain of the future.

ROOTS OF DECLINE: ATTEMPTS AT REFORM

The means by which the Song emperors had secured their control over China did much to undermine their empire in the long run. The weakness they had shown in the face of the Khitan challenge encouraged other nomadic peoples to carve out kingdoms on the northern borders of the Song domains. By the mid-11th century, Tangut tribesmen, who had originally come from Tibet, had established a kingdom named Xi Xia to the northwest of the Khitan kingdom of Liao. The tribute that the Song had to pay to each of these peoples for "protection" of their northern borders was a great drain on the resources of the empire and a growing burden for the Chinese peasantry. Equally burdensome was the cost of the army, numbering nearly one million soldiers by the middle of the 11th century, that the Song had to maintain to guard against invasion from the north.

The emphasis on civil administration and the scholar-gentry and the growing disdain among the Song elite for the military also took their toll. Though Song armies were large, their commanders were rarely the most able men available, and funds needed to upgrade weapons or repair fortifications were often diverted to the scholarly pursuits and entertainments of the court and gentry. At the court and among the ruling classes throughout the empire, painting and poetry, which account for some of the most splendid achievements of the Song era, were cultivated, while the horsemanship and hunting that had so preoccupied earlier rulers and their courtiers went out of fashion.

In the 1070s and early 1080s, Wang Anshi, the chief minister of the Song Shenzong emperor, attempted to ward off the impending collapse of the dynasty through the introduction of sweeping reforms. Wang, who was a celebrated Confucian scholar, ran the government on the basis of the Legalist (see Chapter 5) assumption that an energetic and interventionist state could greatly increase the resources and strength of the dynasty. For 20 years, in the face of strong opposition from the conservative ministers who controlled most of the administrative apparatus, Wang sought to correct the grave defects in the imperial order. He introduced cheap loans and government-assisted irrigation projects to encourage agricultural expansion. He taxed the landlord and scholarly classes who had regularly exempted themselves from military service. Wang used the revenue received to establish well-trained mercenary forces to replace armies that had formerly been conscripted from the unprepared and unwilling peasantry. Wang even sought to reorganize university education and reorient the examination system so that analytical skills were given precedence over the rote memorization of the classics that had long been key to success.

REACTION AND DISASTER: THE FLIGHT TO THE SOUTH

Unfortunately, Wang's ability to propose and enact reforms was totally dependent on continuing support from the Shenzong emperor. In 1085 the Shenzong emperor died, and the new emperor favored the conservative cliques that had long opposed Wang's changes. The neo-Confucians came to power; reform halted and many of Wang's initiatives were reversed. As a result, economic conditions continued to deteriorate and peasant unrest grew throughout the empire. Faced by banditry and rebellion from within, an unprepared military proved no match for the increasing threat from beyond the northern borders of the empire. In 1115, a new nomadic contender, the Jurchens, had overthrown the Liao dynasty of the Khitans and established the Qin kingdom north of the Song Empire. After successful invasions of Song territory, the Jurchens annexed most of the Yellow River basin to what had become the Qin Empire and forced the Song to flee to the south. With the Yangtze River basin as their anchor and their capital transferred to Hangzhou, the Song dynasty would survive for another century and a half. Politically the southern Song dynasty (1127–1279) was little more than a rump state carved out of the much larger domains ruled by the Tang and northern Song. Culturally, its comparatively brief reign was to be one of the most glorious in Chinese history, perhaps in the history of all humankind.

TANG AND SONG PROSPERITY: THE BASIS OF A GOLDEN AGE

In addition to being the era in which China was reunified under strong imperial regimes, the Tang and Song centuries were a time of major transitions in Chinese history. Major shifts in the balance of population within China, new patterns of trade and commerce, renewed urban expansion, novel forms of artistic and literary expression, and a series of further technological breakthroughs all contributed to new directions in the development of Chinese civilization. These shifts became particularly pronounced in the late Tang period and the centuries of rule by the Song dynasty (960–1279). The China that emerged from this era was vastly more wealthy and market oriented and much more bureaucratized, urbanized, and cosmopolitan than the civilization that had first come to fruition in the Han epoch.

THE GROWING IMPORTANCE OF THE SOUTH

The attention given to canal building by the Sui emperors and the Tang rulers who followed them was compelled by a major shift in the population balance within Chinese civilization. The Grand Canal, which Yangdi imperiled his throne to have constructed, was designed to link the original centers of Chinese civilization on the north China plain with the Yangtze River basin over 500 miles to the south. Because the great river systems that were essential to China's agrarian base ran west to east—from the mountains of central Asia to the sea—the movement of people and goods in that direction was much easier than from north to south. Though no major geographical barriers separated the millet-growing areas of northern China from the rice-producing Yangtze basin, travel overland was slow and difficult and the transport of bulk goods like millet or rice was prohibitively expensive. The great increase of the ethnic Chinese population in the southern regions in the later Han and Six Dynasties periods made improving communications between north and south imperative once the two regions were joined by the Sui conquests. Not only did more and more of the emperor's subjects live in the southern regions, but the Yangtze basin and other rice-growing areas in the south were fast becoming the major food-producing areas of the empire. By late Tang and early Song times, the south had surpassed the north in both crop production and total population.

Yangdi's Grand Canal was intended to facilitate control over the southern regions by courts, bureaucracies, and armies centered in ancient imperial centers such as Chan-

This 17th-century engraving illustrates farming methods that were developed in the Song era. Note the overseer, protected by an umbrella from the hot sun.

A NEW AGE OF COMMERCIAL EXPANSION

Tang conquests in central Asia and the building of the canal system did much to promote commercial expansion in the Tang and Song centuries. Tang control deep into central Asia meant that the overland silk routes between China and Persia to the west were reopened and protected, a vital step in the intensification of international contacts in the postclassical period. This facilitated mutually beneficial exchanges between China and Buddhist centers in the nomadic lands, as well as with the Islamic world farther west. Horses, Persian rugs, and tapestries passed to China along these routes, while fine silk textiles, porcelain, and paper were exported to the centers of Islamic civilization. The canal system within China made possible greater regional specialization in products such as tea, copper, and tropical fruits, which could be transported and sold throughout the empire. The access the canals and better roads provided to the ports on the southern coast led to a revival of trade with the coastal kingdoms of Southeast Asia.

As in the Han era, China exported mainly manufactured goods to the "lands beneath the wind (southern monsoons)," while importing mainly luxury products such as aromatic woods and spices. Ships for overseas trade and canal and river transport improved dramatically and multiplied many times in the Tang and Song eras. In late Tang and Song times, Chinese merchants and sailors increasingly carried Chinese trade overseas instead of being content to let foreign seafarers come to them. Along with the dhows of the Arabs, Chinese junks were the best ships in the world in this era. They were equipped with watertight bulkheads, sternpost rudders, oars, sails, compasses, bamboo fenders, and gunpowder-propelled rockets for self-defense. With such vessels, Chinese sailors and merchants became the dominant force in the Asian seas east of the Malayan peninsula. But the elites of the land-based and largely self-sufficient empires of post-Tang China lacked strong motives to sustain overseas exploration or project Chinese power through the military domination of the sea.

The heightened role of commerce and the money economy in Chinese life was readily apparent in the numerous and enlarged market quarters found in all cities and major towns. These were filled with shops and stalls that sold products drawn from local farms, regional centers of artisan production, and entrepôts as distant as the Mediterranean. The Tang and Song governments supervised the hours and methods in these centers, while merchants specializing in products of the same kind banded together in guilds to promote their interests with local officials and to regulate competition within the trading community.

gan and Loyang in the north. The canal made it possible to transport revenue collected in the form of grain from the fertile southern regions and to transfer food from areas in the south to districts threatened by drought and famine in the north. No wonder that Yangdi was quite literally obsessed with canal construction. By the time the Grand Canal was finished, well over one million forced laborers had worked, and many had died, on its locks and embankments.

The completed canal system was an engineering achievement every bit as impressive as the Great Wall. It joined the Yellow River to the cities of the northeast and to the Yangtze basin and the sea on the south-central coast. Most stretches of the canal, which totaled nearly 1200 miles in length, were 40 paces wide, and imperial highways lined with willow trees ran along the banks on both sides. Its construction not only created a bridge to join north and south China, it opened up the south to migration and commercial development on a scale unimaginable in previous centuries. The maintenance of the canal system became a priority for all Chinese regimes from the Tang onward.

This expansion in scale was accompanied by a growing sophistication in commercial organization and forms of credit available in China. The proportion of exchanges involved in the money economy expanded greatly, and *deposit shops,* an early form of bank, were found in many parts of the empire. The first use of paper money also occurred in the Tang era. Merchants deposited their profits in their hometowns before setting out on trading caravans to distant cities. They were given credit vouchers or what the Chinese called *flying money,* which they could then present for reimbursement at the appropriate office in the city of destination. This arrangement greatly reduced the danger of robbery on the often perilous journeys merchants made from one market center to another. In the early 11th century, the government itself began to issue paper money when an economic crisis made it clear that the private merchant banks could no longer handle the demand for the new currency.

THE WORLD'S MOST SPLENDID CITIES

The expansion of commerce and artisan production was complemented by a surge in urban growth in the Tang and Song eras. At nearly two million, the population of the Tang capital and its suburbs at Changan was far larger than that of any other city in the world at the time. The city walls were laid out in a rectangle that extended five miles in width and six miles in length. The imperial city, which was an inner citadel within the walls of Changan, was divided into a highly restricted zone dominated by the palace and audience halls and a section crowded with the offices of the ministries and secretariats of the imperial government. Near the imperial city, but outside Changan's walls, elaborate gardens and a hunting park were laid out for the amusement of the emperors and favored courtiers. The rest of the city was divided into large rectangular and square blocks by wide streets that ran north and south.

The spread of commerce and the increasing population fed urban growth through most of the Tang and Song periods. In the north and especially the south, old cities mushroomed in size as suburbs spread in all directions from the original city walls. Towns grew rapidly into cities, and the proportion of the empire's population living in urban centers grew steadily. China had numerous cities with over 100,000 people, whereas most other preindustrial civilizations were fortunate to have more than a handful of large urban centers and some had none. The number of people living in large cities in China, which may have been as high as ten percent, was also far greater than that found in any civilization until after the Industrial Revolution.

China's cities were more than just large and well planned. They were endowed with markets stocked with products from much of the then-known world; with parks and delightful gardens, both private and public; with numerous baths, where one could also get a massage and a cup of tea or rice wine; and with sumptuous restaurants that specialized in the varied and delicious cuisines of the different regions of China. Of all China's remarkable urban centers in this era, perhaps none surpassed the late Song capital of Hangzhou in size and sophistication. With a population that exceeded one million and a location on the Jiantang River near the East China Sea that allowed it to draw on the wealth and creativity of north and south China and overseas trading centers, Hangzhou has rarely been matched for sheer beauty and the high level of civilization it exemplified.

EXPANDING AGRARIAN PRODUCTION AND LIFE IN THE COUNTRY

The movement of the population southward to the fertile valleys of the Yangtze and other river systems was part of a larger process of agrarian expansion in the Tang and Song period. The expansion of Chinese settlement and agricultural production was promoted by the rulers of both dynasties, who actively encouraged peasant groups to migrate to uncultivated areas or those occupied by shifting cultivators or peoples of non-Chinese descent. The state supported military garrisons in these areas to protect the new settlements and complete the task of pacifying indigenous non-Chinese peoples or driving them from the empire if they would not submit to Chinese rule. State-regulated irrigation and embankment systems also advanced agrarian expansion, and the great canals made it possible for peasants who grew specialized crops such as tea or who cultivated silkworms to market their produce over much of the empire. The introduction of new seeds, such as the famed Champa rice from Vietnam; better use of human, animal, and silt manures; more thorough soil preparation and weeding; and multiple-cropping and improved techniques of water control increased the yields of peasant holdings. Inventions, such as the wheelbarrow, eased somewhat the laborious tasks linked to plowing, planting, weeding, and harvesting that occupied much of the time of the great majority of the Chinese people.

The rulers of both the Sui and Tang dynasties had adopted policies aimed at breaking up the great estates of the old aristocracy and distributing land more equitably among the free peasant households of the empire. These policies were, of course, designed in part to reduce if not eliminate the threat that the powerful aristocracy posed for the new dynasties. They were also intended to bolster the position of the ordinary peasants, whose labors and well-being had long been viewed by Confucian scholars as essential to a prosperous and stable social order. To a point these agrarian measures succeeded. For a time the numbers of the free peasantry increased and the average holding size in many areas rose. The fortunes of many of the old aristocratic families also declined, thus removing many of them as independent centers of power. They were gradually supplanted in the rural areas by the gentry side of the scholar-gentry combination that dominated the imperial bureaucracy.

The extended-family households of the gentry that were found in rural settlements in the Han era increased in size and elegance in the Tang and Song. The widespread use of the graceful curved roofs with upturned corners that one associates with Chinese civilization dates from the Tang period. By imperial decree, curved roofs were reserved for persons of high rank, including the gentry families. With intricately carved and painted roof timbers topped with glazed tiles of yellow or green, the great dwellings of the gentry left no doubt as to the status and power of the families who resided in them. At the same time, their muted colors, wood and bamboo construction and simple lines blended beautifully with nearby gardens and groves of trees.

FAMILY AND SOCIETY IN THE TANG AND SONG ERAS

Though Chinese family organization at various class levels in the Tang and Song centuries closely resembled that found in earlier periods, the position of women showed signs of improving under the Tang and early Song, and then deteriorated steadily in the late Song. As in the classical age, marriages were viewed primarily as alliances between families; extended-family households were preferred but they could normally be afforded only by the upper classes; and the male-dominated hierarchy promoted by Confucius and other early thinkers held sway at all class levels. In the Tang era, the authority of elders and males within the family was buttressed by laws that prescribed beheading as a punishment for children who struck their parents or grandparents in anger and two and one-half years of hard labor for younger brothers or sisters who hit their older siblings.

Over the centuries a very elaborate process of forging marriage alliances developed. Professional go-betweens, who were almost invariably women, assisted both families in negotiating such prickly issues as matching young men and women and the amount of the dowry to be paid to the husband's family. In contrast to India, brides and grooms were generally approximately the same age, probably because of the Confucian abhorrence of mixing generations. Among the lower classes and in rural areas, the age of marriage was generally lower than in the cities and among the scholar-gentry. Some potential sons-in-law were adopted by their prospective parents-in-law at birth, though the marriage ceremony did not actually take place until both parties had at least reached puberty. Among the urban upper classes, marriages were consumated somewhat later. It was not uncommon for the son of a scholar-gentry family, who was busy with studies for the state examinations, to delay his marriage until he was 30 or more years old.

CONTRASTING FATES: THE ROLES OF WOMEN IN THE ELITE AND COMMONER CLASSES

Both within the family and in society at large, women remained clearly subordinate to males. But some of the evidence we have suggests that, at least for women of the upper classes in urban areas, opportunities for personal expression increased in the Tang and early Song. As the example of the empresses Wu and Wei and the concubine Yang Guifei make clear, at the highest levels of Chinese society Tang women could wield considerable power. That they also enjoyed access to a rather broad range of activities, if not career possibilities, is indicated by a surviving pottery figure from the early Tang period of a young woman playing polo.

Some semblance of women's rights is evidenced by provisions in Tang and Song law for divorce by mutual consent of both husband and wife, as well as those prohibiting a man from setting aside his wife if her parents were dead or if he had been poor when they were married and later became rich. These suggest that Chinese wives had more defenses against capricious behavior by their spouses than was the case in India at this time. The practice that was reported in late Song times of wealthy women in large cities like Hangzhou taking lovers (or what were politely called "complementary husbands") with the silent though presumably unwilling complicity of their spouses, also indicates a remarkable degree of female independence.

In Chinese, as in Islamic civilization, court politics in the Tang and Song eras were increasingly complicated by the intense involvement of both women and eunuchs attached to the imperial household. In both cases, the practice by which emperors (and in many instances high court officials) took both an official wife and concubines, who sometimes numbered in the thousands, was the root cause of this growing source of political instability. Not only did both wives and concubines compete for the ruler's favor, they sought to use royal patronage to advance the fortunes of their relatives and friends at court. Very often wives, and sometimes concubines as in the case of Yang Guifei, became central figures in court cliques that vied for power. In fact, some Chinese historians have claimed that Yang encouraged An Lushan, with whom it is suggested she had a romantic involvement, to revolt and overthrow her husband. The need to defend against liaisons between the women of the imperial court and outside males also led to the large-scale employment of eunuchs to keep watch. In both Chinese and Islamic civilizations the eunuchs soon became a major party to palace intrigues, and on numerous occasions dominated weak emperors or caliphs.

The contests between rival cliques became the most intense in struggles for succession to the throne. The fact that neither Muslim peoples nor the Chinese were able to establish a clear order for political succession was, of course, a critical factor in the rise of these disputes. Different wives and concubines sought to gain a ruler's support for their own sons. They and their allies engaged in all manner of plots and resorted to deception, defamation of character, and even murder to have their way. The mother of the caliph al-Rashid, for example, cleared the way to the power for her son by poisoning another royal prince who had been designated heir to the throne by her husband, al-Mahdi. The woman who became Tang Empress Wu began her rise to power as a favored concubine. After her second husband's death, she installed one of her young sons on the throne, intending to rule in his stead. When the youth tried to assert his authority, Wu had him replaced by another, more docile, son. Six years later, she deposed this puppet emperor, claimed the throne outright, and even sought to found a new dynasty.

The actual seizure of the throne by Empress Wu was exceptional, but the deep involvement in imperial politics by women at Islamic, Chinese, Japanese, or Vietnamese courts was not. Despite the fact that she was a very capable monarch, subsequent Chinese historians vilified Wu because she was a woman who dared to rule in her own right. But neither Chinese nor Islamic scholars nor the rulers they served found a lasting answer to the factionalism and intrigue spawned by the multiplication of imperial consorts and the lack of a clear procedure by which succession was determined. As we have seen, this uncertainty and the deep divisions it caused at the highest levels of government led repeatedly to instability and, at times, violent civil strife. These struggles proved costly to the imperial subjects who got caught up in them and left openings for foreign invaders to exploit the empires through raids and often conquest.

Evidence of the independence and legal rights enjoyed by a small minority of privileged women in the Tang and Song eras is all but overwhelmed by broader trends that point emphatically to the worsening condition of Chinese women in general. The assertion of male dominance both within the family and beyond was especially pronounced in the thinking of the neo-Confucian philosophers, who, as we have seen, became a major force in the later Song period. The neo-Confucians stressed the woman's role as housemaker and mother, particularly the bearer of sons to continue the patrilineal family line. They advocated the physical confinement of women and stressed the importance of virginity for young brides, fidelity for wives, and chastity for widows, who like their counterparts in India were discouraged from remarrying. At the same time, men were permitted to have premarital sex without scandal, to take numerous concubines if they could afford it, and to remarry if one or more of their wives died. The neo-Confucians attacked the Buddhists for promoting career alternatives, such as the monastic life and female scholarship, to marriage and raising a family. They drafted laws that favored males in inheritance, divorce, and familial interaction, and they excluded females from the sort of education that would allow them to enter the civil service and rise to positions of political power.

No practice better exemplifies the degree to which women in Chinese civilization had been constricted and subordinated by the end of the Song era as dramatically as foot-binding does. This counterpart of the veil and seclusion in Islam may have had its origins in the delight that one of the emperors had taken in the tiny feet of his favorite dancing girl. Whatever its origins, by the later Song era upper-class males displayed a decided preference for small feet, a preference that later spread to lower-class groups, including the peasantry. In response to male demands, on which the successful negotiation of a young woman's marriage contract might hinge, mothers began to bind the feet of their daughters as early as the age of five or six. The young girl's toes were turned under and bound with silk, which was wound more tightly as the child grew. By the time she reached marriageable age, the woman's foot had been transformed into the "lotus petal" or "golden lily" shapes that were presumably preferred by prospective marriage partners.

Bound feet were not only a constant source of pain for the rest of a woman's life; they greatly restricted her mobility by making it very difficult to walk even short distances. Restricted physical mobility, of course, made it easier for husbands to confine their wives to the family household and impossible for women to engage in most occupations. For the latter reason, the lower classes, whose

This diagram contrasts the bone structure of a normal foot with that of a Chinese woman whose foot has been bound since she was a young girl.

households were often dependent on female labor to make ends meet, were slow to adopt the practice. But once it was in fashion among the scholar-gentry and other elite classes, foot-binding became vital to winning a suitable husband for a young girl. Since a good marriage for her daughters was the primary goal of any self-respecting mother, the practice was unquestioningly passed from one generation of women to the next. Upper-class women came to accept the pain and disfigurement associated with foot-binding because they saw it as essential for a chance to have what they considered a full and happy life. Their constricted vision of the possibilities for self-fulfillment and willingness to endure a painful and unnecessary physical deformity to achieve it say a great deal about the lowly position to which women had been relegated in China by the end of the Song era.

A GLORIOUS AGE: INVENTION AND ARTISTIC CREATIVITY

Perhaps even more than for their political and economic achievements, the Tang and Song eras are remembered as a time of remarkable accomplishment in science and technology, literature and the fine arts. Major technological breakthroughs and scientific discoveries were made under each dynasty. Some of these, particularly those involving the invention of new tools, production techniques, and weapons, would gradually be disseminated to other civilizations and

fundamentally alter the course of human development as a whole. Until recent centuries the arts and literature of China were less well known beyond its borders. Their impact was confined mainly to areas, such as central Asia, Japan, and Vietnam, where Chinese imports had long been a major impetus for cultural advance. But the poetry and short stories of the Tang and the landscape paintings of the Song represent some of the most splendid artistic creations of all human history.

As we have seen, new agricultural implements and innovations, such as banks and paper money, contributed a great deal to economic growth and social prosperity in the Tang and Song eras. In this respect, the engineering feats of the period are particularly noteworthy. In addition to constructing the Grand Canal, Tang and Song engineers made great advances in building dikes and dams and regulating the flow of water in complex irrigation systems. They also devised ingenious new ways to build bridges, long a major focus of engineering efforts in a land dominated by mountains and waterways. From arched and segmented to suspension and trussed, most of the basic bridge types known to humans were pioneered in China.

The single most important of the many technological advances made in the Tang era, the invention of explosive powder, had at first little impact on warfare. For centuries, the Chinese used these potent chemical mixtures mainly for fireworks, which delighted emperors and the masses alike. By the late Song, however, explosive powder was widely employed by the imperial armies in a variety of grenades and bombs that were hurled at the enemy by catapults. Song armies and warships were also equipped with naphtha flamethrowers, poisonous gases, and rocket launchers that were perhaps the most effective weapons the dynasty employed in its losing struggle to check nomadic incursions. On the domestic scene, chairs were introduced into the household, the habit of tea drinking swept the empire, coal was used for fuel for the first time, and the first kite soared into the heavens.

Though the number of major inventions in the Song era was lower than in the Tang, several were pivotal for the future history of all civilizations. Compasses, which had been used since the last centuries B.C. by Chinese military commanders and magicians, were applied to sea navigation for the first time in the Song period. The abacus, the ancestor of the modern calculator, was introduced to help merchants count their profits and tax collectors keep track of the revenues due. And in the middle of the 11th century, a remarkable artisan named Bi Sheng devised the technique of printing using moveable type. Though block printing had been perfected in China in the preceding centuries, the use of moveable type represented a great advance in the production of written records and scholarly books. Combined with paper, which the Chinese had also invented much earlier in the Han period, printing made it possible for them to attain a level of elite literacy that excelled that of any preindustrial civilization.

SCHOLARLY REFINEMENT AND ARTISTIC ACCOMPLISHMENT

The reinvigorated scholar-gentry elite was responsible for much of the artistic and literary creativity of the Tang and Song eras. Buddhist art and architecture had been heavily patronized by the court and wealthy monasteries in the Tang period. But scholar administrators and Confucian teachers wrote much of the literature for which the Tang is best remembered and painted the landscapes that were the most sublime cultural productions of the Song. Confucian thinkers highly esteemed skillful writing and painting, and educated individuals were expected to be involved in these activities on an ongoing basis. The Chinese educational establishment was geared to turning out generalists rather than the specialists who are so revered in our own society. A well-educated man was a *dilettante*, a person who dabbled with varying degrees of success in many fields. Thus, after a hard day at the Ministry of Public Works, a truly accomplished official was expected to spend the evening composing songs on his lute, admiring a new painting or creating his own, or sipping rice wine while composing a poem to the harvest moon. Thus, talented and often well-trained amateurs wrote most of the poems, composed much of the music, and painted the landscapes for which the Tang and Song eras are renowned.

As the Confucian scholar-gentry supplanted the Buddhists as the major producers of art and literature, devotional objects and religious homilies gave way to a growing fixation on everyday life and the delights of the natural world. Much of the short story literature was focused on the doings of the common folk, popular beliefs in witchcraft and demons, ill-fated romances, and even detective stories about brutal murders or deaths that occurred in mysterious circumstances. Tang poetry moved from early verses that dwelt on the "pleasant breezes that envelope[d] the emperor's chair" to a seemingly endless variety of ways of celebrating the natural world. No one was better at the latter than the most famous poet of the Tang era, Li Bo. As the following illustrates, his poems, like those of the great Persian authors, blend images of the mundane world with philosophical musings:

> *The rain was over, green covered the land.*
> *One last cloudlet melted away in the clear sky.*
> *The east wind came home with the spring*
> *Bearing blossoms to sprout on the branches.*
> *Flowers are fading now and time will end.*
> *All mortal men perceive it and their sighs are deep.*
>
> *But I will turn to the sacred hills*
> *And learn from Tao [Dao] and from magic how to fly.*

This intense interest in nature came to full artistic fruition in the landscape paintings of the Song era. Most of these were produced by the cultivated gentlemen of the scholar-gentry class, and they pulled together diverse aspects of Chinese civilization. The brushes and techniques employed were similar to those used in writing the Chinese language, which itself was regarded as a high art form. The paintings were symbolic, intended to teach moral lessons or explore philosophical ideas. The objects depicted were not only beautiful in themselves, but they stood for larger concepts: A crane and a pine tree, for example, rep-

As shown in this ink drawing of Chinese philosophers during the Song dynasty, board games and musical recitals were highly esteemed leisure activities for the scholar-gentry class.

The simplicity of the composition, the use of empty space, and the emphasis on nature are all characteristic of Chinese landscape painting at its height.

resented longevity; bamboo shoots were associated with the scholar-gentry class; and a dragon could call to mind a number of things including the emperor, the cosmos, or life-giving rain. There was an abstract quality to the paintings that gives them a special appeal in the present day. The artists were not concerned with depicting nature accurately but rather with creating a highly personal vision of natural beauty. A premium was placed on subtlety and suggestion. The winner of an imperial contest, for example, painted a lone monk drawing water from an icy stream to depict the subject announced by the emperor: a monastery hidden deep in the mountains during the winter. Song landscapes were often painted on scrolls that could be "read" as the viewer unfolded them bit by bit. Most were accompanied by a poem, sometimes composed by the painter, that complemented the subject matter and was aimed at further elucidating the artist's ideas.

ANALYSIS
ARTISTIC EXPRESSION AND SOCIAL VALUES

In its many forms, artistic creativity provides one of the richest ways of probing the beliefs and values of a civilization. In some cases where the civilization in question did not develop writing or at least writing that we can now decipher, art and architecture provide much of the evidence by which we can learn about the attitudes and life-styles of vanished peoples. Some of the most notable examples include the ancient Indus civilization of South Asia and many of the high civilizations of the Americas and sub-Saharan Africa. Even in civilizations where written records have survived, we can learn a good deal about social structure by discovering who produced the art and for whom it was created; about technology by studying artistic techniques and materials; and about worldview by exploring the messages the art was intended to convey. In comparing some of the major forms of artistic expression of the great civilizations, we can also identify underlying similarities and differences in the values by which the peoples who developed them organized their societies and responded to the natural and supernatural worlds.

The fact that members of the ruling political elite produced many of the landscape paintings of the Song era is a rather exceptional occurrence in the history of civilization. The sculptures that adorned the temples of India or the statues, paintings, and stained glass that graced the cathedrals of medieval Europe were created mainly by specialized and highly trained craftsmen, whose skills were passed down from father to son over many generations. By contrast, the Song artists were often amateurs who painted in their leisure time. Even the most talented, who won sufficient patronage to devote themselves to painting full time, began as Confucian scholars and very often administrators. It is not just the amateur and "master of all fields" ideals that are remarkable here, but the fact that so much art was produced by the men who also ran the country. In most of the other civilizations we have studied, political life has been dominated by warrior and priestly classes, not artistic scholar-bureaucrats like those who governed China. Even in civilizations like those of medieval Europe and Islam, where priests and religious teachers produced fine art in the form of manuscript illuminations, the individuals involved were seldom persons with political responsibilities or power. Thus, the artistic creativity of China's political elite underscores the importance of the preference for civil over military leaders in Chinese society. It also tells us a good deal about the qualities the Chinese associated with a truly civilized and superior person, a person who was deemed worthy to rule the Middle Kingdom.

Song landscapes were aimed at expressing the reactions and ideals of individual persons, whom we can identify by the distinctive seals with which they stamped their paintings. The paintings were clearly elitist, intended for the pleasure and edification of members of the Chinese educated classes, not for museum viewing or mass consumption. Landscape painting served to reinforce the identity and values of this scholarly elite across the vast spaces of the Chinese empire as well as across time. In one of the most famous incidents illustrating the latter, the Confucian philosopher Ju Xi remarked on the nobility and loyalty that he saw so clearly displayed by the calligraphy of scholars from the Warring States era.

This individualism and elitism in the art of Chinese civilization can be contrasted with the anonymous creation of the works of sculpture and religious paintings in Hindu and Buddhist civilizations and medieval Europe, or the mosaic decorations of the mosques of Islam. In each of these, artistic works that adorned temples, cathedrals, and mosques were intended for a mass audience. The moral instruction for the scholarly few that was contained in the Song landscapes had a very different purpose than the religious sculptures or mosaics of other civilizations. The sculptures and mosaics were created to convey a religious message, to remind the viewers of a key event in the life of Christ or the Buddha, or to impress upon them the horrors of hell or the delights of heaven.

Thus, the highest art forms, linked to a common religion, served to bridge the gulf between elites and the masses in Hindu, Buddhist, Christian, and Muslim civilizations. Though imported Buddhist art forms performed this function in some periods in Chinese history, the more enduring Confucian-Daoist artistic creativity, as best exemplified by landscape painting, accentuated the differences that separated the educated scholar-gentry and the common people. Where religion was a central source of legitimacy for elites in most preindustrial civilizations, in China it was present in fertility sacrifices and ancestral veneration, but was much less vital to the legitimacy of the ruling elites. The knowledge and administrative skills of the educated Confucian bureaucrats and their concern for the common people provided the primary justification for their power and privileges.

Questions: What do you think the diminutive size of the people in Chinese landscape paintings can tell us about Chinese views on the relationship between humans and the natural world? What political functions might monumental art like that found in Hindu, Islamic, and Christian civilizations serve beyond reminding the masses of religious ties to the elite? Which forms of artistic expression exact the highest toll from the mass of the people; which best serve their interests? Can you think of American or European politicians who have created great works of art? Do we expect this sort of creativity from our elected officials, and, if not, what does this tell us about the values of our own civilization?

CONCLUSION

THE END OF THE SONG: THE LEGACY OF TWO GREAT DYNASTIES

By retreating to the south, the Song rulers had managed to survive the assaults of the nomads from the north. They could not retreat far enough to escape the onslaught of the most brilliant nomadic commander of them all, Chinggis Khan, who directed perhaps the most powerful military machine the world had seen up to that time. The Song rulers bought time by paying tribute to the Mongol Khan and striking alliances with him against their common enemies, the Tanguts and Jurchens. But once the nomadic dynasties of the north had been beaten, the Song domains lay open to Mongol conquest. This was delayed for a time by the death of Chinggis Khan and struggles for succession. As we shall see in Chapter 20, by the late 1260s, Kubilai, who had long had a strong interest in Chinese civilization, had emerged as the paramount Mongol lord, and he was ready to launch a sustained effort to conquer the southern refuge of the Song dynasty. By 1279, decades after Kubilai Khan had proclaimed himself emperor of China, the south had been completely conquered and the last claimant to the Song throne had drowned attempting to escape to Vietnam. Though nomads once again ruled China, the wisdom of Kubilai and the strength of the early Mongol, or Yuan, regime meant that China was spared the period of division and chaos that had marked earlier transitions from one dynasty to the next.

The long Tang and Song epoch had proved to be truly pivotal in Chinese and world history. Centralized administration and the great Chinese bureaucratic apparatus were not only restored but strengthened. The scholar-gentry elite, which had for so long been the critical binding force for Chinese civilization, triumphed over its aristocratic, nomadic, and Buddhist monastic rivals. Under nomadic and indigenous dynasties, it would continue to define and direct Chinese civilization for the next six and one-half centuries. During the nearly seven centuries of Tang and Song rule, the area that comprised Chinese civilization had grown dramatically, as the south was fully integrated with the north.

From the Tang era onward, the unified population of China would make up approximately one-fourth of humankind. From the Tang and Song eras, the Chinese economy would be one of the world's most advanced in terms of market orientation, volume of overseas trade, productivity per acre, and the sophistication of its tools and techniques of craft production. No civilization, with the possible exception of that of the Romans or the Incas, could match its system of roads and certainly none had such an extensive and sophisticated canal and irrigation network. Until the 18th century, the imperial dynasties of China possessed political power and drew on economic resources unmatched by any other civilization.

The great changes that occurred in the Tang and Song eras caution us against the temptation to equate the remarkable continuity displayed by Chinese civilization with stagnation. China did retain or revive key ideas, institutions, and patterns of political and social organization from the classical age. But it also changed dramatically, in the balance between regions within the empire, in its level of commercial and urban development, in technology, in the impact of outside influences such as Buddhism, and even in the degree to which the scholar-gentry exercised political power and social dominance. Part of the genius of Chinese civilization has clearly arisen from their ability to incorporate far-reaching changes into ancient traditions and time-tested patterns of social interaction and political organization.

As we will see in the next chapter, beyond its borders China continued to dominate culturally the peoples of the East Asian world—Korean, Tibetan, Vietnamese, Japanese, and nomadic—even though it did not control them politically for most of the centuries after the fall of the Tang dynasty. Chinese inventions such as paper, printing, and gunpowder would fundamentally alter the course of development in all other human civilizations, including those as yet unknown in the New World. If the Qin and Han epoch had established and defined the meaning of civilization in China, the Tang and Song had restored and redefined it. The persisting importance of the Tang and Song eras for the Chinese people is indicated by the fact that, even to the present day, they identify themselves as both the "sons of Han" and the "men of Tang."

FURTHER READINGS

In addition to the general histories of China suggested in Chapter 5, there are a number of important works devoted to the Tang and Song eras. The volume, edited by Denis Twitchett, devoted to the Tang and Song in the *Cambridge History of China* is an essential reference work. There are detailed works on the founding of the Tang dynasty by C. P. Fitzgerald (1970) and Woodbridge Bingham (1940), but these should be read in conjunction with the more recent *Mirror to the Son of Heaven* (1974), which provides valuable correctives to the interpretations of these earlier authors. Useful insights into political and cultural

life in the Tang era can be gleaned from the specialized essays in a volume on *Perspectives on the Tang* (1973), edited by Arthur Wright and Denis Twitchett. Much less has been written specifically on society and politics in the Song than the Tang, but Jacques Gernet's, *Daily Life in China on the Eve of the Mongol Invasion, 1250–1276* (1962) is both highly entertaining and informative. On the great social and economic transitions of the Song era, Mark Elvin's *The Pattern of the Chinese Past* (1973) is insightful, provocative, and controversial.

Of the numerous works on Chinese art and painting, perhaps the best place to start is with the standard work by Mai-mai Sze, *The Way of Chinese Painting* (1956), which quotes extensively from Chinese manuals. Of more recent works, the general survey by Laurence Sickman and Alexander Soper, as well as James Cahill's study of landscape painting, stand out. Though there is as yet no full-scale study of gender roles in Tang or Song China, Elisabeth Croll's *Feminism and Socialism in China* (1980) has a superb introductory chapter on the position of women in traditional China, which can be supplemented by the appropriate sections in Gernet and other works on social life in the period. A wonderful sampler of Li Bo's poetry can be found in a volume entitled *Bright Moon, Perching Bird* (1987), edited by J. P. Seaton and James Cryer.

206 B.C.–A.D. 220 Reign of
the Han dynasty in China

222–589 Period of Six
Dynasties in China

618–907 Tang dynasty in China
   646 Taika reforms in Japan
      668 Korea wins indepen-
   dence from Tang conquerors

794 Japanese capital
shifts to Heian (Kyoto)

918–1392 Koryo dynasty in Korea
   939 Vietnam wins its
   independence from China

111 B.C. Vietnam conquered by the Chinese

589–618 Sui dy-
nasty in China

838 Last Japanese embassy to Chinn

109 B.C. Choson (Korea) conquered by Chinese

668–918 Silla kingdom in Korea

A.D. 39 Trung sisters revolt in Vietnam

710–784 Imperial Japanese capital at Nara

857–1160 Period of Fuji-
wara dominance in Japan

19

The Spread of Chinese Civilization: Korea, Japan, and Vietnam

INTRODUCTION. By the time of the Han dynasty (206 B.C.–A.D. 220), the peoples who had come to identify themselves as Chinese had demonstrated a capacity for civilized development that was equaled by few other societies. Not only had the Chinese built one of the largest, most powerful, and most prosperous of all human societies, they had found ways of maintaining their patterns of civilized life over long periods of time. While the great civilizations of Egypt, Mesopotamia, Persia, India, and the Americas rose and fell, China persisted. Sometimes divided, often challenged by the warlike peoples beyond their frontiers, the Chinese managed to preserve a sense of identity, to absorb the nomadic peoples that periodically broke through their defenses, and to build continuously on the institutions, ways of thought, and modes of social organization devised in the last millennium B.C.

The Chinese did much more than endure; they managed to excel in virtually all areas of human endeavor. Their agrarian system was able to support a far larger population, in both absolute terms and per acre, than any other preindustrial civilization. They fashioned centralized administrative systems that effectively controlled a massive empire that dwarfed most of their civilized rivals, who exercised far less control than the Chinese over the territories they claimed as part of their empires. The Chinese led the classical and postclassical world in technological innovation, made great strides in scientific understanding, excelled in engineering and architectural design, supported one of the most advanced educational systems and scholarly elites in the civilized world, and consistently produced brilliant works in literature and the fine arts.

It was not likely that such splendid achievements would go unnoticed by China's neighbors. It was perhaps inevitable that surrounding peoples would strive to emulate the Chinese model of civilized development. As we have seen,

---

980–1009 Le dynasty in Vietnam

1160–1185 Taira clan dominant in Japan

1180–1185 Gempei Wars in Japan

1185–1333 Kamakura Shogunate in Japan

1231–1392 Mongol rule in Korea

1336–1573 Ashikaga Shogunate in Japan

1392–1910 Yi dynasty in Korea

1467–1477 Onin War in Japan

c. 1500 Nguyen dynasty in central/South Vietnam founded

1539–1787 Trinh dynasty in Vietnam/Red River

1600 Founding of the Tokugawa Shogunate in Japan

Japan, which was the most important of these neighbors in terms of its subsequent impact on global history, began to borrow heavily from China in the critical 5th and 6th centuries A.D., when its own pattern of civilization started to coalesce. China's influence upon the nomadic peoples to the north and west and upon areas such as Tibet has also been noted in earlier chapters. But the areas most drawn to the Chinese model over long periods of time were the sedentary, wet-rice growing societies that flanked China on the east—Korea and Japan—and in the south, Vietnam. Developments in these areas in the postclassical period formed vital parts of the expansion of civilization and the spread of world religions. While Chinese example kept this zone of civilization somewhat apart, mutual interaction with the wider world network developed as well.

This chapter will focus on the interaction and exchanges between China and these three regions. In each area Chinese influences were blended with local conditions, preferences, and creativity to produce related but very distinctive patterns of civilized development. In the case of the Japanese, we will examine the strategies they adopted to build on the foundations laid in the first centuries A.D., which were discussed in Chapter 10. For Korea and Vietnam, we will begin with the first contacts between the expansive Chinese and the peoples of these areas, and then examine the quite different paths to civilization each followed. In all these areas Chinese influences and regional reactions to them led to particularly significant patterns of civilized development in the postclassical era. Each case forms an important example of the larger theme of the expansion of civilization and the growing number and depth of the linkages that bound civilized societies across the globe.

Partly due to geography and partly to historical circumstances, each of these three areas interacted with their giant neighbor and common source of civilization in very different ways. Despite intermittent efforts of the Chinese, particularly under the Mongol Yuan dynasty, to assert direct control over the islands, the Japanese managed to retain political independence. This meant that they had much greater control than the Koreans or Vietnamese over which aspects of Chinese civilization they wished to borrow and, equally important, over how these aspects were introduced into Japanese culture. As a result, though Chinese influences continued to shape Japanese life, particularly at the level of the court and aristocracy, distinctive Japanese approaches to social organization, thought, and artistic creativity became more and more pronounced.

In contrast to the Japanese, the Koreans and Vietnamese, both of whom could be reached overland by Chinese forces, were conquered and directly ruled by various Chinese dynasties. This meant that they had less control over the introduction and effects of Chinese cultural influences

than the Japanese. But both peoples managed to preserve a strong sense of their own identity, which was forged to a large extent by prolonged resistance to Chinese political domination and their fear of absorption by their larger neighbor. In the first centuries A.D. the Koreans broke free from the Chinese yoke and managed to remain independent for most of the centuries thereafter. The Vietnamese struggled violently to escape Chinese rule for more than 1000 years. Ethnically and culturally both the Koreans and Vietnamese preserved key elements in their pre-conquest cultures and societies. These were blended with Chinese imports to produce unique variants of a broader East Asian pattern of civilization.

As we shall see, in each of the satellite areas of Chinese civilization, Buddhism in a variety of forms played key roles in the transmission of Chinese civilization and in the development of the indigenous cultures. Because Buddhism originated in India, the layers of cross-cultural interaction in the satellite areas are all the more complex and profound. In each case, ideas and rituals originating in India were filtered through Chinese society and culture before being passed on to Korea, Japan, and Vietnam. Historically, Buddhism also provided a critical link between two of the satellite civilizations, Korea and Japan. Because the satellites received Buddhism from China, the schools that developed in these areas were from the Mahayana rather than the Theravada branch of the faith. Thus, they were on the whole more prone to salvationist teachings that evoked a ready response from the common people. Still, even the more esoteric forms of Buddhism found in Japan or Vietnam originated in China—Japanese Zen, for example, began as the Chinese Chan. As the impact of Zen on Japanese culture in the warlord era perhaps best illustrates, the influence of Buddhism was felt in virtually all spheres of life and at all social levels in each of the satellite civilizations.

Chinese influence in Japan, Korea, and Vietnam meant, finally, that each of these societies emphasized links to China more than links to the wider world network, which was encountered mainly through China itself. This fact, plus the struggle to define some autonomy in relationship to China, imposed considerable isolation on Japan and Korea in terms of wider international contacts. The East Asian zone thus differed from Europe, where contacts were more open-ended, despite basic similarities in the process of borrowing and self-definition.

JAPAN: THE IMPERIAL AGE

By the 7th and 8th centuries A.D., the Japanese court at Nara was awash in Chinese imports. Indigenous cultural influences, particularly those linked to Shinto views on the natural and supernatural world, remained central to Japanese cultural development. But in the Taika (645–710), Nara (710–784), and Heian (794–857) periods, Japanese borrowing from China—though selective—peaked and touched virtually all aspects of Japanese life, particularly at the level of the elites and among the populace of the court towns. In 646, the emperor and his advisors introduced the far-reaching Taika reforms that were aimed at completely revamping the imperial administration along Chinese lines. Japanese court scholars struggled to master thousands of Chinese characters that bore little relationship to the language they spoke. They wrote dynastic histories patterned after those commissioned by the emperors of China, and followed an elaborate court etiquette that somewhat uneasily combined Chinese protocol with ancient Japanese ideas about politeness and decorum. The Japanese aristocracy struggled to master Confucian ways, while they worshiped in Chinese-style temples and admired Buddhist art that was Chinese in subject matter and technique.

Even the common people were affected by the steady flow of influence from the mainland. In the towns they stared in awe at the great Buddhist temples and bowed to passing aristocrats striving to present themselves as Confucian scholars. The peasants turned to Buddhist monks for cures when they were sick or to Buddhist magic when they needed a change of luck. They had begun to mesh the worship of Buddhist deities with that of the ancient *kami*, or nature spirits, of Japan.

Just as Chinese influence in Japan peaked, it began to be challenged—directly by the aristocracy, who increasingly argued for a return to Japanese ways, and silently by the peasantry, who steadily reworked Chinese Buddhism into a distinctly Japanese religion. In part, the erosion of support for Chinese ways reflected the failure of the ambitious reforms introduced by the emperor in 646. That failure led to a gradual seepage of power from the emperor and his administrators to first the aristocratic families in attendance at court and later local lords in the provinces. As this shift of power occurred, those who argued for a revival and strengthening of Japanese traditions at the expense of Chinese influence slowly gained the upper hand. By the 11th and 12th centuries, Japan's political and social systems had been virtually remade. Though important Chinese effects lingered, this new order bore little resemblance to the Chinese Confucian model that had triumphed in the Middle Kingdom under the Tang and Song.

CRISIS AT NARA AND THE SHIFT TO HEIAN (KYOTO)

If they had succeeded, the Taika reforms of 646 would have represented the culmination of centuries of Japanese borrowing from China. The central objectives of the proposed changes were to remake the Japanese monarch into an absolutist Chinese-style emperor (even to the point of adding "Son of Heaven" to the Japanese ruler's many ti-

Japan in the Imperial and Warlord Periods

In this artist's impression, Prince Genji, the hero of Lady Murasaki's novel of the Heian court, is surrounded by ladies of the court. From the elaborate dress and studied poses of Genji and his companions, the carefully cultivated trees, and the tasteful furniture and curtains, one gains a vivid sense of the formality and the attention to aesthetic pleasures that dominated the lives of the Japanese elite in this era.

tles) and to create a genuine professional bureaucracy and peasant conscript army in Japan to match those of Han-Tang China. But the changes necessary for these goals to be achieved were largely frustrated by the resistance of the aristocratic families and the Buddhist monastic orders who dominated both the emperor and the capital as a whole. A century later, the Buddhist monks in particular had grown so bold and powerful that the court and aristocracy lived in fear of street demonstrations by "rowdy monks" and of the escalating demands of the heads of the monastic orders. Their influence even threatened to engulf the throne in the 760s when a clever Buddhist prelate worked his way into the inner circle of the empress Koken. Though his schemes to marry her and claim the throne were uncovered and foiled, it was now clear that measures had to be taken both to ensure that women could never rule Japan and to check the growing influence of the monastic orders at court.

The emperor, Koken's husband, literally fled some 28 miles and established a new capital city at Heian, or what was later called Kyoto. The Buddhists were forbidden to build monasteries in the new capital. To get around this restriction, the monks established monasteries in the hills surrounding the new capital, and they soon reemerged as a potent force at court as royal advisors.

In addition to his efforts to control the Buddhist monks,

the emperor abandoned all pretense of continuing the Taika reforms, which in any case had long been stalled by aristocratic and popular opposition. He fully restored the great aristocratic families, whose power the reforms had been in part intended to curb. The elaborate system of ranks into which the aristocrats were divided (patterned after that in China) was maintained. But like the Koreans, the Japanese broke with Chinese precedent in determining rank primarily by birth and allowing little mobility between the various orders. The aristocrats had already taken over most of the positions in the central government; now their formal right to build up rural estates was restored as well. The emperor also gave up an ambitious scheme to build up a peasant conscript army, patterned after that created in China in the Tang era. In its place, local leaders were ordered to organize militia forces that would soon play a critical role in further eroding the actual control of the imperial household.

ULTRACIVILIZED: COURT LIFE IN THE HEIAN ERA

Though the basis of imperial political power had been severely compromised within decades of the shift to Heian, court culture soared to new levels of refinement. For several centuries more, the Japanese emperors and their courtiers continued to inhabit a closed world of luxury and aesthetic delights. Males and females of the aristocratic classes lived out their lives in accordance with strict codes of polite behavior, under the constant scrutiny of their peers and superiors. In this hothouse atmosphere, social status was everything; love affairs were a major preoccupation; and gossip was rampant. By our standards, life in this constricted and very artificial world was false and suffocating. Yet rarely in human history has so much energy been so focused on the pursuit of beauty, or has social interaction, on the surface at least, been so gracious and well mannered.

In this scene the artist depicts Genji seated with three ladies of the court under a maple tree.

At the Heian court, members of the imperial household and the leading aristocratic families lived in a complex of palaces and gardens. The buildings were of unpainted wood, which Japanese taste found the most appealing, with sliding panels, matted floors, and wooden walkways running between the separate residences where the many dignitaries lived. Fish ponds, man-made lakes with waterfalls, and fine gardens were interspersed among the courtiers' living quarters. Life in this sheltered world is depicted in the diaries and fiction written by a number of courtiers, but none captured its charm as well as its underlying tensions and sadness as wonderfully as Lady Murasaki's *Tale of Genji*. In this, the first novel in any language, she relates the life history of a prominent and amorous son of the emperor and the fate of his descendants.

As the story makes clear, Genji's life is almost wholly devoted to the pursuit of aesthetic enjoyment, whether this be found in affairs with beautiful women or in musical entertainments in a garden scented with blooming flowers. Uncouth commoners and distasteful things, such as dirt, cheap pottery, and rough popular entertainments, are to be avoided at all costs. When her rivals at the court wish to insult Genji's mother, they leave spoiled fruit in the passages where she or her maid servants must pass. An encounter with a shriveled piece of fruit contributes to the illness that leads to her premature death. Everyone who matters in Genji's world is obsessed with social conventions that govern everything, from which gown is proper for a given ceremony to the composition of a suitable poem to woo a potential lover or win the emperor's favor. Indeed, writing original verse was perhaps the most valued of arts at the court. The poems, which were often written on painted fans or scented paper and sometimes sent in little boats down the streams that ran through the palace grounds, were brief and full of allusions to Chinese and Japanese verse and classical writings. Genji, for example, expresses his disappointment at being denied access to a pretty young girl in the following poem:

Having come upon an evening blossom
The mist is loath to go with the morning sun.

Partly to accommodate the need for literary expression of this nature, the written script the Japanese had borrowed from the Chinese was simplified in this period, making it more compatible with spoken Japanese. One result of these changes was an outpouring of poetic and literary works that were more and more distinctively Japanese. In addition to novels like Lady Murasaki's, some of the most elegant poetry in the Japanese language was written in this era. Again it is characteristically sparing in words but rich in imagery and allusions to the natural world:

> *This perfectly still*
> *Spring Day bathed in the soft light*
> *From the spread-out sky,*
> *Why do the cherry blossoms so restlessly scatter down?*

> *Although I am sure*
> *That he will not be coming*
> *In the evening light*
> *When the locusts shrilly call*
> *I go to the door and wait.*

As the female authorship of this poem clearly illustrates, at the court women were expected to be as poised and cultured as men. They too wrote poems, played flutes or stringed instruments in informal concerts, and became embroiled in elaborate schemes to snub or disgrace rivals. Like their counterparts in China and the Islamic world, they also became involved in palace intrigues and power struggles, as the plotting against Genji's mother makes clear. Though it was unseemly for women to openly pursue princely lovers, some of them did—if we are to believe the *Tale of Genji* and other court memoirs—take the initiative. It was not unheard of for a highborn woman to spurn a suitor and humiliate him in front of her maidservants.

THE DECLINE OF IMPERIAL POWER

While the emperor and his courtiers admired the plum blossoms and the newest fashions in court dress, some of the aristocratic families at court were busy running the rapidly shrinking imperial bureaucracy. By the middle of the 9th century, one of these families, the Fujiwara, exercised exceptional influence over imperial affairs. They not only packed the upper administration with family members and the sons of allied households and shaped imperial policy, they increasingly married Fujiwaras into the imperial family. By the middle of the 10th century, one aged Fujiwara chief minister had seen four of his daughters married to emperors.

Families like the Fujiwara also took advantage of the wealth and influence their high office ensured to buy up large estates that provided a stable financial base for their growing power. Especially in the vicinity of the capital, they had to compete in these purchases with the Buddhist monasteries. But both could work together in the steady campaign to whittle down imperial control and increase their own. As the lands under their control expanded, both

the monks and court nobility greatly increased the number of peasants and artisans they effectively ruled. Cooperation between monastic orders and court aristocrats was promoted by the introduction of the secret texts and ceremonies of esoteric Buddhism in this period. These teachings and techniques to achieve salvation through prayers and meditation, which were focused by mystical diagrams and special hand positions, were the rage among the Heian elite. As aristocrats and monks steadily built up their own power in the capital, however, they failed to reckon with the growing power of the local lords.

THE RISE OF THE PROVINCIAL WARRIOR ELITE

The pursuit of landed estates that increasingly preoccupied the court aristocracy was also taken up by elite families in the provinces. Some of these were originally from aristocratic origins, but most had risen to power as landowners, estate managers, or local state officials. These families not only came to control land and labor and to deny these resources to the court, but they gradually carved out little kingdoms, ruled by "house" governments, in various parts of the islands. They ruled their kingdoms within the larger Japanese state from small fortresses surrounded by wooden or earthen walls and moatlike ditches. The local lord and his retainers were housed within the fortress, constantly on the alert for an attack by a neighboring lord or the forces of one of the powerful families at court. Granaries for storing the rice provided by local peasants, blacksmith forges and stables, wells for water, and even armories made the fortresses self-contained worlds.

Within the little kingdoms ruled from the forts, the warrior leaders, or *bushi*, administered law, supervised public works projects, and collected revenue—for themselves, not the court. The failure of the court's plans to build conscript armies also left the way open for the bushi to build up their own armies, which soon became the most effective military forces in the land. Though these mounted troops, or *samurai*, were loyal to the local lord, not to the court or high aristocratic officials, they were increasingly called in to protect the emperor and his retainers and keep the peace in the capital. As the imperial government's control over the country weakened in the 11th and 12th centuries, bandits freely roamed the countryside and the streets of the capital. Buddhist monasteries employed armed toughs to protect themselves and strike at rival sects. In this atmosphere of rampant crime and civil strife, both the court and high officials hired provincial lords and their samurai retainers to serve as bodyguards and to protect their palaces and mansions from robbery and arson.

The imposing presence of a fully armed samurai warrior is captured in this pen-and-ink drawing.

These trends proved critical to the emergence of a warrior class. Counting on peasant dependents to supply them with food and other necessities, the bushi and samurai devoted their lives to hunting, riding, archery practice, and other activities that sharpened their martial skills. Until the 12th century, the main weapons of the mounted warriors were powerful longbows, though they also carried straight swords. From the 12th century, they increasingly relied in combat on the superbly forged, curved steel swords that we commonly associate with the Japanese samurai. The bushi and the samurai warriors who served them rode into battles that increasingly hinged on the man-to-man duels of great champions. These combats represented heroic warfare in the extreme. The time and location of battles were elaborately negotiated beforehand, and each side strove to demonstrate the justice of its cause and the perfidy of its enemies. Before charging into battle, Japanese warriors would proudly proclaim their family lineage and its notable military exploits to their adversaries, who often missed the details because they were shouting back their own.

A warrior code developed that stressed family honor and death rather than retreat or defeat. Beaten or disgraced warriors turned to ritual suicide, which they called *seppuku* (disembowelment) but which is commonly known in the West by the more vulgar *hara-kiri* (belly splitting), to prove their courage and restore their family's honor. Battles were chaotic affairs—lots of shouting and clashing but relatively few fatalities—that were won or lost depending on the performance of the champions on each side. Though a full chivalric code did not develop until some centuries later, Japan was steadily moving toward a feudal order that was remarkably similar to that developing in western Europe in this era.

The rise of the samurai frustrated all hopes of creating a free peasantry. In fact, Japanese peasants were reduced in the next centuries to the status of serfs, bound to the land they worked and treated as the property of the local lord. They were also separated by rigid class barriers from the warrior elite, which was physically set off by its different ways of dressing and by prohibitions against the peasants carrying swords or riding on horseback. In their growing poverty and degradation, the peasants turned to popular Buddhism in the form of the salvationist "pure lands" sect, which offered the promise of bliss in heaven for those who lived upright lives on earth. Colorful figures, such as the dancing monk Kuya, and Genshin, whose *Essentials of Salvation* outlined in great detail the pleasures of paradise and the horrible tortures of hell, strove to make Buddhist teachings comprehensible and appealing both to the peasantry and the artisans in the towns. The latter were concentrated at the court center in Heian and the fortress towns of some of the more powerful bushi. Though their skills in pottery making, painting, and textile manufacture were celebrated by subsequent generations, the artisans were paid almost as poorly as the peasants and accorded little status. In contrast to China, where these activities were often pursued by the scholar-gentry, in Japan they were usually undertaken by professional craftsmen who inherited their skills from their fathers.

The horrible demons waiting to inflict torture on those who violate Buddhist teachings and fall into sin are graphically depicted in this painting of hell.

🙚 THE ERA OF WARRIOR DOMINANCE

As the power of the provincial lords grew, that of the imperial household *and* court aristocracy declined. Increasingly powerful families at the court, such as the Fujiwara, depended on alliances with regional lords to bolster them in disputes with their rivals. By the 11th and 12th centuries, the provincial families had begun to pack the court bureaucracy and contest power in their own right. By the mid-12th century, competition turned to open feuding between the most powerful of these families, the Taira and the Minamoto. For a time, the Taira gained the upper hand by controlling the emperor and dominating at court. But when rivalry turned to open warfare in the early 1180s, the Minamoto commanders and their powerful network of alliances with provincial lords in various parts of the country proved vastly superior to the leaders or allies the Taira could muster. More fundamentally, the Tairas' concentration of their power grabbing efforts in the capital led to the breakdown of critical links with rural notables, who often sided with the Minamoto in the factional struggles.

For five years, the Gempei Wars raged in the heartland of the main island of Honshu, much to the grief of the peasantry, whose farmlands were ravaged and who fought, forcibly conscripted but poorly armed and untrained, against each other, while the samurai clashed in their ritual combats. By 1185, the Taira house faction had been destroyed. The Minamoto then established the *bakufu*, which literally means "tent," or the military government at Kamakura in their base area on the Kanto plain, far east of the capital at Heian. The emperor and his court were preserved—in fact all the military houses would derive their legitimacy from the descendants of the sun goddess—but real power now rested with the Minamoto and their samurai retainers. The feudal age in Japan had begun.

ANALYSIS
COMPARING FEUDALISMS

Two societies in the world developed fully feudal political systems in the postclassical period: western Europe and Japan. To heighten the coincidence, they both did so at approximately the same time. Both used feudal relationships in situations where they could not sustain more complex political forms. The West had the example of Rome's empire, but medieval leaders could simply not reconstruct the elements that had allowed the empire to exist and flourish. They could not organize or afford the necessary armies; they could not generate agreement on standardized laws; and they could not produce an independent bureaucracy that could cut across tribes and language groups except through the important but somewhat specialized mechanism of the Church. The Japanese had the example of the Chinese imperial system available to them, and did briefly attempt a comparable kind of bureaucratic development, using Confucianism to promote the proper political attitudes. But again, the system did not take root in Japanese soil.

Both the West and Japan would develop more elaborate political forms, with the Japanese again making great use of Confucianism after the 16th century. But these innovations came late, after intermediate experience with feudal monarchy or the shogunate, and they had to incorporate centuries of feudal heritage, which meant, among other things, that they still did not replicate the imperial political structures of Rome or China.

In one sense the existence of feudalism requires no elaborate assessment. Many societies generated only weak central government structures simply because they lacked the resources, the shared political values, and the bureaucratic experience to develop alternatives. China under the Zhou dynasty is sometimes called feudal. The Russian kings from Rurik onward exercised only loose overlordship over powerful landlords. Kings in the divine monarchy systems of sub-Saharan Africa, which flourished from about the 9th until the 19th century in various parts of the continent, similarly relied on deals and compromises with local and regional leaders. Indeed, African historians have often noted with some justice that kingdoms, such as Ghana or Mali, were ruled about as effectively as were Western monarchies during the Middle Ages. A comparison of this sort reminds us that feudal systems were in many ways early, somewhat unsophisticated versions of political societies that were gradually moving from purely local toward more elaborate organization, and that almost all civiliza-

tions have experienced long periods of this sort of semicentralized rule. In all such cases, including the feudal cases, claims of central authorities are not matched by effective power (which is why central authorities so often rely on the idea of divine backing). Regional leaders have armies of their own and do much of the effective administration of their localities. Kings have to make deals with such leaders, relying on personal negotiation and pledges of mutual respect, marriage alliances, lots of negotiation, and a willingness to give the local princes much free rein in practice.

The feudal systems that arose in the West and Japan had some features that were different from the many other decentralized cases they admittedly resemble. These differences make it desirable, analytically, not to call all such cases *feudal*, lest a term extremely useful for comparison be diluted beyond recognition. Russia, for example—while it was often decentralized and frequently saw its rulers, whatever their grandiose claims, make concessions to regional nobles because they depended on their loyalty and service to rule—never developed a real feudal tradition, which is one of the features that distinguished it from the West. The same holds true for China in comparison with Japan, or for sub-Saharan Africa.

Japan and the medieval West developed in feudalism a set of political values that did, however imperfectly, embrace most of the participants in the system—primarily, of course, the aristocratic landlords. The idea of mutual ties and obligations, and the rituals and institutions that expressed them, went beyond more casual local deals and compromises. In both cases, feudalism was exceedingly militaristic. Both the medieval West and Japan went through long centuries of unusually frequent and bitter internal warfare, based in large part on feudal loyalties and rivalries. In both cases fighting was largely confined to the landlord class, and feudalism summed up a host of military virtues—bravery, allegiance in battle—that long discouraged more stable, centralized government. The military aura of feudalism in both cases survived the feudal era, giving Japan problems of dealing with its samurai class after the worst periods of internal conflict had passed (by the 17th century), and giving the West a strong belief that one purpose of the state was to make war and provide opportunities for military leaders to demonstrate their prowess.

The heritage of feudalism was not simply military, however. The idea of mutual ties as a foundation of political activity would continue to affect political life and institutions in both the West and Japan, even after the specifically feudal period ended. Here is where feudalism, with its elaborate rituals and the requirement that young leaders be initiated into its value system, differed most markedly from other decentralized systems.

Adding complexity, however, the heritages of feudalism in Japan and in the West were not identical. Western feudalism emphasized contractual ideas more strongly than did Japanese. While mutual ties were sincerely preached, the idea was that individuals contracted with each other with fairly careful assurance of the advantages they would extract from the situation as individuals. Japanese feudalism stressed group loyalties more purely. Probably for this reason the clearest ongoing legacy of feudalism in the West proved to be parliamentary institutions, where individual aristocrats (and townsmen and clergy) could join to defend interests against the central monarch. In Japan, feudalism's legacy involved a less institutionalized group consciousness, propelling individuals to function as part of collective decision-making teams that ultimately could be linked to the state. In both cases, feudalism helped shape a distinctive political style that would be combined with later centralizing tendencies; but the styles themselves were not the same.

Can the common fact of a feudal heritage be used to explain another similarity between the West and Japan that emerged clearly only in the 20th century? Both societies have proved to be unusually successful in industrial development, leading the world in this regard by the final quarter of our own century. It would certainly be tempting, and convenient, to point to feudalism, the medieval feature the two societies uniquely shared, as a partial explanation for the otherwise unexpected 20th-century resemblance.

By limiting the growth of a central state, feudalism may in both societies have provided important latitude for other forces, such as merchants, to develop independent expression. The interest in military prowess extended to a concern for technological innovation, which could fuel broader economic change. The somewhat chaotic vigor of feudalism might, though in admittedly obscure ways, generate the kinds of dynamism that would later feed industrial development. Connections of this sort are tantalizing, yet they cannot be pressed too far. A great deal of diverse history must be added before we can pretend to relate medieval politics to modern economic forms, for neither in the West nor in Japan were political characteristics immutably set by the 14th century.

When the Japanese talent for group cohesion is identified so strikingly as an ingredient in 20th-century economic success, or when Western nations painfully win political stability through use of parliamentary forms, it surely seems legitimate to point to some persistent threads that, though greatly altered with new circumstances, run through the experience of the two societies. Whether one can push further, to treat the common experience of feudalism as a common basis for later economic dynamism, is

a matter for speculation. It need not, however, be excluded from a list of provocative uses of comparative analysis simply because the links are challenging.

Questions: Do you think characteristics of feudalism help explain the later success of Western and Japanese societies? What other factors must be considered? Why might Arab or Chinese historians be skeptical about claims for feudalism's special importance in world history? ☸

THE DECLINING INFLUENCE OF CHINA

As the power of the imperial house weakened and that of the aristocracy grew, the relevance of Chinese precedents and institutions for the Japanese diminished. Pretensions to a heavenly mandate and centralized power became ludicrous; the emergence of a scholar-gentry elite was stifled by the reassertion of aristocratic power and prerogatives. Grand designs for an imperial bureaucracy never materialized. The central Confucian precept that civilian administrators should rule and soldiers serve and keep out of the way was utterly violated by the growing influence of the provincially based bushi elite and their samurai retainers. Even Buddhism, which from the outset had been a central channel for the transmission of Chinese influence, was increasingly transformed by both aristocrats and peasants into a distinctively Japanese religion.

With the decline of the Tang and a return to decades of political uncertainty and social turmoil in China, the China model seemed even less relevant to the Japanese. As early as 838, the Japanese court decided to discontinue its embassies to the much-reduced Tang court. Japanese monks and traders continued to make the dangerous sea crossing to China, but the emperor's advisors no longer deemed official visits and groveling before the Son of Heaven worth all the bother.

THE BREAKDOWN OF BAKUFU DOMINANCE AND THE AGE OF THE WARLORDS

Yoritomo, the leader of the victorious Minamoto, gravely weakened the Kamakura regime due to his obsessive fear of being overthrown by members of his own family. Close relatives, including his brother Yoshitsune, whose courage and military genius had much to do with the Minamoto triumph over the Taira, were murdered or driven into exile. Fear of spies and uncertainty about what one could do in order to be above suspicion lent an element of paranoia to elite life under the first of the Kamakura *shoguns,* or the military leaders of the bakufu. Though Yoritomo's rule went unchallenged, the measures he had adopted to protect his throne left him without an able heir. His death and the weakness of those who succeeded him led to a scramble on the part of the bushi lords to build up their own power and enlarge their domains. The Hojo, one of the warrior families that had long been closely allied to the Minamoto, soon dominated the Kamakura regime, though they were content to leave the Minamoto as the formal rulers. Thus, a curious and confusing three-tiered system arose with real power resting in the Hojo family, who manipulated the Minamoto shoguns, who in turn claimed to rule in the name of the emperor who resided at Kyoto.

In the early 14th century, the situation became murkier still when the head of one of the branches of the Minamoto family, named Ashikaga Takuaji, led a revolt of the bushi that overthrew the Kamakura regime and established the Ashikaga Shogunate (1336–1573) in its place. Because the emperor at the time of Ashikaga's seizure of power refused to recognize the usurper and sought to revive imperial power, he was driven from Kyoto to the mountain town of Yoshino. There, with the support of a number of warlords, he and his heirs fought against the Ashikaga faction and the puppet emperors they placed on the throne at Kyoto for much of the rest of the 14th century.

Though the Ashikaga were finally successful in destroying the rival Yoshino center of imperial authority, the long period of civil strife seriously undermined both whatever authority the emperor had left and that of the shogunate. The bushi vassals of the warring factions were free to crush local rivals and seize the lands of the peasantry as well as the agents of the old aristocracy and the competing warlords. As the power of the warlords grew, the court aristocracy, which was impoverished by its inability to defend its estates, was virtually wiped out. The lands the warlords acquired were parceled out to their samurai retainers, who in turn pledged their loyalty and were expected to provide military support whenever their lord called on them. Though the pledge was formal, it did not involve the legal contract that bound lord and vassal in Europe in this period. Because most of the warlord's vassals were no longer linked to him by family ties, vows of loyalty counted for a good deal less than in earlier centuries. Vassals frequently struck deals with rival lords whom they believed to be on the rise or who promised to reward them more handsomely for their services. Acts of betrayal,

including shifting sides on the battlefield, were more and more common, and unscrupulous upstarts rose and fell in rapid succession.

The collapse of any semblance of centralized authority was sharply accelerated by the outbreak of the Onin War, which raged for over a decade between 1467 and 1477. Rival heirs to the Ashikaga Shogunate called on the warlord chiefs to support their claims. Samurai flocked to the rival headquarters in different sections of Kyoto, where feuding soon broke into all-out warfare. Within a matter of years, the old imperial capital had been reduced to rubble and weed-choked fields. While the shogunate self-destructed in the capital, the provincial lords continued to amass power and plot new coalitions to destroy their enemies. Japan was divided into nearly 300 little states, whose warlord rulers (the successors of the bushi) were called *daimyos.* Unlike the bushi domains of earlier centuries, the daimyos' holdings, which varied greatly in size, were consolidated into unified and bounded ministates. In the place of mud-walled forts, there arose the massive wood and stone castles that would dominate the Japanese landscape for centuries. To discourage betrayal by their vassals, the daimyo required them to live in the towns that developed around the castles, or at least to leave members of their families there as hostages to ensure their good behavior.

TOWARD BARBARISM? MILITARY DIVISION AND SOCIAL CHANGE

Though the rituals became more elaborate, the armor heavier, and the swords more superbly forged, the chivalrous qualities of the bushi era deteriorated noticeably in the 15th and 16th centuries. Spying, sneak attacks, ruses, and timely betrayals became the order of the day. The pattern of warfare was fundamentally transformed as large numbers of peasants armed with pikes became a critical component of daimyo armies. Battles hinged less and less on the outcome of samurai combat. Victory depended on the size and organization of a warlord's forces and on how effectively his commanders employed them in the field. The scarcely trained and poorly fed peasant forces became a major source of the growing misery of the common people. As they marched about the countryside to fight the incessant wars of their overlords, they looted and pillaged with impunity. Often in response to the depredations of warlord armies, the peasantry in different areas sporadically rose up in hopeless but often ferocious revolts that fed the trend toward brutality and destruction. It is no wonder that contemporary accounts of the era, as well as those written in

Himeji Castle was one of the most formidable of the many fortresses that dominated the Japanese landscape in the age of warlord dominance. Though the inner buildings were often built of wood, these more vulnerable structures were defended by walls and long, fortified passageways made of stone at the entrances.

later centuries, are dominated by a sense of pessimism and foreboding—a conviction that Japan was reverting from civilized life to barbarism.

Despite the chaos and suffering of the warlord period, there was much economic and cultural growth. Most of the daimyos clearly recognized the necessity of building up their petty states if they were to be strong enough to survive in the long run. Within the domains of the more able daimyos, attempts were made to stabilize village life by introducing regular tax collection, supporting the construction of irrigation systems and other public works, and building strong rural communities. Incentives were offered to encourage the settlement of unoccupied areas, and new tools, the greater use of draft animals, and new crops—especially soybeans—contributed to the well-being of the peasantry in the better-run domains. Peasants were also encouraged to produce items such as silk, hemp, paper, dyes, and vegetable oils, which were highly marketable and thus potential sources of household income. Daimyos vied with each other to attract merchants to their growing castle towns, and a new and quite wealthy commercial class emerged as the purveyors of goods for the military elite and the intermediaries in trade between Japan and overseas areas, especially China. As in medieval Europe, guild organizations for both craftsmen (carpenters, thatchers, smiths, potters, etc.) and merchants were strong in this era. They helped provide social solidarity and group protection in a time of political breakdown and insecurity.

There is considerable evidence that the growth of commerce and the handicraft industries gave a minority of Japanese women opportunities to avoid the sharp drop in status that most experienced in the age of the warring daimyos. Women in merchant and artisan families apparently exercised a fair degree of independence that was reflected in their participation in guild organizations, business management, and the fact that their positions were sometimes inherited by their daughters. But the position of the women in the emerging commercial classes contrasted sharply with that of women of the warrior elites. In earlier centuries the wives and daughters of the provincial bushi households learned to ride and to use a bow and arrow, and often joined in the hunt. By the 14th and 15th centuries, however, the trend among the daimyo families toward *primogeniture*, or the restriction of inheritance to the eldest son, dealt a heavy blow to women among the elite classes. Wives and daughters of warrior households, who had hitherto shared in the division of the family estate, now received little or no land or income.

Disinheritance was part of a larger pattern that saw women increasingly treated as defenseless appendages of their warrior fathers or husbands. They were given in marriage to cement alliances between warrior households, raised to anticipate their warrior husband's every desire, and taught to slay themselves rather than dishonor the family line by being defiled by illicit suitors or enemy soldiers. That the restrictions and loss of status felt by women at the level of the warrior elite were shared by Japanese women more generally is suggested by their loss of the role of the celebrant in village religious ceremonies and their replacement in Japanese theatrical performances by males specially trained to impersonate women.

Fears that the constant wars between the swaggering samurai might drag Japan back to barbarism were somewhat mollified by continuing cultivation of the arts in the warring-houses era. Zen Buddhism, which due to its stress on simplicity and discipline had a special appeal to the warrior elite, played a critical role in securing the place of the arts in an era of strife and destruction. Zen monasteries provided key points of renewed diplomatic and trade contacts with China, which in turn led to a revival of Chinese influence in Japan, at least at the cultural level. Though much of the painting of the era imitated contemporary Chinese work, the monochrome ink sketches of Japanese artists were both brilliant and original. Also notable were screen and scroll paintings, some of which capture the natural beauty of Japan, while others provide us with invalu-

Patronage of landscape painting and the other fine arts made it possible for artistic expression to survive in the long centuries of political division and civil war.

able glimpses into Japanese life in this period. Zen sensibilities are also prominent in some of the splendid architectural works of this period, including the Golden and Silver Pavilions that two of the Ashikaga shoguns had built in Kyoto. Each pavilion is designed to blend into the natural setting in which it is placed, to create a pleasing shelter from which one might contemplate nature.

This contemplative mood is also evident in the design of some of the more famous gardens that were laid out in this era, such as that at the Ryoanji Temple that consists entirely of islands of volcanic rock set amid white sand that is periodically raked into varying patterns. The influence of Zen and the related Japanese ability to find great beauty in the rough and simple were also present in the tea ceremony that developed in the era of warrior dominance. The graceful gestures, elaborate rituals, and subtly shaped and glazed

The Golden Pavilion, also called the Kinkaku-ji Pavilion, is a relic of the cultural golden age of the 15th century.

pots and cups that came to be associated with the service of tea on special occasions all lent themselves to composure and meditation. Walking the paths near the Golden Temple or sitting in the wooden gallery that looks out into the garden at Ryoanji, it is hard to imagine that places of such beauty were created in an era so dominated by violence and civil strife.

SEEDS OF UNITY AND JAPANESE NATIONHOOD

The economic and cultural growth of the warlord era demonstrated that Japan would not slip back into chaos and barbarism. Interestingly, these developments, combined with measures taken by the daimyos to improve administra-

tion within their domains, laid the basis for the lasting unification of Japan. Though often tied to particular lords and castle towns, the emerging commercial and artisan classes would in later centuries readily transfer their capital reserves and talents to building a unified economy under political leaders determined to break down regional trade barriers and to create a unified currency and system of weights and measures. Though it was long disguised by the rivalries and warfare between the daimyo lords, the legal and administrative systems established within each of the feudal domains could, if linked together, provide the bureaucratic infrastructure for a unified Japanese state. Within the domains, there also began to emerge professional government functionaries who were slowly acquiring the skills that would eventually enable them to man a centralized bureaucracy.

What was needed, of course, was a leader or coalition of leaders capable of politically and economically unifying the many parts into which Japan had fragmented. Amid the warfare and famine that ravaged Japan in the 15th century, there seemed to be little hope of such leadership emerging. But within a century a succession of three able military and political leaders would again establish a central authority in the islands. Though the daimyo divisions, somewhat reduced in numbers, remained, Japan was on its way to becoming a unified nation-state.

KOREA: BETWEEN CHINA AND JAPAN

Of all the areas to which the Chinese formula for civilized development spread, Korea was the most profoundly influenced for the longest period of time. Because the Korean peninsula is no more than a physical extension of the Chinese mainland, and because historically Korean kingdoms were dwarfed by their giant neighbor to the west, most observers have treated Korea as little more than an appendage of China. In fact, this was a view often adopted by the Koreans themselves, as they sought to memorize Chinese classics or faithfully imitate the current style in Chinese poetry or essay writing. But lumping Korea together with China overlooks the fact that the peninsula was ruled by indigenous dynasties through most of its history, even though these dynasties often paid tribute to the reigning Chinese emperor. Equally important, the Korean people, like the Vietnamese and Japanese, developed a separate identity that was expressed in distinctive forms of dress, cuisine, material culture, and a class system that varied significantly from that in China.

Korean development was also strongly affected by interchange with the nomadic peoples of Manchuria to the north and Japan across the sea to the east. In these contacts, the Koreans sometimes played active roles as civilizers in their own right. They were, for example, instrumental in the transmission of Buddhist teachings and art forms to Japan. Therefore, in tracing Korea's rise as one of the major satellite civilizations of China, we must be careful not to neglect the initiatives and remarkable creativity of the Korean people themselves.

DIVISION AND CHINESE DOMINANCE

The peoples who occupied the Korean peninsula represented quite a different ethnic blend than those who came some centuries earlier to identify themselves as Chinese. The Koreans descended from the hunting and herding peoples of eastern Siberia and Manchuria, rather than the Mongolian and Turkic-speaking tribes to the west. By the 4th century B.C., those who moved into the Korean peninsula had begun to acquire sedentary farming and metalworking techniques from the Chinese. From this point onward the Koreans played a role in the dynastic struggles that preoccupied the peoples of the north China plain. In 109 B.C. the earliest Korean kingdom, Choson, was conquered by the Han emperor Wudi, and parts of Korea were colonized by Chinese settlers who would remain for nearly four centuries. These colonies soon became a channel by which Chinese influences began to filter into Korean culture in the critical centuries of its early development. A small Japanese enclave in the southeast of the peninsula provided contacts with the islands as well, though cultural influences in this era ran overwhelmingly east from China to Korea and then on to Japan.

The Korean Peninsula during the Three Kingdoms Era

Despite conquest and colonization under the Han, the tribal peoples of the peninsula, particularly the Koguryo in the north, soon rose in resistance to Chinese rule. As Chinese control weakened, the Koguryo established an independent state in the northern half of the peninsula that was soon at war with two southern rivals, Silla and Paekche. Divisions within Korea permitted periodic nomadic incursions and interventions by the nomadic dynasties that ruled China in the era of disunity following the collapse of the Han Empire. Contacts between the splinter kingdoms of North China and Koguryo resulted in the first wave of *Sinification*—that is, the extensive adoption of Chinese culture—in Korea. As was the case in Japan, Buddhism supplied the key links between Korea and the successors of the Han dynasty in northeast China. Korean rulers patronized Buddhist artists and financed the building of monasteries and pagodas. Korean scholars traveled to China and a select few went to the source of the Buddhist faith, India.

In addition to Sinified variants of Buddhism, Chinese writing was introduced, even though the spoken Korean language was as ill-suited for adaptation to the Chinese characters as the Japanese language had been. The Koguryo monarch imposed a unified law code patterned after that of Han China. He established universities, where Korean youths struggled to master the Confucian classics and their teachers wrote histories of China rather than their own land. With the intent of expanding his power and improving revenue collection, the Koguryo ruler also attempted to put together a Chinese-style bureaucracy. But the noble families who supported him had little use for a project that posed such an obvious threat to their own power. Without their support the monarch did not have the resources for such an ambitious undertaking. Thus, the full implementation had to wait for a more powerful dynasty to emerge some centuries later.

THE FULL ADOPTION OF THE CHINESE MODEL UNDER THE SILLA AND KORYO

Centuries of warfare between the three kingdoms weakened each without giving paramount power in the peninsula to any. Internal strife also left Korea vulnerable to further attacks from the outside, this time by the Sui ruler, Wendi, who viewed the conquest of Korea as a vital part of his campaign to reconstruct the Chinese Empire as it had been under the Han. As we have seen, Wendi's campaigns in Korea were not only unsuccessful, they were so mishandled and costly that they led to his overthrow and the replacement of the short-lived Sui by the Tang dynasty. The founders of the Tang also included Korea in the territories they staked out for their empire, but it was some decades before one of them could finally mount a successful invasion. The stubborn warriors of the Koguryo kingdom bore the brunt of the Tang assaults, just as they had those launched by the Sui rulers. Finally, Tang strategists hit on the idea of taking advantage of Korean divisions to bring the troublesome region into line. Striking an alliance with the rulers of the Silla kingdom to the southeast, they destroyed the Paekche kingdom and then defeated the Koguryo and put an end to the long-lived dynasty that had played such a key role in Korea's early development.

The Chinese conquerors now began to quarrel with their Silla allies over how to divide the spoils. When the Silla proved able to fight the larger Chinese forces in the peninsula to a standstill and revolts broke out in the former Paekche and Koguryo territories already conquered, the Tang decided it was time to strike a deal. In return for the Silla monarch's submission as a vassal of the Tang emperor and regular tribute payments, the Chinese withdrew their armies in 668, leaving the Silla in effect the independent rulers of a united Korea. Despite brief lapses, the Koreans were to maintain this independence and roughly the same boundaries established by the Silla until the occupation of their land by the Japanese in the early 20th century.

SINIFICATION: THE TRIBUTARY LINK

Under the Silla monarchs, who ruled from 668 until the late 9th century, and the Koryo dynasty (918–1392) that followed, Chinese influences peaked and Korean culture achieved its first full flowering. The Silla rulers consciously strove to turn their kingdom into a miniature of the Tang Empire. They regularly sent embassies and tribute to the Tang court, where Korean scholars collected Chinese texts and noted the latest fashions in court dress and etiquette. The Koreans' regular attendance on the Chinese emperors was a key manifestation of their prominent and enduring participation in the Chinese tribute system. At various times, the participants in the system included nomads from central and North Asia, the Tibetans, many of the kingdoms of Southeast Asia, and the emperors of Japan. None of these participants was more committed to the tributary arrangements than the Koreans. Rather than attempt to conquer the Koreans and other surrounding peoples, most Chinese emperors were content to receive embassies from them. These emissaries both offered tribute in the form of splendid gifts and acknowledged the superiority of the Son of Heaven by their willingness to kowtow to him (kowtowing involved a series of ritual bows in which the supplicant prostrated himself before the throne).

To most of the peoples involved, this seemed a small price to pay for the benefits they received from the Middle Kingdom. Not only did submission and tribute guarantee continuing peace with the Chinese, it brought far richer gifts in return for those offered to the Chinese ruler, plus privileged access to Chinese learning, art, and manufactured goods. Tribute missions normally included merchants, whose ability to buy up Chinese manufactures and sell their own goods in the lucrative Chinese market hinged on their country's participation in the tribute system. Missions from heavily Sinified areas, such as Japan, Korea, and Vietnam, also included contingents of scholars, who studied at Chinese academies or Buddhist monasteries and busily purchased Chinese scrolls and works of art to fill the libraries and embellish the palaces back home. Thus, the tribute system became a major channel of trade and intercultural exchange between China and its neighbors. Until forcibly dismantled by the European powers in the 19th century, the system was virtually the only means by which the Middle Kingdom maintained ongoing relations with the Sinified (and thus civilized) states and the "barbarian" peoples who surrounded it on all sides.

THE SINIFICATION OF KOREAN ELITE CULTURE

The Silla rulers rebuilt their capital at Kumsong on the Kyongju plain to look like its Tang counterpart. The streets were laid out on a regular grid; there were central markets, parks and lakes, and a separate district to house the imperial family. Fleeing the tedium of the backward rural areas and provincial capitals, the aristocratic families who surrounded the throne and dominated imperial government crowded their mansions in the areas around the imperial palace. With their large extended families and hundreds of slaves and hangers-on, they made up a sizeable portion of the capital's population. Some of the aristocracy studied in Chinese schools, and a minority even submitted to the rigors of the Confucian examination system introduced under the Silla rulers. Most of the aristocracy opted for the artistic pursuits and entertainments available in the capital. They could do so because most positions in the government continued to be occupied by members of the aristocratic families, by virtue of their birth and family connections rather than their knowledge of the Confucian classics. In this and other respects, the attempt to duplicate the Chinese bureaucratic apparatus was a failure under the Silla. Though the Koryo monarchs were somewhat more successful in this regard, the aristocratic clans continued to dominate Korean politics and society as a whole.

Partly out of self-interest, the Korean elite continued to favor Buddhism over Confucianism. They and the Korean royal family lavishly endowed monasteries and patronized works of art, which became major forms of Korean cultural creativity. The capital at Kumsong soon became crowded with Buddhist temples, which were usually built of wood; Buddhist monks were constantly in attendance on the ruler as well as members of the royal family and the more powerful aristocratic households. But the schools of Buddhism that caught on among the elite were Chinese; Korean artwork and monastic design reproduced, sometimes splendidly, Chinese prototypes; and even the location of monasteries and pagodas in high places followed Chinese ideas about the need to mollify local spirits and balance supernatural forces.

Sometimes the Koreans borrowed from the Chinese and then outdid their teachers. Most notable in this regard was the pottery produced in both the Silla and Koryo eras. The Koreans first learned the techniques of porcelain manufacture from the Chinese. But in the pale green-glazed celadon bowls and vases of the late Silla and Koryo, they created masterworks that even Chinese connoisseurs admired and collected. They also pioneered in making oxide glazes that were used in the manufacture of the black- and rust-colored stoneware of this era, which is still recognized as some of the finest pottery ever crafted.

CIVILIZATION FOR THE FEW

With the exception of Buddhist sects like the "pure lands" that had strong appeal to the ordinary people, imports from China in this and later eras were all but monopolized by the tiny elite. The aristocratic families were divided into several ranks that neither intermarried nor socialized with each other, much less the rest of the population. They not only filled most of the posts in the Korean bureaucracy, but also dominated the social and economic life of the entire kingdom. Much of Korea's trade with the Chinese and Japanese was oriented to providing the aristocrats with the fancy clothing, special teas, scrolls, and artwork that occupied such an important place in their idle lives. In return, Korea exported mainly raw materials, such as forest products and metals like copper, which was mined by virtual slaves who lived in horrendous conditions. Some manufactures, including pottery, ink, paper, and painted fans, also found their way into Korea's trade with China and Japan. Often members of the royal family and the aristocratic households financed artisan production for export or the supply of the court; some backed mercantile expeditions and even engaged extensively in money-lending. All of this, of course, constricted the activities of artisans and traders. The former were usually considered low in status and were poorly paid for their talents and labor. The latter were so weak that they did not really form a distinct class.

The aristocratic "ranks" were the only people who really counted for anything in Korean society. The classes beneath them were oriented to their service. These included government functionaries, who were recognized as a separate social category; commoners, who were mainly peasants; and virtual slaves, who were known as the "low born" and ranged from miners and artisans to servants and entertainers. Persons from these social groups benefited little from contacts with China, and most lived lives of drudgery and poverty that were scarcely, if at all, enlivened by extensive cultural borrowing from China.

A real Chinese civil service never developed in Korea to provide the services to the masses that the Confucians had envisioned as essential responsibilities of the privileged elite. Buddhist festivals periodically relieved the monotony of the lives of the common people, and Buddhist salvationist teachings gave them hope for bliss in the afterlife. But much of what the peasants, artisans, and miners produced went to support the outsized court and aristocracy in the capital, where the wealth and cultural creativity of an otherwise impoverished and backward land was concentrated.

KORYO COLLAPSE: DYNASTIC RENEWAL

Periodically, the common people and the "low born" found their lot too much to bear and rose up against a ruling class that was obviously much more devoted to pursuing its own pleasures than to their well-being. Most of these risings were local affairs that were ruthlessly repressed by armies of the ruling class. But collectively they weakened both the Silla and Koryo regimes, and in combination with quarrels between the aristocratic households and outside invasions they contributed to the fall of both dynasties. In the absence of real alternatives, the aristocratic families managed to survive these crises and elevate one of their number above the others to the royal throne. After nearly a century and a half of conflict and turmoil triggered by the Mongol invasion in 1231, the Yi dynasty was established in 1392; remarkably, it would rule Korea until 1910. Though there would be some modifications, the Yi quickly restored the aristocratic dominance and links to China that had predominated under their predecessors. Of all of the peoples who received higher civilization from China, none would be as content to live in the shadow of the Middle Kingdom as the Koreans.

These Korean ceramic cups, formed in the shape of lotus flowers with decorative stands, are from the time of the Korai dynasty (924–1392).

✾ BETWEEN CHINA AND SOUTHEAST ASIA: THE MAKING OF VIETNAM

From the Chinese point of view, the Red River valley, which became the heartland of the Vietnamese people in the 1st millennium A.D., was just another rice-growing area to be annexed to their ever expanding civilization. So much territory and so many peoples had already been absorbed in the fertile southern regions that it was natural to anticipate the same fate for the Red River area and its inhabitants. But the Viets, who lived there, differed in critical ways from the other "southern barbarians" the Chinese had encountered. For one thing, their homeland was farther away from the main centers of Chinese political power on the northern plains than any people whom the Chinese had sought to absorb up to that point. For another, the Viets had already developed a fairly sophisticated and, as it turned out, very resilient culture of their own—a culture that shared much with the other peoples of Southeast Asia.

This culture in turn gave them a strong sense of themselves as a distinct people with a common heritage that they did not want to see overwhelmed by an expanding China. Thus, though the Viets were well aware of the benefits they derived from the superior technology, modes of political organization, and ideas they received from China, their gratitude was tempered by their fear of losing their own identity, of becoming just another part of China's massive civilization. This ambivalence is perhaps the central theme of the first two millennia of Vietnamese history, in which the Vietnamese admired and extensively adopted Chinese culture while they fiercely resisted Chinese rule.

FIRST CONTACTS: THE CHINESE AND THE "SOUTHERN BARBARIANS"

The Viets first came into history as a group of "southern barbarians" mentioned by Chinese scholars in accounts of Qin raids in South China in the 220s B.C. At that time their kingdom, which the Chinese called Nam Viet, meaning "people in the south," extended along the southern coastal area of what is now China. The initial raids by Qin forces left little lasting Chinese presence, but they probably gave a boost to the lively trade that had been conducted between the Viets and the peoples of South China for centuries. In exchange for silk manufactured by the Chinese, the Viets traded ivory, tortoise shells, pearls, peacock feathers, aromatic woods, and other exotic products drawn from the sea and tropical forests. Some decades after the Qin raids, the Viet rulers defeated the feudal lords who controlled the Red River valley and brought their lands under the control of the Viet kingdom. In the following centuries the Viets intermarried and blended with the Mon-Khmer and Tai-speaking peoples who occupied the Red River area. This proved to be a crucial step in the formation of the Vietnamese as a distinct ethnic group.

As the Viets' willingness to intermarry with ethnic groups like the Khmers (today's Cambodians) and the Tais suggests, before their conquest by the Han they possessed a culture that exhibited many features characteristic of Southeast Asia. Their spoken language was not related to Chinese. They enjoyed a strong tradition of village autonomy, physically symbolized by bamboo hedges that surround northern Vietnamese villages to the present day. The Vietnamese favored the nuclear family to the extended household preferred by the Chinese, and they never developed the clan networks that have been such a prominent feature of south Chinese society. Vietnamese women have historically possessed greater freedom and more influence, both within the family and in society at large, than their Chinese counterparts.

Vietnamese customs and cultural forms also differed very significantly from Chinese. The Vietnamese dressed quite differently; women, for example, preferred long skirts to the black pants nonelite women wore in China. The Vietnamese delighted in the archetypical Southeast Asian pastime, the cockfight; chewed betel nut, which the Chinese found disgusting; and blackened their teeth, which the Chinese also considered repulsive. In the centuries when they were dominated by the Chinese politically, the Vietnamese managed to preserve most of these original features of their society. They also became much more fervently attached at the grass roots level to Buddhism and developed art and literature, especially poetry, that was refined and quite distinct from that of the Chinese.

CONQUEST AND SINIFICATION

As the Han rulers who succeeded the Qin sought to incorporate South China into their empire, they inevitably came into conflict with the Viets. Though the Han emperor initially settled for the Viet ruler's admission of his vassal status and periodic payments of tribute, by 111 B.C. the Han thought it best to conquer the feisty Viets outright and to govern them directly by Chinese officials. The Red River area was garrisoned by Chinese troops, and Chinese administrators set to work co-opting the local lords and encouraging them to adopt Chinese culture. Because the Viet elite realized that they had a great deal to learn from their powerful neighbors to the north, they cooperated with the agents of the new regime. Sensing that they had found another barbarian people ripe for assimilation, the Chinese eagerly introduced essential elements of their own culture into the southern lands.

South China and Vietnam on the Eve of the Han Conquest

In the centuries after the Chinese conquest, the Vietnamese elite were drawn into the bureaucratic machine that the Han emperors and the shi had developed to hold together the empire won by the Qin. They attended Chinese-style schools, where they wrote in the Chinese script and read and memorized the classical Chinese texts of Confucius and Mencius. They took exams to qualify for administrative posts whose responsibilities and privileges were defined by Chinese precedents. They introduced Chinese cropping techniques and irrigation technology, which soon made Vietnamese agriculture the most productive in Southeast Asia. This meant that Vietnamese society, like Chinese, could support larger numbers of people—resulting in the high population density characteristic of the Red River valley and the lowland coastal areas to the south. The Vietnamese also found that Chinese political and military organization gave them a decisive edge over the Indianized peoples to the west and south, with whom they increasingly clashed over the control of lands to settle and cultivate. Over time, the Vietnamese elite adopted the extended family ideal and took to venerating their ancestors in the Confucian manner. Their Chinese overlords had every reason to assume that the barbarians were well on their way to becoming civilized—that is, like the Chinese.

DOCUMENT

LITERATURE AS A MIRROR OF THE EXCHANGES AMONG CIVILIZED CENTERS

The following passages from Lady Murasaki's classic Japanese account of court life, *The Tale of Genji* (Vintage Press, ed., 1985), and perhaps the most popular and beloved work of Vietnamese literature, Nguyen Du's *The Tale of Kieu* (Vintage Press, ed., 1973), provide superb examples of the important and far-reaching exchanges between the civilizations of South and East Asia. Not surprisingly, Chinese influences, including numerous allusions to Chinese writings and historical events, are paramount, but Buddhist (hence originally Indian) themes are pervasive in both works. As one of the following passages illustrates, there is also evidence of significant exchanges between the satellite civilizations of China.

[Kieu] dreamed a girl appeared hard by her side
and murmured: "Kieu! Your Karma's still undone.
How can you shirk your debt of grief to fate?
You yet have to play out your woman's role."

The moderator was a man of considerable learning. There was much of interest in his exchanges with the Korean. There were also exchanges of Chinese poetry, and in one of his poems the Korean succeeded most skillfully in conveying his joy at having been able to observe such a countenance on this the eve of his return to his own land. . . . Summoning an astrologer of the Indian school, the emperor was pleased to learn that the Indian view coincided with the Japanese and the Korean; and so he concluded that the boy should become a commoner with the name of Minamoto or Genji.

Looking at the keepsakes Myobu had brought back, [Genji] thought what a comfort it would be if some wizard were to bring him, like that Chinese emperor, a comb from the world where his lost love was dwelling. . . . There are limits to the powers of the most gifted artist. The Chinese lady in the paintings did not have the luster of life. Yang Kuei-fei was said to have resembled the lotus of the Sublime Pond, the willows of the Timeless Hall. No doubt she was very beautiful in her Chinese finery.

"You are well-famed as a lute-player," he
said.
"Like Chung Tzu-ch'i I've longed to hear
you play."
    . . . Now [Kieu] began to play. A battle
scene—
oh how they clashed and clanged, Han and Ch'u
swords!
The Ssu-ma tune, *A Phoenix Seeks His Mate*—
it sounded like an outburst of pure grief.
Then Hsi K'ang's masterpiece, *Kuang-ling*, was
heard:
it rushed on like a stream or flew like clouds.
Next came what Chao-chin played—she mourned
her Prince
and all her kinsfolk she must leave behind
as she crossed the Great Wall to wed a Hun.

The [abbot] talked of this ephemeral world and of the world to come. His own burden of sin was heavy, thought Genji, that he had been lured into an illicit and profitless affair. He would regret it all his life and suffer even more terribly in the life to come. What a joy to withdraw to such a place [a mountain monastery] as this!

When one must weigh and choose between one's love
and filial duty, which will turn the scale?
Kieu brushed aside her solemn vows to [the young
student] Kim—
she'd pay a daughter's debt before all else.
Resolved on what to do, she spoke her mind:
"Hands off my father, please! I'll sell myself and
ransom him."

"A happy home where love will reign," said Kieu,
"who does not dream of it? But I believe
a bride must bring her man the purity
of an unopened flower, the perfect shape
of a full moon. Priceless is chastity."

Questions: From these passages can you identify Chinese precedents in terms of place names and historical personages, allusions to Chinese literary works, and attitudes toward gender or social organization more generally that can be traced to Chinese models? Can you detect passages that convey Buddhist ideas about the nature of the world and human existence?

ROOTS OF RESISTANCE

Sporadic revolts, led by members of the Vietnamese aristocracy, and the failure of Chinese cultural imports to make much of an impression on the Vietnamese peasantry ultimately frustrated Chinese hopes for the absorption of the Viets. Though they had learned much from the Chinese, the Vietnamese lords chafed under their overlordship, in part because the Chinese often found it difficult to conceal their disdain for local customs in what they considered a backward and unhealthy outpost of the empire. Vietnamese literature attests to the less than reverent attitudes Vietnamese collaborators felt toward Chinese learning and culture. In the following poem a teacher mocks himself and doubts his usefulness to the people he serves:

> I bear the title "Disciple of Confucius."
> Why bother with blockheads, wearing such a label?
> I dress like a museum piece:
> I speak only in learned quotations (poetry and prose);
> Long since dried out, I still strut like a peacock;
> Failed in my exams, I've been dropped like a shrivelled root.
> Doctorate, M. A.: all out of reach,
> So why not teach school, and beat the devil out of my students.

Elsewhere in Vietnamese writings, self-doubts and mockery turn to rage and a fierce determination to resist Chinese dominance, whatever the cost. The following sentiments of a Vietnamese caught up in resistance to the reimposition of rule from China by the Mongols in the 13th century provides a dramatic case in point.

> I myself often forget to eat at mealtime, and in the middle of the night I wake up and caress my pillow. My intestines hurt me incessantly, as if they had been cut off, and tears flow abundantly from my eyes. My only grief is that I have not yet succeeded in hacking apart the enemy's body, peeling off his skin, swallowing his liver, drinking his blood.

The intensity and ferocity contained in this passage give some sense of why the Chinese failed in the end to hold or assimilate the Vietnamese. They also failed because the peasantry rallied again and again to the call of their own lords to rise up and drive off the alien rulers. The fact that the most famous of these risings was that led in A.D. 39 by the Trung sisters, who were children of a deposed local leader, points to the importance of the contrasting position of women in Chinese and Vietnamese society as a source of resistance to Chinese domination.

Vietnamese women were understandably hostile to the Confucian codes and family system that would have confined them to the household and subjected them to male authority figures. We do not know if this resentment figured in the Trung sisters' decision to revolt, but poetry written in later centuries by female authors leaves little doubt about the reactions of Vietnamese women to Confucian norms or male dominance. One of the most famous of these writers, Ho Xuan Huong, flaunts Confucian decorum in her ribald verse and mocks her male suitors:

> Careful, careful where are you going:
>   You group of know-nothings!
> Come here and let your older sister
>   teach you to write poems.
> Young bees whose stingers itch
>   rub them in wilted flowers.
> Young goats who have nothing to do with their horns
>   butt them against sparse shrubbery.

In the following poem, entitled "Sharing a Husband," Huong ridicules those who advocate the practice of polygamy, a practice favored by any self-respecting Confucian:

> One wife is covered by a quilted blanket, while one wife
>   is left in the cold.
> Cursed be this fate of sharing a common husband.
> Seldom do you have an occasion to possess your husband,
> Not even twice in one month.
> You toil and endure hardships in order to earn your
>   steamed rice, and then the rice is cold and tasteless.
> It is like renting your services for hire, and then
>   receiving no wages.
> How is it that I have turned out this way,
> I would rather suffer the fate of remaining unmarried
>   and living alone by myself.

WINNING INDEPENDENCE

In addition to a strong sense of prior identity and motives for resistance that crossed class and gender barriers, the Vietnamese struggle for independence was assisted by the fragility of the links that bound them to China. Great distances and mountain barriers created nightmare conditions for Chinese administrators responsible for supplying military expeditions to the far south. Only small numbers of Chinese—mostly bureaucrats, soldiers, and merchants—resided in the Red River area, and few of them remained on a permanent basis. Most critically, Chinese control over the distant Vietnamese depended on the strength of the ruling dynasties in China itself.

The Vietnamese were quick to take advantage of political turmoil and nomadic incursions in northern China to assert their independence. After failing to completely free themselves on several occasions, they mounted a massive rebellion during the period of chaos in China following the fall of the Tang dynasty in 907. By 939 they had won political independence from their northern neighbors. Though both the Mongol and Ming rulers of China later attempted to reassert control over the Vietnamese, both efforts ended in humiliating retreats. From 939 until the conquests of the French in the 19th century, the Vietnamese were masters of their own land.

THE CONTINUING CHINESE IMPACT

Though the Chinese political hold was broken, Chinese cultural exports continued to play central roles in Vietnamese society. A succession of Vietnamese dynasties beginning with the Le (980–1009), which became the source of legitimacy for the rest, built Chinese-style palaces in the midst of forbidden cities patterned after those in Changan and Beijing. They ruled through a bureaucracy that was a much smaller copy of the Chinese administrative system, with secretariats, six main ministries, and a bureau of censors to keep graft and corruption in check. Civil service exams were reintroduced, and an administrative elite schooled in the Confucian classics sought the emperor's favor and commanded deference from the common people. But the Vietnamese equivalent of the Chinese scholar-gentry never enjoyed as much power or influence. For one thing their control at the village level was much less secure than that of their Chinese counterparts. Much more than those in China, local Vietnamese officials tended to identify with the peasantry rather than with the court and higher administrators. To a much greater degree, they looked out for local interests and served as leaders in village risings against the ruling dynasty if its demands on the common people became too oppressive.

As in China during the period of division following the fall of the Han, the power of the scholar-bureaucrats in Vietnam was also limited in the reign of many dynasties by competition from well-educated Buddhist monks. The fact that the Buddhists sought and gained much stronger links with the Vietnamese peasantry than the monastic orders had in China strengthened them in their struggles with the Confucian scholars. The relatively high esteem in which women were held in Buddhist teachings and institutions also enhanced the popularity of the monks in Vietnam. Thus, countervailing centers of power and influence prevented most Vietnamese dynasties from enjoying the authority of their Chinese counterparts. They also frustrated

efforts by Confucian bureaucrats to control the peasantry as firmly as the Chinese scholar-gentry whom they sought to emulate.

THE VIETNAMESE DRIVE TO THE SOUTH

However watered down, the Chinese legacy gave the Vietnamese great advantages in the struggles within Indochina that became a major preoccupation of independent Vietnamese rulers. Because the Vietnamese refused to settle in the malarial highlands that fringed the Red River area and rose abruptly from the coastal plains farther south, their main adversaries were the Chams and Khmers, who occupied the lowland areas to the south that the Vietnamese coveted themselves. The Vietnamese launched periodic expeditions to retaliate for raids on their villages by the hill peoples. They also regularly traded with the hill dwellers for forest products, but the Vietnamese sought to minimize cultural exchange with these hunters and shifting agriculturists, whom they regarded as "nude savages."

As they moved out in the only direction left to them—south along the narrow plain between the mountains and the sea—the Vietnamese made good use of the larger population and superior bureaucratic and military organization that the Chinese connection had done much to foster. From the 11th to the 18th centuries, they fought a long series of generally successful wars against the Chams, an Indianized people living in the lowland areas along the coast. Eventually the Chams were driven into the highlands, where their descendants, in much diminished numbers, live to the present day. Having beaten the Chams and settled on their former croplands, the Vietnamese next clashed with the Khmers, who had begun to move into the Mekong delta region during the centuries of the Vietnamese drive south. Again Indianized armies, this time marching under Khmer rulers, whose power had declined markedly from that of the monarchs who had overseen the building of the great temples of Angkor Wat and the Bayon, proved no match for the Chinese-inspired military forces and weapons of the Vietnamese. By the time the French arrived in force in the Mekong area in the late-18th century, the Vietnamese had occupied much of the upper delta and were beginning to push into territory that today belongs to Cambodia.

EXPANSION AND DIVISION

As Vietnamese armies and peasant colonists moved farther and farther from the capital at Hanoi, the dynasties centered there found it increasingly difficult to control the commanders and peasants fighting and living in the frontier areas. As the southerners intermarried with and

As this view of the moat and part of the palace of the Vietnamese emperors at Hue illustrates, Chinese taste and architectural style strongly influenced the construction and decoration of Vietnamese court centers.

adopted some of the customs of the Chams and Khmers, differences in culture and attitude developed between them and the northerners. Though both continued to identify themselves as Vietnamese, the northerners (much like their counterparts in the United States) came to see the Vietnamese who settled in the frontier south as less energetic, slower in speech and movement. As the hold of the Hanoi-based dynasties over the southern regions slipped, regional military commanders grew less and less responsive to orders from the north and slower in remitting taxes due to the court. Bickering turned to violent clashes, and by the end of the 16th century a rival dynasty, the Nguyen, had emerged to challenge the legitimacy of the Trinh family that ruled the north.

The territories of the Nguyen at this point in time were centered on the narrow plains that connected the two great rice bowls of Vietnam along the Red and Mekong rivers. Their capital was at Hue, far north of the Mekong delta region that in this period had scarcely been settled by the Vietnamese. For the next two centuries these rival dynastic houses fought for the right to rule Vietnam. None accepted the division of Vietnam as permanent; each sought to unite all of the Vietnamese people under a single monarch. This long struggle not only absorbed much of the Vietnamese energies, it also prevented them from recognizing the growing external threat to their homeland. For the first time in history, the danger came not from the Chinese giant to the north, but from a distant land and religion about which the Vietnamese knew and cared nothing—France and the conversion-minded Roman Catholic church.

CONCLUSION

DIVERGENT PATHS IN EAST ASIAN DEVELOPMENT

The 1st millennium A.D. was a pivotal epoch in the history of the peoples of East Asia. The spread of ideas, organizational models, and material culture from a common Chinese center spawned the rise of three distinct satellite civilizations in Japan, Korea, and Vietnam. In contrast to the lands of the nomadic peoples who had long been in contact with China from the north and west, each of these regions contained fertile and well-watered lowland areas that were suited to sedentary cultivation, which was essential to the spread of the Chinese pattern of civilized development. Each in fact provided an ideal environment for the cultivation of wet rice, which was increasingly replacing millet and other grains as the staple of China.

Common elements of Chinese culture, from modes of writing and bureaucratic organization to religious teachings and art, were transmitted to each satellite. In all three cases, Chinese imports, with the important exception of popular Buddhism, were all but monopolized by court and provincial elite groups, the former prominent in Japan and Korea, the latter in Vietnam. In all three cases, Chinese thought patterns and modes of social organization were actively and willingly cultivated by these local elites, who were well aware that they were the key to a higher level of development.

Thus, for a time at least, all three satellites shared prominent aspects of political organization, social development, and intellectual creativity. But the differing ways in which Chinese influences were transmitted to each area resulted in very divergent outcomes in terms of the mix of Chinese-derived and indigenous elements that were blended to produce distinctive variations of a common pattern of civilized life. In Korea, where the period of direct Chinese rule was relatively brief but China's physical presence and military power all too apparent, the need for symbolic political submission was obvious and the desire for long-term cultural dependence firmly implanted. In Vietnam, where Chinese conquest and control lasted over a thousand years, a hard-fought struggle for political independence gave way to a growing attachment to Chinese culture as a counterbalance to the Indian influences that had brought civilization to the Southeast Asian rivals of the Vietnamese.

In Japan, where all attempts by Chinese dynasties to assert direct control had failed miserably, Chinese culture was emulated by the courtly elite that first brought civilization to Japan. But the rise of a rival aristocratic class, which was based in the provinces and championed military values that were fundamentally opposed to Chinese Confucianism, led to the gradual limitation of Chinese influence in Japanese culture and society and the reassertion of Japanese traditional ways. Japanese political patterns in particular formed a marked contrast with the predominance of rule by a centralized bureaucracy in China. Nonetheless, in Japan as in the rest of East Asia, China remained the epitome of civilized development; Chinese ways were the standard by which all peoples ought to be judged.

In Korea and Japan, as in China itself, preoccupation with interaction in the East Asian sphere led to many beneficial exchanges that were similar to those occurring in other centers of civilized life during the postclassical centuries. In East Asia, however, these exchanges occurred in semi-isolation, with a lower level of awareness of larger world currents than was the case among the peoples of the Islamic empires, Christian Europe, or the Buddhist kingdoms of mainland Southeast Asia. Thus, East Asia provides an important variant on the general theme of cross-cultural contact that was a dominant feature of the postclassical age.

FURTHER READINGS

In comparison with Korea, there is a wealth of good secondary works on early Japanese and Vietnamese history. The most accessible works on Korea are William Henthorn's *History of Korea* (1971), which gives some attention to the arts in addition to rather standard accounts of political and social changes; Hatada Takashi's *A History of Korea* (1969); and the sections by Albert Craig in Fairbank and Reischauer's *East Asia: The Modern Transformation*

(1965). The best introductory works to Japanese history and culture are the writings of Reischauer in J. W. Hall's *Japan from prehistory to modern times* (1970), and Mikisio Hane's superb overview, *Japan: A Historical Survey* (1972). H. Paul Varley's *Japanese Culture: A Short History* (1973) has fine sections on the arts, religion, and literature in the warlord era. Also good on this period are Peter Du-us's *Japanese Feudalism* (1969); Varley's *Samurai* (1970), which was coauthored with Ivan and Nobuko Morris; and the first and second volumes of George Sansom's *A History of Japan* (1958, 1960).

For an understanding of the Chinese impact on Vietnam, there is no better place to begin than Alexander Woodsides' *Vietnam and the Chinese Model* (1971). The best works on the earliest period in Vietnamese history are translations of the writings of the French scholar Georges Coedes and the superspecialized *Birth of Vietnam* (1983) by Keith Taylor. Thomas Hodgkin's survey of Vietnamese history has the virtues of being highly readable plus making extensive use of Vietnamese literature. Troung Buu Lam's edited volume of *Patterns of Vietnamese Response to Foreign Intervention* (1967), along with the Genji and Kieu tales cited in the "Document" of this chapter, provides wonderful ways for the student to get inside Japanese or Vietnamese culture.

1130–c. 1250 Almohads rule North Africa and Spain

1215 First Mongol attacks on
North China; Beijing captured

1236–1240 Mongol
conquest of Russia

1234 Mongols take all of North
China; End of Qin dynasty

1037–1194 Seljuk Turks dominant in the Middle East

1235–1279 Mongol conquest of South
China; End of southern Song dynasty

1115–1234 Jurchens (Qin
dynasty) rules North China

1227 Death of Chinggis Khan;
Ogedei named successor

907–1118 Khitan conquest of North China

1219–1223 First Mongol invasions
of Russia and the Islamic world

1126 Song dynasty flees to South China

1206 Temujin takes the name of Chinggis Khan; Mongol state is founded

20 The Last Great Nomadic Challenges: From Chinggis Khan to Timur

INTRODUCTION. From the first explosion of Mongol military might from the steppes of central Asia in the early decades of the 13th century to the death of Timur in 1405, the nomads of central Asia made a last, stunning return to center stage in world history. Mongol invasions ended or interrupted many of the great empires of the postclassical period, while also extending the world network that had increasingly defined the period. Under Chinggis Khan— who united his own Mongol tribesmen and numerous nomadic neighbors into the mightiest war machine the world had seen to that time—central Asia, northern China, and eastern Persia were brought under Mongol rule. Under Chinggis Khan's sons and grandsons, the rest of China, Tibet, Persia, Iraq, much of Asia Minor, and all of southern Russia were added to the vast Mongol imperium. Though the empire was divided between Chinggis Khan's sons after his death in 1227, the four *khanates* or kingdoms— which emerged in the struggles for succession—dominated most of Asia for the next one and one-half centuries. The Mongol conquests and the empires they produced represented the most formidable nomadic challenge to the growing global dominance of the sedentary peoples of the civilized cores since the great nomadic migrations in the first centuries A.D. Except for Timur's devastating but short-lived grab for power at the end of the 14th century, nomadic peoples would never again mount a challenge as massive and sweeping as that of the Mongols.

1240–1241 Mongol invasion of western Europe

1271–1368 Reign of the Yuan (Mongol) dynasty in China

1271–1295 Journey of Marco Polo to central Asia, China, and Southeast Asia

1258 Mongol destruction of Baghdad

1274, 1280 Failed Mongol invasions of Japan

1253 Mongol victory over Seljuk Turks; rise of Ottoman Turks in Middle East

1290s First true guns used in China

1260–1294 Reign of Kubilai Khan in China

1260 Mameluk (slave) rulers of Egypt defeat Mongols at Ain Jalut; End of drive west

1368 Yuan dynasty overthrown; Ming period in China begins

1336–1405 Life of Timur

c. 1370 Gunpowder weapons effectively deployed in China and Europe

mid-14th century Spread of the Black Death in Eurasia

1380 Russian victory at Kulikova; power of the (Mongol descended) Golden Horde is broken

In most histories, the Mongol conquests have been depicted as a savage assault by backward and barbaric peoples on many of the most ancient and developed centers of human civilization. Much is made of the ferocity of Mongol warriors in battle, their destruction of great cities, such as Baghdad, in reprisal for resistance to Mongol armies, and their mass slaughters of defeated enemies. Depending on the civilization from whose city walls a historian recorded the coming of the Mongol "hordes," they were depicted as the scourge of Islam, devils bent on the destruction of Christianity, persecutors of the Buddhists, or defilers of the Confucian traditions of China. Though they were indeed fierce fighters and capable of terrible acts of retribution against those who dared to defy them, the Mongols' conquests brought much more than death and devastation.

At the peak of their power, the domains of the Mongol *khans*, or rulers, made up a vast realm in which once-hostile peoples lived together in peace and virtually all religions were tolerated. From the Khanate of Persia in the west to the empire of the fabled Kubilai Khan in the east, the law code first promulgated by Chinggis Khan ordered human interaction. The result was an important new stage in international contact. From eastern Europe to southern China, merchants and travelers could move across the well-policed Mongol domains without fear for their lives or property. The great swath of Mongol territory that covered or connected most of Europe, Asia, and the Middle East served as a bridge between the civilizations of the Eastern Hemisphere. The caravans and embassies that crossed the Mongol lands transmitted new foods, inventions, and ideas

from one civilized pool to the others and from civilized pools to the nomadic peoples who served as intermediaries. Like the Islamic expansion that preceded it, the Mongol explosion did much to lay the foundations for more human interaction on a global scale, extending and intensifying the world network that had been building since the classical age.

This chapter will explore the sources of the Mongol drive for a world empire and the course of Mongol expansion. Particular attention will be given to the nomadic basis of the Mongol war machine and the long-standing patterns of nomadic-sedentary interaction that shaped the character, direction, and impact of Mongol expansion. After a discussion of the career and campaigns of Chinggis Khan, separate sections of this chapter will deal with Mongol conquest and rule in Russia and eastern Europe, the Middle East, and China. The chapter will conclude with an assessment of the meaning of the Mongol interlude for the development of civilization and the growth of cross-cultural interaction on a global scale. In both their destructive and constructive roles, the Mongols generated major changes within the framework of global history.

THE MONGOL EMPIRE OF CHINGGIS KHAN

Mongol legends suggest that the ancient ancestors of the Mongols were forest-dwelling hunters, and the hunt persisted as a central element in Mongol culture. By the time the Mongols are first mentioned in the accounts of the sedentary peoples, who traded with them and periodically felt

The First Mongol Empire of Chinggis Khan

the fury of their lightning raids, most of them had adopted the life-style of the herding, horse-riding nomads of the central Asian steppes (see Chapter 4). In fact, in most ways the Mongols epitomized nomadic society and culture. Their survival depended on the well-being of the herds of goats and sheep they drove from one pasture area to another according to the cycle of the seasons. Their staple foods were the meat and milk products provided by their herds, supplemented in most cases by grain and vegetables gained through trade with sedentary farming peoples. They also traded hides and dairy products for jewelry, weapons, and cloth manufactured in urban centers. They dressed in sheepskins, made boots from tanned sheep hides, and lived in round felt tents that were processed from wool sheared from their animals. The tough little ponies they rode to round up their herds, hunt wild animals, and make war, were equally essential to their way of life. Both male and female Mongol children could ride as soon as they were able to walk. Mongol warriors could literally ride for days on end, sleeping and eating in the saddle. Ponies were the Mongols' most prized possessions. Deprived of their horses on the harsh and vast steppes, tribespeople could not survive long. Thus, horse stealing became a major object of interclan and tribal raids and an offense that brought instant death if the original owners caught up with the thieves.

Like the Arabs and other nomadic peoples we have encountered, the basic unit of Mongol society was the tribe, which was divided into kin-related clans whose members camped and herded together on a regular basis. When threatened by external enemies or in preparation for raids on other nomads or invasions of sedentary areas, clans and tribes could be combined in great confederations. Depending on the skills of their leaders, these confederations could be held together for months or even years. But when the threat had passed or the raiding was done, clans and tribes invariably drifted back to their own pasturelands and campsites. At all organizational levels leaders were elected by the free males of the group. Though women exercised considerable influence within the family and had the right to be heard in tribal councils, males dominated positions of leadership. The elected leaders normally exhibited the qualities and skills that were essential to survival in the steppe environment where rash action or timid hesitation could lead to the destruction of a leader's kinsmen and dependents.

Courage in battle, usually evidenced from youth by bravery in the hunt, and the capacity to forge alliances and attract dependents were vital leadership skills. A strong leader could quickly build up a large following of chiefs from other clans and tribal groups. Some of these subordinates might be defeated rivals who had been enslaved by

Though it was a cumbersome process, even large Mongol tents could be moved when mounted on huge wagons, which were pulled by large teams of oxen.

the victorious chief, though often the life-style of master and slave differed little. Should the leader grow old and feeble or suffer severe reverses, his once-loyal subordinates would quickly abandon him. He expected this to happen, and the subordinates felt no remorse. Their survival and that of their dependents hinged on attaching themselves to a strong tribal leader.

THE MAKING OF A GREAT WARRIOR: THE EARLY CAREER OF CHINGGIS KHAN

Indo-European and then Turkic-speaking nomads had dominated the steppes and posed the principal threat to Asian and European sedentary civilizations in the early millennia of recorded history. But peoples speaking Mongolian languages had enjoyed moments of power and actually carved out regional kingdoms in north China in the 4th and 10th centuries A.D. In fact, in the early 12th century, Chinggis Khan's great-grandfather, Kabul Khan, had led a Mongol alliance that had won glory by defeating an army sent against them by the Qin kingdom of north China. Soon after this victory, Kabul Khan became ill and died, and his successors could neither defeat their nomadic enemies nor hold the Mongol alliance together. Divided and beaten, the Mongols fell on hard times.

Chinggis Khan, who as a youth was named Temujin, was born in the 1170s into one of the splinter clans that fought for survival in the decades after the death of Kabul Khan. Temujin's father was an able leader, who managed to build up a decent following and negotiate a promise of marriage between his eldest son and the daughter of a stronger Mongol chief. Just when the family fortunes seemed to be on the upswing, Temujin's father was poisoned by the agents of a rival nomadic group, according to Mongol accounts. Suddenly, Temujin, who was still a teenager, was thrust into a position of leadership. But most of the chiefs who had attached themselves to his father refused to follow a mere boy, whose prospects of survival appeared to be slim.

In the months that followed, his much-reduced encampment was threatened and finally attacked by a rival tribe. Temujin was taken prisoner in 1182, locked into a wooden collar, and led in humiliation to the camp of his enemies. After a daring midnight escape, Temujin rejoined his mother and brothers and found refuge for his tiny band of followers deep in the mountains. Facing extermination, Temujin did what any sensible nomad leader would have done: he and his people joined the camp of a more powerful Mongol chieftain, who had once been aided by Temujin's father. With the support of this powerful leader, Temujin revenged the insults of the clan that had enslaved him and another that had taken advantage of his weakness

to raid his camp for horses and women. These successes and Temujin's growing reputation as a warrior and military commander soon won him allies and clan chiefs eager to attach themselves to a leader with a promising future. Within a decade, the youthful Temujin had defeated his Mongol rivals and routed the forces sent to crush him by the Tartars and other nomadic peoples. In 1206, at a *kuriltai*, or meeting of all of the Mongol chieftains, Temujin—renamed Chinggis Khan—was elected the *khaghan*, or supreme ruler, of the Mongol tribes. United under a strong leader, the Mongols prepared to launch a massive assault on an unsuspecting world.

BUILDING THE MONGOL WAR MACHINE

The men of the Mongol tribes that had elevated Chinggis Khan to leadership were in many ways natural warriors. Trained from youth not only to ride but also to hunt and fight, they were physically tough, mobile, and accustomed to killing and death. They wielded a variety of weapons, including lances, hatchets, and iron maces. None of their weapons was as demoralizing for enemy forces as their powerful short bows. A Mongol warrior could fire a quiver of arrows with stunning accuracy without breaking the stride of his horse. He could hit enemy soldiers as distant as 400 yards (compared to a range of 250 yards for the English longbow) while charging straight ahead, ducking under the belly of his pony, or leaning over the horse's rump while retreating from superior forces. The fact that the Mongol armies were entirely cavalry meant that they possessed speed and a mobility that were demoralizing to enemy forces. Leading two or three horses to use as remounts, Mongol warriors could spend more than one week in the saddle and, when pressed, cover 80 or 90 miles per day. They could strike before their enemies had prepared their defenses, hit unanticipated targets, retreat back to the steppes after suffering temporary reverses, and then suddenly reappear in force.

To a people whose very life-style bred mobility, physical courage, and a love of combat, Chinggis Khan and his many able subordinate commanders brought organization, discipline, and unity of command. The old quarrels and vendettas between clans and tribes were overridden by loyalty to the khaghan, and energies once devoted to infighting were now directed toward conquest and looting in the civilized centers that fringed the steppes on all sides. The Mongol forces were divided into armies made up of basic fighting units called *tumens*, consisting of 10,000 cavalrymen. Each tumen was further divided into units of 1000, 100, and 10 warriors. Commanders at each level were responsible for the training, arming, and discipline of the cavalrymen under their charge. The tumens were also

This Chinese painting of a Mongol warrior clearly enjoying hunting small game suggests the well-deserved reputation the Mongols had earned for their skills as riders and archers.

divided into heavy cavalry, which carried lances and wore some metal armor, and light cavalry, which relied primarily on the bow and arrow and leather helmets and body covering. Even more lightly armed and protected were the scouting parties that rode ahead of Mongol armies and, using flags and special signal fires, kept the main force apprised of the enemy's movements.

Chinggis Khan also created a separate messenger force, whose bodies were tightly bandaged to allow them to remain in the saddle for days, switching from horse to horse to carry urgent messages between the khaghan and his commanders. Military discipline had long been secured by personal ties between commanders and ordinary soldiers. Mongol values, which made courage in battle a prerequisite for male self-esteem, were also buttressed by a formal code that dictated the immediate execution of a warrior who deserted his unit. Chinggis Khan's swift executions left little doubt about the fate of traitors to his own cause or turncoats who abandoned enemy commanders in his favor. His generosity to brave foes was also legendary. The most famous of the latter, a man named Jebe, nicknamed "the arrow," won the khaghan's affection and high posts in the Mongol armies by standing his ground after his troops had been routed and fearlessly shooting Chinggis Khan's horse out from under him.

A special unit supplied Mongol armies with excellent maps of the areas they were to invade, based largely on information supplied by Chinggis Khan's extensive network of spies and informers. New weapons, including a variety of flaming and exploding arrows, gunpowder projectiles, and later bronze cannons, were also devised for the Mongol forces. By the time his armies rode east and west in search of plunder and conquest in the second decade of the 13th century, Chinggis Khan's warriors were among the best armed and trained and the most experienced, disciplined, and mobile soldiers in the world.

CONQUEST: THE MONGOL EMPIRE UNDER CHINGGIS KHAN

When he was proclaimed the khaghan in 1206, Temujin was probably not yet 40 years old. At that point, he was the supreme ruler of nearly one-half million Mongol tribesmen and the overlord of one to two million more nomadic tribesmen who had been defeated by his armies or had voluntarily allied themselves with this promising young commander. But Chinggis Khan had much greater ambitions. He once remarked that his greatest pleasure in life was making war, defeating enemies, forcing ". . . their beloved [to] weep, riding on their horses, embracing their wives and daughters." He came to see himself and his sons as men marked for a special destiny; warriors born to conquer the known world. In 1207, he set out to fulfill this ambition. His first campaigns humbled the Tangut kingdom of Xi-Xia in northwest China, whose ruler was forced to declare himself a vassal of the khaghan and pay a hefty tribute. Next the Mongol armies attacked the much more powerful Qin Empire, which the Manchu-related Jurchens had established a century earlier in north China.

This 14th-century miniature painting from Rashid al-Din's, *History of the World*, depicts Mongol horsemen charging into battle against retreating Persian forces.

In these campaigns, the Mongol armies were confronted for the first time with large, fortified cities their adversaries assumed could easily withstand the assaults of these uncouth tribesmen from the steppes. Indeed, at first the Mongol invaders were thwarted by the intricate defensive works that the Chinese had perfected over the centuries to deter nomadic incursions. But the adaptive Mongols, with the help of captured Chinese artisans and military commanders, soon devised a whole arsenal of siege weapons. These included battering rams, catapults that hurled rocks and explosive balls, and bamboo rockets that spread fire and fear in besieged towns.

Chinggis Khan and the early Mongol commanders had little regard for these towns, whose inhabitants they regarded as soft and effete. Therefore, when resistance was encountered, the Mongols adopted a policy of terrifying retribution. Though the Mongols often spared the lives of famed scholars—whom they employed as advisors—and artisans with particularly useful skills, towns that fought back were usually sacked once they had been taken. The townspeople were slaughtered or sold into slavery; their homes, palaces, mosques, and temples were reduced to

rubble. Towns that surrendered without a fight were usually spared this fate, though they were required to pay tribute to their Mongol conquerors as the price of their deliverance.

FIRST ASSAULT ON THE ISLAMIC WORLD; CONQUEST IN CHINA

Having established a foothold in north China and solidified his empire in the steppes, Chinggis Khan sent his armies westward against the Kara-Khitai Empire established by a Mongolian-speaking people a century earlier. Having overwhelmed and annexed the Kara-Khitai, in 1219 Chinggis Khan sent envoys to demand the submission of Muhammad Shah II, the Turkic ruler of the Khwarazm Empire to the west. Outraged by the audacity of the still little-known Mongol commander, one of Muhammad's subordinates had some of Chinggis Khan's later envoys killed and sent the rest with shaved heads back to the khaghan. These insults, of course, meant war, a war in which the Khwarazm were overwhelmed. Their great cities fell to the new siege weapons and tactics the Mongols had perfected in their north China campaigns. Their armies were repeatedly routed in battles with the Mongol cavalry. Again and again, the Mongols used their favorite battle tactic in these encounters. Cavalry was sent to attack the enemy's main force. Feigning defeat, the cavalry retreated, drawing the opposing forces out of formation in the hopes of a chance to slaughter the fleeing Mongols. Once the enemy's pursuing horsemen had spread themselves over the countryside, the main force of Mongol heavy cavalry, until then concealed, attacked them in a devastating pincers formation.

Like the Russians, Hungarians, Chinese, and numerous other adversaries, the Khwarazm never seemed to catch on to these well-executed ruses, and many a proud and much larger army was destroyed in the Mongol trap. Within two years, his once flourishing cities in ruin, his kingdom in Mongol hands, Muhammad Shah II, having retreated across his empire, died on a desolate island near the Caspian Sea. In addition to greatly enlarging his domains, Chinggis Khan's victories meant that he could incorporate tens of thousands of Turkic horsemen into his armies. With his forces greatly enlarged by these new recruits, he once again turned eastward, where in the last years of his life his armies destroyed the Xi-Xia kingdom and overran the Qin Empire of north China. By 1227, the year of his death, the Mongols ruled an empire that stretched from eastern Persia to the North China Sea.

LIFE UNDER THE MONGOL YOKE

Despite their fury as warriors and the horrible destruction they could unleash on those who resisted their demands for submission and tribute, the Mongols proved remarkably astute and tolerant rulers. Chinggis Khan himself set the standards in this regard, and most of these were followed by his more able successors. He was a complex man. He was capable, as we have seen, of gloating over the ruin of his enemies, but was also open to new ideas and committed to building a world where the diverse peoples of his empire could live together in peace. Though illiterate, Chinggis Khan was neither the ignorant savage nor the cultureless vandal often depicted in the accounts of civilized writers—usually those who had never met him. Once the conquered peoples had been subdued, he took a keen interest in their arts and learning, though he refused to live in their cities. Instead he established a new capital at Karakorum on the steppes and summoned the wise and clever from all parts of the empire to the lavish palace of tents with gilded pillars where he lived with his wives, closest advisors, and personal bodyguards that now numbered over a thousand of the best and most loyal troops.

At Karakorum, Chinggis Khan consulted with Confucian scholars about how to rule China; with Muslim engineers about how to build siege weapons and improve trade with the lands farther west; and with Daoist holy men, whom he hoped could provide him with an elixir that would make him immortal. Though he himself followed the shamanistic (focused on the propitiation of nature spirits) beliefs of his ancestors, all religions were tolerated in his empire. He was visited by Muslim mullahs, Buddhist and Daoist monks, and Christian missionaries. The followers of these faiths, as well as smaller religious communities, such as the Jews and Zoroastrians, worshipped without fear of persecution throughout his empire.

Chinggis Khan and his advisors sought to establish the basis for lasting peace and prosperity in his domains. Drawing on the advice and talents of both Muslim and Chinese bureaucrats, an administrative framework was created. A script was devised for the Mongolian language in order to facilitate record keeping and the standardization of laws. Chinggis Khan promulgated a legal code that was enforced by a special police force. Much of the code was aimed at putting an end to the divisions and quarrels that had so long occupied the Mongols. Grazing lands were systematically allotted to different tribes, and harsh penalties were established for rustling livestock or stealing horses. On the advice of his Chinese counselors, Chinggis Khan resisted the temptation to turn the cultivated lands of north China into a vast grazing area, which of course would have meant the destruction of tens of millions of peasants. Instead he ordered that the farmers be regularly taxed to support his courts and future military expeditions.

Above all, the Mongol conquests brought a peace to much of Asia that in some areas persisted for generations. In the towns of the empire, handicraft production and scholarship flourished and artistic creativity was allowed free expression. Chinggis Khan and his successors actively promoted the growth of trade and travelers by protecting the caravans that made their way across the ancient Asian silk routes and by establishing rest stations for weary merchants and fortified outposts for those harassed by bandits. One Muslim historian wrote of the peoples within the domains of the khaghan that they "enjoyed such a peace that a man might have journeyed from the land of sunrise to the land of sunset with a golden platter upon his head without suffering the least violence from anyone." Secure trade routes made for prosperous merchants and wealthy, cosmopolitan cities. They also facilitated the spread of foods such as sorghum, sugar, citrus fruits, and grapes; inventions such as firearms, printing, and windmills; and techniques ranging from those involving papermaking to those for improving irrigation from one civilization to an-other. Paradoxically, Mongol expansion, which began as a "barbarian" orgy of violence and destruction, had become a major force for economic and social development and the enhancement of civilized life.

THE DEATH OF CHINGGIS KHAN AND THE DIVISION OF THE EMPIRE

When the Mongols had moved west to attack Kara Khi-tai in 1219, support was demanded from the vassal king of Xi-Xia. The Tangut ruler had impudently responded that if the Mongols were not strong enough to win wars on their own, they were best advised to refrain from attacking others. In 1226, his wars in the west won, Chinggis Khan turned east with an army of 180,000 warriors to punish the Tanguts and complete a conquest that he regretted hav-ing left unfinished over a decade earlier. After routing a much larger Tangut army in a battle fought on the frozen waters of the Yellow River, the Mongol armies overran Xi-Xia, plundering and burning and mercilessly hunting down any Tangut survivors. As his forces closed in on the Tangut capital and last refuge, Chinggis Khan, who had been injured in a skirmish some months earlier, fell griev-ously ill. After impressing upon his sons the dangers of quarreling among themselves for the spoils of the empire, the khaghan died in August of 1227.

With one last outburst of Mongol wrath, this time di-rected against death itself, his body was carried back to Mongolia for burial. The Mongol forces escorting the fu-neral procession hunted down and killed every human and animal in its path. As Chinggis Khan had instructed, his armies also treacherously slaughtered the unarmed inhabit-ants of the Tangut capital after a truce and surrender had been arranged.

The vast pasturelands the Mongols now controlled were divided between Chinggis Khan's three remaining sons and Batu, a grandson and heir of the khaghan's recently de-ceased son Jochi. Towns and cultivated areas like those in north China and parts of Persia were considered the com-mon property of the Mongol ruling family. A kuriltai was convened at Karakorum, the Mongol capital, to select a successor to the great conqueror. In accordance with Chinggis Khan's preference, Ogedei, his third son, was elected grand khan. Though not as capable a military leader as his brothers or nephews, Ogedei was a crafty dip-lomat and deft manipulator, skills much needed if the am-bitious heads of the vast provinces of the empire were to be kept from each others' throats.

For nearly a decade, Ogedei directed Mongol energies into further campaigns and conquests. The areas that were targeted by this new round of Mongol expansion paid the

This portrait of Ogedei, who was elected to succeed Chinggis Khan as the grand khan of the Mongols, is from a 13th-century album of Chinese emperors.

price for peace within the Mongol Empire. The fate of the most important victims—Russia and eastern Europe, the Islamic heartlands, and China—will be the focus of much of the rest of this chapter. As we shall see, the Mongols were by no means finished with their efforts to build a world empire and to alter the course of global history.

THE MONGOL DRIVE TO THE WEST

While in pursuit of the Khwarazm ruler, Muhammad Shah II, the Mongols had made their first contacts with the rich kingdoms to the west of the steppe heartlands of Chinggis Khan's empire. Raids of reconnaissance into Georgia and across the Russian steppe convinced the Mon-gol commanders that the Christian lands to the west were theirs for the taking. Russia and Europe were added to their agenda for world conquest. The subjugation of these regions became the project of the armies of the Golden Horde, which was named after the golden tent of the early khans of the western sector of the Mongol Empire. The territories of the Golden Horde, which covered much of what is today south-central Russia, made up the four great khanates into which the Mongol Empire had been divided at the time of Chinggis Khan's death. The khanate to the

The Four Khanates of the Divided Mongol Empire, c. 1290

south, called the Ilkhan Empire, claimed the task of completing the conquest of the Muslim world that had begun with the invasion of the Khwarazm domains. Though neither Europe nor the Islamic heartlands were ultimately subdued, Mongol successes on the battlefield and the fury of their assaults affected the history of the regions that came under attack, particularly Russia and the Islamic world.

THE INVASION OF RUSSIA

In a very real sense the Mongol assault on Russia was a side campaign, a chance to fine-tune the war machine and win a little booty while en route to the real prize, western Europe. As we saw in Chapter 15, in the first half of the 13th century when the Mongol warriors first descended, a more united Russia had been divided into numerous petty kingdoms, centered on trading cities such as Novgorod and Kiev. By this time Kiev, which had originally dominated much of central Russia, had been in decline for some time. As a result there was no paramount power to rally Russian forces against the invaders. Despite the dire warnings spread by those who had witnessed the crushing defeats suffered by the Georgians in the early 1220s, the princes of Russia refused to cooperate. They preferred to fight alone and be routed individually.

In 1236, Chinggis Khan's grandson Batu led a Mongol force of upwards of 120,000 cavalrymen into the Russian heartlands. From 1237 to 1238 and later in 1240, these "Tartars," as the Russian peoples called them, carried out the only successful winter invasions in Russian history. In fact, the Mongols preferred to fight in the winter. The frozen earth provided good footing for their horses and

frozen rivers gave them access rather than blocking the way to their enemies. One after another, the Mongol armies defeated the often much larger forces of local nomadic groups and the Russian princes. Cities such as Rizan, Moscow, and Vladimir, which resisted the Mongol command to surrender, were razed to the ground; their inhabitants were slaughtered or led into slavery. As a contemporary Russian chronicler observed, "no eye remained to weep for the dead." Just as it appeared that all of Russia would be ravaged by the Mongols, whom the Russians compared to locusts, Batu's armies withdrew. The largest cities, Novgorod and Kiev, appeared to have been spared. Russian priests thanked God; the Mongol commanders blamed the spring thaw, which slowed the Mongol horsemen and raised the risk of defeat in the treacherous mud.

Salvation yielded to further disasters when the Mongols returned in force in the winter of 1240. In this second campaign, even the great walled city of Kiev, which had reached a population of over 100,000 by the end of the 12th century, fell. Enraged by Kievan resistance—its ruler had ordered the Mongol envoys thrown from the city walls—the Mongols reduced the greatest city in Russia to a smoldering ruin. The cathedral of Saint Sophia was spared, but the rest of the city was systematically looted and destroyed, its inhabitants smoked out and slaughtered. Novgorod again braced itself for the Mongol onslaught. Again it was, according to the Russian chroniclers, "miraculously" spared. In fact it was saved largely due to the willingness of its prince, Alexander Nevskii, to submit, at least temporarily, to Mongol demands. In addition, the Mongol armies were eager to move on to the main event, the invasion of western Europe.

RUSSIA IN BONDAGE

The crushing victories of Batu's armies initiated nearly two and one-half centuries of Mongol dominance in Russia. Russian princes were forced to submit as vassals of the khan of the Golden Horde and to pay tribute or risk the ravages of Mongol raiders. Mongol exactions fell particularly heavily on the Russian peasantry, who had to yield up their crops and labor to both their own princes and the Mongol overlords. Impoverished and ever fearful of the lightning raids of Mongol marauders, the peasants fled to remote areas or became, in effect, the serfs (see Chapter 16) of the Russian ruling class in return for protection.

The decision on the part of many peasants to become the lifetime laborers of the nobility resulted in a major change in the rural social structure of Russia. Until the mid-19th century, the great majority of the population of Russia would be tied to the lands they worked and bound to the tiny minority of nobles who owned these great estates. Some Russian towns made profits on the increased trade Mongol links made possible, and sometimes the gains exceeded the tribute they paid to the Golden Horde. No town benefited from the Mongol presence more than Moscow. Badly plundered and partially burned in the early Mongol assaults, the city was gradually rebuilt and its ruling princes steadily swallowed up nearby towns and surrounding villages. After 1328, Moscow also profited from its status as the tribute collector for the Mongol khans. Its princes not only used their position to fill their own coffers, they annexed further towns as punishment for falling behind on the payment of their tribute.

As Moscow grew in strength, the power of the Golden Horde declined. Mongol religious toleration benefited both the Orthodox church and Moscow. The *Metropolitan*, or head of the Orthodox church, was made the representative of all the clergy in Russia, which did much to enhance the church's standing. The choice of Moscow as the seat of the Orthodox leaders brought new sources of wealth to its princes and buttressed Muscovite claims to be Russia's leading city. In 1380, those claims received an additional boost when the princes of Moscow shifted from being tribute collectors to being the defenders of Russia. In alliance with other Russian vassals, they raised an army that defeated the forces of the Golden Horde at the battle of Kulikova. Their victory and the devastating blows Timur's attacks dealt the Golden Horde two decades later effectively broke the Mongol hold over Russia. Mongol forces raided as late as the 1450s, and the princes of Muscovy did not formally renounce their vassal status until 1480. But from the end of the 14th century, Moscow was the center of political power in Russia, and it was armies from Poland and Lithuania that posed the main threat to Russian peace and prosperity.

Though much of the Mongol impact was negative, their conquest proved in a number of ways a decisive turning point in Russian history. In addition to their meaning for Moscow and the Orthodox church, Mongol contacts led to changes in Russian military organization and tactics and the political style of Russian rulers. Claims that the Tartars were responsible for Russian despotism, either Tsarist or Stalinist, are clearly overstated. Still, the Mongol example may have influenced the desire of Russian princes to centralize their control and minimize the limitations placed on their power by the landed nobility, the clergy, and wealthy merchants. By far the greatest effects of Mongol rule, however, were those resulting from Russia's relative isolation from Christian lands farther west. On the one hand, the Mongols protected a divided and weak Russia from the attacks of much more powerful kingdoms such as Poland, Lithuania, and Hungary as well as the "crusades" of militant Christian orders like the Teutonic Knights, which were determined to stamp out the Orthodox heresy. On the other hand, Mongol overlordship cut Russia off from key transformations in western Europe that were inspired by the Renaissance and led ultimately to the Reformation. The Orthodox clergy, of course, would have had little use for these influences, but their absence severely reduced the options available for Russian political, economic, and intellectual development.

MONGOL INCURSIONS AND THE RETREAT FROM EUROPE

Until news of the Mongol campaigns in Russia reached European peoples such as the Germans and Hungarians farther west, Christian leaders had been quite pleased by the rise of a new military power in central Asia. Rumors and reports from Nestorian Christians, chafing under what they perceived as the persecution of their Muslim overlords, convinced many in western Europe that the Mongol Khan was none other than Prester John. Prester John was the name given to a mythical, rich and powerful Christian monarch whose kingdom had supposedly been cut off from Europe by the Muslim conquests of the 7th and 8th centuries. Sometimes located in Africa, sometimes in central Asia, Prester John loomed large in the European imagination as a potential ally who could strike the Muslim enemy from the rear and join up with European Christians to destroy their common adversary. The Mongol assault on the Muslim Khwarazm Empire appeared to confirm the speculation that Chinggis Khan was indeed Prester John.

The assault on Christian, though Orthodox, Russia made it clear that the Mongol armies were neither the legions of Prester John nor more partial to the Christians than any other people who stood in their way. The rulers of Europe were nevertheless slow to realize the magnitude of the threat the Mongols posed to western Christendom. When Mongol envoys, one of whom was an Englishman, arrived at the court of King Bela of Hungary demanding that he surrender a group of nomads who had fled to his domains after being beaten by the Mongols in Russia, he contemptuously dismissed them and Batu's demand that he submit to Mongol overlordship. Bela reasoned that he was the ruler of a powerful kingdom, while the Mongols were just another ragtag band of nomads in search of easy plunder. As had so often been the case in the past, his foolish refusal to negotiate provided the Mongols with a pretext to invade. Their ambition remained the conquest and pillage of all western Europe. That this goal was clearly attainable was demonstrated by the sound drubbing they gave to first the Hungarians in 1240 and then to a mixed force of Christian knights led by the German ruler, King Henry of Silesia. In both battles, the Mongols used the time-tested tactic of retreat and envelopment. In the first engagement 70,000 Christian soldiers perished; in the second, 40,000 Europeans died, many of them the elite of eastern European knighthood.

These victories left the Mongols free to raid and pillage from the Adriatic Sea region in the south to Poland and the German states of the north. It also left the rest of Europe open to Mongol conquest. Just as the kings and clergy of the western portions of Christendom were beginning to fear the worst, the Mongol forces disappeared. The death of the Khaghan Ogedei, in the distant Mongol capital at Karakorum, forced Batu to withdraw in preparation for the struggle for succession that was under way. The campaign for the conquest of Europe was never resumed. Perhaps Batu was satisfied with the huge empire of the Golden Horde that he ruled from his splendid new capital at Sarai; most certainly the Mongols had found richer lands to plunder in the following decades in the Muslim empires of the Middle East. Whatever the reason, Europe was spared the full fury of the Mongol assault. Of the civilizations that fringed the steppe homelands of the Mongols, only India would be as fortunate.

THE MONGOL ASSAULT ON THE ISLAMIC HEARTLANDS

After the Mongol conquest of the Khwarazm Empire, it was only a matter of time before they struck westward against the far wealthier Muslim empires of Mesopotamia and North Africa. The conquest of these areas became the main project of Hulegu, another grandson of Chinggis Khan and the ruler of the Ilkhan portions of the Mongol Empire. As we saw in Chapter 12, one of the key results of Hulegu's assaults on the Muslim heartlands was the cap-

ture and destruction of Baghdad in 1258. The murder of the Abbasid caliph, one of some 800,000 people who were reported to have been killed in Mongol retribution for the city's resistance, brought an end to the dynasty that had ruled the core regions of the Islamic world since the middle of the 8th century. A major Mongol victory over the Seljuk Turks in 1243 also proved critical to the future history of the region, because it opened up Asia Minor to conquest by a different Turkic people, the Ottomans, who would be the next great power in the Islamic heartlands.

The opening sieges of Hulegu's campaigns had also destroyed the Assassins, who had posed a major threat to Sunni Muslims for centuries. The hundreds of mountain fortresses of the sect were captured and destroyed. One of these, Alamut, held out for three years despite the Mongol siege engines. Finally, the leader of the sect was taken prisoner and sent to the khaghan at Karakorum. Refused an audience, the last of the Assassins' commanders was murdered by his captors.

Despite the removal of the Assassin menace, it is understandable that Muslim historians treated the coming of the Mongols as one of the great catastrophes in the history of Islam. The murder of the caliph and his family left the faithful without a central authority; the sack of Baghdad and numerous other cities from central Asia to the shores of the Mediterranean devastated the focal points of Islamic civilization. The Mongols had also severely crippled Muslim military strength, much to the delight of the Christians, especially those like the Nestorians who lived in the Middle East. Some Christians offered assistance in the form of information; others, especially the Nestorians from inner Asia, served as commanders in Hulegu's armies. One contemporary Muslim chronicler, Ibn al-Athir, found the tribulations the Mongols had visited on his people so horrific that he apologized to his readers for recounting them and wished that he had not been born to witness them. He lamented that:

> . . . in just one year they seized the most populous, the most beautiful, and the best cultivated part of the earth whose inhabitants excelled in character and urbanity. In the countries that have not yet been overrun by them, everyone spends the night afraid that they may yet appear there, too. . . . Thus, Islam and the Muslims were struck, at that time, by a disaster such as no people had experienced before.

Given these reverses, one can imagine the relief the peoples of the Muslim world felt when the Mongols were finally defeated in 1260 by the armies of the *Mameluk*, or slave, dynasty of Egypt at Ain Jalut. Ironically, Baibars, the commander of the Egyptian forces, and many of his

The Abbasid capital at Baghdad had long been in decline when the Mongols besieged it in 1258. The Mongols' capture and sack of the city put an end to all pretense that Baghdad was still the center of the Muslim world.

lieutenants had been enslaved by the Mongols some years earlier and sold in Egypt, where they rose to power through military service. The Muslim victory was won with the rare cooperation of the Christians, who allowed Baibars's forces to cross unopposed through their much diminished, crusader territories in Palestine. Hulegu was in central Asia, engaged in yet another succession struggle, when the battle occurred. Upon his return, he was forced to reconsider his plans for conquest of the entire Muslim world. The Mameluks were deeply entrenched and growing stronger; Hulegu was threatened by his cousin Berke, the new khan of the Golden Horde to the north, who had converted to Islam. After openly clashing with Berke and learning of Baibars's overtures for an alliance with the Golden Horde, Hulegu decided to settle for the sizeable kingdom he already ruled, which stretched from the frontiers of Byzantium to the Oxus River in central Asia.

THE MONGOL IMPACT ON EUROPE AND THE ISLAMIC WORLD

Though much of what the Mongols wrought on their westward march was destructive, some benefits were reaped from their forays into Europe and conquests in Muslim areas. By example, they taught new ways of making war and

impressed on their Turkic and European enemies the effectiveness of gunpowder. As we have seen, Mongol conquests facilitated trade between the civilizations at each end of Eurasia, making possible the exchange of foods, tools, and ideas on an unprecedented scale. The revived trade routes brought great wealth to traders such as those from north Italy, who set up outposts in the eastern Mediterranean, along the Black Sea coast, and as far east as the Caspian Sea. Because the establishment of these trading empires by the Venetians and Genoese provided precedents for the later drives for overseas expansion by peoples such as the Portuguese and English, they are of special significance in global history.

Perhaps the greatest long-term impact of the Mongol drive to the west was indirect and unintended. In recent years a growing number of historians have become convinced that the Mongol conquests played a key role in transmitting the fleas that carried bubonic plague from central Asia to Europe and the Middle East. The fleas may have hitched a ride on the livestock the Mongols drove into the new pasturelands won by their conquests or on the rats who nibbled the grain transported by merchants along the trading routes the Mongol rulers fostered between east and west. Whatever the exact connection, the Mongol armies unknowingly paved the way for the spread of the dreaded *Black Death* across the steppes to the Islamic heart-lands and from there to most of Europe in the mid-14th century. In so doing, they unleashed possibly the most fatal epidemic in all human history. From mortality rates higher than half the population in some areas of Europe and the Middle East to the economic and social adjustments that the plague forced wherever it spread, this accidental, but devastating, side effect of the Mongol conquests influenced the course of civilized development in Eurasia for centuries to come.

THE MONGOL INTERLUDE IN CHINESE HISTORY

Soon after Ogedei was elected as the great khan, the Mongol advance into China was resumed. Having conquered Xi-Xia, the Mongol commanders now turned to the Qin Empire to the east, which had proven the most resistant of all the kingdoms assaulted under the leadership of Chinggis Khan. During the Mongol campaign, the Chinese Song ruler to the south, seeing a chance to weaken the long-standing "barbarian" threat from the northeast, made the mistake of allowing Mongol armies to pass through his lands to attack the Qin and even sent troops to help with the siege of the Qin capital. By 1234 the Qin had been overwhelmed, and the buffer between the Song and the Mongols had been all but destroyed. But the Mongols still did not occupy most of the Qin domains or attempt to govern them directly. The Song rulers then betrayed the Mongol alliance by attempting to garrison some of the cities they had jointly besieged. The Mongols returned in force, making short work of the rump state of Qin and sweeping onward into the Song-ruled south.

In the campaigns against the Song, the Mongol forces were directed by Kubilai Khan, one of the grandsons of Chinggis Khan and a man who would play a pivotal role in Chinese history for the next half century. Even under a decadent dynasty that had long neglected its defenses, south China proved one of the toughest areas for the Mongols to conquer. From 1235 to 1279, the Mongols were continually on the march; they fought battle after battle and besieged seemingly innumerable, well-fortified Chinese cities. In 1260, Kubilai assumed the title of the great khan, much to the chagrin of his cousins who ruled other parts of the empire. A decade later in 1271, on the recommendation of Chinese advisors, he changed the name of the Mongol dynasty to the Sinicized Yuan. Though he was still nearly a decade away from fully defeating the last-ditch efforts of Confucian advisors and Chinese generals to save the Song dynasty, Kubilai ruled most of China, and he now set about the task of establishing Mongol control on a more permanent basis.

KUBILAI KHAN AND THE MONGOL PRESENCE IN CHINA

Kubilai had long been fascinated by Chinese civilization. Even before he had begun the conquest of the Song Empire, Kubilai had surrounded himself with Chinese advisors, some Buddhist, others Daoist or Confucian. His capital at Tatu in the north (present-day Beijing) was built on the site occupied by earlier dynasties, and he introduced Chinese rituals and classical music into his own court. But he did not then, nor later when he had conquered the south, listen to the pleas of his Confucian advisors to reestablish the civil service exams, which had been discontinued by the Qin rulers. Thus, from the outset, Kubilai was ambivalent in his attitude toward the ancient civilization that was slipping piecemeal under Mongol control. He was determined to preserve Mongol separateness and to keep the scholar-gentry from gaining too much power—hence the refusal to reintroduce the exams. But he also adopted a Chinese life-style, was anxious to follow Chinese precedents, and became a major patron of the arts and a promoter of Chinese culture in general. Despite his efforts to preserve Mongol identity, Kubilai's choice of China as the site of his capital and his deep involvement in Chinese affairs signaled, in effect, the passing of an overarching command of the far-flung Mongol Empire. From the late 13th century onward, the main divisions of the empire were ruled and governed as virtually independent realms.

THE MONGOL ELITE

Kubilai promulgated many laws to preserve the distinction between Mongol and Chinese. He forbade Chinese scholars to learn the Mongol script, which was used for records and correspondence at the upper levels of the imperial government. Mongols were forbidden to marry ethnic Chinese, and only women from nomadic families were selected for the imperial harem. Even friendships between the two peoples were discouraged. Mongol religious ceremonies and customs were retained, and a tent encampment in the traditional Mongol style was set up in the imperial city, even though Kubilai usually resided in a Chinese-style palace. Kubilai and his successors continued to enjoy key Mongol pastimes such as the hunt, and Mongol military forces remained separate from Chinese.

In the Yuan era, a new social structure was established in China with the Mongols on top and their central Asian nomadic and Muslim allies right below them in the hierarchy. These two groups occupied most of the offices at the highest levels of the bureaucracy. Beneath them came the north Chinese and below them the ethnic Chinese and the minority peoples of the south. Though ethnic Chinese from both north and south ran the Yuan bureaucracy at the regional and local levels, they could ordinarily exercise power at the top only as advisors to the Mongols or other nomadic officials. At all levels, their activities were scrutinized by Mongol functionaries from an enlarged and much-strengthened censors' bureau.

GENDER AND THE CULTURAL BARRIERS

Mongol women in particular remained aloof from Chinese culture, at least Chinese culture in its Confucian guise. Like their counterparts in the Tang era, some of the wives of the emperors exercised considerable political power at the court. Perhaps the most notable in this regard was Kubilai's wife, Chabi, who not only gave him critical

Chabi, the spirited wife of the Mongol conqueror and emperor of China, Kubilai Khan, is depicted in this portrait.

advice on how to counter the schemes of his ambitious brother but also promoted the interests of the Buddhists in the highest circles of government. At one point, she intervened to frustrate a plan to turn cultivated lands near the capital into pasturelands for the Mongols' ponies. After the conquest of the Qin, Chabi convinced Kubilai that lenient treatment of the survivors of the defeated royal family was the best way to reconcile the peoples of north China to Mongol rule.

It was not just the imperial consorts who enjoyed a remarkable degree of influence and freedom compared to their Chinese counterparts. Mongol women refused to adopt the practice of foot-binding that so constricted the activities of Chinese women. They retained their rights to property and control within the household and the capacity to move freely about town and countryside. No more striking evidence can be found than accounts that describe Mongol women riding to the hunt, both with their husbands and at the head of their own hunting parties. The daughter of one of Kubilai's cousins even went to war, and she refused to marry until one of her many suitors proved able to throw her in a wrestling match. Unfortunately, the Mongol era was too brief to reverse the trends that were lowering the position of Chinese women. As neo-Confucianism gained ground under Kubilai's successors, the arguments for the confinement of women multiplied.

MONGOL ADOPTION OF CHINESE WAYS

Though Kubilai Khan was much more taken with Chinese culture and eager to adopt Chinese ways than most of his Mongol followers, those who settled down in China invariably became Sinified to varying degrees. This was perhaps inevitable when one considers that at most there were only a few hundred thousand Mongols residing in the midst of a Chinese population of perhaps 90 million. Much to the dismay of Mongol purists fresh from the steppes, Kubilai modeled much at his capital and court at Tatu after Chinese precedents. His palace was laid out like those of Chinese emperors and made up primarily of Chinese-style buildings, despite the tents in the parklands and altars for sacrifices to the Mongol deities. The upper levels of the bureaucracy were organized and run, minus the civil service exams, along Tang-Song lines. Kubilai put the empire on the Chinese calendar, listened to Chinese music, and offered sacrifices to his ancestors at a special temple in the imperial city. He also summoned the best Confucian scholars to give his son a proper Chinese education, a move that perhaps more than any other demonstrated his determination to civilize his Mongol followers.

CHAPTER 20 THE LAST GREAT NOMADIC CHALLENGES: FROM CHINGGIS KHAN TO TIMUR

MONGOL TOLERANCE AND FOREIGN CULTURAL INFLUENCES

Like Chinggis Khan and a number of other Mongol overlords, Kubilai had an unbounded curiosity and very cosmopolitan tastes. His generous patronage drew to his splendid court scholars, artists, artisans, and office seekers from many lands. Some of the most favored came from regional Muslim kingdoms to the east that had also come under Mongol rule. Muslims were included in the second highest social grouping, just beneath the Mongols themselves. Persians and Turks were admitted to the inner circle of Kubilai's administrators and advisors. Muslims designed and supervised the building of his Chinese-style imperial city and proposed new systems for the more efficient collection of taxes. Persian astronomers imported more advanced Middle Eastern instruments for celestial observations, corrected the Chinese calendar, and made some of the most accurate maps that the Chinese had ever seen. Muslim doctors ran the imperial hospitals and added translations of 36 volumes on Muslim medicine to the imperial library. Though some of Kubilai's most powerful advisors were infamous for their corrupt ways, most served him well and did much to advance Chinese learning and technology through the transmission of texts, instruments, and weapons from throughout the Muslim world.

In addition to the Muslims, Kubilai welcomed travelers and emissaries from many foreign lands to his court. Like his grandfather, Kubilai displayed a strong interest in all religions and insisted on toleration in his domains. Buddhists, Nestorian Christians, Daoists and Latin Christians made their way to his court. The most renowned of the latter were members of the Polo family from Venice in northern Italy, who traveled extensively in the Mongol Empire in the middle of the 13th century. Marco Polo's account of Kubilai Khan's court and empire is perhaps the most famous travel account written by a European. Marco accepted fantastic tales of grotesques and strange customs, and he may have cribbed parts of his account from other sources. Still, his descriptions of the palaces, cities, and wealth of Kubilai's empire enhanced European interest in the "Indies" and helped to inspire efforts by navigators like Columbus to find a water route to these fabled lands.

This 15th-century English manuscript painting shows Marco Polo and his fellow merchants about to leave from Venice on their lengthy journey to Asia.

As his account makes clear, Marco Polo was very impressed with the number and size of cities in China. In the following passages, he writes about Hangzhou, the capital of the south Song dynasty, which he called Kin-sai and ranked among the most splendid.

At the end of three days you reach the noble and magnificent city of Kin-sai, a name that signifies "the celestial city," and which it merits from its preeminence to all others in the world, in point of grandeur and beauty, which might lead an inhabitant to imagine himself in paradise. According to common estimation, this city is a hundred miles in circuit. Its streets and canals are extensive, and there are squares, or market-places, which, being necessarily proportioned in size to the prodigious concourse of people by whom they are frequented, are exceedingly spacious. It is situated between a lake of fresh and very clear water on the one side, and a river of great magnitude on the other, the waters of which, by a number of canals, large and small, are made to run through every quarter of the city, carrying with them all the filth into the lake, and ultimately the sea. This, whilst it contributes much to the purity of the air, furnishes a communication by water, in addition to that by land, to all parts of the town; the canals and streets being of sufficient width to allow of boats on the one, and carriages in the other, conveniently passing, with articles for the consumption of the inhabitants. It is commonly said that the number of bridges, of all sizes, amounts to twelve thousand. Those which are thrown over the principal canals and are connected with the main streets, have arches so high, and built with so much skill, that vessels with their masts can pass under them, whilst at the same time, carts and horses are passing over their heads. . . .

On each side of the principal street, already mentioned as extending from one end of the city to the other, there are houses and mansions of great size, with their gardens, and near to these, the dwellings of the artisans, who work in shops, at their several trades; and at all hours you see such multitudes of people passing and repassing, on their various avocations, that the providing of food in sufficiency for their maintenance might be deemed an impossibility; but other ideas will be formed when it is observed that, on every market-day, the squares are crowded with tradespeople, who cover the whole space with the articles brought by carts and boats, for all of which they find a sale. . . .

The natural disposition of the native inhabitants of Kin-sai is pacific, and by the example of their former kings, who were themselves unwarlike, they have been accustomed to habits of tranquillity. The management of arms is unknown to them, nor do they keep any in their houses. Contentious broils are never heard among them. They conduct their mercantile and manufacturing concerns with perfect candor and probity. They are friendly towards each other, and persons who inhabit the same street, both men and women, from the mere circumstance of neighborhood, appear like one family.

Questions: What aspects of the city impressed Marco Polo? Were any of the things he found particularly noteworthy related to prominent features of his own hometown? Do you think that his readers back in Europe were also interested in these aspects of the city? Why? How might this description have spurred European explorers to set out overseas in search of the land where the city was located?

SOCIAL POLICIES AND SCHOLAR-GENTRY RESISTANCE

Kubilai's efforts to promote Mongol adaptation to Chinese culture were overshadowed in the long run by countervailing measures to preserve Mongol separateness. The ethnic Chinese, particularly in the south, who made up the vast majority of his subjects were never really reconciled to Mongol rule. Despite Kubilai's cultivation of Confucian rituals and his extensive employment of Chinese bureaucrats, most of the scholar-gentry regarded the Mongol overlord and his successors as uncouth barbarians whose policies endangered Chinese traditions. As it was intended to do, Kubilai's refusal to reinstate the examination route to administrative office prevented Confucian scholars from dominating politics. The favoritism he showed Mongol and other foreign officials further alienated the scholar-gentry.

To add insult to injury, Kubilai went to great lengths to bolster the position of the artisan classes, who had never enjoyed high standing, and the merchants, whom the Confucian thinkers had long dismissed as parasites. The Mongols had from the outset shown great regard for artisans, often sparing them the slaughter meted out to their fellow city dwellers because of their useful skills. During the Yuan period in China, merchants also prospered and commerce boomed, partly owing to Mongol efforts to improve transportation and expand the supply of paper money. The Mongols developed—with amazing speed for a people who had no prior experience with seafaring—a substantial navy that played a major role in the conquest of the Song Empire. After the conquest of China was completed, the great Mongol war fleets were used to put down pirates, who threatened river and overseas commerce, and, toward the end of Kubilai's reign, for overseas expeditions of conquest and exploration. Thus, during the Yuan period, artisans and traders enjoyed a level of government backing and social status that was never again equaled in Chinese civilization.

Ironically, despite the Mongol's ingrained suspicion of cities and sedentary life-styles, both flourished in the Yuan era. The urban expansion begun under the Tang and Song dynasties continued, and the Mongol elite soon became addicted to the diversions of urban life. Though traditional Chinese artistic endeavors, such as poetry and essay writing, languished under the Mongols in comparison with their flowering in the Tang-Song eras, popular entertainments, particularly musical dramas, flourished. Perhaps the most famous of Chinese dramatic works, *The Romance of the West Chamber*, was written in the Yuan period, and dozens of major playwrights wrote for the court, the rising merchant classes, and the well-heeled Mongol elite. Actors and actresses, who had long been relegated by the Confucian scholars to the despised status of "mean people," achieved celebrity and some measure of social esteem. All of this rankled the scholar-gentry, who bided their time, waiting for the chance to restore Confucian decorum and what they believed to be the proper social hierarchy for a civilized people like the Chinese.

Initially at least, Kubilai Khan pursued policies toward one social group, the peasants, that the scholarly class would have heartily approved. He issued edicts forbidding Mongol cavalrymen from turning croplands into pasture and restored the granary system for famine relief that had been badly neglected in the late Song. Kubilai also sought to reduce peasant tax and corvée-labor burdens, partly by redirecting peasant payments from local non-official tax farmers directly to government officials. He and his advisors also formulated a revolutionary plan to establish elementary education at the village level. Though the level of learning they envisioned was rudimentary, such a project—if it had been enacted—would have provided a major challenge to the elite-centric educational system that hitherto had dominated Chinese civilization.

If the scholar-gentry were upset over reports of the impending educational reforms, the peasants grew disgruntled about a further rural project that was put into effect. All peasant households were organized into 50-unit clusters that were intended to enhance peasant cooperation, improve farming techniques, and increase productivity. Because each cluster was supervised by state officials and each household was responsible for reporting misdeeds by members of the others, the scheme was also clearly a device for asserting state control. Because in practice its control functions were favored at the expense of its potential for agrarian improvement, the reorganization was increasingly resented by the peasants, whose discontent had much to do with the rapid demise of the Yuan dynasty.

THE FALL OF THE HOUSE OF YUAN

Historians often remark on the seeming contradiction between the military prowess of the Mongol conquerors and the short life of the dynasty they established in China. Kubilai Khan's long reign encompassed a good portion of the nine decades that the Mongols ruled all of China. Already by the end of his reign, the dynasty was showing signs of weakening. Song loyalists raised the standard of revolt in the south, and popular hostility toward the foreign overlords was expressed more and more openly. The Mongol aura of military invincibility was badly tarnished by Kubilai's rebuffs at the hands of the military lords of Japan and the failure of the expeditions that he sent to punish them, first in 1274 and a much larger effort that was mounted in 1280. The defeats suffered by Mongol forces engaged in similar expeditions to Vietnam and Java in this same period further undermined the Mongols' standing.

Kubilai's dissolute life-style in his later years, partly brought on by the death of his favorite wife Chabi and, five years later, the death of his favorite son, set the tone for a general softening of the Mongol ruling class as a whole. Kubilai's successors lacked his capacity for leadership and cared little for the tedium of day-to-day administrative tasks. Many of the Muslim and Chinese functionaries to whom they entrusted the finances of the

empire enriched themselves through flagrant graft and corruption. This greatly angered the hard-pressed peasantry
who had to bear the burden of rising taxes and demands
for forced labor. The scholar-gentry played on this discontent by calling on the people to rise up and overthrow the
"barbarian" usurpers.

By the 1350s, the signs of dynastic decline were apparent. Banditry and piracy were widespread, and the government's forces were too feeble to curb them. Famines hit
many regions and spawned local uprisings that grew to engulf large portions of the empire. Secret religious sects,
such as the White Lotus Society, were formed that were
dedicated to the overthrow of the dynasty. Their leaders'
claims that they had magical powers to heal their followers
and to confound their enemies helped prompt further peasant resistance against the Mongols. As had been the case in
the past, rebel leaders quarreled and fought with each
other. For a time chaos reigned as the Yuan regime dissolved, and those Mongols who could escape the fury of
the mob retreated back into central Asia. The restoration of
peace and order came from an unexpected quarter. Rather
than a regional military commander or aristocratic lord, a
man from an impoverished peasant family, Ju Yuanzhang,
emerged to found the Ming dynasty that would rule China
for most of the next three centuries.

ANALYSIS

THE ECLIPSE OF THE NOMADIC WAR MACHINE

As the shock waves of the Mongol and Timurid explosions
amply demonstrated, nomadic incursions into the civilized
cores have had an impact on global history that far exceeds
what one would expect, given the relatively small numbers
of nomadic peoples and the limited resources of the regions
they inhabited. From the time of the great Indo-European
migrations in the formative epoch of civilized development
in the 3d and 2d millennia B.C. (see Chapters 2, 3 and 4)
through the classical and postclassical eras, nomadic peoples
periodically emerged from their steppe, prairie, and desert
fringe homelands to invade, often build empires, and settle
in the sedentary zones of Eurasia, Africa, and the Americas. Their intrusions have significantly altered political history by destroying existing polities and even—as in the
case of Assyria and Harappa—whole civilizations. They
have also generated major population movements, sparked
social upheavals, and facilitated critical cultural and economic exchanges across civilizations. As the Mongols' stunning successes in the 13th century illustrate, the capacity of

nomadic peoples to break through the defenses of the much
more populous civilized zones and to establish control over
much richer and more sophisticated peoples arose primarily
from the advantages the nomads possessed in waging war.

A reservoir of battle-ready warriors and mobility have
from ancient times proven the key to success for expansion-
minded nomads. Harsh environments and ongoing intertribal and interclan conflicts for survival within them
produced tough, resourceful fighters who could live off the
land on the march and who regarded combat as an integral
part of their lives. The horses and camels on which pastoral peoples in Eurasia and Sudanic Africa relied gave them
a degree of mobility that confounded the sedentary peoples
who sought to ward off their incursions. The mounted
warriors of nomadic armies possessed the advantages of
speed, surprise, and superior intelligence, which was gathered by mounted reconnaissance patrols. The most successful nomadic invaders, such as the Mongols, also proved
willing to experiment with and adapt to technological innovations with military applications. Some of these, such as
the stirrup and various sorts of harnesses, were devised by
the nomads themselves. Others, such as gunpowder and the
siege engines—both Muslim and Chinese—that the Mongols used to smash the defenses of walled towns, were borrowed from sedentary peoples and adapted to the nomads'
fighting machines.

Aside from the considerable military advantages that ac-
crued from nomadic life-styles and social organization,
their successes in war owed much to the weaknesses of
their adversaries in the sedentary, civilized zones. The
great empires that provided the main defense for agricultural peoples against nomadic incursions were even in the
best circumstances diverse and overextended polities, in
which imperial control—and protection—diminished
steadily as one moved away from the capital and core provinces. Imperial boundaries were usually fluid, and the
outer provinces were consistently vulnerable to nomadic
raids, if not conquest.

Classical and postclassical empires, such as the Egyptian
and Han and the Abbasid, Byzantine, and Song enjoyed
great advantages over the nomads in terms of the populations and resources they controlled. But their armies were,
almost without exception, too slow, too low on firepower,
and too poorly trained to resist large and well-organized
forces of nomadic intruders. In times of dynastic strength
in the sedentary zones, well-defended fortress systems and
ingenious weapons—such as the cross bow, which could be
fairly easily mastered by the peasant conscripts—proved
quite effective against nomadic incursions. Nonetheless,
even the strongest dynasties depended heavily on "protection" payments to nomad leaders and the divisions among

the nomadic peoples on their borders for their security. And even the strongest sedentary empires were periodically shaken by nomadic raids into the outer provinces. When the empires weakened or when large numbers of nomads were united under able leaders, such as Muhammad and his successors or Chinggis Khan, nomadic assaults made a shambles of sedentary armies and fortifications.

In the centuries after the Mongol and Timurid explosions, which in many ways represented the apex of nomadic power and influence on world history, this age-old pattern of interaction between nomads and farming town-dwelling peoples was fundamentally transformed. This transformation resulted in the growing ability of sedentary peoples to first resist and then dominate nomadic peoples, and it marks a major watershed in the history of the human community. Some of the causes of the shift were immediate

In 1398 Timur-i Lang's central Asian armies left Delhi completely destroyed and India politically fragmented.

and specific. The most critical of these was the devastation wrought by the Black Death on the nomads of Central Asia in the 14th century. Though the epidemic proved catastrophic for large portions of the civilized zones as well, it dealt the relatively sparse nomadic populations a blow from which they took centuries to recover. The more rapid *demographic*—relating to population trends—resurgence of the sedentary peoples greatly increased their already considerable numerical advantage over the nomadic peoples in the following centuries. The combination of this growing numerical advantage, which in earlier epochs the nomads had often been able to overcome, with key political and economic shifts and technological innovations proved critical in bringing about the decline of the nomadic war machine.

In the centuries after the Mongol conquests, the rulers of sedentary states found increasingly effective ways of centralizing their political power and mobilizing the manpower and resources of their domains for war. Some improvements in this regard were made by the rulers of China and the empires of the Islamic belt. But the sovereigns of the nascent states of western Europe surpassed all other potentates in advances in these spheres. Stronger control and better organization allowed a growing share of steadily increasing national wealth to be channeled toward military ends. The competing rulers of Europe also invested heavily in technological innovations with military applications, from improved metalworking techniques to the development of ever more potent gunpowder and firearms. From the 15th and 16th centuries, the discipline and training of European armies also improved markedly. With pikes, muskets, fire drill, and trained commanders, European armies were more than a match for the massed nomad cavalry that had so long terrorized sedentary peoples.

With the introduction early in the 17th century of light, mobile field artillery into European armies, the nomads' retreat began. States such as Russia, which had centralized power on the western European model, as well as the Ottoman Empire in the eastern Mediterranean and the Qing in China, which had shared many of the armament advances of the Europeans, moved steadily into the steppe and desert heartlands of the horse and camel nomads. Each followed a conscious policy of settling part of its rapidly growing peasant population in the areas taken from the nomads. Thus, nomadic populations were not only brought under the direct rule of sedentary empires, their pasturelands were plowed and planted wherever the soil and water supply permitted.

These trends suggest that the nomadic war machine had been in decline long before the new wave of innovation that ushered in the Industrial Revolution in the 18th century. But that process sealed its fate. Railways and repeating rifles allowed sedentary peoples to penetrate even the most wild and remote of the nomadic refuges and subdue even the most determined and fierce of nomadic warriors, from the Plains Indians of North America to the bedouin of the Sahara and Arabia. The periodic nomadic incursions into the sedentary zones, which had reoccurred sporadically for millennia, had come to an end.

Questions: What are some of the major ways in which nomadic peoples and their periodic expansions have affected the course of global history? Which of their movements and conquests do you think were the most important? Why were the Mongols able to build a much greater empire than any previous nomadic contender? Why did the Mongol Empire collapse so rapidly, and what does its fall tell us about the underlying weaknesses of the nomadic war machine?

CONCLUSION

THE MONGOL LEGACY AND AN AFTERSHOCK: THE BRIEF RIDE OF TIMUR

As we have seen, the Mongol impact on the many areas where they raided and conquered varied considerably. The sedentary peoples on the farms and in the cities, who experienced the fury of their assaults and the burden of their tribute exactions, understandably emphasized the destructive side of the Mongol legacy. But the Mongol campaigns also decisively influenced the course of human history in the ways they altered warfare and the political repercussions they generated in invaded areas. Mongol armies, for example, provided openings for the rise of Moscow as the central force in the creation of a Russian state, they put an end to Abbasid and Seljuk power, and they opened the way for the Mameluks and the Ottomans. The Mongol Empire promoted trade and important exchanges among civilizations, though, as the spread of the black death illustrates, the latter were not always beneficial. Mongol rule also brought stable, at times quite effective, government and religious toleration to peoples over much of Asia. On balance, it can be argued that the cost of these by-products of Mongol expansion was far too high. However high the price, there can be little doubt that the Mongol interlude

changed the course of human history in major ways. It represented the most significant involvement of nomadic peoples in the development of civilization since the transition to sedentary agriculture in the Neolithic epoch.

Just as the peoples of Eurasia had begun to recover from the upheavals caused by Mongol expansion, a second nomadic explosion from central Asia plunged them again into fear and despair. This time the nomads in question were Turks, not Mongols, and their leader, Timur-i Lang or Timur the Lame, was from a noble landowning clan, not a tribal, herding background. Timur's was a decidedly divided personality. On the one hand, he was a highly cultured individual who delighted in the fine arts, lush gardens, and splendid architecture, and who could spend days conversing with great scholars such as the Muslim historian Ibn Khaldun. On the other, he was a ruthless conqueror, apparently indifferent to human suffering and capable of commanding his troops to commit atrocities on a scale that would not be matched in the human experience until the 20th century. Beginning in the 1360s, his armies moved out from his base at Samarkand to conquests in Persia, the Fertile Crescent, India, and southern Russia.

If his empire did not begin to compare with that of the Mongols in size, he outdid them in the ferocity of his campaigns. In fact, Timur is remembered for little more than truly barbaric destruction—for the pyramids of skulls he built with the heads of the tens of thousands of people slaughtered after the city of Aleppo in Asia Minor was taken, or the thousands of prisoners he had massacred as a warning to the citizens of Delhi in north India not to resist his armies. In the face of this wanton slaughter, the fact that he spared artisans and scientists to embellish his capital city at Samarkand counts for little. Unlike the Mongols, his rule brought neither increased trade and significant cross-cultural exchanges nor internal peace. Mercifully, his reign was as brief as it was violent. After his death in 1405, his empire was pulled apart by his warring commanders and old enemies anxious for revenge. With his passing, the last great challenge of the steppe nomads to the civilizations of Eurasia came to an end.

FURTHER READINGS

A substantial literature has developed on the Mongol interlude in global history. The most readable and reliable biography of Chinggis Khan is René Grousset's *Conqueror of the World* (1966). Grousset has also written a broader history of central Asia entitled *The Empire of the Steppes* (1970). Peter Brent's more recent *The Mongol Empire* (1976) provides an updated overview and wonderful illustrations. Berthold Spuler's *The Mongols in History* (1971) makes some attempt to gauge their impact on world history, and his *History of the Mongols* (1968) supplies a wide variety of firsthand accounts of the Mongols from the founding of the empire to life in the successor states. T. Allsen's *Mongol Imperialism* provides the best account of the rise and structure of the empires built by Chinggis Khan and his successors.

For specific areas, George Verdansky's *The Mongols in Russia* (1953) remains the standard, though some of its views are now contested; Morris Rossabi's recent *Kubilai Khan: His Life and Times* (1988) is by far the best work on the Mongols in China; James Chambers's *The Devil's Horsemen* (1979) and Denis Sinor's, *History of Hungary* (1957) contain good accounts of the Mongol incursions into eastern and central Europe. The fullest and most accessible summary of the links between Mongol expansion and the spread of the Black Death can be found in William H. McNeill's *Plagues and Peoples* (1976).

c. 1266–1337 Giotto

1275–1292 Marco Polo in China   **1304–1374** Petrarch; development of Italian Renaissance

1348–1375 Plague spreads in Europe including Russia

1320s Spread of bubonic plague in Gobi desert

1258 Mongol conquest of Bagh-   **1291** First Italian expedi-   **1320s** First European use of cannon in warfare   **1348** Peak of Black
dad; fall of Abbasid caliphate   tion seeks route to Indies   Death in Middle East
                                                          1330s Black Death
1290–1317 New famines in Europe   reaches China   **1347** Plague reaches Sicily

A.D. 1250   A.D. 1300   A.D. 1350

21

The West and the Changing World Balance

INTRODUCTION. By the year 1400, partly as a result of the Mongol invasions and their aftermath, it was becoming clear that the balance among civilizations in the world was beginning to change dramatically. This chapter summarizes the leading developments in this new world balance, building on the coverage of specific civilizations in preceding chapters.

This period of transition in the 14th and early 15th centuries involves three major components. First, the conditions that opened the possibility of a rebalancing must be surveyed. This involves particularly a reminder of the decline of Arab strength—symbolized by the fall of the last Arab caliphate in 1258—and the disruptions caused elsewhere in Asia and eastern Europe by the Mongol incursions. These developments opened new confusions and opportunities within the international network that had been established in the postclassical centuries, particularly through the expansive power of Arab religion, trade, and politics. Various candidates emerged to take a new international role, including for a short time China in the early stages of the Ming dynasty that replaced the Mongol overlords during the 14th century.

The most dynamic new contender for international power was western Europe, and the conditions that propelled Western civilization toward a new position around 1400 form the second major theme of this chapter. The West was not yet the world's major power; it did not replace the Arabs as international leaders quickly or easily. The first stages of the rise of the West were accompanied by important changes within Western civilization itself, also taking shape by around 1400. At this point Italy, Spain, and Portugal took a new leadership role in the West, which they would hold for about two centuries.

1439 Portugal takes over Azores; increasing expeditions into Atlantic, along northwest African coast

1469 Union of Aragon and Castile; rise of Spanish monarchy

1400 End of Polynesian migrations

1368 Mongols expelled from China; Ming dynasty

1405 Chinese trading expeditions begin

1453 Ottomans capture Constantinople; fall of Byzantine empire

1433 End of Chinese expeditions

The third major component to introduce in this world status report involves the civilizations that were largely or completely outside the international network. Important civilizations in parts of Africa, as well as in the Americas and Polynesia, were independent of larger world connections; yet changes they were experiencing by 1400 would feed into the international equation that was taking shape in the 15th century.

After presenting the three main ingredients working toward a new world balance, we can summarize the state of the world in the decades after 1400 by talking about the overall characteristics of a key period of transition in world history. This transition can be compared to the previous time of change, as in the decline of the great classical empires, and to a subsequent time of transition as well. Interestingly, the 15th-century transition bears some marked resemblances to the international flux of the 20th century.

THE DECLINE OF THE OLD ORDER

The first steps in the new world order that was beginning to emerge by 1400 involved modifications in the bases of the previous world order that had prevailed from the 7th until the 14th centuries. Here, the most obvious ingredients involved the major reshuffling in the Middle East and North Africa. In 1200 this region was still described by two powerful empires, the Byzantine in the northwest and the Islamic caliphate through much of the Middle Eastern heartland. By 1400 this structure was in full disarray. The Byzantine Empire still existed, but it was on its last legs, pressed by invading Ottoman Turks. The imperial capital, Constantinople, would fall to the Turks in 1453, effectively ending the empire. Two centuries earlier, the caliphate, long sapped by increasing reliance on foreign troops and advisors, including the omnipresent Turks, fell to Mongol invasion. Arabs have never since been able to unite a significant portion of their homeland under their own rule.

SOCIAL AND CULTURAL DECLINE IN THE MIDDLE EAST

The decline of the Arabs and the caliphate went beyond politics. Increasingly, by around 1300 religious leaders in the Islamic Middle East gained the upper hand over poets, philosophers, and scientists. An earlier tension among diverse cultural elements yielded to the predominance of the faith. The new piety associated with the rising Sufi movement was both the cause and the result of this development. In literature, emphasis on secular themes, such as the joys of feasting and hunting, gave way to more strictly

This Persian-style painting depicts the Ottoman Turks as they assail the Hungarians with troops and cannons in a battle in 1526.

religious ideas. Persian poets, writing now in their own language instead of Arabic, led the way, and religious poetry—not poetry in general—became part of the education of upper-class children. In philosophy, the rationalistic current encountered new attack. In Muslim Spain the philosopher Ibn-Rushd (Averroës) espoused Greek rationalism, but his efforts were largely ignored in the Middle East. European scholars were in fact more heavily influenced by his work. In the Middle East proper, a more typical philosopher now claimed to use Aristotle's logic to show that it was impossible to discover religious truth by human reason—in a book revealingly, if not subtly, entitled *The Destruction of Philosophy*.

Increasingly, then, Middle Eastern scholarship focused on religion and the Islamic legalistic traditions. Some interest in science remained, though it too began to fade. In its place, many Sufi scholars wrote excitingly of their mystical contacts with God and the stages of their religious passion, which could lead to dramatic new statements of Islam.

This shift and narrowing of Middle Eastern cultural life had less impact on the arts. Artisans' production continued to flourish in many centers, maintaining the Middle East's distinctive commitment to richly decorated rugs, leather goods, and other wares.

Changes in society and the economy were still more subtle than, but in many ways as ominous as, the shifts in politics and intellectual life. As the authority of the caliphate declined, landlords seized power over the peasantry. From about 1100 onward, Middle Eastern peasants increasingly lost their freedom, becoming serfs on large estates. This loss was not the peasants' alone, for agricultural productivity suffered as a result. Landlords turned to sucking what they could from their estates, rather than trying to develop a more vital agriculture, and peasants had scant incentive and no means to do better. This was no sudden crisis, but simply a gradual, partial deterioration; with it came fewer tax revenues for the state and less basis for flourishing trade. And indeed Arab and other Middle Eastern traders began to lose ground. Few Arab coins have been found in Europe dating from later than 1100. European merchants began to control their own turf and to challenge the Arabs in other parts of the Mediterranean; initiative in this vital trading area was passing to their hands. Arab and Persian commerce remained active in the Indian Ocean, but the time was not too distant when it would face new competition there as well.

CONTINUING STRENGTHS

The decline of the Islamic caliphate and its economy was gradual and incomplete. It cannot be compared with the dramatic fall of the Roman Empire in the West many centuries before—another, more subtle model is needed. The reduction of dynamism in trade, for example, linked to weaker or more limited political and cultural forms, by no means took the Arabs out of major world markets.

Finally, the political fragmentation of the Arab world did not produce durable confusion in the Middle East. The emerging Ottoman Turkish state soon mastered most of the lands of the old caliphate as well as the Byzantine corner, expanding into southeastern Europe. (See Chapter 26 for the development of the new Ottoman Empire.) It is important to realize, further, that the empire was far more powerful, politically and militarily, than the caliphate had

been for many centuries—and proportionately more frightening to observers in neighboring civilizations such as western Europe.

Nevertheless, even the rise of the Ottoman Empire did not restore the full international vigor that the Islamic caliphate had possessed at the height of its powers. Turkish rulers—rather scornful of their Arab subjects though sharing their religion—did not promote trade, particularly maritime trade, as vigorously as in the past. While they patronized Arab and Persian artists and craftsmen, they also did not encourage the same kind of general cultural flowering as had occurred at the height of the caliphates. Scientific and philosophical development tended to stagnate in the Middle East. The expansionist power of the Ottoman Empire was very real, and would persist into the 17th century, but its bases were somewhat limited. Military activity gained a new lease on life, but cultural and commercial impact outside the new empire was modest. The empire could not serve as the sole hub of an international network, as the Arab caliphate was a few centuries before.

A VACUUM OF POWER IN INTERNATIONAL LEADERSHIP

The result, particularly given the Arab decline in international trade, was something of a power vacuum beyond the borders of the Ottoman Empire. A single replacement for the Arabs as hub of the loose international network was not perhaps inevitable, and no other civilization deliberately set out to advance a candidacy as a matter of explicit policy, but in fact a sorting-out process was well under way by 1400, with the West beginning to emerge as the leading beneficiary.

There were several limitations to the list of possible replacements for the Arabs as leading international actors. The Ottoman Empire emphasized trade and cultural dynamism too little. Japan simply did not think in terms of major expansion. India was divided into regional kingdoms that largely reacted to foreign contacts (particularly from Islamic invaders), rather than initiating them. Russia would be a source of new expansion beginning late in the 15th century.

THE CHINESE THRUST

This left, effectively, only two contenders for the mantle of leading international manipulator: China and the West. China clearly had the edge and for a time took full advantage of the new opportunities in international trade. In a conscious policy decision, however, the new Ming dynasty took itself out of the main international arena, returning to

**Major Boundary
Changes in Asia,
1350–1500**

long-standing traditions in the civilization that urged concentration on developing the Middle Kingdom and its evolving internal strengths.

Rebellions in China drove out the deeply resented Mongol overlords in 1368. A rebel leader, born of peasant stock, seized the Mongol capital of Beijing and proclaimed a new Ming—meaning "brilliant"—dynasty that was to last until 1644. This dynasty began with a burst of unusual expansionism. As in earlier dynasties, initial Ming rulers pressed to secure the borders of the Middle Kingdom. This meant pushing the Mongols far to the north to the plains of what is now Mongolia. It meant reestablishing influence over neighboring governments and winning tribute payments from states in Korea, Vietnam, and Tibet—reviving much of the East Asian regional structure set up by the Tang dynasty. Far more unusual was a new policy, adopted soon after 1400, of mounting huge, state-sponsored trading expeditions to southern Asia and beyond.

A first fleet sailed in 1405 to India, with 62 ships carrying 28,000 men. Later voyages reached the Middle East

and the eastern coast of Africa, bringing chinaware and copper coinage in exchange for local goods. Chinese shipping at its height consisted of 2700 coastal vessels, 400 armed naval ships, and at least as many long-distance ships. Nine great "treasure ships," the most sophisticated in the world at the time in their size and provisions as well as the improved compasses they used for navigation, explored the Indian Ocean, the Persian Gulf, and the Red Sea, establishing regular trade with all parts of southern Asia and the Middle East. Seven trips were made in all, commanded by a Chinese Muslim eunuch named Cheng Ho.

There is no question that the course of world history might have been immeasurably altered had the Chinese thrust continued, for the tiny European expeditions that began to creep down the western coast of Africa at about the same time would have been no match for this combination of merchant and military organization. But the emperors called the expeditions to a halt in 1433. The bureaucrats had long opposed the new trade policy, out of rivalry with other officials such as Cheng Ho, but there were deeper reasons as well. The costs seemed unacceptable given continuing expenses of the campaigns against the Mongols and the desire to build a luxurious new capital city in Beijing. This assessment was not, of course, inevitable. It reflected a preference for traditional expenditures rather than distant foreign involvements. Chinese merchant activity continued to be extensive in Southeast Asia. Chinese trading groups established permanent settlements in the Philippines, Malaysia, and Indonesia, where they added to the cultural diversity of the area and maintained a disproportionate role in local and regional trading activities into the 20th century. China's chance to become a dominant world trading power was lost, however, at least for some centuries, with a decision that in essence confirmed the relatively low status of trade within the official Chinese scheme of things.

EVALUATING THE CHINESE WITHDRAWAL

To Western eyes, accustomed to judging a society's dynamism by its ability to reach out and gain new territories or trade positions, China's decision may seem hard to understand, the precursor to some inevitable decline. In Chinese terms, of course, it was the brief trading flurry that was unusual, not its cessation. China had long emphasized internal development, amid some international isolation, while maintaining suspicion of merchant values and any policy that would unduly elevate commercial activity. Despite the intensity of internal trade, undue policy emphasis was shunned. And China did not clearly suffer from the decision to pull back, at least not in the short run. It did not need foreign products. Ming emperors consolidated their rule over the empire's vast territory. Internal economic development continued as well. Industry expanded, with growth in the production of textiles and porcelain; ongoing trade with Southeast Asia enriched the port cities; agricultural production and population both increased. Cultural activity showed the clearest hints of declining creativity. Intellectuals focused on summing up expanding knowledge in medicine, agriculture, and technology, maintaining interest in drama and poetry, and pursuing philosophical training in Confucianism.

The shift in Chinese policy unintentionally cleared the way for another, in most ways decidedly inferior, civilization to work toward a new international position. With the Arabs in partial eclipse and with China briefly moving into the resulting trade vacuum but then retreating, hesitant Western expansionism, launched before 1400, began to take on new significance. Within a century, Western explorers and traders had begun directly to seize international trading dominance and had expanded the international network to include parts of the Americas for the first time.

 ## THE RISE OF THE WEST

The West's gradual emergence into larger world contacts during the 15th century was surprising in many respects. The Western nations lacked the political coherence and organizing ability of several other societies. Westerners remained awed, and rightly so, by the powerful bureaucracies and opulent treasuries of empires in the traditional civilization centers such as Constantinople. Furthermore, the West was changing in some painful ways. Staples of medieval culture at its high point were under new question by 1400. The Church, long one of the organizing institutions of Western civilization, was under new attack. Many popes seemed more interested in advancing their wealth and political position than in religious leadership. On another front powerful national rulers, such as the king of France, claimed increasing authority in religious matters and defied Church rulings directly, even imprisoning a recalcitrant pope. Medieval philosophy had passed its creative phase. Warrior aristocrats, long a key leadership group in feudal society, increasingly softened their style of life as military technology began to pass them by, preferring court rituals and jousting tournaments and adopting military armor so cumbersome that real fighting was difficult.

Even more striking, the lives and economic activities of ordinary Europeans were in serious disarray. This was a time of crisis, and Europe's expanding world role by no means reversed the fundamental challenges to internal economic and demographic structure. Europeans began to suffer from recurrent famine after 1300, as population had outstripped food supply and no new techniques were discovered to alter the equation. A pattern of cold weather also set in, causing unexpected freezes and reduced food output for almost two centuries. Famine conditions in turn reduced disease resistance, making Europe more vulnerable to the bubonic plagues that spread from Asia.

Bubonic plague, or Black Death, surfaced in various parts of Asia in the 14th century. In China it reduced the population by nearly 30 percent by 1400. Following trade routes, it then spread into India and the Middle East, causing thousands of deaths per day in the larger cities. The plague's worst European impact occurred between 1348 and 1375, by which time 30 million people, one-third of Europe's population, had died.

Population loss of this magnitude inevitably caused further economic dislocation. Labor shortages prompted wage increases, which brought efforts at limitation and control; these in turn produced bitter strikes and peasant risings. Finally, France and England devoted much of the same period, between the mid-14th and mid-15th centuries, to their costly Hundred Years' War, which devastated parts of France and drained the revenues of both nations.

SOURCES OF DYNAMISM: MEDIEVAL VITALITY

How, then, could the West be poised for a new international role? The answer to that question must embrace several ingredients. First, several key advances of medieval society were not really reversed amid the troubles of the decades around 1400. The strengthening of feudal monarchy, for example, provided more effective national or regional governments for much of the West. The Hundred Years' War stimulated innovations in military organization, including nonaristocratic soldiers recruited and paid directly by the royal government, that enhanced central political power. Strong regional monarchies took hold in parts of Spain and in Portugal, as Christian leaders drove back the Muslim rulers of this region. Along with more effective political rule, the growth of cities and urban economies continued to spur the commercial side of Western society. Even the Church had made its peace with key principles of capitalism such as profit seeking.

Technology continued to advance, particularly in ironwork—used for bells and weapons—and timekeeping. Here too, the Hundred Years' War added demands for guns and munitions, spurring this industrial sector. Even in culture, medieval interests in furthering human understanding continued to support advances in scientific research in areas such as optics. The first element of an explanation of new Western vigor involves an understanding that some of the gains the West had achieved during the Middle Ages continued, even as certain characteristic medieval forms wavered.

DEMOGRAPHIC VIGOR

One key durable trend involved population growth, which, beginning around the 9th century, had been a key symptom and cause of other changes in the medieval West. As commerce expanded, agriculture improved, and internal warfare declined, Western population continued to grow. Indeed, between A.D. 1000 and 1700 Western population expanded at a more rapid rate than that of any other continent. Agricultural shortages and the Black Death temporarily pushed population growth back in the West, but the overall trend was toward expansion. The West's population was still smaller, in absolute terms, than that of the other major civilizations, but it was gaining ground relatively. By the end of the postclassical era, European population had already surpassed that of the Middle East. Demographic vigor of this sort helps explain Europe's thirst for expansion and contributed to its growing sense of confidence.

TABLE 21.1

Population Levels (in millions)

Continents	Years				
	1000	1700	1800	1900	1975
Europe	36	120	180	390	635
Asia (includes Middle East)	185	415	625	970	2300
Africa	33	61	70	110	385
Americas	39	13	24	145	545
Oceania (includes Australia)	1.5	2.25	2.5	6.75	23
Totals	294.5	611.25	901.5	1621.75	3888

Note: Estimates for the earlier dates are only that; they are not precise figures. They indicate comparative magnitudes with reasonable precision.

Source: Adapted from Dennis H. Wrong, ed., *Population and Society* (1977).

TABLE 21.2

Percentages or Proportions of Total World Population

Continents	Years				
	1000	1700	1800	1900	1975
Europe	12.2	19.6	19.7	24	16.3
Asia	62.9	67.6	69.3	59.8	59.2
Africa	11.2	10.0	7.8	6.8	9.9
Americas	13.4	2.1	2.7	8.9	14.0
Oceania	0.4	0.4	0.3	0.3	0.6

Source: Adapted from Dennis H. Wrong, ed., *Population and Society* (1977).

PLAYING TO CATCH UP

Continuities from medieval dynamism, however, whether in commercial growth or population expansion, are not the whole story. A second ingredient of the West's surge involves the status of the civilization itself. Western leaders knew they remained inferior to other world powers, particularly to the advancing Ottoman Turks. One of the motives for ongoing explorations into routes that would allow the West direct contact with southern and eastern Asia, without passing through Muslim lands or Muslim traders, involved recognition of weakness and even a concern that further Muslim inroads were impending.

A third ingredient of the West's surge involves a certain amount of world-historical luck. The West had been spared the confusion of a Mongol invasion, largely because of accidental distractions of Mongol politics in Asia (see Chapter 20). Yet the Mongol Empire established in Asia and eastern Europe provided, in the late 13th and early 14th centuries, new access to Asian knowledge and technology. Political stability and an openness to foreign visitors by the great khans, along with continued trade through the Mediterranean, helped Westerners learn of Asian technologies ranging from printing to the compass and explosive powder. Because of a combination of heightened contact and Western eagerness to learn, particularly where technology had military implications, Western technology drew closer to the highest world levels by the early 15th century. Soon it would begin to surpass these levels.

Finally, as the fourth major ingredient of the West's surge, the West itself began to change, not only in challenging medieval forms but in developing some constructive alternatives. The decline of medieval society, far from complete in any event, did not signal a narrowing of Western culture or politics, but rather an opportunity to innovate. Important dislocations did exist, but they did not prevent some vital new directions. The fact that key innovations occurred in places like Italy, where medieval forms such as Gothic architecture or scholastic philosophy had less intense impact, helps explain how the West was able to begin to change its skin.

THE EARLY RENAISSANCE

Italy, in 1400, was in the midst of a vital cultural and political movement known as the *Renaissance,* or rebirth, and this in turn provided the clearest indication that the West was renewing its society, not really declining. This was a cultural movement above all, though it rested on the urban vitality and expanding commerce Italians had developed during the postclassical period. The early phases of the Renaissance, taking shape during the 14th century, involved literature and art friendlier to things of this world, not in opposition to religious goals but with distinctly more secular priorities. Religious art remained dominant but with more realistic portrayals of people and nature, and some nonreligious themes surfaced outright. The doings of human beings deserved attention for their own sake, in the Renaissance view, not as they reflected a divine plan. The goals of artists and writers became more openly ambitious for personal reputation and glory.

THE ITALIAN CONTEXT

Italy was the center of initial Renaissance cultural definitions because it retained more contact with Roman tradition than did the rest of Europe and because it led the West, by the 14th century, in banking and trade. Active commerce and considerable urban manufacturing gave Italian cities the wealth to sponsor new cultural activities, contacts with some foreign scholars particularly in Byzantium, and a more optimistic view of the power of human endeavor and the validity of earthly goals. Italy was not spared some of the crises of the late Middle Ages, including the massive death rates caused by the epidemic of bubonic plague, but cultural innovation proceeded despite these constraints.

Special political characteristics in Italy contributed to the Renaissance surge, along with classical traditions and capitalist enterprise. Although northern Italy technically fell into the territory controlled by the German emperors, in fact key city-states had long exercised effective government power in the major regions. Feudal relationships were not dominant. Rather, city-state governments were made up of successful military entrepreneurs, who translated their heroic exploits into political control, or of individual merchants or merchant councils. These governments lacked the

Giotto's 14th-century Renaissance painting preserves Christian themes in the lamentation over the dead Christ, but with new attention to naturalism and expression in the human figures.

support of tradition and had to woo popular backing and undertake an array of new functions, from grain supply to policing, in order to retain power. Furthermore, the city-states were intensely competitive, and while this led to many wars as well as commercial rivalry, it also encouraged sponsorship of cultural achievements as badges of urban greatness. Finally, the attention to government and diplomacy led intellectuals and political leaders to their emphasis on "this worldly" culture. One of the reasons for the new interest in classical Roman culture was its emphasis on republican virtues, oratorical ability, and other skills useful in successful administration. The Renaissance was very definitely an urban phenomenon, but it also was a result of the special role and organization of Italian cities.

RENAISSANCE CULTURE

For all its political and commercial roots, the Renaissance was first and foremost a cultural movement, launched in Florence and manifesting itself in literature and various arts. The Renaissance focused on a new interest in stylistic grace, an exploration of "this worldly" themes such as romance and nature, and a concern for practical ethics and codes of behavior for urban gentlemen. One leading 14th-century writer, Francesco Petrarch, not only took pride in his city and his age, but explored the glories of personal achievement with new confidence. The tone of innovation—in style, subject matter, and implicit view of human powers—predominated in the many writings of 14th-century Florentines.

Innovation increasingly prevailed in the visual arts and music as well. The subject matter of art moved toward nature and people, including both cityscapes and the inevitable portraits of the rich and powerful, whether the themes were religious or secular. The Florentine painter Giotto led the way, departing from medieval formalism and stiffness. Other painters, beginning later in the 14th century, started to introduce perspective while also using new colors and other materials. In architecture, favor shifted away from the Gothic to a classicism derived from the styles of Greece and Rome. Vivid, realistic statues complemented the new palaces and public buildings.

As a massive shift in cultural emphases, the impact of the early Renaissance must not be exaggerated. It had little influence, as yet, outside of Italy. Even in Italy it focused on high culture, not popular outlook. And while it built on distinctive political and economic forms, it did not constitute a full break from medieval tendencies. Even in Italian intellectual life, important work on science, at places such as the University of Padua, maintained medieval impulses and would gradually lead to later scientific advance, outside of the most popular cultural themes of the Renaissance.

Nevertheless, the advent of new cultural currents was an important innovation in Western history. The full ramifications of the Renaissance feed into the next period of both world and Western history (see Chapter 22). The movement was only getting started by 1400. Yet, in combination with some larger medieval trends, the early Renaissance had some interesting implications for Europe's position in the world. The wide range of Italian commerce and shipping proved to be one of the building blocks of European outreach. By the 14th century, ships, particularly from Genoa, which was less well-placed than Venice for eastern Mediterranean trade, were ready for new roles. Ambitious city-state governments encouraged new ventures, eager for greater tax money and unembarrassed about promoting commerce as one of their explicit functions. A larger, if poorly defined "Renaissance spirit" could also spur innovation. While people like Petrarch defined human ambition mainly in cultural terms, other urban and commercial leaders, including seafaring men like Genoa's Christopher Columbus, might translate some of the same desire for personal glory and confidence in individual ability and in the validity of secular goals to different areas—such as exploration or conquest. It was no accident that Marco Polo, the European who brought new knowledge of China to his civilization, was an Italian inspired by the urban culture of the early Renaissance.

THE IBERIAN SPIRIT

Western civilization by 1400 was a complex mixture of old and new. Medieval forms predominated in many ways, and in many parts of Europe the most important changes involved the new problems medieval institutions were encountering. Yet the advent of the Renaissance suggested important alternatives and a vital ability to strike out in new directions that would soon overtake the confusions of medieval decline. Finally, there were other important innovations, different both from medieval stagnation and Renaissance brashness. Along with Italy a key center for change by the 14th century was the Iberian Peninsula, where Christian military leaders had for several centuries been pressing back the boundaries of the Muslim state in Spain. Soon after 1400 major regional monarchies had been established in the provinces of Castile and Aragon, which would be united through royal marriage in 1469, and the Muslims had been pushed out of the entire peninsula save for the region around Granada.

DOCUMENT
ITALIAN RENAISSANCE CULTURE

Writers in the first phase of the Italian Renaissance were aware that they were defining a culture quite different from that of medieval theologians and philosophers. In the passages that follow, Petrarch (1304–1374) writes about his priorities in literature, including the kind of classical examples he revered, first in a letter to another major writer, Boccaccio, and then in a poem. Petrarch's cultural interests and his definition of personal goals form part of a movement called *humanism* (see Chapter 22). Judging by the following documents, what defined a Renaissance humanist?

FROM PETRARCH, LETTER TO BOCCACCIO (1362)

Neither exhortations to virtue nor the argument of approaching death should divert us from literature; for in a good mind it excites the love of virtue, and dissipates, or at least diminishes, the fear of death. To desert our studies shows want of self-confidence rather than wisdom, for letters do not hinder but aid the properly constituted mind which possesses them; they facilitate our life, they do not retard it. . . . If it were otherwise, surely the zeal of certain persons who persevered to the end could not have roused such admiration. Cato, I never forget, acquainted himself with Latin literature as he was growing old, and Greek when he had really become an old man. Varro, who reached his hundredth year still reading and writing, parted from life sooner than from his love of study. Livius Drusus, although weakened by age and afflicted with blindness, did not give up his interpretation of the civil law, which he carried on to the great advantage of the state. . . .

Besides these and innumerable others like them, have not all those of our own religion whom we should wish most to imitate devoted their whole lives to literature, and grown old and died in the same pursuit? Some, indeed, were overtaken by death while still at work reading or writing. To none of them, so far as I know, did it prove a disadvantage to be noted for secular learning. . . .

While I know that many have become famous for piety without learning, at the same time I know of no one who has been prevented by literature from following the path of holiness. The apostle Paul was, to be sure, accused of having his head turned by study, but the world has long ago passed its verdict upon this accusation. If I may be allowed to speak for myself, it seems to me that, although the path to virtue by the way of ignorance may be plain, it fosters sloth. The goal of all good people is the same, but the ways of reaching it are many and various. Some advance slowly, others with more spirit; some obscurely, others again conspicuously. One takes a lower path, another takes a higher path. Although all alike are on the road to happiness, certainly the more elevated path is the more glorious. Hence ignorance, however devout, is by no means to be put on a plane with the enlightened devoutness of one familiar with literature. Nor can you pick me out from the whole array of unlettered saints, an example so holy that I cannot match it with a still holier one from the other group.

FROM PETRARCH, THE SONNETS (c. 1535)

To A Friend, Encouraging Him to Pursue Poetry

Torn is each virtue from its earthy throne
By sloth, intemperance, and voluptuous ease;
Far hence is every light celestial gone,
That guides mankind through life's
*   perplexing maze . . .*
Who now would laurel, myrtel-wreaths obtain?
Let want, let shame, Philosophy attend!
Cries the base world, intent on sordid gain.
What though thy favourite path be trod by few;
Let it but urge thee more, dear gentle friend,
Thy great design of glory to pursue.

Questions: What are the key purposes of intellectual activity, according to Petrarch? How can these purposes be reconciled with Christianity? To what extent does Petrarch's humanism suggest a more "modern" outlook than that of medieval Western culture?

Even before the marriage of Ferdinand and Isabella, Spanish and Portuguese rulers had developed a vigorous military and religious agenda. They supported effective armies, including infantry and feudal cavalry. And they believed that government had a mission to promote Christianity by converting Arabs and Jews or expelling those who held back, and by maintaining doctrinal purity within the Church itself. Close links between church and state provided revenues and officials for the royal government. In return, the government supported church courts in their quest for moral and doctrinal purity. Later in the 15th century this interaction would lead to the reestablishment of church-run courts of the Inquisition in Spain, designed to enforce religious orthodoxy and punish deviants. Spain and Portugal, in other words, were developing effective new governments with a special sense of religious mission and religious support. These changes, too, would feed the West's surge into wider world contacts.

European Exploration of the Atlantic around Africa

WESTERN EXPANSION: THE EXPERIMENTAL PHASE

The picture of the world in 1400, as painted thus far, is not yet complete, partly because areas of the world not in the previous Asia-Europe-North Africa network have not been sketched in, and partly because one final ingredient in western Europe's own position has yet to be defined.

A CRISIS IN ECONOMIC POSITION

The fact was, by 1400, that western Europe was in serious international economic difficulties. These related to the general problems of relative Western weakness amid the older civilizations of Asia, but they had a specific twist. From the Crusades onward, Western elites had become accustomed to increasing consumption of Asian luxury products, including spices such as cinnamon and nutmeg, silks, sugar, perfumes, and jewels. In exchange for the luxury items, Europeans mainly had cruder goods to offer—wool, tin, copper, honey, and salt. The value of European exports almost never equaled the value of what was imported from Asia. The resulting unfavorable balance of trade had to be made up in gold, but Western people had only a limited gold supply. By 1400, the constant drain to Asia was creating a gold famine that threatened the whole European economy with collapse.

Furthermore, there were legitimate fears of a new Muslim threat. The Ottoman Empire was taking shape. Even before this the Muslim capture of the last Crusader stronghold (the city of Acre in the Middle East) in 1291 had

been a disaster for the Christian faith, but it also gave Muslim traders—particularly Egyptians—new opportunities to serve as middlemen in the oriental trade, for there were no Western-controlled ports left in the eastern Mediterranean. One response to this was a series of conquests by the city-state of Venice along the eastern coast of the Adriatic. A more important and durable response was to begin explorations of alternative routes to Asia that would bypass the Middle East and the feared and hated Muslim realms altogether.

EARLY EXPLORATIONS

As early as 1291 two Italian brothers, the Vivaldis from Genoa, sailed with two galleys through the Straits of Gibraltar, seeking a Western route to the "Indies." They were never heard from again, and though they proved to be precursors of a major Western thrust into the southern Atlantic, it is not even entirely clear what they meant by the "Indies."

Early in the 14th century other explorers from Genoa rediscovered the Canary Islands, populated by a hunting-and-gathering people; these islands had been known vaguely since classical times but had never before been directly opened by Europeans. Genoese sailors also visited the Madeiras and probably reached the more distant Azores by 1351. Soon after this, ships from northeastern Spain, based in the port of Barcelona, sailed along the African coast as far south as present-day Sierra Leone.

Further efforts were impossible until after 1430 because of technological barriers. European shipping could not risk wider ventures into the Atlantic because they lacked adequate navigation instruments. They also needed better ships than the shallow-drafted, oar-propelled Mediterranean galleys. Shipbuilding adaptations were under way, however, toward developing an oceangoing sailing vessel. At the same time the crucial navigational problems were met by new knowledge of the compass and the astrolabe, used to determine latitude at sea by reckoning from the stars. Contacts with Arab merchants (who had learned from the Chinese) provided knowledge of these devices. European mapmaking, improving steadily during the 14th century, was also a key innovation. Because of these advances, Europeans were ready soon after 1400 to undertake voyages impossible just a century before.

COLONIAL PATTERNS

Even as these voyages began—in a familiar pattern detailed in Chapter 23—Westerners, led by the Spanish and Portuguese, began to take advantage of the new lands they had already discovered. Portugal by 1439 had taken control of the Azores and granted land to colonists. Soon Spaniards and Portuguese had wholly conquered and colonized the Madeiras and Canaries, bringing in, among other things, Western plants, animals, weapons, and diseases. The result was something of a laboratory for the larger European imperialism that would soon take shape, particularly in the Americas. European colonists quickly set up large agricultural estates designed to produce cash crops that could be sold on the European market. First they introduced sugar, an item once imported from Asia but now available in growing quantities from Western-controlled sources. The new supply of sugar launched a progressive Western conversion to a sweet-tooth consumption that remains vigorous to the present day. Ultimately other crops, such as cotton and tobacco, were also introduced to the Atlantic islands. To produce these market crops, the new colonists brought in slaves from northwestern Africa, mainly in Portuguese ships—the first examples of a new commercial version of slavery that the West would soon expand, and the first sign that Western expansion could have serious impact on other societies as well.

These developments around 1400 remained modest, even in their consequences for Africa. They serve mainly to illustrate how quickly Western conquerors decided what to do with lands and peoples newly in their grasp. The ventures were easily successful enough to motivate more extensive probes into the southern Atlantic as soon as tech-

Columbus is supposed to have had a copy of this world map in Spain. The map, dating from about 1489, shows the Old World as Europeans were increasingly coming to know it.

nology permitted. Indeed, voyages of exploration down the coast of Africa and across the Atlantic began to occur as the island colonies were being fully settled. The ventures summed up the swirl of forces that were beginning to reshape the West's role in the world: inferiorities and fears, particularly vis-à-vis the Muslims; new energies of Renaissance merchants and Iberian rulers; economic pressures and a long-standing population surge.

ANALYSIS
THE PROBLEM OF ETHNOCENTRISM

Many cultures encourage an ethnocentric outlook, and American culture is certainly one of them. Ethnocentrism, however, generates problems in interpreting world history. The dictionary definition of ethnocentrism is "a habitual disposition to judge foreign peoples or groups by the standards and practices of one's own culture or ethnic group." Most of us take pride in many of our own institutions and values, and it is tempting to move from this pride to a certain amount of disapproval of other peoples when they clearly do not share our behaviors and beliefs. Many Americans have a difficult time understanding how "other" peoples have failed to establish the stable democratic political structure that we can point to in our own country. Even liberals who pride themselves on a sophisticated appreciation of different habits in some areas may adopt an ethnocentric shock at the seemingly clumsy oppression (by current American standards) of women that is visible in certain societies today or in the past. Indeed, unless a person is almost totally alienated from his or her own society, some tendency to ethnocentric reactions is hard to avoid.

Nevertheless, unexamined ethnocentrism can be a barrier in dealing with world history. Because world history after its early phases often consists of an inquiry into the establishment and evolution of civilizations different from our own, its meaning can be distorted by too much editorializing. We will grasp other times and places better, and perhaps use our own values more intelligently, if we do not too readily dismiss cultures in which "objectionable" practices occur.

Controlling ethnocentrism does not mean abandoning all standards, as if any social behavior is as good as any other. It does involve a certain open-mindedness and sophistication. Reducing distracting levels of ethnocentrism can be aided by some specific procedures. It is important to realize that few cultures behave irrationally over long periods of time. They may differ from our taste, but their patterns respond to valid causes and problems. Our own values are not without complexity. We sometimes believe things about our own society that are not as true as we wish; or, in judging other societies, we forget about drawbacks in our own surroundings. Perspective on our own habits, including awareness of how other cultures might judge us, helps restrain ethnocentrism.

Ethnocentrism may become a particularly strong impulse, however, in dealing with some of the changes in world history taking shape around 1400. The West was gaining strength. Since many Americans identify with Western civilization, it will be tempting to downplay some of the subtleties and disadvantages involved in this process or to exaggerate the extent to which the West began to organize world history more generally.

The balance of power among civilizations was beginning to shift around 1400, and it is legitimate, and not simply ethnocentric, to note that the West's rise was one of the leading aspects of this change with ultimately international significance. It is unnecessary to neglect the many other patterns continuing or emerging—including new vigor in several other societies—or to gloss over the mixture of motives and results that the West's rise entailed. Ethnocentric impulses can profitably be monitored in grasping the complexity of change in world history, particularly as Western values altered somewhat and at the same time became more important on the world stage.

Questions: Why can ethnocentrism complicate interpretations in world history? How can one balance disapproval and understanding in dealing with practices such as female infanticide? How might a Chinese or Muslim observer have judged some of the cultural innovations of the early Italian Renaissance?

OUTSIDE THE WORLD NETWORK

The international framework that had developed during the postclassical period embraced most of Asia and Europe, North Africa, and selected portions of Africa south of the Sahara. This network left out important groups and regions. Developments in the Americas, Polynesia, and several parts of sub-Saharan Africa were simply not affected by the new international exchange. During the next period of world history these regions would all be pulled into a new level of international contact, but a world balance sheet in 1400 must emphasize their separateness.

At the same time, several of the societies outside the international network were experiencing some new problems during the 15th century that would leave them unusually vulnerable to outside interference thereafter. These problems were entirely coincidental, and they had no larger world significance until Western expeditions redefined the international network. Problems included new political strains in the leading American civilizations and a fragmentation of the principal island groups in Polynesian culture after several centuries of internal migration and exchange.

THE AMERICAS AND AFRICA

As discussed in Chapter 17, both the Aztec and the Inca empires ran into increasing difficulties not long after 1400. These difficulties had nothing to do with international context, but resulted from internal dynamics of the two states and societies. Aztec exploitation of subject peoples—their exactions of gold, slaves, and religious sacrifices—roused great resentment. What would have happened to the Aztec Empire had Spaniards not intervened after 1500 is not clear, but it is obvious that disunity created opportunities for outside intervention that might not otherwise have existed. The Inca system, though far less brutal than the Aztecs, involved an ongoing tension between central leadership and local initiative that was hard to sustain given the vast expanse of the Inca domains. Here too, probable overextension made change likely by the 1500s—indeed, the empire was already receding somewhat—even aside from European intervention. At the same time, other cultures were developing in parts of the Americas that might well have been candidates for new political leadership, had the dynamics of American history continued to unfold without the complication of contacts with the wider world.

Patterns in sub-Saharan Africa were more complex. The vast continent displayed great diversity. Several regional kingdoms were in decline by 1400, again with little or no involvement with wider world currents. Thus Zimbabwe began its collapse, while the great Sudanic empire of Mali yielded increasingly to attacks from regional rivals. Another Muslim kingdom, Songhay, soon rose to take Mali's place, however, flourishing between 1464 and 1591, and it increased the effectiveness of the central state by raising royal armies directly instead of depending on alliances with local lords. There was no sense, certainly, that African history was poised in 1400 for major change.

Indeed, in many respects African history continued a pattern of independent evolution long after the 15th century. Well-organized regional kingdoms maintained substantial control in many areas, even in most of the cases where European traders increasingly intervened. The fact that African society had previously interacted with Mediterranean and Asian cultures precluded the worst potential consequences of isolation. A few European contact points long huddled along the coast, at the suffrance of local rulers and with little interior penetration. Yet soon after 1500 some important shifts were introduced from the outside. Trade patterns increasingly redirected in West Africa, from overland contact with the Mediterranean to concentration on opportunities along the Atlantic, and relatedly from Muslim to European hands. Seizure of slaves for European use, already introduced into Spanish and Portuguese island colonies before 1500, touched many regions deeply.

This 18th-century engraving portrays Vasco da Gama's audience with the Indian ruler of Calicut in 1498.

Even politics would be affected, as European weapons and troops played an increasing role in regional conflicts including the attacks that, at the end of the 16th century, brought down Songhay.

POLYNESIA

A third culture area long remote from world contacts, but soon to be pulled into the expanding world network, comprised the islands of Polynesia. Here, as in the Americas, important changes had taken place during the postclassical era, but with no relationship to developments in societies elsewhere in the world. The key Polynesian theme from the 7th century to 1400 was expansion, spurts of migration, and conquest that implanted Polynesian culture well beyond the initial base in the Society Islands—as Tahiti, Samoa, and Fiji groups are called collectively (see Chapter 9).

One channel of migration pointed northward to the islands of Hawaii. The first Polynesians reached these previously uninhabited islands before the 7th century, traveling in the great war canoes. From the 7th century until about 1300 or 1400, recurrent contacts remained between the Hawaiian islands and the larger Society Islands group, allowing periodic new migration. From about 1400 until the arrival of European explorers in 1778, Hawaiian society was cut off even from Polynesia.

Polynesians in Hawaii spread widely across the islands, in agricultural clusters and fishing villages amid the volcanic mountains. There were no cities. Hawaiians proved inventive in using local vegetation for construction purposes, weaving fabrics as well as making materials and fishing nets from grass. They also imported pigs from the Society Islands, a vital source of meat though a source of devastation to many plant species unique to Hawaii. Politically, Hawaii was organized into regional kingdoms, highly warlike. Society was structured into a caste system, with priests and nobles at the top, reserving many lands for their exclusive use. Commoners were viewed almost as a separate people, barred from certain activities.

Thus with a neolithic technology, the Hawaiians created a complex culture on their islands. Lacking a written language, their legends and oral histories, tracing the genealogies of chiefly families back to the original war canoes, were remarkable achievements that formed and preserved their culture.

THE MAORIS

A second direction of Polynesian migration aimed thousands of miles to the southwest of the Society Islands, perhaps as early as the 8th century when canoe or raft crews discovered the two large islands that today make up New Zealand. The original numbers of people were small but were supplemented over the following centuries by additional migrations from the Polynesian home islands.

The Polynesians in New Zealand, called Maoris, successfully adapted to an environment considerably colder and harsher than the home islands. They developed the most elaborate of all Polynesian art and produced an expanding population that may have reached 200,000 people by the 18th century, primarily on the northern of the two islands. As in Hawaii, tribal military leaders and priests held great power in Maori society; each tribe also included a group of slaves, drawn from prisoners of war and their descendants. Frequent warfare defined much of Maori culture, as leaders had to demonstrate military prowess and young men proved their worth as warriors.

Overall, Polynesian society not only spread but developed increasing complexity in the centuries of the postclassical era. Maoris and others produced a rich oral tradition in which fascinating legends combined with an emphasis on oratorical skill. Woodworking and decoration advanced steadily. The Polynesians did not work metals, but they

Polynesian Expansion

produced a vigorous economy by combining imported crops and animals with vegetation native to the new settlements. All of these achievements, however, were accomplished in isolation—total isolation from the rest of the world, and particularly after 1400 substantial isolation of each major island grouping from the rest of the Polynesian world. Polynesians were the last of the major isolated cultures to encounter larger world currents brought forcefully by European explorers in the 18th century. When this encounter did come, it produced the same effects that had burdened the Americas: vulnerability to disease, weakness in the face of superior weaponry and technology, and considerable cultural disintegration.

CONCLUSION

ADDING UP THE CHANGES

The decades that clustered around the year 1400 clearly constituted a time of transition in world history as well as in the development of many individual civilizations. Shifts in international trade leadership, a rebalancing of power and dynamism, and the impact of spreading technologies all worked to change not just particular societies but the world framework as well.

As a time of transition, the 15th century may be loosely compared with the later 20th century. In each case a growing series of international contacts, capped by a century of far-flung empires, yielded to a time of rebalancing. The predominant powers of the previous period—the Arabs, and now the West—were challenged by new and more dynamic upstarts. Major changes and dislocations occurred within the rising societies as they prepared, partly unwittingly and partly quite consciously, for unfamiliar world roles. Ordinary people in many parts of the world suffered from new hardships as a result of devastating plagues or wars. At the same time previous international contacts helped spread technological innovations initially developed by older centers.

The similarities between the 15th century and the present as times of change within world history cannot be pressed too far, particularly since we cannot know exactly where present shifts are heading and how much rebalancing will occur, or how fast. And there is irony in the fact that the challenger for new power emerging after 1400, Western civilization, becomes at the next point of major world transition the challenged. The fact is that the world history framework that began to take shape after 1400 con-stituted the most important alteration since the fall of the classical empires almost a thousand years before, and it was to last in broad outline until close to our own time. Comparing the nature and causation of this transition with those few similar shifts before and after can aid in grasping the nature not only of past change, but to some extent of changes yet to come.

FURTHER READINGS

Crucial changes in the Middle East are covered in F. Babinger's *Mehmed the Conqueror and His Times* (1978) on the Ottoman leader who captured Constantinople, and Bernard Lewis's *The Arabs in History* (4th ed., 1958), which offers a brisk interpretation of Arab decline. See also H. Islamoglu-Inan, ed., *The Ottoman Empire and the World Economy* (1987). On China under the early Ming dynasty, see Charles O. Hucker's *The Ming Dynasty: Its Origins and Evolving Institutions* (1978).

An important, highly readable interpretation of the West's rise in a world context, is C. Cipolla's *Guns, Sails and Empires: Technological Innovation and the Early Phases of European Expansion, 1400–1700* (1985). See also J. H. Parry's *Age of Reconnaissance* (1963) and *The Discovery of the Sea* (1981). An important interpretation of new Western interests is S. W. Mintz's *Sweetness and Power: The Place of Sugar in Modern History* (1985).

On the Black Death and economic dislocation, see M. W. Dols's *The Black Death in the Middle East* (1977), W. H. McNeill's *Plagues and Peoples* (1976), and the very readable B. Tuchman's *A Distant Mirror: The Calamitous 14th Century* (1979). A provocative study of relevant Western outlook is P. Ariès's *The Hour of Our Death* (1981).

J. Huizinga's *Waning of the Middle Ages* (1973) deals with the decline of medieval forms in Europe. The early Renaissance is treated in D. Hay's *The Italian Renaissance* (1977); for more cultural emphasis, see C. Trinkhaus's *The Scope of Renaissance Humanism* (1983). On Spain, see F. Braudel's *The Mediterranean and the Mediterranean World* 2 vols. (1978) and R. Altimira's *A History of Spain* (1949).

An excellent overview of the period is Janet L. Abu-Lughod's *Before European Hegemony: The World System A.D. 1250–1350* (1989).

1434–1498 Portuguese expeditions down West African coast

1390 Ming restrictions
on overseas trade

1492 Columbus expeditions

1368 Ming dynasty in China

1281 Founding of Ottoman dynasty

1480 Moscow region
free of Mongol control

1405–1423 Chinese
expedition period

1350s Ottoman invasion
of southeastern Europe

1453 Ottoman conquest of Constantinople

1441 Beginning of European slave trade in Africa

The gun was introduced into Japan in 1542 through the Portuguese. By 1562, 10,000 Japanese soldiers carried muskets. The scenes depicted here are from a military manual written by one of the greatest generals of the period, Nobunaga.

1500–1600 Europe's
commercial revolution   **1519–1521** Magellan circumnavigates globe

1552 Russia begins expansion in
central Asia and western Siberia

1509 Spanish colonies on American mainland

1498–1499 Vasco da Gama
expedition opens seas to Asia

1570 Portuguese colony
of Angola (Africa)

1520–1566 Suleiman the Magnificent (Ottoman)

1510–1511 Portugal conquers Goa (India), Malacca (Malaysia)

1526 Babur conquest in northern India (Mughal)

1501–1510 Safavid
conquest of Iran   **1517–1541** Protestant Reformation (Europe)

1590 Hideyoshi
unifies Japan

1548 Portuguese government in Brazil

1533 Pizarro wins Peru   **1591** Fall of Songhay (Africa)

1519–1524 Cortes conquers Mexico   **1571** Ottoman naval defeat at Lepanto

1600–1690 Scientific revolution (Europe)
1603 Tokugawa shogunate

1608 First French North American colonies

1637 Russian pioneers to Pacific
1600 Dutch and British merchants begin activity in India

1607 First British colonies
in North America

1644 Qing
dynasty, China

1642–1727 Isaac Newton
1641 Dutch colonies in Indonesia
1640s Japan isolation

PART
4

The World Shrinks, 1450–1750

A number of developments highlighted the three centuries of world history after 1450, marking a major new period—the early modern period—in the global experience. As in most new world history periods, the balance of power among major civilizations shifted; the West became the most dynamic force worldwide. Largely under Western aegis, contacts among many civilizations intensified; the world became smaller, as international trade affected many diverse societies and the speed and range of sailing ships increased. Finally, based mainly on new weaponry, particularly gunpowder, new or revamped empires formed important regional political units in many parts of the world—a set of developments especially significant in Asia. The West built a new colonial empire in various parts of the world, using its new maritime muscle combined with naval gunnery. Land-based empires emerged in Russia—now a rapidly rising power; under the Ottoman Turks, in the Middle East, southwestern Europe, and to an extent North Africa; as well as in India, Persia, and China where this was already a familiar pattern. Gunpowder empires showed new capacities for political integration of substantial territories and cut into traditionally independent areas notably in central Asia.

The rise of the West, the intensification of international contacts on literally a global scale, and the formation of new empires marked off the early modern centuries from the previous postclassical period in world history. The period was launched during the 15th century when Western countries, headed by Portugal and Spain, began new explo-

1689–1725 Peter the Great (Russia)

1652 Dutch colony South Africa

1682–1699 Turks driven from Hungary

1722 Fall of Safavid dynasty (Iran)

1759–1788 Reforms of Latin American colonial administration

1792 Slave uprising in Haiti

1763 Britain acquires "New France"

1772–1795 Partition of Poland

1775–1783 American Revolution

1658–1707 Aurangzeb reign, beginning of Mughal decline

1713 New Bourbon dynasty, Spain

1764 British East India Company controls Bengal (India)

1781 Indian revolts in New Granada and Peru (Latin America)

1756–1763 Seven Years' War

1770s European-Bantu conflicts in southern Africa

---

rations and soon new colonization efforts around Africa to Asia and to the Americas. It was launched, also, by the formation of the powerful new Ottoman Empire in the Middle East and the emergence of Russia from two centuries of Mongol control.

ON THE EVE OF THE EARLY MODERN PERIOD: THE WORLD AROUND 1450

Important new or expanded civilization areas developed in the postclassical period, in contact with the leading centers. Russia was one such case, as a Russian monarchy formed. Western Europe, slowly recovering from the 5th-century collapse of the Roman Empire, failed to gain political unity. West Europeans built important regional kingdoms, while expanding the role of commerce and city life and establishing an elaborate artistic and philosophical culture around Catholic Christianity. In sub-Saharan Africa, another set of regional kingdoms formed, though there were vital areas organized more loosely; African trade and artistic expression gained ground steadily. Areas in contact with China, finally, built increasingly elaborate societies. Japan, like western Europe, emphasized a rather decentralized, militaristic feudal system in politics, but it copied many aspects of Chinese culture and some social principles, including a more patriarchal approach to the status of women.

A third area of the world featured civilizations or elaborate cultures developing in isolation from any international contacts. This was true of parts of sub-Saharan Africa and of the expanding Polynesian zone in the Pacific Islands. It characterized the brilliant, populous civilizations of the Americas, focused in Central America (under the Aztecs) and in the Andes (by the 15th century under the vast Inca realm).

The structure of the postclassical world began to shift between the 13th and 15th centuries, setting the stage for the new world history period. The isolated civilizations were not affected by these changes, precisely because they were isolated; they continued to follow their own dynamic, which culminated in the great Aztec and Inca empires, both of which were showing signs of strain and overextension by the later 15th century. In Asia, Africa, and Europe, the key development was the decline of Arab political power and cultural dynamism. Islam continued to expand, but its political and commercial units fragmented. At the same time, a new round of invasions from central Asia, under the Mongols, attacked China, the Middle East, and eastern Europe, disrupting established political boundaries and allowing new contacts between Asia and Europe.

By 1400 the Mongol threat was receding, though only slowly in Russia. A new empire emerged in China. The Arab caliphate had perished, but a new Islamic political force, under the Ottoman Turks, was taking shape, unifying much of the Middle East and poised to destroy the venerable Byzantine Empire. Utilizing their growing commercial vigor, but also terrified by the emergence of a new Islamic power, west Europeans cast about for ways to gain greater control over their international trade, while possibly winning new areas for the Christian faith and new territories for the competing regional kingdoms. China briefly experimented with a dominant international role early in the 15th century, sending out a series of mighty trading expeditions across the Indian Ocean, but then it pulled back, deciding to concentrate on its traditions of internal political, cultural, and commercial development. This, as it turned out, left the way open for the west European probes, as Western leaders benefited from a number of technologies newly learned from China and Islam—such as the compass and explosive powder—while adding important innovations such as guns and faster oceangoing ships.

THE RISE OF THE WEST

Between 1450 and 1750 the West, headed initially by Spain and Portugal, then by Britain, France, and Holland, gained control of the key international trade routes. It established colonies in the Americas and, on a much more limited basis, in Africa and parts of Asia.

At the same time, partly because of its new international position and the growing impact of commerce, the West itself changed rapidly, becoming an increasingly unusual kind of agricultural civilization. Commerce began to alter the social structure and also affected basic attitudes toward family life and the natural environment. A host of new ideas, some of them springing from religious reformers, created a novel cultural climate in which scientific principles increasingly held pride of place; the scientific revolution gradually reshaped Western culture as a whole. More effective political structures emerged by the 17th century, as Western monarchs began to introduce bureaucratic principles similar to those pioneered long before in China.

A vital facet of the early modern period, then, consisted of the West's expansion as an international force and its simultaneous internal transformation. Like the previous world-class civilization, Arab Islam, the West developed a diverse and dynamic culture and society, which was both a result and a cause of its ascending international position.

THE WORLD ECONOMY AND GLOBAL CONTACTS

It was as a result of initiatives mainly from the West that the world network set up in the previous period intensified and took on new dimensions. The change involved more than the fact that the Europeans, not the Muslims, dominated international trade. It involved an expansion of the world network to literally global proportions, well beyond the geographical scope of previous linkages. Far more of Africa, and above all the Americas, were brought into contact with other cultures and included in international exchanges for the first time. At the end of the period, in the 18th century, Polynesian and Australian societies began to undergo the same painful integrating experience.

Effectively, by 1750 there were no more fully isolated societies of any great size. The new globalism of human contacts had a host of vital consequences that ran through early modern centuries. The human disease pool became fully international for the first time, and peoples who had previously been isolated from most of the rest of the world suffered immensely from their exposure to diseases for which they had developed no immunities. The global network also permitted a massive exchange of plants and animals. Cows and horses were introduced to the Americas, prompting substantial changes in American Indian habits in economy and warfare alike. American food crops were spread around the world, bringing sweet potatoes, corn, and manioc to China, corn to Africa, potatoes and tobacco to Europe—innovations that in many places prompted great changes in agricultural production. One result through most of the world, beginning in Asia as well as western Europe, was a rapid population expansion that quickly attained unprecedented levels.

Even globalization, though its impact was vast, did not exhaust the changes wrought in the world network during the three centuries after 1450. Far more than in the postclassical era, the period between 1450 and 1750 saw a set of definite and highly unequal relationships established among a number of civilizations. During the postclassical millennium, A.D. 450–1450, a few areas had contributed relatively inexpensive raw materials (including labor power in the form of slaves) to more advanced societies, notably China and the Islamic world; this was true for the West and parts of Africa and Southeast Asia. Though economic relationships in these instances were unequal, they did not constrain the "raw-materials-producing" societies too severely, because international trade was simply not of overriding importance yet. After 1450 or 1500, as Western commerce expanded internationally, the West began to set up relationships with a number of areas that produced pronounced dependence and subordination in the international economy. Areas such as Latin America depended heavily on sales to export merchants, on imports of processed goods, and on Western ships and merchants to handle international trade. Dependence of this sort might have political ramifications in creating weak governments open to foreign intervention; it certainly affected labor relations by encouraging commercial exploitation of slaves and serfs; and it even tied in with cultural impositions from the West on some of the dependent areas. It is vital to stress that much of the world, particularly in the great Asian civilizations, remained outside this set of relationships, but there was a growing tendency to draw closer toward it, as occurred in India and much of Indonesia by the 18th century, as the level of Western overseas expansion increased steadily. The establishment of a new set of international economic relationships, based on Western preeminence, is discussed explicitly in Chapter 23, but it undergirds analysis of many individual civilizations as well.

The linked themes of the rise of the West and the intensification and transformation of the world network accurately convey key international trends during the period

World Boundaries, about 1453

after 1450, supplemented as they were by new food and disease exchanges and resultant population shifts. As before, no simple set of features covers the complexities of developments in the many and diverse areas involved in world history. Particularly because the West's influence varied in different parts of the world, and the relationships between African, Asian, or Amerindian peoples to the Western-dominated international economy varied as well, it is vital to note two other developments that were larger than individual civilizations, but not fully subsumed under the emergence of the Western world system either.

THE GUNPOWDER EMPIRES

The centuries after 1450 could also be designated "the age of the gunpowder empires." The development of cannons and muskets in the 15th and 16th centuries, through the combination of Western technology with previous Chinese invention, obviously spurred the West's expansion. Ship-based artillery was fundamental to the West's mastery of international sea lanes and many ports and islands. But gunnery was picked up by other societies as well. The Ottoman Turks used Hungarian-built cannons to aid their successful siege of Constantinople in 1453. The subsequent Ottoman Empire relied heavily on land-based guns to supplement trained cavalry. The rise of a new Russian Empire after 1480 also built on growing use of guns, and the Rus-

sian economy was subsequently reshaped to provide the manufacturing basis for the new military hardware. Three other key empires—the Mughal in India, the Safavid in Persia, and the 17th-century Manchu dynasty in China— relied on the new strength of gun-supported land armies. Guns also played a role in Japanese and African history during the period.

Clearly, guns supported important military changes that in turn supported new political organization—colonial empires in the case of the West, where naval strength played a particularly important role, and new land agglomerations through much of Asia and eastern Europe and, to an extent, in Africa. Here were developments largely independent of Western influence, save for some of the initial technologies, and which in fact counterbalanced the growth of Western power to a considerable degree. The rise of the Russian Empire ran through the whole period, and while not as important as the rise of the West it was certainly a vital theme, involving among other things the progressive elimination of an independent central Asia. The rise of the Ottomans, Safavids, and Mughals was a bit shorter-lived, but echoed through the first two centuries of the period and, in the case of the Ottomans, created one of the most durable empires known in world history.

To the labels "rise of the West" or "new world economy," then, the phrase "age of the gunpowder empires" could quite legitimately be added to describe 1450–1750.

World Boundaries, about 1700

It reflects developments that affected a massive number of people and long overshadowed, at least in the eyes of most Asian leaders, the Western surge.

portant for the world today? What parts of the world look very different today, in terms of the boundaries of major political units, from the form they had achieved by the 18th century?

ANALYSIS
MAP

The period of 1450–1750 saw an unusual number of boundary changes in world history. The spread of Western colonies was the most obvious development, but the establishment or extension of a number of large land-based empires was almost as significant. Compare the two maps by tracing the areas of Western penetration. You will see the different forms this penetration took in different parts of the world. Note also what parts of the world offered particular opportunities for rivalries among the leading Western colonial powers, and what parts were particularly immune to Western expansion of any major sort.

Look also to the land-based empires. What empires were particularly new as they took shape between the 15th and 18th centuries? What parts of the world had the most stable boundaries during these centuries? Why?

Of the boundary changes you can trace during this three-century period, which changes seem particularly im-

COMMERCE AND ITS OUTREACH

One other development deserves note: This was also an age of world commercialization. Market exchange played an increasing role in shaping economic activity. The world remained predominantly agricultural, but agriculture was now modified more than ever by specializations that depended on market transactions, as well as by the activities of merchants and the lure of money. Heightened commercial activity was one of the means by which rising populations could be sustained in advance of major technological change in the means of production. Commerce not only spread knowledge of new foodstuffs, but also allowed increased specialization in production that could heighten output, as some regions concentrated on goods they were best suited to grow or manufacture, relying on trade for other materials.

The intensification of international trade, under the sponsorship of Western traders but also involving merchants in other societies, played an important part in the general expansion of commerce. Not only did many Latin Americans produce precious metals and agricultural products for sale to the West; many more Latin Americans produced foods and clothes to sell to workers in the export sectors. Internal trade increased within Latin America, particularly by the 18th century. International trade activities prompted increasing numbers of Westerners, as well, to engage in market activities, at home as well as abroad. Similar patterns emerged in West Africa. Earlier international trade routes, oriented toward North Africa, were diverted to a new Atlantic commerce organized by European merchants. African kings and merchants organized goods to sell in this trade, particularly slaves, and received manufactured products, including guns, in exchange. Again the West was encouraged in its own commercial expansion, as considerable profits could be realized in the slave trade; the Americas were transformed through the introduction of new African populations and a new kind of slavery; and Africa itself was diversely affected by the new exchange.

The spread of commerce went beyond these Western-dominated transactions, however. Both China and Japan witnessed the rapid growth of market exchanges within their own boundaries, as production and sale of foodstuffs, beverages, and the like expanded. A general trend—the Western-dominated international economy and its growth—was thus supplemented by some parallelisms in some other parts of the world, where internal trade far outweighed international exchange. And this meant not only a surprisingly widespread commercial and urban surge, but also some broader effects in terms of culture and society. In most cases without toppling the land-based aristocracy, merchants in a number of societies, not just the West, gained new influence. Growing trade also played a role in some societies (in the West but also, for instance, in Japan) in encouraging some groups to reduce their commitment to religion and other worldly goals in favor of a focus on secular pursuits. The expansion of commerce, in other words, though not producing a uniform new version of an agricultural economy or society, had some wider potential reverberations in many parts of the world.

EVOLUTION OF THE EARLY MODERN PERIOD: CIVILIZATIONS AND LARGER TRENDS

As in earlier world history epochs, many developments during these early modern centuries occurred within individual civilizations, with little or no relationship to more general world trends. Only the Americas came close to being overwhelmed by outside influences. Many of the following chapters, correspondingly, will focus on particular societies.

Nevertheless, the impact of the four international trends—Western expansion, intensification and globalization of the world network, the military and political results of gunpowder, and the spread of commerce—affected patterns in the separate societies in many ways, for the force of international trends was growing. These four trends generate the central questions to be addressed to each major civilization, to see how it fit the larger world picture. Response to the key trends ranged from eager embrace of new international currents, to self-conscious isolation, to forced compliance. A new set of diversities described major societies precisely because of the heightened potency of real or potential international contacts.

The tensions between the West's expansion and its attributes versus more general forces of change—population growth in several societies, commercial expansion, and the power of gunpowder empires—allowed many societies to evolve with scant reference to what the West and its colonies were up to. The period's beginning date—1450—embraces both patterns. It was after 1450 that Western exploration and maritime expansion began to take off with particular rapidity, and it was also then that two of the most important new land-based empires, the Ottoman and the Russian, fully emerged. This already suggests the need to treat these centuries as involving more than the West and world reactions to the West. The balance between Western-sponsored change and more general patterns of development did tend to shift over time, particularly in the final century before 1750.

By 1700 the West's activities were looming larger not just in key areas such as the Americas, the Asian island groups, and the coast of West Africa, but in Asia and eastern Europe as well. A new Russian urge selectively to copy aspects of the West and the establishment of growing British control in parts of India expressed two facets of this shift. Even Japan, which had responded to the new world economy by effective isolation, began to show modest new openness, rescinding a ban on translating Western books.

By 1750 it is fair, with all the advantages historians have of knowing how their stories turn out, to note that civilizations that were not in a position to react effectively to the West's new world role were verging on decline—whereas a mere century before, this would have been a considerable distortion of a more complex international balance. After 1750, in large part because of another major transformation within the West—the emergence of a revolutionary industrial economy—the theme of Western predominance took on new meaning, which is why the periodization of world history breaks at this point once again.

The acceleration of economic change in the West was clearly underway by 1750, but it is important to note that its effects on other societies lagged a bit. In many ways the themes of the early modern period persisted in places, such as Russia and Asia, for a few decades more, which means that chapters covering these societies push beyond 1750 in some respects. Worldwide transition to the effects of pioneering industrialization in western Europe was not an overnight affair, though it was widely underway by 1800.

The chapters in this unit focus first on changes within the West and the emergence of Western colonies and Western-dominated world trade. Then two chapters deal with two societies that had particular links with the West—Russia, whose expansion was such an important theme in its own right, and a new kind of emerging civilization in Latin America. The final group of chapters deals with major societies in Asia and Africa where contacts with the West and the new world economy were significant, particularly as the early modern period wore on, but where separate patterns of activity remained vital.

1450–1600 Northern Renaissance

1490s France and Spain invade Italian
city-states; beginning of Italian decline   1541–1564 Calvin in Geneva

1475–1514   1515–1547 Francis I of France
Michelangelo

1517 Luther's 95 theses; beginning of Protestant Reformation

1300–1450 Italian Renaissance   1469–1527 Machiavelli   1534 Beginning of Church of England

1452–1519 Leonardo da Vinci

1455 First European   1500–1600 "Commercial revolution"
printing press in
Mainz, Germany   1543 "Copernican revolution";
Copernicus' work on astronomy

A.D. 1300   A.D. 1450

22 The Transformation of the West, 1450–1750

INTRODUCTION. During the three centuries after 1450, Western civilization—particularly its core areas such as France, Britain, the Low Countries, and much of Germany—changed in dramatic ways. Still a largely agricultural society in 1750, the West had become unusually commercially active and had laid out a growing manufacturing sector. Government powers had expanded, while new political ideas and challenges complicated the picture. Beliefs had altered. Science came to form the centerpiece of Western intellectual life for the first time in the history of any society. The popular outlook, including ideas about personality and family as well as concepts of nature, also had shifted substantially.

In a variety of ways and at various social levels, the West was becoming an unusual kind of agricultural civilization compared to most others in the world at the time. In some areas the West in this period may be seen as incorporating developments, such as increased bureaucratization in the central state, that other more advanced civilizations had already instituted. But in other areas, such as popular belief and family structure, the West was striking out in new directions. Certainly, Western civilization changed more fundamentally in this period than any of the established societies in Asia, and its innovations prepared further changes—notably, the Industrial Revolution—for the future.

Even before 1450 Western culture and the Western economy had been changing. Initially, change focused on Italy and Spain, the former being the leader in cultural innovation, the latter spearheading Europe's overseas expan-

---

17th century Scientific revolution

1642–1727 Newton

1730–1850 European population boom

1643–1715 Louis XIV in France; absolute monarchy

18th century Enlightenment

1609 Independence of Netherlands

1776 Adam Smith's *Wealth of Nations*

1688–1690 Glorious Revolution in Britain; parliamentary monarchy; some religious toleration; political writing of John Locke

1555–1603 Elizabeth I, England

1588 Defeat of Spanish Armada by English

1780–1790 Joseph II, Austria and Hungary

1733 James Kay invents flying shuttle loom

1736 Beginnings of Methodism

1550–1649 Religious wars in France, Germany, and Britain

1670–1692 Decline of witchcraft trials

1642–1649 English civil wars

1792 Mary Wollstonecraft's *Vindication of the Rights of Women*

1712–1786 Frederick the Great of Prussia; enlightened despotism

1682–1699 Habsburgs drive Turks from Hungary

1564–1642 Galileo

1647–1648 Culmination of popular rebellion

1618–1648 Thirty Years' War

1756–1763 Seven Years' War: France, Britain, Prussia, and Austria sion along with Portugal. Increasingly, after 1450, change became more general through Western society, and the center of activity shifted northward to France, Britain, and surrounding areas. Changes within Europe, finally, constantly interacted with overseas expansion and the fruits of European dominance of international trade; Europe's steady evolution resulted from its new world power, and furthered this power in turn.

EPISODES IN THE LARGER PATTERNS OF CHANGE

The new directions taken up in the West were reflected in a host of subperiods, most of which are staples of European history in what is rightly called the West's early modern period. During the 15th century the Renaissance took full shape, spreading to northern Europe from its initial home in Italy. Then came the disruption of religious unity in the West, with the Protestant Reformation and Catholic response. Then came the rise of absolute monarchy in the 17th century and also the scientific revolution. By 1730 this was followed by the Enlightenment and a rather modest, but widely trumpeted, modification of absolute monarchy called *enlightened despotism*.

Key developments occurred at different points; there was no coordinated evolution. The proliferation of subperiods, many with famous labels such as Renaissance or Reformation, suggests that change in the West involved a number of specific stages, each with its own characteristics. Relatedly, change was not uniform or always consistent, nor was it always terribly rapid. The Renaissance, as a cultural movement, suggested more secular art and literature; its writers and artists esteemed human achievements and the human form. The leaders of the Reformation reasserted the primacy of religious values, attacking Renaissance secularism and covering portions of Renaissance paintings that had celebrated the human form too vividly. Changes thus moved unevenly. Overall, Europe's early modern period saw a reduction in the importance of religion, but there were many countercurrents. Amid this complexity, it is important to seize on the four major trends of the period:

- First, the Western economy became steadily more commercial, and this commercialization began to transform the social structure.
- Second, Western culture shifted gears at both the elite and popular levels. This revolution in beliefs had stages and was certainly a gradual process, but its main outlines moved through several of the subperiods of early modern history. People began to look at nature and human society in new ways.

- Third, soon after the economic and cultural changes were launched, the West moved from feudal monarchy as a typical political form to the nation-state unit, with characteristically stronger governments and greater contacts between the state and ordinary people.
- Accompanying these three changes was the major alteration in the West's position in the wider world. From a backwater area, the West became a world trader and colonizer. This role is taken up in Chapter 23, but it must be remembered as, from the West's own standpoint, a fourth major change intertwined with the other three.

FROM RAGS TO RICHES

Western Europe in 1450 was in many ways a poor candidate for great new dynamism. It was politically divided with regional governments rather decentralized through the powers of the Church and feudal aristocracy; feudalism had involved a network of mutual restraints and obligations among landowners, many with their own armies, that seriously constrained even the strongest monarchies. Its economy, though no longer purely agricultural, lagged well behind the major civilizations in technology and commercial experience. Medieval culture had, furthermore, passed its high point. Theology had become less vibrant, more wrapped up in petty debates over trivial definitions. Population and economy had been weakened by major plagues and an inability to produce enough food to sustain previous population growth. Some of these weaknesses, in fact, spurred innovation—including new efforts, through voyages of exploration, to find ways to overcome the West's inferiority in world trade.

The results of change, gradually accumulated, overrode many characteristics of the medieval past. These results explain why the West was able to seize a new world role. They explain also why other societies would seek to copy some of the characteristics the West was now pioneering. Russia launched a selective imitation as early as 1700, and other societies would confront similar agendas after 1800. The transformation of the West, in sum, without defining the whole of subsequent world history, had repercussions well beyond the West.

THE FIRST BIG CHANGES: CULTURE AND COMMERCE

The West's initial moves away from its earlier ideas and institutions as well as the stagnation that had developed in the 14th and early 15th centuries focused on art, religion, popular beliefs, and trade. These changes built on traditional elements, including religious fervor and the important merchant activities that had arisen with the cities of the postclassical period in Europe. The new trends extended from the late 15th century through the subsequent century, embracing thus the Renaissance, Reformation, and Catholic response and what is aptly known as a 16th-century commercial revolution. Some political and technological shifts accompanied the more sweeping developments. By 1600 the West had reluctantly abandoned religious unity, and some people had found religious certainty reduced as well. It had begun to define a new social structure that could accommodate greater commercial activity; new groups of propertyless workers had no choice but to provide labor for profit-seeking merchants. Elements of this social structure continue to describe Western society even today. Its genesis also provoked a massive popular outcry in the name of older values—a sign of the major transformation and disruption involved.

THE RENAISSANCE

The process of moving away from earlier patterns began with the Renaissance, which first developed in Italy during the 14th and 15th centuries. The significance of this "rebirth" should not be exaggerated: more fundamental changes came later and somewhat separately. But the Renaissance did challenge medieval intellectual values and styles. It suggested a certain amount of political innovation and built on a more commercialized economy. The Renaissance also sketched a new, brasher spirit that may have helped create a new Western interest in exploring strange waters or urging that old truths be reexamined.

Italy was already well launched in the development of Renaissance culture by the 15th century, based on its unusually extensive urban, commercial economy and its competitive city-state politics. Writers such as Petrarch and Boccaccio had trumpeted classical literary canons against medieval logic and theology, writing in Italian as well as the traditional Latin and emphasizing secular subjects such as love and pride. Painting turned to new realism and a host of classical and human-centered themes. Religion declined as a central focus.

The Italian Renaissance blossomed further in the 15th century. This was a great age of Western art, as Leonardo da Vinci advanced the realistic portrayal of the human body while Michelangelo applied classical styles in both painting and sculpture. In political theory Niccolo Machiavelli emphasized realistic discussions of how to seize and maintain power; his work *The Prince* resembled earlier Chinese legalism in urging that rulers do what they must do, without

scruple, in order to control undisciplined subjects. Like the artists, Machiavelli bolstered his realism with abundant use of Greek and Roman examples. In history, scholars portrayed a past unencumbered by divine intervention and established new critical standards that could be used to disprove traditional Church claims.

Overall, Italian Renaissance culture stressed themes of humanism—a focus on humankind as the center of intellectual and artistic endeavor. Religion was not attacked, but its principles were no longer predominant. Humanists clearly touted the superiority of classical forms over medieval styles. As individuals they could proclaim a pride in their own achievements, which implied an ability of talented people to progress, to advance on the basis of human effort alone.

This religious painting from 15th-century Renaissance Italy depicts the Martyrdom of St. Sebastian. Realism in human figures and careful perspective mark this painting, attributed to Pollaiuolo.

These Renaissance themes had some bearing on politics and commerce. Renaissance merchants improved banking techniques and became more unabashedly capitalist in their profit-seeking than their medieval counterparts had been. City-state leaders experimented with new political forms and functions. They justified their rule not on the basis of heredity or divine guidance, but more on the basis of what they could do to advance general well-being. Thus they sponsored cultural activities and tried to improve the administration of the economy. They also developed more professional armies, for wars among the city-states were common, and gave new attention to military tactics and training. They also rethought the practice of diplomacy, introducing the regular exchange of ambassadors for the first time in the West. Clearly, the Renaissance encouraged innovation, though it could also produce some slavish dependence on classical models.

THE RENAISSANCE MOVES NORTHWARD

Italy began to decline as a Renaissance center by about 1500. French and Spanish monarchs invaded the peninsula, cutting down on political independence. At the same time new Atlantic trade routes reduced the importance of Mediterranean ports, a huge blow to the Italian economy.

As Renaissance creativity faded in its Italian birthplace, it passed northward. The northern Renaissance—focused in France, the Low Countries, Germany, and England—opened up after 1450. Classical styles in art and architecture became the rage. Knowledge of Greek and Latin literature gained ground, though most northern humanists wrote in their vernacular languages. Northern humanists were more religious than their Italian counterparts, trying to blend secular interests with continued Christian devotion. Renaissance writers such as Shakespeare in England, or Rabelais in France, also mixed classical themes with an earthiness, a joy in bodily functions and human passions, that maintained elements of medieval popular culture. Renaissance literature established a new set of classics for literary traditions in the major Western languages: Shakespeare for England, Cervantes for Spain, and so on.

The northern Renaissance produced some political change. Renaissance kings increased their pomp and ceremony. Kings such as Francis I in France became patrons of the arts, even importing Italian sculptors and architects for their classical-style palaces, as these in turn replaced

Western Europe during the Renaissance and Reformation

fortified castles. Many Renaissance monarchs tried to impose new controls over the Catholic church, and they also developed some new functions in the areas of economy and welfare. Many monarchs, by the late 16th century, were sponsoring trading companies and colonial enterprises. Interest in military conquest became more blatant than in the Middle Ages. Francis I was even willing to ally in principle with the Ottoman sultan, the key Muslim leader. His goal was to distract his main enemy, the Habsburg ruler of Austria and Spain. In fact the alliance was in name only, but it illustrated how power politics was beginning to emerge without some of the feudal or religious justifications that had previously clothed it in the West.

Through most of the West, the Renaissance signaled some vital changes in cultural life. The classical styles favored by Renaissance leaders long prevailed over the medieval Gothic. Upper-class education changed, becoming defined in terms of classical precepts—such as Cicero's advice on moderate morals and devotion to the public good—plus literary study as well as an appropriate dose of Christian morality. Elements of this education would continue to describe the experience of upper-class Westerners into the 20th century. A Renaissance spirit of individual excellence and defiance of tradition influenced other facets of life in the West, including new scientific endeavor.

Yet the impact of the Renaissance should not be overdone, particularly outside Italy. Renaissance kings had new ceremonies, but they were still confined by the political powers of feudal landlords—a really new political form had yet to emerge. Ordinary people were little touched by Renaissance values; the life of most peasants and artisans went on much as before. Economic life, too, was little altered, particularly outside the Italian commercial centers. Rural people were sometimes pressed for new taxes to support cities and kings. Women, even in the upper classes, sometimes encountered new limits as Renaissance leaders touted men's public bravado over women's domestic roles.

THE COMMERCIAL ECONOMY

More fundamental changes were brewing in Western society by 1500, beneath the glittering surface of the Renaissance. Spurred by trading contacts with Asia, workers in the West improved the quality of pulleys and pumps in mines and learned how to forge stronger iron products. Printing was introduced in the 15th century, as the German Johannes Gutenberg invented movable type, a much more flexible system than Chinese block printing. Soon books were distributed in new quantities in the West, which helped expand the audience for Renaissance writers but particularly served to disseminate religious ideas. Liter-

acy began to gain ground, a fertile source of new kinds of thinking. Technology clearly began to spur a variety of changes.

Family structure was also changing. A European-style family pattern came into being by the 15th century. It involved, for ordinary people, a relatively late marriage age and a primary emphasis on nuclear families of parents and children, rather than extended families characteristic of most agricultural civilizations. These changes emphasized the importance of husband-wife relations. It also linked the family to individual property holdings with new intensity, for most people could not marry until they had appropriate access to property. Late marriage also provided a certain amount of birth control, which prevented vast overcrowding even as economic activity began to speed up again in the West. By the 16th century most ordinary Europeans did not marry until they were 26 or 27—late by the standards of most societies. Newly formed families were largely independent of older parents, however, which could encourage some sense of division between family and community.

Winds of change were blowing from several directions by the early 16th century. New family habits unseated traditions at one level; new cultural interests challenged them at another. Both elites and ordinary people generated innovation, though in somewhat different manners. It was in the 16th century, however, with religious upheaval and a new commercial surge, that the directions of change began to be more fully defined.

RELIGIOUS AND ECONOMIC LIFE

In 1517 a German monk named Martin Luther nailed a document containing 95 *theses*, or propositions, to the door of the castle church in Wittenberg. He was specifically protesting claims made by a papal representative in selling *indulgences*, or grants of salvation, for money, but in fact his protest went deeper. Luther's reading of the Bible convinced him that only faith could gain salvation. Pious actions or Church sacraments were not the path, for God could not be manipulated. Luther's protest, rebuffed by the papacy, soon led him to challenge many Catholic beliefs, including the authority of the pope himself. Luther would soon argue that monasticism was wrong, that priests should marry (as he did), and that the Bible should be translated from Latin so ordinary people might have direct access to the teachings of the faith. Luther did not want to break Christian unity, but the church he wanted should be on his terms (or, as he would have argued, the terms of the true faith).

THE REFORMATION

Disputes and heresies were not new in Western Christianity, but always before the Catholic church had ultimately managed to contain them. The Renaissance papacy, however, was not interested in compromise as it tried to force Luther to back down. At the same time Luther picked up wide support for his views during the middle decades of the 16th century and beyond. Many Germans resented the authority and taxes of the Roman pope, in something of a nationalist reaction. German princes saw an opportunity to gain more power, for their nominal leader, the holy Roman emperor, remained Catholic. Princes who turned Protestant could increase their independence; they also had an excuse to seize Church lands. The Lutheran version of Protestantism (as the general wave of religious dissent was called) urged state control of the church as an alternative to papal authority, and this had obvious political appeal.

There were reasons for ordinary people to shift as well. Some German peasants saw Luther's attack on authority as a sanction for their own social rebellion against landlords, though Luther specifically renounced this reading. Some townspeople were drawn to Luther's approval of work in the world; since faith gained salvation, Lutheranism could sanction money-making and other earthly pursuits more wholeheartedly than did traditional Catholicism.

Once Christian unity was breached, other Protestant groups sprang forward. In England Henry VIII set up an Anglican church initially to challenge papal attempts to enforce his first marriage, which had failed to produce a male heir. (Henry would ultimately have six wives in sequence, executing two of them.) Henry was also attracted to some of the new doctrines, and his most durable successor, his daughter Elizabeth I, was Protestant outright. The Anglican church became increasingly, though broadly, Protestant in doctrine as well as a separate form of church government. Still more important were the churches inspired by Jean Calvin, a Frenchman who set his base in the Swiss city of Geneva. Calvinism insisted on God's *predestination*, or prior determination, of those who would be saved. Nothing humans could do, and certainly no sacraments, could win God's favor. At the same time those elected to God's grace had the obligation to encourage others to behave morally and to gain knowledge of the Bible. Calvinist ministers became moral guardians and preachers of God's Word. Calvinists sought the participation of all believers in local church administration, which had political implications in encouraging the idea of a wider access to government. They also promoted wider popular education so that more people could read the Bible. Calvinism was accepted not only in part of Switzerland but also in

portions of Germany and France (where it produced strong minority groups), in the Netherlands, and in England and Scotland. By the early 17th century it also spread to North America.

The Catholic church did not sit still under Protestant attack. It did not restore religious unity, but it defended southern Europe, Austria, Poland, Hungary, and key parts of Germany for the Catholic faith. Under a Catholic Reformation, Church councils revived Catholic doctrine and refuted key Protestant tenets such as the idea that priests had no special sacramental power and could marry. They also attacked popular superstitions and remnants of animism, which meant that Catholics and Protestants alike were trying to find new ways to shape the outlook of ordinary folk. A new religious order, the Jesuits, became active in politics, education, and missionary work, regaining some parts of Europe for the Church. Jesuit fervor would also sponsor Catholic missionary activity in Asia and the Americas.

THE END OF CHRISTIAN UNITY IN THE WEST

The Protestant and Catholic Reformations had a number of results within Europe during the later 16th and early 17th centuries. Most obvious was an important series of religious wars. France was a scene of bitter battles between Calvinist and Catholic forces, intertwined with new rebellions by landed nobles against royal authority. These disputes ended only with the granting of tolerance to Protestants through the edict of Nantes in 1598—though in the next century French kings progressively cut back on Protestant rights. Wars raged recurrently in Germany, punctuated by efforts to agree on which states could be Protestant, which Catholic. In 1618 the Thirty Years' War broke out, pitting German Protestants and allies such as Lutheran Sweden against the holy Roman emperor, backed by Spain. The war was so devastating that it reduced German power and prosperity for a full century. It was ended only by the 1648 Treaty of Westphalia that agreed to the territorial tolerance concept, with some princely states and cities choosing one religion, some another. The treaty also reduced Spain's power, after decades in which Spanish armies had been the most powerful in Europe, in favor of France, which had backed the Protestant side. This treaty also finally settled a rebellion of the Protestant Netherlands against Spain, giving the former its full independence.

Religious fighting, finally, punctuated British history, first before the reign of Elizabeth in the 16th century, then in a civil war in the 1640s. Here too religious issues conjoined with other problems, particularly in a battle between the claims of parliament to rights of controlling royal actions and some rather tactless assertions of authority by a new line of English kings. The fighting of the civil war ended in 1660 (after one king had been beheaded), but full resolution came only in 1688 to 1689, when limited religious toleration was granted to most Protestant (but not Catholic) faiths.

Religious issues thus dominated European politics for almost a century. The religious wars led generally to a grudging and limited acceptance of the idea of religious pluralism: Christian unity could not be restored, though in most individual countries (the Netherlands came closest to a full exception) any idea of full religious liberty was still in the future. The religious wars persuaded some people that religion itself was suspect; if there was no dominant single truth, why all the cruelty and carnage? The wars, finally, affected the power balance and political structure of

Europe. France, after a period of weakness during its internal strife, was on the upswing. The Netherlands and Britain were galvanized toward a growing international role. Spain, briefly ascendant, fell back. Internally some kings and princes benefited from the decline of papal authority by taking a stronger role in religious affairs. This was true in many Catholic as well as Protestant domains. In some cases, however, Protestant dissent and Protestant-derived political theory that challenged the idea of one-man rule encouraged popular political movements and enhanced parliamentary power.

The impact of religious change went well beyond politics. The way people thought and acted in daily life began to shift toward new forms. Popular mentalities changed most in Protestant areas, but Catholic reform produced new impulses as well. Several basic shifts were set in motion. Western people gradually became less likely to see an intimate connection between God and nature. Protestants believed fervently in God's power—and in important ways the role of religion in popular belief gained ground for at least a century—but they did not focus on miracles or other disruptive interventions in nature's course. Protestant churches, as physical structures, were more isolated than their Catholic counterparts from market activities in the cities, encouraging an idea that religion and daily life were separate. Many Westerners, in sum, gained a new sense of distinction between religious and other activities and tended to see nature in desacralized terms. This could affect, for example, their approach to health problems, encouraging (very gradually) a greater tendency to turn strictly to secular healers rather than religious or religiouslike practitioners when ill.

Religious change also promoted greater concentration on family life. Protestant and Catholic leaders began to talk of the family in more positive terms, not simply as an institution necessary because of human lust. Love between husband and wife was encouraged. As one English writer put it, "When love is absent between husband and wife, it is like a bone out of joint: there is no ease, no order." This promotion of family had ambiguous implications for women. Protestantism, abolishing religious convents, made marriage more necessary for women than before; there were fewer alternatives for women who could not marry. On the other hand, within the family women's emotional role improved with the new emphasis on affection.

Religious change accompanied and promoted growing literacy along with the spread of the printing press. In the town of Durham, England, around 1570 only 20 percent of all people were literate, but by 1630 the figure had climbed to 47 percent. Growing, though still limited, lit-

Hans Holbein's "The Dance of Death" was encouraged by the continuing plague as well as religious clash.

eracy opened people to additional new ideas and ways of thinking. It may have encouraged a new independence, a new belief in the powers of the individual to seek truth. This in turn promoted the idea of the self as a distinct entity, separate from church or community.

Without producing sudden or complete revolution in outlook, religious change obviously stimulated a considerable reorientation of the mental map of many ordinary people in the West. This reorientation followed from the important divisions that opened up in formal religious affiliations and the reduced political power of the Christian churches.

THE COMMERCIAL REVOLUTION

Concurrent with religious upheaval during the 16th century, the economic structure of the West underwent fundamental redefinition. The level of European trade rose sharply, and many Europeans had new goods available to them. Involvement with markets and merchants increased. At the same time western Europe's growing role in international trade furthered the role of commerce at home.

A basic spur to greater commercialization was a substantial price inflation that occurred throughout western Europe during the 16th century. The massive import of gold and silver from Spain's new colonies in Latin America forced prices up. New wealth heightened demand for products to sell both in the colonies and in Europe, but Western production could not keep pace—hence the price inflation. Inflation, in turn, while it hurt groups such as landlords who faced fixed rents, encouraged merchants to take new risks, for borrowing was cheap when money was losing value.

Inflation and the new colonial opportunities led to the formation of great trading companies, often with government backing in Spain, England, the Netherlands, and France. Governments granted regional monopolies to these giant concerns; thus the Dutch East Indies Company long dominated trade with the islands of Indonesia. European merchants increasingly pushed out Arab and Indian traders in East Asia and the Indian Ocean. They brought new profits back to Europe and developed new managerial skills and banking arrangements.

Colonial markets and generally increasing trade stimulated manufacturing. Most peasants continued to produce mainly for their own needs, but agricultural specialty areas developed in the production of wines, cheeses, wool, and the like. Some of these encouraged commercial farming and the use of paid laborers on the land. Shoemaking, pottery, metalworking, and other manufacturing specializa-

tions arose both in rural villages and in the cities. Technical improvements followed in many branches of manufacture, particularly in metals and mining.

The spread of markets and considerable manufacturing had a number of sweeping effects. Population grew by about 20 percent between 1500 and 1650, reversing a long period of decline. Several large urban centers arose. Prosperity increased for ordinary people as well as for the great merchants. English farmers, for example, enjoyed pewter tableware, more feather beds, and other amenities.

One historian has estimated that by around 1600 the average Western peasant or artisan owned five times as many "things" as his or her counterpart in southeastern Europe. Landowning peasants began to commission painters to decorate cabinets and other furnishings, in a popular art style that spread through western and central Europe. People were aware of the change in material standards at the time. A 16th-century Englishman noted that whereas in the past a peasant and his family slept on the floor, having only a pan or two as kitchenware, by the final decades of the century a farmer might have "a fair garnish of pewter in his cupboard, three or four feather beds, so many coverlets and carpets of tapestry, a silver salt, a bowl for wine . . . and a dozen spoons." It was around this time that French peasants began to enjoy wine on a fairly regular basis, rather than simply at special occasions—the result of higher productivity and better trade and transport facilities.

There were victims of change as well, however. Growing commercialization created the beginnings of a new proletariat in the West—people without access to producing property. Population growth and rising food prices hit hard at the poor, and many people had to sell their small plots of land. Some proletarians became manufacturing workers, depending on orders from merchant capitalists to keep their tools busy in their cottages. Others became paid labor on agricultural estates, where landlords were eager for a more manipulable work force to take advantage of sales opportunities in the cities. Others pressed into the cities, and a growing problem of wandering poor and beggars began to affect Western society; a new, tough attitude toward poverty crystallized that has lasted to some extent to the present day. New methods of disciplining elements of the proletariat, including institutional prisons, emerged to counter those features of proletarianization that impacted unfavorably on the rest of society. Government began to organize some aid to the poor, an important new function.

Commercialization, besides moving European society farther away from older traditions of community solidarity, had other results. Growing prosperity for some groups helped support a more elaborate family life. Better furnishings encouraged people to spend more time at home, at family meals for example, and many women were prompted to become regulators of domestic social routine. More market involvement encouraged greater belief in personal achievement and in the demystification of nature. Economic change, in other words, intertwined with some of the alterations in mentalities also wrapped up in the religious upheaval.

Finally, the shifts in popular economic and cultural traditions provoked important outcry, for these were fundamental challenges to sanctioned behaviors and values. A huge wave of popular protest in western Europe developed at the end of the 16th century, extending until about 1650. Peasants and townspeople alike rose in defense of noncommercial economic motives and greater protection from poverty and proletarianization. The risings did not deflect the basic currents of change, but they revealed the massive dislocation involved. Not directed against established governments, the riots showed real hatred of the rich merchant classes as well as a sense of popular democracy that would reemerge in the 18th century.

A huge outburst against suspected witches arose in the same decades in various parts of western Europe and also in New England. More than 100,000 suspected witches were accused and killed. The witchcraft hysteria reflected new resentments against the poor, often accused of witchcraft by communities unwilling to accept responsibility for their poverty. The hysteria also reflected new uncertainties about religious truth, for the trials were particularly common in areas converted to Protestantism. It even showed new tensions about family life and the role of women, who were the most common targets of persecution.

The West, in sum, was moving toward new economic structures and a new belief system, both of which promised further change in the future. Many people greeted the changes with dismay and sought ways of expressing their insecurity and fear, for the changes reached deeply into personal life and intimate beliefs.

NEW SOCIAL DIVISIONS

Renaissance, Reformation, and economic change had combined to produce a number of new divisions in western Europe. The Renaissance created some new wedges between the educated elite and the mass of ordinary people. Traditionally, Europe's aristocracy had shared in popular culture, enjoying peasant festivals and an earthiness that embraced ribald jokes and even public urination—as in

This 1514 woodcut portrays the European view of witches, concocting an ointment to be used for flying to the Sabbath.

Wales where a young man might urinate on his betrothed's dress as a sign of possession. By the 16th century many aristocrats and religious leaders began to pull away from popular culture, urging more refined manners and/or a purer religious spirit. Both the Protestant and the Catholic Reformation picked up on this latter tone, attacking popular dancing and other customs that had mixed in with religious ceremonies.

In response to elite disapproval and to the growth of a propertyless proletariat, popular rebellions throughout Europe signaled important social tension. Peasant songs expressed such sentiments as this: "The whole country must be overturned, for we peasants are now to be the lords, it is we who will sit in the shade." Risings in 1648 produced demands for a popular political voice; an English group called the Levelers gained 100,000 signatures on a petition for political rights. Elsewhere common people praised the kings while attacking their "bad advisors" and high taxes. One English agitator said that "we should cut off all the gentlemen's heads . . . we shall have a merrier world shortly." In France Protestant and Catholic peasants rose together against landlords and taxes: "They seek only the ruin of the poor people for our ruin is their wealth."

New social divisions were not, however, completely straightforward, which is one reason the popular risings ul-timately failed. Growing wealth spread to property-owning peasants and craftsmen, who also gained increasing literacy. These people might be attracted to some of the new ideas, urged by religious leaders, about tighter family structures. These groups could readily share the suspicions of government leaders about the irresponsibility of the poor. Western social alignments were in flux, which most obviously produced impressive popular protest and new divisions over beliefs, but which also generated audiences for various other new ideas.

DOCUMENT
CONTROVERSIES ABOUT WOMEN

Changes in family structure and some shifts in the economic roles of women, plus ambivalent Protestant promptings about women that emphasized the family context but urged affection and respect between wives and husbands, touched off new gender tensions in Western society by the 17th century. Some of these tensions showed in witchcraft trials, so disproportionately directed against women. Other tensions showed in open debate about women's relationship to men, in which new male hostility toward women not content with a docile wifeliness vied with new claims of virtue and prowess by some women. Though the debate centered in the upper class of Protestant nations such as England, it may have had wider ramifications; some of these ramifications, though quieter during the 18th century, would burst forth again in arguments about inequality and family confinement in the 19th century, when a more durable feminist movement took shape in the West. In the selections below, the antiwoman position is set forth in a 1615 pamphlet by Joseph Swetnam; the favorable view implicitly urging new rights is in a 1640 pamphlet pseudonymously authored by "Mary Tattle-well and Ioane Hit-him-home, spinsters."

SWETNAM'S "ARRAIGNMENT OF WOMEN"

Men, I say, may live without women, but women cannot live without men: for Venus, whose beauty was excellent fair, yet when she needed man's help, she took Vulcan, a clubfooted Smith. . . .
For women have a thousand ways to entice thee and ten thousand ways to deceive thee and all such fools as are suitors unto them: some they keep in hand with promises, and some they feed with flattery, and some they delay with dalliances, and some they please with kisses. They lay out the folds of their hair to entangle men into their love; betwixt their breasts is the vale of destruction; and in their beds there is hell, sorrow, and repentance. Eagles eat not men till they are dead, but women devour them alive. . . .

It is said of men that they have that one fault, but of women it is said that they have two faults: that is to say, they can neither say well nor do well. There is a saying that goeth thus: that things far fetched and dear bought are of us most dearly beloved. The like may be said of women; although many of them are not far fetched, yet they are dear bought, yea and so dear that many a man curseth his hard pennyworths and bans his own heart. For the pleasure of the fairest woman in the world lasteth but a honeymoon; that is, while a man hath glutted his affections and reaped the first fruit, his pleasure being past, sorrow and repentance remaineth still with him.

TATTLE-WELL AND HIT-HIM-HOME'S "WOMEN'S SHARP REVENGE"

But it hath been the policy of all parents, even from the beginning, to curb us of that benefit by striving to keep us under and to make us men's mere Vassals even unto all posterity. How else comes it to pass that when a Father hath a numerous issue of Sons and Daughters, the sons forsooth they must be first put to the Grammar school, and after perchance sent to the University, and trained up in the Liberal Arts and Sciences, and there (if they prove not Blockheads) they may in time be book-learned? . . .

When we, whom they style by the name of weaker Vessels, though of a more delicate, fine, soft, and more pliant flesh therefore of a temper most capable of the best Impression, have not that generous and liberal Education, lest we should be made able to vindicate our own injuries, we are set only to the Needle, to prick our fingers, or else to the Wheel to spin a fair thread for our own undoing, or perchance to some more dirty and debased drudgery. If we be taught to read, they then confine us within the compass of our Mother Tongue, and that limit we are not suffered to pass; or if (which sometimes happeneth) we be brought up to Music, to singing, and to dancing, it is not for any benefit that thereby we can engross unto ourselves, but for their own particular ends, the better to please and content their licentious appetites when we come to our maturity and ripeness. And thus if we be weak by Nature, they strive to make us more weak by our Nurture; and if in degree of place low, they strive by their policy to keep us more under.

Now to show we are no such despised matter as you would seem to make us, come to our first Creation, when man was made of the mere dust of the earth. The woman had her being from the best part of his body, the Rib next to his heart, which difference even in our complexions may be easily decided. Man is of a dull, earthy, and melancholy aspect, having shallows in his face and a very forest upon his Chin, when our soft and smooth Cheeks are a true representation of a delectable garden of intermixed Roses and Lilies. . . .

Man might consider that women were not created to be their slaves or vassals; for as they had not their Original out of his head (thereby to command him), so it was not out of his foot to be trod upon, but in a *medium* out of his side to be his fellow feeler, his equal, and companion. . . .

Thus have I truly and impartially proved that for Chastity, Charity, Constancy, Magnanimity, Valor, Wisdom, Piety, or any Grace or Virtue whatsoever, women have always been more than equal with men, and that for Luxury, Surquidant obscenity, profanity, Ebriety, Impiety, and all that may be called bad we do come far short of them.

Questions: Why did such different views about women develop in the 17th century? Why did some women defy patriarchal culture, and what were their main arguments? Did the new arguments in favor of women suggest that their conditions were improving?

SCIENCE AND POLITICS: THE NEXT PHASE OF CHANGE

Religious disruptions had produced major changes in Western intellectual life, and the related shifts in popular mentality involved even more fundamental new directions. It was the revolution in science, culminating in the 17th century, that set the seal on the cultural reorientation of the West. While the scientific revolution most obviously affected formal intellectual life, it also furthered some of the key changes in wider mentalities.

At the same time, after the political upheavals occasioned by the Reformation, a more decisive set of new government forms arose in the West, centering on the emergence of the nation state. The functions of the state and its contacts with popular loyalties expanded. The Western nation state was not a single form, as key variants emerged such as absolute monarchies and parliamentary regimes, but there were some common patterns beneath the surface. Continued cultural change, then, and new roles for the state defined the second major phase in the transformation of the early modern West during the late 17th and early 18th centuries.

SCIENCE

During the 16th century important scientific research had continued the traditions of the later Middle Ages, although the results were somewhat obscured by the more striking developments in art and religion. A Polish monk, Copernicus, used astronomical observation and mathematical calculation to disprove the Hellenistic belief that the earth was the center of the universe. Rather, the earth moved around the sun. Also in the 16th century, anatomical work by the Belgian Vesalius overturned many medical ideas. These key discoveries not only advanced knowledge; they also implied a new power for scientific research in its ability to test and often overrule accepted ideas.

These implications won full attention in a dizzying series of empirical advances and wider theoretical generalizations from the 1590s onward. New instruments such as the microscope and improved telescopes allowed gains in biology and astronomy. Scientists throughout the Western world participated in a surge of excited discovery. The Italian Galileo publicized Copernicus's discoveries while adding his own basic findings about the laws of gravity and planetary motion. Condemned by the Catholic church for his innovations, Galileo nevertheless definitively proved the inadequacy of traditional ideas about the universe. He also showed the new pride in scientific achievement, writing modestly how he, "by marvelous discoveries and clear demonstrations, had enlarged a thousand times" the knowledge produced by "the wise men of bygone ages." Chemical research advanced understanding of the behavior of gases. The English physician John Harvey demonstrated the circular movement of the blood in animals, with the heart as the "central pumping station."

The advances in knowledge were accompanied by important methodological statements about science and its impact. Francis Bacon urged the value of careful empirical research and predicted that scientific knowledge could steadily advance, producing improvements in technology as well. René Descartes established the importance of a skepti-

This 40-foot reflecting telescope was built in Britain in 1789.

cal review of all received wisdom, arguing that human reason could then develop laws that would explain the fundamental workings of nature. Descartes included a proof of God in his rationalistic generalizations, but this system allowed no real room for divine interventions.

The capstone to the 17th-century scientific revolution came with Isaac Newton's publication of his *Principia* in 1687, for this drew the various astronomical and physical observations and wider theories together in a neat framework of natural laws. Newton set forth the basic, simple principles of all motion: that a body in motion maintains uniform momentum unless affected by outside forces, that changes in rates of motion are proportional to the outside force, and that to every action there is always opposed an equal reaction. Newton defined the forces of gravity in great mathematical detail and showed that the whole universe responded to these forces, which among other things explained the planetary orbits. Finally, Newton stated the basic scientific method in terms of a mixture of rational hypothesis and generalization and careful empirical observation and experiment. Here was a vision of a natural universe that could be captured in relatively simple laws (though increasingly complex mathematics accompanied the findings). Here was a vision of a method of knowing that might do away with blind reliance on tradition or an acceptance of the need for religious faith.

The scientific revolution was quickly popularized among educated Westerners, though not yet the wider populace. New scientific institutes were set up, often with government aid, to advance research and disseminate findings. Lectures and easy-to-read manuals publicized the latest advances and communicated the excitement researchers themselves shared. The results fed into some of the wider shifts in outlook, at least among literate, urban people. Attacks on beliefs in witchcraft became more common, and magistrates grew increasingly reluctant to entertain witchcraft accusations in court; the public hysteria began to die down after about 1670. There were growing signs of a new belief that people could control and calculate their environment. Insurance companies sprang up to help guard against risk. Doctors increased their attacks on popular healers in the name of a more scientific diagnosis of illness. Newsletters, an innovation by the late 17th century, began to advertise lost and found items, for there was no point leaving this kind of problem to blind chance.

The scientific revolution had important implications beyond science in terms of how and what people could know. By the 1680s writers affected by the new science, though not themselves scientists, began to attack traditional religious ideas such as miracles, for in the universe of the scientific revolution there was no room for disruption of nature's laws. Some intellectuals held out a new conception of God, called "Deism," arguing that while there might be a divinity its role was simply to set natural laws in motion, not to regulate them once the process was launched. Faith came under direct scrutiny. John Locke, in England, argued that people, through their senses and reason, could learn everything they needed to know; faith was irrelevant. Christian beliefs in human sinfulness crumbled in the view of the ascendant intellectuals, for human nature was basically good, given the capacity to learn. Finally, scientific advance created wider assumptions about the possibility of human progress. If knowledge could advance through concerted human effort, why not progress in other domains? Even literary authorities joined this parade—the idea that past styles set timeless standards of perfection came under growing criticism.

The scientific revolution by no means monopolized the West's intellectual life around 1700. There were important movements in art with the continued reliance on classical styles. Religious authorities were hardly silent, and many attacked the brashness of the new science. Unquestionably, however, the balance of intellectual interests was shifting, and science, with its presumed implications for other kinds of knowledge, increasingly ruled the roost.

This realignment was a first in human history. Science had never before been central to intellectual life. Science had played important roles in other civilizations, as in China, classical Greece, and Islam. Generally, however, wider religious or philosophical interests predominated. In China most notably, despite some real interest in generalizations about the physical universe derived from Daoism, science continued to be construed mainly in terms of practical, empirical advances. Chinese science piled up concrete information about astronomy or medicinal drugs. The Western passion for combining empiricism with more sweeping rational formulations—the idea of general laws of nature—clearly built on specific traditions that had come from Greek thought as mediated by Christian theology and Islamic philosophy during the postclassical period. The West, in sum, was not alone in developing crucial scientific data, but it had become the most vibrant center for scientific advance and its leading thinkers stood alone, for some time, in seeing science as the key to gaining and defining knowledge.

THE NATION-STATE

The feudal monarchy—that balance between king and nobles—that had defined Western politics since the High Middle Ages finally came undone in the 17th century. In most countries, after the passions of religious wars finally cooled, monarchs gained new powers, curtailing the tradition of noble pressure or revolt. At the same time, more ambitious military organization, in states that defined war as a central purpose, required more careful administration and improved tax collection.

The prototype for this new pattern was France, now the West's most important nation. French kings steadily built up their power in the 17th century. They stopped calling the medieval parliament, passing laws as they saw fit, though some provincial councils remained strong. They blew up the castles of dissident nobles, another sign of how gunpowder undercut the military basis of feudalism. They appointed a growing bureaucracy, drawn from the merchants and lawyers. They sent direct representatives to the outlying provinces. They professionalized the army, giving more formal training to officers, providing uniforms and logistical support, and creating military hospitals and pensions. The French kings had larger and more reliable military forces than ever before in Western history.

So great was the power of the monarch, in fact, that the French system became known as *absolute monarchy*. Its most glorious royal proponent, King Louis XIV, summed up its principles succinctly: "I am the state." Louis became a major patron of the arts, giving government a cultural role beyond any previous levels in the West. His academies not only encouraged science but worked to standardize the French language. A sumptuous palace at Versailles was used to keep nobles busy with social functions, so that they could not interfere with affairs of state.

More substantively, using the new bureaucratic structure, Louis and his ministers developed additional functions for the state. They cut down on internal tariffs barriers to trade and created new, state-run manufacturing. The reigning economic theory, called *mercantilism,* held that governments should promote the internal economy in order to improve tax revenues and to limit imports from other nations, lest money be lost to enemy states. Hence absolute monarchs like Louis XIV set tariffs on imported goods, tried to encourage their merchant fleets, and sought colonies to provide raw materials and a guaranteed market for manufactured goods produced at home.

The basic structure of absolute monarchy developed in other states besides France. Spain, after its 17th century decline, tried to imitate French principles in the 18th century, which resulted among other things in efforts to tighten control over its Latin American colonies. The most important spread of absolute monarchy occurred, however, in the central European states that were gaining in importance. A series of kings in Prussia, in eastern Germany, built a strong army and bureaucracy. They promoted economic activity and also began to develop a state-sponsored school system. Habsburg kings in Austria-Hungary, though still officially rulers of the Holy Roman Empire, in fact concentrated increasingly on developing a stronger monarchy in the lands under their direct control. The power of these Habsburg rulers increased after they pushed back the last Turkish invasion threat late in the 17th century, and then added the kingdom of Hungary to their domains.

Absolute monarchy and the classical style in architecture are symbolized by Louis XIV's great 17th-century palace at Versailles.

Absolute monarchy formed a domestic system of government. Most absolute monarchs saw a strong military as a key political goal, and many hoped for territorial expansion. Louis XIV used his strong state as the basis for a series of wars from the 1680s onward. The wars yielded some new territory for France but finally attracted an opposing alliance system that blocked further advance. Prussian kings, though long cautious in exposing their proud military to the risk of major war, turned in the 18th century to a series of conflicts that won new territory.

Britain and the Netherlands, both growing commercial and colonial powers, stood apart from the trend toward absolute monarchy in the 17th century. They, too, emphasized the role of the central state, but they also firmed up parliamentary regimes in which the kings shared power with representatives selected by the nobility and upper urban classes. The English civil wars produced a final political settlement in 1688 and 1689 (the so-called Glorious Revolution) in which parliament won basic sovereignty over the king. The English parliament no longer depended on the king to convene, for regular sessions were now

scheduled, and it held assured rights to approve taxation that allowed it to monitor or initiate most major policies.

Furthermore, a growing body of political theory arose in the 17th century that built on these parliamentary ideas. John Locke and others argued that power came basically from the people, not from a divine right to royal rule. Kings should therefore be restrained by institutions that protected the popular interest, including certain general rights to freedom and property. A right of revolution could legitimately oppose unjust rule.

Overall, while the West developed important diversity in political forms, between absolute monarchy and a new kind of *parliamentary monarchy,* a characteristic tension remained between government growth and the idea that there should be some limits to state authority. This tension was expressed in new forms, but it recalled some principles that had originated in the Middle Ages.

Government growth itself should not be exaggerated. While absolute monarchs had torn down some of the characteristic institutions of feudal days, they lacked the means to gain detailed control over their subjects. Nobles in fact

Europe under Absolute Monarchy, 1715

A De koningh gheeft d'Ordre van S. Joris
an D. Jucob B. de koningh an't Block
C.D. Juxon D. Colnel Tomelinson
E.Colonel Hacker F. De twee Beuls

White Hall

BANCKET HAVS

Civil war resulted in the execution of Charles I in London, England, in 1649.

continued to play a considerable role in affairs of state. Furthermore, many of the innovations that did occur simply brought to the West the kinds of bureaucratic structures that other civilizations, particularly China, had developed long before.

It was significant, nevertheless, that at a time in world history when governments in many civilizations were entering a period of decline, those in the West were on the upswing. It was significant also that Western governments gained new powers to influence wider spheres of activity. They affected economic life and the treatment of the poor. They increasingly defined the way prisoners should be treated. They played some role in cultural trends. They also gave merchants a political role, as bureaucrats or parliamentary representatives, that was unusual in world history to that point.

Furthermore, both the absolute monarchies and the parliamentary monarchies shared important characteristics as nation-states. Unlike the great empires of many other civi-

lizations, they ruled peoples who shared a common culture and language, some important minorities apart. They thus could appeal for a certain loyalty that linked cultural and political bonds. This was as true of England, where the idea of special rights of Englishmen helped feed the parliamentary movement, as of France. Not surprisingly, ordinary people in many nation-states, even though not directly represented in government, showed increasing belief that government should act for their interests. Thus Louis XIV faced recurrent popular riots predicated on the assumption that, when bad harvests drove up food prices, it was the obligation of government to help people out. Thus the English parliamentary system, though monopolized by the upper classes, opened the way to frequent popular petitions about various grievances.

Nation-states, in sum, developed a growing list of functions, particularly under the banner of mercantilism whose principles were shared by monarchists and parliamentary leaders alike. They also promoted new political values and loyalties that were somewhat less common among the political traditions of other civilizations. They certainly kept the West divided politically and frequently at war.

ANALYSIS
ELITES AND MASSES

What caused the end of witchcraft hysteria in the West by the later 17th century? One explanation focuses on new efforts by elites, such as local magistrates, to discipline mass impulses. Authorities stopped believing in demonic disruptions of natural processes, and so forced an end to persecutions. But many ordinary people were also thinking in new ways. Without converting fully to a scientific outlook, they became open to new ideas about how to handle health problems, reducing their belief in magical remedies; they needed witches less. Early attacks on witches may have changed popular habits, contributing to the reduction of hysteria. Older women, for example, threatened by growing community suspicion, learned to maintain a lower profile, emphasizing benign, grandmotherly qualities rather than seeking a more independent role. Some Western people still believed in witches, and a few believed they were witches themselves. (A few still do, in the later 20th century in the West.) But witchcraft beliefs, once a key element in the Western mentality, and the hysteria specifically characteristic of the 16th and 17th centuries, both declined. This decline reflected new ways of thinking about strangeness and disruption. It involved complex interactions among various segments of Western society—magistrates and villagers, scientists and priests, husbands and widows.

The transformation of Western society after 1450 raises fascinating questions about the role of elites—particularly powerful groups and creative individuals—versus the ordinary run of folk in causing change. The growing importance of social history has called attention to ordinary people, as we have seen, but it has not answered all the questions about their actual role. This role varies, of course, by place and time. But some social historians tend generally to see ordinary people as victims of change, bumped and beleaguered by the power groups. Others, in contrast, tend generally to stress the positive historical role of ordinary people in partly shaping the context of their own lives and affecting the larger course of history as well.

Massive religious change, for example, such as the spread of Islam or the Protestant Reformation in Europe, involved the needs and opportunities of ordinary people in contact with extraordinary religious leaders. Such change has always involved conversion of ordinary people—by persuasion or coercion—the activities of rulers, and indeed a combination of popular impulses and traditions with formal religious doctrine.

It is easy to read the early modern transformation of western Europe as an operation shaped by elites, with the masses as passive or futilely protesting clay. Not only the Renaissance and Reformation, but also the commercial revolution, entailed decisive action by key leadership groups. Leading merchants spurred economic change, and they ultimately began to farm out manufacturing jobs. Resultant proletarianization—which tore a growing minority of west Europeans away from property and so from economic control of their lives—graphically illustrated the disparities of power in Western society, as capitalist merchants and landowners gained a more manipulable labor force. Ordinary people knuckled under or protested, but they were reacting, not initiating.

The rise of science rivets attention on the activities of extraordinarily creative individuals, such as Newton, and elite institutions such as the scientific academies. Some historians have suggested that the rise of science forged a new gap between the way educated upper classes and masses thought.

Yet the ordinary people of western Europe were not inert, nor did they simply and abortively protest change in the name of the tried and true. Widespread shifts came from repeated decisions by nameless peasants and artisans, not just from those at the top. The steady technological improvements in manufacturing thus flowed upward from practicing artisans, not downward from formal scientists. The European-style family, an innovation by ordinary people the elite long ignored, encouraged new parent-child relations, new tensions between young adults and the old, that might spur other innovations—including a willingness to settle distant colonies in search of property. The fact that young people often had to wait to marry until their property-owning fathers died could spur many to seek new lands or new economic methods. Ordinary people, in other words, changed their habits too. They created a new climate for generating as well as receiving new ideas about medicine or witchcraft or about how to handle emotions in the family. They created new motives and rhythms for work. In mentalities, changes at the popular level clearly related to elite currents, despite clashes and discontinuities.

Finally, the dichotomy of elites and ordinary people was bridged in important new ways during the early modern centuries, and particularly after about 1650. The spread of literacy facilitated interchange, first in religion and then in science. While the rise of a proletarian minority constituted a new rift, growing prosperity and commercial mindedness among many middle-level property owners complicated any claim to growing economic inequality overall. Gender divisions increased in some respects, as women became more fully associated with domestic functions, but the emphasis on family values encouraged men and women to participate in some shared experiences. Western society was generating some new middle ground in outlook and power. Commercial contacts even eased, without fully eliminating, one of the oldest divisions in agricultural civilization, that between country and town. Rural people gained access to new (sometimes disturbing) urban habits and leisure forms.

The new Western patterns were obviously complex, as any sweeping transformation must be. Changes emanated from various levels, moved in various directions, and created new groupings as well as new disparities. The active involvement of ordinary people warrants comparison with transformations in other key junctures of world history. It also explains why other civilizations, later seeking to imitate certain features of the new Western society, faced important choices about whether and how to involve the masses—choices in which the masses would have their own contributions to make.

Questions: Did elites gain new power over the masses in early modern Western society? Are ordinary people more conservative by nature, more suspicious of change, than groups at the top? Can you describe at least two other historical cases in which it is important whether change was imposed on ordinary people from above, or whether ordinary people themselves produced important innovations? ✸

THE WEST BY 1750

The three great currents of change—commercialization, cultural reorientation, and the rise of the nation-state—continued to operate in the West after 1700, along with the growing international influence of the West. Each strand, in fact, produced new ramifications that furthered the overall transformation of the West.

POLITICAL PATTERNS

On the whole, during the middle decades of the 18th century political changes seemed least significant. During much of the century English politics settled into a rather turgid parliamentary routine, in which key political groups competed for influence without major policy differences. Some popular concern for greater representation surfaced in the 1760s, as a movement for democracy surged briefly, but there was as yet no consistent reform current. Absolute monarchy in France changed little institutionally, but it became progressively less effective. It was unable to force changes in the tax structure that would give it more solid financial footing, because aristocrats refused to surrender their traditional exemptions.

Political developments were far livelier in central Europe. In Prussia Frederick the Great, building on the military and bureaucratic organization of his predecessors, introduced greater freedom of religion while expanding the economic functions of the state. His government actively encouraged better agricultural methods, as in promoting use of the potato as a staple crop. It also codified its laws toward greater commercial coordination and greater equity; harsh traditional punishments were cut back. Later in the 18th century an Austrian emperor, Joseph II, tried a similar program of state-sponsored improvements, including a major effort to roll back the power of the Catholic church. Rulers of this sort claimed to be enlightened despots, wielding great authority but for the good of society at large.

Enlightened or not, the policies of the major Western nation-states produced recurrent warfare. France and Britain squared off in the 1740s and again in the Seven Years' War (1756–1763); their conflicts focused on battles for colonial empire. Austria and Prussia also fought, with Prussia gaining new land. Wars in the 18th century were carefully modulated, without devastating effects, but they demonstrated the continued linkage between statecraft and war characteristic of the West.

ENLIGHTENMENT THOUGHT

In culture, the aftermath of the scientific revolution spilled over into a new movement known as the *Enlightenment*, centered particularly in France but with adherents throughout the Western world. Enlightenment thinkers continued to support scientific advance. While there were no Newton-like breakthroughs, chemists gained new understanding of major elements and biologists developed a vital new classification system for the natural species.

The Enlightenment also pioneered in applying scientific methods to the study of human society, sketching the modern social sciences. The basic idea here was that rational laws could describe social as well as physical behavior, and that knowledge could be used to improve policy. Thus criminologists wrote about how brutal punishments failed

Enlightenment efficiency and old-fashioned public punishment caused the construction of this "mass production" scaffold, which sped up executions at the Old Bailey, London. Other reformers opposed capital punishment, however quick and humane.

to deter crime, whereas a decent society would be able to rehabilitate criminals through education. Political theorists wrote about the importance of carefully planned constitutions and controls over privilege, though they disagreed about what political form was best. A new school of economists developed. The Scottish philosopher Adam Smith set forth a number of invariable principles of economic behavior, based on the belief that people act according to their self-interest but, through competition, work to promote general economic advance. Government should avoid regulation in favor of the operation of individual initiative and market forces. Here was an important specific statement of economic policy and an illustration of the growing belief that general models of human behavior could be derived from rational thought.

More generally still, the Enlightenment produced a set of basic principles about human affairs. Human beings are naturally good and can be educated to be better. Reason was the key to truth, and religions that relied on blind faith or refused to tolerate diversity were wrong. Enlightenment thinkers attacked the Catholic church with particular vigor. Progress was possible, even inevitable, if people could be set free. Society's goals should center on improvements in material and social life.

Enlightenment thinkers showed great interest in technological change, for greater prosperity was a valid and achievable goal. Coercion and cruelty could be corrected, for the Enlightenment encouraged a humanitarian outlook that was applied in condemnations of slavery and war.

Though not typical of the Enlightenment's main thrust, a few thinkers applied the general principles to other areas. A handful of socialists argued that economic equality and the abolition of private property must become important goals. A few feminist thinkers, such as Mary Wollstonecraft in England, argued that new political rights and freedoms should extend to women, against the general male-centered views of most Enlightenment thinkers.

The Enlightenment, summing up and extending earlier intellectual changes, became an important force for political and social reform. It did not rule unchallenged. Important popular religious movements, such as Methodism in England, showed the continued power of spiritual faith. Many writers, particularly those experimenting with the novel as a new literary form in the West, rebelled against Enlightenment rationality to urge the importance of sentimentality and emotion. These approaches, too, encouraged rethinking of traditional styles.

The popularization of new ideas encouraged further changes in the habits and beliefs of many ordinary people. Reading clubs and coffeehouses allowed many urban artisans and businessmen to discuss the latest reform ideas. Leading writers and compilations of scientific and philosophical findings, such as the *Encyclopaedia Britannica,* won a wide audience and, in a few cases, a substantial fortune due to the sale of books. Groups and individuals formed to promote better agricultural or industrial methods, or bent on winning new political rights, referred directly to Enlightenment thinking. Some groups of artisans and peasants also turned against established churches and even withdrew from religious belief, as secular values gained ground.

Other changes in popular outlook paralleled the new intellectual currents, though they had deeper sources than philosophy alone. Attitudes toward children began to shift in many social groups. Older methods of physical discipline were criticized, in favor of more restrained behavior that would respect the goodness and innocence of children. Swaddling began to decline, as parents were interested in freer movement and greater interaction for young children; no longer were infants tightly wrapped during their first months. Among wealthy families, educational toys and books for children reflected the idea that childhood should be a stage for learning and growth. At the most basic level, parents became increasingly likely to give young children names at birth and to select names different from those of older relatives—a sign of a new affection for children and new belief in their individuality. These changes were gradual, and they involved more adult control of children as well as a more humane outlook. The idea of shaping children and instilling guilt-stimulated consciences gained ground. Unquestionably, the net effect was to alter parent-child relations and also to produce novel personality ideals for adults themselves.

Family life generally was altered by a growing sense that old hierarchies needed to be rethought, toward somewhat greater equality in the treatment of women and children within the home. Love among family members gained new respect, and an emotional bond in marriage became more widely sought. Parents, for example, grew more reluctant to force a match on a son or daughter if the emotional vibrations were not right. Here was a link not only with Enlightenment ideas of proper family relations but with the novels that poured out a sentimental view of life.

Ongoing economic change, finally, paralleled the ferment in popular culture and intellectual life. Commerce continued its spread. Ordinary Westerners began to buy processed products, such as refined sugar and coffee or tea obtained from Indonesia and the West Indies, for daily use. Here was a sign of the growing importance of Europe's new colonies for ordinary life and of the beginnings of mass consumerism in Western society. Another sign of change was the growing use of paid, professional entertainment as part of popular leisure even in rural festivals. Not accidentally, circuses, first introduced in France in the 1670s, began to redefine leisure to include spectatorship and a taste for the bizarre.

Agriculture began to change. Until the later 17th century Western Europe had continued to rely largely on the methods and techniques characteristic of the Middle Ages—a severe economic constraint in a still agricultural society. Now, first in the Netherlands and then elsewhere, new procedures for draining swamps added available land. Nitrogen-fixing crops were introduced to reduce the need to leave land fallow. Stockbreeding improved, and new techniques like seed-drills or simply the use of scythes instead of sickles for harvesting heightened productivity. Some changes spread particularly fast on large estates, which was one reason that in England more and more land was enclosed, with ordinary farmers serving as tenants or laborers rather than owners. Other changes affected ordinary peasants as well. Particularly vital in this category was the spread of the potato from the late 17th century onward. A New World crop, the potato had long been shunned because it was not mentioned in the Bible and was held to be the cause of plagues. Enlightened government leaders and peasant desire to win greater economic security and better nutrition led to widespread adoption of this efficient crop. The West, in sum, improved its food supply and also its agricultural efficiency, leaving more labor available for other pursuits.

These changes, along with the steady growth of colonial trade and internal commerce, spurred increased manufacturing. The 18th century witnessed a rapid spread of household production of textiles and metal products, mostly by rural workers who alternated manufacturing with some agriculture. Hundreds of thousands of people were drawn into this domestic system in which capitalist merchants distributed supplies and orders and workers ran the production process for pay. While manufacturing tools were still hand operated, the spread of domestic manufacturing spurred important technical innovations designed to improve efficiency. In 1733 James Kay in England introduced the flying shuttle, which permitted automatic crossing of threads on looms; with this, an individual weaver could do the work of two. Improvements in spinning soon followed, as the Western economy began to escalate toward a full-fledged Industrial Revolution.

Finally, agricultural changes, commercialism, and manufacturing combined, particularly after about 1730, to produce a rapidly growing population in the West. With better food supplies, more people survived—the potato was a crucial ingredient here. More commercial motives helped prompt landlords and some ambitious peasants to acquire more land and to push unneeded labor off, heightening proletarianization but also reducing the restraints some parents could impose over the sexual behavior of their children: In essence, as some groups grew unsure of inheritance, they sought more immediate pleasures and also hoped to use the labor of the resultant children. Finally, new manufacturing jobs helped landless people support themselves, promoting in some cases earlier marriage and sexual liaisons. Growing population, in turn, promoted further economic change, heightening competition and producing a more manipulable labor force. The West's great population revolution, which would continue into the 19th century, both caused and reflected the civilization's dynamism, though it also produced great strain and confusion.

Western society was still essentially agricultural by the mid-18th century. Decisive new political forms had yet to be introduced, and in many ways government policies failed to keep pace with cultural and economic change after 1700. Established churches were forces to be reckoned with still. Even new developments, such as the spread of domestic manufacturing, functioned because they allowed so many traditional habits to persist. Thus while new market relationships described this growing system, the location and many of the methods of work as well as the association of family with production were not altered. Western society hovered between older values and institutions and the full flowering of change. Decades of outright political and economic revolution, which would build on these tensions and cause a fuller transformation, were yet to come.

CONCLUSION

INNOVATION AND INSTABILITY

Nevertheless, despite important continuities from the past, Western society had by the 18th century become increasingly accustomed to change. Population pressure and the force of new ideas generated additional stimuli. All levels of society were involved. The traditional aristocratic upper class had to think about new values and the challenge of commercial habits; it was also faced with population growth in its own ranks, which raised concern about what to do with surviving younger sons and daughters. Proletarians had to adjust to work without property; they also picked up new ideas about sex and children, and possibly new expectations about government responsibilities.

It was also notable that, by the 18th century, the various strands of change began to intertwine in Western civilization. Stronger governments promoted agricultural improvements that helped prod population growth. Changes in mentalities were fed by new economic structures; both encouraged a reevaluation of the family and the roles of children. New beliefs raised new political challenges. Enlightenment ideas about liberty and some fundamental human equality could obviously be directed against existing regimes. New family practices might have political implications as well. Children, raised with less adult restraint or encouraged to value their individual worth through parental love and careful education, might see traditional political limitations in new ways. There was no perfect fit, no inevitable match, in the three strands of change that had been transforming the West for two centuries or more—the commercial, the cultural, and the political. Clearly, however, by 1750, all were in place. The combination had already produced an unusual version of an agricultural civilization, and it promised more upheaval in the future.

The Western package of change had also produced a society unusually dynamic in the world at large. Two cautions here. First, other societies had changed rapidly before, and some displayed great vigor after 1450; the West in no sense invented change. Second, Western change depended heavily on the position it won in the wider world. Commercialization, for example, built on the West's ability to extract wealth from other societies. It remained true that internal shifts helped explain the West's course in the wider world, and here the key connection was the West's instability and tension, not its smooth course.

Religious disputes, political rivalries, and economic dislocations all helped explain why Westerners reached out, as individuals and in groups, for new roles in international trade, explorations, or colonies. International activity flowed not from serene strength, but from recurrent disruption, and this activity in turn served the West as a vital outlet. Only in the 20th century have Westerners faced the obvious resultant question: What will happen to the West and its crosscurrents once the civilization's international role meets new challengers?

FURTHER READINGS

For an overview of developments in Western society during this period, with extensive bibliographies, see Sheldon Watts's *A Social History of Western Europe, 1450–1720* (1984) and Peter N. Stearns's *Life and Society in the West: The Modern Centuries* (1988). Charles Tilly's *Big Structures, Large Processes, Huge Comparisons* (1985) offers an analytical framework based on major change; see also Tilly's edited volume, *The Formation of National States in Western Europe* (1975).

On more specific developments and periods, J. H. Plumb's *The Italian Renaissance* (1986), F. H. New's *The Renaissance and Reformation: A Short History* (1977), O. Chadwick's *The Reformation* (1983), and Stephen Ozment's *The Age of Reform, 1520–1550* (1980) are fine introductions to early changes. See also Hubert Jedin and John Dolan, eds., *Reformation and Counter Reformation* (1980). Later political changes are sketched in G. Clark's *Early Modern Europe* (1960), M. Beloff's *The Age of Absolutism* (1967), and R. Hatton's *Europe in the Age of Louis XIV* (1979).

Key aspects of social change in this period can be approached through Peter Burke's *Popular Culture in Early Modern Europe* (1978), Keith Thomas's *Religion and the Decline of Magic* (1971), and Lawrence Stone's *The Family, Sex and Marriage in England 1500–1800* (1977). On popular protest, see Charles Tilly's *The Contentious French* (1986) and H. A. F. Kamen's *The Iron Century: Social Change in Europe 1550–1660* (1971).

On science, A. R. Hall's *From Galileo to Newton, 1630–1720* (1982) is a fine introduction. Relations between science and technology are covered in C. Cipolla's *Before the Industrial Revolution* (1976).

1434 Portugal extends expeditions down West African coast

1519–1521 Magellan circumnavigates globe

1562 Britain begins
its slave trade

1497–1498 Vasco da Gama to India

1542 Portuguese reach Japan

1514 Expedition to Indonesia

1571 Ottoman
fleet defeated in
Battle of Lepanto

1394–1460 Prince Henry the Navigator

1488 Portuguese round Cape of Good Hope

1433 China ends great expeditions

1492 Columbus's first expedition

1534 First French explorations in Canada

1509 First Spanish colonies on Latin American mainland

A.D. 1400   A.D. 1500

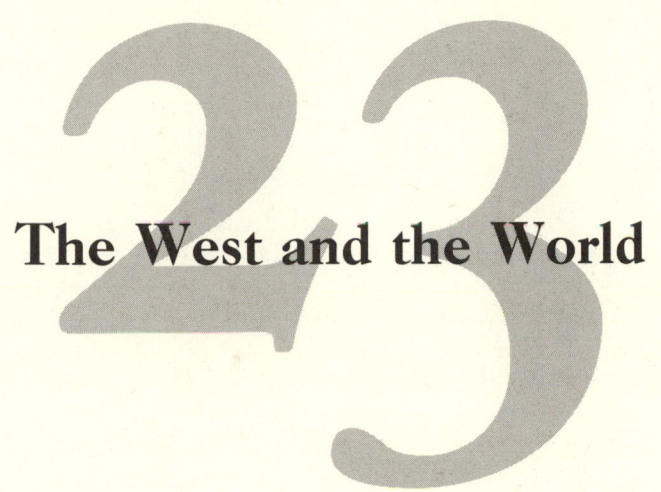

The West and the World

INTRODUCTION. One of the ways Westerners long have used history to make themselves feel good involves the recounting of the great explorations and conquests accomplished by Western stalwarts from the late 15th century onward. School children are steeped in the voyages of Columbus, the empires hacked out in Central and South America by Spanish conquerors, and the work of Christian missionaries in Asia and the New World.

The West did become steadily more important in the world in the centuries after 1450. It entered into some contact with every major society, it spurred and largely controlled a growing volume of international trade, and it set up colonies in key areas and outposts in others. The rise of the West between the 15th and the 18th centuries was also wrapped up in other developments of crucial importance in world history: the heightening and redefinition of interchanges among world societies and civilizations.

Previous periods had witnessed important steps toward greater diffusion of goods and ideas. During the classical era, most attention was given to the development of larger regional economies and cultural zones, such as the whole Chinese Middle Kingdom or the Mediterranean basin. Wider international contacts existed, as in the silk trade from China westward or the interaction between India and Hellenistic outposts following the conquests of Alexander the Great; few of these contacts, however, were of fundamental importance to the societies involved.

The level and significance of contacts increased during the postclassical era. Missionary religions spilled across civilizational boundaries, as with Buddhism in eastern and Southeast Asia and above all with Islam. The Indian Ocean became the center for a thriving international trade, which created new feeder regions—notably in East Africa—for the dominant centers in the Middle East. For the Middle East, parts of Africa, and much of India, international trade became an important feature of the basic economic structure, with some regions garnering particular profits. In other cases wider regional economies developed, notably in trade from the Mediterranean northward in Europe or in the new regional economic zone in eastern Asia. Therefore, these varied economic and cultural exchanges sped up the pace of transfering technology among civilizations—a major boon to Europe in gaining access to earlier Chinese discoveries.

These previous intensifications of world interchange must not be neglected. It remains true, nevertheless, that the kind of world relationships that developed after 1450, mainly though not exclusively sponsored by Western leaders, spelled a new period in world history. Most obviously, new areas of the world were for the first time brought into the international complex, particularly the Americas, but also new parts of Africa and ultimately Polynesia. The rate and impact of international trade also increased in some portions of the Old World, such as the islands of Southeast Asia and India. Further, international trade now became so significant that it forged different relationships among key societies based on the kind of goods and amount of control contributed to the surging world economy. These new economic relationships, in turn, prompted some societies to reconsider older political and cultural traditions in light of patterns—again, particularly those of the West—that seemed compellingly successful. This kind of differential interchange had occurred before in world history—witness the Japanese imitation of China or the impact of Islam in East Africa—but it now spread more widely, more literally internationally.

The rise of the West, important in itself, was thus part of a larger reshuffling of world relationships. The intensification of an international framework became a factor, in some cases a determining factor, in the development of individual societies. Complexity remained. The traditions of individual civilizations, even those most affected by international pressures and Western incursions, were not totally effaced. More important, different civilizations forged different relationships to the international framework, creating various levels of involvement and impact. The story of the rise of the West must be cast in terms of its relationship to new international systems and the distinctions that arose within these systems.

This chapter, accordingly, deals with several interrelated developments during the centuries between about 1450 and 1750—the same centuries when the West was changing rapidly within its own borders. Topic one is simply the West's next explorations and acquisitions as it became the world's leading international trader and colonial power. Topic two involves the larger international economic system the West created, which turned out to have a life of its own. New contacts in terms of exchanges of ideas, foods, and diseases followed from the emergence of this new system. Topic three, finally, involves sorting out the different kinds of responses generated outside the West to the new economic framework and the West's role, ranging from attempts at isolation to outright subjection. The possibilities were considerable, and no society's history was fully described by Western activities or international economics. The new developments did, however, set part of the environment in which individual civilizations continued to evolve.

THE WEST'S FIRST OUTREACH

Various Western leaders, particularly merchants but also some princes and churchmen, had become increasingly aware of the larger world around them since the High Middle Ages. Cultural contacts with Islam and the Byzantine Empire formed part of this new awareness. The Crusades brought knowledge of Islam's superior economic levels and the goods that could be imported, for the delectation of the West's increasingly sophisticated aristocracy, from the Middle East and Asia. The Mongol Empire, which sped up exchanges among the civilizations of Asia, also spurred European interest. The fall of the Khans in China disrupted this interchange, as China became once again a land of mystery as far as Europeans were concerned. Europe's upper classes had by this time become accustomed to imported products from Southeast Asia and India, particularly spices. These goods were transported by sea to the Middle East in Arab ships, then brought overland where they were loaded again onto vessels (mainly from Genoa and Venice, in Italy) for the Mediterranean trade.

Europe entered into this era of growing contacts with the wider world network with a number of disadvantages. Their ignorance of the wider world remained vast. To be sure, Viking adventurers from Scandinavia had crossed the Atlantic in the 10th century, reaching Greenland and then North America, which they named Vinland. They quickly lost interest beyond establishing settlements on Greenland and Iceland, however, in part because they encountered Indian warriors whose weaponry was good enough to cause them serious problems. And many Europeans continued to believe that the earth was flat, though scientists in more advanced civilizations knew otherwise; their beliefs made them fearful of distant voyages, lest they fall off the world's edge.

Europeans did launch a more consistent effort at expansion from 1291 onward, as was discussed in Chapter 21. They were spurred by a new commercial and venturesome spirit, linked to Christian missionary zeal and Renaissance confidence alike. They were also pressed by new problems: fear of the strength of the emerging Ottoman Empire, a major new Muslim power, and the lack of gold to pay for Asian imports. Initial settlements in island groups in the south Atlantic fed hopes for further gains. Though Europeans failed to find the gold explorers kept claiming existed in great abundance somewhere in Africa—playing off the fabled treasures of the kings of Mali and some outright myths—early enterprises did have some concrete economic results. The first expeditions were limited, however, by the small, oar-propelled ships used in the Mediterranean trade, for these could not press far into the oceans.

NEW TECHNOLOGY: A KEY TO POWER

During the 15th century a series of technological improvements began to change the equation. Europeans developed deep-draft, round-hulled sailing ships for the Atlantic, capable of carrying heavier armaments than the ships they or most other societies had previously used. They also began to use a compass for navigation (an instrument they copied from the Arabs, who in turn had gained it from the Chinese). Mapmaking and other navigational devices improved as well. Finally, European knowledge of explosives, another Chinese invention, was adapted into gunnery. European metalwork, steadily advancing in sophistication, allowed Western craftsmen to devise the first guns and cannon. European technology, initially employed to produce bells, had introduced heavier castings than the finer Asian or African metalwork, and those castings were adaptable to gunnery. Though not initially very accurate, this weaponry was awesome by the standards of the time (and more than a bit terrifying to many Europeans, who had reason to fear the new destructive power of their own armies and navies). The West began to forge a weapons advantage over all other civilizations of the world, at first primarily on the seas—an advantage it would retain into the 20th century. With an unprecedented ability to kill and intimidate from a distance, the West was ready for its big push.

PORTUGAL AND SPAIN LEAD THE PACK

The specific initiative came from the small kingdom of Portugal. The rulers of this country had just finished driving out the Muslims, who still threatened from North Af-

rica. This threat, the surge of energy that sometimes accompanies expulsion of an occupation force, and Christian missionary zeal prompted the Portuguese to look for conquests in Africa during the 15th century. Portugal's rulers were drawn by the excitement of discovery, the harm they might cause to the Muslim world, and a thirst for wealth—a potent mix. A Portuguese prince, Henry the Navigator, directed a series of expeditions along the African coast and also outward to islands such as the Azores. Beginning in 1434 the Portuguese began to press down the African coast, each expedition going a little farther than its predecessor. They brought back some slaves, spices such as pepper, and many stories of gold hordes they had not yet been able to find.

Later in the 15th century, Portuguese sailors ventured around the Cape of Good Hope planning to find India, where direct contact would give Europeans easier access to

Prince Henry the Navigator of Portugal sent annual expeditions down the western coast of Africa.

luxury cloths and spices, and also to reach the African east coast, held to be the source of gold. They rounded the Cape in 1488, but weary sailors forced the expedition back before it could see India. Then, after news of Columbus's discovery of America for Spain in 1492, Portugal redoubled its efforts, hoping to stave off the new Spanish competition. Vasco da Gama's fleet of four ships reached India, with the aid of a Hindu pilot picked up in East Africa, in 1497. The Portuguese mistakenly believed that the Indians were Christians, for they were confused by the Hindu temples they saw and thought they were churches. They faced the hostility of Muslim merchants, who had long dominated trade in this part of the world, but they managed to return with a small load of spices.

This success set in motion an annual series of Portuguese voyages to the Indian Ocean. One expedition, blown off course, reached Brazil where it proclaimed Portuguese sovereignty. With growing experience and rapidly improving maps, both Portuguese and Spanish expeditions became increasingly comfortable with voyages in the South Atlantic and the Indian Ocean. Portugal began to set up forts on the African coast and also in India—the forerunners of such Portuguese colonies as Mozambique, in East Africa, and Goa, in India. By 1514 the Portuguese had reached the islands of Indonesia, the center of spice production, and also China. By 1542 one Portuguese expedition arrived in Japan, where a missionary effort was launched that met with some success for several decades. In the space of

This is the earliest European sketch of American Indians at the time of a Portuguese expedition to northern South America about 1500. "The people are thus naked, handsome, brown. . . . They also eat each other, . . . and hang the flesh of them in the smoke. They become a hundred and fifty years of age, and have no government."

roughly a century, Portugal had traveled to almost every part of the world; as a Portuguese poet later said, "And if there had been more world they would have found it."

Meanwhile, only a short time after the Portuguese quest began, the Spanish reached out with even greater force. Here too was a country only recently freed from Muslim rule, full of missionary zeal and a desire for riches. The Spanish had traveled into the Atlantic during the 14th century. Then in 1492—the same year that the final Muslim fortress was captured in Spain—the Italian navigator Christopher Columbus, sailing in the name of the newly united Spanish monarchy and its rulers Ferdinand and Isabella, set sail for a westward route to India, convinced that the round earth would make his quest possible. As is well known, he failed, reaching the Americas instead and mistakenly naming their inhabitants Indians. Although Columbus believed to his death that he had sailed to India, later Spanish expeditions brought a firm realization that they had voyaged to a region in which Europeans and Asians had not traveled previously. One expedition, headed by Amerigo Vespucci, gave the New World its name. Spain,

eager to claim this new land, won papal approval for Spanish dominion over most of what is now Latin America, though a later treaty awarded Brazil to Portugal.

Finally, a Spanish expedition under Ferdinand Magellan set sail westward in 1519, passing the southern tip of South America and sailing across the Pacific, reaching the Indonesian islands in 1521 after incredible hardships. It was on the basis of this voyage, ultimately the first trip around the world, that Spain claimed the Philippines, which were to be Spanish territory until 1898.

Portugal emerged from this first round of exploration with coastal holdings in parts of Africa and in the Indian port of Goa, a lease on the Chinese port of Macao, short-lived interests in trade with Japan, and, finally, the claim on Brazil. Spain asserted its hold on the Philippines, various Pacific islands, and the bulk of the Americas. During the 16th century, the Spanish moved to back up these claims by military expeditions to Mexico and South America. The Spanish also held Florida and sent expeditions northward from Mexico into California and other parts of what later became the southwestern United States.

Spain and Portugal: Explorations and Colonies, about 1600

In the first passage, Columbus writes to the Spanish monarchy on his way home from his 1492 expedition. In the second passage, the brother of Francisco Pizarro, the Spanish conqueror of Peru, describes in 1533 how the Inca ruler, Atahuallpa, was defeated.

DOCUMENT
WESTERN CONQUERORS: TACTICS AND MOTIVES

COLUMBUS'S 1492 EXPEDITION

SIR, Believing that you will take pleasure in hearing of the great success which our Lord has granted me in my voyage, I write you this letter, whereby you will learn how in thirty-three days' time I reached the Indies with the fleet which the most illustrious King and Queen, our Sovereigns, gave to me, where I found very many islands thickly peopled, of all which I took possession without resistance for their Highnesses by proclamation made and with the royal standard unfurled. To the first island that I found I gave the name of *San Salvador,* in remembrance of His High Majesty, who hath marvelously brought all these things to pass; the Indians call it *Guanaham.* . . .

Espanola is a wonder. Its mountains and plains, and meadows, and fields, are so beautiful and rich for planting and sowing, and rearing cattle of all kinds, and for building towns and villages. The harbours on the coast, and the number and size and wholesomeness of the rivers, most of them bearing gold, surpass anything that would be believed by one who had not seen them. There is a great difference between the trees, fruits, and plants of this island and those of *Juana.* In this island there are many spices and extensive mines of gold and other metals. The inhabitants of this and of all the other islands I have found or gained intelligence of, both men and women, go as naked as they were born, with the exception that some of the women cover one part only with a single leaf of grass or with a piece of cotton, made for that purpose. They have neither iron, nor steel, nor arms, nor are they competent to use them, not that they are not well-formed and of handsome stature, but because they are timid to a surprising degree. . . .

Although I have taken possession of all these islands in the name of their Highnesses, and they are all more abundant in wealth than I am able to express

. . . yet there was one large town in *Espanola* of which especially I took possession, situated in a locality well adapted for the working of the gold mines, and for all kinds of commerce, either with the main land on this side, or with that beyond which is the land of the great Khan, with which there is great profit. . . .

I have also established the greatest friendship with the king of that country, so much so that he took pride in calling me his brother, and treating me as such. Even should these people change their intentions towards us and become hostile, they do not know what arms are, but, as I have said, go naked, and are the most timid people in the world; so that the men I have left could, alone, destroy the whole country, and this island has no danger for them, if they only know how to conduct themselves. . . . Finally, and speaking only of what has taken place in this voyage, which has been so hasty, their Highnesses may see that I shall give them all the gold they require, if they will give me but a very little assistance; spices also, and cotton, as much as their Highnesses shall command to be shipped; and mastic, hitherto found only in Greece . . . slaves, as many of these idolators as their Highnesses shall command to be shipped. . . .

But our Redeemer hath granted this victory our illustrious King and Queen and their kingdoms, which have acquired great fame by an event of such high importance, in which all Christendom ought to rejoice, and which it ought to celebrate with great festivals and the offering of solemn thanks to the Holy Trinity with many solemn prayers, both for the great exaltation which may accrue to them in turning so many nations to our holy faith, and also for the temporal benefits which will bring great refreshment and gain, not only to Spain, but to all Christians.

WHY AND HOW ATAHUALLPA WAS DEFEATED

The messengers came back to ask the Governor to send a Christian to Atahuallpa, that he intended to come at once, and that he would come unarmed. The Governor sent a Christian, and presently

Atahuallpa moved, leaving the armed men behind him. He took with him about five or six thousand Indians without arms, except that, under their shirts, they had small darts and slings with stones.

He came in a litter, and before him went three or four hundred Indians in liveries, cleaning the straws from the road and singing. Then came Atahuallpa in the midst of his chiefs and principal men, the greatest among them being also borne on men's shoulders. . . . A Dominican Friar, who was with the Governor, came forward to tell him, on the part of the Governor, that he waited for him in his lodgings, and that he was sent to speak with him. The Friar then told Atahuallpa that he was a Priest, and that he was sent there to teach the things of the Faith, if they should desire to be Christians. He showed Atahuallpa a book . . . and told him that that book contained the things of God. Atahuallpa asked for the book, and threw it on the ground, saying: "I will not leave this place until you have restored all that you have taken in my land. I know well who you are, and what you have come for. . . ." The Friar went to the Governor and reported what was being done, and that no time was to be lost. The Governor sent to me; and I had arranged with the Captain of the artillery that, when a sign was given, he should discharge his pieces, and that, on hearing the reports, all the troops should come forth at once. This was done, and as the Indians were unarmed, they were defeated without danger to any Christian. Those who carried the litter, and the chiefs who surrounded Atahuallpa, were all killed, falling round him. The Governor came out and seized Atahuallpa, and in protecting him, he received a knife cut from a Christian in the hand. The troops continued the pursuit as far as the place where the armed Indians were stationed, who made no resistance whatever, because it was night. All were brought into town, where the Governor was quartered.

Next morning the Governor ordered us to go to the camp of Atahuallpa, where we found forty thousand pesos worth of gold and two or three pounds of silver. . . . The Governor said that he had not come to make war on the Indians, but that our Lord the Emperor, who was Lord of the whole world, had ordered him to come that he might see the land, and let Atahuallpa know the things of our Faith. . . . The Governor also told him that that land, and all other lands, belonged to the Emperor, and that he must acknowledge him as his Lord. He replied that he was content, and, observing that the Christians had collected some gold, Atahuallpa said to the Governor that they need not take such care of it, as if there was so little; for that he could give them ten thousand plates, and that he could fill the room in which he was up to a white line, which was the height of a man and a half from the floor.

Questions: What were the main bases for initial European judgments about the characteristics of American Indians? How might the Indians have judged the Europeans? What motives does Columbus appeal to in trying to interest Spanish rulers in the new land?

NORTHERN EUROPEAN EXPEDITIONS

Later in the 16th century, the lead in further exploration passed to northern Europe, as newly strong monarchies, such as France and England, got into the act, and zealous Protestants in Britain and Holland strove to rival Catholic gains. In part this shift in dynamism occurred because Spain and Portugal were busy digesting the gains they had already made; in part it was because northern Europeans, particularly the Dutch and the British, improved the design of oceanic vessels, producing lighter, faster ships than those of their Catholic adversaries. Britain won a historic sea battle with Spain in 1588, in which the British navy and adverse weather routed a massive Spanish Armada. From this point onward, the British, the Dutch, and to an extent the French vied for dominance on the seas, though in the Americas they mainly aimed northward because they could not challenge the Spanish and Portuguese colonies. Only in the sugar-rich West Indies did northern Europe seize islands initially claimed by Spain.

French explorers crossed the Atlantic first in 1534, reaching Canada, which was claimed in France's name. French voyages increased in the 17th century, as various expeditions pressed down from Canada into the Great Lakes region and the Mississippi valley.

The British also turned their attention to North America, starting with a brief expedition as early as 1497. The English hoped, in vain, to discover a northwest passage to India, and in fact accomplished little beyond exploration of the Hudson Bay area of Canada during the 16th century. England's serious work began in the 17th century, with the colonization of the east coast of North America. Holland also had holdings in North America and, for a time, in Brazil.

The Dutch entered the picture after winning independence from Spain, and Holland quickly became a major competitor with Portugal in Southeast Asia. The Dutch sent substantial numbers of sailors and ships to the region, ousting the Portuguese from the Indonesian islands by the early 17th century. Voyagers from the Netherlands explored the coast of Australia, though without much immediate result. Finally, toward the middle of the 17th century, Holland established a settlement on the southern tip of Africa, mainly to provide a relay station for its ships bound for the East Indies.

Dutch and British exploration and trade were sponsored by the government, but unlike the Spanish, the Portuguese, and to some extent the French expeditions, they owed much to the private initiative of merchant groups. The Netherlands, Britain, and France all chartered great trading companies such as the Dutch East India Company or the British firm of similar name. These companies were given government monopolies of trade in the regions des-

ignated, but they were not rigorously supervised by their own states. Thus semiprivate companies, formed by pooling merchant capital and amassing great fortunes in commerce, long acted almost like independent governments in the regions they claimed. For some time a Dutch trading company virtually ruled the island of Taiwan off the coast of China; the British East India Company played a similar role in parts of India during much of the 18th century. Companies in North America traded actively in furs.

ANALYSIS

CAUSATION AND THE WEST'S EXPANSION

Because of their central interest in social change, historians inevitably deal with causation. What prompted the fall of Rome? Why did Islam spread so widely? What factors explain why most agricultural civilizations developed patriarchal family structures?

Historical causation differs from the kinds of causation many scientists test. When experiments or observations can be repeated, scientists can gain a relatively precise understanding of the factors that produce a phenomenon and their exact priority: Remove an ingredient and the product changes. Historical causation is slipperier. Major develop-

French, British, and Dutch Holdings, about 1700

ments may resemble each other but they never happen the same way twice, and so definitive proof that factor X explains 40 percent of the spread of Buddhism in East Asia is impossible. Despite the fact that historians cannot prove definitively that they have their causation right—and hence often disagree—the attempt to fathom the process continues, for if precision is impossible, high probability is not. Further, probing causation helps explore the phenomenon itself. We know more about the nature of Western expansion in the 15th and 16th centuries if we discuss what caused it.

Some historians and other social scientists posit a systematic causation. They look to one kind of cause as the key to explanation in a variety of circumstances. Some anthropologists are cultural determinists. They judge that a basic set of cultural factors, usually assumed to be very durable, causes the ongoing differences among societies: Chinese on average respond differently to emotional stimuli from Greeks because of their cultural conditioning. Some historians, in explaining change, also look to the primacy of cultural causation, assuming that a change in ideas or values leads to other developments such as revolutions or inventions. More common is a technological or economic determinism. Some historians regularly look to technological change as setting other changes in motion. Others, including Marxists, argue that economic arrangements, in terms of the way the economy is structured and what groups control it, produce at least the basic framework for innovations in culture, politics, or family life.

At another pole, some historians used to look to "great men" as the prime movers in history. The causes of change thus became Chinggis Khan or Ashoka, with no need to look much farther. While the "great man" approach is less popular today, as most historians prefer more sweeping forces within which individual leaders operate, it has been dressed up by attempts to probe the special psychology of certain movers and shakers such as Martin Luther. One American historian has recently argued that we should pay more attention to great people as causes because we can thus inspire our youth to believe they can shape their destinies and national development through rational planning and ethical behavior.

Various approaches to causation have been applied to the West's explorations and colonial conquests in the early modern period. There is room, certainly, for a great man analysis. Many descriptive accounts that dwell on explorers and conquerors—Vasco da Gama and Cortez, for example—and on leaders who sponsored them—such as Henry the Navigator—implicitly suggest that the key cause of the West's new world role stemmed from the daring and vision of exceptional individuals.

Cultural causation can also be invoked. Somehow Europe's expansion must relate to the wonders of innovation introduced by the Renaissance. A society that spawned humanistic fascination with the power of individuals to achieve and innovate, to challenge past constraints, also yielded efforts to challenge the spatial limits of Western civilization. Not accidentally, key early explorers came from the same kind of Italian city-states as the Renaissance centers. The link with Christian culture is even easier to prove, for a missionary spirit quickly supplemented the efforts of early explorers, leading to more voyages and settlement in Asia and the Americas.

Political causation enters in, if not in causing the initial surge, at least in confirming it. Through the 16th century and beyond, rivalries among the nation-states helped impel a continuing quest for new trade routes and colonies.

There is also room, however, for a simpler, technologically determinist approach. Europe's gains, in this view, came from a handful of new inventions. Benefiting from knowledge of advances in China and the Middle East, Europeans gained improved navigational techniques (the compass). They also adapted explosives by introducing gunnery with special effect in naval cannon. Along with steady improvements in ship design, new techniques explain why Europe gained as it did. Save in the Americas, where they had larger technical and organizational advantages, Europeans advanced in areas they could reach by sea and dominate by ships' cannon—port cities, islands, and trade routes—and not elsewhere. In the simplest rendering of technological determinism, Europe gained simply through these few technical edges.

Like all determinisms, however, this technological approach raises as many questions as it answers. Why were Europeans so ready to adopt new inventions? Why did other societies, such as China, quickly aware of Europe's innovations, show little interest in imitation? Chinese policy successfully aimed at containing Europe's penetration by political arrangements, especially in granting limited access through Macao; it deliberately scorned any adoption of Western naval techniques. Here a different outlook, plus China's past decision not to expand its seaborne trade, determined a reaction different from that of the West. Technology and culture went hand in hand. Clearly, some combined causal framework is required in this case, with room for individual factors such as the special position of Spain and Portugal after the expulsion of the Muslims.

Finally, the world history context requires the addition of causes resulting from the West's ambiguous position in the interchanges among key civilizations by the 15th century. Europe expanded from special weakness as well as some new strengths. Explorations were goaded by a fear of

Muslim superiority, heightened by the impact of the Turkish conquest of Constantinople. Westerners wanted trade routes that would free them from any dependence on the Islamic powerhouse. They also needed new trading strength, for their economic inferiority required them to pay in gold for costly goods such as spices—hence the greed for precious metals that drove so many early expeditions. The results of expansion changed Europe's economic position in the world dramatically, but these should not be confused with initial causation.

All students of history can sort through the factors involved in a development as complex as the West's expansion to refine the list and try to set priorities. Or they can ponder more sweeping theories about what propels a society to new dynamism in world history. We cannot expect uniform agreement on a precise ordering of causation, but we can expect fruitful debate—the kind of debate that already has moved our understanding beyond surface causation, like the powerful personalities of a few people, to a grasp of more underlying context.

Questions: If you had to choose a single determinism (cultural, technological, or economic) as basic to social change, which one would you pick? Why? In what ways might the professed motives of Western explorers and colonists have differed from their real motives? Would they necessarily have been aware of the discrepancy?

TOWARD A WORLD ECONOMY

By the late 16th century, West Europeans had gained control of most of the world's seas. They were moving freely across the Atlantic Ocean and with some regularity across the vast Pacific as well—the first time in world history these oceans had opened to regular human use. Europe's maritime dominance, in turn, had three great effects in world history: It created a new international pool for basic exchanges of foods, diseases, and a few manufactured products. It created a new world economy, involving of course the fuller inclusion of Africa and the first embrace of the Americas in international trade, but setting a different framework even for Europe and Asia. And it created the conditions for direct Western penetration of some parts of the world through the formation of colonies. The consequences of Western colonization, though immense, were largely regional at this point, whereas the first two results more literally recast the framework for much of world history.

THE "COLOMBIAN EXCHANGE" OF DISEASE AND FOOD

The impact of wider exchange became visible quite quickly. Just as earlier European contacts with Asia, a few centuries previously, had helped spread new plagues, so the extension of international interaction facilitated disease. Here the tragic victims were millions of American Indians who had not previously been exposed to diseases such as smallpox and measles and who therefore had no natural immunities. During the 16th and into the 17th centuries, they died in huge numbers. Overall, in North and South America, well over half the native population would perish; some estimates run as high as 80 percent. Whole island populations in the West Indies were wiped out. Here was a major blow to earlier forms of civilization in the Americas, as well as an opportunity for Europeans to forge a partially new population from their own ranks and the ranks of slaves imported from Africa. The devastation occurred over a 150-year period, though some areas were depleted quickly. When Europeans gained contact with north Pacific coast Indians in the 18th century, the same dreadful pattern played out—again cutting back a vibrant culture.

Other exchanges were less dire. New world crops were spread rapidly via Western merchants. American corn was taken up widely in China (where merchants learned of it from Spaniards in the Philippines), the Mediterranean, and parts of Africa. In some cases this productive new crop, along with local agricultural improvements, triggered substantial population increases. China, for example, began to experience long-term population pressure in the 17th century, and new crops played a key role. Europe itself, ironically, was slower to take advantage of new crops. The use of tobacco, sugar, and coffee spread, but corn and particularly the potato began to win adoption only in the late 17th century, at which point they spurred major population upheaval in Europe as well.

Animal husbandry became more similar across the world, as European or Asian animals, such as horses and cattle, were introduced to the New World. Dissemination of basic products and diseases, then, formed an important backdrop to world history from the 16th century on as a phenomenon never before experienced on such a wide scale, and never with such quick and massive results on population structures in various regions.

THE WEST'S COMMERCIAL OUTREACH

The development of a new kind of world economy related more directly to European naval advantages. Here, in turn, the key point was the ability of the Europeans to dominate most international trade while steadily increasing its overall levels. Westerners did not displace all Asian shipping from the coastal waters of China and Japan, nor did they completely monopolize the Indian Ocean (see Chapter 28). Along the East African coast, while a few European bases were established, Muslim traders remained active and the orientation of commerce continued to veer toward the Middle East. Generally, however, the West dominated a great deal of oceanic shipping, even muscling in on trade between other societies (as between India and southeast Asia). This greatly improved Europe's overall profit situation, because even before terms of trade improved in the West's direction with the development of manufacturing exports, profits came back simply for handling commerce. The longer-range result was increased European ability to determine the framework for international trade, based on disproportionate control of the relevant carriers and the companies experienced in the field.

Europe gained its shipping position, of course, through the combination of technology and force that had propelled its initial explorations and conquests. Experienced merchant marines and superior ship design helped undercut competition from other societies. Naval gunnery did the rest. In the Mediterranean, for example, a Spanish-directed fleet inflicted a decisive defeat on the navy of the Ottoman Empire in the battle of Lepanto in 1571. With this setback, any hope of successful Muslim rivalry against European naval power ended. The Turks rebuilt their fleet and continued activity in the eastern Mediterranean just as India and China maintained a stake in Asian shipping, but they could not challenge the Europeans on the larger international routes. Here, competition for international trade continued, but among European powers, not across civilizations. Spaniards vied with English merchant shippers and pirates, and then as Spanish shipping declined, competition among English, Dutch, and French shippers heated up.

Sheer control of the seas and the bulk of international trade involved other incursions of Western power. While the West did not conquer much inland territory in Africa or Asia, it did seek a limited network of secure harbors. Led by Spain and Portugal, then followed by the various northern powers, European ports spread along the west coast of Africa, several parts of the Indian subcontinent, and the islands of Southeast Asia by the 17th century. Even in China, where unusually strong governments limited European ability to seize harbors outright, the Portuguese won effective control over the island port of Macao.

European-controlled ports, in turn, brought some fortifications, plus supplies for the omnipresent shipping. They also served as contact areas with overland traders (usually local merchants) and so brought access to inland goods not directly within the reach of the West.

Where scattered ports were not feasible because of effective governments that did not want this kind of foreign interference, European influence and the lure of the trade involved led to the formation of special Western enclaves in existing cities, where Western traders won special rights including, often, the ability to regulate themselves rather than be subject to local law. This was the pattern in the Ottoman Empire, where Western merchants set up virtual colonies within Constantinople, and also in Russia, where Western factors (shipping agents) set up first in Moscow and then in St. Petersburg. Elements of this system even emerged in Japan after a firm isolationist policy was launched around 1600, as Dutch traders had some special access to the port of Nagasaki. The point was obvious: Virtually worldwide, international trade gained growing importance in supplementing regional economies. Since the West now ran this trade, the West won special rights of access.

IMBALANCES IN WORLD TRADE

What was emerging by the 17th century was a new layering of the world economy, with key Western nations on top, along with the greater extent and volume of world trade. Leading trading states ruled the roost. Spain briefly held this position in the 16th century as it brought in silver from the New World. However, its own economy and banking system could not easily accommodate this new wealth—among other things, there was not enough local manufacturing to meet demand—so Spain, like Portugal, declined in economic vitality even while continuing to administer huge colonial empires. The more durable economically dominant powers emerged with the second round of exploration and commercial expansion led by England, France, and Holland. These nations pulled in the lion's share of profits from world trade. Supremacy as world merchants brought additional earnings through control of international banking and other commercial services. Furthermore, these nations and some other parts of western Europe quickly expanded their manufacturing operations so that they were able to export relatively expensive, processed goods—such as guns or manufactured cloth—as well as some high-fashion artisan products in return for cruder unprocessed goods, such as silver or sugar, traded by many other societies. Here, too, was a tidy profit margin.

These dominant core areas in the new world system supplemented their growing economic prowess by self-serving political policies. The doctrines of *mercantilism*, which urged that a nation-state not import goods from outside its own empire but sell exports as widely as possible in its own ships, both reflected and encouraged the new world system. Tariff policies, designed to discourage manufacturing in colonial areas as well as to compete with other Western nation-states, actively furthered the new layering of the world economy.

Around the core nations of northwestern Europe grew up a hinterland of other European states that did not dominate banking or manufacturing but might still benefit somewhat from the new world system. Spain, even after its post-1600 decline, continued to produce some specialty items, such as high-quality wool, that won it some benefits from the international market. Italy was another area, now lagging somewhat because of political divisions and the decline of the Mediterranean as a commercial focal point, that nevertheless maintained a middle level in world-economic operations.

Beyond this zone, in turn, lay areas that were increasingly enmeshed in the world economy but on a strictly dependent basis. These areas produced low-cost goods in growing quantity—precious metals, cash crops such as sugar and tobacco (and later cotton) from the Americas, or spices and tea from plantations in Southeast Asia and India. These goods were of course carried in European vessels, with shipping arranged by European agents. In a special, though vitally important case, human labor was the item of exchange. Parts of sub-Saharan Africa entered the new world economy mainly on the basis of supplying slaves. In return for relatively unprocessed products—including human beings—Europeans traded their manufactured items while profiting from their control of commercial and shipping services.

The rise of core and dependent economic zones was a vitally important development in world history in the 16th and 17th centuries. It was not absolutely without precedent, though the West had never before been in the economic driver's seat. Greece and Rome had imported cheap foods in return for processed goods in their relationship with colonies elsewhere in the Mediterranean, as in North Africa; in Rome's case this relationship had even encouraged such excessive farming in North Africa that soil quality was permanently damaged. The Muslim Middle East developed a set of dependent areas in Africa that provided slaves or salt or other relatively cheap goods. In this case, Arab "core" traders also organized the ships or caravans in a pattern quite like what the West developed after 1500.

These had been regional relationships, not worldwide, however, and they usually had less impact on the economies involved than the New World economy did. Europe's New World economy uprooted many older trade patterns. In West Africa the earlier orientation toward trading across the Sahara yielded to a dominant focus on the Atlantic, and therefore to activities organized by Western shippers. Some parts of West Africa suffered dearly from the decline of the old routes.

A SYSTEM OF INTERNATIONAL INEQUALITY

Disruptive as they often were at first, the new world economic relationships proved highly durable. Most of the areas established as dependent by the 17th century still, in the late 20th century, suffer some special burdens in world trade. Core and dependent statuses tended to reinforce each other, making it hard to break out of their grasp.

The core-dependent system should not of course be exaggerated, quite apart from the fact that, as we will see, most of the world was not yet fully embraced in it. While the core areas of northwestern Europe drew great profits from international trade and became increasingly commercialized as a result, the benefits were not evenly distributed. Growing interest in commercial production and manufacturing encouraged the growth of a poor, wage-earning proletariat, juxtaposed with the rising standard of living of great merchants and many property owners. Core status was linked to a deterioration of life for some people in the core as well as in the dependent areas.

In dependent areas like Latin America or the slave-supplying parts of Africa, not all people were mired in deepest poverty. African slave traders and princes who taxed the trade might grow rich. In Latin America the silver mines and commercial estates required regional merchants and farmers who supplied food; not all market activity was directly ensnared in Western-dominated world trade, which means that internal social and economic structures could be fairly complex. Further, there were many peasants in Latin America, and even more in Africa, not yet involved in a market economy at all—regional or international—but rather producing for local subsistence with traditional motives and methods. It was true, however, that important minorities were wrapped up in production for the world market. It was also true that most African or Latin American merchants and landlords did not fully control their own terms of trade. They might prosper, but their wealth did not stimulate much local manufacturing or general economic advance. Rather, they tended to import European-made goods, including (in the case of American planters) art objects and luxury items.

Moreover, dependence in the world economy had implications beyond the economy itself. It helped determine a coercive labor system. Because dependent economies relied on cheap production of unprocessed goods, there was an inevitable tendency to build a system of forced labor that would cost relatively little even when the overall labor supply was a bit precarious. In the Americas, given the population loss due to disease, this led to the massive importation of African slaves, which brought Africa as well as the Americas into the dependent economic network. Also in the Americas, for many Indians and *mestizos*, or people of mixed European and Indian blood, systems of estate management developed that exacted large amounts of labor service and high rents (usually through payments in kind). Systems of this sort not only generated marketable foods, such as sugar, but also staffed the great silver mines in the Andes. While outright slavery and coercive estate systems developed most fully in the Americas and West Indies, more limited examples of estate agriculture, with peasants forced into labor without the legal freedom to leave, arose also for the production of spices in the Dutch East Indies and, by the 18th century, in British-dominated agricultural operations in India.

Forced labor plus the high degree of European influence in economic affairs tended to generate or maintain relatively weak government structures in the dependent areas. Weak governments in Latin America, for example, allowed estates a relatively free hand in regulating their labor force, while substantial poverty among the masses limited the tax revenues available to governments—and so limited the effective outreach of governments themselves. In contrast core states, with growing trade revenues, tended to generate increasing government strength, as in France's absolute monarchy or the nation-state operations of Britain or Holland.

Core and dependent areas thus differed in politics, class structure, and labor systems, as well as in their ability to draw profits from the new world trading relationships. The differences resulted from distinctive trading positions, including who actually controlled the shipping and international business operations, but they also reinforced these differences, confirming the framework with each passing decade. During the 16th and 17th centuries, furthermore, the gap between core and dependent areas showed starkly in population trends. In other words, while West Europe's population modestly expanded, the population of Latin America—hit by disease—declined; the population of sub-Saharan Africa, depleted by the huge trade in slaves, at best stagnated.

HOW MUCH WORLD IN THE WORLD ECONOMY?

The idea of a new world economy arising with the West's commercial expansion is not universally accepted by all interested historians. Some historians object that the world-economy notion distracts us from other developments in places like Latin America or (even more) sub-Saharan Africa, as if Western capitalists were calling all the shots. Certainly many people and activities were not directly involved in the world economy. Still more important was the fact that huge areas of the world were not caught up in any intense contact with the world economy. In these areas the new framework did not significantly influence politics or culture, nor did it prevent vigorous regional economic life. The societies that were external to the New World system certainly did not gain ground as rapidly as the core areas of Europe, because they did not have the profit opportunities in international trade. Their commercial operations expanded less rapidly and they did not have the same spurs to additional technological change in transport and manufacturing. Their lag, at least until the 18th century, was relative, not direct; it did not force any particular response, and indeed the societies involved were often blissfully unaware of the gradual shift in relative economic balance.

Dependent economic relationships arose mainly in areas where civilizations had developed late and in some isolation, with resultant technological lags behind the Eurasian world. The leading Asian civilizations, in contrast, had ample political strength and economic sophistication to avoid dependent status. They had little need for goods manufactured in Europe. They might be attracted to some products brought by European shippers, such as a few agricultural items grown in other regions that were not locally available. But the trade that resulted in return for some spices or artistic products, such as Chinese porcelain, even though handled mainly by Western merchants, was not substantial enough to have a major impact on the regional economy. Most trade and production, in other words, was either aimed at local consumption or was destined for regional markets, carried by local shippers overland, by river, or in coastal waters.

East Asia constituted the civilization that remained most fully and consciously external to the burgeoning world economy. The Chinese government, having renounced large-scale international trade of its own early in the 15th century when the great Indian Ocean expeditions were halted just before western Europe began its surge, was resolutely uninterested in elaborate involvement with international trade on someone else's terms. It did copy some firearms manufacturing from the Europeans, though at a fairly low level. Beyond this it depended on extensive government regulation, backed up by a coastal navy, to keep European activities in check. Most of the limited trade that existed was channeled through Macao. European visitors wrote scornfully of China's disdain for military advances—a Jesuit wrote that "The military . . . is considered mean among them"—and for their addiction to tradition. One Western missionary in the 17th century described how, in his opinion, the Chinese could not be persuaded "to make use of new instruments and leave their old ones without an especial order from the Emperor to that effect. They are more fond of the most defective piece of antiquity than of the most perfect of the modern, differing much in that from us who are in love with nothing but what is new."

The German Jesuit missionary Johann Adam Schall became the official astronomer at the Chinese court in the mid-17th century.

So China opted out, not keeping up with European developments but also not subservient to European merchants. The world economy thus had little to do with Chinese history through the 18th century. Indeed at the end of the 18th century a famous British mission, appealing to the government to open the country to greater trade, was treated to a perfectly accurate rebuff, as the imperial court, after insisting on the most abject abasement by the British envoy, haughtily informed him that the Chinese had no need for outside goods. European eagerness for Chinese goods—attested to by the habit adopted in the 17th century of calling fine porcelain "china"—was simply not matched by Chinese enthusiasm, though a trickle of trade continued. Westerners compensated in part by developing their own porcelain industry by the 18th century, which fed into the early Industrial Revolution, particularly in Britain; still there were hopes for commercial entry to China that remained unfulfilled.

Japan, though initially attracted by Western expeditions in the 16th century, also quickly pulled back. The Japanese displayed some openness to Christian missions and they were also fascinated by Western advances in gunnery and shipping. Guns had particular relevance amid Japan's ongoing feudal wars, for there was no disdain here for military life. Yet Japanese leaders soon worried about undue Western influence and the impact this could have on internal divisions among warring lords, as well as the threat guns posed to samurai military dominance. They encouraged a local gun making industry that matched existing European muskets and small cannon fairly readily, but having achieved this they cut off all but the most vestigial contact with any world trade. Japanese were forbidden to travel or trade abroad, the small Christian minority was suppressed and, from the 17th until the 19th centuries, Japan entered a period of almost complete isolation. Important internal changes continued, including expanding national commerce; but only indirectly, by the decision to halt a previous policy of selective imitation and regional trade in East Asia, had the rise of the world economy affected Japan.

Several other societies remained substantially untouched by new world trade, participating if at all at levels too low for significant internal impact. The rulers of India's new Mughal Empire in the 16th century were interested in some contact with Western traders and even encouraged the establishment of small port colonies, but the bulk of their attention was riveted on internal development; world trade was but a sideline. The same held true for the Ottoman and Safavid empires in the Middle East through the 17th

Japanese artists in the 16th century depicted the Europeans and their African slaves as exotic and unfamiliar.

century; the essential dynamics had nothing to do with the West's trading activities, despite the presence of small European enclaves in key cities. Russia also lay outside the world economic orbit. A substantially agricultural society, Russia conducted much of its trade with nomadic peoples in central Asia, which further cushioned it against West European demands. Finally, much of Africa, outside the slave-trading orbit in western regions, was simply untouched by world trade patterns.

Clearly, the salience of the world economic network should not be read as some sudden or complete globalization of the dynamic of history. Societies that remained outside any intense world economic involvement might themselves be expanding as a result of new use of gunpowder for land armies and superior political organization, or they might stagnate or fluctuate, as with the fortunes of several African kingdoms. Whatever their trajectory, they responded primarily to regional changes, not international ones.

THE EXPANSIONIST TREND

Yet the world economy was itself not stationary; it tended to gain ground over time. While South America, the West Indies, a part of North America, and some regions in West Africa were first staked out as dependencies beginning in the 16th century, the list subsequently expanded. Portions of Southeast Asia that produced for world markets, under the dominance of the great Western trading companies, were brought into the orbit by the 17th century.

By the late 17th century Western traders were advancing in India, as the Mughal Empire began falling apart. British and French East India Companies staked out increasing roles in internal trade and administration. Early in the 18th century, Britain began to apply legislation to India clearly designed to fit Britain's holdings into a dependent status in the world economy. Notably, tariffs were passed against the import of cotton cloth manufactured in

534 PART 4 THE WORLD SHRINKS, 1450–1750

India as a means of protecting Britain's own infant cotton textile industry. The intent was to beat down Indian manufacturing that might have export potential in favor of using India as a market for British-processed goods and a source of relatively cheap cash crops such as tea—or as a source of outright payments of gold, which the British were exacting in some quantity by the later 18th century. Indian observers were themselves quite aware of the shifting balance. An 18th century account noted:

> But such is the little regard which they [the British] show to the people of this kingdom, and such their apathy and indifference for their welfare, that the people under their dominion groan everywhere, and are reduced to poverty and distress.

India maintained a complex regional economy still, with much internal manufacturing and trade; it was not forced into such complete dependency as, say, Latin America. Nor did coerced labor become as widespread. Clearly, however, what had initially been a position external to the world economy was being modified, and on the whole to India's disadvantage.

Some similar tendencies emerged in the Ottoman Empire, though they were less marked. Western traders played a growing role by the 18th century, and pressed steadily for further advantages. The stagnation of technology through the Middle East and southeastern Europe contrasted with steady Western gains. The great Ottoman problem, to be sure, was not the world economy but Russia's rising military power, backed as it was by superior artillery. Nevertheless, world economic forces played an increasing role.

Eastern Europe constituted a final area brought into a growing relationship with the world economy and the West European core. The growth of manufacturing in the West, with considerable attendant expansion of cities, created a growing market for imported grains by the 18th century. Much of this market was filled by East European growers, particularly in Prussia and Poland but also to an extent in Russia. Export grains, in turn, were produced mainly on large estates by serfs who were subjected to increasingly coercive controls including prolonged periods of labor service. The exports in turn were handled by Western shippers who also imported Western-made products, including art objects and furnishings for aristocrats. There was no small resemblance between this relationship and that which prevailed in Latin America, with one exception: Outside of Poland, East European governments were considerably stronger than their Latin American counterparts.

The rise and evolution of the world economy thus set a partial, but increasingly important, framework for world history in the centuries after 1500. Along with purely regional developments, as in Japan, it extended the importance of commercial arrangements in many otherwise different societies. It definitely set up a new pecking order among world societies, with the Western core, a number of external societies that lagged compared to the West, and a growing number of societies in considerable economic dependency. Never before had a single economic system exerted so much effect on such a variety of civilizations, while still, admittedly, falling short of fully determining regional patterns.

COLONIAL EXPANSION

Along with the larger world economic system, a new wave of colonialism took shape following the early Spanish and Portuguese explorations. Key Western nations developed direct overseas empires. Their outreach began at the same time as Russian expansion plus the spread of the Ottoman and Mughal empires, which also had vital consequences. But the Western colonial pattern, based as it was on naval supremacy, was unusual in bringing considerable Western dominance over a variety of peoples and cultures. It also reinforced the larger world economy, for most colonial areas were quickly placed in dependent status, with colonial administrations encouraging the production of unprocessed materials and the development of cheap labor systems. The world economic system did not in fact necessitate outright colonies, for certain areas could be brought into partial dependency while retaining their own governments; but colonialism helped, and many Western leaders believed that direct control was the only sure way of guaranteeing markets for European products and assured access to cheap supplies of precious metals, cash crops, timber, and other vital items.

THE AMERICAS

Opportunities for colonies were particularly inviting in the Americas, where European guns, horses, and iron weapons offered special advantages and where in many cases political disarray, soon exacerbated by the population losses caused by new disease, provided openings (see Chapter 25). Spain moved first. The Spanish colonized several West Indian islands soon after Columbus's first voyage, starting with Hispaniola and then extending to Cuba, Jamaica, and Puerto Rico. Only in 1509 did they begin settlement on the mainland, in search of gold; the first colony was established under an able if unscrupulous adventurer, Balboa. Several expeditions fanned out in Central America, and then a separate expedition from Cuba launched the Spanish conquest of the Aztecs in Mexico. Explorations and some settlements in northern Mexico and what is now the American Southwest followed. Another expedition headed toward the Inca realm in the Andes in 1531, where hard fighting was needed before ultimate victory. From this base several colonial expeditions spread to Colombia, other parts of the Andes, and portions of Argentina.

Portugal moved more slowly in Brazil, initially content with a few small coastal settlements. The need to protect their claim against other European powers like the Dutch,

plus gradual realization of the wealth that could be found in the interior, caused more substantial settlement and a more formal administration.

Early colonies in the Americas were typically developed by small bands of Europeans, often loosely controlled by colonial administrations in the mainland. Thirst for gold drew many adventurers, whose behavior toward each other, as well as toward American Indians, was frequently violent and duplicitous. Where Indian populations were substantial and not totally decimated by disease, the colonial rulers often established only loose controls at first, content to exact tribute without imposing detailed administration and sometimes leaving existing leaders in place. Gradually somewhat

Europeans in Florida during the 1590s scorned American Indians for worshiping a column set up by an earlier explorer.

more formal administration spread, as agricultural settlements were established and official colonial systems took shape under control of bureaucrats sent from Spain or Portugal. Active missionary endeavor, which formed parish churches and a host of missions designed to Christianize the Indians, added another layer of detailed administration throughout the Spanish holdings in North and South America.

France, Britain, and Holland, though latecomers to the Americas, also staked out colonial settlements. French explorations along the St. Lawrence River in Canada led to small colonies around Quebec, from 1608 onward, plus explorations in the Mississippi River basin. Dutch and English settlers moved into portions of the Atlantic coastal regions early in the 17th century. Also in the 17th century all three countries seized and colonized several West Indian islands, which they soon involved in the growing slave trade.

AFRICA AND ASIA

While Europeans for the most part contented themselves with small coastal fortresses in Africa, negotiating with African kings and merchants but without attempting to claim large territories on their own, there were two important exceptions. From initial coastal settlements, Portugal sent expeditions into Angola in search of slaves. These expeditions had more direct and more disruptive impact in this part of southwestern Africa than was characteristic elsewhere along the Atlantic coast. More important still was a colony planted by the Dutch on the Cape of Good Hope in 1652. The intent was to form another coastal station in order to supply Dutch ships bound for Asia. But some Dutch farmers were sent out, and these Boers (the Dutch word for farmers) began to fan out on large farms in a region still lightly populated by Africans. They clashed with local hunting groups, enslaving some of them. Only after 1770 did the expanding Boer settlements directly conflict with Bantu farmers, opening a long battle for control of southern Africa that still rages today in the nation of South Africa. South Africa was exceptional, however, because of its mild climate and scant population. Generally, Europeans were deterred by climate, disease, and unnavigable rivers from trying to reach into the interior. The real scramble to colonize Africa came later.

European colonies in Asia were also exceptional. Spain set up an administration for the Philippines, while the Dutch East India company, one of the great government-chartered trading units that sprung up all over western Europe, ousted the Portuguese and administered portions of the main islands of present-day Indonesia and also Taiwan, off the China coast. These holdings, while economically important, did not compel extensive government efforts or substantial settlements from Europe, though the Spanish in the Philippines also mounted a substantial and successful missionary effort in the name of the Catholic church.

Colonization in Asia entered a new phase as the British and French began to struggle for control of India, beginning in the late 17th century when the Mughal Empire weakened. Even before the Mughals faltered after their last great emperor Aurangzeb, who died in 1707, French and British forts dotted the east and west coasts, along with Portuguese Goa. (Dutch presence, briefly a factor, had declined given the Netherlands' primary focus in the East Indies.) As Mughal inefficiency increased, with a resultant surge of regional states ruled by Indians, portions of the subcontinent became an arena for the growing international rivalry between Britain and France.

The British East India Company had two advantages in this competition. Through negotiation with local princes it had gained a station at Calcutta, which gave it some access to the great wealth of the Ganges valley. Further, the company had enormous influence over the British government and, through Britain's superior navy, excellent communication on the ocean routes. Its French rivals, in contrast, had less political clout at home, where the government was often distracted by European land wars. The French were also more interested in missionary work than the British, who like most Protestants became deeply committed to efforts at conversion in colonial territories only in the 19th century. Before then, the British were content to leave Hindu customs alone and devote themselves to commercial profits.

French-British rivalry raged bitterly through the middle decades of the 18th century. Each side recruited Indian princes and troops as allies. Outright warfare erupted in 1744 and then again during the Seven Years' War. British officials had become alarmed at growing French influence with local princes and troops. They were also roused by the capture of Calcutta in 1756 by an Indian official, who imprisoned English captives in a "black hole"—an underground chamber originally used as a jail by the English themselves; many English officials suffocated. The East India Company's army recaptured Calcutta and then seized additional French and Indian territory, aided by abundant bribes distributed to many regional princes. French power in India was destroyed, and England was committed—without plan or clear intent as the East India Company dragged the government in its wake—to administration of the region called Bengal, which stretched inland from Calcutta. Soon after this, the British also gained the island of Ceylon from the Dutch. Although the British military force remained small, its superior weaponry, including field artillery, plus tight military organization and alliances with many local leaders had proved decisive in battles with hostile Indian rulers. At the same time, more sophisticated naval power allowed Britain to outdistance its European rivals. Thus, from 1764 onward, a British empire in India was truly launched. Along with Indonesia and the Americas, India became one of the great territorial acquisitions of the West prior to 1800.

This Indian portrait of two ladies in European dress illustrates the English influence in 18th-century India.

The full history of British India did not begin until late in the 18th century when the British government took a more active hand in Indian administration, supplementing the quasi-government of the East India Company. Indeed, British control of the subcontinent was incomplete. The Mughal Empire remained, though it was increasingly hollow and controlled scant territory, as did other regional kingdoms including the Sikh state. Britain gained some new territories by force of arms, but was also content to ally with local princes without disturbing their internal administration.

British, and to an extent French and Dutch, commercial activities in India had an important effect even before the full implications of India's new colonial status were worked out. Throughout the 18th century, much of India was increasingly drawn into the world trading patterns dominated by the West. Like Indonesia, but unlike the Americas, India offered a well-developed manufacturing economy along with a vast population and a solid agricultural base. European merchants were eager to exploit India's wealth, but were concerned lest India compete with their own manufacturing capabilities. This caused the tariff barriers on Indian exports. By limiting Indian access to a British market, London effectively reduced India's opportunities in world trade. British-made goods, including textiles, were widely sold on the subcontinent. In turn, the Indians exported gold and also agricultural products, such as tea, which were grown on commercial estates staffed by low-paid laborers and set up so that Europe might shake off dependence on Chinese-grown tea. British agents also took growing command over Indian textile production, dictating wages and conditions to the workers, while the British East India Company exported Indian gold as a payment for their costs of administration.

By the late 18th century major European colonial holdings had spread through key parts of southern and southeastern Asia as well as the Americas. The Middle East and East Asia were untouched, as was most of Africa. In Africa, however, the expanding Dutch settlement in the south was joined by Portuguese claims in Angola (where effective administration remained confined to coastal regions), and several key ports in West Africa were beginning to develop as urban centers, with some conversions to Christianity and other signs of interest in European culture among a small number of urbanized Africans. French coastal holdings in what is now the nation of Senegal, for example, were beginning to radiate a certain amount of influence.

In most cases European administration of African and Asian colonies remained rather loose. Colonial officials were few in number, backed by small armed forces plus the omnipresent navies that could rush in as enforcers in case of emergency. Most administrations depended heavily on deals with local princes; they did not interfere directly in regional affairs or in most village life. Political and, in many cases, cultural impacts were limited in this situation. In Africa established kingdoms still held sway. In Asia, significant conversions to Christianity occurred only in the Philippines, and they were limited still in Africa. European influence was too small, and attachment to established beliefs too great, to effect extensive change. The chief result of colonial acquisitions for the world at large involved the redirection of economic patterns, as the new colonies were fit into the world economy.

Few colonies received much European settlement. In Asian holdings, a few merchants and planters joined the sketchy governmental staffs and missionary groups. Dutch South Africa was unusual in that an initially small settler group multiplied, joined by some new European immigration (including French Protestants) in the later 17th and 18th centuries. Most West Indian islands drew only small European settlements of plantation owners and the like—though in a few cases, such as Bermuda (previously unpopulated), a larger European percentage lived alongside imported African slaves. Latin America drew somewhat larger groups of Spaniards and Portuguese, and by the 17th century their intermarriage with Indian groups created the largest population segment, the mestizos. People of "pure" European stock continued to hold a special place in Latin American economic and political life, but they were a small minority compared to mestizos, Indians, and (in many areas) imported African slaves. Western impact in terms of sheer numbers of settlers, then, was also limited throughout most of the new colonial holdings.

IMPACT ON WESTERN EUROPE

Western Europe, of course, was affected by its own colonial success not only economically but also diplomatically. Colonial rivalries and wars added to the endemic hostilities among key nation-states. England and Holland early turned against Spanish success, with great effect. The Dutch and the English competed, with many skirmishes in the 17th century. Then attention turned to the growing competition among the British and French. This contest had such extensive geographical ramifications, with the Seven Years' War fought in Europe, India, and North America, that it presaged later world wars precipitated in Europe. Economically, colonies supplemented the effects of the overall world economy by bringing new wealth into Europe, encouraging a merchant class, and promoting domestic manufacturing.

There were humbler effects in European society. For example, from the mid-17th century onward, the use of colonially produced sugar spread widely, particularly in countries like Britain with relatively cold climates. Previously, sugar had been a costly, upper-class item. Now for the first time, except for salt, a basic product available to ordinary people was being traded over long distances. The spread of sugar had cultural as well as social and economic significance in giving ordinary Europeans an ability to obtain pleasurable sensations in relatively quick doses, an interesting foreshadowing of later features of Western consumer behavior.

In the world at large, however, the impact of European expansion must be treated in terms of interaction, not simple Western dominance. European penetrations affected the history of key civilizations, such as India, but they did not bring these civilizations even close to a Western framework. Nor was there any intention of doing so, for the goal was economic differentiation between the West and its colonies, not a merger of equals. Even in Latin America, where the Western impact was far greater than in Africa or Asia, a separate historical record must be written in which the Western share forms only part of a complex story. Western colonialism was an important development in world history by the 18th century, in part because of its role in creating the new world economic system, but it by no means dictated this history even in the regions where it was most pervasive.

BRITISH AND FRENCH NORTH AMERICA

One set of colonies stands out from the general pattern in that a fuller development of Western institutions and values took place as part of the colonial experience. In essence, with important modifications suitable to the new location, Western civilization was extended to the Atlantic coast of North America, in French and particularly British colonies, from the 17th century onward.

Colonial holdings in North America—aside from Spain's crucial Mexican colony with its northerly extensions—were generally of least interest to Western colonial powers in the 17th and even the 18th centuries. The Dutch had settlements in what is now New York and New Jersey, but were more attached to their Asian colonies. British and French leaders valued West Indian holdings well above their North American colonies. North America was judged in terms of mercantilism and the world economy and was regarded as a source of crude goods, such as timber or furs, and as a market for costlier imports. But the fact was that the value of North American products was not nearly as great as those available from the Indies or

Latin America, and so much less attention was given to careful controls—a crucial ingredient in allowing some merchant and manufacturing activities to emerge among new Americans themselves.

North America remained relatively unimportant in world history through the 18th century. The American colonies that would become the United States had a population of a mere three million, far smaller than the powerful colonies in Latin America. The value of imports and exports also remained relatively insignificant. Southern colonies that produced tobacco and sugar, and then cotton, did win importance. Patterns emerged there quite similar to those of Latin America, with large estates based on imported slave labor, a wealthy planter class bent on importing luxury products from western Europe, and relatively weak formal governments. Still, in world historical terms the Atlantic colonies in North America remained something of a backwater amid the larger colonial holdings staked out in the early modern centuries.

Yet, partly because unimportance permitted some freedom of maneuver, the extent to which Western civilization was spread to this new land was important for the future. Driven by religious dissent, ambition, and other motives, a number of Europeans, many from the British Isles, colonized the Atlantic coastal region, where Indian populations were quickly reduced by disease and war. The society that developed in the British colonies was far closer to West European forms than was that of Latin America. The colonies operated their own assemblies, which provided considerable political experience. Local town governments were also active, as in many cases were Calvinist church assemblies that gave governing power to groups of elders or wider congregations. Many colonists thus had reason to share with some West Europeans a sense of the importance of representative institutions and self-government. They were also avid consumers of political theories written in Europe, such as those of John Locke.

Trade and some manufacturing developed widely. While most international trade was carried in British ships, merchants in the mid-Atlantic colonies and New England made forays of their own. By the late 18th century some were even trading with China, their ships picking up medicinal herbs along the Pacific coast and exchanging these for Chinese artifacts and tea. Great Britain attempted to impose firmer limits on this modestly thriving local economy, trying to win greater tax revenues and guarantee markets for British goods and traders, but the effort came too late and helped encourage rebellion in key colonies. Unusually among the West's colonies, North America developed a merchant class and some stake in manufacturing in a pattern similar to that taking shape in western Europe.

North American colonists also retained vigorous cultural ties with western Europe, particularly with Britain and France where so much of the cultural action centered in the 17th and 18th centuries. Thanks to Protestant encouragement, an unusual percentage of the colonists were literate, which promoted this kind of cultural exchange. Most Americans focused primarily on religious writings, but even these gave some link to European religious currents including such later Protestant movements as Methodism. There was also wide reading and discussion of Enlightenment materials, and institutions like the American Philosophical Society formed in the 18th century in deliberate imitation of European scientific institutes. Hundreds of North Americans contributed scientific findings to the British Royal Society. The colonies remained somewhat modest in certain cultural attainments. Art was rather primitive, though stylistic cues came largely from Europe. There was no question that in formal culture North American leaders saw themselves as part of a larger Western world.

The spread of Western values in the Atlantic colonies and in British and French settlements in Canada was also facilitated by the relatively slight ongoing impact of American Indians in these settled areas. The Indian population of this part of North America had always been less dense than in Central America or the Andes region. Because few Indian groups in these regions practiced settled agriculture, instead combining hunting with a slash-and-burn corn-growing complement, European colonists found it relatively easy to displace them from large stretches of territory. The ravages of European-imported disease reduced the Indian population greatly. Further, some Indian groups moved out of the coastal forests spontaneously, from the mid-17th century onward, heading for the plains farther west. Various plains Indians began to adopt the horse after Indians in Mexico first gained its use from the Spanish conquerors. The horse (once known in North America but becoming extinct just as the first Indian settlers arrived from Asia) gave Indian hunters immense advantages in killing bison, and, combined with European pressure on the coasts, this induced many forest people to abandon agriculture. Many territorial wars resulted among North American Indian groups. The net result of all these factors was that, while colonists certainly interacted with Indians, learned from them, and feared and misused them, they did not combine with them to forge a new cultural amalgam as occurred in much of Latin America.

By 1700 the importation of African slaves proved to be a more important modification of Western habits, particularly in the southern colonies. The practice of slave-holding and interactions with African culture would mark off North American life from its European counterpart.

British naval power allowed the light infantry to scale the French Fort from the St. Lawrence
River and capture Quebec in 1759.

NORTH AMERICA AND WESTERN CIVILIZATION

On balance, most white settlers intended to transplant
key Western habits into their new setting and managed to
do so. Family patterns, for example, were similar. American colonists were able to marry slightly earlier than ordinary West Europeans because of greater abundance of
land, and they had larger families. Still, they reproduced
most features of the European-style family, including primary emphasis on the nuclear unit. The new Americans
did display unusual concern for children, if only because
they depended so heavily on their work in a labor-scarce
environment. European visitors commented on the child-
centeredness of American families and the freedom of children to speak up. These variations, while significant,
played on trends also becoming visible in Europe, with the
new emphasis on family affection. In other respects, as
coastal colonies became more crowded in the 18th century,
American families reverted more closely to European patterns, as in marrying later in order to limit the pressure of
large numbers of children on property. In basic features of
life, then, such as family behavior, North American colonists and their European counterparts moved from essentially the same base in very similar directions.

Americans were conscious of some distinctiveness. They
lacked Europe's elaborate art and great cities, though they
were eager to imitate. They felt somewhat inferior to the
more-powerful mother countries, but also took pride in
what they claimed was greater freedom (slavery conve-

niently set apart in a highly racist culture that judged by conditions of whites alone) and a more youthful vigor. The habit of looking to Europe, plus the spontaneous parallels between key European and American developments in economic, social, and intellectual life, modified the claims to a totally new civilization. Even when key colonies rebelled against European control, as they did in 1776, they moved in the name of Western political ideas and economic goals against the dependency the British belatedly tried to impose, and they proceeded to establish a government that, though it pioneered some distinctive features, remained within the range of Western political values.

Crucial diversities arose among the Atlantic colonies. The most important divided the cash-crop, slave-holding colonies, clearly enmeshed as dependents in the European-dominated world economy, and those to the north. There were divisions as well between the colonies that would become the United States and those in Canada.

In Canada, the first substantial European settlements were launched by the French government under Louis XIV. The initial plan involved setting up manorial estates under great lords whose rights were carefully restricted by the state. French peasants were urged to emigrate, though it proved difficult to develop an adequate labor force. However, birth rates were high and by 1755 New France had about 55,000 settlers in a peasant society that proved extremely durable as it fanned out around the fortress of Quebec. Strong organization by the Catholic church completed this partial replica of French provincial society. France lost its colony under the terms of the Treaty of Paris that in 1763 settled the Seven Years' War. France eagerly regained its West Indian sugar islands, along with trading posts in Africa, while Britain took control of Canada and the Mississippi basin. Relations between British officials and the French-Canadian community remained strained as British settlements developed in eastern Canada and in Ontario; the flight of many American loyalists after the 1776 revolution added to the English-speaking contingent in Canada.

Many English colonies along the Atlantic seaboard began much as the French in Canada had begun, with grants of land to major proprietors, such as William Penn, who then set about recruiting settlers. New England was an exception, with its early base in Calvinist refugees from religious tensions in Britain. New York began as a Dutch settlement, but was taken over easily by an English expedition in 1664. Whatever the initial origins, however, the thirteen colonies ultimately set up along the coast all developed local representative assemblies with considerable influ-

ence over the governors appointed by the English crown. Economic conditions were considerably more equal than in Europe, and there was no formal aristocracy; only the 23 percent of the population held as slaves stood clearly apart from the mass. This was a new kind of colonial setup, based on significant settlement and displacement, rather than use or conversion, of the original Indian population. This fact, combined with the loose rule of the British crown, assured a trajectory for this part of North America considerably different from that of the other European holdings. One of the first concrete results of this difference came in the rebellious reaction of many colonists when Britain did at last, after its expenses in the Seven Years' War, attempt to treat these colonies more similarly to its other vast holdings in order to win clearer economic advantages and also to recoup administrative costs.

CONCLUSION

THE IMPACT OF A NEW WORLD ORDER

Important as Europe's colonies were in bringing Western influences or a Western outcropping to new areas of the world, the larger development of the world economy stands as the West's most important, and in some ways most durable, incursion onto the world scene during the centuries after 1500. Like all major shifts in human history, the world economy brought both advantages and disadvantages in its wake. Some societies definitely suffered as economic inequalities increased among key regions. Latin America, major parts of Africa, and even the southern colonies of what became the United States were drawn into the world economy as inferiors, with harsh labor systems and political limitations as a result. Many of these economic inferiorities proved to be self-perpetuating, for few of the initially dependent regions have even today fully achieved economic parity with world economic leaders or substantial control over their own economic destinies. Correspondingly the West, ultimately to include much of North America, became a long-term beneficiary in world economic relationships, in a pattern that still substantially prevails today.

The world economy also created new links, mainly through rising commerce, among key societies. Knowledge of new foodstuffs as well as increased trade helped many agricultural societies expand their populations and deal with some problems of scarcity that had previously been irremediable.

Above all, the creation of the world economic framework presented key challenges to virtually every civilization in the world. While not yet a dominant factor in all regions, the world economy, supplemented by the West's military advantages and thirst for colonies, did raise new questions about how to react. Even when the choice involved a new effort at isolation, some innovation was required. The West's new world role, in sum, unleashed an important force for change. Responses varied because of varying conditions and prior traditions, and other changes developed that had little to do with the West one way or the other. Even societies that sought stability above all, however, found their environment shifting, so that some new policies were essential simply to try to stand still.

new trade relationships and their impact on politics and social structure is Immanuel Wallerstein's *The Modern World System: Capitalist Agriculture and the Origins of the European World Economy in the Sixteenth Century* (1974) and *The Modern World System: Mercantilism and the Consolidation of the European World Economy 1600–1750* (1980); see also his *Politics of the World Economy: The States, the Movements and the Civilizations* (1984).

For discussions on where colonial North America fits in this period of world history, see Jack Greene and J. R. Pole, eds., *Colonial British America: Essays on the New History of the Early Modern Era* (1984).

FURTHER READINGS

Excellent discussions of Western exploration and expansion are Carlo Cipolla's *Guns, Sails and Empires: Technological Innovation and the Early Phases of European Expansion 1400–1700* (1965) and J. H. Parry's *The Age of Reconnaissance* (1982). Somewhat more specific facets are treated in D. K. Fieldhouse's *The Colonial Empires* (1971), J. H. Parry's *The Discovery of South America* (1979), and C. R. Boxer's *Four Centuries of Portuguese Expansion* (1969). A vital treatment of the international results of new trading patterns of foods and disease is Alfred Crosby's *The Columbian Exchange: Biological and Cultural Consequences of 1492* (1972).

On slavery and its trade, see Eric Williams's *Capitalism and Slavery* (1964), Orlando Patterson's *Slavery and Social Death: A Comparative Study* (1982), and D. B. Davis's *Slavery and Human Progress* (1984)—the last two being important comparative and analytical statements in a major field of recent historical study. See also Philip D. Curtin's *Atlantic Slave Trade* (1972) and his edited volume, *Africa Remembered: Narratives by West Africans from the Era of the Slave Trade* (1967). A good recent survey of developments in Africa and in the period is Paul Bohannan and Philip Curtin's *Africa and Africans* (3d ed., 1988).

New world-trading patterns are discussed in K. N. N. Shanduri's *Trade and Civilization in the Indian Ocean* (1985) and Philip Curtin's *Cross-Cultural Trade in World History* (1984). A controversial theoretical statement about

1462 Much of Russia freed from
Tartars by Ivan III (Ivan the Great)

1480 Moscow region free; Russian
expansion presses south

1533–1584 Ivan IV (Ivan the Terrible),
first to be called tsar; boyar power reduced

1552–1556 Russian expansion in central Asia, western Siberia

1613–1917 Romanov dynasty

1604–1613 Time
of Troubles

1637 Russian
pioneers to
Pacific

24

The Rise of Russia

INTRODUCTION. World history between 1450 and 1750 was defined by the rise of several empires besides that of the West. New military technologies, particularly the growing use of gunpowder by imperial armies, provided the common means for these expansions. The non-Western empires, however, were largely acquired over land and contiguous, therefore, to their original bases. While they had important economic implications, the commerce of these empires was regional in scope; thus they lacked the worldwide economic influences the Western powerhouses were carving out. Some of the empires, in fact, despite their impressive military and political structures, became enmeshed in the Western-dominated world economy on unfavorable terms.

Of these surging overland empires, the one with the most lasting success and whose achievements changed the map of Europe and Asia most substantially was the new Russian empire. Russian leaders, casting off Tartar domination between 1450 and 1480, proceeded on a fairly steady course of expansion. Much of their new territory was Asian, but their growth soon gave Russia the leading role in eastern Europe as well. Smaller kingdoms remained in eastern Europe, and many of them differed from Russian characteristics in important ways. But Russia was now the focal point, as it became a significant force in world history for the first time.

Russia had been a minor actor on the world stage before the 15th century. Russian culture had developed in close connection with the Byzantine Empire, from roughly the 9th century onward. Russia had also converted to Orthodox Christianity, with its vibrant cultural traditions and rich art (see Chapter 15). Russia's regional kingdom resembled other loose kingdoms in eastern Europe during the postclassical period, such as Lithuania and Hungary. Russia's kingdom weakened, however, as the Byzantine Empire began to collapse, and in the 13th century it was overrun by Mongol invaders. The ensuing two centuries of Mongol,

1649 Law enacted making serfdom hereditary	**1689–1725** Peter the Great	**1762–1796** Catherine the Great	**1785** Law enacted tightening landlord power over serfs
	1700–1721 Wars with Sweden	**1773–1775** Pugachev revolt	
	1703 Founding of St. Petersburg	**1772, 1793, 1795** Partition of Poland	

A.D. 1750

or Tartar, rule had reduced Russia's cities and trade and lowered its cultural and educational levels. Christianity remained, as did the memory of political independence. However, Tartar rule confirmed Russia's substantial separation from activities in western Europe, and also reduced Russian vitality precisely at a point when Western economic and political institutions were beginning to spring forward.

Russia's evolution after 1450 compels our attention not simply because of territorial expansion and growing importance, but because of the fascinating transformation the nation undertook as part of its surge onto the world scene. Building on older East European traditions, including the glories of the Byzantine Empire, and on a strong sense of separate identity, the Russians also entered into new contacts with Western society. The result established new complexities in the definition of the two European civilizations, for more contacts and more outright imitation developed than had been true prior to 1450. Yet Russia, though the first society consciously and by its own volition to mimic the West, did not become Western. It could not, among other things, gain equality within the world economy, nor did it really strive to do so at this point. In this respect and in the social structure that underlay its economy, Russia and most of eastern Europe drew apart from Western patterns during these centuries. A tension arose concerning Western influence—whether to embrace it, select from it, or shun it—that has continued in Russian culture to this day.

The period from 1450 to 1750, in sum, formed many of the characteristics of East European civilization that have lasted into our own time: the dominance of Russia and the formation of a Eurasian Russian Empire; the capacity for change but a dynamic force rather different from that of the West in the same era; the ambivalence toward the West itself. All of these characteristics became more significant as part of larger world history, as the region moved into greater power and prominence.

This chapter deals with one of the great regional empires formed during the early modern period. Russia's rise was novel, and it involved substantial territorial redefinitions not only in eastern Europe, but also in central and northeastern Asia. Russia's development also brought new contacts with Western civilization and a first case of *Westernization*, as Russia borrowed selectively from Western economic and political techniques and from Western culture, while remaining a distinctive civilization overall. Here was an important forerunner of later developments elsewhere in the world, and also a vital new ingredient in Russian culture that continues to play a role.

 RUSSIA'S EXPANSIONIST POLITICS
UNDER THE TSARS

Russia's emergence as a new power, first in eastern Europe and central Asia and ultimately on a still-larger scale, initially depended on gaining freedom from Mongol (Tartar) control. The Duchy of Moscow served as the center for the liberation effort beginning in the 14th century. Local princes began to carve out greater autonomy, and the effectiveness of Mongol control began to diminish. Ironically, the Moscow princes initially gained political experience as tax collectors for the Mongols, but gradually they moved toward regional independence. Under Ivan III, or Ivan the Great, who claimed succession from the Rurik dynasty and the old Kievan days, a large part of Russia was freed after 1462. Ivan organized a strong army, giving the new government a military emphasis it would long retain. He also used loyalties to the Orthodox Christian faith and to Russia—that is, to a blend of vague nationalism with religion—to win support for his campaigns. By 1480 Moscow had been freed from any payment to the Mongols and had gained a vast territory running from the borders of the Polish kingdom, in the west, to the Ural mountains.

THE NEED FOR REVIVAL

Mongol control had never reshaped basic Russian values, for the rulers had been interested in tribute, not full government. Many Russian landlords did adopt Mongol styles of dress and social habits. However, most Russians had remained Christians, and many recalled the earlier times in which Russia had ruled itself. Most local administrative issues remained in the hands of regional princes, landlords, or peasant villages. In these senses Russia was set to resume many of its earlier trajectories when full independence was achieved. On the other hand the Mongol period had reduced the vigor of Russian cultural life—worsening, for example, the levels of literacy among the priesthood. An earlier literary and artistic tradition had partially atrophied. Economic life deteriorated as well, with trade down and manufacturing limited; Russia had become a purely agricultural economy, dependent on peasant labor. In these senses independence brought a challenge for revival and reform.

Ivan the Great restored the earlier tradition of centralized rule, which went back to the Rurik dynasty and Byzantine precedents. He added to this a new sense of imperial mission. He married the niece of the last Byzantine emperor, which gave him the chance to claim supervision of all Orthodox churches whether in Russia or not.

Encouraged by his advisors, Ivan also insisted that Russia had succeeded Byzantium as a "third Rome," with all that this implied in terms of grandeur and expansionist potential. Ivan accordingly entitled himself tsar, or Caesar—the "autocrat of all the Russians."

The next important tsar, Ivan IV, justly called Ivan the Terrible, continued the policy of Russian expansion. He also placed still greater emphasis on confirming the power of the tsarist autocracy, earning his nickname by attacking many Russian nobles, or boyars, whom he suspected of conspiracy, and killing a number of them. This obviously reduced potential competition for governing rights. Russian aristocrats lacked the tradition of political assertion of their counterparts in western Europe, and Ivan's policies of terror confirmed this fact.

PATTERNS OF EXPANSION

The territorial expansion policy focused particularly on central Asia. It was motivated by a desire to push the former Mongol overlords farther back as a reaction to previous invasions common in human history, and thus was quite sensible from a strategic point of view. Russia was a country of vast plains, with few natural barriers to invasion. The early tsars turned this drawback to an advantage by pushing southward toward the Caspian Sea; they also moved east, into the Ural mountains and beyond. Both Ivan III and Ivan IV recruited peasants to migrate to the newly seized lands, particularly in the south. These peasant-adventurers, or *cossacks*, were Russian pioneers, com-

bining agriculture with daring military feats on horseback. Expansion territories long had a rough-and-ready frontier quality, only gradually settling down to more regular administration. The cossack spirit provided volunteers to implement further expansion, for many of the pioneers—like their American westward-moving analogies in the 19th century—chafed under detailed tsarist control and were eager to move on to new settlements. During the 16th century the cossacks not only completed the conquest of the Caspian Sea area but also moved into western Siberia, across the Urals, beginning the gradual takeover and settlement of these vast plains, previously sparsely inhabited by nomadic Asian peoples.

Russia's expansionist policy, firmly set by the 16th century, resulted thus from an initial impulse to chase previous overlords farther away, building on the kind of energy that seems often to follow a national liberation (compare, for example, China after periods of foreign control, or Spain and Portugal after the expulsion of the Muslims). The policy was maintained by the development of a powerful military-settler force and spirit. It was also justified by the heady tsarist sense that Russia had succeeded to the mantle of the great Rome. Russia's Christianity and sense of Orthodox mission also provided ideological motivation, although some of the conquered peoples were not brought into a Christian fold; here, nevertheless, was an expansionist element similar to that operating in the West during the same period. Expansion also offered tsars a means of rewarding loyal noblemen and bureaucrats by giving them estates in new territories, and it provided not only new ag-

Russian Expansion under the Early Tsars, 1462–1598

ricultural areas but also sources of labor—Russia utilized slaves for certain kinds of production work into the 18th century. While Russia never became as dependent on expansion for social control and economic advance as the later Roman Empire or the Ottoman Empire had, it certainly had abundant reasons to continue the policy. The zeal for conquest, the easy geographic access to surrounding territory, and the economic and technical advantages Russia had over many central and northeast Asian groups facilitated the policy in turn. Russia, though not possessed of advanced manufacturing techniques, did create substantial trading connections with its new Asian territories and their neighbors.

Russia's early expansion, along with that of the Ottoman Empire to the south, eliminated independent central Asia, that age-old source of nomadic cultures and periodic invasions in both the east and the west. The same expansion, while driven by the movement of Russian peasants and landlords to new areas, also added to Russia a diversity of new peoples, making this empire, like that of the Mughals and Ottomans, a real multicultural entity. Particularly important was the addition of a large Muslim minority, overseen by the tsarist government but not pressed to integrate with Russian culture.

RUSSIA AND THE WEST

Along with expansion and enforcement of tsarist primacy, the early tsars added one final policy ingredient to their overall approach: some carefully managed contacts with the West. The tsars realized that Russia's cultural and economic lag under the Mongols had put them at a disadvantage relative to the West, whose commercial expansion and, with the Renaissance, cultural drive could not fail to impress. Ivan III was eager to launch diplomatic missions to the leading Western states, as an emblem of Russia's renewed independence and a sign that it wanted contact with the Western network of international relations. During the

These icons depict Mary and the Christ child, one from the early 15th century, the other from 1655. The Russian icon tradition used styles passed from Byzantine art that under Western influence became more naturalistic by the 17th century.

reign of Ivan IV, British merchants established trading contacts with Russia, selling manufactured products in exchange for furs and other raw materials. Soon, outposts of Western merchants were established in Moscow and other centers. The tsars also imported Italian artists and craftsmen to design church buildings and the magnificent royal palace in the Kremlin in Moscow. The foreign architects modified Renaissance styles to take Russian building traditions into account, producing the ornate, onion-shaped domes that became characteristic of Russian (and other East European) churches and creating a distinctive form of classicism. Nevertheless, the tradition of looking to the West, particularly for emblems of upper-class art and status, was beginning to emerge by the 16th century, along with some reliance on Western commercial initiative.

Ivan IV died, little mourned, without an heir. This set off the Time of Troubles early in the 17th century. The boyars tried to use the vacuum of power to gain governing rights for themselves, in an effort reminiscent of battles between throne and nobility in the West. Several neighboring states, led by Sweden and Poland, also captured Russian territory, for they had worried about the growth of a giant neighbor to their east. In 1613, however, an assembly of boyars chose a member of the Romanov family as tsar. This family was to rule Russia until the great revolution of 1917. While many individual Romanov rulers were weak and tensions with noble claims recurred at various points, the Time of Troubles did not produce any lasting constraints on tsarist power, as did the parliaments that were gaining ground in some Western states at this time.

The first Romanov, Michael, did have to accept a few noble claims, for the autocracy was not fully restored until late in the 17th century, but he established internal order without great difficulty. He also drove out the foreign invaders and resumed the expansionist policy of his predecessors. A successful war against Poland brought Russia part of the Ukraine, including Kiev, and in the south Russia's boundaries were stretched to meet those of the Ottoman Empire. Expansion at this point, obviously, was beginning to suggest new diplomatic implications as Russia encountered other established governments and began to move eastward as well as into parts of Asia.

Alexis Romanov abolished the assemblies of nobles and gained new powers over the Russian church. He was eager to purge the Church of many superstitions and errors that, in his judgment, had crept in during Mongol times. His policies resumed the Orthodox tradition of state control over the Church. It also created new tensions within Russian religion, as hundreds of thousands of Russians, attached to the rituals and beliefs Alexis attacked, tried to resist what they viewed as dangerous innovation. The government, in turn, exiled thousands of these "old believers" to Siberia or to southern Russia, where they maintained their religion but also extended Russia's colonizing activities.

 ## PETER THE GREAT AND WESTERNIZATION

By the end of the 17th century Russia had become, territorially, one of the great land empires, spanning major parts of Europe and Asia. European Russia alone was the largest political unit on this continent. Tsarist autocracy, briefly threatened, had been reasserted. Economically, however, Russia remained unusually agricultural by the standards of the commercializing West and of the great Asian civilizations. A strong Russian cultural voice had yet to redevelop, despite important contacts with the West and a rich popular tradition in music and storytelling.

The reign of Peter I, the son of Alexis and known with some justice as Peter the Great, built a number of new features into this framework between 1689 and 1725. In essence Peter extended his predecessors' policies of building up tsarist control and expanding Russian territory. He added a more definite interest in changing selected aspects of Russian economy and culture through imitation of Western forms.

Peter the Great was an energetic leader of exceptional intelligence and ruthless energy. A giant himself, standing 6 feet 8 inches, he was eager to move his country more fully into the Western diplomatic and cultural orbit, without making it fully Western. He traveled widely in the West, incognito, seeking Western allies for a crusade against Turkish power in Europe—for which he found little enthusiasm. He also visited many Western manufacturing centers, even working as a ship's carpenter in Holland; through these activities he gained an interest in Western science and technology. He brought scores of Western artisans back with him to Russia.

TSARIST AUTOCRACY

In politics Peter was a clear autocrat. He put down revolts against his rule with great cruelty, in one case executing some of the ringleaders personally. He had no interest in the parliamentary features of Western centers such as Holland, seizing instead on the absolutist currents in the West at this time. Peter enhanced the power of the Russian state by using it as a reform force, trying to show that even aristocratic habits could be modified by state decree. Peter also extended an earlier policy of recruiting bureaucrats from outside aristocratic ranks and giving them noble titles to reward bureaucratic service. Here was a key means

This piece of art portrays Peter the Great in heroic pose with his subordinates and his military technology.

of freeing the state from exclusive dependence on aristocratic officials, who might maneuver from their separate power base. Peter imitated Western military organization, creating a specially trained fighting force that put down local militias.

Furthermore, Peter the Great set up a secret police to prevent dissent and to supervise the bureaucracy, here paralleling an earlier Chinese innovation but going well beyond the bureaucratic-control impulses of Western absolutists at this time. Peter's Chancery of Secret Police was to survive, though under different names and with changing functions, to the present day, reinstituted after 1917 by a revolutionary regime that in other respects worked to undo key features of the tsarist regime.

Peter's foreign policy maintained many well-established lines. He attacked the Ottoman Empire (no crusade was involved, but more of a power quest), though he won no great victories. He warred with Sweden, at the time one of the leading northern powers in Europe, and gained territory on the eastern coast of the Baltic Sea, which reduced Sweden to second-rate military status. Russia now had a window on the sea, including an ice-free port, and from this time onward Russia became a major factor in European diplomatic and military alignments. The tsar commemorated both Russia's shift of interests westward and his desire to reform Russia in some Western directions by moving his capital from Moscow to a new Baltic city that he named St. Petersburg.

WHAT WESTERNIZATION MEANT

As a reformist, Peter concentrated on improvements in political organization, on selected economic development, and on cultural change. Peter attempted to streamline Russia's small bureaucracy and alter military structure to take Western organizational principles into account. He created a clearer military hierarchy, while developing separate, functionally specialized bureaucratic departments. He also improved the army's weaponry and, with aid from Western advisors, created the first Russian navy. He completed the elimination of old noble councils, creating a set of advisors under his control. Provincial governors were appointed from St. Petersburg, and while town councils were elected, here too a tsar-appointed magistrate served as final authority. The Russian church was placed still more firmly under state control, with the tsar as head of the church directing a committee of bishops who ran detailed religious affairs. Peter's ministers systematized law codes to extend through the whole empire, and the tax system was revised with taxes on ordinary Russian peasants increasing steadily. New training institutes were established for aspiring bureaucrats and officers, which was one way for more talented nonnobles to be brought into the system.

Peter's economic efforts concentrated on building up metallurgical and mining industries, using Russia's extensive iron holdings that could feed state-run munitions and shipbuilding facilities. Without urbanizing extensively or developing a large commercial class, Peter's reforms did alter the Russian economy. Landlords were rewarded for using serf labor to staff new manufacturing operations. The result gave Russia not a Western-level manufacturing base, but a sufficiently independent operation that avoided the need for imports for military purposes. This was a limited goal, but a very important one in giving Russia the internal economic means of maintaining a substantial military presence for almost two centuries.

Finally, Peter was eager to make Russia culturally respectable in Western eyes. Cultural change would supplement bureaucratic training and provide greater technical expertise—it was not all window dressing. Peter was also eager to cut the Russian elite off from its traditions, to enhance state power, and to commit the elite to new identities. Thus he issued edicts requiring nobles to shave off their beards and wear Western dress; in symbolic ceremonies he cut off the long, Mongol-type sleeves and pigtails that were characteristic of the boyars. Here was the first of many instances in which traditional appearance was forcibly altered as part of Western-oriented change, though in this case only the upper class was involved. Of greater sub-stance were attempts to provide more education in mathematics and other technical subjects for the nobility. Under Peter and his successors scientific institutes and academies were founded along Western lines, and serious discussion of the latest scientific and technical findings became common. At the elite level, indeed, Peter succeeded in building Russia into the Western cultural zone, with fads and fashions extending easily into the glittering new capital city. Ballet, for example, initially encouraged in the French royal court, was imported and made something of a Russian specialty.

This first case of Westernization embodied several features that would be visible in other societies later on. In the first place the changes envisaged were selective. Peter did not try to touch the ordinary people of Russia or to involve them in the kinds of technologies or mentalities becoming current in the West. New manufacturing involved labor that was partially coerced, not the more independent (though not necessarily richly rewarding) system of wage

This contemporary Russian cartoon lampoons Peter the Great's order to his nobility to cut off their beards.

labor spreading in the West. There was no interest in building the kind of worldwide export economy characteristic of the West. Peter wanted economic development to support military strength, rather than for wider commercial goals. Westernization was meant, finally, to encourage the autocratic state, not to challenge it with some of the new political ideas circulating in the West at this time. This was real change, but it did not fold Russia into Western civilization outright; selectivity was crucial, and there was no interest in abandoning particularly Russian goals.

Furthermore, the Westernization that did occur brought hostile response. Many peasants resented the Westernized airs and expenses of their landlords, some of whom no longer even knew Russian but spoke only French. Elements of the elite opposed Peter's thirst for change, arguing that Russian traditions were superior to those of the West and that emphasis should be placed on Russia's distinctive culture, not on its ability to mimic. This tension would continue in Russian history from this point forward, leading to important oscillations between enthusiasm and revulsion where Western values were concerned.

RUSSIA IN THE 18TH CENTURY

The death of Peter the Great in 1724 was followed by several decades of weak rule, dominated in part by power plays among army officers who guided the selection of several ineffective emperors and empresses. The weakness of tsardom in these years encouraged new grumblings about undue Westernization and also some new initiatives by church officials eager to gain more freedom of maneuver, but no major new policy directions were set. Russian territorial expansion continued, with several clashes with the Ottoman Empire and further exploration and settlement in Siberia.

In 1762 Peter III, nephew of Peter the Great's youngest daughter, reached the throne. He was retarded, but his wife, a German-born princess who changed her name to Catherine—later, Catherine the Great—soon took matters in hand and continued to rule as empress after Peter III's death. Catherine resumed Peter the Great's interests in several respects. She defended the powers of the central monarch. She put down a vigorous peasant uprising, led by Emelian Pugachev, butchering Pugachev himself. She used the Pugachev rebellion as an excuse to extend the powers of the central government in regional affairs.

Catherine was also a Westernizer. She flirted vigorously with the ideas of the French Enlightenment, importing several French philosophers for visits and playing the patroness of arts and sciences. She summoned various reform commissions to discuss new law codes and other Western-style measures, including reduction of traditionally severe punishments.

There was more than a bit of facade in Catherine's internal programs, however. A centralizer she was, and certainly an advocate of a strong tsarist hand. But Catherine also gave new powers to the nobility over their serfs, maintaining a kind of trade-off that had been developing over the previous two centuries in Russia. In this trade-off, nobles would acquiesce in strong central government prerogatives and would staff the government as bureaucrats and officers. They were in this sense a service aristocracy, not an independent force. They would also accept into their ranks newly ennobled officials chosen by the tsars. In return, however, most of the actual administration over local peasants, except for those on government-run estates, was wielded by the noble landlords. These landlords could requisition peasant labor, tax in money and in kind, and even exact punishments for crimes since local justice was administered by landlord-dominated courts. Catherine increased the harshness of punishments nobles could decree for their serfs, thus ensuring that, for the majority of the Russian people, government remained effectively decentralized despite the tsarist superstructure.

The central government taxed the peasants and recruited some peasants for military service, but its contacts with many ordinary people were limited. The extensive government tradition of empires, such as China or the more activist governments beginning to develop in the West, were not paralleled in Russia, which combined a real monopoly of formal politics by a central tsarist administration with limited functions and personnel in the outlying provinces. Tsarist administrations controlled some land directly, where labor was performed by state serfs, but its hold over estates owned by nobles was almost nonexistent.

Catherine's Westernization program was extremely shallow, though it did represent a real desire to appear progressive in the eyes of Western intellectuals. The new law codes, when enacted, were not really put into effect. Confirmation of landlord power over serfs moved, in fact, in opposite directions to those preached in Enlightenment theory. Catherine did patronize Western-style art and architecture, continuing to build St. Petersburg in the classical styles popular at the same time in the West and encouraging leading nobles to tour the West or even send children for some Western education. But she also sought to avoid contagion from the West. When political turmoil hit the West in the form of the great French Revolution of 1789, Catherine was quick to close Russia's doors to the "seditious" writings of liberals and democrats. She also censored

The Western fashion and Western painting style that won the Russian elite are shown in this 1762 painting of Catherine the Great.

a small but emerging band of Russian intellectuals who urged reforms along Western lines, prohibiting the publication of critiques of serfdom or the autocratic political system. One of the first Western-inspired radicals, a nobleman named Radishev who sought abolition of serfdom and more liberal political rule, was vigorously harassed by Catherine's police, his writings banned.

Catherine pursued the tradition of Russian expansion with vigor and success. She resumed campaigns against the Ottoman Empire, winning considerable new territories in central Asia including the Crimea, bordering the Black Sea. The Russian-Ottoman contest became a central diplomatic issue for both powers, with Russia increasingly ascendant. She sped the colonization of Russia's holdings in Siberia and encouraged further exploration, claiming the territory of Alaska in Russia's name. Russian explorers also moved down the Pacific coast of North America into what is now northern California, while tens of thousands of pioneers spread over Siberia.

Another sign of Russian expansion was the establishment by a Russian trading company of several forts on the northernmost Hawaiian island around 1800. These forts

Russia's Holdings by 1800

and trade around them flourished only until 1817 (when a newly unified Hawaiian kingdom under British influence expelled them), but they raised a hope briefly of yet another Russian acquisition. In combination with Russia's push down the North American Pacific coast, these Pacific expeditions showed a dynamism not matched again for one and one-half centuries, as Russia after 1815 would enter a period of growing internal tensions and constraint.

Finally, Catherine pressed Russia's interests in Europe, playing power politics along with Prussia and Austria though without risking major wars. She stepped up Russian interference in Polish affairs. The Polish government was extremely weak, almost paralyzed by a parliamentary system that let noble landowners veto any significant measure, and this invited interest by more powerful neighbors. Russia was able to win agreements with Austria and Prussia to partition Poland. Three partitions, in 1772, 1793, and 1795, eliminated Poland as an independent state, and Russia held the lion's share of the spoils. The basis for further Russian involvement in European affairs had obviously been created, and this would show in Russia's ultimate role in putting down the French armies of Napoleon after 1812, the first time Russian troops moved into the heartland of western Europe.

By the time of Catherine's death in 1796, Russia had passed through three centuries of extraordinary development. It had won independence and constructed a strong central state, though one that had to balance the local political and economic interests of a powerful nobility. It had infused new elements into Russia's culture and economy, in part by borrowing from the West. And it had extended its control over the largest land empire in the world. In the east it now bordered China, where an 18th-century Amur River agreement set new frontiers. It had pressed into central Asia in the south, and was now pushing against the much weaker Ottoman Empire and in fact stimulating its further decline. And of course it had moved west, into the Baltic region and now Poland; by 1796 it was bumping against the borders of Prussia and Habsburg Austria, with most smaller nations of eastern Europe now eliminated. A tradition of careful but successful military aggrandizement had been established, along with a real pioneering spirit of settlement. It is no small wonder that not too long after 1800 a perceptive French observer, Alexis de Tocqueville, would liken the expanded and more important Russia to the new country emerging in the Western hemisphere, the United States of America, as the two new giants of emerging world history.

DOCUMENT
THE NATURE OF WESTERNIZATION

Peter the Great and Catherine the Great were the two chief reformist rulers in Russia before 1800. In the first of the following edicts, Peter focuses on educational change; his approach reflected a real desire for innovation, Russia's autocratic tradition in government, and its hierarchical social structure. Catherine's *Instruction* borrowed heavily from Western philosophers and was hailed by one French intellectual as "the finest monument of the century." This document, too, showed distinctively Russian traditions and problems. Furthermore, the reforms in law and punishment were not put into practice, and indeed the document itself was banned as subversive by Catherine's successor, as Russia's rulers began to fear the subversive qualities of Western influence following the French Revolution.

DECREES ON COMPULSORY EDUCATION OF THE RUSSIAN NOBILITY, JANUARY 12 AND FEBRUARY 28, 1714

Send to every *gubernia* [region] some persons from mathematical schools to teach the children of the nobility—except those of freeholders and government clerks—mathematics and geometry; as a penalty [for evasion] establish a rule that no one will be allowed to marry unless he learns these [subjects]. Inform all prelates to issue no marriage certificates to those who are ordered to go to schools. . . .

The Great Sovereign has decreed: in all *gubernias* children between the ages of ten and fifteen of the nobility, of government clerks, and of lesser officials, except those of freeholders, must be taught mathematics and some geometry. Toward that end, students should be sent from mathematical schools [as teachers], several into each *gubernia*, to prelates and to renowned monasteries to establish schools. During their instruction these teachers should be given food and financial remuneration of three *altyns* and two *dengas* per day from *gubernia* revenues set aside for that purpose by personal orders of His Imperial Majesty. No fees should be collected from students. When they have mastered the material, they should then be given certificates written in their own handwriting. When the students are released they ought to pay one ruble each for their training.

Without these certificates they should not be allowed to marry nor receive marriage certificates.

THE "INSTRUCTION" OF 1767

6. Russia is a European State.

7. This is clearly demonstrated by the following Observations: The Alterations which *Peter the Great* undertook in Russia succeeded with the greater Ease, because the Manners, which prevailed at that Time, and had been introduced amongst us by a Mixture of different Nations, and the Conquest of foreign Territories, were quite unsuitable to the Climate. *Peter the First*, by introducing the Manners and Customs of Europe among the European People in his Dominions, found at that Time such Means as even he himself was not sanguine enough to expect.

8. The Possessions of the Russian Empire extend upon the terrestrial Globe to 32 Degrees of Latitude, and to 165 of Longitude.

9. The Sovereign is absolute; for there is no other Authority but that which centers in his single Person, that can act with a Vigour proportionate to the Extent of such a vast Dominion.

10. The Extent of the Dominion requires an absolute Power to be vested in that Person who rules over it. It is expedient so to be, that the quick Dispatch of Affairs, sent from distant Parts, might make ample Amends for the Delay occasioned by the great Distance of the Places.

11. Every other Form of Government whatsoever would not only have been prejudicial to Russia, but would even have proved its entire Ruin.

12. Another Reason is: That it is better to be subject to the Laws under one Master, than to be subservient to many.

13. What is the true End of Monarchy? Not to deprive People of their natural Liberty; but to correct their Actions, in order to attain the *supreme Good*. . . .

272. The more happily a People live under a government, the more easily the Number of the Inhabitants increases. . . .

519. It is certain, that a *high* Opinion of the *Glory* and *Power* of the Sovereign, would *increase* the *Strength* of his Administration; but a *good Opinion of his Love of Justice, will increase it at least as much.*

520. All this will never please those Flatterers, who are daily instilling this pernicious Maxim into all the Sovereigns on Earth, *That their People are created for them only.* But *We* think, and esteem it *Our* Glory to declare, "That *We* are created for *Our* People; and, for this Reason, *We* are obliged to Speak of Things just as they

ought to be." For God forbid! That, after this Legislation is finished, any Nation on Earth should be more just; and, consequently, should flourish, more than Russia; otherwise the Intention of *Our* Laws would be totally frustrated; an Unhappiness *which I do not wish to survive.*

Questions: In what sense did reformist measures strengthen Russian autocracy? Why might 18th-century Western thinkers admire reformist tsars? What relationships to the West did the reform measures suggest?

THEMES IN EARLY MODERN RUSSIAN HISTORY

Our attention easily rests on tsarist policies and the series of wars and diplomatic maneuverings that created the great empire. However, the 17th and 18th centuries were also crucial in the development of key features of Russian social and economic life. It was here, more than in the political sphere, that the differences between Russia (plus much of the rest of eastern Europe) and the West were particularly manifest, widening in fact just as political and cultural contacts increased. A key theme running through social and economic relationships and cultural life involved the great gap between Russia's ruling classes and its peasant masses, in a society where only small urban populations existed to provide any intermediary social diversity.

Because of its great estates, its local political power, and its service to the state, the Russian nobility maintained a vital—indeed, unusually important—position in Russian society. In Russia and in eastern Europe generally, landed nobles tended to divide between a minority of great magnates, who lived in major cities and provided key cultural patronage, and smaller landowners whose culture was less Westernized, and whose life-style was considerably less opulent. Despite important periods in which nobles sought an independent political voice, notably during the Time of Troubles early in the 17th century, Russia's nobility did not win a separate institutional role in the central state. Rather, their politics were expressed through service in the tsarist state and the preeminent political power they wielded over the peasant serfs.

SERFDOM: THE LIFE OF EAST EUROPE'S MASSES

This power, furthermore, increased fairly steadily during the 17th and 18th centuries. Again in common with much of eastern Europe, Russia saw a progressive intensi-

fication of serfdom during these centuries, precisely as the West was tending toward a relaxation of this institution in favor of different labor systems. Prior to the Mongol conquest Russian peasants had been largely free farmers, their legal position superior to that of their medieval Western counterparts. After the expulsion of the Tartars, however, increasing numbers of Russian peasants fell into debt and had to accept servile status to the noble landowners when they could not repay. They retained access to much of the land, in other words, but not primary ownership. The Russian government actively encouraged this process from the 16th century onward. Serfdom gave the government a means of conciliating the nobility and of regulating peasants when the government itself lacked the means—financial and bureaucratic—to extend controls directly over the common people. As new territories were added to the empire, the system of serfdom was extended accordingly, sometimes after a period of free farming. By 1800 half of Russia's peasantry was enserfed to the landlords, and much of the other half owed comparable obligations to the state. Laws passed during the 17th and 18th centuries tied the serfs to the land and increased the legal rights of the landlords. An act in 1649 fixed the hereditary status of the serfs, so that people born to that station could not legally escape it.

Russia was in the process of setting up a system of serfdom very close to outright slavery in that serfs could be bought and sold, gambled away, as well as punished by their masters. Prompted in part by a labor shortage in the vast, expanding empire, the system constituted a very unusual case in which a people essentially enslaved many of its own number—in contrast to most slave systems, which focused on identifiable "outsiders."

While Russian serfdom was unusually harsh, rural conditions in many other parts of eastern Europe were quite similar. Nobles maintained estate agriculture in Poland, Hungary, and elsewhere. They used the system to support

The tsar's agents collected taxes from the oppressed peasantry in the 17th century.

their political control and distinctive life-style, as in Russia, though the landlord class was divided between sophisticated, Westernized magnates and provincial, cruder gentry types. The intensification of estate agriculture and serf labor also reflected eastern Europe's growing economic subordination to the West. Coerced labor was used to produce grain surpluses sold to Western merchants, to be transported in Western ships to the growing cities of Britain and Holland, as well as other parts of Western Europe. In return, Western merchants brought in manufactured goods, including the luxury furnishings and clothing essential to the aristocratic life-style. This unequal economic relationship, and its dependence on cheap, manipulated serf labor, was more pronounced in Poland and Hungary than in

Russia, where economic dependence on the West was less complete, but it increasingly defined aspects of the Russian economy during the 18th century.

Serfs on the estates of eastern Europe were taxed and policed by their landlords and were even bought and sold like ordinary property. In Russia, whole villages were thus sold as manufacturing labor, a process Peter the Great, eager to spur the economy but unable to recruit workers otherwise, actively encouraged. Peasants were not literally slaves. They continued actively to use village governments to regulate many aspects of their lives, relying more heavily on community ties than their analogues in the Western countryside. Yet most peasants were quite poor and illiterate. They paid high taxes or obligations in kind, and they owed extensive labor service to the landlords or the government—a source not only of agricultural production but also of mining and manufacturing. The labor obligation, or *obruk,* could take up to one-tenth of the total work time the serfs had, and it tended to increase. This was the labor that produced grain available for export and that serviced the mines and metallurgical operations. Both the economic and the legal situation of the peasantry continued to deteriorate. While Catherine the Great sponsored a few model villages to display her enlightenment to Western-minded friends, in fact she turned the government of the serfs over to the landlords more completely than ever before. A law of 1785 allowed landlords to punish harshly any serfs convicted of major crimes or rebellion.

Peasant conditions formed both the setting for most peoples' lives and Russia's most pressing social issue by the later 18th century. Peasant rebellions recurred from the 17th century onward, but the Pugachev uprising of the 1770s was unusually menacing. Pugachev, a cossack chieftain who claimed to be the legitimate tsar, promised an end to serfdom, taxation, and military conscription, along with the abolition of the landed aristocracy. His forces roamed over southern Russia until they were finally defeated in pitched battles. Pugachev himself was brought to Moscow in a case and cut into quarters in a public square. The triumph of Catherine and the nobility did not resolve the issue, though it did highlight the mutual dependence of government and upper class. Liberal reformers such as Radishev, though imprisoned for their views, kept the issue alive as they interviewed discontented peasants. Radishev, finding peasants barely able to find enough time to work their own plots of land and sometimes tortured to work harder, thought he saw the handwriting on the wall: "Tremble, cruelhearted landlord! On the brow of each of your peasants I see your condemnation written."

TRADE AND ECONOMIC DEPENDENCE

In between serfs and landlords, Russian society offered scant layering. Cities were small, as 95 percent of the population remained rural. (Most manufacturing, obviously, took place in the countryside; hence there was no well-defined artisanal class.) Government growth encouraged some nonnoble bureaucrats and professionals. Small merchant groups existed as well, though most of Russia's European trade was handled by Westerners posted to the main Russian cities and relying on Western shipping. During the 18th century, logically following on Peter the Great's economic development program, an increase of internal trade occurred, which briefly spurred the growth of local merchants, many drawn from peasant origins. But the no-

After the great serf revolt, Pugachev was imprisoned and then executed.

bility—concerned about this potential social competition—managed to reduce this group, and a substantial merchant class with any sense of more than local identity simply did not develop.

This meant that much of the task of economic direction outside of agriculture fell either to foreign traders or to the state. The government thus took the leadership in organizing mining, munitions factories, and related iron-processing works, playing a considerably greater relative role in the economy than was common in the more commercially developed West. International trade was organized by Western merchant companies that maintained important privileges in St. Petersburg.

Russia's social and economic system, though distinctive by Western standards, worked well in many respects. It produced enough revenue to support an expanding state and empire. It underwrote the aristocratic magnates and their glittering, Westernized culture. The system, along with Russia's expansion, yielded significant population growth—Russia's inhabitants doubled during the 18th century to 36 million. For an empire burdened by a harsh climate in most regions, this was no small achievement. Periodic famines, as well as epidemics, bedeviled Russia still, but there was no question that the overall economy had advanced.

Yet the system suffered from important limitations. Most agricultural methods were highly traditional, and there was little motivation among the peasantry for improvement—since increased production would likely be taken by state or landlord. Landlords themselves, though like their Western counterparts they debated agricultural improvements in their academies, had little reason to take the trouble of trying to change. For them increased production meant placing greater burdens on the peasantry, not trying to sponsor new methods. Manufacturing, similarly, lagged by Western standards, despite the important extension developed under Peter the Great; again, cheap, unfree labor, not great technical sophistication, served as the key to success.

Russia did have enough economic strength to avoid the elaborate dependence in the world economy characteristic of other world regions, such as Latin America. It did not need massive Western imports; here Peter the Great's promotion of self-sufficiency in metals and weapons was a crucial move. Russia was able to trade in furs and other commodities with areas in central Asia outside its boundaries, which meant that its export economy was not totally oriented toward the more dynamic West. Yet increasing involvement with the Western-dominated world economy, and at an obvious disadvantage, was emerging by the 18th century. Western merchants expanded their operations. Russia did export increasing amounts of raw materials, notably furs, grain, and timber products, to the West, again through Western agents and ships. These exports were crucial to finance the artistic imports cherished by the upper aristocracy, as well as some other manufactured goods. This pattern bore real similarities to the clearly dependent relationships the West had encouraged in other parts of the world. It was marked also by the reliance on cheap, servile labor, with Russian peasants playing a role similar to that of Latin American *hacienda* workers (see Chapter 25).

There is no need to oversimplify. Russia's economy had strength and diversity. Russia's political independence and growing power marked it off from the more fully subordinate areas in the world economy. Other parts of eastern Europe, notably Poland, that converted more fully to grain exports to the West based on serf labor, fell into a dependent role more completely. Still, the trends of the 18th century suggested not only a growing economic weakness, but also a tendency to rigidify internal labor arrangements for world-economic as well as internal political reasons.

SOCIAL UNREST

Russia's economic and social system certainly generated important protest. By the end of the 18th century a small but growing number of Western-oriented aristocrats like Radishev were criticizing the regime's backwardness, urging measures as far-reaching as the abolition of serfdom. Here were the seeds of a radical intelligentsia that, despite government repression, would grow with time.

More significant still were the recurring peasant rebellions. Russian peasants were for the most part politically loyal to the tsar, but they harbored bitter resentments against their landlords, seen as having taken lands that were rightfully theirs. Periodic rebellions, such as those of the mid-17th century or the Pugachev uprising under Catherine, saw peasants destroy manorial records, seize land, and sometimes kill landlords and their officials. Here too was a current of discontent that would grow in the 19th century, again producing important government repression that could prevent peasant gains but could not prevent recurrent outbreaks. Peasants had the sense of grievance and the tight community structure and group traditions ideal for popular rural protest. They maintained strong family ties, extending among collateral relatives, and they preserved active village institutions—both providing a political basis for action.

By the 18th century Russia had developed what would soon be recognized as a "peasant problem" that limited its economic options because of the inflexible labor organization involved. This challenged political and social stability and embarrassed those Russians persuaded by the standards of the Western Enlightenment that a society should work toward greater human freedom and equality. Not surprisingly, it would prove difficult to decide what to do about the peasant issue, even when the issue was recognized.

RUSSIAN CULTURE AND THE TENSIONS OF WESTERNIZATION

Russia's social organization, finally, had important cultural ramifications. Russia's most obvious cultural history, beginning with the Ivans and their contact with Renaissance art and extending through the more pervasive Westernization of taste in the 18th century, involved growing participation in Western cultural forms. By the 18th century increasing numbers of Russians provided an audience for Western literature and philosophy, as well as art, music, and dance. Russia's main contributions to these mainstream Western styles lay in the future; the first great Russian poets and novelists, using Russian themes but largely Western genres, were just emerging in 1800. The same held true in musical composition, where Russia was to win such an important role in the 19th and early 20th centuries. Nor were there, as yet, major scientific contributions, though here too educated Russians attended to the achievements of the Enlightenment.

The movement toward Western cultural forms was not, however, the whole story. In addition, Orthodox priests and some nobles produced objections, fearing outside influence and arguing in the name of special Russian institutions and values. As one priest wrote to tsar Alexis, "You feed the foreigners too well, instead of bidding your folk to cling to the old customs." The attempt to define and preserve a Russian soul would remain a durable part of Russia's cultural development, building on Russia's undeniably distinctive social structure and on the separate Orthodox tradition.

Most ordinary Russians remained far removed from both Westernizing and articulately anti-Western currents. A substantial cultural gap opened between the elite and the masses. Ordinary Russian culture during the early modern centuries meant the Orthodox religion and traditional oral expressions—the heroic epics, rich musical life, and often witty proverbs designed to explain life's vagaries. The carefully structured rituals of the Orthodox church and the worship of saints allowed ordinary Russians to pray for victories or for protection from disease and famine. They represented the focal point of an elaborate system of festivals, more numerous in Russia than in the West, in which feasting and celebration contrasted with the ordinary work routine. Icon painting, resumed as a major art form after the Mongol expulsion and lasting until the later 17th century (at which point Westernizing currents began to capture artistic creativity), linked more formal culture to the popular currents, as did the revival of religious chronicles written by monks.

Religion aside, peasant cultural values also emphasized the importance of community and an earthy appreciation of life's foibles and pleasures. Community harmony was facilitated by informal village government run by peasants themselves. Most villages worked hard to regulate disputes among peasants, often using liberal doses of liquor, consumed before the village court convened, to smooth the process. Strong patriarchal control over the extended family also served as an organizing principle in peasant life. Unlike West European peasants, Russian peasants tended to marry early, through arrangements made by parents; the new household became part of the larger family economy run by the groom's father.

This peasant culture, though linked to the Orthodox church, was largely untouched by the more formal developments sponsored by the tsar. Westernized aristocrats, as a result, might point with horror at the coarseness and su-

perstitiousness of the peasantry, but there were few efforts to bridge the gap by directly challenging traditional popular beliefs. Here too was a significant difference from the admittedly complex elite-popular cultural mixture in the West during the same centuries. Despite Westernization, or almost because of its concentration within the elite, Russia maintained a distinctive, highly traditional peasant culture into the 20th century.

ANALYSIS
RUSSIAN HISTORY AND THE COLD WAR

It is always difficult fully to appreciate traditions other than our own. It is hard to grasp the meanings of ideas and habits that differ from what we're used to, and harder still, in most cases, not to find the differences we do grasp as somehow inferior. Thus China, in not separating state and society as we in the West deem proper, can be criticized for bureaucratic heavy-handedness and lack of innovation—despite the fact that during long historical periods the Chinese record of initiatives and flexibility is considerable.

Consideration of Russian history amplifies the normal problems of interpreting distinctiveness, for Russians can easily be seen not only as different from us in the West, but also as particularly backward and hostile. Since 1947, and to an extent since Russia's communist revolution in 1917, many Westerners have regarded Russia as an overwhelming threat to world peace and independence. In 1947 a "cold war" arose that pitted the Soviet Union and its East European allies in a tense, militarized competition with the West, particularly with the United States. Diplomatic alliances and arms races stood at the core of this competition, but there were also rivalries in economic growth rates, in international sports, and in the arts. While the tensest cold-war mood eased after the 1950s, and lightened still further after the mid-1980s, it continues to affect mutual judgments between Russia and the West.

These judgments can easily spill over into historical interpretation. Recent rivalry between the United States and the Soviet Union might make it comforting to see Russia as traditionally backward, doomed always to lag behind the West. This backwardness judgment picks up earlier Western ideas, dating from before the cold war, that reflected the West's pride in its commercial superiority. Westerners have long seen Russia as underdeveloped, by the West's own standards. Backwardness judgments were also encouraged by a tendency among some Westernized Russians to hold up foreign standards and condemn their own society on this basis.

The cold-war legacy also promotes a more specific tendency toward oversimplification of the Russian past, as if it were locked into institutions and habits different from those in the West and predictive of what many Westerners dislike about what they understand to be Soviet communism. Thus Russians may be dismissed in cold-war commentary as almost inherently docile to authority or suspiciously closed-minded. Important features of Russian history, such as the absence of a Western-style church-state separation, may be magnified into generalizations about the unendingly authoritarian qualities of Russian government.

There are three controls for these kinds of facile generalizations, none of which oversimplifies in the other direction by ignoring the real differences in traditions—the fact that Russia did participate in a civilization distinct from that of the West—that did exist. The first check on simplistic characterizations of the Russian past involves a recognition of diversity and tension. Russia was not a simple society. It was autocratic in government form during the early modern centuries, but it also had a strong popular protest tradition that demonstrated an ability to shake off deference to authority. Russians did manifest some suspicions of foreign influences, but they were also open to selective imitation; again, the cultural qualities were (and remain) complex. Diversity led to many outright disagreements between Westernizers and their opponents, peasants and landlords, conservatives and radicals.

Secondly, Russia could and did change. The powers of tsarist autocrats varied over time. Reformist interests oscillated, rising and falling depending on the personality of the tsar and the larger social context. Russia after Peter the Great was quite different, culturally and economically, from its 17th-century predecessor. The capacity to change would flower again in the 19th century, as part of Russia's successful industrialization, and of course abundantly in the revolutionary era after 1920. Russia's capacity to change blossomed again after 1985. Since the 15th century Russia has probably been one of the more adaptable of the world's societies, without, however, seeking to become thoroughly Western.

Finally, Russia's relationship to the West has not been constant. The movement of Byzantine influence into Russia from the 9th century onward set a base largely separate from the West. But new and abundant contacts opened up from the late 15th century onward. Many Westerners easily accepted Russia as part of a common cultural and political tradition by the 18th century, because of shared Enlightenment beliefs at the elite level and also because of parallel developments in government. Russian absolutists had much in common with counterparts in France and Prussia. Historical patterns in the 19th century tended to reemphasize some distance, despite participation in a common diplomatic framework. Russian politics, like Russian society earlier, did not march to the Western drum at this point. The nature as well as the extent of Russian-Western distinctions were not constant, for the two civilizations had important kinship. Even in the late 20th century some leading West European conservatives, no friends to communism, argued that Russia was more fully a part of a real European tradition than was the brash, consumer-minded United States.

Russian history, in sum, overlaps Western history without merging with it. Its distinctiveness should not be confused with unusual changelessness. Twentieth-century judgments that try to oversimplify Russia's past to argue that a particularly feared regime, such as the Stalinist police state, is an inevitable expression of Russianness risk being as silly as any other culturally determinist approach that fails to allow either for change or for the diversities of the past itself.

Questions: Is there any sense in which Russia and the West were bound to clash as a result of developments visible by the 18th century? What are the best arguments for holding that Russia is a variant of a basic European civilization, not a separate entity?

CONCLUSION

RUSSIA AND EASTERN EUROPE

Russian history did not describe the whole of eastern Europe after the 15th century, though Russia's expansion, particularly its final acquisition of much of Poland, did merge much of the larger region into the Russian embrace. Regions west of Russia continued nevertheless to form something of a fluctuating borderland between West European and East European influences, aside from the Balkan lands that remained part of the Ottoman Empire. Even in this last case, by the 18th century growing trade with the West sparked some new cultural exchange, as Greek merchants, for example, picked up some Enlightenment ideas.

Areas such as present-day Poland or Czechoslovakia were more fully a part of the Western cultural orbit than was Russia, even by the 18th century. Thus a Polish scientist such as Copernicus participated early on in fundamental discoveries in what became the scientific revolution. Western currents such as the Reformation also echoed in parts of east-central Europe such as Hungary.

It was true that the smaller East European nationalities tended to lose political autonomy during the early modern era. Hungary, freed from the Turks, became part of the German-dominated Habsburg Empire. This empire also took over Czechoslovakia (then called Bohemia). Prussian territory pushed eastward into Polish lands. These developments meant also that much of eastern Europe even outside of Russia was described by the trends of absolute monarchy, largely immune to the political diversities and the new political theories current in the West at the same time.

The decline of Poland was particularly striking. In 1500 Poland, formed in 1386 by a union of the regional kingdoms of Poland and Lithuania, was the largest state in eastern Europe aside from Russia. Polish cultural life, linked through shared Roman Catholicism with the West, flourished in the 16th century. By 1600, however, economic and political setbacks mounted. Polish aristocrats, charged with electing the king, began deliberately to choose weak figures. The central government became powerless, while aristocrats ran roughshod over impoverished peasants. As in Russia, urban centers, and thus a merchant class, were lacking. The aristocratic parliament vetoed any reform efforts. As Polish power dwindled, it became ripe for the division by Prussia, the Habsburgs, and particularly Russia, which erased it as an independent country.

Separate cultures survived in the East European borderlands, even if political independence did not. Poles, Czechs, Hungarians, and the southern Slavs under Turkish rule preserved prior religion, language, and folkways, refusing assimilation into the larger empires that had swallowed them up.

At the same time, however, eastern Europe shared with Russia key social and economic patterns that distinguished the region as a whole from western Europe. The landed aristocracy loomed large. Most agriculture was controlled by large estates, with rigid serfdom providing the labor in a pattern pervasive from Prussia eastward through the Russian steppes and southward through Hungary and the Balkans. Western merchants gained increasing roles in eastern Europe because a native commercial class and a significant urban culture were largely absent—stronger in some cases than in Russia but far weaker than in the West.

Despite vital diversities, then, something of an East European economy had emerged by the 18th century that would significantly shape subsequent political and social change, despite internal political and cultural boundaries. For its part, Russia had become more than an East European power. Its achievement of empire was one of the key developments of the centuries after 1500. Here, Russia deserves comparison not so much with the West, whose imperial attainments were rather different, but with the other

great landed empires of the period. Like the Mughals or Ottomans, Russia established rule through its armies. Also like these empires, the Russian Empire embraced a number of diverse, indeed potentially conflicting cultures. Expansion into Siberia brought contact with relatively small hunting-and-gathering groups. The movement into southern and central Asia gained Russia its large Muslim minority and a number of distinct racial groups. Fewer Russians moved into central Asia than into Siberia, a fact that sustained great diversity within this multinational empire. Finally, penetration farther into Europe produced control over several different Slavic minorities and some Germans. Many of these minorities were Catholic, not Orthodox Christian.

Russia's push westward also brought it a large Jewish population. Jews, excluded from Russia for religious reasons until the 18th century, were finally admitted as Russia pushed West. Catherine promised some tolerance but, bowing to Christian prejudices, did not allow Jews in key centers such as Moscow. Here, as in other cases, Russia's diversity suggested tensions for the future. Jews did fan out into many other parts of Russia, becoming an important, though often deeply resented, minority element of the multinational empire.

The multicultural character of the new empire proved a lasting feature. Yet Russia's fate obviously differed from that of other such empires in the early modern period, such as the Ottomans or the Mughals. The Russian Empire lasted longer, its vigor lasted longer still. The ethnic Russian presence was larger, for Ottomans and Mughals ruled over a majority of people from other cultures (the Arabs in the Ottoman Empire) or religions (the Hindus in the Mughal realm). Ethnic Russians with their high birthrate formed a larger percentage of the empire's total population. Russia also actively pushed pioneer settlements, which brought Russian presence, and in some cases dominance, in many of the new regions. Economic development, for all its hesitations, was also backed more vigorously, which gave the new empire some coherence and no small energy. Russia, in sum, became not only the new boy on the imperial block during the centuries after 1500, but one of history's unusual imperial success stories—still going strong, though much changed, at least until the end of the 20th century.

The early modern period was obviously a crucial formative era for Russia and for its role in Asia and Europe, despite important traditions from before the Mongol invasions. Tensions and ambiguities in Russia's contacts with the West, created in this period, continue to define Russian society. Questions raised by a multinational empire of the sort Russia so successfully created in this same period rose again to haunt the Russian state at the end of the 20th century. Issues of economic development, and whether or not to define it in strictly Russian terms, were recast in the 20th century, but they retained some of the overtones initially imparted by Peter the Great. Because of the importance Russia also began to acquire in world affairs in the early modern period, Russian questions could easily become issues affecting many other societies around the world.

FURTHER READINGS

For excellent survey coverage on this period, plus additional bibliography, see Nicholas Riasanovsky's *History of Russia* (4th ed., 1984). Two excellent source collections for this vital period of Russian history are T. Riha, ed., *Readings in Russian Civilization*. Vol. II, *Imperial Russia 1700–1917* (1969) and Basil Dmytryshyn's *Imperial Russia: A Sourcebook 1700–1917* (1967).

On important regimes, see J. L. I. Fennell's *Ivan the Great of Moscow* (1961), R. Massie's *Peter the Great* (1981), and N. V. Riasanovsky's *The Image of Peter the Great in Russian History and Thought* (1985). This last book is a very interesting interpretive effort. On Catherine, see I. de Madariaga's *Russia in the Age of Catherine the Great* (1981).

Three good studies deal with cultural history: H. Rogger's *National Consciousness in Eighteenth Century Russia* (1963), Marc Raeff's *Origins of the Russian Intelligentsia: The Eighteenth Century Nobility* (1966), and Marc Raeff, ed., *Russian Intellectual History* (1986).

For economic and social history, A. Kahan's *The Knout and the Plowshare: Economic History of Russia in the 18th Century* (1985) is a major treatment. For the vital peasant question, see Jerome Blum's *Lord and Peasant in Russia from the Ninth to the Nineteenth Century* (1961); see also Richad Hellie's *Slavery in Russia, 1450–1725* (1982). For an analytical overview, see Marc Raeff's *Understanding Imperial Russia; State and Society in the Old Regime* (1984).

1493–1520 Exploration and settlement in the Caribbean

1494 Treaty of Tordesillas

1540–1542 Coronado explores southwestern United States

1519–1524 Cortés leads conquest of Mexico

1580–1640 Spain and Portugal united under same rulers

1549 Royal government established in Brazil

1492 Fall of Granada, last Muslim kingdom in Spain; expulsion of the Jews; Columbus landfall in the Caribbean

1541 Santiago, Chile founded

1493 Columbus's second expedition; beginnings of settlement in the Indies

1630 1654 Dutch capture northeastern Brazil

1500 Cabral lands in Brazil   **1533** Cuzco, Peru falls to Francisco Pizarro

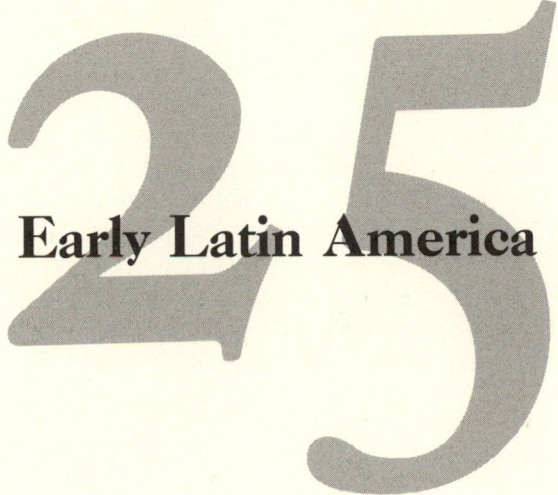

Early Latin America

INTRODUCTION. As Russia began to define its new empire in eastern Europe and Asia during the 15th and 16th centuries, other empires took shape in Central and South America—created and controlled by Spain and Portugal. In contrast to Russia, these were dependent empires, and both their economies and their cultural relationships to the West differed accordingly.

The new Latin American empires, like Russia by the 18th century, maintained special contacts with the West—and, as with Russia, this fact has continued to shape key characteristics to the present day. Whereas Russian leaders decided what to borrow, however, Western forms were simply imposed on many Latin American people. The new empires were examples also of the potency of gunpowder, which the conquerors used to establish their sway. Spanish and Portuguese conquerors, however, had advantages besides gunpowder: metal equipment, horses, and the fearsome power of European diseases. This explains why the conquerors were able to force highly unequal relationships on the subject populations.

Latin America was immediately drawn into the New World economy, playing a central role in providing silver, new crops, and other goods. The new hierarchy of world economic relationships, correspondingly, shaped conditions in this new civilization for several centuries.

The societies of Latin America also generated important new political and cultural forms, as conquering Spaniards and Portuguese mixed with Native Americans and their earlier civilization forms, and were influenced by imported African slaves. The formative period for Latin American civilization—the newest on the world's list—extended from initial contacts in the 1490s through the 18th century when colonial structures began to decline. This span ran slightly longer than the early modern period in Europe—

1695 Gold discovered in Brazil

1702–1713 War of the Spanish succession; Bourbon dynasty rules Spain

1654 English take Jamaica

1759–1788 Charles III rules Spain; Bourbon reforms

1763 Brazilian capital moved to Rio de Janeiro

1767 Jesuits expelled from Spanish America

1756–1763 Seven Years' War

1755–1776 Marquis of Pombal, Prime minister of Portugal

1759 Jesuits expelled from Brazil

1781 Comunero revolt in New Granada; Tupac Amaru rebellion in Peru

1788 Conspiracy for independence in Minas Gerais, Brazil the early 1800s, rather than 1750, is the appropriate terminal point. This period also embraced a number of discrete stages, from raw conquest to growing economic and political complexity by the 18th century.

The landfall of Columbus on a Caribbean island in October 1492 began the process of conquest and settlement of what was to become Latin America. New societies, created by the intrusion of Spaniards and Portuguese and by the incorporation or destruction of indigenous Native Americans and their cultures, arose throughout the American continents. Both Europeans and Indians drew heavily on their previous experiences and understandings as they grappled with the problems created by their encounter with each other. Much of what the Iberians (the Spaniards and Portuguese) did in the Americas followed the patterns and examples of their European traditions. The life-styles of Indians who survived, although battered and profoundly transformed, showed a vitality and resiliency that shaped the subsequent societies in many ways. What resulted drew on European and Indian precedents, but was something new—the world's latest addition to the list of distinctive civilizations.

The various European nations essentially sought the same ends in the New World—economic gain and social mobility. The Portuguese, English, Spanish, and French all created large landed estates, or *plantations*, worked by coerced laborers, ultimately African slaves, wherever tropical conditions and European demand combined to make such enterprises feasible. The Europeans exploited precious metals when they were discovered, and those Europeans who did not find the metals followed rumors of gold or emeralds hopefully. The goals and desires formed similar plots, but the stages, settings, and actors differed.

The chronology of events in the areas conquered and colonized by the Spaniards and Portuguese falls roughly into three periods during the early modern centuries. These are: an era of conquest from 1492 to about 1570 during which the main lines of administration and economy were set out; a second phase of consolidation and maturity to about 1700 in which the colonial institutions and societies took their definite form; and finally, during the 18th century, a period of reform and reorganization in both Spanish America and Portuguese Brazil that intensified the colonial relationship and planted the seeds of dissatisfaction and revolt.

SPANIARDS AND PORTUGUESE: BACKGROUND TO CONQUEST

The peoples who inhabited the Iberian peninsula had long lived at the frontier of Mediterranean Europe. The peninsula had known many inhabitants—Phoenicians,

Carthaginians, Romans, and Goths—and during the Middle Ages it had become a cultural frontier between Christianity and Islam. Conflict along that frontier created a strong tradition of military conquest and rule over peoples of other beliefs and customs—a tradition that became part of the Iberian experience. A number of Christian kingdoms had emerged. Of these the most important were Portugal on the Atlantic coast, and in the center of the peninsula, Castile, the largest of all. By the mid-15th century, the religious and ethnic diversity in these kingdoms was being submerged by a process of political and religious unification. In 1452, the marriage of Ferdinand—the Prince of Aragon—and Isabella—the Princess of Castile—brought the crowns of Aragon and Castile into close alliance, and in 1492 with the fall Granada, the last Muslim kingdom, the cross had triumphed throughout the peninsula. Political savvy and religious fervor moved Isabella. Immediately upon the fall of Granada, Isabella (now Queen of Castile) ordered the Jews of her realm to convert or leave the country. As many as 200,000 may have left, severely disrupting some aspects of the Castilian economy. It was also in 1492, with the Granada War at an end and religious unification established, that Isabella and Ferdinand were willing to support the project of a Genoese mariner named Christopher Columbus, who hoped to reach the East Indies by sailing westward around the globe.

IBERIAN SOCIETY AND TRADITION

Spanish and Portuguese society had a number of distinctive features that would become part of the American ventures. Like many Mediterranean people they were heavily urban, with many peasants not scattered across the countryside but living in small towns and villages. The desire to live in an urban setting helped set up a pattern of Spanish cities amid a largely Indian countryside in many parts of the Americas.

Emphasis on nobility ran strong in Iberian society, and many Spanish and Portuguese commoners who came to America as conquerors sought to recreate themselves as a new nobility, with Indians as their serfs. Few former Iberian peasants wanted a life of farming in the New World. Patriarchal ideals were also heavily emphasized, though women had an active role in family life. The patriarchal family was readily adapted to Latin America, where large estates and grants of Indian laborers, or *encomiendas*, provided the framework for relations based on economic dominance. The Iberian peninsula maintained a tradition of holding slaves—part of its experience as an ethnic frontier—in contrast to most of medieval Europe, and African slaves had been imported from the trans-Sahara trade. The extension of slavery to America built upon this tradition.

Portugal and Castile were well launched by the 15th century on political centralization and the creation of a professional bureaucracy. Legally trained bureaucrats formed the basis of Iberian rule in Latin America in a process worth comparing with China and other great empires. Religion and the Church served as the other pillar of Iberian politics; close links between Church and state resulted from the reconquest of the peninsula from the Muslims, and these links, including royal nomination of Church officials, were also extended to the New World.

Spanish and particularly Portuguese merchants also shaped traditions that became relevant in the American colonies. Portugal had been pushing down the African coast since 1415, establishing forts for commercial exchange rather than outright colonies. In the Atlantic islands, however, more extensive estates were established, leading to a slave trade with Africa and a highly commercial agricultural system based on sugar. Brazil would extend this pattern, starting out as a trade factory but then shifting, as in the Atlantic islands, to plantation agriculture.

THE CONQUEST OF THE NEW WORLD

The period from 1492 to about 1600 witnessed a remarkable spurt of human energy in destruction and creation. During roughly a century, vast areas of two continents and millions of people were brought under European control. The bases of an economic system that linked these areas to an emerging Atlantic economy were created, and a flow of immigration and commerce was set in motion. These processes were accompanied and made

possible by the conquest and destruction of many Indian societies and the transformation of others, as well as by the introduction in some places of forced immigrants, the African slaves. Mexico and Peru, with their large sedentary populations and mineral resources, attracted the Spaniards and became, after the short initial Caribbean stage, the focus of immigration and institution building. Other conquests radiated outward from the Peruvian and Mexican centers.

THE CARIBBEAN CRUCIBLE

The Caribbean experience served Spain as a model for its actions elsewhere in the Americas. From this crucible the foundations of the empire were forged. After Columbus's original voyage in 1492, a return expedition in the next year established a colony on the island of Santo Domingo (Hispaniola). From there and from Spain, expeditions carried out new explorations and conquests. Puerto Rico (1508) and Cuba (1511) fell under Spanish control and by 1513 settlements existed in Panama and on the northern coast of South America.

In the Caribbean, Columbus's attempt to keep the Mediterranean and West African model of trade forts, private investment under royal contract, and a trade in gold and slaves proved unworkable, and a more extensive colonization pattern quickly developed. The agricultural Taino Indians of the islands provided enough surplus labor to make their distribution to individual Spaniards feasible, and thus began what would become the encomienda, or grants of Indians to individual Spaniards in a kind of serfdom. Gold

St. Augustine, Florida, the oldest city in the United States (founded in 1565), reflects its Spanish heritage in the central plaza and the checkerboard layout that can be seen in this 18th-century engraving.

hunting, slaving, and European diseases rapidly depopulated the islands, and there was little left there to hold Spanish attention by the time of Hernán Cortés's conquest of Mexico. A few strongly fortified ports, such as Havana, San Juan, and Santo Domingo, guarded Spain's commercial lifeline, but on the whole the Caribbean became a colonial backwater for the next two centuries until sugar and slaves provided the basis of its resurgence.

In the short period of 40 years between the first voyage of Columbus and the conquest of Mexico by Cortés, the Caribbean served as a testing ground. Iberian-style cities were established. Spaniards had to adapt them to American realities. Hurricanes and Indians caused a number of towns to be moved or abandoned, but the New World also provided opportunities to implant new ideas and forms. Unlike cities in Europe, Spanish American cities were usually laid out according to a grid plan or checkerboard form with the town hall, major church, and governor's palace in the central plaza. Spanish conquerors and administrators applied classical models and rational town planning ideas to the new situation. Using the Caribbean experience, the model of town foundation was carried throughout the Americas, and in 1570 Spain issued a basic set of instructions for setting up towns. Conquest came to imply settlement.

A move from the private control of Columbus and his family to royal administration was marked by the creation of administrative institutions: the governorship, the treasury office, and the royal court of appeals, or *audiencia*, staffed by professional magistrates. Spanish legalism was part of the institutional transfer. Notaries accompanied new expeditions, and a body of laws was developed based on those of Spain and augmented by American experience. The Church, represented at first by individual priests and then by contingents of missionaries such as the Dominicans, participated in the enterprise and by 1530, a cathedral was being built on Hispaniola with a university to follow. The new area had to be provisioned and its commerce regularized. The Genoese participated in this process at first, but by the turn of the century the Board of Trade (*Casa de Contratación*) was operating in Seville and Spanish merchants were fully involved.

Rumors and hopes stimulated immigration from Spain, and by the 1510s this included larger numbers of Spanish women. Also, Spanish and Italian merchants began to import African slaves to work on the few sugar plantations that operated on the islands. The arrival of both Spanish women and African slaves represented a shift from an area of conquest to one of settlement. The same process would be noted elsewhere in the Indies. The gold hunting phase had given out in the islands by the 1520s and was replaced by the establishment of ranches and sugar plantations. The

adventurous, the disappointed, and the greedy repeated the pattern. Expeditions spun off in new directions, repeating the processes already set in motion, although in each case drawing on the experience already gained.

Among these experiences was the virtual annihilation of the Indians of the Caribbean. Depopulation of the laboring population led to slaving in other islands, and in a sadly remarkable period of 30 years or so, most of the Indian population had died or been killed. The fewer, less sedentary, and more warlike Caribs of the lesser Antilles (whom the Spanish accused of cannibalism and who were thus always subject to enslavement) held out longer because their islands were less attractive to European settlement. The pattern of European concentration on areas of denser Indian populations was already forming. The destruction of the Indians led to further expeditions toward the mainland; it also caused a transformation of the islands' economies toward activities like sugar production, which called forth the African slave trade.

As early as the 1510s the mistreatment and destruction of the Indians led to attempts by clerics and royal administrators to end the worst abuses. The activities of men such as the Dominican friar Bartolomé de Las Casas (1484–1566), a conquistador turned priest, initiated the struggle for justice that was also to repeat itself elsewhere in the Indies. He became an ardent supporter of conversion through kindness and peaceful means, an opponent of forced labor, and an advocate of Indian rights. His position actually won some support from a Spanish crown interested in limiting the power of the emerging conquistador aristocracy.

Expeditions, formed by a cross section of Spanish society, leapt from island to island. Leadership was personalist, investment was private, and division of spoils was made on a shares basis. An expedition's successful leader quickly sought to ignore the authority of whomever had sent him out and asked for direct power in the king's name. By the time Cortés looked upon the Aztec capital of Tenochtitlan, the techniques of conquest and settlement were already well established. Where the Indian peoples and cultures were more resilient, their impact on the subsequent societies was greater than in the Caribbean, but the process of contact was similar.

By the time of the conquest of Mexico in the 1520s and Peru in the 1530s, all the elements of the colonial system of Latin America were in place. Even in Brazil, which the Portuguese began to exploit after 1500, a period of bartering with the Indians was slowly replaced by increasing royal control and development of a sugar plantation economy. There, as in the Caribbean, Indian resistance and subsequent depopulation led to the importation of African laborers.

CONQUESTS AND CONQUERORS

No other race can be found that can penetrate through such rugged lands, such dense forests, such great mountains and deserts and cross such broad rivers as the Spaniards have done . . . solely by the valor of their persons and the forcefulness of their breed.

These words, written in the 16th century by Pedro Cieza de Leon, one of the conquistadores of Peru, underlined the pride of the Spaniards in their accomplishments. In less than a century, a large portion of two continents and islands in an inland sea, inhabited by millions of people, was brought under Spanish control. Spanish expeditions, usually from 50 to 500 men, provided the spearhead of conquest, and in their wake followed the women, missionaries, administrators, and artisans who began to form civil society.

The conquest was not a unified movement, but rather a series of individual initiatives that usually operated with government approval. After Columbus's settlement of Santo Domingo, the conquest of the Americas was two-pronged: One prong was directed toward Mexico and the other aimed at South America. From Santo Domingo, expeditions moved to Cuba and then on to Mexico.

We can use the well-documented campaign in Mexico as an example of the conquest. In 1519 Hernán Cortés, a man of some education and considerable ability as a leader, led an expedition of some 600 men to the coast of Mexico. After hearing rumors of a great kingdom in the interior, he destroyed his ships to leave no route of retreat, established a base at Veracruz on the coast, and then began to strike inland. A number of pitched battles were fought with towns subject to the Aztec Empire, but after gaining these victories, Cortés was able to enlist the Indians' support against their overlords. With the help of the Indian allies, Cortes eventually reached the great Aztec island capital of Tenochtitlan. By a combination of deception, boldness, courage, ruthlessness, and luck, the Aztec emperor Moctezuma II was made a captive and then killed. Cortés and his followers were forced to flee the Aztec capital and retreat toward the coast, but with the help of the Aztecs' traditional enemies, Tenochtitlan was cut off and besieged. Although the Aztec confederacy put up a stiff resistance, disease, starvation, and battle brought the city down. The Aztec poets later remembered:

> We are crushed to the ground,
> we lie in ruins.
> There is nothing but grief and suffering
> in Mexico and Tlatelolco,
> where once we saw beauty and valor.

By 1521, the Spaniards had broken organized Aztec opposition and were beginning to construct their capital, the city of Mexico, on the ruins of Tenochtitlan. By 1535 most of central Mexico with its network of towns and its dense, agricultural populations had been brought under Spanish control as the kingdom of New Spain. From there, the Spanish pushed their conquest southward into Guatemala and Honduras and northward into the area of the nomadic Indians of North-central Mexico.

The second trajectory of conquests led from the Caribbean outposts to the coast of northern South America and Panama. From Panama, the Spaniards followed rumors of a rich kingdom to the south. In 1535, after a false start, Francisco Pizarro led his men to the conquest of the Inca Empire, which was already weakened by a long civil war. Once again, using guile and audacity, fewer than 200 Spaniards and their Indian allies brought a great Indian empire down. The Inca capital of Cuzco, high in the Andes, fell in 1533, but the Spanish decided to build their major city, Lima, closer to the coast. By 1540 most of Peru was under Spanish control, although an active resistance continued in remote areas for another 30 years.

From the conquests of the sedentary Indians' densely populated areas, such as Mexico and Peru, where there were considerable surpluses in food and potential laborers, Spanish expeditions spread out in search of further riches and strange peoples. The conquest of the sedentary Chibcha Indians of New Granada (modern Colombia) in northern South America took place between 1536 and 1538, carried out by expeditions from both the Caribbean and Peru. Spanish expeditions penetrated the zones of semisedentary and nomadic peoples who often offered stiff resistance. Expeditions from Mexico moved into the northern frontiers inhabited by the nomadic Chichimecs. From 1540 to 1542 in one of the most famous expeditions, Francisco Vázquez de Coronado, searching for mythical cities of gold, penetrated what is now southwestern United States as far as Kansas. At the other end of the Americas, Pedro de Valdivia conquered the tenacious Araucanian Indians of central Chile and set up the city of Santiago in 1541, although the Araucanians continued to fight long after. Buenos Aires at the southern end of the continent, founded by an expedition from Spain in 1536, was abandoned because of Indian resistance and only refounded in 1580. Expeditions like that led by Gonzalo Pizarro (1541–1542) penetrated the Amazon basin, and others explored the tropical forests of Central and South America during these years, but there was little there to attract permanent settlement. By the 1550s a string of settlements had been created from Venezuela to Argentina and Chile. By 1570 there were 192 Spanish cities and towns throughout the Americas, one-third of which were in Mexico and Central America.

THE CONQUERORS

We can make some general statements about the conquerors and the organization of conquest. Leadership in the conquests was based on reputation and past achievement. The captains led by force of will and personal power. "God in the sky, the king in Spain, and me here," was the motto of one captain, and sometimes absolute power could lead to tyranny. Usually, an agreement was drawn up between the leader of the conquest and the representatives of the Spanish crown that granted authority for the expedition in return for a promise to pay one-fifth of all treasure or other gains to the crown. Men signed up on a shares basis; those who brought horses or who had special skills might get double shares. Rewards were made according to the contract, with premiums paid for special service and valor. There was a tendency for leaders to reward their friends, relatives, and men from their home province more liberally than others, so that after each conquest there was always a group of unhappy and dissatisfied conquerors ready to organize for a new expedition. As one observer put it, "if each man was given the governorship, it would not be enough."

Few of the conquerors were professional soldiers; they represented all walks of Spanish life, including a scattering of gentlemen. Some of the later expeditions included a few Spanish women such as Ines Suarez, the heroine of the conquest of Chile, but such cases were rare. In general, the conquerors were men on the make, hoping to better themselves and serve God by converting the heathen at the same time. Always on the lookout for treasure, most conquerors were satisfied by grants of Indians who could be taxed or put to work. They took a distinct pride in the fact that they were not paid soldiers, but rather volunteers who risked their lives for king and Church. These adventurous men, many of humble origins, came to see themselves as a new nobility entitled to dominion over a new peasantry—the Indians.

The reasons for Spanish success were varied. Horses, firearms, and more generally steel weapons gave them a great advantage over the stone technology of the Indians. This technological edge, combined with effective and ruthless leadership, produced remarkable results. Europeans were also aided by the silent ally, epidemic disease, which sometimes even preceded a conquest and weakened the In-

Population Decline in New Spain

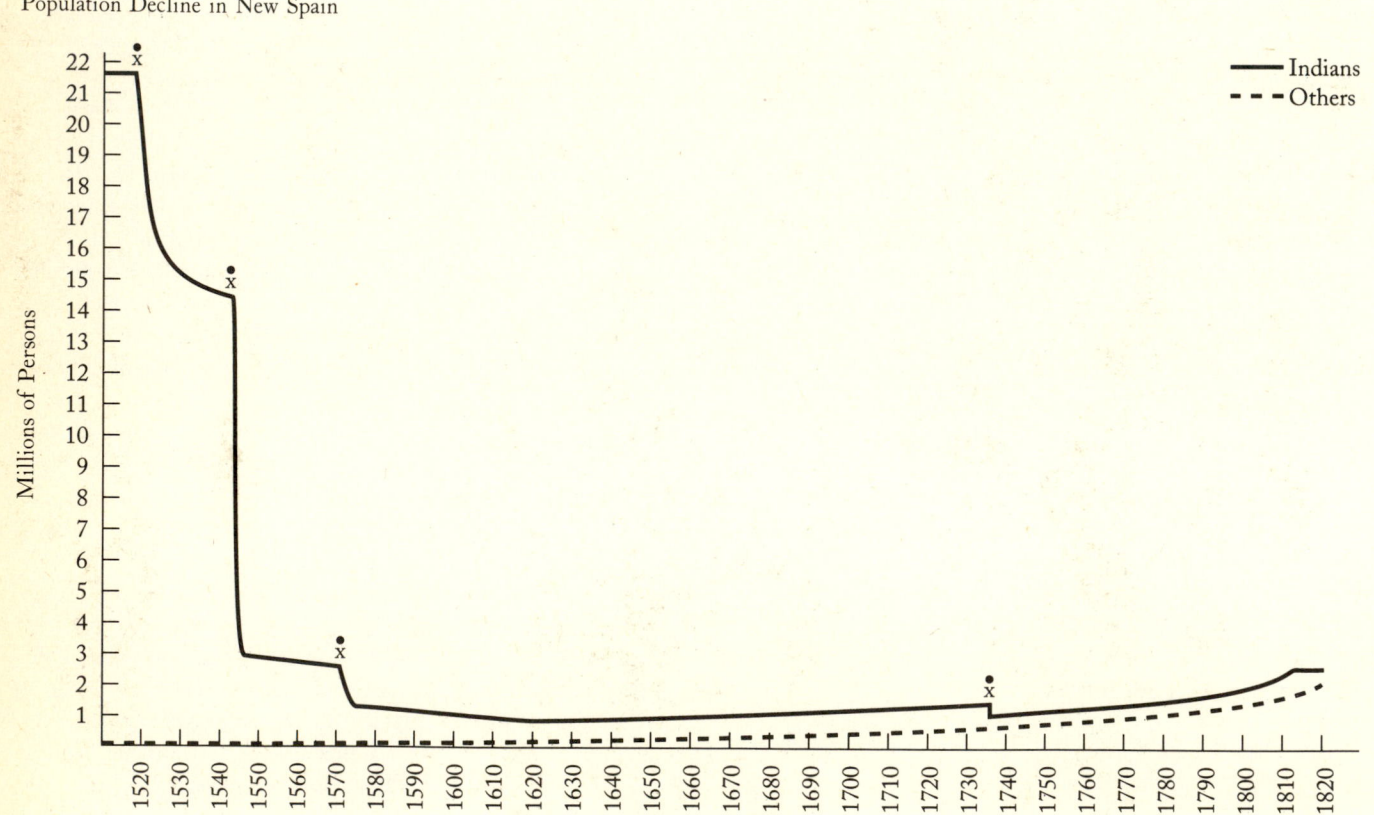

dian resistance. Finally, internal divisions and rivalries within Indian empires and their high levels of centralization made the great civilizations particularly vulnerable. It is not accidental that the Indian peoples who offered the stiffest and most continuous resistance were usually the mobile and tough nomadic tribes rather than the centralized states composed of a sedentary peasantry.

By about 1570, the age of the conquest was coming to a close and the generation of the conquerors was replaced by bureaucrats, merchants, and colonists as the institutions of colonial rule and the basis of the economy were regularized. The transition was not easy. In Peru a civil war erupted in the 1540s, and in Mexico there were grumblings from the old followers of Cortés, but when viceroys were established in the two main colonies and law courts were created in the main centers, the presence and effectiveness of royal government greatly increased. Spanish America became a colony rather than a conquest.

 ## THE DESTRUCTION AND TRANSFORMATION OF INDIAN SOCIETIES

The various Indian peoples responded in many ways to the invasion of America and the transformation of their societies. All of them suffered a severe decline of population. This was a demographic catastrophe of incredible proportions. On the main islands of the Caribbean, the Indian population had virtually disappeared by 1540, a result of slaving, mistreatment, and disease. In central Mexico, war, destruction, and above all disease brought the population from an estimated 25 million in 1519 to less than two million in 1580. In Peru, a similar process brought a loss from 10 million to 1.5 million between 1530 and 1590. Elsewhere in the Americas a similar but less well-documented process took place. Smallpox, influenza, and even measles wreaked havoc on the Indian population, which had developed no immunities against these diseases.

A Comparison of Human and Livestock Populations in Central Mexico

Indian Population

Cattle, Sheep, and Goats

Millions

Year

While epidemic disease was the major cause of depopulation, the destruction of the conquest and the weakening of indigenous societies contributed to the mortality and made the Indian populations more susceptible to disease. Population losses of this size disrupted Indian societies in many ways. For example, in central Mexico the contraction of the Indian population led the Spanish to concentrate the remaining population in fewer towns, and this led in turn to the seizure of former communal farming lands by Spanish landowners. Demographic collapse made the maintenance of traditional social and economic structures very difficult.

The case of Mexico is particularly stark. The tremendous decline of the Indian population was matched by the rapid increase in European livestock. Cattle, sheep, and horses flourished on the newly created Spanish farms or on unclaimed lands. In a way, the Indian population of Mexico was replaced by European livestock.

EXPLOITATION OF THE INDIANS

Spanish desires to exploit the Indians as laborers or to extract a tribute from them led to Spanish attempts to maintain those aspects of Indian life that served colonial goals or at least did not openly conflict with Spanish authority or religion. Thus, in Mexico and Peru, while the old Indian religion and its priestly class were eliminated, the traditional Indian nobility remained in place, supported by Spanish authority, as middlemen between the tax and labor demands of the new rulers and the majority of the population.

The enslavement of Indians, except those taken in war, was prohibited by the mid-16th century in most of Spanish America. Instead, different forms of labor or taxation were imposed. At first, encomiendas were given to the individual conquerors of a region. The holders of these grants, or *encomenderos,* were able to use their Indians as workers and servants or to tax them. While in the Inca and Aztec empires commoners had owed tribute or labor to the state, the new demands were arbitrary, often excessive, and usually devoid of the reciprocity of obligation and protection characteristic of the Indian societies. Encomiendas were introduced after the initial conquest of a region from New Mexico in the north to Chile in the south. In general, the encomiendas proved to be destructive to Indian societies, and as depopulation continued, the holders of the grants became dissatisfied. Finally, the Spanish crown, unwilling to see a new nobility arise in the New World among the conquerors with their grants of Indian serfs, moved to end the institution in the 1540s. The crown limited the inheritability of encomiendas and prohibited the right to demand certain kinds of labor from the Indians. While encomien-

das continued to exist in marginal regions at the fringes of the empire, in the central areas of Mexico and Peru they were all but gone by the 1620s. With the disappearance of the encomienda, the colonists and descendants of the conquerors increasingly sought grants of land rather than Indians as the basis of wealth.

Meanwhile, the colonial government increasingly extracted Indian labor and tax through local royal officials. In many places, communities were required to send groups of laborers to work on state projects, such as church construction or road building, or in labor gangs for mining or agriculture. This forced labor, called the *mita* in Peru, mobilized thousands of Indians to work in the mines and on other projects. While the Indians were paid a wage for this work, there were many abuses of the system by the local officials, and community labor requirements were often disruptive and destructive to Indian life. By the 17th century, many Indians left their villages to avoid the labor and tax obligations, preferring instead to work for Spanish landowners or to seek employment in the cities. This process eventually led to the growth of a wage labor system in which Indians, no longer resident in their villages, worked for wages on Spanish-owned mines and farms or in the cities.

In the wake of this disruption, Indian culture also demonstrated considerable resiliency in the face of Spanish institutions and forms, adapting and modifying them to Indian ways. In New Spain, the Spanish municipal councils established in Indian towns were staffed by the Indian elite, and their operations reflected preconquest patterns within European forms. In Peru and Mexico, Indians learned to use the legal system and the law courts so that litigation became a way of life. At the local level, many aspects of Indian life remained, and Indians proved to be selective in their adaptation of European foods, technology, and culture.

ANALYSIS
THE GREAT EXCHANGE

The arrival of the Spaniards and the Portuguese in the Americas initiated one of the most extensive and profound changes in the history of humankind. The New World, which had existed in relative isolation since the end of the last Ice Age, was now brought into continual contact with the Old World. The peoples and cultures of Europe and Africa came to the Americas through voluntary or forced immigration. Between 1500 and 1850 perhaps 10 to 15 million Africans and five million Europeans crossed the Atlantic and settled in the Americas as part of the great migratory movement. Contact also initiated a broader biological and ecological exchange that changed the face of both the Old World and the New World—the way people lived, what they ate, and how they died—as the animals, plants, and diseases of the two hemispheres were transferred. Historian Alfred Crosby has called this process the "Columbian exchange," and he has pointed out its profound effects as the first stage of the "ecological imperialism" that accompanied the expansion of the West.

In this chapter we have discussed the devastating impact of Old World disease on Indian peoples. Long separated from the populations of the Old World and lacking immunities to diseases such as measles and smallpox, Indian populations throughout the Americas suffered disastrous losses after initial contact. Not only among the dense populations in Peru and Mexico, but in the forests of Brazil and the woodlands of North America, contact with Europeans and Africans resulted in epidemics that devastated the Indian populations. Only after a number of generations did immunities build up in the remaining population that allowed it to withstand the diseases.

Disease may have also moved in the other direction. Some authorities believe that syphilis had an American origin and was brought to Europe only after 1492. In general, however, forms of life in the Old World—diseases, plants, and animals—were more complex than those that existed in the Americas and thus displaced the New World varieties in open competition. The diseases of Eurasia and Africa had a greater impact on America than vice versa.

With animals also, the major exchange was from the Old World to the New World. From the beginning of contact, Europeans noted with curiosity the strange fauna of America, so different from Europe. The birds were a hit. Parrots were among the first things brought to Europe from America. Many early observers commented on the smaller size of the mammals in the New World and the absence of certain types, not realizing that mastodons, horses, camels, and other animals that had once roamed the Americas had long since disappeared. American Indians had domesticated dogs, guinea pigs, some fowl, and the llama, but in general domesticated animals were far less important in the Americas than in the Old World. Protein resources were thus also more restricted. The absence of cattle and horses had also left the peoples of the Americas without suitable beasts of burden except for the llamas of the Andes.

In the first years of settlement in the Caribbean, the Spanish introduced horses, cattle, sheep, chickens, and domestic goats and pigs, all of which were considered essen-

tial for civilized life as the Iberians understood it. Some of these animals thrived in the New World. In the scrub brush and prairies of North America, in the tropical grasslands of Venezuela, and on the South American *pampas* vast herds of cattle began to roam freely. A hundred head of cattle abandoned by the Spanish in the Rio de la Plata area in 1587 had become 100,000 head 20 years later. Both for the consumption of meat, tallow, and hides in the Americas and eventually for the export of hides and meat to Europe and the rest of the world, the arrival of cattle in the Americas was a revolutionary occurence. In Mexico, livestock and Spanish haciendas grew as rapidly as the Indian population declined and Indian communities contracted. The replacement of Indians by cattle became a metaphor of the conquest of Mexico.

The success of other European livestock was no less impressive. In the Andes and in Mexico, sheep thrived and supported an active textile industry which eventually supplied most of the local needs. Horses were quickly adopted by the nomadic peoples of North and South America. This adaptation transformed their societies and gave them added mobility, allowing them to meet the Europeans on an almost equal basis. With horses, the Apaches of Arizona and the Indians of the Argentine pampas were able to hold off the Europeans for 300 years.

European livestock and even animals such as the humble pigs and chickens transformed Indian life in America. Indians acquired some animals, such as oxen, slowly, but other animals, such as horses and sheep, had obvious benefits. The Indian chieftain who answered that the greatest benefit Spain had brought to his people was the chicken egg may have disappointed his questioner, but it reflected a keen appreciation of the importance of the interchange. The newly introduced animals changed the ecological balance in the New World. Not only animals that were purposefully introduced, but species such as the sparrow and the brown rat, whose arrival was unplanned, changed the nature of life in the Americas.

The Europeans also brought their crops. It was hard for Iberians to live without the Mediterranean necessities: wheat bread, olive oil, and wine. Columbus on his second voyage in 1499 had introduced wheat, peas, melons, onions, grapes, and probably olives, as well as sugar cane. Some crops, like sugar cane, thrived and provided the basis for the rise of plantation economies; other crops like wheat, olives, and grapes needed cooler or drier environments and had to wait until the Spanish reached the more temperate zones before they flourished. Subsequently, Europeans introduced all of their own crops and even some crops—bananas, coconut trees, coffee, and breadfruit—that they had encountered in Africa, Asia, and the Pacific.

In the exchange of foods and stimulants, the contribution of America probably outweighed that of Europe, however. It is difficult today to imagine the diet of the Old World prior to the discovery of America. New World plants, such as the tomato, squash, sweet potatoes, types of beans, and peppers, became essential foods in Europe. Tobacco and cacao, or chocolate, both American in origin, became widely distributed throughout the world.

Even more important were basic crops, such as the potato, maize, and manioc, all of which yielded more calories per acre than all the Old World grains except rice. The high yield of calories per acre of maize and potatoes had supported the high population densities of the American civilizations. After the Columbian voyages, these foods began to produce similar effects in the rest of the world. Manioc or casava (we know it as tapioca) was a basic Indian food in the Caribbean and tropical South America. Particularly well-suited to the tropics, manioc was never popular in Europe, but it spread widely in Asia and Africa, where it became a basic food by the 18th century. The potato, a staple of the Andean civilizations, was easy to grow and yielded large numbers of calories. By the 18th century it was well known from Ireland to Russia. Maize was the great success story. It yielded as many calories per acre as rice but it was easier to grow and could flourish in a wide variety of situations. By the 17th century it had spread to Spain and France, and by the 18th century it was found in Italy, Turkey, Greece, and Russia. The Europeans also introduced it to West Africa and China. Maize became a staple across the globe. At present, at least one-third of the crops raised to feed the world's population are of New World origin.

In the period after 1750 the population of the world experienced a dramatic rise. The reasons for this expansion were many, but the contribution of the American foodstuffs with their high yields was a central aspect. Manioc, potatoes, sweet potatoes, and maize—to say nothing of peanuts, beans, and tomatoes—greatly expanded the food resources available to men and women throughout the world and continue to do so today. The balance sheet of the "Columbian exchange" was mixed, but the world was undeniably different after it began.

Questions: Why and in what ways was the "Columbian exchange" a particularly significant case of global contact? Was western Europe the chief beneficiary of the exchange? What balance was there between the economic dependency of the Americas and the ideas, technology, and goods they received from Europe?

COLONIAL ECONOMIES AND GOVERNMENTS

Spanish America was an agrarian society in which the vast majority of people, perhaps 80 percent of the population, lived and worked on the land. Yet in terms of America's importance to Spain, mining was the essential activity and the basis of Spain's rule in the Indies. Until the 18th century, the whole Spanish maritime commercial system was essentially organized around the mining economy and the exchange of America's precious metals for manufactured goods from Europe. It was this exchange that began to fit Latin America into the New World economy as a somewhat dependent area producing unprocessed exports to trade with western Europe.

While the booty of conquest provided some wealth, most of the precious metal sent across the Atlantic came from the postconquest mining industry. Gold was found in the Caribbean, Colombia, and Chile, but it was silver far more than gold that formed the basis of Spain's wealth in America.

THE SILVER HEART OF EMPIRE

The major silver mining strikes were made in Mexico between 1545 and 1565 and in Peru at roughly the same time. Great silver mining towns developed. Potosí in Upper Peru (in what is now Bolivia) was the largest mine of all, producing about 80 percent of all the Peruvian silver. In the early 17th century over 160,000 people lived and worked in the town and its mine. Peru's Potosí and Mexico's Zacatecas became wealthy mining centers with opulent churches and a luxurious way of life for some, but as one viceroy of Peru commented, it was not silver that was sent to Spain, "but the blood and sweat of Indians."

Mining labor was provided by a variety of workers. The early use of Indian slaves and encomienda workers in the 16th century was gradually replaced by a system of labor drafts. By 1572 the mining mita in Peru was providing about 13,000 workers a year to Potosí alone. Similar labor drafts were also used in Mexico, but by the 17th century the mines in both places also had large numbers of wage workers willing to brave the dangers of mining in return for the relatively good wages.

Although Indian methods were used at first, most mining techniques were European in origin. After 1580, silver mining depended on a process of amalgamation with mercury to extract the silver from the ore-bearing rock. The discovery of a mountain of mercury at Huancavelica in Peru aided American silver production. Potosí and Huancavelica became the "great marriage of Peru" and the basis of silver production in South America.

According to Spanish law, all subsoil rights belonged to the crown, but the mines and the processing plants were owned by private individuals who were permitted to extract the silver in return for paying one-fifth of production to the government, which also profited from its monopoly of the mercury needed to produce the silver.

Although there is considerable debate about Spanish American mining output, some points seem clear. Silver production expanded rapidly after 1580 and crested by 1640. In this period, production from Peru outstripped that in Mexico. Both areas then experienced a steady decline caused by disruption of the mercury supply and mismanagement, although the crisis seems to have been more silver failing to reach Spain rather than difficulties in production. Still, there was decline in silver output until the mid-18th century, when there was a new mining boom. Mexico's mines emerged as the leader of American production.

Mining served as a stimulus to many other aspects of the economy, even in areas far removed from the mines. Workers had to be fed and the mines supplied. In Mexico, where most of the mines were located beyond the area of settled preconquest Indian population, large Spanish-style farms developed to raise cattle, sheep, and wheat. To Peruvian mines high in the Andes from distant regions ran a steady stream of supplies: mercury, mules, food, clothing, and even coca leaves, used to deaden hunger and make the work at high altitudes less painful. From Spain's perspective, mining was the heart of the colonial economy.

HACIENDAS AND VILLAGES

While mining gave America meaning to Spain's colonial enterprise, Spanish America remained predominantly an agrarian economy. In highland Peru, Mexico, Guatemala,

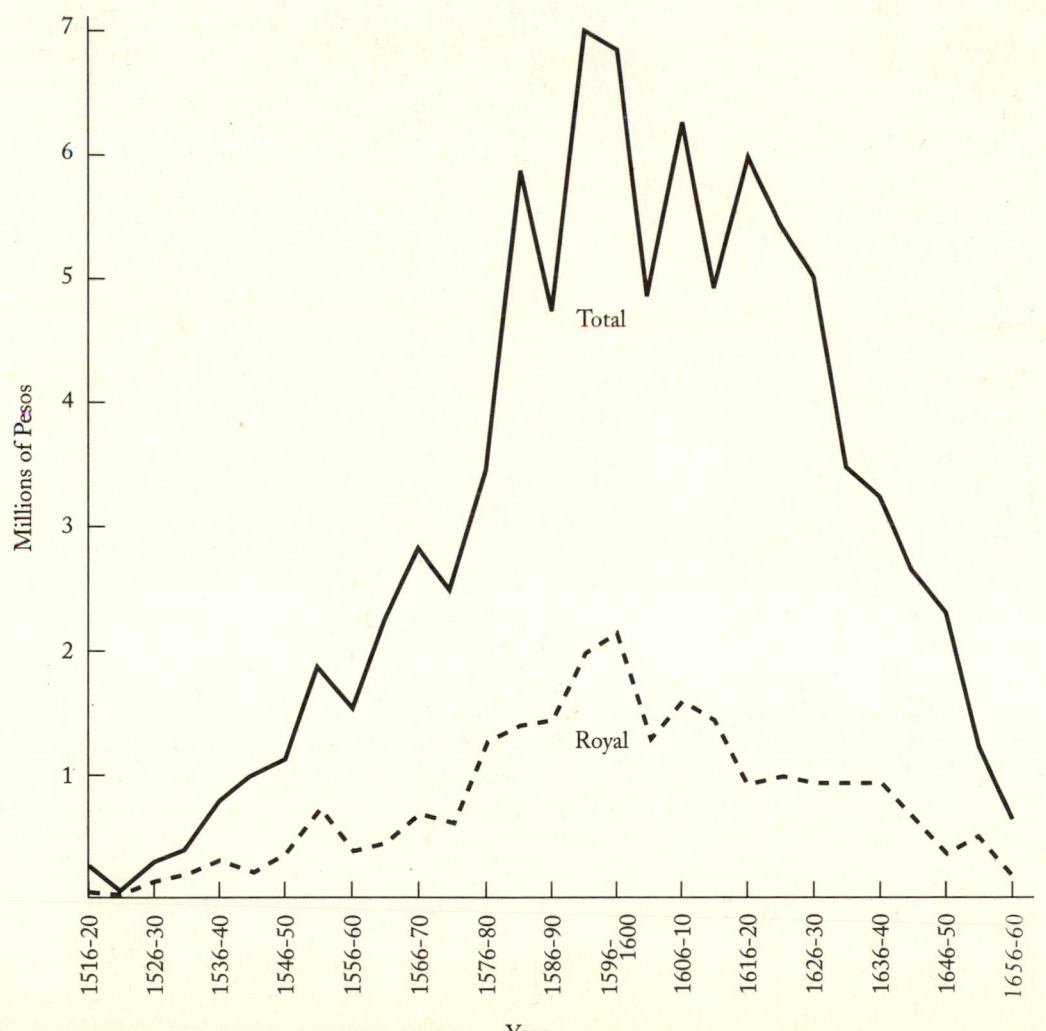

Silver Production in Spanish America, 1516–1660

and New Granada where large sedentary populations existed, Indian communal agriculture of traditional crops continued. As populations dwindled, Spanish ranches and farms began to emerge to feed the populations of the cities. The colonists, faced with declining Indian populations, also found landownership more attractive. Rural estates, based on family ownership and which produced grains, grapes, and livestock, developed throughout the central areas of Spanish America. Most of their labor force came from Indians who had left their communities and from people of mixed Indian and European heritage. These rural estates, or *haciendas*, producing primarily for consumers in America, became the basis of wealth and power for the local aristocracy in many regions. Although some plantation crops, such as sugar and later cacao, were exported to Europe from Spanish America, they made up only a small fraction of the value of the exports in comparison to silver. In some regions where Indian communities continued to hold traditional farming lands, an endemic competition between haciendas and village communities emerged.

INDUSTRY AND THE COMMERCIAL SYSTEM

Industry was not lacking. Sheep raising in areas, such as Ecuador, New Spain, and Peru, led to the development of small textile sweatshops, or *obrajes*, where common cloth was produced, usually by Indian women workers. America became self-sufficient for its basic foods and material goods and looked to Europe only for fine (and costly) luxury items not locally available.

Still, from Spain's perspective and that of the larger world economy taking shape in the early modern centuries, the American "kingdoms" had a silver heart and the whole Spanish commercial system was organized around that fact. Spain took an exclusivist position, essentially allowing only Spaniards to trade with America and even then under tight restrictions. All American trade from Spain after the mid-16th century was funneled through the city of Seville and, later, the nearby port of Cádiz. The Board of Trade in Seville registered ships and passengers, kept charts, collected duties, and in general controlled the Indies trade. It often worked in conjunction with a merchant guild, or *consulado*, in Seville that had virtual monopoly rights over goods shipped to America and handled much of the silver received in return. Linked to branches in Mexico City and Lima, the consulados kept tight control over the trade and were able to keep prices high in the colonies. For most of the 17th century, for example, the consulado had such power that most goods moving from Spain to the Río de la Plata on the Atlantic coast of South America had to be

Women in colonial Latin America were engaged in agriculture and in manufacturing, especially in textile workshops, but social ideology still reserved the household and the kitchen as the proper sphere for women, as seen in a kitchen of a large Mexican home.

shipped to Panama, carried across the isthmus, reshipped to Lima, and then carried across the Andes, a trip that greatly added to their cost and to the profits of the merchant guild.

As the trade of the Indies grew and the precious metals flowed to Spain, other Europeans looked on with envious eyes. To discourage foreign rivals and pirates, the Spanish eventually worked out a convoy system in which two fleets sailed annually from Spain, traded their goods for precious metals in Mexico and Panama, as well as silver from Peru, and then rendezvoused at Havana, Cuba, before returning to Spain.

The fleet system was well planned and included a number of elements. The fleets were made possible by the development of the large, heavily armed ships called galleons that were used to carry the silver belonging to the crown. Two great galleons a year also sailed from Manila in the Philippines to Mexico loaded with Chinese silks, porcelain, and lacquer. These goods were then transshipped on the convoy to Spain along with the American silver. In the

Caribbean, heavily fortified ports, such as Havana and Cartegena (Colombia), provided shelter for the treasure ships, while coastguard fleets cleared the waters of potential raiders. Although cumbersome, the convoys (which continued until the 1730s) were relatively successful. While pirates and Spain's European enemies sometimes captured individual ships, and although some ships were lost to storms and other disasters, only one fleet was lost, to the Dutch in 1627.

In general, the supply of American silver to Spain was continuous and made the colonies seem worth the effort, but the reality of American treasure was more complicated. Much of the wealth flowed out of Spain to pay for Spain's European wars, its long-term debts, and the purchase of manufactured goods to be sent back to the Indies. Probably less than half of the silver remained in Spain itself. The arrival of American treasure also contributed to a sharp rise in prices and a general inflation, first in Spain and then throughout western Europe during the 16th century. At no time did the American treasure make up more than one-fourth of Spain's state revenues, which is to say that the wealth of Spain depended more on the taxes levied on its own population than it did on the exploitation of its Indian subjects. The seemingly endless supply of silver did, however, stimulate bankers to continue to loan money to Spain, because the prospect of the great silver fleet was always enough to offset the falling credit of the Spanish rulers and of the sometimes bankrupt government. As early as 1619, Sancho de Moncada wrote that "the poverty of Spain resulted from the discovery of the Indies," but there were few who could see the long-term costs of empire.

DOCUMENT
A VISION FROM THE VANQUISHED

History is usually written by the victors, so it is rare when we have a detailed statement from the vanquished. In the 17th century, Guaman Poma de Ayala, an acculturated Peruvian Indian who claimed to trace his lineage to the provincial nobility of Inca times, composed a memorial outlining the history of Peru under the Incas and reporting on the current conditions under Spanish rule. Guaman Poma was a Christian and a loyal subject. He hoped that his report would reach King Phillip III of Spain who might then order an end to the worst abuses, among which were the Spanish failure to recognize the rank and status of Indian nobles like himself. His book was not published in his lifetime and was only recovered in the 20th century.

In addition to his class pride, Guaman Poma was also an educated, bilingual Indian who spoke Quechua as well as Spanish and who had a profound understanding of Andean culture. His book is remarkable for its revelations of Indian life, for its detailed criticism of the abuses suffered by the Indians, and especially because Guaman Poma illustrated his memorial with a series of drawings that give his words a visual effect. The illustrations also reveal the world view of this interesting character. The drawings and text offer a critical inside view not of the laws, but of the workings of Spain's empire in America from an Indian point of view.

MINERS

At the mercury mines of Huancavelica the Indian workers are punished and illtreated to such an extent that they die like flies and our whole race is threatened with extermination. Even the chiefs are tortured by being suspended by their feet. Conditions in the silver-mines of Potosí and Chocllococha, or at the gold-mines of Carabaya are little better. The managers and supervisors, who are Spaniards or mestizos have virtually absolute power. There is no reason for them to fear justice, since they are never brought before the courts.

Beatings are incessant. The victims are mounted for this purpose on a llama's back, tied naked to a round pillar or put in stocks. Their hair is cut off and they are deprived of food and water during detention.

Any shortage in the labor gangs is made an excuse for punishing the chiefs as if they were common thieves or traitors instead of the nobility of the country. The work itself is so hard as to cause permanent injury to many of those who survive it. There is no remuneration for the journey to the mines and a day's labor is paid at the rate for half a day.

PROPRIETORS

Your Majesty has granted large estates, including the right to employ Indian labor, to a number of individuals of whom some are good Christians and the remainder are very bad ones. These *encomenderos*, as they are termed, may boast about their high position, but in reality they are harmful both to the labor force and to the surviving Indian nobility. I therefore propose to set down the details of their life and conduct.

They exude an air of success as they go from their card games to their dinners in fine silk clothes. Their money is squandered on these luxuries, as well it may, since it costs them no work or sweat whatever. Although the Indians ultimately pay the bill, no concern is ever felt for them or even for Your Majesty or God himself.

Official posts like those of royal administrator and judge ought not to be given to big employers or mine-owners or to their obnoxious sons, because these peoples have enough to live on already. The appointments ought to go to Christian gentleman of small means, who have rendered some service to the Crown and are educated and humane, not just greedy.

Anybody with rights over Indian labor sees to it that his own household is well supplied with servant girls and indoor and outdoor staff. When collecting dues and taxes, it is usual to impose penalties and detain Indians against their will. There is no redress since, if any complaint is made, the law always favours the employer.

The collection of tribute is delegated to stewards, who make a practice of adding something in for themselves. They too consider themselves entitled to free service and obligatory presents, and they end up as bad as their masters. All of them, and their wives as well, regard themselves as entitled to eat at the Indians' expense.

The Indians are seldom paid the few reales a day which are owed to them, but they are hired out for the porterage of wine and making rope or clothing. Little rest is possible either by day or night and they are usually unable to sleep at home.

It is impossible for servant girls, or even married women, to remain chaste. They are bound to be corrupted and prostituted because employers do not feel any scruple about threatening them with flogging, execution, or burial alive if they refuse to satisfy their master's desires.

The Spanish grandees and their wives have borrowed from the Inca the custom of having themselves conveyed in litters like the images of saints in processions. These Spaniards are absolute lords without fear of either God or retribution. In their own eyes they are judges over our people, whom they can reserve for their personal service or their pleasure, to the detriment of the community.

Great positions are achieved by favour from above, by wealth or by having relations at Court in Castile. With some notable exceptions, the beneficiaries act without consideration for those under their control.

The *encomenderos* call themselves conquerors, but their Conquest was achieved by uttering the words: *Ama mancha noca Inca*, or 'Have no fear. I am the Inca.' This false pretense was the sum total of their performance.

Questions: What are the main abuses Guaman Poma complains about? What remedies does he recommend? What relationship do his views have to traditional Inca values? How might a white landlord or colonial official have answered his attacks?

RULING AN EMPIRE

Spain controlled its American empire through a carefully regulated administrative and bureaucratic system. Sovereignty rested with the crown, based not on the right of conquest, but on a papal grant that awarded the Indies to Castile in return for its services in bringing those lands and peoples into the Christian community. Some Indians found this curious and could not understand how the pope could assign to Castile what was not his in the first place. Some European theologians agreed, but Spain was careful to bolster its rule in other ways. The Treaty of Tordesillas (1494) between Castile and Portugal clarified the spheres of influence and right of possession of the two kingdoms by drawing a hypothetical north-south line around the globe and reserving to Portugal newly discovered lands (and their route to India) to the east of the line and to Castile all lands to the west. Thus, Brazil fell within the Portuguese sphere. France, England, and other European nations would later raise their own objections to the Spanish and Portuguese claims.

The Spanish Empire became a great bureaucratic system built on a juridical core and staffed to a large extent by *letrados*, or university-trained lawyers from Spain. The modern division of powers was not clearly defined in the Spanish system, so that judicial officers also exercised legislative and administrative authority. Spanish society was highly legalistic and the formulation of law was a major attribute of authority. The body of laws for the Indies was so large and varied that it took almost a century to complete a great law code, the *Recopilación* (1681), which despite its defects and inconsistencies became the basis of law in the Indies.

THE STATE AND THE CHURCH

The king ruled through the Council of the Indies in Spain that issued the laws and advised him on all matters dealing with the colonies. Within the Indies, Spain created two viceroyalties in the 16th century, one based on Mexico City and the other on Lima. Viceroys, high-ranking nobles who were direct representatives of the king, wielded broad military, legislative, and, when they had legal training, judicial powers. The viceroyalties of New Spain and Peru were then subdivided into ten judicial divisions controlled by superior courts, or audiencias, staffed by professional royal magistrates who helped to make law as well as apply it. At the local level, royally appointed magistrates in the towns and villages were the direct representatives of the state, applying the laws, collecting taxes, and assigning the work requirements on Indian communities. It is little

wonder that they often were highly criticized for bending the law and taking advantage of the Indians under their control. Below them was a myriad of minor officials, customs and tax collectors, municipal officers, and inspectors who made bureaucracy both a living and a way of life.

To some extent the clergy formed another branch of the state apparatus, although, of course, it had other functions and goals as well. The conquest of America had been a remarkable missionary as well as military effort. Catholic religious orders such as the Franciscans, Dominicans, and Jesuits carried out the widespread conversion of the Indians, establishing churches in the towns and villages of sedentary Indians and setting up missions in frontier areas.

Taking seriously the pope's admonition to Christianize the peoples of the new lands as the primary justification for Spain's rule, some of the early missionaries became ardent defenders of Indian rights and even admirers of aspects of Indian culture. For example, the Franciscan priest Fray Bernardino de Sahagún (1499–1590) became an expert in the Nahuatl language and composed a bilingual encyclopedia of Aztec culture, which was based on methods very similar to those used by modern anthropologists. Other clerics wrote histories, grammars, and studies of Indian language and culture. Some were like Diego de Landa, Bishop of Yucatán (1547), who admired much about the culture of the Maya but who so detested their religion and feared its survival that he burned all their ancient books and tortured many Maya suspected of backsliding from Christianity. The recording and analysis of Indian cultures were designed primarily to provide tools for conversion.

In the core areas of Peru and New Spain, the missionary church was eventually replaced by an institutional structure of parishes and bishoprics. Archbishops sat in the major capitals, and a complicated church hierarchy developed, which reflected the demographic and economic realities of each area. Since the holders of all ecclesiastical positions were nominated by the Spanish crown, the clergy tended to be a major support of state policy as well as a primary influence on it. It was no accident that in the *Recopilación*, the great law code of the Indies, the first section dealt with "the Holy Catholic Faith."

The Catholic church profoundly influenced the cultural and intellectual life of the colonies in many ways. The construction of churches, especially the great baroque cathedrals of the capitals, stimulated the work of architects and artists, usually reflective of European models but sometimes taking up local themes and subjects. The printing presses, introduced to America in the early 16th century, always published a high percentage of religious books, as well as works of history, poetry, philosophy, law, and language.

Much intellectual life was organized around religion. Schools—such as those of Mexico City and Lima, founded in the 1550s—were run by the clergy and universities and were created to provide training primarily in law and theology, the foundations of state and society. Eventually, over 70 universities flourished in Spanish America. A stunning example of colonial intellectual life was the nun, Sor Juana Inés de la Cruz (1651–1695), author, poet, musician, and social thinker, who was welcomed at the court of the viceroy in Mexico City where her beauty and intelligence were celebrated. She eventually gave up secular concerns and her library, at the urging of her superiors, to concentrate on purely spiritual matters. Even secular authors were heavily influenced by baroque Catholicism. To control the morality and orthodoxy of the population, the tribunal of the Inquisition set up offices in the major capitals, although Indians were usually exempt from its jurisdiction. Overall, church and state combined to create an ideological and political framework for the society and economy of Spanish America.

Sor Juana Inés de la Cruz was the remarkable Mexican poet and writer whose talents won her recognition rarely given to women for intellectual achievements in colonial Latin America.

BRAZIL: THE FIRST PLANTATION COLONY

The search for gold and silver was a constant theme in overseas expansion, but there were other European demands the New World could also satisfy, which contributed to its growing involvement in the Western-dominated world economy. While Spanish America seemed to fulfill dreams of mineral wealth, Brazil—Portugal's American colony—became the first major plantation zone, organized to produce a tropical crop—sugar—in great demand and short supply in Europe.

Although the Portuguese had already set up small plantation colonies on the little Atlantic islands of Madeira and Sao Tomé, the move toward plantation agriculture in Brazil was gradual. The first official Portuguese landfall on the South American coast took place in 1500 when Pedro Álvares Cabral, leader of an expedition to India, stopped briefly on the tropical Brazilian shore, celebrated a mass, and bartered with the Indians. There was little at first to attract European interest except for the dyewood trees that grew in the forests, and thus for 30 years the Portuguese crown paid little attention to Brazil, preferring instead to grant licenses to merchants who agreed to exploit the dyewood in return for tax benefits and services. Pressure from French merchants also interested in dyewood finally moved the Portuguese crown to military action. The coast was cleared of the French and a new system of settlement was established in 1532. Minor Portuguese nobles were given strips of land along the coast to colonize and develop. The nobles who held these *capitaincies* combined broad, seemingly "feudal" powers with a strong desire for commercial development. Most of them lacked sufficient capital to carry out the colonization and some had continual problems with the local Indian population. In a few places, towns were established, colonists were brought over, relations with the Indians were relatively peaceful, and, most importantly, sugar plantations were established using first Indian, and then imported African, slaves.

The limited success of the captaincies caused the Portuguese crown in 1549 to send a governor general and other royal officials and to create a royal capital at Salvador. The first Jesuit missionaries also arrived. By 1600 Indian resistance had been broken in many places either by military action, missionary activity, or by epidemic disease. A string of settlements extended along the coast, centered on port cities such as Salvador and Rio de Janeiro. These served the roughly 150 sugar plantations, a number which would double by 1630. The plantations were increasingly worked by African slaves. By 1600 the Brazilian colony had about 100,000 inhabitants: 30,000 Europeans, 15,000 black slaves, and the rest Indians and people of mixed origin.

Divisions of the Tordesillas

SUGAR AND SLAVERY

During most of the next century, Brazil held its position as the world's leading sugar producer. Sugar cane had to be processed in the field—cut, pressed in large mills, and the juice then heated before it would crystallize into sugar. This combination of agriculture and industry in the field demanded large amounts of capital for machinery and large quantities of labor for the backbreaking work. While there were always some free workers who had skilled or artisan occupations, slaves did most of the work. During the 17th century, about 7000 slaves a year were imported from Africa. By the end of the century, Brazil had about 150,000 slaves—about half its total population.

Based on a single crop produced by slave labor, Brazil became the first great plantation colony and a model that would later be followed by other European nations in their own Caribbean colonies. Even after the Brazilian economy became more diverse, Brazil's society still reflected its plantation and slave origins. Slavery and the plantation system imposed a strong social hierarchy. The white planter families became an aristocracy that controlled local social and political life. Linked by interest and marriage to resident merchants and to the few Portuguese bureaucrats and officials, this class dominated local institutions. At the bottom of society were the slaves, distinguished by their color and their servile condition as property. There was, however, a growing segment of the population composed of people of mixed origins, the result of miscegenation between whites, Indians, and Africans who—alongside poorer whites, freed blacks, and free Indians—served as artisans, small farmers, herdsmen, and free laborers. In many ways, society as a whole reflected the hierarchy of the plantation.

Like Spain, Portugal created a bureaucratic structure that integrated this colony within an imperial system. A governor general ruled from Salvador, but the governors in each captaincy often acted with independence and reported directly to the overseas council in Lisbon. The missionary orders were particularly important in Brazil, especially the Jesuits. Their extensive cattle ranches and sugar mills supported the construction of churches and schools as well as a network of missions with thousands of Indian residents.

As in Spanish America, royal officials trained in the law formed the core of the bureaucracy. Unlike the Spanish Empire, which was, with the exception of the Phillipines, almost exclusively American, the Portuguese Empire included colonies and outposts in Asia, Africa, and Brazil. Only gradually in the 17th century did Brazil become the predominant Portuguese colony. Even then, Brazil's ties to Portugal were in some ways stronger and more dependent than those between Spanish America and Spain. Unlike Spanish America, neither universities nor printing presses existed in Brazil. Thus intellectual life was always an extension of Portugal, and Brazilians seeking higher education and government offices or hoping to publish always had to turn to the mother country. The general economic dependency of Latin America was matched by an intellectual subordination more intense in Brazil than in Spanish America.

BRAZIL'S AGE OF GOLD

As overseas extensions of Europe, the American colonies were particularly susceptible to changes in European politics. For 60 years (1580–1640), Spain and Portugal were

Sugar was introduced to the Caribbean in 1493, but Brazil became the greatest producer by the next century. Sugar plantations using enslaved workers characterized Brazil and the Caribbean. This early European engraving is wrong in some details, but it does convey an image of the almost factorylike conditions in the sugar mills.

ruled by the same monarchs, a situation that sponsored their cooperation and gave the Habsburg kings of Spain and Portugal a worldwide empire. From 1630 to 1654, as part of a global struggle against Spain, the Dutch seized a portion of northeastern Brazil and controlled its sugar production. Although the Dutch were expelled from Brazil in 1654, by the 1680s the Dutch, English, and French had established their own plantation colonies in the Caribbean and were producing sugar, once again with slave laborers. This competition—which led to a rising price for slaves and a falling world price for sugar—undercut the Brazilian sugar industry, and the colony entered into hard times. Eventually, each European nation tried to establish an integrated set of colonies that included plantations (the Caribbean, Brazil), slaving ports (Africa), and food producing areas (New England, southern Brazil).

Although Brazil's domination of the world sugar market was lost, throughout the 17th century *Paulistas*, hardy backwoodsmen from São Paulo (an area with few sugar plantations), had been exploring the interior, capturing Indians and searching for precious metals. These expeditions not only established Portuguese claims to much of the interior of the continent, but were eventually successful in

their quest for wealth. In 1695, gold strikes were made in the mountainous interior in a region that came to be called Minas Gerais (General Mines), and the Brazilian colony experienced a new boom.

A great gold rush began. People deserted coastal towns and plantations to head for the gold washings, and they were soon joined by waves of about 5000 immigrants a year who came directly from Portugal. Labor in the mines, as in the plantations, was provided mostly by slaves. By 1720 there were over 35,000 slaves in Minas Gerais, and by 1775 there were over 150,000 (out of a total population of 300,000 for the region). Wild mining camps and a wide-open society eventually coalesced into a network of towns like the administrative center of Ouro Prêto, and the government, anxious to control the new-found wealth, imposed a heavy hand to collect taxes and reign in the unruly population. Gold production reached its height between 1735 and 1760 and averaged about three tons a year in that period, making Brazil the greatest source of gold in the Western world.

The discovery of gold was a mixed blessing in the long run. Further discovery of gold—and later of diamonds— opened the interior to further settlement, once again with disastrous effects on the Indian population and with the expansion of slavery. The early disruption of coastal agriculture caused by the gold strikes was overcome by government control of the slave trade, and exports of sugar and tobacco continued to be important to the colony. Mining did stimulate the opening of new areas to ranching and farming, to supply the new markets in the mining zone. Cattle ranches appeared in the interior of northeast Brazil, while large herds spread over the grassy plains of the south. Rio de Janeiro, the port closest to the mines, grew in size and importance. It became capital of the colony in 1763. In Minas Gerais a distinctive society developed in the mining towns, where the local wealth was used to sponsor the building of churches, which in turn stimulated many artisan activities and the work of artists, architects, and composers. Like the rest of Brazil, however, the hierarchy of color and the legal distinctions of slavery marked life in the mining zones, which were populated by large numbers of slaves and free persons of color.

Finally, gold allowed Portugal to continue economic policies that were detrimental in the long run. With access to gold, Portugal could purchase the manufactured goods it needed for itself and its colonies. Few industries were developed in the mother country and, with pressures from Portuguese wine producers, a treaty was signed with England in 1703 that guaranteed a trading arrangement with that country. As a result much of the Brazilian gold flowed from Portugal to England to pay for manufactured goods and to compensate for a trade imbalance, since the value of English manufactures was greater than that of Portuguese wine. After 1760 as the supply of gold began to dwindle, Portugal was again in a difficult position, in some ways an economic dependency of England.

MULTIRACIAL SOCIETIES

The conquest and settlement of Latin America created the conditions for the formation of multiethnic societies on a large scale. The three major groups—Indians, Europeans, and Africans—had been brought together under very different conditions: the Europeans as conquerors and voluntary immigrants, the Indians as conquered peoples, and the Africans as slaves. This situation created hierarchies of masters and servants, Christians and pagans that reflected the relationships of power and the colonial condition. In some places like central Mexico, where an Indian nobility had existed, aspects of preconquest social organization were maintained because these served the ends of Spanish government. In theory, there was a separation between the "republic of the Spaniards," which included all non-Indians, and the "republic of the Indians," which was supposed to

have its own social rankings and its own rules and laws. This separation was never a reality, however, and the "republic of the Indians" always formed the base on which all society rested. Indians paid tribute, something not required of others in society.

THE SOCIETY OF CASTAS

Spaniards had an idea of society drawn from their own medieval experience, but American realities soon altered that concept. The key was miscegenation. The conquest had involved the sexual exploitation of Indian women as well as occasional alliances formed by the giving of concubines and female servants. Marriages with Indian women, especially with the Indian nobility, were not unknown, and as early as 1516 the Spanish crown tried to sponsor mixed marriages, although later it sought to limit opportunities for mixed offspring. With few European women available, especially in frontier regions, mixed marriages and informal unions were common. The result was the growth of a large population of mixed background, the so-called mestizos. Although always suspected of illegitimacy, their status, especially in the early years, was higher than that of Indians. More acculturated than the Indians, able to operate in two worlds, mestizos became an intermediate category, not fully accepted as equals to Spaniards and yet expected to live according to the standards of Spanish society and often acting as auxiliaries to it. A similar process took place in areas like Brazil and the Caribbean coasts where large numbers of African slaves were imported. Slave owners exploited their female slaves or took slave women as mistresses, and then sometimes freed their mulatto children. The result was the growth of a large population of mixed background, often illegitimate in its origins.

Throughout the Spanish Indies, European categories of noble, priest, and commoner continued, as did hierarchies based on wealth and occupation. But American realities created new distinctions in which race and place of birth played a crucial role. This was the *sociedad de castas*, based on racial origins, in which Europeans or whites were at the top, black slaves or Indians were at the bottom, and the many kinds of mixes filled the intermediate categories. The sexual fusion and mixing accompanied the great cultural fusion in the formation of Latin America.

From the three original ethnic categories, many combinations and crosses were possible: mestizos, mulattoes, zambos (Indian-African parents), castizos (mestizo-Spanish origins), etc. By the 18th century, this segment of the population had grown rapidly and there was much confusion and local variation in terminology. A whole genre of painting developed simply to identify and classify the various

By the 18th century a genre of painting developed to portray the various racial mixtures. In this canvas a *mestizo* father and his Spanish wife are shown with their *castizo* (three-fourths white) daughter. These paintings are also interesting because they show relations between men and women and between adults and children.

combinations. Together, the people of mixed origins were called the *castas*, and they constituted a large and troublesome population; relegated to secondary status, considered dangerous, pushy, and untrustworthy, restricted from certain positions and honors, not fully accepted by Spanish society, and yet needed by it to fill many of the essential positions of artisans, craftsmen, shopkeepers, and small farmers. In 1650 the castas made up perhaps 5 to 10 percent of the population of Spanish America, but by 1750, with considerable regional variation, they constituted 35 to 40 percent. In Brazil, still dominated by slavery, free people of color made up about 28 percent of the population, a proportion equal to that of whites. Together, however, free and slave blacks and mulattoes made up two-thirds of the inhabitants of Brazil in the late 18th century.

As the mixed population grew in Spanish America, increasing restrictions were placed on them, but their social mobility could not be halted. The "racial" labels, in fact, were changed by individuals as their occupations, wealth, or marital status changed. A successful Indian might call himself a mestizo; a mestizo who married a Spanish woman might be called a white. The ranks of the castas were also swelled by former slaves who had been given or

had bought their freedom and by Indians who left their communities, spoke Spanish, and lived within the orbit of the Hispanic world. Thus, physical characteristics were only one among many criteria of rank and status, but color and ethnicity mattered and created a pseudoracial hierarchy. European or white status was a great social advantage. Not every person of European background was wealthy, but most of the wealthy merchants, landowners, bureaucrats, and miners were white. As one visitor wrote: "In America, every white is a gentleman."

Originally, all whites had shared the privileged status of Spaniards regardless of the continent of their birth, but over time distinctions developed between *peninsulares*, or those actually born in Spain, and *Creoles*, or those born in the New World. Creoles thought of themselves as loyal American Spaniards, but with so many mestizos around, the shadow of an Indian forbearer and illegitimacy always made their status suspect as far as the Europeans were concerned. Still, creoles dominated the local economies, held sway over large numbers of dependents at their haciendas and mines, and with the exception of the peninsulares, stood at the top of society. Increasingly, they developed a sense of identity and pride in their accomplishments, and

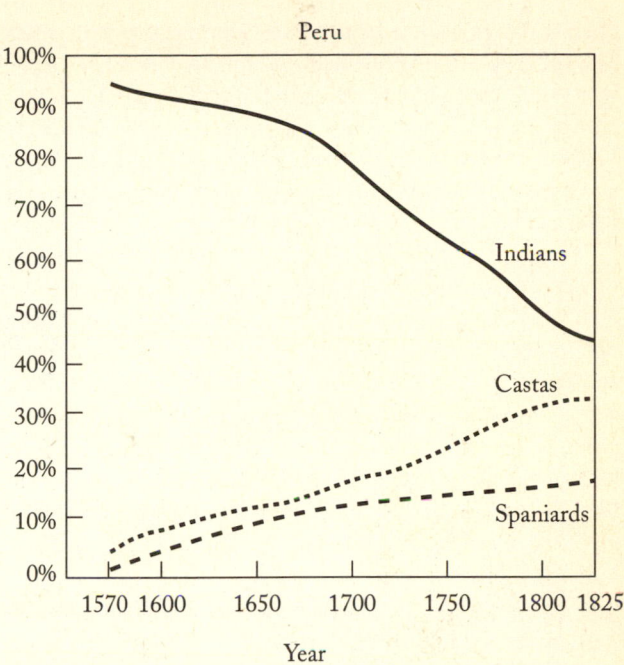

Changing Ratios of Ethnic Categories in Mexico and Peru

they were sensitive to any suggestion of inferiority or to any discrimination because of their American birth. That growing sense of self-identity eventually contributed to the movements for independence in Latin America.

The hierarchy of race intersected with traditional Iberian distinctions based on gender, age, and class. The father of a family had legal authority over his children until age 25. Women were in a subordinate position; they could not serve in government and were expected to assume the duties of motherhood and household. After marriage, women came under the authority of their husbands, but many widows assumed the direction of their family's activities. Lower-class women often controlled small-scale commerce in towns and villages, worked in the fields, or labored at the looms of small factories. Marriages were often arranged and accompanied by the payment of a dowry that remained the property of the women throughout the marriage. Women also had full rights to inheritance. Upper-class women who did not marry at a young age were placed in convents to prevent contacts or marriages with partners of unsuitable backgrounds.

THE 18TH CENTURY REFORMS

No less than in the rest of Europe, the 18th century was a period of considerable intellectual change and ferment in Spain and Portugal as well as in their empires. In

Spain and its colonies, small clubs and associations, calling themselves *amigos del país*, or friends of the country, met in many cities to discuss and plan all kinds of improvements and reform. Their programs were for material benefits and improvements, not political changes, and they sometimes had the direct sponsorship of high officials and even the king himself. In Portugal, foreign influences and ideas created a group of progressive thinkers and bureaucrats open to new ideas in economy, education, and philosophy. Much of the change that came in both empires resulted as much from the changing European economic and demographic realities as from new ideas. The expansion of population and economy in Europe and increased demands for American products, along with the long series of wars in the 18th century, gave the American colonies a new importance. The result was a resuscitation of both the Spanish and Portuguese empires, but with some long-term results that eventually led to the disruption and fall of both.

THE SHIFTING BALANCE OF POLITICS AND TRADE

By the 18th century it was clear the colonial system that had linked America to Spain had become outmoded and that Spain's exclusive hold on the Indies was no longer secure. To some extent the problem lay in Spain itself. The

Spanish kings were relatively weak by the late 17th century and did not provide adequate leadership. Beset by foreign wars, increasing debt, declining population, and internal revolts, a weakened Spain was threatened by a powerful France and by the rising mercantile strength of England and Holland, whose intransigent Protestantism also made them natural rivals of Catholic Spain.

Since the 16th century French, Dutch, and English ship captains had combined contraband trade with raiding in the Spanish Empire, and while Spain's European rivals could not seize Mexico or Peru, the sparsely populated islands and coasts of the Caribbean became likely targets. Buccaneers, owing allegiance to no nation, raided the Caribbean ports in the late-17th century. Meanwhile, the English took Jamaica in 1654, the French took control of western Hispaniola (Haiti) by 1697, and other islands fell to the English, French, and Dutch. The age of the buccaneers came to a close in the early 18th century when the other Europeans also had an interest in stopping their raids, but by then Spain and Portugal had permanent rivals in the Americas. Many of the islands turned to sugar production and the creation of slave and plantation colonies much like those in Brazil. These settlements were part of a general process of colonization, in which the English settlement of eastern North America and French occupation of Canada and the Mississippi valley were another part.

Less apparent than the loss of territories, but equally important, was the failure of the Spanish mercantile and political system. Traditional ideas that national wealth consisted primarily of the amount of silver and gold in the royal treasury were no longer adequate, and in England and France they had been replaced by mercantilist concepts in which national wealth was based on the volume of trade. Spain was slow to move toward these new ideas even though the flow of precious metal from the Indies had fallen off. The annual fleets became irregular. Silver remittances from America declined, while most goods shipped to the Indies and even the ships that carried them were non-Spanish in origin. The colonies became increasingly self-sufficient in basic commodities, and as central government became weaker, local aristocrats in the colonies exercised increasing control over the economy and government of their regions, often at the expense of the Indian and the lower-class populations. Graft and corruption were rampant in many branches of government. The empire seemed to be crumbling. What is most impressive is that Spain was able to retain its American possessions for another century.

Even with Spain in decline, the Indies still seemed an attractive prize coveted by other powers, and the opportunity to gain them was not long in coming. A final crisis was set in motion in 1701 when the Spanish king, Charles II, died without an heir. Other European nations backed various claimants to the Spanish throne, hoping to win the prize of the Spanish monarchy and its American colonies. Philip of Anjou, a Bourbon and thus a relative of the king of France, was named successor to the Spanish throne; the possibility of a powerful union of Spain and France threatened England and Austria, France's rivals. The War of the Spanish Succession (1702–1713) ensued, and the result at the Treaty of Utrecht (1713) was recognition of a branch of the Bourbon family as rulers of Spain. The treaty also recognized the loss of some territory, such as Gibraltar, to England as well as commercial concessions that allowed French merchants to operate in Seville and permitted England to trade slaves in Spanish America (and even to send one ship per year to trade for silver in the Americas). Spain's commercial monopoly was now being broken, not just by contraband trade, but by legal means as well.

THE BOURBON REFORMS

In the face of territorial loss and commercial weakness, the new and vigorous Bourbon dynasty in Spain launched a series of reforms aimed at strengthening the state and its economy. In this age of "enlightened despotism" the Spanish Bourbon monarchs, especially Charles III (1759–1788), moved by economic nationalism and a desire for strong centralized government instituted fiscal, administrative, and military reforms in Spain and its empire. The goal of these rulers and their progressive ministers, such as the Count of Floridablanca (1728–1808), was to resuscitate Spain within the framework of its traditional society by applying the principles of rational and planned government. Thus the aim was to make government more effective and more powerful, better able to direct the economy. Certain groups or institutions that opposed these measures or stood in the way might be punished or suppressed. The Jesuit order, for example, with its special allegiance to Rome, its rumored wealth, and its missions in the New World (which controlled almost 100,000 Indians in Paraguay alone) was a prime target. The Jesuits were expelled from Spain and its empire in 1767 as they had been from the Portuguese empire in 1759. In general, however, the entrenched interests of the Church and nobility were not frontally attacked so long as they did not conflict with the authority of the crown. The reforms aimed at material improvements and a more powerful state, not social or political upheaval.

French bureaucratic models were introduced. In Spain, the councils of government were supplanted by ministers who took direct responsibility for policy. The system of

Charles III, King of Spain (1759–1788), ruled Spain and its empire during the most important of the Bourbon reforms.

trade to many ports in Spain and the Indies, although trade was still restricted to Spaniards or ships sailing under Spanish license. Still, the more open policy undercut the monopoly of the consulados, and by stimulating trade made contraband less attractive.

In the Indies, the Bourbons initiated a broad program of reform. New viceroyalties were created in New Granada (1739) and the Rio de la Plata (1778) to provide better administration and defense to the growing populations of these regions. Royal investigators were sent to the Indies. The most important investigator, José de Gálvez, spent six years in Mexico before returning to Spain to become Minister of the Indies and a chief architect of reform. His investigations as well as reports by others revealed the worst abuses of graft and corruption, which implicated the local magistrates and the Creole American landowners and aristocracy. Gálvez moved to eliminate the Creoles from the upper bureaucracy of the colonies. New offices were created. After 1780 the *corregidores*, or local magistrates, were removed from the Indian villages and that office was replaced by a new system of *intendants*, or provincial governors, based on French models. This intendancy system was introduced throughout the Indies. These well-paid and experienced Spaniards took direct responsibility for tax collection, military matters, and economic development in their regions. Such measures did improve the collection of taxes and made government more effective, but these reforms also disrupted the patterns of influence and power especially among the Creole bureaucrats, miners, and landowners as their political power declined.

Many of the reforms in America were directly linked to defense and military matters. During the century, Spain was often allied with France and the global struggle between England and France for world hegemony made Spain's American possessions a logical target for English attack. During the Seven Years' War (1756–1763) the loss of Florida and the English seizure of Havana shocked Spain into action, particularly because when England held Havana in 1762, Cuban trade boomed. Regular Spanish troops were sent to New Spain, and militia units, led by local Creoles who were given military rank, were created throughout the empire. Frontiers were expanded and previously unoccupied or loosely controlled regions, such as California, were settled by a combination of missions and small frontier outposts. In the case of the Rio de la Plata, foreign competitors were resisted by military means. Spain sought every means to strengthen itself and its colonies.

During the Bourbon reforms the government took an active role in the economy. State monopolies were established on essential items such as tobacco and gunpowder. Whole new areas of Spanish America were opened to de-

taxation was tightened. The navy was reformed and new ships built. The convoy fleet system was abandoned and new ports were opened in Spain and America for the Indies trade. In 1778 the policy of *commercio libre* opened velopment. Monopoly companies were granted exclusive rights to develop certain colonial areas in return for developing the economies of those regions. The Caracas Company, formed in 1728, stimulated the development of cacao production in Venezuela and assured Spain an inexpensive supply of chocolate, but by eliminating contraband and controlling the price of imports it also provoked complaints and even rebellion from the colonists.

The commerce of the Caribbean greatly expanded under the more liberal trading regulations. Cuba now became another full-scale plantation and slave colony, exporting sugar, coffee, and tobacco and importing large numbers of Africans. Buenos Aires on the Río de la Plata proved to be a great success story. Its population had grown rapidly in the 18th century, and by 1790 it had a booming economy based on ranching and on the export of hides and salted beef. The liberalization of commerce meant that Buenos Aires no longer had to depend on the old established trade routes from Peru, and a newly prosperous merchant community in Buenos Aires now dominated the region's trade.

The commercial changes were a double-edged sword. As Spanish and English manufactures became cheaper and more accessible, they undercut locally produced goods so that some regions, such as the interior of the Río de la Plata and Ecuador, that had specialized in producing cloth or other goods now were unable to compete with the European imports. Links to international trade tightened as the diversity of Latin America's economy decreased. Later conflicts between those who favored "free trade" and those who wanted to limit imports and protect local industry were often as much about regional interests as about economic philosophy.

Finally, and most important, the major centers of the Spanish Empire also experienced considerable growth in the second half of the 18th century. As part of the general policy of reform, mining inspectors and experts had been sent to Peru and New Spain to suggest reforms and to introduce new techniques. This plus the discovery of new veins allowed for an expansion of production, especially in New Spain where silver output reached new heights, far outstripping Peru, which itself witnessed increased production.

All in all, the Bourbon reforms must be seen from two vantage points: Spain and America. Undoubtedly, in the short run the restructuring of government and economy resuscitated the Spanish Empire and gave it new life. In the long run, the removal of Creoles from government, the creation of a militia with a Creole officer corps, the opening of commerce, and other such changes contributed to a growing sense of dissatisfaction among the elite, which only their relative well-being and the existing social tensions of the sociedad de castas kept in check.

POMBAL AND BRAZIL

The Bourbon reforms in Spain and Spanish America were paralleled in the Portuguese world during the administration of the Marquis of Pombal (1755–1776), Portugal's authoritarian prime minister. Pombal had lived as ambassador in England and had observed the benefits of mercantilism first hand. He hoped to use these same techniques along with state intervention in the economy to break England's hold on the Portuguese economy, especially on the flow of Brazilian gold from Portugal to England. This became crucial as the production of Brazilian gold began to decline after 1760. In another example of "enlightened despotism," Pombal brutally suppressed any group or institution that stood in the way of royal power and his programs. He developed a particular dislike for the Jesuits because of their allegiance to Rome and their semi-independent control of large areas in Brazil. Pombal expelled the Jesuits from the Portuguese Empire in 1759.

Pombal made Brazil the centerpiece of his reforms. Vigorous administrators were sent to the colony to enforce the changes. Fiscal reforms aimed at eliminating contraband, gold smuggling, and tax evasion. Monopoly companies were formed to stimulate agriculture in older plantation zones and were given the right to import large numbers of slaves. New crops were introduced. Just as in Spanish America, in Brazil new regions began to flourish under the impetus of reform. Rio de Janeiro became the capital and its hinterland was the scene of agricultural growth. The undeveloped Amazonian region, long dominated by Jesuit missionaries, received new attention. A monopoly company was created to develop the region's economy, and it stimulated the development of cotton plantations and the export of wild cacao from the Amazonian forests. These new exports joined the traditional sugar, tobacco, and hides as Brazil's main products.

Pombal was willing to do some social tinkering as part of his project of reform. He abolished slavery in Portugal in order to assure a steady supply of slaves to Brazil, the economic cornerstone of the empire. Because Brazil was vast and needed to be both occupied and defended, he removed Indians from missionary control in the Amazon and encouraged whites to marry them. Immigrant couples from Portugal and the Azores were sent to colonize in the Amazon and the plains of southern Brazil, which now began to produce quantities of wheat and cattle. In 1778 a treaty between Spain and Portugal established the frontier between their American colonies. Like the Bourbons in Spain, Pombal hoped to revitalize the colonies as a way of strengthening the mother country. While new policies were instituted, little changed within society. Brazil was just as profoundly based on slavery in the late 18th century as it had ever been, as levels of slave imports reached 20,000 a year.

Even in the long run Pombal's policies were not fully effective. Although he considerably reduced Portugal's trade imbalance with England in this period, Brazilian trade suffered because demand for its products on the world market remained low. This was a classic problem for the American colonies. Their economies were so tied to the sale of their products on the European market and so controlled by policies in the metropolis that the colonies' range of action was always limited. While for all his efforts Pombal's policies were not immediately successful, they did set the stage and provided the structure for an economic boom in the last 20 years of the 18th century.

REFORMS, REACTIONS, AND REVOLTS

By the middle of the 18th century the American colonies of Spain and Portugal, like the rest of the world, were experiencing considerable growth in population and productive capacity. Scholars disagree on the role of the Bourbon and Pombaline reforms in this process, but the growth was undeniable. By the end of the century, Spanish America had a population of close to 13 million. Between 1740 and 1800 the population of Mexico, the most populous area, increased from 3.5 to almost 6 million, about half of which were Indians. In Brazil, the population reached about 2 million by the end of the century. This overall increase was due to declining mortality rates, increasing fertility levels, increasing immigration from Europe, and the thriving slave trade. The opening of new areas to development and Europe's increasing demand for American products accompanied the growth of population. The American colonies were experiencing a boom in the last years of the 18th century.

Reformist policies, tighter tax collection, and the presence of a more activist government in both Spanish America and Brazil disrupted old patterns of power and influence, raised expectations, and sometimes provoked violent colonial reactions. Urban riots, tax revolts, and Indian uprisings were not unknown before 1700, but after that date serious and more protracted rebellions broke out. In New Granada, popular complaints against the government's control of tobacco and liquor consumption, and rising

prices as well as new taxes, led to the widespread Comunero Revolt in 1781. A royal army was defeated, the viceroy fled from Bogotá, and a rebel army almost took the capital. Only tensions among the various racial and social groups and concessions by the government brought an end to the rebellion.

At the same time in Peru, an even more threatening revolt erupted. A great Indian uprising took place under the leadership of Jose Gabriel Condorcanqui, Tupac Amaru. A mestizo with a direct link to the family of the Incas, Tupac Amaru led a rebellion against "bad government." For almost three years the whole viceroyalty was thrown into turmoil as over 70,000 Indians, mestizos, and even a few Creoles joined in rebellion against the worst abuses of the colonial regime. Tupac Amaru was captured and brutally executed, but the rebellion smoldered until 1783. It failed mostly because the Creoles, though they had their own grievances against the government, feared that a real social upheaval might take place.

This kind of social upheaval was not present in Brazil, where a government attempt to collect back taxes in the mining region led in 1788 to a plot against Portuguese control. A few bureaucrats, intellectuals, and miners planned an uprising for independence, but their conspiracy was discovered. The plotters were arrested, and one conspirator, a militia officer nicknamed Tiradentes, was hung.

These movements despite their various social bases, indicated that the activist government increased dissatisfaction in the American colonies. The new prosperity of the late 18th century contributed to a sense of self-confidence and economic interest among certain colonial classes, which made them sensitive to restrictions and control by Spain and Portugal. Different groups had different complaints, but the sharp social and ethnic divisions within the colonies acted as a barrier to common effort and tended to undercut revolutionary movements. Only when the Spanish political system became disrupted by a crisis of legitimacy at the beginning of the 19th century did real separation and independence from the mother countries become a possibility.

CONCLUSION

THE DIVERSE INGREDIENTS OF LATIN AMERICAN CIVILIZATION

During the course of three centuries, Spain and Portugal had created large colonial empires in the Americas. These American colonies had provided a basis of power to their

Iberian mother countries and had taken a vital place in the expanding world economy as suppliers of precious minerals and certain crops to the growing economy of Europe. By the 18th century, the weakened positions of Spain and Portugal within Europe had allowed England and France to benefit directly from the Iberian trade with American colonies.

To their American colonies, the Iberian nations had transferred and imposed their language, laws, forms of government, religion, and institutions. Large numbers of immigrants, first as conquerors and later as settlers, had come to the colonies. Eventually, the whole spectrum of Iberian society was recreated in the New World as men and women came to seek a better life, bringing with them their customs, ideas, religion, laws, and ways of life. By government and individual action, a certain homogeneity was created, both in Spanish America and in Brazil. That seeming unity was most apparent among the Europeanized population.

Underlying the apparent continuity with Spain and Portugal and homogeneity among the various colonies were great variations. Latin America, with its distinct environments, its various economic possibilities, and its diverse Indian peoples imposed new realities. In places like Mexico and Peru, Indian cultures had emerged from the shock of conquest, battered but still vibrant. Indian communities adapted to the new colonial situation. A distinctive multiethnic and multiracial society developed, drawing on Iberian precedents but also dependent on the nature of the Indian population and the proportion of various mixed racial categories. In areas where slavery predominated, African cultures also played a major role. Argentina with few Indians, Cuba with its slaves and plantations, and Mexico with its large rural Indian population all shared the same Hispanic traditions and laws and all had a predominantly white elite, but their social and economic realities made them very different places. Latin America developed as a composite civilization—distinct from the West though related to it—combining in a series of local variations aspects of European and Indian culture and society, or creating the racial hierarchies of slave societies in places like Brazil.

From the perspective of the world economy, despite the decline in production of precious metals, Latin American products remained in great demand in Europe's markets, and as Latin Americans began to seek political independence in the early 19th century, they were confronted by this basic economic fact and by their continued dependence on trade with the developing world economy. Latin America's world economic position, with its labor force organiza-

tion and outside commercial control, was yet another difference between this new civilization and that of western Europe.

FURTHER READINGS

James Lockhart and Stuart B. Schwartz's *Early Latin America* (1982), provides an interpretation and overview. Lyle N. Macalister's *Spain and Portugal in the New World* (1984) is particularly good on the Iberian background and on the formation of societies in Latin America. John H. Parry's *The Spanish Seabourn Empire* (1966) is well written and particularly good on commerce and government.

On the conquest period there are excellent regional studies. Geographer Carl O. Sauer's *The Early Caribbean* (1966), describes the discovery, settlement, and conquest of that region with much attention to Indian culture. James Lockhart's *Spanish Peru* (1968) is a model reconstruction of conquest society while his *Men of Cajamarca* (1972) is an in-depth look at a group of conquistadores. The conquest of Mexico can be seen from two different angles in Bernal Díaz del Castillo's *The Discovery and Conquest of Mexico*, trans. A. P. Maudsley (1956), and in Miguel López-Portilla's *The Broken Spears. The Aztec Account of the Conquest of Mexico* (1962).

The transformation of Indian societies has been studied in books such as Steve J. Stern's *Peru's Indian Peoples and the Challenge of Spanish Conquest* (1982) on the early colonial era, and William B. Taylor's *Drinking, Homicide, and Rebellion in Colonial Mexican Villages* (1979) on the 18th century. Another approach to the impact of conquest is presented in Noble David Cook's *Demographic Collapse. Indian Peru, 1520–1620* (1981), while Murdo MacLeod's *Spanish Central America* (1973), presents an integrated regional study of society and economy. Particularly sensitive to Indian views is Nancy Farriss's *Maya Society under Colonial Rule* (1984).

Social and economic history have received considerable attention. The establishment of colonial economies has been studied in detail in books such as François Chevalier's *Land and Society in Colonial Mexico* (1963), Stuart Schwartz's *Sugar Plantations and the Formation of Brazilian Society* (1985), and Peter J. Bakewell's *Silver Mining and Society in Colonial Mexico* (1971). Very good social history is now being written. For example, Silvia Arrom's *The Women of Mexico City, 1790–1857* (1985) examines the changing role of women. In Louisa Schell Hoberman and

Susan Migden Socolow, eds., *Cities and Society in Colonial Latin America* (1986), urban social types are examined. A different kind of social history that examines popular thought can be seen in Jacques Lafaye's *Quetzalcóatl and Guadalupe* (1974).

The best starting place on the Bourbon reforms is David Brading's *Miners and Merchants in Bourbon Mexico*

(1971), while John L. Phelan's study of the Comunero Revolt, *The People and the King* (1978), examines the Bourbon reforms' unintended effects. Dauril Alden's *Royal Government in Colonial Brazil* (1968) shows Pombal's effects on Brazil.

Ottoman Empire	1281 Founding of the Ottoman dynasty	1453 Ottoman capture of Constantinople	1507 Portuguese victory over Ottoman-Arab fleet at Diu in the Indian Ocean	1520–1566 Rule of Suley-man the Magnificent; con-struction of the Suleymaniye mosque in Constantinople
	1350s Ottoman invasion of Europe; conquest of much of the Balkans and Hungary	c. 1450s Beginning of large-scale recruitment of Janissary troops		1514 Ottoman victory over Safavids at Chaldiran
	1243 Mongol invasion of Asia Minor　1402 Timur's invasion; Ottoman setbacks under Bayazid			1517 Ottoman capture of Syria and Egypt
Safavid Dynasty	1334 Death of the first Safavid Sufi master at Ardabil	c. 1450s Shi'ite influences enter Safavid teachings	1501–1510 Safavid conquest of Persia (present-day Iran)	
			1514 Safavid defeat by Ottomans at Chaldiran	
Mughal Dynasty				

26 The Muslim Empires

INTRODUCTION. Early modern developments in the Islamic world—the Middle East, North Africa, parts of India and island Southeast Asia, and (in terms of political control) southeastern Europe—differed greatly from the dynamics of the new civilization that was developing in Latin America. Muslim civilization encompassed a diverse combination of age-old civilized centers, now reorganized in terms of political boundaries but predominantly Islamic in religion and cultural influences. Intensified trading contacts, the continuing spread of the Islamic faith, and the growth of three great empires dominated the 1450-1750 period in the overall history of the Muslim zone. The rise of the West and the growing world economic links that had been so central to developments in Latin American societies had much less of an impact on Muslim peoples and cultures in this era. But from the eastern Mediterranean to the Java Sea, the expansive Europeans were establishing commercial and military beachheads that would serve as the bases for their growing dominance over some parts of the Islamic world from the early 18th century onward.

The great nomadic invasions by the Mongols in the first half of the 13th century and by the armies of Timur in the last decades of the 14th century had made a shambles of much of the Muslim world. The

---

1529 First Ottoman siege of Vienna

1571 Battle of Lepanto

1699 Treaty of Carlowitz; Ottomans cede territories in Europe

1730 Ottoman armies are defeated by Persian forces under Nadir Khan (later Nadir Shah, emperor of Persia)

1727 First Turkish-language printing press founded

1683 Last Ottoman siege of Vienna

1730s First Western-modeled military schools established

1540–1545 Mughal ruler Humayan in exile at Safavid court

1588–1629 Reign of Abbas I (the Great)

1736–1747 Reign of Nadir Shah

1722 Fall of the Safavid dynasty

1556–1605 Reign of Akbar

1631–1653 Construction of the Taj Mahal

1657–1658 Great war of succession between sons of Shah Jahan

1540–1545 Humayan in exile at the Safavid court

1640s Rise of Maratta resistance to Mughals in western India

1739 Nadir Shah invades India from Persia, sacks the Mughal capital at Delhi

1540 Babur's successor, Humayan, driven from India

1526 Battle of Panipat; Babur's conquest of India

1582 Akbar's proclamation of his new religion

1556 Mughal Empire reestablished in North India

c. 1600s Arrival of Dutch and English merchants in the Mughal Empire

1680s Rajput and peasant revolts in North India

1658–1707 Reign of Aurangzeb

pretence of Muslim unity, which had been preserved by the Seljuk Sultans' retention of the powerless caliphs after 1055, was shattered in 1258 by the conquest and sacking of the Abbasid capital and the extinction of the long-lived caliphate. Regional dynasties in areas as distant as Asia Minor and India were also crushed by nomadic armies, and many splendid Islamic cities were laid to waste. But in the wake of the last and greatest incursions of the nomadic peoples of central Asia into the civilized heartlands of Eurasia, three new Muslim dynasties arose that collectively produced a new flowering of Islamic civilization. Competition between them also led to important political divisions and periodic military clashes, especially between the Ottomans and Safavids, within the Muslim world.

The largest of the three empires, the Ottoman, stretched at its peak in the 17th century from North Africa to southern Russia, and from Hungary to the port of Aden on the southern end of the Red Sea. To the east in what is now Iran and Afghanistan, the Safavid dynasty arose to challenge the Ottomans for leadership of the Islamic world. Finally, in India yet another Muslim empire, centered like most of the earlier ones on the Delhi region of the Gangetic plain, was built under the leadership of a succession of remarkable Mughal rulers.

The combination of these three empires—Ottoman, Safavid, and Mughal—produced the greatest political and military power the Islamic world had yet attained. The Ottomans' armies captured Byzantium in 1453, thus putting an end to the Eastern Roman Empire. They reduced Hungary to vassalage and threatened Austria as late as the end of the 17th century. Farther east, Mughal forces conquered much of the Indian subcontinent, thus building a far larger empire than any previous Muslim or even

Hindu dynasty. Muslim naval power was felt in the Mediterranean and the Indian Ocean until late in the 16th century. With those of China, the Ottoman navies were the only ones that stood a chance of blocking European global expansion by sea.

In addition to political and military power, the three empires produced an artistic renaissance in the Islamic world. Particularly in painting, architecture, and literature, the 16th and 17th centuries, when each of the empires peaked in power, were a time of stunning achievement. Though new breakthroughs in the sciences paled in comparison with earlier Muslim discoveries, there were advances in military technology and engineering, and medical treatment and hospital care continued to compare favorably with what was available in Europe and China. The strength and splendor of the three great empires contributed to the continued expansion of Islam, mainly through peaceful conversion in Africa, India, Southeast and central Asia, as well as in some of the European bastions of Christendom.

There were striking similarities among the three empires that are the focus of this chapter. Each empire had its origins in the Turkic nomadic cultures of the central Asian steppe. Religious fervor and zeal for Islamic conversion were central to the rise of both the Ottoman and Safavid dynasties. Though the founders of the Mughal Empire were displaced princes in search of a new kingdom rather than religious zealots, their successors were frequently preoccupied with questions of how far to push conversion efforts aimed at the Hindu majority of the peoples of India. Each empire was based on military conquest, and, at least in its early stages, oriented to the support of its armies and military classes. Both the early conquests and continued strength of each of the dynasties depended on its effective use of firearms on the battlefield and in siege warfare. Each of the Muslim empires was ruled by a succession of absolute monarchs whose imperial pretensions and courtly rituals were patterned in varying degrees after those of earlier Islamic kingdoms. Support of the ever-expanding bureaucracies and military establishments of each empire was drawn primarily from taxes levied on the peoples of the ancient agrarian societies that each empire conquered and ruled. Under each dynasty unique styles of artistic and literary expression developed, which drew both on earlier Islamic expression and on the skills and sensibilities of the conquered peoples, both Muslim and non-Muslim.

These similarities were counterbalanced by significant differences between the rival Muslim empires. Although each dynasty was Muslim, the Mughals, for example, ruled a predominantly non-Muslim population. Thus the political tactics and social policies followed by the Mughal rulers in India differed fundamentally from those pursued

The Ottoman, Safavid, and Mughal Empires

by their Safavid rivals in Persia, whose subjects were for the most part followers of Islam. The Ottoman situation in this respect was midway between the Mughals and Safavids. For the first centuries of Ottoman rule, their subjects were largely Christian. Though extensive conversions to Islam from the 15th century onward resulted in a Muslim majority, throughout their reign the Ottoman sultans had to keep the interests and reactions of the empire's large Christian minority in mind. The empires were also divided by the Sunni-Shi'a split that, as we have seen, emerged in the early decades of Islamic history and persisted through the centuries. Enmity was particularly intense between the Ottoman champions of Sunni Islam and the Shi'ite Safavids. These neighboring powers frequently warred over territory and persecuted the adherents of their rivals' brand of Islam. Sunni and Shi'a differences also led to varying religious practices, legal codes, and social organization in each of the Islamic empires.

THE OTTOMANS: FROM FRONTIER WARRIORS TO EMPIRE BUILDERS

For centuries before the rise of the Ottoman dynasty in the 13th and 14th centuries, Turkic-speaking peoples from central Asia had played key roles in Islamic civilization as soldiers and administrators, often in the service of the Abbasid caliphs. In fact, the collapse of the Seljuk Turkic kingdom of Rum in eastern Anatolia in Asia Minor, following the invasion by the Mongols in 1243 described in Chapter 20, opened the way for the Ottomans' rise to power. The Mongols raided but did not directly rule Anatolia, which fell into a chaotic period of warfare between petty, would-be successor states to the Seljuk sultans. Turkic peoples, both those fleeing the Mongols and those in search of easy booty, flooded into the region in the last decades of the 13th century. One of these peoples, called the Ottomans after an early leader named Osman, came to dominate the rest, and within decades they had begun to build a new empire based in Anatolia.

By the 1350s, the Ottomans had advanced from their strongholds in Asia Minor across the Bosporus straits into Europe. Thrace was quickly conquered and by the end of the century large portions of the Balkans had been added to their rapidly expanding territories. The Ottoman rise to power was severely, but only temporarily set back in 1402, when the armies of Timur swept into Anatolia and defeated the Ottoman sultan Bayazid at Angora. For nearly a decade thereafter the region was torn by civil war between Bayazid's sons, each hoping to occupy his father's throne. The victory of Mehmed I led to the reunification of the empire and new conquests in both Europe and Asia Minor.

In moving into Europe in the mid-14th century, the Ottomans had bypassed rather than conquered the great city of Constantinople, long the capital of the once-powerful Byzantine Empire. By the mid-15th century, the Ottomans, who had earlier alternated between alliances and warfare with the Byzantines, were strong enough to undertake the capture of the well-fortified city. For seven weeks in the spring of 1453, the army of Mehmed II, "The Conqueror," which numbered well over 100,000, assaulted the triple ring of land walls that had protected the city for centuries. The undermanned forces of the defenders repulsed attack after attack until the sultan ordered his gunners to batter a portion of the walls with their massive siege cannon. Wave after wave of Ottoman troops struck at

This illuminated French manuscript from the 15th century shows the Ottoman siege of Constantinople in 1453. The Muslim capture of the great eastern bastion of Christian Europe aroused fears throughout the continent, resulting in demands for Crusades to recapture the city.

the gaps in the defenses that had been cut by the guns, overwhelmed the defenders, and raced into the city to loot and pillage for the three days that Mehmed had promised as their reward for victory.

In the two centuries after the conquest of Constantinople, the armies of a succession of able Ottoman rulers extended the empire into Syria and Egypt, across North Africa, thus bringing under their rule the bulk of the Arab world. The empire also spread through the Balkans into Hungary in Europe, and around the Black and Red Seas. The Ottomans also became a formidable naval power in the Mediterranean Sea. Powerful Ottoman galley fleets made it possible to capture major island bases on Rhodes, Crete, and Cyprus; to drive the Venetians and Genoese from much of the eastern Mediterranean; and to threaten southern Italy with invasion on a number of occasions. From their humble origins as frontier vassals, the Ottomans had risen to become the protectors of the Islamic heartlands and the scourge of Christian Europe. As late as 1683, Ottoman armies were able to lay siege to the capital of the Austrian Habsburg dynasty at Vienna. Even though the Ottoman Empire was in decline by this point in time and the threat the assault posed to Vienna was far less serious than a previous attack in the early 16th century, the Ottomans remained a major force in European politics until the late 19th century.

A STATE GEARED TO WARFARE

Befitting an empire that had been founded and extended to spread Islam through the waging of the jihad, or holy war, military leaders played a dominant role in the Ottoman state and the economy of the empire was geared to warfare and expansion. The Turkic cavalrymen, who were chiefly responsible for the Ottomans' early conquests from the 13th to the 16th centuries, gradually developed into a warrior aristocracy. They were granted control over land and peasant producers in annexed areas for the support of their often sizeable households and numerous military retainers. From the 15th century onward, members of the warrior class also vied with religious leaders and administrators drawn from other social groups for control of the ever-expanding Ottoman bureaucracy. As the power of the warrior aristocracy shrank at the center, they sought to build up regional and local bases of support that inevitably competed with the sultans and central bureaucracy for revenue and labor control.

A considerable portion of the economic resources that the Ottoman sultans managed to control themselves was funneled into maintaining the massive armies required both to sustain expansion and protect the territories the Ottomans had won from rivals in all directions. From the mid-15th century, the imperial armies were increasingly

The Ottoman Empire at Its Peak in the 17th Century

dominated by infantry divisions made up of troops called *Janissaries*. Most of the Janissaries had been forcibly conscripted as adolescent boys in conquered areas, such as the Balkans, where the majority of the population retained its Christian faith. Sometimes the boys' parents had willingly turned their sons over to the Ottoman recruiters because of the opportunities for advancement that came with service to the Ottoman sultans. Though legally slaves, the youths were given fairly extensive schooling for the time and converted to Islam. Some of them went on to serve in the palace or bureaucracy, but most became Janissaries.

Because the Janissaries controlled the artillery and firearms that became increasingly vital to Ottoman success in warfare with both Christian and Muslim adversaries, they rapidly became the most powerful component in the Ottoman military machine. Their growing importance was another factor contributing to the steady decline of the role of the aristocratic cavalrymen. Just like the mercenary forces that had earlier served the caliphs of Baghdad, the Janissaries eventually sought to translate military service into political influence. By the late 15th century they were deeply involved in court politics; by the mid-16th century they had the power to depose sultans and decide which one of a dying ruler's sons would mount the throne.

THE SULTANS AND THEIR COURT

The sultans were nominally absolute monarchs, but even the most powerful sultan maintained his position by playing factions in the warrior elite off each other and the warriors as a whole against the Janissaries and other groups. Chief among the latter were the Islamic religious scholars and legal experts, who retained many of the administrative functions they had held under the Arab caliphs of earlier centuries. In addition to Muslim traders, commerce within the empire was in the hands of Christian and Jewish trading groups, who as dhimmis, or "peoples of the Book," were under the protection of the Ottoman rulers. The sultans were also responsible for the prosperity of their subjects and for upholding Islamic law within their domains. Though they have often been depicted as brutal and corrupt despots in Western writings, the Ottoman sultans, especially in the early centuries of their sway, were frequently very capable rulers. Ottoman conquest often meant effective administration and tax relief for the peoples of areas annexed to the empire. This was true for the peasants throughout much of the Balkans, whose Christian overlords had oppressed them with excessive tax and service demands in the decades before the Ottoman takeover.

Like the Abbasid caliphs, the Ottoman sultans grew more and more distant from their subjects as their empire increased in size and wealth. In their splendid marble palaces and pleasure gardens, surrounded by large numbers of slaves and the many wives and concubines of their harems, Ottoman rulers followed elaborate court rituals based on those of earlier Byzantine, Persian, and Arab dynasts. Day-to-day administration was carried out by a large bureaucracy headed by a grand *vizier* (*wazir* in Arabic), the overall head of the imperial administration, who often held more real power than the sultan himself. Early sultans took an active role in political decisions and often personally led their armies into battle. Their sons were usually made provincial administrators or military commanders. This practice gave the potential successors to the ruler vital leadership training, and it does much to explain the high quality of many of the Ottoman monarchs until the late 16th century.

Like earlier Muslim dynasties, however, the Ottomans suffered greatly because they inherited Islamic principles of political succession that remained vague and contested. The existence of many talented and experienced claimants to the throne meant constant danger of civil strife. The death of a sultan could, and increasingly did, lead to protracted warfare among his sons. Defeated claimants sometimes fled to the domains of Christian or Muslim rulers hostile to the Ottomans, thereby becoming rallying points for military campaigns against the son who had managed to gain the throne. The uncertainty of succession and threat of civil strife led some of the early sultans to have all their brothers and other potential family rivals put to death at the time of their accession to the throne. The extent to which fratricide was practiced, however, was greatly exaggerated by the Ottomans' Christian adversaries. From about 1600, rival princes and other possible claimants to the throne were usually confined to the palace and harem, rather than being put to death.

CONSTANTINOPLE RESTORED AND THE FLOWERING OF OTTOMAN CULTURE

An empire that encompassed so many and diverse cultures from Europe, Africa, and Asia naturally varied greatly from one province to the next in its social arrangements, artistic production, and physical appearance. But the Ottomans' ancient and cosmopolitan capital at Constantinople richly combined the disparate elements of their extensive territories. Like the Byzantine Empire as a whole, Constantinople had fallen on hard times in the centuries before the Ottoman conquest in 1453. Soon after Mehmed II's armies had captured and sacked the city, however, the Ottoman ruler set about restoring its ancient glory. He had the cathedral of Saint Sophia converted into one of the grandest mosques in the Islamic world, and new mosques and palaces were built throughout the city, benefiting from architectural advances the Ottomans derived from the Byzantine heritage. Aqueducts were constructed from the surrounding hills to supply the growing population with water, markets were reopened, and the city's defenses were repaired. Each of the sultans who ruled in the centuries after Mehmed strove to be remembered for his efforts to beautify the capital. The most prominent additions were further mosques that represent some of the most sublime contributions of the Ottomans to Islamic and human civilization. The most spectacular of these was the Suleymaniye, built by one of the most successful of the sultans, Suleyman the Magnificent (1520–1566). Though it smacks a good deal of hometown pride, the following description by a 17th-century Ottoman chronicler of the reaction of some Christian visitors to the mosque conveys a sense of the awe that the structure still evokes:

The humble writer of these lines once himself saw ten Frankish infidels skilful [sic] in geometry and architecture, who, when the door-keeper had changed their shoes for slippers, and had introduced them into the mosque for the purpose of showing it to them, laid their finger on their mouths, and each bit his finger from astonishment when they saw the minarets; but when they beheld the dome they tossed up their hats and cried Maria! Maria! and on observing the four arches which supported the dome . . . they could not find terms to express their admiration, and the ten . . . remained a full hour looking with astonishment on those arches. [One of them said] that nowhere was so much beauty, external and internal, to be found united, and that in the whole of Frangistan [Christian Europe] there was not a single edifice which could be compared to this.

In addition to the mosques, sultans and powerful administrators built mansions, rest houses, religious schools, and hospitals throughout the city. Both public and private gardens further beautified the capital, which Ottoman writers were inclined to compare to paradise itself. The city and its suburbs stretched along both sides of the Bosporus, the narrow strait that separates Europe from Asia. Its harbors and the Golden Horn, a triangular bay that formed the northern boundary of the city, were crowded with merchant ships from ports throughout the Mediterranean and the Black Sea. Constantinople's great bazaars were filled with merchants and travelers from throughout the empire and places as distant as England and Malaya. They offered the seasoned shopper all manner of produce from the spices of the East Indies and the ivory of Africa to slaves and forest products from Russia and fine carpets from Persia. Coffeehouses—places where males gathered to smoke to-

bacco (introduced from America in the 17th century by English merchants), gossip, do business, and play chess—were found in all sections of the city and were pivotal to the social life of the capital. The coffeehouses also played a major role in the cultural life of Constantinople as centers where poets and scholars could congregate, read their latest works aloud, and debate about politics and the merits of each other's ideas.

Beneath the ruling classes a sizeable portion of the population of Constantinople and other Ottoman cities belonged to the merchant and artisan classes. The Ottoman regime closely regulated both commercial exchanges and handicraft production. Government inspectors were employed to ensure that standard weights and measures were used, to license the opening of new shops and regulate the entry of apprentice artisans into the trades, and to inspect the quality of the goods they produced. Like their counterparts in medieval European towns, the artisans were organized into guilds. Guild officers set craft standards, arbitrated disputes between their members, provided financial assistance for needy members, and even arranged popular entertainments, which were often linked to religious festivals. The guilds of Ottoman towns were much more closely supervised by government officials, and a wider array of occupational groups—including entertainers, prostitutes, and even ordinary laborers—were organized into guilds than was normally the case in Europe.

The early Ottomans had written in Persian, while Arabic remained an important language for works on law and religion throughout the empire's history. But by the 17th century the Turkish language of the Ottoman court had become the preferred mode of expression for poets and historians as well as the language of the Ottoman bureaucracy. In writing, as in the fine arts, the Ottomans' achievements have been somewhat overshadowed by those of their contemporary Persian and Indian rivals. Nonetheless, the authors, artists, and craftsmen of the Ottoman Empire have left a considerable legacy, particularly in poetry, ceramics, carpet manufacturing, and above all in architecture.

THE PROBLEM OF OTTOMAN DECLINE

Much of the literature on the Ottoman Empire concentrates on its slow decline from the champion of the Muslim world and the great adversary of Christendom to the "sick man" of Europe in the 18th and 19th centuries. This approach provides a very skewed view of Ottoman history as a whole. Traced from its origins in the late 13th century, the Ottoman state is one of the great success stories in human political history. Vigorous and expansive until the late 17th century, the Ottomans were able to ward off the powerful enemies that surrounded their domains on all sides for nearly four centuries. The dynasty endured for over 600 years—a feat matched by no other in all human history.

From one perspective the long Ottoman decline, which officials and court historians actively discussed from the mid-17th century onward, reflects the great strength of the institutions on which the empire was built. Despite internal revolts and periodic conflicts with such powerful foreign rivals as the Russian, Austrian, Spanish, and Safavid empires, the Ottomans ruled into the 20th century. Yet centuries earlier the empire had reached the limits of its expansive power, and by the late 17th century the long retreat from Russia, Europe, and the Arab lands had begun. In a sense, some contraction was inevitable. Even when it was at the height of its power, the empire was too large to be maintained given the resource base that the sultans had at their disposal and the primitive state of transport and communications in the preindustrial era.

INTERNAL WEAKNESSES AND IMPERIAL DECLINE

The Ottoman state had been built on war and steady territorial expansion. As possibilities for new conquests ran out and lands began to be lost to the Ottomans' Christian and Muslim enemies, the means of maintaining the over-sized bureaucracy and army shrank markedly. The decline in the effectiveness of the administrative system that held the empire together was signaled by the rampant growth of corruption among Ottoman officials. The venality and incompetence of state bureaucrats in turn prompted regional and local officials—in provinces where the population was predominantly European and Arab as well as those with a Turkish majority—to retain increasing amounts of revenue for their own purposes. Revenues that were retained at the local and regional level were, of course, lost to those who sought to run and defend the empire as a whole.

Poorly regulated by the central government, many local officials, who also controlled large landed estates, squeezed the peasants and the laborers who worked their lands for additional taxes and services. At times the oppressive demands of local officials and estate owners sparked rebellions. But more frequently they caused the hard-pressed peasantry to abandon their holdings and flee to those of less rapacious lords or to become vagabonds, bandits, or beggars in the cities. Both responses resulted in the abandonment of cultivated lands and social dislocations that further drained the resources of the empire.

From the 17th century on, the forces that undermined the empire from below were compounded by growing problems at the center of imperial administration. The practice of assigning the royal princes administrative or military positions, in order to prepare them to rule, died out. Instead, possible successors to the throne were kept like hostages in special sections of the palace, where they remained until one of them ascended the throne. The other princes and potential rivals were also, in effect, imprisoned for life in the palace. Though it might have made the reigning sultan more secure, this solution to the problem of contested succession produced monarchs far less prepared to rule than those in the formative centuries of the dynasty. The great warrior-emperors of early Ottoman history gave way, with some important exceptions, to weak and indolent rulers, addicted to drink, drugs, and the pleasures of the harem. In many instances the later sultans were little more than pawns in the power struggles between the viziers and other powerful officials, and the leaders of the increasingly influential Janissary corps. Because the imperial apparatus had been geared to strong and absolute rulers, the decline in the caliber of Ottoman emperors had devastating effects on the strength of the empire as a whole. Civil strife increased and the discipline and leadership of the armies on which the empire depended for survival deteriorated.

MILITARY REVERSES AND THE OTTOMAN RETREAT

Debilitating changes within the empire were occurring at a time when challenges from without were growing rapidly. The Ottomans had made very effective use of artillery and firearms in building their empire. But their addiction to huge siege guns and the Janissaries' determination to block all military changes that might jeopardize the power they had been able to gain within the state caused the Ottomans to fall farther and farther behind their European rivals in the critical art of waging war. With the widespread introduction of light field artillery into the armies of the European powers in the 17th century, Ottoman losses on the battlefield multiplied rapidly and the threat they posed for the West began to recede.

On the sea the Ottomans were eclipsed as early as the 16th century. The end of their dominance was presaged by their defeat by a combined Spanish-Venetian fleet at Lepanto in 1571. Though the Ottomans had completely rebuilt their war fleet within a year after the battle and soon launched an assault on North Africa that preserved that area for Islam, their control of the eastern Mediterranean had been lost. Even more ominously, in the decades before Lepanto, the Ottomans and the Muslim world had been outflanked by the Portuguese seafarers down and then around the coast of Africa. The failure in the early 1500s of the Ottomans and their Muslim allies in the Indian Ocean to drive the Portuguese from Asian waters proved far more disastrous than Ottoman defeats in the Mediterranean.

The clash of the galley fleets at Lepanto was one of the great sea battles in history. But despite devastating losses, the Ottomans managed to replace most of their fleet and go back on the offensive against their Christian adversaries within a year.

Portuguese naval victories in the Indian Ocean revealed the obsolescence of the Ottoman galley fleets and Mediterranean-style warships more generally. The trading goods, particularly spices, that the Portuguese carried back to Europe around Africa enriched the Ottomans' Christian rivals. In addition, the fact that a sizeable portion of the flow of these products was no longer transmitted to European ports through Muslim trading centers in the eastern Mediterranean meant that merchants and tax collectors in the Ottoman Empire lost critical profits and revenues. As if this were not enough, from the late 16th century on, large amounts of silver flowed into the Ottomans' lands from mines worked by Amerindian laborers in the Spanish possessions of the New World. This sudden influx of bullion into the rather rigid and slow growing economy of the Ottoman Empire set off a long-term inflationary trend that further undermined the finances of the empire.

Several able sultans took measures to shore up the crumbling imperial edifice in the 17th century. The collapse of the Safavid dynasty in Persia and conflicts between the European powers at this time also gave the Ottomans

hope that their earlier dominance might be restored, but their reprieve proved temporary. With the scientific, technological, and commercial changes occurring in Europe and the overseas expansion that these innovations had made possible, the Ottomans were falling at an accelerating rate behind their Christian rivals in most areas of endeavor, but most critically in trade and making war. The sense the Ottomans inherited from their Arab, Persian, and Turkic predecessors that little of what happened in Europe was important prevented them from taking seriously the revolutionary changes transforming western Europe. The intense conservatism of powerful groups like the Janissaries and, to a lesser extent, the religious scholars reinforced this fatal myopia. Through much of the 17th and 18th centuries, these groups proved able to block most of the Western-inspired innovations that reform-minded sultans or their advisors sought to introduce. As a result of this narrow and potentially dangerous view, the isolated and increasingly fossilized Ottoman imperial system proved incapable of checking the forces that were steadily making for its dismemberment.

DOCUMENT
AN ISLAMIC
TRAVELER LAMENTS
THE MUSLIMS'
INDIFFERENCE TO
EUROPE

Though most of the travelers and explorers in this era were Europeans who went out to Africa, Asia, and the Americas, a few individuals from these lands visited Europe. One of these, Abu Taleb, was a scholar of mixed Turkic-Persian descent whose family had settled in India. At the end of the 18th century, Abu Taleb traveled in Europe for three years and later wrote an account in Persian of his experiences there. Though his was one of the few firsthand sources of information about Europe available to Muslim scholars and leaders, Abu Taleb was deeply disturbed by the lack of interest shown by other Muslims in his observations and discoveries.

. . . when I reflect on the want of energy and the indolent dispositions of my countrymen, and the many erroneous customs which exist in all Mohammedan countries and among all ranks of Mussulmans, I am fearful that my exertions [in writing down his experiences in Europe] will be thrown away. The great and the rich intoxicated with pride and luxury, and puffed up with the vanity of their possessions, consider universal science as comprehended in the circle of their own scanty acquirements and limited knowledge; while the poor and common people, from the want of leisure, and overpowered by the difficulty of procuring a livelihood, have not time to attend to their personal concerns, much less to form desires for the acquirement of information of new discoveries and inventions, although such a passion has been implanted by nature in every human breast, as an honor and an ornament to the species. I therefore despair of their reaping any fruit from my labors, being convinced that they will consider this book of no greater value than the volumes of tales and romances which they peruse merely to pass away their time, or are attracted thereto by the easiness of the style. It may consequently be concluded, that as they will find no pleasure in reading a work which contains a number of foreign names, treats on uncommon subjects, and alludes to other matters which cannot be understood at first glance, but require a little time for consideration, they will, under pretense of zeal for their religion, entirely abstain and refrain from perusing it.

Questions: What reasons does Abu Taleb give for the Muslims' indifference to his account of Europe? What other factors can be added as a result of our study of long-standing Islamic attitudes toward Europe and conditions in the Ottoman Empire in this period? In what ways might the Muslims' neglect of events in Europe hinder their efforts to cope with this expansive civilization in the following centuries?

ABBASID COMPARISONS AND THE OTTOMAN ACHIEVEMENT

We have encountered many of the forces that led to the decline of the Ottoman Empire in earlier Islamic history. In fact, in many ways the Ottoman decline seems to be a replay of the earlier fall of the Abbasid caliphate. At the center of both empires, the forces that sapped their strength included the decreasing ability and reduced powers of the rulers, court intrigues and succession disputes, the growing involvement of mercenary soldiers in politics, and bureaucratic corruption. Away from the capitals at Baghdad and Constantinople, revolts by peasants and townsmen oppressed by the landed classes, the loss of territory to internal rebels, and defeats in wars by foreign powers all contributed to imperial decline.

Though these parallels are striking, they should not blind us to crucial differences between the two cases. These differences arise in part from changes in the international and domestic conditions that each dynasty, which were widely separated in time, had to face. The growing military and economic competition of European rivals, for example, had much more to do with the Ottoman decline than the Abbasid, in which (despite the Crusades) the Europeans did not play a critical role. But they also suggest that the Ottomans had learned a good deal from Abbasid mistakes and improved considerably upon their predecessors' performance.

To begin with, the real power of the Ottoman rulers persisted much longer than that of the Abbasid caliphs—two to three centuries as opposed to three or four generations. In part this was due to the higher caliber of the early Ottoman sultans, which can be traced to the better training that the princes of the royal house were given in the first phase of Ottoman history. In addition, the Ottoman bureaucracy was larger, better organized, and more dedicated than its Abbasid counterpart. It was therefore better able to administer effectively the various parts of the empire and funnel resources to the central government, at least in the early centuries of Ottoman rule. The Ottoman military machine was much better prepared, disciplined, and led than the motley alliance of forces that had brought the Abbasids to power. In the early centuries of Ottoman expansion, a military elite from a single ethnic stock, committed to a common project of religious expansion, directed military operations and discouraged infighting. By contrast, the Abbasid alliance soon broke apart, with Sunni fighting Shi'a and individual commanders seeking to create their own kingdoms. In both cases mercenary forces, which were employed to strengthen the military establishment, became deeply embroiled in politics. But the Janissaries were, initially at least, more effectively controlled by the Ottoman rulers. They also took much longer to become a major political force than the Turkic mercenaries who threatened the Abbasid throne soon after they first entered the service of the caliphate.

Interestingly, the greater political and military success of the Ottomans did not translate into a higher level of intellectual or artistic achievement. Though the Abbasid dynasty was weaker and far less expansive than the Ottoman, its reign witnessed a burst of creativity in the arts, sciences, and philosophy that has seldom been matched by any human society. Though the Ottomans made significant contributions to Islamic architecture, literature, and various crafts, their accomplishments lacked the range, originality, and sheer magnitude of those of the Abbasid age. In the broadest sense, the Ottoman legacy was one in which the restoration and preservation of the Islamic heritage was foremost. For centuries, Ottoman power brought a high level of internal peace and protection from outside invaders to the Islamic heartlands. But the price of security was an inflated bureaucracy and military establishment that proved both an increasing burden for peasants and merchants and a major barrier to creativity and innovation. With the Muslims' old adversaries, the Europeans, forging ahead, the price paid would prove a very high one indeed.

THE SHI'ITE CHALLENGE OF THE SAFAVIDS

Like the Ottomans, the Safavid dynasty arose from the struggles of rival Turkic nomadic groups in the wake of the Mongol and Timurid invasions of the 13th and 14th centuries. Also like the Ottomans, the Safavids rose to prominence as the frontier-warrior champions of a highly militant strain of Islam. But unlike the Ottomans, who became the champions of the Sunni majority of the Muslim faithful, the Safavids espoused the Shi'ite variant of Islam. As we saw in Chapter 12, in the early decades of Muslim expansion a split developed in the community of the faithful between the Sunnis, who recognized the legitimacy of the first three successors to Muhammad (Abu Bakr, Umar, and Uthman) and the Shi'ites, who believed that only the fourth successor (Ali, Muhammad's cousin and son-in-law) had the right to succeed the prophet. Over time, differences in doctrine and ritual were added to the disagreements over succession that had originally divided the Islamic community. Divisions have also arisen within both the Shi'ite and Sunni groupings, but bitter hostility and violent conflict have most often developed along Sunni-Shi'a lines. The long rivalry between the Sunni Ottomans and the Shi'ite Safavids proved to be one of the most pivotal episodes in the long history of these sectarian struggles.

In the first years of the 16th century after decades of warfare against established Muslim states, rival sects, and Christian communities in what is today southern Russia, the Safavids founded a dynasty and conquered the region that comprises the present-day nation of Iran. From that point onward, Iran has been one of the strongest and most enduring centers of Shi'ism within the Islamic world. Under the Safavid dynasty, which lasted until 1722, the Iranian region was also restored as a center of political power and cultural creativity at a level that it had rarely enjoyed since the collapse of the Sassanid Empire in the middle of the 7th century. With the Ottoman and Mughal empires that bordered it on the west and east, Safavid Iran was one of the three core regions of Islamic civilization in the gunpowder age.

SAFAVID BEGINNINGS

The Safavid dynasty had its origins in a family of Sufi mystics and religious preachers, whose shrine-center was at Ardabil near the Caspian Sea. In the early 14th century, one of these Sufis, Safi al-Din, who gave the dynasty its name, began a militant campaign to purify and reform Islam and spread Muslim teachings among the Turkic tribes of the region. In the chaos that followed the collapse of Mongol authority around the mid-14th century, Safi al-Din and other Safavid Sufi leaders gained increasing support. But as the numbers of the "Red Heads" (as the Safavids' followers were called after their distinctive headgear) grew, and as they began in the mid-15th century to preach Shi'ite doctrines, their enemies multiplied. After decades of fierce local struggles in which three successive Safavid leaders perished, a surviving Sufi commander, Ismail, led his Turkic followers to a string of victories on the battlefield. In 1501 Ismail's armies took the city of Tabriz, where he was proclaimed shah, or emperor.

In the next decade, Ismail's followers conquered most of Persia, drove the Safavid's ancient enemies—the Ozbegs, a neighboring nomadic people of Turkic stock—back into the central Asian steppes, and advanced into what is now Iraq. The Safavid successes and the support their followers received in the Ottoman borderlands from Turkic-speaking peoples inevitably brought them into conflict with Ottoman rulers. In August of 1514, at Chaldiran in northwest Persia, the armies of the two empires met in one of the most fateful battles in Islamic history.

Chaldiran was more than a struggle between dynasties: it was a clash between the most powerful adherents of the Shi'a and Sunni variants of Islam. The fervor with which both sides fought the battle was enhanced by the long-standing Safavid persecutions of the Sunnis and the recent slaughter, by the forces of the Ottoman sultan Selim, of the Shi'ias in Anatolia on whom his soldiers could lay their hands. At Chaldiran the Safavid cavalry, which made up the bulk of Ismail's forces, proved no match for the musketeers and cannon of the Ottomans. The Safavids were dealt a devastating defeat that checked the westward advance of Shi'ism and decimated the ranks of the Turkic warriors who had built the Safavid Empire. But the Ottomans were unable to follow up their victory with an occupation that would have put an end to the Safavids. The latter's capital at Tabriz was too far from Ottoman supply areas to be held through the approaching winter. The with-

drawal of the Ottoman forces gave the Safavids the breathing space they needed to regroup their forces and reoccupy much of the territory they had originally conquered. Though the two empires would fight wars periodically over the next centuries, Chaldiran had more or less set the limits to which each could expand and extend its variant of the Islamic faith.

POLITICS AND WAR UNDER THE SAFAVID SHAHS

After his defeat at Chaldiran, Ismail, who had once been a courageous warrior and popular leader, retreated to his palace and sought to escape his troubles through drink. His seclusion, and struggles between factions backing each of his sons for the right to succeed him, left openings for subordinate Turkic chiefs to attempt to seize power. After years of turmoil, a new shah, Tahmasp I (1534–1576), won the throne and set about restoring the power of the dynasty. The Turkic chiefs were foiled in their bid for supreme power, and the Ozbegs were again and again driven from the Safavid domains. Under Shah Abbas I (1587–1629) the empire reached the height of its strength and prosperity, though the territories it controlled remained roughly equivalent to those ruled by Ismail and Tahmasp I.

Under Tahmasp I and his successors repeated efforts were made to bring the Turkic chiefs under control. They were gradually transformed into a warrior nobility comparable to that in the Ottoman domains. Like their Ottoman counterparts, the Safavid warrior nobles were assigned vil-

This Persian miniature from 1680 depicts a Safavid notable, probably Shah Suleiman I (1667–1693), with a group of courtiers, which includes (on the right-hand side of the central horseman) a European visitor bearing presents for the Persian leader.

lages, whose peasants were required to supply them and their troops with food and labor. The most powerful of the warrior leaders occupied key posts in the imperial administration, and from the defeat at Chaldiran onward they posed a constant threat to the Safavid monarchs. To counterbalance this threat, Safavid rulers recruited Persians for positions both at the court and in the rapidly expanding imperial bureaucracy. The tug-of-war for power and influence between Turkic and Persian notables was further complicated by the practice, initiated by Ismail's successor Tahmasp I, of recruiting into the bureaucracy and army slave boys, who were captured in campaigns in southern Russia. Like the Janissaries in the Ottoman Empire, many of these slaves rose to positions of considerable power. Also like the Janissaries, the slave regiments soon became a major force in Safavid political struggles.

Of all of the Safavid shahs, Abbas I made the greatest use of the youths captured in Russia, then educated and converted to Islam. They not only came to form the backbone of his military forces, but they were granted provincial governorships and high offices at court. Like the Janissaries, "slave" regiments, which were wholly dependent on Abbas's support, monopolized the firearms that had become increasingly prominent in Safavid armies. The Persians had artillery and handguns long before the arrival of the Portuguese by sea in the first decades of the 16th century. But Abbas and his successors showed little reluctance to call upon the knowledgeable but infidel Europeans for assistance in their wars with the Ottomans. Abbas turned to European advisors, particularly the Sherley brothers from England, for instruction in the casting of cannon and the training of his slave infantrymen and a special regiment of musketeers recruited from the Iranian peasantry. By the end of his reign, Abbas had built up a standing army of nearly 40,000 troops and an elite bodyguard. These measures to strengthen his armies and his victories on the battlefield appeared to promise security for the Safavid domains for decades to come—a promise that was not to be fulfilled.

STATE AND RELIGION

The Safavid family was originally of Turkic stock, and early shahs like Ismail wrote in Turkish, in ironic contrast to their Ottoman rivals who preferred to write in Persian. After Chaldiran, however, Persian gradually supplanted Turkish as the language of the court and bureaucracy. Persian influences were also felt in the organization of court rituals and in the more and more exalted posture of the Safavid shahs. Abandoning all pretense to the egalitarian

comradery that had marked their earlier dealings with the warrior chiefs, the Safavids took grand titles, such as *padishah* or king of kings, often derived from those used by the ancient Persian emperors. Like the Ottoman rulers, the Safavids presided from their high thrones over opulent palace complexes, crowded with servants and courtiers. The pattern of palace life was set by elaborate court rituals and social interaction governed by a refined sense of etiquette and decorum. Though the later Safavid shahs played down claims to divinity that had been set forth under Ismail and his predecessors, they continued to claim descent from one of the Shi'ite *imams*, or successors of Ali.

Changes in the status accorded to the Safavid rulers were paralleled by shifts in the religious impulses that had been so critical to their rise to power. The militant, expansive cast of Shi'ite ideology was modified as the faith became a major pillar of dynasty and empire. The early Safavids imported Arabic-speaking religious experts of the Shi'a persuasion, but later shahs came to rely on Persian religious scholars who entered into the service of the state and were paid by the government. *Mullahs*, who were both local mosque officials and prayer leaders, were also supervised by and given some support from the state. All religious leaders were required to curse the first three caliphs and mention the Safavid ruler in the Friday sermon. Teaching in the mosque schools was also planned and directed by state religious officials.

Through these agents the bulk of the Iranian population was gradually converted to Shi'ism during the centuries of Safavid rule. Sunni Muslims, Christians, Jews, Zoroastrians and—ironically, given the Safavids' origins—the followers of Sufi preachers were pressured, and sometimes persecuted, to induce them to convert to Shi'ism. Shi'a religious festivals, such as that commemorating the martyrdom of Husayn that involved public flagellation and passion plays, and pilgrimages to Shi'a shrines, such as that at Karbala in central Iraq, became the focal points of popular religion in Iran. Thus, Shi'ism not only provided ideological and institutional support for the Safavid dynasty, it came to be an integral part of Iranian identity, setting the people of the region off from most of their Arab and Turkic neighbors.

When the dynasty weakened, some of the religious experts and mullahs grew more independent. They found support in their local communities and voiced interpretations of the sacred texts that were based more on their own study than on the dictates of Safavid functionaries. Some religious scholars disputed the legitimacy of the dissolute shahs who occupied the throne in the latter stages of the dynasty. But it would be wrong to equate the power of these religious thinkers with that the *ayatollahs,* or highest religious authorities, have gained in present-day Iran. None tried to seize power in his own right. Most continued to serve the dynasty or the rulers who succeeded the Safavids, or they withdrew from political affairs altogether.

ELITE AFFLUENCE AND ARTISTIC SPLENDOR

Though earlier rulers had erected or restored mosques and religious schools and financed public works projects, Abbas I surpassed them all. After securing his political position with a string of military victories, Abbas I set about the task of establishing his empire as a major center of international trade and Islamic culture. He had a network of roads and rest houses constructed and strove to make merchants and travelers safe within his domains. He set up workshops to manufacture the silk textiles and splendid Persian carpets that then, as now, were in great demand. Abbas I sought to encourage Iranian merchants to trade not only with their Muslim neighbors and India and China to the east, but also with the Portuguese—and later the Dutch and English—whose war and merchant ships were becoming a familiar sight in the Persian Gulf and Arabian Sea.

Though Abbas I undertook building projects throughout his empire, he devoted special attention to his capital at Isfahan. The splendid seat of Safavid power was laid out around a great square, which was lined with two-storied shops interspersed with great mosques, government offices, and soaring arches that opened onto formal gardens. Abbas I oversaw the construction of numerous public baths and rest houses, and founded several colleges. He patronized workshops where intricately detailed and brilliantly colored miniatures were produced by master painters and their apprentices.

It was above all the great mosques Abbas I had built at Isfahan that were the glory of his reign. The vividly colored ceramic tiles, which Iranian builders had begun to use centuries earlier, turned the massive domes and graceful minarets of Safavid mosques and royal tombs into creations of stunning beauty. Geometric designs, floral patterns, and verses from the Quran written in stylized Arabic added movement and texture to the deep blue tiles that distinguished the monumental construction of the Safavid era. Gardens and reflecting pools were built near the mosques and rest houses. By combining graceful arches, greenery, and colorful designs, Persian architects and artisans sought to create lush and cool refuges (perhaps duplicating heaven itself as it is described in the Quran) in a land that is dry, dusty, and predominately gray-brown for much of the year.

SOCIETY AND GENDER ROLES: OTTOMAN AND SAFAVID COMPARISONS

Though the Ottomans and Safavids were bitter political rivals and religious adversaries, the social systems that developed under the two dynasties had much in common. Both were dominated, particularly in their earliest phases, by warrior aristocracies, which shared power with the theoretically absolutist monarchs of each empire and enjoyed the prestige and luxury of elite life in the capital and on rural estates. In both cases the warrior aristocrats gradually retreated to the estates, making life increasingly difficult for the peasants on whom they were dependent for the support of their grand households and many retainers. During the early phases of Safavid and Ottoman rule, the strength of the court and traditional peasant defenses such as the underreporting of crop yields and the threat of flight more or less kept in check the demands of the warrior elite, now predominantly a rural landowning class. But as the real

The great square of the Safavid capital at Isfahan was built by Abbas I to project the splendor and power of his empire. The buildings of the square made up one of the most splendid architectural complexes of the early modern era.

power of the rulers of each empire diminished and population increases reduced the uncultivated lands to which peasants might flee, the exactions of the landlord class grew harsher. Foreign invasions, civil strife, and the breakdown in vital services once provided by the state added to the growing misery of the peasantry. The resulting spread of banditry, peasant uprisings, and flight from the land further drained the resources of each empire and undermined the legitimacy of the rival dynasties.

The early rulers of both the Ottoman and Safavid empires sought to encourage the growth of handicraft production and trade in their realms. Both dynasties established imperial workshops where products ranging from miniature paintings and rugs to weapons and metal utensils were manufactured. The rulers of each empire lavishly patronized public works projects that provided reasonably well-paid work for engineers, stonemasons, carpenters, and other sorts of artisans. Some of the more able emperors of each dynasty also pursued policies that they believed would increase both internal and international trade. In these endeavors, the Ottomans gained in the short run from the fact that large-scale traders in their empire were often from minority groups, such as the Christians and Jews, who had extensive contacts with overseas traders that the bazaar merchants of the Safavid realm normally lacked. Though Safavid cooperation with Portuguese traders remedied this shortcoming to some extent, the Safavid economy remained much more constricted, less market oriented, and more technically backward than that of their Ottoman rivals.

Significantly, the Ottomans' advantages in trade and handicraft production were only relative; they were reversed when comparisons were made with European kingdoms to the west. While European techniques and technology were changing dramatically—even before 1750 and the beginnings of the Industrial Revolution—Ottoman manufacturing stagnated, and its most dynamic trade sectors, still controlled by non-Muslim minorities, developed in increasing isolation from Ottoman society as a whole and often in defiance of imperial restrictions.

Women in Islamic societies under Ottoman or Safavid rule faced legal and social disadvantages that were comparable to those we have encountered in most civilized areas. Within the family women were subordinated to their fathers and husbands; they seldom exercised political or religious power in their own right; and they had surprisingly meager outlets for artistic or scholarly expression. To some extent the great nomadic influx into the Islamic heartlands on the part of both Mongol and Turkic peoples from the 12th to the 15th centuries offset these trends. As we have seen, women generally enjoyed more personal freedom and

higher social status in the nomadic societies than in the sedentary societies of the Middle East and central Asia. Much of this was eventually, if not immediately, sacrificed by women of Turkic or Mongol backgrounds when they settled in the towns of conquered areas. There the dictates of increasingly male-centric codes and restrictive practices such as seclusion and veiling were imposed on the women of all classes, but most strictly on those of the elite.

Recent evidence suggests, however, that many women in the Islamic heartlands in this era, perhaps clinging to the memory of the lives their nomadic predecessors had led, struggled against these restrictions. Travelers to Persia in the time of Abbas I remarked on the brightly colored robes worn by women in the capital and elsewhere, and noted that many women made no effort to cover their faces in public. At both the Ottoman and Safavid courts, the wives and concubines of the rulers and royal princes continued to exert considerable influence behind the throne and remained deeply involved in palace conspiracies. More important for ordinary women in each of these societies was the fact that many women were active in trade and some in moneylending. Court records also suggest that women were often able to invoke provisions in Islamic law that protected their rights to inheritance, decent treatment by their spouses, and even divorce in situations that had become intolerable.

How typical these instances of female assertion and fulfillment were is not at all clear. Though some women were a good deal better off than we had once thought and perhaps as well or better off than their counterparts in China and western Europe, most women very likely lived unenviable lives. Limited largely to contacts with their own families and left with little more than household chores and domestic handicrafts like embroidery to occupy their time, the overwhelming majority of women in effect disappeared from the history of two of the great centers of Islamic civilization.

THE RAPID DEMISE OF THE SAFAVID EMPIRE

Given the power and splendor the Safavid Empire had achieved by the end of the reign of Abbas I, its collapse was stunningly rapid. Abbas's fears of usurpation by one of his sons, which were fed by plots on the part of several of his closest advisors, had led during his reign to the death or blinding of all who could legitimately succeed him. A grandson, who was weak and thus thought by high state officials to be easily manipulated, was placed on the throne following Abbas's death. From this point the dynasty's fortunes declined markedly. As was true of the Ottomans, the practice of confining the princes to the atmosphere of luxury and intrigue that permeated the court led to a sharp fall in the quality of Safavid rulers. Able shahs, such as Abbas II (1642–1666), were too few to halt the rot within the imperial administration or to deal effectively with the many foreign threats to the empire. Factional disputes and rebellions shook the empire from within, while nomadic raiders and Ottoman and Mughal armies steadily reduced the territory the Safavids could tap for manpower and revenue.

By March of 1722, Isfahan was besieged by Afghani tribesmen. In October, after over 80,000 of the capital's inhabitants had perished of starvation and disease, the city fell and Safavid power was effectively ended. One of those who fought for the throne in the decade of war and destruction that followed claimed descent from the Safavid line. But a soldier-adventurer named Nadir Khan Afshar eventually emerged victorious from these bloody struggles. Though he began as a champion of Safavid restoration, Nadir Khan proclaimed himself shah in 1736. Despite the title, his dynasty and those that followed were short-lived. The area that had once made up the Safavid Empire was reduced for generations to a battleground for its powerful neighbors and a tempting target for nomadic raiders.

THE MUGHALS AND THE APEX OF MUSLIM CIVILIZATION IN INDIA

Despite the fact that the founder of the Mughal dynasty, Babur, traced his descent on one side from the Mongol khans, the Mughal in the dynasty's name had little to do with the earlier nomadic conquerors. Babur was also descended from Turkic warriors like Timur, and most of his followers were from Turkic or mixed-nomadic origins. Unlike the Ottomans and Safavids, Babur's motives for conquest and empire building had little to do with religious fervor. He led his followers into India in 1526 because he had lost his original kingdom centered on Farghana in central Asia in the preceding decades. On his father's death in 1498, Babur, then only a boy of 16, was thrown into a fierce struggle with the Ozbeg tribesmen for control of his ancestral realm. By 1504 Babur and his supporters had been driven back to Kabul in what is now Afghanistan. Originally, he directed raids into the fertile and heavily populated plains of India only to gain booty to support his campaigns to win back Farghana. Though India had much greater potential as a base on which to build an empire, Babur cared little for the green and well-watered subcontinent. Even after he later conquered India, he con-

tinued to long for the arid steppe and blue-domed mosques of his central Asian birthplace. But after decades of wars that repeatedly ended in defeat, he was forced to give up his dream of reclaiming his homeland and to turn his full energies to the conquest of northern India.

In 1526 Babur—by then a seasoned military commander—entered India at the head of a veteran and well-organized army. At Panipat north of Delhi, his army of 12,000 met the huge force of over 100,000 sent to crush it by the last ruler of the Muslim Lodi dynasty, which then ruled much of northern India. Employing gun carts, movable artillery, and cavalry tactics similar to those that had brought the Ottomans victory at Chaldiran, Babur routed the Lodi army. In addition to the superior firepower and mobility of his forces, their victory owed a great deal to the tactic of frightening the hundreds of war elephants that led the Lodi army into battle. The elephants stampeded, trampling thousands of Lodi infantrymen or sending them into flight. A year later, Babur's forces, again vastly outnumbered, decisively defeated a confederation of Hindu warrior-kings at Khanua. Within two years he had conquered large portions of the Indus and Gangetic plains and founded a dynasty that would last over 300 years.

SUCCESSION AND NEAR FATAL IMPERIAL CRISIS

The founder of the Mughal dynasty was a truly remarkable man. A fine military strategist and fierce fighter who went into battle alongside his troops, Babur also managed, in the decades when he was continually fighting for his very life, to cultivate a taste for the arts and music. He wrote one of the great histories of India, was a fine musician, and designed wonderful gardens for his new capital at Delhi. But he proved a better conqueror than administrator. He did little to reform the very ineffective Lodi bureaucracy he had taken over, a project that would have solidified the Mughals' hold on the empire that Babur was soon to pass on to his much-loved son, Humayan. In 1530, at the age of 48, Babur suddenly fell ill and died, leaving Humayan to inherit the newly founded kingdom.

Like his father, Humayan was a good soldier; in fact he had won his first battle at the age of 18. But Babur's death was the signal for his enemies to strike from all sides. One of Humayan's brothers disputed his succession, and armies from Afghanistan and the Rajput states of western India marched on his capital. By 1540, with his armies shattered, Humayan was forced to flee to Persia, where he remained in exile, an embarrassed guest at the Safavid court, for nearly a decade. Having gained a foothold at Kabul in 1545, Humayan launched a series of campaigns into India that restored Mughal rule to the northern plains by 1556. But Humayan did not live to savor his victory. Shortly after entering Delhi in triumph, he was hurrying down his library steps, his arms full of books, to answer the call to prayer. He stumbled and fell, hitting his head. He was dead within days.

AKBAR AND THE BASIS FOR A LASTING EMPIRE

Humayan's sudden death once again imperiled the Mughal dynasty. His son and successor, Akbar, was only 13 years old, and the Mughals' enemies moved quickly to take advantage of what they viewed as a very favorable turn of events. Their expectations were soon dashed because in Akbar, two gifted monarchs were succeeded by one of the great leaders of all history. Interestingly, Akbar's reign was contemporaneous with those of a number of other remarkable monarchs, including Elizabeth I of England, Philip of Spain, and the Muslim rulers, Suleyman the Magnificent and Abbas I. Akbar was a match for any of these very formidable rivals.

Like his father and grandfather, Akbar was a fine military commander who possessed great personal courage. But unlike his predecessors, Akbar also had a vision of empire and sense of mission that hinged on uniting India under his rule. A workaholic who seldom slept more than three hours a night, Akbar personally oversaw the building of the military and administrative systems that would form the backbone of the Mughal Empire for centuries. He also patronized the arts, personally entered into complex religious and philosophical discussions with learned scholars from throughout the Muslim, Christian, and Hindu worlds, and still found time to carry out social reforms and invent his own universalistic religion. Though illiterate— there had been little time for book learning when his father fought for survival in the wilderness—Akbar had an insatiable curiosity and incredible memory. By having others read aloud to him, he became a learned man in a number of fields.

At first with the help of senior advisors but soon on his own, Akbar routed the enemies who had hoped to capitalize on the Mughals' misfortunes. In the decades after 1560, when he took charge of the government, Akbar's armies greatly extended the empire with conquests throughout north and central India. It was Akbar's social policies and administrative genius that made it possible to establish the foundations of a lasting dominion in the subcontinent. He pursued a policy of reconciliation and cooperation with the Hindu princes and the Hindu majority of the population of his realm. He encouraged intermarriage between the Mughal aristocracy and the families of the Hindu Rajput rulers. Akbar also abolished the much-hated head taxes that earlier Muslim rulers had levied on Hindu unbelievers. He promoted Hindus to the highest ranks in the government, ended a long-standing ban on the building of new Hindu temples, and ordered Muslims to respect cows, which the Hindu majority viewed as sacred. Despite all this, Akbar considered his new religion, the Din-i-Ilahi, which blended elements of the many faiths with which he was familiar, as the long-term key to his efforts to reconcile Hindus and Muslims. If he could persuade the adherents of each religion to embrace the common faith he had devised, sectarian quarrels and even violent conflict could be brought to an end.

The Muslim and Hindu warrior aristocracy that formed the core of the supporters of the Mughal dynasty were, like their counterparts in the Ottoman and Safavid empires, granted villages for their support. In turn they were required to maintain a specified number of cavalrymen and

The Growth of the Mughal Empire, from Akbar to Aurangzeb

This engraving from a late 16th-century German traveler's account of India shows a European artist's impression of an Indian widow committing *sati*. Not surprisingly, this practice of immolating high-caste widows on their deceased husbands' funeral pyres was frequently described at great length by European visitors in this era.

to be on call should the emperor require their services. The court and central bureaucracy were supported by revenues drawn both from the tribute paid by the military retainers and (especially) from taxes on lands—mostly near the twin capitals at Delhi and Agra—set aside for the support of the imperial household. Due to a shortage of manpower, in most areas local notables, many of whom were Hindu, were left in place as long as they swore allegiance to the Mughal rulers and paid their taxes on time. These arrangements left the control and welfare of the village population largely in the hands of the military retainers of the dynasty and local power brokers. Depending on the leader in a given locality, this could result in strict but paternalistic administration of peasant affairs or blatant corruption and the exploitation of the village population.

SOCIAL REFORM AND SOCIAL CHANGE

In addition to his administrative reforms, Akbar pushed for social changes that he believed would greatly benefit his subjects. Beyond the public works that were typically favored by able Muslim rulers, Akbar sought to improve the calendar, establish living quarters for the rather large population of beggars and vagabonds in the large cities, and

regulate the consumption of alcohol. Whatever success the latter campaign may have had in Indian society as a whole, it apparently failed in Akbar's own household for one of his sons was reputed to drink 20 cups of double-distilled wine per day.

More than any of Akbar's many reform efforts, those involving the position of women demonstrated how far the Mughal ruler was in advance of his time. He sought to encourage widow remarriage, at that point taboo for both Hindus and Muslims, and to discourage child marriages. The latter were so widespread among the upper classes that he did not attempt to outlaw them, and it is doubtful that his disapproval did much to curb the practice. Akbar did legally prohibit sati, or the immolation of high-caste Hindu women on their husbands' funeral pyres, even though this custom was deeply entrenched among the Rajput princes and warrior classes that were some of his most faithful allies. Akbar was so determined to eradicate sati, particularly in cases where the widow was pressured to agree to be burned alive, that he once personally rescued a young girl despite the protestations of her angry relatives. He also sought to provide relief for women trapped in *purdah*, or the seclusion from public viewing, by encouraging the merchants of Delhi and other cities to set aside special market days for women only. Even prostitutes were a matter of concern for the emperor. He had special sections in Mughal towns set aside for their brothels; he appointed inspectors to check abuses against both the prostitutes and their clientele; and he even had records kept of those who frequented houses of prostitution, perhaps to discourage the practice.

MUGHAL SPLENDOR AND EARLY EUROPEAN CONTACTS

Despite his many successes and the civil peace and prosperity his reign brought to much of northern India, Akbar died a lonely and discouraged man. By 1605 he had outlived most of his friends and faced revolts by sons eager to claim his throne. Above all, he died knowing that the Din-i-Ilahi, the religion that he had created to reconcile his Hindu and Muslim subjects, had been rejected by both.

Though neither of his successors, Jahangir (1605–1627) or Shah Jahan (1627–1658), added much territory to the empire Akbar had left them, in their reigns Mughal India reached the peak of its splendor. European visitors marveled at the size and opulence of the chief Mughal cities of Delhi, Agra, and Lahore. The huge Mughal armies, replete with elephant and artillery corps, dwarfed those of even the most powerful European rulers at the time. European ambassadors to the great Mughal's court were literally dazzled by the jewel-encrusted palaces of white marble and red sandstone and the large numbers of courtiers who vied for the emperor's favor. Some of the more perceptive of the European observers, such as Francois Bernier, also noted the abject poverty in which the lower classes in both town and countryside lived and the lack of discipline and training of most of the soldiers in the Mughal armies. Perhaps most ominously, Bernier added that in invention and the sciences India had fallen far behind western Europe in most areas. Until the 18th century, however, criticisms by writers like Bernier were drowned out by exclamations of wonder on the part of the merchants, adventurers, and missionaries who visited the empire.

Beyond the (as it turned out false) promise of tens of millions of converts that Mughal India offered to Christian missionaries, it became in the reigns of Akbar's successors one of the major overseas centers for European traders. French, Dutch, and English merchants brought products from throughout Asia, though little from Europe itself, to exchange for a variety of Indian products, particularly the subcontinent's famed cotton textiles. The trade gap that the demand for Indian cotton cloth and clothing had created in the West in Roman times persisted millennia later. The

17th- and 18th-century rage for Indian textile products is reflected in the following ditty from *Prince Butler's Tales*, written in England in 1696:

> *Our ladyes all were sent a gadding*
> *After these toys they ran a madding*
> *And nothing then would please their fancies*
> *Nor dolls, nor joans [cotton caps]*
> *Nor wanton nancies.*
> *Unless it be of Indian making.*

The importance of the Indian textile trade is also indicated by the names we still use for different kinds of cotton cloth, from calico (after the Indian port city of Calicut) to chintz and muslin, as well as by our names for cotton apparel such as pajamas.

Because they were easily washed and relatively inexpensive, Indian textiles first won a large market among the working and middle classes in Britain and elsewhere in Europe. In the reigns of Queen Mary and Queen Anne, fine Indian cloth came into fashion at the court as well. An incident from the reign of the Mughal emperor Aurangzeb, who succeeded Shah Jahan, suggests just how fine the cloth in question was. Aurangzeb, a religious zealot and a bit of a prig, chastised his favorite daughter for appearing in his presence in garments that revealed so much of her body. The daughter protested that she had on three layers of fine cotton clothing. It is thus no wonder that even after industrialization had revolutionized cotton textile manufacture in England, European visitors to India continued to observe and write in great detail about the techniques used by Indian artisans to weave and dye cotton cloth. The popularity of so-called "madras" cloth today demonstrates that this interest has by no means died out.

ARTISTIC ACHIEVEMENT IN THE MUGHAL ERA

Both Jahangir and Shah Jahan continued Akbar's policy of tolerance toward the Hindu majority and retained most of the alliances he had forged with Hindu princes and local leaders. They made little attempt to alter significantly the administrative apparatus they had inherited from Akbar, and fought their wars in much the same way the founders of the dynasty had. Both mounted campaigns to crush potential enemies and in some cases to enlarge the empire, but neither was as interested in conquest and politics as he was in enjoying the good life. Both were fond of drink, dancing girls, and the pleasure gardens they had laid out from Kashmir to Allahabad. Both were delighted

This miniature painting by Bishndas depicts the birth of Prince Jahangir. The mixed reactions of the other members of Akbar's harem, the presence of musicians, and the varied activities of the courtiers in the courtyard below provide wonderful insights into the nature of court life at the height of the Mughal age.

by polo matches (a game invented by the princes of India), ox and tiger or elephant fights, and games of parchesi, which they played on life-sized boards with dancing girls as chips. Both took great pleasure in the elaborate court ceremonies that blended Indian and Persian precedents, in lavish state processions, in their palaces and jewel-studded wardrobes, and in the scented and sweetened ices that were rushed from the cool mountains in the north to their capitals on the sweltering plains.

Jahangir and Shah Jahan are best remembered not for their pleasure-loving ways but as two of the foremost patrons of the fine arts in human history. They expanded the painting workshops that had been started by the early Mughals to the point where thousands of exquisite miniatures could be produced during their reigns. Some of these paintings show the influence of European painting: at times superficial, as in the addition of halos and cherubs to por-

traits of Jahangir; at times more fundamental, as when Indian artists attempted to introduce true perspective or Christian religious themes into their work. Most of the miniatures, however, are devoted to more traditional Islamic subjects, such as key battles and scenes of life at court or portraits of Mughal noblemen and wonderfully detailed paintings of animals and plants. As these choices of subject matter indicate, Indian artists, such as those in Persia, ignored the prohibition against depicting the human figure that was pushed by some religious authorities from the earliest centuries of Islam. Manuscript illumination was a highly valued art form that was carried to near perfection by the draftsmen and painters at the Mughal court.

Both Jahangir and Shah Jahan also devoted a good deal of personal attention and vast revenues and manpower to building some of the most stunning architectural works of all time. The best known of these is the Taj Mahal, which has come to be a symbol for India itself, as witnessed by Air India advertisements and lists of the wonders of the

Perhaps no single building has come to symbolize Indian civilization more than the Taj Mahal. The grace and elegance of the tomb that Shah Jahan built in his wife's honor provide an enduring source of aesthetic delight.

world. But structures, such as the audience hall in the Red Fort at Delhi, Akbar's tomb at Sikandra, and the tomb of Itimad al-Dowleh at Agra, rival the Taj Mahal in design and perhaps surpass it in detail and decoration.

At its best, Mughal architecture blends what is finest in the Persian and Hindu traditions. It fuses the Islamic genius for domes, arches, and minarets and the balance between them with the Hindu love of ornament. In place of the ceramic tiles the Persians used to finish their mosques and tombs, Indian artisans substituted gleaming white marble that was inset with semiprecious stones arranged in floral and geometric patterns. Extensive use was also made of marble reflecting pools, the most famous of which mirrors the beauty of the Taj Mahal. When these pools were inlaid with floral patterns and provided with fountains, the rippling water appeared to give life to the stone plant forms. Like the architects and artisans of the Ottoman Empire and Safavid Persia, those who served the Mughal rulers sought to create paradise on earth—an aspiration that was carved in marble on the audience hall of the Red Fort at Delhi. Around the ceiling of the great hall, it is written "If there is paradise on earth—It is here . . . it is here."

COURT POLITICS AND THE POSITION OF ELITE AND ORDINARY WOMEN

Not surprisingly, two rulers who were so absorbed in the arts and the pursuit of pleasure left most of the mundane tasks of day-to-day administration largely in the hands of subordinates. In both cases strong-willed wives took advantage of their husbands' neglect of politics to win positions of considerable power and influence at the Mughal court. Jahangir's wife, Nur Jahan, continually amassed power as he became more and more addicted to wine and opium. She packed the court with able male relatives, and her faction dominated the empire for much of the later years of Jahangir's reign. Nur Jahan was a big spender, but not only on pomp and luxury. She became a major patron of much-needed charities in the major cities. Despite her considerable success at pursuits that were normally reserved for males, she was defeated in the end by the roles of wife and mother to which many felt she should confine herself. She died giving birth to her 19th child.

Shah Jahan's consort, Mumtaz Mahal, also became actively involved in court politics. But Shah Jahan was a much more engaged and able ruler than Jahangir, and thus her opportunities to amass power behind the throne were more limited. Mumtaz Mahal is remembered not for her political acumen but for the love and devotion that Shah Jahan bestowed upon her—a love literally enshrined in the Taj Mahal, the tomb where she is buried. Shah Jahan's plans to build a companion tomb in black marble across

the Jumna River were foiled by the revolt of his sons and his imprisonment. He is buried next to his wife in the Taj Mahal. But her tomb is central and far larger than that of her emperor-husband.

Though the position of women at the Mughal court improved in the middle years of the dynasty's power, that of women in the rest of Indian society declined markedly. Child marriage grew more popular and the age limit was even lowered. It was not unheard of for young girls to be married at the age of nine. Widow remarriage among Hindus virtually died out. Seclusion was more and more strictly enforced for upper-caste women, both Hindu and Muslim. Muslim women rarely ventured forth from their homes unveiled, and those who did risked verbal and even physical abuse. The governor of one of the provinces of the Mughal Empire divorced his wife because she was seen scrambling for her life, but unveiled, from an elephant that had run amuck. Among upper-caste Hindus, the practice of sati spread despite Shah Jahan's renewal of efforts to outlaw it. The dwindling roles left to women and the correspondingly limited productivity permitted them, combined with the burden of the dowry that had to be provided to marry them off, meant that the birth of a girl was increasingly viewed as an inauspicious event. At court or in the homes of ordinary villagers only the birth of a son was greeted with feasting and celebrations.

THE BEGINNINGS OF IMPERIAL DECLINE

Aurangzeb, Shah Jahan's son and successor, seized control of an empire that was threatened by internal decay and growing dangers from external enemies. For decades the need for essential administrative, military, and social reforms had been ignored. The Mughal bureaucracy had grown bloated and excessively corrupt, the army was equally bloated and woefully backward in weaponry and tactics, and the peasants and urban workers had seen their productivity and living standards fall steadily. The Taj Mahal and other wonders of the Mughal artistic imagination had been paid for by the mass of the people at a very high price.

Though far from being the cruel bigot that he is often portrayed as, Aurangzeb was not the man to restore the dynasty's declining fortunes. Courageous, honest, intelligent, and hardworking, he seemed an ideal successor to two rulers who had so badly neglected affairs of state. But Aurangzeb was driven by two ambitions that proved disastrous to his schemes to strengthen the empire. He was determined to extend Mughal control over the whole of the Indian subcontinent, and he believed that it was his duty to purify Indian Islam, to rid it of the Hindu influences he was convinced were steadily corrupting it.

The first ambition increased the number of the empire's adversaries, strained the allegiance of its vassals and allies, and greatly overextended its huge but ponderous and obsolescent military forces. By the time of his death in 1707, after a reign of nearly 50 years, Aurangzeb had conquered most of the subcontinent and extended Mughal control as far north as Kabul in what is now Afghanistan. But the almost incessant warfare of his years in power drained the treasury and further enlarged an already flabby and inefficient bureaucracy and army without generating corresponding increases in revenues to support them.

Equally critical, the long wars occupied much of Aurangzeb's time and energies, diverting him from administrative tasks and reforms essential to the dynasty's continued strength. While he was leading his massive armies in the south, there were peasant uprisings and revolts by Muslim and Hindu princes in the north. Perhaps even more fundamentally harmful to the imperial system was the growing autonomy of local leaders, who were able to divert more and more revenue from the central administration into their own coffers. On the northern borders, incursions by Persian and Afghan warrior bands were on the increase.

While Aurangzeb's military campaigns strained the resources of the empire, his religious policies gravely weakened the internal alliances and disrupted the social peace Akbar had so skillfully established. Aurangzeb continued to employ Hindus in the imperial service—in fact, he did not have the Muslim replacements to do without them. But non-Muslims were given far fewer posts at the upper levels of the bureaucracy and their personal contact with the emperor was severely restricted. Aurangzeb also took measures that he and his religious advisors felt would help rid their Muslim faith and culture of the Hindu influences that had permeated it over the centuries. He forbade the building of new temples and had several demolished. He put an end to Hindu religious festivals at court and strove to reinstate the hated head tax on unbelievers, a measure he hoped might prod them to convert to Islam. The tax fell heavily on the Hindu poor and in some cases drove them to support sectarian movements that rose up to resist Aurangzeb's proselytizing zeal.

By the end of Aurangzeb's reign the Mughal Empire was far larger than it had been under any of the earlier emperors, but it was also a good deal more unstable. Internal rebellions by those such as the Marattas of western India, who claimed to be defending Hinduism against Muslim persecution, put an end to effective Mughal control over large areas. The rise of new sects, such as the Sikhs in the northwest, further strained the declining resources of an imperial system that was clearly overextended. The early leaders of the Sikhs had originally sought to bridge the differences between Hindu and Muslim. But Mughal persecution of the new sect, which was seen as religiously heretical and a political threat to the dynasty, eventually transformed Sikhism into a staunchly anti-Muslim force within the subcontinent. In addition, Muslim kingdoms in the Deccan and Bengal regions continued to resist Mughal hegemony, and Islamic invaders waited at the poorly guarded passes through the Himalayas to strike and plunder once it was clear that the Mughals could no longer effectively fend them off.

From the first decades of the 18th century onward, control and state revenues passed increasingly from the Mughal court and bureaucracy to regional lords, who had once served as Mughal governors but now gave little more than lip service and token tribute payments to the Mughal emperors. As centralized political control broke down and warfare increased markedly throughout much of the subcontinent, these regional lords became the keys to social coherence and cultural creativity. In a sense this shift from fairly centralized to regional political control marked a return to a pattern that had long been predominant in South Asian civilization. However, the fragmentation of political power in the early decades of the 18th century left tempting openings in many parts of India for foreign intervention and the economic exploitation of Indian artisans and peasants by local lords and foreign and local merchants. None would take fuller advantage of these opportunities than the English, who began the century as just one of many Asian and European contenders for the fallen crown of the Mughal emperors. (On England's expansion in India, see Chapters 23 and 30.)

ANALYSIS

THE DECLINE OF EMPIRES—MUSLIM VARIATIONS ON A UNIVERSAL THEME

In their rise and decline, each of the Muslim gunpowder dynasties exhibited common patterns that can tell us a great deal about the dynamics of preindustrial political systems and the difficulties of sustaining empires more generally. Each of the Muslim empires owed its existence to the courage and fighting abilities of frontier warriors, whose nomadic life-style provided extensive training in the arts of war and a high degree of mobility. In each case a succession of strong leaders was able to forge a disciplined and unified military force from disparate bands of fractious herdsmen. The success of these forces in establishing lasting imperial dynasties depended on their combination with regiments equipped with handguns and artillery.

Each of the dynasties was also continuously challenged by the warrior peoples that had been so critical to their rise to power. Measures taken by the rulers of each empire to offset the power of the warrior aristocrats that developed, such as the Safavid and Ottoman recruitment of slave soldiers and Mughal alliances with Hindu princes, eventually contributed to the downfall of their empires. These attempts to develop alternative bases of power weakened the loyalty of the warrior peoples and, by reducing their importance to the state, contributed to a gradual decline in their military preparedness.

Because each of the Muslim empires was built on military conquest and expansion, each was increasingly confronted by a dilemma that none was able to solve. On the one hand, continued wars and annexations were essential to the maintenance of ever larger bureaucracies and military establishments. On the other hand, the preindustrial weaponry and communications technology available made it difficult to control effectively the far-flung territories each claimed. Russia, another gunpowder empire, here gained strengths—by innovations in military technology under rulers like Peter the Great—that the Muslim empires ignored. Efforts to hold the Muslim empires together often used up more resources than new territories generated—again in contrast to the Russian and Western empires in the early modern period. Wars of expansion sustained hostilities with peoples bordering on the empires or created new foes. They also diverted the rulers of each of the empires from much-needed reforms at home and allowed internal competitors to amass strength. When external enemies and logistical limitations blocked its capacity to expand farther, each empire entered into a phase of decline.

Though religious fervor was a key factor in the emergence of only two of the empires, the Ottoman and Safavid, it became an increasingly important factor in the Mughal Empire as well. The frontier-warrior holy war appeals of Osman and the holy men of Ardabil go far to explaining the victories of their followers over often superior armies. Once their successors were established in power, religious justifications for their rule grew hollow as missionary zeal gave way to officially sponsored treatises on Islamic precedents for absolutist rule. The varying strains of Islam the Ottomans and Safavids espoused led to intermittent warfare between the two empires. These clashes further drained their resources and prevented them from paying sufficient attention to other threats, particularly those from an expanding Europe.

The Mughals, who professed the Sunni variant of Islam, clashed on occasion with the Shi'ite Safavids, but their chief religious problems were of a different sort. Despite the heroic efforts of Akbar, no lasting rapprochement could be found with the Hindu majority or minority sects.

Thus, key alliances with Hindu princes remained uncertain and religiously inspired rebellions increasingly shook the Mughal imperium. This problem was less serious for the Ottomans and Safavids, but both had to deal with sectarian enemies within their domains and worry about the reliability of support rendered by Christian minorities.

Consistent with the pattern of Islamic political history as a whole, none of the three gunpowder empires solved the critical problem of political succession. Each of the empires was periodically racked by bitter civil wars between the forces backing rival claimants to the throne, who were usually the sons of a recently deceased or gravely ill ruler. Emperors were often forced to kill off or blind (the latter act was sufficient in Muslim law to bar them from succession) their most able sons, who had attempted or were suspected of plotting to attempt to seize their thrones by force. Efforts to establish less violent modes of determining succession, such as the virtual captivity of the Ottoman princes in the palace complex, resulted in other, perhaps more serious problems. The many untested, harem-ridden sultans this seclusion produced from the 17th century onward led to a marked decline in the quality of the sultans—a serious consequence in a system so dependent upon effective autocratic rule.

Questions: To what extent do the forces that led to decline in the Muslim gunpowder empires correspond to those discussed for the civilizations of the classical world? Which of these causes are unique to the Islamic world? Is the larger crisis set in motion by the rising power of the West something new or a phenomenon we have encountered before in global history?

CONCLUSION

THE RISE OF EUROPE AND THE ECLIPSE OF ISLAMIC CIVILIZATION AS THE PIVOT OF THE WORLD ORDER

The causes of decline outlined above were probably in themselves sufficient to destroy each of the great gunpowder empires of Islam. But each was also undermined by further weaknesses that would have profound significance for Islamic civilization as a whole. Captivated by their rivalries with each other and the problems of holding together their empires, none of the dynasties took the rising threat from Europe seriously. Though they called on travelers and missionaries for advice in casting cannon or military tactics, none of the Islamic emperors systematically monitored technological advances in Europe, much less attempted to adopt them on a wide scale. This failure to take strong measures to meet the challenges that European overseas expansion was creating for Islamic civilization as a whole was also responsible for the weakening of the economic basis of each of the empires. Key tax revenues and merchant profits were drained off by the rise of European trading empires in Asia (see Chapter 23). Spiraling inflation and the resulting devaluation of Ottoman currency, brought on by the unchecked importation of precious metals from European colonies in the Americas, priced Ottoman handicraft goods out of the world market and disrupted the agrarian economy throughout their domains. Minority peoples within the Muslim gunpowder empires, from the Christian and Jewish merchants of the Ottoman lands to the Hindu traders of India, increasingly oriented their commercial activities to the more dynamic economies of European nations, overseas colonies, and trading outposts. The Europeans' gains in ways to generate wealth and economic growth meant increasing losses for Muslim societies and political systems, losses that would eventually prove critical to the failure of their efforts to compete successfully with their Christian neighbors and long-standing rivals.

Equally critical, Muslim rulers and scholars continued to take little interest in European learning. Thus, they were largely oblivious to the scientific ideas that were transforming the European world view and steadily enhancing the Westerners' ability to tap new sources of power for production, communications, and war. The Muslims' contempt for the Europeans and their culture was centuries old, but by the 16th century it was also a dangerous anachronism. In the 18th and 19th centuries Muslim peoples and cultures would pay a high price for this arrogance and their leaders' failure to inquire into and match the intellectual and material accomplishments of the West.

FURTHER READINGS

The Lapidus survey suggested in the earlier chapters on Islam provides a fine introduction to the empires that are the focus of this chapter. The best detailed studies of the Ottoman Empire can be found in the works of Halil Inalcik, especially his chapters in *The Cambridge History of Islam*. For a rather different perspective on the Ottomans, see Stanford Shaw's *History of the Ottoman Empire and Modern Turkey*, vol. I (1280–1808) (1976). See Bernard Lewis's *Istanbul and the Civilization of the Ottoman Empire* (1963) for internal views of life at the center of the Ottoman Empire, and Peter F. Sugar's *Southeastern Europe under Ottoman Rule, 1354–1804* (1977) for life in the Christian portions of the Ottoman Empire.

R. M. Savory's writings, including his chapters in *The Cambridge History*, are the most reliable of a very limited literature on the Safavid period. Though quite specialized, Michel Mazzaoui's *The Origins of the Safavids* (1972) provides the fullest account of the origins and rise of the Safavid dynasty. The contributions to the volume that Savory edited on *Islamic Civilization* (1976) include good discussions of the arts and society in the Turkic and Persian sectors of the Islamic heartland. The introductory sections of Nikki Keddi's *Roots of Revolution* (1981) provide a good discussion of the relationship between religion and the state in the Safavid period.

The Ikram and Ahmad books cited in the earlier chapter on Islam in India are also good on the Mughals. Though specialized, the works of Muhammad Habib and Athar Ali on the Mughal Empire are also critical. Of the many works on Mughal art and architecture, the volume by Gavin Hambly on *Mughal Cities* (1968) has some of the better color plates and an intelligent commentary.

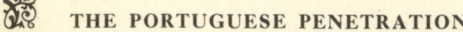

1441 First shipment of African slaves brought directly from Africa to Portugal

1591 Fall of Songhay Empire

1481 Portuguese fort established at El Mina

1562 Beginnings of English slave trade

1415 Portuguese capture Ceuta (Morocco); beginning of European expansion

1570 Portuguese establish colony in Angola

A.D. 1400   A.D. 1500   A.D. 1600

27

Africa and the Africans in the Age of the Atlantic Slave Trade

INTRODUCTION. While the new empires dominated the core areas of the Muslim world during the early modern centuries, sub-Saharan Africa, previously linked to the Muslim world in many ways, pulled into a different orbit. Islam remained important, and in eastern Africa so did trade with western Asia, but the rise of the West and of the Western-dominated world economy proved to be a powerful force in recasting the framework of African history.

The strength of earlier African cultural and political traditions persisted in many places, but the impact of the West was the newest influence in Africa, and in some respects an immensely powerful one.

African history had its own pace and rhythm and so this chapter will exceed the chronological boundaries of the early modern period. The external influences of Islam and the West initiated or intensified processes of religious conversion, political reorganization, and social transformation that persisted, in some cases, to the 19th century. The distinctive nature and chronology of African history should not blind us, however, to its role in world history.

During the age of European maritime and commercial expansion, large areas of Africa were brought into the orbit of the expanding world economy and were influenced by the transformation taking place. Not all parts of Africa were influenced in the same way nor at the same time. During the period after 1450, the growing and often bitter contacts between Europeans and Africans, primarily through the slave trade, linked the destiny of Africa to broader external trends and resulted in a diaspora of millions of Africans to the Middle East, Europe, and especially the Americas. Not all European contact with Africa was centered on the slave trade, nor was the desire for slaves the only impulse behind European explorations, but the slave trade after 1600 came to predominate other activities until the mid-19th century.

1700–1717 Osei Tutu unifies the Asante kingdom

1792 Slave uprising in Haiti

1818–1828 Shaka forges Zulu power and expansion; *Mfecane* under way

1834 Boers make "great trek" into Natal

1652 Dutch establish colony at Cape of Good Hope

1720s Rise of the kingdom of Dahomey

1815 Cape colony comes under formal British control

1833 Great Britain abolishes slavery in the West Indies

1713 English get right to import slaves to Spanish Empire

1790s Abolitionist movement gains strength in England

1804 Usuman Dan Fodio leads Hausa expansion

This process had a direct impact on certain areas of Africa, and it also made Africans an important element in the changing balance of world civilizations. The forced movement of Africans as captive laborers and the creation of slave-based societies in the Americas were major aspects of the formation of the modern world and the growth of the economies of western Europe. In a way, this forced migration was part of the international exchange of foods, diseases, animals, and ideas that marked the era, and which, as we saw in the case of the Americas, had a profound influence on the indigenous peoples in various regions. Moreover, in large areas of the Americas, colonized by Europeans, where slavery came to be the predominant form of labor, African culture was transferred, contributing to the creation of new cultural forms. In this chapter we will examine, in some detail, the history of parts of Africa in the age of the slave trade and the creation of slave societies in the Atlantic world as part of the general process of European expansion and the creation of a world economy.

While much of the analysis in this chapter emphasizes the increasing linkage between Africa and the wider world, it should be made clear at the outset that many fundamental processes of African development discussed in Chapters 10 and 14 continued throughout this period. It is vital to realize that almost all of Africa remained independent of outside political control and that most cultural development was autonomous as well. Africa differed profoundly from Latin America in these aspects during the early modern centuries.

A variety of trends affected various parts of the sub-Saharan region. Islam consolidated its position in East Africa and the Sudan. In Ethiopia, the Christian kingdom of the highlands continued to hold off its Muslim rivals. In many places in Africa, as in Europe, a tendency for independent states to form and expand in size continued, perhaps as a result of a population expansion that followed the diffusion of iron tools and improved agriculture. Kingdoms spread to new areas. Scholars hold differing opinions on the extent to which these long-term developments were affected by Europeans and the rise of the Atlantic slave trade. Some have argued that the enlarged political scale—the growth of large kingdoms through much of the sub-continent—was the dominant theme of the period, with slavery one of its by-products. Others see European demand as a major impulse in political expansion. In this chapter we emphasize the impact of slavery and the slave trade because our focus is not simply the geographical region of Africa, but the African peoples who were swept into the expanding international economy.

THE PORTUGUESE PENETRATION

As we have seen, the Portuguese were the first Europeans to begin direct contact with black Africa. The Portuguese knew that much of the gold that arrived in North Africa came from beyond the Sahara, and during the difficult years of the 15th century following the Black Death, they were anxious to acquire direct access to this gold. Beginning in 1415, after seizing the Moorish stronghold of Ceuta in Morocco, Portuguese ships began to push down the West African coast in search of gold, ivory, pepper, and other exotic commodities. These voyages were usually private ventures, but were sometimes sponsored and financed by important nobles, such as Prince Henry (called "The Navigator")—a younger son of the Portuguese king—who also seems to have gathered mapmakers, mariners, and scholars together in order to plan and prepare for further voyages. Prince Henry financed about one-third of the voyages personally and granted licenses for most of the others before his death in 1460. Moved also by curiosity and by hopes of finding the fabled Christian kingdom of Prester John, which might eventually have aided in a war against Islam, Portuguese exploration and voyages continued to be primarily commercial in nature.

THE EARLY ATLANTIC SLAVE TRADE

Ships pushed down the West African coast into the region of Senegal and Guinea, and finally reached the Cape of Good Hope in 1487. Along the coast, the Portuguese established trade forts and trading posts with resident merchants. The most important of these was El Mina (1482) in the heart of the gold-producing region of the forest zone. These forts assured arriving ships of a secure landing place where goods could be traded. They also allowed for the exercise of some control or influence with minimum investment of manpower. Although some raiding was carried out by the early voyages, once out of range of their canons, the Portuguese were simply not powerful enough to enforce their will on the larger West African states. Most of the forts, therefore, were established with the agreement or license of local rulers who benefited from the access to European commodities and sometimes from the military support the Portuguese provided in local wars.

Africans acquired cloth, iron, copper, brass, horses, and guns from the Portuguese, who also sometimes provided African rulers with slaves brought from other stretches of the coast. In return the Portuguese received ivory, pepper, animal skins, and gold. From El Mina, Accra, and other trade forts, routes led directly into the gold-producing regions of the interior so that the Portuguese eventually traded with Mande and Soninke merchants from Mali and Songhay. Much of the Portuguese success was due to their ability to penetrate the already existing African trade routes, to which they could also add specialized items. Portuguese and African-Portuguese mulatto traders and middlemen struck out into the interior to establish trade contacts and collection points. These isolated *lançados* provided essential links between the economies of the African interior and the nodules of European mercantilism on the coast.

Trade was the basis of Portuguese relations with Africans but in the wake of commerce came political, religious, and social relations. The small states of the Senegambian coast did not impress the Portuguese, and they were particularly suspicious of Muslims since Iberian Catholics considered Islam a traditional enemy. When they reached the area of the Gold Coast (modern Ghana) and encountered the kingdom of Benin, they were impressed both by the power of the ruler and by the magnificence of his court. Other large African states also provoked similar responses.

Missionary efforts were made to convert the rulers of Benin, Kongo, and other African kingdoms. The Portuguese contacted the Kongo kingdom south of the Zaire River about 1484. The missionaries achieved a major success in Kongo, where members of the royal family were converted and eventually the ruler, Nzinga Mvemba, took the title Afonso I. During his reign (1507–1543) he sought, with the help of Portuguese advisors and missionaries, to convert the whole kingdom to Christianity. Attempts were made to "Europeanize" the kingdom. Portugal and Kongo exchanged ambassadors and dealt with each other with a certain equality in this early period, but eventually enslavement of his subjects led Afonso to attempt to end the slave trade and limit Portuguese activities. In this he was only partially successful because of Portugal's control of Kongo's ability to communicate with the outside world and its dominance over Kongo's trade.

These first contacts were marked by preconceptions as well as an appreciation or curiosity. Africans found the newcomers strange and at first tried to fit them into their existing concepts of the spiritual and natural world. Images of Portuguese soldiers and traders began to appear in the bronzes of Benin and the carved ivory sculptures of other African peoples. The Portuguese looked on Africans as savages and pagans, who were, however, capable of civilized behavior and conversion. African arts were appreciated. Carved elephant tusks, ivory salt cellars, and other items done by African artists in a distinctive Afro-Portuguese style became an item of trade with Europe.

African artists were impressed by the Europeans and sometimes incorporated them in their own work, as can be seen in the headpiece of this beautifully carved ivory head of a Benin monarch. Europeans in turn employed African craftsmen to produce decorative luxury goods.

Portuguese exploration continued southward toward the Cape of Good Hope and beyond in the 16th century. Early contacts were made with the Mbundu peoples south of Kongo in the 1520s, and a more permanent Portuguese presence was established there in the 1570s with the foundation of Luanda on the coast. This became the basis for the Portuguese colony of Angola. We have already seen that, after Vasco da Gama rounded the Cape and reached the trading cities of East Africa on his way to India, the Portuguese sought to impose themselves on the existing trading system of the African ports in the Indian Ocean and Red Sea. They established a base on Mozambique island and then secured bases at Kilwa, Mombasa, Sofala, and other ports that gave them access to the gold trade from Monomotapa (Mwenemutapa) in the interior. In East Africa as on the West African coast, the number of permanent Portuguese settlers was minimal. The Portuguese effort was primarily commercial and military, although it was always accompanied by a strong missionary effort.

The Portuguese were the first Europeans to establish a permanent presence in Africa and as such they established the patterns that were to characterize such contacts for the next 200 years. In the 17th century, other Europeans— the Dutch, English, French, and others—competed with the Portuguese and displaced them to some extent, but the system of fortified trading stations, the combination of force and diplomacy, alliances with local rulers, and the predominance of commercial relations continued as the principal pattern of European contact with Africa.

Portuguese Expansion and Major African Kingdoms

Although for a long time Portugal's major interest was in gold, pepper, and other products, a central element in this pattern was the slave trade. Slavery as an institution had been extensive in the Roman Empire, but had died out in most of Europe during the Middle Ages as it had been replaced by serfdom. In the Mediterranean and in Iberia, however, where there was an active military frontier between Christians and Muslims, it had remained important. Moreover, the trans-Saharan slave trade had brought small numbers of black Africans into the Mediterranean throughout the period. The Portuguese voyages now opened a direct channel to sub-Saharan Africa. The first slaves brought directly to Portugal from Africa arrived in 1441, and after that date slaves became a growing item in trade. The Portuguese and later other Europeans raided for slaves along the coast, but the numbers acquired in this way were comparatively small and after initial raids Europeans found that trade was a much more secure and profitable way to get these human cargoes. The Portuguese, for example, sent about 50 slaves per year to Portugal prior to 1450 when raiding was prevalent, but by 1460 some 500 slaves per year arrived in Portugal as a trade with African rulers developed. Acquired by raiding or trade, the effects on the victims were similar. An eyewitness to the unloading of slaves in Portugal in 1444 wrote:

> But what heart could be so hard as not to be pierced with piteous feelings to see that company? For some kept their heads low and their faces bathed in tears, looking one upon another; others stood groaning very dolorously, looking up to the height of heaven, fixing their eyes upon it, crying out loudly, as if asking help of the Father of Nature.

The trade was given an added impetus when the Portuguese and the Spanish began to develop sugar plantations on the Atlantic islands of Madeira (Portugal), the Canaries (Spain), and off the African coast on Portuguese São Tomé. Sugar production demanded many workers and constant labor under difficult conditions, usually in a tropical or subtropical environment. The plantation system of organization associated with sugar, in which managers were able to control and direct laborers over long periods with little restraint, was later extended to America and then to other crops. While it did not depend only on Africans, they became the primary plantation laborers in the Atlantic world. The slave trade grew significantly in volume and complexity after 1550 as the American plantation colonies, especially Brazil, began to develop. By 1600 the slave trade predominated over all other kinds of commerce on the African coast.

THE STRUCTURE OF THE ATLANTIC SLAVE TRADE

Although considerable debate and controversy surrounds many aspects of the history of slavery, it is perhaps best to start with the numbers. Estimates of the volume of the trade have varied widely and scholars still debate the figures and their implications, but the range of calculations has been narrowed by recent research. Between 1450 and 1850 it is estimated that about 12 million Africans were shipped across the Atlantic, and with a mortality rate of 10 to 20 percent on the ships, about ten or eleven million Africans actually arrived in the Americas. How many people died in Africa as a result of the slaving wars or in the forced marches to the coast is unknown, but estimates have been as high as one-third of the total captured.

TREND TOWARD EXPANSION

The volume changed over time. In the 16th century, numbers were relatively small, but they increased to perhaps 16,000 per year in the 17th century. The 18th century was the great age of the Atlantic slave trade; probably over seven million slaves, or over 80 percent of all those embarked, were exported between 1700 and 1800. By the latter date about three million slaves resided in the Americas. Even in the 19th century, when slavery was under attack, the trade continued in volume to some places. Cuba received some 700,000 slaves and Brazil took over one million in that century alone.

The high volume of the slave trade was a necessity because in most of the slave regimes in the Caribbean and Latin America slave mortality was high and fertility was low (partly because more men than women were imported). Thus, over time there was usually a loss of population. The only way to maintain or expand the number of slaves was by importing more from Africa. The one exception to this pattern was the southern United States, where the slave population had a positive rate of growth due perhaps to the temperate climate and the fact that few worked in dangerous and unhealthy occupations like sugar and mining. By 1860 almost six million slaves worked in the Americas, but about four million of them lived in the southern United States, an area that depended more on natural population growth than on the Atlantic slave trade. In terms of total population, however, slaves in British North America were never more than one-fourth of the whole population, while in the British and French Caribbean they made up between 80 and 90 percent of the population.

The dimensions of the trade varied over time, reflecting the economic and political situation in the Americas. From 1530 to 1650, Spanish America and Brazil received the majority of African slaves, but after the English and French began to cultivate sugar in the Caribbean, the islands of Jamaica, Barbados, and St. Domingue (Haiti) became important terminals for the slavers. By the 18th century, Virginia and the Carolinas in North America had also become major destinations, although they never rivaled the Caribbean or Brazil.

If we view the whole history of the slave trade from about 1550 to 1850, it is possible to see the relative proportions of the trade. Brazil alone received between 3.5 and 5 million Africans, or about 42 percent of all those who reached the New World. The Caribbean islands, dedicated to sugar production, were the other major destination of Africans. The island colonies of St. Domingue and Jamaica each received over one million slaves in the 18th century alone.

It should be emphasized that these figures represent only the volume in the Atlantic slave trade. The older trans-Sahara, Red Sea, and East African slave trades in the hands of Muslim traders continued throughout the period and added another three million people to the total of Africans exported as slaves in this period.

The Atlantic trade drew slaves from across the continent and its concentration shifted over time. In the 16th century, the majority of slaves were exported from the Senegambia region but by the 17th century West-central Africa (modern Zaire and Angola) was the major supplier. It was joined by the areas of the Gold Coast and the Slave Coast—Dahomey and Benin—at the end of the century

TABLE 27.1

Slave Exports from Africa (1500 to the 19th Century)

Region	1500–1600 (1000s)	%	1600–1700 (1000s)	%	1700–1800 (1000s)	%	1800–1900 (1000s)	%	TOTALS (1000s)	%
Red Sea	200	17	200	7	200	3	450	8	1,050	6
Trans-Sahara	550	47	700	24	700	9	1,200	22	3,150	19
East Africa and Indian Ocean	100	9	100	4	400	5	442	8	1,042	6
Trans-Atlantic	325	28	1,868	65	6,133	83	3,330	61	11,656	69
									16,898	

Source: Adapted from Paul Lovejoy, *Transformations in Slavery. A History of Slavery in Africa* (1983).

TABLE 27.2

Destinations of African Slaves in the Atlantic Slave Trade

Region	Number in 1000s	%
British North America	523	5
Spanish America	1,687	15
British Caribbean	2,443	21
French Caribbean	1,655	15
Dutch Caribbean	500	4
Danish Caribbean	50	0.4
Brazil	4,190	37
Old World	297	2.6
	11,345	

Source: James Rawley, *The Transatlantic Slave Trade* (1981), 428.

when Benin alone was exporting over 10,000 slaves per year. In the following century, wars for control of the interior created the large states of Asante among the Akan peoples of the Gold Coast and of Dahomey among the Fon peoples. These wars were both the cause and the result of increasing slave exports from these regions.

DEMOGRAPHIC PATTERNS

The demographic patterns of the Atlantic slave trade also merit discussion. The trans-Saharan slave trade had carried a majority of women to be used as concubines and domestic servants in North Africa and the Middle East, but the Atlantic slave trade concentrated on men. The slave ships carried mostly young men. To some extent this was because planters and mine owners in the Americas were seeking workers for heavy labor and were not anxious to risk the purchase of children due to high levels of mortality. On the other hand, African societies that sold captives into slavery often preferred to sell the men and keep the women and children as domestic slaves or to extend existing kin groups.

The Atlantic trade seems to have had a demographic impact on at least certain parts of West and central Africa. One estimate is that the population of about 25 million in 1850 in those regions was about one-half what it would have been had there been no slave trade. It is true that the trans-Atlantic trade carried more men than women and more women than children, but captive women and children who remained in Africa swelled the numbers of enslaved people and skewed the proportion of women to men

in the African enslaving societies. Finally, as the Atlantic trade developed, new crops, such as maize and manioc, were introduced to Africa that provided new food resources for the population and helped it recover from the losses to the slave trade.

ORGANIZATION OF THE TRADE

The patterns of contact and trade established by the Portuguese were at first followed by rival Europeans on the African coast. Control of the slave trade or a portion of it generally reflected the political situation in Europe. For one and one-half centuries until about 1630, the Portuguese controlled most of the coastal trade and were the major suppliers of their own colony of Brazil and the Spanish settlements in America. The growth of slave-based plantation colonies in the Caribbean and elsewhere led other Europeans to compete with the Portuguese. The Dutch became major competitors when they seized El Mina in 1637 and temporarily took Angola (1641–1648) in order to supply their conquests in northeastern Brazil. By the 1660s the English were anxious to have their own source of slaves for their growing colonies in Barbados, Jamaica, and Virginia. The Royal African Company was chartered for that purpose. The French made similar arrangements in the 1660s, but it was not until the 18th century that France became a major carrier. Even smaller European nations like Denmark had its agents and forts on the African coast. Each nation established merchant towns or trade forts at places such as Axim, Nembe, Bonny, Whydah, and Luanda from which a steady source of captives could be obtained.

For the Europeans stationed on the coast, Africa was also a graveyard because of the tropical diseases encountered. Less than ten percent of the employees of the Royal Africa Company who went to Africa ever returned to England, and the majority died in the first year out. European mortality among the crews of slave ships was also very high due to tropical diseases like malaria. The slave trade proved deadly to all involved, but at least for some of the Europeans there was choice, while for the enslaved Africans there was none.

European agents for the companies often had to deal directly with local rulers, paying a tax or offering "gifts." Various forms of currency were used: iron bars, brass rings, cowrie shells. Traders calculated slaves and European goods in units of these currencies. The Spanish developed a complicated system in which a healthy adult male was called an "Indies piece," while children and women were valued at fractions of that value. Slaves were brought to the coast by a variety of means. Sometimes, as in Angola, European military campaigns produced captives for slaves or African and mulatto agents would purchase captives at interior trade centers. In Dahomey, a royal monopoly was established to control the flow of slaves. Some groups used their position to tax or control the movement of slaves from the interior to the coast. Although African and European states sought to establish monopolies over the trade, often private merchants circumvented restrictions.

Clearly, the slave trade was a trade that involved both Europeans and Africans. It was also not always clear which side was in control. One group of English merchants on the Gold Coast complained of African insolence in 1784 because in negotiations the Africans had emphasized that "the country belongs to them." In any case, the result of this collaboration was to send millions of Africans into bondage in foreign lands.

Historians have long debated the profitability of the slave trade. Some have argued that the profits were so great and constant that they constituted a major element in the rise of commercial capitalism and, later, the origins of the Industrial Revolution. Undoubtedly, many people derived a profit from the trade in Africans. An individual slaving voyage might gain a profit of as much as 300 percent and merchants in the ports that specialized in fitting out ships for the slave trade, such as Liverpool, England, or Nantes, France—as well as African suppliers—derived a profit from the slave trade. But the slave trade also involved considerable risks and costs, so that in the long run profitability levels did not maintain such high returns. In the late 18th century, profitability in the English slave trade probably ran between five and ten percent on the average and in the French and Dutch trades it was slightly lower. The slave trade was little more profitable in the long run than most business activities of the age, and as such it alone was not a major source for the capital needed in the Industrial Revolution.

It is more difficult, however, to calculate the full economic importance of slavery to the economies of Europe because it was so directly linked to the plantation and mining economies of the Americas. During some periods a "triangular" trade existed in which slaves were carried to the Americas; sugar, tobacco, and other goods were then carried to Europe; and then European products were sent to the coast of Africa to begin the triangle again. Were profits from the slave trade accumulated in Liverpool invested in the nascent textile industry of England? And if so, how important were these for the growth of that industry? The value of goods produced in Europe for exchange in the slave trade as well as the profits derived from the colonies would need to be calculated in order to adequately measure the importance of slavery to the growth of the Eu-

ropean economies. Still, the very persistence of the trade indicates its viability. The slave trade surely contributed to the formation of emerging capitalism in the Atlantic world and made Africa very much a part of the process. In Africa itself, the slave trade often had the effect of deforming economies into dependence on trade with Europeans and suppressing the growth of alternative economic activities.

The debate over the slave trade continues. Whatever its long-range implications, by the late 18th century it is clear that the slave trade and slavery were essential aspects of the economy of the Atlantic basin, and their importance was increasing. Over 40 percent of all the slaves that crossed the Atlantic embarked in the century after 1760, and the plantation economies of Brazil, the Caribbean, and the southern United States were booming in the early 19th century. The slave trade was profitable enough to keep merchants in it, and it contributed in some way to the expanding economy of western Europe. It was also the major way in which Africa was linked to the increasingly integrated economy of the world.

AFRICAN SOCIETIES, SLAVERY, AND THE SLAVE TRADE

Europeans in the age of the slave trade sometimes justified enslavement of Africans by pointing out that slavery already existed on that continent. However, while forms of bondage were ancient in Africa, and the Muslim trans-Saharan and Red Sea trades were long-standing, the Atlantic trade interacted with and transformed these earlier aspects of slavery.

African societies had developed many forms of bondage and servitude that varied from a kind of peasant status to something much more like chattel slavery in which people are considered things—"property with a soul," as Aristotle put it. African states were usually nonegalitarian and since in many African societies all land was owned by the state or the "ruler," the control of slaves was one of the few, if not the only way, in which individuals or lineages could increase their wealth and status. Slaves were employed in many ways as servants, concubines, soldiers, administrators, and field workers. In some cases, as in the ancient empire of Ghana and in Kongo, there were whole villages of enslaved dependents who were required to pay tribute to the ruler. The Muslim traders of West Africa who linked the forest region to the savanna had slave porters as well as villages of slaves to supply their caravans. In a number of situations, these forms of servitude were relatively benign and were an extension of lineage and kinship systems. In others, however, they were exploitative economic and social relations that reinforced the hierarchies of various African

The size of African cities and the power of African rulers often impressed European observers. Here the city of Loango, capital of a kingdom on the Congo coast, is depicted as a bustling urban center. At this time it was a major port in the slave trade.

societies and allowed the nobles, senior lineages, and rulers to exercise their power. Among the forest states of West Africa, such as Benin, and in the Kongo kingdom in central Africa slavery was already an important institution prior to the European arrival, but the Atlantic trade opened up new opportunities for expansion and intensification of slavery in those societies.

Despite considerable variation in African societies and the fact that slaves sometimes attained positions of command and trust, in most cases slaves were denied choice about their lives and actions. They were placed in dependent or inferior positions, and they were often considered aliens. It is important to remember that the enslavement of women was a central feature of African slavery. Although slaves were used in many ways in African societies, domestic slavery and extension of lineages through the addition of female members remained a central feature in many places. Some historians believe that the excess of women led to polygyny and the creation of large harems by rulers and merchants, whose power was increased by this process while the position of women was lowered in some societies.

In the Sudanic states of the savanna, Islamic concepts of slavery had been introduced. Slavery was viewed as a legitimate fate for nonbelievers but an illegal treatment for Muslims. Despite the complaints of legal scholars like the Ahmad Baba of Timbuktu (1556–1627) against the enslavement of Muslims, many of the Sudanic states enslaved their captives both pagan and Muslim. In the Niger Valley many slave communities produced agricultural surpluses for the rulers and nobles of Songhay, Gao, and other states. Slaves were used for gold mining and salt production, and as caravan workers in the Sahara. Slavery was a widely diffused form of labor control and wealth in Africa.

The existence of slavery in Africa and the preexisting trade in people allowed Europeans to mobilize the commerce in slaves relatively quickly by tapping existing routes and supplies. In this venture they were aided by the rulers of certain African states who were anxious to acquire more slaves for themselves and to supply slaves to the Europeans in exchange for aid and commodities. In the 16th century Kongo kingdom, the ruler had an army of 20,000 slaves as part of his household, and this gave him greater power than any Kongo ruler had ever held. In general, African rulers did not enslave their own people, except for crimes or in other unusual circumstances, but rather sought to enslave their neighbors. Thus, expanding, centralizing states were often the major suppliers of slaves to the Europeans as well as to societies in which slavery was an important institution.

SLAVING AND AFRICAN POLITICS

As one French agent put it, "the trade in slaves is the business of kings, rich men, and prime merchants." European merchants and royal officials were able to tap existing routes, markets, and institutions, but the new and constant demand also intensified enslavement in Africa and perhaps changed the nature of slavery itself in some African societies.

In the period between 1500 and 1750 as the gunpowder empires and expanding international commerce of Europe penetrated sub-Saharan Africa, existing states and societies were often transformed. Although, as we saw in Chapter 14, the empire of Songhay controlled a vast region of the western savanna until its defeat by a Moroccan invasion in 1591, for the most part the many states of central and western Africa were relatively small and fragmented. This led to a situation of instability caused by competition and warfare as states sought to expand at the expense of their neighbors or to consolidate power by incorporating subject provinces. The warrior or soldier emerged in this situation as an important social type in states such as the Kongo kingdom and Dahomey, as well as along the Zambezi River. The incessant wars promoted the importance of the military and made the sale of captives into the slave trade an extension of the politics of regions of Africa. Sometimes, as among the Muslim states of the savanna or the Lake Chad region, wars took on a religious overtone of believers against nonbelievers, but in much of West and central Africa that was not the case. Some authors see this situation as an endemic aspect of African politics; others feel it is the result of European demand for new slaves. In either case, the result was the capture and sale of millions of human beings. While increasing centralization and hierarchy could be seen in the enslaving African societies, a contrary trend of self-sufficiency and antiauthoritarian ideas developed among those peoples who bore the brunt of the slaving attacks.

One result of the presence of Europeans on the coast was a shift in the locus of power within Africa. Whereas states like Ghana and Songhay in the savanna had taken advantage of their position as intermediaries between the gold of the West African forests and the trans-Saharan trade routes, now those states closer to the coast or in contact with the Europeans could play a similar role. Those right on the coast tried to monopolize the trade with Europeans, but European meddling in their internal affairs and European fears of any coastal power that became too strong blocked the creation of centralized states under the shadow of European forts. Just beyond the coast it was different. With access to European goods, especially firearms, iron, horses, cloth, tobacco, and other goods, West and central African kingdoms began to redirect trade toward the coast and to expand their influence. Some historians have written of a gun and slave cycle in which increased firepower allowed these states to expand over their neighbors, producing more slaves that then could be exchanged for more guns. The result was unending warfare and the disruption of societies as the search for slaves pushed ever farther into the interior.

ASANTE AND DAHOMEY

Perhaps the effects of the slave trade on African societies are best seen in some specific cases. A number of large states developed in West Africa during the slave trade era. Each, in its own way, represented a response to the realities of the European presence and to the process of state formation long under way in Africa. Rulers in these states grew in power and often surrounded themselves with ritual authority and a luxurious court life as a way of reinforcing the position that their armies had won.

In the area called the Gold Coast by the Europeans, the empire of Asante (Ashanti) rose to prominence in the period of the slave trade. The Asante were members of the Akan people (the major group of modern Ghana) who had settled in and around Kumasi, a region of gold and kola nut production that lay between the coast and the Hausa and Mande trading centers to the north. There were at least 20 small states based on the matrilineal clans that were common to all the Akan peoples, but those of the Oyoko clan predominated. Their cooperation and their access to firearms after 1650 initiated a period of centralization and expansion. Under the vigorous Osei Tutu (d. 1717) the title of *asantehene* was created as supreme civil and religious leader. His golden stool became the symbol of an Asante union that was created by linking the many Akan clans under the authority of the asantehene but recognizing the autonomy of subordinate areas. An all-Asante council advised the ruler, and an ideology of unity was was used to overcome the traditional clan divisions. With this new structure and a series of military reforms, conquest of the area began. By 1700 the Dutch on the coast realized that a new power had emerged, and they began to deal directly with it.

With control of the gold-producing zones and a constant supply of prisoners to be sold as slaves for more firearms, Asante maintained its power until the 1820s as the dominant state of the Gold Coast. Although gold continued to be a major item of export, by the end of the 17th century the value of slaves made up almost two-thirds of Asante's trade.

Farther to the east in the area of the Bight of Benin (between the Volta and Benin rivers on what the Europeans called the Slave Coast), a number of large states developed in the slave trade era. The kingdom of Benin was at the height of its power when the Europeans arrived. It traced its origins to the city of Ife and to the Yoruba peoples that were its neighbors, but it had become a separate and independent kingdom with its own well-developed political and artistic traditions, especially in the casting of bronze. As early as 1516 the ruler, or oba, limited the slave trade from Benin, and for a long time most of the trade with Europeans was controlled directly by the king and was in pepper, textiles, and ivory rather than slaves. Eventually European pressure and the goals of the Benin nobility combined to generate a significant slave trade in the 18th century, but Benin never made the slave trade its primary source of revenue or state policy.

The kingdom of Dahomey, which developed among the Fon (or Aja) peoples, used a different strategy of response to the European presence. It began to emerge as a power in the 17th century from its center at Abomey about 70 miles from the coast. Its kings ruled with the advice of councils that had considerable power, but by the 1720s access to firearms allowed the rulers to create an autocratic and sometimes brutal political regime based on the slave trade. In the 1720s, under king Agaja (1708–1740), the

kingdom of Dahomey moved toward the coast, seizing in 1727 the port town of Whydah, which had attracted a large number of European traders. Although Dahomey became to some extent a subject of the powerful neighboring Yoruba state of Oyo, whose cavalry and archers made it strong, Dahomey maintained its autonomy and turned increasingly to the cycle of firearms and slaves. The trade was controlled by the royal court, whose armies (including a regiment of women) were used to raid for more captives. As Dahomey expanded it eliminated the royal families and customs of the areas it conquered and imposed its own traditions. This resulted in the formation of a unified state that proved more lasting than some of its neighbors.

Well into the 19th century, Dahomey was a slaving state. Dependence on the trade in human beings had negative effects on the society as a whole. The large-scale sacrifice of human victims in the annual renewal festival, or Customs, at the royal court was one example of the cheapening of life that the trade produced. Historians argue about whether the expansion of Dahomey was driven by the desire for more slaves or by an attempt to unify all the Aja peoples, but in any case, slavery played a central role in the history of the area. Over 1.8 million slaves were exported from the Bight of Benin between 1640 and 1890.

Emphasis on the slave trade should not obscure the creative process within many of the African states. The growing devine authority of the rulers paralleled in some ways the rise of absolutism in Europe. It led to the development of new political forms, some of which had the power to limit the role of the king. In the Yoruba state of Oyo, for example, a governing council shared power with the ruler. In some states, a balance of offices kept central power in check. In Asante the traditional village chiefs and officials whose authority was based on their lineage were increasingly challenged by new officials appointed by the asantehene, as a state bureaucracy began to form.

The creativity of these societies was also seen in traditional arts. In many places, crafts such as bronze casting, woodcarving, and weaving flourished. Guilds of artisans developed in a number of societies and their specialization produced crafts executed with great skill. In Benin and the Yoruba states, for example, remarkable and lifelike sculptures in wood and ivory continued to be produced. Often, however, the best artisans labored for the royal court, producing objects designed to honor the ruling family and reinforce the civil and religious authority of the king. This was true in architecture, weaving, and the decorative arts as well. Much of this artistic production also had a religious function or contained religious symbolism as African artists made the spiritual world visually apparent.

EAST AFRICA AND THE SUDAN

West Africa was obviously the region most directly influenced by the trans-Atlantic slave trade, but there and elsewhere in Africa, long-term patterns of society and economy continued and intersected with the new external influences.

On the East Coast of Africa, the Swahili trading cities continued their commerce in the Indian Ocean and the Arabian Sea, accommodating to the military presence of the Portuguese and the Ottoman Turks. Trade to the interior continued to bring ivory, gold, and a steady supply of slaves. Many of these slaves were destined for the harems and households of Arabia and the Middle East, but also a small percent were carried away by the Europeans for their plantation colonies. The Portuguese and Indo-Portuguese settlers along the Zambezi River in Mozambique made use of slave soldiers to increase their territories, and certain groups in interior East Africa specialized in supplying ivory and slaves to the East African coast. Europeans did establish some plantation-style colonies on islands like Mauritius in the Indian Ocean, and these depended on the East African slave trade.

On Zanzibar and other offshore islands, and later on the coast itself, Swahili, Indian, and Arabian merchants actually followed the European model and set up plantations producing cloves, using African slave laborers. Some of the plantations were large, and by the 1860s Zanzibar had a slave population of around 100,000. The sultan of Zanzibar alone owned over 4000 slaves in 1870. Slavery became an extensive feature of the East African coast, and the slave trade from the interior to these plantations and to the traditional slave markets of the Red Sea continued until the end of the 19th century.

Much less is known about the interior of eastern Africa. The well-watered and heavily populated region of the great lakes of the interior supported large and small kingdoms. Bantu-speakers predominated but a number of peoples inhabited the region. Linguistic and archeological evidence suggests that pastoralist Nilotic peoples from the Upper Nile Valley with a distinctive late iron age technology had moved southward into what is today western Kenya and Uganda where they came into contact with Bantu-speakers and with the farmers and herdsmen who were speakers of another group of languages called Cushitic. The Bantu states absorbed the immigrants, even when at times the newcomers established ruling dynasties. Later Nilotic migrations, especially of the Luo peoples, resulted in the construction of a number of related dynasties among the states in the area of the large lakes of east-central Africa. At Bun-

yoro, the Luo eventually established a ruling dynasty among the existing Bantu population. This composite kingdom exercised considerable power in the 16th and 17th centuries. Other related and similar states formed in the region. In Buganda, near Lake Victoria, a strong monarchy ruled a heterogeneous population and dominated the region in the 18th century. These developments in the interior, as important as they were for the history of the region, were less influenced by the growing contact with the outside world than were other regions of Africa.

Across the continent in the northern savanna at the end of the 18th century, the process of Islamization, which had been important in the days of the empires of Mali and Songhay, entered a new and violent stage that not only linked Islamization to both the external slave trades and the growth of slavery in Africa, but also produced other long-term effects in the region. After the break up of Songhay in the 16th century, a number of successor states had developed. Some, such as the Bambara kingdom of Segu, were pagan. Others, such as the Hausa kingdoms in Northern Nigeria, were ruled by Muslim royal families and urban aristocracies but continued to contain large numbers of animist subjects, most of whom were rural peasants. In these states the degree of Islamization was slight, and an accommodation between Muslims and animists was achieved. Beginning in the 1770s Muslim reform movements began to sweep the western Sudan. Religious brotherhoods advocating a purifying Sufi variant of Islam extended their influence throughout the Muslim trade networks in the Senegambia region and the western Sudan. This movement had an intense impact on the Fulani (Fulbe), a pastoral people who were spread across a broad area of the western Sudan.

In 1804 Usuman Dan Fodio, a studious and charismatic Muslim Fulani scholar, began to preach the reformist ideology in the Hausa kingdoms. His movement became a revolution when in 1804, seeing himself as God's instrument, he preached a jihad against the Hausa kings whom he felt were not following the teachings of the Prophet. A great upheaval followed in which the Fulani took control of most of the Hausa states of northern Nigeria in the western Sudan. A new kingdom, based on the city of Sokoto, developed under Dan Fodio's son and brother. The Fulani expansion was driven not only by religious zeal but by political ambitions, as the attack on the well-established Muslim kingdom of Bornu demonstrated. The result of this upheaval was the creation of a powerful Sokoto state under a caliph, whose authority was established over cities such as Kano and Zaria and whose rulers became emirs of provinces within the Sokoto caliphate.

By the 1840s the effects of Islamization and the Fulani expansion were felt across much of the interior of West Africa. New political units were created, a reformist Islam that sought to eliminate pagan practices was spread, and social and cultural changes took place in the wake of these changes. Literacy, for example, became more widely dispersed and new centers of trade, such as Kano, emerged in this period. Later jihads established other new states along similar lines. All of these changes had long-term effects on the region of the western Sudan.

These upheavals—moved by religious, political, and economic motives—were not unaffected by the external pressures on Africa. They fed into the ongoing processes of the external slave trades and the development of slavery within African societies. Large numbers of captives resulting from the wars were exported down to the coast for sale to the Europeans, while another stream of slaves crossed the Sahara to North Africa. In the western and central Sudan the level of slave labor rose, especially in the larger towns and along the trade routes. Slave villages, supplying royal courts and merchant activities as well as a sort of plantation system, developed to produce peanuts and other crops. Slave women spun cotton and wove cloth for sale, slave artisans worked in the towns, and slaves served the caravan traders, but most slaves did agricultural labor. By the late 19th century regions of the savanna contained large slave populations—in some places as much as 30 to 50 percent of the whole population. From the Senegambia region of Futa Jallon, across the Niger and Senegal basins, and to the east of Lake Chad, slavery became a central feature of the Sudanic states and remained so through the 19th century.

WHITE SETTLERS AND AFRICANS IN SOUTHERN AFRICA

One area of Africa little affected by the slave trade in the early modern period was the southern end of the continent. As we saw in Chapter 17 this region was still occupied by non-Bantu hunting peoples, the San (Bushmen), and by the Khoikhoi (Hottentots) who lived by hunting and sheep herding, and, after contact with the Bantu, cattle-herding peoples as well. Peoples practicing farming and using iron tools were living south of the Limpopo River by the 3d century A.D. Probably Bantu-speakers, they spread southward and established their villages and cattle herds in the fertile lands along the eastern coast, where rainfall was favorable to their agricultural and pastoral way of life. The drier western regions toward the Kalahari Desert were left to the Khoikhoi and San. Mixed farming

and pastoralism spread throughout the region in a complex process that involved migration, peaceful contacts, and warfare.

By the 16th century, Bantu-speaking peoples occupied much of the eastern regions of southern Africa. They practiced agriculture and herding; worked iron and copper into tools, weapons, and adornments; and traded with their neighbors. They spoke related languages such as Tswana, Sotho, as well as the Nguni languages such as Zulu and Xhosa. Among the Sotho, villages might have contained as many as 200 people, but the Nguni lived in hamlets made up of a few extended families. Men served as artisans and herdsmen; women did the farming and housework, and sometimes organized their labor communally. Politically, chiefdoms of various sizes—many small, but a few with as many as 50,000 inhabitants—characterized the southern Bantu peoples. Chiefs held power with the support of relatives and with the acceptance of the people, but there was considerable variation in chiefly authority. The Bantu-speaking peoples' pattern of political organization and the splitting off of junior lineages to form new villages created a process of expansion that led to competition for land and absorption of newly conquered groups. This situation became intense at the end of the 18th century, either because of the pressures and competition for foreign trade through the Portuguese outposts on the East African coast or because of the growth of population among the southern Bantu. In any case, the result was farther expansion southward into the path of another people who had arrived in southern Africa.

In 1652 the Dutch East India Company established a colony at the Cape of Good Hope to serve as a provisioning ground for ships sailing to Asia. On the fertile lands around this colony relatively large farms developed. The Cape colony depended on slave labor brought from Indonesia and Asia for a while, but it soon enslaved local Africans as well. The expanding colony and its labor needs led to a series of wars with the San and Hottentot populations, who were pushed farther to the north and west. By the 1760s the Dutch, or Boer, farmers had crossed the Orange River in search of new lands. They viewed the fertile plains and hills as theirs, and they saw the Africans only as intruders and as a possible source of labor. Competition and warfare resulted. Around 1800 the Cape colony had about 17,000 settlers (or Afrikaners as they came to be called), 26,000 slaves, and 14,000 Khoikhoi.

At the same time that the Boers were pushing northward, the southern Bantu were extending their movement to the south. Matters were also complicated by European events when Great Britain seized the Cape colony in 1795 and then took it under formal British control in 1815. While the British government helped the settlers to clear out Africans from potential farming lands, government attempts to limit the Boer settlements and their use of African labor were unsuccessful. Meanwhile competition for farming and grazing land led to a series of wars between the settlers and the Bantu during the early 19th century.

Various government measures, the increasing arrival of English-speaking immigrants, and the lure of better lands caused groups of Boers to move to the north. These "voortrekkers" moved into lands occupied by the southern Nguni, eventually creating a number of autonomous Boer states. After 1834, when Britain abolished slavery and imposed restrictions on landholding, groups of Boers staged a "great trek" far to the north to be free of government interference. This movement eventually brought them across the Orange River and into Natal on the more fertile east coast, which the Boers believed to be only sparsely inhabited by Africans. They did not realize at the time that the lack of population was due to a great military upheaval taking place among the Bantu peoples of the region.

THE "MFECANE" AND THE ZULU RISE TO POWER

Among the Nguni peoples, major changes had taken place. A process of unification had begun among some of the northern chiefdoms, and a new military organization had emerged. In 1818 leadership fell to Shaka, a brilliant military tactician who reformed the loose forces into regiments organized by lineage and age. Iron discipline and new tactics were introduced, including the use of a short stabbing-spear to be used at close range. The army was made a permanent institution, and the regiments were housed together in separate villages. The fighting men were only allowed to marry after their service had been completed. Shaka's own Zulu chiefdom became the center of this new military and political organization that began to absorb or destroy its neighbors. Shaka demonstrated considerable talents as a politician, destroying the ruling families of those groups he incorporated into the growing Zulu state. He ruled with an iron hand, destroying his enemies, acquiring their cattle, and crushing any opposition. His policies brought power to the Zulu, but his erratic and cruel behavior also earned him enemies among his own people. Though he was assassinated in 1828, Shaka's reforms remained in place and his successors built on the structure he had created. Zulu power was still growing in the 1840s, and the Zulu remained the most impressive military force in black Africa until the end of the century.

The rise of the Zulu and other Nguni chiefdoms was the beginning of the *mfecane*, or wars of crushing and wandering. As Zulu control expanded, a series of campaigns and forced migrations led to incessant fighting, as other peoples sought to survive by fleeing, emulating, or joining the Zulu. Groups spun off to the north and south, raiding the Portuguese on the coast, clashing with the Europeans to the south, and fighting with neighboring chiefdoms. New African states, such as the Swazi, that adapted aspects of the Zulu model emerged among the survivors. One state, Lesotho, successfully resisted the Zulu example. It combined Sotho and Nguni speakers and defended itself against Nguni armies. It eventually developed as a kingdom far less committed to military organization and one in which the people exercised considerable influence on their leaders.

The whole of the southern continent, from the Cape colony to Lake Malawi, had been thrown into turmoil by raiding parties, remnants, and refugees. Superior firepower allowed the Boers to continue to hold their lands, but it was not until the Zulu Wars of the 1870s that Zulu power was crushed by Great Britain—and even then only at great cost. During the process, the basic patterns of conflict between Africans and Europeans in the largest settler colony on the continent were created. These patterns included a competition between settlers and Africans for

This Zulu royal kraal drawn in the 1830s gives some idea of the power of the Zulu at the time that Shaka was forging Zulu dominance during the *mfecane*.

land, the expanding influence of European governmental control, and the desire of Europeans to make use of Africans as laborers.

ANALYSIS
SLAVERY AND HUMAN SOCIETY

Slavery is a very old and pervasive institution. It has been found at different times all over the globe, among relatively simple societies and in the great centers of civilization. In some of these societies, it has been an essentially marginal or secondary form of labor, while in others it became the predominant labor form or "mode of production" (in the jargon of Marxist analysis). The need for labor beyond the capacity of the individual or the family unit is very old, and as soon as authority, law, or custom could be established to set the conditions for coercion, the tribe, the state, the priests, or some other group or institution extracted labor by force. Coerced labor, of course, could take different forms. There are important distinctions between indentured servants, convict laborers, debt-peons, and chattel slaves.

While most societies placed some limits on the slaveholder's authority or power, the denial of the slave's control over his or her own labor and life choices was characteristic of this form of coercion throughout history. In most societies that had a form of chattel slavery, the slave was denied a sense of belonging in the society, the idea of kinship. The honor associated with family or lineage was the antithesis of slavery. Joseph in Egypt, the viziers of the sultans of Turkey might rise to high positions, but the fact that they were slaves meant that they were essentially instruments of their masters' will. In fact, because they were slaves and thus unconstrained by kinship or other ties and obligations, they could be trusted in positions of command.

Because slaves became nonpersons, or as one modern author has put it, because they suffered a "social death," it was always easier to enslave "others" or "outsiders," those who were different in some way. Hebrews enslaved Canaanites, Greeks enslaved "barbarians," and Muslims made slaves of nonbelievers. If the difference between slave and master was readily seen, it made enforcement of slave status that much easier. Racism as such did not cause modern slavery, but differences in culture, language, color, or other physical characteristics had always facilitated

enslavement. The familiarity of Europeans and Muslims with black Africans in an enslaved status contributed to the development of modern racism. To paraphrase the English historian Charles Boxer, no people can enslave another for 400 years without developing an attitude of superiority.

Slavery was not only a general phenomenon that existed in many societies; rarely questioned on any grounds, it was recognized as a necessary and "natural" phenomenon. Slavery appears and is accepted in the texts of ancient India, the Old Testament, and the writings of 5th century Greece. Aristotle specifically argued that some people were born to rule and others to serve. In Christian theology, while all people might be free in spirit in the kingdom of God, in the real world, servitude was a necessary reality. Voices might be raised arguing for fair treatment or against the enslavement of a particular group, but the condition of servitude itself was usually taken as part of the natural order of the world.

In this context, the attack on slavery in Western culture that grew from the Enlightenment and the social and economic changes in western Europe and its Atlantic colonies at the end of the 18th century was really a remarkable turning point in world history. Whether one believes that slavery was an atavistic labor form that was incompatible with industrial capitalism and was, therefore, abolished or that it was destroyed essentially because its immorality became all too obvious, its demise was relatively quick. In about one and one-half centuries, the moral and religious underpining of chattel slavery was cut away and its economic justifications seriously questioned. Although slavery lingered on in at least a few places well into the 20th century, few people were willing to defend the institution publicly.

While slavery historically existed in many places it has become intimately associated with Africa because of the scope of the Atlantic slave trade and the importance of slavery in the formation of the modern world system. There was nothing inevitable about Africa becoming the primary source of laborers in the modern world. Europeans did make use of American Indians and European indentured workers when they could, but historical precedents, maritime technology, and availability all contributed to the process which made Africa the source of labor for the expanding plantation colonies of Europe.

African slavery obviously played an important role in the shaping of the modern world. The African slave trade was one of the first truely international trades, and it created an easy access to labor that enabled Europeans to carry out the exploitation of the Americas. Some have argued that it was an important, even a necessary feature in the rise of capitalism and the international division of labor. Others are less convinced. In this question, as in virtually every other question regarding modern slavery, controversies still abound.

In the context of African history, the interpretation of slavery is still in the process of rapid change. The estimate of the volume involved in the Atlantic trade (10–12 million) has been seriously questioned, especially by African scholars who see these new figures as an attempt to lessen the extent of the exploitation of Africa. Another debate centers on the impact of the trade on the population and societies within Africa. The slave trade was important to the economy of the Atlantic, but how important was this external trade in Africa itself? Early researchers, reacting to the preabolitionist European self-justifications that the slave trade was no great crime because Africans were long familiar with slavery and were selling already enslaved individuals, argued that African "slavery" was often an extension of kinship or other forms of dependency and was quite unlike the chattel slavery of western Europe. But further research has demonstrated that in many African societies, slavery was an integral and essential part of the economy and that while specific conditions might vary considerably from the Americas, the servile condition in Africa had much in common with chattel slavery. The Sokoto caliphate in the 19th century, for example, had a proportion of slaves similar to Brazil or the southern United States. Slave societies did exist in Africa.

Now controversy rages over the extent to which the development of African slavery resulted from the long-term impact of the slave trade and European demand for captive labor. African societies did not live in isolation from the pressures and examples of the wider world economy into which they were drawn. The extent to which that contact transformed slavery in Africa is now in question. These controversies among historians reflect current concerns and a realization that the present social and political situation in Africa and in many places in the Americas continues to bear the burden of a historical past in which slavery played an essential role. In the evaluation of slavery as in all other historical questions, what we think about the present shapes our inquiry and interpretation of the past.

Questions: Why did Africa become the leading source of slaves in the early modern world economy? What are some of the leading issues in the interpretation of African slavery? What were the roles of Africans and Europeans in the early modern slave trade?

THE AFRICAN DIASPORA

The slave trade was the means by which the history of the Americas and Africa became linked and a principal way in which African societies were drawn into the world economy. The import into Africa of European firearms, Indian textiles, Indonesian cowrie shells, and American tobacco in return for African ivory, gold, and especially slaves demonstrated Africa's integration into the mercantile structure of the world. Africans involved in the trade learned to deal effectively with this situation. The price of slaves rose steadily in the 18th century and the terms of trade increasingly favored African dealers. In many African ports, such as Whydah, Porto Novo, and Luanda, an African or Afro-European community developed that specialized in the slave trade and used their position as middlemen to advantage.

SLAVE LIVES

For those carried in the trade, such considerations had little meaning. For them slavery meant destruction of their villages or capture in war, separation from friends and family, and then the forced march to an interior trading town or to the slave pens at the towns or forts of the coast. Conditions during the process were deadly and perhaps as many as one-third of the captives died along the way or in the slave pens. Eventually the slaves were loaded onto the ships. Cargo size varied and could go as high as 700 slaves packed and crowded into the dank, unhealthy conditions of the slave ships, but most cargoes were smaller and overcrowding was less of a factor in mortality than the length of the voyage or the point of origin in Africa—the Bights of Benin and Biafra being particularly unhealthy. The average rate of mortality for slaves varied over time but ran at about 18 to 20 percent until the 18th century when it declined somewhat. Still, on individual ships losses could be catastrophic, as on a Dutch ship of 1737 where 700 of the 716 slaves perished on the voyage.

The so-called Middle Passage, or slave voyage to the Americas, was a traumatic experience for the slaves. Taken from their homes, branded, confined, and shackled, they faced not only the dangers of poor hygiene, dysentery, disease, and bad treatment, but also the fear of being eaten or worse by the Europeans. Their situation led sometimes to suicide or to resistance and mutiny on the ships. However traumatic, the Middle Passage certainly did not strip Africans of their culture, and they arrived in the Americas with their languages, beliefs, artistic traditions, and strong memories of their past.

During the era of the slave trade a number of enslaved Africans by one means or another succeeded in telling their stories. These accounts with their specific details of the injustice and inhumanities of slavery became particularly useful in the abolitionist crusade. The biography of Frederick Douglas is perhaps the most famous of these accounts.

The biography of Olaudah Equiano, an Ibo from what is today eastern Nigeria on the Niger River, presents a personal description of the enslavement process in Africa and the terrors of the Middle Passage. Equiano and his sister were kidnapped in 1756 by African slave hunters and sold to British slave traders. Separated from his sister, he was carried to the West Indies and later to Virginia where he became servant to a naval officer. He traveled widely on his master's military campaigns and was later sold to a Philadelphia Quaker merchant who eventually allowed him to buy his freedom. Later in life, he moved to England and became an active member in the movement to end slavery and the slave trade. His biography was published in 1789. The political uses of this kind of biography and Equiano's association with the abolitionists should caution us to take some care in accepting the account at face value, but it does convey the personal shock and anguish of those caught in the slave trade's web.

The first object which saluted my eyes when I arrived on the coast was the sea, and a slaveship, which was riding at anchor, and waiting for its cargo. These filled me with astonishment, which was soon converted into terror, which I am yet at a loss to describe, nor the then feelings of my mind. When I was carried on board I was immediately handled, and tossed up, to see if I were sound, by some of the crew; and I was now persuaded that I had got into a world of bad spirits, and that they were going to kill me. Their complexions too differing so much from ours, their long hair, and the language they spoke, which was very different from any I had ever heard, united to confirm me in this belief. Indeed, such were the horrors of my views and fears at that moment, that if ten thousand worlds had been my own, I would have freely parted with them all to have exchanged my condition with that of the meanest slave in my own country. When I looked round the ship too, and saw a large furnace or copper boiler, and a multitude of black people of ev-

ery description chained together, every one of their countenances expressing dejection and sorrow, I no longer doubted my fate; and, quite overpowered with horror and anguish, I fell motionless on the deck and fainted. When I recovered a little, I found some black people about me, who I believed were some of those who brought me on board, and had been receiving their pay; they talked to me in order to cheer me, but all in vain. I asked them if we were not to be eaten by those white men with horrible looks, red faces, and long hair. They told me I was not. . . . I now saw myself deprived of all chance of returning to my native country, or even the least glimpse of hope of gaining the shore, which I now considered as friendly; and I even wished for my former slavery, in preference to my present situation, which was filled with horrors of every kind, still heightened by my ignorance of what I was to undergo. I was not long suffered to indulge my grief; I was soon put down under decks, and there I received such a salutation in my nostrils as I had never experienced in my life; so that with the loathsomeness of the stench, and the crying together, I became so sick and low that I was not able to eat, nor had I the least desire to taste anything. I now wished for the last friend, death, to relieve me; but soon, to my grief two white men offered me eatables; and on my refusing to eat, one of them held me fast by the hands, and laid me across, I think, the windlass, and tied my feet while the other flogged me severely. I had never experienced anything of this kind before; and, although not being used to the water, I naturally feared that element the first time I saw it; yet, nevertheless, could I have got over the nettings, I would have jumped over the side; but I could not; and, besides the crew used to watch us very closely who were not chained down to the decks, lest we should leap into the water; and I have seen some of these poor African prisoners most severely cut for attempting to do so, and hourly whipped for not eating. This, indeed was often the case with myself. In a little time after amongst the poor chained men, I found some of my own nation, which in a small degree gave ease to my mind. I inquired of them what was to be done with us? They gave me to understand we were to be carried to these white people's country to work for them. I then was a little revived, and thought, if it were no worse than working, my situation was not so desperate: but still I feared I should be put to death, the white people looked and acted, as I thought, in so savage a manner; for I had never seen among any people such instances of brutal cruelty; and this was not only shown to us blacks, but also to some of the whites themselves. . . .

At last when the ship we were in had got in all her cargo, they made ready with many fearful noises, and we were all put under deck, so that we could not see how they managed the vessel. But this disappointment was the least of my sorrow. The stench of the hold while we were on the coast was so intolerably loathsome, that it was dangerous to remain there for any time, and some of us had been permitted to stay on deck for the fresh air; but now the whole ship's cargo was confined together, it became absolutely pestilential. The closeness of the place, and the heat of the climate, added to the number in the ship, which was so crowded that each had scarcely room to turn himself, almost suffocated us. This produced copious perspirations, so that the air soon became unfit for respiration, from a variety of loathsome smells, and brought on a sickness amongst the slaves, of which many died, thus falling victims to the improvident avarice, as I may call it, of their purchasers. This wretched situation was again aggravated by the galling of the chains, now become insupportable; and the filth of the necessary tubs, into which the children fell, and were almost suffocated. The shrieks of the women, and the groans of the dying, rendered the whole a scene of horror almost inconceivable. . . .

Questions: In what ways does Equiano's description alter an understanding of the slave trade? What opportunities existed for the captives to resist? What effect might the experience of Africans on the slave ships have on their perceptions of each other and of the Europeans?

AFRICANS IN AMERICA

The destination of the slaves carried across the Atlantic was principally the plantations and mines of America. Landed estates using large amounts of often coerced labor became characteristic of American agriculture, at first in the production of sugar, and later for rice, cotton, and tobacco. The plantation system already used for producing sugar on the Atlantic islands of Spain and Portugal was transferred to the New World. After attempts to use Indian laborers in places like Brazil and Hispaniola, Africans were brought in. West Africans, in fact, coming from societies in which herding, metallurgy, and intensive agriculture were widely practiced were sought by Europeans for the specialized tasks of making sugar. In the English colonies of Barbados and Virginia, indentured servants from England were eventually replaced by enslaved Africans when either new crops, such as sugar, were introduced or when indentured servants became less available. In any case, the plantation system of farming with a dependent or enslaved work force characterized the production of many tropical and semitropical crops in demand in Europe, and thus the plantation became the locus of African and Afro-American life.

Slaves did many other things as well. As we saw in Chapter 24, gold mining in Brazil made extensive use of black slaves and the Spanish used slaves in the silver mines of Mexico. Urban slavery was characteristic of Latin American cities, where slaves were often artisans, street vendors, and household servants. In early 17th century Lima, Peru, capital of Spain's colony in South America, blacks outnumbered Europeans. Later cities, such as Charleston and New Orleans, would also develop a large slave and free Afro-American population. In short, there was virtually no occupation that slaves did not perform, although the vast majority lived their lives as agricultural laborers.

AMERICAN SLAVE SOCIETIES

Each American slave-based society reflected the variations of its European origin and its component African cultures, but there were certain similarities and common features. Each recognized distinctions between African-born "salt water" slaves who were almost invariably black (by European standards) and their American-born descendants, the Creole slaves, some of whom were mulattoes as a result of sexual exploitation of slave women or the process of miscegenation. In all the American slave societies, a hierarchy of status evolved in which free whites were at the top, slaves were at the bottom, and free people of color had an intermediate position. In this sense color and "race" played a role in American slavery it had not played in Africa. Among the slaves, slaveholders also created a hierarchy based on origin and color. Creole and especially mulatto slaves were given more opportunities to acquire skilled jobs

Africans were set to all kinds of labor in the Americas, from domestic service to mining and shipbuilding, but the vast majority worked on plantations like this sugar mill in the Caribbean.

or to work in the house as servants rather than in the fields or mines. They were also more likely to win their freedom by manumission.

This system of hierarchy was a creation of the slave-holders and did not necessarily reflect perceptions among the slaves. There is evidence that important African nobles or religious leaders, who for one reason or another were sold into slavery, continued to exercise authority within the slave community. Still, the distinctions between Creole and African slaves tended to divide that community, as did the distinctions between different African groups who maintained their ties and affiliations in America. Many of the slave rebellions in the Caribbean and Brazil were organized along African ethnic and political lines. In Jamaica there were a number of Akan-led rebellions in the 18th century and the largest escaped-slave community in 17th century Brazil was apparently organized and led by Angolans.

While economic organization and European concepts of hierarchy imposed a certain similarity in the various colonies in which Africans formed a part, the slave-based societies also varied in their composition. In the 18th century, for example, on the Caribbean islands where the Indian population had died out or had been exterminated and where few Europeans settled, Africans and their descendants formed the vast majority. In Jamaica and St. Domingue, slaves made up over 80 percent of the population, and because mortality levels were so high, a large proportion were African-born. Brazil also had large numbers of imported Africans, but its more diverse population and economy, as well as a tradition of manumitting slaves and high levels of miscegenation, meant that slaves made

up only about 35 percent of the population. Free people of color, the descendants of former slaves, however, made up about another one-third, so that together slaves and free colored constituted two-thirds of the total population.

The Caribbean and Brazil differed significantly from the southern colonies of British North America, which depended less on imported Africans because of a positive rate of growth among the slave population. There, Creoles predominated but manumission was less common and free people of color were less than ten percent of the total Afro-American origin. The result was that slavery in North America was less influenced directly by Africa: By the mid-18th century, the slave population in most places in North America was reproducing itself. By 1850 less than one percent of the slaves there were African-born. The combination of natural growth and the relatively small direct trade from Africa reduced the degree of African cultural reinforcement in comparison with Cuba or Brazil.

THE PEOPLE AND GODS IN EXILE

Africans brought as slaves to America faced a peculiar series of problems. Working conditions were exhausting and life for most slaves was often "nasty, brutish, and short." Family formation was made difficult because of the general shortage of women carried in the slave trade, a situation made even worse where the ratio of men to women was sometimes as much as three to one. To this was added the insecurity of slave status in which family members might be separated by sale or by the masters' whim. Still, most slaves lived in family units even if their marriages were not always sanctioned by the religion of their masters.

Throughout the Americas, wherever Africans were brought, aspects of their language, religion, artistic sensibilities, and other elements of culture survived. To some extent the amount of continuity depended on the intensity and volume of the slave trade from a particular area. Yoruba culture, for example, was particularly strong in northeastern Brazil because the trade between it and the Bight of Benin was heavy and continuous in the early 19th century. During certain periods, Akan peoples predominated in Jamaica, while Ewe or Dahomeans predominated in Haiti. Some slaveholders tried to mix up the slaves on their plantations so that strong African identities would be lost, but colonial dependence on slavers who dealt continually with the same region tended to undercut such policies. In the reality of slavery in the Americas, Africans had to adapt and change and to incorporate other African peoples and their ideas and customs. Moreover, there were also the ways and customs of the masters that were both imposed and adopted. Thus, what emerged as Afro-American culture reflected specific African roots adapted to a new reality. Afro-American culture was dynamic and creative in this sense.

Religion was an obvious example of continuity and adaptation. Slaves were converted to Catholicism by Spaniards and Portuguese, and slaves were capable of fervent devotion as members of Black Catholic brotherhoods some of which were organized by African origins. Still, African religious ideas and practices did not die out, and many African slaves were accused of "witchcraft" by the Inquisition in those colonies. In the English islands, *obeah* was the name given to the African religious practices, and the men and women knowledgeable in them were held in high regard within the community. In Brazilian *candomble* (Yoruba) and Haitian *Vodun* (Aja), rather fully developed versions of African religion flourished and continue until the present, despite attempts to suppress them.

The reality of the Middle Passage meant that religious ideas and concepts were easier to transfer than the institutional aspects of religion. Without religious specialists or a priestly class, aspects of African religions were changed or transformed by contact with other African peoples as well as with colonial society. In many cases slaves held their new faith in Christianity and their African beliefs at the same time, and sought to fuse the two. For Muslim Africans this was less possible. In 1835 in Bahia, the largest slave rebellion in Brazil was organized by Muslim Yoruba and Hausa slaves and directed against the whites and against nonbelievers.

Resistance and rebellion were other aspects of African-American history. Recalcitrance, running away, and direct confrontation were present wherever slaves were held. As early as 1508 African runaways disrupted communications on Hispaniola, and in 1527 a plot to rebel was uncovered in Mexico City. Throughout the Americas communities of

The cultures of Africa brought to the Americas were transformed in the new setting. African religions that were transferred to Brazil, for example, survived and were combined with local elements to form vibrant new faiths. Here a participant who has been "possessed" by one of the goddesses dances in her regalia.

runaway slaves formed. In Jamaica, Colombia, Venezuela, Haiti, and Brazil runaway communities were continuous and persistent. In Brazil, during the 17th century, Palmares, an enormous runaway slave kingdom with numerous villages and a population of perhaps 8,000 to 10,000 people, resisted Portuguese and Dutch attempts to destroy it for a century. Although its inhabitants were both Creoles and Africans of various backgrounds, its origins, organization, and leadership were Angolan. In Jamaica, the runaway "Maroons" were able to gain some independence and a recognition of their freedom. So-called ethnic slave rebellions organized by a particular African group were relatively common in the Caribbean and Brazil in the 18th century. In North America where reinforcement from the slave trade was less important, resistance was also important, but it was based less on African origins or ethnicities.

Perhaps, the most remarkable story of African American resistance is found in the forests of Suriname, a former Dutch plantation colony. There large numbers of slaves ran off in the 18th century and mounted an almost perpetual war in the rain forest against the various expeditions sent to hunt them down. Those captured were brutally executed, but eventually a truce developed. Today about 50,000 Maroon descendants still live in Suriname and French Guiana. The Suriname Maroons maintained many aspects of their West African background in terms of language, kinship relations, and religious beliefs, but these were fused with new forms and ways drawn from European and American Indian contacts resulting from their New World experience. From this fusion based on their own creativity, a truly Afro-American culture was created.

AFRICA AND THE END OF THE SLAVE TRADE

The end of the Atlantic slave trade and the abolition of slavery in the Atlantic world resulted from economic, political, and religious changes in Europe and in its overseas American colonies and former colonies. These changes, which were manifestations of the Enlightenment, the Age of Revolution, Christian revivalism, and perhaps the Industrial Revolution, were basically external to Africa but once again they determined the pace and nature of transformations within the African continent.

Like much else about the history of slavery, there is considerable disagreement about the end of the slave trade. It is true that some African societies began to export new "legitimate" commodities, such as peanuts, cotton, and palm oil, which made their dependence on the slave trade less important, but the supply of slaves to European mer-

African or American, or both? In Suriname, descendants of escaped slaves maintain many aspects of African culture but have adapted, modified, and transformed them in many ways. This wooden door shows the imaginative skills of African-American carvers.

chants was not greatly affected by this development. In general, the British plantation economies were booming in the period from 1790 to 1830, and plantations in Cuba, Brazil, and the South of the United States flourished in the following decades. Thus, it is difficult to find a direct and simple link between economic self-interest and the movement to suppress the slave trade.

Opponents of slavery and the brutality of the trade had appeared in the mid-18th century, in relation to new intellectual movements in the West. The philosopher Jean Jacques Rousseau in France and the political economist Adam Smith in England had both written against it. Whereas in ancient Rome during the spread of Christianity and Islam or in 16th century Europe, enslavement of "barbarians" or nonbelievers was viewed as a positive benefit, a means to civilize others. Slavery during the European Enlightenment and bourgeois revolution came to be viewed as unprogressive, retrograde, and immoral. The slave trade was particularly criticized. It was the symbol of slavery's inhumanity and cruelty.

England, as the major maritime power of the period, was the key to the end of the slave trade. Under the leadership of religious humanitarians, such as John Wesley and William Wilberforce, an abolitionist movement gained strength against its opponents made up of merchants and the "West Indies interests." After considerable parliamentary debate, the British slave trade was abolished in 1807. Having set out on this course, Britain sought to impose abolition of the slave trade on other countries throughout the Atlantic. Spain and Portugal were pressured to gradual suppression, and the British navy was used as a means to enforce these agreements by capturing illegal slave ships, though the full end of slavery in the Americas occurred only in 1888.

CONCLUSION

THE IMPACT OF SLAVERY
ON AFRICA

Africa had been drawn into the world economy in the era of the slave trade, at first slowly, but after 1750 with increasing intensity. Its incorporation produced differing effects on African societies, reinforcing authority in some places, creating new states in others, and sometimes provoking social, religious, and political reactions. While many aspects of African life followed traditional patterns, the contact with the world economy forced many African societies to adapt and adjust in ways that often placed them at a later disadvantage and facilitated Europe's eventual colonization of Africa in the 19th century. Well into the 20th century, as forced labor continued in Africa itself under European direction, the legacy of the slave trade era proved slow to die.

FURTHER READINGS

Aside from the general books on Africa already mentioned in the bibliographical suggestions for previous chapters, there are some specific readings that are particularly useful. Martin Hall's *The Changing Past. Farmers, Kings, and Traders in Southern Africa* (1987) discusses the use of archeological evidence in African history. D. Birmingham and Phyllis Martin, eds., *History of Central Africa*, 2 vols. (1983) presents extended essays on a number of regions. On West Africa in the age of the slave trade, a good introduction is J. F. A. Ajayi and Michael Crowder, eds., *History of West Africa*, 2 vols. (1971), especially volume 1. On southern Africa, Leonard Thompson's *A History of South Africa* (1990) presents a broad survey, while J. D. Omer-Cooper's *The Zulu Aftermath* (1969) is a classic account.

There are many histories of the slave trade, but James Rawley's *The Transatlantic Slave Trade* (1981) provides an intelligent overview. On the quantitative aspects of the slave trade, Philip Curtin's *The Atlantic Slave Trade. A Census* (1969) is the proper starting point. Roger Anstey's *The Atlantic Slave Trade and British Abolition* (1975) deals with the economic and religious aspects of the end of the trade.

On Africa, Paul Lovejoy's *Transformations in Slavery. A History of Slavery in Africa* (1983) and Patrick Manning's *Slavery and African Life* (1990) provide comprehensive overviews, while J. E. Inikori's *Forced Migration. The Impact of the Export Slave Trade on African Societies* (1982) brings together essays by leading scholars. Joseph Miller's *Way of Death* (1989) is a detailed study of the effects of the slave trade on Angola and a fine example of an in-depth study of one region.

Walter Rodney's essay, "Africa in Europe and the Americas," *Cambridge History of Africa*, vol. 4, 578–622 is a succinct overview of the African diaspora. Herbert Klein's *African Slavery in Latin America and the Caribbean* (1987) is an up-to-date survey.

On the general theoretical issues of slavery, Orlando Patterson's *Slavery and Social Death* (1982) is a broad comparative sociological study. David B. Davis's *Slavery and Human Progress* (1984) takes a historical approach to many of the same questions and then places the abolitionist movement in context.

1405–1423 Zhenghe expeditions from China to Southeast Asia, India, and East Africa

1511 Portuguese conquer Malacca on the tip of Malayan peninsula

1510 Portuguese conquest of Goa in western India

1573–1620 Reign of the Wanli emperor

1590 Hideyoshi unifies Japan

1368–1398 Reign of the Hongwu emperor

1498–1499 Vasco da Gama opens the sea route around Africa to Asia

1592 First Japanese invasion of Korea

1403–1424 Reign of the Yunglo emperor in China

1573 End of the Ashikaga Shogunate

1540s Francis Xavier makes mass converts in India

1390 Ming restrictions on overseas commerce

1368 Ming dynasty comes to power in China

1507 Portuguese defeat a combined Muslim war fleet at Diu off the coast of western India

1580s Jesuits arrive in China

A.D. 1350   A.D. 1500

Asian Transitions in an Age of Global Change

28

INTRODUCTION. Trends in East and Southeast Asia during the early modern centuries, while highly diverse, compare interestingly with developments in other regions. Island areas, such as Ceylon (or what is today Sri Lanka), Java and the "spice islands" of the Indonesian archipelago, and the Philippines, were quickly involved in the West's overseas expansion and its efforts to redefine the world economy. The results were distinctive, but they can be compared to patterns emerging in parts of Latin America and, by the 18th century, India. China and Japan, however, followed a different path. Like other centers of well-established civilization, such as those in the Middle East, China and Japan were not fundamentally reshaped by the rise of the West in the early modern era. Political consolidation and social and intellectual revival marked most of East Asia during these centuries. In contrast to the Islamic world, however, East Asia not only developed new political and social strengths, but its peoples also pursued a more explicit policy of isolation in response to global trends. This distinctive reaction had great implications for Asian as well as global history in the succeeding centuries.

When Vasco da Gama's ships returned to Lisbon in 1499, it was clear that tiny Portugal rather than mighty Spain had won the race to the fabled Indies. Though Columbus's voyages to the Americas with the support of the Spanish rulers opened up new worlds to the civilizations of Europe, Asia, and Africa, da Gama's voyages accomplished the task that was the ultimate aim of all the explorations launched by the Europeans as early as the 14th century. Da Gama had found a sea link between an expansive and insecure Europe and the Asian sources of power and wealth that the rulers of Christendom hoped to tap to strengthen them in their struggles with the Muslims and their European rivals.

1597 Second Japanese invasion of Korea

1619–1620 Dutch East India Company established at Batavia on Java

1654–1722 Reign of the Kangxi emperor in China

1644 Nomadic Manchus put an end to the Ming dynasty; Manchu Qing dynasty rules China

1755–1757 Dutch reign as the paramount power on Java; Qing conquest of Mongolia

1614 Christianity banned in Japan

1603 Tokugawa Shogunate established

1640s Japan moves into self-imposed isolation

1641 Dutch capture Malacca from the Portuguese; Dutch confined to Deshima Island off Nagasaki

c. 1600s Dutch and British assault on Portuguese Empire in Asia; decline of Portuguese power

1658 Dutch conquer Portuguese areas on Ceylon

Though da Gama's voyage from 1498 to 1499 marked a major turning point for much of western Europe, its impact on most of Asia was a good deal less decisive, at least in the 16th and 17th centuries. The Portuguese and the Dutch, French, and English who followed them into Asia soon found that they had little to offer the Asians in exchange for the silks and spices they risked their lives to carry back to Europe and sell at exorbitant prices. They were disappointed to find that few of the Asian peoples were interested in converting to Christianity, which they deemed the one true religion and sought to spread wherever their ships sailed. They also quickly realized that however feisty and well-armed they might be, they were far too few in numbers to make much headway against even the smaller kingdoms of Asia, such as Siam or Vietnam, much less against mighty empires like those ruled by the Chinese or the Mughals.

The Europeans used their sea power to control the export of specific products like spices and the seaborne commerce found in some sections of the vast Asian trading network that stretched from the ports of the Red Sea to South China. But efforts at trade control proved expensive and were difficult to sustain in the face of widespread Asian resistance. The Portuguese—and after them the Dutch and English—found that it was better to fit themselves into the Asian system rather than to attempt to capture it. They also concluded that they gained a good deal more by doing homage to and serving Asian monarchs than by quarreling with them or becoming involved in madcap schemes to capture their kingdoms or forcibly convert their subjects to Christianity.

For their part, most of the Asian peoples were only marginally, if at all, affected by the coming of the Europeans in the two centuries after da Gama's voyage. The Europeans concentrated their efforts on Ceylon (present-day Sri Lanka) and island Southeast Asia, where the spices were concentrated and where their sea power was the most effective. They also traded in India, mainland Southeast Asia, Persia, and, to a much lesser extent, China and Japan. But they neither controlled the commerce of these areas nor significantly altered the course of their social, economic, or political development. As was the case with the Mughal and Safavid empires (see Chapter 26), the central themes in the history of Asian civilizations in the 16th and 17th centuries often had little or nothing to do with European expansion. They emerged from long-term processes that were rooted in the inner workings of these ancient civilizations and their interaction with neighboring states and nomadic peoples. For example, the Europeans had nothing to do with the impressive expeditions by which the Chinese sought in the first decades of the 14th

century, to initiate their own global expansion. A century later, threats from elsewhere in Asia, not Europe, convinced the rulers of China to attempt to shut their kingdom off from the world. Though European missionaries and firearms played important roles in the civil wars that raged in Japan in the 16th century, these struggles were part of a pattern of feudal fragmentation and a quest for political unity that long preceded the coming of the Europeans.

Thus, though the European presence was felt in each of the areas considered in this chapter, the impact of Europe's global expansion remained of secondary importance except in island Southeast Asia, which is the focus of the first section of this chapter. The sections on China and Japan that follow emphasize the longer-term unfolding of the pattern of civilization within each of these areas and the effects of their interaction on each other. The continuing importance of nomadic challenges to Chinese civilization also is stressed. Though fascinating in their own right, European responses to and activities in China and Japan are worked into these larger patterns because this perspective more accurately conveys the actual situation in this era. European seafarers may have sailed out across much of the globe, but European peoples had not yet gained the military strength and economic power to dominate the civilizations of Asia or alter the course of their historical development.

THE ASIAN TRADING WORLD AND THE COMING OF THE EUROPEANS

Vasco da Gama and his Portuguese crew received a rather rude shock soon after arriving in India in 1498. Still congratulating themselves on having found a sea route around Africa, which Portuguese explorers had been seeking for generations, they successfully made their way across the Arabian Sea to India. At Calicut, a prosperous commercial center on the southwest coast, they went ashore to trade for the spices, fine textiles, and other Asian products that were among the main objectives of the voyages of exploration. Reveling in the fine quality and abundance of the products from all over Asia available in the town's great marketplace, the Portuguese were startled to learn that none of the merchants was interested in the products they had brought along to swap for Asian goods. In fact, their cast-iron pots, coarse cloth, and coral beads elicited little more than sneers of contempt from the savvy merchants they approached. Suddenly da Gama and his crews faced the humbling prospect of returning home with little proof that they had actually reached Asia and begun to tap its fabled wealth. Reluctantly, they concluded that they had little choice but to make use of the small supply of silver bullion they had brought along for emergency situations. They found that the Asian merchants were quite willing to take their precious metal, but also that their meager provision did not go very far toward filling the holds of their ships with Asian treasures. Nonetheless, at least there was tangible evidence that they had indeed reached Asia, that Portuguese sailors had succeeded where Columbus and the ships of Spain had failed.

Much of the European enterprise in Asia in the 16th and 17th centuries was devoted to working out the implications of that first encounter in Calicut. The very fact of da Gama's arrival demonstrated both the needs and curiosity that had driven the Europeans halfway around the world as well as the seaworthiness of their ships. The encounter at Calicut introduced the Europeans to the vast and sophisticated trading network that had linked the civilizations of Asia since ancient times. It had made them aware that if they were going to break into that system, they would either have to empty the Portuguese royal treasury of precious metals, an unthinkable alternative at the time, or apply military force to obtain the products they desired. The latter option soon became a major preoccupation of the Portuguese and of the Dutch and English who followed them into Asia in the 17th century.

Their stops at Calicut and other ports on the eastern coast of Africa also made the Portuguese acutely aware of the fact that their old rivals the Muslims had arrived in East Africa and South and Southeast Asia well ahead of them. This unpleasant discovery promised resistance to Portuguese trading and empire building in Asia and major obstacles to their designs for the mass conversion of the peoples of the area to Roman Catholicism. But the Portuguese also observed that the Muslims and the Asian peoples as a whole were deeply divided among themselves, and that they were rarely able to comprehend the potential threat posed by what was after all a handful of strangers from across the world.

BONDS OF COMMERCE: THE ASIAN SEA-TRADING NETWORK, C. 1500

As subsequent voyages by Portuguese fleets quickly revealed, Calicut and the ports of East Africa, which da Gama had encountered on the initial foray into Asia, made up only a small segment of a larger network of commercial exchange and cultural interaction. This trading system stretched thousands of miles from the Middle East and Africa along all the coasts of the giant Asian continent. Both the products exchanged in this network and the main routes followed by those who sailed it had been established for centuries, in many cases millennia.

In general, the trading system can be broken down into three main zones, each of which was focused on major centers of handicraft manufacture. In the west was an Arab zone anchored on the glass, carpet, and tapestry manufacturing Islamic heartlands at the head of the Red Sea and Persian Gulf. India, with its superb cotton textiles, dominated the central portions of the system; and China, which excelled in the production of paper, porcelain, and silk textiles, formed the eastern pole. In between or on the fringes of the three great manufacturing centers were areas such as Japan, the mainland kingdoms and island states of Southeast Asia, and the port cities of East Africa that fed mainly raw materials—precious metals and forest products—into the trading network.

Many products circulated throughout the system. Cotton textiles from India were sold from Egypt (and Europe) to Africa and eastward throughout Southeast Asia. Chinese silks and porcelains were in high demand throughout Asia and on the African coast and found their way, at hugely inflated prices, to the Middle East and Italy. Of the raw materials circulating in the system, the broadest demand and highest prices were paid for spices—such as pepper, cinnamon, nutmeg, and mace—that came mainly from Ceylon and the islands at the eastern end of what is today the Indonesian archipelago. African ivory also found lucrative markets from India to China and Japan. Some products, such as Indian elephants, Arabian horses, European glassware, and African slaves reached only more limited regional markets. Long-distance trade was largely in high-priced commodities such as spices, ivory, and precious stones, but silk and cotton textiles were also traded over long distances. Bulk items, such as rice, livestock, and timber, were normally exchanged between the ports within each of the main trading zones. Though less profitable than luxury commodities, bulk staples made up a substantial portion of the volume of goods traded in some segments of the system.

Since ancient times monsoon winds and the nature of the ships and navigational instruments available to sailors had dictated the main trade routes in the Asian network. Much navigation was of the coasting variety, that is sailing along the shoreline and charting distances and location with reference to towns and natural landmarks. Peoples like the Arabs and Chinese, who possessed compasses and large and well-built ships, could cross large expanses of open water such as the Arabian and South China seas. But even they preferred established coastal routes to navigating in the largely uncharted and less predictable open seas. As the Portuguese quickly discerned, there were a number of crucial points where segments of the trade converged or where geography funneled it into narrow confines. The mouths of

Routes and Major Products Exchanged in the Asian Trading Network, c. 1500

the Red Sea and Persian Gulf were two of these points, as were the straits of Malacca that separated mainland from island Southeast Asia. What had been centers of cross-cultural interaction and exchange in the millennia before da Gama's arrival would become strategic nodes of the sea empires the Europeans sought to build from the 16th to the 18th centuries.

Two general characteristics of the trading system at the time of the Portuguese arrival were critical to subsequent European attempts to regulate and dominate it: There was no central or overall control, and military force was usually absent from commercial exchanges. Though Arab sailors and merchants were found in ports throughout much of the network, they had no sense of common cause. They sailed and traded to provide for their own livelihood and to make profits for individual princes or specific merchants who financed their expeditions. The same was true for the Chinese, Southeast Asian, and Indian merchants and sailors who were concentrated in particular segments of the whole trading complex. Because all the peoples participating in the network had something to exchange for the products they desired from others, exchanges within the system were largely peaceful. Trading vessels were lightly armed, in case they should be attacked by pirates. Though Asian coastal states like Shrivijaya sometimes used war fleets to control trade in limited segments of the network, their ef-

forts were usually short-lived and resented by other participants in the system. The great powers of Asia, such as the Chinese and Safavid empires, were too wealthy and self-sufficient to consider resorting to naval warfare in order to control a trading system in which they already played such prominent roles.

TRADING EMPIRE: THE PORTUGUESE RESPONSE TO THE ENCOUNTER AT CALICUT

The Portuguese were simply not prepared to abide by the informal rules that had evolved over the centuries for commercial and cultural exchanges in the great Asian trading complex. It was apparent after the sobering trip to the market in Calicut that the Portuguese had little, other than gold and silver, to exchange with Asian peoples. In an age where prominent economic theorists, called *mercantilists*, taught that a state's power depended heavily on the amount of precious metals a monarch had in his coffers, a steady flow of bullion to Asia was unthinkable. It was particularly objectionable because it would enrich and thus strengthen merchants and rulers from rival kingdoms and religions, particularly the heretical Muslims, whose position the Portuguese had deliberately set out to undermine through their overseas enterprises. Unwilling to forgo the possibilities for profit that pioneering a sea route to Asia presented, the Portuguese resolved to take by force what they could not get through fair trade.

To a large degree the Portuguese decision to resort to force to extract spices and other market commodities from Asia resulted from their realization that they could offset their lack of numbers and trading goods with their superior ships and weaponry. Though the Chinese had ships that were much larger and in some respects better built, none of the Asian peoples possessed oceangoing vessels that were as swift and maneuverable as the caravels that had carried the Portuguese around Africa. These slender, long-hulled vessels with many triangular, or lateen, sails, which made them highly maneuverable and allowed them to sail against the wind, were a match for any of the vessels they encountered in Asian waters. Navigational advantages combined with the fact that Portuguese ships were increasingly well armed whereas Asian ships were rarely so, made it possible for the Portuguese to build a trading empire in Asia within decades of da Gama's voyage.

Excepting the huge war fleets of Chinese junks, no Asian people could muster fleets able to withstand the firepower and maneuverability of the Portuguese squadrons. Their sudden appearance in Asian waters and their interjection of sea warfare into a trading system that had been overwhelmingly peaceful gained the European intruders an element of surprise that kept their adversaries off balance in the critical early years of empire building. The Portuguese, whose forces were small in numbers but united in their drive for wealth and religious converts, also took advantage of the deep divisions that separated their Asian competitors and their inability to combine their forces effectively in battle. Thus, when da Gama returned on a second expedition to Asian waters in 1502, he was able to force ports on both the African and Indian coasts to submit to a Portuguese tribute regime and to bombard with impunity those towns that refused to cooperate. When a combined Egyptian-Indian fleet was finally sent in reprisal in 1509, it was decisively defeated off Diu on the western Indian coast. The Portuguese would not have to face so formidable an alliance of Asian sea powers again.

The Portuguese soon found that sea patrols and raids on coastal towns were not sufficient to control the trade in the items, especially spices, they desired. Thus, from 1507 onward, the Portuguese strove to capture towns and build fortresses at a number of strategic points on the Asian trading network. In that year they took Ormuz at the southern end of the Persian Gulf; in 1510 they captured Goa on the western Indian coast; and, most critical of all, in the next year they successfully stormed Malacca on the tip of the

In the 15th and 16th centuries, the port of Lisbon in tiny Portugal was one of the great centers of international commerce and European overseas exploration. Though aspects of the early, streamlined caravel design can be detected in the ships pictured here, additional square sails, higher fore and aft castles, and numerous cannons projecting from holes cut in the ships' sides exemplify a later stage of naval development.

Malayan peninsula. These ports served as both naval bases for Portuguese fleets patrolling Asian waters and as "factories" or points where spices and other products could be stored until they were transhipped to Europe to be sold at hefty profits. Ships and naval stations became the key components of a Portuguese trading empire that was financed and directed by the kings of Portugal.

The aim of the empire was to establish Portuguese monopoly control over key Asian products, particularly spices. Ideally, all the spices produced were to be shipped in Portuguese galleons to Asian or European markets. There they would be sold at prices the Portuguese could dictate because they controlled the total supply of these goods. The Portuguese also sought, with little success, to impose a licensing system on all merchant ships that traded in the Indian Ocean from Ormuz to Malacca. The combination of monopoly and the licensing system, backed by force, was intended to give the Portuguese control of a sizeable portion of the Asian trading network.

PORTUGUESE VULNERABILITY AND THE RISE OF THE DUTCH AND ENGLISH TRADING EMPIRES

The plans for empire that the Portuguese drew up on paper were never even close to being translated into reality. Though they managed for some decades to control much of the flow of spices, such as nutmeg and mace that were grown in very limited locales, a corner on the market in key condiments, such as pepper and cinnamon, eluded them. Despite draconian punishments—they were not above cutting off the hands of the rival traders and ships' crews caught transporting spices in defiance of their monopoly—the Portuguese did not have the manpower or the ships to sustain either their monopolies or the even more ambitious licensing system. With just over a million people in all of Portugal and never more than 15,000 Portuguese in Asia at one time, the manpower of the trading empire was stretched thin indeed. Even this relatively small community soon became deeply divided, and many of the Portuguese who went out to serve in the empire became independent traders in defiance of the crown monopoly. The resistance of Asian rivals, military indiscipline, rampant corruption among crown officials, and heavy losses to Portuguese shipping due to overloading and poor design had taken a heavy toll on the empire by the end of the 16th century.

The overextended and declining Portuguese trading empire proved no match for the Dutch and English rivals whose war fleets challenged it in the early decades of the 17th century. The position of the Portuguese had grown so weak that they proved unable to exploit the deep hostility and frequent clashes between their northern European rivals. Of the two, the Dutch emerged, at least in the short term, as the victors. They captured the critical Portuguese port and fortress at Malacca and built a new port of their own in 1620 at Batavia on the island of Java. The latter location, which was much closer to the island sources of key spices, reflected not only the much improved European knowledge of Asian geography but also the Dutch decision to concentrate on the monopoly control of certain spices rather than Asian trade more generally. The English, who fought hard but lost the struggle for control of the spice islands, were forced to fall back on India. At the time this appeared to be a disheartening reversal. In the 18th century, however, when the demand for Indian textiles soared and India emerged as the keystone of Britain's global empire, it came to be seen as an incredible stroke of good fortune.

The Dutch trading empire was made up of the same basic components as those of the Portuguese: fortified towns and factories, warships on patrol, and monopoly control of a very limited number of products. But the Dutch had more numerous and better armed ships and went about the business of monopoly control in a much more systematic fashion. To regulate the supply of cloves, nutmeg, and mace, for example, they uprooted the plants that produced these spices on islands they did not control. They also forcibly removed or wiped out island peoples who cultivated these spices without Dutch supervision and dared to sell them to trading rivals of the Dutch.

Though the very impressive profits from the sale of these spices in Europe in the middle decades of the 17th century helped sustain Holland's golden age, the Dutch found that the greatest profits in the long-run could be gained from peacefully working themselves into the long established Asian trading system. As the demand for spices declined and their futile efforts to gain control over crops, such as pepper, that were grown in many places became more and more expensive, the Dutch came to rely on the fees they charged for transporting products from one area in Asia to another. They also depended on profits gained from buying Asian products, such as cloth, in one area and trading them in other areas for goods that could be sold in Europe at inflated prices. The English also adopted these trading patterns, though their enterprises were concentrated along the coasts of India and on the cloth trade rather than on the spices of Southeast Asia. For both the Dutch and the English peaceful commerce came to be more profitable than forcible control, and monopolistic measures were increasingly aimed at European rather than Asian rivals.

GOING ASHORE: EUROPEAN TRIBUTE SYSTEMS IN ASIA

Although their ships and guns allowed the Europeans to force their way into the Asian trading network in the 16th and 17th centuries, as they moved inland, away from the sea, their military advantages and capacity to dominate Asian peoples rapidly disappeared. Because the vastly superior numbers of Asian armies offset the limited edge the Europeans possessed in weapons and organization for waging war on land, even relatively small kingdoms like those found on Java and throughout mainland Southeast Asia proved able to resist European inroads into their domains. In the larger empires like those in China, India, and Persia—or when confronted by martial cultures like that of Japan—the Europeans quickly learned their place. That they were often reduced to kowtowing or humbling themselves before the thrones of Asian potentates is clearly demonstrated by the following instructions given by a Dutch envoy regarding the proper behavior for a visit to the Japanese court:

Our ministers have no other instruction to take there except to look to the wishes of that brave, superb, precise nation in order to please it in everything, and by no means to think on anything which might cause greater antipathy to us. . . . That consequently the Company's ministers frequenting the scrupulous state each year must above all go armed in modesty, humility, courtesy, and amity, always being the lesser.

In certain situations, however, the Europeans were drawn inland away from their forts, factories, and war fleets in the early centuries of their expansion into Asia. The Portuguese, and the Dutch after them, felt compelled to conquer the coastal areas of Ceylon in order to control the production and sale of cinnamon, which grew in the forests of the southern portions of that island. The Dutch moved slowly inland from their base at Batavia into the highlands of western Java. They discovered that this area was ideal for the cultivation of coffee, which was in great demand in Europe by the 17th century. By the middle of

This photograph, taken in the era of British colonial rule, shows Sinhalese workers peeling the bark from the branches of cinnamon trees. Much the same techniques were used by cinnamon peelers in the pre-European, the Portuguese, and the Dutch periods to extract the sticks and powder that were in great demand in Europe.

the 18th century, the Dutch not only controlled the coffee-growing areas, but were the paramount power on the island of Java. The Treaty of Gijanti in 1757 reduced the remaining Javanese princes to vassals of the Dutch East Indian Company. The Spanish, taking advantage of the fact that the Philippine islands lay in the half of the world the pope had given them to explore and settle in 1493, invaded the islands in the 1560s. The conquest of Luzon and the northern islands was facilitated by the fact that the animistic peoples inhabiting them lived in small states the Spanish could subjugate one by one. The repeated failure of Spanish expeditions to conquer the southern island of Mindanao, which was ruled by a single kingdom whose Muslim rulers were determined to resist Christian dominance, dramatically underscores the limits of the Europeans' ability to project their power on land in this era.

In each of the areas where the Europeans went ashore in the early centuries of expansion, they set up tribute regimes that closely resembled those the Spanish imposed on the Amerindian peoples of the New World (see Chapter 25). The European overlords were content to let the indigenous peoples live in their traditional settlements, which were controlled largely by hereditary leaders drawn from their own communities. In most areas little attempt was made to interfere in the daily lives of the conquered peoples as long as their leaders met the tribute quotas set by the European conquerors. The tribute was paid in the form of agricultural products that were cultivated by the peasantry under forced labor systems supervised by the peasants' own elites. The Philippines, where a major missionary effort was launched after the conquest, provided an important exception to the pattern of minimal intervention. In some cases the indigenous peoples continued to harvest crops they had produced for centuries, such as the bark of the cinnamon plant demanded of special villages in southwestern Ceylon. In other areas new crops, such as coffee or sugarcane, were introduced. But in all cases, tribute demands took into account the local peasants' need to raise the crops on which they themselves subsisted.

SPREADING THE FAITH: THE MISSIONARY ENTERPRISE IN SOUTH AND SOUTHEAST ASIA

Though the Protestant Dutch and English were little interested in winning converts to Christianity in the early centuries of overseas expansion, the spread of Roman Catholicism was a fundamental part of the global mission of the Portuguese and Spanish. After the widespread conversion of Amerindian peoples, the rather meager returns from the Iberian missionary offensive in Asia were disappointing. The fact that Islam had arrived in much of maritime South and Southeast Asia centuries before da Gama's arrival had much to do with the indifference or open hostility the Portuguese encountered when they attempted to convert the peoples to Christianity. The dream of a Christian Asia joining the Iberian crusade against the Muslims was also dealt a setback by the discovery that the Hindus, whom da Gama and some of his entourage had originally believed to be Christians, possessed a sophisticated and deeply entrenched set of alternative religious ideas and rituals. As a result, widespread conversion in South and Southeast Asia was limited to outcaste groups in Indian coastal areas and peoples, such as the northern Filipinos, who had not previously been exposed to a world religion like Islam or Buddhism and who came under the direct rule of the Europeans.

In India from the 1540s onward, Francis Xavier and his coworkers, who were willing to bring food and care to the poor and low-caste fisherfolk and pariahs along the southwest coast, brought initial conversions in the tens of thousands. But the Franciscans and other missionary orders soon realized that they were making little headway among high-caste groups and, in fact, low-caste conversions made it virtually impossible to even approach upper-caste groups.

In the early 1600s, an Italian Jesuit, Robert di Nobili, attempted a rather different approach. He learned a number of Indian languages, including Sanskrit (which allowed him to read the sacred texts of the Hindus), donned the garments of an Indian brahman, and adopted a vegetarian diet. All of these measures were calculated to win over the upper-caste Hindus in South India where he was based. His strategy to Christianize the Hindus by first converting the elite groups, who, he argued, would then bring the lower Hindu classes into the fold, was to be widely adopted by Jesuits working in various parts of Asia. Despite some early successes, in India di Nobili's strategy was undone by the high-caste Hindus' refusal to worship with low-caste groups and to give up their traditional beliefs and religious rituals. Citing these trends, rival missionaries denounced his approach. Eventually di Nobili was recalled to Rome and his mission collapsed.

Because they had conquered the northern Philippines and then governed them as part of their vast intercontinental empire, the Spanish could take a much more conventional approach to conversion in the islands. Once areas had been "pacified" by Spanish conquistadores, the administration of the Filipinos, or at least of those who lived outside the capital at Manila, was turned over to the missionary orders. The *friars*, as the priests and brothers who went out to convert and govern the rural populace were called, became the main channel for the transmission of European influences. The friars first converted and then administered through local Filipino leaders. These leaders were usually persuaded to order their followers to construct new settlements that were centered, like those in Iberia and the New World, on town squares where the local church, the residences of the missionary fathers, and government offices (if there were any) were located. Beyond tending to the spiritual needs of the villagers in their congregation, the friars in effect served as government officials. They dispensed justice, oversaw the collection of the tribute payments and public works projects, and were responsible for what little education rural Filipinos received. Very often friars were the only Europeans the great majority of the Philippines' population saw for years or even decades.

Like the Amerindian peoples of Spain's New World empire, most of the Filipinos were formally converted to Catholicism. But also like the Amerindians, the Filipinos' brand of Christianity represented a creative blend of their traditional beliefs and customs and the religion preached by the friars. Since key tenets of the Christian faith were taught in Spanish for fear that they would be corrupted if put in the local languages, it is doubtful that most of the converts had a very good grasp of Christian beliefs. Many converted because Spanish dominance and their own leaders' co-optation gave them little choice; others adopted the new faith because they believed that the Christian God could protect them from illness or because they were taken with the notion that they would be equal to their Spanish overlords in heaven.

Almost all Filipinos clung to their traditional ways and in the process seriously compromised Christian beliefs and practices. Most attended confession, for example, at best once a year to be absolved of all the "heathenish" sins the missionaries accused them of committing. Catholic saints easily fused with preconquest idolatry, and Christian miracles were easily assimilated into indigenous magical practices. The Filipinos continued public bathing, which the missionaries condemned as immodest; refused to give up ritual drinking; and continued to commune with deceased members of their families, often in sessions that were disguised as public recitations of the rosary. Thus, even in the Asian area where European control was the strongest and pressures for acculturation to European ways the greatest, much of the preconquest way of life and approach to the world was maintained.

MODEST RETURNS: THE EARLY IMPACT OF EUROPEANS IN MARITIME ASIA

In 1700, after two centuries of European involvement in South and Southeast Asia, most of the peoples of the area had been little affected by efforts to build trading empires and win Christian converts. European sailors had added a number of new routes to the Asian trading net-

work, the most important being the link around the Cape of Good Hope between Europe and the Indian Ocean and the connection between the Philippine islands and Mexico in the New World. The Europeans' need for safe harbors and storage areas had led to the establishment or rapid growth of trading centers, such as Goa, Calcutta, and Batavia, as well as the gradual decline of existing rival centers, such as many of the Gujarati cities in western India, several Muslim centers in East Africa, and, after the arrival of the Dutch, the fortress town of Malacca. Though Europeans reaped most of the profits, they did introduce the principle of sea warfare into what had been a peaceful commercial world. But the Asian trading system as a whole survived the initial shocks, and the Europeans eventually concluded that they were better off accommodating than dismantling the existing commercial arrangements.

Because Europe and Asia had been exchanging plants and diseases for millennia, few new plants and diseases were spread in the era of expansion (except for the New World plants brought to Asia by European merchants), particularly in comparison with the catastrophic exchange between Europe and Africa and the New World. Mostly Europeans died of diseases like new strains of malaria and dysentery that they contracted in Asia. They spread diseases only to the more isolated parts of Asia, such as the Philippines, where the coming of the Spanish was accompanied by a devastating smallpox epidemic. The impact of European ideas, inventions, and modes of social organization was also very limited in the first centuries of expansion. Key European devices, such as clocks, were regarded as toys by Asian rulers to whom they were given as presents. Christianity aroused more hostility than interest from the adherents of the ancient faiths of Asia and the more recent converts to Islam.

 ### MING CHINA: A GLOBAL MISSION REFUSED

With the restoration of ethnic Chinese rule and the reunification of the country under the Ming dynasty in 1368, Chinese civilization seemed ready for a new age of splendor. China's endowment in terms of both human and natural resources was indeed impressive. Its population was the largest of any center of civilization at the time, probably exceeding that of all western Europe combined. Its resources were vast, and it had some of the most advanced technology as well as large numbers of skilled engineers and artisans to put its rich soils and mineral wealth to productive use. China's centralized bureaucracy was the best organized and most efficient in the world. Though the firearms of its armies were somewhat behind those of the West, in numbers, organization, and leadership China possessed a formidable military establishment. A return to the examination system under the Ming rulers ensured that the Chinese elite was one of the largest and best educated of any major civilization. These developments within Chinese civilization will be the focus of the early sections on Ming China.

As China's achievements multiplied and its advantages over neighboring civilizations grew, there was every reason to expect that its internal prosperity and dynamism would be translated into external expansion. In earlier periods, strong dynasties, such as the Han and the Tang, had pursued territorial and commercial expansion overland into central and Southeast Asia and overseas. The century of Mongol rule from 1260 to 1368 reinforced these expansive tendencies by opening China to outside influences from places as distant as the Middle East and Europe and through Mongol military forays in East and Southeast Asia. At the time of the Ming dynasty's assumption of power, however, China had not yet expanded on a global scale. Some of its technology had been widely disseminated, but the spread of the Chinese pattern of civilization had been confined mainly to areas bordering the Middle Kingdom—the nomadic steppe to the north and west, the rice valleys to the east and south, and the Japanese islands off China's northern coast.

In the early Ming era it appeared that China would break out of these regional confines to become one of the great global powers of the coming age. In fact, in the early decades of the 15th century, when the Portuguese had not yet begun to probe the African coastline in search of a route to Asia, a series of major sea expeditions (see Chapter 21) carried the Chinese across the Java Sea and Indian Ocean to the coast of Africa. The hundreds of ships and tens of thousands of officials, sailors, soldiers, and merchants involved in these voyages unquestionably demonstrated China's capacity to expand; to become perhaps the premier global power. These expeditions and China's involvement with the outside world more generally are the focus of the later sections on the Ming period.

If the leaders of China had chosen to follow up on these early initiatives to project the power of their empire and civilization overseas, the subsequent history of the world would have been dramatically altered. At the very least, there would have been, certainly in Asia and perhaps in East Africa, a major countervailing force to check the expansive drive and rise to global dominance of western Europe. Chinese war fleets, for example, which at the time of the Ming were more than a match for those from Europe, might have been able to ward off European attempts to transform key segments of the open, peaceful Asian commercial network into closed trading empires. But the leaders of China did not choose to follow up on these early expeditions. A combination of factors, including old concerns with enemies in the interior of Asia and political rivalries at the Ming court, put an end to Chinese overseas expansion. Significantly, the past successes and the high degree of self-sufficiency of Chinese civilization played vital roles in the decisions to withdraw. In contrast to the Europeans, who had strong motives for their exploration and colonization efforts (see Chapter 23), there seemed to be little China needed from the rest of the world. What little there was, the Chinese could get through peaceful trade with people who were eager to come to China rather than wait for the Chinese to go out to them.

RESTORATION: THE BEGINNINGS OF THE MING ERA

The founding of the Ming dynasty, which would reign for nearly three centuries between 1368 and 1644, meant a good deal more than the restoration of ethnic Chinese rule after yet another period of nomadic dominance. The early Ming emperors sought both to restore key Chinese institutions and practices that had been set aside or neglected by the Mongols and to reform the Chinese polity in major ways. Zhu Yuanzhang, a military commander of peasant origins who was the founder of the Ming dynasty, had suffered a great deal under the Mongol yoke. Both of his parents and two brothers had died in a plague in 1344, and he and a remaining brother were reduced to begging for the land to bury the rest of their family. Threatened with the prospect of starvation in one of the many famines that ravaged the countryside in the later, corruption-riddled reigns of the Mongols, Zhu alternated between begging and living in a Buddhist monastery to survive. When the neighboring countryside rose in rebellion in the late 1340s, Zhu left the monastery to join a rebel band. His courage in combat and natural capacity as a leader had soon made him one of the more prominent of a number of rebel warlords seeking to overthrow the Yuan dynasty. After protracted military struggles against rival rebel claimants to the throne and the Mongol rulers themselves, Zhu's armies conquered most of China, and he declared himself the Hongwu emperor in 1368. He would reign for 30 years.

Immediately following his seizure of the throne, Zhu launched a concerted effort to rid China of all traces of the "barbarian" Mongols. Mongol dress was discarded, Mongol names were both dropped by those who had adopted them and removed from buildings and court records, and Mongol palaces and administrative buildings in some areas were raided and sacked. The nomads themselves fled or were driven beyond the Great Wall, where Ming military expeditions pursued them on a number of occasions in order to raid and intimidate them.

THE SCHOLAR-GENTRY REVIVAL

Because the Hongwu emperor, like the founder of the earlier Han dynasty, was from a peasant family and thus poorly educated, he viewed the scholar-gentry with some suspicion. But he also realized that their cooperation was essential to the full revival of Chinese civilization. Scholars well-versed in the Confucian classics were again appointed to the very highest positions in the imperial government. The generous state subsidies that had provided support for the imperial academies in the capital and the regional colleges were fully restored. Most critically, the civil service examination system, which the Mongols had discontinued, was reinstated and greatly expanded. In the Ming era and the Qing that followed, the examinations played a greater role in determining entry into the Chinese bureaucracy than had been the case under any earlier dynasty. At times, as many as half of all government officials had earned their positions through success in the exam competitions. Though this left many positions to be won by virtue of being born into the right family or of timely "gifts" to high officials, the exams ensured that there was a high level of education and talent for Ming administrators as a whole.

In the Ming era the examination system was routinized and made more complex than before. Prefectural or county exams were held in two of every three years to award the lowest degree, which allowed successful candidates to compete for higher degrees (and positions) and, less commonly, to win appointments to minor offices. Competition was fierce since there could be only 20 to 30 successful candidates. The exams were given in large compounds, surrounded by walls and watch towers from which the examiners could keep an eye on the thousands of candidates. Each candidate was provided with a small cubicle, where he struggled to answer the questions posed, and slept and ate over the several days that it took to complete the exams.

Those who passed and received the lowest degree were eligible to take the next level of exams that were given in the provincial capitals every three years. Only the most gifted and ambitious went on because the odds against success were even higher than at the beginning level. Each province had a quota—in some cases 4000 candidates competed for 150 degrees. Success at the provincial level brought a considerable rise in status and opened the way for appointments to positions in the middle levels of the imperial bureaucracy. It also permitted a particularly talented scholar to take the imperial examinations, which were given in the capital every three years. Those who passed the imperial exams were eligible for the highest posts in the realm and were the most revered of all Chinese, excepting members of the royal family.

This 19th-century engraving shows the cubicles in which Chinese students and bureaucrats took the imperial civil service examinations that were given in the capital at Beijing. Examinees were confined to the cubicles for days and completed their exams under the constant surveillance of official proctors.

DOCUMENT
EXAM QUESTIONS AS A MIRROR OF CHINESE VALUES

The subjects and specific learning tested on the Chinese civil service exams give us great insight into behavior and attitudes expected of the literate, ruling classes of what was perhaps the best educated preindustrial civilization. A reading of sample test questions from these exams can tell us a good deal about what sorts of knowledge were considered important and what kinds of skills were necessary for those who aspired to successful careers in the most prestigious and potentially the most lucrative field open to Chinese youths—administrative service in the imperial bureaucracy. The very fact that such a tiny portion of the Chinese *male* population could take the exams and an even smaller number could successfully pass them says a lot about gender roles and elitism in Chinese society. In addition, the often decisive role of a student's calligraphy, the skill with which he was able to brush the Chinese characters, reflects the emphasis the Chinese elite placed on a refined sense of aesthetics.

Question 1—Provide the missing phrases and elaborate on the meaning of the following:

The Duke of She observed to Confucius: "Among us there was an upright man called Kung who was so upright that when his father appropriated a sheep, he bore witness against him." Confucius said . . .

(The missing phrases are:

"The upright men among us are not like that. A father will screen his son and a son his father—yet uprightness is to be found in that.")

Question 2—Write an eight-legged essay [one consisting of eight sections] on the following:
Scrupulous in his own conduct and lenient only in his dealings with the people.

Question 3—First unscramble the following characters and then comment on the significance of the quotation from the classics:

Beginning, good, mutually, nature, basically, practice, far, near, men's

(The correct answer is:

Men's beginning nature is basically good.
Nature mutually near.
Practice mutually far.)

Questions: Looking at the actual content of these questions, what else can we learn about Chinese society and attitudes? Where, for example, do the Chinese look for models to orient their social behavior? What kinds of knowledge are important to the Chinese? Do they stress specialist skills or the sort of learning that we associate with a "broad liberal arts education"? If we take SAT exams as equivalent gauges of our social values, how would you compare Ming China and modern America? What are the advantages and drawbacks of each system?

REFORM: HONGWU'S EFFORTS TO ROOT OUT ABUSES IN COURT POLITICS

Though mindful of his dependence on a well-educated and loyal scholar-gentry for the day-to-day administration of the empire, Hongwu sought to put clear limits on their influence over the emperor and to institute reforms that would check the abuses of other factions at court. Early in his reign he abolished the position of chief minister, which had formerly been the key link between the many ministries of the central government. The very considerable powers that had been amassed by members of the scholar-gentry class who occupied this office were transferred to the emperor himself, who now worked through the Grand Secretary with the heads of each of the secretariats, the six main government departments, and the head of the Censorate. Hongwu also sought to impress all officials with the honesty, loyalty, and discipline he expected from them by introducing the practice of public beatings for bureaucrats found guilty of corruption or incompetence. Officials charged with misdeeds were paraded before the assembled courtiers and beaten a specified number of times on their bare buttocks. Many died of the wounds they received in the ordeal. Those who survived never recovered from the humiliation, which was to a certain extent shared by all the scholar-gentry by virtue of the very fact that such degrading punishments could be meted out to them.

Hongwu also introduced measures to cut down on the court factionalism and never ending conspiracies that had done much to erode the power of earlier dynasties. He decreed that the emperor's wives should come only from humble family origins, in order to put an end to the power plays of the consorts from high-ranking families who built palace cliques that were centered on their influential aristocratic relatives. He warned against allowing eunuchs to occupy positions of independent power and sought to limit their numbers within the Forbidden City. To prevent plots against the ruler and fights over succession, Hongwu established the practice of exiling all the potential rivals to the throne to estates in the provinces, and he forbade them to become involved in political affairs. On the darker side, Hongwu condoned thought control, as when he had some sections from Mencius's writings that displeased him deleted forever from the writings included on the imperial exams. Though many of these measures went far to keep peace at court under Hongwu and his strong successor, the Yunglo emperor (1403–1424), they were allowed to lapse under later, less capable, emperors with devastating consequences for the Ming Empire.

CONTINUITY AND CHANGE: FAMILY, CLASS, AND GENDER UNDER THE MING

Perhaps because his lowly origins and personal suffering made him sensitive to the plight of the peasantry, Hongwu sought to introduce measures that would improve the lot of the common people. Like most strong emperors, he promoted public works projects, including dike building and the extension of irrigation systems aimed at improving the farmers' yields. In order to bring new lands under cultivation and encourage the growth of a peasant class that owned the lands it toiled so hard to bring into production, Hongwu decreed that unoccupied lands would become the tax-exempt property of those who cleared and cultivated them. He also sought to lower forced labor demands on the peasantry by both the government and members of the gentry class, and to promote silk and cotton cloth production and other handicrafts that provided supplemental sources of income for peasant households.

Though these measures led in the short run to some improvement in the peasants' condition, they were all but offset by the growing power of rural landlord families, buttressed by alliances with kinsmen in the imperial bureaucracy. Gentry households with members in government service were exempted from land taxes and enjoyed special privileges, such as permission to be carried about in sedan chairs by their growing retinues of slaves and the right to use fans and umbrellas. Many gentry families engaged in moneylending on the side; some even ran lucrative gambling dens. Almost all sought to add to their estates either by buying up lands held by peasant small landholders or through the foreclosure on loans made to cultivators in times of need in exchange for mortgages on their family plots. Peasants displaced in these ways had little choice but to become tenants of large landowners or landless laborers moving about in search of employment.

More land meant ever larger and more comfortable households for the gentry class, who sought to justify the growing gap between their wealth and the general impoverishment of the peasantry by contrasting their foresight and industry with the lazy and wasteful ways of the ordinary cultivators. The virtues of the gentry class were celebrated in stories and popular illustrations. These show, for example, members of gentry households hard at work weaving and storing grain to see them through the cold weather, while commoners, who neglected these tasks, wandering during the winter months cold and hungry past the walled compounds and closed gates of gentry households.

At most levels of Chinese society, the Ming period saw the continuation of the subordination of youths to elders and women to men that had been steadily intensifying in earlier periods. If anything, neo-Confucian thinking was even more influential than under the late-Song and Yuan dynasties. The remedies of some of its advocates for challenges to the increasingly rigid allocation of social status and roles were truly draconian. Students, for example, were expected to venerate and follow the instructions of their teachers, no matter how muddle-headed or tipsy the latter might be. A terrifying lesson in proper decorum was drawn from an incident in which a student at the imperial academy dared to dispute the findings of one of his instructors. The student was beheaded, and his severed head was hung on a pole at the entrance to the academy. Not surprisingly, this rather unsubtle solution to the problem of keeping order in the classroom merely drove student protest underground. Anonymous letters critical of poorly prepared teachers continued to circulate among the student body.

In a sense women were also driven to underground activities to ameliorate their subordination and, if they dared, expand their career opportunities. At the court, they continued, despite Hongwu's measures, to play strong roles behind the scenes. Even strong rulers like Hongwu were swayed by the advice of favorite wives or dowager mothers and aunts. On one occasion Hongwu chided the empress Ma for daring to inquire into the condition of the common people. She replied that since he was the father of the people, then she was the mother and thus it was quite proper for her to be concerned for the welfare of her children. Weak emperors like Wanli (1573–1620) could become so embroiled in disputes arising from rivalry between their wives and concubines and their allies at court that the rulers' ability to govern was seriously impaired.

Even within the palace, however, the plight of most women was grim. Hundreds, sometimes thousands of comely young women were brought to the court in the hope that they would catch the emperor's fancy and become one of his concubines or perhaps even be elevated to the status of wife. Because few actually succeeded, many spent their lives in loneliness and inactivity, just waiting for the emperor to glance their way.

In society at large, women had to settle for whatever status and respect they could win within the family. As before, their success in this regard hinged largely on being able to bear male children and, when they were married, moving from the status of daughter-in-law to mother-in-law. But the daughters of upper-class families were often taught to read and write by their parents or male siblings, and many composed poetry, painted, or played musical instruments. As in earlier centuries, even well-read women were barred from taking the civil service exams and obtaining positions in the bureaucracy. Though women from the nonelite classes still worked the fields and in some areas sold goods in the local market, the main avenues for some degree of independence and self-expression remained becoming courtesans or entertainers. The former should be clearly distinguished from prostitutes in that they served a very different clientele and were literate and often quite accomplished in painting, music, and poetry writing. Though even the most successful courtesans made their living by gratifying the needs of upper-class males for uninhibited sex and companionship, they often enjoyed lives of considerable luxury and much greater personal freedom than even women from scholar-gentry households.

AN AGE OF GROWTH: AGRICULTURE, POPULATION, COMMERCE, AND THE ARTS

The first decades of the Ming period were an age of buoyant economic growth in China that was both fed by and resulted in unprecedented contacts with other civilizations overseas. The territories controlled by the Ming emperors were never as extensive as those ruled by the Tang emperors. But in the Ming era, the great commercial

The varied diversions of the wives and many concubines of Ming emperors are depicted in this scene of court life. In addition to court intrigues and maneuvers to win the emperor's favor, women of the imperial household occupied themselves with dance, music making, games, and polite conversation.

boom and population increase that had begun in the late-Song was renewed and accelerated. The peopling of the Yangtze region and the areas to the south was given a great boost by the importation, through Spanish and Portuguese merchant intermediaries, of new food crops from the Americas, particularly root crops from the Andes highlands. Three plants—maize (our corn), sweet potatoes, and peanuts—were especially important. Because they could be grown on inferior soils that did not require irrigation, the cultivation of these crops spread quickly through the hilly and marginal areas that bordered on the irrigated rice plots of southern China. They became vital supplements to the staple rice or millet diet of the Chinese people as a whole, but particularly those of the rapidly growing southern regions. Because these plants were less susceptible to drought, they also became an important hedge against famine. The introduction of these new crops was an important factor behind the great surge in population growth that was under way by the end of the Ming era. By 1600 the population of China had risen to about 120 million from 80 to 90 million in the 14th century. Two centuries later in 1800, it had more than doubled and surpassed 300 million.

Agrarian expansion and population increase were paralleled in early Ming times by a renewal of commercial growth. The market sector of the domestic economy became ever more pervasive, and overseas trading links multiplied, particularly to areas in Southeast Asia such as Siam and the Philippines. Because China's advanced handicraft industries produced a wide variety of goods, from silk textiles and tea to fine ceramics and lacquerware that were in high demand throughout Asia and in Europe, the terms of trade ran very much in China's favor. In addition to the Arab and Asian traders, who had long risked arduous and dangerous overland or overseas journeys to trade in China, Europeans arrived in increasing numbers at the only two places—Macao and, somewhat later and more sporadically, Canton—where they were officially allowed to do business in Ming China. From Japan, from the European trading empires in South and Southeast Asia, and especially from Manila in the Spanish-held Philippines, there was a steady flow of precious metals, particularly silver, into China. Though some inflation was inevitable, the vast and sophisticated Chinese economy was much more equipped to handle this influx of new wealth than societies such as Spain and the Ottoman Empire, which had far less-developed market and manufacturing sectors.

Not surprisingly, the merchant classes, particularly those engaged in long-distance trade, reaped the biggest profits from the economic boom. But a good portion of their gains was transferred to the state in the form of taxes and to the scholar-gentry in the form of "gifts" for official favors. Much of the merchant wealth was invested in land, rather than being plowed back into trade or manufacturing, because landowning, not commerce, remained the surest route to social status in China. Though the pattern was not as pronounced as it would become in the Qing era that followed the Ming, the state and scholar-gentry were also enriched by the money paid by prominent merchants to have their sons educated so that they might pass the civil service exams. In some cases, large sums were paid to ensure that merchants' offspring did well; in others, offices were simply bought outright.

Ming prosperity was reflected in the fine arts, which found generous patrons both at court and among the scholar-gentry class more generally. Though the monochro-

Like the Ming courtiers shown here admiring a scroll painting in a carefully arranged garden setting, accomplished members of the scholar-gentry elite cultivated a taste for fine literature and the arts and interacted in accordance with an elaborate code of ritual and etiquette.

matic simplicity of the work of earlier dynasties was sustained by the ink-brush paintings of artists, such as Xuwei, much of the Ming output was busier and more colorful. Portraits and scenes of court, city, or country life were more prominent, though the Chinese delight in depicting individual scholars or travelers—contemplating the beauty of mountains, lakes, and marshes that dwarf the human observers—continued unabated.

While the painters of the Ming era concentrated mainly on developing established techniques and genres, major innovation in the arts came in literature with the full development of the Chinese novel, which had its beginnings in the writings of the Yuan era. The novel was given great impetus by the spread of literacy among the upper classes in the Ming era and by the growing availability of books that had resulted from the spread of woodblock printing from the 10th century onward. Ming novels, such as *The Water Margin, Monkey,* and *The Golden Lotus,* were recognized as classics in their own time and continue to set the standard for Chinese prose literature to the present day. Thus, though Chinese inventiveness of a more technical nature seems to have slowed at a critical point in time, given the great advances in science and technology in contemporary Europe, Ming achievements in the fine arts were impressive, even in comparison with those of the glorious Tang and Song eras.

AN AGE OF EXPANSION: THE ZHENGHE EXPEDITIONS

The seemingly boundless energy of the Chinese in early decades of Ming rule drove them far beyond the traditional areas of expansion in central Asia and the regions south of the Yangtze. In the reign of the third Ming emperor, Yunglo, they launched a series of expeditions that had no precedent in Chinese history. Between 1405 and 1423, a court eunuch named Zhenghe, who was one of Yunglo's most trusted subordinates, led seven major expeditions overseas. A mix of motives, including a desire to explore other lands and proclaim the glory of the Ming Empire to the wider world, prompted the voyages. The early expeditions were confined largely to Southeast Asian seas and kingdoms; the last three expeditions reached as far as Persia, southern Arabia, and the east coast of Africa, distances comparable to those covered by the Portuguese in their early voyages around Africa.

The ships and fleets involved in each of the overseas missions were truly impressive. The initial fleet contained 62 ships—compared to 3 for Columbus in 1492 and 4 for da Gama 6 years later—that accommodated nearly 28,000

Ming China and the Zhenghe Expeditions, 1405–1423

sailors, merchants, and soldiers—compared to 150 for da Gama's first voyage around Africa. Some of the larger ships in Zhenghe's fleet were over 400 feet long and displaced up to 1500 tons of water; the largest of da Gama's caravels cannot have been much more than 60 feet in length and displaced around 300 tons of water. Taken together, the expeditions led by Zhenghe leave little doubt that the Chinese had the capacity to expand on a global scale at least a century before the Europeans rounded the Cape of Good Hope and entered Asian waters.

Though they possessed ample means, the Chinese were more than a little ambivalent about the worth of the voyages. It was gratifying to have "barbarian" peoples from the southern seas do homage to the emissaries of the Ming ruler; also, the giraffes and other curious animals that were carried home made interesting additions to the imperial zoo. But there were few tangible returns from what were very expensive undertakings. The scholar-gentry rivals of Zhenghe and other court eunuchs could convincingly argue that the voyages were a luxury that the empire simply could not afford. When they noted that the Mongols were once again restless beyond the defenses of the Great Wall (which was in need of repair and reinforcements), it was hard to refute their insistence that the defense of the empire must come before seemingly frivolous overseas exploration. Though there was one more voyage after the death of Yunglo in 1424, his successors shared little of his enthusiasm for the voyages, and consequently they were abandoned in the early 1430s. China's spectacular entry onto the world stage proved a short run indeed.

ANALYSIS

MEANS AND MOTIVES FOR OVERSEAS EXPANSION: EUROPE AND CHINA COMPARED

Given China's demonstrated capacity for overseas expansion and the fateful consequences for global history that resulted from the fact that Europe, not China, eventually took the lead in this sort of endeavor, the reasons for the Chinese failure to follow up on their early voyages of exploration merit serious examination. The explanations for the Chinese refusal to commit to overseas expansion can be best understood if they are contrasted with the forces that drove the Europeans with increasing determination into the outside world. In broad terms such a comparison underscores the fact that, though both the Europeans and the Chinese had the means to expand on a global scale, only the Europeans had strong motives for doing so.

The social and economic transformations that occurred in European civilization during the late Middle Ages and the early Renaissance had brought it to a level of development that compared favorably with China in many areas (see Chapters 21, 22, and 23). Though the Chinese empire was far vaster and more populous than tiny nation-states, such as Portugal, Spain, and Holland, European kingdoms had grown more efficient at mobilizing their more limited resources. Rivalries between the states of a fragmented Europe had also made for a greater aggressiveness and sense of competition on the part of the Europeans than the rulers of the Chinese monolith could even imagine. China's armies were far larger than those of any of the European kingdoms, but European soldiers were on the whole better led, armed, and disciplined. Chinese wet-rice agriculture was more productive than European dry-land farming, and the Chinese rulers had a far larger population to cultivate their fields, build their dikes and bridges, work their mines, and manufacture tools, clothing, and weapons. But on the whole, the technological innovations of the medieval period had given the Europeans a decided advantage over the Chinese in the animal and machine power they could generate—a capacity that did much to make up for their manpower deficiencies.

Despite differences, both civilizations possessed the means for sustained exploration and expansion overseas, though the Chinese were ready to undertake such enterprises some centuries earlier than the Europeans. As the voyages of da Gama and Columbus on the one side and Zhenghe on the other side demonstrated, both civilizations possessed the shipbuilding and navigational skills and tech-nology to tackle such ambitious undertakings. Why then were the much more impressive Zhenghe expeditions a dead end, while the much more modest probes of Columbus and da Gama were the beginning of a half-millennia of European overseas expansion and global dominance?

The full answer to this question is as complex as the societies it asks us to compare. We can learn a good deal by looking at the groups pushing for expansion within each civilization and the needs that drove them into the outside world. There was widespread support for exploration and overseas expansion in seafaring European nations such as Portugal, Spain, Holland, and England. European rulers financed expeditions they hoped would bring home precious metals and trade goods that could be sold at great profits. Both treasure and profits could be translated into warships and armies that would strengthen these rulers in their incessant wars with both European rivals and, in the case of the Iberian kingdoms, their Muslim adversaries. European traders looked for much the same benefits from overseas expansion. Rulers and merchants also hoped that explorers would find new lands whose climates and soils were suitable for the cultivation of crops, such as sugar, that were in high demand and thus would bring big profits. Leaders of rival branches of the Christian faith believed that overseas expansion would give their missionaries access to unlimited numbers of heathens to be converted, or would put them in touch with the legendary lost king, Prester John, who would ally with them in their struggle with the infidel Muslims.

By contrast, the Chinese Zhenghe expeditions were very much the project of a single emperor and a favored eunuch whose Muslim family origins may go a long way toward accounting for his wanderlust. Yunglo appears to have been driven by little more than curiosity and the vain desire to impress his greatness and that of his empire on peoples whom he considered inferior. Though some Chinese merchants went along for the ride, most felt little need for the voyages. They already traded on favorable terms for all the products that Asia, and in some cases Europe and Africa, could offer. The merchants had the option of waiting for other peoples to come to them, or, if they were a bit more ambitious, of going out in their own ships to maritime Southeast Asia.

The scholar-gentry were actively hostile to the Zhenghe expeditions. The voyages strengthened the position of the much-hated eunuchs who vied with the scholar-gentry for the emperor's favor and the high posts that went with it. In addition, the scholar-gentry saw the voyages as a foolish diversion of resources that the empire could not afford. They believed it would be better to direct the wealth and talents of the empire to building armies and fortifications to keep out the hated Mongols and other nomads. The memory of foreign rule was, after all, quite fresh.

As the foregoing makes clear, the elites of western European nations had very good reasons for pushing voyages of exploration and projects of overseas expansion. The rulers and bureaucrats of China, on the other hand, had no reasons that were very convincing. In fact, there were very persuasive reasons, rooted in centuries of struggle against the nomads, for diverting resources that might have gone into overseas expeditions into projects on the home front. As so often before in their history, the Chinese were drawn inward, fixated on internal struggles and the continuing threat from central Asia. As the Chinese retreated, the Europeans exploded outward. It is difficult to exaggerate the magnitude of the consequences for both civilizations and all humankind.

Questions: How might history have been changed if the Chinese had mounted a serious and sustained effort to project their power overseas in the decades before da Gama rounded the Cape of Good Hope? Why did the Chinese fail to foresee the threat that European expansion would pose for the rest of Asia and finally for China itself? Are there other civilizations that had the capacity for global expansion in this era? What prevented them from launching expeditions similar to those of the Chinese and Europeans? In terms of motivation for overseas expansion, were peoples such as the Muslims, Indians, and Amerindians more like the Europeans or the Chinese?

CHINESE RETREAT AND THE ARRIVAL OF THE EUROPEANS

Just over a half century after the last of the Zhenghe expeditions, China consciously had moved from the position of a great power reaching out overseas to an increasingly isolated empire. In 1390 the first imperial edict aimed at limiting Chinese overseas commerce was issued. In the following centuries, the Ming war fleet declined dramatically in the number and quality of its ships, and strict limits were placed on the size and number of masts with which a seagoing ship might be fitted out. As the Chinese shut themselves in, the Europeans probed ever farther across the globe and were irresistibly drawn to the most legendary of all overseas civilizations, the Middle Kingdom of China. In addition to the trading contacts noted above, Christian missionaries infiltrated Chinese coastal areas and

sought to gain access to the court, where they hoped to curry favor with the Ming emperors. While religious orders, such as the Franciscans and Dominicans, toiled to win converts among the common people and made modest progress that could be counted in the tens of thousands, the Jesuits adopted the "top down" strategy that di Nobili had pursued in India. In China, however, a single individual, the Ming emperor, instead of a whole caste, sat at the top of the social hierarchy, and for that reason the rulers and their chief advisors became the prime targets of the Jesuit mission.

Some Chinese scholars showed interest in Christian teachings and Western thinking more generally. But the Jesuit missionaries who managed to make their way to Beijing clearly recognized that their scientific knowledge and technical skills were the keys to maintaining a presence at the Ming court and eventually interesting the Chinese elite in Christianity. Beginning in the 1580s a succession of brilliant Jesuit scholars, such as Matteo Ricci and Adam Schall, spent most of their time in the imperial city correcting faulty calendars, forging cannon, fixing clocks imported from Europe, and astounding the Chinese literati with the accuracy of their instruments and their ability to predict eclipses. They won a few converts among the scholar-gentry, but most of the highest court officials were suspicious of these strange looking "barbarians" with large noses and hairy faces and sought to limit their contacts with the imperial family. Some at the court, especially the scholar-officials, who were humiliated by the foreigners' corrections to their calendars, and many of the eunuchs, were openly hostile to the Jesuits. Despite serious harassment, however, the later Ming emperors remained sufficiently fascinated by these very learned and able visitors that they allowed a handful to remain at court. When the Ming were overthrown by the Manchu nomads from the north, the Jesuits were able to hold and even strengthen their position at court.

MING DECLINE AND THE CHINESE PREDICAMENT

By the late 1500s the Ming retreat from overseas involvement had become just one facet of a familiar pattern of dynastic decline. The highly centralized, absolutist political structure, which had been established by Hongwu and run well by able successors such as Yunglo, became a major liability under the mediocre or incompetent individuals who occupied the throne through much of the last two centuries of Ming rule. Decades of rampant official corruption, exacerbated by the growing isolation of weak rulers by the thousands of eunuchs who gradually came to dominate life within the Forbidden City, eventually eroded the very foundations on which the empire was built.

Public works projects, including the critical dike works on the Yellow River, fell into disrepair, and floods, drought, and famine soon ravaged the land. Peasants in afflicted districts were reduced to eating the bark from trees or the excrement of wild geese. Some peasants sold their children into slavery to keep them from starving, and peasants in some areas resorted to cannibalism. Rapacious local landlords built huge estates by taking advantage of the increasingly desperate peasant population. As in earlier phases of dynastic decline, cultivators who had been turned off their land and tortured for taxes, or had lost most of the crop they had grown, turned to flight, banditry, and finally open rebellion to confiscate food and avenge their exploitation by avaricious landlords and corrupt officials.

True to the pattern of dynastic rise and fall, internal disorder resulted in and was intensified by foreign threats and renewed assaults by nomadic peoples from beyond the Great Wall. One of the early signs of the seriousness of imperial deterioration was the inability of Chinese bureaucrats and military forces to put an end to the epidemic of Japanese (and ethnic Chinese) pirate attacks that ravaged the southern coast in the mid-16th century. Despite an official preoccupation with the Mongols early in the Ming era and with the Jurchens or Manchus to the northeast of the Great Wall in later times, the dynasty was finally toppled in 1644 not by the Mongols in the west but by rebels from within. By that point in time, the administrative apparatus had become so feeble that the last Ming emperor, Chongzhen, did not realize how serious the rebel advance was until enemy soldiers were scaling the walls of the Forbidden City. After watching his wife withdraw to her chambers to commit suicide and bungling an attempt to kill his young daughter, the ill-fated Chongzhen retreated to the imperial gardens and hanged himself rather than face the ignominy of capture.

Though they managed to topple the dynasty, none of the divided rebel forces that challenged the Ming in the 1640s proved a viable replacement. A political vacuum within China once again opened the way for invasions and conquest by a nomadic people from beyond the Great Wall. This time, the Jurchens or Manchus, not the Mongols, seized power following a series of military victories and the capture of the imperial capital. The Manchu leader, Nurhaci, established a new dynasty, the Qing, that would rule China for nearly 3½ centuries and prove to be the last of a succession of imperial houses that extended back more than two millennia. Roughly the first half of the Qing reign, extending to the 1780s, was a time of renewed political strength, economic prosperity, and cultural development for Chinese civilization. Between 1644 and the mid-18th century, China's influence over surrounding areas in East Asia was restored. But by the end of the 18th century, a combination of internal crises and growing external challenges, particularly on the part of the increasingly aggressive European powers, gave rise to fundamental challenges that not only threatened the Qing dynasty but the very foundations of Chinese civilization. In Chapters 32 and 41, we will see how these challenges profoundly shaped the history of Chinese civilization throughout the past two centuries and how they continue to affect it to the present day.

FENDING OFF THE WEST: JAPAN'S REUNIFICATION AND THE FIRST CHALLENGE

Given the deep divisions of the country that resulted from the rise of the warring daimyo households, Japan was fortunate that it appeared to have little to attract the Europeans in the early centuries of their expansion. The islands were off the main trading routes and, compared to their Chinese and Southeast Asian neighbors, had few products to tempt European merchants. In fact, Japan, like Europe, contributed mainly raw materials, especially silver, to the Asian trading system the Europeans were striving to dominate. In comparison with China, the Japanese were few in number. Thus, though Francis Xavier thought them the "best people [the Europeans] had yet discovered," the prospect of their conversion paled in comparison with missionary hopes for Christianizing the multitudes of China or India. In addition, the Europeans soon discovered that the relatively small population of the islands was ruled by one of the most disciplined and fierce military elites that they had encountered anywhere in the world. It is hard to know how the Portuguese or Spanish would have fared if they had attempted to invade the islands as they did the Philippines and coastal Sri Lanka. As European visitors to Japan readily acknowledged, even divided the Japanese would make formidable adversaries.

Fortunately for the Japanese, their ability to defend their island home was not to be tested in the early centuries of expansion. In the decades just after the Europeans began to arrive in the islands in the 1540s, the Japanese found the leaders who had the military and diplomatic skills and ruthlessness needed to restore the shogunate and force the daimyo to acknowledge a supreme commander, if not a true sovereign. By the early 1600s with the potential threat from the Europeans looming ever larger in the Japanese imagination, the new Tokugawa shoguns had gained sufficient control to gradually shut down contacts with outsiders and put into effect a self-imposed isolation of the islands that would last nearly 2½ centuries. One of the main casualties of this move into isolation was the Christian missionary effort, which in the 1580s seemed on the verge of converting the shogun and the majority of his subjects. One of the great advantages of withdrawal from the Japanese point of view was the time it provided for them to recover from the long years of civil war and to build the political and economic infrastructure that was essential for lasting internal peace and the defense of Japan from outside invaders.

THE SHOGUNATE REVIVED: TOWARD THE RETURN OF INTERNAL ORDER

By the 16th century, the daimyo stalemate and the pattern of recurring civil war were so entrenched in Japanese society that it required a succession of three rather remarkable military leaders to restore a semblance of unity and internal peace. Nobunaga, the first of these leaders, was from a minor warrior household, but his skills as a military leader soon vaulted him into prominence in the ongoing struggles for power among the daimyo lords. As a leader Nobunaga combined daringness, a willingness to innovate, and ruthless determination—some would say outright cruelty. He was quite prepared to launch a surprise attack against an enemy that outnumbered him ten to one, and he

was one of the first of the daimyos to make extensive use of the firearms that the Japanese had begun to acquire from the Portuguese in the 1540s. The measures Nobunaga took in reprisal against those who resisted him, such as the slaughter of thousands of monks and villagers attached to the Buddhist monastery at Mount Hiei near Kyoto, may well have cowed some of the weaker daimyos into submission. In 1573 Nobunaga deposed the last of the Ashikaga shoguns, who had long ruled in name only, and by 1580 he had unified much of central Honshu under his command. As his armies drove against the powerful western daimyo in 1582, Nobunaga was caught off guard by one of his vassal generals and killed when the Kyoto temple where he had taken refuge was burned to the ground.

At first it appeared that Nobunaga's campaigns to restore central authority to the islands might be undone. But his ablest general, Toyotomi Hideyoshi, moved quickly to punish those who had betrayed Nobunaga and to renew the drive to break the power of the daimyos who had not yet submitted to him. Though the son of a peasant, Hideyoshi matched his master in military prowess and was far more skillful at diplomacy. A system of alliances and a string of victories over the last of the resisting daimyos made Hideyoshi the military master of Japan by 1590.

The ambitious overlord had much more grandiose schemes of conquest in mind. He dreamed of ruling China and even India, though he knew little about either place,

Japan: The Rise of the Tokugawa Shogunate

In this late 16th-century portrait Hideyoshi (1536–1598) grasps the sword that catapulted him to power and exudes the discipline and self-confidence that did much to further his campaigns to unify Japan.

and threatened, among others, the Spanish in the Philippines. Apparently as the first step toward fulfilling this vision of empire-building on a grand scale, Hideyoshi launched two attacks on Korea in 1592 and 1597, each of which involved nearly 150,000 soldiers. After initial successes both campaigns stalled: The first ended in defeat; the second was still in progress when Hideyoshi died in 1598.

Though Hideyoshi had sought to ensure that he would be succeeded by his son, the vassals whom he had appointed to carry out his wishes sought to seize power for themselves after his death. One of these vassals, Tokugawa Ieyasu, who had originally come from a minor daimyo house but as an ally of Hideyoshi, had been able to build up a powerful domain on the heavily populated Kanto plain and emerged triumphant from the renewed warfare that resulted. Rather than continue Hideyoshi's campaigns of overseas expansion, Ieyasu concentrated on consolidating power at home. In 1603 he was granted the title of shogun by the emperor, an act which formally inaugurated 2½ centuries of rule by the Tokugawa family. Under Ieyasu's direction, the remaining daimyos were reorganized. Most of the lands in central Honshu were either controlled directly by the Tokugawa family, who now ruled the land from the city of Edo (later Tokyo), or were held by daimyos who were closely allied with the shoguns. Though many of the outlying or vassal daimyos retained their domains, they were carefully controlled and required to pledge their personal allegiance to the shogun. Over a period of time the estates of numerous vassal daimyos were reduced in size or broken up and absorbed by the Tokugawa family or their close allies. It was soon clear that the Tokugawas' victory had put an end to the civil wars and brought a semblance of political unity to the islands.

DEALING WITH THE EUROPEAN CHALLENGE

All through the decades when the three unifiers were struggling to bring the feisty daimyos under control, they also had to contend with a totally new force in Japanese history, the Europeans. From the time in 1543 when shipwrecked Portuguese sailors were washed up on the shore of Kyushu island, European traders and missionaries visited the islands in increasing numbers. The traders brought the Japanese mainly goods produced in India, China, and Southeast Asia and exchanged them for silver, copper, pottery, and lacquerware. Perhaps more important, the European traders and the missionaries who followed them to the islands brought firearms, printing presses, and other Western devices such as clocks. The firearms, which the Japanese could themselves manufacture within years and were improving in design within a generation, revolutionized Japanese warfare and contributed much to the victories of the unifiers. Commercial contacts with the Europeans also encouraged the Japanese to venture overseas to trade in nearby Formosa and Korea and places as distant as the Philippines and Siam.

Soon after the merchants, Christian missionaries arrived in the islands and set to work converting the Japanese to Roman Catholicism. Beginning in the outlying daimyos' domains, the missionaries worked their way toward the political center that was beginning to coalesce around Nobunaga and his followers by the 1570s. Seeing Christianity as a counterforce to the militant Buddhist orders that were resisting his rise to power, Nobunaga took the missionaries under his protection and encouraged them to preach their faith to his people. The Jesuits, adopting the same "top down" strategy of conversion that they had followed in India and China, converted a number of the daimyos and many of their samurai retainers. Some of the Jesuits were also convinced that they were on the verge of

This 16th-century screen painting shows the arrival of Francis Xavier and his entourage in Japan. The painting conveys a sense of the Japanese perception of these strangers from distant lands as exotic, awkward, and curiously dressed.

winning over Nobunaga, who delighted in wearing Western clothes, encouraged his artists to copy Western paintings of the Virgin Mary and scenes from the life of Christ, and permitted the missionaries to build churches in towns throughout the islands. The missionaries were persuaded that Nobunaga's conversion would bring the whole of the Japanese people into the Christian fold. Even without it, they reported converts in the hundreds of thousands by the early 1580s. After all of the frustrations that the missionaries had experienced as a result of their efforts in India, China, and elsewhere, Japan looked for a time to be the most promising candidate in all of Asia for widespread conversion.

In the late 1580s, quite suddenly, the missionaries saw their carefully mounted conversion campaign collapse. Nobunaga was murdered, and his successor, Hideyoshi, though not yet openly hostile, was lukewarm toward the missionary enterprise. In part the missionaries' fall from favor resulted from the fact that the resistance of the Buddhist sects had been crushed. More critically, Hideyoshi and his followers were alarmed by reports of converts refusing to obey commands, which they believed conflicted with their newly adopted Christian beliefs, from their daimyo overlords or their own parents. Thus, the threat that the new religion posed for the established social order was growing more apparent. That threat was compounded by signs that the Europeans might follow up their commercial and missionary overtures with military expeditions aimed at the conquest of the islands. The Japanese had been strongly impressed with the firearms and pugnacity of the Europeans, and they were therefore not inclined to take threats of invasion lightly.

JAPAN'S SELF-IMPOSED ISOLATION

Growing doubts about European intentions and fears that both merchants and missionaries might subvert the existing social order led, beginning in the late 1580s, to official measures to restrict foreign activities in Japan. First, the Christian missionaries were ordered by Hideyoshi to leave the islands—an order that was not rigorously enforced, at least at the outset. By the mid-1590s, Hideyoshi was actively persecuting both Christian missionaries and converts. His successor Ieyasu continued this persecution and then officially banned the faith in 1614. European missionaries were driven out of the islands; those who remained underground were hunted down and killed or expelled. Japanese converts were compelled to renounce their faith; those who refused, including women and children, were imprisoned, tortured, and executed. By the 1630s the

persecutions, even against Christians who attempted to practice their faith in secret, had become so intense that thousands of converts in the western regions joined in hard-fought, but hopeless, rebellions against the local daimyo and the forces of the *shogun*. With the suppression of these uprisings Christianity in Japan was reduced to an underground faith of isolated communities. As in India and China, a promising start toward conversion had come to little.

Under Ieyasu and his successors the persecution of the Christians grew into a broader campaign to utterly isolate Japan from outside influences. In 1616 foreign traders were confined to a handful of cities; in the 1630s all Japanese ships were forbidden to trade or even sail overseas. One after another different European nations were either officially excluded from Japan (the Spanish) or concluded that trading there was no longer worth the considerable risk (the English). By the 1640s only a limited number of Dutch and Chinese ships were allowed to call at and carry on commerce in the small island of Deshima in Nagasaki Bay. The export of silver and copper was greatly restricted, Western books were banned to prevent Christian ideas from reentering the country, and foreigners were permitted to live and travel only in very limited areas.

By the mid-17th century Japan's retreat into almost total isolation was completed. Much of the next century was spent in consolidating the internal control of the Tokugawa Shogunate by extending bureaucratic administration into the vassal daimyo domains throughout the islands. In the 18th century, a revival of neo-Confucian philosophy, which had marked the period of the Tokugawa's rise to power, increasingly gave way to the influence of thinkers who championed the school of "National Learning." As its name implies, the new ideology laid great emphasis on Japan's unique historical experience and the revival of indigenous culture at the expense of Chinese imports such as Confucianism. In the following centuries, through contacts with the small Dutch community at Deshima, members of the Japanese elite also followed developments in the West. Their avid interest in the achievements of the Europeans contrasted sharply with the indifference of the Chinese scholar-gentry in this period to the doings of the "hairy barbarians" from Europe.

The openings the Japanese left to the outside world meant than when the second push by the Western powers for entry into Japan came, beginning in the 1850s, the Japanese knew much more clearly than the Chinese what they were up against. Chinese indifference left them blind to the intentions and power of their European adversaries, and thus unable to deal effectively with European demands and ultimately military incursions in the middle decades of the 19th century. After much debate within the daimyo elite, the Japanese first followed a policy of concession and evasion in the face of the Western challenge, then concentrated on building up their strength by adopting European innovations they had monitored over the centuries through contacts with the Dutch at Deshima.

CONCLUSION

ASIA AND THE FIRST PHASE OF EUROPE'S GLOBAL EXPANSION

During the early modern period in global history, the West's surge in exploration and commercial expansion touched most of Asia only peripherally. This was particularly true of East Asia, where the political cohesion and military strength of the vast Chinese empire and the Japanese warrior-dominated states blocked all hope of European domination. Promising missionary inroads in the 16th century were stifled by hostile Tokugawa shoguns in the early 17th century and carefully contained by the Ming emperors and the nomadic Qing dynasty that succeeded in the mid-1600s. Strong Chinese and Japanese rulers also limited trading contacts with the aggressive Europeans and confined European merchants to one or two ports — Macao and Canton in China, Deshima in Japan — that were remote from their respective capitals. These restrictions and the strength of the regimes and societies able to impose them meant that the European impact on East Asian civilizations was highly selective and limited in the first three centuries of European overseas expansion. Change in China, Japan, Korea, or central Asia was generated mainly by internal factors; continuity was ensured by the persistence of centuries-old cultural and social patterns and techniques of handling alien intruders like the European seafarers.

Even in most of South and Southeast Asia, where the European impact in the early centuries of Western overseas expansion was much more pronounced, Asians retained control over their own destinies and their history was shaped far more by long-standing indigenous patterns of development than by impulses from a vibrant but distant Europe. European control was limited to the island periphery of great empires, such as that built by the Mughals in India, and the kingdoms of mainland and island Southeast Asia. Sea power allowed the Portuguese, and after them the Spanish, Dutch, and English, to control trading outposts in ports such as Goa, Malacca, Batavia, and Bombay, and even to conquer parts of island kingdoms, such as the southwest corner of Ceylon or the northwest end of Java. But little European headway was made until well into the 18th century against even some of the weaker kingdoms of South or Southeast Asia, and Christian missionaries won few converts except in areas, such as the northern Philippines, where one of the major Asian religions had not previously spread. Even in commerce and seafaring, where the influence of the West in Asia was the greatest, the Europeans found that it was better to blend into the existing networks and cooperate with local rulers and merchants than to build expensive and vulnerable trading empires.

Only in the 18th century were first the Dutch and later the English able to begin to dominate some of the core areas of South and Southeast Asian civilization. Even then, as we shall see in Chapter 30, the domination was as much a product of Asian divisions and weaknesses as of decisive European advantages in making war or running bureaucracies.

FURTHER READINGS

C. G. F. Simkins's *The Traditional Trade of Asia* (1968) provides an able overview of the Asian trading network from ancient times until about the 18th century. Much more detailed accounts of specific segments of the system, as well as the impact of the Dutch and Portuguese on it, can be found in the works of J. C. van Leur, M. A. P. Meilink-Roelofsz, K. N. Chaudhuri, Ashin Das Gupta, and Michael Pearson. C. R. Boxer's *The Portuguese Seaborne Empire* (1969) and *The Dutch Seaborne Empire* (1965) are still essential reading, though the latter has little on the Europeans in Asia. Boxer's *Race Relations in the Portuguese Colonial Empire, 1415–1825* (1963) provides a stimulating, if contentious, introduction to the history of European social interaction with overseas peoples in the early centuries of expansion. G. B. Sansom's *The Western World and Japan* (1968) includes a wealth of information on the interaction between Europeans and, despite its title, peoples throughout Asia, and it has good sections on the missionary initiatives in both China and Japan.

The period of the Ming dynasty has been the focus of broad but detailed studies to a greater extent than the dynasties that preceded it. An important early work is Charles O. Hucker's *The Censorial System of Ming China*

(1966). Two essential recent works are Albert Chan's *The Glory and Fall of the Ming Dynasty* (1982) and Edward Dreyer's more traditional political history entitled *Early Ming China, 1355–1435* (1982). There are also wonderful insights into daily life at various levels of Chinese society in Roy Huang's very readable *1587: A Year of No Significance; The Ming Dynasty in Decline* (1981), and into the interaction between the Chinese and the Jesuits in Jonathan Spence's *The Memory Palace of Matteo Ricci* (1984). Frederic Wakeman Jr.'s *The Great Enterprise*, 2 vols. (1985), is essential to an understanding of the transition from Ming to Manchu rule. The early chapters of Jonathan Spence's *The Search for Modern China* (1990) also provides an illuminating overview of that process.

Perhaps the best introductions to the situation in Japan in the early phase of European expansion are provided by G. B. Sansom's survey, *A History of Japan, 1615–1867* (1963), and Conrad Totman's *Politics in the Tokugawa Bakufu, 1600–1843* (1967). Numerous studies on the Europeans in Japan include those by Donald Keene, Grant Goodman, Noel Perrin, and C. R. Boxer. Intellectual trends in Japan in this era are the most fully treated in H. D. Harootunian's *Toward Restoration: The Growth of Political Consciousness in Tokugawa Japan* (1970).

1770 James Watt's steam engine;
beginning of Industrial Revolution

1808–1825 Latin-American wars of independence

1789–1815 French Revolution and Napoleon

1730–1850 Population
boom in western Europe

1805–1849 Muhammed Ali rules Egypt

1776–1783 American Revolution

1823 Monroe Doctrine

1812 Napoleon's failed invasion of Russia

1786–1790 First British reforms in India

1822 Brazil declares independence

1815 Vienna settlement

1788 Australian
colonization begins

1798 Napoleon's
invasion of Egypt

1815 British annexation of Cape
Town and region of southern Africa

The Crystal Palace in Hyde Park, London, was constructed for the 1851 World's Fair. The building is almost all glass and was one of the industrial wonders of the time.

1839–1876 Reforms in Ottoman Empire

1848 ff. Beginnings   **1860–1868** Civil strife in Japan
of Marxism

1840 Semiautonomous government in Canada   **1861–1865** American
Civil War   **1870–1910** Acceleration
of "demographic transi-
tion" in western Europe

1853 Perry expedition   and the United States
to Edo Bay in Japan   **1863** Emancipation
of slaves in U.S.

1839–1841 Opium War with China

1830, 1848 Revolutions in Europe   **1854–1856**

1835 English education in India   Crimean War   **1867** Union of central and eastern Canada

1826 New Zealand
colonization begins   **1838** Ottoman trade treaty with Britain   **1868–1912** Meiji (reform) era in Japan

1850–1864 Taiping
rebellion in China

1864–1871 German   **1870–1910** Expansion of

1825–1855 Repression in Russia   unification   commercial export economy in Latin America

1846–1848 Mexican-   **1858** British Parliament
American War   assumes control over India   **1870** Establishment of
Japanese Ministry of
1861 Emancipation of serfs   Industry
in Russia; reform era begins

PART 5

Industrialization and Western Global Hegemony, 1750–1914

The period of world history that spans almost two centuries after 1750 was marked by unusually clear characteristics. These were the decades in which Western civilization (now embracing much of North America as well as western Europe) experienced the Industrial Revolution, which transformed the bases of production through new technology and new sources of power. Building on earlier Western developments, including the scientific revolution, industrialization brought massive changes to the West's economy and society.

Largely on the basis of industrialization the West attained a genuine, if fleeting, hegemony over most other civilizations in the world. In contrast to the early modern period, when Western power away from the seas was characteristically limited, particularly in and around most of Asia, no area could now escape the possibility of extensive European or United States penetration. Thus Africa, previously able to accommodate to Western power while strengthening internal political units, was now carved up into a patchwork of colonies. The West's new hegemony was also expressed through the rapid expansion of Western imperialism and the intensification of colonial controls even in many older holdings such as India. It was expressed through growing commercial penetration of areas such as much of China and the Ottoman Empire, not directly held as colonies. Western hegemony also continued to constrain Latin America, which ran against the tide in achieving independence from colonial

1884–1914 Russian
industrialization

1898–1901 Boxer Rebellion in China

1871–1912 High
point of European
imperialism

1882 British
takeover of Egypt

1890s Partition of East Africa

1911–1912 Revolution in China; abolition of empire

1903 Construction of Panama Canal begins

1890s European leases in China

1877–1878 Ottomans out of most
of Balkans; Treaty of San Stefano

1898 Formation of Marxist Social Democratic Party in Russia

1908 Young Turk rising

1914 World War I

1879–1890s Partition of West Africa

1894–1895 Sino-Japanese War

1904–1905 Russo-Japanese War

1910 Japan annexes Korea

1886–1888 Slavery abolished in Cuba and Brazil

1905–1906 Revolution in Russia; limited reforms

1895 Cuban revolt against Spain

1901 Commonwealth of Australia

1885 Formation of National
Congress Party in India

1898 Spanish-American War; U.S.
acquires the Philippines, Puerto Rico,
and Hawaii; U.S. intervenes in Cuba

1890 Japanese constitution

rule early in the 19th century. Finally, Western hegemony was expressed by the need of every civilization to come to terms with Western institutions and values, by figuring out what to try to imitate and how.

In a sense, the dominant themes of the imperialist era amplified tendencies already discernible in the early modern centuries. International commercial contacts increased, largely through Western merchant activity and shipping, enhanced now by major technological innovations in the transportation field—notably the steamship, railroad, and telegraph. Cultural contacts reflected Western power as well. Just as Christianity and commercial penetration had gone hand in hand in Latin America during the early modern period, by the end of the 19th century substantial

Industrial Development in Key Regional Centers, about 1900

religious conversion began to accompany Western political and economic entry into Africa's heartlands.

Geographical rebalancing, in terms of the most obvious border shifts, also maintained the Western preeminence theme. Along with new levels of international exchange, boundary changes constitute one of the key criteria for defining a major period in world history, and during the 19th century they reflected the rise of Western power above all.

The decades of imperialism were not, however, simply a continuation of early modern trends in colonialism and the world economy. The dramatic new ingredient was the West's Industrial Revolution, which set the key themes of 19th-century world history by massively increasing the imperialist power of the West and by intensifying world economic contacts under the West's commercial sponsorship. By the 1850s the leading issues in all civilizations began to revolve around what to do about the West's new power—how and whether to resist, and what could or should be imitated. Western commercial interests generated the most obvious enhancement of international contacts, but missionary and other cultural conversion efforts played a role. These patterns, plus some common efforts at response, produced new parallels among major societies—as in growing interest in establishing new kinds of schools and, in a

number of cases, even parliaments and constitutions. New geography, new contacts, and new parallels constitute the common stuff of world history periods, and in the 19th century they all took shape under Western influence.

CHRONOLOGY: FROM INDUSTRIAL REVOLUTION TO THE BEGINNINGS OF A WESTERN BREAKDOWN

The beginning point of this new period, 1750, focuses on no particular event, though it is true that the war that opened in that decade, pitting France against Britain as colonial powers and producing battles in Europe, North America, and India as well as on the seas, has some claim to being history's first global conflict. More important is the fact that it was during the 1750s that the forces that directly produced Europe's Industrial Revolution began to take shape: rapid population growth, expansion of manufacturing, a surge of new inventions. A real Industrial Revolution is properly dated a few decades later, but the second half of the 18th century captures its formative stages.

With Western industrialization under way, signs of its impact on the wider world followed relatively quickly. In 1798 a modest French expeditionary force seized Egypt from its Muslim rulers—a clear sign of a new power bal-

Main Colonial Holdings, about 1914

ance in the eastern Mediterranean and a warning, as a few Muslim leaders recognized even in the retreating Ottoman Empire, of a need to innovate in response. In the 1820s Britain's hold over India began to intensify. In the 1830s the West forced open China's markets, using the insistence on the right to sell opium in China as the unsavory entering wedge. In the 1850s Britain and France defeated Russia in a war in its own Crimean backyard, while the United States and Britain pried open Japanese markets under threat of naval bombardment. The American Civil War (1861–1865) saw the industrial north prevail over the slaveholding south. Also in the 1860s, the scramble for new African colonies effectively began. In the 1870s a new level of commercial penetration started to transform the Latin American economy and social relationships. Between the 1850s and 1900, the islands of Polynesia were brought under Western control as colonies; the Maoris of New Zealand were subjected to a government of European settlers.

Western industrialization and imperialism, supplemented by major policy changes in the Western states, led to huge shifts in the population structures of various parts of the world. In the West, including the United States, the birthrate began to decline to historically low levels, beginning in some cases before 1800 and accelerating after 1870. This "demographic transition" to low birthrates reflected the fact that child labor was being displaced by machines; children were far less useful than they had been in agricultural societies. Child death rates also declined in the West, especially after 1880, as a result of better living conditions—which caused a further reduction in birthrates. The changes in the definitions of children's purposes and emphasis on their lovableness also supported the demographic transition. With high birthrates continuing elsewhere in the world, the West's percentage of total world population began to slip by 1900, even as the West's world power reached its brief peak.

Industrialization drew workers from populous agricultural regions to the new factory centers. European areas that were slow to industrialize, especially in southern and eastern Europe, sent hundreds of thousands of immigrants to centers in Germany and France, and especially to the United States, Australia, and Canada. Italians, Portuguese, and Spanish immigrants also flooded to the more prosperous Latin American nations in the late 19th century. The slave trade from Africa was ended under British leadership early in the 19th century; only a trickle continued, mainly to the Middle East. Humanitarian considerations, plus the new abilities demonstrated by industrial factories to organize "free" workers more effectively for production, fed this development.

Various immigration patterns arose to replace the slave trade. European immigrants, as well as Asian immigrants, were recruited. New Asian minorities became important factors in various parts of the world, beginning a pattern that would continue in the 20th century. Though not slaves, most immigrants were poorly paid and often restricted by harsh contracts and employer controls that might include obligatory company-owned stores, where workers were required to shop at often inflated prices. Despite poor conditions, many eastern and southern Asian immigrants were able to rise as shopkeepers and other commercial agents in their new societies, another development that heightened the importance of the great population movements of the 19th century.

Demographic and immigration patterns reflected the strength of the basic causation that determined the leading developments in world history from 1750 to 1914. Western power allowed recruitment of labor from other societies without the crudeness of slavery. Western industrialization, causing major demographic redefinitions in the West itself, began to attract workers from other, poorer societies still locked in agricultural economies.

The industrial-imperialist period drew to a close with the outbreak of World War I in 1914 quite simply because, in the wake of this massive conflict, the West's world hold began to recede, and a new, if gradual and complex, pattern of global relationships began to take shape. Revolutions in Russia, Japanese expansion, and the beginnings of colonial revolt signaled the end of the undisputed dominance of the industrial West.

DIVERSITIES IN THE AGE OF WESTERN DOMINANCE

Western industrialization and imperialist expansion were not the only major developments in the world between 1750 and 1914. A major surge of popular conversion to Islam began in sub-Saharan Africa at the end of the 18th century, marking an important shift in the continent's religious map. Latin American nations, for the most part winning freedom from Spain and Portugal by the 1820s after a series of wars for independence, launched an important process of new-nation building that requires emphasis in its own right. Latin America and the United States formed the world's first examples of societies working to forge stable institutions and identities after Western colonial dominance. Significant developments elsewhere echoed more traditional themes. Thus in China, major social unrest in the mid-19th century recalled earlier periods of dynastic decline, in which rural elements rose against population pressure and unchecked landlord control.

The 19th century must not be simplified into the results of Western imperialist pressure alone. Nevertheless, the period's central themes are inescapable. The West's industrially fueled expansion did not command every trend, but it affected most of them.

The principal complexity in dealing with the period from 1750 to 1914 lies not in identifying the common international forces centered around the West's new expansion, but in detailing the diversities of reactions to the dominant trends. Amid growing Western influence and powerful pressures or inducements to imitate, the world remained diverse, and civilization boundaries continued to define distinctive experiences.

One reaction was incorporation into an expanded Western civilization. The West expanded during the 19th century through the emergence of strong immigrant societies in the United States, Canada, Australia, and New Zealand, each with its own important modifications of basic Western patterns.

Elsewhere, several other responses to the rise of the West predominated, and they revealed unexpected similarities among otherwise diverse societies. Two societies, Russia and Japan, undertook a substantial internal transformation amid great stress, which permitted them to imitate key Western gains without becoming Western outright. Another set of civilizations grappled more tentatively with reform, producing less definitive results amid growing weakness. A third set of societies were colonies outright and faced the twin issues of change and domination.

China and the Ottoman Empire both lost territories to Western imperialism, but preserved a degree of independence amid growing weakness, outside interference, and agonizing indecision about the most effective way to counter the challenge from the West. Latin American nations that were newly independent also grappled with reform currents but amid particularly intense economic constraints.

Most of the rest of the world, including North Africa, was either colonized outright or, as with Latin America, reduced to economic dependence on Western trade. Colonial rule was not a constant, having somewhat different effects in India, for example, than in Africa, where imperialism was a later arrival and where in some cases a harsher racism affected Western policy.

The different kinds of reactions to the industrial, imperialist West constituted an additional source of geographical change in the 19th century, helping to define the period particularly in its later phases. Areas that had previously cohered, at least loosely, as a single civilization zone now split apart.

Diverse responses to the West's fierce surge reflected prior civilization traditions. Some societies found it easier than others to imitate or to concentrate on technological change on the basis of preexisting cultural values or political forms. Diversity followed from different power bases in terms of political institutions and the extent and rapidity of Western economic penetration.

Finally, different patterns of response resulted also from changes in the West itself, in a chaotic if exhilarating period of Western history. What was the West: Was it Christianity or one of the newer political faiths such as nationalism or socialism? Was the Western political message liberal, or did it consist of tighter bureaucratic organization and more effective military force—both definite aspects of the West's 19th-century experience? Different Western faces would obviously appeal to different prior experiences, depending on the civilization involved and the manner in which the West was now encountered.

The analytical challenge of world history in the age of industrialization and Western global hegemony from 1750 to 1914 consists less in tracing the main themes, than in tracing, explaining, and assessing the significance of diverse responses to these themes. Only through this analysis can the dynamic of the 19th century history be grasped, as it ranged from eager embrace of what the West seemed to represent to horrified rejection. And only through this comparative analysis can the next stage of world history be properly anticipated; for in the 20th century world-historical trends became once again more complex with the decline of formal Western power amid the potent lingering effects of the West's economic and cultural examples and amid the worldwide impact of the industrial economy.

Chapters covering the industrial-imperialist age begin with the huge transformation of the West, where political upheavals associated with an age of democratic revolution joined the fundamental impact of the world's first industrial revolutions. The effects of industrialization on imperialism are presented in Chapter 30, with the new colonial patterns in India and Southeast Asia and the rapid acquisition of new swaths of territory from the Pacific to North Africa. The special pattern of Latin America stands in complex contrast to the various colonial settings, as economic dependence coexisted with newly independent nations. The two old civilizations not colonized outright, but faced with agonizing adjustment problems, China and Islam, are juxtaposed next. Finally, the startling responses of Russia and Japan, where Western pressures were deeply felt but actively countered, are compared. This concludes the treatment of a short period of world history made unusually dramatic by the economic revolution whose impact, reverberating around the globe, created important new economic inequalities from one society to the next along with new and intense connections.

Western Europe				
		1800–1850 Romanticism in literature and art		
	1789–1799 French Revolution		**1832** Reform Bill of 1832 (England)	
		1815 Congress of Vienna; more conservative period		
1730 ff. Massive population rise	**1793–1794** Radical phase	**1820** Revolutions in Greece and Spain; rise of liberalism and nationalism		
c. 1770 James Watt's steam engine; beginning of Industrial Revolution	**1799–1815** Reign of Napoleon			
			1830, 1848 Revolutions in several European countries	

Extensions of Western Civilization				
	1789 Washington, first president of the U.S.	**1826–1837** Begin active European colonization in New Zealand		
	1788 First convict settlement in Australia	**1820s ff.** Industrialization in U.S.		
		1810–1826 Rise of democratic suffrage in U.S.		
	1793 First free European settlers in Australia			
	1803 The Louisiana Purchase (U.S.)	**1829** Jackson, seventh president of the U.S.		
	1790 ff. Begin per capita birthrate decline	**1823** First legislative council in Australia		

29 The Industrialization of the West, 1760–1914

INTRODUCTION. In the century and a half after 1760, Western society went through a dizzying series of changes. A combustion of political and social revolutions reverberated throughout the society. The French Revolution of 1789 was in essence the first great modern revolution in world history, but it was paralleled by uprisings in North America and many other European states in a pattern that lasted through 1848. Dramatic new cultural styles developed, some challenging 18th-century Enlightenment thought, some building on it through scientific research or political theory. Changes in popular culture occurred as well, and ordinary Westerners thought and behaved quite differently in 1900 than in the mid-18th century. A host of diplomatic upheavals accompanied internal change. New Western states rose to power—the surge of Germany was particularly noteworthy—and at the end of the period a new alliance system brought the West to a catastrophic war.

The greatest change of all involved the West's industrialization. The Industrial Revolution featured the creation of radical new technological and economic structures, transforming agricultural society much as the Neolithic revolution had once transformed hunting-and-gathering cultures. The force of the industrial upheaval spilled over into all facets of Western life, changing intimate popular habits such as sexuality and family life and basic social processes such as the making of war.

	1859–1870 Unification of Italy	**1871–1914** High point of European imperialism
		1864–1871 German unification
1848 ff. Writings of Karl Marx; rise of socialism		**1870–1879** Institution of French Third Republic
	1859 Darwin's *Origin of Species*	**1870s ff.** Rapid birthrate decline
		1870s ff. Spread of compulsory education laws

1843–1848 First Maori War in New Zealand   **1860–1870** Second Maori War

1852 New constitution in New Zealand; elected councils

1837–1842 U.S.-Canada border clashes
1837 Rebellion in Canada   **1867** British North America Act, unites eastern and central Canada

1846–1848 Mexican-American War

1840 Union act reorganizes Canada, provides elected legislature   **1861–1865** American Civil War

1850 Australia's Colonies Government Act allows legislature and more autonomy

1839 New British colonial policy   **1863** Emancipation of slaves

This fundamental transformation of Western society, during what was by historical standards a surprisingly short span of time, had obvious significance for wider world history. The West was already established as one of the world's vigorous civilizations, so basic change had automatic importance simply as part of the ongoing human panorama. The West did not shake off all previous characteristics, but all traditions—for example, parliamentary political forms—had to be rethought and adapted.

More obviously still, the changes of the industrial period further enhanced Europe's power in the world. Important extensions of Western civilization arose not only in the young United States but also in Canada, Australia, and New Zealand. By the end of the 19th century, literally all areas were touched by Western economic and military strength, so that reactions to the West's transformation became a fundamental part of world history.

Finally, the changes the West experienced during these decades foreshadowed some of the issues and patterns that would affect other societies later on, even into our own day. The struggle to industrialize, to create appropriate new political forms, and to alter traditional family life would not take exactly the same shape everywhere, but some common themes were usually involved. In this sense, as in viewing the great French Revolution as the first of many modern revolutions around the world, change in the West can be used as an analogy, a base for comparison with other major civilizations from the late 19th century onward.

The Western pattern of change, partly because it had no full parallels in earlier human history—no society had ever industrialized before, no society had ever pulled the majority of its population into cities, no society had ever virtually eliminated death among young children—was inevitably complex. Not all changes easily related to each other. Political revolution, for example, began as a development separate from industrialization; in contrast the Industrial Revolution, taking shape first in Britain, occurred in a society that remained relatively stable (though not unchanging) in politics. Only gradually did the strands of political and industrial transformation merge.

The best way to untangle the complexity of the Western transformation is, not surprisingly, to proceed historically—that is, to identify key subperiods within the longer span. These subperiods involve a growing crisis, late in the 18th century, that helped create changes in a variety of areas from sex to machinery; then a phase of experimentation, roughly 1789 to 1850, in which political revolution vied for attention with the initial thrust of industrialization; and finally, from 1850 to 1914, a more mature stage in which the implications of industrial society were more fully worked out. This final subperiod seemed at the time tranquil after the alarms and excitements of the revolutionary decades, but it embodied subterranean tensions that would burst forth in the most dreadful war the world had ever known.

Through these three subperiods virtually every aspect of western Europe changed, with Britain, France, and Germany leading the way. Science gained ground, art was revolutionized by new styles, and religion on the whole declined further. Women's conditions were redefined, as was basic social structure. Recreation shifted from reliance on popular festivals, to a period of repression in the name of more diligent work habits, to an explosion of commer-

1879–1907 Alliance system: Germany-Austria (1879); Germany-Austria-Russia (1881); Germany-Italy-Austria (1882); France-Russia (1891); Britain-France (1904); Britain-Russia (1907)

1912–1913 Balkan Wars

1880s ff. High point of impressionism in art

1914 Beginning of World War I

1881–1889 German social insurance laws enacted

1881–1914 Build Canadian Pacific Railway

1893 U.S. annexes Hawaii

1899 U.S. acquires part of Samoa

1907 New Zealand dominion status in British Empire

1917 U.S. enters World War I

1891–1898 Australia and New Zealand restrict Asian immigration

1901 Commonwealth of Australia, creates national federation

1882 U.S. excludes Chinese immigrants

1893 Women's suffrage in New Zealand

1898 Spanish-American War; U.S. acquires Puerto Rico, Guam, Philippines cialized mass leisure outlets at the end of the 19th century. Amid all these developments, two strands of change stand out, adding to the forces—such as the scientific revolution—that had already been reshaping the West. First, dramatic new technologies, the heart of the Industrial Revolution, transformed production and with it many other aspects of life. Second, new political forces brought a basic redefinition of the state and of peoples' relationships to the state.

THE CRISIS OF THE LATE 18TH CENTURY AND THE FRENCH REVOLUTION

The industrial transformation of Western society raises an obvious conundrum: Did it flow naturally from the previous shifts in this civilization, or was it a brutal jolt? The answer is "both." Western society had been changing rapidly since the 15th century through commercialization, the growth of the nation-state, and cultural redefinition. This is why the West was able to industrialize first, with no prior models to follow. At the same time, industrialization did involve important new directions that caused great strain, some of which continue to cause strain even in the late 20th century. This is why it is vital to see how a period of upheaval emerged, partly as a result of previous shifts and partly as a result of new factors that forced further, and sometimes agonizing, innovation.

FORCES OF CHANGE

The explosion of political revolution in France and the Industrial Revolution in Britain at the end of the 18th century seemed to some Western observers particularly startling in that so much of the previous century had been placid, at least on the surface. Western nations had quarreled over colonies, but most of the 18th-century wars had been fairly sedate, and the ascending position of the West in the wider world was unchallenged. Few major popular rebellions challenged the absolute monarchs of the continent, though it was true that the French monarchy, unable to reform a tax structure marked by exemptions for nobles and the Church, showed signs of stress. Parliamentary politics in Britain drew wide consensus, save for some agitation for wider voting rights in the 1760s.

Intellectual ferment, however, ran high. Enlightenment thinkers challenged regimes that did not grant full religious freedom, or that insisted on aristocratic privilege, and a few called for widespread popular voice in government. A gap had opened between leading intellectuals and established institutions, and this would play a role in the revolutions that lay ahead (as would a similar gap in revolutions elsewhere in the world after 1900).

Enlightenment thinkers agreed that traditional inequalities in law, which gave certain groups rights by birth, were wrong. They wanted governments to serve the general good and to protect various freedoms. Some also wanted governments to be open to participation by the people at large, through some kind of democratic vote. These ideas, a fundamental challenge to Europe's absolute monarchies, established churches, and privileged upper classes, lay behind much of the political agitation that drew the 18th century to a close.

A second source of disruption was occurring more quietly, at all social levels. Western Europe experienced a huge population jump after about 1730. Within half a century the population of France rose by 50 percent, that of Britain and Prussia rose a full 100 percent. This population revolution was itself caused by relatively stable conditions, including better border policing by the efficient nation-state governments that reduced the movement of disease-bearing animals. More important still was improved nutrition resulting from the growing use of the potato and other crops of American origin. Westerners had long resisted these new crops, but now shifted to them in order to allow more secure subsistence, often on smaller plots of land. The potato was particularly important because of the calories it yielded on limited acreage. These various factors reduced the death rate, particularly for children; instead of over 40 percent of all children dying by age two, the figure by the 1780s was nearer 33 percent. More children surviving also meant more people living to have children of their own, so the birthrate increased as well.

Population pressure at this level always has dramatic impact. In China recurrent population pressure had historically produced growing popular unrest, often leading to the collapse of a dynasty. In medieval Europe population growth had ultimately outstripped available resources, leading to subsequent decline. The 18th-century population surge, however, produced more innovative responses, though it certainly heightened popular grievances as well. Upper-class families, faced with more surviving children, tried to tighten their grip on existing offices. It became harder, in the later 18th century, for a nonaristocrat to gain a high post in the Church or state. This reaction helped feed demands for change by other groups. Business families faced with more children often decided to expand their operations, sometimes adopting new equipment in order to spur business success. Here was a source of a new willingness to take risks. For some ordinary peasants, population pressure caused a new interest in expanding market agriculture, as some peasants began to acquire more land and employ wage labor in order to take advantage of new opportunities. Above all, population pressure drove many people into the working-class proletariat, as they lost any real chance of inheriting property. These people were eager to take advantage of new labor opportunities simply to survive. They thus formed the nucleus of a new working class in agriculture and, above all, in manufacturing.

The population growth of the 18th century prompted a rapid expansion of domestic manufacturing throughout western Europe and also, by 1800, in the United States. Hundreds of thousands of people became full- or part-time producers of textile and metal products, working at home but in a capitalist system in which materials, work orders, and ultimate sales depended on urban merchants. This development has been called a process of *protoindustrialization* because of the importance of new market relationships and sheer manufacturing volume in advance of the technological revolution associated with industrialization. Some societies in the 20th century, still predominantly rural, may be in a somewhat analogous protoindustrial phase, so the concept may have wider applicability.

Population upheaval and the spread of a propertyless class working, where possible, for money wages certainly had a sweeping impact on a variety of behaviors in Western society, including North America. Many villagers began to modify their dress in favor of more urban styles— suggesting an early form of new consumer interest. Among groups with little or no property, the authority of parents began to decline because the traditional threat of denying inheritance now had no meaning. Youthful independence became more marked, and while this showed particularly in economic behavior as many young people now looked for jobs on their own, the new defiance of authority might have had political implications as well.

Sexual behavior changed as the West began, around 1780, to experience something of a sexual revolution particularly among the lower classes in cities and countryside. More young people began to have sex before marriage— resulting, among other things, in a rapid increase in the percentage of illegitimate births, which rose to as much as 10 percent of all births. There were more general signs that sexual expression was becoming more important, at least to young men, who now sought sexual pleasures to compensate for some of the uncertainties of life in other respects. Some women, saddled with unwanted children, may have suffered from this sexual revolution in which they often participated in hope of marriage, but others may have seen sex as a new badge of individual pleasure seeking. Certainly, traditional rules seemed to be changing.

The upheavals triggered by population growth plus the continuing spread of Enlightenment ideas had two more sweeping consequences, both of which became visible during the 1780s. First, the surge of revolutionary protest de-

veloped essentially because new grievances and changing beliefs butted against institutions that were incapable of major change, such as France's lackluster absolute monarchy, and against the inflexibility of many existing leaders who focused on closing off opportunities for people in other social layers. Second, the economic changes involved in protoindustrialization turned to outright economic revolution with a spate of fundamental new inventions developed primarily in Britain.

 ## DECADES OF FERMENT: THE TIDE OF REVOLUTION, 1789–1830

The placid politics of the 18th century was shattered by a series of revolutions that took shape in the 1770s and 1780s. The wave of revolutions reflected the disparity between social and ideological change on the one hand, and business-as-usual politics on the other. It also caught up a large number of social groups with very diverse motives, some eager to use revolution to promote further change, some hoping that the same revolution would allow them to turn back the clock and recover older values.

THE AMERICAN REVOLUTION

The first concrete development occurred when Britain's Atlantic colonies rebelled in 1775 in what was primarily a war for independence rather than a full-fledged revolution. A significant minority of American colonists resisted Britain's attempt to impose new taxes and trade controls on the colonies after 1763. Many settlers also resented restrictions on free movement into the frontier areas. Britain's moves also triggered objections in principle, as colonists invoked British political theory to argue that they should not be taxed without representation. Resentment against British rule and advocacy of national independence and self-government, were supplemented by internal grievances. Crowding along the eastern seaboard led some younger men to seek new opportunities, including political office, that turned them against the older colonial leadership. Growing commerce and money-making antagonized some farmers and artisans, who sought ways to defend older values of greater social equality and community spirit.

Colonial rebels set up a new government that issued the Declaration of Independence in 1776 and also authorized a formal army to pursue its war. The persistence of the revolutionaries (who introduced some tactics such as informal guerrilla-type raids on the more structured British army— tactics that would be developed more fully in 20th-century independence wars) combined with British strategic mistakes and significant aid from the French government designed to embarrass its key enemy. After several years of fighting the United States won its freedom, and in 1787 set up a new constitutional structure based on Enlightenment principles, with checks and balances between the legislature and the executive and formal guarantees of individual liberties. Voting rights, though limited, were widespread, and the new regime was for a time the most radical in the world. Socially, the revolution accomplished less; slavery was untouched in its strongholds. And new American leaders, bent on solidifying their nation, deliberately shunned elaborate contacts with the Old World of Europe. Nevertheless, American success did spur many Europeans to a sense that political upheaval could pay off.

1789

The next step in the revolutionary spiral focused on France. It was the French Revolution that most clearly set in motion the political restructuring of western Europe. Several factors conjoined in the 1780s in what became something of a classic pattern of revolutionary causation. Ideological insistence on change won increasing attention from the mid-18th century onward. Enlightenment thinkers urged the need to limit the powers of the Catholic church, to weaken the hold of the aristocracy—including their tax privileges—and possibly to give new political voice to the common man. They attacked the inefficiency and arbitrary behavior of the monarchy. Social changes reinforced the ideological challenge. Some middle-class people, proud of their business or professional success, wanted a greater political role. Many peasants, pressed by population growth, wanted fuller freedom from landlord exactions, while resenting the large estates directly controlled by aristocrats and the Church. These grievances added up to a social attack on remnants of manorialism and the privileged position of the Church.

At the same time growing commercial activity produced its own discontent. Many peasants were upset by the expansion of a minority of villagers, bent on buying land and dividing village common holdings in the name of market exploitation. Many craftworkers resisted the commercial motives of some artisans, who tried to speed their labor in order to take advantage of sales opportunities. The revolution, in other words, would combine protest by people rising in the market economy, who sought commensurate political voice, with protest by people who were suffering and who sought a return to older values—a "moral economy" in which commercial profit seeking and individualism would be set aside.

Amid the ferment, the government and upper classes proved incapable of reform. Aristocrats indeed tightened their grip in response to their own population pressure, while the government proved increasingly ineffective—a key ingredient in any successful revolution. Finally, a sharp economic slump in 1787 and 1788, triggered by bad harvests, set the seal on revolution.

The French king, Louis XVI, called a meeting of the traditional parliament in order to consider tax reform for his financially pinched regime. But middle-class representatives, inspired by Enlightenment ideals, insisted on turning this assembly (which had not met for 1½ centuries) into a modern parliament, with voting by head rather than by estate and within majority representation for nonnoble property owners. The fearful king caved in after some street riots in Paris in the summer of 1789, and the revolution was underway.

Events in the summer were crucial. The new assembly, with its middle-class majority, quickly turned to devising a new political regime. A stirring Declaration of Rights of Man and the Citizen proclaimed freedom of thought. A popular riot stormed a political prison, the Bastille, on July 14, in what became the Revolution's symbol—though ironically, almost no prisoners were in fact to be found. Soon after this, peasants, stirred by rumors of brigandage, but also correctly afraid that Paris would ignore their needs, seized manorial records and many landed estates. This triggered a general proclamation abolishing manorialism, giving peasants clear title to much land and also establishing equality under the law. While aristocrats survived for some time, the principles of aristocratic rule were undercut.

Amid all this excitement, the French uprising, like most revolutions, went through an initial moderate phase, and in this case (unlike 20th-century revolts where this first phase was typically short-lived) many lasting gains were pushed through. Peasants did not get all the land, but they were free from all traces of serfdom. Not only was aristocratic privilege abolished, but the privileges of the Church were also attacked, and Church property was seized. A new constitution proclaimed individual rights, including freedom of religion, press, and property. A strong parliament was set up to limit the king, with about one-half the adult male population—those with property—eligible to vote.

Here, then, was a sketch of a new political system, with an elected legislature in charge of policy and a constitution limiting arbitrary state action. At the same time, traditional local barriers to government authority—such as aristocratic courts—were torn down, so government officials won greater contact with ordinary citizens.

THE FRENCH REVOLUTION: RADICAL CHORDS AND AUTHORITARIAN CONSOLIDATION

By 1792 the liberal regime began to turn more radical. Initial reforms provoked massive opposition in the name of church and aristocracy, and civil war broke out in several parts of France. Monarchs in Britain, Prussia, and Austria trumpeted their opposition to this revolutionary nightmare, and France soon faced European war as well. The revolutionary leadership was also beleaguered by economic chaos at home, which caused further popular rioting. All these pressures led to a takeover by radical leaders, who wanted to press the Revolution further and to set up firmer authority in the Revolution's defense. The monarchy was abolished and the king was decapitated on the guillotine—a new device introduced, Enlightenment-fashion, to provide more humane executions but instead became a symbol of revolutionary bloodthirst. The radical leadership also attacked enemies at home and abroad. Several thousand people were executed in what was named the Reign of Terror—even though by later standards it was relatively mild.

Besides stiffening the Revolution and becoming a symbol of revolutionary excess, this radical phase introduced a new rhetoric. Its new constitution, never fully put into practice, proclaimed universal adult male suffrage. It discussed mass education and social reform, though it never envisaged an attack on private property. More concretely, the radicals introduced a metric system of weights and measures, the product of the rationalizing genius of the Enlightenment. They also proclaimed universal military conscription, on grounds that now that all citizens were free, they owed loyalty and service to the government that assured their freedom. And revolutionary armies, swelled by new numbers and also new officers who had not been able to rise in the aristocrat-dominated forces of the old regime, began to win major success. Not only were France's enemies driven out, but the revolution began to win new territory in the Low Countries, Italy, and Germany—spreading revolutionary gains still farther in western Europe.

A new spirit of popular nationalism surfaced during the Revolution's radical phase. Many French people felt an active loyalty to the new regime, to a state they believed they

Napoleon's Empire in 1812

helped create. Nationalism could replace older loyalties to church or locality.

Radical leadership was itself toppled in 1795, and after four years of more moderate government the final phase of the Revolution was ushered in with the victory of Napoleon Bonaparte, a leading general who soon converted the revolutionary republic to an authoritarian empire. Under Napoleon parliament was reduced to a rubber stamp, while a powerful police system limited freedom of expression. However, Napoleon confirmed other liberal gains, including religious freedom, while enacting substantial equality—though for men, not women—in a series of new law codes. To train bureaucrats, a centralized system of secondary schools and universities developed.

Goaded by insatiable ambition, Napoleon devoted most of his attention not to consolidation of the Revolution at home, though this was one of his key achievements, but to expansion abroad. A series of wars brought France against all of Europe's major powers, including Russia. At its height around 1812, the French empire directly held or controlled as satellite kingdoms most of western Europe, and its success spurred some reform measures even in Prussia and Russia. The French Empire crumbled after this point. An attempt to invade Russia in 1812 failed miserably, as French armies perished in the cold Russian winter even as they pushed deep into the empire. An alliance system organized by Britain crushed the emperor definitively in 1814 and 1815. Yet Napoleon's campaigns had done more than dominate European diplomacy for 1½ decades. They had also spread key revolutionary legislation—the idea of equality under the law, the attack on privileged institutions such as aristocracy, church, or craft guilds—throughout much of western Europe.

The Revolution and Napoleon encouraged popular nationalism outside of France as well as within. French military success continued to draw great excitement at home. Elsewhere, French armies tore down local governments, as in Italy and Germany, which whetted appetites for national unity. And the sheer fact of French invasion made many people more conscious of loyalty to their own nation; popular resistance to Napoleon, in parts of Spain and Germany, played a role in the final French defeat.

A CONSERVATIVE SETTLEMENT AND THE REVOLUTIONARY LEGACY

The allies who had brought the proud emperor down met at Vienna in 1815 to reach a peace settlement that would make further revolution impossible. They did not try to punish France too sternly, on grounds that the Euro-

pean balance of power should be restored. This act of generosity helped promote peace in Europe for many decades. Still, a series of stronger powers were established around France, which meant gains for Prussia within Germany and for the hitherto obscure nation of Piedmont in northern Italy. Italian and German nationalists were disappointed, but the old map was not restored and the realignments did ultimately facilitate unifications. Britain gained new colonial territories, confirming its lead in the scramble for empire in the wider world. Russia, newly important in European affairs as its own expansionist momentum resumed, confirmed its hold over most of Poland.

These territorial adjustments kept Europe fairly stable for almost half a century, a major achievement given the crisscrossed rivalries that long characterized Western society. But the Vienna negotiators were much less successful in promoting internal peace. The idea was to restore monarchy in France and to link conservative powers in a new war on revolutionary radicalism. A more formal conservative sentiment grew up in reaction to the quarter century of upheaval, urging the importance of king and church and arguing that change should come slowly and gradually, not through protest or rationalistic constitution-making.

The revolutionary era had stirred forces that could not be contained by the Vienna settlement or the conservative alliance formed by Napoleon's opponents. New political movements arose to challenge conservatism. All the forces promoted by the French Revolution, many of them following from Enlightenment political ideas, grew into more formal political movements during the 1820s and 1830s throughout the Western world.

Liberals focused primarily on issues of political structure, as they sought ways to limit state interference in individual life and also representation of propertied people in government. Liberals urged the importance of constitutional rule and protection for freedoms of religion, press, and assembly. They wanted parliaments to represent middle-class voters and check the power of kings. Many liberals also sought economic reforms, including better education that would promote industrial growth.

Radicals accepted the importance of most liberal demands, but they also wanted wider voting rights. Some advocated outright democracy. They also urged some social reforms in the interest of the lower classes. A smaller current of socialism urged an attack on private property in the name of equality and an end to capitalist exploitation of the working man.

Nationalists, finally, though often allied with one of the other "isms" urged the importance of national unity and glory. Nationalists spoke of their nation's liberty, and easily joined the wider liberal current, but they valued a collective identity that could conflict with liberal individualism.

Each of the new political movements gained ground in pressing Europe's established order; each would have a long life in Western political history. The key Western political issues shifted from the development of absolute monarchy to constitutional structure and political participation. While most articulate political agitators were drawn from the middle class and related student groups who sought a new voice for themselves as opposed to continued aristocratic dominance, popular protesters picked up new political demands as well. Many urban artisans in particular, worried about the continued inroads of commercialism on their older values of cooperation and skill and conscious of a growing threat from industrial machines that might unseat the artisans altogether, provided a recurrent force in the streets, matching the ideological leadership offered by the middle class. Artisans had a solid tradition of organization, and they could draw demands from the sense of traditional justice they now saw under attack; they were an ideal revolutionary force.

Revolutions broke out in several places in 1820 and again in 1830. The 1820 revolts involved a nationalist uprising in Greece against Ottoman rule—a key step in gradually dismantling the Ottoman Empire in the Balkans—and a rebellion in Spain. Revolutions in 1830 struck closer to the heart of Western society. The French rebelled again, installing a different king and a somewhat more liberal monarchy, though not producing a final balance among the conflicting ingredients of French politics. Risings also occurred in key states in Italy and Germany, though without durable result; a revolution in Belgium produced a liberal regime and a newly independent nation.

The Belgian Revolution of 1830 was a classic example of how new political forces could combine. Belgium had been placed under Dutch rule at the Congress of Vienna. Belgian nationalists, building on religious and language differences, found national independence an obvious target. Liberals chafed under Dutch restrictions on freedom of the press and teaching. Urban artisans, worried about rapid commercial change as Belgium began to develop factory production, sought new political rights.

Britain and the United States also participated in the process of political change, though without revolution. Key states in the United States granted universal adult male suffrage and other political changes in the 1820s, leading to the election of a popular president, Andrew Jackson, in 1828. In Britain the Reform Bill of 1832, prodded by considerable popular agitation, gave the parliamentary vote to most members of the middle class. This change ushered in a period in which urban governments gained new powers as they came under control of business leaders, while the aristocrats who still controlled the national ministries began to adopt measures that increasingly favored commercial development.

Through the 1830s the tides of revolution and the larger impact of new political movements had produced important changes in Western society. Regimes in France, Britain, Belgium, the United States, and several other countries now had solid parliaments (Congress in the United States), at least some guarantees for individual rights against arbitrary state action, considerable religious freedom not only for various Christian sects but also for Jews, and a voting system ranging from democratic (for men) to upper middle-class. Even more widely, movements representing liberal and other political views had spread throughout Western society, operating as political parties in the liberalized states, as agitators in central Europe. The revolutionary sequence had not ended—a major outburst was still to come in 1848—but it had already begun to interact with the other great Western transformation, the rise of industrialization.

THE INDUSTRIAL REVOLUTION

The essence of the Industrial Revolution was technological change, particularly the application of coal-powered engines (or, later, engines powered by other fossil fuels) to the production process. The new engines replaced people and animals as the key sources of energy in many branches of production. They were joined by new production equipment that could apply power to manufacturing through more automatic processes. Thus spindles were invented that wrapped fiber automatically into thread, and looms mixed thread automatically without direct human intervention. Hammering and rolling devices allowed application of power machinery to metals. And while in early industrialization textile and metallurgical production received primary attention, engines were also used in sugar refining, printing, and other processes.

The British Industrial Revolution resulted from a host of factors, including favorable natural resources and strong capital reserves won from previous trade. Industrialization was fed, also, by the late 18th-century crisis. Population pressure forced innovations at all social levels. Enlightenment beliefs encouraged faith in progress and in human ability to dominate nature. They also sanctioned a devotion to improving material life. Here were motivations for inventing new processes and applying them widely.

At the same time, the Industrial Revolution built on previous trends in Western society, including the large manufacturing sector and the huge advantages in world trade. Earlier commercialization played a role; British aristocrats were unusually tolerant of commerce, which helped center initial changes in the British Isles. Prior development of science set a basis for artisans to widen their efforts at technical innovation. Governments, already committed to policies of economic growth, also supported industrialization by instituting laws encouraging new inventions and new trading and banking systems.

ORIGINS OF INDUSTRIALIZATION, 1770–1840

The key inventions of early industrialization developed in Britain during the 18th century. Automatic machinery in textiles was initially intended for manual use in the domestic system. Then in the 1770s the Scottish artisan James Watt devised a steam engine that could be used for production, and the Industrial Revolution was off and running. Within a decade in Britain, the domestic production of key materials, such as cotton thread, was converted to factory-housed machines, at the expense of thousands of home workers, mostly women. Changes of this sort spurred the creation of new industries, to build machines, and also the rapid expansion of coal mining to fuel the new productive fires.

Additional inventions followed on the heels of the original set, for a key feature of the Industrial Revolution was recurrent technological change. Early machine spindles were expanded, so that a given worker could supervise even vaster output. American inventors devised a production system of interchangeable parts, initially for rifles, that helped standardize and so mechanize the production of machinery itself. Metallurgy advanced by use of coal and coke, instead of charcoal, for smelting and refining, allowing the creation of larger furnaces and greater output.

Technological change was quickly applied to transportation and communication, essential areas now that there were more goods to be moved and more distant markets to contact. The development of the telegraph, steam shipping, and the railway, all early in the 19th century, provided new speed in the movement of information and goods. These inventions were vital in facilitating a new stage in Western penetration of world affairs; they also kept the Industrial Revolution going in the West, by promoting mass-marketing techniques and providing direct orders for rails and other industrial goods.

While technological change lay at the heart of industrialization, several basic economic changes were inherent in the process as well. The Industrial Revolution depended on improvements in agriculture. Industrialization concentrated increasing amounts of manufacturing in cities, where power sources could be brought together with labor. City growth was dizzying during the first decades of industrial-

ization, with sleepy villages—such as Manchester, England—growing to cities of several hundred thousand people. This kind of growth depended on better agricultural production, accomplished through improved equipment and seeds, plus growing use of fertilizers. Better agriculture freed up a growing percentage of the labor force for nonagricultural pursuits, and fairly soon in vigorous industrializers, such as Britain, manufacturing output surpassed that of farming in importance.

Industrialization also meant a factory system. Steam engines had to be concentrated, for their power could not be widely diffused until the later application of electricity. Factory labor separated work from the home—one of the basic human changes inherent in the Industrial Revolution. It also allowed manufacturers to introduce greater specialization of labor and more explicit rules and discipline, which along with the noisy machines permanently changed the nature of human labor.

Industrialization required new amounts of capital, which meant steady improvements in banking, and it required new marketing systems to handle rapidly growing output. Prices of manufactured goods fell because of new technologies that encouraged mass sales. The bigger industrial concerns began to set up nationwide, even with international sales organizations. Shops spread to villages where only occasional peddlers had previously brought in goods—as peasants began to produce more for urban markets, they tended to specialize and, thus, to buy clothing and equipment they once had made themselves. The first department stores opened in Paris in the mid-1830s, another response to the need for sophisticated marketing.

Overall, industrialization also promoted the development of increasingly large firms, though small operations might also benefit for a time from the Industrial Revolution's energy. Through the 19th century, large firms tended to promote more efficient use of engines and equipment, while also amassing needed stores of capital and developing efficient marketing and purchasing arrangements. Industrialization gradually promoted an economic organization that featured concentration, bureaucratic management, and a certain impersonality in directing the labor force.

Once Britain launched industrialization, other Western nations quickly saw the need to imitate. Britain's industrial power helped the nation hold out against Napoleon and led to huge profits for successful businessmen by the early 19th century. Hence both governments and individual entrepreneurs, in places such as Belgium, Germany, or New England, soon rushed to copy. Since most of the general factors that permitted industrialization were present in these areas as well, including population pressure and an ideology of material progress, industrialization proceeded relatively swiftly throughout much of the Western world.

On the European continent, French revolutionary laws helped unleash industrialization by destroying local restrictions on trade, protecting private property, and abolishing artisan guilds that had often tried to defend older production techniques. With guilds and manors destroyed, propertyless workers were commodities, to be used and paid as the market required.

Belgium and France began to industrialize in the 1820s, the United States and Germany followed soon thereafter. Industrialization did not immediately sweep all before it, even in Britain; artisan production actually expanded for a time as cities grew, and rural labor remained vital. But the forms of the Industrial Revolution gained ground steadily once implanted in the West, and factory workers and their managers became evermore important minorities in the general labor force.

THE DISRUPTIONS OF INDUSTRIAL LIFE

The causes of Western industrialization should not mislead us. Even though the phenomenon can be explained through earlier shifts in Western business, outlook, government policy, and labor supply—shifts that also explain why the Industrial Revolution occurred first in the West and often proved difficult to reproduce in other civilizations—the changes involved were massive, and they did not come easily.

The Industrial Revolution involved huge movements of people from countryside to city. Families were disrupted in this process, as young adults proved to be the prime migrants. Cities themselves, poorly equipped to begin with and now crowded beyond all precedent, became hellholes for many new residents. Health conditions worsened in poor districts because of packed housing and inadequate sanitation. Crime increased for a time. New social divisions opened up, as middle-class families sought to move away from the center-city poor, beginning a pattern of suburbanization that continued into the later 20th century.

Work became more unpleasant for many people. Not only was it largely separated from family, the new machines and factory rules compelled a rapid pace and coordination that pulverized traditional values of leisurely, quality production. First in Britain, then elsewhere, groups of workers responded to the new machines by outright attack; for example, Luddite protests, named after a mythical British machine-breaker called Ned Ludd, failed to stop industrialization, but they showed the stress involved. Many business and farm families were also appalled by the noise, dirt, and sheer novelty involved in the Industrial Revolution.

The early Industrial Revolution also forced new constraints on traditions of popular leisure. Factory owners, bent on getting as much work as possible from their labor

Population growth, factory-promoted unemployment, and the growing potency of industrially produced alcoholic drinks helped create a slum life in English cities in the 18th and early 19th centuries.

force to help pay for expensive machines, deliberately reduced recreational aspects of work: They tried to ban singing, napping, drinking, and other customary frivolities on the job. Off the job, new business-led city governments, backed by expanding police forces, attacked popular festivals, animal contests, and gambling in the name of proper discipline and good order. Attempts were made to reduce social drinking as well, but they largely failed in light of workers' insistence on some recreational outlets. Nevertheless, the Industrial Revolution considerably reduced key leisure traditions and community ties, which made the early phases of the experience still more disorienting and grim for many people involved.

Family life changed, and in changing revealed some of the wider stresses of the industrialization process. Middle-class people quickly moved to enhance the redefinition of the family already begun in the early modern centuries: The family for them served as an image of affection and purity. Children and women were to be sheltered from the storms of the new work world. Women, traditionally active partners to merchants, now withdrew from formal jobs. They gained new roles in caring for children and the home, and their moral stature in many ways improved, but their sphere was more radically separate from that of men than had been true before. Children, too, were redefined. The middle class led in seeing education, not work and apprenticeship, as the logical role for children to prepare them for a complex future and, it was hoped, to maintain their innocence until they were prepared to cope with business or professional life.

The working-class family changed as well, though it could not afford all these indulgences. Young children, increasingly unnecessary on the job, were often sent to school. Women worked from adolescence until marriage, when they were often pulled away because of the demands of shopping, home care, and motherhood. Even when on the job, working-class women were more likely to be sent into domestic service in middle-class households than to factories, though there was an important minority of female factory hands. The working class, in sum, developed its own version of separate spheres, in part simply to com-pensate for the new distinction between jobs and home. Family life became more important than ever before, to provide homemaking services but also to offer some hope of emotional satisfaction in a confusing world. Marriages encountered new stresses, but the marriage rate went up fairly steadily.

The changes in family roles and values show how deeply the Industrial Revolution could reach into personal life, particularly for factory workers but also for other groups. The changes were not all bad, and many people found ways to use family satisfactions or community institutions such as neighborhood taverns to help compensate for a loss of power at work. Yet considerable confusion and anxiety remained; even businessmen, actively building the new industrial world, might be fearful of the effects of change. As a leading French industrialist noted, "Progress is not necessarily progressive. If it were not inevitable, it might be better to stop it."

DOCUMENT
WOMEN IN THE INDUSTRIAL REVOLUTION

The West's Industrial Revolution changed the situation of women in many ways. Some of the changes have occurred more recently in other civilizations, others were particularly characteristic of the 19th-century West. Industrialization cut into women's traditional work and protest roles (for example, in spearheading bread riots as attention shifted to work-based strikes), but it tended to expand educational opportunities. Some new work roles and protest outlets, including feminism, developed by 1914. Important changes occurred in the home as well. New ideas and standards at once elevated women's position and set up more demanding tasks. Relations among women were also affected by the growing use of domestic servants (the most common urban job for working-class women) and new attitudes by middle- and lower-class women alike. The first document that follows sketches the idealization of middle-class women; it comes from an American moral tract of 1837, anonymously authored, probably by a man. The second document, written by a woman in an English woman's magazine, shows new household standards of another sort, with a critical tone also common in middle-class literature. Finally, a British housewife discusses her servant problems, reflecting yet another facet of women's lives. How could women decide what their domestic roles were and whether they brought satisfaction or not?

WOMEN AS CIVILIZERS (1837)

As a sister, she soothes the troubled heart, chastens and tempers the wild daring of the hurt mind restless with disappointed pride or fired with ambition. As a mistress, she inspires the nobler sentiment of purer love, and the sober purpose of conquering himself for virtue's sake. As a wife, she consoles him in grief, animates him with hope in despair, restrains him in prosperity, cheers him in poverty and trouble, swells the pulsations of his throbbing breast that beats for honorable distinction, and rewards his toils with the undivided homage of a grateful heart. In the important and endearing character of mother, she watches and directs the various impulses of unfledged genius, instills into the tender and susceptible mind the quickening seeds of virtue, fits us to brave dangers in time of peril, and consecrates to truth and virtue the best affections of our nature.

MOTHERHOOD AS POWER AND BURDEN (1877)

Every woman who has charge of a household should have a practical knowledge of nursing, simple doctoring and physicianing. The professional doctor must be called in for real illness. But the Home

Doctor may do so much to render professional visits very few and far between. And her knowledge will be of infinite value when it is necessary to carry out the doctor's orders. . . .

THE MOTHER BUILDER

It is a curious fact that architects who design and builders who carry out their plans must have a training for this work. But the Mother Builder is supposed to have to know by instinct how to put in each tiny brick which builds up the "human." The result of leaving it to "instinct" is that the child starts out with bad foundations and a jerry-built constitution. . . .

When one considers that one child in every three born dies before the age of five years, it is evident how wide-spread must be the ignorance as to the feeding and care of these little ones. It is a matter of surprise to those who understand the constitution and needs of infants that, considering the conditions under which the large number of them are reared, the mortality is not greater. . . .

THE RISKS BABIES RUN

To begin with, the popular superstition that a young baby must be "hungry" because it lives on milk, and is on this plea the recipient of scraps and bits of vegetables, potato and gravy, crusts, and other heterogeneous articles of diet, has much to answer for. Then, the artistic sense of the mother which leads her to display mottled necks, dimpled arms, and chubby legs, instead of warmly covering these charming portions of baby's anatomy, goes hugely to swell the death-rate. Mistakes in feeding and covering have much to answer for in the high mortality of infants.

THE SERVANT "PROBLEM" (1860)

So we lost Mary, and Peggy reigned in her stead for some six weeks. . . .

But Peggy differed greatly from her predecessor, Mary. She was not clean in her person, and my

mother declared that her presence was not desirable within a few feet. Moreover she had no notion of putting things in their places, but always left all her working materials in the apartment where they were last used. It was not therefore pleasant, when one wanted a sweeping brush, to have to sit down and think which room Peggy had swept the last, and so on with all the paraphernalia for dusting and scrubbing. But this was not the worst. My mother, accustomed to receive almost reverential respect from her old servants, could not endure poor Peggy's familiar ways. . . .

Now, though I am quite willing to acknowledge the mutual obligation which exists between the employer and employed, I do *not* agree with my charwoman that she is the only person who ought to be considered as conferring a favor. I desire to treat her with all kindness, showing every possible regard to her comfort, and I expect from her no more work than I would cheerfully and easily perform in the same time. But when I scrupulously perform my part of the bargain, both as regards food and wages, not to mention much thought and care in order to make things easy for her and which were not in the agreement at all, I think she ought not only to keep faith with me if possible, but to abstain from hinting at the obligation she confers in coming.

It is not pleasant, as my mother says, to beg and pray for the help for which we also pay liberally. But it is worse for my kitchen helper to be continually reminding me that she need not go out unless she likes, and that it was only to oblige me she ever came at all. I do not relish this utter ignoring of her wages, etc., or her being quite deaf because I choose to offer a suggestion as to the propriety of dusting out the corners, or when I mildly hint that I should prefer her doing something in my way. . . .

But if I were to detail all my experiences, I should never have done. I have had many good and willing workers; but few on whose punctuality and regularity I could rely.

Questions: In what ways did industrialization increase differences between women and men in the 19th century West? What were the main changes in women's roles and ideals? How did middle-class and working-class women differ?

INDUSTRIAL REVOLUTION AND POLITICAL REVOLUTION

The strands of political and industrial upheaval, initially somewhat separate, began to intertwine in the West by the 1830s. Both revolutions had of course responded to some of the same changes and crises in Western society. But their courses had not at first overlapped: Industry centered in Britain where politics was relatively stable, while political revolution elsewhere had actually detracted from economic development.

Yet there were important links. In the first place, political revolution helped clear the way for industrialization in places such as France. Revolutionaries did not deliberately plan industrial development, but many of them did hope for a more favorable business climate. By attacking the aristocracy, they increased the prestige of business life. By abolishing manorialism and guilds they created a labor force more open to market activities and freer to move to new work locations. Standardized law codes and more rational systems of measurement also promoted economic change. As in Russia early in the 20th century, the West's era of revolution resulted from the slowness of change at the top and created the conditions for more rapid innovation thereafter.

The early phases of industrialization, in turn, had strong political implications. Groups that benefited from industrial change usually sought a growing voice in government. This was a key pressure behind the British Reform Bill of 1832 that enfranchised the middle classes and gave them a means of representing their own interests in Parliament and in city administrations. A key result was a new tariff system in Britain that reduced protection for agriculture (and by facilitating food imports helped keep wages low). Other groups became more politically active as a slightly less obvious adjustment to industrialization. Lawyers, for example, and in many places also doctors, sought through political life a prestige and income that would help them compensate for the growing wealth and prestige of leading businessmen. Professional groups also pressed governments to provide better training and licensing facilities, in order to reduce competition from "unauthorized" practitioners.

Governments at various levels had to consider the process of industrialization in other respects. All major Western states shifted their economic policies to some extent during the first half of the 19th century. Some were not eager to embrace the Industrial Revolution outright, but all saw the need to sponsor certain activities that would help keep pace with Britain. All Western governments, for example, encouraged railway development; Prussia built many lines directly, while the United States government gave large land grants to promote a national rail system. All governments began to organize technical fairs and to promote engineering and science education. Most governments took an interest in education more generally, on grounds that a more literate work force would be more productive. Thus France, soon after the Revolution of 1830, began to encourage (though not yet require) primary schools throughout the nation, while state governments in the northern United States moved soon thereafter to make education compulsory. Another area that cried out for government attention involved urban conditions. Again by the 1830s, governments began to build new sewer systems, to promote some housing regulation and in general to launch the process of making the new cities minimally habitable. They also developed formal urban police forces, another vital extension of government power.

Important groups in the 19th century argued, in one version of the new liberal movement, that government activities should on balance decline. Many revolutionaries urged that governments should pull out of religious affairs, reduce economic regulation in the interest of promoting free competition, and even let the poor fend for themselves. In fact, only two Western governments actually scaled down their activities in the early 19th century: Britain and Norway. Other governments responded to political and industrial pressures by rebalancing their functions—with a net increase in the government role.

Political and industrial revolution intertwined in one final respect in the first half of the 19th century. Some lower-class groups, already mobilized through an interest in political rights, began to turn to the government as a means of compensating for industrial change and to revolt when the government seemed unresponsive. Artisans and workers in Britain generated a new movement to gain the vote in the 1830s and 1840s; this Chartist movement hoped that a democratic government would regulate new technologies and promote popular education. Artisans in France and Germany increased their revolutionary ardor because of their growing fears of displacement through industrialization. The political mood of the West became more fervent by the 1840s under the twin impact of unfulfilled popular revolutionary demands and the pressures and anxieties promoted by early industrialization.

THE 1848 REVOLUTIONS

The result was a final, extraordinary wave of revolutions in 1848 and 1849. Paris was again the center. In a popular uprising that began in February 1848, the French monarchy was once again expelled, this time for good, and a democratic republic was briefly established. Urban artisans pressed for serious social reform—perhaps some version of socialism and certainly government-supported jobs for the unemployed; groups of women schoolteachers, though fewer in number, agitated for the vote and other rights for women. This revolution, then, started on a more radical basis than had the great uprising of 1789, with a wider array of social demands and a democratic, rather than simply liberal, political platform.

Moreover, revolution quickly spread to other centers. Major revolts occurred in Germany, Austria, and Hungary. Revolutionaries in these areas sought liberal constitutions to modify conservative monarchies; artisans pressed for social reforms that would restrain industrialization; peasants sought a complete end to manorialism. Revolts in central Europe also pressed for nationalist demands, with German nationalists seeking the unity of their country, and various nationalities in Austria-Hungary, including Slavic groups, seeking greater autonomy. A similar liberal-nationalist revolt occurred in various parts of Italy. Significant agitation developed in other parts of western Europe.

The revolutionary fires burned only briefly. Nowhere did revolution win the kind of success the great French Revolution had achieved, partly because significant political changes had already been introduced. The social demands put forth by artisans and some factory workers, either for socialist gains or for a return to older guild structures, were quickly put down; not only conservatives but middle-class liberals opposed these efforts. Nationalist agitation also failed for the moment, as the armies of Austria-Hungary and Prussia restored the status quo to central Europe and Italy. Democracy persisted in France, but a nephew of the great Napoleon soon replaced the liberal republic with an authoritarian empire that lasted until 1870. Peasant demands were met, and serfdom was now fully abolished throughout western Europe. Many peasants, uninterested in other gains, now supported conservative forces.

The substantial failure of the revolutions of 1848 drew the revolutionary era in western Europe to a close. Failure taught many liberals and working-class leaders that revolution was too risky; more gradual methods should be used instead. Improved transportation reduced the chance of food crises, the traditional trigger for revolution in West-

In 1848 crowds, mainly urban artisans, stormed the military arsenal in Berlin during the last great revolution in the industrial West.

ern history. Bad harvests in 1846 and 1847 had driven up food prices and helped promote insurgency in the cities, but famines of this sort did not recur in the West. Many governments also installed better riot control police.

The ongoing social changes brought by industrialization also played a role in ending political revolution in the West. The artisan class, whose sense of organization and older values had been crucial to revolts, began to decline as factory industry continued to gain ground. Artisans did not disappear, but they lost some of their sense of mission. Many began to concentrate on personal advancement, or a solid but moderate craft trade unionism that sought improvements within the system rather than a different system. While many grievances continued on the part of new and old social groups, the belief that political upheaval could stem the tide of industrialization began to fade.

Finally, the experience of decades of recurrent revolution, plus industrialization itself, created new social divisions that made uprisings more difficult. The period of revolution had been predicated on old-style social divisions that pitted commoners against the privileges of the aristocracy, and on other institutions, such as unreconstructed monarchies or established churches that did not give ordinary people a voice. Divisions of interest obviously existed among commoners, depending on wealth or on urban as opposed to rural residence, but there could also be some shared interest in attacking the structures of the old regime. By 1850 an industrial class structure had come to predominate. Earlier revolutionary gains had reduced the legal privileges of the aristocracy, while the rise of business had eroded aristocrats' economic dominance. With industrialization social structure came to rest less on privilege and birth, and more on money. Key divisions by 1850 pitted middle-class property owners against workers of various sorts. The old alliances that had produced the revolutions were now dissolved. New social cleavages would produce important unrest, but not in the classic revolutionary mold. An era of transition had ended. Through intended and unanticipated results of earlier revolutions and the steady gains of an industrial economy, a new society had been created in the West—a society that, somewhat surprisingly, made revolution almost obsolete in the West from 1850 through the later 20th century.

THE CONSOLIDATION OF THE INDUSTRIAL ORDER, 1850–1914

In most respects, the 65 years after 1850 seemed calmer than the frenzied period of political upheaval and initial industrialization. Many people became accustomed to change. City growth continued in the West, and indeed several

countries, starting with Britain, neared the 50 percent mark in urbanization, the first time in human history that more than a minority of a population had lived in cities. But the rate of city growth slowed. Furthermore, city government began to gain ground on the pressing problems growth had created. Sanitation improved, and death rates fell below birthrates for the first time in urban history. Parks, museums, effective regulation of food and housing facilities, more efficient police forces—all added to the safety and the physical and cultural amenities of urban life. Hosts of problems remained, but the horror stories of early industrialization did begin to abate. Revealingly, crime rates began to stabilize or even drop in several industrial areas, a sign of more effective social control but also a more disciplined population.

ADJUSTMENTS TO INDUSTRIAL LIFE

The theme of adjustment and stabilization applied to family life. Illegitimacy rates stopped rising—until 1960—which suggested that some earlier disruption in personal habits was easing. Within families, birthrates began to drop as Western society initiated a substantial *demographic transition* to a new system that promoted fairly stable population levels through a new combination of relatively low birthrates as well as low death rates. Led initially by the middle classes, the low birthrate involved a reassessment of the purposes of children. Children were now seen as a source of emotional satisfaction and considerable parental responsibility, not as contributors to a family economy. This meant that individual children would be highly valued, but the total number would be reduced. Other social groups soon bought into this reassessment, which reflected the progressive disappearance of child labor and promoted the economic well-being of all family members. Family life might still prove difficult, as expectations for improvements in standards of living or for emotional rewards might outpace reality. Merely effecting lower birthrates could be challenging, for while artificial birth control devices began to spread after 1850, they were still unfamiliar and not fully reliable, which meant that many families had to practice new levels of sexual restraint. Nevertheless, some of the starkest pressures did begin to yield in family life, as a result of significant adjustments to new realities.

Material conditions generally improved after 1850. There were important fluctuations; the industrial economy was unstable, and frequent depressions caused falling wages and unemployment. Huge income gaps also continued to divide various social groups. Nevertheless, the general trend was upward. By 1900 probably two-thirds of the

Western population enjoyed conditions above the subsistence level; people could afford a few amenities such as newspapers or family outings, and their diet and housing improved. Health got better. The decades from 1880 to 1920 saw a real revolution in children's health, thanks in part to better hygiene during childbirth and better parental care. Infancy and death separated for the first time in human history: Instead of one-third or more of all children dying by age 10, rates fell to under 10 percent and continued to plummet. Adult health also benefited from better nutrition and improved work safety. Discovery of germs by Louis Pasteur led by the 1880s to more conscientious sanitary regulations and procedures by doctors and other health care specialists; this reduced the deaths of women in childbirth. Women now began to outlive men by a noticeable margin, but men's health also improved.

While material life gained in several measurable respects, the workplace recurrently challenged established habits. Industrial jobs continued to involve a fast pace and severe limitations on worker autonomy. These characteristics worsened after 1850. New machines in textiles and metallurgy sped up work while reducing skill levels. The typical industrial worker was now semiskilled, trained in very limited areas that involved little sense of pride or creativity. New methods of supervision, often pioneered in the United States, involved detailed calculations by efficiency engineers designed to spur output and limit wasted motion. From this base, managers in industries such as automobile production introduced assembly-line procedures early in the 20th century, with workers deliberately reduced to machinelike repetitions.

Yet, as workers suffered under these new conditions—some to the point of severe depression—there were new ways to compensate. Important labor movements took shape among industrial workers by the 1890s, with massive strike movements by miners, metalworkers, and others from the United States to Germany. The new trade-union movement stressed the massed power of workers, and while often defeated by management-government coalitions, it did win some important gains and gave workers some sense of voice and dignity. Furthermore, both within the labor movement and as individuals, many workers learned to react to the new systems of work instrumentally. The instrumentalist reaction urged workers to regard their jobs not as ends in themselves, but as vehicles for other goals. Many workers, as instrumentalists, learned to bargain for better pay and shorter hours, so that less of their lives would be invested in the work process.

The theme of adjustment extended also to the countryside. Many European peasants gained new ability to use market conditions to their own benefit. Some, as in Holland and Denmark, developed cooperatives to market goods and purchase supplies efficiently; here was a sign of new rural organizing ability. Many peasants specialized in new cash crops such as dairy products. Still more widely, peasants began to send their children to school to pick up new knowledge that would facilitate farming operations. The traditional isolation of rural areas began to decline.

Rural conditions lagged behind those in the cities in many ways. European peasants also faced massive competition from the agricultural exports of the United States, Canada, Australia, and Argentina, which began to flood Western markets as ocean shipping improved and refrigeration was introduced in the 1870s. Here, as with urban labor, the theme of successful adjustment should not be exaggerated. Nevertheless, the raw confrontation with new pressures that had characterized important aspects of the transition decades before 1850 did yield to an extent. And in the countryside, as opposed to the cities, the amount of social protest declined as well, once manorialism was fully removed. Some important strikes by rural laborers occurred after 1890, and in the United States an important populist movement pitted many kinds of farmers against railroads and other manifestations of big business, but for the most part the rural world seemed fairly peaceful—and certainly more peaceful than rural populations in many other parts of the globe in the same decades.

The theme of consolidation is an obvious one, after the turmoil of the revolutionary decades. Vital changes continued—new technologies, the new work systems, new agricultural competition—but they were no longer startling to a population accustomed to the basic framework of industrial society. Adjustments by ordinary people, such as the radically new levels of birth control or the idea of instrumentalism, fed into consolidation as well: People were not being totally manipulated by forces beyond their control. Did adjustment mean that people were more contented than they had been when industrialization was new? Measuring contentment is always difficult, and certainly important expressions of grievance continued in Western society. The development of new expressions of social stress was a final feature of the decades after 1850 in the West.

POLITICAL TRENDS

The consolidation theme clearly applies to Western politics after the failures of the revolutions of 1848. Quite simply, issues that had dominated the Western political agenda for many decades were largely resolved within a generation. The great debates about fundamental constitutions and government structure, which had emerged first in the 17th century with the rise of absolutism and new political theory and then raged during the decades of revolution, at last grew quiet.

Many Western leaders worked to reduce the need for political revolution after 1850. Liberals decided that revolution was too risky and became more willing to compromise. Key conservatives strove to develop a new political consensus that would save elements of the old regime, including power for the landed aristocracy and the monarchy, but, through reform, would not engender resistance down the line. Conservatives realized that they could allow parliaments with limited powers, appeal to workers through limited social reforms, and even extend the vote without necessarily losing power. A British conservative leader, Benjamin Disraeli, thus in 1867 took the initiative of granting the vote to working-class males. Count Camillo di Cavour, in the Italian state of Piedmont, began even earlier to support industrial development and extend the powers of Parliament in order to please liberal forces. In Prussia a new prime minister, Otto von Bismarck, similarly began to work with a parliament and extend the vote to all adult males (though grouping them in wealth categories that protected the country from full democracy). These developments fell short of full liberal demands, in that parliaments did not have basic control over the appointment of ministries, but many groups gained some effective political voice. Other Prussian reforms granted freedom to Jews, extended (without guaranteeing) rights to the press, and promoted mass education. The gap between liberal and conservative regimes narrowed in the West, though it remained significant.

The new conservatives also began to use the force of nationalism to win support for the existing social order. Previously, nationalism had been a radical force, challenging established arrangements in the name of new loyalties. Many liberals continued to defend nationalist causes. Now, however, conservative politicians learned how to wrap themselves in the flag, often promoting an active foreign policy in the interests of promoting domestic calm. Thus British conservatives became champions of expanding the empire, while in the United States by the 1890s the Republican party became increasingly identified with imperialist causes.

The most important new uses of nationalism within the West occurred in Italy and Germany. Cavour, after wooing liberal support, formed an alliance with France that enabled him to attack Austrian control of northern Italian provinces in 1858. The war set in motion a nationalist rebellion in other parts of the peninsula that allowed Cavour to unite most of Italy under the Piedmontese king. This led to a reduction of the political power of the Catholic pope, already an opponent of liberal and nationalist ideas—an important part of the general reduction of Church power in Western politics.

Following Cavour's example, Bismarck in Prussia staged a series of wars in the 1860s that expanded Prussian power in Germany. A final war, against France, led to outright German unity in 1871. The new German Empire boasted a national parliament with a lower house based on uni-

The Unifications of Italy and Germany

versal male suffrage and an upper house that favored conservative state governments. This kind of compromise, plus the dizzying joy of nationalist success, won support for the new regime from most liberals and many conservatives.

Other key political issues were resolved around the same time. The United States fought its bloody Civil War—the first war based extensively on industrial weaponry and transport systems, carefully watched by European military observers—between 1861 and 1865. The war resolved by force the simmering dispute over sectional rights between the North and South in the new nation, and also brought an end to slavery. France, after its defeat by Germany in 1870, overthrew its short-lived echo of the Napoleonic Empire and established a conservative republic—with votes for all adult men, a reduction of Church power, and expansion of education, but no major social reform or tampering with existing property relationships. Just as a conservative Bismarck could be selectively radical, so France proved that liberals could be very cautious.

With these changes, the war between conservatives and liberals yielded to petty skirmishes and sniper attacks. The big issues that divided the two groups were gone. Virtually the entire West now had a parliamentary system, usually a democracy of some sort, in which religious and other freedoms were widely protected. In this system, liberal and conservative ministries could alternate without major changes of internal policy. Indeed, Italy developed a process called *transformismo*, or transformism, in which parliamentary deputies, no matter what platforms they professed, were transformed once in Rome to a single-minded pursuit of political office and support of the status quo.

THE SOCIAL QUESTION AND NEW GOVERNMENT FUNCTIONS

The decline of basic constitutional disputes by the 1870s had two further results: It opened the way for a new set of political issues in the West, and it promoted the fuller development of an industrial-style state. At the same time the unifications of Italy and particularly of Germany had major impact on the diplomacy of western Europe. Germany, once unified, was immediately a dominant European power, with a rapidly expanding industrial base. Its ascendancy, plus the sheer addition of major diplomatic actors on the European stage, inevitably unsettled international relations among the Western states. Here, too, was an agenda item of growing importance after 1870, following many decades in which major diplomatic issues had been downplayed in favor of concentration on internal economic development and political challenge.

Government functions and personnel expanded rapidly throughout the Western world after 1870. All Western governments introduced civil service examinations to test applicants on the basis of talent, rather than on connections or birth alone—thus unwittingly imitating Chinese innovations over a thousand years before. With a growing bureaucracy and improved recruitment, governments began to extend their regulatory apparatus—inspecting factory safety, the health of prostitutes, hospital conditions, and even—through the introduction of passports and border controls—personal travel.

Schooling expanded, becoming generally compulsory up to age 12. Many American states by 1900 began also to require high school education, and most Western nations expanded their public secondary school systems. Here was a huge addition to the ways governments and individuals interacted. The new school systems promoted literacy, long gaining ground in the West and now becoming virtually universal; by 1900, 90 to 95 percent of all adults in western Europe and the United States could read. They promoted numerical skills and other job-related aptitudes. They also encouraged certain social agendas. Girls were carefully taught about the importance of home and women's moral mission; domestic science programs were designed to promote better nutrition and hygiene. Boys and girls alike were taught the advantages of medical science over other health measures, and in general, governments played a major role in promoting the use of doctors. Schools also carefully propounded nationalism, teaching the superiority of the nation's language and history as well as attacking minority or immigrant cultures.

Governments also began to introduce wider welfare measures, again replacing or supplementing traditional groups such as churches and families. Bismarck was a pioneer in this area too in the 1880s, as he sought to wean German workers from their attraction to socialism. His tactic failed, as socialism steadily advanced, but his measures had lasting importance. German social insurance began to provide assistance in cases of accident, illness, and old age. Soon some measures to aid the unemployed were also added, initially in Britain. These early welfare programs were small and their utility limited, but they sketched a major extension of government power.

The growth of government obviously required new financing. Western governments benefited from the advancing prosperity brought by industrialization. They also introduced personal income taxes by 1900, here too starting small but gradually expanding the take.

The industrial-style government widely introduced by Western nations at the end of the 19th century had considerably more contact with ordinary people than any Western government had ever before maintained. It also sought active loyalty, not mere calm. It began to take over many functions previously performed by families and communities, in part because these institutions had weakened or changed under the impact of industrialization.

Accompanying the quiet revolution in government functions was a realignment of the political spectrum in the Western world during the later 19th century that involved the replacement of constitutional issues by social issues— what people of the time called "the social question"—as the key criteria for political partisanship. Socialist and feminist movements surged to the political fore, placing liberals as well as conservatives in a new, though by no means unsuccessful, defensive posture.

The rise of socialism depended above all on the power of grievance of the working class, with allies from other groups. It also reflected a major redefinition of political theory accomplished, from 1848 through the 1860s, by one of the leading intellectuals of the century in the West, Karl Marx. Early socialist doctrine, from the Enlightenment through 1848, had focused on human perfectibility: Set up a few exemplary communities, where work and rewards would be shared, and the evils of capitalism would end as people exercised their rational judgment to choose the better way. Marx's socialism was tough-minded, and he blasted earlier theorists as giddy utopians. Marx saw socialism as the final phase of an inexorable march of history, which could be studied dispassionately and scientifically. History for Marx was shaped by the available means of production and who controlled those means—an obvious reflection of the looming role of technology in the industrial world forming at that time. Class struggle always pitted a group out of power with the group controlling the means of production; hence, in the era just passed, the middle class had battled the feudal aristocracy. Now the middle class had won; it dominated production and, through this, the state and culture as well. But it had created a new class enemy, the propertyless worker proletariat, that would grow until revolution became inevitable. Then, after a transitional period in which proletarian dictatorship would clean up the remnants of the bourgeois social order, full freedom would be achieved. People would benefit justly from their work, as essential equality would prevail, and the state would wither away; the historic class struggle would at last end because classes would be eliminated.

Marx's vision was a powerful one. It clearly identified capitalist evil. It told workers that their low wages were exploitative and unjust. It urged the need for violent action but also assured that revolution was part of the inexorable tides of history. Victory was assured, and the result would be heaven on earth—ultimately, an Enlightenment-like vision of progress.

Marx's message also came at a good time. Earlier socialist movements had withered in the collapse of the revolutions of 1848, partly because they seemed so impractical and partly because of government crackdowns on radical leaders. By the 1860s, when working-class activity began to revive, Marxist doctrine provided encouragement and structure. Marx himself continued to concentrate on ideological development and purity, but leaders in many countries translated his doctrine into practical political parties.

Germany led the way. As Bismarck extended the vote, socialist leaders in the 1860s and 1870s were the first to understand the implications of mass electioneering. Socialist movements were always strong in the provision of grassroots organization, available to constituents not only in election periods; they provided fiery speakers who courted popular support instead of appealing, as many liberals and conservatives did, on the basis of their elevated social station and the respect it deserved. By the 1880s socialists in Germany were cutting into liberal support, and by 1900 the party was the largest single political force in the nation. Socialist parties in Austria, France, and elsewhere followed a roughly similar course, everywhere emerging as a strong minority force. Only in Britain and particularly the United States did socialism lag somewhat, in part because workers already had the habit of looking to liberal movements as their political expression. In Britain, too, socialism became a significant third force by 1914.

The rise of socialism terrified many people in Western society, who took the revolutionary message literally. In combination with major industrial strikes and unionization, it was possible to see social issues portending outright social war. But socialism itself was not unchanging. As socialist parties gained strength, they often allied with other groups to achieve more moderate reforms, and in the main they became firm supporters of parliamentary democracy. A movement called *revisionism* arose, which argued that Marx's revolutionary vision was wrong—it needed revising—because industrial workers were not becoming a full majority and because success could be achieved by peaceful, gradual means. Revisionism was denounced by many socialist leaders, but in fact most behaved in revisionist fashion, putting their energies into building electoral victories rather than plotting violent revolution. Western socialism, in other words, while it reflected bitter grievances and class divisions as against a mood of consolidation and adjustment, worked to a great extent within the democratic political system.

Socialism was not the only challenge to the existing order. By 1900 powerful feminist movements arose, which sought various legal and economic gains for women, such

Agitating for the vote after 1900, militant "suffragettes" blocked public ways in England, provoking many confrontations with police.

as equal access to professions and higher education as well as the right to vote. Feminism won support particularly from middle-class women, who argued that the very moral superiority granted to women in the home should be translated into political voice. Many middle-class women also chafed against the confines of their domestic roles, particularly as family size declined. A small but important group of women entered the professions directly, challenging ideas of inherent male superiority; a still-larger number became teachers and nurses, increasingly dominating semiprofessions that gave women both a new work role, at least before marriage, and a new sense that their opportunities were unjustly limited. In several countries feminism combined with socialism, but in Britain, the United States, Australia, and Scandinavia a separate feminist current arose that petitioned widely and even conducted acts of violence in order to win the vote. Here, too, was a major threat to political adjustment, but here too was a threat that might be managed. Several American states and Scandinavian countries extended the vote to women by 1914, in a pattern that would spread to Britain, Germany, and the whole United States after 1918.

The politics of Western society remained lively, with new forces jostling older interests and assumptions. Outside of formal policy—for example, in some new cultural currents—tensions were even more pronounced, as against the mood of complacency—of confidence in industrial and political progress—that remained widespread around 1900.

POPULAR CULTURE AND HIGH CULTURE

Key developments in popular culture differentiated Western society after 1850 from the decades of initial industrialization. Better wages and the reduction of work hours gave ordinary people new flexibility to express themselves. Changes in social and economic structure also opened new doors. Alongside the working class grew a large white-collar labor force of secretaries, clerks, and salespeople, who serviced the growing bureaucracies of big business and the state. These people, some of them women workers, adopted many middle-class values, but they also insisted on interesting consumption and leisure opportunities. The middle class itself, freed from the work burdens of early industrialization, became more open, though with reservations, to the idea that pleasure could be legitimate.

Furthermore, the economy demanded change. Factories could now spew out goods in such quantity that popular consumption had to be encouraged simply to keep pace with production. Widespread advertising developed to promote a sense of need where none had before existed. Product crazes emerged. The bicycle fad of the 1880s, in which middle-class families flocked to purchase the new machine, was the first of many consumer fads in modern Western history. Bicycles were expensive; they altered previous social habits, as women needed less cumbersome garments and young couples could outpedal any potential chaperon during courtship; and people just had to have them. With consumerism spreading, becoming indeed a basic ingredient of the economy, older hesitations about pleasure seeking declined.

Mass leisure culture began to emerge. Popular newspapers, with bold headlines and compelling human-interest stories, won millions of subscribers in the industrial West. They featured shock and entertainment, more than appeals to reason or political principle. Crime, imperialist exploits, sports, and even comics became the items of the day. Popular theater soared. Comedy routines and musical reviews drew thousands of patrons to music halls; after 1900 some of these entertainment themes dominated the new medium of motion pictures. Vacation trips became increasingly common, and seaside resorts grew more and more to the level of big business.

Leisure outlets of these sorts were designed for fun. They appealed to impulse and escapism. Leisure was now a commodity to be enjoyed regularly, rather than through periodic festivals as in traditional society. With work increasingly disciplined, leisure was seen by many not as a chance for restraint and self-improvement, as the middle class still sometimes tried to insist, but as release.

The rise of team sports readily expressed the complexities of the late 19th century leisure revolution. Here was another Western-wide development, though one that soon had international impact. Soccer, football, and baseball all surged into new prominence, at both amateur and professional levels. These new sports reflected industrial life. Though based on traditional games, they were organized with rules and umpires. They taught the virtues of coordination and discipline, and could be viewed as useful preparation for work or military life. They were suitably commercial: Sports equipment, based on the ability to mass-produce rubber balls, and professional teams and stadia quickly became major businesses. But sports also expressed impulse and violence. They expressed irrational community loyalties and even, as Olympic Games were reintroduced in 1892, nationalist passions.

Overall, new leisure interests suggested a complex set of attitudes on the part of ordinary people in Western society. They demonstrated growing secularism. Religion still counted for something among some groups, but religious practice had declined markedly as people looked increasingly for worldly entertainments and gave allegiance to secular faiths such as nationalism or socialism or simply the growing prestige of science. Many people would have agreed that progress was possible on this earth, through rational planning and individual self-control. Yet mass leisure also suggested a more impulsive side to popular outlook, one bent on display of passion or at least, as spectators, vicarious participation in emotional release.

SCIENCE AND ART

A similar dualism, though a more formal one, developed in intellectual life in the West, with roots going back to the early 19th century. On the one hand, science continued to gain ground; on the other hand, a bewildering array of intellectual movements attempted to provide alternate views of reality and a less structured approach to human understanding. There were some common basic themes. The size of the intellectual and artistic community in the West expanded steadily, with rising prosperity and advancing educational levels. A growing audience existed for various intellectual and artistic products, making it more possible than ever before to hope to earn a living through painting or writing or scientific research. The bulk of the new activity was resolutely secular. Though new churches were built as cities grew, and missionary activity reached new heights outside the Western world, the churches no longer served as centers for the most creative intellectual life.

A major portion of Western cultural activity built on the traditions of rationalism that had been firmed up by the Enlightenment. Major political theories, such as liberalism,

Middle class and working class excursionists made trips to the seaside popular before costumes fully adjusted, as can be seen in this scene from Yarmouth, England.

assumed that people were basically rational and improvable, and that human society could be grasped through investigation of fundamental social laws. Thus liberals urged the importance of education and freedom of inquiry, while also urging that economic activity, for example, could be grasped through basic operations of supply and demand. Karl Marx, though arguing that large historical forces dominated individual action, also urged rational investigation, claiming that his revolutionary society would place rational human nature and benevolence in full command at last.

Continuing advances in science kept alive the rationalist tradition. Universities and other research establishments increasingly applied science to practical affairs, linking science and technology in the popular mind under a general aura of progress. Improvements in medical pathology and the germ theory linked science and medicine, though no breakthrough therapies as yet resulted. Science was applied to agriculture, with Germany and then the United States in the lead, through studies of seed yields and chemical fertilizers.

The great advance in theoretical science came in biology, with the evolutionary theory of Charles Darwin (whose major work was published in 1859). On the basis of careful observation, Darwin argued that all living species had evolved into their present form through the ability to adapt in a struggle for survival. Biological development could be scientifically understood as a process taking place over time, with some animal and plant species disappearing and others evolving from earlier forms. Darwin's ideas clashed with traditional beliefs that God had fashioned humankind as part of initial creation, and the resultant debate further weakened the intellectual hold of religion. Darwin's advance also created a more complex picture of nature than Newton's simple physical laws had suggested. Nature now worked through random struggle, and people were seen as animals with large brains, not as supremely rational. The theory of evolution confirmed the link between science and advancement of knowledge, and Darwin's theory was in fact compatible with a continued belief in progress.

Developments in physics continued as well, with work on electromagnetic behavior and then, around 1900, increasing knowledge of the behavior of the atom and its major components. New theories arose, based on complex mathematics, to explain the behavior of planetary motion and the movement of electrical particles, where Newtonian laws seemed too simple. After 1900 Albert Einstein's theory of relativity formalized this new work by adding time as a factor in physical measurement. Again, science seemed to be steadily advancing in its grasp of the physical universe, though it was also important to note that its complexity now surpassed the grasp even of educated laypeople.

The social sciences also continued to advance, on the basis of observation, experiment, and rationalist theorizing. Great efforts went into compilations of statistical data concerning populations, economic patterns, and health conditions. Sheer empirical knowledge about human affairs had never been more extensive. At the level of theory, leading economists tried to explain business cycles and the causes of poverty, while social psychologists studied the behavior of crowds. Toward the end of the 19th century the Viennese physician Sigmund Freud began to develop his theories of the workings of the human unconscious, arguing that much behavior is determined by impulses but that emotional problems can be relieved if they are brought into the light of rational discussion. Social scientists were thus complicating the traditional Enlightenment view of human nature by studying the animal impulses and unconscious strivings of human beings. Still, they continued to rely on standard scientific methods in their work, believing that human behavior can be described in rational categories; most social scientists asserted that ultimately human reason would pre-

Romantic painters delighted in evocative scenes and a mysterious Gothic presence, as depicted by Joseph Turner in "Tinturn Abbey."

vail. Social scientists claimed that personal and social problems alike could be reduced through knowledge and logical planning, and indeed the role of social science experts in advising governments and even individual families increased steadily.

Yet there was a second approach in the Western culture that developed in the 19th century. This approach emphasized artistic values and often glorified the irrational. To be sure, many novelists, such as Charles Dickens in England, bent their efforts toward realistic portrayals of human problems, believing that they could inform as well as improve the world around them. Many painters built on the discoveries of science, using knowledge of optics and color. Nevertheless, the central artistic vision, beginning with *romanticism* in the first half of the century, held that emotion and impression, not reason and generalization, were the keys to the mysteries of human experience and nature. Artists sought to portray intense passions, even madness, not calm reflection. Romantic novelists wanted to move readers to tears, not philosophical debate; painters sought empathy with the beauties of nature or the storm-tossed tragedy of shipwreck, not structured portrayal. Romantics and their successors after 1850 also deliberately endeavored to violate traditional Western artistic standards. Poetry did not have to rhyme; drama did not necessarily need plot; painting

could be evocative, not literal (for literal portrayals, painters could now argue, use a camera). Each generation of artists proved more defiant than the last. By 1900 painters and sculptors were becoming increasingly abstract, while musical composers worked with atonal scales that defied long-established conventions. Some artists talked of an art for art's sake—arguing essentially that art had its own purposes, regardless of the larger society around it.

The development of modern artistic styles brought constant innovation into literature and art. This linked art to other facets of Western society where change and novelty were the name of the game, but it distressed many people who hoped art would confirm traditional values. After 1900 the new styles began to have an international influence, but they also pulled into the Western experience stylistic lessons from African and East Asian art, newly accessible as a result of growing cultural links.

Within the West itself, the split between rationalists and nonrationalists assured continued debate about the nature of truth. The debate had institutional implications: Most scientists and social scientists by 1900 worked in or around growing research universities, whereas artists often had no set institutional apparatus. Scientists were viewed as bastions of progress, as an essential part of industrial society, whereas artists might be seen as dangerous experimenters

Impressionists sought to escape literal representation, in favor of visual impressions of natural settings. This painting, *On the Seine at Bennecourt*, was completed by Claude Monet (1868) as the experimental style was getting underway.

or immoral vagabonds. Despite the imbalance, the modern art impulse continued to expand, which meant that many creative Westerners required a vision different from that of the established order and that elements of a wider public also wanted an outlet that would express some of the confusion of modern life and the human personality.

At neither the formal nor the popular levels, then, did Western culture produce a clear synthesis in the 19th century. New discipline and rationalism warred with impulse, even evocations of violence. The earlier certainties of Christianity or even the Enlightenment gave way to greater debate. The debate could be vigorous, and it seemed to reflect different facets of the industrial experience in the West; but some observers worried that it also expressed tensions that could become dangerous, between different kinds of observers or between different facets of the same modern mind. Perhaps the Western world was not put together quite so neatly as the adjustments and consolidations after 1850 might suggest.

ANALYSIS
THE UNITED STATES IN WORLD HISTORY

World history surveys often have some problems in integrating the United States, after some coverage of colonial origins as part of Western explorations and trade. World history already offers a full menu. American students always take some separate United States history courses. So why not simplify life and leave the United States out of world surveys?

This approach gains added support from the fact that until the late 19th century the United States, relatively isolated save for the arrival of immigrants, was not particularly important in the larger stream of world history. American preoccupation lay in internal development, including westward expansion. This brought clashes with Mexico, an important foretaste of the rebalancing in power between the United States and Latin America. Westward expansion also brought some posturing against European nations tempted to interfere in the Western hemisphere. The Monroe Doctrine (1820) warned against meddling in Latin America. In fact it was British policy and naval power that kept the hemisphere largely free from new colonialism.

The United States counted for little in world diplomacy. The nation's population, though growing, was small. Its economy, though developing, exported little until the great surge of agricultural exports followed by an industrial output.

flow in the 1870s and 1880s. The United States was a debtor nation, depending on loans from European banks for much of its development until 1914. The nation did play an important role in receiving European immigrants, just as it earlier had affected African history through its role in the slave trade. And the nation symbolized, especially to some Europeans, a land of freedom and prosperity; revolutionaries in 1848, for example, invoked American institutions, just as Latin American independence fighters had done around 1820. But while the United States depended on world currents of immigration, loans, and culture, it had yet to contribute much in detail.

By the end of the 19th century the tentativeness and isolation of the United States in world affairs, though they still affected American perceptions in promoting a belief that the nation could be shielded from international involvements, had really passed. American agriculture poured goods into the markets of Europe. American industry was rising, along with that of Germany, to the top of world output rankings. The United States had clearly become, along with western Europe, part of the dominant economic core in world trade. American naval power led to the acquisition of important colonies in Asia and the West Indies. As it gained in international impact, the United States, while retaining some of its earlier image as a revolutionary new nation, became increasingly similar to major west European powers in defending existing world power alignments.

Since the international importance of the United States did grow, leaving the nation out of world history until the late 19th century risks missing significant early patterns. But building United States history in, even after 1870, raises some conceptual as well as practical problems.

There is a legitimate historical question about whether to treat the United States as a separate civilization (along perhaps with Canada and other places that mixed dominant Western settlement with frontier conditions). Latin America, because of the peculiarities of its colonial experience, its ongoing position in the world economy, and above all its blending of European, Indian, and African influences, cannot be subsumed as part of an expanding Western civilization. Does the same hold true for the United States?

Because the United States is so often treated separately in history courses there is a ready assumption of American uniqueness. The United States had purer diplomatic motives than did western Europe—look at the idealism of Woodrow Wilson. It had its own cultural movements, such as the religious "great awakening" of the 18th century or transcendentalism in the 19th. The United States had the unique experience of wave after wave of immigrants reaching its shores, contributing great cultural diversity but also promoting considerable cultural and social integration under the banners of "Americanization." Many of these assumptions of uniqueness are mere reflexes, not supported by serious comparative study. There is, however, a more careful school of historians who argue for American *exceptionalism*—that is, the United States as its own civilization, not part of larger Western patterns. American exceptionalism need not contend that the United States was immune from contact with western Europe, which would be ridiculous, but it argues that this contact was incidental to the larger development of the United States on its own terms.

American exceptionalists can point to a number of factors that caused the development of a separate United States civilization. The Atlantic colonies gained political and cultural characteristics in relative isolation—they were, among other things, unusually democratic (among white males) compared to Europe at the time. Though colonial immigrants often intended to duplicate European styles of life, the vastness and wealth of the new land quickly forced changes. As a result American families gave greater voice to women and children, abundant land created a class of independent farmers rather than a traditionalist peasantry with its tight-knit villages. Even after the colonial era, distinctive institutions, created by the successful revolution and its federal Constitution, would continue to shape a political life different from that of western Europe. The frontier, which lasted until the 1890s and had cultural impact even beyond that date, would continue to make Americans unusually mobile and restless, while draining off some of the social grievances that arose in western Europe.

Distinctive causes, furthermore, produced distinctive results. There is no question that the United States, into the 20th century, had a different agricultural setup from that of western Europe. American politics—with the huge exception of the Civil War—emphasized relatively small disagreements between two major political parties, with third party movements typically pulled into the mainstream rather quickly. There was less political fragmentation and extremism than in western Europe, and more stability (some would add boredom). No strong socialist movement took shape. Religion was more important in American than in European life by the later 19th century. Religion served immigrants as a badge of identity and helped all Americans, building a new society, retain some sense of moorings. The absence of established churches in the United States kept religion out of politics, in contrast to Europe where churches got caught up in more general attacks on the political establishment.

The American exceptionalist argument often appeals particularly to things Americans like to believe about themselves—more religious, less socialistic, full of the

competence that came from taming a frontier—but it must embrace some less savory distinctiveness as well. The existence of slavery, and then the racist attitudes and institutions that arose following its abolition, created ongoing issues in American life that had no direct counterpart in western Europe. Europe, correspondingly, had less direct contact with African culture; jazz was one of the key products of this aspect of American life.

The exceptionalist argument is powerful, particularly because Americans (and Europeans) are normally schooled to think of the United States history as a largely separate line of development. Yet from a world history standpoint, the United States must be seen also, and perhaps primarily, as an offshoot of Western civilization. The colonial experience showed the powerful impact of Western political ideas, culture, and even family styles. American history in the 19th century followed patterns common in western Europe. The development of parliamentary life and the spread of democracy, though unusually early in the United States, fits a larger Western trajectory. American industrialization was a direct offshoot of Europe and followed a basically common dynamic. American intellectuals kept in close contact with European developments, and there were few purely American styles. Conditions for women and wider patterns of family life, in areas such as birth control or disciplining children, were similar on both sides of the North Atlantic, which shows that the United States not only imitated western Europe but paralleled it.

In some important cases, because the United States was freer from peasant and aristocratic traditions, it pioneered developments that would soon surface in western Europe. This was true to an extent in politics; it was true in the development of mass consumer culture and mass media (for example, the popular press and popular films). In these areas the United States can be seen, not as distinctive to the point of forming a separate civilization, but as anticipating some developments that would become common in Western civilization in part because of American example.

American exceptions remain—the Civil War and racial issues, the absence of serious socialism (but not of trade unionism and bitter labor strife, quite similar to West European patterns), and the importance of religion. American distinctiveness remains in another respect: The United States was rising to world power just as key European nations, notably Britain, began to decline. The trajectory of American history is somewhat different from that of western Europe, and the 20th century revealed growing American ability to play power politics in western Europe itself. Just as American exceptionalists must admit special Western influences, so those who argue the United States as part of the West must work in special features and dynamics.

While the shared Western experience provides the most accurate framework, given not only mutual influence but so many common impulses, the main point is to analyze American history in careful comparative terms as part of removing the nation's history from the isolation in which it is so often taught and viewed.

There is, finally, one other vantage point, not definitive but suggestive, that uses the world history framework in the form of analogy. The United States here is Rome compared to West Europe's Greece. Like classical Greece, western Europe produced the basic cultural creativity of the civilization and its first expansion (the Atlantic of course replaced the Mediterranean). Like Greece, western Europe could never really unite, and its empires were fragile as a result. Like Rome, the United States went through a republican period in considerable isolation, full of stern virtue and the strengths of a solid farming community. It initially feared Western culture as corrupting. But as the United States gained power, like Rome, its initial political and social institutions gave way to a more powerful state, larger armies, and huge corporations (the equivalent of Rome's great estates). American power, like Roman, soon eclipsed the power of the civilization's source. Yet the United States never matched Europe's cultural creativity; its strength lay in highways, stadia, organizational ability, and brash self-confidence. Here, then, in analogy, is a restatement of American participation in Western history, but also of a distinctive American role. Is the analogy useful? Does it suggest the same last chapter: an American collapse that will affect the whole of Western civilization save perhaps for a "third Rome" somewhere else?

Questions: Which argument has the greater strength in describing 19th century history, the United States as a separate civilization, or the United States as part of the West? Have the United States and western Europe become more or less similar in the 20th century? Why?   ❧

❧ THE EXPANSION OF THE WEST AND WESTERN DIPLOMACY

The Industrial Revolution, plus related improvements in bureaucratic organizing ability and science, prompted a major expansion of the West's power in the world. Western nations could pour out far more processed goods than before, which meant that they needed new markets. They also required new raw materials and agricultural products, which spurred the development of more commercial agri-

culture in places such as Africa and Latin America. The West's dominance in the world economy was greatly enhanced, and more areas of the world were brought into some kind of dependent relationship to it. The vast ships and communications networks created by industrial technology merely spurred the intensification of the Western-led world economy, while bringing additional profits back to Europe in the form of banking fees and merchant commissions.

Industrialization also extended the West's military advantage in the wider world. Steamships could navigate previously impassable river systems, bringing Western guns inland as never before. Invention of the repeating rifle and machine gun gave small bands of Western troops immense superiority over masses of local troops. These new means combined with new motives: European nations rivaled for new colonies as part of their nationalistic competition, businessmen sought new chances for profit, and missionaries sought opportunities for conversion. Haltingly before 1860, then rapidly, Europe's empires spread through Africa and Southeast Asia, plus parts of China and the Middle East.

Western dominance did not mean absolute sovereignty, and world history still had to be written in terms of the staying power of key civilizations even as they interacted with Western values. The working out of the West's imperialist century, then, must be treated not as part of Western history but as part of the civilizations affected.

NEW EUROPEAN SETTLEMENTS

In several areas, because of sparse previous settlement, Western expansion in the 19th century meant an extension of Western society itself, and not primarily a new cultural interchange. Already Britain's colonies on the Atlantic coast of North America had established an identifiable Western culture amid important new influences resulting from new interracial contacts and the frontier experience. During most of the 19th century the westward expansion of the new United States brought the American version of Western society across a whole continent. Early in the century Jefferson's purchase of Louisiana had opened a frontier across the Mississippi, and subsequent settlement plus war with Mexico had pushed the new nation to the Pacific coast.

At the same time, Canada, Australia, and New Zealand also filled with immigrants from Europe and established parliamentary legislatures and vigorous commercial economies that placed them in the general dynamic of Western civilization. Like the United States, these new nations looked primarily to Europe for cultural styles and intellec-

19th-Century Settlement and Consolidation in the United States, Canada, Australia, and New Zealand

tual leadership. They also followed common Western patterns in such areas as family life, the valuation of women, and the extension of mass education and culture. Unlike the United States, however, these nations remained part of the British Empire, though with growing autonomy.

Canada, won by Britain in wars with France in the 18th century, had been preserved from the contagion of the American Revolution. Religious differences between French Catholic settlers and British rulers and settlers troubled the area recurrently, and a number of uprisings occurred early in the 19th century. Determined not to lose this colony as it had lost the United States, the British began in 1839 to grant increasing self-rule. Canada set up its own Parliament and laws, while remaining attached to the larger empire. Initially this system applied primarily to the province of Ontario, but other provinces were included, creating a federal system that describes Canada to this day. French hostilities were eased somewhat by the creation of a separate province, Quebec, where the majority of French speakers were located. Massive railroad building, beginning in the 1850s, brought settlement to western territories and a great expansion of mining and commercial agriculture in the vast plains. As in the United States to the south, new immigrants from southern and particularly eastern Europe poured in during the last decades of the century, attracted by Canada's growing commercial development and spurring further gains.

Britain's Australian colonies originated in 1788 when a ship deposited convicts to establish a penal settlement at Sydney. Australia's only previous inhabitants had been a hunting-and-gathering people called the aborigines, and they were in no position to resist European settlement and exploration. By 1840 Australia had 140,000 European in-

habitants, based mainly on a prosperous sheep-growing agriculture that provided needed wool for British industries. Exportation of convicts ceased in 1853, by which time most settlers were free immigrants. Discovery of gold in 1851 spurred further pioneering, leading to a population of over a million by 1861. As in Canada, major provinces were granted self-government with a multiparty parliamentary system. A unified federal nation was proclaimed on the first day of the 20th century. By this time considerable industrialization, a growing socialist party, and significant welfare legislation had occurred.

Finally, New Zealand, discovered by the Dutch in the 17th century and explored by the English in 1770, began to receive British attention after 1814. Here the Polynesian hunting-and-gathering people, the Maoris, were well organized politically. Missionary efforts converted many of them to Christianity between 1814 and the 1840s. The British government, fearful of French interest in the area, moved to take official control in 1840, and considerable European immigration followed. New Zealand settlers relied heavily on agriculture (including sheep growing), selling initially to Australia's booming gold-rush population and then to Britain. Wars with the Maoris plagued the 1860s, but after the Maori defeat, generally good relations were established, with Maoris winning some representation in Parliament. As in Canada and Australia, a parliamentary system was created that allowed the new nation to rule itself as a dominion of the British Empire, without interference from the mother country.

Like the United States, Canada, New Zealand, and Australia each had distinct national flavors and national issues. These new countries were far more dependent on the European, particularly the British, economy than was the

United States. Industrialization did not overshadow commercial agriculture and mining, even in Australia, so that exchanges with Europe remained unusually important. Nevertheless, despite their distinctive features, these countries followed basic patterns of Western civilization from this point onward, from political forms to key leisure activities. Currents of liberalism, socialism, modern art, and scientific education that described Western civilization to 1900 and beyond, thus largely characterized these important new extensions.

It was these areas, finally, along with the United States and part of Latin America, particularly Brazil and Argentina, that received new waves of European emigrants during the 19th century. Though Europe's population growth rate slowed after 1800, it still advanced rapidly on the basis of previous gains—that is, as more children reached adulthood and had children of their own. Europe's expansion was in fact greater than Asia's in percentage terms, with both continents relying heavily on the use of foodstuffs initially discovered in the New World, and Europe's export of people helped explain how Western societies could take shape in such distant areas.

The extension of Western society through most of North America as well as Australia and New Zealand depended on the fortuitous absence of large previous populations, compounded by the continued ravages of Western-imported diseases on the people who were present. Other parts of the world, more thickly inhabited, had quite different experiences under the impact of Western influence and some outright settlement. The spread of the West also reflected the new power of Western industrialization. Huge areas could now be settled quickly thanks to steamships and rails, while remaining in close contact with the Western home base in Europe. The expansion of the West revealed the power of Western values and institutions, as colonists deliberately introduced most of the patterns that had prevailed in Europe, from parliaments to Western-defined standards for women and children.

As a new century dawned in 1900, newspapers throughout the Western world—the new segments as well as the old—trumpeted the progress that had occurred during the past century and the bright prospects for the future. They noted the rise of mass education, improvements in material standards and health care, and the assurance of political freedoms and representation—the list seemed endless. Not all Westerners shared this rosy vision. Many workers as well as many women judged that progress had passed them by, though some expected to join the parade in the near future. Adjustments to industrial society had produced a noisy confidence on the part of many groups in the West.

The same confidence showed in the facile implantation of essentially Western societies in other key parts of the world.

DIPLOMATIC TENSIONS

Western expansion had its limits, however, and these limits were beginning to tell on the Western heartland by 1900. The rise of new parts of the Western world, particularly the growing strength and assertiveness of the United States, added to the sense of national competition. Along with Germany's new-found muscle, American presence on the world diplomatic scene made rivalries for empire and trade more intense.

More important still at this point was the fact that by 1900 there were few parts of the world available for Western seizure. Latin America was independent but under extensive United States influence, so that a new intrusion of colonialism was impossible. Africa was almost entirely carved up. The few final colonies taken after 1900—Morocco by France and Tripoli (Libya) by Italy—caused great diplomatic furor on the part of other colonial powers worried about the balance of force on that continent. China and the Middle East were technically independent, but were in fact crisscrossed by rivalries among the Western powers and Russia (and in China's case, Japan). No agreement was possible on further takeovers.

Yet for several decades the growth of empire had served as a vital outlet for Western diplomatic and military energies. The tensions among the Western nation-states had escalated dangerously after the unifications of Italy and Germany. Bismarck, the architect of German unity, cleverly devised an alliance system during the 1870s and 1880s that neutralized France, a "natural enemy" that feared the growing power of the German neighbor and resented the loss of territories after the war in 1870–1871. Germany allied directly with Austria and Italy, and had had a separate understanding with Russia. This intricate alliance system was in fact preserved by the interest key nations took in overseas expansion. France worried less about the rivalry with Germany than about gaining new colonies in Africa and Indochina, while Germany itself entered the imperialist game by seizures in Africa and East Asia. Britain remained primarily preoccupied with colonial expansion.

Imperialist expansion, however, fed the sense of rivalry among key nation-states. Britain, in particular, grew worried about Germany's overseas drive, supplemented after 1890 by the construction of a large navy. Economic competition between a surging Germany and a lagging Britain added fuel to the fire. France, eager to escape the Bismarck-engineered isolation, was willing to play down traditional rivalries with Britain. The French also took the opportunity to ally with Russia, when after 1890 Germany dropped this particular alliance because of Russian-Austrian enmity.

By 1907 most major European nations were paired off in two alliance systems: Germany, Austria-Hungary, and Italy formed the Triple Alliance, while Britain, Russia, and France constituted the newer Triple Entente. Three against three seemed fair, but in fact Germany grew increasingly concerned about facing potential enemies both to the east (Russia) and west (France). All the powers steadily built up their military arsenals in what turned out to be the first of several arms races in the 20th century. All

powers save Britain had instituted peacetime military conscription, to provide large armies and even larger trained reserves. Artillery levels and naval forces built steadily—the addition of a new kind of battleship, the Dreadnaught, to naval arsenals was a key escalation—while discussions about reducing armament levels got nowhere.

Each alliance system, furthermore, was dependent on an unstable partner. Russia suffered a revolution in 1905, and its allies worried that any further diplomatic setbacks might paralyze the eastern giant. Austria-Hungary was plagued by nationalities disputes, particularly by minority Slavic groups; German leaders fretted that a diplomatic setback might bring chaos. Both Austria and Russia were heavily involved, finally, in maneuverings in the Balkans—the final piece in what became a nightmare puzzle.

The arms race began around 1900. The massive "Dreadnought" battleship of 1911 was developed in Britain but provoked German buildup in response.

Small Balkan nations had won independence from the Ottoman Empire during the 19th century; as Turkish power declined, local nationalism rose, and Russian support for its Slavic neighbors paid off. But the nations were intensely hostile to each other. Furthermore, Balkan nationalism threatened Austria, which had a large southern Slav population. Russia and Austria nearly came to blows on several occasions over Balkan issues, for Austria felt that it must keep the Slavs in line while Russia looked to the Balkans as a place where it might pick up needed diplomatic prestige. Then in 1912 and 1913 the Balkan nations engaged in two internal wars, which led to territorial gains for several states but satisfied no one. Serbia, particularly, which bordered Austria to the south, had hoped for greater stakes. At the same time Austria grew nervous over the gains Serbia had achieved. In 1914 a Serbian nationalist assassinated an Austrian archduke on behalf of Serbian claims. Austria vowed to punish Serbia. Russia rushed to the defense of her little Slavic brother and mobilized its troops against Austria. Germany, worried about Austria and also eager to be able to strike against France before Russia's cumbersome mobilization was complete, called up her reserves, and then declared war on August 1. Britain hesitated briefly, then joined its allies. World War I had begun, and with it came a host of new problems for Western society.

CONCLUSION

DIPLOMACY AND SOCIETY

The tensions that spiraled into major war are not easy to explain. Diplomatic maneuverings can seem quite remote from the central concerns of most people, if only because key decisions—for example, with whom to ally—are made by a specialist elite. Even as the West became more democratic, few ordinary people placed foreign affairs high on their election agendas.

The West had long been characterized by political divisions and rivalries. This was, by comparison with some other civilizations, an endemic weakness of the Western political system. In a sense, what happened by the late 19th century was that the nation-state system got out of hand, encouraged by the absence of serious challenge from any other civilizations. The details of this development, involving the rise of Germany and the new tensions in the Balkans, are obviously important, but the link with a longer-term Western problem area should not be forgotten.

At the same time, the diplomatic escalation also had some links with the strains of Western society under the impact of industrialization. Obviously the fact that modern war proved so horrible, as had already been suggested in the American Civil War, stemmed directly from the destructive power of modern factory-produced weaponry, from massive new guns and ships to steady improvements in the explosive power of chemical combinations. The causes of war, also, related to industrial patterns.

Most obviously, established leadership in the West continued to worry about social protest and the growing visibility of the masses. Leaders tended as a result to seek diplomatic successes in order to distract. This procedure worked nicely for a few decades when imperialist gains came easily. But then it proved a straitjacket: German officials around 1914, fearful of the power of the socialists, wondered if war would not aid national unity, while British leaders, beset by feminist as well as labor unrest, failed to think through their own diplomatic options. Leaders also depended on military buildups for economic purposes. Modern industry, pressed to sell the soaring output of its factories, found naval purchases and army equipment a vital supplement.

The masses themselves had some role to play. Though some groups, particularly in the socialist camp, were hostile to the alliance system and to imperialism, many workers and clerks found the diplomatic successes of their nations exciting. In an increasingly disciplined and organized society, with work frequently routine if not downright boring, the idea of violence and energy, even of war, could find appeal. Mass newspapers that fanned nationalist pride with stories of conquest and tales of the evils of rival nations, helped shape this belligerent popular culture.

The consolidation of industrial society in the West, in other words, had continued to generate strain at various levels. Consolidation meant more powerful armies and governments, a more potent industrial machine. It also meant continued social frictions and an ongoing tug of war between rational restraint and a desire to break out, to dare something wild.

Thus it was that, just a few years after celebrating a century of material progress and relative peace, ordinary Europeans went to war almost gaily in 1914. Troops departed for the front convinced that war would be exciting with quick victories, their departure hailed by enthusiastic civilians who draped their trains with flowers. Four years later almost everyone would have agreed that war had been unmitigated hell. The complexities of industrial society were such, however, that war's advent seemed almost a welcome breath of the unexpected, a chance to get away from the disciplined stability of everyday life.

FURTHER READINGS

Two excellent studies survey Europe's industrial revolution: Sidney Pollard's *Peaceful Conquest: The Industrialization of Europe* (1981) and David Landes's *The Unbound Prometheus: Technological Change and Industrial Development in Western Europe from 1700 to the Present* (1969). See also Phyllis Dean's *The First Industrial Revolution* (1980), on Britain. On the demographic experience, see Thomas McKeown's *The Modern Rise of Population* (1977).

For the French Revolution and political upheaval, O. Connelly's *French Revolution—Napoleonic Era* (1979) is a useful introduction. Lynn Hunt's *Politics, Culture and Class in the French Revolution* (1984) is an important recent study. Other revolutionary currents are treated in George Rudé's *The Crowd in History: Popular Disturbances in France and England* (1981) and Peter Stearns's *1848: The Revolutionary Tide in Europe* (1974).

Major developments concerning women and the family are covered in Louise Tilly and Joan Scott's *Women, Work and Family* (1978) and Steven Mintz and Susan Kellogg's *Domestic Revolutions: A Social History of American Family Life* (1989). See also R. Evans's *The Feminists: Women's Emancipation in Europe, America and Australia* (1979). An important age group is treated in John Gillisk's *Youth and History* (1981).

For an overview on social change, see Peter Stearns and Herrick Chapman's *European Society in Upheaval* (1991). On labor history, see Michael Hanagan's *The Logic of Solidarity* (1981) and Albert Lindemann's *History of European Socialism* (1983). Eugen Weber's *Peasants into Frenchmen: The Modernization of Rural France* (1976) and Harvey Graff, ed., *Literacy and Social Development in the West* (1982) deal with important special topics.

On political and cultural history, see Gordon Wright's *France in Modern Times* (1981), Gordon Craig's *Germany, 1866–1945* (1978), and Louis Snyder's *Roots of German Nationalism* (1978). J. H. Randall's *The Making of the Modern Mind* (1976) is a useful survey; see also O. Chadwick's *The Secularization of the European Mind in the Nineteenth Century* (1976). On major diplomatic developments, see D. K. Fieldhouse's *Economics and Empire, 1830–1914* (1970) and David Kaiser's *Politics and War: European Conflict from Philip II to Hitler* (1990).

1661 British port-trading center founded at Bombay

1620s Sultan of Mataram's
attacks on Batavia fail

1690 Calcutta established at center of British activities in Bengal

1619 Dutch establish trading post at Batavia in Java

1707 Death of Mughal
emperor, Aurangzeb; beginning of imperial breakdown

1652 First Dutch settlement in
South Africa at Cape Town

1740–1748 War of Aus-
trian Succession; global
British-French struggle
for colonial dominance

1756–1763 Seven Years' War,
British-French global warfare

1757 Battle of Plassey; British
dominant power in Bengal

1739 Nadir Shah's invasion of India from Persia

1750s Civil war and division of Mataram;
Dutch become the paramount power on Java

1775–1782 War for independence by American colonists;
another British-French struggle for global preeminence

1786–1790
Cornwallis's
political re-
forms in India

1769–1770 Great Famine in Bengal

A.D. 1600   A.D. 1700   A.D. 1750

30

Industrialization and Imperialism: The Making of the European Global Order

INTRODUCTION. The process of industrialization that began to transform western European societies in the last half of the 18th century fundamentally altered the nature and impact of European overseas expansion. In the centuries of expansion before the industrial era, the Europeans went overseas because they sought material things they could not produce themselves and because they were threatened by powerful external enemies. They initially sought precious metals for which they traded in Africa and waged wars of conquest to control in the Americas. In the Americas they also seized land on which they could grow high-priced commercial crops such as sugar and coffee. In Asia, European traders and adventurers sought either manufactured goods, such as cotton and silk textiles (produced mainly in India, China, and the Middle East), or luxury items, such as spices, that would improve the living standards of the aristocracy and rising middle classes.

In the Americas, Africa, and Asia missionaries from Roman Catholic areas, such as Spain and Portugal, sought to convert what were regarded as "heathen" peoples to Christianity. Both the wealth gained from products brought home from overseas and the souls won for Christ were viewed as ways of strengthening Christian Europe in its long struggle with Muslim empires that threatened Europe from the south and east. Only on the eve of Columbus's voyage in 1492 were the Muslims driven from Spain into North Africa; and the Ottoman Empire remained a formidable foe of the European powers throughout the first two centuries of overseas expansion.

1790–1815 Wars of the Revolution and Napoleonic era

1835 Decision to give state support for English education in India; English adopted as the language of Indian law courts

c. 1879–1890s Partition of West Africa

1867 Diamonds discovered in the Orange Free State

1914 Outbreak of World War I

1899–1902 Anglo-Boer War in South Africa

1853 First railway line constructed in India

1815 British annex Cape Town and surrounding area

1857 Calcutta, Madras, and Bombay universities founded

1879 Zulu victory over British at Isandhlwana; defeat at Rourke's Drift

1858 British Parliament assumes control over India from the East India Company

1798 Napoleon's invasion of Egypt

1885 Indian National Congress Party founded in India; gold discovered in the Transvaal

1850s Boer republics established in the Orange Free State and Transvaal

1882 British invasion of Egypt

1830 Start of the Boers' Great Trek in South Africa

1869 Opening of the Suez Canal

1890s Partition of East Africa

1898 British-French crisis over Fashoda in the Sudan

1857–58 "Mutiny" or Great Rebellion in north India

In the industrial era, from roughly 1800 onward, the things that Europeans sought in the outside world as well as the source of the insecurities that drove them there changed dramatically. Raw materials—metals, vegetable oils, dyes, cotton, and hemp—needed to feed the machines of Europe, not spices or manufactured goods, were the main products the Europeans sought overseas. Industrialization made Europe for the first time the manufacturing center of the world, and overseas markets for machine-made European products became a key concern of those who pushed for colonial expansion. Christian missionaries, by then as likely to be Protestant as Roman Catholic, still sought to win converts overseas. But unlike the rulers of Portugal and Spain in the early centuries of expansion, European leaders in the industrial age rarely took initiatives overseas to promote Christian proselytization. In part this reflected the fact that western Europe itself was no longer seriously threatened by the Muslims or any other non-European people. The fears that fueled European imperialist expansion in the industrial age arose from internal rivalries between the European powers. Overseas peoples might resist the European advance, but the Europeans feared each other far more than even the largest non-European empires.

The contrast between European expansion in the preindustrial era and in the age of industrialization was also reflected in the extent to which the Europeans were able to sail to overseas areas, go ashore, and move inland. In the early centuries of overseas expansion, European conquests were concentrated in the Americas, whose long isolation left their peoples particularly vulnerable to the technology and diseases of the expansive Europeans (see Chapter 25). In much of the rest of the world (see Chapters 23, 26, and 28), European traders and conquistadores were confined largely to the sea-lanes, islands, and coastal enclaves. Now, industrial technology and techniques of organization and discipline associated with the increasing mechanization of the West gave the Europeans the capacity to reach and infiltrate any foreign land. From the populous, highly centralized, and technologically sophisticated Chinese Empire to small bands of hunters and gatherers struggling to survive in the harsh environment of Tierra del Fuego on the southern coast of South America, few peoples were remote enough to be out of reach of the steamships and railways that carried the Europeans to and across all continents of the globe. No culture was strong enough to remain untouched by the European drive for global dominance in this era, and none could long resist the profound changes unleashed by European conquest and colonization.

The shift from the preindustrial to the industrial phase of European overseas expansion was gradual and cumulative, extending roughly from 1750 to 1850. By the middle decades of the 19th century, few who were attuned to international events could doubt that a watershed had been crossed. The first section of this chapter will explore the initial stages of this momentous transformation. It will trace the advance of the Dutch inland on Java and the rise in India of what can be seen as the first empire of the industrial era. The middle sections of this chapter will be devoted to the forces in Europe and the outside world that led to the great burst of imperialist expansion, which was a dominant feature of global history in the last decades of the 19th century. The final sections will explore the patterns of European conquest and rule that persisted from earlier colonization efforts as well as the innovations that were dictated by the ambitions and aspirations of the European and American champions of the "new" imperialism. Special attention will be given to some of the key consequences of European domination for the societies and cultures of the colonized peoples of Africa and Asia.

THE SHIFT TO LAND EMPIRES IN ASIA

Though we usually use the term "partition" to refer to the European division of Africa at the end of the 19th century, the Western powers had actually been carving up the globe into colonial enclaves for centuries. In the early going, this process was haphazard and often quite contrary to the interests and designs of those in charge of European enterprises overseas. The "Directors," for example, who ran the Dutch and English East India Companies (which were granted monopolies of the trade between their respective countries and "the East" in the 17th and 18th centuries), had little interest in territorial acquisitions. In fact, they were actively opposed to involvement in the political rivalries of the Asian princes. Wars were expensive, and direct administration of African or Asian possessions was even more so. Both cut deeply into the profits gained through participation in the Asian trading system, and profits not empires were the chief concern of the Dutch or English Directors.

Whatever policies company Directors may have instructed their agents in Africa and Asia to follow, these men-on-the-spot were inevitably drawn into local power struggles. They had, after all, to defend their forts, warehouses, and occasionally their ships from the attacks of local lords who resented their competition or laid claim to the land that the Europeans occupied. Though the company Directors had to learn to write off these political entanglements as part of the overhead of their trading empires, they continued to resist initiatives by their overseas agents that would involve them in governing large numbers of Asians or Africans. But before the Industrial Revolution produced the telegraph and other methods of rapid com-

European Colonial Territories, before and after 1800

munication, company Directors or prime ministers in Europe had very little control over those who actually ran their trading empires. In the 18th century a letter took months to reach Calcutta from London; the reply took many more months. Thus, commanders in the field had a great deal of leeway. They could and did conquer whole provinces or kingdoms before home officials even learned that their armies were on the move. Thus, the land empires the European powers began to build were very much the product of initiatives by men-on-the-spot, often acting against the wishes and belated orders of their superiors in Europe.

PROTOTYPE: THE DUTCH ADVANCE ON JAVA

One of the earliest empires to be built in this fashion was that pieced together in the late 17th and 18th centuries by the Dutch in Java, the most populous of the chain of hundreds of islands that today makes up the country of Indonesia. In the early years after the Dutch established their Asian headquarters at Batavia on the northwest coast of the island in 1619, it was a struggle just to survive. After beating back major attacks against Batavia launched in the late 1620s by Sultan Agung—the ruler of the kingdom of

The great pride that 17th-century Dutch took in their overseas commerce and trading empire is evident in this portrait of a Dutch East India Company official and his wife—accompanied by a Western attired Javanese servant and large, Javenese-style umbrella—pointing to the fort and harbor of Batavia (present-day Jakarta) in Java.

Mataram, which controlled most of the Javanese interior—the Dutch were content to become the vassals of Mataram and pay an annual tribute. In the following decades, the Dutch concentrated on gaining monopoly control over the spices produced on the smaller islands of the Indonesian archipelago to the east. In the 1670s, however, an attempt by one of the vassals of the ruler of Mataram to seize the throne embroiled the Dutch in Javanese politics. Content with the security they had gained as a tributary of the Mataram sultans, the Dutch backed the threatened sultan and, when he was driven from his palace and died, his young son. In return for their support, the Dutch were ceded the Preanger territories south of Batavia in 1677.

This episode was the first of a long series of Dutch interventions in the wars of succession between the princes of Mataram. Dutch armies mainly comprised troops recruited from the island peoples of the eastern archipelago, who were led by Dutch commanders. Their superior organization and discipline, even more than their firearms, made the Dutch a potent ally of whichever prince was able to win them to his side. But the price the Javanese rulers paid was very high. Each succession dispute and Dutch intervention led to more and more land being ceded to the increasingly land-hungry Europeans. By the mid-18th century, the sultans of Mataram controlled only the south central portions of Java. A failed attempt by Sultan Mangkubumi to restore Mataram's control over the Dutch in the 1750s ended with a Dutch-dictated division of the kingdom that signified Dutch paramountcy over the entire island. Thus, just about the time the British were beginning to build a land empire in India, the Dutch had completed the capture of Java, which would be the heart of their Asian empire for the next 200 years.

PIVOT OF WORLD EMPIRE: THE RISE OF THE BRITISH RAJ IN INDIA

In many ways, the rise of the British as a land power in India resembled the Dutch capture of Java. The directors of the English East India Company were as hostile as the Dutch financiers to territorial expansion. But British agents of the company in India were repeatedly drawn into local wars, and all the more so as the great Mughal Empire disintegrated from the middle decades of the 18th century. In their wars of conquest, the British, adopting a practice pioneered by the French, relied heavily on Indian troops, called *sepoys*, recruited from peoples throughout the subcontinent. As had been the case in Java, Indian princes long regarded the British as allies that they could use *and* control to crush Indian rivals or put down usurpers who sought to seize their thrones. As had happened in Java, the European pawns gradually emerged as first a serious rival to the established Indian rulers and eventually the paramount power in the continent.

Partly because the struggle for India came later in time, there were also important differences between the patterns of colonial conquest in India and Java as well as the global repercussions of each. In contrast to the Dutch march in-

The Stages of Dutch Expansion in Java

land, which resulted largely from responses to local threats and opportunities, the rise of the British Raj in India owed much to the fierce global rivalry between the British and the French. In the 18th century the British and French found themselves on opposite sides in five major wars. These struggles were global in a very real sense. On land and sea, the two old adversaries not only fought in Europe, but they also squared off in the Caribbean where each had valuable plantation colonies, in North America, and on the coasts and bays of the Indian Ocean. With the exception of the American War of Independence (1775–1782), these struggles ended in British victories. The British loss of the American colonies in that ill-fated effort was more than offset by earlier victories in the Caribbean and especially in India, which gradually gave the British control of the entire South Asian subcontinent.

Though the first victories of the British over the French and the Indian princes came in the south in the late 1740s, their rise as a major land power in Asia hinged on victories won in Bengal to the northeast. The key battle at Plassey in 1757, in which fewer than 3000 British troops and Indian sepoys defeated an Indian army of nearly 50,000, is traditionally pictured as a heroic triumph of a handful of brave and disciplined Europeans over a horde of ill-trained and poorly led Asians. The battle pitted the *Nawab* Sirāj-ud-daula, who was then the ruler of Bengal, against Robert Clive, the architect of the British victory in the south. The

prize was control of the fertile and populous kingdom of Bengal. The real reasons for Clive's famed victory, however, tell us a good deal more about the process of empire building in Asia and Africa than this white-hero-in-the-tropics cliché.

The numbers on each side and maneuvers on the field tell us little about a battle that was in a sense over before it had begun. Clive's well-paid Indian spies had given him detailed accounts of the divisions in Sirāj-ud-daula's ranks in the months before the battle. With money provided by Hindu bankers who were anxious to get back at the Muslim prince for unpaid debts and for confiscating their treasure on a number of occasions, Clive proceeded to buy off the Nawab's chief general and several of his key allies. Even the Nawab's leading spy was on Clive's payroll, which somewhat offset the fact that the main British spy had been bribed by Sirāj-ud-daula. The backing Clive received from the Indian bankers also meant that his troops were well paid, while those of the Nawab were not. Thus, when the understandably uneasy ruler of Bengal rode into battle on June 23, 1757, his fate had already been sealed. Though the troops under the French and one Indian commander fought well, the Nawab's major Indian allies defected to the British or remained stationary on his flanks when the two sides were locked in combat. These defections more or less wiped out the Nawab's numerical advantage, and Clive's skillful leadership and the superiority of his artillery did the rest. The British victors had once again foiled their French rivals, and they soon took over

Indian soldiers, or *sepoys*, made up a large portion of the rank-and-file troops in the armies of British India. Commanded by European officers, and armed, uniformed, and drilled according to European standards, troops like those pictured here were recruited from the colonized peoples and became one of the mainstays of all European colonial regimes.

The Growth of the British Empire in India, from the 1750s to 1858

the direct administration of the sizeable Bengal-Bihar region. The foundations of Britain's Indian and global empire had been laid.

THE CONSOLIDATION OF BRITISH RULE

In the decades after Plassey, the British officials of the East India Company repeatedly went to war with Indian princes whose kingdoms bordered on the company's growing possessions, or, like the Dutch on Java, they became involved in succession disputes and ended up controlling the kingdoms being contested. All of these pulls grew stronger and stronger as the Mughal Empire broke down in the last decades of the century. In its ruins, regional Indian princes fought incessantly to defend or expand their territories at the expense of their neighbors. Involvement in these conflicts or assaults on war-weakened Indian kingdoms allowed the British to advance steadily inland from their three trading towns on the Indian coast—Madras, Bombay, and Calcutta. These cities became the administrative centers of the three Presidencies that eventually made up the bulk of the territory they ruled directly in India. In many areas, the British were content to leave defeated or allied Indian princes on their thrones and to control their kingdoms through agents stationed at the rulers' courts. By

the time the British government took over direct control of India from the expiring East India Company in 1858, these "Princely States" made up over one-third of the British Indian Empire.

The British conquest of the Indian subcontinent was not completed until the 1850s. Thus, in the early industrial era the British took a century to colonize an area that was considerably smaller than the continent of Africa—an area that the more fully industrialized European powers would carve up in a matter of decades in the late 19th century. It is fashionable to downplay the role of industrialization in Britain's conquest of India. But there is little question that British armies, both those made up of soldiers recruited in Europe and those consisting of Indian sepoys, gained great advantage from modes of organization and bodily discipline promoted by industrialization. By the early 19th century, their more reliable field guns and the uniformity of their hand weapons also reflected advances in European metallurgy and machine tooling that their Indian adversaries were unable to match.

In attempting to prevent the conquest of their kingdoms by these forces, the princes of India, like those before them in Java, were handicapped in a number of critical ways. Because there was no India or sense of Indian national identity, it was impossible to appeal to the defense of the homeland or the need for unity to drive out the foreigners. Indian princes continued to fear and fight with each other despite the ever growing power of the British Raj. Old grudges and hatreds ran deeper than the new threat of the British, and there was a sense that the British would someday just go away. Many ordinary Indians were eager to serve in the British regiments, which had better weapons, brighter uniforms, and higher and more regular pay than all but a handful of the armies of the Indian rulers. The British were equally eager to recruit these volunteers, especially those drawn from Indian peoples whom the British deemed especially warlike, such as the Gurkhas of Nepal and the Sikhs of the Punjab. By the mid-19th century, Indian soldiers in the pay of the British outnumbered British officers and enlisted men in India by almost five to one.

From the first decades of the 19th century, India was clearly the pivot of the great empire being built by Britain on a global scale. Older colonies with large numbers of white settlers, such as Canada and Australia, contributed more space to the total square miles of empire the British were so fond of calculating, but India had by far the largest share of colonized peoples. Britain's largest and most powerful land forces were the armies recruited from the Indian peoples, and these were rapidly becoming the policemen of the entire British Indian Empire. In the middle of the 19th century, Indian soldiers were sent to punish the Chinese and Afghans, conquer Burma and Malaya, and begin the conquest of South and East Africa.

Indian ports were essential to British sea power east of the Cape of Good Hope, and the famous gunboats, which were a key instrument of British diplomacy in the 19th century, were more likely to sail from Bombay and Calcutta than from the British Isles. As the century progressed, India became the major outlet for British overseas investments and manufactured goods as well as a major source of key raw materials. India was the envy of the French and the Germans, and the acknowledged symbol of Britain's global empire, the largest that any people had ever built.

EARLY COLONIAL SOCIETY IN INDIA AND JAVA

Though they slowly emerged as the political masters of Java and India, the Dutch and British were at first content to leave the social systems of the peoples they now ruled pretty much as they had found them. The small numbers of European traders and company officials who actually lived in the colonies for any length of time simply formed a new class atop the social hierarchies that already existed

in Java and different parts of India. Beneath them the aristocratic classes and often the old ruling families were preserved and left in charge of the day-to-day administration at all but the top levels. In most cases, European backing actually strengthened the control of the Javanese and Indian lords and middlemen over the peasantry, which continued to make up nearly 90 percent of the population in each area. Though Dutch monopolies and attacks by the sultans of Mataram on the northern coastal towns had decimated the Javanese trading classes, Chinese and Chinese-Javanese mestizo (mixed race) merchants soon emerged to take their place and increasingly allied themselves with the Dutch overlords. As we have seen, in India the links between East India Company officials and traders and Indian merchants and bankers were even more highly developed. Indian merchants and middlemen also recruited and controlled the handicraft laborers who produced the cotton textiles that remained the Company's chief export from India.

In order to survive in the hot tropical environments of South and Southeast Asia, the Dutch and English were forced to accommodate themselves to the ancient and sophisticated host cultures of their Asian colonies. After establishing themselves at Batavia, for example, the Dutch initially sought to create a little Holland in Java. They built high, close-packed houses overlooking canals, just like those they had left behind in Amsterdam and Rotterdam. But they soon discovered that the canals were splendid breeding grounds for insects and microbes that (though the Europeans did not make the connection until somewhat later) carried debilitating or lethal diseases like dysentery, malaria, and typhoid. By the late 17th century, the prosperous merchants and officials of Batavia had begun to move away from the unhealthy center of the city to villas in the suburbs, which were set in gardens and separated by rice paddies and palm groves. The tall houses of the inner city gave way to low, sprawling dwellings with many open spaces to catch the tropical breezes as well as long porches with overhanging roofs to block the heat and glare of the sun. Similar dwellings, from which we get our term *bungalow*, came into fashion in India in the 18th century.

Europeans living in the tropical colonies also adopted, to varying degrees, the dress, eating and work habits, and even the political symbols and styles of the Asian peoples they ruled. Though some Englishmen refused to give up their tight-fitting, woolen clothing—at least in public— many (one suspects most of those who survived) took to wearing looser fitting, cotton clothing. Dutch gentlemen even donned the long skirt-like *sarongs* of the Javanese aristocrats. British and Dutch officials learned to appreciate the splendid cuisines of India and Java, a taste that the Dutch would never lose and the British would revive at home in the postindependence era. Englishmen smoked Indian *hookahs*, or water pipes, and delighted in performances of Indian dancing girls. Adjusting to the heat of the colonies, both the Dutch and English worked hard in the relative cool of the morning, took a long lunch break (often with a siesta), and then returned to the office for the late afternoon and early evening. Impressive retinues followed Dutch colonial officials as they paraded about under umbrellas, which like those of the Javanese elite were colored and decorated in accordance with their rank. British governors rode about on lavishly attired elephants and received visitors in settings that would have done justice to the throne rooms of the more ostentatious Asian princes.

Though the Europeans usually lived in separate quarters within the factory towns or in villas in the countryside, they mingled quite freely with the indigenous peoples. They were waited on by large numbers of Asian servants, from cooks and coachmen to wet nurses and nannies who tended to their children. Dutch and British officials also struck up friendships with their peers among the subject populations. British officers and Indian princes played polo and enjoyed such "exotic" Indian pastimes as tiger and elephant fights.

Because the Europeans who went to Asia until the mid-19th century were overwhelmingly male, Dutch and British traders and soldiers commonly had liaisons with Asian women. In some cases these involved little more than visits to the local brothel, but very often European men lived with Asian women, and sometimes they married them. The mixed-blood Eurasian children who resulted from these liaisons were often abandoned by their fathers and ended up in orphanages when their destitute mothers proved unable to support them. Before the end of the 18th century, however, mixed marriages on the part of prominent traders or officers were widely accepted, particularly in Java. Some Eurasian children remained with their parents and found a place in the European sectors of the colonial world. Though examples of racial discrimination against the subject peoples on the basis of their physical appearance can certainly be found during the early decades of European overseas empire, the frequency of liaisons that cut across racial boundaries suggests a social fluidity and a degree of interracial interaction that would be unthinkable by the last half of the 19th century.

EDUCATION AND REFORM

Until the early 19th century neither the Dutch nor the British had much desire to push for changes in the social or cultural life of their Asian subjects. The British sanc-

The close alliances that the European colonizers often struck with the "native" princes of conquered areas are graphically illustrated by this photo of the Susuhunan of Surakarta, a kingdom in central Java, standing arm-in-arm with a high Dutch official.

tioned and enforced the rigid divisions of the Hindu caste system, and both the British and Dutch made it clear that they had little interest in spreading Christianity among the Indians or Javanese. In fact, for fear of offending Hindu or Muslim religious sentiments, the British refused to allow Christian missionaries to preach in their territories until the second decade of the 19th century.

Beginning in the 1770s, however, rampant corruption on the part of company officials forced the British Parliament to enact significant reforms in the administration of the East India Company and its colonies. By that time most of those who served in India viewed their brief tenure as a chance to strike it rich quickly. They made great fortunes by cheating the company and exploiting the Indian peasants and artisans. The bad manners and conspicuous consumption of these upstarts, whom contemporaries scornfully dubbed *nabobs*, were satirized by novelists of the age, such as William Thackeray.

When the venality and misgovernment of the nabobs resulted in the catastrophic Bengal famine of 1770, when as much as one-third of the population of that once-prosperous province died, their abuses could no longer be ignored. Parliament passed a number of acts that restructured the company hierarchy and made it much more accountable to the British government. A succession of political reforms culminated in sweeping measures taken in the 1790s by the same Lord Cornwallis whose surrender at Yorktown had sealed Britain's loss of the American colonies. By cleaning up the courts and reducing the power of local British administrators, Cornwallis did much to check the widespread corruption that had hitherto made a sham of any pretence to good government on the part of the British. Unfortunately, because of his mistrust of Indians, his measures also severely constricted their participation in governing the empire.

In this same period forces were building, both in India and England, that caused a major shift in British policy regarding social reform among the subject peoples. The Evangelical religious revival, which had seen the spread of Methodism among the English working classes, soon spilled over into Britain's colonial domains. Evangelicals were in the vanguard of the struggle to put an end to the slave trade, and by the early years of the 19th century, they added the eradication of Indian social abuses to their campaigns for human improvement. Their calls for reforms were warmly supported by utilitarian philosophers such as Jeremy Bentham and James Mill, who believed that there were common principles by which human societies ought to be run if decent living conditions were to be attained by people at all class levels. Mill and other utilitarians were convinced that, though flawed, British society was far more advanced than Indian society. Thus, they pushed for the introduction of British institutions and ways of thinking in India as well as the eradication of what they considered Indian superstitions and social abuses.

Though the utilitarians had little use for the spread of Christianity that the Evangelicals saw as the ultimate solution to India's ills, both agreed that Western education was the key to revitalizing an ancient but decadent Indian civilization. Both factions had little use for Indian learning—the influential British historian, Thomas Babington Macaulay, put it most bluntly when he declared in the 1830s that one shelf of an English gentleman's library was

worth all the writings of Asia. Consequently the Evangelicals and utilitarians pushed for the introduction of English language education for the children of the Indian elite. In one sense, their advocacy of English was very self-serving. The British were in great need of Indians who were fluent in English to serve as clerks in their counting houses and as lower-level bureaucrats. But both Evangelicals and utilitarians also had more elevated motives. They firmly believed that English education would expose the Indian elite to Western learning in critical areas such as ethics, the sciences, and the creative arts. They envisioned this new class of English-educated Indians enlightening and reforming those beneath them in Indian society and thus playing critical roles in bringing India into the "modern" era.

The utilitarian and Evangelical determination to change Indian society went far beyond the introduction of Western learning. Officials of this persuasion pushed for major reforms in Indian society and advocated a large-scale infusion of Western technology. The period of their greatest influence was in the 1830s when they pushed through a number of reforms to correct major abuses that did in fact exist in Indian society. Ritual banditry, whose practitioners were known as thugs, was repressed, and human sacrifice among some of the hill peoples and certain Hindu sects was ended. A major effort was launched to end female infanticide, which was practiced by some high-caste groups who were fearful of financial ruin as the result of the huge expense of their daughters' marriage dowries.

The set piece of the reformers' campaign was the effort to put an end to sati, which, as we have seen, was the ritual immolation of Hindu widows on the funeral pyres of their deceased husbands. This practice, which was clearly a corruption of Hindu religious beliefs, had spread fairly widely among upper-caste Hindu groups by the era of the Muslim invasions in the 11th and 12th centuries A.D. In fact, the wives of proud warrior peoples, such as the Rajputs, had been encouraged to commit mass suicide rather than risk dishonoring their husbands by being captured and molested by Muslim invaders. By the early 19th century, some Brahmin castes and even lower-caste groups in limited areas had adopted the practice of sati.

In the 1830s, bolstered by the strong support and active cooperation of Western-educated Indian leaders such as Ram Mohun Roy, the British outlawed sati. A confrontation between the British and those affected by their efforts to prevent widow burnings provides a wonderful illustration of the confidence of the reformers in the righteousness of their cause and the sense of moral and social superiority over the Indians that the British in general felt in this era. A group of Brahmins complained to a British official,

Charles Napier, that his refusal to allow them to burn the widow of a prominent leader of their community was a violation of their social customs. Napier replied:

> The burning of widows is your custom. Prepare the funeral pyre. But my nation also has a custom. When men burn women alive, we hang them and confiscate all their property. My carpenters shall therefore erect gibbets on which to hang all concerned when the widow is consumed. Let us all act according to our national customs.

The range and magnitude of the reforms the British enacted in India in the first decades of the 19th century marked a watershed in global history. In these years the alien British, who had become the rulers of one of humankind's oldest centers of civilization, consciously began to transmit the ideas and inventions, modes of organization, and technology associated with western Europe's scientific and industrial revolutions to the peoples of the non-Western world. English education, social reforms, and railways and telegraph lines were only part of a larger project by which the British sought to remake Indian society along Western lines. India's croplands were measured and registered; its forests were set aside for "scientific" management; and its people were drawn more and more into the European-dominated global market economy. British officials promoted policies they believed would teach the Indian peasantry the merits of thrift and hard work. British educators lectured the children of India's rising middle classes on the importance of emulating their European masters in matters as diverse as being punctual, exercising their bodies, and mastering the literature and scientific learning of the West. Here was a far more sweeping, but also less spontaneous, Westernization process than Russia had attempted in the 19th century. The scientific and technological breakthroughs that had radically transformed western European civilization had begun to profoundly affect the lives of all the peoples of the globe.

ANALYSIS
WESTERN EDUCATION AND THE RISE OF AN AFRICAN AND ASIAN MIDDLE CLASS

To varying degrees and for many of the same reasons as the British in India, all European colonizers sought to educate the children of African and Asian elite groups in Western-language schools. The early 19th-century debate over education in India was paralleled, for example, by an equally hard-fought controversy among French officials and missionaries regarding the proper schooling for the peoples of Senegal in West Africa. The Dutch did not develop European language schools for the sons of the Javanese elite until the middle of the 19th century, and many young Javanese males continued to be educated in the homes of the Dutch residing in the colonies until the end of the century. Like the British, the French and Dutch needed administrative assistants and postal clerks, and they could neither recruit enough Europeans to fill these posts nor afford the wages European employees would have demanded.

One of the chief advantages of having Western-educated African and Asian subordinates—for they were always below European officials or managers in the office or on the parade ground—was that their salaries were considerably lower than what Europeans would have been paid for doing the same work. The Europeans had no trouble rationalizing this inequity. Africans and Asians served in their own lands and were thus accustomed to life in the hot, humid, insect- and disease-ridden tropics. For the Europeans who worked in the colonies, life in these environments was deemed difficult, even dangerous. Higher pay was thought to compensate them for the "sacrifices" involved in colonial service. The Europeans also had a higher standard of living than Africans or Asians, and colonial officials assumed that European employees would be more hardworking and efficient.

Beyond the need for government functionaries and business assistants, each European colonizer stressed different objectives in designing Western-language schools for the children of upper-class families. As we have seen, the transmission of Western scientific learning and production techniques was a high priority for the British in India. Educational policymakers, such as Macaulay, also sought to teach the Indians Western literature and manners and to instill in them a Western sense of morality. As Macaulay put it, they hoped that English-language schools would turn out brown English gentlemen, who would in turn teach their countrymen the ways of the West.

The French, at least until the end of the 19th century, went even further. They stressed the importance of Africans and other colonial students mastering the French language and the subtleties of French culture. When the lessons had been fully absorbed and the students fully assimilated to French culture, they could become full citizens of France, no matter what their family origins or the color of their skin. Though only a tiny minority of the population of any French colony had the opportunity for the sort of schooling that would qualify them for French citizenship, there were thousands of Senegalese and hundreds of

Vietnamese or Tunisians who could carry French passports, vote in French elections, and even run for seats in the French Parliament. Other European colonial powers adopted either the British or the French approach to education and its aims. The Dutch and Germans, for example, followed the British pattern, while the Portuguese pushed assimilation for even smaller numbers of the elite classes among the peoples they colonized.

Western education in the colonies succeeded in producing both clerks and railway conductors, and brown Indian gentlemen and black French citizens. It also had effects that those who shaped colonial educational policy did not intend, effects that would within a generation or two produce major challenges to the continuation of European colonial dominance. The population of most colonized areas was divided into many different ethnic, religious, and language groups with separate histories and identities. Western language schools gave the sons (and in limited instances, the daughters) of the leading families a common language in which to communicate. The schools also inculcated common attitudes and ideas and imparted to the members of diverse groups a common body of knowledge. In all European colonial societies, Western education led to similar occupational opportunities—in government service, with Western business firms, or as professionals (lawyers, doctors, journalists, etc.). Thus, within a generation after their introduction, Western-language schools had in effect created a new middle class in the colonies that had no counterpart in precolonial African or Asian societies.

Occupying social strata and economic niches in the middle range between the European colonizers and the old aristocracy on the one hand, and the peasantry and urban laborers on the other, Western-educated Africans and Asians within each colony became increasingly aware of the interests and grievances they had in common. They often found themselves at odds with the traditional rulers or the landed gentry, who ironically were often their fathers or grandfathers. Members of the new middle class also felt alienated from the peasantry, whose beliefs and way of life were so different from those they had learned in Western-language schools. For over a generation they clung to their European tutors and employers. Eventually, however, they grew increasingly resentful of their lower salaries, of European competition for scarce jobs, and of their social segregation from the Europeans, who often made little effort to disguise their contempt for even the most accomplished of the African or Asian students of Western ways. Thus, members of the new middle class in the colonies were caught between two worlds: the traditional ways and teachings of their fathers and the "modern" world of their European masters. Finding that they would be fully admitted

to neither world, they rejected the first and set about supplanting the Europeans and building their own modern world.

Questions: Why did the Europeans continue to provide Western-language education for Africans and Asians once it was clear they were creating a class that might challenge their position of dominance? Why were challenges from this new class much more effective than resistance on the part of the peasantry or movements led by the traditional religious and political elites? Do you think the European colonial order would have lasted longer if Western-language education had been denied to colonized peoples?

INDUSTRIAL RIVALRIES AND THE PARTITION OF THE WORLD, C. 1870–1914

The spread of the Industrial Revolution from the British Isles to Continental Europe and North America greatly increased the already considerable advantages the Western powers possessed in manufacturing capacity and the ability to wage war relative to all other peoples and civilizations. These advantages resulted in ever higher levels of European—and American—involvement in the outside world and culminated in the virtually unchallenged domination of the globe by the Western powers by the last decades of the 19th century. Beginning in the 1870s, the Europeans indulged in an orgy of overseas conquests that reduced most of Africa, Asia, and the Pacific Ocean region to colonial possessions by the time of the outbreak of the First World War in 1914. During each year of that time period, an area larger than France was added to the empires of the different Western powers. By 1914 Europe and its colonial possessions occupied over 80 percent of the inhabitable lands of the earth. Areas not annexed directly, such as China and Persia, were forcibly "opened" to European trade and investment, and divided into informal "spheres of influence" of the various Western nations. The remaking of the world economic order to industrial Europe's specifications was completed. According to the new global division of labor, Europe and increasingly North America provided finance and machine capital, entrepreneurial and managerial talent, and manufactured goods. The rest of the world provided raw materials for Europe's factories, cheap labor, and abundant, if not always fertile, land. Thus, it was not without reason that the Europeans ultimately came to regard themselves as the "lords of humankind."

The Partition of Africa to 191[...]

Though science and industry gave the Europeans the capacity to run roughshod over the rest of the world, they also heightened economic competition and political rivalries between the European powers. In the first half of the 19th century industrial Britain, with its seemingly insurmountable naval superiority, was left alone to dominate overseas trade and empire building. By the last decades of the century, Belgium, France, and especially Germany and the United States were challenging Britain's industrial supremacy and actively building (or in the case of France, adding to) colonial empires of their own. Many of the political leaders of these expansive nations viewed the possession of colonies as an essential attribute of states that aspired to great-power status. Colonies were also seen as insurance against raw material shortages and the loss of overseas market outlets to European or North American rivals.

Quarrels over the division of the colonial spoils were cited by those who sought to justify the arms buildup and general militarism of the age. Colonial rivalries greatly intensified the growing tension and paranoia that dominated great power interaction in the decades before World War I. As Europe divided into armed camps, successive crises over control of the Sudan, Morocco, and the Balkans (which the great powers treated very much like colonies) had much to do with the alliances that formed and the crisis mentality that contributed so much to the outbreak of the conflict in August, 1914.

MOTIVES BEHIND THE GLOBAL
SCRAMBLE FOR COLONIES

Through much of the 20th century, historians have argued about the reasons for the unprecedented drive for colonial expansion that seized Europe and, to a lesser extent, the United States in the last decades of the 19th century. The majority of those engaged in this often heated debate have tended to join one of two camps: those who favor a political explanation for the outburst of territorial aggrandizement, and those who argue that it was fundamentally economic in origin. The truth may well be found by combining the two views—by recognizing that political leaders, not just businessmen, had to take into account economic concerns when deciding to intervene in disputes or to annex territories in Africa, Asia, or the South Pacific.

The Partition of Southeast Asia and the Pacific Islands to 1914

The British obsession with protecting strategic overseas naval stations, such as those in Malaya and in South Africa, for example, was linked to an underlying perception of growing threats to their Indian Empire. That empire was in turn more than just their "garrison in the east" and largest colonial possession. It was a major source of raw materials for British industries and a key outlet for both British manufactured goods and British overseas investment. Thus, political and economic motives were often impossible to separate; doing so unnecessarily oversimplifies and distorts our understanding of the forces behind the scramble for empire in the late 19th century.

It would also be a mistake to see a complete break between the pattern of European colonial expansion before and after 1870. Though a good deal more territory was annexed per year after that date, there were numerous colonial wars and additions to both the British and French empires all through the middle decades of the 19th century. One of the key differences between the two periods was that before 1870, Britain had only a weak France with which to compete in the outside world. This meant that the British were less likely than at the end of the century to be pushed into full-scale invasions and annexations because they feared that another European power was about to seize potentially valuable colonies. It also allowed the British to

rely heavily on threats and gunboat raids rather than outright conquest to bring African kings or Asian emperors into line. With its "white" settler colonies (Canada, Australia, and New Zealand) and India, plus enclaves in Africa and Southeast Asia, the British already had all the empire they could handle. Most British politicians were cautious about or firmly opposed to adding more colonies. The British were wary of French advances in various parts of the globe, which were usually made to restore France's great-power standing following setbacks in Europe. But the French were far too weak economically and too politically divided to contest Britain's naval mastery or its standing as the greatest colonial power.

Once Germany was united in 1871, and the German Empire and the United States began to pass Britain as industrial powers, the situation was significantly altered. India and the rest of the empire were now seen as essential to Britain's maintenance of its great-power standing. British politicians worried that if Britain stood still while the rest of the powers built up overseas empires, it would soon be supplanted as the number one naval and colonial power. The concern here was economic as well as strategic. The last decades of the 19th century were a period of recurring economic depressions in Europe and the United States. The leaders of the newly industrialized nations had little

This engraving from the popular *Illustrated London News* shows British warships and gunboats bombarding the East
African port of Mombasa in 1874. As in the early centuries of European expansion, sea power remained a critical way
for the British and other colonizers to project their power overseas throughout the 19th century.

experience in handling the overproduction and unemployment that came with each of these economic crises. They
were understandably deeply concerned about the social unrest and in some cases what appeared to them to be stirrings of revolution, that each phase of depression
engendered. Some political theorists argued that as destinations to which unemployed workers might migrate and as
potential markets for surplus goods, colonial possessions
could serve as safety values to release the pressure built up
in times of industrial slumps.

Thus, although a colony seemed to be of little economic
value when it was annexed, it could prove a valuable asset
later on. Industrial Europe's growing need for raw materials gave added credence to this line of reasoning. Each
power felt compelled to conquer and annex vast territories—which often consisted of scantily populated, arid
lands—because it feared that otherwise a rival would take
them. In letting a competitor grab what might prove to be
a mineral-rich colony, Britain or Germany might be fore-
closing on its future chances to remain a global power.

Competition among the great powers had much to do
with another major cause of the late 19th-century scramble
for colonial possessions. Britain's successful application of
gunboat diplomacy and indirect control over African and
Asian kingdoms in the early 19th century depended heavily
on the existence of reasonably strong African and Asian
leaders who could enforce the demands made by the Europeans. With the intensification of European rivalries in the

late 19th century, these leaders attempted to play the powers off each other. This reduced the value of their cooperation and often prompted one of the powers to invade their
lands, remove them from power, and find less troublesome
collaborators. In addition, in many areas, but particularly
in Africa, decades and even centuries of European economic penetration and political interference resulted in the
disintegration of indigenous governments and societies as a
whole. Lack of a local center of power through which to
exert their control as well as threats by growing social dislocations in areas where one or more of the powers had a
strong strategic or economic stake caused European policymakers to conclude that military intervention and formal
annexation were their only option.

As these motives suggest, in the era of the scramble for
colonial possessions, political leaders in Europe played a
much more prominent role in decisions to annex overseas
territories than they had earlier, even in the first half of
the 19th century. In part, this was due to improved communications. Telegraphs and railways not only made it possible to transmit orders from the capitals of Europe to
men-on-the-spot in the tropics much more rapidly, they allowed ministers in Europe to play a much more active role
in the ongoing governance of the colonies. More than politicians were involved in late 19th-century decisions to add
to the colonial empires. The jingoistic "penny" press and
the extension of the vote to the lower middle and working
classes through much of industrial Europe and in the

United States made public opinion a major factor in foreign policy. Though stalwart explorers might on their own initiative make treaties with local African or Asian potentates who assigned their lands to France or Germany, these annexations had to be ratified by the home government. In most cases, ratification meant fierce parliamentary debates that often spilled over into press wars and popular demonstrations. Empires were no longer the personal projects of private trading concerns and ambitious individuals; they were the property and pride of the nations of Europe and North America.

UNEQUAL COMBAT: COLONIAL WARS AND THE APEX OF IMPERIALISM

Industrial change not only justified the Europeans' grab for colonial possessions, it made them much easier to acquire. By the last decades of the 19th century, scientific discoveries and technological innovations had catapulted the Europeans far ahead of all other peoples in the capacity to wage war. The Europeans could tap mineral resources that most peoples did not even know existed, and European chemists mixed ever more deadly explosives. Advances in metallurgy made possible the mass production of light and mobile artillery pieces that rendered suicidal the massed cavalry or infantry charges that were the mainstay of Asian and African armies. Advances in artillery were matched by great improvements in hand arms. Much more accurate and faster firing, breech-loading rifles replaced the clumsy muzzle-loading muskets of the first phase of empire building. By the 1880s, after decades of experimentation, the machine gun had become an effective battlefield weapon. Railroads gave the Europeans the mobility of the swiftest African or Asian horsemen as well as the ability to supply large armies in the field for extended periods of time. On the sea, Europe's already formidable advantages were awesomely increased by industrial transformations. After the opening of the Suez canal in 1869, steam power supplanted the sail, iron hulls replaced wood, and massive guns, capable of hitting enemy vessels miles away, were introduced into the fleets of the great powers.

The dazzling array of new weaponry with which the Europeans set out on their expeditions to the Indian frontiers or the African "bush" made the wars of colonial conquest very lopsided affairs. This was particularly true when the Europeans encountered resistance from peoples, such as those in the interior of Africa or the Pacific islands, who had been cut off from most preindustrial advances in technology and thus fought the European machine guns with spears, arrows, and leather shields. One African leader, whose people struggled with little hope to halt the German advance into East Africa, resorted to natural imagery to account for the power of the invaders' weapons:

> On Monday we heard a shuddering like Leviathan, the voice of many cannon; we heard the roar like waves of the rocks and rumble like thunder in the rains. We heard a crashing like elephants or monsters and our hearts melted at the number of shells. We knew that we were hearing the battle of Pangani; the guns were like a hurricane in our ears.

Not even peoples with advanced preindustrial technology and sophisticated military organization, such as the Chinese and Vietnamese, could stand against, or really comprehend, the fearful killing devices of the Europeans. In advising the Vietnamese emperor to give in to European demands, one of his officials, who had led the fight against the French invaders, warned:

> Nobody can resist them. They go where they choose. . . . Under heaven, everything is feasible to them, save only the matter of life and death.

Despite the odds against them, African and Asian peoples often fiercely resisted the imposition of colonial rule. West African leaders, such as Samory and Ahmadou Sekou, held back the European advance for decades, and when rulers, such as the Vietnamese emperors, refused to fight, local officials organized guerrilla resistance in defense of the traditional regime. Martial peoples, such as the Zulus in South Africa, had the courage and discipline to face and defeat sizeable British forces in set piece (or conventional and critical) battles, such as that at Isandhlwana in 1879. But conventional resistance eventually ended in defeat: The guerrilla bands in Vietnam were eventually run to the ground; even at Isandhlwana, 3000 Zulus lost their lives in the massacre of 800 British and 500 African troops. In addition, within days of the Zulu victory, a tiny force of 120 British troops held off an army of three or four thousand Zulus. Given the European advantages in conventional battles, guerrilla resistance, sabotage, and, in some cases, banditry proved the most effective means of fighting the Europeans' attempts to assert political control. Religious leaders were often in the forefront of these struggles. The magic potions and divine assistance they offered for the protection of their followers seemed to be the only way to offset the demoralizing killing power of the Europeans' weapons.

However admirable the courage of those who resisted the European advance and despite temporary setbacks, by the eve of World War I in 1914 there was very little of

This rather romantic depiction of the 1879 battle of Isandhlwana in the Natal province of South Africa shows that, despite their superior firepower, the Europeans could be defeated, if only temporarily, by well-organized and determined African or Asian resistance forces.

the earth left for the Europeans to conquer. Excepting Ethiopia, all of Africa had been divided between the European powers. Maps of the continent became a patchwork of colors—red for Great Britain, green for France, blue for Germany, and so on. In Southeast Asia, only Siam remained independent, in part because Britain and France could not decide which of them should have it. The Americans had replaced the Spanish as the colonial overlords of the Philippines, and the Dutch were completing the conquest of the "outer islands" of the Indonesian archipelago. Even the island clusters of the Pacific had been divided among the hungry industrial powers. China, Persia, and the Middle East had not yet been occupied, but many believed that the "informal" political and economic influences the European powers exerted in these areas were the prelude to formal annexation.

What was perhaps most striking was how easy this division of the world had been. There had been prolonged resistance in desolate places, such as the Sudan and the rain forests of Vietnam, but overall the Europeans had conquered most of the earth in a matter of decades with a remarkably low level of expense and loss of European lives. They had divided the world with little thought for the reactions of the peoples who came under their rule. European leaders quarreled and bargained at green, felt-topped tables in Paris or Berlin over lands they scarcely knew anything about. It was like a colossal game of *Diplomacy* or *Risk*, with armies and fleets moved, and colonies won, lost, and traded at the gaming tables of the European diplomats. To expand on an image offered by the arch-imperialist King Leopold of the Belgians, industrial technology had turned the world into a giant *gateau*, or cake, to be sliced up and divided between the European powers.

PATTERNS OF DOMINANCE: CONTINUITY AND CHANGE

By the end of the 19th century, the European colonial order was made up of two, quite different, kinds of colonies. The greater portion of the European empires consisted of "true" colonies in Africa, Asia, and the South Pacific in which small numbers of Europeans ruled large numbers of non-Western peoples. The true colonies represented a vast extension of the pattern of dominance the British, Dutch, and French had worked out earlier in India, Java, and African enclaves such as Senegal. Most of these had been brought, often quite suddenly, under European rule in the last decades of the 19th century and the first years of the 20th century. The following sections devoted to this form of colonization focus on the new forms of colonial rule and changing patterns of social interaction between colonizer and colonized that emerged in the decades of imperialist expansion before World War I.

Settlement colonies made up the second major type of European overseas possession, but within this type there were two different patterns of European settlement and indigenous response. The first pattern was exhibited by colonies such as Canada and Australia, which the British labeled the "White Dominions." The White Dominions accounted for a good portion of the land area but only a tiny minority of the population of Britain's global empire. The descendants of European settlers made up the overwhelming majority of the population in these colonies, in which small numbers of native inhabitants had been decimated by diseases and wars of conquest. These patterns of substantial European settlement and the precipitous decline of the indigenous population were also found in those portions of

North America that came to form the United States. Though Canada and Australia remained within the British Empire, each moved steadily toward self-government and parliamentary rule in the late 19th century.

In some areas where large numbers of Europeans had migrated, a second major variation on the settlement type of colony developed. Both in regions that had been colonized as early as North America, such as South Africa, and in those the Europeans and Americans had begun to occupy only in the mid- or late 19th century, such as Algeria, Kenya, New Zealand, and Hawaii, the key demographic characteristics of both the settler and the "true" colonies were combined. Temperate climates and relatively mild disease environments in these areas made it possible for tens or hundreds of thousands of Europeans to settle on a permanent basis. Despite the Europeans' arrival, large indigenous populations survived and then began to increase rapidly. As a result, in these areas for which the label *contested settler colonies* seems most apt, Europeans and indigenous peoples increasingly clashed over land rights, resource control, social status, and cultural differences. From the 19th century onward, the history of contested settler societies has been dominated by the interaction between European settlers and indigenous peoples. The last sections of this chapter are devoted to case studies of three of the most important and representative examples of the contested settler variation on the settlement colony pattern: South Africa, New Zealand, and Hawaii. Because the pattern of colonization involved in the White Dominions has been considered in some depth in Chapter 23, developments in Canada and Australia are covered largely through comparisons to patterns in South Africa and other contested settlement areas.

COLONIAL REGIMES AND AFRICAN AND ASIAN PEOPLES

As the Europeans imposed their rule over tens of millions of additional Africans and Asians in the late 19th century, they drew heavily on precedents set in older colonies, particularly India, in establishing administrative, legal, and educational systems. As in India (or in Java and Senegal), the Europeans exploited long-standing ethnic and cultural divisions between the peoples of their new African or Asian colonies to put down resistance and maintain control. In West and East Africa in particular, they used the peoples who followed animistic religions (those that focused on the propitiation of nature or ancestral spirits) or those who had converted to Christianity against the Muslim communities that existed in most colonies. In official reports and censuses, colonial administrators rigidified and enhanced existing ethnic differences by dividing the peoples in each colony into "tribes." The label itself, with its connotations of primitiveness and backwardness, says a great deal about general European attitudes toward the peoples of sub-Saharan Africa. In Southeast Asia, the colonizers sought to use hill dwelling "tribal" minorities against the majority populations that lived in the lowlands. In each colonial area, favored minorities, often Christians, were recruited into the civil service and police. Their collaboration not only resulted in a sense of loyalty to the colonizers, it antagonized less-favored ethnic and religious groups, thus bolstering the divide and rule strategy of the Europeans.

As had been the case in India, Java, and Senegal small numbers of Europeans, who lived mainly in the capital city and major provincial towns, oversaw the administration of the African and Asian colonies, which was actually carried out at the local level mainly by hundreds or thousands of African and Asian subordinates. Some of these—normally those in positions of the greatest authority—were Western educated, but the majority were recruited from indigenous elite groups, including village headmen, local notables, and regional lords. In Burma, Malaya, and East Africa, numerous Indian administrators and soldiers assisted the British in ruling new additions to their empire. The Europeans also recruited promising male youths in the newly colonized areas for Western schooling that would make them fit for jobs as government clerks or railway mechanics.

In contrast to Java and India, where schools were heavily state-supported, Western-language education in Africa was left largely to Protestant and Catholic missionaries. As a result of deep-seated racial prejudices held by virtually all the colonizers, higher education was not promoted in Africa, and in Africa college graduates were rare compared to India, the Dutch East Indies, or even smaller Asian colonies such as Burma and Vietnam. Of course, this policy stunted the growth of a middle class in black Africa, a consequence that European colonial officials increasingly intended. As nationalist agitation spread among the Western-educated classes in India and other Asian colonies, colonial policymakers warned against the dangers posed by college graduates. Those with advanced educations among the colonized, according to this argument, aspired to jobs that were beyond their capacity and were understandably disgruntled when they could not find employment.

CHANGING SOCIAL RELATIONS BETWEEN COLONIZER AND COLONIZED

In both long-held and newly acquired colonies, the growing tensions between the colonizers and the rising African and Asian middle classes reflected a larger shift in

This pointedly dramatized engraving of the submission in 1896 of King Prempeh of the powerful Asante kingdom in present-day Ghana underscores the importance European colonizers placed on alliances with or the forced submission of indigenous African rulers and local leaders.

European social interaction with the colonized peoples. This shift had actually begun long before the scramble for colonies in the late 19th century. Its causes are complex, but the growing size and changing makeup of European communities in the colonies were critical factors. As more and more Europeans went to the colonies, they tended to keep to themselves on social occasions rather than mixing with the "natives." New medicines and increasingly segregated living quarters made it possible to bring to the colonies the wives and families of government officials and European military officers (but not of the rank-and-file until well into the 20th century). Wives and families further closed the social circle of the colonized, and European women looked disapprovingly on liaisons between European men and Asian or African women. Brothels were put off-limits for upper-class officials and officers, and mixed marriages or living arrangements met with more and more vocal disapproval both within the constricted world of the

colonial communities and back home in Europe. The growing numbers of missionaries and pastors for European congregations in the colonies obviously served to strengthen these taboos.

European women were once held to be the chief culprits in the growing social gap between colonizer and colonized, but male officials may well have been mainly responsible. They established laws restricting or prohibiting miscegenation and other sorts of interracial liaisons, and they pushed for housing arrangements and police practices designed specifically to keep social contacts between European women and the colonized at a minimum. These measures locked European women in the colonies into an almost exclusively European world. They still had lots of "native" servants and "native" nannies for their children, but they rarely came into contact with men or women of their own social standing from the colonized peoples. Occasions when they did were highly public and strictly formal.

The trend toward social exclusivism on the part of Europeans in the colonies and their open disdain for the culture of colonized peoples were reinforced by notions of white racial supremacy, which peaked in acceptance in the decades before the First World War. It was widely believed that the mental and moral superiority of whites over the rest of humankind, which was usually divided into racial types according to the crude criterion of skin color, had been demonstrated by scientific experiments. Because the inferior intelligence and weak sense of morality of non-Europeans were believed to be inherent and permanent, there seemed little motivation for Europeans to socialize with the colonized and lots of good reasons for fighting the earlier tendency to adopt elements of the culture and lifestyle of subject peoples. As photos from the late 19th century reveal, stiff collars and ties for men, and corsets and long skirts for women became obligatory for the respectable colonial functionaries and their wives. The colonizers' houses were filled with the overstuffed furniture and bric-a-brac that the late Victorians loved so dearly. European social life in the colonies revolved around the infamous clubs, where the only "natives" allowed were the servants. In the heat of the summer months, most of the administrators and virtually all of the colonizers' families retreated to the hill stations, where the cool air and the quaint architecture made it seem almost as if they were home again—or at least in a Swiss mountain resort.

SHIFTS IN METHODS OF ECONOMIC EXTRACTION

The relationship between the colonizers and the mass of the colonized remained much as it had been before. District officers, with the help of many "native" subordinates, continued to do their paternal duty to settle disputes between peasant villagers, punish criminals, and collect taxes. European planters and merchants still relied on African or Asian overseers and brokers to manage laborers and purchase crops and handicraft manufactures. But late 19th century colonial bureaucrats and managers sought to instruct African and Asian peasants in "scientific" farming techniques and to compel the colonized peoples more generally to work harder and more efficiently. Here was an important extension of dependent status in the Western-dominated world economy, as pressure for new work habits supported the drive for cheap raw materials (exports) and drew in a growing segment of the colonial labor force.

A wide range of incentives was devised in response to the expansion of production for export and also the abolition of prior forms of slavery. Some of these incentives benefited the colonized peoples, such as the cheap consumer goods that could be purchased with cash earned producing marketable crops or laboring on European plantations. In many instances, however, colonized peoples were simply forced to produce crops or raw materials that the Europeans desired for little or no remuneration. Head and hut taxes were imposed that could only be paid in ivory, palm nuts, or wages earned working on European estates. Villagers were forced to grow market produce on lands they normally devoted to food crops. Under the worst of these forced-labor schemes, such as those inflicted on the peoples of the Belgian Congo in the final decades of the 19th century, villagers were flogged and killed if they failed to meet production quotas, and women and children were held hostage to ensure that their menfolk would deliver the products demanded on time. Whether out of self-interest or fear, the colonial overlords were determined to draw their subjects into fuller participation in the European-dominated global market economy.

As increasing numbers of the colonized peoples were drawn into the production of crops or minerals intended for export to Europe, colonized areas in Africa, India, and Southeast Asia were reduced to dependence on the industrializing European economies. Roads and railways were built primarily to facilitate the movement of farm produce and raw materials from the interior of colonized areas to port areas where they could be shipped to Europe. Benefiting from Europe's technological advances, mining sectors grew dramatically in most of the colonies. Vast areas that were previously uncultivated or (more commonly) had been planted in food crops were converted to the production of commodities—such as cocoa, palm oil, rubber, and hemp—in great demand in the markets of Europe and, increasingly, the United States.

The profits from the precious metals and minerals extracted from Africa's mines or the rubber grown in Malaya went mainly to European merchants and industrialists. The raw materials themselves were shipped to Europe to be processed and sold or used in the manufacture of industrial products. The finished products were intended mainly for European consumers, whether these be members of middle and working class families or government contractors. The African and Asian laborers who produced these products were generally poorly paid—if indeed they were paid at all. The laborers and colonial economies as a whole were steadily reduced to dependence on the European-dominated global market. Thus, economic dependence complemented the political subjugation and social subordination of colonized African and Asian peoples in a world order loaded in favor of the expansionist nations of western Europe.

DOCUMENT
CONTRARY IMAGES:
THE COLONIZER VS.
THE COLONIZED ON
THE "CIVILIZING
MISSION"

Each of the following passages from novels written in the colonial era expresses a different view of the reasons behind and the consequences of European colonization in Africa and Asia. The first is taken from an adventure story written by John Buchan entitled *Prestor John*, a favorite in the pre-World War I decades among English schoolboys—many of whom would go out as young men to administer in the colonies. Davie, the protagonist in the story, is a "tall, square-set lad . . . renown [for his] prowess at Rugby football." He summarizes key elements of the "civilizing mission" credo by which so many European thinkers and political leaders attempted to justify their colonization of most of the rest of the world.

I knew then [after Davie's struggle to thwart a "native" rising in South Africa] the meaning of the white man's duty. He has to take all the risks, reck-[on]ing nothing of his life or his fortunes and well content to find his reward in the fulfillment of his task. That is the difference between white and black, the gift of responsibility, the power of being in a little way a king; and so long as we know this and practise it, we will rule not in Africa alone but wherever there are dark men who live only for the day and their own bellies. Moreover the work made me pitiful and kindly. I learned much of the untold grievances of the natives and saw something of their strange, twisted reasoning.

The second passage is taken from René Maran's *Batouala*, which was first published in 1921 just after the First World War. Though a French colonial official in West Africa, Maran was an African-American, born in Martinique, who was highly sensitive to the plight of the colonized in Africa. Here his protagonist, a local African leader named Batouala, complains of the burdens rather than the benefits of colonial rule, and mocks the self-important European agents of the vaunted civilizing mission.

But what good does it do to talk about it? It's nothing new to us that men of white skin are more delicate than men of black skin.

One example of a thousand possible. Everyone knows that the whites, saying that they are "collecting taxes," force all blacks of a marriageable age to carry voluminous packages from when the sun rises to when it sets.

These trips last two, three, five days. Little matter to them the weight of these packages which are called "sandoukous." They don't sink under the burden. Rain, sun, cold? They don't suffer. So they pay no attention. And long live the worst weather, provided the whites are sheltered.

Whites fret about mosquito bites. . . . They fear mason bees. They are also afraid of the "prakongo," the scorpion who lives, black and venomous, among decaying roofs, under rubble, or in the midst of debris.

In a word, everything worries them. As if a man worthy of the name would worry about everything which lives, crawls, or moves around him.

The whites, aha! The whites . . . didn't everyone know that their feet were just a stinking mass? And what a ridiculous idea to encase feet in black, white, or banana-colored skins! And if it were only their feet which stank! *Lalala*—their whole body smelled like a corpse.

Questions: What sorts of roles does Davie assume that the Europeans must play in the colonies? What benefits accrue to colonized peoples from their rule? What impression does he convey of the thinking and behavior of the colonized peoples? In what ways do Batouala's views of the Europeans conflict with Davie's assumptions about himself and other colonizers? Does Batouala agree with Davie's conviction that colonial rule is beneficial for the Africans? What sorts of burdens does Batouala believe it imposes? According to Batouala what advantages do Africans have over Europeans?

SETTLER COLONIES AND WHITE DOMINIONS: SOUTH AFRICA

The contested settler colonies that developed in Africa and the Pacific in the 19th century were in important ways similar to the White Dominions. In fact, the early history of South Africa, one of the largest of the contested settler colonies, exhibited interesting comparisons and contrasts with that of Canada and Australia, the largest of the White Dominions. European settlers began to move into the southwest corner of South Africa and eastern Canada in the middle decades of the 17th century, long before the settlement of Australia got under way in the 1840s. The initial Dutch colony at Cape Town was established to provide a way station where Dutch merchant ships could take on water and fresh foods in the middle of their long journey from Europe to the East Indies. In contrast to Canada, where French fur trappers and missionaries quickly moved into the interior, the small community of Dutch settlers stayed near the coast for decades after their arrival. But like the settlers in Australia, the Boers (or farmers), as the Dutch in South Africa came to be called, eventually began to move into the vast interior regions of the continent. Though the settlers in each of the three areas were confronted by wild, uncharted, and in some ways inhospitable frontier regions, they also found a temperate climate in which they could grow the crops and raise the livestock they were accustomed to in Europe. Equally important, they encountered a disease environment they could withstand.

The Boers and Australians found the areas into which they moved sparsely populated. In this respec t their experience was somewhat different from that of the settlers in Canada, where the Amerindian population, though far from dense, was organized into powerful tribal confederations. The Boers and Australians faced much less resistance as they took possession of the lands once occupied by hunting-and-gathering peoples. The Boer farmers and cattle ranchers enslaved these peoples, the Khoikhoi, while at the same time integrating them into their large frontier homesteads. Extensive miscegenation between the Boers and Khoikhoi in these early centuries of European colonization produced the sizeable "colored" population that exists in South Africa today, which is regarded as quite distinct from the black or African majority. The Australian and Canadian settlers drove the "aborigines" they encountered into the interior, eventually leaving those who survived their invasions the uneasy occupants of remote tracts of waste, which were not worth settling. In both cases, but particularly in Canada, the indigenous population was also decimated by many of the same diseases that had turned contacts with the Europeans into a demographic disaster for the rest of the Americas in the early centuries of expansion.

Thus, until the first decades of the 19th century, the process of colonization in South Africa paralleled that in Canada and Australia quite closely. Small numbers of Europeans had migrated into lands that they considered "empty" or undeveloped. After driving away or subjugating the indigenous peoples, the Europeans farmed, mined, and grazed their herds on these lands, which they claimed as their own. But while the settler societies in Canada and Australia went on to develop, rather peacefully, into loyal and largely self-governing dominions of the British empire, the arrival of the same British overlords in South Africa in the early 19th century sent the Boers reeling onto a very different historical course. The British captured Cape Town during the wars precipitated by the French Revolution in the 1790s when Holland was overrun by France, thus making its colonies subject to British attack. The British held the colony during the Napoleonic conflicts that followed and annexed it permanently in 1815 as a vital link on the route to India.

Made up mainly of people of Dutch and French Protestant descent, the Boer community differed from the British newcomers in almost every way possible. The Boers spoke a different language, and they lived mostly in isolated rural homesteads that had missed the scientific, industrial, and urban revolutions that had transformed British society and attitudes. Most critically, the Evangelical missionaries who entered South Africa under the protection of the new British overlords were deeply committed to eradicating slavery. They made no exception for the domestic pattern of enslavement that had developed in Boer homesteads and communities. By the 1830s missionary pressure and increasing British interference in their lives drove a handful of Boers to open, but futile, rebellion, and drove many of the remaining Boers to flee the Cape Colony.

In the decades of the Great Trek that followed, tens of thousands of Boer farmers migrated in covered wagons pulled by oxen, first east across the Great Fish River and then over the mountains into the *veld*, or rolling, grassy plains that make up much of the South African interior. In these areas, the Boers collided head-on with populous, militarily powerful, and well-organized African states built by Bantu peoples such as the Zulus and the Xhosa. Throughout the middle decades of the 19th century, the migrating Boers clashed again and again with the Bantu peoples, who were determined to resist the seizure of the lands where they pastured their great herds of cattle and grew subsistence foods. The British in effect followed the Boer pio-

This 1864 engraving shows well-to-do Afrikaner homes near Cape Town in South Africa. The abundance of mulatto servants, shown in the foreground, was typical of Boer homesteads, where color lines were quite permeable and miscegenation was not uncommon until well into the 19th century.

neers along the southern and eastern coast, eventually establishing a second major outpost at Durban in Natal. Tensions between Boers and Britain remained high, but the British were often drawn into the frontier wars against the Bantu peoples, even though they were not always formally allied to the Boers.

In the early 1850s the hard-liners among the Boers established two republics, the Orange Free State and the Transvaal, in the interior, which they sought to keep free of British influence. For over a decade they managed to keep the British out of their affairs. But when diamonds were discovered in the Orange Free State in 1867, British entrepreneurs, such as Cecil Rhodes, and prospectors began to move in, and tensions between Boers and British began to build anew. In 1880 and 1881, these tensions led to a brief war in which the Boers were victorious. The tide of British immigration into the republics, however, rose even higher after gold was discovered in the Transvaal in 1885.

Though the British had pretty much left the Boers to deal with the African peoples who lived in the republics as they pleased, British migrants and financiers grew more and more resentful of Boer efforts to limit their numbers and curb their civil rights. British efforts to protect the settlers and bring the feisty and independent Boers into line led to the republics' declaration of war against the British in late 1899, and Boer attacks on British bases in Natal, the Cape Colony, and elsewhere. The Boer War that resulted raged until 1902 and began the process of decoloni-

zation for the European settlers of South Africa, while at the same time it opened the way for their dominance over the African majority.

PACIFIC TRAGEDIES

The territories the Europeans, Americans, and Japanese claimed throughout the South Pacific in the 19th century were in some cases outposts of true empire, in others contested settler colonies. In both situations, however, the coming of colonial rule resulted in demographic disasters and social disruptions of a magnitude that had not been seen since the first century of European expansion into the Americas. Like the Amerindian peoples of the New World, the peoples of the South Pacific had long lived in isolation. This meant that like the Amerindians they had no immunities to many of the diseases European explorers and later merchants, missionaries, and settlers carried to their island homes from the 1760s onward. In addition, their cultures were extremely vulnerable to the corrosive effects of outside influences, such as new religions, different sexual mores, more lethal weapons, and sudden influxes of cheap consumer goods. Thus, whatever the intentions of the incoming Europeans and Americans—and they were by no means always benevolent—their contacts with the peoples of the Pacific islands almost invariably ushered in periods of social disintegration and widespread human suffering.

Of the many cases of contact between the expansive peoples of the West and the long isolated island cultures of the South Pacific, the confrontations in New Zealand and Hawaii are among the most informative. As we saw in Chapters 10 and 21, quite sophisticated cultures and fairly complex societies had developed in each of these areas. In addition, the two island groups contained, at the time of the European explorers' arrivals, some of the largest concentrations of population in the whole Pacific region. Both areas were subjected to European influences carried by a variety of agents from whalers and merchants to missionaries and colonial administrators. After the first decades of contact, the peoples of both New Zealand and Hawaii experienced a period of crisis so severe that their continued survival was in doubt. In both cases, however, the threatened peoples and cultures rebounded and found enduring solutions to the challenges from overseas that combined accommodation to outside influences and revivals of traditional beliefs and practices.

NEW ZEALAND.   The Maoris of New Zealand actually went through two periods of profound disruption and danger. The first began in the 1790s when timber merchants and whalers established small settlements on the New Zealand coast. Maoris living near these settlements were afflicted with alcoholism and the spread of prostitution. In addition, they traded wood and food for European firearms that soon revolutionized Maori warfare—in part by rendering it much more deadly—and upset the existing balance among different tribal groups. Even more devastating was the impact of diseases, such as smallpox, tuberculosis, and even the common cold, that ravaged Maori communities throughout the north island. By the 1840s only eighty to ninety thousand Maoris remained of a population that had been as high as 130,000 less than a century earlier. But the Maoris survived these calamities and began to adjust to the imports of the foreigners. They took up farming with European implements, and grazed cattle purchased from European traders. They cut timber, built windmills, and traded extensively with the merchants who frequented their shores. Many even converted to Christianity, which the missionaries began to proselytize after their first station was established in 1814, though observers noted the Maoris' continuing adherence to their old beliefs and rituals.

The arrival of British farmers and herders in search of land in the early 1850s and the British decision to claim the islands as part of their global empire, again plunged the Maoris into misery and despair. Backed by the military clout of the colonial government, the settlers occupied some of the most fertile areas of the north island. The warlike Maori fought back, sometimes with temporary successes, but they were steadily driven back into the interior of the island. In desperation in the 1860s and 1870s, they flocked to religious prophets who promised them magical charms and supernatural assistance in their efforts to drive out the invaders. When the prophets also failed them, the Maoris seemed for a time to face extinction. In fact, some British writers, heavily influenced by the work of "social Darwinists," such as Herbert Spencer, predicted that within generations the Maoris, like the Arawaks and Tasmanians before them, would die out.

The Maoris displayed surprising resilience. As they built up immunities to new diseases, they also learned to use European laws and political institutions to defend themselves and preserve what was left of their ancestral lands. Because the British had in effect turned the internal administration of the islands over to the settlers' representatives, the Maoris' main struggle was with the invaders who had come to stay. Western schooling and a growing ability to win British colonial officials over to their point of view eventually enabled the Maoris to hold their own in their ongoing legal contests and daily exchanges with the settlers. A multiracial society has now evolved in which there is a reasonable level of European and Maori accommodation and interaction, and which has allowed the Maori to preserve much of value in their traditional culture.

HAWAII.   The conversion of Hawaii to settler colony status followed familiar basic imperialist patterns, but with a number of specific twists. Hawaii did not become a colony until the United States proclaimed annexation in 1898, though an overzealous British official had briefly declared the islands for his nation in 1843. Hawaii came under increasing Western influence, however, from the late 18th century onward—politically at the hands of the British, culturally and economically from the United States whose westward surge quickly spilled into the Pacific Ocean.

While very occasional contact with Spanish ships during the 16th and 17th centuries is probable, Hawaii was effectively opened to the West through the voyages of Captain James Cook from 1777 to 1779. Cook was first welcomed as a god, partly because he had the good luck to land during a sacred period when war was forbidden. A later and less well-timed visit brought Cook's death, as Hawaiian warriors sought to take over his ship with its metal nails, much prized by a people whose elaborate culture rested on a Neolithic technology. Cook and later British expeditions convinced a young Hawaiian prince, Kamehameha, that some imitation of Western ways could produce a unified kingdom under his leadership, replacing the small and warring regional units that had previously prevailed. A series of vigorous wars, backed by British weapons and advisors, won Kamehameha his kingdom between 1794 and 1810. The new king and his successors promoted economic change, encouraging Western merchants to establish export trade in Hawaiian goods in return for increasing revenues to the royal treasury.

Hawaiian royalty began to imitate Western habits, in some cases traveling to Britain and often building Western-style palaces. Two powerful queens advanced the process of change by insisting that traditional taboos subordinating women be abandoned. In this context vigorous missionary efforts from Protestant New England, beginning in 1819, brought extensive conversions to Christianity. As with other conversion processes, religious change had wide implications. Missionaries railed against traditional Hawaiian costumes, insisting that women cover their breasts, and a new garment, the muumuu, was fashioned from homespun American nightgowns with the sleeves cut off. Backed by the Hawaiian monarchy, missionaries also quickly established an extensive school system, by 1831 serving 50,000 students from a culture that had not previously developed writing.

The combination of Hawaiian interest and Western intrusion produced creative political and cultural changes, though inevitably at the expense of previous values. Demographic and economic trends had more insidious effects. Western-imported disease, particularly venereal disease and tuberculosis, had the usual tragic consequences for a previously isolated people: By 1850 only about 80,000 Hawaiians remained of a prior population of about half a million. Westerners more consciously exploited the Hawaiian economy. Whalers helped create raucous seaport towns. Western settlers from various countries (called *haoles* by the Hawaiians) experimented with potential commercial crops, soon concentrating particularly on sugar. Many missionary families turned to leasing land or buying it outright, impatient with the subsistence habits of Hawaiian commoners. They did not entirely forget their religious motives—among other things, many American missionaries had a strong antislavery background and shunned the most intense forms of exploitation; but it remained true that many families who came to Hawaii to do good ended by doing well.

Western businesses were mainly encouraged by the Hawaiian monarchy, eager for revenues and impressed by the West's military power. In 1848 an edict called the Great Mahele imposed Western concepts of property on Hawaiian land that had previously been shared by commoners and aristocrats. Most of the newly defined private property went to the king and the nobles, who gradually sold most of it to investors from the West. As sugar estates spread,

increasing numbers of Americans moved in to take up other commercial and professional positions—hence an increasingly "settler" pattern even in a technically independent state. Given Hawaiian population decline, it was also necessary to import Asian workers to staff the estates. The first Chinese contract workers were actually brought in before 1800, and after 1868 a larger current of Japanese swelled the immigrant throng.

Literal imperialism came as an anticlimax. The abilities of Hawaiian kings declined after 1872, in one case because of problems of disease and alcoholism. Under a weakened state, powerful planter interests pressed for special treaties with the United States that would promote their sugar exports, and the American government claimed naval rights at the Pearl Harbor base by 1887. As the last Hawaiian monarchs turned increasingly to the promotion of culture, writing a number of lasting Hawaiian songs but also spending considerable money on luxurious appointments, American planters concluded that their economic interests required outright United States control. An "annexation committee" persuaded American naval officers to "protect American lives and property" by posting troops around Honolulu in 1893, and the monarchy was disbanded. An imperial-minded United States Congress obligingly took over the islands in 1898.

As in New Zealand, Western control combined with considerable respect for Polynesian culture. Americans in Hawaii did not apply the same degree of racism that had described earlier relations with North American Indians or with African slaves. Hawaii's status as a settler colony was further complicated by the arrival of so many Asian immigrants. Nevertheless, Western cultural and particularly economic influence extended steadily, and the ultimate political seizure merely ratified the colonization of the islands.

CONCLUSION

THE PATTERN OF THE AGE OF IMPERIALISM

Though the basic patterns of domination in European colonial empires remained similar to those worked out in Java and India in the early industrial period, the style of colonial rule and patterns of social interaction between colonizer and colonized changed considerably in the late 19th century. Racism and social snobbery became pervasive in contacts between the colonizers and their African and Asian subordinates. The Europeans consciously renounced the ways of dressing, eating habits, and pastimes that had earlier been borrowed from or shared with the peoples of the colonies. The colonizers no longer saw themselves simply as the most successful competitors in a many-sided struggle for political power. They were convinced that they were inherently superior beings, citizens of the most powerful, civilized, and advanced societies on earth. Colonial officials in the age of "high imperialism" were much more concerned than earlier administrators to pull the peasants, who made up the overwhelming majority of the population of all colonized societies, into the market economy and teach them the value of hard work and discipline. Colonial educators were determined to impress upon the children of the colonized elite classes the superiority of Western learning and of everything from political organization to fashions in clothing.

In striving for these objectives, the European colonizers started with the assumption that it was their duty to impose their own views and ways of doing things, rather than learn from others—to remake the world, insofar as the abilities of the "natives" would allow, in the image of industrial Europe. But in pushing for change within colonized societies that had ancient, deeply rooted cultures and patterns of civilized life, the Europeans frequently aroused resistance to specific policies and to colonial rule more generally. Though the colonizers were able to put down protest movements led by displaced princes and religious prophets, much more enduring and successful challenges to their rule came, ironically, from the leaders their social reforms and Western-language schools had done much to nurture. These nationalists reworked European ideas and resurrected those of their own cultures, borrowed European organizational techniques, and made use of the communications systems and common language the Europeans had introduced into the colonies to contest European dominance. The overwhelming dependence of the Europeans on the collaboration of colonized peoples to govern and police their empires rendered the Europeans particularly vulnerable to these challenges from within.

FURTHER READINGS

There is vast literature on various aspects of European imperialism. Useful general histories on the different empires include Bernard Porter's *The Lion's Share: A Short History of British Imperialism 1850–1970* (1975), Raymond Betts's *Tricouleur* (1978), James J. Cooke's *The New French Imperialism, 1880–1910* (1973), and Woodruff D.

Smith's *The German Colonial Empire* (1978). There is no really satisfactory general history of the growth of Dutch power on Java or the British Empire in India, but Edward Thompson and G. T. Garratt provide a reasonably lively chronology in the *Rise and Fulfillment of British Rule in India* (1962), which can be supplemented by the essays in R. C. Majumdar, ed., *British Paramountcy and Indian Renaissance* part I, (1963). More recent accounts of specific aspects of the rise of British power in India are available in C. A. Bayley's *Indian society and the making of the British Empire* (1988) and P. J. Marshall's *Bengal: The British Beachhead, 1740–1828* (1987), both part of *The New Cambridge History of India*.

Of the many contributions to the debate over late 19th century imperialism, some of the most essential are those by D. C. M. Platt, Hans-Ulrich Wehler, William Appleman Williams, Jean Stengers, D. K. Fieldhouse, and Henri Brunschwig, plus the earlier works by Lenin and J. A. Hobson. Winfried Baumgart's *Imperialism* (1982) provides a good overview of the literature and conflicting arguments. Very different perspectives on the partition of Africa can be found in Jean Suret-Canale's *French Colonialism in Tropical Africa, 1900–1945* (1971) and Ronald Robinson and John Gallagher's *Africa and the Victorians* (1961).

Most of the better studies on the impact of imperialism and social life in the colonies are specialized monographs, but Percival Spear's *The Nabobs* (1963) is a superb place to start on the latter from the European viewpoint, while the works of Frantz Fanon, Albert Memmi, and O. Mannoni provide much information on the plight of the colonized. The impact of industrialization and other changes in Europe on European attitudes toward the colonized are treated in a number of works, including Philip Curtin's *The Image of Africa* (1964), William B. Cohen's *The French Encounter with Africans* (1980), and Michael Adas's *Machines as the Measure of Men* (1989). Ester Boserup's *Women's Role in Economic Development* (1970) provides a good overview of the impact of colonization on African and Asian women and families, but it should be supplemented by more recent monographs on the position of women in colonial settings. One of the best of these is Jean Taylor's *The Social World of Batavia* (1983).

1792 Slave rebellion in
St. Domingue (Haiti)

1804 Haiti declares independence

1808–1825 Spanish-American
wars of independence

1810 In Mexico, Father Hidalgo
initiates rebellion against Spain

1808 Portuguese court flees Napoleon,
arrives in Brazil; French armies invade Spain

1822 Brazil declares independence;
empire established under Dom Pedro I
1823 Monroe Doctrine indicates U.S. opposition to European ambitions in the Americas

1830 Bolívar dies; Gran Colombia dissolves into separate countries of Venezuela, Colombia, and Equador
1821 Mexico declares independence; empire under Iturbide lasts to 1823

1829–1852 Juan Manuel de Rosas rules Rio de la Plata

1854 Benito Juárez
leads reform in Mexico

1846–1848 Mexican-American War

1847–1855 Caste War in Yucatan

1850s Beginnings of rail-
road construction in
Cuba, Chile, and Brazil

3I

The Consolidation of Latin America, 1830–1920

INTRODUCTION. The spread of Western imperialism, along with its consolidation in prior holdings such as Indonesia, had carved up much of the world during the 19th century. Africa, both north and south of the Sahara, was almost entirely swallowed up, in contrast to the much more limited colonial patterns established before 1800. Australia, New Zealand, and all the clusters of smaller Pacific islands, including Polynesia, were seized. Southeast Asia was taken, and in combination with earlier acquisitions this meant a solid colonial swatch from India in the west to the Philippines in the east.

Four major parts of the world, however, were not caught up in the full imperialist scramble, even though they were not "Western." Russia, most of the Middle East, and much of East Asia were exempt, though imperialist rivalries cut into the latter two civilizations to some extent. Vestiges of inherited political strength and/or new initiatives prevented Western control. The fourth exception, Latin America, was the most surprising of all, for in a century of imperialism this society cast off previous colonial controls. The force of the industrial West was deeply felt—like other non-Western and noncolonial areas, Latin America was substantially reshaped by the dominant international forces of the day. New and independent political and cultural initiatives also formed a major part of this civilization's 19th-century experience.

It was early in the 19th century that most of the nations of Latin America gained their political independence. These former American colonies of Spain and Portugal were swept by the same winds of change that brought about the transformation of Europe's society and economy and led to the separation of England's North American colonies. Although at present Latin America is sometimes

---

1862–1867 French intervention in Mexico

1876–1911 Porfirio Díaz rules Mexico

1868–1878 Ten year war against Spain in Cuba

1889 Fall of Brazilian Empire; republic established

1903 Panamanian independence; beginning of Panama Canal (opens in 1914)

1865–1870 War of the Triple Alliance (Argentina, Brazil, and Uruguay against Paraguay)

1886–1888 Cuba and Brazil finally abolish slavery

1895–1898 Cuban Spanish-American War; U.S. acquires Puerto Rico and Philippines

1869 First school for girls in Mexico

considered part of the "Third World" along with many Asian and African nations, in reality its political culture was formed in the 18th century by the ideas of the Western Enlightenment and the crisis of the traditional monarchy and social structure. Thus Latin-American leaders in the 19th century, despite their many differences, often shared with Western political figures a firm belief in the virtues of "progress," reform, representational and constitutional government, and the "sacred" rights of private property. At the same time Latin-American leaders were often faced with insurmountable problems different from those of Europe and the United States. The colonial heritage had left little tradition of participatory government among the majority of the Latin-American population. A highly centralized colonial state had intervened in many aspects of life and had created not only a dependence on central authority but a resentment of it as well. Class and regional interests deeply divided the new nations, and wealth was very unequally distributed. Finally, the rise of European industrial capitalism created an economic situation that often placed the new nations in a weak or dependent position. These problems and tensions will serve as the focus for our examination of Latin America in the 19th century.

FROM COLONIES TO NATIONS

By the late 18th century, the Creole elites expressed a growing self-consciousness as they began to question the policies of Spain and Portugal and the very necessity of remaining in a colonial relationship. At the same time, these elites were joined by the majority of the population in resentment of the increasingly heavy hand of government as expressed in the new taxes and administrative reforms of the 18th century. But the shared resentment was not enough to overcome class conflicts and divisions. Early movements for independence usually failed because of the reluctance of the colonial upper classes to enlist the support of the Indian, mestizo, and mulatto masses who might later prove too difficult to control. The actual movements were only set in motion when events in Europe precipitated actions in America.

CAUSES OF POLITICAL CHANGE

Latin-American political independence was achieved as part of the general Atlantic revolution of the late 18th and early 19th centuries, and Latin-American leaders were moved by the same ideas and influenced by the same trends as those seeking political change elsewhere in the Atlantic world. Four external events had a particularly strong im-

pact on political thought in Latin America. The American Revolution from 1776 to 1783 provided a model of how colonies could break with the mother country. George Washington and Thomas Jefferson seemed to be examples of "Creole" leaders, and the revolutionary ideas of Jefferson, Thomas Paine, and the Declaration of Independence were eventually smuggled into Latin America. The French Revolution of 1789 provoked great interest in Latin America, and its slogans of "liberty, equality, and fraternity" appealed to some sectors of the population. As that revolution became increasingly radical, it was rejected by the Creole elites who could not support regicide, rejection of the Church's authority, and the social leveling implied by the Declaration of the Rights of Man.

The third external event was really an extension of the French Revolution. Torn by internal political conflict during the turmoil in France, the whites and free people of color in St. Domingue—France's great island sugar colony in the Caribbean—became divided. The slaves siezed the moment in 1791 to stage a great general rebellion. Under able leadership provided by Toussaint L'Overture and other blacks, various attempts to subdue the island were defeated and in 1804 the independent republic of Haiti was proclaimed. For Latin-American elites, Haiti was an example to be avoided. The spectre of general social upheaval and of slaves becoming their own masters so frightened them that they became even more unwilling to risk political change. It was not accidental that neighboring Cuba and Puerto Rico, with plantations and slaves and acutely aware of events in Haiti, were among the last of Spain's colonies to eventually gain independence. For slaves and free people of color throughout the Americas, however, Haiti became a symbol of freedom and hope.

What eventually precipitated the movements for independence in Latin America was the confused Iberian political situation caused by the French Revolution and its aftermath. Portugal was invaded by the French in 1807, and in 1808 Napoleon placed the king of Spain and his son Ferdinand VII under arrest and forced them to abdicate in favor of his brother Joseph Bonaparte who then sought to rule Spain backed by French bayonets. A general insurrection erupted in 1808 and was followed by a long guerrilla war. During the fighting a central committee, or *junta central*, ruled in Ferdinand's absence, in opposition to Napoleon's brother who also claimed to be king.

Who was the legitimate ruler? By 1810 the confusion in Spain had provoked a crisis in the colonies. In a number of places such as Caracas, Bogotá, and Mexico, Creoles pretending to be loyal to captive Ferdinand set up juntas to rule in his name, but they effectively ruled on their own behalf. "The mask of Ferdinand" fooled few people and soon the more conservative elements of the population, those still loyal to Spain and royal officials, opposed the movements for autonomy and independence. A crisis of legitimacy reverberated throughout the American colonies.

SPANISH-AMERICAN INDEPENDENCE STRUGGLES

The independence movements divided into three major theaters of operation. In Mexico, a conspiracy among leading Creoles moved one of the plotters, the priest Father Miguel de Hidalgo, to call for help from the Indians and mestizos of his region in 1810. He won a number of early victories, but eventually lost the support of the Creoles who feared social rebellion more than they desired independence. Hidalgo was captured and executed, but the insurgency smoldered in various parts of the country. Eventually, after 1820 when events in Spain weakened the king and the central government, conservative Creoles in Mexico were willing to move toward independence by uniting with the remnants of the insurgent forces. Augustín de Iturbide, a Creole officer at the head of an army that had been sent to eliminate the insurgents, drew up an agreement with them instead, and the combined forces of independence occupied Mexico City in September, 1821. Soon thereafter, with the support of the army, Iturbide was proclaimed emperor of Mexico.

This was a conservative solution. The new nation of Mexico was born as a monarchy, and little recognition was given to the social aspirations and programs of Hidalgo and his movement. Central America was briefly attached to the Mexican Empire, which collapsed in 1824. Mexico became a republic, and the Central American states, after attempting union until 1838, split apart into independent nations.

In South America and the Caribbean the chronology of independence was a mirror image of the conquest of the 16th century. Formerly secondary areas like Argentina and Venezuela, slowest to be settled in the 16th century, were among the first to opt for independence and the best able to achieve it, while the old colonial center in Peru was among the last to break with Spain. The Caribbean islands of Cuba and Puerto Rico—among the first of Spain's American possessions—fearful of slave rebellion and occupied by large Spanish garrisons, remained loyal until the end of the 19th century.

In northern South America, a movement for independence centered in Caracas had begun in 1810. After early reverses, Simón Bolívar, a wealthy Creole officer, emerged as the leader of the revolt against Spain. With considerable military skill and a passion for independence, he eventually

mobilized support, and between 1817 and 1822 he won a series of victories in Venezuela, Colombia, and Ecuador. Until 1830 these countries were united into a new nation called Gran Colombia. Political differences and regional interests led to the breakup of Gran Colombia. Bolívar became disillusioned and fearful of anarchy. "America is ungovernable," he said, and "those who have served the revolution have plowed the sea." To his credit, however, Bolívar rejected all attempts to crown him as king and remained until his death in 1830 firmly committed to the cause of independence and republican government.

Meanwhile in southern South America another movement had coalesced under José de San Martín in the Rio de La Plata. Buenos Aires had become a booming commer-

Simón Bolívar led the struggle for political independence in northern South America. Son of a wealthy Creole family, he became an ardent proponent of independence and a firm believer in the republican form of government.

cial center in the late 18th century and its residents, called *porteños*, particularly resented Spanish trade restrictions. Pushing for freedom of trade, they opted for autonomy in 1810 but tried to keep the outlying areas, such as Paraguay, under their control. The myth of autonomy rather than independence was preserved for a while. By 1816, however, the independence of the United Provinces of the Rio de la Plata had been proclaimed, although the provinces were far from united. Upper Peru (Bolivia) remained under Spanish control, Paraguay declared independence in 1813, and the Banda Oriental (Uruguay) resisted the central authority of Buenos Aires.

In Buenos Aires, José de San Martín had emerged as a military commander willing to speak and act for independence. From Argentina his armies crossed the Andes to Chile to help the patriot forces in that colony. With victories there, the patriot forces looked northward. Peru, the seat of the old viceroyalty and the scene of the Indian rebellion of Tupac Amaru in the 1780s, remained under Spanish rule. Its upper class was deeply conservative and little attracted to the movements for independence. San Martín's forces entered Peru and Creole adherence was slowly won. With victories like the battle of Ayacucho in 1824, royalist forces were defeated. By 1825 all of Spanish South America had gained its political independence. Despite various plans and programs to create some form of monarchy in many of the new states, all of them emerged as independent republics with representative governments. The nations of Spanish America were born of the Enlightenment and the ideas of 19th century liberalism.

BRAZILIAN INDEPENDENCE

Although the movement for independence in Brazil was roughly contemporaneous to those in Spanish America and many of the causes were similar, independence was achieved by quite a different process. By the end of the 18th century, Brazil had grown in population and economic importance and had clearly become the dominant part of the Portuguese colonial system. The expansion of European demand for colonial products, such as sugar, cotton, and cacao, contributed to that growth and also to the intensification of slave imports to the colony. While Brazilian planters, merchants, and miners sometimes longed for more open trade and fewer taxes, they feared that any upsetting of the political system might lead to a social revolution or, even worse, a Haitian-style general slave uprising. Thus incipient movements for independence in Minas Gerais in 1788 and Bahia in 1798 were unsuccessful. As one official said, "Men established in goods and property were unwilling to risk political change."

The Napoleonic invasions provoked a different outcome in Portugal than in Spain. When in 1807 French troops invaded Portugal, the whole Portuguese royal family and court were able to flee the country and, under the protection of British ships, sailed to Brazil. A new court was established at Rio de Janeiro, which then became the effective capital of the Portuguese Empire. Brazil was raised to equal status with Portugal, and all the functions of royal government were set up in the colony. As a partial concession to England and to colonial interests, the ports of Brazil were opened to world commerce, thus satisfying one of the main desires of the Brazilian elites. Unlike Spanish America, where the Napoleonic invasions provoked a crisis of authority and led Spanish Americans to consider ruling in their own name, in Brazil the transfer of the court brought royal government closer and tended to reinforce the colonial relationship.

From 1808 to 1820 the Portuguese king, Dom João VI, resided in Brazil and ruled his empire from there. Rio de Janeiro was transformed into a capital city with a public library, botanical gardens, and other improvements. Printing presses began to operate in the colony for the first time, schools were created, and commerce, especially with England, boomed in the newly opened ports. The Brazilian elite were given noble titles and offices in order to win their loyalty to the government, but the arrival of many Portuguese bureaucrats and nobles with the court also created jealousy and resentment. Still, during this period Brazil was transformed into the seat of empire, a fact not lost on its most prominent citizens.

Matters changed drastically in 1820 when, after the defeat of Napoleon in Europe and a liberal revolution in Portugal, the king was recalled and a parliament convoked. João VI, who loved Brazil, was reluctant to leave, but realizing that his return was inevitable, he left his young son Pedro as regent, warning him that if independence had to come, he should lead the movement and not some "adventurer." Although Brazilians were allowed representation at the Portuguese Parliament, it became clear that Brazil's new status was doomed and that it would be "recolonized." After demands that the prince regent also return to Europe, Pedro refused, and in September 1822 declared Brazilian independence. He became Dom Pedro I, constitutional emperor of Brazil. Fighting against Portuguese troops lasted a year, but Brazil avoided the long wars of Spanish America. Brazil's independence did not upset the existing social organization based on slavery nor did it radically change the political structure. With the brief exception of Mexico, all of the former Spanish-American colonies became republics, but Brazil became a monarchy under a member of the Portuguese ruling house.

NEW NATIONS CONFRONT OLD AND NEW PROBLEMS

By 1830 the former Spanish and Portuguese colonies had become independent nations. The roughly 20 million inhabitants of these nations looked hopefully to the future. Born in the crisis of the old regime and Iberian colonialism, many of the leaders of independence shared the ideals of representative government, careers open to talent, freedom of commerce and trade, the right to private property, and a belief in the individual as the basis of society. Generally there was a belief that the new nations should be sovereign and independent states, large enough to be economically viable and integrated by a common set of laws.

On the issue of freedom of religion and the position of the Church, however, there was less agreement among the leadership. Roman Catholicism had been the state religion and the only one allowed by the Spanish crown. While most leaders sought to maintain Catholicism as the official religion of the new states, some sought to end the exclusion of other faiths. The defense of the Church became a rallying cry for the conservative forces.

The ideals of the early leaders of independence were often egalitarian. Bolívar had received aid from Haiti and had promised in return to abolish slavery in the areas he liberated. By 1854 slavery had been abolished everywhere except Spain's remaining colonies of Cuba and Puerto Rico as well as in Brazil (all places where the economy was profoundly based on it). Early promises to end Indian tribute and taxes on people of mixed origin came much slower because the new nations still needed the revenue such policies produced. Egalitarian sentiments were often tempered by fears that the mass of the population was unprepared for self-rule and democracy. Early constitutions sought to balance order and popular representation by imposing property or literacy restrictions. Invariably, voting rights were reserved for males. Women were still disenfranchised and usually unable to hold public office. The Creole elite's lack of trust was based on the fact that in many places the masses had not demonstrated a clear preference for the new regimes and had sometimes fought in royalist armies mobilized by traditional loyalties and regional interests. While some mestizos had risen to leadership roles in the wars of independence, the old casta, or color distinctions, did not disappear easily. In Mexico, Guatemala, and the Andean nations, the large Indian population remained mostly outside of national political life. The mass of the Latin-American population—Indians and people of mixed origins—waited to see what was to come, and they were suspicious of the new political elite who were often drawn from the old colonial aristocracy but were now also joined by a new commercial and urban bourgeoisie.

POLITICAL FRAGMENTATION

The new nations can be grouped into a number of regional blocks. Some of the early leaders for independence had dreamed of creating a unified nation in some form, but regional rivalries, economic competition, and political divisions soon made that hope, and even more modest versions of it, impossible. Mexico emerged as a short-lived monarchy until a republic was proclaimed in 1823, but its government remained unstable until the 1860s because of military coups, financial failures, foreign intervention, and political turmoil. Central America broke away from the Mexican monarchy and did form a union, but regional antagonisms and resentment of Guatemala, the largest nation in the region, eventually led to dissolution of the union in 1838. Spain's Caribbean colonies, Cuba and Puerto Rico, suppressed early movements for independence and remained outwardly loyal. The Dominican Republic was occupied by its neighbor Haiti, and after resisting its neighbor as well as France and Spain, it finally gained independence in 1844. The Dominican example and the fear of a Haitian-style slave revolt tended to keep the Creole leaders of Cuba and Puerto Rico quiet.

In South America, as mentioned previously, the old colonial viceroyalty of New Granada became the basis for Gran Colombia—the large new state created by Bolívar that included modern Ecuador, Colombia, Panama, and Venezuela. The union, made possible to some extent by Bolívar's personal reputation and leadership, disintegrated as his own standing declined, and it ended in 1830, the year of his death. In the south, the viceroyalty of the Río de la Plata served as the basis for a desired state that the peoples of Argentina hoped to lead. Other parts of the region resisted these hopes. Paraguay declared and maintained its autonomy under Dr. José Rodríguez de Francia, who ruled his isolated and landlocked country as a dictator until 1840. Modern Uruguay was formed by a revolution for independence against the dominant power of its large neighbors Argentina and Brazil. It became an independent buffer between those two nations in 1828. The Andean nations of Peru and Bolivia, with their large Indian populations and conservative colonial aristocracies, flirted with union from 1829 to 1839 under the mestizo general Andrés Santa Cruz, but once again regional rivalries and the fears of their neighbors undermined the effort. Finally, Chile, somewhat isolated and blessed by the opening of trade in the Pacific, followed its own political course in a relatively stable fashion.

Most attempts at consolidation and union failed. Enormous geographical barriers and great distances separated nations and even regions within nations. Roads were poor and transportation rudimentary. To move goods 200 miles from Guayaquil on the coast to Quito in the Andes was an enormous task, and to send a message from Mexico City to Monterrey, California, took weeks. Geography, regional interests, and political divisions were too strong to overcome. Then too, the colonial heritage, in which the Spanish crown had protected some interests and regions at the expense of others and had left the mass of the population outside the political process, carried over into the new regimes. The problems of national integration were daunting. What is striking is not that Spanish America became 18 separate nations, but that it did not separate into even more.

"CAUDILLOS," POLITICS, AND THE CHURCH

The problems confronting the new nations were many. Over a decade of warfare in places, such as Venezuela, Colombia, and Mexico, had disrupted the economies and devastated wide areas. The mobilization of large armies whose loyalty to regional commanders was often based on their personal qualities, rather than their rank or politics, led to the rise of *caudillos,* independent leaders who dominated local areas by force in defiance of national policies and who sometimes seized the national government itself to impose their concept of rule. In situations of intense division among civilian politicians, a powerful regional commander of the army became the arbiter of power, leading sometimes to a situation of "praetorian politics" in which the army made and unmade governments. Keeping the army in the barracks became a preoccupation of governments, and the amount of money spent on the military in national budgets far exceeded needs.

Military commanders and regional or national caudillos were usually interested in power for their own sake, but they could represent or mobilize different groups in society. Many often defended the interests of regional elites, usually landowners, but others were populists who mobilized and claimed to speak for Indians, peasants, and the poor and sometimes received their unquestioning support. A few, such as the conservative Rafael Carrera, who ruled Guatemala from 1839 to 1865, sincerely took the interest of the Indian majority to heart, but in other matters there was a disregard for the normal workings of an open political system and the rule of law among these personalist leaders.

Other common issues confronted many of the new nations. With the exception of Brazil and briefly Mexico, the political leaders were agreed on the republic as the basic form of government, but what kind of republic? A struggle often developed between centralists—who wished to create strong, centralized national governments with broad powers—and federalists—who wanted policies, especially fiscal and commercial ones, to be set by regional governments. Other tensions developed between liberals and conservatives. Liberals stressed the rights of the individual and attacked the corporate (membership in a group or organization) structure of colonial society. They dreamed of a secular society and looked to the models of the United States or France. Often they wanted a decentralized or federalist form of government. Conservatives usually believed in a strong centralized state, and they often wished to maintain aspects of colonial society. They believed that a structure in which corporate groups (such as the Indians), artisan guilds, or institutions (such as the Church) provided the most equitable basis of social action should be recognized in law. Rather than a society based on open competition and individualism, society for the conservatives was organic—each group was linked to the other like parts of a body whose health depended on the proper functioning of each part. Not all conservatives resisted change, and some—such as the Mexican intellectual and politician, Lucas Alamán—were among the most "enlightened" leaders in terms of economic and commercial reforms, but as a group the conservatives were skeptical of secularism and individualism and strove to keep the Catholic Iberian heritage alive.

The role of the Church became a crucial issue in politics. The secularization of society and the role of the Church was a key matter that divided pro-clerical conservatives from the more secular liberals. In Mexico, for example, the Church had played a major role in education, the economy, and politics. Few questioned its dogma, but liberals sought to limit its role in civil life. The Church fought back with the aid of its pro-clerical supporters and with the power of the Papacy, which until the 1840s refused to fill vacant positions in the hierarchy or to cooperate with the new governments.

Political parties, often calling themselves Liberal or Conservative, sprang up throughout Latin America. They struggled for power and sought to impose their vision of the future on society. Their leadership, however, was usually drawn from the same social class of landowners and urban bourgeoisie with little to differentiate them except their position in the Church or on the question of federalism vs. centralization. The general population might be mobilized by the force and personality of a particular leader such as Juan Manuel de Rosas in Argentina or Antonio López de Santa Anna in Mexico, but political ideology was rarely an issue for most of the population.

The result was political turmoil and insecurity in much of Latin America in the first 50 years following independence. Presidents came and went with sad rapidity. Written constitutions, which both Liberals and Conservatives thought were a positive thing, were often short-lived and overturned with a change in government because the margin for interpretation of the constitution was slight. To some extent this was due to the Roman legal heritage that pervaded Hispanic law and emphasized written laws rather than the more interpretative common-law tradition. Great efforts were made to make constitutions precise, specific, and definitive, but this resulted in an attempt to change or at least modify the constitution each time there was a change in government. Some nations avoided the worst aspects of instability. Chile, after enacting a constitution in 1833 that gave the president broad powers, established a functioning political system that allowed for compromise. Brazil with its monarchical rule, despite a period of turmoil from 1832 to 1850, was able to maintain a political system of compromise, although it was dominated by the Conservatives who were favored by the emperor. Its 1824 constitution remained in force until 1889.

It is fair to say that in much of Latin America the basic questions of government and society remained unresolved after independence. Some observers attributed these problems to personalism, a lack of civic responsibility, and other defects in the "Latin" character. Nevertheless, the parallel experience of later emerging nations in the 20th century suggests that these problems were typical of former colonial dependencies searching for order and economic security in a world in which their options were constrained by their own potential and by external conditions.

LATIN-AMERICAN ECONOMIES AND WORLD MARKETS, 1820–1870

The former colonies of Spain and Portugal now entered the world of diplomatic relations and international commerce. The new nations sought diplomatic recognition and security. In the 1820s, while Europe was undergoing the post-Napoleonic conservative reaction and monarchies were being restored, various plans to help Spain recolonize Latin America were put forward. Great Britain, however, generally opposed these ideas, and since Great Britain was the dominant power at sea, its recognition of Latin-American sovereignty was crucial. Moreover, the newly independent United States also felt an affinity and sympathy for the new nations to the south. The Monroe Doctrine of 1823 stated clearly that any attempt of a European power to colonize in the Americas would be considered an unfriendly act by the United States. The United States at the time probably could have done little to prevent such actions, but Britain could, and its support of Latin-American independence provided needed protection.

There was a price for this support. During the turmoil of the 1820s, British foreign minister Lord Canning had once said, "Spanish America is free and if we do not mismanage our affairs sadly, she is English." He was referring to the broad economic and commercial advantages that the new nations offered. British commerce had penetrated the area in the 18th century when various concessions for trade had been won from the Spanish government, and Britain had profited from illegal trade as well. Now it could afford to offer its diplomatic recognition in exchange for the freedom to trade with the new nations. While little capital was directly invested in Latin America prior to 1850, Latin-American governments turned to foreign governments and banks for loans. Meanwhile, Britain became a major consumer of Latin-American products. In return Britain sold about £5 million of manufactured goods to the new nations each year, about half of which went to Brazil where British merchants were especially strong. While some historians argue that this was a rather small portion of Britain's overseas trade, it was crucial for Latin America. In some ways Britain replaced Spain as a dominant economic force over the area in a sort of neocolonial commercial system. Although other nations, notably France and the United States, also traded with Latin America, prior to 1860 Britain remained predominant.

Open ports and the influx of foreign goods, often of better quality and cheaper than local products, benefited the port cities that controlled customhouses and the large landowners whose hides, sugar, and other products were exported. But these policies tended to damage local industries or regions that had specialized in producing for internal markets. Little capital was available for investment in local industries, and often the governments controlled by liberal free traders or conservative landowners refused or were unable to impose tariffs on imports needed to protect or stimulate local industry. Latin America became increasingly dependent on foreign markets and foreign imports, and as it did, it reinforced the old colonial economic heritage in which land was the basis of wealth and prestige.

MID-CENTURY STAGNATION

From about 1820 to 1850 the economy of Latin America was stagnant. Its mining sector was slow to recover after the wars of independence, its transportation network and port facilities were still underdeveloped, and it lacked capital for investment or found that so much capital was tied up in land that it was unavailable for investment in industry. Only Cuba with its booming sugar economy experienced expansion, but Cuba was still a colony of Spain. After 1850, however, this situation began to change as the expansion of the European economy created new demands for Latin-American products. Coffee cultivation in Brazil, hides and beef in Argentina, and minerals and grains in Chile provided the basis of growth and allowed some Latin-American governments to address social issues. Peru, for example, exploited enormous guano (bird droppings) deposits on islands off its coast. Between 1850 and 1880, exports of this fertilizer earned Peru over £10 million, and this income allowed the government to end Indian tribute and to abolish slavery by compensating the owners. Latin-American cities began to grow and provide good internal markets, and the introduction of steamships and railroads began to overcome the old problems of transportation. By the 1840s steamship lines improved communications within countries and opened up new possibilities for international commerce, and by the 1860s railroads were being constructed, usually to link export-producing regions to the ports. Landed wealth and exports continued to characterize the economies of the region as they had in the colonial era,

and as the levels of exports and the governments' dependence on them increased, the vulnerability of Latin America to the vagaries of the world economy increased as well.

Without detailing all the complex changes within the Latin-American nations during the 19th century, a few general patterns can be discerned. After the turmoil of independence, a number of Liberal reformers attempted to institute a series of programs in the 1820s and 1830s intended to break the patterns of the colonial heritage and to follow the main social and economic trends of western Europe. These ideas were often imposed on societies and economies unprepared for drastic change, especially since the strength of opposing institutions, such as the Church and the army, remained intact. By the 1840s Conservatives had returned to power in many places to slow or stop the reform measures. Some of them attempted to speak for the lower classes or Indians, who wished to see the paternal aspects of the old colonial state reimposed to protect them from the reforms of the liberals. In some ways, an alliance

The drive for progress made Latin-American nations anxious to accept foreign investment. Railroads were important for economic growth in that they often linked key exports to the ports and were designed principally to serve the needs of foreign capital.

between the landowners and the peasantry emerged in opposition to the changes suggested by the middle class and urban "modernizers."

ECONOMIC RESURGENCE AND LIBERAL POLITICS

By the last quarter of the century, as the world economy entered into a phase of rapid expansion, there was a shift in attitude and possibilities in Latin America. Liberals returned to power in many places in Latin America and initiated a series of changes that began to transform their nations. The ideological basis of the new liberal surge was also changing. Based on the ideas of *positivism* of the French philosopher Auguste Comte, who stressed observation and a scientific approach to the problems of society, Latin-American politicians and intellectuals found a guiding set of principles and a justification of their quest for political stability and economic growth.

This shift was due in large part to the general economic expansion of the "second" Industrial Revolution and the age of imperialism. The application of science to industry created new demands for Latin-American products, such as copper and rubber, to accompany the increasing demand for its consumer products such as wheat, sugar, and coffee. The population of Latin America doubled to over 43 million inhabitants in the 60 years between 1820 and 1880. After 1850 economies grew rapidly. Timing, of course, varied greatly but the expansion of exports in places, such as Colombia, Argentina, and Brazil, stimulated prosperity for some and a general belief in the advantages of the Liberal programs. The desire to participate in the capitalist expansion of the Western economy dominated the thinking of Latin-American leaders. Foreign entrepreneurs and bankers joined hands with philosophical liberals, landowners, and urban merchants in Latin America to back the Liberal programs, which now became possible because of the increased revenues generated by exports.

The leaders of the post-1860 governments were a new generation of politicians who had matured, not in the age of independence, but during the chaotic years of postindependence politics. Their inspiration came from England, France, and the United States. They were firm believers in progress, education, and free competition within a secular society, but they were sometimes distrustful of the mass of their own people, who seemed to represent an ancient "barbarism" in contrast to the "civilization" of progress. That distrust and their sometimes insensitive application of foreign models to a very different reality in their own countries — what one Brazilian author has called "ideas out of place" — prevented many from achieving the progress they so ardently desired.

Economic growth and "progress" were costly. Responding to international demand, landowners increased their holdings, often aided by the governments they controlled or influenced. Peasant lands were expropriated in Chile, Peru, and Bolivia; small farmers were displaced in Brazil and Costa Rica; and Church lands were seized in Mexico. Labor was needed. Immigrants from Europe flooded into Argentina and Brazil, while in other countries new forms of tenancy, peonage, and disguised servitude developed.

DOCUMENT
CONFRONTING THE HISPANIC HERITAGE: FROM INDEPENDENCE TO CONSOLIDATION

Simón Bolívar (1783–1830) "The Liberator" was a man of determination and perception. His campaigns for independence were defeated on a number of occasions, yet he did not despair. In 1815 while in exile on the island of Jamaica, he penned a letter to a newspaper that gave his evaluation of Latin America's situation and his vision for the future for its various parts. He advocated a republican form of government and rejected monarchy, but he warned against federalism and against popular democracies that might lead to dictatorships. "As long as our countrymen do not acquire the abilities and political virtues that distinguish our brothers to the north, wholly popular systems, far from working to our advantage, will, I greatly fear, bring about our downfall." Spain had left America unprepared, and in this letter Bolívar summarized many of the complaints of Latin Americans against Spanish rule and underlined the difficulty of the tasks of liberation — political, social, and economic. The famous "Letter of Jamaica" is one of the most candid writings by a leader of Latin-American independence. The following excerpts suggest its tone and content.

"BOLÍVAR'S JAMAICA LETTER" (1815)

We are a young people. We inhabit a world apart, separated by broad seas. We are young in the ways of almost all the arts and sciences, although, in a certain manner, we are old in the ways of civilized society. I look upon the present state of America as similar to that of Rome after its fall. Each part of Rome adopted a political system conforming to its interest and situation or was led by the individual ambitions of certain chiefs, dynasties, or associations. But this important difference exists: those dispersed parts later reestablished their ancient nations, subject to the changes imposed by circumstances or events. But we scarcely retain a vestige of what once was; we are, moreover, neither Indian nor European, but a species midway between the legitimate proprietors of this country and the Spanish usurpers. In short, although Americans by birth we derive our rights from Europe, and we have to assert these rights against the rights of the natives, and at the same time we must defend ourselves against the invaders. This places us in a most extraordinary and involved situation. . . .

The role of the inhabitants of the American hemisphere has for centuries been purely passive. Politically they were nonexistent. We are still in a position lower than slavery, and therefore it is more difficult for us to rise to the enjoyment of freedom. . . . States are slaves because of either the nature or the misuse of their constitutions; a people is therefore enslaved when the government, by its nature or its vices infringes on and usurps the rights of the citizen or subject. Applying these principles, we find that America was denied not only its freedom but even an active and effective tyranny. . . .

We have been harassed by a conduct which has not only deprived us of our rights but has kept us in a sort of permanent infancy with regard to public affairs. If we could have at least managed our domestic affairs and our internal administration, we could have acquainted ourselves with the processes and mechanics of public affairs. We should also have enjoyed a personal consideration, thereby commanding a certain unconscious respect from the people, which is so necessary to preserve amidst revolutions. That is why I say we have even been deprived of an active tyranny, since we have not been permitted to exercise its functions.

Americans today, and perhaps to a greater extent than ever before, who live within the Spanish system occupy a position in society no better than that of serfs destined to labor, or at best they have no more status than that of mere consumers. Yet even this status is surrounded with galling restrictions, such as being forbidden to grow European crops, or to store products which are royal monopolies, or to establish factories of a type the Peninsula (Spain) itself does not possess. To this add the exclusive trading privileges, even in articles of prime necessity, and the barriers between the American provinces, designed to prevent all exchange of trade, traffic, and understanding. In short, do you wish to know what our future held?—simply the cultivation of the fields of indigo, grain, coffee, sugar cane, cacao, and cotton; cattle raising on the broad plains, hunting wild game in the jungles; digging in the earth to mine its gold—but even these limitations could never satisfy the greed of Spain. So negative was our existence that I can find nothing comparable in any other civilized society. . . .

By mid-century Latin American political leaders were advocating "progress" and seeking to bring Latin America closer to the norms of life set by Europe. For liberals like the Argentine soldier, statesman, and author Domingo F. Sarmiento (1811–1888) his nation's task was to overcome the "barbarism" of rural life and implant the "civilization" of the Europeanized cities. Sarmiento saw in the bands of mounted rural workers, or *gauchos*, and their caudillo leaders an anachronistic way of life that held the nation back. His comparison of the gauchos, to the Berbers of North Africa demonstrates the ancient hostility of "civilized" urban-dwellers to the nomadic way of life. In a way, Sarmiento saw the dictatorship of Juan Manuel de Rosas as a result of the persistence of the gauchos and the manipulation of the lower classes, a sort of living example of what Bolívar had warned against. The following excerpt from Sarmiento's classic *Life in the Argentine Republic in the Days of the Tyrants or Civilization and Barbarism* (1868) demonstrates his admiration for European culture including that of Spain, and his desire it model his nation on it. That such a program might involve economic and cultural dependency did not concern Sarmiento and others like him.

THE SEARCH FOR PROGRESS

Before 1810 two distinct, rival, and incompatible forms of society, two differing kinds of civilization existed in the Argentine Republic: one being Spanish, European, and cultivated, the other barbarous,

American, and almost wholly of native growth. The revolution which occurred in the cities acted only as the cause, the impulse, which set these two distinct forms of national existence face to face, and gave occasion for a contest between them, to be ended, after lasting many years, by the absorption of one into the other.

I have pointed out the normal form of association, or want of association, of the country people, a form worse a thousand times, than that of a nomad tribe. I have described the artificial associations formed in idleness, and the sources of fame among the gauchos—bravery, daring, violence and opposition to regular law, to the civil law, that is, of the city. These phenomena of social organization existed in 1810, and still exist, modified in many points, slowly changing in others, and yet untouched in several more. These foci about which were gathered the brave, ignorant, free, and unemployed peasantry, were found by thousands through the country. The revolution of 1810 carried everywhere commotion and the sound of arms. Public life, previously wanting in this Arabo-Roman society, made its appearance in all the taverns, and the revolutionary movement finally brought about provincial, warlike associations, called *montoneras* [mounted gaucho guerrilla bands] legitimate offspring of the tavern and the field, hostile to the city and to the army of revolutionary patriots. As events succeed each other, we shall see the provincial montoneras headed by their chiefs; the final triumph, in Facundo Quiroga [a caudillo leader], of the country over the cities throughout the land; and by their subjugation in spirit, government, and civilization, the final formation of the central consolidated despotic government of the landed proprietor, Don Juan Manuel de Rosas, who applied the knife of the gaucho to the culture of Buenos Aires, and destroyed the work of centuries—of civilization, law, and liberty. . . .

They [revolutions for independence] were the same throughout America, and sprang from the same source, namely, the progress of European ideas. South America pursued that course because all other nations were pursuing it. Books, events, and the impulses given by these, induced South America to take part in the movement imparted to France by North American demands for liberty, and to Spain by her own and French writers. But what my object requires me to notice, is, that the revolution—except in its external symbolic independence of the king—

was interesting and intelligible only to the Argentine cities, but foreign and unmeaning to the rural districts. Books, ideas, municipal spirit, courts, laws, statutes, education, all points of contact and union existing between us and the people of Europe, were to be found in the cities, where there was a basis of organization, incomplete and comparatively evil, perhaps, for the very reason it was incomplete, and had not attained the elevation which it felt itself capable of reaching, but it entered into the revolution with enthusiasm. Outside the cities, the revolution was a problematical affair, and [in] so far [as] shaking off the king's authority was shaking off judicial authority, it was acceptable. The pastoral districts could only regard the question from this point of view. Liberty, responsibility of power, and all the questions which the revolution was to solve, were foreign to their mode of life and to their needs. But they derived this advantage from the revolution, that it tended to confer an object and an occupation upon the excess of vital force, the presence of which among them has been pointed out, and was to add a broader base of union than that to which throughout the country districts the men daily resorted. These Spartan constitutions, that warlike nature hitherto ill-satisfied by the free use of the dagger, that Roman-like idleness which could only be exchanged for the activity of the battle-field, that utter impatience of judicial control, were all to have at last a fit sphere of action in the world. . . .

Its [the caudillo band's] essence was individual action; its exclusive weapon, the horse; its stage, the vast pampas. The Bedouin hordes which in our day disturb the Algerian frontier by their war-cries and depredations, give us an exact idea of the Argentine montonera, which has been made use of by men of sagacity, as well as by noted desperadoes. In Africa, at the present day, there exists the same struggle between civilization and barbarism: the Bedouin band and the montonera are distinguished by the same characters, the same spirit, the same undisciplined strategy. . . .

The only explanation of the montonera is to be discovered in the examination of the society from which it proceeded. Artigas [caudillo leader of the Uruguayan rebels] the scout and outlaw, at war with the authorities of the city, but bought over as provincial commandant and chief of equestrian bands, presents a type reproduced with little change in each provincial commandant who came to be like a partisan leader. Like all civil wars in which deep differences in education, belief, and motives divide the parties engaged in them, the internal warfare of the Argentine Republic was long and obstinate, until one of the elements of the strife was victorious. The Argentine Revolutionary War was twofold: first, a civilized warfare of the cities against Spain; second, a war against the cities on the part of the country chieftains with the view of shaking off all political subjugation and satisfying their hatred of civilization. The cities overcame the Spaniards, and were in their turn overcome by the country districts. This is the explanation of the Argentine Revolution, the first shot of which was fired in 1810, and the last is still to be heard.

Questions: To what extent did the leaders of independence see their problems as a result of their Hispanic heritage? What would have been the reaction of the mass of the population to Sarmiento's idea of progress? Were the leaders naive about Latin America's possibilities for political democracy?

MEXICO: INSTABILITY AND FOREIGN INTERVENTION

After the short monarchical experiment, a Mexican republic was established. Its constitution of 1824, based on the examples of France, the United States, and Spain was a federalist document that guaranteed basic civil rights. Nevertheless, this constitution did not address the nation's continuing social problems and needs: the maldistribution of land, the status of the Indians, the problems of education, and the situation of vast numbers of indigent poor among the approximately seven million people in Mexico, the most populous of the new nations. Politics soon became a complicated struggle between the Conservative centralists and the Liberal federalists and was made even more complicated by the rival jockeying for advantage by commercial agents of Great Britain and the United States. Control by the Conservatives led to some financial and economic improvements under the intelligent and innovative Lucas Alamán, but General Antonio López de Santa Ana staged a coup and then, after being elected president, turned the government over to the Liberals. For a short period from 1832 to 1835, the Liberals, led by Valentín Gómez Farías, were in control and tried to institute a series of sweeping social and economic reforms, but their attack on the Church led to violent reaction and the return of Santa Ana—this time as a defender of the Church.

The mercurial Santa Ana remained until his death the maker of Mexican politics. He was an archetype of the caudillo; the personalist, autocratic leader. But Mexico's instability was not only due to his personality. Santa Ana was merely the symptom of deeper problems.

These in fact were many. Mexico's instability and financial difficulties made it a target for foreign intervention. A Spanish invasion was repulsed in 1829, and a French expedition landed to collect unpaid debts in 1838. More serious, Texas, the vast area of Mexico's northern frontier was increasingly occupied by Anglo-American settlers who brought their language, customs, and religion despite restrictions on the latter. Although the Texans at first sought more autonomy as federalists within the Mexican nation, as had been done in Yucatán and other Mexican provinces, ethnic and religious differences as well as Santa Ana's attempts to suppress the Texans in 1836 led to widespread fighting and the declaration of Texan independence. Santa Ana, captured for a while by the Texans, returned to dominate Mexican politics, but the question of Texas festered and became acute when in 1845 the United States, with its eye on California and moved by "manifest destiny"—a belief that it was destined to rule the continent from coast to coast—voted to annex Texas.

The result was war. A border dispute and the breakdown of negotiations over California led to hostilities in 1846. Santa Ana, who had been in exile, returned to lead the Mexican forces, but United States armies seized California, penetrated northern Mexico, and eventually occupied the Mexican capital. Mexico was forced to sign the disadvantageous Treaty of Guadalupe-Hidalgo (1848) in which the United States acquired about one-half of Mexico's national territory—but less than five percent of its population. The Mexican-American War and the treaty left a bitter legacy of distrust of the northern neighbor, not only in Mexico but throughout the region. For Mexico there was also a serious loss of economic potential, but the heroic battle against the better-equipped Americans produced a sense of nationalism and a desire to confront the nation's serious internal problems, which also bore some responsibility for the war and the defeat.

Politics could not return to the situation before the war. Santa Ana did return to office for a while, more mercurial and despotic than ever, but now he was opposed by a new generation of Liberals: intellectuals, lawyers, and some rural leaders, many of them from middle class backgrounds, some of them mestizos and even a few Indians. Perhaps the most prominent of them was Benito Juárez (1806–1872), a humble Indian who had received a legal education and who had eventually become the governor of his state. He shared the Liberal vision of a secular society based on the rule of law in which the old privileges of the Church and the army would be eliminated as a way of promoting economic change and growth. The Liberal revolt, called *La Reforma*, began in 1854, and within a year the Liberals had taken Mexico City. In a series of laws integrated into a new constitution in 1857, the Liberals set the basis for their vision of society. Military and clerical privileges were curtailed and Church property was placed on sale. Indian communal lands were also restricted, and the government forced the sale of these lands to individuals—it was hoped to Indians. The goal of these programs was to create a nation of small independent farmers. The lands, however, were often bought up by speculators or already wealthy hacendados, and the result, in fact, was that the peasants and Indians lost what land they had. By 1910 about half of Mexico's rural population was landless. Good intentions had brought disastrous results.

The Liberal program produced the expected Conservative reaction. The Church threatened to excommunicate those who upheld the new constitution. Civil war erupted, and in reaction, Juárez, now president, pushed forward even more radical measures, including confiscation of Church properties and the secularization of marriage and burial. Losing ground in the war, the Conservatives turned to Europe and convinced Napoleon III of France to intervene. Attracted by possible economic advantage, dreams of empire, and a desire to please Catholic opinion in France, Napoleon III justified French intervention by claims of a shared "Latin" culture (this was the origin of the term "Latin America"). Under cover of a joint expedition, French forces landed in 1862 and soon took the capital. At French urging Maximilian von Habsburg, an Austrian archduke, was convinced to take the throne of Mexico. Well-intentioned but ineffective, Emperor Maximilian tried to get the support of Juárez and the Liberals and even kept many of the laws of the *Reforma* in place, to the dismay of his Conservative supporters. But Juárez absolutely rejected the idea of a foreign prince ruling Mexico. French bayonets and the United States' preoccupation with its own Civil War allowed Maximilian and his Empress Carlota to rule until 1867. When French troops were withdrawn, however, the regime crumbled. Maximilian and his loyal generals were captured and executed in 1867.

Juárez returned to office, but his administration was increasingly autocratic—a reality that he felt was unavoidable after so long a period of instability. By his death in 1872,

Benito Juárez, an Indian from southern Mexico, rose to the presidency and began a series of sweeping reforms designed to break the old colonial structures. His uncompromising resistance to foreign intervention and monarchy has made him a symbol of Mexican sovereignty and independence. Here he is portrayed in a mural by Diego Rivera.

the force of his personality, his concern for the poor, and his nationalist position against foreign intervention had identified Liberalism with nationalism in Mexico and made Juárez a symbol of the nation. By 1880 Mexico was poised on the edge of a period of strong central government and relative political stability, which under the virtual dictator Porfirio Díaz led to rapid economic growth, penetration of the economy by foreign capital, the expansion of the large landed estates, political repression, and a revolution.

ARGENTINA: THE PORT AND THE NATION

Whereas Mexico and its silver had been the core of Spain's empire in America, the rolling plains, or pampas, of the Rio de la Plata in southern South America had been a colonial backwater until the 18th century when direct trade had begun to stimulate its economy. The Rio de la Plata was dominated by the port of Buenos Aires and its merchants, but the other areas of the region had their own interests and resented the power and growth of the port city and its surrounding countryside. The United Prov-

inces of the Rio de la Plata, which declared their independence in 1816, soon split apart, and local caudillos, able to call on the support of gauchos, dominated each region. In Buenos Aires, the Liberals gained control in the 1820s and under Bernardino Rivadavia (1780–1857), a Europeanized lawyer, instituted a series of broad reforms in education, finance, agriculture, and immigration. These included a program of public land sales that stimulated the growth of cattle ranches and the power of the rancher class.

In many ways the secular and progressive program of Rivadavia in Argentina paralleled the program of Gómez Farias in Mexico and produced a similar negative reaction from Conservatives and the Church, especially when Church lands were confiscated and freedom of religion was legislated. But Rivadavia's main sin was centralism, a desire to create a strong national government. Centralists (called Unitarians in the Argentine context) provoked the reaction of the federalists, who by 1831 had taken power under Juan Manuel de Rosas, who commanded the loyalty of the gaucho employees of the stockmen.

Under Rosas the federalist program of a weak central

Emperor Maximilian was finally captured after his attempt with French help to reestablish a monarchy in Mexico. Well-meaning, he eventually lost the support of the conservatives, and Juárez refused to spare his life, as a warning to other ambitious nations that Mexico would remain independent.

government and local autonomy was instituted, but Rosas's federalism favored the ranchers of the Buenos Aires province and the merchants of the great port. He campaigned against the Indians to the south in order to open new lands to the cattle ranchers. Exports of hides and salted meat increased, but the revenues collected at the port were not shared with the other provinces. Although popular with the gauchos and the urban poor and remembered today as a nationalist who resisted British and French economic pressure, Rosas proved to be a despotic leader, crushing his opponents and forcing people to display his slogan, "Death to the savage, filthy Unitarians." His brand of populist, authoritarian, personalist politics drove Liberal opponents into exile where they plotted his overthrow. Meanwhile his policies continued to favor the ranching and meat exporting interests of Buenos Aires. Eventually, the Liberal exiles joined forces with the caudillos who, while federalists, resented Rosas's brand of federalism that had so favored the Buenos Aires province. In 1852 this coalition defeated Rosas and drove him from power.

There followed a confused decade of rival governments, because the questions of federalism and the role of Buenos Aires within the nation remained unresolved. A new constitution was issued in 1853 under the influence of Juan Bautista Alberdi, an able and progressive journalist who was also a strong believer in the need to encourage immigration. This constitution incorporated the programs of the federalists but guaranteed national unity through the power of the presidency over the provincial governors. By 1862 after considerable fighting, a compromise was worked out and the new, unified nation, now called the Argentine Republic, entered into a period of prosperity and growth under a series of Liberal presidents whose programs paralleled the *Reforma* in Mexico. The age of the Liberals was now in full swing.

Between 1862 and 1890, able and intelligent presidents, such as Bartolomé Mitre (1821–1876) and Domingo F. Sarmiento (1811–1888), initiated a wide series of political reforms and economic measures designed to bring "progress" to Argentina. Sarmiento was an archetype of the liberal reformers of the mid-century. A great admirer of England and the United States, a firm believer in the value of education, and an ardent supporter of "progress," Sarmiento had been a constant opponent of Rosas and had been driven into exile. During that time, he had written *Facundo*, a critique of the caudillo politics of the region, in which the "barbarism" of the gauchos and their leaders was contrasted to the "civilization" of the liberal reformers. (See the document in this chapter.)

Now in power, Sarmiento and the other liberal leaders were able to put their programs into practice. They were aided by a number of factors. Political stability made investment more attractive to foreign banks and merchants. The expansion of the Argentine economy, especially exports of beef, hides, and wool, created the basis for prosperity. Foreign trade in 1890 was five times as great as it had been in 1860. The population tripled to over three million as the agricultural expansion, high wages, and opportunities for mobility attracted large numbers of European immigrants. With increased revenues the government could initiate reforms in education, transportation, and other areas, often turning to foreign models and foreign investors. Then too there was an increased feeling of national unity. A long and bloody war waged by Argentina, Brazil, and Uruguay against their neighbor Paraguay from 1865 to 1870 created a sense of unity and national pride that was previously absent.

That sense was also heightened by the final defeat of the Indians south of Buenos Aires by 1880 as more land was opened to ranching and agriculture. At about the same time as in the United States, the railroad, the telegraph, and the repeating rifle brought an end to Indian resistence and opened their lands to settlement. The Indians, who were pushed far to the south, and the gauchos, whose way of life was displaced by the tide of immigrants, received little sympathy from the Liberal government. By 1890 Argentina seemed to represent the achievement of a Liberal program for Latin America.

THE BRAZILIAN EMPIRE

It was sometimes said that, despite its monarchical form, Brazil was the only functioning republic in South America in the 19th century. At first glance it seemed that Brazil did avoid much of the political instability and turmoil found elsewhere in the continent, and that through the mediation of the emperor a political compromise was worked out. Beneath that facade, however, problems and patterns similar to those in Spanish America were apparent. The transition to nationhood was relatively smooth, and thus the basic foundations of Brazilian society—slavery, large landholdings, and an export economy—remained securely in place, reinforced by a new Brazilian nobility created for the new empire.

Brazilian independence had been declared in 1822, and by 1824 a relatively liberal constitution had been issued by Dom Pedro I, the young Brazilian monarch, although not without resistance from those who wanted a republic or at least a very weak constitutional monarch. But Dom Pedro I was an autocrat, still surrounded by Portuguese courtiers, and when his expansionist policies in the Rio de la Plata and his scandalous personal life began to wear away his

The tremendous boom in the Argentine economy was reflected in the growth of Buenos Aires, the so-called "Paris of the Americas," as a cosmopolitan urban center.

popularity, pressures built up against him. In 1831 he was forced to abdicate in favor of his young son, Pedro (later to become Dom Pedro II), but the boy was too young to rule and a series of regents directed the country in his name. What followed was an experiment in republican government, although the facade of monarchy was maintained.

The next decade was as tumultuous as any in Spanish America. The issues of liberalism vs. conservatism were complicated by the existence of monarchist and antimonarchist factions in Brazil. The centralism of the government in Rio de Janeiro was opposed by the provinces, and a series of regional revolts erupted, some of which took on aspects of social wars as slaves, peasants, and free people of color were mobilized in the fighting. The southernmost province of Brazil, Rio Grande do Sul, attempted to break away and declare its independence over federalist issues. In northeastern Brazil, a strong republican tradition had led to rebellions in 1817 and 1824, and now the region generated a series of revolts against the central government. All of these were suppressed by the imperial government, and the territorial unity of Brazil remained intact. By 1840, however, the politicians were willing to see the young Dom Pedro II begin to rule in his own name.

Meanwhile, Brazil had been undergoing an economic transformation brought about by a new export crop, coffee. Brazil had long been an exporter of minerals and agricultural products, a position reinforced by the trade agreements made with Great Britain in the 19th century. Coffee provided a new basis for agricultural expansion in southern Brazil. In the provinces of Rio de Janeiro and then São Paulo, coffee estates, or *fazendas*, began to spread toward the interior as new lands were opened. By 1840 coffee made up over 40 percent of Brazil's exports, and by 1880 that figure reached 60 percent.

Along with the expansion of coffee growing came an intensification of slavery, Brazil's primary form of labor. For a variety of humanitarian and economic reasons Great Britain pressured Brazil to end the slave trade from Africa during the 19th century, but the slave trade continued on an enormous scale up to 1850. Over 1.4 million Africans were imported in the last 50 years of the trade, and even after the trans-Atlantic slave trade ended, slavery continued. At mid-century about one-fourth of Brazil's population were still enslaved. While some reformers were in favor of ending slavery, a real abolitionist movement did not develop in Brazil until after 1870. Brazil did not finally abolish slavery until 1888.

As in the rest of Latin America, the years after 1850 witnessed considerable growth and prosperity in Brazil. Dom Pedro II proved to be an enlightened man of rather bourgeois middle-class habits who was anxious to reign over a tranquil and progressive nation, even if that tranquility was based on slave labor. Dom Pedro II favored the Conservatives in his appointment of ministers, but Liberals were given enough access to government to avoid direct confrontations. The trappings of a monarchy, a court, and noble titles kept the elite attached to the regime. Meanwhile railroads, steamships, and the telegraph began to change the nature of communication and transportation. Foreign companies invested in these projects as well as in banking and other activities. In growing cities like Rio de Janeiro and São Paulo merchants, lawyers, and a middle and urban working class began to exert pressure on the government. Less wedded to landholding and to slavery, these new groups were a catalyst for change, even though the right to vote was still very limited. Moreover, the nature of the labor force was changing.

After 1850 a tide of immigrants, mostly from Italy and Portugal, began to reach Brazil's shores, increasingly attracted by government immigration schemes. Between 1850 and 1875 over 300,000 immigrants arrived in Brazil and over two-thirds of them went to work in the coffee trees of southern Brazil. Their presence lessened the dependence on slavery, and by 1870 the abolitionist movement was gaining strength. A series of laws freeing children and the aged, the sympathy of Dom Pedro II himself, the agitation by abolitionists (both black and white), and the efforts of the slaves (who began to overtly resist and run away in large numbers) brought in 1888 an end to slavery in Brazil, the last nation in the Western Hemisphere to abolish it.

The Brazilian monarchy rested on the support of the planter aristocracy, but after 1870 their commitment and that of other groups began to wither. The long war of the Triple Alliance against Paraguay (1865–1870) had become unpopular, and the military began to take an active role in politics. Squabbles with the Church undercut support from the clergy. The planters now turned increasingly to immigrants for their laborers, and some began to modernize their operations. The ideas of positivism, a modernizing philosophy that sought to bring about material progress through the application of scientific principles to government and society, attracted many intellectuals and key members of the army. Politically, a Republican party, formed in 1871, began to gather support in urban areas from a wide spectrum of the population. The Brazilian monarchy could not survive the abolition of slavery. In 1889 a virtually bloodless military coup deposed the emperor and established a republic under military men strongly influenced by positivist intellectuals and Republican politicians.

SOCIETIES IN SEARCH OF THEMSELVES

As colonial subjects of Spain and Portugal, the elites of Latin America had shared the culture and values of Europe. Recognition of that shared experience continued among the upper classes who still looked to Europe for their inspiration, but political independence also provoked feelings of Americanism and at least a partial separation from, and rejection of, the old forms. Many times, however, this was simply a denial of the Hispanic traditions associated with the old colonial status and an acceptance of English and French models that seemed to represent the new age.

CULTURAL LIFE AND POLITICS

In Latin America, there was little separation between intellectual life and politics. The *pensador*, or thinker, who might write poetry, history, essays, and novels and combine that activity with political action, public office, and military command, was a common and highly respected figure.

The end of colonial rule opened up Latin America to direct influences from the rest of Europe. Scientific observers, travelers, and the just plain curious often accompanied by artists came to see and record, and while doing so introduced new ideas and fashions. Artistic and cultural missions were sometimes brought directly from Europe by Latin-American governments.

The tastes and fashions of Europe were adopted by the elite in the new nations. The battles and triumphs of independence were celebrated in paintings, hymns, odes, and theatrical pieces in the neoclassical style in an attempt to use Greece and Rome as a model for the present. In this Latin Americans followed the lead of Europe, especially France. The same neoclassical tradition was also apparent in the architecture of the early 19th century.

In the 1830s the generation that came of age after independence turned to romanticism and found the basis of a new nationality in historical images, the Indian, and local customs. This generation often had a romantic view of "liberty." They emphasized the exotic as well as the distinctive aspects of American society. In Brazil, for example, the poet Antônio Gonçalves Dias (1823–1864) used the Indian as a symbol of Brazil and America. In Cuba, novels sympathetic to slaves began to appear by mid-century. In Argentina, writers celebrated the pampas and its lonely open spaces. Sarmiento's critical account of the caudillos in *Facundo* described in depth the life of the gauchos, but it was José Hernández who wrote *Martín Fierro* in 1872, a romantic epic poem about the end of the way of the gaucho. Historical themes and the writing of history itself became a political act, because the analysis of the past became a way of setting out a proper program for the present. Many of Latin America's leading politicians were also excellent historians—Mitre in Argentina, Alamán in

Mexico, and a remarkable group of liberal Chilean historians deeply influenced by positivism.

By the 1870s a new realism emerged in the arts and literature more in line with the scientific approach of positivism and the modernization of the new nations. As the economies of Latin America surged forward, novelists appeared who were unafraid to deal with human frailties such as corruption, prejudice, and greed. The Chilean Alberto Blest Gana and the Brazilian mulatto J. Machado de Assis (1839–1908) wrote critically about the social mores of their countries during this era.

Throughout the century, the culture of the mass of the population had been little affected by the trends and taste of the elite. Popular arts, folk music, and dance flourished in traditional settings, demonstrating a vitality and adaptability to new situations that was often lacking in the more imitative fine arts. Sometimes authors in the romantic tradition or poets like Hernández turned to themes for their subject and inspiration, and in that way increasingly brought these traditions to the attention of their class and of the world. For the most part, however, popular artistic expressions were not appreciated or valued by the traditional elites, by the modernizing urban bourgeoisie, or by the newly arrived immigrants.

GENDER, CLASS, AND RACE

While significant political changes make it appealing to deal with the 19th century as an era of great change and transformation in Latin America, it is necessary to recognize the persistence of old patterns and sometimes their reinforcement. Changes took place to be sure, but their effects were not felt equally by all classes or groups in society, nor were all groups attracted by the promises of the new political regimes and their views of progress.

Women, for example, gained little ground during most of the century. They had participated actively in the independence movements. Some had taken up arms or aided the insurgent forces, and some—such as the Colombian Policarpa (La Pola) Salvatierra, whose final words were "Do not forget my example"—had paid for their activities on the gallows. Following independence, there was virtually no change in the predominant attitudes toward women's proper role. Expected to be wives and mothers, women could not vote, hold public office, become lawyers, or, in some places, testify in a court of law. While there were a few exceptions, unmarried women less than 25 years of age remained under the power and authority of their fathers. Once married they could not work, enter into contracts, or control their own estates without permission of their husbands. As in the colonial era, marriage, poli-

Machado de Assiz (1839–1908) was a gifted African-Brazilian author of humble origins whose psychological short stories and novels won him acclaim as Brazil's greatest novelist of the 19th century.

tics, and the creation of kinship links were essential elements in elite control of land and political power, and thus women remained a crucial resource in family strategies.

Lower-class women had more economic freedom—often controlling local marketing—and also more personal freedom than elite women under the constraints of powerful families. In legal terms, however, their situation was no better—and in material terms, much worse—than their elite sisters. Still, women were by the 1870s an important part of the work force.

The one area in which the situation of women began to change significantly was in public education. There had already been a movement in this direction in the colonial era; at first the idea behind it was that since women were responsible for the education of their children, they should be educated so that the proper values could be passed to the next generation. By 1842 Mexico City required girls and boys of age 7 to 15 to attend school, and in 1869 the first girls' school was created in Mexico. Liberals in Mexico wanted secular public education to prepare women for an enlightened role within the home, and similar sentiments were expressed by liberal regimes elsewhere. Public schools appeared throughout Latin America, although their impact was limited. Brazil, for example, had a population of 10 million in 1873 but only about one million men and half that number of women were literate.

The rise of secular public education created new opportunities for women. The demand for teachers at the primary level created the need for schools in which to train teachers. Since most teachers were women, these teacher training schools provided women access to advanced education; and while the curriculum often emphasized traditional female roles, an increasing number of educated women began to emerge who were dissatisfied with the legal and social constraints on their lives. By the end of the 19th century these women were becoming increasingly active in advocating womens' rights and other political issues.

The new nations, in most cases, legally ended the old "society of castes" in which legal status and definition depended on color and ethnicity, but in reality much of that system continued. The stigma of skin color and former slave status created barriers to advancement. Indians in Mexico, Bolivia, and Peru often continued to labor under poor conditions and to suffer the effects of government failures. There was conflict. In Yucatán, a great rebellion broke out, pitting the Maya against the central government and the whites, in 1839 and then again in 1847. It smoldered for ten years. Despite the intentions of governments, Indians proved resistant to changes imposed from outside their communities and willing to defend their traditional ways. The word "Indian" was still an insult in most places in Latin America. For some mestizos and others of mixed origin, the century presented opportunities for advancement in the army, professions, and commerce, but these cases were exceptions.

In many places expansion of the export economy resulted in a continuation and intensification of old patterns. Liberalism itself changed during the century, and once its program of secularization, rationalism, and rights of property were implanted as law, it displayed a more restrictive nature. Positivists of the end of the century still hoped for economic growth, but some were willing to gain it at the expense of individual freedoms. The motto, "Order and Progress," chosen for the flag of the Brazilian republic reflected that willingness. The positivists were generally convinced of the benefits of international trade for Latin America, and large landholdings increased in many areas at the expense of small farms or Indian communal lands as a result. A small, white Creole, landed upper class controlled the economies and politics in most places and they were sometimes joined in the political and economic functions by a strata of urban middle class merchants, bureaucrats, and other bourgeois types. The landed and mercantile elite tended to merge over time to create one group that, in most places, controlled the government. Meanwhile, there were new social forces at work. The flood of immigration, beginning in earnest in the 1870s, to Argentina, Brazil, and a few other nations began to alter the social composition of those places. Increasingly, rapid urbanization also changed the nature of these societies. Still, Latin America, though politically independent, began the 1880s as a group of predominantly agrarian nations with rigid social structures and a continuing dependency on the world market.

ANALYSIS
EXPLAINING UNDERDEVELOPMENT

Whether we use the word *underdeveloped*, the more benign *developing*, or the old-fashioned *backward*, it is usually clear that the term describes a large number of nations in the world that seem to be beset by a series of economic and social problems. Because Latin America was the first part of what we now call the Third World to establish its independence and begin to compete within the world economy, it had to confront the reasons for its relative position and problems quite early and without many alternative models to follow. The documents included in this chapter offer two visions of Latin America's early problems that are similar because both emphasize the Hispanic cultural heritage, as well as its supposed deficiencies or strengths, as a key explanation for the region's history. Such cultural explanations were popular among 19th-century intellectuals and political leaders, and they continue today, though other general theories based on economics and politics have become more popular.

At the time of Latin-American independence the adoption of European models of economy, government, and law seemed to offer great hope. But as "progress," republican forms of government, free trade, and liberalism failed to bring about general prosperity and social harmony, Latin Americans and others began to search for alternative explanations of their continuing problems as a first step in resolving them. Some critics condemned the Hispanic cultural legacy; others saw the materialism of the modern world as the major problem and called for a return to religion and idealism. By the 20th century, Marxism provided a powerful analysis of Latin America's history and present reality—though Marxists themselves could not decide if Latin-American societies were essentially feudal and needed first to become capitalist, or if they were already capitalist and ready for socialist revolution.

Throughout these discussions and debates Latin Americans often implicitly compared their situation to that of the United States and tried to explain the different economic positions of the two regions. At the beginning of the 19th century both regions were still primarily agricultural, and while a few places in North America were starting small industries, the mining sector in Latin America was far stronger than that of its northern neighbor. In 1850 Latin America had a population of 33 million in comparison to 23 million in the United States, and the per capita income in both regions was roughly equal; by 1940, however, Latin America's population was much larger, and its economic situation far worse than in the United States. Why and how this disparity arose preoccupied observers. Was there some flaw in the Latin-American character, or were the explanations to be found in the economic and political differences of the two areas and how could these differences be explained? The answers to these questions were not easy to obtain, but increasingly they were sought not in the history of individual countries but in analyses of a world economic and political system.

While there had long been a Marxist critique of colonialism and imperialism, the modern Latin-American analysis of underdevelopment grew from different origins. During the 1950s, a number of European and North American scholars developed the concept of "modernization," or "Westernization." Basing their ideas on the historical experience of Western Europe, they believed that development was a matter of increasing per capita production in any society, and that as development took place various kinds of social changes would follow. The more industrialized, urban, and modern a society became, the more social change and improvement were possible as traditional patterns and attitudes were abandoned or transformed. Technology, communications, and the diffusion of material goods were the means by which the transformation would take place. Some scholars also believed that as this process occurred, there would be a natural movement toward more democratic forms of government and popular participation.

Modernization theory held out the promise that any society could move toward a brighter future by essentially following the path taken earlier by Western Europe. Its message was one of improvement through gradual rather than radical or revolutionary change, and thus it tended to be politically conservative. It also tended to disregard cultural differences, internal class conflicts, and struggles for power within nations. Moreover, it was sometimes adopted by military regimes that believed, that by imposing order, they could best promote the economic changes necessary for modernization.

The proponents of modernization theory had a difficult time convincing many people in the "underdeveloped" world, where the historical experience had been considerably different from that of western Europe. In 19th century Latin America, for example, early attempts to develop industry had been faced with competition from the cheaper and better products of already industrialized nations such as England and France, and so a similar path to development was impossible. Critics argued that each nation did not operate individually, but was part of a world system that operated to keep some areas "developed" at the expense of others.

These ideas were first and most cogently expressed in Latin America. After World War II, the United Nations established an Economic Commission for Latin America (ECLA). Under the leadership of the Argentine economist Raul Prebisch, the ECLA began to analyze the Latin-American economies. Prebisch argued that "unequal exchange" between the developed nations at the center of the world economy and those like Latin America created structural blocks to economic growth. The ECLA suggested various policies to overcome the problems, especially the development of industries that would overcome the region's dependence on foreign imports.

From the structural analysis of the ECLA and from more traditional Marxist critiques, a new kind of explanation, usually called *dependency theory*, began to emerge in the 1960s. Rather than seeing underdevelopment or the lack of economic growth as the result of failed modernization, some scholars in Latin America began to argue that development and underdevelopment were not stages but part of the same process. They believed that the development and growth of some areas, such as Western Europe and the United States, were achieved at the expense of, or because of, the underdevelopment of dependent regions such as Latin America. Agricultural economies at the periphery of the world economic system were always at a disadvantage in dealing with the industrial nations of the center, and would thus become relatively poorer as the industrial nations got richer. The industrial nations would continually draw products, profits, and cheap labor from the periphery. This basic economic relationship of dependency meant that production, capital accumulation, and class relations in a dependent country were all essentially determined by external forces. Some theorists went even further and argued that Latin America and other nations of the Third World were also culturally dependent in their consumption of ideas and concepts. Both modernization theory and Mickey Mouse were seen as the agents of a cultural domination that was simply an extension of economic reality. These theorists usually argued that socialism was the only hope to break out of the dependency relationship.

These ideas, which dominated Latin-American intellectual life, were broadly appealing to other areas of Asia and Africa that had recently emerged from colonial control. Forms of dependency analysis became popular in many areas of the world in the 1960s and 1970s. By the 1980s, however, dependency theory was loosing its appeal. As an explanation of what had happened historically in Latin America, it was useful; but as a theory that could predict what might happen elsewhere and what to do, it provided little help. Marxists argued that it overemphasized the circulation of goods (trade) rather than how things were produced and that it ignored the class conflicts they felt were the motor force of history. Moreover, with the rise of multinational corporations the nature of capitalism itself was changing, and thus an analysis based on trade relationships between countries became somewhat outdated.

Whether development can be widely diffused as modernization theory argued or whether the underdevelopment of some countries is inherent in the nature of the capitalist world economy as the dependency theorists believe, is still a matter of dispute, but recent events in Eastern Europe have thrown the socialist alternative into question as well. A search for new explanations and new solutions to the problems of development will characterize the decade of the 1990s as peoples throughout the world seek to improve their lives.

Questions: In what sense was 19th-century Latin America a dependent economy? Which explanation or prediction about dependency best fits world economic trends today? ☙

 THE GREAT BOOM, 1880–1920

Between 1880 and 1920 Latin America, like certain areas of Asia and Africa, experienced a tremendous spurt of economic growth, stimulated by the increasing demand in industrializing Europe and the United States for raw materials, foodstuffs, and specialized tropical crops. Latin America was well prepared for this export-led economic expansion. The Liberal ideology of individual freedoms, an open market, and limited government intervention in the

operation of the economy had triumphed in many places. Whereas this ideology had been the expression of the middle class in Europe, in Latin America it was adopted not only by the small urban middle sectors of lawyers, retailers, bureaucrats, and professionals, but also by the large landowners, miners, and export merchants linked to the rural economy and the traditional patterns of wealth and landowning. In a number of countries a political alliance was forged between the traditional aristocracy of wealth and the new urban elements. Together they controlled the presidential offices and the congresses and imposed a business-as-usual approach to government at the expense of peasants and a newly emerging working class.

The expansion of Latin American economies was led by exports. Each nation had a specialty: bananas and coffee from Central America; tobacco and sugar from Cuba; rubber and coffee from Brazil; henequen (a fiber for making rope), copper, and silver from Mexico; wool, wheat, and beef from Argentina; and copper from Chile. In this era of strong demand and good prices these nations experienced high profits. This allowed for the import of large quantities of foreign manufactures, and it provided funds for the beautification of cities and other government projects. But export-led expansion was always risky because the world-market prices of Latin-American commodities were ultimately determined by conditions outside the region. In that sense, these economies were particularly vulnerable and in some ways dependent.

The expansion of Latin-American trade was remarkable. It increased by about 50 percent between 1870 and 1890. Argentina's trade was increasing at about 5 percent a year in this period, one of the highest rates of growth ever recorded for a national economy. "As wealthy as an Argentine," became an expression in Paris, reflecting the fortunes that wool, beef, and grain were earning for some in Argentina. In Mexico an "oligarchic dictatorship," which maintained all the outward attributes of democracy but imposed "law and order" under the dictator Porfirio Díaz, created the conditions for unrestrained profits. Mexican exports doubled between 1877 and 1900. Similar figures could be cited for Chile, Costa Rica, and Bolivia.

This rapidly expanding commerce attracted the interest of foreign investors anxious for high returns on their capital. British, French, German, and North American businessmen and entrepreneurs invested in mining, railroads, public utilities, and banking. Over half the foreign investments in Latin America were British, which alone increased to over £750 million by 1913, or to ten times as much as had been invested in 1870. But British leadership was no longer uncontested; Germany and increasingly the United States provided competition. The United States was particularly active in the Caribbean region and Mexico, but not until after World War I would United States capital predominate in the region.

Foreign investments provided Latin America with needed capital and services, but tended to place key industries, transportation facilities, and services in foreign hands. These were thus vulnerable to external influences and decisions. Foreign investments also constrained Latin-American governments in the social, commercial, and diplomatic policies which they could follow.

MEXICO AND ARGENTINA

We can use these two large Latin-American nations as examples of different responses within the same general pattern. In Mexico the Liberal triumph of Juárez had set the stage for economic growth and constitutional government. In 1876 Porfirio Díaz, one of Juárez's generals, was elected president and for the next 35 years he dominated politics either as president or as the power behind the scenes. Díaz suppressed regional rebellions and imposed a strong centralized government. Using foreign capital, the railroad system grew rapidly, providing a new way of integrating Mexican regional economies, moving goods to the ports for export, and allowing the movement of government troops to keep order. Industrialization began to take place. Foreign investment was encouraged in mining, transportation, and other sectors of the economy, and financial policies were changed to promote investments. United States investments, for example, expanded from about 30 million pesos in 1883 to over 1 billion by 1911.

The forms of Liberal democracy were maintained but were subverted in order to keep Díaz in power and to give his development plans an open track. Behind these policies were a number of Díaz's advisors, who were strongly influenced by positivist ideas and who wished to impose a scientific approach on the national economy. These *cientificos* set the tone for Mexico while the government suppressed any political opposition to these policies. Diaz's Mexico projected an image of modernization led by a Europeanized elite who greatly profited from the economic growth and the imposition of order under Don Porfirio.

Growth was often bought at the expense of Mexico's large rural peasantry and its growing urban and working classes. This population was essentially native, since unlike in Argentina and Brazil few immigrants came to Mexico. They participated very little in the prosperity of export-led growth. The expansion of henequen production in Yucatán displaced peasants, and their attempts at resistence led to arrests and deportation as convict laborers to Cuba. Indian rebellions in the north were similarly crushed. In Morelos in central Mexico, modernization of sugar production with the use of steam-powered mills increased the capacity of the haciendas. Their expansion at the expense of peasants and Indian communal lands created a volatile situation.

Strikes and labor unrest increased, particularly among railroad workers, miners, and textile workers. An especially violent strike took place at the American-owned Cananea Copper mines from 1906 to 1908. In the countryside a national police force, the *Rurales*, maintained order and the army was mobilized when needed. At the regional level political bosses linked to the Díaz regime in Mexico City delivered the votes in rigged elections.

For 35 years Díaz reigned supreme and oversaw the transformation of the Mexican economy. His opponents were arrested or driven into exile while the small middle class, the landowners, miners, and foreign investors celebrated the progress of Mexico. In 1910, however, a middle-class movement with limited political goals seeking electoral reform began to mushroom into a more general uprising in which the frustrations of the poor, the workers, the peasants, and nationalist intellectuals of various political persuasions erupted in a bloody ten-year civil war, the Mexican Revolution.

At the other end of the hemisphere Argentina followed an alternate path of economic expansion. By 1880 the Indians on the southern pampa had finally been conquered and vast new tracts of land opened to ranching. The strange relationship between Buenos Aires and the rest of the nation had finally been resolved when Buenos Aires had been made a federal district. With a rapidly expanding economy it became "the Paris of South America," an expression that reflected the drive by wealthy Argentines to establish their credentials as a modern nation. By 1914 Buenos Aires had over two million inhabitants, or about one-fourth of the national population. Its political leaders, the "Generation of 1880," were the inheritors of the Liberal program of Sarmiento and Mitre, and they were able to enact their programs because of the high levels of income generated by the expanding economy.

Technological changes contributed to Argentine prosperity. Refrigerated ships allowed fresh beef to be sent directly to Europe, and this along with wool and wheat provided the basis of expansion. Labor was provided by a flood of immigrants. Some were *golondrinas,* which literally means swallows, who were able to work one harvest in Italy and then a second in Argentina because of the differences in seasons in the two hemispheres, but many immigrants elected to stay. Almost 3.5 million immigrants stayed in Argentina between 1857 and 1930, and unlike in Mexico, by 1914 about one-third of the Argentine population was foreign-born. Italians, Germans, Russians, and

Jews came to "hacer America"—that is, "to make America"—and remained. In a way, quite unlike Mexico they really did Europeanize Argentina, introducing the folkways and ideologies of the European rural and working classes. The result was a fusion of cultures that produced not only a radical workers' movement, but also the distinctive music of the "tango" which combined Spanish, African, and other musical elements in the cafés and red-light districts of Buenos Aires. The tango became the music of the Argentine urban working class.

As the immigrant flood increased, workers began to seek political expression. A Socialist party was formed in the 1890s, seeking to elect representatives to office. Anarchists hoped to smash the political system and called for strikes and walkouts. Moved to some extent by European ideological battles, the struggle spilled into the streets. Violent strikes and government repression characterized the decade after 1910, culminating in a series of strikes in 1918 that led to extreme repression. Development had its social costs.

The Argentine oligarchy was capable of some internal reform, however. Critics of corruption emerged within the political system, and a new party representing the emerging middle class began to organize. It was aided by an electoral law in 1912 that called for secret ballots, universal male suffrage, and compulsory voting. With this change the Radical party, promising political reform and more liberal policies for workers, came to power in 1916, but faced with labor unrest it acted as repressively as its predecessors. The oligarchy made room for middle-class politicians and interests, but the problems of Argentina's expanding labor force remained unresolved, and Argentina's economy remained closely tied to the international market for its exports.

With considerable variations, similar patterns of economic growth, political domination by oligarchies formed by traditional aristocracies and "progressive" middle classes, and a rising tide of labor unrest or rural rebellion can be noted elsewhere in Latin America. Modernization and "progress" were not welcomed by all sectors of society. Messianic religious movements in Brazil, Indian resistance to the loss of lands in Colombia, and banditry in Mexico were all to some extent reactions to the changes being forced on the societies by national governments tied to the ideology of progress and often insensitive to its effects.

UNCLE SAM GOES SOUTH

After its Civil War, the United States began to take a more direct and active interest in the politics and economic situation of Latin America. Commerce and investments began to expand rapidly in this period, especially in Mexico and Central America. American industry was seeking new markets and raw materials, while the growing population of the United States created a demand for Latin-American products. Attempts were made to create inter-American cooperation, but a major turning point came in 1898 with the outbreak of war between Spain and the United States, which now began to join the nations of western Europe in the age of imperialism.

The war centered on Cuba and Puerto Rico, Spain's last colonies in the Americas. The Cuban economy had boomed in the 19th century based on its exports of sugar and tobacco grown with slave labor. A ten-year civil war for independence beginning in 1868 had failed in its main objective but had won the island some autonomy. A number of ardent Cuban nationalists, such as the journalist and poet José Marti, had gone into exile to continue the struggle. Fighting erupted again in 1895 and the United States joined in 1898, declaring war on Spain and occupying Cuba, Puerto Rico, and the Philippines.

In fact, United States investments in Cuba had been rapidly increasing prior to the war, and the United States had become a major market for Cuban sugar. The Cuban Spanish-American War now opened the door to direct United States involvement in the Caribbean. The Cuban army was treated poorly by its American allies, and a United States government of occupation was imposed on Cuba and Puerto Rico. When the occupation ended in 1902, a series of onerous conditions were imposed on independent Cuba that made it a virtual American dependency, a status that was, in fact, legally imposed in Puerto Rico.

For strategic, commercial, and economic reasons Latin America, particularly the Caribbean and Mexico, began to attract American interest at the turn of the century. These considerations lay behind the drive to construct a canal across Central America that would shorten the route between the Atlantic and Pacific. When Colombia proved reluctant to meet American proposals, the United States backed a Panamanian movement for independence and then signed a treaty with its representative that granted the United States extensive rights over a trans-isthmus canal. President Theodore Roosevelt was a major force behind the canal, which opened to traffic in 1908.

The Panama Canal was a remarkable engineering feat and a fitting symbol of the technological and industrial strength of the United States. North Americans were proud of these achievements and hoped to demonstrate the superiority of the "American way," a feeling fed to some extent by racist ideas and a sense of cultural superiority. Latin Americans were now wary of American power and intentions in the area. A number of intellectuals cautioned against the expansionist designs of the United States and

José Martí (1853–1895), an ardent Cuban patriot, used his talents as a poet, journalist, and lawyer for the cause of Cuban independence. While living a long exile in the United States, he became critical of U.S. ambitions in the Caribbean. He died in the early stages of the Spanish-American War.

against what they viewed as the materialism of American culture. The Uruguayan José Enrique Rodó, in his essay *Ariel* (1900), compared the spirituality of Hispanic culture to the materialism of the United States. Others, elsewhere in Latin America, offered similar critiques.

Latin-American criticism had a variety of origins: nationalism, a Catholic defense of traditional values, and also some socialist attacks on expansive capitalism. In a way,

Latin America, which had achieved its political independence in the 19th century and had been part of European developments, was able to articulate clearly the fears and the reactions of the areas that had become the colonies and semicolonies of western Europe and the United States in the age of empire.

CONCLUSION

NEW NATIONS, OLD PROBLEMS

During the 19th century the nations of Latin America moved from the status of colonies to that of independent nation-states. The process was sometimes exhilarating and often painful, but during the course of the century, these nations were able to construct governments and begin to address many social and economic problems. These problems were inherited from the colonial era and intensified by internal political and ideological conflicts and by foreign intervention. Moreover, the Latin-American nations also had to resuscitate their economies after the struggles for independence and to confront their position within the world economic system as suppliers of agricultural products and consumers of manufactured goods.

The heritage of the past weighed heavily in Latin America. Political and social changes were many, and pressures for these changes came from a variety of sources such as progressive politicians, modernizing military men, a growing urban population, dissatisfied workers, and disadvantaged peasants. Still, in many ways Latin America remained remarkably unchanged. Revolts were frequent but revolutions that altered the structure of society or the distribution of land or wealth were few, and the reforms intended to do this were usually unsuccessful. The elite controlled most of the economic resources, a growing but still small urban sector had emerged politically but either remained weak or had to accommodate the elite, and the vast majority of the population continued to labor on the land with little hope of improvement. Latin America was a distinctive civilization—culturally and politically sharing much of the Western tradition, yet economically functioning more like areas of Asia and Africa. Latin America was the first non-Western area to face the problems of decolonization, and many aspects of its history that seemed so distinctive in the 19th century proved to be previews of what would follow—decolonization and nation-building elsewhere in the world in the 20th century.

FURTHER READINGS

Stanley J. and Barbara Stein's *The Colonial Heritage of Latin America* (1970) is a hard-hitting interpretation of colonial and 19th-century Latin America that emphasizes its continued dependency and its neocolonial status after independence. David Bushnell and Neil Macauley's *The Emergence of Latin America in the Nineteenth Century* (1988) provides an excellent overview that is critical of the dependency thesis. The classic study from the dependency perspective is Fernando Henrique Cardoso and Enzo Faletto's *Dependency and Development in Latin America* (1979). Roberto Cortés Conde's *The First Stages of Modernization in Spanish America* (1974) provides a good economic analysis. The movements for independence are described in John Lynch's *The Spanish American Revolutions* (1973). Tulio Halperin Donghi's *The Aftermath of Revolution in Latin America* (1973) analyzes the first half of the 19th century. Claudio Veliz's *The Centralist Tradition in Latin America* (1980) tries to explain the divergent development of Latin America and western Europe, while E. Bradford Burns's *Poverty or Progress. Latin America in the Nineteenth Century* (1973) provides a challenging attack on the liberal programs and a defense of a "folk" political tradition. Jean Franco's *The Modern Culture of Latin America. Society and the Artist* (1967) is a lively discussion of literature and the arts. Volumes 3 to 5 of the *Cambridge History of Latin America* (1985–1986) contain up-to-date essays on major themes and individual countries. A good essay from the collection is Robert Freeman Smith's "Latin America, the United States, and the European Powers, 1830–1930," vol. IV, 83–120.

There are an enormous number of single-volume country histories as well as monographs on particular topics. David Rock's *Argentina* (1985), E. B. Burns' *A History of Brazil* (1980), Michael Meyer and William Sherman's *The Course of Mexican History* (1979), and Herbert Klein's *Bolivia* (1982) are good examples of national histories. There are excellent rural histories, such as Stanley Stein's *Vassouras. A Brazilian Coffee County*, (2d ed., 1989), Charles Berquist's *Coffee and Conflict in Colombia, 1886–1910* (1978), and Arnold Bauer's *Chilean Rural Society* (1975). Silvia Arrom's *The Women of Mexico City* (1985) is a fine example of the growing literature in women's history, some of which is also seen in June Nash and Helen Safa, eds., *Sex and Class in Latin America* (1980). Hobart Spalding, Jr.'s *Organized Labor in Latin America* (1977) surveys urban labor, while Charles Berquist's *Labor in Latin America* (1986) is a comparative interpretive essay.

32 Civilizations in Crisis: The Ottoman Empire, the Islamic Heartlands, and Qing China

INTRODUCTION. Conditions in those parts of Asia that were not outright European colonies differed in many ways from those in Latin America during the century and a half after 1750. Problems of political decline and reactions of highly successful traditional cultures to new challenges predominated, particularly in the great empires of China and the Middle East. The threat of Western imperialism was more menacing, though larger problems of dealing with the West's industrial lead and the intensified world economy overlapped with issues in Latin America.

By the early decades of the 18th century, it appeared that two of the civilizations—Middle Eastern Islamic and Chinese—still capable of contesting the European drive for global dominance were headed in very different directions. Under the Manchu rulers, whose seizure of the Chinese throne in the mid-17th century was noted in Chapter 28, China was enjoying yet another early dynastic period of growth and general prosperity. The territory controlled by the Manchus was greater than that claimed by any Chinese dynasty since the Tang in the 7th century. China's population was growing steadily, and its trade and agricultural production were keeping pace. China's border defenses were strong; its huge armies, led by the elite "banner" units made up of ethnic Manchu soldiers, appeared capable of defending the empire against any outside threat. Like other "barbarian" peoples, the Europeans were closely controlled by the functionaries of the ruling Qing dynasty. European traders were confined to the ports of Macao and Canton on China's south coast. In the early 18th century, the Qing emperor had severely curtailed

---

1849–1905 Life of Muhammad Abduh

1870 Ottoman legal code reformed

1908 Young Turks seize power in Istanbul

1898–1901 Boxer Rebellion in China; 100 Days of Reform in China

1883 Mahdist victory over British-led Egyptian expeditionary force at Shakyan

1882 British invasion and occupation of Egypt; failed revolt led Orabi in Egypt

1850–1864 Taiping rebellion in China

1876 Constitution promulgated for Ottoman Empire

1869 Opening of the Suez Canal

1877 Treaty of San Stefano; Ottomans driven from most of the Balkans

1905 Fatherland Party established in Egypt

1856–1860 Anglo-French war against China

1866 First railway begun in Ottoman Empire

1889 Young Turks established in Paris

1898 British-Egyptian army defeats the Mahdist army at Omdurman

1854–1856 Crimean War

1876–1908 Reign of Ottoman Sultan Abdul Hamid

missionary activities in China without fear of foreign reprisals. Thus, despite signs of growing poverty and social unrest in some districts, the Manchus appeared not only to have restored good government and the well-being of the general populace but to have carried China to a new level of political and cultural dominance in East Asia.

At the other end of Asia, the fate of the Ottomans appeared to be exactly the reverse. After centuries of able rule and expansion at the expense of their Christian and Muslim neighbors (see Chapter 26), the Ottomans were in full retreat by the first decades of the 18th century. From the west the Austrian Habsburgs chipped away at the Ottomans' European possessions, while a revived Russia closed in from the north. Muslim kingdoms in North Africa broke away from the empire, and imperial governors and local notables throughout the Arab portions of the Middle East grew more and more independent of the ruling Sultan in Istanbul. Political decline was accompanied by rising economic and social disruption. Inflation was rampant throughout much of the empire, and European imports were rapidly destroying what was left of the already battered Ottoman handicraft industries. The empire was racked by social tensions, crime, and rebellion in some areas. The divided Ottoman elite could not agree on a strategy to reinvigorate state and society or to drive back the Christian infidels whose advance was undoing centuries of hard-won conquests. With its Ottoman defenders reduced, the very heartlands of the Islamic world were increasingly at risk.

In a little over a century, the very different paths these two civilizations appeared to be following suddenly converged, and then the Ottomans gained strength as China fell apart. A combination of internal weaknesses and growing pressure from the industrializing European powers threw China into a period of prolonged crisis in the early 19th century. If anything, Chinese civilization was revealed as even more exposed and vulnerable than the Islamic world the Ottomans sought to defend in the face of internal decay and European inroads. While the Ottomans began to find new sources of leadership and to introduce reforms on the basis of Western precedents, the Manchus were paralyzed by the shock of devastating defeats at the hands of the European "barbarians." Overpopulation, drug addiction—particularly that which afflicted members of the scholar-gentry elite—and massive rebellions sapped China's strength from within, while European gunboats and armies broke down its outer defenses. By the end of the 19th century, internal disruptions and external pressures had literally demolished the foundations of Chinese civilization, a civilization whose development we have traced over nearly four millennia.

As old China died, its leaders struggled to find a new and viable system to put in its place. That struggle would be carried on throughout a half century (roughly from 1898 to 1949) of foreign invasion, revolution, and social and economic breakdown that produced suffering on a scale unmatched in all human history. In sharp contrast, by the end of the 19th century new leaders had emerged in the Ottoman Empire who were able to overthrow the sultanate with a minimum of bloodshed and to begin the process of nation making in the Turkish portions of the empire (largely the present-day nation of Turkey). Unfortunately, Ottoman weaknesses in earlier decades left the rest of the Middle East exposed to European inroads, and a larger Islamic crisis proved impervious to Turkish solutions.

The early sections of this chapter will focus on attempts to revive the declining Ottoman Empire and the emergence of groups within the Ottoman elite dedicated to the overthrow of the sultanate and the establishment of a new state on the basis of Turkish nationalism. In dealing with these patterns we will also look at developments in the central Islamic lands, from the great changes set in motion by Napoleon's invasion of Egypt in 1798, to the differing responses of Islamic thinkers and political leaders, to the growing threat of industrial Europe. The second half of the chapter will concentrate on the forces that led to the collapse of Chinese civilization in the last half of the 19th century. We will also look at some of the early Chinese responses to the profound crisis engendered by this collapse and examine the legacy of the fall of the Qing, China's last imperial dynasty, in the first years of the 20th century.

ANALYSIS
WESTERN DOMINANCE AND THE DECLINE OF CIVILIZATIONS

With Europe's emergence as the dominant global power from the 18th century onward, the patterns of the rise and fall of civilizations established in the classical age were fundamentally altered. As we have seen in our examination of the forces that have led to the breakup of the great civilizations in human history, each civilization has a unique history, but a number of general patterns, such as those set out in Chapter 11, have been associated with the decline of civilizations. Both internal weaknesses and external pressures have acted over a period of time to erode the institutions and break down the defenses of even the largest and most sophisticated civilizations that humans have created. In the preindustrial era, slow and vulnerable communications systems were a major barrier to the long-term cohesion of the political systems that held civilizations together. Ethnic, religious, and regional differences, which were overridden by the confidence and energy of the founders of civilizations, reemerged as self-serving corruption and the pursuit of pleasure gradually eroded the sense of purpose of the elite groups that played a pivotal role in civilized development. The deterioration in governance and military strength that followed both exacerbated social tensions and undermined rather fragile preindustrial economies.

Growing social unrest from within was paralleled by increasing threats from without. A major factor in the fall of virtually every great civilization, from those of the Indus valley and Mesopotamia to Rome and the civilizations of Mesoamerica, was an influx of nomadic peoples, whom the civilized peoples invariably regarded as barbarians. Nomadic assaults not only revealed the ineptness of the ruling elites and destroyed their military base, but barbarian raids disrupted the agricultural routines and smashed the public works on which all civilizations rested. Normally, the nomadic invaders stayed on as the rulers of the sedentary peoples they had conquered, as happened repeatedly in China, Mesoamerica, and the Islamic world. Elsewhere, as after the destruction of the Indus valley civilization in India and the fall of Rome, the vanquished civilization was largely forgotten or lay dormant for centuries. But over time the invading peoples living in its ruins managed to restore patterns of civilized life that were quite different from, though sometimes influenced by, the civilization their incursions had helped to destroy centuries earlier.

Neighboring civilizations sometimes clashed in wars on their frontiers, but it was rare for one civilization to play a major part in the demise of another. In areas like Mesopotamia, where civilizations were crowded together in space and time in the last millennia B.C. (see Chapter 2), older, long dominant civilizations had been overthrown and absorbed by upstart rivals. In most cases, however, and often in Mesopotamia, external threats to civilizations came from nomadic peoples. This was true even of Islamic civilization, which proved the most expansive before the emergence of Europe and whose rise and spread brought about the collapse of a number of long-established civilized centers. The initial Arab explosion from Arabia that felled Sassanid Persia and captured Egypt was very much a nomadic enterprise. But the incursions of the Arab bedouins differed from earlier and later nomadic assaults on neighboring civilizations because the new religion that they carried with them from Arabia provided the basis for a new civilization which incorporated the older ones they conquered. Thus, like other nomadic conquerors, they borrowed heavily from the civilizations they overran.

The emergence of western Europe as an expansive global force radically altered the patterns of interaction between civilizations as well as between civilizations and nomadic peoples. From the first years of overseas exploration, the aggressive Europeans proved a threat to other civilizations. Within decades of Columbus's arrival in 1492, European military assaults had destroyed two of the great centers of high civilization in the Americas—the Aztec and Inca empires. The previous isolation of the Amerindian societies and their consequent susceptibility to European diseases and weapons made them more vulnerable than most of the peoples the Europeans encountered overseas. Thus, in the first centuries of expansion, most of the existing civilizations in Africa and Asia proved quite capable of standing up to the Europeans—except on the sea. With the scientific discoveries and especially the technological innovations that transformed Europe in the 17th and 18th centuries, all of this gradually changed. The unparalleled extent of the western Europeans' mastery of the natural world gave them new sources of power for resource extraction, manufacture, and war. By the end of the 18th century, this power was being translated into the economic, military, and increasingly the political domination of other civilizations.

A century later, the Europeans had either conquered most of these civilizations outright or reduced them to spheres they controlled indirectly and threatened to annex. The adverse effects of economic influences emanating from the West and Western political domination proved highly corrosive to the very fabric of civilizations as diverse as those of West Africa, the Islamic heartlands, and China. For a span of several decades before the First World War, it appeared that the materially advanced and expansive West would level all other civilized centers. In that era, most leading European, and some African and Asian, thinkers and political leaders believed that the rest of humankind had no alternative (except perhaps a reversion to savagery or barbarism) but to follow the path of development pioneered by the West.

As we shall see in this chapter and the ones that follow, the many challenges European global domination posed for other civilizations provoked a wide variety of responses. These ranged from those that stressed a retreat into an idealized past free of European influences to responses that presumed the need for the extensive transformation of non-Western societies along European lines. The leaders and thinkers of all non-Western peoples debated how extensively their societies must adopt Western ways to survive the onslaught of the European imperialist powers and whether it would be possible to confine Western influences to certain spheres. They also struggled to come up with ways of mobilizing popular support for movements aimed at resisting the advance of the European powers and driving them from areas in Africa and Asia where they were already in control. As we shall see in the examples drawn from the Middle East and China in the sections that follow, some of these modes of resistance were more successful than others— some civilizations managed to adapt and survive, while others collapsed entirely. But all non-Western peoples became preoccupied with coping with the powerful challenges the industrial West posed for the survival of their civilized past and the course of their future development.

Questions: Can you think of instances where one preindustrial civilization was a major factor in the collapse of another? Why do you think such an occurrence was so rare? Discuss the advantages that the Amerindians' isolation from civilizations in Europe, Africa, and Asia gave the European intruders in the 16th century. What kinds of advantages did the scientific and industrial revolutions give the Europeans over all other civilized peoples from the 18th century onward? Is the West losing these advantages today, and, if so, what do you think the consequences will be? ✪

BETWEEN THE WESTERN POWERS: THE STRUGGLE OF THE OTTOMAN EMPIRE FOR SURVIVAL

By the early 18th century, the days of the Ottoman Empire appeared numbered. In part the crisis was brought on by a succession of weak rulers within a political and social order that was centered on the sultan at the top. Inactive or inept sultans opened the way for seemingly endless power struggles between rival ministers, religious experts, and the commanders of the Janissary corps. Competition between factions of the elite further eroded effective leadership within the empire, exposing it to external assaults by its European enemies and weakening its control over the population and resources it claimed to rule. Provincial officials colluded with the local landowning classes, the ayan, to cheat the sultan of a good portion of the taxes due him, and they skimmed all the revenue they could from the already impoverished peasantry in the countryside. As in other preindustrial civilizations, the peasants responded to these threats to their livelihood with flight (if open lands or less exacting landlords were within reach), banditry, and outright rebellions in various parts of the empire.

At the same time, the position of the artisan workers in the towns deteriorated due to competition from imported manufactures from Europe. This led, particularly in the 18th and early 19th centuries, to urban riots in which members of artisan guilds or young mens' associations often took a leading role. Merchants within the empire, especially those who belonged to minority religious communities, such as the Jews and Christians, grew more and more dependent on commercial dealings with their European counterparts. This pattern accelerated the influx of Western manufactured goods that was steadily undermining handicraft industries within the empire, thereby increasing Ottoman economic dependence on some of its most threatening European political rivals.

With the Ottoman leaders embroiled in internal squabbles and their armies deprived of the resources needed to match the great advances in weaponry and training made by European rivals, the far-flung Ottoman possessions proved an irresistible temptation for their neighbors. In the early decades of the 18th century, the Austrian Habsburg dynasty was the main beneficiary of Ottoman decadence. The long-standing threat to Vienna was forever vanquished, and the Ottomans were pushed out of Hungary and the northern Balkans.

In the later 1700s, the Russian Empire, strengthened by Peter the Great's forced Westernization (see Chapter 24), became the main threat to the Ottomans' survival. As military setbacks mounted and the Russians advanced across the steppes toward warm water ports in the Black Sea, the Ottomans' weakness was underscored by their attempts to forge alliances with other Christian powers. As the Russians gobbled up poorly defended Ottoman lands in the

The Ottoman Empire in the Late 18th Century

Caucasus and Crimea, the subject Christian peoples of the Balkans grew more and more restive under Ottoman rule. In 1804 a major uprising broke out in Serbia that was repressed after years of difficult and costly military campaigns. Military force could not quell the Greek revolt that broke out in the early 1820s, and by 1830 the Greeks had regained their independence after centuries of Ottoman rule. By 1867 Serbia was also free, and by the late 1870s the Ottomans had been driven from virtually the whole of the Balkans and thus most of the European provinces of their empire. In the following decades Istanbul itself was repeatedly threatened by Russian armies or those of the smaller Balkan States.

REFORM AND SURVIVAL

Despite almost two centuries of unrelieved defeats on the battlefield and steady losses of territory, the Ottoman Empire somehow managed to survive into the 20th century. In part this was due to divisions between the European powers, each of which feared that the others would gain more from the total dismemberment of the empire. In fact the British concern to prevent the Russians from controlling Istanbul—thus gaining direct access to and threatening British naval dominance in the Mediterranean—led them to prop up the tottering Ottoman regime repeatedly in the last half of the 19th century. Ultimately, the Ottomans' survival depended on reforms from within—reforms initiated by the sultans and their advisors at the top of the imperial system and carried out in stages over most of the 19th century. At each stage, reform initiatives intensified tensions within the ruling elite: Some advocated far-reaching change along European lines; others argued for reforms based on precedents from the early Ottoman period; and still others had a vested interest in blocking change of any sort.

These deep divisions within the Ottoman elite rendered reform a dangerous enterprise. Though modest innovations, including the introduction of the first printing press in 1727, had been enacted in the 18th century, Sultan Selim III (1789–1807) believed that bolder initiatives were required if the dynasty and empire were to survive. But his reform efforts, which were aimed at improving administrative efficiency and building a new army and navy capable of reversing a century of defeats at the hands of the European powers, angered powerful factions within the bureaucracy. They were also viewed by the Janissary corps, which had long been the dominant force within the Ottoman military (see Chapter 26), as a direct and vital threat. Selim's modest initiatives cost him his throne—he was toppled by a Janissary revolt in 1807—and his life.

The European view of the Ottoman Empire as an exotic and bizarrely antique land is captured in this late 18th-century engraving of the Ottoman sultan entertaining the French ambassador and his entourage.

Two decades later, a more skillful sultan, Mahmud II, succeeded where Selim III had failed. After secretly building a small professional army with the help of European advisors, in 1826 Mahmud II ordered his agents to incite a mutiny of the Janissaries. This began when the angry Janissaries overturned the huge soup kettles in their mess area. With little thought of preparation, the Janissaries poured into the streets of Istanbul, more a mob than a military force, where they were shocked to be confronted by the sultan's well-trained new army. The confrontation ended in the slaughter of the Janissaries, their families, and the Janissaries' religious allies.

After cowing the ayan or provincial notables into at least formal submission to the throne, Mahmud II launched a program of much more far-reaching reforms than Selim III had attempted. Though the ulama, or religious experts, and some of Mahmud's advisors argued for self-strengthening through a return to the Ottoman and Islamic past, Mahmud II patterned his reform program on Western precedents. After all, the Western powers had made a shambles of his empire. He established a diplomatic corps on Western lines and exchanged ambassadors with the European powers. The Westernization of the army was expanded from Mahmud's secret force to the whole military establishment. European military advisors, both army and navy, were imported to supervise the overhaul of Ottoman training, armament, and officers' education.

In the following decades, Western influences were pervasive at the upper levels of Ottoman society, particularly during the period of the Tanzimat reforms between 1839 and 1876. University education was reorganized on Western lines, including the introduction of training in the European sciences and mathematics. State-run postal and telegraph systems were introduced in the 1830s and railways were begun in the 1860s. Newspapers were established in the major towns of the empire, extensive legal reforms were enacted, and in 1876 a constitution, based heavily on European prototypes, was promulgated. These legal reforms greatly improved the position of minority religious groups, whose role in the Ottoman economy increased steadily.

Some groups were adversely affected by these changes that opened the empire more and more to Western influences. This was especially true of the artisans, whose position was gravely weakened by an 1838 treaty with the British that removed import taxes and other barriers to foreign trade that had protected indigenous producers from competition from the West. Other social groups gained little from the Tanzimat reforms. This was particularly true of women. Though proposals for women's education and the end to seclusion, polygamy, and veiling were debated in Ottoman intellectual circles from the 1860s onward, few improvements in the position of women—even among the elite classes—were won until after the fall of the dynasty in 1908.

REPRESSION AND REVOLT

Though the reforms initiated by the sultans and their advisors did improve somewhat the Ottomans' ability to fend off, or at least deflect, the assaults of foreign aggressors, they increasingly threatened the dynasty responsible for them. Western-educated bureaucrats, military officers, and professionals came increasingly to view the sultanate as a major barrier to even more radical reforms—some of which involved proposals for constitutional checks on the rulers' authority—and the full transformation of society. The new elites also clashed with conservative but powerful groups, such as the ulama and ayan, who had a vested interest in preserving as much as possible of the old order. There were also divisions within the new elite between those who had derived great benefit from the early reforms and were wary of further changes, and those who saw the reforms already enacted as the entering wedge for a much more radical restructuring of Ottoman institutions and society.

The Ottoman Sultan Abdul Hamid responded to the growing threat from Westernized officers and civilians by attempting to return to despotic absolutism during his long reign from 1878 to 1908. He nullified the constitution, restricted civil liberties, particularly the freedom of the press, and deprived Westernized elite groups of the considerable initiative they had gained in the formulation of imperial policies. Legal safeguards were flaunted as dissidents or even suspected troublemakers were summarily imprisoned, and sometimes tortured and killed. But the deep impact that decades of reform had made upon the empire was demonstrated by the fact that even Abdul Hamid continued to push for Westernization in certain areas. The military continued to adopt European arms and techniques, increasingly under the instruction of German advisors. In addition, railways, including the famed line that linked Berlin to Baghdad, and telegraph lines were constructed between the main population centers, more often than not under the aegis of German investors and supervisors. Western-style educational institutions continued to grow, and judicial reforms continued. Under Abdul Hamid the old bureaucratic apparatus remained largely in place and social reforms were minimal, but the military and communications infrastructure for a modern state was established.

The despotism of Abdul Hamid came to an abrupt end in the nearly bloodless coup of 1908. Resistance to his authoritarian rule had led exiled Turkish intellectuals and political agitators to found an organization, the Ottoman Society for Union and Progress, in Paris in 1889. Though professing their loyalty to the Ottoman regime, the Young Turks, as members of the society came to be known, were determined to restore the 1876 constitution and resume far-reaching reforms within the empire. Clandestine printing presses operated by the Young Turks turned out tracts denouncing the regime and outlining the further steps to be taken to modernize and thus save the empire. Assassinations were attempted and coups plotted, but until 1908 all were undone by a combination of divisions within the ranks of the Westernized dissidents and police countermeasures.

The fascination that the Young Turks and what appeared to be their revolutionary movement held for European intellectuals is reflected in the cover drawing and story of a 1909 edition of the popular French periodical *Le Petit Parisien*. It is also suggested by the radical or avant-garde connotations that the label "Young Turk" has had from the early 20th century to the present day.

Sympathy within the military for the 1908 coup had much to do with its success, as did the fact that only a handful of the sultan's supporters were willing to die defending the regime. Though a group of officers came to power, they restored the constitution and press freedoms and promised reforms in education, administration, and even the status of women. The sultan was retained as a political figurehead and the highest religious authority in Islam.

Unfortunately, the officers soon became embroiled in factional fights that took up much of the limited time remaining before the outbreak of World War I. In addition, their hold on power was shaken as they lost a new round of wars in the Balkans and against Italy over the Ottomans' last remaining possession in North Africa, Libya. Just as the sultans had before them, however, the Young Turk officers managed to stave off the collapse of the empire with last-gasp military victories and by playing the hostile European powers against each other.

Though it is difficult to know how the Young Turks would have fared if it had not been for the outbreak of the First World War, their failure to resolve a number of critical issues did not bode well for the future. They had overthrown the sultan, but they could not bring themselves to give up the empire ruled by Turks for over 600 years. The peoples most affected by their decision to salvage what was left of the empire were the Arabs of the Fertile Crescent and coastal Arabia who still remained under Ottoman control. Arab leaders in Beirut and Damascus had initially favored the 1908 coup because they believed it would bring about the end of their long domination by the Turks. To their dismay, the Arabs discovered that the Young Turks not only meant to continue their subjugation, but that they were determined to enforce state control to a degree unthinkable to the later Ottoman sultans. The quarrels between the leaders of the Young Turk coalition and the growing resistance in the Arab portions of what was left of the Ottoman Empire were quite suddenly cut short by a much larger global crisis brought on by the outbreak of general war in Europe in August 1914. Turkish entry into and defeat in the First World War brought about the dissolution of the Ottoman Empire. This also gave rise to the leader, Mustafa Kemal or Ataturk, and some of the forces that proved critical in the emergence of the modern nation of Turkey from the ruins of the empire. However able a military commander he might have been, Ataturk's successes would not have been possible without the struggles and reforms of the last century and a half of the Ottoman Empire.

WESTERN INTRUSIONS AND THE CRISIS IN THE ARAB ISLAMIC HEARTLANDS

By the early 1800s, the Arab peoples of the Fertile Crescent, Egypt, coastal Arabia and North Africa had lived for centuries under Ottoman-Turkish rule. Though most Arabs resented Turkish domination, they could identify with the Ottomans as fellow Muslims, who were both ardent defenders of the faith and patrons of Islamic culture. Still, the steadily diminishing capacity of the Ottomans to defend the Arab Islamic heartlands left them exposed to the danger of conquest by the aggressive European powers. The European capture of outlying, but highly developed, Islamic states from those in the Indonesian archipelago and India to Algeria in North Africa engendered a sense of crisis among the Islamic faithful in the Middle Eastern heartlands. From the terror of Christendom and the encirclers of its European bastion, the Muslims had become the besieged. Islam had been displaced by

Europe as the leading civilization in a wide range of endeavors from scientific inquiry to monumental architecture. Much of the Muslim community was forced to live under infidel European overlords; what remained was threatened by European conquest.

The profound crisis of Islamic confidence brought on by successive reverses and the ever-increasing strength of their old European rivals gave rise to a wide variety of responses in the Islamic world. Islamic thinkers debated the best way of reversing the decline and driving back the Europeans. Some argued for a return to the Islamic past; others favored a large-scale adoption of Western ways; while still others sought to find ways to combine the two approaches. Reformist leaders, such as those in 19th-century Turkey, tried to graft on elements of Western culture while preserving the old state and society pretty much intact. Religious leaders, sometimes proclaiming themselves divinely appointed prophets, rose up to lead their followers in jihads, or holy wars, against the advancing Europeans. Though it is not possible to examine all of these responses in each of the Islamic lands, the following sections focus on key responses on the part of Arab peoples in Egypt and the Sudan in the 19th century. In these areas, European involvement was intense and the growing challenges posed by the West generated important attempts to find ways of reversing the decline of Islamic civilization and restoring it to its former glory.

FRENCH INVASION AND MAMLUK DEFEAT

Though it did not establish a permanent European presence in the Islamic heartlands, Napoleon's invasion of Egypt in 1798 sent shock waves across what remained of the Muslim world. Significantly, Napoleon's motives for launching the expedition had little to do with designs for empire in the Middle East itself. Rather he saw the Egyptian campaign as the prelude to the destruction of British power in India, where, as we have seen, the French had come out on the short end of earlier wars for empire. Whatever his calculations, Napoleon managed to slip his fleet past the British blockade in the Mediterranean and put ashore his armies in July 1798. There followed one of the most lopsided military clashes in modern history. As they advanced inland, Napoleon's forces were met by tens of thousands of cavalrymen bent on defending the Mamluk regime that then ruled Egypt as a vassal of the Ottoman sultans. The term Mamluk literally meant slave, and it suggested the Turkic origins of the regime in Egypt. Beginning as slaves who served Muslim overlords, the Mamluks had centuries earlier risen in the ranks as military commanders to the point where they were able to seize power in their own name. Murad, the head of the coalition of Mamluk households that shared power in Egypt at the time of Napoleon's arrival, dismissed the invader as a donkey boy whom he would soon drive from his lands.

Though courageous and determined to drive back the French invaders at the Battle of the Pyramids, the undisciplined Mamluk cavalrymen proved no match for the drilled marksmen and massed artillery of Napoleon's armies.

Murad's contempt for the talented young French commander was symptomatic of the profound ignorance of events in Europe that was characteristic of many leaders of the Islamic world at that time. Murad's ignorance led to a series of crushing defeats, the most famous of which came in a battle fought beneath the pyramids of the ancient Egyptian pharaohs. In the brief but bloody battle, the disciplined firepower of the French legions devastated the ranks of Mamluk horsemen clad in medieval armor, wielding spears against the artillery Napoleon used with such devastating effect.

Because the Mamluks had long been regarded as fighters of great prowess in the Islamic world, their rout was literally traumatic. It brutally revealed just how vulnerable even the Muslim core areas were to European aggression and how far the Muslims had fallen behind the Europeans in the capacity to wage war. Ironically, the successful invasion of Egypt brought little advantage to Napoleon or the French. The British caught up with the French fleet and sunk most of it at the Battle of Aboukir in August of 1798. With his supply line cut off, Napoleon was forced to abandon his army and sneak back to Paris, where his enemies were attempting to use his reverses in Egypt to put an end to his rise to power. Thus, Egypt was spared European conquest—for a time. The reprieve brought little consolation, since the British, not Egypt's Muslim defenders, had been responsible for the French retreat.

THE RISE OF MUHAMMAD ALI

In the chaos that followed the French invasion and eventual withdrawal in 1801, the Mamluk survivors fought with local notables for political control. The unexpected winner of these struggles was a young officer of Albanian origins named Muhammad Ali. He was a member of the Ottoman expeditionary force that had been sent to drive the French from Egypt. Having consolidated his base in the Cairo area by 1805, Muhammad Ali was master of Egypt after his soldiers slaughtered 300 Mamluk chieftains in 1811. Deeply impressed by the weapons and discipline of the French armies, the Albanian upstart devoted his energies and the resources of the land that he had brought under his rule to building an up-to-date European-style military force. He introduced Western-style conscription among the Egyptian peasantry, hired French officers to train his troops, imported Western arms, and adopted Western tactics and modes of organization and supply. Within years he had put together the most effective fighting force in the Middle East. With it, he flaunted the authority of his nominal overlord, the Ottoman sultan, by successfully invading Syria and building a modern war fleet that threatened Istanbul on a number of occasions.

By the 1830s Muhammad Ali's armies had been so successful that they were threatening the Ottoman regime itself. Twice, intervention by European powers was necessary to rescue the regime at Istanbul and foil Muhammad Ali's dreams of becoming the paramount lord of the Arab Muslim heartlands. Once again, the Europeans, not Muslim leaders, emerged as the arbiters of the destiny of the Arab world.

Though Muhammad Ali's efforts to introduce reforms patterned after Western precedents were not confined to the military, they fell far short of a fundamental transformation of Egyptian society. To shore up his economic base, he ordered the Egyptian peasantry to expand their production of cotton, hemp, indigo, and other crops that were in growing demand in industrial Europe. Efforts to improve Egyptian harbors and extend irrigation works met with some success and led to modest increases in the revenues that could be devoted to the continuing modernization of the military. Attempts to reform education were ambitious but limited in what was actually achieved. Many of the most significant innovations in schooling were linked to Muhammad Ali's military projects. His frequent schemes to build up an Egyptian industrial sector were eventually frustrated by the opposition of the European powers and by the intense competition from imported, Western-manufactured goods.

To secure his home base, Muhammad Ali also found that he had little choice but to ally with the powerful rural landlords, the ayan, to control the peasantry. He eliminated the tax farmers and claimed all land as state property, but despite these measures within decades a hereditary landlord class was firmly entrenched in the rural areas. His forcible confiscations of the peasants' produce to pay for the rising costs of the military establishment and for his foreign entanglements further impoverished an already hard-pressed rural population.

The limited scope of Muhammad Ali's reforms ultimately checked his plans for territorial expansion and left Egypt open to inroads by the European powers. He died in 1848, embittered by the European opposition that had prevented him from mastering the Ottoman sultans and well aware that his empire beyond Egypt was crumbling. Lacking his ambition and ability, his successors were content to confine their claims to Egypt and the Sudanic lands that stretched away from the banks of the Upper Nile to the south. Intermarrying with Turkish families that had originally come to Egypt to govern in the name of the Ottoman sultans, Muhammad Ali's descendants provided a succession of rulers, known as khedives after 1867, who were the formal rulers of Egypt until they were overthrown by the military coup that brought Nasser to power in 1952.

BANKRUPTCY, EUROPEAN INTERVENTION, AND STRATEGIES OF RESISTANCE

Muhammad Ali's successors made a muddle of his efforts to reform and revitalize Egyptian society. While cotton production increased and the landlord class grew fat, the great majority of the peasants went hungry or starved. The long-term consequences of these developments were equally troubling. The great expansion of cotton production at the expense of food grains and alternative market crops rendered Egypt dependent on a single export and vulnerable to fluctuations in demand on the European markets to which most of it was exported. Some further educational advances were made, mainly at elite schools where French was the language of instruction. But the advances were too limited to benefit the populace by making government more efficient or stimulating public works projects and improved health care.

Much of the revenue the khedives managed to collect, despite the resistance of the ayan, was wasted on extravagant pastimes and fruitless military campaigns to assert Egyptian authority over the Sudanic peoples along the Upper Nile. The increasing inability of the khedives to balance their books led in the middle decades of the 19th century to their growing indebtedness to European financiers. The latter lent money to the profligate khedives and members of the Turkish elite because the financiers desired both continued access to Egypt's cheap cotton and, by the 1850s, a share in the potentially lucrative schemes to build a canal across the Isthmus of Suez that would connect the Mediterranean and Red seas. The completion of the Suez Canal in 1869 shortened the distance by sea between Europe and Asia and allowed steamboats to replace sailing vessels, which had earlier proven better able to weather the rough passage around Africa.

The ineptitude of the khedival regime and the Ottoman sultans, who were their nominal overlords, prompted a good deal of discussion among Muslim intellectuals and political activists as to how they might find the leadership and means to ward off the growing European menace. Egypt, and particularly Cairo's ancient Muslim University of al-Azhar, became in the middle decades of the 19th cen-

The construction of a canal over the desert wastes of the Isthmus of Suez was a remarkable engineering feat. As this contemporary photo illustrates, a massive investment in up-to-date technology was essential to the success of the venture.

tury one of the key meeting places of these thinkers from throughout the Islamic world. Some prominent Islamic scholars called for a jihad to drive the infidels from Muslim lands. They also argued that the Muslim world could be saved only by a return to the patterns of religious observance and social interaction that they believed had existed in the "golden age" of the Prophet.

Other thinkers, such as al-Afghani (1839–1897) and his disciple Muhammad Abduh (1849–1905), stressed the need for Muslims to borrow scientific learning and technology from the West and to revive their earlier capacity to innovate. They argued that Islamic civilization had once taught the Europeans much in the sciences and mathematics, including such critical concepts as the Indian numerals. Thus, it was fitting that Muslims learn from the advances the Europeans had made with the help of Islamic borrowings. Those who advocated this approach also stressed the

One of the oldest universities in the world, al-Azhar in Cairo has been one of the main centers of Muslim intellectual ferment in the modern era.

importance of the tradition of rational inquiry in Islamic history. They strongly disputed the views of fundamentalist theorists who contended that the Quran was the source of all truth and should be interpreted literally.

Though both fundamentalists and those who stressed the need for imports from the West agreed on the need for Muslim unity in the face of the growing European threat, they could not reconcile their very different approaches to Islamic revival. Their differences and the uncertainties they have injected into Islamic efforts to cope with the challenges of the West remain central problems in the Muslim world today.

The mounting debts of the khedival regime and the strategic importance of the canal gave the European powers, particularly Britain and France, a growing stake in the stability and accessibility of Egypt. French and British bankers, who had bought up a good portion of the khedive's shares in the canal, urged their governments to intervene militarily when the khedives proved unable to meet their loan payments. At the same time, French and British diplomats quarreled over how much influence their nations should exercise within Egypt. In the early 1880s a genuinely nationalist challenge to both the puppet khedival regime and the European powers prompted the British to intervene militarily to the chagrin of the French, who at that point were in no position to do likewise.

The challenge was mounted by the supporters of a charismatic young Egyptian officer named Achmad Orabi. The son of a small farmer in lower Egypt, Orabi had attended Quranic school and studied under the reform-minded Muhammad Abduh at al-Azhar. Though a native Egyptian, Orabi had risen in the ranks of the khedival army and had become increasingly critical of the fact that the officer corps was dominated by Turks with strong ties to the khedival regime. An attempt by the khedive to save money by disbanding Egyptian regiments and dismissing Egyptian officers sparked a revolt led by Orabi in the summer of 1882. Riots in the city of Alexandria, associated with mutinies in the Egyptian armies, drove the frightened khedive to seek British assistance. After bombarding coastal batteries set up by Orabi's troops, the British sent ashore an expeditionary force that crushed Orabi's rebellion and secured the position of the khedive. Though Egypt was not formally colonized, the British intervention began decades of dominance by both British consuls, who ruled through the puppet khedives, and British advisors to all high-ranking Egyptian administrators. British officials controlled Egypt's finances and foreign affairs, and British troops ensured that their directives were heeded by Egyptian administrators. Direct European control over the Islamic heartlands had begun.

JIHAD: THE MAHDIST REVOLT IN THE SUDAN

As Egypt fell under British control, the invaders were inevitably drawn into the turmoil and conflict that gripped the Sudanic region to the south in the last decades of the 19th century. Egyptian efforts to conquer and rule the Sudan, beginning in the 1820s, were fiercely resisted, particularly by the camel and cattle herding nomads who occupied the vast, arid plains that stretched west and east from the Upper Nile. The sedentary peoples who worked the narrow strip of fertile land along the river were more easily dominated. Thus, Egyptian authority, insofar as it existed at all, was concentrated in these areas and in river towns such as Khartoum, which was the center of Egyptian administration.

Even in the riverine areas Egyptian overlordship was greatly resented. The Egyptian regime was notoriously corrupt and its taxes placed a heavy burden on the peasants compelled to pay them. The Egyptians were clearly carpetbagging outsiders, and the favoritism they showed some of the Sudanic tribes was guaranteed to alienate the others. In addition, virtually all groups in the Muslim areas in the north Sudan were angered by Egyptian attempts in the 1870s to eradicate the slave trade. The trade had long been a great source of profit for both the merchants of the Nile towns and the nomads, who attacked non-Muslim peoples, such as the Dinka in the south, in order to capture slaves. British advisors at the khedive's court had strongly pushed for the antislavery effort, and an English commander, George Gordon, had taken charge of the campaign and on occasion employed very heavy-handed methods to suppress the trade.

By the late 1870s Egyptian oppression and British intervention had aroused deep resentment and hostility, particularly among the Muslim peoples of the northern Sudan. But a leader was needed to unite the diverse and often divided peoples of the region and to provide an ideology that would give focus and meaning to rebellion. The son of a boat builder named Muhammad Achmad, who had been educated by the holy man head of a local Sufi brotherhood, proved to be that leader. The fact that his family claimed descent from the Prophet and that he had the physical signs—a cleft in his teeth and a mole on his right cheek—that the local people associated with the promised deliverer did much to advance his reputation. The visions he began to experience, after he had broken with his Sufi master and established his own sectarian following, also suggested that a remarkable future was in store. What was seen to be a miraculous escape from a bungled Egyptian effort to capture and imprison Muhammad Achmad soon led to his widespread acceptance as a divinely appointed leader of revolt against the foreign intruders.

The jihad that Muhammad Achmad, who was known to his followers as the Mahdi (the promised deliverer), proclaimed against both the Egyptian heretics and British infidels was one of a number of such movements that had swept sub-Saharan Africa since the 18th century. It represented the most extreme and violent Islamic response to what was perceived as the dilution of Islam in the African environment and the growing threat of Europe. Muhammad Achmad promised to purge Islam of what he viewed as superstitious beliefs and degrading practices that had built up over the centuries and to return Islam to what he claimed was its original purity. He led his followers in a violent assault on the Egyptians, whom he believed professed this corrupt version of the faith, and the European infidels. At one point, his successors dreamed of toppling the Ottoman sultans and invading Europe itself.

The Mahdi's skillful use of guerrilla tactics and the confidence his followers placed in his blessings and magical charms earned his forces a number of stunning victories over the Egyptians. In 1883 the Mahdi's commanders drew a force of 8000 Egyptians, led by British officers, deep into the desert wilderness and ambushed and destroyed it in a desolate valley called Shaykan. By the end of 1883 the Mahdi's forces controlled most of the northern Sudan and were besieging the Egyptians' last major stronghold at Khartoum. In both ignorance and arrogance, the British sent a single officer, General Gordon, who had earlier overseen the suppression of the slave trade, up the Nile to Khartoum to command the Egyptian garrison and put down the Mahdist rebellion. Just under a year after Gordon's arrival, the city was taken and he was killed by the Mahdi's followers. The Mahdists had driven off the Egyptians, slaughtered their British commanders, and were now the masters of the Sudan.

At the peak of his power, the Mahdi fell ill from typhus and died just months after the capture of Khartoum. In contrast to many movements of this type, which have collapsed rapidly after the death of their prophetic leaders, the Mahdists found a capable successor to Muhammad Achmad in the Khalifa Abdallahi, one of his most skillful military commanders. Under Abdallahi, the Mahdists built a strong, expansive state and a closely controlled society, where smoking, dancing, and alcoholic drink were forbidden and theft, prostitution, and adultery were severely punished. For nearly a decade, Mahdist armies attacked or threatened neighboring states on all sides, including the Egyptians to the north, whose territories the Mahdists planned to invade. But in the fall of 1896, famed British General Kitchener was sent with an expeditionary force to put an end to what was one of the most serious threats to European domination in Africa. The spears and magical garments of the Mahdist forces proved no match for the machine guns and artillery of Kitchener's columns, and at the battle of Omdurman in 1898 the bulk of the Mahdist cavalry and Abdallahi himself were slaughtered. The Mahdist state collapsed and British power advanced still farther into the interior of Africa.

RETREAT AND ANXIETY: ISLAM IMPERILED

The 19th century was a time of severe reverses for the peoples of the Islamic world. Outflanked and outfought by their old European rivals, Islamic leaders either became puppets of European overlords or their lands passed under the rule of infidel colonial rulers. Diverse forms of resistance, from the reformist path taken by the Ottoman sultans to the prophetic rebellions of leaders such as Muhammad Achmad, slowed but could not halt the European advance. European products and demands steadily eroded the economic fabric and heightened social tensions in Islamic lands. The stunning military and economic successes of the Christian Europeans cast doubts on Muslim claims to possession of the one true faith. By the century's end it was clear that neither the fundamentalists, who called for a return to a purified Islam free of Western influences, nor the reformers, who argued that some borrowing from the West was essential for survival, had come up with a successful formula for dealing with the powerful challenges posed by the industrial West. Failing to find ad-

equate responses and deeply divided within, the Islamic community grew increasingly anxious over the dangers that lay ahead. Islamic civilization was by no means defeated, but its continued viability was clearly threatened by the powerful neighbor that had become master of the world.

THE LAST DYNASTY: THE RISE AND FALL OF THE QING EMPIRE IN CHINA

By the early decades of the 19th century a major collision between the aggressive and ever-expanding European industrial powers and the largest and most enduring of preindustrial civilizations, China, was unavoidable. For centuries the rulers of China had superciliously resisted European attempts to "open up" their rich lands and vast population to Christian missionary campaigns or the market economy the Europeans had extended over much of the globe. European traders were confined to two ports, Macao, which had been established by the Portuguese in the 16th century, and Canton, where their activities were strictly supervised by Chinese officials. The Chinese refused to accept European ambassadors or even to recognize nations, such as Britain and France, as their equals. Chinese officials treated European merchants and emissaries with the contempt that they felt the "southern (because they came by sea from the south) barbarians" deserved. Because they believed the Europeans had little to offer in the way of civilized attainments, the rulers of China made little ef-

China during the Qing Era

fort to learn about the nation-states they represented. They knew next to nothing about the Renaissance and Reformation, and not much more about the scientific and industrial revolutions. As a result, when the Chinese were confronted by armed intervention of the European powers in the first decades of the 19th century, they struck out in blindness against adversaries whose motives they could not understand and whose power they were not at all prepared to reckon with.

Though China had been strong enough to get away with its policies of isolation and attitudes of disdain in the early centuries of expansion, by the late 18th century these were outmoded and dangerous. Not only had the Europeans grown incomparably stronger than they had been in the early centuries of expansion, but Chinese society was crumbling from within. Over a century of strong rule by the Manchus and a high degree of social stability, if not prosperity, for the Chinese people gave way to rampant official corruption, severe economic dislocations, and social unrest by the last decades of the 18th century. Each of these phases will be considered in the first sections of the following discussion of Chinese history in the Qing era. The next sections will be devoted to the growing tensions between the Chinese and the Europeans, particularly the British, and the series of 19th-century wars that resulted. The remaining portions of this chapter on the crises of Europe's two greatest rival civilizations, Islam and China, will explore the consequences of Europe's forcible entry into China and the slow demise of the last Chinese dynasty.

THE MAKING OF THE MANCHU IMPERIUM

Though the Manchu nomads had been building an expansive state of their own north of the Great Wall for decades, their conquest of China was both unexpected and sudden. A local leader named Nurhaci (1559–1626) was the architect of unity among the quarrelsome Manchu tribes. He combined the male warriors of each tribe into extremely cohesive fighting units within eight banner armies, named after the flags that identified each. In the first decades of the 17th century, Nurhaci brought much of Manchuria, including a number of non-Manchu peoples, under his rule. Though he remained the nominal vassal of the Chinese Ming emperor, Nurhaci's forces continually harassed the Chinese who lived north of the Great Wall, steadily driving them southward or in some cases incorporating them into his growing state. In this period, the Manchu elite's adoption of Chinese ways, which had begun much earlier, was greatly accelerated. The Manchu bureaucracy was organized along Chinese lines, Chinese court

ceremonies were adopted, and numerous Chinese scholar-officials found lucrative employment in the growing barbarian state north of the Great Wall. Though less affected by Chinese influences, Manchu commoners had some exposure to Chinese ways, and though most remained nomadic herders, a fair percentage had become sedentary farmers by the time of the conquest of China proper.

The weakness of the declining Ming regime, rather than the Manchus' own strength, provided the opportunity to seize control in China. The Manchu entry into China resulted from a bit of luck. In 1644 an official of the Ming government in charge of the northern defenses called in the Manchus to help him put down a widespread rebellion in the region near the Great Wall. Having allowed the Manchus to pass through the wall, the official found that they were even a greater threat than the rebels. Exploiting the political divisions and social unrest that were in the process of destroying what was left of Ming authority, the Manchus boldly advanced on the Ming capital at Beijing, which they captured within the year. Though it took nearly two decades before centers of Ming and rebel resistance in the south and west were destroyed by the banner armies, the Manchus soon found themselves the masters of China.

They quickly proved that they were up to the challenge of ruling the largest empire in the world. Their armies forced submission by nomadic peoples far to the west and compelled tribute from kingdoms such as Vietnam and Burma to the south. Within decades, the Manchu regime, which had taken the dynastic name Qing before their conquest of China, ruled an area larger than any previous Chinese dynasty with the exception of the Tang.

To reconcile the ethnic Chinese who made up the vast majority of their subjects, the Manchu rulers shrewdly retained much of the political system of their Ming predecessors. They added to the court calendar whatever Confucian rituals they did not already observe. They made it clear that they wished the scholar-officials who had served the Ming to continue in office, and the Manchus even pardoned many who had been instrumental in prolonging resistance to their conquest. At the same time, however, the new rulers assumed a much more direct role in the appointment of local officials than had the Ming, and somewhat reduced the tax exemptions and privileges of these functionaries. For much of the first century of the dynasty, Chinese and Manchu officials were paired in appointments to most of the highest posts of the imperial bureaucracy, and Chinese officials predominated at the regional and local levels. Though Manchus, who made up less than two percent of the population of the Qing Empire, occupied a dis-

This Western engraving after a Chinese drawing portrays the first Manchu emperor, Kangxi, whose long reign between 1654 and 1722 brought such power and prosperity to China that European writers like Voltaire compared him to the philosopher-king who was the ideal of Plato.

proportionate number of the highest political positions, there were few limits as to how high talented ethnic Chinese could rise in the imperial bureaucracy.

Unlike the Mongol conquerors who abolished it, the Manchus retained the examination system and had their own sons educated in the Chinese classics. The Manchu emperors styled themselves the Sons of Heaven and rooted their claims to be the legitimate rulers of China in their practice of the traditional Confucian virtues. The early Manchu rulers were generous patrons of the Chinese arts and at least one, Kangxi (1661–1722), was a significant Confucian scholar in his own right. Kangxi and other Manchu rulers employed thousands of scholars to compile great encyclopedias of Chinese learning.

Despite the Manchus' high degree of Sinification and efforts to conciliate the Chinese scholar-gentry elite, resentment of them persisted. The burden of maintaining garrisons of their troops in the major cities of the empire was a very real one, and many ethnic Chinese never forgave the Manchus the humiliation of an edict that forced all Chinese males to shave their foreheads and wear their hair braided in the back. When the empire was strong and prosperous, most of the Manchus' subjects were willing to put up with these burdens. But when the Qing dynasty went into decline in the late 18th century, its foreign origins became a rallying point for risings from below.

ECONOMY AND SOCIETY IN THE EARLY CENTURIES OF QING RULE

The Manchu determination to preserve much of the Chinese political system was paralleled by an equally conservative approach to Chinese society as a whole. In the early centuries of their reign the writings of Zhu Xi, which had been so influential in the preceding dynastic eras, continued to dominate official thinking. Thus, long-nurtured values such as respect for rank and acceptance of hierarchy—that is, old over young, male over female, scholar-bureaucrat over commoner—were emphasized in education and imperial edicts. Among the elite classes, the extended family remained the core unit of the social order, and the state grew increasingly suspicious of any forms of social organization, such as guilds and especially secret societies, that rivaled it.

The lives of women at all social levels remained centered or wholly confined to the household, where the dominance of elder males was upheld by familial pressures and the state. Male control was enhanced by the practice of choosing brides from families slightly lower in social status than those of the grooms. Because they were a loss to their parents' household at marriage and usually required a sizeable dowry, daughters continued to be much less desirable than sons. Despite the poor quality of the statistics relating to the practice, there are indications that the incidence of female infanticide rose in this period. In the population as a whole males considerably outnumbered females—the reverse of the balance between the two in contemporary industrial societies.

Beyond the family compound the world pretty much belonged to men, though women from lower-class families continued to labor in the fields and sell produce in the local markets. The best a married woman could hope for was strong backing from her father and brother after she had gone to her husband's home, as well as the good luck in the first place to be chosen as the wife rather than as a second or third partner in the form of a concubine. If they bore sons and lived long enough, wives took charge of running the household, and in elite families they exercised considerable control over other females and even younger males. In contrast to India where widow remarriage was all but prohibited, especially among the higher castes, in China it was permitted since widows were seen as a burden on family resources.

Some of the strongest measures the Manchus took after conquering China were aimed at alleviating the rural distress and unrest that had become so pronounced in the last years of Ming rule. Taxes and state labor demands were lowered, and incentives, such as tax-free tenure, were offered to those willing to resettle lands that had been abandoned in the turmoil of the preceding decades. A sizeable chunk of the imperial budget (up to ten percent in the early years of the dynasty) was devoted to the repair of existing dikes, canals, and roadways and the extension of irrigation works. Peasants were encouraged to plant new crops, including those for which there was a considerable market demand, and to grow two or even three crops per year on their holdings. Like a number of the earlier dynasties, the Qing sought to check the accumulation of great estates by rural landlords or, failing that, to at least strengthen the position of the tenant classes.

Given the growing pressure of population on the available cultivable acreage and the virtual disappearance in most areas of open lands that could be settled, the regime had very little success in these laudable endeavors. After several decades of holding steady, the landed classes found that they could add to their estates with impunity by calling in loans to peasants or simply buying them out. With a surplus of laborers desirous of their positions, tenants had less and less bargaining power in their dealings with landlords. If they objected to the share of the crop the landlords offered, they were turned off the land and replaced by those willing to accept even less. As a result of these patterns, the gap between the rural gentry and ordinary peasants, not to mention the impoverished laborers, in-

creased noticeably. One could not miss the old and new rich in the rural areas, as they rode, decked out in silks and furs, to make social calls on their peers. To further impress their superior social standing upon those whom they encountered, many males of the gentry class let their nails grow long to demonstrate that they never engaged in physical labor.

The sector of Chinese society over which the Qing were able to exercise the least control was also the most dynamic. The commercial and urban expansion that had begun in the Song era gained new strength in the long peace China enjoyed during the first century and a half of Manchu rule. Regional diversification in crops such as tea was matched by the development of new ways of financing agricultural and artisan production. Until the end of the 18th century, both the state and the mercantile classes profited enormously from the great influx of silver that poured into China in payment for its exports of tea, porcelain, and silk textiles. European and other foreign traders flocked to Canton, and Chinese merchants, freed from the restrictions against overseas travel of the late Ming, found lucrative market outlets in the Philippines, Siam, and elsewhere in Southeast Asia. The influx of silver meant some inflation, but until the latter half of the 18th century the much more market-oriented and sophisticated Chinese economy was better able to handle rising prices than its Islamic counterparts were. Overseas trading links gave rise to a wealthy new group of merchants, the *compradors*, who specialized in the import-export trade on China's south coast. In the 19th century, these merchants proved to be one of the major links between China and the outside world. The inability of the Qing regime to control this growing commercial class effectively both undermined the regime's attempts to prohibit the import of harmful substances, such as opium, and deprived the regime of substantial tax revenues.

ROT FROM WITHIN: BUREAUCRATIC BREAKDOWN AND SOCIAL DISINTEGRATION

By the late 18th century, it was clear that, like so many Chinese dynasties of the past, the Qing was in decline. The signs of decline were pervasive and familiar. The bureaucratic foundations of the Chinese Empire were rotting from within. The exam system, which had done well in selecting able and honest bureaucrats in the early decades of the dynasty, had become riddled with cheating and favoritism. Despite formal restrictions, sons of high officials were often ensured a place in the ever-growing bureaucracy. Even more disturbing was the fact that virtually anyone with enough money could buy a post for sons or brothers.

Impoverished scholars could be paid to take the exams for poorly educated or not so bright relatives, and examiners could be bribed to approve their credentials or look the other way when candidates consulted cheat sheets while taking their exams. In one of the most notorious cases of cheating, a merchant's son won high honors, despite the fact that he had spent the days of testing in a brothel hundreds of miles from the examination.

Cheating had become so blatant as early as the first decades of the 18th century that in 1711 students who had failed the exams at Yangzhou held a public demonstration to protest bribes given to the exam officials by wealthy salt merchants. The growing influx of merchant and poorly educated landlords' sons into the bureaucracy was particularly troubling because few of these had received the classical Confucian education that stressed the responsibilities of the educated ruling classes and their obligation to serve the people. Increasingly, positions in the bureaucracy were regarded by the wealthy as a means of exerting influence over local officials and judges as well as a way of enhancing family fortunes without regard for the effects of bureaucratic decisions on the peasantry and urban laborers.

Over a period of decades, the diversion of revenue from state projects to the enrichment of individual families had a devastating impact on Chinese society. For example, funds needed to maintain the armies and fleets that defended the huge empire fell off sharply, resulting in a noticeable drop in the training and armament of the military. Even more critical for the mass of the people were reductions in spending on public works projects. Of these, the most vital were the great dikes that confined the Yellow River in northern China. Over the millennia, the silting of the river bottom and the constant repair of and additions to the dikes created a situation where river and dikes were raised high above the densely populated farmlands through which they passed. Thus, when neglected for lack of funds and proper official supervision of repairs, leaking dikes and rampaging waters of the great river meant catastrophe for much of northeastern China.

Nowhere was this disaster more apparent than in the region of the Shandong peninsula. Before the mid-19th century, the Yellow River emptied into the sea south of the peninsula. By the 1850s, however, the neglected dikes had broken down over much of the area and the river had flooded hundreds of square miles of heavily cultivated farmland. By the 1860s the main channel of the river flowed north of the peninsula. The lands in between had been flooded and the farms wiped out. Peasants in the millions were left without livestock or land to cultivate; tens, perhaps hundreds, of thousands of peasants died of famine and disease.

As the condition of the peasantry deteriorated in many parts of the empire, further signs of dynastic decline appeared. Food shortages and landlord exactions prompted mass migrations; vagabond bands clogged the roads and beggars crowded the city streets. Banditry, long seen by the Chinese as one of the surest gauges of the extent of dynastic decline, became a major problem in many districts. As the following verse from a popular ditty of the 1860s illustrates, the government's inability to deal with the bandits was seen as a further sign of Qing weakness:

> When the bandits arrive, where are the troops?
> When the troops come, the bandits have vanished.
> Alas, when will the bandits and troops meet?

The assumption then widely held by Chinese thinkers—that the dynastic cycle would again run its course with the Manchus being replaced by a new and vigorous dynasty—was belied by the magnitude of the problems confronting the leaders of China. The belief that China's future could be predicted by the patterns of its past history ignored the fact that, in a number of ways, there were no precedents for the critical changes that had occurred in China under Manchu rule. Some of these changes had their roots in the preceding Ming era (see Chapter 28) in which, for example, food crops from the New World had set in motion a population explosion. An already large population had nearly doubled to reach a total of over 200 million in the first century (c. 1650–1750) of Manchu rule; in the following century it doubled again to reach 410 to 415 million. However successful they had been in the past, Chinese social and economic systems were simply not capable of carrying a population of this magnitude. China desperately needed innovations, breakthroughs in technology and organization that would increase its productivity to the point where its exploding population could be supported at a reasonable level. The corrupt and highly conservative late-Manchu regime was increasingly an obstacle to, rather than a source of, these desperately needed changes.

BARBARIANS AT THE SOUTHERN GATES

A second major difference between the forces sapping the strength of the Manchus and those that had brought down earlier dynasties was the nature of the so-called barbarians who threatened the empire from outside. As we have seen, nomadic incursions had traditionally played a large role in the dynastic cycle. Their bolder and more frequent incursions into the agrarian regions protected by the Great Wall was one of the surest signs of the impending end of a dynasty. But in the past the nomads, even when—like the Manchus—they had established themselves as the new rulers of China, had soon been assimilated to China's more sophisticated culture and society and absorbed into the much larger Chinese population.

Though the Chinese, out of ignorance, treated the Europeans much like the nomads and other peoples whom they regarded as barbarians, the Europeans presented a very different sort of challenge. They came from a civilization that was China's equal in sophistication and complexity. In fact, though European nation-states like Great Britain were much smaller in population (in the early 19th century England had seven million people to China's 400 million), they could, thanks to the scientific and industrial revolutions, compensate for their smaller numbers with better organization and superior technology. As tensions built up between the Europeans—who demanded that restrictions on their trading and religious proselytization in China be removed—and the Chinese—who were determined to limit foreigners' activities within the empire— the Europeans' advantages in technology and knowledge of the wider world became increasingly decisive. When violent clashes between the two led to wars between 1839 and 1842 as well as 1856 and 1860, the underlying vulnerabilities of Chinese civilization were brutally exposed.

DOCUMENT
THE LETTER OF THE QIANLONG EMPEROR TO KING GEORGE III

One of the most fascinating and important documents from the early decades of European imperialist involvement in China was the letter sent in 1793 from the emperor of China to King George III of England. Excerpts of the letter follow:

We have perused the text of your state message and the wording expresses your earnestness. From it your sincere humility and obedience can clearly be seen. . . . As to what you have requested in your message, O King, namely to be allowed to send one of your subjects to reside in the Celestial Empire to look after your country's trade, this does not conform to the Celestial Empire's ceremonial system, and definitely cannot be done. . . . If it is said that your object, O King, is to take care of trade, men from your country have been trading at Macao for some time and have always been treated favorably. For instance, in the past Portugal and Italy and other countries have several times sent envoys to the Celestial Empire with requests to look after their trade, and the Celestial Empire, bearing in mind their loyalty, treated them with great kindness. Whenever any matter concerning trade has arisen which affected those countries it has always been fully taken care of.

The Celestial Empire, ruling all within the four seas [the world], simply concentrates on carrying out the affairs of the Government properly, and does not value rare and precious things. Now you, O King, have presented various objects to the throne, and mindful of your loyalty in presenting offerings from afar, we have specially ordered the Department of Foreign tribute to receive them. In fact, the virtue and power of the Celestial Dynasty has penetrated afar to the myriad kingdoms, which have come to render homage, and so all kinds of precious things from "over mountain and sea" have been collected here, things which your chief envoy and others have seen for themselves. Nevertheless, we have never valued ingenious articles, nor do we have the slightest need of your country's manufactures. Therefore, O King, as regards your request to send someone to remain at the capital, while it is not in harmony with the regulations of the Celestial Empire we also feel very much that it is of no advantage to your country. Hence we have issued these detailed instructions and have commanded your tribute envoys to return safely home. You, O King, should simply act in conformity with our wishes by strengthening your loyalty and swearing perpetual obedience so as to ensure that your country may share the blessings of peace.

Questions: What do these excerpts tell you about the Chinese view of themselves, the English, and the wider world at the time? How well do these attitudes correspond to the actual situation? Why were they likely to cause serious problems for the Chinese?

THE ORIGINS OF THE OPIUM WAR

The issue that was responsible for the initial warfare between China and the British did little credit to the latter. For centuries British merchants had eagerly exported silks, fine porcelains, tea, and other products from the Chinese Empire. Finding that they had little in the way of manufactured goods or raw materials that the Chinese were willing to take in exchange for these products, the British were forced to surrender growing amounts of silver bullion to obtain the products they wanted. Unhappy about the unfavorable terms of trade in China, British merchants hit on a possible solution in the form of opium that was grown in the hills of eastern India. Though opium was also cultivated in China, the Indian variety was far more potent and soon in great demand in the Middle Kingdom. By the first decades of the 19th century an average of 4500 chests of opium, each weighing 133 pounds, were sold, either legally or illicitly, to merchants on the south China coast. By 1839, on the eve of the Opium War, nearly 40,000 chests were imported by the Chinese.

Though the British had found a way to reverse the trade balance in their favor, the Chinese soon realized that the opium traffic was a major threat to their economy and social order. Within years China's favorable trade balance with the outside world was reversed and silver began to flow in large quantities out of the country. As sources of capital for public works and trade expansion decreased, agricultural productivity stagnated or declined and unemployment spread, especially in the hinterlands of the coastal trading areas. Wealthy Chinese, who could best afford it,

squandered increasing amounts of China's wealth to support their opium habits, and opium dens spread in the towns and villages of the empire at an alarming rate. By 1838, it has been estimated, one percent of China's better than 400 million people were addicted to the drug. Strung out officials neglected their administrative responsibilities, the sons of prominent scholar-gentry families lost their ambition, and even laborers and peasants abandoned their work for the debilitating pleasures of the squalid opium dens.

From early in the 18th century, Qing emperors had issued edicts forbidding the traffic, but little had been done to enforce them. By the first years of the 19th century, it was clear to the court and high officials that the opium trade must be stopped. When serious efforts were finally undertaken in the early 1820s, they only served to drive the opium dealers from Canton to nearby islands and other clandestine locations on the coast. Finally, in the late 1830s the emperor sent one of the most distinguished officials in the empire, Lin Zexu, with orders to use every means available to stamp out the trade. Lin, who was famed for his incorruptibility, took his charge quite seriously. After being rebuffed in his attempts to win the cooperation of European merchants and naval officers in putting an end to the trade, Lin ordered the European trading areas in Canton blockaded, their warehouses searched, and all the opium that was confiscated destroyed.

Not surprisingly, these actions enraged the European merchants, and they demanded military action to avenge their losses. Arguing that Lin's measures violated both the property rights of the merchants and principles of free

This mid-19th-century European engraving depicts the criminal atmosphere and dissolution associated with Chinese opium dens. Victorian sensibilities made it difficult for contemporary artists to capture fully the depths of despair and degradation that addicts reached in these centers of unchecked vice.

trade, the British ordered the Chinese to put an end to their antiopium campaign or risk military intervention. When Lin persisted, war broke out in late 1839. In the conflict that followed the Chinese were first routed on the sea, where their now-antiquated war junks were no match for British gunboats; then they were soundly defeated in their attempts to repel an expeditionary force the British sent ashore. With British warships and armies threatening the cities of the Yangze River region, the Qing emperor was forced to sue for peace and send Lin into exile in a remote province of the empire.

Their victories in the Opium War and a second conflict, which erupted in the late 1850s, allowed the European powers to force China to open trade and diplomatic exchanges. After the first war, Hong Kong was established as an additional center of British commerce, and European trade was permitted at five other ports, where the Europeans were given land to build more warehouses and living quarters. By the 1890s, 90 ports of call were available to over 300,000 European and American traders, missionaries, and diplomats. Britain, France, Germany, and Russia had won long-term leases over several ports and surrounding territory, as imperialist expansion pressed China directly.

Though the treaty of 1842 made no reference to the opium trade, following China's defeat the drug poured unchecked into China. By the middle of the century, China's foreign trade and customs were overseen by British officials. They were careful to ensure that European nationals had favored access to China's markets and that no protective tariffs, such as those the Americans were using at the time to protect their young industries, were established by the Chinese. Most humiliating of all for the Chinese was the fact that they were forced to accept European ambassadors at the Qing court. Not only were ambassadors traditionally (and usually quite rightly) regarded as spies, but the exchange of diplomatic missions was a concession that European nations were equal in stature to China. Given the deeply entrenched Chinese conviction that their Middle Kingdom was the civilized center of the earth and that all other peoples were barbarians, this was indeed a very difficult concession to make. European battleships and firepower gave them little choice.

A CIVILIZATION AT RISK: REBELLION, FAILED REFORMS, AND THE FALL OF THE QING

Though it was not immediately apparent, China's defeat in the Opium War greatly contributed to a building crisis that threatened not just the Qing dynasty but Chinese civilization as a whole. Defeat and the dislocations in south China brought on by the growing commercial encroachments of the West spawned a massive rebellion that convulsed much of south China in the 1850s and early 1860s, and at one point threatened to overthrow the Qing dynasty. Led by a mentally unstable, semi-Christianized prophet named Hong Xiuquan, the Taiping rebellion exacerbated the already considerable stresses within Chinese society and further drained the diminishing resources of the ruling dynasty. Though widespread peasant risings, incited by the members of secret societies like the White Lotus, had erupted as early as the 1770s, the Taiping movement was the first to pose a serious alternative not only to the Qing dynasty but to Confucian civilization as a whole. In contrast to a number of contemporary rebellions to the west of China, the Taipings offered sweeping programs for social reform, land redistribution, and the liberation of women. They also attacked the traditional Confucian elite and the learning on which its claims to authority rested. Taiping rebels smashed ancestral tablets and shrines, and proposed a simplified script and mass literacy that would have undermined one of the scholar-gentry's chief sources of power.

Their attack on the scholar-gentry, in fact, was one of the main causes of the Taipings' ultimate defeat. Left no option but to rally to the Manchu regime, the provincial gentry became the focus of resistance to the Taipings. Honest and able Qing officials, such as Zeng Guofan, raised more effective, provincially based military forces just in time to beat off the Taiping assault on northern China. Zeng and his allies in the government also sought to carry out much-needed reforms to root out corruption in the bureaucracy and revive the stagnating Chinese economy.

In the last decades of the 19th century, these dynamic provincial leaders were the most responsible for China's self-strengthening movement, which was aimed at countering the challenge from the West. They encouraged Western investment in railways and even factories in the areas they governed, and sought to modernize their armies. Combined with the breakdown of Taiping leadership and the declining appeal of a movement that could not deliver on the promises it made to its followers, the efforts of the gentry brought about the eventual but very bloody suppression of the Taiping rebellion. Other movements were also crushed and banditry was brought under control for a time. But like the Ottoman sultans and their advisors, the Chinese gentry introduced changes that they viewed as limited, aimed at preserving the existing order, not fundamentally transforming it. They continued to profess loyalty to the gravely weakened Manchu regime because they saw it as a defender of the traditional order. At the same time, their own power grew to the point that the Manchus could control them only with great difficulty. Resources were increasingly drained from the court center to the provincial governors, whose growing military and political power posed a potential threat to the Qing court. The basis of China's political fragmentation was building behind the crumbling facade of Manchu rule.

Despite their clearly desperate situation by the last decades of the 19th century, including a shocking loss in a war with Japan in 1894 and 1895, the Manchu rulers stubbornly resisted the far-reaching reforms that were the only hope of saving the regime, and, as it turned out, Chinese civilization. Manchu rulers on occasion moved to back those officials who pushed for extensive political and social reforms, some of which were inspired by the example of the West. But their efforts were repeatedly frustrated by the backlash of members of the imperial household who allied themselves to the great majority of the scholar-gentry, who were determined to preserve the old order with only minor changes and to make no concessions to the West.

The last decades of the dynasty were dominated by the ultra-conservative dowager empress Cixi, who became the power behind the throne. In 1898 she and her faction crushed the most serious move toward reform from the top. Her nephew, the emperor, was imprisoned in the Forbidden City, and leading advocates for reform were executed or driven from China. On one occasion, Cixi flaunted the Westernizers by rechanneling funds that had been raised to build modern warships to defend China into the building of a huge marble boat in one of the lakes in the imperial gardens. With genuine reform blocked by Cixi and her faction, the Manchus relied on divisions between the provincial officials as well as between the European powers to maintain their position. The involvement of members of the Qing household in popular outbursts aimed at forcibly expelling the foreigners from China—such as the Boxer Rebellion that broke out in 1898 and was only put down through the intervention of the imperialist powers in 1901—resulted in further military setbacks and enhanced the control of the Europeans and the power of the provincial officials.

By the first years of the 20th century, the days of the Manchus were clearly numbered. With the defeat of the Taipings, resistance to the Qing came to be centered in rival secret society organizations such as the Triads and the Society of Elders and Brothers. These underground organizations inspired numerous local risings against the dynasty in the last decades of the 19th century, which failed for lack of coordination and sufficient resources. But some of the secret society cells became a valuable training ground

that prepared the way for a new sort of resistance to the Manchus. By the end of the 19th century, the sons of some of the scholar-gentry and especially of the comprador merchants in the port cities were becoming more and more involved in secret society operations and other activities aimed at the overthrow of the regime. Because many of these young men had received European-style educations, their resistance was aimed at more than just getting rid of the Manchus. They envisioned power passing to Western-educated, reformist leaders who would build a new and strong nation-state in China patterned after those of the West, rather than simply establishing yet another imperial dynasty. For aspiring revolutionaries such as Sun Yat-sen, who emerged as one of their most articulate spokesmen, their seizure of power was also seen as a way of enacting desperately needed social programs to relieve the misery of the peasantry and urban workers.

Though they drew heavily on the West for ideas and organizational models, the revolutionaries from the rising middle classes were deeply hostile to the involvement of the imperialist powers in Chinese affairs and condemned the Manchus for their failure to control the foreigners. The young rebels cut off their queues in defiance of Manchu order that all ethnic Chinese wear their hair in this fashion, and joined in uprisings fomented by the secret societies or plotted assassinations and acts of sabotage on their own. Attempts to coordinate an all-China rising floundered on a number of occasions due to personal animosities or amateurish incompetence. But in late 1911, opposition to the government's reliance on the Western powers for railway loans led to secret society uprisings, student demonstrations, and mutinies on the part of imperial troops. When a number of key provincial officials refused to put down the spreading rebellion, the Manchus had no choice but to abdicate. In February of 1912 the last emperor of China, a small boy named Puyi, was deposed, and one of the more powerful of the provincial lords was asked to establish a republican government in China.

THE END OF A CIVILIZATION?

The revolution of 1911 toppled the Qing dynasty, but in many ways a more important watershed for Chinese civilization was crossed in 1905. In that year the civil service exams were given for the last time. Reluctantly, even the ultraconservative advisors of the empress Cixi had concluded that solutions to China's predicament could no longer be found in the Confucian learning the exams tested. The abandonment of the exams in effect signaled the end of a pattern of civilized life the Chinese had nurtured, improved, and held to for nearly 2500 years. The mix of philosophies and values that had come to be known as the Confucian system, the massive civil bureaucracy, rule by an educated and cultivated scholar-gentry elite, and even the artistic accomplishments of the old order were to come under increasing criticism in the early years of the 20th century. Many of these hallmarks of the most enduring civilization that had ever existed would be vehemently discarded, violently destroyed. As we shall see in Chapter 41, however, even though Confucian civilization like so many before it passed into history, many of its ideas, attitudes, and ways of approaching the world survived. Some of these played critical roles in the violent and painful struggle of the Chinese people to build a new civilization to replace the one that had failed them. The challenge of blending and balancing the two remains to the present day.

CONCLUSION

ISLAMIC AND CHINESE RESPONSES TO THE CHALLENGE OF THE WEST COMPARED

Though both Chinese and Islamic civilizations were severely weakened by internal disruptions in the 18th and 19th centuries, each was thrown into prolonged crisis by the growing challenges posed by the West. A number of key differences in the interaction between each civilization and the West do much to explain why Islam, though badly shaken, survived, while Chinese civilization collapsed under the burden of domestic upheavals and foreign aggression. For the Muslims, who had been warring and trading with Christian Europe since the Middle Ages, the Western threat had long existed. What was new was the much greater strength of the Europeans in the ongoing contest, which resulted from their global expansion and their scientific and industrial revolutions. For China, the challenges from the West came suddenly and brutally. Within decades, the Chinese had to revise their estimate of their empire as the center of the world and the source of civilization itself to take into account severe defeats at the hands of peoples they once dismissed as barbarians.

The Muslims could also take comfort from the fact that in the Judeo-Christian and Greek traditions they shared much with the ascendant Europeans, and that elements of their own civilization had played critical roles in the rise of the West. This made it easier to justify Muslim borrowing from the West, which in any case could be set in a long tradition of exchanges with other civilizations. Though some Chinese technology had passed to the West, Chinese and Western leaders were largely unaware of early exchanges but deeply impressed by the profound differences between their societies. For the Chinese, borrowing from the barbarians required a painful reassessment of their place in the world—a reassessment many were unwilling to make.

In countering the thrusts from the West, the Muslims gained from the fact that they had many centers to defend—the fall of a single dynasty or regime did not mean the end of Islamic independence. The Muslims also gained from the more gradual nature of the Western advance. They had time to learn from earlier mistakes and try out different responses to the Western challenges. For the Chinese, the defense of their civilization came to be equated with the survival of the Qing dynasty—a line of thinking that the Manchus did all they could to promote. When the dynasty collapsed in the early 20th century, the Chinese lost faith in the formula for civilization they had successfully followed for over two millennia. Again timing was critical. The crisis in China seemed to come without warning. Within decades, the Qing went from the arrogant controller of the barbarians to a defeated and humbled pawn of the European powers.

When the dynasty failed and it became increasingly clear that the barbarians had outdone the Chinese in so many fields of civilized endeavor, the Chinese had little to fall back on. Like the Europeans, they had excelled in social and political organization and mastery of the material world. Unlike the Hindus or the Muslims, they had no great religious tradition with which to counter the European conceit that worldly dominance could be equated with inherent superiority. In the depths of their crisis, Muslim peoples clung to the conviction that they possessed the true faith, the last and fullest of God's revelations to humankind. That faith became the basis of their resistance and of their strategies for renewal, the key to the survival of Islamic civilization and its continuing efforts to meet the challenges of the West in the 20th century.

FURTHER READINGS

The best general introductions to the Ottoman decline and the origins of the nation of Turkey remain Bernard Lewis's *The Emergence of Modern Turkey* (1961) and the chapter on "The Later Ottoman Empire" by Halil Inalcik in the *Cambridge History of Islam*, vol. 1 (1973). Other recent studies of importance on specific aspects of this process include C. V. Findley's studies of Ottoman bureaucratic reform and the development of a modern civil service in what is today Turkey, Ernest Ramsaur's *The Young Turks* (1957), Stanford Shaw's *Between Old and New* (1971), and David Kusher's essay on *The Rise of Turkish Nationalism* (1977). On Egypt and the Islamic heartlands in this period, see P. M. Holt's *Egypt and the Fertile Crescent, 1516–1922* (1965) or P. J. Vatikiotis's *The History of Egypt* (1985). On the Mahdist movement in the Sudan see P. M. Holt's *The Mahdist State in the Sudan* (1958) or the fine summary by L. Carl Brown in Robert Rotberg and Ali Mazrui, eds., *Protest and Power in Black Africa* (1970). The latter also includes many informative articles on African resistance to European conquest and rule. On women and changes in the family in the Ottoman realm, see Nermin Abadan-Unat's *Women in Turkish Society* (1981), and in the Arab world, see Nawal el Saadawi's *The Hidden Face of Eve* (1980).

On the Manchu takeover in China, see Frederic Wakeman, Jr.'s *The Great Enterprise* (1985) and Jonathan Spence and John E. Willis, eds., *Ming to Ch'ing* (1979). On Qing rule, among the most readable and useful works are Spence's *Emperor of China: Portrait of K'ang-hsi* (1974) and the relevant sections in his recent study on *The Search for Modern China* (1990); Susan Naquin and Evelyn Rawski's *Chinese Society in the 18th Century* (1987); and the essays in John Fairbank, ed., *Cambridge History of China: Late Ch'ing 1800–1911* (1978). A good survey of the causes and course of the Opium War is provided by Chang Hsin-pao's *Commissioner Lin and the Opium War* (1964). The Taiping rebellion is covered in Jen Yu-wen's *The Taiping Revolutionary Movement* (1973), and the first stages of the Chinese nationalist movement are examined in the essays in Mary Wright, ed., *China in Revolution: The First Phase* (1968). The early sections of Elisabeth Croll's *Feminism and Socialism in China* (1980) provide an excellent overview of the status and condition of women in the Qing era.

RUSSIA'S REFORMS AND INDUSTRIAL ADVANCE

 PROTEST AND REVOLUTION

JAPAN

Russia

1829–1878 Serbia gains increasing autonomy
in Ottoman Empire, then independence
1831 Greece wins independence
after revolt against Ottomans

1812 Failure of Napoleon's invasion

1830–1831 Polish nationalist revolt repressed
1833, 1853 Russian-Ottoman wars

1815 Russia reacquires Poland
through the Treaty of Vienna;
Alexander I and the Holy Alliance

1825 Decembrist Revolt

1825–1855 Heightening of
repression by Tsar Nicholas I

Japan

1800–1850 Growth of "Dutch school"

1720 End ban on Western books

1841–1843 Brief
shogun reform effort

33

Russia and Japan: Industrialization Outside the West

INTRODUCTION. Two important nations defied the common pattern of growing Western domination during the 19th century: Russia and Japan. Both did so only after a heightened threat of Western interference, and both had to accept Western advisors and other intrusions. Russia and Japan did, however, manage to launch significant industrialization by 1914, along with other changes designed to strengthen their political and social systems and preserve national independence. Neither Russia nor Japan rivaled the industrial might of the West at this point; both were trying to catch up after a late start. Their achievement was economic autonomy—not yet a share in the West's core position—which enabled both nations to gain sufficient power to wield important political and military influence, participating in the imperialist scramble of the late 19th century.

Most of the non-Western world, as we have seen, was described largely in terms of growing vulnerability in the face of Western advance during the 19th century. A host of territories were either newly seized colonies or existing colonies controlled with new rigor. Latin America, a special case, won independence and admittedly enjoyed some growing economic success by the later 19th century, but amid firm commercial and diplomatic constraints from western Europe and the United States. China and the Islamic Middle East, technically independent amid important territorial loss, hesitated in their response to new

---

1881–1905 Growing repression, attacks on minorities

1860s–1870s Alexander II reforms

1898 Formation of Marxist Social Democratic Party

1875–1877 Russian-Ottoman war, Russia wins new territory

1861 Russian emancipation of serfs

1884–1887 New gains in central Asia

1904–1905 Loss in Russo-Japanese War

1854–1856 Crimean War

1884–1914 Beginnings of Russian industrialization; near-completion of trans-Siberian railway (full linkage 1916)

1914 World War I

1867 Russia sells Alaska to U.S.

1905–1906 Revolution results in peasant reforms and duma

1917 Revolution and Bolshevik victory

1856 Romania gains virtual independence

1878 Bulgaria gains independence

1892–1903 Sergey Witte, minister of finance

1865–1876 Russian conquests in central Asia

1881 Anarchist assassination of Alexander II

1860–1868 Civil strife

1870–1940 Population growth

1890 New constitution and legal code

1904–1905 Russo-Japanese War

1870 Ministry of Industry established

1902 Loose alliance with Britain

1916–1918 Seizure of former German holdings in Pacific and China

1853 Perry expedition to Edo Bay

1872 Universal military service established

1910 Annexation of Korea

1854 Follow-up American and British fleet visits

1868–1912 Meiji period

1877 Final samurai rising

1894–1895 Sino-Japanese war

1912 Growing party strife in Parliament

1867 Mutsuhito, emperor of Japan

1914 Entry to World War I

Western power, though Turkish reformers and Arab nationalists sketched some promising alternatives by 1900. Russia and Japan were different, though they too experienced new Western threats.

The early industrial revolutions of Japan and Russia as well as the forces that prompted them constitute important phenomena in that here were major cases of change in significant societies. These changes are also interesting in showing what societies could do, and had to do, in order to launch the kind of transformation the West had pioneered—without becoming fully Western.

Yet the distinctiveness of the Russian and Japanese patterns must also be recognized. These were the only societies outside the West to begin a wholesale process of industrialization before the 1960s. Other societies changed in many ways, but for various reasons, including Western interference, their transformations did not include this economic centerpiece. This means, in turn, that some special factors must be grasped in Japan and Russia, involving not just their industrialization but also their earlier history and their evolution during the early 19th century, in order to explain their unusual reactions to the West's industrial example.

The pairing of Russia and Japan was in many ways unexpected. The two societies had little to do with each other in the past, and they had scant contact even as they began to industrialize. Furthermore, their processes of change were quite different, based on different institutional structures and cultures. Japan displayed much more political flexibility than Russia did, and, once committed to reforms, Japan undertook a more sweeping transformation. Change in Russia more obviously heightened social strains, leading to a significant revolution in 1905 and a major upheaval in 1917. Japan had no outright revolution, which in a way made its ability to change all the more remarkable.

Japan must also be compared to other East Asian societies, particularly China, with which it shared many characteristics—the fruit of earlier imitation—but from which it began to diverge. Simply put, Japanese industrialization and related reforms seemed less expected in light of previous patterns than did Russia's, where an awareness of Western models and an interest in selective borrowing had developed by 1700. Japan pulled away from its larger civilization area at least for a time, whereas Russia continued a pattern of expanding influence in eastern Europe and central Asia.

Nevertheless, while Russia and Japan cannot be dealt with in a single sketch, their pairing is not random. Industrialization involved some common processes, and as late industrializers—chasing a considerable Western lead—Japan and Russia displayed still more similarities. Further,

while Japan avoided revolution it did not escape serious strain; its differentiation from Russia should be not exaggerated on this score. Reactions to the West's Industrial Revolution obviously could shake up earlier civilizational alignments—such as in pulling Japan farther away from Chinese patterns.

Finally, in general but important ways Russia and Japan did have some common characteristics, which help explain why both could maintain economic and political independence during the West's century of power. They both had prior experience of imitation, Japan from China, Russia from Byzantium and then the West. They knew that learning from outsiders could be profitable and need not necessarily destroy their native cultures. They both had improved their political effectiveness during the 17th and 18th centuries, through the Tokugawa shogunate and tsarist empire. This would aid both in dealing with change from the basis of some political strength, though it did not deflect a need for further political reform, and it would allow both nations to use the state to sponsor changes that in the West had rested in part with private groups such as businessmen.

Ironically, soon after the reform period began in both countries, Russia and Japan met in new ways, as expansionist interests brought a clash over influence in Korea. The resultant Russo-Japanese War symbolized the growing importance of both societies in world affairs and their common involvement in unsettling change, though it also showed Japan's greater success in military modernization. The war promoted further change, convincing Japanese leaders that they were on the right course, while weakening a beleaguered Russian establishment.

RUSSIA'S REFORMS AND INDUSTRIAL ADVANCE

Neither Russia nor Japan generated significant changes during the first half of the 19th century. Both countries were bent on maintaining the status quo, though in Russia's case this involved pulling apart from Western patterns more fully than had been necessary in the previous century. Yet the early 19th century in both countries must be briefly probed in order to explain the ability and willingness to react decisively to a new Western challenge after 1850.

RUSSIA BEFORE REFORM

Russia's new fearfulness about Western patterns started in the governing elite and it was rooted in the shock generated by the French Revolution. Russian rulers, beginning with Catherine the Great in her later years, sought means to protect the country from Western revolutionary contagion, and in the process the sense that Western policies might serve as models for Russia faded dramatically. Napolean's 1812 invasion of Russia also produced new concern with defense. This turn toward renewed isolation was supported by conservative intellectuals who seized the opportunity to vaunt Russian values over those of the chaotic West. In the eyes of these aristocratic writers, Russia knew the true meaning of community and stability. The system of serfdom provided ignorant peasants with the guidance and protection of paternalistic masters—an inaccurate social analysis, but a comforting one. To combat Napoleon's pressure early in the 19th century some improvements in bureaucratic training were introduced, and city administrations were granted somewhat greater authority. A new tsar, Alexander I, flirted with liberal rhetoric, but he also sponsored the Holy Alliance idea at the Congress of Vienna that grouped the conservative monarchies of Russia, Prussia, and Austria in defense of religion and the established order. The idea of Russia as a bastion of sanity in a Europe gone mad was an appealing one.

The defense of the status quo produced some important new tensions, however. A number of intellectuals remained fascinated with Western progress, though they typically criticized certain aspects of it. Some praised political freedom and educational and scientific advance, while deploring the West's neglect of social issues amid the squalor of early industrialization. Others focused more purely on Western cultural styles. Early in the 19th century, Russia began to contribute creatively to European cultural output. The poet Pushkin, for example, descended from an African slave, used romantic styles to celebrate the beauties of the Russian soul and the tragic dignity of the common people. Because of its compatibility with the use of folklore and a sense of nationalism, the romantic style took deep root in eastern Europe. Russian musical composers would soon begin their contributions, again using folk themes and sonorous sentimentality within an essentially Western stylistic context.

While Russia's ruling elite continued to welcome Western artistic styles and took great pride in Russia's growing cultural respectability, they increasingly censored intellectuals who tried to incorporate liberal or radical political values. Many intellectuals were jailed or exiled to the West, in a pattern that to some extent has continued until very recently.

Western values also inspired a minor but disturbing political revolt, the Decembrist uprising in 1825. A group of middle-level army officers, many of whom had served in western Europe during the Napoleonic wars and who de-

plored Russia's backwardness compared to Western bureaucratic efficiency and political liberalism, rose up in the name of change. The officers were not well organized, and they were divided between a majority who wanted political improvements and nothing more and a minority who talked vaguely of more sweeping social change including peasant reforms. The revolt was easily put down, but it inspired the new tsar, Nicholas I, to still more adamant conservatism. Repression of political opponents stiffened, and the secret police expanded. Newspapers and schools, already confined to a small minority, were tightly supervised. What political criticism there was flourished mainly in exile in places such as Paris or London, and had little impact on Russia.

Partly because of political repression, Russia was spared the wave of revolutions that spread through Europe in 1830 and 1848. There was no substantial middle class to spearhead liberal protest, and police activity prevented the kind of ideological buildup that preceded revolution in the West. The artisan class was small and lacked strong organizational traditions. The huge peasant majority had grievances aplenty, and it continued to break out in periodic regional revolts against landlord exactions, but these revolts were not substantial enough to trigger a larger uprising. Russia seemed to be operating in a different political orbit from that of the West, to the great delight of most Russian officials. In its role as Europe's conservative anchor, Russia even intervened in 1849 to help Austria put down the nationalist revolution in Hungary—a blow in favor of monarchy but also a reminder of Russia's eagerness to flex its muscles in wider European affairs.

In the military Decembrist revolt in St. Petersburg, Loyalist troops ultimately put down the revolting regiments in 1825.

Russian Expansion, 1815–1914

While turning more fiercely conservative than it had been in the 18th century, Russia maintained its tradition of territorial expansion. Russia had confirmed its hold over most of Poland at the Congress of Vienna in 1815 after Napoleon had briefly sponsored a separate Polish duchy. While technically a separate entity under the tsar, the Polish territory was ruled with a heavy hand. Nationalist sentiment, inspired by the growth of romantic nationalism in Poland and backed by many Polish landowners with ties to the West, roused recurrent Polish opposition to Russian rule. An uprising occurred in 1830 and 1831, triggered by news of the revolutions in the West and led by liberal aristocrats and loyal Catholics who chafed under the rule of an Orthodox power. Tsar Nicholas I put down this revolt with great brutality, driving many leaders into exile.

Russia was clearly bent on maintaining full authority over its new European holdings. At the same time the Russians continued pressure on the Ottoman Empire, whose weakness attracted eager attention. A war in the 1830s led to some territorial gains, though Western powers, fearful of a Russian advance on Constantinople that would provide easy access to the Mediterranean, forced some limitations. France and Britain recurrently tried to prop up Ottoman authority in the interest of countering Russian aggression. Russia also supported many nationalist movements in the Balkans, including the Greek indepen-

dence war in the 1820s—a desire to cut back the Turks here outweighed Russia's commitment to conservatism. Overall, while no massive acquisitions marked the early 19th century, Russia continued to be a dynamic diplomatic and military force.

ECONOMIC AND SOCIAL PROBLEMS: THE PEASANT QUESTION

Russia's economic position, however, did not keep pace with its diplomatic aspirations. As the West industrialized and central European powers, such as Prussia and Austria, introduced at least the beginnings of industrialization, including some rail lines, Russia largely stood pat—this meant that it began to fall increasingly behind the West in technology and trade. The patterns of the 18th century, which had suggested growing Russian economic dependence on the West, resumed with a vengeance. Russian landlords eagerly took advantage of Western markets for grain, but they increased their exports not by improving their techniques but by tightening the labor obligations on their serfs. This was a common pattern in much of eastern Europe in the early 19th century, as Polish and Hungarian nobles also increased labor service in order to gain ground in the export market. In return for low-cost grain exports, Russia and other East European areas imported some

Western machinery and other costly equipment, as well as luxury goods for the great aristocrats to display as badges of cultured respectability. A few isolated factories were opened up using Western equipment, but there was no significant change in overall manufacturing or transportation mechanisms. Russia remained a profoundly agricultural society based on essentially unfree labor, but it was now a visibly stagnant society as well. Many Russian leaders were aware of the West's great economic innovation and dynamism, but they papered over the differences by their enthusiastic embrace of European cultural styles, keeping up to date on the latest in costume, dance, or painting, while in some cases offering criticisms of the social injustice of industrialization.

The widening gap between Russia and the West was dramatically driven home by a fairly minor war in the Crimea between 1854 and 1856. Nicholas I had provoked conflict with the Ottoman Empire in 1853, arguing among other things that Russia had the responsibility for protecting Christian interests in the Holy Land and that the Ottomans were not assuring the rights of churches and monasteries there. Essentially this attack resumed the longstanding Russian attempt to gain ground in the area. This time, however, France and Britain were not content with diplomatic maneuverings to limit Russian gains, but came directly to the sultan's aid. Britain was increasingly worried about any great power advance in the region that might threaten its hold on India, while France sought diplomatic glory and also represented itself as the Western champion of Christian rights. The resultant Crimean War was fought directly in Russia's backyard on the Black Sea, yet the Western forces won, driving the Russian armies from their entrenched positions. The loss was shocking and profoundly disturbing to Russian leadership, for the West won this little war not because of great tactics or inspired principles, but essentially because of their industrial advantage. They had the ships to send masses of military supplies long distances, and their artillery and other weapons were vastly superior to Russia's home-produced models. Here was a severe blow to a regime that prided itself on military vigor, and a frightening portent for the future.

The Crimean War helped convince Russian leaders, including the new tsar, Alexander II, that it was time for a change. Reform was essential not to copy the West, but to allow sufficient economic adjustments for Russia to keep pace in the military arena. And reform meant, first and foremost, some resolution of Russia's leading social issue, the issue that most distinguished Russian society from that of the West: serfdom. Only if the status of serfs changed could Russia develop a more vigorous and mobile labor force and so be able to contemplate some version of industrialization. Russian concern paralleled attacks on slavery in the Americas in the same period, reflecting a desire to meet Western humanitarian standards and a need for cheap, flexible labor.

Other factors argued for reform of the serfs as well. Some aristocrats were convinced that a freer labor system would motivate serfs to work hard and thus produce higher agricultural profits. Several leaders were also stung by repeated Western-inspired criticisms of the injustice of Russian society, which focused on the harsh conditions of servile labor. Even more aristocrats were concerned by the periodic peasant uprisings that focused on lack of freedom, undue obligations, and lack of land. Stability required some dramatic new moves that would protect the essentials of the social order while contenting the peasantry to a greater degree. Peasant uprisings increased in the 1850s, triggered in part by some bad harvests—unlike the West at this point, Russia was still vulnerable to famine when crops failed—and in part by the discontents of returning peasant veterans from the Crimea.

So Russia returned, for two decades, to a policy of reform, based in part on Western standards and examples—manorialism had been fully abolished in western Europe after 1789 and in east-central regions such as Prussia and Hungary, in the aftermath of the revolutions of 1848. As before, however, the intention was not to duplicate Western measures down the line, but to protect distinctive Russian institutions including the landed aristocracy and tightly knit peasant communities. The result was an important series of changes that, with tragic irony, created more grievances than they resolved while opening the way to further economic change.

THE REFORM ERA AND EARLY INDUSTRIALIZATION

The final decision to emancipate the serfs in 1861 came at roughly the same time that the United States and, soon, Brazil decided to free slaves. Neither slavery nor rigorous serfdom suited the economic needs of a society seeking an independent position in Western-dominated world trade.

In some ways the emancipation of the serfs was more generous than the liberation of slaves in the Americas. While aristocrats retained part of the land, including the most fertile holdings, the serfs got most of it—in contrast to slaves who received their freedom but nothing else. Russian emancipation, however, was careful to preserve essential aristocratic power; the tsar was not interested in destroying the nobility, who remained his most reliable political ally and the source of most bureaucrats. Even more, emancipation was designed to retain the tight grip of the tsarist state. The serfs obtained no new political rights at a national level. They were still tied to their villages until they could pay for the land they were given—the redemption money going to the aristocrats to help preserve this class. Redemption payments added greatly to peasants' material hardship, and they were infuriating, for peasants thought the land belonged to them with no need to pay for its return. Enforcement of redemption obligations meant many peasants could still not move freely or even sell their land, though some became more mobile. High redemption payments, in addition to state taxes that increased as Russia sought funds to build railroads and factories, kept most Russian peasants miserably poor.

Emancipation did bring change; it helped create a larger urban labor force. But it did not spur a revolution in agricultural productivity, as most peasants continued to use traditional methods on their small plots. And it did not bring contentment: Indeed, peasant uprisings became more common as hopes for a brighter future now seemed dashed by the limits of change. Rural unrest in Russia was furthered also by substantial population growth, as some of the factors that had earlier swelled the West's population now spread to Russia, including growing use of the potato. Peasant crowding would by itself have created hardship, while also providing new migrants in search of other work; in combination with grievances about emancipation, it was a truly explosive force.

Russia, in sum, provided after 1861 a classic case of a society in the midst of rapid change where reform did not go far enough—perhaps, given traditions and established interests, it could not go far enough—to satisfy key protest groups. Peasants used their village structures so often praised by Russian conservatives to provide organization and goals for recurrent attacks on landlords and state tax officials, while usually still professing loyalty to the tsar.

To be sure, the reform movement did not end with emancipation. Alexander II introduced a host of further measures in the 1860s and early 1870s. New law codes cut back traditional punishments now that serfs were legally free in the eyes of the law (though subject to important transitional restrictions). The tsar created local political councils, the *zemstvoes*, that had a voice in regulating roads, schools, and other regional policies. Some form of local government was essential now that the nobles no longer directly ruled the peasantry. The zemstvoes gave some Russians, particularly middle-class people such as doctors and lawyers, new political experience, and they undertook important inquiries into local problems. The coun-

This roadside scene in the late 19th century depicts the poverty of a Russian peasant village.

cils, however, had no influence on national policy, where the tsar resolutely maintained his own authority and that of his extensive bureaucracy. Another important area of change was the army, where the Crimean War had shown the need for reform. The officer corps were improved through promotion by merit and a new organization of essential services. Recruitment was extended, and many peasants learned new skills, including literacy, through their military service. Some strides were made also in providing state-sponsored basic education, though schools spread unevenly.

These adjustments, like emancipation itself, were important. They imitated some Western principles; the new law codes, for example, included a more humanitarian approach to punishment for crime as well as technical equality before the law. The reforms were sufficient to spur the beginnings of Russian industrialization. They were not sufficient to provide a stable social base for this inherently traumatic economic upheaval.

From the reform era onward, literacy spread rapidly in Russian society. A new market developed for popular reading matter that had some similarities to the mass reading culture developing in the West. Interestingly, Russian pot-boiler novels, while displaying a pronounced taste for excitement and exotic adventure, also attested to distinctive values; Russian "bad guys" for example were never glorified in the end, but always were either returned to social loyalty or condemned for their obduracy, a clear sign of the limits to individualism. Women gained new positions in the climate of change. Some won access to higher education, and, as in the West, a minority of women mainly from the upper classes began to penetrate professions such as medicine.

As these examples suggest, Russia had been launched on a process of considerable transformation, going well beyond the official political reforms. Even sexual habits began to change, as had occurred in the West a century before. Fathers' control over their children's behavior loosened a bit, particularly where non-agricultural jobs were available, and sexual activity before marriage increased.

The move toward industrialization was part of the wider process of change. The tsar's government was not always in agreement over industrialization goals, with some conservatives rightly fearing the impact of economic change on the existing social and political structure. On the whole, however, state support for industrialization continued even after the reform era ended in the late 1870s. And state support was vital for this shift toward industrialization, for Russia lacked a preexisting middle class and substantial capital; state enterprises had to make up part of the gap, in the tradition of economic activity that went back to Peter the Great.

The first step toward industrialization came with railroads, a clear necessity for military and political coordination as well as economic development in the vast land. Russia began to create an extensive railroad network in the 1870s. The establishment of the trans-Siberian railroad, which connected European Russia with the Pacific, was the crowning achievement of this drive when it was substantially completed by the end of the 1880s. The railroad boom directly stimulated expansion of Russia's iron and coal sectors. Rails also allowed fuller utilization of Russia's rich holdings in both minerals, for in contrast to England and Germany (and to an extent the United States) Russia lacked waterways that could do the job, as the north-south flow of rivers did not link up coal and iron deposits. Railroad development also stimulated the export of grain to the West, which now became essential to earn foreign currency needed in payment for advanced Western machinery. The railroads also opened Siberia up to new development, which in turn brought Russia into a more active and contested Asian role.

By the 1880s, when Russia's railroad network had almost quintupled compared to 1860, modern factories were beginning to spring up in Moscow, St. Petersburg, and several Polish cities, and an urban working class was growing apace. Printing factories and metalworking shops expanded the skilled artisanry in the cities, while new works in metallurgy and textiles created a still-newer, semiskilled industrial labor force from the troubled countryside.

Under Count Witte, minister of finance from 1892 to 1903 and an ardent economic modernizer, the government enacted high tariffs to protect new Russian industry, improved its banking system, and encouraged Western investors to build great factories with advanced technology. As Witte put it, "The inflow of foreign capital is . . . the only way by which our industry will be able to supply our country quickly with abundant and cheap products." By 1900 approximately half of Russian industry was foreign-owned and much of it was foreign-operated, with British, German, and French industrialists taking the lead. Russia became a debtor nation as huge industrial development loans piled up. And while an important class of Russian industrialists emerged, the early phases of Russian industrialization did not clearly improve Russia's autonomy in the world economy. Witte and others were confident that strong government controls could keep the foreigners in line rather than converting Russia into a new imperialist playground, and certainly foreign influence over basic government policy was not extensive. While the foreign presence and foreign profit-taking created resentments from workers and conservatives alike, there was some clear payoff: By 1900 Russia had surged to fourth rank in the world in steel production, and was second to the United States in the newer area of petroleum production and refining. Russian textile output was also impressive. Long-standing Russian economic lags were beginning to yield.

This was still an industrial revolution in its early stages. Russia's world rank was a function more of its great size and population, along with its very rich natural resources, than of really thorough mechanization. Many Russian factories were vast—on average, the largest in the world—but they were not usually up to Western technical standards, nor was the labor force highly trained. Many workers continued to go back and forth from factory to countryside, which helped ease the adjustment to often appalling urban and factory conditions but did not encourage full conversion to new work regimes. Agriculture also remained backward, as peasants, often illiterate, had neither capital nor motives to change their ways. Poor agriculture limited the growth of cities—which did surge forward impressively nevertheless—and made famine a recurrent threat.

Other reforms also produced ambiguous results. Russia remained a traditional peasant society in many ways. Beneath official military reorganization, many peasant-soldiers continued to regard their officers as landlord-patrons. Discipline and military efficiency were lax. It was not clear that the Russian masses had experienced the kinds of attitudinal changes that had occurred in the West around the time of initial industrialization or even before. Even more obvious was the absence of a large, self-confident middle class of the sort that had arisen earlier in the West. Businessmen and professional people grew in numbers, but they were often dependent on state initiatives—through zemstvo employment for doctors, or economic guidance for businessmen—and simply lacked the class size and tradition to become as assertive as their Western counterparts had been, for example, in challenging aristocratic power and values. The limitations of change in Russia reflected the recency of the process; by 1914 Russia was really only

Early Russian industrialization is depicted in this 1888 photo of the commercial department of the Abrikosova and Son factory.

DOCUMENT
RUSSIAN CONSERVATISM AND THE WEST

Russian conservatives continued to define a special Russian tradition in contrast to Westernizing initiatives up to the 1917 revolution. Their arguments help explain why Russia avoided basic political change; their assumptions about popular support seem somewhat fanciful in light of ultimate revolution. Yet the attempt to argue for an alternative to Western forms was important, not only in explaining Russian policies for several decades, but in suggesting reasons that people in various societies—including Russia itself even after 1917—might seek to avoid a strict Western model. The statement that follows, written in the shock of Alexander II's assassination in 1881, comes from a speech by a leading Slavophile, Ivan Aksakov.

The Emperor is murdered; the same Emperor who was the greatest benefactor to his country, who emancipated, bestowing upon them human and civil rights, tens of millions of Russian peasants. He is murdered; not from personal vengeance, not for booty, but precisely because he is the Emperor, the crowned head, the representative, the first man of his country, that vital, single man, who personified the very essence, the whole image, the whole strength and power, of Russia. From time immemorial that power constituted the strength of the country. The attempt directed against the person of the Tsar is al-

ways directed against the whole people; but in this case the whole historical principle of the national life has been attacked, the autocratic power bestowed upon the Emperor by the country itself. Who are those who dared to bring that awful shame upon the people, and, as if by mockery, in the name of the people? . . .

Can it be anything else but the logical, extreme expression of that Westernism which, since the time of Peter the Great, demoralized both our government and our society, and has already marred all the spiritual manifestations of our national life? Not content to profit by all the riches of European thought and knowledge, we borrowed her spirit, developed by a foreign history and foreign religion. We began idolizing Europe, worshiping her gods and her idols! Who is to be blamed? Some forty years ago has not Khomiakov warned us, threatening us with Divine punishment for 'deserting all that is sacred to our hearts'? But really, what are these 'Anarchists,' 'Social Democrats,' and Revolutionists, as they call themselves? Have they the smallest particle of Russian spirit in all their aspirations and aims? Is there the slightest shade in their teachings of a protest against the real shortcomings of which Russia is suffering? Just the opposite; what they despise most is precisely the Russian people. . . .

Our peasantry, forming almost eighty per cent of the whole realm, now possess land, organization, and the most complete self-government. To this very day, that fourth class is the keeper of our historical instinct, of our religion, and of the whole element of our political organism. They, and not the so-called 'Intelligentsia,' are the real supporters of our country. . . . Who accepts the causes has also to accept their logical consequences. Who accepts the Western Constitution has also to bear the last expression of Western political life, viz., social revolution with all its manifestations.

Worse than all the external calamities was the moral treason of its leading class, powerful through knowledge and development. The reforms of Peter the Great weakened our memory and disabled us from understanding our own history—so very different from that of the West. Conquest is not at the bottom of our historical life, as is the case in all the Western countries. Our history begins with quite a voluntary and rational appeal to power. The same appeal was repeated much later, in 1612, and gave the foundation to the present reigning dynasty, empowered with autocracy, and nothing and nobody could induce the country to alter that shape of government. Such was the will, such was the inspiration of the national spirit.

Our history does not possess, therefore, that fundamental fact, which characterizes the political life of the Western powers of Europe, the antagonism between the people and a power imposed by conquest. That antagonism, however, is the very foundation of Western constitutionalism. It is a mere agreement; a compromise between two camps hostile to each other, mistrusting each other; a kind of treaty, surrounded with all sorts of conditions. To evade those conditions *without contradicting the letter of the agreement*, constitutes the great talent of the rulers as well as of those who are ruled. Struggle for power—that is the real sense of the political life of European countries. The foundation of their administration is a kind of mechanical apparatus; the center of power and mind, or an *unlimited power*, belongs to the majority of voices based upon the numbers of the representatives. Thus some ten voices—often bribed and bought—automatically decide the destinies of the people, forming the actual majority, in comparison of which the parliamentary majority is a few grains of sand compared to the sandy wilderness of Sahara. But that autocrat, composed of several numerical units, bears no moral responsibility before its conscience and the country, responsibility which falls heavily on the one personal representative of the supreme power.

During the First Republic the French Representative Assembly declared—quite legally as far as the form was concerned, and in the name of the people—that worship addressed to God was null, and replaced by adoration of the 'Goddess of Reason'; and all that in the face of tens of millions of true believers, but of men deprived of any legal voice, and thus unable to protest at all. The same thing happened in France the other day. It is ordered now to put in all the primary schools, instead of the word God, the word *Nature*. Is this not a study illustrative of popular Western representation? What is the use of political rights which allow, in the name of liberty and law, such a revolting infraction of freedom and truth?

Such are the kinds of freedom promised to Russia by worshipers of European liberal institutions. But the instincts and the notions of freedom in the Russian people are higher and broader than in any part of the world, because they are free from the conventional and formal element, and are based on *moral truth*. They are easily traced in our self-government, the broadest of Europe, and in the largest application of the *elective element*. . . .

The Russian people has not entrusted full power to a heartless, soulless, mechanical apparatus, but to the 'holiest of beings'—to a man with a human soul, with a Russian heart, and a Christian conscience. The people know, and know well, the drawbacks of every human institution, but feel at the same time the power to overcome and improve them. And our former Tsars have not deceived their hopes and confidence; they held majestically and rigorously their imperial tide. . . . There was no mentioning any political rights, or supporting any kind of political doctrine. It was the regular, the natural manifestation of national life itself. Neither the people nor the autocratic Tsar ever thought themselves otherwise than in a constant moral and intellectual alliance of unity.

Questions: In what ways does Aksakov define the special Russian spirit? Why, in this judgment, are Western values inferior to Russian traditions? What kind of political system, according to this view, works best in Russia?

in its third decade of outright industrial revolution. It also reflected distinctive features of the process itself, and of earlier Russian tradition.

PROTEST AND REVOLUTION

A rising tide of unrest accompanied Russia's period of transformation. Alexander II's reforms, plus economic change with the greater population mobility it involved, helped encourage demands by minority nationalities in the great empire. Intellectuals explored the cultural traditions of Ukrainians and other groups. This cultural nationalism could lead to political demands, particularly at a point when state power, through military recruitment and school expansion, was beginning to increase. Nationalist beliefs were initially imported from western Europe, but here, and elsewhere in eastern Europe, they encouraged divisive minority agitation that multinational states, such as Russia or Austria-Hungary, found very hard to handle. Nationalist pressures were not the main problem in Russia, but in combination with other kinds of protest and given Russia's mainstream nationalist insistence on the distinctive superiorities of a Russian tradition, they did cause problems.

A RANGE OF DISCONTENT

Social protest was more vigorous still, and it was heightened not only by the limitations of reform but by industrialization itself. Peasant discontent was not a constant force, but it continued to burst forth. Recurrent famines regularly provoked uprising. Peasants deeply resented redemption payments and taxes and frequently attacked and burned the records that indicated what they "owed." Peasants' sense of natural justice, heightened by population pressure, also turned them against aristocratic estates.

Many educated Russians, including some aristocrats, also clamored for revolutionary change. Two strands developed. Many business and professional people, while not extremely aggressive, began to seek a fuller political voice and new rights such as greater freedom in the schools and press; they thus argued for liberal reforms. At the same time a group of radical *intelligentsia*—a Russian term denoting articulate intellectuals as a class—building on earlier intellectual discontent, became increasingly active. The intelligentsia formed a self-conscious group bent on radical change; the group was more distinct than in the West if only because the middle-class reform tradition, to which intellectuals might attach their efforts, was so limited. As Russian universities expanded, student groups grew as well, and many were extremely impatient with Russia's slow development and with the visible restrictions on political activity.

Some intellectuals later toned down their goals as they entered the bureaucracy or business life. But many remained inspired by radical doctrines, and more than a few devoted their lives to a revolutionary cause. This kind of intellectual alienation, while it utilized some of the principles that had earlier disturbed intellectuals in the West, went deeper in the Russian case. It was the first example of a kind of intellectual radicalism, capable of motivating outright terrorism, that would characterize other societies caught in uncompleted change during the 20th century. The goals and motives of the Russian intelligentsia varied, but in general they wanted political freedom and deep social reform while maintaining a Russian culture different from that of the West, which they saw as hopelessly plutocratic and materialistic. Their radicalism may have stemmed from the demanding task they set themselves: simultaneously to attack key Russian institutions while building a new society that would not reproduce the injustices and crippling limitations of the Western world.

The radical intelligentsia claimed that a spirit of community lay deep in the Russian soul, and this could serve both as the basis for social justice in Russia and as the foundation for an egalitarian society free from the exploitation and competitive individualism of the capitalist West. Many Russian radicals were anarchists, who sought the abolition of all formal government. While anarchism was not unknown in the West, it took on particular force in Russia in opposition to unyielding tsarist autocracy. Many early anarchists in the 1860s hoped that they could triumph by winning peasant support, and a host of upper-class radicals fanned out to teach the peasantry the beauties of political activism. They found however that peasants were largely uninterested in political change and not at all eager to take lessons from upper-class leaders, revolutionary or not. This failure led many anarchists to violent methods, forming the first large terrorist movement in the modern world. Given the lack of popular support and of other political outlets, assassinations and bombings seemed the only way to attack the existing order. Anarchist tactics indeed often focused more on destruction than on coherent political goals for the future; terrorism could become an end in itself. As the anarchist leader Bakunin put it:

> We have only one plan—general destruction. We want a national revolution of the peasants. We refuse to take any part in the working out of schemes to better the conditions of life; we regard as fruitless solely theoretical work. We consider destruction to be such an enormous and difficult task that we must devote all our powers to it, and we do not wish to deceive ourselves with the dream that we will have enough strength and knowledge for creation.

Not surprisingly, the recurrent waves of terrorism merely confirmed the tsarist regime in its resolve to avoid further political change, in what became a vicious circle in 19th-century Russian politics.

By the late 1870s Alexander II was pulling back from his reform interest, fearing that change was getting out of hand. Censorship of newspapers and political meetings tightened; many dissidents were arrested and sent to Siberia. Alexander II was assassinated by a terrorist bomb in 1881, after a series of botched attempts. His successors, while escalating the effort to industrialize, continued to oppose further political reform. New measures of repression were also directed against minority nationalities, partly to dampen their unrest but partly to gain the support of upper-class conservatives who were wary of the industrialization process and could be contented only by vigorous backing for Russian dominance in language and culture. The Poles and other groups were carefully supervised. Russian language instruction was forced on people such as the Ukrainians. Persecution of the large Jewish minority was stepped up, resulting in many executions—called *pogroms*—and seizures of property; as a consequence, many Russian Jews emigrated. The regime also tried to Christianize many Jewish children by force. All of this, of course, spurred additional, underground protest among various nationalities.

By the 1890s the protest currents were complicated by two other ultimately related developments. In the first place, Marxist doctrines spread from the Western socialist movement to a segment of the Russian intelligentsia. There was no unity here, and anarchists and other peasant-oriented revolutionaries bitterly disputed Marxist insistence on careful revolutionary organization and a focus on the working class. Nevertheless small Marxist groups formed, some in exile, committed to a tightly organized proletarian revolution. One of the most active Marxist leaders was Vladimir Ilyich Ulyanov, known as Lenin. Lenin, from a bureaucratic family whose brother had been killed by the political police, introduced important innovations in Marxist theory to make it more appropriate for the Russian scene. He argued that, because of the spread of international capitalism, a proletariat was developing worldwide in advance of industrialization. Russia, then, could have a proletarian revolution without going through a distinct middle-class phase. Lenin also insisted on the importance of disciplined revolutionary cells that could maintain doctrinal purity and effective action even amid severe police repression. Small but dedicated revolutionary cadres, not the mass electioneering of the Western socialist parties whose revisionism Lenin detested, would be the path to the future. Lenin's approach animated the group of Russian Marxists known as *Bolsheviks,* or majority party (though ironically they were actually a minority in the Russian Marxist movement as a whole, much of which remained more wedded to the idea of an initial middle-class revolution). The approach proved ideal for Russian conditions.

Working-class unrest in the cities developed apace with the new currents among the intelligentsia. Russian workers became far more radical than their Western counterparts. They formed unions and conducted strikes—all illegal—but many of them also had firm political goals in mind. Their radicalism stemmed partly from the absence of legal political outlets. They stemmed partly from rural unrest, for these new workers pulled in peasant grievances against the existing order. They stemmed partly from the severe conditions of early industrialization, exacerbated by large factories and frequent foreign ownership. While many workers were not linked to any particular doctrine, some became interested in one of the revolutionary agendas—including Bolshevism—and they were urged on by passionate organizers.

By 1900 the contradictory currents in Russian society may have made revolution inevitable. The forces demanding change were not united, but the importance of mass protest both in countryside and city, plus the radical intelligentsia, made it difficult to find a compromise position that might content some while isolating others. Furthermore, the regime remained resolutely uninterested in compromise. Vigorous conservative ministers urged a policy of resistance and repression; this kept most uprisings in hand, but it fed further pressure from below.

THE REVOLUTION OF 1905

Military defeat in 1904 and 1905 finally lit this tinderbox. Russia had maintained its expansionist foreign policy through the later 19th century, in part because of tradition and in part because diplomatic success might draw the venom from some internal unrest. It also wanted to match the imperialist strides of the Western great powers. A war with the Ottoman Empire in the 1870s brought substantial gains, which were then pushed back at the insistence of France and Britain. Russia also successfully aided the creation of new Slavic nations in the Balkans, such as Serbia and Bulgaria, the "little Slavic brothers" that filled nationalist hearts with pride. Some conservative writers even talked in terms of a Pan-Slavic movement that would unite the Slavic people, under Russian leadership of course. Russia participated vigorously in other Middle Eastern and central Asia areas. Russia and Britain both increased their influence in Persia and Afghanistan, reaching some uneasy truces that divided spheres of activity early in the 20th century. Russia was also active in China. The development of the trans-Siberian railroad encouraged Russia to incorporate some northern portions of Manchuria, violating the 18th century Amur River agreement. Russia also joined Western powers in obtaining long-term leases to Chinese territory during the 1890s.

These were important gains, but they did not satisfy growing Russian ambitions, and they also brought trouble. Russia risked now an overextension, as its diplomatic aspirations were not backed by real increases in military power. The problem first came to a head in 1904. Japan, increasingly powerful in its own right, became worried about further Russian expansion in northern China and efforts to extend influence into Korea. War broke out in 1904. Against all expectation, save Japan's, the Japanese won. Russia could not move her fleet quickly to the Pacific, and her military organization in general proved too cumbersome to oppose more effective Japanese maneuvers. Japan gained the opportunity to move into Korea, as the balance of power in the Far East began to shift.

Unexpected defeat in war unleashed massive protests on the home front in the Revolution of 1905. Urban workers mounted well-organized general strikes designed above all for political gains. Peasants produced a tumultuous series of insurrections, while liberal groups also agitated. After first trying brutal police repression—which only infuriated the urban crowds—and worried about the reliability of the peasant-based army, the tsarist regime had to change course. It granted little to the workers, for new rights for unions and Marxist political parties were almost immediately stripped away—though not before worker organizations gained further ground. But liberals were wooed through the creation of a national parliament, the *duma*. And the minister Stolypin introduced an important series of reforms for the peasantry. The emancipation system was greatly loosened. Peasants gained greater freedom from redemption payments and village controls. They could buy and sell land quite liberally. The goal here was to create a stratified, market-oriented peasantry in which successful farmers would move away from the peasant masses, becoming rural capitalists. Indeed, peasant unrest did die down, and a minority of aggressive entrepreneurs, called *kulaks*, began to increase agricultural production and buy additional land. Yet the reform package overall quickly came unglued. Not only were workers' rights withdrawn, triggering a new series of strikes and underground activities, but the duma was progressively stripped of power. Nicholas II, a weak man who was badly advised, simply could not surrender the tradition of autocratic rule, and the duma became a hollow institution, representing and satisfying no one. Police repression also resumed, creating new opponents to the regime.

Pressed in the diplomatic arena by the closing of the Far Eastern theater through Japanese advance, yet eager to counter paralyzing internal pressures by some foreign policy success, the Russian government turned once again to the Ottoman Empire and the Balkans. Various stratagems to acquire new rights of access to the Mediterranean and to back Slavic allies in the Balkans yielded no concrete results, but they did stir the pot in this vulnerable area and helped lead to World War I. And this war, in which Russia participated in order to maintain her diplomatic standing and live up to the billing of Slavic protector while hoping for new territorial gains, led to one of the great revolutions of modern times.

RUSSIA AND EASTERN EUROPE

Russia was not the whole of eastern Europe, of course, but in many respects Russian patterns were paralleled in smaller states such as Hungary (joined to Austria but autonomous after 1866), Romania, Serbia, Bulgaria, and Greece. These were new nations—unlike Russia—and emerging after long Ottoman dominance, they had no access to the diplomatic influence of their giant neighbor. Most of the new nations established parliaments, in imitation of Western forms, but carefully restricted voting rights and parliamentary powers. Kings—some of them new, as the Balkan nations had set up monarchies after gaining independence from the Ottoman Empire—ruled without much check. Most East European nations followed Russia's lead in emancipating serfs, but landlord power remained more extensive than in Russia, and the usual result of recurrent peasant unrest followed. Most of the smaller East European nations industrialized much less extensively than Russia, and so they remained, as agricultural exporters, far more dependent on Western markets.

Yet amid all the problems, eastern Europe enjoyed a period of glittering cultural productivity in the late 19th century, with Russia in the lead. Utilization of the romantic tradition and other Western styles continued. National dictionaries and histories helped the smaller Slavic nations gain a sense of their heritage, along with the collection of folk tales and music. The Russian novel enjoyed a period of unprecedented brilliance. Westernizers such as Turgenev wrote realistic novels that vaunted what they saw as modern values, while writers such as Tolstoy and Dostoevsky displayed more ambiguity about Western values and tried to portray a special Russian spirit. Russian music moved from the romanticism of Tchaikovsky to more innovative, atonal styles early in the 20th century. Polish composers such as Chopin and Liszt also made an important mark. Russian painters began participating in modern art currents, producing important abstract work. Finally, scientific work advanced at levels of fundamental importance. A Czech scientist, Gregor Mendel, advanced the understanding of genetics, while a Russian physiologist, Ivan Pavlov, experimenting on conditioned reflexes, explained unconscious responses in human beings.

Eastern Europe thus participated more fully than ever before in a cultural world shared with the West, though with some distinctive emphases. This fruitful juncture was not matched by comparable developments in the political and social spheres, however, and it was complicated by attempts to define a special Russian or Slavic essence.

Furthermore, the masses in eastern Europe, mainly peasant, remained firmly attached to a largely separate popular culture, including the Orthodox religion, that was different from the traditions of the West and from those of the partially Westernized upper classes. Peasant culture was not unchanging, as the openness to some new radical loyalties demonstrated, but it was not easily manipulable. And popular resentment against growing Western cultural as well as economic influence contributed to the revolutionary tides during and after World War I.

By 1900, then, Russia and much of the rest of eastern Europe represented a distinctive amalgam of tradition and change. Principles of authoritarian rule remained virtually unaltered, but they were now joined with diverse political opposition bent in the main on sweeping revolution rather than on purely liberal reforms. The tradition of territorial expansionism, though checked by resistance from the West and Japan, still ran strong. Pan-Slavic sentiments indeed encouraged new Russian influence in southeastern Europe. Massive social change had resulted from emancipation and industrialization, but East European society continued to be more agricultural and in many ways more traditionalist than its Western counterpart. Finally, a larger ambivalence toward Western values persisted. East European intellectuals contributed creatively to general European artistic and scientific work, but a desire to define distinctive features and to resist full Westernization remained lively in many quarters, both elite and popular. Eastern Europe was, in sum, developing its own pattern of change as it entered the industrial age. This pattern would soon embrace a distinctive kind of revolution as well.

  JAPAN

Like Russia, Japan faced new pressure from the West during the 1850s, though it took the form of a demand for more open trade rather than outright military conflict.

Japan's response was more direct than Russia's and, on the whole, more immediately successful. Despite its long history of isolation, Japanese society was better adapted than Russia's to the challenge of industrial change. Market forms were more extensive, reaching into peasant agriculture; levels of literacy were higher. Nevertheless, Japan had to rework many of its institutions during the final decades of the 19th century, and the process produced significant strain. The result, by 1900, was different both from purely Western patterns and from the more obvious tensions of Russian society.

THE FINAL DECADES OF THE SHOGUNATE

On the surface, Japan experienced little change during the first half of the 19th century, and certainly this was a quiet time, compared to the earlier establishment of the Tokugawa shogunate or the transformation introduced after the 1850s. Some scholars have argued that the shogunate was becoming less effective, and there were some signs of deterioration. It is also important to note ongoing currents of change that continued from the 17th and early 18th centuries. These developments help explain why Japan was able to adjust so quickly when a new challenge, requiring major adjustments, became apparent.

During the first half of the 19th century, the shogunate continued to combine a central bureaucracy with semifeudal alliances between the regional daimyos and the samurai. The government recurrently ran into financial problems. Its taxes were based on agriculture, despite the growing commercialization of the Japanese economy; this was a severe constraint. At the same time, maintaining the feudal shell was costly. The samurai were paid government stipends in return for their loyalty. Loans from merchants frequently bridged the gap between expenditure and income, but this system also required periodic reform movements that would limit the budget and introduce greater stringency. These reform periods would then yield to a more openhanded mood. A long reform spurt late in the 18th century built a successful momentum for a time, but a shorter effort between 1841 and 1843 was notably unsuccessful. This weakened the shogunate into the 1850s and hampered its response to the crisis induced by Western pressure. Until that point, however, the balance between central bureaucrats and regional lords had lasted surprisingly well, with neither group trying to undercut the authority of the other. It was true that bureaucratization advanced in some spheres, as in the collection of taxes from the samurai domains (on the basis of which the government paid the samurai) and in a proliferation of administrative codes and attendant hierarchies of offices and paperwork. But the bureaucracy itself was reserved for the samurai, which eased the tension between the principles of centralization and ongoing feudal privilege.

Japanese intellectual life and culture also continued to develop under the Tokugawa regime, though the major literary figures of earlier centuries were not equaled. Confucianism continued to gain, among the ruling elite, at the expense of Buddhist fervor. Japan became more secular, though gradually and particularly among the upper classes: This was an important precondition for the nation's response to the Western challenge in that it precluded a strong religious-based resistance to change. Various Confucian schools actively debated into the mid-19th century, which kept Japanese intellectual life relatively creative—in contrast to the increasing sterility, including rote, examination-based memorization, characteristic of China in the same decades. Schools and academies expanded, reaching well below the upper class through commoner schools, or *terakoya*, that taught reading, writing, and the rudiments of Confucianism to ordinary people. By 1859 over 40 percent of all adult men and over 15 percent of all women were literate—a far higher percentage than anywhere else in the world outside the West, including Russia, and on a par with some of the fringe areas of the West (including the American South). Here was a fruitful basis for the development of new attitudes that could shape labor activities as well as official policies when the Western challenge arrived.

While Confucianism remained the dominant intellectual strand, there were important rivals. Tensions between traditionalists and reformist intellectuals were emerging, as in Russia in the same decades. A national studies group praised Japanese traditions, including the office of emperor, over the fascination with Chinese values and the institutions of the shogunate. Here was a seedbed for a special nationalist feeling, including praise for the Shinto tradition—Japan's indigenous animist, ceremonial religion—and scorn for Chinese narrowness and artificiality. One national studies writer expressed a typical sentiment late in the 18th century: "The 'special dispensation of our Imperial Land' means that ours is the native land of the Heaven-Shining Goddess who casts her light over all countries in the four seas. Thus our country is the source and fountainhead of all other countries, and in all matters it excels all the others." The influence of the national studies school grew somewhat in the early 19th century and played some role in promoting the office of emperor during the subsequent Meiji restoration; more important, it helped inspire ultranationalist sentiment at the end of the century and beyond.

A second minority group consisted of what the Japanese called Dutch Studies. While major Western works had been banned when the policy of isolation was adopted, a group of Japanese translators kept alive knowledge of Dutch in order to deal with the traders at Nagasaki. The ban on Western books was ended in 1720, and thereafter a group of Japanese scholars interested in "Dutch medicine" created a new interest in Western scientific advance—based on the realization that Western anatomy texts were superior to the Chinese. In 1850 there were schools of Dutch studies in all major cities, and their students urged freer exchange with the West and an attack on Chinese medicine and culture. "Our general opinion was that we should rid our country of the influences of the Chinese altogether. Whenever we met a young student of Chinese literature, we simply felt sorry for him." Here, obviously, was the basis for a much fuller interest in the West, including Western science, in later decades, for already a knowledge of Western physics, geography, and chemistry were entering Japan along with the knowledge of medicine. Not surprisingly, the Dutch schools expanded rapidly in reaction to the concern aroused by the visit of Western fleets after 1853.

Just as Japanese culture showed an important capacity for lively debate and fruitful internal tension, so the Japanese economy continued to develop into the 19th century. Commerce continued to expand, as big merchant companies established monopoly privileges in many centers. Manufacturing gained ground in the countryside, in such consumer-goods industries as soy sauce and silks, and much of this was organized by city merchants. Some of these developments were comparable to slightly earlier changes in the West and have given rise to arguments that, economically, Japan had a running start on industrialization once the Western challenge showed the necessity of further economic change. Obviously also, the Japanese economy was significantly more commercial than that of Russia, and not at all touched before the 1850s by any dependency on cheap exports; here too was an advantage in coping with subsequent change that helps explain the absence of severe revolutionary pressures.

The Japanese economy was not growing rapidly by the 1850s, however; its earlier surge had trailed off somewhat. Some scholars have, as a result, stressed Japan's backwardness compared to the West. The population was stagnant because of constraints on agricultural expansion given available technology. Frequent infanticide plus abortion and birth control achieved this result, which limited the strain on resources but also provided little motive for rapid growth. Poor families, especially, were careful to restrict their effective birthrate. At the same time rural riots in-

creased in many regions, from the late 18th century onward. They were not overtly political, but rather directed
against wealthy peasants, merchants, and landlord controls;
they included resentment against commercial practices. Increasingly violent protests, which extended into the 1860s,
weakened the Tokugawa shogunate and helped explain its
demise. While authorities put down unrest with little difficulty, the protests contributed to a willingness to consider
change when they were joined by challenge from the outside.

THE CHALLENGE

Some Japanese had become increasingly worried about
potential outside threats. In 1791 a book was issued advocating a strong navy. Fears about the West's growing
power and particularly Russia's Asian expansion fed these
concerns in subsequent decades.

Fear became reality in 1853, when the American commodore Matthew Perry arrived with a fleet in Edo Bay
near Tokyo and insisted by threats of bombardment that
Americans be allowed to trade. The United States, increasingly an active part of the West's core economy, thus
launched for Japan the same kind of pressure the Opium
War had created for China—due to the heightened military superiority of the West and its insistence on opening
markets for its burgeoning economy. In 1854 Perry returned and won the right to station an American consul in
Japan; through a formal treaty, two ports were opened to
commerce. Britain, Russia, and Holland quickly won similar rights. As in China this meant that Westerners living
in Japan would be governed by their own representatives,
not by Japanese law. Other privileges soon followed. Leading Western nations simply insisted on their need and right
to trade as part of the expanding world economy, while
also seeking fishing rights in Japanese waters. Russian pressure was a problem as well, as the nation's eastward expansion had already produced a few small clashes over control
of islands in the north Pacific.

The bureaucrats of the shogunate had seen no alternative
but to open up Japan, given the superiority of Western
navies now including steamships. And there were of course
Japanese who had grown impatient with strict isolation,
whose numbers swelled as Dutch schools began to expand.
On the other hand the daimyos, intensely conservative,
were opposed to the new concessions, which forced the shogun to appeal to the emperor for support. Soon, samurai
opponents of the bureaucracy were also appealing to the
emperor, who began to emerge from his centuries-long
confinement as a largely religious and ceremonial figure.
While most daimyos defended the status quo, samurai were

This Japanese cartoon portrays American Admiral Perry as a
greedy warlord.

more divided, some seeing opportunity in change including
unseating the shogunate. The fact was that the complex
shogunate system had depended on the isolation policy: It
could not survive the stresses of foreign influence and internal reactions. The result was not immediate collapse; indeed into the late 1850s Japanese life seemed to go on
much as before.

In the 1860s a political crisis came into the open, involving a clash between the feudal lords and the shogunate
exacerbated by disagreements over the appointment of a
new shogun. The crisis was spiced by samurai attacks on
foreigners, including one murder of a British official,
matched by Western naval bombardments of feudal forts.
Virtual civil war broke out in 1866 as the samurai eagerly
armed themselves with American Civil War surplus weapons, causing Japan's aristocracy to come to terms with the
superiority of Western armaments. When the samurai de-

feated a shogunate force, a number of Japanese finally were shocked out of their traditional reliance on their own superiority, with one author arguing that the nation was, compared to the West with its technology, science, and humane laws, only half-civilized.

This multifaceted crisis came to an end in 1868, with the proclamation of rule by a new emperor named Mutsuhito but commonly called Meiji, or Enlightened One. Backed by some samurai leaders, the new emperor managed to put down the troops of the shogunate and gradually built up support. The crisis period had been shocking enough to allow further changes in Japan's basic political structure—changes that went much deeper at the political level than those introduced by Russia from 1861 onward. One reason Japan avoided political revolution as part of its transformation process involved this early crisis and its sweeping results. Unlike Russia, Japan joined restructuring of the central state and the upper class to its other reforms.

ANALYSIS

THE SEPARATE PATHS OF JAPAN AND CHINA

Japan's ability to change in response to new Western pressure contrasted strikingly with the sluggishness of Chinese reactions into the 20th century. The contrast draws particular attention because China and Japan had been part of the same civilization orbit for so long, which means that some of the assets Japan possessed in dealing with change were present in China as well. Indeed Japan turned out to benefit, by the mid-19th century, from having become more like China in key respects during the Tokugawa period. The link between Chinese and Japanese traditions should not be overdrawn, of course, and earlier differences help explain the divergence that opened so clearly in the later 19th century. A problem of interpretation remains, however, as the East Asian world now split apart, with Japan seizing eagerly on Chinese weakness to target a series of attacks from the 1890s to 1945—which of course merely made China's troubles worse.

Japan and China had both chosen isolation from larger world currents from about 1600 until the West forced new openings between 1830 and 1860. Japan's isolation was the more complete. Both countries lagged behind the West because of their self-containment, which was why Western industrialization caught them unprepared. China's power and wealth roused Western greed and interference first, which gave Japan some relative leeway.

China, however, surpassed Japan in some areas that should have aided it in reacting to the Western challenge. Its leadership, devoted to Confucianism, was more thoroughly secular and bureaucratic in outlook. There was no need to brush aside otherworldly commitments or feudal distractions in order to deal with the West's material and organizational power. Government centralization, still an issue in Japan, had a hoary history in China. With a rich tradition of technological innovation and scientific discovery in its past as well, China might appear to be a natural to lead the Asian world in responding to the West.

That role, however, fell to Japan. Several aspects of Japanese tradition turned out to give it a flexibility that China lacked. It already knew the benefits of imitation, which China, save for its period of attraction to Buddhism, had never acknowledged. Japan's slower government growth had allowed a stronger, more autonomous merchant tradition, even as both societies became more commercial in the 17th and early 18th centuries. Feudal traditions, though declining under the Tokugawa shogunate, also limited the heavy hand of government controls while stimulating some sense of competitiveness—as in the West. China's government, in contrast, probably tried to control too much by the 18th century and squashed initiative in the process.

China was also oppressed by massive population growth from the 17th century onward. This population pressure consumed great energy, leaving scant capital for more fundamental economic initiatives. Japan's population stability into the 19th century, though a sign of economic sluggishness, was more manageable and pressed resources less severely. Japan's island status made the nation more sensitive to Western naval pressures.

Finally, China and Japan were enmeshed in somewhat different trajectories when the Western challenge intruded in the mid-19th century. China was suffering one of its recurrent dynastic declines. Government became less efficient, intellectual life stagnated, and popular unrest surged. Quite possibly a cycle of renewal would have followed, with a new dynasty seizing more vigorous reins. But Western interference distorted this process, complicating reform and creating various new discontents that ultimately overturned the imperial office. China's sluggish leadership, convinced of the nation's superiority, finally provoked reformers to radical action as they saw their country torn apart by foreign imperialists.

Japan, in contrast, maintained considerable political and economic vigor into the 19th century. There were some new political challenges and an increase of peasant revolt. Whereas by the late 19th century China ironically needed Western guidance simply to handle such bureaucratic affairs as tariff collection or repression of peasant rebellion, Japan suffered no such breakdown of authority, using foreign advisors far more selectively.

Once a different pattern of response was established, every decade increased the gap. Western exploitation of Chinese assets as well as dilution of government power made conditions more chaotic, while Japanese strength steadily grew after a very brief period of uncertainty. By the 20th century the two nations were not only enemies—with Japan, for the first time, the stronger—but seemed to be in different orbits. Japan was an increasing industrial success, with a conservative state that would yield after World War II to a more fully parliamentary form. China, after decades of revolution, finally won its 20th century political solution, in communism.

Yet today, near the arrival of the 21st century, it becomes possible to wonder if East Asia was split as permanently as 19th and early 20th century developments had suggested. Japan's industrial lead remains, but China's economy begins perhaps to stir, along with other innovations along Asia's Pacific coast. Common cultural habits of group cooperation and decision making remind us that beneath different political systems, a fruitful shared heritage continues to operate—a heritage quite different from that of the West, but seemingly fully adaptable to the demands of economic change. And so Westerners begin to wonder if a Pacific century is about to dawn.

Questions: What civilization features had Japan and China shared before the 19th century? In what ways were Japanese political institutions more adaptable than Chinese institutions? Why was Russia able to change earlier and more fundamentally than 19th-century China?

THE MEIJI STATE AND INDUSTRIAL DEVELOPMENT

The new Meiji government promptly set about abolishing feudalism, replacing the domains of the daimyos in 1871 with a system of nationally appointed prefects (carefully chosen from different regions). Political power was effectively centralized, and from this base in turn the Meiji rulers—the emperor and his close advisors drawn from loyal segments of the aristocracy—began to expand the power of the state to effect economic and social change.

Quickly, the Japanese government sent samurai officials abroad, to western Europe and the United States, to study economic and political institutions and technology. These samurai, deeply impressed by what they saw, pulled back

from the earlier antiforeign mood and gained increasing voice over other officials in the government. Their basic goal was Japan's domestic development, accompanied by a careful diplomatic policy that would avoid antagonizing the West.

POLITICAL CHANGE

The restructuring of the state and its new policy commitments were accompanied by a fundamental improvement in government finance. Between 1873 and 1876 the Meiji ministers introduced a real social revolution. They abolished the samurai class and the stipends this group had received. The tax on agriculture was converted to a wider tax, payable in money. The samurai were conciliated by government-backed bonds, but these decreased in value and most samurai became impoverished. This development sparked renewed conflict, with a final samurai uprising in 1877. However, the government had by this point introduced an army based on national conscription, and by 1878 the nation was militarily secure. Individual samurai found new opportunities in political and business areas, as they amplified their reaction to change. The continued existence of the samurai—reflecting Japan's lack of outright revolution—would leave diverse results in subsequent Japanese history.

The final capping of the process of political reconstruction came in 1889. Many former samurai had organized political parties, which had room to operate in district assemblies established in 1878. At the same time, Meiji leaders traveled abroad to gain suggestions about appropriate modern political forms. In 1884 they created a new conservative nobility, stocked by former nobles and Meiji leaders, that would operate a British-style House of Peers. Next the bureaucracy was reorganized, insulated from political pressures, and opened to talent on the basis of civil service examinations. The bureaucracy simultaneously began rapidly to expand; it would grow from 29,000 officials in 1890 to 72,000 in 1908. Finally, the constitution, issued in 1889, assured major prerogatives for the emperor along with limited powers for the lower house of the Diet (as the new Parliament was called). Here Germany provided the model, for the emperor commanded the military directly (served by a German-style general staff) and also directly named his ministers. The Diet could pass laws (upon agreement of both houses) and could approve budgets, but failure to pass a budget would simply reinstate the budget of the previous year. Parliament could thus advise government, but it could not control it. Finally, the conservative tone of this parliamentary experiment was confirmed by high property qualifications set for voting rights.

Only about five percent of the adult male population had enough wealth to be allowed to vote for representatives to the lower house.

Japan's political structure thus came to involve centralized imperial rule, wielded by a handful of Meiji advisors, combined with limited representative institutions copied from the West. This combination gave great power to an oligarchy of wealthy businessmen and former nobles, who influenced the emperor and also pulled strings within Parliament. The structure was radically new, and it greatly strengthened government authority while opening opportunities to new people. But it also retained a traditional flavor by relying on cooperation at the top rather than persistent political competition, and by building in a great deal of deference to the authority of the upper classes. Political parties arose, but a coherent oligarchy overrode their divisions into the 20th century. Japan thus followed its new policy of imitating the West, but it retained its own identity. It also devised a structure that appeased many former samurai, by giving them a voice in Parliament, while creating the effective central government necessary to reorganize military and economic affairs. Finally, the Japanese political solution compared interestingly to Russian institutions after Alexander II's reforms: Both states were centralized and authoritarian, but Japan's institution had incorporated business leaders into its governing structure while Russia defended a more traditional social elite.

JAPAN'S INDUSTRIAL REVOLUTION

Political decisions were essential following the crisis of the 1860s, but they were soon matched by other initiatives. The new army, based on the universal conscription of young men, was further improved by formal officer training—as older feudal fighting traditions were put aside—and by upgrading armaments according to Western standards. With the aid of Western advisors, a modern navy was established.

Attention also focused on creating the conditions necessary for industrialization. New banks were created by the government to fund growing trade and to provide capital for industry. State-built railroads spread across the country, and the islands were connected by rapid steamers. The market emphasis in agriculture increased, as new methods were introduced to raise output to feed the people of the growing cities.

The new economic structure depended on destruction of many older restrictions. Guilds and internal road tariffs were abolished to create a national market. Land reform created clear individual ownership for many farmers,

which helped motivate expansion of production and the introduction of new fertilizers and equipment. Rice production grew rapidly. Rural Japan included progressive landlords, enterprising peasants, and a growing group of tenants—a class stratification not totally unlike that of the West, though based on different crops and more labor-intensive methods.

Government initiative dominated manufacturing, not only in the creation of transportation networks but also in state operation of mines, shipyards, and metallurgical plants. Scarce capital and the unfamiliarity of new technology seemed to compel state direction—as occurred in Russia at the same time. Government control also helped check the many foreign advisors early Japanese industry required, and here Japan maintained closer supervision than its Russian neighbor. Japan established the Ministry of Industry in 1870, and it quickly became one of the key government agencies, setting overall economic policy as well as operating specific sectors. By the 1880s model shipyards, arsenals, and factories, though not yet capable of substantial output, provided experience in new technology and disciplined work systems for many Japanese. Finally, by expanding technical training and education, setting up banks and post offices, and also by regularizing commercial laws the government provided a structure within which Japan could develop on many fronts. Measures in this area largely copied established practices in the West, but with adaptation suitable for Japanese conditions; thus, well before any European university, Tokyo Imperial University had a faculty of agriculture.

Private enterprise quickly played a role in Japan's growing economy, particularly in the vital textiles sector. Some businessmen came from older merchant families, though some of the great houses had been ruined along with the financial destruction of the samurai class. There were also newcomers, some rising from peasant ranks. Shuibuzawa Eiichi, for example, born a peasant, became a merchant and then an official of the Finance Ministry. He turned to banking in 1873, using other people's money to set up cotton-spinning mills and other textile operations. Chemicals, construction material, and food products (including beer) were other areas dominated by private entrepreneurs, many of whom however had government experience. By the 1890s huge new industrial combines, later known as *zaibatsu*, were being formed as the result of accumulations of capital and far-flung merchant and industrial operations.

By 1900 the Japanese economy was fully launched in an industrial revolution. It rested on a political and social structure different from that of Russia, and one that had in most respects changed more substantially. Japan's success in

This silk factory, based on imported technology and designed mainly for the burgeoning export trade to the West, is representative of early Japanese industrialization.

organizing industrialization, including its careful management of foreign advice and models, proved to be one of the great developments of later 19th-century history. Toward the end of the 20th century many Americans, pressed by Japanese competition, would fondly imagine that Japan's economic success was due to American guidance and generosity after 1945. The fact was that industrialization came about through largely Japanese efforts, as indeed must be the case given the fundamental transformation involved.

It is important to keep these early phases of Japanese industrialization in perspective. Pre–World War I Japan was far from the West's equal. It depended on substantial imports of Western equipment, and also of raw materials such as coal—for Japan was, for industrial purposes, a resource-poor nation. While economic growth and careful government policy allowed Japan to avoid Western domination, Japan was newly dependent on world economic conditions and often at a disadvantage in the process. Exports were vital to pay for machine and resource imports, and these in turn required hordes of inexpensive labor. Silk production grew rapidly, the bulk of it destined for Western markets. Much of this production was based on poorly paid workers laboring at home or in sweatshops, not in mechanized factories. Correspondingly the Japanese economy, in this fragile transition period, had little leeway for

expansive social measures. A few big companies provided social organizations and other benefits for their employees, which helped maintain low-wage policies but also translated group loyalty traditions from the feudal past. Most workers, however, were given a poor salary and nothing more. Efforts at labor organization or other means of protest were greeted by vigorous repression. This exploitative mood was not a permanent feature of Japanese industrialization, but it was widely characteristic of this first period, which meant that the social impact of Japan's industrial revolution had much in common with its earlier counterpart in the West or in contemporary Russia.

In some respects, Japan's early industrialization was distinctive, compared either to the West or to Russia. The need to rely on low-paid labor to produce manufacturing exports had some similarity to Western practice during the 18th century, but the fact that Japan had no prior capital built up from earlier foreign trade sharpened this characteristic. The export momentum also differed from the Russian case, for Russia's industrialization could utilize earnings from grain exports; Russia's industry was not geared in this direction. The Russian focus rested on heavy industry and production for domestic use, including government purchases for rails and military expansion. Japan produced ships and heavy industrial goods and built up its military forces; but it was inevitably more involved, because of its lack of domestic energy sources, in a vigorous drive to sell manufactured goods abroad, even though this was a very new enterprise for the Japanese. These differences between Japanese and Russian industrial patterns would have ongoing implications in the 20th century, affecting relationships with the wider world as well.

SOCIAL AND ECONOMIC EFFECTS OF INDUSTRIALIZATION

The industrial revolution and the wider extensions of manufacturing and commercial agriculture, along with political change, had significant ramifications within Japanese

In the Meiji era in the late 19th century, Japanese women learned Western musical forms and how to play Western instruments. Note the Western impact on Japanese fashions.

culture and society. The Japanese government introduced a universal education system, providing primary schools for all. This education stressed the discipline of science and the importance of technical subjects along with political loyalty to the nation and emperor. Elite students at the university level also took courses that emphasized science, and many of the Japanese students went abroad to study technical subjects in other countries. The rapid assimilation of a scientific outlook built on and enhanced the earlier secularization of Japanese elite culture, but it was a major new ingredient.

As in the West earlier, industrialization altered social structure. While an important group of aristocrats and people from the samurai warrior class entered the ranks of successful businessmen and officials, a new elite was formed that embraced leading entrepreneurs for the first time. Among the masses, the rise of a huge, propertyless class of urban workers was a new development. Both peasants and workers endured low wages and high taxes, as Japanese leaders required profits and tax revenue to amass the capital needed for further investment. Japan's industrial success did not come easily as far as the lower classes were concerned. And while the new elite did not cultivate the luxurious life-style of Western business magnates, being content with lower profit rates, it did insist on retaining power. Unions and lower-class political parties began to emerge by 1900 but made only slow headway, and a militant socialist movement was outlawed. Periodic strike movements were brutally repressed, though a legacy of serious class bitterness remained.

Japanese society was also disrupted by massive population growth. Better nutrition and new medical provisions reduced death rates, while the upheaval of the rural masses cut into traditional restraints on births. The result was a steady population surge that strained Japanese resources and stability, though it also assured an ongoing supply of low-cost labor.

Many Japanese copied Western fashions as part of the effort to become modern. Western-style haircuts replaced the samurai shaved head with a top knot—another example of the fascinating pattern of the Westernization of hair in world history. Western standards of hygiene spread, and the Japanese became enthusiastic toothbrushers and consumers of patent medicines. Japan also adopted the Western calendar and the metric system. Few Japanese converted to Christianity, however, and despite fads for Western popular culture, the Japanese managed to preserve an emphasis on their own values. What the Japanese wanted and got from the West involved practical techniques; they planned to infuse these with a distinctively Japanese spirit. As an early Japanese visitor to the American White House wrote in a self-satisfied poem that caught part of the national mood:

> We suffered the barbarians to look upon
> The glory of our Eastern Empire of Japan.

Western-oriented enthusiasms, in other words, were not meant to destroy a distinctive Japanese spirit.

Japanese family life retained many traditional emphases. The birthrate dropped as rapid population growth forced increasing numbers of people off the land. Meanwhile the rise of factory industry, separating work from home, made the labor of children less useful. Here was a trend, developed earlier in the West, that seems inseparable from successful industrialization. There were new signs of family instability as well. Many men moved to cities, leaving wives behind in rural manufacturing. The result in 1900, until legal changes made procedures more difficult, was the highest divorce rate in the world. On the more traditional side, however, the Japanese were eager to maintain the inferiority of women in the home. The position of Western women repelled them. Japanese government visitors to the United States were appalled by what they saw as the bossy ways of women: "The way women are treated here is like the way parents are respected in our country." Standards of Japanese courtesy also contrasted with the more open and boisterous behavior of Westerners—particularly Americans. "Obscenity is inherent in the customs of this coun-

try," noted another samurai visitor to the United States. Other basic features of Japanese life, including diet, were maintained in the face of Western influence. Certain Japanese religious values were also preserved. Buddhism lost some ground, though it remained important, but Shintoism, which appealed to the new nationalist concern with Japan's distinctive mission and the religious functions of the emperor, won new interest.

Japan's transformation had not brought the country to Western levels, and the Japanese remained intensely fearful for their independence. Economic change and the tensions, as well as the power it generated, did, however, produce a shift in Japanese foreign policy. With only one previous exception, the Japanese had never before been interested in territorial expansion, but by the 1890s they joined the ranks of imperialist powers. Partly this shift was an imitation of Western models, and at the same time an effort to prevent Western encroachment. Imperialism also relieved some strains within Japanese society, giving displaced samurai a chance to exercise their military talents elsewhere and providing symbols of nationalist achievement for the populace as a whole. The Japanese economy also required access to markets and raw materials. Because Japan was poor in many basic materials, including coal and oil for energy, the pressure for expansion was particularly great.

Japan's quick victory over China, in the quarrel for influence over Korea in 1894 and 1895, was a first step toward expansion. Japan convincingly demonstrated its new superiority over all other purely Asian powers. Humiliated

Japanese Colonial Expansion to 1914

by Western insistence that it abandon the Liaotung peninsula it had just won, the Japanese planned a war with Russia as a means of striking out against the nearest European power. A 1902 alliance with Britain was an important sign of Japan's arrival as an equal nation in the Western-dominated world diplomatic system. The Japanese were also eager to dent Russia's growing strength in East Asia, after the development of the trans-Siberian railroad. Disputes over Russian influence in Manchuria and Japanese influence in Korea led to the Russo-Japanese War in 1904, which Japan won handily on the basis of its superior navy. Japan annexed Korea in 1910; with this annexation, Japan was now not only a modern industrial power, but a new imperialist power as well.

THE STRAIN OF MODERNIZATION

Japan's success in a scant three decades was amazing. Its victories over China and then Russia surprised virtually every outside observer. There is no question that Japan's rapid transformation, like its more recent success in becoming one of the most advanced industrial societies in the world, constitutes a unique achievement. Furthermore, the Japanese—unlike Russia or major parts of the West—prepared the groundwork for industrialization without serious threat of revolution.

Yet this achievement, even blended as it was with substantial continuities from earlier Japanese culture and political styles, had its costs. Many Japanese conservatives resented the passion some of their countrymen displayed for Western fashions. Their concern helped assure that Japanese women, initially the subject of some reform interest, would be mainly confined to family roles. Nevertheless, disputes between generations, with the old clinging to traditional standards and the young more interested in Western styles, were commonplace, and very troubling in a society that stressed the importance of parental authority. Social tensions added to the strain, as expectations rose more rapidly than standards of living. Crowded conditions in the growing cities produced misery at least as great as in earlier Western slums. The high divorce rates showed another kind of strain.

Some tension entered political life. Political parties in Japan's Parliament clashed with the emperor's ministers over rights to determine policy. The government frequently had to dissolve the Diet and call for new elections, seeking a more workable parliamentary majority. Political assassinations and attempted assassinations reflected grievances, including direct action impulses in the samurai tradition.

Another kind of friction emerged in intellectual life. Many Japanese scholars copied Western philosophies and literary styles, and there was enough adaptation to prevent the emergence of a full, Russian-style intelligentsia. In addition to their interest in more traditional forms, other intellectuals expressed a deep pessimism about the loss of identity in a changing world. Some wanted the government to become more fully Western; many were concerned about jobs, as universities tended to turn out more graduates than the economy could handle. The underlying theme was confusion about a Japan that was no longer traditional, but not Western either. What was it? Thus some writers spoke of Japan heading for a "nervous collapse from which we will not be able to recover." Others dealt with more personal conflicts like those in the following poem:

> Do not be loved by others; do not accept their charity, do not promise anything. . . . Always wear a mask. Always be ready for a fight—be able to hit the next man on the head at any time. Don't forget that when you make friends with someone you are sooner or later certain to break with him.

As an antidote to social and cultural insecurity, Japanese leaders urged national loyalty and devotion to the emperor, and with considerable success. The official message promoted Japanese virtues of obedience and harmony that the West lacked. School texts thus stressed:

> Our country takes as its base the family system: the nation is but a single family, the imperial family is our main house. We the people worship the unbroken imperial line with the same feeling of respect and love that a child feels toward his parents. . . . The union of loyalty and filial piety is truly the special character of our national polity.

Nationalism was a partially new force in Japan, and of course it was common in the West and other parts of the world. But Japanese nationalism built on traditions of superiority and cohesion, and deference to rulers, as well as on the new tensions generated by rapid change. It became a deep force, probably in Japan more than elsewhere, that played a unique role in justifying sacrifice and struggle in a national mission to preserve independence and dignity in a hostile world. Nationalism, along with firm police repression of dissent and the sweeping changes of the early Meiji years, certainly helps explain why Japan avoided the revolutionary pressure that hit Russia, China, and other countries after 1900, and also avoided the kind of unrest that had characterized early Western industrialization around 1848.

Japan's traditions thus enabled it to foster rapid change through initiatives by the state and the elite, without the need for revolution. The result by 1900 was a dynamic country newly powerful on the world scene, shaping a distinctive kind of industrial society.

Yet Japan's very success reminds us of how unusual it was. No other society outside the Western world was yet able to match its achievements. Russia, responding to Western example in its own way, continued its growth as a world power, but amid such social disarray that further upheaval was inevitable. Most of the rest of the world, including independent Latin America, was not yet in a position to ask the Japanese question—how to industrialize without losing essential values—as it faced the more immediate concern of adjusting to or combating Western dominance. Even today, when classic Western imperialism has become largely a thing of the past and many societies are striving toward greater industrialization, the ability to emulate the Japanese pattern of rapid change seems very limited—concentrated, interestingly enough, in other small East Asian and Southeast Asian nations.

CONCLUSION

JAPAN, RUSSIA, AND WORLD WAR I

The beginnings of serious industrialization in Russia and Japan, and the unprecedented entry of Japan into world affairs, contributed important new ingredients to the world diplomatic picture by the early 20th century. Developments in both countries, along with the rise of the United States, added to the growing sense of rivalry among the established Western powers. Japan's surge, and particularly its surprising military victories, promoted a fear in the West of a new "yellow peril" that should be opposed through greater imperialist efforts. Outright colonial acquisitions by the new powers added directly to the competitive atmosphere, particularly in the Far East. Japan, to be sure, was not yet a major world player, but it was beginning to make its muscle felt.

Furthermore, the strains of early industrialization, including the need to appease embittered conservative aristocrats as well as aggrieved masses, made both Russia and Japan increasingly dependent on diplomatic success. After

1912, for example, Japan faced growing political party competition in Parliament, with frequent if futile parliamentary defiance of the emperor's ministers. Massive popular protest added fuel to the fire as Japanese workers and peasants developed new political expectations and allegiances. It was in this setting that Japan joined the Allied side in World War I, hoping not for a significant military role but for the chance to seize German colonies in the Pacific—which it quickly gobbled up. Russia, of course, launched into the war from the outset, as a central actor, as its narrowing diplomatic options combined with internal pressures to preclude any alternative. Japan and Russia were not unique in finding diplomacy affected by new domestic rifts—the Western industrial leaders faced some similar tensions—but they were unquestionably caught up in a new spiral.

THE STRAINS OF WAR

The war itself, finally, exacerbated problems in both countries. Japan's participation as an ally to Britain and France encouraged new liberal and democratic sentiments along with an increased pro-Western sentiment. This alarmed conservatives, who were also disappointed that Japan did not win full great-power status from the war. Here were seeds of new political tensions in Japan.

Involvement in World War I was no mere prelude in Russia: Building on the existing tensions in Russian society, it brought major revolution. Russia fared badly in the war, losing important territory to Germany. Furthermore, the Russian economy, after an initial year of solid performance, simply could not sustain the effort of a modern total war. Hunger became widespread and, along with military setbacks and the incompetence of the tsar and his advisors, this produced by 1916 a growing wave of strikes and discontent. Yet in 1916 the tsar adjourned the duma and proceeded to rule alone, making even moderate political groups discontent. Then in March 1917 strikes broke out in the major cities, backed by growing unrest in the peasant countryside. The duma had to be recalled and soon took over the government, while Marxists and other radical leaders improved their organization among the urban workers. The Russian Revolution was under way.

Russia and soon Japan were thus embroiled in new adventures in the wake of World War I. Their new directions reflected the stresses of rapid change in the context of a complicated world diplomatic and economic system. Given the importance of the nations and their newfound industrial power, changes both in Russia and in Japan would have major repercussions in the world.

THE WORLD IN 1914

As World War I broke out, despite the industrial stir-rings of the latecomers, the world was still largely under the Western thumb. Japan and Russia had figured out their own special relationship to the West's industrially driven surge, which gave them unusual freedom of action. Their increasing industrialization would progressively challenge unadulterated Western domination, and it constituted an important qualification to Western triumphs even in 1914. It remained true that the world's most important quarrels in 1914 were among Western powers, not between the West and other societies—simply because of Western economic, political, and military power.

Western imperialism and economic outreach had operated as the major forces in world history for a full century by 1914, substantially altering world patterns and the dynamic of individual societies. Significant divisions opened between societies directly under imperialist control and those, such as China and the Ottoman Empire, touched by imperialism but technically independent. New distinctions arose in East Asia, between China's sluggish response to the new world environment and Japan's modernization surge. Russia continued its own rise to greater power, now grafting early industrialization onto this process. Latin America was another scene of important change, as political independence and cultural identity were combined with the growing commercialization of a dependent economy. As a result of imperialism plus reactions to Western example, some common changes were beginning to take shape around the world. Educational systems spread in most societies. Traditional forms of unfree labor, including rigorous serfdom and slavery, largely disappeared, though low-paying wage labor on estates and in factories provided new thralls for many workers. A new element of nationalism surfaced almost everywhere.

Yet in 1900, the world's diversity remained striking, as it blended long-standing differences in cultural and political traditions with the variety of responses to Western imperialism and industrial example. Some of the divisions taking shape between industrializers, including "early late-comers" such as Japan, and more dependent economies would have continuing influence in world history. Other divisions between an India open to forced Western influence and a more traditionalist China would be complicated or superseded by later developments. What was becoming clear was the new set of divisions among civilizations, based no longer on evolving tradition alone, but also on response to change and challenge. What would become clear when war broke out in 1914 was that rivalries within the West, tragically played out on battlefields in Europe, would combine with new reactions elsewhere to close the era of Western supremacy. The new chapter that then opened in world history would give fuller rein to changes and diversities in other societies, including the new power bases being prepared in Russia and Japan.

FURTHER READINGS

Several studies deal with Russian industrialization. W. Blackwell's *The Industrialization of Russia* (1982) provides useful overview. An older collection deals with Russian change in terms of modernization theory: C. Black, ed., *The Transformation of Russian Society* (1960). Economic backwardness and latecomer reactions are taken up in A. Gerschenkron's *Economic Backwardness in Historical Perspective* (1962).

A number of historians have advanced understanding of Russia's workers: See R. Zelnik's *Labor and Society in Tsarist Russia, 1855–1870* (1971) and Victoria Bonnell, ed., *The Russian Worker: Life and Labor under the Tsarist Regime* (1983). On rural conditions, see T. Emmons's *The Russian Landed Gentry and the Peasant Emancipation of 1861* (1968). Political agitation is discussed in A. B. Ulam's *Russia's Failed Revolutionaries* (1981). Army service and protest form the subject of John Bushnell's *Mutiny and Repression: Russian Soldiers in the Revolution of 1905–1906* (1983). Barbara Engel's *Mothers and Daughters: Women of the Intelligentsia in Nineteenth Century Russia* (1983) takes up another vital topic. Finally, on popular culture, see Jeffrey Brooks's *When Russia Learned to Read: Literacy and Popular Culture* (1987) and Ben Eklof's *Russian Peasant Schools: Officialdom, Village Culture, and Popular Pedagogy, 1864–1914* (1986).

For general coverage of Japan in the period, consult G. Akita's *Foundations of Constitutional Government in Modern Japan, 1868–1900* (1967) and W. G. Beasley's *The Meiji Restoration* (1973). Several books cover economic trends: G. C. Allen's *A Short Economic History of Modern Japan* (1958), W. W. Lockwood's *The Economic Development of Japan* (1954), and R. Dore, ed., *Aspects of Social Change in Modern Japan* (1967).

Japanese industrial structure has received much recent attention from worried Americans: See J. C. Abegglen's *The Japanese Factory: Aspects of Its Social Organization* (1985), Hugh Patrick, ed., *Japanese Industrialization and*

Its Social Consequences (1973), and the careful study by Andrew Gordon, *The Evolution of Labor Relations in Japan* (1985). On culture, E. O. Reischauer's *Japan, the Story of a Nation* (1981) is unusually readable, and M. Miyoshi's *Accomplices of Silence: The Modern Japanese Novel* (1974) is good. See also R. H. Myers and M. R. Beattie, eds., *The Japanese Colonial Empire 1895–1945* (1984).

1910–1920 Mexican Revolution

1914–1918 World War I

1917 Russian Revolution

1919 Versailles peace settlement; League of Nations

1921 Foundation of Chinese Communist party

1912 African National Congress party formed in South Africa

1920 Treaty of Sèvres reorganizes Middle East

1917 United States' entry to World War I

1919 Revolt in Egypt; first Pan-African Nationalist Congress

1912 Fall of Qing dynasty in China; beginning of Chinese revolution

1917 Balfour Declaration promises Jews a homeland in Palestine

1916 Arab revolts against Ottomans

1930–1945 Vargas regime in Brazil

1933–1939 New Deal in United States

1933 Nazis rise to power in Germany

1931–1947 Gandhi-led resistance in India

1934–1940 Cárdenas reform period in Mexico

1929–1933 Height of Great Depression

1937 Army officers in power in Japan; invasion of China

1931 Japan invades Manchuria

1927–1928 Stalin heads Soviet Union; five-year plans and collectivization

1935 German rearmament; Italy conquers Ethiopia

On July 26 and 27, 1941 the night skies over the Kremlin were illuminated during German air raids.

1946–1974 Decolonization in Asia, Africa, and Oceania

1948 Division of Korea

1939–1945 World War II

1960s Civil rights movement in U.S.; revival of feminism

1945 Formation of United Nations

1949 Formation of NATO

1959 Cuban Revolution

1968–1973 Student protests in West

1948 Israel-Palestine partition; first Arab-Israeli war

1942–1945 Holocaust

1957 Ghana becomes first independent African nation

1950–1953 Korean War

1951 End U.S. occupation of Japan

1965–1968 Cultural revolution in China

1945–1948 Soviet takeover of Eastern Europe

1939 Nazi-Soviet pact

1955 Bandung conference; nonaligned movement

1947 India and Pakistan gain independence

1956 Partial end of Stalinism

1945 Atomic bomb

1949 Communist victory in China

1941 United States enters war

1947–1975 Cold war; Marshall Plan

1946 Philippines proclaim independence

1957 European Economic Community (Common Market)

1965–1973 U.S. military intervention in Vietnam

1945 Communists proclaim Vietnam independence

1947 Peronism in Argentina

1955 Warsaw Pact

1962 Algeria declares independence

PART

The 20th Century in World History

6

Pinpointing the 20th century as a time period is one of the most challenging tasks facing a historian, particularly a world historian. We are so close to the patterns involved that reasoned judgment is difficult. Previous periods, though they generate continued debate, at least constitute stories whose endings are known. We can easily see, for example, that the Industrial Revolution ushered in profound changes for the West and some other parts of the world by 1900. We can even more easily see that during the 19th century Western nations gained unprecedented power in the world at large, building on earlier colonialism but also measurably surpassing it. It is not difficult, in other words, to define the 19th century in terms of its contrasts with the early modern period, to see what its new ingredients were and how many of them turned out.

We ourselves are engaged in the 20th century, which makes judgment far more tentative. In the 19th century, for example, many people were not explicitly aware of the Industrial Revolution, even when they were involved in it. They would be much more likely to point to some recent political event or cultural current in defining their era. Most historians, however, now take a different view, and argue that what people thought was significant may have been somewhat less vital than the underlying processes of which contemporaries were only dimly aware. Knowing this, we must admit uncertainty in trying to pinpoint our own age. How significant in world history, for example, was the surge of Nazism of the 1930s? Here was a fearsome new political movement that at the time seemed to

1975–1989 Democratic regimes spread in Latin America

1989 Reform movement in South Africa

1980–1988 Iran-Iraq War

1990 Reunification of Germany

1973, 1979 Oil crises;
height of OPEC power

1985 ff. Gorbachev heads Soviet Union;
reforms and unrest through Eastern Europe

1976 Death of Mao; new reform pattern in China

1992 Full economic integration
of Common Market

1979 Iranian Revolution; spread
of Islamic fundamentalism

1990–1991 Iraq invades Kuwait; Persian
Gulf crisis; U.S.-Allied defeat of Iraq

1975 Communist victory in Vietnam

1989 New regimes throughout Eastern Europe

---

threaten some permanent changes in political trends and that disrupted two decades and, through World War II, contributed to undeniably important shifts in many parts of the world. Almost any historian, at least in the Western world, writing in the 1950s would have seen the rise of Nazism as a major turning point. Yet from the vantage point of the 1990s Nazism seems one of a number of developments that mark a key subperiod, rather than a fundamental feature of the whole century, though some similar racist movements still survive. Many Americans in the 1990s would rate the rise of Japan to the status of industrial superpower far more important in creating a novel international context for our century than Nazism was. Nazism's decisive focus has diluted with the passage of time—which is another way of reminding us that our judgment of the 20th century in terms of world history periodization is highly conditioned by how we feel about world conditions now.

Given the problems of perspective, two contradictory impulses can affect historians' efforts to place their century as part of a larger scheme of periodization. One impulse is to emphasize the continuities, lest we be misled into exaggerating the novelty of our time and perhaps forget the importance of the past. At the end of the 1980s, amid a host of changes in Russia and Eastern Europe, nationalist sentiment revived in the Balkans and a number of other ethnic regions. Bulgaria tried to eliminate a Turkish minority (by expelling them or making them adopt Bulgarian names); Romanians clashed with Hungarians. Despite more than 50 years of war, revolution, and massive attendant political change in this region, passions dating from at least the 19th century remained lively. Which is more important: all the new developments or the fact that, in the minds of many, basic loyalties had changed so little?

At the other extreme, some historians and many other observers caught in a modern culture that emphasizes rapid and fundamental change as a condition of contemporary life are prone to see the 20th century as a decisive new stage in human history. They write of the 20th century as a "third revolution," comparable only to the Neolithic and Industrial Revolutions of the past in setting up basic new conditions for human existence. Or they see the 20th century defined by the final exhaustion of human frontiers (at least on this planet), as a result of massive population growth and new technologies. As the remaining tropical forests are being chopped down at a fearsome rate, and as human crowding reaches proportions never before imagined, these historians stress the extent to which the 20th century has altered the human condition in ways that have no clear precedent at all. We are moving into uncharted waters. It is certainly useful to discuss whether 20th-century developments can be compared to a few key changes in the past (like the previous transformations of economic modes) or whether they are moving toward unprecedented novelty. We will discuss some of these extremely important and complex contemporary issues in the final chapter of this final unit of the text.

For the moment, however, it seems safest to avoid the most extreme predictions, most of which pick up on fairly recent developments (for example, advent of computers in the postindustrial revolution model) or on catastrophes that have not yet definitively occurred, and recognize that at most points in world history a balance of continuity and change must be embraced to capture reality. This has been the case heretofore—even during the throes of the Industrial Revolution—and may prove to characterize the 20th century as well, regardless of all the real and apparent innovations.

The key question, to make the change and continuity formula more precise, is whether the 20th century opened up a new basic period in world history, or whether it added lots of modifications to the fundamental patterns of the 19th century without, however, altering the basic framework. Here, despite all the appropriate caveats about not exaggerating change, the answer seems clear: The 20th century has provided one of those relatively rare breaks in world history, comparable in scope to the 15th century or to the 5th century. The contemporary period in world history is just taking shape even in the 1990s, and so it is harder to define than earlier watersheds; we cannot be sure of some ultimate directions. It may prove distinctive also in that some unprecedented force—a sweeping new technology or environmental degradation—will pull the 20th century away from prior historical patterns. It is, however, assessable as a period in world history, and this can prepare a more extended inquiry.

Previous periods in world history, at least since the great classical age, have met three criteria: They have involved basic geographic rebalancing among major civilization areas; they have measurably increased the intensity and extent of contact among civilizations; and they have, partly as a result of new contacts, demonstrated some new and roughly parallel patterns among many if not all of these major civilizations. The 20th century fits this definition, as a result of developments that can be traced to the events involved in World War I and its aftermath; this is why its position as the launching pad for a new periodization schema seems secure.

THE REPOSITIONING OF THE WEST

The 20th-century shift in balance among civilizations has featured the relative decline of the West. This resulted in part from the two intensely destructive internal wars fought in the West between 1914 and 1945, which in each case expanded into global conflict. The West's relative decline also reflected the patterns of change and development in a number of other societies (including of course the two—Russia and Japan—that had begun an industrial revolution even before 1900). The rise of the United States to new international importance maintained Western influence to some extent, but this merely enhanced Western Europe's relative decline and did not prevent the relative slippage of the West as a whole. Despite great Western strength, including European revival after 1945 and again in the 1990s, the pattern of the 19th century prevailed no more. The rise of the West to steadily more powerful international positions—militarily, commercially, and politi-

cally—stopped and then reversed during the 20th century, even with the United States added to the West's leadership ranks.

The West's relative decline showed in several areas. Western population (including that of the United States), began to fall back rapidly as a percentage of world totals, reversing a pattern that had begun to develop in the 12th century. Western birth control (matched to be sure in a few other areas, such as the Soviet Union and Japan) combined with rapid population growth rates elsewhere to produce this result. What the long-term outcome of the West's population slide will be remains unclear; many analysts argue that since the Industrial Revolution, rapid population growth is a source of weakness, not a strength. At the very least, the West's population stagnation opened Europe and the United States to rapid immigration from other societies. Here was a new pattern that might either add to Western dynamism or lead to crippling new tensions.

More specific than population rebalancing was the decline and then virtual end of the great Western empires, a process clearly under way by the 1920s and then culminating after 1945. The West, which dominated most of the world directly or indirectly by 1920, ruled little beyond its own borders by 1980. Its influence remained very great—change in this area was complex; but literal political control unquestionably receded, again reversing a centuries-long trend. Monopoly over the most advanced weapons systems, a key Western advantage since the 16th century, also ended, though key Western nations—led after 1945 by the United States—retained a major share in leadership. Japan and then the Soviet Union joined the West as world military giants, while other societies though not quite as advanced, gained ground. Further, alternate forms of warfare—particularly guerrilla tactics used in colonial struggles, but to some extent terrorism as well—allowed certain technologically inferior regions to counter Western military supremacy. In terms of warfare, the world (from a Western standpoint) became more complicated, after centuries of a steadily advancing edge in raw power.

In 1991 the United States and various allies decisively defeated the nation of Iraq in the Persian Gulf War, using a variety of high-technology weaponry. Clearly, Western-dominated military advances were again demonstrated, as only a few hundred allied soldiers died in combat compared to possibly 100,000 Iraqis. But even this war showed how the 20th century had become more complex than the easy days of Western imperialism. It took months of military buildup, a force of over half a million men and women, plus expenditures of over $50 billion to defeat (overwhelmingly, to be sure) a medium-sized Arab state.

The West also lost its unchallenged preeminence as world trader and manufacturer. Of course, much of the world economic system established in the 16th century persisted. Important regions still sent cheap raw materials—based on low-paid labor—into international trade, which constrained not only their economic levels but also their political independence. Nations with heavy international debts thus faced substantial outside intervention in a 20th-century version of international inequality. Only a few societies won the bulk of the profits from international trade because they ran the shipping and banking facilities and produced the most expensive processed products. In this basic sense, there was substantial continuity from earlier periods in world history. But the actors changed, which is where the West's relative decline showed up. While the West continued to be among the dominant economic agents, it was joined, by the 1960s, by Japan and an increasing number of other East Asian centers.

Clearly, on a number of fronts the rise of the West, one of the leading processes in world history since the 15th century, leveled off, with the 1920s and 1930s forming a key turning point. The results of this change were diffuse. No single civilization emerged by the 1990s to claim the kind of growing world leadership the West had long produced. In part this was because the West itself still remained quite strong with its influence pervasive on many international fronts. Parts of East Asia now matched the West economically, but other areas generated new international influence in military or cultural sectors. As with the decline of Arab civilization earlier in world history, a number of new centers of power emerged. Perhaps one center will ultimately take primary leadership as the West had ultimately done after Arab recession, but this is not inevitable and is not likely to be speedy.

More obvious was the increased autonomy the West's relative decline made possible for a number of regional centers. This allowed places such as Brazil, India, and the Middle East to develop new combinations of tradition and change that had some relationship to Western models but were not dictated by them. The proliferation of new nations around the world in the decades after 1945 was a revealing index of opportunities for political innovation; a host of states had to establish political legitimacy and decide on appropriate state structures. Even in the economic area, where Western and Japanese prominence remained extremely influential, a number of world regions managed to generate substantial internal economic growth and win a place as exporters of manufactured goods. Brazil, for example, became the world's fourth largest computer exporter by the 1990s, behind only the high-tech leaders: Japan, the United States, and Western Europe. These patterns will be explored in the chapters that follow.

World Distribution of Manufacturing, 1930

(Values for Europe are approximate.)

INTERNATIONAL CONTACTS

Along with rebalancing among civilizations, with a vigorous West now challenged by great vitality in other regions, came intensifying international contacts. A few areas pulled back into relative isolation: This was true of the Soviet Union from the late 1920s through the 1970s when a largely independent national economy was forged with little involvement in wider world trade; it also characterized China, especially in the decades after 1956. Nevertheless, even relative isolation was difficult, for the dominant trends urged increasing interaction. Technology was critical: Innovations included faster communication via wireless radio and, later, satellite and computer; faster transport, using the airplane; and larger capacity for both communication and movement of goods. World-trade levels steadily increased, and more and more corporations (particularly from the West and Japan) operated on an international basis.

World wars and peacetime alliances demonstrated the new levels of international contact on other fronts. Great diversity of interests remained, but diplomatic contacts were internationalized as never before; thus the intensity and importance of United States-Chinese diplomacy, to choose one example, rivaled the relationships between Britain and Germany a century before. International cultural influences also increased in tandem with improved communications and the efforts of multinational corporations. Films, scientific research, and artistic styles all spread widely at both popular and elite levels. The result was not a single world culture, for extent of penetration and regional reactions varied widely. But most cultures had to come to some terms with the impact of Hollywood movies, Parisian art, or British-American popular music. International sports interest constituted another unprecedented development across civilization lines: soccer football won mass enthusiasm virtually everywhere; the Olympic Games, which were reestablished in the 1890s and gradually shifted from an initial Western dominance to global participation, both symbolized and promoted this facet of new cultural contacts.

INTERNATIONAL CHALLENGES IN POLITICS AND CULTURE

Parallelisms in patterns of change resulted partly from outright imitation, particularly of Western models, but also from regional efforts to push back Western dominance. One result was a sweeping pattern of political change. Almost no society aside from some of the more stable Western nations (United States, Britain, and Scandinavia) had the same form of government by 1990 that it had maintained in 1900. Monarchies crumbled, replaced by democracies, totalitarian governments, or authoritarian regimes. The results were varied, but the fact of innovation was virtually universal, as major civilizations tried to come to terms with Western example while also developing governments vigorous enough to gain or maintain independence. More concretely, revolutions and decolonization compelled political experiments almost everywhere outside the West as well as in key areas within Western society. Moreover, along with new political forms came new functions. Governments generally took on new roles in trying to further economic growth. They also accepted new and unprecedented responsibilities in areas such as education and health care, and their contact with masses of citizens increased greatly as a result. Regardless of prior political traditions and ongoing diversity, the governments of the 20th century world innovated in several common directions.

Changes or modifications in previous belief systems formed another current that swept over many national and civilizational boundaries. Most of the world's people in 1850 adhered to one of the great religions or philosophical systems created during the classical or postclassical eras: Confucianism, Christianity, Islam, and the like. These systems were still lively in 1950 and some were even winning new converts. In most parts of the world, however, they had been modified or challenged by new systems of beliefs that were more strictly secular in orientation, such as liberalism, nationalism, or communism. Quite widely, they were also challenged by growing interest in science, a staple of the burgeoning mass education systems. As with politics, belief changes took no single direction, but the encounter with fundamentally novel ideas was a genuinely international experience—and one of the key developments of 20th-century world history.

Changes in ideas and politics related to a third general international current: the displacement of long-standing beliefs in rigid social inequalities. All the great agricultural civilizations had developed highly structured systems of inequality, though some of the civilizations complicated these systems through religious beliefs in the spiritual equality of all souls. Western ideas, expressed in great movements such as the French Revolution of 1789, had attacked assumptions of structured inequality and legal privilege. Also, the abolition of slavery through most of the world in the 19th century signaled the end of another traditional institution of inequality. The further spread of Western ideas plus new movements such as Russian and Chinese communism and the nationalisms of Asia and Africa brought a more widespread attack on rigid inequalities in the 20th century. Caste systems and aristocracies "officially" crumbled, with only rare exceptions. Societies turned to new efforts at equality or at least equality of opportunity, including widespread voting rights, though countercurrents such as racist beliefs or gender inequalities complicated the picture. Inequality did not end, but older ideas that had sanctified it did yield to new beliefs.

Patterns of economic change were more diverse: Despite a general interest in improving production levels, some societies remained largely agricultural, while others began to move into industrial ranks. Nevertheless, efforts at change as well as the influence of international corporations and trade prompted some widespread social effects. Most societies witnessed new levels of social mobility, as earlier caste or class lines loosened. The social status of women was almost everywhere reconsidered, as a result of new levels of education and new involvement in work outside the home, though again specific results varied.

No single world society existed, even in embryo, by the 1990s. Differences among civilizations remained great: Some of them reached deep into earlier traditions, while others reflected diverse experiences in the 20th century itself. India and China differed, thus, because of patterns inherited from the classical and postclassical eras and because one society underwent revolution while the other experienced a somewhat less traumatic decolonization in the middle decades of the 20th century. The developments highlighted in this unit on the contemporary era must be evaluated both in terms of the distinctive features of major civilizations, old features as well as new ones, and in terms of their common participation in international phenomena such as political change or gender redefinition.

USING THE 20TH CENTURY AS A NEW PERIOD IN WORLD HISTORY

Understanding the 20th century as the starting point of a new period in world history, comparable to a few key transition periods in the past, helps explain why the last eight decades have been so very dramatic, not simply in one or two particularly dynamic or troubled areas, but almost across the board. Other shaping factors add ingredients to the sense of overall global change: the impact of massive, though somewhat uneven, population growth; environmental change in an unprecedentedly populous, mechanized, urbanized, and interconnected human community; new and potentially devastating forms of warfare, involving nuclear weapons and rocketry; and what may turn out to be a radically novel technological framework as postindustrial systems replace the steam-driven machinery of an industrial age. Any one of these ingredients, and particu-

The World in 1991

![Map of the world in 1991 showing areas of recent conflict and unrest marked with dots, including: ESTONIA, LATVIA, LITHUANIA, ARMENIA AND AZERBAIJAN, AFGHANISTAN, YUGOSLAVIA, IRAQ, KUWAIT, INDIA AND PAKISTAN, TIBET, CHINA, WEST BANK AND GAZA STRIP, CHAD, ETHIOPIA AND ERITREA, BURMA, CAMBODIA, PHILIPPINES, SRI LANKA, LIBERIA, HAITI, PERU, WALVIS BAY, SOUTH AFRICA. Oceans labeled: ATLANTIC OCEAN, PACIFIC OCEAN, INDIAN OCEAN. SOVIET UNION labeled.]

Areas of recent conflict and unrest

larly their combination, may turn out to dwarf the civilizational rebalancings and parallelisms discussed here. Or, more probably, these processes can be seen in conjunction with the new world history framework, enhancing international contacts and creating additional impulses toward change.

The 20th century as a new period in world history unfolded in at least two phases. Between 1914 and 1945 the world was shaken by a series of catastrophic events—two world wars and an international depression—that can be seen as the birth pains of the new international order, causing and reflecting the West's relative decline and facilitating the emergence of new centers of activity. Several political revolutions accompanied the West's crises, ushering in new regimes in Russia, Mexico, China, and (if a top-down revolution may be included) Turkey. After 1945 the West began to adjust to a new world order in which decolonization created a host of novel governments. These were the decades in which new social mobility, changes in gender relations, and redefinitions of government functions moved to center stage, although some had been suggested during the crisis period as well.

The following chapters deal first with the crisis era, in terms of basic international events and processes of the decades of war and depression. Then individual civilizations are treated: first the West and its most obvious rivals for power—the Soviet Union and Eastern Europe as well as the Pacific Rim states dominated by Japan. Latin America is something of a special case in that decolonization had already occurred, but industrialization remained elusive; nevertheless, the 20th century was a period of fundamental change in this region, including a number of key revolutions in Mexico, Cuba, and several Andes nations. Areas dominated by decolonization and the formation of new nations include much of southern Asia, the Middle East, and Africa, where the hold of distinctive traditions reflected continued diversity in combination with some common problems and opportunities. China and its neighbors require separate treatment because of the special importance of complex revolutionary processes. Finally, some trends and prospects for the later 20th century and beyond return to the more general dynamic of world history in its emerging new period.

One basic corollary of 20th-century periodization must be kept in mind. Many people in the world today argue that change has accelerated, and this may be true; nevertheless, most new periods in world history have taken at least two centuries or more to clarify. The history of the 20th century allows us to see the forces overturning the old framework; it permits only glimpses of what the new one will be. We know that the new period will not be Western-dominated to the extent the previous one turned out to be, but we cannot be sure whether a successor will emerge, or what the successor will be. Precisely because of the uncertainties of transition, many pundits offer beguiling simplicities: Will the next West be East Asia or, perhaps, Brazil? Then again everyone will be computer-linked anyway so separate traditions won't matter much. The chapters in this unit flesh out a periodization scheme for the 20th century, describing frameworks applicable to many different areas. These frameworks, however, also demonstrate that the century has been exceedingly complex thus far, its implications diverse. Grasping what has happened already in the most recent period of world history is the best basis for discussing what may yet come.

1914–1918 World War I   1919–1939 Period of United States isolation

1917 British Balfour Declaration promises Jews a homeland in Palestine

1923 Treaty of Lausanne recognizes independence of Turkey

1918 German emperor abdicates

1916 Beginning of Arab revolt against Ottoman Empire

1920 Treaty of Sèvres dissolves Ottoman Empire; French and British mandates set up in Middle East

1917 Russian Revolution

1918 Treaty of Brest-Litovsk; Russia withdraws from war

1919 Versailles conference and treaty; League of Nations established

1915 Italy enters war

1919 Treaty of St. Germain recognizes Czechoslovakia, Yugoslavia, Poland, and Hungary

1917 United States enters war

One-half Century of Crisis, 1914–1945

INTRODUCTION. This chapter focuses on key developments in international military, diplomatic, and economic spheres in the crucial time period framed by the two world wars and filled by an agonizing global economic depression.

These developments illustrate the extent to which the world network had intensified. There had been previous wars with international ramifications—European conflict in the Seven Years' War spilled over to struggles in the colonies in North America and India, as well as on the seas; the same held true for the battles against Napoleon early in the 19th century. The two world wars, however, were more genuine international conflicts in that they directly covered a larger portion of the globe and, though heavily centered on struggles within Europe, involved nations from several different civilizations as major combatants as well as victims. The explosion of the international economy was perhaps less novel since many regions of the world already had been tied to each other economically, but the sudden embroilment of so many different economies in the Great Depression had qualities of its own.

This chapter, in other words, covers key disruptions in the international framework, at a point in which the importance of this framework requires assessment before turning to developments in individual civilizations. International crises lay behind new directions in the world economy and massive political change, marking the 20th century as a crucial break in global periodization.

The international framework was still skewed by the fact that some civilizations were economically and militarily more powerful than others. World War I was mainly a

---

1929–1939 Great Depression

1936–1939 Spanish Civil War

1933 Nazis to power in Germany

1937 New Japanese attack on China; beginning of war in Asia

1931 Japan invades Manchuria

1938 Germany's union (Anschluss) with Austria; Germany invades Czechoslovakia; Munich conference

1935 Germany rearms; Italy invades Ethiopia

1939 World War II begins; Germany and Soviet Union invade Poland

1942–1945 Allied conferences in Teheran, Yalta, Potsdam

1940 Axis agreement (Germany, Italy, Japan)

1941 German invasion of Soviet Union

1939 Nazi-Soviet Pact

1940 Fall of France

1942 Tide begins to turn in both war theaters; Soviet Union repulses attack on Stalingrad; Allies invade North Africa

1945 Atomic bomb dropped on Japan

1945 United Nations established

1941 Japanese attack Pearl Harbor; United States enters war

1944 Invasion of France by Allies

1945 End of World War II

1946 United States grants Philippines independence

1947 Cold war begins between United States and Soviet Union

1947 Wider decolonization begins with independence of India and Pakistan

European conflict, though it involved participants from the colonies and had independent areas of operations in the Pacific region and the Middle East. The Great Depression was more generally international, as it stemmed from economic problems in various parts of the world; here again, however, the focus of the collapse was on western Europe and the United States. World War II, finally, saw decisive activity in Asia and Europe as well as on the high seas. International events, in other words, drew in a growing number of active participants, most notably Japan and the United States (along with Europe including Russia), but also other parts of Asia and portions of Africa. The impact of international events was wider yet, even when, as in both depression and war, some areas were primarily victims of other areas' disasters rather than being directly responsible.

The chapter does not attempt to cover all major aspects of world historical development between 1914 and 1945; subsequent chapters will turn to the major individual civilizations. Each society was marked, however, by the great international events that are the focus of this chapter. Grasping these events is vital to tracing their more particular impacts that would last well beyond 1945.

THE RISE OF THE UNITED STATES

The growing international role of the United States was a crucial ingredient of the new century. American power had been building since the 1870s. By then, the nation's sectional conflict had ended and overland expansion to the West was nearing completion. Fueled by new immigration, population levels soared. Most important, the United States became a major player in the international economy, sending both farm and factory exports abroad. From 1890 until after 1960, exports consistently exceeded imports. Though still a debtor nation until World War I, the United States expanded its investments abroad, more than quadrupling the level between 1897 and 1914. Finally, national confidence soared. American missionaries worked in Africa and Asia; the number in China alone rose from 436 in 1874 to 5462 in 1914. American nationalist pride easily kept pace with the nation's religious sense.

These developments propelled the United States into the imperialist scramble by the 1890s. Following involvement by merchants and missionaries, Hawaii and some other Pacific islands were seized. The Spanish-American War brought the Philippines plus vital territory in the Caribbean under the United States' protection. The United States' intervention in Central America became commonplace, leading among other things to construction and control of the Panama Canal. American muscle began to affect

great power diplomacy. Theodore Roosevelt sponsored the conference that ended the Russo-Japanese War, winning the Nobel Peace Prize for his efforts and also signaling American concern about Japanese expansion.

Full American entry into world affairs awaited World War I. Even then, many Americans remained unsure of their international role, eager to continue to benefit from world trade but inclined to return to diplomatic isolation at crucial junctures. The first half of the 20th century was an experimental period for the United States internationally. Even apart from debates over involvement, Americans also oscillated between conventional great-power maneuvers and some desire to bring a special idealism to the diplomatic process. It was not always easy for other parts of the world to adjust to the American style; here too, the period from 1900 to 1950 required experimentation.

DECADES OF DISASTER

Despite innovative developments, such as the new United States' role in the world, the overriding tone of the period from 1900 to 1950 must be gloomy. Wars became bloodier and more international in scope. The 20th century showed that man's ability to kill man, woman, and child had reached new levels of gruesome sophistication. The depression devastated not only whole economies, but countless personal lives. This was a time of troubles in world history.

This chapter will reflect and explain how so many disasters occurred. Here, however, oversimplification is dangerous. As in earlier periods of world history, international trends were not uniform and certainly could vary in their impact. This half-century was a period of exciting—if sometimes chaotic and bloody—revolution in a number of countries. Societies in revolution, particularly Soviet Russia, were assuredly affected by the larger international trends but in distinctive ways. Even where the theme of hardship more fully predominated, clouds could have silver linings. Latin America, for example, profoundly hurt by worldwide depression (though not by the international wars), was able to respond to the disaster by new and constructive forms of government policy, opening a new chapter in the civilization's political history and at least a modification of its long-standing inferiority in international trade.

The disasters of the age particularly affected the West's power position in the world, and this meant opportunities for many dependent or colonial societies to strike out in new ways. Nationalism in India and the Middle East became more confident and effective. Here too, the international framework—though undeniably difficult—offered novel hopes, not crushing despair. Correspondingly the most agonized reactions to the half-century of crisis were voiced in the West, by people who suffered directly and who forecast further decline in their civilization.

Yet even in the West, the crisis half-century was not the final historical word. The results did diminish the West's role in the world, opening a complex rebalancing among civilizations after 1945. Nevertheless, Western society rebounded, creating a political and economic vitality that contrasted markedly with the agonies of the previous 40 years. Thus, while some people (particularly in the West) who lived through the decades of crisis thought that civilization was coming to an end, and while crises did reflect and cause huge changes in the international framework, they did not dictate the tone for world history after 1945. This tone will be discussed in Chapter 42.

For now, the key point to note is the complexity of the results of worldwide crises. These events created a new set of problems but also important new opportunities. The ensuing agenda can be summed up after dealing with the crises themselves, starting with World War I.

THE FIRST WORLD WAR

To many Western observers shortly before 1914, the main trends in world history seemed both clear and benign. During the previous century or more, Western society had become unquestionably richer and by many measurements more open and just. Mass education had become a fact of life. Health had improved, and the death of infants, long a constant in human history, was becoming increasingly rare. New political rights gave most adult men a direct voice in government, while protecting freedoms of religion and press. Knowledge advanced steadily, with increasing understanding of the physical universe. Dark corners of the universe existed still, but it was reasonable to assume that scientific planning, leavened by humanitarian concern, could reduce them steadily. Certainly, in this vision, catastrophic war had no place—people and governments should be too enlightened to allow more than minor discord.

CONFIDENCE AND INTERNATIONALISM ON THE WAR'S EVE

The optimism of many Westerners focused mainly on what they saw as progress in their own civilization, but there was also an international dimension to their belief in progress. Imperialists believed that Western leadership was bringing new enlightenment to the inferior peoples of the rest of the world, though they did not make it clear

whether these peoples might someday learn enough to take care of themselves according to Western standards. Beyond outright imperialism, there had been during the later 19th century some interesting first steps at international organization, which might foreshadow a more smoothly and peacefully functioning world.

In 1851, for example, an International Statistical Congress began meeting to standardize the practices of statistical services of the European governments. A more informal committee met in 1863 to prepare policies on the rights of neutral parties to aid the wounded during wars, and an official diplomatic conference redrafted these policies in 1864 at the Geneva Convention, establishing the Red Cross, an international agency for humanitarian service in wartime. The Telegraphic Union of 1865 blazed a new trail, followed ten years later by the Postal Union—both unions set agreed-upon international procedures for regular exchanges of letters and messages. Some of these steps constituted serious modifications of the idea that an individual national government could do as it pleased, and the practical agreements certainly facilitated the further development of international business arrangements. The habit of thinking internationally seemed to spread increasingly. Scientists met often in international conferences; industrialists showed their wares at international fairs and exhibitions, starting with London's great Crystal Palace display in 1851 and extending through regular world's fairs in various parts of Europe and the United States. Western socialists formed an international movement, based on the idea that working peoples should unite across national boundaries. Athletes gained a new forum for international competition with the establishment of the modern Olympic Games in 1890.

These various moves toward internationalization constituted an important development in world history, both recognizing and furthering the intensification of the world network. Many of the international systems and habits established from the later 19th century still facilitate world exchanges today—some, like easy international mailing, are so routine that they barely merit thought.

Despite genuine significance, however, the international movement had two related weaknesses. First, it was heavily based on Western dominance and control of empires. A few other governments fit in—from North America, Latin America, and Asia—but most of the initial arrangements were primarily set by Europeans and for Europeans. The process of weaning internationalism from Western control would be a long and painful one, focused particularly on the decades after 1945. Internationalization, furthermore, gained ground at the same time that European nationalism was at a height, as well as at a time when the idea of national independence and pride was spreading to new areas such as India. Here was another limit on internationalist thinking, quickly visible in areas such as the Olympic Games, which turned into an international forum for fierce athletic competition among rival nations.

The limits on internationalism showed clearly when the movement turned away from economic and goodwill areas to more directly political matters. In 1898 the Russian tsar urged the calling of a peace conference, designed to seek agreement on reducing armaments levels among the world's great powers. The move was prompted in part by Russia's economic problems, as a nation just beginning to industrialize, and its difficulty in keeping up with the arms costs escalating among the Western nations. Nevertheless, the discussions, held in The Hague in 1899, amplified international agreements on the treatment of war prisoners, temporarily prohibited weapons thrown from balloons, and banned gas warfare and some other new technologies (these latter measures were ignored in the great world war that broke out 15 years later). Disarmament and the idea of a compulsory arbitration of international disputes were shunted aside. But a permanent court of arbitration was established that nations could use to settle disputes. This court, now called the World Court, still sits in The Hague and has ruled on conflicts in such areas as economic rights or minor boundary questions. Obviously, however, the promising move toward more genuine international discussion of the issues that might cause war was not possible, given intense national rivalries at the time and since.

It remains true that an optimistic observer before 1914 could legitimately believe that a more rational approach toward international problems was in the works. The strides that had occurred in setting up international mechanisms were limited but not entirely illusory. Interestingly, though the international movement did not prevent massive 20th-century war, it also did not die—it was reinvoked, indeed, as part of the effort to settle World War I.

Still, the main point is the gap between confident assumptions in the West, about internal and international progress alike, and the disaster that beckoned in 1914. How did the West collapse into near-total war, dragging much of the world along with it? The advent of an unprecedented kind of war seemed to make a mockery of widely held optimism, causing all the more havoc because so many people had fervently believed that such man-made catastrophes were impossible.

THE ONSET OF WORLD WAR I

Diplomatic tensions had escalated fairly steadily among the major European powers—Britain, France, Russia, Germany, and Austria-Hungary—since the 1890s (see

Chapter 29). Two rival alliances had formed, theoretically pitting the first three nations against the last two plus Italy. Rapid imperialist gains in Africa and Asia had accustomed all the European nations to territorial expansion and easy diplomatic prestige, yet by 1900 most of the world's available territory had already been carved up. Inevitably, tensions within Europe became prominent once again. Many nations tended to use military growth—such as the big battleship-building rivalry that seized Britain and Germany—and diplomatic victories as a means of distracting people from difficult social tensions at home. This was particularly tempting in central and eastern Europe. Austria-Hungary was beset by bitter national struggles among a number of Slavic groups against the control of German and Hungarian leadership. Russia faced a revolutionary mood among workers and peasants—revolution had burst out directly in 1905—producing a belief that diplomatic success was essential. More stable nations, such as France, were so burdened by fears of rivals, such as Germany, that they refused to pull back from their less stable allies. The two alliance systems focused increasingly on the leading European trouble spot, the Balkans in the southeast, where a number of bitterly competitive small nations fought two wars in 1912 and 1913. Russia was directly interested in these struggles because of her vaunted kinship with other Slavic peoples; Austria-Hungary was interested because it feared the same south-Slavic nationalism.

The stage for war, in other words, was set by a combination of explicitly diplomatic rivalries and an unusually inflexible, though theoretically defensive, alliance system. It was also fed by the social tensions of industrial Europe among Western powers, who had become accustomed to big armaments expenses as one means of supporting heavy industry, and among several East European nations caught in the stresses of an earlier phase of industrialization. It was fed finally by ethnic tensions in eastern Europe, where a variety of Slavic groups and small nations, such as in the Balkans, competed for influence and tried to undermine multinational empires like Austria-Hungary.

The spark for war occurred, not surprisingly, in the troubled Balkans. In July 1914 a Serbian nationalist shot the Austrian archduke Ferdinand, the emperor's nephew, hoping to strike a blow for Serbian acquisition of Slavic territories controlled by Austria. After years of tension, this was the last straw for Austria-Hungary: Serbia had to be attacked. Germany supported Austria, partly out of loyalty to a weak ally and partly because some leaders believed that world war was inevitable and sooner was better than later, because both France and Russia were in early stages of military reforms that would strengthen them in the long run. Russia refused to let Austria bully Serbia, lest it lose all Balkan influence, and France vowed to support Russia come what might. When Austria declared war on Serbia on July 28, Russia declared a general mobilization—Russia believed it had to prepare because its procedures were slow. Mobilization frightened Germany, whose strategy called for a quick defeat of France before turning to Russia, so Germany declared war on both allies on August 1. Britain hesitated, hoping for peace, but in fact the nation was heavily committed to France and then was frightened and offended by Germany's invasion of Belgium, which was part of Germany's plan to knock France out quickly by attacking from the north as well as the east. Britain entered the fray on August 4. After a century of considerable peace in Europe, the nation-states had once again launched a general war. But this one, fed by the new powers of the state, by new nationalist passions, and by the devastating armaments produced by industrialization, would have far more awesome consequences than any previous struggle.

PATTERNS OF WAR IN EUROPE

Quickly, two major fronts were established as hostilities opened. One, mainly in France, pitted attacking German troops against French and British defenders. The second developed in eastern Europe, particularly in Russian Poland, where German armies battled Russian forces while trying also to support the weaker Austrian-Hungarian army to the south. After 1915 when Italy entered the war on the

side of France and Britain, wooed by promises of territory to be seized from Austria and in the Middle East, a third front developed between Italians and Austrians. There was also an important contest for the seas. The large German surface fleet was bottled up by the British for most of the war, but German submarines played havoc with Atlantic sea-lanes, particularly through 1916. German attacks on United States ships bringing people and supplies to Britain were the most important single cause of American entry into the war in 1917.

FIELDS OF BATTLE

France thrust briefly into Germany in the late summer of 1914, but on the western front, the German conquest of Belgium and advance through northern France were the big news. For a brief moment, as French forces pulled back in panic from their own offensive, it looked as though German hopes for a quick Western settlement might be met. But France rallied, aided by British reinforcements and by heroic civilian support, including a famous troop convoy organized by Parisian cabdrivers. Soon northern France was pockmarked with trenches, from which little advance was possible. The awesome technology of modern war was revealed in all its power, as devastating artillery, the withering fire of machine guns, barbed-wire fences, and the use of poison gas defined the deadening stalemate. By 1916 stagnation on the western front had

World War I Fronts in Europe and the Middle East

The horrors of trench warfare are clearly visible in this photo from World War I.

turned into a nightmare as the Germans lost 850,000 men, the French 700,000, and the British 410,000— without any appreciable change in the lines of battle. A German novelist later described life in the rat-infested trenches:

> The front is a cage in which we must await fearfully whatever may happen. We lie under the network of arching shells and live in a suspense of uncertainty. Over us Chance hovers.

Other fronts were slightly more mobile, although they too took huge tolls in lives. The Italian front also produced trench warfare, though it moved back and forth in northeastern Italy. In eastern Europe, Germany fought off a Russian offensive but had to aid Austria-Hungary, which was outclassed by Russian troops. Most of the fighting on the eastern front took place in the western portions of Russia, with some momentous battles. Fighting also spread to the Balkans, where Austria crushed Serbia and the other small states aligned variously in hopes of local advantage.

Along both the western and eastern fronts, the intensity of involvement among the combatants ran high. The conscripted and professional soldiers of the mass armies were

most heavily engaged, of course, and even those who survived would long be marked by physical and psychological scars, often including a resentment against civilian authorities, politicians above all, who could not have known what the horror of war was. Yet civilian commitment was considerable, as each nation-state showed its power of mobilization to the fullest. Governments increasingly organized the major sectors of the economy to ration resources and production and to prevent crippling labor disputes. Whole industrial sectors, such as railroads in the United States, were administered outright by the state. Within government, the executive branch increasingly took over from parliament—particularly in Germany, where by 1917 a top general virtually ran the country. Governments also leaned heavily on public opinion. Dissent was censored, and dissenters were arrested. Newspapers and other media were manipulated to create the most favorable public opinion possible. Thus the British (and through them, the Americans) were regaled with exaggerated stories of German violence, while Germans were so carefully shielded from military setbacks after 1917 that many did not know they were losing until the end actually came. The power of governments to command resources and also beliefs and passions made this truly the first total war.

The war in essence sped up many developments already visible in industrial society. The power of organization increased, particularly through the new interventions of governments. To keep the social peace, socialists and trade unions were given new recognition, serving on governing boards for industry and the like. By the same token, however, many labor leaders also became more involved in the existing system, which heightened revolutionary discontent among a minority of workers and others. Women's participation in the labor force increased greatly, although this proved to be a fragile trend as men recaptured many jobs at the war's end. At the same time, the war brought material shortages, even famine, to many people in the belligerent nations, while imposing great tensions on soldiers and civilians alike. These hardships, plus feverish hopes for a better world after war had ended, brought a revolutionary or near-revolutionary mood to many European nations after four years of struggle.

THE WAR OUTSIDE EUROPE

World War I was essentially a European conflict, a particularly cruel result of the political divisions and rivalries that had long marked the Western experience and had been exacerbated by nationalism and other new forces during the 19th century. Nevertheless, given the West's world dominance, it was inevitable that the war spilled over into other areas, or that it had some of its most important effects outside Europe proper.

British dominions, notably Canada, Australia, and New Zealand, were drawn into the war effort early on as loyal members of the British Empire. Forces from these countries fought bravely on several fronts and in the process brought their new nations into greater world involvements.

World War I also brought the United States into world power politics as a major player, culminating a development that had been brewing for some time. By 1914 the United States was turning decisively away from a largely regional diplomatic role, with its Asian empire, centering on Hawaii and the Philippines, complementing its forceful activities in Central America and the West Indies. The advent of world war, however, caught the United States in a mood of considerable ambivalence. Distant from these battlefields, Americans also disagreed over which side, if either, was in the right. American businessmen, in the meantime, profited greatly from the war by selling goods to the various combatants and taking advantage of European distraction to gain new ground in other world markets. Rapidly rising exports, combined with loans to European governments that needed credit in order to buy war materials and food, converted the United States from an international debtor to a creditor nation essentially for the first time in the nation's history. Despite all the gains resulting from noninvolvement, American leadership was on balance decidedly pro-British. Clumsy German attempts to influence American opinion as well as the submarine warfare that affected American ships, including passenger vessels, moved the country toward a more interventionist mood. In 1917 the United States entered the war, soon sending fresh troops as well as needed supplies to the western front, and unquestionably helping to turn the tide against the Germans. The United States also brought into the war a new current of idealism, choosing to see their unaccustomed role as a battle for international justice and democracy; this input, too, would play an important role in the war's results.

AFRICA AND ASIA

The involvement of the United States and the British Commonwealth was only part of the war's international story. Minor skirmishes in the war were fought around the German colonies in Africa, but the major African involvement came in the use by Britain and France of many African troops in their armies on the European front. Britain also used important contingents from India. Experience in

fighting in a European war could be an important one for the Africans and Asians involved, by increasing awareness of European standards and the contradiction between fierce nationalist pride in Europe and the subjection of their own peoples. It was no accident that the first Pan-African Nationalist Congress occurred in 1919, as emerging African leaders pursued nationalist goals similar to those they had seen in Europe, though without the internal divisiveness.

The war also spread to East Asia, where it fit into a new pattern of conflict. Japan entered the war on the side of Britain and France, honoring its previous alliance with Britain. The main Japanese purpose was to seize Germany's Far Eastern colonies—Pacific islands and holdings in China—to advance its imperialist role and strengthen itself in relation to China. Australia and New Zealand seized German Samoa to forestall Japanese advance to the south. China declared war on Germany in 1917, hoping not to be ignored by the European powers. But Japan was the big gainer in the region, moving into German holdings in China's Shantung province and presenting additional demands for Chinese concessions. World War I in the Far East, then, advanced already aggressive Japanese policy, setting the stage for further conflict.

Large numbers of troops from India fought for the British in Europe. Indian nationalists backed the war effort, hoping that a British victory would promote India's freedom. Allied wartime declarations about national liberation inspired hope in India as in Africa and elsewhere, again promoting new issues for the future.

World War I had wider ramifications still in the Middle East. The Ottoman Empire, long attached to German military advisors, joined Germany in the war effort. The Germans even hoped that the Turks could sponsor a Muslim uprising against British and French holdings in North Africa, though this did not materialize. Rather, the war weakened the already feeble Ottoman state. Britain sponsored an attack on the Dardanelles, near Constantinople, hoping to open an additional front to rescue the smaller Balkan states. The campaign was a failure, yet it cost 150,000 British and colonial troops. Nevertheless, the British did sponsor Arab nationalists against their Ottoman overlords, winning important allies along the eastern Mediterranean. They also promised support to Jewish settlers in Israel, in the Balfour Declaration of 1917. Allied actions set in motion various forces hostile to Ottoman rule and eager for some kind of independence, though they also encouraged contradictory goals in the Middle East itself.

Overall, the war's international ramifications constituted a substantial diminution of Europe's world power. Two new players, the United States and Japan, gained ground, winning new prestige or new territory. Europe's need for colonial support and its devotion to belligerent nationalism encouraged many other people in India, Africa, and the Middle East to a higher level of awareness of their own national rights and merits.

THE WAR'S END

The international context, save for the United States' entry, did not play a massive role in the central theaters of war, where attention riveted once more on the two major fronts by 1917. In March 1917, the pressures of war, added to the earlier massive strains in Russian society, caused a major revolution that toppled the tsarist government (see Chapter 36). The new government, strongly committed to Western-style liberalism, vowed to live up to Russian obligations under the alliance, but in fact the Russian war effort began to falter even further. Moreover, popular hostility to the impositions of war helped produce more radical agitation, aided by the activities of communist leaders such as Lenin who had been transported to Russia from a Swiss exile by the German government precisely in hopes of fomenting trouble. The result was a new revolt, in October 1917, that brought Lenin and the communists to power. This leadership, bent on restructuring Russian society, wanted to escape the pressures of war. In March 1918 it signed the Brest-Litovsk treaty with the Germans, giving the Germans substantial territories in western Russia in return for peace.

This proved to be the peak of German success, however, and indeed the treaty was a partial mistake. The Germans had to commit more troops to occupying its new territory than was sensible, reducing the abilities of a thoroughly war-torn nation to push new energy into the crucial western front. Heavy fighting there during 1917 caused massive losses on both sides, prior to the arrival of fresh American troops. A last-ditch German offensive in 1918 failed, leaving the nation with no reserves. Then a French-British-American counteroffensive pressed forward, aided by the collapse of Austrian forces in Italy and the Balkans. The German military generals, by now effectively running the country, installed a new civilian government so that blame for defeat would not fall directly on their forces. This government, led ultimately by socialists when the German emperor abdicated, had no choice but to sue for peace in November 1918.

THE PEACE AND THE AFTERMATH

Settlement of the war was difficult, even with the military apparatus of Germany temporarily dismantled or underground. Diplomats of the victorious nations convened at Versailles, near Paris, where they debated the fate of much of the world, with Russia, Germany, and indeed most of the world unrepresented. France was bent on revenge against Germany and assurance that Germany would be so weakened that it could not attack a third time. It got back the provinces surrendered after its 1871 war loss, but not the security it yearned for. Italy wanted new territory in abundance; it received some, but not enough and emerged unsatisfied as well. Japan hoped for a great power role but was largely ignored, which heightened Japanese discontent despite concrete war gains. The United States, led by President Woodrow Wilson, espoused great ideals, hoping for just settlement of all nationalist issues—particularly in eastern Europe where many nationalities struggled for recognition—and a new League of Nations to deal with future disputes and to make war unnecessary. But ideals were hard to put into practice amid the welter of conflicting interests, and opinion back home prevented the United States from taking a consistently active role. The nation did not even join the League of Nations its representatives had devised. American isolationism contributed to French and British fears for the future, in a peacetime that was badly born.

The big losers at Versailles were of course Germany and Austria-Hungary in Europe. In Asia China suffered particularly because of its losses to a surging Japan and internal unrest that followed the war, as China refused to sign away the Shantung province to Japan but was powerless to resist. The Austro-Hungarian Empire collapsed entirely, as nationalist groups carved out the new nations of Czechoslovakia and Hungary, plus Yugoslavia as an enlarged south Slavic state—leaving a somewhat fragile Germanic Austria, cut off from its traditional markets, as one of many small countries in a weakened region of Europe. Germany lost Alsace-Lorraine to France, as well as territory to a revived Polish state in the east. It was also blamed for causing the war and faced huge reparation payments to the Allies, particularly France and Belgium. The level of military forces was limited, and the region west of the Rhine was supposed to remain demilitarized entirely. These various impositions created huge discontent in Germany, with many leaders vowing revenge on France as the leader of the punitive peacemakers. Russia, ignored as a communist pariah after its revolution in 1917, was also cut back through the creation of additional small states in eastern Europe at its expense—Poland and several Baltic republics. Here too was potential for future trouble. The Versailles peace settlement thus set up important preconditions for future diplomatic strife in Europe by creating new categories of discontented great powers, insecure or disappointed victors, and a new series of small states in parts of eastern Europe that might tempt future expansionists.

LARGER DISLOCATIONS

The legacy of World War I involved more, however, than a difficult diplomatic heritage. The war had devastated Europe's economy and society. More than ten million people had died, meaning that almost every European family had a death to mourn. Never before had a war approached this level of devastation. Countries such as France and Serbia, particularly hard hit, lost over one-tenth of their total populations. Truly, this war was "the blood red dawn of the 20th century." The loss of young men was an economic as well as a psychological blow, for these men were the potential cream of the upcoming labor force and leadership groups. Loss of men also hampered the European birthrate, for families that might have formed now could not start. Massive destruction of industrial property and agricultural land temporarily dislocated many economies, leading to a period of postwar instability that ended only in 1923. More serious than these largely repairable setbacks was an imbalance produced by the methods of financing the war. Most combatant regimes had borrowed heavily, unwilling to raise taxes too much lest civilian morale be destroyed. Even during the last years of war, despite government restrictions, prices began to rise because of the inflationary impact of increased government spending and money supply. And after the war, in many countries infla-

tion soared. Although some groups could profit from rapidly rising prices, many people with fixed savings were nearly wiped out, while others, such as many farmers, were encouraged to borrow unwisely, which would later leave them strapped for funds and wondering how to solve their economic problems. In various ways, then, the war introduced basic dislocations that promised, and later produced, further trouble.

The peace settlement also set in motion the forces that would launch western Europe's decline in the wider world. To be sure, there was little outright loss of colonies, and indeed the 1920s constituted (on paper) the apogee of Western imperialism. Germany's African colonies were taken over and much of the Middle East was divided between France and Britain, but the new "colonies" were held as mandates of the League of Nations, not outright possessions. The implication was that, although colonial administrations might in fact be established, they were only temporarily responsible, with an obligation under international scrutiny to prepare for independence. In the Middle East and elsewhere, nationalist leaders seized on Wilsonian principles of self-determination, asking why they were applied only within Europe and not to the wider world. Here was a vital pressure for heightened agitation against imperialist rule.

The Postwar World in 1920

Leadership in the peace settlements also passed from strictly European hands. The United States role, though ultimately confused by isolationism, was vital. Japan gained international status as a wartime ally of Britain and France, though Japanese leaders emerged (like almost everyone else) dissatisfied with their rewards and infuriated at exclusion from the European-United States great power conclaves, eager to resume a quest for expansion.

A crucial area of change involved the Middle East. The Ottoman Empire effectively collapsed. Italy and Greece led an initial effort to carve up even those areas around Constantinople where Turks were in the majority, but a vigorous new Turkish republic by 1923 repulsed these efforts through war and negotiation. The rest of the Ottoman holdings, however, were divided up as mandates of the League of Nations, with Britain taking Palestine and Iraq, and France gaining Syria and Lebanon. A few new monarchies, notably the kingdom of Saudi Arabia, sprang up outside the old Ottoman domains. The Middle East was recreated as a series of separate fragments—a legacy that would burn through world affairs later in the 20th century. Here, as in central Europe, the settlement simply asked for further trouble.

Beyond the peace settlement itself, the international economic results of the war continued to reverberate. American and Japanese businessmen had captured many European export markets, which complicated Europe's immediate postwar recovery and, even when the continent had regained greater health, forced an unprecedented amount of international competition. Britain, particularly, never recovered the export position on which its eminence had so long depended. Debts to impatient United States creditors further complicated the international economic mix.

Overall, the results of the war and its settlement, in addition to provoking a host of new tensions within Europe, set the stage for further change in the larger world balance. The European nations remained major actors, their role exaggerated by Russian preoccupation with its internal revolution and the United States' refusal to attend consistently to international affairs. Nationalist agitation in the colonies, new economic imbalances, and the heightened power of Japan and the United States all portended a new world structure that was not, however, clearly defined.

The war also sketched a new international organization. The League of Nations established a number of subsidiary groups, dealing with issues such as protecting minimum

At the Paris Peace Conference of 1919, the Arabs sought a new voice. The Arab representations included Prince Feisel of Jordan and an Iraqi general. The Arabs did not win full application of the principles of national self-determination to their homelands.

working conditions, that effectively gathered information and focused international social concerns. The league itself, however, proved to be little more than a discussion group, as real diplomacy continued on a nation-to-nation basis. Several disarmament conferences held in the 1920s, designed particularly to reduce naval competition, were ultimately ineffective as well. The international idea advanced, in sum, but it lacked muscle.

The peace settlement after World War I is routinely and correctly criticized for its failure to handle European tensions well. Too many small countries were created near dissatisfied great powers, notably the Soviet Union and Germany. Further conflict was inevitable. The peace settlement took insufficient account of Europe's reduced position in the world, blithely assuming in fact that imperialism was at most slightly modified. In fact, the war had roused nationalist ambitions virtually worldwide, and this was perhaps its most lasting legacy. The war taught Africans, Arabs, Jews, and a host of different Asians that nationalism was legitimate; by creating new European weakness it also held out the hope that non-European nationalisms might also be feasible.

 THE GREAT DEPRESSION

The next step in a mounting spiral of international crisis came with the onset of a global economic depression, which hit the headlines with the crash of key Western banks in 1929 but which in fact had begun, sullenly, in many parts of the world economy even earlier.

The depression resulted from new problems in the industrial economy of Europe and the United States, combined with the long-term weakness in economies, like those of Latin America, that depended on sales of cheap exports in the international market. The result was a worldwide collapse that spared only a few economies and brought political and economic pressures on virtually every society.

CAUSATION

The impact of the First World War on the European economy had led to several rocky years into the early 1920s. War-induced inflation was a particular problem in Germany, as prices soared daily and ordinary purchases required huge quantities of currency. Forceful government action finally resolved this crisis in 1923, but only by a massive devaluation of the mark, which did nothing to restore lost savings. More generally, a sharp, brief recession in 1920 and 1921 had reflected other postwar dislocations, though by 1923 production levels had regained or surpassed prewar levels. Great Britain, an industrial pioneer that was already victim of a loss of dynamism before the

war, recovered more slowly, in part because of its unusually great dependence on an export market now open to wider competition.

Structural problems affected other areas of Europe besides Britain and lasted well beyond the predictable readjustments to peacetime. Farmers throughout much of the Western world including the United States faced almost chronic overproduction of food and resulting low prices. Food production had soared in response to wartime needs, and then during postwar inflation many farmers, both in western Europe and in North America, borrowed heavily to buy new equipment, overconfident that their good markets would be sustained. But rising European production combined with large imports from the Americas sent prices down, which made debts harder to repay. One response was continued flight from the countryside, as urbanization continued. Remaining farmers were hard-pressed and unable to sustain high demand for manufactured goods.

Thus, although economies in nations such as France and Germany seemed to have recovered by 1925, there were continued problems: the fears inflation had generated, which in turn limited the capacity of governments to respond to other problems, plus the weaknesses in the buying power of key groups. In this situation, part of the mid-decade prosperity rested on exceedingly fragile grounds. Loans from United States banks to various European enterprises helped sustain demand for goods, but on condition that additional loans pour in to help pay off the resultant debts.

Furthermore, most of the dependent areas in the world economy, colonies and noncolonies alike, were suffering badly. Pronounced tendencies toward overproduction developed in the smaller nations of eastern Europe, which sent agricultural goods to western Europe, as well as among tropical producers in Africa and Latin America. Here, continued efforts to win export revenue drove local estate owners to drive up output in such goods as coffee, sugar, and rubber. As European governments and businessmen organized their African colonies for more profitable exploitation, they set up large estates devoted to goods of this type. Again, production frequently exceeded demand, which drove prices and earnings down not only in Africa but also in Latin America. This meant in turn that many colonies and dependent economies were unable to buy many industrial exports, which weakened demand for Western products precisely when output tended to rise amid growing United States and Japanese competition.

Governments of the leading industrial nations provided scant leadership during the emerging crisis of the 1920s. Knowledge of economics was often feeble amid a Western leadership group not noteworthy for its quality even in more conventional areas. Nationalistic selfishness predominated. Western nations were more concerned about insisting on repayment of any debts owed to them or about constructing tariff barriers to protect their own industries than in facilitating balanced world economic growth. Protectionism, in particular, as practiced even by traditionally free-trade Great Britain and by the many new nations in eastern Europe, simply reduced market opportunities and made a bad situation worse. By the later 1920s employment in key export industrial sectors in the West—coal (also beset by new competition from imported oil), iron, and textiles—began to decline, the foretaste of more general collapse.

THE DEBACLE

The formal advent of depression occurred in October 1929, when the New York stock market crashed. Stock values tumbled, as investors quickly lost confidence in issues that had been pushed ridiculously high. United States banks, which had depended heavily on their stock investments, rapidly echoed the financial crisis, and many institutions failed, dragging their depositors along with them. Even before this collapse, Americans had begun to call back earlier loans to Europe. Yet the European credit structure depended extensively on American loans, which had fueled some industrial expansion but also less productive investments such as German reparation payments and the construction of fancy town halls and other amenities. In Europe, as in the United States, many commercial enterprises existed on the basis not of real production power but of continued speculation. When one piece of the speculative spiral was withdrawn, the whole edifice quickly collapsed. Key bank failures in Austria and Germany followed the American crisis. Throughout most of the industrial West, investment funds dried up as creditors went bankrupt or tried to pull in their horns.

With investment receding, industrial production quickly began to fall, beginning in the industries that produced capital goods and extending quickly to consumer products fields. Falling production—levels dropped by as much as one-third by 1932—meant falling employment and lower wages, which in turn withdrew still more demand from the economy and led to further hardship. The existing weakness of some markets, such as the farm sector or the nonindustrial world, was exacerbated as demand for foods and minerals plummeted. New and appalling problems developed among workers—now out of jobs or suffering from reduced hours and reduced pay—as well as the middle classes. The depression, in sum, fed on itself, growing steadily worse from 1929 to 1933. Even countries initially less hard hit, such as France and Italy, saw themselves drawn into the vortex by 1931.

In itself, the Great Depression was not entirely unprecedented. Previous periods had seen slumps triggered by bank failures and overspeculation, yielding several years of falling production, unemployment, and real hardship. But the intensity of the Great Depression had no precedent in the brief history of industrial societies. Its duration was also unprecedented; in many countries full recovery came only after a decade, and only with the forced production schedules provoked by World War II. The depression was also more marked than its antecedents because it came on the heels of so much other distress—the economic hardships of war, for example, and the catastrophic inflation of the 1920s—and because it caught most governments utterly unprepared to cope.

The depression was more, of course, than an economic event. It reached into countless lives, creating hardship and tension that would be recalled even as the crisis itself eased. Loss of earnings, loss of work, or simply fears that loss would come could devastate people at all social levels. The suicides of ruined investors in New York were paralleled by the vagrants' camps and begging that spread among displaced workers. The statistics were grim: up to one-third of all blue-collar workers in the West lost their jobs for prolonged periods. White-collar unemployment, though not quite as severe, was also unparalleled. In Germany 600,000 of four million white-collar workers had lost their jobs by 1931. Graduating students could not find work or had to resort to jobs they regarded as insecure or demeaning. Figures of six million overall unemployed in Germany and 22 percent of the labor force unemployed in Britain were statistics of stark misery and despair. Families were disrupted, as men felt emasculated at their inability to provide and women and children were disgusted at authority figures whose authority was now hollow. In some cases wives and mothers found it easier to gain jobs in a low-wage economy than their husbands did, and although this development had some promise in terms of new opportunities for women, it could also be confusing for standard family roles. Again, the agony and personal disruption of the depression constituted no short shock. For many it was desperately prolonged, with renewed recession around 1937 and with unemployment still averaging ten percent or more in many countries by 1939.

Just as World War I had been, the depression was an event that blatantly contradicted the optimistic assumptions of the later 19th century. To many, it showed the fragility of any idea of progress, any belief that Western civilization was becoming more humane. To still more it challenged the notion that standard Western governments—the parliamentary democracies—were able to control their own destinies. And because it was a second catastrophic event within a generation, the depression led to even more ex-

A United States woman reflects unemployment and poverty during the Great Depression.

treme results than the war itself had done—more bizarre experiments, more paralysis in the face of deepening despair.

WORLDWIDE IMPACT

Just as the depression had been caused by a combination of specifically Western problems and wider weaknesses in the world economy, so its effects had both Western twists and international repercussions.

A few economies were buffered from the depression. The Soviet Union, busy building an industrial society under communist control, had cut off all but the most insignificant economic ties with other nations under the heading "socialism in one country." The result placed great hardships on many Russian people, called to sustain rapid industrial development without outside capital, but it did prevent anything like a depression during the 1930s. Soviet leaders pointed with pride to the lack of serious unemployment and steadily rising production rates, in a telling contrast with the miseries of Western capitalism at the time.

For most of the rest of the world, however, the depression worsened an already bleak economic picture. Western markets could absorb fewer commodity imports as production fell and incomes dwindled. Hence the nations that produced foods and raw materials saw prices and earnings drop even more than before. Unemployment rose rapidly in the export sectors of the Latin American economy, creating a major political challenge not unlike that faced by the Western leaders.

Japan, as a new industrial country still heavily dependent on export earnings for financing its imports of essential fuel and raw materials, was hit hard too. The Japanese silk industry, an export staple, was already suffering from the advent of artificial silk-like fibers produced by Western chemical giants. Now luxury purchases collapsed, leading to severe unemployment and, again, a crucial political crisis.

Between 1929 and 1931, the value of Japanese exports plummeted by 50 percent. Workers' real income dropped by almost one-third, and there were over three million unemployed. Depression was compounded by bad harvests in several regions, leading to rural begging and near-starvation.

The Great Depression, though most familiar in its Western dimensions, was a truly international collapse, a sign of the tight bonds and serious imbalances that had developed in world trading patterns. The results of the collapse, and particularly the varied responses to it, are best traced in individual cases. For Latin America, the depression marked a pronounced stimulus to new kinds of effective political action, and particularly greater state involvement in planning and direction. New government vigor did not cure the economic effects of the depression, which escaped the control of most individual states, but it did set an important new phase in the civilization's political evolution. For Japan, the depression increased suspicions of the West and helped promote new expansionism designed among other things to win more assured markets in Asia. In the West the depression led to new welfare programs that stimulated demand and helped restore confidence, but it also led to radical social and political experiments such as German Nazism. What was common in this welter of reactions was the intractable global quality of the depression itself, which made it impossible for any purely national policy to restore full prosperity. Even Nazi Germany, which boasted of regaining full employment, continued to suffer from low wages and other dislocations aside from its obvious and growing dependence on military production.

The reactions to the depression, including a sense of weakness and confusion in many quarters inside and outside policy circles, finally helped to bring the final great crisis of the first half of the 20th century: a second, and more fully international, world war.

In March 1939 Joseph Stalin, uncontested leader of the Soviet state, spoke to the 18th Communist Party Congress on the state of the world and the implications for the Soviet Union. His evaluation of the nature of the depression and its implications were central to his overall policy statement.

NEW ECONOMIC CRISIS IN THE CAPITALIST COUNTRIES. INTENSIFICATION OF THE STRUGGLE FOR MARKETS AND SOURCES OF RAW MATERIAL, AND FOR A NEW REDIVISION OF THE WORLD

The economic crisis which broke out in the capitalist countries in the latter half of 1929 lasted until the end of 1933. After that the crisis passed into a depression, and was then followed by a certain revival, a certain upward trend of industry. But this upward trend of industry did not develop into a boom, as is usually the case in a period of revival. On the contrary, in the latter half of 1937 a new economic crisis began which seized the United States first of all and then England, France and a number of other countries.

The capitalist countries thus found themselves faced with a new economic crisis before they had even recovered from the ravages of the recent one.

This circumstance naturally led to an increase of unemployment. The number of unemployment in capitalist countries, which had fallen from 30,000,000 in 1933 to 14,000,000 in 1937, has now again risen to 18,000,000 as a result of the new crisis.

A distinguishing feature of the new crisis is that it differs in many respects from the preceding one, and, moreover, differs for the worse and not for the better.

Firstly, the new crisis did not begin after an industrial boom, as was the case in 1929, but after a depression and a certain revival, which, however, did not develop into a boom. This means that the present crisis will be more severe and more difficult to cope with than the previous crisis.

Further, the present crisis has broken out not in time of peace, but at a time when a second imperialist war has already begun; when Japan, already in the second year of her war with China, is disorganizing the immense Chinese market and rendering it almost inaccessible to the goods of other countries; when Italy and Germany have already placed their national economies on a war footing, squandering their reserves of raw material and foreign currency for this purpose; and when all the other big capitalist powers are beginning to reorganize themselves on a war footing. This means that capitalism will have far less resources at its disposal for a normal way out of the present crisis than during the preceding crisis.

Lastly, as distinct from the preceding crisis, the present crisis is not universal, but as yet involves chiefly the economically powerful countries which have not yet placed themselves on a war economy basis. As regards the aggressive countries, such as Japan, Germany and Italy, who have already reorganized their economies on a war footing, they, because of the intense development of their war industry, are not yet experiencing a crisis of overproduction, although they are approaching it. This means that by the time the economically powerful, nonaggressive countries begin to emerge from the phase of crisis the aggressive countries, having exhausted their reserves of gold and raw material in the course of the war fever, are bound to enter a phase of very severe crisis. . . .

The Soviet Union is the only country in the world where crises are unknown and where industry is continuously on the upgrade. Naturally, such an unfavorable turn of economic affairs could not but aggravate relations among the powers. The preceding crisis had already mixed the cards and sharpened the struggle for markets and sources of raw materials. The seizure of Manchuria and North China by Japan, the seizure of Abyssinia by Italy—all this reflected the acuteness of the struggle among the powers. The new economic crisis was bound to lead, and is actually leading, to a further sharpening of the imperialist struggle. It is no longer a question of competition in the markets, of a commercial war, of dumping. These methods of struggle have long been recognized as inadequate. It is now a question of a new redivision of the world, of spheres of influence and colonies, by military action. It is a distinguishing feature of the new imperialist war that it has not yet become universal, a world war. The war is being waged by aggressor states, who in every way infringe upon the interests of the nonaggressive states, primarily Britain, France and the U.S.A., while the latter draw back and retreat, making concession after concession to the aggressors.

Thus we are witnessing an open redivision of the world and spheres of influence at the expense of the nonaggressive states, without the least attempt at resistance, and even with a certain connivance, on their part.

Incredible, but true.

To what are we to attribute this one-sided and strange character of the new imperialist war?

How is it that the nonaggressive countries, which possess such vast opportunities, have so easily and without resistance abandoned their positions and their obligations to please the aggressors?

Is it to be attributed to the weakness of the nonaggressive states? Of course not! Combined, the nonaggressive, democratic states are unquestionably stronger than the fascist states, both economically and militarily.

To what then are we to attribute the systematic concessions made by these states to the aggressors?

It might be attributed, for example, to the fear that a revolution might break out if the nonaggressive states were to go to war and the war were to assume world-wide proportions. The bourgeois politicians know, of course, that the first imperialist world war led to the victory of the revolution in one of the largest countries. They are afraid that the second imperialist world war may also lead to the victory of the revolution in one or several countries.

Questions: How did Stalin compare his nation's economy to that of the capitalist leaders? How did he relate the depression to the diplomatic crisis? Was his judgment accurate, or was it unduly biased by communist theory? What would be the implications of this kind of analysis for Soviet foreign policy by 1939?

WORLD WAR II

World War II, which broke out formally in 1939 but was actually prepared by a series of wars and clashes through the 1930s, was fed by two active agents and an excessively passive one. Deliberate strides toward military expansion on the part of new regimes in Japan and Germany formed the active causes, bringing the clouds of war to Asia and the Pacific as well as to Europe and the Mediterranean quite directly. The passivity centered on the most logical opponents to the new aggressors—the other powerful states in Europe and North America. Here, nationalistic and ideological divisions, including widespread Western suspicion of the communist regime in the Soviet Union, limited an ability to act. So did weak leadership and paralyzing internal political disputes, which made positive response difficult until a late hour. Amid ineffective responses, the inability of the League of Nations to take more than rhetorical action was a foregone conclusion, and the league progressively withered as a policy instrument during the prewar decade.

Underlying all the factors contributing to war was the prior experience of war and economic depression. The aggressive regimes resulted from the tensions in Germany and Japan caused by economic collapse, supplemented in Germany's case by the wounds of prior defeat and a harsh

peace. Western passivity followed also from the confusions engendered by prior crises. World history, or at least those facets dominated by the great powers, seemed locked in a spiral of growing tragedy.

THE NEW REGIMES

The first scenes of this new tragedy involved the advent of new, militaristic governments as key national actors plus an important supporting player. The early phases of the depression had triggered growing political fragmentation in Japan, particularly through the rise of various ultranationalist groups. Some opposed Western values in the name of Shintoism and Confucianism, while others urged a Nazi-style authoritarian government free from parliamentary restraint and undue tradition. A military group, backed by many younger officers, urged a "defense state" under their control. It was this group in 1932 that attacked key government and business offices and killed the prime minister. The result, satisfactory to no major group, was four years of moderate military rule under an older admiral, followed in 1936 and 1937 by a tougher military regime after another officer rebellion had failed. Japanese voters continued to prefer more moderate parties, but effective leadership fell increasingly into militaristic hands.

The advent of military rule developed in a context of regional diplomatic crisis. During the later 1920s, Chinese nationalist forces seemed to be gaining ground in their effort to unify their chaotic nation after the 1911 revolution. Their success worried Japan's army leaders, who wanted to be able to influence the Manchurian province of China as a buffer between their colony of Korea and the Soviet Union. Japan had, in fact, dominated the Manchurian warlord since its victory over Russia in 1905. Fearful of losing ground, and unimpeded by the weak civilian government in Tokyo, the Japanese army marched into Manchuria in 1931, proclaiming it an independent state. Japan's action was condemned by the League of Nations—which, however, was unable to take effective action—and in consequence Japan simply withdrew from the league. The resulting atmosphere of crisis aided the military's advance in domestic politics, for other leaders were reluctant to damage national military strength, and this advance in turn set the scene for the next round of crisis—effectively, the outbreak of World War II in the Far East—in 1937.

In the meantime, however, a more decisive change of regime had occurred in Germany. Here too, a trend toward growing conservatism and suspicion of parliamentary government had developed by the late 1920s, and then the advent of full depression triggered near-chaos politically. The National Socialist (Nazi) party, led by Adolf Hitler, began to pick up strength after nearly fading from existence during the mid-1920s. Nazis advocated many things, but among their leading goals were an authoritarian state under a single leader as well as an aggressive foreign policy that would reverse the humiliation of the Versailles treaty and gain Germany military glory and new territory for expansion. As German parliamentary leaders bickered among themselves and failed to provide decisive policies to address the depression, and as communist strength grew on the left, Nazis were able to win a growing minority of votes in general elections, while also disrupting normal political meetings and winning quiet support from many business and military leaders. Sponsored by conservatives who erroneously thought they could control him, Hitler was able to take power legally in 1933, and soon abolished the parliamentary regime and constructed a totalitarian state with himself at the helm.

The Nazi state was a radically new kind of regime. Hitler attacked competing sources of power within Germany, abolishing free trade unions as well as opposition political parties. Many political opponents were placed in concentration camps, and new political police added to the terror. Attacks on Jews, the so-called enemies of true Germans, mounted steadily, as part of Hitler's racist ideology. During World War II these attacks escalated into what Hitler called his "final solution," as millions of Jews were forced into concentration camps and then murdered in gas chambers. Nazism also meant construction of a war machine. Hitler expanded armaments production, creating new jobs in the process, and also built up the army and separate Nazi military forces. In Hitler's view, the essence of the state was authority, and the function of the state was war.

Hitler's advent galvanized the authoritarian regime of a near-great power, Italy. Here, a fascist state had been formed in the 1920s, led by Benito Mussolini. Mussolini had, like Hitler, promised an aggressive foreign policy and new nationalist glories, but in fact his first decade had been rather moderate diplomatically. With Hitler in power, however, Mussolini began to experiment more boldly, if only to avoid being overshadowed completely. Here, then, was another destabilizing element in world politics.

THE STEPS TOWARD WAR

Hitler moved first. He suspended German reparation payments, thus renouncing this part of the Versailles settlement; he walked out of a disarmament conference and withdrew from the League of Nations. In 1935 he announced German rearmament and in 1936 brought military forces into the Rhineland—both moves in further violation of Versailles. When these challenges were greeted by loud verbal protests from France and Britain, but nothing more serious, Hitler was poised for the further buildup of German strength and further diplomatic adventures that would ultimately lead to World War II.

In 1935 Mussolini attacked Ethiopia, planning to avenge Italy's failure to conquer this ancient land during the imperialist surge of the 1890s. Again the League of Nations condemned the action, but again neither it nor the democratic powers in Europe and North America took action. Consequently, after some hard fighting, the Italians won their new colony.

In 1936 a civil war engulfed Spain, pitting authoritarian and military leaders against republicans and leftists. Germany and Italy quickly moved to support the Spanish right, sending in supplies and troops, gaining not only new glory but also precious military training in such specialties as bombing civilian targets. France, Britain, and the United States, in contrast, though vaguely supporting the Spanish republic, could agree on no concrete action. Only the Soviet Union sent effective government support, and by 1939 the republican forces had been defeated.

In 1938 Hitler proclaimed a long-sought union, or *Anschluss*, with Austria as a fellow German nation. Western powers complained and denounced but did nothing. In the same year Hitler marched into a German-speaking part of Czechoslovakia. War threatened, but a conference at Munich convinced French and British leaders that Hitler might be satisfied with acquiescence. Czechoslovakia was dismembered and the western (Sudeten) region was turned over to Germany, as the British prime minister, Neville Chamberlain, duped by Hitler's apparent eagerness to compromise, proclaimed that his appeasement had won "peace in our time." ("Our time" turned out to be slightly over a year.) Emboldened by Western weakness, in March 1939 Hitler took over all of Czechoslovakia and began to press Poland for territorial concessions. He also concluded an agreement with the Soviet Union, which was not ready for war with Germany and had despaired of Western resolve. The Soviets also coveted parts of Poland, the Baltic states, and Finland for their own, and when Hitler invaded Poland, Russia launched its own war to undo the Versailles settlement. Hitler attacked Poland on September 1, 1939, not necessarily expecting general war but clearly prepared to risk it; Britain and France, now convinced that nothing short of war would stop the Nazis, made their own declaration in response.

War had already broken out in China. Japan, continuing to press the ruling Chinese government lest it gain sufficient strength to threaten Japanese gains, became involved in a skirmish with Chinese forces in the Beijing area in 1937. Fighting spread, initially quite unplanned. Most Japanese military leaders opposed more general war, arguing that the nation's only interest was to defend Manchuria and Korea. However, influential figures on the General Staff held that China's armies should be decisively defeated to prevent trouble in the future. This view prevailed, and Japanese forces quickly occupied the cities and railroads of eastern China. The Chinese army refused to give in, and a stalemate resulted that lasted in effect until 1945, with neither side capable of major new advance.

In 1940 the two main areas of conflict, Europe and the Pacific, drew together, when Germany and Italy (already uneasy allies) signed an agreement with Japan. Japanese leaders had long admired Germany and welcomed Hitler's basic hostility to the Soviet Union and communism. Full alliance was prevented by the Nazi-Soviet agreement, which briefly drove Japan to try to resolve disputes with the United States. But the United States insisted that the Japanese evacuate China, so full reconciliation was impossible. Meanwhile, early German successes in the European war and Japanese realization that expansion in the Pacific would pit them against the United States combined to argue for a more formal alliance. A Tripartite Pact was signed by Germany, Japan, and Italy in September 1940. In fact, Japan and Germany never collaborated closely.

Notably, Japan refused to participate in Germany's ultimate war with the Soviet Union, despite long-standing opposition to Russian strength. Nevertheless, the union of the aggressor states, however hollow in practice, seemed to align the powers of the world between those on the attack and those legitimately on the defense—a symbolism particularly influential for the United States.

As war broke out from 1937 to 1939, the powers most interested in preserving the status quo remained unprepared, hopeful that war could be deflected by talk and concessions. France and Britain continued to feel the debilitating effects of World War I and were not eager for another conflict. Depression-induced tensions made it difficult to agree on any active policy, and political leftists and conservatives even disagreed over which was the greater enemy, Germany or the Soviet Union. The United States was less polarized, but eager to maintain its policy of isolationism in order not to complicate the delicate process of constructing a new set of government programs to fight the depression. Only by late 1938 did Western leaders begin to admit that war was likely, launching some measures of military preparedness including army expansion and aircraft production. Britain took the lead here, and its efforts proved vital in allowing successful defense of the nation in the first stages of the war with Germany, but the Western effort was too little and too late to stop war itself.

THE COURSE OF THE WAR: JAPAN'S ADVANCE AND RETREAT

The background to World War II made it obvious that war would be fought in two major centers—the Pacific and the European regions, the latter spilling over into North Africa and the Middle East. The background also made it inevitable that the first years of the war would feature almost unremitting German and Japanese success against ill-prepared opponents. Only in 1942 and 1943 did the tide begin to change, based on the fact that the powers that had been drawn into war were essentially more powerful, economically and in population size, than their ambitious taunters.

The bitter war in Asia, pitting Japan against the United States with Britain in an important supporting role, followed a fairly simple course of thrust and counterthrust. Stalemated in China, Japan used the outbreak of war in Europe as an occasion to turn its attention to other parts of Asia. It seized Indochina from France's troops. The alliance with Germany and Italy, along with continued expansion in Southeast Asia as the Japanese attacked Malaya and Burma, put the Japanese on a collision course with the United States, which as a Pacific power was unwilling to

The Main Theaters of World War II

allow Japan to become a predominant force in the Far East. United States' holdings in Hawaii and the Philippines, plus American attempts to withhold materials necessary to Japan's war economy, convinced Japanese leaders that a clash was inevitable. Negotiations with the United States broke down with American insistence that Japan renounce all gains acquired since 1931. It was in this setting that the Japanese attacked Pearl Harbor on December 7, 1941, and then in the following months seized American

Japan's military buildup included marine machine-gun squads such as this one in occupied Shanghai, China.

possessions in the eastern Pacific, including the Philippine Islands. Only toward the end of 1942 did the United States begin to gain the initiative, using its greater numbers and superior level of industrialization. Scattered islands were reconquered in 1943, and the Philippines were regained in 1944, while massive air raids began an onslaught on Japan itself. Meanwhile American, British, and Chinese forces continued to tie down a considerable Japanese army on the Asian mainland.

GERMANY OVERREACHES

In Europe the early years of World War II carried key trends of the 1930s toward even deeper tragedy. Germany seemed unstoppable and the Western democracies suffered accordingly. German strategy focused on the *blitzkrieg*, or "lightning war," involving rapid movement of troops, tanks, and mechanized carriers. With this the Germans crushed Poland and, after a brief lull, pushed early in 1940 into Denmark and Norway. The next targets were Holland, Belgium, and France, with invasion prepared by massive bombardments of civilian targets. Rotterdam, for example, was flattened at the cost of 40,000 lives.

German dynamism was matched, again as in the 1930s, by Allied weakness. France fell surprisingly quickly, partly because the French were unprepared for war and reliant on

These Japanese soldiers were captured by Chinese forces in the interior of China after a bitter battle in 1942.

an outdated defensive strategy, and partly because French troops were quickly demoralized due to the deep tensions within their own society. By the summer of 1940 most of France lay in German hands, while a semifascist collaborative regime, based in the city of Vichy, ruled the remainder. Only Britain stood apart, able to withstand Hitler's air offensive and win the contest for its skies known as the Battle of Britain. Imaginative air force tactics combined with solid new leadership, under a coalition government headed by Winston Churchill, as well as the iron resolve on the part of British citizens to resist the devastating air raids. Hitler's hopes for a British collapse were dashed.

In 1940 Germany controlled the bulk of the European continent. It aided its ally, Italy, in a conquest of Yugoslavia and Greece. It moved into North Africa to press British and French holdings. Conquered territories were forced to supply materials, troops, and compulsory slave labor to the German war machine. Hitler also stepped up his campaign against the Jews, aiming at a "final solution" that meant mass slaughter in Germany as well as its tribute territories. Even as Germany ground out its war effort, it forced six million Jews from all parts of Europe into concentration camps and gas chambers. This holocaust was the most shocking aspect of the war, an attempt at genocide on an unprecedented scale.

The balance in the war began to shift slightly in 1941. Blocked from invasion of Britain, Hitler turned toward the tempting target of Russia, viewed as an inferior Slavic state in Nazi racial ideology. Germany's attack began in June, all pretense of alliance abandoned, and the Germans easily penetrated into central Russia. Yet the Soviet forces, while giving ground amid massive loss of life, did not collapse. They moved back, relocating Soviet industry eastward. As with Napoleon's invasion attempt over a century before, weather also came to the Russians' aid, as a harsh winter caught the Germans off guard, counting on another quick victory. As in Britain, civilian morale in Russia greatly aided the war effort, and although German forces continued to advance through 1942, the knockout blow eluded them. The invasion attempt also stretched German resources very thin, revealing how ill-prepared Hitler's economy was for a long-haul effort and how inefficient the economy was in many aspects of war production.

Late 1941 also brought the United States' entry into the war, spurred initially by the Japanese attack on Pearl Harbor, which in fact took place against German wishes. The United States' leadership had already supported Britain with loans and supplies, and they now eagerly used the bombing of Pearl Harbor to enter the war in Europe and Asia against what seemed a clear threat to Western democracy, perhaps to Western civilization itself. American involvement, delayed because of lack of full prior preparation, began to make itself felt in 1942 when American and British forces challenged the Germans in North Africa. The Soviet Union, in the same year, pushed back an intensive German siege of the city of Stalingrad, which if successful might have opened the way to the Ural Mountains and Russia's new industrial heartland. Over one-third of the German force surrendered, and the Red armies began a gradual push westward that would take them past their own borders, through eastern Europe, and by 1945 deep into Germany itself.

In the meantime, British and American forces moved into the Italian peninsula from North Africa, ousting Mussolini, while also bombing German industrial and civilian targets. Then in 1944 the Allies invaded France, again pushing the Germans back with the aid of French forces hostile to fascism. Amid bitter fighting—Hitler decided to resist as fiercely as possible, goaded in part by Allied insistence that Germany surrender without conditions—the Anglo-American forces gradually surged into western Germany. In late April 1945, Russian and American troops met on the Elbe River. On April 30 Hitler committed suicide in his Berlin bunker, and in the following month German military commanders surrendered their country to the victorious invaders.

Within months after this the war in the Pacific also ended. This conflict had become primarily a duel between Japan and the United States, but British and Chinese forces were also engaged and, after the European theater of operations closed, the Soviet Union turned its attention eastward as well. Japan's surrender was precipitated by

American use of atomic bombs on two cities, Hiroshima and Nagasaki, which forced a full Japanese surrender and a period of American occupation.

HUMAN COSTS

World War II had been a huge killer, with wanton cruelty adding to the effect of unprecedented weapons. Japanese troops in China had killed hosts of civilians, often after torturing them, when they captured cities that had tried to hold out; in Nanking, for example, as many as 300,000 were killed after the city had fallen. Hitler's decision to eliminate Jews throughout Europe led to six million dead in the gas chambers of the Holocaust. Hitler's forces also deliberately attacked civilian centers through bombing raids, in the usually mistaken belief that such destruction would destroy morale. Allied forces, as they became more powerful, paid back in kind. The British air force firebombed the German city of Dresden in retaliation for earlier German raids. Firebombing of Japanese cities led to as many as 80,000 dead in a single raid. The American decision to drop its newly developed atomic bomb on Japan was taken in this atmosphere. American officials wanted to force Japan to surrender without needlessly costly invasion, and they also hurried to prevent Soviet advance in Asia. Bombing of Hiroshima killed over 78,000 civilians, and the raid on Nagasaki two days later also killed tens of thousands. Radiation fallout ultimately killed thousands more, as the new American President, Harry Truman, termed the bombing "the greatest thing in history." Overall, at least 35 million people were killed in the war—20 million in the Soviet Union alone.

ANALYSIS
TOTAL WAR

In the earlier history of civilization—quite clearly by the classical period—the nature of war changed, losing its ritual characteristics and becoming more commonly an all-out battle in which any tactics and weapons that would aid in victory were now countenanced. War, in other words, became less restrained than it had been among more "primitive" peoples who often enjoyed bluff and scare more than all-out violence. All sorts of wars were fought between the classical era and the 20th century, as weapons and military organization changed and varied. Particularly bloody episodes often involved peoples from different cultures, including Westerners battling what they conveniently

regarded as "savages." Sometimes, at the other extreme, a ritual element might return, as in the carefully uniformed parades of troops who fought Europe's battles in the 18th century, recognizing the importance of stylized maneuvers over random bloodshed.

It was the 20th century, however, that most clearly saw the introduction of a fundamentally new kind of war—total war, in which vast resources and emotional commitments of the belligerent nations were marshaled to support military effort. The two world wars were thus novel not only in their geographical sweep, but in their mobilization of the major combatants. The features of total war also fed some regional conflicts later in the 20th century, such as the long Iran-Iraq War in the Middle East in the 1980s. They also colored other forms of struggle, helping to explain brutal guerrilla and terrorist acts among groups not powerful enough to mount total wars but nonetheless affected by their methods and passions.

Total war can be seen as resulting from the impact of industrialization on military effort, reflecting both the technological innovation and the organizational capacity that accompanied the industrial economy from its early stages. Key steps in the development of total war thus emerged in the West from the end of the 18th century onward. The French Revolution, building new power for the state in contact with ordinary citizens, introduced mass conscription of men, forming larger armies than had ever before been possible. New citizen involvement was reflected in incitements to nationalism and stirring military songs including—a new idea itself—aggressive national anthems. Industrial technology was first applied to war on a large scale in the American Civil War. Railroads allowed wider movement of mass armies, while mass-produced guns and artillery made a mockery of earlier cavalry charges and might redefine the kind of personal bravery needed to fight in war.

It was World War I, however, that fully revealed the nature of total war. Steadily more destructive technology included battleships, submarines, tanks, airplanes, poison gas (this theoretically banned by international agreement prior to the war), machine guns, and long-range artillery. Organization for war included not only massive, compulsory recruitment—the draft—but also government control of economic activity, via obligatory planning and rationing, that altered management policy, labor relations, and personal consumption options. It included unprecedented control of media, not only through effective censorship and the jailing of dissidents but through powerful propaganda designed to incite passionate, all-out commitment to the national cause and deep, unreasoned hatred of the enemy. Vivid posters, flaming speeches and outright falsehood combined in the emotional mobilization effort. All of these features returned with a vengeance, of course, in World War II, from the new technology of bombing, rocketry, and ultimately the atomic bomb to the enhanced economic mobilization effort organized by government planners.

The people most affected by the character of total war were the troops themselves, who directly endured—bled from and died from—the new technology. But one measure of total war was a blurring of the distinction between military and civilians, a distinction that had often restrained war's impact earlier in world history. Whole civilian populations, and not just those unfortunate enough to be near front lines, were now forced into certain types of work, urged to certain types of beliefs. The bombing raids, including the German rockets directed against British cities late in World War II, subjected civilians to some of the most lethal weapons available, as many belligerents

deliberately focused attacks on densely populated cities. Correspondingly psychological suffering, though less common among civilians than among frontline soldiers, could arise quite widely in the populations involved in war.

Total war, like any major historical development, had mixed results. Greater government economic direction often included new measures to protect workers and give them a voice on management boards. Labor force mobilization often produced at least temporary breakthroughs for women. And intense efforts to organize technological research often produced side results of more general economic benefit, as in the invention of new materials such as synthetic rubber.

Still, total war was notable especially for its devastation. The idea of throwing all possible resources into a military effort and having the organizational ability and transporta-

This British government cartoon appealed for loans from the public. It shows a simple, almost sportive and jocular war, with a British Tommy confronting a ridiculous German emperor.

tion capacity to do so made war typically more economically disruptive than had been the case before, at least in terms of short-term impact. The possibilities unleashed in total war produced embittered veterans who might vent their anger by attacking established political values. It certainly made postwar diplomacy more difficult. One result of total war was a tendency to be inflexible in negotiations at war's end: People who fought so hard found it difficult to treat enemies generously, and the results of a quest for vengeance often produced new tensions that led directly, and quickly, to further conflict. War-induced passions and disruptions could also spark new violence at home, as crime rates often soared not only right after the war ended (a traditional result), but more durably. Trying to determine how much the passions sparked by total war altered basic processes, such as diplomacy, crime, or even family life, yields a set of key questions about wider aspects of 20th-century history. How much of the nature of life has been determined by the consequences of total war?

Questions: How did being a soldier in a total war differ from being a soldier in a more traditional war? How did the experience of total war affect social and political patterns after the war's end? Why do many historians believe that total war made rational peacetime settlements more difficult than earlier in history?

THE SETTLEMENT OF WORLD WAR II

World War II did not produce the sweeping peace settlement, untidy as it was, that had officially ended World War I. The major Allies opposed to Germany and Japan did meet on several occasions, earnestly trying to construct a peace that would avoid the mistakes of Versailles. There was agreement that a new international organization, the United Nations, should be set up, with better representation than had characterized the League of Nations. The United States pledged to join, and indeed ultimately it housed the United Nations headquarters in New York. The Soviet Union was included, and China (represented by the Nationalist government) attained great power status for the first time in modern history. Britain and France rounded out the key group of great powers that would have a permanent seat on the Security Council—the steering committee for the new organization. Internationalism now moved beyond the conventional Western orbit, though the Western leaders sought to retain dominance. Like the league, the United Nations had as its primary mission pro-

vision of a forum for negotiating disputes, but it also took over the apparatus of more specialized international agencies that addressed world problems in agriculture, labor, and the like.

Beyond agreeing on a new, if ultimately fairly modest, international apparatus, the wartime Allies found it increasingly difficult to reach accord on the shape of the postwar world. Some leaders wanted virtually to destroy Germany's industrial structure, to prevent any recurrence of threat from this quarter, but others held out for milder measures—though all agreed that Hitler's regime must go and that Germany must surrender unconditionally, a stance that may have discouraged some peace movements within the German military. The key problem that emerged involved growing tension between the Soviet Union and the United States along with British representatives who feared Soviet ambitions.

Initial discussions among United States, British, and Soviet governments began in 1942, focusing at first on purely military issues. Heads of the three states met in 1943, in Teheran, Iran, where the Soviet government pressed the Western powers to open a new front in France, which was of course done with the invasion of Normandy in 1944. The decision to focus on France rather than moving up from the Mediterranean in effect gave the Soviet forces a free hand to move through the smaller nations of eastern Europe as they pushed the Nazi armies back. Britain negotiated separately with the Soviets to assure Western preponderance in postwar Greece as well as equality in Hungary and Yugoslavia, with Soviet control of Romania and Bulgaria—but the United States resisted this kind of un-Wilsonian scorn for the rights of small nations.

With the war nearly over, the next settlement meeting took place in Yalta in the Soviet Crimea early in 1945. Franklin Roosevelt of the United States was eager to press the Soviet Union for assistance against Japan, and to this end the Soviets were promised important territorial gains in Manchuria and the northern Japanese islands. The organization of the United Nations was confirmed. As to Europe, however, agreement was more difficult. The three powers easily arranged to divide Germany into four occupation zones (liberated France getting a chunk), which would be disarmed and purged of Nazi influence. Britain, however, resisted Soviet zeal to eliminate German industrial power, seeing a viable Germany as a potential ally in a subsequent Western-Soviet contest. Bitter disagreement also raged over the smaller nations of Eastern Europe. That they should be friendly to their Soviet neighbor was uncontested, but the Western leaders also wanted them to be free and democratic. Stalin, the Soviet leader, had to make some concessions by including noncommunist leaders in what was already a Soviet-controlled government in liberated Poland—concessions that he soon violated.

The final postwar conference occurred in Potsdam, a Berlin suburb, in July 1945. Russian forces now occupied not only most of Eastern Europe but eastern Germany as well. This de facto situation prompted agreement that the Soviet Union could take over much of what had been eastern Poland, with the Poles gaining part of eastern Germany in compensation. Germany was divided pending a final peace treaty (which was not to come for over 40 years). Austria was also divided and occupied, gaining unity and independence only in 1956 on condition of neutrality between the United States and the Soviet Union. Amid great difficulty, treaties were worked out for Germany's other allies, including Italy, but the United States and, later, the Soviet Union signed separate treaties with Japan.

All these maneuvers had several results. Japan was occupied by the United States. Its wartime gains were stripped away, and even Korea, taken earlier, was freed—but divided between United States and Soviet zones of occupation (the basis for the North-South Korea division still in effect today). Former Asian colonies were returned to their old "masters," though often quite briefly as new independence movements quickly challenged the control of the weakened imperialist powers. China regained most of its former territory, though here too stability was quickly challenged by renewed fighting between communist and Nationalist forces within the nation, aided by the Soviet Union and the United States, respectively.

The effort to confirm old colonial regimes applied also to the Middle East, India, and Africa. Indian and African troops had fought for Britain during the war, though Britain imprisoned key nationalist leaders and put independence plans on hold. African leaders had participated constructively in the French resistance to its authoritarian wartime government. The Middle East and North Africa had been shaken by German invasions and Allied counterattacks. Irritability increased, and so did expectations for change. With Europe's imperial powers further weakened by their war effort, adjustments seemed inevitable, as in those parts of Asia invaded by the Japanese.

In Europe the boundaries of the Soviet Union pushed westward, with virtually all the losses after World War I erased. Independent nations created in 1918 were for the most part restored (though the former Baltic states of Latvia, Lithuania, and Estonia became Soviet provinces because they had been Russian provinces before World War I). Except for Greece and Yugoslavia, the new nations

The World after World War II

quickly fell under Soviet domination, with communist governments forced upon them and Soviet troops in occupation. The nations of Western Europe were free to set up or confirm democratic regimes, but most of them lived under the shadow of growing United States influence, manifested in continued occupation by American troops, substantial economic aid and coordination, and no small amount of outright policy manipulation.

The stage was set, in other words, for two of the great movements that would shape the ensuing decades in world history: the challenges by subject peoples to the tired vestiges of control by the great European empires—the movement known as decolonization that in a few decades would create scores of new nations in Asia, Africa, and the West Indies; and the confrontation between the two great powers that emerged from the war, the United States and the Soviet Union, each with new international influence and new military might. This confrontation was dubbed the "cold war," and many believed it would soon become a war in a more literal and devastating sense. That these trends constituted a peace settlement was hard to imagine in 1945 or 1947, yet they seemed the best that could be done.

CONCLUSION

A BRUTAL TRANSITION, 1914–1945

The framework for world history established through the two world wars and the Great Depression was only that—a framework. It must be explored by more detailed consideration of developments in key individual areas during the first half of the 20th century. Understanding of the framework itself requires more detailed probing. War and depression, for example, did not inevitably produce the horrors of Nazism in Germany; other factors must be explored even in the connections between war, depression, and renewed war.

The consequences of the war-torn international framework must also be explored by probing the major trends of the century's second half, which were by no means all anticipated by the tense war settlement that emerged after 1945. Then, after examining individual regions of the world both before and after 1945, we can return to the question of the kind of overarching global context that has taken shape in recent decades—a context that is freer from the ascending spiral of disaster that seemed to engulf the world between 1914 and 1945.

The best way to capture the essential results of the many events that marked the first half of the 20th century is to view them as part of an exceedingly painful transition from Western world dominance to a different kind of world order. Whether this transition would have occurred had the major powers of Europe not tried twice to destroy each other, oblivious to the impact on their wider world role, cannot be determined. Certainly the transition would not have occurred so quickly.

The world wars weakened and distracted the nations that had long formed the core of Western civilization. They allowed new powers—the United States and the Soviet Union, as well as Japan despite the crushing defeat in 1945—to gain new roles. They allowed new independence movements and revolutionary uprisings. The Japanese forces that invaded Vietnam, the Philippines, and Indonesia during the early 1940s were often cordially detested by their new subjects, but they did teach that the Western overlords could be defeated and that a nonwhite people could put the West on the run. The lessons were important in supporting nationalist demands that had already stirred. World wars and depression broke the political framework western Europe had established during the preceding century, without at all restoring what had been before; and they dented, though less simply and decisively, the older

Western-dominated world economic framework as well. The major events of the decades after 1914 constituted the death throes of one world order and the bloody birth pains of a new one.

This is why, for each of the individual societies still operating during the 20th century, a set of common questions can be asked. How did world wars and resultant international rebalancing affect the society? What was the impact of depression in shaping new political and social responses?

Yet the world wars, particularly, had one further long-range result beyond stirring new expectations and resentments and reducing Europe's world role. They also raised the specter of war itself to a new level.

Two world wars in a single generation had to haunt the world's people in 1945, particularly those in Europe, China, Japan, the Soviet Union, and even the United States (spared direct combat on its own soil) who had lived through one or both wars so directly. The lack of complete settlement after World War II was profoundly troubling as well, because it resulted from the almost immediate crescendo of a new conflict between the United States and the Soviets. Finally, war had become increasingly terrible, its destructive power mounting with every passing year. Again, the end of World War II, with the inauguration of the two atomic bombs dropped on Japan, could only stir a feeling of dread. Even optimistic Americans went through at least six years of pressing anxiety, as they tried to come to terms with the nuclear monster they had created.

Yet the end of World War II brought new leadership to almost every part of the globe as a result of new elections, toppling of colonial regimes, the discrediting of defeated governments, and a new revolutionary surge in China. Many new leaders vowed to undo some of the mistakes of the past, though they disagreed profoundly over what the mistakes had been and how they should be remedied. How new leadership confronted the issues that had brought depression and war to world dominance during the first half of the 20th century raises another set of questions that must be addressed to almost every major society in exploring its most recent history.

FURTHER READINGS

A number of important books have dealt with the origins of World War I. L. Lafore's *The Long Fuse* (1965) is a very readable introduction; see also James Joll's *Origins of World War I* (1984), which is slightly more up to date. A controversial interpretation is F. Fischer's *Germany's Aims in the First World War* (1967); see also P. Kennedy's *The Rise of the Anglo-German Antagonism 1860–1914* (1980). I. Geiss's *July 1914* (1967) is a collection of documents on the subject.

For a wider perspective, G. Barraclough's *An Introduction to Contemporary History* (1968) is extremely interesting. On the war's cultural impact, P. Fussell's *The Great War and Modern Memory* (1975) is a brilliant treatment. See also R. J. Sontag's *A Broken World, 1919–1939* (1971) for a survey of the period, mainly dealing with Europe. On the war itself see K. Robbins's *The First World War* (1984); see also J. Williams's *The Other Battleground: The Home Fronts, Britain, France, and Germany, 1911–1918* (1972) and R. Wohl's *The Generation of 1914* (1979). On the peace settlement, see A. J. Mayer's *The Politics and Diplomacy of Peacemaking* (1968).

On the depression, C. Kindleberger's *The World in Depression, 1929–1939* (1973), is a solid introduction. See also J. Galbraith's *The Great Crash of 1929* (1980) and, for a useful collection of articles, W. Laqueur and G. L. Mosse, eds., *The Great Depression* (1970). Japan's experience is covered in I. Morris, ed., *Japan, 1931–1945: Militarism, Fascism, Japanism?* (1963).

A good introduction to World War II is Gordon Wright's *The Ordeal of Total War, 1939–1945* (1968); see also W. Murray's *The Change in the European Balance of Power* (1984). On the war itself, see B. H. Liddell Hart's *History of the Second World War*, vol. 2 (1971). The United States' role is the subject of R. A. Divine's *The Reluctant Belligerent: American Entry into World War II* (1979). On the Asian front, see J. H. Boyle's *China and Japan at War, 1937–1945* (1972) and R. Butow's *Japan's Decision to Surrender* (1954). See also S. Ienaga's *The Pacific War* (1978) and Chi Hsi-sheng's *Nationalist China at War* (1982).

On the war's immediate aftermath, see H. Feis's *From Trust to Terror: The Onset of the Cold War, 1945–1950* (1970) and Martin Sherwin's *A World Destroyed: The Atomic Bomb and the Grand Alliance* (1975). For a more general assessment of war's role in the 20th century, see Raymond Aron's *Century of Total War* (1985).

1918–1923 Postwar adjustments; new republic in Germany; economic recession and
recovery; emergence of communist movement

1933–1957 New Deal
in United States

1947–1974 Decolonization

1933 Hitler becomes
chancellor of Germany

1947–1960s Emergence and
most intense phase of cold war

1930 Rapid rise of Nazi party

1945 End of World War II

1936 Popular
Front govern-
ment in France

1945–1948 New constitutions in Italy,
Germany, and France; Labour party victory
in Britain; basic measures of welfare states

1925 Locarno agreements regularize Germany's diplomatic relations

1942 Hitler decides on extermination of European Jews

1922 Mussolini takes power in Italy

1947 Marshall Plan

1948 Publication of *The Second Sex*

1935 Nuremberg laws deprive German Jews of citizenship

1928 Kellogg-Briand Pact

1948 East and West German regimes established

1938 Attacks on Ger-
man Jews increase

1949 North Atlantic Treaty Organization established

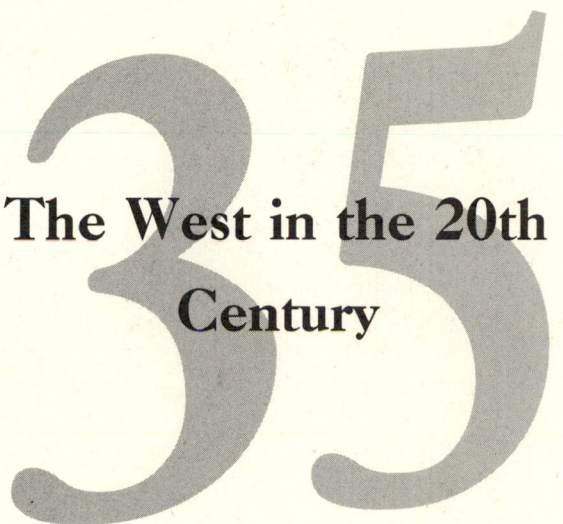

The West in the 20th Century

INTRODUCTION. The theme of Western history during the last part of the 19th century was a new consolidation of political and social forms as the industrialization process matured. Tensions among social classes worked in part within the existing system, while the state took on new functions that met some pressing needs and also allowed new kinds of discipline through schools and military recruitment.

With the shock of World War I and its unsettling results, the consolidation focus was replaced by new confusions, bordering on the chaotic. The three decades after 1914 are among the most troubled in Western history. Political forms that had seemed so successful, revolving around some kind of representative institutions, were cast aside in favor of new radical regimes, or simply stopped functioning with any efficacy. Cultural emphases dating from the Enlightenment and building on beliefs in human rationality were challenged by new movements that deliberately appealed to the vicious and impulsive traits in human nature.

During the decades between the world wars, conflicts and paralysis within western Europe encouraged the development of new challenges to the West's world supremacy. European power within Western civilization also declined, in favor of the surging United States—which, however, was not ready to take a leadership role directly. These rebalancing effects within the West, and for the West in the world, proved durable and were only enhanced by the results of renewed struggle during World War II.

1979 Thatcher and new conservatism in Britain

1960s Civil rights movement in U.S.

1973, 1979 Oil crises

1981 Reagan president in U.S.

1958 De Gaulle's Fifth Republic in France

1970s Democratic regimes in Spain, Portugal, and Greece

1992 End of economic restrictions within Common Market

1957 Establishment of European Economic Community (Common Market)

1968–1973 Massive student protests

1979 Significant recession

1960s Emergence of new feminist movement

Other elements of the West's interwar experience, however, proved less persistent. The dominant events of world history between 1914 and 1945 did not set a rigid framework for the internal development of the West thereafter. Western society, both in Europe and the United States, found new sources of dynamism after 1945 as older themes combined with new departures in politics, while a new economic and social structure was gradually developed. The West was hardly problem-free in the decades after World War II, among other things because adjustments to its new world position raised uncertainties and concrete issues. But the level of conflict and confusion was far less great, with a newly constructive spirit dominating the 1950s and 1960s, and people responding positively in the workplace to this constructive strain.

Western history in the 20th century thus divides into two periods in which marked deterioration contrasts with considerable resurgence. Western history was dominated, between 1914 and 1945, by the impact or imminence of wars and depression, but somewhat surprisingly it shook off much of this context after 1945. Despite the West's decline in the world at large—a decline partially balanced by the emergence of the United States as a world power—Western patterns continued to play a disproportionate role in world affairs. The West's problems during the 1920s and 1930s gave other regions an opportunity to assert new independence. Western revival after 1945, while it did not stem the loss of colonies, maintained the West as a pacesetter in culture, technology, and to a degree in political style. Thus, even in a period of world history when the West lost its 19th-century preeminence, it is logical to begin the examination of recent world patterns by examining the recent, and oddly complex, evolution of this civilization.

Western development, particularly since the late 1940s, reminds us that the West's position in the world has slipped only relatively during the 20th century, given new economic competition from the Pacific Rim states and the independence and regional political strength of many former colonies. Important adjustments occurred in diplomatic and political forms that, despite many new problems, greatly heightened the West's internal strengths. Both the United States (plus Canada, Australia, and New Zealand) and the leading nations of Western Europe displayed considerable flexibility in dealing with major political and economic issues. The West also continued to provide leadership in scientific research and in the elaboration of popular consumer culture. In these various areas Western patterns continued to have influence well beyond the borders of the civilization itself.

THE WEST'S DISARRAY, 1914–1945

World War I quickly shattered the confidence many Europeans had maintained around the turn of the century. It also brought serious structural damage to the European economy, diplomatic relations among Western states, and political systems in many individual countries.

While the ultimate effects of World War I involved Europe's world position, it also brought tremendous dislocation within Europe, and though some of the damage was quickly repaired, much persisted for the subsequent two decades. The key battlegrounds for four bloody years had been in Europe. The sheer rate of death and maiming, as well as the frustration of nearly four years of virtual stalemate, had a devastating material and psychological impact on the European combatants. More than ten million Europeans had died. In key countries, such as Britain, France, and Germany, the percentage killed had a serious demographic impact, reducing the number of young men available. Vast amounts of property had been destroyed. Most governments had failed to tax their populations enough to pay for the war effort—lest they weaken domestic support—so huge debts accumulated, leading to inflationary pressure even before the war was over. Key prewar regimes were toppled when the German emperor abdicated and the Habsburg Empire collapsed.

THE ROARING '20s

Despite all the disruptions, a brief period of stability, even optimism emerged in the mid-1920s. Diplomatic tensions eased somewhat within Europe, as Germany made some moves to accommodate its reduced position in return for partial relief from the reparations payments. While Germany refused definitively to accept its new eastern boundaries, it did promise friendship all around. Hopes that the Versailles settlement could be permanent ran so high that an American and a French leader coauthored a treaty outlawing war forever (the Kellogg-Briand Pact of 1928, which a number of nations dutifully ratified)—a sign of the shallow hopes of the decade.

Internal politics also seemed to calm. The war's end and immediate economic dislocations, plus the impact of the Russian Revolution, had inspired a new political polarization in many countries. Many veterans joined groups on the far right that wanted an authoritarian government and recovery of national honor; the labor movement on the left split, with a minority wing becoming communist, taking cues from the revolutionary regime in the Soviet Union. Both radical factions scared each other, further complicating parliamentary life. Germany produced an admirable constitution for its new democratic republic, but many groups did not accept it and there were understandable fears for its life. Even Britain, long known for its political stability, saw a major shift as the Labour party replaced the Liberals as the second major political force. Generally, the liberal middle sector of European politics was weakened. Nevertheless, the middle years of the 1920s brought a brief respite, as the extremist groups declined in force. Few leaders of great stature emerged, as even in the United States a series of colorless presidents captured the political timidity of the decade.

Economic prosperity buoyed hopes in the middle of the decade. The worst inflationary pressures were resolved at the cost of wiping out the value of savings for many propertied groups. Industrial production boomed, though more markedly in the United States than in western Europe. Mass consumption standards rose for several years. New products such as rayon, an artificial fiber, and radios spread widely. Particularly in the United States, the automobile

This magazine cover by John Held, Jr., depicts the coed of 1926 as a combination of sweetness and sophistication.

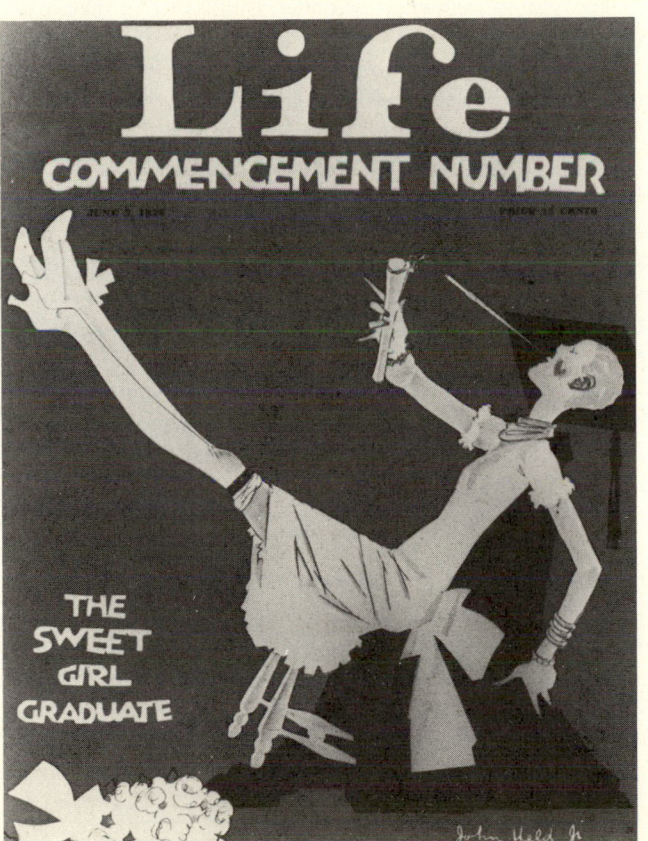

became a mass consumption item, with effects ranging from reducing rural isolation to changing teenage dating habits. Household appliances proliferated, as technology's impact on daily life reached a new level.

Finally, the 1920s saw a burst of cultural creativity in many parts of the West. Filmmakers experimented with this genre for artistic expression as well as mass entertainment. Modern artists developed geometrical cubist styles and other innovations. Writers and playwrights pioneered new forms, reducing plot lines and, in the case of drama, often seeking audience involvement. In retrospect the mood of the 1920s, in terms of high culture and popular culture alike, seemed somewhat frenzied, as if people sought escape from the tragic destiny that awaited. There was, however, no denying major new strides in art and science, as well as a significant development of mass consumer habits.

Women, particularly in the middle class, registered important change. Women's involvement in the labor force during the war was short-lived as men pushed them out at war's end. However, postwar legislation granted suffrage in Britain, Germany, and the United States. Further, prosperity and the still falling birthrate gave many women the chance to develop new leisure habits and less restrictive fashions. Young women in the United States began to date more freely, as a preliminary to courtship. Wives in Britain wrote of new interests in sexual pleasure, while maintaining commitment to marriage. Here were developments, like the more general rise of consumerism, that would gain momentum later on.

THE DEPRESSION'S IMPACT

All the hopeful signs seemed to vanish with the onset of depression in 1929—and the Great Depression revealed that neither the economic nor the political achievements of the mid-20s had been as solidly based as had been hoped. Political consequences were inevitable, with so many people out of work or threatened. The relatively weak Western governments responded to the onset of the catastrophe counterproductively. National tariffs were raised to keep out the goods of other countries, but this merely worsened the international economy and weakened sales for everyone. Most governments tried to cut spending, because with falling production their own revenues went down. They were concerned about avoiding renewed inflation, but in fact their measures further reduced economic stimulus and pushed additional workers—government employees—out of jobs. Confidence in the normal political process deteriorated. And the depression in many countries heightened political polarization. People sought solutions from radical parties or movements, both on the left and the right. Support for communist parties went up in many countries, and in important cases an authoritarian movement on the radical right gained increased attention. Even in relatively stable countries, such as Britain, battles between conservative and labor movements made decisive policy difficult.

There were a few cases of constructive political response. Scandinavian states, directed by moderate socialist movements, increased government spending, providing new levels of social insurance against illness and unemployment and foreshadowing the modern welfare state. In the United States, Franklin Roosevelt's New Deal, from 1933 onward, enacted a number of social insurance measures and used government spending to stimulate the economy. The New Deal did not cure the American depression, but it alleviated the worst effects and provided new hope that forestalled persistent political pressure against the established order. The New Deal also brought the United States more in line with the government traditions of other Western nations by increasing the power of the state in what had been, by European standards, a rather loosely governed society. Under Roosevelt the government became much more active, regulating banks and other economic activities and sponsoring huge public works. A new social security system provided some assistance to the unemployed and retirees; older people began, correspondingly, to expect less economic support from their families, and more from the state.

In key cases, however, the Great Depression led to one of two effects: a parliamentary system that became increasingly incapacitated, unable to come to grips with the new economic dilemma and too divided to take vigorous action even in more familiar areas such as foreign policy; or the outright overturning of the parliamentary system itself.

France was a prime example of the first pattern. The French government responded sluggishly to the depression. Voters responded to the depression by moving toward political extremes. Socialist and then Communist parties expanded. Rightist movements calling for a strong leader and fervent nationalism grew, often disrupting political meetings in order to discredit the parliamentary system. In response, Liberal, Socialist, and Communist parties allied in a Popular Front in 1936, winning the election. The Popular Front government, however, was unable to take strong measures of social reform because of the ongoing strength of conservative republicans and the authoritarian right. The same paralysis crept into foreign policy, as Popular Front leaders, initially eager to support the new liberal regime in Spain that was attacked by conservative army leaders in the Spanish Civil War, found themselves forced to pull back. The Popular Front fell in 1938, but even before this France was close to a standstill.

FASCISM

In Germany, the impact of the depression led directly to the new fascist regime. Germany had suffered the shock of loss in World War I, enhanced by treaty arrangements that cast blame for the war on the German nation. This was a country in which modern parliamentary traditions were recent and shaky. A number of factors combined to make Germany a breeding ground for fascism, though it took the depression to bring this current to the fore.

Fascism was a product of the war. The movement's advocates, many of them former veterans, attacked the weakness of parliamentary democracy and the corruption and class conflict of Western capitalism. They proposed a strong state ruled by a powerful leader, who would revive the nation's forces through vigorous foreign and military policy. Fascists vaguely promised social reforms to alleviate class antagonisms, and their attacks on trade unions as well as Socialist and Communist parties pleased landlords and business groups. A first fascist regime took power in Italy in 1923, and Fascist parties complicated the political process in a number of other nations during the 1920s and beyond. It was the advent of the National Socialist, or Nazi, regime in Germany under Adolf Hitler that made this new political movement a major force in world history. Here, a modern Western commitment to liberal, democratic political forms was challenged and reversed.

In his vote-gathering campaigns, Hitler repeated standard fascist arguments about the need for unity and the hopeless weakness of parliamentary politics. The state should provide guidance, for it was greater than the sum of individual interests, and the leader should guide the state. Hitler promised many groups a return to more traditional ways; thus many artisans voted for him in the belief that preindustrial economic institutions, such as the guilds, would be revived. Middle-class elements, including big business leaders, were attracted to Hitler's commitment to a firm stance against socialism and communism. Hitler also focused grievances against various currents in modern life, from big department stores to feminism, by attacking Jewish influences in Germany. And he promised a glorious foreign policy to undo the wrongs of the Versailles treaty. Finally, Hitler represented a hope for effective action against the depression. While the Nazis never won a majority vote in a free election, his party did win the largest single slice in 1932, and this enabled Hitler to make arrangements with other political leaders for his rise to power legally in 1933.

Once in power, Hitler quickly set about constructing a *totalitarian* state—that is, a new kind of government that would exercise massive, direct control over virtually all the activities of its subjects. Hitler eliminated all opposition

German Nazis moved the orchestrated mass rally to a high art form, profoundly influencing those who participated as well as those who could feel its power and solidarity through the radio or the movie screen.

parties; he purged the bureaucracy and military, installing loyal Nazis in many posts. His secret police, the *Gestapo*, arrested hundreds of thousands of political opponents. Trade unions were replaced by government-sponsored bodies that tried to appease low-paid workers by offering full employment and various welfare benefits. Government economic planning helped restore production levels, with particular emphasis on armaments construction. Hitler cemented his regime by constant, well-staged propaganda bombardments, strident nationalism, and an incessant attack on Germany's large Jewish minority.

Hitler's hatred of Jews ran deep; he blamed them for various personal misfortunes and also for movements such as socialism and excessive capitalism that in his view had weakened the German spirit. Obviously, anti-Semitism served as a catchall for a host of diverse dissatisfactions, and as such it appealed to many Germans. Anti-Semitism also played into Hitler's hands by providing a scapegoat that could rouse national passions and distract the population from other problems. Measures against Jews became more and more severe, as they were forced to wear special emblems, their property was attacked and seized, and increasing numbers were sent to concentration camps. After 1940 Hitler's policy insanely turned to the literal elimination of European Jewry, as the Holocaust raged in the concentration camps of Germany and conquered territories.

Hitler's foreign and military policies were based on preparation for war. He wanted not only to recoup Germany's World War I losses but to create a land empire that would extend across much of Europe, particularly toward the east against what he saw as the inferior Slavic peoples. Progressively Hitler violated the limits on German armaments and annexed neighboring territories, provoking only weak response from the Western democracies. When war finally resulted in 1939, Hitler's forces pressed forward for three years before his opponents were able to regroup. By late 1942 Soviet armies had recovered from German invasion, with some assistance in the form of armaments from the United States, and pressed inexorably toward Germany's eastern borders. American and British forces, aided by resistance movements against Nazi occupation, drove Germany first from North Africa, then gradually from Italy. In 1944 a massive invasion moved across the English Channel into France, and within a year the Allies entered Germany from the west, finally meeting Soviet forces along the Elbe River—Germany's new divide. Hitler committed suicide, and the war in Europe drew to a close.

The years from one world war through the next read like a tragic drama in Western history. One dire event led almost inexorably to the next, with none of the major participants able to tamper with fate.

PATTERNS IN WESTERN HISTORY, 1914–1945

Amid this sequence of events it is important to discern some key patterns. In the first place, the relentless unfolding of the Western tragedy had three key sources. The escalation of national conflicts, visible already in the later 19th century, was one such source. World War I, creating new grievances and imbalances, simply enhanced this nationalist tension within Western civilization. Secondly, the nature of war now changed, with the advent of total war, and had more sweeping effects on societies involved in combat than earlier wars had done. Propaganda bombarded civilians, often raising false hopes and encouraging new hatreds of foreign enemies as well as internal suspects such as leftists or capitalist profiteers. The economy was massively enmeshed in the war effort, making subsequent recovery difficult. Also, the weaponry of war involved unprecedented capacity to kill and damage. Finally, weaknesses in Western democracy and industrialization, exacerbated by war, came home to roost. From an economic standpoint the Western economies tolerated too much poverty, in addition to depending on exports to poor countries, to be entirely secure: Sales could easily plummet. From a social standpoint a number of groups continued to be suspicious of industrial conditions, eager in a crisis either to attack capitalism in the name of socialism or to urge a return to older values and authority.

Conditions of women, for example, continued to provoke fundamental disagreements from both genders. Some women were delighted with new consumer and life-style opportunities that opened up during the 1920s (along, in many countries, with the right to vote). Women began to smoke and drink in public and to enjoy new dance crazes and other leisure options. Yet other women continued to protest the limitations on women's roles, and particularly their inequality in work opportunities, as a brief wartime surge of female employment was pushed back during the 1920s. These feminist grievances, though less pronounced than before World War I, could feed leftist sentiment. Still other Westerners were aghast at the changes that had arrived, urging that women return to more purely domestic roles and traditional, modest costumes and habits. This sentiment provided some support for fascist movements. The West, in sum, remained deeply affected by the innovations brought by industrialization, and the resultant divisions helped sharpen political dispute.

Industrialization, however, continued to advance. The interwar decades saw continued gains for assembly-line production and big business forms. Huge combines developed in key industries, both in Europe and the United States, while managers learned new ways to coordinate and discipline masses of workers in factories, offices, and sales outlets. Major new product lines developed with artificial fibers and other consumer goods, including British-pioneered television production in the 1930s. In terms of industrial development and big business, Nazi Germany, despite anticapitalist rhetoric, promoted change as well, somewhat ironically weakening many of the more conservative sectors of German society. Capitalist control of industry and marketing advanced under Hitler, further reducing the role of small shops and artisans, while peasant agriculture was squeezed by support for large estates. The Nazi regime did dispute dominant Western cultural trends. It attacked modern art, urging more realistic, heroic styles often in the classical mode, and even challenged scientific education with praise for sports and physical training over intellectual life.

In the main, however, Western culture continued to develop along earlier lines. Fundamental discoveries in physics confirmed the earlier work of Einstein and led to additional work on atomic structure—which Nazi Germany supported because of its relevance to military power—while new discoveries in medicine advanced understanding of tissues and glands. The link between science and progress was confirmed as medicine introduced new inoculations for childhood diseases and new therapies, based at first on sulfa drugs, that greatly reduced the death rates from respiratory disease. The interwar period, in sum, did not see a total reversal of technical and intellectual development, even as dire events accumulated and a special mood of despair gripped Westerners—particularly in Europe—at many social levels.

In most countries occupied by Nazi Germany, resistance movements sprang up during the war to contest the short-lived empire. Resistance fighters in Holland, France, and elsewhere also formulated plans for a new Europe after the war that would redress the social and diplomatic tensions that had bedeviled the West for decades. This resistance spirit was far from fully realized as Europe rebuilt after 1945, but it helps explain some of the West's new directions and unexpected comeback. The first of the following selections comes from a document adopted by the French National Resistance Council in 1944, representing various movements. The second selection contains excerpts from underground newspapers in the previous year.

THE RESISTANCE COUNCIL PLEDGED TO REMAIN UNITED AFTER THE WAR

In order to assure: the establishment of the broadest possible democracy by allowing the people to voice their desires through the reestablishment of universal suffrage; full liberty of thought, conscience and expression; freedom of the press—an honest press, independent of the State, powerful economic interests and foreign influences; freedom of association, freedom to meet and demonstrate; the inviolability of the home and of private correspondence; respect for the individual; absolute equality of all citizens before the law.

In order to effect the necessary reforms:
a. Economic: the establishment of a true economic and social democracy, with the requisite eviction of the great economic and financial feudatories from the direction of the economy; rational organization of the economy, assuring the subordination of special interests to the general interest, and freed from the professional dictatorship installed in the image of the fascist states; the development of national production following a state plan, established after consultation with the representatives of all interested groups; the return to the nation of the great monopolies, fruits of the labor of all, of energy resources, of the underground riches of the country, of the insurance companies and the major banks; the development and support of producers', buyers', and sellers' cooperatives in both agriculture and manufacturing; the right of qualified workers to rise to administrative and management positions in businesses, and workers' participation in the running of the economy.
b. Social: the right to work and the right to leisure, in particular by the reestablishment and the improvement of labor contracts; a major readjustment of wages and the guarantee of a level of wages and working conditions which will assure every worker and his family security, dignity, and the chance of a decent life; a complete social security system, providing all citizens with the means of existence when they are unable to secure it themselves—a system whose management is shared by those concerned and by the State; a meaningful opportunity for all French children to have the benefits of education and access to the best of French culture, whatever their family's financial status, so that the highest positions in society are truly open to all those with the capacity to fill them, thus bringing into being a real elite, of merit rather than of birth, constantly renewed from the people.

FROM LA REVUE LIBRE AND L'ECOLE D'URIAGE, 1943

The visible causes of the war are not the main causes: racist imperialism, megalomania of the totalitarian leaders, etc. All these factors stem from an essential main cause, to wit the need for people to adapt their social and economic organization to the progress of science and technology. . . .

Like it or not, this war is revolutionary, in several senses.

First, it destroys the last vestiges of the decaying capitalist order. . . . Under the Nazi oppression the masses in Europe, long so apathetic, are gradually regaining the taste for liberty. To use their energies we must give this war a goal, which can rouse their enthusiasm, to win their agreement to the construction of a world where they are no longer pariahs, but with the completion of democracy, truly sovereign. . . .

As to France, we think that some kind of Western grouping effected with us, mainly on an economic basis and as extensive as possible, can offer great advantages. Such a grouping, extended in Africa, in close relations with the Orient and notably the Arab states which legitimately seek to unite their interests, and for which the English Channel, the Rhine, the Mediterranean will be like arteries, can constitute a chief center in the worldwide organization of production, exchange and security.

Questions: What did resistance leaders identify as Europe's big problems? How might resistance thinking help explain European recovery after 1945?

AFTER WORLD WAR II: INTERNATIONAL SETTING FOR THE WEST

World War II was fully as total a war as its predecessor, and it left Western Europe in shambles. The sheer physical destruction, caused particularly by bombing raids, disrupted housing and transportation. Downed bridges and rail lines complicated food shipments, leaving many people in places such as France and Germany ill-fed and unable to work at full efficiency. German use of forced foreign labor plus the many boundary changes generated hundreds of thousands of refugees trying to return home or find a new home. For at least two years after 1945, it was unclear that recovery would be possible, as sheer survival proved difficult enough. In the long run, Europe's postwar weakness, after three decades of strife, helped trigger a crescendo of nationalist sentiment directed against the West, plus the fuller emergence of the United States and the Soviet Union, whose size and building industrial strength finally overshadowed Europe's proud nation-states.

EUROPE AND ITS COLONIES

Two larger changes provoked by the war quickly intruded on the West: decolonization and the cold war. Colonies outside Europe, roused by the war, proved increasingly restive. Colonial powers returned where they had been dislodged—such as the British to Malaya and the Dutch to Indonesia—but they found a more hostile climate, with well-organized nationalist resistance. It was soon clear that many colonies could be maintained only at great cost, and in the main the European nations decided that the game was not worth the candle. A few cases proved messy. France tried to defend its holdings in Vietnam against communist guerrillas, yielding only in 1954 after some major defeats. The French clung even more fiercely to Algeria, its oldest African colony, and one with a large European minority. The French military joined Algerian settlers in insisting on a war to the death against nationalist forces, and bitter fighting went on for years. Tension even threatened civil war in France, until a new president, Charles de Gaulle, realized the hopelessness of the struggle and negotiated Algeria's independence in 1962.

Overall, decolonization proceeded more smoothly than in Algeria between the late 1940s and the mid-1970s, without prolonged fighting that might drain the Western nations themselves. Western governments typically retained important cultural relations with their former colonies and sometimes provided administrative and military help as well. Both France and Belgium, for example, frequently intervened in Africa after decolonization was officially complete. Finally, Western economic interests remained strong in most former colonies—particularly in Africa, which exploited mineral and agricultural resources in a pattern of trade not radically different from colonial days.

The impact of decolonization on the West should not, however, be minimized. Important minorities of former settlers and officials came home embittered, though except briefly in France they were not a significant political force. Europe's overt power in the world was dramatically reduced. Efforts by Britain and France to attack independent Egypt in 1956, to protest Egypt's nationalization of the Suez Canal, symbolized the new state of affairs. The United States and the Soviet Union forced a quick end to hostilities, and what was once a colonial lifeline came under non-Western hands. Yet, while decolonization was a powerful change in world affairs, it did not, at least in the short run, overwhelm the West, as neither economic growth nor internal political stability suffered greatly.

THE COLD WAR

The final new ingredient of Europe's diplomatic framework, the cold war between the United States and the Soviet Union, had a more durable ongoing influence on politics and society within the West. The conflict shaped up between 1945 and 1947. The last wartime meetings among the leaders of Britain, the United States, and the Soviet Union had rather vaguely staked out the dimensions of postwar Europe, which were certainly open to varied interpretations. By the war's end Russian troops firmly occupied most Eastern European countries, and within three years the Russians had installed communist regimes to their liking, while excluding opposition political movements. Thus an *eastern bloc* shaped up that included Poland, Czechoslovakia, Bulgaria, Romania, and Hungary. And Soviet boundaries themselves had pushed west, reversing the decisions of the post-World War I Versailles conference. The Baltic states disappeared, and Poland lost territory to Russia, gaining some former German lands as compensation. Finally, Soviet occupation of the eastern zone of Germany gave Russia a base farther toward the heart of Europe than the tsars had ever dreamed possible.

Offended by Russia's heavy-handed manipulation of Eastern Europe, United States and British policymakers tried to counter. The new American president, Harry Truman, was less eager for smooth relations with the Soviets than Franklin Roosevelt had been; he was emboldened by the United States' development in 1945 of the atomic bomb. Britain's wartime leader, Winston Churchill, had long feared communist aggression; it was he in 1946 who coined the phrase *iron curtain* to describe the division between free and repressed societies that he saw taking shape in Europe. But Britain frankly lacked the power to resist Soviet pressure, and under the Labour government it explicitly left the initiative to the United States.

The United States responded to Russia's power plays with vigor. It criticized Russian policies and denied Russian applications for reconstruction loans. It bolstered regimes in Iran, Turkey, and Greece that were under Soviet pressure. In Greece, particularly, Americans took over British resistance to a powerful communist guerrilla campaign. Then in 1947 the United States proclaimed its Marshall Plan, a program of substantial loans that was designed to aid Western nations in rebuilding from the war's devastation. In Soviet eyes, the Marshall Plan was a vehicle for American economic dominance, and indeed there is little question that in addition to humanitarian motives the United States intended to beat back domestic communist movements in countries such as France and Italy by promoting economic growth.

The focal point of the cold war in these early years was in Germany. Soviet policy in Germany initially concentrated on seizing goods and factories as reparation. The Western Allies soon prevented Russian intervention in their own zones and turned to some rebuilding efforts in the interests of playing a modest "German card" against growing Soviet strength in the east. That is, although the West, led by the United States, did not intend to resurrect a powerful Germany, it soon began to think in terms of constructing a viable political and economic entity. Allied collaboration started building a unified West Germany in 1946, and local followed by more national political structures were established through elections. When in 1947 the West moved to promote German economic recovery by creating a stable currency, the Soviet Union responded by blockading the city of Berlin, the divided former capital that sat in the midst of the Russian zone. The United States responded with a massive airlift to keep the city supplied, and the crisis finally ended in 1948, with two separate Germanies—East and West—beginning to take clear shape along a tense, heavily fortified frontier.

Cold war divisions spread from Germany to Europe more generally with the formation of two rival military alliances. The North Atlantic Treaty Organization (NATO) was formed in 1949, under United States' leadership, to group most of the Western European powers plus Canada in a defensive alliance against possible Soviet aggression. The NATO pact soon legitimated some rearmament of West Germany in the context of resistance to communism. It also legitimated the continued maintenance of a substantial United States military presence in Germany and in other member nations. In response, the Soviet Union organized the Warsaw Pact among its Eastern European satellites, and when in 1949 the Soviets developed their own nuclear capability, the world—particularly, the European world—seemed indeed divided between two rival camps, each in turn dominated by its own superpower. Numerous American and Soviet military units were permanently stationed in Europe on either side of the cold war divide.

The cold war had a number of implications for Western Europe. It brought new pressures from the United States on internal as well as foreign policy. Americans pressed, through the 1950s and beyond, for acceptance of German rearmament (though under some agreed-upon limits); it lobbied for higher military expenditures in its old allies France and Britain; and it pressed for acceptance of American forces and weapons systems. The United States' wishes were not always met, but the Americans had vital negotiating leverage in the economic aid they offered (and might withdraw), in the troops they stationed in Europe, and in the nuclear "umbrella" they developed (and might, in theory, also withdraw). The nuclear weapons seemed to offer the only realistic protection should the Soviet Union venture direct attack. The Soviets, for their part, influenced Western Europe not only through perceived aggressive intent, but also by funding and supporting substantial communist movements in France and Italy, which in turn affected but did not overwhelm the political process.

The cold war did not maintain the intensity it reached in its early years. Centers of conflict shifted in part outside Europe as Korea, then Vietnam, and recurrently the Middle East became flashpoints. A few European states, in special circumstances, managed to stay out of strict cold war alignment. Sweden and Switzerland maintained traditions of neutrality; Finland, a capitalist democracy on Soviet borders, was neutral perforce. Austria regained independence in 1956—in a period of lessening cold war dispute—on condition of neutrality; and Yugoslavia, though communist, pulled away increasingly from the Soviet camp. Finally, the main Western powers themselves, once launched on recovery, found increasing room to maneuver. After 1958, France became more and more restive under what it viewed as Anglo-American dominance of NATO, and it finally withdrew its forces from the joint NATO command, requiring also that American troops leave French soil. In the 1970s Germany opened new negotiations with the Soviet Union and eastern bloc countries, toward increasing export opportunities and reducing diplomatic tension.

The fact was that the cold war and the resultant alliance system continued to describe much of the framework of East-West relations in Europe from the end of World War II into the 1990s. France might have gained partial independence from NATO, but it did not withdraw entirely. Although tensions often receded after the high point of the late 1940s, fear of possible Soviet aggression remained; for this reason the United States' military presence was deemed essential by leading policymakers, if not the entire European public. Western Europe could no longer plan on defending itself against a major outside enemy. Although Great Britain and, after 1958, France developed small nuclear capabilities, they simply could not afford the massive stockpiles and rockets of the two superpowers. To some extent, indeed, Western Europeans ultimately grew rather comfortable in their reliance on United States' protection. Not only during the lean postwar recovery years, but even after prosperity returned, European nations kept military budgets relatively modest, compared to United States or Soviet spending, which meant a degree of vulnerability to outside military and diplomatic pressures that had no precedent in modern European history.

A vital feature of this diplomatic realignment obviously involved the rise of the United States to preeminence within the West. This was a development long in the making. America's industrial surge had already brought it new influence by the late 19th century, as key United States firms—Singer sewing machines, for example—quickly established a worldwide base with branches heavily influencing the economies of several European nations. Economic power was enhanced by agricultural exports and, after World War I, the power of American banking and credit. Following World War II, when the dollar became standard international currency, the economic supremacy of the United States among the Western nations seemed assured, and for a time many experts worried that Europe would never regain economic autonomy, doomed always to poor relative status vis-à-vis the giant American cousin. This situation proved temporary, as we will see, but even in the 1980s the economic power of the United States continued to surpass that of Western Europe.

The diplomatic and military ascendancy of the United States showed more checkered progress. The nation flexed its muscles during the First World War but then pulled back; only after 1941 did its full international potential stand revealed. The leadership role played by the United States in the postwar Western alliance—while it produced grievances and protests within Europe from various groups, both conservative nationalists and leftist supporters of nuclear disarmament—was never seriously challenged. The rise of the United States qualified the general pattern of declining world power for the West, though there were those by the late 1980s who argued that this nation, too, had become overcommitted and was destined to pull back. This same rise signaled the reduced status of what had been the Western heartland in Europe and raised questions about whether the West would remain coherent, not just diplomatically but also culturally, under unfamiliar American leadership.

The shifting balance between America and Europe produced a crisscrossing of military relationships, whatever the larger implications of the shift. As Western Europe abandoned military preeminence, the United States, never before a major peacetime military power, devoted growing resources to its military capacity and gave a growing voice to its military leaders. Regardless of the political party in power, the percentage of the United States government budget going to the military remained stable from the 1950s to the 1980s—when it went up. In contrast, some European leaders boasted that their societies had made a transition toward preeminence of civilian values and goals. Although American and European values and institutions became more similar in key respects after World War II, the difference in military roles signaled ongoing distinctions within Western society.

AFTER WORLD WAR II: NEW DIRECTIONS IN THE WEST

While the shifts in the West's external environment triggered by World War II were not catastrophic, they constituted major readjustments. Ironically, Western Europe's domestic development in this same period was considerably more positive, a strong contrast not only to the reduction in world status but also to the massive troubles that had followed World War I. Immediately after the war, Western Europe suffered tremendous dislocation, amid grinding poverty and painful rebuilding, made worse by the new cold war division of the European map and strong fears of a new superpower clash.

Though postwar problems left their mark, Western Europe demonstrated surprising resiliency. A new set of leaders emerged in many countries, some from wartime resistance movements eager to avoid the mistakes that had led to depression and war. While their vision was not always realized, from 1945 onward Western Europe did move forward on three important fronts: the extension of democratic political systems; a modification of nation-state rivalries within Europe; and a commitment to rapid economic growth that reduced previous social and gender tensions.

THE SPREAD OF LIBERAL DEMOCRACY

In politics, defeat in war greatly discredited fascism and other rightist movements that had opposed parliamentary democracy. Vestiges of these movements continued, periodically surfacing in countries such as France and Italy, but rarely with much muscle. At the same time, key leftist groups, including the strong communist movements that emerged from the war in France and Italy, were committed to democratic politics. While social protest continued, outright revolutionary sentiment declined. Finally, several new political movements surfaced, notably an important Christian Democratic current, which was wedded to democratic institutions and moderate social reform. While great national variations existed, in general Western Europe experienced a shift in the political spectrum toward fuller support for democratic constitutions and greater agreement on the need for government planning and welfare activities.

New regimes had to be constructed in Germany and Italy after the defeat of fascist and Nazi leadership, while France established a new republic once occupation ended. In Germany, political reconstruction was delayed by the division of the nation by the victorious Allies. As the cold war took shape, however, France, Britain, and the United States progressively merged their zones into what became the Federal Republic of Germany (West Germany), encouraging a new constitution that would avoid the mistakes of Germany's earlier Weimar Republic by outlawing extremist political movements. The new constitutions set up after 1945 in many European countries, while varied in particulars, uniformly established effective parliaments with universal (now always including female) suffrage. And the

regimes endured. Only France, pressed by the Algerian War, changed its constitution in 1958, forming a Fifth Republic, still democratic but with stronger presidential authority.

Western Europe's movement toward more consistent democracy was extended in the 1970s when Spain and Portugal shifted from their authoritarian, semifascist constitutions, following the deaths of longtime strongmen to democratic, parliamentary systems. Greece, increasingly linked to the West, followed the same pattern. By the 1980s Western Europe had become more politically uniform than ever before in history. Party dominance shifted, with conservatives including Christian Democrats alternating with Socialist coalitions, but all major actors agreed on the constitutional system itself.

THE WELFARE STATE

The consolidation of democracy also entailed a general movement toward a welfare state. Resistance ideas and the shift leftward of the political spectrum helped explain the new activism of the state in economic policy and welfare issues. Wartime planning in the British government had pointed to the need for new programs to reduce the impact of economic inequality and to reward the lower classes for their loyalty. Not surprisingly, the governments that emerged at the war's end—Britain's Labour party and communist-socialist-Christian Democrat coalitions in France and Italy—quickly moved to set up a new government apparatus that would play a vigorous role in economic planning and develop new social activities as well. By 1948 the basic nature of the modern welfare state had been established throughout Western Europe, as not only the new regimes but also established reformists (as in Scandinavia) extended a variety of government programs. The United States, though somewhat more tentative in welfare measures, added to its New Deal legislation in the 1960s, under President Lyndon Johnson's *Great Society* programs, creating medical assistance packages for the poor and the elderly. Canada enacted a still more comprehensive medical insurance plan.

The welfare state elaborated a host of social insurance measures. Unemployment insurance was improved. Medical care was supported by state-funded insurance or, as in Britain where it became a centerpiece to the new Labour program, the basic health-care system was nationalized. State-run medical facilities provided free care to the bulk of the British population from 1947 onward, although some small fees were later introduced. Family assistance was another category, not entirely new, that was now greatly expanded. All Western European governments provided payments to families with several children, the amount increasing with family size. Because the poor now tended to have the largest families, family-aid programs both encouraged population growth—of particular concern to countries such as France—and helped redistribute some of the general tax revenues toward the neediest groups. In the 1950s a French worker's family with low earnings and five children (admittedly an unusual brood by this point) could improve its income by as much as 40 percent through family aid. Governments also became more active in the housing field—a virtual necessity given wartime destruction and postwar population growth. Britain embarked on an ambitious program of *council housing,* providing many single-family units that deliberately mixed working-class and middle-class families in new neighborhoods. By the 1950s over one-fourth of the British population was housed in structures built and run by the government.

The welfare state that emerged in the postwar years was a compromise product. It recognized a substantial private sector and tried to limit and cushion individual initiative rather than replace it with state action alone as in the communist system. It provided aid for citizens at many income levels. Middle-class people might benefit from family assistance, and they certainly used state medical insurance. They also disproportionately benefited from the expanded educational systems and university scholarships that developed along with the welfare state. In other words, although the welfare state focused particularly on problems of workers and the poor, it won support from other groups by dealing with some of their special needs as well.

Relatedly, although some aspects of the welfare state redistributed income, the welfare state did not generally make a huge dent on Western Europe's unequal class system. Though taxes rose, they were not always steeply graduated. Furthermore, starting with France, a supplementary tax system was installed, beginning in the late 1950s, that was not graduated at all. This "value-added" tax system, which quickly spread through Europe, levied taxes on each stage of the production process, operating essentially as a super-sales tax ultimately paid by consumers.

The welfare state was, in sum, an important new definition of government functions, but hardly a device for social revolution. It cushioned citizens against big expenses and unusual hardships, rather than rearranging overall social structure. It protected the purchasing power of the very poor against catastrophe, and it contributed to improved health conditions generally. It also, of course, increased contacts between government and citizen, and it produced a host of new regulations that framed European life.

Despite many criticisms from both the left and the right, the welfare state initially seemed to win wide acceptance. The British, for example, became quickly attached to their new health system, making major revision impossible. For the most part political debate centered on tinkering with the welfare state, not revolutionizing it in any particular direction. Socialist parties, when in power, extended welfare measures by improving their coverage and benefits. Conservative parties, for their part, often cut back a bit and promised more efficient administration. Into the 1970s, no major political movement attacked the new state root and branch.

The welfare state was undeniably expensive. It greatly expanded government bureaucracies, in addition to channeling tax monies to new purposes. By the 1950s, up to 25 percent of the gross national product of countries such as France or Holland was going to welfare purposes, and the figure tended to rise with time. As military expenses began to stabilize, welfare commitments became far and away the largest component of Western government budgets outside the United States. Here was a clear indication of the extent to which the Western European state had altered its relationship to the wider society.

An increased governmental role in economic policy paralleled the welfare state. Most postwar governments nationalized some sectors of industry outright. Most European countries also set up new planning offices, responsible for developing multiyear economic projections and for setting goals and the means to meet them. By coordinating tax concessions and directing the flow of capital from state banks, government planners had genuine power to shape, although not directly to run, economic activity. Planning extended to agriculture as well as industry. Planning offices regulated crop sizes and encouraged consolidation of land for greater efficiency, and they could require farmers to participate in cooperatives that would improve marketing and purchasing procedures.

Planning involved European governments more directly than ever before in commitments to economic growth, full employment, and avoidance of damaging recessions. It was also aimed at improving the economic development of laggard regions. Italy thus tried to direct increasing industrialization toward the south while France industrialized toward the west, in both cases with partial success.

Of the Western nations, only the United States shunned an economic planning office, though it maintained government regulation of the financial system. American government growth consisted more of expanding military activities and piecemeal welfare measures, though American elections, like European, usually hinged on the electorate's judgment of how well the nation was doing economically.

Despite important variations, the role of the state loomed unprecedentedly large throughout the West from the 1940s onward. A new breed of bureaucrat, often called a *technocrat* because of intense training in engineering or economics and because of a devotion to the power of national planning, came to the fore in the offices of the government. Some state initiatives undoubtedly reflected the potential overzealousness of the new breed. Housing authorities forced workers out of old but comfortable slums into anonymous high-rise structures that, however elegant on paper, never felt right to residents. Peasants, no friend of distant central governments even before, often lamented heavy-handed requirements. Yet here too, as with the welfare state, no particularly coherent political disputes took shape, at least until the 1960s. The new state seemed to work well enough that it was difficult to attack categorically.

POLITICAL STABILITY AND THE QUESTION MARKS

The fact was that big, contentious political issues were notable for their absence through most of Europe during the 1950s and 1960s, except for the polarizing experience of the Algerian War in France. Reformist governments of the immediate postwar years tended to give way to more conservative regimes during the 1950s. Labour, for example, lost the 1951 election in Britain and, even earlier, communists had been forced out of coalitions in France and Italy. But the conservative regimes were generally content to support the existing definition of state functions. Also, when socialist or labor governments gained renewed access to power, as in Britain in the 1960s, they too, typically, had no dramatic new programs to offer. For better or worse, Europeans seemed to accept the state's new social and economic role as well as its constitutional structure. Political debates were often fierce, and partisan loyalties intense, but few sweeping issues were raised.

The Western pattern of political compromise around the mechanisms of parliamentary democracy and the welfare state were, however, severely jolted by a series of student protests that developed in the late 1960s. Even before this, in the United States a vigorous civil rights movement had developed to protest unequal treatment of African Americans. Massive demonstrations, particularly in southern cities, attacked segregation and limitations on African-American voting rights.

Campus unrest was a Western-wide phenomenon in the 1960s. At major American universities, campus unrest focused on the nation's involvement in the war in Vietnam. Young people in Europe and the United States also targeted the materialism of their societies, including the stodginess of the welfare state, seeking more idealistic goals and greater justice. Student uprisings in France in 1968 created a near revolution. By the early 1970s, new rights for students as well as other reforms, combined with police repression, ended the most intense student protests, while passage of civil rights legislation in the United States ultimately reduced urban rioting and demonstrations. The flexibility of postwar Western democracy seemed triumphant. Some additional political concerns, including a new

During the civil rights movement in the United States, African-American leaders pressed for voting rights and other movements toward legal and educational equality through vivid demonstrations. Here, a voter registration drive in 1965 features a march from Selma to Montgomery, Alabama.

wave of feminism focusing on economic rights and dignity for women and environmentalist movements, entered the arena during the 1970s, partly as an aftermath of the student explosion. The rise of the Green movement in several countries in the 1970s signaled a new political tone, hostile to uncontrolled economic growth; Green parliamentary deputies in Germany refused even to wear coats and ties in their efforts to defy established political habits.

Observers in many countries speculated that a shift in basic political alignments might be in the making if old parties failed to deal adequately with the new issues. In some West European countries, also, a terrorist movement, targeting political and business leaders, caused recurrent anxiety. As economic growth slowed in the 1970s, and the Western world faced its greatest economic recession since the immediate postwar years, other signs of political change emerged. New leadership sprang up within the British Conservative party and the United States Republican party. In 1979 British Conservative leader Margaret Thatcher began the longest-running prime-ministership in history, working to cut welfare and housing expenses and to promote free enterprise. Neither she nor her American counterpart, Ronald Reagan, fully dismantled the welfare state, but they did reduce its impact.

Despite all the portents of change, however, the main lines of postwar government persisted into the 1990s. Democratic institutions often failed to command great excitement, as voting levels went down throughout the West (particularly in the United States), but they roused no widespread, coherent resistance either. New political movements, while interesting, had yet to dislodge mainstream Conservative and Socialist (or, in the United States, liberal) parties. The Western world has unquestionably remained freer from major political upheavals than have most other civilizations in the postwar decades, and freer than Western society itself had been during the 1920s and 1930s. Has Western society achieved a durable new harmony, or were the postwar decades a period of deceiving tranquility before some yet-to-be-defined storm?

THE DIPLOMATIC CONTEXT

Along with the extension of democracy and the development of the welfare state, the West showed postwar vigor in addressing some traditional diplomatic problems, notably the recurrent bugbear of nationalistic rivalry plus specific manifestations such as French-German enmity. United States guidance combined with innovative thinking in the new European governments.

Many resistance leaders had, during the war, tempered their hatred of Nazism with a plea for a reconstruction of the European spirit. The Christian Democratic movement,

particularly, produced important new advocates of harmony among European nations. Early postwar reforms, however, concentrated primarily on internal changes. While cold war rivalries prevented a formal European peace settlement, initial impulses on the part of the victorious Allies suggested a harsh treatment of Germany, possibly a permanent dismemberment, as the means of avoiding a repetition of the two previous world wars—not a more fundamental rethinking of Western conventions.

Yet the demands of the cold war and pressure from the United States forced second thoughts, which ultimately revived elements of resistance idealism. By 1947, as American leaders grew eager to spur Western Europe's economic recovery, they judged that coordination across national boundaries was an essential precondition. Thus the American Marshall Plan required discussion of tariffs and other development issues among recipient nations. With simultaneous American insistence on the partial rearmament of Germany and German participation in NATO, the framework for diplomatic reform was complete.

Faced with these pressures and aware of the failure of nationalistic policies between the wars, several French statesmen took a lead in proposing coordination between France and Germany as a means of setting up a new Europe. The nations of the Low Countries and Italy were soon linked in these activities. The idea was to tie German economic activity to an international framework so that the nation's growing strength would not again threaten European peace. Institutions were established to link policies in heavy industry and later to develop atomic power. A measure to establish a united European military force proved too ambitious and collapsed under nationalist objections. But in 1958 the six West European nations (West Germany, France, Italy, Belgium, Luxembourg, and the Netherlands) set up the European Economic Community, or Common Market, to begin to create a single economic entity across national political boundaries. Tariffs were progressively reduced among the member nations, while a common tariff policy was set for the outside world. Free movement of labor and investment was encouraged. A Common Market bureaucracy was established, ultimately in Brussels, to oversee these operations. The Common Market set up a court system to adjudicate disputes and prevent violations of coordination rules; it also administered a development fund to spur economic growth in laggard regions such as southern Italy or western France.

The Common Market did not move quickly toward a single government. Important national disputes limited the organization's further growth. France and Germany, for example, routinely quarreled over agricultural policy, with France seeking more payments to farmers as a matter of obvious self-interest. The establishment of the Fifth Re-

The Common Market and Its Growth; NATO Boundaries and Neutral Nations

public in France, under Charles de Gaulle, indeed signaled an increase of French nationalism. But while the Common Market did not turn into full unity, it did survive and, on the whole, prosper. It even established an advisory international Parliament, ultimately elected by direct vote. Further, in the 1980s, firm arrangements were made to dismantle all trade and currency exchange barriers among member states in 1992, creating essentially complete economic unity. And the Common Market's success expanded its hold within Western Europe. After long hesitations, Britain, despite its tradition of proud island independence, decided to join, as did Ireland, Denmark, and later Greece, Spain, and Portugal. Nationalist tensions within Europe receded to a lower point than ever before in modern European history. After the worst scares of the cold war, focused mainly on the division between the communist East and the semicapitalist West, Europe became a diplomatically placid continent, enjoying one of the longest periods of complete internal peace in its history.

ECONOMIC EXPANSION

Accompanying political and diplomatic change was striking economic growth, after a short, if agonizing, postwar rebuilding. The welfare state and Common Market may have encouraged this growth by improving purchasing power for the masses and facilitating market expansion across national boundaries; economic growth encouraged the success of new political and diplomatic systems.

There was no question that, by the mid-1950s, Western Europe had entered a new economic phase. Agricultural production and productivity increased rapidly as peasant farmers, backed by the technocrats, adopted new equipment and seeds. European agriculture was still less efficient than that of North America, which necessitated some hotly debated tariff barriers by the Common Market. But food production easily met European needs, often with some to spare for export. Retooled industries poured out textiles and metallurgical products. Expensive consumer products such as automobiles and appliances supported rapidly growing factories. Western Europe also remained a leading center of weapons production, trailing only the United States and the Soviet Union in exports.

Overall growth in gross national product surpassed the rates of any extended period since the Industrial Revolution began; it also surpassed the growth rates of the United States economy during the 1950s and 1960s. The German economy, once some basic reconstruction and currency stabilization had occurred by 1948, took off at a six percent annual expansion during the 1950s; with few modest setbacks this pace continued into the early 1970s. France attained an eight percent growth rate by the late 1950s, maintained almost this level during the 1960s, and returned to rates of over seven percent annually by the early 1970s. By 1959 the Italian economy, a newcomer to the industrial big leagues, was expanding at an 11 percent annual rate. These were, admittedly, the clearest success stories. Scandinavian growth was substantial but more modest, and Britain, also expanding but falling rapidly in rank among the European national economies, managed at best a four percent increase annually. Even this, however, contrasted markedly with the stagnation of the 1920s and early 1930s.

Growth rates of the sort common in Western Europe, their impact heightened by the absence of major depressions, depended on rapid technological change. Europe's rising food production was achieved with a steadily shrinking agricultural labor force. France's peasant population—16 percent of the labor force in the early 1950s—fell to 10 percent two decades later, but overall output was much higher than before. During the 1950s the industrial work force grew as part of factory expansion, but by the 1960s, despite rising production, the relative proportion of factory workers also began to drop. Workers in the service sector, filling functions as teachers, clerks, medical personnel, insurance and bank workers, and performers and other "leisure industry" personnel, rose rapidly in contrast. Europe, like the United States, began to convert technological advance into the provision of larger bureaucracies and service operations without jeopardizing the expanding output of goods. In France, by 1968 half of all paid workers were in the service sector, and the proportion rose steadily thereafter.

The high rates of economic growth also assured relatively low unemployment after the immediate postwar dislocations passed. Even Britain, with lagging development, averaged no more than four percent unemployment per year during the 1950s and 1960s, while countries such as France and Germany featured rates of two percent to three percent a year. Indeed, many parts of the continent were labor-short and had to seek hundreds of thousands of workers from other areas—first from southern Europe, then, as this region industrialized, from Africa, the Middle East, and parts of Asia. The rise of immigrant minorities was a vital development in Western Europe and also the United States, where the influx of Asian and Latin-American immigrants stepped up markedly.

Unprecedented economic growth plus low unemployment meant unprecedented improvements in incomes, even with the taxation necessary to sustain welfare programs. Per-capita disposable income rose 117 percent in the United States between 1960 and 1973, while soaring 258 percent in France, 312 percent in Germany, and 323 percent in Denmark. Scandinavia, Switzerland, and the Federal Republic of Germany indeed surpassed the United States in standards of living by the 1980s, while France, long an apparent laggard in modern economic development, pulled even. New spending money rapidly translated

In the United States, as well as in Japan and Western Europe, advertisements increasingly evoked a good life to be fulfilled through buying the right goods. The newest car was associated with a prosperous home, a loving family, and even happy pets.

into huge increases in the purchase of durable consumer goods, as virtually the whole of Western civilization became an "affluent society." By 1969 two of every ten people in Britain, Sweden, West Germany, and France owned an automobile. Ownership of television sets became virtually universal. France and other countries indulged in a mania for household appliances. Shopping malls and supermarkets, the agents of affluence and extensive but efficient shopping that had first developed in the United States, spread widely, at the expense of more traditional, specialist small shops. A West German company, in fact, took over a key American grocery chain in the late 1970s, on grounds that Europeans now knew mass marketing as well as or better than the American consumer pioneers.

Europe had unquestionably developed a framework of affluent consumerism as fully as had the United States, with at least as much impact on basic social patterns and

TABLE 35.1

Two Measures of Rising Consumer Prosperity in Europe, 1957 and 1965

Automobiles	1957	1965
France	3,476,000	7,842,000
Germany (Federal Republic)	2,456,288	8,103,600
Italy	1,051,004 (1956)	5,469,981
The Netherlands	375,676	1,272,890
Sweden	796,000	1,793,000

Televisions	1957	1965
France	683,000	6,489,000
Germany	789,586	11,379,000
Italy	367,000	6,044,542
The Netherlands	239,000	2,113,000
Sweden	75,817	2,110,584

Sources: Adapted from *The Europa Year Book 1959* (London: Europa Publications, 1959) and *The Europa Year Book 1967*, vol. 1 (London: Europa Publications, 1967).

habits of thought. Advertising was not quite as ubiquitous in Europe as across the Atlantic, particularly because most television channels were state-run and noncommercial. But promptings to buy, to smell good, to look right, to express one's personality in the latest car style, began quickly to describe European life. The frenzy to find good vacation spots was certainly intense. Literally millions of Germans poured annually into Italy and Spain, seeking the sun. Britons thronged to Spanish beaches. Europeans were bent on combining efficient work with indulgent leisure.

The West's economic advance was not without some dark spots. Inflation was a recurrent headache, when demand outstripped production. And inflation in the 1970s, affecting even the cautious Germans who were eager to avoid this specter from the past, caused serious dislocation. Pockets of unemployment were troubling. Many immigrant workers from Turkey, North Africa, Pakistan, and the West Indies suffered very low wages and unstable employment. These immigrants, euphemistically labeled "guest workers," were often residentially segregated and victims of discrimination by employers and police, as racism continued to be an important factor in Western society.

More troubling still was the slowing of economic growth in the 1970s. In 1973 the oil-producing states of the Middle East cut their production and raised prices, initially in response to a Middle Eastern war with Israel.

Many nations were hit hard by higher energy prices, but Western Europe, heavily dependent on imports, was particularly pressed. A second orchestrated oil crisis in 1979 led to a severe recession throughout Western society, with unusually high rates of unemployment. Growing competition from East Asia and other areas cut into traditional staples such as steel and automobile production, making it difficult to recover the dynamism of the two postwar decades.

Western leaders were able to respond to new crises with some success. Conservation measures reduced dependence on imported oil, and by the 1980s energy prices fell back. Several European nations embarked on rapid development of nuclear energy production. European productivity rates continued to improve, with nations such as France introducing the use of robots on assembly lines at a particularly rapid pace. The economic climate had become tighter, however. This spurred some renewed labor agitation, directed, for example, at governments that closed inefficient factories. Yet even by 1990, the ongoing impact of dramatic economic growth lingered, giving Western Europe as well as the United States a source of new satisfactions and interests, as well as a vigorous presence in the world power structure even as colonies disappeared and sheer military dominance receded.

THE SOURCES OF WESTERN VITALITY

No single factor explained the post-1945 vigor of Western society in political, diplomatic, and economic structure. The West, including the United States, continued to benefit from technological leadership in the world economy even as it faced new competition from Japan. It built on its existing industrial base, in contrast to most other societies still trying to industrialize for the first time. It also spread and adapted democratic and parliamentary traditions, another heritage from the 19th century and before. Emphasis on scientific training, particularly strong in Europe, followed from prior intellectual change; it made Westerners open to new ideas and techniques.

The West was not involved in revolutionary adaptation, even as it pulled out of the doldrums of the decades from 1914 to 1945. Yet there were major changes resulting from innovative leadership—the fruit of new groups ascending to power after World War II plus the role of the United States in influencing key adjustments. The reduction of nationalism in favor of regional cooperation was a basic step. So was the more active posture of the state in promoting and guiding change. Even as Western politics became less contentious, political leadership became more central in shaping the patterns of Western society.

CULTURE AND SOCIETY IN THE WEST

Political and economic changes in Western society progressively altered the contours of earlier industrial development. They also smoothed out a number of earlier differences within Western society, particularly between the United States and Western Europe, as the two key Western spaces converged in many respects. The West became the first example of an advanced industrial society, especially from the 1950s onward, and both the United States and Western Europe shared in leading facets of change.

SOCIAL STRUCTURE

Economic growth, bringing increasing prosperity to most groups, eased some earlier social conflicts throughout the West. Workers were still propertyless, but they had substantial holdings as consumers. Social lines were also blurred by rapid social mobility, as educational opportunities opened further and the size of the white-collar sector expanded. Much unskilled labor was left to immigrants. Economic and political change also altered conditions for West Europe's peasantry. Peasants became commercial, eager for improvements in standards of living, and, through car trips and television, participants in urban culture. They also became more attuned to bureaucracies, as state regulations pushed them into cooperative organizations.

Social distinctions remained, to be sure. Middle-class people had more abundant leisure opportunities and a more optimistic outlook than did most workers. Signs of tension continued. Crime rates went up throughout Western society after the 1920s, though the levels were particularly high in the United States. Race riots punctuated American life in the 1950s and 1960s and exploded in immigrant sections of British cities in the 1980s.

There were strong signs that what was happening in Western society, at least by the 1960s, was not so much a resolution of older issues—how to fit peasants into modern society or what to do about worker grievances—as the establishment of a new social system, a second version of industrial society or, as some held, a postindustrial society. The majority of the labor force in the West was now engaged in services and management hierarchies, not working as producers in either farm or factory. It was drawn less to the older ethic of hard work than to new ideas of high consumption and expressive leisure. The West, in sum, continued to change, whether for good or ill.

THE WOMEN'S REVOLUTION

A key facet of postwar change involved women and the family, and again both Western Europe and the United States participated fully in this upheaval. While family ideals persisted in many ways—with workers, for example, urging that "a loving family is the finest thing, something to work for, to look to and to look after"—the realities of family life changed in many ways. Family leisure activities expanded. Extended family contacts were facilitated by telephones and automobiles. More years of schooling increased the importance of peer groups for children, and the authority of parents undoubtedly declined.

The clearest innovation in family life came through the new working patterns of women. World War II brought increased factory and clerical jobs for women, as the earlier world war had done. After a few years of downward adjustment, the trends continued. From the early 1950s onward, the number of working women, particularly married women, rose steadily both in Western Europe and in the United States and Canada. Women's earlier educational gains had improved their work qualifications; the growing number of service jobs created a need for additional workers—and women, long associated with clerical jobs and paid less than men, were ideal candidates. Many women also sought entry into the labor force as a means of adding to personal or family income, to afford some of the consumer items now becoming feasible but not yet easy to buy, or as a means of personal fulfillment in a society that associated worth with work and earnings.

The growing employment of women, which by the 1970s brought the female segment of the labor force up to 44 percent of the total in most Western countries, represented particularly the employment of adult women, most of them married and many with children. Teenage employment dropped as more girls stayed in school, but long-term work commitments rose steadily. This was not, to be sure, a full stride to job equality. Women's pay lagged behind men's pay. Most women were concentrated in clerical jobs rather than spread through the occupational spectrum, despite a growing minority of middle-class women who were entering professional and management ranks. Clearly, however, the trends of the 19th-century Industrial Revolution, to keep women and family separate from work outside the home, had yielded to a dramatic new pattern.

Other new rights for women accompanied this shift. Where women had lacked the vote before, as in France, they now got it; only Switzerland, of the West European nations, doggedly refused this concession at the national level until 1971. Gains in higher education were considerable, though again full equality remained elusive. Women constituted 23 percent of German university students in 1963, and under socialist governments in the 1970s the figure rose. Preferred subjects, however, remained different from those of men, as most women stayed out of engineering, science (except medicine), and management. Family rights improved, at least in the judgment of most

The feminist movement focused particularly on economic gains for women and a rejection of purely domestic roles. The movement first gained momentum in the United States in the late 1960s, in the wake of civil rights agitation, but soon spread to Western Europe.

women's advocates. Access to divorce increased, which many observers viewed as particularly important to women. Abortion law eased, though more slowly in countries of Catholic background than in Britain or Scandinavia; it became increasingly easy for women to regulate their birthrate. Development of new birth-control methods, such as the contraceptive pill introduced in 1960, plus growing knowledge and acceptability of birth control, decreased unwanted pregnancies. Sex and procreation became increasingly separate considerations. Although women continued to differ from men in sexual outlook and behavior—over twice as many French women as men, for example, hoped

to link sex, marriage, and romantic love, according to 1960s polls—more women than before tended to define sex in terms of pleasure.

Predictably, of course, changes in the family, including the roles of women, brought new issues as well as redefined ideals of companionship. The first issue involved children. A brief increase in the Western birthrate ended in the early 1960s, and a rapid decline ensued. Women working and the desire to use income for high consumer standards mitigated against children, or very many children, particularly in the middle class, where birthrates were lowest. Those children born were increasingly sent, often at an early age, to day-care centers, one of the amenities provided by the European welfare state and particularly essential where new fears about population growth began to surface. European families had few hesitations about replacing maternal care with collective care, and parents often claimed that the result was preferable for children. At the same time, however, some observers worried that Western society, and the Western family, were becoming indifferent to children in an eagerness for adult work and consumer achievements. American adults, for example, between the 1950s and 1980s, shifted their assessment of family satisfaction away from parenthood by concentrating on shared enjoyments between husbands and wives.

Family stability also opened new cracks. Pressures to readjust family roles, women working outside the family context, and growing legal freedoms for women, caused men and women alike to turn more readily to divorce. In 1961 nine percent of all British marriages ended in divorce; by 1965 the figure was 16 percent and rising. By the late 1970s one-third of all British marriages ended in divorce, and the United States' rate was higher still.

Finally, even aside from divorce, the changing roles of women raised questions about family values. Expectations lagged behind reality. Polls taken of German women in the 1960s indicated that a solid majority believed mothers with children under 12 should stay home; yet in fact a solid majority of such mothers were working. Gaps of this sort, between ideals and practice, suggested that, like Western society generally, the family was in a new transition, its end state far from clear.

The development of a new surge of feminist protest, although it reflected far wider concerns than family life alone, showed the strains caused by women's new activities and continued limitations. Growing divorce produced many cases of impoverished women combining work and child care. New work roles revealed the persistent earnings gap between men and women. More generally, many women sought supporting values and organizations as they tried to define new identities less tied to the domestic roles and images of previous decades.

A new feminism began to take shape with the publication in 1949 of *The Second Sex* by the French intellectual Simone de Beauvoir. Echoed in the 1950s and 1960s by other works, such as American Betty Friedan's *The Feminine Mystique,* a new wave of women's rights agitation arose after three decades of relative calm. The new feminism tended to emphasize a more literal equality that would play down special domestic roles and qualities; therefore, it promoted not only specific reforms but more basic redefinitions of what it meant to be male or female.

The new feminism did not win all women, even in the middle class, which was feminism's most avid audience. It also did not cause some of the most sweeping practical changes that were taking place, as in the new work roles. But it did support the revolution in roles. From the late 1960s onward it pressed Western governments for further change, raising issues that were hard to fit into established political contexts. The movement both articulated and promoted the gap between new expectations and ongoing inequalities in gender. And the new feminism expressed and promoted some unanswered questions about family functions. In a real sense, later 20th-century feminism seemed to respond to the same desire for individuality and work identity in women that had earlier been urged on men as part of the new mentality suitable for a commercialized economy. Family remained important in the evolving outlook of women, although some feminist leaders attacked the institution outright as hopelessly repressive. Even for many less ideological women, however, family goals were less important than they had been before.

Thus, even as social class tensions declined in the West, compared to the century of industrialization, new divisions surged forward. Gender conflict was an obvious new issue, but so was the gap between racial minorities, new or old, and established white populations.

ANALYSIS
THE DECLINE OF THE WEST?

At various points in the 20th century, various kinds of Westerners have worried about the decline of Western society. Sometimes their concern focuses on the undeniable relative decline of the West in the world, which sets the 20th century off from the periods in world history between 1450 and 1920. In the 1980s, for example, various United States news magazines began to trumpet the idea of an emerging "Pacific century," dominated by East Asian powers, that would replace the period of Western (and recently, American) preponderance.

The idea of absolute decline has had its proponents as well. The West's relative loss of power over the past 60 years, with decolonization and the rise of Japanese exports, may produce absolute decline compared to earlier Western leadership. Some societies—such as the Roman Empire or the Ottoman Empire—depended on continued expansion to provide labor or booty for the upper class and then began to lose their vitality when further growth became impossible. The West no longer requires colonies to provide slaves, but it might have become so dependent on its ability to dominate other economies that relative decline will spell the beginning of a new period of internal woes.

Furthermore, there have been numerous periods in which developments within the West provoked gloom. Early in the 20th century, pondering the growing pleasure seeking of Western culture and its internal divisions, a German philosopher named Oswald Spengler wrote a book called the *Decline of the West* in which he predicted that Western civilization was going the way of Rome, doomed to fall before the onslaught of such vigorous but less civilized peoples as the Russians or the Americans. His book was hugely popular after World War I, when it looked as if Western nations had indeed inflicted grievous injury on their own society. Other historians, though somewhat less cosmically pessimistic than Spengler, have picked up the theme of what they see as an inevitable decline of societies following periods of vigor. The theme seemed to fit Western Europe again immediately after World War II, when both victors and vanquished were suffering through the immense problems of reconstruction. It was revived again in the late 1980s, when the world dominance of the United States seemed in retreat.

Other observers, though less systematic, discerned internal decay. Some focused on cultural trends, bemoaning the lack of standards in art—the tendency to play with novel styles, however frivolous, simply to win attention. Or they might bemoan popular culture for what they claimed was a shallow materialism and vulgar sexuality; some critics saw analogies between Western commercialism and the Roman "bread and circuses" approach to the urban masses that, they argued, had weakened the empire's moral fiber and reduced its capacity for work and military valor.

Analogies, however, are inexact, and the role of moral decline in causing Rome's downfall is debatable in any event. One of the problems in comparing current Western trends to past cases of decline—even subtler cases, such as the gradual reduction of Arab vitality in the later postclassical era—is that modern conditions as shaped by industrialization may weaken the applicability of past standards.

Western demography is a case in point. There is no question that the demographic vitality of the West weakened in the late 19th and 20th centuries, with the baby boom era, from 1943 to 1963, a brief if interesting exception. Birthrates have gone down fairly steadily, in the 1930s and again by the 1980s reaching a point close to bare reproduction. Indeed some Western nations, such as Germany, were by the 1980s coming close to falling beneath reproduction levels, with birthrates so low that population decline would soon set in unless compensated by further immigration. Moreover, slow or zero population growth was accompanied by increased aging, the result of advancing life expectancy combined with the relatively small number of children being born. In most historic situations, slowing population growth has signaled a general decrease in vitality, causing further decline as competition and the opportunity provided by population increase waned. Unquestionably, the West's demographic trends reduced its percentage of world population, which might relate to its relative decline and certainly opened it to new immigration from various parts of the world. But the total package was hard to measure, for in the context of an industrial society, which provided a variety of technical aids to human labor and was a heavy consumer of resources, stable populations might prove a source of strength, not weakness, while rapid population increase might be a fateful burden that limited effective development.

Judgments about decline, finally, are complicated by the cycles of Western history during the 20th century and the nature of modern Western expectations. Periods of great disarray, like the 1930s, have not thus far led to long-term chaos, as Western nations have seemed able to bounce back. Other decades roused anxieties mainly because of the heavy Western commitment to steady progress. Thus during the 1970s, when economic growth slowed, many polls showed that Americans had stopped believing that their society would advance in the future (though interestingly they still believed that their own lives would get better). Yet the 1970s brought no huge crisis, simply a slowing in the pace of improvement. The Western habit of expecting steady economic advance could easily lead to temporary exaggerations of what 1970s Americans called "malaise."

Clearly, to paraphrase Mark Twain, reports of the death of the West seemed premature. Yet past examples from world history suggest one other caution: Social decline, if it does set in, typically takes a long time to work through. Rome declined for three centuries before it "fell"; the Ottoman Empire began to turn downward two centuries before it became known as "sick." The first century of decline may be hard to perceive, yet particularly important to monitor in case restorative measures are necessary.

Question: Has the West shown signs of cultural decline in the 20th century? What is the best case for arguing that 20th-century Western history does <u>not</u> suggest cultural decline? If the West is in decline by the late 20th century, what might be done about it? Does world history suggest that decline is reversible?   ◉

WESTERN CULTURE

As with leading social trends, Western culture in the 20th century displayed important creativity and change, but also signs of tension. Artists and composers stressed stylistic innovation, as against older traditions and even the efforts of the previous generation. Scientific work flourished, as the West remained the center of most fundamental inquiry in the theoretical sciences. But complex discoveries, such as the principle of relativity in physics, qualified older ideas that nature can be captured in a few sweeping scientific laws. And the sheer specialization of scientific research removed much of it from ready public understanding. Because no clear unifying assumptions captured the essence of formal intellectual activity in the contemporary West, neutral terms such as *modern* or *postmodern* were used even in the artistic field. Disciplines that once provided an intellectual overview, such as philosophy, declined in the 20th century or were transformed into specialized research fields; many philosophers, for example, turned to the scientific study of language, while sweeping political theory virtually disappeared. And while work in theology continued among both Catholic and Protestant thinkers, it no longer commanded center stage in intellectual life. No emphasis was placed on an integrated approach, as Western intellectual life developed with specialized branches, and no agreement was reached on what constitutes an essential understanding of human endeavor.

The dynamism of scientific research continued to form the clearest central thread in Western culture after 1920. Growing science faculties commanded greatest prestige in the expanding universities. Individual scientists made striking discoveries, while a veritable army of researchers cranked out more specific findings than scientists had ever before produced. In addition, the wider public continued to maintain a faith that science held the keys to understanding nature and society and to improving technology and human life. Finally, while scientific findings varied widely, a belief in a central scientific method persisted: Form a rational hypothesis, test that hypothesis through experiment or observation, and emerge with a generalization that will show regularities in physical behaviors and thus provide human reason with a means of systematizing and even predicting such behaviors. No other approach to understanding in Western culture has had such power or widespread adherence.

By the 1930s, physicists began to experiment with bombarding basic matter with *neutrons*, or particles that carry no electric charge; this work was to culminate during World War II in the development of the atomic bomb. Research in physics continued after World War II with a combination of increasingly sophisticated means of observation, made possible by improved telescopes, atom smashers, and then lasers and space satellites, and the complex mathematical theories facilitated by the theory of relativity. Astronomers made substantial progress in identifying additional galaxies and other phenomena in space; the debate also continued about the nature of matter.

Breakthroughs in biology primarily involved genetics. The identification in the 1860s of principles of inheritance received wide attention only after 1900. By the 1920s, researchers who used the increasingly familiar fruit fly had exact rules for genetic transmission. Discovery in the 1950s by British and American scientists of the structure of the basic genetic unit, the famous "double helix" pattern of deoxyribonucleic acid (DNA), advanced the understanding of how genetic information is transmitted and how it can be altered.

Fundamental discoveries in physics and biology, though hard to grasp even by the educated public, promoted the idea of science as penetrating the mysteries of the universe. They also furthered the relationship between science and technology. Physicists spearheaded research into atomic weaponry and atomic power. During and after World War II, they helped develop missiles and other spacecraft. Biologists produced major improvements in health care. New drugs, beginning with penicillin in 1928, revolutionized the treatment of common diseases, while immunization virtually eliminated scourges such as diphtheria. Genetics itself, by the 1970s, gave rise to a host of industries that utilized scientific principles to produce new medicines, seeds, and pesticides.

The new science displayed some troubling features, even apart from its use in the weapons of destruction or its sheer complexity. The physical world was no longer considered to be neatly regulated as it had been by Newtonian physics. Many other phenomena came to be perceived as relative and unpredictable. Genetics made it clear that evolution proceeded by a series of random accidents, not through any consistent pattern. Use of the rational, scientific method thus has not produced the kind of tidy world view that was prevalent a century or so ago, and the resultant uncertainties have influenced some artists in their attempts to convey an irrational, relativist universe. Yet in the public mind, partly because the new science is so hard to understand, the belief in progress, defined both as better technology and as rational penetration of nature, largely persisted.

The rational method, broadly conceived, also advanced in the social sciences from 1920 onward. In economics, while sweeping theories were downplayed, quantitative models of economic cycles or business behavior increasingly gained ground. Work by the British economist John Keynes, stressing the importance of government spending to compensate for loss of purchasing power during a depression, played a great role in the policies of the American New Deal and efforts by European planners to control the economic cycles after World War II. In psychology, the work by Sigmund Freud on the human unconscious and its role in mental disturbance gained increasing attention; while no single psychological theory predominated, the idea of using research to probe both conscious thought and irrational impulse won growing acceptance.

Like the sciences, the social sciences became increasingly diverse and specialized. Like the sciences also, many social scientists sought practical applications for their work. Psychologists became involved, for example, not only in dealing with mental illness but in trying to promote greater work efficiency. Governments called on economists for their advice, particularly after World War II when their forecasting attempts formed the basis of economic planning. Great diversity existed within the social sciences, and many individual researchers, like their scientific counterparts, worked on small problems of data gathering and manipulation. The rise of anthropology in the 1920s, and the development of social history as a branch of inquiry into human behavior, swam against the social scientific current by pointing to the importance of diversity and chronology in understanding human life. Most leading social scientists, however, continued to emphasize the quest for consistency in human and social behavior. After World War II the increasing use of mathematical models and laboratory experiments in the social sciences enhanced this emphasis.

Most 20th-century artists, concerned with capturing the world through impressions, worked against the grain of science and social science. Painting became increasingly nonrepresentational. The cubist movement, headed by Pablo Picasso, rendered familiar objects as geometrical shapes; after cubism, modern art moved even further from normal perception, stressing purely geometrical design or wild swirls of color. The focus was on mood, the individual reaction of viewers to the individual reality of the artist. Musical composition involved the use of dissonance and experimentation with new scales; after World War II, a growing interest in electronic instrumentation added to this diversity. In poetry the use of unfamiliar forms, ungrammatical constructions, and sweeping imagery continued the movement of the later 19th century. In literature the novel remained dominant, but it turned toward the exploration of moods and personalities.

Marcel Duchamp, using a modified cubist style, sought dramatic visual effect in an approach characteristic of Western art from the 1920s onward.

The arts in the 20th-century West were thus characterized by unprecedented diversity, by a conscious effort to seek new forms, and by a focus on the individual and mood, rather than on some agreed-upon objective reality. These emphases, as noted earlier, joined with science in certain ways: They provided the artistic equivalent of relativity, and they certainly stressed the importance of the unconscious. But a vast gulf grew between the scientific approach and the artistic framework as to how reality can be captured and, to an extent, what constitutes reality.

Many people ignored the leading modern artists and writers in favor of more commercial artistic productions and popular stories. The gap that had opened earlier be-

tween avant-garde art and public taste generally continued. Some politicians, including Adolf Hitler, campaigned against what they saw as the decadence and immorality of modern art, urging a return to more traditional styles. And certainly art did not hold its own against the growing prestige of science.

Yet the artistic vision was not simply a preoccupation of artists. Designs and sculptures based on abstract art began to grace public places from the 1920s onward; furnishings and films also reflected the modernist themes. Most revealing of a blend between art, modern technology, and public taste was the development of a characteristic 20th-century architectural style, the "modern" or "international" style. Use of new materials, such as reinforced concrete and massive sheets of glass, allowed the abandonment of much that was traditional in architecture. Need for new kinds of buildings, particularly for office use, and the growing cost of urban space also encouraged the introduction of new forms such as the skyscraper, pioneered in the United States. In general, the modern style of architecture sought to develop individually distinct buildings—sharing the goal of modern art to defy conventional taste and cultivate the unique—while conveying a sense of space and freedom from natural constraints. Soaring structures, free-floating columns, and new combinations of angles and curves were features that described leading Western buildings in the 20th century. Following World War II, when reconstruction in Europe and the expansion of new centers in the West and Southwest of the United States provided massive opportunities for building, the face of urban space in Western society was greatly transformed.

Artistic innovation thus played an important role in Western society in the 20th century. Inherently controversial, it seemed to provide an alternative to the regularized world of mechanized industry and rationalistic science. The result has been no unified culture, but a set of tensions and options that can be creative for society as a whole, as well as meaningful to many individuals.

There have been a few unifying themes between the artistic and the scientific approaches, as both explored elements of the human unconscious or reflected a growing uncertainty about the benevolence and clear rationality of nature and human nature. A constant quest for the new has been another feature, as artists sought new styles and scientists sought new discoveries. Furthermore, Western culture in the 20th century, both in art and in science, has become largely secular. Individual artists, writers, and scientists may proclaim religious faith, but the churches have long since lost control over basic style or content. In Western Europe, despite an important reform movement within the Catholic church that cut down traditional ceremonies in favor of more direct contact between priests and worshipers,

The skyscraper, launched first in the United States, became a major expression of artistic innovation and dramatic new structural materials, including novel uses of glass. This Chicago tower was designed by the European master, Ludwig Mies van der Rohe.

religion played a minor role in both formal and popular culture. Regular church attendance fell, attracting only five percent of the British population, for example, by the 1970s. Increasing use of cremation, rather than burial, showed radical change in traditional Christian approaches to death. In the United States, religion maintained a greater hold, and both church attendance and popular belief remained at higher levels than elsewhere in Western society. The United States also saw, both in the 1920s and again after World War II, a greater variety of popular revival movements and attempts to use religion to maintain or restore traditional values.

On the whole, however, Western people participated in ongoing change in beliefs in the 20th century, with the secular focus predominating. Here was one area where the West actively participated in and helped to shape larger world trends. Before 1950 new beliefs often came in the form of political ideologies, with passionate commitments to fascist nationalism or to communism. More pervasive was the growing attachment to consumer goods and to a scientific outlook. Feminism, for example, strived for the same kind of material rewards and opportunities for individual expansion for women as for men. Growing use of doctors and hospitals showed a desire to place illness and death in a scientific framework, as Western nations began, after 1945, to pay up to 15 percent of their total incomes into efforts to stave off disease. While sweeping ideologies declined in the West, the commitment to a secular value system advanced steadily.

Western culture was not a monopoly of European civilization in the 20th century. Western art forms, particularly in architecture, spread widely, because of their practicality and their currency in what remained a highly influential society. The achievements of Western science, at least those related to technology and medicine, often had to be taken into account by societies seeking their own industrial development. Western art and science were, by the same token, greatly enriched by many practitioners from other cultures—by Japanese artists, for example, or Indian medical researchers and computer scientists. Elements of Western culture thus have now become international, and we will have to trace their interweaving into a number of other civilizations. Yet no other culture, not even the Japanese, created quite the same balance between an overwhelming interest in science and a frenzied concern for stylistic innovation and individual expression in the arts.

CONCLUSION

WILL THE REAL WEST PLEASE STAND UP?

To some observers the West in the 20th century was dominated by the futilities and barbarianisms of the interwar years: No superficial recovery could undo these wounds or make good these failures. This despairing judgment might be compounded by the renewed uncertainties of Western life in the 1970s and 1980s and the growing impact of the decline in world dominance that the interwar years had launched.

Other observers saw Western trends in terms of some ongoing dilemmas raised by industrialization. They noted the dualism present in formal culture and popular outlook

since the 19th century. Western intellectuals thus insisted on the primacy of rational inquiry, while relying on artistic forms that seemed bent on portraying a world gone mad. Ordinary Europeans and Americans accepted a disciplined work environment that stressed control over emotion while reveling in scenes of violence and sexual ecstasy in their leisure hours, sometimes embellished as well by the use of drugs.

ADJUSTING TO INDUSTRIAL SOCIETY

Contemporary Western society reflected tensions between industrial values and Western traditions that were exacerbated in the 20th century. On the one hand, the society encouraged children to think of themselves as individuals, to rise above their parents' achievements if possible, to adjust to new work opportunities. Leisure interests appealed to individual pleasure seeking. But individualism was severely curtailed by the growing bureaucratization of society. Most jobs involved routine activities, controlled by an elaborate supervisory apparatus; individual initiative counted for little in factories as well as in the offices of giant corporations. Leisure, appealing to individual self-expression in one sense, generally meant mass, commercially manipulated outlets for all but a handful of venturesome souls. By the 1950s television watching had become far and away the leading recreational interest of Western peoples, and most television fare was deliberately standardized. Ironically, individualism and its outlets in consumer behavior often made collective protest against bureaucratization and routine extremely difficult. One of the reasons for the decline of organized labor throughout the West was workers' growing need to spend time earning money for a new car or using the new car they had.

To critics within Western society and without, Western society at times seemed badly confused. Poverty and job boredom coexisted with affluence and continued appeals to the essential value of work. Youth protest—including defiant costumes and pulsating rock music—family instability, and growing crime might be signs of a fatally flawed society. Rising rates of suicide and increasing incidence of mental illness were other troubling symptoms. At the least, Western society continued to display the strains of change.

Western civilization, in sum, continued to be distinctive for a mixture of old and new reasons. Headed by the United States, it led the world, by the 1960s, in the use of mind-altering drugs. The burgeoning leisure culture involved many Westerners with an interest in sexuality and sexual symbolism profoundly shocking to people from many other societies. The West also maintained a distinctive commitment to liberal democracy, and when Latin America and then Eastern Europe looked to political change in the 1970s and 1980s, they turned largely to Western models. Germany reunited in 1990, for example, as East Germans sought both the affluence and the political freedom they saw among their western cousins.

The West also remained closely tied to larger world currents. It continued to organize much world trade, as its economy fairly steadily expanded. Western developments in technology, science, and popular culture continued to have international impact. Western feminism, a newer force, helped inspire feminist interests in other societies, such as Japan. At the same time, growing rates of immigration to the West and the increasing impact of economic competition from industry in other societies made it clear that the West's links to the rest of the world were not entirely determined by the West itself.

A POSTINDUSTRIAL AGE?

Many people in Western society, indeed, believe they are facing greater changes than ever before, whether for better or for worse. By the late 1960s a new concept of a postindustrial society took shape both in Western Europe and in North America. The idea was that Western society was leading in a transformation as fundamental as the Industrial Revolution had been. The rise of a service economy, according to this argument propounded by people in different strata of the country, promised as many shifts as the rise of an industrial economy had done. Control of knowledge, rather than control of goods, would be the key to the postindustrial social structure. Technology would allow expansion of factory production with a shrinking labor force, and attention would shift to the generation and control of information. The advent of new technology, particularly the computer, supported the postindustrial concept by applying to knowledge transmission the same potential technological revolution the steam engine had brought to manufacturing.

Changes in the role of women paralleled the postindustrial concept, and some observers began to talk of a postindustrial family in which two equal spouses would pool their earnings in a high-consumption life-style. Postindustrial cities would increasingly become entertainment centers, as most work could now be decentralized in suburbs, linked by the omnipresent computer. Postindustrial politics were less clearly defined, though some commentators noted that the old party structure might loosen as new, service-sector voters sought issues more appropriate to their interests. The rise of environmental and feminist concerns,

which cut across older political alignments, thus might prove an opening wedge to an unpredictable future for the West.

The postindustrial society is not established fact, of course. Important continuities with earlier social forms, including political values and cultural directions, suggest that new technologies might modify rather than revolutionize Western industrial society. It is clear, however, that Western society has taken on important new characteristics, ranging from age brackets to occupational structure, that differentiate it from the initial industrial patterns generated in the 19th century. And this fact, even if more modest than the visions of some postindustrial forecasters, raises a vital question for the West and the world: How would a rapidly changing, advanced industrial society fit in a world that has yet fully to industrialize? How could the concerns of an affluent, urban, fad-conscious Westerner coexist with the values of the world's peasant majority?

FURTHER READINGS

For an excellent general survey see Robert Paxton's *Europe in the 20th Century* (1985). See also Morris Janowitz's *The Last Half Century: Social Change and Politics in America* (1978). A good factual compendium is Tony Howarth's *Twentieth-Century History: The World Since 1900* (1979).

Some excellent national interpretations enhance coverage. See A. F. Havighurst's *Twentieth-Century Britain* (1982) and John Ardagh's highly readable *The New French Revolution: A Social and Economic Survey of France* (1968) plus *France in the 1980's* (1982). Volker Berghahn's *Modern Germany: Society, Economy and Politics in the 20th Century* (1983) is also useful.

On Europe between the wars, Charles Maier's *Recasting Bourgeois Europe* (1975) is a penetrating comparative approach. On fascism and Nazism, see F. Carsten's *The Rise of Fascism* (1980) and S. Payne's *Fascism: Comparison and Definition* (1984). David Schoenbaum's *Hitler's Social Revolution* (1980) is an excellent study of how Nazism worked in practice. See also Gerald Fleming's *Hitler and the Final Solution* (1984), on the holocaust. R. Stromberg's *Intellectual History of Modern Europe* (1966) and K. D. Bracher's *Age of Ideologies: A History of Political Thought in the Twentieth Century* (1989) provide a factual framework in a complex area. See also H. S. Hughes's *Consciousness and Society* (1976).

On post–World War II social and economic trends see C. Kindleberger's *Europe's Postwar Growth* (1967); V. Bogdanor and R. Skidelsky, eds., *The Age of Affluence* (1970); and R. Dahrendorf, ed., *Europe's Economy in Crisis* (1982). On the welfare state, see Stephen Cohen's *Modern Capitalist Planning: The French Model* (1977) and E. S. Einhorn and J. Logue's *Welfare States in Hard Times* (1982).

Important overviews of recent European history are Walter Laqueur's *Europe Since Hitler* (1982), R. von Albertini's *Decolonization* (1982), Helen Wallace and others' *Policy-Making in the European Community* (1983), and Alfred Grosser's *The Western Alliance* (1982).

1918–1919 Independent smaller nations in eastern Europe

1923 New constitution in Russia

1928 Beginning of collectivization of agriculture and five-year plans

1927 Stalin in full power

1917 Russian Revolution; Bolshevik takeover (October)

1921 Lenin's New Economic Policy

1936–1938 Stalin's great purges

1939 Signing of Russo-German pact; Soviet invasion of eastern Poland and Finland

1943 Soviet army pushes west

1941 German invasion of Soviet Union

1945–1948 Soviet takeover of Eastern Europe

1949 Soviet Union develops atomic bomb

1955 Formation of Warsaw Pact

1956 Stalinism attacked by Khrushchev

1953 Stalin's death

1956 Hungarian revolt and its suppression

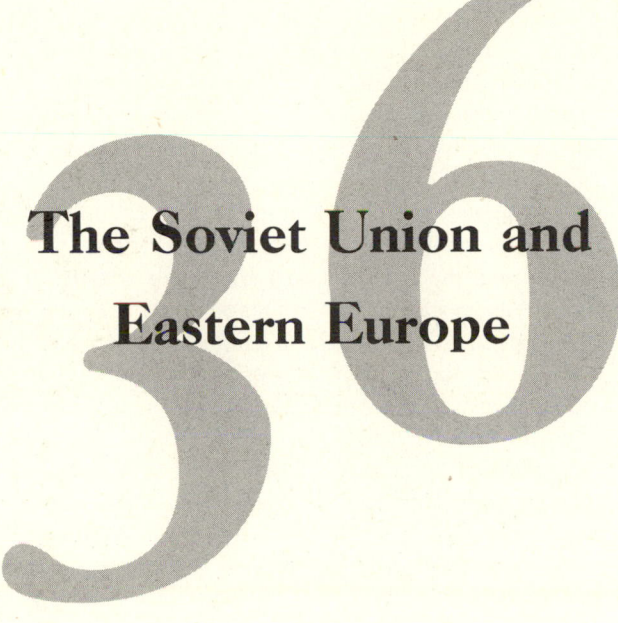

The Soviet Union and Eastern Europe

INTRODUCTION. East European history in the 20th century has been dominated by the glare of Russia's 1917 revolution, one of the great upheavals of modern times. The varied discontents that had swelled during the later 19th century, heightened by the stresses of early industrialization, partial reform, and an inept tsarist administration, came together in a rush in 1917, under the further pressure of world war. Much of Russian history thereafter, particularly during the 1920s and 1930s but to some extent into the 1990s, derived from the revolution's impact and the attempt to build a society on new, communist principles.

Russia's history merged unprecedentedly with that of the rest of Eastern Europe after 1945, as Soviet-dominated regimes were installed in most of the smaller countries after a confused interwar period. Soviet control was not complete, and important discontents boiled to the surface particularly after 1985, but there were more common directions in East European institutions than ever before in the region's history.

There are two reasons why Soviet history also had an unprecedented importance in wider world history during the 20th century. The Russian Revolution seemed to many people, in many parts of the world, a vital beacon; the example of the revolution, as well as the rise of communist movements to some extent patterned after and guided by Russian leadership, played a vital role in the history of most societies after 1917. China and Cuba used Russian models though adding their own twists; revolutionaries elsewhere in Latin America and Asia, and also in Africa and the West, drew inspiration from the Soviet system.

Spurred by the revolution and ongoing industrialization, the new Soviet Union also emerged after 1945 as one of the two great world powers. Soviet economic and military

---

1962 Cuban missile crisis

1961 Berlin Wall erected

1968 Revolt in Czechoslovakia and its repression; Soviet policy (Brezhnev doctrine) proclaims right to intervene in any Socialist country

1979 Uprisings in Poland and their suppression

1979 Soviet invasion of Afghanistan

1985 Gorbachev to power

1988–1989 Liberalization movements throughout Eastern Europe; new constitutions, economic reforms; nationalities agitation in Soviet Union

1990 Gorbachev selected as President; new elections throughout much of Eastern Europe; economic unification in Germany

1988 New Soviet constitution; establishment of the Congress of People's Deputies influence burst beyond Europe and Asia to have direct effects literally around the globe, as a Soviet-United States rivalry set a basic framework for world diplomacy in the post-World War II decades. The Soviet role must thus be added to the factors considered in the intensifying world exchange of the 20th century. For several decades after 1945, as Western colonial controls receded, Soviet ideological influence seemed to rival the West's cultural outreach in the world at large.

Soviet history during the century involves several major themes. Russia, already an important civilization, should be examined in relationship to its own past. The revolution commands analysis in its own right as one of the great phenomena in contemporary history. The Soviet role as world power must be assessed, but so should its failure to match Western economic dynamism after the 1950s, as Eastern Europe, though industrialized, settled into growing stagnation. Finally, an explosion of new uncertainties, opening up after 1985, raises vital questions not only about the Soviet Union, but about the cold war, Eastern Europe, and the future of revolution.

One means of sorting out the complex history of the Soviet Union and its 20th-century role involves division into four subperiods. The years from 1917 to 1928 were dominated by the revolution and its initial installation. Then, from 1928 to 1945, the dictatorship of Joseph Stalin commandeered the revolutionary process. During the first part of this period, the Soviet Union attempted considerable isolation from wider world contacts, and the aftermath of this isolation affected later Soviet history. The years from 1945 to 1985, as Stalinism was modified, saw the emergence of the Soviet Union as a world superpower and the incorporation of Eastern Europe into the Soviet empire. Finally, since 1985 a host of innovations and uncertainties have shaken the Soviet system, dissolved its empire, and raised questions about survival of the Soviet state itself.

THEMES IN EASTERN EUROPE

The Russian Revolution of 1917 and the spread of communism throughout most of Eastern Europe after World War II embraced several subsidiary themes. The revolution redefined Russia's relationship with Western civilization, but it did not end the ambivalent attraction-rejection reactions that had surfaced earlier. The theme of Russian expansion resumed in the postrevolutionary decades, after a retreat during an initial consolidation period. To Western eyes Russian expansion seemed an obvious resumption of older tsarist goals, though to Soviet leaders themselves a different set of criteria, including the importance of spreading revolutionary truth and the need to prevent a recurrence of German attack, seemed more salient.

Revolutionary Russia also resumed and quickened the process of industrialization, at the same time temporarily removing Russia from the intricate involvements with the world economy that had been taking shape during the 19th century. Russian industrialization after 1917 resembled industrializations elsewhere in many ways, with some common social results including the rapid growth of cities and changes in family styles. It was also a unique product, however, concentrating unusually on heavy industry and designed to protect Russia's independence from the world economy and Western modes of exchange, rather than to gain new power within the world commercial network. As the Soviets built their society and completed the basic industrialization framework, they greatly enhanced their strength in world affairs, but on somewhat distinctive foundations.

The theme of change dominates East European history during the 20th century, because of the great revolution that opened the contemporary era in this region and then the extension of Russian influence to virtually the entire civilization. Yet even great changes must be balanced against continuities from the past. Earlier political and foreign policy traditions intertwined with the effects of revolution within the Soviet Union. Communist rule and industrialization greatly altered the lives of Russian peasants, but a peasant problem remained, in an interesting if muted echo from tsarist days. Aspects of Western culture were embraced more eagerly than before, particularly in scientific areas, but new ambiguities surfaced in relation to Western art and popular culture—again a redefinition of an older theme. The smaller East European nations also recalled their past in different kinds of relationships with Soviet military dominance and political guidance. Seldom had conditions of life changed as rapidly in Eastern Europe as they did in the decades after 1917, yet earlier values persisted as well, including intense ethnic identities. The ferment after 1985 showed how many traditional impulses had survived, even as another new era dawned.

EASTERN EUROPE AND THE WORLD

The Russian Revolution and the later extension of Soviet control over Eastern Europe isolated this region in world affairs to some extent. Russian revolutionaries, initially hopeful of sparking risings elsewhere, pulled back by the later 1920s, arguing that they could build an industrial, socialist society by themselves. Russia's post–World War II empire in Eastern Europe, correspondingly, was closed off by walls and fences.

Yet developments in Eastern Europe had considerable impact on the 20th-century world. The example of the Russian Revolution inspired many radicals in Asia, Africa, and Latin America—as well as in the West—as a sign that a society could throw off a Western aura and carve out its own path to independence and justice. The Soviet Union's superpower status after World War II brought it into new economic, cultural, and diplomatic contact with various regions of the world. Smaller East European nations participated in this outreach as well. Russian influence on China, Vietnam, Cuba, and other regions was considerable and constituted a new force in contemporary world history.

By the same token Russian isolation could not ultimately be preserved. It contradicted the Soviet Union's far-flung activities as a superpower. The growing strength of international economic and cultural contacts attracted many Russians—leaders and ordinary people alike—who gained some sense of the wider world around them. When the Soviet empire exploded in the 1980s, its collapse resulted in part from expectations fed by international contacts, and it opened the whole region to unprecedented new international influences.

East European history in the 20th century has an undeniable flavor of its own, combining earlier traditions and distinctive events in the region. At the same time, East European developments helped shape the new world framework and was shaped by it in turn.

THE RUSSIAN REVOLUTION

In March 1917, strikes and food riots broke out in Russia's capital, St. Petersburg (later renamed Leningrad, briefly known as Petrograd in an effort to Rus-

sianize and secularize its original name, and renamed St. Petersburg in 1991). The outbursts, spurred by wartime misery but more basically protesting the conditions of early industrialization set against incomplete rural reform and an unresponsive political system, quickly assumed revolutionary proportions. The rioters called not just for more food and work but for a new political regime. A council of workers, called a *soviet*, took over the city government and arrested the tsar's ministers, after some brutal attempts at military repression. Unable to rely on his own soldiers the tsar abdicated, thus ending the long period of imperial rule.

LIBERALISM TO COMMUNISM

For eight months a liberal provisional government struggled to rule the country. Russia seemed thus to launch its revolution on a basis similar to France in 1789, where a liberal period set change in motion. Like Western liberals, revolutionary leaders such as Alexander Kerensky were eager to see genuine parliamentary rule, religious and other freedoms, and a host of political and legal changes. But liberalism was not deeply rooted in Russia, if only because of the small middle class, so the analogies with the first phase of the French Revolution cannot be pressed too far. Furthermore, Russia's revolution took place in far more adverse circumstances, given the pressures of participation in the world war. The initial liberal leaders were eager to maintain their war effort, which associated their link with democratic France and Britain. Yet the nation was desperately war weary, and prolongation drastically worsened economic conditions while public morale plummeted. Liberal

Moscow workers guard the Bolshevik headquarters during the Russian Revolution of 1917.

leaders also held back from the massive land reforms expected by the peasantry, for in good middle-class fashion they respected existing property arrangements and did not wish to rush into social change before a legitimate new political structure could be established. Hence serious popular unrest continued, and in November (October, by the Russian calendar) a second revolution took place that expelled liberal leadership and soon brought to power the radical, Bolshevik wing of the Social Democratic party (soon renamed the Communist party) and Lenin, its dynamic chief.

The revolution was a godsend to Lenin, though he had long been writing of Russia's readiness for a communist revolt because of the power of international capitalism and its creation—even in a society that had not directly passed through middle-class rule—of a massive proletariat. Lenin quickly gained a strong position among the urban workers' councils in the major cities. This corresponded to his rooted belief that revolution should come not from literal mass action, but from tightly organized cells whose leaders boasted a coherent plan of action.

Once the liberals were toppled, Lenin and the Bolsheviks faced several immediate problems. One problem, the war, they handled by signing a humiliating peace treaty with Germany that gave up huge sections of western Russia in return for an end of hostilities. This treaty was soon nullified by Germany's defeat at the hands of the Western allies, but Russia was ignored at the Versailles peace conference—treated as a pariah by the fearful Western powers—and found considerable territory converted into nation-states. A revived Poland built heavily on land Russia had controlled for over a century, and new, small Baltic states cut into even earlier acquisitions. Still, while Russia harbored deep grievances against the Versailles treaty, which would later help motivate renewed expansionism, the early end to the war was vital to Lenin's consolidation of power.

The second problem faced at the end of 1917 was that Lenin and the Bolsheviks, though they had gained a majority role in the leading urban soviets, were not the most popular revolutionary party. The November seizure of power had created the Council of People's Commissars, headed by Lenin and drawn from soviets across the nation, to govern the state. But a parliamentary election had already been called, and this produced a clear majority for the Social Revolutionary party, which emphasized peasant support and rural reform. Lenin, however, shut down the Parliament, replacing it with a Bolshevik-dominated Congress of Soviets. He pressed the Social Revolutionaries to disband, arguing that "the people voted for a party which

Other voices of revolution were heard at a 1917 women's demonstration. Well into the 1920s, revolutionary committees debated major reforms in the lives of women, and a variety of women's groups added strong voices to the ferment of change.

Eastern Europe and the Soviet Union, 1919–1939

no longer existed." Russia was thus to have no Western-style, multiparty system but rather a Bolshevik monopoly in the name of the true people's will. Indeed, Communist control of the government apparatus persisted from this point to 1989, a record for continuity far different from the fate of revolutionary groups earlier in the Western past.

Russia's revolution did, however, produce a familiar backlash that revolutionaries in other eras would have recognized quite easily: foreign hostility and, even more important, domestic resistance. The world's leading nations were appalled at the Communist success, which threatened principles of property and freedom they cherished deeply. They also, as settled regimes, disliked the unexpected, and some were directly injured by Russia's renunciation of its heavy foreign debts. So there was an attempt at intervention, recalling the attacks on France in 1792. Britain, France, the United States, and Japan all sent troops, but this intervention, while it heightened Russian suspicion of outsiders, did relatively little damage. The Western powers, exhausted by World War I, pulled out quickly, and even Japan, though interested in lingering in Asiatic Russia, stepped back fairly soon.

The internal civil war, which foreign troops slightly abetted, was a more serious matter, as it raged from 1918 to 1921. Tsarist generals, religiously faithful peasants, and many minority nationalities made common cause against the communist regime. Their efforts were aided by continuing economic distress, the normal result of revolutionary disar-

Civil war and peasant resistance to collectivization measures dramatically reduced food supplies, ultimately forcing a temporary change in government policy. Children were the victims of the famine of 1922.

ray but heightened by earlier communist measures. Lenin had quickly decreed a redistribution of land to the peasantry and also launched a *nationalization,* or state takeover, of basic industry. Many already landed peasants resented the loss of property and incentive, and in reaction lowered food production and the goods sent to markets. Industrial nationalization somewhat similarly disrupted manufacturing. Famine and unemployment created more economic hardship than the war had generated, which added fuel to the civil war fires. Even workers revolted in several cities, threatening the new regime's most obvious social base as well as its ideological mainstay.

STABILIZATION OF THE NEW REGIME

Order was restored, however, on several key foundations. First, a powerful new army was constructed under the leadership of Leon Trotsky, which recruited able generals and masses of loyal conscripts. This Red Army was an early beneficiary of two ongoing sources of strength for Communist Russia: a willingness to use people of humble background but great ability, who could rise to great heights under the new order but who had been doomed to immobility under the old system; and a capacity to inspire mass loyalty in the name of an end to previous injustice and a promise of a brighter future. Next, economic disarray was reduced in 1921 when Lenin issued his New Economic Policy (NEP). Intended as a stopgap measure in recognition of the real-life barriers to immediate construction of communism, the NEP promised considerable freedom of action for small businessmen and peasant landowners. The state continued to set basic economic policies, but its efforts were now combined with individual initiative. Under this temporary policy, food production began to recover and the regime gained time to prepare the more durable structures of the Communist system.

By 1923 the Bolshevik Revolution was an accomplished fact. A new constitution set up a federal system of socialist republics. This system recognized the multinational character of the nation, known now not as Russia but the Union of Soviet Socialist Republics. The dominance of ethnic Russians was preserved in the central state apparatus, however, and certain groups, notably Jews, were given no distinct representation. Since the separate republics were firmly controlled by the national Communist party, and since basic decisions were as firmly centralized, the impact of the new nationalities policy was somewhat mixed. It was also true, however, that direct nationalities protest declined notably from the 1920s until the late 1980s.

The apparatus of the central state was another mixture of appearance and reality. A Supreme Soviet had many of the trappings of a parliament and was elected by universal suffrage. But competition in elections was normally prohibited, which meant that the Communist party easily controlled this body that, in any event, served mainly to ratify decisions made by the party's central executive. Parallel systems of central bureaucracy and party bureaucracy further confirmed the Communist monopoly on power and the ability to control major decisions from the center. The Soviet political system was elaborated over time. A new constitution in the 1930s spoke glowingly of human rights. In fact, the Communists had quickly reestablished an authoritarian system, making it more efficient than its tsarist predecessor had been, complete with updated versions of political police to assure loyalty.

Along with its political and constitutional construction, the Soviet regime grappled with other key definitional issues early in the 1920s. Rivalries among leaders at the top had to be sorted out. Lenin sickened and then died in 1924, creating an unexpected leadership gap. A number of key lieutenants jostled for power, including the Red Army's flamboyant Trotsky and a Communist party stalwart of worker origins who had taken the name Stalin, meaning steel. After a few years of jockeying, Stalin emerged as undisputed leader of the Soviet state, his victory a triumph also for party control over other branches of government. Stalin's accession was more than a personal bureaucratic issue, however, for Stalin represented a strongly nationalist version of communism, in contrast to the more ideological and international visions of many rivals. At the revolution's outset Lenin had believed that the Russian rising would be merely a prelude to a sweeping Communist upheaval throughout the Western, industrial world. Many revolutionary leaders actively encouraged Communist parties in the West and set up a *Comintern,* or Communist International office, to guide this process. But revolution did not spill over, despite a few brief risings in places such as Hungary and Germany right after World War I. Under Stalin, the revolutionary leadership, while still committed in theory to an international movement, pulled back to concentrate on Russian developments pure and simple—building "socialism in one country," as Stalin put it. Stalin in many ways represented the anti-Western strain in Russian tradition, though in new guise. Rival leaders were killed or expelled, and rival visions of the revolution were downplayed.

The Russian Revolution was one of the most successful uprisings in human history. Building on widespread if diverse popular discontent and a firm belief in centralized leadership, the Bolsheviks beat back powerful odds to create a new, though not totally unprecedented, political regime. They used features of the tsarist system, but they managed to propel a wholly new leadership group to power not only at the top, but at all levels of the bureaucracy and army. The tsar and his hated ministers were gone, mostly executed, but so was the overweening aristocratic class that had loomed so large in Russian history for centuries. And after the first years the revolutionaries never had to look backward; they avoided even a partial restoration of the "old regime" as had occurred in England after its 17th-century Civil War as well as in France after Napoleon's defeat. The Bolsheviks, in contrast, managed to create a new political, economic, and cultural structure without serious internal challenge between the initial, chaotic years and the late 1980s.

Serious revolutions, however, do not end quickly. While the formal revolutionary period consumed but a few vivid years, the actual force of the revolution continued easily until the mid-1930s—that is, through a period of fascinating experimentation during the 1920s and into the establishment of a full Stalinist regime from 1928 onward.

ANALYSIS
20TH-CENTURY REVOLUTIONS

Never in world history have there been as many revolutions, in not one but a host of different civilizations, as in the 20th century. The roster includes a minor and a major revolution in Russia; one or perhaps two major revolutions in China (the question concerns whether to view the whole span from 1911 to 1947 as a single revolutionary process or a sequence of two outbreaks); a major upheaval in Mexico; then, much later, significant revolutions in Cuba, Bolivia, and Nicaragua; and quite recently a revolution in Iran. In addition to these major cases, other possible candidates include the Philippines, where the replacement of strongman rule in 1986 had revolutionary overtones but where it remains too soon to judge whether significant changes in social arrangements are involved. These revolutions do not count the important shifts to and from authoritarian and democratic regimes in other Latin-American countries, as well as in Africa and the Middle East, where the heavy popular involvement characteristic of a revolution as opposed to a coup d'etat was not fully present. Also omitted are the recent, largely nonviolent transformations in Eastern Europe.

The abundance of 20th-century revolutions raises vital questions about possible patterns and common causation, which are easier, however, to evoke than to answer. Contemporary revolutions occur in societies where significant changes are under way—such as the earliest phases of industrialization in Russia, the economic development undertaken by the prerevolutionary regime in Iran, or the initial political and educational changes in China—but where these changes have not yet had a chance to coalesce. The revolutionary moment, in other words, sees some groups antagonized by the shifts that have occurred and other groups eager for still more rapid change. Relatedly, 20th-century revolutions, like earlier revolts, always involve a number of different groups with diverse demands and revolutionary attributes, some capable of assuming political controls, others willing to participate in street violence or rural uprisings. Most of the 20th-century revolutions have a strong peasant component and take place where landlord controls had helped spur rural grievances (in contrast to poor regions where peasant ownership predominated).

The wave of 20th-century revolutions has always involved a prior intellectual buildup. Doctrines of democracy and liberalism, nationalism, or some form of socialism (most often Marxism) have provided the most common ideological spurs, but the Iranian revolution—one of the most distinctive in the group—was dominated by Islamic fundamentalism. Revolutions also, though this is an obvious point, require an absence of effective political outlets for key groups plus a weakening of the established state; strong governments can repress discontent, though it is always possible that too many years of repression will raise new doubts and uncertainties and so lead to a softening of the established order. Most revolutionary cases involve a government structure strong in principle but recently deteriorated due to weak new leaders (the tsarist case, for example) or the aging of an authoritarian figure (as in Mexico, Cuba, and Iran).

Some historians have sought to develop a standard revolutionary dynamic, based, however, on earlier Western models more than 20th-century cases. In this model, revolutions begin with initially liberal impulses, seeking greater freedom and control from below. Then as economic problems continue, and often civil strife and even foreign intervention, the liberal phase gives way to greater authority, even outright dictatorship. Elements of this pattern are visible in several 20th-century cases (such as China, Russia to an extent, Mexico, and Iran briefly) but the authoritarian strand in most instances emerges very quickly. This in turn often reflects an absence of a significant basis for liberalism in the host society, the decline of liberalism as a revolutionary doctrine, and the presence of more experienced revolutionary leaders who know that they must seize the state and use its power if the revolution is to have a chance.

An important common ingredient of 20th-century revolutions is the need to come to terms with Western influence and often to reassert greater national autonomy. Mexico, Russia, and China all grappled with growing Western economic control and cultural influence in the early 20th century, and all tried to come up with alternative development models. Though an array of internal issues is involved in each revolution, the problem of reacting to the West, as well as the objections to the responses developed by the existing regime (often friendlier to Western involvement or at least weaker in its face than the revolutionaries desire), serves as a common bond. Many revolutions thus heighten anti-Western sentiment, at least for a time, and all try to reduce the Western power to interfere with internal affairs. Thus the Russian Revolution reduced foreign business involvement, while Stalinism went on the attack against "decadent" Western cultural influence.

This revolutionary feature helps explain why 20th-century revolutions have generally occurred in societies that had not been Western colonies, at least in their recent past, for in such colonies national independence movements could serve some of the purposes revolutions served elsewhere. Colonial administration often brought some of the changes revolutionaries sought elsewhere, in unseating old-fashioned monarchies for example; independence movements brought new leaders to power and gave larger groups a sense of national pride that made revolution for a time less salient. This may explain why India and most of Africa have avoided revolution to date in the 20th century (just as Latin America did during its first century of independence after 1820).

No sense of a schema for 20th-century revolutions should, however, ignore two basic points. First, each revolution, including of course the Russian, had its own flavor—its own specific causes, its own outcomes. Individual flavor came from distinctive cultural traditions, social balances, and individual leadership. Not every revolution, for example, had a Lenin who could unify and galvanize the whole experience. Second, while 20th-century revolutions share some common ingredients, including previous government heavy-handedness, ideological buildup, peasant or other mass discontent, and anti-Western reactions, it remains impossible to predict where revolution will strike next. Understanding what revolutions are like once they occur, as well as grasping certain common features such as a period of radical isolation and truculence with foreign intervention, is possible on the basis of a sketch of the common revolutionary dynamic. And it is possible to suggest that certain societies are unlikely to face revolution because of the strength of government, social balance, or recency of major change. But revolutions involve enough accident, a sufficiently unusual blend of factors, that precise forecasting defies expertise—whether the expertise comes from the historian or the intelligence community employed by one of the established powers fearful of revolutionary explosion. Right before World War I, an Austrian banker urged investment in the Russian Empire because it had endured so well compared to the harassed regimes of Western Europe; right before the Iranian Revolution, the American Central Intelligence Agency sent back rosy reports of the government's solidity. Revolutions do have patterns, and these patterns suggest a great deal about the dynamic of 20th-century world history in which the phenomenon of revolution has loomed so large. Revolutions must also be evaluated through their spontaneous qualities, their capacity to make predictions look ridiculous.

Questions: How do 20th-century revolutions compare with "liberal" Western revolutions from 1789 to 1848? Will revolutions affect other societies in the 21st century, or has the revolutionary movement exhausted itself?

BUILDING SOVIET SOCIETY

The mid-1920s constituted a lively, experimental period in Soviet history, partly because of jockeying for power at the top of the power pyramid. Despite the absence of Western-style political competition, a host of new groups found a voice. The Communist party, though not eager to recruit too many members lest it lose its tight organization and elite status, encouraged all sorts of subsidiary organizations. Youth movements, women's groups, and particularly organizations of workers all actively debated problems in their social environment and what directions future planning should take. Workers were able to influence management practices, while women's leaders helped carve legal equality and new educational and work opportunities for their constituents.

The atmosphere of excited debate spilled over into such areas as family policy. At various points Soviet policy seemed to downplay the importance of family in favor of individual rights, thus making it easy to obtain divorces or abortions. Ultimately, by the 1930s the pendulum swung back toward greater conservatism, featuring protection of the family unit and an effort to encourage the birthrate, but only after some fascinating fluctuations and experimentalism. One key to the creative mood of these years was the rapid spread of education promoted by the government, plus educational and propaganda activities sponsored by various adult groups. Literacy gained ground quickly. The new educational system was also bent on reshaping popular culture away from older peasant traditions and, above all, religion, and toward beliefs in Communist political analysis and in science. Access to new information, new modes of inquiry, and new values encouraged controversy.

STALINISM

The experimental mood began to fade after 1927, when Joseph Stalin acquired full power over potential rivals. Stalin, eager for authoritarian control, was also anxious to renew the momentum toward socialism that had been deflected by the New Economic Policy and the surge of discussion among many mass organizations. By this point the bulk of the land lay in the hands of a minority of wealthy, commercially oriented peasants, the *kulaks*, who were particularly attuned to a profit-based market agriculture. Rural Russia seemed inclined to parallel earlier Western experience, in dividing the peasantry among relatively innovative owners and a mass of laborers—and this was not socialism. Even in industry, state-run enterprises and planning had only limited effect, as opposed to small private businesses. Stalin devoted himself to a double task: to make the Soviet Union a fully industrial society, and to do so under full control of the state, rather than through private initiative and individual ownership of producing property. In essence, Stalin wanted modernization, but with a revolutionary, noncapitalist twist. And while he was willing to borrow Western techniques and advice, importing a small number of foreign engineers for example, he insisted on Russian control and largely Russian endeavor.

ECONOMIC POLICIES

A massive program to collectivize agriculture began in 1928. *Collectivization* meant the creation of large, state-run farms rather than individual holdings as in the West. Communist party agitators pressed peasants to join in collectives. The collective movement was not only distinctively socialistic; it further offered, at least in theory, the chance to mechanize agriculture most effectively, as collective farms could group scarce equipment such as tractors and harvesters. Collectivization also allowed more efficient control over peasants themselves, as the Soviet state continued (in radical new form) a Russian reluctance to leave peasants to their own devices. Government and party control was desirable not only for political reasons, but also because Stalin's hopes for a speedup of industrialization required that resources be taken from peasants, through taxation, in order to provide capital for industry.

The Russian peasantry responded to collectivization with a decidedly mixed voice. Many laborers, resentful of kulak wealth, initially welcomed the opportunity to have more direct access to land. But most kulaks refused to cooperate voluntarily, often destroying livestock and other property rather than submit to collectivization. Devastating famine resulted from Stalin's insistence on pressing forward. In addition, millions of kulaks were killed or deported to Siberia during the early 1930s, in one of the most brutal oppressions of what turned out to be a brutal century in world history. Gradually, rural resistance collapsed and production began to increase once again; the decimation of the kulaks may indeed have weakened opportunities to oppose Stalin's increasingly authoritarian hold for a generation or more. But collectivization, though increasingly thorough, was not a smash success, for even those peasants who participated often seemed relatively unmotivated. While the collective farms allowed peasants small plots of their own, plus job security and considerable propagandizing by the omnipresent party members, they created an atmosphere of factory-like discipline and rigid planning from above that antagonized many. The centralized planning process allowed few incentives for special efforts and often complicated a smooth flow of supplies and equipment, a problem also exacerbated by the Stalinist regime's priority concentration on the industrial sector. Agricultural production remained a major weakness in the Soviet economy, demanding a higher percentage of the labor force than was common under industrialization.

The collective farms did, however, allow normally adequate if minimal food supplies once the messy transition period had ended, and they did free excess workers to be channeled into the ranks of urban labor. The late 1920s and early 1930s saw a massive flow of unskilled workers into the cities, as Russia's industrialization shifted into high gear.

If Stalin's approach to agriculture had serious flaws, his handling of industry was in most ways a smashing success. A system of five-year plans under the state planning commission began to set clear priorities for industrial development, including expected output levels and new facilities. The government constructed massive factories in metallurgy, mining, and electric power to make Russia an industrial country independent of Western-dominated world banking and trading patterns, with the productive infrastructure also suitable for modern war. There was more than a hint of Peter the Great's policies here, in updating the economy without really Westernizing it, save that industrialization constituted a more massive departure than anything Peter had contemplated. The focus, as earlier, was on heavy industry, which built on Russia's great natural resources and also served to prepare for possible war with Hitler's anti-Communist Germany. This distinctive industrialization, which slighted consumer goods production, was to remain characteristic of the Soviet version of industrial society. Further, Stalin sought to create an alternative not simply to private business ownership but to the profit-oriented market mechanisms of the West. Thus he relied not on price competition but on formal, centralized resource allocation to distribute equipment and supplies. This led to many bottlenecks and considerable waste, as quotas for individual factories were set in Moscow, but there was no question that rapid industrial growth occurred. During the first two five-year plans, to 1937—that is, during the same period the West was mired in the depression—Russia's output of machinery and metal products grew fourteenfold. Russia had become the world's third industrial power, behind Germany and the United States. A long history of backwardness seemed to have ended.

TOWARD AN INDUSTRIAL SOCIETY

The Russian industrialization process, for all its distinctive features, produced many results similar to those in the West. Increasing numbers of Russians were crowded into cities, often cramped in inadequate housing stock—for Russian planners, like earlier Western capitalists, were reluctant to put too many resources into mass housing. Factory discipline was strict as Communist managers sought to instill new habits in a peasant-derived work force. Incentive procedures were introduced to motivate higher production. Particularly capable workers received bonuses and also elaborate public awards for their service to society. At the same time, Communist policy quickly built up a network of welfare services, surpassing the West in this area as well as reversing decades of tsarist neglect. Workers had meeting houses and recreational programs, plus protection in cases of illness and old age. Soviet industrial society provided only modest standards of living at this point, but a host of collective activities compensated to some degree. Finally, while Soviet industry was directed from the top, with no legal outlet for worker grievances—strikes were outlawed, and the only trade union movement was controlled by the party—worker concerns were studied, and identified problems were addressed. Stalinist Russia used force and authority, but it also recognized the importance of maintaining worker support—so, informally, it consulted as well.

TOTALITARIAN RULE

Stalin combined his industrialization program with a new intensification of government police procedures, as he used the party and state apparatus to monopolize power, even more thoroughly than Hitler's totalitarian state attempted. Opponents and imagined opponents of his version of communism were executed. During the great purge of party leaders that culminated in 1937 and 1938, hundreds of people were intimidated into confessing imaginary crimes against the state, and most of them were put to death. Many thousands more were sent to Siberian labor camps. Any possibility of vigorous internal initiative was crushed, as both the state and the Communist party were bent under Stalin's suspicious will. News outlets were monopolized by the state and the party, and informal meetings also risked a visit from the ubiquitous secret police, renamed the MVD (Ministry of Internal Affairs) in 1934. Party congresses and meetings of the executive committee, or *Politburo*, became mere rubber stamps. An atmosphere of terror spread in Russian society.

Stalin's purges, which included top army officials, ironically weakened the nation's ability to respond to growing foreign policy problems, notably the rising threat of Hitler. Soviet diplomatic initiatives after the revolution had been unwontedly modest, given the nation's traditions, largely because of the intense concentration on internal development. Diplomatic relations with major nations were gradually reestablished, as the fact of Communist leadership was accepted, and the Soviet Union was allowed into the League of Nations. A few secret military negotiations, as with Turkey in the early 1920s, showed a flicker of interest in more active diplomacy, and of course the nation continued to encourage and often guide internal Communist party activities in many other countries.

Hitler's rise was a clear signal that more active concern was necessary. A strong Germany was inevitably a threat to Russia from the west, and Hitler was vocal about his scorn for Slavic peoples and communism, about his desire to create a "living room" for Germany to the east. Stalin initially hoped that he could cooperate with the Western democracies in blocking the German threat. The Soviet Union thus tried to participate in a common response to German and Italian intervention during the Spanish civil war in 1936 and 1937. But France and Britain were incapable of forceful action and were in any event almost as suspicious of the Soviets as of the Nazis. So the Soviet Union, unready for war and greatly disappointed in the West, signed the historic agreement with Hitler in 1939. This pact bought some time for greater war preparation, and also enabled Russian troops to attack eastern Poland and Finland in an effort to regain territories lost in World War I. Here was the first sign of a revival of Russia's long interest in conquest, which would be intensified by the experience of World War II.

The awkward honeymoon with Hitler did not last. The Nazis, having completed their sweep of France but blocked from invading Britain, quickly regained their eastern appetites, sharpened by concern about the Soviet Union's territorial gains. The invasion of the Soviet Union was launched in 1941 and soon brought a new Soviet alliance with the Western powers including, by the end of the year, the United States.

The war itself was devastating but also exhilarating for the Soviet Union. Russia's new industrial base, hastily relocated in the Ural Mountains and beyond, proved vital in providing the material needed for war, but the effort was extremely costly. Great cities such as Leningrad and Stalingrad were besieged by the Germans for months, with huge loss of life. The war heightened Russia's age-old fear of invasion and foreign interference, already enhanced by World War I and Western intervention during the revolution. But as the Red Army pressed westward after 1943, finally penetrating to the Elbe River in Germany, there was new opportunity for aggrandizement. Russia was able to regain its former western boundaries at the expense of nations such as Poland; some small states set up by the Treaty of Versailles were swallowed entirely. Larger eastern European states were allowed to remain intact, but their regimes were quickly brought under the control of Communist parties backed by the Soviet occupation forces.

DOCUMENT
SOCIALIST REALISM

One of the most fascinating features of the Soviet system was the attempt to create a distinctive art, different from Western culture now regarded as decadent, and appropriate to the Communist mission. This effort involved a great deal of censorship and forced orthodoxy, but it constituted also an attempt to resolve earlier Russian problems of relating formal culture to the masses and of trying to preserve distinctiveness amid the seductions of Western influence. The following effort to define Soviet artistic policy was written by Andrey Zhdanov in 1934, the year Stalin made him the party's spokesman at the Congress of Soviet Writers.

. . . There is not and never has been a literature making its basic subject-matter the life of the working class and the peasantry and their struggle for socialism. There does not exist in any country in the world a literature to defend and protect the equality of rights of the working people of all nations and the equality of rights of women. There is not, nor can there be in any bourgeois country, a literature to wage consistent war on all obscurantism, mysticism, hierarchic religious attitudes and threats of hell-fire, as our literature does.

Only Soviet literature could become and has in fact become such an advanced, thought-imbued literature. It is one flesh and blood with our socialist construction. . . .

What can the bourgeois writer write or think of, where can he find passion, if the worker in the capitalist countries is not sure of his tomorrow, does not know whether he will have work, if the peasant does not know whether he will be working on his bit of land or thrown on the scrap heap by a capitalist crisis, if the working intellectual is out of work today and does not know whether he will have work tomorrow?

What can the bourgeois author write about, what source of inspiration can there be for him, when the world, from one day to the next, may be plunged once more into the abyss of a new imperialist war?

The present position of bourgeois literature is such that it is already incapable of producing great works. *The decline and decay of bourgeois literature derive from the decline and decay of the capitalist system and are a feature and aspect characteristic of the present condition of bourgeois culture and literature.* The days when bourgeois literature, reflecting the victories of the bourgeois system over feudalism, was in the heyday of capitalism capable of creating great works, have gone, never to return. Today a degeneration in subject matter, in talents, in authors and in heroes, is in progress. . . .

A riot of mysticism, religious mania and pornography is characteristic of the decline and decay of bourgeois culture. The "celebrities" of that bourgeois literature which has sold its pen to capital are today thieves, detectives, prostitutes, pimps and gangsters. . . .

The proletariat of the capitalist countries is already forging its army of writers and artists — revolutionary writers, the representatives of whom we are glad to be able to welcome here today at the first Soviet Writers' Congress. The number of revolutionary writers in the capitalist countries is still small but it is growing and will grow with every day's sharpening of the class struggle, with the growing strength of the world proletarian revolution.

We are firmly convinced that the few dozen foreign comrades we have welcomed here constitute the kernel, the embryo, of a mighty army of proletarian writers to be created by the world proletarian revolution in foreign countries. . . .

Comrade Stalin has called our writers "engineers of the human soul." What does this mean? What obligations does such an appellation put upon you?

It means, in the first place, that you must know life to be able to depict it truthfully in artistic creations, to depict it neither "scholastically" nor lifelessly, nor simply as "objective reality," but rather as reality in its revolutionary development. The truthfulness and historical exactitude of the artistic image must be linked with the task of ideological transformation, of the education of the working people in the spirit of socialism. This method in fiction and literary criticism is what we call the method of socialist realism.

Our Soviet literature is not afraid of being called tendentious, for in the epoch of class struggle there is not and cannot be "apolitical" literature.

And it seems to me that any and every Soviet writer may say to any dull-witted bourgeois, to any philistine or to any bourgeois writers who speak of the tendentiousness of our literature: "Yes, our Soviet literature is tendentious and we are proud of it, for our tendentiousness is to free the working people—and the whole of mankind—from the yoke of capitalist slavery."

To be an engineer of the human soul is to stand four-square on real life. And this in turn means a break with oldstyle romanticism, with the romanticism which depicted a non-existent life and non-existent heroes, drawing the reader away from the contradictions and shackles of life into an unrealizable and utopian world. Romanticism is not alien to our literature, a literature standing firmly on a materialistic basis, but ours is a romanticism of a new type, revolutionary romanticism.

We say that socialist realism is the fundamental method of Soviet fiction and literary criticism, and this implies that revolutionary romanticism will appear as an integral part of any literary creation, since the whole life of our Party, of the working class and its struggle, is a fusion of the hardest, most matter-of-fact practical work, with the greatest heroism and the vastest perspectives. The strength of our Party has always lain in the fact that it has united and unites efficiency and practicality with broad vision, with an incessant forward striving and the struggle to build a communist society.

Soviet literature must be able to portray our heroes and to see our tomorrow. This will not be utopian since our tomorrow is being prepared by planned and conscious work today. . . .

Questions: What were the reasons for culture according to Stalinist intellectuals? How did Soviet cultural leaders analyze Western intellectual life?

THE SOVIET UNION AS A SUPERPOWER

By 1945 Soviet foreign policy had several ingredients. Desire to regain tsarist boundaries (though not carried through regarding Finland) joined with traditional interest in expansion and in playing an active role in European diplomacy. Genuine revulsion at Germany's two invasions prompted a feverish desire to set up buffer zones under Soviet control. As a result of Soviet industrialization and its World War II push westward, the nation also emerged as a world power, like the newcomer United States. Continued concentration on heavy industry and weapons development, plus strategic alliances and links to Communist movements in various parts of the world, helped maintain this status.

Russian participation in the late phases of the war against Japan brought an opportunity to seize some islands in the northern Pacific. Russia established a protectorate over the Communist regime of North Korea to match the American protectorate in South Korea. Russian aid to the victorious Communist party in China brought new influence in that country for a time, and in the 1970s Russia was to gain a new ally in Communist Vietnam, which among other things provided naval bases for the Russian fleet. Russia's growing military and economic strength gave the postwar Soviet Union new leverage in the Middle East, Africa, and even parts of Latin America; alliance with newly Communist Cuba was a key step here during

Soviet and East European Boundaries by 1948

The small nations of eastern Europe, mostly new or revived after World War I, had gone through a troubled period between the world wars, and this helped make them vulnerable to Nazi and then Soviet advances. Most were consumed by nationalist excitement at independence by 1918, as well as by intense grievances about territories not acquired. Hence there were bitter rivalries among the East European states, which weakened them diplomatically and economically. Most of the new nations began the interwar period with some form of parliamentary democracy in imitation of the West but soon converted to authoritarian rule, either through a dictator (as was the pattern in Poland) or by a monarch's seizure of new power (as in Yugoslavia, the new nation expanded from Serbia). This political pattern resulted from more underlying social tensions. Most East European countries remained primarily agricultural and heavily dependent on sales to western Europe. They were hard hit by the collapse of agricultural prices in the 1920s, and then they were further damaged by the depression. Furthermore, most countries also refused to undertake serious land reform, despite widely professed intentions. Aristocratic estate owners thus sought desperately to repress peasant movements, which brought them to the support of authoritarian regimes complete, often, with vaguely fascist trappings. Peasant hunger to own land and continued problems of poverty and illiteracy were simply not addressed in most cases.

Only Czechoslovakia stood as an exception, where an unusually advanced industrialization process and extensive urban culture, combined with substantial land reform, produced the basis for an effective parliamentary-democratic regime. Only Czechoslovakia, relatedly, clearly maintained the East European borderland impulse to look primarily to the West for models and interaction. Most of the rest of eastern Europe remained caught between Western patterns that seemed impossible or irrelevant and a revolutionary Soviet Union now feared for its communism as well as its Russian strength. The situation was predictably impossible. While the interwar experience served to enhance nationalist loyalties, it did not create a viable economic or diplomatic system for the region.

Then came the Nazi attack and ineffective Western response. Czechoslovakia, Poland, and Yugoslavia were seized by German or Italian forces. Several other East European authoritarians allied directly with Hitler, because of shared ideological leanings and a fear of the Soviet Union plus Germany's great economic voice as primary importer and exporter. Eastern Europe fell under Nazi control for four years, compelled to provide troops and labor and brought under Hitler's holocaust attack on the Jews.

the 1960s. The Soviet Union's superpower status was confirmed by its development of the atomic and then hydrogen bombs from 1949 onward and by its deployment of missiles and naval forces to match the rapid expansion of United States arsenals. Russia had become a world power.

THE NEW SOVIET EMPIRE IN EASTERN EUROPE

While the Soviet Union, as a superpower, developed increasing worldwide influence, with trade and cultural missions on all inhabited continents and military alliances with several Asian, African, and Latin-American nations, the clearest extension of the Soviet sphere developed right after World War II in Eastern Europe, and here the Soviets made it clear that they intended to stay, pushing Russia's effective sphere of influence farther to the west than ever before in history. Soviet insistence on this empire helped launch the cold war, as the Soviet Union demonstrated its willingness to confront the West rather than relax its grip.

The Red Armies came next, directly liberating all of eastern Europe plus the eastern part of Germany to the Elbe River, except for Greece and Yugoslavia, remaking the East European map. Through the combination of Soviet military might and collaboration with local Communist movements in the nations that remained technically independent, opposition parties were crushed and non-Communist regimes were forced out by 1948. Only three East European nations stood out from the common pattern: Greece, which moved toward the Western camp in diplomatic alignment and political and social systems; Albania, which formed a rigid Stalinist regime that ironically brought it into disagreement with Russia's post-Stalinist leaders; and Yugoslavia, where a Communist regime formed under the resistance leader Tito quickly proclaimed its neutrality in the cold war, defying Soviet direction and trying to form a more open-ended, responsive version of the Communist economic and social system.

Through most of Eastern Europe, after the essential Soviet takeover, a standard development dynamic emerged by the early 1950s. The new Soviet-sponsored regimes attacked possible rivals for power, including where relevant the Roman Catholic church. Mass education and propaganda outlets were quickly spread. Collectivization of agriculture ended the large estate system without creating a property-owning peasantry. Industrialization was pushed through successive five-year plans, though with some limitations due to Soviet insistence on access to key natural resources (such as Romanian oil) on favorable terms. After the formation of NATO in Western Europe, the relevant East European nations were also enfolded in a common defense alliance, the Warsaw Pact, and a common economic planning organization. Soviet troops continued to be stationed in most East European states both to confront the Western alliance and to monitor the new regimes and their loyalty to the common cause.

The imposition of the Soviet system, while it responded to many social problems in the smaller nations of Eastern Europe as well as to the desire of the Soviet Union to expand its influence and guard against German or more general Western attack, created obvious tensions. Dissatisfaction with particularly tight controls in East Germany brought a workers' uprising in 1953, vigorously repressed by Soviet troops, and widespread exodus to West Germany until a Berlin wall was built in 1961 to contain the flow. All along the new borders of Eastern Europe barbed wire fences and armed patrols served to keep the people in. Relaxation of Stalinism within the Soviet Union in 1956 created new hopes that controls might be loosened. More liberal Communist leaders arose in Hungary and Poland, with massive popular backing, seeking to create states that, while Communist, would permit greater diversity and certainly more freedom from Soviet domination. In Poland, the Russians accepted a new leader more popular with the Polish people; among other results, Poland was allowed to halt agricultural collectivization, establishing widespread peasant ownership in its place, while the Catholic church, now the symbol of Polish independence, gained greater tolerance. A new regime in Hungary, however, was cruelly crushed by the Russian army and replaced by hard-line Stalinist leadership.

Yet Soviet control over Eastern Europe did loosen slightly overall, for the heavy-handed repression cost considerable prestige. East European governments were given a freer hand in economic policy and were allowed limited room to experiment with greater cultural freedom. Several countries thus began to outstrip the Soviet Union in industrialization levels and consumer prosperity. Contacts with the West expanded in several cases, with greater trade and tourism. Eastern Europe remained, with the Soviet Union, a somewhat separate economic bloc in world trade, but there was room for limited diversity. Individual nations such as Hungary developed new intellectual vigor, while experimenting with slightly less centralized economic planning. The Communist political system remained in full force, however, with its single-party dominance and strong police controls, and diplomatic and military alignment with the Soviet Union remained essential.

The limits of experimentation in Eastern Europe were brought home again in 1968, when a more liberal regime came to power in Czechoslovakia. Again the Russian army responded, expelling the reformers and setting up a particularly rigid leader in their stead. A challenge came again from Poland in the late 1970s in the form of widespread Catholic unrest plus an independent labor movement called Solidarity, all against the backdrop of a stagnant economy and low morale. Here response was slightly more muted, though key agitators were arrested; the Polish army took over the state, under careful Soviet supervision.

Eastern Europe had, by the 1980s, been vastly transformed by several decades of Communist rule. Important national diversity remained, visible both in industrial levels and in political styles. Important discontents remained as well. Yet a Communist-imposed social revolution had brought considerable economic change and real social upheaval, through the abolition of the once-dominant aristocracy and the remaking of the peasant masses through collectivization and industrial, urban growth. Earlier cultural ties with the West, though still greater than in the Soviet Union itself, had been lessened; Russian, not French or English, was the first foreign language learned.

The expansion of Soviet influence answered important foreign policy goals, both traditional and new. The Soviets retained military presence deep in Europe, which among

As Soviet troops moved into Hungary to crush the revolt of 1956, freedom fighters in Budapest headed for the front with whatever weapons they could find.

other things reduced very real anxiety about yet another German threat. East European allies aided Soviet ventures in other parts of the world, providing supplies and advisors for activities in Africa, Latin America, and elsewhere. The recurrent unrest in Eastern Europe served as something of a check on Soviet policy as well; the need for continued military presence may have diverted Soviet leaders from emphasizing expansionist ambitions in other directions, particularly where direct commitment of troops might be involved.

EVOLUTION OF DOMESTIC POLICIES

Within the Soviet Union, the Stalinist system remained intact during the initial postwar years. The war encouraged growing use of nationalism as well as appeals for Communist loyalty, as millions of Russians responded heroically to the new foreign threat. Elements of this mood were sustained as the cold war with the United States took shape after 1947, with news media blasting America as an evil power and a distorted society. Many Russians, fearful of a new war that American aggressiveness seemed to threaten, agreed that strong government authority remained necessary. This attitude helped sustain the difficult rebuilding

efforts after the war, which proceeded rapidly enough for the Soviet Union to regain its prewar industrial capacity and then proceed, during the 1950s, to impressive annual growth rates. The attitude also helped support Stalin's rigorous efforts to shield the Soviet population from extensive contact with foreigners or foreign ideas. Strict limits on travel, outside media, or any uncensored glimpse of the outside world kept the Soviet Union unusually isolated in the mid-20th century world; its culture, like its economy, was largely removed from world currents.

Stalin's political structure continued to emphasize central controls and the ever-present party bureaucracy, leavened by the adulation accorded to Stalin himself and the aging leader's endemic suspiciousness. Moscow-based direction of the national economy, along with the steady extension of education, welfare, and police operations, expanded the bureaucracy both of the government and of the parallel Communist party. Recruitment from the ranks of peasant and worker families continued into the 1940s, as educational opportunities, including growing secondary school and university facilities, allowed talented young people to rise from below. Party membership was the ticket to bureaucratic promotion, and the party deliberately kept its membership low, at about six percent of the population, to assure selection of the most dedicated elements. New candidates for the party, drawn mostly from the more broadly based Communist youth organizations, had to be nominated by at least three party members. They vowed unswerving loyalty and group consciousness. A 1939 party charter stated the essential qualities:

> The Party is a united militant organization bound together by a conscious discipline which is equally binding on all its members. The Party is strong because of its solidarity, unity of will and unity of action, which are incompatible with any deviation from its program and rules, with any violation of Party discipline, with fractional groupings, or with double-dealing. The Party purges its ranks of persons who violate its program, rules or discipline.

Through the party apparatus, the Soviet system became characterized by careful hierarchy and elaborate bureaucracy. The party was run by the Politburo, consisting of 20 people who were the real power brokers in the nation—operating, of course, under Stalin's watchful eye. Most Politburo members also held key ministries or top positions in the secret police or army. The Politburo apparatus helped coordinate these various branches and balance their interests and ambitions. Both party and state, as overlapping governing bodies, spread gradations of authority from the top committees through the regional governments to local industries, cities, and collective farms. Decisions were made at the top, often in secret, and then transmitted to lower levels for execution; little reverse initiative, with proposals coming from lower bureaucratic agencies, was encouraged.

The Stalinist version of this system, indeed, engendered particular bureaucratic caution. Innovative proposals, much less criticisms, were risky. Top officials who kept their posts tended to be colorless figures, competent but above all extremely loyal both to official ideology and to Stalin as leader. One durable foreign minister, Molotov, for example, was described by Stalin as having a "mind like a file clerk."

The Communist government built on the precedent of tsarist authoritarianism. As with the tsars, political contests and open-ended agencies such as multiparty parliaments were shunned. Carefully worded constitutions gave Russians the vote and required participation in elections, but mainly to rubber-stamp official candidates and policies. The Supreme Soviet, like the earlier duma, had no power to initiate legislation or block official decisions; it served to ratify and praise.

SOVIET CULTURE: PROMOTING NEW BELIEFS

The Soviet government was also a new product, and an impressive one. It carried on a much wider array of functions than the tsars had ventured, not only in fostering industrialization but also in reaching out for the direct loyalties of individual citizens. The direction of agriculture was itself a new initiative that the tsars had never attempted. The government and party also maintained an active cultural agenda. While this had been foreshadowed by the church-state links of tsarist days, it had no full precedent. The regime quickly declared war on the Orthodox church and other religions, seeking to shape a secular population that would maintain a Marxist, scientific orthodoxy; vestigial church activities remained but under tight government regulation. Artistic and literary styles, as well as purely political writings, were carefully monitored to assure the party line. The educational system was used to train and recruit technicians and bureaucrats, as well as to create a loyal, right-thinking citizenry. New mass ceremonies, such as May Day parades, stimulated devotion to Russia and communism.

While the new regime did not attempt to abolish the Orthodox church outright, it greatly limited the church's outreach. Thus the church was barred from giving religious instruction to anyone under the age of 18, while state schools vigorously preached that religion is mere superstition. While loyalties to the church persisted, they now seemed concentrated in a largely elderly minority. The Soviet regime also limited freedom of religion for the Jewish minority, often holding Jews up as enemies of the state in what was, in fact, a manipulation of traditional Russian anti-Semitism. The larger Muslim minority was given greater latitude, on condition of careful loyalty to the regime. On the whole, the traditional religious orientation of Russian society was severely tested in favor of a scientific outlook and Marxist explanations of history in terms of class conflict.

The Soviet state also opposed the strong Western cultural orientation of the 19th-century tsarist elite, which had never widely touched the masses in any event. Modern Western styles of art and literature were attacked as decadent. Earlier styles, appropriated as Russian, were maintained. Thus Russian orchestras performed a wide variety of classical music, and the Russian ballet, though rigid and conservative by 20th-century Western norms, commanded wide attention and enforced rigorous standards of excellence. Soviet culture emphasized a new style of "Socialist realism" in the arts, bent on glorifying heroic workers, soldiers, and peasants. A vigorous strand of modern art in prerevolutionary and 1920s Russia was repulsed under Stalin in favor of grandiose, neoclassical paintings and sculpture. Russian architecture, though careful to preserve older buildings, emphasized functional, classical lines, with a pronounced taste for the monumental. Socialist realist principles spread to Eastern Europe after World War II, particularly in public displays and monuments. With some political loosening and cold war thaw after 1950, however, Soviet and East European artists began to interact somewhat more with Western styles. At the popular level, jazz and rock music bands began to emerge by the 1980s, though official suspicion persisted.

Russian literature remained diverse and creative, despite official controls sponsored by the Communist-dominated Writers' Union. Leading Russian authors wrote movingly of the travails of the civil war and World War II, maintaining the earlier tradition of sympathy with the Russian people, great patriotism, and a concern for the Russian soul.

In his 1949 painting, *Creative Fellowship*, Shcherbakov shows the cooperation of scientists and workers in an idealized factory setting.

The most creative Soviet artists, and particularly the writers, often skirted a fine line between conveying some of the sufferings of the Russian people in the 20th century and courting official disapproval. Their freedom also varied, depending on leadership mood; thus censorship eased after Stalin, and then tightened somewhat though not to previous levels. Yet even authors critical of aspects of the Soviet regime maintained distinctive Russian values. Aleksandr Solzhenitsyn, for example, who was exiled to the West because of publication of his trilogy on Siberian prison camps, *Gulag Archipelago*, found the West too materialistic and individualistic for his taste. Though barred from his homeland, he continued to seek some alternative both to Communist policy and to Westernization, with more than a hint of a continuing belief in the durable solidarity and faith of the Russian common people and the national soul.

Along with interest in the arts and a genuine diversity of expression despite official party lines, Soviet culture placed strong emphasis on science and social science. Scientists enjoyed great prestige and wielded considerable power. Social scientific work, heavily colored by Marxist theory, nonetheless produced important analyses of current trends and history. Scientific research was even more heavily funded, and Soviet scientists generated a number of fundamental discoveries in physics, chemistry, and mathematics. At times scientists felt the heavy hand of official disapproval. Biologists and psychiatrists, particularly, were urged to reject Western theories that called human rationality and social progress into question. Thus Freudianism was banned, and under Stalin biologists who overemphasized the uncontrollability of genetic evolution were jailed. But Russian scientists overall enjoyed considerable latitude as well as real prestige. As in the West, their work was often linked with advances in technology and weaponry. After the heyday of Stalinism, scientists gained greater freedom from ideological dictates, and exchanges with Western researchers became more common in what was, at base, a common scientific culture.

Shaped by substantial state control, 20th-century Soviet culture overall proved neither traditional nor Western. Considerable ambivalence about the West remained, as Russians continued to utilize many art forms they developed in common with the West, such as the ballet, while instilling a comparable faith in science. Fear of cultural pollution, particularly of course through non-Marxist political tracts but also through modern art forms, remained lively, as Soviet leaders sought a culture that would enhance their goals of building a socialist society separate from the capitalist West.

In this example of Socialist realism, heroic women workers labor at a bustling, productive factory. Their stalwart energy was an inspiration to the Soviet people.

ECONOMY AND SOCIETY

The Soviet Union became a fully industrial society between the 1920s and 1950s. Rapid growth of manufacturing and the rise of city populations to over 50 percent of the total were measures of this development. Most of the rest of Eastern Europe was also fully industrialized by the 1950s. East European modernization, however, had a number of distinctive features. State control of virtually all economic sectors was one key element. No other industrialized society gave so little leeway to private initiative. The unusual imbalance between heavy industrial goods and consumer items was another distinctive aspect. The Soviet Union lagged in the priorities it placed on consumer goods—not only Western staples such as automobiles, but also housing construction and simple items such as bathtub plugs. Consumer-goods industries were poorly funded and did not achieve the advanced technological level that characterized the heavy manufacturing sector. The Soviet need to amass capital for development, in a traditionally poor society, helped explain the inattention to consumer goods; so did the need to create a massive armaments industry to ri-

val that of the United States, in a society that remained poorer overall. Thus, despite an occasional desire to beat the West at its own affluent-society game, Eastern Europe did not develop the kind of consumer society that came to characterize the West. Living standards improved greatly, and extensive welfare services provided security for some groups that was lacking in the West, but complaints about poor consumer products and long lines to obtain desired goods remained a feature of Soviet life.

The Communist system throughout Eastern Europe also failed to resolve problems with agriculture. Capital that might have gone into farming equipment was often diverted to armaments and heavy industry. The arduous climate of northern Europe and Asia was a factor as well, dooming a number of attempts to spread grain production to Siberia, for example. It also seemed clear that the East European peasantry continued to find the constraints and lack of individual incentive in collectivized agriculture a deterrent to maximum effort. Thus, Eastern Europe had to retain a larger percentage of its labor force in agriculture than was true of the industrial West and still encountered problems with food supply and quality.

Despite the importance of distinctive political and economic characteristics, Eastern European society echoed a number of the themes of contemporary Western social history—simply because of the shared fact of industrial life. Work rhythms, for example, became roughly similar. Industrialization in Russia brought massive efforts to speed the pace of work and introduce regularized supervision. The incentive systems designed to encourage able workers resembled those used in Western factories. Along with similar work habits came similar leisure activities. Sports provided excitement for the peoples of Eastern Europe, as did mass media such as films and television. Family vacations to the beaches of the Black Sea became cherished respites. Here too there were some distinctive twists, as the Communist states boosted sports efforts as part of their political program (in contrast to the Western view of sports as a combination of leisure and commercialism).

East European social structure also grew closer to that of the West, despite the continued importance of the rural population and despite the impact of Marxist theory. Particularly interesting was a tendency to divide urban society along class lines, between workers and a better-educated, managerial middle class. Wealth divisions remained much less great than in the West, to be sure, but the perquisites of managers and professional people—particularly if they were Communist party members—set them off from the standard of living of the masses.

Finally, the Soviet family reacted to some of the same pressures of industrialization the Western family experienced. Massive movement to the cities and crowded housing focused the nuclear family unit, as ties to a wider network of relatives loosened. The birthrate dropped. Official Soviet policy on birthrates varied for a time, but the basic pressures became similar to those in the West. Declining infant death rates due to improved diets and medical care, plus growing periods of schooling and some increase in consumer expectations, made large families less desirable than before. Wartime dislocations contributed to birthrate decline as well. By the 1970s the Russian growth rate was about the same as that of the West. As in the West, also, some minority groups, particularly Muslims in southern Russia, maintained higher birthrates than the majority ethnic group—in this case, ethnic Russians—a differential that caused some concern about maintaining Russian cultural dominance in the future.

Patterns of child rearing showed some similarities to those in the West, as parents, especially in the managerial middle class, devoted great attention to promoting their children's education and assuring good jobs for the future. At the same time children were more strictly disciplined than in the West, both at home and in school, with an emphasis on authority that had political implications. Russian families never afforded the domestic idealization of women that had prevailed in the West during industrialization. Most married women worked, an essential feature of an economy struggling to industrialize and offering relatively low wages to individual workers. As in the peasant past, women performed many heavy physical tasks. They also dominated some professions, such as medicine, though these were far lower in status than their male-dominated counterparts in the West. Russian propagandists took pride in the constructive role of women and their official equality, but there were signs that many women suffered burdens from demanding jobs with little help from their husbands at home.

The features Russian society shared with the West, because of common urban and industrial experience, showed in aspects of popular culture. Concerns about acquisition, romance, and school success could have a very Western, or more properly modern-industrial, ring. Thus 1970s graffiti on a church wall in Leningrad—a traditional site of wish lists since the last tsarist days—displayed familiar personal aspirations:

"Lord, grant me luck, and help me to be accepted into the Art Academy in four years."—"Happiness and health to me and Volodya."—"Lord strangle Tarisyn."—"Lord, help me get rid of Valery."—"Lord, help me in love."—"Lord make Charlotte fall in love with me."—"Lord, I'm hungry."—"Lord, help me pass the exam in political economics."—"Lord, help me pass the exam in: (1) electrical technology; (2) electrical vacuum instruments; (3) Marxism-Leninism."—"Help me pass my driver's license test, Lord."—"Lord, take the arrogance out of my wife."—"Lord, help me win a transistor radio, model AP-2-14, in the lottery." (Added on by another person:) "All we have is P-20-1. Archangel Gabriel."

Overall, Soviet society and culture displayed a distinctive blend of basic features. Several key traditions persisted, like beliefs in a Russian soul. Revolutionary emphases produced unique artistic forms (though later imitated in other Communist societies) and the large bureaucratic class. Industrialization generated many familiar forms of urban life, even in such intimate areas as family behavior and personal aspirations.

DE-STALINIZATION

The rigid government apparatus, created by Stalin and sustained after World War II by frequent arrests and exiles to forced labor camps, was put to a major test after Stalin's death in 1953. The results gradually loosened, without totally reversing, Stalinist cultural isolation.

Focus on one-man rule might have created immense succession problems, and indeed frequent jockeying for power did develop among aspiring candidates. Yet the system held together. Years of bureaucratic experience gave most Soviet leaders a taste for coordination and compromise, along with a reluctance to strike out in radical new directions that might cause controversy or arouse resistance from one of the key power blocs within the state. Stalin's death was answered by a ruling committee that balanced interest groups, notably the army, the police, and the party apparatus. This mechanism encouraged conservatism, as each bureaucratic sector defended its existing prerogatives, but it also assured fundamental stability.

In 1956, however, a new Soviet leader, Nikita Khrushchev, emerged from the committee pack to gain primary power, though without seeking to match Stalin's eminence. Khrushchev indeed attacked Stalinism for its concentration of power and arbitrary dictatorship, in a stirring speech delivered to the party congress. Khrushchev condemned Stalin for his treatment of political opponents, for his narrow interpretations of Marxist doctrine, even for his failure adequately to prepare for World War II. The implications of this startling blast modified the Soviet political climate and led to some decentralization of decision making. Little concrete institutional reform occurred, however. Political trials became less common, and the most overt police repression eased. A few intellectuals were allowed to raise new issues, dealing for example with the purges and other Stalinist excesses. Outright critics of the regime were less likely to be executed and more likely to be sent to psychiatric institutions or, in the case of internationally visible figures such as a handful of novelists, exiled to the West or confined to house arrest. Party control and centralized economic planning remained intact. Khrushchev indeed planned a major extension of state-directed initiative by opening new Siberian land to cultivation; his failure in this costly effort, plus his antagonization of many Stalinist loyalists, led to his quiet downfall.

After the de-Stalinization furor and Khrushchev's fall from power, patterns in the Soviet Union remained stable into the 1980s, verging at times on stagnant. Economic growth continued, but with no dramatic breakthroughs and with recurrent worries over sluggish productivity and especially over periodically inadequate harvests, which compelled expensive grain deals with Western nations including the United States. A number of subsequent leadership changes occurred, as party chieftains aged and died, but the transitions were handled smoothly.

Cold war policies eased somewhat upon Stalin's death. Khrushchev vaunted Soviet ability to outdo the West at its own industrial game, bragging on a visit to the United States that "we will bury you." The Khrushchev regime did produce one of the most intense moments of the cold war with the United States, as it probed for vulnerabilities. Exploiting the new alliance with Cuba the Soviets installed missiles there, yielding only to firm American response in 1962. Khrushchev had no desire for war, and both before and after the Cuban missile crisis he promoted a new policy of peaceful coexistence. He hoped to beat the West economically and actively expanded the Soviet space program: Sputnik, the first manned spacecraft, was sent into space in 1957, well in advance of the United States' equivalent. Khrushchev maintained a competitive tone, but he shifted away from the exclusive military emphasis. Lowered cold war tensions with the West permitted a small influx of Western tourists by the 1960s, plus greater access to the Western media and a variety of cultural exchanges that gave some Russians a renewed sense of contact with a wider world and restored some of the earlier ambiguities about Russia's relationship to Western standards.

At the same time the Soviet leadership continued a steady military buildup, adding increasingly sophisticated rocketry and bolstered by its unusually successful space program. The Soviets maintained a lead in manned space flights into the late 1980s. Both in space and in the arms race the Soviet Union demonstrated great technical ability combined with a willingness to settle for somewhat simpler systems than those the United States attempted, which helped explain how it could maintain superpower parity even with a less prosperous overall economy. An active sports program, resulting in a growing array of victories in Olympic Games competition, also showed the Soviet Union's new ability to compete on an international scale and its growing pride in international achievements.

The nation faced a number of new foreign policy problems, while maintaining superpower status. A growing rift with China, from the mid-1950s onward, pitted against each other two great Communist nations who also shared a massive border. Successful courtship of many other nations—such as Egypt, a close diplomatic friend during the 1960s—often turned sour, though these developments sometimes were balanced by new alignments elsewhere. The rise of Muslim awareness in the 1970s was deeply troubling to the Soviet Union, with its own large Muslim minority; this prompted an invasion of Afghanistan, to promote a friendly puppet regime, which bogged down amid guerrilla warfare into the late 1980s. On balance, the Soviet Union played a normally cautious diplomatic game, almost never engaging directly in warfare but maintaining a high level of preparedness.

Problems of work motivation and discipline loomed larger in Russia than in the West by the 1980s, after the heroic period of building an industrial society under Stalinist exhortation and threat. With highly bureaucratized and centralized work plans, plus an absence of abundant consumer goods, many workers found little reason for great diligence. High rates of alcoholism, so severe as to cause an increase in death rates particularly among adult males, also burdened work performance and caused great concern to Soviet leaders. More familiar were problems of youth agitation. While Russian statistics tended to conceal crime problems, it was clear that many Russian youths became impatient with the disciplined life and were eager to have greater access to Western culture, including rock music and blue jeans.

Russian output continued to grow, though the Russian economy by 1980 was lagging behind the West and Japan in adopting new technologies such as computers (aside from military application). Military and space technology still kept pace with Western levels, as both sides fed the arms race. A higher percentage of Russian output had to go to military use than in the West because of the continued differential in per capita wealth, but until the 1980s most Russians seemed to accept that the higher percentage was necessary, given what they were told about the West's aggressive intentions and their own memory of invasion in World War II.

Some skepticism about the existing system showed in the minority of beleaguered intellectuals who occasionally ventured criticisms of domestic and foreign policies, including armaments policies. Cynicism cropped up also in humor magazines and popular jokes, which poked fun at the luxurious living of Communist officials and the inefficiencies of the bureaucracy. Humor may at the same time have provided some outlet for grievances that might otherwise have festered.

 ## THE EXPLOSION OF THE 1980S AND 1990S

From 1985 onward, the Soviet Union entered a period of intensive reform. This was soon matched by a host of new political movements in Eastern Europe that effectively dismantled the Soviet Empire. The initial cause of this extraordinary and unanticipated upheaval lay in the deteriorating Soviet economic performance, intensified by the costs of military rivalry with the United States.

THE ECONOMIC SETTING

There were reasons for pride in the Soviet system, and many observers believed that public attitudes by the 1980s were shaped much less by terror than by satisfaction with the Soviet Union's world prestige and the improvements the Communist regime had fostered in education and welfare. But to a degree unperceived outside the Soviet Union

the economy was grinding to a standstill. Forced industrialization had produced extensive environmental deterioration throughout Eastern Europe. According to Soviet estimates, half of all rivers were severely polluted, and over 40 percent of all agricultural land was endangered by the late 1980s; over 20 percent of Soviet citizens lived in regions of "ecological disaster." Rates and severity of respiratory and other diseases rose, impairing both morale and economic performance. Infant mortality rates also rose in several regions, sometimes matching the highest levels anywhere in the world.

More directly still, industrial production began to stagnate and even drop as a result of rigid central planning, health problems, and poor worker morale. Growing inadequacy of housing and common goods resulted, yet further worsened motivation. As economic growth stopped, the percentage of resources allocated to military production escalated toward one-third of all national income. This reduced funds available for other investments or for consumer needs. Younger leaders began to recognize, at first privately, that the system was near collapse.

THE AGE OF REFORM

The Soviet system was not changeless, despite its heavy bureaucratization. Problems and dissatisfactions, though controlled, could provoke response beyond renewed repression. In 1985, after a succession of leaders whose age or health precluded major initiatives, the Soviet Union brought a new, younger official to the fore. Mikhail Gorbachev quickly renewed some of the earlier attacks on Stalinist rigidity and replaced some of the old-line party bureaucrats. He conveyed a new and more Western style, dressing in fashionable clothes (and accompanied by his wife who did the same), holding relatively open press conferences, and even allowing Soviet media to engage in active debate and report on problems affecting the country as well as successes.

Gorbachev also further altered the Soviet Union's modified cold war stance. He urged a reduction in nuclear armament, and in 1987 negotiated a new agreement with the United States that limited medium-range missiles in Europe. He ended the war in Afghanistan, bringing Soviet troops home. Internally, Gorbachev proclaimed a policy of *glasnost*, or openness, which implied new freedom to comment and criticize. He pressed particularly for a reduction in bureaucratic decision making and the use of some market incentives to stimulate greater output. The sweep of Gorbachev's reforms, as opposed to an undeniable new tone in Soviet public relations, remained difficult to assess. Strong limits on political freedom persisted, and it was unclear whether Gorbachev could cut through the centralized planning apparatus that controlled the main lines of the Soviet economy. There was also uncertainty about how well the new leader could balance reform and stability.

Questions about Gorbachev's prospects, indeed, recalled many basic issues in Russian as well as Soviet history. In many ways Gorbachev's policies constituted a return to a characteristic ambivalence about the West as he reduced Soviet isolation while continuing to criticize aspects of Western political and social structure. Gorbachev clearly hoped to use some Western management techniques and was open to certain Western cultural styles, without intending to abandon basic controls of the Communist state. Western analysts wondered if the Soviet economy could improve worker motivations without embracing a Western-style consumerism, or whether computers could be more widely introduced without admitting wider freedom to information exchange.

Gorbachev also sought to open the Soviet Union to fuller participation in the world economy, recognizing that isolation in a separate empire had restricted access to new technology and limited motivation to change. While the new leadership did not rush to make foreign trade or investment too easy—considerable suspicion persisted—the economic initiatives brought symbolic changes, such as the opening of a McDonald's restaurant in Moscow, and a whole array of new contacts with foreigners for various Soviet citizens.

Gorbachev's initial policies, while not successful in quickly stirring the Soviet economy, had immediate political impacts—some of which the reform leader had almost certainly not anticipated. The keynote of the reform program was *perestroika*, or economic restructuring, which Gorbachev translated into more leeway for private ownership and decentralized control in industry and agriculture. Farmers, for example, won the chance to lease land for 50 years with rights of inheritance, while industrial concerns were authorized to buy from either private or state operations. Foreign investment was newly encouraged. Gorbachev pressed for reductions in Soviet military commitments, particularly through agreements with the United States on troop reductions as well as limitations on nuclear weaponry, in order to free resources for consumer goods industries. He urged more self-help among the Russians, including a reduction in drinking, arguing that he wanted to "rid public opinion of . . . faith in a 'good Tsar,' the all powerful center, the notion that someone can bring about order and organize perestroika from on high." Politically, he encouraged a new constitution in 1988, giving considerable power to a new Parliament, the Congress of People's Deputies, and abolishing the Communist monopoly on elections. Important opposition groups developed

both inside and outside the party, pressing Gorbachev between radicals wanting faster reforms and conservative hard-liners. Gorbachev was elected to a new, powerful Presidency of the Soviet Union in 1990.

Reform, amid continued economic stagnation, provoked agitation among minority nationalities in the Soviet Union from 1988 onward. Muslims and Armenian Christians rioted in the south, both against each other and against the central state. Baltic nationalists and other European minorities also stirred, some insisting on independence (notably in Lithuania), some pressing for greater autonomy. In early 1991 a number of regions, including Lithuania as well as Georgia in the south, voted for independence, though their efforts were at least temporarily thwarted by the central state. Again, results of this diverse unrest were hard to forecast, but some observers predicted the end to Russian control of central Asia and the European borderlands.

Even social issues were given uncertain new twists. Gorbachev noted that Soviet efforts to establish equality between the sexes had burdened women with a combination of work and household duties. His solution—to allow women to "return to their purely womanly missions" of housework, child rearing, and "the creation of a good family atmosphere"—had a somewhat old-fashioned ring to it.

DISMANTLING THE SOVIET EMPIRE

Gorbachev's new approach, including his desire for better relations with Western powers, prompted more definitive results outside the Soviet Union than within, as the smaller states of Eastern Europe uniformly moved for greater independence and internal reforms. Bulgaria opted for economic liberalization in 1987 but was held back by the Soviets; pressure resumed in 1989 as the Bulgarian party leader was ousted and free elections were arranged. Hungary changed leadership in 1988 and installed a non-Communist president. A new constitution and free elections were planned in Hungary as the Communist party renamed itself Socialist. Hungary also reviewed its great 1956 uprising, formally declaring it "a popular uprising . . . against an oligarchic system . . . which had humiliated the nation." Hungary moved rapidly toward a free-market economy.

Poland installed a non-Communist government in 1988 and again worked quickly to dismantle the state-run economy; prices rose rapidly as government subsidies were withdrawn. The Solidarity movement, born a decade before through a merger of non-Communist labor leaders and Catholic intellectuals, became the dominant political force. East Germany displaced its Communist government in 1989, expelling key leaders and moving rapidly toward

During the revolts of the late 1980s, Lithuanians demonstrated for national independence from the Soviet Union, in the capital city of Vilnius.

unification with West Germany. The Berlin wall was dismantled, and in 1990 non-Communists won a free election. Full German unification occurred toward the end of 1990. Czechoslovakia installed a new government in 1989, headed by a playwright, and again sought to introduce free elections and a more market-driven economy.

While mass demonstrations played a key role in several of these political upheavals, only in Romania was there outright violence, as an exceptionally authoritarian Communist leader was swept out by force. As in Bulgaria, the Communist party retained considerable power, though under new leadership, and reforms moved less rapidly than in places such as Hungary and Czechoslovakia.

New divergences in the nature and extent of reform in Eastern Europe were exacerbated by clashes among nationalities—as in the Soviet Union itself. Change and uncertainty brought older attachments to the fore. Romanians and ethnic Hungarians clashed, while Bulgarians attacked a Turkish minority left over from the Ottoman period. Yu-

goslavia witnessed bitter clashes among rival Slavic groups.

Amid this rapid and unexpected change, prospects for the future were in many ways very unpredictable. Few of the new governments fully defined their constitutional structures, while amid innovation the range of new political parties almost compelled later consolidations. Like the Soviet Union itself, all the East European states suffered from sluggish production, and economic problems might well lead to new political discontents. Environmental issues were also massive. Diplomatic linkages among small states—a critical problem area between the two world wars—also had yet to be resolved. What was clear was the massive change in Soviet policy. Gorbachev reversed postwar imperialism completely, stating that "any nation has the right to decide its fate by itself." In several cases, notably Hungary, Soviet troops were rapidly withdrawn, and generally it seemed unlikely that a change of heart, toward a repressive attempt to reestablish empire, would be possible.

SHOCKS IN 1991

The uncertainties of the situation within the Soviet Union were confirmed in the summer of 1991, when an attempted coup was mounted by military and police elements. Gorbachev's presidency and democratic decentralization were both threatened. Massive popular demonstrations, however, asserted the strong democratic current that had developed in the Soviet Union since 1986. The contrast with earlier Soviet history and with the suppression of democracy in China two years before was striking.

The failed coup led to new attacks on the Communist party and to new independence movements by minority nationalities. The Baltic republics declared independence again, this time with wide international recognition. How many other regions might split away, even from a loose union, and what political forces might replace the Communist party in organizing the political process within the huge Russian republic moved to the top of the agenda in an ongoing process of change and redefinition.

CONCLUSION

WHAT NEXT?

Inevitably, Soviet and East European history in the 1990s is dominated by the surprising events of the most recent periods, and by huge uncertainties about their consequences. Recent events made clear that much less had changed in this region during the 20th century than had been recognized—even by Soviet citizens themselves. Soviet law had long trumpeted women's equality, and indeed Soviet women played vital roles in the labor force, but inequality in household chores continued while unavailability of reliable birth-control devices—a result of shoddy consumer goods production—forced a high rate of abortions. Soviet constitutions had featured a system of federated republics, but in fact central government control and Russian ethnic dominance spurred minority nationalism, and nationalist hostilities burned brightly. Nationalism in the Soviet Union and among newly independent East European nations threatened to divide the region profoundly.

Religion also remained a vital force, despite decades of secularization. Catholicism in the smaller nations and in the Western republics of the Soviet Union plus Islam in central Asia provided important loyalties.

Revolution and a totalitarian state had gained limited impact, despite theories of absolute control and undeniable police terror in key periods. The same system had made

less of a dent in traditional attraction to Western values and standards than might have been imagined. Several East European states indeed rushed to proclaim a Western-style devotion to individual liberty as well as a market economy. Though nationalist loyalties and economic lags might well limit openness to Westernization in the long run, it seemed unlikely that isolation could be resumed—a sign both of older East European interests in the West and the new intensity of international contacts.

The excitement of recent change, however, and the huge uncertainties of Eastern Europe's future are not the whole story of the 20th century. The Soviet Union had been an expansionist state, building on an older Russian tradition of expansionism. It had been a cautious superpower in most respects, avoiding outright war after 1945, save in Afghanistan—more careful in this respect than the United States. Economic problems prompted a pullback under Gorbachev, but questions remained about the permanence of this reorientation. Concern about outside threats, plus the temptation to use military means to defend a beleaguered empire, might change Soviet moderation in the future, and undue rigidity by the United States might have the same effect. Alternatively, some observers worried that the Soviet Union might split into hostile republics, several with sophisticated atomic weaponry; this would be novel, but at least as threatening as former cold war maneuvering.

Communist domestic policies might also survive the turmoil of transition. The conservative Soviet bureaucracy remains suspicious of loss of control. Gorbachev tried to construct a powerful presidency, legally protected from public "insult," to balance greater political freedom, thus displaying strong attachment to authoritarian structure, as have new leaders in Bulgaria and Romania. Use of the Soviet army to put down dissident nationalities within the Soviet Union in 1991—particularly in Lithuania and Georgia— increased the conservative strain in the new Soviet regime. Even other areas, such as Poland, might return to authoritarianism, as they had before World War II, if economic pressures should persist, for liberal experience is limited. Change in several areas brought new opportunities for ruthless ambition, and the prospects for democratic leadership were by no means secure.

Continuities or potential continuities are not confined to leadership ranks. East Europeans and Soviet citizens value the welfare protections of Communist society and the limitations on social inequality. Many hope to combine elements of collective protection with a larger dollop of capitalism. Many continue to attack aspects of Western individualism that seem unattractive—such as high crime rates and youth unrest—even as these very trends gain ground in East European society. And many citizens appreciate the earlier achievements of the Soviet system, in destroying the landlord class, for example, and in revolutionizing educational access. Soviet people also display antagonism to blatant individual profiteering, maintaining earlier communal traditions that predated communism; for some, equality in poverty seems preferable to individual self-seeking.

Prospects in Eastern Europe remain unclear not only because of the shock of recent changes and the magnitude of economic and environmental issues, but also because of holdovers from earlier revolutionary institutions and the expectations they had fostered. The restructuring born in the fires of earlier revolution is open to drastic change, but it is unlikely to be obliterated. Tensions in relationships with Western values, an old theme redefined under communism, may persist as well.

Eastern Europe had been a dynamic factor in world history for centuries, which means that the questions about its future, unanswerable in the early 1990s, affect far more than the region itself. Throughout the turmoil of 20th-century war and revolution, the Soviet Union retained a pivotal position in European and Asian power balances, and ultimately in world affairs more widely. Is this role to be redefined, or will it gradually recede—and with what consequences?

FURTHER READINGS

On the Russian Revolution, Sheila Fitzpatrick's *The Russian Revolution, 1917–1932* (1982) is a recent overview with a rich bibliography. See also A. Rabinowitch's *The Bolsheviks Come to Power* (1976), Robert Tucker's *Stalin as Revolutionary* (1972), and R. Conquest's *The Great Terror* (1968). Edmund Wilson's *To the Finland Station* (1972) offers a dramatic account of the revolution's early phase. On nationalities issues see R. Pipes's *The Formation of the Soviet Union* (1964).

More recent Soviet history is treated in Richard Barnet's *The Giants: Russia and America* (1977); A. Rubinstein's *Soviet Foreign Policy Since World War II* (1981); Alec Nove's *The Soviet Economic System* (1980); Stephen Cohen and others, eds., *The Soviet Union Since Stalin*; and Ben Eklof's *Gorbachev and the Reform Period* (1988).

Other parts of Eastern Europe are treated in H. Setson Watson's *Eastern Europe between the Wars* (1962), F. Fetjo's *History of the People's Democracies: Eastern Europe Since Stalin* (1971), J. Tampke's *The People's Republics of Eastern Europe* (1983), Timothy Ash's *The Polish Revolution: Solidarity* (1984), H. G. Skilling's *Czechoslovakia: In-* *terrupted Revolution* (1976) (on the 1968 uprising), and B. Kovrig's *Communism in Hungary from Kun to Kadar* (1979).

A major interpretation of the Communist experience is T. Skocpol's *States and Social Revolutions* (1979). On the early signs of explosion in Eastern Europe, see K. Dawisha's *Eastern Europe, Gorbachev and Reform: The Great Challenge* (1988). Bohdan Nahaylo and Victor Swoboda's *Soviet Disunion: A History of the Nationalities Problem in the USSR* (1990) provides important background. On women's experiences, see Barbara Engel and Christine Worobec, eds., *Russia's Women: Accommodation, Resistance, Transformation* (1990).

1931 Rebellion in Korea; Japanese repression

1923 Tokyo earthquake

1931 Rise of nationalism, new hostility to West

1936 Assassination of several Japanese political leaders; young army officer rebellion

1938 Japan's war budget; state control of economic life

1923 Defeat of Japanese bill for universal suffrage

1931 Height of depression, impact on Japan; bad harvests

1937 Increasingly open rule by military officers; arrest of opposition politicians

Japan and the Pacific Rim

INTRODUCTION. The rise of coastal areas in eastern Asia to world importance forms one of the major facets of the rebalancing of major societies in the 20th century. Unmarked by formal revolution—in contrast to Russia—the Pacific Rim gained momentum as an economic rather than a military superpower, particularly following the upheaval of World War II. The dynamism of Asia's Pacific Coast centered in several societies long in China's shadow as East Asian civilization was redivided and redefined, and the same societies began to influence international patterns in unprecedented ways. Societies that had been shaped by Confucian influence began to take very different paths.

This chapter covers several political units in eastern Asia—Japan, Korea, Taiwan, and the city-states of Singapore and Hong Kong—that are joined by their common ability to generate unusual economic growth during the second half of the 20th century. The Pacific Rim states also reflect some common heritage that had included considerable Chinese influence. The Pacific Rim category was still tentative by the 1990s, for it was not clear how much these different nations would prove to have in common, or how permanent their splitting away from other East Asian societies would be, notably China and Vietnam (see Chapter 41). Yet the Pacific Rim states were undeniably important in their own right, becoming along with the West the center of the world's greatest economic strength, and challenging the West through new competition. The Pacific Rim states also shared a fascinating effort to blend successful industrial forms with a distinctive cultural and political tradition—providing the clearest alternative to the West of what a vigorous modern society might look like.

The key actor was Japan, which had diverged from Chinese patters in the previous period. Japan's rise to new eminence had been launched in the 19th century with the

---

1946–1948 Kuomintang (Nationalist) regime consolidates in Taiwan

1955 Japanese production reaches prewar levels

1948 Korea divided

1951 American occupation ends in Japan

1965 Growing Hong Kong autonomy

1959 Singapore declares independence

1961 Military regime in South Korea

1945 Japan defeated; American occupation

1954 U.S.-Taiwan defense treaty

1955 Merger forms Liberal Democratic party in Japan

1950–1953 Korean War after invasion of North Korea

1988–1989 Growing student agitation for liberal political reform in South Korea; elected civilian government installed

1980 End U.S.-Taiwan treaty alliance

1984 British-Chinese agreement to return Hong Kong to China in 1999

reforms of the Meiji era, the beginnings of industrialization, and then the military push that brought Japanese victories over China and Russia and profitable participation on the Allied side in World War I. During the 1930s the Japanese military surge continued with attacks on China and big stretches of southeast Asia and the Pacific. After defeat in World War II and a new series of internal reforms, Japanese influence returned, this time in the guise of dynamic economic growth that by the 1960s made Japan a major world competitor—the first Asian nation to reach this position since the onset of the Industrial Revolution. Japan became a leading factor in international markets of all sorts—in banking, in foreign investment both in raw materials areas and in the United States, and in foreign economic aid—as the relatively small, resource-poor island nation reached toward control of almost one-fifth of total world trade. Japanese competition challenged the United States and Western Europe, while its demand for raw materials figured prominently in Canada, Latin America, and the Middle East as well as Asia.

After World War II, Japan's success was mirrored by the rapid rise of other centers in eastern Asia, some of which became the first successful entrants to the ranks of industrial economies for virtually a century—since Japan and Russia had begun their surge. South Korea, Taiwan, and the city-states of Hong Kong and Singapore, though not yet attaining Japanese levels of prosperity and influence, gained ground rapidly, challenging the Japanese lead in certain export sectors and making a profound impact on international markets.

The rise of the Pacific Rim nations commands attention in 20th-century history because of their success in breaking the previous Western monopoly on industrial leadership—not only in sheer volume of production and export trade, but in technological innovation as well. Many observers predicted that coastal East Asia, perhaps joined by parts of China and other areas, would replace the West in world leadership. This has not yet occurred by the early 1990s, though the Pacific Rim unquestionably generates significant new competition. It was revealing, nevertheless, that many Western businesses and political leaders advocated imitation of certain Japanese methods of organization and personality style, on grounds that the Japanese had leapfrogged over the West in the habits essential to successful modern life. "Japanization" has not become a word, and Japan's ability to provoke imitation has not yet reached Westernization levels in the world at large; Japan, indeed, continues its earlier interest in selective adoption of Western attributes even as it serves as a model in other respects. Nevertheless, the Pacific Rim's presence seems to increase with every

passing year during the final quarter of the 20th century. Japan has begun to earn the combination of envy and resentment the West itself had produced during its period of growing influence.

The emergence of a Pacific Rim also commands interest because it has formed such a challenging exception to the general difficulty faced by 20th-century societies that were still to enter into a genuine industrial revolution. And it commands interest because successful industrialization has not led to full Westernization. In political styles and a host of personal values, the Pacific Rim states, headed by Japan, have provided a laboratory for testing what social features were inherent in industrial advance, and what features could diverge from Western patterns on the basis of distinctive traditions and ongoing experience. Japan and increasingly other nations such as South Korea were at once highly industrial, setting new standards for the most advanced versions of industrial society, and highly Asian, adapting a host of regional traditions quite different from contemporary Western patterns.

Overall, the Pacific Rim has formed a distinctive grouping of societies amid the larger patterns of the 20th-century world, particularly after the upheavals of World War II and its immediate aftermath. Pacific Rim societies differ from the West, from Eastern Europe, and from most of the rest of Asia.

DECADES OF TURMOIL: THE WORLD WARS AND THEIR CONSEQUENCES

During the initial decades of the 20th century, Japan concentrated heavily on diplomatic and military gains plus the difficult process of adjusting to the parliamentary, constitutional government established during the Meiji period. During the 1890s the various branches of the central government had faced serious problems of cooperation, while opposition parties in the Parliament tried to gain ground at the expense of the executive ministries. In 1900 the government leaders formed their own political party, winning a majority in the lower house of Parliament. Over the next 22 years the leadership party struggled to maintain a working majority against various opposition factions. Japan was by this point an expansionist power; it formally annexed Korea in 1910. Japan ruled its new Asian colonies firmly, exacting considerable taxes and raw materials while securing markets for its growing industrial output. In no sense did the new Japanese empire lead directly to a united or vigorous Pacific Rim, though the disruption of established dependence on China did add an important new ingredient to Korean development.

JAPAN'S ONGOING DEVELOPMENT

Along with international gains came continued industrial advance. Japanese industry continued to lag behind Western levels, relying heavily on low-wage labor and the export of a relatively small number of items such as silk cloth; silk production, at 16 million pounds in 1900, soared to 93 million pounds in 1929. Agricultural productivity improved steadily, led by progressive landlords who introduced fertilizers and new equipment. Rice production more than doubled between the 1880s and the 1930s. Modern industry advanced more slowly, though it passed well beyond the pilot phase of the late 19th century. Great industrial combines—the *zaibatsu*—sponsored rapid expansion in fields such as shipbuilding, usually relying heavily on tight links with the government bureaucracy, but there were daring individual entrepreneurs as well. Between 1905 and 1918, Japan enjoyed a considerable industrial boom, with rapid advances not only in light industries such as silk, but also in electrical power, iron, and coal. Japanese life expectancy began to improve, fueled by a higher standard of living. A popular consumer culture was sketched, at least in the cities, as workers began to attend movies and read newspapers. Education advanced rapidly, with primary-school attendance universal in the relevant age groups by 1925. Enrollments in secondary schools and technical colleges swelled, improving the capacity to assimilate the newer Western technologies.

Limits on Japanese economic advance included vulnerability to economic conditions abroad. Because Japan exported relatively few items to the West, but continued to require considerable imports of raw materials, including fuels, as well as sophisticated equipment, a slump in demand for a product such as silk cloth could be disastrous. In this sense, Japan bore some resemblance to dependent economies in the world, despite industrial progress. Population growth was another burden, or at least a mixed blessing. Japan's population soared from 30 million in 1868, to 45 million in 1900, and then to 73 million by 1940. This was a tribute to agricultural advance, as the size of the farm population remained constant, and it facilitated a low-wage industrial economy. It also restricted further improvements in standard of living and created social dislocation in the crowded, migrant-filled cities. Periodic protests through strikes, demonstrations, and some socialist agitation were met with vigorous police response. Conditions worsened (see Chapter 34) in the first phase of the Great Depression of the 1930s. The economy recovered quickly, however, under the twin stimuli of a new export boom and government-organized military procurement as Japan began to beef up its war machine.

By 1937 Japan boasted the third largest and the newest merchant marine in the world. The nation became self-sufficient in machine tools and scientific equipment, the fruit of the growth in technical training. The quality of Japanese industrial goods rose, producing the first Western outcry against Japanese exports—even though in 1936, the Japanese controlled only 3.6 percent of world trade. The basis had been set for the more significant economic surge of the later 20th century, delayed by Japan's dash into World War II.

POLITICAL CRISIS

While the economy gained, however, political crisis seized center stage, leading in turn to a new and risky round of military and diplomatic experiments that culminated in World War II. Social tensions played a role in this transition, as Japan moved further from its basic tradition of noninvolvement in elaborate foreign ventures. Tokyo was virtually destroyed by an earthquake in 1923, and 100,000 people died. Six years later, the initial impact of the depression caused great misery, as exports fell by two-thirds. Half of all factories were idled by 1931. Widespread poverty and fears of social unrest helped produce an atmosphere in which new measures, including military aggression, seemed essential. In some areas in 1931, children were reduced to begging for food from passing trains, while farmers were forced to eat the inner bark of pine trees. Despite these dire conditions, social protest did not surge to dangerous proportions and the depression was soon successfully countered by an active government policy; Japan suffered far less, as a result, than many Western nations did during the depression decade as a whole. Under the 1930s minister of finance, Korekiyo Takahashi, the government increased its spending to provide jobs, which in turn generated new demands for food and manufactured items, yielding not only the export boom but also the virtual elimination of unemployment by 1936. The same policy helped support government military purchasing, but it is not clear that this constituted an essential response.

The key to Japan's new initiatives rested rather with ongoing difficulties in assimilating a generally accepted political structure—difficulties that had not been resolved during the first decades of the 20th century. Military leaders began to take a growing role in setting general diplomatic policy from the mid-1920s onward, at the expense of the civilian parties and politicians. Japan's oligarchic political structure, in which elite groups negotiated with each other for appropriate policy rather than fully yielding to any single agency, such as Parliament, permitted this kind of realignment. From the Meiji period onward, military leaders, though weaned fully from the samurai tradition, had remained separate from the civilian bureaucracy. They were trained in separate schools and regarded themselves as true guardians of the modern Japanese state as well as older traditions. They reported not to civilian authority, but directly to the emperor. Like military leaders in the West during the 1920s, but with greater vigor, they resented what they regarded as the selfishness and accommodation to special interests of the political parties, as the latter increasingly converted to mass political campaigns and vote-getting strategies. Reduction of military budgets during the 1920s hit military leaders hard, and army prestige declined to the point that officers wore civilian clothing when off base. Naval officers, at the same time, were appalled at decisions accepted from a great power Naval Conference in 1930 that limited fleet levels. In essence, Japan experi-

mented during the 1920s with a liberal political pattern, which seemed to give primacy to party maneuverings and electoral appeals, but which also antagonized the military (and other conservative elite groups) while failing to subject them to new controls. This was the context in which military officials began to make separate decisions about Manchuria, leading to the 1931 seizure of this key Chinese region, while the civilian government tried to equivocate.

Then, as political divisions increased in response to the initial impact of the depression, a variety of nationalist groups emerged, some advocating a return to Shintoist or Confucian principles against the more Western values of urban Japan. This was more than a political response to the depression. As in Germany, a variety of groups used the occasion for a more sweeping protest against parliamentary forms; nationalism here seemed a counterpoise to alien Western values. Older military officers joined some bu-

During the early stages of World War II in Asia, Shanghai, China, was bombed by the Japanese in 1937.

reaucrats in urging a more authoritarian state that could ignore party politics; some wanted further military expansion to protect Japan from the uncertainties of the world economy by providing secure markets.

In May 1932, a group of younger army officers attacked key government and banking officers and murdered the prime minister. They did not take over the state directly, but for the next four years moderate military leaders headed the executive branch, frustrating both the military firebrands and the political parties. Another attempted military coup in 1936 was put down by forces controlled by the established admirals and generals, but this group, including the vigorous General Tojo Hideki, increasingly interfered with civilian cabinets, blocking the appointment of most liberal bureaucrats. The result, after 1936, was a series of increasingly militaristic prime ministers.

Japan gained a great deal of novel political experience during the 1920s and 1930s, and moderate political parties won widespread support. The Japanese electorate, though strongly nationalistic and loyal to the emperor, were not enthusiastic expansionists. These ingredients would reemerge in Japanese politics after World War II. For the moment, however, the military superseded civilian politics, particularly when renewed wars broke out between Japan and China in 1937. By the end of 1938, Japan controlled a substantial regional empire including Manchuria, Korea, and Taiwan, within which the nation sold half its exports and from which it bought over 40 percent of all imports, particularly food and raw materials. Both the military leadership, eager to justify further modernization of Japan's weaponry and to consolidate political control, and economic leaders, interested in rich resources of other parts of Asia—such as the rubber of British Malaya or the oil of the Dutch East Indies—soon pressed for wider conquests as Japan surged into World War II.

OTHER AREAS IN THE PACIFIC RIM

During the interwar decades, the experiences of other parts of eastern Asia were diverse. Japan's firm control over Korea created important resentments, and Japanese economic policies did little to stimulate major new developments in the Korean economy. The period of Japanese rule did have important results in disrupting Korean traditions, including the tendency to look toward Chinese superiority and the fact of monarchy itself. The Korean king, prior to full Japanese annexation in 1910, had attempted to protest growing interference, but Western powers had ignored his appeals. The Japanese had replaced the monarch with his feebleminded son in 1908, and then, when a Korean patriot assassinated the resident general in 1909, they abol-

ished the monarchy altogether. Korea's elaborate court aristocracy was undermined in this process. Colonial status, which lasted until Japan's World War II defeat in 1945, prevented the generation of new, alternative institutions, but there was new potential for innovation after the long centuries of Yi dynasty rule.

Economically and culturally, the Japanese annexation of Korea ushered in an era of virtually unchecked exploitation of its land and people. For most of the 3½ decades the Japanese ruled the peninsula, it was governed by military leaders who put down all resistance quite brutally. Almost from the outset, the Japanese launched a concerted effort to suppress Korean culture and promote adoption of Japanese ways. Korean language newspapers were banned, Korean teachers were required to wear Japanese uniforms and carry swords, and Japanese money, weights and measures, and language instruction were introduced throughout the country. Korean resources were put at the disposal of Japanese industrialists, many of whom invested in factories in the new colony. The Korean peasantry was compelled to concentrate on rice production for export to Japan and other foreign markets. With much of their labor devoted to producing rice for others to eat, the impoverished Koreans increasingly found that they could only afford millet (a grain they had traditionally considered quite inferior to rice) for their own consumption. In the Great Depression when the world market for rice contracted rapidly and the price plunged as a consequence, the concentration on rice production proved disastrous. The long-suffering Korean peasant bore the brunt of the misery caused by Japanese miscalculations.

Peasants also bore the brunt of the Japanese effort to speed up exploitation of Korea's resources and labor as the Japanese advanced into China in the late 1930s and the Pacific war with America approached. Korea became the strategic pivot of Japanese empire building in East Asia, a vast warehouse devoted to supplying Japanese military forces. Army officers instructed the dreaded Japanese military police to forcibly conscript increasing numbers of Korean youths for labor gangs and troops to support their expanding war effort. The population was exhorted to join the Japanese people in "training to endure hardship." Japanese military rituals were given great prominence and the cult of the Japanese god-emperor was celebrated in schools and community centers across the colony. Throughout the 1930s and early 1940s, the Korean people were forced to endure hardships and the loss of tens of thousands of youth for an emperor who had usurped the powers of their own and a cause that had nothing to do with them. The state in which the long Japanese occupation left the country only prolonged the suffering and multiplied the casualties.

In March 1919 the Korean people declared their independence and rose in revolt against Japanese imperialism. Many Koreans were executed by Japanese police during the movement.

Singapore, a city with a largely Chinese population held as part of Britain's colony of Malaya, underwent important development during the late 1930s as the British tried to build it into an "invulnerable" naval base. Singapore served as a growing international seaport linked by road and rail to the rubber- and tin-producing areas of Malaya, though its people remained separate in identity and loyalty from the Muslim Malays themselves. It suffered greatly during the Japanese World War II occupation, emerging with massive unemployment and poverty.

Overall, the first decades of the 20th century brought important changes to various parts of East Asia, largely though not exclusively as the result of new Japanese initiatives. China, long the dominant East Asian force, was con-sumed by its complex process of internal revolution and was of course itself beset by the Japanese; it lost much of its traditional regional hold in the process. Japan led the way in economic development, despite difficulties and set-backs, gaining new international as well as regional impor-tance—witness its unusual ability to bounce back from the depression as most Western nations foundered. World War II obviously increased pressures for change in the region, as the Japanese temporarily dislodged Western colonial rule in places such as Malaya. Japan's defeat, and the hostility it had generated in its colonies along with admiration for its ability to defy the West, challenged the patterns that had developed by 1945, while assuring the need for further change.

DOCUMENT
JAPAN AND THE LOSS
IN WORLD WAR II

Japan's defeat obviously brought a great deal of moral as well as material confu-sion. The government was so uncertain of the intentions of the victorious Americans that it evacuated its female employees to the countryside. The following document, from the 1945 diary of Miss Yoshizawa Hisako (who became a writer on home economics), indicates something of more popular attitudes and the mixed ingredients that com-posed them. The passage also suggests how the American occupation force tried to present itself and the reception it received.

August 15. As I listened to the Em-peror's voice announcing the surrender, every word acquired a special meaning and His Majesty's voice penetrated my mind. Tears streamed down my cheeks. I kept on telling myself that we must not fight ourselves and work hard for our common good. Yes, I pledged myself, I must work [for Japan's recovery].

The city was quiet.

I could not detect any special expression in people's faces. Were they too tired? However, somehow they seemed brighter, and I could catch an expression showing a sign of relief. It could have been a reflection of my own feelings. But I knew I could trust what I saw. . . .

The voluntary fighting unit was disbanded, and I was no longer a member of that unit. Each of us burned the insignia and other identifications.

I cannot foresee what kind of difficulty will befall me, but all I know is that I must learn to survive relying on my health and my will to live.

August 16. People do not wear expressions any different from other days. However, in place of a "good morning" or "good afternoon," people are now greeting each other with the phrase "What will become of us?"

During the morning, the city was still placed under air-raid alert.

My company announced that until everything becomes clearer, no female employees were to come to work, and urged all of us to go to the countryside, adding that we should leave forwarding addresses. This measure was taken to conform to the step already taken by governmental bureaus. Are they thinking that the occupation army will do something to us girls? There are so many important questions we have to cope with, I cannot understand why governmental officials are so worried about these matters.

We did not have enough power and lost the war.

The Army continued to appeal to the people to resist the enemy to the end. This poses a lot of problems. People can show their true colors better when they are defeated than when they win. I just hope we, as a nation, can show our better side now.

Just because we have been defeated, I do not wish to see us destroying our national characteristics when we are dealing with foreign countries.

August 17. It was rumored that a number of lower echelon military officers were unhappy with the peace, and were making some secret moves. There were other rumors, and with the quiet evacuation of women and children from the cities, our fear seemed to have intensified. After all we have never experienced a defeat before. Our fear may simply be the manifestation of fear of the unknown.

Our airplanes dropped propaganda leaflets.

One of the leaflets was posted at the Kanda Station which said: "Both the Army and Navy are alive and well. We expect the nation to follow our lead." The leaflet was signed. I could understand how those military men felt. However, we already have the imperial rescript to surrender. If we are going to rebuild, we must open a new path. It is much easier to die than to live. In the long history of our nation, this defeat may become one of those insignificant happenings. However, the rebuilding after the defeat is likely to be treated as a far more important chapter in our history.

We did our best and lost, so there is nothing we have to say in our own defense. Only those people who did not do their best may now be feeling guilty, though.

Mr. C. said that everything he saw in the city was so repugnant that he wanted to retreat to the countryside. I was amazed by the narrowness of his thought process. I could say that he had a pure sense of devotion to the country, but that was only his own way of thinking. Beautiful perhaps, but it lacked firm foundation. I wish men like him would learn to broaden their perspectives.

August 18. Rationed bread distribution in the morning. I went to the distribution center with Mrs. A.

August 21. We heard that the allied advance units will be airlifted and arrive in Japan on the 26th. And the following day, their fleet will also anchor in our harbors. The American Army will be airlifted and land in Atsugi airport.

According to someone who accompanied the Japanese delegation which went to accept surrender conditions, Americans behaved like gentlemen. They explained to the Americans that certain conditions were unworkable in light of the present situation in Japan. The Americans immediately agreed to alter those conditions. They listened very carefully to what the Japanese delegation had to say.

An American paper, according to someone, reported that meeting as follows: "We cooked thick beefsteak expecting seven or eight Japanese would appear. But seventeen of them came, so we had to kill a turkey to prepare for them. We treated them well before they returned. . . ." When I hear things like this, I immediately feel how exaggerated and inefficient our ways of doing things are. They say that Americans will tackle one item after another at a conference table, and do not waste even 30 seconds. . . .

In contrast, Japanese administration is conducted by many chairs and seals. For example when an auxiliary unit is asked to undertake a task for a governmental bureau, before anything can be done, twenty or thirty seals of approval must be secured. So there is no con-

cept of not wasting time. Even in war, they are too accustomed to doing things the way they have been doing, and their many seals and chairs are nothing but a manifestation of their refusal to take individual responsibilities.

The fact of a defeat is a very serious matter and it is not easy to accept. However, it can bring some positive effects, if it can inculcate in our minds all the shortcomings we have had. I hope this will come true some day, and toward that end we must all endeavor. Even if we have to suffer hunger and other tribulations we must strive toward a positive goal.

Questions: How did Japanese attitudes in defeat help prepare Japan for postwar redevelopment? What other kinds of reactions might have been expected? How would you explain the rather calm and constructive outlook the passage suggests? Would American reactions to a Japanese victory have been similar?

EAST ASIA IN THE POSTWAR SETTLEMENTS

The victors in World War II had some reasonably clear ideas about how East Asia was to be restructured. Korea, was divided between a Russian zone of occupation in the north and an American zone in the south. Taiwan was restored to China, which was in principle ruled by a Kuomintang government headed by Chiang Kai-shek. The United States regained the Philippines, with a pledge to grant independence quickly—retaining some key military bases. European powers restored controls over their holdings in Vietnam, Malaya, and Indonesia. Japan was occupied by American forces bent on introducing major changes that would prevent a recurrence of military aggression.

NEW DIVISIONS AND THE END OF EMPIRES

Not surprisingly, given the complex impact of the war plus the complication of the new cold war struggle between the United States and the Soviet Union, the Pacific regions

of Asia did not quickly settle into agreed-upon patterns. A decade after the war's end, not only the Philippines but also Indonesia and Malaya were independent—part of the postwar tide of decolonization. Taiwan was still ruled by Chiang Kai-shek, but the Chinese mainland was in the hands of a new and powerful Communist regime. Chiang's Nationalist regime claimed a mission to recover China, but in fact Taiwan was now a separate republic. Korea remained divided, but had undergone a brutal north-south conflict in which only United States intervention preserved South Korea's independence. Japan, rather ironically, was one of the few Pacific regions where matters had proceeded somewhat according to plan, as the nation began to recover while also adjusting to a considerably altered political structure.

East Asia's postwar turmoil forms a complex story, only part of which is directly relevant to the emergence of the Pacific Rim economy. The Communist phase of China's revolution maintained a separation between China and the parts of its traditional regional hinterland that showed little interest in communism; Vietnam's decolonization struggles also demand special attention. The Pacific Rim turned out

The United States advanced on Japan with the invasion and capture of Okinawa in March, 1945.

to be composed of areas traditionally influenced to some degree by Chinese culture but not brought under Communist control. This somewhat complex definition was forged in part by the actual experience of key Pacific regions during the period of postwar confusion.

JAPANESE RECOVERY

Japan in 1945 was in shambles. Its cities were burned, its factories destroyed or idle, its people impoverished and also shocked by the fact of surrender and by the trauma of bombing, including the atomic devastation of Hiroshima and Nagasaki. However, like the industrial nations of the West, Japan was capable of reestablishing a vigorous economy with surprising speed. And its occupation by United States forces, eager to reform Japan but also eager to avoid punitive measures, provided an opportunity for a new period of selective Westernization.

The American occupation government, headed by General Douglas MacArthur, worked quickly to tear down Japan's wartime political structure. The military forces were disbanded, the police decentralized, a number of officials removed, and political prisoners released. For the long run, American authorities pressed for a democratization of Japanese society by giving women the vote, encouraging labor unions, and abolishing Shintoism as a state religion.

Several economic reforms were also introduced, breaking up landed estates for the benefit of small farmers, who quickly became politically conservative, and dissolving the holdings of the zaibatsu combines, a measure that had little lasting effect as Japanese big business quickly regrouped.

A new constitution tried to cut through older limitations by making Parliament the supreme government body, from which the cabinet was appointed; a variety of civil liberties were guaranteed, along with gender equality in marriage and collective bargaining rights; military forces with "war potential" were abolished forever, making Japan a unique major nation in its limited military strength; and the emperor was made merely a symbolic figurehead, without political power and with no claims to Shinto divinity. Even as Japan accepted many political and legal concepts, it inserted its own values into the new constitution. Thus a 1963 law inscribed special social obligations to the elderly, in obvious contrast to Western approaches to this subject, at the statutory level: "The elders shall be loved and respected as those who have for many years contributed toward the development of society, and a wholesome and peaceful life shall be guaranteed to them. . . ."

These new constitutional measures were in the main embraced by the Japanese people, many of whom became avid opponents of any hint of military revival. Japan did ultimately create a self-defense force and military capacity qui-

The Pacific Rim Areas by 1960

etly grew well beyond what the constitution intended, but military expenditures remained a minuscule part of the overall budget. Military power and responsibility in the region were retained by the United States, which long after the occupation period kept important bases in Japan. Many of the political features of the new constitution worked smoothly, in large part, of course, because the Japanese had experienced parliamentary and political party activity for extended periods in previous decades. Two moderate parties, both with substantial prewar traditions, vied for power during the late 1940s, with the Liberal party holding sway; in 1947 a minority Socialist party gained ground by winning 26 percent of the vote in the first postwar elections. The Socialist threat indeed spurred a 1955 merger of the moderate parties into the new Liberal Democratic party that would monopolize Japan's government into the 1990s.

Amid political reconstruction, Japan's economy gradually recovered. By 1955 production in the major industrial branches regained prewar levels. At that point many experts anticipated a moderation of growth, but in fact a huge surge ensued that propelled Japan into the first rank of world industrial powers. By this point, of course, the post-

war adjustment period was clearly past, a fact expressed by the signing in 1951 of a peace treaty between Japan and 48 of its former wartime opponents; American occupation ended in the following year, with an agreement on postwar bases. The Soviet Union, now locked in the cold war (which in fact had spurred the United States to convert Japan from defeated enemy to dependent ally) did not officially make peace, and its continued occupation of former Japanese islands was a source of serious friction. Nevertheless the Soviets acquiesced in the new arrangements de facto, leaving Japan free from major diplomatic distractions.

KOREA: INTERVENTION AND WAR

Korea's postwar adjustment period was far more troubled than Japan's. Leaders of the great Allied powers during World War II had agreed in principle that Korea should be restored as an independent state. But United States' eagerness to obtain Soviet help against Japan, plus long-standing Russian interest in the area, determined that the northern part of the peninsula was occupied by the Soviet Union after the war. As the cold war intensified, American and Soviet authorities could not agree on unification of the zones, and in 1948 the United States sponsored a Republic of Korea in the south, matched by a Soviet-dominated People's Democratic Republic of Korea in the north. North Korea's regime drew on an earlier Korean Communist party founded in exile in the 1920s. North Korea quickly became a Communist state with Stalinist-type emphasis on the power of the leader, Kim Il-Sung. The South Korean regime, bolstered by ongoing American military presence, was headed by the nationalist Syngman Rhee, another politician who had earlier worked in exile against Japanese occupation. Rhee's South Korea developed parliamentary institutions in form, but maintained a strongly authoritarian tone.

In June 1950, North Korean forces attacked the south, hoping to impose unification on Communist terms. The United States, eager to maintain South Korea as protection for its deeper interests in Japan, reacted quickly (after some confusing signals about whether or not South Korea was inside the United States' "defense perimeter"). President Truman insisted on drawing another line against Communist aggression, and orchestrated United Nations sponsorship of a largely American "police action" in support of South Korean troops. Under General MacArthur's leadership, Allied forces pushed North Korea back, driving on toward the Chinese border; this in turn roused concern on the part of China's Communist regime, which sent "volunteers" that drove American troops back toward the south. The front stabilized in 1952 near the original north-south border. The stalemate dragged on until 1953, when a new American administration was able to agree to an armistice.

Korea then continued its dual pattern of development. North Korea produced an unusually isolated version of one-man rule, as Kim concentrated powers over the only legal political party, the military, and the government. Even Soviet liberalization in the late 1980s brought little change. South Korea and the United States concluded a mutual defense treaty in 1954; American troops levels were reduced, but the South Korean army gained more sophisticated military equipment and the United States poured considerable economic aid into the country, initially to prevent starvation in a war-ravaged land. The political tenor of South Korea continued to be authoritarian, but with sporadic protests in behalf of a more genuine democracy. In 1961 army officers took over effective rule of the country, though sometimes a civilian government served as a facade. Economic change, however, began to gain ground in the south, ushering in a new phase of activity and international impact. Tensions between the two Koreas continued to run high, with many border clashes and sabotage, but outright warfare was avoided.

TAIWAN, HONG KONG, AND SINGAPORE

Postwar adjustments in Taiwan involved yet another set of issues. As the Communist revolutionary armies gained the upper hand in mainland China, between 1946 and 1948 the Kuomintang (Nationalist) regime prepared to fall back on its newly reacquired island, which the Communists could not threaten because they had no navy. The result was imposition over the Taiwanese majority of a new leadership, bureaucracy, and massive military force drawn from the mainland and, particularly in its early years but in principle for several decades, devoted to the task of regaining mainland authority from the Communists.

The authoritarian political patterns the Nationalists had developed in China, centered on Chiang Kai-shek's personal control of the government, were amplified by the

This tank unit of the North Korean Peoples Army assembled in September 1950.

need to keep disaffected Taiwanese in check. Tensions with the Communist regime across the Taiwan Strait ran high. In 1950 the United States sent its Seventh Fleet to protect the island, and in 1954 a mutual defense treaty was signed (ended only in 1980, in the aftermath of United States diplomatic recognition of the Communist regime). In 1955 and 1958 the Communists bombarded two small islands controlled by the Nationalists, Quemoy and Matsu, and wider conflict threatened as the United States backed up its ally. Tensions were defused when China agreed to fire on the islands only on alternate days, while United States ships supplied them on the off-days, thus salvaging national honor. Finally, the United States induced Chiang to renounce any intentions of attacking the mainland, and conflict eased into mutual bombardments of propaganda leaflets. During this period, as in South Korea, the United States devoted considerable economic aid to its Taiwanese ally, ending assistance only in the 1960s when growing prosperity (and increasing competition with United States firms in the manufacture of inexpensive consumer items) seemed assured.

Two other ultimate participants in Pacific Rim economic advance were distinguished by special ties to Britain. Hong Kong remained a British colony after World War II; only in the 1980s was an agreement reached between Britain and China for its 1997 return to the Chinese fold. Hong Kong gained increasing autonomy from direct British rule. Its Chinese population, already considerable, swelled at various points after 1946 as a result of flights from Communist rule. Singapore retained a large British naval base until 1971, when Britain abandoned all pretense of significant power in East Asia. Even before this a merger with independent Malaya (granted self-government in 1957) collapsed on racial grounds. Because Singapore's presence made the Chinese in the whole of Malaysia a plurality (44 percent to the Malay 41 percent), Malay nationalists rejected the association with Singapore, which gained independence as a vigorous free port in 1959.

Overall, by the end of the 1950s a certain stability had emerged in the political situation of the smaller East Asian nations with the vital exception of Vietnam and its neighbors in Indochina. Despite unresolved problems, such as Korean unity or Taiwanese-Chinese relations, a number of nations had acquired de facto independence or, like Japan, had accepted important alterations in previous political and military structures. Several of these nations in turn had received special Western attention and economic support during this same adjustment period. It was from the 1960s onward that some of these same areas, combining Western contacts with important earlier traditions of group activity

and vigorous group loyalty, moved from impressive economic recovery to new international influence on the basis of manufacturing and trade.

JAPAN, INCORPORATED

As Japanese politics developed under its postwar constitution, its chief emphasis lay in a rather conservative stability. The Liberal Democratic party, formed by the merger of two conservative units in response to Socialist challenge, held the reins of government from 1955 onward. This meant that Japan, uniquely among the democratic nations of the postwar world, had no experience with shifts in party administration. Changes in leadership, which at times were frequent, were handled through negotiations among the Liberal Democratic elite, not directly as a result of shifts in voter preference.

THE DISTINCTIVE POLITICAL STYLE

Clearly, this system revived many of the oligarchic features of Meiji Japan and the Japan of the 1920s, in which parliamentary rule was mediated through the close ties among the members of the elite. The system also encouraged cooperation between government bureaucracy and big business combines, based on shared participation in the leadership group. The Liberal Democrats also revived some other features of Japan's previous political tradition. In the late 1950s, for example, it recentralized the police force. Socialist opponents of these programs reacted bitterly, protesting what they termed a revival of authoritarianism; Japan's political atmosphere for a time turned venomous, and there were many strikes and street demonstrations to protest government policies. During the 1960s, however, the Liberal Democrats shifted to avoid needless confrontations, and they strongly emphasized policies of economic development. During the prosperous 1970s and 1980s, economic progress plus the Liberal Democrats' willingness to consult opposition leaders about major legislation reinforced Japan's effective political unity. Only at the end of the 1980s, when a number of Liberal Democratic leaders were branded by corruption of various sorts and Socialist strength revived somewhat, were new political questions raised.

Japan's distinctive political atmosphere, even under a Western-influenced constitution, showed clearly in the array of functions the government undertook in cooperation with business leaders. Economic planning was extensive, and the state set production and investment goals while actively lending public resources to encourage investment and limit imports. There was scant sense of division between public and private spheres, another reminder of older Japanese traditions in this case encouraged by Confucian principles. The government-business coordination to promote economic growth and export expansion prompted the half-admiring, half-derisory Western label of "Japan, Incorporated."

Close business and political interaction resulted in part from the needs of postwar reconstruction and from Japan's precarious resource position, as the nation needed to import petroleum and most other vital raw materials and so depended on success in the export sector to an unusual degree. Government initiative extended also to the demographic sphere, as postwar leaders realized that, with Japanese imperial expansion ended, it was vital to control population size. The government actively campaigned to promote birth control and abortion, and demographic growth, though still somewhat higher than Western levels, slowed notably. Here again was a product of the strong national tradition of group cohesion: While it did not prevent strong political party differences, this tradition united many Japanese in a sense of common purpose with the government. Later, however, Japan's aging population prompted the government to try to limit birth control by making a number of common methods illegal; here Japan's people proved more recalcitrant, as high costs of living kept families small.

Expansion of the educational system was another practical contact between state and citizens. The extensive school system developed from the Meiji era was further expanded, giving many more Japanese an opportunity to attend secondary schools and universities, which in turn were strongly oriented toward technical subjects. Japanese children were encouraged to achieve academic success, with demanding examinations for entry into universities defining much of the youth of ambitious men and women. The scientific and technical focus encouraged further secularization in Japanese culture, with strong emphasis on rational inquiry and practical knowledge. Not only growing creativity in science and technology, as Japan began to generate innovative discoveries instead of specializing in clever imitation of ideas developed elsewhere, but the unusually high I.Q. scores of Japanese children, showed the deep impact of this cultural focus. Again, traditional elements entered the picture, as education stressed somewhat mechanical group learning, based on disciplined memorization, over more eccentric individual achievements.

Japanese culture more generally preserved other important traditional elements that provided aesthetic and spiritual satisfactions amid rapid economic change and an ongoing interest in Western forms. Customary styles in po-

The hot sand baths at Kyushu exemplify traditional practices of health and relaxation in Japan.

etry, painting, tea ceremonies, and flower arrangements continued; each New Year's Day, for example, the emperor presided at a poetry contest, and masters of traditional arts were honored by being designated as "Living National Treasures." Kabuki and No theater also flourished. Japanese films and novels often recalled earlier history, including the age of the samurai warriors; they also stressed group loyalties, as opposed to individuality or strong assertions of will. Japanese painters and architects participated actively in the "international style" pioneered in the West, but they often infused it with earlier Japanese motifs such as stylized nature painting. City orchestras played the works of Western composers, both classical and contemporary, and also native compositions with passages played on the Japanese flute and zither. Both Buddhism and Shinto-

Traditional settings are found in modern Japan. The yomei-mon gateway, at the mausoleum of Ieyasu in Nikko, is a traditional place for contemplation.

ism remained significant forces in Japanese life as well, despite the strong secular emphasis. Overall, Japan in the later 20th century blended new cultural interests, which allowed the Japanese to incorporate many Western forms, with distinctive recollections of strictly national ways. At the same time, aside from interior decoration and film, Japanese contributions to world culture were negligible; this was not where national creativity showed an international face.

THE ECONOMIC SURGE

Particularly after the mid-1950s, it was rapid economic growth that produced Japan's clearest mark internationally and commanded the most intense energies at home. By 1983 the total national product was equal to the combined totals of China, both Koreas, Taiwan, India, Pakistan, Australia, and Brazil. Per capita income, though still slightly behind the leading Western nations such as West Germany, had passed that of many centers, including Britain. Annual economic growth reached at least 10 percent

regularly from the mid-1950s onward, surpassing the regular levels of every other nation during the 1960s and 1970s, as Japan became one of the top two or three economic powers in the world. Leading Japanese corporations, such as the great automobile manufacturers and electronic equipment producers, became known not simply for their volume of international exports but for the high quality of their goods.

A host of factors fed this astounding economic performance. Active government encouragement was a vital ingredient, as the government made economic growth its top priority. Cheap loans for technological innovations and direct technical research in government laboratories, as well as carefully favorable international trade policies, translated this priority directly. Educational expansion played a vital role, as Japan began to turn out far more engineers than did more populous competitors such as the United States. Foreign policy also played a role. Japan was able to devote virtually its whole capital to investment in productive technology, for its military expenses were negligible given reliance on United States' protection. Labor was a central feature. Japan had a growing available labor force based on continued if slower population growth and a rapid reduction of the agricultural population (from 47 percent in 1945 to the standard advanced-industrial rate of about 10 percent by the mid-1980s).

Workers were not only abundant but highly organized mainly, however, in company unions that engaged in important social activities and some serious bargaining for improved benefits but remained careful not to impair their companies' productivity. Leading corporations solidified this cooperation, which spurred zealous work from most employees. Few days were lost to strikes because of paternalistic policies that provided important benefits to workers despite wages that remained slightly low by Western standards. Social activities promoted and expressed group loyalty (including group exercise sessions before the start of the working day), and managers displayed active interest in suggestions by employees. The Japanese system also assured lifetime employment to an important part of the labor force, a policy aided by economic growth, low average unemployment rates, and a relatively early retirement age. This network of policies and attitudes made Japanese labor seem both less class-conscious and less individualistic than labor forces in the advanced industrial nations of the West; it reflected older traditions of group solidarity in Japan, going back to feudal patterns. Other popular habits encouraged economic growth, including a high (20 percent) savings rate born of a cautious attitude toward materialist acquisitiveness and the need to set aside money for old age. The result was considerable capital for investment in further innovation.

Japanese management displayed a distinctive spirit, again the result of adapting older traditions of leadership. There was more group consciousness, including a willingness to abide by collective decisions once made, and less concern for quick personal profits than was characteristic of the West and particularly the United States. Few corporate bureaucrats changed firms, which meant that their own efforts concentrated on their company's success.

Japan, in other words, produced a distinctive economic culture that was clearly compatible with impressive results, that responded to particular Japanese needs and traditions, and that differed in important ways from Western norms. It had costs: Workers faced intense pressure to produce and were deprived of much protest outlet. Personal consumer standards did not rise as rapidly as national output did, because of the concentration on savings and group benefits and the government-sponsored push to promote exports rather than drain output toward internal use. Leisure life remained meager by Western standards, and many Japanese even proved reluctant to take regular vacations.

Not surprisingly, the society that developed under the rapid industrial spurt showed features similar to the West's slightly earlier experience. Japanese women, though increasingly well educated and experiencing an important decline in birthrates, did not follow Western patterns precisely. A feminist movement was confined to a small number of intellectuals. Women's work outside the home was slightly less common and considerably more segregated than in the postwar West. Within the family, women shared fewer leisure activities with their husbands, concentrating more heavily on domestic duties and intensive child rearing than was true in the West by the 1970s. Divorce rates were lower (merely one-third of United States levels), a sign of Japanese family stability after the disruptions of earlier stages of modernization, but this stability was predicated on the acceptance of considerable differences in gender roles and power.

Japanese methods of child rearing reflected distinctive family values. Conformity to group standards was emphasized far more than in the West or in Communist China. A comparative study of nursery schools thus showed Japanese teachers bent on effacing their own authority in the interests of developing strong bonds among the children themselves. Shame was directed toward nonconformist behaviors—a disciplinary approach the West had largely abandoned in the early 19th century. Japanese television game shows, superficially copied from the West, accordingly imposed elaborate, dishonoring punishment on losing contestants.

The same group-oriented culture shone through in diverse facets of Japanese life. The nation had few lawyers, for it was assumed that people could make and abide by firm arrangements through mutual agreement. In the psychological area, psychiatrists reported far fewer problems of loneliness and individual alienation than in the West, as the Japanese remained devoted to group activities. Conversely, situations that promoted competition among individuals, such as the university entrance tests, produced far higher stress levels than did analogous Western experiences. The Japanese had particular ways to relieve tension, as well. Bouts of heavy drinking were more readily tolerated than in the West, as a time when normal codes of conduct could be suspended under the helpful eyes of friends. Businessmen and some politicians had recourse to traditional geisha houses for female-supplied cosseting, as a normal and publicly accepted activity. Japanese teenagers participated in higher rates of sexual activity than was common in the West, another sign perhaps of a distinctive Japanese combination of hard work with recreational release.

Japanese popular culture was not static, both because of ongoing attraction to Western standards and because of rapid urbanization and economic growth. The United States' presence after World War II brought a growing fascination with baseball, and a number of professional teams were set up. Individual Japanese athletes began also to excel in such sports as tennis and golf. In popular as well as more formal culture, change and Westernization continued to cause concern among conservatives who worried that vital traditions might be lost for good. In the mid-1980s the government, appalled to discover that a majority of Japanese children did not use chopsticks to eat (preferring knives and forks in order to eat more rapidly), invested considerable money to promote chopstick training in the schools—a minor development, but indicative of the ongoing tension between change, with its Western connotations, and a commitment to Japanese identity. At the end of the 1980s a new assertion of women's political power against some Japanese politicians who kept mistresses suggested the possibility that a more Western-style feminist consciousness might gain ground as part of Japan's ongoing evolution and its growing awareness, through cultural imports and also growing tourism abroad, of the standards of other societies. Veneration of old age was challenged by some youthful assertiveness and also by the sheer cost of the rapidly growing percentage of older people—for Japan relied heavily on family support for elders. Questions abounded about how Japan would combine distinctiveness with its industrial achievement in the future, but to Western eyes the Japanese ability to adapt traditions to change and imitation remained the most striking characteristic of the nation as the end of the 20th century neared.

Japan's continued success in international competition remained the dominant theme. Many nations both in the West and Asia resented Japanese competition and the Japanese reluctance to open their own markets to outside goods. Calls for retaliation by erecting tariff barriers against Japan were a recurrent threat, and the Japanese tried to respond—for example by increasing their economic aid to developing nations and by investing directly in the United States and Europe—without changing their policies entirely. By the 1960s, pollution became a serious problem as cities and industry expanded rapidly; traffic police, for example, sometimes wore protective masks to protect their lungs, though the government (eager to preempt a potential opposition issue) paid increasing attention to environmental issues after 1970. Some Japanese experts, worried that the nation's economic vigor would prove fragile amid such problems as growing fuel costs, foreign hostility, and internal problems, wrote articles with such titles as "The Short, Happy Life of Japan as a Superpower." Western

Crowding and commerce in contemporary Japan are depicted in this photo of the lively Shinjuku district of Tokyo at night.

observers continued at times to expect that Japan would soon become like the West, that is, would experience the same level of crime, strikes, individualism, family instability, youth unrest, and feminist assertiveness as the West had come to know. This expectation combined a certain amount of wishful thinking—that a wider array of problems would slow Japan up—with an implicit belief that industrialization must in the long run produce the same kinds of society regardless of the starting point.

Increasing recognition developed, however, that Japan must be understood in its combination of change with distinctiveness. Some observers even advocated that the West copy key Japanese values, particularly in the areas of diligence and group loyalty. Quite possibly, now that advanced industrialization had ceased being a Western monopoly, Japanese models would gain an increasing audience, though how much the West could or would imitate remained unclear. What was obvious, though confusing to many in the West, was Japan's achievement in reaching full economic equality—in becoming a genuine economic superpower—without adopting all Western forms of politics, family life, or personal values.

THE PACIFIC RIM: NEW JAPANS?

Economic and to some extent political developments in several other middle-sized nations and city-states on Asia's Pacific coast mirrored important elements of Japan's 20th-century history, though at a slightly later date. Political authoritarianism was characteristic, though usually with periodic bows to parliamentary forms and with recurrent protest from dissident elements who wanted greater freedom. Government functions extended to careful economic planning and promotion and to rapid expansions of the educational system, with the emphasis on technical training. Group loyalties promoted diligent labor and a willingness to work hard for relatively low wages. Economic growth burgeoned.

THE KOREAN MIRACLE

South Korea was the most obvious exemplar of the spread of new economic dynamism to other parts of the Pacific Rim. The Korean government rested normally in the hands of a political strongman, usually from army ranks. Syngman Rhee was forced out of office by massive student demonstrations in 1960, but a year later a military general, Chung-hee, seized power. He retained his authority until his assassination in 1979 by his director of intelligence. Then another general seized power. Intense student protest, backed by wider popular support, pressed the military from power at the end of the 1980s, but a conservative politician won the ensuing general election and it was not clear how much the political situation had changed. Opposition activity was possible in South Korea, though usually heavily circumscribed with many leaders jailed. There was some freedom of the press except for publications from Communist countries.

As in postwar Japan, the South Korean government from the mid-1950s onward placed its primary emphasis on economic growth, which in this case started from a much lower base after the Korean War and previous Japanese exploitation. Huge industrial firms were created by a combination of government aid and active entrepreneurship. Exports were actively encouraged and by the 1970s, when Korean growth rates began to match those of Japan, Korea was competing successfully, in the area of cheap consumer goods as well as in steel and automobiles, in a variety of international markets. In steel, Korea's surge—based on the most up-to-date technology, a skilled engineering sector, and low wages—indeed pushed past Japan. The same held true in textiles, where Korean growth (along with that of Taiwan) erased almost one-third of the jobs held in the industry in Japan.

Huge industrial groups like Daewoo and Hyundai resembled the great Japanese holding companies before and after World War II and wielded great political influence. Hyundai, for example, is the creation of the entrepreneur Chung Ju Yung, a modern folk hero who walked 150 miles to Seoul, South Korea's capital, from his native village to take his first job as a day laborer at the age of 16. By the 1980s, when Chung was in his sixties, his firm had 135,000 employees and embraced 42 overseas offices throughout the world. Hyundai virtually governed Korea's southeastern coast. It built ships, including petroleum supertankers; it constructed thousands of housing units given to relatively low-paid workers at below-market rates; it built schools, a technical college, and an arena for the practice of the traditional Korean martial art, Tae Kwon Do. With their lives carefully provided for, Hyundai workers responded in kind, putting in six-day weeks with three vacation days per year and participating in almost-worshipful ceremonies when a fleet of cars was shipped abroad or a new tanker launched.

South Korea's rapid entry into the ranks of newly industrialized countries produced a host of more general changes. Population growth soared, as by the 1980s over 40 million people lived in a nation about the size of the state of Indiana, producing the highest population density on earth, about 1000 people per square mile. Here was

one reason that, even amid growing prosperity, many Koreans emigrated, while the government gradually began to encourage couples to limit their birthrates. Seoul expanded to embrace nine million people, with intense air pollution and a hothouse atmosphere of deals and business maneuvers. Per capita income advanced despite demography, rising almost ten times from the early 1950s to the early 1980s—but to a level still only one-ninth of that of Japan. Huge fortunes coexisted with massive poverty in this setting, though the poverty itself had risen well above levels characteristic of less-developed nations.

ADVANCES IN TAIWAN AND THE CITY-STATES

The Republic of China, as the government on Taiwan came to call itself, experienced a rate of economic development similar to that in Korea, though slightly less impressive in terms of outright industrialization. Productivity in both agriculture and industry increased rapidly, the former spurred by substantial land reform that benefited small commercial farmers. The government concentrated increasingly on economic gains, as its involvement in plans for military action against the mainland Communist regime declined. As in Japan and Korea, formal economic planning reached high levels, though not at the expense of considerable latitude for private business. Massive investments were also poured into education, with basic literacy rates and levels of technical training rising rapidly. The result was important cultural and economic change for the Taiwanese people. Traditional medical practices and ritualistic popular religion remained lively, but expanded to allow simultaneous use of modern, Western-derived medicine and some of the urban entertainment forms popular elsewhere.

The assimilation of rapid change gave the Taiwanese government considerable stability despite a host of new concerns. United States recognition of the People's Republic of China brought with it a steadily decreasing official commitment to Taiwan. In 1978 the United States severed diplomatic ties with the Taiwanese regime, though unofficial contacts—through the American Institute in Taiwan and the Coordination Council for North American Affairs established by the republic in Washington—remained strong. The Taiwanese also built important regional contacts with other governments in eastern and southeastern Asia that facilitated trade; Japan, for example, served as the nation's most important single trading partner, purchasing foodstuffs, manufactured textiles, chemicals and other industrial goods.

Taiwan also developed some informal links with the Communist regime in Beijing, though the latter continued to claim the island as part of its territory. The republic survived the death of Chiang Kai-shek and the accession of his son, Chiang Ching-kuo, to power in 1978. The young Chiang emphasized personal authority less than his father had, and reduced somewhat the gap between mainland-born military personnel and native Taiwanese in government ranks. A strong authoritarian strain, however, continued, and political diversity was not encouraged.

Conditions in the city-state of Singapore, though less enveloped in echoes of great-power politics, resembled those in Taiwan in many ways. The prime minister, Lee Kuan Yew, took office in 1959, when the area first gained independence, and held power for the next three decades. The government established tight controls over its citizens—here going beyond anything attempted elsewhere in the Pacific Rim. Sexual behavior and potential economic corruption, as well as more standard aspects of municipal regulation and economic planning, were carefully scrutinized, as the government proclaimed the necessity of unusual discipline and restraint given a large population crowded into limited space. One result was unusually low reported crime rates; another was a limitation on tensions between the Chinese majority and other ethnic groups; and still another was the virtual impossibility of serious political protest. The authoritarian strain in politics developed increasingly, after an initially democratic constitution; the dominant People's Action party suppressed opposition movements, though there was some easing in the late 1980s. Authoritarian politics were rendered somewhat more palatable by extraordinarily successful economic development, based on a combination of government controls and initiatives and free enterprise. Already the world's fourth largest port, Singapore saw manufacturing and banking surpass shipping as sources of revenue. Electronics, textiles, and oil refining joined shipbuilding as major sectors. By the 1980s Singapore's population enjoyed the second highest per capita income in Asia. Educational levels and health conditions improved commensurately. Government regulation and propaganda combined to reduce population growth, which leveled off notably.

Finally, Hong Kong retained its status as a major world port and branched out increasingly as a center of international banking, serving as a bridge between the Communist regime in China and the wider world. Export production combined high-speed technology with low wages and long hours for the labor force, yielding highly competitive results. While textiles and clothing formed 39 percent of total exports by the 1980s, other sectors, including

heavy industry, had developed impressively as well. As in other Pacific Rim nations, a large and prosperous middle class had developed, with cosmopolitan links to many other parts of the world, Western and Asian alike.

COMMON THEMES IN THE PACIFIC RIM

Overall, the Pacific Rim states, including Japan as a special case of advanced industrial success, had more in common than their rapid growth rates and expanding exports. They all stressed group loyalties against excessive individualism and in support of hard work and somewhat limited consumer demands. Confucian morality was often utilized, implicitly or explicitly, as part of this effort, for all the Pacific Rim states were either Chinese or had been strongly influenced by Chinese values. Pacific Rim areas thus sought to merge rapid change and considerable imitation of Western ways with preservation of core standards that were distinctly East Asian. Pacific Rim states also shared, despite diverse specific political systems, considerable reliance on government planning and direction, amid limitations on dissent and instability.

ANALYSIS
THE PACIFIC RIM AS A UNITED STATES POLICY ISSUE

Whenever power balances change among nations or larger civilizations, a host of policy issues arise for all parties involved. The rise of the Pacific Rim economies posed some important dilemmas for the West, and particularly, because of its military role in the Pacific as well as its world economic role, for the United States. The United States had actively promoted economic growth in Japan, Korea, and Taiwan as part of its desire to sponsor solid regional development that would discourage the spread of communism. While American aid was not alone responsible for Pacific Rim advance, and while it tapered off by the 1960s, the United States took some satisfaction in the fruits of its efforts and in the demonstration of the vitality of non-Communist economies. The United States was also not eager to relinquish its military superiority in the region, which gave it a stake in continued conciliation of Asian opinion; it did not want to see tensions translated into outright hostility that might threaten American bases (as in South Korea) or lead to independent military efforts (a potential in the case of Japan).

Yet the threats posed by growing Pacific Rim economic competition, if more subtle than the military challenges more characteristic of changing power balances, were real and growing. Japan seemed to wield a permanent balance of payments superiority; exports to the United States regularly exceeded imports by the 1970s and 1980s, which contributed greatly to the United States' unfavorable overall trade balance. Japanese investment in American companies and real estate, while helping to bridge the international payments deficit by bringing yen for dollars, increased the United States' growing indebtedness to foreign nations. Symbolic problems were real as well. Japanese observers pointed out with some justice that Americans seemed more worried about Japanese investments than about larger British holdings in the United States — an imbalance that smacked of racism. Certainly Americans found it harder to accept Asian competition than they did European, if only because it was less familiar. Thus a Korean advertisement for a major firm, placed in a 1984 copy of Fortune magazine, featured tales of technological prowess and also pictures of three leading executives wearing the sweatshirts of their American university alma maters (MIT, Wisconsin, and Cal Tech) — a combination that rankled many Americans both because of the boasts and because of the partially justified sense that the United States' know-how was being used against it. More concretely, Japanese ability to gain near-monopolies in key industries such as electronic recording systems — in some of which initial inventions still came from the United States, but their successful implementation shifted to Asia — and the growing Korean challenge in steel and automobiles meant or seemed to mean loss of jobs and perhaps a threat of more fundamental economic decline in years to come.

Several general lines of response were suggested to deal with the new competitive balance between the United States and the Pacific Rim. Some observers downplayed any sense of crisis. They argued that some readjustment was acceptable — the United States did not have to maintain its brief economic superiority worldwide and could not indeed do so. They urged that acceptance of Japanese economic vigor in tandem with American military strength in East Asia was a viable combination — each society specialized in areas it had talent for, to the benefit of both.

Other observers, far more concerned about a worsening economic imbalance, urged American imitation of the bases of Pacific Rim success: The United States should open more partnerships between government and private industry and do more economic planning; it should teach managers to commit themselves to group harmony rather than individual profit seeking; and it should build a new con-

cord between management and labor based on mutual respect, greater job security and cooperative social programs. Some United States' firms did introduce certain Japanese management methods, including more consultation with workers, with some success.

A final set of observers, also concerned about long-term erosion of American power on the Pacific Rim, urged a more antagonistic stance. A few wanted the United States to pull out of costly Japanese and Korean bases, so that the Pacific Rim would be forced to shoulder more of its own defense costs. Others wanted to mount tariffs against Asian goods, at least until Pacific Rim nations made it easier for American firms to compete in Asian markets. Some limits on Asian competition were introduced by law during the 1980s, and Japan occasionally agreed to stabilize exports lest more hostile restrictions ensue. Aggrieved American workers sometimes smashed imported cars and threatened Asian immigrants, though many Americans, as consumers, continued to prefer Pacific Rim products and many American firms set up production in Japan or Korea — with an eye toward export back to the home market — in order to maintain profits while using superior Pacific Rim technology and advantageous labor costs. The options were complex, and American policy continued to veer among them.

Pacific Rim nations also faced choices about orientation toward the West, and here too particularly the United States'. Questions that had arisen earlier about what Western patterns to copy and what to avoid continued to be important — as the Japanese concern about forks and chopsticks suggests. Added now were issues about how to express pride and confidence in modern achievements against what was seen as Western tendencies to belittle and patronize. In 1988 the summer Olympic Games were held in South Korea, a sign of Korea's international advance and a source of great national satisfaction. During the games, a great deal of Korean nationalism flared against United States' athletes and television commentators, based on real or imagined tendencies to seek out faults in Korean society. South Korea, like Japan, continued to look heavily toward Western markets and United States military assistance, but there was clearly a desire to put the relationship on a more fully equal footing. This desire reflected widespread public opinion, and it could have policy implications.

Questions: How great were the challenges posed by the Pacific Rim to the United States' world position and well-being? What are the most likely changes in American-Pacific Rim relations over the next two decades?

PACIFIC RIM AS EXCEPTION
OR AS MODEL

The rise of the Pacific Rim nations was based on a combination of several factors. First, the nations shared in aspects of the Chinese cultural and political heritage, mediated, as in Japan, by many prior adaptations and additions. A roughly common culture helped account for similar tendencies to emphasize cooperation, to build tight links between state and society, and to seek to maintain distinctive identity even amid change and imitation of aspects of Western technical and social forms. Second, the Pacific Rim nations shared some special contacts with the West through unusually intense interaction with the British or through postwar dealings with the United States. These contacts provided a certain amount of economic and/or military support at key junctures, and also some unusual opportunities to grasp aspects of the West's technology, politics, and even popular culture. Finally, the principal Pacific Rim centers, including Japan, had been rocked by 20th-century events, which virtually forced considerable rethinking and innovation.

The shared features of the Pacific Rim were very general. The region was not unified geographically or in any other way, though growing mutual trade provided an important bond in some instances. Japan was far more advanced industrially than the rest of the Pacific Rim. Political structures and diplomatic and military contexts varied considerably. The apparent similarities of Pacific Rim nations might therefore prove temporary. Certainly, even in the short run, there was mutual rivalry, most obviously in the economic competition between Japan and Korea exacerbated by mutual memories of Japanese occupation.

At least for an important moment in the later 20th century, however, the emergence of the Pacific Rim nations involved important innovations both in the cultural and political map of East Asia, newly divided between Communist and other, and in the economic map of the world as a whole. The Pacific Rim, headed by Japan but joined by the self-sustaining industrializations achieved elsewhere, provided the clearest challenge to the West's long international economic leadership. Though not wedded to commensurate military prowess, the Pacific Rim's economic surge might foreshadow wider international influence later on, as cultural forms and values, for example, begin spreading both ways instead of primarily mainly west to east. And what of China, and possibly Vietnam, where different issues dominated much of the 20th century but

where many features were shared or could be resurrected that would mesh with the factors responsible for Pacific Rim dynamism? As China experimented with new economic forms in the late 1970s and early 1980s, many observers wondered if this Asian giant, or at least its coastal cities, would soon join in the Pacific Rim ascendancy. What would happen, for example, when Hong Kong was rejoined to China in 1997, assuming the Communist regime kept its pledge to give the city-state considerable latitude? Would this encourage more general Chinese adaptation to a more mixed economic structure that in turn could propel more rapid economic growth?

Certainly the success of the Pacific Rim states after World War II raised substantial questions about the contrast to China, questions that linked history to present patterns. Confucian traditions were clearly not only compatible with rapid industrial advance but could actually contribute to it. Chinese zest for commerce showed directly in Hong Kong, Taiwan, and Singapore. Huge population pressure and a long period of foreign exploitation did not hold South Korea back. Was East Asia durably divided between industrial states and societies that, while changing, remained largely agricultural, or between non-Communist and Communist? Here is a key question for Hong Kong as it prepares to accept Chinese rule in 1997. And here is a larger question for the future, where recent experience and long-term tradition suggest different answers.

The possibility also exists that economic dynamism similar to that of the Pacific Rim states may take hold in other small, non-Communist societies in southeast Asia, even though religious traditions and ethnic makeup differ from the Pacific Rim proper. By the 1980s economic growth rates in Malaysia and Thailand spurted forward, suggesting the possibility of an industrialization process beyond more piecemeal technological change.

Ongoing evolution within the Pacific Rim states raises a final set of questions. Both Japan and South Korea continue to express tension between change and considerable imitation of Western forms, on the one hand, and periodic traditionalist-nationalist reactions. Usually, to be sure, a compromise has prevailed that maintains distinctive social forms without preventing rapid change. Japan's interwar experience, and some of the political frustrations visible in South Korea late in the 1980s, remind us that adaptive compromise might not always be successful.

Even without these speculations for the future, the entry of the Pacific Rim into the mainstream of international trade represented a vital new development both for the region itself and for the world economy. Unsupported by military might after World War II and not joined as yet by any missionary culture of the sort that helped propel the

Arabs or West Europeans in the past, the rise of the Pacific Rim was an unusual development in world history, quite apart from its contrast with the region's substantial isolation in earlier eras. It is not surprising that it provokes questions about a wider ultimate international role. If a choice has to be made for the next internationally dominant region—and it is not clear that it is sensible to project a choice in the early 1990s—East Asia seems the most obvious single candidate.

Paul Kuznets's *Economic Growth and Structure in the Republic of Korea* (1977), and Dennis McNamara's *The Colonial Origins of Korean Enterprise 1910–1945* (1990).

For a fascinating exploration of cultural change and continuity in Taiwan around issues in health and medicine, see Arthur Kleinman's *Patients and Healers in the Context of Culture* (1979). On Singapore, Janet W. Salaff's *State and Family in Singapore* (1988) is an excellent study; see also R. N. Kearney, ed., *Politics and Modernization in South and Southeast Asia* (1975).

FURTHER READINGS

The best account of contemporary Japanese society and politics is E. O. Reischauer's *The Japanese* (1988). For a recent history, see M. Howe's *Modern Japan: A Historical Survey* (1986). On the economy, consult H. Patrick and H. Rosovsky's *Asia's New Giant: How the Japanese Economy Works* (1976); E. F. Vogel's *Japan as Number One: Lessons for America* (1979); and K. Ohkawa and H. Rosovsky's *Japanese Economic Growth: Trend Acceleration in the Twentieth Century* (1973).

Several novels and literary collections are accessible and useful. J. Tanizaki's *The Makioka Sisters* (1957) deals with a merchant family in the 1930s; see also H. Hibbett, ed., *Contemporary Japanese Literature: An Anthology of Fiction, Film and Other Writing Since 1945* (1977). An important study of change, focusing on postwar rural society, is G. Bernstein's *Haruko's World: A Japanese Farm Woman and Her Community* (1983). Another complex 20th-century topic is assessed in R. Storry's *The Double Patriots: A Story of Japanese Nationalism* (1973).

On the Pacific Rim concept and its implications in terms of the world economy, see David Aikman's *Pacific Rim: Area of Change, Area of Opportunity* (1986); Philip West and others, eds., *Pacific Rim and the Western World: Strategic, Economic and Cultural Perspectives* (1987); Stephen Haggard and Chung-in Moon's *Pacific Dynamics: The International Politics of Industrial Change* (1988); Ronald A. Morse and others' *Pacific Basin: Concept and Challenge* (1986); and Staffan B. Linder's *Pacific Century: Economic and Political Consequences of Asian-Pacific Dynamism* (1986).

Excellent introductions to recent Korean history are Bruce Cumings's *The Two Koreas* (1984) and David Rees's *A Short History of Modern Korea* (1988). A variety of special topics are addressed in Marshall R. Pihl, ed., *Listening to Korea* (1973). See also David Steinberg's *The Republic of Korea: Economic Transformation and Social Change* (1989),

1920–1940 Mexican muralist movement active

1910–1920 Mexican Revolution

1934–1940 President Cárdenas enacts many of
the reforms promised by the Mexican Revolution

1917 Mexican Constitution
includes revolutionary changes

1932 Women win voting rights in Cuba and Brazil

1929 Women
get the right to
vote in Ecuador

1910 Madero's revolt

1933 Death of Augusto César Sandino, leader
of Nicaraguan resistance to U.S. occupation

1911 Zapata promises land reform

1930 Revolution in Brazil brings Getúlio Vargas to power

1914 Panama Canal opens

1930 Military takes control of the Argentine government

A.D. 1910   A.D. 1920   A.D. 1930

Latin America: Revolution and Reaction in the 20th Century

INTRODUCTION. The focus of the previous three chapters—the West, Eastern Europe, and the Pacific Rim—involved societies with very different 20th-century institutions and experiences, but with one common bond: the experience of industrialization or its elaboration. The following chapters deal with societies grouped in what is sometimes termed the Third World in contrast to the capitalist industrial nations of the First World and the Communist industrial nations of the Second World. Third World societies displayed great diversity, depending on political tradition—the presence or absence of revolutionary experience, for example—and on cultural emphasis. They all, however, faced issues of economic development and inequality—of relating to economically more powerful societies—as part of their 20th-century history.

Latin America fit the Third World definition closely, despite great regional variety, but it also demonstrated how very loose this definition was. During the 20th century, Latin America continued to demonstrate its intermediate position between the nations of the North Atlantic and the developing countries of Asia and Africa. While Latin America shared many problems with these other areas of the Third World, its earlier political independence and its often more Western social and political structures placed it in a distinct category. During the course of the century, the Latin-American elites led their nations into closer ties with the growing international capitalist economy, although admittedly over increasing objections from critics within their nations. Investments and initiative often came from Europe and the United States, and Latin-American economies continued their concentration on exports. As a result, Latin America became increasingly vulnerable to changes in the world financial system.

1938 Mexico nationalizes its petroleum resources

1942 Brazil joins the Allies; sends troops to Europe

1944–1954 Arevalo and Arbenz reforms in Guatemala

1947 Juan Peron elected president of Argentina

1952–1964 Bolivian Revolution

1954 Arbenz overthrown with help from U.S.

1959 Castro leads revolution in Cuba

1961 U.S.-backed invasion of Cuba is defeated

1964 Military coup topples Brazilian government

1970–1973 Salvador Allende, Socialist government in Chile; overthrown and assassinated by the military in 1973

1979 Sandinista Revolution takes control in Nicaragua

1982 Argentina and Great Britain clash over the Falkland Islands (Malvinas Islas)

1983 U.S. invades Grenada

1989 Sandinistas lose election in Nicaragua

1989 U.S. invades Panama, deposes General Noriega

A.D. 1940   A.D. 1960   A.D. 1980

For many Latin Americans, this "dependency" on the markets, the financial situation, and economic decisions made outside the region was also reflected in a political and even cultural dependency in which foreign influence and foreign models shaped all aspects of national life.

Throughout the century, Latin Americans grappled with the problem of finding a basis for social justice, cultural autonomy, and economic security either by adopting ideologies from abroad or by developing a specifically Latin-American approach to the problem. Thus, in Latin America the struggle for decolonization has been primarily one of economic disengagement and a search for political and cultural forms appropriate to Latin-American realities, rather than being a process of political separation and independence as in Asia and Africa.

New groups began to appear on the political stage. While Latin America continued its 19th-century emphasis on agrarian and mineral production, there was also a growth of an industrial sector in some places, and as this movement gathered strength, worker organizations began to emerge as a political force. Industrialization was accompanied by continued immigration to some countries and urban growth in many places. A growing urban middle class linked to commerce, industry, and the expanding state bureaucracies also began to play a role in the political process.

With considerable variation from country to country, overall the economy and the political process were subject to a series of broad shifts. There was a pattern to these shifts, with economic expansion (accompanied by relatively conservative regimes that, although sometimes willing to make gradual reforms, hoped to maintain a political status quo) alternating with periods of economic crisis during which various attempts were made to provide social justice or to break with old social and political patterns. Thus the political pendulum swung broadly across the region and often affected a number of countries at roughly the same time, indicating the relationship between international trends and the internal events in these nations.

Latin Americans have long debated the nature of their societies and the need for change. While much of the rhetoric of Latin America has stressed radical reform and revolutionary change in the 20th century, the fact is that the region has remained remarkably unchanged as the old institutions and patterns of politics and economy have adapted to new situations and provided a sometimes disheartening continuity. Revolutionaries have not been lacking, but the task of defeating the existing political and social order and creating a new one upon which the majority of the population will agree is a difficult one, especially when this must be done within an international as well as a national context. Thus the few revolutionary political changes that have had long-term effects stand in marked contrast to the general trends of the region's political history. At the same time, however, there have been significant changes in education, social services, the position of women, and the role of industry that have taken place over the course of the century and have gradually begun to transform many areas of Latin-American life.

 ## THE MEXICAN REVOLUTION AND THE GREAT WAR

Two cataclysmic events launched Latin America into the 20th century and set in motion trends that would determine much of the region's subsequent history. The first of these events was the ten-year civil war and political upheaval of the Mexican Revolution, which erupted because of the internal situation in that country. Eventually, however, the Mexican Revolution was also influenced by the other major event, the outbreak of World War I. While most Latin-American nations avoided direct participation in the Great War, as World War I was called at the time, the disruption of traditional markets for Latin-American exports and the elimination of European sources of manufactures caused a realignment of the economies of a number of nations in the region. Forced to rely on themselves, a spurt of manufacturing continued the process begun after 1870, and some small steps were taken to overcome the traditional dependence on outside supply. Finally, at the end of World War I, the United States emerged as the dominant foreign power in the region replacing Great Britain in both economic and political terms. That position created a reality that Latin Americans could not ignore and that greatly influenced economic and political options in the region.

MEXICO'S UPHEAVAL

The event that announced a new age in Latin America and launched it into the 20th century was the Mexican Revolution of 1910. The regime of Porfirio Díaz had been in power since 1876 and seemed unshakable. During the Díaz dictatorship, tremendous economic changes had been made, and foreign concessions in mining, railroads, and other sectors of the economy had created a sense of prosperity among the Mexican elite. This progress, however, had been bought at considerable expense. Foreigners controlled large sectors of the economy. The hacienda system of extensive landholdings dominated certain regions of the country. The political system was wholly corrupt and any complaint was stifled. The government took repressive measures against workers, peasants, and Indians who opposed the alienation of their lands or the unbearable working conditions. Political opponents were often imprisoned or forced into exile. In short, Díaz ruled with an iron fist through an effective political machine.

By 1910, however, Díaz was 80 years old and seemed willing to allow some political opposition. Francisco Madero, a wealthy son of an elite family, proposed to run against Díaz. Madero was no radical, but he believed that some moderate democratic political reforms would relieve social tensions and allow the government to continue its "progressive" economic developments with a minimum of popular unrest. Madero's moderate challenge was not much, but it was more than Díaz could stand. Madero was arrested, a rigged election put Díaz back in power; and things returned to normal. When Madero was released from prison, he called for a revolt.

A general rebellion developed. In the north, small farmers, railroaders, and cowboys coalesced under the colorful former bandit and able commander, Pancho Villa. In Morelos, an area of old conflicts between Indian communities and large sugar estates, a peasant-based guerrilla movement began under Emiliano Zapata whose goal of land reform was expressed in his motto "Tierra y Libertad" (Land and Liberty). Díaz was driven from power by this coalition of forces, but it soon became apparent that Madero's moderate programs would not resolve Mexico's continuing social problems. Zapata rose in revolt demanding a sweeping land reform and Madero steadily lost control of his subordinates. In 1913, with at least tacit agreement of the American ambassador in Mexico, a military coup removed Madero from government and he was then assassinated.

General Victoriano Huerta sought to reimpose a Díaz-type dictatorship supported by the large landowners, the army, and the foreign companies, but the tide of revolution could not be stopped so easily. Villa and Zapata rose again against the government and were joined by other middle-class political opponents of Huerta's illegal rule. By 1914 Huerta was forced from power, but the victorious leaders now began to fight over the nature of the new regime and the mantle of leadership. An extended period of warfare followed as the tides of battle continually shifted. The railroad lines built under Díaz now moved large numbers of troops and their accompanying women *soldaderas* who sometimes shouldered arms. Matters were also complicated by United States intervention and by diplomatic maneuverings after the outbreak of World War I in Europe. Villa and Zapata remained in control in their home territo-

ries, but they could not wrest the government from control of the more moderate political leaders in Mexico City. Alvaro Obregón, an able general who had learned the new tactics of machine guns and trenches from the war raging in Europe and had beaten Villa's cavalry in a series of bloody battles in 1915, emerged as leader of the government.

As much as the Mexican Revolution had its own internal dynamic, it is interesting to note that it was roughly contemporaneous with revolutions in other agrarian societies which had also just undergone a period of rapid and disruptive modernization. The Boxer Rebellion in China (1899–1901) and the toppling of the emperor in 1911, the 1905 revolution in Russia and a revolution in Iran in the same year underlined the rapid changes in these societies, all of which had received large foreign investments from either the United States or western Europe. In each of these countries governments had tried to establish strong

The Mexican Revolution mobilized large segments of the population, both men and women. The Villista forces shown here included soldaderas among the railroad workers, peasants, cowboys, and townsfolk who took up arms in northern Mexico.

centralized control and had sought rapid modernization, but in doing so had made their nations increasingly dependent on foreign investments and consequently on world financial markets. Thus a world banking crisis like that of 1907 and 1908 cut Mexico and these other countries off from their needed sources of capital and created severe strains on their governments. This kind of dependency, and the fact that in Mexico over 20 percent of the nation's territory was owned directly by United States' citizens or companies, fed a growing nationalism that spread through many sectors of society. That nationalist sentiment played a role in each of these revolutions.

By 1920 the period of civil war was ended and Mexico began to consolidate the changes that had taken place in the previous confused and bloody decade. Obregón was elected president in that year, and he was then followed by a series of presidents from the new "revolutionary elite" who sought to consolidate the new regime. There was much to be done. The revolution had devastated the country: one-half million people had died, major industries were destroyed, ranching and farming were disrupted. But there was great hope because the revolution also promised (although it did not always deliver) real changes.

What were some of these changes? A new constitution of 1917 promised land reform, limited the foreign ownership of key resources, guaranteed the rights of workers, placed restrictions on clerical education and Church ownership of property, and promised educational reforms. The workers who had been mobilized were organized in a national confederation and were given representation in the government. The promised land reforms were slow in coming, but under President Lázaro Cárdenas (1934-1940) over 40 million acres were distributed, most of it in the form of *ejidos,* or communal holdings. The government launched an extensive program of primary and especially rural education.

CULTURE AND POLITICS IN POSTREVOLUTIONARY MEXICO

Nationalism and *indigenism,* or the concern for the Indians and their contribution to Mexican culture, lay beneath many reforms. Having failed to integrate the Indians into national life for a century, Mexico now sought to "Indianize" the nation through secular schools that emphasized nationalism and a vision of the Mexican past that glorified its Indian heritage and denounced Western capitalism. Artists such as Diego Rivera and José Clemente Orozco recaptured that past and outlined a social program for the future in stunning murals on public buildings designed to inform, convince, and entertain at the same time. The Mexican muralist movement had a wide impact on artists throughout Latin America even though, as Orozco himself stated, it sometimes created simple solutions and strange utopias by mixing a romantic image of the Indian past with Christian symbols and Communist ideology. Novelists

During and after the Mexican Revolution, artists like David Alfaro Siqueiros called for murals in public places, worker neighborhoods, and sport stadiums, as well as on large buildings to record the history of Mexico and to emphasize the actions of the people. Siqueiros's *Struggle for the Banner* (1957) portrays workers and peasants seizing the national flag from the hands of oppressors.

such as Mariano Azuela found in the revolution itself a focus for the examination of Mexican reality. Popular culture celebrated the heroes and events of the revolution in scores of ballads that were sung to celebrate and inform. In literature, music, and the arts, the revolution as well as its themes provided a stimulus to a tremendous burst of creativity.

The gains of the revolution were not made without considerable opposition. While it had preceded the Russian Revolution of 1917 and had no single ideological model, many of the ideas of Marxian socialism were held by leading Mexican intellectuals and a few politicians. The secularization of society and especially education met strong opposition from the Church and the clergy, especially when in some states Socialist rhetoric and anticlericalism was extreme. In the 1920s a conservative peasant movement backed by the Church erupted in central Mexico. These "Cristeros," backed also by conservative politicians, fought to stop the slide toward secularization. Fighting lasted for years until a compromise was reached.

The United States had intervened diplomatically and militarily during the revolution. An incident provoked a short-lived United States seizure of Veracruz in 1914, and when Pancho Villa's forces had raided across the border,

the United States sent an expeditionary force into Mexico to catch him. The mission failed. For the most part, however, the war in Europe had distracted American foreign policy until 1918. The United States was suspicious of the new government and a serious conflict arose when American-owned oil companies ran into problems with workers. The companies called for United States intervention or pressure when President Cárdenas expropriated the companies in 1934. An agreement was worked out, however, and Mexico nationalized its petroleum industry in a state-run monopoly. This nationalization of natural resources was considered a declaration of economic independence. It symbolized the nationalistic basis of many of the revolution's goals.

As in any revolution, the question of continuity arose when the fighting ended. The revolutionary leadership hoped to institutionalize the new regime by creating a one-party system. This organization, presently called the Party of the Institutionalized Revolution (PRI), developed slowly during the 1920s and 1930s into a dominant force in Mexican politics. It incorporated labor, peasant, military, and middle class sectors and proved flexible enough to incorporate new interest groups as they developed. While Mexico became in theory a multiparty democracy, in real-

These graphs reflect party membership by sectors. Note that the population shifted away from rural areas and that labor remained fairly steady.

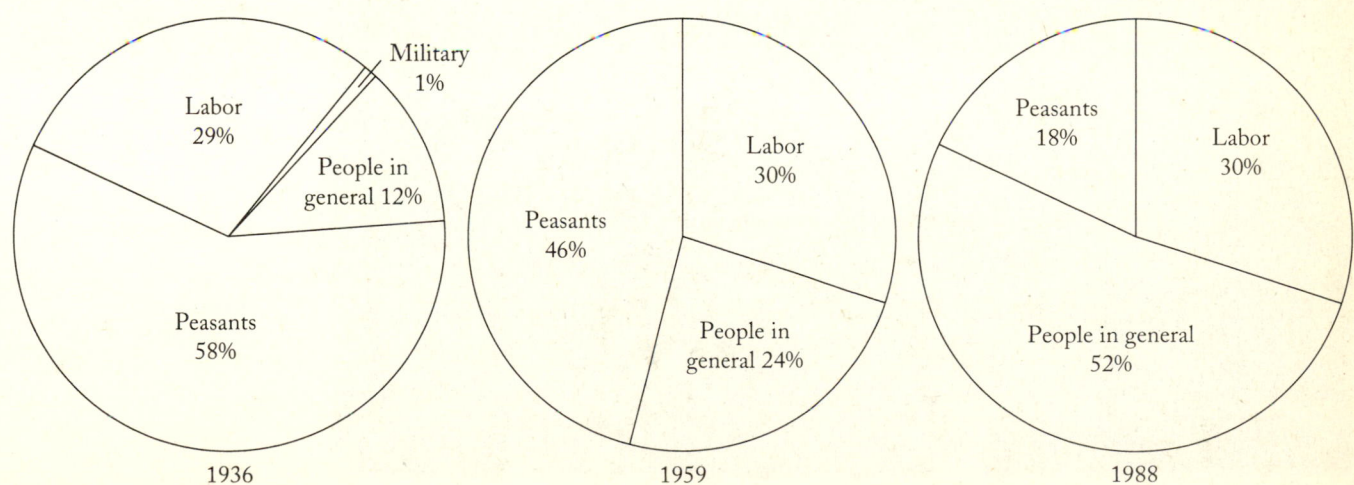

1936

Labor 29%
Military 1%
People in general 12%
Peasants 58%

1959

Labor 30%
Peasants 46%
People in general 24%

1988

Peasants 18%
Labor 30%
People in general 52%

ity the PRI controlled politics and, by accomodation and sometimes repression, maintained its hold on national political life. Some presidents governed much like the strong men in the 19th century had done, but the party structure and the need to incorporate various interests within the government coalition limited the worst aspects of caudillo, or personalist, rule. Presidents were strong, but the policy of limiting the presidency to one six-year term ensured some change in leadership. The question of whether a revolution could be institutionalized remained in debate. By the last decades of the century, many Mexicans believed that little remained of the principles and programs of the revolutionaries of 1910.

LATIN-AMERICAN ECONOMIES AND WORLD WAR I

The Mexican Revolution had a limited immediate impact beyond the borders of Mexico, but the outbreak of World War I affected most of the region directly. Throughout much of Latin America, the effects of the economic boom of the late 19th century had continued into the first decades of the 20th century. Each nation had its specialized crop or set of exports—coffee for Colombia,

Brazil, and Costa Rica; minerals from Bolivia, Chile, and Peru; bananas from Ecuador and Central America; and sugar from Cuba. As long as European demand remained high, groups in control of these exports greatly profited.

For a while, World War I produced some immediate effects on the Latin-American economies. Cut off from supplies of traditional imports, a spurt of industrial growth took place in what economists call "import substitution industrialization." Latin Americans had to produce for themselves some of what they had formerly imported. Most of this involved "light" industry such as textiles. Latin America continued to suffer from a lack of capital, limited markets (because so many people had so little to spend), and low technological levels. Still, changes had taken place. Moreover, during the war there was also increased European demand for some products. World War I had provided a stimulus to the economy but it was a false start. After the war a general inflationary trend meant that the real wages of the working classes declined and their worsening condition contributed to increasing political unrest.

That unrest also resulted from population growth, which was rapid in some countries. Immigrants continued to pour into Argentina, Brazil, and some of the other temperate countries, swelling the ranks of the rural and urban

Latin America experienced industrial growth with light industries such as textiles. This painting of a Mexican factory is from the mid-19th century.

working classes. Cities grew in size and importance. Often the old pattern of a capital city and its port dominating the rest of the country became reinforced during this period. This has been a continuing problem in Latin America, where cities such as Lima, Montevideo, Quito, and Mexico City have so dominated the economic and political resources of their countries that growth outside the capital has been difficult. By 1920, for example, 20 percent of Argentina's total population lived in Buenos Aires; 14 percent of the population of Chile and Cuba lived in their capitals of Santiago and Havana. Latin America had a strong urban tradition since colonial times, but in the 20th century rapid urban growth created a series of social problems that reflected the transformation of Latin America from basically agrarian to industrializing societies.

NEW POLITICAL ACTORS: LABOR AND THE MIDDLE CLASS

The rising importance of an urban labor force and the growth of an urban middle class led to changes in the political structure of some Latin-American nations. The traditional landowning oligarchy in countries such as Argentina, Chile, and Brazil began to open up the political system in order to meet the desire of the growing middle class to share political power. In Argentina, for example, a new electoral law in 1912 resulted in the 1916 triumph of the middle-class-based Radical party. After some preliminary attempts to forge an alliance with workers, however, that strategy was abandoned in favor of closer ties with the traditional elites. In Brazil, after the establishment of a republic in 1889, a series of conservative presidents from the Republican party in the wealthiest and most powerful states held control of the government. This alliance of traditional landed interests and urban middle classes maintained political stability and a business-as-usual approach to government, but it began to encounter a series of opponents during the 1920s. Reformist military officers, disaffected state politicians, social bandits, and millenarian peasant movements seeking a return to a golden age, all acted in different ways against the political system and the system of export-import capitalism that seemed to produce increasing inequality while it produced great wealth. Similar criticisms were voiced elsewhere throughout Latin America.

As in western Europe, in Latin America the growing industrial and urban labor forces began to exert some influence on politics in the first decades of the century. Not surprisingly, many of these workers were engaged in the production of exports or in related transportation activities. Immigrants from Spain, Italy, and elsewhere in Europe

sometimes came with well-developed political goals and ideologies from anarchism, which wished to smash the state entirely by using the weapon of the general strike to gain power, to syndicalism, which hoped to use the organization of labor to achieve that goal. Railroad, dock, and mining workers were often among the most radical and the first to organize and were usually met with force. Hundreds of miners in Iquique, Chile, striking against awful conditions in 1907, were shot down by government forces. Between 1914 and 1930 a series of general strikes and labor unrest swept through much of Latin America. Sometimes, as in Argentina in 1919 during the "Tragic Week" government reaction to "revolutionary workers," many of whom were foreign-born, led to brutal repression under the guise of nationalism.

A growing sense of class conflict developed in Latin America as it had in western Europe in this period. Some gains were made, however, as it became increasingly clear that governments now had to consider organized labor as a force that had to be confronted or incorporated. It should be emphasized that, unlike in western Europe, the vast majority of workers in Latin America were still agrarian and for the most part were not organized. Thus, the history of the labor movement tells only a small part of the story.

IDEOLOGY AND SOCIAL REFORM

In the 1920s and 1930s the failures of liberalism were becoming increasingly apparent. A middle class had emerged and had begun to enter politics, but unlike its western European counterpart, it gained power only in conjunction with the traditional oligarchy and/or the military. In Latin America the ideology of liberalism we discussed in Chapter 31 was not an expression of the strength of this class, but rather a series of ideas, "out of place," not particularly suited to the realities of Latin America where large segments of the population were landless, uneducated, and destitute. Increasing industrialization did not dissolve the old class boundaries, nor did public education and other classic liberal programs produce as much social mobility as had been expected.

Disillusioned by liberalism and by the destruction of Europe in the Great War, artists and intellectuals who had looked to Europe for inspiration turned to Latin America's own populations and history for values and solutions to Latin-American problems. Increasingly, during the 1920s intellectuals complained that Latin America was embarked on a race to nowhere. Books such as Paulo Prado's *Portrait of Brazil* (1928) or the Argentine Eziquiel Martínez's

X-Ray of the Pampa (1933) examined the pseudo-European regimes, the corruption, and the seeming failure of these "co-optive democracies" that provided the forms of democratic government but little of the substance to the vast majority of the population. In literature and the arts the ideas of rationality, progress, and order associated with liberalism were under attack.

Ideas of reform and social change were in the air. University students in Cordoba, Argentina, began a reform of their university system that gave the university more autonomy and students more power within it. This movement soon spread to other countries. Movements for social reform gathered strength in Brazil, Chile, and Uruguay. Many of those who criticized the failure of the Liberal regimes claimed that Latin America should seek its own solutions and paths rather than import ideas and models from Europe. There were other responses as well. Socialist and Communist parties were formed or grew in strength in a number of Latin American nations in this period, especially after the Russian Revolution of 1917. The strength of these parties of the left originated in local conditions, but was sometimes aided by the international Communist movement. While criticism of existing governments and of liberalism as a political and economic philosophy came from these left-leaning parties, it also came from traditional elements in society such as the Roman Catholic church, which disliked the secularization a capitalist society represented.

POPULIST POLITICS: THE CASE OF PERU

We can use Peru as an example of this ferment. That Andean nation, with its predominantly Indian population, had followed the general trend of export-oriented development based on nitrates and a few agricultural products. The foreign capital that was invested controlled many crucial transportation facilities and vital industries. The elites profited from economic expansion, but a war with Chile (the War of the Pacific, 1879–1883) led to the loss of territory and nitrate resources. Many peasants were landless and government graft and corruption were rampant. By the 1920s critics had emerged. José Carlos Mariateguí (1895–1930), a young essayist, wrote nationalistic analyses of Peru's ills from a Socialist perspective that glorified the Indian past and denounced political and economic conditions in Peru. His *Seven Essays of Peruvian Reality* (1928) became a classic of social criticism.

Another young Peruvian, Victor Raul Haya de la Torre (1895–1979) created a new party called American Popular Revolutionary Alliance (APRA) in 1924. This party, drawing on the models of the Mexican Revolution, socialism, and nationalism, as well as some aspects of Mussolini's fascism, aimed at being an international party throughout the hemisphere. Its greatest success, however, was in Peru itself where by the 1930s its members had made an impact on politics. Anti-imperialist, nationalistic, and in favor of nationalizing lands and basic industries, APRA's program won wide support. Haya de la Torre depended on his own personal charisma and on middle-class and proletarian support for the success of APRA. This was a mix of personal qualities and programs that could be seen in a number of Latin-American regimes in the period. Electoral battles and a virtual political war between right and left in the 1930s kept APRA from power. Although opposed by the military and other sectors of society, *Apristas* remained a force in Peruvian politics and finally gained the presidency in 1985 with the victory of Alan García, but the origins of the movement were tied to the political disillusionment of the period between the wars.

APRA represented the new populist political parties in Latin America that began to mobilize mass support among workers, small farmers, and urban sectors under the direction of personalist leaders. Populism was usually nationalist and seemingly antiestablishment. It gained broad support from urban masses and rural peasants, but it was often led by politicians from the military or the elites who channeled this support into policies that did not challenge the structure of government. With an emphasis on personal charisma, direct appeals to the masses, and the political mobilization of people previously excluded from politics, Populist leaders, such as Juan Perón in Argentina, became powerful forces in the region.

THE GREAT CRASH AND LATIN-AMERICAN RESPONSES

The economic dependency of Latin America and the internal weaknesses of the Liberal regimes were made abundantly clear by the great world financial crisis of 1929. After the crash, the foreign investments so essential to the continued growth of the Latin-American economies ceased, and purchases of the region's products declined. Unemployment and economic dislocation were general. The Liberal political and economic programs that had brought the changes of the late 19th and early 20th centuries were now literally bankrupt. Within three years, there were violent military coups in 12 countries as new alternatives were sought to the deepening crisis of the area. Among these alternatives were various adaptations of socialism or *corporatism*, a political ideology that emphasized the organic nature of society and made the state a mediator, adjusting the interests of different social groups. This philosophy often appealed to conservative groups in society and to the military because it stressed cooperation and the avoidance of class conflict and because it placed the state at the center of power. Moreover, the fact that corporatism was adopted by Catholic European regimes, such as Italy, Spain, and Portugal, contributed to its popularity in Latin America. Aspects of Italian and later German fascism also appealed to conservatives in Latin America. During the 1930s Fascist groups formed, complete with their own militant rhetoric and uniforms, and sometimes gained considerable political power in Brazil, Mexico, and Chile.

Unrestrained capitalism had created deep social divisions. By the 1930s many Western societies, including Latin America, began to moderate the principles and policies of unbridled laissez-faire capitalism by attempting to provide some kind of social reform in order to provide a broader basis for governments. The New Deal in the United States and the corporatist governments of Italy and Spain were responses to the failures and problems of capitalism. Latin America also participated in this trend.

PROMISES OF SOCIAL REFORM

New regimes or a new concern with social problems characterized much of Latin America in the 1930s. We have already mentioned the reforming administration of President Cárdenas (1934–1940) in Mexico, when land reform and many of the social aspects of the revolution were finally initiated on a large scale. Cárdenas distributed over 40 million acres of land and created communal farms and a credit system to support them. He expropriated foreign oil companies that refused to obey Mexican law and created a state oil monopoly. He expanded rural education programs. These measures made him broadly popular in Mexico and seemed to give the promise of the revolution substance.

Cárdenas was perhaps the most successful example of the new political tide in Latin America. In Cuba, for example, a Nationalist revolution in 1933 aimed at social reform and breaking the tutelage of the United States took power, and although it soon was taken over by moderate elements, important changes and reforms did take place. To some extent such new departures underlined both the growing force of nationalism and the desire to integrate new forces into the political process. Nowhere was this more apparent than in the populist regimes of Brazil and Argentina.

THE VARGAS REGIME IN BRAZIL

In Brazil, a contested political election in 1929 in which the state elites could not agree on the next president, resulted in a short civil war and the emergence of Getúlio Vargas (1872–1954) as the new president. The Brazilian economy, based on coffee exports, was a shambles due to the impact of the 1929 crash on coffee exports. Vargas had promised liberal reforms and elimination of the worst abuses of the old system. Once in power, he launched a new kind of centralized political program, imposing federal administrators over the state governments. He held off attempted coups by the Communists in 1935 and by the green-shirted Fascist "Integralists" in 1937. With the support of the military, Vargas then imposed a new constitution in 1937 that established the *Estado Novo* (New State), based on ideas from Mussolini's Italy. It imposed an authoritarian regime within the context of nationalism and economic reforms, limiting immigration and eliminating parties and groups that resisted national integration or that opposed the government.

For a while Vargas played off Germany and the Western powers in hopes of securing armaments and favorable trade arrangements. Despite Vargas's authoritarian sympathies, he eventually joined the Allies, supplied bases to the United States, and even sent troops to fight against the Axis powers in Italy. In return, Brazil obtained arms, financial support for industrial development, and trade advantages. Meanwhile, Vargas ran a corporatist government allowing some room for labor negotiations, but under strict government supervision. Little open opposition to the government was allowed. The state, moreover, organized many other aspects of the economy. Opposition to Vargas and his repressive policies was building in Brazil by 1945, but by then he was turning increasingly to the left, seeking support from organized labor and coming to terms with the Communist party leaders whom he had imprisoned.

In 1945 Vargas was deposed by a military coup, but he did not disappear from Brazilian political life. After an interim of five years, Vargas returned to the presidency, this time on a program of nationalism and with support from the left and from a new Workers' party (PTB). Under his supporter, João Goulart, the party mobilized the urban labor force. Limitations were put on foreign profit-making in Brazil. As in Mexico and Argentina, a state monopoly of petroleum was established. Vargas's Nationalist and Populist stance had a broad appeal, but his policies were often more conservative than his statements. Under attack and criticism from both the political right and left, Vargas committed suicide in 1954. His suicide note emphasized his Populist ties and blamed his death on Brazil's enemies:

Once more the forces and interests which work against the people have organized themselves again and emerge against me. . . . I was a slave to the people, and today I am freeing myself for eternal life. But this people whose slave I was will no longer be slave to anyone. My sacrifice will remain forever in their souls and my blood will be the price of their ransom. . . .

Much of Brazilian history since Vargas has been a struggle over his mantle of leadership. In death, Vargas became a martyr and a Nationalist hero even to those groups that he had repressed and imprisoned in the 1930s.

ARGENTINA: POPULISM, PERÓN, AND THE MILITARY

Argentina was somewhat of an anomaly. In Argentina, the middle-class Radical party that had held power during the 1920s fell when the economy collapsed in 1929. A military coup backed by a strange coalition of Nationalists, Fascists, and Socialists seized power, hoping to return Argentina to the golden days of the great export boom of the 1890s. The coup failed. Argentina became more dependent, as foreign investments increased and markets for Argentine products declined. Industry, however, was growing, and with it grew the numbers and strength of industrial workers, many of whom had migrated from the countryside. By the 1940s the workers were organized in two major labor federations. Conservative governments backed by the traditional military held power through the 1930s, but in 1943 a military group once again took control of government.

The new military rulers were Nationalists who wished to industrialize and modernize Argentina and make it the dominant power of South America. Some were admirers of the Fascist powers and their programs. While many of them were distrustful of the workers, the man who became the dominant political force in Argentina recognized the need to create a broader basis of support for the government. Colonel Juan D. Perón (1895–1974) emerged as a power in the government. Using his position in the Ministry of Labor, he appealed to workers, raising their salaries, improving their benefits, and generally supporting their demands. Attempts to displace him failed, and he increasingly gained popular support, aided by his wife Eva Duarte, known as Evita. She became a public spokesperson for Perón among the lower classes. During World War II Peron's admiration for the Axis powers was well known. In 1946 Perón successfully manipulated an attempt by the United States to discredit him because of his pro-Fascist sympathies into Nationalist support for his presidential campaign.

Perón forged an alliance of interest among the workers, the industrialists, and the military. Like Vargas, he learned the effectiveness of the radio, the press, and public speeches in mobilizing public support. He depended on his personal charisma and on repression of opponents to main-

The populist politics of Juan Perón and his wife Evita brought new forces, especially urban workers, into Argentine politics. Their personal charisma attracted great support among groups formerly excluded from politics but eventually led to opposition from the Argentine military and Perón's overthrow in 1955.

tain his rule. The Peronist program was couched in nationalistic terms. The government nationalized the foreign-owned railroads and telephone companies as well as petroleum resources. The foreign debt was paid off and for a while the Argentine economy boomed in the immediate postwar years. But by 1949, there were economic problems again. Meanwhile Perón ruled by a combination of inducements and repression while his wife Evita became a symbol to the *descamisados,* or the poor and downtrodden who saw in Peronism a glimmer of hope. Her death in 1952 at age 33 was the cause for national mourning.

Perón's regime was a populist government with a broader base than had ever been attempted before in Argentina. Nevertheless, holding the interests of the various components of the coalition together became increasingly difficult as the economy worsened. A democratic opposition developed and complained of Perón's control of the press and his violation of civil liberties. Industrialists disliked the strength of labor organizations. The military worried that Perón would arm the workers, and so they feared Perón would begin to cut back on the military's gains. The Peronist party became more radical and began a campaign against the Catholic church. In 1955 anti-Perón military officers drove him into exile.

Argentina then lived the next 20 years in the shadow of Perón. The Peronist party was banned, and a succession of military-supported civilian governments tried to resolve the nation's economic problems and continuing political instability. But Peronism could survive even without Perón, and the mass of urban workers and the strongly Peronist unions continued to agitate for his programs, especially as austerity measures began to affect living conditions of the working class. Perón and his new wife Isabel returned to Argentina in 1973, and they won the presidential election in that year (she as vice president). When he died the following year, however, it was clear that Argentina's problems could not be solved by the old formulas. Argentina slid once more into military dictatorship.

RADICAL OPTIONS IN THE 1950S

The Argentine and Brazilian cases begun by Vargas and Perón were symptomatic of the continuing problems of Latin America, but their personalistic authoritarian solutions were only one possible response. By the 1940s frustration had built up considerable pressure for change throughout much of Latin America. Across the political spectrum there was a desire to improve the social and economic conditions throughout the region and a general agreement that "development" and economic strength were the keys to a better future. How to achieve those goals, however, remained in question. In Mexico, one-party rule continued, and the "Revolution" became increasingly conservative and interested in economic growth rather than social justice. In a few countries, such as Venezuela and Costa Rica, reform-minded democratic parties were able to win elections in an open political system. In other places such a solution was less likely or less attractive to

those who wished to bring about reform. Unlike the Mexican revolutionaries of 1910 through 1920, those seeking change in the post-World War II period could turn to the well-developed political philosophy of Marxian socialism as a guide. Such models, however, were fraught with dangers because of the context of the cold war and the ideological struggle between Western Europe and the Soviet bloc.

Throughout Latin America, the failures of political democratization, economic development, and social reforms led to the consideration of radical and revolutionary solutions to national problems. During the 1950s, three major attempts at radical change were made in Latin America with very different results.

GUATEMALA: REFORM AND UNITED STATES INTERVENTION

The first place where more radical solutions were tried was Guatemala. This predominantly Indian nation suffered from some of the worst features of the region's problems. Its population was mostly illiterate and suffered poor health conditions and high rates of mortality. Land and wealth were very unequally distributed, and the whole economy depended on the highly volatile prices for its main exports of coffee and bananas. In 1944 a coalition of middle class and labor elected a reformer, Juan José Arevalo as president. With a new constitution he began a series of programs within the context of "spiritual socialism" that included land reform and an improvement in the rights and conditions of rural and industrial workers. An income tax, the first in the nation's history, was projected and educational reforms were planned. These programs and his sponsorship of an intense nationalism brought the Arevalo government into direct conflict with foreign interests operating in Guatemala, especially the United Fruit Company, the largest and most important foreign concern there. That company had operated in Guatemala from the turn of the century and had acquired extensive properties. It also controlled transportation and shipping facilities. Its workers were often better paid than the average, and their health and other benefits were more extensive, but because it was a foreign company with such a powerful role in Guatemala, United Fruit was the target of nationalistic anger.

In 1951, after a free election, the presidency passed to Colonel Jacobo Arbenz, whose Nationalist program was more radical and whose public statements against foreign economic interests and the landholding oligarchy were more extreme than under Arevalo. Arbenz announced a number of programs to improve or to nationalize the transportation network, the hydroelectric system, and other areas of the economy. A move to expropriate unused lands on large estates in 1953 provoked opposition from the landed oligarchy and from United Fruit, which was eventually threatened with the loss of almost half a million acres of "reserve" land. The United States government, fearing "Communist" penetration of the Arbenz government and under considerable pressure from United Fruit Company, denounced the changes and began to impose economic and diplomatic restrictions on Guatemala. At the same time, the level of Nationalist rhetoric intensified and the government increasingly received the support of the political left in Latin America and in the Socialist bloc.

In 1954, with the help of the Central Intelligence Agency, a dissident military force was organized and invaded Guatemala. The Arbenz government fell, and the pro-American regime that replaced it then turned back the land reform and negotiated a settlement favorable for United Fruit. The reform experiment was thus brought to a halt. In retrospect, by the standards of the 1960s, the programs of Arevalo and Arbenz seemed rather mild, although undoubtedly Arbenz's statements and his acceptance of arms from eastern Europe had contributed to the United States' intervention. The reforms promised by the United States-supported governments were minimal. Guatemala continued to be characterized by a low standard of living, especially for its Indian population. The series of military governments following the coup failed to address the nation's social and economic problems. That failure led to continual violence and political instability. A coalition of coffee planters, foreign companies, and the military controlled political life. A guerrilla movement grew and provoked brutal military repression, which once again fell particularly hard on the rural Indian population. Guate-

U.S. fears of Soviet influence in Guatemala and sweeping land reforms that threatened U.S. interests led to the coup of 1954. Members of the U.S.-supported "Liberation Army" train their guns on an effigy of the overthrown leftist president, Arbenz. The sign on the effigy reads, "I am going back to Russia with Arevalo."

mala's attempt at radical change, an attempt that began with an eye toward improving the conditions of the people, failed because of external intervention.

THE BOLIVIAN REVOLUTION: A LOSS OF DIRECTION

Another predominantly Indian nation, Bolivia, was the scene of a similar movement for revolutionary change, but its outcome differed. Long characterized by political instability, and with an economy considerably weakened after the loss of territory and access to the sea in the War of the Pacific against neighboring Chile (1879–1883), Bolivia experienced a period of expansion in the 1920s as demands for its major products, silver and tin, increased. Foreign companies, such as Standard Oil of New Jersey, secured concessions to exploit its major resources, and the government took large loans from United States banks to finance various projects. With the world financial crisis of 1929 and a drop in the price of tin, the Bolivian economy was thrown into crisis. To make matters worse, a war broke out with neighboring Paraguay over the disputed region of the Chaco, which blocked Bolivia's access to the rivers leading to the Atlantic and which was thought to contain rich petroleum deposits. The Chaco War (1932–1935) led to high casualties on both sides and more political instability in Bolivia, as defeat by Paraguay led to disillusionment.

Through the 1920s and 1930s, despite rhetoric to the contrary, little was done to lessen the great social gap between the mass of the Indian population and the urban elites or to improve the conditions of the miners, the backbone of the nation's work force. As late as 1950 over 90 percent of the land was owned by six percent of the population, and Indians were often treated like serfs. Conditions in the mines were abysmal, and to a large extent three foreign-owned or controlled mining companies regulated that sector of the economy. Little could be done to change this situation. Because of literacy requirements and gender exclusion for voting, less than seven percent of the population was entitled to cast a ballot.

After an army coup to forestall the electoral victory of a Reformist and Nationalist political coalition called the National Revolutionary Movement (MNR), a revolt erupted in 1952. Although initially an urban political movement, it soon became a real revolution as Indian peasants and mining workers joined in, taking up arms and seizing lands and mines. This was a violent social movement in which armed workers and peasants joined with students and radical middle class interests against the army, the mine owners, and the landed elite. Winning the government, the

MNR initiated a series of reforms including universal suffrage, nationalization of the mines, land expropriation and redistribution, and the movement of population from the Andes to unused lands in the nation's eastern lowlands. The mines, long-controlled by three great companies, were nationalized, and the government raised wages and benefits. Land redistribution was extensive. With militant and armed worker and peasant organizations, the government cut back on support for the military, whose power was greatly reduced for a while. The United States, faced with these revolutionary changes, acted cautiously, but since the level of Socialist rhetoric was relatively muted and there seemed to be no direct "external" involvement, the United States recognized the revolutionary government and offered financial assistance, sometimes in large amounts.

The momentum of revolutionary change could not be maintained, however. The mining and agricultural sectors were disrupted by the changes and by poor world prices in the 1960s for tin and other Bolivian minerals. Fearing the radical unions, the government allowed the military to regain some of its power, and then the MNR began to maneuver to ensure its continuance in power. By 1964 the military stepped in again. Since then a series of military governments has ruled for most of the time. While a few of the governments have promised reforms and continuation of the principles of the 1952 revolution, most have been more interested in the maintenance of order. By the 1980s little was left of the revolutionary program, and, more sinisterly, new cartels of cocaine producers linked to the government and the military emerged. The Bolivian Revolution did not fail because of outside intervention as much as it did from the mistakes of its leadership, the weight of the nation's past, and its problems that continued to the present day.

THE CUBAN REVOLUTION: SOCIALISM IN THE CARIBBEAN

The differences between Cuba and Bolivia or Guatemala underline the diversity of Latin America. The island nation had a population of about six million, most of whom were the descendants of Spaniards and the African slaves who had been imported to produce the sugar, tobacco, and hides that were the colony's mainstays. Cuba had a relatively large middle class, and levels of literacy and health care were better than in most of the rest of the region. Rural areas lagged behind in these matters, however, and there the working and living conditions were poor, especially for the workers on the large sugar estates. Always in the shadow of the United States, Cuban politics and economy were rarely free of American interests. By the 1950s about three-fourths of what Cuba imported came from the United States; American investments in the island were heavy during the 1940s and 1950s. While the island experienced periods of prosperity, fluctuations in the world market for Cuba's main product, sugar, revealed the tenuous basis of the economy. Moreover, the disparity between the countryside and the growing middle class in Havana underlined the nation's continuing problems.

From 1934 to 1944 Cuba had been ruled by Fulgencio Batista, a strong-willed, authoritarian reformer who had risen from the lower ranks of the army. Among his reforms were a democratic constitution of 1940 that promised major changes, nationalization of natural resources, full employment, and land reform. Batista's programs of reform, however, began to founder on the shoals of graft and corruption, and when in 1952 he returned to the presidency, there was little left of the reformer but a great deal of the dictator. Opposition developed in various sectors of society. Among the regime's opponents was Fidel Castro, a young lawyer, experienced in leftist university politics and an ardent critic of the Batista government and the ills of Cuban society. On July 26, 1953, Castro and a few followers launched an unsuccessful attack on some military barracks. Captured, Castro faced a trial, an occasion he used to expound his revolutionary ideals, which were mostly aimed at a return to democracy, social justice, and the establishment of a less-dependent economy.

Released from prison, Castro fled to exile in Mexico where, with the aid of Ernesto "Che" Guevara, a militant Argentine revolutionary, a small military force was gathered. They landed in Cuba in 1956 and slowly began to gather strength in the mountains. By 1958 the "26th of July Movement" had found support from students, some labor organizations, and rural workers and was able to conduct operations against Batista's army. The bearded rebels, or *barbudos*, won a series of victories. The dictator, under siege and isolated by the United States (which refused to support him any longer), was driven from power, and the rebels took Havana amid wild scenes of genuine joy and relief.

What happened next is highly debatable, and Castro himself has offered alternate interpretations at different times. Whether Castro was already a Marxist-Leninist and had always intended to introduce a Socialist regime (as he now claims), or whether the development of this program was the result of a series of pragmatic decisions is in question. Rather than simply returning to the Constitution of 1940 and enacting moderate reforms, Castro launched a program of sweeping change that altered the nature of Cuba. Foreign properties were expropriated, farms were

Fidel Castro and his guerrilla army finally brought the downfall of the Batista government in January 1959, to the wild acclaim of many Cubans. Castro began to initiate sweeping reforms in Cuba that eventually led to the creation of a socialist regime and the hostility of the U.S.

collectivized, and a centralized Socialist economy was put in place. Most of these changes were accompanied by a Nationalist and anti-imperialist foreign policy. Relations with the United States were broken off in 1961, and Cuba increasingly depended on the financial support and arms of the Soviet Union to maintain its revolution. With that support in place, Castro was able to survive the increasingly hostile reaction of the United States. That reaction included a disastrous United States sponsored invasion by Cuban exiles in 1961 and an embargo on trade with Cuba. Dependence on the Soviet Union led to a crisis in 1962, when Soviet nuclear missiles were discovered in Cuba and a confrontation between the superpowers ensued. Despite these problems, to a large extent the Cuban Revolution survived because the politics of the cold war provided Cuba with a protector and a benefactor.

The results of the revolution have been mixed. The social programs were extensive. Education, health, and housing have greatly improved and rank Cuba among the world's leaders—quite unlike most other nations of the region. This is especially true in the long-neglected rural areas. A wide variety of social and educational programs has mobilized all sectors of the population. To some extent the achievements have been accompanied by severe restrictions of basic freedoms.

Attempts to diversify and strengthen the economy have been less successful. An effort to industrialize in the 1960s failed, and Cuba turned again to its ability to produce sugar. The world's falling sugar and rising petroleum prices led to a disastrous situation. Only a subsidy for Cuban sugar and the supply of petroleum below the world price has enabled the Soviet Union to maintain the Cuban economy, which has become increasingly dependent on the Soviet Union and the nations of Eastern Europe. Despite these problems, the Cuban Revolution has offered an example that has proven attractive to those seeking the transformation of Latin-American societies. Early direct attempts to spread the model of the Cuban Revolution, such as Che Guevara's guerrilla operation in Bolivia where he lost his life in 1967, were failures, but the Cuban model and the island's ability to resist the pressure of a hostile United States has proven attractive to other nations in the Caribbean and Central America, such as Grenada and Nicaragua that have also sought the revolutionary option.

DOCUMENT
THE PEOPLE SPEAK

Scholarly analysis of general trends often cannot convey the way in which historical events and patterns affect the lives of people, or the fact that history is made up of the collective experience of individuals. It is often very difficult to know about the lives of common people in the past or to learn about their perceptions of their lives. In recent years in Latin America, however, a growing literature of autobiographies, interpreted autobiographies (when another writer puts the story down and edits it), and collections of interviews have provided a vision of the lives of common people. These statements, like any historical document must always be used carefully because their authors or editors sometimes have political purposes, because they reflect individual opinions, or because the events they report may be atypical. Nevertheless, these personal statements do put flesh and blood on the bones of history and provide an important perspective from those whose voice in history is often lost.

A BOLIVIAN WOMAN DESCRIBES HER LIFE

Domitilia Barrios de Chungara was a miner's wife who became politically active in the mine workers' political movement. Her presence at the United Nations-sponsored International Woman's Year Tribunal in 1975 moved a Brazilian journalist to organize her statements into a book about her life. This excerpt provides a picture of the everyday struggle for life.

My day begins at four in the morning, especially when my compañero is on the first shift. I prepare his breakfast. Then I have to prepare *salteñas* [small meat pastries] because I make about one hundred *salteñas* every day and I sell them on the street. I do this in order to make up for what my husband's wage doesn't cover in terms of our necessities. The night before, we prepare the dough and at four in the morning I make the *salteñas* while I feed the kids. The kids help me.

Then the ones that go to school in the morning have to get ready, while I wash the clothes left soaking over night.

At eight I go out to sell. The kids that go to school in the afternoon help me. We have to go to the company store and bring home the staples. And in the store there are immensely long lines and you have to wait there until eleven in order to stock up. You have to line up for meat, for vegetables, for oil. So it's just one line after another. Since everything is in a different place, that's how it has to be.

From what we earn between my husband and me, we can eat and dress. Food is very expensive: 28 pesos for a kilo of meat, 4 pesos for carrots, 6 pesos for onions. . . . Considering that my compañero earns 28 pesos a day, that's hardly enough is it?

We don't ever buy ready made clothes. We buy wool and knit. At the beginning of each year, I also spend about 2,000 pesos on cloth and a pair of shoes for each of us. And the company discounts some of that each month from my husband's wage. On the pay slips that's referred to as the "bundle." And what happens is that before we finish paying the "bundle" our shoes are worn out. That's how it is.

Well, from eight to eleven in the morning I sell

salteñas. I do the shopping in the grocery store, and I also work at the Housewives Committee, talking with the sisters who go there for advice.

At noon, lunch has to be ready because the rest of the kids have to go to school.

In the afternoon I have to wash clothes. There are no laundries. We use troughs and have to get the water from a pump.

I've got to correct the kids' homework and prepare everything I'll need to make the next day's *salteñas*.

FROM PEASANT TO REVOLUTIONARY

Rigoberta Menchú, a Quiché Indian from the Guatemalan highlands, came from a peasant family that had been drawn into politics during the repression of Indian communities and human rights in the 1970s. In these excerpts she reveals her disillusionment with the government and her realization of the ethnic division between Indians and *ladinos*, or mestizos, that complicates political action in Guatemala.

The CUC [Peasant Union] started growing; it spread like wildfire among the peasants in Guatemala. We began to understand that the root of all our problems was exploitation. That there were rich and poor and that the rich exploited the poor — our sweat, our labor. That's how the rich got richer and richer. The fact that we were always waiting in offices, always bowing to the authorities was part of the discrimination that we Indians suffered.

The situation got worse when the murderous generals came to power although I did not actually know who was the president at the time. I began to know them from 1974 when General Kjell Langerud came to power. He came to our region and said: "We're going to solve the land problem. The land belongs to you. You cultivate the land and I will share it out among you." We trusted him. I was at the meeting when [he] spoke. And what did he give us? My father tortured and imprisoned.

Later I had the opportunity of meeting other Indians. Achi Indians, the group that lives closest to us. And I got to know some Mam Indians too. They all told me: "The rich are bad. But not all *ladinos* are bad." And I started wondering: "Could it be that not all *ladinos* are bad? . . ." There were poor *ladinos* as well as rich *ladinos*, and they were exploited as well. That's when I began recognizing exploitation. I kept on going to the *finca* [large farm] but now I really wanted to find out, to prove if that was true and learn the details. There were poor *ladinos* on the *finca*. They worked the same, and their children's bellies were swollen like my little brother's. . . . I was just beginning to speak a little Spanish in those days and I began to talk to them. I said to one poor *ladino*: "You are a poor *ladino*, aren't you?" And he nearly hit me. He said: "What do you know about it, Indian?" I wondered: "Why is that when I say poor *ladinos* are like us, I'm spurned?" I didn't know then that the same system which tries to isolate us Indians also puts barriers between Indians and *ladinos*. . . . Soon afterwards, I was with the nuns and we went to a village in Uspantán where mostly *ladinos* live. The nun asked a little boy if they were poor and he said: "Yes, we're poor but we're not Indians." That stayed with me. The nun didn't notice, she went on talking. She was foreign, she wasn't Guatemalan. She asked someone else the same question and he said: "Yes, we're poor but we're not Indians." It was very painful for me to accept that an Indian was inferior to a *ladino*. I kept on worrying about it. It's a big barrier they've sown between us, between Indian and *ladino*. I didn't understand it.

Questions: What was distinctive about lower-class life and outlook in late 20th-century Latin America? How had life of the lower class changed from the 19th century?

 ### THE SEARCH FOR REFORM AND THE MILITARY OPTION

The revolutionary attempts of the 1950s, the durability of the Cuban Revolution, and the general appeal of Marxist doctrines in the Third World underlined Latin America's proclivity for revolutionary change, so long as real reforms in its economic and social structures remained unchanged. How could the traditional patterns of inequality and international dependency be overcome? What was the best path to the future?

For some, the answer was political stability, imposed if necessary, in order to assure conditions for capitalist economic growth. The one-party system of Mexico demonstrated its capacity for repression when student dissidents were brutally killed during disturbances in 1968. Mexico enjoyed some prosperity from its petroleum resources in the 1970s, but poor financial planning, corruption, and foreign debt had again caused problems by the 1980s, and the PRI seemed to be loosing its ability to maintain control of Mexican politics.

For others the Church, long a power in Latin America, provided a guide. Christian Democratic parties formed in Chile and Venezuela in the 1950s, hoping to bring reforms through popularly based mass parties that would preempt the radical left. The Church, in fact, was often divided politically, but the clergy took an increasingly "engaged" position, arguing for social justice and human rights, often in support of government opponents. A few, such as Father Camilo Torres in Colombia, actually joined armed revolutionary groups in the 1960s.

More common was the emergence within the Church hierarchy of an increased concern for social justice. By the 1970s a "Liberation theology" combined Catholic theology and Socialist principles in an effort to bring about improved conditions for the poor. When criticized for promoting communism in his native Brazil, Dom Helder da Camara, archbishop of Pernambuco, remarked: "The trouble with Brazil is not an excess of Communist doctrine, but a lack of Christian justice." The position of the Church in Latin-American societies was changing, but there was no single program for this new stance nor even agreement among the clergy about its validity. Still, this activist position provoked attacks against clergymen such as the courageous Archbishop Oscar Romero of El Salvador who was assassinated in 1980. The Church also played an important role in the fall of the Paraguayan dictatorship in 1988.

OUT OF THE BARRACKS: SOLDIERS TAKE POWER

The success of the Cuban Revolution also impressed and worried those who feared revolutionary change within a Communist political system. The military forces in Latin America had been involved in politics since the days of the caudillos in the 19th century, and in a number of nations military interventions had been relatively common. As the Latin-American military became more professionalized, however, a new philosophy underlay the military's involvement in politics. The soldiers began to see themselves as above the selfish interests of political parties and as the "true" representatives of the nation. With considerable technical training and organizational skills, military officers by the 1920s and 1930s believed that they were best equipped to solve their nations' problems, even if that meant sacrificing the democratic processes and imposing martial law.

In the 1960s the Latin-American military establishments, made nervous by the Cuban success and the swing to leftist or Populist regimes, began to intervene directly in the political process, not simply to clean out a disliked president or party, as they had done in the past, but to take over government itself. In 1964 the Brazilian military (with the compliance of the United States and supported by the middle class) overthrew the elected president after he threatened a number of sweeping social reforms. In Argentina, growing polarization between the Peronists and the middle class led to a military intervention in 1966. In Chile, the Socialist government of President Salvador Allende was overthrown in 1973 by the Chilean military, which until then had remained for the most part out of politics. Allende had nationalized industries and banks and had sponsored peasant and worker expropriations of lands and factories. His government was caught in an increasing polarization between groups trying to halt these changes and those pushing for faster and more radical reforms. By 1973 the economy was in serious difficulty, undermined by resistence in Chile and by United States policies designed to isolate the country. Allende was killed during the military coup against him, and throughout Latin America there were demonstrations against the military and United States involvement. But Chile was not alone. Similar coups took place in Uruguay in 1973 and in Peru in 1968.

The soldiers in power imposed a new type of "bureaucratic authoritarian regime." Their governments were supposed to stand above competing demands of various sectors and establish economic stability. Now, as arbiters of politics, the soldiers would place the national interest above "selfish interests" by imposing dictatorships. Government was essentially a presidency controlled by the military in which policies were formulated and applied by a bureaucracy organized like a military chain of command. Political repression and torture were used to silence critics, and stringent measures were imposed in order to control inflation and strengthen the economies. While laws limited political freedoms, repression often was brutal and illegal. In Argentina, violent opposition to military rule led to a counteroffensive and a "dirty war" in which thousands of people were "disappeared" [kidnapped] and brutally tortured or killed by government security forces.

Government economic policies fell heaviest on labor and the working class. The goal of the military in Brazil and Argentina was "development" and to some extent, in Brazil at least, considerable economic improvements took place, although income distribution became even more unequal than it had been. Inflation was reduced, industrialization increased, and gains were made in literacy and health, but basic structural problems such as landownership and social conditions for the poorest members of society remained unchanged.

There were variations within these military regimes. All were nationalistic. The Peruvian military tried to create a mass base for its programs and sought to mobilize popular support among the peasantry. It had a real social program, including extensive land reform, and was not simply a surrogate for the conservatives in Peruvian society. In Chile and Uruguay, the military was fiercely anti-Communist. In Argentina, nationalism and a desire to gain popular support in the face of a worsening economy led to a confrontation with Great Britain over the Falkland Islands (Islas Malvinas), which both nations claimed. A short war in 1982 resulted in an Argentine defeat and a loss in the military's credibility that contributed to its loss of authority.

THE NEW DEMOCRATIC TREND

In Argentina and elsewhere in South America, by the mid-1980s, the military had begun to return government to civilian politicians. Continuing economic problems and the pressures of containing opponents wore heavily on the military leaders, who began to realize that their solutions were no more destined to success than those of civilian governments. Moreover, the Populist parties, such as the Peronists and Apristas, seemed less of a threat, and the fear of Cuban-style communism had diminished. In Argentina, elections were held in 1983. Brazil began a process to restore democratic government after 1985 and in 1989 chose its first popularly elected president since the military takeover. The South American military bureaucrats and modernizers were returning to their barracks.

The process of redemocratization was not easy, nor was it universal. In Peru, "Sendero Luminoso (Shining Path)," a long-sustained leftist guerrilla movement controlled areas of the countryside and tried to disrupt national elections in 1990. In Central America, the military cast a long shadow over the government in El Salvador. After the elections of 1990, which removed the Sandinistas from control in Nicaragua, an uneasy truce continued between them and the centralist government of Violeta Chamorro, the newly elected president. The United States demonstrated its continuing power in the region in its invasion of Panama and the arrest of its strongman leader Manuel Noriega.

Latin-American governments in the 1980s faced tremendous problems. Large foreign loans taken in the 1970s for the purposes of development, sometimes for unnecessary projects, had created a tremendous level of debt that threatened the economic stability of countries such as Brazil, Peru, and Mexico. High rates of inflation provoked social instability as real wages fell. Pressure from the international banking community to curb inflation by cutting government spending and reducing wages often ignored the social and political consequences of such actions. Programs to control inflation, such as that introduced by Brazilian president Fernando Collor de Mello, were shock treatments that often disrupted the economy as a whole.

By the late 1980s an international commerce in drugs, which produced tremendous profits, stimulated criminal activity and created powerful international cartels that could even threaten national sovereignty as they did in Colombia. In countries as diverse as Cuba, Panama, and Bolivia the narcotics trade penetrated the highest government circles.

THE UNITED STATES AND LATIN AMERICA

As a backdrop to the political and economic story we have traced thus far stands the continuing presence of the United States. After World War I, the United States had emerged as the predominant power in the hemisphere, a position it had already begun to assume at the close of the 19th century with the Cuban-Spanish-American War and the building of the Panama Canal. European nations were displaced as the leading investors in Latin America by the United States. In South America, private investments by American companies and entrepreneurs, as well as loans from the American government, were the chief means of United States influence. United States investments rose to over five billion dollars by 1929, or over one-third of all United States investments abroad.

In Cuba and Puerto Rico, of course, there was direct United States involvement and almost a protectorate status. But in the Caribbean and Central America, the face of United States power, economic interest, and disregard for the sovereignty of weaker neighbors was most apparent. Military interventions to protect United States-owned properties and investments became common. There were over 30 prior to 1933. Haiti, Nicaragua, the Dominican Republic, Mexico, and Cuba all witnessed one or more direct interventions by United States troops. Central America was a peculiar case because the level of United States private investments of companies such as United Fruit was very high and the economies of these countries were so closely tied to the United States. Those who resisted the United States' presence were treated as "bandits" by expeditionary forces. In Nicaragua Augusto Sandino led a resistance movement against occupying troops until his assassination by the United States-trained Nicaraguan National Guard in 1934. His struggle against American intervention made him a hero and the figurehead of the Sandinista party, which carried out a Socialist revolution in Nicaragua in the 1980s.

Intervention in Central America and the Caribbean, 1898–1981

The grounds for these interventions were economic, political, strategic, and ideological. The direct interventions were usually followed by the creation or support of conservative governments, often dictatorships that would be "friendly" to the United States. These became "Banana Republics," a reference not only to their dependence on the export of tropical products, but also to their often subservient and corrupt governments.

Foreign interventions contributed to a growing Nationalist reaction. Central America with its continuing political problems became a symbol of Latin America's weakness in the face of foreign, especially United States, influence and interference. The Nobel Prize-winning Chilean Communist poet Pablo Neruda, in his poem "The United Fruit Co."

(1950), spoke of the dictators of Central America as "circus flies, wise flies, learned in tyranny" who buzzed over the graves of the people. He wrote the following eight lines with passion:

When the trumpet sounded, all was prepared in the
   land,
and Jehovah divided the world between Coca Cola Inc.,
Anaconda, Ford Motors, and other companies:
United Fruit Co. reserved for itself the juiciest part,
the central coast of my land,
the sweet waist of America
and baptized again its lands
as Banana Republics. . . .

The actions of the United States changed considerably after 1933, when President Roosevelt introduced the Good Neighbor Policy that promised to deal more fairly with Latin America and to stop direct interventions. After World War II, however, the United States' preoccupation with containment of the Soviet Union and communism as an ideology led to new strategies in Latin America. These included participation in regional organizations, the support of governments that at least expressed democratic or anti-Communist principles, the covert undermining of governments considered unfriendly to United States interests, and, when necessary, direct intervention. Underlying much of this policy was also a firm belief that economic development would eliminate the conditions that contributed to radical political solutions. Thus, United States programs such as the Alliance for Progress, begun in 1961, aimed at the development of the region as an alternative to those solutions. The alliance had only limited success despite good intentions and over ten billion dollars of aid. Because of its record, Latin Americans and North Americans both began to question the assumption that "development" was basically a problem of capital and resources, and that appropriate strategies would lead to social and economic improvement, which in turn would forestall revolution.

During the 1970s and 1980s, United States policy was often "pragmatic," accepting Latin America "as it was," which meant dealing on friendly terms with the military dictatorships. President Jimmy Carter (1976-1980) made a new initiative to deal with Latin America and to influence governments there to observe civil liberties. Most significantly, a treaty was signed with Panama ceding to that nation eventual control of the Panama Canal.

Increasing violence in Central America in the 1980s and the more conservative presidencies of Ronald Reagan and George Bush have led the United States back to policies based on strategic, economic, and defense considerations in which direct intervention or support of counterrevolutionary forces have played a part. Thus in 1989 and 1990 the United States toppled a government in Panama—authoritarian but defiant of United States policies, including control of drug smuggling—replacing it with a cooperative regime backed by American troops.

ANALYSIS
HUMAN RIGHTS IN THE 20TH CENTURY

In Latin America the question of "human rights" became a burning issue in the decade of the 1960s and continued thereafter. The use of torture by repressive governments, the mobilization of death squads and other vigilante groups with government acquiescence, and the employment of terrorism against political opponents by the state and by groups opposed to the state became all too common in the region. Latin America's record on violation of human rights was no worse than that of some other areas of the world. However, the demonstrations by the Argentine "Mothers of the Plaza del Mayo" to focus attention on their disappeared children; the publication of prison memoirs recounting human rights violations in Brazil, Cuba, and Argentina; and films dramatizing events such as the assassination of Archbishop Oscar Romero in El Salvador have all focused attention on the problem in Latin America. Moreover, because Latin America shares in the cultural heritage of Western societies it is difficult to make an argument that human rights there have a different meaning or importance than in Europe or North America.

The concept of "human rights," that is, certain universal rights enjoyed by all people because these are justified by a moral standard that stands above the laws of any individual nation, may go back to ancient Greece. The concept of "natural law" and the protection of religious or ethnic minorities also moved nations in the 19th century toward a defense of human rights. To some extent the international movement to abolish the slave trade was an early human rights movement. In modern times, however, the concept of human rights has been strongly attached to the foundation of the United Nations. In 1948, that body, with the experience of World War II in mind, issued a Universal Declaration of Human Rights and created a commission to oversee the human rights situation. The Universal Declaration, which guaranteed basic liberties and freedoms regardless of color, sex, or religion, proclaimed that it should be the "common standard for all peoples and nations." One critic has stated, however, that of the 160 nations in the United Nations, only about 30 have a consistently good record on the matter of human rights.

A major problem for the international community has been enforcement. The United Nations commission did not have any specific powers of enforcement, and much debate subsequently has taken place on the power of the United Nations to intervene in the internal affairs of any nation. More recently, various regional organizations have tried to establish the norms that should govern human rights and to create institutions to enforce these norms. The European community established a body to deal with human rights in the 1950s. Since 1969, under the auspices of the Organization of American States, the American Convention on Human Rights has been active in the Americas. More recently, in the 1980s, the Organization of African Unity has created a similar body. In addition there are private groups such as Amnesty International, which seeks to investigate and reveal abuses. Throughout much of the world there is a growing feeling that the issue of human rights transcends national boundaries.

One specialist has claimed that "human rights is the world's first universal ideology." The defense of human rights would seem to be a cause that most people and governments would be able to accept without hesitation, but the question is, in fact, a complex one. While the rights to life, liberty, security, and to be free from torture or degrading punishment are generally accepted in principle by all nations, other "rights" remain open to question. What is a "right," and to what extent are definitions of "rights" determined by culture?

The question of universality versus relativism quickly emerged in the debate over human rights. What seemed to be obvious human rights in Western societies were less obvious in other parts of the world where other priorities were held. Laws prohibiting child labor, for example, were enforced by most Western societies, but throughout the world perhaps 150 million children worked, often in unhealthy and exploitative conditions. They worked often because of economic necessity but in some societies they also worked because such labor was considered moral and proper. Such cultural differences have led to a position of relativism, which recognizes that there are profound cultural variations in what is considered moral and just. Critics of the original Universal Declaration, for example, have contended that its advocacy of the right to own property and the right to vote imposed Western political and economic values as universals, which in fact they were not. Cultural relativism had the advantage of recognizing the variety of cultures and standards in the world, but it has at times also been used as a shield to deflect criticism and to continue to violate human rights.

The definition of human rights is also political. The West has placed considerable emphasis on civil and political rights of the individual. The Socialist nations have placed social and economic justice above individual rights, although by the 1990s movements in Eastern Europe and China indicated that there was considerable pressure to modify this approach. In the Third World an argument for "peoples' rights" has emerged in which the "right to development," which calls for a major structural redistribution of the world's resources and economic opportunities, is a central concept. As Leopold Senghor of Senegal put it: "Human rights begin with breakfast"; or as a report on Ghana stated: "'One man, one vote,' is meaningless unless accompanied by the principle of 'one man, one bread.'" Needless to say, while the "right to development" is seen as a human right in the Third World, it is viewed instead as a political and economic demand in wealthier nations of the West.

Another dimension of human rights is the extent to which it influences national foreign policies. Governments may make statements pledging respect for human rights in their foreign policy, but often considerations of national defense, sovereignty, or goals, such as the maintenance of peace, may move human rights concerns into a secondary position. Sometimes disputes over the role of human rights in foreign policy have been posed as a conflict between "moralistic utopians" who see the world as it should be and "pragmatists" who see the world as it is. Neither approach necessarily denies the importance of human rights, but there are differences in priority and strategy. Pragmatists might argue that it is better to maintain relations with a nation violating human rights in order to be able to exercise some influence over it in the future, or that other policy considerations must be weighed along with those of human rights in establishing foreign policy. Moralists would hope to bring pressure by isolating and condemning a nation that violates international standards.

These different approaches have been reflected in United States policy shifts toward Latin America. In the 1950s human rights considerations were secondary to opposing the spread of communism in the hemisphere, and the United States was willing to support governments that violated human rights so long as they were staunch anti-Communist allies. During the 1960s this policy continued, but increasing and systematic abuses by military regimes in Brazil, Uruguay, Chile, Nicaragua, and elsewhere in Latin America began to elicit some changes. In 1977 President Carter initiated a new policy in which human rights considerations would be given high priority in United States foreign policy. The United States' refusal to support or aid governments that violated human rights contributed to the weakening of some regimes and stimulated resistance to human rights violations in Latin America, but by the 1980s a more pragmatic approach had returned to United States policy. Criticism of human rights violations was sometimes made selectively, dismissing abuses in "friendly" governments. The extent to which human rights concerns must be balanced against issues such as security, the maintenance of peace, and nonintervention continues to preoccupy policymakers.

During the 1990s attention to human rights will play an increasingly important role in international affairs. Problems of definition still remain and there is no universal agreement on the exact nature of human rights. Controversy on the relative weight of political and civil rights and social, cultural, and economic ones continues to divide richer and poorer nations. Still, the United Nations Declaration of Human Rights, to which 160 nations are signatories, provides a basic guideline and an outline for the future.

Questions: Why might various regimes oppose human rights, and on what basis? Is the human rights movement a Western replacement for imperialism as a means of international political influence? Have international human rights movements produced political change?   ☯

SOCIETIES IN SEARCH OF CHANGE

Despite the structural, political, and international conditions that have frustrated Latin-American attempts at profound reform there have been considerable changes during the 20th century. Problems of ethnicity, gender, and class continue to influence many of these societies. The movement of populations and their settlement has also been a major feature of the century. These two aspects of social life represent just two of the continuing historical processes of Latin America.

Social and gender relations have changed during the century. We have already seen how countries such as Mexico, Peru, and Bolivia sought to enfranchise their Indian populations during this century in different ways and with differing degrees of success. National ideologies and actual practice are often not the same, and discrimination on the basis of ethnicity continues in many places. To be called "Indian" is still an insult in many places in Latin America. While ethnic and cultural mixture characterizes many Latin-American populations and makes Indian and African elements important features of national identity, relations with Indian populations often continue to be marked by exploitation and discrimination in nations as diverse as Brazil, Nicaragua, and Guatemala.

WOMEN'S ROLES

The role of women has changed considerably but relatively slowly. In the years following World War I, women in Latin America continued to live under disabilities in the work place and in politics. Women were denied the right to vote anywhere in Latin America until Ecuador enfranchised women in 1929 and Brazil and Cuba did the same in 1932, but throughout most of the region those examples were not followed until the decades of the 1940s and 1950s. In some nations, the traditional associations of women with religion and the Catholic church in Hispanic life made reformers and revolutionaries fear that women would become a conservative force in national politics. This attitude, combined with traditional male attitudes that women should be concerned only with home and family, led to a continued exclusion of women from political life.

In response, women formed various associations and clubs and began to push for the vote and other issues of particular interest to them.

Feminist organizations, suffrage movements, and international pressures eventually combined to bring about change. In Argentina 15 bills for female suffrage were introduced into the senate before the vote was won in 1945. Sometimes the victory was a matter of political expediency for those in power. In a number of places such as the Dominican Republic, enfranchisement of women was a strategy used by conservative groups to add more conservative voters to the electorate in an effort to hold off political change. In Argentina recently enfranchised women became a major pillar of the Peronist regime, although that regime was not averse to suppressing female political opponents such as Victoria Ocampo, editor of the important literary magazine, *Sur*.

Women eventually discovered that the ability to vote did not by itself guarantee political rights or the ability to have their specific issues heard. After achieving the vote, women tended to join the national political parties, where traditional prejudices against women in public life limited their ability to influence political programs. In Argentina, Brazil, Colombia, and Chile, for example, the integration of women into national political programs has been slow, and women have not participated in proportion to their numbers. In a few cases, however, such as in the election of Perón in Argentina in 1946 and Eduardo Frei in Chile in 1964, or in the popular opposition to Salvador Allende in 1973, women played a crucial role.

Some of the earliest examples of mobilization of women and their integration into the national labor force of various Latin-American nations came in the period just before the First World War and continued thereafter. The classic roles of women as homemakers, mothers, and part of the agricultural work force were increasingly expanded as women entered the industrial labor force in growing numbers. By 1911 in Argentina, for example, women made up almost 80 percent of the textile and clothing industry's workers. But women found that their salaries were often below those of comparable male workers and that their jobs, no matter the skill levels demanded, were considered "unskilled" and thus less well paid. Under these conditions women, like other workers, joined the Anarchist, Socialist, and other labor unions and organizations.

Labor organizations are only a small part of the story of women in the labor force. In countries such as Peru, Bolivia, and Ecuador, market women control much small-scale commerce and have become increasingly active politically. In the growing service sectors women have also become an important part of the labor force. Shifts in attitudes about women's roles have come more slowly than political and economic changes. Even in revolutionary Cuba, where a Law of the Family guaranteed equal rights and responsibilities within the home, enforcement has been difficult.

By the mid-1980s, the position of women in Latin America stood closer to the status of women in Western Europe and North America than it did to the other areas of the world. Women made up nine percent of the legislators in Latin America, a percentage higher than in any other region of the world. They also held nine percent of the cabinet posts, a figure only behind North America (12 percent). In terms of demographic patterns, health, education, and place in the work force, the comparative position of women reinforced Latin America's intermediate position between the "developed nations" and the Third World.

THE MOVEMENT OF PEOPLE

In 1950 the populations of North America (United States and Canada) and Latin America were both about 165 million, but by 1985 Latin America's population had grown to over 400 million compared to 165 million for North America. Declining mortality and continuing high fertility were responsible for this situation.

While at the beginning of the 20th century the major trend of population movement was immigration to Latin America, the region has long experienced internal migration and the movement of people within the hemisphere. By the 1980s this movement had reached significant levels, fed by the flow of workers seeking jobs, the demands of capital for cheap labor, and the flight of political refugees seeking basic freedoms. Large numbers of West Indians from Jamaica, Barbados, and other islands have migrated to Great Britain or the United States. In the 1920s Mexican workers crossed the border to the United States in large numbers at the same time that Guatemalans crossed the border to Mexico to work on coffee estates. During World War II government programs to supply laborers were set up between the United States and Mexico, but these were always accompanied by a considerable amount of extralegal migration, which fluctuated with the economy. Conditions for migrant laborers were often deplorable, although the extension of social welfare to them in the 1960s began to address some of the problems. By the 1970s over 750,000 illegal Mexican migrants a year were crossing the border—some more than once—as the United States continued to attract migrants.

This internationalization of the labor market was comparable in many ways to the movement of workers from poorer countries such as Turkey, Morocco, Portugal, and Spain to the stronger economies of West Germany and France. In Latin America it also reflected the fact that in-

dustrialization in the 20th century depended on highly mechanized industry that did not create enough new jobs to meet the needs of the growing population. Much of the migration has been to the United States, but there has also been considerable movement across Latin-American frontiers, as Haitians migrate to work in the Dominican Republic or Colombians illegally migrate to Venezuela. By the 1970s about five million people per year were migrating in Latin America and the Caribbean.

Politics has also been a major impulse for migration. Haitians fleeing political repression and abysmal conditions have risked great dangers in small open boats to reach the United States. One of the great political migrations of the century has been caused by the Cuban Revolution. Beginning in 1959 with the middle class fleeing socialism, but continuing into the 1980s with the flight of Cuban workers, close to one million Cubans have left the island. The revolutionary upheaval in Nicaragua and political violence in Central America have contributed to the flight of refugees. Often, it is difficult to separate political and economic factors in the movement of people from their homelands.

International migration is only part of the story. During the century there has been a marked movement in Latin America from rural to urban areas. While in the 19th century Latin America had been an agrarian region, by the 1980s about one-half of the population lived in cities of over 20,000, and over 25 of these cities had populations of over one million. Some of these cities had reached enormous size. In 1988 Mexico City had over 16 million inhabitants, São Paulo had 10 million, and Buenos Aires had 8 million. Latin America was by far the most urbanized area of the developing world and only slightly less urbanized than Western Europe.

The problem is not one simply of size but of the rate of growth. The urban populations have grown at a rate about three times that of the population as a whole, which itself was growing rapidly. Urban economies have not been able to create enough jobs for the rapidly increasing population. Often recent migrants lived in marginal neighborhoods or in shantytowns, which have become characteristic of the rapid urban growth of Latin America. These *favelas*, to give the Brazilian term for them, have created awful living conditions, but over time some have become poorer neighborhoods within the cities in which community cooperation and action have taken place to secure basic urban services.

In Socialist Cuba, a concerted effort to de-emphasize Havana and other large cities and reverse the rural-urban migration pattern was made, but in most of the region, urbanization has continued as growing populations seek better opportunities. In part, this movement is explained by a general population growth rate of over 2.5 percent per year since the 1960s.

TABLE 38-1

Population of Capital Cities as a Percentage of Total Population in Ten Latin-American Nations

	Nation	Capital	1880	1905	1930	1960	1983
1.	Brazil	Rio	3	4	4	7	(4)
2.	Mexico	Mexico City	3	3	5	15	20
3.	Argentina	Buenos Aires	12	20	20	32	34
4.	Colombia	Bogotá	1	2	2	8	11
5.	Peru	Lima	3	3	5	19	27
6.	Chile	Santiago	6	10	13	22	37
7.	Uruguay	Montevideo	12	30	28	31	40
8.	Venezuela	Caracas	3	4	7	20	18
9.	Cuba	Havana	13	15	15	18	20
10.	Panama	Panama City	7	14	16	25	20

( ) = no longer capital city

Source: From J. P. Cole, *Latin America: An Economic and Social Geography* (1965), 417.

While Latin-American urbanization has increased rapidly since 1940, the percentage of its people living in cities is still less than in Western Europe but more than in Asia and Africa. Unlike the 19th-century European experience, the lack of employment in Latin-American cities has kept rural migrants from becoming part of a laboring class with a strong identification with fellow workers. Those who do succeed in securing industrial jobs often join paternalistic labor organizations that are linked to the government. Thus there is a separation between the chronically underemployed urban lower class and the industrial labor force. Whereas industrialization and urbanization promoted a strong class solidarity in 19th-century Europe that led to the gains of organized labor, in contemporary Latin America Nationalist and Populist politics have weakened the ability of the working class to operate effectively in politics.

CULTURAL REFLECTIONS OF DESPAIR AND HOPE

Latin America remains an amalgamation of cultures and peoples seeking to adjust to changing world realities. Protestant denominations have made some inroads, but the vast majority of Latin Americans are still nominally Roman Catholics. Hispanic traditions of family, gender relations, business, and social interaction influence everyday life and help to determine responses to the modern world.

Latin-American popular culture remains vibrant. It draws on African and Indian traditional crafts, images, and techniques but arranges them in new ways. Also part of popular culture are various forms of Latin-American music. The Argentine tango of the turn of the century developed from the music halls of lower-class working districts of Buenos Aires into an international craze. The African-influenced Brazilian *samba* and the Caribbean *salsa* have been widely diffused, a Latin-American contribution to world civilization.

The struggle for social justice, economic security, and political formulas in keeping with the cultural and social realities of their nations has provided a dynamic tension that has produced tremendous artistic achievements. Latin-American poets and novelists have gained worldwide recognition. We have already noted the artistic accomplishments of the Mexican Revolution. In 1922 Brazilian artists, composers, and authors staged a Modern Art Week in São Paulo, which emphasized a search for a national artistic expression that reflected Brazilian realities.

That theme also preoccupied authors elsewhere in Latin America. The social criticism of the 1930s produced powerful realist novels that revealed the exploitation of the poor, the peasantry, and the Indians. Whether in the heights of the Andes or in the dark streets of the growing urban slums, the plight of the common folk provided a generation of authors with themes worthy of their effort. Social and political criticism has remained a central feature

Latin-American artists such as Colombian Fernando Botero (b. 1932) used surrealism and irony to depict Latin-American realities. The dominance of military regimes in the 1970s called forth the imaginative parody of the soldiers reflected in this painting.

of Latin-American literature and art and has played an important role in the development of newer art forms such as filmmaking.

The inability to bring about social justice or to influence politics has also sometimes led Latin-American artists and intellectuals to follow other paths. In the 1960s a "boom" of literature took place in which novels that mixed the political, the historical, the erotic, and the fantastic were produced by a generation of authors who found the reality of Latin America too absurd to be described by the traditional forms or logic. Writers such as the Argentine Jorge Luis Borges (b. 1899) and the Colombian Gabriel García Marquez (b. 1928) won acclaim throughout the world for their literary ability. García Marquez's *One Hundred Years of Solitude* (1967) used the history of a family in a mythical town called Macondo as an allegory of Latin America and traced the evils that befell the family and the community as they moved from naive isolation to a maturity that included oppression, exploitation, war, revolution, and natural disaster, but which never subdued the spirit of its people. In that way, his book outlined the trajectory of Latin America in the 20th century.

CONCLUSION

STRUGGLING TOWARD THE FUTURE

By the last decade of the 20th century Latin America continued to search for economic growth, social justice, and political stability. No easy solutions were available. In many ways, Latin-American societies remained "unrevolutionary," unable to bring about needed changes because of deeply entrenched class interests, international conditions, or power politics. The struggle for change had, however, produced some important results. The Mexican and Cuban revolutions brought profound changes in those countries and had a broad impact over the rest of the hemisphere, either as models to copy or dangers to be avoided. Other nations, such as Bolivia, Peru, and Nicaragua, attempted their own versions of radical change with greater or lesser success. New forms of politics, sometimes Populist and sometimes militarist, were tried and new political and social ideas like those of "Liberation Theology" grew out of the struggle to find a just and effective formula for change. Latin-American authors and artists served as a conscience for their societies and received worldwide recognition for their depiction of the sometimes surreal reality they observed. While tremendous problems continued to face the region, Latin America remained the most advanced part of the developing world.

FURTHER READINGS

There is a considerable literature in many disciplines that deals with Latin America as a whole, as well as many country-specific studies. Two good introductory texts, both of which present variations of the "dependency" interpretation, are E. Bradford Burns's *Latin America: A Concise Interpretative History* (4th ed., 1986) and Thomas E. Skidmore and Peter H. Smith's *Modern Latin America* (1989). An excellent overview of Latin-American literature and art is provided by Jean Franco's *The Modern Culture of Latin America* (2d ed., 1970). Aspects of population history are discussed in Nicholas Sánchez-Albornoz's *The Population of Latin America* (1970) and Magnus Morner's *Adventurers and Proletarians: The Story of Migrants in Latin America* (1985). The role of women is presented briefly in June Hahner's *Women in Latin American History* (1976).

The economic history of Latin America is summarized in the classic by Brazilian economist Celso Furtado, *Economic Development of Latin America* (2d ed., 1976) and in John Sheahan's *Patterns of Development in Latin America* (1987). Two excellent studies of labor that have essentially different emphases are Hobart Spalding, Jr.'s *Organized Labor in Latin America* (1977) and Charles Berquist's *Labor in Latin America* (1986).

There are many good studies of Latin American politics, but Guillermo O'Donnell's *Modernization and Bureaucratic Authoritarianism* (1973) has influenced much recent scholarship. The role of the United States is discussed in Abraham Lowenthal's *Partners in Conflict: The United States and Latin America* (1987). Lester D. Langley's *The United States and the Caribbean in the Twentieth Century* (4th ed., 1989) gives a clear account of the recent history in that region, while Walter La Feber's *Inevitable Revolutions* (1984) is a critical assessment of United States policy in Central America. Lars Schoultz's *Human Rights and United States Policy toward Latin America* (1981), details how human rights have influenced foreign policy.

A few good monographs on important topics can serve to indicate the high level of scholarship on Latin America. Alan Knight's *The Mexican Revolution*, 2 vols. (1986) and John M. Hart's *Revolutionary Mexico* (1987) provide excellent analyses of that event. Florencia Mallon's *The Defense of Community in Peru's Central Highlands* (1983) looks at national change from a community perspective. Robert Potash's *The Army and Politics in Argentina 1945–1962* (1980) is one of the best in-depth studies of a Latin-American military establishment, while Richard Gott's *Guerilla Movements in Latin America* (1972) presents analysis and documents on the movements seeking revolutionary change.

1876 Madras famine in India

1890s First Egyptian political parties formed

1904–1905 Japanese victory over Russia; British partition of the province of Bengal in India

1885 Founding of the Indian Congress party

1897 World Zionist Organization founded; West African Aborigines Rights Protection Society founded

1906 Dinshawai incident in Egypt; Muslim League founded in India

1882 Orabi revolt in Egypt; British occupation of Egypt

39

Decolonization and the Decline of the European World Order

INTRODUCTION. All of the great civilizations of Asia and Africa had been shaken to their foundations by Europe's rise to global hegemony in the 18th and 19th centuries. European political, economic, and later cultural dominance forced the thinkers and leaders of ancient centers of civilized development—from China and the Islamic heartlands to South Asia and Sudanic Africa (see Chapters 29, 30 and 32)—to reappraise their own beliefs, institutions, and traditions. However reluctantly, many of these thinkers and politicians came to the realization that if their civilizations were to be revitalized and freed from European domination, hard decisions had to be made as to what could be preserved of their own cultures and what could be rejected, what needed to be borrowed from the Europeans and what could be refused.

Most accounts of African and Asian solutions to these dilemmas stress ideas such as nationalism and modes of political organization that the colonized peoples borrowed from the Europeans. But African and Asian responses, which eventually forced the Europeans to relinquish their colonial empires, were also deeply rooted in their own religions, long-standing patterns of political mobilization, and other facets of their traditions of civilization. Reinvigorating and reformulating these distinctive civilized traditions has proven one of the central challenges for 20th-century African and Asian leaders, both in the era of decolonization and the postcolonial period that followed.

In the decades at the end of the 19th century when Europe's global domination peaked, forces were beginning to build that would eventually lead to the loss of its colonial empires and bring its world domination to an end. Some

---

1914–1918 World War I; main theaters of war in European colonies: Mesopotamia, Arabia and Palestine, and Africa

1915–1916 McMahon-Hussein correspondence

1909 Morley-Minto political reforms in India

1913 Rabindranath Tagore wins the Nobel Prize for literature

1917 Balfour Declaration

1920s Pan-African Congresses in Paris; beginnings of the négritude movement

1922 British granted the League of Nations mandate for Palestine; first stage in Egyptian independence

1921 René Maran wins the French Prix Goncourt for *Batouala*

1919 Revolt in Egypt, women a major force in demonstrations; Montagu-Chelmsford reforms in India; Rowlatt Act in India; first all-India civil disobedience movement

1930s Great Depression

1931 Gandhi-led Salt March revives Indian Nationalist movement; strikes and rebellion in Sierra Leone

1927 Simon Commission in India

1935 Government of India Act

1936–1939 Arab risings in Palestine

of these forces came from within the colonies as a sense of community and common cause began to build among the Western-educated, middle-class groups that emerged in colonized Asia and Africa (see Chapter 30). The political organizations established by these groups and their efforts to arouse mass nationalist sentiments increasingly challenged the right of the Europeans to subjugate African and Asian lands and peoples.

Though violence was sometimes employed, particularly in colonial societies with settler populations, African and Asian nationalists relied mainly on peaceful mass demonstrations, economic boycotts, and constitutional maneuvers in their struggles for independence. In these struggles, leaders such as Mohandas Gandhi and Kwame Nkrumah deftly turned the Europeans' own principles and values, such as those stressing human dignity and civil rights, against the colonial overlords. At the same time they employed indigenous religious beliefs and traditional symbols of legitimacy to rally mass support to their cause. The fact that European colonial regimes had been built in collaboration with indigenous elite groups—including princes, landlords, and the new middle classes—and depended for their survival on these groups, as well as on soldiers and policemen recruited from the colonized peoples, rendered them particularly vulnerable to growing challenges from within.

In addition to internal forces that eroded the European colonial order, growing conflicts between the Western powers dealt heavy blows to the imperial edifice. The rivalries between the great powers that helped cause the late 19th-century scramble for colonies also contributed to the outbreak of the series of global conflicts that set the framework for 20th-century global history. Thus, World War I cast doubt on the Europeans' claims that they were the fittest of all peoples to rule. It also strengthened the arguments of nationalist leaders who sought to disprove prevailing myths of European invincibility and superiority.

Even before 1914 those myths had been badly damaged by the rise of Japan as an industrialized, global power. Japan's decisive victory over the Russians in the Russo-Japanese War of 1904 and 1905 thrilled nationalists from Vietnam to Egypt and gave them confidence that the European colonizers could be overcome.

The social and economic disruptions caused by the war in key colonies, such as Egypt, India, and the Ivory Coast, made it possible for nationalist agitators to build a mass base for their anticolonial movements. The Great Depression of the 1930s, which hit most of the colonies very hard, gave further strength to the nationalist cause. It also brought on harsh repression in many colonies on the part of European administrators, who became deeply worried about their capacity to preserve European dominance in Africa and Asia. Despite the ultimate victory of the old colonial powers over Nazi Germany and Japan, World War II dealt a series of crushing blows to the European colonial order. Within decades of the end of that conflict, most of Africa and Asia had been liberated from European rule.

This chapter will explore each of these phases of the decolonization process, beginning with the first stirrings of nationalism in India and Egypt in the late 19th century. The sections that follow will examine the interplay between international events, such as those associated with the two world wars and the Great Depression, and conditions and movements in the colonies. Since it is impossible to relate the history of the independence struggles in each of the colonies, key movements, such as those in India, Egypt, and British and French West Africa, will be considered in some depth. These specific movements will then be related to broader patterns in African and Asian decolonization or, in the case of South Africa, the winning of independence for a small minority of the colonial population. The case of Vietnam, which makes an interesting comparison with its equally revolutionary neighbor, China, will be considered in Chapter 41.

1941–1945 World War II; main theaters of war in European colonies: North Africa, Southeast Asia, and Pacific Islands

1958 Afrikaner Nationalist party declares independence of South Africa

1948 Israel-Palestine partition, first Arab-Israeli war; beginning of apartheid legislation in South Africa

1962 Algeria wins independence

1942 Cripps Mission to India; Quit India movement

1957 Ghana established as first independent African nation

1947 India and Pakistan gain independence

1941 Fall of Singapore to the Japanese

1960 Congo granted independence from Belgian rule

A.D. 1940   A.D. 1950   A.D. 1960

THE INDIAN PROTOTYPE: THE MAKINGS OF THE NATIONALIST CHALLENGE TO THE BRITISH RAJ

Because India and much of Southeast Asia had been colonized long before Africa, movements for independence arose in Asian colonies somewhat earlier than in their African counterparts. By the last years of the 19th century, the Western-educated minority of the colonized had been organized politically in India and the Philippines for decades and were beginning to form associations to give voice to their political concerns in Burma and the Netherlands Indies. Because of India's size, the pivotal role it played in the British Empire (by far the largest of the European imperialist empires) as a whole, and the large numbers and sophistication of India's Western-educated elite, the Indian nationalist movement pioneered patterns of nationalist challenge and European retreat that were later followed in many other colonies. Local conditions elsewhere in Asia and in Africa made for important variations on the sequence of decolonization worked out in India. But key themes, such as the lead taken by Western-educated elites, the importance of charismatic leaders in the spread of the anticolonial struggle to the peasant and urban masses, and a reliance on nonviolent forms of protest, were repeated again and again in other colonial settings, often in conscious emulation of strategies that had achieved great success in India.

The Indian Congress party, which led the Indians to independence and has governed through most of the postcolonial era, grew out of regional associations of Western-educated Indians that were more like study clubs than political organizations in any meaningful sense of the term. These associations were centered in the cities of Bombay, Poona, Calcutta, and Madras. The Congress party that Indian leaders formed in 1885 had the blessing of a number of high-ranking British officials. These officials viewed it as a forum through which the opinions of educated Indians could be made known to the government, thereby heading off potential discontent and political protest.

For most of its first decades, the Congress party served these purposes quite well. The organization had no mass base and very few ongoing staff members or full-time politicians who could sustain lobbying efforts on issues raised at its annual meetings. Some members of the Congress party voiced concern for the growing poverty of the Indian masses and the drain of wealth from the subcontinent to Great Britain. But the Congress party's debates and petitions to the government were dominated by elite-centric issues such as the removal of barriers to Indian employment in the colonial bureaucracy and increased Indian representation in all-Indian and local legislative bodies. Most of the members of the early Congress party were firmly loyal to the British rulers and confident that once their grievances were made known to the government, they would be remedied.

British India in the Nationalist Era

As this photograph of some of the leaders of the "Non-Cooperative" Congress party illustrates, by the early 1920s even moderate Indian nationalist leaders were moving away from loyalty to the British and extensive Anglicization. In the next decades the mix of Western coats and ties and Indian headgear and dhotis increasingly gave way to apparel that was entirely Indian, even among highly Anglicized nationalist families like the Nehrus.

Many Western-educated Indians were increasingly troubled, however, by the growing virulence of British racism, which they were convinced had much to do with their poor salaries and limited opportunities for advancement in the colonial administration. In their annual meetings, members of the Congress party, who were now able to converse and write in a common English language, discovered that from wherever they came in India, they were treated in a similar fashion. The Indians' common grievances, their similar educational and class backgrounds, and their growing contacts through the Congress party gave rise to a sense of common Indian identity that had never existed before among the diverse linguistic and religious groups in the Indian subcontinent.

SOCIAL FOUNDATIONS OF A MASS MOVEMENT

By the last years of the 19th century, the Western-educated elites had also begun to grope for causes that would draw a larger segment of the Indian population into their growing nationalist community. Over a century of British rule had generated in many areas of India the social and economic disruptions and the sort of discontent that produced substantial numbers of recruits for the nationalist campaigns. Indian businessmen, many of whom would become major financial backers of the Congress party, were

angered by the favoritism the British rulers showed to British investors in establishing trade policies in India. Tariffs or taxes on British imports into India were set low, which kept the price of British goods down and made it difficult for Indian producers of such competing products as cotton textiles to shift to modern industrial techniques. Indian investors were also incensed by advantages, in the form of tax incentives and contracts, given to their British rivals. In their ever sharper attacks on British policies, Indian political leaders increasingly stressed these inequities and the more general loss to the Indian people resulting from what they termed the "drain" of Indian resources under colonial rule. Though the British rebutted that a price had to be paid for the peace and good government that had come with colonial rule, nationalist thinkers pointed out that the cost was very high indeed.

A large portion of the government of India budget went to cover the expenses of the huge army that mainly fought wars elsewhere in the British Empire that had little to do with the welfare of the Indian people. The Indian people also paid for the very high salaries and pensions of British administrators, who manned posts that Indians themselves could have managed at much lower wages. Whenever possible, such as in the purchase of railway equipment or steel for public works projects, the government bought goods manufactured in Great Britain. This practice not only served to buttress a British economy that was fast losing ground to the United States and Germany; it ensured that the classic colonial relationship between a manufacturing European colonizer and its raw-material-producing overseas dependencies was maintained.

In the villages of India, the shortcomings of British rule were equally apparent by the last decades of the 19th century. The needs of the British home economy had often dictated policies that pushed the Indian peasantry toward the production of cash crops such as cotton, jute, and indigo. The decline in food production that invariably resulted played a major role in the regional famines that struck repeatedly in the pre-World War I period. Radical Indian nationalists frequently charged that the British were callously indifferent to the suffering caused by food shortages or outbreaks of epidemic disease, and that they did far too little to alleviate the suffering that resulted. In many areas landlessness and chronic poverty, already a problem before the establishment of British rule, increased markedly. In most places, British measures to control indebtedness and protect small landholders and tenants were too little and came too late.

One clear symptom of the worsening condition of the agrarian classes was the rash of localized riots and rebellions against moneylenders and landlords that shook the imperial peace in the late 19th century. Ironically, discontent among agrarian groups was most pronounced among the more prosperous smallholders and tenants, whose hard work and shrewdness had made them major beneficiaries of great increases in market production in the last half of the 19th century. When the global demand for many kinds of Indian agricultural produce fell at the end of the century, these groups began to rethink their loyalty to the British overlords and respond to the organizational appeals of the Indian nationalists. In many parts of India, these market producers were to provide the key organizers and the ongoing core of the popular support aroused by Gandhi and other nationalist leaders in the war years and decades thereafter.

THE RISE OF MILITANT NATIONALISM

While the issues, such as cow protection, that nationalist leaders selected in their campaigns to build a mass base had great appeal to devout Hindus, they often strongly alienated other religious groups, especially the Muslims, who made up nearly one-fourth of the population of the Indian Empire. Some leaders, such as B. G. Tilak, were little concerned by this split. They believed that since Hindus made up the overwhelming majority of the Indian population, nationalism should be built on appeals to Hindu religiosity. Tilak worked to promote the restoration and revival of what he believed to be the ancient traditions of Hinduism. On this basis, he opposed women's education and the raising of the (very low) marriage age for women.

Despite widespread railway construction, government relief measures often proved too little and too late to avert horrific famines in the Indian countryside in the late 19th century. As in Ireland in the same period, British ineptitude in providing famine relief provided Indian nationalist leaders with compelling arguments for the struggle to end alien colonial rule.

Tilak also turned festivals for Hindu gods into occasions for mass political demonstrations. He broke with more moderate leaders of the Congress party by demanding (long before Gandhi) the boycott of British-manufactured goods and insisting that Indians refuse to serve in the colonial administration and military. He demanded full independence, with no deals or delays, and threatened violent rebellion if the British failed to comply.

Tilak's oratorical skills and religious appeals made him the first Indian nationalist leader with a genuine mass following, though that was confined mainly to his home base in Bombay and surrounding areas in western India. At the same time, his strong views alienated most of the moderates, and his promotion of a very reactionary sort of Hinduism offended and frightened Muslims, progressive Hindus, and the followers of other religions such as Sikhism. When evidence was found connecting Tilak's writings to underground organizations that advocated violent revolt, the British, who had grown increasingly uneasy about his radical demands and mass appeal, arrested and imprisoned him. Though mass protests against Tilak's conviction and six-year jail term erupted in western India, they were quickly suppressed. Six years in a prison in Burma, during which Tilak's wife died, took much of the fire out of India's first populist leader.

The other major threat to the British in India before World War I also came from Hindu communalists who advocated the violent overthrow of the colonial regime. But unlike Tilak and his followers, those who joined the terrorist movement favored clandestine operations over mass demonstrations. Though terrorists were active in several parts of India by the last decade of the 19th century, those in Bengal built perhaps the most extensive underground network. Considerable numbers of young Bengalis, impatient with the gradualist approach advocated by moderates in the Congress party, were attracted to secret societies led by quasi-religious, guru-style leaders who exhorted them to build up their physiques with Western-style calisthenics and learn how to use firearms and make bombs. British officials and government buildings were the major targets of terrorist assassination plots and sabotage, though on occasion the young revolutionaries also struck at European civilians and collaborators among the Indian population. But the terrorists' small numbers and limited support among the colonized populace as a whole rendered them highly vulnerable to British repressive measures. The very considerable resources the British devoted to crushing these violent threats to their rule had broken or greatly weakened the secret organizations by the outbreak of the First World War.

The alternative approaches to protest, which Gandhi developed first in South Africa in the early 1900s and then in India in the years after the war, further sapped the strength of violent populists, such as Tilak, as well as the communalist terrorists. Tilak's removal and the repression campaigns against the terrorists strengthened the hand of the more moderate politicians of the Congress party in the years before the war. Western-educated Indian lawyers came to be the dominant force in nationalist politics, and—as the careers of Gandhi, Jinnah, and Nehru demonstrated—they would provide many of the movement's key leaders throughout the struggle for independence.

The approach of those who advocated a peaceful, constitutionalist route to decolonization was given added appeal by timely political concessions on the part of the British. The Morley-Minto reforms of 1909 provided educated Indians with considerably expanded opportunities to elect and to serve on local and all-India legislative councils. The moderates also sought ways to expand their political base by both backing local protest movements and increasing their criticisms of the economic and social policies of the British colonizers. In addition, they dropped their loyalist attachment to the colonial overlords. By 1914, prominent moderate politicians were actually demanding Home Rule for India—but Home Rule within the larger British Empire. Though mass agitation that was genuinely nationalist rather than communalist only emerged with the rise of Gandhi after World War I, much of the organizational basis for Gandhi's early campaigns had been laid in the prewar decades.

EGYPT AND THE RISE OF NATIONALISM IN THE MIDDLE EAST

Egypt is the one country in the Afro-Asian world in which the emergence of nationalism *preceded* European conquest and domination. The risings touched off by the mutiny of Ahmad Orabi and other Egyptian officers (see Chapter 32), which led to the British occupation in 1882, were aimed at the liberation of the Egyptian people from their alien Turkish overlords as well as the meddling Europeans. In contrast to the other peoples who shared an Arab and Islamic cultural tradition, the Egyptians long had a strong sense of separate identity that was anchored in their view of themselves as the descendants of the builders of the great ancient Egyptian civilizations. The concentration of the Egyptians along the Nile River and their geographical separation from other Islamic centers enhanced this sense of a distinctive identity. After the British occupa-

The Middle East, 1914–1922

tion in 1882, this identity was further reinforced by railway and telegraph systems that were aimed at establishing communication links within the Nile valley rather than with other Islamic centers such as those in Syria-Lebanon and the Fertile Crescent. Egyptian distinctiveness was also strengthened by the growing struggle against the British occupation, which other Arabs had not experienced, and the preoccupation of Arab leaders in Syria-Lebanon and the Fertile Crescent with opposition to Ottoman rule.

SOURCES OF EGYPTIAN NATIONALISM

British occupation meant, in effect, double colonization for the Egyptian people by the Turkish khedives (who were left in power) and their British advisors. In the decades following the British conquest, government policy was dominated by the strong-willed and imperious Lord Cromer, who pushed for much-needed economic reforms that reduced but could not eliminate the debts of the khedival regime, for sweeping reforms in the khedival bureaucracy, and for the construction of irrigation systems and other public works projects. But the prosperity the British congratulated themselves for having brought to Egypt by the first decade of the 20th century favored the tiny middle

and elite classes, often at the expense of the mass of the population. The leading beneficiaries included foreign merchants, the Turco-Egyptian political elite, a small Egyptian bourgeoisie in Cairo and other towns in the Nile delta, and the ayan, the great landlords in the rural areas.

The latter were clearly one of the biggest gainers. The British had been forced to rely heavily on established local, estate-owning notables in extending their control into the rural areas. As a result, the ayan, not the impoverished mass of rural cultivators and laborers, received most of the benefits of the new irrigation works, the spread of the railway, and the increasing orientation of Egyptian agriculture to the production of raw cotton for the export market. Unfettered by legal restrictions for decades, the ayan had greedily amassed ever larger estates by turning smallholder owners into landless tenants and laborers. As their wealth grew, the contrast between the landlords' estate houses and the thatch and mud-walled villages of the great mass of the peasantry became more and more pronounced. Bored by life in the provinces, the well-heeled landed classes spent most of their time in the fashionable districts of Cairo or in resort towns such as Alexandria. Their estates were run by hired managers who, as far as the peasants were concerned, were little more than rent collectors.

DOCUMENT

**LESSONS FOR THE
COLONIZED FROM
THE SLAUGHTER IN
THE TRENCHES**

The prolonged and horrific slaughter of the youth of Europe in the trench stalemate on the western front did much to erode the image of Europeans as superior, rational, and more civilized beings that they had worked hard to propagate among the colonized peoples in the decades before the Great War. The futility of the seemingly endless slaughter cast doubts on the Europeans' rationality and fitness to rule themselves, much less the rest of the world. The destructive uses to which their science and technology were put brought into question the Europeans' long-standing claims that these material advancements tangibly demonstrated their intellectual and organizational superiority over all other peoples. The following quotations, taken from the writings of some of the leading thinkers and political leaders of the colonized peoples of Africa and Asia, reflect their disillusionment with the West as a result of the war and the continuing turmoil in Europe in the postwar era.

1. Rabindranath Tagore, Bengali poet, playwright, and novelist, who was one of the earliest non-European recipients of the Nobel Prize for literature:

> Has not this truth already come home to you now when this cruel war has driven its claws into the vitals of Europe? When her hoard of wealth is bursting into smoke and her humanity is shattered on her battlefields? You ask in amazement what she has done to deserve this? The answer is, that the West has been systematically petrifying her moral nature in order to lay a solid foundation for her gigantic abstractions of efficiency. She has been all along starving the life of the personal man into that of the professional.

2. Mohandas Gandhi, who emerged in the years after the war as India's leading nationalist figure:

> India's destiny lies not along the bloody way of the West, but along the bloodless way of peace that comes from a simple and godly life. India is in danger of losing her soul. . . . She must not, therefore, lazily and helplessly say, "I cannot escape the onrush from the West." She must be strong enough to resist it for her own sake and that of the world. I make

bold to say that the Europeans themselves will have to remodel their outlooks if they are not to perish under the weight of the comforts to which they are becoming slaves.

3. Léopold Sédar Senghor, Senegalese poet and political leader, who is widely regarded as one of the finest writers in the *French* language of the 20th century:

> *Lord, the snow of your Peace is your proposal to a divided world to a divided Europe*
> *To Spain torn apart. . . .*
> *And I forget*
> *White hands that fired the shots which brought the empires crumbling*
> *Hands that flogged the slaves, that flogged You [Jesus Christ]*
> *Chalk-white hands that buffeted You, powdered painted hands that buffeted me*
> *Confident hands that delivered me to solitude to hatred*
> *White hands that felled the forest of palm trees once commanding Africa, in the heart of Africa. . . .*
> (From *Snow Upon Paris*)

4. Aimé Cesaire, West-Indian poet and founder of the *négritude*, or the assertion of black culture, movement in the late 1920s:

> *Heia [Praise] for those who have never invented anything*
> *those who never explored anything*
> *those who never tamed anything*
> *those who give themselves, up to the essence of all things*
> *ignorant of surfaces but struck by the movement of all things*
> (From *Return to My Native Land*)

Questions: On the basis of this sample, what aspects of the West's claims to superiority would you say were called into question by the suicidal conflict of the leading powers within European civilization? What aspects of their own civilizations do these writers, both implicitly and explicitly, champion as alternatives to the ways of the West? Are these writers in danger of stereotyping both the West and their own civilizations?

With the khedival regime and the great landlords closely allied to the British overlords, resistance to the occupation was left mainly to the middle class that had been growing in the towns since the middle of the 19th century. With the memory of Orabi's revolt in 1882 still fresh, the cause of Egyptian independence was taken up mainly by the sons of the *effendi,* the prosperous business and professional urban families. Even nationalist leaders who came from rural ayan families built up their following from among the urban middle classes. In contrast to India where lawyers predominated in the nationalist leadership, in Egypt, journalists (a number of them educated in France) led the way. In the 1890s and early 1900s numerous newspapers in Arabic (and to a lesser extent French and English) vied to expose the mistakes of the British and the corruption of the khedival regime. Egyptian writers also attacked the British for their racist arrogance and their monopolization of well-paying positions in the Egyptian bureaucracy, which could just as well have gone to university-educated Egyptians. In the 1890s the first nationalist party was formed, but, again in contrast to India where the Congress party dominated the nationalist movement from the outset, a variety of rival parties proliferated in Egypt. There were three main alternatives by 1907, and none could be said to speak for the great majority of the Egyptians, who were illiterate, poorly paid, and largely ignored urban laborers and rural cultivators.

NATIONALIST AGITATION BEFORE WORLD WAR I

Despite the failure of the nationalist parties to unite or build a mass base in the decades before the First World War, the extent of the hostility felt by the Egyptian masses was demonstrated by the Dinshawai incident that occurred in 1906. Most Egyptian villages raised large numbers of pigeons, which served as an important supplement to the meager peasant diet. Over the years, some of the British had turned the hunting of the pigeons of selected villages into a holiday pastime. A party of British officers on leave were hunting the pigeons of the village of Dinshawai in the Nile delta when they accidentally hit the wife of the prayer leader of the local mosque. The angry villagers mobbed the greatly outnumbered shooting party, which in panic fired on the villagers. In the scuffle both the villagers and the British soldiers suffered casualties. In reprisal for the death of one of the officers, the British summarily hung four of the villagers and publicly flogged or punished with hard labor numerous others.

The harsh British reprisals in turn aroused a storm of

By the early 1920s, Mohandas Gandhi had become a pivotal figure in Indian politics. The Mahatma attracted crowds whenever he appeared in public, and this mass appeal gave him unprecedented leverage in dealing with the British as well as other nationalist politicians.

protest in the Egyptian press and among the nationalist parties. Some Egyptian leaders later recounted how the incident convinced them that cooperation with the British was totally unacceptable and fixed their resolve to agitate for an end to Egypt's occupation. Popular protests in a number of areas and the emergence of ayan support for the nationalist cause also suggested the possibility of building a mass base for anti-British agitation. In the years before the outbreak of World War I in 1914, heavy-handed British repression was necessary on several occasions to put down student riots or in reprisal for assassination attempts on high British and Turco-Egyptian officials. By 1913, the British had been sufficiently intimidated by the rising tide of Egyptian nationalism to grant a constitution and representation in a parliament elected indirectly by the men of wealth and influence. World War I and the British declaration of martial law put a temporary end to nationalist agitation. But, as in India, the war unleashed forces in Egypt that could not be stopped and that would soon lead to the revival of the drive for independence with even greater strength than before.

 ## WORLD WAR I AND THE POSTWAR CRISIS OF THE EUROPEAN EMPIRES

The nationalist struggle against European colonial domination was given a great boost by the long and devastating war between the great powers of Europe that broke out in 1914. Though the European powers had frequently quarreled over colonial possessions in the late 19th century, during the war they actually fought each other in the colonies for the first time. Major theaters of conflict developed during the war in West and East Africa and especially in the Middle East. British naval supremacy denied the Germans access to their colonies in Africa and the Pacific. With the blockade on their side, the British, French, and Belgians were able to draw heavily on their colonies for soldiers, laborers, and raw materials.

African and Asian soldiers in the hundreds of thousands served both on the western front and in the far-flung theaters of war from Egypt, Palestine, and Mesopotamia to East Africa. The French recruited tens of thousands of African and Asian laborers to replace workers in French industrial centers who had been conscripted into the armies fighting on the western front. The colonies also supplied food for the home populations of the Entente powers and vital raw materials such as oil, jute, and cotton. Contrary to long-standing colonial policy, the hard-pressed British even encouraged a considerable expansion of industrial production in India to supplement the output of their overex-

tended home factories. Thus, the war years contributed to the development in India of the largest industrial sector in the colonized world.

World War I presented the subjugated peoples of Africa and Asia with the spectacle of the self-styled civilizers of humankind sending their young men by the millions to be slaughtered in the horrific and barbaric trench stalemate on the western front. For the first time, African and Asian soldiers were ordered by their European officers to kill other Europeans. In the process, the deep divisions between and the vulnerability of the seemingly invincible Europeans were starkly revealed. During the war years, European troops in the colonies were withdrawn to meet the need for manpower on the many war fronts. The garrisons that remained were dangerously understaffed. The need to recall administrative personnel from both British and French colonies meant that colonial officials were compelled to fill their vacated posts with African and Asian administrators, many of whom enjoyed real responsibility for the first time.

To maintain the loyalty of their traditional allies among the colonized and to win the support of the Western-educated elites or new allies such as the Arabs, the British and French made many promises regarding the postwar settlement. Because these concessions often seriously compromised their prewar dominance or plans for further colonial expansion, the leaders of victorious allies repeatedly reneged on them in the years after the war. The betrayal of these pledges understandably contributed a great deal to postwar agitation against the continuance and spread of European colonial domination.

INDIA: GANDHI AND THE NATIONALIST STRUGGLE

In the months after the outbreak of the war, the British could take great comfort from the way in which the peoples of the empire rallied to their defense. Though already well on the way to independence, their subjects in the White Dominions—Canada, Australia, and New Zealand—lost no time in declaring war on the Central Powers and raising armies. Dominion troops served with distinction in both the Middle Eastern and European theaters of war, though botched campaigns like those at Gallipoli and the costly offensives on the Somme severely strained relations between the British high command and the colonials. Of the many colonies in the "true" empire, none played as critical a role in the British war effort as India. The Indian princes offered substantial war loans; Indian soldiers bore the brunt of the war effort in East Af-

This contemporary photograph shows the hangings that were carried out in reprisal for the attacks on British soldiers at the village of Dinshawai. The conical tower in the distance behind the scaffold was the roost for the pigeons that were the original and intended targets of the ill-fated hunting party.

rica and the Middle East; and nationalist leaders, including Gandhi and Tilak, toured India selling British war bonds. But as the war dragged on and Indians died on the battlefield or went hungry at home to sustain a conflict that had little to do with them, signs of unrest spread throughout the subcontinent.

Wartime inflation had adversely affected virtually all segments of the Indian population. Indian peasants were angered at the ceilings set on the price of their market produce, despite rising costs, and often their inability to sell it due to shipping shortages linked to the war. Indian laborers saw their already meager wages drop steadily in the face of rising prices. At the same time, their bosses grew rich from profits earned in war production. Many localities suffered from famines that were exacerbated by wartime transport shortages that impeded relief efforts.

Moderate Indian politicians were frustrated by the British refusal to honor promises that if they continued to support the war effort, India would move steadily after the war to self-government *within the empire*, just as Canada had one-half century earlier. Indian hopes for the fulfillment of these promises were raised by the Montagu-Chelmsford reforms of 1919, which increased the powers of Indian legislators at the all-India level and placed much of the provincial administration of India under local ministries controlled by legislative bodies with substantial numbers of elected Indians. But the concessions granted in the reforms were offset by the passage later in the year of the Rowlatt Act, which placed severe restrictions on key Indian civil rights such as freedom of the press. These conditions fueled localized protest during and immediately after the war; Gandhi soon built the protest into an all-India campaign directed against the policies of the colonial overlords.

Gandhi's remarkable appeal to the masses and the Western-educated nationalist politicians was due to a number of personal traits as well as to the strategy for protest that had been worked out a decade earlier in opposing restrictive laws imposed on the Indian migrant community in South Africa. Gandhi combined the experience of a Western-educated lawyer, having considerable world exposure and a rather astute understanding of the British colonizers, with the attributes of a traditional Hindu holy man, which served as a reminder of the glories of India's past civilizations. The former made it possible for him to build up a strong following among middle-class, Western-educated Indians who, as we have seen, had long been the dominant force behind nationalist campaigns. Gandhi's stress on non-violent, but quite aggressive, protest tactics endeared him both to the moderates and more radical elements within the nationalist movement. His advocacy of peaceful boycotts, strikes, noncooperation, and mass demonstrations — which he labeled collectively *satyagraha*, or truth force — proved a viable way of weakening British control while limiting opportunities for violent reprisals that would allow the British to make full use of their superior military strength.

These tactics also required the involvement of ever-increasing numbers of the Indian people in the nationalist cause. The holy man image Gandhi projected was critical in arousing this mass support from peasants and laborers alike, many of whom walked for miles when Gandhi was on tour to do honor to a saint rather than listen to a political speech. Gandhi's widespread popular appeal in turn gave him even greater influence among nationalist politicians, who were very much aware of the leverage this mass base gave to them in their negotiations with British officials.

THE RISE OF COMMUNALISM AND THE BEGINNINGS OF POLITICAL FRAGMENTATION

Gandhi's holy man side did, however, hamper his efforts to reach out to all Indians. Despite his constant stress on religious tolerance and communal harmony, many Muslims mistrusted this Hindu *guru* and the Congress party politicians who organized his civil disobedience campaigns. The less well-educated Muslim minority had been suspicious of the Hindu-dominated Congress party from the outset, even though a number of Muslims had been and continued to be prominent leaders in the organization. To better support their demands for separate electorates and legislative seats, a number of mostly well-educated and well-to-do Muslims founded a separate party, the Muslim League, in 1906. Though the League represented only a small percentage of even the Muslim minority until the 1940s, its presence signified a dangerous potential division within the Indian national movement. Its intransigence was matched on the Hindu side by a number of extremist, communalist parties that were equally mistrustful of united action and vehemently opposed to Gandhi's call for tolerance and Hindu power sharing with minority religious groups. All the charisma and wisdom Gandhi could muster was not sufficient to bring these fringe groups into the Congress party's mainstream. The Muslims would destroy his vision of a united India; a Hindu extremist would eventually take his life.

The success of Gandhian satyagraha tactics in a number of local protest movements paved the way for his sudden emergence as the central figure in the all-Indian nationalist struggle. The India-wide campaign to repeal the Rowlatt Act demonstrated both the strengths and weaknesses of the Gandhian approach. Congress party organizers rallied mass support for boycotts, noncooperation, and civil disobedience throughout the subcontinent that stunned the British and put them on the defensive. But a lack of time and sufficient numbers of trained followers to instruct protesters in the discipline of passive resistance led inevitably to violent

reprisals for police repression. Convinced that satyagraha could not be truly carried out under these conditions, Gandhi delighted the British and angered other nationalist politicians, such as Nehru, by calling off the anti-Rowlatt campaign. His withdrawal allowed the British to round up and imprison Gandhi and other nationalists whom they had identified as the ring leaders of the movement.

Although it would be nearly a decade before Gandhi and the Congress party would be able to launch a campaign on a scale comparable to the postwar satyagraha, British relief at the successful repression of dissent was short-lived. Throughout the 1920s, urban lawyers and peasant associations made use of Gandhian tactics to protest colonial policies and local abuses by both British and Indian officials. By the early 1930s, British insensitivity and the mounting effects of the global Great Depression paved the way for a revival of the civil disobedience campaign on an all-India basis. The establishment in 1927 of the all-white Simon Commission to consider future government responses to nationalist demands angered and unified, for a brief period, nationalist politicians on both the left and the right and those representing both Hindus and Muslims. The depression left openings for the revival of the mass struggle for decolonization. The sharp fall in the early 1930s in the price of agricultural products hit virtually all segments of the rural population, which made up well over 80 percent of the total Indian population.

Astutely gauging the mood of the Indian masses, Gandhi launched another round of all-India civil disobedience campaigns with the dramatic Salt March and satyagraha in early 1931. The British alternated between mass jailings and forcible repression and roundtable negotiations in the next half decade, but ended by making major concessions to nationalist demands. These were embodied in the Government of India Act of 1935. Though retaining control of the central administration, the British agreed to turn the provincial governments over to Indian leaders who would be chosen by a greatly expanded electorate. Their assumption of office by 1937 brought an end to the already much diminished civil disobedience agitation and a British-nationalist accommodation that lasted until another global war shook the foundations of the European colonial order.

THE MIDDLE EAST: BETRAYAL AND THE GROWTH OF ARAB NATIONALISM

In the years after World War I, resistance to European colonial domination that had been confined largely to Egypt in the prewar years spread to much of the Middle East. With Turkish rule in the area ended by their defeat in the war, Arab nationalists in Beirut, Damascus, and Baghdad turned to face the new threat presented by the victorious Entente powers, France and Britain. Betraying promises to preserve Arab independence that Henry McMahon, the British High Commissioner in Egypt, had made in 1915 and early 1916 to Hussein, the *sherif* of Mecca, French and British forces occupied much of the Middle East in the years after the war. Because Hussein had used these promises to convince Arabs to rise in support of Britain's war against the Turks, who were fellow Muslims, their violation by the Allies humiliated and deeply angered Arabs throughout the Middle East. The occupying European powers faced stiff resistance from the Arabs in each of the mandates they carved out in Syria, Iraq, and Lebanon under the auspices of the League of Nations. The Arabs' sense of humiliation and anger was greatly intensified by the disposition of Palestine, where the British occupation was coupled with promises of a Jewish homeland.

The fact that the British had appeared to promise Palestine, for which they received a League of Nations mandate in 1922, to both the Jewish Zionists and the Arabs during the war greatly complicated an already confused situation. British promises to the Arabs have already been discussed, but some background is necessary to understand their pledge to the Zionists and determination to occupy the area themselves. Zionist aspirations to return to their ancient Middle Eastern homeland had been nurtured by the Jews of the diaspora for millennia. But political organizations, created to restore the Jewish home in Palestine, were largely a product of the persecution of the Jews of eastern Europe in the last decades of the 19th century. Particularly vicious pogroms, or violent assaults on the Jewish communities of Russia and Romania in the 1860s and 1870s, convinced Jewish intellectuals such as Leon Pinsker that assimilation into or even acceptance by Christian European nations was impossible. Pinsker and other thinkers called for a return to the Holy Land. Like-minded individuals founded Zionist organizations, such as the Society for the Colonization of Israel, to promote Jewish migration to Palestine in the last decades of the 19th century. Until World War I, the numbers of Jews returning were small—in the tens of thousands—though Zionist communities were established on lands purchased in Palestine.

Until the late 1890s, the Zionist effort was generally opposed by Jews in Germany, France, and other parts of western Europe, who enjoyed citizenship and extensive civil rights, and many of whom had grown prosperous and powerful in their adopted lands. A major defection to the Zionists occurred in 1894 after Theodor Herzl, an established Austrian journalist, witnessed angry mobs shouting "Death to the Jews" as they taunted the hapless French army officer Alfred Dreyfus, a Jew who had been falsely accused of passing military secrets to the Germans. Soon after this incident, Herzl and a number of other western European Jews joined with prominent eastern Jews in forming the World Zionist Organization in 1897. As Herzl made clear in his writings, the central aim of his increasingly well funded organization was to promote Jewish migration to and settlement in Palestine until the point was reached when a Zionist state could be established in the area. Herzl's nationalist ambitions, as well as his indifference to the Arabs already living in the area, were captured in his often quoted view that Palestine was "a land without people for a people [the Jews] without a land."

British motivations for claiming Palestine in the postwar settlement arose from the dangers posed by Turkish offensives during the war against Britain's crucial lifeline at Suez. These offensives convinced the British of the need to occupy Palestine as an additional buffer zone. The situation was further complicated in 1917 when Lord Balfour, the British foreign secretary, assured prominent Zionist leaders that the British would promote the establishment of a Jewish homeland in the region after the war. Lord Balfour's promises to the Zionists and the British takeover of Palestine struck the Arabs as a double betrayal of McMahon's assurances that Arab support for the Entente powers against the Turks would guarantee them independence after the war. This sense of betrayal was a critical source of the growing hostility the Arabs felt toward Jewish emigration to Palestine and their purchase of land in the area.

Rising Arab opposition convinced many British officials, especially those who actually administered Palestine, to constrict severely the rather open-ended pledges that had been made to the Zionists during the war. This shift only led to Zionist mistrust of and open resistance to British policies, as well as a determination to build up their own defenses against the increasingly violent Arab resistance to the Zionist presence in Palestine. But British attempts to limit Jewish emigration and settlement were not matched by efforts to encourage, through education and consultation, the emergence of strong leadership within the Arab population of Palestine. Consequently, in the critical struggles and diplomatic maneuvers of the 1930s and 1940s, the Arabs of Palestine rarely spoke for themselves. They were represented by Arab leaders from neighboring lands, who did not always understand their needs and desires, and who often acted more in the interest of Syrian or Lebanese Arabs than that of the Arabs of Palestine.

REVOLT IN EGYPT

Because Egypt was already occupied by the British when the war broke out and had been formally declared a protectorate in 1914, it was not included in the promises made by McMahon to the sherif Hussein. As a result, the anti-colonial struggle in Egypt was rooted in earlier agitation and the heavy toll the war had taken on the Egyptian people, particularly the peasantry. During the war, the defense of the Suez Canal was one of the top priorities for the British. To guard against possible Muslim uprisings in response to Turkish calls for a holy war, martial law was declared soon after hostilities began, and throughout the war large contingents of Entente and empire forces were garrisoned in Egypt. These proved a heavy drain on the increasingly scarce food supplies of the area. Forced labor and confiscations by the military of the precious draft animals of the peasantry also led to widespread discontent. As the war dragged on, this dissidence was further inflamed by spiraling inflation and by food shortages and even starvation in some areas. The wartime cotton boom enriched a tiny mercantile elite, which included many Europeans and Egyptian Christians, and further alienated the mass of peasants and workers from the British and their loyal khedival allies.

By the end of the war, Egypt was ripe for revolt. Mass discontent strengthened the resolve of the educated nationalist elite to receive a hearing at Versailles, where the victorious Allies were struggling to reach a postwar settlement. Like many of the leaders of the colonial world, the Egyptians were also inspired by Woodrow Wilson's principle of self-determination. What they failed to understand was that Wilson's belief that subjugated ethnic groups should have the right to freely elect their own leaders and form their own nations was intended only for Poles and Czechs, not Arabs, Indians, or Africans. When a delegation, or *Wafd* in Arabic, of Egyptian leaders was denied permission to travel to France to put the case for Egyptian self-determination to the peacemakers at Versailles, most Egyptians resigned from the government and called for mass demonstrations. What followed shocked even the most nervous British officials. Student-led riots touched off outright insurrection over much of Egypt. At one point Cairo was cut off from the outside world, and much of the countryside was hostile territory for the occupying power. Though the British army was able, at the cost of scores of deaths, to restore control, it was clear that some hearing had to be given to Egyptian demands. The emergence of the newly formed Wafd party under its hard-driving leader Sa'd Zaghlūl provided the nationalists with both unity and a mass base that far excelled any they had attracted in the prewar decades.

When a special British commission, sent to inquire into the causes of the upheaval in Egypt, met with widespread civil disobedience and continuing violent opposition, it recommended that the British begin negotiations for an eventual withdrawal from Egypt. Years of bargaining followed, which led to a highly qualified independence for the Egyptians that came in stages beginning in 1922 and culminating in the British withdrawal to the Suez Canal zone in 1936. The British pulled out of Egypt proper, but the khedival regime was preserved and the British reserved the right to reoccupy should Egypt be threatened by a foreign aggressor.

Though they had won a significant degree of political independence, the Egyptian leaders of the Wafd party, as well as its rivals in the Liberal Constitutionalist and Union parties that were formed in the 1920s, did little to relieve the increasing misery of the great majority of the Egyptian people. Most Egyptian politicians regarded the winning of office as an opportunity to increase their own and their families' fortunes. Many politicians, both those from ayan households and those from the professional and merchant classes, used their influence and growing wealth to amass huge estates, which were worked by landless tenants and laborers. Locked in personal and interparty quarrels, as well as the ongoing contest with the khedival regime for control of the government, few political leaders had the time or inclination to push for the land reforms and public works projects that the peasantry so desperately needed. Though entrepreneurs and landlords were adversely affected by the slump in the cotton market that hit Egypt during the Great Depression, most were able to pass along their losses to laborers and tenants, who had no choice but to accept lower wages or pay higher rents.

The utter social bankruptcy of the 40 years of nationalist political dominance that preceded Nasser's revolution in 1952 is suggested by some revealing statistics compiled by the United Nations in the early 1950s. By that time, nearly 70 percent of Egypt's cultivable land was owned by six percent of the population. Some 12,000 families alone controlled 37 percent of the farmland. As for the mass of the people, 98 percent of the peasants were illiterate; malnutrition was chronic among both the urban and rural population; and an estimated 95 percent of rural Egyptians suffered from eye diseases. Such was the legacy of the very unrevolutionary process of decolonization in Egypt.

THE BEGINNINGS OF THE LIBERATION STRUGGLE IN AFRICA

Although most of Africa had only come under European colonial rule in the decades just before the outbreak of World War I, precolonial missionary efforts had produced small groups of Western-educated Africans in parts of

West and south-central Africa by the end of the 19th century. Like their counterparts in India, most western-educated Africans were staunchly loyal to their British and French overlords during the First World War. With the backing of both Western-educated Africans and the traditional rulers, many of whom found that their powers actually increased under colonial rule, the British and especially the French were able to draw on their African possessions for manpower and raw materials throughout the war. But this reliance took its toll on their colonial domination in the long run. In addition to local rebellions in response to the forcible recruitment of African soldiers and laborers, the war effort seriously disrupted newly colonized African societies. African merchants and farmers suffered from shipping shortages and the sudden decline in demand for crops, such as cocoa, some of which had been heavily dependent on German markets before the war. African villagers were not happy to go hungry so that their crops could feed the armies of the Allies. The sudden removal of European administrators and policemen from the colonies led to widespread and dangerous rumors that the Europeans were withdrawing for good or that they had run out of manpower in Europe itself. As Lord Lugard pointed out, the desperate plight of the British and French also forced them to teach tens of thousands of Africans:

. . . how to kill white men, around whom [they had] been taught to weave a web of sanctity of life. [They] also know how to handle bombs and Lewis guns and Maxims—and [they have] seen the white men budge when [they have] stood fast. Altogether [they have] acquired much knowledge that might be put to uncomfortable use someday.

The fact that the Europeans kept few of the promises of better jobs and public honors after the war, which they had made to induce young Africans to enlist in the armed forces or serve in the colonial administration, contributed a good deal to the unrest of the postwar years. In the French colonies—where opportunities for political organization, much less protest, were severely constricted—there were major strikes and a number of riots in the interwar period. In the British colonies, where there was considerably more tolerance for political organization, there were also strikes and a major uprising in Sierra Leone in 1931, protesting colonial taxes and the hardships caused by the sharp fall in prices paid for cash crops due to the Great Depression. The economic slump brought on by the depression also contributed to the refusal of cocoa producers in the Gold Coast colony (later called Ghana) to market their crops for the much-reduced prices offered by the merchants in the port towns. The growing political involvement of the cocoa farmers and other cash-crop producers was to prove a major factor in the nationalists' ability to build a popular base for anticolonialism in the post–World War II era.

Though Western-educated politicians did not link up with urban workers or peasants in most African colonies until the 1940s, disenchanted members of the emerging African elite began to organize in the 1920s and 1930s. In the early stages of this process, charismatic black American political figures, such as Marcus Garvey and W. E. B. Du Bois, had a major impact on emerging African nationalist leaders, including those who were delegates to international conferences in Paris and other Western capitals. Unlike Indian or Egyptian nationalist leaders, African nationalists had to struggle with the question of the level at which their political energies ought to be focused. In the 1920s much effort was placed into attempts to arouse all-Africa loyalties and build Pan-African organizations. The fact that the leadership of these organizations was more American and West Indian than African, and that African delegates faced very different challenges in different colonies, rendered Pan-Africanism unworkable. But its well-attended conferences did much to arouse anticolonial sentiments among Western-educated Africans.

By the mid-1920s, nationalists from French and British colonies were pretty much going separate ways. Due to restrictions in the colonies and the fact that small, but well-educated, groups of Africans were represented in the French Parliament, French-speaking West Africans concentrated their organizational and ideological efforts in Paris in this period. The négritude literary movement nurtured by these exiles did much to combat the racial stereotyping that had so long held the Africans in psychological bondage to the Europeans. Writers such as L. S. Senghor, Léon Damas, and the West Indian Aimé Cesaire celebrated the beauty of black skin and the African physique. They argued that in the precolonial era African peoples had built societies where women were freer, old people were better cared for, and attitudes towards sex were far healthier than they had ever been in the so-called civilized West. Though there was no literary movement comparable to négritude in the British colonies, authors such as Edward Blyden and J. E. Casely Hayford stressed Africa's contributions to the civilized development of all humankind in their books and essays. These and other writers made good use of the press, which was a good deal freer in the British colonies.

Western-educated Africans in British colonies were also given greater opportunities to organize political associations within Africa itself. Early organizations that linked the

In the post–World War I era, African and African-American intellectuals like Léopold Sédar Senghor (pictured here), W.E.B. Du Bois, and Aimé Césaire explored in their writings the ravages wrought by centuries of suffering inflicted on the people of Africa by the slave trade and the forced diaspora that resulted. These intellectuals sought to affirm the genius of African culture and patterns of social interaction.

emerging nationalists of different British colonies, such as the National Congress of British West Africa, gave way in the late 1920s to political groupings concerned primarily with issues confined to single colonies such as Sierra Leone, the Gold Coast, or Nigeria. After the British granted some representation in colonial advisory councils to Western-educated Africans in this period, these types of political groupings became even more pronounced. Though most of these early political organizations were too loosely structured to be considered true political parties and their members spent most of their energies getting elected to the colonial legislative councils, there was a growing recognition on the part of some leaders of the need to build a

mass base. In the 1930s a new generation of leaders not only made much more vigorous attacks on the policies of the British, but through their newspapers and political associations they sought to reach out to the ordinary African villagers and the young, who had hitherto played little role in nationalist agitation. The disruptions of yet another world war and the emergence of a new generation of much more radical nationalist leaders would turn these early efforts at outreach to the masses into the more broadly supported movements that won independence in both British and French Africa in the 1950s and 1960s.

ANALYSIS

WOMEN IN ASIAN AND AFRICAN NATIONALIST MOVEMENTS

One important, but often neglected, dimension of the liberation struggles that Asian and African peoples waged against their colonial overlords was the emergence of a stratum of educated, articulate, and politically active women in most colonial societies. In this process, the educational opportunities provided by the European colonizers often played as vital a role as they had in the formation of male leadership in nationalist movements. Though confined in the early stages of European involvement in Africa and Asia to the daughters of low-class or marginal social groups, missionary girls' schools had by the end of the 19th century become quite respectable for women from the growing Westernized business and professional classes. In fact, in many cases, some degree of Western education was essential if Westernized males were to find wives with whom they could share their career concerns and intellectual pursuits.

The seemingly insurmountable barriers that separated Westernized Asian and African males from their traditional—and thus usually without formal education—wives became a stock theme in the novels and short stories of the early nationalist era, a theme perhaps best exemplified by the works of Rabindranath Tagore. The problem was felt so acutely by the first generation of Indian nationalist leaders that many took up the task of teaching their wives English and Western philosophy and literature at home. Thus, for many upper-class Asian and African women colonization proved a liberating force. This trend was often offset by the male-centric nature of colonial education and the "domestic" focus of much of the curriculum in women's schools.

Although women played little role in the early, elitist stages of Asian and African nationalist movements, they frequently became more and more prominent as the early study clubs and political associations reached out to build a mass base. In India, women who had been exposed to Western education and European ways, such as Tagore's famous heroine in the novel *The Home and the World*, came out of seclusion and took up supporting roles, though still usually behind the scenes. Gandhi's campaign to supplant imported, machine-made British cloth with homespun Indian cloth, for example, owed much of whatever success it had to female spinners and weavers. As nationalist leaders moved their anticolonial campaigns into the streets, women became involved in mass demonstrations. Throughout the 1920s and 1930s, Indian women braved the *lathi*, or billy club, assaults of the Indian police, suffered the indignities of imprisonment, and launched their own newspapers and lecture campaigns to mobilize female support for the nationalist struggle.

In Egypt, the British made special note of the powerful effect that the participation of both traditional veiled women and more Westernized upper-class women had on mass demonstrations in 1919 and the early 1920s. These outpourings of popular support did much to give credibility to the Wafd's demands for British withdrawal. In both India and Egypt, female nationalists addressed special appeals to British and American suffragettes to support their peoples' struggles for political and social liberation. In India in particular, their causes were advanced by feminists such as the English champion of Hinduism, Annie Besant, who became a major figure in the nationalist movement both before and after the First World War.

When African nationalism became a popularly supported movement in the post-World War II period, women, particularly the outspoken and fearless market women in West Africa, emerged as a major political force. In settler colonies such as Algeria and Kenya, where violent revolt proved necessary to bring down deeply entrenched colonial regimes, women took on the dangerous tasks of messengers, bomb carriers, and guerrilla fighters. As Frantz Fanon argued decades ago, and as it was later beautifully dramatized in the film "The Battle of Algiers," for women who had been in seclusion right up until the time of the revolutionary upsurge this transformation was particularly painful. The cutting of their hair, as well as the wearing of lipstick and Western clothes, often alienated them from their own fathers and brothers, who equated such practices with prostitution.

In many cases, women's participation in struggles for the political liberation of their people was paralleled by campaigns for female rights in societies that, as we have

seen, were dominated by males. Upper-class Egyptian women founded newspapers and educational associations that pushed for raising the age of marriage, educational opportunities for women, and an end to seclusion and veiling. Indian women took up many of these causes and also sought to develop programs to improve hygiene and employment opportunities for lower-caste women. These early efforts, as well as the prominent place of women in nationalist struggles, had much to do with the granting of rights to women, including suffrage and legal equality that were key features of the constitutions of many newly independent Asian and African nations. Though the great majority of women in the new states of Africa and Asia have yet to enjoy most of these rights, their recognition in constitutions and laws provides crucial backing for the struggle for women's liberation in much of the present-day Third World.

Questions: Why might missionary education for women in the colonies have stressed domestic skills? In what ways do you think measures to "modernize" colonial societies might have been oriented to males? Can you think of women who have been or are major political figures in the contemporary Third World? Why have there not been more? What sorts of traditional constraints hamper the efforts of women to achieve economic and social equality and major political roles in the Third World today?

ANOTHER GLOBAL WAR AND THE COLLAPSE OF THE EUROPEAN WORLD ORDER

The effects of a second global conflict, brought on by the expansionist ambitions of Hitler's Germany and imperial Japan, proved fatal to the already badly battered European colonial empires. The Nazi rout of the French and the stunningly rapid Japanese capture of the French, Dutch, British, and American colonies in Southeast Asia put an end to whatever illusions the colonized peoples of Africa and Asia had left about the strength and innate superiority of the colonial overlords. Because the Japanese were non-Europeans, their early victories over the Europeans and Americans played a particularly critical role in destroying the myth of the white man's invincibility. The fall of the "impregnable" fortress at Singapore on the southern tip of Malaya and the Americans' reverses at Pearl Harbor and in the Philippines proved to be blows from which the colonizers never quite recovered, even though they went on to eventually defeat the Japanese. The sight of tens of thousands of British, Dutch, or American troops, struggling under the supervision of the victorious Japanese to survive the "death marches" to prison camps in their former colonies, left an indelible impression on the Asian villagers who saw them pass by. The colonized peoples were also disenchanted by the feeble defense against the Japanese invaders put up by their former masters. The harsh regimes and heavy demands the Japanese conquerors imposed on the peoples of Southeast Asia during the war further strengthened their determination to fight for self-rule and look to their own defenses after the conflict was over.

The devastation of World War II—a total war fought in the cities and countryside over much of Europe—drained the resources of the European powers and sapped their citizens' will to hold increasingly resistant African and Asian peoples in bondage. The war also greatly enhanced the power and influence of the two giants on the European periphery, the United States and the Soviet Union. In Africa and the Middle East, as well as in the Pacific, the United States approached the war as a campaign of liberation. American propagandists made no secret of Franklin Roosevelt's hostility to colonialism in their efforts to win Asian and African support for the Allied war effort. In the Atlantic Charter of 1941, which sealed an alliance between the United States and Great Britain that the latter desperately needed to survive, Roosevelt persuaded a reluctant Churchill to include a clause that recognized the "right of all people to choose the form of government under which they live." The Soviets were equally vocal in their condemnation of colonialism, and even more forthcoming with material support for nationalist campaigns after the war. In the cold war world of the superpowers that emerged after 1945, there was little room for the domination the much-reduced powers of Western Europe had once exercised over much of the globe.

THE WINNING OF INDEPENDENCE IN SOUTH AND SOUTHEAST ASIA

The outbreak of the Second World War soon put an end to the accommodation between the Indian Congress party and the British in the late 1930s. Congress party leaders offered to support the British war effort, if the British would give them a significant share of power at the all-India level and commit themselves to Indian independence once the conflict was over. These conditions were staunchly rejected both by the viceroy in India and at home by Winston Churchill, who headed the coalition government that led Britain through the war. Labour members of the coalition government, however, indicated that they were quite willing to negotiate India's eventual independence. As tensions built between the nationalist leaders and

the British rulers, hard-pressed in the early 1940s by their defeats both in Southeast Asia and the Mediterranean, Sir Stafford Cripps was sent to India in early 1942 to see if a deal could be struck to bring the Indians fully behind the British in the war effort. Indian divisions and British intransigence led to the collapse of Cripps's initiative and the renewal of mass civil disobedience campaigns under the guise of the Quit India movement, which began in the summer of 1942.

The British responded with repression and mass arrests, and for much of the remainder of the war Gandhi, Nehru, and other major Congress party politicians were imprisoned. Of the Indian nationalist parties, only the Communists—who were committed to the anti-Fascist alliance and, more ominously, the Muslim League—rallied to the British cause. The League, now led by a former Congress party politician, the dour and uncompromising Muhammad Ali Jinnah, won much favor from the British for its wartime support. As their demands for a separate Muslim state in the subcontinent hardened, the links between the British, Jinnah, and other League leaders became a key factor in the struggle for decolonization in South Asia.

The Second World War brought disruptions to India similar to those caused by the 1914 to 1918 conflict. Inflation stirred up urban unrest, while a widespread famine in 1943 and 1944, brought on in part by wartime transport shortages, engendered much bitterness in rural India. Though successful, the repression of the nationalists during the war convinced many British politicians and even the viceroy of India in the mid-1940s that they had neither the resources nor the will to hold India by force. Churchill's defeat in the 1945 elections, in large part because of his determination to resist India's move toward independence, brought to power a Labour government ready to deal with the nationalist leaders. With independence in effect conceded in the near future, the process of decolonization between 1945 and 1947 focused on what sort of state or states would be carved out of the subcontinent after the British withdrawal. Jinnah and the Muslim League had begun to build a mass following among the Muslims on the basis of their claims that a single Indian nation would be dominated by the Hindu majority, with the Muslims an oppressed minority. It was therefore essential, they insisted, that a separate Muslim state called Pakistan be created from those areas in northwest and east India where Muslims were in the majority.

As communal rioting, which only the physical presence of Gandhi was capable of checking, spread throughout India, the British and key Congress party politicians reluctantly concluded that only partition—the creation of two nations in the subcontinent, one secular, one Muslim—

could avert a bloodbath. Thus, in the summer of 1947 the British handed power over to the leaders of the majority Congress party, who headed the new nation of India, and to Jinnah, who became the first president of Pakistan. In part because of the haste with which the British withdrew their forces from the deeply divided subcontinent, a bloodbath occurred anyway. Vicious Hindu-Muslim and Muslim-Sikh communal rioting, in which neither women nor children were spared, took the lives of hundreds of thousands in the searing summer heat of the plains of northwest India. Whole villages were destroyed; trains pulled into railway stations that were packed with corpses hacked to death by armed bands of rival religious adherents. These atrocities fed a massive exchange of refugee populations between Hindu-Sikh and Muslim areas that may have totaled ten million people. Those who fled were so terrified that they were willing to give up their land, their villages, and most of their worldly possessions.

Partition was compounded by the fact that there was soon no longer a Gandhi to preach tolerance and communal coexistence. On January 30, 1948, Mohandas Gandhi was shot by a Hindu fanatic while on his way to one of his regular prayer meetings. Ironically, Gandhi's prayer sessions had always begun with prayers from each of the many faiths observed by the peoples of the Indian subcontinent.

In granting independence to India, the British in effect removed the keystone from the arch of an empire that spanned three continents. Burma (known today as Myanmar) and Ceylon (now named Sri Lanka) won their independence peacefully in the following years. India's independence and Gandhi's civil disobedience campaigns, which had done so much to win a mass following for the nationalist cause, also inspired African leaders such as Nkrumah, Kenyatta, and Nyerere in the 1950s and 1960s.

The retreat of the greatest of the imperial powers could not help but contribute to the weakening of lesser empires such as those of the Dutch, French, and Americans. In fact, the process of the transfer of power from United States officials to moderate, middle-class Filipino politicians was well under way before the Second World War broke out. The loyalty to the Americans most Filipinos displayed during the war, as well as the stubborn guerrilla resistance they put up against the Japanese occupation, did much to bring about the rapid granting of independence to the Philippines once the war was ended. The Dutch and French were less willing to follow the British example and relinquish their colonial possessions in the postwar era. From 1945 to 1949, the Dutch fought a losing war to destroy the nation of Indonesia, which nationalists in the Netherlands Indies had claimed when the Japanese hold

over the islands broke down in mid-1945. The French struggle to retain Indochina will be discussed in Chapter 41, which focuses on the Communist revolutions in East Asia that also emerged victorious in the postwar period. No sooner had the European colonizers suffered those losses than they were forced to deal with new threats to the last bastions of the imperial order in Africa.

THE LIBERATION OF NONSETTLER AFRICA

The Second World War proved even more disruptive to the colonial order imposed on Africa than the first global conflict of the European powers. Forced labor and confiscations of crops and minerals returned, and inflation and controlled markets again cut down on African earnings. African recruits in the hundreds of thousands were drawn once more into the conflict and had even greater opportunities to use the latest European weapons to destroy Europeans. African servicemen, who had witnessed British and French defeats in the Middle East and Southeast Asia and fought bravely only to experience again racial discrimination once they returned home, became in some colonies the staunchest supporters of postwar nationalist campaigns. The swift and humiliating rout of the French and Belgians by Nazi armies in the spring of 1940 shattered whatever was left of the colonizers' reputation for military prowess. It also led to a bitter and, in the circumstances, embarrassing struggle between the forces of the puppet Vichy regime and those of de Gaulle's *Free French*, or those who continued fighting the Nazis, which was fought out mainly in France's North and West African colonies.

The wartime needs of both the British and the Free French led to major departures from long-standing colonial policies that had restricted industrial development throughout Africa. Factories to process urgently needed vegetable oils, foods, and minerals were established in West and south-central Africa. These in turn contributed to a growing migration on the part of African peasants to the towns and a sharp spurt in African urban growth. The inability of many of those who moved to the towns to find employment made for a reservoir of disgruntled, idle workers that would be skillfully tapped by nationalist politicians in the postwar decades.

There were essentially two main paths to decolonization in nonsettler Africa in the postwar era. The first was pioneered by Kwame Nkrumah and his followers in the British Gold Coast colony, which, as the nation of Ghana, became the first independent black African state in 1957. Nkrumah epitomized the more radical sort of African leader that emerged throughout Africa after the war. Edu-

The scene depicted in this photo was played out tens of times in the decades after World War II. British Home Secretary R. A. Butler is greeted by Kwame Nkrumah, whom Butler soon installs as the leader of the first independent nation, Ghana, to be carved out of Britain's African colonies.

cated in African missionary schools and the United States, he had established wide contacts with nationalist leaders in both British and French West Africa and civil rights leaders in America prior to his return to the Gold Coast in the late 1940s. He returned to a land in ferment. The restrictions of government-controlled marketing boards and their favoritism for British merchants had led to protests and then, after the police fired on a peaceful demonstration of ex-servicemen, to widespread rioting in 1948. Though both urban workers and cash crop farmers had supported the unrest, Western-educated African leaders were slow to organize their dissidents into a sustained mass movement. Their reluctance arose in part from their fear of losing major political concessions, such as seats on colonial legislative councils, that the British had just made. Sweeping aside the fears of more established political leaders regarding the radical nature of the popular protest, Nkrumah resigned his position as chairman of the dominant political party in the Gold Coast and established his own Convention Peoples party (CPP). Even before the formal break, Nkrumah had signaled the arrival of a new style of politics by organizing

mass rallies, boycotts, and strikes—inspired, as he readily admitted, by the tactics of Gandhi and the Indian nationalists. In the mid-1950s, Nkrumah's growing stature as a leader who would not be deterred by imprisonment or British threats and his mass following won repeated concessions from the British. Educated Africans were given more and more representation in legislative bodies, and gradually they took over administration of the colony. The British acknowledgement of Nkrumah as the prime minister of an independent Ghana in 1957 simply concluded a transfer of power from the European colonizers to the Western-educated African elite that had been under way for nearly a decade.

The peaceful devolution of power to African nationalists—often led by charismatic figures, such as Nkrumah, who were capable of mobilizing mass protest when the British stalled—led to the independence of the British non-settler colonies in black Africa by the mid-1960s. Independence in the comparable areas of the French and Belgian empires in Africa came in a somewhat different way. Pressed by costly military struggles to hold on to their colonies in Indochina and Algeria, the French took a much more conciliatory line in dealing with the many peoples they ruled in West Africa. Ongoing negotiations with leaders, such as Senegal's Senghor and the Ivory Coast's Felix Houphouët-Boigny, led to reforms and political concessions that ensured that moderate African leaders, who were eager to retain French economic and cultural ties, dominated the nationalist movement in French West Africa. Between 1956 and 1960, the French colonies moved by stages toward nationhood, a process that sped up after de Gaulle's return to power in 1958. By 1960, all of France's African colonies, with the exception of Algeria, where there was a European settler community nearly one million strong, had been granted their independence.

In the same year, the Belgians completed an even hastier retreat from their huge colonial possession in the Congo (now called Zaire). Their rapid retreat is evidenced by the fact that there was little in the way of an organized nationalist movement to pressure them into concessions of any kind. In fact, by design there were scarcely any well-educated Congolese to lead resistance to Belgian rule. At independence in 1960, there were only 16 African college graduates in a Congolese population that exceeded 13 million. Though the Portuguese still clung to their impoverished and scattered colonial territories, by the mid-1960s the European colonial era had come to an end.

REPRESSION AND GUERRILLA WAR: THE STRUGGLE FOR THE SETTLER COLONIES

The pattern of relatively peaceful withdrawal by stages that characterized the process of decolonization in most of Asia and Africa proved unworkable in areas such as Algeria, Kenya, and Southern Rhodesia, where substantial numbers of Europeans had gone to settle permanently in the 19th and early 20th centuries, and in South Africa, which had begun to be settled by Europeans centuries earlier. In each case, the presence of European settler communities, varying in size from millions of whites in South Africa and Algeria to tens of thousands in Kenya and Southern Rhodesia, blocked both the rise of indigenous nationalist movements and concessions on the part of the colonial overlords. Because the settlers regarded the colonies to which they had emigrated as their permanent homes, they fought all attempts to turn political control over to the African majority or even to grant them civil rights. They also doggedly refused all reforms by colonial administrators that required them to give up any of the lands they had occupied, often dispossessing the indigenous Africans in the process. Unable to make headway through nonviolent protest tactics, which were forbidden, or negotiations with

British or French officials, who were fearful of angering the highly vocal settler minority, many African leaders turned to violent, revolutionary struggles to win their peoples' independence.

The first of these erupted in Kenya in the early 1950s. Impatient with the failure of the nonviolent approach adopted by Jomo Kenyatta and the leading nationalist party, the Kenya African Union (KAU), an underground organization, coalesced around a number of more radical leaders to win meaningful concessions from the settler-dominated regime. Some of these leaders had fought with the British in Burma and were disgusted by the British failure to reward their services with a fair hearing on such key issues as land confiscations by the settlers. After forming the Land Freedom Army, they mounted, beginning in 1952, a campaign of terror and guerrilla warfare against the British, the settlers, and Africans who were considered collaborators. At the height of the struggle in 1954, some 200,000 rebels were in action in the capital at Nairobi and in the forest reserves of the central Kenyan highlands. The British responded with an all-out effort to crush the guerrilla movement—which was dismissed as an explosion of African savagery and labeled, menacingly, the Mau Mau. In the process they imprisoned Kenyatta and his KAU organizers, thus eliminating the nonviolent alternative to the guerrillas.

Though the rebel movement had been militarily defeated by 1956 at the cost of thousands of lives, the British were now in a mood to negotiate with the nationalists, despite strong objections from the European settlers. Kenyatta was released from prison, and he emerged as the spokesman for the Africans of Kenya. By 1963 a multiracial Kenya had won its independence, and under virtually one-party rule it remained until the mid-1980s one of the most stable and more prosperous of the new African states.

The struggle of the Arab and Berber peoples of Algeria for independence was longer and even more vicious than that in Kenya. Algeria had for decades been regarded by the French as in integral part of France, a department just like Provence or Brittany. The presence of more than one million European settlers in the colony only served to bolster the resolve of French politicians to retain it at all costs. When sporadic rioting in the years after the war turned to sustained guerrilla resistance, led by the National Liberation Front (FLN) in the mid-1950s, the French army saw the defeat of the movement as a way to restore a reputation that had been badly tarnished by recent defeats in Vietnam. As in Kenya, the rebels were defeated in the field, but they gradually negotiated the independence of Algeria after de Gaulle came to power in 1958. The French people soon wearied of the seemingly endless war, and de Gaulle became convinced that he could not restore France to great power status as long as its resources were drained by the Algerian conflict.

In contrast to Kenya, the Algerian struggle was prolonged and brutalized by a violent settler backlash, led after 1960 by the Secret Army Organization (OAS), directed against the Arabs and Berbers as well as Frenchmen who favored independence for the colony. With strong support from elements in the French military, earlier settler resistance had managed to topple the government in Paris in 1958, thereby putting an end to the Fourth Republic. In the early 1960s, the OAS came close to assassinating de Gaulle and overthrowing the Fifth Republic, which his accession to power brought into existence. In the end Algeria was granted its independence in 1962. After the bitter civil war, the multiracial accommodation worked out in Kenya appeared out of the question for the settlers. Over 900,000 left the new nation within months after its birth.

In southern Africa, violent revolutions had also put an end to white settler dominance in the Portuguese colonies of Angola and Mozambique in 1975 and in Southern Rhodesia (now Zimbabwe) by 1980. Only in South Africa has the white minority managed to maintain its position of supremacy. Its ability to do so rests on a number of factors that distinguish it from other settler societies. To begin with, the white population of South Africa, roughly equally divided between the Dutch-descended Afrikaners and the more recently arrived English speakers, was a good deal larger than that of any of the other settler societies. Though only a small minority in a country of 23 million black Africans and 3½ million East Indians and coloreds (mulattos in American parlance), by the mid-1980s South Africa's settler-descended population had reached 4½ million. Unlike the settlers in Kenya and Algeria, who had the option of retreating to Europe as full citizens of France or Great Britain, the Afrikaners in particular have no European homeland to fall back upon. They have lived in South Africa as long as Europeans have lived in North America and consider themselves quite distinct from the Dutch. Over the centuries, the Afrikaners had also built up what was for them a persuasive ideology of white racist supremacy, which, though crude by European or American standards, is far more explicit and elaborate than that developed by the settlers in any other colony. The Afrikaner ideology is grounded in selected biblical

Algerians celebrate in Oran as French barricades, designed to confine the Arab-Berber population to non-European quarters of the city, are torn down by the local militia and civilians just after independence is announced in July 1962.

quotations and the celebration of their historic struggle to "tame a beautiful but hard land" in the face of opposition from both the African "savages" and the British "imperialists."

Ironically, their defeat by the British in the Boer War from 1899 to 1902 (see Chapter 30), also contributed much to the capacity of the white settler minority to maintain its place of dominance in South Africa. A sense of guilt, arising especially from their treatment of Boer women and children during the war—tens of thousands of whom died of disease in what the British called "concentration camps"—led the British to make major concessions to the Afrikaners in the postwar decades. The most important of these was internal political control, which included turning over the fate of the black African majority to the openly racist supremist Afrikaners. Not surprisingly, the continued subjugation of the black Africans became a central aim of the Afrikaner political organizations that emerged in the 1930s and 1940s, culminating in the Afrikaner National party. From 1948, when it emerged as the majority party in the all-white South African legislature, the National party devoted itself to winning complete independence from Britain (which came without violence in 1961) and to establishing lasting white domination over the political, social, and economic life of the new nation.

A rigid system of racial segregation (which will be discussed more fully in the following chapter), called *apartheid* by the Afrikaners, was established after 1948 through the passage of thousands of laws. Among other things, this legislation reserved the best jobs for whites and carefully defined the sorts of contacts permissible between different racial groups. Not only was the vote and political representation denied to the black Africans and ultimately to the coloreds and Indians, it was illegal for them to hold mass meetings or to organize political parties or labor unions. These restrictions, combined with very limited opportunities for higher education for black Africans, obviously hampered the growth of black African political parties and mass mobilization for decolonization efforts. The Afrikaners' establishment of a vigilant and brutal police state to uphold apartheid and their opportunistic cultivation of divisions between the diverse peoples in the black African population also contributed to their ability to preserve a bastion of white supremacy in a liberated continent. Thus far, despite the opening of political dialogue under the current de Klerk regime, decolonization in South Africa has been meaningful only for the privileged white majority. Black, colored, and Indian South Africans struggle to the present day to win their freedom from bondage under a regime that is as exploitative and oppressive as any that existed in the era of European colonial dominance.

CONFLICTING NATIONALISMS: ARABS, ISRAELIS, AND THE PALESTINIAN QUESTION

Though virtually all Arab peoples who were not yet free by the end of the Second World War were liberated by the early 1960s, the fate of Palestine continued to present special problems. Hitler's campaign of genocide against the European Jews had provided powerful support for the Zionists' insistence that the Jews must have their own homeland, which was increasingly conceived in terms of a modern, national state. The brutal persecution of the Jews also won international sympathy for the Zionist cause—in part because the leaders of many nations were reluctant to admit Jews fleeing the Nazi terror into their own countries. As Hitler's henchmen stepped up their race war against the Jews, the tide of Jewish immigration to Palestine rose sharply. But growing Arab resistance to Jewish settlement and land purchases in Palestine, which was often expressed in communal rioting and violent assaults on Zionist communities, led to increasing British restrictions on Jewish entry into the colony. A major Muslim revolt between 1936 and 1939, which the British only managed to put down with great difficulty, both decimated the leadership of the Palestinian Arab community and further strengthened the British resolve to stem the flow of Jewish immigrants to Palestine. Government measures to keep out Jewish refugees from the Holocaust led in turn to violent Zionist resistance to the British presence in Palestine. The Zionist assault was spearheaded by several underground terrorist organizations, including the Stern Gang and the Haganah.

By the end of World War II, the major parties claiming Palestine were locked into a deadly stalemate. The Zionists were determined to carve out a Jewish state in the region. The Palestinian Arabs and their allies in neighboring Arab lands were equally determined to transform Palestine into a multireligious nation, in which the position of the Arab majority would be ensured. Having badly bungled their mandatory responsibilities and under attack from both sides, the British wanted more than anything else to scuttle and run. The 1937 report of a British commission of inquiry supplied a possible solution—partition; the newly created United Nations provided an international body that could give a semblance of legality to the proceedings. In 1948, with sympathy for the Jews running high due to postwar revelations of the horrors of Hitler's Final Solution, the member nations of the United Nations, with the United States and the Soviet Union in rare agreement, approved the partition of Palestine into Arab and Jewish states.

The Arab states that bordered on the newly created nation of Israel had vehemently opposed the United Nation's action and attacked from all sides. Though heavily outnumbered, the Zionists proved to be better armed and much better prepared to defend themselves than almost anyone could have expected. They not only held on to the tiny, patchwork state they had been given by the United Nations, they expanded it at the Arabs' expense. The brief but bloody war that ensued created hundreds of thousands of Arab refugees from Palestine and engendered the abiding hostility between Arabs and Israelis that has been the all-consuming issue in the region and a major international problem throughout the postwar era. In Palestine, conflicting strains of nationalism had collided, and the legacy of colonialism proved even more of a liability to social and economic development than in the rest of the newly independent Third World.

the leaders of West African states continue to pride themselves on their impeccable French, decorate their presidential palaces with French antiques, and keep closely in touch with trends in French intellectual circles.

The liberation of the colonies also did little to disrupt Western dominance of the terms of international trade or the global economic order more generally. In fact, in the negotiations that led to decolonization Asian and African leaders often explicitly promised to protect the interests of Western merchants and businessmen in the postindependence era. As we shall see in the next chapter, these and other limits that sustained Western influence and often dominance, even after freedom was won, greatly reduced the options open to nationalist leaders struggling to build viable and prosperous nations. Though new forces have also played important roles, the postindependence history of the Third World cannot be understood without taking into account the lingering effects of the colonial interlude.

CONCLUSION

THE LIMITS OF DECOLONIZATION

Given the rather fragile foundations on which it rested, the rather rapid demise of the European colonial order is not really surprising. The winning of political freedom in Asia and Africa also represented less of a break with the colonial past than the appearance of many new nations on the map of the world might lead one to assume. The decidedly nonrevolutionary, elite-to-elite transfer of power that was central to the decolonization process in most colonies, even those where there were violent guerrilla movements, limited the amount of change that accompanied the decolonization process. The Western-educated African and Asian classes moved into the offices and jobs, and often the former homes, of the European colonizers. But social gains for the rest of the population in most new nations were minimal or nonexistent. In Kenya, Algeria, and Zimbabwe (formerly Southern Rhodesia), abandoned European lands were distributed to Arab and African peasants and laborers, but in most ex-colonies, especially in Asia, the big landholders were indigenous, and they have held on tenaciously to their holdings. Though educational reforms were carried out to include more sciences in school curricula and the history of Asia or Africa rather than Europe, Western cultural influences have remained strong in almost all of the former colonies. Indians with a higher education continue to communicate in English; some of the most prominent of

FURTHER READINGS

The best introduction to the massive literature that has developed on the Indian nationalist movement, as well as a good general historical chronology of the struggle for independence, can be found in Sumit Sarkar's *Modern India 1885–1947* (1983). Louis Fischer's biography of *Gandhi* (1950) still yields valuable insights into the personality of one of the great nationalist leaders and the workings of nationalist politics; Judith Brown's studies of Gandhi's political career, including *Gandhi's Rise to Power* (1972), provide an approach more in tune with current research. The poems and novels of Tagore yield wonderful insights into the social and cultural life of India through much of this era.

P. J. Vatikiotis's *The History of Egypt* (especially the 1985 edition) has excellent sections on the nationalist era in that country. Interesting, but less reliable, is Jacque Berque's *Colonialism and Nationalism in Egypt* (1972). George Antonius's *The Arab Awakening* (1946) is essential reading on the Palestine question. It can be balanced by Aaron Cohen's *The Arabs and Israel* (1970) and Fred Khouri's survey of the roots of *The Arab-Israeli Dilemma* (1968). The early stages of the nationalist struggle in West Africa are covered by Michael Crowder's *West Africa under Colonial Rule* (1982), while the final drives for decolonization are surveyed by Ali A. Mazrui and Michael Tidy in *Nationalism and New States in Africa* (1984), J. D. Hargreaves's *Decolonization in Africa* (1988), and W. R. Louis and P. Gifford, eds., *Decolonization in Africa* (1984). On specific movements, see Alstair Horne's *A Savage War of Peace* (1977) on Algeria, C. Rosberg and J. Nottingham's *The Myth of 'Mau Mau'* (1966) on Kenya, and the writings of Terrence Ranger on Rhodesia. Of the many works on South Africa, the general histories of S. Throup, B. Bunting, T. D. Moodie, and L. Thompson provide a good introduction to the rise of Afrikaner power.

1930s Free Officers movement develops in Egypt

1947 India and Pakistan
achieve independence

1952 Farouk and khedival regime overthrown
in Egypt; Nasser and Free Officers to power

1951 India's first Five-Year Plan for
economic development launched

1956 Abortive
British-French
intervention in Suez

1912 African National
Congress party formed

1949 Hassan al-Banna assassinated in Egypt

1955 Bandung Confer-
ence; beginning of Non-
Aligned movement

1948 First Arab-Israeli War; Afrikaner
Nationalist party to power in South
Africa; beginnings of apartheid legislation

1928 Founding of the Muslim Brotherhood in Egypt

A.D. 1920   A.D. 1940   A.D. 1950

Africa and Asia in the Era of Independence

40

INTRODUCTION. In Gillo Pontecorvo's moving film on the struggle for independence in Algeria, "The Battle of Algiers," one member of the high command of the National Liberation Front (FLN) reflects on the nature of the revolutionary struggle in a conversation with a young guerrilla fighter, the protagonist of the film. When the young man expresses his anxieties about the outcome of the general strike then taking place in the city of Algiers, the thoughtful leader of the FLN seeks to put the immediate crisis in a larger perspective. Revolutions, he muses, are difficult to get going and even harder to sustain. But the real tests, he concludes, will come when the revolutionary struggle has been successfully concluded, when the makers of the movement must assume power and face the greatest challenges of all—those involved in building viable nations and prosperous societies for peoples disoriented and deprived by decades or in many cases centuries of colonial rule.

These reflections on the process of decolonization anticipated the actual experience of the peoples in the new nations carved out of the ruins of the European colonial empires. Once the European colonizers had withdrawn and the initial euphoria of freedom had begun to wear off, Western-educated nationalist leaders were forced to confront the sobering realities of the fragile state structures and underdeveloped economies they had inherited. With the common European enemy gone, the deep divisions between the different ethnic and religious groups that had been thrown uneasily together in the postcolonial states became more and more apparent and disruptive. The Western-educated leaders soon realized how small a proportion of the population had gen-

---

1958 South Africa completely independent of Great Britain

1960 Sharpeville shootings in South Africa

1966 Nkrumah overthrown by a military coup in Ghana

1966–1970 Biafran secessionist war in Nigeria

1967 Six-Day War between Israel and the Arabs

1970s Peak period for the OPEC cartel

1971 Bangladesh revolt against West Pakistan; Indo-Pakistani War

1972 Bangladesh becomes an independent nation

1973 Third Arab-Israeli War

1979 Shah of Iran overthrown; Khomaini-led Islamic republic declared

1980–1988 Iran-Iraq War

1989 De Klerk charts a path of peaceful reform in South Africa

1990 Nelson Mandela released from prison; Iraqi invasion of Kuwait

1991 First Gulf War

uinely committed themselves to the nationalist identity and goals that had formed the backbone of the drive for independence. They were often startled by how shallow loyalty to a common nation was, even among the Westernized elite classes that had led the decolonization struggle.

The leaders of the new nations found their efforts to spur economic growth constricted by concessions made to the departing colonizers and the very nature of the international economy, in which the terms of investment and trade heavily favored the industrialized nations. They saw their ambitious schemes to improve living standards among formerly colonized peoples frustrated by a shortage of expertise and resources and by population growth rates that quickly ate up whatever modest advances could be made. Many of the nationalist leaders despaired as hungry peasants flocked to the rapidly growing cities where there was little employment to be had, and bad weather and market reverses resulted in famines and mounting debts that left their nations even more at the mercy of the industrialized world. The leaders of the new nations lamented the continuing intellectual and cultural dependence of their societies on the United States and Western Europe. This dependence was reflected in all manner of things from the architecture of African and Asian cities and the literary output of their novelists, playwrights, and movie directors to university curricula and the pop music and blue jeans the children of the elite classes consumed as avidly as their counterparts in the West.

Increasing poverty, official corruption, and a growing concern for the breakdown of traditional culture and social values produced widespread social unrest and often violence between different religious and ethnic groups. Dissent and civil disturbances called into question the leadership abilities of nationalist politicians who had won independence but floundered as heads of new nations. Challenges to the existing order came both from Communist parties on the left and religious revivalist movements on the right. In order to remain in power and to ensure that they would be able to realize their visions of economic and social development in the postcolonial era, Western-educated nationalist leaders adopted various strategies to beat back these threats. These strategies ranged from attempts by leaders such as Sukarno of Indonesia and Nkrumah of Ghana to establish themselves as charismatic strongmen at the head of unopposed populist movements to the state-directed reform and development programs nurtured by Nehru in India, where civil rights and democracy were preserved. As we shall see, these strategies met with widely varying degrees of success. The price for failure was often a fall from power and at times the execution of former nationalist heroes. In many instances, their places were taken by military commanders who assumed dictatorial powers, forcibly silenced dissent, and suppressed interethnic and religious rivalries. In a limited number of cases, the champions of religious revival and resistance to Western influences, most notably those in Iran, swept moderate reformers and dictators from power.

The many nations carved out of the colonial empires were invariably lumped together as members of the Third World. This grouping of what were very diverse societies and political systems reflected the common dilemmas these nations had to face. They became contested ground between the wealthy First World of the West and Japan and the militant and aspiring states of the Second World, the Communist bloc, which was united in the years right after the war behind the Soviet Union and the Peoples Republic of China. The newly independent states of Africa and Asia also shared a common experience of colonization and the struggle for freedom, and they came to independence with underdeveloped economies and consequently high levels of poverty, illiteracy, and population growth.

Though most of the Latin-American countries have often been included in the Third World category, they had actually won their political independence much earlier. Because the Latin-American struggles for development and social justice have been discussed in some depth in Chapter 38, this chapter focuses on responses to these challenges in the newly independent states of Asia and Africa. In some cases similar social and economic problems have produced comparable responses, but it is vital to keep in mind the great diversity of Third World societies—a diversity grounded in the very different precolonial histories and colonial experiences of various African and Asian peoples. For that reason, after the common challenges that faced Third World societies in the early independence era are surveyed in the opening sections of this chapter, the remaining sections will be devoted to the varying solutions different leaders of African and Asian nations devised to deal with the urgent and complex problems they faced.

THE CHALLENGES OF INDEPENDENCE

The nationalist movements that won independence for most of the peoples of Africa and Asia usually involved some degree of mass mobilization. Peasants and working-class townspeople, who hitherto had little voice in politics beyond their village boundaries or local labor associations, were drawn into political contests that toppled empires and established new nations. To win the support of these groups, nationalist leaders promised them jobs, civil rights, and equality once independence was won. The leaders of many nationalist movements nurtured visions of postindependence utopias in the minds of their followers. They were told that once the Europeans, who monopolized the best jobs, were driven away and their exploitative hold on the economies of colonized peoples was brought to an end, there would be enough to give everyone a good life.

Unfortunately, the realities of the postindependence situation in virtually all new African and Asian nations made it impossible for nationalist leaders to fulfill the expectations they had aroused among their followers and in varying degrees the colonized populace at large. Even with the Europeans gone and terms of economic exchange with more developed countries somewhat improved, there was simply not enough to go around. Thus, the socialist-inspired ideologies that had often been embraced by nationalist leaders and propagated to their followers proved misleading. The problem was not just that goods and services were unequally distributed, leaving some people rich and the majority poor. The problem was that there were not sufficient resources to take care of everybody, even if it had been possible to distribute them equitably.

When utopia failed to materialize, personal rivalries and long-standing divisions between different classes and ethnic groups, which had been more or less successfully muted by the common struggle against the alien colonizers, resur-faced or intensified. In almost all of the new states, these rivalries and differences became dominant features of political life. They produced political instability and often threatened the viability of the nations themselves. They also consumed resources that might have been devoted to economic development and blocked—in the name of the defense of subnational interests—measures designed to build more viable and prosperous states. Absorbed by the task of just holding their new nations together, African and Asian politicians neglected problems—such as soaring population increases, uncontrolled urban growth, rural landlessness, and ecological deterioration—that soon loomed as just as great a threat as political instability to their young nations.

BUILDING NATIONS AND NATIONAL IDENTITIES

A pernicious precedent was set at the very beginning of the decolonization process. Neither Gandhi, nor the British, nor the compromises offered by Congress party politicians could break Jinnah's resolve, and in 1947 India

Colonial Division of Africa and the Emergence of New Nations

became two hostile nations rather than a unified state in which Hindus, Muslims, Sikhs and other religious groups strove to live together in peace. The communal rivalries and centuries-old hatred and mistrust that surfaced in the era of decolonization in India could be found in equal or even greater measure in virtually all of the colonies that made up the European overseas empires. The way the empires had been built and their boundaries demarcated ensured that this would be the case. European generals conquered and European explorers staked out claims to territories in ways that rarely, if ever, took into account the interests or history of the peoples who occupied these lands. In most colonies, the pattern that had been set in India prevailed. Peoples who had traditionally lived in separate states and developed very different cultures were thrown together under the same colonial regime. India at least was bound by common institutions, such as the caste system, and Hindus and Muslims had lived together there for centuries before the coming of the British.

In Africa, which was grabbed by the rival European powers in much greater haste, peoples who had little in common except wars over slaves and territory found themselves thrown together as subjects of alien colonizers. As Lord Salisbury, one of the most prominent late 19th century champions of imperialist expansion, confessed in the 1890s, the conquerors knew next to nothing about the lands they divided up around the green-felt tables at conferences in Berlin, Paris, and other European capitals:

> We have been engaged in drawing lines upon maps where no white man's foot ever trod; we have been giving away mountains and rivers and lakes to each other [Europeans] only hindered by the small impediment that we never knew exactly where the mountains and rivers and lakes were. . . .

If they could not locate the mountains and rivers, European diplomats could hardly have been expected to know much about the peoples who lived on or along them. As a consequence, the division of Africa was completely arbitrary. Colonial boundaries cut peoples such as the Yoruba of West Africa and the Somalis of the horn of East Africa apart, and they tossed together tens, sometimes hundreds, of very different—often hostile—African peoples. The roads and railways built by the colonizers, the marketing systems they established, and the educational policies they pursued all hardened the unnatural boundaries and divisions established in the decades of the late 19th century. It was these artificial units, these motley combinations of peoples that defied the logic of history and cultural affinity, that African nationalist leaders had to try to meld into nations in the decades after World War II.

In virtually all of the new states that have emerged from the European colonial empires, ethnic rivalries and communal violence have been endemic. In some cases, the unnatural creations of the colonizers did not long survive the transfer of power to indigenous leaders. The most spectacular collapse of a new state came in Pakistan, the unwieldy patchwork of a nation the British had thrown together at the last minute in 1947 to satisfy Jinnah's demands for majority rule in Muslim areas of the Indian subcontinent. A glance at the map revealed the vulnerability of Pakistan, split into two parts, West and East Pakistan that were separated by over 1000 miles of hostile Indian territory. Some attention to the history of the two halves that made up Pakistan would have made clear the problems in store.

Bengal in the east was a region shaped by the tropical monsoons. Its language was akin to Hindi, one of the official languages of India; it was written in a script derived from ancient Sanskrit, the sacred language of the Hindus. The Muslim Bengalis in East Pakistan followed a less fundamentalist, much more Hindu-influenced variant of the Islamic faith than the Muslim peoples of the other half of Pakistan far to the west. The Bengalis were physically closer to the peoples of south India and parts of Southeast Asia than the lighter-skinned, taller peoples of West Paki-

The Partition of South Asia: The Formation of India, Pakistan, Bangladesh, and Sri Lanka

stan. The latter, molded by the hard, dry climate of the regions they inhabited, were a very different sort of people than the Bengalis. Their main language was Urdu, written in a script derived from Persian; they were more prone to embrace Islamic fundamentalism, more resistant to Hindu influences. Many traced their descent from the Muslim peoples who invaded the Indian subcontinent a millennium earlier. This heritage contrasted sharply with that of the Bengalis, most of whom descended from Hindu and Buddhist peoples who had converted to Islam during the early centuries after the Muslims' arrival. Thus, even the Islamic religion that the people of the two halves of Pakistan shared and that had been responsible for them being combined in the same country in the first place differed significantly from west to east.

Though efforts had been made to bridge differences between the two Pakistans and especially to ensure that political power was shared equally between the two regions, the politicians and military leaders of the West soon gained the upper hand. Though the export of jute and other crops from the East brought in most of the foreign currency earned by Pakistan, the West absorbed a lion's share of state revenues, especially those spent on economic development schemes. West Pakistanis held a far greater portion of positions at the upper levels of the national bureaucracy and in the military forces than they warranted in view of the larger population in East Pakistan. In the 1960s, under a succession of military leaders, West Pakistanis sought to limit civil liberties in and further curtail the political influence of East Pakistanis. By the 1970s, the heavy handed, often outright arrogant policy of the West Pakistanis had generated resistance movements in East Pakistan. A brutal attempt in 1971 by the military strongman Yahya Khan to crush this resistance triggered an all-out revolt in East Pakistan against West Pakistani dominance. Backed by the Indians, always eager to weaken their Pakistani rivals, the East Pakistanis won a war of secession that led to the establishment of the independent nation of Bangladesh in 1972.

The contrasting lush tropical and arid semidesert environments of East and West Pakistan underscore the great differences between the two areas—differences that eventually led to the violent breakaway of East Pakistan and the creation of the nation of Bangladesh.

At various points in their history, most of the new nations of Africa and Southeast Asia have been threatened by similar secessionist movements. In fact, India, which relished the chance to contribute to the breakup of Pakistan, has itself been repeatedly threatened by civil strife between different linguistic, religious, and ethnic groups. At the present time, Sikh guerrillas carry on a violent campaign for separation in the north, and the Indian government has been forced to intervene militarily in the violent struggle between different ethnic and religious groups in Sri Lanka (Ceylon), its neighbor to the south.

In Africa, where there was often even less of a common historical and cultural basis on which to build nationalism than in South or Southeast Asia, separatist movements have been a prominent feature of the political life of new states. Secessionist movements currently rage from Morocco in the northwest to Ethiopia in the east and Angola in the south. Civil wars, such as the current struggle of the non-Muslim peoples of the southern Sudan against the Muslim rulers from the northern parts of that country, have also abounded. Thus far, none of the secessionist movements have succeeded, though that of the Ibo peoples of eastern Nigeria, who proclaimed an independent state of Biafra in 1967, led to three years of bloody warfare in Africa's most populous nation.

Though African leaders have been acutely aware of the injustices and persecutions of minority groups that have often precipitated these conflicts, none has seriously suggested altering the unnatural boundaries established in the colonial era. The reverse, in fact, is the case. These divisions have become sacrosanct, because each African leader fears that a successful secession movement in another country or a redrawing of boundaries elsewhere could provide precedents for dissident minorities in their own country or for neighboring leaders to claim boundary adjustments that would work to their disadvantage.

In all cases, the artificial nature of the new nations of the Third World has proved costly. In addition to internal divisions, boundary disputes between newly independent nations have often led to border clashes and on a number of occasions to open warfare. India and Pakistan have fought three such wars since 1947. Iraq's Saddam Hussein justified his 1990 annexation of Kuwait with the argument that the tiny, but oil-rich, Arab "sheikhdom" was an artificial creation of the British colonizers, who had carved out land that had historically been part of Iraq. These disputes have done much to confirm the West's view of the Third World as a region of unrest and instability. But it is important to remember that "developed" countries, such as the United States, took decades and numerous boundary

In the late 1960s, posters and photos such as this, which graphically depicted the ravages of the Nigerian civil war, served as reminders of the artificiality and instability of the new states that had been hastily carved out of the European colonial empires.

disputes (with, for example, the British over Canada) and outright wars, such as that with Mexico, to reach their current size and contours.

Democracy has often been one of the main victims of the tensions between rival ethnic groups within Africa and Asian nations and threats from neighbors without. Politicians in virtually all of the new states have been quick to play upon ethnic and religious loyalties as well as fears to win votes. The result has been that freely elected legislatures have often been dominated by parties representing these special interests. Suspicions that those in power were favoring their own or allied groups led to endless bickering and stalemated national legislatures, which became tempting targets for the coup attempts of military strongmen. One of the more persuasive reasons these usurpers have given for dictatorial rule was the need to contain communal conflict, which had only been whipped up by democratic election campaigns. Ironically, this was one of the key rationales given by the European colonizers to justify the continuation of colonial rule. The threats from rival ethnic and religious groups felt by those in power have also contributed to exorbitant military spending by Asian and African leaders—spending that their impoverished societies can rarely afford. In countries where civil wars have actually occurred, such as Ethiopia, Mozambique, and Angola, economic development has ground to a virtual standstill, while disease and famine have reduced their peoples to levels of misery and despair that even the most well-funded of international agencies often can do little to alleviate.

THE POPULATION BOMB

The nationalist leaders who led the Third World peoples to independence had firmly committed themselves to promoting rapid economic development once colonial restraints were removed. In keeping with their Western-educated backgrounds, most of these leaders envisioned their nations following the path of industrialization that had brought national prosperity and international power to much of Western Europe and the United States. This course of development was also fostered by representatives of the Soviet bloc, who had emphasized heavy industry in their state-directed drives to "modernize" their backward economies and societies. Of the many barriers to the rapid economic breakthroughs Third World leaders hoped for, the most formidable and persistent were the spiraling increases of population that often overwhelmed whatever economic advances the peoples of the new nations managed to make.

Factors making for sustained population increases in already quite densely populated areas of Asia and Africa had begun to take effect even before the era of high colonialism. Food crops, mostly from the New World, had contributed to dramatic population growth in China and India as early as the 17th century. They also helped sustain high levels of population in areas such as the Niger delta in West Africa, despite heavy losses of both males and females as a result of the slave trade. The coming of colonial rule reinforced these upward trends in a number of ways. It ended local warfare that had caused population losses and, perhaps more significantly, had indirectly promoted the spread of epidemic diseases and famine. The new railroad and steamship links established by the colonizers in order to foster the spread of the market economy also cut down on regional famines that had been a major check against sustained population increase since ancient times.

Large amounts of food could now be shipped from areas where harvests were good to those where drought or floods threatened the local inhabitants with starvation.

With war and famine—two of the main checks that Malthus and others had identified as major barriers to population increase—much reduced, growth began to speed up, particularly in areas such as India and Java that had been under European control for decades. The death rate declined, but the birthrate remained much the same, leaving more and more sizeable net increases. Improved hygiene and medical treatment played little part in this rise until the first decades of the 20th century. From that time, efforts to eradicate tropical diseases, as well as global scourges such as smallpox, and to improve sewage systems and purify drinking water have given further impetus to sharp upswings in population, particularly in sub-Saharan Africa.

Virtually all the leaders of the emerging Third World nations headed states in which the population was increasing at unprecedented levels. This increase continued in the early years of independence. In much of Asia, it has begun to level off in recent decades. But in most of Africa population growth continues at very high rates. In some cases, most notably South Asia, rather moderate growth rates have produced prodigious total populations because they were adding to an already large base. As a result, in the 1970s population experts predicted that at the then-current rates, South Asia's population of over 600 million would more than double by the year 2000. With over one billion people by the late 1980s, the prophecy appears well on the way to fulfillment.

In Africa, by contrast, which began with relatively low population levels, given its large land area, very high birthrates and diminished mortality rates have resulted in population increases of alarming proportions in recent decades. The magnitude of this increase can be envisioned if one considers the predictions of some population experts that, if present growth rates continue, by the middle of the next century Nigeria will have a population equal to that of present-day China and Kenya will have a population double that of the United States in the mid-1980s. Some indication of the size of the human calamities that are likely to result is suggested by the fact that the 400 million peoples of Africa are currently supported by a continental economy with a productive capacity equal to just six percent of the present United States' economy, or roughly equal to that of the state of Illinois.

On the face of it the conquest of the Malthusian checks to sustained population growth throughout much of human history—war, disease, and famine—was one of the great

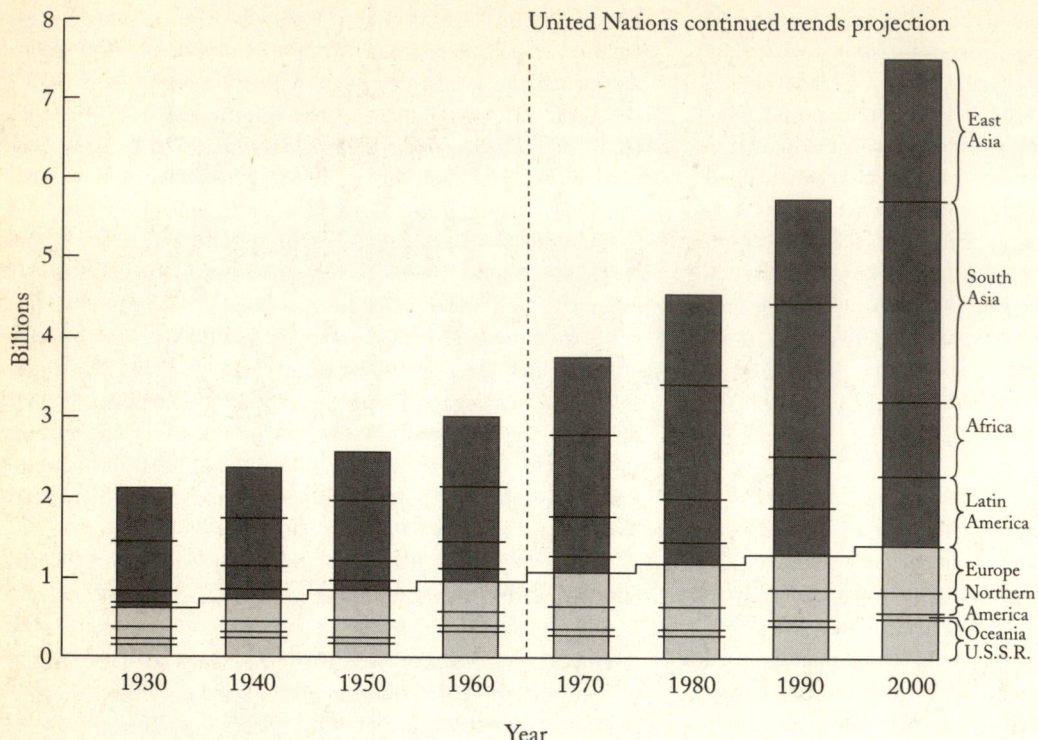

United Nations continued trends projection

Numerical growth of world population, 1930-2000.

achievements of European colonial regimes. It was certainly an accomplishment that colonial officials never tired of citing in defense of the perpetuation of European dominance. But another side of the colonial legacy rendered this increase a trap in which most of the Third World nations were soon to find themselves caught. The European policy of limiting industrialization in their colonial dependencies meant that one of the key ways by which Europe had met its own population boom in the 19th and early 20th centuries was not available to the new nations of the Third World. They lacked the factories to employ the exploding population that moved to the cities from the rural areas, as well as the technology to produce the necessities of life for more and more people. Unlike the Europeans and the Americans, the Third World nations found it difficult to draw food and mineral resources from the rest of the world to feed this ever-proliferating population. In fact, these were the very things the colonized peoples had been set up to sell to the industrialized countries. Even in countries such as India, where impressive advances in industrialization were made in the postcolonial era, gains in productivity were rapidly swallowed up by the population explosion.

In most Third World countries there has been considerable resistance to birth control efforts aimed at bringing runaway population growth in check. Some of this resistance is linked to deeply entrenched social patterns and reli-

gious beliefs. In many Third World societies, procreation is seen as a key marker of male virility, and the capacity to bear children, preferably male children, continues to be critical to the social standing of adult women. In some cases, resistance to birth control is linked to specific cultural norms. Hindus, for example, believe that a deceased man's soul cannot begin the cycle of rebirth until his eldest son has performed special ceremonies over his funeral pyre. This belief both increases the already considerable pressure on Indian women to have children, and it encourages families to have several sons in order to ensure that at least one survives the father.

In Africa children are seen as indispensable additions to the lineage—the extended network of relatives (and deceased ancestors) that, much more than the nuclear family, makes up the core social group over much of the subcontinent. As in India, sons are essential for, among other things, the continuation of the patrilineal family line and the performance of burial and ancestral rites. Their key roles in agricultural production and marketing make female offspring more highly valued in Africa than in many Asian societies, where high dowries and occupational restrictions limit their contribution to family welfare.

Before the 20th century, the high incidence of stillbirths and high rates of infant mortality more generally meant that mothers could expect to lose many of the children to whom they gave birth—ten or 12 deaths of 15 or 16 children conceived was not unheard of. Beyond the obvious psychological scars left by these high death rates, they also fostered the conviction that it was necessary to have many children to ensure that some would outlive the parents. In societies where welfare systems and old-age pensions were meager or unknown, surviving children took on special urgency because they were the only ones who would care for their parents once they could no longer work for themselves. The persistence of these attitudes in recent decades, when medical advances have greatly reduced infant mortality, has been a major factor contributing to soaring population growth.

In the early decades after independence, many Third World leaders were deeply opposed to state measures to promote family planning and birth control. Some saw these as Western attempts to meddle in their internal affairs; others proudly declared that the socialist societies they were building would be able to take care of the additional population. As it has become increasingly clear that excessive population increase renders significant economic advances impossible, many Third World leaders have begun to reassess their earlier attitudes toward birth control. A particular cause for alarm is the fact that in many Third World countries a high percentage of the population is under the age of 15 (as high as 40 percent in some countries) and thus dependent on others for support. But even for those who now wish to actively promote family planning, the obstacles are staggering. In addition to the cultural and social factors making for resistance discussed above, Third World leaders often find they lack sufficient resources and the educated personnel required to make these programs effective. High rates of illiteracy, particularly among women, need to be overcome, but education is expensive. Perhaps no form of financial and technical assistance from the industrialized to the developing world will be as critical in the coming decades as that devoted to family planning to defuse the global population bomb.

PARASITIC CITIES AND ENDANGERED ECOSYSTEMS

As population increase in the rural areas of Third World countries outstripped the land and employment opportunities available to the peasantry, mass migrations to urban areas ensued. The massive movement of population from overcrowded villages to the cities was one of the most dramatic developments in the postcolonial history of most Third World nations. Ambitious youths and the rural poor crowded into port centers and capital cities in search of jobs and a chance to win the "good life" that the big hotels and restaurants and the neon lights of the city center ap-

peared to offer to all comers. But because Third World cities lacked the rapidly expanding industrial sectors that had made possible the absorption (with considerable difficulty) of a similar migrant influx earlier in the West, they were often dead ends for migrants from the rural areas. There were few jobs, and heavy competition for these ensured that wages would remain low for most workers. The growing numbers of underemployed or unemployed turned to street vending, scavenging, huckstering, begging, or petty crime to survive. The idleness and despair of the urban underclass has been a prominent theme in the novels and plays of Third World writers such as Mochtar Lubis of Indonesia, Cyprian Ekwensi of Nigeria, and V. S. Naipaul, who was born of Indian parents in the Caribbean and has written about many Third World countries.

In the independence era, the urban poor has become a volatile factor in the political struggles of the elite, willing for a price to cheer on one contender or jeer down another, ready to riot and loot in times of government crisis. In deeply divided societies, the poor, working-class, or idle youths of the urban areas have often formed the shock troops in communal clashes between rival ethnic and religious groups. Fear of outbursts by urban "mobs" has also forced Third World regimes to expend considerable portions of their scarce resources to subsidize and thus keep low the price of staple foods, such as bread, and other necessities.

The great and sudden influx of population from the rural areas to cities without the jobs or infrastructure to support them has greatly skewed urban growth in the Third World. Within decades, Asian cities have become some of the largest in the world, while African urban areas have sprawled far beyond their modest limits of colonial times. The wealth of the glitzy hotel and high-rise dominated enclaves of the upper- and middle-class minorities in Third World societies contrasts disturbingly with the poverty of the vast slums that stretch in all directions from the city centers. Little or no planning was possible for the slum quarters that expanded as squatters erected makeshift shelters wherever open land or derelict buildings could be found. Originally, most of the slum areas lacked electricity, running water, or even the most elementary sewage facilities. As shanties were gradually converted into ramshackle dwellings, many Third World governments scrapped plans to level slum settlements and sought instead to provide them with some semblance of electrical and sanitary systems. As an increasing number of development specialists have reluctantly concluded, slums often provide the only housing urban dwellers are likely to find for some time to come. Only substantially higher levels of economic growth will give most Third World nations the resources to replace them with planned housing at some future date.

In the urbanized areas of the Third World, the contrast between the wealth of the few and the poverty of the majority is starkly revealed by the juxtaposition of the high-rise apartments of the affluent middle classes and the ramshackle shantytowns of the urban poor.

These conditions have burdened most Third World societies with parasitic rather than productive cities, which are heavily dependent for survival on food and resources drawn from their own countryside or from abroad. In contrast to the cities of Western Europe and North America—even during the decades of rapid urban expansion in the 19th century—few Third World cities have had the manufacturing base required to generate growth in their surrounding regions or the nation as a whole. They take from the already impoverished countryside, but they are able to give little in return, though in the more industrialized societies of the Third World, such as India, cement and steel for dam and road construction and farm implements have made some contribution to rural development. Urban dependence on the countryside further stretches the already overextended resources of the rural areas.

Rural overpopulation in the decades after independence has led to the depletion of soils in many areas that have been worked for centuries or millennia. It has also resulted in an alarming rate of deforestation throughout the Third World, as peasant villagers cut trees for fuel or to clear land for farming and their flocks. Deforestation and overgrazing not only pose major threats to the wild animal life, ranging from tigers to elephants, they also upset the balance in fragile tropical ecosystems, producing further soil depletion and erosion and encouraging desertification. This environmental degradation is intensified by industrial pollution, both from developed countries and Third World nations themselves. Though the industrial sectors in the latter are generally small, pollution tends to be proportionally greater than in the developed world because Third World nations rarely have the means to afford the anti-pollution technology introduced in Western Europe, Japan, and North America.

ANALYSIS
WOMEN AND THE STRUGGLE TO BUILD NEW SOCIETIES IN THE THIRD WORLD

The example of both the Western democracies and the Communist republics of Eastern Europe, where women had won the right to vote in the middle decades of the 20th century, encouraged the founders of the nations of the Third World to write female suffrage into their constitutions. The very active part women played in many nationalist struggles was perhaps even more critical to their earning the right to vote and run for political office. Female activism also produced some semblance of equality in terms of legal rights, education, and occupational opportunities under the laws of many new nations.

The equality that was proclaimed on paper, however, often bore little resemblance to the actual rights that the great majority of African and Asian women could exercise or had little bearing on the conditions under which they lived their daily lives. Despite the media attention given to Third World women such as Indira Gandhi, Corazon Aquino, and Benazir Bhutto who have emerged as national leaders, political life in most African and Asian countries continues to be dominated by males. The overwhelming majority of elected officials and government administrators, particularly at the upper levels of state bureaucracies, are males. Because they are usually less well educated than their husbands, women in societies where genuine elections are held often do not exercise their right to vote, or they simply vote for the party and candidates favored by their spouses. In many Third World societies in which coups or one-party dominance have put an end to democratic politics, female suffrage is meaningless.

Even the rise to power of individual women like Indira Gandhi, who proved to be one of the most resolute and powerful of all Third World leaders, is deceptive. In every case, female heads of state in the Third World entered politics and initially won political support because they were connected to powerful males. Indira Gandhi was the daughter of Jawaharlal Nehru, India's first prime minister; Corazon Aquino's husband was the martyred leader of the Filipino opposition to Ferdinand Marcos; and Benazir Bhutto's father was a domineering Pakistani prime minister who had been toppled by a military coup and was executed in the late 1970s. Lacking these sorts of connections, the vast majority of Third World women have been at best relegated to peripheral political positions, and at worst, they are allowed no participation in the political process whatsoever.

The limited real gains made by Third World women in the political sphere are paralleled by the second-class position to which most are consigned in many societies. In some respects their handicaps are comparable to those that constrict women in the industrialized democracies and communist nations. But the obstacles to female self-fulfillment, and in many cases just survival, in Third World societies are usually much more blatant and fundamental than the child-rearing patterns, educational and job discrimination, and other sexist restrictions women have to contend with in developed societies. To begin with, the fact that early marriage ages for women and large families are still the norm in most Third World societies means that women spend their youthful and middle-age years having children. There is little time to think of higher education or a career.

In many Third World societies, large numbers of women are still confined to the home, a trend that has been reinforced by the spread of religious fundamentalism in recent decades. Even in India, which is officially a secular state, it was estimated that decades after independence in 1947, as high as 20 percent of all women were still in *pur-dah*, or domestic seclusion. In Islamic lands, the proportion of women confined to the home is often a good deal higher. This trend has not been followed in most of sub-Saharan Africa, where women were traditionally more independent and free to follow occupations outside the home. It has also been resisted by women of the middle and elite classes in many Third World countries, who have had the resources to pursue higher education and professional careers. As the experience of the Iranian revolution suggests, "liberated" women from these classes are likely to lose these outlets in areas where religious fundamentalism takes hold.

Because of the low level of sanitation in many Third World communities and food scarcity, all but upper-class women experience endemic anxiety regarding such basic issues as sufficient and nutritional meals for their hungry children and their susceptibility to disease. The persistence of male-centric customs directly affects the health and life expectancy of women themselves. The Indian tradition, for example, which dictates that women first serve their husbands' and sons' meals and then eat what is left, has obvious disadvantages. The quantity and nutritional content of the leftovers is likely to be lower than of the original meals, and in tropical environments flies and other disease-bearing insects are more likely to have fouled the food.

The consequences of these social patterns can be quite injurious for women. In the 1970s, for example, it was estimated that as high as 20 percent of the female population of India was malnourished and that as much as another 30 percent had a diet that was well below acceptable United Nations levels. In sharp contrast to the industrial societies of Japan, North America, and Europe, where women outnumber (because on the average they outlive) men, in India there are only 930 females for every 1000 males.

In most Third World societies, the disadvantages women traditionally faced within the household and in terms of career opportunities were compounded by the prejudices and policies of colonial officials. Whatever education, particularly higher and technical education, that was provided was geared to males. Colonial development schemes and links to the global markets also favored males. Thus, in societies like those of West Africa and Southeast Asia, where women had traditionally played significant roles in farming and marketing, their position actually declined in the colonial era.

Traditional religious restrictions on women often remained after independence, and they lagged far behind men in the degree to which they were able to take advantage of what might have been countervailing educational and occupational opportunities. As late as 1975, for example, there were only 300,000 women in India with bachelors degrees in a total population of some 600 million.

Though the highly secular property and divorce laws many new states promulgated after independence gave women much greater rights, many of these have been ignored in practice, and very often Third World women have neither the education nor the resources to exercise their legal rights. The spread of religious fundamentalism has in many cases further eroded these rights, most notably in Islamic areas, though advocates of a return to tradition often argue that practices such as veiling and stoning for women (but not men) caught in adultery actually enhance the dignity and status of women. Wherever one comes down in these disputes, there is little doubt that most Third World women continue to be dominated by male family members, are much more constricted than males in terms of career opportunities, and are likely to be less well-fed, educated, and healthy than males at a comparable social level.

Questions: In what ways would the persistence of some of the traditional religious beliefs of African and Asian societies, which we have discussed in earlier chapters, contribute to the limitation of women's rights and career opportunities in the Third World? Are there comparable obstacles in the religious and secular belief systems of the West? What sorts of programs and measures could be undertaken by international agencies, such as the United Nations, and Third World governments to speed the liberation of African and Asian women?

"NEOCOLONIALISM," COLD WAR RIVALRIES, AND UNDERDEVELOPMENT

The schemes of nationalist leaders aimed at building an industrial base that would provide adequate support for the rapidly increasing populations of their new nations soon floundered amid the economic realities of the postcolonial world. Not only did most of the nations that emerged from colonialism have little in the way of an industrial base, their means of obtaining one were depressingly meager. In order to buy the machines and hire or train the technical experts they needed to get industrialization going, Third World countries needed to earn capital they could invest for these ends. Some funds could be accumulated by saving a portion of the state revenues collected from the peasantry. In most cases, however, there was precious little left once bureaucrats had been given their salaries, essential public works and the extension of education had been funded, and other state expenses had been met. Thus, most Third World countries have relied on the sale of cash crops and minerals to earn the foreign exchange they need to finance

industrialization. As their leaders soon discovered, the structure of the world market was heavily loaded against them.

The pattern of exchange promoted in the colonial era left most Third World countries dependent on the export production of two or three food or industrial crops—such as cocoa, palm oil, coffee, or jute and hemp—or minerals—such as copper, bauxite, and oil—for which there was a high demand in the industrialized economies of Europe, North America, and increasingly Japan. Since the Second World War, the prices of this sort of export—which economists call primary products—have not only fluctuated widely, they have steadily declined when compared to the prices of most of the manufactured goods Third World countries usually buy from the industrialized nations. Price fluctuations have created nightmares for planners in the Third World. Revenue estimates from the sale of coffee or copper in years when the price is high are used to plan government projects for the construction of roads, factories, and dams. Market slumps can wipe out these critical funds—thereby retarding economic growth—and throw Third World countries deeply into debt. These setbacks are doubly frustrating because in order to get industrialization going, Third World countries are often forced to export precious and finite mineral resources that they themselves will require if they succeed in industrializing.

Except with oil, the leaders and planners of Third World countries have had little success in improving the terms under which they participate in the global market economy. Even the gains made by the oil cartel have tended to be confined to a select few Third World nations and to be temporary. They were also soon rolled back to a large degree by divisions between the oil-producing states. These differences, including those partly responsible for Iraq's invasion of Kuwait in 1990, have made it difficult to maintain the production quotas that were essential to the great rise in the price of oil in the mid-1970s. Third World leaders have been quite ready to blame the legacy of colonialism and what they have termed the "neocolonial" structure of the global economy for the limited returns yielded thus far by their development schemes. Though there is much truth to these accusations, they do not tell the whole story. Third World leaders and elites must also share the responsibility for the slow pace of economic development in much of the Third World. To begin with, few leaders of the new nations had the technical or scientific training to tackle the mundane but complex tasks involved in development. To some extent their deficiencies can be blamed on the low level of technical education available in most colonies. But even in areas like India where it was available, the rising Western-educated classes rarely pursued it, preferring instead the training in Western languages and the humanities that opened to them well-paying careers in government, law, and business.

In addition, members of the educated classes that came to dominate the political and business life of newly independent nations often used their positions to enrich themselves and their relatives at the expense of their societies as a whole. Corruption has been notoriously widespread in most of the new nations. Government controls on the import of goods, such as automobiles, television sets, and stereos, which are luxury items for most of the people, have often been lax. As a result, tax revenues and export earnings that could have fueled development have often gone to provide "the good life" for small minorities within Third World societies. The inability or refusal of many Third World regimes to carry out key social reforms such as land redistribution, which would spread the limited resources available more equitably over the population, has contributed vitally to the persistence of these patterns. Leaders who have defied the interests of the elite classes from which they came and pushed for sweeping reforms have often fallen victim to coups and even assassination plots.

Badly strapped for investment funds and essential technology, Third World nations have often turned to international organizations, such as the World Bank and the International Monetary Fund, and the rival great powers for assistance. Though considerable resources for development have been generated in this way, the price for international assistance has often been high. Both the United States and the Soviet Union, as well as their allies, have normally extracted major concessions in return for their aid. These have ranged from commitments to buy the products of and favor investors from the lending countries to entering into alliances and permitting military bases on the territory of the client state. Loans from international lending agencies have almost invariably been granted only after the needy nation agreed to what are called "conditionalities." These are regulations that determine how the money is to be invested and repaid, and they usually involve promises to undertake major "reforms" in the economy of the borrowing nation.

In recent years, these promises have often included a commitment to remove or reduce state subsidies on food and other essential consumer items. State subsidies were designed to keep prices for staple goods at a level that the urban and rural poor—the great majority of the people in virtually all Third World countries—could afford. When carried through, subsidy reductions have frequently led to widespread social unrest, violent riots, and the collapse or near collapse of Third World regimes. These violent outbursts have served as dramatic reminders both of just how precarious social stability is in much of the Third World, and of how limited and perilous solutions to the problems facing the new states spawned by decolonization have proved.

PATHS TO DEVELOPMENT

However much the leaders of the new Third World countries might have blamed their nations' woes on the recently departed colonizers, they soon felt the need to deliver on the promises of social reform and economic well-being that had done so much to rally support to the nationalist cause. Different leaders adopted different approaches, and some tried one strategy after another. Depending on their own skills, the talents of their advisors and lieutenants, and the resources at their disposal, Third World leaders tackled the awesome task of development with varying degrees of success. Though it is obviously impossible to deal with all of these efforts at nation-building and economic development in depth, the basic elements of several distinctive strategies will be considered in sections that make up the second half of this chapter. Discussion of each strategy will focus on a single, prominent case example, and some attempt will be made to assess the merits and drawbacks of each approach. As this overview clearly reveals, though some countries have done a good deal better than others, successful overall strategies to deal with the challenges facing the nations of the Third World have yet to be devised.

Solutions to specific problems, such as the Green Revolution in agriculture that many development experts credit with averting global famine in the last two decades, have often given rise to new problems. Ways have been found to raise the living standards of some of the population of Third World nations, but these have rarely benefited the majority. Revolutionary movements aimed at genuine redistribution and the benefit of all have thus far floundered due to planning errors and insufficient resources. It may be too early to judge the outcomes of many development schemes, but thus far none has proven a path to the social justice and general economic development that nationalist leaders envisioned as the ultimate outcome of struggles for decolonization.

CHARISMATIC POPULISTS AND ONE-PARTY RULE

One of the least successful responses on the part of Third World leaders who found their dreams for national renewal frustrated was a retreat into authoritarian rule, which was disguised by calculated, charismatic appeals for support from the disenfranchised masses. Perhaps the career of Kwame Nkrumah, the leader of Ghana's independence movement, illustrates this pattern as well as that of any Third World politician. There can be little question that Nkrumah was genuinely committed to social reform and economic uplift for the Ghanaian people during the years of his rise to the position of the first prime minister of Ghana in 1957. After assuming power, he moved vigorously to initiate programs that would translate his high aspirations for his people into reality. But his ambitious schemes for everything from universal education to industrial development soon ran into trouble. Rival political parties, some of them representing regional interests and ethnic groups long hostile to Nkrumah, repeatedly challenged his initiatives and sought to block efforts to carry out his schemes. His leftist leanings won support from the Soviet bloc, but frightened away Western investors who had a good deal more capital to plow into his economy. They also led to growing hostility on the part of the United States, Great Britain, and other influential noncommunist countries. Most devastatingly, soon after independence the price of cocoa, by far Ghana's largest export crop, began to fall sharply. Tens of thousands of Ghanaian cocoa farmers were hard hit and the resources for Nkrumah's development schemes suddenly dried up.

Nkrumah's response to these growing problems was increasingly dictatorial. He refused to give up or cut back on his development plans. As a result, most failed miserably due to lack of key supplies and to official mismanagement. In the early 1960s he forcibly crushed all political opposition by banning rival parties and jailing other political leaders. He assumed dictatorial powers and ruled through functionaries in his own Convention Peoples party.

Nkrumah also sought to hold on to the loyalty of the masses and mobilize their energies by highly stage-managed "events" and the manipulation of largely invented symbols and traditions that were said to be derived from Ghana's past history. Thus, he sought to justify his policies and leadership style with references to a uniquely African brand of socialism and the need to revive African traditions and African civilization. Even before independence he had taken to wearing the traditional garb of the Ghanaian elite. The very name of Ghana, which Nkrumah himself had proposed for the new nation that emerged from the former Gold Coast colony, had been taken from an ancient African kingdom that had actually been centered much farther to the north and had little to do with the peoples of the Gold Coast.

Many monumental statues of Kwame Nkrumah like this one rose in the towns and villages of Ghana as he attempted to cover the failure of his socialist-inspired development programs with dictatorial rule and self-glorification.

Nkrumah went about the country giving fiery speeches, dedicating monuments to the "revolution," which often consisted of giant statues of himself, and taking a prominent role in the nonaligned movement that was then sweeping the Third World. As the French journalist Jean Lacouture reported in the mid-1960s, Nkrumah's posturing had become a substitute for his failed development schemes. His followers' adulation knew no bounds. Members of his captive Parliament compared him to Confucius, Muhammad, Shakespeare, and Napoleon and predicted that his birthplace would serve as a "Mecca" for all of Africa's statesmen. But his suppression of all opposition and his growing ties to the Communist party, coupled with the rapid deterioration of the Ghanaian economy, increased his enemies, who laid low and waited for a chance to strike. That chance came early in 1966 when Nkrumah went off on one of his many trips, this time a peace mission to Vietnam. In his absence, he was deposed by a military coup. Nkrumah died in exile in 1972, and Ghana moved in a very different direction under its new military rulers.

MILITARY RESPONSES: DICTATORSHIPS AND REVOLUTIONS

Nkrumah is just one of many civilian leaders in the Third World who have fallen victim to military coups. In fact, it is far more difficult to find African and Asian (or, as we have seen in Chapter 38, Latin-American) countries that have remained under civilian regimes since independence than those that have experienced military takeovers of varying durations. India, the Ivory Coast, Kenya, Zambia, and Zimbabwe are some of the more notable of the former; much of South and Southeast Asia and the rest of Africa have been or are now governed by military regimes. Given the difficulties confronted after independence by leaders such as Nkrumah and a number of advantages the military have in crisis situations, the proliferation of coups in the Third World is not all that surprising.

The armed forces in Third World countries have at times been divided by the religious and ethnic rivalries that have proved such a disruptive force in new nations. But the regimentation and emphasis on discipline and in-group solidarity in military training have often rendered soldiers more resistant to these forces than other social groups. In conditions of political breakdown and social conflict, the military possesses the monopoly—or near monopoly—of force that is often essential for restoring order. Their occupational conditioning not only makes soldiers more ready than civilian leaders to use the force at their disposal, but less concerned with its destructive consequences. Military personnel also tend to possess some degree of technical training, which as we have seen was usually lacking in the humanities-oriented education of civilian nationalist leaders. Because most military leaders have been staunchly anticommunist, they have often attracted covert technical and financial assistance from Western governments.

Once in control, military leaders have banned civilian political parties and imposed military regimes of varying degrees of repression and authoritarian control. Yet the ends to which these regimes have put their dictatorial powers have differed considerably. At their worst, military regimes—such as those in Uganda, Burma (now Myanmar), and Zaire—have quashed civil liberties, while making little attempt to reduce social inequities or improve living standards. These regimes have existed mainly to enrich the military strongmen, as well as their cronies and lackeys, who control them. Regimes of this sort have been notorious for official corruption and the imprisonment and brutal torture or outright elimination of political dissidents. Understandably uneasy about being overthrown, they have diverted a high proportion of their nations' meager resources that might have gone for economic development into expenditures on expensive military hardware, which the Western democracies and the countries of the Soviet bloc have been only too eager to sell to them. Military leaders of this type have also been ready to use quarrels and sometimes military conflicts with neighboring regimes to divert attention from the bankruptcy of their domestic policies.

In a few cases, military leaders have proven quite radical with regard to economic and social reform. Perhaps none was more so than Gamal Abdul Nasser, who took power in Egypt following a military coup in 1952. As we have seen, the Egyptians had won their independence, except for the lingering British presence in the Suez Canal zone in the mid-1930s. But self-centered civilian politicians and the corrupt khedival regime had done little to improve the standard of living of the mass of the Egyptian people. As conditions worsened and Egypt's governing parties did little but rake in wealth for their limited, largely elitist memberships, two revolutionary forces emerged in Egyptian society.

The first was the Muslim Brotherhood, a party founded by Hasan al-Banna in 1928. Though committed to a fundamentalist approach to Islam, al-Banna's organization was also devoted to social uplift and sweeping reform. The Muslim Brotherhood became involved in a wide range of activities, from promoting trade unions and building medical clinics to educating women and pushing for land reform. By the late 1930s, the Brotherhood's social service had become highly politicized. Al-Banna's followers fomented strikes and urban riots and set up militant youth organizations and paramilitary assassination squads. Though stunned by the murder of al-Banna by the khedive Farouk's hit men in 1949, the members of the Brotherhood continued to expand its influence among both middle-class youth and the impoverished masses into the early 1950s. Its ultimate goal of the seizure of power, however, was thwarted by the second revolutionary force that emerged in this period.

The Free Officers movement, which evolved from a secret organization established by officers in the Egyptian army in the 1930s, was for many decades loosely allied to the Muslim Brotherhood. Founded by idealistic young officers of Egyptian, rather than Turco-Egyptian, descent, the secret Revolutionary Command Council studied conditions in the country and prepared to seize power in the name of a genuine revolution. Following Egypt's humiliating defeats in the first Arab-Israeli War in 1948 and in a clash with the British over the latter's continuing occupation of the Suez Canal zone in 1952, mass anger with a discredited khedival and parliamentary regime gave the officers their chance. In July of 1952, an almost bloodless military coup toppled the corrupt and "well-padded" khedive Farouk from his jewel-encrusted throne.

The revolution had begun. The monarchy was ended, and the Egyptians ruled themselves for the first time since the 6th century B.C. By 1954, all political parties had been disbanded—including the Muslim Brotherhood, which had clashed with its former allies in the military—and had been suppressed after an attempt on the life of Nasser. Nasser was only one of several officers as the head of the Free Officers movement, and by no means was he initially the most charismatic. After months of internal power struggles in the officer corps, however, he emerged as the head of a military government that was deeply committed to revolution.

The growing Egyptian resistance to the continuing British occupation of the Suez Canal zone was dramatically expressed in this effigy of a British soldier that was strung up on a Cairo street corner in January 1952. Within months mass demonstrations and a military coup freed Egypt from the British occupation and the repressive khedival regime.

Nasser and his fellow officers used the dictatorial powers they had won in the coup in an attempt to uplift the long oppressed Egyptian masses. They believed that only the state possessed the power to carry out essential social and economic reforms, and thus they began to intervene in all aspects of Egyptian life. Land reform measures were enacted: limits were placed on how much land an individual could own, and excess lands were seized and redistributed to landless peasants. State-financed education was made available to Egyptians through the college level. The government became Egypt's main employer—by 1980 over 30 percent of Egypt's work force was on the state payroll. State subsidies were used to lower the price of basic food staples such as wheat and cooking oil. State-controlled development schemes were introduced that emphasized industrial growth, just like the Five-Year Plans of the Soviet Union. In order to establish Egypt's economic independence, stiff restrictions were placed on foreign investment, and in some cases foreign properties were seized and redistributed to Egyptian investors. Nasser also embarked on an interventionist foreign policy that stressed the struggle to destroy the newly established Israeli state, forge Arab unity, and foment socialist revolutions in neighboring lands. His greatest foreign policy coup came in 1956, when he rallied international opinion to oust finally the British (and their French allies) from the Suez Canal zone. Despite the setbacks suffered by Egyptian military forces, Nasser made good use of the rare combined backing of the United States and the Soviet Union to achieve his aims in the crisis.

However well-intentioned, many of Nasser's initiatives misfired. Land reform efforts were frustrated by bureaucratic corruption and the clever stratagems devised by the landlord class to hold on to their estates. State development schemes often lacked proper funding and failed due to mismanagement and miscalculations. Even the Aswân Dam project, which was the cornerstone of Nasser's development drive, was something of a fiasco. Egypt's continuing population boom quickly canceled out the additional cultivable lands the dam produced. The dam's interference with the flow of the Nile resulted in an increase in parasites that spread blindness, as well as in a decline in the fertility of farmlands in the Lower Nile delta that were deprived of the rich silt annually washed down by the river. Foreign investment funds from the West, which Egypt desperately needed, soon dried up. Aid from the much poorer Soviet bloc could not begin to match what was lost, and much of this assistance was military. In the absence of sufficient foreign investment and with Egypt's uncontrolled population rising at an alarming rate, the state simply could not afford all the ambitious schemes to which Nasser and the revolutionary officers had committed it. The gap between aspirations and means was increased in the later years of Nasser's reign (in the 1960s) by the heavy costs of his mostly failed foreign adventures, including the disastrous Six-Day War with Israel that Egypt was drawn into in 1967.

Though he had to move slowly at first, Nasser's successor, Anwar Sadat, had little choice but to dismantle the massive state apparatus that had been created. He favored private rather than state initiatives, and during his tenure in office the middle class, which had been greatly restricted by Nasser, emerged again as a powerful force. Sadat also moved, after fighting the Israelis to a stalemate in 1973, to end the costly confrontation with Israel and Egypt's support for revolutionary movements in the Arab world. Sadat expelled the Russians and opened Egypt to aid and investment from the United States and Western Europe.

Sadat's shift in direction has been continued by his successor and the present leader of Egypt, Hosni Mubarak. But neither the attempt at genuine revolution led by Nasser nor the retreat to capitalism and more pro-West positions under his successors has done much to check Egypt's alarming population increases and the corruption of its bloated bureaucracy. Neither path to development has had much effect on the glaring gap between the living conditions of Egypt's rich minority and its impoverished masses.

THE INDIAN ALTERNATIVE: DEVELOPMENT FOR SOME OF THE PEOPLE

Although the approach to nation building and economic development followed by the leaders of independent India has shared the Nasserite emphasis on socialism and state intervention, India's experience has diverged from Egypt's in a number of very significant respects. To begin with, the Indians have managed to preserve civilian rule throughout the four decades since they won their independence from Great Britain. In fact, in India the military has consistently defended secular democracy against religious extremism and other would-be authoritarian trends. In addition, though India, like Egypt, has been saddled with a crushing burden of overpopulation, it came to independence with a larger industrial and scientific sector, a better communications system and bureaucratic grid, and a larger and more skilled middle class in proportion to its total population than any other Third World country.

During the first decades of its freedom, India had the good fortune to be governed by leaders, such as Jawaharlal Nehru and his allies in the Congress party, who were deeply committed to social reform and economic development as well as the preservation of civil rights and democracy. India's success at the latter has been nothing short of remarkable. Despite continuous threats of secession by religious and linguistic minorities, as well as massive poverty,

unemployment, and recurring natural disasters, India remains the world's largest functioning democracy. Except for brief periods of rule by coalitions of opposition parties, the Congress party has ruled at the center for most of the independence era. But opposition parties have controlled many state and local governments, and they remain vocal and active in the national Parliament. Civil liberties, exemplified by a very outspoken press and free elections, have been upheld to an extent that sets India off from much of the rest of the Third World. Their staying power was perhaps most emphatically demonstrated by the heavy political price that Nehru's daughter, Indira Gandhi, and more dictatorially-prone successor paid for attempting to curtail press and political freedoms in the mid-1970s, an attempt that led to the one of the rare election defeats the Congress party has suffered thus far.

Nehru's less dictatorial approach to government and development also differed from Nasser's in his more moderate mix of state and private initiatives. Nehru and his successors pushed state intervention in some sectors, but also encouraged foreign investment from countries in both of the rival blocs in the cold war. As a consequence, India has been able to build on its initial advantages in industrial infrastructure and its skilled managerial and labor endowment. Its significant capitalist sector has encouraged ambitious farmers like those in the Panjab in the northwest to invest heavily in the improved seed strains, fertilizers, and irrigation that are at the heart of the Green Revolution. The new techniques associated with the Green Revolution have produced much higher yields in key crops such as rice, wheat, and corn throughout much of the Third World in recent decades. Considerable industrial and agrarian growth have generated the revenue for the Indian government to promote literacy and village development schemes, as well as family planning, village electrification, and other improvement projects in recent decades.

Despite its very considerable successes, India has suffered from the same gap between needs and resources that all Third World nations have had to face. Whatever the government's intentions—and India has been hit by corruption and self-serving like most polities—there have simply not been the resources to raise the living standards of even a majority of its huge population. The middle class has grown, perhaps as rapidly as that of any Third World nation. Its presence is striking in the affluent neighborhoods of cities like Bombay and Delhi and proclaimed by the Indian film industry, the world's largest, in innumerable sitcoms and dramas about the woes in the lives of yuppies, Indian-style. But as high as 60 percent of India's people have gained little or nothing from the development schemes and economic growth that have occurred since independence.

In part, this has been because population growth has wiped out economic gains. But social reform has been slow in most areas, both rural and urban. Groups like the wealthy landlords, who supported the nationalist drive for independence, have continued to dominate the great mass of tenants and landless laborers, just as they did in the precolonial and colonial eras. Some development measures, most notably those associated with the Green Revolution, have greatly favored those cultivators with the resources to invest in new seeds and fertilizer. They have increased the gap between well-off and poor people over much of rural India. India's literacy rate remains well below that of China (the only rival with which it can be reasonably compared given the size of each and the magnitude of the problems they face), and a far larger proportion of India's population remains malnourished. Thus, the poor have paid and will continue to pay the price for Indian gradualism, and those favoring more revolutionary solutions to India's social inequities and mass poverty have plenty of ammunition with which to attack the ruling parties.

DOCUMENT
CULTURAL CREATIVITY IN THE THIRD WORLD: SOME LITERARY SAMPLES

Despite, or perhaps because of, political instability and chronic economic difficulties, Third World societies have generated a high level of artistic creativity over the past decades. Nowhere has this creativity been more prominent and brilliant than in literary productivity, for which Third World writers have earned Nobel Prizes and deservedly won a wide readership far beyond their own nations. The selections that follow provide only a small sample of the vast and varied talent Third World writers have displayed, from poetry and drama to novels and short stories.

Much of the literature of Third World writers focuses on the predicament of the Western-educated African and Asian elites who dominate the new nations that emerged from the European colonial empires. In the following stanza from the poem "I Run Around with Them," the Indonesian poet, Chairil Anwar, reflects on the lack of purpose and malaise he believed to be widespread among the children of these elite groups.

> I run around with them, what else can I do, now—
> Changing my face at the edge of the street, I use
>   their eyes
> And tag along to visit the fun house:
> These are the facts as I know them
> (A new American flic at the Capitol,
> The new songs they dance to).
> We go home: there's nothing doing
> Though this kind of Death is our neighbor, our
>   friend, now.
> Hanging around at the corner, we wait for the city
>   bus
> That glows night to day like a gold tooth;
> Lame, deformed, negative, we
> Lean our bony asses against lamp poles
> And jaw away the years.

In the next quotation from the novel *No Longer at Ease*, the widely read Nigerian author, Chinua Achebe, identifies another dilemma, the pull between Western culture and the ancient civilization of one's own land.

Nothing gave him greater pleasure than to find another Ibo-speaking student in a London bus. But when he had to speak in English with a Nigerian student from another tribe he lowered his voice. It was humiliating to have to speak to one's countryman in a foreign language, especially in the presence of the proud owners of that language. They would naturally assume that one had no language of one's own. He wished they were here today to see. Let them come to Umuofia [the protagonist's home village] now and listen to the talk of men who made a great art of conversation. Let them come and see men and women and children who knew how to live, whose joy of life had not yet been killed by those who claimed to teach other nations how to live.

Like a number of the more famous Third World novelists, V. S. Naipaul is an expatriot who was born in the Caribbean and now lives in rural England. In his moving account of his return to his Indian ancestral home, entitled *An Area of Darkness*, Naipaul confronts the problem of massive poverty and the responses of foreigners and the Indian elite to it.

. . . to see [India's] poverty is to make an observation of no value; a thousand newcomers to the country before you have seen and said as you. And not only newcomers. Our own sons and daughters, when they return from Europe and America, have spoken in your very words. Do not think that your anger and contempt are marks of your sensitivity. You might have seen more: the smiles on the faces of the begging children, that domestic group among the pavement sleepers waking in the cool Bombay morning, father, mother and baby in a trinity of love, so self-contained that they are as private as if walls had separated them from you; it is your gaze that violates them, your sense of outrage that outrages them. . . . It is your surprise, your anger that denies [them] humanity.

Questions: Can you think of parallels in American history or contemporary society for the situations and responses conveyed in these passages from recent African and Asian writings? Do they suggest that it is possible to communicate even intimate feelings across cultures or do you find them alien, different?

IRAN: RELIGIOUS REVIVALISM AND THE REJECTION OF THE WEST

No path of development adopted by a Third World society has provided more fundamental challenges to the existing world order than revolutionary Iran under the direction of Ayatollah Khomaini. In many respects, the Khomaini revolution of 1979 represents a throwback to the religious fervor of such anticolonial resistance movements as that led by the Mahdi of the Sudan in the 1880s. The emphasis on religious purification and the rejoining of religion and politics that leaders such as the Mahdi and Khomaini have seen as central to the Islamic tradition provided the core motivations for the followers of both movements. The call for a return to the kind of society believed to have existed in the past "golden age" of the prophet Muhammad was central to the policies pursued by both the Mahdist and Iranian regimes once they had gained power. Both movements were aimed at Western-backed governments: the Mahdist at the Anglo-Egyptian presence in the Sudan, and Khomaini's against the autocratic Iranian shah and the Pahlavi dynasty, which were pictured as advocates of secularization and unchecked Westernization as well as puppets of America.

Though from the Sunni and Shi'ite religious traditions respectively, both the Mahdi and Khomaini claimed to be divinely inspired deliverers who would rescue the Islamic faithful from imperialist Westerners and corrupt and heretical leaders within the Muslim world. Both leaders promised their followers magical protection and instant paradise should they fall waging the holy war against the heretics and infidels. Each movement sought to build a lasting state and social order on the basis of what were believed to be Islamic precedents. Thus, each movement aimed at the defense and restoration of what its leaders believed to be the true beliefs, traditions, and institutions of Islamic civilization. The leaders of both movements sought to spread their revolutions to surrounding areas, both Muslim and infidel, and each believed he was setting in motion forces that would eventually sweep the entire globe.

Though proclaimed as an alternate path for development that can be followed by the rest of the Third World, Khomaini's revolution owed its initial success in seizing power to a number of circumstances that were more or less unique to Iran. Like China, Iran had not been formally colonized by the European powers, but rather reduced to a sphere of informal influence, divided between Great Britain and Russia. As a result, neither the bureaucratic nor the communications infrastructures that accompanied colonial takeovers were highly developed there. Nor did a substantial Western-educated middle class emerge. Thus, the impetus for "modernization" came suddenly and was imposed from above by the Pahlavi shahs. The initiatives taken by the second shah in particular, which were supported by Iran's considerable oil wealth, wrenched Iran out of the isolation and backwardness in which most of the nation lived until the mid-20th century. The shah sought to impose economic development and social change by government directives. Though advances occurred, the regime managed to alienate the great mass of the Iranian people in the process.

The shah's dictatorial and repressive regime deeply offended the emerging middle class, whom he considered his strongest potential supporters. His flaunting of Islamic conventions and neglect of Islamic worship and religious institutions enraged the ayatollahs, or religious experts, and mullahs, or local prayer leaders and mosque attendants, who guided the religious and personal lives of the great majority of the Iranian population. The favoritism he showed foreign investors and a handful of big Iranian entrepreneurs, who had personal connections to highly placed officials, angered the smaller bazaar merchants, who had long maintained close links with the mullahs and other religious leaders. The shah's halfhearted land reform schemes alienated the landowning classes without really doing much to improve the condition of the rural poor. Even the urban workers, who benefited most from the boom in construction and light industrialization the shah's development efforts had stimulated, were disaffected in the years before the 1979 revolution by a fall in oil prices that had led to an economic slump and widespread unemployment.

Though he had treated his officers well, the shah had badly neglected the military rank-and-file, especially in the army. So when the crisis came in 1978, the shah found that few of his countrymen were prepared to defend his regime. His armies refused to fire on the growing crowds that demonstrated for his removal and the return of Khomaini, then in exile in Paris. Dying of cancer and disheartened by what he viewed as betrayal by his people and allies such as the United States, the shah fled without much of a fight. Khomaini's revolution triumphed over a regime that looked powerful, but in fact proved to be exceptionally vulnerable.

After coming to power, Khomaini, defying the predictions of most Western "experts" on Iranian affairs, followed through on his promises of radical change. Constitutional and leftist parties allied to the revolutionary movement were brutally repressed. Moderate leaders were quickly replaced by radical religious figures, eager to obey Khomaini's every command. The "satanic" influences of the United States and Western Europe were purged; at the same time Iran also distanced itself from the atheistic communist world. Secular influences in law and government were supplanted by strict Islamic legal codes, which included such punishments as the amputation of limbs for theft and stoning for women caught in adultery, and rule by the mullahs and ayatollahs. Veiling became obligatory for all females, and the career prospects for women of the educated middle classes, who had been among the most favored by the shah's reforms, were suddenly greatly constricted.

Khomaini's planners also drew up grand schemes for land reform, religious education, and economic development that accorded with the dictates of Islam. Most of these measures came to little because soon after the revolution, Saddam Hussein, the military leader of neighboring Iraq, sought to take advantage of the turmoil in Iran by annexing its western, oil-rich provinces. The war that resulted has swallowed up Iranian energies and resources for virtually the entire decade since Khomaini came to power. Though clearly initially the fault of the invading Iraqis, the struggle became a highly personal vendetta for Khomaini, who was determined to destroy Hussein and punish the Iraqis. His refusal to negotiate peace caused heavy losses and untold suffering to the Iranian people. This suffering continued long after it was clear that the Iranians'

Women played a vital role in the mass demonstrations that toppled the shah and brought Ayatollah Khomaini to power. The fundamentalist version of Islam pursued by Khomaini and his allies, expressed, for example, by the return to veiling for women shown here, divided many of the highly Westernized women of the new Iranian middle classes from those of the urban working and merchant classes as well as the peasant class.

aging military equipment and handful of allies were no match for Hussein's more advanced military hardware and an Iraqi war machine bankrolled by its oil-rich Arab neighbors, who were fearful that Khomaini's revolution might spread to their own countries.

As the support of the Western powers, including the United States (despite protestations of neutrality), for the Iraqis increased, the position of the isolated Iranians became increasingly intolerable. Hundreds of thousands of poorly armed and half-trained Iranian conscripts, including tens of thousands of untrained and virtually weaponless boys, died before Khomaini finally agreed to a humiliating armistice in 1988. Peace found revolutionary Iran in shambles: Few of its development initiatives had been pursued, and shortages in food, fuel, and the other necessities of life were widespread.

Iran's decade-long absorption in the war makes it impossible to assess the potential of the religious revivalist, anti-Western option for Third World nations. What had seemed at first to be a viable path to genuinely independent development for African and Asian peoples has become mired in brutal internal repression and littered with the wreckage of a losing war.

SOUTH AFRICA: DEFENDING AND CHALLENGING THE GARRISON STATE

South Africa was by no means the only area still under some form of colonial dominance decades after India became the first of the former European colonies to gain its independence in 1947. Portugal, the oldest and long considered the weakest of the European colonizers, held onto Angola, Mozambique, and its other African possessions until the mid-1970s. Zimbabwe (formerly Southern Rhodesia) was run by white settlers, who had unilaterally declared their independence from Great Britain, until 1980. Southwest Africa only became fully free of South African control in 1989, and some of the smaller islands in the West Indies and the Pacific remain under European or American rule to the present day.

By the 1970s, however, South Africa was by far the largest, most populous, richest, and most strategic area where the great majority of the population had yet to be liberated from colonial domination. Since the 1940s, the white settlers, particularly the Dutch-descended Afrikaners, have solidified their internal control of the country under the leadership of the Nationalist party. In stages and through a series of elections in which the blacks, who made up the great majority of South Africans, were not allowed to vote, the Nationalists won complete independence from Great Britain in 1960. From 1948, when the Nationalist party first came to power, the Afrikaners moved to institutionalize white supremacy and white minority rule by the passage of thousands of laws that, taken together, made up the system of apartheid that dominates all aspects of South African life today.

The system of apartheid was designed not only to ensure a monopoly of political power and economic dominance for the white minority, both British and Dutch descended, but also to impose a system of extreme segregation on all races of South Africa, in all aspects of their lives. Separate and patently unequal facilities were established for different racial groups for recreation, education, housing, work, and medical care. Dating or sexual intercourse across racial lines was strictly prohibited; skilled and high-paying jobs were reserved for white workers; and nonwhites were required to carry passes that listed the parts of South Africa where they were allowed to work and reside. If caught by the police without their passes or in areas where they were not permitted to travel, nonwhite South Africans were routinely given stiff jail sentences.

Spacial separation was also organized on a grander scale by the creation of numerous homelands within South Africa, each designated for the main ethno-linguistic or "tribal" groups within the black African population. Though touted by the Afrikaners as the ultimate solution to the racial "problem," the homelands scheme would leave the black African majority with a small percent of some of the poorest land in South Africa. Because the homelands are overpopulated and poverty stricken, the white minority is guaranteed a ready supply of cheap black labor to work in their factories and mines and on their farms. Denied citizenship in South Africa proper, these laborers are

The blatant segregation of public facilities was a key feature of the apartheid regime in South Africa. The police stood ready to enforce the multitude of laws that confined the blacks to designated areas and a very limited range of low-paying occupational roles.

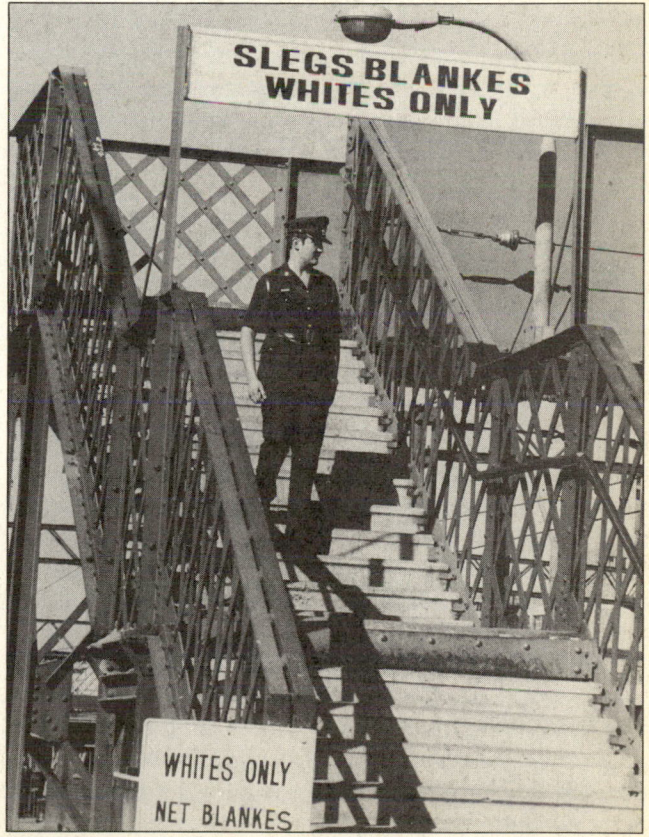

forced eventually to return to the homelands, because they have left their wives and children there while emigrating in search of work.

To maintain the blatantly racist and inequitable system of apartheid, the white minority has had to build a police state and expend a large portion of the federal budget on a sophisticated and well-trained military establishment. Because of the land's great mineral wealth, the Afrikaner nationalists have thus far been able to find the resources to fund their garrison state. Until the late 1980s, the government prohibited all forms of black protest and brutally repressed even nonviolent resistance. Black organizations, such as the African National Congress, were declared illegal, and African leaders, such as Walter Sisulu and Nelson Mandela, were shipped off to maximum-security prisons. Other leaders, such as Steve Biko, one of the young organizers of the Black Consciousness movement, died under very suspicious circumstances while in police custody.

Through spies and police informers, the regime sought to capitalize on personal and ethnic divisions within the black majority community. Favoritism was shown to some leaders and groups to keep them from uniting with others in all-out opposition to apartheid. With all avenues of constitutional negotiation and peaceful protest closed, many advocates of black majority rule in a multiracial society have turned to guerrilla resistance in recent decades. The South African government responded in the 1980s with a state of emergency, which simply intensified the restrictions already in place in the garrison state. The government has repeatedly justified its draconian repression by labeling virtually all black protest as communist inspired and playing on the racial fears of the white minority.

Through most of the 1970s and early 1980s, it appeared that the hardening hostility between the unyielding white minority and the frustrated black majority was building to a major and very violent upheaval. This may still prove the end result of apartheid and the Afrikaners' garrison state. In recent years, however, there have been signs that some Afrikaner leaders are beginning to realize that these solutions are dead ends. Reforms give some hope that apartheid can be dismantled. The release of key black political prisoners, such as the dramatic freeing of Nelson Mandela in 1990, and permission for peaceful mass demonstrations are signs that those in power, most notably the Afrikaner-descended president de Klerk, may finally be willing to listen to and negotiate a settlement with black leaders.

Black African leaders are understandably wary after so many years of oppression and repression, but so far most have been willing to wait and explore peaceful ways to put pressure on the regime. The differences between the two sides remain colossal, and more radical and violence-prone alternatives threaten both those in power and the more moderate leaders of the black majority. Bitter interethnic rivalries within the black majority community, which flared into bloody battles between Zulus and Xhosas in the summer of 1990, also threaten to be a major obstacle to a peaceful settlement. It is still possible for the stalemate to intensify and massive civil war to erupt. Yet for the first time since the white majority won their independence in the 1940s and 1950s, there are signs that the internal colonization that has continued for the great majority of the peoples of South Africa under apartheid may be breaking down. Its demise may well pave the way to the peaceful creation of a truly free, multiracial society in South Africa.

CONCLUSION

THE THIRD WORLD EXPERIENCE IN HISTORICAL PERSPECTIVE

Although the years of independence for the nations that have emerged from the colonial empires have been filled with political and economic crises and social turmoil, it is important to put recent Third World history in a larger perspective. Most of these new nations have been in existence only a few decades, and they came to independence with severe handicaps, many of which were a direct legacy of their colonial experiences. Some observers have been tempted to question whether Africans and Asians are able to govern themselves, given the widespread occurrence of communal violence, civil strife, and military takeovers in the new states. But if we consider that the far smaller, much better resource endowed, and relatively homogenous population that made up the young American republic in the late 18th century was so deeply divided for nearly 100 years that only a massive civil war could salvage the union in the 1860s, the political tensions in Third World nations do not seem so exceptional. If one takes into account the artificial nature of these states, most have held together rather well. This is especially striking if they are compared to European nations, such as Yugoslavia, still shaken periodically by regional and religious clashes, despite the fact that the peoples who make them up have a lot more in common historically and culturally than the populations of most Third World countries.

India's success is particularly striking here. In size—both population and ethnic—as well as in linguistic and religious diversity, India is a continent comparable to Western Europe. Yet, few see Europe's long centuries of national rivalries, quarrels, and wars as a sign that the Europeans are incapable of governing themselves. India's continuing unity contrasts sharply with Europe's disunity, but India's very considerable political achievements are passed over in favor of sensationalist accounts of religious and regional strife in the subcontinent.

What is true in politics is true of all other aspects of the Third World experience. With much lower populations and far fewer or no industrial competitors, as well as drawing on the resources of much of the rest of the world, European and North American nations had to struggle to industrialize and thereby achieve a reasonable standard of living for most of their people. Even with their advantages, the human cost in terms of horrific working conditions and urban squalor was enormous, and we are still paying the high ecological price. Third World countries (and, as you saw in Chapter 33, Japan) have had few or none of the West's advantages. They have begun the "great ascent" to development burdened by excessive and rapidly increasing populations that overwhelm their limited resources, which must be exported to earn the capital to buy food and machines. They struggle to establish a place in the world market system that is heavily loaded in favor of the established industrial powers in terms of pricing and investment. Their efforts to build modest industrial sectors are frustrated by competition from the many nations that have industrialized ahead of them.

Despite the cultural dominance of the West, which was one of the great legacies or burdens of the colonial era, Third World thinkers and artists have achieved a great deal. If much of this—such as African and Asian political organizations and economic planning—has been dependent on Western models, one should not be surprised given the educational backgrounds and personal experiences of the first generations of African and Asian leaders.

The challenge for the coming generations will be to find genuinely Third World solutions to the problems that have stunted political and economic development and to the dependence on the West that once had checked intellectual originality. If the promise Iran once seemed to offer in this respect has faded after a decade of brutal internal repression, economic retreat, and war, the conviction among Third World leaders and thinkers that other options must emerge is growing. The solutions reached are likely to vary a great deal, given the diversity of the nations and societies of the Third World. They are also more likely to be forged from a combination of Western and indigenous influences than from the Iranian Revolution, whose leaders have been so determined to ban and destroy all Western influences, even those that might be critical to building viable and prosperous nations. They are also likely to draw heavily on the ancient and distinguished traditions of civilized life that have been nurtured by African and Asian peoples for millennia.

FURTHER READINGS

Much of the very large literature on political and economic development in the Third World is focused on individual nations, and it is more helpful to know several cases in some depth rather than try to master them all. Robert Heilbroner's writings, starting with his *The Great Ascent* (1961), still provide the most sensible introduction to challenges to the new states in the early decades of independence. Peter Worsley's *The Third World* (1964) provides a provocative, if somewhat disjointed, supplement to Heilbroner's many works. Though focused mainly on South and Southeast Asia, Gunnar Myrdal's *Asian Drama*, 3 vols. (1968), is the best exploration in a single cultural area of the complexities of the challenges to development. A good overview of developments in India can be found in W. N. Brown's *The United States and India, Pakistan, and Bangladesh* (1984 ed.), despite its misleadingly Western-centric title. Michael Brecher's *Nehru: A Political Biography* (1969) is a very readable account of Indian history in the Nehru years after independence. Ali Mazrui and Michael Tidy's *Nationalism and New States in Africa* (1984) gives a good overview of developments throughout Africa. Also useful are S. A. Akintoye's *Emergent African States* (1976) and H. Bretton's *Power and Politics in Africa* (1973). For the Middle East, John Waterbury's *The Egypt of Nasser and Sadat* (1983) provides a detailed account of the politics of development, and Peter Mansfield's *The Arabs* (1978) supplies a decent (if now a bit dated) overview.

On military coups, see Ruth First's *The Barrel of a Gun* (1971) and S. Decalo's *Coups and Army Rule in Africa* (1976). Shaul Bakash's *The Reign of the Ayatollahs* (1984) is perhaps the most insightful of several books that have appeared on Iran since the revolution. Brian Bunting's *The Rise of the South African Reich* (1964) traces the rise of the apartheid regime in great (and polemical) detail, while Gail Gerhart's *Black Power in South Africa* (1978) is one of the better studies devoted to efforts to tear that system down. Among the many fine Third World authors whose works are available in English, some of the best include (for Africa) Chinua Achebe, Wole Soyinka, and Ousmane Sembene; (for India) A. K. Narayan and V. K. Naipaul; (for Egypt) Nawal el Saadawi and Neguib Mahfouz; and (for Indonesia) Mochtar Lubis and P. A. Toer. For white perspectives on the South African situation, the works of Nadine Gordimer and J. M. Coetzee are superb.

1770s Tayson rebellion in Vietnam

1912 Fall of the Qing
dynasty in China

1929 Failed VNQDD-inspired uprising

1925 VNQDD founded in Vietnam; first Communist organization established in Vietnam

1931 Japanese invasion of Manchuria

1858–1862 Beginning of the
French conquest of Vietnam

1921 Communist party
of China founded

1883 French conquest of
Vietnam is completed

1930 Failed Communist
uprising in Vietnam

1919 May Fourth Move-
ment begins; founding of
Guomindang or Nation-
alist party

1911 Revolution
in China

1802 Establishment of the
Nguyen dynasty; Vietnam unified

1927 Nationalists capture
Shanghai; purge of Com-
munists and workers

1937 Japanese inva-
sion of China proper

41

War and Revolution in China and Vietnam

INTRODUCTION. In many respects the recent histories of China and the peoples of Japan, Korea, and Vietnam whose cultures were so profoundly affected by Chinese civilization have been fundamentally different from that of much of the rest of the Third World. Particularly in the past century, the experience of the Japanese has diverged the most from those of other African and Asian peoples (see Chapters 33 and 37). The ethnically homogenous, politically unified, and militarily adept Japanese were not only able to beat off Western imperialist advances against their island home; they have been one of the few non-Western peoples to achieve a high level of industrialization. Within decades of the forced "opening" of Japan by the United States in the 1850s, Japan also became the only African or Asian nation to join the ranks of the great powers, and in imitation of Western rivals, it embarked on its own campaign of imperialist expansion overseas. Though Korea was colonized early in the 20th century by its powerful Japanese neighbor, in the decades since the Second World War it has emerged as one of the new industrial centers on the Pacific Rim (see Chapter 37).

In contrast to industrialized Japan and to Korea in the past two decades or so, with their relatively high standards of living and global economic power, the recent histories of China and Vietnam have had much in common with the rest of the Third World. Both China and Vietnam suffered heavily from the assaults and exploitative terms of exchange imposed by imperialist powers, both Western and Japanese. Each has had to contend with underdevelopment, overpopulation, poverty, and environmental degradation. Moreover, in contrast to most of the rest of the Third World,

1950–1953 Korean War   **1958–1960** "Great Leap Forward" in China   **1975** Communist victory in Vietnam; collapse of the Republic of South Vietnam

1942 Japanese occupation of French Indochina

mid-1950s Build-up of U.S. advisors in South Vietnam

1957 "Let a Thousand Flowers Bloom" campaign in China

1950–1951 Purge of the landlord class in China

1949 Victory of the Communists in China; People's Republic of China established

1965–1968 Era of the Cultural Revolution in China

1963 Beginning of state family planning in China

1953 Beginning of China's first Five-Year Plan

1954 French defeated at Dien Bien Phu; Geneva accords, French withdrawal from Vietnam; beginning of the Sino-Soviet split

1965–1973 Direct U.S. military intervention in Vietnam

1945 Ho Chi Minh proclaims the Republic of Vietnam

1968 Tet offensive in Vietnam

1976 Death of Zhou Enlai and Mao Zedong; purge of the Gang of Four

China and Vietnam have had to deal with these awesome challenges in the midst of the utter collapse of the patterns of civilized life each had followed for thousands of years.

However disruptive imperialist conquest and its effects proved in the rest of the African-Asian world, most colonized peoples managed to preserve much of their precolonial cultures and modes of social organization. The defense and revival of traditional customs, religious beliefs, and social arrangements played a key role in the struggle for decolonization. This was not the case in China and Vietnam, where a combination of external aggression and internal upheavals discredited and destroyed the Confucian system that had long been synonymous with the preservation of civilized life.

With their traditional order in shambles, the peoples of China and Vietnam had no choice but to embark on full-scale revolutions that would clear away the rubble of the failed Confucian system, remove the obstacles posed by imperialist dominance, and provide the means to build new and viable states and societies. In contrast to much of the rest of the colonized world, the countries of China and Vietnam derived few benefits from European domination, either informal or formal. Imperialist pressures eroded and smashed their political institutions, rather than building up a bureaucratic grid and imparting political ideologies that could form the basis for nation building.

For differing reasons, neither China nor Vietnam developed a large middle class, though each had wealthy commercial groups. In each society, the weakness of the bourgeoisie, coupled with the establishment of highly repressive regimes in the region in the late 19th and early 20th centuries, greatly constricted constitutionalist and nonviolent political options. The magnitude of the disruption and hardships the Chinese and Vietnamese peoples endured in this period also discredited gradualism and reformist democracy in the eyes of many emerging intellectuals and political leaders. Young students, such as Mao Zedong (Tsetung) and Nguyen Ai Quoc (alias Ho Chi Minh), became convinced that the salvation of their peoples and the restoration of civilized life in their lands could be won only through armed revolution and radical social transformations.

The distinctive forces that made for revolutionary upheavals in China and Vietnam will be examined in this chapter. Special attention will be given to why revolutionary rather than gradualist, reformist alternatives emerged victorious in each case. In the case of China, which has had a great impact on much of the Third World, we will also explore the history of the period after the revolutionaries took power. In considering these patterns, emphasis will be placed on key themes in the history of Chinese civilization and that of its Vietnamese neighbor over the past century, including the changing position of women; the impact of invasion, civil war, and natural calamities; and the struggle to develop new forms of intellectual and cultural expression. Perhaps more than any other part of the modern world, China and Vietnam provide us with the opportunity to study why civilizations break down and how new civilizations are fashioned from the ruins of the old. An awareness of their experience is crucial to an understanding of present changes and the future course of civilized development in the world as a whole.

THE STRUGGLE FOR CHINA

The abdication of Puyi, the Manchu boy-emperor in 1912, marked the end of a century-long losing struggle on the part of the Qing dynasty to protect Chinese civilization from foreign invaders and revolutionary threats from within like the massive Taiping movement (see Chapter 32). The fall of the Qing opened the way for an extended struggle over which a leader or movement would be able to capture the mandate to rule the ancient society that had for millennia ordered the lives of one-fourth of the population of humankind. The loose alliance of students, middle-class politicians, secret societies, and regional military commanders that overthrew the Manchus quickly splintered into a number of hostile contenders for the right to rule China.

The best positioned of the contenders for power were the military commanders, or warlords, who would play a leading role in Chinese politics for the next three decades. Many of the warlords combined in cliques or alliances, both to protect their own territories and to crush neighbors and annex their lands. The most powerful of these cliques was centered in north China, and headed by the unscrupulous Yuan Shikai, who hoped to seize the vacated Manchu throne and found a new dynasty. By virtue of their wealth, the merchants and bankers of coastal cities like Shanghai and Canton made up a second power center in post-Manchu China. As had been the case in the late-Confucian era, their involvement in politics resulted from their eagerness to bankroll both favored warlords and Western-educated, middle-class politicians like Sun Yat-sen.

Sometimes supportive of the urban civilian politicians, sometimes wary of them, university students and their teachers, as well as independent intellectuals, provided yet another factor in the complex political equation. Though the intellectuals and students played critical roles in shaping new ideologies to rebuild Chinese civilization, they were virtually defenseless in a situation in which force was essential to those who hoped to exert political influence. Deeply

China in the Era of Revolution and Civil War

divided, but very strong in some regions, the secret societies represented another contender for power. Like the military, they envisioned the restoration of monarchical rule, but under a Chinese not a foreign dynasty like that of the Manchus. As if the situation were not already confused enough, it was further complicated by the continuing intervention of the Western powers anxious to profit from China's divisions and weakness. Their inroads, however, were increasingly overshadowed by entry into the contest for the control of China by the newest imperialist power, Japan. From the mid-1890s, when the Japanese had humiliated their much larger neighbor by easily defeating them in war, until 1945, when Japan's surrender ended World War II, the Japanese were a major factor in the long and bloody contest for mastery of China.

THE MAY FOURTH MOVEMENT AND THE FAILURE OF LIBERALISM

Sun Yat-sen, who headed the Revolutionary Alliance, a loose coalition of anti-Qing political groups that had spearheaded the 1911 revolt, claimed that he and the parties of the alliance were rightful successors to the fallen Manchus. But he could do little to assert civilian control in the face of warlord opposition. The Revolutionary Alliance had little power and virtually no popular support outside the urban trading centers of the coastal areas in central and south China. Even in these areas they were at the mercy of the local warlords. The alliance formally elected Sun president at the end of 1911, set up a parliament modeled after those in Europe, and chose cabinets with great fanfare, but their decisions had little effect on warlord-dominated China.

Sun Yat-sen conceded this reality when he resigned the acting presidency in favor of the northern warlord Yuan Shikai in 1912. As the most powerful of the northern clique of generals, Yuan appeared to have the best chance to unify China under a single government. He at first feigned sympathy for the democratic aims of the alliance leaders, but soon revealed his true intentions. He took foreign loans to build up his military forces and buy out most of the bureaucracy in the capital at Beijing. When Sun and other leaders of the Revolutionary Alliance called for a second revolution to oust Yuan in the years after 1912, he made full use of his military power and more underhanded methods, such as assassinations, to put down their opposition. By 1915, it appeared that Yuan was well on his way to realizing his ambition of becoming China's next emperor. His schemes were foiled, however, by the continuing rivalry of other warlords, republican nationalists like Sun, and the growing influence of Japan in China, which increased dramatically as a result of the First World War.

As England's ally according to terms of a 1902 treaty, Japan immediately entered the war on the side of the Entente powers. Moving much too quickly for the comfort of the British and the other Western powers, the Japanese seized German-held islands in the Pacific and occupied the Germans' concessionary areas in China. With all the great powers except the Americans embroiled in war, the Japanese seized the chance to establish a dominant hold over their giant neighbor. In early 1915 they presented Yuan's government with Twenty-One Demands, which, if accepted, would have reduced China to the status of a dependent protectorate. Though Sun and the Revolutionary Alliance lost much support by refusing to repudiate the Japanese demands, Yuan was no more decisive. He neither accepted nor rejected the demands, but concentrated his energies on an effort to trump up popular enthusiasm for his accession to the throne. Disgusted by Yuan's weakness and ambition, one of his warlord rivals plotted his overthrow. Hostility to the Japanese won Yuan's rival widespread support, and in 1916 Yuan was forced to retreat and then resign the presidency. His fall was the signal for a free-for-all power struggle between the remaining warlords for control of China.

As one of the victorious Allies, Japan managed to solidify its hold on northern China by winning control of the former German concessions in the Versailles Treaty of 1919, which ended the war. However, the Chinese had also allied themselves to the Entente powers during the war. Enraged by what they viewed as a betrayal by the Allied powers, students and nationalist politicians organized mass demonstrations in numerous Chinese cities on May 4, 1919. The demonstrations began a prolonged period of protest against Japanese inroads, which included strikes and mass boycotts of Japanese goods. May 4, the day when the resistance began, gave its name to a movement in which intellectuals and students played a leading role. Initially at least, the May Fourth movement was aimed at transforming China into a liberal democracy. Its program was enunciated in numerous speeches, pamphlets, novels, and newspaper articles. Confucianism was ridiculed and rejected in favor of a wholehearted acceptance of all that the Western democracies had to offer. Noted Western thinkers, such as Bertrand Russell and John Dewey, toured China, extolling the merits of science, industrial technology, and democratic government and basking in the cheers of their packed Chinese audiences. Chinese thinkers called for the liberation of women, the simplification of the Chinese script in order to promote mass literacy, and the promotion of Western-style individualism. Many of these themes are

Spearheaded by students and intellectuals in China's urban areas, the May Fourth demonstrations in 1919 proclaimed the end of nearly 2000 years of Confucian dominance in China and the opening of the country to ideologies from the West, both democratic and Marxist.

captured in the literature of the period. In the novel *Family* by Ba Jin, for example, a younger brother audaciously informs his elder sibling that he will not accept the marriage partner the family has arranged for him. He clearly sees his refusal as part of a more general revolt of the youth of China against the ancient Confucian social code.

> Big Brother, I'm doing what no one in our family has ever dared do before—I'm running out on an arranged marriage. No one cares about my fate, so I've decided to walk my own road alone. I'm determined to struggle against the old forces to the end. Unless you cancel the match, I'll never come back. I'll die first. . . .

However enthusiastically the program of the May Fourth movement was adopted by the urban youth of China, it was soon clear that mere emulation of the liberal democracies of the West could not provide effective solutions to China's prodigious problems. Civil liberties and democratic elections were meaningless in a China that was ruled by warlords; gradualist solutions were folly in a nation where the great mass of the peasantry was destitute, much of it malnourished or dying of starvation. Even if fair elections could be held and a Western-style parliament installed as China's effective rulers, China's crisis had become so severe that there was little time for legislators to squabble and debate. The ministers of an elected government with little military clout would hardly have been able to implement well-meaning programs for land redistribution and subsidies for the poor in the face of deeply entrenched regional opposition from the landlords and the military. It soon became clear to many Chinese intellectuals and students, as well as to some of the nationalist politicians, that more radical solutions were needed. In the 1920s this conviction gave rise to the Communist left within the Chinese nationalist movement.

THE RISE OF THE COMMUNIST ALTERNATIVE

The example of the Russian Revolution, not careful readings of the writings of Karl Marx and Fredrich Engels, made a number of Chinese thinkers aware of possible Marxist solutions to China's ills. In fact, before the Russian upheavals of 1917 and Lenin's launching of a state-directed drive for the social and economic transformation of backward Russia, the few Chinese who knew about Marx or even less radical socialist theorists felt they had little to offer impoverished, agrarian societies like China. Marx, after all, had foreseen socialist revolutions occurring in the more advanced industrial societies with well-

developed working classes and a strong proletarian consciousness. He had thought that there would be little chance for revolution in Russia. In China, with its overwhelmingly rural, peasant population (and Marx viewed the peasantry as a reactionary or at best a conservative, petty bourgeois social element), the prospects for revolution looked even more dismal. But the October revolution in Russia that brought Lenin and the Bolsheviks to power changed all of this. For the first time, a Marxist regime governed, and it had come to power in backward, largely peasant Russia, not in western Europe or North America.

The Bolshevik victory and the programs launched to rebuild Russia prompted Chinese intellectuals, such as Li Dazhao, to give serious attention to the works of Marx, Engels, Trotsky, and Lenin and the potential they offered for the regeneration of China. A number of societies devoted to the study of Marxism developed just after the May Fourth movement around thinkers like Li, who headed the study circle at the University of Beijing. Li's borrowings from European communist thinkers placed heavy emphasis on Marxism's capacity for renewal and its ability to harness the energy and vitality of a nation's youth. In contrast to Lenin, Li saw the peasants rather than the urban workers as the vanguard of the revolution. He justified this shift from the orthodox Marxist emphasis on the working classes, which made up only a tiny fraction of China's population at the time, by characterizing Chinese society as a whole as proletarian. All of China, he argued, had been exploited by the bourgeois, industrialized West. Thus, the oppressed Chinese as a whole needed to unite and rise up against their exploiters.

Li's version of Marxism, with alterations or emphasis on elements that made it suitable for China, had great appeal for the students, including the young Mao Zedong, who joined his study circle. They too were angered by what they perceived as China's betrayal by the imperialist great powers. They shared Li's hostility (very much a throwback to the attitudes of the Confucian era) to merchants and commerce, which appeared to dominate the West. They too longed for a return to a political system, like the Confucian, where those who governed were deeply committed to social reform and social welfare, and an authoritarian state was expected to intervene in all aspects of the peoples' lives.

The societies that developed around Li Dazhao and other Marxist intellectuals soon spawned a number of more broadly based, politically activist organizations. The Marxists' capture of prominent periodicals, such as *New Youth* magazine, did much to spread the ideas of Marx and Lenin among the politically active youth of China's coastal cities. With support from Sun Yat-sen, Marxist intellectu-

Though he received no formal military training, Mao Zedong's adoption of a soldier's uniform reflected the importance of force in the highly militarized and deeply divided society that China had become by the early 20th century.

als established the Socialist Youth Corps in 1920, which was dedicated to recruiting the urban working classes. Students like Mao returned to their provincial bases to win supporters for the leftist cause and foment resistance to the oppressive rule of the local warlords.

In the summer of 1921, in an attempt to unify the growing Marxist wing of the nationalist struggle, a handful of leaders from different parts of China met in secret in the city of Shanghai. At this meeting, closely watched by the agents of the local warlord and rival political organizations, the Communist party of China was born. In Paris a year earlier, Zhou Enlai, who like Mao was later to become one of the main Communist leaders, and a number of other Chinese expatriot students had founded the Communist Youth Corps. In Paris and inside China itself,

the development of Communist organizations was supported by both the advisors and funds of the Comintern, the international arm of the Bolshevik or Communist party of the Soviet Union. Though minuscule in terms of the numbers of their supporters, and at this time fixed on a revolutionary program fatally oriented to the working classes, the Communists at least offered a clear alternative to fill the ideological and institutional void left by the collapse of the Confucian order.

THE SEIZURE OF POWER BY THE GUOMINDANG, OR NATIONALIST PARTY

In the years when the Communist movement in China was being put together by urban students and intellectuals, the Guomindang, or Nationalist party, which was to prove the Communists' great rival for the mandate to rule in China, was struggling to survive in the deep south. Sun Yat-sen, who was the acknowledged head of the nationalist struggle from the 1911 revolution until the time of his death in early 1925, had gone into exile in Japan in 1914, while warlords, such as Yuan Shikai, consolidated their regional power bases. After returning to China, Sun and his followers sought in 1919 to join the diverse political organizations struggling for political influence in China by reorganizing the revolutionary movement and naming it the Nationalist Party of China (the Guomindang).

The Nationalists began the slow process of forging alliances with key social groups and building an army of their own, which they now viewed as the only way to rid China of the warlord menace. Sun strove to enunciate a nationalist ideology that gave something to everyone. It stressed the need to unify China under a strong central government, bring the imperialist intruders under control, and enact social reforms that would alleviate peasant poverty and the oppressive working conditions of laborers in China's cities. Unfortunately for the great majority of the Chinese people, for whom social reforms were the main concern, the Nationalist leaders concentrated on political and international issues and neglected internal reforms.

In this early stage, Sun and the Nationalists built their power primarily on the support provided by urban businessmen and merchants in coastal cities such as Canton. Though it received little publicity, the Nationalist party also drew support from local warlords and the criminal underworld, especially the notorious Green Gang headquartered in Shanghai. After much and very time-consuming factional infighting, Sun had more or less secured control over the party, if not the warlords in the neighborhood of Canton. He forged an alliance with the Communists that was officially proclaimed at the first Nationalist party conference in 1924. For the time being at least, the Nationalist leaders were content to let the Communists serve as their major link to the peasants and the urban workers.

Disappointed in their early hopes of assistance from the Europeans and the United States, Nationalist leaders turned to Soviet Russia. Lenin and the Bolsheviks were eager to support a revolutionary movement in neighboring China. They not only sent advisors and gave material assistance, they encouraged the fledgling Communist party to join with the larger and richer Nationalists in a common struggle to seize power.

From 1924, when the Whampoa Military Academy was founded with Soviet help and partially staffed by Russian instructors, the Nationalists added a critical military dimension to their political maneuvering. The first head of the academy was an ambitious young military officer named Chiang Kai-shek. The son of a poor salt merchant, Chiang had fought his way up in the world through the military and by virtue of connections with powerful figures in the Shanghai underworld. He had received some military training in Japan and managed by the early 1920s to work his way into Sun Yat-sen's inner circle of advisors. Chiang was not happy with the Communist alliance but was willing to bide his time until he had the military strength to deal with both the Communists and the warlords, who remained the major obstacles to the Nationalist seizure of power.

Absorbed by all these political machinations, Sun and other Nationalist leaders had little time left for serious attention to the now severe deterioration of the Chinese economy and the huge population whose sufferings mounted as a result. Though urban laborers worked for pitiful wages and lived in appalling conditions, the social condition of the peasantry, which made up nearly 90 percent of China's population, was perhaps the most pressing issue facing China's aspiring national leaders. Patterns of landowning varied considerably in different parts of China. Over a century of corruption and weak Manchu rule, however, and then the Manchu collapse in 1911 and the depredations of the warlords had left the peasantry in many regions of China in misery. Big landlords and rich peasants rapaciously amassed great landholdings, which they rented out at exorbitant rates that left the tenants who worked them little to feed and clothe their families. In times of flood and drought when the crops failed, tenants, landless laborers, and even small landowners simply could not make ends meet. Tenants and smallholders were turned off their lands, and landless laborers could not find crops to harvest. Famine and disease stalked China's heavily populated provinces, while its ancient irrigation systems fell into disrepair. Corrupt warlords and bureaucrats, including those allied to the Nationalist party, colluded with the landlords to extract the maximum taxes and labor services from the peasantry.

As they had for millennia, dispossessed peasants took to banditry or vagabondage to survive. Many joined the hordes of beggars and unemployed in the towns; many more perished—swept away by floods, famine, disease, or the local warlord's armies. Children were sold into slavery by their parents, so that both might have a chance to survive. A growing number of cases of cannibalism were reported, which occurred after the bark and leaves had been stripped off all the trees to make the scarcely digestible "stew" that the peasants ate to put something in their bellies. Many peasants were too poor to perform the most basic of social duties, such as burying their deceased parents, whose bodies were often left to be devoured by vultures and packs of wild dogs. Given the great reverence for family and parents that had been instilled by Confucian teachings for millennia, the psychological scars left by the nonperformance of such critical obligations must have been deep and lasting.

Though rural China cried out for strong leadership and far-reaching economic and social reform, China's leaders bickered and plotted, but did little. Sun gave lip service to the Nationalist party's need to deal with the peasant problem. But his abysmal ignorance of rural conditions was revealed by statements in which he denied that China had large landlords and his refusal to believe that there were "serious difficulties" between the great mass of the peasantry and the landowners. Communists such as Mao Zedong were an exception to the general Nationalist pattern of ignorance and neglect. But the numbers of peasants the Communists could assist were limited by the small size of the party at that time and the obstacles thrown up by the landlords and warlords. Nonetheless, Mao and his fellow Communists persisted in their work of rural reconstruction in areas such as Hunan in south-central China.

Though the son of a fairly prosperous peasant, Mao had rebelled early in his life against his father's exploitation of the tenants and laborers who worked the family fields. Receiving little assistance from his estranged father, Mao was forced to make his own way and educate himself in the history, philosophy, and economic theory that most other nationalist and revolutionary leaders mastered in private schools. Having made his way to Beijing in the post–May Fourth era, Mao came under the influence of thinkers such as Li Dazhao, who placed considerable emphasis on solutions to the peasant problem as one of the keys to China's survival. As the following passage from Mao's early writings reveals, almost from the outset he was committed to revolutionary solutions that depended on peasant support.

A revolution is an insurrection, an act of violence by which one class overthrows another. A rural revolution is a revolution by which the peasantry overthrows the power of the feudal landlord class. Without using the greatest force, the peasants cannot possibly overthrow the deep-rooted authority of the landlords which has lasted for thousands of years.

Throughout most of the 1920s, however, Mao's vision of a rural revolution remained a minority and much repudiated position even with the Communist party. Rivals such as Li Lisan, who favored a more orthodox strategy based on the urban working classes who had formed the core of support for the Bolshevik revolutionaries in Russia, dominated party policy-making. Ironically, the move by Chiang and the Nationalist leaders to destroy all of the Communists in the late-1920s would pave the way for Mao's rise to leadership in the party.

The Nationalists' successful drive for national power began only after Sun Yat-sen's death in 1925 opened the way for their counterparts among the warlords, Chiang Kai-shek and his cronies, to seize control of the party. After winning over or eliminating the military chiefs in the Canton area, Chiang marched north with his newly created armies in a campaign that culminated in the Nationalists' seizure of the Yangtze River valley and Shanghai in early 1927. Later his forces also captured the capital at Beijing and the rest of the Yellow River basin. The refusal of most of the warlords to end their long-standing feuding meant that Chiang could defeat them or buy them out, one by one. By the late 1920s, he was the master of China—in name and international standing, if not in actual fact. He was, in effect, the head of a warlord hierarchy, but most political leaders within China and in the outside world recognized him as the new president of China.

Since there were no elections, the people had no say in the matter. Nor had Chiang's political rivals, whom he ruthlessly purged even while he was still settling scores with the warlords. The most fateful of these purges came while Chiang's armies were occupying Shanghai in the spring of 1927. After clearing the Communists out of the

The Guomindang's brutal suppression of the workers' organizations in Shanghai in 1927 marked a watershed in the history of modern China. The Guomindang-Communist alliance was shattered, and Mao Zedong's call for a peasant-based revolution became imperative as the vulnerability of the small Chinese working class was exposed.

Nationalist Central Committee, where they had been represented since 1924, Chiang ordered his troops and gangster allies in Shanghai to round up the workers, despite the fact that their mass demonstrations had done so much to make possible the city's capture by the Nationalist armies. In some of the most brutal scenes of an era when violence and human suffering were almost commonplace, Chiang's soldiers and hired toughs machine-gunned and beheaded Communist supporters wherever they could be found throughout the city. Though the Communists' Soviet advisors continued to insist that they cooperate with the Nationalists, Chiang's extension of the bloody purge to other cities and into the countryside precipitated an open civil war between the two main branches of the nationalist movement that, despite temporary and halfhearted truces, ended only with the Communist victory in 1949.

REACTION VS. REVOLUTION: THE STRUGGLE FOR CHINA

At the outset, all signs appeared to favor the Nationalist party in its violent contest with the Communists for control of China. Despite the fact that Chiang did not fully control the more powerful regional warlords, as the heir of Sun Yat-sen and the architect of the victorious northern campaign he had the support of the richest and most powerful social groups in China. These included the urban businessmen and merchants, most of the intellectuals, and a large portion of the university students, the rural landlords, and the military. Chiang could also count on the services of the bureaucrats and police throughout China, and he launched a calculated public relations campaign to win sympathy in the United States and the other Western democracies. The urban workers, who preferred the Communists or other radical parties, had been beaten into submission. The peasants, who longed for stable government and state-sponsored relief, were willing, for the time being at least, to wait and see if the Nationalists would act to alleviate their distress.

Despite his ruthless betrayal of the Communists, Chiang continued to receive assistance from the Soviet Union, where Stalin had emerged as the unchallenged dictator of a totalitarian state. Possibly because he preferred a weak China under the Nationalist party to a revolutionary one under the Communists, Stalin gave little assistance to his alleged comrades and continued to push policies that left them at the mercy of Chiang and his henchmen. With what seemed to be insurmountable advantages, Chiang moved to eliminate what was left in the way of rivals for power, most especially the shattered remnants of the Communist party.

The smashing of the workers' movement in Shanghai and other urban centers greatly strengthened Mao's hand in his ongoing struggle with Li Lisan and other orthodox ideologues within the Communist party. Mao and much of what was left of the Communist leadership retreated into the countryside and set to work carrying out land reform and improving life in China's tens of thousands of impoverished villages.

In the late 1920s the center of Communist operations came to be the south-central province of Hunan, where the Communists established soviets (named after the revolutionary workers' and soldiers' organizations in Russia) and "liberated" zones. This area became the main target of a succession of military campaigns that Chiang launched against the Communists in the early 1930s. Though the Communists successfully resisted the early campaigns, Chiang's reliance on German military advisors and his command of the resources and manpower of the rest of China eventually wore the Communists down. By the autumn of 1934, it was clear that if the remaining Communists did not break out of the Nationalist encirclement and escape from Hunan, they would be eliminated. At the head of over 90,000 party stalwarts, Mao set off on the Long March across thousands of miles of the most difficult terrain in China to Shaanxi in northwestern China, where a smaller number of peasant soviets had been established. At the end of the following year, Mao and only about 20,000 followers fought their way into the rugged, sparsely populated terrain of Shaanxi, which was the center of the Communist movement in China until the mid-1940s.

By the end of the Long March, Mao was firmly established as the head of the Chinese Communist party. The heroic and successful struggle for survival in the Long March on the part of those who supported his peasant-based strategy of revolution greatly enhanced his stature and fired his followers with the conviction that whatever the odds, they could not be defeated. Chiang obviously did not agree. Soon after the Communists were established in Shaanxi, he launched a new series of extermination campaigns. Again, the peasant supporters of the Communists fought valiantly, but Chiang's armies were beginning to get the upper hand by early 1937.

Just as he was convinced that he was on the verge of total victory, Chiang's anti-Communist crusade was rudely interrupted by the all-out Japanese invasion of the Chinese mainland. Obsessed with the Communists, Chiang had done little to block the steady advance of Japanese forces in the early 1930s into Manchuria and the islands along China's coast. Even after the Japanese launched their massive assaults aimed at the conquest of all of China, Chiang wanted to continue the struggle against the Communists.

Forced by his military commanders to concentrate on the Japanese threat, Chiang grudgingly formed a military alliance with the Communists. Though he did all he could to undermine the alliance and continue the anti-Communist struggle by underhanded means, for the next seven years the war against Japan took priority over the civil war in the contest for control of China.

Though it brought yet further suffering to the Chinese people, the Japanese invasion proved enormously advantageous for the Communist party. This turned out to be so vital to the ultimate Communist victory that some writers have speculated Mao chose Shaanxi in the northwest partly out of the calculation that it would put his forces in the probable path of the anticipated Japanese advance. Whatever his thinking, the war against the Japanese greatly strengthened his cause, while weakening his Nationalist rivals. The Japanese invaders captured much of the Chinese coast, where the trading cities were the centers of the business and mercantile backers of the Nationalists. Chiang's conventional military forces were pummeled by the superior air, land, and sea forces of the Japanese. The Nationalists' attempts to meet the Japanese in conventional, set-piece battles led to disaster; their inability to defend the coastal provinces lowered their standing in the eyes of the Chinese people. Chiang's hasty and humiliating retreat to Chongqing in the interior of China further eroded his aura as the savior of the nation and rendered him more dependent than ever on his military allies and the rural landlords.

The guerrilla warfare the Communists waged against the Japanese armies proved far more effective than Chiang's conventional approach. With the Nationalist extermination campaigns suspended, the Communists used their anti-Japanese campaigns to extend their control over large areas of north China. By the end of World War II, the Nationalists controlled mainly the cities in the north—they had become (as Mao prescribed in his political writings) islands surrounded by a sea of revolutionary peasants. The Communists' successes and determination to fight the Japanese, while Chiang and his advisors vacillated, won them the support of most of China's intellectuals and many of the students who had earlier looked to the Nationalists for China's salvation. By 1945, the balance of power within China was clearly shifting in the Communists' favor. In the four-year civil war that followed, Communist soldiers, who were well treated and fought for a cause, consistently routed the much-abused soldiers of the Nationalists, who went over in droves to the Communist side. By 1949, it was over. Chiang and what was left of his armies fled to the island of Formosa (renamed Taiwan) off the China coast, and Mao proclaimed the establishment of the Peoples Republic of China in Beijing.

The Japanese invasion proved critical in the Communist drive to victory. But equally important were the Communists' social and economic reform programs that eventually won the great majority of the peasantry, the students and intellectuals, and even many of the bureaucrats to their side. While Chiang, whatever his intentions, was able to do little to improve the condition of the great mass of the people, Mao made the peasants' uplift the central element in his drive for power. Land reforms, access to education, and improved health care gave the peasantry a real stake in Mao's revolutionary movement and good reason to defend the soviets against both the Nationalists and the Japanese. In contrast to Chiang's armies, whose arrival meant theft, rape, and wanton murder to China's villagers, Mao's soldiers were indoctrinated with the need to protect the peasantry and win their support. Lest they forget, harsh penalties were levied, such as execution for so much as stealing an egg.

As guerrilla fighters, Mao's soldiers had a much better chance to survive and advance in the ranks than the forcibly conscripted, brutally treated rank-and-file of the Nationalists. Mao and the commanders around him, such as Lin Biao who had been trained at Chiang's Whampoa Academy in the 1920s, proved far more gifted—even in conventional warfare—than the often corrupt and inept Nationalist generals. Thus, though the importance of the Japanese invasion cannot be discounted, the Communists won the mandate to govern China because they offered solutions to China's fundamental social and economic problems, and they actually put their programs into action in the areas that came under their control. In a situation where revolutionary changes appeared to be essential, the Communists alone convinced the Chinese people that they had the leaders and program that could affect them.

MAO'S CHINA AND BEYOND

In assuming power in 1949, the Communists faced the formidable task of governing a vast nation in ruins. Over a century of foreign invasions, civil warfare, and natural calamities had ravaged China's cities and villages, destroyed much of its economic infrastructure, and left its population physically exhausted and deeply demoralized. The confidence of Mao and the Communist leaders that they could build a better future did much to lift spirits and rally popular support for the ambitious projects of the new regime.

The Communists could also draw on the enthusiastic support of those peasants, students, and soldiers who had already been liberated by the experience of living in Communist-controlled areas during the mid-1930s and the years of Japanese occupation. In these zones, land reforms had already been put into effect, mass literacy campaigns had been mounted, and young people, both male and female, had enjoyed opportunities to rise in the party ranks on the basis of hard work and personal talents. Thus, in contrast to the Bolsheviks, who seized power in 1917 in Russia quite easily but then had to face years of civil war and foreign aggression, the Communists in China claimed a unified nation from which foreign aggressors had been expelled. Unlike the Bolsheviks, the Communist leadership in China could move directly to the tasks of social reform and economic development that China so desperately needed, and they could build on the base they had established in the "liberated" zones during their long struggle for power.

POLITICS AND SOCIAL REVOLUTION

Although deep social divisions remained, the Chinese faced far less serious splits between different religious and ethnic groups than most other new nations of Africa and Asia. Millennia of common history and common cultural development had given the peoples of China a sense of identity and a tradition of political unity. The long struggle against foreign aggressors had strengthened these bonds and impressed upon the Chinese the importance of maintaining a united front against outsiders if they were to avoid future humiliations and exploitation. The Communists' "long march" to power had left the party with a strong political and military organization that was rooted in the party cadres and the Peoples Liberation Army. The continuing importance of the army was indicated by the fact that most of China was administered by military officials for five years after the Communists came to power. But the army remained clearly subordinate to the party, with cadre advisors attached to military contingents at all levels and the central committees of the party dominated by nonmilitary personnel.

With this strong political framework in place, the Communists moved quickly to both assert China's traditional preeminence in East and much of Southeast Asia. Potential secessionist movements were forcibly repressed in Inner Mongolia and Tibet, though resistance in the latter has erupted periodically and continues to the present day. In the early 1950s, the Chinese intervened militarily in the conflict between North and South Korea, an intervention that was critical in forcing the United States to settle for a stalemate and a lasting division of the peninsula. Refusing to accept a similar, but far more lopsided, two-nation outcome of the struggle in China itself, the Communist leadership has periodically threatened to invade the Nationalists' refuge on Taiwan, in a number of cases touching off inter-

national incidents in the process. China also played an increasingly important role in the liberation struggle of the Vietnamese to the south, though that would not peak until the height of American involvement in the conflict in the 1960s.

By the late 1950s, the close collaboration between the Soviet Union and China that marked the early years of Mao's rule had broken down. Border disputes, focusing on territories the Russians had seized during the period of Manchu decline, and the Chinese refusal to play second fiddle to Russia, especially after Stalin was succeeded by the less imposing Khrushchev, were key causes of the split. These causes of the breakdown in collaboration greatly exacerbated differences resulting from the disappointingly meager economic assistance provided by the Soviet "comrades" and Mao's sense that, with the passing of Stalin, he was the number-one theoretician and leader of the communist world. In the early 1960s, the Chinese flexed their very considerable military and technological muscle by thrashing India in a brief war that resulted from a border dispute and more startlingly by exploding the first nuclear device developed by a nonindustrial nation.

On the domestic front, the new leaders of China moved with equal vigor, though with a good deal less success. Their first priority was to complete the social revolution in the rural areas that had been, to some extent, carried through in Communist controlled areas during the wars against the Japanese and Guomindang. Between 1950 and 1952, the landlord class and the large landholders, most of whom had been spared in earlier stages of the revolution, were dispossessed and purged. Village tribunals, overseen by party cadre members, gave tenants and laborers a chance to get even for decades of oppression. Perhaps as many as three million people who were denounced as members of the exploitative landlord class were executed. At the same time, the land taken from the landowning classes was distributed to peasants who had none or little. For a brief time at least, one of the central pledges of the communist revolutionaries was fulfilled: China became a land of peasant smallholders.

Communist planners, however, saw rapid industrialization, not peasant farmers, as the key to successful development. With the introduction of the first Stalinist-style Five-Year Plan in 1953, the Communist leadership turned away from the peasantry, which had brought them to power, to the urban workers as the hope for a new China. With little foreign assistance from either the West or the Soviet bloc, the state resorted to stringent measures to draw resources from the countryside to finance industrial growth. Though some advances were made in industrialization, particularly in heavy industries such as steel, the shift in direction had consequences that were increasingly unacceptable to Mao and his more radical supporters in the party. State planning and centralization were stressed, party bureaucrats greatly increased their power and influence, and an urban-based privileged class of technocrats began to develop. These changes and the external threat to China posed by the American intervention in Korea and continuing United States-China friction led Mao and his followers to force a change of strategies in the mid-1950s.

Mao had long nurtured a deep hostility toward elitism, which he associated with the discredited Confucian system. He had little use for Lenin's vision of revolution from above, led by a disciplined cadre of professional political activists. He distrusted intellectuals, disliked specialization, and clung to his faith in the peasants rather than the workers as the repository of basic virtue and the driving force of the revolution. Acting to stem the trend toward an elitist, urban-industrial focus, Mao and his supporters introduced the Mass Line approach, beginning with the formation of agricultural cooperatives in 1955. In the following year, cooperatives became farming collectives that soon accounted for over 90 percent of China's peasant population. The peasants had enjoyed their own holdings for less than three years. As had occurred earlier in the Soviet Union, the leaders of the revolution that had originally won the land for the mass of the peasants, later took it away from them through collectivization.

In 1957 Mao struck at the intellectuals through what may have been a miscalculation or perhaps a clever ruse. Announcing that he wished to "let a thousand flowers bloom," Mao encouraged professors, artists, and other intellectuals to speak out on the course of development under Communist rule. His request stirred up a storm of angry protest and criticism of communist schemes. Having flushed the critics into the open, if the campaign was indeed a ruse, or having been shocked by the vehemence of the response, the party struck with demotions, prison sentences, and banishment to hard labor on the collectives. The flowers rapidly wilted in the face of this betrayal.

With political opposition within the party and army apparently in check (or in prison), Mao and his supporters launched the Great Leap Forward in 1958. The programs of the Great Leap represented a further effort to revitalize the flagging revolution by restoring its mass, rural base. Rather than huge plants located in the cities, industrialization would be pushed through small-scale projects integrated into the peasant communes. Instead of siphoning off the communes' surplus to build steel mills, industrial de-

The famous backyard steel furnaces became a central symbol of China's failed drive for self-sufficiency during the "Great Leap Forward" in the late 1950s.

velopment would be aimed at producing tractors, cement for irrigation projects, and other manufactures needed by the peasantry. Enormous publicity was given to efforts to produce steel in "backyard" furnaces, relying on labor—rather than machine-intensive techniques. Mao preached the benefits of backwardness and the joys of mass involvement, and looked forward to the withering away of the meddling bureaucracy. Emphasis was placed on self-reliance within the peasant communes, and all aspects of the lives of their members were regulated and regimented by the commune leaders and the heads of the local labor brigades.

Within months after it was launched, all indicators suggested that the Great Leap Forward and rapid collectivization were leading to economic disaster. Peasant resistance to collectivization, the abuses of commune leaders, and the dismal output of the backyard factories combined with the failure of the rains to turn the Great Leap into a giant step backward. The worst famine of the Communist era spread across China. For the first time since 1949 China had to import large amounts of grain to feed its people. And the numbers of Chinese to feed continued to grow at an alarming rate. Defiantly rejecting Western and United Nations proposals for family planning, Mao and like-thinking radicals charged that socialist China could care for its people, no matter how many they were. Birth control was viewed as a symptom of capitalist selfishness and inability to provide a decent living for all of the people.

Like those of India, China's birthrates were actually a good deal lower than many Third World nations. Also like India, however, the Chinese were adding people to a massive population base. At the time of the Communist rise to power, China had approximately 550 million people. By 1965, this had risen to approximately 750 million. If that rate of growth had continued, some experts predicted that China would have 1.8 billion people by the year 2000.

In the face of the environmental degradation and overcrowding that this leap in population inevitably produced, even the party ideologues came around to the view that something must be done to curb the birthrate. Beginning in the mid-1960s, the government launched a nationwide family planning campaign designed to limit urban couples to two children and those in rural areas to one. By the early 1970s, these targets had been scaled back to two children for either urban or rural couples. But by the 1980s, just one child per family was allowed. Though there is considerable evidence of official excesses—undue pressure for women to have abortions, for example—these programs have greatly reduced the birthrate and have begun to slow China's overall population increase. But again, the

base to which new births are added is already so large that China's population will not stabilize until well into the next century when there will be far more people than even now to educate, feed, house, and provide with productive work.

Advances made in the first decade of the new regime were lost through amateurish blunders, excesses of overzealous cadre leaders, and students' meddling. China's national productivity fell by as much as 25 percent. Population increase soon overwhelmed the stagnating productivity of both the agricultural and industrial sectors. By 1960, it was clear that the Great Leap must be ended and a new course of development adopted. Mao lost his position as State Chairman (though he remained the head of the party's Central Committee). The "pragmatists," including Mao's old ally Zhou Enlai along with Liu Shaoqui and Deng Xiaoping, came to power determined to restore state direction and market incentives at the local level.

"WOMEN HOLD UP HALF OF THE HEAVENS"

In Mao's struggles to renew the revolutionary fervor of the Chinese people, his wife, Jiang Qing, played an increasingly prominent role. Mao's reliance on her, which had become dependence by the time of his death in 1976, was quite consistent with the commitment to the liberation of Chinese women he had acted upon throughout his political career. As a young man he had been deeply moved by a newspaper story about a young girl who had committed suicide rather than be forced by her family to submit to the marriage they had arranged for her with a rich but very elderly man. From that point onward, women's issues and the support of women for the Communist movement became important parts of Mao's revolutionary strategy. Here he was drawing on a well-established revolutionary tradition, for women had been very active in the Taiping Rebellion of the mid-19th century, as well as the Boxer revolt in 1900 and the 1911 revolution that had toppled the Manchu regime. One of the key causes taken up by the May Fourth intellectuals, who had a great impact on the youthful Mao Zedong, was women's rights. Their efforts put an end to foot-binding. They also did much to advance campaigns to end female seclusion, win legal rights for women, and open educational and career opportunities to them.

The attempts by the Nationalists in the late-1920s and 1930s to reverse many of the gains made by women in the early revolution brought many women into the Communist camp. Led by Chiang's wife, Madam Chiang Kai-shek, the Nationalist counteroffensive (like comparable movements in the Fascist countries of Europe at the time) sought to return Chinese women to the home and hearth. Madam Chiang proclaimed a special Good Mother's Day, and declared that "virtue was more important [for women] than learning." She taught that it was immoral for a wife to criticize her husband (an ethical precept she herself apparently ignored).

The Nationalist campaign to restore Chinese women to their traditional domestic roles and dependence on males contrasted sharply with the Communists' extensive employment of women to advance the revolutionary cause. Women served as teachers, nurses, spies, truck drivers, and laborers on projects ranging from growing food to building machine-gun bunkers. Though the party preferred to use them in these support roles, in moments of extreme crisis women became soldiers on the front lines, where many won distinction for their bravery under fire. Some rose to become cadre leaders, and many were prominent in the antilandlord campaigns and agrarian reform. Their contribution to the victory of the revolutionary cause truly bore out Mao's early dictum that the energies and talents of women had to be harnessed to the national cause because, after all, "women hold up half of the heavens."

As was the case in many other African and Asian countries, the victory of the revolution brought women legal equality with men—in itself a revolutionary development in a society like China. Women were expected to choose their marriage partners without familial interference. But arranged marriages persist today, especially in rural areas, and the need to have party approval for all marriages represents a new form of control beyond the choice of the couple involved.

Women were also expected to work outside the home. Their opportunities for education and professional careers have greatly improved. As in other Socialist states, however, openings for employment outside the home have proved something of a burden for Chinese women. Until the late 1970s, traditional attitudes toward child rearing and home care prevailed. As a result, women were required not only to hold down a regular job, but also to raise a family, cook meals, clean, and shop—and all without the benefit of the modern appliances available in Western societies. Though considerable numbers of women held cadre posts at the middle and lower levels of the party and bureaucracy, the upper echelons of both were overwhelmingly controlled by males.

As in other developing societies, the rather brief but very considerable power amassed by Mao's wife, Jiang Qing, in the early 1970s runs counter to the overall dominance of males in politics and the military. In any case, like her counterparts elsewhere, Jiang Qing got to the top because she was married to Mao. She exercised power mainly in his name and was toppled soon after his death when she tried to rule in her own right. Women have come far in China, but, as is the case in most other societies in both the "developed" and "developing" worlds, they have by no means attained full equality with males in career opportunities, social status, or political power.

DOCUMENT
WOMEN IN THE REVOLUTIONARY STRUGGLE

Even more than in the nationalist movements in colonized areas such as India and Egypt, women were drawn in large numbers into violent, revolutionary struggles in areas such as China and Vietnam. The breakdown of the political system and social order not only weakened the legal and family restrictions that had subordinated women and limited their career choices, but it ushered in decades of severe crisis and brutal conflict in which the very survival of women depended on them assuming radically new roles and actively involving themselves in revolutionary activities. The following quotations are taken from Vietnamese and Chinese revolutionary writings and interviews with women involved in the revolutionary movements in each country. They express the women's goals, their struggle to be taken seriously in the uncharacteristic political roles they had assumed, and some of the many ways women found self-respect and redress for their grievances as a result of the changes wrought by the spread of the new social order.

1. Women must first of all be masters of themselves. They must strive to become skilled workers . . . and, at the same time, they must strictly observe family planning. Another major question is the responsibility of husbands to help their wives look after children and other housework. . . .

2. We intellectuals had had little contact with the

peasants and when we first walked through the village in our Chinese gowns or skirts the people would just stare at us and talk behind our backs. When the village head beat gongs to call out the women to the meetings we were holding for them, only men and old women came, but no young ones. Later we found out that the land-lords and rich peasants had spread slanders among the masses saying "They are a pack of wild women. Their words are not for young brides to hear."

3. . . . . brave wives and daughters-in-law, untram-melled by the presence of their menfolk, could voice their own bitterness . . . encourage their poor sisters to do likewise, and thus eventually bring to the village-wide gatherings the strength of "half of China" as the more enlightened women, very much in earnest, like to call them-selves. By "speaking pains to recall pains," the women found that they had as many if not more grievances than the men, and that given a chance to speak in public, they were as good at it as their fathers and husbands.

4. In Chingtsun the work team found a woman whose husband thought her ugly and wanted to divorce her. She was very depressed until she learned that under the Draft Law [of the Com-munist party] she could have her own share of land. Then she cheered up immediately. "If he divorces me, never mind," she said. "I'll get my share and the children will get theirs. We can live a good life without him."

Questions: On the basis of these quotations, what tradi-tional roles and attitudes of women (explored in earlier chapters on China and Vietnam) did those who opposed revolutionary movements in China and Vietnam seek to defend? Which of these roles and attitudes do the revo-lutionaries reject? What do they believe is essential if women are to gain equality with men? How similar and different are the demands of the women supporting these revolutionary movements in Asia to those of wom-en's rights advocates in the United States?

MAO'S LAST CAMPAIGN AND THE FALL OF THE "GANG OF FOUR"

Having lost his position as head of state but still power-ful in the Communist party and by far the most charis-matic and popular of the Communist leaders, Mao worked throughout the early 1960s to establish grass roots support for yet another renewal of the revolutionary struggle. He fiercely opposed the efforts of Deng Xiaoping and his pragmatist allies to scale back the communes, promote peasant production on what were in effect private plots, and push economic growth over political orthodoxy. By late 1965, Mao was convinced that his support among the students, peasants, and military was strong enough to launch what would turn out to be his last campaign, the Cultural Revolution. With mass student demonstrations paving the way, he launched an all-out assault on the "cap-italist-roaders" in the party.

Waving "little red books" of Mao's pronouncements on all manner of issues, the infamous Red Guard student bri-gades publicly ridiculed and abused Mao's political rivals. Liu Shaoqui was killed, Deng Xiaoping was imprisoned, and Zhou Enlai was driven into seclusion. The aroused students and the rank and file of the Peoples Liberation Army were used to pull down the bureaucrats from their positions of power and privilege. College professors, plant managers, and the children of the bureaucratic elite were berated and forced to confess publicly their many crimes against "the people." Those who were not imprisoned or, more rarely, killed were forced to do manual labor on ru-ral communes to enable them to understand the hardships endured by China's peasantry. In cities such as Shanghai, the workers seized control of the factories and local bureau-cracy. As Mao had hoped, the centralized state and techno-cratic elites that had grown steadily since the first revolution won power in 1949 were being torn apart by the rage of the people.

However satisfying for an advocate of continuing revo-lution like Mao and supporters like his wife Jiang Qing, who saw her power grow by leaps and bounds as Mao's former compatriots were purged, it was soon clear that the Cultural Revolution threatened to return China to the chaos and vulnerability of the prerevolutionary era. The rank-and-file threat to the leaders of the Peoples Liberation Army proved in the end decisive in prompting counter-measures that forced Mao to call off the campaign by late 1968. The heads of the armed forces moved to bring the rank and file back into line; the student and worker move-

In launching the Cultural Revolution in the mid-1960s, Mao Zedong and his allies sought to restore the revolutionary fervor of the 1930s and 1940s that they felt had been eroded by the growing bureaucratization of China. In this photo a crowd of Mao's young supporters rally in Beijing.

ments were disbanded and in some cases forcibly repressed. By the early 1970s, Mao's old rivals had begun to surface again, and until the mid-1970s a hard-fought struggle was waged at the upper levels of the party and the army for control of the government. The reconciliation between China and the United States negotiated in the early 1970s suggested that, at least in foreign policy, the pragmatists were gaining the upper hand over the ideologues. Deng's growing role in policy formation from 1973 onward also represented a major setback for Jiang Qing and her three allies, who made up the notorious "Gang of Four" that increasingly contested power on behalf of the aging Mao.

The death in early 1976 of Zhou Enlai, who was second only to Mao in stature as a revolutionary hero and who had consistently backed the pragmatists, appeared to be a major blow to those whom the Gang of Four had marked out as "capitalist-roaders" and betrayers of the revolution. But Mao's death later in the same year cleared the way for an open clash between the rival factions. While the Gang of Four plotted to seize control of the government, the pragmatists acted in alliance with some of the more influential military leaders. The Gang of Four were arrested, and their supporters' attempts to foment popular insurrections were easily foiled. Later tried for their crimes against the people, Jiang Qing and the members of her clique were purged from the party and imprisoned for life, after having death sentences commuted.

In the past decade, the pragmatists have been ascendant, and leaders such as Deng Xiaoping have opened China to Western influences and considerable capitalist development, if not yet democratic reform. Under Deng and his allies the farming communes have been discontinued and private peasant production for the market encouraged. Private enterprise has also been encouraged in the industrial sector, and experiments have been made with such arch-capitalist institutions as a stock exchange and foreign hotel chains.

Though it has become fashionable to dismiss the development schemes of the Communist states as misguided failures, the achievements of the Communist regime in China over the past four decades have been considerable. Despite severe economic setbacks, political turmoil, and a low level of foreign assistance, the Communists have managed a truly revolutionary redistribution of the wealth of the country. China's very large population remains poor, but in education, health care, housing, working conditions, and the availability of food, most of it is far better off than it was in the prerevolutionary era. The Chinese have managed to provide a decent standard of living for a higher proportion of their people than perhaps any other large developing country. They have also achieved higher rates of industrial and agricultural growth than neighboring India, with its mixed state-capitalist economy and democratic polity. And the Chinese have done all of this without leaving up to half their people in misery, and with much less foreign assistance than most Third World nations. If the pragmatists remain in power and the champions of the market economy are right, China's growth in the coming decades should be even more impressive. But the central challenge for China's leaders will be how to nurture that growth as well as the improved living standards without a recurrence of the economic inequities and social injustice that made for the revolution in the first place.

 ## DECOLONIZATION AND REVOLUTION IN VIETNAM

Like most of the peoples of the African and Asian world, the Vietnamese, as well as their neighbors in Laos and Cambodia, were brought under European colonial rule in the 19th century. But because the Vietnamese had long modeled their polity on the Confucian system of their giant neighbor to the north and borrowed heavily from China in the social and cultural spheres, their encounter with the expansive West had much in common with that of the Chinese. The Vietnamese were also shocked by the sudden and forcible intrusion into their formerly rather sheltered world by one of the European imperialist powers, in this instance France bent on restoring its world empire after defeats in Europe. As was the case in China, the failure of Vietnam's Confucian emperor and bureaucracy to successfully repel the foreign invaders discredited and eventually led to the complete collapse of the system around which the Vietnamese had organized civilized life for nearly two millennia.

As in China, the Vietnamese nationalists who emerged in the 1890s and early 1900s soon realized that their rejection of the traditional order meant radical solutions rather than gradualist, reformist measures would be required to liberate Vietnam and build a viable social order for its people. The French refusal to encourage the growth of moderate political parties and to tolerate constitutional or peaceful mass agitation also served to channel Vietnamese political energies into revolutionary channels. The highly exploitative nature of French rule in Vietnam, which was excessive even by colonial standards, also gave rise to economic distress and social dislocations that rendered the status quo unbearable for most of the Vietnamese and won widespread support for those who offered revolutionary alternatives. Therefore, in contrast to much of the rest of the colonized

world, the Vietnamese drive to win independence and build a new nation was dominated by violent insurrections, long decades of guerrilla warfare, and far-reaching social and economic transformations.

As if the struggle against the French and reactionary elements in Vietnam itself were not enough, the Vietnamese also had to contend with the intervention of the American goliath in their affairs and nearly a decade of armed struggle against the world's leading military power. Though a tribute to their endurance and dedication, the ultimate victory of the Vietnamese in that struggle left the nation in shambles and isolated from much of the rest of the world.

THE NGUYEN DYNASTY AND THE RISE OF FRENCH COLONIAL DOMINANCE

French interest in Vietnam reached back as far as the 17th century. Driven from Japan by the founders of the Tokugawa Shogunate, French missionaries fell back on coastal Vietnam. Vietnam attracted them both because its Confucian elite seemed deceptively similar to that of the Japanese, and because the continuing wars between rival dynastic houses in the Red River valley and central Vietnam gave the missionaries ample openings for their conversion efforts. From this time onward, French rulers, who styled themselves the protectors of the Catholic missions overseas, took an interest in Vietnamese affairs. As the numbers of converts grew into the tens of thousands and French merchants began to trade at Vietnamese ports, the French stake in the region increased.

By the last decades of the 18th century, French involvement had become distinctly political as a result of the power struggles that convulsed the whole region. In the south, a genuine peasant rebellion, the Tayson, toppled the Nguyen dynasty in the late 1770s. In the following years, the northern rival of the Nguyen, the Trinh dynasty, was also dethroned. The Tayson controlled most of the country, eliminated the Trinh, and all but wiped out the Nguyen. Seeing a chance to win influence in the ruling house, the French head of the Vietnam mission, the Bishop of Adran, threw his support behind the one surviving prince of the southern house, Nguyen Anh.

Anh had fled into the Mekong wilderness with a handful of supporters, thus escaping death at the hands of the Tayson. With the arms and advice of the French, he rallied local support for the dynasty and soon fielded a sizeable army. After driving the Tayson from the south, Nguyen Anh launched an invasion of Tayson strongholds in the north. His task of conquest was made easier by bit-

Vietnam: Divisions in the Nguyen and French Periods

French Control of Indochina
1862
1863
1867
1883
1907

ter quarrels among the Tayson leaders. By 1802 the Nguyen armies had prevailed, and Nguyen Anh proclaimed himself the Gia Long emperor of Vietnam.

Nguyen Anh made the old Nguyen capital at Hue in central Vietnam the imperial capital of a unified Vietnam. His French missionary allies were rewarded with a special place at court, and French traders were given greater access to the port of Saigon, which was rapidly emerging as the leading city of the Mekong River valley region in the south. The Nguyen dynasty was the first in centuries to rule all of Vietnam and the first to rule a Vietnamese kingdom that included both the Red River and Mekong deltas. In fact, the Mekong region had only begun to be settled extensively by Vietnamese in the century or so before Nguyen Anh rose to power.

Nguyen Anh and his successors proved to be arch-traditionalists deeply committed to strengthening Confucianism in Vietnam. Their capital at Hue was intended to be a perfect miniature of the imperial palace at Beijing. The dynasty patronized Confucian schools and built its administration around scholar-bureaucrats well-versed in Confucian learning. The second emperor Minh Mang (1820–1841) prided himself on his knowledge of the Confucian classics and his mastery of the Chinese script. He even had the audacity to criticize the brushwork of the reigning Chinese emperor, who after all was not any more Chinese than Minh Mang but descended from Manchu nomads. All of this proved deeply disappointing to the French missionaries, who had been counting on baptizing Nguyen Anh and

then carrying out the sort of top-down conversion of the Vietnamese the Jesuits had hoped for ever since their arrival in Asia. Things actually got worse. Gia Long's ultra-Confucian successor Minh Mang came to view the Catholics as something of a fifth column, which he believed posed a substantial danger to the dynasty. His persecution of the Vietnamese Catholic community not only enraged the missionaries, but it contributed to the growing political and military intervention of the French government in the region.

Pushed both by political pressures at home and military defeats in Europe, French adventurers and soldiers exploited quarrels with the Nguyen rulers to justify the piecemeal conquest of Vietnam and neighboring Cambodia and Laos, beginning in the late 1840s. By the 1890s, the whole of the country was under French control and the Nguyen dynasty had been reduced to the status of puppet princes. In the following decades, the French concentrated on drawing revenue and resources from Vietnam, while providing very little in return.

The French determination to make Vietnam a colony that was profitable for the homeland exacerbated social and economic problems that were already bad under the Nguyen rulers. Most of the densely packed peasant population of the north lacked enough land to even eke out a subsistence livelihood. French taxes and the burden of obligatory purchases by each village of set amounts of government-sold opium and alcohol drove many peasants into labor in the mines. Even larger numbers left their ancestral villages and migrated to the Mekong region to work on the plantations established there by French and Chinese entrepreneurs, or to become tenants on the great estates that had been carved out of sparsely settled frontier regions by Vietnamese and Chinese landlords. Migration brought little relief. Plantation workers were paid little and treated much like slave laborers. The unchecked demands of the Mekong landlords left their tenants with scarcely enough of the crops they grew to feed, clothe, and house their families. The blatantly exploitative nature of French colonialism in Vietnam was graphically revealed by the statistics the French themselves collected. These showed a sharp drop in the food consumed by the peasantry in all parts of the colony between the early 1900s and the 1930s—a drop that occurred despite the fact that Vietnam became, in these years, one of the world's major rice-exporting areas.

VIETNAMESE NATIONALISM: BOURGEOIS DEAD ENDS AND COMMUNIST SURVIVAL

The failure of the Nguyen rulers after Minh Mang to rally the forces of resistance against the French did much to discredit the dynasty. But from the 1880s into the first decades of the 20th century, guerrilla warfare was waged in various parts of the country in support of the Save the King movement. Because this resistance was localized and small-scale, the French were able to crush it on a piecemeal basis. In any case, French control over the puppet emperors who remained on the throne at Hue left the rebels with little cause worth fighting for. The failure of the Nguyen and the Confucian bureaucratic classes to defend Vietnam against the French did much to discredit the old order in the eyes of the new generations that came of age in the early decades of French rule. Perhaps because it was imported rather than homegrown, the Vietnamese were quicker than the Chinese to reject Confucianism once its failings were clear, and they did it with a good deal less trauma. But its demise left an ideological and institutional vacuum that the Vietnamese, again like the Chinese, would struggle decades to fill.

In the first years of the 20th century, a new Western-educated middle class, similar to that found in other colonial settings (see Chapters 30 and 39) was formed by the children of the traditional Confucian elite and the emerging landlord class in the Mekong region. Some, taking advantage of their parents wealth, went to French schools and emerged speaking fluent French and with a taste for French fashions and frequent holiday jaunts to Paris and the French Riviera. Many of these went to work for the French as colonial administrators, bank managers, and even labor recruiters. Others pursued independent professional careers as lawyers, doctors, and journalists. Many who opted for French educations and French life-styles were soon drawn into nationalist organizations. Like their counterparts elsewhere in the colonies, the members of these organizations initially concentrated on protesting French racism and discrimination, improving their wages, and gaining access to positions in the colonial government held by Frenchmen.

As in other colonies, nationalist newspapers and magazines proliferated. These became the focal point of an extended debate regarding the approach that should be taken

Though violent Vietnamese resistance to French rule never really died out, as this cartoon illustrates, some Vietnamese—mostly from the landlord and commercial middle classes—were willing not only to collaborate with the colonizers but also to adopt their dress and social conventions.

toward winning freedom from French rule and, increasingly, what needed to be done to rebuild Vietnam as a whole. Because the French forcibly repressed all attempts to mount peaceful mass demonstrations or organize constitutional agitation, those who argued for violent resistance eventually gained the upper hand. In the early 1920s the nationalist struggle was centered in the clandestine Vietnamese Nationalist party (Vietnamese Quoc Dan Dong or VNQDD), which was committed to violent revolution against the French colonizers. Though the VNQDD made some attempt to organize urban laborers and peasant villagers, party members were drawn overwhelmingly from the children of the landlord elite and urban professional classes. Their secret codes and elaborate rituals proved little protection against the dreaded Sûreté or French Secret Police. A series of failed uprisings, culminating in a 1929 attempt to spark off a general revolution with the assassination of a much-hated French official in charge of labor recruitment, decimated the party. It was particularly hard-hit by the following all-out French campaign of repression, execution, and imprisonment. From that point onward, the bourgeois nationalists were never again the dominant force in the independence struggle.

The demise of the VNQDD left its major rival, the Communist party, as the main focus of nationalist resistance in Vietnam. As in China and Korea, the Communist wing of the nationalist movement had developed in Vietnam during the 1920s, often at the initiative of leaders in exile. By the late 1920s, the party was dominated by the charismatic, young Nguyen Ai Quoc, who would later be known as Ho Chi Minh. Ho had discovered Marxism while studying in France and Russia during and after World War I. Disillusioned by his failure to gain a hearing for his plea to the victorious Allies at the Versailles Peace Conference for the Vietnamese right to self-determination, Ho dedicated himself to a revolutionary struggle to drive the French from Indochina.

In the early 1930s the Communist party still held to the rigid, though unrealistic, orthodox vision of a revolution based on the urban working classes. Since the workers in Vietnam made up as small a percentage of the population as they had in China, the orthodox strategy made little headway. A sudden shift in the early 1930s to a peasant emphasis, in part to take advantage of widespread but non-Communist inspired peasant uprisings in central Vietnam, led to a disaster almost as great as that which had overtaken the VNQDD a year before. French repression smashed the Communist party hierarchy and drove most of the major Communist leaders into exile. But the superior underground organization of the Communists and the sup-

port they received from Comintern helped them survive a French onslaught. Slowly, during the late 1930s, the discredited Ho reestablished his place in the party, and the party won growing peasant support due to its programs for land reform, higher wages for laborers, mass education, and health care. When the French were weakened by the Japanese invasion of Indochina in 1941, the Communists were ready to use the colonizers' setbacks to advance the struggle for national liberation.

THE WAR OF LIBERATION AGAINST THE FRENCH

During World War II, operating out of bases in south China, the Communist-dominated nationalist movement, known as the Viet Minh, established liberated areas throughout the northern Red River delta. As in Korea, the abrupt end of Japanese rule left a vacuum in Vietnam, which only the Viet Minh was prepared to fill. Its programs for land reform and mass education had wide appeal among the hard-pressed peasants of the north, where they had been propagated during the 1930s and especially the war years. The fact that the Viet Minh actually put their reform and community building programs into effect in the areas they controlled won them very solid support among much of the rural population. The Viet Minh's efforts to provide assistance to the peasants during the terrible famine of 1944 and 1945 also convinced the much-abused Vietnamese people that here at last was a political organization that was genuinely committed to improving their lot.

Under the leadership of General Giap, the Viet Minh skillfully employed guerrilla tactics similar to those devised by Mao in China. These offset the advantages that first the French and then the Japanese enjoyed in conventional firepower. With a strong base of support in much of the rural north and the hill regions, where they had won the support of key non-Vietnamese "tribal" peoples, the Viet Minh forces advanced triumphantly into the Red River delta as the Japanese withdrew. By August, 1945, the Viet Minh were in control of Hanoi, where Ho Chi Minh proclaimed the establishment of the independent nation of Vietnam.

Though the Viet Minh had liberated much of the north, they had very little control in the south, where a variety of Communist and bourgeois nationalist parties jostled for power. The French, anxious to reclaim their colonial empire and put behind them their humiliations at the hands of the Nazis, were quick to exploit this turmoil. With British assistance, the French reoccupied Saigon and much of south and central Vietnam. In March 1946 they denounced the August declaration of Vietnamese independence and moved to reassert their colonial control over the whole of Vietnam and the rest of Indochina. An unsteady truce between the French and the Viet Minh quickly broke down, and Vietnam was soon consumed by a renewal of the Viet Minh's guerrilla war for liberation, as well as bloody infighting between the different factions of the Vietnamese. After nearly a decade of indecisive struggle, the Viet Minh had gained control of much of the Vietnamese countryside, while the French, with increasing American financial and military aid, clung to the fortified towns. In 1954 the Viet Minh decisively defeated the French at Dien Bien Phu in the mountain highlands near the Laotian border. The victory won the Viet Minh control of the northern portions of Vietnam as a result of an international conference at Geneva in the same year. At Geneva, elections throughout Vietnam were promised within two years to decide who should govern a reunited north and the still politically fragmented south.

ANALYSIS
DECOLONIZATION WITH AND WITHOUT SOCIAL REVOLUTION

As we have seen, independence was won in most of the nonsettler colonized world with a minimum of violence and only very limited changes in Africa and Asian economies and social hierarchies. Vietnam provides a sharp contrast to this dominant pattern, despite the fact that it had few French settlers and was colonized by the French in much the same way as the rest of Africa and Asia under European rule. The reasons for the divergent path to independence taken by the Vietnamese tell us much about the origins of revolutionary as opposed to gradualist, reformist political change. They are rooted in the differences between Vietnam, China and its other satellite civilizations in East Asia, and most of the rest of the Afro-Asian world. They are also tied to the extraordinarily exploitative and excessively repressive nature of colonial rule under the French in Vietnam as well as the consequences of the brief period of Japanese control in the area.

Like the other peoples of East Asia, the Vietnamese already had a unified state, a common written and spoken language, and a strong sense of common identity long before the expansive Europeans broke into their comparatively isolated world. There were sharp cultural and political divisions between the lowland-dwelling, wet-rice growing Vietnamese and the multitude of slash-and-burn cultivating peoples who lived in the hills. But the Vietnamese made up an overwhelming majority of the people who occupied the areas that would eventually comprise the nation of Vietnam. French rule promoted Vietnamese dominance over the hill peoples as well as over the lowland peoples of neighboring Laos and Cambodia. It also intensified the traditional Vietnamese sense of identity, both by providing a foreign target for them to resist and by enriching that sense of identity with the European concepts of the nation and patriotism. Like all peoples who had been deeply influenced by China's Confucian tradition, the Vietnamese found their political subjugation to the "barbarian" Europeans intensely galling. Their own long tradition of violent resistance to political foreign domination, whether by the Chinese, the Mongols, or the Manchus, also fed the Vietnamese determination to fight against the French conquest.

In contrast to colonial India, Africa, and most of the rest of Southeast Asia, from the outset Vietnamese cooperation with the French was branded by those who resisted French rule as a betrayal of the Vietnamese people and tradition. Also in contrast to other colonized areas, the Vietnamese continued to violently resist the imposition of French rule long after the initial wars of conquest and "pacification" had ended. There was to be no early colonial period of peace and submissiveness in Vietnam. From the outset, the Vietnamese fought the French encroachments into their country with fierce determination. This violent struggle continued through most of the period of French rule.

The crumbling of the Confucian order and the nature of French rule in Vietnam made it essential for those who sought to mobilize opposition to the French to promise far-reaching social and economic transformations. As in China and Korea, the failure of the Confucian elite in Vietnam to ward off the intrusions of the West led to the rejection of Confucian civilization as a whole. As a result and in contrast to the peoples of most of the rest of the Afro-Asian world, the Vietnamese were left without a "tradition" to defend and to revive as an alternative to European colonialism. Unlike Islam, Hinduism, and Buddhism elsewhere, the depoliticized, eclectic, and rather amorphous variant of Buddhism in Vietnam was simply not seen by the emerging nationalists of the country as a viable base on which to build a postcolonial order. The fact that the breakdown of the Confucian system was paralleled by the worsening condition of the peasantry resulting from French exploitative policies rendered mere political responses insufficient. The substitution of French-educated, middle class, Vietnamese politicians for French colonial officials would do little to alleviate the misery of the peasant farmers of the north or the plantation workers in the south.

In any case, the middle class could make little headway even in the political sphere against determined repression by the French. In contrast to the policies followed in most other nonsettler colonies, the French prohibited all but the most innocuous political organizations. The Vietnamese press was tightly controlled; even moderate political parties were smashed; and mass demonstrations of any kind were strictly prohibited. The French doggedly refused to negotiate seriously with, much less make any significant constitutional concessions to, the bourgeois nationalists, whose collaboration was a major prop of their continued domination in Indochina. Under these circumstances the gradual transfer of power from the colonizers to the nationalists, which had been a key factor in peaceful decolonization in other areas, was out of the question. As a consequence, underground terrorist and guerrilla organizations like the VNQDD and the Communist party dominated the struggle for independence by the 1920s.

Even the Japanese takeover in the 1940s, which proved so crucial to the strengthening of moderate, constitutional nationalist organizations in Burma, Indonesia, the Philippines and other areas they occupied, had the reverse effect in Indochina. For most of the period of occupation, the Japanese were content to let French collaborators, linked to the Nazi-puppet Vichy regime then in power in France (see Chapter 34), continue to run the colony under their supervision. As a result, the policy of repressing nationalist organizations continued. Thus, any hopes for building a nonviolent, moderate party that could rival the Communist-dominated Viet Minh were again crushed. The violent struggle against the Japanese, the French, and later the Americans only served to reinforce the revolutionary orientation of the Vietnamese Communist party.

Questions: Compare the precolonial sense of identity and political unity in Vietnam with the situation found in most of the rest of the colonized world. How have the differences between the two made for very different paths of political development in Vietnam, as opposed to patterns of colonial dominance and nation-building in much of the rest of the Third World? If the French had been more tolerant of moderate nationalist agitation, do you think that revolutionary parties like the Communists would have dominated the independence movement? Why or why not?

THE WAR OF LIBERATION AGAINST THE UNITED STATES

The promise at Geneva that free elections would be held to determine who should govern a united Vietnam was never kept. Like the rest of East Asia, Vietnam had become entangled in the cold war maneuvers of the United States and the Soviet Union. Despite very amicable cooperation between the Viet Minh and United States armed forces during the war against Japan, American support for the French in the First Indochina War and the growing fame of Ho Chi Minh as a Communist leader drove the two further and further into opposition. The anti-Communist hysteria in the United States in the early 1950s fed the perception of influential American leaders that, like South Korea, South Vietnam must be protected from Communist takeover.

The search for a leader to build a government in the south that the United States could prop up with economic and military assistance led to Ngo Dinh Diem. Diem appeared to have impeccable nationalist credentials. In fact, he had gone into exile rather than give up the struggle against the French. His sojourn in the United States in the 1940s and the fact that he was a Catholic also recommended him to American politicians and churchmen. Unfortunately, these same aspects would alienate him from the great majority of his countrymen.

With American backing, Diem was installed as the president of Vietnam, a status he tried to legitimatize in the late-1950s by holding rigged elections in the South, in which the Communists were not permitted to run. Diem also mounted a series of campaigns to eliminate by force all possible political rivals in the South. Because the Communists posed the biggest threat (and were of the greatest concern to Diem's American backers), the suppression campaign increasingly focused on the Communist cadres that remained in the South after Vietnam had been divided at Geneva. By the mid-1950s, the Viet Cong (as the Diem regime dubbed the Communist resistance) were threatened with extermination. In response to this threat, the Communist regime in the north began to pump weapons, advisors, and other resources into the southern cadres, which were reorganized as the National Liberation Front in 1958.

As guerrilla warfare spread and Diem's military responses expanded, both the United States and the North Vietnamese escalated their support for the warring parties. When Diem proved unable to stem the Communist tide in the countryside, the United States gave the go-ahead for the military to overthrow him and take direct charge of the war. When the Vietnamese military could make little headway, the United States stepped up its military intervention.

After decades of struggle against foreign invaders, Vietnamese guerrillas march with the regular forces of the North Vietnamese army into Saigon in May 1975. The capture of the city marked the end of the long wars to free a unified Vietnam.

From thousands of special advisors in the early 1950s, the American commitment rose to nearly 500,000 men and women, who made up a massive force of occupation by 1968. But despite the loss of nearly 60,000 American lives and hundreds of thousands of Vietnamese casualties, the Americans could not defeat the communist movement. In part, their failure resulted from their very presence, which made it possible for the Communists to convince the great majority of the Vietnamese people that they were fighting for their independence from yet another imperialist aggressor.

Though more explosives were dropped on tiny Vietnam, North and South, than in all of the theaters of the Second World War, and America resorted to chemical warfare against the very environment of the South Vietnamese they claimed to be trying to save, the Communists would not yield. The indomitable Vietnamese emerged as the victors of the Second Indochina War. In the early 1970s, American diplomats negotiated an end to direct American involvement in the conflict. Without that support, the unpopular military regime in the South fell apart by 1975.

The Communists united Vietnam under a single government for the first time since the late-1850s. But the nation they governed was shattered and impoverished by decades of civil war, revolution, and armed conflict with two major colonial powers and the most powerful nation of the second half of the 20th century.

CONCLUSION

REVOLUTIONS AND CIVILIZATION IN CHINA AND VIETNAM

There can be little doubt that the ancient civilizations of both China and Vietnam have undergone revolutionary transformations in the 20th century. Monarchies or autocratic colonial regimes have been replaced by Communist party cadres who seized power in the name of the peasants and workers. Whole social classes, such as the scholar-gentry and the large landlords, have been eliminated. Elite-centric education and writing systems have been replaced by mass-oriented schooling and simplified scripts designed to promote general literacy. Women have greatly improved their legal status and position within the family, and a wide range of career opportunities, most of which would have been unthinkable under the prerevolutionary Confucian order, have opened to them. Marxism-Leninism—blended in recent years with experiments in Western-style capitalism—has replaced Confucianism as the state ideology and provided the philosophical underpinnings for the new social order.

The breadth and profundity of these changes might lead one to conclude that the patterns of civilized life China and Vietnam nurtured for over two millennia disappeared as completely as Harappa vanished from the Indian landscape in the 2d millennium B.C. But upon closer examination, it becomes clear that much more has been preserved than these gauges of radical change and the rhetoric of the ruling parties of China and Vietnam might lead one to believe. Both societies, for example, have retained deeply ingrained suspicions of the commercial and entrepreneurial classes. Both continue to stress that those who wield political power are obligated to rule in ways that promote the welfare of the mass of the people. Both China and Vietnam still adhere to ideological systems that stress the secular, social harmony, and life in this world rather than religious concerns and life hereafter. In each case these continuities between the prerevolutionary patterns and those of the post-

revolutionary era exemplify important affinities between Marxist-Leninist and Confucian thought. They explain why Marxism had such a strong appeal to Chinese and Vietnamese intellectuals and revolutionary leaders.

The persistence of the ancient civilized traditions of China and Vietnam extends far beyond areas of agreement between Marxism and Confucianism. At times it runs directly counter to Marxist-Leninist internationalism. The continuing Chinese sense of cultural superiority to even more powerful nations, such as the United States and Japan, and Mao's conviction that he, not Stalin or Trotsky, should be the leading authority on Marxian revolutionary thought are but two notable examples of this persistence. The repeated reassertion of elitist thinking and bureaucratic control over all aspects of social life, which Mao railed against in the last decades of his career, provides additional evidence of the strength of prerevolutionary patterns of civilization. Resistance in both China and Vietnam to the full liberation of women, to restrictions on the number of children each married couple is allowed to have, and to state attempts to break down extended family ties are important manifestations of the persistence of these patterns in society more generally.

These continuities caution us, as we have argued in the introduction to this section on the 20th century, against overstating the extent to which the history of the present century marks a decisive break with the past. Just as the Bolsheviks in Russia drew on the political traditions of the Tsarist era and nationalists in India and Africa invoked the ancient symbols and beliefs of their societies, Chinese and Vietnamese revolutionaries struggled to build "new" societies that owed much to their Confucian past. These continuities also remind us of the resilience of ideas and patterns of civilized life that have been nurtured over centuries and, in the cases of China and Vietnam, over millennia. Civilizations weave dense and complex webs of human interaction. These may be profoundly altered by the sort of revolutionary upheavals that have occurred in the 20th century. But more often than not the changes are less sweeping and much more is preserved than revolutionary leaders would like to admit.

FURTHER READINGS

Some of the best general studies on China in the 20th century include Lucian Bianco's *The Communist Revolution in China* (1967), C. P. Fitzgerald's *The Birth of Commu-*

CHAPTER 41 WAR AND REVOLUTION IN CHINA AND VIETNAM   1015

nist *China* (1964), Wolfgang Franke's *A Century of Chinese Revolution* (1970), and Jonathan Spence's *The Search for Modern China* (1990). For firsthand accounts of conditions in the revolutionary era, see especially Graham Peck's *Two Kinds of Time* (1950), Edgar Snow's *Red Star Over China* (1938), and Theodore White and Analee Jacoby's *Thunder Out of China* (1946). Mark Selden's *The Yenan Way to Revolution in China* (1971) provides the fullest account of the development of the Communist movement after the Long March. Of the growing number of works on China after the Communists came to power, Maurice Meisner's *Mao's China* (1977) and Michael Gasster's *China's Struggle to Modernize* (1987 ed.) are the most useful. Rodney Macfarquhar's two-volume study of the *Origins of the Cultural Revolution* (1974, 1983) is essential for an understanding of the last years of Mao's rule. Elisabeth Croll's *Feminism and Socialism in China* (1978) is by far the best single work on the position of women in revolutionary China.

There is substantial literature on Vietnamese history during the Nguyen and French period, as well as, of course, a large number of works on Vietnam during the Second Indochina War. Alexander Woodside's *Vietnam and the China Model* (1971) remains the place to start on the pre-French period, and Buttinger's *Political History of Vietnam* (1968) also remains useful for general background. Woodside, Huynh Kim Khanh, David Marr, Milton Osborne, William Duiker, and Hue Tam Ho-Tai have all made important contributions to the rise of nationalism and communism in Vietnam. On U.S. intervention in the area, see the works by George Kahin and Lloyd Gardner. On the conduct of the war, Jeffrey Race and Malcolm Browne are among the most insightful of many accounts.

42 Toward the Future: World History Yet to Come

INTRODUCTION   Since the formation of civilizations, the history of the world has involved relatively rapid change—sometimes in directions already set, but sometimes in new trajectories. This pattern obviously continues as we near the 21st century. Indeed, some people would argue that the pace of change has sped up, as new discoveries and new technologies press against older ideas and habits. World history, in other words, offers no convenient stopping point at which one can lean back and say, This is what it all means. Contemporary world history provides no magic vantage point, either, on what is to come. The only thing we know for sure about the future is that we do not know what it will bring.

People in various civilizations have attempted to devise schemes to look beyond their present. From the time of the ancient river-valley civilizations to the 20th century, some people have used astrology or other divinations to predict the future. More systematically, some scholars have assumed that time moves in cycles, so that one could count on repetition of basic patterns. This was a common assumption in Chinese historical thought and also among Muslim historians in the postclassical period. Others, including Christian thinkers and advocates of more secular faiths such as Marxism, have looked toward some great change in the future: the Last Judgment, for example, or the classless society to which history is steadily working. The idea of some master plan guiding history, moving it in a steady direction and toward a purpose, runs deep in the thought of several cultures, including our own. Whatever the approach, the human impulse to know what we cannot definitely know seems inescapable.

Yet all the evidence suggests that our vision of the future remains cloudy at best. It has been calculated that well over 60 percent of all predictions or forecasts offered by serious social scientists in the United States since 1945—called upon to sketch future business cycles, family trends, or political currents, for instance—have been wrong. How many observers just 50 years ago could have predicted such basic recent transformations as decolonization; the rise of new kinds of authoritarianism; fundamental revolutions in China, Iran, and Cuba; the challenge to communist rule in the Soviet Union; the invention of computer and genetic engineering technologies; or the industrial breakthroughs of many Pacific coast regions of Asia? A few of these events could be discerned in advance, to be sure, but many were great surprises. And other developments that were confidently predicted have not come to pass: Americans are not normally riding about in helicopters rather than automobiles (an image of the 1940s), nor have families been replaced by promiscuous communes (a forecast of the 1960s).

Even though we cannot know the future, we can use history to develop a framework for evaluating it and partially anticipating it as it unfolds: We can know what factors to monitor. Recent patterns and their relationship to older themes in world history allow an orientation toward what is to come. This final chapter suggests several vantage points from which to relate past to present to future. We deal with issues of progress and deterioration, with the ongoing tensions between separate civilizations and forces that impact throughout the world, and with trends in the basic political, cultural, economic, and social functions of human society.

This chapter presents several methods of approaching the future, all of which require historical knowledge and analytical skills in assessment. No method offers certainty, which is why some historians refuse to deal with forecasting in any form, lest it corrupt their true craft. All the approaches, however, promote further thinking, not only about the future but about the various kinds of historical trends that are shaping it.

We begin first with the easiest relationship between recent past, present, and future: extrapolating from recent trends. We then turn to two more dramatic forms: the moral evaluation based on judgments of whether world society is getting better or worse and the dramatic forecast based on a revolutionary factor that will provoke a major disruption between future and past. Finally, we look at the future in terms of a set of issues fundamental to world history for many centuries, though taking new form in our own era.

PERIODIZATION: NEW EVENTS AND UNCERTAINTY

What we know about 20th-century history both helps and hinders use of the recent past to organize some sense of the future. It seems clear that in the 1920s and 1930s a new phase in world history began to take shape by the usual periodization criteria: parallel developments in major civilizations, reshuffling of geographical boundaries including changes in the roster of particularly influential civilizations, and intensification of international contacts. More extensive trade, unprecedented worldwide alliance systems, and the new variety of cultural exchanges readily illustrate

the international intensification theme. Geographical changes include the loosening of Western domination through the decolonization movement and the new sources of industrial competition; they also include realignments in the societies of East and Southeast Asia and new configurations of the Middle East and the Indian subcontinent. Developments that cut across diverse societies include shared technologies (despite continuing gaps in overall technological levels), new political forms, and a tendency toward cultural secularization. The patterns add up, as we have seen, to a break in world history at least as great as the one that occurred in the 15th century, as Arab dominance yielded and new empires and trade patterns emerged.

The fact of a major break in world history, and of such recent vintage, means that many patterns familiar from the 19th century will almost surely continue to recede—we need not expect a revival of Western colonial dominance, for example. More positively, it is reasonable to expect continuing intensification of many world contacts: the necessary technology is increasingly available with international computer linkages and air-delivery systems, and the increase in contacts has formed a fairly steady trend in world history for at least 1000 years. Societies in the 20th century that have tried to isolate themselves from larger world currents—the Soviet Union in the 1930s to an extent as well as China under Mao, for example—have usually found it necessary to open somewhat more fully, lest they lose the technological and economic benefits of contact.

The fact that the 20th century launches a major new period, however, automatically limits more precise prediction. We may know that the West's relative dominance has declined, but we do not know whether it will continue to do so. Events in the early 1990s, including the reunification of Germany, hopes for firmer West European unity, and Westernized leadership for many of the newly independent East European nations, point to a European revival—not back to 19th-century imperialist levels, but well beyond what could have been foreseen just two decades ago. Analogies for a Western decline drawn from Roman or even Arab experience in the classical and postclassical periods may be totally misplaced. By the same token, there may be no single center of dominance—of the sort Arab and then Western civilization represented—in this emerging period in world history. The world of the future may continue the present pattern of several major centers of power and influence.

Other forecasts, based on recent trends, are also uncertain. The century has seen growing secularization of belief in otherwise varied societies. Trends are not uniform, given Muslim and Christian missionary activity in Africa as well as the Islamic resurgence elsewhere, but the general point—describing the spread of communism, consumer materialism, and nationalism—has been clear. Yet the idea of a world without dominant religions is so strange to some observers that they predict a major religious revival—perhaps under some new doctrine—for the coming century. Who is to say they are wrong? The point is that a new period in world history inevitably produces doubt about the directions of the future precisely because old patterns are shaken up and emerging trends are hard to gauge.

MAKING SENSE OF RECENT DEVELOPMENTS

Events themselves establish uncertain directions. The biggest political development of the late 1980s involved the explosions in the communist world. China experimented through the entire decade with a range of interactions with the capitalist world and with the introduction of more market devices into its own economy. Consumer interest grew in Chinese cities, while a number of peasant entrepreneurs amassed considerable earnings by catering to market demand in their agricultural production. Gorbachev's ascent to leadership in the Soviet Union in 1985 triggered sharper change (see Chapter 36). Reforms and protest vied within the Soviet Union, and the smaller East European states burst from Soviet Europe.

This was almost unprecedented ferment. Most observers, including seasoned intelligence experts, were astounded at the events throughout the communist system, precisely because they overturned settled assumptions about Soviet power and the hold of what had been effective police states. While it was essential to recast these assumptions, it was not clear how to predict subsequent patterns. Would Gorbachev succeed in reforming Soviet politics and coping with his country's admitted economic doldrums and massive environmental problems? His policies triggered important worker strikes for higher earnings and even more urgent nationalist protests from minority peoples long subject to Russian dominance. Here was a reminder of continuities of cultural identity and political interest, even amid apparent change. Indeed, the demands of regional nationalities in Eastern Europe by 1990 recalled tensions in the area before World War I; not only Soviet groups, but Bulgarians, Turks, Hungarians, Serbs, Croats, and Romanians began to raise intense and conflicting territorial demands. It was possible that the weakening of the Soviet empire would bring new diplomatic and even military turmoil to key parts of the world.

Within the Soviet Union, it was not clear that Gor-bachev could survive the varied sources of discontent, and many predicted that a more authoritarian regime, bent on protecting the integrity of the Soviet empire, would replace him. If Gorbachev fell or changed his policies, what would happen to the new regimes in places such as Poland and Hungary? Further, could Soviet and East European economies break out of a limited industrial framework to the newer technologies and affluence of the advanced industrial societies of the West or of the Pacific Rim?

In China, meanwhile, a massive student demonstration in 1989 in favor of greater democracy was brutally repressed. Would China remain an exception to trends in European communism, or had a seed of liberalization been planted that must someday flower more fully?

Historical understanding aids in sorting out possibilities, but only to a point simply because the future does not cleanly reproduce the past and the past itself offers various models. Some experts emphasized Russia's long authoritarian tradition and the more specific antecedents of Stalinist communism: Gorbachev's reformism must fail, in this view, because it countered Russian officialdom's commitment to a strong state and a controlled social order. Others, however, argued that Gorbachev was reviving an important Russian tradition of looking to partial Western models and experimenting on this base, an impulse visible not only in pre-Soviet experience but during the 1920s. Here was a more optimistic rendering that could be supplemented by the possibility that new factors, including the nation's productivity problems, could wipe away some historical precedents. The failure of the 1991 coup, amid democratic resistance to revived authoritarianism, emphasized the extent of real change in Russian political culture. Prognostication about China was no easier. It was nice to believe that democratic agitation, once launched, could not be permanently repressed, particularly if China continued a policy of economic reforms and contacts with the wider world economy. On the other hand, China's traditions of control and the specific precedents of Maoism might support a long period of suppression. It was also worth noting that student protest movements in 1989 had not precisely called for Western-style politics anyway, for they were directed in part toward smoother and less corrupt bureaucratic procedures, evoking Confucianism as much as Western liberalism.

Upheavals in Eastern Europe and potentially in China raised questions about the future of communism and the world balance of power. The rise of the Soviet Union and the United States had followed on the decline of Western Europe by the late 1940s. However, by the 1990s the Soviet Union was in partial eclipse and the United States, burdened by heavy international debt, found its international activities somewhat constrained. With the cold war and its leading practitioners receding, what global pattern would follow? Analogy could be suggestive: Recall that the first initiative that briefly replaced Arab dominance in the 15th century—the Chinese surge in international trade— proved to be a false start. Perhaps the cold war, with the United States and Soviet international rivalry, would be a similar episode, revealing the decline of the older West European dominance but not providing more than a temporary alternative. This possibility does not, however, predict what patterns may prove more durable, nor does it forecast the extent of Soviet decline or American constraint.

THE TRIUMPH OF THE WEST?

A few popularizers, to be sure, tried to make sense of complex trends as the 20th century neared its close. One writer from the American State Department, briefly popular among official United States government circles, projected an "end to history." He argued that the cold war had ended with a Western victory; all parts of the world were bent on imitating Western institutions. With this development, history with its massive conflicts and ideological competitions had ended. Peace would prevail through a somewhat boring eternity, sparked mainly by marketplace competitions in a thoroughly capitalist world. Such a prospect might be comforting, particularly as it seemed to glorify Western values. Yet the attempt to judge the future on the basis of recent events, while simplifying those events in turn, might also be judged foolhardy. Various Western historians have periodically attempted to postulate an end to the normal ups and downs of history. Middle-class liberals—the British Whig school—argued over a century ago that bourgeois values of education, social mobility, and political rights would lead to such general justice or satisfaction that there would be no reason for further change: All of history had been pointing to this moment of supreme enlightenment. Marx, of course, anticipated an end to historical process through communism's victory, though he did not claim to be quite so clear about the details of the future order. Hopes for a simpler future based on real or imagined recent trends thus has a pedigree; whether it greatly aids understanding or intelligently uses what we know of the past to predict the future, is doubtful.

Indeed the decline of the cold war clearly encouraged realignments in troubled regions, now that superpower rivalry no longer served as constraint. German reunification in 1990, resulting from the expulsion of the Communist regime from East Germany and creating a powerful state in Europe's center, raised some questions about European tensions, though plans for full economic unity in the Common Market proceeded. Iraq's ambitious leader, Saddam Hussein, judged the moment opportune for a more daring realignment in the Middle East. He invaded the small, oil-rich nation of Kuwait and may have hoped to use invasion to spearhead Muslim unity in the whole region, in the tradition of earlier conquerors such as the caliphs or the Ottomans. A United States led coalition defeated Hussein, changing the balance of power in the area but again making future arrangements extremely unpredictable. The victorious American president called for a "new world order" of stability, but the prospects for regional disruptions in the Middle East and elsewhere may have become more likely rather than less, as various leaders probed the decline of superpower rivalry.

TRENDS IN WORLD SOCIETIES

Prediction based on dramatic recent events is both essential and frustrating; the complication of the larger issues of 20th-century periodization recur constantly. One forecasting mode, however, seeks to cut through some of the problems by focusing on processes rather than events and by identifying strong current trends in order to gain some sense of the future's shape or at least of the questions that might be sensibly asked about it.

Trend extrapolation can be quite precise. Within a particular society such as the West or Japan, for example, it is easy to predict an expansion of problems associated with retirement and old age costs in the near future, based on current patterns and the almost-certain further results of low birthrates and growing longevity. The problems are present already, and they will increase. Only unforeseen changes, such as a spurt in the birthrate or new policies that deny medical care for older adults and so reduce longevity gains, can throw such short-term projections off.

Extrapolating vaguer trends, as well as adding an international basis, is obviously riskier. Nevertheless, several common questions or issues had emerged in the later 20th century that provide a valid framework for anticipating ongoing opportunities or problems.

POLITICAL ISSUES

In the political sphere, the changing balance between democracy and other 20th-century government forms, notably communism and authoritarianism, provided the most obvious link between recent trends and future prospects.

Democratic parliamentarianism is now a well-established tradition in much of the West. Extremist movements still challenge it in some countries, and the fact that democratic trends were dislodged by Nazism in Germany scarcely one-half century ago reminds us not to be too complacent. Major economic setbacks might again call the regimes into doubt. But while there are many problems with Western politics, the regimes do seem firmly rooted. They have withstood massive shocks such as loss of colonies. Indian and Japanese democracies are more recent and possibly less rooted in prior political forms; Japanese democracy still combines somewhat uneasily with the tradition of upper-class dominance, while Indian democracy seeks to accommodate the old tendency toward regional fragmentation plus new class and religious tensions. Here too, however, comparative stability has by now described a span of several decades.

More generally, there is no question that a democratic impulse was spreading in the world by the late 1980s, as it had in the first flush of decolonization in the 1940s and 1950s. New currents in the communist world suggested a clear link between democracy and economic reform, which resulted in widespread popular aspiration toward a democratic system.

The authoritarian form of government also showed new weaknesses. Authoritarian forms in the 20th century had resulted from the tensions experienced by many new nations after the destruction of earlier political institutions and from sources of available leadership such as the military. Authoritarianism has a strong base in Latin-American tradition, where it goes back to the 19th century and where it has proved capable of both change and popularity. By the 1980s, however, democratic institutions had effaced authoritarianism in all but a few cases in Latin America. Again in the 1980s attacks on authoritarianism in the Philippines, Korea, and Pakistan raised new doubts about the system's future, though particularly in Korea authoritarian overtones remained even under an elected president. Early in the 1990s new democratic movements challenged authoritarianism in many African states.

Buoyed by the trends, some observers argued that a form of liberal democracy would prove to be the only viable political style for modern nations, because of the prestige it carried and because of the flexibility it allowed in responding to rapid social and economic change. Arguments of this sort were not new, but they gained increasing credibility with the overturning of authoritarian regimes in Latin America during the 1970s and then the upheaval of the communist world. Certainly a worldwide turn to democracy would have simplified political analysis, yet doubts about the forecast remained, because of the distinctiveness—both traditional and recent—of Chinese political systems, for example, or the stubborn persistence of authoritarian regimes in the Middle East.

CULTURAL ISSUES

The idea of a set of cultural issues affecting the world's future is hardly commonplace. We are instead accustomed to thinking about political and military scenarios or the tensions of economic development. Furthermore, many cultural patterns apply primarily to individual civilizations, which are defined more clearly by cultural styles than by any other characteristic.

A few cultural themes cut across civilizations, however, raising questions about what is to come. Many people have periodically wondered or worried about the results of pressures for homogeneity, as the trappings of consumer culture, the popularity of Western fads, and the impact of the leading international artistic and architectural styles continue to spread. It is possible to travel to most of the world's cities today and stay in hotels, eat in restaurants, and buy goods that would scarcely differentiate downtown Chicago from downtown Istanbul. The dissemination of English as a world-currency language for travel, business, and science adds to the impression of growing homogeneity. The popularity of Western-dominated cultural styles has raised issues for Japan, it has added to the confusions of growing up in modern African cities, and it has helped divide Islamic societies. So the issue of balancing international modes and distinctive traditions has wide applicability. To date, most civilizations have maintained their own tone, even as they selectively use international fads and products. But the further spread of global customs will probably intensify the friction between tradition and modernity, while possibly undermining diversity around the world. Further internationalization might also, at the same time, promote greater understanding; already, at their best, the modern Olympic Games, based on an internationalization of key sports, have bridged some gaps that political leaders cannot close.

A more subtle issue involves the role of expressions such as art or music in human life. Industrialization forces such concentration on economic and technical needs and involves such uprooting of established habits through emphasis on technical training that the arts may be pushed to the periphery. This concern, of course, is phrased in various ways, depending on the civilization. Westerners worry that a rich popular cultural tradition has been replaced by commercialized, shallow entertainments designed to sell goods. The most creative artists may have become unusually remote from public taste. Non-Western intellectuals worry that their cultural traditions are being displaced by urban squalor or Westernization, or that government controls bend culture to purposes of political obedience. Japanese intellectuals sometimes lament the materialism of their own

This photo of downtown Lagos, Nigeria, shows the Western influence on international urban architecture.

culture where traditional art survives but, again, may play a less central role than in the past. Some dissident Russian intellectuals have expressed the same concern about their industrial society, while Africans worry that traditional art degenerates into mass-produced trinkets for tourists.

The problem of integrating science with more traditional religious and artistic endeavors constitutes a related theme. Science has long been part of the intellectual arsenal of most civilizations, but it played a role subordinate to religious and esthetic interpretations of nature and human nature. Starting with the West, modern intellectual history has involved a steady upgrading of science, which became linked to the broader process of technical and industrial development. Yet even in the West, science has not satisfied all human needs, and at the same time it has not provided as encompassing a framework as traditional religion once did for relating separate portions of the human cultural experience. The result in the West, during the past two centuries, has been enduring tension, dividing science from the arts or humanistic disciplines. Several societies outside the West have lagged in developing scientific research to match better-established interests in arts, religion, and literature, or, as with Islamic fundamentalism, they have insisted on the primacy of a religious view. Tensions between science and nonscience may be healthy; they certainly seem inevitable; but in various ways in different major cultures, they raise important issues about the integration of intellectual outlook for the future.

World culture in the future must also deal with technological change. The omnipresence of the radio is already an accomplished fact; most villages, not to mention urban families, have their transistors. Television too is becoming a global medium, as over half the world's population has relatively ready access to a TV set. The potential spread of computer-based information systems raises an additional prospect for the future. Most people in the later 20th century are contending with standardized sources of information and with increased amounts of information. The question of the ongoing impact of new transmission technologies on popular culture as well as on creativity in the sciences and nonsciences alike, forms a final open-ended issue for the world's cultural evolution at the end of the 20th century and beyond.

ECONOMIC ISSUES

Economic problems and prospects form the most familiar framework for discussing the future. Will the agricultural civilizations, as in Africa or Latin America, manage to industrialize? Can the environment withstand mounting industrialization? How will the growing parity between the West and East Asia in industrial development work out— will the West decline, or can it live with a new balance? Has East European development, so vigorous earlier in the century, reached a plateau, and if so, what will the results be in terms of Russian politics and diplomacy?

The gap that opened between early industrializing societies—including those initial latecomers, Russia and Japan—and those that are still industrializing remains stubbornly wide. Several major civilizations besides the industrial pioneers—most notably India, China, and Southeast Asia—have been generating economic growth above population increase in recent decades. They have invested substantially in agriculture and in manufacturing. The industrial world continues to undergo change as well, as the advent of postindustrial technologies and labor-force structures attests.

The economic divisions of the contemporary world are more subtle than the convenient dichotomy between industrial and developing nations suggests. Gaps have opened among industrial nations, depending on use of the newest technology; thus Eastern Europe again lags, as in the 18th and 19th centuries, which is an important source of the recent turmoil. Important differences divide nations struggling for agricultural subsistence from those involved in rapid economic transformation. A few smaller nations, particularly on Asia's Pacific Rim, have joined the ranks of industrialized states, while other nations, such as Brazil, have developed strong industrial sectors amid many severe economic problems. Economic inequalities are complex, and they remain a concern. In a world increasingly interconnected, the political and military tensions resulting from economic differences can be acute. Unequal levels of wealth among major civilizations are no novelty in history, but disparities in levels of development in such a tightly linked global economy constitutes a novel combination. The stresses of playing catch-up in the economic development game and the resentments that can result on all sides—including those in wealthy nations seeking to preserve their lead—are an important if incalculable ingredient in the world's future.

Economic imbalances also helped explain other important developments in the later 20th century for which no clear end was in sight. The international drug trade picked up steam from the 1920s onward. Supplies came largely from countries with poor peasantries and desperate need for foreign exchange, plus in some cases weak governments. Between the world wars, countries such as Turkey and China served as key suppliers; after World War II, as these countries moved toward greater economic development, areas such as northwestern Latin America moved toward center stage. Demand for the drugs resulted from tensions in several industrial societies, as the burgeoning trade served as a perverse link among quite different kinds of economies in the interconnected world market.

The world's economic imbalances, plus different rates of population growth, also generated new pressures for immigration. Arabs and South Asians moved toward the oil-rich states of the Middle East. Growing minorities from Africa, Latin America, and Asia gravitated toward the United States and Western Europe. Japan, though leery of immigrants, admitted laborers and also prearranged brides from various Asian countries. The result of these movements has been a cross-civilization mixture of peoples unusual in world history and often associated with considerable tension and confusion. Continued relocation pressures form vital issues for many societies, including those that depend on sending excess labor elsewhere.

SOCIAL ISSUES

Diverse civilizations and unequal levels of industrial and urban development produce radically different social forms. Concern about family stability in the West and Africa contrasts with substantial family stability (and undue traditionalism?) in India and Latin America. Pressures of economic development have called some traditional social forms into question; most societies now attempt to encourage some social mobility as part of an effort to recruit talented leadership, spread education, and promote social justice. But specific social issues continue to vary greatly: India faces persistent, if now informal, gaps among castes, Communist societies uneasily accommodate a managerial or bureaucratic middle class, peasant unrest continues in parts of Latin America, and the West worries about racial tensions surrounding new or traditional minorities. Even relations among the generations vary, with most industrial societies gradually coming to terms with a growing old-age segment, and most agricultural civilizations still focusing on problems of nurturing and educating the young.

A few fundamental questions do apply to all societies. Industrialization has involved city growth, and urbanization now in many cases races ahead of other economic change. City life, in turn, poses some basic challenges, such as problems of dealing with crowding, problems of providing appropriate entertainment, and problems of dealing with psychological stress stemming from the excitement and tension of city life. At times, though not invariably, urbanization brings heightened crime. It certainly reduces traditional community control over behavior, so that other devices, including formal policing, must be extended. The impact of urbanization, both its promise and its difficulties, thus raises global questions for the present and future alike. Urbanization also creates new divisions between rural and urban people, a source of heightened misunderstanding, and, in many societies, a neglect of farming populations and even of agriculture.

Economic change and the spread of mass education also affect the family, including conditions for women and the position of other groups. Young people are subjected to examples other than those of their immediate relatives. Children who are better educated than their parents or who work outside the home often develop a taste for independence—a theme that, in the contemporary world, runs from Hong Kong to Nairobi to St. Louis. While the West, as the first industrializer, faced the changing role of children somewhat earlier than other societies, it has hardly resolved the resulting issues, and some common concerns about youth unrest and family solidarity have cut across a number of cultures, including that of the Soviet Union in recent decades.

Another trend to monitor involves social structure. Control of the land becomes steadily less important as the basis for social position. Aristocracies and landlord classes loom less large in late 20th-century world history than at any time since the dawn of civilization. Urbanized societies tend to place emphasis on wealth, knowledge, and managerial control as the basis of social prestige. This has been the clear pattern in the West and in Communist Eastern Europe; the pattern seems to be emerging in Africa and Asia as well. Division between wealthy managerial classes and laboring groups with little or no property and inferior education forms a set of tensions that cuts across several different civilizations. Educational access and attainment, for example, become everywhere more important as a basis for upward mobility, though this is a less novel phenomenon in Chinese tradition than, say, in Latin American tradition.

In sum: What we know about industrialization patterns and the impact of efforts to industrialize in various parts of the world suggests some ongoing questions about social and family structure that apply to a number of societies despite vastly different specific patterns. The social structures of the world range from remnants of India's caste system to the managerial bureaucracies of China and the Soviet Union, and from highly urbanized Japan to societies where urban elites struggle to control rural majorities. Quite generally, however, tension between expectations of opportunity and ongoing social hierarchies raises another set of leading questions for the future.

THE WORLD'S FUTURE AS PROMISE OR THREAT

Talking about future issues on the basis of recent trends provides a vital connection between what we know about the later 20th century and the issues we can anticipate in the 21st century. The strategy can be applied to a vast range of specific issues and specific societies, beyond the general points raised in the previous section. The approach

lacks flair, however, and many observers prefer a different and more dramatic means of linking society past and society to come.

One mode, and a tempting way to end a world history text, is to offer glowing words of hope about the achievements and bright prospects of humankind. Moral judgments here substitute for precise forecasts. Contemporary Western culture continues to value optimism and to believe that students, especially, should be inspired to think well of the society around them, hopeful as they face their own future. Yet the message of history, including contemporary history, is decidedly ambiguous on the question of hopefulness.

THE BRIGHT SIDE

World history is without question a record of impressive, even inspiring, human achievement. Through art, music, and literature, people have created moments of great beauty. Through religion and science, people have gained new understanding of the world they live in; the daily environment is surely a less fearful and more intelligible habitat for us than it was for our hunting-and-gathering ancestors. Political institutions have been generated that at certain times at least brought impressive stability and mechanisms of justice to many people. Technological mastery of nature has increased fairly steadily in human history. Certainly our species has learned how to support ever greater numbers of people, as agricultural techniques and then industrialization provided more reliable means of subsistence. Humankind, at first a rather frail competitor for survival, now easily outnumbers any of the other complex mammalian species, and thus has, to date, handily passed this basic biological test of success.

The 20th century has contributed at least its share to the record of progress. Advances in industry and agriculture have permitted the birth and survival of more people in our century than in all previous centuries combined. Life expectancy has risen notably in all societies, not just those with a sophisticated industrial apparatus. New seeds and fertilizers in the agricultural "green revolution" have greatly improved food supplies in otherwise "poor" societies such as India. Scientific discoveries add greatly to our knowledge as well as to our technology, though some civilizations continue to value nonscientific ways of viewing the world. Experts in virtually every nation know more about the functioning of the human body, about weather and climate patterns, about astronomy, and indeed about human history than any society has ever known before. The capacity to organize large groups of people has also improved, at least in certain respects. Most societies today can operate larger businesses or school systems or census-taking operations than ever before. Along with this bureaucratic achievement come some probable improvements in certain aspects of social relationships. Slavery has been almost fully eradicated. Although great variety persists, women have been granted new opportunities in many parts of the world in terms of political rights and less complete confinement to domestic functions. No one would argue that injustice has been eliminated, but there may be some measurable gains. The spread of education, another general development in the 20th century, also provides a basis for claiming a genuine increase in human knowledge, not just at the level of advanced research but also among peasants and workers.

Many of these developments provide additional hope for the future. Better medical care and nutrition may broaden the human potential. Mass schooling, still a relative novelty in many societies, may join with electronic technologies, such as radio and television, to bring formal education even to remote regions that remain largely agricultural. Additional research gains seem virtually assured, as physicists, for example, make almost daily discoveries about the nature of the universe. Unquestionably, the human potential remains vast. It seems likely, though not certain, that women in most societies will continue to gain new rights and functions, based on worldwide trends of rising educational levels, falling birthrates and greater legal and suffrage equality. Women's conditions may vary considerably according to the particular standards of each civilization, but there are some general trends away from traditional patriarchy—in Africa, China, and parts of the Middle East as well as in industrial societies.

THE OTHER SIDE

Yet history is also, unquestionably, the record of humankind's inhumanity to its own members. The historical record is peppered with acts of massive cruelty and bitter hatreds that have divided nations and races. While certain civilizations may claim to have tamed some destructive impulses, and while certain cruelties like deliberate human sacrifice have ended, it is hard to argue that the overall record of world history reveals measurable improvements in human relationships.

The 20th century has generated particularly troubling questions about human impulses wedded to awesome technologies and wider contacts among peoples. The century has produced the bloodiest wars on record; 60 million people were killed in World War II alone. Even small wars produced great carnage, such as the 100,000 Iraqis killed by Western bombing in 1991's Persian Gulf conflict. The introduction of sophisticated weaponry, combined with on-going political tensions, has resulted in massive slaughter even aside from formal wars: the deaths of hundreds of thousands as part of revolution in Russia and China; Hitler's insane efforts to exterminate the Jews; and the execution of additional hundreds of thousands stemming from racial or religious conflict in Uganda, Cambodia, and on the Indian subcontinent, for example. Less massive but surely menacing has been the rise of new kinds of terrorism in the West, the Middle East, and parts of Asia, as political fanatics attack civilian populations to dramatize their desire for social revolution or redress of nationalist grievances. The 20th century has been a violent period, surpassing even the most ravaged periods of the past in the sheer volume of slaughter if only because of the availability of technologies for mass killing. A number of societies, as a result of revolutionary or other tensions, developed new nonchalance about killing during key periods of tension. Even India, long a tolerant civilization and known in the 20th century for emphasis on nonviolence, exhibited unusual levels of internal religious warfare, intolerant hatreds, and attendant killing.

Our violent century has also generated a nuclear capability that makes the prospect of future war a new shadow on world history. Humankind may now have the weaponry necessary to destroy itself as a species and to destroy its habitat, planet Earth, as well. The atomic bomb has been used only once, by the United States, and it is possible to hope that the fearsomeness of the nuclear arsenal will teach world leaders to avoid all-out war in the future. But the peace many regions of the world have enjoyed since 1945 rests on a balance of terror more than on demonstrable enlightenment, and most efforts to negotiate serious nuclear disarmament have at best slowed rates of arsenal expansion, not reversed the trend of growing weapons sophistication.

We can hope that further escalation of human violence will not occur. Amid the new economic problems in the Soviet Union and budget pressures in the United States, greater willingness to reduce some weapons stocks emerged at the end of the 1980s, though both superpowers continued research into lasers and space shields. While almost one-half century without direct major-power warfare was encouraging, it hardly offered guarantees for the future. Further, spreading nuclear and chemical warfare capacity in other nations such as Iran, Iraq, and South Africa heightened anxieties about escalating tensions in some future regional conflict. Dependence of nations such as the United States and France on export sales of advanced weaponry added to a host of area arms races. Although most people have learned to carry on their lives without anxieties about nuclear disaster, no one can believe the world is secure.

The first true thermonuclear explosion in 1945 introduced the nuclear age.

The pattern of 20th-century war, terror, and weaponry forms the clearest blot on any idea of overall progress, but there are other nightmares. In the first place, the technologies that allow more people to survive in our world have also generated frightening levels of pollution and created potential imbalances in the natural environment. The daily elimination of acres of natural vegetation in expanding societies, such as those of Latin America and Africa, hinders the natural production of oxygen through photosynthesis, while in other regions industrial plants lower air and water quality and the increased output of human wastes produces still other environmental problems. Our ability to sustain growing populations, though unquestionable in recent history despite warfare, may be jeopardized in the future, or at least the amenities to which many people have become accustomed may be reduced.

Major environmental accidents during the 1980s pointed up the severity of the problems. Many different societies were involved in the generation of these accidents. A Russian nuclear reactor at Chernobyl in the Ukraine experienced partial meltdown, devastating the immediate regions with radiation and increasing radioactive levels in a wide area of Europe. An American chemical plant in Bhopal, India, suffered a huge explosion, killing hundreds of

The rain forest is threatened by each new road through the Amazon. Economic development vs. world ecological balance is a major problem of the region.

people and maiming even more. In 1989 a series of oceanic oil spills around the United States, including a particularly extensive accident in Alaska, severely damaged shorelines and marine life. The 1991 Persian Gulf War resulted in massive oil spills and oil fires. More general findings, about penetration of the ozone layer because of chemical pollution and about widely anticipated global warming because of the growing use of hydrocarbons, demonstrated the international scope of environmental issues and the lag between policy controls and the acceleration of problems.

Other areas of concern more directly involve human relations. Improvements in bureaucratic capacity have brought new means of police control over many people around the world, most obviously in some authoritarian and Communist nations but also in places such as the United States that maintain unusually large prison populations. Human freedom is hard to measure over time, but it would certainly be difficult to assert that it has steadily increased in recent decades. The 20th century also stands open to some attack for its relative neglect of spiritual and esthetic expressions, though here, of course, evaluation is particularly subjective. Crowding, war, and the sheer concentration on economic development may have tended to shunt artistic and religious creativity to the side, reducing the beauty available in many human lives. Critics who worry about the undermining of African cultural traditions

and those who bemoan the mindless mass entertainments of the contemporary West may be identifying an important common problem in our own time and in our future.

New formulations of social and economic inequalities also support a pessimistic rendition of recent history. Slavery and caste systems were officially gone, to be sure. But the deteriorating position of unskilled wage labor, including much immigrant labor, within individual nations such as the United States, and the growing worldwide gaps between labor standards of the industrial and the less developed nations posed troubling new trends. Freedom from want was not uniformly increasing.

A review of both optimistic and pessimistic cases provides useful ways of summing up historical patterns and deciding what one's own standards of evaluation are. But it seems fatuous to pretend that either an optimistic or a pessimistic approach is so clear-cut as to define the meaning of recent world history or the world's probable future. Some of humankind's most hopeful recent endeavors have not worked out particularly well: the United Nations organization, for example, has not produced serious mechanisms for conflict resolution, though it has usefully facilitated discussion. On the other hand, some of humankind's direst recent fears have not come to pass either: world population has not yet overwhelmed the available food supply, the United States and the Soviet Union have not as yet yielded to some inevitable cataclysm, and Nazi-style racism and

The greatest nuclear disaster to date occurred at Chernobyl, Soviet Union, in 1986. The nuclear plant was in ruins after the reactor's explosion.

brutality have not gained ground in the world's repertoire of political movements.

✥ THE ZIPPY FORECAST

Another common approach to the future, sometimes related to optimism or pessimism, involves identification of an overwhelming causal factor that will fundamentally alter the framework in which the societies of the world operate. Just as some historians have long sought a basic factor to explain historical change—through technology, trade levels, or cultural values—so the most dramatic breed of forecasters points to the single emerging revolutionary factor that will make almost everything different. The resultant dramatic forecast differs from general extrapolation from trends by seizing on one decisive ingredient and by anticipating massive contrasts between future and present.

THE OVERCROWDING SCENARIO

In the 1960s and early 1970s, gloomy "population bomb" predictions received a considerable audience. Experts correctly noted the unprecedented size and growth rates of world population, and argued that, unchecked, the sheer number of people would outstrip available resources, produce unmanageable environmental degradation, and cre-

ate rivalries for space that could usher in a series of bitter wars. Concern about world population trends, though still lively, had lessened by 1990, in part because growth rates had slowed. Some experts claimed that resources could expand with population growth, and noted that historically population expansion had often been a major source of innovation and creativity. Some also claimed a racist element in population bomb forecasts, insofar as these involved Western pundits urging people of color to have fewer babies. Population bomb forecasts had not been discounted entirely, and environmentalists picked up some of their concerns. As a tool for gauging the future, however, the "bomb" approach was yesterday's fad, though it remained true in 1990 that world population continued to grow at a rate of 250,000 new people per day.

A variant on the population bomb approach, though less widely publicized, played up the exhaustion of frontiers. Only by the later 20th century, some world historians argued, had human societies fully run out of room to expand—pending as yet unrealized space travel. Each previous period of world history had featured expansions into relatively empty spaces; thus the postclassical period saw movements into eastern Europe and western China plus Bantu migrations southward in Africa, while the 19th century had climaxed the history of human frontiers with the fuller peopling of the Americas and Australia and Rus-

World hunger and international aid. Ethiopian famine victims receive aid at a Red Cross center in 1984.

sian settlement in Siberia. With frontiers gone by the late 20th century, organized societies bumped against each other far more than ever before, while immigration inevitably meant movement not into relatively unsettled terrain, but into highly populous, often suspicious host societies. The implications for potential conflict, environmental exhaustion, and efforts to impede human movement were considerable, if this major factor is viewed as a basic distinction between society future and society past.

A POSTINDUSTRIAL WORLD

Another effort to identify deterministic causation highlights a revolutionary wave of technological change associated with computers, genetic engineering, robotics, and new devices for transmitting energy. According to some popular forecasters, late 20th-century society entered a postindustrial revolution fully as dramatic as the Industrial Revolution two centuries ago or the Neolithic revolution 10,000 years ago—with exactly the same potential for altering the whole framework of human existence. As technology continues to take over production, postindustrial society will feature service occupations dealing with people and information exchange, as not only agriculture but also industrial production is handled largely by machines. Social status will depend on technical knowledge, not money or landed property. Cities will change, becoming centers for meetings and recreation, not basic points of exchange and production. This picture is dramatic, and some observers have claimed to find ample evidence of its accuracy in existing trends. The postindustrial vision is also usually optimistic in assuming that key industrial problems will be resolved in the new order. Routine, repetitive work, for example, will be eliminated by automation, and computers will allow labor to become more varied and individualized.

Critics of the postindustrial vision raise several objections. They are not sure that the transformation discernible in the United States or Western Europe, for example, is as fundamental as the analogies to the Industrial Revolution suggest. Change is occurring, to be sure, but it preserves management and labor structures similar to the patterns of industrial society. There is no relocation of people as massive as industrial-based urbanization had involved and no need for such fundamental shifts in habits of thought. Computers can make work more routine, not less, as rigorous supervision becomes automated. Corporate and government bureaucracies continue to expand. New technology, in other words, does not necessarily change most basic trends, and technological determinism should not be pressed too far. Further, if distinctive postindustrial societies are developing, they concentrate in very few parts of the world—the West and Japan; postindustrialization mainly exacerbates the economic inequalities among major areas that had already arisen as part of the world economy. How useful, then, is the concept for forecasting overall world history?

The computer age comes to life at an office of the International Business Machines corporation.

Dramatic forecasting of this sort—whether imbued with postindustrial optimism or population-bomb gloom, relies heavily on a single basic casual factor—technology or population determines all, and everything falls into place once this factor is established. Yet most historians reject this kind of determinism. The analysis of the past shows the power of considerable continuity, rather than some single-minded transformation. Major changes do occur, but they result from the confluence of several factors, not a single cause. Though some cataclysm is always possible, most historians assume that complexity will continue. Eye-catching forecasts can help organize thinking about what makes history tick and how present relates to past, but there are other orientations toward the future as well.

REGIONS, CIVILIZATIONS, AND WORLD FORCES

A final set of issues for the future returns us to more complex prospects, different from the stark drama of all-or-nothing forecasts and their reliance on one primary source of causation. These final issues really involve another assessment based on current trends but of a special sort that reaches not only into developments of the late 20th century but well back into world history and its fundamental dynamics.

Since the classical period, world history has involved a tension between the operations of individual civilizations and wider international forces that shape the way people think and behave across civilizational boundaries and sometimes almost through the entire world. As a new period in world history, the 20th century raises important new questions about this tension. As usual when large but inherently uncertain interpretive problems are at stake, some polar positions are available. It is possible to predict a new splintering among civilizations, even a new selfish regionalism, with each area emphasizing its own flavor now that the hothouse period of Western dominance is cooling down. There are also new centripetal forces, however, that may reduce the scope for individual cultures in favor of more literally international trends.

THE QUEST FOR SEPARATE IDENTITIES

Because the history of civilization began against a backdrop of widely separated communities, whether agricultural villages or hunting-and-gathering bands, patterns of aggregation and of building larger units form an underlying theme in the larger world-historical process. Yet aggregation into regions or whole civilizations has never been a constant. Empires and even cultural units fragment. The great multinational empires of the early modern period—

the Mughal, Ottoman, and now Russian, for example—all split apart. Events in the 1980s raised the prospect of new fragmentations to a surprising level: Peoples in relatively small regions showed that old loyalties persisted fiercely. Thus Slavic groups in Eastern Europe, even in a single small nation such as Yugoslavia, turned on each other with demands for separation or at least autonomy. French descendants in Quebec, seeking greater independence, encountered hostility from their English-descended neighbors elsewhere in Canada. A host of established units, including of course the Soviet Union, were newly vulnerable to regional ethnic, linguistic, and religious loyalties.

Amid the welter of new or newly recognized issues in the 20th century, it was easy to forget the persistence of many separate traditions. Various societies were grouped under common headings—such as *nonindustrial, overpopulated,* and *authoritarian*—and these labels had real meaning.

Nevertheless, regional patterns still counted, and in some cases they were supplemented by distinctive recent experiences—such as India's interaction with Britain in the 19th and early 20th centuries, compared to China's more complex contacts with the West. Areas where traditional religion remained intense, as in the Middle East and India, might share some results in the relatively low status of women, but they also divided depending on what the religion was. Islam's role in the Middle East thus helped differentiate this region from Hindu-majority India. Artistic styles picked up other long-standing distinctions, as did commitment to political centralization versus emphasis on greater regional autonomy. Even revolutionary China showed the hand of its particular past, despite great changes, in the continued emphasis on an embracing central state and the extensive reliance—interrupted only during Mao's cultural revolution—on elders in political leadership.

Developments after 1950 continued to reflect civilization boundaries. Thus both China and India newly struggled against high birthrates. The Indian government, however, proved relatively ineffective, given traditional resistance to state involvement, whereas Chinese efforts, though far from completely successful against older family habits, could build on earlier patterns of state intervention. Japan's avoidance of lawyers, in favor of reliance on honor and group loyalty, reflected inherited values different from those of the more contract-minded West.

Regions and civilizations have not remained changeless, but they combine distinctive traditions, distinctive recent experiences, and a distinctive filter by which even common experiences are modified. This pattern survives in the later 20th century. Thus the Indian interpretation of the problem of economic development differs from that of the Chinese, while the Chinese interpretation of what a Communist society involves turns out to differ from that of Soviet Russia. Moreover, despite important common themes, including nationalism, mass education, and attempts to improve agricultural and industrial technology, no overriding pattern of modernization has yet obliterated key boundaries among the major civilizations.

A basic theme of 20th-century history, almost certain to extend into the 21st century, thus involves an understanding of how each major civilization will interpret the forces of modern politics and industrialization to create its own amalgam. We can begin to see that this process may well resemble the earlier interplay between the spread of agriculture and local cultures, when a similar force of economic change—in this case, from hunting and gathering to farming—generated a variety of political, religious, and family institutions, all of which differed from the hunting past. Correspondingly, any common international process—for example, the forces that work toward modification of a patriarchal structure for women—must be evaluated specifically for each civilization. Generalization about the whole world could easily misfire in light of separate traditions (such as the specific forms of patriarchy) and distinctive recent experience.

A key result of decolonization and the growing challenge to Western dominance was, in fact, a reassertion of the cultural independence of several civilizations. The end of the cold war enhanced the prospects for new regional separations. This was a strong ingredient both of the Iranian revolution, bent on guiding a reinvigoration of Islam more generally, and of Chinese Communist reactions to the protest currents at the end of the 1980s, where renewed claims to China's separate and superior path surfaced quickly.

The quest for cultural autonomy in several major societies is particularly marked in contrast to the homogenizing impulses of modern mass culture. Indian films reproduce the themes and spirit of the great Hindu sagas in the world's largest movie industry. Islamic societies, quite like other Third World areas in many respects, maintain particularly vigorous religious strains, expressed also in distinctive birthrates and family patterns. Latin-American intellectuals deal with problems of identity and loneliness that derive from this civilization's particular past. Japan uses habits of group loyalty to generate modes of industrial governance different from those of the West, within an equally successful economic framework.

One key theme for the future, then, involves identifying separate paths for major civilizations and regions, including new ingredients and new vitalities as well as outright continuities from the past—as has long been the pattern in world history. It is certainly not possible to predict an international spread of a Western-type women's rights movement, though it is valid to note that conditions for women are changing everywhere. Formal feminism may depend heavily on prior political and cultural traditions, and though Western feminism has had some international echoes, it may not emerge as a strong popular force in Japan or Egypt. Again, each specific civilizational context balances larger world trends.

Yet the emphasis on distinctive civilizations, increasingly conscious of their unique qualities, is not the only focus of world history as we approach the future. In the first place, there is little assurance that the civilization areas identifiable in the late 20th century will remain constant. Societies do collapse and merge, and they may split apart. The differences between China and Japan in recent centuries prevent ongoing reference to a single East Asian pattern, and the emergence of a Pacific Rim adds further complexities. In another case, Turkey at the end of the 1980s applied for admission to the European Common Market. Without renouncing Islam, but building on the special relationship Turks have long maintained with the West, Turkey asked essentially to become part of the West. The application roused great anxieties in Western Europe,

The surge of feminism led to this women's rights rally in the United States in the 1970s.

concerned not only about Turkey's backwardness despite considerable recent industrial advance, but also about its strangeness. Possibly, however, the map of the Middle East was about to be redrawn once again, in terms of a division among separate identities.

The most important question for the future, however, involves the civilizational framework itself, as it has been elaborated over a 5000-year span, and whether it will persist. Civilizations, long functioning as forms that integrated more disparate and smaller regions to some degree, now may see a similar process pulling them into closer synchronism on a global basis.

THE FORCES OF INTERNATIONAL INTEGRATION

Previous crosscutting forces in world history, from agricultural technologies to the great world religions to new foodstuffs or inventions, such as the printing press, all promoted transformation *within* the separate civilizations. Even the rise of Western-dominated world trade did not fuse the civilizations into a single basic pattern. Arab or Western dominance reduced the autonomy of most civilizations only modestly, save in special cases such as Latin America where a prior civilization was substantially destroyed. Even in Latin America international contact brought massive change, but not full merger into Western cultural, political, or economic forms.

This balance, between separate regional and civilizational identities and international pressure, may now be changing decisively. The crosscutting forces of the past century or so have unquestionably stepped up the impact of international forces. One sign of this is the difficulty major societies have in trying to isolate themselves for whatever ideological reason. While the distinct features of individual civilizations can readily be discerned even in the way apparently common ideas, such as feminism, are handled, this may not always be the case. International movements of women, computer hackers, or soccer fans clearly override civilization boundaries, and they may gradually make those boundaries less distinct.

The internationalization of the world embraces a number of familiar ingredients. The speed of modern transportation and communication brings societies closer together, as does the rising volume of world trade. International artistic styles, particularly in urban architecture, have more vitality than ever before. The popularity of Western fads and fashions, from clothes to television to sports, leads to cultural contact among ordinary people in daily activities. In this sense the rise of the West continues to reverberate

even as its relative dominance recedes. The diplomatic framework created for the world by the cold-war rivalry between the United States and Russia touches virtually every regional conflict in ways that no single international pattern ever did before. At the elite level, if not at the level of mass culture, the spread of scientific training cuts across cultural boundaries as no world religion ever did.

The fact of growing world contacts and a spreading array of global forces produced the understandable, but erroneous, attempt a generation ago to simplify recent world history into a study of how rapidly each society yielded to the inevitable impulse to become essentially Western. Thus serious scholars assumed that the Western version of modernization, including industrialization, mass education, democratic parliamentary politics, low birthrate, a consumer society, and greater equality for women, would take hold around the world. Each civilization could thus be measured by the speed at which it generated the standard modern (meaning Western) features. This analytical approach confused some undeniably common impulses, including the desire to alter traditional patterns in the name of nationalism and economic development, with homogeneity. And it did not, moreover, allow for the revived force of traditional values in societies such as Islam.

Still, if the simplest modernization model has proved clearly inaccurate, as the world's civilizations continue to handle certain common impulses distinctively, the sense that a new simplifying framework may be right around the corner persists. Will one of the new technologies taking hold, for example, do the trick? This is a crucial aspect of any postindustrial argument applied at a world level. The spread of computer networks is sometimes held to foreshadow new, common patterns of organization, research, and thinking, bringing far greater similarities to the societies involved than the rhythms of the factory or the farm ever did. Some advocates even believe that agricultural societies can shift to a computer system for production and communication without going through a classic industrial phase. The idea of a computer-generated system of organization providing new common ground among civilizations applies most readily to the West and Japan, where structural changes have already brought similarity without obliterating vital diversities. But technologies have cut across cultural divides before, and possibly the power and speed of the computer revolution will have even more sweeping impacts.

Common cultures generate other forces through which specific international communities are obliterating civilizational distinctions. Scientists and social scientists from almost every society can now meet and discuss common methods and common basic assumptions. Political or other divisions may complicate this harmony, but a fundamental international community exists with a shared frame of reference. At another level, soccer football and a few other sports elicit very similar enthusiasms around much of the world, even though they also express competition among the societies fielding the teams.

International business constitutes another integrating force. As Japanese and Korean firms join Americans and Europeans in setting up branches of production in almost every regional market, and as business leaders strive to imitate each other's organizational forms and labor policies, civilizational boundaries retreat considerably.

On several different fronts, then, the intensification of international networks, itself part of a long and varied process in world history, has proceeded to the point that various scholars could seriously see in the late 20th century the beginning of the end for the civilizational form. World diversities and inequalities will obviously persist amid new international communities, but coherent regional civilizations may gradually pull apart at the seams.

For the moment, separate civilizations are still very much alive. An equilibrium between distinct civilizations and unifying developments provides the most obvious interpretive basis for asking questions about the future. Increasingly rapid and intense contacts around the world have not created a single framework for world history. The pull of regional as well as civilizational loyalties remains strong. The revival of divisive allegiances in many parts of the world in the early 1990s surely reflects a human need to find a way to counterbalance the large, impersonal forces stemming from international developments. The world, in some ways growing smaller, is becoming no less complex. Distinctive traditions continue to modify, sometimes to reverse, seemingly powerful unifying forces, though these forces persist as well.

CONCLUSION

ASKING QUESTIONS

Whatever the vantage point, questions easily outweigh answers in contemplating the future. The power of particular models—such as Western democracy or mass culture—and the international power of industrial business and technology pose new challenges to particular civilizations. This is not a mere replay of earlier tensions between world

currents and separate civilizational traditions. Yet continuities from the past—the surge of religious sentiment in Eastern Europe, for example—and possibly new needs for smaller-scale identities make predictions of an imminent triumph of a single world framework sheer folly. We know that tensions between international forces and needs, as well as the distinct reactions of individual societies, will shape the future, and that the tensions have some different ingredients in this newest period of world history from earlier periods. We know that the resultant interplay will be an important part of the future, along with new technologies and crucial environmental issues—for such interplay between contacts and divisiveness has shaped world history for many centuries. We do not know, however, what the precise results will be.

History contributes more than an understanding of the traditions and patterns that will continue to play some role in the future. Through analogies to past situations—such as earlier interactions between individual societies and a world economy—and through an understanding of changing trends, history improves our ability to ask good questions about the future and to evaluate the major types of forecasting available. We can count on the emerging world future to challenge our understanding, but we can also learn to use a grasp of the world past as a partial guide.

FURTHER READINGS

Several serious books (as well as many more simplistic popularized efforts) attempt to sketch the world's or the West's future. On the postindustrial society concept, see Daniel Bell's *The Coming of Post-Industrial Society* (1974). For other projections, consult R. L. Heilbroner's *An Inquiry into the Human Prospect* (1974) and L. Stavrianos's *The Promise of the Coming Dark Age* (1976).

On environment and resource issues, D. H. Meadows and D. L. Meadows's *The Limits of Growth* (1974) and L. Herbert's *Our Synthetic Environment* (1962) are worthwhile. M. ul Haq's *The Poverty Curtain: Choices for the Third World* (1976) and L. Solomon's *Multinational Corporations and the Emerging World Order* (1978) cover economic issues, in part from a non-Western perspective.

On military and diplomatic issues, A. Sakharov's *Progress Coexistence and Intellectual Freedom*, rev. ed. (1970), is an important statement by a Russian dissident; other useful texts include S. Hoffman's *Primacy or World Order. American Foreign Policy Since the Cold War* (1978),

S. Melman's *The Peace Race* (1961), and W. Epstein's *The Last Chance. Nuclear Proliferation and Arms Control* (1976).

On a leading social issue, see P. Hudson's *Third World Women Speak Out* (1979). A major interpretation of the 20th century world is Theodore von Laue's *The World Revolution of Westernization* (1989).

Glossary

Abbas the Great: Safavid ruler from 1587 to 1629; extended Safavid domain to greatest extent; created slave regiments based on captured Russians who monopolized firearms within Safavid armies; incorporated Western military technology. (26)

Abbasid: Dynasty that succeeded the Umayyads as caliphs within Islam; came to power in A.D. 750. (12)

Abdallahi, Khalifa: Successor of Muhammad Achmad as leader of Mahdists in Sudan; established state in Sudan; defeated by British General Kitchener in 1898. (32)

Abduh, Muhammad: Discipline of al-Afghani; Muslim thinker at end of the 19th century; stressed need for adoption of Western scientific learning and technology, importance of tradition of rational inquiry. (32)

Abdul Hamid: Ottoman sultan who attempted to return to despotic absolutism during reign from 1878 to 1908; nullified constitution and restricted civil liberties; deposed in coup in 1908. (32)

Abelard, Peter: Author of *Yes and No;* university scholar who applied logic to problems of theology; demonstrated logical contradictions within established doctrine. (16)

absolute monarchy: Concept of government developed during rise of nation-states in western Europe during the 17th century; featured monarchs who passed laws without parliaments, appointed professionalized armies and bureaucracies, established state churches, imposed state economic policies. (22)

Adena culture: First of the mound-building cultures; originating in southern Ohio; lasted until A.D. 700 in some regions. (9)

Aeschylus: Greek writer of tragedies. (6)

African National Congress: Black political organization within South Africa; pressed for end to policies of apartheid; sought open democracy leading to black majority rule; until the 1990s declared illegal in South Africa. (40)

Afrikaner National party: Emerged as the majority party in the all-white South African legislature after 1948; advocated complete independence from Britain; favored a rigid system of racial segregation called apartheid. (39)

agrarian revolution: Occurred between 8000 and 5000 B.C.; transition from hunting and gathering to sedentary agriculture. (1)

Ahuitzotl: Aztec emperor under whom the empire reached its greatest extent; based on creation of subject tribute states. (17)

Akbar: Son and successor of Humayan; oversaw building of military and administrative systems that became typical of Mughal rule in India; pursued policy of cooperation with Hindu princes; attempted to create new religion to bind Muslim and Hindu populations of India. (26)

Akhenaton: Egyptian pharaoh of the New Kingdom; attempted to establish a one-god religion, replacing the traditional Egyptian pantheon of gods. (2)

al-Afghani: Muslim thinker at the end of the 19th century; stressed need for adoption of Western scientific learning and technology, importance of tradition of rational inquiry. (32)

al-Ghazali: Brilliant Islamic theologian; struggled to fuse Greek and Quranic traditions; not entirely accepted by ulama. (13)

al-Mahdi: Third of the Abbasid caliphs; attempted but failed to reconcile moderates among Shi'as to Abbasid dynasty; failed to resolve problem of succession. (13)

al-Rashid: Most famous of Abbasid caliphs; renowned for sumptuous and costly living; dependent on Persian advisors early in reign; death led to civil wars over succession. (13)

Alexander the Great: Successor of Philip II; successfully conquered Persian Empire prior to his death in 323 B.C.; attempted to combine Greek and Persian cultures. (6)

Alexandria, Egypt: One of many cities of that name founded by Alexander the Great; site of ancient Mediterranean's greatest library; center of literary studies. (6)

Ali: Cousin and son-in-law of Muhammad; one of orthodox caliphs; focus for Shi'a. (12)

ali'i: High chiefs of Hawaiian society who claimed descent from the gods and rested their claims on their ability to recite in great detail their lineages. (10)

Ali, Muhammad: Won power struggle in Egypt following fall of Mamluks; established mastery of all of Egypt by 1811; introduced effective army based on Western tactics and supply; by 1830s able to challenge Ottoman government in Constantinople; died in 1848. (32)

Allah: Supreme God in strictly monotheistic Islam. (12)

Allende, Salvador: President of Chile; nationalized industries and banks; sponsored peasant and worker expropriations of lands and foreign-owned factories; overthrown in

1973 by revolt of Chilean military with the support of the United States. (38)

Alliance for Progress: Begun in 1961 by the United States to develop Latin America as an alternative to radical political solutions; enjoyed only limited success; failure of development programs led to renewal of direct intervention. (38)

Almohades: A reformist movement among the Islamic Berbers of northern Africa; later than the Almoravids; penetrated into sub-Saharan Africa. (14)

Almoravids: A puritanical reformist movement among the Islamic Berber tribes of northern Africa; controlled gold trade across Sahara; conquered Ghana in 1076; moved southward against African kingdoms of the savanna and westward into Spain. (10, 14)

alpacas: Along with llamas, domesticated animals of the Americas; basis for only form of nomadic pastoralism in the New World until European importation of larger animals in 15th century A.D. (4)

Álvares Cabral, Pedro: Portuguese leader of an expedition to India; blown off course in 1500 and landed in Brazil. (25)

Amaru, Tupac: Mestizo leader of Indian revolt in Peru; supported by many among lower social classes; revolt eventually failed because of Creole fears of real social revolution. (25)

Amaterasu: Sun goddess of the Shinto religion. (10)

American Civil War: Fought from 1861 to 1865; first application of Industrial Revolution to warfare; resulted in abolition of slavery in the United States and reunification of North and South. (29)

American exceptionalism: Historical argument that the development of the United States was largely individualistic; contact with western Europe was incidental to the larger development of the United States on its own terms. (29)

American Revolution: Rebellion of English American colonies along Atlantic seaboard between 1775 and 1783; resulted in independence for former British colonies, eventual formation of United States of America. (29)

amigos del país: Clubs and associations dedicated to improvements and reform in Spanish colonies; flourished during the 18th century; called for material improvements rather than political reform. (25)

anarchists: Political groups that sought the abolition of all formal government; particularly prevalent in Russia; opposed

tsarist autocracy; eventually became a terrorist movement responsible for assassination of Alexander II in 1881. (33)

Anasazi: "The ancient ones"; culture located in southwestern United States; flourished from A.D. 200 to 1200; featured large multistory adobe and stone buildings built in protected canyons or cliffs. (9)

Anglican church: Form of Protestantism set up in England after 1534; established by Henry VIII with himself as head at least in part to obtain a divorce from his first wife; became increasingly Protestant following Henry's death. (22)

animism: A religious outlook that sees gods in many aspects of nature and propitiates them to help control and explain nature; typical of Mesopotamian religions. (2)

Anschluss: Hitler's union of Germany with the German-speaking population of Austria; actually took place in 1938, despite complaint of other European nations. (34)

Antigonids: One of the regional dynasties that followed the death of Alexander the Great; founded in Macedonia. (6)

apartheid: Policy of strict racial segregation imposed in South Africa to permit the continued dominance of whites politically and economically. (40)

appeasement: Policy of Neville Chamberlain, British prime minister; particularly applied to Munich Conference agreements; hoped to preserve peace in the face of German aggression; failed when Hitler invaded Poland in 1939. (34)

Aquinas, Thomas: Creator of one of the great syntheses of medieval learning; taught at University of Paris; author of number of *Summas;* believed that through reason it was possible to know much about natural order, moral law, and nature of God. (16)

Arabic numerals: Actually an Indian system of numerical notation transported by Arabs to West; central to two scientific revolutions. (13)

Aragon: Along with Castile, a regional kingdom of the Iberian peninsula; pressed reconquest of peninsula from Muslims; developed a vigorous military and religious agenda. (21)

Archaic cultures: Hunting-and-gathering groups dispersed over the American continents by 9000 B.C. (9)

Arevalo, Juan José: Elected president of Guatemala in 1944; began series of Socialist reforms including land reform; Nationalist program directed against foreign-owned companies such as United Fruit Company. (38)

Argentine Republic: Replaced state of Buenos Aires in 1862; result of compromise between centralists and federalists. (31)

Aristophanes: Greek writer of comedies; author of *The Frogs.* (6)

Aristotle: Greek philosopher; teacher of Alexander the Great; knowledge based on observation of phenomena in material world. (6)

Arthashastra: Political treatise written during reign of Chandragupta Maurya; advocated use of spies and assassins, bribery, and scientific forms of warfare. (7)

Aryans: Indo-European nomadic pastoralists who replaced Harappan civilization; militarized society. (3)

Asante Empire: Established in Gold Coast among Akan people settled around Kumasi; dominated by Oyoko clan; many clans linked under Osei Tutu after 1650. (27)

asantehene: Title taken by ruler of Asante Empire; supreme civil and religious leader; authority symbolized by golden stool. (27)

Ashoka: Grandson of Chandragupta Maurya; completed conquests of Indian subcontinent; converted to Buddhism and sponsored spread of new religion throughout his empire. (7)

Asian sea trading network: Prior to intervention of Europeans consisted of three zones: Arab zone based on glass, carpets, and tapestries; India with cotton textiles; and China with paper, porcelain, and silks. (28)

Atlantic Charter of 1941: Treaty between the United States and Britain creating an alliance; included a clause that recognized the right of all people to choose the form of government under which they live; indicated sympathy for decolonization. (39)

Atlantic colonies: British colonies in North America; originally restricted to coastline of Atlantic Ocean from New England to Georgia. (23)

audiencia: Royal court of appeals established in Spanish colonies of New World; there were ten in each viceroyalty; part of colonial administrative system; staffed by professional magistrates. (25)

Augustus: Name given to Octavian following his defeat of Mark Anthony and Cleopatra; first emperor of Rome. (8)

Aurangzeb: Son and successor of Shah Jahan in Mughal India; determined to extend Mughal control over whole of subcontinent; wished to purify Islam of Hindu influences; incessant warfare exhausted empire despite military successes; died in 1707. (26)

Austronesian: Family of 30 related languages found in the Philippines, Indonesia, and Southeast Asia; people of this linguistic group migrated throughout Pacific. (10)

Axum: Kingdom located in Ethiopian highlands; replaced Meroe in first century A.D.; received strong influence from Arabian peninsula; eventually converted to Christianity. (10)

ayan: The wealthy landed elite that emerged in the early decades of Abbasid rule. (12)

ayllu: Households in Andean societies that recognized some form of kinship; traced descent from some common, sometimes mythical ancestor. (9)

Aztecs: The Mexica; one of the nomadic tribes that used political anarchy after fall of Toltecs to penetrate into the sedentary agricultural zone of Mesoamerican plateau; established empire after 1325 around shores of Lake Texcoco. (17)

Babur: Founder of Mughal dynasty in India; descended from Turkic warriors; first led invasion of India in 1526; died in 1530. (26)

Babylonian empire: Unified all of Mesopotamia c. 1800 B.C.; collapsed due to foreign invasion c. 1600 B.C. (2)

Baghdad: Capital of Abbasid dynasty; located in Iraq near ancient Persian capital of Ctesiphon. (12)

Baibars: Commander of Mameluk forces at Ain Jalut; originally enslaved by Mongols and sold to Egyptians. (20)

Bakr, Abu: One of Muhammad's earliest converts; succeeded Muhammad as first caliph of Islamic community. (12)

bakufu: Military government established by the Minamoto following the Gempei Wars; centered at Kamakura; retained emperor, but real power resided in military government and samurai. (19)

Balboa: First Spanish captain to begin settlement on the mainland of Mesoamerica in 1509; initial settlement eventually led to conquest of Aztec and Inca empires by other captains. (23)

Balfour Declaration: British minister's promise of support for the establishment of Jewish settlement in Palestine during the First World War; issued in 1917. (34)

Balkan: Peninsula located in southeastern Europe, including Macedonia and Greece, plus what became Bulgaria; controlled by Byzantine Empire. (15)

Balkan nationalism: Movements to create independent nations within the Balkan possessions of the Ottoman Empire; provoked a series of crises between the European alliance system; eventually led to the First World War. (29)

ball games: Ritual elements of many American cultures; played on formal courts; religious significance required that losing teams pay penalty of forfeiture of goods or their lives. (9)

Banana Republics: Term given to conservative governments supported or created by the United States in Latin America; believed to be either corrupt or subservient to U.S. interests. (38)

band: A level of social organization normally consisting of between 20 and 30 people; nomadic hunters and gatherers; labor divided on a gender basis. (1)

Bangladesh: Founded as an independent nation in 1972; formerly East Pakistan. (40)

banner armies: Eight armies of the Manchu tribes identified by separate flags; created by Nurhaci in early 17th century; utilized to defeat Ming emperor and establish Qing dynasty. (32)

Bantu: Originated in eastern Nigeria in West Africa; migrated into central and southern Africa using rivers—particularly the Congo Basin; village dwellers who depended on agriculture and fishing. (10)

Basil: Patriarch at Constantinople in mid-4th century; responsible for development of rule for monasticism in Byzantine Empire. (15)

Batavia: Dutch fortress located after 1620 on the island of Java. (28)

Batista, Fulgencio: Dictator of Cuba from 1934 to 1944; returned to presidency in 1952; ousted from government by revolution led by Fidel Castro. (38)

Battle of River Zab: Victory of Abbasids over Umayyads; resulted in conquest of Syria and capture of Umayyad capital. (12)

Battle of Siffin: Fought in 657 between forces of Ali and Umayyads; settled by negotiation that led to fragmentation of Ali's party. (12)

Batu: Ruler of Golden Horde; one of Chinggis Khan's grandsons; responsible for invasion of Russia beginning in 1236. (20)

Batuta, Ibn: Arabic traveler who described African societies and cultures in his travel records. (14)

bedouin: Nomadic pastoralists of the Arabian peninsula; culture based on camel

and goat nomadism; early converts to Islam. (12)

Belgian Revolution of 1830: Produced Belgian independence from the Dutch; established a liberal constitutional monarchy. (29)

Belisarius: One of Justinian's most important military commanders during period of reconquest of western Europe; commanded in North Africa and in Italy. (15)

Benedict of Nursia: Founder of monasticism in what had been the western half of the Roman Empire; established Benedictine Rule in the 6th century; paralleled development of Basil's rules in Byzantine Empire. (11, 16)

Benin: City-state formed in 14th century under Ewuare the Great (1440–1473); control extended from Niger River to coast near modern Lagos. (14)

Berke: Ruler of the Golden Horde; converted to Islam; his threat to Hulegu combined with the growing power of Mameluks in Egypt forestalled further Mongol conquests in the Middle East. (20)

Berlin Wall: Built in 1961 to halt the flow of immigration from East Berlin to West Berlin; immigration in response to lack of consumer goods, close Soviet control of economy, failed workers' uprising in 1953. (36)

Bernard of Clairvaux: Emphasized role of faith in preference to logic; stressed importance of mystical union with God; successfully challenged Abelard and had him driven from the universities. (16)

bhaktic cults: Groups dedicated to gods and goddesses; stressed the importance of strong emotional bonds between devotees and the god or goddess who was the object of their veneration; most widely worshipped gods were Shiva and Vishnu. (13)

Biafra: Founded as an independent nation in eastern Nigeria where the Ibo people were most numerous; suppressed as an independent state and reincorporated into Nigeria in 1970. (40)

bishops: Headed Christian churches and regional centers and supervised the activities of other churches within the jurisdictional area. (8)

Bismarck, Otto von: Conservative prime minister of Prussia; architect of German unification under Prussian king in 1870; utilized liberal reforms to attract support for conservative causes. (29)

Black Death: Plague that struck Europe in

14th century; significantly reduced Europe's population; affected social structure. (16)

blitzkrieg: German term for lightning warfare; involved rapid movement of troops, tanks, and mechanized carriers; resulted in early German victories over Belgium, Holland, and France. (34)

bodhisattvas: Buddhist holy men; built up spiritual merits during their lifetime; prayers even after death could aid people to achieve reflected holiness. (11)

Body of Civil Law: Justinian's codification of Roman law; reconciled Roman edicts and decisions; comprehensive system made Roman law coherent basis for political and economic life. (15)

Boer republics: Transvaal and Orange Free State; established to assert independence of Boers from British colonial government in Cape Colony in 1850s; discovery of diamonds and precious metals caused British migration into the Boer areas in 1860s. (30)

Boer War: Fought between 1899 and 1902 over the continued independence of the Boer republics; resulted in British victory, but began the process of decolonization in South Africa. (30)

Boers: Dutch settlers in Cape Colony. (23)

Bolívar, Simon: Creole military officer in northern South America; won series of victories in Venezuela, Colombia, and Ecuador between 1817 and 1822; military success led to creation of independent state of Gran Colombia. (31)

Bolsheviks: Literally the majority party; the most radical branch of the Russian Marxist movement; led by V. I. Lenin and dedicated to his concept of social revolution; actually a minority in the Russian Marxist political scheme. (33)

Bonaparte, Joseph: Brother of Napoleon; placed on Spanish throne during Napoleonic Wars; disruption of Spanish monarchy contributed to Latin-American movements for liberation. (31)

Bonaparte, Napoleon: Rose within the French army during the wars of the French Revolution; eventually became general; led a coup that ended the French Revolution and established the French Empire under his rule; defeated and deposed in 1815. (29)

Boxer Rebellion: Popular outburst aimed at expelling foreigners from China; failed due to intervention of armies of Western powers in China; defeat enhanced control of Europeans and the power of provincial officials. (32)

boyars: Russian aristocrats; possessed less political power than did their counterparts in western Europe. (15)

Brest-Litovsk: Treaty signed between the revolutionary government of Russia and Germany in March 1918; Russia withdrew from the First World War and granted substantial territories to Germany in return for peace. (34)

British East India Company: Joint stock company that obtained government monopoly over trade in India; acted as virtually independent government inz regions it claimed. (23)

British Raj: Government of the British East India Company; developed as a result of the rivalry between France and Britain in India. (30)

Bronze Age: From 4000 to 3000 B.C.; increased use of plows, metalworking; development of wheeled vehicles, writing. (1)

Buddha: Creator of major Indian and Asian religion; born in 6th century B.C. as son of local ruler among Aryan tribes located near Himalayas; became an ascetic; found enlightenment under bo tree; taught that enlightenment could be achieved only by abandoning desires for all earthly things. (7)

Bulgaria: Slavic kingdom established in northern portions of Balkan peninsula; constant source of pressure on Byzantine Empire; defeated by Emperor Basil II in 1014. (15)

bushi: Regional warrior leaders in Japan; ruled small kingdoms from fortresses; administered the law, supervised public works projects, and collected revenues; built up private armies. (19)

Buyids: Regional splinter dynasty of the mid-10th century; invaded and captured Baghdad; ruled Abbasid Empire under name of sultan; retained Abbasids as figureheads. (13)

Byzantine Empire: Eastern half of Roman Empire following collapse of western half of old empire; retained Mediterranean culture, particularly Greek; later lost Palestine, Syria, and Egypt to Islam; capital at Constantinople. (11, 15)

Caesar, Julius: Roman general responsible for conquest of Gaul; brought army back to Rome and overthrew republic; assassinated in 44 B.C. by conservative senators. (8)

Calcutta: Headquarters of British East India Company in Bengal in Indian subcontinent; located on Ganges; captured in 1756 during early part of Seven Years'

War; later became administrative center for all of Bengal. (23)

caliph: The political and religious successor to Muhammad. (12)

calpulli: Seven clans in Aztec society, later expanded to more than sixty; divided into residential groupings that distributed land and provided labor and warriors. (17)

Calvin, Jean: French Protestant who stressed doctrine of predestination; established center of his group at Swiss canton of Geneva; encouraged ideas of wider access to government, wider public education; spread from Switzerland to northern Europe and North America. (22)

camel nomads: Nomadic pastoralists dependent on domesticated camels; common to Arabian peninsula and Sudanic Africa; associated with development of major trade routes. (4)

candomble: African religious ideas and practices in Brazil, particularly among the Yoruba people. (27)

cannibal kingdom: Modern interpretation of Aztec society created by Marvin Harris; based on observation that Mesoamerica lacked cattle and sheep that replaced human sacrifice in the Old World. (17)

Canton: One of two ports in which Europeans were permitted to trade in China during the Ming dynasty. (28)

Cape Colony: Dutch colony established at Cape of Good Hope in 1652 initially to provide a coastal station for the Dutch seaborne empire; by 1770 settlements had expanded sufficiently to come into conflict with Bantus. (23)

Cape of Good Hope: Southern tip of Africa; first circumnavigated in 1488 by Portuguese in search of direct route to India. (23)

captaincies: Strips of land along Brazilian coast granted to minor Portuguese nobles for development; enjoyed limited success in developing the colony. (25)

caravels: Slender, long-hulled vessels utilized by Portuguese; highly maneuverable and able to sail against the wind; key to development of Portuguese trade empire in Asia. (28)

Cárdenas, Lázaro: President of Mexico from 1934 to 1940; responsible for redistribution of land, primarily to create ejidos or communal farms; also began program of primary and rural education. (38)

Caribbean: First area of Spanish exploration and settlement; served as experimental region for nature of Spanish colonial experience; encomienda, system of colonial government initiated here. (25)

Carolingians: Royal house of Franks after 8th century until their replacement in 10th century. (16)

Carthage: Originally a Phoenician colony in northern Africa; became a major port and commercial power in the western Mediterranean; fought the Punic Wars with Rome for dominance of the western Mediterranean. (8)

Casa de Contratación: Spanish Board of Trade operated out of Seville; regularized commerce with New World, supplied colonial provisions. (25)

castas: People of mixed origin in Spanish colonial society; relegated to secondary status in social system; constituted potentially revolutionary group. (25)

caste system: Rigid system of social classification first introduced into Indian subcontinent by Aryans. (3)

Castile: Along with Aragon, a regional kingdom of the Iberian peninsula; pressed reconquest of peninsula from Muslims; developed a vigorous military and religious agenda. (21)

Castro, Fidel: Cuban revolutionary; overthrew dictator Fulgencio Batista in 1958; initiated series of reforms to establish Socialist reforms; came to depend almost exclusively on USSR. (38)

Çatal Huyuk: Early urban culture based on sedentary agriculture; located in modern southern Turkey; was larger in population than Jericho, had greater degree of social stratification. (1)

Catherine the Great: German-born Russian tsarina; ruled after assassination of her husband; gave appearance of Enlightened rule; accepted Western cultural influence; converted nobility to service aristocracy by granting them new power over peasantry. (24)

Catholic Reformation: Restatement of Orthodox Catholic beliefs in response to Protestant Reformation; established councils that revived Catholic doctrine and refuted Protestant beliefs. (22)

cattle herders: Nomadic pastoralists dependent on domesticated cattle; common to region from upper reaches of Nile to southern Africa; little impact on civilizations until later date. (4)

caudillos: Independent leaders who dominated local areas by force in defiance of national policies; sometimes seized the national governments to impose their concept of rule; typical throughout newly

independent countries of Latin America. (31)

Cavour, Count Camillo di: Architect of Italian unification in 1858; formed an alliance with France to attack Austrian control of northern Italy; resulted in creation of constitutional monarchy under Piedmontese king. (29)

Celts: Inhabited most of Britain and Ireland; organized in small regional kingdoms; featured mixed agricultural and hunting economies; replaced in most places by Germans. (10)

centralists: Those Latin-American politicians who wished to create strong, centralized national governments with broad powers; often supported by those politicians who described themselves as conservatives. (31)

Chabi: Influential wife of Kubilai Khan; promoted interests of Buddhists in China; indicative of refusal of Mongol women to adopt restrictive social conventions of Chinese. (20)

Chaldiran: Site of battle between Safavids and Ottomans in 1514; Safavids severely defeated by Ottomans; checked western advance of Safavid Empire. (26)

Chams: Indianized rivals of the Vietnamese; driven into the highlands by the successful Vietnamese drive to the south. (19)

Chan Buddhism: Known as Zen in Japan; stressed meditation and appreciation of natural and artistic beauty; popular to members of elite Chinese society. (18)

Chandragupta Maurya: Founder of Maurya dynasty; established first empire in Indian subcontinent; first centralized government since Harappan civilization. (7)

Changan: Capital of Tang dynasty; population of two million, larger than any other city in the world at that time. (18)

Charlemagne: Charles the Great; Carolingian monarch who established substantial empire in France and Germany c. 800. (16)

Charles III: Spanish enlightened monarch; ruled from 1759 to 1788; instituted fiscal, administrative, and military reforms in Spain and its empire. (25)

Chartist movement: Attempt on the part of artisans and workers in Britain to gain the vote during the 1840s; demands for reform beyond the Reform Act of 1832 were incorporated into a series of petitions; the movement failed. (29)

Chavín culture: Appeared in highlands of Andes between 1800 and 1200 B.C.;

typified by ceremonial centers with large stone buildings; greatest ceremonial center was Chavín de Huantar; characterized by artistic motifs. (9)

Chiang Ching-kuo: Son and successor of Chiang Kai-shek as ruler of Taiwanese government in 1978; continued authoritarian government; attempted to lessen gap between followers of his father and indigenous islanders. (37)

Chichen Itzá: Originally a Mayan city; conquered by Toltecs c. 1000 and ruled by Toltec dynasties; architecture featured pyramid of Feathered Serpent (Quetzalcoatl). (17)

chichimecs: American hunting-and-gathering groups; largely responsible for the disruption of early civilizations in Mesoamerica. (4)

chiefdom: Widely diffused pattern of social organization in the Americas; featured chieftains who ruled from central towns over a large territory including smaller towns or villages that paid tribute; predominant town often featured temples and priest class. (9)

Chimu state: Regional Andean chiefdom that flourished from A.D. 800 to 1465; fell to Incas. (9)

chinampas: Beds of aquatic weeds, mud, and earth placed in frames made of cane and rooted in lakes to create "floating islands"; system of irrigated agriculture utilized by Aztecs. (17)

Chinggis Khan: Born in 1170s in decades following death of Kabul Khan; elected khagan of all Mongol tribes in 1206; responsible for conquest of northern kingdoms of China, territories as far west as the Abbasid regions; died in 1227, prior to conquest of most of Islamic world. (13, 20)

Chongzhen: Last of the Ming emperors; committed suicide in 1644 in the face of a Jurchen invasion of the Forbidden City at Beijing. (28)

Choson: Earliest Korean kingdom; conquered by Han emperor in 109 B.C. (19)

Christian Democratic movement: Political movement common to many Western European nations after World War II; wedded to democratic institutions and moderate social reform. (35)

Churchill, Winston: British prime minister during World War II; responsible for British resistance to German air assaults. (34)

Cicero: Conservative Roman senator; Stoic

philosopher; one of great orators of his day; killed in reaction to assassination of Julius Caesar. (8)

cientificos: Advisors of government of Porfirio Díaz who were strongly influenced by positivist ideas; permitted government to project image of modernization. (31)

city-state: A form of political organization typical of Mesopotamian civilizations; consisted of agricultural hinterlands ruled by an urban-based king. (2)

civilization: Societies distinguished by reliance on sedentary agriculture, ability to produce food surpluses, and existence of nonfarming elites, as well as merchant and manufacturing groups. (1)

Cixi: Ultraconservative dowager empress who dominated the last decades of the Qing dynasty; supported Boxer Rebellion in 1898 as a means of driving out Westerners. (32)

Classic: Period in Americas from A.D. 150 to 900; period of greatest cultural achievement. (9)

clientage: The social relationship whereby wealthy Roman landholders offered protection and financial aid to lesser citizens in return for political support and labor. (8)

Clisthenes: Athenian reformer of late 6th century B.C.; established democratic Council of 500 in Athens. (6)

Clive, Robert: Architect of British victory at Plassey; established foundations of British Raj in northern India. (30)

Clovis: Early Frankish king; converted Franks to Christianity c. 496; allowed establishment of Frankish kingdom. (16)

Cluny: Monastery in France; site of religious reform movement aimed at restoring purity of monastic movement and removing secularism. (16)

co-optive democracies: Governments that offered forms of democratic government but little of the substance of democracy to the majority of the population; typical in Latin America in the 20th century. (38)

cold war: The state of relations between the United States and its allies and the Soviet Union and its allies between the end of World War II to 1990; based on creation of political spheres of influence and a nuclear arms race rather than actual warfare. (35)

collectivization: Creation of large, state-run farms rather than individual holdings; allowed more efficient control over peasants; part of Stalin's economic and political planning; occasionally adopted in other Communist regimes. (36)

Colombian exchange: Biological and ecological exchange that took place following Spanish establishment of colonies in New World; peoples of Europe and Africa came to New World; animals, plants, and diseases of two hemispheres transferred. (25)

Columbus, Christopher: Genoese captain in service of king and queen of Castile and Aragon; successfully sailed to New World and returned in 1492; initiated European discoveries in Americas. (23)

Comintern: International office of communism under USSR dominance established to encourage the formation of Communist parties in Western Europe. (36)

commercio libre: Policy established during reign of Charles III; opened trade in ports of Spain and Indies to all Spanish merchants; undercut monopoly of consulados. (25)

Communist party of Vietnam: Originally a wing of the nationalist movement; became primary nationalist party after decline of VNQDD in 1929; led in late 1920s by Nguyen Ai Quoc, alias Ho Chi Minh. (41)

compradors: Wealthy new group of Chinese merchants under the Qing dynasty; specialized in the import-export trade on China's south coast; one of the major links between China and the outside world. (32)

Comte, Auguste: French philosopher; founder of positivism, a philosophy that stressed observation and scientific approaches to the problems of society. (31)

Comunero Revolt: One of popular revolts against Spanish colonial rule in New Granada (Colombia) in 1781; suppressed due to divisions among rebels. (25)

Confucius: Also known as Kung Fuzi; major Chinese philosopher; born in 6th century B.C.; author of *Analects;* philosophy based on need for restoration of order through advice of superior men to be found among the shi. (5)

Congress of Soviets: Lenin's parliamentary institution based on the soviets and Bolshevik domination; replaced the initial parliament dominated by the Social Revolutionary party. (36)

Congress of Vienna: Meeting in the aftermath of the Napoleonic Wars to restore political stability in Europe; at first attempted to restore status quo. (33)

Constantine: Roman emperor from A.D. 312 to 337; established second capital at Constantinople; attempted to use religious

force of Christianity to unify empire spiritually. (11)

consulado: Merchant guild of Seville; enjoyed virtual monopoly rights over goods shipped to America and handled much of the silver received in return. (25)

consuls: Two chief executives or magistrates of the Roman republic; elected by an annual assembly dominated by aristocracy. (8)

contested settler colonies: Featured large-scale European settlement despite the existence of large, indigenous populations; generally resulted in clashes over land rights, resource control, social status, and differences in culture; typical of South Africa, New Zealand, Kenya, Algeria, and Hawaii. (30)

Cook, Captain James: Made voyages to Hawaii from 1777 to 1779 resulting in opening of islands to the West; convinced Kamehameha to establish unified kingdom in the islands. (30)

Copernicus: Polish monk and astronomer; disproved Hellenistic belief that the earth was at the center of the universe. (22)

Copts: Christian sect of Egypt; tended to support Islamic invasions of this area in preference to Byzantine rule. (12)

core nations: Nations, usually European, that enjoyed profit from world economy; controlled international banking and commercial services such as shipping; exported manufactured goods for raw materials. (23)

Corinthian: Along with Doric and Ionian, distinct style of Hellenistic architecture; the most ornate of the three styles. (6)

Cornwallis, Lord Charles: Reformer of the East India Company administration of India in 1790s; reduced power of local British administrators, checked widespread corruption. (30)

Coronado, Francisco Vázquez de: Leader of Spanish expedition into northern frontier region of New Spain; entered what is now United States in search of mythical cities of gold. (25)

corporatism: Political ideology that emphasized the organic nature of society and made the state a mediator, adjusting the interests of different social groups; appealed to conservative groups in Latin-American societies and to the military. (38)

Cortés, Hernán: Led expedition of 600 to coast of Mexico in 1519; conquistador responsible for defeat of Aztec Empire; captured Tenochtitlan. (25)

cossacks: Peasants recruited to migrate to

newly seized lands in Russia, particularly in south; combined agriculture with military conquests; spurred additional frontier conquests and settlements. (24)

Council of Nicaea: Christian council that met in A.D. 325 to determine orthodoxy with respect to persons of Trinity; insisted on divinity of all persons of the Trinity. (11)

Council of People's Commissars: Government council composed of representatives from soviets across Russia and headed by Lenin; form of government initially established after November 1917. (36)

Council of the Indies: Body within the Castilian government that issued all laws and advised king on all matters dealing with the Spanish colonies of the New World. (25)

courage cultures: Cultures dominated by warlike males bound to each other by strong ties of personal loyalty; such cultures place emphasis on personal honor and physical courage; typical among pastoral nomads. (4)

Creole slaves: American-born descendants of "salt water" slaves; result of sexual exploitation of slave women or process of miscegenation. (27)

Creoles: Whites born in the New World; dominated local economies; ranked just beneath peninsulares. (25)

Crimean War: Fought between 1854 and 1856; began as Russian attempt to attack Ottoman Empire; opposed by France and Britain as well; resulted in Russian defeat in the face of Western industrial technology; led to Russian reforms under Tsar Alexander II. (33)

Cristeros: Conservative peasant movement in Mexico during the 1920s; most active in central Mexico; attempted to halt slide toward secularism; movement resulted in armed violence. (38)

Cromer, Lord: British adviser in khedival Egypt; pushed for economic reforms that reduced but failed to eliminate the debts of the khedival regime. (39)

Crusades: Series of military adventures initially launched by western Christians to free Holy Land from Muslims; temporarily succeeded in capturing Jerusalem and establishing Christian kingdoms; later used for other purposes such as commercial wars and extermination of heresy. (13, 16)

cubist movement: 20th-century art style; best represented by Spanish artist Pablo Picasso; rendered familiar objects as geometrical shapes. (35)

Cultural Revolution: Movement initiated in 1965 by Mao Zedong to restore his dominance over pragmatists; used mobs to ridicule Mao's political rivals; campaign was called off in 1968. (41)

culture: Combinations of the ideas, objects, and patterns of behavior that result from human social interaction. (1)

cuneiform: A form of writing developed by the Sumerians using a wedge-shaped stylus and clay tablets. (2)

curacas: Ayllu chiefs with privileges of dress and access to resources; community leaders among Andean societies. (9)

Cyril: Along with Methodius, missionary sent by Byzantine government to eastern Europe and the Balkans; converted southern Russia and Balkans to Orthodox Christianity; responsible for creation of written script for Slavic known as Cyrillic. (15)

Cyrus the Great: Established massive Persian Empire by 550 B.C.; successor state to Mesopotamian empires. (6)

da Gama, Vasco: Portuguese captain who first reached India in 1497; established early Portuguese dominance in Indian Ocean. (23)

Dahomey: Kingdom developed among Fon or Aja peoples in 17th century; center at Abomey 70 miles from coast; under King Agaja expanded to control coastline and port of Whydah by 1727; accepted Western firearms and goods in return for African slaves. (27)

daimyos: Warlord rulers of 300 small states following Onin War and disruption of Ashikaga Shogunate; holdings consolidated into unified and bounded ministates. (19)

Damascus: Capital of Umayyad caliphate. (12)

Daoism: Philosophy associated with Laozi; stressed need for alignment with Dao or cosmic force. (5)

Darwin, Charles: Biologist who developed theory of evolution of species; argued that all living species evolved into their present form through the ability to adapt in a struggle for survival. (29)

Dasas: Aryan name for indigenous people of Indus valley region; regarded as socially inferior to Aryans. (3)

De la Cruz, Sor Juana Inés: Author, poet, and musician of New Spain; eventually gave up secular concerns to concentrate on spiritual matters. (25)

Decembrist uprising: Political revolt in Russia in 1825; led by middle-level army officers who advocated reforms; put down by Tsar Nicholas I. (33)

Declaration of the Rights of Man and the Citizen: Adopted during the liberal phase of the French Revolution; stated the fundamental equality of all French citizens; later became a political source for other liberal movements. (29)

Deism: Concept of God current during the scientific revolution; role of divinity was to set natural laws in motion, not to regulate once process was begun. (22)

Delian league: Alliance formed by Athens after the Persian wars; cities contributed to unified treasury on island of Delos to support alliance fleet; later taken over by Athens and became Athenian Empire. (6)

Demak: Most powerful of the trading states on north coast of Java; converted to Islam and served as point of dissemination to other ports. (13)

Demographic Transition: The change from slow to rapid population growth; often associated with process of industrialization; occurred first in Europe and more characteristic of "developed world." (14)

demography: The study of population. (14)

dependency theory: Belief that development and underdevelopment were not stages but part of the same process; that development and growth of some areas such as western Europe were achieved at the expense of underdevelopment of dependent regions such as Latin America. (31)

dependent economic zones: Those regions within the world economy that produced raw materials; dependent on European markets and shipping; tendency to build system of forced, inexpensive labor. (23)

Descartes, Rene: Established importance of skeptical review of all received wisdom; argued that human reason could then develop laws that would explain the fundamental workings of nature. (22)

Deshima: Island port in Nagasaki Bay; only port open to non-Japanese after closure of the islands in the 1640s; only Chinese and Dutch ships were permitted to enter. (28)

Devi: Mother goddess within Hinduism; widely spread following collapse of Guptas; encouraged new emotionalism in religious ritual. (11)

dharma: The caste position and career determined by a person's birth; Hindu culture required that one accept one's social position and perform occupation to the best of one's ability in order to have a better situation in the next life. (7)

dhimmis: Literally "people of the book"; applied as inclusive term to Jews and Christians in Islamic territories; later extended to Zoroastrians and even Hindus. (12)

dhows: Arab sailing vessels with triangular or lateen sails; strongly influenced European ship design. (12)

Díaz, Porfirio: One of Juárez's generals; elected president of Mexico in 1876; dominated Mexican politics for 35 years; imposed strong central government. (31)

Diem, Ngo Dinh: Political leader of southern Vietnam established as president with the support of the United States in the 1950s; opposed Communist government of northern Vietnam; overthrown by military coup supported by the United States. (41)

Dien Bien Phu: Most significant victory of the Viet Minh over French colonial forces in 1954; gave the Viet Minh control of northern portions of Vietnam. (41)

Diet: Japanese parliament established as part of the new constitution of 1889; part of Meiji reforms; could pass laws and approve budgets; able to advise government, but not to control it. (33)

Din-i-Ilahi: Religion initiated by Akbar in Mughal India; blended elements of the many faiths of the subcontinent; key to efforts to reconcile Hindus and Muslims in India; failed to accomplish reconciliation of religions. (26)

Dinshawai incident: Clash between British soldiers and Egyptian villagers in 1906; arose over hunting accident along Nile River where wife of prayer leader of mosque was accidentally shot by army officers hunting pigeons; led to Egyptian protest movement. (39)

Diocletian: Roman emperor from A.D. 284 to 305; restored later empire by improved administration and tax collection. (11)

direct democracy: Literally rule of the people; as interpreted in Athens, all decisions emanated from popular assembly without intermediation of elected representatives. (6)

Disraeli, Benjamin: Leading conservative political figure in Britain in the second half of the 19th century; took initiative of granting vote to working-class males in 1867; typical of conservative politician making use of popular politics. (29)

Doric: Along with Ionian and Corinthian, distinct style of Hellenistic architecture; the least ornate of the three styles. (6)

Duarte, Eva: Also known as Evita Perón; first wife of Juan Perón; became public spokesperson for Perón among the poor until her death in 1952. (38)

duma: A national parliament created in Russia in the aftermath of the Revolution of 1905; progressively stripped of power during the reign of Tsar Nicholas II; failed to forestall further revolution. (33)

Dutch East India Company: Joint stock company that obtained government monopoly over trade in Asia; acted as virtually independent government in regions it claimed. (23)

Dutch Studies: Group of Japanese scholars interested in implications of Western science and technology beginning in the 18th century; urged freer exchange with West; based studies on few Dutch texts available in Japan. (33)

Dutch trading empire: Based on control of fortified towns and factories, warships on patrol, and monopoly control of limited number of products—particularly spices. (28)

East African trading ports: Urbanized commercial centers sharing common Bantu-based and Arabic-influenced Swahili language and other cultural traits; included Mogadishu, Mombasa, Malindi, Kilwa, Pate, and Zanzibar. (14)

eastern bloc: Nations that remained favorable to the Soviet Union in Eastern Europe—particularly Poland, Czechoslovakia, Bulgaria, Rumania, and Hungary. (35)

eastern front: Most mobile of the fronts established during the First World War; lacked trench warfare because of length of front extending from Baltic to southern Russia; after early successes, military defeats led to downfall of the tsarist government in Russia. (34)

edict of Nantes: Grant of tolerance to Protestants in France in 1598; granted only after lengthy civil war between Catholic and Protestant factions. (22)

Edo: Tokugawa capital city; modern-day Tokyo; center of the Tokugawa shogunate. (28)

effendi: Class of prosperous business and professional urban families in khedival Egypt; as a class generally favored Egyptian independence. (39)

Einstein, Albert: Developed mathematical theories to explain the behavior of planetary motion and the movement of electrical particles; after 1900 issued theory of relativity. (29)

El Mina: Most important of early Portuguese trading factories in forest zone of Africa. (27)

emancipation of the serfs: Tsar Alexander II ended rigorous serfdom in Russia in 1861; serfs obtained no political rights; required to stay in villages until they could repay aristocracy for land. (33)

encomendero: Holder of an encomienda; able to use Indians as workers or to tax them. (25)

encomienda: Grants of Indian laborers made to Spanish conquerors and settlers in Mesoamerica and South America; basis for earliest forms of coerced labor in Spanish colonies. (25)

English Civil War: Conflict from 1640 to 1660; featured religious disputes mixed with constitutional issues concerning the powers of the monarchy; ended with restoration of the monarchy in 1660 following execution of previous king. (22)

Enlightenment: Intellectual movement centered in France during the 18th century; featured scientific advance, application of scientific methods to study of human society; belief that rational laws could describe social behavior. (22)

Epic of Gilgamesh: The first literary epic in Western civilization; written down c. 2000 B.C.; included story of Great Flood. (2)

Ethiopian kingdom: A Christian kingdom that developed in the highlands of eastern Africa under the dynasty of King Lalaibela; retained Christianity in the face of Muslim expansion elsewhere in Africa. (14)

Etruscans: Culture that ruled Rome prior to republic; ruled through powerful kings and well-organized armies; expelled by Romans c. 510 B.C. (8)

eunuchs: Castrated males used within the households of Chinese emperors, usually to guard the emperors' concubines; became political counterbalance to powerful marital relatives during Later Han. (5)

European Economic Community: The Common Market; an alliance of six European nations (Germany, France, Italy, Belgium, Luxembourg, and the Netherlands) set up to begin creation of a single economic entity across national boundaries in 1958; later joined by Britain, Ireland, Denmark, Greece, Spain, and Portugal. (35)

extended families: Consisted of several generations, including the family patriarch's sons and grandsons with their wives and children; typical of Shang China elites. (3)

factories: Portuguese trading fortresses and compounds with resident merchants; utilized throughout Portuguese trading empire to assure secure landing places and commerce. (27)

factory system: Not to be confused with the fortified ports of the commercial revolution; intensification of all processes of production at a single site during the Industrial Revolution; involved greater organization of labor and firmer discipline. (29)

fallow: Fields allowed to remain uncultivated; utilized as a means of restoring fertility to the soil during the Middle Ages; until 8th century normally one-half of fields; after 8th century only one-third of fields. (16)

fascism: Political philosophy that became predominant in Italy and then Germany during the 1920s and 1930s; attacked weakness of democracy, corruption of capitalism; promised vigorous foreign and military programs; undertook state control of economy to reduce social friction. (35)

fazendas: Coffee estates that spread within interior of Brazil between 1840 and 1860; created major export commodity for Brazilian trade; led to intensification of slavery in Brazil. (31)

Federal Republic of Germany: What became the nation of West Germany; created by the merging of the zones of occupation held by France, Britain, and the United States. (35)

federalists: Those Latin-American politicians who wanted policies, especially fiscal and commercial regulations, to be set by regional governments rather than centralized national administrations; often supported by those politicians who described themselves as liberals. (31)

feminist movements: Sought various legal and economic gains for women, including equal access to professions and higher education; came to concentrate on right to vote; won support particularly from middle-class women; more active in western Europe at the end of the 19th century. (29)

Ferdinand of Aragon: Along with Isabella of Castile, monarch of largest Christian kingdoms in Iberia; marriage to Isabella created united Spain; responsible for reconquest of Granada, initiation of exploration of New World. (25)

feudalism: The social organization created during the Middle Ages by exchanging grants of land or fiefs in return for formal oaths of allegiance and promises of loyal

service; typical of Zhou dynasty; greater lords provided protection and aid to lesser lords in return for military service. (3, 16)

final solution: Hitler's term for the genocide of European Jews; led to incarceration of millions of Jews in concentration camps and their eventual slaughter in gas chambers devised for mass executions. (34)

five pillars: The obligatory religious duties of all Muslims; confession of faith, prayer, fasting during Ramadan, zakat, and hajj. (12)

five-year plans: Stalin's plans to hasten industrialization of USSR; constructed massive factories in metallurgy, mining, and electric power; led to massive state-planned industrialization at cost of availability of consumer products. (36)

flying money: Chinese credit instrument that provided credit vouchers to merchants to be redeemed at the end of the voyage; reduced danger of robbery; early form of currency. (18)

foot-binding: Practice in Chinese society to mutilate women's feet in order to make them smaller; produced pain and restricted women's movement; made it easier to confine women to the household. (18)

Forbidden City: Imperial precinct with the capital cities of China; only imperial family, advisors, and household were permitted to enter. (5)

Francia, Dr. José Rodríguez de: Ruler of independent Paraguay; ruled country as dictator until 1840. (31)

Francis I: King of France; regarded as Renaissance monarch; patron of arts, imposed new controls on Catholic church; ally of Ottoman sultan against holy Roman emperor. (22)

Frederick the Great: Prussian king; attempted to introduce Enlightenment reforms into Germany; built on military and bureaucratic foundations of his predecessors; introduced freedom of religion; increased state control of economy. (22)

Free Officers movement: Military nationalist movement in Egypt founded in the 1930s; often allied with the Muslim Brotherhood; led coup to seize Egyptian government from khedive in July 1952. (40)

French Revolution: Revolution in France between 1789 and 1800; resulted in temporary overthrow of Bourbon monarchy; ended with establishment of French Empire under Napoleon Bonaparte;

source of many liberal movements and constitutions in Europe. (29)

French Revolution of 1830: Second rebellion against Bourbon monarchy; essentially a liberal movement resulting in the creation of a bourgeois government under a moderate monarchy. (29)

French Revolution of 1848: Overthrew the monarchy established in 1830; briefly established a democratic republic; failure of the republic led to the reestablishment of the French Empire under Napoleon III in 1850. (29)

Freud, Sigmund: Viennese physician; developed theories of the workings of the human unconscious; argued that behavior is determined by impulses. (29)

Fujiwara: Japanese aristocratic family in mid-9th century; exercised exceptional influence over imperial affairs; aided in decline of imperial power. (19)

Fulani: Pastoral people of western Sudan; adopted purifying Sufi variant of Islam; under Usuman Dan Fodio in 1804, launched revolt against Hausa kingdoms; established state centered on Sokoto. (27)

Galileo: Published Copernicus's findings; added own discoveries concerning laws of gravity and planetary motion; condemned by the Catholic church for his work. (22)

galleons: Large, heavily armed ships used to carry silver from New World colonies to Spain; basis for convoy system utilized by Spain for transportation of bullion. (25)

Gálvez, José de: Spanish Minister of the Indies and chief architect of colonial reform; moved to eliminate Creoles from upper bureaucracy of the colonies; created intendants for local government. (25)

Gandhi, Mohandas K.: Western-educated Indian lawyer and nationalist politician; took on attributes of traditional Indian holy man; stressed nonviolent tactics such as boycotts, strikes, and noncooperation; tactics eventually led to Indian independence; assassinated by Hindu fanatic shortly after Indian independence was achieved. (39)

Gang of Four: Jiang Qing and four political allies who attempted to seize control of Communist government in China from the pragmatists; arrested and sentenced to life imprisonment in 1976 following Mao Zedong's death. (41)

gauchos: Bands of mounted rural workers in the region of the Rio de la Plata; aided local caudillos in splitting apart the United Provinces of the Rio de la Plata after 1816. (31)

Gempei Wars: Waged for five years from 1180, on Honshu between the Taira and Minamoto families; resulted in destruction of Taira. (19)

Germans: Resided outside the northern boundaries of the Roman Empire; featured mixed agricultural and pastoral economies; moved southward into Roman Empire in course of 4th and 5th centuries A.D. (10)

Ghana: First great sub-Saharan state; created by Soninke people; by 9th century A.D. a major source of gold in the Mediterranean world. (10)

Ghazni: Dynasty founded from Turks who were originally slaves; seized power in 962 in Afghanistan north of Indus valley; later invaded Indian subcontinent. (13)

Giap, General Vo Nguyen: Chief military commander of the Viet Minh; architect of the Vietnamese victory over the French at Dien Bien Phu in 1954. (41)

Glorious Revolution: English overthrow of James II in 1688; resulted in affirmation of parliament as having basic sovereignty over the king. (22)

Goa: Portuguese factory or fortified trade town located on western India coast; sites for forcible entry into Asian sea trade network. (28)

Golden Horde: One of the four regional subdivisions of the Mongol Empire after Chinggis Khan's death; territory covered much of what is today south-central Russia. (20)

Good Neighbor Policy: Established by Franklin D. Roosevelt for dealing with Latin America in 1933; intended to halt direct intervention in Latin-American politics. (38)

Gorbachev, Mikhail: USSR ruler after 1985; renewed attacks on Stalinism; urged reduction in nuclear armament; proclaimed policies of glasnost and perestroika. (36)

Gordon, General George: English commander in Sudan and leader of antislavery effort at khedival court of Egypt; killed at Khartoum by forces of Mahdi. (32)

Gothic: An architectural style developed during the Middle Ages in western Europe; featured pointed arches and flying buttresses as external supports on main walls. (16)

Government of India Act of 1935: British agreed to retain control of the central administration in return for turning over the provincial governments to Indian leaders chosen by expanded electorate. (39)

Gracchus, Gaius: Along with Tiberius, tribune who attempted to introduce land and citizenship reform within the Roman republic; killed on the command of the Senate. (8)

Gran Colombia: Independent state created in South America as result of military successes of Simon Bolívar; existed only until 1830 at which time Colombia, Venezuela, and Ecuador became separate nations. (31)

Great Depression: International economic crisis following the First World War; said to have begun with collapse of American stock market in 1929; actual causes began with collapse of agricultural prices in 1920s; included collapse of banking houses in the United States and western Europe, massive unemployment; contradicted optimistic assumptions of 19th century. (34)

Great Leap Forward: Economic policy of Mao Zedong introduced in 1958; proposed industrialization of small-scale projects integrated into peasant communes; led to economic disaster; ended in 1960. (41)

Great Mahele: Hawaiian edict issued in 1848; imposed Western concept of property on Hawaiian land previously shared among Hawaiians; much of private property sold off to Western commercial interests by Hawaiian monarchy. (30)

great trek: Movement of Boer settlers in Cape Colony of southern Africa to escape influence of British colonial government in 1834; led to settlement of regions north of Orange River and Natal. (27)

Great Wall: Chinese defensive fortification intended to keep out the nomadic invaders from the north; initiated during Qin dynasty and reign of Shi Huangdi. (5)

Great Zimbabwe: Bantu confederation of Shona-speaking peoples located between Zambezi and Limpopo rivers; developed after 9th century; featured royal courts built of stone; created centralized state by 15th century; king took title of Mwene Mutapa. (14)

Greek fire: Byzantine weapon consisting of mixture of chemicals that ignited when exposed to water; utilized to drive back the Arab fleets that attacked Constantinople. (15)

Greek Revolution: Rebellion in Greece against the Ottoman Empire in 1820; key step in gradually dismantling the Ottoman Empire in the Balkans. (29)

Green Revolution: Attempt to introduce improved seed strains, fertilizers, and irrigation as a means of producing higher yields in crops such as rice, wheat, and corn; particularly important in the densely populated countries of Asia. (40)

Gregory VII: Pope during the 11th century who attempted to free Church from interference of feudal lords; quarreled with Holy Roman Emperor Henry IV over practice of lay investiture. (16)

griots: Professional oral historians who served as keepers of traditions and advisors to kings within the Mali Empire. (14)

guano: Bird droppings utilized as fertilizer; exported from Peru as a major item of trade between 1850 and 1880; income from trade permitted end to Indian tribute and abolition of slavery. (31)

Guevara, Ernesto "Che": Argentine revolutionary; aided Fidel Castro in overthrow of Fulgencio Batista; died while directing guerrilla movement in Bolivia in 1967. (38)

guilds: Sworn associations of people in the same business or trade in a single city; stressed security and mutual control; limited membership, regulated apprenticeship, guaranteed good workmanship; often established franchise within cities. (16)

guillotine: Introduced as a method of humane execution; utilized to execute thousands during the most radical phase of the French Revolution known as the Reign of Terror. (29)

Guomindang: Chinese Nationalist party founded by Sun Yat-sen in 1919; drew support from local warlords and Chinese criminal underworld; initially forged alliance with Communists in 1924; dominated by Chiang Kai-shek after 1925. (41)

Guptas: Dynasty that succeeded the Kushanas in the 3d century A.D.; built empire that extended to all but the southern regions of Indian subcontinent; less centralized than Mauryan Empire. (7)

gurus: Brahmans who served as teachers for the princes of the imperial court of the Guptas. (7)

Gutenberg, Johannes: Introduced movable type to western Europe in 15th century; credited with greatly expanded availability of printed books and pamphlets. (22)

Habsburg, Archduke Maximilian von: Proclaimed emperor of Mexico following intervention of France in 1862; ruled until overthrow and execution by liberal revolutionaries under Benito Juárez in 1867. (31)

ᵃ

haciendas: Rural estates in Spanish colonies in New World; produced agricultural products for consumers in America; basis of wealth and power for local aristocracy. (25)

Hagia Sophia: New church constructed in Constantinople during reign of Justinian. (15)

hajj: Pilgrimage to the holy city of Mecca to worship at the Ka'ba. (12)

Hajjaj: Umayyad viceroy for eastern provinces; launched punitive campaign against king of Sind in India that resulted in first Islamic conquest in subcontinent. (13)

Hammurabi: The most important ruler of the Babylonian empire; responsible for codification of law. (2)

Han dynasty: Chinese dynasty that succeeded the Qin in 202 B.C.; ruled for next 400 years. (5)

Hangzhou: Capital of later Song dynasty; located near East China Sea; permitted overseas trading; population exceeded one million. (18)

Hannibal: Great Carthaginian general during Second Punic War; successfully invaded Italy but failed to conquer Rome; finally defeated at Battle of Zama. (8)

Hanseatic League: An organization of cities in northern Germany for the purpose of establishing a commercial alliance. (16)

hapu: Primary social unit of Maori society in New Zealand; divisions of tribes consisting of extended families; land allotted to extended families in common. (10)

Harappa: Along with Mohenjo-daro, major urban complex of the Harappan civilization; laid out on planned grid pattern. (3)

Harappan civilization: First civilization of Indian subcontinent; emerged in Indus River valley c. 2500 B.C. (3)

Harsha: Descendant of Guptas in India; briefly constructed a loose empire in northern India between A.D. 616 and 657. (11)

Harvey, John: English physician who demonstrated the circular movement of blood in animals, function of heart as pump. (22)

Hausa states: Combined Muslim and pagan traditions; emerged following the demise of Songhay Empire among the Hausa peoples of northern Nigeria, based on cities such as Kano. (14)

Haya de la Torre, Victor Raul: Peruvian politician; founder of APRA (American Popular Revolutionary Alliance) in 1924; aimed at establishing an international party throughout Western Hemisphere. (38)

Heian: Capital city of Japan under the Yamato emperors, later called Kyoto; built in order to escape influence of Buddhist monks; patterned after ancient imperial centers of China; never fully populated. (10, 19)

Hellenism: Culture derived from the Greek civilization that flourished between 800 and 400 B.C. (6)

Hellenistic: That culture associated with the spread of Greek influence as a result of Macedonian conquests; often seen as the combination of Greek culture with eastern political forms. (6)

helots: Conquered indigenous population of Spartan city-state; provided agricultural labor for Spartan landowners; only semi-free; largest population of Spartan city-state. (6)

Henry the Navigator: Portuguese prince responsible for direction of series of expeditions along the African coast in the 15th century; marked beginning of western European expansion. (23, 27)

Herzl, Theodor: Austrian journalist and Zionist; formed World Zionist Organization in 1897; promoted Jewish migration to Palestine and the formation of a Jewish state. (39)

Hidalgo, Father Miguel de: Mexican priest who established independence movement among Indians and mestizos in 1810; despite early victories, was captured and executed. (31)

Hideyoshi, Toyotomi: General under Nobunaga; succeeded as leading military power in central Japan; continued efforts to break power of daimyos; constructed series of alliances that made him military master of Japan in 1590; died in 1598. (28)

hieroglyphs: The form of writing developed in ancient Egypt; more pictorial than Mesopotamian cuneiform. (2)

hijra: Flight of Muhammad and followers in A.D. 622 from Mecca to Yathrib or Medina; marks first year of Islamic calendar. (12)

Himalaya Mountains: Mountain region marking the northern border of the Indian subcontinent; site of the Aryan settlements that formed small kingdoms or warrior republics. (7)

Hiroshima: One of two Japanese cities on which the United States dropped atomic bombs in 1945; devastation of these cities caused Japanese surrender without invasion of home islands. (34)

Hispaniola: First island in Caribbean settled by Spaniards; settlement founded by Columbus on second voyage to New World; Spanish base of operations for further discoveries in New World. (25)

Hitler, Adolf: Nazi leader of fascist Germany from 1933 to his suicide in 1945; created a strongly centralized state in Germany; eliminated all rivals; launched Germany on aggressive foreign policy leading to World War II; responsible for attempted genocide of European Jews. (34)

Hittites: An Indo-European people who entered Mesopotamia c. 1750 B.C.; destroyed the Babylonian empire; swept away c. 1200 B.C. (2)

Ho Chi Minh: Communist nationalist leader of Vietnam; Western-educated; devoted to violent revolution against French colonialism; shifted to Maoist strategy of basing revolution on peasantry during 1930s; defeated France by 1954; led war to reunite Vietnam against United States. (41)

Hojo: Warrior family closely allied with Minamoto; dominated Kamakura regime and manipulated Minamoto rulers; claimed to rule in name of emperor at Kyoto. (19)

holding ecological adaptation: Human adaptation to an environment in such a way the original environment is drastically transformed and replaced with a new, human-oriented ecology; typical of sedentary agricultural communities. (4)

Holocaust: Term for Hitler's attempted genocide of European Jews during World War II; resulted in deaths of six million Jews. (34)

Holy Alliance: Alliance between Russia, Prussia, and Austria in defense of religion and the established order; formed at Congress of Vienna by most conservative monarchies of Europe. (33)

holy Roman emperors: Emperors in northern Italy and Germany following split of Charlemagne's empire; claimed title of emperor c. 10th century; failed to developed centralized monarchy in Germany. (16)

homelands: Areas in South Africa designated for ethno-linguistic groups within the black African population; such areas tend to be overpopulated and poverty stricken. (40)

Homo sapiens: The species of man that emerged as most successful at the end of the Paleolithic period. (1)

Hong Kong: British colony on Chinese mainland; major commercial center; agreement reached between Britain and

People's Republic of China will return colony to China in 1999. (37)

Hong Xiuquan: Leader of the Taiping rebellion; converted to specifically Chinese form of Christianity; attacked traditional Confucian teachings of Chinese elite. (32)

Hongwu: First Ming emperor in 1368; originally of peasant lineage; original name Zhu Yuanzhang; drove out Mongol influence; restored position of scholar-gentry. (28)

Honshu: Largest of the Japanese islands; most heavily populated. (10)

Hopewell culture: Second of the mound-building cultures; lasted from c. A.D. 200 to 500; more complex than Adena culture. (9)

Horace: Poet who adapted Greek poetic meters to the Latin language; author of lyrical poetry laudatory of the empire; patronized by Augustus. (8)

horned god: Naked male figure; one of the major deities of Harappan civilization; favored by priests and upper classes. (3)

horse nomads: A form of pastoralism dependent on domesticated horses; common to Indo-European peoples of central Eurasia. (4)

Hsiung-nu: Also known as the Huns; horse nomads responsible for disruption of Chinese, Gupta, and Roman civilizations. (4)

huacas: Sacred spirits and powers that resided or appeared in caves, mountains, rocks, rivers, and other natural phenomena; typical of Andean societies. (9)

Huancavelica: Location of greatest deposit of mercury in South America; aided in American silver production; linked with Potosí. (25)

Huang-chao: Revolution in China in the 9th century; named for leader of revolt; engulfed much of China but failed to attract support of Confucian scholar-gentry. (18)

Huanghe River basin: Also known as Yellow River basin; site of the development of sedentary agriculture in China. (1)

Huanghe River valley: River source in Tibetan plateau to mouth in China sea; site of early Chinese sedentary agricultural communities. (3)

Huari: Along with Tihuanaco, large center for regional chiefdoms between A.D. 300 and 900; located in southern Peru; featured large ceremonial center supported by extensive irrigated agriculture; established widely diffused religious and artistic symbols spread all over Andean zone. (9)

Huerta, Victoriano: Sought to reestablish centralized dictatorship in Mexico following the removal of Madero in 1913; forced from power in 1914 by Villa and Zapata. (38)

Huitzilopochtli: Aztec tribal patron god; central figure of cult of human sacrifice and warfare; identified with old sun god. (17)

Hulegu: Ruler of the Ilkhan khanate; grandson of Chinggis Khan; responsible for capture and destruction of Baghdad. (20)

human rights: Certain universal rights enjoyed by all people because these are justified by a moral standard that stands above the laws of any individual nation. (38)

humanism: Focus on humankind as center of intellectual and artistic endeavor; method of study that emphasized the superiority of classical forms over medieval styles, in particular the study of ancient languages. (22)

Humayan: Son and successor of Babur; expelled from India in 1540, but restored Mughal rule by 1556; died shortly thereafter. (26)

Hundred Years War: Conflict between England and France from 1337 to 1453; fought over lands England possessed in France and feudal rights versus the emerging claims of national states. (16)

hunting and gathering: Means of obtaining subsistence by human species prior to the adaptation of sedentary agriculture; normally typical of band social organization. (1)

Hussein, Saddam: Military ruler of Iraq; led Iraq in ten-year war with Iran; attempted to annex Kuwait into Iraq in 1990; defeated by coalition of American, European, and Arabic forces in 1991 in Persian Gulf War. (40)

Hyundai: Example of huge industrial groups that wield great power in modern Korea; virtually governed Korea's southeastern coast; vertical economic organization with ships, supertankers, factories, schools, and housing units. (37)

Ibn Khaldun: A Muslim historian; developed concept that dynasties of nomadic conquerors had a cycle of three generations—strong, weak, dissolute. (4)

iconoclasm: Religious controversy within the Byzantine Empire in the 8th century; emperor attempted to suppress veneration of icons; literally "breaking of images"; after long struggle icon veneration was restored. (15)

icons: Images of religious figures that became objects of veneration within Christianity of the Byzantine Empire; particularly prevalent in eastern monasticism. (15)

ideographic writing: Pictographic characters grouped together to create new concepts; typical of Chinese writing. (3)

Ieyasu, Tokugawa: Vassal of Toyotomi Hideyoshi; succeeded him as most powerful military figure in Japan; granted title of shogun in 1603 and established Tokugawa shogunate; established political unity in Japan. (28)

Ifriqiya: The Arabic term for eastern North Africa. (14)

Iliad and Odyssey: Two Greek epic poems attributed to Homer but possibly the work of many authors; defined gods and human nature that shaped Greek mythos. (6)

Ilkhan khanate: One of four regional subdivisions of the Mongol Empire after Chinggis Khan's death; located south of the Golden Horde; eventually conquered much of territory of Abbasid Empire. (20)

imams: According to Shi'ism, rulers who could trace descent from Ali. (26)

import substitution industrialization: Typical of Latin-American economies; production of products during the 20th century that had previously been imported; led to light industrialization. (38)

Inca: Group of clans centered at Cuzco that were able to create empire in Andean civilization c. 1438. (17)

Inca socialism: A view created by Spanish authors to describe Inca society as a type of utopia; image of the Inca Empire as a carefully organized system in which every community collectively contributed to the whole. (17)

Indian: Misnomer created by Columbus referring to indigenous peoples of New World; implies social and ethnic commonality among Native Americans that did not exist; still used to apply to Native Americans. (17)

Indian Congress party: Grew out of regional associations of Western-educated Indians; originally centered in cities of Bombay, Poona, Calcutta, and Madras; became political party in 1885; focus of nationalist movement in India; governed through most of postcolonial period. (39)

Indies piece: Term utilized within the complex exchange system established by the Spanish for African trade; referred to the value of an adult male slave. (27)

Indra: Chief deity of the Aryans; depicted as a colossal, hard-drinking warrior. (3)

Indus River valley: River sources in Himalayas to mouth in Arabian Sea; location of Harappan civilization. (3)

Industrial Revolution: Series of changes in economy of western Europe between 1740 and 20th century; stimulated by rapid population growth, increase in agricultural productivity, commercial revolution of 17th century, and development of new means of transportation; in essence involved technological change and the application of machines to the process of production. (29)

instrumentalist reaction: Workers began during the Industrial Revolution to regard their jobs not as ends, but as vehicles for other goals; workers learned to bargain for better pay and shorter hours. (29)

intelligentsia: Russian term denoting articulate intellectuals as a class; group bent on radical change in Russian political and social system; wished to maintain a Russian culture distinct from the West. (33)

internationalization: Idea that peoples should unite across national boundaries; gained popularity during the mid-19th century; led to establishment of international Red Cross, Telegraphic Union, Postal Union, series of international fairs. (34)

investiture: Practice of state appointment of bishops; Pope Gregory VII attempted to ban the practice of lay investiture, leading to war with Holy Roman Emperor Henry IV. (16)

Ionian: Along with Doric and Corinthian, distinct style of Hellenistic architecture; more ornate than Ionic, but less than Corinthian. (6)

iron curtain: Phrase coined by Winston Churchill to describe the division between free and repressed societies taking shape in Europe after 1946. (35)

Isabella of Castile: Along with Ferdinand of Aragon, monarch of largest Christian kingdoms in Iberia; marriage to Ferdinand created united Spain; responsible for reconquest of Granada, initiation of exploration of New World. (25)

Isandhlwana: Location of battle fought in 1879 between the British and Zulu armies in South Africa; resulted in defeat of British; one of few victories of African forces over western Europeans. (30)

Isfahan: Safavid capital under Abbas the Great; planned city laid out according to shah's plan; example of Safavid architecture. (26)

Islam: Major world religion having its origins in A.D. 610 in the Arabian peninsula; meaning literally submission; based on prophecy of Muhammad. (12)

Ismail: Sufi commander who conquered city of Tabriz in 1501; first Safavid to be proclaimed shah or emperor. (26)

Italian front: Front established in World War I; generally along Italian border with Austria-Hungary; also produced trench warfare; somewhat greater mobility than on western front. (34)

Iturbide, Augustín de: Conservative Creole officer in Mexican army who signed agreement with insurgent forces of independence; combined forces entered Mexico City in 1821; later proclaimed emperor of Mexico until its collapse in 1824. (31)

Ivan III: Also known as Ivan the Great; prince of Duchy of Moscow; claimed descent from Rurik; responsible for freeing Russia from Mongols after 1462; took title of tsar or Caesar—equivalent of emperor. (24)

Ivan IV: Also known as Ivan the Terrible; confirmed power of tsarist autocracy by attacking authority of boyars; continued policy of Russian expansion; established contacts with western European commerce and culture. (24)

Janissaries: Ottoman infantry divisions that dominated Ottoman armies; forcibly conscripted as boys in conquered areas of Balkans; legally slaves; translated military service into political influence, particularly after 15th century. (26)

Jericho: Early walled urban culture based on sedentary agriculture; located in modern Israeli-occupied West Bank near Jordan River. (1)

Jesuits: A new religious order founded during the Catholic Reformation; active in politics, education, and missionary work; sponsored missions to North America and Asia. (22)

Jesus of Nazareth: Prophet and teacher among the Jews; believed by Christians to be the Messiah; executed c. A.D. 30. (8)

Jiang Qing: Wife of Mao Zedong; one of Gang of Four; opposed pragmatists and supported Cultural Revolution of 1965; arrested and imprisoned for life in 1976. (41)

jihad: Islamic holy war. (12)

Jinnah, Muhammad Ali: Muslim nationalist in India; originally a member of the National Congress party; became leader of Muslim League; traded Muslim support for British during World War II for promises of a separate Muslim state after the war; first president of Pakistan. (39)

jinshi: Title granted to those students who passed the most difficult Chinese examinations on all of Chinese literature; became immediate dignitaries and eligible for high office. (18)

jizya: Head tax paid by all nonbelievers in Islamic territories. (12)

João VI, Dom: Portuguese monarch who established seat of government in Brazil from 1808 to 1820 as a result of Napoleonic invasion of Iberian peninsula; made Brazil seat of empire with capital at Rio de Janeiro. (31)

Jomon culture: Created by early migrants to Japan after 3000 B.C.; hunting-and-gathering people; produced distinctive pottery form. (10)

Joseph II: Enlightened monarch of Austria; attempted to introduce reforms into Austria such as limitation of powers of Catholic church, restructuring of peasantry. (22)

Ju Yuanzhang: Chinese peasant who led successful revolt against Yuan; founded Ming dynasty. (20)

Juárez, Benito: Indian governor of state of Oaxaca in Mexico; leader of liberal rebellion against Santa Ana; liberal government defeated by French intervention under Emperor Napoleon III of France and establishment of Mexican Empire under Maximilian; restored to power in 1867 until his death in 1872. (31)

junks: Chinese ships equipped with watertight bulkheads, sternpost rudders, compasses, and bamboo fenders; dominant force in Asian seas east of the Malayan peninsula. (18)

Jurchens: Founders of the Qin kingdom that succeeded the Liao in northern China; annexed most of Yellow River basin and forced Song to flee to south. (18)

Justinian: Eastern Roman emperor between A.D. 527 and 565; tried to restore unity of old Roman Empire; issued most famous compilation of Roman law. (11)

juula: Malinke merchants; formed small partnerships to carry out trade throughout Mali Empire; eventually spread throughout much of West Africa. (14)

Ka'ba: Most revered religious shrine in pre-Islamic Arabia; located in Mecca; focus of obligatory annual truce among bedouin tribes; later incorporated as important shrine in Islam. (12)

Kabir: Muslim Mystic during 15th century; played down the importance of ritual differences between Hinduism and Islam. (13)

Kamasutra: Written by Vatsayana during Gupta era; offered instructions on all aspects of life for higher caste males including grooming, hygiene, etiquette, selection of wives, and instruction on love-making. (7)

Kamehameha I: Fought series of wars backed by British weapons and advisors resulting in unified Hawaiian kingdom by 1810; as king he promoted economic change encouraging Western merchants to establish export trade in Hawaiian goods. (1, 30)

Kanauj: Capital of Harsha's empire; featured formidable walls, palatial homes, and beautiful gardens. (13)

Kangxi: Confucian scholar and Manchu emperor of Qing dynasty from 1661 to 1722; established high degree of Sinification among the Manchus. (32)

kapu: Complex set of social regulations in Hawaii, which forbade certain activities and regulated social discourse. (10)

Karakorum: Capital of the Mongol Empire under Chinggis Khan. (20)

Karbala: Site of defeat and death of Husayn, son of Ali; marked beginning of Shi'a resistance to Umayyad caliphate. (12)

karma: The sum of merits accumulated by a soul at any given point in time; determined the caste to which the soul would be assigned in the next life. (7)

Kautilya: Political advisor to Chandragupta Maurya; one of authors of *Arthashastra;* believed in scientific application of warfare. (7)

Kellogg-Briand Pact: A treaty coauthored by American and French leaders in 1928; outlawed war forever; ratified subsequently by other nations. (35)

Kenyatta, Jomo: Leader of the nonviolent nationalist party in Kenya; organized the Kenya African Union (KAU); failed to win concessions because of resistance of white settlers; came to power only after suppression of the Land Freedom Army or Mau Mau. (39)

Kerensky, Alexander: Liberal revolutionary leader during the early stages of the Russian Revolution of 1917; sought development of parliamentary rule, religious freedom. (36)

Keynes, John: British economist who stressed importance of government spending to compensate for loss of purchasing power during a depression; played role in the policies of the American

New Deal and European economic planning after World War II. (35)

khagan: Title of the supreme ruler of the Mongol tribes. (20)

khanates: Four regional Mongol kingdoms that arose following the death of Chinggis Khan. (20)

Khartoum: River town that was administrative center of Egyptian authority in Sudan. (32)

khedives: Descendants of Muhammad Ali in Egypt after 1867; formal rulers of Egypt despite French and English intervention until overthrown by military coup in 1952. (32)

Khmers: Indianized rivals of the Vietnamese; moved into Mekong River delta region at time of Vietnamese drive to the south. (19)

Khomaini, Ayatollah: Religious ruler of Iran following revolution of 1979 to expel the Pahlavi shah of Iran; emphasized religious purification; sought to eliminate Western influences and establish purely Islamic government. (40)

Khrushchev, Nikita: Stalin's successor as head of the USSR; attacked Stalinism for concentration of power and arbitrary dictatorship; failure of Siberian development program and antagonism of Stalinists led to downfall. (36)

Kiev: Trade city in southern Russia established by Scandinavian traders in 9th century; became focal point for kingdom of Russia that flourished to 12th century. (15)

kivas: Circular pits in Anasazi communities used for religious meetings by the men in the society. (9)

Koguryo: Tribal people of northern Korea; established an independent kingdom in the northern half of the peninsula; adopted cultural Sinification. (19)

Kongo: Kingdom, based on agriculture, formed on lower Congo River by late 15th century; capital at Mbanza Kongo; ruled by hereditary monarchy. (14)

Korean War: Fought from 1950 to 1953; North supported by USSR and later People's Republic of China; South supported by United States and small international United Nations force; ended in stalemate and continued division of Korea. (37)

Korekiyo Takahashi: Minister of finance in Japan during the 1930s; increased government spending to provide jobs; created export boom and elimination of unemployment by 1936; helped support military purchasing. (37)

Kubilai Khan: Grandson of Chinggis Khan; commander of the Mongol forces responsible for the conquest of China; became khagan in 1260; established Sinicized Mongol Yuan dynasty in China in 1271. (20)

kulaks: Agricultural entrepreneurs who utilized the Stolypin reforms to increase agricultural production and buy additional land. (33)

Kumbi Saleh: Capital of empire of Ghana; divided into two adjoining cities—one for the king, court, and indigenous people, one for the merchants, scholars, and religious leaders. (10)

Kung Fuzi: Also known as Confucius; major Chinese philosopher; born in 6th century B.C.; author of *Analects;* philosophy based on need for restoration of order through advice of superior men to be found among the shi. (5)

kuriltai: Meeting of all Mongol chieftains at which the supreme ruler of all tribes was selected. (20)

Kush: An African state that developed along the upper reaches of the Nile c. 1000 B.C.; conquered Egypt and ruled it for several centuries. (2)

Kushanas: Dynasty that succeeded the Mauryas in northwestern India; sponsors of Buddhism; empire did not extend to Ganges River valley. (7)

L'Overture, Toussaint: Leader of slave rebellion on the French sugar island of St. Domingue in 1791; led to creation of independent republic of Haiti in 1804. (31)

La Reforma: The name given to the liberal rebellion of Benito Juárez against the forces of Santa Ana. (31)

lançados: Collection points for Portuguese trade in the interior of Africa; provided essential links between economies of African interior and factories on the coast. (27)

Land Freedom Army: Radical organization of independence in Kenya; frustrated by failure of nonviolent means, initiated campaign of terror in 1952; referred to by British as the Mau Mau. (39)

Laozi: Major Chinese philosopher; recommended retreat from society into nature; individual should seek to become attuned with Dao. (5)

Las Casas, Bartolomé de: Dominican friar who supported peaceful conversion of the Native American population of the Spanish colonies; opposed forced labor and advocated Indian rights. (25)

League of Nations: International diplomatic and peace organization created in the Treaty of Versailles that ended the First World War; one of the chief goals of President Woodrow Wilson of the United States in the peace negotiations; the United States was never a member. (34)

Lee Kuan Yew: Ruler of Singapore from independence in 1959 to present; established tightly controlled authoritarian government; ruled through People's Action party to suppress political diversity. (37)

Legalists: Chinese school of political thought; served Qin dynasty and subsequent dynasties; stressed need for the absolute power of the emperor; power enforced through strict application of laws. (5)

legions: The basic military unit of the Roman military; developed during the republic. (8)

Lepanto: Naval battle between the Spanish and the Ottoman Empire resulting in a Spanish victory in 1571; demonstrated European naval superiority over Muslims. (23)

Lesotho: Southern African state that survived mfecane; not based on Zulu model; less emphasis on military organization, less authoritarian government. (27)

letrados: University-trained lawyers from Spain in the New World; juridical core of Spanish colonial bureaucracy; exercised both legislative and administrative functions. (25)

Li Bo: Most famous poet of the Tang era; blended images of the mundane world with philosophical musings. (18)

Li Dazhao: Chinese intellectual who gave serious attention to Marxist philosophy; headed study circle at the University of Beijing; saw peasants as vanguard of revolutionary communism in China. (41)

Li Yuan: Also known as Duke of Tang; minister for Yangdi; took over empire following assassination of Yangdi; first emperor of Tang dynasty; took imperial title of Gaozu. (18)

liberal: Political viewpoint with origins in western Europe during the 19th century; stressed limited state interference in individual life, representation of propertied people in government; urged importance of constitutional rule and parliaments. (29)

Liberal Democratic party: Monopolized Japanese government from its formation in 1955 into the 1990s; largely responsible for economic reconstruction of Japan. (37)

Liberation theology: Combined Catholic theology and Socialist principles in effort to bring about improved conditions for the poor in Latin America. (38)

Lin Zexu: Distinguished Chinese official during the early 19th century; charged with stamping out the opium trade in southern China; ordered European trading areas in Canton blockaded and confiscation of opium; sent into exile following Opium War. (32)

Liu Bang: Founder of the Han dynasty in 202 B.C. (5)

Livy: Roman historian who linked empire to traditions of republican past; stressed republican virtues popular in early empire. (8)

llamas: Along with alpacas, domesticated animals of the Americas; basis for only form of nomadic pastoralism in the New World until European importation of larger animals in 15th century A.D. (4)

Locke, John: English philosopher during 17th century; argued that people could learn everything through senses; argued that power of government came from the people, not divine right of kings; offered possibility of revolution to overthrow tyrants. (22)

loess: Fine-grained soil deposited in Ordos bend by winds from central Asia; created fertile soil for sedentary agricultural communities. (3)

long count: Mayan system of dating from a fixed date in the past—3114 B.C.; marked the beginning of a great cycle of 5200 years; allowed precision dating of events in Mayan history. (9)

Long March: Communist escape from Hunan province during civil war with Guomindang in 1934; center of Communist power removed to Shaanxi province; firmly established Mao Zedong as head of the Communist party in China. (41)

Longshan culture: One of the formative Chinese cultures located at Ordos bend c. 2000 to 1500 B.C.; based primarily on cultivation of millet. (3)

Louis XIV: French monarch who personified absolute monarchy. (22)

Louis XVI: Bourbon monarch of France who was executed during the radical phase of the French Revolution. (29)

Loyang: Along with Xian, capital of the Zhou dynasty. (3)

Luanda: Portuguese factory established in 1520s south of Kongo; became basis for Portuguese colony of Angola. (27)

Luddites: Workers in Britain who responded to replacement of human labor by machines during the Industrial Revolution by attempting to destroy the machines; named after a fictional British worker named Ned Ludd. (29)

lunar cycle: One of the principal means of establishing a calendar; based on cycles of moon; differed from solar cycle and failed to provide accurate guide to round of the seasons; required constant revision or intercalation. (9)

Luo: Nilotic people who migrated from Upper Nile valley; established dynasty among existing Bantu population in lake region of central eastern Africa; center at Bunyoro. (27)

Luther, Martin: German monk; initiated Protestant Reformation by nailing 95 theses to door of Wittenberg church; emphasized primacy of faith over works stressed in Catholic church; urged state control of Church. (22)

Luzon: Northern island of Philippines; conquered by Spain during the 1560s; site of major Catholic missionary effort. (28)

Macao: One of two ports in which Europeans were permitted to trade in China during the Ming dynasty. (28)

MacArthur, General Douglas: American commander in Pacific campaign of World War II; headed American occupation government of Japan after the war; later commanded international forces during Korean War. (37)

Macedon: Kingdom located in northern Greece; originally loosely organized under kings, became centralized under Philip II; served as basis for unification of Greece and later Macedonian Empire. (6)

Machiavelli, Niccolo: Author of *The Prince;* emphasized realistic discussions of how to seize and maintain power; one of most influential authors of Italian Renaissance. (22)

Madero, Francisco: Moderate democratic reformer in Mexico; proposed moderate reforms in 1910; arrested by Porfirio Díaz; initiated revolution against Díaz when released from prison; temporarily gained power, but removed and assassinated in 1913. (38)

Magellan, Ferdinand: Spanish captain who in 1519 initiated first circumnavigation of the globe; died during the voyage; allowed Spain to claim Philippines. (23)

Maghrib: The Arabic word for western North Africa. (14)

Magna Carta: Great Charter issued by King John of England in 1215; confirmed feudal rights against monarchical claims; represented principle of mutual limits and obligations between rulers and feudal aristocracy. (16)

Mahabharta: Indian epic; written down in the last centuries B.C.; previously handed down in oral form. (7)

Mahayana: Chinese version of Buddhism; placed considerable emphasis on Buddha as god or savior. (11)

Mahdi: Muhammad Achmad, head of a Sudanic Sufi brotherhood; claimed descent from Prophet; proclaimed both Egyptians and British as infidels; launched revolt to purge Islam of impurities; took Khartoum in 1883. (32)

Mahmud II: Ottoman sultan; built a private, professional army; fomented revolution of Janissaries and crushed them with private army; destroyed power of Janissaries and their religious allies; initiated reform of Ottoman Empire on Western precedents. (32)

Mahmud of Ghazni: Third ruler of dynasty; lead invasions of northern India; credited with sacking one of wealthiest of Hindu temples in northern India; gave Muslims reputation for intolerance and aggression. (13)

maize: One of the staple crops of sedentary agriculturists in the Americas; domesticated by 4000 B.C. in central Mexico. (9)

Malacca: Portuguese factory or fortified trade town located on the tip of the Malayan peninsula; traditionally a center for trade among the southeastern Asian islands. (28)

Malacca: Powerful trading city on mainland of Malaya; established smaller trading empire after fall of Shrivijaya. (13)

Mali: Empire centered between the Senegal and Niger rivers; creation of Malinke peoples; broke away from control of Ghana in 13th century. (14)

Mameluks: Muslim slave warriors; established a dynasty in Egypt; defeated the Mongols at Ain Jalut in 1260 and halted Mongol advance. (20)

mana: Power of ali'i; emanated from their lineages and enabled them to extract labor or tribute from their subjects. (10)

Manchus: Jurchen people from region to the northeast of the Chinese empire; seized power following collapse of Ming dynasty; established Qing dynasty, last of imperial houses. (28)

mandalas: Cosmic diagrams of the Hindu natural and spiritual world; Hindu temple complexes during the Gupta Empire were laid out in this fashion. (7)

mandarins: Title given to scholar-gentry by Western visitors to China; Confucian backbone of Chinese bureaucracy and government. (18)

Mandate of Heaven: The divine source for political legitimacy of Chinese rulers; established by Zhou to justify overthrow of Shang. (3)

mandates: Governments entrusted to European nations in the Middle East in the aftermath of World War I; Britain occupied mandates in Syria, Iraq, Lebanon, and Palestine after 1922. (39)

manifest destiny: Belief of the government of the United States that it was destined to rule the continent from coast to coast; led to annexation of Texas and Mexican-American War. (31)

manioc: One of staple crops of sedentary agriculturists in the Americas; principal crop of peoples of the lowlands of South America and the islands of the Caribbean. (9)

manorialism: System that described economic and political relations between landlords and their peasant laborers during the Middle Ages; involved a hierarchy of reciprocal obligations that exchanged labor or rents for access to land. (16)

Mao Zedong: Communist leader in revolutionary China; advocated rural reform and role of peasantry in Nationalist revolution; influenced by Li Dazhao; led Communist reaction against Guomindang purges in 1920s culminating in Long March of 1934; seized control of all of mainland China by 1949; initiated Great Leap Forward in 1958. (41)

Maoris: Residents of New Zealand; migrated to New Zealand from Society Islands as early as 8th century A.D. (10)

Marius: Successful Roman general during the last century B.C.; introduced the concept of using paid volunteers in his army rather than citizen conscripts; created military force with personal loyalties to commander. (8)

Marquis of Pombal: Prime minister of Portugal from 1755 to 1776; acted to strengthen royal authority in Brazil; expelled Jesuits; enacted fiscal reforms and established monopoly companies to stimulate the colonial economy. (25)

Marshall Plan: Program of substantial loans initiated by the United States in 1947; designed to aid Western nations in rebuilding from the war's devastation; vehicle for American economic dominance. (35)

Martel, Charles: Carolingian monarch of Franks; responsible for defeating Muslims in battle of Tours in 732; ended Muslim threat to western Europe. (16)

Marx, Karl: German socialist; blasted earlier socialist movements as utopian; saw history as defined by class struggle between groups out of power and those controlling the means of production; preached necessity of social revolution to create proletarian dictatorship. (29)

mask of Ferdinand: Term given to movements in Latin America allegedly loyal to the displaced Bourbon king of Spain, Ferdinand VII; actually Creole movements for independence. (31)

mass leisure culture: An aspect of the later Industrial Revolution; based on newspapers, music halls, popular theater, vacation trips, and team sports. (29)

Mass Line: Economic policy of Mao Zedong; led to formation of agricultural cooperatives in 1955; cooperatives became farming collectives in 1956. (41)

Mataram: Kingdom that controlled interior regions of Java in 17th century; Dutch East India Company paid tribute to the kingdom for rights of trade at Batavia; weakness of kingdom after 1670s allowed Dutch to exert control over all of Java. (30)

matrilineal: Family descent and inheritance traced through the female line. (1)

matrilocal: A culture in which young men upon marriage go to live with the brides' families. (1)

Mauryas: Dynasty established in Indian subcontinent in 4th century B.C. following invasion of Alexander the Great. (7)

mawali: Non-Arab converts to Islam. (12)

May Fourth movement: Resistance to Japanese encroachments in China began on this date in 1919; spawned movement of intellectuals aimed at transforming China into a liberal democracy; rejected Confucianism. (41)

Maya: Classical culture emerging in southern Mexico, and Central American contemporary with Teotihuacan; extended over broad region; featured monumental architecture, written language, calendrical and mathematical systems, highly developed religion. (9)

mayeques: Class of agricultural laborers or serfs created to work on lands belonging to the Aztec nobility; controlled no land of their own. (17)

Mecca: City located in mountainous region along Red Sea in Arabian peninsula; founded by Umayyad clan of Quraysh; site of Ka'ba; original home of Muhammad; location of chief religious pilgrimage point in Islam. (12)

Medina: Also known as Yathrib; town located northeast of Mecca; grew date palms whose fruit was sold to bedouins; became refuge for Muhammad following flight from Mecca (hijra). (12)

Mehmed II: Ottoman sultan called the "Conqueror"; responsible for conquest of Constantinople in 1453; destroyed what remained of Byzantine Empire. (26)

Meiji restoration: Restoration of the power of the emperor in Japan in 1868; new emperor named Mutsuhito, but called Meiji or Enlightened One; put down troops of shogunate; marked beginning of creation of centralized Japanese government. (33)

Mencius: Also known as Meng Ko; follower of Confucius; stressed consent of the common people. (5)

Meng Ko: Also known as Mencius; follower of Confucius; stressed consent of the common people. (5)

mercantilism: Economic theory that stressed governments' promotion of limitation of imports from other nations and internal economies in order to improve tax revenues; popular during 17th and 18th centuries. (22)

Mesoamerica: Mexico and Central America; along with Peru, site of development of sedentary agriculture in Western hemisphere. (1)

Mesopotamia: Literally "between the rivers"; the civilizations that arose in the alluvial plain of the Tigris-Euphrates river valleys. (2)

mestizos: People of mixed European and Indian ancestry in Mesoamerica and South America; particularly prevalent in areas colonized by Spain; often part of forced labor system. (23)

Methodius: Along with Cyril, missionary sent by Byzantine government to eastern Europe and the Balkans; converted southern Russia and Balkans to Orthodox Christianity; responsible for creation of written script for Slavic known as Cyrillic. (15)

Metropolitan: Head of the Russian Orthodox church; located at Moscow. (20)

Mexican Constitution of 1917: Promised land reform, limited foreign ownership of key resources, guaranteed the rights of workers, and placed restrictions on clerical education; marked end of Mexican Revolution. (38)

Mexican Revolution: Fought over a period of ten years from 1910; resulted in ouster of Porfirio Díaz from power; opposition forces led by Pancho Villa and Emiliano Zapata. (38)

Mexican-American War: Fought between Mexico and the United States from 1846 to 1848; led to devastating defeat of Mexican forces; loss of about one-half of Mexico's national territory to the United States. (31)

Mexico City: Capital of New Spain; built on ruins of Aztec capital of Tenochtitlan. (25)

mfecane: Wars of crushing and wandering in southern Africa; created by Zulu expansion under Shaka; revolutionized political organization of southern Africa. (27)

Middle Ages: The period in western European history from the decline and fall of the Roman Empire until the 15th century. (16)

Middle Passage: Slave voyage from Africa to the Americas; generally a traumatic experience for black slaves, although it failed to strip Africans of their culture. (27)

Minas Gerais: Region of Brazil located in mountainous interior where gold strikes were discovered in 1695; became location for gold rush. (25)

Mindanao: Southern island of Philippines; a Muslim kingdom that was able to successfully resist Spanish conquest. (28)

Ming dynasty: Succeeded Mongol Yuan dynasty in China in 1368; lasted until 1644; initially mounted huge trade expeditions to southern Asia and elsewhere, but later concentrated efforts on internal development within China. (21)

Minh Mang: Second emperor of a united Vietnam, successor of Nguyen Anh; ruled from 1820 to 1841; sponsored emphasis of Confucianism; persecuted Catholics. (41)

Ministry of Rites: Administered examinations to students from Chinese government schools or those recommended by distinguished scholars. (18)

Minoans: A civilization that developed on the island of Crete c. 1600 B.C.; capital at the palace complex of Knossos. (2)

miscegenation: Practice of interracial marriage; found in virtually all colonial ventures. (30)

Mississippian culture: Last of the mound-building cultures of North America; flourished between A.D. 800 and 1300; featured large towns and ceremonial centers; lacked stone architecture of Central America. (9)

mita: Labor extracted for lands assigned to the state and the religion; all communities were expected to contribute; an essential aspect of Inca imperial control; replaced encomienda system in Spanish colonies during the 16th century; particularly important in providing labor for mines. (17, 25)

mitmaq: Inca colonists in new regions; could be Quechua-speakers; used to pacify new conquest or conquered population moved to new home. (17)

MNR: The National Revolutionary Movement; Reformist and Nationalist political coalition in Bolivia; seized power as a result of a revolution in 1952; initiated series of reforms including universal suffrage, nationalization of mines, land redistribution; cut back power of military; replaced by military government in 1964. (38)

moa: Large, wingless birds native to New Zealand; hunted to extinction by early settlers; extinction established need to develop new sources of protein. (10)

Mochica state: Flourished in Andes north of Chavín culture in Moche valley between A.D. 200 and 700; featured great clay-brick temples; created military chiefdom supported by extensive irrigated agriculture. (9)

Moctezuma II: Last independent Aztec emperor; killed during Hernán Cortés's conquest of Tenochtitlan. (25)

modernization theory: The belief that the more industrialized, urban, and modern a society became, the more social change and improvement were possible as traditional patterns and attitudes were abandoned or transformed; used as a blueprint for development in Latin America. (31)

Mohenjo-daro: Along with Harappa, major urban complex of the Harappan civilization; laid out on planned grid pattern. (3)

moldboard: Heavy plow introduced in northern Europe during the Middle Ages; permitted deeper cultivation of heavier soils; a technological innovation of the medieval agricultural system. (16)

Mongols: Central Asian nomadic peoples; smashed Turko-Persian kingdoms; captured Baghdad in 1258 and killed last Abbasid caliph. (13)

monotheism: The exclusive worship of a single god; introduced by the Jews into Western civilization. (2)

Monroe Doctrine: American declaration stated in 1823; established that any attempt of a European country to colonize in the Americas would be considered an unfriendly act by the United States; supported by Great Britain as a means of opening Latin-American trade. (31)

monsoons: Seasonal winds crossing Indian subcontinent and Southeast Asia; during summer bring rains. (3)

Montagu-Chelmsford reforms: Increased the powers of Indian legislators at the all-India level and placed much of the privincial administration of India under local ministries controlled by legislative bodies with substantial numbers of elected Indians; passed in 1919. (39)

montaña: Located on eastern slopes of Andes mountains; location of cultivation and gathering of tropical fruits and coca leaf. (9)

Monte Alban: Chief center of Zapotec culture in southern Mexico during preclassic period; contemporary with Olmec culture; based on irrigated agriculture, calendrical, and writing systems. (9)

Morley-Minto reforms of 1909: Provided educated Indians with considerably expanded opportunities to elect and to serve on local and all-Indian legislative councils. (39)

Mu'awiya: Leader of Umayyad clan; first Umayyad caliph following civil war with Ali. (12)

Mughal dynasty: Established by Babur in India in 1526; the name is taken from the supposed Mongol descent of Babur, but there is little indication of any Mongol influence in the dynasty; became weak after rule of Aurangzeb in first decades of 18th century. (26)

Muhammad: Prophet of Islam; born c. 570 to Banu Hashim clan of Quraysh tribe in Mecca; raised by father's family; received revelations from Allah in A.D. 610 and thereafter; died in 632. (12)

Muhammad ibn Qasim: Arab general; conquered Sind in India; declared the region and the Indus valley to be part of Umayyad Empire. (13)

Muhammad of Ghur: Military commander of Persian extraction who ruled small mountain kingdom in Afghanistan; began process of conquest to establish Muslim political control of northern India; brought much of Indus valley, Sind, and northwestern India under his control. (13)

Muhammad Shah II: Turkic ruler of Muslim Khwarazm kingdom; attempted to resist Mongol conquest; conquered in 1220. (20)

Muhammad the Great: Extended the boundaries of the Songhay Empire; Islamic ruler of the mid-16th century. (14)

mullahs: Local mosque officials and prayer leaders within the Safavid Empire; agents of Safavid religious campaign to convert all of population to Shi'ism. (26)

mummification: The act of preserving the bodies of the dead; practiced in Egypt to preserve the body for enjoyment of the afterlife. (2)

Munich Conference: Meeting concerning Germany's occupation of portions of Czechoslovakia in 1938; after receiving Hitler's assurances that he would take no more land, Western leaders agreed to the division of Czechoslovakia. (34)

Murad: Head of the coalition of Mamluk households in Egypt; opposed Napoleonic invasion of Egypt and suffered devastating defeat; failure destroyed Mamluk government in Egypt and revealed vulnerability of Muslim core. (32)

Muslim Brotherhood: Egyptian nationalist movement founded by Hasan al-Banna in 1928; committed to fundamentalist movement in Islam; fostered strikes and urban riots against the khedival government. (40)

Muslim League: Founded in 1906 to better support demands of Muslims for separate electorates and legislative seats in Hindu-dominated India; represented division within Indian nationalist movement. (39)

Muslims: Followers of Islam. (12)

Mussolini, Benito: Italian fascist leader; actually created first fascist government based on aggressive foreign policy and new nationalist glories. (34)

Mvemba, Nzinga: King of Kongo south of Zaire River from 1507 to 1543; converted to Christianity and took title of Afonso I; under Portuguese influence attempted to Christianize all of kingdom. (27)

Mycenae: The first civilization to emerge on the Greek mainland; destroyed c. 1000 B.C. (2)

nabobs: Name given to British representatives of the East India Company who went briefly to India to make fortunes through graft and exploitation. (30)

Nadir Khan Afshar: Soldier-adventurer following fall of Safavid dynasty in 1722; proclaimed himself shah in 1736; established short-lived dynasty in reduced kingdom. (26)

Nagasaki: One of two Japanese cities on which the United States dropped atomic bombs in 1945; devastation of these cities caused Japanese surrender without invasion of home islands. (34)

Nahuatl: Language spoken by the Toltecs and Aztecs. (17)

Nara: Along with Heian, capital of the Yamato emperors; patterned after ancient imperial centers of China; never fully populated. (10)

Narmer: First pharaoh of Egyptian Old Kingdom; ruled c. 3100 B.C. (2)

Nasser, Gamal Abdul: Took power in Egypt following a military coup in 1952; enacted land reforms and used state resources to reduce unemployment; ousted Britain from the Suez Canal zone in 1956. (40)

Natal: British colony in South Africa; developed after Boer trek north from Cape Colony; major commercial outpost at Durban. (30)

National Liberation Front (FLN): Radical nationalist movement in Algeria; launched sustained guerrilla war against France in the 1950s; success of attacks led to independence of Algeria in 1958. (39)

National Socialist party: Also known as the Nazi Party; led by Adolf Hitler in Germany; picked up political support during the economic chaos of the Great Depression; advocated authoritarian state under a single leader, aggressive foreign policy to reverse humiliation of the Treaty of Versailles; took power in Germany in 1933. (34)

nationalism: Political viewpoint with origins in western Europe in the 19th century; often allies with one of other "isms"; urged importance of national unity; valued a collective identity based on race or ethnic origin. (29)

Natufian complex: Preagricultural culture; located in present-day Israel, Jordan, and Lebanon; practiced the collection of naturally present barley and wheat to supplement game; typified by large settlement sites. (1)

natural law: General principles of law applicable to all societies; a fundamental concept of the Roman legal system under the empire; related to Stoic ethical theory. (8)

Neanderthals: Species of genus *Homo* that disappeared at the end of the Paleolithic period. (1)

négritude: Literary movement in Africa; sought to combat racial stereotypes of African culture; celebrated the beauty of black skin and African physique; associated with origins of African nationalist movements. (39)

Nehru, Jawaharlal: One of Gandhi's disciples; governed India after independence; committed to program of social reform and economic development; preserved civil rights and democracy. (40)

neocolonial economy: Economy that results from continued dominance of the First and Second World nations of the world's economy; ability of the First and Second World nations to maintain economic colonialism without political colonialism. (40)

Neolithic era: The New Stone Age between 8000 and 5000 B.C.; period in which adaptation of sedentary agriculture occurred; domestication of plants and animals accomplished. (1)

Nestorians: A Christian sect found in Asia; tended to support Islamic invasions of this area in preference to Byzantine rule; cut off from Europe by Muslim invasions. (12, 20)

New Deal: President Franklin Roosevelt's precursor of the modern welfare state; program to combat economic depression enacted a number of social insurance measures and used government spending to stimulate the economy; increased power of the state and the state's intervention in social and economic life. (35)

New Economic Policy: Initiated by Lenin in 1921; state continued to set basic economic policies, but efforts now combined with individual initiative; policy allowed food production to recover. (36)

new feminism: New wave of women's rights agitations dating from 1949; emphasized more literal equality that would play down domestic roles and qualities for women; promoted specific reforms and redefinition of what it meant to be female. (35)

New France: French colonies in North America; extended from St. Lawrence along Great Lakes and down Mississippi River valley system. (23)

New Spain: Spanish colonial possessions in Mesoamerica; included most of central Mexico; based on imperial system of Aztecs. (25)

New Youth: Marxist periodical in China; did much to spread the ideas of Marx and Lenin among the politically active youth of China's coastal cities. (41)

Newton, Isaac: English scientist during the 17th century; author of *Principia*; drew the various astronomical and physical observations and wider theories together in a neat framework of natural laws; established principles of motion; defined forces of gravity. (22)

Nguyen: Rival Vietnamese dynasty that arose in southern Vietnam to challenge traditional dynasty of Trinh in north at Hanoi; kingdom centered on Red and Mekong rivers; capital at Hue. (19)

Nguyen Anh: Last surviving member of Nguyen dynasty following Tayson Rebellion in Vietnam; with French support retook southern Vietnam; drove Tayson from northern Vietnam by 1802; proclaimed himself emperor with capital at Hue. (41)

niche ecological adaptation: Human adaptation to an environment in such a way that there is minimal impact on the ecology; normally typical of hunting-and-gathering groups. (4)

nirvana: The Buddhist state of enlightenment; a state of tranquility. (7)

Nkrumah, Kwame: African nationalist during period of decolonization; responsible for creation of first independent, black African state of Ghana in 1957; established power through his own party—Convention Peoples party (CPP). (39)

Nobili, Robert di: Italian Jesuit missionary; worked in India during the early 1600s; introduced strategy to convert elites first; strategy later widely adopted by Jesuits in various parts of Asia; mission eventually failed. (28)

Nobunaga: Japanese daimyo; first to make extensive use of firearms; in 1573 deposed last of Ashikaga shoguns; unified much of central Honshu under his command; killed in 1582. (28)

Nok: Culture featuring highly developed art style flourishing between 500 B.C. and A.D. 200; located in forests of central Nigeria. (14)

nomads: Cattle- and sheep-herding societies normally found on the fringes of civilized societies; commonly referred to as "barbarian" by civilized societies. (1)

North Atlantic Treaty Organization (NATO): Created in 1949 under United States leadership to group most of the Western European powers plus Canada in a defensive alliance against possible Soviet aggression. (35)

Northern Renaissance: Cultural and intellectual movement of northern Europe; began later than Italian Renaissance c. 1450; centered in France, Low Countries, England, and Germany; featured greater emphasis on religion than Italian Renaissance. (22)

nuclear families: Consisted of husband and wife, their children, and perhaps a grandmother or orphaned cousin; typical of Chinese peasantry. (3)

Nur Jahan: Wife of Jahangir; amassed power in court and created faction of male relatives who dominated empire during later years of Jahangir's reign. (26)

Nurhaci: Architect of Manchu unity; created distinctive Manchu banner armies; controlled most of Manchuria; adopted Chinese bureaucracy and court ceremonies in Manchuria; entered China and successfully captured Ming capital at Beijing. (32)

obeah: African religious ideas and practices in the English islands. (27)

obrajes: Small textile workshops established in Spanish colonies in New World; produced common cloth usually with Indian women's labor; supplied American demand. (25)

Obregón, Alvaro: Emerged as leader of the Mexican government in 1915; elected president in 1920. (38)

obruk: Labor obligations of Russian peasants to either their aristocratic landlords or to the state; typical of increased labor burdens placed on Russian peasantry during the 18th century. (24)

Octavian: Julius Caesar's grandnephew and adopted son; defeated conservative senators following Caesar's assassination; later defeated forces of Mark Anthony and Cleopatra in Egypt; offered title of Augustus by Senate; became first Roman emperor. (8)

Ogedei: Third son of Chinggis Khan; succeeded Chinggis Khan as khagan of the Mongols following his father's death. (20)

old believers: Russians who refused to accept the ecclesiastical reforms of Alexis Romanov; many exiled to Siberia or southern Russia where they became part of Russian colonization. (24)

Olmec culture: Cultural tradition that arose at San Lorenzo and La Venta in Mexico c. 1200 B.C.; featured irrigated agriculture, urbanism, elaborate religion, beginnings of calendrical and writing systems. (9)

Olympic games: One of the pan-Hellenic rituals observed by all Greek city-states; involved athletic competitions and ritual celebrations. (6)

Onin War: War between rival heirs of Ashikaga Shogunate; fought between 1467 and 1477; led to warfare between rival headquarters and Kyoto and destruction of old capital. (19)

Opium War: Fought between the British and Qing China beginning in 1839; fought to protect British trade in opium; resulted in resounding British victory, opening of Hong Kong as British port of trade. (32)

Orabi, Achmad: Student of Muhammad Abduh; led revolt in 1882 against Turkish influence in Egyptian army; forced khedive to call on British army for support. (32)

oracle of Delphi: Person representing the god Apollo; allegedly received cryptic messages from the god that had predictive value if the seeker could correctly interpret the communication. (6)

oracles: Shamans or priests in Chinese society who foretold the future through interpretations of animal bones cracked by heat; inscriptions on bones led to Chinese writing. (3)

Ordos bend: Located on Huanghe River; region of fertile soil; site of Yangshao and Longshan cultures. (3)

Ormuz: Portuguese factory or fortified trade town located at southern end of Persian Gulf; site for forcible entry into Asian sea trade network. (28)

Orozco, José Clemente: Mexican muralist of the period after the Mexican Revolution; like Rivera, his work featured romantic images of the Indian past with Christian symbols and Communist ideology. (38)

Ottoman Empire: Turkic empire established in Asia Minor and eventually extending throughout Middle East; responsible for conquest of Constantinople and end of Byzantine Empire in 1453; succeeded Seljuk Turks following retreat of Mongols. (21)

Ottoman Society for Union and Progress: Organization of political agitators in opposition to rule of Abdul Hamid; also called "Young Turks"; desired to restore 1876 constitution. (32)

Ottomans: Turkic people who advanced from strongholds in Asia Minor during 1350s; conquered large part of Balkans; unified under Mehmed I; captured

Constantinople in 1453; established empire from Balkans that included most of Arab world. (26)

Ovid: Roman poet exiled by Augustus for sensual poetry considered out of touch with the imperial policies stressing family virtues. (8)

Pachakuti: Ruler of Inca society from 1438 to 1471; launched a series of military campaigns that gave Incas control of the region from Cuzco to the shores of Lake Titicaca. (17)

Pacific Rim states: Japan, Korea, Singapore, Hong Kong, Taiwan; typified by rapid growth rates, expanding exports, and industrialization; either Chinese or strongly influenced by Chinese values; considerable reliance on government planning and direction, limitations on dissent and instability. (37)

pahi: Double canoes used for long-distance voyaging; carried a platform between canoes for passengers or cargo. (10)

Paleolithic: The Old Stone Age ending in 12,000 B.C.; typified by use of crude stone tools and hunting and gathering for subsistence. (1)

Palmares: Kingdom of runaway slaves with a population of 8,000 to 10,000 people; located in Brazil during the 17th century; leadership was Angolan. (27)

Panama Canal: An aspect of American intervention in Latin America; resulted from United States support for a Panamanian independence movement in return for a grant to exclusive rights to a canal across the Panama isthmus; provided short route from Atlantic to Pacific Ocean. (31)

parliaments: Bodies representing privileged groups; institutionalized feudal principle that rulers should consult with their vassals; found in England, Spain, Germany, and France. (16)

Partition of Poland: Three separate divisions of Polish territory between Russia, Prussia, and Austria in 1772, 1793, and 1795; eliminated Poland as an independent state; part of expansion of Russian influence in eastern Europe. (24)

Pasteur, Louis: Discoverer of germs; led to more conscientious sanitary regulation by the 1880s. (29)

pastoral nomads: An intermediate form of ecological adaptation dependent on domesticated animal herds that feed on natural environment; typically more populous than shifting cultivation groups. (4)

pastoralism: A nomadic agricultural lifestyle based on herding domesticated animals; tended to produce independent people capable of challenging sedentary agricultural societies. (1)

patriarchate: Societies in which women defer to men; societies run by men and based on the assumption that men naturally directed political, economic, and cultural life. (2)

Paul: One of the first Christian missionaries; moved away from insistence that adherents of the new religion follow Jewish law; use of Greek as language of Church. (8)

Paulistas: Backwoodsmen from São Paulo in Brazil; penetrated Brazilian interior in search of precious metals during 17th century. (25)

Pearl Harbor: American naval base in Hawaii; attack by Japanese on this facility in December 1941 crippled American fleet in the Pacific; caused entry of United States into World War II. (34)

Pedro I, Dom: Son and successor of Dom João VI in Brazil; aided in the declaration of Brazilian independence from Portugal in 1822; became constitutional emperor of Brazil. (31)

Peloponnesian War: War from 431 to 404 B.C. between Athens and Sparta for dominance in southern Greece; resulted in Spartan victory but failure to achieve political unification of Greece. (6)

peninsulares: People living in the New World Spanish colonies but born in Spain. (25)

People's Democratic Republic of Korea: Northern half of Korea dominated by USSR; headed by Kim II-Sung; attacked south in 1950 and initiated Korean War; retained independence as a Communist state after the war. (37)

Peoples Liberation Army: Chinese Communist army; administered much of country under Peoples Republic of China. (41)

Peoples Republic of China: Communist government of mainland China; proclaimed in 1949 following military success of Mao Zedong over forces of Chiang Kai-shek and the Guomindang. (41)

perestroika: Policy of Mikhail Gorbachev calling for economic restructuring in the USSR; more leeway for private ownership and decentralized control in industry and agriculture. (36)

Pericles: Athenian political leader during 5th century B.C.; guided development of

Athenian Empire; died during early stages of Peloponnesian War. (6)

period of the Six Dynasties: Era from 220 to 589; featured endless wars fought by the patchwork of regional kingdoms that followed the fall of the Han in China. (18)

Perón, Evita: Also known as Eva Duarte; first wife of Juan Perón; became public spokesperson for Perón among the poor until her death in 1952. (38)

Perón, Juan D.: Military leader in Argentina who became dominant political figure after military coup in 1943; used position as Minister of Labor to appeal to working groups and the poor; became president in 1946; forced into exile in 1955; returned and won presidency in 1973. (38)

Perry, Matthew: American commodore who visited Edo Bay with American fleet in 1853; insisted on opening ports to American trade on threat of naval bombardment; won rights for American trade with Japan in 1854. (33)

Persian Wars: Two wars fought in early 5th century between Persian Empire and Greek city-states; Greek victories allowed Greek civilization to define identity separate from the Asian empire. (6)

Peter I: Also known as Peter the Great; son of Alexis Romanov; ruled from 1689 to 1725; continued growth of absolutism and conquest; included more definite interest in changing selected aspects of economy and culture through imitation of western European models. (24)

Petrarch, Francesco: One of the major literary figures of the Western Renaissance; an Italian author and humanist. (21)

Philip II: Ruled Macedon from 359 to 336 B.C.; founder of centralized kingdom; later conquered rest of Greece, which was subjected to Macedonian authority. (6)

Phoenicians: Seafaring civilization located on the shores of the eastern Mediterranean; established colonies throughout the Mediterranean. (2)

Pinsker, Leon: European Zionist who believed that Jewish assimilation into Christian European nations was impossible; argued for return to Middle Eastern Holy Land. (39)

pipiltin: Nobility in Aztec society; formed by intermarriage of the Aztecs with the leading families of the Culhuacan who could trace lineage back to the Toltecs; achieved dominance in society as result of conquest of Azcapotzalco. (17)

Pisastratus: Athenian tyrant of the 6th century B.C.; gained popular support against traditional aristocratic councils of Athenian government. (6)

Pizarro, Francisco: Led conquest of Inca Empire of Peru beginning in 1535; by 1540 most of Inca possessions fell to Spanish. (25)

Plassey: Battle in 1757 between troops of the British East India Company and an Indian army under Sirāj-ud-daula, ruler of Bengal; British victory resulted in control of northern India. (30)

Plato: Greek philosopher; knowledge based on consideration of ideal forms outside the material world; proposed ideal form of government based on abstract principles in which philosophers ruled. (6)

plebeians: Ordinary citizens; originally those Roman families that could not trace their relationship to one of the major Roman clans. (8)

pochteca: Special merchant class in Aztec society; specialized in long-distance trade in luxury items. (17)

polis: City-state form of government; typical of Greek political organization from 800 to 400 B.C. (6)

Politburo: Executive committee of the Communist party; 20 members. (36)

polyandry: Marriage practice in which one woman had several husbands; recounted in Aryan epics. (3)

polygamy: Marriage practice in which one husband had several wives; practiced in Aryan society. (3)

Polynesia: Islands contained in a rough triangle whose points lie at Hawaii, New Zealand, and Easter Island. (10)

pope: Bishop of Rome; head of the Christian Church in western Europe. (11)

Popular Front: Combination of Socialist and Communist political parties in France; won election in 1936; unable to take strong measures of social reform because of continuing strength of conservatives; fell from power in 1938. (35)

population revolution: Huge growth in population in western Europe beginning about 1730; prelude to Industrial Revolution; population of France increased 50 percent, England and Prussia 100 percent. (29)

positivism: French philosophy based on observation and scientific approach to problems of society; adopted by many Latin-American liberals in the aftermath of independence. (31)

Potosí: Mine located in upper Peru (modern Bolivia); largest of New World silver mines; produced 80 percent of all Peruvian silver. (25)

Potsdam Conference: Meeting between leaders of the United States, Britain, and the Soviet Union just before the end of the war in 1945; Allies agreed upon Soviet domination in eastern Europe; Germany and Austria to be divided among victorious Allies. (34)

potter's wheel: A technological advance in pottery-making; invented c. 6000 B.C.; encouraged faster and higher-quality ceramic pottery production. (2)

pragmatists: Chinese Communist politicians such as Zhou Enlai, Deng Xiaoping, and Liu Shaoqui; determined to restore state direction and market incentives at the local level; opposed Great Leap Forward. (41)

preclassic: Period in Americas from 2000 to 300 B.C.; period of Olmec culture, also Monte Alban culture in Oaxaca. (9)

Presidencies: Three districts that made up the bulk of the directly ruled British territories in India; capitals at Madras, Calcutta, and Bombay. (30)

Prester John: Name given to a mythical Christian monarch whose kingdom had supposedly been cut off from Europe by the Muslim conquests; Chinggis Khan was originally believed to be this mythical ruler. (20)

PRI: Party of the Institutionalized Revolution; dominant political party in Mexico; developed during the 1920s and 1930s; incorporated labor, peasant, military, and middle-class sectors; controlled other political organizations in Mexico. (38)

primary products: Food or industrial crops for which there is a high demand in industrialized economies; prices of such products tend to fluctuate widely; typically the primary exports of Third World economies. (40)

Princely States: Indian princes allied with the British Raj; agents of the East India Company were stationed at the rulers' courts to ensure compliance; made up over one-third of the British Indian Empire. (30)

proletariat: Class of people without access to producing property; typically manufacturing workers, paid laborers in agricultural economy, or urban poor; product of economic changes of 16th and 17th centuries. (22)

Protestantism: General wave of religious dissent against Catholic church; generally held to have begun with Martin Luther's attack on Catholic beliefs in 1517; included many varieties of religious belief. (22)

protoindustrialization: Preliminary shift away from agricultural economy; workers become full- or part-time producers of textile and metal products, working at home but in a capitalist system in which materials, work orders, and ultimate sales depended on urban merchants; prelude to Industrial Revolution. (29)

Ptolemies: One of the regional dynasties that followed the death of Alexander the Great; founded in Egypt. (6)

Pugachev rebellion: During 1770s in reign of Catherine the Great; led by cossack Emelyan Pugachev who claimed to be legitimate tsar; eventually crushed; typical of peasant unrest during the 18th century and thereafter. (24)

puna: High valleys and steppes lying between the two major chains of the Andes mountains; site of South American agricultural origins, also only location of pastoralism in Americas. (9)

Punic Wars: Fought between Rome and Carthage to establish dominance in the western Mediterranean; won by Rome after three separate conflicts. (8)

pure land Buddhism: Emphasized salvationist aspects of Chinese Buddhism; popular among masses of Chinese society. (18)

Puyi: Last emperor of China; deposed as emperor while still a small boy in 1912. (32)

Pygmies: One of few pure hunting societies left in Africa following Bantu migration. (10)

pyramids: Monumental architecture typical of Old Kingdom Egypt; used as burial sites for pharaohs. (2)

Qin dynasty: Established in 221 B.C. at the end of the Warring States period following the decline of the Zhou dynasty; fell in 207 B.C. (5)

Quetzalcoatl: Toltec deity; Feathered Serpent; adopted by Aztecs as major god. (17)

quipu: System of knotted strings utilized by the Incas in place of a writing system; could contain numerical and other types of information for censuses and financial records. (17)

Quran: Recitations of revelations received by Muhammad; holy book of Islam. (12)

Quraysh: Tribe of bedouins that controlled Mecca. (12)

Qutb-ud-din Aibak: Lieutenant of Muhammad of Ghur; established kingdom in India with capital at Delhi; proclaimed himself Sultan of India. (13)

radical: Political viewpoint with origins in western Europe during the 19th century; advocated broader voting rights than liberals; in some cases advocated outright democracy; urged reforms in favor of the lower classes. (29)

Rajput: Regional princes in India following collapse of empire; emphasized military control of their regions. (11)

Rajputana: Region in south of India divided into patchwork of tiny kingdoms; dominated by warrior elite; remained independent of Harsha's empire. (13)

Rama: Major figure in the popular Indian epic, *Ramayana*. (7)

Recopilación: Body of laws collected in 1681 for Spanish possessions in New World; basis of law in the Indies. (25)

Red Army: Military organization constructed under leadership of Leon Trotsky, Bolshevik follower of Lenin; made use of people of humble background. (36)

Red Guard: Student brigades utilized by Mao Zedong and his political allies during the Cultural Revolution to discredit Mao's political enemies. (41)

Red Heads: Name given to Safavid followers for distinctive red headgear. (26)

Reform Bill of 1832: Legislation passed in Great Britain that extended the vote to most members of the middle class; failed to produce democracy in Britain. (29)

reincarnation: The successive attachment of the soul to some animate form according to merits earned in previous lives. (7)

reindeer herders: Nomadic pastoralists dependent on domesticated reindeer; common to tundra of northern Europe; generally isolated from civilizations. (4)

Renaissance: Cultural and political movement in western Europe; began in Italy c. 1400; rested on urban vitality and expanding commerce; featured a literature and art with distinctly more secular priorities than those of the Middle Ages. (21)

republic: The balanced constitution of Rome from c. 510 to 47 B.C.; featured an aristocratic Senate, a panel of magistrates, and several popular assemblies. (8)

Republic of Korea: Southern half of Korea sponsored by United States following World War II; headed by nationalist Syngman Rhee; developed parliamentary institutions, but maintained authoritarian government; defended by UN forces during Korean War; underwent industrialization and economic emergence after 1950s. (37)

revisionism: Socialist movement that disavowed Marxist revolutionary doctrine; believed social success could be achieved gradually through political institutions. (29)

Revolutions of 1848: Generally refers to those nationalist and liberal movements within the Habsburg Empire—specifically in Italy, Germany, Austria, and Hungary; after temporary success, the revolutions failed. (29)

Rhodes, Cecil: British entrepreneur in South Africa; manipulated political situation in South Africa to gain entry to resources of Boer republics; initiated Boer War as means of destroying Boer independence. (30)

Ricci, Matteo: Along with Adam Schall, Jesuit scholar in court of Ming emperors; skilled scientist; corrected calendars, forged cannons, fixed clocks; won few converts to Christianity. (28)

Ridda: Wars that followed Muhammad's death in 632; resulted in defeat of rival prophets and some of larger clans; restored unity of Islam. (12)

Rio de Janeiro: Brazilian port; close to mines Minas Gerais; importance grew with gold strikes; became colonial capital in 1763. (25)

Rivadavia, Bernardino: Liberal leader in Buenos Aires in 1820s; instituted series of reforms in education, finance, agriculture, and immigration; attempted to create a strong central government. (31)

Rivera, Diego: Mexican artist of the period after the Mexican Revolution; famous for murals painted on walls of public buildings; mixed romantic images of the Indian past with Christian symbols and Communist ideology. (38)

Romance of the West Chamber: Chinese dramatic work written during the Yuan period; indicative of the continued literary vitality of China during Mongol rule. (20)

Romanov, Alexis: Second Romanov tsar; abolished assemblies of nobles; gained new powers over Russian Orthodox church. (24)

Romanov dynasty: Dynasty elected in 1613 at end of Time of Troubles; ruled Russia until 1917. (24)

romanticism: Artistic and literary movement of the 19th century in western Europe; held that emotion and impression, not reason, were the keys to the mysteries of human experience and nature; sought to portray passions, not calm reflection. (29)

Roosevelt, Theodore: American president; sponsored the conference that ended the Russo-Japanese War; winner of the Nobel Peace Prize; efforts indicated first American concern with Japanese expansion in Pacific. (34)

Rosas, Juan Manuel de: Federalist leader in Buenos Aires; took power in 1831; commanded loyalty of gauchos; restored local autonomy. (31)

Rowlatt Act: Placed severe restrictions on key Indian civil rights such as freedom of the press; acted to offset the concessions granted under Montagu-Chelmsford reforms of 1919. (39)

Royal African Company: Chartered in 1660s to establish a monopoly over the slave trade among British merchants; supplied African slaves to colonies in Barbados, Jamaica, and Virginia. (27)

Rurik: Legendary Scandinavian who theoretically established first kingdom of Russia based in Kiev in A.D. 855. (15)

Russian Communist party: The Bolshevik wing of the Social Democratic party in Russia in 1917; came to power under Lenin after the November expulsion of Kerensky's liberal government. (36)

Russian Orthodoxy: Russian form of Christianity imported from Byzantine Empire and combined with local religion; king characteristically controlled major appointments. (15)

Russian Revolution of 1905: Consisted of strikes by urban workers and widespread insurrections among the peasantry; resulted in some temporary reforms such as the creation of the duma. (33)

Russo-Japanese War: War between Japan and Russia over territory in Manchuria beginning in 1905; Japan defeated the Russians, largely due to superior naval power; Japan annexed Korea in 1910 as a result of military dominance. (33)

Sadat, Anwar: Successor of Gamal Abdul Nasser as ruler of Egypt; acted to dismantle costly state programs; accepted peace treaty with Israel in 1973; opened Egypt to investment by Western European nations. (40)

Safavid dynasty: Originally a Turkic nomadic group; family originated in Sufi mystic group; espoused Shi'ism; conquered territory and established kingdom in region equivalent to modern Iran; lasted until 1722. (26)

Safi al-Din: Early 14th century Sufi mystic; began campaign to purify Islam; first member of Safavid dynasty. (26)

Sahara: Desert running across northern Africa; separates the Mediterranean coast from southern Africa. (10)

Sahel: The extensive grassland belt at the southern edge of the Sahara; a point of exchange between the forests to the south and North Africa. (14)

saints: Holy men and women, often martyrs, who were revered in Christianity as models of Christian life-styles; built up treasury of merit that could be tapped by more ordinary Christians. (11)

Saladin: Muslim leader in the last decades of the 12th century; reconquered most of the crusader outposts for Islam. (13)

"salt water" slaves: Slaves transported from Africa; almost invariably black. (27)

samurai: Mounted troops of the bushi; loyal to local lords, not the emperor. (19)

San Martín, José de: Leader of independence movement in Rio de la Plata; led to independence of the United Provinces of the Rio de la Plata by 1816; later led independence movement in Chile and Peru as well. (31)

Sandinista party: Nicaraguan Socialist movement named after Augusto Sandino; successfully carried out a Socialist revolution in Nicaragua during the 1980s. (38)

Sandino, Augusto: Led a guerrilla resistance movement against U.S. occupation forces in Nicaragua; assassinated by Nicaraguan National Guard in 1934; became national hero and symbol of resistance to U.S. influence in Central America. (38)

Sanskrit: The sacred and classical Indian language. (7)

Santa Ana, General Antonio López de: Seized power in Mexico after collapse of empire of Mexico in 1824; after brief reign of liberals, seized power in 1835 as caudillo; defeated by Texans in war for independence in 1836; defeated by United States in Mexican-American War in 1848; unseated by liberal rebellion in 1854. (31)

Santa Cruz, Andrés: Mestizo general who established union of independent Peru and Bolivia between 1829 and 1839. (31)

Sargon I: Ruler of city-state of Akkad; established the first empire in Mesopotamian civilization c. 2400 B.C. (2)

Sarmiento, Domingo F.: Liberal politician and president of Argentine Republic; author of *Facundo*, a critique of

caudillo politics; increased international trade, launched internal reforms in education and transportation. (31)

Sassanid Empire: Replaced Parthian Empire in A.D. 227 in northeastern portion of Middle East; shared border with Byzantine Empire. (11)

sati: Ritual in India of immolating surviving widows with the bodies of their deceased husbands. (13)

satyagraha: Literally "truth-force"; Gandhi's policy of nonviolent opposition to British colonialism. (39)

savages: Societies engaged in either hunting and gathering for subsistence or in migratory cultivation; not as stratified or specialized as civilized and nomadic societies. (1)

Schall, Adam: Along with Matteo Ricci, Jesuit scholar in court of Ming emperors; skilled scientist; corrected calendars, forged cannons, fixed clocks; won few converts to Christianity. (28)

scholar-gentry: Chinese class created by the marital linkage of the local landholding aristocracy with the office-holding shi; superseded shi as governors of China. (5)

scholasticism: Dominant medieval philosophical approach; so-called because of its base in the schools or universities; based on use of logic to resolve theological problems. (16)

school of National Learning: New ideology that laid emphasis on Japan's unique historical experience and the revival of indigenous culture at the expense of Chinese imports such as Confucianism; typical of Japan in 18th century. (28)

scientific revolution: Culminated in 17th century; period of empirical advances associated with the development of wider theoretical generalizations; resulted in change in traditional beliefs of Middle Ages. (22)

Secret Army Organization: Organization of French settlers in Algeria; led guerrilla war following independence during the 1960s; assaults directed against Arabs, Berbers, and French who advocated independence. (39)

secret societies: Chinese peasant organizations; provided financial support in hard times and physical protection in case of disputes with local aristocracy. (5)

Seleucids: One of the regional dynasties that followed the death of Alexander the Great; founded in Persia. (6)

Selim III: Sultan who ruled Ottoman Empire from 1789 to 1807; aimed at improving administrative efficiency and building a new army and navy; toppled by Janissaries in 1807. (32)

Seljuk Turks: Nomadic invaders from central Asia via Persia; staunch Sunnis; ruled in name of Abbasid caliphs from mid-11th century. (13)

Senate: Assembly of Roman aristocrats; advised on policy within the republic; one of the early elements of the Roman constitution. (8)

sepoys: Troops that served the British East India Company; recruited from various warlike peoples of India. (30)

seppuku: Ritual suicide or disembowelment in Japan; commonly known in West as hara-kiri; demonstrated courage and a means to restore family honor. (19)

serfs: Peasant agricultural laborers within the manorial system of the Middle Ages. (16)

Seven Years' War: Fought both in continental Europe and also in overseas colonies between 1756 and 1763; resulted in Prussian seizures of land from Austria, English seizures of colonies in India and North America. (22)

Shah-Nama: Written by Firdawsi in late 10th and early 11th centuries; relates history of Persia from creation to the Islamic conquests. (13)

Shaka: Ruler and reformer of Nguni peoples after 1818; reformed loose forces into regiments organized by lineage and age; created Zulu chiefdom that began to absorb or destroy its neighbors in southern Africa. (27)

Shang: First Chinese dynasty for which archeological evidence exists; capital located in Ordos bend. (3)

Sharia: Islamic law; defined among other things the patrilineal nature of Islamic inheritance. (14)

shaykhs: Leaders of tribes and clans within bedouin society; usually men with large herds, several wives, and many children. (12)

shi: Probably originally priests; transformed into corps of professional bureaucrats because of knowledge of writing during Zhou dynasty in China. (3)

Shi Huangdi: Founder of the brief Qin dynasty in 221 B.C. (5)

Shi'as: Political and theological division within Islam; followers of Ali. (12)

shifting cultivation: An intermediate form of ecological adaptation in which temporary forms of cultivation are carried out with little impact on the natural ecology; typical of rain forest cultivators. (4)

Shinto: Religion of early Japanese culture; devotees worshipped numerous gods and spirits associated with the natural world; offers of food and prayers made to gods and nature spirits. (10)

shoguns: Military leaders of the bakufu. (19)

Shrivijaya: Trading empire centered on Malacca Straits between Malaya and Sumatra; controlled trade of empire; Buddhist government resistant to Muslim missionaries; fall opened up southeastern Asia to Muslim conversion. (13)

siege of Stalingrad: Turning point in Germany's assault on Soviet Union in 1942; despite massive losses, Russians successfully defended the city; over one-third of German army surrendered. (34)

Signet Ring of Rakshasa: One of great dramas produced during the Gupta Empire; dramatized authority of brahmans. (7)

silk route: The most famous of the trading routes established by pastoral nomads connecting the European, Indian, and Chinese civilizations; transmitted goods and ideas among civilizations. (4)

Silla: Independent Korean kingdom in southeastern part of peninsula; defeated Koguryo along with their Chinese Tang allies; submitted as a vassal of the Tang emperor and agreed to tribute payment; ruled united Korea by 668. (19)

Simon Commission: In 1927 considered future Indian colonial government responses to nationalist demands; served to unify nationalist politicians on both right and left of independence movement as well as healed rift between Muslims and Hindus. (39)

Singapore: Originally held by British as part of colony of Malaya; largely Chinese population; British attempted to create invulnerable naval base; captured by Japanese during World War II; emerged after war as independent port. (37)

Sinification: Extensive adaptation of Chinese culture in other regions; typical of Korea and Japan, less typical of Vietnam. (19)

Sino-Japanese War: War fought between Japan and Qing China between 1894 and 1895; resulted in Japanese victory; frustrated Japanese imperial aims due to Western insistence that Japan withdraw from Liaotung peninsula. (33)

Skanda Gupta: Last of the able rulers of the Gupta dynasty; following his reign the empire dissolved under the pressure of nomadic invasions. (7)

slash-and-burn technique: A system of cultivation typical of shifting cultivators; forest floors cleared by fire are then planted. (4)

Slavs: Indo-European group; ultimately dominated much of eastern Europe from the Balkans northward; formed regional kingdoms by 5th century A.D. (10)

Smith, Adam: Established new school of economy; argued that government should avoid regulation of economy in favor of the operation of the laws of market forces. (22)

social question: Issues relating to repressed classes in western Europe during the Industrial Revolution, particularly workers and women; became more critical than constitutional issues after 1870. (29)

Social Revolutionary party: Winners of the parliamentary majority of the first election held following the November 1917 Bolshevik seizure of power; emphasized peasant support and rural reform; expelled in favor of Bolsheviks. (36)

socialism: Political viewpoint with origins in western Europe during the 19th century; urged an attack on private property in the name of equality; wanted state control of means of production, end to capitalist exploitation of the working man. (29)

socialism in one country: Joseph Stalin's concept of Russian communism based solely on the Soviet Union rather than the Leninist concept of international revolution; by cutting off the Soviet Union from other economies, the USSR avoided worst consequences of the Great Depression. (34)

Socialist realism: Attempt within the USSR to relate formal culture to the masses in order to avoid the adoption of Western European cultural forms; begun under Joseph Stalin; fundamental method of Soviet fiction and literary criticism. (36)

Socialist Youth Corps: Formed in 1920 in China; dedicated to recruiting urban working classes to the nationalist revolution in China. (41)

sociedad de castas: American social system based on racial origins; Europeans or whites at top, black slaves or Indians at bottom, mixed races in middle. (25)

Socrates: Athenian philosopher of later 5th century B.C.; tutor of Plato; urged rational reflection of moral decisions; condemned to death for corrupting minds of Athenian young. (6)

solar cycle: Calendrical system based on solar year; typical of all civilizations; variations of solar calendars in Western civilization are Julian and Gregorian calendars; Mayas also constructed solar calendar. (9)

Solidarity: Polish labor movement formed in 1970s under Lech Walesa; challenged USSR-dominated government of Poland. (36)

Solon: Athenian reformer of the 6th century; established laws that eased burden of debt on farmers, forbade enslavement for debt. (6)

Solzhenitsyn, Aleksandr: Russian author critical of the Soviet regime; published trilogy on the Siberian prison camps—*Gulag Archipelago*. (36)

Songhay: Successor state to Mali; dominated middle reaches of Niger valley; formed as independent kingdom under a Berber dynasty; capital at Gao; reached imperial status under Sunni Ali (1464–1492). (14)

Sophocles: Greek writer of tragedies; author of *Oedipus Rex*. (6)

southern Song: Rump state of Song dynasty from 1127 to 1279; carved out of much larger domains ruled by the Tang and northern Song. (18)

soviet: Council of workers formed to seize city government in Petrograd in 1917; basis for early political organization of Russian Revolution. (36)

Spanish Civil War: War between authoritarian and military leaders in Spain against republicans and leftists between 1936 and 1939; Germany and Italy supported the royalists; the Soviet Union supported the republicans; led to victory of the royalist forces. (34)

Spanish-American War: War fought between Spain and the United States beginning in 1898; centered on Cuba and Puerto Rico; permitted American intervention in Caribbean, annexation of Puerto Rico and the Philippines. (31)

split inheritance: Inca practice of descent; all titles and political power went to successor, but wealth and land remained in hands of male descendants for support of cult of dead Inca's mummy. (17)

Sputnik: First manned spacecraft in 1957; sent up during Khrushchev government; initiated space race with the United States. (36)

St. Basil: Founder of Christian monasticism in eastern half of Roman Empire in 4th century A.D. (11)

St. Petersburg: New capital of Russia established during the reign of Peter the Great. (24)

Stalin, Joseph: Successor to Lenin as head of the USSR; strongly nationalist view of communism; represented anti-Western strain of Russian tradition; crushed opposition to his rule; established series of five-year plans to replace New Economic Policy; fostered agricultural collectivization; led USSR through World War II; initiated cold war with Western Europe and the United States; died in 1953. (36)

stateless societies: African societies organized around kinship or other forms of obligation and lacking the concentration of political power and authority associated with states. (14)

stelae: Large memorial pillars erected to commemorate triumphs and events in the lives of Maya rulers. (9)

Stoics: Hellenistic group of philosophers; emphasized inner moral independence cultivated by strict discipline of the body and personal bravery. (6)

Stolypin reforms: Reforms introduced by the Russian minister for which they are named; basically reforms intended to placate the peasantry in the aftermath of the Revolution of 1905; included reduction in redemption payments, attempt to create market-oriented peasantry. (33)

stupas: Stone shrines built to house pieces of bone or hair and personal possessions said to be relics of the Buddha; preserved Buddhist architectural forms. (7)

submarine warfare: Use of the relatively new sea weapon was a major aspect of the German naval effort against the western allies in the First World War; unrestricted submarine warfare was major factor in bringing the United States into active participation. (34)

Sudanic states: Kingdoms that developed during the height of Ghana's power in the region; based at Takrur on the Senegal River to the west and Gao on the Niger River to the east; included Mali and Songhay. (14)

Suez Canal: Built across Isthmus of Suez connecting Mediterranean with the Red Sea in 1869; financed by European investors; with increasing indebtedness of khedives, permitted intervention of British into Egyptian politics to protect their investment. (32)

Sufis: Mystics within Islam; responsible for expansion of Islam to southeastern Asia. (13)

Sui: Dynasty that succeeded the Han in China; emerged from strong rulers in northern China; united all of northern China and reconquered southern China. (11)

Sulla: Conservative military commander during last century B.C.; attempted to reinforce powers of the Senate and to undo influence of Marius. (8)

Sumerians: People who migrated into Mesopotamia c. 4000 B.C.; created first civilization within region; organized area into city-states. (2)

Sun Yat-sen: Head of Revolutionary Alliance, organization that led 1911 revolt against Qing dynasty in China; briefly elected president in 1911, but yielded in favor of Yuan Shikai in 1912; created Nationalist party of China (Guomindang) in 1919; died in 1925. (41)

Sundiata: The "Lion Prince"; a member of the Keita clan; created a unified state that became the Mali Empire; died about 1260. (14)

Sunnis: Political and theological division within Islam; followers of the Umayyads. (12)

Sunzi: Author of *The Art of War*; argued that war was extension of statecraft; taught war according to scientific principles. (5)

Supreme Soviet: Parliament of Union of Soviet Socialist Republics; elected by universal suffrage; actually controlled by Communist party; served to ratify party decisions. (36)

Suriname: Formerly a Dutch plantation colony on the coast of South America; location of runaway slave kingdom in 18th century; able to retain independence despite attempts to crush guerrilla resistance. (27)

Swazi: New African state formed on model of Zulu chiefdom; survived mfecane. (27)

syndicalism: Government based on the organization of labor; imported in Latin America from European political movements; militant force in Latin-American politics. (38)

Tang: Dynasty that succeeded the Sui in A.D. 618; more stable than previous dynasty. (11)

Taika reforms: Attempt to remake Japanese monarch into an absolutist Chinese-style emperor; included attempts to create professional bureaucracy and peasant conscript army. (19)

Taiping rebellion: Broke out in south China in the 1850s and early 1860s; led by Hong Xiuquan, a semi-Christianized prophet; sought to overthrow Qing dynasty and Confucian basis of scholar-gentry. (32)

Taiwan: Island off Chinese mainland; became refuge for Nationalist Chinese regime under Chiang Kai-shek as Republic of China in 1948; successfully retained independence with aid of United States; rapidly industrialized after 1950s. (37)

Taj Mahal: Most famous architectural achievement of Mughal India; originally built as a mausoleum for the wife of Shah Jahan, Mumtaz Mahal. (26)

Takuaji, Ashikaga: Member of Minamoto family; overthrew the Kamakura regime and established Ashikaga Shogunate from 1336 to 1573; drove emperor from Kyoto to Yoshino. (19)

Tale of Genji: Written by Lady Murasaki; first novel in any language; relates life history of prominent and amorous son of the Japanese emperor; evidence for mannered style of Japanese society. (19)

tambos: Way stations used by Incas as inns and storehouses; supply centers for Inca armies on move; relay points for system of runners used to carry messages. (17)

Tangut: Rulers of Xi-Xia kingdom of northwest China, one of regional kingdoms during period of southern Song; conquered by Mongols in 1226. (20)

Tanzimat reforms: Series of reforms in Ottoman Empire between 1839 and 1876; established Western-style university, state postal system, railways, extensive legal reforms; resulted in creation of new constitution in 1876. (32)

Tartars: Mongols; captured Russian cities and largely destroyed Kievan state in 1236; left Russian Orthodoxy and aristocracy intact. (15)

Tatu: Mongol capital of Yuan dynasty; present-day Beijing. (20)

Tayson Rebellion: Peasant revolution in southern Vietnam during the late 1770s; succeeded in toppling the Nguyen dynasty; subsequently unseated the Trinh dynasty of northern Vietnam. (41)

technocrat: New type of bureaucrat; intensely trained in engineering or economics and devoted to the power of national planning; came to fore in offices of governments following World War II. (35)

Teheran Conference: Meeting between leaders of the United States, Britain, and the Soviet Union in 1943; agreed to the opening of a new front in France. (34)

Temple of the Sun: Inca religious center located at Cuzco; center of state religion; held mummies of past Incas. (17)

Tenochtitlan: Founded c. 1325 on marshy island in Lake Texcoco; became center of Aztec power; joined with Tlacopan and Texcoco in 1434 to form a triple alliance that controlled most of central plateau of Mesoamerica. (17)

Teotihuacan: Site of Classic culture in central Mexico; urban center with important religious functions; supported by intensive agriculture in surrounding regions; population of as much as 200,000. (9)

terakoya: Commoner schools founded during the Tokugawa shogunate in Japan to teach reading, writing, and the rudiments of Confucianism; resulted in high literacy rate approaching 40 percent of Japanese males. (33)

Thatcher, Margaret: Conservative British prime minister from 1979 to 1991; held office longer than any other person; worked to cut welfare and housing expenses, promote free enterprise. (35)

third Rome: Russian claim to be successor state to Roman and Byzantine empires; based in part on continuity of Orthodox church in Russia following fall of Constantinople in 1453. (24)

Third World: Those nations outside the capitalist industrial nations of the First World and the industrialized Communist nations of the Second World; generally less economically powerful, but with varied economies. (38)

Thirty Years' War: War within the Holy Roman Empire between German Protestants and their allies (Sweden, Denmark, France) and the emperor and his ally, Spain; ended in 1648 after great destruction with Treaty of Westphalia. (22)

three estates: Typical social organization of Middle Ages after 10th century; included military nobility, clergy, and ordinary people. (16)

three-field system: System of agricultural cultivation by 9th century in western Europe; included one-third of fields in winter grains, one-third in spring grains, one-third fallow. (16)

Tian: Heavan; an abstract conception in early Chinese religion; possibly the combined spirits of all male ancestors; first appeared during Zhou dynasty. (3)

Tiberius: Along with Gaius Gracchus, tribune who attempted to introduce land and citizenship reform within the Roman republic; killed on the command of the Senate. (8)

Tihuanaco: Along with Huari, large center for regional chiefdoms between A.D. 300 and 900; located in southern Peru; featured large ceremonial center supported by extensive irrigated agriculture; established widely diffused religious and artistic symbols spread all over Andean zone. (9)

Tilak, B. G.: Believed that nationalism in India should be based on appeals to Hindu religiosity; worked to promote the restoration and revival of ancient Hindu traditions; offended Muslims and other religious groups; first Populist leader in India. (39)

Timbuktu: Port city of Mali; located just off the flood plain on the great bend in the Niger River; population of 50,000; contained a library and university. (14)

Time of Troubles: Followed death of Ivan IV without heir early in 17th century; boyars attempted to use vacuum of power to reestablish their authority; ended with selection of Michael Romanov as tsar in 1613. (24)

Timur-i Lang: Leader of Turkic nomads; beginning in 1360s from base at Samarkand, launched series of attacks in Persia, the Fertile Crescent, India, and southern Russia; empire disintegrated after his death in 1405. (20)

Tlacaelel: Advisor to Aztec rulers from 1427 to c. 1480; had histories of Mexico rewritten; expanded cult of human sacrifice as effective means of political terror. (17)

Tlaloc: Major god of Aztecs; associated with fertility and the agricultural cycle; god of rain. (17)

Tlatelolco: Originally a separate island city in Lake Texcoco; later incorporated into Tenochtitlan; market remained most important in combined city. (17)

Tojo Hideki: Japanese general; put down attempted military coup in 1936; increasingly interfered with civilian cabinets to block appointment of liberal bureaucrats; helped create increasingly militaristic series of prime ministers after 1936. (37)

Toltec culture: Succeeded Teotihuacan culture in central Mexico; Nahuatl-speaking people; established political control over large territory after A.D. 1000; declined after A.D. 1200. (9)

Toltecs: Nomadic peoples from beyond the northern frontier of the sedentary agricultural area in Mesoamerica; established capital of Tula following migration into central Mesoamerican plateau; strongly militaristic ethic including cult of human sacrifice. (17)

Topiltzin: Religious leader and reformer of the Toltecs; dedicated to god Quetzalcoatl; after losing struggle for power, went into exile in the Yucatan peninsula. (17)

total war: Warfare of the 20th century; vast resources and emotional commitments of the belligerent nations were marshaled to support military effort; resulted from impact of industrialization on the military effort reflecting technological innovation and organizational capacity. (34)

totalitarian state: A new kind of government in the 20th century that exercised massive, direct control over virtually all the activities of its subjects; existed in Germany, Italy, and the Soviet Union. (35)

totem: Most commonly an animal utilized by nomadic tribesmen as a representation of a mythic ancestor of the group; venerated as a progenitor and protector. (4)

Tragic Week: Occurred in Argentina in 1919; government response to general strike of labor forces led to brutal repression under guise of nationalism. (38)

Trajan: Emperor from A.D. 101 to 106; instituted more aggressive imperial foreign policy resulting in expansion of empire to its greatest limits. (8)

trans-Siberian railroad: Constructed in 1870s to connect European Russia with the Pacific; completed by the end of the 1880s; brought Russia into a more active Asian role. (33)

transformismo: Political system in Italy that promoted alliance of conservatives and liberals; parliamentary deputies of all parties supported the status quo. (29)

transhumance: A form of pastoralism common to the Mediterranean basin and the Sahara; involves moving from one region to another according to the season. (10)

transmigration: The belief in the successive reincarnation of the soul in different bodies. (7)

Treaty of Gijanti: Signed in 1757; reduced remaining Javanese princes to vassals of Dutch East India Company; allowed Dutch to monopolize production of coffee on Java. (28)

Treaty of Guadalupe-Hidalgo: Agreement that ended the Mexican-American War; provided for loss of Texas and California to the United States; left legacy of distrust of the United States in Latin America. (31)

Treaty of Paris: Arranged in 1763 following Seven Years' War; granted New France to England in exchange for return of French sugar islands in Caribbean. (23)

Treaty of Tordesillas: Signed in 1494 between Castile and Portugal; clarified spheres of influence and rights of possession in New World; reserved Brazil and all newly discovered lands east of Brazil to Portugal; granted all lands west of Brazil to Spain. (25)

Treaty of Versailles: Ended the First World War; provided for the League of Nations; also punished Germany with loss of territories and the payment of reparations as a result of their "war guilt"; Russia also lost territories with the reestablishment of eastern European nations such as Poland. (34)

Treaty of Westphalia: Ended Thirty Years' War in 1648; granted right to individual rulers within the Holy Roman Empire to choose their own religion—either Protestant or Catholic. (22)

triangular trade: Commerce linking Africa, the New World colonies, and Europe; slaves carried to America for sugar and tobacco transported to Europe. (27)

tribunes: Plebeian representatives in the Roman republic; elected in the Councilium Plebis Tributum on an annual basis. (8)

Trinity: Christian doctrine that held that God had three persons—Father, Son, Holy Ghost—all equally divine. (11)

Tripartite Pact: Alliance of Japan, Germany, and Italy signed in September 1940; created alliance system for World War II. (34)

Triple Alliance: Alliance between Germany, Austria-Hungary, and Italy at the end of the 19th century; part of European alliance system and balance of power prior to the First World War. (29)

Triple Entente: Alliance between Britain, Russia, and France at the outset of the 20th century; part of European alliance system and balance of power prior to the First World War. (29)

true colonies: Western European possessions in Africa, Asia, and the South Pacific in which small numbers of Europeans ruled large numbers of non-Western peoples; mostly brought under European control during the last decades of the 19th century and the first years of the 20th century. (30)

Truman, Harry: American president from 1945 to 1952; less eager for smooth relations with the Soviet Union than Franklin Roosevelt; authorized use of atomic bomb during World War II; architect of American diplomacy that initiated the cold war. (35)

Trung sisters: Leaders of one of the frequent peasant rebellions in Vietnam against Chinese rule; revolt broke out in A.D. 39; demonstrates importance of Vietnamese women in indigenous society. (19)

tsetse fly: Flourished in wet lowlands; carried sleeping sickness that severely limited pastoralism in western and central Africa. (10)

tumens: Basic fighting units of the Mongol forces; consisted of 10,000 cavalrymen; each unit was further divided into units of 1000, 100, and 10. (20)

Tutu, Osei: Member of Oyoko clan of Akan peoples in Gold Coast region of Africa; responsible for creating unified Asante Empire; utilized Western firearms. (27)

Twantinsuyu: Word for Inca Empire; region from present-day Colombia to Chile and eastward to northern Argentina. (17)

ulama: Orthodox religious scholars within Islam; pressed for a more conservative and restrictive theology; increasingly opposed to non-Islamic ideas and scientific thinking. (13)

Ulyanov, Vladimir Ilyich: Better known as Lenin; most active Russian Marxist leader; insisted on importance of disciplined revolutionary cells; leader of Bolsheviks. (33)

Umayyad: Clan of Quraysh that dominated politics and commercial economy of Mecca; clan later able to establish dynasty as rulers of Islam. (12)

umma: Community of the faithful within Islam; transcended old tribal boundaries to create degree of political unity. (12)

Union of Soviet Socialist Republics: Federal system of socialist republics established in 1923 in various ethnic regions of Russia; firmly controlled by Communist party; diminished nationalities protest under Bolsheviks. (36)

United Fruit Company: Most important foreign economic concern in Guatemala during the 20th century; attempted land reform aimed at United Fruit caused U.S. intervention in Guatemalan politics leading to ouster of reform government in 1954. (38)

United Nations: International organization formed in the aftermath of World War II; included all of the victorious Allies; its primary mission was to provide a forum for negotiating disputes. (34)

untouchables: Lowest caste in Indian society; performed tasks that were considered polluting—street sweeping, removal of human waste, and tanning. (7)

Upanishads: Later books of the Vedas; contained sophisticated and sublime philosophical ideas; utilized by brahmans to restore religious authority. (7)

Urban II: Called First Crusade in 1095; appealed to Christians to mount military assault to free the Holy Land from the Muslims. (16)

Uthman: Third caliph and member of Umayyad clan; murdered by mutinous warriors returning from Egypt; death set off civil war in Islam between followers of Ali and the Umayyad clan. (12)

Valdivia, Pedro de: Spanish conquistador; conquered Araucanian Indians of Chile and established city of Santiago in 1541. (25)

Vargas, Getúlio: Elected president of Brazil in 1929; launched centralized political program by imposing federal administrators over state governments; held off coups by Communists in 1935 and Fascists in 1937; imposed a new constitution based on Mussolini's Italy; leaned to Communists after 1949; committed suicide in 1954. (38)

varnas: Clusters of caste groups in Aryan society; four social castes—brahmans (priests), warriors, merchants, and peasants; beneath four Aryan castes was group of socially untouchable Dasas. (3)

vassal retainers: Members of former ruling families granted control over the peasant and artisan populations of areas throughout Shang kingdom; indirectly exploited wealth of their territories. (3)

vassals: Members of the military elite in the Middle Ages who received land or a benefice from a lord in return for military service and loyalty. (16)

Vedas: Aryan hymns originally transmitted orally but written down in sacred books from the 6th century B.C. (3)

vendettas: Blood-feuds between families or clans of nomadic pastoralists; created a major barrier to interclan and tribal cooperation. (4)

Vergil: One of greatest of Roman epic poets during "Golden Age" of Latin literature; patronized by Augustus; author of *Aeneid*. (8)

viceroyalties: Two major divisions of Spanish colonies in New World; one based in Lima, the other in Mexico City; direct representatives of the king. (25)

Vichy: French collaborationist government established in 1940 in southern France following defeat of French armies by the Germans. (34)

Viet Cong: Name given by Diem regime to Communist guerrilla movement in southern Vietnam; reorganized with northern

Vietnamese assistance as the National Liberation Front in 1958. (41)

Viet Minh: Communist-dominated Vietnamese nationalist movement; operated out of base in southern China during World War II; employed guerrilla tactics similar to the Maoists in China. (41)

Vietnamese Nationalist party: Also known as the Vietnamese Quoc Dan Dong or VNQDD; active in 1920s as revolutionary force committed to violent overthrow of French colonialism. (41)

Vikings: Seagoing Scandinavian raiders from Sweden, Denmark, and Norway that disrupted coastal areas of western Europe from the 8th to the 11th centuries. (16)

Villa, Pancho: Mexican revolutionary and military commander in northern Mexico during the Mexican Revolution; succeeded along with Emiliano Zapata in removing Díaz from power; also participated in campaigns that removed Madero and Huerta. (38)

Vivaldis: Two Genoese brothers who attempted to find a Western route to the "Indies"; disappeared in 1291; precursors of thrust into southern Atlantic. (21)

vizier: Ottoman equivalent of the Abbasid wazir; head of the Ottoman bureaucracy; after 15th century often more powerful than sultan. (26)

Vladimir I: Ruler of Russian kingdom of Kiev from 980 to 1015; converted kingdom to Christianity. (15)

Vodun: African religious ideas and practices among descendants of African slaves in Haiti. (27)

Völkerwanderungen: Movement of Germanic peoples southward into the Roman Empire; resulted from population growth, pressure of Asian groups on eastern flanks of Germanic regions. (10)

Wafd party: Egyptian nationalist party that emerged after an Egyptian delegation was refused a hearing at the Versailles Treaty negotiations following World War I; led by Sa'd Zaghlūl; negotiations eventually led to limited Egyptian independence beginning in 1922. (39)

Wang Anshi: Confucian scholar and chief minister of a Song emperor in 1070s; introduced sweeping reforms based on Legalists; advocated greater state intervention in society. (18)

Wang Mang: Member of one of the powerful families related to the Han emperors through marriage; temporarily overthrew the Han between A.D. 9 and 23. (5)

War of the Spanish Succession: Resulted from Bourbon family's succession to Spanish throne in 1701; ended by Treaty of Utrecht in 1713; resulted in recognition of Bourbons, loss of some lands, grants of commercial rights to English and French. (25)

Warring States period: Period of warfare between regional lords following the decline of the Zhou in the 8th century B.C.; ended with rise of Qin. (5)

Water Margin, The; Monkey; and The Golden Lotus: Novels written during the Ming period in China; recognized as classics in their own time; established standards for Chinese prose literature. (28)

Watt, James: Devised a steam engine in 1770s during the Industrial Revolution that could be used for production; utilized in textile industries, mining, and railroads. (29)

wazir: Chief administrative official under the Abbasid caliphate; initially recruited from Persian provinces of empire. (12)

welfare state: New activism of the state in economic policy and welfare issues after World War II; introduced programs to reduce the impact of economic inequality; typically included medical and civil rights program. (35)

Wendi: Member of prominent northern Chinese family during period of Six Dynasties; proclaimed himself emperor; supported by nomadic peoples of northern China; established Sui dynasty. (18)

western front: Front established in World War I; generally along line from Belgium to Switzerland; featured trench warfare and horrendous casualties for all sides in the conflict. (34)

Whampoa Military Academy: Founded in 1924; military wing of the Guomindang; first head of the academy was Chiang Kai-shek. (41)

White Dominions: Colonies in which European settlers made up the overwhelming majority of the population; small numbers of native inhabitants typically reduced by disease and wars of conquest; typical of British colonies in North America and Australia. (30)

White Lotus Society: Secret religious society dedicated to overthrow of Yuan dynasty in China; typical of peasant resistance to Mongol rule. (20)

white racial supremacy: Belief in the inherent mental, moral, and cultural superiority of whites; peaked in acceptance in decades before First World War;

supported by social science doctrines of social Darwinists such as Herbert Spencer. (30)

Wilberforce, William: British statesman and reformer; leader of abolitionist movement in English parliament; led abolition of English slave trade in 1807. (27)

William the Conqueror: Invaded England from Normandy in 1066; extended tight feudal system to England; established administrative system based on sheriffs; established centralized monarchy. (16)

witchcraft hysteria: Reflected resentment against the poor, uncertainties about religious truth; resulted in death of over 100,000 people between 1590 and 1650; particularly common in Protestant areas. (22)

Witte, Count: Russian minister of finance from 1892 to 1903; economic modernizer responsible for high tariffs, improved banking system; encouraged Western investors to build factories in Russia. (33)

Wollstonecraft, Mary: Enlightenment feminist thinker in England; argued that new political rights should extend to women. (22)

World Court: Developed during period of internationalization; permanent court of arbitration established at the Hague in 1899; intended to remove causes of war; failed to resolve problems of international conflict in 20th century. (34)

world economy: Established by Europeans by the late 16th century; based on control of seas including the Atlantic and Pacific; created an international exchange of foods, diseases, and manufactured products. (23)

World War I: Fought between 1914 and 1919; involved almost all European nations and their respective colonies; arose over conflict in the Balkans; resulted in victory of allied countries of Britain, France, Italy, and the United States; ended with Treaty of Versailles. (34)

World War II: Fought from 1939 to 1945 on fronts including western Europe, northern Africa, the Middle East, Eurasia, southwestern Asia, China, and the Pacific; ended with defeat of Germany and Japan in 1945. (34)

Wu: First of the Zhou to be recognized as king, 1122 B.C. (3)

Wuzong: Chinese emperor of Tang dynasty who openly persecuted Buddhism by destroying monasteries in 840s; reduced influence of Chinese Buddhism in favor of Confucian ideology. (18)

Xavier, Francis: Spanish Franciscan missionary; worked in India in 1540s among the outcaste and lower caste groups; made little headway among elites. (28)

Xia: China's first, possibly mythical, kingdom; no archeological sites have been connected to it; ruled by Yu. (3)

Xian: Along with Loyang, capital of the Zhou dynasty. (3)

Xunzi: Follower of Confucius; stressed need for authoritarian government. (5)

Yahweh: The single god of the Hebrews; constructed a covenant with Jews as his chosen people. (2)

Yalta Conference: Meeting between leaders of the United States, Britain, and the Soviet Union in 1945; agreed to Soviet entry into the Pacific war in return for possessions in Manchuria, organization of the United Nations; disputed the division of political organization among the eastern European states to be reestablished after the war. (34)

Yamato: Japanese clan that gained increasing dominance in the 4th and 5th centuries A.D.; created imperial cult around Amaterasu and Shinto; brought most of the lowland plains of the southern islands under control. (10)

yanas: A class of people within Inca society removed from their ayllus to serve permanently as servants, artisans, or workers for the Inca or the Inca nobility. (17)

Yang Guifei: Young woman belonging to harem of Tang prince; raised to status of royal concubine during reign of Xuanzong; introduction of relatives into royal administration led to revolt. (18)

Yangdi: Second member of Sui dynasty; murdered his father to gain throne; restored Confucian examination system; responsible for construction of Chinese canal system; assassinated in 618. (18)

Yangshao culture: One of formative Chinese cultures located at Ordos bend c. 2500 to 2000 B.C.; primarily an intensive hunting-and-gathering society supplemented by shifting cultivation. (3)

Yaroslav: Last of great Kievan monarchs; issued legal codification based on formal codes developed in Byzantium. (15)

Yathrib: Also known as Medina; town located northeast of Mecca; grew date palms whose fruit was sold to bedouins; became refuge for Muhammad following flight from Mecca (hijra). (12)

Yayoi epoch: Last centuries B.C.; featured introduction of wet-rice cultivation, iron

working; produced wheel-turned pottery and sophisticated bronzeware. (10)

yellow peril: Western term for perceived threat of Japanese imperialism; met by increased Western imperialism in region. (33)

Yellow River basin: Also known as Huanghe River basin; site of the development of sedentary agriculture in China. (1)

Yellow Turbans: Chinese Daoists who launched a revolt in A.D. 184 in China promising a golden age to be brought about by divine magic. (11)

Yi: Korean dynasty that succeeded Koryo dynasty following period of Mongol invasions; established in 1392; ruled Korea to 1910; restored aristocratic dominance and Chinese influence. (19)

Yoruba: City-states developed in northern Nigeria c. A.D. 1200; Ile-Ife featured artistic style possibly related to earlier Nok culture; agricultural societies supported by peasantry and dominated by ruling family and aristocracy. (14)

Yu: A possibly mythical Chinese ruler revered for the construction of an effective system of flood control along the Huanghe River valley; founder of the Xia kingdom. (3)

Yuan Shikai: Warlord in northern China after fall of Qing dynasty; hoped to seize imperial throne; president of China after 1912; resigned in face of Japanese invasion in 1916. (41)

Yueh-chih: Nomadic invaders of Indian subcontinent; invasions gave rise to Kushana dynasty. (7)

Yupanqui, Topac: Ruled as Inca from 1471 to 1493; conquered the northern coastal kingdom of Chimor by seizing its irrigation system. (17)

zaibatsu: Huge industrial combines created in Japan in the 1890s as part of the process of industrialization. (33)

zakat: Tax for charity; obligatory for all Muslims. (12)

Zanj: Arabic term for the East African coast. (14)

Zapata, Emiliano: Mexican revolutionary and military commander of peasant guerrilla movement centered in Morelos; succeeded along with Pancho Villa in removing Díaz from power; also participated in campaigns that removed Madero and Huerta; demanded sweeping land reform. (38)

zemstvoes: Local political councils created as part of reforms of Tsar Alexander II;

gave some Russians, particularly middle-class professionals, some experience in government; councils had no impact on national policy. (33)

Zhao Kuangyin: Founder of Song dynasty; originally a general following fall of Tang; took title of Taizu; failed to overcome northern Liao dynasty that remained independent. (18)

Zhenghe expeditions: Series of seven overseas trade expeditions under third Ming emperor, Yunglo; led by court eunuch Zhenghe between 1405 and 1423; last Chinese attempt to create worldwide trade empire. (28)

Zhou: Originally a vassal family of Shang China; possibly Turkic in origin; overthrew Shang and established second historical Chinese dynasty. (3)

Zhu Xi: Most prominent of neo-Confucian scholars during the Song dynasty in China; stressed importance of applying philosophical principles to everyday life and action. (18)

ziggurats: Massive towers usually associated with Mesopotamian temple complexes. (2)

Zionism: Movement originating in eastern Europe during the 1860s and 1870s that argued that the Jews must return to a Middle Eastern Holy Land; eventually identified with the settlement of Palestine. (39)

Zoroastrianism: Animist religion that saw material existence as battle between forces of good and evil; stressed the importance of moral choice; righteous lived on after death in "House of Song"; chief religion of Persian Empire. (6)

Credits

CHAPTER 17

Map of Inca Empire from *Atlas of Ancient America* by Coe, Snow & Benson, p. 196. Copyright © 1986. Reprinted by permission of Andromeda Oxford Ltd., Abington, UK.

CHAPTER 18

Cited in *Chinese Civilization* translated by Janet Seligman. Copyright © 1969 by Faber & Faber.

CHAPTER 19

From *The Tale of Genji* translated by Edward G. Seidensticker. Copyright © 1976 by Edward G. Seidensticker. Reprinted by permission of Alfred A. Knopf, Inc.

From *The Tale of Kieu* translated by Huynh Sanh Thong. Copyright © 1973 by Huynh Sanh Thong. Reprinted by permission of Vintage Books, a Division of Random House, Inc.

Poem by Ki no Tomonori from *Japanese Literature from the Earliest Era to the Nineteenth Century* edited by Donald Keene. Copyright © 1955 by Grove Press, Inc. Used by permission of Grove Press, Inc.

Poem by Ki no Tsurayuki from *Japanese Culture* by H. Paul Varley. Copyright © 1977 by H. Paul Varley. Reprinted by permission of Henry Holt and Company, Inc.

Poem by Ho Xuan cited in *Vietnam and the Chinese Model* by A. Woodside. Cambridge, MA.: Harvard University Press, 1971, p. 48.

Poem cited in *From the Vietnamese: Ten Centuries of Poetry* translated by Burton Raffel. Copyright © 1968 by October House.

From *Cultural Atlas of Japan* by Martin Collcutt, et al., 1988. Copyright © 1988. Reprinted by permission of Andromeda, Oxford Ltd., Abington UK.

Adaptation of Map V "Nam Viet" cited in *The Smaller Oragon: A Political History of Vietnam* by J. Buttinger. Copyright © 1958 by Joseph Buttinger.

CHAPTER 21

Adaptation of Map "The Old World." Copyright © 1970 George Philip & Son Ltd. Reprinted by permission.

CHAPTER 24

From *Documents of Catherine the Great* edited by W. F. Reddaway, pp. 216, 258 & 293. Copyright © 1931 by Cambridge University Press. Reprinted by permission.

Cited in *Imperial Russia: A Source Book, 1700–1917* edited by Basil Dymtryshyn. Copyright © 1967 by Harcourt, Brace, Jovanovich.

CHAPTER 25

From *Florentine Codex*, Book VI. Reprinted by permission of The University of Utah Press.

CHAPTER 27

From *Africa Remembered* by Philip D. Curtin, pp. 92–94. Copyright © 1967 by the Regents of The University of Wisconsin. Reprinted by permission.

Table from *Transformations in Slavery* by Paul E. Lovejoy, pp. 45 & 47. Copyright © 1983 Cambridge University Press. Reprinted by permission.

CHAPTER 28

From *Cultural Atlas of Japan* by Martin Collcutt, et al., 1988. Copyright ©1988. Reprinted by permission of Andromeda Oxford Ltd., Abington, UK.

PART 5

Adaptation of map "The Development of the World Economy" cited in *The Times Atlas of World History* edited by G. Barraclough. Copyright © 1985 by Times Books Ltd.

CHAPTER 30

From *Britain and Germany in Africa* edited by P. Gifford et al, p. 670. Copyright ©1967 Yale University Press. Reprinted by permission.

Cited in *Patterns of Vietnamese Response to Foreign Intervention: 1858–1900* by Truong Buu Lam. Copyright ©1967 by Yale Southeast Asia Studies.

Map "Dutch Penetration in Java, 1619–1830" cited in *A Short History of Indonesia* by Ailsa Zainu'ddin. Copyright © 1968 by Greenwood Publishing.

CHAPTER 33

From *Cultural Atlas of Japan* by Martin Collcutt, et al., 1988. Copyright © 1988. Reprinted by permission of Andromeda Oxford Ltd., Abington, UK.

PART 6

Adaptation of map "Industrialization Outside Europe and North America" cited in *The Times Atlas of World History* edited by G. Barraclough. Copyright © 1985 by Times Books Ltd.

CHAPTER 36

From *Readings in Russian Civilization*, V.III edited by Thomas Riha. Copyright © 1969 The University of Chicago Press. Reprinted by permission.

Adaptation of Map "The Civil War" from *The World Atlas of Revolutions* by Andrew Wheatcroft. Text copyright © 1983 by Andrew Wheatcroft, Cartography © 1983 by Hamish Hamilton Ltd. Reprinted by permission of Simon & Schuster.

CHAPTER 39

From Poem "Snow Upon Paris" from *Selected Poems* by Léopold Sédar Senghor, Translated and Introduced by John Reed and Clive Wake. Copyright © 1974 Oxford University Press. Reprinted by permission of Oxford University Press.

Excerpt of poem cited in *Return to My Native Land* by Aime Cesaire. Copyright © 1956 by Penguin Books Ltd.

CHAPTER 40

Abridgement of "I Run Around With Them" cited in *The Complete Poetry and Prose of Chairil Anwar* edited & translated by Burton Raffel. Copyright © 1970 by State University of New York Press.

CHAPTER 41

Letter "Big Brother" from *Family* by Pa Chin, Copyright © 1972 by Doubleday.

Adaptation of map "The Northern Expedition 1926–27" cited in *The Times Atlas of World History*, revised edition edited by G. Barraclough. Copyright © 1985 by Times Books Ltd.

Adaptation of Map from *Histoire du Vietnam* par André Masson, p. 86. Copyright © 1949 Presses Universitaires de France. Reprinted by permission.

PHOTO CREDITS

Unless otherwise acknowledged, all photographs are the property of ScottForesman. Page abbreviations are as follows: (T)top, (C)center, (B)bottom, (L)left, (R)right.

PART 1

xxxii Scala/Art Resource, NY; 4 Tokyo National Museum

CHAPTER 1

6 Arch.Phot.Paris/S.P.A.D.E.M.; 10 Reprinted from LIFE: INTRODUCTION TO BIOLOGY 3E by Beck, Liem &

Simpson, (c)1991, Reprinted by permission HarperCollinsPublishers, Inc.; **11** Musée de L'Homme, Paris; **14** Lauros-Giraudon/ Art Resource, NY; **15** from PAST WORLDS: ARCHAEOLOGY, TIME Books, London; **18** from W. Buttler and W. Haberey, DIE BANDKERMISCHE ANSIEDLUNG BEI FORSCHUN, Vol. II; **20** Lee Boltin; **21T** ATLAS DE/ 'ARCHEOLOGIE/ENCYCLO-PAEDIA UNIVERSALIS, PARIS; **21BL** from THE NEOLITHIC OF THE NEAR EAST by James Mellaart; **21BR** Ara Guler; **22** from THE NEOLITHIC OF THE NEAR EAST by James Mellaart

CHAPTER 2

24 The Metropolitan Museum of Art; **30L** The University Museum, University of Pennsylvania; **30R** The University Museum, University of Pennsylvania; **33T** Directorate General of Antiquities, Baghdad, Iraq; **33B** Courtesy Hirmer Fotoarchiv, Munich; **34** Louvre, Paris/Art Resource, NY; **38** Robert Frerck/Odyssey Productions, Chicago; **39** Lespius, Denkmaler; **40** Oriental Institute, The University of Chicago; **44** Princeton University Press/Art Resource, NY

CHAPTER 3

48 National Museum of New Delhi; **51** Karachi Museum/Robert Harding Picture Library Ltd., London; **52** Festival of Britain Trustees; **56** The Granger Collection, New York; **59** East Asian Library, Columbia University; **60** Wan-go Weng; **61** Musée Cernuschi, Paris; **68** Erich Lessing/Magna Photos

PART 2

72 The Granger Collection, New York

CHAPTER 4

74 Hermitage, Leningrad/Novosti Press Agency; **80B** G. Popov/SOVFOTO; **80T** F.A.O. Photo, Rome; **83** Standard Oil Company, New Jersey; **84** Bibliothèque Nationale; **89** Four by Five/SUPER-STOCK

CHAPTER 5

92 Wan-go H. C. Weng; **95** Field Museum of Natural History, Chicago; **100** Henri Cartier-Bresson/Magnum Photos; **101** SUPERSTOCK; **105** Wan-go H. C. Weng; **106** Nelson Galler of Art/Atkins Museum, Kansas City, Mo.; **107** Wan-go H. C. Weng; **109** Wan-go H. C. Weng

CHAPTER 6

114 The Metropolitan Museum of Art; **117** Oriental Institute, The University of Chicago; **118** Robert Sheridan Picture Library/Ancient Art & Architecture Collection; **122** Loyola University of Chicago/Raymond V. Schoder, S. J.; **124** Alinari/Art Resource, NY; **128TL** Alinari/Art Resource, NY; **128TR** Robert Frerck/Odyssey Productions, Chicago; **128BL** The Metropolitan Museum of Art; **128BR** Art Resource, NY; **129** Alinari/Art Resource, NY

CHAPTER 7

138 Shostal/SUPERSTOCK; **143** Percy Brown's INDIAN ARCHITECTURE: BUDDHIST & HINDU PERIOD PUBL-DB Tapaporevala Sons & Co. Ltd. Bombay; **150** Nickerson Fund/Photo: Jim Ballard/The Art Institute of Chicago. All Rights Reserved; **153** Government of India Tourist Office; **155** JH Wade Fund/The Cleveland Museum of Art; **157** Eliot Elisofon/Life Magazine Time Warner Inc.; **159** Jahangir Gazdar/Woodfin Camp & Associates

CHAPTER 8

165 Alinari/Art Resource, NY; **168** Alinari/Art Resource, NY; **171** Robert Sheridan Picture Library/Ancient Art & Architecture Collection; **177** Alinari/Art Resource, NY; **180** The Granger Collection, New York; **181** Stab. D Anderson-Roma

CHAPTER 9

184 Courtesy, Museum of Fine Arts, Boston; **192** Emil Muench; **194** M Mattson/SUPERSTOCK; **195** Lee Boltin; **196** Lee Boltin; **203** Lee Boltin; **205** Cornell Capa/Magnum Photos

CHAPTER 10

208 The British Library; **210** Garneau and Provost/SUPERSTOCK; **215** Philip Jones Griffith/Magnum Photos; **219** Aero Films Library; **221** Suzanne Engelmann/SUPERSTOCK; **224** Tokyo National Museum

CHAPTER 11

234 Robert Hardin Picture Library Ltd., London; **239** Photograph Cliche Pelliot/Archives Musée Guimet; **241** Victor Kenney/Robert Harding Picture Library Ltd., London; **242** Kinnari & Apsoros/Borromeo/Art Resource, NY; **246** Courtesy of the Trustees of the British Museum; **251** Giraudon/Art Resource, NY; **252** The Granger Collection, New York

PART 3

256 Courtesy of The Newberry Library, Chicago

CHAPTER 12

264 Freer Gallery of Art, The Smithsonian Institution, Wash., D.C.; **267** Exclusive News Agency/Popperfoto; **269** The Granger Collection, New York; **272** The Spencer Collection/New York Public Library, Astor, Lenox and Tilden Foundations; **273** Alice Shalek/Three Lions/SUPERSTOCK; **281** The Granger Collection, New York; **284TL** Jane Van Eps 1988/SUPERSTOCK; **284BL** Robert Frerck/Odyssey Productions, Chicago; **284TR** M Koonce/SUPERSTOCK; **284BR** Shostal/SUPERSTOCK

CHAPTER 13

288 Bibliothèque Nationale; **292** The Harvard University Art Museums, gift of John Goelet, formerly Collection of Louis J Cartier; **296** Photogrique Yan; **297** Rogers Fund 1951/The Metropolitan Museum of Art; **298** Nelson Gallery of Art/Atkins Museum, Kansas City, Mo.; **299** The Granger Collection, New York; **307** British Library/Art Resource, NY

CHAPTER 14

312 Photographic Archives/The University Museum, University of Pennsylvania; **317** Floyd Norgaard/Ric Ergenbright; **319** The British Library; **320** E. Streichan/SUPERSTOCK; **328** Lent by The Guennol Collection/Courtesy The Brooklyn Museum

CHAPTER 15

332 Biblioteca Nacional, Madrid; **337** Alinari/Art Resource, NY; **338** The Granger Collection, New York; **340** Erich Lessing/Magnum Photos; **341** from "MINIATURES ARMENIENNES," (c)1960 Editions Cercle d'Art, Paris; **344L** Staatsbibliothek Preubischer Kulturbesitz, Berlin; **345** Biblioteca Nacional, Madrid; **347** Novosti Press Agency

CHAPTER 16

350 Städelsches Kunstinstitut/Photograph: Ursula Edelmann, Frankfurt am Main; **355** Giraudon/Art Resource, NY; **357** Giraudon/Art Resource, NY; **360** The British Library; **365** Ewing Galloway; **368** Giraudon/Art Resource, NY; **373** The Bettmann Archive; **374** Courtesy of The Newberry Library, Chicago

CHAPTER 17

378 Lee Boltin; **382** Peter Menzel; **385** Institute Nacional de Anthopologia e Historia; **386** Library of Congress; **387** from "The Chinampas of Mexico," by Michael Coe, July 1964, Copyright (c) SCIENTIFIC AMERICAN, Inc. All rights reserved.; **388** NEED XEROX/ Courtesy of The Newberry Library, Chicago; **393** Ric Ergenbright; **395** American History

Index

Dharma, 144
Díaz, Porfirio, 750, 916
di Cavour, Count Camillo, 687
Dickens, Charles, 693
Diet, 795
Din-i-Ilahi, 608, 610
di Nobili, Robert, 646
Diocletian, 245
Dionysos, 150
Disease, 528, 534, 569, 571-72, 573, 580, 622, 709, 724-26
Disraeli, Benjamin, 687
Divorce, 799, 800, 857, 907
Dominicans, 568, 579
Dostoevsky, Feodor, 790
Douglass, Frederick, 632
Drama, Yuan dynasty, 467
Dreadnaught, 699
Dreyfus, Alfred, 953
Duarte, Eva, 924
Du Bois, W. E. B., 955
Duma, 790
Dutch East India Company, 526, 536, 628-29, 646, 704
Dutch Studies, 792

Eastern Bloc, 847
Economic Commission for Latin America (ECLA), 749
Economic determinism, 527
Edict of Nantes, 502
Edo, 659
Education
  in China's Tang and Song dynasties, 407, 413
  in classical China, 105-106
  in classical Rome, 169-70
  in early modern Europe, 683
  in early modern India, 710-13
  in early modern Japan, 792
  in Latin America, 747
  in medieval Europe, 358, 363
  in modern Europe, 688
  in modern Japan, 798
  in Mongolian society, 467
  in Ottoman Empire, 760
  western, in Asia and Africa, 712-13
  in the Yuan dynasty, 467
Egypt
  ancient, 3-5, 35-40
  compared to early Africa, 214
  compared with Mesopotamia, 39-40
  ideas and art, 37-38
  patterns of society, 36-37
  technical and cultural heritage, 43
  women in, 40-41
  modern, 946-47, 950, 953-54, 981-83
Einstein, Albert, 692, 844
El Mina, 618, 622

El Salvador, 193, 932
Elites, 513-14
Elizabeth I, 502
Emancipation of the serfs (Russia), 783-84
Encomenderos, 572
Encomiendas, 566
Encyclopaedia Britannica, 515
England. See also Britain
  absolute monarchy, 510-13
  Henry VIII, 502
  Hundred Years War, 359, 371
  literature, 364, 366
  Reformation, 502-504
  Renaissance, 500-501
  Seven Years' War, 514
  trading and banking, 367
  William the Conquerer, 358
English civil wars, 506, 511
Enlightened despotism, 498, 586-88
Enlightenment, 514-16
  Encyclopaedia Brittannica, 515
  and religion, 515
  and women and children, 515-16
Epic of Gilgamesh, 33
Equiano, Olaudah, 632
Ethiopia, 828
  Christian state in, 316-17
Ethnocentrism, 484
Etruscans, 165
Euclid, 127
European Economic Community. See Common Market
Evangelicals, 711
Exceptionalism, 695
Expeditions
  Northern European, 525-26
  Portuguese and Spanish, 521-23, 524-25
Ezekiel, 147

Family, 60
  in ancient India, 146, 158-59
  in Aztec society, 389
  in China's Tang and Song dynasties, 417
  in classical China, 106
  in classical Greece, 135
  in classical Rome, 177
  in early Africa, 320, 325
  in early America, 205-206
  in early Japan, 430, 431, 437
  in early Korea, 440
  in early modern Europe, 501
  in the first Industrial Revolution, 680-82, 685
  in medieval Europe, 369
  Mesoamerican, 197
  in Mesopotamia and Egypt, 39-41
  in modern Japan, 800
  nomadic, 84-85

in North American colonies, 540
in pre- and early-Islamic Arabia, 269-70, 277-78
and the Reformation, 503-504
after World War II, 856-58
Famine, 477
  Russia, 559, 788
Farghana, 607
Fascism, 828, 842-44
Feminine Mystique, The, (Friedan), 858
Feminist movement, 506, 689-90, 844, 857-58, 936-37
Ferdinand of Aragon, 359
Ferdinand VII (Spain), 523, 566, 730
Ferdinand, Archduke Franz, 816
Fertile Crescent, 27
Fertility, 53
Feudal order, 63
  comparison of Japanese and European, 433-34
  in Japan, 431
  in medieval western Europe, 354, 356, 358-59, 360, 370-71
  in Zhou dynasty, 63-64
Fiefs, 63
Fifth Republic, 852-53
Final solution, 828
Firdawsi, 298
Five Year Plans (USSR), 837, 1001-1002
Florence, in the Renaissance, 480
Forbidden City, 651, 656
France, medieval, 355, 357, 367
  feudal order, 358-59, 360
  Hundred Years War, 359, 371
France, early modern
  absolute monarchy, 510-13
  colonies in North America, 538-39, 541
  colonization of India, 536-38
  legacy of the Revolution, 677-78
  Renaissance in, 500-501
  Revolution of 1789, 675-77
France, modern, 846, 854
  colonial rule in Southeast Asia, 1007, 1008-1011
  origins of World War I, 698-700
  Revolution of 1848, 683-85
  World War I, 817-18
  World War II, 829-35
Francis I, 500, 501
Franciscans, 360, 579
Franks, 354-55
Frederick II, "the Great" (Prussia), 514
Free French, 959
Free Officers movement, 981
French National Resistance Council, 845-46
Freud, Sigmund, 32, 692, 860
Friars, 646
Friedan, Betty, 858
Fujiwara family, 430